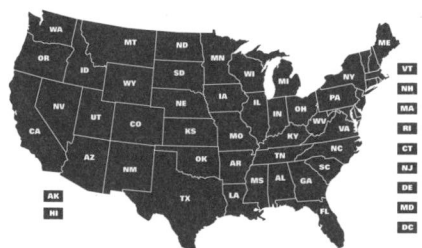

McDougal Littell

Pre-Algebra

Teacher's Edition

Contents

Larson Boswell Kanold Stiff

McDougal Littell
A DIVISION OF HOUGHTON MIFFLIN COMPANY
Evanston, Illinois • Boston • Dallas

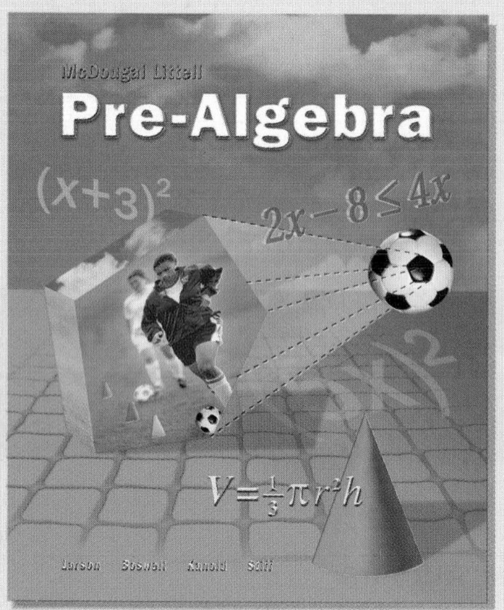

About Pre-Algebra

McDougal Littell Pre-Algebra will give your students a strong foundation in algebra while also preparing them for future study of geometry, probability, and data analysis. The clearly written lessons make even difficult math concepts and methods understandable by providing numerous stepped-out examples. Each lesson's exercise set includes a wide variety of exercises, ranging from basic exercises that help students develop and practice skills to challenging exercises that involve logical reasoning and problem solving.

This book will also help your students become better at taking notes and taking tests. Look for a notetaking strategy at the beginning of each chapter as well as helpful marginal notes throughout each chapter. The marginal notes give your students support in keeping a notebook, studying math, reading algebra and geometry, doing homework, using technology, and reviewing for tests. Also look for instruction and practice that prepare your students for taking standardized tests with questions in multiple choice, short response, and extended response formats. In all these ways—and many more—*McDougal Littell Pre-Algebra* puts your students on the road to success in mathematics.

Contributing Authors and Reviewers

The authors wish to thank the following individuals for their contributions to this Teacher's Edition.

Differentiating Instruction *(pp. T48–T50, 2E–2F)*—Donna Foley, Curriculum Specialist for Math, Chelmsford Middle School, Chelmsford, MA; Mark Johnson, Mathematics Assessment Specialist, Massachusetts Department of Education, Malden, MA

Reading, Writing, Notetaking; CRISS *(pp. T51–T53)*—Kit Granat, Master CRISS Trainer, Former Language Arts Supervisor, Miami-Dade County Public Schools, Miami, FL; Joan Smathers, National CRISS Trainer, Former Language Arts Supervisor, Brevard County, FL; Marie Pettet, Reading and Language Arts Curriculum Specialist, Former K–12 Language Arts Coordinator, Fulton County, GA

Universal Access *(pp. T56–T59)*—Catherine Barkett, Vice President, Director of Training, Calabash Professional Learning Systems, Sacramento, CA

English Learners *(pp. T60–T61, 2E–2F)*—Olga Bautista, Vice Principal, Will C. Wood Middle School, Sacramento, CA; Judy Lewis, Director, State and Federal Programs, Folsom Cordova Unified School District, CA

Printed in China

ISBN-13: 978-0-618-80077-3

ISBN-10: 0-618-80077-8 456789–0940–13 12 11 10

Internet Web Site: http://www.mcdougallittell.com

ABOUT THE AUTHORS

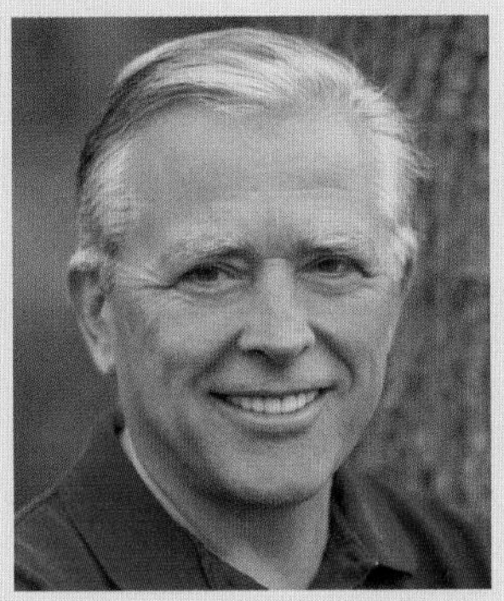

RON LARSON

Ron Larson is a professor of mathematics at Penn State University at Erie, where he has taught since receiving his Ph.D. in mathematics from the University of Colorado. Dr. Larson is well known as the author of a comprehensive program for mathematics that spans middle school, high school, and college courses. Dr. Larson's numerous professional activities keep him in constant touch with the needs of teachers and supervisors. He closely follows developments in mathematics standards and assessment.

LAURIE BOSWELL

Laurie Boswell is the mathematics department chair at Profile Junior-Senior High School in Bethlehem, New Hampshire. A recipient of the Presidential Award for Excellence in Mathematics Teaching, she has also been a Tandy Technology Scholar. She serves on the National Council of Teachers of Mathematics Board of Directors. She speaks frequently on topics related to instructional strategies and course content.

TIMOTHY KANOLD

Timothy Kanold is the superintendent of Adlai E. Stevenson High School District 125 in Lincolnshire, Illinois, where he served as a teacher and the Director of Mathematics for 16 years. He has a Ph.D. from Loyola University Chicago. Dr. Kanold is a recipient of the Presidential Award for Excellence in Mathematics and Science Teaching and served on The Academy Services Committee for NCTM. He is a frequent speaker at mathematics meetings where he shares his in-depth knowledge of mathematics teaching and curriculum.

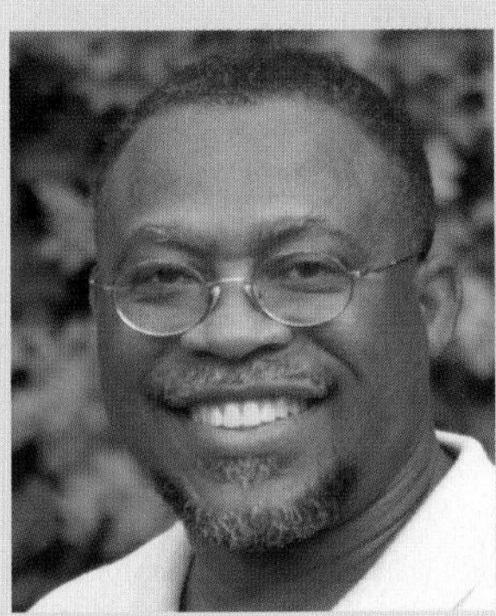

LEE STIFF

Lee Stiff is a professor of mathematics education in the College of Education of North Carolina State University at Raleigh. His extensive experience in mathematics education includes teaching at the middle school and high school levels. He has received the W. W. Rankin Award for Excellence in Mathematics Education, and was Fulbright Scholar to the Department of Mathematics of the University of Ghana. He served as President of the National Council of Teachers of Mathematics (2000–2002).

ADVISERS AND REVIEWERS

Curriculum Advisers and Reviewers

Donna Foley
Curriculum Specialist for Math
Chelmsford Middle School
Chelmsford, MA

Barbara Nunn
Secondary Mathematics Specialist
Broward County Schools
Fort Lauderdale, FL

Wendy Loeb
Mathematics Teacher
Twin Groves Junior High School
Buffalo Grove, IL

Tom Scott
Resource Teacher
Duval County Public Schools
Jacksonville, FL

Teacher Panels

Florida Panel

Kathy Adams
Mathematics Teacher
Allapattah Middle School
Miami, FL

Micki Hawn
Mathematics Teacher
Pompano Beach Middle School
Pompano Beach, FL

Barbara Schober
Mathematics Department Chair
Okeeheelee Middle School
West Palm Beach, FL

Sue Carrico-Beddow
Mathematics Teacher
Bayonet Point Middle School
New Port Richey, FL

Pat Powell
Mathematics Department Chair
Stewart Middle School
Tampa, FL

Laurie St. Julien
Mathematics Teacher
Oak Grove Middle School
Clearwater, FL

Melissa Grabowski
Mathematics Teacher
Stone Middle School
Melbourne, FL

Kansas and Missouri Panel

Linda Cordes
Department Chair
Paul Robeson Middle School
Kansas City, MO

Rhonda Foote
Mathematics Department Chair
Maple Park Middle School
North Kansas City, MO

Jan Rase
Mathematics Teacher
Moreland Ridge Middle School
Blue Springs, MO

Linda Dodd
Mathematics Department Chair
Argentine Middle School
Kansas City, KS

Cas Kyle
District Math Curriculum Coordinator
Richard A. Warren Middle School
Leavenworth, KS

Dan Schoenemann
Mathematics Teacher
Raytown Middle School
Kansas City, MO

Melanie Dowell
Mathematics Teacher
Raytown South Middle School
Raytown, MO

Texas Panel

Judy Carlin
Mathematics Teacher
Brown Middle School
McAllen, TX

Judith Cody
Mathematics Teacher
Deady Middle School
Houston, TX

Lisa Hiracheta
Mathematics Teacher
Irons Junior High School
Lubbock, TX

Kay Neuse
Mathematics Teacher
Wilson Middle School
Plano, TX

Louise Nutzman
Mathematics Teacher
Sugar Land Middle School
Sugar Land, TX

Clarice Orise
Mathematics Teacher
Tafolla Middle School
San Antonio, TX

Wonda Webb
Mathematics Teacher
William H. Atwell Middle School and Law Academy
Dallas, TX

Karen Young
Mathematics Teacher
Murchison Elementary School
Pflugerville, TX

Teacher Reviewers

Debra Dean
Oberon Middle School
Arvada, CO

Linda Gojak
John Carroll University
University Heights, OH

Stephen Goodly
McDonough 35 Senior High School
New Orleans, LA

Debbie Gray
Carter G. Woodson Learning Academy
New Orleans, LA

Chris Kelly
Adlai Stevenson High School
Lincolnshire, IL

Donna Simpson Leak
Revere Elementary Accelerated School
Chicago, IL

Wendy Loeb
Twin Groves Junior High School
Buffalo Grove, IL

Nina McGibney
Jefferson County School District R-1
Golden, CO

Rick Nelson
Eastmont Junior High School
East Wenatchee, WA

Karen Tripoli
Lexington Public Schools
Lexington, MA

CHAPTER 1

Variables, Expressions, *and* Integers

Add integers to find a diver's position, pp. 29-30

PLANNING

You can use *Appendix 1: Absolute Value Equations,* on page 824, after completing Lesson 2.6.

CHAPTER 2

Solving Equations

Internet Resources
CLASSZONE.COM
eEdition Plus Online
eWorkbook Plus Online
eTutorial Plus Online
State Test Practice
More Examples

Reading, Writing, and Notetaking
Vocabulary, 62, 66, 73, 80, 87, 93, 99, 105, 108
Reading Algebra, 71, 80, 85, 91
Writing, 67, 75, 81, 88, 90, 94, 96, 101, 106
Notetaking, 62, 64, 78

Student Help
Study Strategy, 64, 74, 79, 103
Homework Help, 66, 74, 81, 87, 93, 99, 105
Tech Help, 83
Student Reference: Perimeter and Area, 69; Rates and Unit Analysis, 76

Problem Solving
Guided Problem Solving, 87, 99, 105
Extended Problem Solving, 67, 75, 81, 88, 94, 100, 106
Challenge, 68, 75, 82, 89, 95, 101, 106

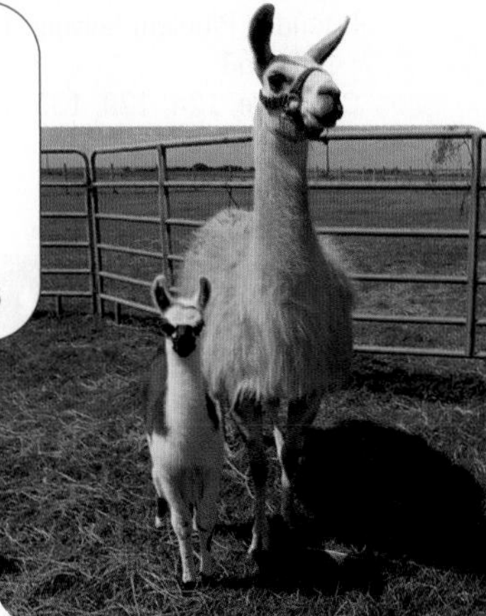

Use algebra to find dimensions of a llama pen, p. 75

CHAPTER

3

Multi-Step Equations *and* Inequalities

Use an equation to find rafting costs, p. 123

CHAPTER 4

Factors, Fractions, *and* Exponents

Use fractions to compare snowboarding data, p. 188

CHAPTER

5

Rational Numbers *and* Equations

Multiply fractions to extend a recipe, p. 241

PLANNING

You can use *Appendix 2: Proportion Applications,* on page 826, after completing Lesson 6.3.

CHAPTER 6

Ratio, Proportion, *and* Probability

Internet Resources
CLASSZONE.COM
eEdition Plus Online
eWorkbook Plus Online
eTutorial Plus Online
State Test Practice
More Examples

Reading, Writing, and Notetaking
Vocabulary, 268, 272, 277, 282, 290, 295, 302, 309, 315, 318
Reading Algebra, 275, 281, 300, 306, 308, 310
Reading Geometry, 288
Writing, 278, 283, 292, 310, 316
Notetaking, 268, 282, 290

Student Help
Study Strategy, 289, 294, 307, 314
Homework Help, 272, 278, 283, 291, 295, 302, 309, 315
Tech Help, 312
Student Reference: Basic Geometry Concepts, 285

Problem Solving
Guided Problem Solving, 272, 282, 295, 302, 309, 315
Extended Problem Solving, 273, 284, 292, 310
Challenge, 274, 279, 284, 292, 297, 304, 311, 317

Use a proportion to find how much an elephant eats, pp. 275, 277

PLANNING

You can use *Appendix 3: Using Small and Large Percents,* on page 828, after completing Lesson 7.3.

CHAPTER 7

Percents

Apply percents to chess, p. 332

CHAPTER 8

Linear Functions

Use a graph to find the speed of a wakeboarder, p. 406

PLANNING

You can use *Appendix 4: Operations with Square Roots,* on page 830, after completing Lesson 9.2.

You can use *Appendix 5: Symbolic Notation and Truth Tables,* on page 833, after completing Lesson 9.3.

Real Numbers *and* Right Triangles

CLASSZONE.COM
eEdition Plus Online
eWorkbook Plus Online
eTutorial Plus Online
State Test Practice
More Examples

Reading, Writing, and Notetaking

Vocabulary, 452, 455, 460, 467, 472, 479, 485, 491, 496, 500
Reading Algebra, 458, 466, 476, 492
Reading Geometry, 489
Writing, 457, 461, 464, 468, 473, 482, 486, 488, 492, 497
Notetaking, 452, 454, 484

Study Strategy, 453, 466, 470, 471, 477, 484
Homework Help, 456, 460, 467, 473, 479, 486, 491, 497
Tech Help, 454, 490, 499
Student Reference: Triangles, 462

Problem Solving

Guided Problem Solving, 455, 467, 496
Extended Problem Solving, 457, 461, 469, 474, 481, 486, 493, 498
Challenge, 457, 461, 469, 474, 481, 487, 493, 498

Apply square roots to determine film speeds, p. 456

CHAPTER

10

Measurement, Area, *and* Volume

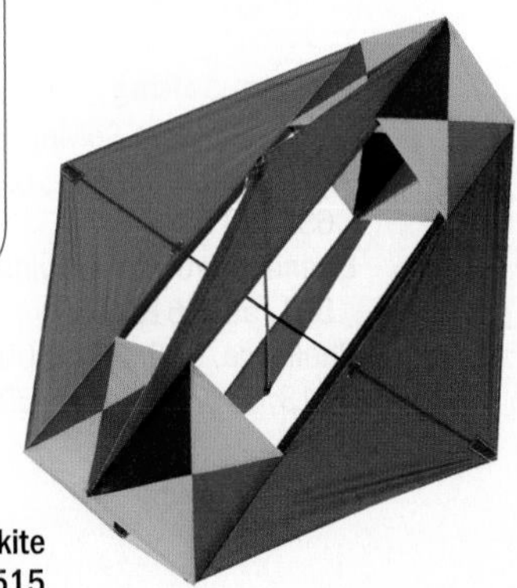

Use geometry to find kite dimensions, p. 515

PLANNING

You can use *Appendix 6: Using Venn Diagrams*, on page 835, after completing Lesson 11.3.

CHAPTER

11

Data Analysis *and* Probability

CLASSZONE.COM

eEdition Plus Online
eWorkbook Plus Online
eTutorial Plus Online
State Test Practice
More Examples

Reading, Writing, and Notetaking

Student Help

Problem Solving

Apply combinations to count basketball matchups, p. 620

CHAPTER 12

Polynomials *and* Nonlinear Functions

Internet Resources
CLASSZONE.COM
eEdition Plus Online
eWorkbook Plus Online
eTutorial Plus Online
State Test Practice
More Examples

Reading, Writing, and Notetaking
Vocabulary, 650, 653, 659, 664, 670, 676, 682, 689, 695, 698
Reading Algebra, 652, 687
Writing, 654, 660, 665, 667, 671, 677, 683, 689, 695
Notetaking, 650, 669, 687

Student Help
Study Strategy, 651, 680, 681, 686, 693, 694
Homework Help, 654, 660, 664, 670, 677, 682, 689, 695
Tech Help, 685

Problem Solving
Guided Problem Solving, 664, 682, 689
Extended Problem Solving, 655, 660, 665, 672, 678, 684, 690, 696
Challenge, 655, 661, 666, 672, 678, 684, 691, 697
Focus on Problem Solving: Looking Back, 704

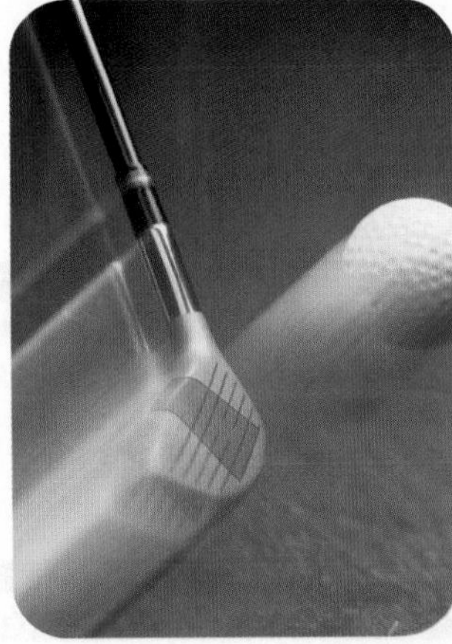

Use polynomials to find the height of a golf ball, p. 654

PLANNING

You can use *Appendix 7: Linear and Nonlinear Relations and Functions* on page 836, after completing Lesson 12.7.

CHAPTER

13

Angle Relationships *and* Transformations

Analyze angles in chair design, p. 719

Contents *of* Student Resources

McDougal Littell

Pre-Algebra

The right math, the right way, the right results

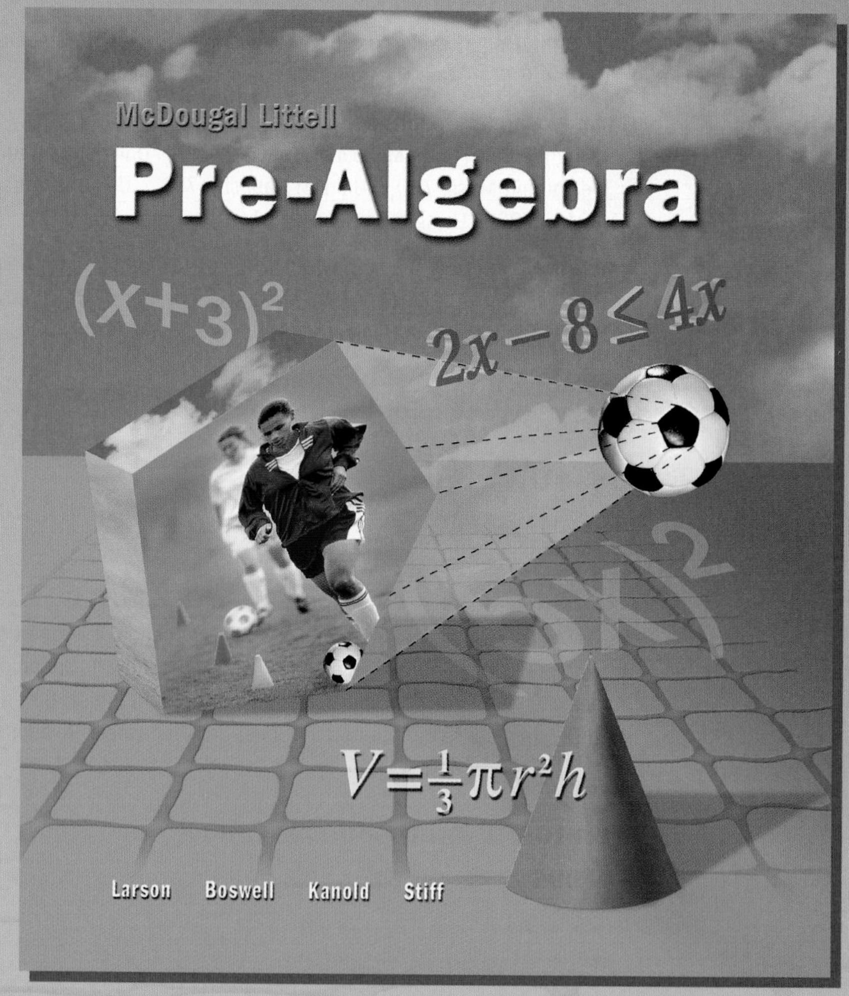

McDougal Littell Pre-Algebra provides the foundation in algebra, geometry, and problem solving that is needed for success in more advanced courses. Built-in study and notetaking strategies help students develop their learning skills.

$2x - 8 \leq 4x$

Prepare

Clear presentation of key concepts and challenging problem-solving practice prepare students for algebra courses.

$V = \frac{1}{3}\pi r^2 h$

Develop

Notetaking strategies, vocabulary review, and margin notes guide students to develop study skills and conceptual understanding.

Achieve

Practice with test-taking strategies and varied question formats, in print and integrated technology resources, builds the confidence and problem-solving skills needed to achieve success.

$(x + 3)^2$

Prepare
Clear, Focused Content

This Pre-Algebra program features the algebra prerequisites students need to understand key concepts.

Read It!
New concepts are introduced using algebraic symbols, words, and numbers.

Prepare for It!
Lesson openers prepare students to learn by connecting new skills to prior learning.

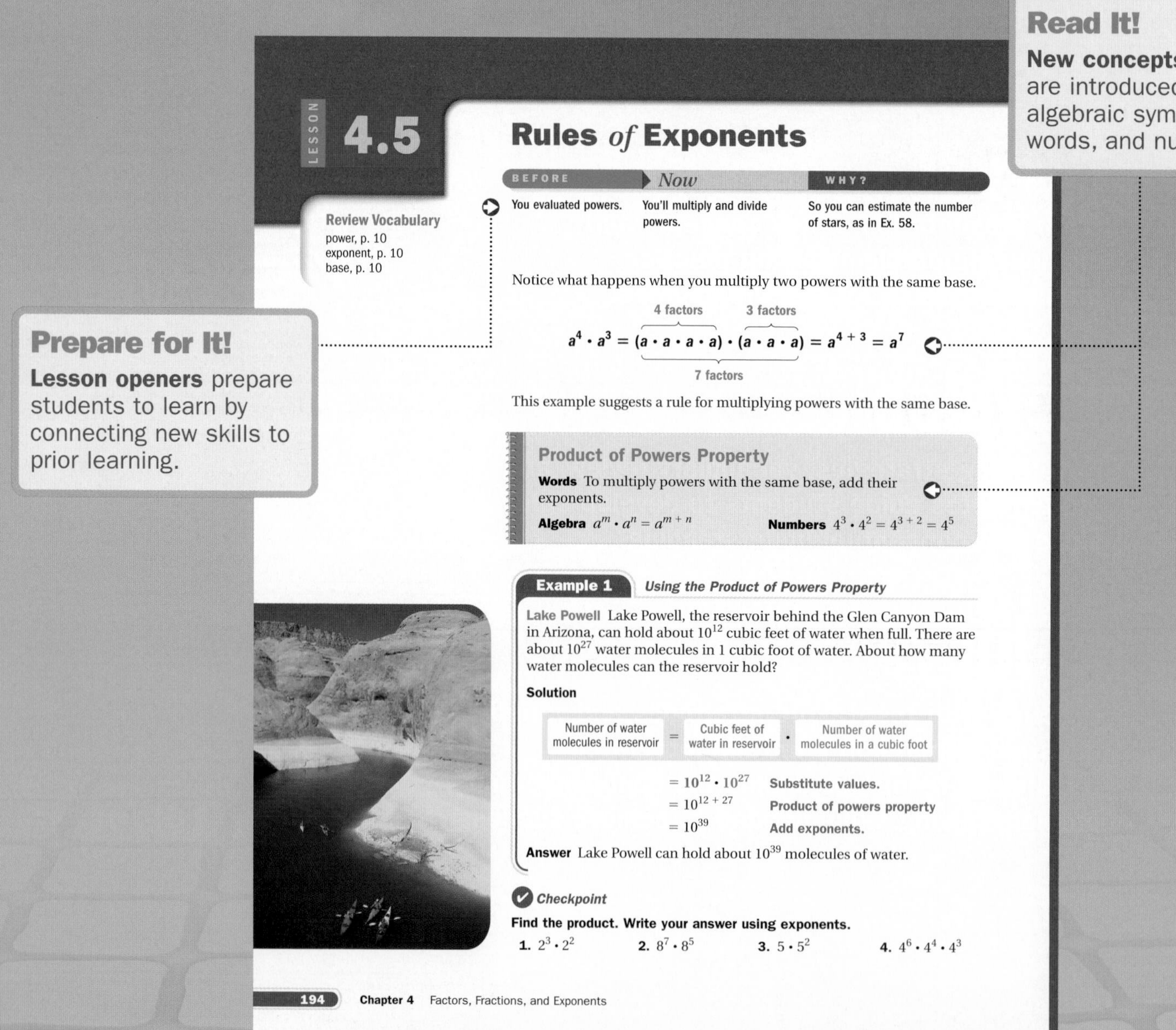

LESSON 4.5
Rules of Exponents
BEFORE
You evaluated powers.
Now
You'll multiply and divide powers.
WHY?
So you can estimate the number of stars, as in Ex. 58.
Review Vocabulary
power, p. 10
exponent, p. 10
base, p. 10
Notice what happens when you multiply two powers with the same base.
4 factors
3 factors
$a^4 \cdot a^3 = (a \cdot a \cdot a \cdot a) \cdot (a \cdot a \cdot a) = a^{4+3} = a^7$
7 factors
This example suggests a rule for multiplying powers with the same base.
Product of Powers Property
Words To multiply powers with the same base, add their exponents.
Algebra $a^m \cdot a^n = a^{m+n}$
Numbers $4^3 \cdot 4^2 = 4^{3+2} = 4^5$
Example 1 Using the Product of Powers Property
Lake Powell Lake Powell, the reservoir behind the Glen Canyon Dam in Arizona, can hold about 10^{12} cubic feet of water when full. There are about 10^{27} water molecules in 1 cubic foot of water. About how many water molecules can the reservoir hold?
Solution
Number of water molecules in reservoir = Cubic feet of water in reservoir • Number of water molecules in a cubic foot
$= 10^{12} \cdot 10^{27}$ Substitute values.
$= 10^{12+27}$ Product of powers property
$= 10^{39}$ Add exponents.
Answer Lake Powell can hold about 10^{39} molecules of water.
Checkpoint
Find the product. Write your answer using exponents.
1. $2^3 \cdot 2^2$
2. $8^7 \cdot 8^5$
3. $5 \cdot 5^2$
4. $4^6 \cdot 4^4 \cdot 4^3$
194 Chapter 4 Factors, Fractions, and Exponents

Note Worthy

When taking notes about Example 2, be sure to write a verbal description next to each step in the calculation.

Example 2 *Using the Product of Powers Property*

a. $x^6 \cdot x^9 = x^{6+9}$ — Product of powers property

$= x^{15}$ — Add exponents.

b. $3x \cdot 5x^5 = 3 \cdot 5 \cdot x^1 \cdot x^5$ — Commutative property of multiplication

$= 3 \cdot 5 \cdot x^{1+5}$ — Product of powers property

$= 3 \cdot 5 \cdot x^6$ — Add exponents.

$= 15x^6$ — Multiply.

Quotients of Powers There is a related rule you can use for dividing powers with the same base. The following example suggests this rule.

$$\frac{a^5}{a^2} = \frac{\overbrace{a \cdot a \cdot a \cdot a \cdot a}^{5\text{ factors}}}{\underbrace{a \cdot a}_{2\text{ factors}}} = \frac{a \cdot a \cdot a \cdot a \cdot a}{a \cdot a} = \underbrace{a \cdot a \cdot a}_{3\text{ factors}} = a^{5-2} = a^3$$

Quotient of Powers Property

Words To divide powers with the same base, subtract the exponent of the denominator from the exponent of the numerator.

Algebra $\frac{a^m}{a^n} = a^{m-n}$, where $a \neq 0$ **Numbers** $\frac{6^8}{6^5} = 6^{8-5} = 6^3$

Example 3 *Using the Quotient of Powers Property*

a. $\frac{7^6}{7^2} = 7^{6-2}$ — Quotient of powers property

$= 7^4$ — Subtract exponents.

b. $\frac{4x^8}{10x^2} = \frac{4x^{8-2}}{10}$ — Quotient of powers property

$= \frac{4x^6}{10}$ — Subtract exponents.

$= \frac{2x^6}{5}$ — Divide numerator and denominator by 2.

Checkpoint

Find the product or quotient. Write your answer using exponents.

5. $b^7 \cdot b^2$ **6.** $a \cdot a^5 \cdot a^2$ **7.** $2n^{11} \cdot 6n^8$ **8.** $2m^4 \cdot 7m^5$

9. $\frac{6^9}{6^4}$ **10.** $\frac{10^{11}}{10^7}$ **11.** $\frac{z^8}{z^3}$ **12.** $\frac{12n^5}{8n^2}$

Try It!

Checkpoint exercises, closely tied to examples, help ensure understanding.

Apply It!

A variety of exercises provides students practice with concepts, skills, and critical thinking.

This printer can print pages several feet wide.

60. Extended Problem Solving Inkjet printers spray droplets of ink onto paper. The volume of a single droplet is about 10 picoliters. Some printers spray as many as 10^6 droplets to completely cover a square inch of paper.

a. Find the volume of ink in picoliters needed to completely cover a square inch of paper.

b. There are 10^{12} picoliters in a liter. Find the volume of ink in liters needed to completely cover a square inch of paper.

c. Estimate Find the area of a 8.5 inch by 11 inch piece of paper and round this number to the nearest power of 10. Then estimate the volume of ink (in liters) needed to completely cover an entire piece of paper.

d. Apply Suppose an inkjet cartridge contains 60 milliliters of ink. About how many pages can this cartridge print if each page is 8.5 inches by 11 inches and is covered completely in ink?

61. Challenge One way to develop the definitions of zero and negative exponents is to use the quotient of powers property.

a. Consider $\frac{a^n}{a^n}$. First, simplify using the quotient of powers property.

b. Then simplify the expression in part (a) in a different way: Write the numerator and denominator as a product of *a*'s and divide out common factors. Which definition of exponents have you developed?

c. Now consider $\frac{a^0}{a^n}$. First, simplify using the quotient of powers property.

d. Then simplify the expression in part (c) by using the definition of a zero exponent. Which definition of exponents have you developed?

Mixed Review

Algebra Basics Solve the equation using mental math. *(Lesson 2.4)*

62. $9 + x = 17$ **63.** $8 - x = 3$ **64.** $-3x = 36$ **65.** $\frac{x}{-8} = 6$

66. Amusement Parks You must be at least 46 inches tall to ride the bumper cars at an amusement park. Write and graph an inequality to show the heights for which you can ride the bumper cars. *(Lesson 3.4)*

Find the product or quotient. Write your answer using exponents. *(Lesson 4.5)*

67. $3^2 \cdot 3^2$ **68.** $5^4 \cdot 5$ **69.** $\frac{2^9}{2^4}$ **70.** $\frac{10^8}{10^5}$

Standardized Test Practice

71. Multiple Choice Which expression is *not* equivalent to $x^2 \cdot x^{-6}$?

A. x^{-4} **B.** $x^{-2} \cdot x^6$ **C.** $\frac{1}{x^4}$ **D.** $\frac{x^2}{x^6}$

72. Multiple Choice Which expression is equivalent to $\frac{24a^6}{3b^2}$?

F. $24a^{-6}b^2$ **G.** $24a^6b^{-2}$ **H.** $8a^6b^{-2}$ **I.** $8a^{-6}b^2$

Review It!

Standardized test practice in every lesson prepares students for different types of test formats.

Develop
Algebra and Study Skills

Integrated skill-building tools aid students in developing understanding.

Develop It!

Prerequisite skills review opens each chapter and helps students develop algebraic thinking.

CHAPTER

4

Chapter Prerequisite Skills

Review Vocabulary
power, p. 10
base, p. 10
exponent, p. 10
positive integer, p. 22
negative integer, p. 22
numerator, p. 777
denominator, p. 777

PREREQUISITE SKILLS QUIZ

Preparing for Success **To prepare for success in this chapter, test your knowledge of these concepts and skills. You may want to look at the pages referred to in blue for additional review.**

1. Vocabulary Label the power, the base, and the exponent in the expression 9^3.

Write the mixed number as an improper fraction. *(p. 778)*

2. $5\frac{1}{3}$ **3.** $6\frac{2}{5}$ **4.** $3\frac{7}{9}$ **5.** $8\frac{5}{6}$

Find the product. *(p. 780)*

6. $20 \times \frac{3}{5}$ **7.** $32 \times \frac{7}{8}$ **8.** $\frac{2}{3} \times 27$ **9.** $\frac{9}{10} \times 50$

Write the power in words and as a repeated multiplication. Then evaluate the power. *(p. 10)*

10. 5^4 **11.** 12^3 **12.** $(1.3)^3$ **13.** $(0.2)^2$

Note It!

Integrated notetaking features prompt students to record important ideas in their notebooks.

NOTETAKING STRATEGIES

Note *Worthy*

You will find a notetaking strategy at the beginning of each chapter. Look for additional notetaking and study strategies throughout the chapter.

RECORDING THE PROCESS When copying examples in class, be sure to write a verbal description next to each step in a calculation. Then you can refer to the example when solving similar exercises.

Calculation step:	Verbal description:
$-5x - 8 = -23$	Write original equation.
$-5x - 8 + 8 = -23 + 8$	Add 8 to each side.
$-5x = -15$	Simplify.
$\frac{-5x}{-5} = \frac{-15}{-5}$	Divide each side by -5.
$x = 3$	Simplify.

The strategy above will be helpful in Lesson 4.5 when you are simplifying variable expressions with powers.

170

Know It!

A **vocabulary list** at the beginning of each lesson previews key terms students need to know.

LESSON **4.2**

Greatest Common Factor

BEFORE	Now	WHY?
You found all the factors of a whole number.	You'll find the GCF of two or more whole numbers.	So you can organize bands at a music camp, as in Ex. 32.

Vocabulary
common factor, p. 177
greatest common factor (GCF), p. 177
relatively prime, p. 178

Music Choir A choir director wants to divide a choir into smaller groups. The choir has 24 sopranos, 60 altos, and 36 tenors. Each group will have the same number of each type of voice. What is the greatest number of groups that can be formed? How many sopranos, altos, and tenors will be in each group?

A **common factor** is a whole number that is a factor of two or more nonzero whole numbers. The greatest of the common factors is the **greatest common factor (GCF)**.

Example 1 *Finding the Greatest Common Factor*

For the choir described above, the greatest number of groups that can be formed is given by the GCF of 24, 60, and 36. You can use one of two methods to find the GCF.

Method 1 List the factors of each number. Identify the greatest number that is on every list.

Factors of 24: 1, 2, 3, 4, 6, (12), 24
Factors of 60: 1, 2, 3, 4, 5, 6, 10, (12), 15, 20, 30, 60
Factors of 36: 1, 2, 3, 4, 6, 9, (12), 18, 36

The common factors are 1, 2, 3, 4, 6, and 12. The GCF is 12.

Method 2 Write the prime factorization of each number. The GCF is the product of the common prime factors.

$24 = 2 \cdot 2 \cdot 2 \cdot 3$
$60 = 2 \cdot 2 \cdot 3 \cdot 5$
$36 = 2 \cdot 2 \cdot 3 \cdot 3$

The common prime factors are 2, 2, and 3. The GCF is the product $2 \cdot 2 \cdot 3 = 12$.

Answer The greatest number of groups that can be formed is 12. Each group will have $24 \div 12 = 2$ sopranos, $60 \div 12 = 5$ altos, and $36 \div 12 = 3$ tenors.

Checkpoint

Find the greatest common factor of the numbers.

1. 12, 30 **2.** 21, 42 **3.** 16, 32, 40 **4.** 27, 45, 90

Study It!

Margin notes provide study strategies to build effective learning skills.

Study *Strategy*

The table lists all the factors of each number. However, to determine whether a number is composite, you need to find only one factor other than the number itself and 1.

Prime and Composite Numbers A **prime number** is a whole number that is greater than 1 and has exactly two whole number factors, 1 and itself. A **composite number** is a whole number that is greater than 1 and has more than two whole number factors. The number 1 is neither prime nor composite.

Examples of Prime and Composite Numbers

Number	Factors	Prime or composite?
24	1, 2, 3, 4, 6, 8, 12, 24	Composite
41	1, 41	Prime
51	1, 3, 17, 51	Composite
89	1, 89	Prime
121	1, 11, 121	Composite

Prime Factorization When you write a number as a product of prime numbers, you are writing its **prime factorization**. You can use a diagram called a **factor tree** to write the prime factorization of a number.

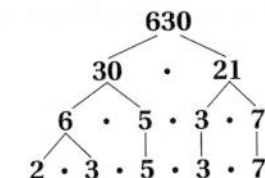

Note *Worthy*

It is helpful to include diagrams in your notes. Include a different factor tree for the number 630 in your notes.

Example 2 *Writing a Prime Factorization*

Write the prime factorization of 630.

One possible factor tree:

630 — Write original number.
$30 \cdot 21$ — Write 630 as $30 \cdot 21$.
$6 \cdot 5 \cdot 3 \cdot 7$ — Write 30 as $6 \cdot 5$. Write 21 as $3 \cdot 7$.
$2 \cdot 3 \cdot 5 \cdot 3 \cdot 7$ — Write 6 as $2 \cdot 3$.

Another possible factor tree:

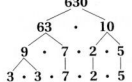

630 — Write original number.
$63 \cdot 10$ — Write 630 as $63 \cdot 10$.
$9 \cdot 7 \cdot 2 \cdot 5$ — Write 63 as $9 \cdot 7$. Write 10 as $2 \cdot 5$.
$3 \cdot 3 \cdot 7 \cdot 2 \cdot 5$ — Write 9 as $3 \cdot 3$.

Both trees give the same result: $630 = 2 \cdot 3 \cdot 3 \cdot 5 \cdot 7 = 2 \cdot 3^2 \cdot 5 \cdot 7$.

Answer The prime factorization of 630 is $2 \cdot 3^2 \cdot 5 \cdot 7$.

Checkpoint

Tell whether the number is *prime* or *composite*. If it is composite, write its prime factorization.

5. 32 **6.** 56 **7.** 59 **8.** 83
9. 101 **10.** 175 **11.** 180 **12.** 420

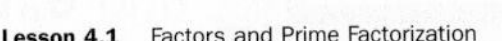

See It!

Clear, stepped-out examples help students understand concepts and skills.

Achieve Assessment Preparation and Practice

Assessment tips and practice opportunities help students achieve algebra success.

Achieve It!
Frequent assessment practice helps students master skills.

CHAPTER 4

Mid-Chapter Quiz

Tell whether the number is *prime* or *composite*. If it is composite, write its prime factorization using exponents.

1. 46 2. 57 3. 61 4. 89

Factor the monomial.

5. $25m^3$ 6. $14n^4$ 7. $19a^2b$ 8. $64f^2g^2$

Find the greatest common factor of the numbers. Then tell whether the numbers are relatively prime.

9. 9, 16 10. 12, 51 11. 18, 49 12. 56, 75

13. **Soccer** A soccer league has 180 members. The league consists of 24 eight-year-olds, 96 nine-year-olds, and 60 ten-year-olds. You want to divide the members into teams that have the same number of eight-year-olds, nine-year-olds, and ten-year-olds. What is the greatest number of teams that can be formed? How many ten-year-olds will be on each team?

Write the fraction in simplest form.

14. $\frac{18}{48}$ 15. $\frac{42}{81}$ 16. $\frac{32a}{8a^2}$ 17. $\frac{15b}{39b^4}$

Find the least common multiple of the numbers.

18. 4, 11 19. 10, 24 20. 15, 45 21. 30, 54

Use the LCD to determine which fraction is greater.

22. $\frac{3}{8}, \frac{4}{9}$ 23. $\frac{7}{10}, \frac{18}{25}$ 24. $\frac{5}{12}, \frac{9}{20}$ 25. $\frac{11}{18}, \frac{13}{24}$

Fraction Scramble

Rearrange the numerators and denominators in the five fractions shown to create five new fractions that are all equivalent to each other. Numerators can become denominators and vice versa. The question mark can be any positive integer.

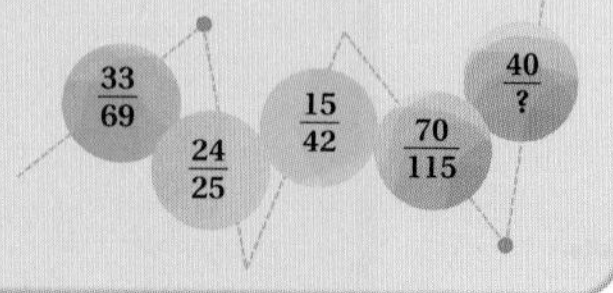

Chapter Standardized Test

Test-Taking Strategy **Be sure to completely read the question and all answer choices before choosing an answer.**

1. Which number is *not* prime?
   A. 7 **B.** 37 **C.** 53 **D.** 57
2. Which expression is the prime factorization of 168?
   F. $2^2 \cdot 3^2 \cdot 7$ **G.** $2 \cdot 3 \cdot 7^2$ **H.** $2^3 \cdot 3 \cdot 7$ **I.** $2^3 \cdot 3 \cdot 7^2$
3. What is the greatest common factor of $14x^2$ and $38x^3$?
   A. $2x^3$ **B.** $2x^2$ **C.** $266x^3$ **D.** $532x^2$
4. Which numbers are relatively prime?
   F. 25, 36 **G.** 12, 20 **H.** 24, 28 **I.** 45, 84
5. Which fraction is *not* in simplest form?
   A. $\frac{1}{2}$ **B.** $\frac{21}{32}$ **C.** $\frac{35}{54}$ **D.** $\frac{54}{72}$
6. In a florist's window, 30 of 36 plants are flowering. Write the fraction of flowering plants in simplest form.
   F. $\frac{5}{6}$ **G.** $\frac{10}{12}$ **H.** $\frac{15}{18}$ **I.** $\frac{30}{36}$
7. What is the LCM of 16 and 80?
   A. 8 **B.** 80 **C.** 160 **D.** 320
8. Which fraction is greater than $\frac{17}{60}$?
   F. $\frac{4}{15}$ **G.** $\frac{7}{30}$ **H.** $\frac{19}{45}$ **I.** $\frac{29}{120}$
9. Which expression is equivalent to $8x^4 \cdot 5x^3$?
   A. $20x^7$ **B.** $40x^7$ **C.** $20x^{12}$ **D.** $40x^{12}$
10. Which expression is equivalent to $\frac{15b^9}{25b^3}$?
    F. $\frac{3b^3}{5}$ **G.** $\frac{3}{5b^3}$ **H.** $\frac{3b^6}{5}$ **I.** $\frac{3}{5b^6}$
11. Which expression is *not* equivalent to $\frac{1}{64}$?
    A. 2^{-6} **B.** 4^{-4} **C.** 8^{-2} **D.** 64^{-1}
12. Which expression is equivalent to $3^{-4}x^0$?
    F. $\frac{1}{81}$ **G.** 3^4 **H.** $\frac{1}{81x}$ **I.** $\frac{x}{81}$
13. Which list of numbers is in order from least to greatest?
    A. $1.4 \times 10^6, 3.28 \times 10^3, 6.3 \times 10^2, 8.2 \times 10^3$
    B. $6.3 \times 10^2, 8.2 \times 10^3, 3.28 \times 10^3, 1.4 \times 10^6$
    C. $1.4 \times 10^6, 6.3 \times 10^2, 3.28 \times 10^3, 8.2 \times 10^3$
    D. $6.3 \times 10^2, 3.28 \times 10^3, 8.2 \times 10^3, 1.4 \times 10^6$
14. **Short Response** A certain type of bacteria has been found in lengths 0.000018 meter, 7.5×10^{-6} meter, and 2.5×10^{-6} meter. Order these lengths from least to greatest.
15. **Extended Response** You have a wooden board that measures 54 centimeters by 90 centimeters. You want to cut the board into identical square pieces with integer side lengths and use all of the wood.
    a. Make a sketch of the board. Find three possible side lengths for the squares
    b. What is the largest side length you can choose? Explain.
    c. How many square pieces will you have?

Assess It!
Multiple-choice, short-response, and **extended-response questions** help students succeed on tests.

Reinforce It!

Rubrics and stepped-out strategies strengthen assessment skills to ensure students' best performance on high-stakes tests.

Unit 2
Chapters 4–7

Building Test-Taking Skills

Strategies for Answering
Short Response Questions

Scoring Rubric

Full Credit
- answer is correct, *and*
- work or reasoning is included

Partial Credit
- answer is correct, but reasoning is incorrect, *or*
- answer is incorrect, but reasoning is correct

No Credit
- no answer is given, *or*
- answer makes no sense

Problem A CD player is on sale at a store for 25% off the retail price of $120. If you buy the CD player at the store, you pay a 5% sales tax on the sale price. An identical CD player is on sale at an Internet site for 30% off the retail price of $120. If you buy the CD player online, you pay a $20 shipping cost. Which is less, the total cost at the store or the total cost online?

Full credit solution

The total cost at the store is the sum of the sale price and a 5% sales tax on the sale price.

The steps of the solution are clearly written.

Sale price = Retail price − Discount
= 120 − 25% • 120 = 120 − 0.25 • 120 = 90

The correct calculations are performed to find the total cost at the store and the total cost online.

Total cost at store = Sale price + Sales tax
= 90 + 5% • 90 = 90 + 0.05 • 90 = 94.50

The total cost online is the sum of the sale price and the shipping cost.

Sale price = Retail price − Discount
= 120 − 30% • 120 = 120 − 0.3 • 120 = 84

Total cost online = Sale price + Shipping cost
= 84 + 20 = 104

The question asked is answered correctly.

The total cost at the store, $94.50, is less than the total cost online, $104.

Partial credit solution

The total cost at the store and the total cost online are correct.

Total cost at store = $90 + $4.50 = $94.50
Total cost online = $84 + $20 = $104

There are no explanations to support the student's calculations.

Because $94.50 is less than $104, the total cost at the store is less than the total cost online.

374 **Unit 2** Rational Numbers and Proportions

eEdition Plus Online provides an interactive, online version of the text that engages students and facilitates teaching.

eWorkbook Plus Online includes interactive practice opportunities that correspond to the text.

eTutorial Plus Online offers an Internet tutorial that makes it easier than ever to help students master skills and concepts.

State Test Practice helps support students as they prepare to achieve their goals on state tests.

More Examples include additional, online support that helps students master new concepts.

Teacher's Resource Package

This package is conveniently organized and includes a variety of materials to help you adapt the program to your teaching style and to the specific needs of your Pre-Algebra students!

Teacher's Resource Package includes:

Chapter Resource Books
(one for each chapter, organized by lesson)

Assessment Book

Notetaking Guide Teacher's Edition

Practice Workbook Teacher's Edition

Teacher Survival Kit
(includes the Professional Development Book, the Special Activities Book, and Posters)

Warm-Up Transparencies with Daily Homework Quiz

Worked-Out Solution Key

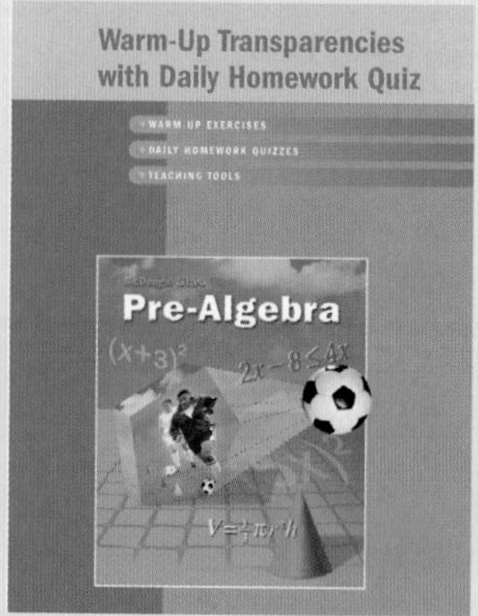

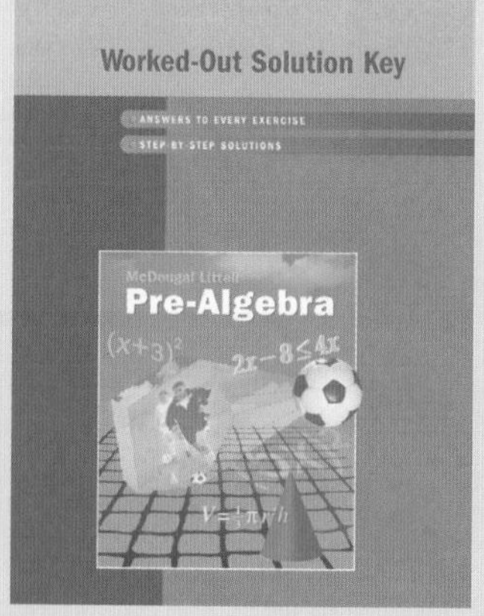

Complete daily resources, organized to save you time!

Chapter Resource Books

Chapter Resource Books allow you to carry the resources you have for a chapter in one manageable book. The materials in each Chapter Resource Book are organized by lesson so that you can easily see everything you have available.

Chapter Resource Books include:

- Tips for New Teachers
- Parents as Partners
- Games Support Master
- Lesson Plans
- Lesson Plans for Block Scheduling
- Activity Masters
- Technology Activities and Keystrokes
- Practice (Levels A, B, and C)
- Study Guide
- Real-World Problem Solving
- Challenge Practice
- Chapter Review Games and Activities
- Real Life Project with Teacher's Notes
- Cooperative Project with Teacher's Notes
- Independent Extra Credit Project with Teacher's Notes
- Cumulative Practice
- Resource Book Answers

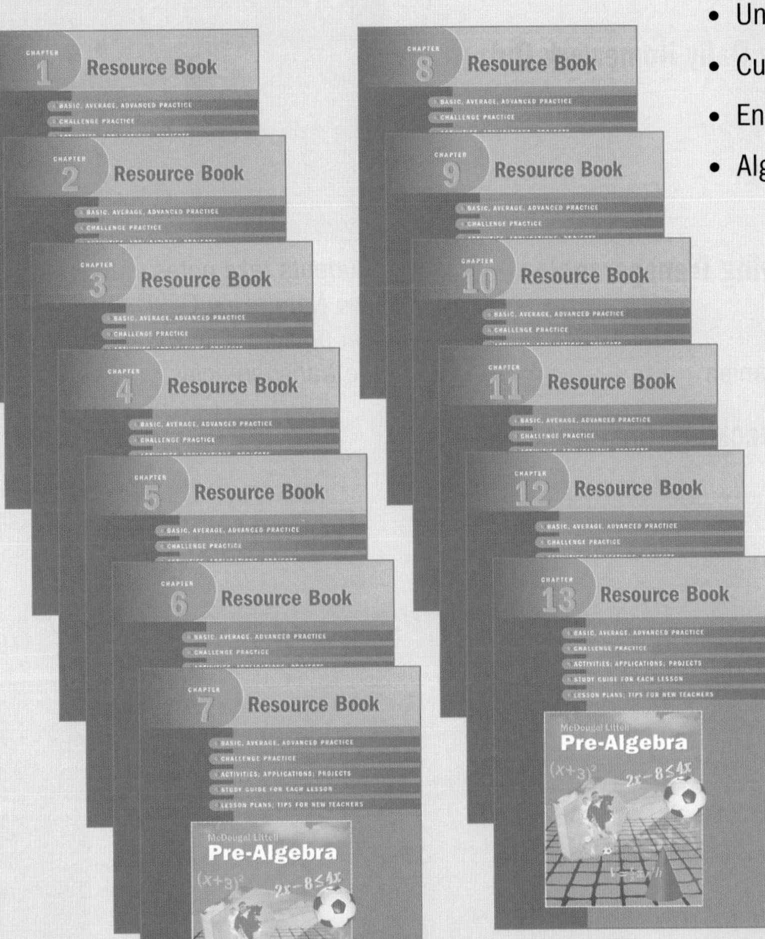

Assessment Book

- Diagnostic Pre-Course Test
- Quizzes
- Chapter Tests (Levels A, B, and C)
- Standardized Tests
- Alternative Assessment with Math Journal and Rubric
- Unit Tests
- Cumulative Tests
- End-of-Course Test
- Algebra Readiness Test

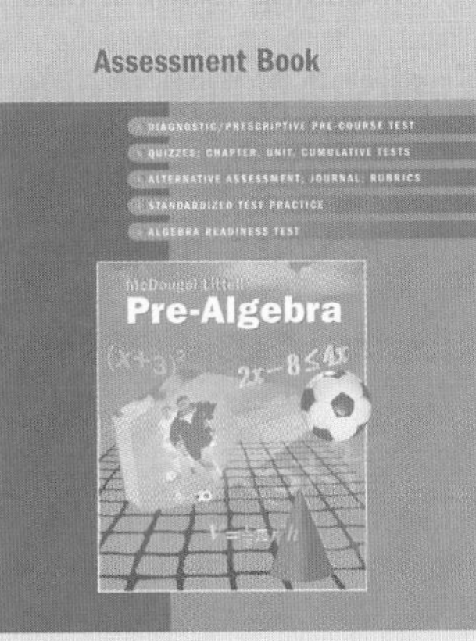

Transparency Packages

The transparency packages give you many easy-to-use options for reviewing homework, starting class, and teaching notetaking and problem solving strategies.

Notetaking Guide Transparencies

- Promote notetaking skills
- Reinforce key concepts

Warm-Up Transparencies with Daily Homework Quiz

- Warm-Up Exercises
- Daily Homework Quizzes
- Teaching Tool Transparencies

English-Spanish Problem Solving Transparencies

- Worked-Out Problems
- Presented in English and Spanish

Answer Transparencies for Checking Homework

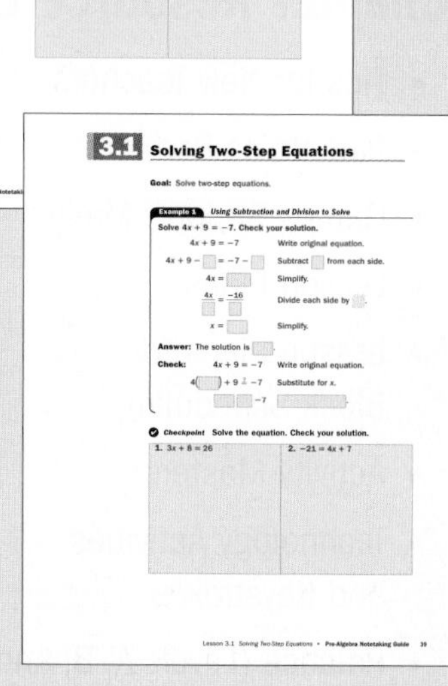

Students take notes in their own Notetaking Guide as you present a lesson using the transparencies.

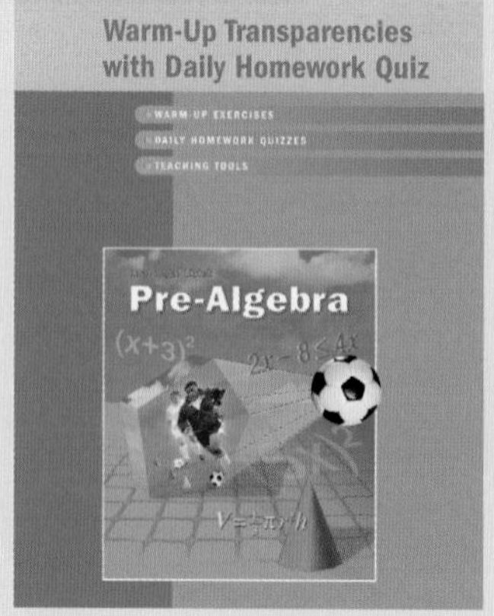

Teacher Survival Kit

This kit provides professional development ideas, helpful activities, and materials to enhance your classroom environment.

Teacher Survival Kit includes:

- Professional Development Book
- Special Activities Book
- Posters

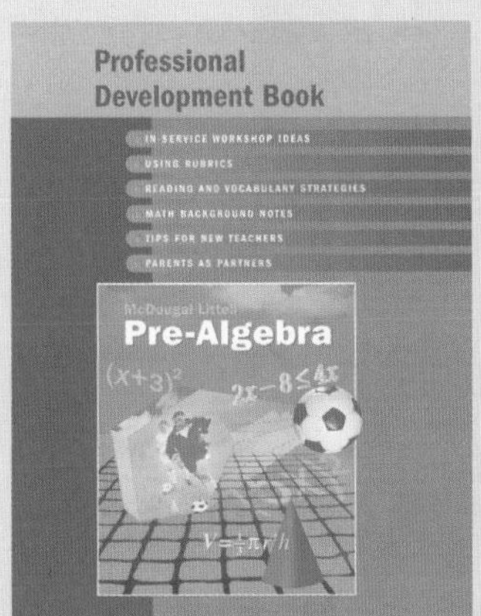

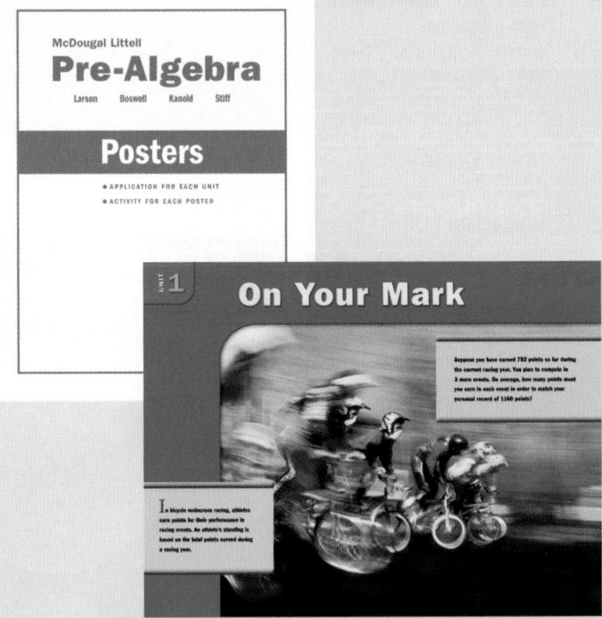

Math Tutor Place

Math Tutor Place helps students practice and master essential math topics. The instruction and practice are provided by 104 cards divided into five main categories:

- Whole Numbers and Decimals
- Fractions
- Ratio, Proportion, and Percent
- Geometry and Measurement
- Algebra

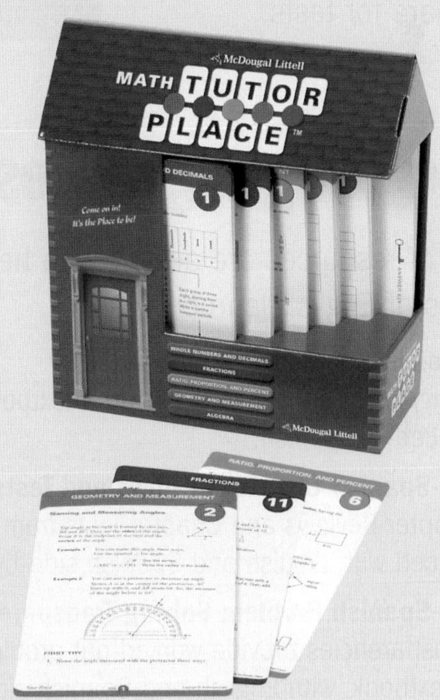

Manipulative Kits

The Student Manipulative Kit contains rulers, protractors, compasses, and algebra tiles. The Teacher's Overhead Manipulative Kit gives you tools to demonstrate key concepts.

Notetaking Guide

This workbook promotes notetaking skills and helps build understanding by providing students with a framework for recording the key concepts of every lesson. This workbook is also useful in helping students review and prepare for tests.

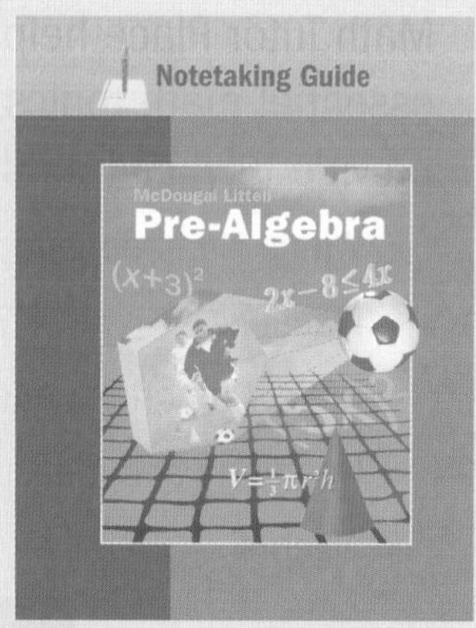

Practice Workbook

The Practice Workbook includes practice exercises for every lesson.

World Languages Resources

A variety of resources are available to help you address the needs of English learners.

Exercises in Spanish
The exercises in each lesson from the textbook are reproduced in Spanish.

English-Spanish Chapter Reviews and Tests
The Chapter Reviews and Chapter Tests from the textbook are reproduced with English and Spanish side-by-side.

English-Spanish Problem Solving Transparencies
The transparencies provide worked-out problems, correlated to the textbook, with English and Spanish side-by-side.

Spanish Study Guide
The Study Guide pages and Parents as Partners pages from the Chapter Resource Books are reproduced in Spanish.

Multi-Language Visual Glossary
A visual math glossary is translated into 9 languages.

Chapter Audio Summaries CDs
Available in English, Spanish, and Haitian Creole.

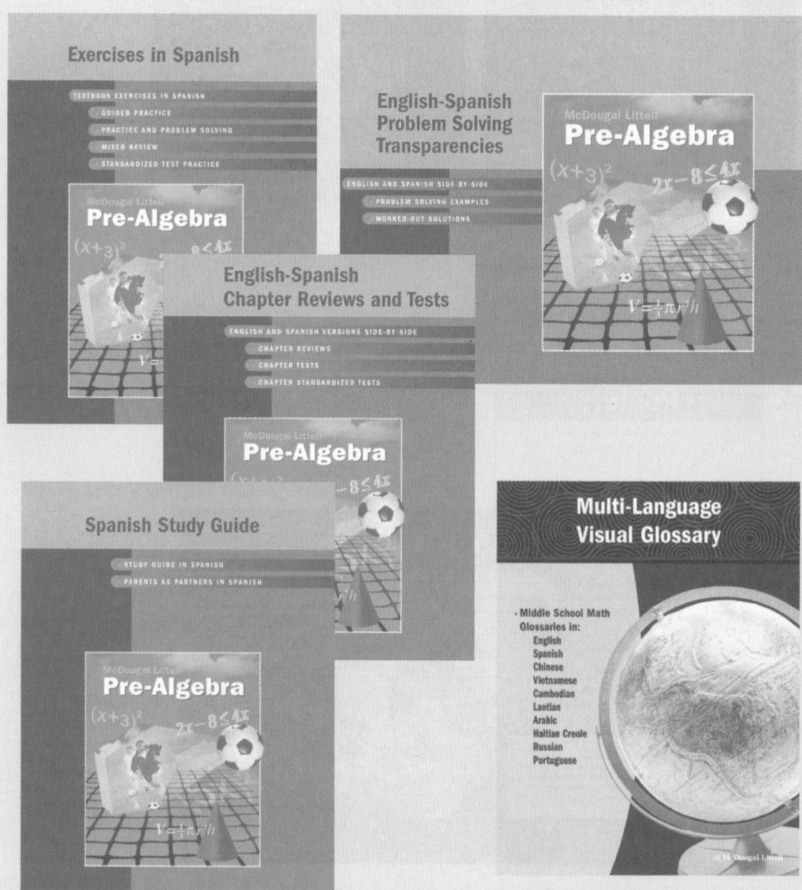

Technology Resources

McDougal Littell offers resources online and on CD-ROM to enhance lessons and help students build understanding.

Online Resources:

Online resources at www.classzone.com are linked together and provide instruction, practice, and learning support.

- **eEdition Plus Online** This electronic version of the book is enhanced by interactive extensions that allow students to explore concepts and self-assessment questions that check understanding. Reports on individual student performance help you track student progress.
- **eWorkbook Plus Online** This interactive software presents students with algorithmically generated problems correlated directly to the lessons and tracks their performance for your review. The problems can be accessed straight from the eEdition or directly from the Web site.
- **eTutorial Plus Online** An interactive program provides students additional material and reinforces key skills. The tutorial can be accessed straight from the eEdition or directly from the Web site.
- **Chapter-Based Support** State test practice, vocabulary support, self-quizzes, and other engaging student activities are provided online.
- **EasyPlanner Plus Online** This planner provides you access to all materials that come along with the program. It allows you to organize them into lesson plans and provides correlations to your state standards.

Other CD-Rom Resources include:

- **Chapter Audio Summaries CDs** These CDs summarize the key concepts of each chapter in English, Spanish, and Haitian Creole.
- **eEdition CD-ROM**
- **eTutorial CD-ROM**
- **EasyPlanner CD-ROM**
- **Power Presentations CD-ROM** PowerPoint™ slides help you walk through key concepts in a stepped out lesson presentation.
- **Test and Practice Generator** The power of the Internet and the computer lab are available to you with this new generation of software.

eEdition Plus Online

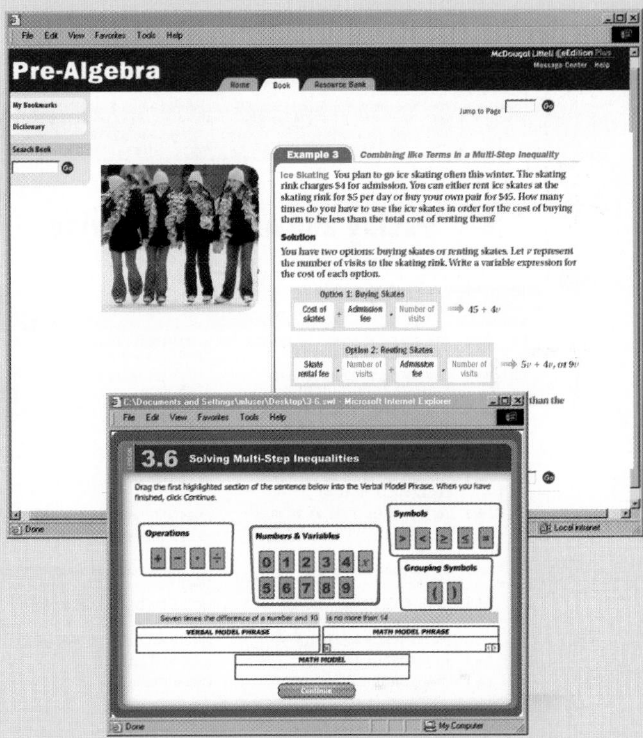

eTutorial Plus Online

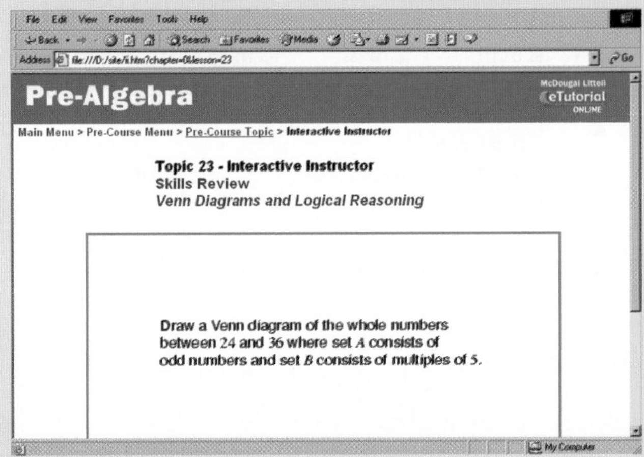

Planning the Chapter

- Regular and Block schedules for pacing the course

- A handy guide for integrating resource materials into your lessons

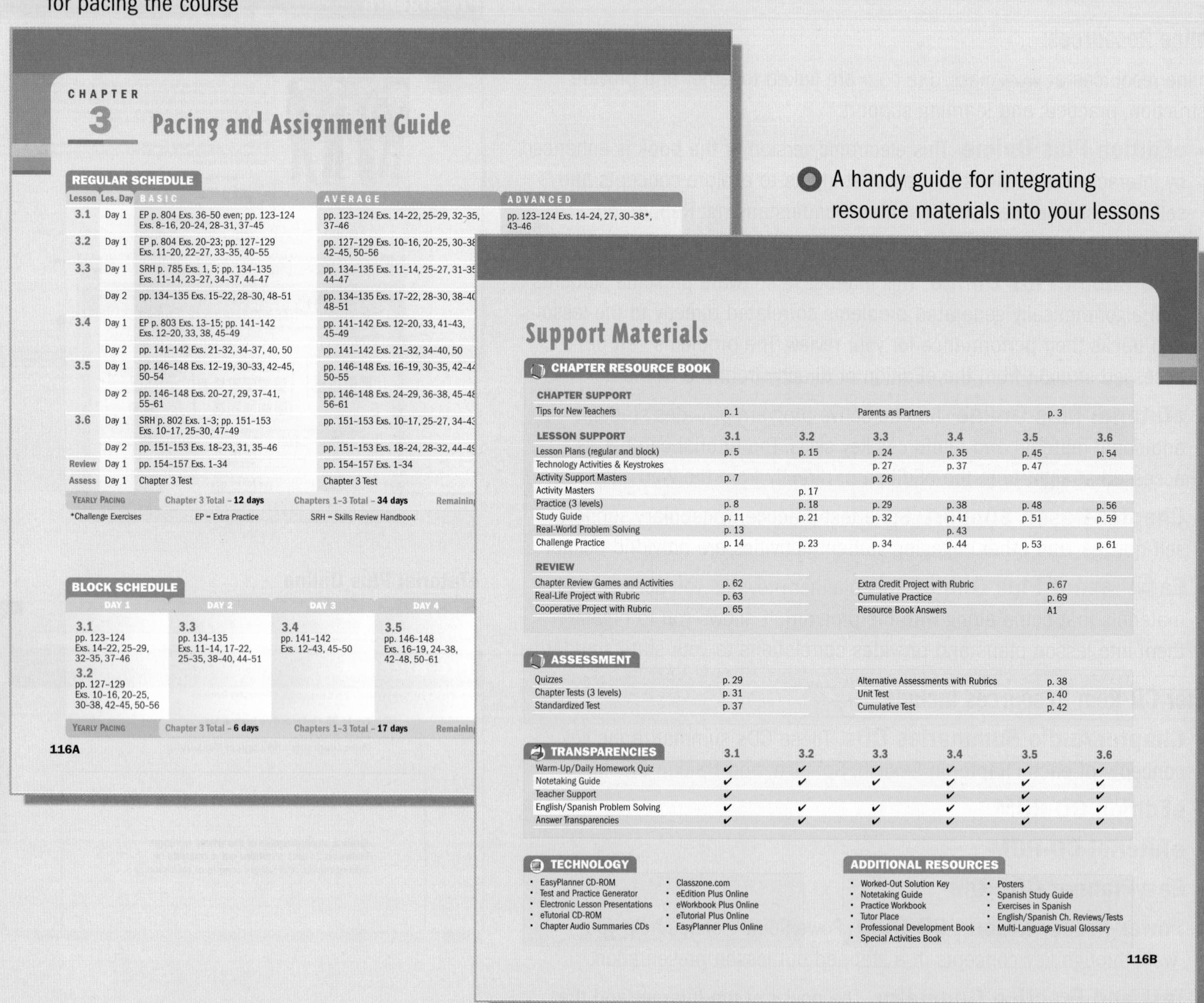

CHAPTER 3

Pacing and Assignment Guide

REGULAR SCHEDULE

Lesson	Les. Day	BASIC	AVERAGE	ADVANCED
3.1	Day 1	EP p. 804 Exs. 36-50 even; pp. 123-124 Exs. 8-16, 20-24, 28-31, 37-45	pp. 123-124 Exs. 14-22, 25-29, 32-35, 37-46	pp. 123-124 Exs. 14-24, 27, 30-38*, 43-46
3.2	Day 1	EP p. 804 Exs. 20-23; pp. 127-129 Exs. 11-20, 22-27, 33-35, 40-55	pp. 127-129 Exs. 10-16, 20-25, 30-38 42-45, 50-56	
3.3	Day 1	SRH p. 785 Exs. 1, 5; pp. 134-135 Exs. 11-14, 23-27, 34-37, 44-47	pp. 134-135 Exs. 11-14, 25-27, 31-35 44-47	
	Day 2	pp. 134-135 Exs. 15-22, 28-30, 48-51	pp. 134-135 Exs. 17-22, 28-30, 38-40 48-51	
3.4	Day 1	EP p. 803 Exs. 13-15; pp. 141-142 Exs. 12-20, 33, 38, 45-49	pp. 141-142 Exs. 12-20, 33, 41-43, 45-49	
	Day 2	pp. 141-142 Exs. 21-32, 34-37, 40, 50	pp. 141-142 Exs. 21-32, 34-40, 50	
3.5	Day 1	pp. 146-148 Exs. 12-19, 30-33, 42-45, 50-54	pp. 146-148 Exs. 16-19, 30-35, 42-44 50-55	
	Day 2	pp. 146-148 Exs. 20-27, 29, 37-41, 55-61	pp. 146-148 Exs. 24-29, 36-38, 45-48 56-61	
3.6	Day 1	SRH p. 802 Exs. 1-3; pp. 151-153 Exs. 10-17, 25-30, 47-49	pp. 151-153 Exs. 10-17, 25-27, 34-43	
	Day 2	pp. 151-153 Exs. 18-23, 31, 35-46	pp. 151-153 Exs. 18-24, 28-32, 44-49	
Review	Day 1	pp. 154-157 Exs. 1-34	pp. 154-157 Exs. 1-34	
Assess	Day 1	Chapter 3 Test	Chapter 3 Test	
YEARLY PACING		Chapter 3 Total – **12 days**	Chapters 1-3 Total – **34 days**	Remaining

*Challenge Exercises EP = Extra Practice SRH = Skills Review Handbook

BLOCK SCHEDULE

DAY 1	DAY 2	DAY 3	DAY 4
3.1 pp. 123-124 Exs. 14-22, 25-29, 32-35, 37-46 **3.2** pp. 127-129 Exs. 10-16, 20-25, 30-38, 42-45, 50-56	**3.3** pp. 134-135 Exs. 11-14, 17-22, 25-35, 38-40, 44-51	**3.4** pp. 141-142 Exs. 12-43, 45-50	**3.5** pp. 146-148 Exs. 16-19, 24-38, 42-48, 50-61

YEARLY PACING	Chapter 3 Total – **6 days**	Chapters 1-3 Total – **17 days**	Remaining

116A

Support Materials

CHAPTER RESOURCE BOOK

CHAPTER SUPPORT			
Tips for New Teachers	p. 1	Parents as Partners	p. 3

LESSON SUPPORT	3.1	3.2	3.3	3.4	3.5	3.6
Lesson Plans (regular and block)	p. 5	p. 15	p. 24	p. 35	p. 45	p. 54
Technology Activities & Keystrokes			p. 27	p. 37	p. 47	
Activity Support Masters	p. 7		p. 26			
Activity Masters		p. 17				
Practice (3 levels)	p. 8	p. 18	p. 29	p. 38	p. 48	p. 56
Study Guide	p. 11	p. 21	p. 32	p. 41	p. 51	p. 59
Real-World Problem Solving	p. 13			p. 43		
Challenge Practice	p. 14	p. 23	p. 34	p. 44	p. 53	p. 61

REVIEW			
Chapter Review Games and Activities	p. 62	Extra Credit Project with Rubric	p. 67
Real-Life Project with Rubric	p. 63	Cumulative Practice	p. 69
Cooperative Project with Rubric	p. 65	Resource Book Answers	A1

ASSESSMENT

Quizzes	p. 29	Alternative Assessments with Rubrics	p. 38
Chapter Tests (3 levels)	p. 31	Unit Test	p. 40
Standardized Test	p. 37	Cumulative Test	p. 42

TRANSPARENCIES	3.1	3.2	3.3	3.4	3.5	3.6
Warm-Up/Daily Homework Quiz	✔	✔	✔	✔	✔	✔
Notetaking Guide	✔	✔	✔	✔	✔	✔
Teacher Support	✔			✔	✔	✔
English/Spanish Problem Solving	✔	✔	✔	✔	✔	✔
Answer Transparencies	✔	✔	✔	✔	✔	✔

TECHNOLOGY

- EasyPlanner CD-ROM
- Test and Practice Generator
- Electronic Lesson Presentations
- eTutorial CD-ROM
- Chapter Audio Summaries CDs
- Classzone.com
- eEdition Plus Online
- eWorkbook Plus Online
- eTutorial Plus Online
- EasyPlanner Plus Online

ADDITIONAL RESOURCES

- Worked-Out Solution Key
- Notetaking Guide
- Practice Workbook
- Tutor Place
- Professional Development Book
- Special Activities Book
- Posters
- Spanish Study Guide
- Exercises in Spanish
- English/Spanish Ch. Reviews/Tests
- Multi-Language Visual Glossary

116B

Complete planning support preceding each chapter

Math background and teaching strategies provide suggestions to help you present each lesson and to increase student understanding

CHAPTER 3 **Math Background and Teaching Strategies**

Lesson 3.1

MATH BACKGROUND

As with one-step equations, the goal when solving two-step equations is to isolate the variable on one side of the equation. The method remains to undo what has been done to the variable by using inverse operations. For two-step equations, however, students will need to apply an appropriate property of equality twice during the solution process instead of just once.

TEACHING STRATEGIES

You may want to show students that it does not matter whether the addition/subtraction step is performed first or the multiplication/division step is performed first when solving a two-step equation. For example, the equation $3x - 6 = 9$ can be solved as shown below:

$3x - 6 = 9$

$\frac{3x}{3} - \frac{6}{3} = \frac{9}{3}$ Divide each term on both sides by 3.

$x - 2 = 3$ Simplify.

$x = 5$ Add 2 to each side.

Students must realize, though, that *both* terms on the left side of the original equation must be divided by 3. Also, point out that if the equation were $3x - 5 = 10$, which has the same solution, dividing both sides by 3 first would create fractions that would then have to be added, making the calculations more difficult than if 5 were added to each side before dividing by 3. With these examples, students should see that their first goal in solving a two-step equation should be to isolate the variable term on one side of the equation. Then they can isolate the variable in the next step.

Lesson 3.2

MATH BACKGROUND

Until this lesson, solving one- and two-step equations has involved using the properties of equality to perform the same operation on each side of an equation. Students now encounter equations that first need simplification on one side. To do this, they need to use the distributive property, either explicitly, as when simplifying the product of a number and an expression in parentheses, or implicitly, as when combining like terms, or both.

TEACHING STRATEGIES

Work the following additional example with students. Point out to students that as they solve more complicated equations, they are not doing anything new, but are just applying properties they already know: the properties of addition, the associative property, the commutative property, and the distrib

$8w - 3(-4 +$

$8w + 12 -$

$2w +$

$2w + 12 -$

Lesson 3.

MATH BACKGR

VARIABLES O

equation have

remains to isol

so that it conta

the additive in

subtraction pr

from one side

term on the si

variable term i

or divide each

the next step.

TEACHING STR

Have students

both sides usi

Make sure stu

process they h

1-tiles from ea

Strategies for enabling all students to learn mathematics

CHAPTER 3 **Differentiating Instruction**

Strategies for Underachievers

USE MODELS

MANIPULATIVES Concept Activities 3.1 and 3.3, which use algebra tiles to solve equations, will be especially helpful to underachievers. Provide each student her or his own set of algebra tiles. In Concept Activity 3.3, make sure students recognize that they are using the same process with x-tiles that they used with 1-tiles in Concept Activity 3.1. Students should have access to algebra tiles for as long as the tiles are helpful to them. You may need to guide students' work with the tiles so they do not become confused by trying to solve equations that are not easily modeled with algebra tiles.

IDENTIFY KEY TERMS

WORD PROBLEMS In this chapter, students will be faced with many word problems that require them to write equations or inequalities to represent different situations. Students may benefit from returning to the list of words and expressions indicating mathematical operations that was mentioned in the "Strategies for Underachievers" notes preceding Chapter 2. Encourage students to add any new words or expressions that they encounter to their lists. For example, as they begin solving inequalities in Lesson 3.4, students should identify words or phrases that indicate order relations and add them to their lists. You may want to encourage students to write the words/phrases from their lists on index cards for quick reference.

DEVELOP PROBLEM SOLVING MODELS

The methods for solving increasingly complex linear equations in Lessons 3.1–3.3 proceed in discrete steps, building on the methods for solving one-step equations in Chapter 2. This step-by-step process is then repeated for solving linear inequalities in Lessons 3.4–3.6. Encourage students to create posters or notebook entries that detail each new step in increasing complexity, beginning with solving one-step equations. In Lesson 3.2, students might need some guidance in realizing that the basic step presented is to simplify one side of the equation (by combining like terms, using the distributive property, and so on) before using the properties of equality. For each step, students should give examples and give the order of the steps that they need to carry out. Help students see how the same basic equation-solving strategy applies at each level of complexity even though additional steps may be added.

USE CALCULATORS

As they encounter more difficult equations, especially those involving decimals or greater coefficients and constants, some students may benefit from the use of calculators so that their focus remains on the equation-solving process rather than on computational skills. Students should still be required to show each step used in the process.

USE SCAFFOLDING

You may wish to provide students with templates similar to the one below to guide their work as they solve equations.

$-2(x + 5) + 6x = 30$	
___ + ___ + $6x$ = 30	Distributive property
___x _ ___ = 30	Combine like terms.
___x ______ = ______	+/− property of equality
___x = ___	Simplify.
___ = ___	×/÷ property of equality
x = ___	Simplify.

Alternatively, you may want to provide students with several model problems for which you have shown all the necessary steps. Students can then use these models to guide them when working problems on their own.

USE REPETITION

REVERSING INEQUALITIES Plan on repeating Concept Activity 3.5 on page 143 with several additional examples in order to help underachievers become comfortable solving inequalities using multiplication or division. The concept of multiplying or dividing an inequality by a negative number is confusing for many underachievers. Take extra time here to answer any student questions about when and why the direction of the inequality is reversed.

Planning the Lesson

1 PLAN

Skill Check

1. $4 \cdot (-4) = \underline{?}$ −16
2. $25 \div (-5) = \underline{?}$ −5
3. $-7 \cdot (-8) = \underline{?}$ 56
4. $-22 \div (-4) = \underline{?}$ 5.5

LESSON OBJECTIVE

Solve inequalities using multiplication or division.

PACING

Suggested Number of Days
Basic Course: 2 days
Average Course: 2 days
Advanced Course: 2 days
Block: 1 block

TEACHING RESOURCES

For a complete list of Teaching Resources, see page 116B.

TRANSPARENCY

Warm-Up Exercises for this lesson are available on a transparency. A support transparency is available for Checkpoint Exercises 1–4.

2 TEACH

MOTIVATING THE LESSON

Share information about other migratory birds with students.

TIPS *for* NEW TEACHERS

Point out that solving inequalities is the same as solving equations except that sometimes you must reverse the inequality symbol. Stress that the symbol is reversed whenever each side is multiplied or divided by a negative number. See Tips for New Teachers in the *Chapter 3 Resource Book.*

144

LESSON 3.5

Solving Inequalities Using Multiplication *or* Division

BEFORE: You solved two-step equations.
Now: You'll solve inequalities using multiplication or division.
WHY?: So you can find how fast you should bike, as in Ex. 38.

Review Vocabulary
inequality, p. 138
equivalent inequalities, p. 139

Geese Migration Some flocks of Canada geese can fly nonstop for up to 16 hours. In this time, a flock can migrate as far as 848 miles. At what average speeds can such a flock fly during migration? In Example 3, you will see how to answer this question by solving an inequality.

As shown below, when each side of the inequality $2 < 8$ is multiplied by a positive number, the inequality remains true. When each side is multiplied by a negative number, the inequality sign must be reversed.

$2 < 8$ $2 < 8$

$4 \cdot 2 \overset{?}{<} 4 \cdot 8$ $-4 \cdot 2$

$8 < 32$ -8

These examples suggest the followin

Multiplication Property o

Words Multiplying each side of a number produces an equivalent

Multiplying each side of an ineq *reversing the direction of the ineq* equivalent inequality.

Algebra If $a < b$ and $c > 0$, then a

If $a < b$ and $c < 0$, then a

Example 1 *Solving an Ineq*

$\frac{m}{-3} > 3$ Original ineq

$-3 \cdot \frac{m}{-3} < -3 \cdot 3$ Multiply eac Reverse ine

$m < -9$ Simplify.

TEACH

- A Motivating the Lesson note at the beginning of each lesson
- Extra Example for each example in the book
- Concept Check question at the end of each lesson
- Teaching Tips, Common Error notes ... AND MORE

Division The rules for solving an inequality using division are like the rules for solving an inequality using multiplication.

Study *Strategy*

The multiplication and division properties of inequality are also true for inequalities involving $>$, $\le$, and $\ge$.

Division Property of Inequality

Words Dividing each side of an inequality by a *positive* number produces an equivalent inequality.

Dividing each side of an inequality by a *negative* number and *reversing the direction of the inequality symbol* produces an equivalent inequality.

Algebra If $a < b$ and $c > 0$, then $\frac{a}{c} < \frac{b}{c}$.

If $a < b$ and $c < 0$, then $\frac{a}{c} > \frac{b}{c}$.

Example 2 *Solving an Inequality Using Division*

$-10t \ge 34$ Original inequality

$\frac{-10t}{-10} \le \frac{34}{-10}$ Divide each side by −10. Reverse inequality symbol.

$t \le -3.4$ Simplify.

Checkpoint

Solve the inequality. Graph your solution. 1–4. See margin for art.

1. $\frac{n}{6} > 7$ $n > 42$
2. $\frac{t}{-4} \le 8$ $t \ge -32$
3. $2x > -8$ $x > -4$
4. $-7s \le 14$ $s \ge -2$

In the **Real World**

Geese Migration In North America, not all Canada geese migrate. About 3.6 million "resident" geese live in urban and suburban areas, such as parks, throughout the year. Resident Canada geese outnumber migrating Canada geese. Write an inequality that compares the numbers of migrating geese and resident geese. $m < 3.6$ million

Example 3 *Writing and Solving an Inequality*

Find the average speeds at which the flock of Canada geese described on page 144 can fly during migration.

Solution

Let s represent the average flight speeds. Write a verbal model.

Flight time · Average flight speeds ≤ Maximum flight distance

$16s \le 848$ Substitute.

$\frac{16s}{16} \le \frac{848}{16}$ Divide each side by 16.

$s \le 53$ Simplify.

Answer The flock of Canada geese can fly at average speeds of 53 miles per hour or less during migration.

Extra Examples

Example 1 Solve $\frac{k}{-8} \ge -5$. $k \le 40$

Example 2 Solve $-18y < 72$. $y > -4$

Example 3 On average, a customer service representative helps at most 160 customers during an 8-hour workday. Write and solve an inequality to find the average number of customers c she can help each hour during one of her workdays. $8c \le 160$, $c \le 20$; she can help 20 customers or less each hour.

NOTETAKING

Have students record the multiplication and division properties of inequality using either words or algebra. Then have them record a few examples. Urge students to highlight steps they found confusing and to write a note about how they came to understand these steps.

COMMON ERROR

Expect some students to occasionally forget to reverse the inequality symbol when they multiply or divide an inequality by a negative number.

CONCEPT CHECK

When does the inequality symbol need to be reversed when solving an inequality? whenever each side of the inequality is multiplied or divided by a negative number

DAILY PUZZLER

If $a < b$, which is greater, $\frac{a}{b}$ or $\frac{-b}{-a}$? $\frac{-b}{-a}$

1–4. See Additional Answers beginning on page AA1.

145

PLAN

- Skill Check
- Lesson Objective
- Pacing summary
- Teaching Resources
- Transparency support

Convenient, point-of-use support for each lesson

3 APPLY

ASSIGNMENT GUIDE

Basic Course
Day 1: pp. 146-148 Exs. 12-19, 30-33, 42-45, 50-54
Day 2: pp. 146-148 Exs. 20-27, 29, 37-41, 55-61

Average Course
Day 1: pp. 146-148 Exs. 16-19, 30-35, 42-44, 50-55
Day 2: pp. 146-148 Exs. 24-29, 36-38, 45-48, 56-61

Advanced Course
Day 1: pp. 146-148 Exs. 16-19, 32-35, 42-46, 54-58
Day 2: pp. 146-148 Exs. 24-29, 36-38, 47-51*, 59-61

Block
pp. 146-148 Exs. 16-19, 24-38, 42-48, 50-61

EXTRA PRACTICE
- Student Edition, p. 805
- Chapter 3 Resource Book, pp. 48-50
- Test and Practice Generator

TRANSPARENCY
Even-numbered answers are available on transparencies. A support transparency is available for Exercises 3-10, 12-27, 39-44, and 55-58.

HOMEWORK CHECK
When you review students' homework for this lesson, go over the following exercises to check understanding of key concepts.
Basic: 12, 14, 22, 26, 29
Average: 17, 19, 24, 27, 29
Advanced: 17, 19, 25, 27, 37

3.5 Exercises

More Practice, p. 805

INTERNET eWorkbook Plus CLASSZONE.COM

Guided Practice

Vocabulary Check
1. Which property would you use to solve the inequality $-7y \le 49$? division property of inequality
2. Explain how solving $2x > -14$ is different from solving $-2x > 14$. See margin.

Skill Check **Solve the inequality. Graph and check your solution.** 3–10. See margin for art.

3. $\frac{v}{-2} < -8$ $v > 16$ 4. $8b > 32$ $b > 4$ 5. $\frac{u}{6} \ge 3$ $u \ge 18$ 6. $-6s \le 54$ $s \ge -9$
7. $5a < -35$ $a < -7$ 8. $\frac{p}{7} > 6$ $p > 42$ 9. $3r \ge 21$ $r \ge 7$ 10. $\frac{t}{4} \le -9$ $t \le -36$

Guided Problem Solving
11. Training While training for a marathon, you try to consume at least 2400 Calories each day. For one meal, you like to eat at least 500 Calories. You choose to eat pasta that has 200 Calories per cup. How many cups of pasta should you eat?
   1) Let c represent the number of cups of pasta. Write an inequality based on the verbal model given below. $200 \cdot c \ge 500$
   Calories per cup • Nu...
   2) Solve the inequality. c ...
   3) Explain what the soluti... *Sample answer:* You must e... get the desired number of c...

2. *Sample answer:* In $2x > -14$, you divide each side by 2, which is positive, so the direction of the inequality symbol does not change, but in $-2x > 14$, you divide each side by -2, which is negative, so you must reverse the direction of the inequality symbol.

Practice and Problem Solving

Homework Help

Example	Exercises
1	12-27
2	12-27
3	29, 36-38

Online Resources CLASSZONE.COM
- More Examples
- eTutorial Plus

Solve the inequality. Graph your...

A 12. $\frac{a}{2} < -9$ $a < -18$ 13. $\frac{b}{7} > 7$ b...
16. $5z < 65$ $z < 13$ 17. $\frac{d}{-11} \le 6$ $d \ge -66$
20. $\frac{t}{9} < -12$ $t < -108$ 21. $\frac{h}{-6} \le 13$ $h \ge -78$
24. $-7s \ge -84$ $s \le 12$ 25. $4m < -6...$ $m < -1...$
28. **Error Analysis** Describe a... correct the error in solving... the inequality $9x > -45$.
Since each side was divided by... positive, the direction of the ine... symbol should not have been re... second statement. It should be ... followed by $x > -5$.

APPLY

- Assignment Guide
- Extra Practice references
- Transparency support
- Homework Check exercises

ASSESS AND FOLLOW-UP

- Assessment Resources
- Mini-Quiz for each lesson
- Diagnosis/Remediation
- English Learner Support
- Challenge

4 ASSESS

ASSESSMENT RESOURCES
For more assessment resources, see:
- Assessment Book
- Test and Practice Generator

MINI-QUIZ
Solve. Graph your solution.
1. $14m \ge -56$ $m \ge -4$
2. $\frac{a}{-3} < 9$ $a > -27$
3. Write the following verbal sentence as an inequality. Then solve the inequality.
Six times a number is no more than −96. $6x \le -96$; $x \le -16$
4. **Challenge** Megan is ordering tacos for her office staff. They cost \$2.25 each, including tax, and there is a \$6 delivery charge. How many tacos can she buy if she has \$42? at most 16 tacos

5 FOLLOW-UP

DIAGNOSIS/REMEDIATION
- Study Guide in Chapter 3 Resource Book, pp. 51-52
- Tutor Place, Algebra Cards 14-16
- eTutorial Plus Online
- Extra Practice, p. 805
- Lesson Practice in Chapter 3 Resource Book, pp. 48-50

ENGLISH LEARNER SUPPORT
- Spanish Study Guide
- Multi-Language Visual Glossary
- Chapter Audio Summaries CDs

CHALLENGE
- Challenge Practice in Chapter 3 Resource Book, p. 53
- Teacher's Edition, p. 116F

55–58. See Additional Answers beginning on page AA1.

C 48. **Critical Thinking** The inequalities $2x < 3$ and $4x < 6$ are equivalent inequalities. Write a third inequality equivalent to $2x < 3$ and $4x < 6$. *Sample answer:* $10x < 15$

49. **Challenge** An underwater camera can withstand pressures up to 1500 pounds per square inch. The formula $P = 14.7 + 0.45d$ can be used to find the water pressure P (in pounds per square inch) at depth d (in feet) underwater. Find the depths at which the camera can be used. at or above $3300\frac{2}{3}$ ft, or 3300 ft 8 in.

Mixed Review Algebra Basics **Solve the equation. Check your solution.** *(Lesson 2.7)*

50. $x + 3.5 = 9.2$ 5.7 51. $x - 6.7 = 5.8$ 12.5 52. $44.72 = 5.2x$ 8.6 53. $\frac{x}{7.6} = 9.5$ 72.2

54. Find the perimeter of the square. *(Lesson 3.3)* 40 units

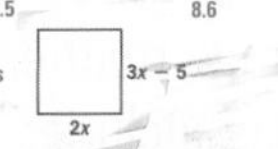

Solve the inequality. Graph your solution. *(Lesson 3.4)* 55–58. See margin for art.

55. $x + 12 > 96$ $x > 84$ 56. $x + 17 \ge 44$ $x \ge 27$ 57. $x - 26 \le 33$ $x \le 59$ 58. $x - 14 < 29$ $x < 43$

Standardized Test Practice

59. **Multiple Choice** Which number is *not* a solution of $\frac{t}{-9} \ge 3$? D
   A. −35 B. −30 C. −27 D. −25
60. **Multiple Choice** Which number is a solution of $\frac{x}{-7} < 6$? I
   F. −100 G. −56 H. −42 I. −14
61. **Multiple Choice** Which inequality is equivalent to $-18 \le 3p$? C
   A. $p \ge -54$ B. $-54 \ge p$ C. $p \ge -6$ D. $-6 \ge p$

Brain GAME — *Youngest to Oldest*

Use the given information to list the six cousins in order from least to greatest age and give their ages. No two cousins are the same age.

Erika is 4 years old.
Charlie's age is greater than 4 times Dawn's age.
All the girls' ages are greater than Anthony's age.
All the cousins' ages are less than or equal to 13.
Matthew is older than exactly three cousins.
Stephanie is 6 years older than Erika.
All the cousins' ages are greater than or equal to 2.
Erika is 1 year older than Dawn.
One boy is 6 years old.

Anthony: 2 y, Dawn: 3 y, Erika: 4 y, Matthew: 6 y, Stephanie: 10 y, Charlie: 13 y

Pacing the Course

The Pacing Chart below shows the number of days allotted for each chapter. The Regular Schedule requires 160 days. The Block Schedule requires 80 days. These time frames include days for review and assessment: 2 days per chapter for the Regular Schedule and 1 day per chapter for the Block Schedule. Semester and trimester divisions are indicated by blue and green rules, respectively.

	Semester 1							Semester 2					
Chapter	**1**	**2**	**3**	**4**	**5**	**6**	**7**	**8**	**9**	**10**	**11**	**12**	**13**
Regular Schedule	10	12	12	10	14	12	10	14	14	12	14	14	12
Block Schedule	5	6	6	5	7	6	5	7	7	6	7	7	6
	Trimester 1					Trimester 2				Trimester 3			

Assignments are provided with each lesson for a basic course, an average course, an advanced course, and a block-schedule course. Each of the four courses covers all thirteen chapters.

Basic Course

The basic course is intended for students who enter with below-average mathematical and problem-solving skills. Assignments include:

- spiral review of pre-course and on-level topics through Skills Review Handbook and Extra Practice references
- substantial work with the skills and concepts presented in the lesson
- straightforward applications of these skills and concepts
- test preparation and mixed review exercises

Average Course

The average course is intended for students who enter with typical mathematical and problem-solving skills. Assignments include:

- substantial work with the skills and concepts presented in the lesson
- applications of these skills and concepts
- test preparation and mixed review exercises

Advanced Course

The advanced course is intended for students who enter with above-average mathematical and problem-solving skills. Assignments include:

- substantial work with the skills and concepts presented in the lesson
- more complex applications and challenge exercises
- test preparation and mixed review exercises
- optional extra challenge exercises provided in the Teacher's Edition and in the Chapter Resource Books

Block-Schedule Course

The block-schedule course is intended for schools that use a block schedule. It covers the same content as the regular-schedule course. The exercises assigned are comparable to the exercises for the average course.

Pacing and daily assignments for 4 courses

The Pacing and Assignment Guide for each chapter is located on the interleaved pages preceding the chapter. Part of the Pacing Chart for Chapter 3 is shown here.

Regular-Schedule Chart

This chart provides pacing for the basic, average, and advanced courses.

Lesson	Les. Day	BASIC	AVERAGE	ADVANCED
3.1	Day 1	EP p. 804 Exs. 36-50 even; pp. 123-124 Exs. 8-16, 20-24, 28-31, 37-45	pp. 123-124 Exs. 14-22, 25-29, 32-35, 37-46	pp. 123-124 Exs. 14-24, 27, 30-38*, 43-46
3.2	Day 1	EP p. 804 Exs. 20-23; pp. 127-129 Exs. 11-20, 22-27, 33-35, 40-55	pp. 127-129 Exs. 10-16, 20-25, 30-38, 42-45, 50-56	pp. 127-129 Exs. 10-13, 17-29, 32-39*, 44-47, 52-56
3.3	Day 1	SRH p. 785 Exs. 1, 5; pp. 134-135 Exs. 11-14, 23-27, 34-37, 44-47	pp. 134-135 Exs. 11-14, 25-27, 31-35, 44-47	pp. 134-135 Exs. 11-14, 25-27, 31-33, 39-45*
	Day 2	pp. 134-135 Exs. 15-22, 28-30, 48-51	pp. 134-135 Exs. 17-22, 28-30, 38-40, 48-51	pp. 134-135 Exs. 17-22, 28-30, 36-38, 46-51

YEARLY PACING — Chapter 3 Total – **12 days** — Chapters 1–3 Total – **34 days** — Remaining – **126 days**

*Challenge Exercises EP = Extra Practice SRH = Skills Review Handbook

Block-Schedule Chart

This chart provides pacing for the block-schedule course.

DAY 1	DAY 2	DAY 3	DAY 4	DAY 5	DAY 6
3.1 pp. 123-124 Exs. 14-22, 25-29, 32-35, 37-46 **3.2** pp. 127-129 Exs. 10-16, 20-25, 30-38, 42-45, 50-56	**3.3** pp. 134-135 Exs. 11-14, 17-22, 25-35, 38-40, 44-51	**3.4** pp. 141-142 Exs. 12-43, 45-50	**3.5** pp. 146-148 Exs. 16-19, 24-38, 42-48, 50-61	**3.6** pp. 151-153 Exs. 10-15, 18-32, 34-49	**Review** pp. 154-157 Exs. 1-34 **Assess** Chapter 3 Test

YEARLY PACING — Chapter 3 Total – **6 days** — Chapters 1–3 Total – **17 days** — Remaining – **63 days**

Assignment Guide

An assignment guide for each lesson is provided at the beginning of the exercise set. Assignments are given for basic, average, advanced, and block-schedule courses.

ASSIGNMENT GUIDE

Basic Course
Day 1: EP p. 804 Exs. 36-50 even; pp. 123-124 Exs. 8-16, 20-24, 28-31, 37-45

Average Course
Day 1: pp. 123-124 Exs. 14-22, 25-29, 32-35, 37-46

Advanced Course
Day 1: pp. 123-124 Exs. 14-24, 27, 30-38*, 43-46

Block Schedule
pp. 123-124 Exs. 14-22, 25-29, 32-35, 37-46

Professional Articles

Meeting your planning and teaching needs

The following pages include information about the *Pre-Algebra* program and explain how it reflects current research in mathematics instruction.

Letter from the Authors

Dear Colleagues,

While writing this Pre-Algebra book, we kept two goals in mind. First, we wanted to help your students learn the concepts and skills they need to be successful in mathematics. Second, we wanted to make your work easier by providing a comprehensive selection of teaching resources.

With these goals in mind, we reviewed many state curriculum and assessment guidelines, as well as those of the National Council of Teachers of Mathematics. This will ensure that students have the opportunity to learn the mathematics required to succeed in this course and on important assessments. We also used our extensive teaching experience to plan the course so that students are well prepared for succeeding courses.

Our philosophy is to write books that are mathematically correct, student friendly, and pedagogically sound. Our books also reflect the valuable input from the many teachers and students nationwide who have used earlier editions or pilot materials in the classroom. We believe that a balance of teaching approaches is effective. Thus, we offer clear, straightforward instruction in concepts and skills, combined with engaging student activities, motivating real-world applications, and useful problem solving and communication strategies.

As an author team that has written together for more than 14 years, we are committed to setting high mathematics standards for all students. We are committed to creating textbooks that have the support that students need, whether this is differentiated instruction for underachieving students, helpful study tips and worthwhile practice for most students, or thoughtful challenges for advanced students and other interested students.

We wish you the best in your pursuit of a quality mathematics education for every student in your classroom.

Laurie Boswell

Ron Larson

Lee Stiff

Tim Kanold

A Program *you can* trust

The right math, presented in the right way

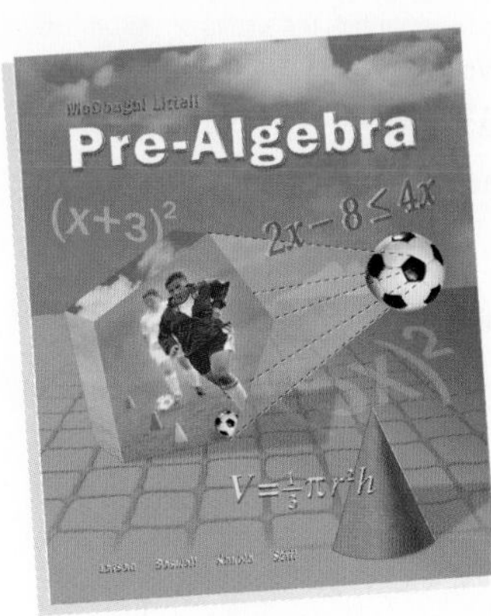

McDougal Littell Pre-Algebra is a program you can count on to teach the mathematical concepts and methods that your students need to know in order to meet high curriculum standards and succeed on high-stakes tests. Including the appropriate content, however, is not enough. The math must be presented in a way that students can understand and that will motivate them to learn. The distinguished author team of *McDougal Littell Pre-Algebra* and the thorough, research-based planning and development process ensure that this program both includes the right math and teaches the math in the right way, so that students gain conceptual understanding and achieve success on important assessments.

DISTINGUISHED AUTHOR TEAM

The experienced, expert author team of Ron Larson, Laurie Boswell, Timothy Kanold, and Lee Stiff brings a wealth of mathematical expertise, writing talent, and classroom teaching and curriculum planning experience from middle school through college to the creation of this program. Lead author Ron Larson has been writing highly-respected and widely-used textbooks for more than 20 years, and each new book benefits from the comments of the many teachers and students who used earlier editions.

STANDARDS-BASED INSTRUCTION AND ASSESSMENT

State and National Standards In planning the outlines and writing the textbook, the authors paid careful attention to state curriculum standards and state assessment objectives from all states to make sure that the important mathematical concepts and skills were included and given appropriate emphasis. The authors also made sure that the outline and course content fully addressed the standards of national organizations such as the National Council of Teachers of Mathematics (NCTM) and the National Assessment of Educational Progress (NAEP). A correlation to the NAEP objectives appears on page T62 and a correlation to the NCTM Standards can be found on page T63.

SUPPORTING BEST PRACTICES FROM RESEARCH

Educational and Cognitive Research Recent research studies have confirmed strategies for increasing student achievement. These strategies, which reflect the best practices of successful teachers, can help all students learn more effectively. The authors kept this research in mind as they planned and wrote *Pre-Algebra*, so that the content, organization, and instructional strategies in the program would make it easy for you to implement best-practice instruction in your classroom.

...validated by research

COMPREHENSIVE RESEARCH AND REVIEW

About three years prior to the publication of this book, the authors and teams of editors, consultants, graphic designers, professional researchers, and experts in content, instruction, and technology began gathering and analyzing the extensive data on which the plans for this program are based. Data were gathered in the following ways:

- **Classroom Visits** Discussions and classroom observations took place in schools throughout the country to determine the key needs of teachers and students, the obstacles that they face in achieving their goals, and the types of materials that can help them achieve success.

- **Nationwide Research Surveys** Comprehensive mail surveys on Pre-Algebra curriculum needs, instructional practices, student achievement levels, and teacher preferences regarding instructional materials were conducted early in the development process to guide the planning of the program.

- **Teacher Panels** Panels of expert teachers from different areas of the country participated in the development of the program by identifying instructional and curriculum needs, reviewing prototype outlines and sample materials for both print and electronic materials, and providing suggestions for teaching-support publications.

- **Student Discussion Groups** Discussion groups were held with Pre-Algebra students to determine the textbook characteristics that make it easy or hard for them to learn and the extent to which they have access to and feel comfortable using electronic products.

- **Focus Tests** Focus tests in which teachers discussed their instructional goals and evaluated sample student and teacher materials were held in different areas of the country. The teachers participating in the focus groups were chosen to represent the wide range of types of schools, philosophies of instruction, and teacher characteristics (like number of years of teaching) in the teaching population. The feedback from these diverse groups of teachers was used to revise and refine the project plans prior to writing.

- **Curriculum Advisers and Reviewers** The Curriculum Advisers and Reviewers listed on page T4 participated in planning the program and read all the proof for the student edition in detail with regard to clarity, accuracy, and appropriateness for classroom use. Other teacher reviewers read selected chapters for these characteristics.

- **Learner Verification** The *Middle School Math Research-Based Framework and Learner Verification* book provides information about the instructional research on which the program was based as well as classroom research demonstrating the effectiveness of the *Middle School Math* program.

The Bigger Picture of Mathematics

by Dr. Ron Larson,
Lead Author of the Larson Mathematics Series

Ron Larson

What is Mathematics? You would think that this is an easy question to answer. But, it isn't.

Was mathematics discovered or was it invented? Is mathematics a logical system that exists devoid of applications or is mathematics a problem solving language whose very essence is solving real-life problems? Is correct calculation an important part of mathematics or is it only important to be able to "set the problem up" correctly? Is mathematics a system of rules or is mathematics a way of thinking?

As mathematics teachers, it is important for us to realize that mathematics is all of these things. We need to be careful to pass this understanding on to our students so that they will not have a narrow answer to the question "What is Mathematics?" We need to show them the bigger picture of mathematics.

MATHEMATICS AS CALCULATION

Most people equate mathematics with calculation. While this view of mathematics is too limited, it is still true that calculation plays a critical role in mathematics.

I worry when I hear educators dismissing calculation as "something best left to calculators" or even worse, as "drill and kill." I prefer to think about other phrases that describe the importance of calculation, such as "practice makes perfect."

When I drive across a bridge, I am thankful that the teacher of the civil engineer who designed the bridge believed in the importance of correct calculation.

The point is that part of our job as mathematics teachers is to help prepare skilled professionals who can fly planes, prescribe medicines, and do any of thousands of other technically difficult jobs.

But, there may be a stronger reason for teaching students to calculate correctly. It is simply the way that students learn best. They learn specific examples first. Generalization comes later.

After a career in mathematics, it is clear to me that we derive important insights into a mathematical theory when we see how it relates to actual calculations.

...in our world

MATHEMATICS AS A FIELD OF STUDY

Mathematics, of course, is not simply a collection of techniques for calculating sums, products, slopes, and so on. Mathematics has content. It has a vocabulary of defined and undefined terms. It has a collection of axioms and theorems.

The vocabulary and rules of mathematics comprise much of the curriculum we teach from grade school through high school.

Like it or not, the vocabulary of mathematics is formal. It has to be in order to provide for clear communication. It is important that students know the difference between an expression and an equation. We *evaluate* an expression. We *solve* an equation.

The rules of mathematics are also formal—they are rigid and unforgiving. We don't do students favors when we allow them to approach mathematics in a sloppy manner. Mathematics must be approached carefully, with the confidence that comes from knowing its rules.

MATHEMATICS AS A MODELING LANGUAGE

It is difficult to know which of the many faces of mathematics was the first to show itself on our planet. Surely, one of the first was the use of symbols and calculations to model and solve real-life problems.

To me, the perennial debate about the virtues of applied versus pure mathematics isn't productive. From a historical point of view, it seems clear that both must be taught—hand-in-hand—from grade school through high school.

To be good at mathematics, students must understand the various types of models we use: linear, quadratic, cubic, radical, rational, exponential, logarithmic, and trigonometric. They must learn to translate real-life situations to mathematical models, obtain mathematical solutions, and then translate those solutions back into the context of the real-life application.

MATHEMATICS AS LOGICAL THOUGHT

Perhaps the most difficult task we face as mathematics teachers is to teach our students to think logically.

The real world is filled with logical fallacy —such as some advertisements and political slogans that contain illogical arguments. As mathematics teachers, we can improve our nation and our world by teaching careful logical thought to our students.

In light of all these things, I hope that this text helps your students get a view of the bigger picture of mathematics.

The Bigger Picture in *Pre-Algebra*

The following chart shows how the various ways of looking at the mathematics described in the article on pages T44–T45 are developed across the *Pre-Algebra* book.

Because these strands of thought are integrated throughout the book, the lesson references here are selected examples in each category, not a comprehensive listing.

MATHEMATICS AS CALCULATION	
Performing calculations	Evaluating expressions (1.1), operations with integers (1.5, 1.6, 1.7), solving two-step equations (3.1), solving proportions using cross products (6.3), finding slope (8.4), finding areas and volumes (10.3, 10.4, 10.7, 10.8), finding permutations and combinations (11.6, 11.7)

MATHEMATICS AS A FIELD OF STUDY	
Using mathematical vocabulary	Definitions of the coordinate plane (1.8), equations (2.4), rational numbers (5.1), ratios and rates (6.1), similar and congruent figures (6.4), polygons (10.2), polynomials (12.1)
Knowing mathematical principles	Order of operations (1.3), properties of addition and multiplication (2.1), distributive property (2.2), properties of equality (2.5, 2.6), properties of inequality (3.4, 3.5), rules of exponents (4.5, 12.5)

MATHEMATICS AS A MODELING LANGUAGE	
Using mathematical models	Writing equations in one variable from verbal models (2.4, 2.5, 2.6, 3.1, 3.2, 3.3), indirect measurement (6.5), simple and compound interest (7.7), predicting with best-fitting lines (8.6), exponential growth and decay (12.7)
Translating real-life situations to mathematical models, obtaining solutions, and then translating solutions back into real-life contexts	Finding the weight of a horse (2.5), triathlon times (3.4), breaking records (3.6), shopping (5.7), investing (7.7), female physicians (8.6), high-speed Internet service (8.8), surface area of a pizza box (10.5), area of a corral (12.3), depreciation (12.7)

MATHEMATICS AS LOGICAL THOUGHT	
Thinking logically	Inductive reasoning (1.6), recognizing relevant, irrelevant, and missing information (Focus on Problem Solving, Chapter 1), deductive reasoning (6.3), converse of a statement (9.3), counterexample (Skills Review Handbook)

Preparing for Algebra and Geometry

McDougal Littell Pre-Algebra provides a strong foundation for future courses in Algebra and Geometry, as shown below. *Pre-Algebra* has a strong focus on algebraic concepts and reasoning, starting with Chapter 1, followed immediately by two chapters devoted entirely to equations and inequalities. This focus continues throughout the text. Geometry topics appear throughout the book, with special emphasis given to geometry in Chapters 10 and 13.

PREPARING FOR ALGEBRA	PREPARING FOR GEOMETRY
Writing • algebraic expressions • equations and inequalities • proportions • linear functions • systems of linear equations **Evaluating** • algebraic expressions • formulas **Simplifying expressions** • combining like terms • using rules of exponents • using properties of square roots **Solving** • equations and inequalities • proportions • systems of linear equations **Graphing** • equations and inequalities • systems of linear equations • quadratic and exponential functions **Ordering** • rational and irrational numbers **Applying** • negative and zero exponents • the percent equation • the Pythagorean theorem • distance and midpoint formulas • arithmetic and geometric sequences **Identifying** • relations and functions **Performing** • operations with polynomials	**Understanding** • basic geometric concepts **Applying** • similarity and congruence • the Pythagorean theorem • properties of triangles • properties of quadrilaterals • trigonometric ratios • transformations **Exploring** • special right triangles • angle relationships • angles and parallel lines • angles and polygons **Finding** • distances in a coordinate plane • coordinates of a midpoint • perimeter and area of polygons • circumference and area of circles • surface area and volume **Connecting to algebra** • slope • parallel and perpendicular lines **Justifying** • geometric properties using algebra **Constructing** • an angle congruent to a given angle • angle bisectors • perpendicular bisectors

Differentiating Instruction

No Child Left Behind

The federal law known as *No Child Left Behind* (NCLB) highlights the need to ensure that all students, whether they are struggling, average, or advanced learners, have opportunities to make continuing progress in developing the skills they need to become successful adults. This law charges the states with the responsibility of establishing statewide accountability systems based on challenging standards, annual assessment in Grades 3–8, and annual statewide progress objectives.

McDougal Littell Pre-Algebra supports the goals of NCLB. The program is based on challenging state curriculum standards and assessment objectives *(see page T42)*. It provides you with helpful materials for diagnosing how well students understand the material, for differentiating instruction to reach all students, for assessing student progress, and for providing remediation. It also emphasizes important test-taking skills and problem-solving strategies.

ONGOING DIAGNOSIS AND PRESCRIPTION

Materials to diagnose student understanding are provided before, during, and following each chapter and lesson.

- **Pre-Course Tests** in the Student Edition and the Assessment Book help you diagnose how well students have mastered key prerequisite skills for the course.
- **Math in the Real World** and **Chapter Prerequisite Skills** exercises at the beginning of each chapter provide two different mechanisms for reviewing pre-chapter skills and vocabulary.
- **Skill Check** exercises in the Teacher's Edition and **Warm-Up** exercises on transparencies provide practice with prerequisite skills for the upcoming lesson.
- **Checkpoint** and **Guided Practice** exercises in the Student Edition, along with **Concept Check** items in the Teacher's Edition, help you to monitor how well students are grasping the vocabulary, skills, and concepts as you present each lesson.
- **Homework Check** boxes in the Teacher's Edition identify exercises from the homework assignment that you can use to determine whether or not students have mastered the key skills and concepts.
- You can also use the **Test and Practice Generator** to create online practice sheets and see a report of the results to monitor individual progress.

...in the diverse classroom

DIFFERENTIATED INSTRUCTION AND PRACTICE

Being able to differentiate instruction and practice can help you reach all students. The list below highlights a few components of *Pre-Algebra* that are designed to help you in this effort. You can use **EasyPlanner Plus Online** to preview and select the resources as you develop your lesson plans. *(See also pages T56–T61 and the E and F pages preceding each chapter.)*

Instruction

- Concept Activities in the Student Edition and a Special Activities Book
- Visualize and Multiple Representation notes in the Teacher's Edition
- Notetaking Guide workbook and transparencies
- English-Spanish Problem Solving Transparencies
- Chapter Audio Summaries CDs (in English, Spanish, and Haitian Creole)
- Power Presentations (electronic lesson presentations)
- Online Activities and Vocabulary Support

Practice

- Leveled exercises labeled in the Teacher's Edition; leveled homework assignments; leveled practice worksheets
- Challenge exercises in the Student Edition; Daily Puzzlers in the Teacher's Edition; and Challenge Practice worksheets in the Chapter Resource Books *(See also page IN28.)*
- Math Tutor Place cards with practice on essential math topics
- Cooperative Learning Projects in the Chapter Resource Books
- Textbook exercises in Spanish
- Spanish Study Guide

ASSESSMENT

Pre-Algebra provides diagnostic, formative, and summative assessment resources for measuring student progress on an ongoing basis.

- The **Student Edition** has test-practice questions at the end of every exercise set, including multiple choice, short response, and extended response items. Also included are quizzes, reviews, traditional and standardized chapter tests, and an end-of-course test.
- The **Teacher's Edition** has a quiz for every lesson. An alternate quiz is available on a transparency.
- The **Assessment Book** has alternate forms of all of the quizzes and tests in the textbook, PLUS leveled chapter tests, alternative assessments, unit tests, and cumulative tests.
- You can use the **Test and Practice Generator** to create your own customized quizzes and tests. **Online quizzes** and **State Test Practice** are available at www.classzone.com.

BUILDING TEST-TAKING SKILLS

It is more important than ever for students to build strong test-taking skills in order to be successful on annual assessments required by the NCLB Act. *Pre-Algebra* provides instruction and practice with test-taking skills at the end of every unit in the textbook.

- **Multiple Choice Questions** Students are encouraged to use number sense and estimation skills to decide whether answer choices are reasonable.
- **Short Response Questions** Students are given guidance about how to write complete answers and show their work.
- **Context-Based Multiple Choice Questions** Students practice answering multiple-choice questions that involve interpreting diagrams and graphs.
- **Extended Response Questions** Students learn how to write complete answers to multi-step problems.

Continued

RETEACHING AND REMEDIATION

Students sometimes need reteaching in order to understand concepts better or additional practice in order to master key skills. *Pre-Algebra* provides a variety of resources to help students achieve success. These same resources can also be used by absent students to help them catch up.

- **Student Edition** Includes **Review Help** notes that direct students to appropriate review materials, **Mid-Chapter Quizzes** that practice key vocabulary and skills from the first half of the chapter, **Chapter Reviews** with more vocabulary and skill practice, **Cumulative Practice** at the end of every unit, a **Skills Review Handbook** with reteaching and practice for pre-book skills, and **Extra Practice** for every lesson.
- **Teacher's Edition** Includes **Extra Examples** and **Common Error** notes that can be used to help clarify understanding.
- **Chapter Resource Books** Include **Practice** masters (Levels A, B, C), **Challenge Practice** masters, **Cumulative Practice** masters, **Study Guide** masters with worked-out examples, and **Chapter Review Games and Activities.**
- **Math Tutor Place** Includes 104 cards organized by mathematical strand to give students reteaching and practice on important concepts.
- **Technology Resources** Include a variety of interactive and engaging materials for reteaching and practice. *(See page T33 for descriptions.)*

PROBLEM SOLVING STRATEGIES

Questions on state and national tests are often posed as word problems. In order for students to demonstrate their mastery of computational skills, they must be able to read and interpret word problems and apply appropriate problem solving strategies to solve them. *Pre-Algebra* incorporates problem solving strategies and word problems throughout the book to help students learn to apply computational skills in context. (*See also the Professional Development Book, the Chapter Resource Books, and the English-Spanish Problem Solving Transparencies.*)

- **Problem Solving Plan** A four-step problem solving plan, where students read, plan, solve, and look back, is introduced in Chapter 1.
- **Focus on Problem Solving** These features help students develop problem solving strategies for identifying relevant and irrelevant information, using multiple strategies, solving problems with many or no solutions, and finally extending and generalizing solutions.
- **Word Problems at All Levels** Word problems appear at all three exercise levels and in the Guided Practice section.
- **Multi-Step Problems** Guided Problem Solving, scaffolded to help students get started, and Extended Problem Solving exercises help students prepare for multi-step problems on state and national tests.
- **Challenge Problems** Challenge problems in each exercise set help students develop their reasoning and writing skills for state and national tests. *(See also* Mathematical Rigor and Challenge *on page IN28.)*
- **Test Practice** Test-practice exercises at the end of each lesson, chapter, and unit are stated in words.

Reading, *Writing,* Notetaking

VITAL SKILLS FOR TODAY AND THE FUTURE

Vital Skills Today more than ever, students need strong skills in reading, writing, and notetaking in mathematics in order to understand course content, be successful on important state and national assessments, and develop the ability to become independent learners. Acquiring these skills in a Pre-Algebra course will build an important foundation for more advanced courses and for adult life. *McDougal Littell Pre-Algebra* provides many opportunities in the textbook and in the teacher's materials to help students develop their reading, writing, and notetaking skills.

Recent Research Recent brain research and classroom research in reading and writing have provided new insights into learning and also confirmed the value of well-known practices of successful teachers. Although the focus of this research is often on reading in language arts and social studies, many of the strategies also help those reading mathematical material. Two important aspects of reading addressed by research are vocabulary development and reading comprehension. *Pre-Algebra* offers substantial learning support in these core areas.

VOCABULARY DEVELOPMENT

The textbook provides strong support to students in learning, practicing, and reviewing vocabulary. On the Chapter Prerequisite Skills page at the start of each chapter, key review words are listed and are practiced in the Vocabulary exercises. Then, at the beginning of each lesson, the key vocabulary for the lesson appears under the Vocabulary list, and new vocabulary in the lesson is emphasized by boldface type with yellow highlighting. Reading Algebra and Reading Geometry notes in the margin serve as a built-in vocabulary, reading, and problem solving tutor. In the Teacher's Edition, Reading Strategy and other notes suggest ways teachers can help students read and learn new vocabulary words. ***See pp. 118, 178, 306, 453, 652; TE pp. 65, 72, 195.***

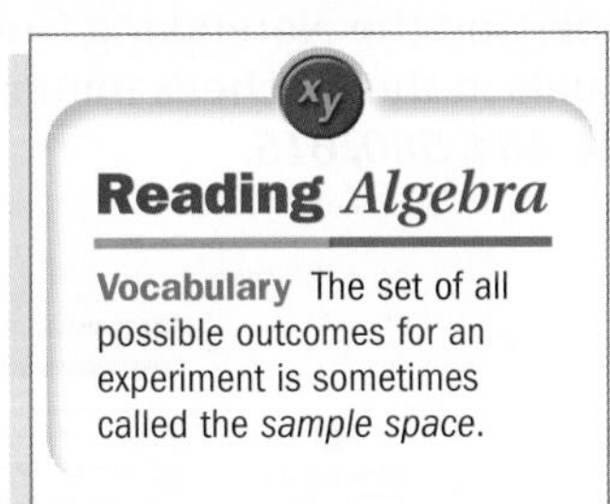

Reading Algebra
Vocabulary The set of all possible outcomes for an experiment is sometimes called the sample space.

In the Exercises, the Guided Practice exercises (which help students get ready for homework) include vocabulary as well as skill and guided problem solving practice. The Chapter Reviews provide a list of key vocabulary and include vocabulary exercises. In addition, there is a complete Glossary that includes examples and diagrams at the back of the book. ***See pp. 93, 258, 442, 824.***

The teacher's materials give specific suggestions for helping students understand and remember vocabulary. ***See, in particular, the Professional Development Book, pp. 13–20.***

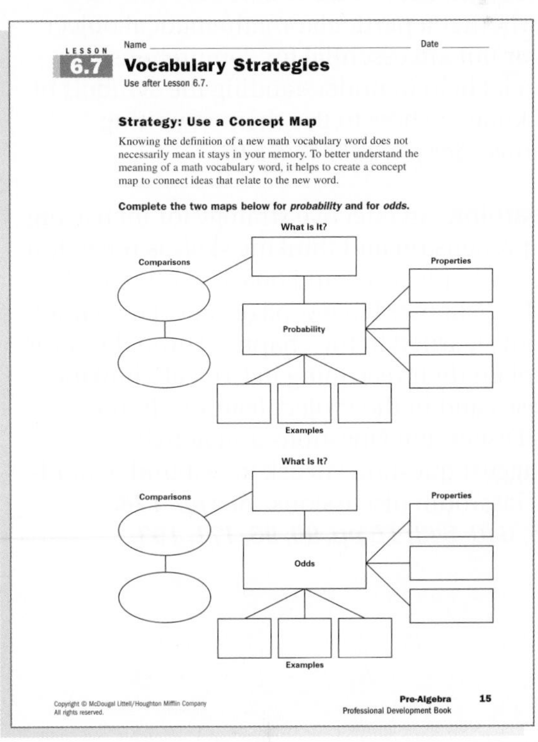

LESSON 6.7 Name ______ Date ______

Vocabulary Strategies

Use after Lesson 6.7.

Strategy: Use a Concept Map

Knowing the definition of a new math vocabulary word does not necessarily mean it stays in your memory. To better understand the meaning of a math vocabulary word, it helps to create a concept map to connect ideas that relate to the new word.

Complete the two maps below for *probability* and for *odds*.

Copyright © McDougal Littell/Houghton Mifflin Company All rights reserved.

Pre-Algebra Professional Development Book 15

Continued

READING COMPREHENSION

Student Handbook The Student Handbook gets students off to a good start with reading the textbook by giving tips for identifying the main idea, understanding the vocabulary, knowing what's important in a lesson, being an active reader, and reading word problems. ***See pp. xx-xxv.***

Establishing a Context A useful comprehension strategy supported by both brain and classroom research is connecting new learning to prior knowledge. This strategy is incorporated throughout *Pre-Algebra* in the Before/Now/Why lists at the beginnings of chapters and the beginnings of lessons; in the Math in the Real World chapter-opening applications that review prerequisite skills; and in the Chapter Prerequisite Skills pages at the start of each chapter. In the Teacher's Edition, Motivating the Lesson notes in some lessons help teachers give students a real-life context to help them anticipate the math facts covered in the lesson. ***See pp. 4, 182, 328, 588; TE pp. 71, 91, 172, 177.***

Facilitating Understanding In order to create a student-friendly book, the authors kept these principles in mind as they wrote: Students can learn new concepts more easily when they are presented in short sentences that use simple syntax and are accompanied by appropriate tables, charts, and diagrams. Clear definitions that enable students to determine easily whether a particular mathematical object fits the definition or not are essential for comprehension. Students need special help in understanding the symbols of mathematics and knowing how to use them in writing algebraic expressions. ***See pp. 145, 458, 516.***

Reflecting on Learning An effective strategy for increasing both reading comprehension and thinking skills is reflection on what has been read or learned and *how* it was learned (metacognition). The Chapter Review pages in each chapter review what students learned in the chapter. Throughout the book, students explain their reasoning in Critical Thinking and Writing exercises and in the Project features. In the Teacher's Edition, Discussion Questions and Activity Assessments all suggest questions to ask to test understanding and promote classroom discussions. ***See pp. 128, 210–213, 316, 525, 640–643; TE pp. 90, 96, 171, 193.***

Using Graphic Organizers Graphic organizers such as charts, Venn diagrams, or concept maps can be especially helpful for classifying mathematical objects such as types of numbers or types of geometric figures. These organizers are used throughout the textbook, and suggestions on how to use them are given to the student in lessons and in the Notetaking Strategies sections on Chapter Prerequisite Skills pages. ***See pp. 62, 268, 328, 452, 510, 580.***

WRITING OPPORTUNITIES

In order to become good writers, students need frequent opportunities to practice their writing skills. These opportunities occur throughout the textbook in the Critical Thinking, Logical Reasoning, Writing exercises, Concept Activities, and Projects. ***See pp. 106, 115, 135, 202, 303, 305, 310, 457.***

EFFECTIVE NOTETAKING

Taking effective notes is an important reading, learning, and review strategy, and yet math teachers throughout the country report that many students enter a Pre-Algebra course with few if any notetaking skills. Thus, the authors identified the goal of helping students develop their notetaking skills as an important objective of the program, and they have incorporated many notetaking aids into the program. See, especially, the Notetaking Strategies notes on Chapter Prerequisite Skills pages, the Note Worthy boxes in many lessons in the textbook, and the Notetaking Guide workbooks and overhead visuals in the teacher's materials. ***See pp. 118, 132, 282, 290, 384, 404, 580, 615.***

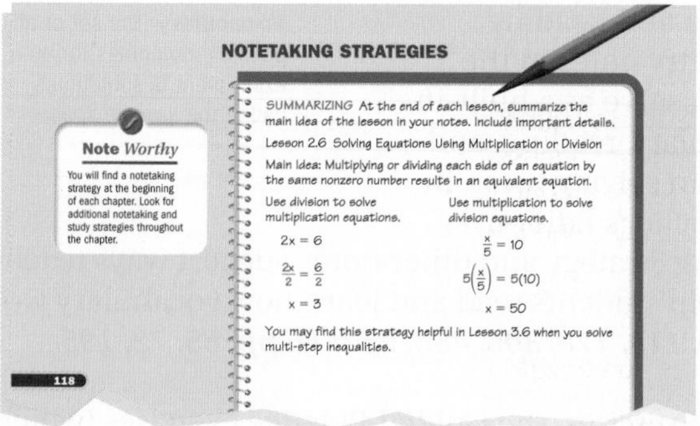
NOTETAKING STRATEGIES

Note *Worthy*

You will find a notetaking strategy at the beginning of each chapter. Look for additional notetaking and study strategies throughout the chapter.

SUMMARIZING At the end of each lesson, summarize the main idea of the lesson in your notes. Include important details.

Lesson 2.6 Solving Equations Using Multiplication or Division

Main Idea: Multiplying or dividing each side of an equation by the same nonzero number results in an equivalent equation.

Use division to solve multiplication equations.

$2x = 6$

$\frac{2x}{2} = \frac{6}{2}$

$x = 3$

Use multiplication to solve division equations.

$\frac{x}{5} = 10$

$5\left(\frac{x}{5}\right) = 5(10)$

$x = 50$

You may find this strategy helpful in Lesson 3.6 when you solve multi-step inequalities.

118

Further reading: A helpful reference is *Teaching Reading in Mathematics,* by Mary Lee Barton and Clare Heidema, published by Mid-continent Research for Education and Learning (MCREL), Aurora, Colorado.

CRISS: *CR*eating *I*ndependence through *S*tudent-owned *S*trategies

Project CRISS was founded to help develop thoughtful, independent readers and learners through instruction based on strategies arising from scientifically-based cognitive and social learning research of the past 25 years. The chart below lists the key CRISS principles, together with examples from *McDougal Littell Pre-Algebra* that support them.

Background Knowledge Background knowledge is a powerful determinant of reading comprehension. Look for introductory materials that both activate prior knowledge and provide background knowledge.	Math In the Real World, 3, 117, 327, 579; Chapter Prerequisite Skills, 4, 118, 328, 510, 650; Before/Now/Why, 78, 168, 247, 362, 382, 581; Review Help, 65, 189, 304, 511; Student Reference, 39–40, 285–286, 462–463, 714–715; Skills Review Handbook, 770–802
Active Involvement Good readers are engaged with the text and with their learning. Look for methods and activities that involve higher level thinking and motivate students to learn.	Notetaking Strategies, 4, 118, 268, 384, 580; Chapter Review, 108–111, 210–213, 368–371, 564–567; Worked-Out Examples, 86, 122, 248, 313, 413; Concept Activities, 90, 171, 287, 403, 608, 740; Brain Games, 38, 87, 198, 297, 350, 614; Projects, 324–325
Discussion Students need many opportunities to talk with one another about their reading and about what they are learning. Look for activities that open doors for discussion, in pairs, in groups, and with the whole class.	Concept Activities, 608, 626; Brain Games, 304, 350, 361, 625; Projects, 114–115, 324–325, 506–507, 646–647
Metacognition Good readers are metacognitive. They are goal-directed, and they know how to interact with print to construct meaning. Look for opportunities to help teach students to become more aware of their own learning through discussion and writing as they reflect on the *how* and *why* of their understanding.	Throughout the text, students reflect on their learning and explain their reasoning. Examples include: Writing, 13, 28, 33, 106, 181, 190, 283, 316 (Ex. 16), 389 (Ex. 23), 424, 613; Critical Thinking, 26, 128, 190, 305, 310, 356, 439, 480, 515, 519, 726; Challenge, 38, 186, 198, 235, 390, 481, 592; Interpret and Apply, 123, 152, 390, 409; Notetaking Strategies, 118, 170, 218, 510
Writing Students need multiple opportunities to write about what they are learning. Look for activities that occur naturally throughout the textbook and activities in teacher's materials that are correlated to the textbook.	Notetaking Strategies, 62, 170, 328, 452, 650; Notetaking, 132, 150, 282, 560; Short Response, 82, 224, 349, 447; Extended Response, 20, 159, 208, 373; Writing, 67, 181, 250, 338
Understanding the Author's Craft Students learn that an author's style of presentation aids in comprehension. Students use this knowledge as a basis for studying and writing strategies. Look for examples of structure that show intentional placement of items such as vocabulary, content examples, and assessment, helping students become aware of the author's approach.	Throughout the text, the lesson, chapter, unit, and overall book structure promote student comprehension. Examples include: Student Handbook, xx–xxv; Student Reference, 14–15, 69–70, 285–286, 410–411, 462–463; Student Help margin notes (e.g. Study Strategies, Homework Help, Review Help), 64, 134, 173, 189; Notetaking Strategies, 62, 170, 268, 452; Focus on Problem Solving, 58, 264, 448, 704; Cumulative Practice, 164, 378, 574, 762
Organizing for Learning Good readers know a variety of ways to organize information for learning. Look for suggestions for use of tables, charts, graphic organizers, and other devices that help students organize and interpret their learning.	Notetaking Strategies, 62, 268, 328, 384, 452; Focus on Problem Solving, 58, 264, 448, 704; Notetaking, 47, 78, 173, 290; Study Strategies, 17, 175, 221; Graphic organizers, 62, 219, 313, 364, 452, 470, 510, 560, 580, 615, 626
Explanation and Modeling Students become strategic when teachers model processes. Look for modeling that explains the *why* of a method or strategy.	Worked-out Examples, 6, 71, 122, 238; Focus on Problem Solving, 58, 264, 448, 704; Technology Activities, 136, 312, 397, 499; Critical Thinking, 128, 185, 224, 297, 333, 367, 432, 585, 733; Problem Solving Strategies, 795–802
Teaching for Understanding Students come to understand by doing a variety of activities. Look for a rich variety and choice of activities, exercises, and projects.	Extended Problem Solving, 9, 67, 223, 273, 585; Critical Thinking, 13, 148, 356, 480; Challenge, 82, 191, 304, 390; Brain Games, 84, 181, 297, 344; Concept Activities, 90, 143, 171, 287; Short Response, 75, 124, 229, 274; Extended Response, 107, 246, 304, 390; Projects, 114–115, 324–325, 506–507, 646–647

Research-Based *Solutions*

The *McDougal Littell Pre-Algebra* program reflects current research in education. The Student Edition (SE), Teacher's Edition (TE), Chapter Resource Books (CRB), and other ancillary materials provide opportunities for teachers and students to experience a number of different learning strategies both in school and at home.

One group of instructional strategies used in this program are the instructional strategies presented in *Classroom Instruction that Works**, a publication from the Association for Supervision and Curriculum Development. The nine strategies discussed in that publication are summarized below, along with some specific instances of the strategy's use in the *McDougal Littell Pre-Algebra* program.

1. Identifying Similarities and Differences

This strategy includes comparing and classifying and suggests representing comparisons in graphic or symbolic form.

Pre-Algebra examples include *compare* exercises throughout the chapters, showing relationships between types of numbers, contrasting units of measure and types of geometric figures, making concept maps and Venn diagrams.

See, for example, SE88, SE305, SE452, SE786, SE793, TE118, TE144, CRB1 pp. 72, 75

2. Summarizing and Notetaking

This strategy includes deciding when to delete, substitute, or keep information in writing a summary and using a variety of notetaking formats—e.g., outlines, webbing, or a combination technique—and suggests encouraging students to use notes as a study guide for tests.

Pre-Algebra examples include the entire Notetaking Guide; Notetaking Strategies, Note Worthy, Notebooks, Study Strategy (SE); Notetaking Strategies, Notetaking (TE)

See, for example, SE4, SE64, SE118, SE314, SE521, TE62, TE178, TE218, CRB1 p. 3

3. Reinforcing Effort and Providing Recognition

This strategy includes making the connection between effort and achievement clear to students and providing recognition for attainment of specific goals to stimulate motivation.

Pre-Algebra examples include Checkpoint, Guided Practice, Guided Problem Solving (SE); Motivating the Lesson, Concept Check, Mini Quiz (TE)

See, for example, SE178, SE179, TE138, TE142, TE341, CRB2 p. 4

4. Homework and Practice

This strategy includes making the purpose of homework assignments clear to students and focusing practice assignments on specific elements of a complex skill.

Pre-Algebra examples include Practice Workbook; Math Tutor Place; Homework Help, Practice and Problem Solving, Chapter Review, Extra Practice (SE); Skill Check, Extra Examples, Extra Practice, Homework Check, Diagnosis/Remediation (TE); Practice A, B, C (CRB)

See, for example, SE74, SE318–321, SE805, TE335, TE336, TE337, TE339, CRB1 pp. 41–43, CRB2 pp. 26–28

* Marzano, Robert J., Debra J. Pickering, and Jane E. Pollock, *Classroom Instruction that Works: Research-Based Strategies for Increasing Student Achievement* and its accompanying handbook. Alexandria, Virginia: Association for Supervision and Curriculum Development, 2001.

...for your classroom

5. Nonlinguistic Representations

This strategy includes creating nonlinguistic representations—including creating graphic organizers, making physical models, generating mental pictures, drawing pictures and pictographs, and engaging in kinesthetic activity—to help students understand content in a whole new way.

Pre-Algebra examples include Notetaking Strategies, Note Worthy, Brain Games (SE); Differentiating Instruction, Visualize, Multiple Representations, Alternative Strategy (TE)

See, for example, SE62, SE484, SE520, TE72, TE119, TE183, TE239

6. Cooperative Learning

This strategy includes a description of the five defining elements of cooperative learning—positive interdependence, face-to-face interaction, individual and group accountability, interpersonal and group skills, and group processing—and gives suggestions for grouping techniques.

Pre-Algebra examples include Concept Activities, Projects (SE); Grouping, Classroom Management, Differentiating Instruction (TE); Cooperative Projects (CRB); see also the Special Activities Book

See, for example, SE506, SE608, TE221, TE646, TE718, CRB1 p. 77

7. Setting Objectives and Providing Feedback

This strategy includes using instructional goals to narrow what students focus on and suggests providing feedback that is specific to a criterion and encouraging students to personalize their teacher's goals and to provide some of their own feedback.

Pre-Algebra examples include Prerequisite Skills Quiz, Before/Now/Why in student lessons, Activity Goals, and scoring rubrics on Building Test-Taking Skills pages (SE); Lesson Objectives, Key Discovery (TE); goals and objectives given on Activity Master and Technology Activity pages and rubrics provided with projects (CRBs); discussion of rubrics in the Professional Development Book; Online self-assessment quizzes

See, for example, SE131, SE218, SE374, SE403, TE193, TE219, CRB2 pp. 16, 74

8. Generating and Testing Hypotheses

This strategy includes using a variety of structured tasks to guide students through generating and testing hypotheses, using induction or deduction, and suggests asking students to clearly explain their hypotheses and their conclusions to help deepen their understanding.

Pre-Algebra examples include Concept Activities, Logical Reasoning, Critical Thinking, Predict, and Writing exercises throughout book (SE); Activity/Key Discovery, Algebraic Reasoning (TE)

See, for example, SE9, SE45, SE171, SE198, SE305, TE92, TE143, TE233

9. Cues, Questions, and Advance Organizers

This strategy includes asking questions or giving explicit cues before a learning experience to provide students with a preview of what they are about to experience; using verbal and graphic advance organizers, or having students skim information before reading as an advance organizer.

Pre-Algebra examples include Math in the Real World at beginning of chapters, Before/Now/Why at start of lessons, pre-reading lesson elements such as Vocabulary lists and Example heads throughout book, problem solving plan (SE); Motivating the Lesson (TE); discussion of problem solving in the Professional Development Book

See, for example, SE14–15, SE61, SE398, TE71, TE149, TE182, TE329

PROFESSIONAL ARTICLES

Providing *Universal Access*

With careful planning, you can help *all* students

DIVERSE STUDENTS

In most classrooms, students present a variety of achievement levels, skills, and needs. The goal for all students is the same: We want them to develop sufficient computational, procedural, and problem solving skills to provide a solid foundation for further study in mathematics. However, all students do not arrive at these competencies at the same time or in the same way. In this article we suggest research-based strategies teachers can use to modify curriculum and instruction for special needs students. The basic instructional plan in *Pre-Algebra* is designed for students who are achieving at near grade level; but just prior to each chapter we include specific suggestions for students who are achieving above and below grade level, and for students who are not fluent in English (see also the article titled "Adapting Curriculum and Instruction for English Learners").

Student Groups Teachers may find it helpful to view students as members of four basic groups, as shown on the facing page. (English learners can be found in all four groups.) Teachers do not need to place students in these groups; the categories are suggested so teachers can plan ahead to meet different needs of students. Note the use of the term *underachievers.* This term is not synonymous with special education. It may include some special education pupils but includes many more students whose low achievement levels are the result of inadequate prior schooling or attendance, high mobility rates, or a host of other reasons that have nothing to do with their abilities or disabilities. The term *underachievers* is not meant to be a negative term. On the contrary, we believe that students achieving below grade level can be successful in mathematics given carefully designed instruction.

SETTING THE RIGHT TONE

There are three key strategies recommended for teachers as they adapt any program to students' needs:

- Use frequent assessment as a way to determine what each student does or does not know, and use that assessment as the basis for planning.
- Plan modifications of curriculum and instruction ahead of time so that you are ready to differentiate as the need arises.
- Use a variety of grouping strategies to facilitate learning. A combination of whole class instruction and temporary groupings of students, with groups organized around students' needs, will facilitate management of the variety of achievement levels and learning needs in the classroom.

Assessment, planning, and flexible grouping are essential to ensuring that your students have the optimal chance for success. In addition to these three key strategies, general guidelines for establishing a classroom designed to meet students' needs are:

1. Establish an atmosphere where students feel comfortable asking questions and are rewarded for asking about things they don't understand.
2. Maintain the same goals for all students. Allow additional time and practice for students who need it, and provide challenging alternatives for those who are ready to move more quickly.
3. Clearly identify the skill, concept, or standards you are working on and measure progress toward those ends.
4. Have students show their work. It is much easier for teachers to understand where a student gets confused if they have evidence of the student's thought process.
5. Try small modifications in curriculum and instruction before more drastic ones.
6. Don't persist with a strategy that is not working. Try something else.
7. Encourage effort and persistence, and celebrate successes with your students.

VARYING CURRICULUM AND INSTRUCTION

1. Time Most students whose achievement is below grade level will need more time. Students who are not fluent in English will need more time. The contents of this book might be offered over a two-year period, or two periods a day. Perhaps the day can be extended through study hall, regular homework assignments, tutoring, or Saturday, summer, or "off track" catch-up sessions. Advanced students might "test out" of portions of the book and complete the material in half a year, or they may compact two courses into one.

2. **Presentation** Instructing in a variety of ways and taking a single concept and explaining it verbally and visually with concrete and abstract examples provide students multiple opportunities for understanding. Area, for example, is a key concept in geometry. In earlier grades students have found areas of simple objects, both by using tiles to cover an area, and by applying algorithms. Later, students practice with unusual shapes, dividing them into simpler ones. Finally, students tackle sophisticated examples like finding the shape with the maximum area given a fixed perimeter, using both trial and error and more abstract methods.

3. **Task parameters** Multi-step problems can be especially difficult for students. These types of problems are just combinations of simpler problems and can be broken down into those simpler steps, with additional help and practice at each step. Confusing elements can be minimized and extraneous material eliminated. For advanced students, simpler problems can be eliminated and more challenging ones (as suggested in each chapter) substituted.

4. **Methods of assessment** Students learning English may be able to demonstrate on paper what they cannot yet verbalize. Students with physical challenges may be unable to draw a graph but may be able to select the right graph from a series of options or verbally describe the graph so that someone else can draw it. Allow students to demonstrate their knowledge in a variety of ways while helping all students to master the skills and knowledge necessary to exhibit their understanding in standard ways.

Pre-Algebra is organized so that much of the differentiation for special needs students is built into the design of the program. Note that simpler concepts are introduced before more complex ones. Ample practice is provided. Challenge exercises are included throughout the pupil text. Activities provide students with models for conceptual understanding of the mathematical reasoning behind each key concept. Mathematical reasoning is stressed throughout each chapter. Vocabulary words, examples, and Guided Practice exercises are

FOUR BASIC STUDENT GROUPS

Advanced Group

Advanced students have already completed some of the grade-level material. They make rapid progress and become bored with repetition. They may or may not have been formally identified as gifted or talented in the area of mathematics.

Suggested Plan

1. Assess what these students already know.
2. Allow these students to "test out" of chapters or assignments.
3. Substitute challenging assignments for easier ones.
4. Modify instruction so that it is more complex or more in-depth.

Grade Level Group

Students achieving at grade level may have minor, occasional difficulties but they can be assisted to maintain their progress with extra practice and individual or group assistance on an ad hoc basis.

Suggested Plan

1. Assess what these students already know.
2. Progress through *Pre-Algebra* at the recommended pace and sequence.
3. On an ad hoc basis, review or provide additional practice as needed.

Underachieving Group

These learners are not achieving at expected grade level but can, with a carefully designed program that provides targeted assistance. Systematic differentiation such as preteaching, reteaching, and additional instructional time should be planned for these students, as suggested in each chapter.

Suggested Plan

1. Assess what these students already know.
2. Provide additional scaffolding and the instructional variations suggested in this book.
3. Focus on the key concepts and present material systematically.
4. Vary the kinds of instruction so that students have several opportunities to understand.
5. Provide additional practice homework.

Intensive Needs Group

Intensive needs students are those whose performance is two or more standard deviations below the mean on standardized measures. These students will probably already be eligible for special education services. This is a very small percentage of the general population.

Suggested Plan

1. Assess what these students already know.
2. Determine if these students have an IEP.
3. Refer students for special education testing or child study team discussion; enlist the help of specialists.
4. Carefully consider each student's most appropriate placement in mathematics.
5. Use the specific suggestions for underachieving learners.

Continued

standard features of each chapter. Each lesson includes Mixed Review exercises so that students recall and use skills and understandings from previous chapters. These features were designed to help you meet the needs of your class.

FOR STUDENTS WHO HAVE TROUBLE PAYING ATTENTION

Some students in your classroom may be formally identified as having Attention Deficit Hyperactivity Disorder (ADHD) or Attention Deficit Disorder (ADD). Others may exhibit the same learning challenges but may not be formally identified. Whether formally identified or not, students who have trouble paying attention generally share these characteristics:

- Trouble paying attention is not just occasional. It occurs most or all of the time, across content areas, and is inappropriate for the age of the child.
- Forgetfulness, memory problems, losing things, disorganization
- Restlessness, fidgeting
- Socially inappropriate behavior such as excessive talking, interrupting others, and difficulty waiting their turn

These students may be very bright and capable in mathematics but have a hard time staying focused for long periods of time. They need to be taught strategies for organizing their work and keeping track of where they are. In general, students with attention problems need to be helped to develop coping strategies. The teacher should approach the student in a problem solving mode: "Let's find ways to help you concentrate and organize your work," rather than using one of the following strategies in a punitive way.

1. **Present the work in smaller chunks over smaller time periods** and then gradually increase expectations. If students have trouble completing long tests, for example, break the material into smaller quizzes and increase the length of the quizzes as the year progresses.
2. **Use cumulative review and practice.** Have students periodically review what they learned in previous chapters and provide additional practice if they have forgotten.
3. **Make it more obvious what the student should focus on.** For example, use the test generator to put only four problems on each page; use a large font; or use an index card or piece of cardboard with a hole cut out of the middle to place on the page so that the student can focus on one problem at a time. A pencil, finger, highlighter, or sticky paper can also be used by the student to keep track of which problem he or she is working on.
4. **Have students race against the clock.** For some students, racing against the clock to see how many problems can be completed accurately within a five-minute time period is more motivating than doing the same number of problems at their leisure. The time period can be extended gradually.
5. **Help students develop simple strategies for bringing work to and from class.** A two-pocket folder, where homework goes home in the left pocket and comes back in the right, is a simple way to keep track of assignments.
6. **Allow movement and schedule breaks.**
7. **Minimize distractions by seating students that are easily distracted near the teacher** and away from hallway noise. Tables with several students at a table are more distracting than rows of desks. When students are to work quietly, offer headphones to block out noise. Headphones can be set to play quiet music or "white noise," or can be used just as earplugs to help block out noise.
8. **Graphic organizers** such as Venn diagrams, tree diagrams, lists, outlines, tables, and charts can all provide structures for organizing and remembering information. Mental images, choral responses, or even hand signals can help students remember. Highlighters can be used to make sure that decimal points are lined up. Graph paper is excellent for keeping homework problems neat, even when a graph is not required.
9. **Keep instructions simple and clear, especially at the beginning of the year.** Establish routines (e.g., the week's homework is always due on Thursday; assignments are written in a specific place on the board; the last ten minutes of class is used to make sure everyone understands what homework is expected and how to do it). Students who know the routine find it easier to work independently.

FOR STUDENTS WHO HAVE TROUBLE UNDERSTANDING THE CONCEPTS

Success in mathematics, as in music, sports, or other areas, comes for most students only with hard work and persistent effort. Concepts may seem difficult at first, but with repeated teaching and practice virtually all students can master the mathematics they need to graduate from high school, access a variety of jobs, and lay the foundation for further study in mathematics or a related field.

Several strategies can help students make steady progress in mathematics. These include:

1. Focus on key mathematical concepts.
2. Review key concepts and skills from earlier lessons, chapters, or years.
3. Preteach key concepts and vocabulary.
4. Anticipate problem areas.
5. Provide scaffolding (guided practice) for students who need extra help.
6. Think out loud to show hidden steps.
7. Provide a sample problem to which students can return when they get stuck.
8. Break problems into simpler components.
9. Explicitly teach students a variety of problem solving strategies and help them select one that fits the situation.
10. Present concepts in a variety of ways: visually, verbally, concretely, abstractly, etc.
11. Encourage students to draw a picture or use a visual aid such as a number line, graph, or diagram.
12. Provide sufficient practice.

Finally, good teachers are perpetual students themselves. They are always looking for ways to deepen their understanding of mathematics and for good ways to explain and teach mathematics to others.

FOR ADVANCED STUDENTS

Occasionally students can demonstrate mastery of all the mathematics expected to be learned in a given grade level. Repeating previously learned material for a year is deadly to these students. It can make them dislike mathematics. For these students, moving them up a grade level for math is a simple and cost-effective solution.

Most advanced students, however, are advanced in some areas but not in others. They tend to learn quickly and need more instructional material, as well as more difficult material. The student edition, teacher's edition, and ancillaries for this program provide challenging exercises that can be used when students have demonstrated competence in a particular area. These challenge exercises should be substituted for the easier exercises in a homework assignment or lesson. When they have the time and interest, all students should be encouraged to work the challenge exercises.

General strategies for differentiating the curriculum for advanced learners include:

1. **Vary the pacing.** Allow advanced students some flexibility in how they progress through the course. Students who can demonstrate mastery of the objectives for a given lesson or chapter can be working on challenge exercises. Advanced students may become fascinated with a particular aspect of mathematics and want to spend *more* time on it.
2. **Differentiate in terms of depth.** Encourage advanced students to delve more in depth into mathematics. Looking at the details and the patterns; studying the language of the discipline; and looking at trends, themes, properties, theorems, proofs, and unanswered questions can enrich the curriculum for advanced students.
3. **Differentiate in terms of complexity.** Advanced students may be ready to connect ideas across disciplines in ways characteristic of older students or adults. Encourage them to investigate relationships between mathematics and art, history, science, and music, and to look at the development of mathematics over time.

USING GROUPING TO BENEFIT ALL STUDENTS

Grouping advanced learners together for investigations of challenge problems can provide you with time to work more closely with a group of students who need help in a particular area. Alternatively, while students who need more help are working on additional reinforcement activities or practice, you can work with a group of advanced students on a challenge project. Groups can be organized and revised daily, weekly, or by lesson according to how proficient students are with the concepts and skills targeted for that day, week, or lesson. At times you may have only one student who is ready for a challenge problem; at other times the whole class may be ready. Flexible grouping is the key to ensuring that students do not become "tracked." Asking advanced students to report to the whole class on their progress on challenge problems can provide the opportunity for the whole class to engage in more abstract and theoretical thinking.

Adapting Curriculum and Instruction *for* English Learners

English learners come to the classroom with all the variety of English speakers in regard to mathematics achievement. They may be at, behind, or ahead of grade expectations in mathematics. They may be gifted or eligible for special education services. They may have been born in the United States, or they may have arrived in this country very recently. They may speak one or more languages, and they may be literate in one or more languages other than English. They may be nearly fluent in English or have beginning or intermediate levels of understanding and production. They have in common one characteristic: They are all learning English.

Teachers can maximize success for English learners in the mathematics classroom by assessing each student's competencies in mathematics and English to form a basis for program planning.

GETTING TO KNOW YOUR STUDENTS

Before school starts, check the cumulative folder on each student in your class to determine which ones are learning English. See if there is recent testing. Two types of testing are most useful: mathematics achievement and reading achievement levels. If no recent test information is available, you may instead administer a pre-course math test and ask English learners to write a dictated paragraph in English to assess their reading and writing skills. Make sure students understand that the testing is for diagnosis only, not for a numerical grade. Use the chart on the facing page as a guide to understanding student assessment data.

SUGGESTIONS FOR MATHEMATICS TEACHERS OF ENGLISH LEARNERS

1. Allocate additional time for mathematics. Many students will be translating from English to their primary language and back again. When you ask questions, allow extra time for students to respond. Reading mathematics textbooks and understanding what is asked for in a word problem will be slower.
2. Use student's background knowledge. Some English learners will have developed substantial background in mathematics; others will have very little. Find out what students know and then build on more.
3. Reduce the amount and sophistication of the English language used. This may be done by reordering the lessons in each chapter to begin with key vocabulary, followed by problems with a minimum of written English, followed by at least one word problem each day. Choose word problems that don't rely on assumed background knowledge. Keep your questions direct and simple. Speak more slowly, avoid idioms and slang, be precise and concise, and use short sentences and simple vocabulary. Using hand gestures and pictures as well as words aids communication.
4. Develop predictable routines. Introduce one concept per day. Keeping the focus simple will aid students in understanding the point of the lesson.
5. Use different methods for getting a point across. Presenting concepts verbally and visually, with concrete examples and in abstract mathematical symbols, and using pictures, graphs, diagrams, and charts will enhance a student's chance of understanding at least one of the presentations. As you introduce a new word, rule, or property, write it down.
6. Provide opportunities for English learners to interact with their English-speaking peers. Students who are learning a language need to hear native speakers using the language, and they need opportunities to use their new mathematics vocabulary in their speech and in their writing.
7. Provide opportunities for English learners to discuss their understandings with each other, confirm the homework assignments, or ask questions of each other in whatever language they may have in common. (Well-schooled parents can also help by explaining concepts/procedures in their home language.)

8. Allow English learners to demonstrate what they know in a variety of ways. When students first learn a language, they generally understand the spoken language before they can produce it themselves. Also, students may be able to read in English but not speak it themselves. Allow students to point, nod, gesture, draw a picture, or work math problems without words as they learn English.
9. Extend mathematics instructional time through homework, an extra class period, summer school, or tutoring. Many of the suggestions for English learners in this series can be carried out in collaboration with language arts teachers or other specialists, and are well-suited for discussion in a language arts class, English as a second language class, or in a a tutorial.
10. Keep on hand picture dictionaries, foreign language dictionaries, and multi-language math glossaries.

SPECIFIC SUGGESTIONS

Prior to each chapter you will find suggestions to help you modify curriculum and instruction so that the content is accessible to English learners. The suggestions and activities in these sections are designed to (1) teach mathematical vocabulary; (2) explain mathematical concepts in a variety of ways; and (3) dissect the structure of word problems. Much of the vocabulary study in this book may be review for some of your students. In that case, work as quickly as possible through the activities. For those students who need more systematic study, progressing through the activities as indicated will ensure that students understand basic terms prior to statewide testing that generally occurs toward the end of each school year. We recommend that if you have English learners in your classroom, you skim all the chapter suggestions for English learners so that you may use them as you need them.

ENGLISH LEARNERS

	Low Mathematics Achievement: Who is this student?	Low Mathematics Achievement: What to do?	High Mathematics Achievement: Who is this student?	High Mathematics Achievement: What to do?
Low Reading Achievement	Student may be new to the class, school, or country. Student may have had inadequate schooling. Student may have moved a lot. Student may be unmotivated or have test anxiety. Low reading achievement may be depressing mathematics scores. Student may have gaps and holes in knowledge. Student may need special education assistance.	Examine cumulative folder for other testing, notes, etc. Ask questions about language use and prior schooling. Delay any testing for a week or two. Help student feel comfortable in the class during that period of time. Administer mathematics achievement test and reading test, preferably in an individual setting. Assess this student at weekly intervals and monitor classroom work to determine if progress is being made. Look at the English Learners suggestions in each chapter.	Student has had good prior mathematics instruction. Mathematics is an area where this student can excel. Math achievement level may actually be higher than scores indicate. (Limited English reading skills affect mathematics achievement as well.) Word problems will be especially difficult.	Mathematics instruction should proceed at normal or near normal pace. Student should be involved in a systematic English language development program and intensive reading program outside of mathematics class. Spend part of each class period on mathematics vocabulary study. Provide student with a bilingual dictionary or math glossary and a mathematics text in the home language. Look at the English Learners suggestions in each chapter for those that are most useful.
High Reading Achievement	Student may have been designated as an English learner because oral skills lag behind reading skills. Student may not test well in mathematics. Most students can make rapid progress in mathematics; a few may have learning difficulties that require the help of a specialist.	Assess mathematics achievement in a variety of ways. Concentrate on developing oral fluency. Focus on vocabulary specific to mathematics. Use a student's reading ability to improve his or her math scores.	Student may be ready for designation as a fluent English speaker. May need extra study in the specialized vocabulary of mathematics. Complex syntax may present obstacles to performance. Given systematic instruction, this student should be able to achieve at or above grade level.	Scan all of the suggestions for English learners in each chapter and progress through the ones the student needs as quickly as possible. Monitor carefully to make sure this student continues to progress at a reasonable pace.

NAEP: National Assessment of Educational Progress

The NAEP is used to assess student understanding of math across the nation. The chart below lists the topics assessed by the NAEP, and lessons and features from McDougal Littell Pre-Algebra *that address them.*

NUMBER PROPERTIES AND OPERATIONS	
1) Number sense	1.4 through 1.6, 2.5 Act., 2.6 Act., 3.1 Act., 3.3 Act., 3.4, 3.5. 3.6, 4.3, 4.4, 4.6, 4.7, 5.1, 5.3, 5.4, 6.1, 7.1 through 7.4, 7.5 Act., 8.1, 9.3 Act., 9.4, 11.1, 12.5, Skills Rev. Handbook
2) Estimation	1.2 (Ex. 29), 1.5 (Exs. 42–44), 2.7 (Chkpt. 7), 4.6, 7.1 (Ex. 57), 7.4 (Ex. 28), 7.6 (Ex. 27), 8.2, 8.3 (Ex. 29), 8.5 (Ex. 20), 8.6, 8.8, 8.9, 9.1, 10.4, 10.5, 10.6, 10.7, 10.8, Skills Rev. Handbook
3) Number operations	1.2, 1.3, 1.5 through 1.7, 2.1, 2.5, 2.6, 2.7, 3.5, 4.5, 4.6, 4.7, 5.2 through 5.5, 5.6, 6.2, 6.3, 6.4, 6.5, 6.6, Ch. 7, 12.5, Skills Rev. Handbook
4) Ratios and proportional reasoning	5.6 (Ex. 9), 6.1, 6.2, 6.3, 6.4, 6.5, 6.6, 7.1, 7.2, 7.3 through 7.6, 8.4, 9.7, 9.8, 10.1, 10.7 Tech. Act., 11.3 Stud. Ref., 12.8, 13.7
5) Properties of number and operations	1.2 (Ex. 37), 1.3, 1.5 (Exs. 54–56), 2.1, 2.2, 2.5, 2.6, 3.4, 3.5 Act. (Ex. 1), 3.5, 4.1 through 4.4, 4.5, 4.6, 4.7 (Exs. 38, 53), Unit 3 Focus on Problem Solving, 9.2, 9.3 Act., 12.5

MEASUREMENT	
1) Measuring physical attributes	1.2, 2.2 Stud. Ref., 2.2, 3.2, 3.3, 6.2 through 6.5, 6.6, 7.5 Act., 8.4, 8.5, 8.6, 9.5, 9.7, 9.8, 10.1, 10.3, 10.4, 10.5 through 10.8, 13.2 Stud. Ref., 13.3 Act., 13.6 Act., Skills Rev. Handbook
2) Systems of measurement	1.6 (Ex. 34), 6.2 (Ex. 28), 6.6, 8.2 (Exs. 32–34), 10.3 through 10.8, Skills Rev. Handbook

GEOMETRY	
1) Dimension and shape	6.6 Act., 8.5 Stud. Ref., 9.3 Stud. Ref., 9.3 (Ex. 31), 9.5, 9.6, 10.1, 10.2, 10.4, 10.5 Stud. Ref., 10.5, 10.7 Act., 13.2 Stud. Ref., 13.6 Act., Skills Rev. Handbook
2) Transformation of shapes and preservation of properties	6.4, 6.5, 6.6, 9.3 Stud. Ref., 9.3 Act., 9.7 Act., 10.6 (Exs. 10–12, 30), 13.4, 13.5, 13.6, 13.7
3) Relationships between geometric figures	8.5 Stud. Ref., 8.5, 8.8, 9.3 Stud. Ref., 9.3 through 9.6, 9.7, 9.8, Ch. 10, 13.1 through 13.4
4) Position and direction	8.5, 8.8, 9.5, 10.5 (Ex. 19), 13.2 Stud. Ref., 13.4 through 13.6
5) Mathematical reasoning	13.3 Act., 13.3 (Ex. 27)

DATA ANALYSIS AND PROBABILITY	
1) Data representation	1.8, 7.1 (Ex. 57), 7.2 (Ex. 22), 7.3 (Ex. 60), 7.5 (Ex. 25), 8.1 (Ex. 22), 8.6, 11.1 through 11.3, 11.4 Tech. Act., 11.5, Skills Rev. Handbook
2) Characteristics of data sets	1.7 Stud. Ref., 1.7, 8.6, 11.1, 11.2, 11.3
3) Experiments and samples	11.4, 11.5 Act., 11.5
4) Probability	6.7 Act., 6.7, 6.8, 7.1, 11.6 through 11.9

ALGEBRA	
1) Patterns, relations, and functions	1.7 Act., 1.8, 3.4, 4.2 (Ex. 52), 4.5 Act., 8.1 through 8.7, 12.6 through 12.8, 13.4 through 13.7
2) Algebraic representations	1.1, 1.8, 2.3, 2.4 through 2.7, 3.1 through 3.6, 5.6, 5.7, 6.2, 6.3, 6.4, 6.5, 6.6, 7.2, 7.4, 7.5, 7.6, 7.7, Ch. 8, 9.5, 12.6 through 12.8, 13.4 through 13.7
3) Variables, expressions, and operations	1.1, 2.3 through 2.7, Ch. 3, 4.5, 4.6, 5.3, 5.4, 5.6, 5.7, 6.2, 6.3, 6.4, 6.5, 6.6, 7.2, 7.4 through 7.7, 8.3, 8.5, 8.6, 8.7, 9.1 through 9.6, 10.1, 12.1 through 12.5, 12.8, 13.4 through 13.7
4) Equations and inequalities	1.2, 2.2 Stud. Ref., 2.2, 2.3 Stud. Ref., 2.4, 2.5, 2.6, 2.7, Ch. 3, 5.6, 5.7, 6.2, 6.3, 6.4, 6.5, 6.6, 7.2, 7.4, 7.5, 7.6, 7.7, 8.2 through 8.9, 9.3, 9.5, 9.7, 9.8, Ch. 10, 12.7, 13.3

NCTM: National Council of Teachers of Mathematics

The chart below lists the lessons and other features in the textbook that address the NCTM Standards.

CONTENT STANDARDS	
1) Number and Operations Understand numbers, ways of representing numbers, relationships among numbers, and number systems; understand meanings of operations and how they relate to one another; compute fluently and make reasonable estimates.	1.1, 1.2, 1.3 through 1.7, 2.1, 2.2, 2.3, 2.5, 2.6, 2.7, 3.1, 3.2, 3.3, 3.4 through 3.6, 4.1 Act. through 4.7 Tech. Act., 5.1 through 5.7, 6.1, 7.1, 7.3, 7.4, 7.5, 7.6, 7.7, 9.1, 9.2, 9.4, 12.5, Appendices 1, 3, and 4
2) Algebra Understand patterns, relations, and functions; represent and analyze mathematical situations and structures using algebraic symbols; use mathematical models to represent and understand quantitative relationships; analyze change in various contexts.	1.1, 1.2, 2.1, 2.2 Student Reference, 2.2, 2.3 through 2.7, 3.1 Act. through 3.4, 3.5, 3.6, 4.1 Act., 4.2, 4.4 through 4.6, 5.5 Act., 5.6, 5.7, 6.2, 6.3, 6.4, 6.5, 6.6, 7.2 Act., 7.2, 7.4, 7.5 Act., 7.7, 7.7 Tech. Act., 8.1, 8.2, 8.3 through 8.4, 8.5, 8.6, 8.7 through 8.9, 9.3, 9.6, 10.1, 10.2, 10.7 Tech. Act., 11.6, 11.7, 12.1, 12.2, 12.3, 12.4 through 12.8, 13.1, 13.3 Act., 13.3, Appendices 1, 2, 3, and 7
3) Geometry Analyze characteristics and properties of two- and three-dimensional geometric shapes and develop mathematical arguments about geometric relationships; specify locations and describe spatial relationships using coordinate geometry and other representational systems; apply transformations and use symmetry to analyze mathematical situations; use visualization, spatial reasoning, and geometric modeling to solve problems.	1.8, 6.4 Student Reference, 6.4 Act., 6.4, 6.5, 8.5 Student Reference, 9.3 Student Reference, 9.3 Act., 9.3, 9.5 through 9.8, 10.1, 10.2, 10.3, 10.4, 10.5 Student Reference, 10.5 through 10.7, 10.8, 13.1 through 13.7
4) Measurement Understand measurable attributes of objects and the units, systems, and processes of measurement; apply appropriate techniques, tools, and formulas to determine measurements.	2.2 Student Reference, 2.3 Student Reference, 6.1, 9.3 Student Reference, 10.3 through 10.4, 10.5 Act., 10.5, 10.6, 10.7, 10.8
5) Data Analysis and Probability Formulate questions that can be addressed with data and collect, organize, and display relevant data to answer them; select and use appropriate statistical methods to analyze data; develop and evaluate inferences and predictions that are based on data; understand and apply basic concepts of probability.	1.7 Student Reference, 1.8, 6.7 Act., 6.7, 6.7 Tech Act., 8.6, 8.6 Tech. Act., 11.1 through 11.5, 11.8, 11.9 Act., 11.9, Appendix 6

PROCESS STANDARDS	
6) Problem Solving Build new mathematical knowledge through problem solving; solve problems that arise in mathematics and in other contexts; apply and adapt a variety of appropriate strategies to solve problems; monitor and reflect on the process of mathematical problem solving.	1.3 Student Reference, 6.1, 6.2, 6.3, 6.4, 6.5, 6.8, 7.1, 7.2, 7.4, 7.5, 7.6, 7.7, 8.2 Tech. Act., 8.3, 8.5, 8.7, 8.8, 8.9, 9.7, 9.8, 9.8 Tech. Act., 10.1, 10.3, 10.4, 10.5, 10.6, 10.7, 10.7 Tech. Act., 10.8, 11.6, 11.7, 11.9, 12.1, 12.2, 12.8, 13.1, Appendices 2 and 3
7) Reasoning and Proof Recognize reasoning and proof as fundamental aspects of mathematics; make and investigate mathematical conjectures; develop and evaluate mathematical arguments and proofs; select and use various types of reasoning and methods of proof.	Occurs throughout. E.g.: Critical thinking exs.: 4.5, 8.7, 9.4, 10.2, 12.2, 13.3; Error analysis exs.: 2.1, 4.1, 7.5, 8.9, 10.2; Short/extended response exs.: 3.1, 5.5, 6.7, 8.5, 10.6, 13.2, Appendix 5
8) Communication Organize and consolidate their mathematical thinking through communication; communicate their mathematical thinking coherently and clearly to peers, teachers, and others; analyze and evaluate the mathematical thinking and strategies of others; use the language of mathematical ideas precisely.	Occurs throughout. E.g.: Explain exs.: 1.5, 3.2, 4.6, 6.3, 8.9, 9.5, 11.3, 13.1; Notetaking help: 2.1, 4.2, 5.3, 7.2, 8.4, 10.8, 12.7, 13.2; Writing exs.: 1.3, 2.6, 5.7, 6.7, 9.2, 11.4, 11.5, 12.1, Appendix 5
9) Connections Recognize and use connections among mathematical ideas; understand how mathematical ideas interconnect and build on one another to produce a coherent whole; recognize and apply mathematics in contexts outside of mathematics.	9.3 Act., 9.3, 9.7 Act., 9.7, 9.8, 9.8 Tech. Act.
10) Representation Create and use representations to organize, record, and communicate mathematical ideas; select, apply, and translate among mathematical representations to solve problems; use representations to model and interpret physical, social, and mathematical phenomena.	1.4, 1.5, 1.6, 1.8, 5.3 Act., 6.4 Student Reference, 6.6 Act., 6.6, 6.8, 8.1, 8.2, 8.2 Tech. Act., 8.4 Act., 8.4, 10.5 Student Reference, 10.5 Act., 10.7 Act., 11.3 Student Reference, 11.3, 11.8 Act., 11.8, 12.2 Act., 12.4 Act., 12.4, Appendix 6

Student Handbook

Help with Taking Notes

One of the most important tools for success in mathematics is organizing what you have learned. Writing down important information in a notebook helps you remember key concepts and skills. You can use your notebook as a reference when you do your homework or when you study for a test.

Vocabulary
Your notebook is a good place to include definitions for vocabulary terms that appear at the beginning of each chapter and each lesson.

Notetaking Strategies
You'll find a different notetaking strategy at the beginning of each chapter.

Note Worthy
Look for notes in each chapter that provide helpful hints about notetaking.

Taking Notes
Your textbook displays important ideas and definitions on a notebook. You'll want to include this information in your notes.

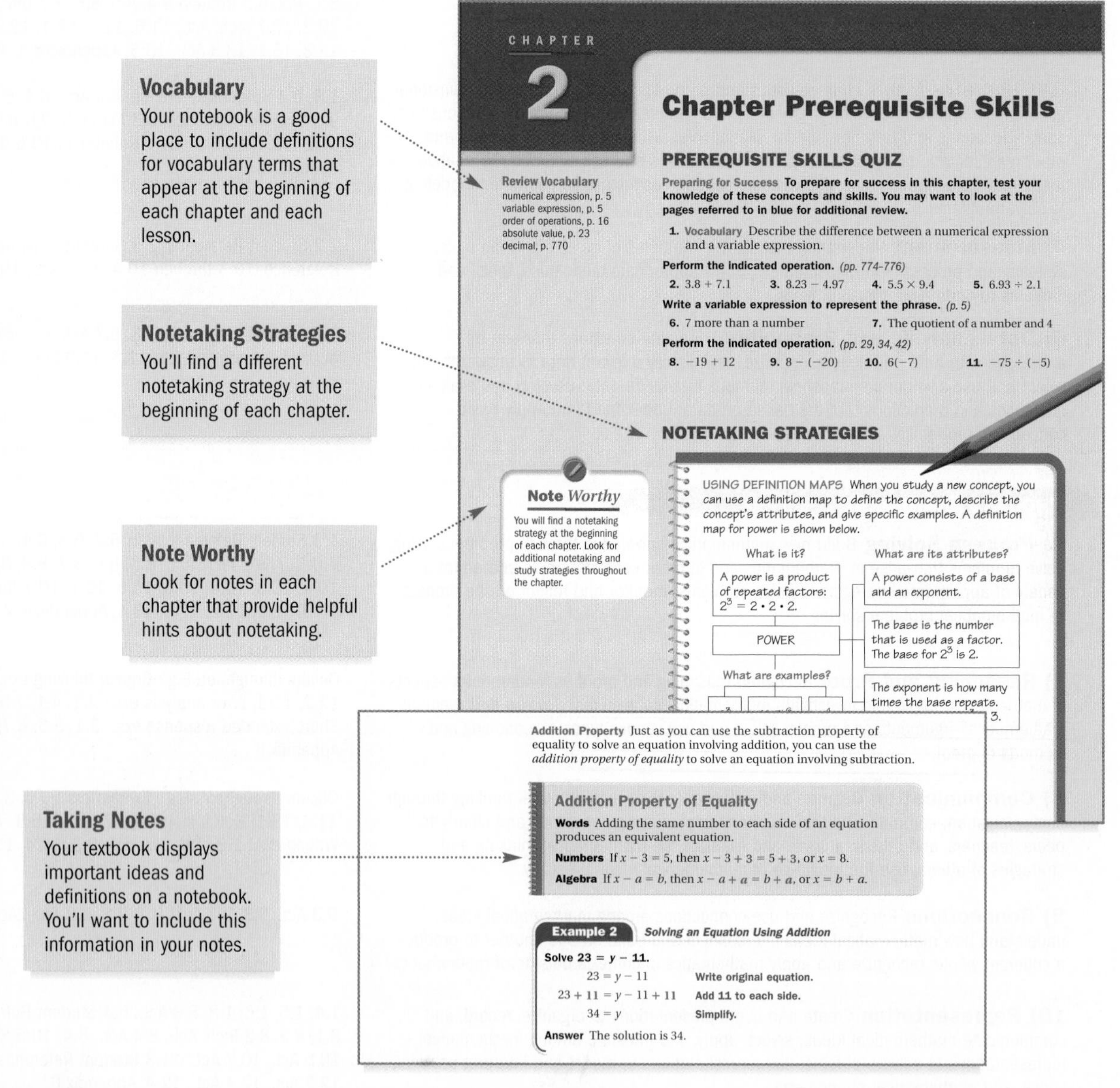

CHAPTER 2

Chapter Prerequisite Skills

PREREQUISITE SKILLS QUIZ

Review Vocabulary
numerical expression, p. 5
variable expression, p. 5
order of operations, p. 16
absolute value, p. 23
decimal, p. 770

Preparing for Success **To prepare for success in this chapter, test your knowledge of these concepts and skills. You may want to look at the pages referred to in blue for additional review.**

1. **Vocabulary** Describe the difference between a numerical expression and a variable expression.

Perform the indicated operation. *(pp. 774–776)*

2. $3.8 + 7.1$ 3. $8.23 - 4.97$ 4. 5.5×9.4 5. $6.93 \div 2.1$

Write a variable expression to represent the phrase. *(p. 5)*

6. 7 more than a number 7. The quotient of a number and 4

Perform the indicated operation. *(pp. 29, 34, 42)*

8. $-19 + 12$ 9. $8 - (-20)$ 10. $6(-7)$ 11. $-75 \div (-5)$

NOTETAKING STRATEGIES

USING DEFINITION MAPS When you study a new concept, you can use a definition map to define the concept, describe the concept's attributes, and give specific examples. A definition map for power is shown below.

What is it?
A power is a product of repeated factors: $2^3 = 2 \cdot 2 \cdot 2$.
POWER
What are examples?
What are its attributes?
A power consists of a base and an exponent.
The base is the number that is used as a factor. The base for 2^3 is 2.
The exponent is how many times the base repeats.

Note *Worthy*
You will find a notetaking strategy at the beginning of each chapter. Look for additional notetaking and study strategies throughout the chapter.

Addition Property Just as you can use the subtraction property of equality to solve an equation involving addition, you can use the *addition property of equality* to solve an equation involving subtraction.

Addition Property of Equality
Words Adding the same number to each side of an equation produces an equivalent equation.
Numbers If $x - 3 = 5$, then $x - 3 + 3 = 5 + 3$, or $x = 8$.
Algebra If $x - a = b$, then $x - a + a = b + a$, or $x = b + a$.

Example 2 *Solving an Equation Using Addition*

Solve $23 = y - 11$.

$23 = y - 11$ **Write original equation.**
$23 + 11 = y - 11 + 11$ **Add 11 to each side.**
$34 = y$ **Simplify.**

Answer The solution is 34.

Help with Learning Mathematics

Your textbook helps you succeed in mathematics. Keep your eye out for notes that help you with understanding important concepts, reading algebra and geometry, and doing your homework. Some examples of the types of notes you'll see are shown below.

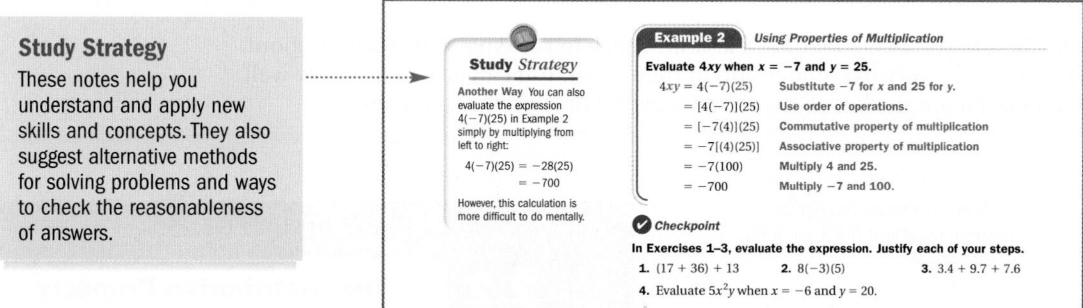

Study Strategy

These notes help you understand and apply new skills and concepts. They also suggest alternative methods for solving problems and ways to check the reasonableness of answers.

Study *Strategy*

Another Way You can also evaluate the expression $4(-7)(25)$ in Example 2 simply by multiplying from left to right:

$4(-7)(25) = -28(25)$
$= -700$

However, this calculation is more difficult to do mentally.

Example 2 *Using Properties of Multiplication*

Evaluate $4xy$ when $x = -7$ and $y = 25$.

$4xy = 4(-7)(25)$	Substitute -7 for x and 25 for y.
$= [4(-7)](25)$	Use order of operations.
$= [-7(4)](25)$	Commutative property of multiplication
$= -7[(4)(25)]$	Associative property of multiplication
$= -7(100)$	Multiply 4 and 25.
$= -700$	Multiply -7 and 100.

Checkpoint

In Exercises 1–3, evaluate the expression. Justify each of your steps.

1. $(17 + 36) + 13$ **2.** $8(-3)(5)$ **3.** $3.4 + 9.7 + 7.6$

4. Evaluate $5x^2y$ when $x = -6$ and $y = 20$.

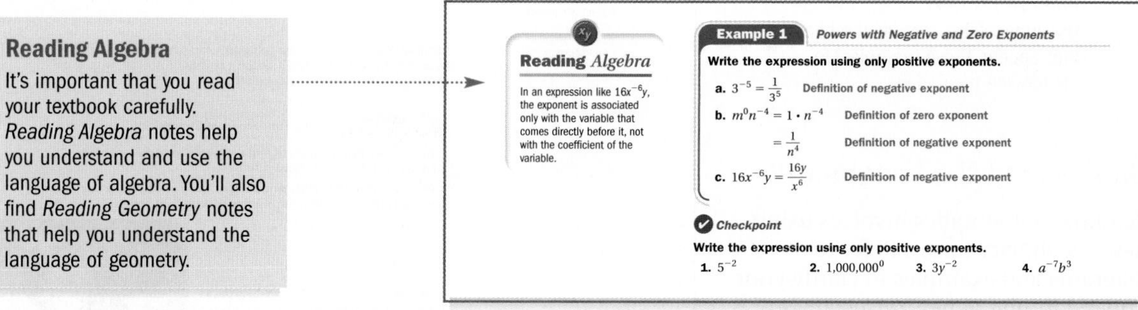

Reading Algebra

It's important that you read your textbook carefully. *Reading Algebra* notes help you understand and use the language of algebra. You'll also find *Reading Geometry* notes that help you understand the language of geometry.

Reading *Algebra*

In an expression like $16x^{-6}y$, the exponent is associated only with the variable that comes directly before it, not with the coefficient of the variable.

Example 1 *Powers with Negative and Zero Exponents*

Write the expression using only positive exponents.

a. $3^{-5} = \frac{1}{3^5}$ Definition of negative exponent

b. $m^0n^{-4} = 1 \cdot n^{-4}$ Definition of zero exponent

$= \frac{1}{n^4}$ Definition of negative exponent

c. $16x^{-6}y = \frac{16y}{x^6}$ Definition of negative exponent

Checkpoint

Write the expression using only positive exponents.

1. 5^{-2} **2.** $1{,}000{,}000^0$ **3.** $3y^{-2}$ **4.** $a^{-7}b^3$

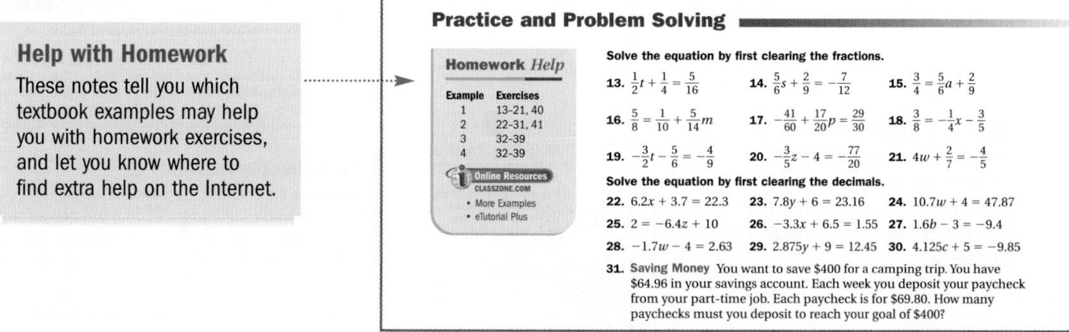

Help with Homework

These notes tell you which textbook examples may help you with homework exercises, and let you know where to find extra help on the Internet.

Practice and Problem Solving

Homework *Help*

Example	Exercises
1	13-21, 40
2	22-31, 41
3	32-39
4	32-39

Online Resources
CLASSZONE.COM
- More Examples
- eTutorial Plus

Solve the equation by first clearing the fractions.

13. $\frac{1}{2}t + \frac{1}{4} = \frac{5}{16}$ **14.** $\frac{5}{6}s + \frac{2}{9} = -\frac{7}{12}$ **15.** $\frac{3}{4} = \frac{5}{6}a + \frac{2}{9}$

16. $\frac{5}{8} = \frac{1}{10} + \frac{5}{14}m$ **17.** $-\frac{41}{60} + \frac{17}{20}p = \frac{29}{30}$ **18.** $\frac{3}{8} = -\frac{1}{4}x - \frac{3}{5}$

19. $-\frac{3}{2}t - \frac{5}{6} = -\frac{4}{9}$ **20.** $-\frac{3}{5}z - 4 = -\frac{77}{20}$ **21.** $4w + \frac{2}{7} = -\frac{4}{5}$

Solve the equation by first clearing the decimals.

22. $6.2x + 3.7 = 22.3$ **23.** $7.8y + 6 = 23.16$ **24.** $10.7w + 4 = 47.87$

25. $2 = -6.4z + 10$ **26.** $-3.3x + 6.5 = 1.55$ **27.** $1.6b - 3 = -9.4$

28. $-1.7w - 4 = 2.63$ **29.** $2.875y + 9 = 12.45$ **30.** $4.125c + 5 = -9.85$

31. Saving Money You want to save $400 for a camping trip. You have $64.96 in your savings account. Each week you deposit your paycheck from your part-time job. Each paycheck is for $69.80. How many paychecks must you deposit to reach your goal of $400?

Continued

Student Handbook

Reading Your Textbook

You need special skills to read a math textbook. These skills include identifying the main idea, learning new vocabulary, and focusing on the important concepts in a lesson. Most important, you need to be an active reader.

Identify the Main Idea

Even before you begin reading a lesson, check to see what the lesson is about. Then you'll know what to focus on in the lesson. You can also assess how well you understand the lesson content when you finish reading the lesson.

Lesson Opener
Look at the lesson opener for information about the main idea of the lesson.

Example Heads
Use other clues, such as the heads that appear above examples, to identify the main idea.

Understand the Vocabulary

Reading mathematics involves using new vocabulary terms. Refer to diagrams and examples to clarify your understanding of new terms. If you forget what a term means, look back at previous lessons or use the Glossary, which starts on page 824.

Vocabulary
New vocabulary terms are highlighted within a lesson. In addition, the Vocabulary list at the beginning of the lesson lists the important vocabulary terms in the lesson.

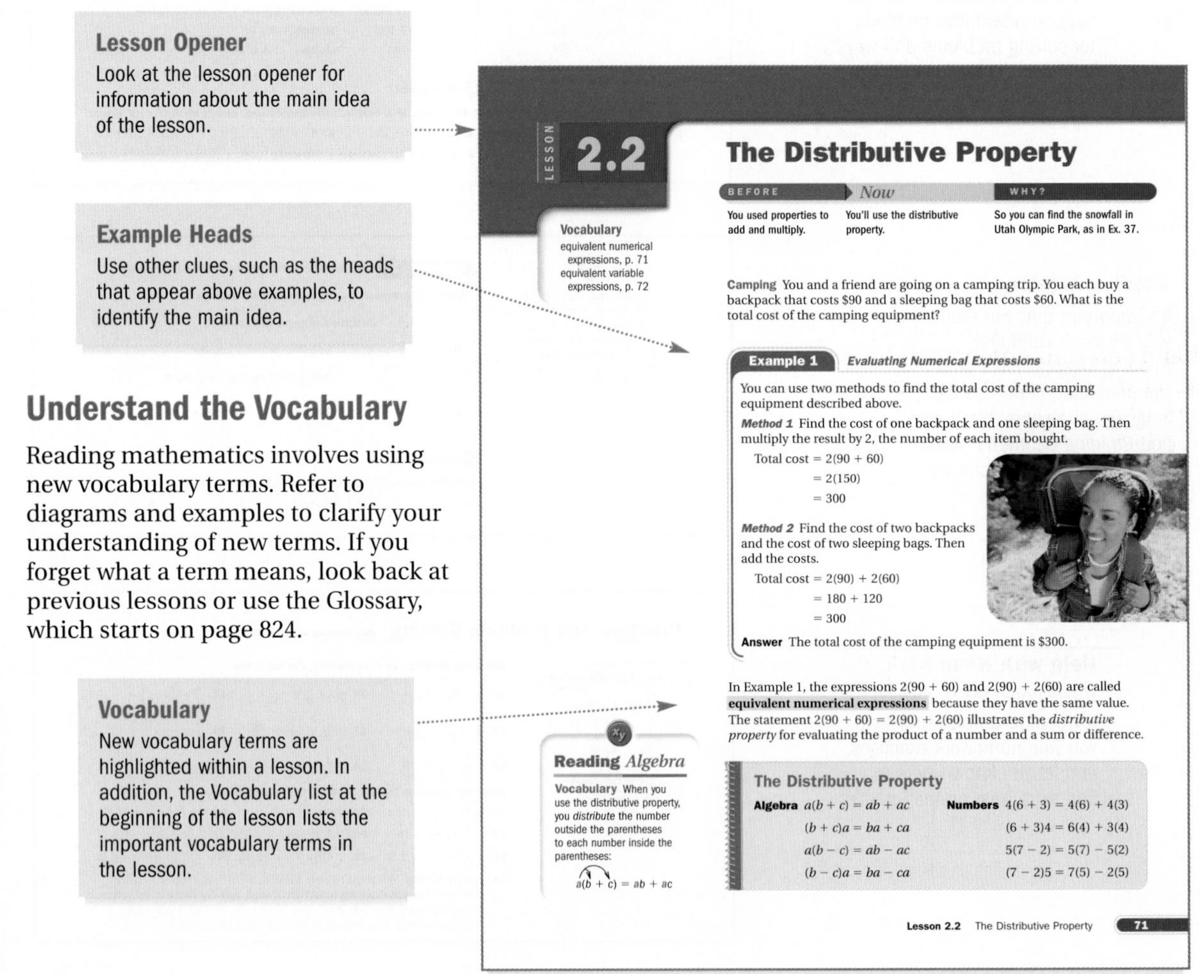

LESSON 2.2

The Distributive Property

BEFORE	Now	WHY?
You used properties to add and multiply.	You'll use the distributive property.	So you can find the snowfall in Utah Olympic Park, as in Ex. 37.

Vocabulary
equivalent numerical expressions, p. 71
equivalent variable expressions, p. 72

Camping You and a friend are going on a camping trip. You each buy a backpack that costs \$90 and a sleeping bag that costs \$60. What is the total cost of the camping equipment?

Example 1 *Evaluating Numerical Expressions*

You can use two methods to find the total cost of the camping equipment described above.

Method 1 Find the cost of one backpack and one sleeping bag. Then multiply the result by 2, the number of each item bought.

Total cost $= 2(90 + 60)$
$= 2(150)$
$= 300$

Method 2 Find the cost of two backpacks and the cost of two sleeping bags. Then add the costs.

Total cost $= 2(90) + 2(60)$
$= 180 + 120$
$= 300$

Answer The total cost of the camping equipment is \$300.

In Example 1, the expressions $2(90 + 60)$ and $2(90) + 2(60)$ are called **equivalent numerical expressions** because they have the same value. The statement $2(90 + 60) = 2(90) + 2(60)$ illustrates the *distributive property* for evaluating the product of a number and a sum or difference.

Reading Algebra
Vocabulary When you use the distributive property, you *distribute* the number outside the parentheses to each number inside the parentheses:
$a(b + c) = ab + ac$

The Distributive Property

	Algebra	Numbers
	$a(b + c) = ab + ac$	$4(6 + 3) = 4(6) + 4(3)$
	$(b + c)a = ba + ca$	$(6 + 3)4 = 6(4) + 3(4)$
	$a(b - c) = ab - ac$	$5(7 - 2) = 5(7) - 5(2)$
	$(b - c)a = ba - ca$	$(7 - 2)5 = 7(5) - 2(5)$

Lesson 2.2 The Distributive Property 71

Know What's Important

Focus on the important information in a lesson. Pay attention to highlighted vocabulary terms. Be on the lookout for definitions, properties, formulas, and other information displayed on a notebook. Make sure that you understand the worked-out examples.

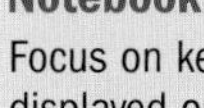

Notebook
Focus on key ideas that are displayed on a notebook.

Worked-Out Examples
Do the worked-out examples to make sure you know how to apply new concepts.

Be an Active Reader

As you read, keep a pencil in your hand and your notebook ready so that you can write down important information, practice new skills, and jot down questions to ask in class.

Checkpoint
Solve the Checkpoint exercises to make sure you understand new material.

Use Your Notebook
As you solve the examples yourself, you may find it helpful to describe the steps you follow. Write down any questions you have so you can ask them in class.

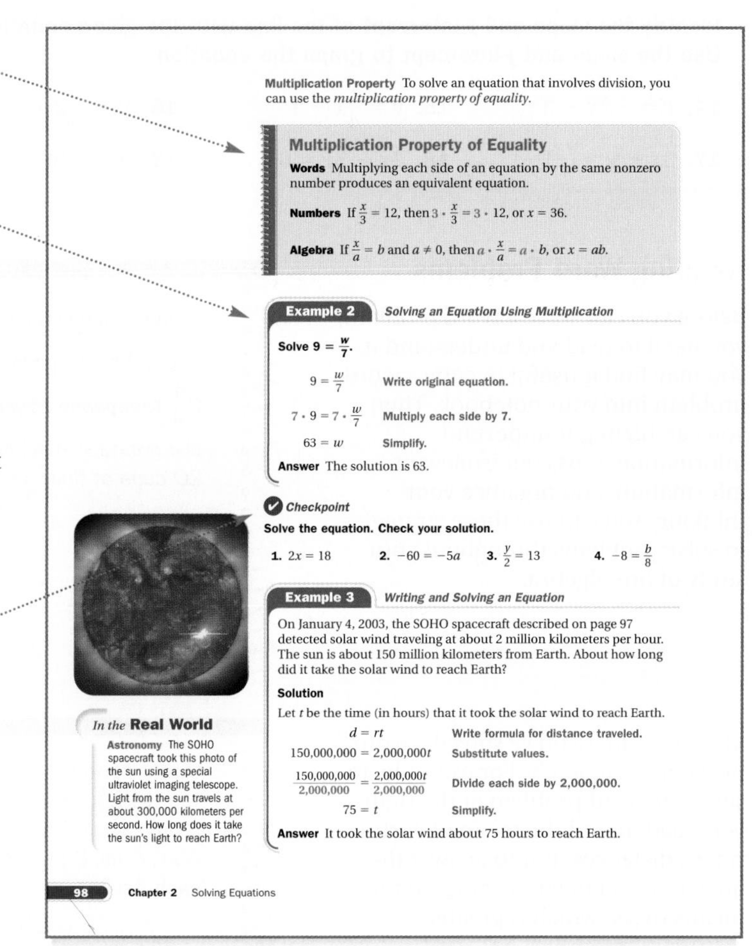

Multiplication Property To solve an equation that involves division, you can use the *multiplication property of equality.*

Multiplication Property of Equality

Words Multiplying each side of an equation by the same nonzero number produces an equivalent equation.

Numbers If $\frac{x}{3} = 12$, then $3 \cdot \frac{x}{3} = 3 \cdot 12$, or $x = 36$.

Algebra If $\frac{x}{a} = b$ and $a \neq 0$, then $a \cdot \frac{x}{a} = a \cdot b$, or $x = ab$.

Example 2 *Solving an Equation Using Multiplication*

Solve $9 = \frac{w}{7}$.

$9 = \frac{w}{7}$ Write original equation.

$7 \cdot 9 = 7 \cdot \frac{w}{7}$ Multiply each side by 7.

$63 = w$ Simplify.

Answer The solution is 63.

Checkpoint

Solve the equation. Check your solution.

1. $2x = 18$ **2.** $-60 = -5a$ **3.** $\frac{y}{2} = 13$ **4.** $-8 = \frac{b}{8}$

Example 3 *Writing and Solving an Equation*

On January 4, 2003, the SOHO spacecraft described on page 97 detected solar wind traveling at about 2 million kilometers per hour. The sun is about 150 million kilometers from Earth. About how long did it take the solar wind to reach Earth?

Solution

Let t be the time (in hours) that it took the solar wind to reach Earth.

$d = rt$ Write formula for distance traveled.

$150{,}000{,}000 = 2{,}000{,}000t$ Substitute values.

$\frac{150{,}000{,}000}{2{,}000{,}000} = \frac{2{,}000{,}000t}{2{,}000{,}000}$ Divide each side by 2,000,000.

$75 = t$ Simplify.

Answer It took the solar wind about 75 hours to reach Earth.

In the **Real World**

Astronomy The SOHO spacecraft took this photo of the sun using a special ultraviolet imaging telescope. Light from the sun travels at about 300,000 kilometers per second. How long does it take the sun's light to reach Earth?

98 Chapter 2 Solving Equations

Continued

Student Handbook

Reading and Problem Solving

The language in your math textbook is precise. When you do your homework, be sure to read carefully. For example, the direction line below from Chapter 8 asks you to do two things for each of the exercises: find the slope and y-intercept of a line, and then use the slope and y-intercept to graph an equation.

Identify the slope and *y*-intercept of the line with the given equation. Use the slope and *y*-intercept to graph the equation.

14. $y = -2x + 3$ **15.** $y = \frac{1}{4}x + 1$ **16.** $y = -2$

17. $3x + y = -1$ **18.** $2x - 3y = 0$ **19.** $5x - 2y = -4$

Reading Word Problems

Before you can solve a word problem, you need to read and understand it. You may find it useful to copy a word problem into your notebook. Then you can highlight important information, cross out irrelevant information, and organize your thinking. You can use these strategies to solve problems throughout your study of pre-algebra.

To make dough for two pizzas, you need 4 cups of flour, ~~2 tablespoons of olive oil, $1\frac{1}{2}$ teaspoons of salt,~~ $2\frac{1}{4}$ teaspoons of yeast, ~~and $1\frac{1}{2}$ cups of water.~~ What is the greatest number of pizzas you can make if you have 20 cups of flour and 6 teaspoons of yeast?

Ingredient	Needed (for 2 pizzas)	Already have
Flour	4 c	20 c
Yeast	$2\frac{1}{4}$ tsp	6 tsp

Make sure that you've solved a word problem completely. For example, to solve the word problem at the right, you need to find the mean of each rider's distances. But to answer the question, you need to compare the means to see which is greater.

Over a period of 4 days, you rode these distances on your bike: 10 mi, 12 mi, 11 mi, 8 mi. Over a period of 5 days, your friend rode these distances: 11 mi, 14 mi, 8 mi, 8 mi, 8 mi. On average, which of you rode farther each day?

You: $\frac{10 + 12 + 11 + 8}{4} = 10.25$ miles each day

Your friend: $\frac{11 + 14 + 8 + 8 + 8}{5} = 9.8$ miles each day

On average, you rode farther than your friend each day.

Additional Resources in Your Textbook

Your textbook contains many resources that you can use for reference when you are studying or doing your homework.

Skills Review Handbook Use the Skills Review Handbook on pages 770–802 to review material learned in previous courses.

Student Reference Pages Use the Student Reference pages that appear throughout the book to review key material for use in upcoming lessons.

Tables Refer to the tables on pages 816–823 if you need information about mathematical symbols, measures, formulas, and properties.

English and Spanish Glossaries Use the glossaries on pages 840–865 and 866–893 to look up the meanings of math vocabulary terms. Each glossary entry also tells where in your book a term is covered in more detail.

Index Use the Index on pages 894–922 as a quick guide for finding out where a particular math topic is covered in the book.

Selected Answers Use the Selected Answers starting on page SA1 to check your work or to see whether you are on the right track in solving a problem.

TEXTBOOK Scavenger Hunt

Get some practice using your textbook. Use the additional resources described above to answer each question. Give page numbers to show where you found the answer to the question.

1. What is a rational number? **See p. 857. (For Spanish, see p. 884.)**
2. On what page of the book can you find selected answers for Lesson 1.1? **See p. SA1.**
3. What formula can you use to find the surface area of a cone? **See p. 818.**
4. Tell what each of these symbols means: $m\angle B$, $|a|$, $\leq$. **See p. 816.**
5. Where can you find a statement of the associative property of multiplication? **See p. 820.**
6. What is a scatter plot? **See p. 859. (For Spanish, see p. 886.)**
7. How many pounds are there in one ton? **See p. 817.**
8. On what page can you review the skill of classifying angles? **See p. 793.**
9. What is the freezing point of water in degrees Fahrenheit? in degrees Celsius? **See p. 817.**
10. On what pages can you review the topics *mean*, *median*, *mode*, and *range*? **See pp. 39 and 40.**

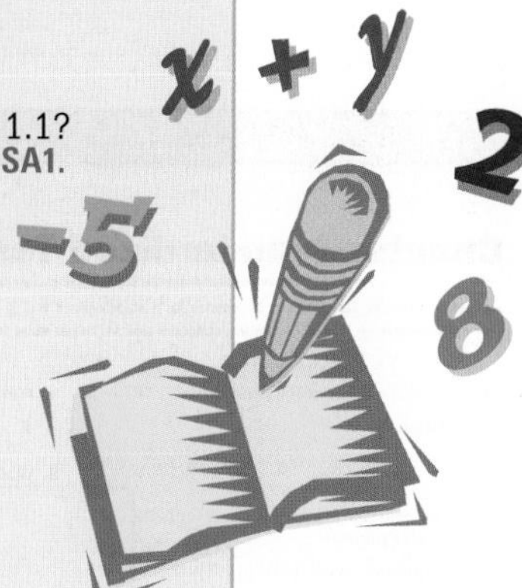

Assessing Progress

Strategies for Success on Tests

Your book will help you succeed on tests. At the end of each unit, a *Building Test-Taking Skills* section guides you, step by step, through strategies for solving common types of test questions, including multiple choice, short response, context-based multiple choice, and extended response questions. You'll also learn how to evaluate your work using a scoring rubric. You can practice test-taking skills in every lesson, in every chapter, and in every unit.

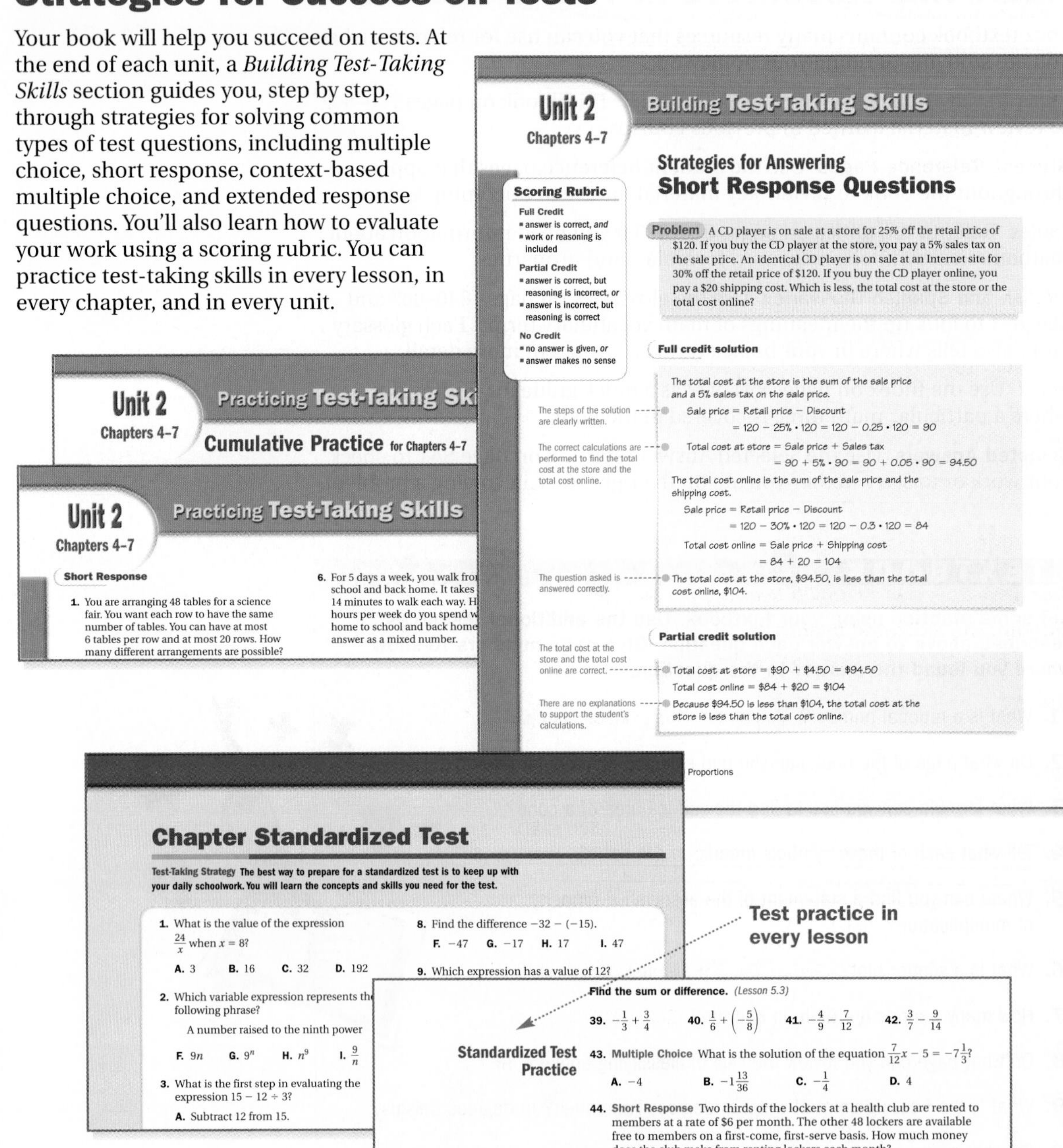

Unit 2 Chapters 4–7 — Building **Test-Taking Skills**

Strategies for Answering **Short Response Questions**

Scoring Rubric

Full Credit
- answer is correct, *and*
- work or reasoning is included

Partial Credit
- answer is correct, but reasoning is incorrect, or
- answer is incorrect, but reasoning is correct

No Credit
- no answer is given, or
- answer makes no sense

Problem A CD player is on sale at a store for 25% off the retail price of \$120. If you buy the CD player at the store, you pay a 5% sales tax on the sale price. An identical CD player is on sale at an Internet site for 30% off the retail price of \$120. If you buy the CD player online, you pay a \$20 shipping cost. Which is less, the total cost at the store or the total cost online?

Full credit solution

The total cost at the store is the sum of the sale price and a 5% sales tax on the sale price.

Sale price = Retail price − Discount
= 120 − 25% • 120 = 120 − 0.25 • 120 = 90

Total cost at store = Sale price + Sales tax
= 90 + 5% • 90 = 90 + 0.05 • 90 = 94.50

The total cost online is the sum of the sale price and the shipping cost.

Sale price = Retail price − Discount
= 120 − 30% • 120 = 120 − 0.3 • 120 = 84

Total cost online = Sale price + Shipping cost
= 84 + 20 = 104

The total cost at the store, \$94.50, is less than the total cost online, \$104.

The steps of the solution are clearly written.

The correct calculations are performed to find the total cost at the store and the total cost online.

The question asked is answered correctly.

Partial credit solution

Total cost at store = \$90 + \$4.50 = \$94.50
Total cost online = \$84 + \$20 = \$104
Because \$94.50 is less than \$104, the total cost at the store is less than the total cost online.

The total cost at the store and the total cost online are correct.

There are no explanations to support the student's calculations.

Proportions

Unit 2 Chapters 4–7 — Practicing **Test-Taking Ski**

Cumulative Practice for Chapters 4–7

Unit 2 Chapters 4–7 — Practicing **Test-Taking Skills**

Short Response

1. You are arranging 48 tables for a science fair. You want each row to have the same number of tables. You can have at most 6 tables per row and at most 20 rows. How many different arrangements are possible?

6. For 5 days a week, you walk fro school and back home. It takes 14 minutes to walk each way. H hours per week do you spend w home to school and back home answer as a mixed number.

Chapter Standardized Test

Test-Taking Strategy **The best way to prepare for a standardized test is to keep up with your daily schoolwork. You will learn the concepts and skills you need for the test.**

1. What is the value of the expression $\frac{24}{x}$ when $x = 8$?
   A. 3 **B.** 16 **C.** 32 **D.** 192
2. Which variable expression represents th following phrase?
   A number raised to the ninth power
   F. $9n$ **G.** 9^n **H.** n^9 **I.** $\frac{9}{n}$
3. What is the first step in evaluating the expression $15 - 12 \div 3$?
   A. Subtract 12 from 15.

8. Find the difference $-32 - (-15)$.
   F. −47 **G.** −17 **H.** 17 **I.** 47
9. Which expression has a value of 12?

Test practice in every lesson

Standardized Test Practice

Find the sum or difference. *(Lesson 5.3)*

39. $-\frac{1}{3} + \frac{3}{4}$ 40. $\frac{1}{6} + \left(-\frac{5}{8}\right)$ 41. $-\frac{4}{9} - \frac{7}{12}$ 42. $\frac{3}{7} - \frac{9}{14}$

43. **Multiple Choice** What is the solution of the equation $\frac{7}{12}x - 5 = -7\frac{1}{3}$?
    A. −4 **B.** $-1\frac{13}{36}$ **C.** $-\frac{1}{4}$ **D.** 4

44. **Short Response** Two thirds of the lockers at a health club are rented to members at a rate of \$6 per month. The other 48 lockers are available free to members on a first-come, first-serve basis. How much money does the club make from renting lockers each month?

Pre-Course Test

Estimation

Place Value and Rounding *(Skills Review, p. 770)*

Give the place and value of the red digit. Then round the number to that place.

1. 49.21 tenths, 0.2; 49.2
2. 1097.253 tens, 90; 1100
3. 352,453.349 hundred thousands, 300,000; 400,000
4. 7482.9154 thousandths, 0.005; 7482.915

Estimating *(Skills Review, pp. 771–772)*

Estimate the sum or difference by rounding each number to the place of its leading digit.

5. 93,120 + 28,643 120,000
6. 87,302 − 32,218 60,000
7. 59,265 − 14,794 50,000
8. 78,942 + 41,678 120,000

Find a low and high estimate for the product or quotient. 9–12. Estimates may vary.

9. 823×26 16,000; 27,000
10. 4897×872 3,200,000; 4,500,000
11. $7231 \div 82$ 80; 100
12. $5461 \div 64$ 70; 100

Decimals

Comparing and Ordering Decimals *(Skills Review, p. 773)*

13. Order the numbers 0.2, 0.25, 0.02, and 0.252 from least to greatest. 0.02, 0.2, 0.25, 0.252

Decimal Operations *(Skills Review, pp. 774–776)*

Perform the indicated operation.

14. 5.6 + 9.2 14.8
15. 12.87 + 4.58 17.45
16. 5.1 − 2.67 2.43
17. 4.21 − 3.78 0.43
18. 0.86×0.3 0.258
19. $61.95 \div 3.5$ 17.7
20. $455.7 \div 9.8$ 46.5
21. 0.04×9.8 0.392

Fractions

Fractions, Mixed Numbers, and Improper Fractions *(Skills Review, pp. 777–778)*

Write the mixed number as an improper fraction or the improper fraction as a mixed number.

22. $4\frac{1}{8}$ $\frac{33}{8}$
23. $5\frac{4}{9}$ $\frac{49}{9}$
24. $\frac{23}{3}$ $7\frac{2}{3}$
25. $\frac{61}{7}$ $8\frac{5}{7}$

Fraction Operations *(Skills Review, pp. 779–780)*

Perform the indicated operation.

26. $\frac{2}{5} + \frac{1}{5}$ $\frac{3}{5}$
27. $\frac{5}{9} + \frac{2}{9}$ $\frac{7}{9}$
28. $\frac{3}{17} + \frac{11}{17}$ $\frac{14}{17}$
29. $\frac{14}{15} - \frac{1}{15}$ $\frac{13}{15}$
30. $\frac{14}{19} - \frac{10}{19}$ $\frac{4}{19}$
31. $\frac{3}{8} \times 24$ 9
32. $12 \times \frac{5}{6}$ 10
33. $\frac{3}{10} \times 20$ 6

38. 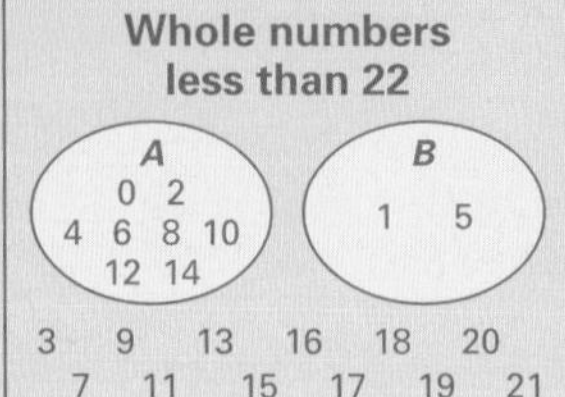

45.

Data Analysis

Reading Graphs *(Skills Review, pp. 781–783)*

In Exercises 34 and 35, use the bar graph, which shows the results of a survey of 120 people asked about their favorite summer activity.

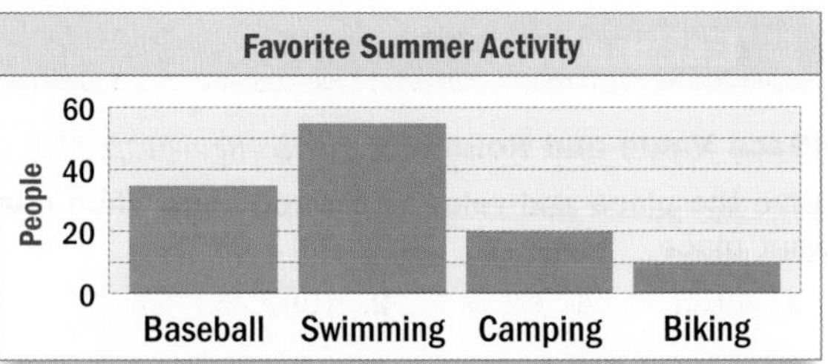

34. How many people said camping is their favorite summer activity? **20 people**

35. What summer activity did the greatest number of people say is their favorite? **swimming**

In Exercises 36 and 37, use the circle graph, which shows the results of a survey of 300 people asked about their favorite fruit.

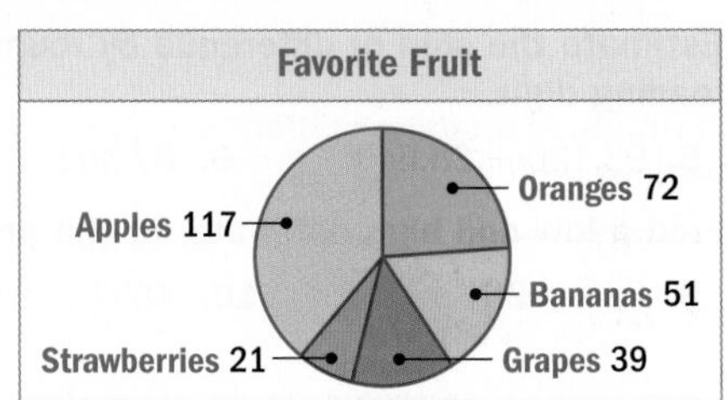

36. What type of fruit did the greatest number of people say is their favorite? **apples**

37. How many more people chose oranges as their favorite fruit than chose grapes as their favorite fruit? **33 more people**

Venn Diagrams and Logical Reasoning *(Skills Review, p. 784)*

38. Using the whole numbers less than 22, draw a Venn diagram showing set A, which consists of even numbers less than 15, and set B, which consists of numbers that are factors of 5. **See margin.**

Geometry and Measurement

Basic Geometric Figures *(Skills Review, p. 785)*

39. What is the perimeter of a rectangle with a length of 7 centimeters and a width of 4 centimeters? **22 cm**

Measurement *(Skills Review, pp. 786–791)*

In Exercises 40–42, copy and complete the statement.

40. 15 yards = _?_ feet **45**

41. 25 kilograms = _?_ grams **25,000**

42. 32 ounces = _?_ pounds **2**

43. Find the area of the square. **81 in.^{2}**

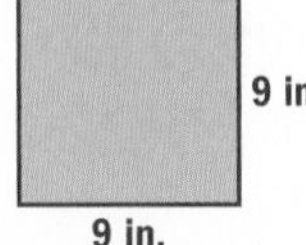

44. Find the volume of the cube. **3375 m^3**

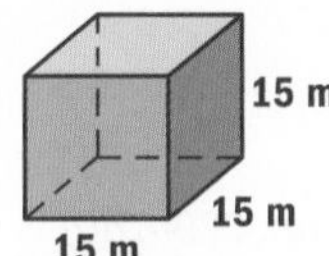

Using a Protractor and Compass *(Skills Review, pp. 792–794)*

45. Use a protractor to draw an angle with a measure of 86°. Classify the angle as *acute, right, obtuse,* or *straight.* **See margin for art; acute.**

46. Use a compass to draw a circle with a radius of 4 centimeters. **Check students' work.**

3. hundred thousands, 300,000; 400,000

6. ten millions, 10,000,000; 310,000,000

Pre-Course Practice

Estimation

Place Value and Rounding *(Skills Review, p. 770)*

Give the place and value of the red digit. Then round the number to that place.

1. 0.598 tenths, 0.5; 0.6
2. 63.9721 thousandths, 0.002; 63.972
3. 356,418 See margin.
4. 12,590.6 thousands, 2000; 13,000
5. 15,213.04 tens, 10; 15,210
6. 312,145,203 See margin.
7. 213.392 tenths, 0.3; 213.4
8. 214,986.32 ones, 6; 214,986

Estimating *(Skills Review, pp. 771–772)*

Estimate the sum or difference by rounding each number to the place of its leading digit.

9. 781 + 615 1400
10. 58,498 + 34,215 90,000
11. 23,619 + 78,278 100,000
12. 815 − 478 300
13. 81,592 − 79,902 0
14. 324,981 − 142,243 200,000

Find a low and high estimate for the product or quotient. 15–20. Estimates may vary.

15. 467 × 47 16,000; 25,000
16. 758 × 312 210,000; 320,000
17. 9738 × 852 7,200,000; 9,000,000
18. 823 ÷ 32 20; 28
19. 4516 ÷ 77 50; 70
20. 62,491 ÷ 16 3100; 6300

Decimals

Comparing and Ordering Decimals *(Skills Review, p. 773)*

Copy and complete the statement using <, >, or =.

21. 0.32 _?_ 0.3 >
22. 5.0 _?_ 5 =
23. 6.02 _?_ 6.2 <
24. 78.3 _?_ 77.8 >
25. 0.54 _?_ 0.45 >
26. 2.323 _?_ 2.3230 =

Order the numbers from least to greatest.

27. 1.2, 2.1, 2.15, 1.9 — 1.2, 1.9, 2.1, 2.15
28. 7.7, 7.77, 6.77, 7.71 — 6.77, 7.7, 7.71, 7.77
29. 0.5, 0, 0.25, 0.51 — 0, 0.25, 0.5, 0.51
30. 9.4, 9.43, 9.5, 9.3 — 9.3, 9.4, 9.43, 9.5
31. 3.4, 3.04, 3.41, 3.14 — 3.04, 3.14, 3.4, 3.41
32. 10.01, 1.01, 10.1, 11 — 1.01, 10.01, 10.1, 11

Decimal Operations *(Skills Review, pp. 774–776)*

Perform the indicated operation.

33. 4.3 + 9.2 13.5
34. 6.5 + 7.6 14.1
35. 5.04 + 9.27 14.31
36. 8.98 + 1.76 10.74
37. 8.4 + 3.15 11.55
38. 4.8 − 2.3 2.5
39. 18.954 − 13.785 5.169
40. 24.6 − 19.83 4.77
41. 54.1 − 39.806 14.294
42. 9.2 × 0.4 3.68
43. 5.3 × 9.8 51.94
44. 2.12 × 4.65 9.858
45. 8.343 ÷ 2.7 3.09
46. 62.685 ÷ 3.5 17.91
47. 11.7 ÷ 1.3 9

Fractions

Fractions, Mixed Numbers, and Improper Fractions *(Skills Review, pp. 777–778)*

Write a fraction or mixed number to represent the shaded region.

48. $1\frac{4}{9}$

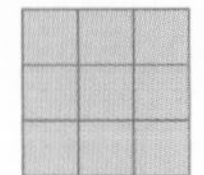
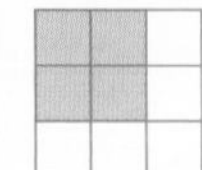

49. $\frac{5}{8}$

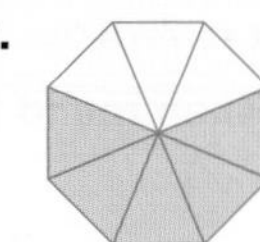

Write the mixed number as an improper fraction.

50. $1\frac{5}{9}$ $\frac{14}{9}$ **51.** $4\frac{3}{4}$ $\frac{19}{4}$ **52.** $9\frac{7}{12}$ $\frac{115}{12}$ **53.** $15\frac{2}{3}$ $\frac{47}{3}$

Write the improper fraction as a mixed number.

54. $\frac{23}{6}$ $3\frac{5}{6}$ **55.** $\frac{83}{8}$ $10\frac{3}{8}$ **56.** $\frac{59}{6}$ $9\frac{5}{6}$ **57.** $\frac{53}{2}$ $26\frac{1}{2}$

Fraction Operations *(Skills Review, pp. 779–780)*

Find the sum or difference.

58. $\frac{4}{7}+\frac{2}{7}$ $\frac{6}{7}$ **59.** $\frac{9}{13}+\frac{3}{13}$ $\frac{12}{13}$ **60.** $\frac{7}{11}+\frac{2}{11}$ $\frac{9}{11}$ **61.** $\frac{10}{21}+\frac{1}{21}$ $\frac{11}{21}$

62. $\frac{2}{3}-\frac{1}{3}$ $\frac{1}{3}$ **63.** $\frac{7}{17}-\frac{3}{17}$ $\frac{4}{17}$ **64.** $\frac{11}{23}-\frac{5}{23}$ $\frac{6}{23}$ **65.** $\frac{12}{25}-\frac{4}{25}$ $\frac{8}{25}$

Find the product.

66. $6\times\frac{2}{3}$ 4 **67.** $\frac{5}{11}\times 22$ 10 **68.** $\frac{2}{7}\times 7$ 2 **69.** $12\times\frac{1}{4}$ 3

Data Analysis

Reading Graphs *(Skills Review, pp. 781–783)*

In Exercises 70–72, use the bar graph, which shows the most popular boys' names given to babies in 2001.

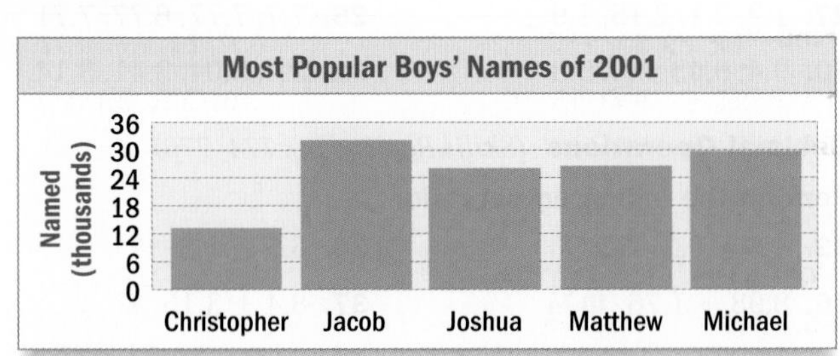

70. What was the most popular boys' name in 2001? **Jacob**

71. What two names were given to about the same number of boys? **Joshua and Matthew**

72. About how many more boys were given the name Michael than were given the name Christopher? **about 16,000 more boys**

In Exercises 73–75, use the line graph, which shows the first year sales at a store.

73. Between what two months did sales increase the most? **months 3 and 4**

74. Between what two months did sales decrease the most? **months 6 and 7**

75. Between what two months did sales stay the same? **months 4 and 5**

In Exercises 76–78, use the circle graph, which shows the results of a survey of 200 people asked about favorite places to vacation.

76. What is the most favorite place to vacation? **ocean**

77. What is the least favorite place to vacation? **city**

78. How many more people prefer visiting a lake than prefer visiting a city? **24 more people**

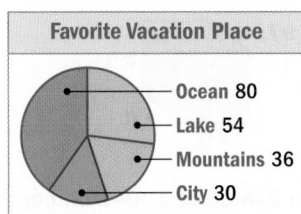

Favorite Vacation Place

Ocean 80
Lake 54
Mountains 36
City 30

Venn Diagrams and Logical Reasoning *(Skills Review, p. 784)*

Draw a Venn diagram of the sets described. **79–80. See margin.**

79. Of the whole numbers less than 20, set A consists of numbers less than 15 and greater than 8, and set B consists of even numbers.

80. Of the odd whole numbers less than 50, set A consists of multiples of 3, and set B consists of multiples of 5.

Use the Venn diagram you drew in Exercise 80 to tell whether the statement is *true* or *false*. Explain your reasoning.

81. More than one odd whole number less than 50 is a multiple of 3 and 5. **See margin.**

82. All odd whole numbers less than 50 are multiples of 3. **False. *Sample answer:* There are many odd numbers less than 50 that are not multiples of 3, such as 7, 25, and 31; these numbers are located outside of the oval representing set A.**

Geometry and Measurement

Basic Geometric Figures *(Skills Review, p. 785)*

Find the perimeter of the figure described.

83. A square with sides 2 in. long **8 in.**

84. A triangle with sides 3 cm, 5 cm, and 6 cm long **14 cm**

Measurement *(Skills Review, pp. 786–791)*

Copy and complete the statement.

85. 48 inches = _?_ feet **4**

86. 24 ounces = _?_ pounds **$1\frac{1}{2}$, or 1.5**

87. 5 kilograms = _?_ grams **5000**

Use a ruler to draw a segment with the given length. **88–91. Check students' work.**

88. $4\frac{3}{8}$ inches

89. $\frac{1}{2}$ inch

90. 3.2 centimeters

91. 4.8 centimeters

79.

Whole numbers less than 20

A: 9 11 13
A and B: 10 12 14
B: 0 2 4 6 8 16 18
Outside: 1 3 5 7 15 17 19

80.

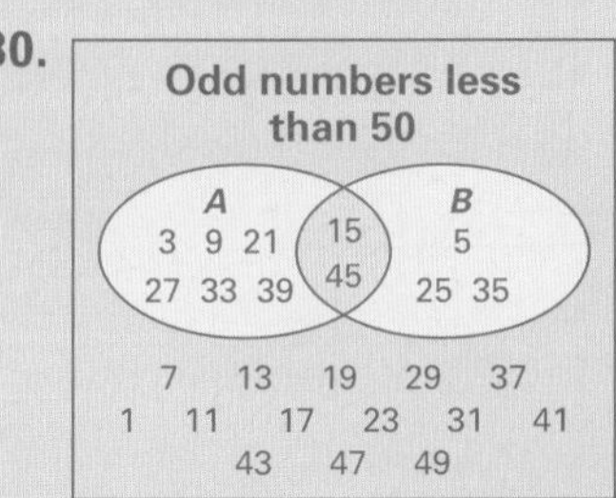

81. True. *Sample answer:* Both 15 and 45 are odd multiples of 3 and 5 that are less than 50; they are located in the overlap of the ovals representing sets A and B.

105.

106.

107.

108.

Use a ruler to find the length of the segment in inches and in centimeters.

92. ______ about $1\frac{11}{16}$ in., about 4.3 cm **93.** ______ about $2\frac{3}{8}$ in., about 6.1 cm

Find the area of the square.

94. 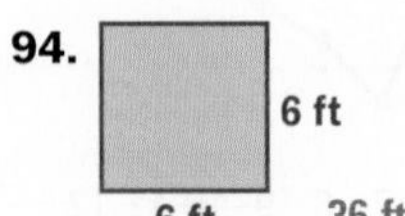

36 ft²

95. 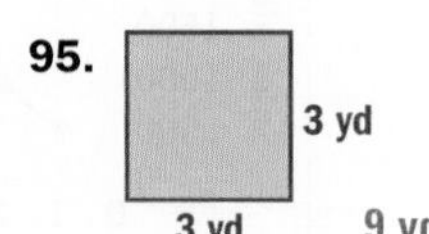

9 yd²

96. 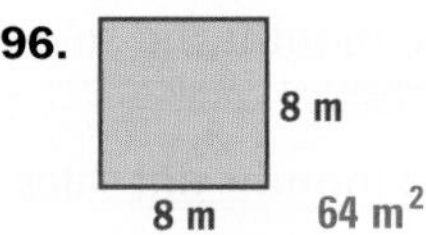

64 m²

Find the volume of the cube.

97. 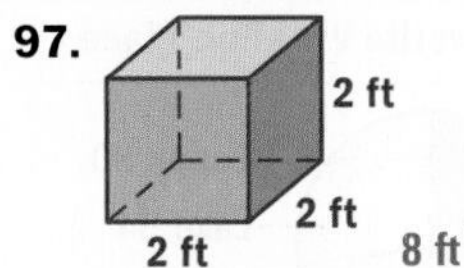

8 ft³

98. 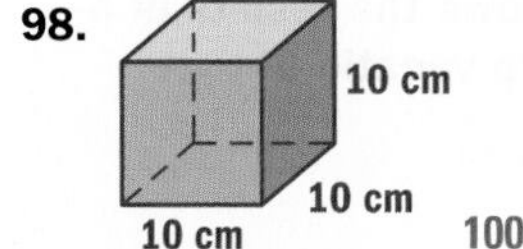

1000 cm³

99. 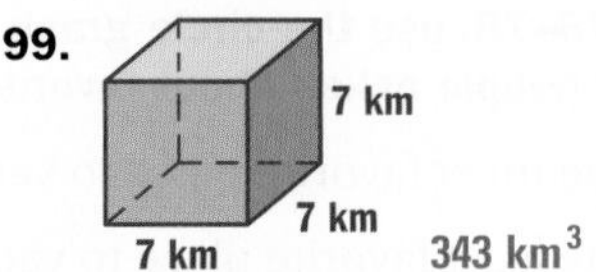

343 km³

In Exercises 100–102, copy and complete the statement using <, >, or =.

100. 3.5 tons _?_ 7500 lb < **101.** 14 lb _?_ 220 oz > **102.** 437 g _?_ 4.3 kg <

103. Find the weight of the cheese. $1\frac{1}{2}$ lb, or 1 lb 8 oz

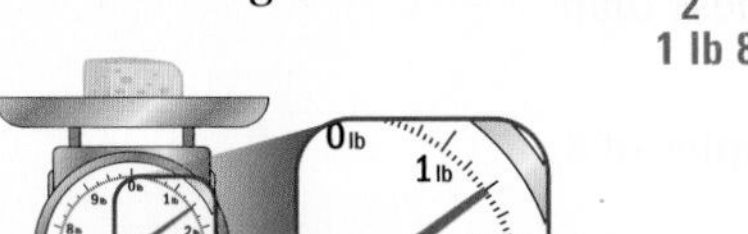

104. Find the amount of liquid in the measuring cup. 350 mL

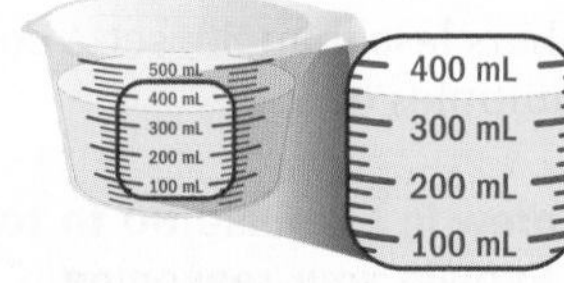

Using a Protractor and Compass *(Skills Review, pp. 792–794)*

Use a protractor to draw an angle with the given measure. 105–108. See margin.

105. 45° **106.** 175° **107.** 180° **108.** 93°

Find the measure of the angle. Classify the angle as *acute, right, obtuse,* or *straight*. Measures may vary. Accept reasonable measures.

109. 60°; acute

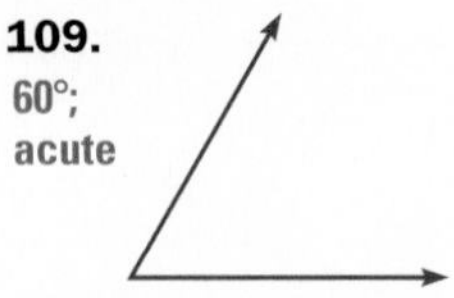

110. 144°; obtuse

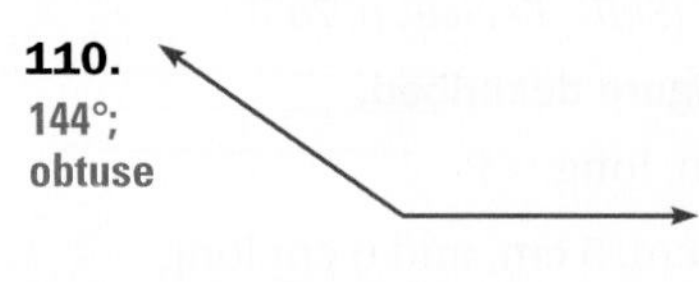

Use a compass to draw a circle with the given radius. 111–114. Check students' work.

111. 3 inches **112.** 5 centimeters **113.** 2 centimeters **114.** 2.5 inches

115. Use a straightedge and a compass to draw a segment whose length is the *sum* of the lengths of the two given segments. Check students' work.

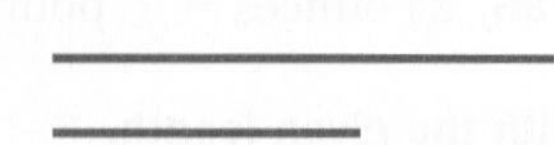

UNIT 1

Integers, Equations, *and* Inequalities

Chapter 1 Variables, Expressions, and Integers

- Write and evaluate variable expressions.
- Perform operations with integers.
- Plot points in a coordinate plane.

Chapter 2 Solving Equations

- Use mathematical properties to simplify variable expressions.
- Write and solve one-step equations.
- Perform operations with positive and negative decimals.

Chapter 3 Multi-Step Equations and Inequalities

- Write and solve multi-step equations.
- Write and solve inequalities.

From Chapter 2, p. 100
How long does it take a gray whale to migrate?

UNIT RESOURCES

These resources are provided to help you prepare for the unit and to customize review materials:

 ***Chapter Resource Books***
- Chapter 1
- Chapter 2
- Chapter 3

 ***Assessment Book***
- Chapters 1–3, pp. 7–45

 ***Technology***
- EasyPlanner CD-ROM
- Test and Practice Generator
- Electronic Lesson Presentations CD-ROM
- eTutorial CD-ROM

 ***Internet***
- Classzone
- eEdition Plus Online
- eWorkbook Plus Online
- eTutorial Plus Online
- EasyPlanner Plus Online

ENGLISH LEARNER SUPPORT

- Spanish Study Guide
- Multi-Language Visual Glossary
- Chapter Audio Summaries CDs
- Teacher's Edition
  Chapter 1, pp. 2E–2F
  Chapter 2, pp. 60E–60F
  Chapter 3, pp. 116E–116F

CHAPTER 1

Pacing and Assignment Guide

REGULAR SCHEDULE

Lesson	Les. Day	BASIC	AVERAGE	ADVANCED
1.1	Day 1	pp. 7-9 Exs. 12-27, 32-43, 49, 50, 57-67	pp. 7-9 Exs. 16-27, 32-38, 40, 45-55, 57-67	pp. 7-9 Exs. 16-19, 28-56*, 59-67
1.2	Day 1	SRH p. 789 Exs. 1, 2, 5, 6; pp. 12-13 Exs. 13-33, 36, 39-48	pp. 12-13 Exs. 17-37, 39-49	pp. 12-13 Exs. 17-20, 25-29, 32-38*, 43-49
1.3	Day 1	SRH p. 774 Exs. 1-4, p. 775 Exs. 1-4; pp. 19-20 Exs. 10-35, 40-44	pp. 19-20 Exs. 12-18, 23-38, 40-44	pp. 19-20 Exs. 13-18, 23-30, 32-44*
1.4	Day 1	pp. 25-26 Exs. 18-51, 54-56, 66-76	pp. 25-26 Exs. 21-37, 42-53, 57-62, 66-76	pp. 25-26 Exs. 21, 24, 25, 30-34, 39, 42-71, 75, 76*
1.5	Day 1	pp. 32-33 Exs. 14-38, 41-44, 47-51, 61-67	pp. 32-33 Exs. 18-23, 27-56, 58, 61-68	pp. 32-33 Exs. 21-23, 27-32, 36-66*, 68
1.6	Day 1	pp. 36-38 Exs. 12-33, 35-44, 55-66	pp. 36-38 Exs. 18-23, 26-48, 51, 52, 55-66	pp. 36-38 Exs. 20-23, 28-55*, 59-66
1.7	Day 1	SRH p. 781 Exs. 1-3; pp. 45-46 Exs. 12-25, 27-39, 45-51	pp. 45-46 Exs. 18-41, 45-52	pp. 45-46 Exs. 20-28, 33-52*
1.8	Day 1	pp. 49-51 Exs. 8-24, 27-29, 35-44	pp. 49-51 Exs. 12-31, 35-44	pp. 49-51 Exs. 14-16, 21-44*
Review	Day 1	pp. 52-55 Exs. 1-64	pp. 52-55 Exs. 1-64	pp. 52-55 Exs. 1-64
Assess	Day 1	Chapter 1 Test	Chapter 1 Test	Chapter 1 Test
YEARLY PACING		Chapter 1 Total – **10 days**	Chapter 1 Total – **10 days**	Remaining – **150 days**

*Challenge Exercises EP = Extra Practice SRH = Skills Review Handbook

BLOCK SCHEDULE

DAY 1	DAY 2	DAY 3	DAY 4	DAY 5
1.1 pp. 7-9 Exs. 16-27, 32-38, 40, 45-55, 57-67 **1.2** pp. 12-13 Exs. 17-37, 39-49	**1.3** pp. 19-20 Exs. 12-18, 23-38, 40-44 **1.4** pp. 25-26 Exs. 21-37, 42-53, 57-62, 66-76	**1.5** pp. 32-33 Exs. 18-23, 27-56, 58, 61-68 **1.6** pp. 36-38 Exs. 18-23, 26-48, 51, 52, 55-66	**1.7** pp. 45-46 Exs. 18-41, 45-52 **1.8** pp. 49-51 Exs. 12-31, 35-44	**Review** pp. 52-55 Exs. 1-64 **Assess** Chapter 1 Test

YEARLY PACING	Chapter 1 Total – **5 days**	Chapter 1 Total – **5 days**	Remaining – **75 days**

Support Materials

CHAPTER RESOURCE BOOK

CHAPTER SUPPORT								
Tips for New Teachers	p. 1			Parents as Partners			p. 3	
LESSON SUPPORT	**1.1**	**1.2**	**1.3**	**1.4**	**1.5**	**1.6**	**1.7**	**1.8**
Lesson Plans (regular and block)	p. 5	p. 14	p. 22	p. 31	p. 39	p. 48	p. 57	p. 65
Technology Activities & Keystrokes	p. 7		p. 24					
Activity Support Masters								
Activity Masters						p. 50		
Practice (3 levels)	p. 8	p. 16	p. 25	p. 33	p. 41	p. 51	p. 59	p. 67
Study Guide	p. 11	p. 19	p. 28	p. 36	p. 44	p. 54	p. 62	p. 70
Real-World Problem Solving					p. 46			p. 72
Challenge Practice	p. 13	p. 21	p. 30	p. 38	p. 47	p. 56	p. 64	p. 73

REVIEW

Chapter Review Games and Activities	p. 74	Extra Credit Project with Rubric	p. 79
Real-Life Project with Rubric	p. 75	Cumulative Practice	p. 81
Cooperative Project with Rubric	p. 77	Resource Book Answers	A1

ASSESSMENT

Quizzes	p. 7	Alternative Assessments with Rubrics	p. 16
Chapter Tests (3 levels)	p. 9	Unit Test	p. 40
Standardized Test	p. 15	Cumulative Test	p. 42

TRANSPARENCIES

	1.1	1.2	1.3	1.4	1.5	1.6	1.7	1.8
Warm-Up/Daily Homework Quiz	✔	✔	✔	✔	✔	✔	✔	✔
Notetaking Guide	✔	✔	✔	✔	✔	✔	✔	✔
Teacher Support				✔	✔			✔
English/Spanish Problem Solving	✔		✔	✔	✔	✔	✔	
Answer Transparencies	✔	✔	✔	✔	✔	✔	✔	✔

TECHNOLOGY

- EasyPlanner CD-ROM
- Test and Practice Generator
- Electronic Lesson Presentations
- eTutorial CD-ROM
- Chapter Audio Summaries CDs
- Classzone.com
- eEdition Plus Online
- eWorkbook Plus Online
- eTutorial Plus Online
- EasyPlanner Plus Online

ADDITIONAL RESOURCES

- Worked-Out Solution Key
- Notetaking Guide
- Practice Workbook
- Tutor Place
- Professional Development Book
- Special Activities Book
- Posters
- Spanish Study Guide
- Exercises in Spanish
- English/Spanish Ch. Reviews/Tests
- Multi-Language Visual Glossary

CHAPTER 1

Math Background and Teaching Strategies

Lesson 1.1

MATH BACKGROUND

A **numerical expression** consists of numbers and operations. An expression does not contain an equal sign or a comparison symbol, such as > or <. A **variable** is any symbol, usually a letter, that represents an unknown value. A **variable expression** is an expression that contains one or more variables. To **evaluate** a variable expression, substitute a number for each variable and then find the value of the resulting numerical expression.

TEACHING STRATEGIES

Make a list of at least four different numerical quantities that relate to sports played in school, such as the numbers of baseball, soccer, volleyball, and track participants. Have students choose letters, such as b, s, v, and t, to represent the quantities. Then have them write variable expressions to represent quantities that involve these variables, such as $b + s + v$ to represent the total number of baseball, soccer, and volleyball participants, or $t + 3$ to represent the total number of track participants after 3 new students sign up.

Lesson 1.2

MATH BACKGROUND

When a number, even a small one like 3, is multiplied by itself over and over, the product gets very large, very fast. Some bacteria can grow into a colony of billions in a matter of hours by doubling every 20 minutes. To describe such situations, mathematicians use **powers**. A power consists of a **base**, the factor that is used repeatedly, and the **exponent**, which tells how many times the base is used as a factor.

TEACHING STRATEGIES

Have students work in pairs. Each pair should have two number cubes and a calculator. Have the students roll the number cubes successively, using the first value rolled as the base and the second value as the exponent. Have students write each power in exponential form and then evaluate the power, using the calculator as needed for higher powers.

Lesson 1.3

MATH BACKGROUND

The **order of operations** is not an intrinsic property of our number system. It was developed to ensure that everyone gets the same result when evaluating any expression.

TEACHING STRATEGIES

Write several numerical expressions on the board for students to evaluate using the order of operations. Have them check their work using a calculator. You may want to challenge students to develop their own mnemonics for remembering the order of operations, such as "**G**eorge's **P**arachute **M**akes **D**iving **A**lmost **S**afe" (grouping symbols, powers, multiplication, division, addition, subtraction).

Lesson 1.4

MATH BACKGROUND

By expanding the set of natural numbers to include zero, we form the whole numbers. Expanding the set of whole numbers to include the opposite of each whole number forms the **integers**. The integers have an additive inverse property as well as the additive identity property inherited from the whole numbers. We can use a number line that extends infinitely in two directions to represent and order the integers. We can then understand the **absolute value** of an integer as its distance from zero on the number line. Because a number and its opposite are the same distance from zero on the number line, they have the same absolute value.

TEACHING STRATEGIES

Draw a large number line on the board and have students help label the number line with the integers. Alternatively, have students help assemble a number line that can be displayed on a wall by joining together pieces of paper or poster board on which they have drawn sections of the number line. Have students use the number line to locate, compare, and order integers, as well as to investigate the concepts of opposites and absolute value.

Lesson 1.5

MATH BACKGROUND

Students are used to adding natural numbers. Adding integers, however, introduces the concept of direction to addition, and so can be much more difficult for students. Since direction is involved in adding integers, the number line provides a critical visual model.

TEACHING STRATEGIES

Use a large number line as mentioned in the Teaching Strategies for Lesson 1.4. Have students create arrows whose lengths match the magnitudes of smaller natural numbers, such as 1 to 6. Have students model the addition of pairs of integers using these arrows pointed in the proper directions. Use arrows for *both* of the integers, with the beginning of the arrow for the first integer placed at zero, and the beginning of the second arrow placed at the tip of the arrowhead of the first arrow.

Lesson 1.6

MATH BACKGROUND

When subtracting integers, a new possibility appears that did not exist with whole numbers—namely, that a difference can be greater than both numbers. The concept of adding the opposite provides an explanation of this fact. Using a number line model, subtracting an integer is represented by flipping its arrow in the opposite direction and then performing addition.

TEACHING STRATEGIES

Continue working with a classroom number line to illustrate integer subtraction. Begin by having students represent subtracting a positive number. Remind them that because subtraction is equivalent to adding the opposite, and because the arrows for a number and its opposite point in opposite directions, they will need to reverse the arrow for the number being subtracted. After students are adept at modeling subtracting a positive number, have them model subtracting a negative number. As an extension, challenge students to find pairs of numbers that have a particular difference. For example, have them find a pair of negative numbers whose difference is 3.

Lesson 1.7

MATH BACKGROUND

Multiplying and dividing integers is the same as performing these operations on whole numbers, except for determining the sign of the product or quotient. The guidelines for making this determination are the same for both operations: if two integers have the same sign, their product or quotient is positive; if two integers have different signs, their product or quotient is negative.

TEACHING STRATEGIES

Have students use a pair of positive integers to investigate the sign possibilities when multiplying and dividing integers, as shown below.

Showing multiplication as repeated addition:

$4 \cdot 3 = 12 \rightarrow + \cdot + = +$

$4 \cdot (-3) = (-3) + (-3) + (-3) + (-3) = -12 \rightarrow + \cdot - = -$

$-4 \cdot 3 = 3 \cdot (-4) = (-4) + (-4) + (-4) = -12 \rightarrow - \cdot + = -$

$-4 \cdot (-3) = -1 \cdot 4 \cdot (-3) = -1 \cdot (-12) = 12 \rightarrow - \cdot - = +$

Using multiplication/division fact families:

$4 \cdot 3 = 12 \rightarrow 12 \div 4 = 3 \rightarrow + \div + = +$

$4 \cdot (-3) = -12 \rightarrow -12 \div 4 = -3 \rightarrow - \div + = -$

$(-4) \cdot 3 = -12 \rightarrow -12 \div (-4) = 3 \rightarrow - \div - = +$

$-4 \cdot (-3) = 12 \rightarrow 12 \div (-4) = -3 \rightarrow + \div - = -$

Lesson 1.8

MATH BACKGROUND

The **coordinate plane** allows us to visualize the relationship between two quantities. Assigning an **ordered pair** of numbers to each point in the coordinate plane allows us to express geometric concepts and derive geometric results using the language of algebra.

TEACHING STRATEGIES

On the board or on a wall, have a large coordinate grid, with axes and quadrants labeled, available for class use. Before having students practice finding and identifying points, begin by asking questions such as the following. "A point has a negative x-coordinate—where could it be located?" "A point has a positive x-coordinate and a negative y-coordinate—where could it be located?" "A point has x-coordinate 0 and a negative y-coordinate—where could it be located?"

CHAPTER

1 Differentiating Instruction

At the start of each chapter, we will outline modifications of curriculum and instruction designed to address the unique needs of Underachieving Students, English Learners, and Advanced Learners. Underachievers are those whose mathematics achievement is below grade level who need strategic and sustained assistance in order to be successful in mathematics. English Learners are those who are not yet fluent in English. Advanced Learners are those whose mathematics achievement is above grade level. Each class of students is different, and you may find your whole class benefits from some of these suggestions. Most of the activities for Underachievers and English Learners would best be done in a second class period, as homework, or in a tutorial, since both groups of students need increased instructional time in mathematics. Some of the activities, particularly those involving vocabulary development, would fit nicely into a language arts period. The Challenge problems for Advanced Learners are provided as extra challenge problems in addition to those in the exercise sets.

Strategies for Underachievers

EMPHASIZE NOTETAKING STRATEGIES

Most students at this level are not naturally good notetakers. Good notetaking is a strategy that must be developed and practiced. Encourage students to pay special attention to the Notetaking Strategies at the beginning of each chapter.

FOCUS ON VOCABULARY

Beginning with the first lesson in this text, students are presented with numerous vocabulary terms. These terms are crucial to understanding the material and completing the exercises. Incorporate these terms frequently into classroom discussion, pausing when necessary to make sure students understand the terms. Insist that students use new mathematical vocabulary accurately in all written and oral communication. Encourage students to keep a glossary or make note cards that contain frequently-used vocabulary terms, along with examples that clarify their meaning.

USE TOOLS AND MANIPULATIVES

Beginning in Lesson 1.4 and continuing throughout all appropriate lessons, it will be especially helpful to underachievers to have a large number line, including positive and negative integers, displayed on the board or a wall. For some students, smaller number lines affixed to the tops of their desks can be helpful.

INTEGER ADDITION AND SUBTRACTION In Lessons 1.5 and 1.6, the number line(s) just mentioned can help underachievers learn to add and subtract integers, but as an alternative, you may want to have positive and negative counters available for students to manipulate. Allow students who prefer concrete modeling using number lines or counters to use them as long as necessary. They will naturally break from modeling when they have developed sufficient skill to perform these operations abstractly.

USE SCAFFOLDING

ORDER OF OPERATIONS In Lesson 1.3, you may wish to provide templates to guide students through a few complicated order of operations exercises to reinforce their understanding. An example is shown below.

$$\begin{aligned}
&7[2.5 + 3(12 - 7)]\\
&= \underline{\quad\quad}[\underline{\quad\quad} + \underline{\quad\quad}(\underline{\quad\quad})]\\
&= \underline{\quad\quad}(\underline{\quad\quad} + \underline{\quad\quad})\\
&= \underline{\quad\quad}(\underline{\quad\quad})\\
&= \underline{\quad\quad}
\end{aligned}$$

INCORPORATE MNEMONIC DEVICES

ORDER OF OPERATIONS Different mnemonic schemes have been developed for remembering the order of operations presented in Lesson 1.3. Probably the best known is "**P**lease **E**xcuse **M**y **D**ear **A**unt **S**ally," where the "P" stands for "parentheses" and the "E" stands for "exponents." A mnemonic for which "grouping" replaces "parentheses" and "powers" replaces "exponents" is given in the Teaching Strategies note for this lesson on page 2C.

Strategies for English Learners

REWORD PROBLEMS

At the beginning of the year (or whenever English learners enroll in your class) you may want to focus on using math problems that require little or no reading in English. As the year goes on and the constant emphasis on vocabulary study results in improved reading skills, you can increase the number of problems that require reading and increase the length of word problems. Many math problems can be rewritten in an "if . . . then" format. For example, students could be asked to "Evaluate the variable expression when $x = 4$," and given four problems to solve. At the beginning of the year, the English can be minimized so that the student can do the mathematics if he or she can read the word *if*, understand the equal sign, and understand that a letter represents a number. It can read:

If $x = 4$,
$3x = \underline{?}$
$9 + x = \underline{?}$
$\frac{16}{x} = \underline{?}$
$x - 1 = \underline{?}$

PRETEACH VOCABULARY

Vocabulary development in this chapter can focus on words that express opposites. Remind students of what the word *opposite* means with some simple examples such as *big* and *little*, *over* and *under*, *inside* and *outside*. Ask students to generate other common pairs of opposites. Call on volunteers and make a list. There are examples in the chapter you can point out, such as on page 23, where students are asked to state the opposite of a number. As homework, you might ask English learners to list all the pairs of opposites they can find on a page. Pick a page with word problems or descriptions. In fact, you may want English learners to do this for the entire chapter and create an opposites list for their notebooks as well. This would also be a good approach to use with synonyms.

Strategies for Advanced Learners

PROVIDE REAL-WORLD CONNECTIONS

VARIABLE EXPRESSIONS In conjunction with Lesson 1.1, you may wish to supply students with blank copies of federal or state income tax forms. (Forms are usually downloadable from agency websites.) Have students search these forms for algorithms that are used in determining tax amounts, for example, "subtract line 34 from line 22" or "multiply $3000 by the total number of exemptions claimed on line 6d." Have students write variable expressions for these algorithms and then evaluate the expressions for different values of the variables. Students can also create questions that require the use of these expressions, and then exchange and answer each other's questions.

In conjunction with Lessons 1.5 and 1.6, encourage advanced students to monitor daily high or low temperatures for several days. At the end of the period, have these students find the differences in the temperatures from day to day and then find the sum of these differences. Ask them how this sum relates to the difference in the temperatures on the last and first days of the period.

INCREASE DEPTH AND COMPLEXITY

POWERS In Lesson 1.2, you may wish to have advanced students list the first several powers of small natural numbers, such as 2 though 10. Have them look for patterns in the sequences of powers. As a way to help students start, you may want to ask them to look for patterns in the ones digit of each set of powers.

In Lesson 1.3, some advanced students may wish to explore the concept of roots, how they are related to exponents, and how they fit into the order of operations.

In conjunction with Lesson 1.7, advanced students can explore powers that have negative bases. Ask them to draw conclusions about any patterns they see.

CHAPTER 1

Differentiating Instruction: Resource Materials

Differentiating Practice

McDougal Littell *Pre-Algebra* offers teachers a wide variety of practice for all levels of students. Pictured on these pages are facsimiles of the Level A, Level C, and Challenge Practice pages from the *Chapter 1 Resource Book*, pages from the *Practice Workbook*, and the *Test and Practice Generator*.

RESOURCE BOOK

The *Chapter Resource Books* contain three levels of practice, A (Basic), B (Average), and C (Advanced), for each lesson in the textbook. Also included is a page of Challenge practice for each lesson for your most advanced students.

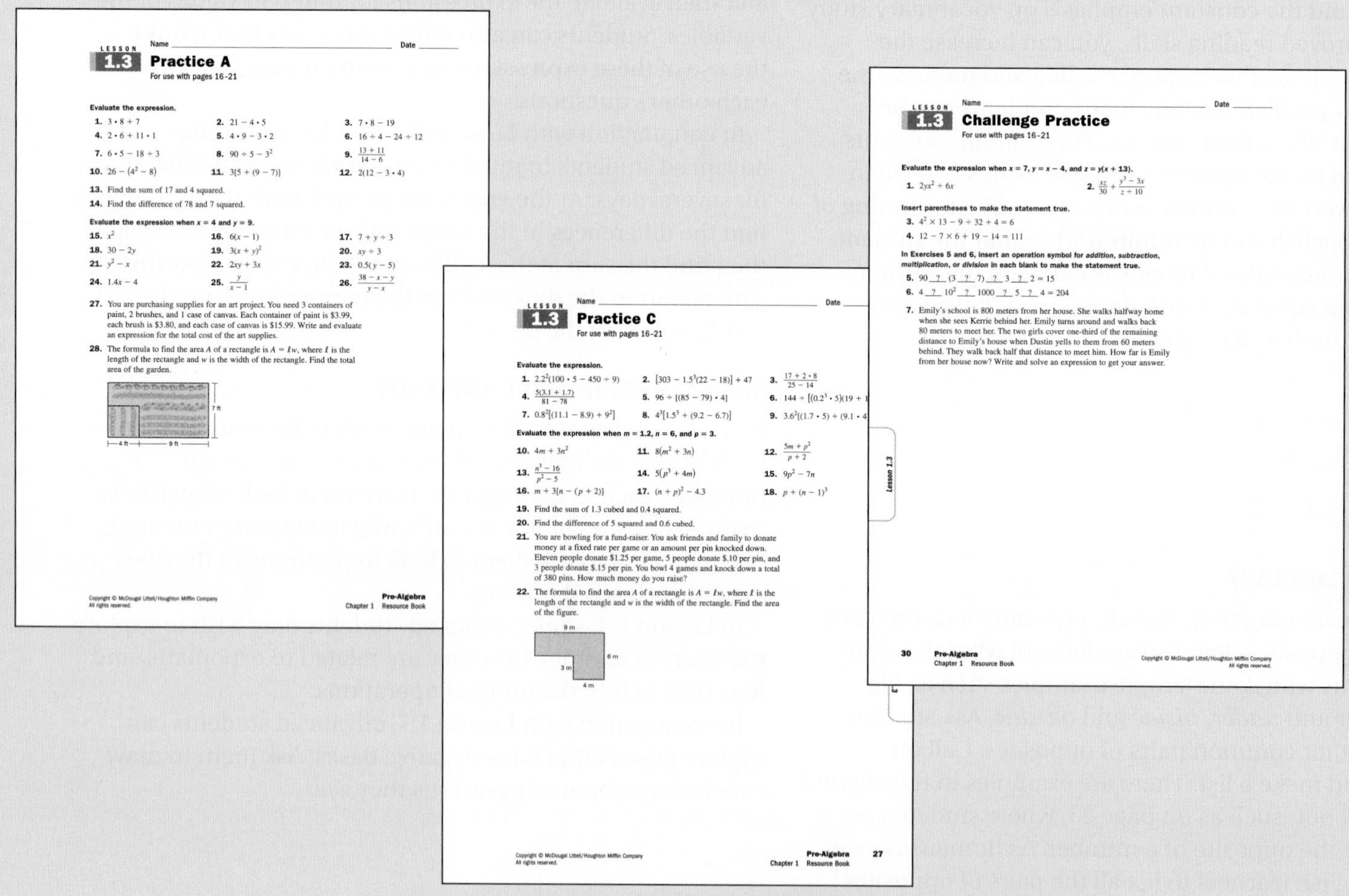

LESSON 1.3 Name ______ Date ______

Practice A

For use with pages 16-21

Evaluate the expression.

1. $3 \cdot 8 + 7$
2. $21 - 4 \cdot 5$
3. $7 \cdot 8 - 19$
4. $2 \cdot 6 + 11 \cdot 1$
5. $4 \cdot 9 - 3 \cdot 2$
6. $16 \div 4 - 24 \div 12$
7. $6 \cdot 5 - 18 \div 3$
8. $90 \div 5 - 3^2$
9. $\frac{13 + 11}{14 - 6}$
10. $26 - (4^2 - 8)$
11. $3[5 + (9 - 7)]$
12. $2(12 - 3 \cdot 4)$
13. Find the sum of 17 and 4 squared.
14. Find the difference of 78 and 7 squared.

Evaluate the expression when $x = 4$ and $y = 9$.

15. x^2
16. $6(x - 1)$
17. $7 + y \div 3$
18. $30 - 2y$
19. $3(x + y)^2$
20. $xy \div 3$
21. $y^2 - x$
22. $2xy + 3x$
23. $0.5(y - 5)$
24. $1.4x - 4$
25. $\frac{y}{x - 1}$
26. $\frac{38 - x - y}{y - x}$
27. You are purchasing supplies for an art project. You need 3 containers of paint, 2 brushes, and 1 case of canvas. Each container of paint is $3.99, each brush is $3.80, and each case of canvas is $15.99. Write and evaluate an expression for the total cost of the art supplies.
28. The formula to find the area A of a rectangle is $A = \ell w$, where ℓ is the length of the rectangle and w is the width of the rectangle. Find the total area of the garden.

7 ft
4 ft
9 ft

LESSON 1.3 Name ______ Date ______

Practice C

For use with pages 16-21

Evaluate the expression.

1. $2.2^2(100 \cdot 5 - 450 \div 9)$
2. $[303 - 1.5^3(22 - 18)] + 47$
3. $\frac{17 + 2 \cdot 8}{25 - 14}$
4. $\frac{5(3.1 + 1.7)}{81 - 78}$
5. $96 \div [(85 - 79) \cdot 4]$
6. $144 \div [(0.2^3 \cdot 5)(19 + 1$
7. $0.8^2[(11.1 - 8.9) + 9^2]$
8. $4^3[1.5^3 + (9.2 - 6.7)]$
9. $3.6^2[(1.7 \cdot 5) + (9.1 \cdot 4$

Evaluate the expression when $m = 1.2$, $n = 6$, and $p = 3$.

10. $4m + 3n^2$
11. $8(m^2 + 3n)$
12. $\frac{5m + p^2}{p + 2}$
13. $\frac{n^3 - 16}{p^2 - 5}$
14. $5(p^3 + 4m)$
15. $9p^2 - 7n$
16. $m + 3[n - (p + 2)]$
17. $(n + p)^2 - 4.3$
18. $p + (n - 1)^3$
19. Find the sum of 1.3 cubed and 0.4 squared.
20. Find the difference of 5 squared and 0.6 cubed.
21. You are bowling for a fund-raiser. You ask friends and family to donate money at a fixed rate per game or an amount per pin knocked down. Eleven people donate $1.25 per game, 5 people donate $.10 per pin, and 3 people donate $.15 per pin. You bowl 4 games and knock down a total of 380 pins. How much money do you raise?
22. The formula to find the area A of a rectangle is $A = \ell w$, where ℓ is the length of the rectangle and w is the width of the rectangle. Find the area of the figure.

9 m
6 m
3 m
4 m

Lesson 1.3

LESSON 1.3 Name ______ Date ______

Challenge Practice

For use with pages 16-21

Evaluate the expression when $x = 7$, $y = x - 4$, and $z = y(x + 13)$.

1. $2yx^2 \div 6x$
2. $\frac{xz}{30} + \frac{y^3 - 3x}{z \div 10}$

Insert parentheses to make the statement true.

3. $4^2 \times 13 - 9 \div 32 + 4 = 6$
4. $12 - 7 \times 6 + 19 - 14 = 111$

In Exercises 5 and 6, insert an operation symbol for *addition, subtraction, multiplication,* or *division* in each blank to make the statement true.

5. 90 __?__ (3 __?__ 7) __?__ 3 __?__ 2 = 15
6. 4 __?__ 10^2 __?__ 1000 __?__ 5 __?__ 4 = 204
7. Emily's school is 800 meters from her house. She walks halfway home when she sees Kerrie behind her. Emily turns around and walks back 80 meters to meet her. The two girls cover one-third of the remaining distance to Emily's house when Dustin yells to them from 60 meters behind. They walk back half that distance to meet him. How far is Emily from her house now? Write and solve an expression to get your answer.

PRACTICE WORKBOOK

The *Practice Workbook* contains the average B-level practice for each lesson reformatted in workbook form to allow students to show their work for each exercise.

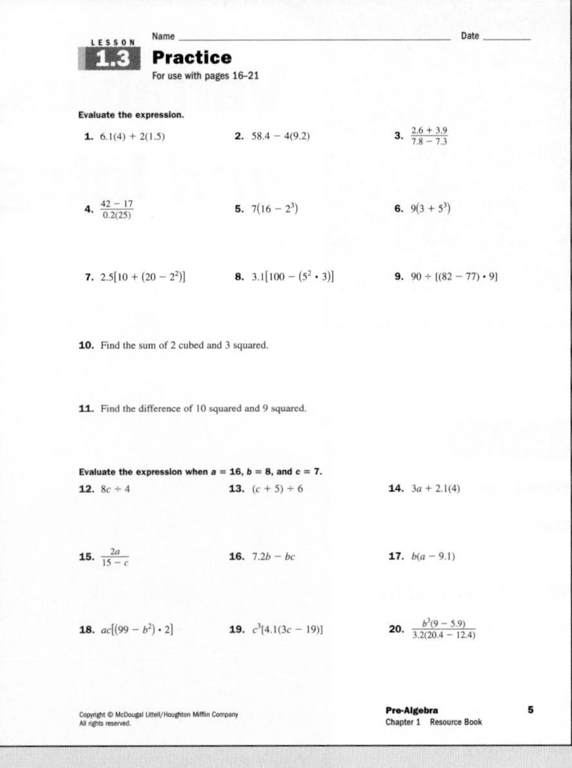

LESSON 1.3 Name ______________________ Date ________

Practice

For use with pages 16-21

Evaluate the expression.

1. $6.1(4) + 2(1.5)$ **2.** $58.4 - 4(9.2)$ **3.** $\frac{2.6 + 3.9}{7.8 - 7.3}$

4. $\frac{42 - 17}{0.2(25)}$ **5.** $7(16 - 2^3)$ **6.** $9(3 + 5^3)$

7. $2.5[10 + (20 - 2^2)]$ **8.** $3.1[100 - (5^2 \cdot 3)]$ **9.** $90 \div [(82 - 77) \cdot 9]$

10. Find the sum of 2 cubed and 3 squared.

11. Find the difference of 10 squared and 9 squared.

Evaluate the expression when $a = 16$, $b = 8$, and $c = 7$.

12. $8c \div 4$ **13.** $(c + 5) \div 6$ **14.** $3a + 2.1(4)$

15. $\frac{2a}{15 - c}$ **16.** $7.2b - bc$ **17.** $b(a - 9.1)$

18. $ac[(99 - b^2) \cdot 2]$ **19.** $c^3[4.1(3c - 19)]$ **20.** $\frac{b^3(9 - 5.9)}{3.2(20.4 - 12.4)}$

Pre-Algebra
Chapter 1 Resource Book 5

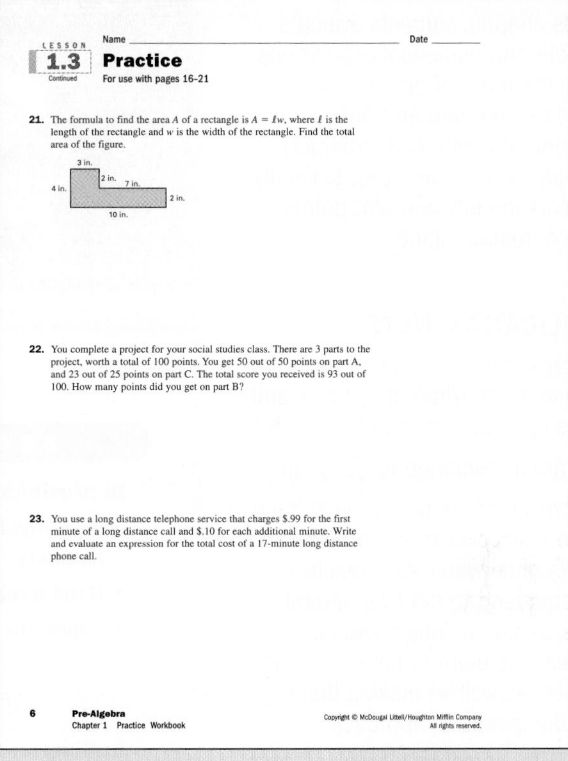

LESSON 1.3 Continued Name ______________________ Date ________

Practice

For use with pages 16-21

21. The formula to find the area A of a rectangle is $A = \ell w$, where ℓ is the length of the rectangle and w is the width of the rectangle. Find the total area of the figure.

22. You complete a project for your social studies class. There are 3 parts to the project, worth a total of 100 points. You get 50 out of 50 points on part A, and 23 out of 25 points on part C. The total score you received is 93 out of 100. How many points did you get on part B?

23. You use a long distance telephone service that charges \$.99 for the first minute of a long distance call and \$.10 for each additional minute. Write and evaluate an expression for the total cost of a 17-minute long distance phone call.

6 Pre-Algebra
Chapter 1 Practice Workbook

TEST AND PRACTICE GENERATOR CD-ROM

The *Test and Practice Generator* allows you to create practice worksheets for each lesson using both static and algorithmic exercises.

Chapter 1 Practice **Page 1**

1. Use mental math to solve the equation. [A] −6 [B] −4 [C] 4 [D] 6
   $-2(-6)x = -48$
2. Find the sum. [A] −70 [B] 148 [C] −54 [D] 70
   $-62 + 39 + (-47)$
3. You drop a pebble off of a cliff. At time t seconds, the rock has fallen $16t^2$ feet. It takes 3 seconds for the pebble to hit the ground. How high is the cliff?
4. Find the product. [A] −96 [B] −86 [C] 86 [D] 96
   $-8 \bullet |-12|$

Evaluate the expression.

5. $135 \div (14 - 11)^2$ [A] 22.5 [B] 18 [C] 15 [D] 1.8
6. $7.2 \div (11 - 3)$
7. Use a number line to find the sum.
   $3 + (-6)$
8. Evaluate the expression.
   $\frac{14 + 30}{13 - 2}$
9. Solve the equation using mental math. [A] 12 [B] −6 [C] 0 [D] −12
   $-6 = 6 + k$

Find the sum.

10. $44 + (-46)$
11. $-74 + 22$

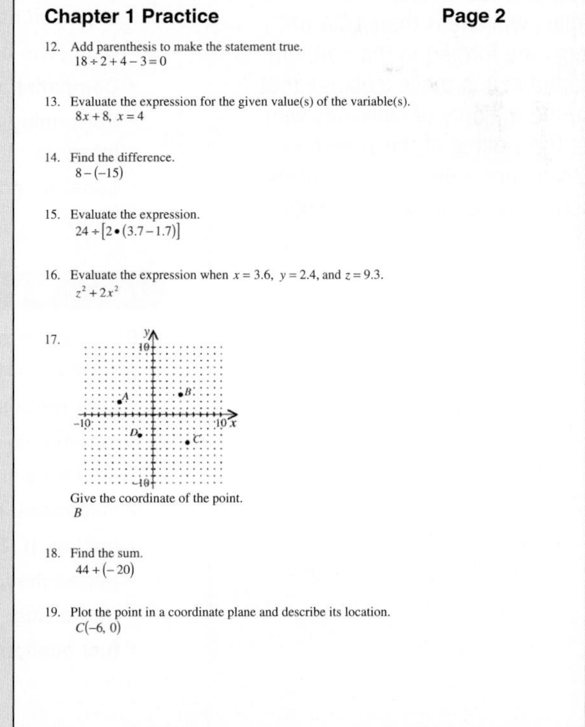

Chapter 1 Practice **Page 2**

12. Add parenthesis to make the statement true.
    $18 \div 2 + 4 - 3 = 0$
13. Evaluate the expression for the given value(s) of the variable(s).
    $8x + 8,\ x = 4$
14. Find the difference.
    $8 - (-15)$
15. Evaluate the expression.
    $24 \div [2 \bullet (3.7 - 1.7)]$
16. Evaluate the expression when $x = 3.6$, $y = 2.4$, and $z = 9.3$.
    $z^2 + 2x^2$
17.

    Give the coordinate of the point.
    B
18. Find the sum.
    $44 + (-20)$
19. Plot the point in a coordinate plane and describe its location.
    $C(-6, 0)$

OVERVIEW

MAIN IDEAS

In this chapter, students evaluate variable and numerical expressions using the order of operations. Students compare and order integers. Students add, subtract, multiply, and divide integers. Finally, students identify and plot points in a coordinate plane.

APPLICATION NOTE

Icebergs can take years to melt, depending on where they travel and the temperature of the ocean water they are in. Since up to $\frac{9}{10}$ of an iceberg's mass is below the surface of the ocean, most of the melting occurs underwater. As a result, icebergs tend to flip over several times as the melting takes place. This causes them to have fantastic shapes, as well as making them very dangerous to approach.

Over 90% of icebergs break off from the edges of ice sheets in the Antarctic. While less than 10% of icebergs are formed in the northern hemisphere, it is these icebergs that cause the majority of collisions with ships. The sinking of the *Titanic* in 1912 was only one of many sinkings caused by collisions with icebergs.

CHAPTER 1

Variables, Expressions, *and* Integers

BEFORE

In previous courses you've . . .

- **Performed operations on whole numbers**
- **Read bar graphs and line graphs**
- **Found the mean of a set of data**

Now

In Chapter 1 you'll study . . .

- **Evaluating and writing variable expressions**
- **Using the order of operations**
- **Comparing and ordering integers**
- **Performing operations on integers**
- **Locating points in a coordinate plane**

WHY?

So you can solve real-world problems about . . .

- **DVD rentals, p. 8**
- **aquariums, p. 13**
- **basketball, p. 19**
- **volcanoes, p. 24**
- **hockey, p. 32**
- **avalanches, p. 37**
- **free diving, p. 45**
- **fuel economy, p. 50**

How tall is an iceberg?

CHAPTER 1

INTERNET Preview

CLASSZONE.COM

- eEdition Plus Online
- eWorkbook Plus Online
- eTutorial Plus Online
- State Test Practice
- More Examples

MATH In the **Real World**

Icebergs Icebergs like this one in LeConte Bay, Alaska, typically float with most of their mass below sea level. In this chapter, you will use *integers* to describe distances above and below sea level.

What do you think? Suppose the highest point on an iceberg is 45 feet above the water's surface. The lowest point is 357 feet below the surface. Find the vertical distance between these two points. 402 ft

Chapter Resources

These resources are provided to help you prepare for the chapter and to customize review materials:

Chapter 1 Resource Book

- Tips for New Teachers, pp. 1–2
- Lesson Plan, pp. 5, 14, 22, 31, 39, 48, 57, 65
- Lesson Plan for Block Scheduling, pp. 6, 15, 23, 32, 40, 49, 58, 66

Technology

- EasyPlanner CD-ROM
- Test and Practice Generator
- Electronic Lesson Presentations CD-ROM
- eTutorial CD-ROM

Internet

- Classzone
- eEdition Plus Online
- eWorkbook Plus Online
- eTutorial Plus Online
- EasyPlanner Plus Online

English Learner Support

- Spanish Study Guide
- Multi-Language Visual Glossary
- Chapter Audio Summaries CDs
- Teacher's Edition, pp. 2E–2F

PREPARE

DIAGNOSIS/REMEDIATION

Prerequisite Skills Quiz

The Prerequisite Skills Quiz can help you diagnose whether students have the following skills needed in Chapter 1:

- Use vocabulary (Exs. 1–2)
- Find the sum or difference of two decimal numbers (Exs. 3–6)
- Find the product or quotient of two decimal numbers (Exs. 7–10)

 ***Chapter 1 Resource Book***

- Study Guide (Lessons 1.1–1.8)

 ***Tutor Place***

NOTETAKING STRATEGIES

Stress that students should use their notebook to record information that is important for their own study purposes, organized in a manner that will help them review the material later. Emphasize that each student's notebook will differ from those of other students. Further suggestions for keeping a notebook can be found on pages 10, 16, and 47.

For more support on notetaking, see:

- Notetaking Guide Workbook
- Notetaking Transparencies

CHAPTER 1

Chapter Prerequisite Skills

Review Vocabulary

sum, p. 771
difference, p. 771
product, p. 772
quotient, p. 772
factor, p. 772

PREREQUISITE SKILLS QUIZ

Preparing for Success **To prepare for success in this chapter, test your knowledge of these concepts and skills. You may want to look at the pages referred to in blue for additional review.**

Vocabulary **Copy and complete the statement using a review word.**

1. In the multiplication equation $12 \cdot 5 = 60$, 12 and 5 are called _?_ and 60 is called the _?_. **factors, product**
2. When you divide one number by another, the result is called the _?_. **quotient**

Find the sum or difference. *(p. 774)*

3. $7.2 + 13.7$ **20.9** **4.** $2.41 + 34.6$ **37.01** **5.** $10.5 - 7.3$ **3.2** **6.** $27.1 - 18.6$ **8.5**

Find the product or quotient. *(pp. 775, 776)*

7. 3.2×1.4 **4.48** **8.** 0.5×27 **13.5** **9.** $27.88 \div 8.2$ **3.4** **10.** $11.9 \div 1.7$ **7**

NOTETAKING STRATEGIES

KEEPING A NOTEBOOK Some useful items to put in your notebook include the following.

- assignments
- vocabulary
- formulas
- symbols
- rules and properties
- worked-out examples

When you copy examples into your notebook, you may find it helpful to draw a diagram. Include comments that make the solution process clear. For example, a diagram can help you to order the numbers 3.2, 3.09, 3, 3.15, 3.12, and 3.02 from least to greatest.

Draw a number line and graph the numbers:

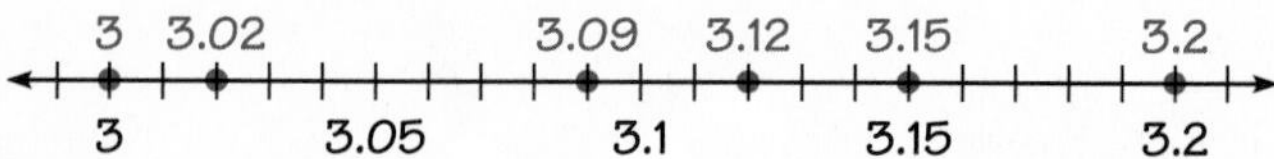

Write the numbers in the order in which they appear from left to right: 3, 3.02, 3.09, 3.12, 3.15, 3.2.

In Lesson 1.8, you may want to include a diagram of a coordinate plane in your notebook.

Note *Worthy*

You will find a notetaking strategy at the beginning of each chapter. Look for additional notetaking and study strategies throughout the chapter.

LESSON

1.1 Expressions *and* Variables

BEFORE	*Now*	WHY?
You evaluated numerical expressions.	You'll evaluate and write variable expressions.	So you can find the amount left on a gift card, as in Ex. 39.

Vocabulary

numerical expression, p. 5
variable, p. 5
variable expression, p. 5
evaluate, p. 5
verbal model, p. 6

Blue Whales During its summer feeding season, a blue whale eats about 4 tons of food every day. To find about how many tons of food a blue whale eats in a given number of days, you can multiply the number of days by 4, as shown in the table.

Days	Tons of food eaten
1	$4 \cdot 1$
2	$4 \cdot 2$
10	$4 \cdot 10$
d	$4 \cdot d$

A **numerical expression** consists of numbers and operations. In the table, the expression $4 \cdot 10$ is a numerical expression. It can also be written as 4×10 or $4(10)$.

A **variable** is a letter used to represent one or more numbers. A **variable expression** consists of numbers, variables, and operations.

One way you can use a variable expression is to generalize a pattern, as in the table. The variable expression $4 \cdot d$ represents the amount of food a blue whale can eat in d days. You can also write $4 \cdot d$ as $4d$.

To **evaluate** a variable expression, substitute a number for each variable and evaluate the resulting numerical expression.

Study *Strategy*

When you write a variable expression involving multiplication, avoid using the symbol $\times$. It may be confused with the variable x.

Example 1 *Evaluating a Variable Expression*

Evaluate the expression $4 \cdot d$ when $d = 120$ to find about how many tons of food a blue whale eats in a feeding season of 120 days.

Solution

$4 \cdot d = 4 \cdot 120$ **Substitute 120 for *d*.**

$= 480$ **Multiply.**

Answer A blue whale eats about 480 tons of food in 120 days.

NCTM CURRICULUM STANDARDS
Standard 1: Understand meanings of operations
Standard 2: Represent situations using algebraic symbols; Analyze situations using algebraic symbols

1 PLAN

Skill Check

1. $16 + 8 = \underline{?}$	**24**
2. $13 \times 4 = \underline{?}$	**52**
3. $34 - 19 = \underline{?}$	**15**
4. $96 \div 6 = \underline{?}$	**16**

LESSON OBJECTIVE

Evaluate and write variable expressions.

PACING

Suggested Number of Days
Basic Course: 1 day
Average Course: 1 day
Advanced Course: 1 day
Block: 0.5 block with 1.2

TEACHING RESOURCES

For a complete list of Teaching Resources, see page 2B.

TRANSPARENCY

Warm-Up Exercises for this lesson are available on a transparency.

2 TEACH

MOTIVATING THE LESSON

Ask a science teacher to talk to the class about blue whales. Ask students how many pounds are equivalent to 1 ton. **2000 lb**

TIPS *for* NEW TEACHERS

Students may be more familiar with using x as a variable than other letters. Point out the advantage of using a letter with a connection to the quantity it represents. See Tips for New Teachers in the *Chapter 1 Resource Book.*

Extra Examples

Example 1 Evaluate the expression 3 • s when $s = 60$ to find how many miles Doug drives in 3 hours at a speed of 60 miles per hour. **180 mi**

Example 2 Evaluate the expression when $x = 5$ and $y = 8$.
a. $y + x$ **13** **b.** $y - x$ **3**

Example 3 You plan to provide 8 carrot sticks for each of h hikers to take as a snack. Write a variable expression for the number of carrot sticks you will need if you know the number of hikers. **8*h***

Reading Strategy

Discuss the use of color in Example 1. Point out how both the variable d and the value 120 being substituted for d are shown in red. Then point out how two colors are used in Example 2 in order to help students visualize the two substitutions being made.

Concept Check

How is a variable useful in writing a numerical pattern? ***Sample answer:* You can write a variable expression that generalizes the pattern of numbers.**

Daily Puzzler

Madison, Mike, Christine, and Kenny live on four different floors of a 4-story apartment building. Mike lives above Kenny, Christine lives below Madison, and Kenny lives between Madison and Christine. Who lives on which floor? **1st floor: Christine; 2nd floor: Kenny; 3rd floor: Madison; 4th floor: Mike**

Example 2 *Evaluating Expressions with Two Variables*

Evaluate the expression when $x = 10$ and $y = 4$.

a. $x + y = 10 + 4$ **Substitute 10 for *x* and 4 for *y*.**
$= 14$ **Add.**

b. $xy = 10(4)$ **Substitute 10 for *x* and 4 for *y*.**
$= 40$ **Multiply.**

Checkpoint

Evaluate the expression when $x = 6$ and $y = 12$.

1. $y + 8$ 20 **2.** $9 - x$ 3 **3.** $y - x$ 6 **4.** xy 72

Writing Variable Expressions You can solve a real-world problem by creating a *verbal model* and using it to write a variable expression. A **verbal model** describes a problem using words as labels and using math symbols to relate the words. The table shows common words and phrases that indicate mathematical operations.

Common Words and Phrases that Indicate Operations			
Addition	**Subtraction**	**Multiplication**	**Division**
plus	minus	times	divided by
the sum of	the difference of	the product of	divided into
increased by	decreased by	multiplied by	the quotient of
total	fewer than	of	
more than	less than		
added to	subtracted from		

Watch *Out*

Order is important in subtraction and division expressions. "The difference of a number and 7" means $n - 7$, *not* $7 - n$. "The quotient of a number and 5" means $\frac{n}{5}$, *not* $\frac{5}{n}$.

Example 3 *Writing a Variable Expression*

Baseball You plan to divide the 120 players in a baseball league into teams with the same number of players. Use a verbal model to write a variable expression for the number of teams if you know the number of players on each team.

Solution

Let p represent the number of players on each team. The word *divide* indicates division.

Number of teams = Number of players in league ÷ Number of players on each team

$= 120 \div p$

Answer The number of teams is $120 \div p$, or $\frac{120}{p}$.

Reading *Algebra*

When you write a variable expression involving division, use a fraction bar instead of the division symbol ÷. For example, write "the quotient of n and 12" as $\frac{n}{12}$.

1.1 Exercises

More Practice, p. 803

Guided Practice

Vocabulary Check

1. Identify the variable in the expression $21 + d$. d

2. Compare and contrast the expressions $2 + x$ and $2 + 3$. $2 + x$ is a variable expression and $2 + 3$ is a numerical expression.

Skill Check

Evaluate the expression when $x = 4$.

3. $10 - x$ 6 **4.** $x + 7$ 11 **5.** $2x$ 8 **6.** $\frac{32}{x}$ 8

Evaluate the expression when $m = 5$ and $n = 6$.

7. $\frac{n}{2}$ 3 **8.** $m + n$ 11 **9.** $n - m$ 1 **10.** mn 30

Guided Problem Solving

11. Astronauts In 2002, astronauts Carl Walz and Dan Bursch spent 196 days in orbit. How many sunrises did they see?

1) An astronaut in orbit circles Earth every 90 minutes and sees 16 sunrises each day. Let d be the number of days an astronaut is in orbit. Write a variable expression for the number of sunrises seen in d days. $16d$

2) Identify the value of d for Walz's and Bursch's 2002 space flight. 196

3) Find the number of sunrises Walz and Bursch saw. 3136 sunrises

Practice and Problem Solving

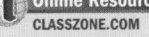

Homework Help

Example	Exercises
1	12-19, 39
2	20-31, 40
3	32-38, 40

Online Resources
CLASSZONE.COM
- More Examples
- eTutorial Plus

Evaluate the expression when $x = 6$.

A **12.** $x + 3$ 9 **13.** $15 - x$ 9 **14.** $2x$ 12 **15.** $\frac{x}{3}$ 2

16. $20x$ 120 **17.** $\frac{24}{x}$ 4 **18.** $30 - x$ 24 **19.** $15 + x$ 21

Evaluate the expression when $a = 4$, $b = 2$, and $c = 16$.

20. $a + b$ 6 **21.** $c - a$ 12 **22.** ab 8 **23.** $\frac{a}{b}$ 2

24. bc 32 **25.** $\frac{c}{a}$ 4 **26.** $a - b$ 2 **27.** $\frac{c}{b}$ 8

28. $b + c$ 18 **29.** $c - b$ 14 **30.** ac 64 **31.** $a + c$ 20

3 APPLY

ASSIGNMENT GUIDE

Basic Course

Day 1: pp. 7-9 Exs. 12-27, 32-43, 49, 50, 57-67

Average Course

Day 1: pp. 7-9 Exs. 16-27, 32-38, 40, 45-55, 57-67

Advanced Course

Day 1: pp. 7-9 Exs. 16-19, 28-56*, 59-67

Block

pp. 7-9 Exs. 16-27, 32-38, 40, 45-55, 57-67 (with 1.2)

Extra Practice

- Student Edition, p. 803
- Chapter 1 Resource Book, pp. 8-10
- Test and Practice Generator

Transparency

Even-numbered answers are available on transparencies.

Homework Check

When you review students' homework for this lesson, go over the following exercises to check understanding of key concepts.
Basic: 13, 16, 20, 23, 32
Average: 16, 18, 27, 36, 40
Advanced: 17, 28, 30, 39, 40

Common Error

In Exercise 33, watch for students who are unsure whether "the difference of a number and 1" is represented by $n - 1$ or $1 - n$. Likewise, in Exercise 36, watch for students who are unsure whether "the quotient of a number and 3" is represented by $n \div 3$ or $3 \div n$. Stress that the order of the words in the phrase dictates the order in which the values are subtracted and divided; $n - 1$ and $n \div 3$ are the correct expressions because the word "number" appears before 1 and 3, respectively, in the two exercises.

Cross-Curriculum

Music After discussing Exercise 40, you may wish to discuss other expressions that could be related to music situations. For example, expressions to represent the number of beats in b bars or to represent the cost of an instrument rental for w weeks. Invite music students to suggest other expressions.

Teaching Tip

In Exercise 49, if students need help, ask them how many inches are in 1 foot, 2 feet, and 3 feet. Students may need help deciding if the expression is $12x$ or $\frac{x}{12}$.

Write a variable expression to represent the phrase.

32. The product of 72 and a number $72m$

33. The difference of a number and 1 $q - 1$

34. 13 more than a number $r + 13$

35. The sum of a number and 9.4 $n + 9.4$

36. The quotient of a number and 3 $\frac{s}{3}$

37. A number divided by 41 $\frac{n}{41}$

38. Error Analysis Describe and correct the error in writing a variable expression for the difference of a number and 31. "The difference of a number and 31" means $p - 31$, not $31 - p$.

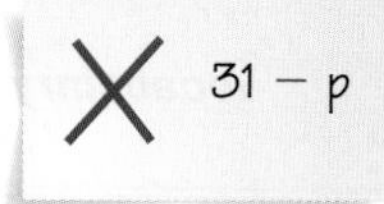

39. Gift Card You can evaluate the expression $50 - d$ to find the amount you have left on a \$50 gift card after you have spent d dollars. Find the amount left after you have spent \$18. \$32

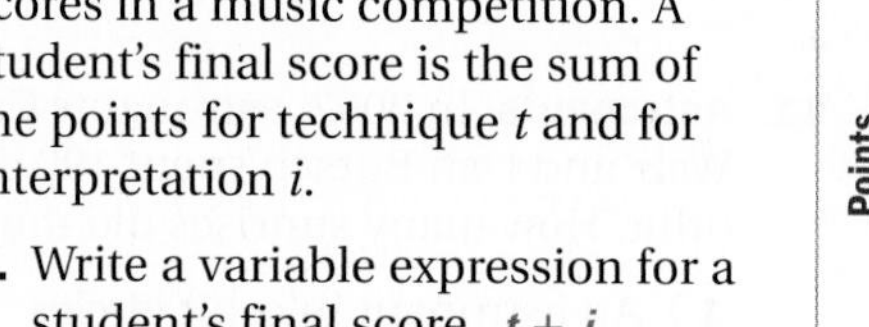

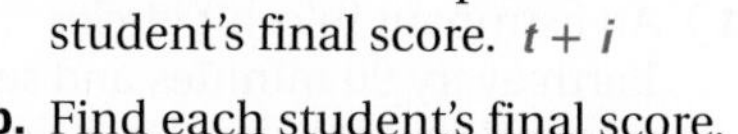

40. Music Competition The double bar graph shows three students' scores in a music competition. A student's final score is the sum of the points for technique t and for interpretation i.

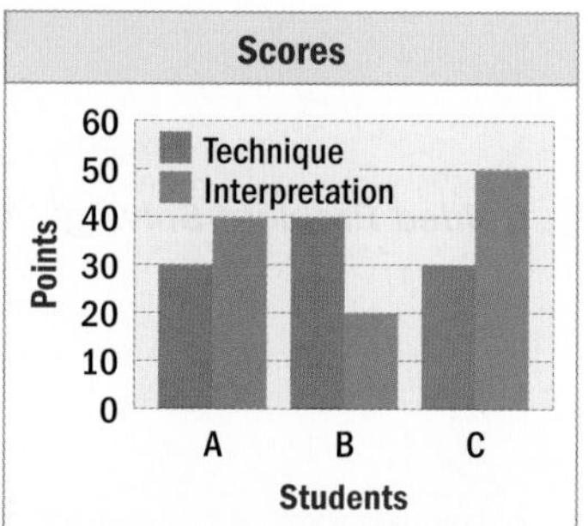

a. Write a variable expression for a student's final score. $t + i$

b. Find each student's final score. A: 70; B: 60; C: 80

c. Interpret You earn 35 points for technique. At least how many points must you earn for interpretation to have a higher score than students A, B, and C? 46 points

Evaluate the expression when $a = 2.5$, $b = 15$, and $c = 3.5$.

B **41.** $a + b$ 17.5 **42.** $b - c$ 11.5 **43.** bc 52.5 **44.** $a + c$ 6

45. $\frac{b}{a}$ 6 **46.** $c - a$ 1 **47.** $\frac{c}{a}$ 1.4 **48.** ac 8.75

Review Help

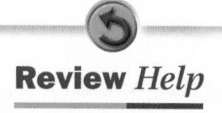

For help with units of length, see p. 786. For help with units of weight and mass, see p. 790.

Write a variable expression to represent the phrase.

49. The number of inches in x feet $12x$

50. The number of pounds in y ounces $\frac{y}{16}$

51. DVD Rentals You belong to an online DVD rental service. Your yearly rental budget is \$200. Each rental costs \$4.

a. Copy and complete the table.

DVDs	Cost (dollars)	Amount left (dollars)
1	4	196
2	8	192
3	? 12	? 188
4	? 16	? 184

b. Write a variable expression for the cost of r rentals. $4r$

c. Write a variable expression for the amount of your budget left after r rentals. $200 - 4r$

d. *Writing* How many DVDs will you be able to rent before the \$200 is spent? Explain how you found your answer.
50 rentals. *Sample answer:* Find the greatest value of r so that $200 - 4r$ is not less than zero.

52. Extended Problem Solving In football, each field goal (FG) is worth 3 points. Each kicked point after touchdown (PAT) is worth 1 point. The table shows career totals for three leading kickers.

Player	FGs	PATs
George Blanda	335	943
Nick Lowery	383	562
Norm Johnson	366	638

a. Let p be the number of points after touchdown that a kicker scored, and let f be the number of field goals. Write a variable expression for the total number of points. $p + 3f$

b. Evaluate Find the total number of points for each kicker. Blanda: 1948 points; Lowery: 1711 points; Johnson: 1736 points

c. Compare List the players in order from least total number of points to greatest. Lowery, Johnson, Blanda

53. Critical Thinking Are there any values of the variable a for which the expressions $2 + a$ and $2a$ have the same value? Explain. Yes; when $a = 2$, the value of $2 + a$ is 4 and the value of $2a$ is 4.

Logical Reasoning Describe the pattern shown in the table. Then write a variable expression involving *n* to complete the table. In the table, the three dots indicate that the pattern continues.

The cost with tax is 1.05 times the cost of the item; $1.05n$.

C **54.**

Cost of item (dollars)	1.00	2.00	3.00	4.00	...	n
Cost with tax (dollars)	1.05	2.10	3.15	4.20	...	?

Review *Help*

For help with looking for a pattern, see p. 796.

55.

Cost of item (dollars)	1.00	1.50	2.00	2.50	...	n
Cost with coupon (dollars)	0.50	1.00	1.50	2.00	...	?

The cost with a coupon is \$.50 less than the cost of the item; $n - 0.50$.

56. Challenge The plastic tips on the ends of a shoelace are called aglets. Suppose a sneaker factory produces p pairs of shoes each hour and is in operation for h hours each day. Write a variable expression for the number of single aglets the factory uses each day. Evaluate the expression when $p = 200$ and $h = 24$. Explain what your answer means. $4ph$; 19,200; the factory uses 19,200 aglets each day.

Mixed Review

Find the sum or difference. *(p. 774)*

57. $3.2 + 4.7$ 7.9 **58.** $5.1 + 6.8$ 11.9 **59.** $7.3 - 2.1$ 5.2 **60.** $9.9 - 5.4$ 4.5

Find the product or quotient. *(pp. 775, 776)*

61. $8(13.2)$ 105.6 **62.** $\frac{12.5}{5}$ 2.5 **63.** $\frac{24.32}{3.2}$ 7.6 **64.** $(6.5)(4.3)$ 27.95

65. Order the decimals from least to greatest: 8.9, 8.79, 7.98, 9.87, 7.8, 9.78. *(p. 773)* 7.8, 7.98, 8.79, 8.9, 9.78, 9.87

Standardized Test Practice

66. Multiple Choice Write a variable expression for a length of time in minutes if you know the number s of seconds. B

A. $s + 60$ **B.** $\frac{s}{60}$ **C.** $60s$ **D.** $\frac{60}{s}$

67. Multiple Choice Evaluate the expression $x - y$ when $x = 12.8$ and $y = 4$. G

F. 3.2 **G.** 8.8 **H.** 12.4 **I.** 13.2

4 ASSESS

ASSESSMENT RESOURCES

For more assessment resources, see:

- Assessment Book
- Test and Practice Generator

MINI-QUIZ

Evaluate the expression when $x = 8$, $y = 2$, and $z = 6$.

1. $x + z$ **14** **2.** $\frac{z}{y}$ **3**

3. $z - y$ **4** **4.** xy **16**

5. Write a variable expression to represent the amount Stephan earns in w weeks if he earns \$110 each week. **110*w***

6. Challenge A company makes inline skates that have 4 wheels on each skate. Suppose the company produces p pairs of inline skates each hour and is in operation for h hours each day. Write a variable expression for the number of wheels the company uses each day. Evaluate the expression for $p = 40$ and $h = 16$. **8*ph*; 5120**

5 FOLLOW-UP

DIAGNOSIS/REMEDIATION

- Study Guide in Chapter 1 Resource Book, pp. 11–12
- Tutor Place, Algebra Cards 1, 4
- eTutorial Plus Online
- Extra Practice, p. 803
- Lesson Practice in Chapter 1 Resource Book, pp. 8–10

ENGLISH LEARNER SUPPORT

- Spanish Study Guide
- Multi-Language Visual Glossary
- Chapter Audio Summaries CDs

CHALLENGE

- Challenge Practice in Chapter 1 Resource Book, p. 13
- Teacher's Edition, p. 2F

1 PLAN

Skill Check

1. $4 \cdot 4 \cdot 4 = \underline{?}$ 64
2. $10 \cdot 10 \cdot 10 = \underline{?}$ 1000
3. $(0.7)(0.7) = \underline{?}$ 0.49
4. $2 \cdot 2 \cdot 2 \cdot 2 = \underline{?}$ 16

LESSON OBJECTIVE

Use powers to describe repeated multiplication.

PACING

Suggested Number of Days
Basic Course: 1 day
Average Course: 1 day
Advanced Course: 1 day
Block: 0.5 block with 1.1

TEACHING RESOURCES

For a complete list of Teaching Resources, see page 2B.

TRANSPARENCY

Warm-Up Exercises for this lesson are available on a transparency.

2 TEACH

MOTIVATING THE LESSON

Write the sum $8 + 8 + 8 + 8 + 8$ on the board. Show students how this sum can be rewritten as the product $8 \cdot 5$. Then ask how the product $8 \cdot 8 \cdot 8 \cdot 8 \cdot 8$ might be rewritten. 8^5

TIPS *for* NEW TEACHERS

Stress to students to write exponents neatly so that they do not confuse powers with whole numbers, such as confusing 4^3 with 43. See Tips for New Teachers in the *Chapter 1 Resource Book*.

LESSON 1.2

Powers *and* Exponents

BEFORE	*Now*	WHY?
You multiplied whole numbers and decimals.	You'll use powers to describe repeated multiplication.	So you can find the total number of e-mails sent, as in Ex. 29.

Vocabulary
power, p. 10
base, p. 10
exponent, p. 10

A **power** is the result of a repeated multiplication of the same factor. For example, the number 125 is a power because $125 = 5 \cdot 5 \cdot 5$. A power can be written in a form that has two parts: a number called the **base** and a number called the **exponent**. The exponent shows the number of times the base is used as a factor.

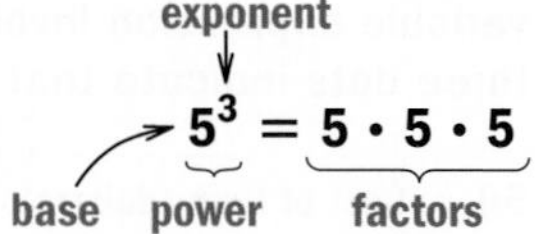

The base 5 is used as a factor 3 times.

The table shows how to read and write powers. Numbers raised to the first power, such as 12^1, are usually written without the exponent.

Power	In words	Value
12^1	12 to the first power	$12^1 = 12$
$(0.5)^2$	0.5 to the second power, or 0.5 squared	$(0.5)(0.5) = 0.25$
4^3	4 to the third power, or 4 cubed	$4 \cdot 4 \cdot 4 = 64$
8^4	8 to the fourth power	$8 \cdot 8 \cdot 8 \cdot 8 = 4096$

Note *Worthy*

Write additional examples of your own in your notebook. For each product, identify the base and the exponent, then write the product using an exponent.

Example 1 *Using Exponents*

Write the product using an exponent.

a. $13 \cdot 13 \cdot 13 \cdot 13 = 13^4$ **The base 13 is used as a factor 4 times.**

b. $(0.2)(0.2)(0.2) = (0.2)^3$ **The base 0.2 is used as a factor 3 times.**

c. $n \cdot n \cdot n \cdot n \cdot n \cdot n = n^6$ **The base *n* is used as a factor 6 times.**

d. $t \cdot t \cdot t \cdot t \cdot t = t^5$ **The base *t* is used as a factor 5 times.**

Checkpoint

Write the product using an exponent.

1. $10 \cdot 10 \cdot 10$ 10^3 **2.** $(4.3)(4.3)$ $(4.3)^2$ **3.** $x \cdot x \cdot x \cdot x$ x^4

4. Critical Thinking Evaluate each power: $0^2, 0^3, 0^4$. Use your results to write a rule for the value of 0 raised to any nonzero whole number exponent.

4. 0, 0, 0; zero raised to any nonzero whole number exponent is zero.

NCTM CURRICULUM STANDARDS
Standard 1: Understand meanings of operations; Compute fluently
Standard 2: Represent situations using algebraic symbols

Example 2 *Evaluating Powers with Variables*

Evaluate the expression x^4 when $x = 0.5$.

$x^4 = (0.5)^4$	**Substitute 0.5 for *x*.**
$= (0.5)(0.5)(0.5)(0.5)$	**Use 0.5 as a factor 4 times.**
$= 0.0625$	**Multiply.**

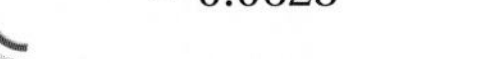

Checkpoint

Evaluate the expression when $m = 3$.

5. m^2 9 **6.** m^3 27 **7.** m^4 81 **8.** m^5 243

Review *Help*

For help with area and volume, see p. 789.

Using Formulas A formula describes a relationship between quantities. Some formulas involve powers. For example, you can use a formula to find the area of a square or the volume of a cube.

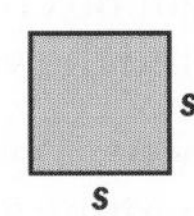

Area *A* of a square

$A = s^2$

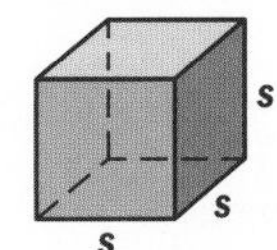

Volume *V* of a cube

$V = s^3$

Area is measured in square units, such as square feet (ft^2) or square centimeters (cm^2). Volume is measured in cubic units, such as cubic inches ($in.^3$) or cubic meters (m^3).

In the **Real World**

Ice Sculpture A cubic inch of ice weighs about 0.03 pound. If the artist carves away about 2000 cubic inches from the block in Example 3, about how much does the resulting sculpture weigh? **180 lb**

Example 3 *Using Powers in Formulas*

Ice Sculpture An artist uses a cube-shaped block of ice to make an ice sculpture for a competition. Find the volume of the block of ice.

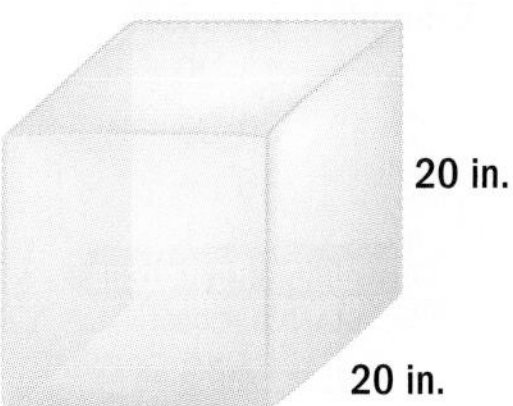

Solution

Use the formula for the volume of a cube.

$V = s^3$	**Write the formula.**
$= (20)^3$	**Substitute 20 for *s*.**
$= 8000$	**Evaluate power.**

Answer The volume of the block of ice is 8000 cubic inches.

Checkpoint

Find the area of a square with the given side length.

9. 9 meters $81\ m^2$ **10.** 11 inches $121\ in.^2$ **11.** 1.5 centimeters $2.25\ cm^2$

Extra Examples

Example 1 Write the product using an exponent.

a. 19 • 19 • 19 19^3

b. (1.7)(1.7)(1.7)(1.7)(1.7) $(1.7)^5$

c. $p \cdot p \cdot p \cdot p$ p^4

d. $w \cdot w \cdot w \cdot w \cdot w \cdot w \cdot w$ w^7

Example 2 Evaluate the expression y^3 when $y = 2.1$. **9.261**

Example 3 A store is displaying copies of a new bestselling book. The display is a stack of books that forms a cube that measures 5 feet on each side. Find the volume of the stack of books. **125 ft^3**

Reading Strategy

In this lesson, point out how the multiplication symbol × is no longer used. In Checkpoint Exercise 3 on page 10, stress how confusing it would be to use the multiplication symbol × with the variable *x*. Encourage students to use multiplication dots or pairs of parentheses, as in Example 2, when they are writing multiplication expressions.

Teaching Tip

In Example 2, point out how 0.5 is written in parentheses and stress that it should not be written as 0.5^4.

Concept Check

How would you write the product $b \cdot b \cdot b \cdot b$ using an exponent? b^4

Daily Puzzler

If $x = 2^2$, what is the value of x^2? **16**

3 APPLY

ASSIGNMENT GUIDE

Basic Course

Day 1: SRH p. 789 Exs. 1, 2, 5, 6; pp. 12-13 Exs. 13-33, 36, 39-48

Average Course

Day 1: pp. 12-13 Exs. 17-37, 39-49

Advanced Course

Day 1: pp. 12-13 Exs. 17-20, 25-29, 32-38*, 43-49

Block

pp. 12-13 Exs. 17-37, 39-49 (with 1.1)

EXTRA PRACTICE

- Student Edition, p. 803
- Chapter 1 Resource Book, pp. 16-18
- Test and Practice Generator

TRANSPARENCY

Even-numbered answers are available on transparencies.

HOMEWORK CHECK

When you review students' homework for this lesson, go over the following exercises to check understanding of key concepts.

Basic: 14, 19, 30, 31, 36

Average: 18, 19, 31, 32, 36

Advanced: 18, 20, 32, 33, 36

TEACHING TIP

In Exercises 13-18, remind students that they do not need to evaluate the expressions but just write them using exponents.

1.2 Exercises

More Practice, p. 803

Guided Practice

Vocabulary Check

1. Identify the base and the exponent in the expression 13^5. base: 13; exponent: 5
2. How are the expressions 3^4 and 4^3 different? 3^4 means $3 \cdot 3 \cdot 3 \cdot 3$ and 4^3 means $4 \cdot 4 \cdot 4$.

Skill Check

Write the power in words and as a repeated multiplication. Then evaluate the power.

3. 12^2 4. $(0.3)^3$ 5. $(1.2)^3$ 6. 5^4

3. 12 squared; $12 \cdot 12$; 144
4. 0.3 cubed; (0.3)(0.3)(0.3); 0.027
5. 1.2 cubed; (1.2)(1.2)(1.2); 1.728
6. 5 to the fourth power; $5 \cdot 5 \cdot 5 \cdot 5$; 625

Evaluate the expression when $k = 6$.

7. k^2 36 8. k^3 216 9. k^4 1296 10. k^5 7776

11. **Gift Box** A gift box has the shape of a cube with an edge length of 14 inches. Find the volume of the box. 2744 in.^{3}

12. **Error Analysis** Describe and correct the error in writing 2^3 as a repeated multiplication. 2^3 means $2 \cdot 2 \cdot 2$.

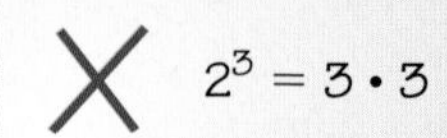

21. 8 cubed; $8 \cdot 8 \cdot 8$; 512
22. 2 to the fifth power; $2 \cdot 2 \cdot 2 \cdot 2 \cdot 2$; 32
23. 10 to the sixth power; $10 \cdot 10 \cdot 10 \cdot 10 \cdot 10 \cdot 10$; 1,000,000
24. 12 cubed; $12 \cdot 12 \cdot 12$; 1728

Practice and Problem Solving

Homework *Help*

Example	Exercises
1	13-29
2	30-33
3	36

Online Resources
CLASSZONE.COM
- More Examples
- eTutorial Plus

Write the product using an exponent.

A 13. $32 \cdot 32$ 32^2 14. $11 \cdot 11 \cdot 11$ 11^3 15. $6 \cdot 6 \cdot 6 \cdot 6 \cdot 6$ 6^5 16. $2 \cdot 2 \cdot 2 \cdot 2$ 2^4

17. $(5.6)(5.6)(5.6)$ $(5.6)^3$ 18. $(1.7)(1.7)$ $(1.7)^2$ 19. $z \cdot z \cdot z$ z^3 20. $n \cdot n \cdot n \cdot n$ n^4

Write the power in words and as a repeated multiplication. Then evaluate the power. 21–28. See margin.

21. 8^3 22. 2^5 23. 10^6 24. 12^3

25. 9^3 26. 4^4 27. $(0.2)^2$ 28. $(0.6)^4$

25. 9 cubed; $9 \cdot 9 \cdot 9$; 729
26. 4 to the fourth power; $4 \cdot 4 \cdot 4 \cdot 4$; 256
27. 0.2 squared; (0.2)(0.2); 0.04
28. 0.6 to the fourth power; (0.6)(0.6)(0.6)(0.6); 0.1296

29. **Extended Problem Solving** You send an e-mail to 4 friends. Each friend sends the e-mail to 4 more friends. Each of those friends sends it to 4 friends, and so on.

Stage	E-mails sent, as a power	Value of power
1	4^1	4
2	4^2	16
3	? 4^3	? 64
4	? 4^4	? 256

a. Copy and complete the table.

b. **Calculate** Find the number of e-mails sent at stage 9. 262,144 e-mails

c. **Estimate** Estimate the stage at which more than 1,000,000 e-mails will be sent. Use a calculator to check your estimate. stage 10

34. *Sample answer:* The area of a square with side s is s^2 and the volume of a cube with side s is s^3.

Evaluate the expression when $n = 7$ and when $n = 0.4$.

30. n^2 49; 0.16 **31.** n^3 343; 0.064 **32.** n^4 2401; 0.0256 **33.** n^5 16,807; 0.01024

B **34.** *Writing* The *square* of a number is the second power of the number. The *cube* of a number is the third power of the number. Explain why these names are reasonable.

35. Critical Thinking Explain why 1 raised to any power is equal to 1. See margin.

36. Aquariums An aquarium has a square base with a side length of 15 inches. You fill the aquarium with water to a height of 15 inches.

a. Find the volume of the water in the aquarium. 3375 in.^{3}

b. A cubic inch of water weighs approximately 0.036 pound. Find the approximate weight of the water in the aquarium. 121.5 lb

C **37. Patterns** The table shows sums of odd numbers.

n	Sum of first n odd numbers
1	1
2	$1 + 3 = 4$
3	$1 + 3 + 5 = ?$
4	$1 + 3 + 5 + 7 = ?$
5	?

a. Copy and complete the table. Identify any pattern that you see. See margin.

b. Write a variable expression for the sum of the first n odd numbers. n^2

c. Use your expression from part (b) to find the sum of the first 100 odd numbers. 10,000

35. *Sample answer:* If you use the base 1 as a factor any number of times, the product is 1.

37a. Row 3: 9; Row 4: 16; Row 5: $1 + 3 + 5 + 7 + 9 = 25$; the sum of the first n odd numbers equals n squared.

38. Challenge Find values of x, y, and z so that each of the expressions x^2, y^3, and z^6 has a value of 64. $x = 8$, $y = 4$, $z = 2$

Mixed Review

Find the product or quotient. *(pp. 775, 776)*

39. (2.5)(7.1) 17.75 **40.** (2.3)(8.4) 19.32 **41.** $1.2 \div 2.4$ 0.5 **42.** $5.2 \div 1.25$ 4.16

43. Olympics The bar graph shows the number of gold medals won by the four countries with the most gold medals in the 2000 Olympic Summer Games. How many gold medals did the four countries win in all? *(p. 781)* 115 gold medals

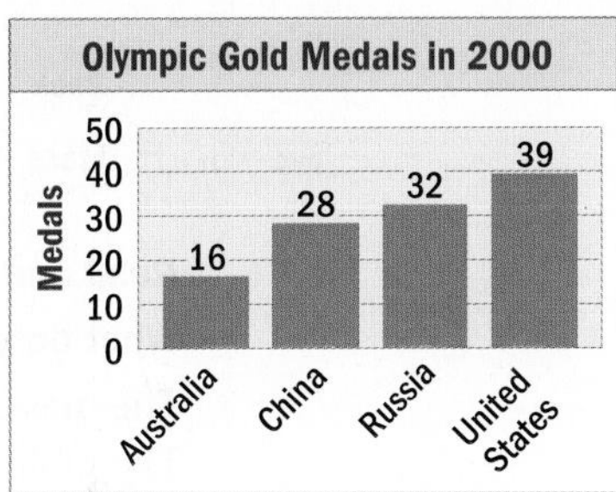

Evaluate the expression when $x = 15$. *(Lesson 1.1)*

44. $x + 4$ 19 **45.** $200 - x$ 185 **46.** $x - 11$ 4 **47.** $3x$ 45

Standardized Test Practice

48. Multiple Choice Which expression has a value of 81? B

A. 4^3 **B.** 3^4 **C.** 2^8 **D.** 27^3

49. Short Response Compare each number in the top row of the table with the number below it. Describe any pattern you see. Complete the table with a variable expression involving n.

1	2	3	4	...	n
1	8	27	64	...	?

The number in the bottom row is the cube of the number in the top row; n^3.

4 ASSESS

Assessment Resources

For more assessment resources, see:

- Assessment Book
- Test and Practice Generator

Mini-Quiz

Write the product using an exponent.

1. $41 \cdot 41 \cdot 41$ 41^3

2. $k \cdot k \cdot k \cdot k \cdot k$ k^5

Evaluate the expression when $m = 3$ and when $m = 0.8$.

3. m^3 27; 0.512

4. m^4 81; 0.4096

5. Challenge Find the values of a and c so that both of the expressions a^3 and c^6 have a value of 729. $a = 9, c = 3$

5 FOLLOW-UP

Diagnosis/Remediation

- Study Guide in Chapter 1 Resource Book, pp.19–20
- Tutor Place, Geometry and Measurement Cards 11, 21, Algebra Cards 2, 4, 13
- eTutorial Plus Online
- Extra Practice, p. 803
- Lesson Practice in Chapter 1 Resource Book, pp. 16–18

English Learner Support

- Spanish Study Guide
- Multi-Language Visual Glossary
- Chapter Audio Summaries CDs

Challenge

- Challenge Practice in Chapter 1 Resource Book, p. 21
- Teacher's Edition, p. 2F

1 PLAN

Skill Check

1. 1.4 + 2.1 = ? **3.5**
2. 3.8 + 1.9 = ? **5.7**
3. 2.5 + 2.1 = ? **4.6**
4. 3.8 + 2.1 = ? **5.9**

LESSON OBJECTIVE

Prepare for solving problems.

2 TEACH

TEACHING TIP

To help students visualize the different combinations of books that are possible, have them write the mass of each book on a slip of paper and then arrange the papers into groups on their desks.

Extra Examples

Example 1 On a school night, Travis goes to bed at 10 P.M. This evening, he has three homework assignments that will each take 45 minutes to complete, plus chores that will take 1 hour to finish, and he needs to allow 45 minutes for dinner. What time should he start all these tasks in order to be ready for bed at 10 P.M.? **6 P.M.**

Student Reference

A Problem Solving Plan

▶ **Review** this topic in preparation for solving problems in Lesson 1.3. For a review of problem solving strategies, see pp. 795–802.

A Problem Solving Plan

You can use the following 4-step plan to solve a problem.

1. ***Read and Understand*** Read the problem carefully. Identify the question and any important information.
2. ***Make a Plan*** Decide on a problem solving strategy.
3. ***Solve the Problem*** Use the problem solving strategy to answer the question.
4. ***Look Back*** Check that your answer is reasonable.

Reading and Planning

Example You plan to ship 5 books to a friend. The table shows the masses of the books. Is it possible to ship the books in 2 boxes, each with a mass of 6 kilograms or less? Explain.

Book	A	B	C	D	E
Mass (kg)	1.4	2.1	3.8	1.9	2.5

Read and Understand

What do you know?

The mass of each box must be 6 kilograms or less.
The table gives the mass of each book.

What do you want to find out?

Is it possible to put the books in 2 boxes so that each box has a mass of 6 kilograms or less?

Make a Plan

How can you relate what you know to what you want to find out?

Check that the total mass of the books doesn't exceed 12 kilograms. If it does, you can't divide the books as you want.
Use the strategy *guess, check, and revise* to choose books for each box.

NCTM CURRICULUM STANDARDS
Standard 6: Apply/adapt strategies to solve problems

Solving and Looking Back

To solve the problem from page 14 about shipping books, carry out the plan. Then check the answer.

Solve the Problem

The total mass of the books is 1.4 + 2.1 + 3.8 + 1.9 + 2.5 = 11.7 kg, so it may be possible to ship the books as you want.

Now use the strategy *guess, check, and revise.* Put the 3 lightest books in one box and the 2 heaviest in the other. The mass of the second box is more than 6 kg.

Books	Total mass (kg)
A, D, B	1.4 + 1.9 + 2.1 = 5.4
C, E	3.8 + 2.5 = 6.3

Try switching books B and E. The mass of each box is less than 6 kg.

Books	Total mass (kg)
A, D, E	1.4 + 1.9 + 2.5 = 5.8
C, B	3.8 + 2.1 = 5.9

Answer It is possible to ship the books in 2 boxes, each with a mass of 6 kg or less. Put books A, D, and E in one box and books C and B in the other.

Look Back

It makes sense that the box with 3 books contains the 2 lightest books and the box with 2 books contains the heaviest book. So, the answer is reasonable.

Checkpoint

▶ **Test** your knowledge of the problem solving plan by solving these problems.

1. **Pool Schedules** A community pool offers 3 swim sessions each Saturday morning. Each session lasts 35 minutes, with 10 minutes between sessions. The final session ends at 11:05 A.M. At what time does the first session begin? **9:00 A.M.**
2. **Theater Seating** The center section of a theater has 10 rows. There are 41 seats in row 10, 38 seats in row 9, 35 seats in row 8, and so on. How many seats are in row 1? **14 seats**
3. **Movie Marathon** You have invited friends over to watch movies. You have rented 4 movies: one action, one science fiction, one comedy, and one animated. In how many different orders can you watch the movies? **24 orders**

Common Error

Arithmetic errors in this example will prevent students from finding the correct answer. Suggest that once students have assigned the books to the two boxes, they find the mass of each box and then find the combined mass of the two boxes to confirm that they total 11.7 kilograms.

3 APPLY

Transparency

Even-numbered answers are available on transparencies.

Common Error

In Exercise 1, stress that there is more than one 10-minute break each Saturday morning.

Teaching Tip

In Exercise 3, suggest that students make an organized list of the orders in which the movies can be watched.

1 PLAN

Skill Check

1. 5 • 44,200 = ? **221,000**
2. 144,500 + 96,800 = ? **241,300**
3. 15.1 − 6.4 = ? **8.7**
4. 50.4 ÷ 8 = ? **6.3**

Lesson Objective

Use order of operations to evaluate expressions.

Pacing

Suggested Number of Days
Basic Course: 1 day
Average Course: 1 day
Advanced Course: 1 day
Block: 0.5 block with 1.4

Teaching Resources

For a complete list of Teaching Resources, see page 2B.

Transparency

Warm-Up Exercises for this lesson are available on a transparency.

2 TEACH

Motivating the Lesson

Before students open their books, write the expression for the total number of plants on the board. Ask students to offer suggestions on how to evaluate the expression.

TIPS *for* NEW TEACHERS

Stress that operations of equal importance, such as multiplication and division, should be performed in order from left to right. See Tips for New Teachers in the *Chapter 1 Resource Book.*

LESSON **1.3**

Order *of* Operations

BEFORE	*Now*	WHY?
You performed basic operations.	You'll use order of operations to evaluate expressions.	So you can find the height of a boojum, as in Ex. 28.

Vocabulary
order of operations, p. 16

Flower Flag There are about 2000 plants in each of the 50 stars of this flower flag. There are about 64,100 plants in each of the 7 short stripes and 106,700 plants in each of the 6 long stripes. The blue region contains about 198,900 plants. You can approximate the total number of plants by evaluating the expression

$$50 \cdot 2000 + 7 \cdot 64{,}100 + 6 \cdot 106{,}700 + 198{,}900.$$

To evaluate expressions involving more than one operation, mathematicians have agreed on a set of rules called the **order of operations**.

Note *Worthy*

You should include material that appears on a notebook like the one shown in your own notebook.

Order of Operations

1. Evaluate expressions inside grouping symbols.
2. Evaluate powers.
3. Multiply and divide from left to right.
4. Add and subtract from left to right.

Example 1 ***Using Order of Operations***

To approximate the total number of plants in the flower flag described above, use the order of operations to evaluate the expression $50 \cdot 2000 + 7 \cdot 64{,}100 + 6 \cdot 106{,}700 + 198{,}900$.

$50 \cdot 2000 + 7 \cdot 64{,}100 + 6 \cdot 106{,}700 + 198{,}900$	**Write expression.**
$= 100{,}000 + 448{,}700 + 640{,}200 + 198{,}900$	**Multiply.**
$= 1{,}387{,}800$	**Add.**

Answer There are approximately 1,387,800 plants in the flower flag.

NCTM CURRICULUM STANDARDS
Standard 1: Understand meanings of operations; Understand how operations are related; Compute fluently

Grouping Symbols Parentheses ( ), brackets [ ], and fraction bars are common grouping symbols. Grouping symbols indicate operations that should be performed first. For example, compare the expressions $3 \cdot 2 + 5$ and $3(2 + 5)$. To evaluate $3 \cdot 2 + 5$, you multiply first, then add. To evaluate $3(2 + 5)$, you add first, then multiply.

Example 2 *Using Grouping Symbols*

Evaluate the expression.

a. $8(17 - 2.3) = 8(14.7)$ **Subtract within parentheses.**

$= 117.6$ **Multiply.**

b. $\frac{14 + 6}{12 - 7} = (14 + 6) \div (12 - 7)$ **Rewrite fraction as division.**

$= 20 \div 5$ **Evaluate within parentheses.**

$= 4$ **Divide.**

c. $5 \cdot [36 - (13 + 9)] = 5 \cdot [36 - 22]$ **Add within parentheses.**

$= 5 \cdot 14$ **Subtract within brackets.**

$= 70$ **Multiply.**

Watch *Out*

When grouping symbols appear inside other grouping symbols, as in part (c) of Example 2, work from the innermost grouping symbols out.

Checkpoint

Evaluate the expression.

1. $28 - 63 \div 7$ **19** **2.** $52 + 12.5 \cdot 4$ **102** **3.** $9 \cdot 6 + 27 \div 3$ **63**

4. $10(1.5 + 0.6)$ **21** **5.** $\frac{70 - 9.2}{3 + 5}$ **7.6** **6.** $72 \div [(11 - 7) \cdot 2]$ **9**

Example 3 *Evaluating Variable Expressions*

Evaluate the expression when $x = 2$ and $y = 5$.

a. $4(x + y) = 4(2 + 5)$ **Substitute 2 for x and 5 for y.**

$= 4(7)$ **Add within parentheses.**

$= 28$ **Multiply.**

b. $3(x + y)^2 = 3(2 + 5)^2$ **Substitute 2 for x and 5 for y.**

$= 3(7)^2$ **Add within parentheses.**

$= 3(49)$ **Evaluate power.**

$= 147$ **Multiply.**

Study *Strategy*

You can use the first letters of the words of the sentence *Please Excuse My Dear Aunt Sally* to help you remember the order of operations.

P parentheses
E exponents
M } multiplication and
D } division
A } addition and
S } subtraction

Checkpoint

Evaluate the expression when $x = 4$ and $y = 2$.

7. $1.2(x + 3)$ **8.4** **8.** $1.2x + 3$ **7.8** **9.** $3x - 2y$ **8**

10. $0.5[y - (x - 2)]$ **0** **11.** $x^2 - y$ **14** **12.** $2(x - y)^2$ **8**

Extra Examples

Example 1 Kamini is buying breakfast for herself and 6 friends. The group orders 3 vegetable omelets at a cost of \$5.50 each, and 4 shrimp omelets at a cost of \$7.50 each. To determine how much money Kamini spent for the group's breakfast, use the order of operations to evaluate the expression $3 \cdot 5.50 + 4 \cdot 7.50$. **\$46.50**

Example 2 Evaluate the expression.

a. $3(7.4 + 2.2)$ **28.8**

b. $\frac{23 - 5}{4.2 + 4.8}$ **2**

c. $10 \cdot [6 + (8 \cdot 2)]$ **220**

Example 3 Evaluate the expression when $x = 4$ and $y = 9$.

a. $10(y - x)$ **50**

b. $3[(x^2 - y) + 6]$ **39**

Common Error

In part c of Example 2, stress that students must evaluate within grouping symbols beginning from the innermost pair and working outward. Watch for students who evaluate $36 - (13 + 9)$ as if it is $36 - 13 + 9$.

Notetaking

When students record the order of operations in their notebooks, have them record the "Please Excuse My Dear Aunt Sally" mnemonic given on this page or encourage them to create a mnemonic that they like better.

Teaching Tip

Draw students' attention to Checkpoint Exercises 7 and 8. Ask students to describe the difference between the two given expressions.

Extra Examples

Example 4 You buy a CD player costing \$24.75, three CDs costing \$12.99 each, and two packages of batteries costing \$4.86 each. Find the total cost.
\$73.44

CONCEPT CHECK

In what order should you evaluate expressions? **Evaluate inside grouping symbols first, followed by evaluating powers, then multiply and divide from left to right, and finally add and subtract from left to right.**

DAILY PUZZLER

Replace each ® with an operation symbol to make the sentence true.
[3 ® 3 ® (3 ® 3)] ® 3 = 1
$[3 \cdot 3 - (3 + 3)] \div 3 = 1$

Example 4 *Using a Problem Solving Plan*

Sewing You buy a pattern and enough material to make two pillows. The pattern costs \$5. Each pillow requires \$3.95 worth of fabric and a button that costs \$.75. Find the total cost.

Solution

Read and Understand You buy one pattern plus fabric and buttons for two pillows. You are asked to find the total cost.

Make a Plan Write a verbal model.

Total cost = Cost of pattern + Number of pillows • Cost of each pillow

Solve the Problem Write and evaluate an expression.

Total cost $= 5 + 2(3.95 + 0.75)$	**Substitute values into verbal model.**
$= 5 + 2(4.70)$	**Add within parentheses.**
$= 5 + 9.40$	**Multiply.**
$= 14.40$	**Add.**

Answer The total cost is \$14.40.

Look Back Use estimation to check that the answer is reasonable. The cost of materials for each pillow is about \$4 + \$1 = \$5. The total cost is about \$5 + 2(\$5) = \$15. The answer is reasonable.

1.3 Exercises

More Practice, p. 803

Guided Practice

Vocabulary Check

1. Give three examples of grouping symbols. ***Sample answer:*** **Fraction bar, parentheses, brackets**
2. Describe in order the steps you would take to evaluate the expression $12(x - 3)^2$ when $x = 5$. **See margin.**

Skill Check **Evaluate the expression.**

3. $15 - 3 \cdot 4$ **3**
4. $48 \div 6 + 2$ **10**
5. $3 \cdot 8 + 5 \cdot 4$ **44**
6. $\frac{18 + 12}{7 - 2}$ **6**
7. $17 - (3^2 - 2)$ **10**
8. $4[15 - (2 + 5)]$ **32**

9. **Twin Convention** The table shows the numbers of sets of twins, triplets, quadruplets, and quintuplets registered at a twin convention. Write and evaluate an expression for the total number of people who registered at the convention.
2(2697) + 3(29) + 4(2) + 5(1) = 5494 people

Type	Sets
Twins	2697
Triplets	29
Quadruplets	2
Quintuplets	1

2. $12(x - 3)^2$	
$= 12(5 - 3)^2$	**Substitute 5 for *x*.**
$= 12(2)^2$	**Subtract within parentheses.**
$= 12(4)$	**Evaluate power.**
$= 48$	**Multiply.**

Practice and Problem Solving

Homework *Help*

Example	Exercises
1	10-13
2	14-18
3	19-27
4	28-31

Online Resources
CLASSZONE.COM
- More Examples
- eTutorial Plus

Evaluate the expression.

A **10.** $47.7 - 12 \cdot 3$ 11.7 **11.** $11 \cdot 7 - 9 \cdot 5$ 32 **12.** $14 \div 7 + 36 \div 4$ 11

13. $5.8(3) + 3(1.1)$ 20.7 **14.** $\frac{36 - 12}{2 + 6}$ 3 **15.** $\frac{9.8 + 2.2}{7 - 5}$ 6

16. $5(21 - 3^2)$ 60 **17.** $7[2.5 + 3(12 - 7)]$ 122.5 **18.** $84 \div [(18 - 16) \cdot 3]$ 14

Evaluate the expression when $x = 3$, $y = 4$, and $z = 5$.

19. $0.25y + x$ 4 **20.** $0.25(y + x)$ 1.75 **21.** $4(z - x)$ 8

22. $\frac{6.5y}{x - 1}$ 13 **23.** $x + \frac{24.4}{y}$ 9.1 **24.** $7z - x^2$ 26

25. $x + 2[z - (y - 1)]$ 7 **26.** $(x + y)^2 - 3.6$ 45.4 **27.** $y + (z - 1)^2$ 20

28. Plants A boojum is a very slow-growing cactus. One fifty-year-old boojum is 1.5 meters tall and has been growing about 0.03 meter each year. Assume the growth pattern continues.

a. Write an expression for the height in meters of the boojum y years from now. $1.5 + 0.03y$

b. Apply How tall will the boojum be in 50 years? 3 m

29. Craft Fair Your school is setting up a row of 5 tables for a craft fair. Each table is 72 inches long. The space between each pair of neighboring tables must be 48 inches. Write and evaluate an expression to find the length of the space needed for the tables from the beginning of the first table to the end of the last table. $5 \cdot 72 + 4 \cdot 48$; 552 in.

30. Basketball In basketball, players score points by making free throws worth 1 point each, field goals worth 2 points each, and field goals worth 3 points each. A player scores 4 free throws, 7 two-point field goals, and 2 three-point field goals. Write and evaluate an expression for the total number of points the player scores. $4(1) + 7(2) + 2(3)$; 24 points

31. Movies You buy 4 videotapes for \$14.99 each and 3 DVDs for \$19.99 each. Find the total cost of the movies. \$119.93

Evaluate the expression when $x = 4$ and $y = 3$.

B **32.** $5x^2 + 2y$ 86 **33.** $7(x^2 - 5y)$ 7 **34.** $\frac{x^2 + 9}{y + 2}$ 5 **35.** $\frac{6.5y + 2}{x + 1}$ 4.3

36. Cell Phone You and your sister share cell phone service. You divide the bill equally, including the monthly fee of \$39 plus \$.30 for each additional minute beyond your free minutes.

a. Write an expression for your share of the bill in a month when you are charged for m extra minutes. $\frac{39 + 0.3m}{2}$ or $19.5 + 0.15m$

b. Apply One month, you are charged for 125 additional minutes. Find your share of the bill. \$38.25

3 APPLY

ASSIGNMENT GUIDE

Basic Course

Day 1: SRH p. 774 Exs. 1-4, p. 775 Exs. 1-4; pp. 19-20 Exs. 10-35, 40-44

Average Course

Day 1: pp. 19-20 Exs. 12-18, 23-38, 40-44

Advanced Course

Day 1: pp. 19-20 Exs. 13-18, 23-30, 32-44*

Block

pp. 19-20 Exs. 12-18, 23-38, 40-44 (with 1.4)

EXTRA PRACTICE

- Student Edition, p. 803
- Chapter 1 Resource Book, pp. 25-27
- Test and Practice Generator

TRANSPARENCY

Even-numbered answers are available on transparencies.

HOMEWORK CHECK

When you review students' homework for this lesson, go over the following exercises to check understanding of key concepts.
Basic: 10, 14, 20, 24, 28
Average: 12, 15, 23, 25, 29
Advanced: 13, 17, 26, 27, 30

COMMON ERROR

In Exercise 32, watch for students who write $54^2 + 23$ and evaluate this expression. Urge these students to rewrite expressions containing variables by putting parentheses around the variables, for example $5(x)^2 + 2(y)$. Then have them rewrite the expressions with the given values substituted for the variables inside the parentheses.

4 ASSESS

ASSESSMENT RESOURCES

For more assessment resources, see:
- Assessment Book
- Test and Practice Generator

MINI-QUIZ

Evaluate the expression.

1. $\frac{30 - 8}{9 + 2}$ **2**
2. $6[14 - (2.7 - 1.8)]$ **78.6**

Evaluate the expression when $a = 8$ and $b = 4$.

3. $0.5(a + b)$ **6**
4. $5b + (a - 3)^2$ **45**
5. **Challenge** The measure, in degrees, of each angle in a regular polygon with n sides is given by the expression $\frac{180(n - 2)}{n}$. Find the measure of each angle in a regular polygon with 8 sides. **135 degrees**

5 FOLLOW-UP

DIAGNOSIS/REMEDIATION

- Study Guide in Chapter 1 Resource Book, pp. 28–29
- Tutor Place, Whole Numbers and Decimals Card 18, Algebra Cards 3, 4
- eTutorial Plus Online
- Extra Practice, p. 803
- Lesson Practice in Chapter 1 Resource Book, pp. 25–27

ENGLISH LEARNER SUPPORT

- Spanish Study Guide
- Multi-Language Visual Glossary
- Chapter Audio Summaries CDs

CHALLENGE

- Challenge Practice in Chapter 1 Resource Book, p. 30
- Teacher's Edition, p. 2F

39c. See Additional Answers beginning on page AA1.

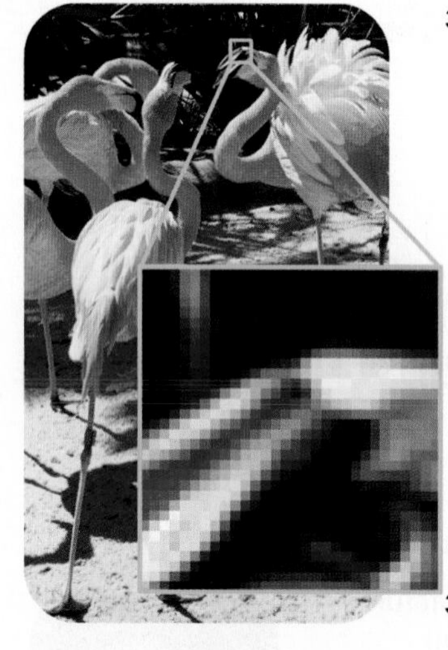

In the **Real World**

Digital Images A digital image with m megapixels requires approximately $2.86m$ megabytes (MB) of storage. Suppose you have 64 MB of storage. About how many 1.2 megapixel images can you store? **18 images**

37c. No; $\frac{1.3}{8 \cdot 10} \approx 0.016$, $0.016 < 0.017$ so the print will not be clear.

37. **Extended Problem Solving** Digital cameras capture images in rows and columns of *pixels*, which are small rectangular colored dots. The more pixels in a given space, the greater the detail of the image.

    a. **Calculate** The total number of pixels in an image is the product of the number of pixels in a row and the number of pixels in a column. Your camera produces an image that has 1280 pixels in a row and 1024 pixels in a column. Find the total number of pixels. **1,310,720 pixels**

    b. A megapixel is 1,000,000 pixels. Find, to the nearest tenth, the number of megapixels in the image in part (a). **1.3 megapixels**

    c. **Apply** Let m be the number of megapixels in an image, and let l and w be the length and width in inches of a printed photo. A print is clear if the value of the expression $\frac{m}{lw}$ is 0.017 or greater. Can you make a clear 8 inch by 10 inch print of the image in part (a)? Explain. **See margin.**

38. **Museum Cost** A group of 20 members and 5 nonmembers visited a museum. The admission cost was \$6 for members and \$10 for nonmembers. The group decided to divide the total cost evenly among all 25 people. What did each person pay? **\$6.80**
C

39. **Challenge** You are decorating a square mouse pad. You place a colored sticker at each corner. If you have r different colors available, the number of possible patterns is the value of the expression $\frac{r^4 + 2r^3 + 3r^2 + 2r}{8}$. Two patterns are different if you cannot produce either pattern by turning the other around.

    a. *Writing* Tell whether the patterns shown are the same. Explain. **See margin.**

    b. You decide to use two colors. Find the number of possible patterns. **6 possible patterns**

    c. Sketch all the possible patterns for two different colors. **See margin.**

39a. They are the same; turn either pattern a quarter turn to get the other pattern.

Mixed Review

Copy and complete the statement using $<$, $>$, or $=$. *(p. 773)*

40. 1.99 _?_ 1.98 $>$
41. 0.56 _?_ 0.65 $<$
42. 0.32 _?_ 0.23 $>$
43. **Color Monitor** The *bit depth* of a color monitor is the number of colors it can display and is expressed as a power of 2. A 32 bit monitor can display 2^{32} colors. Write and evaluate an expression for the number of colors an 8 bit monitor can display. *(Lesson 1.2)* 2^8; **256 colors**

Standardized Test Practice

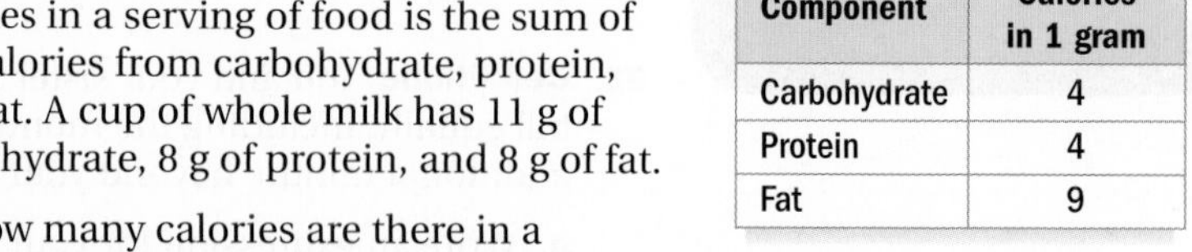

44. **Extended Response** The number of calories in a serving of food is the sum of the calories from carbohydrate, protein, and fat. A cup of whole milk has 11 g of carbohydrate, 8 g of protein, and 8 g of fat.

Component	Calories in 1 gram
Carbohydrate	4
Protein	4
Fat	9

    a. How many calories are there in a cup of whole milk? **148 Calories**

    b. If you drank enough whole milk to get 20 g of protein, how many calories would it provide? Explain how you found your answer.

44b. 370 Calories; if a serving of whole milk contains 20 g of protein, the serving is $\frac{20}{8} = 2.5$ cups, and $2.5(148) = 370$ calories.

1.3 Using Order of Operations

Goal Use a calculator to evaluate expressions using the order of operations.

Example

Baseball Alex Rodriguez played for the Texas Rangers during the 2002 baseball season. Use the following information to calculate his batting average for that season.

To find a baseball player's batting average, you divide the number of hits he made by the number of times he was at bat and round the quotient to the nearest thousandth. The table gives Alex Rodriguez's 2002 batting statistics.

2002 season	Hits	At bats
Before All-Star Game	100	328
After All-Star Game	87	296

Solution

Divide the total number of hits by the total number of times at bat. Use parentheses around each sum.

Keystrokes

(100 + 87) ÷

(328 + 296) =

The arrow indicates that the display does not show the entire entry.

(100+87)÷(328→
0.299679487

Answer Alex Rodriguez's batting average for the entire season was 0.300, which is usually written as .300.

Draw Conclusions

Use a calculator to evaluate the expression.

1. $50 + 21 \div 3$ **57**
2. $15 \times (24 + 8)$ **480**
3. $(8 + 10) \div 2$ **9**
4. $(5 + 2)^2 - 3^2$ **40**
5. $(24 - 16) \div 2$ **4**
6. $(12 - 7)^2 - 1$ **24**
7. $38 \div (2 + 17)$ **2**
8. $(8 + 3)^2 + 2$ **123**
9. **Critical Thinking** What result would you get in the example above if you didn't use parentheses when entering the expression? Why?
10. **Baseball** Barry Bonds played for the San Francisco Giants during the 2002 season. Use the information in the table to calculate his batting average for the entire 2002 season. **.370**

2002 season	Hits	At bats
Before All-Star Game	80	232
After All-Star Game	69	171

Tech *Help*

The keystrokes shown may not be the same as on your calculator. See your calculator's instruction manual for alternative keystrokes. For additional keystroke help, visit the website below.

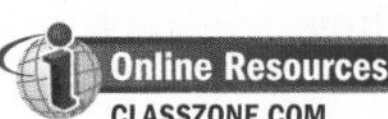

CLASSZONE.COM

- Keystroke Help

9. 396.2652439; for the expression $100 + 87 \div 328 + 296$, the calculator will first do the division $87 \div 328$, then do the additions.

1 PLAN

Learn the Method

- Students will use a calculator to evaluate expressions using the order of operations.
- Students can practice their calculator skills by revisiting some of the exercises and examples presented in Lesson 1.3. Students should verify that they can get the correct value and the correct sign for each expression when evaluating it using a calculator.

2 TEACH

Tips for Success

Students can add the number of hits, add the number of at bats, and then divide in three steps. They can then perform the operations again in one step using parentheses. Finally, they can compare the results they obtain from the two procedures.

Extra Examples

Example Evaluate $(84 + 24) \div (351 + 179)$. **about 0.2**

3 CLOSE

Assessment

Use a calculator to evaluate the expression.

1. $96 \div (37 + 11)$ **2**
2. $(6 + 9)^2 + 35$ **260**

NCTM CURRICULUM STANDARDS

Standard 1: Understand how operations are related

1 PLAN

Skill Check

Which number is greater?

1. 99 or 101 **101**
2. 3.14 or 3.15 **3.15**
3. 2.5 or 2.49 **2.5**

LESSON OBJECTIVE

Compare and order integers.

PACING

Suggested Number of Days

Basic Course: 1 day
Average Course: 1 day
Advanced Course: 1 day
Block: 0.5 block with 1.3

TEACHING RESOURCES

For a complete list of Teaching Resources, see page 2B.

TRANSPARENCY

Warm-Up Exercises for this lesson are available on a transparency. A support transparency is available for Examples 1-3.

2 TEACH

MOTIVATING THE LESSON

Have students research the record low temperature for each month in the United States. After completing Example 1, have students put these temperatures in order.

TIPS *for* NEW TEACHERS

Expect some students to be confused by the fact that, for example, $3 > 1$ but $-3 < -1$. You may wish to display a large number line to which students can refer when comparing integers. See Tips for New Teachers in the *Chapter 1 Resource Book*.

LESSON 1.4

Comparing *and* Ordering Integers

Vocabulary

integer, p. 22
negative integer, p. 22
positive integer, p. 22
absolute value, p. 23
opposite, p. 23

BEFORE	Now	WHY?
You compared and ordered decimals.	You'll compare and order integers.	So you can compare two volcanoes, as in Ex. 17.

Supercooled Insects Water freezes at 0°C, but some animals can resist freezing by producing a chemical that lowers the temperature at which the water in their bodies freezes. This temperature is called the supercooling point. Which of the insects listed in the table has the lowest supercooling point?

Insect	Supercooling point (°C)
Arctic beetle	−54
Gall beetle	−35
Goldenrod gallfly	−9
Snow flea	−19
Wooly bear caterpillar	−70

The numbers in the table are *negative integers*. The **integers** are the numbers . . . , −3, −2, −1, 0, 1, 2, 3, ... (The dots indicate that the numbers continue without end in both the positive and negative directions). **Negative integers** are integers that are less than 0. **Positive integers** are integers that are greater than 0.

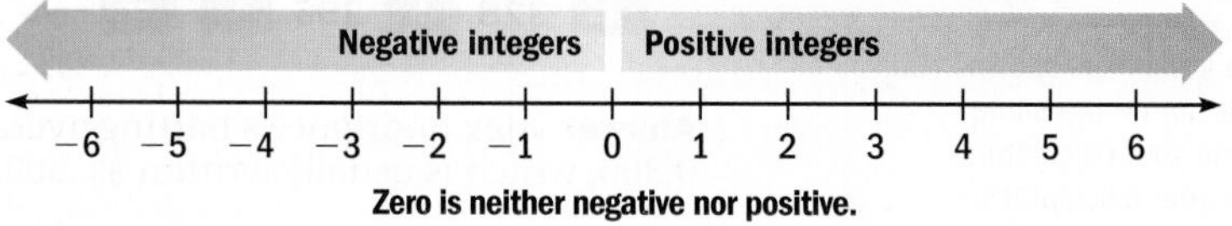

Wooly bear caterpillar

Example 1 *Graphing and Ordering Integers*

To determine which insect in the table above has the lowest supercooling point, graph the integers on a number line.

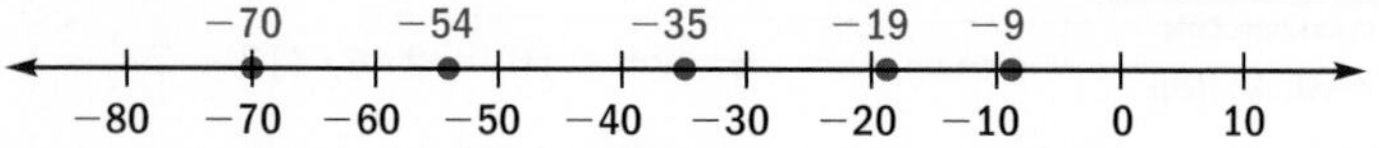

Read the numbers from left to right: −70, −54, −35, −19, −9.

Answer At −70°C, the wooly bear caterpillar has the lowest supercooling point.

Checkpoint

1. Use a number line to order these integers from least to greatest: −8, 5, −4, 2, 0, 6. **−8, −4, 0, 2, 5, 6**

NCTM CURRICULUM STANDARDS

Standard 1: Understand numbers; Understand relationships among numbers
Standard 10: Use representations to communicate ideas

Absolute Value The **absolute value** of a number is its distance from 0 on a number line. The absolute value of a number a is written as $|a|$. You can use a number line to find the absolute value of a number.

Example 2 ***Finding Absolute Value***

State the absolute value of the number.

a. 5 **b.** -7

Solution

a.

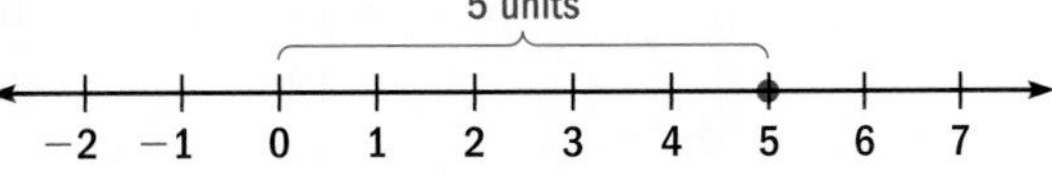

The distance between 5 and 0 is 5. So, $|5| = 5$.

b.

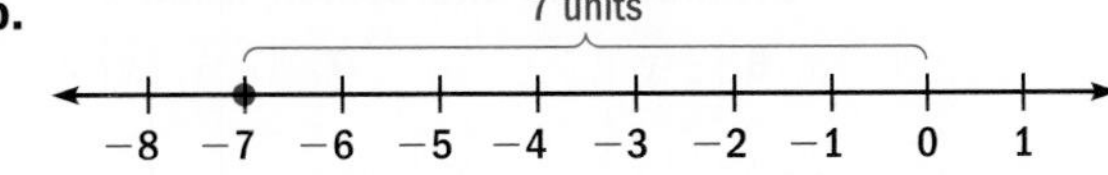

The distance between -7 and 0 is 7. So, $|-7| = 7$.

Reading *Algebra*

The expression $-a$ is always read as "the opposite of a" and *not* as "negative a." If a is a positive number, then $-a$ is a negative number. If a is a negative number, then $-a$ is a positive number.

Opposites Two numbers are **opposites** if they have the same absolute value but different signs. For example, -10 and 10 are opposites. The expression -10 can be read as "the opposite of 10" or as "negative 10." The expression "$-a$" is read as "the opposite of a."

Example 3 ***Finding Opposites***

State the opposite of the number.

a. 6 **b.** -15

Solution

a.

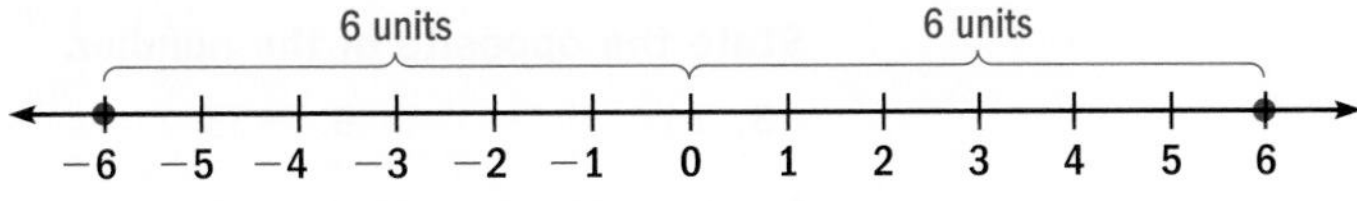

The opposite of 6 is -6.

b.

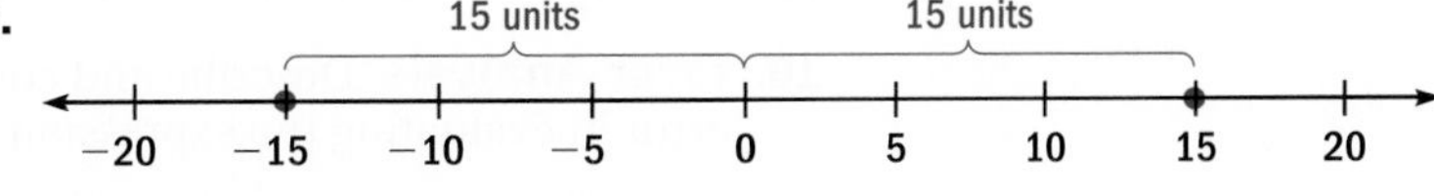

The opposite of -15 is 15.

Checkpoint

State the absolute value and the opposite of the number.

2. 3 3; -3 **3.** -1 1; 1 **4.** 10 10; -10 **5.** -11 11; 11

Extra Examples

Example 1 Use a number line to order these integers from least to greatest: 3, -4, 0, -9, 4, 1. **-9, -4, 0, 1, 3, 4**

Example 2 State the absolute value of the number.
a. -4 **4** **b.** 6 **6**

Example 3 State the opposite of the number.
a. 8 **-8** **b.** -7 **7**

Teaching Tip

Use Example 3 to stress that a number and its opposite are always the same distance from zero. Also, point out that 0 is the only number that is its own opposite.

Algebraic Reasoning

Write the variable x on the board. Make sure students understand that x could represent any number, including a negative integer such as -3. Now write "$-x$" on the board and evaluate $-x$ when x is each of the values 3, 0, and -3. **-3, 0, 3** Stress that the expression $-x$ does not always have a negative value.

Differentiating Instruction

Alternative Teaching Strategy
Give each student a sheet of number lines labeled with integers and several counters. Have them place a counter on a number line at any integer, place a finger at 0, and then find the distance between their finger and the counter. Have students find the distance from 0 to both positive and negative integers to see that the distance, represented by absolute value, is always positive.

Extra Examples

Example 4 Evaluate the expression when $k = -4$.
a. $-k$ 4
b. $8 \div |k|$ 2

 **COMMON ERROR**

In Example 4, watch for students who evaluate $-y$ as -5 instead of 5. Encourage these students to write the variable y in parentheses before substituting -5 for it. Then instruct them to read the expression $-(-5)$ as "the opposite of negative 5."

 **CONCEPT CHECK**

What are opposites? **two numbers that have the same absolute value but different signs**

 **DAILY PUZZLER**

On a number line, which of the integers from 1 to 5 is farthest from its opposite? **5**

Example 4 *Evaluating Variable Expressions*

Evaluate the expression when $y = -5$.

a. $-y$ **b.** $17 - |y|$

Solution

a. $-y = -(-5)$ **Substitute −5 for *y*.**
$= 5$ **The opposite of −5 is 5.**

b. $17 - |y| = 17 - |-5|$ **Substitute −5 for *y*.**
$= 17 - 5$ **The absolute value of −5 is 5.**
$= 12$ **Subtract.**

 ***Checkpoint***

Evaluate the expression when $x = -4$.

6. $-x$ 4 **7.** $12 - |x|$ 8 **8.** $|x| + 9$ 13 **9.** $|x| - 1$ 3

1.4 Exercises

More Practice, p. 803

Guided Practice

Vocabulary Check

1. Which of these numbers is *not* an integer: -31, 74, 22.5, -7, or 19? **22.5**

2. Explain why the absolute value of a number is never negative. **See margin.**

Skill Check

3. Write the integers in order from least to greatest: -9, 12, 6, -3, 0, -5. **See margin.**

2. The distance between a number and zero is never a negative value.

3. $-9, -5, -3, 0, 6, 12$

State the absolute value of the number.

4. 1 **1** **5.** -9 **9** **6.** 15 **15** **7.** -12 **12**

State the opposite of the number.

8. 14 **−14** **9.** -33 **33** **10.** -24 **24** **11.** 81 **−81**

Evaluate the expression when $x = -3$.

12. $|x| + 8$ **11** **13.** $|x| + |-1|$ **4** **14.** $20 - |x|$ **17** **15.** $|50| - |x|$ **47**

16. Error Analysis Describe and correct the error in evaluating the expression $|-17|$.
The distance between −17 and zero is 17, so $|-17| = 17$.

X $|-17| = -17$

17. Volcanoes The elevation of the top of a volcano relative to sea level is called the summit elevation. The summit elevation of Kilauea in Hawaii is 1222 meters. The summit elevation of the underwater volcano Loihi in the Pacific Ocean is -980 meters. Which is farther from sea level, the top of Kilauea or the top of Loihi? **the top of Kilauea**

Practice and Problem Solving

Homework *Help*

Example	Exercises
1	18-25, 38, 42, 51
2	26-33, 52
3	34-41, 52
4	43-50

Online Resources
CLASSZONE.COM
- More Examples
- eTutorial Plus

Copy and complete the statement using < or >.

A **18.** $-8 \underline{?} 3$ < **19.** $-9 \underline{?} -12$ > **20.** $0 \underline{?} -4$ > **21.** $-15 \underline{?} -7$ <

Graph the integers on a number line. Then write the integers in order from least to greatest. 22–25. See margin for art.

22. $-12, 4, -6, 0, -1$ $-12, -6, -1, 0, 4$ **23.** $15, -8, -4, 7, -5$ $-8, -5, -4, 7, 15$

24. $35, 60, -10, -5, 40$ $-10, -5, 35, 40, 60$ **25.** $-22, -30, -25, -16$ $-30, -25, -22, -16$

State the absolute value of the number.

26. -22 22 **27.** 7 7 **28.** 21 21 **29.** -40 40

30. 38 38 **31.** -42 42 **32.** -73 73 **33.** 105 105

State the opposite of the number.

34. 6 -6 **35.** 9 -9 **36.** -2 2 **37.** -11 11

38. -31 31 **39.** -67 67 **40.** 81 -81 **41.** 100 -100

42. Neptune's Moons In 1989, data collected by the Voyager spacecraft showed the surface temperature of Triton, Neptune's largest moon, to be about −392°F. Eight years later, data from the Hubble telescope showed the temperature to be about −389°F. Did the Hubble data indicate a temperature *less than* or *greater than* the one based on the Voyager data? greater than

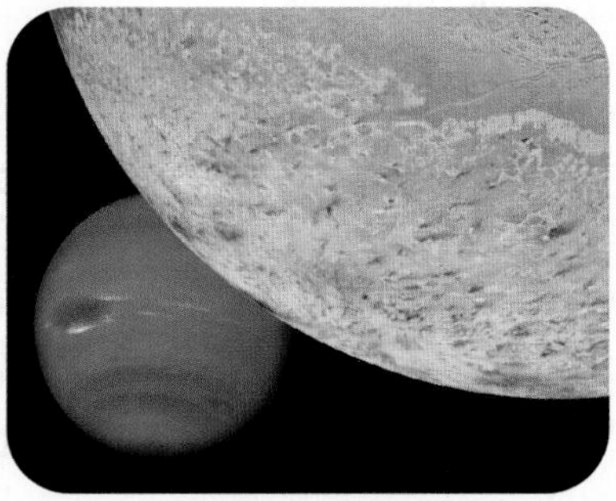

Neptune and Triton

Evaluate the expression when $x = -8$.

43. $-x$ 8 **44.** $|x| - 1$ 7 **45.** $32 - |x|$ 24 **46.** $-x - 2$ 6

47. $5|x|$ 40 **48.** $-x - 3$ 5 **49.** $5 + (-x)$ 13 **50.** $|x| + 10$ 18

51. Underwater Cities Archaeologists have discovered underwater ruins of ancient cities. The table shows the elevation relative to sea level of the deepest point of ruins at several sites.

Site	Elevation relative to sea level
Helike, Greece	3 meters below
Heraklion, Egypt	8 meters below
Port Royal, Jamaica	12 meters below
Unnamed city, Bay of Bengal	37 meters below

a. Write an integer to represent each elevation in the table. $-3, -8, -12, -37$

b. Graph the integers on a number line. See margin.

c. Identify the site whose deepest point is farthest from sea level. Unnamed city, Bay of Bengal

d. Compare The elevation of the modern-day Greek city of Polónia is 1 meter above sea level. Is Polónia *closer to* or *farther from* sea level than the deepest point of the ruins of Helike? closer to

Stoneware cups found at Port Royal, Jamaica

3 APPLY

ASSIGNMENT GUIDE

Basic Course
Day 1: pp. 25-26 Exs. 18-51, 54-56, 66-76

Average Course
Day 1: pp. 25-26 Exs. 21-37, 42-53, 57-62, 66-76

Advanced Course
Day 1: pp. 25-26 Exs. 21, 24, 25, 30-34, 39, 42-71, 75, 76*

Block
pp. 25-26 Exs. 21-37, 42-53, 57-62, 66-76 (with 1.3)

EXTRA PRACTICE

- Student Edition, p. 803
- Chapter 1 Resource Book, pp. 33-35
- Test and Practice Generator

TRANSPARENCY

Even-numbered answers are available on transparencies. A support transparency is available for Exercises 22-25.

HOMEWORK CHECK

When you review students' homework for this lesson, go over the following exercises to check understanding of key concepts.
Basic: 18, 22, 26, 35, 44
Average: 21, 24, 28, 37, 47
Advanced: 25, 32, 40, 50, 52

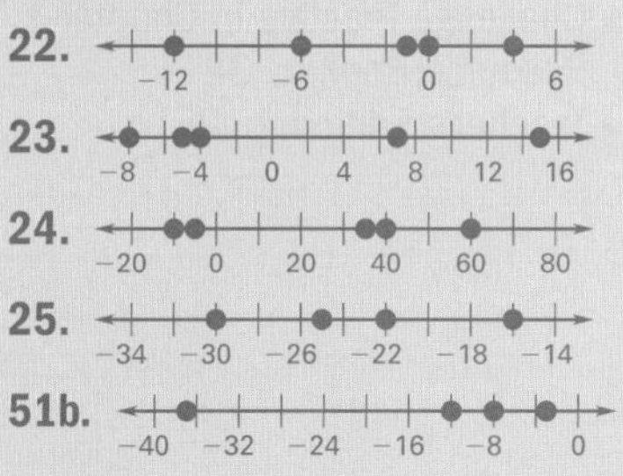

4 ASSESS

Assessment Resources

For more assessment resources, see:
- Assessment Book
- Test and Practice Generator

Mini-Quiz

State the absolute value of the number.

1. −27 **27** **2.** 18 **18**

State the opposite of the number.

3. −100 **100** **4.** 31 **−31**

5. Evaluate the expression $|y| - 2$ when $y = -5$. **3**

6. Challenge If $-7 < x < -2$, then what is the range of values for $|x|$? $2 < |x| < 7$

5 FOLLOW-UP

Diagnosis/Remediation

- Study Guide in Chapter 1 Resource Book, pp. 36–37
- Tutor Place, Algebra Card 4
- eTutorial Plus Online
- Extra Practice, p. 803
- Lesson Practice in Chapter 1 Resource Book, pp. 33–35

English Learner Support

- Spanish Study Guide
- Multi-Language Visual Glossary
- Chapter Audio Summaries CDs

Challenge

- Challenge Practice in Chapter 1 Resource Book, p. 38
- Teacher's Edition, p. 2F

---

52. *Writing* Explain why the absolute value of 0 is 0. **See margin.**

B **53. Extended Problem Solving** The table shows the daily high temperature at Alaska's Barrow Observatory over a seven-day period.

Day	Temperature
Sunday	−19°C
Monday	−17°C
Tuesday	−14°C
Wednesday	−9°C
Thursday	−13°C
Friday	−18°C
Saturday	−21°C

a. Did the temperature *increase* or *decrease* from Sunday to Monday? **increase**

b. Did the temperature *increase* or *decrease* from Friday to Saturday? **decrease**

c. Compare Which day's high temperature was highest for the week? Which was lowest? **Wednesday; Saturday**

d. Interpret and Apply Describe any periods of two or more days during the week when the daily high temperature consistently increased or decreased. **See margin.**

52. The absolute value of a number is its distance from 0, and 0 is 0 units from 0.

53d. The high temperature consistently rose from Sunday through Wednesday and consistently fell from Wednesday through Saturday.

60. Yes; yes; if $x > 0$, then $-x < 0$ and $-x$ is less than x. If $x < 0$, then $-x > 0$ and $-x$ is greater than x.

Evaluate the expression when $a = -2$ and $b = -13$.

54. $|a| + |b|$ **15** **55.** $-a + (-b)$ **15** **56.** $-a + |b|$ **15**

57. $|b| - |a|$ **11** **58.** $-|b|$ **−13** **59.** $|-a|$ **2**

60. Critical Thinking Are there values of x for which $-x$ is less than x? Are there values of x for which $-x$ is greater than x? Explain. **See margin.**

Evaluate the expression when $x = -7$.

C **61.** $|-x|$ **7** **62.** $|x| + |-x|$ **14** **63.** $|x| - |-x|$ **0** **64.** $-|-x|$ **−7**

65. Challenge Copy and complete using x or $-x$: If $x > 0$, then $|x| = \underline{?}$. If $x < 0$, then $|x| = \underline{?}$. **x, $-x$**

Mixed Review

Estimation Estimate the sum or difference by rounding each number to the place of its leading digit. *(p. 771)* **66–68. Estimates may vary.**

66. 278 + 119 + 602 **1000** **67.** 588 − 131 **500** **68.** 112 + 193 + 583 **900**

Find a low and high estimate for the product or quotient. *(p. 772)*

69. 62 × 708 **70.** 31,217 ÷ 218 **71.** 371 × 47

69. between 42,000 and 56,000

70. between 100 and 200

71. between 12,000 and 20,000

Evaluate the expression when $x = 2$ and $y = 8$. *(Lesson 1.3)*

72. $6(x + y)$ **60** **73.** $xy + 1$ **17** **74.** $\frac{x + 22}{y}$ **3**

Standardized Test Practice

75. Multiple Choice Which list of integers is in order from least to greatest? **C**

A. 2, 16, −17, 21, −35 **B.** 2, −16, −17, −21, −35

C. −35, −17, 2, 16, 21 **D.** 21, 16, 2, −17, −35

76. Multiple Choice Which of the following is the value of the expression $|x| + |-5|$ when $x = 5$? **I**

F. −5 **G.** 0 **H.** 5 **I.** 10

Mid-Chapter Quiz

Evaluate the expression when $x = 2$ and $y = 14$.

1. $x + 5$ **7**
2. $y - 2$ **12**
3. $x + y$ **16**
4. $\frac{y}{x}$ **7**
5. **Word Processing** Your computer's word-processing program fits about 250 words on one page. Let p represent the number of pages in a report. Write a variable expression for the approximate number of words in the report. **250*p***

Write the product using an exponent.

6. $11 \cdot 11 \cdot 11 \cdot 11$ 11^4
7. $(2.6)(2.6)(2.6)$ $(2.6)^3$
8. $s \cdot s \cdot s \cdot s$ s^4
9. $y \cdot y \cdot y \cdot y \cdot y$ y^5

Evaluate the expression.

10. $18 - 3 \cdot 2$ **12**
11. $27 \div 3 + 6$ **15**
12. $\frac{20 + 12}{11 - 3}$ **4**
13. $4(20 - 3^2)$ **44**

Evaluate the expression when $x = 20$ and $y = 5$.

14. $0.5x + y$ **15**
15. $\frac{x + 5}{y}$ **5**
16. $3(x - y)$ **45**
17. $y^2 - x$ **5**
18. Graph the integers $-18, 4, -20, -2, -6, 0$ on a number line. Then write the integers in order from least to greatest. **See margin for art; −20, −18, −6, −2, 0, 4.**

State the absolute value and the opposite of the number.

19. -24 **24, 24**
20. 8 **8, −8**
21. 31 **31, −31**
22. -17 **17, 17**
23. Evaluate the expression $44 - |x|$ when $x = -10$. **34**

Brain GAME

Take 5

Use each of the digits 1, 2, 3, 4, and 5 exactly once in each statement to make a true statement.

$(? + ? - ? \times ?) \div ? = 1$

$(4 + 3 - 2 \times 1) \div 5 = 1$

$(? \div ? + ? - ?) \times ? = 8$

$(3 \div 1 + 5 - 4) \times 2 = 8$

$(? + ? \times ?) \div ? - ? = 0$

$(5 + 3 \times 1) \div 4 - 2 = 0$

Additional Resources

The following resources are available to help review the materials in Lessons 1.1–1.4.

Chapter 1 Resource Book
- Lesson Practice
- Study Guide

Assessment Book
- Chapter 1 Quiz 1

Technology
- Test and Practice Generator
- eTutorial CD-ROM

Internet
- Classzone
- eWorkbook Plus Online
- eTutorial Plus Online

English Learner Support

- Spanish Study Guide
- Multi-Language Visual Glossary
- Chapter Audio Summaries CDs

18. 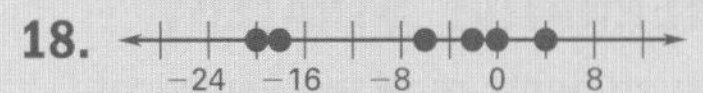

1 PLAN

INVESTIGATE THE CONCEPT

- Students will add integers on a number line.
- This activity leads into the study of adding integers in Lesson 1.5.

MATERIALS

Each student will need paper and pencil. A support transparency is available for this activity.

RECOMMENDED TIME

Work activity: 10 min
Discuss results: 5 min

GROUPING

Students should work individually.

2 TEACH

ALTERNATIVE STRATEGY

Have students read the Investigate instructions aloud one sentence at a time while you perform the actions in front of the class on the board.

3 CLOSE

KEY DISCOVERY

When adding a positive integer to another integer, move to the right on a number line and read the integer at the final position to find the sum. When adding a negative integer to another integer, move to the left on a number line and read the integer at the final position to find the sum.

ASSESSMENT

On a number line, how do you model $4 + (-5)$? **Start at 0 and move 4 units to the right. Then move 5 units to the left. The final position is -1, so $4 + (-5) = -1$.**

13. See Additional Answers beginning on page AA1.

Concept *Activity*

1.5 Adding Integers on a Number Line

Goal
Add integers on a number line.

Materials
- paper
- pencil

Investigate

Use a number line to find the sum of two integers.

 Add $-3 + 7$.

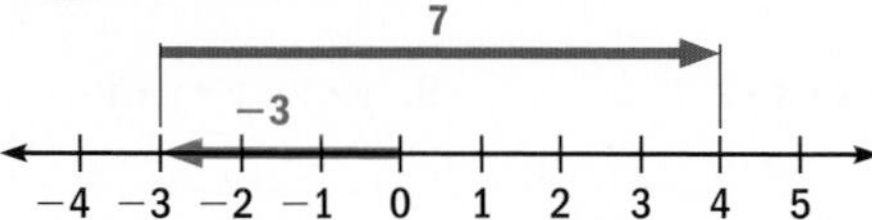

Draw a number line. Place a pencil at 0 and move 3 units to the left to reach -3. Then move 7 units to the right to show addition of 7. Find your final position on the number line.

Copy and complete the statement:

$-3 + 7 = \underline{?}$. 4

2 Add $-1 + (-7)$.

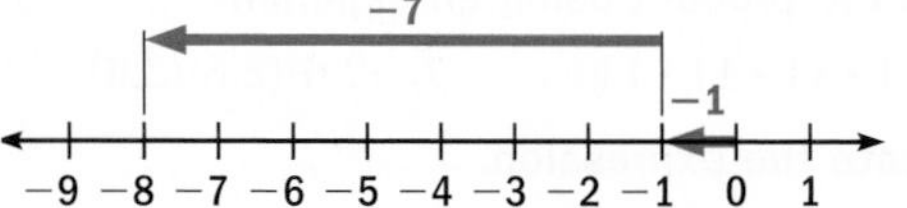

Draw a number line. Place a pencil at 0 and move 1 unit to the left to reach -1. Then move 7 units to the left to show addition of -7. Find your final position on the number line.

Copy and complete the statement:

$-1 + (-7) = \underline{?}$. -8

Draw Conclusions

Use a number line to find the sum.

1. $-6 + 13$ 7 **2.** $-5 + 10$ 5 **3.** $-8 + 4$ -4 **4.** $-1 + 6$ 5

5. $10 + (-6)$ 4 **6.** $10 + (-12)$ -2 **7.** $9 + (-3)$ 6 **8.** $-9 + (-3)$ -12

9. $10 + (-7)$ 3 **10.** $8 + (-11)$ -3 **11.** $-7 + (-8)$ -15 **12.** $4 + (-8)$ -4

13. *Writing* Suppose you are adding a positive integer and a negative integer. Explain how you can tell without actually adding whether the sum of the integers is *positive, negative,* or *zero* by considering the lengths of the arrows that represent the integers. **See margin.**

14. Critical Thinking Another way to add integers on a number line is to start at the first number in the sum and to move a distance and direction determined by the second integer. Identify the addition expression represented in the diagram and find the sum. $4 + (-9)$; -5

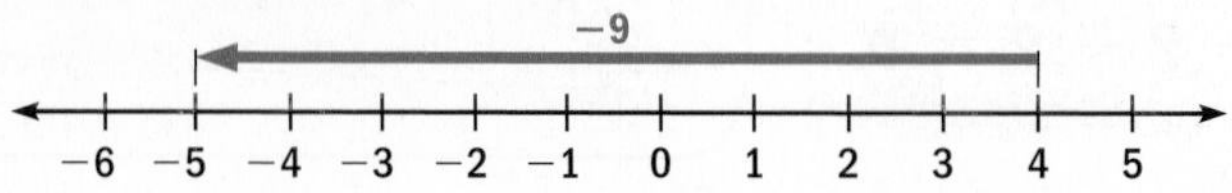

NCTM CURRICULUM STANDARDS
Standard 1: Understand meanings of operations

LESSON

1.5 Adding Integers

BEFORE	Now	WHY?
You added decimals.	You'll add integers.	So you can find a hockey player's plus-minus rating, as in Ex. 40.

Vocabulary
additive inverse, p. 30

Scuba Diver A scuba diver studying marine life is 4 feet below sea level. From that depth, the diver descends 72 feet to the ocean floor and then rises 61 feet. The diver rests there to avoid decompression illness. Where is the diver relative to sea level? In Example 3, you will see how to answer this question by adding integers.

One way to add integers is to use a number line.

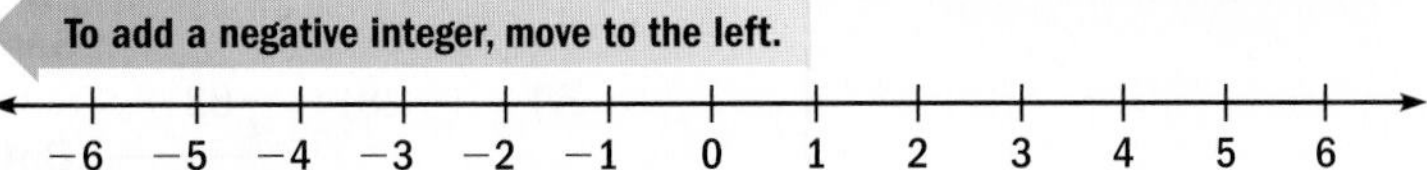

Example 1 *Adding Integers Using a Number Line*

Use a number line to find the sum.

a. $3 + (-9)$

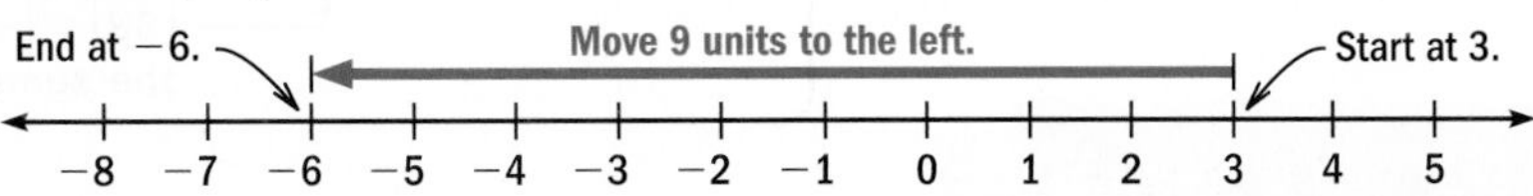

Answer The final position is -6. So, $3 + (-9) = -6$.

b. $-5 + 3$

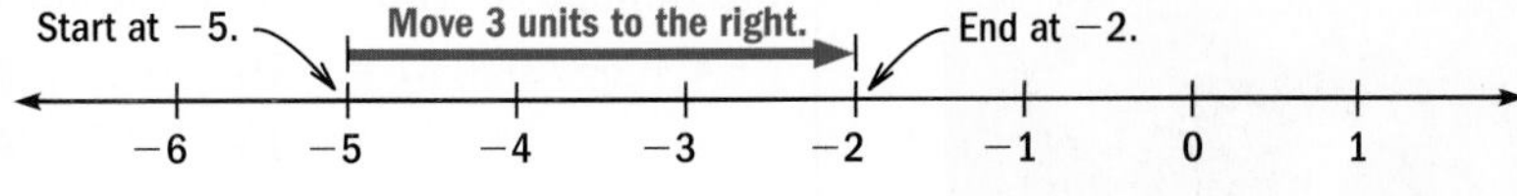

Answer The final position is -2. So, $-5 + 3 = -2$.

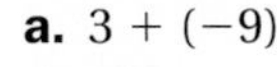

Study *Strategy*

In the activity on page 28, you used two arrows to add two integers on a number line. The first arrow started at 0 and ended at the first number in the sum. In Example 1, you see that you can draw only one arrow if you start at the first number in the sum.

Checkpoint

Use a number line to find the sum.

1. $-11 + 6$ -5 **2.** $-1 + (-8)$ -9 **3.** $10 + (-5)$ 5

NCTM CURRICULUM STANDARDS
Standard 1: Understand numbers; Understand meanings of operations
Standard 10: Use representations to communicate ideas

1 PLAN

Skill Check

1. $18 + 11 = \underline{?}$ 29
2. $26 + 45 = \underline{?}$ 71
3. $79 + 55 = \underline{?}$ 134
4. $7 + 8 + 6 = \underline{?}$ 21

Lesson Objective

Add integers.

Pacing

Suggested Number of Days
Basic Course: 1 day
Average Course: 1 day
Advanced Course: 1 day
Block: 0.5 block with 1.6

Teaching Resources

For a complete list of Teaching Resources, see page 2B.

Transparency

Warm-Up Exercises for this lesson are available on a transparency. A support transparency is available for Example 1.

2 TEACH

Motivating the Lesson

You may want to set up a vertical number line to show students where the diver is at each stage of the dive described in the opening paragraph.

TIPS *for* NEW TEACHERS

Emphasize the rules for adding integers with the "same signs" and adding integers with "different signs" presented on this page. Point out that this focus on same and different signs will occur again in the lesson on multiplying and dividing integers. See Tips for New Teachers in the *Chapter 1 Resource Book*.

Extra Examples

Example 1 Use a number line to find the sum.

a. $-5 + 7$ **2**

b. $-4 + (-8)$ **−12**

Example 2 Find the sum.

a. $-38 + (-14)$ **−52**

b. $-21 + 29$ **8**

Example 3 Find the sum $10 + (-12) + (-8)$. **−10**

MULTIPLE REPRESENTATIONS

In the "Adding Integers" box at the top of this page, note that the instructions for adding integers are given both in words and using numbers. Make sure students recognize that the sums shown beside each verbal description are examples of that rule.

TEACHING TIP

As you discuss adding integers with different signs in part b of Example 2, demonstrate on a number line why the technique of subtracting the lesser absolute value from the greater absolute value works.

Absolute Values You can use absolute values to find the sum of two or more integers.

Adding Integers

Words	Numbers
1. Same Sign Add the absolute values and use the common sign.	$8 + 12 = 20$ $-6 + (-4) = -10$
2. Different Signs Subtract the lesser absolute value from the greater absolute value and use the sign of the number with greater absolute value.	$5 + (-8) = -3$ $-11 + 13 = 2$
3. Opposites The sum of a number and its opposite is 0.	$7 + (-7) = 0$

Additive Inverse Property The opposite of a number is also called its **additive inverse**. Item 3 in the notebook can be written algebraically as $a + (-a) = 0$ and is called the *additive inverse property*.

Example 2 *Adding Two Integers*

a. Find the sum $-54 + (-28)$.

$-54 + (-28) = -82$

Same sign: Add $|-54|$ and $|-28|$.

Both integers are negative, so the sum is negative.

b. Find the sum $38 + (-17)$.

$38 + (-17) = 21$

Different signs: Subtract $|-17|$ from $|38|$.

$|38| > |-17|$, so the sum has the same sign as 38.

Example 3 *Adding More Than Two Integers*

To answer the question about the position of the scuba diver at the top of page 29, you can find the sum $-4 + (-72) + 61$.

$-4 + (-72) + 61 = -76 + 61$ **Add −4 and −72.**

$= -15$ **Add −76 and 61.**

Answer The sum is -15, so the diver is 15 feet below sea level.

Checkpoint

Find the sum.

4. $-41 + 26$ **−15** **5.** $-19 + (-11)$ **−30** **6.** $52 + (-30) + (-46)$ **−24**

Watch *Out*

When you substitute a negative number for a variable, you may have to enclose the number in parentheses, as in part (b) of Example 4, to avoid confusion with an operation sign.

Example 4 ***Evaluating Variable Expressions***

Evaluate the expression when $x = -22$ and $y = -12$.

a. $x + (-9)$ **b.** $x + 17 + y$

Solution

a. $x + (-9) = -22 + (-9)$ **Substitute −22 for *x*.**

$= -31$ **Add.**

b. $x + 17 + y = -22 + 17 + (-12)$ **Substitute for *x* and for *y*.**

$= -5 + (-12)$ **Add −22 and 17.**

$= -17$ **Add −5 and −12.**

 ***Checkpoint***

Evaluate the expression when $a = -18$ and $b = -3$.

7. $a + (-8)$ **−26** **8.** $32 + a$ **14** **9.** $a + b + 30$ **9**

1.5 Exercises

More Practice, p. 803

Guided Practice

Vocabulary Check

1. Copy and complete: To add two integers without using a number line, you need to use the _?_ of each number. **absolute value**

2. How can you tell whether the sum of −71 and 43 is positive or negative without actually finding the sum? **$|-71| > |43|$, so the sum will have the same sign as −71.**

Skill Check **Use a number line to find the sum.**

3. $-9 + 11$ **2** **4.** $-2 + (-13)$ **−15** **5.** $15 + (-7)$ **8**

Find the sum.

6. $24 + (-16)$ **8** **7.** $-15 + 3$ **−12** **8.** $-11 + (-2)$ **−13**

Evaluate the expression when $x = -9$.

9. $x + 3$ **−6** **10.** $-6 + x$ **−15** **11.** $x + (-3)$ **−12**

12. Food Science Food scientists tested the effects that freezing and thawing have on the texture of a cheese filling for ravioli. The filling was frozen to a temperature of −18°C. The temperature was then raised 108°C. What was the final temperature of the filling? **90°C**

13. Error Analysis Describe and correct the error in using a number line to find the sum of −2 and 5.

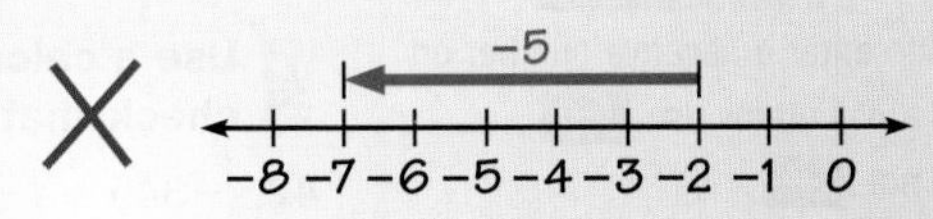

The arrow should start at −2 and go 5 units in the positive direction; −2 + 5 = 3.

Extra Examples

Example 4 Evaluate the expression when $g = -15$ and $h = -8$.

a. $12 + g$ **−3**

b. $h + g + 2$ **−21**

Reading Strategy

Be sure that students have read the Watch Out! feature to the left of Example 4 before discussing part b of that Example.

 **Common Error**

In Example 4, watch for students who omit the negative sign when substituting for *x* and *y* in the given expressions.

 **Concept Check**

How do you add two integers that have different signs? **Subtract the lesser absolute value from the greater absolute value, and attach the sign of the integer with the greater absolute value to the result.**

 **Daily Puzzler**

If you find the sum of two opposite numbers with different signs, what is the sign of the sum? **The sum is 0, which has no sign.**

3 APPLY

ASSIGNMENT GUIDE

Basic Course

Day 1: pp. 32-33 Exs. 14-38, 41-44, 47-51, 61-67

Average Course

Day 1: pp. 32-33 Exs. 18-23, 27-56, 58, 61-68

Advanced Course

Day 1: pp. 32-33 Exs. 21-23, 27-32, 36-66*, 68

Block

pp. 32-33 Exs. 18-23, 27-56, 58, 61-68 (with 1.6)

EXTRA PRACTICE

- Student Edition, p. 803
- Chapter 1 Resource Book, pp. 41-43
- Test and Practice Generator

TRANSPARENCY

Even-numbered answers are available on transparencies. A support transparency is available for Exercises 3-5 and 15-23.

HOMEWORK CHECK

When you review students' homework for this lesson, go over the following exercises to check understanding of key concepts.

Basic: 14, 16, 25, 30, 33
Average: 18, 27, 31, 33, 36
Advanced: 32, 36, 39, 40, 41

TEACHING TIP

In Exercise 41, you may wish to discuss the possible consequences of being overdrawn at a bank.

39. 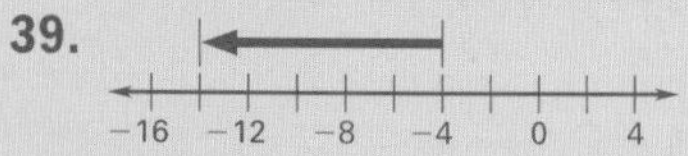

Practice and Problem Solving

Homework Help

Example	Exercises
1	14-23, 39
2	24-29, 40
3	30-32, 41
4	33-38

Online Resources
CLASSZONE.COM
- More Examples
- eTutorial Plus

39. See margin for art. *Sample answer:* The length of the arrow is the absolute value of the second number. The direction of the arrow is right if the second number is positive and left if the second number is negative.

A **14.** Match the correct sum with the addition shown on the number line. A

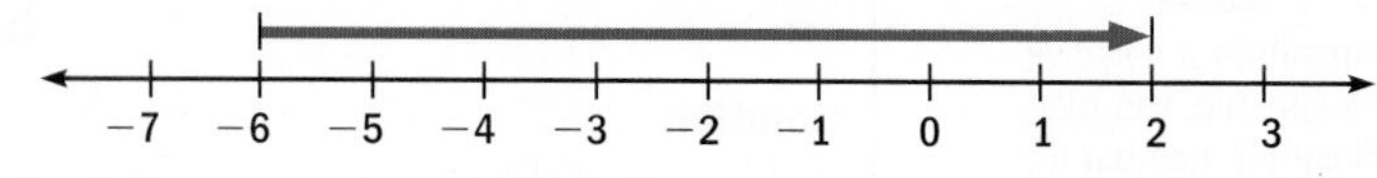

A. $-6 + 8$ **B.** $6 + (-8)$ **C.** $-6 + (-8)$

Use a number line to find the sum.

15. $1 + (-17)$ −16 **16.** $-4 + 13$ 9 **17.** $-7 + (-3)$ −10

18. $13 + (-3)$ 10 **19.** $-9 + (-5)$ −14 **20.** $-6 + (-7)$ −13

21. $8 + (-2)$ 6 **22.** $-3 + 6$ 3 **23.** $-5 + (-4)$ −9

Find the sum.

24. $-54 + 40$ −14 **25.** $-20 + (-32)$ −52 **26.** $66 + (-16)$ 50

27. $19 + (-45)$ −26 **28.** $-32 + 17$ −15 **29.** $-72 + (-30)$ −102

30. $7 + (-9) + 15$ 13 **31.** $-40 + 33 + 12$ 5 **32.** $55 + (-28) + (-6)$ 21

Evaluate the expression when $x = -8$, $y = 4$, and $z = -5$.

33. $x + 15$ 7 **34.** $y + (-75)$ −71 **35.** $-19 + z$ −24

36. $x + y$ −4 **37.** $x + z$ −13 **38.** $y + z$ −1

39. Critical Thinking Use a single arrow on a number line to represent the sum $-4 + (-10)$. What does the length of the arrow indicate? What does the direction of the arrow indicate?

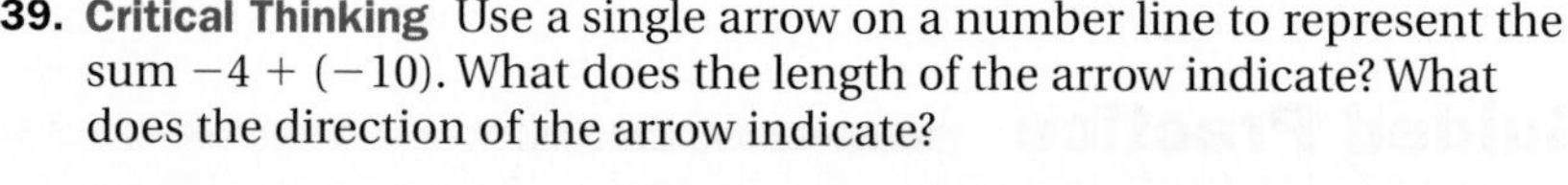

40. Hockey In the National Hockey League, a player is assigned a positive point each time his team scores while he is on the ice. He is assigned a negative point each time the opposing team scores while he is on the ice. (No points are assigned if the scoring team has more players on the ice than the other team.) The sum of the positive and negative points is called the player's plus-minus rating. The table shows the points awarded to a player in two games.

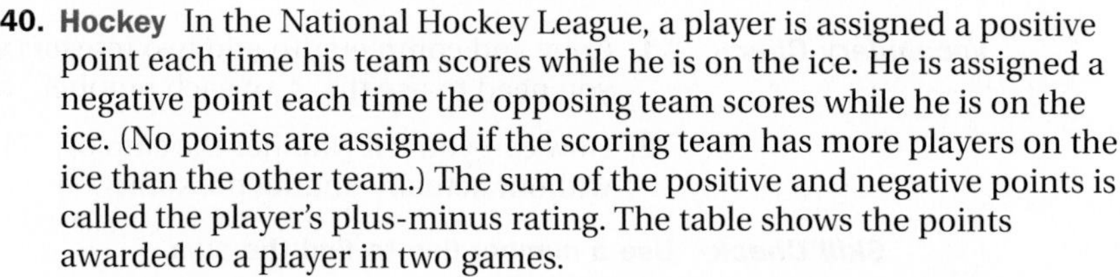

a. Find the player's plus-minus rating for game 1. 2

b. Find the player's plus-minus rating for game 2. −3

Game	Positive points	Negative points
1	3	−1
2	2	−5

c. Find the total plus-minus rating for the two games. −1

d. Interpret and Apply Did the player have a better plus-minus rating in game 1 or in game 2? Explain. Game 1; the greater the plus-minus rating, the better the rating.

41. Overdraft Your checking account shows an *overdraft*, or a negative balance. Your present balance is −\$25. You deposit \$100, then write a check for \$12. What is your new balance? \$63

Tech Help

To enter a negative number on a calculator, use (−), not −.

Use a calculator to find the sum. Estimate the sum by rounding to check that your answer is reasonable.

42. $-345 + (-978)$ −1323 **43.** $2172 + (-4087)$ −1915 **44.** $-1117 + 539$ −578

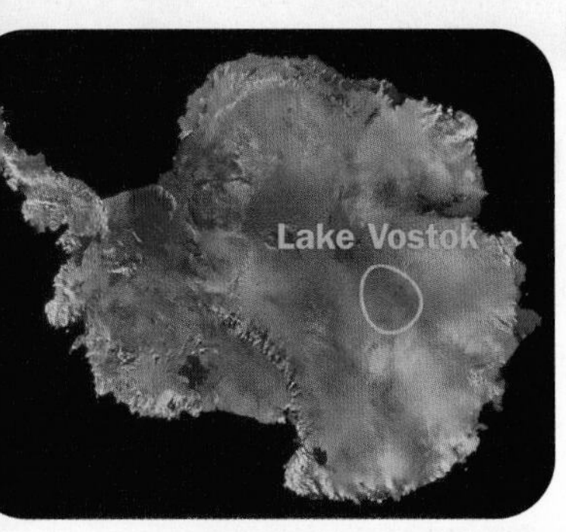

In the **Real World**

Lake Vostok The lowest temperature ever recorded on Earth, about −89°C, was recorded in the region of Lake Vostok. The lowest temperature ever recorded in the United States was about 27°C higher. What was the record low temperature in the United States? **−62°C**

46. ***Sample answer:*** **1 and −25; 2 and −26, 3 and −27; I selected any integer for the first integer, then I found a second integer so the sum of the two integers was −24.**

54. Even; the sum of two even numbers is even.

55. Even; the sum of two odd numbers is even.

56. Odd; the sum of an even number and an odd number is odd.

57. $x \le 0$**; if** $x < 0$**, then** $|x|$ **and** x **are opposites so their sum is 0; if** $x = 0$**, then** $|x|$ **and** x **are both 0 so their sum is 0.**

59. If *a* and *b* have the same sign or if *a* or *b* is 0

60. If *a* and *b* have different signs and neither *a* nor *b* is 0

B **45. Lake Vostok** Lake Vostok, an unfrozen lake buried under Antarctic ice, is about 1200 meters deep. Scientists drilled down 3623 meters into the ice to test for signs of life, but stopped 120 meters above the top of the lake to avoid contaminating it.

Vostok Station
Ice Sheet
Bedrock
Lake

a. Find the position of the top of the lake relative to the ice surface. **−3743 m**

b. Find the position of the bottom of the lake relative to the ice surface. **−4943 m**

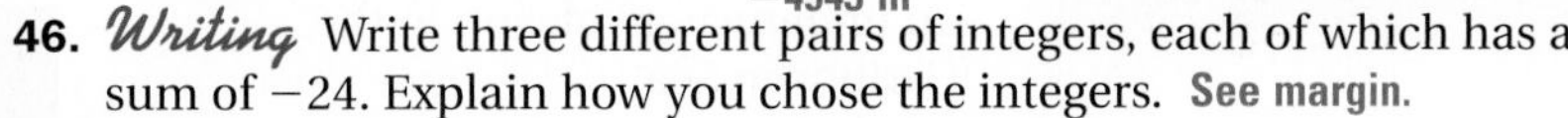

46. ***Writing*** Write three different pairs of integers, each of which has a sum of −24. Explain how you chose the integers. **See margin.**

Find the sum.

47. $-35 + 16 + (-12) + 7$ **−24**

48. $-2 + 10 + (-3) + 5$ **10**

49. $90 + (-24) + (-6) + 5$ **65**

50. $-9 + 16 + (-12) + 3$ **−2**

Evaluate the expression when $a = -14$, $b = 5$, and $c = -8$.

51. $a + b + c$ **−17**

52. $-15 + b + c$ **−18**

53. $8 + a + (-4) + c$ **−18**

Critical Thinking **Using the given information and the fact that *x* and *y* are integers, tell whether the sum $x + y$ is *even* or *odd*. Explain your reasoning.** **54–56. See margin.**

54. x and y are even.

55. x and y are odd.

56. x is even; y is odd.

C **57.** For what values of x is $|x| + x = 0$? Explain. **See margin.**

58. Absolute value bars are grouping symbols. Use the order of operations to evaluate the expression $-3 + |-x + 2|$ when $x = 12$. **7**

59, 60. See margin.

Challenge **Find values of *a* and *b* for which the statement is true.**

59. $|a + b| = |a| + |b|$

60. $|a + b| < |a| + |b|$

Mixed Review

Write a variable expression to represent the phrase. *(Lesson 1.1)*

61. The sum of a number and 14.5 $n + 14.5$

62. The difference of a number and 2.75 $m - 2.75$

63. Area You are building a house on a square-shaped lot. The side length of the lot is 70 yards. Find the area of the lot. *(Lesson 1.2)* **4900 yd²**

Copy and complete the statement using <, >, or =. *(Lesson 1.4)*

64. $|15| \underline{?}\ 15$ =

65. $-12 \underline{?}\ |12|$ <

66. $|-2| \underline{?}\ -2$ >

Standardized Test Practice

67. Multiple Choice What is the value of the expression $x + |y|$ when $x = -3$ and $y = 12$? **C**

A. −15 **B.** −9 **C.** 9 **D.** 15

68. Short Response For what integer value(s) of x is the value of the expression $-10 + |x|$ greater than 0? Explain your reasoning.
$x > 10$ **or** $x < -10$**; if** $x > 10$ **or** $x < -10$**, then** $|x| > 10$ **and** $-10 + |x| > 0$**.**

4 ASSESS

Assessment Resources

For more assessment resources, see:

- Assessment Book
- Test and Practice Generator

Mini-Quiz

Find the sum.

1. $-14 + (-32)$ **−46**

2. $-8 + 22$ **14**

3. $27 + (-16) + (-12)$ **−1**

Evaluate the expression when $p = -7$ and $s = 15$.

4. $p + (-16)$ **−23**

5. $p + s$ **8**

6. Challenge Find the values of a, b, and c for which the statement $|a + b + c| = |a| + |b| + |c|$ is true. **All the values that are not zero have the same sign or they are all 0.**

5 FOLLOW-UP

Diagnosis/Remediation

- Study Guide in Chapter 1 Resource Book, pp. 44-45
- Tutor Place, Algebra Card 4
- eTutorial Plus Online
- Extra Practice, p. 803
- Lesson Practice in Chapter 1 Resource Book, pp. 41-43

English Learner Support

- Spanish Study Guide
- Multi-Language Visual Glossary
- Chapter Audio Summaries CDs

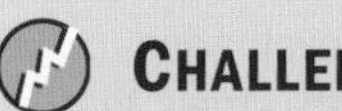

Challenge

- Challenge Practice in Chapter 1 Resource Book, p. 47
- Teacher's Edition, p. 2F

1 PLAN

Skill Check

1. $47 - 18 = \underline{?}$ 29
2. $65 - 48 = \underline{?}$ 17
3. $103 - 88 = \underline{?}$ 15

LESSON OBJECTIVE

Subtract integers.

PACING

Suggested Number of Days
Basic Course: 1 day
Average Course: 1 day
Advanced Course: 1 day
Block: 0.5 block with 1.5

TEACHING RESOURCES

For a complete list of Teaching Resources, see page 2B.

TRANSPARENCY

Warm-Up Exercises for this lesson are available on a transparency.

2 TEACH

MOTIVATING THE LESSON

Ask students what they know about volcanoes, and how an underwater volcano could be growing. Ask them if the top of the volcano would be approaching or getting farther away from the surface. **approaching**

TIPS *for* NEW TEACHERS

When discussing evaluating change on page 35, stress that the order of the subtraction is important. Suggest that students remember the verbal model "current value minus original value." See Tips for New Teachers in the *Chapter 1 Resource Book*.

LESSON **1.6**

Subtracting Integers

Review Vocabulary
opposite, p. 23
difference, p. 771

BEFORE	Now	WHY?
You subtracted decimals.	You'll subtract integers.	So you can find the difference in road elevations, as in Ex. 11.

Earth Science Kick-'em-Jenny is an underwater volcano in the Caribbean Sea.

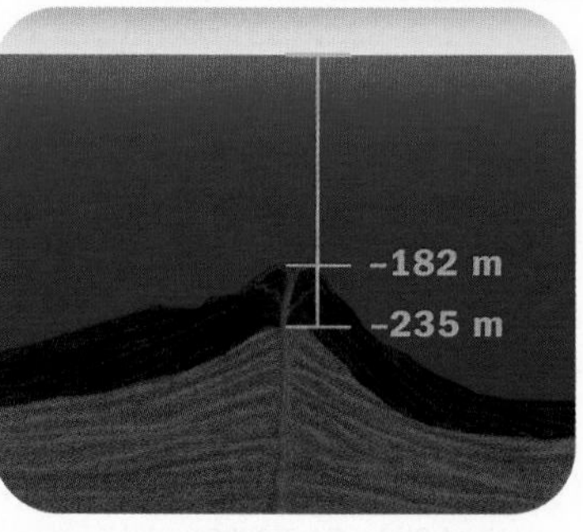

Eruptions have caused the volcano to grow. In 1962, the summit elevation of Kick-'em-Jenny was −235 meters. In 2002, the summit elevation was −182 meters. By how many meters did the elevation of the volcano change? Example 3 uses integer subtraction to answer this question.

As you can see from the number lines below, the expressions $5 - 4$ and $5 + (-4)$ have the same value, 1.

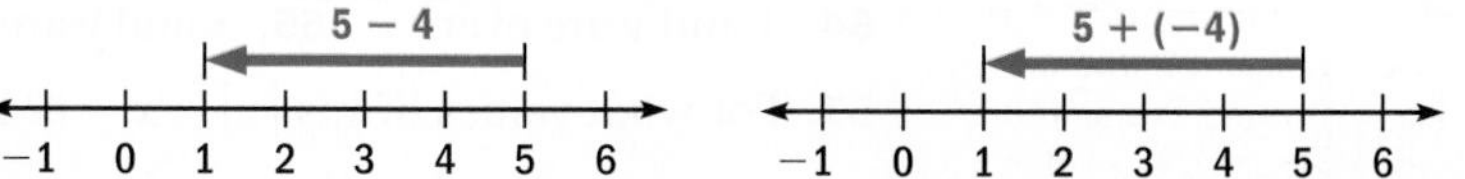

These equivalent expressions suggest the following rule for subtracting integers.

Reading *Algebra*

Check to see that other pairs of expressions, such as $8 - 3$ and $8 + (-3)$, also have the same value. The process of looking at specific examples and drawing a general conclusion is called *inductive reasoning*.

Subtracting Integers

Words To subtract an integer, add its opposite.

Numbers $3 - 7 = 3 + (-7) = -4$ **Algebra** $a - b = a + (-b)$

Example 1 *Subtracting Integers*

a. $4 - 10 = 4 + (-10)$ **To subtract 10, add its opposite, −10.**
$= -6$ **Add 4 and −10.**

b. $7 - (-5) = 7 + 5$ **To subtract −5, add its opposite, 5.**
$= 12$ **Add 7 and 5.**

c. $-2 - (-9) = -2 + 9$ **To subtract −9, add its opposite, 9.**
$= 7$ **Add −2 and 9.**

NCTM CURRICULUM STANDARDS
Standard 1: Understand numbers; Understand meanings of operations
Standard 10: Use representations to communicate ideas

Example 2 *Evaluating Variable Expressions*

Evaluate the expression when $x = -9$.

a. $x - (-40)$ **b.** $7 - x$

Solution

a. $x - (-40) = -9 - (-40)$ **Substitute −9 for *x*.**

$= -9 + 40$ **To subtract −40, add 40.**

$= 31$ **Add −9 and 40.**

b. $7 - x = 7 - (-9)$ **Substitute −9 for *x*.**

$= 7 + 9$ **To subtract −9, add 9.**

$= 16$ **Add 7 and 9.**

 ***Checkpoint***

Find the difference.

1. $2 - 6$ **−4** **2.** $3 - (-8)$ **11** **3.** $-7 - 4$ **−11** **4.** $-1 - (-13)$ **12**

Evaluate the expression when $y = -14$.

5. $y - 3$ **−17** **6.** $25 - y$ **39** **7.** $y - 10$ **−24** **8.** $-9 - y$ **5**

Evaluating Change You can use subtraction to find the change in a variable quantity such as elevation or temperature. Subtract the original value of the quantity from the value after the change.

In the Real World

Earth Science After four years of eruptions, an underwater volcano off the coast of Iceland broke through the ocean's surface. The eruptions began 130 meters below sea level. The volcano became the island of Surtsey, with an elevation of 174 meters. What was the change in elevation? **304 m**

Example 3 *Evaluating Change*

To answer the question on page 34 about the change in elevation of the volcano Kick-'em-Jenny, you can subtract the elevation in 1962 from the elevation in 2002. Write a verbal model.

Change in elevation	=	Elevation in 2002	−	Elevation in 1962

$= -182 - (-235)$ **Substitute values.**

$= -182 + 235$ **To subtract −235, add 235.**

$= 53$ **Add −182 and 235.**

Answer The difference is 53, so the summit elevation of Kick-'em-Jenny increased by 53 meters from 1962 to 2002.

 ***Checkpoint***

Find the change in temperature.

9. From 32°F to −10°F **−42°F** **10.** From −45°F to −80°F **−35°F**

11. From 8°C to −3°C **−11°C** **12.** From −2°C to 15°C **17°C**

Extra Examples

Example 1 Find the difference.
a. 6 − 13 **−7**
b. −12 − 4 **−16**
c. −5 − (−15) **10**

Example 2 Evaluate the expression when *d* = −3.
a. *d* − 5 **−8**
b. −15 − *d* **−12**

Example 3 Find the change in elevation of a diver who descends to −52 feet from −37 feet. **−15 ft**

Common Error

When using the rule for subtracting integers, some students may change both integers to their opposites. While discussing Example 1, stress that only the number being subtracted is to be changed to its opposite.

Concept Check

Explain how you subtract one integer from another? **Add the opposite of the integer being subtracted to the first integer.**

Daily Puzzler

What is 11 − 12 + 13 − 14 + 15 − 16? **−3**

3 APPLY

ASSIGNMENT GUIDE

Basic Course

Day 1: pp. 36–38 Exs. 12–33, 35–44, 55–66

Average Course

Day 1: pp. 36–38 Exs. 18–23, 26–48, 51, 52, 55–66

Advanced Course

Day 1: pp. 36–38 Exs. 20–23, 28–55*, 59–66

Block

pp. 36–38 Exs. 18–23, 26–48, 51, 52, 55–66 (with 1.5)

EXTRA PRACTICE

- Student Edition, p. 803
- Chapter 1 Resource Book, pp. 51–53
- Test and Practice Generator

TRANSPARENCY

Even-numbered answers are available on transparencies.

HOMEWORK CHECK

When you review students' homework for this lesson, go over the following exercises to check understanding of key concepts.

Basic: 14, 20, 24, 26, 33
Average: 18, 22, 28, 29, 35
Advanced: 22, 23, 29, 30, 34

COMMON ERROR

After completing Exercises 24 and 25, some students may think that the value of m is always replaced by its opposite. Then in Exercise 26, they will write $6 + (-7)$ rather than $-6 + (-7)$ before doing the computation. Stress that students should make the substitution for m first, and then they should rewrite the resulting subtraction as an addition statement before computing the result.

1.6 Exercises

More Practice, p. 803

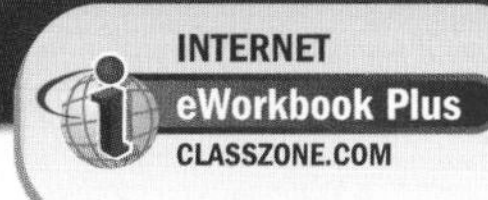

INTERNET
eWorkbook Plus
CLASSZONE.COM

Guided Practice

Vocabulary Check

1. Write the phrase as a variable expression: the difference of -15 and a number x. $-15 - x$

2. Explain how you would find the difference of -45 and -60. Add the opposite of -60 to -45 to obtain $-45 + 60 = 15$.

Skill Check **Find the difference.**

3. $3 - 8$ -5 **4.** $6 - (-2)$ 8 **5.** $-9 - 4$ -13 **6.** $-5 - (-1)$ -4

Evaluate the expression when $m = -6$.

7. $m - 4$ -10 **8.** $m - 16$ -22 **9.** $7 - m$ 13 **10.** $-7 - m$ -1

Guided Problem Solving

11. The Big Dig Boston's Central Artery Project, called "The Big Dig," is one of the most complex highway projects in American history. The project includes an underground highway and a tunnel. The lowest point of the highway is 110 feet below sea level. The lowest point of the tunnel is 90 feet below sea level. What is the difference in these two elevations?

1) Write an integer to represent the elevation of the lowest point of the highway. -110

2) Write an integer to represent the elevation of the lowest point of the tunnel. -90

3) Find the difference of the elevations in Steps 1 and 2. -20 ft

Practice and Problem Solving

Homework *Help*

Example	Exercises
1	12–23, 32
2	24–31
3	33–38

Online Resources
CLASSZONE.COM
- More Examples
- eTutorial Plus

Find the difference.

A **12.** $8 - 9$ -1 **13.** $1 - (-8)$ 9 **14.** $-10 - 6$ -16 **15.** $-5 - (-17)$ 12

16. $0 - 15$ -15 **17.** $2 - (-37)$ 39 **18.** $-20 - 4$ -24 **19.** $-1 - (-53)$ 52

20. $24 - 41$ -17 **21.** $-39 - 32$ -71 **22.** $79 - (-98)$ 177 **23.** $-86 - (-34)$ -52

Evaluate the expression when $m = -6$.

24. $17 - m$ 23 **25.** $4 - m$ 10 **26.** $m - 7$ -13 **27.** $-16 - m$ -10

28. $m - 19$ -25 **29.** $m - 3 - 10$ -19 **30.** $20 - m - 5$ 21 **31.** $14 - 30 - m$ -10

32. Error Analysis Describe and correct the error in finding the difference of -2 and -5.
To subtract a number, add the opposite number; so $-2 - (-5) = -2 + 5 = 3$.

X
$-2 - (-5) = -2 + (-5)$
$= -7$

33. Temperatures The most extreme temperature change in Canadian history occurred when the temperature in Pincher Creek, Alberta, rose from $-19°C$ to $22°C$ in one hour. Find the change in temperature. 41°C

TEACHING TIP

In Exercises 35 and 36, have students first think about whether the temperature rises or falls. Lead them to understand that if the temperature rises then the change in temperature is positive, and if it falls then the change is negative. A similar discussion about Exercises 37 and 38 will also be helpful.

34. Extended Problem Solving There are four stages in the production of ice cream. First, the mix is pasteurized to destroy bacteria. Next, the temperature of the mix is lowered for aging. Flavors are added and the temperature is lowered even more to harden the ice cream. Finally, the ice cream is stored in a freezer. The graph shows the temperature at each stage.

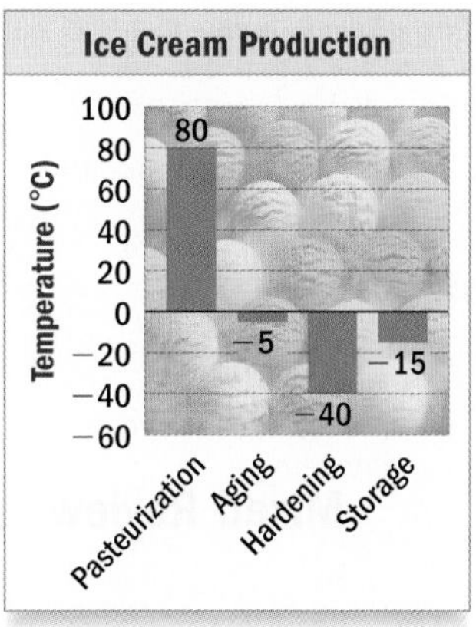

a. Calculate Find the change in temperature between each two consecutive stages. Then find the absolute value of each change.

34a. pasteurization to aging: −85°C, aging to hardening: −35°C, hardening to storage: 25°C; 85°C, 35°C, 25°C

b. Compare Between which two consecutive stages is the absolute value of the temperature change the greatest? pasteurization to aging

c. Estimate You can use the formula $C = \frac{5(F - 32)}{9}$ to convert a temperature F in degrees Fahrenheit to a temperature C in degrees Celsius. Suppose the temperature in your mouth is about 99°F. Use mental math to estimate the temperature in your mouth in degrees Celsius. About how much greater is the temperature in your mouth than the temperature of ice cream just out of a freezer? Estimates may vary; about 52°C.

Find the change in temperature or elevation.

35. From −15°C to 10°C 25°C

36. From −5°F to −13°F −8°F

37. From −120 feet to −90 feet 30 ft

38. From 30 meters to −70 meters −100 m

Find the value of the expression.

B **39.** −15 − 75 − 100 −190

40. −402 + 74 − 281 −609

41. −10 − (−525) − 280 235

42. 118 − (−2) − 315 −195

Evaluate the expression when $x = -5$, $y = 14$, and $z = -7$.

43. $-3 - y - x$ −12

44. $y - (-9) - z$ 30

45. $z - y - x$ −16

46. $x - y - z$ −12

47. Chemistry Ethylene glycol is a chemical that can be added to water to lower its freezing point, the temperature at which it freezes. The freezing point of solution A, which is one part ethylene glycol and three parts water, is −12°C. The freezing point of solution B, which is two parts ethylene glycol and two parts water, is −36°C. Which solution has a lower freezing point? How much lower is it? solution B; 24°C lower

48. Avalanches An avalanche may occur when the temperature keeps snow crystals from sticking together. The room temperature in an avalanche research lab is −30°C. Scientists study changes in snow crystals by melting snow on a hot plate that heats to only −1°C. In a regular lab, the room temperature is about 18°C and a hot plate heats to about 300°C. How many degrees warmer is the hot plate than the room temperature in each lab? Which difference is greater? How much greater? 29°C, 282°C; regular lab; 253°C

4 ASSESS

ASSESSMENT RESOURCES

For more assessment resources, see:
- Assessment Book
- Test and Practice Generator

MINI-QUIZ

Find the difference.

1. $15 - 19$ **−4**

2. $-8 - 7$ **−15**

3. $-11 - (-20)$ **9**

Evaluate the expression when $t = -10$.

4. $22 - t$ **32**

5. $7 - t - 26$ **−9**

6. Challenge If a is a positive integer and b is a negative integer, is the value of the expression $a - b$ a *positive* or a *negative* integer? Explain. **Positive; when changed to the sum of a and the opposite of b, the result is the sum of two positive integers whose sum will be positive.**

5 FOLLOW-UP

DIAGNOSIS/REMEDIATION

- Study Guide in Chapter 1 Resource Book, pp. 54-55
- Tutor Place, Algebra Card 4
- eTutorial Plus Online
- Extra Practice, p. 803
- Lesson Practice in Chapter 1 Resource Book, pp. 51-53

ENGLISH LEARNER SUPPORT

- Spanish Study Guide
- Multi-Language Visual Glossary
- Chapter Audio Summaries CDs

CHALLENGE

- Challenge Practice in Chapter 1 Resource Book, p. 56
- Teacher's Edition, p. 2F

49. No; if $b = 0$, then $a + b = a - b$ and if $b < 0$, then $a + b < a - b$.

54a. Negative; $a < 0$ and $b > 0$, so $-b < 0$ and $a - b = a + (-b)$ is the sum of two negative integers.

54b. Positive; $b > 0$ and $a < 0$, so $-a > 0$ and $b - a = b + (-a)$ is the sum of two positive integers.

54c. Positive; $|a|$ and $|b|$ are both positive.

54d. Negative; $-|a|$ and $-|b|$ are both negative, and $-|a| - |b| = -|a| + (-|b|)$ is the sum of two negative integers.

49. Critical Thinking Let a and b be integers. Is the value of the expression $a + b$ always greater than the value of the expression $a - b$? Explain.

Evaluate the expression $3 - (-x) + 8 - 10$ for the given value of x.

C **50.** 18 **19** **51.** 5 **6** **52.** −2 **−1** **53.** −3 **−2**

54. Challenge If a is a negative integer and b is a positive integer, tell whether the expression represents a *positive* or a *negative* integer. Explain your thinking.

a. $a - b$ **b.** $b - a$ **c.** $|a| + |b|$ **d.** $-|a| - |b|$

Mixed Review

55. Work Backward You want to arrive at school at 7:45 A.M. It takes you half an hour to shower and get dressed, 15 minutes to eat breakfast, and 20 minutes to walk to school. What is the latest you can get up and still arrive at school on time? *(p. 801)* **6:40 A.M.**

Evaluate the expression when $x = 6$ and $y = 12$. *(Lesson 1.3)*

56. $5x - y$ **18** **57.** $3x + y$ **30** **58.** $3(x + y)$ **54**

59. $\frac{x + y}{3}$ **6** **60.** $x + \frac{y}{3}$ **10** **61.** $7x - (y + 1)$ **29**

Find the sum. *(Lesson 1.5)*

62. $89 + (-14)$ **75** **63.** $-104 + 53$ **−51** **64.** $-67 + (-303)$ **−370**

Standardized Test Practice

65. Multiple Choice Which expression has a value closest to 0? **A**

A. $23 - 25$ **B.** $23 - (-22)$ **C.** $-23 - 23$ **D.** $23 - (-25)$

66. Multiple Choice The top of a cliff overlooking the ocean is 1250 feet above sea level. The sea floor at the foot of the cliff is 40 feet below sea level. A rock falls off the cliff and drops to the sea floor. Which expression represents the change in elevation of the rock? **F**

F. $-40 - 1250$ **G.** $40 - 1250$ **H.** $1250 - 40$ **I.** $1250 - (-40)$

Brain Game. ***Sample answer:*** **$-4 + (-3) + (-2) - (-1) = -8$; $-4 + (-3) + (-1) - (-2) = -6$, $-2 + (-4) - (-3) + (-1) = -4$, $-1 + (-3) - (-4) + (-2) = -2$, $-4 - (-3) - (-2) + (-1) = 0$.**

-10 and Counting

In the expression $-1 + (-2) + (-3) + (-4)$, each of the integers -1, -2, -3, and -4 appears exactly once. The value of the expression is -10.

Use each of the integers -1, -2, -3, and -4 exactly once to write an expression that involves addition or subtraction or both and has a value of -8. You may use grouping symbols as needed.

Use the same rules to write four more expressions with values of -6, -4, -2, and 0.

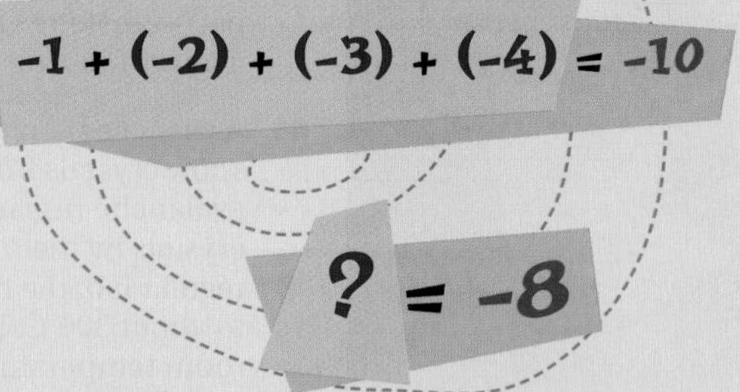

Student Reference

Mean, Median, Mode, *and* Range

▶ **Review** these topics in preparation for solving problems that involve mean, median, mode, and range in Lesson 1.7.

Mean

Data are numbers or facts. The **mean** of a data set is the sum of the values divided by the number of values. The mean is a *measure of central tendency*, that is, an average.

Example The numbers of trails at ten Colorado ski resorts are listed below. Find the mean of the data.

76, 61, 112, 146, 65, 139, 43, 125, 85, 28

First, add the ten values. Then divide by 10, the number of values.

$$\text{Mean} = \frac{76 + 61 + 112 + 146 + 65 + 139 + 43 + 125 + 85 + 28}{10}$$

$$= \frac{880}{10} = 88$$

Answer The mean of the data is 88.

Median

The *median* is another measure of central tendency. The **median** of a data set is the middle value when the values are written in numerical order. If a data set has an even number of values, the median is the mean of the two middle values.

Example The numbers of ski lifts at ten Colorado ski resorts are listed below. Find the median of the data.

8, 5, 4, 13, 2, 25, 7, 23, 14, 5

First, write the values in order from least to greatest.

2 4 5 5 7 8 13 14 23 25

The data set has an even number of values, so the median is the mean of the two middle values, 7 and 8.

$$\text{Median} = \frac{7 + 8}{2} = \frac{15}{2} = 7.5$$

Answer The median of the data is 7.5.

Continued

NCTM CURRICULUM STANDARDS

Standard 5: Use proper statistical methods to analyze data

1 PLAN

Skill Check

Write the numbers in order from least to greatest.

1. 8, 5, 4, 13, 7, 2 **2, 4, 5, 7, 8, 13**

2. 25, 7, 23, 14 **7, 14, 23, 25**

Divide.

3. 275 ÷ 25 **11**

4. 92 ÷ 10 **9.2**

LESSON OBJECTIVE

Prepare for solving problems that involve mean, median, mode, and range.

2 TEACH

COMMON ERROR

Watch for students who omit duplicate values when writing data values in order from least to greatest.

TEACHING TIP

Ask students to explain how the median of the ski lift data is a decimal value even though all the data values are whole numbers.

Extra Examples

Example 1 The weights of six dogs at a dog show are 32 pounds, 84 pounds, 38 pounds, 32 pounds, 42 pounds, and 60 pounds. Find the mean of the data.
48 lb

Example 2 Find the median of the data in Extra Example 1.
40 lb

Extra Examples

Example 3 Find the mode of the dog weights given in Extra Example 1. **32 lb**

Example 4 Find the range of the dog weights given in Extra Example 1. **52 lb**

TEACHING TIP

Stress that there can be no mode, one mode, or more than one mode for any given set of data. Provide data sets on the board with each of these characteristics.

3 APPLY

TRANSPARENCY

Even-numbered answers are available on transparencies.

TEACHING TIP

In Exercises 1–4, urge students to write each data set in order before finding the mean, median, mode, and range. Demonstrate how ordering the data is even helpful when determining the mean, mode, and range, not just the median.

Student Reference Continued

Mode

The *mode* is another measure of central tendency. The **mode** of a data set is the value that occurs most often. A data set can have no mode, one mode, or more than one mode.

Example **Ten Colorado ski resorts have scheduled openings in the following months. Find the mode of the data.**

November, November, December, November, October, October, December, November, November, December

The month that occurs most often is November.

Answer The mode of the data is November.

Range

The *range* of a data set is a *measure of dispersion,* that is, an indicator of how spread out the data are. The **range** of a data set is the difference of the greatest value and the least value.

Example **The average annual snowfall amounts (in inches) for ten Colorado ski resorts are listed below. Find the range of the data.**

300, 367, 300, 307, 410, 300, 200, 280, 300, 240

Range = Greatest value − Least value = 410 − 200 = 210

Answer The range of the data is 210 inches.

Checkpoint

Test your knowledge of mean, median, mode, and range by solving these problems.

Find the mean, median, mode(s), and range of the data.

1. 85, 96, 72, 88, 95, 80, 86 **86; 86; no mode; 24**
2. 7, 11, 13, 9, 7, 8, 9, 12 **9.5; 9; 7 and 9; 6**
3. 0.8, 0.5, 0.5, 0.7, 0.3, 0.9, 0.5 **0.6; 0.5; 0.5; 0.6**
4. 90, 112, 105, 118, 96, 128, 110, 133 **111.5; 111; no mode; 43**
5. **Birds** The table shows the numbers of bird species observed in five national parks. Find the mean, median, mode(s), and range of the data. **183; 178; no mode; 104**

National Park	Species
Joshua Tree	239
Mesa Verde	216
North Cascades	178
Yosemite	147
Nez Perce	135

Concept *Activity*

1.7 Multiplying Integers

Goal
Use patterns to multiply integers.

Materials
- paper
- pencil

Investigate

Use patterns to multiply integers.

Expression	Product
3(3)	9
3(2)	6
3(1)	3
3(0)	? 0
3(−1)	? −3
3(−2)	? −6

Identify a pattern in the second column of the table. Copy the table and use the pattern to complete the table. Then copy and complete the following statement:

The product of a positive integer and a negative integer is _?_. **negative**

Expression	Product
2(−3)	? −6
1(−3)	? −3
0(−3)	? 0
−1(−3)	? 3
−2(−3)	? 6
−3(−3)	? 9

Copy the table. Apply your results from Step 1 to complete rows 1–3. Identify a pattern in the second column. Use that pattern to complete the table. Then copy and complete the following statement:

The product of two negative integers is _?_. **positive**

Draw Conclusions

Find the product.

1. $3(-3)$ **−9** **2.** $3(-4)$ **−12** **3.** $-3(5)$ **−15** **4.** $-5(6)$ **−30**

5. $10(-2)$ **−20** **6.** $4(-7)$ **−28** **7.** $-8(-5)$ **40** **8.** $-3(-12)$ **36**

9. When one factor in a product is a positive integer, you can think of multiplication as repeated addition. For example, the product $3(-1)$ is equal to the sum $-1 + (-1) + (-1)$. Use this idea to justify the statements $4(-2) = -8$ and $-3(5) = -15$.

9. $4(-2) = (-2) + (-2) + (-2) + (-2) = -8$; $-3(5) = (-3) + (-3) + (-3) + (-3) + (-3) = -15$

10. Critical Thinking Suppose that a and b are positive integers. Exercise 9 showed that if you multiply a by the opposite of b, or b by the opposite of a, the result is the opposite of ab. That is, if a and b are positive integers, then $(-a)b = -ab$ and $a(-b) = -ab$. Suppose you apply this rule to the product $(-a)(-b)$ twice:

$$(-a)(-b) = -[(-a)b] = -(-ab).$$

What is the opposite of the opposite of ab? Use your answer to copy and complete this statement: $(-a)(-b) = $ _?_. **The opposite of the opposite of ab is ab; ab.**

NCTM CURRICULUM STANDARDS
Standard 1: Understand meanings of operations

1 PLAN

Investigate the Concept

- Students will use patterns to multiply integers.
- This activity leads into the study of multiplying integers in Lesson 1.7. Students will learn how the signs of the factors determine the sign of their product. These results will be stated formally on page 42 in Lesson 1.7.

Materials

Each student will need paper and pencil.

Recommended Time

Work activity: 10 min
Discuss results: 5 min

Grouping

Students should work individually.

2 TEACH

Tips for Success

In the table for Step 1, look for students who incorrectly write the products as all positive integers and do not recognize that 9, 6, 3, 0, 3, 6 is not a pattern.

3 CLOSE

Key Discovery

The product of a positive integer and a negative integer is a negative integer, while the product of two negative integers is a positive integer.

Assessment

1. If $a > 0$ and $b < 0$, what is the sign of ab? **negative**
2. If $a < 0$ and $b < 0$, what is the sign of ab? **positive**

1 PLAN

Skill Check

1. $4 \times 7 = ?$ 28
2. $9 \times 6 = ?$ 54
3. $18 \times 0 = ?$ 0
4. $12 \times 3 = ?$ 36

LESSON OBJECTIVE

Multiply and divide integers.

PACING

Suggested Number of Days
Basic Course: 1 day
Average Course: 1 day
Advanced Course: 1 day
Block: 0.5 block with 1.8

TEACHING RESOURCES

For a complete list of Teaching Resources, see page 2B.

TRANSPARENCY

Warm-Up Exercises for this lesson are available on a transparency.

2 TEACH

MOTIVATING THE LESSON

Be certain students know that a utility is a company that provides an essential service such as electricity, gas, or water. Ask students if they think investing in a utility is a good idea or a bad idea.

TIPS *for* NEW TEACHERS

Be sure to stress the similarity between the rules for multiplying two integers and the rules for dividing two integers. See Tips for New Teachers in the *Chapter 1 Resource Book*.

LESSON

1.7 Multiplying *and* Dividing Integers

Review Vocabulary
mean, p. 39

BEFORE	Now	WHY?
You multiplied and divided decimals.	You'll multiply and divide integers.	So you can find the position of a submarine, as in Ex. 27.

Stock Market You own shares of stock in a computer company and in a utility. The value of the shares changes over time. The table shows the number of shares of each type of stock you own and the change in the value of each share over a one-year period. What was the total change in the value of your shares of stock? In Example 2, you will see how to multiply integers to answer this question.

Stock Portfolio

Stock	Shares	Change in value of one share
Computer	200	Decreased \$3
Utility	150	Increased \$2

In the activity on page 41, you may have recognized patterns in the products of integers. These patterns suggest the following rules.

Multiplying Integers

Words	Numbers	
The product of two integers with the same sign is positive.	$2(4) = 8$	$-2(-4) = 8$
The product of two integers with different signs is negative.	$2(-4) = -8$	$-2(4) = -8$
The product of any integer and 0 is 0.	$2(0) = 0$	$-2(0) = 0$

Example 1 *Multiplying Integers*

a. $-3(-12) = 36$ **Same sign: Product is positive.**

b. $-7(9) = -63$ **Different signs: Product is negative.**

c. $-24(0) = 0$ **The product of any integer and 0 is 0.**

NCTM CURRICULUM STANDARDS

Standard 1: Understand meanings of operations; Understand how operations are related; Compute fluently

Example 2 *Multiplying Integers*

To find the total change in the value of the shares of stock described on page 42, first multiply the number of shares of each type of stock by the change in the price of each share. Then add the results.

Total change	=	Computer shares	·	Change in 1 share	+	Utility shares	·	Change in 1 share

$= 200(-3) + 150(2)$ **Substitute values.**

$= -600 + 300$ **Multiply.**

$= -300$ **Add.**

Answer The total change in value was -300. The value of the stocks decreased by \$300.

In the **Real World**

Stock Market Stock brokers buy and sell shares of stock. Suppose a broker charges \$12 for each purchase of stock. If a client buys 10 shares of stock selling for \$52.95 for each share, what is the total cost of the transaction? **\$541.50**

Dividing Integers Because $3(-4) = -12$, you know that $-12 \div 3 = -4$ and $-12 \div (-4) = 3$. This relationship between products and quotients suggests that the rules for dividing integers are like the rules for multiplying integers.

Dividing Integers

Words	Numbers	
The quotient of two integers with the same sign is positive.	$8 \div 4 = 2$	$-8 \div (-4) = 2$
The quotient of two integers with different signs is negative.	$-8 \div 4 = -2$	$8 \div (-4) = -2$
The quotient of 0 and any nonzero integer is 0.	$0 \div 4 = 0$	$0 \div (-4) = 0$

Watch *Out*

You cannot divide a number by 0.

Example 3 *Dividing Integers*

a. $-48 \div (-6) = 8$ **Same sign: Quotient is positive.**

b. $56 \div (-8) = -7$ **Different signs: Quotient is negative.**

c. $0 \div 9 = 0$ **The quotient of 0 and any nonzero integer is 0.**

Checkpoint

Find the product or quotient.

1. $9(-11)$ **−99** **2.** $-6(-8)$ **48** **3.** $0(-100)$ **0** **4.** $-4(-8)$ **32**

5. $-24 \div 3$ **−8** **6.** $0 \div (-25)$ **0** **7.** $-35 \div (-7)$ **5** **8.** $24 \div (-6)$ **−4**

Extra Examples

Example 1 Multiply.
a. $-4(-10)$ **40**
b. $15(-3)$ **−45**
c. $0(22)$ **0**

Example 2 The change in Tara's rent was −\$50 per month when she moved to a ground floor apartment, and it changed +\$10 per month when she bought a cat and began paying a pet fee with her rent. Find the total change in rent for one year. **−\$480**

Example 3 Divide.
a. $-60 \div (-12)$ **5**
b. $-77 \div 7$ **−11**
c. $0 \div (-10)$ **0**

Teaching Tip

While introducing the rules for multiplying integers, remind students that 0 does not have a sign.

Visualize

Have students use colored pencils or pens with different colors of ink to create posters illustrating the rules for multiplying positive and negative integers. Have students assign one color to each rule and write examples in the same color. The posters can be displayed in the classroom to assist students in their study of the rules.

Extra Examples

Example 4 Herbie recorded turtles at the following depths, in feet, while he was snorkeling in Kauai. Find the mean of the depths. −10, −15, −12, −20, −8 **−13 ft**

DIFFERENTIATING INSTRUCTION

Advanced Students Challenge students to think of a company or a product that they think would be a good investment. Then have them use the Internet to research the company's stock value. Have students learn the company's current stock price, and its price 1 year, 5 years, and 10 years ago. Have students write 3–5 math problems using the data they collect.

CONCEPT CHECK

Two integers have different signs. What is the sign of their quotient? **negative** Two integers have the same sign. What is the sign of their product? **positive**

DAILY PUZZLER

When can the square of a negative integer be negative? Explain. **Never; the product of two negative integers (even when they are the same integer) is always positive.**

Example 4 *Finding a Mean*

Antarctic Temperatures The table shows record low monthly temperatures from June to November at McMurdo Station in Antarctica. Find the mean of the temperatures.

Month	June	July	Aug.	Sept.	Oct.	Nov.
Temperature (°F)	−42	−59	−57	−47	−40	−19

Solution

To find the mean of the temperatures, first add the temperatures. Then divide by 6, the number of temperatures.

$$\text{Mean} = \frac{-42 + (-59) + (-57) + (-47) + (-40) + (-19)}{6}$$

$$= \frac{-264}{6} = -44$$

Answer The mean of the temperatures is −44°F.

1.7 Exercises

More Practice, p. 803

INTERNET eWorkbook Plus CLASSZONE.COM

Guided Practice

Vocabulary Check

1. Explain what the mean of a data set is. **See margin.**
2. If a and b are integers and the expression ab is positive, what do you know about the signs of a and b? **The signs are the same.**

Skill Check **Tell whether the product or quotient is *positive* or *negative*.**

3. $-238(-17)$ **positive**
4. $\frac{920}{-23}$ **negative**
5. $465(-147)$ **negative**
6. $\frac{-256}{-32}$ **positive**
7. $-1209 \div 31$ **negative**
8. $-65(219)$ **negative**
9. $-98 \div (-2)$ **positive**
10. $-99(-716)$ **positive**

Guided Problem Solving

11. **Electronics** An electronic device is tested to determine how it reacts to changes in temperature. The device is placed in a test chamber at 22°C. After each minute, the temperature in the chamber is lowered 3°C. What is the temperature in the chamber after 9 minutes?

   1) Write an integer that represents the change in temperature in the chamber in one minute. **−3**
   2) Write a product of integers that represents the total change in temperature in 9 minutes. Then evaluate the product. **9(−3); −27**
   3) Find the temperature in the chamber after 9 minutes. **−5°C**

1. The mean of a data set is the sum of the values divided by the number of values.

Practice and Problem Solving

Homework *Help*

Example	Exercises
1	12-26, 29-34
2	27
3	12-25, 29-34
4	28

Online Resources
CLASSZONE.COM
- More Examples
- eTutorial Plus

Find the product or quotient.

A **12.** 12(5) 60 **13.** 28 ÷ 14 2 **14.** 65 ÷ (−5) −13 **15.** 6(−22) −132

16. −7(50) −350 **17.** −26 ÷ 13 −2 **18.** −72 ÷ (−36) 2 **19.** 12(−30) −360

20. $\frac{175}{-25}$ −7 **21.** $\frac{-51}{-3}$ 17 **22.** −17(−20) 340 **23.** $\frac{-840}{7}$ −120

24. Error Analysis Describe and correct the error in multiplying −5 and −12, then dividing by −4. See margin.

X $\frac{-5(-12)}{-4} = \frac{-60}{-4} = 15$

25. Compare and Contrast Tell how the rules for multiplying and dividing integers are alike and how they are different. See margin.

26. Critical Thinking The table below gives expressions involving the multiplication of integers.

Expression	Number of integers	Product	Sign of product
−1(−2)	? 2	? 2	? +
−1(−2)(−3)	? 3	? −6	? −
−1(−2)(−3)(−4)	? 4	? 24	? +
−1(−2)(−3)(−4)(−5)	? 5	? −120	? −

a. Copy and complete the table.

b. *Writing* Write a rule for the sign of the product of more than two negative integers. See margin.

c. Number Sense Suppose that in part (b) the product included positive integer factors as well. Would your rule change? Explain. See margin.

27. MIR Submersible A MIR submersible is a type of submarine. As a MIR dives, its elevation changes by −100 feet each minute.

a. From the surface, a MIR takes about 200 minutes to reach the lowest point to which it can dive. What is its elevation at that point? −20,000 ft

b. How long would a MIR take to dive to 1000 feet below sea level? 10 min

28. Free Diving *Free diving* means diving without breathing equipment. The graph shows the position with respect to sea level for five record free dives.

a. Find the mean of the positions. −49 m

b. Find the median of the positions. −48 m

c. Compare Does the mean or the median represent a lower position? mean

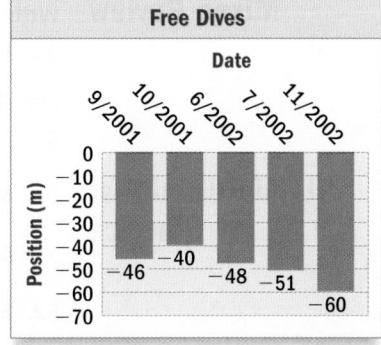

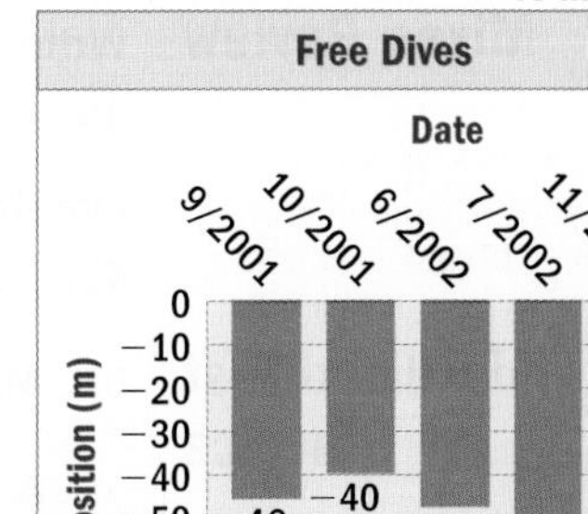

24. The numerator should be positive; $\frac{-5(-12)}{-4} = \frac{60}{-4} = -15$.

MIR submersible being launched

25. *Sample answer:* The rules are alike in that if the two signs are alike the product or quotient is positive and if the two signs are different the product or quotient is negative. The rules are different for zero: for multiplication, if either factor is zero then the product is zero, but for division you have to check that the divisor is not zero.

3 APPLY

ASSIGNMENT GUIDE

Basic Course

Day 1: SRH p. 781 Exs. 1-3; pp. 45-46 Exs. 12-25, 27-39, 45-51

Average Course

Day 1: pp. 45-46 Exs. 18-41, 45-52

Advanced Course

Day 1: pp. 45-46 Exs. 20-28, 33-52*

Block

pp. 45-46 Exs. 18-41, 45-52 (with 1.8)

EXTRA PRACTICE

- Student Edition, p. 803
- Chapter 1 Resource Book, pp. 59-61
- Test and Practice Generator

TRANSPARENCY

Even-numbered answers are available on transparencies.

HOMEWORK CHECK

When you review students' homework for this lesson, go over the following exercises to check understanding of key concepts.

Basic: 12, 15, 18, 27, 28
Average: 18, 20, 22, 27, 28
Advanced: 27, 28, 29, 33, 34

26b. If the number of negative signs is even, then the product is positive; if the number of negative signs is odd, then the product is negative.

26c. No; the sign of the product depends on whether the number of negative signs is even or odd.

4 ASSESS

Assessment Resources

For more assessment resources, see:

- Assessment Book
- Test and Practice Generator

Mini-Quiz

Find the product or quotient.

1. $-6(-8)$ **48**
2. $7(-12)$ **−84**
3. $84 \div (-2)$ **−42**
4. $-36 \div (-12)$ **3**
5. $-200(0)$ **0**
6. **Challenge** Tell whether the following statement is *always*, *sometimes*, or *never* true. Explain your answer.

   If k is less than -1 and n is any integer, then nk is less than n. **Sometimes; nk is less than n only when n is positive.**

5 FOLLOW-UP

Diagnosis/Remediation

- Study Guide in Chapter 1 Resource Book, pp. 62-63
- Tutor Place, Whole Numbers and Decimals Card 19
- eTutorial Plus Online
- Extra Practice, p. 803
- Lesson Practice in Chapter 1 Resource Book, pp. 59-61

English Learner Support

- Spanish Study Guide
- Multi-Language Visual Glossary
- Chapter Audio Summaries CDs

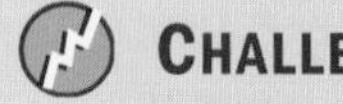

Challenge

- Challenge Practice in Chapter 1 Resource Book, p. 64
- Teacher's Edition, p. 2F

In the **Real World**

Baseball A baseball hit by a player in the major leagues can leave the bat at a speed of 110 miles per hour. Suppose a batter hits a ball at that speed directly back to the pitcher's mound, about 61 feet from home plate. To the nearest tenth of a second, how long does it take the ball to reach the mound? **0.4 sec**

Simplify.

B 29. $-5(-10)(-25)$ **−1250**

30. $16(-4)(-8)$ **512**

31. $360 \div (-36) \div (-2)$ **5**

32. $-72 \div 12 \div 3$ **−2**

33. $-2(-14) \div (-7)$ **−4**

34. $20(-45) \div (-9)$ **100**

Number Sense Without performing the indicated divisions, copy and complete the statement using >, <, or =.

35. $-738 \div 82 \ \underline{?}\ -192 \div (-32)$ **<**

36. $288 \div (-36) \ \underline{?}\ 756 \div 18$ **<**

37. **Sports** A batter hits a baseball. The ball's height h (in feet) above the ground t seconds after it is hit is given by the equation $h = -16t^2 + 80t + 3$. Find the height of the ball 4 seconds after it is hit. **67 ft**

In Exercises 38–41, evaluate the variable expression when $x = -4$.

Example *Evaluating Variable Expressions*

$$-7x^2 = -7(-4)^2 \quad \text{Substitute } -4 \text{ for } x.$$
$$= -7(16) \quad \text{Evaluate power.}$$
$$= -112 \quad \text{Multiply.}$$

Answer When $x = -4$, $-7x^2 = -112$.

38. $-10x^2$ **−160**

39. $\frac{72}{x^2}$ **4.5**

40. $-6x^2$ **−96**

41. $\frac{4x^2}{-10}$ **−6.4**

C 42. For what value of n is $\frac{-4 + (-3) + 5 + 4 + (-3) + n}{-7} = 0$ true? **1**

43. **Explain** You know that for any positive integer n, $1^n = 1$. Is the statement $(-1)^n = -1$ true for any positive integer n? Explain.

44. **Challenge** Tell whether the statement is *always*, *sometimes*, or *never* true. Explain your answer.

    a. If k is any integer and n is less than 0, then nk is less than n.

    b. If k is any integer and n is greater than 1, then nk is greater than n.

43. No; the product of an odd number of negative factors is negative, while the product of an even number of negative factors is positive, so $(-1)^n = -1$ is true for any odd positive integer. For example $(-1)^3 = -1$ but $(-1)^4 = 1$.

44a. Sometimes; if $k = 5$ and $n = -2$, then $nk = -10$ and $-10 < -2$. If $k = -5$ and $n = -2$, then $nk = 10$ and $10 > -2$.

44b. Sometimes; if $k = 5$ and $n = 2$, then $nk = 10$ and $10 > 2$. If $k = -5$ and $n = 2$, then $nk = -10$ and $-10 < 2$.

Mixed Review

Write the integers in order from least to greatest. *(Lesson 1.4)*

45. −12, −21, 31, 0, −5, 13 **−21, −12, −5, 0, 13, 31**

46. −45, −54, −22, −16, −70 **−70, −54, −45, −22, −16**

Find the sum or difference. *(Lessons 1.5, 1.6)*

47. $-27 + 51$ **24**

48. $-17 + (-12)$ **−29**

49. $-18 - 33$ **−51**

50. $-41 - (-9)$ **−32**

Standardized Test Practice

51. **Multiple Choice** Which expression has a positive value? **C**

    A. $\frac{-16(-5)}{4(-9)}$ **B.** $-7^2 - 2$ **C.** $5 - 4(-6)$ **D.** $19 - 6(7)$

52. **Short Response** Find the mean of these temperatures: −12°F, 7°F, −22°F, −11°F, 20°F, −6°F. Describe the steps you used.
    −4°F; Step 1: Add the values to get −24°F. Step 2: Count the values to get 6. Step 3: Divide −24°F by 6 to get −4°F.

LESSON

1.8 The Coordinate Plane

BEFORE	Now	WHY?
You used number lines.	You'll identify and plot points in a coordinate plane.	So you can compare the fuel economy of cars, as in Ex. 27.

Vocabulary
coordinate plane, p. 47
ordered pair, p. 47
scatter plot, p. 48

A **coordinate plane** is formed by the intersection of a horizontal number line called the ***x*-axis** and a vertical number line called the ***y*-axis**. The axes meet at a point called the **origin** and divide the coordinate plane into four **quadrants**.

Each point in a coordinate plane is represented by an **ordered pair**. The first number is the ***x*-coordinate**, and the second number is the ***y*-coordinate**.

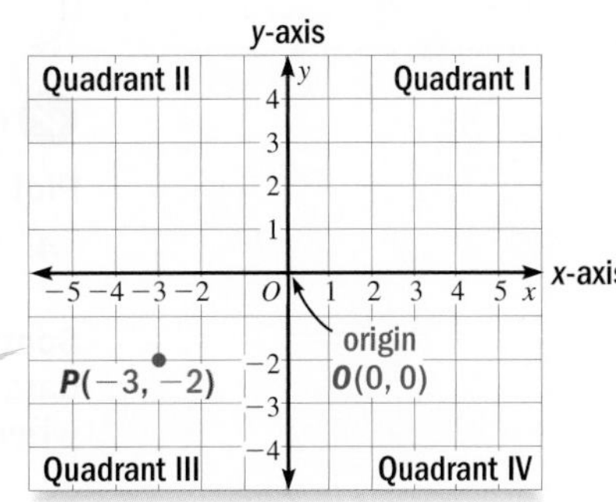

Point P is represented by the ordered pair $(-3, -2)$. Point P is in Quadrant III.

Note Worthy

You may find it helpful to draw a coordinate plane in your notebook. Label the origin and the axes. Use colored arrows as in Example 1 to illustrate how to find the coordinates of a point.

Example 1 Naming Points in a Coordinate Plane

Give the coordinates of the point.

a. A **b.** B

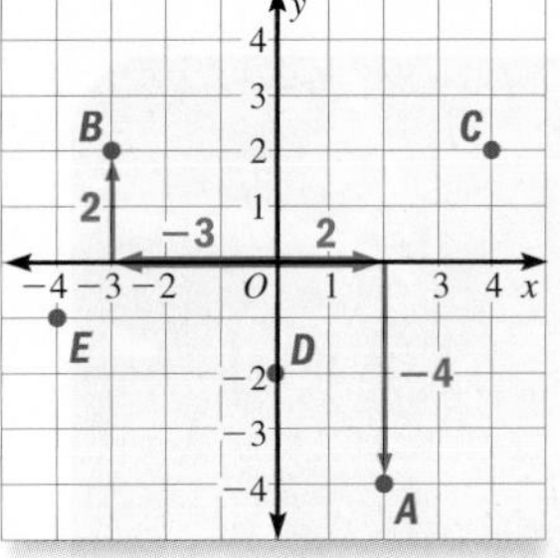

Solution

a. Point A is 2 units to the right of the origin and 4 units down. The x-coordinate is 2, and the y-coordinate is -4. The coordinates are $(2, -4)$.

b. Point B is 3 units to the left of the origin and 2 units up. The x-coordinate is -3, and the y-coordinate is 2. The coordinates are $(-3, 2)$.

Checkpoint

Use the coordinate plane in Example 1. Give the coordinates of the point.

1. C (4, 2) **2.** D (0, −2) **3.** E (−4, −1)

NCTM CURRICULUM STANDARDS
Standard 3: Specify locations using coordinate geometry
Standard 5: Collect, organize, and display data
Standard 10: Use representations to communicate ideas

1 PLAN

Skill Check

1. Graph −3, 2, −1, and 0 on a number line.

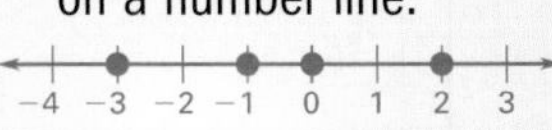

LESSON OBJECTIVE

Identify and plot points in a coordinate plane.

PACING

Suggested Number of Days
Basic Course: 1 day
Average Course: 1 day
Advanced Course: 1 day
Block: 0.5 block with 1.7

TEACHING RESOURCES

For a complete list of Teaching Resources, see page 2B.

TRANSPARENCY

Warm-Up Exercises for this lesson are available on a transparency. A support transparency is available for Examples 1–3.

2 TEACH

MOTIVATING THE LESSON

Show students a road atlas and explain the grid system used to label locations on the map. Then have students look up a city in the index and find it using its grid label.

TIPS *for* NEW TEACHERS

Create a large coordinate grid on a wall or the floor. Give students sticky notes with coordinates on them and have them practice placing the notes at the correct location on the coordinate grid. See Tips for New Teachers in the *Chapter 1 Resource Book*.

Extra Examples

Example 1 Give the coordinates of the point.

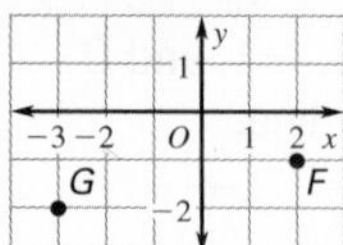

a. F **(2, −1)** **b.** G **(−3, −2)**

Example 2 Plot the point in a coordinate plane. Describe the location of the point.

a. $K(1, -1)$ **Quadrant IV**
b. $L(-1, 0)$ ***x*-axis**
c. $M(-4, 2)$ **Quadrant II**

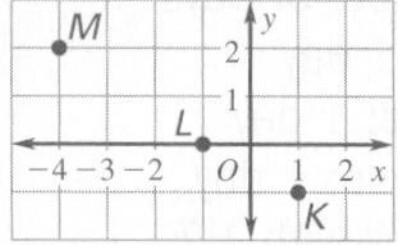

Example 3 A pizza delivery person recorded the total prices and tips received for one evening. Make a scatter plot of the data shown in the table and describe any relationship you see.

Total	Tip	Total	Tip
$10	$1	$15	$1.50
$15	$2	$17	$2
$17	$3	$20	$2
$20	$3	$20	$4

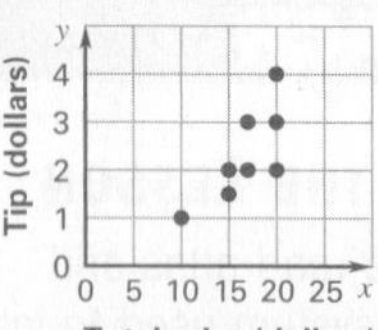

As the total pizza cost increases, the tip also increases.

Concept Check

How is a point in a coordinate plane represented? **by an ordered pair**

Daily Puzzler

What point is halfway between (5, 5) and (−5, −5)? **(0, 0)**

4–7. See Additional Answers beginning on page AA1.

Reading *Algebra*

Points on the *x*-axis or on the *y*-axis are not in any quadrant.

Example 2 *Plotting Points in a Coordinate Plane*

Plot the point in a coordinate plane. Describe the location of the point.

a. $A(4, 1)$ **b.** $B(0, -3)$ **c.** $C(-2, -5)$

Solution

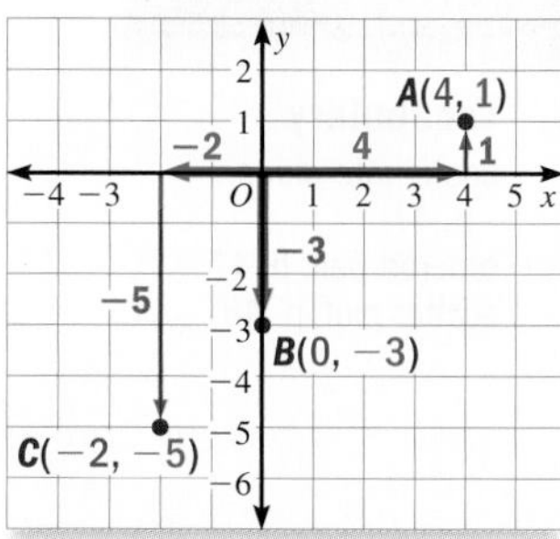

a. Begin at the origin and move 4 units to the right, then 1 unit up. Point *A* is in Quadrant I.

b. Begin at the origin and move 3 units down. Point *B* is on the *y*-axis.

c. Begin at the origin and move 2 units to the left, then 5 units down. Point *C* is in Quadrant III.

Checkpoint

4–7. See margin for art.

Plot the point in a coordinate plane. Describe the location of the point.

4. $P(-1, 1)$ **Quadrant II** **5.** $Q(4, -5)$ **Quadrant IV** **6.** $R(0, 0)$ **origin** **7.** $S(-2, 0)$ ***x*-axis**

Scatter Plots A **scatter plot** uses a coordinate plane to display paired data. Each data pair is plotted as a point. A scatter plot may suggest whether a relationship exists between two sets of data.

Example 3 *Making a Scatter Plot*

Fish A biologist measured the lengths and masses of eight rainbow trout. Make a scatter plot of the data shown in the table and describe any relationship you see.

Length (millimeters)	405	360	413	395	247	280	265	351
Mass (grams)	715	557	754	584	184	248	223	506

Solution

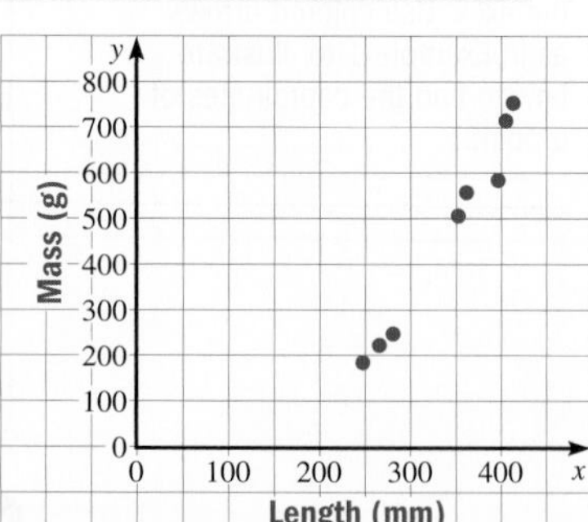

1. Write the data as ordered pairs. Let the *x*-coordinate represent the length, and let the *y*-coordinate represent the mass: (405, 715), (360, 557), (413, 754), (395, 584), (247, 184), (280, 248), (265, 223), (351, 506)

2. Plot the ordered pairs in a coordinate plane. You need only the first quadrant.

Notice that the points rise from left to right. You can conclude that as the lengths of the rainbow trout increase, their masses tend to increase.

1.8 Exercises

More Practice, p. 803

Guided Practice

Vocabulary Check

1. What is the x-coordinate of the point $(-12, 7)$? What is the y-coordinate? **−12; 7**

2. No; you can only determine that the point is either in Quadrant II or in Quadrant IV.

2. A point has one positive coordinate and one negative coordinate. Can you determine in which quadrant the point lies? Explain.

Skill Check

Plot the point in a coordinate plane. Describe the location of the point. 3–6. See margin for art.

3. $J(2, 3)$ Quadrant I
4. $K(-5, -1)$ Quadrant III
5. $L(0, -3)$ y-axis
6. $M(4, -4)$ Quadrant IV

Guided Problem Solving

7. **Earth Science** Scientists studying the Columbia River in Washington measured the speed of the water at one location in the river, but at different depths. The table shows the results. Is there any relationship between the depth of the water and its speed?

Depth (inches)	8	24	31	71	88	103	119	127	134
Speed (inches per second)	19	13	17	14	11	7	7	5	3

7. Step 1: (8, 19), (24, 13), (31, 17), (71, 14), (88, 11), (103, 7), (119, 7), (127, 5), (134, 3)

1) Write the data as ordered pairs. Let the x-coordinate represent depth, and let the y-coordinate represent speed.

2) Make a scatter plot of the data. **See margin.**

3) Does the scatter plot suggest any relationship between the depth of the water and its speed? Explain. **The points generally fall from left to right. We can conclude that as the depth increases the speed tends to decrease.**

Practice and Problem Solving

Homework Help

Example	Exercises
1	8-15
2	16-26
3	27

Online Resources
CLASSZONE.COM
- More Examples
- eTutorial Plus

Give the coordinates of the point.

A
8. A (−4, 2)
9. B (0, 3)
10. C (0, 0)
11. D (4, 0)
12. E (−2, −4)
13. F (3, −3)
14. G (4, 4)
15. H (−3, −2)

16. *Writing* Explain how to plot the point $(6, -3)$ in a coordinate plane. **Begin at the origin and move 6 units to the right and 3 units down.**

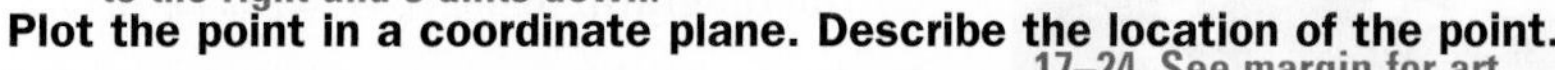

Plot the point in a coordinate plane. Describe the location of the point. 17–24. See margin for art.

17. $P(5, 5)$ Quadrant I
18. $Q(-1, 0)$ x-axis
19. $R(8, -4)$ Quadrant IV
20. $S(2, -4)$ Quadrant IV
21. $T(-3, -6)$ Quadrant III
22. $U(0, -5)$ y-axis
23. $V(-4, -1)$ Quadrant III
24. $W(6, -5)$ Quadrant IV

3 APPLY

ASSIGNMENT GUIDE

Basic Course
Day 1: pp. 49-51 Exs. 8-24, 27-29, 35-44

Average Course
Day 1: pp. 49-51 Exs. 12-31, 35-44

Advanced Course
Day 1: pp. 49-51 Exs. 14-16, 21-44*

Block
pp. 49-51 Exs. 12-31, 35-44 (with 1.7)

EXTRA PRACTICE
- Student Edition, p. 803
- Chapter 1 Resource Book, pp. 67-69
- Test and Practice Generator

TRANSPARENCY

Even-numbered answers are available on transparencies. A support transparency is available for Exercises 3-7, 17-24, and 27-29.

HOMEWORK CHECK

When you review students' homework for this lesson, go over the following exercises to check understanding of key concepts.
Basic: 8, 14, 18, 21, 27
Average: 12, 13, 20, 22, 27
Advanced: 14, 15, 16, 23, 27

COMMON ERROR

In Exercises 9 and 11, watch for students who write the coordinates of an ordered pair in the wrong order when a point is located on one of the axes.

3-6, 7 (Step 2), 17-24. See Additional Answers beginning on page AA1.

ALGEBRAIC REASONING

Exercise 29 introduces students to the concept of *linear function*, a topic that will be covered in detail in Chapter 8. You may wish to strengthen this introduction by giving students other linear expressions and asking them to repeat Exercise 29 for those expressions. Although you may not wish to use the terms at this point, you may want to see if students can make a connection between the constant term of the expression and the *y*-intercept of the line, and between the coefficient of *x* and the slope of the line.

25. The first number refers to left/right and the second number refers to up/down; the point (2, −8) is 2 units to the right of the origin and 8 units down.

26. If an ordered pair contains one zero and that zero is the second number, the point is on the *x*-axis; if that zero is the first number, the point is on the *y*-axis. If both numbers are zero, the point is the origin, and would be on both the *x*-axis and the *y*-axis.

27a.

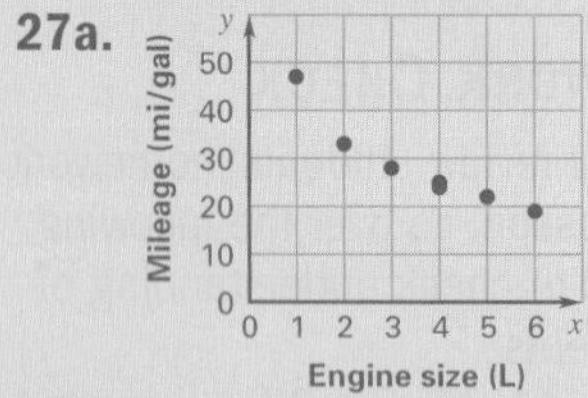

28a.

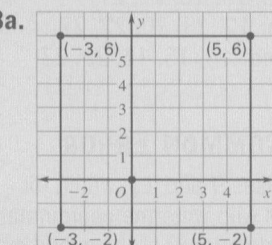

29c. See Additional Answers beginning on page AA1.

In the Real World

Fuel Economy The hybrid car powered by the combined gas engine and electric motor shown has a fuel economy of 46 miles to the gallon in city driving and 51 miles to the gallon on the highway. Suppose you drive the hybrid car about 10,000 miles in the city each year. If you pay $1.75 for one gallon of gas, how much do you pay for gas in a year? **about $380.43**

25. **Error Analysis** Describe and correct the error in locating the point (2, −8). **See margin.**

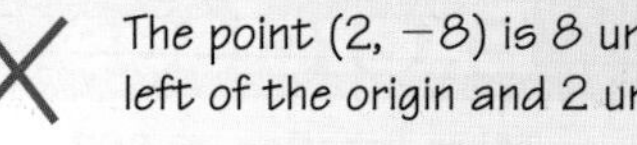

The point (2, −8) is 8 units to the left of the origin and 2 units up.

26. **Critical Thinking** How can you tell by looking at the coordinates of a point whether the point is on the *x*-axis? on the *y*-axis? **See margin.**

27. **Fuel Economy** The table shows the engine sizes of several cars and the average highway mileage for each car.

Engine size (liters)	3	6	2	4	1	4	5
Mileage (miles per gallon)	28	19	33	25	47	24	22

a. Make a scatter plot of the data. **See margin.**

b. **Interpret** Does the scatter plot suggest any relationship between the size of the engine in a car and the car's average highway mileage? Explain. **The points generally fall from left to right, so we can conclude that as the engine size increases the mileage tends to decrease.**

B 28. **Geometry** Use a coordinate plane.

a. Plot the points (−3, −2), (−3, 6), (5, 6), and (5, −2). Connect the points in order. Connect the last point to the first. **See margin.**

b. Identify the figure. Explain your reasoning. **Square; all four sides are the same length and all four angles are right angles.**

29. **Geometry** Use the variable expression $2x + 1$.

a. Evaluate the expression when $x = -3, -2, -1, 0, 1, 2,$ and 3. **−5, −3, −1, 1, 3, 5, 7**

b. Use your results from part (a) to write a list of ordered pairs in the form $(x, 2x + 1)$. **(−3, −5), (−2, −3), (−1, −1), (0, 1), (1, 3), (2, 5), (3, 7)**

c. Plot the order pairs $(x, 2x + 1)$ from part (b) in a coordinate plane. **See margin.**

d. ***Writing*** Describe what you notice about the points. **The points lie on a line.**

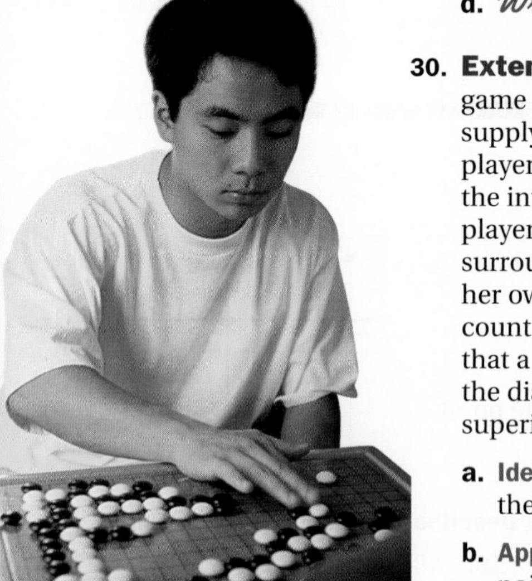

30. **Extended Problem Solving** In the game *Go,* each player begins with a supply of black or white stones. Each player in turn places a stone on a grid at the intersection of two grid lines. A player captures another player's stone by surrounding it on four sides with his or her own stones. (Diagonals do not count.) For example, the diagram shows that a black stone has been captured. In the diagram, coordinate axes have been superimposed on part of a *Go* board.

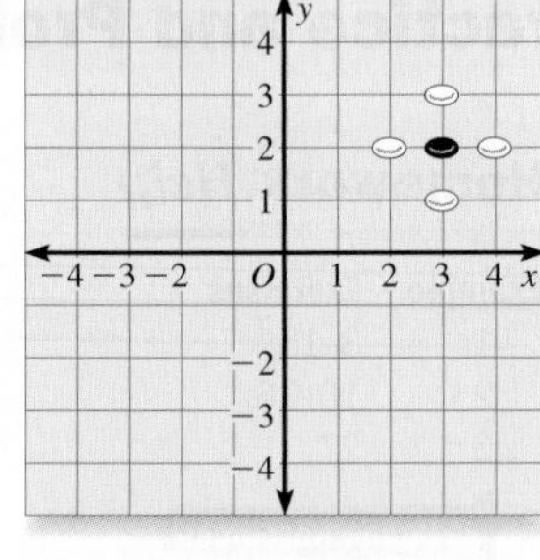

a. **Identify** Give the coordinates of each of the stones shown in the diagram. **B: (3, 2); W: (2, 2), (3, 1), (3, 3), (4, 2)**

b. **Apply** A white stone is placed at (−3, 2). Give the coordinates of the points that a player must cover with black stones to capture the white stone. **(−4, 2), (−3, 1), (−3, 3), (−2, 2)**

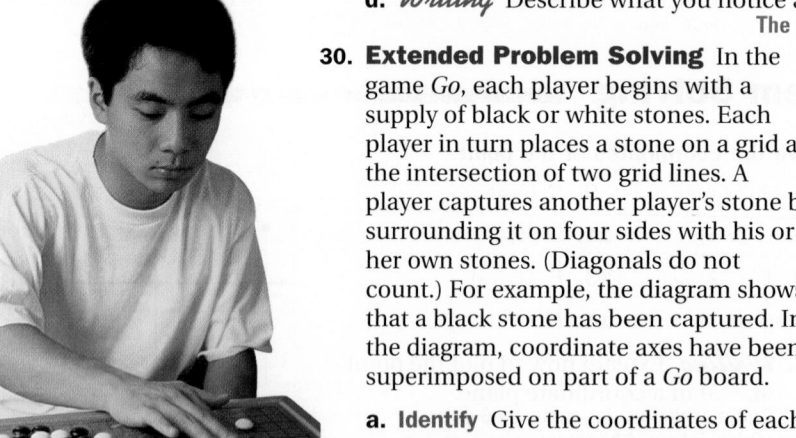

31. *Sample answer:* P(5, 0), Q(5, 5), R(0, 5); the distance from O to P is 5 units, the distance from P to Q is 5 units, the distance from Q to R is 5 units, the distance from R to O is 5 units.

C **31. Geometry** Point O is the origin of a coordinate plane. Choose points P, Q, and R so that O, P, Q, and R are the corners of a square with a side length of 5 units. Identify the coordinates of P, Q, and R. Explain your reasoning.

Challenge The point (a, b) is in Quadrant II of a coordinate plane. Describe the location of the point with the given coordinates.

32. (b, a) Quadrant IV **33.** (a, a) Quadrant III **34.** (b, b) Quadrant I

Mixed Review

35. Movie Tickets Let c represent the cost in dollars of a ticket at the local movie theater. You use a \$20 bill to pay for two tickets. Write a variable expression for the amount of change you receive. *(Lesson 1.1)* $20 - 2c$

Tell whether the sum is *always*, *sometimes*, or *never* negative. *(Lesson 1.5)*

36. The sum of two negative integers always

37. The sum of two positive integers never

38. The sum of a negative integer and a positive integer sometimes

Find the product or quotient. *(Lesson 1.7)*

39. $-15(3)$ -45 **40.** $-252 \div 12$ -21 **41.** $-63 \div (-3)$ 21 **42.** $9(-17)$ -153

Standardized Test Practice

43. Multiple Choice In which quadrant is the point $(-22, 35)$ located? B

A. Quadrant I **B.** Quadrant II **C.** Quadrant III **D.** Quadrant IV

44. Multiple Choice What are the coordinates of point A? G

F. $(-3, 1)$ **G.** $(1, -3)$

H. $(3, -1)$ **I.** $(-1, 3)$

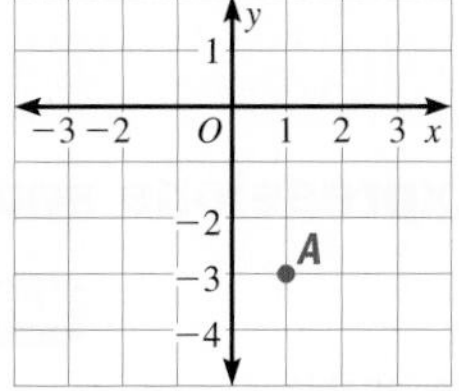

What Is It?

Plot each pair of points on a coordinate grid and connect the two points to solve the riddle:

What force and strength cannot get through, it with a gentle touch can do. And many in the street would stand, were it not a friend at hand. What is it? A KEY

- $(-1, 3)$ and $(-1, -1)$
- $(3, 1)$ and $(4, 3)$
- $(-4, 1)$ and $(-2, -1)$
- $(-8, 3)$ and $(-6, -1)$
- $(-1, 3)$ and $(1, 3)$
- $(3, -1)$ and $(3, 1)$
- $(2, 3)$ and $(3, 1)$
- $(-1, 1)$ and $(1, 1)$
- $(-1, -1)$ and $(1, -1)$
- $(-4, 3)$ and $(-4, -1)$
- $(-9, 1)$ and $(-7, 1)$
- $(-4, 1)$ and $(-2, 3)$
- $(-10, -1)$ and $(-8, 3)$

4 ASSESS

Assessment Resources

For more assessment resources, see:
- Assessment Book
- Test and Practice Generator

Mini-Quiz

Give the coordinates of the point.

1. F (3, −2)

2. G (−2, −1)

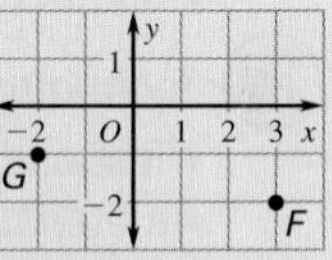

Plot the point in a coordinate plane. Describe the location of the point.

3. $K(2, -2)$ Quadrant IV

4. $L(0, 2)$ y-axis

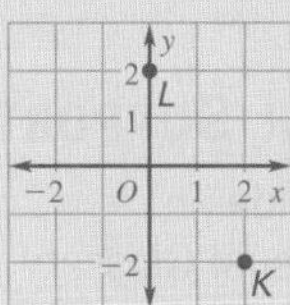

5. Challenge The point (a, b) is in Quadrant IV of a coordinate plane. Describe the location of the point (b, a). Quadrant II

5 FOLLOW-UP

Diagnosis/Remediation

- Study Guide in Chapter 1 Resource Book, pp. 70–71
- Tutor Place, Algebra Card 17
- eTutorial Plus Online
- Extra Practice, p. 803
- Lesson Practice in Chapter 1 Resource Book, pp. 67–69

English Learner Support

- Spanish Study Guide
- Multi-Language Visual Glossary
- Chapter Audio Summaries CDs

Challenge

- Challenge Practice in Chapter 1 Resource Book, p. 73
- Teacher's Edition, p. 2F

ADDITIONAL RESOURCES

The following resources are available to help review the materials in Lessons 1.5–1.8.

Chapter 1 Resource Book
- Lesson Practice
- Study Guide

Assessment Book
- Chapter 1 Quiz 2

Technology
- Test and Practice Generator
- eTutorial CD-ROM

Internet
- Classzone
- eWorkbook Plus Online
- eTutorial Plus Online

ENGLISH LEARNER SUPPORT
- Spanish Study Guide
- Multi-Language Visual Glossary
- Chapter Audio Summaries CDs

1.

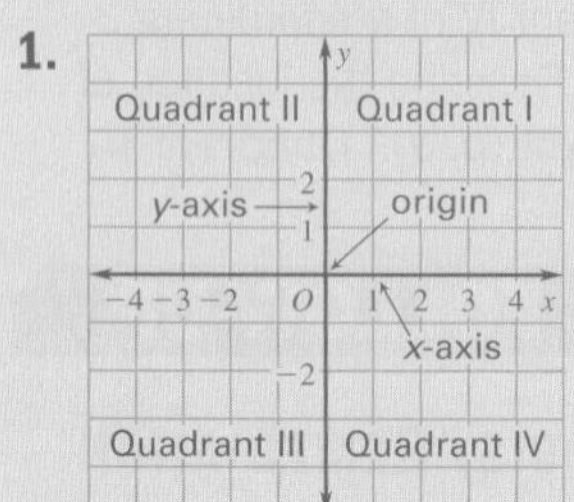

2. *Sample answer:* **In the expression $5^2 = 25$, 5^2 is a power, 5 is the base, and 2 is the exponent.**
3. **The opposite of a nonzero integer has the same absolute value but a different sign. The opposite of zero is zero.**

CHAPTER 1

Chapter Review

Vocabulary Review

numerical expression, p. 5	base, p. 10	absolute value, p. 23	origin, p. 47
variable, p. 5	exponent, p. 10	opposite, p. 23	quadrant, p. 47
variable expression, p. 5	order of operations, p. 16	additive inverse, p. 30	ordered pair, p. 47
evaluate, p. 5	integer, p. 22	coordinate plane, p. 47	*x*-coordinate, p. 47
verbal model, p. 6	negative integer, p. 22	*x*-axis, p. 47	*y*-coordinate, p. 47
power, p. 10	positive integer, p. 22	*y*-axis, p. 47	scatter plot, p. 48

1. Draw a coordinate plane. Label the *x*-axis, the *y*-axis, the origin, and the quadrants. **See margin.**
2. Explain how these vocabulary terms are related: power, base, exponent. **See margin.**
3. Describe how to find the opposite of an integer. **See margin.**
4. What is a variable expression? **A variable expression consists of numbers, variables, and operations.**

1.1 Expressions and Variables

Examples on pp. 5–6

Goal

Evaluate variable expressions.

Example **Evaluate the expression *xy* when $x = 12$ and $y = 3$.**

$xy = 12(3)$ **Substitute 12 for *x* and 3 for *y*.**

$= 36$ **Multiply.**

Evaluate the expression when $p = 12$ and $q = 1.5$.

5. $35 - p$ 23 **6.** $q + 2$ 3.5 **7.** $\frac{60}{p}$ 5 **8.** $16q$ 24

9. $p + q$ 13.5 **10.** $p - q$ 10.5 **11.** $\frac{p}{q}$ 8 **12.** pq 18

1.2 Powers and Exponents

Examples on pp. 10–11

Goal

Evaluate powers.

Example **Evaluate the power $(0.4)^3$.**

$(0.4)^3 = (0.4)(0.4)(0.4)$ **Use 0.4 as a factor 3 times.**

$= 0.064$ **Multiply.**

Evaluate the power.

13. 10^4 10,000 **14.** $(0.3)^3$ 0.027 **15.** $(12.5)^2$ 156.25 **16.** 3^5 243

17. 5^5 3125 **18.** 15^2 225 **19.** $(1.2)^3$ 1.728 **20.** $(0.8)^4$ 0.4096

1.3 Order of Operations

Examples on pp. 16–18

▸ *Goal*

Use the order of operations to evaluate expressions.

Example **Evaluate the expression $800 - 7(2 + 3)^2$.**

$800 - 7(2 + 3)^2 = 800 - 7(5)^2$ **Add within parentheses.**

$= 800 - 7(25)$ **Evaluate power.**

$= 800 - 175$ **Multiply.**

$= 625$ **Subtract.**

Evaluate the expression.

21. $20 \cdot 5 + 7 \cdot 3$ 121 **22.** $\frac{5 + 4}{3} - 2$ 1 **23.** $28 \div (5 - 1) \cdot 3$ 21

1.4 Comparing and Ordering Integers

Examples on pp. 22–24

▸ *Goal*

Compare and order integers.

Example **Graph the integers −2, 3, 0, 2, −3 on a number line. Then write the integers in order from least to greatest.**

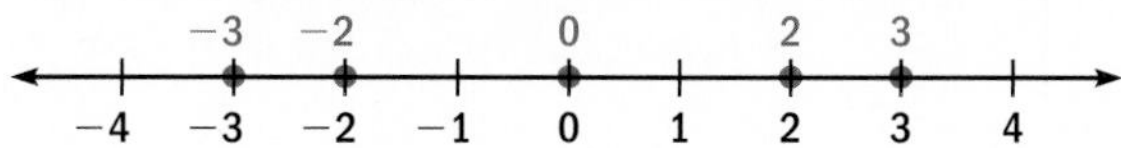

Write the integers from left to right: −3, −2, 0, 2, 3.

Example **State the absolute value and the opposite of −2.**

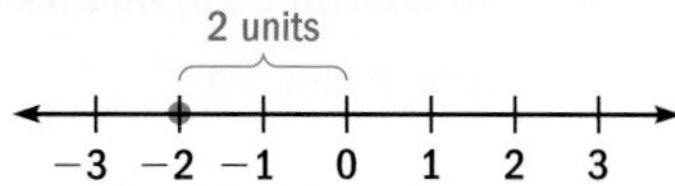

The absolute value of −2 is 2.

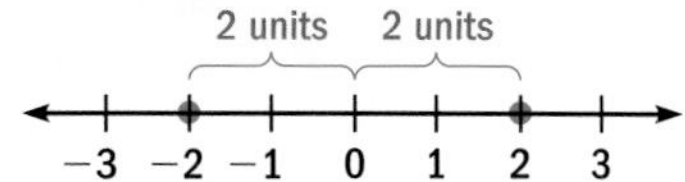

The opposite of −2 is 2.

Graph the integers on a number line. Then write the integers in order from least to greatest. 24–26. See margin for art.

24. 4, 0, −3, 7, −6 −6, −3, 0, 4, 7 **25.** 2, −4, −3, 6, 5, −6 −6, −4, −3, 2, 5, 6 **26.** −8, −12, 4, −7, 1 −12, −8, −7, 1, 4

State the absolute value and the opposite of the number.

27. 18 18, −18 **28.** −9 9, 9 **29.** 4 4, −4 **30.** −100 100, 100

The following resources are available to help review the materials in this chapter.

Chapter 1 Resource Book
- Chapter Review Games and Activities, p. 74
- Cumulative Practice, Ch. 1

English/Spanish Chapter Reviews and Tests

Chapter Audio Summaries CDs

eTutorial CD-ROM

eWorkbook Plus Online

eTutorial Plus Online

24. 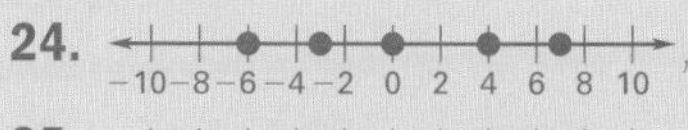

25. 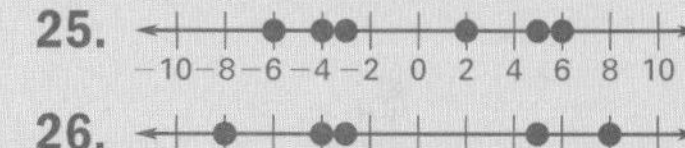

26. −12 −8 −4 0 4

1.5 Adding Integers

Examples on pp. 29–31

Goal

Add Integers.

Example **Find the sum.**

a. $-42 + (-17)$

These integers have the same sign.

$-42 + (-17) = -59$

Add $|-42|$ and $|-17|$.

Both integers are negative, so the sum is negative.

b. $-51 + 63$

These integers have different signs.

$-51 + 63 = 12$

Subtract $|-51|$ from $|63|$.

$|63| > |-51|$, so the sum is positive.

Find the sum.

31. $12 + (-18)$ -6 **32.** $-8 + (-7)$ -15 **33.** $-27 + 38$ 11 **34.** $-11 + (-18)$ -29

35. $61 + (-44)$ 17 **36.** $-13 + (-21)$ -34 **37.** $-21 + 9$ -12 **38.** $-22 + (-7)$ -29

39. At 6:00 A.M., the temperature was −5°F. By 2:00 P.M., the temperature had risen 22°F. What was the temperature at 2:00 P.M.? 17°F

1.6 Subtracting Integers

Examples on pp. 34–35

Goal

Subtract Integers.

Example **Find the difference.**

a. $7 - 15 = 7 + (-15)$ **To subtract 15, add its opposite, −15.**

$= -8$ **Add 7 and −15.**

b. $-9 - (-11) = -9 + 11$ **To subtract −11, add its opposite, 11.**

$= 2$ **Add −9 and 11.**

Find the difference.

40. $0 - 8$ -8 **41.** $-2 - (-2)$ 0 **42.** $-46 - 29$ -75 **43.** $6 - (-13)$ 19

44. $-15 - (-17)$ 2 **45.** $31 - 40$ -9 **46.** $-16 - 9$ -25 **47.** $20 - (-11)$ 31

48. Find the difference of an elevation of 30 feet below sea level and an elevation of 118 feet above sea level. −148 ft

61–64.

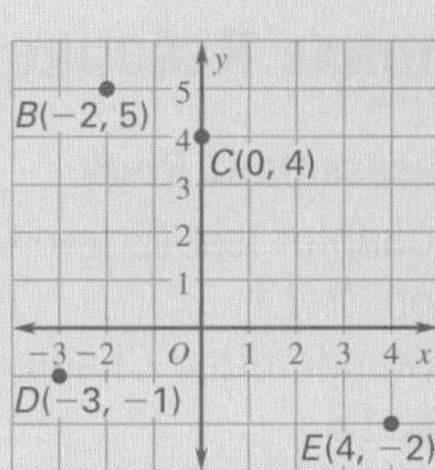

1.7 Multiplying and Dividing Integers

Examples on pp. 42–44

Goal

Multiply and divide integers.

Example **Find the product or quotient.**

a. $-4(-15) = 60$ **Same sign: Product is positive.**

b. $-6(14) = -84$ **Different signs: Product is negative.**

c. $-42 \div (-7) = 6$ **Same sign: Quotient is positive.**

d. $20 \div (-5) = -4$ **Different signs: Quotient is negative.**

✔ **Find the product or quotient.**

49. $-9(-12)$ 108 **50.** $52 \div (-4)$ −13 **51.** $-17(3)$ −51 **52.** $90 \div (-15)$ −6

53. $\frac{-80}{-16}$ 5 **54.** $20(-12)$ −240 **55.** $\frac{48}{-16}$ −3 **56.** $-33(-3)$ 99

1.8 The Coordinate Plane

Examples on pp. 47–48

Goal

Identify and plot points in a coordinate plane.

Example **Give the coordinates of point *P*.**

Point P is 4 units to the left of the origin and 1 unit up. The x-coordinate is -4, and the y-coordinate is 1. The coordinates of point P are $(-4, 1)$.

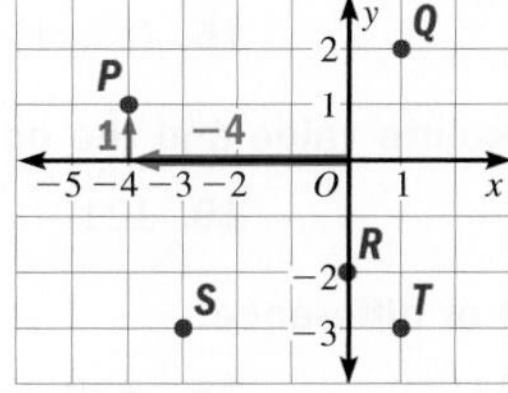

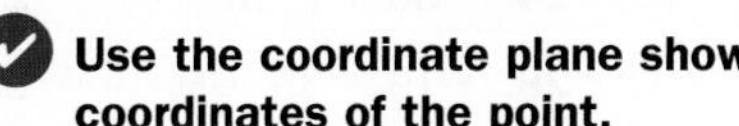

✔ **Use the coordinate plane shown in the example. Give the coordinates of the point.**

57. Q (1, 2) **58.** R (0, −2) **59.** S (−3, −3) **60.** T (1, −3)

Example **Plot the point *A*(1, −3) in a coordinate plane. Describe the location of the point.**

Begin at the origin and move 1 unit to the right, then 3 units down. Point A is in Quadrant IV.

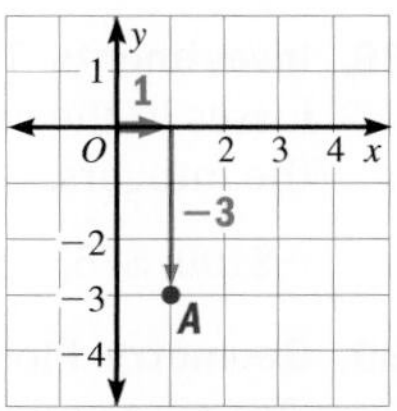

✔ **Plot the point in a coordinate plane. Describe the location of the point.** 61–64. See margin for art.

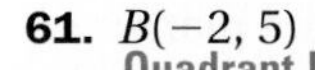

61. $B(-2, 5)$ Quadrant II **62.** $C(0, 4)$ *y*-axis

63. $D(-3, -1)$ Quadrant III **64.** $E(4, -2)$ Quadrant IV

ADDITIONAL RESOURCES

Assessment Book

- Chapter Test (3 levels), pp. 9–14
- Standardized Chapter Test, p. 15
- Alternative Assessment, pp. 16–17

Test and Practice Generator

5. 8 squared; 8 • 8; 64
6. 2 to the seventh power; 2 • 2 • 2 • 2 • 2 • 2 • 2; 128
7. 0.2 to the fifth power; (0.2)(0.2)(0.2)(0.2)(0.2); 0.00032
8. 0.7 to the fourth power; (0.7)(0.7)(0.7)(0.7); 0.2401

39.

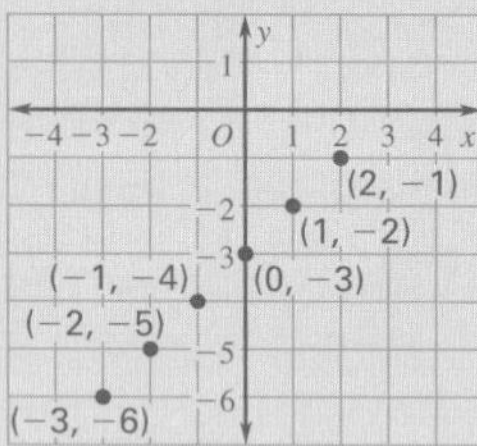

CHAPTER 1

Chapter Test

Evaluate the expression when $y = 16$ and $z = 4$.

1. $y + 9$ 25 **2.** $11 - z$ 7 **3.** $\frac{y}{z}$ 4 **4.** yz 64

Write the power in words and as a repeated multiplication. Then evaluate the power. 5–8. See margin.

5. 8^2 **6.** 2^7 **7.** $(0.2)^5$ **8.** $(0.7)^4$

9. Sewing You are making a beanbag footstool in the shape of a cube with an edge length of 50 centimeters. In order to fill the footstool with plastic beads, you need to know its volume. Find the volume of the footstool. 125,000 cm^3

Evaluate the expression.

10. $70.2 + 4(3.5)$ 84.2 **11.** $\frac{75 - 39}{4 \cdot 3}$ 3 **12.** $90 \div 5 + 4$ 22 **13.** $18 + 30 \div 6$ 23

Evaluate the expression when $r = 4$ and $s = 6$.

14. $3.5s + r$ 25 **15.** $(r + 1)^2 - s$ 19 **16.** $4r + s^2$ 52 **17.** $2(r^2 - 15)$ 2

State the absolute value and the opposite of the number.

18. −78 78, 78 **19.** 121 121, −121 **20.** −33 33, 33 **21.** 19 19, −19

Find the sum or difference.

22. $35 + (-11)$ 24 **23.** $-28 + (-40)$ −68 **24.** $-38 + (-8)$ −46 **25.** $43 + (-22)$ 21

26. $5 - (-16)$ 21 **27.** $-60 - 7$ −67 **28.** $-19 - 35$ −54 **29.** $-48 - (-72)$ 24

Find the product or quotient.

30. $-20(32)$ −640 **31.** $\frac{-76}{4}$ −19 **32.** $-25(-30)$ 750 **33.** $840 \div (-24)$ −35

34. $18(-4)$ −72 **35.** $700 \div (-35)$ −20 **36.** $-12(-16)$ 192 **37.** $\frac{-270}{-18}$ 15

38. Investments The integers below represent the monthly gains and losses in the value of an investment over one year. Find the mean of the integers. −$4

−$190, $75, −$65, $100, $72, −$54, −$62, −$87, $92, $81, −$73, $63

39. Geometry Plot the points listed below in the same coordinate plane. Describe any pattern you see in the graph. See margin for art; the points lie on a line.

(−3, −6), (−2, −5), (−1, −4), (0, −3), (1, −2), (2, −1)

Chapter Standardized Test

Test-Taking Strategy **The best way to prepare for a standardized test is to keep up with your daily schoolwork. You will learn the concepts and skills you need for the test.**

1. What is the value of the expression $\frac{24}{x}$ when $x = 8$? **A**

A. 3 **B.** 16 **C.** 32 **D.** 192

2. Which variable expression represents the following phrase? **H**

A number raised to the ninth power

F. $9n$ **G.** 9^n **H.** n^9 **I.** $\frac{9}{n}$

3. What is the first step in evaluating the expression $15 - 12 \div 3$? **B**

A. Subtract 12 from 15.

B. Divide 12 by 3.

C. Subtract 3 from 15.

D. Divide 15 by 3.

4. What is the value of the expression $x + y^2$ when $x = 3$ and $y = 5$? **H**

F. 64 **G.** 34 **H.** 28 **I.** 13

5. Which expression has a value of -4? **D**

A. $-(-4)$ **B.** $|-4|$ **C.** $|4|$ **D.** $-|4|$

6. Which list of integers is in order from least to greatest? **H**

F. $-4, -7, 0, 2$ **G.** $0, 2, -4, -7$

H. $-7, -4, 0, 2$ **I.** $2, 0, -7, -4$

7. What is the value of the expression $-11 + 24 + (-32)$? **B**

A. -67 **B.** -19 **C.** 19 **D.** 67

8. Find the difference $-32 - (-15)$. **G**

F. -47 **G.** -17 **H.** 17 **I.** 47

9. Which expression has a value of 12? **A**

A. $\frac{-144}{-12}$ **B.** $\frac{36}{-3}$

C. $2(-6)$ **D.** $-3(4)$

10. In a coordinate plane, point P is 8 units to the left of the origin and 6 units up. What are the coordinates of point P? **I**

F. $(6, -8)$ **G.** $(-6, 8)$

H. $(8, -6)$ **I.** $(-8, 6)$

11. **Short Response** The integers -6, 12, -2, and -16 represent yards gained or lost by a football team on 4 plays. Describe the steps you would use to find the mean of the integers. Then find the mean. **See margin.**

12. **Extended Response** The table lists the thicknesses of the trunks of 6 loblolly pine trees and their heights.

a. Make a scatter plot of the data. **See margin.**

b. Describe any relationship the scatter plot suggests. Explain your thinking. **See margin.**

Thickness (inches)	Height (feet)
6	36
9	44
10	46
12	52
15	61
16	67

Additional Resources

Assessment Book

- Standardized Chapter Test, p. 15

Test and Practice Generator

11. Step 1: Add the integers to get -12. Step 2: Count the number of integers to get 4. Step 3: Divide -12 by 4 to get -3.

12a.

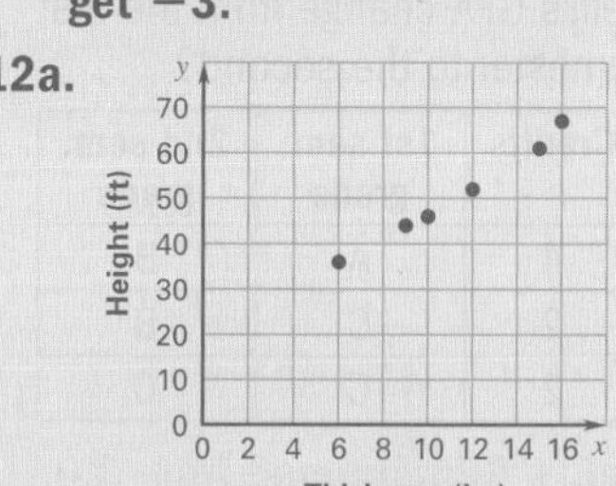

12b. The points rise as you go from left to right, so we can conclude that as the thickness increases the height tends to increase.

1 PLAN

Background Focus

When students solve word problems, they should identify relevant information and be aware that some information may be irrelevant. Students should also be able to decide when there is insufficient information to solve a problem and what information is needed.

2 TEACH

Guiding Students' Work

Students who do not know football terminology may immediately think that they cannot solve the problem. Ask volunteers who are familiar with football to explain the terms used.

Extra Examples

Example Kelli took a 4-credit course and two 2-credit courses both semesters last year. The table shows her grades for these courses. When calculating her grade point average (GPA), an A is worth 4 points, a B is worth 3 points, and a C is worth 2 points. The sum of these points is then divided by the total credits. How much did Kelli's GPA change from the first semester to the second?

Credits	1st sem. grade	2nd sem. grade
4	A	B
2	C	B
2	C	C

Kelli's GPA dropped from 3.0 to 2.75.

Unit 1 *Focus On* Problem Solving

Reading *the* Problem

Recognizing Relevant, Irrelevant, and Missing Information

When you read a problem, you should decide what information you need to solve the problem.

Problem In football, the turnover margin for a team is given by the expression $t - g$, where t is the number of times the team takes the ball away from an opposing team through an interception or a fumble and g is the number of times the team gives the ball to an opposing team through an interception or a fumble. Information about a team is given in the table below. Did this team improve its turnover margin from 2000 to 2001? from 2001 to 2002?

Season	Games played	Takes ball		Gives ball	
		Intercep.	Fumbles	Intercep.	Fumbles
2000	16	11	8	20	13
2001	16	13	15	26	11

1 What information is relevant?

To solve the problem, you need all the information given in the table except for the number of games played. That information is irrelevant for finding turnover margins.

2 Is any information missing?

The table gives you enough information to find the turnover margins for 2000 and 2001 but not for 2002. So, you can determine whether the team improved its turnover margin from 2000 to 2001 but not whether it improved its turnover margin from 2001 to 2002.

3 How is the problem solved?

Find the turnover margins for 2000 and 2001 by evaluating the expression $t - g$. To find t, add the number of interceptions and the number of fumbles for "Takes ball." Likewise, to find g, add the number of interceptions and the number of fumbles for "Gives ball."

2000 season: $t - g = (11 + 8) - (20 + 13)$
$= 19 - 33$
$= -14$

2001 season: $t - g = (13 + 15) - (26 + 11)$
$= 28 - 37$
$= -9$

Answer Because $-9 > -14$, you can conclude that the team improved its turnover margin from 2000 to 2001. You need information about the team's turnovers for 2002 to determine whether the team improved its turnover margin from 2001 to 2002.

3 APPLY

TRANSPARENCY

Even-numbered answers are available on transparencies.

TEACHING TIP

In Exercise 5, suggest that students draw a diagram that breaks the total time until the show into three parts: the time waiting for the ride, the time on the ride, and the time it takes to walk to the show.

SUGGESTED STRATEGIES

You may wish to suggest the following strategies for the problems in the Problem Solving Practice:

- Exercise 1: Solve a Simpler Problem; Guess, Check, and Revise
- Exercise 2: Break into Parts; Work Backward
- Exercise 3: Guess, Check, and Revise; Act It Out
- Exercise 4: Break into Parts
- Exercise 5: Break into Parts; Draw a Diagram; Work Backward
- Exercise 6: Break into Parts
- Exercise 7: Break into Parts

2. 2 boxes; there is not enough information to determine how many cookies can be made.

3. 5 c. *Sample answer:* You can find the information in a dictionary or almanac, or on the Internet.

6. No; there is not enough information to determine the team's average points scored per game in 2002.

Problem Solving Practice

1. **Apples** You buy 10 apples that weigh a total of 4 pounds for $3.92. What is the cost of a pound of apples? How much would 6 pounds of apples cost? **$.98; $5.88**

2. **Baking** You are baking cookies that require 6 cups of cereal for each batch. Use the nutrition facts below to find the number of boxes of cereal you will need to make 3 batches of cookies. Then determine how many cookies you can make. **See margin.**

Nutrition Facts

Serving size: $1\frac{1}{2}$ cups (40 g)

Servings per package: 10

3. **Lemonade** You are making lemonade that requires 2 quarts of water. If you have already added 3 cups of water, how much more do you need to add? (If you do not know how many cups are in a quart, where can you find this information?) **See margin.**

4. **Vacation** Your family is going on a vacation. Your destination is 880 miles away. Your family is driving there at an average speed of 55 miles per hour for 8 hours a day. The car gets 28 miles per gallon of gas, and the car's gas tank holds 10 gallons of gas. If you start your vacation with a full tank of gas, how many times will your family have to stop to fill the gas tank on your way to your destination? **3 times**

5. **Roller Coaster** A roller coaster takes a group of 24 people every 5 minutes. The ride lasts 3 minutes. There are 52 people in front of you. It takes 10 minutes to walk from the roller coaster to the concert stage, where you have reservations for the 2:00 show. If it is 1:30 now, can you ride the roller coaster and still make it to the show on time? **yes**

6. **Football** Use the information on the previous page along with the 2002 information below to determine if the team improved its turnover margin from 2001 to 2002. What was the team's average points scored per game in 2002? **See margin.**

Games played	Takes ball		Gives ball	
	Intercep.	Fumbles	Intercep.	Fumbles
18	7	12	25	12

7. **Temperature** To find the departure from normal temperature, you can use the expression $a - n$, where a is the actual average temperature for the day and n is the normal, or average, temperature historically. Use the table below to find the departure from normal temperature for each day. Then find the mean departure from normal temperature for the week.

Day	Normal temp.	Actual temp.	Precipitation
Sunday	39°F	33°F	0.0 in.
Monday	38°F	42°F	0.1 in.
Tuesday	38°F	25°F	0.5 in.
Wednesday	37°F	24°F	0.0 in.
Thursday	37°F	38°F	0.0 in.
Friday	37°F	29°F	1.6 in.
Saturday	36°F	36°F	0.3 in.

Sun.: −6°F, Mon.: +4°F, Tues.: −13°F, Wed.: −13°F, Thu.: +1°F, Fri.: −8°F, Sat.: 0°F; −5°F

CHAPTER 2

Pacing and Assignment Guide

REGULAR SCHEDULE

Lesson	Les. Day	BASIC	AVERAGE	ADVANCED
2.1	Day 1	SRH p. 786 Exs. 1–6; pp. 66–68 Exs. 16–19, 24–27, 36, 37, 40–47, 60–63	pp. 66–68 Exs. 17–19, 25–27, 36, 37, 40–43, 49–51, 60–65	pp. 66–68 Exs. 18–25, 36, 37, 45–49, 56–59
	Day 2	pp. 66–68 Exs. 20–23, 28–35, 38, 39, 53–59	pp. 66–68 Exs. 21–23, 30–35, 44–48, 53–59	pp. 66–68 Exs. 30–33, 38–42, 50–52*, 60–65
2.2	Day 1	SRH p. 785 Exs. 2–8 even; pp. 74–75 Exs. 12–15, 20–31, 36–43, 46, 51–61	pp. 74–75 Exs. 16–31, 36–38, 42–49, 53–61	pp. 74–75 Exs. 16–23, 30–38, 41–51*, 55–62
2.3	Day 1	SRH p. 795 Exs. 1–3; pp. 81–82 Exs. 10–24, 31–34, 39–41, 44–53	pp. 81–82 Exs. 13–18, 25–27, 31–37, 39–45, 48–54	pp. 81–82 Exs. 13–18, 28–39*, 42–49, 52–54
2.4	Day 1	pp. 87–89 Exs. 8–15, 32, 41–51	pp. 87–89 Exs. 10–15, 32, 41–46, 48–54	pp. 87–89 Exs. 10–15, 32, 37–42*, 44–50
	Day 2	pp. 87–89 Exs. 16–31, 33–35, 52–54	pp. 87–89 Exs. 16–27, 33–39	pp. 87–89 Exs. 16–19, 24–31, 33–36, 51–54
2.5	Day 1	EP p. 808 Exs. 20–27; pp. 93–95 Exs. 11–19, 24–28, 32–38, 46–64	pp. 93–95 Exs. 17–22, 26–34, 38–44, 48–64	pp. 93–95 Exs. 17–19, 23–31, 35–45*, 48–53, 56–65
2.6	Day 1	EP p. 803 Exs. 28–31; pp. 99–101 Exs. 8–19, 24, 28–33, 40–57	pp. 99–101 Exs. 16–30, 34–38, 40–51, 56–58	pp. 99–101 Exs. 16–27, 31–43*, 50–58
2.7	Day 1	pp. 105–107 Exs. 12–17, 24–29, 36, 39–41, 48–51	pp. 105–107 Exs. 12–17, 24–29, 36, 39–41, 45, 50–53	pp. 105–107 Exs. 14–17, 24–29, 36, 39–41, 46–49*
	Day 2	pp. 105–107 Exs. 18–23, 30–35, 37, 38, 42–44, 52–55	pp. 105–107 Exs. 18–23, 30–35, 37, 38, 42–44, 47, 54–56	pp. 105–107 Exs. 20–23, 30–35, 37, 38, 42–45, 54–56
Review	Day 1	pp. 108–111 Exs. 1–47	pp. 108–111 Exs. 1–47	pp. 108–111 Exs. 1–47
Assess	Day 1	Chapter 2 Test	Chapter 2 Test	Chapter 2 Test

Yearly Pacing Chapter 2 Total – **12 days** Chapters 1–2 Total – **22 days** Remaining – **138 days**

*Challenge Exercises EP = Extra Practice SRH = Skills Review Handbook

BLOCK SCHEDULE

DAY 1	DAY 2	DAY 3	DAY 4	DAY 5	DAY 6
2.1 pp. 66–68 Exs. 17–19, 21–23, 25–27, 30–37, 40–51, 53–65	**2.2** pp. 74–75 Exs. 16–31, 36–38, 42–49, 53–61 **2.3** pp. 81–82 Exs. 13–18, 25–27, 31–37, 39–45, 48–54	**2.4** pp. 87–89 Exs. 10–27, 32–39, 41–46, 48–54	**2.5** pp. 93–95 Exs. 17–22, 26–34, 38–44, 48–64 **2.6** pp. 99–101 Exs. 16–30, 34–38, 40–51, 56–58	**2.7** pp. 105–107 Exs. 12–45, 47, 50–56	**Review** pp. 108–111 Exs. 1–47 **Assess** Chapter 2 Test

Yearly Pacing Chapter 2 Total – **6 days** Chapters 1–2 Total – **11 days** Remaining – **69 days**

Support Materials

CHAPTER RESOURCE BOOK

CHAPTER SUPPORT							
Tips for New Teachers	p. 1		Parents as Partners			p. 3	

LESSON SUPPORT	2.1	2.2	2.3	2.4	2.5	2.6	2.7
Lesson Plans (regular and block)	p. 5	p. 14	p. 23	p. 32	p. 42	p. 50	p. 59
Technology Activities & Keystrokes			p. 25	p. 34			p. 61
Activity Support Masters							
Activity Masters		p. 16					
Practice (3 levels)	p. 7	p. 17	p. 26	p. 36	p. 44	p. 52	p. 62
Study Guide	p. 10	p. 20	p. 29	p. 39	p. 47	p. 55	p. 65
Real-World Problem Solving	p. 12					p. 57	
Challenge Practice	p. 13	p. 22	p. 31	p. 41	p. 49	p. 58	p. 67

REVIEW			
Chapter Review Games and Activities	p. 68	Extra Credit Project with Rubric	p. 73
Real-Life Project with Rubric	p. 69	Cumulative Practice	p. 75
Cooperative Project with Rubric	p. 71	Resource Book Answers	A1

ASSESSMENT

Quizzes	p. 18	Alternative Assessments with Rubrics	p. 27
Chapter Tests (3 levels)	p. 20	Unit Test	p. 40
Standardized Test	p. 26	Cumulative Test	p. 42

TRANSPARENCIES

	2.1	2.2	2.3	2.4	2.5	2.6	2.7
Warm-Up/Daily Homework Quiz	✔	✔	✔	✔	✔	✔	✔
Notetaking Guide	✔	✔	✔	✔	✔	✔	✔
Teacher Support	✔					✔	
English/Spanish Problem Solving			✔	✔			✔
Answer Transparencies	✔	✔	✔	✔	✔	✔	✔

TECHNOLOGY

- EasyPlanner CD-ROM
- Test and Practice Generator
- Electronic Lesson Presentations
- eTutorial CD-ROM
- Chapter Audio Summaries CDs
- Classzone.com
- eEdition Plus Online
- eWorkbook Plus Online
- eTutorial Plus Online
- EasyPlanner Plus Online

ADDITIONAL RESOURCES

- Worked-Out Solution Key
- Notetaking Guide
- Practice Workbook
- Tutor Place
- Professional Development Book
- Special Activities Book
- Posters
- Spanish Study Guide
- Exercises in Spanish
- English/Spanish Ch. Reviews/Tests
- Multi-Language Visual Glossary

CHAPTER

2 Math Background and Teaching Strategies

Lesson 2.1

MATH BACKGROUND

Most people know intuitively that the order in which you add or multiply two numbers is not important. However, they may not know that these number facts are called the commutative property of addition and the commutative property of multiplication. Using the commutative and associative properties, which allow different groupings of addends or factors, you can often rearrange expressions so that evaluating them is easier. The identity property of addition (adding 0 to a number does not change it) and the identity property of multiplication (multiplying a number by 1 does not change it) also allow flexibility in evaluating expressions. The identity property of multiplication allows *unit analysis*, which uses multiplication by one or more forms of 1 to convert between measurements that use different units.

TEACHING STRATEGIES

Have students brainstorm to come up with expressions that might look difficult to evaluate, but that can be evaluated simply without the use of a calculator by employing various number properties, such as the commutative and associative properties, identity properties, and the multiplication property of 0. A few examples are shown below.

$5 \cdot 5 \cdot 5 \cdot 5 \cdot 5 \cdot 2 \cdot 2 \cdot 2 \cdot 2 = 5(5 \cdot 2)(5 \cdot 2)(5 \cdot 2)(5 \cdot 2) = 50{,}000$
$(64.2)(37.6)(0)(111.8) = 0$
$131 + 983 + 65 + 869 + 17 + 435 = (131 + 869) + (983 + 17) + (65 + 435) = 2500$

Lesson 2.2

MATH BACKGROUND

The distributive property allows the separation of the multiplication of the sum or difference of two terms into two multiplications, one for each of the terms. Like the number properties introduced in Lesson 2.1, the distributive property allows you to write equivalent expressions to help you simplify a given expression. For example, when multiplying 817 and 12, you are utilizing the fact that $(817)(12) = (817)(2 + 10) = 817(2) + 817(10)$.

TEACHING STRATEGIES

Students often have difficulty when distributing a negative number, especially if subtraction is involved. Work through the following problems to help students clarify the role of negative and minus signs in the distributive property.

(1) $4(2x + 7) = 4(2x) + 4(7) = 8x + 28$
(2) $4(2x - 7) = 4(2x) - 4(7) = 8x - 28$
(3) $-4(2x + 7) = (-4)(2x) + (-4)(7) = -8x - 28$
(4) $-4(2x - 7) = (-4)(2x) - (-4)(7) = -8x + 28$

Make sure students carefully observe the contrast between the initial expressions and final, simplified results for these pairs of problems: (1) and (3), (2) and (4), and (3) and (4).

Lesson 2.3

MATH BACKGROUND

The distributive property also allows you to write a sum of products as the product of a number and a sum. Using this fact, you can combine **like terms** by adding or subtracting the coefficients of the like terms and using the same variable part. For example, $8x^3 - 11x^3 = (8 - 11)x^3$, so simplifying gives $8x^3 - 11x^3 = -3x^3$.

TEACHING STRATEGIES

Have students use algebra tiles to model the simplification of expressions by combining like terms. Besides helping students identify what like terms are, this will help re-familiarize students with algebra tiles before they use them to model equations in Lessons 2.5 and 2.6. Be sure students understand the concept of zero pairs so they can combine the coefficients of like terms by removing zero pairs when possible.

Lesson 2.4

MATH BACKGROUND

In an **equation**, an equal sign is placed between two expressions to form a complete mathematical sentence. One way to understand and solve a simple equation is to rewrite the given sentence as a question, where you are looking for an unknown number represented by a variable.

TEACHING STRATEGIES

Translating between words and mathematical expressions and equations is a key skill needed for solving real-world problems. Work with students to identify key words or phrases that represent mathematical operations, such as *more than, decreased by, difference, total,* and so on. When students approach a real-world problem, encourage them to use the following steps.

1. Identify the question being asked and the quantity being sought.
2. Define a variable to represent the quantity being sought.
3. Go back through the problem and identify the words or phrases that indicate mathematical operations.

By following these steps, students will be able to write a verbal model and then an equation for the problem.

Lesson 2.5

MATH BACKGROUND

For solving equations, the metaphor of keeping a scale in balance is very helpful. The addition and subtraction properties of equality provide the means for keeping the scale in balance. The concept of **inverse operations** is used when applying the properties of equality. By using inverse operations and the properties of equality to get the variable alone on one side of the equation, you can find a solution for the equation.

TEACHING STRATEGIES

You may want to have a poster in front of the class listing the following key elements for solving equations:

(1) Get the variable alone on one side of the equation.
(2) Identify what has been "done to" the variable so you can "undo" it by using inverse operations.
(3) To keep the equation in balance, make sure you do the same thing to both sides of the equation.

Work through these key elements with students to solve an equation such as $13 = x + 7$. Ask students their goal, what has been done to the variable, and how it can be "undone." To reinforce the balance scale metaphor, have students imagine a scale with a small pebble and 7 identical weights on one side and 13 more identical weights on the other side. Ask them how they can get the pebble alone, and what would happen if they removed weights from only one side.

Lesson 2.6

MATH BACKGROUND

Just as the addition and subtraction properties of equality justify performing inverse operations to solve equations involving addition or subtraction, the multiplication and division properties of equality justify performing inverse operations to solve equations involving multiplication or division. The goal remains to isolate the variable on one side of the equation, and the method remains to undo what has been done to the variable by using inverse operations.

TEACHING STRATEGIES

Remind students of the three equation-solving elements listed in the Teaching Strategies for Lesson 2.5. Work through these elements with students to solve an equation such as $3y = 18$. To reinforce the balance scale metaphor, have students imagine a scale with three identical stones on one side and 18 identical weights on the other side. Ask them how they could get a single stone alone on one side of the scale, and how they would keep the scale in balance while doing so.

Lesson 2.7

MATH BACKGROUND

Operations with positive and negative decimals follow all the same rules as operations with positive and negative integers. There is no difference in solving equations with decimal coefficients or constants than in solving equations with integer coefficients or constants besides the fact that the calculations may be more tedious when decimals are involved.

TEACHING STRATEGIES

Work through the following word problem, which involves solving an equation containing decimals, with students.

> Martin's telephone company charges him $.08 a minute for in-state long-distance calls, and rounds the time of a call to tenths of a minute. If Martin is billed $1.16 for the call, how long did the call last?

Have students choose a variable and create a verbal model for the problem. Then have them write an equation. Ask them what operation is necessary to solve the equation, and why. Solving the equation will give students a chance to review division involving decimals.

CHAPTER

2 Differentiating Instruction

Strategies for Underachievers

EMPHASIZE NOTETAKING STRATEGIES

Beginning in Lesson 2.1, this chapter introduces many properties that are critical in simplifying expressions and solving equations: the commutative and associative properties, the identity properties, the distributive property, and the properties of equality. You may wish to encourage underachievers to keep note cards of these properties, complete with worked-out examples for each property. It may also help these students to create a poster of all the properties so that they can compare them at a glance.

FOCUS ON VOCABULARY

Students may need to be reminded of the difference between an *expression* and an *equation*, as well as how the terms *simplify* and *solve* apply to them. Students must also understand when expressions or equations are *equivalent*, and which pairs of operations are *inverse operations*. Also, since students will be writing "word problems" in this lesson, you may want to have them list the different words or expressions that indicate the operations of addition, subtraction, multiplication, and division.

USE MANIPULATIVES AND TOOLS

SOLVING ONE-STEP EQUATIONS In Concept Activities 2.5 and 2.6, students use algebra tiles to model one-step equations. It may help concrete learners to have individual sets of algebra tiles available that they can use throughout Lessons 2.5 and 2.6. Since all the exercises that require division to solve equations have integer answers, students will be able to use tiles to model these equations. Point out to students, however, that algebra tiles will not be useful when solving equations that require multiplication.

Also for these lessons, you may want to allow some students to use calculators, though of course students must be required to show all steps in their solutions, especially those that involve the properties of equality. Though the exercises are not computationally difficult, it may help some students to focus only on the equation-solving process by shifting their attention away from computation.

USE SCAFFOLDING

As students solve equations in Lessons 2.5–2.7, you may wish to provide them with templates to help them organize their work in a step-by-step fashion. Templates for solving the same addition equation using both a horizontal and a vertical format are shown below.

$$\begin{aligned} x + 33 &= 87 \\ x + 33 - \underline{\quad} &= 87 - \underline{\quad} \\ x &= \underline{\quad} \end{aligned}$$

$$\begin{array}{r} x + 33 = 87 \\ \underline{-\ \underline{\quad} = -\ \underline{\quad}} \\ x = \underline{\quad} \end{array}$$

It may be helpful to some students to use grid paper when they solve equations to help them keep their work aligned and organized.

Strategies for English Learners

DISSECT WORD PROBLEMS

With your students, examine the following word problem:

TICKET PRICE You buy five tickets for a sports event that you and your friends want to attend. The total charge for all of the tickets is $100. Write and solve an equation to find the price of one ticket.

Point out the features shown in the following charts:

Heading (optional)	A word or short phrase at the beginning gives you a clue about something in the problem. In this case it gives you a context for the problem but is not needed to solve the problem. In other cases the title may give you a clue as to the concepts or skill you will use (for example, Mental Math, see page 88, starting with Exercise 20) or the type of problem (for example, Multiple Choice, see page 101, Exercise 58.)
TICKET PRICE	

First sentence	
You buy five tickets for a sports event that you and your friends want to attend.	Sometimes the first sentence is a background sentence that provides more context, but usually it provides the first fact or number you will need to work with, in this case *five*. Usually that refers to a number of something that is named in the sentence, often immediately following, in this case tickets.
Second sentence *The total charge for all of the tickets is $100.*	The second sentence usually gives you the second fact or number you will be working with, in this case $100. You need to see what 100 refers to somewhere in the sentence, in this case the total charge.
Third sentence *Write and solve an equation to find the price of one ticket.*	The last sentence or two sentences often contain one of the following words or phrases: *find, who, what, when, where, why, which, how many, how much, how long*. These signal words are usually followed closely by a description of what you are supposed to provide in your answer, in this case the price of one ticket.

Strategies for Advanced Learners

INCREASE DEPTH AND COMPLEXITY

After completing Lesson 2.1, you may wish to have some advanced students extend their work in Exercise 49, in which they determine whether subtraction and division are commutative and associative operations. Have these students perform additional examples that involve negative integers. After students have determined that subtraction and multiplication are not commutative, challenge them to explain their results by rewriting the subtraction and division expressions in terms of addition or multiplication.

In Lesson 2.6, to stress that you cannot divide both sides of an equation by 0, you may want to have advanced students attempt to explain why, for example, $0 \div (-5) = 0$, but $(-5) \div 0$ is undefined. Students can use the fact that the division problem $a \div b = c$ has the related multiplication problem $b \times c = a$ to show that, in the first case, $0 \times (-5) = 0$, as expected, but in the second case, attempting to write a related multiplication problem gives $\underline{?} \times 0 = -5$, and there is no number that when multiplied by 0 gives -5.

The following problems can be used with **Lesson 2.2**:

- **Challenge** Refer to Exercise 50 on page 75.
  - **a.** Do all of the rectangular pens that can be created with 500 feet of fencing have the same area? If not, what are the dimensions and area of the pen with the greatest area? no; 125 ft by 125 ft, 15,625 ft^2
  - **b.** If the length of each side is a multiple of 25, what are the dimensions and area of the pen with the least area? 25 ft by 225 ft, 5625 ft^2

The following problems can be used with **Lesson 2.3**:

- **Challenge** Refer to Exercise 38 on page 82.
  - **a.** If you have a budget of $50 for 20 fish and you buy each type of fish only in pairs, what is the maximum number of angelfish that you can buy? 2 angelfish
  - **b.** Give two examples of combinations of fish you can buy if you spend $60 on 20 fish and you buy each type of fish only in pairs. *Sample answer:* 2 angelfish, 4 swordtails, and 14 tetras or 4 angelfish, 8 swordtails, and 8 tetras

CHAPTER 2

Differentiating Instruction: Resource Materials

Differentiating Assessment

McDougal Littell *Pre-Algebra* offers a wide variety of assessment. This includes Level A, Level B, and Level C Chapter Tests, Standardized Tests, Cumulative Tests, and Quizzes from the *Assessment Book*, Daily Homework Quizzes from the *Warm-Up Transparencies*, and the *Test and Practice Generator*.

ASSESSMENT BOOK

The *Assessment Book* contains two quizzes, three levels of chapter tests, A (Basic), B (Average), and C (Advanced), and a standardized test for each chapter in the textbook. Also included are cumulative tests and unit tests.

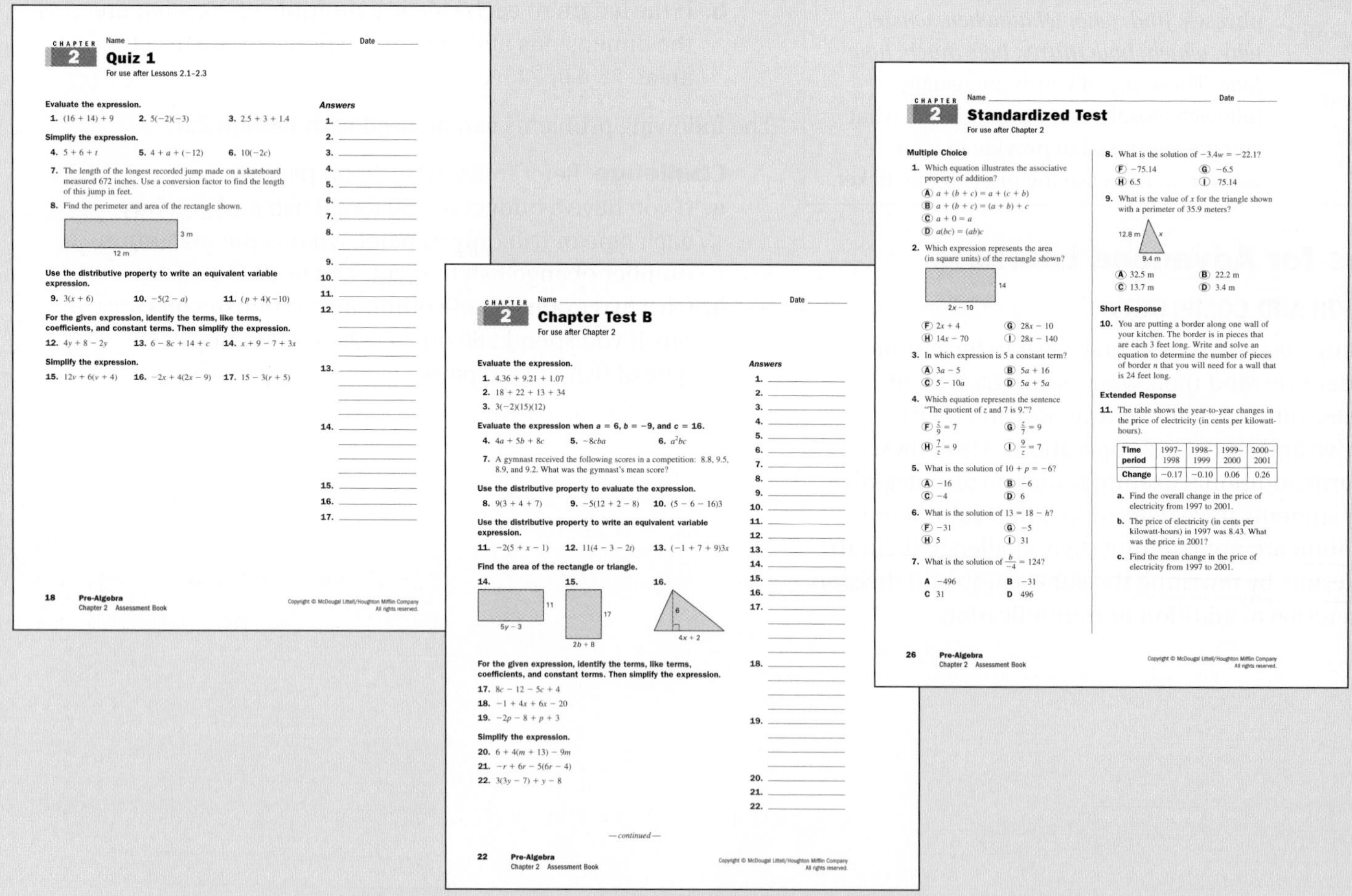

CHAPTER 2 Name ______ Date ______

Quiz 1

For use after Lessons 2.1–2.3

Evaluate the expression.

1. (16 + 14) ÷ 9
2. 5(−2)(−3)
3. 2.5 + 3 + 1.4

Simplify the expression.

4. 5 + 6 + t
5. 4 + a + (−12)
6. 10(−2c)
7. The length of the longest recorded jump made on a skateboard measured 672 inches. Use a conversion factor to find the length of this jump in feet.
8. Find the perimeter and area of the rectangle shown.

3 m; 12 m

Use the distributive property to write an equivalent variable expression.

9. 3(x + 6)
10. −5(2 − a)
11. (p + 4)(−10)

For the given expression, identify the terms, like terms, coefficients, and constant terms. Then simplify the expression.

12. 4y + 8 − 2y
13. 6 − 8c + 14 + c
14. x + 9 − 7 + 3x

Simplify the expression.

15. 12v + 6(v + 4)
16. −2x + 4(2x − 9)
17. 15 − 3(r + 5)

Answers 1.–17.

18 Pre-Algebra Chapter 2 Assessment Book

Copyright © McDougal Littell/Houghton Mifflin Company All rights reserved.

CHAPTER 2 Name ______ Date ______

Chapter Test B

For use after Chapter 2

Evaluate the expression.

1. 4.36 + 9.21 + 1.07
2. 18 + 22 + 13 + 34
3. 3(−2)(15)(12)

Evaluate the expression when a = 6, b = −9, and c = 16.

4. 4a + 5b + 8c
5. −8cba
6. a^2bc
7. A gymnast received the following scores in a competition: 8.8, 9.5, 8.9, and 9.2. What was the gymnast's mean score?

Use the distributive property to evaluate the expression.

8. 9(3 + 4 + 7)
9. −5(12 + 2 − 8)
10. (5 − 6 − 16)3

Use the distributive property to write an equivalent variable expression.

11. −2(5 + x − 1)
12. 11(4 − 3 − 2t)
13. (−1 + 7 + 9)3x

Find the area of the rectangle or triangle.

14. 11; 5y − 3
15. 17; 2b + 8
16. 6; 4x + 2

For the given expression, identify the terms, like terms, coefficients, and constant terms. Then simplify the expression.

17. 8c − 12 − 5c + 4
18. −1 + 4x + 6x − 20
19. −2p − 8 + p + 3

Simplify the expression.

20. 6 + 4(m + 13) − 9m
21. −r + 6r − 5(6r − 4)
22. 3(3y − 7) + y − 8

Answers 1.–22.

—*continued*—

22 Pre-Algebra Chapter 2 Assessment Book

Copyright © McDougal Littell/Houghton Mifflin Company All rights reserved.

CHAPTER 2 Name ______ Date ______

Standardized Test

For use after Chapter 2

Multiple Choice

1. Which equation illustrates the associative property of addition?
   (A) a + (b + c) = a + (c + b)
   (B) a + (b + c) = (a + b) + c
   (C) a + 0 = a
   (D) a(bc) = (ab)c
2. Which expression represents the area (in square units) of the rectangle shown?
   14; 2x − 10
   (F) 2x + 4 (G) 28x − 10
   (H) 14x − 70 (I) 28x − 140
3. In which expression is 5 a constant term?
   (A) 3a − 5 (B) 5a + 16
   (C) 5 − 10a (D) 5a + 5a
4. Which equation represents the sentence "The quotient of z and 7 is 9."?
   (F) $\frac{z}{9} = 7$ (G) $\frac{z}{7} = 9$
   (H) $\frac{7}{z} = 9$ (I) $\frac{9}{z} = 7$
5. What is the solution of 10 + p = −6?
   (A) −16 (B) −6
   (C) −4 (D) 6
6. What is the solution of 13 = 18 − h?
   (F) −31 (G) −5
   (H) 5 (I) 31
7. What is the solution of $\frac{h}{-4} = 124$?
   A −496 B −31
   C 31 D 496
8. What is the solution of −3.4w = −22.1?
   (F) −75.14 (G) −6.5
   (H) 6.5 (I) 75.14
9. What is the value of x for the triangle shown with a perimeter of 35.9 meters?
   12.8 m; x; 9.4 m
   (A) 32.5 m (B) 22.2 m
   (C) 13.7 m (D) 3.4 m

Short Response

10. You are putting a border along one wall of your kitchen. The border is in pieces that are each 3 feet long. Write and solve an equation to determine the number of pieces of border n that you will need for a wall that is 24 feet long.

Extended Response

11. The table shows the year-to-year changes in the price of electricity (in cents per kilowatt-hours).

Time period	1997–1998	1998–1999	1999–2000	2000–2001
Change	−0.17	−0.10	0.06	0.26

a. Find the overall change in the price of electricity from 1997 to 2001.

b. The price of electricity (in cents per kilowatt-hours) in 1997 was 8.43. What was the price in 2001?

c. Find the mean change in the price of electricity from 1997 to 2001.

26 Pre-Algebra Chapter 2 Assessment Book

Copyright © McDougal Littell/Houghton Mifflin Company All rights reserved.

WARM-UP TRANSPARENCIES WITH DAILY HOMEWORK QUIZ

The *Warm-Up Transparencies with Daily Homework Quiz* contains a daily homework quiz for each lesson in the textbook. Each quiz appears with a set of warm-up exercises.

LESSON **2.2** **Warm-Up Exercises**

For use before Lesson 2.2, pages 71–75

Evaluate the expression.

1. 24 + 7 + 6 **2.** 2(8)(5)

3. 7 + 0 + 13 **4.** 3(1)(20)

Find the area of the figure.

5.

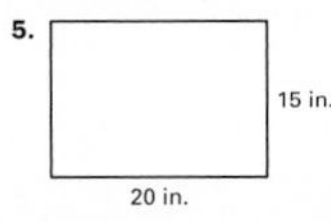

6.

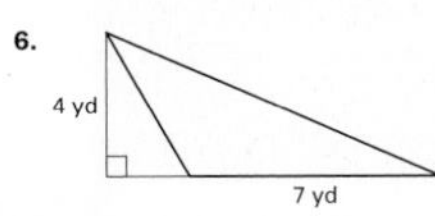

Daily Homework Quiz

For use after Lesson 2.1, pages 63–68

Simplify the expression.

1. 14 + b + 16 **2.** (18n)(5)

Identify the property that the statement illustrates.

3. $k^2 \cdot 1 = k^2$ **4.** $w + (2w + 38) = (w + 2w) + 38$

5. Challenge Find the sum of the numbers from 11 to 20 using mental math. Explain.

ANSWERS

Warm-Ups: 1. 37 **2.** 80 **3.** 20 **4.** 60 **5.** 300 in.^{2} **6.** 14 yd^2

Daily Homework Quiz: 1. $b + 30$ **2.** $90n$

3. identity property of multiplication **4.** associative property of addition

5. 155; *Sample answer:* 11 + 20 = 31, 12 + 19 = 31, 13 + 18 = 31, 14 + 17 = 31, 15 + 16 = 31, and 5(31) = 155

10

LESSON **2.4** **Warm-Up Exercises**

For use before Lesson 2.4, pages 85–89

Write the verbal phrase as an algebraic expression.

1. 5 less than x **2.** The quotient of 14 and y

3. 11 subtracted from p **4.** 7 times q

Evaluate the expression when $x = 19$ and $y = -8$.

5. $8 - x$ **6.** $\frac{64}{y}$ **7.** $-3x$

Daily Homework Quiz

For use after Lesson 2.3, pages 78–83

1. Identify the terms, like terms, coefficients, and constant terms of the expression $4n + 6 - 5n$.

Simplify the expression.

2. $7a - 2 + 9a - 8$ **3.** $3(w - 5) + 4w$ **4.** $-5(3 - 2d) + 3d + 18$

5. Challenge Brianna had \$100. She spent s dollars on sneakers, ℓ dollars on laces, and then spent the rest of the money on tennis balls. Write and simplify an expression in terms of s and ℓ for the cost of the tennis balls.

ANSWERS

Warm-Ups: 1. $x - 5$ **2.** $\frac{14}{y}$ **3.** $p - 11$ **4.** $7q$ **5.** -11 **6.** -8 **7.** -57

Daily Homework Quiz: 1. terms: $4n$, 6, $-5n$; like terms: $4n$ and $-5n$; coefficients: 4, -5; constant: 6 **2.** $16a - 10$ **3.** $7w - 15$ **4.** $13d + 3$ **5.** $(100 - s - \ell)$ dollars

12

TEST AND PRACTICE GENERATOR CD-ROM

The *Test and Practice Generator* can be used to create numerous quizzes and tests for each lesson and for each chapter using both static and algorithmic exercises.

Chapter 2 Test **Page 1**

1. Use the properties of addition and multiplication to find the missing number. Name the property.
   $(3.56 \bullet 4) \bullet 7.65 = \underline{?} \bullet (4 \bullet 7.65)$

2. Simplify the expression by combining like terms.
   $4(x-8) - 8(x+6)$
   [A] $12x - 80$ [B] $-4x - 80$ [C] $-4x + 16$ [D] $12x + 16$

3. You receive \$15 for babysitting for 6 hours. Which equation can you use to find how much you charge per hour?
   [A] $15x = 6$ [B] $6x = 15$ [C] $\frac{x}{6} = 15$ [D] $x = \frac{6}{15}$

4. Simplify the expression.
   $12 \bullet m \bullet 20$

5. You are saving money to buy a new football which costs \$53. You have \$34 saved. How much more money do you need to save? Write a verbal model. Then write and solve an algebraic model for the problem.

6. Simplify the expression by combining like terms.
   $4.2(2x + 3y) + 2.1(3x - 4y) - 2x$

7. Solve the equation. [A] -5 [B] 10 [C] 18.75 [D] 5
   $x + 2.5 = 7.5$

Use the properties of addition and multiplication to find the missing number. Name the property.

8. $(7 + \underline{?}) + 6 = 7 + (9 + 6)$

9. $3.06 \bullet (2 \bullet 2.4) = 3.06 \bullet (\underline{?} \bullet 2)$
   [A] 2.4; associative property of multiplication
   [B] 3.06; commutative property of multiplication
   [C] 2.4; commutative property of multiplication
   [D] 3.06; associative property of multiplication

Chapter 2 Test **Page 2**

10. Solve the equation. [A] -12 [B] 12 [C] -54 [D] 54
    $x - 21 = 33$

11. Solve the equation. Check your solution.
    $\frac{d}{-2.5} = 10$
    [A] -250 [B] -25 [C] -4 [D] 4

Solve the equation.

12. $7.35 + s = 11.26$

13. $c - 8 = 23$ [A] 31 [B] 15 [C] 41 [D] 25

14. Identify the property illustrated in the equation.
    $r + (8 + 3) = (r + 8) + 3$
    [A] Commutative property of addition [B] Commutative property of multiplication
    [C] Associative property of addition [D] Associative property of multiplication

15. A person-hour is a unit of measure representing one person working for one hour. A supervisor estimates that it will take 2200 person-hours to complete a project. If 8 workers are available at the same time, how many hours will it take to complete the project?

16. Solve the equation.
    $p + 6 = 40$

17. Solve the equation. Check your solution.
    $\frac{b}{16} = 11$

18. Tell whether the equation correctly represents the real-life problem. If not, correct the equation.
    Your aunt is four years older than your mother. Your aunt is 43. How old is your mother?
    $y - 4 = 43$

OVERVIEW

MAIN IDEAS

In this chapter, students use properties of addition and multiplication as well as the distributive property to evaluate expressions. Students simplify variable expressions. Students first use mental math to solve equations and then use addition, subtraction, multiplication and division to solve them. Finally, students perform operations with positive and negative decimals, including solving equations involving decimals.

APPLICATION NOTE

In 2002, Tim Montgomery broke the men's world record for the 100-meter dash, running the race in 9.78 seconds. The women's world record for the 100-meter dash is 10.49 seconds, set back in 1988 by Florence Griffith-Joyner. During his record-breaking race, Montgomery ran an average of just more than 10 meters every second. If an athlete could maintain a speed of 10 meters every second, the world records for other races would be quite different than they are today.

Imagine that a runner could maintain a pace of 10 meters per second for an entire 1000-meter race. Such a runner would finish the race in 100 seconds, or 1 minute 40 seconds. This would shatter the men's world record of 2 minutes 11.96 seconds for the 1000-meter race, which was set in 1999.

CHAPTER 2

Solving Equations

How far can an athlete run in 10 seconds?

BEFORE

In the previous chapter you've . . .

- **Performed operations with integers**
- **Written and evaluated variable expressions**

Now

In Chapter 2 you'll study . . .

- **Using addition, multiplication, and distributive properties**
- **Simplifying variable expressions**
- **Solving equations using mental math**
- **Solving equations using addition, subtraction, multiplication, or division**
- **Solving equations with decimals**

WHY?

So you can solve real-world problems about . . .

- **dinosaurs, p. 67**
- **giant pumpkins, p. 74**
- **fitness, p. 81**
- **aviation, p. 89**
- **mountain climbing, p. 94**
- **computers, p. 100**
- **baseball, p. 106**

CHAPTER 2

INTERNET Preview

CLASSZONE.COM

- eEdition Plus Online
- eWorkbook Plus Online
- eTutorial Plus Online
- State Test Practice
- More Examples

MATH In the Real World

Track Race The world's fastest athletes can run 100 meters in under 10 seconds. In this chapter, you will use equations to solve problems like finding the average rate at which an athlete runs a race.

What do you think? Suppose an athlete runs at an average rate of 10.5 meters per second for 10 seconds. Use the formula *distance* = *rate* × *time* to find the distance the athlete runs. **About 105 m**

CHAPTER RESOURCES

These resources are provided to help you prepare for the chapter and to customize review materials:

Chapter 2 Resource Book

- Tips for New Teachers, pp. 1–2
- Lesson Plan, pp. 5, 14, 23, 32, 42, 50, 59
- Lesson Plan for Block Scheduling, pp. 6, 15, 24, 33, 43, 51, 60

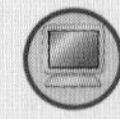

Technology

- EasyPlanner CD-ROM
- Test and Practice Generator
- Electronic Lesson Presentations CD-ROM
- eTutorial CD-ROM

Internet

- Classzone
- eEdition Plus Online
- eWorkbook Plus Online
- eTutorial Plus Online
- EasyPlanner Plus Online

ENGLISH LEARNER SUPPORT

- Spanish Study Guide
- Multi-Language Visual Glossary
- Chapter Audio Summaries CDs
- Teacher's Edition, pp. 60E–60F

PREPARE

DIAGNOSIS/REMEDIATION

Prerequisite Skills Quiz

The Prerequisite Skills Quiz can help you diagnose whether students have the following skills needed in Chapter 2:

- Use vocabulary (Ex. 1)
- Perform operations with decimals (Exs. 2–5)
- Write a variable expression to represent a phrase (Exs. 6–7)
- Perform operations with integers (Exs. 8–11)

Chapter 2 Resource Book

- Study Guide (Lessons 2.1–2.7)

Tutor Place

NOTETAKING STRATEGIES

Another way of making a definition map is to write the concept in a circle in the center of a sheet of paper and then connect the circle with lines to ovals and boxes surrounding the circle that contain attributes, examples, and further explanations for the defined word. Further suggestions for keeping a notebook can be found on pages 64 and 78.

For more support on notetaking, see:

- Notetaking Guide Workbook
- Notetaking Transparencies

CHAPTER 2

Chapter Prerequisite Skills

Review Vocabulary

numerical expression, p. 5
variable expression, p. 5
order of operations, p. 16
absolute value, p. 23
decimal, p. 770

1. *Sample answer:* A numerical expression consists only of numbers and operations, while a variable expression must also contain at least one variable.

PREREQUISITE SKILLS QUIZ

Preparing for Success To prepare for success in this chapter, test your knowledge of these concepts and skills. You may want to look at the pages referred to in blue for additional review.

1. **Vocabulary** Describe the difference between a numerical expression and a variable expression.

Perform the indicated operation. *(pp. 774–776)*

2. $3.8 + 7.1$ 10.9 **3.** $8.23 - 4.97$ 3.26 **4.** 5.5×9.4 51.7 **5.** $6.93 \div 2.1$ 3.3

Write a variable expression to represent the phrase. *(p. 5)*

6. 7 more than a number $n + 7$ **7.** The quotient of a number and 4 $\frac{n}{4}$

Perform the indicated operation. *(pp. 29, 34, 42)*

8. $-19 + 12$ -7 **9.** $8 - (-20)$ 28 **10.** $6(-7)$ -42 **11.** $-75 \div (-5)$ 15

NOTETAKING STRATEGIES

USING DEFINITION MAPS When you study a new concept, you can use a definition map to define the concept, describe the concept's attributes, and give specific examples. A definition map for power is shown below.

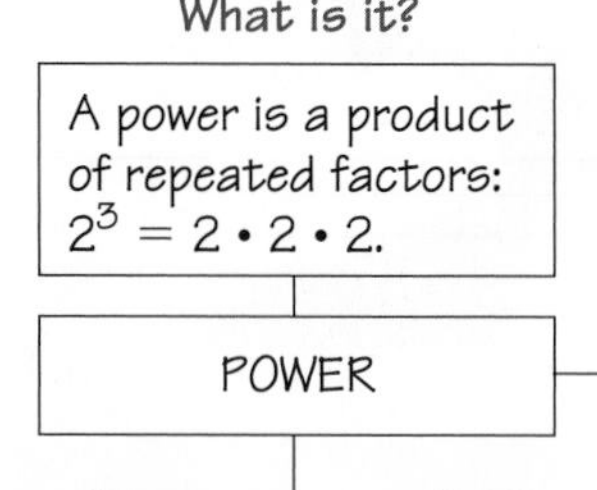

What is it?
A power is a product of repeated factors: $2^3 = 2 \cdot 2 \cdot 2$.
POWER
What are examples?
2^3
$(0.5)^6$
n^4
What are its attributes?
A power consists of a base and an exponent.
The base is the number that is used as a factor. The base for 2^3 is 2.
The exponent is how many times the base repeats. The exponent for 2^3 is 3.

A definition map will be helpful in Lesson 2.3.

Note *Worthy*

You will find a notetaking strategy at the beginning of each chapter. Look for additional notetaking and study strategies throughout the chapter.

LESSON

2.1 Properties *and* Operations

BEFORE — You found sums and products of numbers.

Now — You'll use properties of addition and multiplication.

WHY? — So you can compare the lengths of two fish, as in Ex. 48.

Vocabulary
additive identity, p. 64
multiplicative identity, p. 64

In English, *commute* means to change locations, and *associate* means to group together. These words have similar meanings in mathematics. *Commutative* properties let you change the positions of numbers in a sum or product. *Associative* properties let you group numbers in a sum or product together.

Commutative and Associative Properties

Commutative Property of Addition	Commutative Property of Multiplication
Words In a sum, you can add the numbers in any order.	**Words** In a product, you can multiply the numbers in any order.
Numbers $4 + (-7) = -7 + 4$	**Numbers** $8(-5) = -5(8)$
Algebra $a + b = b + a$	**Algebra** $ab = ba$
Associative Property of Addition	**Associative Property of Multiplication**
Words Changing the grouping of the numbers in a sum does not change the sum.	**Words** Changing the grouping of the numbers in a product does not change the product.
Numbers $(9 + 6) + 2 = 9 + (6 + 2)$	**Numbers** $(3 \cdot 10) \cdot 4 = 3 \cdot (10 \cdot 4)$
Algebra $(a + b) + c = a + (b + c)$	**Algebra** $(ab)c = a(bc)$

Example 1 *Using Properties of Addition*

Music You buy a portable CD player for \$48, rechargeable batteries with charger for \$25, and a CD case for \$12. Find the total cost.

Solution

The total cost is the sum of the three prices. Use properties of addition to group together prices that are easy to add mentally.

$48 + 25 + 12 = (48 + 25) + 12$ **Use order of operations.**

$= (25 + 48) + 12$ **Commutative property of addition**

$= 25 + (48 + 12)$ **Associative property of addition**

$= 25 + 60$ **Add 48 and 12.**

$= 85$ **Add 25 and 60.**

Answer The total cost is \$85.

NCTM CURRICULUM STANDARDS
Standard 1: Understand numbers; Understand meanings of operations
Standard 2: Understand patterns

1 PLAN

Skill Check

1. $7 \cdot 3 = \underline{?}$ — 21
2. $-6 \cdot 8 = \underline{?}$ — −48
3. $23 + 45 = \underline{?}$ — 68
4. $3.7 + 1.3 = \underline{?}$ — 5

Lesson Objective

Use properties of addition and multiplication.

Pacing

Suggested Number of Days
Basic Course: 2 days
Average Course: 2 days
Advanced Course: 2 days
Block: 1 block

Teaching Resources

For a complete list of Teaching Resources, see page 60B.

Transparency

Warm-Up Exercises for this lesson are available on a transparency.

2 TEACH

Motivating the Lesson

Have students brainstorm for words that begin with *commut-* or *assoc-* and use the words to help students make a distinction between the commutative and associative properties.

TIPS *for* NEW TEACHERS

You may wish to create a handout showing the commutative, associative, and identity properties all listed together on one page. See Tips for New Teachers in the *Chapter 2 Resource Book*.

Extra Examples

Example 1 Mr. Newman collects homework papers in three classes from 28 students, 25 students, and 22 students. How many papers did he collect altogether? **75 papers**

Example 2 Evaluate $5mp$ when $m = 9$ and $p = -12$. **−540**

Example 3 Simplify the expression.
a. $7 + k + 5$ **$k + 12$**
b. $(10b)10$ **$100b$**

Teaching Tip

While discussing Example 1, point out to students that the numbers are being regrouped so the sum of one pair is a multiple of 10. This step makes the final addition step one that can be done mentally.

Differentiating Instruction

Less Proficient Students In Checkpoint Exercise 2, some students may not recognize that $40(-3)$ will be easier to compute than $-24(5)$. Work with students to recognize those initial sums and products that result in an easier second computation.

Cross-Curriculum

Physical Education In triathlons, the order of the three events can be rearranged without having any effect on the total distance covered by the athletes. Point out that this is analogous to the associative properties where the sum or product is unchanged by the order in which the computations are done.

1–3. See Additional Answers beginning on page AA1.

Study *Strategy*

Another Way You can also evaluate the expression $4(-7)(25)$ in Example 2 simply by multiplying from left to right:

$$4(-7)(25) = -28(25)$$
$$= -700$$

However, this calculation is more difficult to do mentally.

Example 2 *Using Properties of Multiplication*

Evaluate $4xy$ when $x = -7$ and $y = 25$.

$4xy = 4(-7)(25)$	**Substitute −7 for *x* and 25 for *y*.**
$= [4(-7)](25)$	**Use order of operations.**
$= [-7(4)](25)$	**Commutative property of multiplication**
$= -7[(4)(25)]$	**Associative property of multiplication**
$= -7(100)$	**Multiply 4 and 25.**
$= -700$	**Multiply −7 and 100.**

Checkpoint

In Exercises 1–3, evaluate the expression. Justify each of your steps. 1–3. See margin.

1. $(17 + 36) + 13$ **2.** $8(-3)(5)$ **3.** $3.4 + 9.7 + 7.6$

4. Evaluate $5x^2y$ when $x = -6$ and $y = 20$. **3600**

Example 3 *Using Properties to Simplify Variable Expressions*

Simplify the expression.

a.
$x + 3 + 6 = (x + 3) + 6$	**Use order of operations.**
$= x + (3 + 6)$	**Associative property of addition**
$= x + 9$	**Add 3 and 6.**

b.
$4(8y) = (4 \cdot 8)y$	**Associative property of multiplication**
$= 32y$	**Multiply 4 and 8.**

Checkpoint

Simplify the expression.

5. $m + 5 + 9$ **$m + 14$** **6.** $6(3k)$ **$18k$** **7.** $4 + x + (-1)$ **$x + 3$** **8.** $(2r)(-5)$ **$-10r$**

Identity Properties When 0 is added to any number, or when any number is multiplied by 1, the result is *identical* to the original number. These properties of 0 and 1 are called *identity properties*, and the numbers 0 and 1 are called *identities*.

Note *Worthy*

In your notebook, be sure to include important properties such as those from this lesson. You may find it helpful to write each property using words, numbers, and algebra, as shown at the right.

Identity Properties	
Identity Property of Addition	**Identity Property of Multiplication**
Words The sum of a number and the **additive identity**, 0, is the number.	**Words** The product of a number and the **multiplicative identity**, 1, is the number.
Numbers $-6 + 0 = -6$	**Numbers** $4 \cdot 1 = 4$
Algebra $a + 0 = a$	**Algebra** $a \cdot 1 = a$

Example 4 *Identifying Properties*

	Statement	Property Illustrated
a.	$(-5)(1) = -5$	Identity property of multiplication
b.	$2 + (-9) = -9 + 2$	Commutative property of addition
c.	$y^2 + 0 = y^2$	Identity property of addition
d.	$2(pq) = (2p)q$	Associative property of multiplication

Review *Help*

To write the conversion factor $\frac{1 \text{ foot}}{12 \text{ inches}}$, you need to know that 1 foot = 12 inches. To help you convert measures, see the Table of Measures on p. 817.

Unit Analysis You can use *unit analysis* to find a *conversion factor* that converts a given measurement to different units. A conversion factor, such as $\frac{1 \text{ foot}}{12 \text{ inches}}$, is equal to 1:

$$\frac{1 \text{ foot}}{12 \text{ inches}} = \frac{12 \text{ inches}}{12 \text{ inches}} = 1$$

So, the identity property of multiplication tells you that multiplying a measurement by a conversion factor does not change the measurement.

Example 5 *Multiplying by a Conversion Factor*

Roller Coasters The Steel Dragon 2000 is the world's longest roller coaster. Its length is 2711 yards. How long is the roller coaster in feet?

Solution

1. Find a conversion factor that converts yards to feet. The statement 1 yard = 3 feet gives you two conversion factors.

   Factor 1: $\frac{1 \text{ yard}}{3 \text{ feet}}$ **Factor 2:** $\frac{3 \text{ feet}}{1 \text{ yard}}$

   Unit analysis shows that a conversion factor that converts yards to feet has feet in the numerator and yards in the denominator:

   $$\cancel{\text{yards}} \cdot \frac{\text{feet}}{\cancel{\text{yards}}} = \text{feet}$$

   So, factor 2 is the desired conversion factor.

2. Multiply the roller coaster's length by factor 2 from Step 1.

   $2711 \text{ yards} = 2711 \cancel{\text{yards}} \cdot \frac{3 \text{ feet}}{1 \cancel{\text{yard}}}$ **Use the conversion factor. Divide out common unit.**

   $= 8133 \text{ feet}$ **Multiply.**

Answer The roller coaster is 8133 feet long.

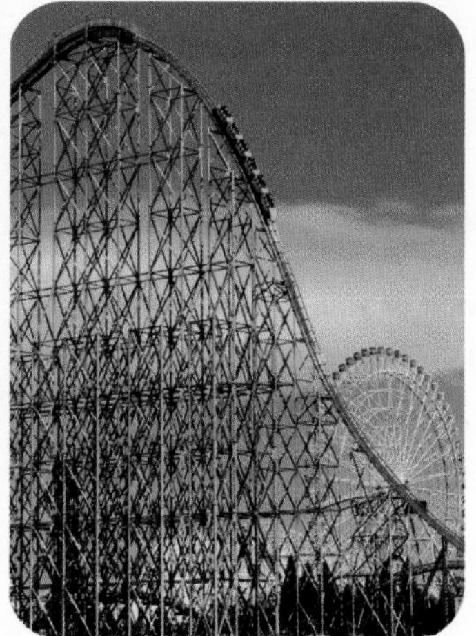

The Steel Dragon 2000, located in Nagashima, Japan

✔ Checkpoint

9. Identify the property illustrated by the statement $z^4 \cdot 1 = z^4$. **identity property of multiplication**

10. Use a conversion factor to convert 400 centimeters to meters. **4 m**

Extra Examples

Example 4 Identify each property.

a. $3a + 0 = 3a$ **identity property of addition**

b. $7(st) = (7s)t$ **associative property of multiplication**

c. $-19(1) = -19$ **identity property of multiplication**

d. $5 + (-12) = -12 + 5$ **commutative property of addition**

Example 5 The Boston Marathon is 26.2 miles long. It is run each year on the third Monday in April. How long is the marathon in feet? **138,336 ft**

Common Error

Students may think that 0 and 1 are both additive identities and multiplicative identities. Ask students to suggest quick ways to remember which value is which identity.

Reading Strategy

As you name the property shown in each of the four parts of Example 4, have students refer back to the definition of that property, read the property silently to themselves, and then examine the example again.

Concept Check

Why is 0 called the additive identity? **When 0 is added to any number, the sum is the original number.**

Daily Puzzler

What is $\frac{20}{10}$? **2** What is $\frac{20}{\frac{10}{5}}$? **10**

3 APPLY

ASSIGNMENT GUIDE

Basic Course

Day 1: SRH p. 786 Exs. 1-6; pp. 66-68 Exs. 16-19, 24-27, 36, 37, 40-47, 60-63

Day 2: pp. 66-68 Exs. 20-23, 28-35, 38, 39, 53-59

Average Course

Day 1: pp. 66-68 Exs. 17-19, 25-27, 36, 37, 40-43, 49-51, 60-65

Day 2: pp. 66-68 Exs. 21-23, 30-35, 44-48, 53-59

Advanced Course

Day 1: pp. 66-68 Exs. 18-25, 36, 37, 45-49, 56-59

Day 2: pp. 66-68 Exs. 30-33, 38-42, 50-52*, 60-65

Block

pp. 66-68 Exs. 17-19, 21-23, 25-27, 30-37, 40-51, 53-65

EXTRA PRACTICE

- Student Edition, p. 804
- Chapter 2 Resource Book, pp.7-9
- Test and Practice Generator

TRANSPARENCY

Even-numbered answers are available on transparencies. A support transparency is available for Exercises 60-63.

HOMEWORK CHECK

When you review students' homework for this lesson, go over the following exercises to check understanding of key concepts.

Basic: 16, 24, 28, 32, 37

Average: 17, 26, 30, 33, 46

Advanced: 18, 25, 31, 38, 46

2.1 Exercises

More Practice, p. 804

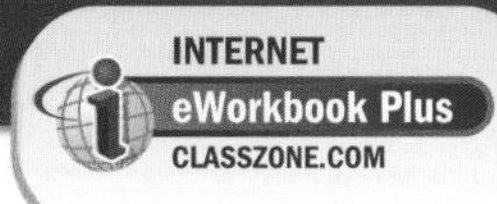

Guided Practice

Vocabulary Check

1. Which property allows you to write $4 + (3 + 9) = (4 + 3) + 9$? **associative property of addition**

2. Explain how the commutative and associative properties of multiplication can help you evaluate the product $5 \cdot 17 \cdot 2$ mentally. **See margin.**

Skill Check

Mental Math Evaluate the expression. Justify each of your steps.

3. $(26 + 18) + 34$ **4.** $-4(9)(-5)$ **5.** $(3.45)(6.26)(0)$ **3–5. See margin.**

Evaluate the expression when $x = 5$ and $y = -2$.

6. $33xy$ **−330** **7.** $x \cdot 11 \cdot y^2$ **220** **8.** $x^2 + y^3 + 15$ **32**

Simplify the expression.

9. $x + 6 + 11$ **$x + 17$** **10.** $9(-5a)$ **$-45a$** **11.** $-2 + y + 8$ **$y + 6$**

Identify the property that the statement illustrates.

12. $n + q = q + n$ **13.** $-4ab = -4ba$ **14.** $(3 \cdot 8) \cdot 2 = 3 \cdot (8 \cdot 2)$

15. Error Analysis Describe and correct the error in converting 80 ounces to pounds.

$$80 \text{ ounces} = 80 \text{ ounces} \cdot \frac{16 \text{ ounces}}{1 \text{ pound}} = 1280 \text{ pounds}$$

12. commutative property of addition

13. commutative property of multiplication

14. associative property of multiplication

15. *Sample answer:* The conversion factor should be $\frac{1 \text{ pound}}{16 \text{ ounces}}$ so that the common factor of ounces can be divided out. This gives 80 ounces = 80 ounces $\cdot \frac{1 \text{ pound}}{16 \text{ ounces}}$ = 5 pounds.

Practice and Problem Solving

Homework *Help*

Example	Exercises
1	16-23, 36, 41-47
2	16-23, 37, 41-46, 48
3	24-27
4	28-31
5	32-35, 38, 39, 48

- More Examples
- eTutorial Plus

16–19. See margin.

Mental Math Evaluate the expression. Justify each of your steps.

A **16.** $32 + 16 + 8$ **17.** $15(-9)(2)$ **18.** $7 \cdot 1 + 0$ **19.** $45 + 29 + 55$

Evaluate the expression when $a = 9$ and $b = -4$.

20. $5ab$ **−180** **21.** $b(25a^2)$ **−8100** **22.** $11 + 4b + a$ **4** **23.** $3a + b^2 + 13$ **56**

Simplify the expression.

24. $x + 17 + 12$ **$x + 29$** **25.** $3 + j + (-9)$ **$j - 6$** **26.** $-8(6c)$ **$-48c$** **27.** $(5y)(26)$ **$130y$**

Identify the property that the statement illustrates.

28. $mn + 0 = mn$ **identity property of addition**

29. $19 \cdot 5^3 = 5^3 \cdot 19$ **commutative property of multiplication**

30. $(2x + 3y) + z = 2x + (3y + z)$ **associative property of addition**

31. $(-7u)(1) = -7u$ **identity property of multiplication**

Use a conversion factor to perform the indicated conversion.

32. 4 miles to feet **21,120 ft** **33.** 7.5 kilograms to grams **7500 g**

34. 360 seconds to minutes **6 min** **35.** 432 square inches to square feet **3 ft^2**

36. **Nutrition** The calories in a breakfast sandwich come from three sources: 144 Calories are from carbohydrates, 108 Calories are from fat, and 56 Calories are from protein. Use properties of addition to find the total number of calories in the sandwich. **308 Cal**

37. **Summer Job** During the summer, you work 4 hours each day as a cashier and earn $7 each hour. Use properties of multiplication to find how much money you earn during a 5 day work week. **$140**

38. **Dinosaurs** Scientists believe that the heaviest dinosaur was *Argentinosaurus*, which weighed about 110 tons. Use a conversion factor to find the weight of *Argentinosaurus* in pounds. **220,000 lb**

39. **Tennis** The area of a regulation tennis court is 2808 square feet. Use a conversion factor to find the area of a tennis court in square yards. **312 yd^2**

40. ***Writing*** Are putting on your socks and putting on your shoes commutative activities? Explain. **No. *Sample answer:* You must always put on your socks before you put on your shoes.**

Mental Math Evaluate the expression. Justify each of your steps. **41–43. See margin.**

B 41. $1.25 + 1.38 + 0.75$ 42. $44 + 19 + 16 + 31$ 43. $4(20)(25)(-5)$

Evaluate the expression when $x = -5$, $y = 3$, and $z = 2$.

44. x^2yz^2 **300** 45. $15yxz$ **−450** 46. $2x + 9y + 5z$ **27**

47. **Surveying** A surveyor measures the depth of a river at three different points and obtains depths of 4.7 meters, 8.5 meters, and 6.3 meters.
   a. Use properties of addition to find the sum of the surveyor's measurements. **19.5 m**
   b. **Analyze** What is the mean depth? **6.5 m**

48. **Extended Problem Solving** One type of fish eaten by swordfish is the mackerel. A swordfish can grow to a length of about 5 yards, while the length of an adult mackerel is about 18 inches.
   a. Copy and complete:
   $$5 \text{ yards} = 5 \text{ yards} \cdot \frac{? \text{ feet}}{1 \text{ yard}} \cdot \frac{? \text{ inches}}{1 \text{ foot}}$$
   3, 12
   b. **Evaluate** Use properties of multiplication to evaluate the product in part (a). What is the length of a swordfish in inches? **180 in.**
   c. **Compare** A swordfish is how many times as long as a mackerel? **10 times**

49. **Logical Reasoning** Copy and complete the table. Use the results in each row to decide whether subtraction and division are commutative or associative operations. Explain your reasoning.

Expression	Result	Expression	Result
$8 - 3$	? 5	$3 - 8$	? −5
$10 \div 5$	? 2	$5 \div 10$	? $\frac{1}{2}$
$(15 - 9) - 4$	? 2	$15 - (9 - 4)$	? 10
$(48 \div 6) \div 2$	? 4	$48 \div (6 \div 2)$	? 16

50. **Critical Thinking** When you divide any number a by 1, what is the result? Write an algebraic statement that expresses this property. a; $\frac{a}{1} = a$

In the Real World

Dinosaurs A replica of an *Argentinosaurus* skeleton was built in the Fernbank Museum of Natural History in Atlanta, Georgia. The skeleton is 42 yards long. What is the skeleton's length in feet? **126 ft**

41. $1.25 + 1.38 + 0.75 =$
$(1.25 + 1.38) + 0.75$
Use order of operations.
$= (1.38 + 1.25) + 0.75$
commutative property of addition
$= 1.38 + (1.25 + 0.75)$
associative property of addition
$= 1.38 + 2$
Add 1.25 and 0.75.
$= 3.38$
Add 1.38 and 2.

49. No. *Sample answer:* The results of evaluating each expression after attempting to apply a commutative or associative property are different from those before applying the property.

Teaching Tip

In Exercises 28–31, point out that students only need to identify the property illustrated, not try to solve the given "equation."

Common Error

In Exercise 44, watch for students who omit the exponents when they simplify. Encourage students to begin by rewriting the expression as $(x)^2(y)(z)^2$ and then substituting the given values for the variables.

2. *Sample answer:* By the commutative property of multiplication, $5 \cdot 17 \cdot 2 = 17 \cdot 5 \cdot 2$, which can be written as $17 \cdot (5 \cdot 2)$ by the associative property of multiplication. It is easy to use mental math to multiply 5 and 2 to get 10, and then to multiply 17 and 10 to get 170.

3. $(26 + 18) + 34$
$= (18 + 26) + 34$ commutative property of addition
$= 18 + (26 + 34)$ associative property of addition
$= 18 + 60$ Add 26 and 34.
$= 78$ Add 18 and 60.

4. $-4(9)(-5)$
$= [-4(9)](-5)$ Use order of operations.
$= [9(-4)](-5)$ commutative property of multiplication
$= 9[(-4)(-5)]$ associative property of multiplication
$= 9(20)$ Multiply −4 and −5.
$= 180$ Multiply 9 and 20.

5. $(3.45)(6.26)(0)$
$= [(3.45)(6.26)](0)$ Use order of operations.
$= 0$ multiplication property of zero

16–19, 42, 43. See Additional Answers beginning on page AA1.

4 ASSESS

ASSESSMENT RESOURCES

For more assessment resources, see:
- Assessment Book
- Test and Practice Generator

MINI-QUIZ

Simplify the expression.

1. $14 + b + 16$ **$b + 30$**

2. $(18n)(5)$ **$90n$**

Identify the property that the statement illustrates.

3. $k^2 \cdot 1 = k^2$ **identity property of multiplication**

4. $w + (2w + 38) = (w + 2w) + 38$ **associative property of addition**

5. Challenge Find the sum of the numbers from 11 to 20 using mental math. Explain. **155; *Sample answer:* 11 + 20 = 31, 12 + 19 = 31, 13 + 18 = 31, 14 + 17 = 31, 15 + 16 = 31, and 5(31) = 155**

5 FOLLOW-UP

DIAGNOSIS/REMEDIATION

- Study Guide in Chapter 2 Resource Book, pp. 10-11
- Tutor Place, Algebra Cards 4, 5
- eTutorial Plus Online
- Extra Practice, p. 804
- Lesson Practice in Chapter 2 Resource Book, pp. 7-9

ENGLISH LEARNER SUPPORT

- Spanish Study Guide
- Multi-Language Visual Glossary
- Chapter Audio Summaries CDs

CHALLENGE

- Challenge Practice in Chapter 2 Resource Book, p. 13
- Teacher's Edition, p. 60F

60–63. See Additional Answers beginning on page AA1.

C **51. Fundraising** To raise money for a charitable organization, 10 members each sell x boxes of greeting cards for \$12 a box. Each box costs the organization \$4.

a. The profit on each box of cards sold is the difference of the selling price and the organization's cost. What is the profit on each box? **\$8**

b. Use properties of multiplication to write a simplified variable expression for the organization's total profit from card sales. **$80x$**

c. Apply What is the total profit if each member sells 25 boxes of cards? **\$2000**

52. Challenge When mathematician Carl Friedrich Gauss was a child, his teacher is said to have asked Gauss and his classmates to add up the integers 1 through 100. Gauss found the answer almost immediately. He first wrote the sum forwards and backwards, as shown.

$$\begin{array}{ccccccccccccc} 1 & + & 2 & + & 3 & + & \cdots & + & 98 & + & 99 & + & 100 \\ 100 & + & 99 & + & 98 & + & \cdots & + & 3 & + & 2 & + & 1 \end{array}$$

Stamp from 1977 honoring Carl Friedrich Gauss

a. You can pair each number in the top sum with the number below it in the bottom sum. What is the sum of the numbers in each pair? **101**

b. How many pairs of numbers are there? **100**

c. Use your answers from parts (a) and (b) to complete this statement: If S is the sum of the integers 1 through 100, then $2S =$ __?__. **10,100**

d. Interpret What is the sum of the integers 1 through 100? Explain.

52d. 5050. *Sample answer:* The sum of all the pairs shown, 2S, is 10,100. But because this represents the sum of the integers 1 through 100 written twice, the sum of the integers 1 through 100 is half of 2S, or 10,100 ÷ 2 = 5050.

Mixed Review

Evaluate the expression. *(Lessons 1.2, 1.3)*

53. 3^4 **81**   **54.** 2^5 **32**   **55.** 10^3 **1000**

56. $2 + 3 \cdot 8$ **26**   **57.** $7 + 6^2 \div 9$ **11**   **58.** $19 + 5 \cdot 11 - 4$ **70**

59. Groceries At a grocery store, you buy 3 boxes of spaghetti for \$1.19 each and 4 jars of spaghetti sauce for \$2.39 each. What is the total cost of your items? *(Lesson 1.3)* **\$13.13**

Plot the point in a coordinate plane. Describe the location of the point. *(Lesson 1.8)* **60–63. See margin for art.**

60. $P(4, 3)$ **Quadrant I**   **61.** $Q(2, -2)$ **Quadrant IV**   **62.** $R(-5, 0)$ ***x*-axis**   **63.** $S(-1, -4)$ **Quadrant III**

Standardized Test Practice

64. Multiple Choice Which conversion factor would you use to find the number of pints in 3 quarts? **B**

A. $\frac{1 \text{ quart}}{2 \text{ pints}}$ **B.** $\frac{2 \text{ pints}}{1 \text{ quart}}$ **C.** $\frac{2 \text{ quarts}}{1 \text{ pint}}$ **D.** $\frac{1 \text{ pint}}{2 \text{ quarts}}$

65. Multiple Choice Identify the property illustrated by this statement: **H**

$$2 \cdot (9 \cdot 17) = (2 \cdot 9) \cdot 17$$

F. Identity property of multiplication

G. Commutative property of multiplication

H. Associative property of multiplication

I. Associative property of addition

Student Reference

Perimeter *and* Area

▶ **Review** these topics in preparation for solving problems that involve perimeter and area in Lessons 2.2–2.7. You will learn more about area in Chapter 10.

Perimeter

Below are formulas for the perimeter of several basic geometric figures.

Triangle

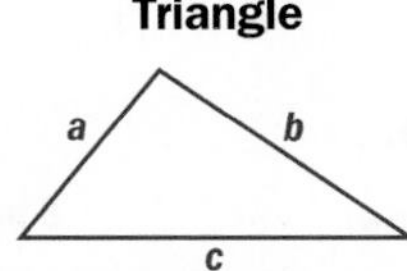

$P = a + b + c$

Square

s

s

$P = 4s$

Rectangle

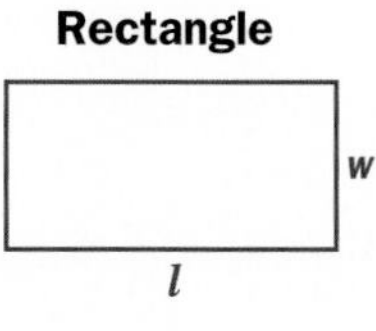

$P = 2l + 2w$

Example **Find the perimeter of the square.**

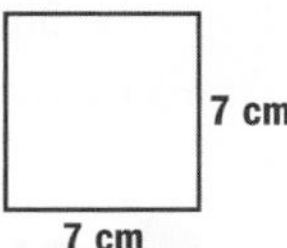

$P = 4s$ — Write formula for perimeter.

$= 4(7)$ — Substitute 7 for *s*.

$= 28$ cm — Multiply.

Area of a Square or Rectangle

Below are formulas for the area of a square and a rectangle.

Square

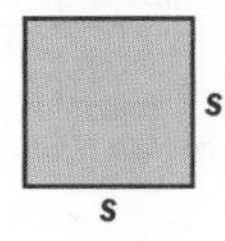

Area = (Side length)^2

$A = s^2$

Rectangle

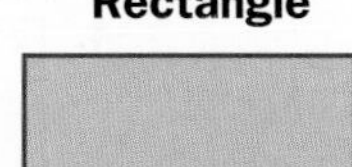

Area = Length × Width

$A = lw$

Example **Find the area of the rectangle.**

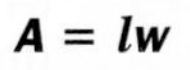

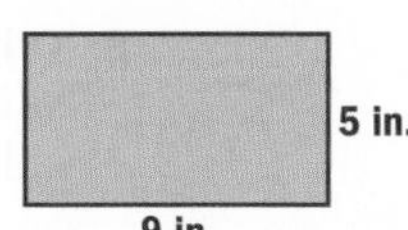

$A = lw$ — Write formula for area.

$= 9(5)$ — Substitute 9 for *l* and 5 for *w*.

$= 45 \text{ in.}^2$ — Multiply.

Continued

NCTM CURRICULUM STANDARDS

Standard 2: Represent situations using algebraic symbols

Standard 4: Apply proper formulas to find measures

1 PLAN

Skill Check

1. $4(8) = \underline{?}$ 32
2. $\frac{1}{2}(10)(6) = \underline{?}$ 30
3. $4(11) = \underline{?}$ 44
4. $\frac{1}{2}(7)(8) = \underline{?}$ 28

Lesson Objective

Prepare for solving problems that involve perimeter and area.

2 TEACH

Teaching Tip

Usually, only the lengths of two sides of a rectangle are labeled. Remind students that the perimeter of a rectangle is the sum of the lengths of all four sides.

Extra Examples

Example 1 Find the perimeter of the triangle. **60 in.**

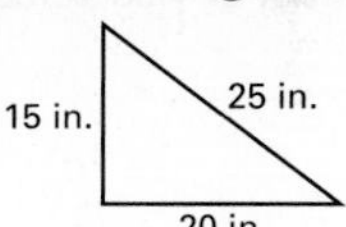

Example 2 Find the area of the rectangle. **800 cm^2**

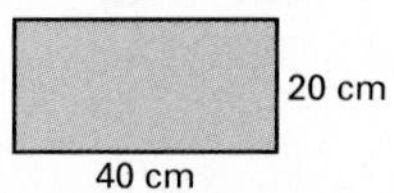

Extra Examples

Example 3 Find the area of the triangle. **60 m²**

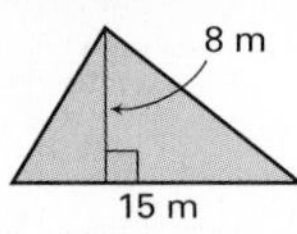

Common Error

Watch for students who find the area of a triangle mentally by halving both the base and the height, and then multiplying the two results. Urge students to write down each step rather than trying to do several steps mentally.

3 APPLY

Transparency

Even-numbered answers are available on transparencies.

Common Error

Watch for students who calculate the perimeter of a figure when they are asked to find its area, or vice versa.

Student Reference Continued

Area of a Triangle

You can find a triangle's area if you know its base and its height.

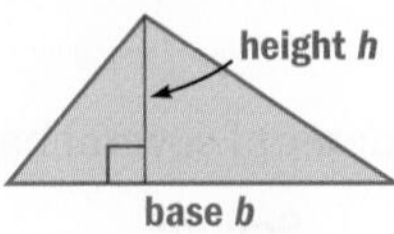

Area $= \frac{1}{2} \times$ **Base** $\times$ **Height**

$A = \frac{1}{2}bh$

Example **Find the area of the triangle.**

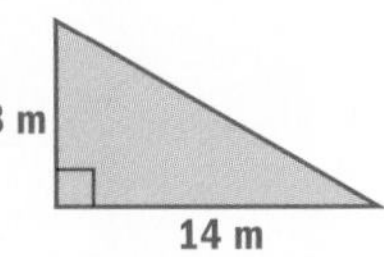

$A = \frac{1}{2}bh$ **Write formula for area.**

$= \frac{1}{2}(14)(8)$ **Substitute 14 for *b* and 8 for *h*.**

$= 56 \text{ m}^2$ **Multiply.**

Checkpoint

▶ **Test** your knowledge of perimeter and area by solving these problems.

Find the perimeter of the triangle, square, or rectangle.

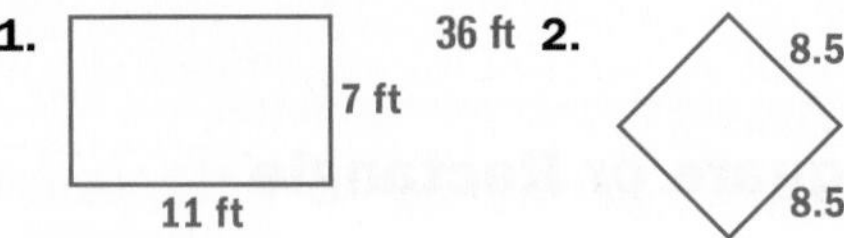

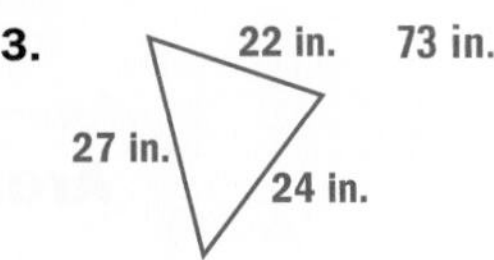

Find the area of the triangle, square, or rectangle.

4. 18 in. × 18 in. **324 in.²** **5.** 30 cm × 20 cm **600 cm²** **6.** triangle, height 6 m, base 10 m **30 m²**

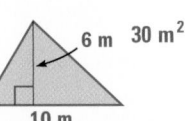

7. Basketball A regulation high school basketball court is a rectangle 84 feet long and 50 feet wide. Find the perimeter and the area of the basketball court. **268 ft, 4200 ft²**

8. Critical Thinking The sides of square B are twice as long as the sides of square A, as shown.

Square A: 3 ft × 3 ft; Square B: 6 ft × 6 ft

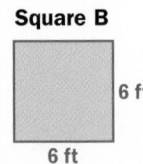

a. Find the perimeter of each square. **square A: 12 ft, square B: 24 ft**

b. Find the area of each square. **square A: 9 ft², square B: 36 ft²**

c. Compare How are the perimeters of the squares related? How are the areas of the squares related? ***Sample answer:*** **The perimeter of square B is twice that of square A. The area of square B is 4 times that of square A.**

LESSON **2.2**

The Distributive Property

BEFORE	Now	WHY?
You used properties to add and multiply.	You'll use the distributive property.	So you can find the snowfall in Utah Olympic Park, as in Ex. 37.

Vocabulary

equivalent numerical expressions, p. 71
equivalent variable expressions, p. 72

Camping You and a friend are going on a camping trip. You each buy a backpack that costs \$90 and a sleeping bag that costs \$60. What is the total cost of the camping equipment?

Example 1 *Evaluating Numerical Expressions*

You can use two methods to find the total cost of the camping equipment described above.

Method 1 Find the cost of one backpack and one sleeping bag. Then multiply the result by 2, the number of each item bought.

$$\text{Total cost} = 2(90 + 60)$$
$$= 2(150)$$
$$= 300$$

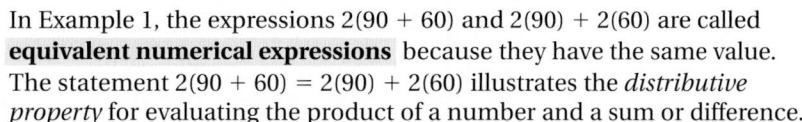

Method 2 Find the cost of two backpacks and the cost of two sleeping bags. Then add the costs.

$$\text{Total cost} = 2(90) + 2(60)$$
$$= 180 + 120$$
$$= 300$$

Answer The total cost of the camping equipment is \$300.

In Example 1, the expressions $2(90 + 60)$ and $2(90) + 2(60)$ are called **equivalent numerical expressions** because they have the same value. The statement $2(90 + 60) = 2(90) + 2(60)$ illustrates the *distributive property* for evaluating the product of a number and a sum or difference.

Reading *Algebra*

Vocabulary When you use the distributive property, you *distribute* the number outside the parentheses to each number inside the parentheses:

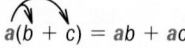

$$a(b + c) = ab + ac$$

The Distributive Property

Algebra	**Numbers**
$a(b + c) = ab + ac$	$4(6 + 3) = 4(6) + 4(3)$
$(b + c)a = ba + ca$	$(6 + 3)4 = 6(4) + 3(4)$
$a(b - c) = ab - ac$	$5(7 - 2) = 5(7) - 5(2)$
$(b - c)a = ba - ca$	$(7 - 2)5 = 7(5) - 2(5)$

NCTM CURRICULUM STANDARDS

Standard 1: Understand numbers; Understand how operations are related

Standard 2: Understand patterns

1 PLAN

Skill Check

1. $3(4) + 8(6) = \underline{?}$ **60**
2. $\frac{1}{2}(15)(20) = \underline{?}$ **150**
3. Find the area of a rectangle with length 3 inches and width 5 inches. **15 in.^{2}**

LESSON OBJECTIVE

Use the distributive property.

PACING

Suggested Number of Days
Basic Course: 1 day
Average Course: 1 day
Advanced Course: 1 day
Block: 0.5 block with 2.3

TEACHING RESOURCES

For a complete list of Teaching Resources, see page 60B.

TRANSPARENCY

Warm-Up Exercises for this lesson are available on a transparency.

2 TEACH

MOTIVATING THE LESSON

Ask students who have camped to name other items (and their costs) that would be purchased for a camping trip. Use these items to create extra examples for students to solve.

TIPS *for* NEW TEACHERS

While discussing the distributive property box at the bottom of this page, spend some extra time on the second and fourth lines of the algebra forms. See Tips for New Teachers in the *Chapter 2 Resource Book*.

Extra Examples

Example 1 At the laundromat, John uses two washing machines costing $1.75 each and two dryers costing $1.25 each. What was John's total cost for doing his laundry? **$6**

Example 2 Connie bought 4 video games costing $19.95 each. Use the distributive property and mental math to find the total cost of the games. **$79.80**

Example 3 Use the distributive property to write an equivalent variable expression.

a. $9(10 - k)$ $\mathbf{90 - 9k}$
b. $(y + 12)(-3)$ $\mathbf{-3y - 36}$
c. $-8(4z + 6)$ $\mathbf{-32z - 48}$

TEACHING TIP

Introduce the distributive property by asking students the meaning of the word *distribute*.

VISUALIZE

Write $a(b + c)$ on the board using white chalk for everything except the variables b and c. Use a second color for b and a third color for c. Then in corresponding colors, draw a large arc from a to b and another large arc from a to c. Encourage students to imagine colored arcs like these when they are applying the distributive property.

COMMON ERROR

In Checkpoint Exercises 9-12, watch for students who do not distributive the "outer" value to both values inside the parentheses.

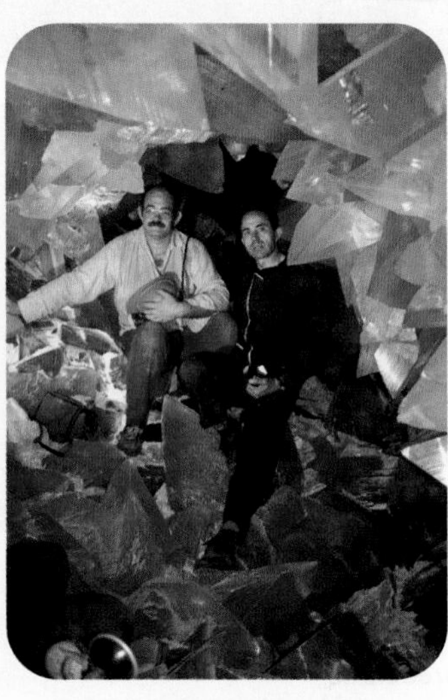

In the Real World

Geodes A geode is a hollow rock whose interior is lined with crystals. Many geodes are small enough to fit in your hand, but a giant geode in Spain is 26 feet long and can hold 10 people inside. How does this geode's length compare with the length of your hand? ***Sample answer:*** **My hand is about 6 inches long, and the geode's length is 26 • 12 = 312 inches, so the geode is about 312 ÷ 6 = 52 times as long as my hand.**

Example 2 *Using the Distributive Property*

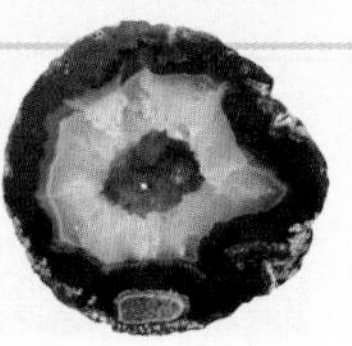

Geodes After touring a cave, you visit the gift shop and buy 3 geodes. Each geode costs $5.95. Use the distributive property and mental math to find the total cost of the geodes.

Solution

Total cost $= 3(5.95)$	**Write expression for total cost.**
$= 3(6 - 0.05)$	**Rewrite 5.95 as 6 − 0.05.**
$= 3(6) - 3(0.05)$	**Distributive property**
$= 18 - 0.15$	**Multiply using mental math.**
$= 17.85$	**Subtract using mental math.**

Answer The total cost of the geodes is $17.85.

Checkpoint

Use the distributive property to evaluate the expression.

1. $3(8 + 5)$ **39** **2.** $(2 + 9)2$ **22** **3.** $6(11 - 4)$ **42** **4.** $(3 - 14)(-5)$ **55**

Evaluate the expression using the distributive property and mental math.

5. $4(105)$ **420** **6.** $3(97)$ **291** **7.** $5(2.9)$ **14.5** **8.** $8(7.02)$ **56.16**

Two variable expressions that have the same value for all values of the variable(s) are called **equivalent variable expressions**. You can use the distributive property to write equivalent variable expressions.

Example 3 *Writing Equivalent Variable Expressions*

Use the distributive property to write an equivalent variable expression.

a. $3(x + 7) = 3(x) + 3(7)$	**Distributive property**
$= 3x + 21$	**Multiply.**
b. $(n + 4)(-2) = n(-2) + 4(-2)$	**Distributive property**
$= -2n + (-8)$	**Multiply.**
$= -2n - 8$	**Definition of subtraction**
c. $-5(2y - 3) = -5(2y) - (-5)(3)$	**Distributive property**
$= -10y - (-15)$	**Multiply.**
$= -10y + 15$	**Definition of subtraction**

Checkpoint

Use the distributive property to write an equivalent variable expression.

9. $8(x + 2)$ $\mathbf{8x + 16}$ **10.** $(7 - t)(-4)$ $\mathbf{-28 + 4t}$ **11.** $9(3m + 5)$ $\mathbf{27m + 45}$ **12.** $-2(6y - 4)$ $\mathbf{-12y + 8}$

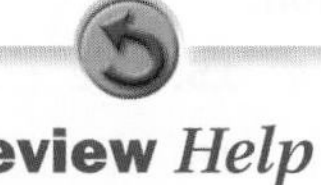

Review *Help*

For help with basic geometric figures, see p. 785.

Example 4 *Finding Areas of Geometric Figures*

Find the area of the rectangle or triangle.

a.

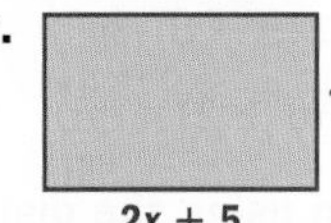

b.

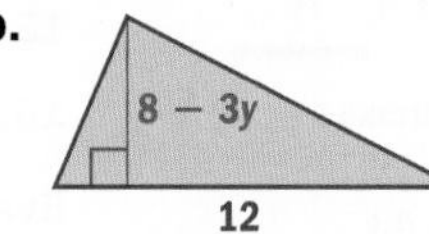

Solution

a. Use the formula for the area of a rectangle.

$A = lw$
$= (2x + 5)(7)$
$= 2x(7) + 5(7)$
$= 14x + 35$

Answer The area is $(14x + 35)$ square units.

b. Use the formula for the area of a triangle.

$A = \frac{1}{2}bh = \frac{1}{2}(12)(8 - 3y)$
$= 6(8 - 3y)$
$= 6(8) - 6(3y)$
$= 48 - 18y$

Answer The area is $(48 - 18y)$ square units.

2.2 Exercises

More Practice, p. 804

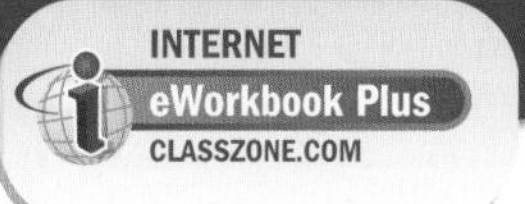

Guided Practice

Vocabulary Check

1. What property is illustrated by the statement $3(4 - 9) = 3(4) - 3(9)$? distributive property
2. Are $2(x + 1)$ and $2x + 1$ equivalent variable expressions? Explain. See margin.

2. No. *Sample answer:* By the distributive property, $2(x + 1) = 2(x) + 2(1) = 2x + 2$, which is not equivalent to $2x + 1$.

Skill Check

Evaluate the expression using the distributive property and mental math.

3. $3(96)$ 288
4. $6(103)$ 618
5. $2(8.95)$ 17.9
6. $4(7.09)$ 28.36

Use the distributive property to write an equivalent variable expression.

7. $2(x - 6)$ $2x - 12$
8. $(y + 11)(-3)$ $-3y - 33$
9. $5(4k + 9)$ $20k + 45$
10. $-4(2n - 7)$ $-8n + 28$

11. **Game Room** You are building a game room adjacent to your living room. The widths of the two rooms must be the same. There are no restrictions on the game room's length l.

	Living room	Game room
15 ft		
	20 ft	l

   a. Write an expression for the total area of both rooms by multiplying their common width by their combined length. $15(20 + l)$
   b. Write a second expression for the total area by finding the area of each room separately and then adding the two areas. $300 + 15l$
   c. Show that the expressions from parts (a) and (b) are equivalent. $15(20 + l) = 15(20) + 15(l) = 300 + 15l$

Extra Examples

Example 4 Find the area of the rectangle or triangle.

a.

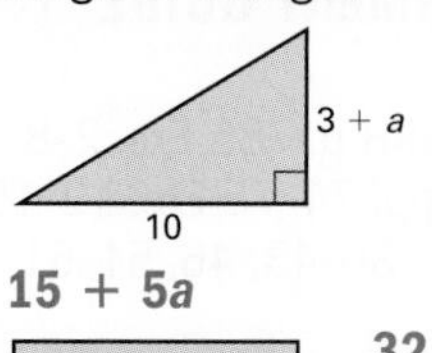

$15 + 5a$

b.

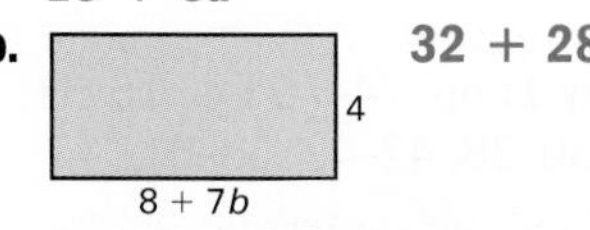

$32 + 28b$

Differentiating Instruction

Advanced Students Encourage students to write expressions with multiple levels of parentheses that can be simplified using the distributive property, such as $1 + 2(3 + 4(5 + 6) + 1)$. Have students trade their expression with a classmate, evaluate the expression they receive, and then check their partner's work.

Concept Check

Explain how to use the distributive property to write an equivalent variable expression for $4(10 + x)$. **First multiply 4 times 10 and then add the product of 4 and x. The equivalent expression is $40 + 4x$.**

Daily Puzzler

You are given that $19 \cdot 100 = 1900$ and $19 \cdot 30 = 570$. How could you use these two equations to find the product $19 \cdot 70$? ***Sample answer:*** **Recognize that $19 \cdot 70$ is equivalent to $19(100 - 30)$, and then use the given equations and the distributive property to evaluate this expression.**

3 APPLY

ASSIGNMENT GUIDE

Basic Course

Day 1: SRH p. 785 Exs. 2-8 even; pp. 74-75 Exs. 12-15, 20-31, 36-43, 46, 51-61

Average Course

Day 1: pp. 74-75 Exs. 16-31, 36-38, 42-49, 53-61

Advanced Course

Day 1: pp. 74-75 Exs. 16-23, 30-38, 41-51*, 55-62

Block

pp. 74-75 Exs. 16-31, 36-38, 42-49, 53-61 (with 2.3)

EXTRA PRACTICE

- Student Edition, p. 804
- Chapter 2 Resource Book, pp. 17-19
- Test and Practice Generator

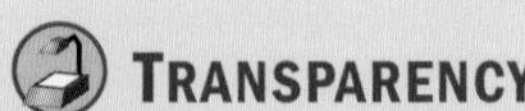

TRANSPARENCY

Even-numbered answers are available on transparencies.

HOMEWORK CHECK

When you review students' homework for this lesson, go over the following exercises to check understanding of key concepts.

Basic: 12, 20, 28, 36, 38

Average: 16, 22, 31, 37, 38

Advanced: 18, 23, 33, 38, 44

TEACHING TIP

Before students begin Exercises 24-27, refer them to Example 2 to review how to rewrite decimals as equivalent sums or differences in order to be able to use the distributive property.

Practice and Problem Solving

Homework *Help*

Example	Exercises
1	12-19, 36, 41-43
2	20-27, 37
3	28-35, 44, 45
4	38-40

Online Resources
CLASSZONE.COM
- More Examples
- eTutorial Plus

37. 295 in./year ≈ 300 in./year, so the total snowfall will be about 5(300) = 1500 in.; 5(295) = 5(300 − 5) = 5(300) − 5(5) = 1500 − 25 = 1475 in., which is close to the answer obtained by the estimation.

Use the distributive property to evaluate the expression.

A **12.** $2(5 + 3)$ 16 **13.** $5(9 - 3)$ 30 **14.** $(4 - 10)7$ −42 **15.** $(7.2 + 1.9)2$ 18.2

16. $-10(18 + 8)$ −260 **17.** $(6 + 21)(-3)$ −81 **18.** $(12 - 7)(-4)$ −20 **19.** $6(-2.3 + 3.8)$ 9

Evaluate the expression using the distributive property and mental math.

20. $4(98)$ 392 **21.** $7(109)$ 763 **22.** $(211)(-3)$ −633 **23.** $-5(396)$ −1980

24. $8(3.1)$ 24.8 **25.** $2(1.99)$ 3.98 **26.** $-6(10.95)$ −65.7 **27.** $(4.02)(-9)$ −36.18

Use the distributive property to write an equivalent variable expression.

28. $4(x - 2)$ $4x - 8$ **29.** $3(y + 9)$ $3y + 27$ **30.** $-2(3 - r)$ $-6 + 2r$ **31.** $(s + 20)(-7)$ $-7s - 140$

32. $6(2p + 1)$ $12p + 6$ **33.** $-5(5q - 4)$ $-25q + 20$ **34.** $9(11 - 6m)$ $99 - 54m$ **35.** $(-2n - 3)(-8)$ $16n + 24$

36. Basketball There are 29 teams in the National Basketball Association (NBA). Each team can have a maximum of 12 healthy players plus 3 players on injured reserve. Use the distributive property to find the maximum number of players who can be in the NBA. 435 players

37. Snowfall Utah Olympic Park, site of the 2002 Olympic Winter Games, gets an average of 295 inches of snow each year. Use estimation to predict the total snowfall in Utah Olympic Park over a 5 year period. Justify your answer using the distributive property and mental math.

Geometry Find the area of the rectangle or triangle.

38.

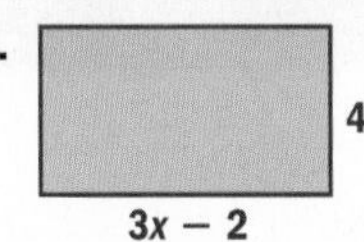

$(12x - 8)$ units^2

39.

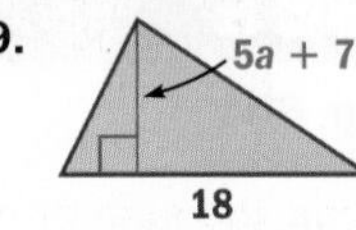

$(45a + 63)$ units^2

40.

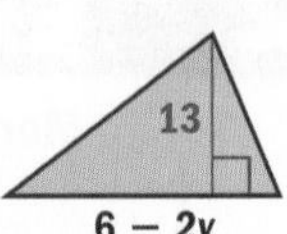

$(39 - 13y)$ units^2

Use the distributive property to evaluate the expression.

B **41.** $5(7 + 2 + 4)$ 65 **42.** $-3(9 - 1 + 6)$ −42 **43.** $(21 - 11 - 3)4$ 28

Study *Strategy*

In Exercises 41-44, you can use an extended version of the distributive property. For example, an expression of the form

$a(b + c + d)$

can be written as

$ab + ac + ad$.

44. Giant Pumpkins A giant pumpkin can be difficult to weigh directly on a scale. To estimate the weight, you can first measure the distances a, b, and c (in inches) as shown below. The weight W (in pounds) can then be approximated using the formula $W = 1.9(a + b + c)$.

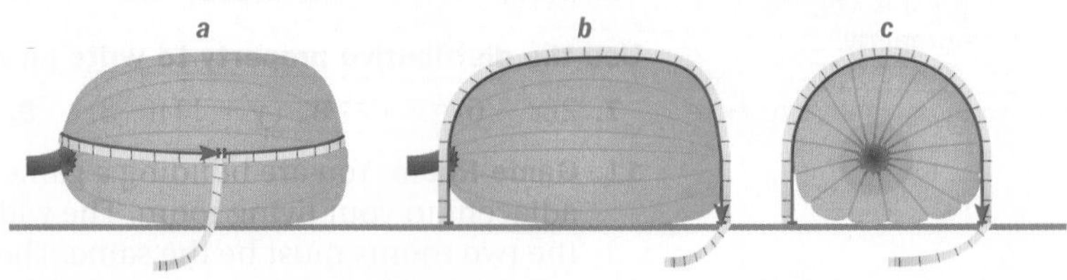

a. Use the distributive property to write the given formula without parentheses. $W = 1.9a + 1.9b + 1.9c$

b. For a certain pumpkin, $a = 132$ inches, $b = 91$ inches, and $c = 85$ inches. Approximate the weight of the pumpkin to the nearest pound. 585 lb

50a. $\frac{1}{2}(500 - 2x)$. *Sample answer:* The perimeter is a sum that includes twice the length, so I subtracted twice the length from the perimeter to find an expression for the distance remaining around the pen. I knew that the remaining distance is twice the width, so I multiplied the entire expression by $\frac{1}{2}$ to find the width.

45. Extended Problem Solving For a cylindrical corn silo with the dimensions shown, the weight W (in pounds) of the corn silage inside is typically given by $W = 4400(40 - d)$, where d is the distance (in feet) from the top of the corn to the top of the silo.

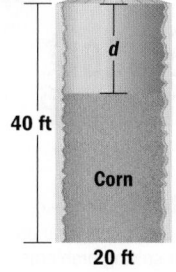

d
40 ft
Corn
20 ft

a. Use the distributive property to write the given formula without parentheses. $W = 176{,}000 - 4400d$

b. Calculate Suppose $d = 15$ feet. What is the weight of the corn in the silo? **110,000 lb**

c. Interpret and Apply How many days will the amount of corn from part (b) last if it is used to feed a herd of 100 cows and each cow eats 10 pounds of corn a day? **110 days**

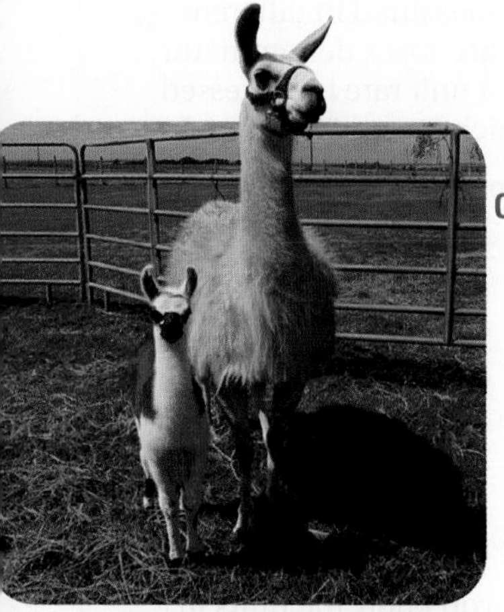

Use the distributive property to write an equivalent variable expression.

C **46.** $x(x + 9)$ $x^2 + 9x$ **47.** $m(5 - m)$ $5m - m^2$ **48.** $(2u - 7)u$ $2u^2 - 7u$ **49.** $-3y(y + 8)$ $-3y^2 - 24y$

50. Challenge Llamas are often raised as pets or to carry supplies in mountainous areas. Suppose you are building a rectangular pen for a herd of llamas. You use 500 feet of fencing for the pen. Let x represent the pen's length (in feet).

a. *Writing* Write an expression for the width of the pen. Explain the steps you used to find the expression. **See margin.**

b. Use the distributive property to write an expression without parentheses for the area of the pen. $250x - x^2$

c. Find the width and the area of the pen if the length is 160 feet. **90 ft, 14,400 ft²**

Mixed Review

Find the sum or difference. *(Lessons 1.5, 1.6)*

51. $20 + (-9)$ **11** **52.** $-34 + 16$ **−18** **53.** $-81 - 58$ **−139** **54.** $65 - (-27)$ **92**

55. Temperature Find the mean of the following temperatures: −15°F, −7°F, 8°F, 3°F, −9°F. *(Lesson 1.7)* **−4°F**

Identify the property that the statement illustrates. *(Lesson 2.1)*

56. $(x + 5y) + 2 = x + (5y + 2)$ **associative property of addition**

57. $3m + 2n = 2n + 3m$ **commutative property of addition**

58. $r^2s = sr^2$ **commutative property of multiplication**

59. $c^7 \cdot 1 = c^7$ **identity property of multiplication**

Standardized Test Practice

62. *Sample answer:* One method is to add to find the cost of a ticket and a popcorn-and-drink combo for one person and then multiply this sum by two to find the total cost. Another method is to find the cost of two tickets and the cost of two popcorn-and-drink combos and add the results. The total amount spent is $28.50.

60. Multiple Choice Which expression is equivalent to $-3(-7 + 2x)$? **A**

A. $21 - 6x$ **B.** $21 + 2x$ **C.** $21 + 6x$ **D.** $-21 - 6x$

61. Multiple Choice What is the area (in square units) of the rectangle shown? **I**

F. $4y + 13$ **G.** $8y + 26$

H. $20y + 8$ **I.** $20y + 40$

62. Short Response You and a friend go to the movies. You each buy a ticket for $9.00 and a popcorn-and-drink combo for $5.25. Describe two methods you can use to find the total amount of money you and your friend spend. What is the total amount spent?

4 ASSESS

Assessment Resources

For more assessment resources, see:

- Assessment Book
- Test and Practice Generator

Mini-Quiz

Use the distributive property to write an equivalent variable expression.

1. $-8(x + 3)$ $\mathbf{-8x - 24}$

2. $9(-4 - m)$ $\mathbf{-36 - 9m}$

Use the distributive property to evaluate the expression.

3. $5(-3.6 + 7.2)$ **18**

4. $10(16 + 3 - 22)$ **−30**

5. Challenge The length l of a rectangle is 10 units more than the width w. Write an expression without parentheses for the area of the rectangle in terms of w. $\mathbf{w^2 + 10w}$

5 FOLLOW-UP

Diagnosis/Remediation

- Study Guide in Chapter 2 Resource Book, pp. 20–21
- Tutor Place, Geometry and Measurement Cards 12, 13, Algebra Cards 4, 6, 13
- Extra Practice, p. 804
- Lesson Practice in Chapter 2 Resource Book, pp. 17–19

English Learner Support

- Spanish Study Guide
- Multi-Language Visual Glossary
- Chapter Audio Summaries CDs

Challenge

- Challenge Practice in Chapter 2 Resource Book, p. 22
- Teacher's Edition, p. 60F

1 PLAN

Skill Check

1. $200 \div 4 = \underline{?}$ 50
2. $55(3) = \underline{?}$ 165
3. $140 \div 4 = \underline{?}$ 35
4. $65 \cdot 2 = \underline{?}$ 130

LESSON OBJECTIVE

Prepare for solving problems that involve rates and unit analysis.

2 TEACH

COMMON ERROR

Students often think that the only rates are unit rates. For example, they might think that $\frac{90 \text{ miles}}{3 \text{ hours}}$ is not a rate. Point out that this is indeed a rate and that the equivalent unit rate is $\frac{30 \text{ miles}}{1 \text{ hour}}$.

Extra Examples

Example 1 Write each unit rate as a fraction.

a. 20 feet per second $\frac{20 \text{ ft}}{1 \text{ sec}}$

b. $1.70 per gallon $\frac{\$1.70}{1 \text{ gal}}$

Example 2 At a grocery store, oranges are being sold at a price of 3 for $1. What is the cost of two dozen oranges? **$8**

Example 3 While driving, Maurice averages a speed of 45 miles per hour. Write an expression for the distance he would cover in *h* hours. **45*h* mi**

Student Reference

Rates *and* Unit Analysis

▶ **Review** these topics in preparation for solving problems that involve rates and unit analysis in Lesson 2.3. You will learn more about these topics in Lesson 6.1.

Writing Unit Rates

A **rate** is a comparison, using division, of quantities measured in different units. Rates are often expressed as fractions. A **unit rate** has a denominator of 1 unit when the rate is written as a fraction. When a unit rate is expressed as a verbal phrase, it often contains the word *per,* which means "for every."

Example	Unit rate as a phrase	Unit rate as a fraction
a.	45 miles per hour	$\frac{45 \text{ mi}}{1 \text{ h}}$
b.	$3 per square foot	$\frac{\$3}{1 \text{ ft}^2}$

Rates and Unit Analysis

You can include unit analysis in a calculation so that you know the units in the answer.

Example **At a grocery store, the price of bananas is $1.19 per pound. What is the cost of 3 pounds of bananas?**

Total cost = Price per pound × Number of pounds

$= \frac{\$1.19}{1 \not{\text{lb}}} \times 3 \not{\text{lb}}$ **Substitute. Divide out common unit.**

$= \$3.57$ **Multiply.**

Answer The cost of the bananas is $3.57.

Rates and Variable Expressions

You can use a rate to write a variable expression.

Example **You fill a pool with water at a rate of 20 gallons per minute. Write an expression for the volume of water in the pool after *t* minutes.**

Volume = Gallons per minute × Number of minutes

$= 20t$

Answer The volume of water in the pool is $20t$ gallons.

NCTM CURRICULUM STANDARDS

Standard 4: Understand the units of measurement; Apply proper formulas to find measures

Using a Formula

Many rate problems involve units of distance and time. The formula below relates distance traveled to the rate of travel and the travel time.

$$\text{Distance} = \text{Rate} \times \text{Time}$$

$$d = rt$$

In problems about distance, rate, and time, the word *speed* means the same thing as *rate*.

Example An ocean liner travels at a constant speed of 36 miles per hour. How far does the ocean liner travel in 4.5 hours?

$d = rt$	**Write formula for distance traveled.**
$= \frac{36 \text{ mi}}{1 \cancel{h}} \times 4.5 \cancel{h}$	**Substitute. Divide out common unit.**
$= 162$ mi	**Multiply.**

Answer The ocean liner travels 162 miles.

Checkpoint

▶ **Test** your knowledge of rates and unit analysis by solving these problems.

Write the rate as a fraction.

1. 17 meters per second $\frac{17 \text{ m}}{1 \text{ sec}}$
2. \$360 per ounce $\frac{\$360}{1 \text{ oz}}$
3. 1.5 inches per hour $\frac{1.5 \text{ in.}}{1 \text{ h}}$
4. 0.75 pound per square foot $\frac{0.75 \text{ lb}}{1 \text{ ft}^2}$
5. **Cows** A milk cow grazing in a field eats about 30 pounds of grass per day. How many pounds does the cow eat in 5 days? **150 lb**
6. **Snails** A snail travels at a speed of about 23 inches per hour. How far can a snail travel in 4 hours? **92 in.**
7. **Carpeting** You want to carpet a rectangular bedroom that is 5 yards long and 4 yards wide. You buy the carpet for \$11.50 per square yard. What is the total cost of the carpet? **\$230**
8. **Space Probe** In 1989, the space probe *Magellan* was launched. It traveled toward the planet Venus at a speed of about 25,000 miles per hour. How far did *Magellan* travel in one day? **600,000 mi**
9. **Nutrition** A certain brand of salsa contains 15 Calories per ounce. Write an expression for the number of calories in x ounces. **15x Cal**
10. **Skiing** You ski down a hill at a speed of 70 feet per second. Write an expression for the distance you travel in t seconds. **70t ft**

Extra Examples

Example 4 A python is slithering at a constant speed of 20 feet per minute. How far will the python travel in 0.5 hour? **600 ft**

Teaching Tip

When discussing Example 4, be sure students know what the speed "36 miles per hour" means. They may recognize that this is a speed but not truly understand that it means an object will travel 36 miles each hour it is moving at this speed.

3 APPLY

Transparency

Even-numbered answers are available on transparencies.

Teaching Tip

In Exercise 4, students may not be familiar with the rate "pounds per square foot." Show students a piece of newspaper about one square foot in area, or draw a square that measures 1 foot on each side on the board. Ask students to suggest items that would weigh about 0.75 pound. Have them imagine that every square foot of space on the classroom floor is covered by one of these items.

1 PLAN

Skill Check

Simplify.

1. $x(27 + 13)$ $40x$
2. $4(k - 2)$ $4k - 8$
3. $3(8 + 2w)$ $24 + 6w$
4. $(z - 2)(-5)$ $-5z + 10$

LESSON OBJECTIVE

Simplify variable expressions.

PACING

Suggested Number of Days
Basic Course: 1 day
Average Course: 1 day
Advanced Course: 1 day
Block: 0.5 block with 2.2

TEACHING RESOURCES

For a complete list of Teaching Resources, see page 60B.

TRANSPARENCY

Warm-Up Exercises for this lesson are available on a transparency.

2 TEACH

MOTIVATING THE LESSON

Ask students to offer suggestions for ways to write $3x + 7 + 4x - 5$ in a simpler form. Discuss any suggestions with the class.

TIPS *for* NEW TEACHERS

Before discussing Example 1, have students write their own variable expressions and identify the parts. See Tips for New Teachers in the *Chapter 2 Resource Book*.

LESSON 2.3

Simplifying Variable Expressions

Vocabulary

term, p. 78
coefficient, p. 78
constant term, p. 78
like terms, p. 78

BEFORE	*Now*	WHY?
You wrote variable expressions.	You'll simplify variable expressions.	So you can find the weight of a freight train's cargo, as in Ex. 32.

Fitness You work out each day after school by jogging around a track and swimming laps in a pool. In Example 4, you'll see how to write and simplify a variable expression that describes the number of calories you burn.

The parts of an expression that are added together are called **terms**. In the expression below, the terms are $5x$, $4x$, and 7. The **coefficient** of a term with a variable is the number part of the term.

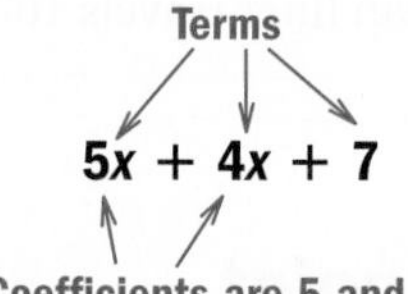

A **constant term**, such as 7, has a number but no variable. **Like terms** are terms that have identical variable parts. In the expression above, $5x$ and $4x$ are like terms. Two or more constant terms are also considered like terms.

Note *Worthy*

In your notebook, make a definition map for *variable expression*, a concept you first studied in Lesson 1.1. Your definition map should discuss terms, coefficients, constant terms, and like terms.

Example 1 *Identifying Parts of an Expression*

Identify the terms, like terms, coefficients, and constant terms of the expression $y + 8 - 5y - 3$.

Solution

1) Write the expression as a sum: $y + 8 + (-5y) + (-3)$.

2) Identify the parts of the expression. Note that because $y = 1y$, the coefficient of y is 1.

Terms: $y, 8, -5y, -3$ **Like terms:** y and $-5y$; 8 and -3

Coefficients: $1, -5$ **Constant terms:** $8, -3$

NCTM CURRICULUM STANDARDS

Standard 1: Understand how operations are related
Standard 2: Understand patterns; Represent situations using algebraic symbols

Simplifying Expressions You can use the distributive property to write an expression such as $7x + 4x$ as a single term:

$$7x + 4x = (7 + 4)x = 11x$$

The like terms $7x$ and $4x$ have been *combined*, and the expression $7x + 4x$ has been *simplified*. A variable expression is simplified if it contains no grouping symbols and all like terms are combined.

Example 2 *Simplifying an Expression*

$4n - 7 - n + 9 = 4n + (-7) + (-n) + 9$	**Write as a sum.**
$= 4n + (-n) + (-7) + 9$	**Commutative property**
$= 4n + (-1n) + (-7) + 9$	**Coefficient of $-n$ is -1.**
$= [4 + (-1)]n + (-7) + 9$	**Distributive property**
$= 3n + 2$	**Simplify.**

Checkpoint

For the given expression, identify the terms, like terms, coefficients, and constant terms. Then simplify the expression.

1. $3x + 2 + 5x$ **2.** $-7b + 3 + b - 10$ **3.** $5 + 8w - 6 - w$

1. terms: $3x$, 2, $5x$; like terms: $3x$ and $5x$; coefficients: 3, 5; constant term: 2; $8x + 2$

2. terms: $-7b$, 3, b, -10; like terms: $-7b$ and b, 3 and -10; coefficients: -7, 1; constant terms: 3, -10; $-6b - 7$

3. terms: 5, $8w$, -6, $-w$; like terms: 5 and -6, $8w$ and $-w$; coefficients: 8, -1; constant terms: 5, -6; $7w - 1$

A quick way to combine like terms containing variables is to add their coefficients mentally. In Example 2, for instance, $4n + (-n) = 3n$ because $4 + (-1) = 3$. This shortcut will be used from now on in this book.

Study *Strategy*

When you use the distributive property in part (b) of Example 3, you can think of $3k - 8(k + 2)$ as $3k + (-8)(k + 2)$ and then distribute -8 through the parentheses. You can use a similar method in part (c).

Example 3 *Simplifying Expressions with Parentheses*

a. $2(x - 4) + 9x + 1 = 2x - 8 + 9x + 1$	**Distributive property**
$= 2x + 9x - 8 + 1$	**Group like terms.**
$= 11x - 7$	**Combine like terms.**
b. $3k - 8(k + 2) = 3k - 8k - 16$	**Distributive property**
$= -5k - 16$	**Combine like terms.**
c. $4a - (4a - 3) = 4a - 1(4a - 3)$	**Identity property**
$= 4a - 4a + 3$	**Distributive property**
$= 0 + 3$	**Combine like terms.**
$= 3$	**Simplify.**

Checkpoint

Simplify the expression.

4. $4(x + 1) + 2x + 5$ $6x + 9$ **5.** $10y - 3(6 - y)$ $13y - 18$ **6.** $8c + 2 - (c + 2)$ $7c$

Extra Examples

Example 1 Identify the terms, like terms, coefficients, and constant terms of the expression $13c - 4 - 5c - 6$.
terms: $13c$, -4, $-5c$, -6; like terms: $13c$ and $-5c$, -4 and -6; coefficients: 13, -5; constant terms: -4, -6

Example 2 Simplify the expression $12k - 9 - 7k + 20$.
$5k + 11$

Example 3 Simplify the expression.

a. $5(6 + b) + 4b - 9$ **$9b + 21$**

b. $4m + 12 - 3(2m + 2)$ **$-2m + 6$**

c. $15x - (10 + 15x)$ **-10**

NOTETAKING

Encourage students to record in their notebooks several examples of like terms, as well as several examples of pairs of terms that are not like terms. Suggest that they also include a worked-out simplification problem like those shown in Example 3, with justifications for each step of the simplification.

COMMON ERROR

Write the expression $4x + 4 + 7 + 7x$ on the board. Ask students which term is like $7x$. Make sure they recognize that $4x$ and $7x$ are like terms, not $7x$ and 7.

Extra Examples

Example 4 Mary charges \$16 per hour for piano lessons and \$8 per hour for the time to drive to and from the student's home.

a. Let p be the amount of time (in hours) that Mary spends giving a student her piano lesson. Write an expression in terms of p for the cost of just the lesson. **$16p$**

b. Suppose Mary gives a lesson for 2 hours and the drive to and from the student's home takes 0.5 hour. How much will Mary charge the student? **\$36**

DIFFERENTIATING INSTRUCTION

Alternative Teaching Strategy
As you discuss Example 4, show students how variables can be used to write notes about the problem. Students can first define the variables they will use. For example, they could record "j = minutes of jogging and s = minutes of swimming." Then they could write "$j + s = 45$" to summarize the total minutes spent doing the workout.

CONCEPT CHECK

Explain how to simplify an expression that has several terms.
Sample answer: **Identify the terms that are like terms. Then combine each group of like terms and write an expression using the results. Check this expression to be sure there are no remaining like terms that can be combined.**

DAILY PUZZLER

Write an expression with six terms that simplifies to $10a - 4$.
Sample answer: **$15a + 8 + 6a - 10 - 11a - 2$**

Reading *Algebra*

An expression written *in terms of* a variable contains that variable and no others.

Example 4 — *Writing and Simplifying an Expression*

During your workout described on page 78, you spend a total of 45 minutes jogging and swimming. You burn 14 Calories per minute when jogging and 8 Calories per minute when swimming.

a. Let j be the time you jog (in minutes). Write an expression in terms of j for the total calories you burn during your workout.

b. Find the total number of calories burned if you jog for 20 minutes.

Solution

a. Write a verbal model for the total number of calories burned.

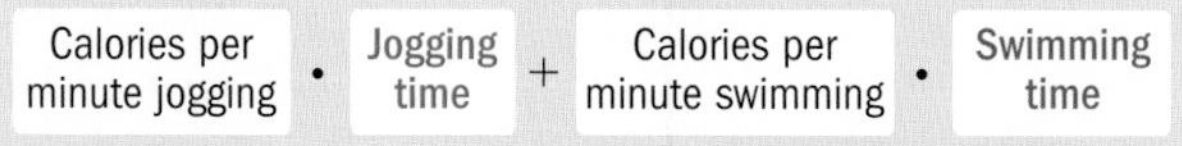

Use the verbal model to write a variable expression, then simplify it. Note that because your entire workout lasts 45 minutes and your jogging time is j, your swimming time must be $45 - j$.

$14j + 8(45 - j) = 14j + 360 - 8j$ **Distributive property**

$= 14j - 8j + 360$ **Group like terms.**

$= 6j + 360$ **Combine like terms.**

b. Evaluate the expression in part (a) when $j = 20$.

$6j + 360 = 6(20) + 360 = 480$ Calories

2.3 Exercises

More Practice, p. 804

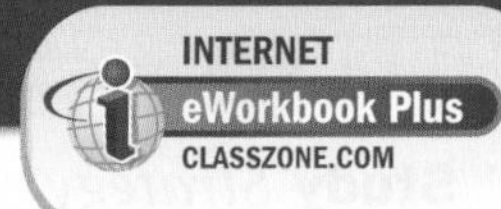

Guided Practice

Vocabulary Check

1. What are terms that have a number but no variable called? **constant terms**

2. What is the coefficient of y in the expression $8 - 3y + 1$? **-3**

Skill Check

For the given expression, identify the terms, like terms, coefficients, and constant terms. Then simplify the expression.

3. $6x + x + 2 + 4$ **4.** $-4k - 12 + 3k$ **5.** $5n + 1 - n - 8$ **See margin.**

3. terms: $6x$, x, 2, 4; like terms: $6x$ and x, 2 and 4; coefficients: 6, 1; constant terms: 2, 4; $7x + 6$

4. terms: $-4k$, -12, $3k$; like terms: $-4k$ and $3k$; coefficients: -4, 3; constant term: -12; $-k - 12$

Simplify the expression.

6. $5x + 2 + 3(x - 1)$ **$8x - 1$**   **7.** $-7(2r + 3) + 11r$ **$-3r - 21$**   **8.** $p + 6 - 6(p - 2)$ **$-5p + 18$**

9. Error Analysis Describe and correct the error in simplifying $5a - (3a - 7)$. **See margin.**

X $5a - (3a - 7) = 5a - 3a - 7$
$= 2a - 7$

Practice and Problem Solving

Homework Help

Example	Exercises
1	10-15
2	10-20
3	21-30
4	31-36

Online Resources CLASSZONE.COM
- More Examples
- eTutorial Plus

For the given expression, identify the terms, like terms, coefficients, and constant terms. Then simplify the expression. 10–15. See margin.

A **10.** $10x + 7 + 3x$ **11.** $4y + 23 - y - 6$ **12.** $-19 - 11a + a + 16$

13. $2b - 8 + 4b - 6b$ **14.** $9 + n - 1 - 7n$ **15.** $8p - 5p + 5 - p - 2$

Simplify the expression.

16. $4x + 2x$ $6x$ **17.** $10a - 3a$ $7a$ **18.** $b - 9b$ $-8b$

19. $x + 2x + 3x$ $6x$ **20.** $9c^2 - 4c^2 + 2c^2$ $7c^2$ **21.** $3(2y + 5y)$ $21y$

22. $4(d + 3) + 7d$ $11d + 12$ **23.** $5(k - 7) - k + 7$ $4k - 28$ **24.** $-2(2m - 1) + 4m$ 2

25. $8n - (n - 3)$ $7n + 3$ **26.** $20u - 6(u + 5)$ $14u - 30$ **27.** $-w + 4 - (3w - 13)$ $-4w + 17$

28. $p - 5(2 - 3p) + 1$ $16p - 9$ **29.** $3(q + 4) + 4q + 1$ $7q + 13$ **30.** $-7(r^2 + 2) + 3r^2$ $-4r^2 - 14$

31. Fitness Look back at Example 4 on page 80. Let s represent the time (in minutes) that you spend swimming. Write and simplify an expression in terms of s for the total number of calories you burn during your workout. $14(45 - s) + 8s$, $630 - 6s$

32. Trains A freight train with 80 cars transports coal and iron ore. Each car carries either 100 tons of coal or 90 tons of iron ore.

a. Let c represent the number of cars carrying coal. Write and simplify an expression in terms of c for the total weight of the freight transported by the train. $100c + 90(80 - c)$, $7200 + 10c$

b. Suppose 28 of the train's cars carry coal. What is the total weight of all the freight? 7480 tons

Geometry Write and simplify an expression for the perimeter of the triangle or rectangle. 33–35. See margin.

B **33.**

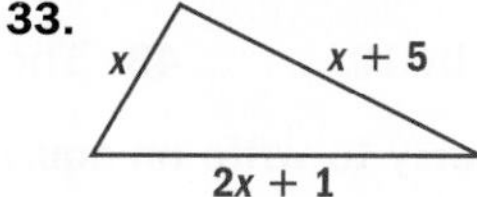

34.

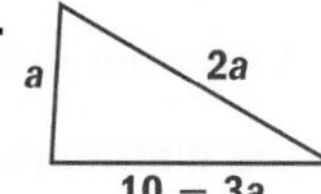

35.

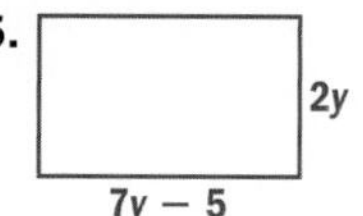

36. Extended Problem Solving You are making a rectangular rug. You want the rug to be twice as long as it is wide. Let w represent the width (in feet) of the rug.

a. Write an expression in terms of w for the perimeter of the rug. $2(2w) + 2w$, or $6w$

b. Write an expression in terms of w for the area of the rug. $2w(w)$, or $2w^2$

c. Calculate Copy and complete the table. Row 2: 6, 12, 24, 48, 96; Row 3: 2, 8, 32, 128, 512

Width (feet)	1	2	4	8	16
Perimeter (feet)	?	?	?	?	?
Area (square feet)	?	?	?	?	?

d. *Writing* Explain how doubling the width of the rug affects the perimeter and the area. Doubling the width of the rug doubles its perimeter and multiplies its area by 4.

10. terms: $10x$, 7, $3x$; like terms: $10x$ and $3x$; coefficients: 10, 3; constant term: 7; $13x + 7$

11. terms: $4y$, 23, $-y$, -6; like terms: $4y$ and $-y$, 23 and -6; coefficients: 4, -1; constant terms: 23, -6; $3y + 17$

12. terms: -19, $-11a$, a, 16; like terms: -19 and 16, $-11a$ and a; coefficients: -11, 1; constant terms: -19, 16; $-10a - 3$

13. terms: $2b$, -8, $4b$, $-6b$; like terms: $2b$, $4b$, and $-6b$; coefficients: 2, 4, -6; constant term: -8; -8

14. terms: 9, n, -1, $-7n$; like terms: 9 and -1, n and $-7n$; coefficients: 1, -7; constant terms: 9, -1; $-6n + 8$

15. terms: $8p$, $-5p$, 5, $-p$, -2; like terms: $8p$, $-5p$, and $-p$; 5 and -2; coefficients: 8, -5, -1; constant terms: 5, -2; $2p + 3$

33. $x + (x + 5) + (2x + 1)$, $4x + 6$

34. $a + 2a + (10 - 3a)$, 10

35. $2(7y - 5) + 2(2y)$, $18y - 10$

3 APPLY

ASSIGNMENT GUIDE

Basic Course

Day 1: SRH p. 795 Exs. 1-3; pp. 81-82 Exs. 10-24, 31-34, 39-41, 44-53

Average Course

Day 1: pp. 81-82 Exs. 13-18, 25-27, 31-37, 39-45, 48-54

Advanced Course

Day 1: pp. 81-82 Exs. 13-18, 28-39*, 42-49, 52-54

Block

pp. 81-82 Exs. 13-18, 25-27, 31-37, 39-45, 48-54 (with 2.2)

EXTRA PRACTICE

- Student Edition, p. 804
- Chapter 2 Resource Book, pp. 26-28
- Test and Practice Generator

TRANSPARENCY

Even-numbered answers are available on transparencies.

HOMEWORK CHECK

When you review students' homework for this lesson, go over the following exercises to check understanding of key concepts.
Basic: 10, 12, 16, 21, 31
Average: 14, 18, 26, 27, 32
Advanced: 15, 18, 28, 35, 36

TEACHING TIP

In Exercises 21-30, remind students to use the distributive property before combining like terms.

5. terms: $5n$, 1, $-n$, -8; like terms: $5n$ and $-n$, 1 and -8; coefficients: 5, -1; constant terms: 1, -8; $4n - 7$

9. See Additional Answers beginning on page AA1.

4 ASSESS

Assessment Resources

For more assessment resources, see:
- Assessment Book
- Test and Practice Generator

Mini-Quiz

1. Identify the terms, like terms, coefficients, and constant terms of the expression $4n + 6 - 5n$. **terms: $4n$, 6, $-5n$; like terms: $4n$ and $-5n$; coefficients: 4, -5; constant: 6**

Simplify the expression.

2. $7a - 2 + 9a - 8$ **$16a - 10$**
3. $3(w - 5) + 4w$ **$7w - 15$**
4. $-5(3 - 2d) + 3d + 18$ **$13d + 3$**
5. **Challenge** Brianna had $100. She spent s dollars on sneakers, l dollars on laces, and then spent the rest of the money on tennis balls. Write and simplify an expression in terms of s and l for the cost of the tennis balls. **$(100 - s - l)$ dollars**

5 FOLLOW-UP

Diagnosis/Remediation

- Study Guide in Chapter 2 Resource Book, pp. 29–30
- Tutor Place, Algebra Card 1
- eTutorial Plus Online
- Extra Practice, p. 804
- Lesson Practice in Chapter 2 Resource Book, pp. 26–28

English Learner Support

- Spanish Study Guide
- Multi-Language Visual Glossary
- Chapter Audio Summaries CDs

Challenge

- Challenge Practice in Chapter 2 Resource Book, p. 31
- Teacher's Edition, p. 60F

C **37. Agriculture** A farmer grows tomatoes and cucumbers in the field shown. The annual cost of growing tomatoes is $.27 per square foot. The annual cost of growing cucumbers is $.10 per square foot. Let x represent the width (in feet) of the tomato portion of the field.

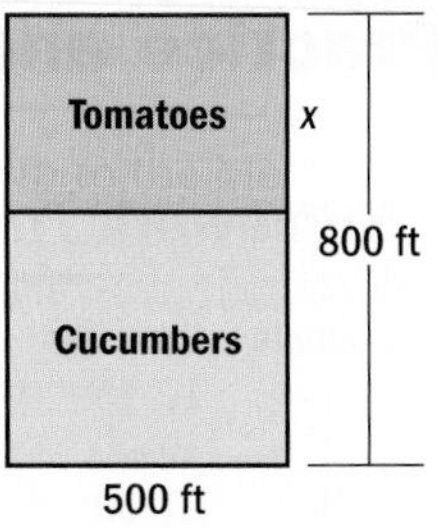

a. In terms of x, what is the area of the tomato portion? of the cucumber portion? **$500x$; $500(800 - x)$, or $400{,}000 - 500x$**

b. Write and simplify an expression in terms of x for the annual cost of growing both crops. **$0.27(500x) + 0.10(400{,}000 - 500x)$, $85x + 40{,}000$**

c. Find the annual cost of growing both crops if the width of the tomato portion is 350 feet. **$69,750**

38. Challenge You want to stock your aquarium with three types of fish: angelfish, swordtails, and tetras. Each angelfish costs $5, each swordtail costs $2, and each tetra costs $3. You plan to buy 20 fish.

a. Let a be the number of angelfish and s be the number of swordtails you buy. In terms of a and s, how many tetras do you buy? **$20 - (a + s)$, or $20 - a - s$**

b. Write and simplify an expression in terms of a and s for the total cost of your fish. **$5a + 2s + 3(20 - a - s)$, $2a - s + 60$**

c. Of the 20 fish you buy, 4 are angelfish and 10 are swordtails. Use your expression from part (b) to find your total cost. **$58**

Mixed Review

54. *Sample answer:* Write a verbal model for the total weight of the canteen and water.
Total weight = Weight of canteen + Weight per fluid ounce • Ounces remaining
$= 0.25 + 0.065(32 - x)$ Substitute.
$= 0.25 + 2.08 - 0.065x$ Distributive property
$= 2.33 - 0.065x$ Combine like terms.

39. Cubing a Number When a number x is cubed, the result is 2744. Use the problem solving strategy *guess, check, and revise* to find the value of x. *(p. 797)* **$x = 14$**

Write a variable expression to represent the phrase. *(Lesson 1.1)*

40. The product of 8 and a number **$8n$**
41. 3 less than a number **$n - 3$**
42. A number increased by 10 **$n + 10$**
43. The quotient of a number and 6 **$\frac{n}{6}$**

Use the distributive property to write an equivalent variable expression. *(Lesson 2.2)*

44. $4(a + 2)$ **$4a + 8$**
45. $-2(x + 3)$ **$-2x - 6$**
46. $7(p - 4)$ **$7p - 28$**
47. $(m - 5)(-6)$ **$-6m + 30$**
48. $5(2q + 11)$ **$10q + 55$**
49. $8(3t - 7)$ **$24t - 56$**
50. $-4(1 - 5u)$ **$-4 + 20u$**
51. $(8w + 9)(-3)$ **$-24w - 27$**

Standardized Test Practice

52. Multiple Choice Which terms are *not* like terms? **C**

A. $8y$ and $-4y$ B. 2 and 3.14 C. x^2 and x^5 D. x^2 and $5x^2$

53. Multiple Choice Which expression is equivalent to $8t - 6(2t - 1)$? **I**

F. $4t + 6$ G. $-4t - 6$ H. $-4t - 1$ I. $-4t + 6$

54. Short Response You have a canteen that holds 32 fluid ounces and weighs 0.25 pound when empty. Water weighs 0.065 pound per fluid ounce. You begin a hike with a full canteen of water. Write and simplify an expression for the weight of the canteen and water after you drink x fluid ounces. Show and justify each step of your solution. **See margin.**

2.3 Simplifying Expressions

Goal Use a graphing calculator to check simplified variable expressions.

Example

Simplify the expression $5x - 2(x - 4)$. Use a graphing calculator to check the result.

1 Simplify the given expression.

$5x - 2(x - 4) = 5x - 2x + 8$ **Distributive property**

$= 3x + 8$ **Combine like terms.**

2 To check the result from Step 1, first enter the original expression and the simplified expression into the calculator.

Keystrokes

[Y=] 5 [x] [−] 2
[(] [x] [−] 4 [)]
[ENTER] 3 [x] [+] 8

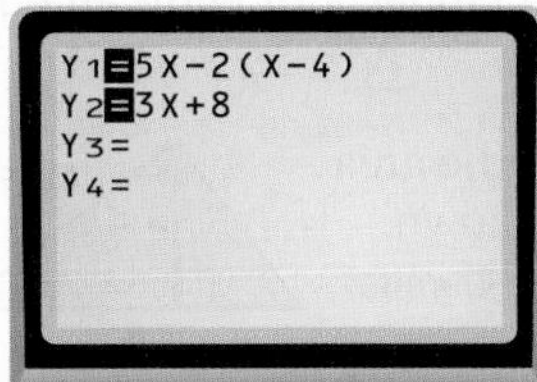

3 Use the calculator's *table* feature to evaluate the original and simplified expressions for different values of x. Press [2nd] **[TBLSET]** and enter the settings shown in the first screen below. Then press [2nd] **[TABLE]** to display the table shown in the second screen.

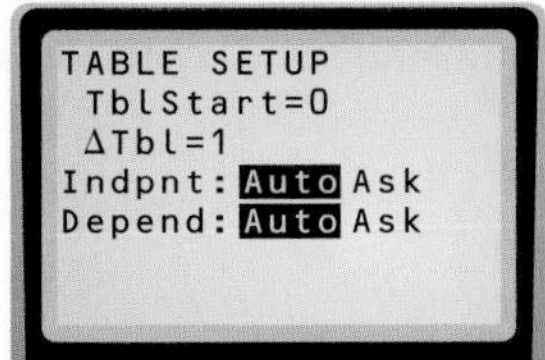

X	Y1	Y2
0	8	8
1	11	11
2	14	14
3	17	17
4	20	20
5	23	23

X=0

4 Compare the values of the original expression in the column for Y1 with the values of the simplified expression in the column for Y2. The values are the same, so the simplification is correct.

Draw Conclusions

Simplify. Use a graphing calculator to check the result.

1. $7(x + 2)$ **$7x + 14$**

2. $2x + 4x + 6x$ **$12x$**

3. $3x - 9 - 8x + 5$ **$-5x - 4$**

4. $-6(x - 3) + 5x$ **$-x + 18$**

5. $11x - 3(x + 5)$ **$8x - 15$**

6. $2(3x + 4) - 6x$ **8**

7. Critical Thinking Show that $2(x - 1) + x$ and $4x - 2$ are equal when $x = 0$. Are the expressions equivalent? Explain.

Tech *Help*

In the TABLE SETUP screen, TblStart is the first value of x in the table, and ΔTbl is the amount by which x increases from one value to the next.

• Keystroke Help

7. When $x = 0$, $2(x - 1) + x = 2(0 - 1) + 0 = 2(-1) = -2$ and $4x - 2 = 4(0) - 2 = 0 - 2 = -2$; no. *Sample answer:* Let Y1 = 2(X − 1) + X and Y2 = 4X − 2. The pairs of values in each row of the table are not always the same, so the two expressions are not equivalent.

NCTM CURRICULUM STANDARDS

Standard 2: Analyze situations using algebraic symbols

1 PLAN

Learn the Method

- Students will use a graphing calculator to check simplified variable expressions.
- Students can use the skills in this activity to verify some of their answers for the exercises in Lesson 2.3.

Grouping

Students should work individually.

2 TEACH

Discussion

As students are working, you may wish to ask them how they can tell from the table in Step 3 that the two expressions are equivalent. **The two y values are the same for each x value in the table.** Ask: "Could the two y values be the same for one value of x and different for all other values of x? What does that tell you about the two expressions?" **Yes; the two expressions are not equivalent.**

Extra Examples

Example Simplify the expression $3(2x + 1) - 4x$. Use a graphing calculator to check the result. **$2x + 3$**

3 CLOSE

Assessment

Simplify. Use a graphing calculator to check the result.

1. $5x - 4 + 3x + 7$ **$8x + 3$**

2. $6x + 2 - (5x + 3)$ **$x - 1$**

Additional Resources

The following resources are available to help review the materials in Lessons 2.1–2.3.

Chapter 2 Resource Book
- Lesson Practice
- Study Guide

Assessment Book
- Chapter 2 Quiz 1

Technology
- Test and Practice Generator
- eTutorial CD-ROM

Internet
- Classzone
- eWorkbook Plus Online
- eTutorial Plus Online

English Learner Support

- Spanish Study Guide
- Multi-Language Visual Glossary
- Chapter Audio Summaries CDs

1–4. See Additional Answers beginning on page AA1.

15. terms: $12x$, 5, $3x$; like terms: $12x$ and $3x$; coefficients: 12, 3; constant term: 5; $15x + 5$

16. terms: 9, a, -2, $-7a$; like terms: 9 and -2, a and $-7a$; coefficients: 1, -7; constant terms: 9, -2; $-6a + 7$

17. terms: $-8c$, 3, $-c$, 1; like terms: $-8c$ and $-c$, 3 and 1; coefficients: -8, -1; constant terms: 3, 1; $-9c + 4$

18. terms: $6n$, $-4n$, $-2n$; like terms: $6n$, $-4n$, and $-2n$; coefficients: 6, -4, -2; constant terms: none; 0

Mid-Chapter Quiz

Evaluate the expression. Justify each of your steps. 1–4. See margin.

1. $29 + 18 + 21$ **2.** $1.3 + 6.8 + 2.7$ **3.** $4(9)(-25)$ **4.** $5(-7)(-12)$

5. Swimming In 1998, Susie Maroney set a record for the longest ocean swim without flippers. She swam 122 miles from Mexico to Cuba. Use a conversion factor to find this distance in feet. **644,160 ft**

Use the distributive property to evaluate the expression.

6. $-3(8 + 5)$ **−39** **7.** $(11 - 4)6$ **42** **8.** $5(98)$ **490** **9.** $7(4.03)$ **28.21**

Use the distributive property to write an equivalent variable expression.

10. $2(x - 3)$ **$2x - 6$** **11.** $-5(y + 4)$ **$-5y - 20$** **12.** $4(9p + 7)$ **$36p + 28$** **13.** $(6 - 2m)(-3)$ **$-18 + 6m$**

14. Geometry Find the area of the triangle shown. **$(12x + 4)$ units^2**

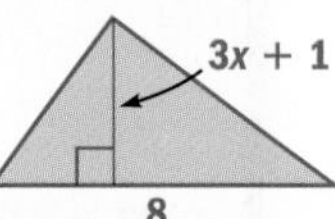

For the given expression, identify the terms, like terms, coefficients, and constant terms. Then simplify the expression. 15–18. See margin.

15. $12x + 5 + 3x$ **16.** $9 + a - 2 - 7a$ **17.** $-8c + 3 - c + 1$ **18.** $6n - 4n - 2n$

Simplify the expression.

19. $3(x + 7) + 2x$ **$5x + 21$** **20.** $y - 2(y - 6)$ **$-y + 12$** **21.** $4(r - 1) + 5r + 3$ **$9r - 1$** **22.** $8s - 4(2s + 3)$ **-12**

Word Scramble

For each statement in the table, identify the type of property the statement illustrates and write the corresponding letter. Unscramble the letters to solve this riddle:

What word has six letters, but when you subtract one, twelve remain?

E, D, N, S, O, Z; DOZENS

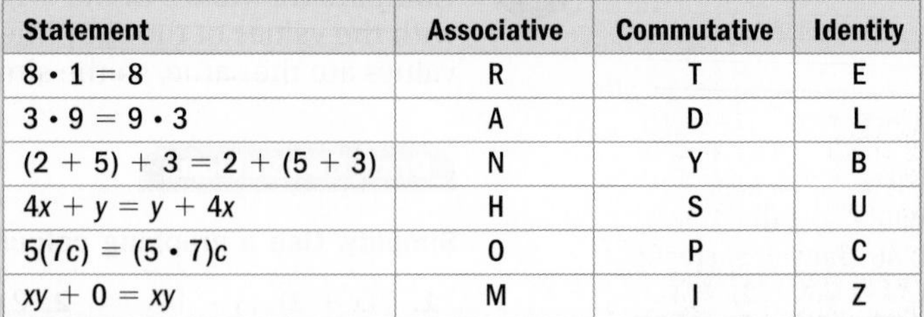

Statement	Associative	Commutative	Identity
$8 \cdot 1 = 8$	R	T	E
$3 \cdot 9 = 9 \cdot 3$	A	D	L
$(2 + 5) + 3 = 2 + (5 + 3)$	N	Y	B
$4x + y = y + 4x$	H	S	U
$5(7c) = (5 \cdot 7)c$	O	P	C
$xy + 0 = xy$	M	I	Z

LESSON **2.4**

Variables *and* Equations

BEFORE	Now	WHY?
You evaluated variable expressions.	You'll solve equations with variables.	So you can find worldwide sales of computers, as in Ex. 33.

Vocabulary
equation, p. 85
solution of an equation, p. 85
solving an equation, p. 86

Biology Lotus flowers like the one shown can be grown from seeds hundreds of years old. In Example 4, you'll see how an *equation* can be used to estimate the year when an ancient lotus seed was formed.

An **equation** is a mathematical sentence formed by placing an equal sign, =, between two expressions. A **solution** of an equation with a variable is a number that produces a true statement when it is substituted for the variable.

Example 1 *Writing Verbal Sentences as Equations*

Verbal Sentence	Equation
a. The sum of x and 6 is 9.	$x + 6 = 9$
b. The difference of 12 and y is 15.	$12 - y = 15$
c. The product of -4 and p is 32.	$-4p = 32$
d. The quotient of n and 2 is 9.	$\frac{n}{2} = 9$

Reading *Algebra*

Symbol	Meaning
$=$	is equal to
$\stackrel{?}{=}$	is equal to?
$\neq$	is not equal to

In general, when you see a question mark above a relation symbol (such as =), a question is being asked. A relation symbol with a slash through it has the opposite meaning of the same symbol without the slash.

Example 2 *Checking Possible Solutions*

Tell whether 9 or 7 is a solution of $x - 5 = 2$.

a. Substitute 9 for x.

$x - 5 = 2$

$9 - 5 \stackrel{?}{=} 2$

$4 \neq 2$

Answer 9 is not a solution.

b. Substitute 7 for x.

$x - 5 = 2$

$7 - 5 \stackrel{?}{=} 2$

$2 = 2$ ✓

Answer 7 is a solution.

Checkpoint

In Exercises 1 and 2, write the verbal sentence as an equation.

1. The sum of 3 and z is -10. $3 + z = -10$
2. The quotient of m and 6 is 4. $\frac{m}{6} = 4$
3. Tell whether -5 or 5 is a solution of $-8y = 40$. **-5 is a solution.**

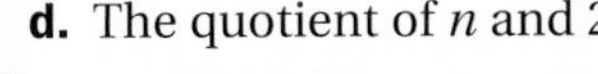

NCTM CURRICULUM STANDARDS
Standard 2: Represent situations using algebraic symbols; Analyze situations using algebraic symbols

1 PLAN

Skill Check

1. $-72 \div (-9) = \underline{?}$ 8
2. $24(-3) = \underline{?}$ -72
3. $-18 + 32 = \underline{?}$ 14
4. $-9 - 17 = \underline{?}$ -26

LESSON OBJECTIVE
Solve equations with variables.

PACING
Suggested Number of Days
Basic Course: 2 days
Average Course: 2 days
Advanced Course: 2 days
Block: 1 block

TEACHING RESOURCES
For a complete list of Teaching Resources, see page 60B.

TRANSPARENCY
Warm-Up Exercises for this lesson are available on a transparency.

2 TEACH

MOTIVATING THE LESSON
Have students write four different number sentences involving the number 100. Each number sentence should contain an equal sign and one operation symbol.

TIPS *for* NEW TEACHERS
Some students may have difficulty solving equations when the variable appears on the right side. Suggest that students rewrite these equations so the variables are on the left. See Tips for New Teachers in the *Chapter 2 Resource Book.*

Extra Examples

Example 1 Write the verbal sentence as an equation.

a. The sum of b and 9 is 17. $\mathbf{b + 9 = 17}$

b. The difference of z and 23 is -7. $\mathbf{z - 23 = -7}$

c. The product of 12 and $-k$ is -60. $\mathbf{12(-k) = -60}$

d. The quotient of t and 5 is 11. $\mathbf{t \div 5 = 11}$

Example 2 Tell whether 52 or 60 is a solution of $\frac{x}{4} = 13$. **52**

Example 3 Solve the equation using mental math.

a. $-49 = 7g$ **−7**

b. $54 - h = 48$ **6**

c. $\frac{x}{-3} = 12$ **−36**

d. $12 + y = 25$ **13**

Example 4 An animal shelter charges $75 to adopt a puppy. One week they collected $1500 in adoption fees. How many puppies were adopted that week? **20 puppies**

Teaching Tip

In Example 2, ask students to explain why there can only be one solution to the equation.

Concept Check

What is an equation? **A mathematical sentence formed by placing an equal sign between two expressions.**

Daily Puzzler

Solve the equation $5(4(3(2 + x))) = 60$. **−1**

Solving Equations Finding all solutions of an equation is called **solving the equation**. You can use mental math to solve a simple equation by thinking of the equation as a question.

Example 3 *Solving Equations Using Mental Math*

	Equation	Question	Solution	Check
a.	$x + 3 = 11$	What number plus 3 equals 11?	8	$8 + 3 = 11$ ✓
b.	$16 - m = 9$	16 minus what number equals 9?	7	$16 - 7 = 9$ ✓
c.	$20 = 5t$	20 equals 5 times what number?	4	$20 = 5(4)$ ✓
d.	$\frac{y}{6} = -3$	What number divided by 6 equals −3?	−18	$\frac{-18}{6} = -3$ ✓

 **Checkpoint**

Solve the equation using mental math.

4. $x - 10 = 7$ **17** 5. $2 + n = -6$ **−8** 6. $3w = -15$ **−5** 7. $4 = \frac{36}{s}$ **9**

Example 4 *Writing and Solving an Equation*

From 1998 to 2002, biologist Jane Shen-Miller grew several lotus plants from ancient seeds she found in China. The oldest seed was about 500 years old. Estimate the year when this seed was formed.

Solution

First write a verbal model for this situation.

Year seed was formed + Age of seed when it sprouted = Year seed sprouted

Let x represent the year when the seed was formed. Because you are only trying to estimate x (rather than determine x precisely), you can use 2000 for the year when the seed sprouted. This year simplifies mental calculations and lies within the given time period, 1998–2002.

$x + 500 = 2000$ **Substitute for quantities in verbal model.**

$1500 + 500 = 2000$ **Use mental math to solve for x.**

Answer Because $x = 1500$, the seed was formed around the year 1500.

Jane Shen-Miller with lotus plants

 **Checkpoint**

8. Go-cart rides cost $5 each at a county fair. During the first day of the fair, the go-cart operator takes in a total of $1000. How many times did people ride the go-carts that day? Write and solve an equation to find the answer. **200 times; $5x = 1000$, $x = 200$**

2.4 Exercises

More Practice, p. 804

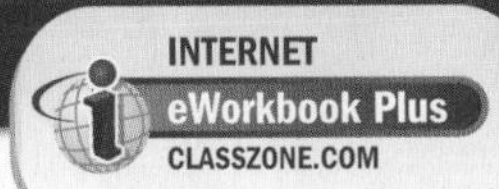

Guided Practice

Vocabulary Check

1. Copy and complete: A(n) _?_ of an equation is a number that produces a true statement when it is substituted for the variable. **solution**

2. What question would you ask yourself if you want to solve the equation $-4t = 28$ mentally?
Sample answer: -4 times what number equals 28?

Skill Check

Write the verbal sentence as an equation. Then tell whether 5 is a solution of the equation.

3. The sum of x and 10 is 15. $x + 10 = 15$; yes

4. The difference of 3 and x is 2. $3 - x = 2$; no

5. The product of -6 and x is 54. $-6x = 54$; no

6. The quotient of -40 and x is -8.

6. $\frac{-40}{x} = -8$; yes

Guided Problem Solving

7. Appetizers You are having a party and are serving quesadillas as appetizers. There will be 12 people at the party. Each quesadilla will be cut into 4 wedges, and you expect each person to eat 3 wedges. How many quesadillas do you need to make?

1) Let x represent the number of quesadillas you need. Write an expression for the number of wedges in x quesadillas. $4x$

2) How many quesadilla wedges do you need to feed 12 people? 36 wedges

3) Use your answers from Steps 1 and 2 to write an equation that you can use to find the number of quesadillas needed. $4x = 36$

4) Solve your equation to find how many quesadillas you need. 9 quesadillas

Practice and Problem Solving

Homework Help

Example	Exercises
1	8-11
2	12-15
3	16-31
4	32-36, 38

Online Resources
CLASSZONE.COM
- More Examples
- eTutorial Plus

Write the verbal sentence as an equation.

A **8.** The difference of x and 8 is -4. $x - 8 = -4$

9. The sum of 26 and y is 43. $26 + y = 43$

10. The quotient of p and 7 is 16. See margin.

11. The product of 14 and m is 56. $14m = 56$

10. $\frac{p}{7} = 16$

Tell whether the given value of the variable is a solution of the equation.

12. $x + 9 = 12; x = -3$ no

13. $21 - z = -4; z = 25$ yes

14. $91 = 7c; c = 13$ yes

15. $\frac{y}{4} = -8; y = 32$ no

Match the equation with the corresponding question. Then solve.

16. $n + 3 = 12$ C; 9

17. $3n = 12$ A; 4

18. $3 = n + 12$ D; -9

19. $\frac{n}{3} = 12$ B; 36

A. 3 times what number equals 12?

B. What number divided by 3 equals 12?

C. What number plus 3 equals 12?

D. 3 equals what number plus 12?

3 APPLY

ASSIGNMENT GUIDE

Basic Course
Day 1: pp. 87-89 Exs. 8-15, 32, 41-51
Day 2: pp. 87-89 Exs. 16-31, 33-35, 52-54

Average Course
Day 1: pp. 87-89 Exs. 10-15, 32, 41-46, 48-54
Day 2: pp. 87-89 Exs. 16-27, 33-39

Advanced Course
Day 1: pp. 87-89 Exs. 10-15, 32, 37-42*, 44-50
Day 2: pp. 87-89 Exs. 16-19, 24-31, 33-36, 51-54

Block
pp. 87-89 Exs. 10-27, 32-39, 41-46, 48-54

EXTRA PRACTICE
- Student Edition, p. 804
- Chapter 2 Resource Book, pp. 36-38
- Test and Practice Generator

TRANSPARENCY

Even-numbered answers are available on transparencies.

HOMEWORK CHECK

When you review students' homework for this lesson, go over the following exercises to check understanding of key concepts.
Basic: 8, 10, 12, 16, 32
Average: 10, 12, 18, 27, 32
Advanced: 11, 15, 24, 36, 38

TEACHING TIP

In Exercise 8, point out that the difference of x and 8 describes the expression $x - 8$, not $8 - x$. Similarly, in Exercise 10, stress that the quotient of p and 7 describes the expression $p \div 7$, not $7 \div p$.

CROSS-CURRICULUM

Science Before assigning Exercise 36, consider asking a science teacher to provide the class with some background information about the use of the Kelvin temperature scale.

In the **Real World**

Insects The dragonfly's main source of food is the mosquito. A dragonfly can eat as many as 300 mosquitoes in a single day. How many mosquitoes can a dragonfly eat in a week? **2100 mosquitoes**

Mental Math Solve the equation using mental math.

20. $x + 6 = 13$ **7** **21.** $x - 8 = 20$ **28** **22.** $0 = t + 79$ **−79** **23.** $-4 + y = -9$ **−5**

24. $11 - p = 19$ **−8** **25.** $-2 = r - 7$ **5** **26.** $7x = 63$ **9** **27.** $-10a = 130$ **−13**

28. $-54 = -9g$ **6** **29.** $\frac{x}{5} = 6$ **30** **30.** $\frac{48}{u} = -3$ **−16** **31.** $1 = \frac{n}{231}$ **231**

In Exercises 32–34, use an equation to solve the problem.

32. Insects The dragonfly is the fastest flying insect. It can move at a speed of about 50 feet per second. Find the approximate time it takes a dragonfly to travel 400 feet. **about 8 sec**

33. Computers From 2000 to 2001, annual worldwide sales of personal computers declined by about 6 million. In 2001, about 128 million personal computers were sold. Find the approximate number of personal computers sold in 2000. **about 134 million personal computers**

34. Snacks You divide a bag of trail mix into 8 portions for you and your friends to have as snacks on a bike ride. Each portion weighs 3 ounces. Find the total weight of the trail mix originally in the bag. **24 oz**

B **35. Geometry** The perimeter of the figure shown is 35 centimeters.

9 cm, 8 cm, 5 cm, 9 cm, x

a. Write an equation that you can use to find x. $x + 9 + 8 + 5 + 9 = 35$, or $x + 31 = 35$

b. Solve your equation. What is the value of x? **4 cm**

36. Extended Problem Solving Scientists often use the Kelvin scale to measure temperature. The temperature K in kelvins (K) is related to the temperature C in degrees Celsius (°C) by this formula:

$$K = C + 273$$

a. *Writing* Explain in words how to find the Kelvin temperature that is equivalent to a given Celsius temperature. ***Sample answer:*** **Add 273 to the temperature in degrees Celsius.**

b. The lowest possible temperature a substance can have is 0 K, which is called absolute zero. What is absolute zero in degrees Celsius? **−273°C**

c. The table shows the melting points of several chemical elements in kelvins. Find each melting point in degrees Celsius.

Element	Nitrogen	Chlorine	Gallium	Radium
Melting point (K)	63	172	303	973
Melting point (°C)	?	?	?	?

−210°C **−101°C** **30°C** **700°C**

d. Interpret and Apply Based on your results from parts (b) and (c), explain in words how to find the Celsius temperature C that is equivalent to a given Kelvin temperature K. Then write a formula that gives C in terms of K. ***Sample answer:*** **Subtract 273 degrees from the temperature in kelvins; $C = K - 273$.**

37. Compare and Contrast Describe the difference between an equation and an expression. Give an example of each.

37. *Sample answer:* An expression consists of numbers and/or variables and operations, but has no equal sign or inequality signs. An example is $24x - 7$. An equation uses an equal sign to show that an expression is equal to a number or another expression. An example is $24x - 7 = 17$.

38. Crafts You make a decorative paper chain with n links by cutting a 9 inch by 12 inch sheet of construction paper into n strips.

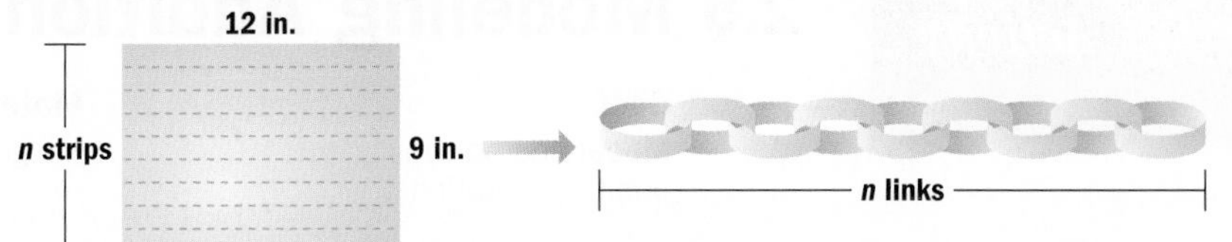

a. Write an expression in terms of n for the width of each paper strip. $\frac{9}{n}$

b. Suppose you want each strip to be 0.75 inch wide. Use the problem solving strategy *guess, check, and revise* to find the number of links your paper chain will have. **12 links**

C **39. Aviation** The Thunderbirds are a United States Air Force team of pilots who fly in air shows around the world. The type of plane they fly, the F-16 Falcon, can climb at a rate of about 800 feet per second.

a. Suppose the Thunderbirds perform a straight-up climb from an altitude of 200 feet to an altitude of 13,000 feet. Let x represent the time (in seconds) that it takes to complete this maneuver. Use the verbal model below to write an equation you can use to find x. **$200 + 800x = 13{,}000$**

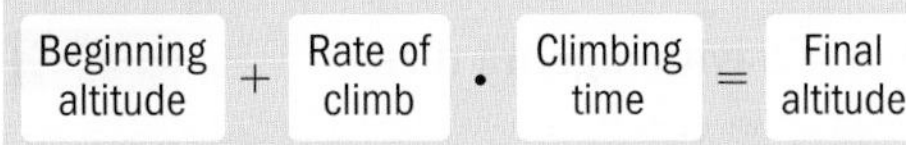

b. Use the *table* feature on a graphing calculator to evaluate the left side of your equation for different values of x. What is the solution of the equation? How long does it take the Thunderbirds to complete the climb? **See margin for art; 16; 16 sec.**

Thunderbirds

40. Challenge Solve the equation $2x + 3 = 11$ using mental math. Explain the reasoning you used to find the solution. **See margin.**

40. 4. *Sample answer:* First, I thought of $2x$ as an unknown number and asked myself, "3 more than what number is 11?" Because this number is 8, I knew that $2x$ must be equal to 8. Then I asked myself, "Twice what number is 8?" This number is 4, the solution of the original equation.

Mixed Review

Evaluate the expression when $x = -5$ and $y = -3$. *(Lessons 1.5, 1.6)*

41. $x + y$ **−8** **42.** $x - y + 6$ **4** **43.** $-x + 2 + 3y$ **−2**

Evaluate the expression using the distributive property and mental math. *(Lesson 2.2)*

44. 8(104) **832** **45.** 5(197) **985** **46.** 4(2.8) **11.2**

Simplify the expression. *(Lesson 2.3)*

47. $5c + 2 + 7c$ **$12c + 2$** **48.** $13k - 8k - k$ **$4k$** **49.** $6x - 3 + 4x + 1$ **$10x - 2$**

50. $3(y + 7) + 11y$ **$14y + 21$** **51.** $p - 6 - (4 + p)$ **−10** **52.** $2n - 7(n - 8)$ **$-5n + 56$**

Standardized Test Practice

53. Multiple Choice Two more than a number is 8. Which equation can you solve to find the number? **B**

A. $2x = 8$ **B.** $x + 2 = 8$ **C.** $x + 8 = 2$ **D.** $2 + 8 = x$

54. Multiple Choice What is the solution of the equation $12p = 60$? **H**

F. 3 **G.** 4 **H.** 5 **I.** 6

4 ASSESS

Assessment Resources

For more assessment resources, see:

- Assessment Book
- Test and Practice Generator

Mini-Quiz

Solve the equation using mental math.

1. $a + 11 = 19$ **8**

2. $34 - b = 27$ **7**

3. $-3c = 12$ **−4**

4. $\frac{63}{d} = 7$ **9**

5. Challenge Solve the equation $3y - 2 = 13$. **5**

5 FOLLOW-UP

Diagnosis/Remediation

- Study Guide in Chapter 2 Resource Book, pp. 39–40
- Tutor Place, Algebra Card 7
- eTutorial Plus Online
- Extra Practice, p. 804
- Lesson Practice in Chapter 2 Resource Book, pp. 36–38

English Learner Support

- Spanish Study Guide
- Multi-Language Visual Glossary
- Chapter Audio Summaries CDs

Challenge

- Challenge Practice in Chapter 2 Resource Book, p. 41
- Teacher's Edition, p. 60F

39b. *Sample:*

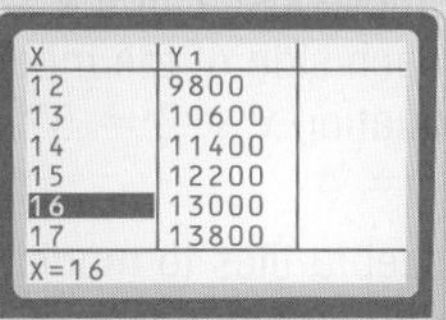

X | Y1
12 | 9800
13 | 10600
14 | 11400
15 | 12200
16 | 13000
17 | 13800
X=16

1 PLAN

Investigate the Concept

- Students will model and solve addition equations.
- This activity leads into solving equations using addition or subtraction in Lesson 2.5.

Materials

Each student will need algebra tiles. A support transparency is available in the Teaching Tools section of the *Warm-Up Transparencies with Daily Homework Quiz*.

Recommended Time

Work activity: 10 min
Discuss results: 10 min

Grouping

Students should work individually.

2 TEACH

Discussion

As students are working, you may wish to ask them why three 1-tiles are removed from each side instead of one or two 1-tiles. **If only one or two 1-tiles are removed, then the *x*-tile is not by itself.**

3 CLOSE

Key Discovery

Simple addition equations can be solved by using subtraction to isolate the variable on one side.

Assessment

1. What equation results when you remove just 1 of the 1-tiles from each side of the model for the equation $x + 3 = 5$? $x + 2 = 4$
2. Use algebra tiles to model and solve the equation $9 = x + 4$. **5**

10, 11. See Additional Answers beginning on page AA1.

Concept *Activity*

2.5 Modeling Addition Equations

Goal
Model and solve addition equations.

Materials
- algebra tiles

You can use algebra tiles to model and solve simple addition equations.

x-tile — An x-tile represents the variable x.

1-tile — A 1-tile represents the number 1.

Investigate

Use algebra tiles to solve $x + 3 = 5$.

1 Model $x + 3 = 5$ with algebra tiles.

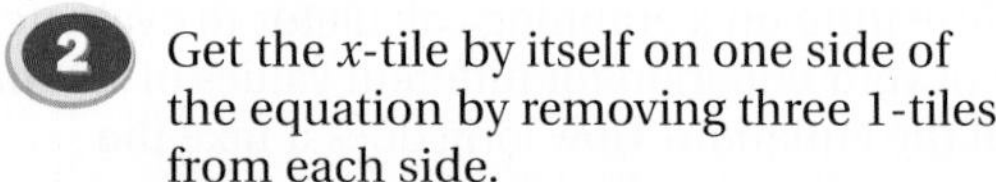

2 Get the x-tile by itself on one side of the equation by removing three 1-tiles from each side.

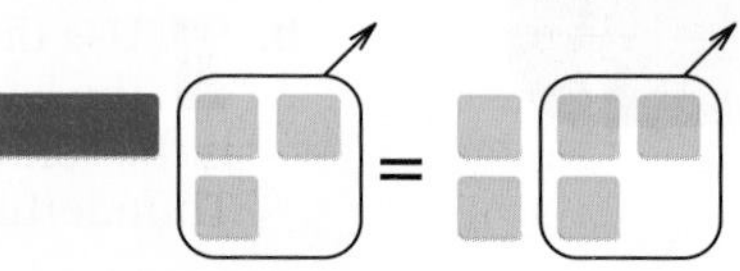

3 The x-tile is equal to two 1-tiles. So, the solution of $x + 3 = 5$ is 2.

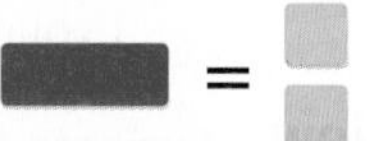

Draw Conclusions

1. Which model would you use to represent the equation $x + 2 = 4$? **A**

A.

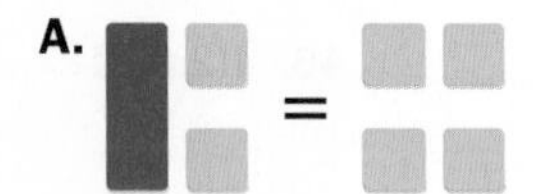

B.

Use algebra tiles to model and solve the equation.

2. $x + 1 = 4$ **3**
3. $x + 2 = 6$ **4**
4. $x + 5 = 7$ **2**
5. $x + 4 = 10$ **6**
6. $3 + x = 8$ **5**
7. $2 + x = 11$ **9**
8. $8 = x + 7$ **1**
9. $16 = 9 + x$ **7**
10. ***Writing*** In Step 2, why is it necessary to subtract three 1-tiles from *each* side of the equation, rather than from just the left side? **See margin.**
11. **Critical Thinking** Describe how you can use algebra tiles to solve the equation $2 + x + 4 = 9$. Then solve. **See margin.**

NCTM CURRICULUM STANDARDS
Standard 2: Use models to understand relationships; Use models to represent relationships

LESSON

2.5 Solving Equations Using Addition *or* Subtraction

Vocabulary
inverse operations, p. 91
equivalent equations, p. 91

BEFORE	*Now*	WHY?
You solved equations using mental math.	You'll solve equations using addition or subtraction.	So you can determine the size of a star, as in Ex. 30.

Horses One method for weighing a horse is to put it in a trailer of known weight and weigh the horse and trailer together on a truck scale. As you'll see in Example 3, the horse's weight can then be found by using an *inverse operation* to solve an equation.

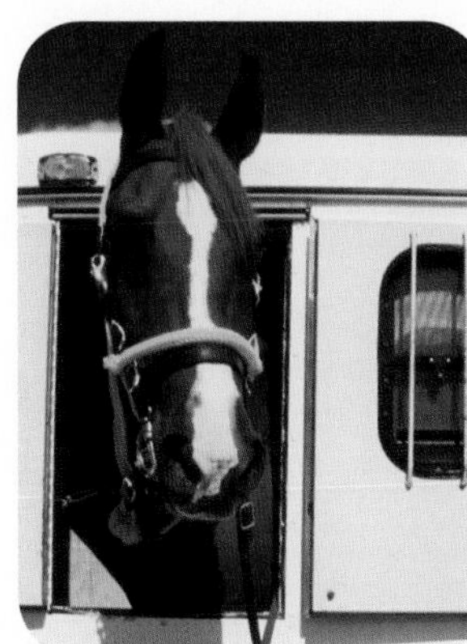

Inverse operations are two operations that undo each other, such as addition and subtraction. When you perform the same inverse operation on each side of an equation, you obtain an *equivalent equation*. **Equivalent equations** have the same solution.

Subtraction Property of Equality

Words Subtracting the same number from each side of an equation produces an equivalent equation.

Numbers If $x + 3 = 5$, then $x + 3 - 3 = 5 - 3$, or $x = 2$.

Algebra If $x + a = b$, then $x + a - a = b - a$, or $x = b - a$.

Reading *Algebra*

Vocabulary When you solve an equation, your goal is to write an equivalent equation that has the variable by itself on one side. This process is called *solving for the variable*.

Example 1 *Solving an Equation Using Subtraction*

Solve $x + 9 = -3$.

$x + 9 = -3$	**Write original equation.**
$x + 9 - 9 = -3 - 9$	**Subtract 9 from each side.**
$x = -12$	**Simplify.**

Answer The solution is -12.

✓ **Check**	$x + 9 = -3$	**Write original equation.**
	$-12 + 9 \stackrel{?}{=} -3$	**Substitute -12 for x.**
	$-3 = -3$ ✓	**Solution checks.**

NCTM CURRICULUM STANDARDS
Standard 1: Understand meanings of operations; Understand how operations are related
Standard 2: Represent situations using algebraic symbols

1 PLAN

Skill Check

1. $-4 + 11 = \underline{?}$ **7**
2. $-12 + (-8) = \underline{?}$ **−20**
3. $2 + (-16) = \underline{?}$ **−14**
4. $-7 - (-3) = \underline{?}$ **−4**

Lesson Objective

Solve equations using addition or subtraction.

Pacing

Suggested Number of Days
Basic Course: 1 day
Average Course: 1 day
Advanced Course: 1 day
Block: 0.5 block with 2.6

Teaching Resources

For a complete list of Teaching Resources, see page 60B.

Transparency

Warm-Up Exercises for this lesson are available on a transparency.

2 TEACH

Motivating the Lesson

Ask students: "If a box containing a book weighs 3 pounds and the box alone weighs 1 pound, how much does the book weigh?" **2 lb** Have students explain how they determined their answer.

TIPS *for* NEW TEACHERS

Draw students' attention to the Reading Algebra box to the left of Example 1. Throughout this lesson, continually remind students of this goal. See Tips for New Teachers in the *Chapter 2 Resource Book*.

Extra Examples

Example 1 Solve $k + 22 = -10$. **-32**

Example 2 Solve $62 = m - 15$. **77**

Example 3 Last month, Tyrone's bill for long-distance phone calls and Internet service was \$55.25. The Internet service charge was \$19.95. What was the cost of Tyrone's long-distance calls? **\$35.30**

ALGEBRAIC REASONING

Prior to Example 1, discuss the subtraction property of equality. Write the equation $x + 3 = 5$ on the board and solve it, writing one line below the other, so students can see how the subtraction property is applied. Then repeat this work, using the equation $x + a = b$, to lead students to think in more general, algebraic terms.

CONCEPT CHECK

How is the addition property of equality used to solve an equation? ***Sample answer:*** **The property justifies the addition of the same number to each side of an equation to produce an equivalent equation that is simpler than the original.**

DAILY PUZZLER

Playing with a balance scale, Angela finds that 3 carrot sticks and 1 tangerine weigh the same as 10 celery sticks. She also finds that 1 carrot stick and 6 celery sticks weigh the same as 1 tangerine. How many celery sticks would weigh the same as 1 tangerine? **7 celery sticks**

Addition Property Just as you can use the subtraction property of equality to solve an equation involving addition, you can use the *addition property of equality* to solve an equation involving subtraction.

Addition Property of Equality

Words Adding the same number to each side of an equation produces an equivalent equation.

Numbers If $x - 3 = 5$, then $x - 3 + 3 = 5 + 3$, or $x = 8$.

Algebra If $x - a = b$, then $x - a + a = b + a$, or $x = b + a$.

Example 2 *Solving an Equation Using Addition*

Solve $23 = y - 11$.

$23 = y - 11$	**Write original equation.**
$23 + 11 = y - 11 + 11$	**Add 11 to each side.**
$34 = y$	**Simplify.**

Answer The solution is 34.

Example 3 *Writing and Solving an Equation*

You weigh a horse using the method described on page 91. The weight of the trailer alone is 2150 pounds. The combined weight of the horse and trailer is 3375 pounds. What is the weight of the horse?

Solution

Let w represent the horse's weight (in pounds). Write a verbal model. Then use the verbal model to write an equation.

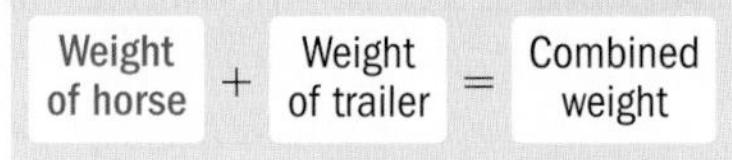

$w + 2150 = 3375$	**Substitute.**
$w + 2150 - 2150 = 3375 - 2150$	**Subtract 2150 from each side.**
$w = 1225$	**Simplify.**

Answer The weight of the horse is 1225 pounds.

In the **Real World**

Horses One of the smallest horses is the Shetland pony. If a typical Shetland pony is weighed using the trailer in Example 3, the combined weight of the pony and trailer would be about 2550 pounds. About how much does a Shetland pony weigh? **400 lb**

 ***Checkpoint***

Solve the equation. Check your solution.

1. $x + 8 = 19$ **11** **2.** $-7 = y + 13$ **-20** **3.** $n - 4 = -11$ **-7** **4.** $26 = p - 61$ **87**

5. While holding his cat, Ben steps on a scale. The scale reads 161 pounds. Ben weighs 148 pounds. What is the weight of the cat? **13 lb**

2.5 Exercises

More Practice, p. 804

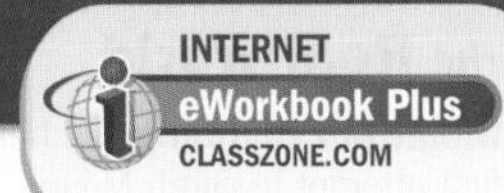

Guided Practice

Vocabulary Check

1. Copy and complete: Addition and subtraction are _?_ operations. inverse
2. Which property of equality would you use to solve $x - 5 = 7$? Explain. See margin.

Skill Check **Solve the equation. Check your solution.**

3. $x + 4 = 10$ 6
4. $t + 9 = -5$ −14
5. $u - 3 = 6$ 9
6. $y - 7 = -2$ 5
7. $16 = a + 25$ −9
8. $-70 = b - 30$ −40
9. **Error Analysis** Describe and correct the error in solving $x + 8 = 10$. See margin.

$x + 8 = 10$
$x + 8 - 8 = 10 + 8$
$x = 18$

10. **Population** From 1990 to 2000, the population of Cresco, Iowa, increased by 236. The population in 2000 was 3905. Use an equation to find the population in 1990. 3669 people

2. Addition property of equality. *Sample answer:* 5 is subtracted from *x*, so I need to perform the inverse operation of subtraction, which is addition, to get *x* alone on one side of the equation. I must add 5 to each side of the equation.

Practice and Problem Solving

Homework Help

Example	Exercises
1	11-25, 32-37
2	11-25, 32-37
3	26-30, 38-42

- More Examples
- eTutorial Plus

Solve the equation. Check your solution.

A
11. $x + 7 = 12$ 5
12. $y + 9 = 0$ −9
13. $-2 = z + 6$ −8
14. $a - 5 = 8$ 13
15. $b - 14 = -3$ 11
16. $37 = c - 29$ 66
17. $21 + m = 4$ −17
18. $n - 72 = 72$ 144
19. $p - 24 = -53$ −29
20. $q + 8 = 57$ 49
21. $r - 23 = -6$ 17
22. $28 = g + 28$ 0
23. $-13 + t = 10$ 23
24. $216 = u - 129$ 345
25. $177 = 403 + w$ −226
26. **Rebates** The advertised price of a DVD player is $185 after a $30 mail-in rebate. Using the verbal model below, write and solve an equation to find the price of the DVD player before the rebate is applied. $x - 30 = 185$, $215

Price before rebate	−	Rebate amount	=	Price after rebate

27. **Biology** When attacked by a giant hornet, Japanese honeybees cluster together to form a ball around the hornet and then generate heat by buzzing. The honeybees can endure temperatures of up to 48°C, which is 3°C greater than the hornet can tolerate. Find the maximum temperature tolerated by a Japanese giant hornet. 45°C
28. **Archaeology** The Great Pyramid in Egypt was built around 2560 B.C. Over the years, it has lost 30 feet of height off its top and is now 451 feet tall. Find the original height of the Great Pyramid. 481 ft

9. The number 8 was subtracted from the left side of the equation, but added to the right side. It should have been subtracted from each side, giving $x + 8 - 8 = 10 - 8$, which simplifies to $x = 2$.

3 APPLY

ASSIGNMENT GUIDE

Basic Course

Day 1: EP p. 803 Exs. 20-27; pp. 93-95 Exs. 11-19, 24-28, 32-38, 46-64

Average Course

Day 1: pp. 93-95 Exs. 17-22, 26-34, 38-44, 48-64

Advanced Course

Day 1: pp. 93-95 Exs. 17-19, 23-31, 35-45*, 48-53, 56-65

Block

pp. 93-95 Exs. 17-22, 26-34, 38-44, 48-64 (with 2.6)

Extra Practice

- Student Edition, p. 804
- Chapter 2 Resource Book, pp. 44-46
- Test and Practice Generator

Transparency

Even-numbered answers are available on transparencies.

Homework Check

When you review students' homework for this lesson, go over the following exercises to check understanding of key concepts.
Basic: 11, 14, 26, 32, 33
Average: 17, 21, 27, 34, 40
Advanced: 17, 19, 28, 37, 41

Teaching Tip

In Exercise 22, the correct answer is 0. Students may be unsure that 0 is an acceptable answer.

TEACHING TIP

Be certain that students are doing Exercises 32–37 in an efficient manner. Suggest that they combine the constant terms on the side with the variable before using the subtraction or addition property of equality to solve the equation.

COMMON ERROR

In Exercise 40, students who give an answer of 242 for *x* used only two sides of the rectangle as the perimeter. Remind students that the perimeter of a rectangle involves all four sides and that the opposite sides are equal in length.

In the Real World

Mountain Climbing On her first attempt to climb Mount Everest, Stacy Allison (shown below) was trapped in a cave for 5 days during a storm. The cave was at an altitude of 23,500 feet. How far from the summit was the cave? **5535 ft**

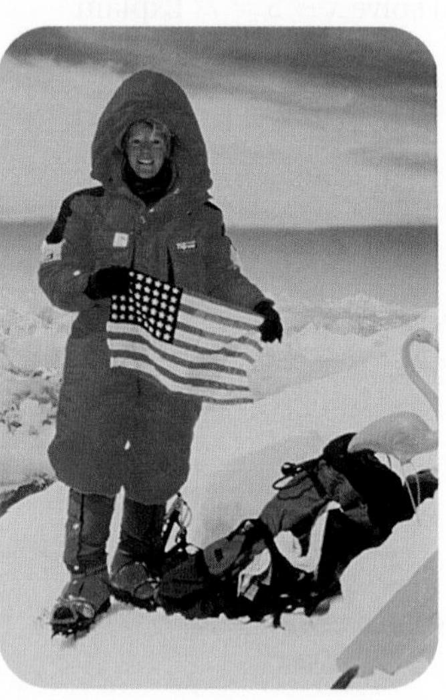

29. Mountain Climbing In 1988, Stacy Allison became the first woman from the United States to reach the summit of Mount Everest, which is 29,035 feet high. One year earlier, she and a team of Americans had attempted to climb Mount Everest but were forced to turn back at an altitude of 26,000 feet due to severe storms. How close to the summit did Stacy Allison get on her first attempt? **3035 ft**

B **30. Astronomy** Cepheid stars appear to pulsate because they expand and contract in size. In its contracted phase, the Cepheid star Zeta Geminorum is 51 million miles across. This is 5 million miles less than the star's distance across in its expanded phase. Find the distance across Zeta Geminorum in its expanded phase. **56 million miles**

31. *Writing* In Example 1 on page 91, the subtraction property of equality is used to solve $x + 9 = -3$. Explain how you can also solve this equation using the addition property of equality. **You can add −9 to each side of the equation.**

Solve the equation. Check your solution.

32. $a + 5 + 8 = 20$ **7** **33.** $3 + c + 6 = -9$ **−18** **34.** $9 + x - 4 = 2$ **−3**

35. $n - 6 - 1 = 5$ **12** **36.** $0 = r + 7 - 32$ **25** **37.** $-5 = -17 + y + 8$ **4**

Geometry Find the value of *x* for the given triangle or rectangle.

38. Perimeter = 34 in. **9 in.**

39. Perimeter = 59 cm **24 cm**

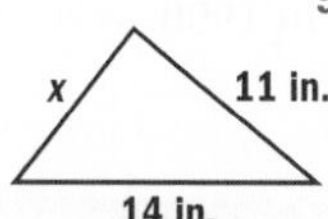

40. Perimeter = 352 ft **66 ft**

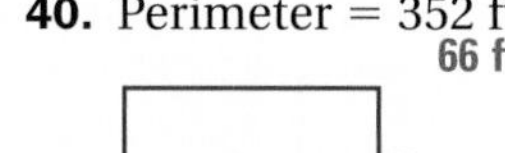

x, 11 in., 14 in. | x, 110 ft

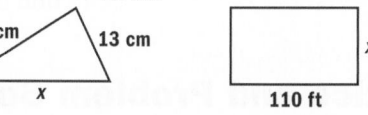

41. Extended Problem Solving Doctors measure the cholesterol in your blood to see if you are at risk for heart disease. The formula below gives your total cholesterol level in terms of your LDL (or "bad") cholesterol, your HDL (or "good") cholesterol, and your triglycerides.

$$\text{Total cholesterol} = \text{LDL} + \text{HDL} + \frac{\text{Triglycerides}}{5}$$

All values are measured in milligrams per deciliter (mg/dL) of blood.

41a. $190 = x + 45 + \frac{125}{5}$

a. When your cholesterol is checked by a doctor, the total cholesterol, HDL cholesterol, and triglycerides are measured directly. The LDL cholesterol is then calculated from these values. Write an equation that you can use to find the LDL level for the patient whose lab results are shown.

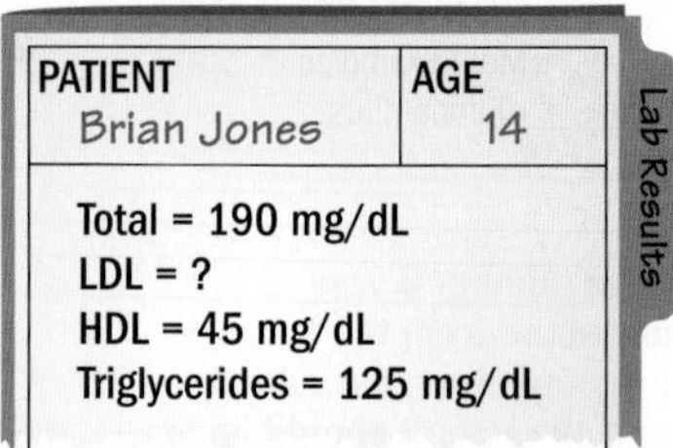

PATIENT
Brian Jones
AGE
14
Total = 190 mg/dL
LDL = ?
HDL = 45 mg/dL
Triglycerides = 125 mg/dL
Lab Results

b. Solve Find the patient's LDL level by solving your equation from part (a). **120 mg/dL**

c. Interpret For teenagers, LDL levels below 110 mg/dL are considered acceptable. Levels from 110 mg/dL to 129 mg/dL are borderline, and levels of 130 mg/dL or greater are too high. Classify the LDL level of the given patient as *acceptable, borderline,* or *too high.* **borderline**

Vasa **Museum in Stockholm, Sweden**

42. History In 1628, the Swedish ship *Vasa* sank in Stockholm Harbor in 105 feet of water. In 1959, salvagers used pontoons and cables to move the *Vasa* to a shallower depth of 50 feet. Underwater repairs were then made to strengthen the ship, and in 1961 the *Vasa* was lifted to the surface.

a. Find the change in the *Vasa*'s position with respect to sea level as a result of the salvage work done in 1959. **55 ft**

b. Find the number of years the *Vasa* remained underwater. **333 y**

43. Critical Thinking In Example 2 on page 92, you saw that the equation $34 = y$ is equivalent to $23 = y - 11$. Write an equation that has $y + 5$ as its right side and is also equivalent to $23 = y - 11$. **$39 = y + 5$**

C **44. Quilting** You are making a quilt and have \$150 to spend on materials. To make the main body of the quilt, you buy 5 yards of solid-color fabric for \$4 per yard and 12 yards of printed fabric for \$8 per yard. You also buy 2 yards of batting (material used to stuff the quilt) for \$11 per yard. How much can you spend on fabric for a decorative border? **\$12**

45. Challenge In the United States, annual sales of tennis shoes increased by \$4 million from 1996 to 1997, decreased by \$30 million from 1997 to 1998, decreased by \$10 million from 1998 to 1999, and increased by \$15 million from 1999 to 2000. In 2000, sales of tennis shoes were \$520 million. Find the sales of tennis shoes in 1996. **\$541 million**

Mixed Review

Write the product using an exponent. *(Lesson 1.2)*

46. $6 \cdot 6 \cdot 6 \cdot 6$ **6^4** **47.** $(0.3)(0.3)$ **0.3^2** **48.** $x \cdot x \cdot x$ **x^3** **49.** $t \cdot t \cdot t \cdot t \cdot t \cdot t$ **t^6**

Evaluate the power. *(Lesson 1.2)*

50. 2^6 **64** **51.** 7^4 **2401** **52.** $(0.8)^2$ **0.64** **53.** $(2.5)^3$ **15.625**

State the opposite of the number. *(Lesson 1.4)*

54. 8 **−8** **55.** −27 **27** **56.** 0 **0** **57.** 144 **−144**

Evaluate the expression when $x = 4$ and $y = -7$. *(Lesson 1.4)*

58. $|x|$ **4** **59.** $|y|$ **7** **60.** $|y| + |-y|$ **14** **61.** $|y| - |-x|$ **3**

62. Dolphins A dolphin can swim at a constant speed of 20 miles per hour for long periods of time. How long does it take a dolphin to swim 60 miles? *(Lesson 2.4)* **3 h**

Standardized Test Practice

63. Multiple Choice What is the solution of $x + 18 = -13$? **A**

A. −31 **B.** −5 **C.** 5 **D.** 31

64. Multiple Choice What is the solution of $-21 = a - 47$? **H**

F. −68 **G.** −26 **H.** 26 **I.** 68

65. Short Response A company hired 140 employees during a year in which 93 employees retired or left the company for other reasons. At the end of the year, the company had 816 employees. Find the number of employees the company had at the beginning of the year. Show and justify each step of your solution. **See margin.**

4 ASSESS

Assessment Resources

For more assessment resources, see:
- Assessment Book
- Test and Practice Generator

Mini-Quiz

Solve the equation.

1. $b + 12 = 31$ **19**
2. $24 + c = -9$ **−33**
3. $d - 19 = 20$ **39**
4. $-44 = f - 6$ **−38**
5. Challenge During May, Shawna deposited \$500 into her account, and withdrew \$120, \$60, and \$40. Her balance at the end of May was \$410. What was her balance at the beginning of May? **\$130**

5 FOLLOW-UP

Diagnosis/Remediation

- Study Guide in Chapter 2 Resource Book, pp. 47–48
- Tutor Place, Algebra Cards 7–9, 12
- eTutorial Plus Online
- Extra Practice, p. 804
- Lesson Practice in Chapter 2 Resource Book, pp. 44–46

English Learner Support

- Spanish Study Guide
- Multi-Language Visual Glossary
- Chapter Audio Summaries CDs

Challenge

- Challenge Practice in Chapter 2 Resource Book, p. 49
- Teacher's Edition, p. 60F

65. See Additional Answers beginning on page AA1.

1 PLAN

Investigate the Concept

- Students will model and solve multiplication equations.
- This activity leads into solving equations using multiplication or division in Lesson 2.6.

Materials

Each student will need algebra tiles. A support transparency is available in the Teaching Tools section of the *Warm-Up Transparencies with Daily Homework Quiz*.

Recommended Time

Work activity: 10 min
Discuss results: 10 min

Grouping

Students should work individually.

2 TEACH

Tips for Success

Make sure students understand that in any equation, a variable such as x represents an unknown number. In the equation $3x = 12$, point out that the x-tile represents an unknown number of 1-tiles.

3 CLOSE

Key Discovery

Simple multiplication equations can be solved by dividing each side by the coefficient of x.

Assessment

1. How many x-tiles would you need in order to model the equation $4x = 20$? **4**
2. To solve the equation $4x = 20$, into how many groups would you divide the x-tiles and the 1-tiles? **4 groups each**

10. See Additional Answers beginning on page AA1.

Concept Activity

2.6 Modeling Multiplication Equations

Goal
Model and solve multiplication equations.

Materials
- algebra tiles

You can use algebra tiles to model and solve simple multiplication equations. For a description of algebra tiles, see page 90.

Investigate

Use algebra tiles to solve $3x = 12$.

1. Model $3x = 12$ with algebra tiles.

2. There are three x-tiles, so divide the x-tiles and 1-tiles into three equal groups.

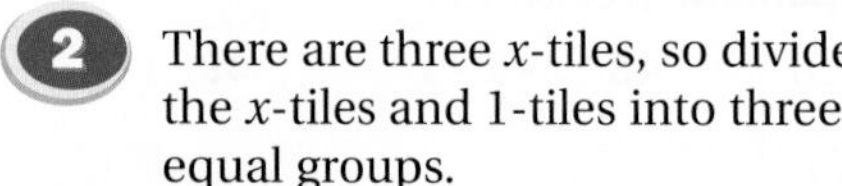

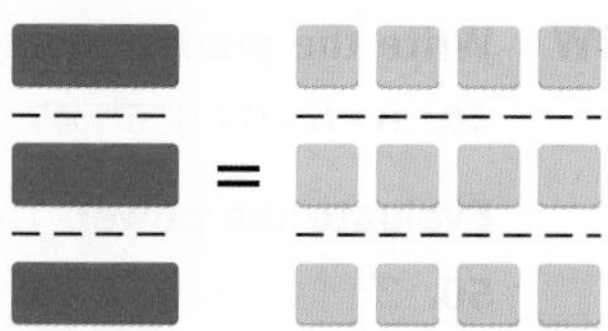

3. One x-tile is equal to four 1-tiles. So, the solution of $3x = 12$ is 4.

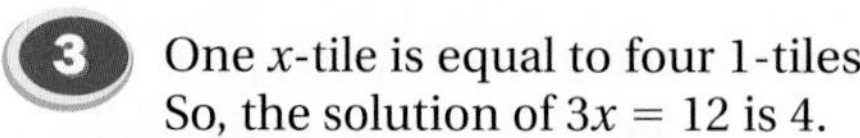

Draw Conclusions

Use algebra tiles to model and solve the equation.

1. $2x = 4$ **2**
2. $2x = 10$ **5**
3. $3x = 18$ **6**
4. $4x = 12$ **3**
5. $6x = 6$ **1**
6. $5x = 20$ **4**
7. $21 = 7x$ **3**
8. $21 = 3x$ **7**
9. *Writing* For each algebra-tile equation in the example shown above, write a corresponding algebraic equation. Based on your results, describe an algebraic method that you can use to solve $8x = 56$. Then use your method to find the equation's solution.
10. **Critical Thinking** Describe how you can use algebra tiles to solve the equation $2x + 3x = 15$. Then solve. **See margin.**

9. Step 1: $3x = 12$; Step 2: $\frac{3x}{3} = \frac{12}{3}$; Step 3: $x = 4$. *Sample answer:* Model $8x = 56$ with algebra tiles. There are eight x-tiles, so divide the x-tiles and 1-tiles into eight equal groups. One x-tile is equal to seven 1-tiles. The solution is $x = 7$.

NCTM CURRICULUM STANDARDS
Standard 2: Use models to understand relationships; Use models to represent relationships

LESSON

2.6 Solving Equations Using Multiplication *or* Division

Review Vocabulary
solving an equation, p. 86
inverse operations, p. 91
equivalent equations, p. 91

BEFORE	Now	WHY?
You solved addition and subtraction equations.	You'll solve equations using multiplication or division.	So you can find how long it takes whales to migrate, as in Ex. 35.

Astronomy In 1995, the Solar and Heliospheric Observatory (SOHO) was launched into space. SOHO studies the sun, including high-speed gas called solar wind that is ejected from the sun and travels throughout the solar system.

In Example 3, you'll see how to use a multiplication equation to find how long it takes solar wind to reach Earth. You can use division to solve such an equation, because multiplication and division are inverse operations.

Division Property of Equality

Words Dividing each side of an equation by the same nonzero number produces an equivalent equation.

Numbers If $3x = 12$, then $\frac{3x}{3} = \frac{12}{3}$, or $x = 4$.

Algebra If $ax = b$ and $a \neq 0$, then $\frac{ax}{a} = \frac{b}{a}$, or $x = \frac{b}{a}$.

Watch *Out*

Remember that you cannot divide a number or an expression by 0.

Example 1 *Solving an Equation Using Division*

Solve $-6x = 48$.

$-6x = 48$ **Write original equation.**

$\frac{-6x}{-6} = \frac{48}{-6}$ **Divide each side by −6.**

$x = -8$ **Simplify.**

Answer The solution is −8.

✓Check $-6x = 48$ **Write original equation.**

$-6(-8) \stackrel{?}{=} 48$ **Substitute −8 for *x*.**

$48 = 48$ ✓ **Solution checks.**

NCTM CURRICULUM STANDARDS
Standard 1: Understand meanings of operations; Understand how operations are related
Standard 2: Represent situations using algebraic symbols

1 PLAN

Skill Check

1. $56 \div (-8) = ?$ −7
2. $96 \div 12 = ?$ 8
3. $(-9)8 = ?$ −72
4. $-13(-4) = ?$ 52

LESSON OBJECTIVE

Solve equations using multiplication or division.

PACING

Suggested Number of Days
Basic Course: 1 day
Average Course: 1 day
Advanced Course: 1 day
Block: 0.5 block with 2.5

TEACHING RESOURCES

For a complete list of Teaching Resources, see page 60B.

TRANSPARENCY

Warm-Up Exercises for this lesson are available on a transparency.

2 TEACH

MOTIVATING THE LESSON

Ask students if they have ever needed to divide a large group of items, like marbles, among several people. Ask them to describe the method they used to accomplish the task. Stress the use of division in the techniques that they describe.

TIPS *for* NEW TEACHERS

It may be necessary to remind students frequently during the lesson that the goal is to solve the equation for the variable. See Tips for New Teachers in the *Chapter 2 Resource Book*.

Extra Examples

Example 1 Solve $12w = -96$. **-8**

Example 2 Solve $\frac{a}{12} = 11$. **132**

Example 3 Li-Shyung bicycled at an average speed of 4 miles per hour to get to a post office that was 1 mile from home. How long did it take her to reach the post office? **15 min**

TEACHING TIP

As you discuss the division property of equality, make sure students understand why the value of the denominator cannot be 0.

CONCEPT CHECK

Which property would you use to solve the equation $\frac{x}{2} = 10$? Explain how the property is used to find the solution. **Multiplication property of equality. *Sample answer:* The property justifies multiplying both sides of the equation by the same number, in this case 2. The left side becomes x and the right side becomes 20. So the solution is $x = 20$.**

DAILY PUZZLER

Replace each variable in the expression $\frac{a}{b} + \frac{c}{d} + \frac{e}{f}$ with one of the numbers 4, 5, 6, 7, 8, and 9 so that the expression has the greatest possible value. Give the value. $\frac{9}{4} + \frac{8}{5} + \frac{7}{6}$; $\frac{301}{60}$ **or** $5\frac{1}{60}$

Multiplication Property To solve an equation that involves division, you can use the *multiplication property of equality.*

Multiplication Property of Equality

Words Multiplying each side of an equation by the same nonzero number produces an equivalent equation.

Numbers If $\frac{x}{3} = 12$, then $3 \cdot \frac{x}{3} = 3 \cdot 12$, or $x = 36$.

Algebra If $\frac{x}{a} = b$ and $a \neq 0$, then $a \cdot \frac{x}{a} = a \cdot b$, or $x = ab$.

Example 2 *Solving an Equation Using Multiplication*

Solve $9 = \frac{w}{7}$.

$9 = \frac{w}{7}$ **Write original equation.**

$7 \cdot 9 = 7 \cdot \frac{w}{7}$ **Multiply each side by 7.**

$63 = w$ **Simplify.**

Answer The solution is 63.

Checkpoint

Solve the equation. Check your solution.

1. $2x = 18$ 9 **2.** $-60 = -5a$ 12 **3.** $\frac{y}{2} = 13$ 26 **4.** $-8 = \frac{b}{8}$ -64

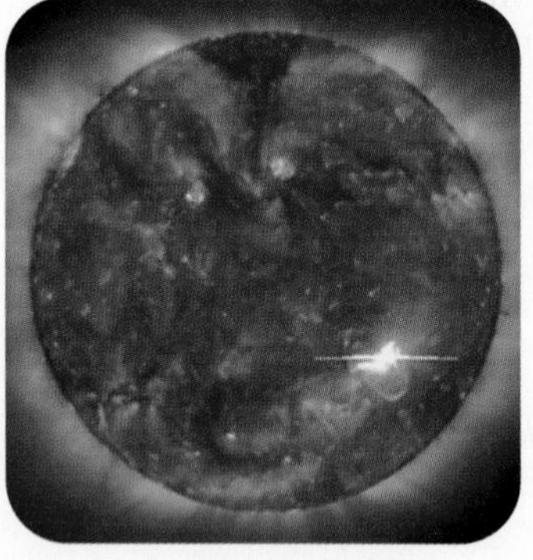

In the **Real World**

Astronomy The SOHO spacecraft took this photo of the sun using a special ultraviolet imaging telescope. Light from the sun travels at about 300,000 kilometers per second. How long does it take the sun's light to reach Earth? **about 500 sec, or 8 min 20 sec**

Example 3 *Writing and Solving an Equation*

On January 4, 2003, the SOHO spacecraft described on page 97 detected solar wind traveling at about 2 million kilometers per hour. The sun is about 150 million kilometers from Earth. About how long did it take the solar wind to reach Earth?

Solution

Let t be the time (in hours) that it took the solar wind to reach Earth.

$d = rt$ **Write formula for distance traveled.**

$150{,}000{,}000 = 2{,}000{,}000t$ **Substitute values.**

$\frac{150{,}000{,}000}{2{,}000{,}000} = \frac{2{,}000{,}000t}{2{,}000{,}000}$ **Divide each side by 2,000,000.**

$75 = t$ **Simplify.**

Answer It took the solar wind about 75 hours to reach Earth.

2.6 Exercises

More Practice, p. 804

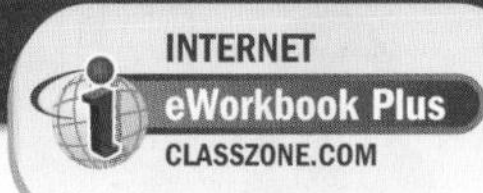

Guided Practice

Vocabulary Check

1. Copy and complete: Multiplication and _?_ are inverse operations. **division**

2. Which property of equality would you use to solve $\frac{x}{5} = 12$? Explain. **See margin.**

Skill Check

Solve the equation. Check your solution.

3. $5c = -15$ **−3** 4. $54 = 9x$ **6** 5. $6 = \frac{u}{4}$ **24** 6. $\frac{y}{-10} = 7$ **−70**

Guided Problem Solving

2. Multiplication property of equality. ***Sample answer:*** **x is divided by 5, so I need to perform the inverse operation of division, which is multiplication, to get x alone on one side of the equation. I must multiply each side of the equation by 5.**

7. **Printers** You buy the inkjet printer shown in the advertisement. You use it to print a 40 page document in black and white and a 20 page document in color. How long does it take to print both documents?

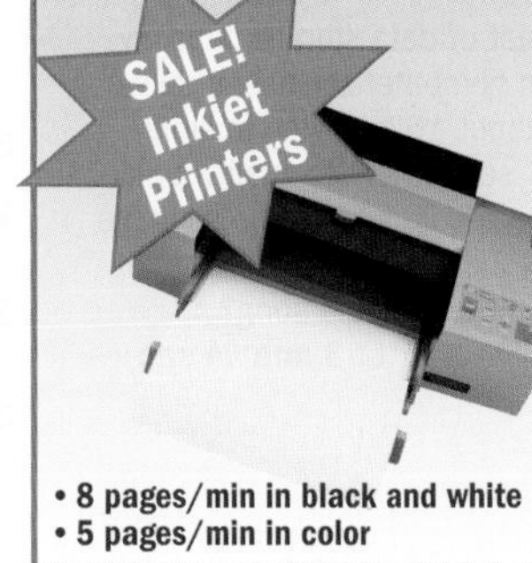

SALE!
Inkjet
Printers
• 8 pages/min in black and white
• 5 pages/min in color

(1) Write and solve an equation to find the time it takes to print the black and white document. **$8x = 40$, 5 min**

(2) Write and solve an equation to find the time it takes to print the color document. **$5x = 20$, 4 min**

(3) Find the time it takes to print both documents. **9 min**

Practice and Problem Solving

Homework Help

Example	Exercises
1	8-23, 28-33
2	8-23, 28-33
3	24-27, 34, 36

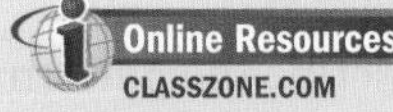

- More Examples
- eTutorial Plus

Solve the equation. Check your solution.

A 8. $3x = 27$ **9** 9. $4y = 52$ **13** 10. $-65 = 13u$ **−5** 11. $84 = -21v$ **−4**

12. $\frac{x}{7} = 5$ **35** 13. $\frac{y}{-3} = 8$ **−24** 14. $16 = \frac{p}{6}$ **96** 15. $-7 = \frac{q}{11}$ **−77**

16. $-23a = 0$ **0** 17. $-95 = -5b$ **19** 18. $-r = 38$ **−38** 19. $301 = 43s$ **7**

20. $\frac{c}{-2} = -91$ **182** 21. $17 = \frac{d}{17}$ **289** 22. $9 = \frac{m}{-36}$ **−324** 23. $\frac{n}{62} = -54$ **−3348**

24. **Football** During the 2002 regular season of the National Football League, running back Michael Bennett played in 16 games and averaged 81 rushing yards per game. Find his total rushing yards by using the verbal model below to write and solve an equation. **$81 = \frac{x}{16}$, 1296 yd**

Average rushing yards per game $=$ $\frac{\text{Total rushing yards}}{\text{Number of games played}}$

3 APPLY

ASSIGNMENT GUIDE

Basic Course

Day 1: EP p. 803 Exs. 28-31; pp. 99-101 Exs. 8-19, 24, 28-33, 40-57

Average Course

Day 1: pp. 99-101 Exs. 16-30, 34-38, 40-51, 56-58

Advanced Course

Day 1: pp. 99-101 Exs. 16-27, 31-43*, 50-58

Block

pp. 99-101 Exs. 16-30, 34-38, 40-51, 56-58 (with 2.5)

Extra Practice

- Student Edition, p. 804
- Chapter 2 Resource Book, pp. 52-54
- Test and Practice Generator

Transparency

Even-numbered answers are available on transparencies. A support transparency is available for Exercise 35.

Homework Check

When you review students' homework for this lesson, go over the following exercises to check understanding of key concepts.

Basic: 8, 13, 24, 28, 30
Average: 16, 22, 26, 28, 34
Advanced: 16, 23, 27, 33, 36

TEACHING TIP

Be certain that students solve Exercises 28–33 in an efficient manner. For example, in Exercise 32, point out to students that 6 and 11 should be added before applying the multiplication property of equality.

READING STRATEGY

For multi-part problems, such as Exercise 35, suggest students read the entire exercise before attempting to solve each part. This will give them an overall view of the exercise and help them determine how the various parts are related. For instance, in Exercise 35, part b is dependent on the result of part a, part c is dependent on part b, part d on part c, and part e on part d.

35c–d.

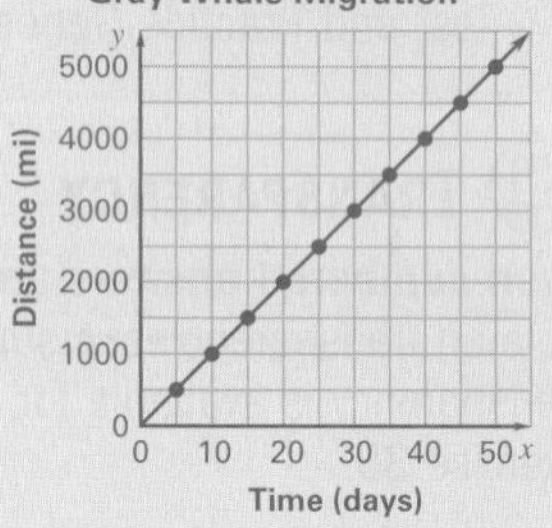

In the Real World

Computers A kilobyte is a unit of data storage capacity in computer science. It takes about 16 kilobytes to store 1 second of CD-quality music on a computer. If the song file in Ex. 27 is CD-quality, about how long is the song? **224 sec, or 3 min 44 sec**

34.a. $8x + (\frac{1}{2})(x)(6)$, $11x$

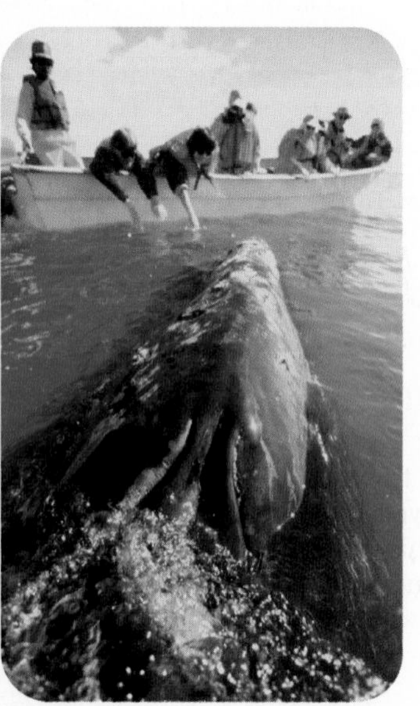

25. **Drilling** One type of thermal ice drill can drill through ice at a rate of 15 feet per minute by using heat to melt the ice. Find the time it takes the drill to melt through a sheet of ice 75 feet thick. **5 min**

26. **Reforestation** In 1998, fire destroyed 100 acres of the Oakwood National Wildlife Refuge in Arkansas. The U.S. Fish and Wildlife Service reforested this area by planting tree seedlings at a density of 300 seedlings per acre. Find the total number of seedlings planted. **30,000 seedlings**

B 27. **Computers** Your favorite rock band distributes one of its songs for free on its website. The size of the song file is 3584 kilobytes (KB). The table shows the maximum speed at which files can be downloaded using each type of Internet service offered in your town.

Type of service	Dial-up	DSL	Cable
Download speed (KB/sec)	7	96	188

To the nearest second, how long does it take to download the song file using dial-up service? using DSL service? using cable service? **512 sec, or 8 min 32 sec; 37 sec; about 19 sec**

Solve the equation. Check your solution.

28. $7x - 3x = 24$ **6**
29. $-110 = 12y + 10y$ **−5**
30. $-4(9g) = 252$ **−7**
31. $150 = 6(5h)$ **5**
32. $-3 = \frac{z}{6 + 11}$ **−51**
33. $\frac{w}{8} = 9 - (-4)$ **104**

34. **Geometry** The figure shown is composed of a triangle and a rectangle.

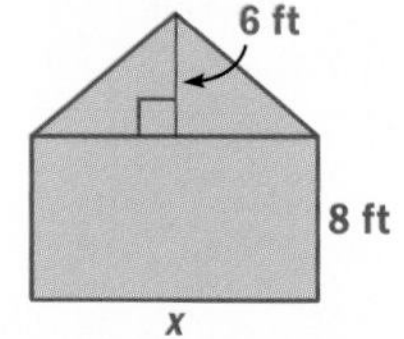

   a. Write and simplify an expression in terms of x for the area of the figure.
   b. What is the value of x if the area of the figure is 154 square feet? **14 ft**

35. **Extended Problem Solving** Each year gray whales migrate about 5000 miles from the Baja Peninsula of Mexico to their feeding grounds near Alaska. The whales travel about 100 miles per day.

   a. Write an expression for the distance the whales travel in x days. **100x mi**
   b. Copy and complete the table using your expression from part (a).

Travel time (days)	0	5	10	15	20	25
Distance traveled (miles)	?	?	?	?	?	?

0 500 1000 1500 2000 2500

   c. Make a scatter plot of the data in the table. Show travel time on the x-axis and distance traveled on the y-axis. Describe the pattern formed by the points in the scatter plot. **See art in part (d).** ***Sample answer:*** **The points all lie on a straight line that passes through the origin.**
   d. **Apply** Extend the pattern you described in part (c) by plotting points for $x = 30$, 35, and so on until you plot a point whose y-coordinate is 5000. How many days does it take the whales to migrate from the Baja Peninsula to Alaska? **See margin for art; 50 days.**
   e. **Reasonableness** Justify your solution to part (d) by solving the equation $100x = 5000$.
   Solving the equation $100x = 5000$ gives an answer of 50, so the answers are the same.

37. *Sample answer:* The Montoyas expect to average 50 miles per hour on their trip to the coast. If it is 400 miles to the coast, how long will the trip take? The solution is 8 hours.

36. Watches A wristwatch has a built-in digital camera with a rectangular viewfinder. An image shown by the viewfinder consists of 6240 tiny rectangular dots called pixels arranged in rows and columns. The viewfinder has 80 rows of pixels. How many columns does it have? **78 columns**

37. ***Writing*** Describe a real-life problem that can be solved using the equation $50x = 400$. Then solve the problem.

C **38. Lightning** On July 1, 2001, a Pennsylvania weather station detected an average of 80 lightning strikes per minute over a 24 hour period. Find the total number of lightning strikes detected during that time. **115,200 lightning strikes**

39. Challenge The problem below is a variation of one that appears in the ancient Chinese text *Nine Chapters on the Mathematical Art.* (In the problem, a *tou* is a Chinese unit of measure.)

> A goat, a horse, and a cow mistakenly enter a farmer's wheat field and eat some stalks of wheat. The horse eats twice as many stalks as the goat, and the cow eats twice as many stalks as the horse. The farmer demands 5 tou of wheat from the owners of the animals to replace what was eaten. How much wheat should be replaced by the goat's owner? by the horse's owner? by the cow's owner?

a. Let x be the amount of wheat (in *tou*) that should be replaced by the goat's owner. What is an expression in terms of x for the amount that should be replaced by the horse's owner? by the cow's owner? **$2x$; $4x$**

b. Write and solve an equation to find x. To the nearest tenth of a *tou*, how much wheat should be replaced by each animal's owner?
$x + 2x + 4x = 5$, $x \approx 0.714$; goat: 0.7 tou, horse: 1.4 tou, cow: 2.9 tou

Mixed Review

Perform the indicated operation. *(pp. 774–776)*

40. $2.9 + 8.4$ **11.3** **41.** $7.63 + 5.18$ **12.81** **42.** $13.8 - 9.3$ **4.5** **43.** $3.239 - 1.74$ **1.499**

44. 4.6×2.3 **10.58** **45.** 6.51×9.22 **60.0222** **46.** $53.6 \div 6.7$ **8** **47.** $8.16 \div 3.4$ **2.4**

Perform the indicated operation. *(Lessons 1.5–1.7)*

48. $-19 + 40$ **21** **49.** $-26 + (-7)$ **−33** **50.** $3 - 18$ **−15** **51.** $-12 - (-10)$ **−2**

52. $5(-14)$ **−70** **53.** $-23(-8)$ **184** **54.** $-90 \div 15$ **−6** **55.** $-36 \div (-4)$ **9**

56. Plants From 1994 to 2001, the number of plant species classified as endangered increased by 177. There were 593 endangered plant species in 2001. Find the number of endangered plant species in 1994. *(Lesson 2.5)* **416 endangered plant species**

Standardized Test Practice

57. Multiple Choice What is the solution of $\frac{x}{-2} = -8$? **D**

A. -16 **B.** -4 **C.** 4 **D.** 16

58. Multiple Choice Starting with a full tank of gas, your family's car is driven 420 miles and then refueled. It takes 12 gallons of gas to fill the car's tank. How many miles per gallon did the car get? **H**

F. 25 mi/gal **G.** 30 mi/gal **H.** 35 mi/gal **I.** 40 mi/gal

4 ASSESS

Assessment Resources

For more assessment resources, see:
- Assessment Book
- Test and Practice Generator

Mini-Quiz

Solve the equation.

1. $7k = 42$ **6**
2. $-11x = 66$ **−6**
3. $\frac{y}{20} = 7$ **140**
4. $21 = \frac{t}{-5}$ **−105**
5. **Challenge** Alison, Barone, and Chad shared a pizza that was cut into 12 slices. Barone had twice as many slices as Alison, while Chad had 4 more slices than Alison. How many slices did Alison have? **2 slices**

5 FOLLOW-UP

Diagnosis/Remediation

- Study Guide in Chapter 2 Resource Book, pp. 55–56
- Tutor Place, Algebra Cards 7, 10–13
- eTutorial Plus Online
- Extra Practice, p. 804
- Lesson Practice in Chapter 2 Resource Book, pp. 52–54

English Learner Support

- Spanish Study Guide
- Multi-Language Visual Glossary
- Chapter Audio Summaries CDs

Challenge

- Challenge Practice in Chapter 2 Resource Book, p. 58
- Teacher's Edition, p. 60F

1 PLAN

Skill Check

1. $2 + (-7) = \underline{?}$ -5
2. $-4 - (-9) = \underline{?}$ 5
3. $-10 + (-3) = \underline{?}$ -13
4. $8 - (-12) = \underline{?}$ 20

Lesson Objective

Solve equations involving decimals.

Pacing

Suggested Number of Days
Basic Course: 2 days
Average Course: 2 days
Advanced Course: 2 days
Block: 1 block

Teaching Resources

For a complete list of Teaching Resources, see page 60B.

Transparency

Warm-Up Exercises for this lesson are available on a transparency.

2 TEACH

Motivating the Lesson

Create a large number line on the board. Ask students to name some decimals between each pair of consecutive integers.

TIPS *for* NEW TEACHERS

Remind students that decimal operations are the same as integer operations with the exception that they need to place the decimal point correctly. See Tips for New Teachers in the *Chapter 2 Resource Book*.

LESSON **2.7**

Decimal Operations *and* Equations *with* Decimals

Review Vocabulary
absolute value, p. 23
solving an equation, p. 86
decimal, p. 770

BEFORE
You solved equations involving integers.

Now
You'll solve equations involving decimals.

WHY?
So you can find the speed of an airplane, as in Ex. 47.

Hibernation When a chipmunk hibernates, its heart rate decreases, its body temperature drops, and the chipmunk loses weight as its stored body fat is converted to energy. In Example 5, you'll see how to use an equation with decimals to describe a chipmunk's weight loss during hibernation.

You already know how to perform operations with positive decimals. However, just as there are negative integers, such as -2, there are also negative decimals, such as -2.5. The number line below shows several positive and negative decimals.

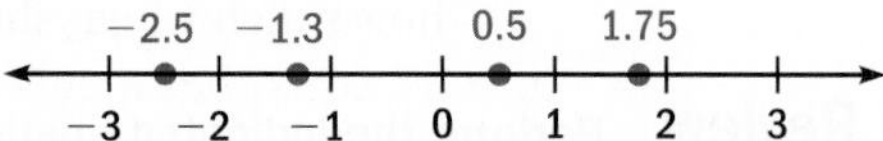

The rules for performing operations with decimals are the same as those you learned for integers in Chapter 1.

Review *Help*
For help with decimal operations, see pp. 774–776.

Example 1 ***Adding and Subtracting Decimals***

a. Find the sum $-2.9 + (-6.5)$.

Use the rule for adding numbers with the same sign.

$$-2.9 + (-6.5) = -9.4$$

Add $|-2.9|$ and $|-6.5|$.

Both decimals are negative, so the sum is negative.

b. Find the difference $-25.38 - (-42.734)$.

First rewrite the difference as a sum: $-25.38 + 42.734$. Then use the rule for adding numbers with different signs.

$$-25.38 + 42.734 = 17.354$$

Subtract $|-25.38|$ from $|42.734|$.

$|42.734| > |-25.38|$, so the sum has the same sign as 42.734.

NCTM CURRICULUM STANDARDS
Standard 1: Understand how operations are related; Compute fluently
Standard 2: Represent situations using algebraic symbols

 **Checkpoint**

Find the sum or difference.

1. $-1.3 + (-4.2)$ **−5.5** **2.** $10.57 + (-6.89)$ **3.68** **3.** $9.817 - (-1.49)$ **11.307**

Example 2 *Multiplying and Dividing Decimals*

Perform the indicated operation.

a. $-0.7(18.4)$ **b.** $-4.5(-9.25)$

c. $-29.07 \div (-1.9)$ **d.** $16.83 \div (-3.3)$

Solution

a. $-0.7(18.4) = -12.88$ **Different signs: Product is negative.**

b. $-4.5(-9.25) = 41.625$ **Same sign: Product is positive.**

c. $-29.07 \div (-1.9) = 15.3$ **Same sign: Quotient is positive.**

d. $16.83 \div (-3.3) = -5.1$ **Different signs: Quotient is negative.**

Study Strategy

Reasonableness You can use estimation to check the results of operations with decimals. In part (c) of Example 2, for instance, notice that $-29.07 \div (-1.9)$ is about $-30 \div (-2)$, or 15. So, an answer of 15.3 is reasonable.

Checkpoint

Find the product or quotient.

4. $3.1(-6.8)$ **−21.08** **5.** $-11.41 \div (-0.7)$ **16.3** **6.** $-15.841 \div 2.17$ **−7.3**

7. Critical Thinking Explain how you can use estimation to check that your answer to Exercise 4 is reasonable. ***Sample answer:*** **3.1(−6.8) is about 3(−7), or −21, so an answer of −21.08 is reasonable.**

Solving Equations You can use what you know about decimal operations to solve equations involving decimals.

Example 3 *Solving Addition and Subtraction Equations*

Solve the equation.

a. $x + 4.7 = 3.5$ **b.** $y - 6.91 = -2.26$

Solution

a.

$x + 4.7 = 3.5$ **Write original equation.**

$x + 4.7 - 4.7 = 3.5 - 4.7$ **Subtract 4.7 from each side.**

$x = -1.2$ **Simplify.**

b.

$y - 6.91 = -2.26$ **Write original equation.**

$y - 6.91 + 6.91 = -2.26 + 6.91$ **Add 6.91 to each side.**

$y = 4.65$ **Simplify.**

Study Strategy

Always check your solution when solving an equation. To check the solution in part (a) of Example 3, for instance, substitute −1.2 for *x* in the original equation.

$x + 4.7 = 3.5$

$-1.2 + 4.7 \stackrel{?}{=} 3.5$

$3.5 = 3.5$ ✓

Checkpoint

Solve the equation. Check your solution.

8. $x + 3.8 = 5.2$ **1.4** **9.** $a + 10.4 = -1.17$ **−11.57** **10.** $6.29 + c = 4.01$ **−2.28**

11. $y - 7.8 = 22.3$ **30.1** **12.** $r - 0.88 = -0.56$ **0.32** **13.** $-9.34 = t - 2.75$ **−6.59**

Extra Examples

Example 1

a. Find the sum $-14.2 + (-17.6)$. **−31.8**

b. Find the difference $4.75 - (-12.5)$. **17.25**

Example 2 Perform the indicated operation.

a. $7.2(-1.5)$ **−10.8**

b. $-9.2(-4.1)$ **37.72**

c. $43.29 \div (-4.5)$ **−9.62**

d. $-71.05 \div (-3.5)$ **20.3**

Example 3 Solve the equation.

a. $12.6 + m = 9.2$ **−3.4**

b. $r - 2.3 = -1.7$ **0.6**

Teaching Tip

In Example 1, students may be overwhelmed by the directive "Add $|-2.9|$ and $|-6.5|$." Consider breaking this instruction into simpler steps. For example, show how to find $29 + 65 = 94$, then $-29 + (-65) = -94$, and finally $-2.9 + (-6.5) = -9.4$.

Common Error

In Checkpoint Exercise 3, watch for students who line up the decimal points incorrectly.

Extra Examples

Example 4 Solve the equation.

a. $-12.2t = 9.76$ **-0.8**

b. $\frac{c}{-4} = -10.5$ **42**

Example 5 The trip odometer on a car showed 229.5 miles before a salesperson left for a sales meeting. When she reached her destination, the trip odometer read 273.2 miles. How far did she have to drive to attend the meeting? **43.7 mi**

CONCEPT CHECK

What is $-1.5 + (-1.5)$? **-3**

DAILY PUZZLER

Lauren needs to measure 1 ounce of flour for a recipe but she can only find the 2-ounce and 5-ounce weights for her balance scale. How can she measure the flour? ***Sample answer:*** **Place the 2-ounce and 5-ounce weights on opposite sides and measure 3 ounces of flour. Then remove the 5-ounce weight and replace it with the 2-ounce weight. Using the 3 ounces of flour, measure 2 ounces. What remains in the cup after 2 ounces are measured is 1 ounce.**

Example 4 *Solving Multiplication and Division Equations*

Solve the equation.

a. $-0.6m = -5.1$ **b.** $\frac{n}{-8} = 1.75$

Solution

a.

$-0.6m = -5.1$	**Write original equation.**
$\frac{-0.6m}{-0.6} = \frac{-5.1}{-0.6}$	**Divide each side by -0.6.**
$m = 8.5$	**Simplify.**

b.

$\frac{n}{-8} = 1.75$	**Write original equation.**
$-8\left(\frac{n}{-8}\right) = -8(1.75)$	**Multiply each side by -8.**
$n = -14$	**Simplify.**

Checkpoint

Solve the equation. Check your solution.

14. $7x = 40.6$ **5.8** **15.** $-1.8u = 6.3$ **-3.5** **16.** $\frac{y}{11.5} = 0.4$ **4.6** **17.** $-9.1 = \frac{v}{-5.9}$ **53.69**

In the **Real World**

Hibernation During hibernation, a chipmunk's body temperature drops to 37.4°F, which is 61.2°F below the normal body temperature for a chipmunk. What is a chipmunk's normal body temperature? **98.6°F**

Example 5 *Writing and Solving an Equation*

When a chipmunk hibernates, its weight decreases by about 0.31 pound. After hibernation, a chipmunk weighs about 0.35 pound. Find the weight of a chipmunk before hibernation.

Solution

Let w represent a chipmunk's weight (in pounds) before hibernation. Write a verbal model. Then use the verbal model to write an equation.

Weight before hibernation − Weight loss = Weight after hibernation

$w - 0.31 = 0.35$	**Substitute.**
$w - 0.31 + 0.31 = 0.35 + 0.31$	**Add 0.31 to each side.**
$w = 0.66$	**Simplify.**

Answer A chipmunk weighs about 0.66 pound before hibernation.

Checkpoint

18. You use an automated teller machine (ATM) to deposit a check for $122.94 into your savings account. Your receipt from the ATM shows a balance of $286.59 after the deposit. Find the balance of your savings account before the deposit. **$163.65**

2.7 Exercises

More Practice, p. 804

Guided Practice

Vocabulary Check

1. Copy and complete: The sum of a positive decimal and a negative decimal has the same sign as the decimal with the greater _?_. absolute value

2. Describe how you would solve the equation $-7.9x = 86.9$. *Sample answer:* Divide each side of the equation by -7.9 to get x alone on one side of the equation.

Skill Check

Perform the indicated operation.

3. $-6.2 + 4.5$ -1.7 **4.** $1.9 - (-9.1)$ 11 **5.** $-0.4(-8.3)$ 3.32 **6.** $7.35 \div (-2.1)$ -3.5

Solve the equation. Check your solution.

7. $x - 2.2 = 3.2$ 5.4 **8.** $y + 0.6 = -1$ -1.6 **9.** $\frac{n}{-7.1} = 5.8$ -41.18 **10.** $-5.2a = -1.3$ 0.25

Guided Problem Solving

11. Earth Science The table shows the year-to-year changes in the mean January water level of Lake Superior during the period 1997–2001. Positive changes represent increases in the water level, while negative changes represent decreases. In 2001, the water level was 182.98 meters. What was the water level in 1997?

Time period	1997 to 1998	1998 to 1999	1999 to 2000	2000 to 2001
Change (meters)	−0.19	−0.28	0.04	−0.18

(1) Find the overall change in the water level from 1997 to 2001 by adding the changes in the table. -0.61 m

(2) Write an equation that you can use to find the water level in 1997. $x - 0.61 = 182.98$

(3) Solve your equation. What was Lake Superior's water level in 1997? 183.59 m

Practice and Problem Solving

Homework Help

Example	Exercises
1	12-17, 45
2	18-23, 45
3	24-29
4	30-35
5	37, 38, 42-44

Online Resources
CLASSZONE.COM
- More Examples
- eTutorial Plus

Perform the indicated operation.

A **12.** $7.8 + (-9.3)$ -1.5 **13.** $-1.25 + 14.4$ 13.15 **14.** $-2.583 + (-5.399)$ -7.982

15. $6.1 - 18.7$ -12.6 **16.** $-3.72 - 4.58$ -8.3 **17.** $-0.62 - (-0.741)$ 0.121

18. $-4.8(0.1)$ -0.48 **19.** $-11.7(-6.82)$ 79.794 **20.** $2.03(-1.66)$ -3.3698

21. $34.1 \div (-5.5)$ -6.2 **22.** $-0.63 \div 0.7$ -0.9 **23.** $-7.532 \div (-2.69)$ 2.8

Solve the equation. Check your solution.

24. $x + 8.5 = 13.7$ 5.2 **25.** $a + 4.8 = 2.29$ -2.51 **26.** $-3.36 = b + 5.12$ -8.48

27. $y - 1.3 = -7.4$ -6.1 **28.** $g - 6.27 = 10.63$ 16.9 **29.** $-0.504 + h = -0.18$ 0.324

30. $8w = 75.2$ 9.4 **31.** $-0.96j = -0.72$ 0.75 **32.** $3.498 = -0.53k$ -6.6

33. $\frac{z}{6.9} = -3$ -20.7 **34.** $\frac{r}{0.4} = 0.8$ 0.32 **35.** $-9.1 = \frac{s}{-7.12}$ 64.792

3 APPLY

ASSIGNMENT GUIDE

Basic Course

Day 1: pp. 105-107 Exs. 12-17, 24-29, 36, 39-41, 48-51

Day 2: pp. 105-107 Exs. 18-23, 30-35, 37, 38, 42-44, 52-55

Average Course

Day 1: pp. 105-107 Exs. 12-17, 24-29, 36, 39-41, 45, 50-53

Day 2: pp. 105-107 Exs. 18-23, 30-35, 37, 38, 42-44, 47, 54-56

Advanced Course

Day 1: pp. 105-107 Exs. 14-17, 24-29, 36, 39-41, 46-49*

Day 2: pp. 105-107 Exs. 20-23, 30-35, 37, 38, 42-45, 54-56

Block

pp. 105-107 Exs. 12-45, 47, 50-56

EXTRA PRACTICE

- Student Edition, p. 804
- Chapter 2 Resource Book, pp. 62-64
- Test and Practice Generator

TRANSPARENCY

Even-numbered answers are available on transparencies.

HOMEWORK CHECK

When you review students' homework for this lesson, go over the following exercises to check understanding of key concepts.

Basic: 12, 18, 24, 30, 37

Average: 15, 20, 25, 32, 38

Advanced: 17, 23, 28, 34, 44

COMMON ERROR

In Exercise 22, students may have more difficulty finding the correct answer when both terms have leading zeros. Urge students to check their work carefully by multiplying the solution by 0.7 to check that they get -0.63.

TEACHING TIP

In Exercise 38, clarify for students that the phrase "batted 692 times" corresponds to the denominator of the term on the right side of the verbal model given.

36. 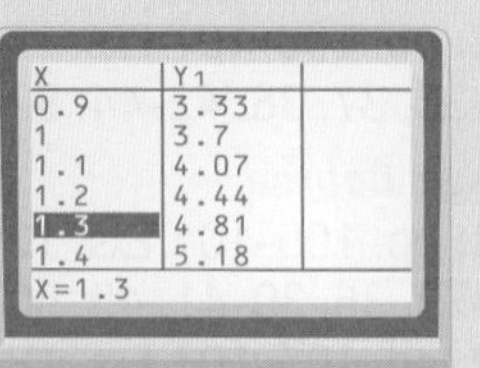

36. Use the *table* feature on a graphing calculator to evaluate $3.7x$ for different values of x. Set TblStart to 0 and ΔTbl to 0.1. Scroll through the table to find the solution of $3.7x = 4.81$. **See margin for art; 1.3.**

W.M. Keck Observatory

37. **Telescopes** The W.M. Keck Observatory, located on top of the dormant volcano Mauna Kea in Hawaii, has two telescopes. Each telescope has a mirror composed of 36 identical sections that are fitted together. The total area of the mirror is about 75.8 square meters. Find the area of each section of the mirror to the nearest tenth of a square meter. **2.1 m²**

38. **Baseball** A baseball player's batting average is defined by the verbal model below. During the 2001 Major League Baseball season, Ichiro Suzuki of the Seattle Mariners batted 692 times and had a batting average of .350. How many hits did Suzuki have? **242 hits**

$$\text{Batting average} = \frac{\text{Number of hits}}{\text{Number of times at bat}}$$

Simplify the expression.

B 39. $2.6x - 7.1x$ **$-4.5x$**

40. $-3.5(4a + 1.9)$ **$-14a - 6.65$**

41. $0.8(3 - 11n) + 1.4n$ **$2.4 - 7.4n$**

Geometry Find the value of *x* for the given triangle or rectangle.

42. Perimeter = 10 m **2.7 m**

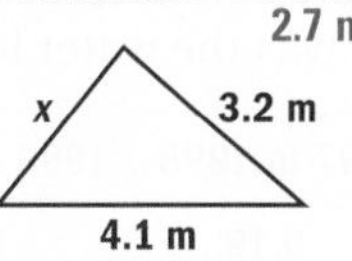

43. Area = 75.52 ft² **6.4 ft**

44. Area = 15.75 cm² **4.2 cm**

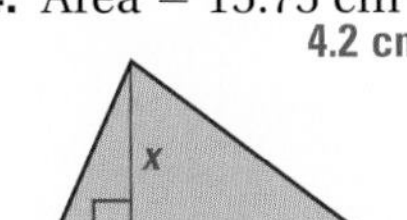

45. **Extended Problem Solving** The table shows the difference between the amount of money the U.S. government received and the amount it spent for the years 1995–2000. Positive amounts, called surpluses, mean that the government received more than it spent. Negative amounts, called deficits, mean that it received less than it spent.

Year	1995	1996	1997	1998	1999	2000
Surplus or deficit (billions of dollars)	−164.0	−107.5	−22.0	69.2	124.6	236.4

a. *Writing* Without performing any calculations, tell whether the U.S. government received *more money* or *less money* than it spent over the entire period 1995–2000. Explain how you got your answer.

b. Check your answer from part (a) by calculating the overall surplus or deficit for 1995–2000. **$136.7 billion surplus**

c. To the nearest tenth of a billion dollars, what was the mean annual surplus or deficit for 1995–2000? **$22.8 billion surplus**

d. **Compare** Find the median annual surplus or deficit for 1995–2000. Compare the median with the mean. **$23.6 billion. *Sample answer:* The median and the mean are almost the same.**

45a. More money. *Sample answer:* Each year of deficit can be paired with a year in which the surplus was greater than the absolute value of the deficit: 1995 with 2000, 1996 with 1999, and 1997 with 1998.

Review *Help*

For help with mean and median, see p. 39.

C 46. **Challenge** Solve the equations $0.1x = 1$, $0.01x = 1$, $0.001x = 1$, and $0.0001x = 1$. What happens to the solutions as the coefficients of x get closer to 0? **10; 100; 1000; 10,000. *Sample answer:* As the coefficients get closer to zero, the solutions become increasingly greater.**

47. **Aviation** The Mach number for an airplane is the speed of the airplane divided by the speed of sound. The speed of sound depends on altitude. The table shows the typical Mach numbers of several airplanes and the speed of sound at each airplane's cruising altitude.

Airplane	Mach number at cruising altitude	Speed of sound at cruising altitude (mi/h)
Cessna Skyhawk	0.19	740
Boeing 747	0.86	663
Concorde	2.04	660

a. Find each airplane's speed at its cruising altitude by solving an equation. Round your answers to the nearest mile per hour. **Cessna Skyhawk: 141 mi/h; Boeing 747: 570 mi/h; Concorde: 1346 mi/h**

b. To the nearest tenth of an hour, how long does it take each airplane to fly 550 miles? **Cessna Skyhawk: 3.9 h; Boeing 747: 1.0 h; Concorde: 0.4 h**

Mixed Review

For the given expression, identify the terms, like terms, coefficients, and constant terms. Then simplify the expression. *(Lesson 2.3)*

48. $5x + 11 + 8x$

49. $-3p + 2 + p - 4$

50. $7w - w + 9 - 6w$

51. $8 + 2y - 1 - 9y + 3$

Solve the equation. Check your solution. *(Lessons 2.5, 2.6)*

52. $x + 12 = 5$ **−7**
53. $y - 9 = -4$ **5**
54. $32c = 192$ **6**
55. $\frac{d}{19} = -8$ **−152**

48. terms: $5x$, 11, $8x$; like terms: $5x$ and $8x$; coefficients: 5, 8; constant term: 11; $13x + 11$

49. terms: $-3p$, 2, p, -4; like terms: $-3p$ and p, 2 and -4; coefficients: -3, 1; constant terms: 2, -4; $-2p - 2$

Standardized Test Practice

56. **Extended Response** When you watch waves pass an anchored boat or other stationary point, the elapsed time between waves is called the period. In deep water, the period T (in seconds) and the wave speed s (in miles per hour) are related by the formula $s = 3.49T$.

a. Suppose a storm near Antarctica generates a series of waves with a period of 11 seconds. Find the speed of the waves. **38.39 mi/h**

b. Waves from Antarctic storms can reach the coast of Alaska, 8000 miles away. How many hours does it take the waves from part (a) to reach the Alaskan coast? How many days does it take? **about 208 h; about 8.7 days**

50. terms: $7w$, $-w$, 9, $-6w$; like terms: $7w$, $-w$, and $-6w$; coefficients: 7, -1, -6; constant term: 9; 9

51. terms: 8, $2y$, -1, $-9y$, 3; like terms: 8, -1, and 3, $2y$ and $-9y$; coefficients: 2, -9; constant terms: 8, -1, 3; $10 - 7y$

Runoff

How long is a marathon? **26.2 mi**

To find the answer, first solve equation 1. Then substitute the solution of equation 1 for a in equation 2, and solve equation 2. Finally, substitute the solution of equation 2 for b in equation 3, and solve equation 3. The solution of equation 3 is a marathon's length in miles.

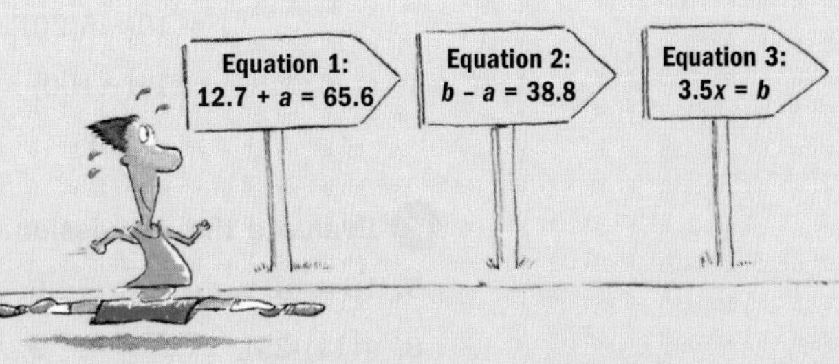

4 ASSESS

Assessment Resources

For more assessment resources, see:
- Assessment Book
- Test and Practice Generator

Mini-Quiz

Solve the equation.

1. $9.5 + b = 11.2$ **1.7**
2. $d - 0.08 = -0.18$ **−0.1**
3. $-3.2h = -11.2$ **3.5**
4. $\frac{m}{-1.5} = 7.5$ **−11.25**
5. **Challenge** Solve the equation $-0.002y = 0.03$. **−15**

5 FOLLOW-UP

Diagnosis/Remediation

- Study Guide in Chapter 2 Resource Book, pp. 65–66
- Tutor Place, Whole Numbers and Decimals Cards 6, 8, 9, 12, 13, Algebra Cards 7–12
- eTutorial Plus Online
- Extra Practice, p. 804
- Lesson Practice in Chapter 2 Resource Book, pp. 62–64

English Learner Support

- Spanish Study Guide
- Multi-Language Visual Glossary
- Chapter Audio Summaries CDs

Challenge

- Challenge Practice in Chapter 2 Resource Book, p. 67
- Teacher's Edition, p. 60F

Additional Resources

The following resources are available to help review the materials in Lessons 2.4–2.7.

Chapter 2 Resource Book

- Lesson Practice
- Study Guide

Assessment Book

- Chapter 2 Quiz 2

Technology

- Test and Practice Generator
- eTutorial CD-ROM

Internet

- Classzone
- eWorkbook Plus Online
- eTutorial Plus Online

English Learner Support

- Spanish Study Guide
- Multi-Language Visual Glossary
- Chapter Audio Summaries CDs

2. *Sample answer:* Divide each side of the equation by a to get x alone on one side of the equation, and then simplify.

5. $16 + 18 + 14$
$= (16 + 18) + 14$ Use order of operations.
$= (18 + 16) + 14$ commutative property of addition
$= 18 + (16 + 14)$ associative property of addition
$= 18 + 30$ Add 16 and 14.
$= 48$ Add 18 and 30.

6. $38 + 23 + (-8)$
$= (38 + 23) + (-8)$ Use order of operations.
$= (23 + 38) + (-8)$ commutative property of addition
$= 23 + [38 + (-8)]$ associative property of addition
$= 23 + 30$ Add 38 and −8.
$= 53$ Add 23 and 30.

CHAPTER 2

Chapter Review

Vocabulary Review

additive identity, p. 64
multiplicative identity, p. 64
equivalent numerical expressions, p. 71
equivalent variable expressions, p. 72
term, p. 78
coefficient, p. 78
constant term, p. 78
like terms, p. 78
equation, p. 85
solution of an equation, p. 85
solving an equation, p. 86
inverse operations, p. 91
equivalent equations, p. 91

1. What number is the additive identity? What number is the multiplicative identity? 0; 1
2. Describe how you would solve an equation of the form $ax = b$ where $a \neq 0$. See margin.
3. Copy and complete: The expressions $2(8 + 3)$ and $2(8) + 2(3)$ are _?_. equivalent numerical expressions
4. In the expression $5 - 9n$, what is the coefficient of n? What is the constant term? −9; 5

2.1 Properties and Operations

Examples on pp. 63–65

Goal

Use properties of addition and multiplication.

Example Evaluate the expression.

a. $57 + 28 + 13 = (57 + 28) + 13$ Use order of operations.
$= (28 + 57) + 13$ Commutative property of addition
$= 28 + (57 + 13)$ Associative property of addition
$= 28 + 70$ Add 57 and 13.
$= 98$ Add 28 and 70.

b. $-5(19)(20) = [-5(19)](20)$ Use order of operations.
$= [19(-5)](20)$ Commutative property of multiplication
$= 19[-5(20)]$ Associative property of multiplication
$= 19(-100)$ Multiply −5 and 20.
$= -1900$ Multiply 19 and −100.

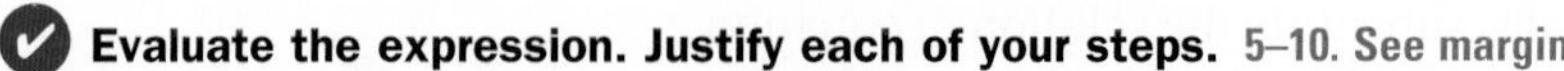

Evaluate the expression. Justify each of your steps. 5–10. See margin.

5. $16 + 18 + 14$
6. $38 + 23 + (-8)$
7. $4.7 + 2.5 + 2.3$
8. $4(11)(25)$
9. $5(-3)(12)$
10. $6(13)(0.5)$

2.2 The Distributive Property

Examples on pp. 71–73

Goal

Use the distributive property.

Example **Use the distributive property to evaluate 5(204).**

$5(204) = 5(200 + 4)$ Rewrite 204 as 200 + 4.

$= 5(200) + 5(4)$ Distributive property

$= 1000 + 20$ Multiply.

$= 1020$ Add.

Example **Write an expression equivalent to $4(3x - 2)$.**

$4(3x - 2) = 4(3x) - 4(2)$ Distributive property

$= 12x - 8$ Multiply.

Use the distributive property to evaluate the expression.

11. 3(106) 318 **12.** 6(99) 594 **13.** 8(5.2) 41.6 **14.** (7.95)4 31.8

Write an equivalent variable expression.

15. $-2(x + 4)$ $-2x - 8$ **16.** $5(y - 8)$ $5y - 40$ **17.** $4(7a + 2)$ $28a + 8$ **18.** $(6 - 11c)(-3)$ $-18 + 33c$

2.3 Simplifying Variable Expressions

Examples on pp. 78–80

Goal

Simplify variable expressions.

Example **Identify the terms, like terms, coefficients, and constant terms of the expression $7n - 5 - 3n + 2$.**

Terms: $7n, -5, -3n, 2$ **Like terms:** $7n$ and $-3n$; -5 and 2

Coefficients: $7, -3$ **Constant terms:** $-5, 2$

Example **Simplify the expression $3p + 5 - 8(p + 2)$.**

$3p + 5 - 8(p + 2) = 3p + 5 - 8p - 16$ Distributive property

$= 3p - 8p + 5 - 16$ Group like terms.

$= -5p - 11$ Combine like terms.

Identify the terms, like terms, coefficients, and constant terms.

19–21. See margin.

19. $4t + 13t + 2$ **20.** $x + 5 - 3x - 1$ **21.** $12 - 7k + 9 - k$

Simplify the expression.

22. $5x - 9 - x + 2$ $4x - 7$ **23.** $3(u + 1) + 4u + 1$ $7u + 4$ **24.** $8a - 2(7a - 3)$ $-6a + 6$

The following resources are available to help review the materials in this chapter.

Chapter 2 Resource Book

- Chapter Review Games and Activities, p. 68
- Cumulative Practice, Chs. 1–2

English/Spanish Chapter Reviews and Tests

Chapter Audio Summaries CDs

eTutorial CD-ROM

eWorkbook Plus Online

eTutorial Plus Online

7. 4.7 + 2.5 + 2.3
= (4.7 + 2.5) + 2.3 Use order of operations.
= (2.5 + 4.7) + 2.3 commutative property of addition
= 2.5 + (4.7 + 2.3) associative property of addition
= 2.5 + 7 Add 4.7 and 2.3.
= 9.5 Add 2.5 and 7.

8. 4(11)(25)
= [4(11)](25) Use order of operations.
= [11(4)](25) commutative property of multiplication
= 11[(4)(25)] associative property of multiplication
= 11(100) Multiply 4 and 25.
= 1100 Multiply 11 and 100.

9, 10. See Additional Answers beginning on page AA1.

19. terms: $4t$, $13t$, 2; like terms: $4t$ and $13t$; coefficients: 4, 13; constant term: 2

20. terms: x, 5, $-3x$, -1; like terms: x and $-3x$, 5 and -1; coefficients: 1, -3; constant terms: 5, -1

21. terms: 12, $-7k$, 9, $-k$; like terms: 12 and 9, $-7k$ and $-k$; coefficients: -7, -1; constant terms: 12, 9

2.4 Variables and Equations

Examples on pp. 85–86

Goal

Use mental math to solve equations.

Example **Solve the equation using mental math.**

	Equation	Question	Solution	Check
a.	$x + 7 = 11$	What number plus 7 equals 11?	4	$4 + 7 = 11$ ✓
b.	$y - 9 = 5$	What number minus 9 equals 5?	14	$14 - 9 = 5$ ✓
c.	$3n = 21$	3 times what number equals 21?	7	$3(7) = 21$ ✓
d.	$-6 = \frac{30}{w}$	−6 equals 30 divided by what number?	−5	$-6 = \frac{30}{-5}$ ✓

✓ **Solve the equation using mental math.**

25. $x + 10 = 23$ 13 **26.** $7 - y = -1$ 8 **27.** $36 = -4a$ −9 **28.** $\frac{b}{5} = 8$ 40

29. Trip Your family drives 150 miles to an amusement park at an average speed of 50 miles per hour. How long does the trip take? 3 h

2.5 Solving Equations Using Addition or Subtraction

Examples on pp. 91–92

Goal

Use addition or subtraction to solve equations.

Example **Solve $x + 19 = 6$.**

$x + 19 = 6$ **Write original equation.**

$x + 19 - 19 = 6 - 19$ **Subtract 19 from each side.**

$x = -13$ **Simplify.**

Example **Solve $m - 42 = -15$.**

$m - 42 = -15$ **Write original equation.**

$m - 42 + 42 = -15 + 42$ **Add 42 to each side.**

$m = 27$ **Simplify.**

✓ **Solve the equation. Check your solution.**

30. $x + 8 = 21$ 13 **31.** $-9 = t + 16$ −25 **32.** $p - 7 = -8$ −1 **33.** $29 = r - 64$ 93

34. Salary An engineer receives a promotion that includes a raise of $4500 in her annual salary. Her new salary is $50,750. What was the engineer's salary before the promotion? $46,250

2.6 Solving Equations Using Multiplication or Division

Examples on pp. 97–98

Goal

Use multiplication or division to solve equations.

Example Solve $\frac{r}{-13} = -5$.

$\frac{r}{-13} = -5$	Write original equation.
$-13\left(\frac{r}{-13}\right) = -13(-5)$	Multiply each side by −13.
$r = 65$	Simplify.

Solve the equation. Check your solution.

35. $-5x = 45$ −9 **36.** $-54 = -3y$ 18 **37.** $\frac{a}{8} = 4$ 32 **38.** $9 = \frac{c}{-9}$ −81

39. Craft Fair You divide a stack of fliers for a craft fair into 6 smaller stacks for volunteers to distribute. Each smaller stack contains 15 fliers. What is the total number of fliers distributed? 90 fliers

2.7 Decimal Operations and Equations with Decimals

Examples on pp. 102–104

Goal

Use positive and negative decimals.

Example Perform the indicated operation.

a. $9.74 + (-3.31) = 6.43$	Add using rule for different signs.
b. $-4.2 - 7.9 = -4.2 + (-7.9)$	Rewrite as a sum.
$= -12.1$	Add using rule for same signs.
c. $-2.6(8.4) = -21.84$	Different signs: Product is negative.
d. $-17.67 \div (-3.1) = 5.7$	Same sign: Quotient is positive.

Example Solve $-1.9k = 0.76$.

$-1.9k = 0.76$	Write original equation.
$\frac{-1.9k}{-1.9} = \frac{0.76}{-1.9}$	Divide each side by −1.9.
$k = -0.4$	Simplify.

Perform the indicated operation.

40. $-6.6 + 1.4$ −5.2 **41.** $2.8 - (-4.7)$ 7.5 **42.** $-9.4(-5.31)$ 49.914 **43.** $7 \div (-2.5)$ −2.8

Solve the equation. Check your solution.

44. $x + 6 = 1.8$ −4.2 **45.** $2.4h = -8.4$ −3.5 **46.** $\frac{n}{-5} = -7.3$ 36.5 **47.** $u - 4.6 = 3.7$ 8.3

ADDITIONAL RESOURCES

Assessment Book

- Chapter Test (3 levels), pp. 20–25
- Standardized Chapter Test, p. 26
- Alternative Assessment, pp. 27-28

Test and Practice Generator

1. $48 + 25 + 22$
$= (48 + 25) + 22$ Use order of operations.
$= (25 + 48) + 22$ commutative property of addition
$= 25 + (48 + 22)$ associative property of addition
$= 25 + 70$ Add 48 and 22.
$= 95$ Add 25 and 70.

2–4. See Additional Answers beginning on page AA1.

5. commutative property of multiplication
6. identity property of addition
7. commutative property of addition
8. associative property of multiplication

18. terms: $4x$, 2, $5x$; like terms: $4x$ and $5x$; coefficients: 4, 5; constant term: 2; $9x + 2$
19. terms: $-a$, $3a$, 7, -4; like terms: $-a$ and $3a$, 7 and -4; coefficients: -1, 3; constant terms: 7, -4; $2a + 3$
20. terms: $8k$, -5, $-2k$, 1; like terms: $8k$ and $-2k$, -5 and 1; coefficients: 8, -2; constant terms: -5, 1; $6k - 4$
21. terms: y, $7y$, -9, $-3y$; like terms: y, $7y$, and $-3y$; coefficients: 1, 7, -3; constant term: -9; $5y - 9$

CHAPTER 2

Chapter Test

Evaluate the expression. Justify each of your steps. 1–4. See margin.

1. $48 + 25 + 22$
2. $15(-7)(4)$
3. $5.9 + 10.4 + 2.1$
4. $36 \cdot 1 + 0$

Identify the property that the statement illustrates. 5–8. See margin.

5. $-8(5) = 5(-8)$
6. $4 + 0 = 4$
7. $x^2 + y = y + x^2$
8. $7(xy^2) = (7x)y^2$

9. **Waves** The highest ocean wave ever reliably measured was sighted by the U.S.S. *Ramapo* during a typhoon in 1933. The wave was about 37 yards high. Use a conversion factor to find this height in feet. 111 ft

Use the distributive property to evaluate the expression.

10. $7(8 - 3)$ 35
11. $(4 + 6)(-6)$ -60
12. $5(309)$ 1545
13. $8(4.95)$ 39.6

Geometry Find the area of the rectangle or triangle.

14. $(5x + 15)$ units^2
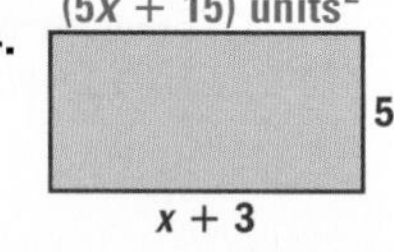

15. $(24a - 30)$ units^2
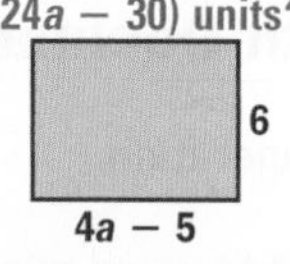

16. $(28 - 4c)$ units^2
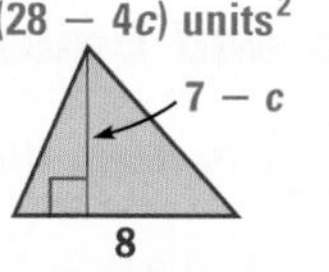

17. $(12n + 60)$ units^2
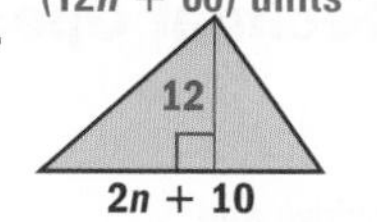

For the given expression, identify the terms, like terms, coefficients, and constant terms. Then simplify the expression. 18–21. See margin.

18. $4x + 2 + 5x$
19. $-a + 3a + 7 - 4$
20. $8k - 5 - 2k + 1$
21. $y + 7y - 9 - 3y$

Simplify the expression.

22. $2(x - 7) - 3x$ $-x - 14$
23. $-4(n + 1) + 15n$ $11n - 4$
24. $8p + 4 - (p + 4)$ $7p$
25. $9t - 3(3t - 2)$ 6

Write the verbal sentence as an equation. Tell whether 12 is a solution.

26. The difference of 17 and x is 4. $17 - x = 4$; 12 is not a solution.
27. The quotient of a and 4 is 3. $\frac{a}{4} = 3$; 12 is a solution.

Solve the equation.

28. $x + 12 = 9$ -3
29. $-4 = h - 20$ 16
30. $-3r = 87$ -29
31. $\frac{s}{7} = 13$ 91

32. **Books** You buy a book that is 540 pages long. You can read about 30 pages per hour. How long does it take you to read the book? 18 h

Perform the indicated operation.

33. $-3.1 + (-7.3)$ -10.4
34. $5.85 - 9.47$ -3.62
35. $-6.2(-0.9)$ 5.58
36. $7.15 \div (-1.3)$ -5.5

Solve the equation.

37. $x + 6.5 = -4.5$ -11
38. $c - 2.59 = 1.48$ 4.07
39. $-9.12 = -2.4y$ 3.8
40. $\frac{m}{-3.4} = 8.3$ -28.22

Additional Resources

Assessment Book

- Standardized Chapter Test, p. 26

Test and Practice Generator

Chapter Standardized Test

Test-Taking Strategy **For difficult questions, first try eliminating answer choices that you know are *not* correct.**

1. Which equation illustrates the identity property of multiplication? C

A. $(xy)z = x(yz)$ **B.** $x \cdot 0 = 0$

C. $x \cdot 1 = x$ **D.** $x + 0 = x$

2. The average height of a male giraffe is 17 feet. What is this height in inches? I

F. 29 inches **G.** 51 inches

H. 170 inches **I.** 204 inches

3. Which expression represents the area (in square units) of the triangle shown? B

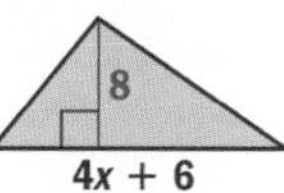

A. $32x + 48$ **B.** $16x + 24$

C. $4x + 14$ **D.** $32x + 6$

4. Which number is *not* a coefficient of n in the expression $3n + 8 - n + 4n$? G

F. -1 **G.** 1 **H.** 3 **I.** 4

5. Which expression is equivalent to $5a + 8 - 2(a + 4)$? A

A. $3a$ **B.** $3a + 4$

C. $3a + 12$ **D.** $3a + 16$

6. Which equation represents the sentence "The difference of 9 and x is 5."? H

F. $9 = x - 5$ **G.** $9 = 5 - x$

H. $9 - x = 5$ **I.** $x - 9 = 5$

7. Which equation does *not* have 6 as a solution? D

A. $t + 5 = 11$ **B.** $3 - t = -3$

C. $7t = 42$ **D.** $\frac{24}{t} = 3$

8. What is the solution of $y + 31 = 19$? G

F. -50 **G.** -12 **H.** 12 **I.** 50

9. What is the solution of $-20 = g - 4$? B

A. -24 **B.** -16 **C.** 5 **D.** 80

10. What is the solution of $\frac{x}{-3} = -18$? I

F. -54 **G.** -6 **H.** 6 **I.** 54

11. What is the value of $-4.85 - (-6.32)$? C

A. -11.17 **B.** -1.47

C. 1.47 **D.** 11.17

12. What is the solution of $5.2w = -2.08$? G

F. -2.5 **G.** -0.4 **H.** 0.4 **I.** 2.5

13. Short Response Once a week, you either rent a movie for \$4 or see a movie in a theater for \$9. Let r represent the number of movies you rent in a year (52 weeks). Write and simplify an expression in terms of r for the total amount you spend on movies during the year. $4r + 9(52 - r)$, $-5r + 468$

14. Extended Response You have been hired to mow a rectangular lawn that is 300 feet long and 150 feet wide. You want to earn \$12 per hour of work, and you can mow about 20,000 square feet per hour.

a. What is the area of the lawn? 45,000 ft^2

b. About how long will it take you to mow the lawn? about 2.25 h

c. How much money should you charge for mowing the lawn? \$27

OVERVIEW

Mathematical Goals

In this project, students will measure with a ruler. They will write and solve an equation. Students will convert between units of measurement, and they will compare measurements.

Managing the Project

Classroom Management
Students can work individually or in groups of two. In groups, students can each perform Step 1 and compare their answers. Group members can work Steps 2–4 together. They should compare the heights and write their explanations as a group.

Guiding Students' Work
In Step 1, students may find it easier to measure taller stacks of pennies. You might suggest that they repeat Steps 1–3 for several stacks of pennies of different heights. Urge students to look up how to convert millimeters to meters if they are unsure how to do this.

Concluding the Project
Students should clearly explain how they found the height of one million pennies and include their measurements and equations. You can use questions like the following for class discussion:

- Why did you measure at least 10 pennies rather than 1 penny?
- A recent news story reported that if the power cords from all the desktop computers in the United States were laid end to end, they would reach halfway from Earth to the moon. If you measured the length of a typical computer cord, how could you estimate how many cords are in the United States?

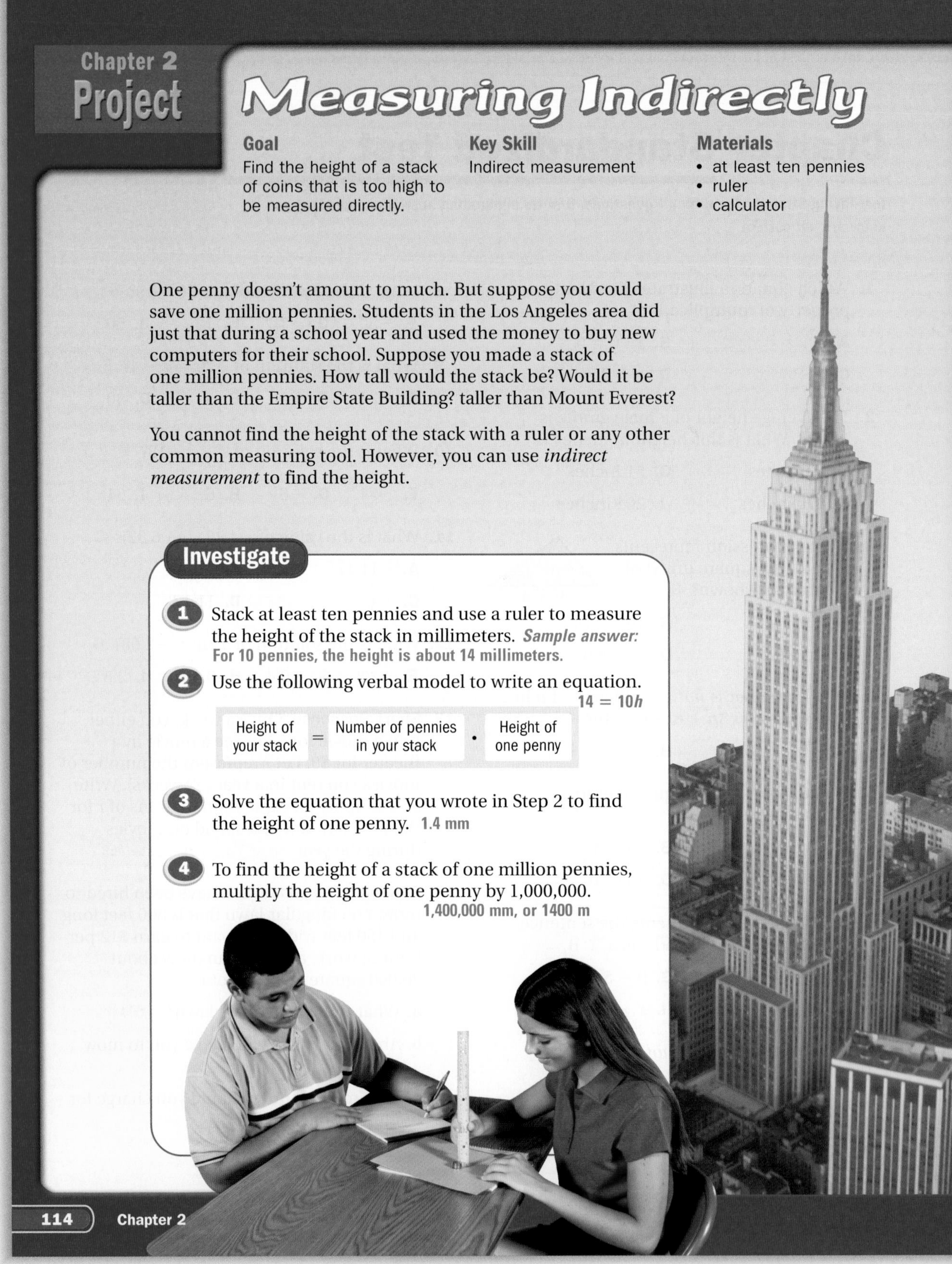

Chapter 2 Project

Measuring Indirectly

Goal
Find the height of a stack of coins that is too high to be measured directly.

Key Skill
Indirect measurement

Materials
- at least ten pennies
- ruler
- calculator

One penny doesn't amount to much. But suppose you could save one million pennies. Students in the Los Angeles area did just that during a school year and used the money to buy new computers for their school. Suppose you made a stack of one million pennies. How tall would the stack be? Would it be taller than the Empire State Building? taller than Mount Everest?

You cannot find the height of the stack with a ruler or any other common measuring tool. However, you can use *indirect measurement* to find the height.

Investigate

1. Stack at least ten pennies and use a ruler to measure the height of the stack in millimeters. ***Sample answer:*** **For 10 pennies, the height is about 14 millimeters.**
2. Use the following verbal model to write an equation. **$14 = 10h$**

Height of your stack	=	Number of pennies in your stack	•	Height of one penny

3. Solve the equation that you wrote in Step 2 to find the height of one penny. **1.4 mm**
4. To find the height of a stack of one million pennies, multiply the height of one penny by 1,000,000. **1,400,000 mm, or 1400 m**

Consider and Decide

Compare the height of a stack of one million pennies with the heights of the Empire State Building and Mount Everest. Consider the following:

- The Empire State Building is 381 meters tall. Mount Everest is 8850 meters tall.
- What unit of measurement did you use to write the height of a stack of one million pennies? Is this unit appropriate? Convert the unit if necessary.

Present Your Results

Write a short explanation of how you found the height of a stack of one million pennies. Include your measurements and equations. Describe how the height of the stack compares with the height of the Empire State Building and the height of Mount Everest.

Research: 2002 data: 7,288,855,000 pennies worth $72,888,550; 1,230,480,000 nickels worth $61,524,000; 2,567,000,000 dimes worth $256,700,000; 3,313,704,000 quarters worth $828,426,000; combined value: $1,219,538,550; to find the values of each coin, I multiplied the number of pennies by $.01, the number of nickels by $.05, the number of dimes by $.10, and the number of quarters by $.25, then I added to find the combined value.

Experiment: Based on an official thickness of about 0.0043 inch or 0.11 millimeter, 17 million $1 bills would have a height of about 6100 feet, or about 1900 meters. Students' answers will likely be higher because of wrinkled bills.

Project Extensions

The U.S. Mint produces coins. Use the Internet to find out how many pennies, nickels, dimes, and quarters were produced by the U.S. Mint last year. Find the total value (in dollars) of each coin type produced. Then find the combined value. Explain how you found your answers.

Experiment Every day about 17 million $1 bills are printed, most of which are used to replace bills already in circulation. Use indirect measurement to find the thickness of a $1 bill. Suppose you made a stack of all the $1 bills printed in one day. How tall would this stack be? Explain the steps you took to find your answers.

Career The U.S. Mint has facilities in Washington, D.C., San Francisco, Fort Knox, and other locations. Employees of the U.S. Mint work to produce and protect American currency. Find out more about careers at the U.S. Mint.

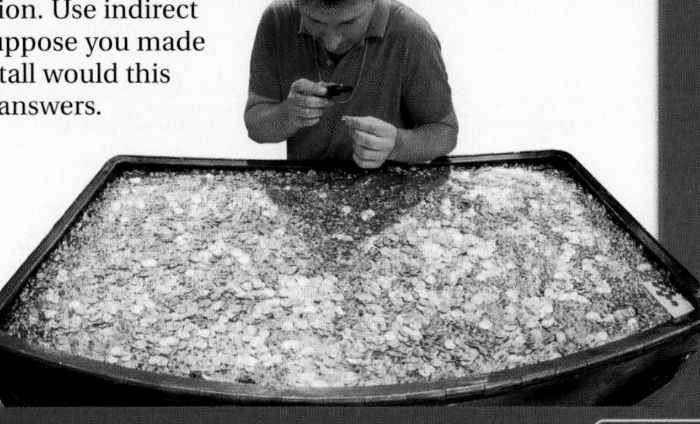

Grading the Project

A well-written project will have the following characteristics:

- The results of Steps 1–4 are complete and reasonable.
- The unit of measure has been converted to meters correctly.
- An explanation of the work that includes measurements, equations, and comparisons is included.

CHAPTER 3

Pacing and Assignment Guide

REGULAR SCHEDULE

Lesson	Les. Day	BASIC	AVERAGE	ADVANCED
3.1	Day 1	EP p. 804 Exs. 36–50 even; pp. 123–124 Exs. 8–16, 20–24, 28–31, 37–45	pp. 123–124 Exs. 14–22, 25–29, 32–35, 37–46	pp. 123–124 Exs. 14–24, 27, 30–38*, 43–46
3.2	Day 1	EP p. 804 Exs. 20–23; pp. 127–129 Exs. 11–20, 22–27, 33–35, 40–55	pp. 127–129 Exs. 10–16, 20–25, 30–38, 42–45, 50–56	pp. 127–129 Exs. 10–13, 17–29, 32–39*, 44–47, 52–56
3.3	Day 1	SRH p. 785 Exs. 1, 5; pp. 134–135 Exs. 11–14, 23–27, 34–37, 44–47	pp. 134–135 Exs. 11–14, 25–27, 31–35, 44–47	pp. 134–135 Exs. 11–14, 25–27, 31–33, 39–45*
	Day 2	pp. 134–135 Exs. 15–22, 28–30, 48–51	pp. 134–135 Exs. 17–22, 28–30, 38–40, 48–51	pp. 134–135 Exs. 17–22, 28–30, 36–38, 46–51
3.4	Day 1	EP p. 803 Exs. 13–15; pp. 141–142 Exs. 12–20, 33, 38, 45–49	pp. 141–142 Exs. 12–20, 33, 41–43, 45–49	pp. 141–142 Exs. 14–20, 33, 41–48*
	Day 2	pp. 141–142 Exs. 21–32, 34–37, 40, 50	pp. 141–142 Exs. 21–32, 34–40, 50	pp. 141–142 Exs. 25–32, 34–40, 49, 50
3.5	Day 1	pp. 146–148 Exs. 12–19, 30–33, 42–45, 50–54	pp. 146–148 Exs. 16–19, 30–35, 42–44, 50–55	pp. 146–148 Exs. 16–19, 32–35, 42–46, 54–58
	Day 2	pp. 146–148 Exs. 20–27, 29, 37–41, 55–61	pp. 146–148 Exs. 24–29, 36–38, 45–48, 56–61	pp. 146–148 Exs. 24–29, 36–38, 47–51*, 59–61
3.6	Day 1	SRH p. 802 Exs. 1–3; pp. 151–153 Exs. 10–17, 25–30, 47–49	pp. 151–153 Exs. 10–17, 25–27, 34–43	pp. 151–153 Exs. 12–17, 25–27, 39–46
	Day 2	pp. 151–153 Exs. 18–23, 31, 35–46	pp. 151–153 Exs. 18–24, 28–32, 44–49	pp. 151–153 Exs. 18–24, 28–34*, 47–49
Review	Day 1	pp. 154–157 Exs. 1–34	pp. 154–157 Exs. 1–34	pp. 154–157 Exs. 1–34
Assess	Day 1	Chapter 3 Test	Chapter 3 Test	Chapter 3 Test

YEARLY PACING Chapter 3 Total – **12 days** Chapters 1–3 Total – **34 days** Remaining – **126 days**

*Challenge Exercises EP = Extra Practice SRH = Skills Review Handbook

BLOCK SCHEDULE

DAY 1	DAY 2	DAY 3	DAY 4	DAY 5	DAY 6
3.1 pp. 123–124 Exs. 14–22, 25–29, 32–35, 37–46 **3.2** pp. 127–129 Exs. 10–16, 20–25, 30–38, 42–45, 50–56	**3.3** pp. 134–135 Exs. 11–14, 17–22, 25–35, 38–40, 44–51	**3.4** pp. 141–142 Exs. 12–43, 45–50	**3.5** pp. 146–148 Exs. 16–19, 24–38, 42–48, 50–61	**3.6** pp. 151–153 Exs. 10–15, 18–32, 34–49	**Review** pp. 154–157 Exs. 1–34 **Assess** Chapter 3 Test

YEARLY PACING Chapter 3 Total – **6 days** Chapters 1–3 Total – **17 days** Remaining – **63 days**

Support Materials

CHAPTER RESOURCE BOOK

CHAPTER SUPPORT						
Tips for New Teachers	p. 1		Parents as Partners		p. 3	

LESSON SUPPORT	3.1	3.2	3.3	3.4	3.5	3.6
Lesson Plans (regular and block)	p. 5	p. 15	p. 24	p. 35	p. 45	p. 54
Technology Activities & Keystrokes			p. 27	p. 37	p. 47	
Activity Support Masters	p. 7		p. 26			
Activity Masters		p. 17				
Practice (3 levels)	p. 8	p. 18	p. 29	p. 38	p. 48	p. 56
Study Guide	p. 11	p. 21	p. 32	p. 41	p. 51	p. 59
Real-World Problem Solving	p. 13			p. 43		
Challenge Practice	p. 14	p. 23	p. 34	p. 44	p. 53	p. 61

REVIEW			
Chapter Review Games and Activities	p. 62	Extra Credit Project with Rubric	p. 67
Real-Life Project with Rubric	p. 63	Cumulative Practice	p. 69
Cooperative Project with Rubric	p. 65	Resource Book Answers	A1

ASSESSMENT

Quizzes	p. 29	Alternative Assessments with Rubrics	p. 38
Chapter Tests (3 levels)	p. 31	Unit Test	p. 40
Standardized Test	p. 37	Cumulative Test	p. 42

TRANSPARENCIES

TRANSPARENCIES	3.1	3.2	3.3	3.4	3.5	3.6
Warm-Up/Daily Homework Quiz	✔	✔	✔	✔	✔	✔
Notetaking Guide	✔	✔	✔	✔	✔	✔
Teacher Support	✔			✔	✔	✔
English/Spanish Problem Solving	✔	✔	✔	✔	✔	✔
Answer Transparencies	✔	✔	✔	✔	✔	✔

TECHNOLOGY

- EasyPlanner CD-ROM
- Test and Practice Generator
- Electronic Lesson Presentations
- eTutorial CD-ROM
- Chapter Audio Summaries CDs
- Classzone.com
- eEdition Plus Online
- eWorkbook Plus Online
- eTutorial Plus Online
- EasyPlanner Plus Online

ADDITIONAL RESOURCES

- Worked-Out Solution Key
- Notetaking Guide
- Practice Workbook
- Tutor Place
- Professional Development Book
- Special Activities Book
- Posters
- Spanish Study Guide
- Exercises in Spanish
- English/Spanish Ch. Reviews/Tests
- Multi-Language Visual Glossary

CHAPTER 3

Math Background and Teaching Strategies

Lesson 3.1

MATH BACKGROUND

As with one-step equations, the goal when solving two-step equations is to isolate the variable on one side of the equation. The method remains to undo what has been done to the variable by using inverse operations. For two-step equations, however, students will need to apply an appropriate property of equality twice during the solution process instead of just once.

TEACHING STRATEGIES

You may want to show students that it does not matter whether the addition/subtraction step is performed first or the multiplication/division step is performed first when solving a two-step equation. For example, the equation $3x - 6 = 9$ can be solved as shown below:

$3x - 6 = 9$	
$\frac{3x}{3} - \frac{6}{3} = \frac{9}{3}$	Divide each term on both sides by 3.
$x - 2 = 3$	Simplify.
$x = 5$	Add 2 to each side.

Students must realize, though, that *both* terms on the left side of the original equation must be divided by 3. Also, point out that if the equation were $3x - 5 = 10$, which has the same solution, dividing both sides by 3 first would create fractions that would then have to be added, making the calculations more difficult than if 5 were added to each side before dividing by 3. With these examples, students should see that their first goal in solving a two-step equation should be to isolate the variable term on one side of the equation. Then they can isolate the variable in the next step.

Lesson 3.2

MATH BACKGROUND

Until this lesson, solving one- and two-step equations has involved using the properties of equality to perform the same operation on each side of an equation. Students now encounter equations that first need simplification on one side. To do this, they need to use the distributive property, either explicitly, as when simplifying the product of a number and an expression in parentheses, or implicitly, as when combining like terms, or both.

TEACHING STRATEGIES

Work the following additional example with students. Point out to students that as they solve more complicated equations, they are not doing anything new, but are just applying properties they already know: the properties of addition, the associative property, the commutative property, and the distributive property.

$8w - 3(-4 + 2w) = 6$	
$8w + 12 - 6w = 6$	Distributive property
$2w + 12 = 6$	Combine like terms.
$2w + 12 - 12 = 6 - 12$	Subtract 12 from each side.
$2w = -6$	Simplify.
$\frac{2w}{2} = \frac{-6}{2}$	Divide each side by 2.
$w = -3$	Simplify.

Lesson 3.3

MATH BACKGROUND

VARIABLES ON BOTH SIDES Sometimes both sides of an equation have one or more variable terms. As before, the goal remains to isolate the variable. Once each side is simplified so that it contains only one variable term, students can use the additive inverse of one of the terms and the addition or subtraction property of equality to eliminate the variable term from one side of the equation. It is best to isolate the variable term on the side of the equation where the coefficient of the variable term is greater; doing so allows students to multiply or divide each side of the equation by a positive number in the next step.

TEACHING STRATEGIES

Have students model solving equations with variables on both sides using algebra tiles, as in the Concept Activity 3.3. Make sure students realize that they are following the same process they have used when removing the same number of 1-tiles from each side of an equation. That is, they are using the subtraction property of equality. Notice that the example in the Concept Activity can be used to reinforce isolating the variable term on the side with the greater coefficient.

Lesson 3.4

MATH BACKGROUND

INEQUALITIES A linear equation expresses a relationship of equality, while a **linear inequality** expresses a relationship of order. While a linear equation has a single solution (unless it is a contradiction or an identity), the solution of a linear inequality is a *range* of numbers. Instead of its graph being a single point on the number line, the graph of the solution of a simple inequality is a ray, although the endpoint of the ray may or may not be included. Adding the same number to each side or subtracting the same number from each side of an inequality does not affect the order relationship.

TEACHING STRATEGIES

To emphasize the addition and subtraction properties of equality, you can perform the following activity with students. Have two students who obviously vary in height stand in front of the classroom. Have students identify and write down the order relationship that they observe, for example, "Bob > Betty." Then give the two students identical hats to place on their heads, and again have students write an order relationship, in this case, "Bob + hat > Betty + hat." Students should realize that the relationship is not changed by "adding" the hat to each "side."

Lesson 3.5

MATH BACKGROUND

While the addition and subtraction properties of inequality are directly parallel to their corresponding properties of equality, this is true for the multiplication and division properties of inequality only when the multiplication or division is by a positive number. When the multiplication or division is by a negative number, students must reverse the direction of the inequality.

TEACHING STRATEGIES

It takes practice for students to write equivalent inequalities correctly when multiplication or division by a negative number is involved, so they will need a lot of practice at this skill. To help them see why the direction of the inequality is reversed, you can use the diagram below, which shows how the order relationship of the opposites of two numbers differs from the order relationship of the two numbers. Students should notice how multiplying each number by −1 "flips" it over the point 0 on the number line.

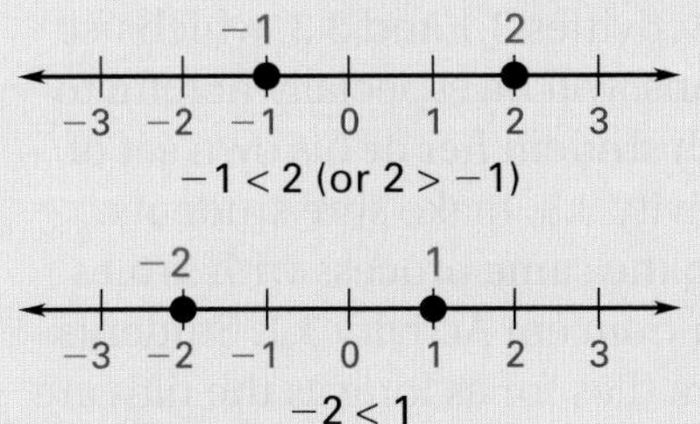

Lesson 3.6

MATH BACKGROUND

The only differences between solving multi-step inequalities and solving multi-step equations involve the nature of the solution sets and what happens when you multiply or divide each side by a negative number. Because of the complication when multiplying or dividing by a negative number, for inequalities where there are variable terms on both sides of an inequality it can be very helpful to isolate the variable on the side of the inequality where the coefficient of the variable term is greater. By doing this, students can avoid having to worry about reversing the direction of the inequality.

TEACHING STRATEGIES

Reassure students that solving inequalities is just like solving equations with the two exceptions listed above, so they should not be intimidated. Remind students that they can check their answers by substitution to make sure that the direction of the inequality symbol is correct. It may help some students to see an inequality worked step-by-step alongside its corresponding equation so that they can see that the process is similar.

CHAPTER 3 Differentiating Instruction

Strategies for Underachievers

USE MODELS

MANIPULATIVES Concept Activities 3.1 and 3.3, which use algebra tiles to solve equations, will be especially helpful to underachievers. Provide each student her or his own set of algebra tiles. In Concept Activity 3.3, make sure students recognize that they are using the same process with x-tiles that they used with 1-tiles in Concept Activity 3.1. Students should have access to algebra tiles for as long as the tiles are helpful to them. You may need to guide students' work with the tiles so they do not become confused by trying to solve equations that are not easily modeled with algebra tiles.

IDENTIFY KEY TERMS

WORD PROBLEMS In this chapter, students will be faced with many word problems that require them to write equations or inequalities to represent different situations. Students may benefit from returning to the list of words and expressions indicating mathematical operations that was mentioned in the "Strategies for Underachievers" notes preceding Chapter 2. Encourage students to add any new words or expressions that they encounter to their lists. For example, as they begin solving inequalities in Lesson 3.4, students should identify words or phrases that indicate order relations and add them to their lists. You may want to encourage students to write the words/phrases from their lists on index cards for quick reference.

DEVELOP PROBLEM SOLVING MODELS

The methods for solving increasingly complex linear equations in Lessons 3.1–3.3 proceed in discrete steps, building on the methods for solving one-step equations in Chapter 2. This step-by-step process is then repeated for solving linear inequalities in Lessons 3.4–3.6. Encourage students to create posters or notebook entries that detail each new step in increasing complexity, beginning with solving one-step equations. In Lesson 3.2, students might need some guidance in realizing that the basic step presented is to simplify one side of the equation (by combining like terms, using the distributive property, and so on) before using the properties of equality. For each step, students should give examples and give the order of the steps that they need to carry out. Help students see how the same basic equation-solving strategy applies at each level of complexity even though additional steps may be added.

USE SCAFFOLDING

You may wish to provide students with templates similar to the one below to guide their work as they solve equations.

$-2(x + 5) + 6x = 30$	
____ + ____ + $6x = 30$	Distributive property
____x __ ____ $= 30$	Combine like terms.
____x ________ = ________	+/− property of equality
____x = ____	Simplify.
____ = ____	×/÷ property of equality
x = ____	Simplify.

Alternatively, you may want to provide students with several model problems for which you have shown all the necessary steps. Students can then use these models to guide them when working problems on their own.

USE REPETITION

REVERSING INEQUALITIES Plan on repeating Concept Activity 3.5 on page 143 with several additional examples in order to help underachievers become comfortable solving inequalities using multiplication or division. The concept of multiplying or dividing an inequality by a negative number is confusing for many underachievers. Take extra time here to answer any student questions about when and why the direction of the inequality is reversed.

USE A CO-TEACHING MODEL

This chapter requires much reading and analyzing of sentences. You may wish to work with a Special Educator who can help underachievers with reading strategies, especially with strategies for identifying the important information in each problem.

Strategies for English Learners

VOCABULARY AND SYMBOLS

Since this chapter has students working with inequalities, have students review the symbols used and their meanings. You can use shapes or simple equations to get the point across.

is equal to	$=$
is not equal to	$\neq$
is approximately equal to	$\approx$
is less than	$<$
is greater than	$>$
is less than or equal to	$\leq$
is greater than or equal to	$\geq$

You can use antonyms such as: *equal* : *unequal*
same : *different*
approximate : *exact*
equivalent : *unequivalent*
(or *not equivalent*)

Students can also review in terms of synonyms: *equal, same, congruent, equivalent, identical.* You may wish to have students begin a symbols list in their notebooks and then add to it as the year progresses.

Strategies for Advanced Learners

INCREASE DEPTH AND COMPLEXITY

In Lesson 3.6, you can extend Exercise 34 on page 153 by having students research local health clubs and then write inequalities to help them compare the costs of different plans to find which clubs offer the best deals for given conditions. Some other real-world situations that can be analyzed similarly are video rental plans or music clubs through which you buy CDs. Long-distance telephone plans also have various combinations of monthly fees and per-minute costs that can be compared using inequalities. Since a great number of students now have cell phones, it can be very useful for them to compare the costs of different plans and providers. Though cell phone plans tend to have many variables that can make it difficult to compare costs directly, students can still collect data from local service providers to make conclusions about which plan would be best for their personal situations.

You may wish to have advanced learners extend their exposure to compound inequalities from Exercise 44 on page 142 by guiding them as they attempt to solve and graph compound inequalities that require two or more steps, such as those shown below. These examples also expose students to the compact form for writing "and" inequalities.

$$-6 < 3x - 9 < 12$$
$$-12 \leq -4(2x - 5) \leq -4$$

USE CROSS-CURRICULAR CONNECTIONS

Chapter 3 is filled with real world situations, some of which can be adapted into cross-curricular activities. These include class trip planning (Exercise 35 on page 124) and school-related fundraising (Exercise 46 on page 142). For example, if your class will be going on a class trip, this is an excellent opportunity to involve students as much as possible in investigating and/or planning the process. Areas of investigation could include, but are not limited to, additional information about the destination, costs, collecting money, writing informational notes to parents, and writing articles for a school newspaper.

CHAPTER 3

Differentiating Instruction: Resource Materials

Differentiating Alternative Assessment

McDougal Littell *Pre-Algebra* offers teachers a wide variety of alternative assessment for all levels of students. Pictured here are facsimiles of the alternative assessment pages from the *Assessment Book*, and the various types of chapter projects available in the *Chapter 3 Resource Book*.

ASSESSMENT BOOK

The *Assessment Book* contains two pages of alternative assessment for each chapter in the textbook.

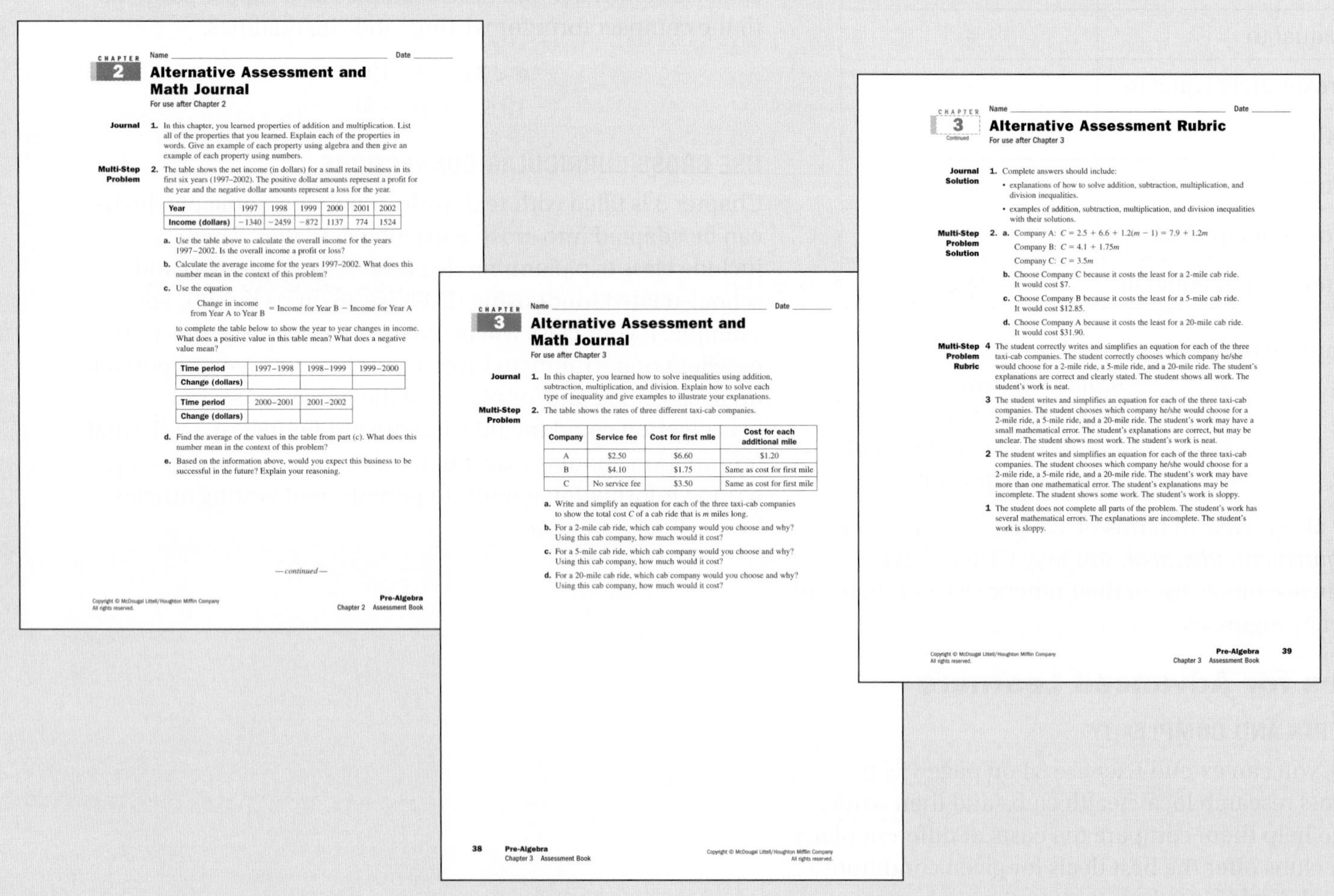

CHAPTER 2 Name ______ Date ______

Alternative Assessment and Math Journal

For use after Chapter 2

Journal 1. In this chapter, you learned properties of addition and multiplication. List all of the properties that you learned. Explain each of the properties in words. Give an example of each property using algebra and then give an example of each property using numbers.

Multi-Step Problem 2. The table shows the net income (in dollars) for a small retail business in its first six years (1997–2002). The positive dollar amounts represent a profit for the year and the negative dollar amounts represent a loss for the year.

Year	1997	1998	1999	2000	2001	2002
Income (dollars)	−1340	−2459	−872	1137	774	1524

a. Use the table above to calculate the overall income for the years 1997–2002. Is the overall income a profit or loss?

b. Calculate the average income for the years 1997–2002. What does this number mean in the context of this problem?

c. Use the equation

Change in income from Year A to Year B = Income for Year B − Income for Year A

to complete the table below to show the year to year changes in income. What does a positive value in this table mean? What does a negative value mean?

Time period	1997–1998	1998–1999	1999–2000
Change (dollars)			

Time period	2000–2001	2001–2002
Change (dollars)		

d. Find the average of the values in the table from part (c). What does this number mean in the context of this problem?

e. Based on the information above, would you expect this business to be successful in the future? Explain your reasoning.

—continued—

CHAPTER 3 Name ______ Date ______

Alternative Assessment and Math Journal

For use after Chapter 3

Journal 1. In this chapter, you learned how to solve inequalities using addition, subtraction, multiplication, and division. Explain how to solve each type of inequality and give examples to illustrate your explanations.

Multi-Step Problem 2. The table shows the rates of three different taxi-cab companies.

Company	Service fee	Cost for first mile	Cost for each additional mile
A	$2.50	$6.60	$1.20
B	$4.10	$1.75	Same as cost for first mile
C	No service fee	$3.50	Same as cost for first mile

a. Write and simplify an equation for each of the three taxi-cab companies to show the total cost C of a cab ride that is m miles long.

b. For a 2-mile cab ride, which cab company would you choose and why? Using this cab company, how much would it cost?

c. For a 5-mile cab ride, which cab company would you choose and why? Using this cab company, how much would it cost?

d. For a 20-mile cab ride, which cab company would you choose and why? Using this cab company, how much would it cost?

CHAPTER 3 Continued Name ______ Date ______

Alternative Assessment Rubric

For use after Chapter 3

Journal Solution 1. Complete answers should include:

- explanations of how to solve addition, subtraction, multiplication, and division inequalities.
- examples of addition, subtraction, multiplication, and division inequalities with their solutions.

Multi-Step Problem Solution 2. a. Company A: $C = 2.5 + 6.6 + 1.2(m - 1) = 7.9 + 1.2m$

Company B: $C = 4.1 + 1.75m$

Company C: $C = 3.5m$

b. Choose Company C because it costs the least for a 2-mile cab ride. It would cost $7.

c. Choose Company B because it costs the least for a 5-mile cab ride. It would cost $12.85.

d. Choose Company A because it costs the least for a 20-mile cab ride. It would cost $31.90.

Multi-Step Problem Rubric

4 The student correctly writes and simplifies an equation for each of the three taxi-cab companies. The student correctly chooses which company he/she would choose for a 2-mile ride, a 5-mile ride, and a 20-mile ride. The student's explanations are correct and clearly stated. The student shows all work. The student's work is neat.

3 The student writes and simplifies an equation for each of the three taxi-cab companies. The student chooses which company he/she would choose for a 2-mile ride, a 5-mile ride, and a 20-mile ride. The student's work may have a small mathematical error. The student's explanations are correct, but may be unclear. The student shows most work. The student's work is neat.

2 The student writes and simplifies an equation for each of the three taxi-cab companies. The student chooses which company he/she would choose for a 2-mile ride, a 5-mile ride, and a 20-mile ride. The student's work may have more than one mathematical error. The student's explanations may be incomplete. The student shows some work. The student's work is sloppy.

1 The student does not complete all parts of the problem. The student's work has several mathematical errors. The explanations are incomplete. The student's work is sloppy.

RESOURCE BOOK

The *Chapter Resource Books* contain three different projects for each chapter: Real Life, Cooperative, and Independent Extra Credit. Each project is accompanied by a scoring rubric. A complete discussion of rubrics is available in the *Professional Development Book*.

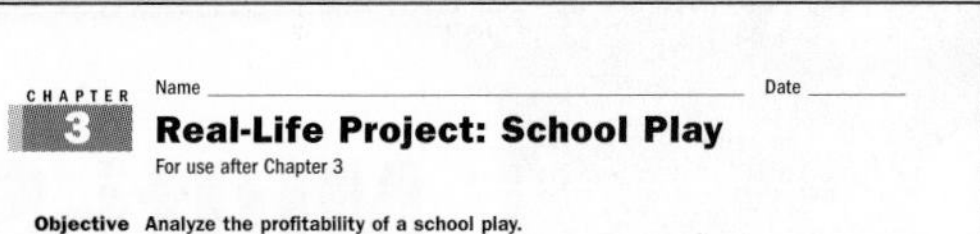

CHAPTER 3 Name ______ Date ______

Real-Life Project: School Play

For use after Chapter 3

Objective **Analyze the profitability of a school play.**

Materials pencil, paper, access to the Internet

Investigation *Getting Going* Your school has an annual play to raise money. You are the supervisor of a committee to organize the play. You decide to have three nights of performances, on Friday, Saturday, and Sunday. The income depends on the number of people that attend the play and pay the admission price. The profit that the school makes is the income minus the expenses. Expenses consist of the costs for snacks and refreshments, spotlight rental, and materials for the costumes and scenery.

Questions

1. The committee decides to charge the same admission fee for students and adults. The table shows the attendance for each night of the play. Write an expression to find the admission income. Let f represent the admission fee. Then evaluate the expression when the admission fee is $4.

Night	Attendance
Friday	216
Saturday	268
Sunday	300

2. Suppose the committee charges admission fees of $5 for adults and $3 for students. The admission profits are shown in the table. Solve the equation $5a + 3(216 - a) = 888$ to find the number of adults a and the number of students that attended the play Friday night.

Night	Admission Profits
Friday	$888
Saturday	$1084
Sunday	$1240

3. You make a list of expenses for the play. The school has $1000 budgeted for expenses. Solve the inequality $3(230 + s) + 80 + 110 \le 1000$ to determine how much money you have remaining to spend on spotlight rentals for each night.

Expense	Cost
Snacks/refreshments	$230/night
Spotlight rentals	s/night
Costume materials	$80
Scenery materials	$110

4. Find the school's profit from the play. Use the table in Exercise 2 and assume the entire budget is spent.
5. Suppose the committee charges $3 for adults and $1.50 for students. Use the table from Exercise 1 and the table shown to find the number of adults and students that attended the play each night.

Night	Admission Profits
Friday	$511.50
Saturday	$603
Sunday	$694.50

6. Using the same expenses, compare the profits for both sets of admission prices. What conclusions can you make? Explain in detail any changes you might make.
7. Choose a partner and organize your own play. Set your own admission prices and use the Internet to research costs for expenses. Set up equations for your partner to solve to find the number of adults and students that attended your play. Compare profits from both plays.

Review and Projects

CHAPTER 3 Continued Name ______ Date ______

Teacher's Notes for School Play Project

For use after Chapter 3

Project Goals
- Add, subtract, and multiply integers.
- Simplify and evaluate expressions.
- Solve equations and inequalities using the distributive property.
- Write and solve equations using addition, subtraction, and division.
- Write and solve equations involving decimals.

Managing the Project *Guiding Students' Work* Encourage students to show all of their work when solving the exercises. Question 5 may be a little difficult to set up the equations for Friday, Saturday, and Sunday, but explain that these are modeled after the equation in Question 2, which should make writing the equations clearer.

When organizing their play, remind students to think economically about the expenses and to maximize the profit. You can also encourage students to possibly include new expenses or new ways to earn income at the play. An example of a new expense might be to hire a disc jockey for music for the play.

Rubric for Project **The following rubric can be used to assess student work.**

4 All of the expressions are correct. The student has written the correct equations and solved them correctly. The student has compared the profits and made insightful conclusions. If changes were made, the changes are reasonable and clearly stated. The student organizes his or her own play with reasonable admission prices, expenses and profit. The equations are then written correctly and solved. The student's work is neat.

3 All of the expressions are correct. The student has written the correct equations and solved them correctly, but some steps may be missing. The student has correctly compared the profits but the conclusions are a little unclear. The student organizes his or her own play and sets up the equations, but there are some minor errors. The student's work is neat.

2 The student's expressions may have minor errors. The equations are written but not solved correctly in some cases. The student has compared the profits but no conclusions are given. The student organizes his or her own play and sets up the equations, but there are some errors. The student's work is sloppy or incomplete.

1 The student's work has several mathematical errors. The equations are incorrect, making the solutions invalid. The student does not correctly calculate the profits and compare them. No attempt is made to organize his or her own play. The student's work is incomplete or sloppy.

Review and Projects

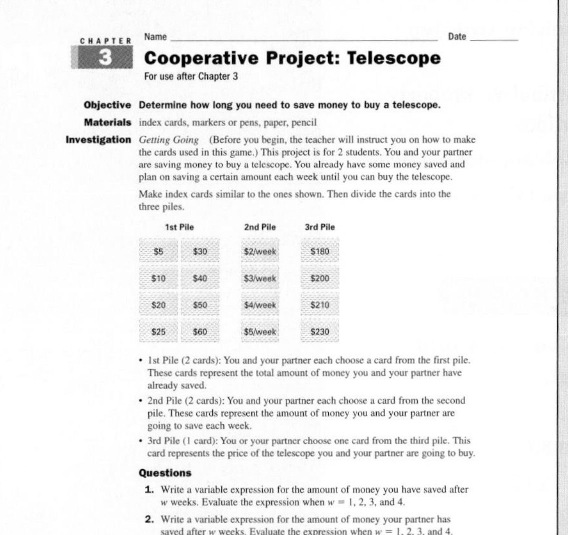

CHAPTER 3 Name ______ Date ______

Cooperative Project: Telescope

For use after Chapter 3

Objective **Determine how long you need to save money to buy a telescope.**

Materials index cards, markers or pens, paper, pencil

Investigation *Getting Going* (Before you begin, the teacher will instruct you on how to make the cards used in this game.) This project is for 2 students. You and your partner are saving money to buy a telescope. You already have some money saved and plan on saving a certain amount each week until you can buy the telescope.

Make index cards similar to the ones shown. Then divide the cards into the three piles.

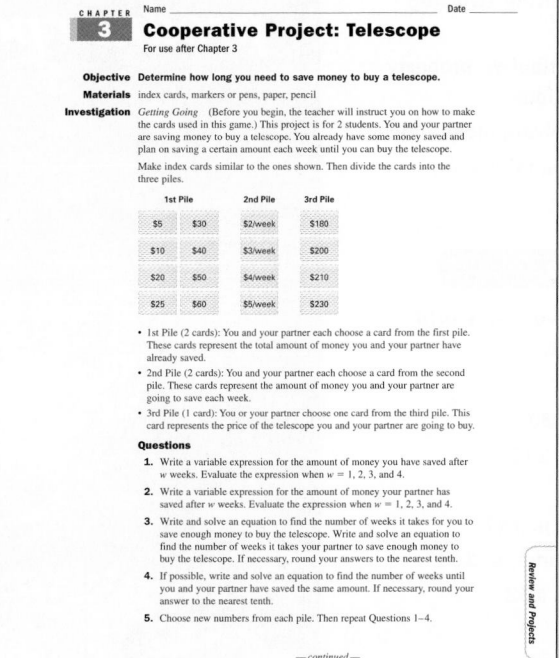

1st Pile		2nd Pile	3rd Pile
$5	$30	$2/week	$180
$10	$40	$3/week	$200
$20	$50	$4/week	$210
$25	$60	$5/week	$230

- 1st Pile (2 cards): You and your partner each choose a card from the first pile. These cards represent the total amount of money you and your partner have already saved.
- 2nd Pile (2 cards): You and your partner each choose a card from the second pile. These cards represent the amount of money you and your partner are going to save each week.
- 3rd Pile (1 card): You or your partner choose one card from the third pile. This card represents the price of the telescope you and your partner are going to buy.

Questions

1. Write a variable expression for the amount of money you have saved after w weeks. Evaluate the expression when $w = 1, 2, 3,$ and 4.
2. Write a variable expression for the amount of money your partner has saved after w weeks. Evaluate the expression when $w = 1, 2, 3,$ and 4.
3. Write and solve an equation to find the number of weeks it takes for you to save enough money to buy the telescope. Write and solve an equation to find the number of weeks it takes your partner to save enough money to buy the telescope. If necessary, round your answers to the nearest tenth.
4. If possible, write and solve an equation to find the number of weeks until you and your partner have saved the same amount. If necessary, round your answer to the nearest tenth.
5. Choose new numbers from each pile. Then repeat Questions 1–4.

—*continued*—

Review and Projects

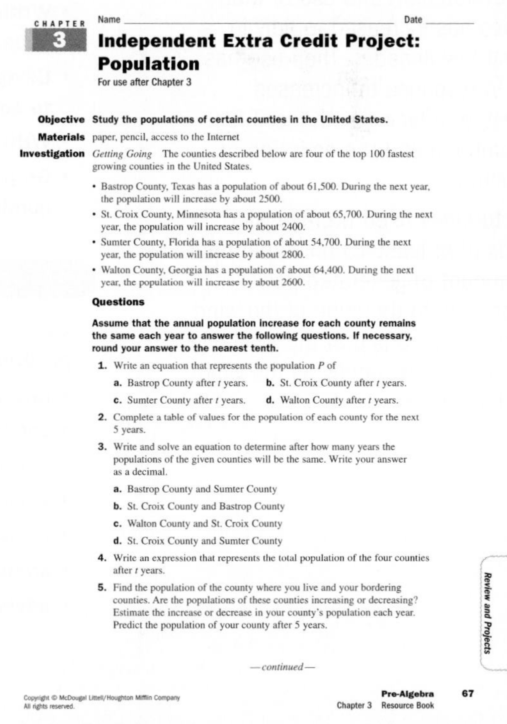

CHAPTER 3 Name ______ Date ______

Independent Extra Credit Project: Population

For use after Chapter 3

Objective **Study the populations of certain counties in the United States.**

Materials paper, pencil, access to the Internet

Investigation *Getting Going* The counties described below are four of the top 100 fastest growing counties in the United States.

- Bastrop County, Texas has a population of about 61,500. During the next year, the population will increase by about 2500.
- St. Croix County, Minnesota has a population of about 65,700. During the next year, the population will increase by about 2400.
- Sumter County, Florida has a population of about 54,700. During the next year, the population will increase by about 2800.
- Walton County, Georgia has a population of about 64,400. During the next year, the population will increase by about 2600.

Questions

Assume that the annual population increase for each county remains the same each year to answer the following questions. If necessary, round your answer to the nearest tenth.

1. Write an equation that represents the population P of
   a. Bastrop County after t years. b. St. Croix County after t years.
   c. Sumter County after t years. d. Walton County after t years.
2. Complete a table of values for the population of each county for the next 5 years.
3. Write and solve an equation to determine after how many years the populations of the given counties will be the same. Write your answer as a decimal.
   a. Bastrop County and Sumter County
   b. St. Croix County and Bastrop County
   c. Walton County and St. Croix County
   d. St. Croix County and Sumter County
4. Write an expression that represents the total population of the four counties after t years.
5. Find the population of the county where you live and your bordering counties. Are the populations of these counties increasing or decreasing? Estimate the increase or decrease in your county's population each year. Predict the population of your county after 5 years.

—*continued*—

Review and Projects

OVERVIEW

Main Ideas

In this chapter, students write and solve two-step equations, equations having like terms and involving parentheses, and equations with variables on both sides. Students then write and solve inequalities using addition, subtraction, multiplication, and division. Students graph the solutions of inequalities on a number line. Finally, students solve multi-step inequalities.

Application Note

Wind power has been used for thousands of years. Windmills were used to pump water more than 2000 years ago in China. In the 1800's, windmills were used extensively throughout rural areas of the United States to pump water. Today, large wind turbines built by utility companies can exceed 300 feet in height, with blades more than 100 feet long.

The development and use of wind turbines has increased rapidly in the last few decades. Their use has been in response to increased interest in reducing both fossil fuel consumption and the emission of air pollutants.

Wind turbines need average wind speeds of at least 13 miles per hour. The amount of generated power is proportional to the cube of the wind speed. This means that the available power increases rapidly as the wind speed increases.

CHAPTER 3

Multi-Step Equations *and* Inequalities

BEFORE

In previous chapters you've . . .

- **Written and evaluated variable expressions**
- **Used the distributive property to simplify variable expressions**
- **Solved one-step equations**

Now

In Chapter 3 you'll study . . .

- **Writing and solving two-step equations**
- **Using the distributive property to solve equations**
- **Writing and solving inequalities**
- **Graphing inequalities on a number line**

WHY?

So you can solve real-world problems about. . .

- **rafting, p. 123**
- **shopping, p. 133**
- **astronauts, p. 140**
- **skiing, p. 142**
- **in-line skates, p. 147**
- **amusement parks, p. 151**
- **advertising, p. 152**

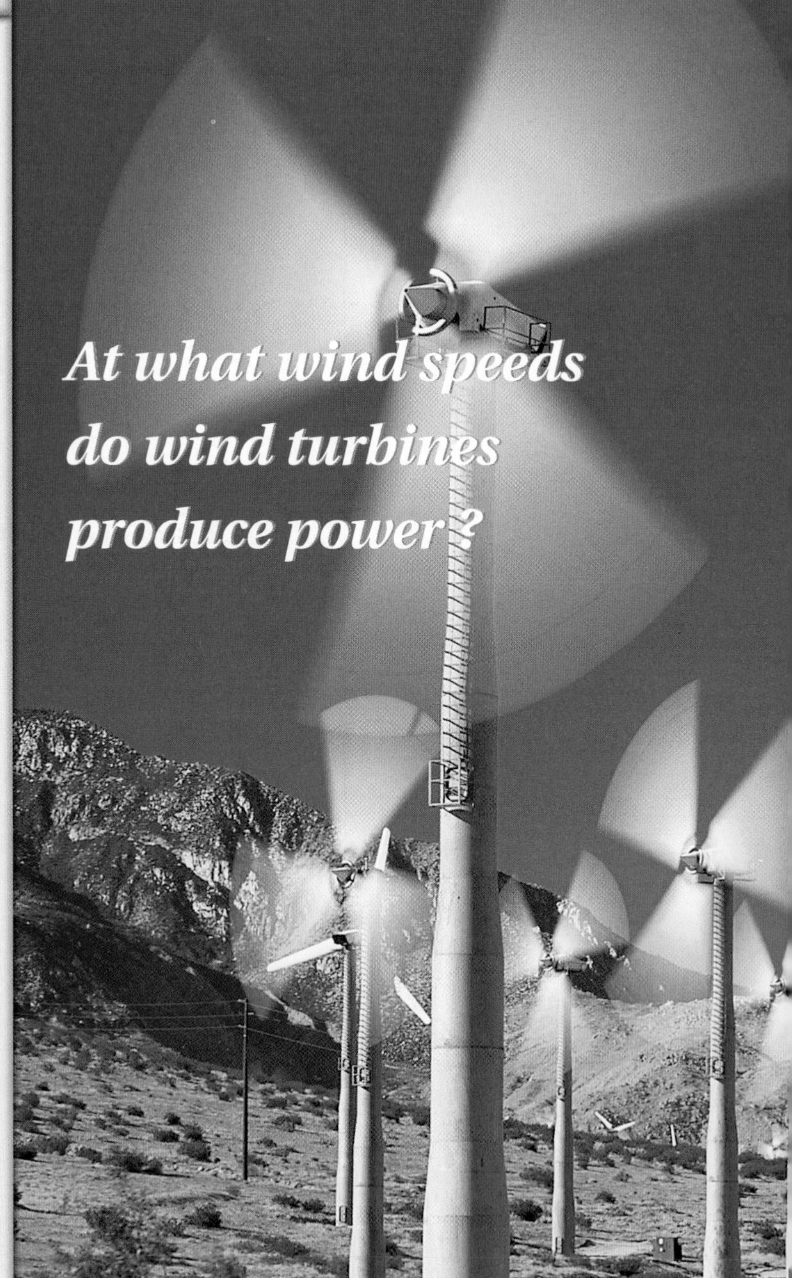

At what wind speeds do wind turbines produce power?

CHAPTER 3

INTERNET Preview

CLASSZONE.COM

- eEdition Plus Online
- eWorkbook Plus Online
- eTutorial Plus Online
- State Test Practice
- More Examples

MATH In the Real World

Wind Power These wind turbines near Palm Springs, California, produce power when the wind turns their blades. In this chapter, you will use inequalities to describe quantities like wind speed.

What do you think? Suppose a turbine begins producing power when the wind speed is at least 10 miles per hour, and shuts down when the wind speed exceeds 65 miles per hour. Plot 10 and 65 on a number line. Shade the number line to show the speeds at which the turbine produces power.

See margin.

CHAPTER RESOURCES

These resources are provided to help you prepare for the chapter and to customize review materials:

Chapter 3 Resource Book

- Tips for New Teachers, pp. 1–2
- Lesson Plan, pp. 5, 15, 24, 35, 45, 54
- Lesson Plan for Block Scheduling, pp. 6, 16, 25, 36, 46, 55

Technology

- EasyPlanner CD-ROM
- Test and Practice Generator
- Electronic Lesson Presentations CD-ROM
- eTutorial CD-ROM

Internet

- Classzone
- eEdition Plus Online
- eWorkbook Plus Online
- eTutorial Plus Online
- EasyPlanner Plus Online

ENGLISH LEARNER SUPPORT

- Spanish Study Guide
- Multi-Language Visual Glossary
- Chapter Audio Summaries CDs
- Teacher's Edition, pp. 116E–116F

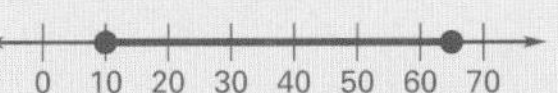

PREPARE

DIAGNOSIS/REMEDIATION

Prerequisite Skills Quiz

The Prerequisite Skills Quiz can help you diagnose whether students have the following skills needed in Chapter 3:

- Use vocabulary (Ex. 1)
- Use the distributive property (Exs. 2–5)
- Simplify expressions (Exs. 6–9)
- Solve equations (Exs. 10–13)

 ***Chapter 3 Resource Book***

- Study Guide (Lessons 3.1–3.6)

 ***Tutor Place***

NOTETAKING STRATEGIES

Stress that lesson topics build on each other. Students might wish to record in their notebooks how a new lesson skill is similar to a skill they already know. Further suggestions for keeping a notebook can be found on pages 132 and 150.

For more support on notetaking, see:

- Notetaking Guide Workbook
- Notetaking Transparencies

CHAPTER 3

Chapter Prerequisite Skills

Review Vocabulary

like terms, p. 78
equation, p. 85
solution of an equation, p. 85
inverse operations, p. 91
equivalent equations, p. 91

PREREQUISITE SKILLS QUIZ

Preparing for Success To prepare for success in this chapter, test your knowledge of these concepts and skills. You may want to look at the pages referred to in blue for additional review.

1. **Vocabulary** Explain what an equation is. Then give an example of an equation with a variable in it.

1. *Sample answer:* An equation is a mathematical sentence that is formed by placing an equal sign between two expressions, for example, $5x - 3 = 22$.

Use the distributive property to write an equivalent variable expression. *(p. 71)*

2. $9(x - 4)$ **$9x - 36$**
3. $8(z - 7)$ **$8z - 56$**
4. $-6(-m + 12)$ **$6m - 72$**
5. $-10(n - 5)$ **$-10n + 50$**

Simplify the expression. *(p. 78)*

6. $c + 4 - c$ **4**
7. $9b - 12b + 3$ **$-3b + 3$**
8. $4(a + 2) + a$ **$5a + 8$**
9. $2(2d + 5 + d)$ **$6d + 10$**

Solve the equation. Check your solution. *(pp. 91, 97, and 102)*

10. $x + 13 = 7$ **-6**
11. $\frac{h}{6} = -8$ **-48**
12. $q - 9.6 = 2$ **11.6**
13. $65 = -13b$ **-5**

NOTETAKING STRATEGIES

Note *Worthy*

You will find a notetaking strategy at the beginning of each chapter. Look for additional notetaking and study strategies throughout the chapter.

SUMMARIZING At the end of each lesson, summarize the main idea of the lesson in your notes. Include important details.

Lesson 2.6 Solving Equations Using Multiplication or Division

Main Idea: Multiplying or dividing each side of an equation by the same nonzero number results in an equivalent equation.

Use division to solve multiplication equations.

$$2x = 6$$
$$\frac{2x}{2} = \frac{6}{2}$$
$$x = 3$$

Use multiplication to solve division equations.

$$\frac{x}{5} = 10$$
$$5\left(\frac{x}{5}\right) = 5(10)$$
$$x = 50$$

You may find this strategy helpful in Lesson 3.6 when you solve multi-step inequalities.

Concept *Activity*

3.1 Modeling Two-Step Equations

Goal
Model and solve two-step equations.

Materials
• algebra tiles

Investigate

Use algebra tiles to solve $3x + 6 = 12$.

1. Model $3x + 6 = 12$ using algebra tiles.

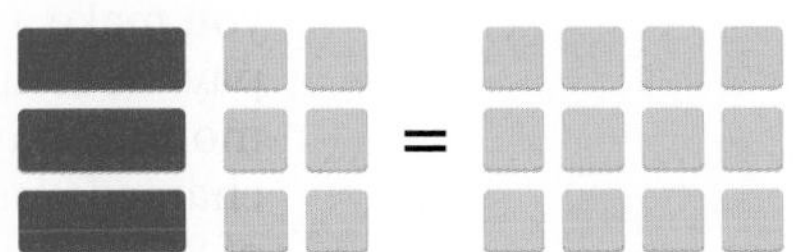

2. Remove six 1-tiles from each side.

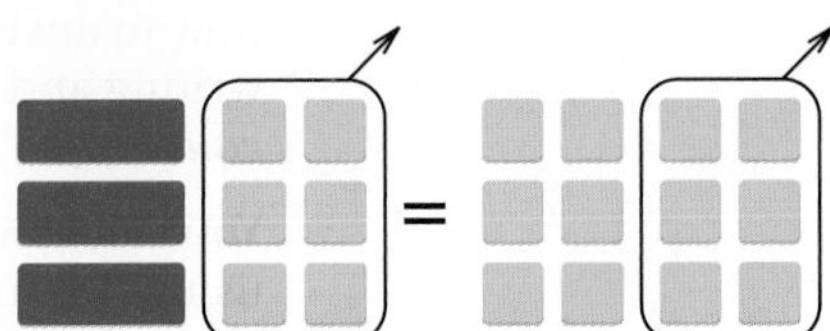

3. Divide the remaining tiles into three equal groups. Each x-tile is equal to two 1-tiles. So, the solution is 2.

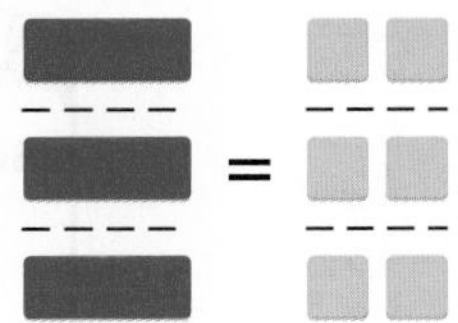

Draw Conclusions

Use algebra tiles to model and solve the equation.

1. $1 + 2x = 9$ 4
2. $4x + 1 = 5$ 1
3. $2x + 2 = 8$ 3
4. $9 = 2x + 5$ 2
5. $11 = 2 + 3x$ 3
6. $5x + 3 = 8$ 1

7. Critical Thinking What property of equality is used in Step 2? in Step 3? **subtraction property of equality; division property of equality**

8. ***Writing*** For each algebra-tile model shown above, write a corresponding algebraic equation. **Step 1: $3x + 6 = 12$; Step 2: $3x = 6$; Step 3: $x = 2$**

9. Interpret Describe the steps you would take to solve $2x + 1 = 5$ without using algebra tiles.
Sample answer: **First I would subtract 1 from each side to obtain $2x = 4$. Then I would divide each side by 2 to obtain $x = 2$.**

NCTM CURRICULUM STANDARDS
Standard 2: Use models to understand relationships; Use models to represent relationships

1 PLAN

Investigate the Concept
- Students model and solve two-step equations.
- This activity leads into solving two-step equations in Lesson 3.1.

Materials
Each student will need algebra tiles. See the Activity Support Master in the *Chapter 3 Resource Book*. A support transparency is also available.

Recommended Time
Work activity: 10 min
Discuss results: 5 min

Grouping
Students should work individually.

2 TEACH

Alternative Strategy
Model the activity for the class by having 21 students act as "algebra tiles." Have three students model x-tiles by giving them a large sheet of brightly colored paper to hold. The other students each represent a 1-tile. Group the students according to the steps in the activity.

3 CLOSE

Key Discovery
Two-step equations can be solved using the properties of equality.

Assessment
1. Why were six 1-tiles removed from each side of the equation in step 2? **So the x-tiles will be alone on one side of the equation.**

1 PLAN

Skill Check

1. $-4 - 8 = \underline{?}$ -12
2. $-7 + 17 = \underline{?}$ 10
3. $-36 \div (-6) = \underline{?}$ 6
4. $5 \cdot \frac{1}{5} = \underline{?}$ 1

Lesson Objective

Solve two-step equations.

Pacing

Suggested Number of Days
Basic Course: 1 day
Average Course: 1 day
Advanced Course: 1 day
Block: 0.5 block with 3.2

Teaching Resources

For a complete list of Teaching Resources, see page 116B.

 **Transparency**

Warm-Up Exercises for this lesson are available on a transparency.

2 TEACH

Motivating the Lesson

Have a volunteer explain the meaning of the term *down payment*. Ask: "After the down payment for the drum set is made, what is the balance due?" **$345**

TIPS *for* NEW TEACHERS

Encourage students to show every step when solving an equation, because these steps are important for diagnosing errors. See Tips for New Teachers in the *Chapter 3 Resource Book*.

LESSON **3.1**

Solving Two-Step Equations

BEFORE	Now	WHY?
You solved one-step equations.	You'll solve two-step equations.	So you can find the cost of a rafting trip, as in Ex. 21.

Review Vocabulary
verbal model, p. 6
equation, p. 85
inverse operations, p. 91

Drum Set You are buying a drum set that costs \$495. The music store lets you make a down payment. You can pay the remaining cost in three equal monthly payments with no interest charged. You make a down payment of \$150. How much is each monthly payment? In Example 4, you will see how to answer this question by writing and solving a *two-step equation.*

You can solve a two-step equation by using two inverse operations.

Example 1 *Using Subtraction and Division to Solve*

Solve $3x + 7 = -5$. Check your solution.

$3x + 7 = -5$	Write original equation.
$3x + 7 - 7 = -5 - 7$	Subtract 7 from each side.
$3x = -12$	Simplify.
$\frac{3x}{3} = \frac{-12}{3}$	Divide each side by 3.
$x = -4$	Simplify.

Answer The solution is -4.

✓**Check** $3x + 7 = -5$	Write original equation.
$3(-4) + 7 \stackrel{?}{=} -5$	Substitute -4 for x.
$-5 = -5$ ✓	Solution checks.

Checkpoint

Solve the equation. Check your solution.

1. $4x + 1 = 5$ 1
2. $3n + 8 = 2$ -2
3. $1 = 2r + 9$ -4
4. $2 = 6h + 20$ -3
5. **Critical Thinking** How is solving $3x - 7 = -5$ different from solving $3x + 7 = -5$?

5. *Sample answer:* When solving $3x - 7 = -5$, 7 would be added to each side of the equation, while when solving $3x + 7 = -5$, 7 would be subtracted from each side of the equation.

NCTM CURRICULUM STANDARDS
Standard 1: Understand meanings of operations; Understand how operations are related
Standard 2: Represent situations using algebraic symbols

Example 2 *Using Addition and Multiplication to Solve*

Solve $\frac{x}{2} - 3 = 1$. Check your solution.

$\frac{x}{2} - 3 = 1$	**Write original equation.**
$\frac{x}{2} - 3 + 3 = 1 + 3$	**Add 3 to each side.**
$\frac{x}{2} = 4$	**Simplify.**
$2\left(\frac{x}{2}\right) = 2(4)$	**Multiply each side by 2.**
$x = 8$	**Simplify.**

Answer The solution is 8.

✓**Check** $\frac{x}{2} - 3 = 1$	**Write original equation.**
$\frac{8}{2} - 3 \stackrel{?}{=} 1$	**Substitute 8 for *x*.**
$1 = 1$ ✓	**Solution checks.**

 ***Checkpoint***

Solve the equation. Check your solution.

6. $\frac{b}{4} - 8 = 1$ 36 **7.** $\frac{c}{6} - 2 = 6$ 48 **8.** $2 = \frac{d}{5} - 1$ 15 **9.** $12 = \frac{f}{2} - 8$ 40

Example 3 *Solving an Equation with Negative Coefficients*

Solve $7 - 4y = 19$. Check your solution.

$7 - 4y = 19$	**Write original equation.**
$7 - 4y - 7 = 19 - 7$	**Subtract 7 from each side.**
$-4y = 12$	**Simplify.**
$\frac{-4y}{-4} = \frac{12}{-4}$	**Divide each side by −4.**
$y = -3$	**Simplify.**

Answer The solution is −3.

✓**Check** $7 - 4y = 19$	**Write original equation.**
$7 - 4(-3) \stackrel{?}{=} 19$	**Substitute −3 for *y*.**
$19 = 19$ ✓	**Solution checks.**

Reading *Algebra*

When you subtract 7 from the left side of the equation in Example 3, you are left with the equation $0 - 4y = 12$. This equation is equivalent to $0 + (-4y) = 12$, or $-4y = 12$.

 ***Checkpoint***

Solve the equation. Check your solution.

10. $12 - 4s = -12$ 6 **11.** $6 - 2m = 8$ −1 **12.** $-2 = 5 - n$ 7

Extra Examples

Example 1 Solve $8x + 7 = 47$. Check your solution. **5**

Example 2 Solve $\frac{y}{4} - 2 = 1$. Check your solution. **12**

Example 3 Solve $9 - 6a = 45$. Check your solution. **−6**

Reading Strategy

After working through Examples 1–3, focus students' attention on the subtitle appearing to the right of each "Example" heading. Have students read the subtitle, review the example, and summarize what they have learned.

Teaching Tip

Before discussing Example 1, review the meaning of the term *inverse operations*. Also remind students that when solving an equation, the intent is to isolate the variable on one side of the equation. For two-step equations, once the variable is isolated, either multiplication or division can then be used to obtain a coefficient of 1 for the variable.

Common Error

In Example 3, watch for students who add 4 to each side of $-4y = 12$ to get $y = 16$. Remind students that $-4y = -4 \cdot y$, not $-4 + y$.

Extra Examples

Example 4 Travis makes a down payment of \$1100 on a motorcycle costing \$2300. If no interest is charged, how many monthly payments of \$200 must he make until he has finished paying for the motorcycle? **6 payments**

CROSS-CURRICULUM

Science Science experiments often involve situations that require solving a two-step equation.

DIFFERENTIATING INSTRUCTION

Advanced Students Have students divide every term in a given equation by 10. For example, dividing each term in the equation $3x + 7 = -5$ yields the equivalent equation $0.3x + 0.7 = -0.5$. Then have students solve the "new" equation. Ask students how solving equations involving decimals is different from solving equations involving only whole numbers, and how it is similar.

CONCEPT CHECK

Explain how you solve the equation $11 - 4p = -1$. ***Sample answer:*** **First subtract 11 from each side, then divide both sides of the resulting equation by −4. The solution is 3.**

DAILY PUZZLER

Jacob has lived one fourth of his life in Michigan, one fifth of his life in Texas, one third of his life in Hawaii, and he has been living in Ohio for the past 13 years. How old is Jacob? **60 years old**

Example 4 *Writing and Solving a Two-Step Equation*

Find the monthly payment for the drum set described on page 120.

Solution

Let p represent the monthly payment. Write a verbal model.

Total cost of drum set	=	Amount of down payment	+	Number of months	•	Monthly payment

$495 = 150 + 3p$	**Substitute.**
$495 - 150 = 150 + 3p - 150$	**Subtract 150 from each side.**
$345 = 3p$	**Simplify.**
$\frac{345}{3} = \frac{3p}{3}$	**Divide each side by 3.**
$115 = p$	**Simplify.**

Answer The monthly payment is \$115.

3.1 Exercises

More Practice, p. 805

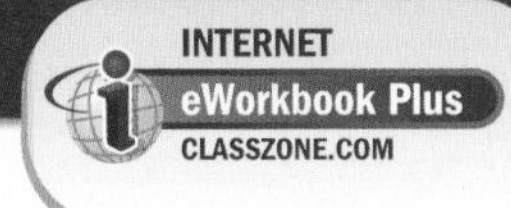

Guided Practice

Vocabulary Check

1. Copy and complete: You can use two _?_ operations to solve a two-step equation. **inverse**
2. Describe the steps you would use to solve the equation $9 + 2s = 15$. **See margin.**

Skill Check **Solve the equation. Check your solution.**

3. $5c + 6 = 31$ **5**
4. $-2 = \frac{t}{3} - 11$ **27**
5. $-9z + 4 = -5$ **1**
6. $-8 - 8d = 64$ **−9**

Guided Problem Solving

7. **Car Repair** The total cost of repairing a car is the sum of the amount paid for parts and the amount paid for labor. You paid \$78 for parts and \$45 for each hour of labor. The total cost to repair the car was \$168. How many hours did it take to repair the car?

   1) Copy and complete the verbal model.

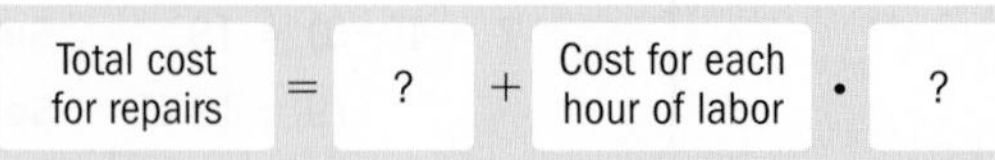

Total cost for repairs
=
?
+
Cost for each hour of labor
•
?

   Cost for parts **Number of hours of labor**

   2) Let h represent the number of hours spent on labor. Write an equation based on your verbal model. **168 = 78 + 45*h***

   3) Solve the equation to find how many hours it took to repair the car. **2 h**

2\. ***Sample answer:*** **First I would subtract 9 from each side to obtain $2s = 6$. Then I would divide each side by 2 to obtain $s = 3$.**

Practice and Problem Solving

Homework Help

Example	Exercises
1	8-19
2	8-19
3	8-19
4	20-22

Online Resources
CLASSZONE.COM
- More Examples
- eTutorial Plus

20a. given: initial gallons of gas in tank, final gallons of gas in tank, gallons of gas used per hour; to find out: in how many hours you will need to stop to refuel

27c. No. *Sample answer:* A heifer and two pigs cost $\$500 + 2 \cdot \$120 = \$740$. This leaves $\$755 - \$740 = \$15$, which is less than the $20 cost of a flock of chicks.

Solve the equation. Check your solution.

A **8.** $12k + 7 = 31$ 2 **9.** $13n + 42 = 81$ 3 **10.** $56 = 17p - 29$ 5

11. $\frac{w}{4} - 21 = -3$ 72 **12.** $\frac{h}{9} - 19 = -10$ 81 **13.** $\frac{d}{12} + 25 = 29$ 48

14. $12 = \frac{a}{36} + 17$ −180 **15.** $18 - r = 42$ −24 **16.** $80 = 23 - 3v$ −19

17. $-2q - 63 = 47$ −55 **18.** $-\frac{x}{2} + 4 = 12$ −16 **19.** $-5 = -19 - \frac{x}{7}$ −98

20. Driving Your family is taking a long-distance car trip. You begin with 16 gallons of gasoline in the fuel tank. Your car uses 3 gallons of gasoline per hour of driving. You will stop to refuel when there is exactly 1 gallon of gasoline remaining in the tank.

a. Analyze List the information you are given and the information you need to find.

b. Write a verbal model. Then write an equation based on your verbal model. ***Sample answer:*** **Initial gallons of gas − Gallons used per hour • Number of hours = Final gallons of gas; $16 - 3n = 1$**

c. After how many hours will you need to stop to refuel? Justify your solution by making a table. 5 h; see margin for table.

21. Rafting A group of 9 friends takes a white-water rafting trip. The total price of the trip before any discounts is \$810. Each person in the group receives a student discount. The total price with the discount is \$729. How much is the discount per person? \$9

22. Trains A train consisting of 50 cars and one locomotive weighs a total of 4725 tons. The locomotive weighs 125 tons. All of the cars have the same weight. Find the weight (in tons) of one car. 92 tons

Write the verbal sentence as an equation. Then solve the equation.

B **23.** Five minus the product of 2 and a number is 7. $5 - 2n = 7$; −1

24. Thirty-two minus the product of 9 and a number is 140. $32 - 9n = 140$; −12

25. Thirteen plus the product of 6 and a number is 67. $13 + 6n = 67$; 9

26. Negative 8 minus the product of 3 and a number is 19. $-8 - 3n = 19$; −9

27. Extended Problem Solving Your class has raised \$755 for a hunger relief organization. The organization provides farm animals that people can use to produce food. Your class plans to buy animals for a family recovering from an earthquake.

a. Calculate One heifer (a young cow) costs \$500, and each flock of chicks costs \$20. If your class buys one heifer, how many flocks of chicks can your class buy? 12 flocks

b. Calculate Your class can also buy pigs for \$120 each. If your class buys a heifer for \$500, how many pigs can your class buy? 2 pigs

c. Interpret and Apply If your class decides to buy the heifer and pigs as described in part (b), does your class have enough money to also buy a flock of chicks? Explain your reasoning.

3 APPLY

ASSIGNMENT GUIDE

Basic Course
Day 1: EP p. 804 Exs. 36–50 even; pp. 123–124 Exs. 8–16, 20–24, 28–31, 37–45

Average Course
Day 1: pp. 123–124 Exs. 14–22, 25–29, 32–35, 37–46

Advanced Course
Day 1: pp. 123–124 Exs. 14–24, 27, 30–38*, 43–46

Block
pp. 123–124 Exs. 14–22, 25–29, 32–35, 37–46 (with 3.2)

EXTRA PRACTICE

- Student Edition, p. 805
- Chapter 3 Resource Book, pp. 8–10
- Test and Practice Generator

TRANSPARENCY

Even-numbered answers are available on transparencies. A support transparency is available for Exercise 35.

HOMEWORK CHECK

When you review students' homework for this lesson, go over the following exercises to check understanding of key concepts.
Basic: 8, 11, 14, 16, 20
Average: 14, 16, 17, 19, 21
Advanced: 14, 17, 19, 20, 22

20c.

Hours driven	Gallons left
1	13
2	10
3	7
4	4
5	1

4 ASSESS

Assessment Resources

For more assessment resources, see:
- Assessment Book
- Test and Practice Generator

Mini-Quiz

Solve the equation.

1. $9b + 8 = 80$ 8
2. $\frac{z}{7} - 5 = -3$ 14
3. $-10 = 20 - 6c$ 5
4. $11 - \frac{b}{6} = 23$ −72
5. **Challenge** Solve $\frac{8 + k}{5} = 3$. 7

5 FOLLOW-UP

Diagnosis/Remediation

- Study Guide in Chapter 3 Resource Book, pp. 11–12
- eTutorial Plus Online
- Extra Practice, p. 805
- Lesson Practice in Chapter 3 Resource Book, pp. 8–10

English Learner Support

- Spanish Study Guide
- Multi-Language Visual Glossary
- Chapter Audio Summaries CDs

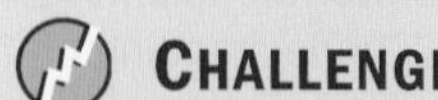

Challenge

- Challenge Practice in Chapter 3 Resource Book, p. 14
- Teacher's Edition, p. 116F

34, 35b, 35d, 36, 46. See Additional Answers beginning on page AA1.

Solve the equation. Check your solution.

28. $54.7 = -9.3n + 8.2$ −5

29. $-5.7 + 2.6d = -14.02$ −3.2

30. $3.2r + 14.7 = -6.74$ −6.7

31. $9.1 = \frac{k}{3.7} + 4.1$ 18.5

32. $11.3 - \frac{p}{2.8} = 1.5$ 27.44

33. $-6.8 - \frac{c}{1.2} = -2.9$ −4.68

34. Compare and Contrast Your friend solved the equation $18 - 2x = -36$ by first adding $2x$ to each side of the equation. You solved the equation by subtracting 18 from each side as the first step. Compare and contrast the two methods. What do you notice? **See margin.**

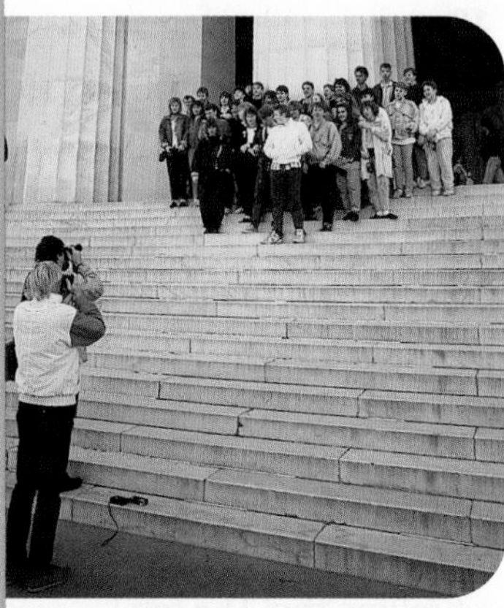

35. Class Trip You are saving money for a class trip to Washington, D.C. You need \$850 for the trip. You have saved \$278. You can save an additional \$50 each month.

Number of months from now	Amount of money saved
0	\$278
1	? \$328
2	? \$378
3	? \$428
4	? \$478

a. Write a variable expression to represent the total amount of money you have saved after m months. Evaluate your expression for whole-number values of m. Record your results in a table like the one shown. $278 + 50m$

b. Analyze Use the data in your table to make a scatter plot. Put months on the horizontal axis and savings on the vertical axis. What pattern do you notice in your graph? How can you use the graph to find the number of months it will take you to save enough money for the trip?

35b. See margin for art. ***Sample answer:*** **The points lie along a straight line; you can extend the scatter plot either by plotting more points as shown or by drawing a line through the plotted points and estimating what value along the horizontal axis corresponds to a value of \$850 on the vertical axis.**

c. Write and solve an equation to find the number of months it will take you to save enough money for the trip. $278 + 50m = 850$, 12 mo

d. Compare List some advantages and disadvantages of the methods you used in parts (a), (b), and (c). **See margin.**

C **36. Challenge** Solve $\frac{x + 2}{4} = 2$. Explain how you solved the equation and how you know your solution is correct. **See margin.**

Mixed Review

Use the distributive property to write an equivalent variable expression. *(Lesson 2.2)*

37. $11(6z + 14)$ $66z + 154$

38. $-9(2x + 12)$ $-18x - 108$

39. $12(3 - 5y)$ $36 - 60y$

40. $8(4 - 7w)$ $32 - 56w$

Algebra Basics **Solve the equation. Check your solution.** *(Lesson 2.5)*

41. $c + 12 = 23$ 11

42. $b + 14 = 91$ 77

43. $x - 17 = -45$ −28

44. $d - 22 = -43$ −21

Standardized Test Practice

45. Multiple Choice What is the solution of the equation $15y - 63 = 57$? B

A. −8 **B.** 8 **C.** 9 **D.** 10

46. Short Response You purchase a video game system for \$150. You make a down payment of \$25. You pay the rest of the money you owe in 5 equal monthly payments with no interest. How much is each monthly payment? Show how you found your answer. **See margin.**

LESSON

3.2 Solving Equations Having Like Terms *and* Parentheses

Review Vocabulary
like terms, p. 78

BEFORE	*Now*	WHY?
You used the distributive property.	You'll solve equations using the distributive property.	So you can budget for fishing rods, as in Ex. 20.

School Spirit Your school's basketball team is playing in the championship game. For the game, the cheerleaders want to buy a banner that costs \$47. They also want to buy small items to give to students in the stands. Pompoms cost \$5.20 each. Noisemakers cost \$.80 each. The cheerleaders have a total budget of \$377 for the game. If they buy equal numbers of pompoms and noisemakers, how many can they afford to buy?

Example 1 *Writing and Solving an Equation*

Find how many pompoms and noisemakers the cheerleaders can afford to buy, as described above.

Solution

Let n represent the number of pompoms and the number of noisemakers. Then $5.20n$ represents the cost of n pompoms, and $0.80n$ represents the cost of n noisemakers. Write a verbal model.

Cost of n pompoms + Cost of n noisemakers + Cost of banner = Total budget

$5.20n + 0.80n + 47 = 377$ **Substitute.**

$6.00n + 47 = 377$ **Combine like terms.**

$6n + 47 - 47 = 377 - 47$ **Subtract 47 from each side.**

$6n = 330$ **Simplify.**

$\frac{6n}{6} = \frac{330}{6}$ **Divide each side by 6.**

$n = 55$ **Simplify.**

Answer The cheerleaders can afford to buy 55 pompoms and 55 noisemakers.

NCTM CURRICULUM STANDARDS
Standard 1: Understand meanings of operations; Understand how operations are related
Standard 2: Represent situations using algebraic symbols

1 PLAN

Skill Check
Use the distributive property.
1. $8(x - 4)$ **$8x - 32$**
2. $-3(a + 2)$ **$-3a - 6$**
3. $4(7 + b)$ **$28 + 4b$**
4. $-5(8 - k)$ **$-40 + 5k$**

Lesson Objective
Solve equations using the distributive property.

Pacing
Suggested Number of Days
Basic Course: 1 day
Average Course: 1 day
Advanced Course: 1 day
Block: 0.5 block with 3.1

Teaching Resources
For a complete list of Teaching Resources, see page 116B.

 **TRANSPARENCY**
Warm-Up Exercises for this lesson are available on a transparency.

2 TEACH

Motivating the Lesson
Bring a catalog of party supplies, office supplies, or something similar to class. Choose several items from the catalog, give students a budget amount, and have them use the catalog items to create two examples similar to Example 1.

TIPS *for* NEW TEACHERS
Some students may be overwhelmed by the increased number of terms in the equations in this lesson. Stress that some of the terms will be combined. See Tips for New Teachers in the *Chapter 3 Resource Book.*

Extra Examples

Example 1 A bookstore spent \$241 to send a group of students to a reading competition. Each student who won was given a \$5 gift certificate and a personalized bookmark that cost \$2. Included in the \$241 was \$45 for the salary of a staff member who accompanied the students to the competition. How many students won prizes? **28 students**

Example 2 Solve the equation.
a. $26 = 2(x - 6)$ **19**
b. $-2(17 - 3k) = -22$ **2**

Example 3 Solve $4k - 3(8k - 60) = -20$. **10**

COMMON ERROR
In the second line of part a in Example 2, watch for students who see the two occurrences of the digits "21" and think that $7x = 0$.

CONCEPT CHECK
What should be your first step when you are solving the equation $10b - 3(4 + b) = 2$? **Apply the distributive property to obtain the equation $10b - 12 - 3b = 2$.**

DAILY PUZZLER
Simplify $a(1 + b[2 + c(3 + d)])$.
$a + 2ab + 3abc + abcd$

Review Help
For help with using the distributive property, see p. 71.

Distributive Property You can use the distributive property to solve equations involving parentheses.

Example 2 ***Solving Equations Using the Distributive Property***

Solve the equation.

a. $-21 = 7(3 - x)$ **b.** $-3(8 - 4x) = 12$

Solution

a.

$-21 = 7(3 - x)$	**Write original equation.**
$-21 = 21 - 7x$	**Distributive property**
$-21 - 21 = 21 - 7x - 21$	**Subtract 21 from each side.**
$-42 = -7x$	**Simplify.**
$\frac{-42}{-7} = \frac{-7x}{-7}$	**Divide each side by −7.**
$6 = x$	**Simplify.**

Answer The solution is 6.

b.

$-3(8 - 4x) = 12$	**Write original equation.**
$-24 + 12x = 12$	**Distributive property**
$-24 + 12x + 24 = 12 + 24$	**Add 24 to each side.**
$12x = 36$	**Simplify.**
$\frac{12x}{12} = \frac{36}{12}$	**Divide each side by 12.**
$x = 3$	**Simplify.**

Answer The solution is 3.

Example 3 ***Combining Like Terms After Distributing***

Solve $5x - 2(x - 1) = 8$.

$5x - 2(x - 1) = 8$	**Write original equation.**
$5x - 2x + 2 = 8$	**Distributive property**
$3x + 2 = 8$	**Combine like terms.**
$3x + 2 - 2 = 8 - 2$	**Subtract 2 from each side.**
$3x = 6$	**Simplify.**
$\frac{3x}{3} = \frac{6}{3}$	**Divide each side by 3.**
$x = 2$	**Simplify.**

Solve the equation. Check your solution.

1. $3n - 40 + 2n = 15$ **11** **2.** $2(s - 1) = 6$ **4** **3.** $13 = 2y - 3(y + 4)$ **−25**

3.2 Exercises

More Practice, p. 805

Guided Practice

Vocabulary Check

1. What property do you use when you rewrite the equation $6(x + 1) = 12$ as $6x + 6 = 12$? **distributive property**

2. Identify the like terms you would combine to solve the equation $-3x + 5 - 2x + 8 = 12$. **$-3x$ and $-2x$, 5 and 8**

Skill Check

Solve the equation. Check your solution.

3. $4 + x + 7 = 10$ **−1**
4. $3x + 2x = 25$ **5**
5. $21 = 4x - 9 - x$ **10**
6. $3(x + 1) = 6$ **1**
7. $16 = 8(x - 1)$ **3**
8. $5 + 2(x - 2) = 19$ **9**

Guided Problem Solving

9. Geometry The perimeter of the rectangle shown is 28 units. The length is 10 units. What is the width of the rectangle?

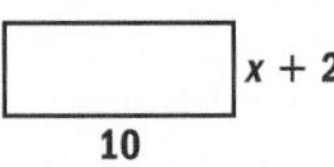

1) Write an equation for the perimeter of the rectangle in terms of x. **$2(10) + 2(x + 2) = 28$**

2) Solve the equation to find the value of x. **2**

3) Find the width of the rectangle using the value of x. **4 units**

4) Check your answer. **$2(10) + 2(x + 2) = 2(10) + 2(2 + 2) = 2(10) + 2(4) = 20 + 8 = 28$**

Practice and Problem Solving

Homework *Help*

Example	Exercises
1	11-13, 20, 21
2	14-19
3	22-31

Online Resources
CLASSZONE.COM
- More Examples
- eTutorial Plus

A **10. Error Analysis** Describe and correct the error in solving the equation $-2(5 - n) = 2$.

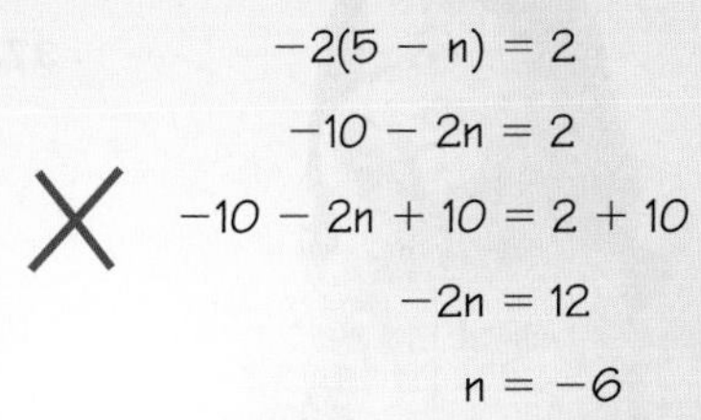

Sample answer: **The distributive property was not applied correctly with −2. Because $-2(5 - n) = -2(5) - (-2)(n) = -10 + 2n$, the steps should be $-2(5 - n) = 2$, $-10 + 2n = 2$, $-10 + 2n + 10 = 2 + 10$, $2n = 12$, and $n = 6$.**

Solve the equation. Check your solution.

11. $13t - 7 - 10t = 2$ **3**
12. $22 + 4y - 14 = 0$ **−2**
13. $2d + 24 + 3d = 84$ **12**
14. $4(x + 5) = 16$ **−1**
15. $3(7 - 2y) = 9$ **2**
16. $-2(z + 11) = 6$ **−14**
17. $-5(3n + 5) = 20$ **−3**
18. $-30 = 6(f - 5)$ **0**
19. $12 = 3(m - 17)$ **21**

20. Fishing A family of five people has $200 to spend on fishing rods and fishing licenses. They spend a total of $20 on licenses. Assuming they buy 5 identical rods, what is the maximum amount they can spend on each rod? **$36**

3 APPLY

ASSIGNMENT GUIDE

Basic Course
Day 1: EP p. 804 Exs. 20-23; pp. 127-129 Exs. 11-20, 22-27, 33-35, 40-55

Average Course
Day 1: pp. 127-129 Exs. 10-16, 20-25, 30-38, 42-45, 50-56

Advanced Course
Day 1: pp. 127-129 Exs. 10-13, 17-29, 32-39*, 44-47, 52-56

Block
pp. 127-129 Exs. 10-16, 20-25, 30-38, 42-45, 50-56 (with 3.1)

EXTRA PRACTICE

- Student Edition, p. 805
- Chapter 3 Resource Book, pp. 18-20
- Test and Practice Generator

TRANSPARENCY

Even-numbered answers are available on transparencies.

HOMEWORK CHECK

When you review students' homework for this lesson, go over the following exercises to check understanding of key concepts.
Basic: 11, 14, 15, 20, 22
Average: 12, 14, 15, 21, 24
Advanced: 11, 17, 19, 24, 29

Common Error

In Exercises 22–31, some students may begin to attempt to solve the equations mentally, resulting in mistakes in the solution process. Continue to urge students to write out every step of the process, drawing their attention to those times when they made errors due to omitting one or more steps.

Teaching Tip

Before Exercises 33–36, consider reviewing the formulas for area and perimeter for each figure shown in order to be sure students are not confusing the two formulas.

38. For part (a), the solution is 7. For part (b), the solution is $\frac{23}{12}$. *Sample answer:* The solution is the same whether division or the distributive property is used first. In part (a), the number outside of the parentheses was a factor of the number on the right side, and dividing first was easiest. In part (b), the number outside of the parentheses was not a factor of the number on the right side, and using the distributive property first was easiest. So, I think I would divide first if the number outside the parentheses is a factor of the number on the other side otherwise I would use the distributive property first.

21. Karaoke You want to organize a group of friends to go to a karaoke studio this Friday night. You must pay \$30 to reserve a private karaoke room plus \$5 for each person in the group. You also want to have snacks for the group at a cost of \$2 per person. How many people can be in the group in order for the total cost to be \$65? **5 people**

Solve the equation. Check your solution.

B **22.** $-5(2w + 1) = 25$ **−3**

23. $4(5 - p) = 8$ **3**

24. $-40 - (2x + 5) = -61$ **8**

25. $2 = 4(3k - 8) - 11k$ **34**

26. $42 = 18t + 4(t + 5)$ **1**

27. $-3(2z - 8) + 10z = 16$ **−2**

28. $-5g - (8 - g) = 12$ **−5**

29. $-5 = 0.25(4 + 20r) - 8r$ **2**

30. $2m + 0.5(m - 4) = 9$ **4.4**

31. $-12 = -2h + 0.2(20 - 6h)$ **5**

32. Photograph The perimeter of a rectangular photograph is 22 inches. The length of the photograph is 1 inch more than the width. What are the dimensions of the photograph? **6 in. by 5 in.**

Geometry Find the value of *x* for the given triangle, rectangle, or square.

33. Perimeter = 40 units **11**

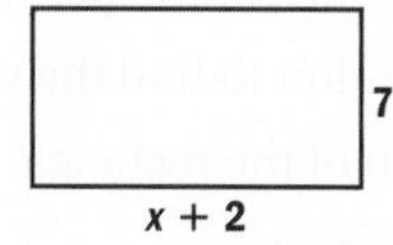

34. Perimeter = 22 units **8**

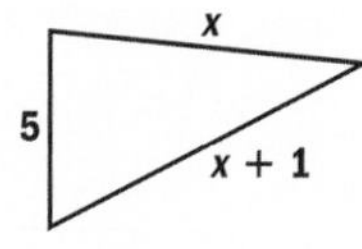

35. Perimeter = 104 units **15**

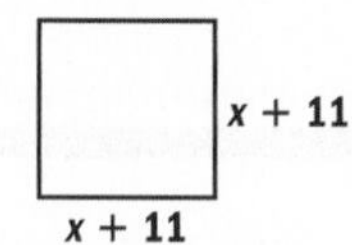

36. Perimeter = 32 units **2**

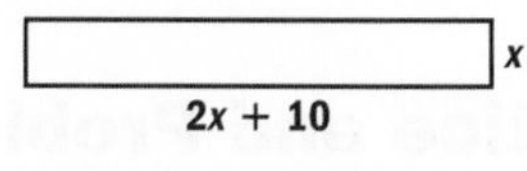

37. Cell Phones Your cell phone provider charges a monthly fee of \$19.50 for 200 minutes. You are also charged \$.25 per minute for each minute over 200 minutes. Last month, your bill was \$29.50.

a. Let *m* represent the total number of minutes you used last month. Use the verbal model below to write an equation. **$29.50 = 19.50 + 0.25(m - 200)$**

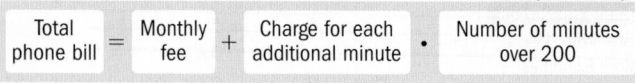

Total phone bill	=	Monthly fee	+	Charge for each additional minute	•	Number of minutes over 200

b. Solve the equation you wrote in part (a). **240**

c. How many additional minutes did you use last month? **40 min**

C **38. Critical Thinking** Solve each equation by first dividing each side of the equation by the number outside the parentheses. Then solve each equation by first using the distributive property. What do you notice? When would you recommend using each method? Explain. **38a–b. See margin.**

a. $3(x + 7) = 42$

b. $4(6x - 8) = 14$

39. **Challenge** The figure shown is composed of a triangle and a rectangle. The figure has a total area of 1258 square units. Find the value of x. **11**

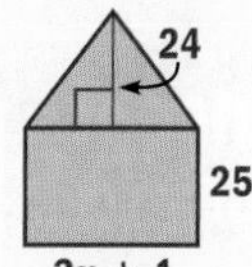

Mixed Review

Plot the point in a coordinate plane. Describe the location of the point. *(Lesson 1.8)* **40–47. See margin for art.**

40. $J(-3, 8)$ **Quadrant II**
41. $K(8, -3)$ **Quadrant IV**
42. $L(4, -4)$ **Quadrant IV**
43. $M(-1, -1)$ **Quadrant III**
44. $N(0, 2)$ **y-axis**
45. $P(5, 1)$ **Quadrant I**
46. $Q(-9, 0)$ **x-axis**
47. $R(-5, -8)$ **Quadrant III**

Simplify the expression. *(Lesson 2.3)*

48. $a - 2 - (3 + a)$ **-5**
49. $3b + 8 + 2(b - 4)$ **$5b$**
50. $-2x + 5 - 7(x + 1)$ **$-9x - 2$**
51. $2y - 4 + 3(y + 1)$ **$5y - 1$**
52. $-(2x + 3) + 4(x + 2)$ **$2x + 5$**
53. $3(2x - 7) + 8(4 - x)$ **$-2x + 11$**
54. **Family Party** A family wants to hold a dinner party at a restaurant. The restaurant charges \$150 to rent space for the party. The food cost for each person at the party is \$18. How many people can come to the party if the family has \$600 to spend? *(Lesson 3.1)* **25 people**

Standardized Test Practice

55. **Multiple Choice** What is the solution of the equation $-3(2x - 1) = -21$? **D**

A. -4 **B.** -3 **C.** 3 **D.** 4

56. **Short Response** The length of a rectangle is 5 feet less than twice its width. The perimeter of the rectangle is 38 feet. Let w represent the width. Write an equation for the perimeter of the rectangle in terms of w. Then solve the equation to find the length and width of the rectangle. **$38 = 2(2w - 5) + 2w$; length: 11 ft, width: 8 ft**

Patent Puzzle

Solve each equation. In each group, there are two equations that have the same solution. Write the value of this solution in the corresponding letter's blank to find the year blue jeans were patented. **1873**

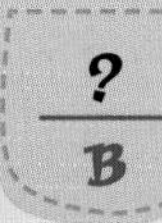

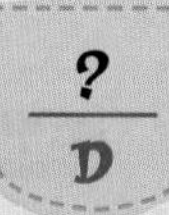

A. $10x + 7 = 17$
$2(7x + 6) = 40$
$-(x - 11) = 10$

B. $8x - 15 = -47$
$6(2x - 1) = 90$
$-7x + 4x = -24$

C. $-5x + 4x = -6$
$7x - (-12) = 61$
$7(x + 2) = 63$

D. $2(6x + 7) = 50$
$-5x - 3x = -56$
$-11x - 9 = -42$

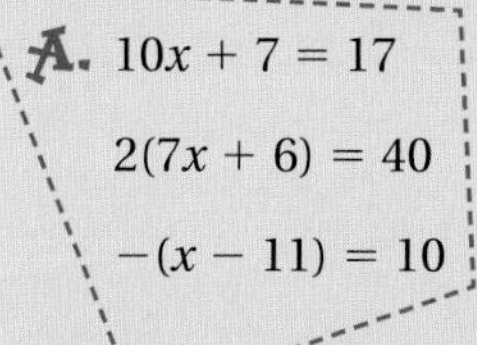

4 ASSESS

Assessment Resources

For more assessment resources, see:
- Assessment Book
- Test and Practice Generator

Mini-Quiz

Solve the equation.

1. $-2(a + 3) = -24$ **9**
2. $7g + 14 - 3g = 6$ **-2**
3. $-11j - (2 - 8j) = -14$ **4**
4. $4 = 6(3 - 2w) - 14$ **0**
5. **Challenge** The figure shown is composed of two triangles. The figure has a total area of 29 square units. Find the value of x. **5**

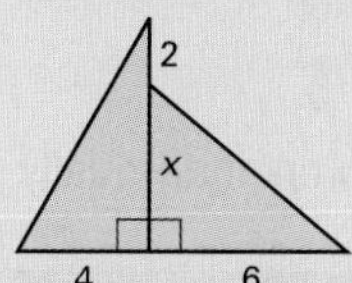

5 FOLLOW-UP

Diagnosis/Remediation

- Study Guide in Chapter 3 Resource Book, pp. 21–22
- eTutorial Plus Online
- Extra Practice, p. 805
- Lesson Practice in Chapter 3 Resource Book, pp. 18–20

English Learner Support

- Spanish Study Guide
- Multi-Language Visual Glossary
- Chapter Audio Summaries CDs

Challenge

- Challenge Practice in Chapter 3 Resource Book, p. 23
- Teacher's Edition, p. 116F

40–47. See Additional Answers beginning on page AA1.

1 PLAN

INVESTIGATE THE CONCEPT

- Students solve equations using algebra tiles.
- This activity leads into solving equations with variables on both sides in Lesson 3.3.

MATERIALS

Each student will need algebra tiles. See the Activity Support Master in the *Chapter 3 Resource Book*. A support transparency is also available.

RECOMMENDED TIME

Work activity: 10 min
Discuss results: 5 min

GROUPING

Students should work individually.

2 TEACH

ALTERNATIVE STRATEGY

Write the equation from the Investigate section on the board. As students complete each step at their desk, have volunteers describe their work and then demonstrate how to perform this same step on the equation written on the board.

3 CLOSE

KEY DISCOVERY

Solving equations with variables on both sides is similar to solving equations with the variable on one side.

ASSESSMENT

1. How do you remove x-tiles from the model of an equation without making the resulting equation incorrect? **Be sure to remove the same number of x-tiles from each side.**

4, 5. See Additional Answers beginning on page AA1.

Concept *Activity*

3.3 Modeling Equations with Variables on Both Sides

Goal
Solve equations using algebra tiles.

Materials
- algebra tiles

Investigate

Use algebra tiles to solve $4x + 6 = 10 + 2x$.

1. Model $4x + 6 = 10 + 2x$ using algebra tiles.

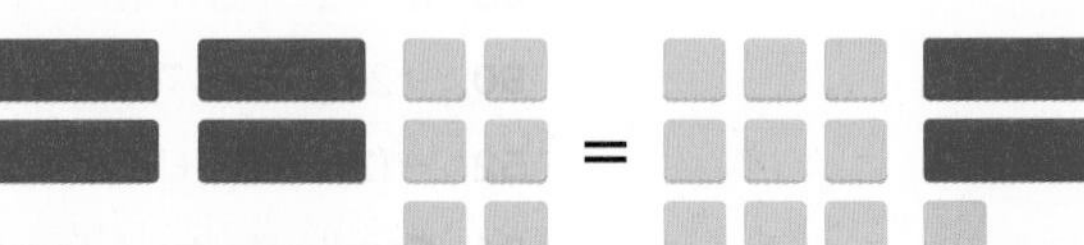

2. Remove two x-tiles from each side.

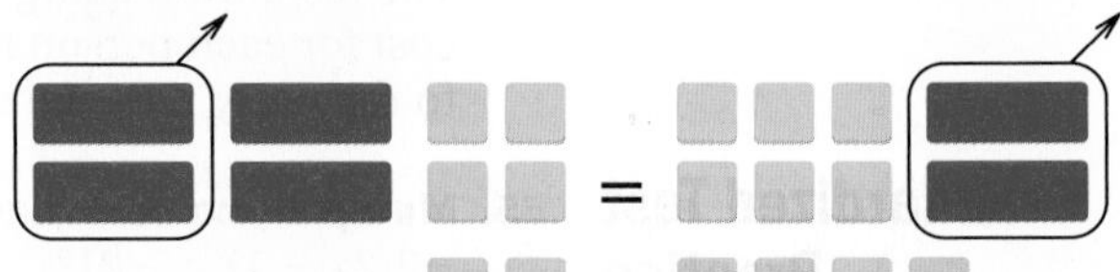

3. Remove six 1-tiles from each side.

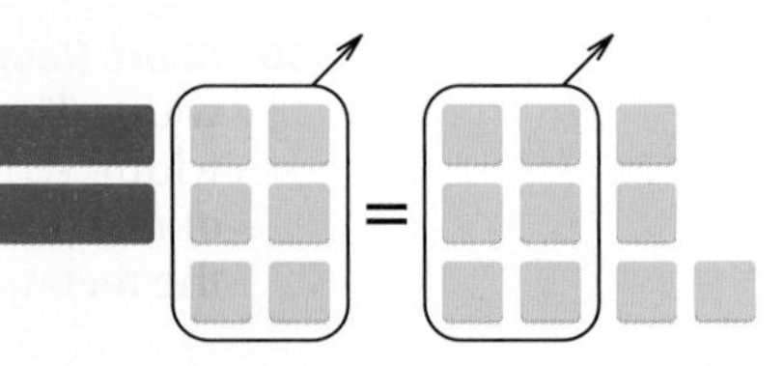

4. Divide the remaining tiles into two equal groups. Each x-tile is equal to two 1-tiles. So, the solution is 2.

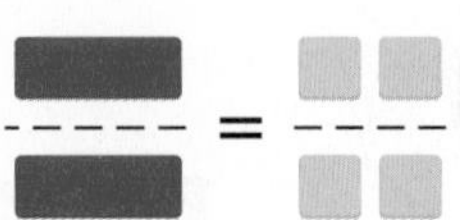

Draw Conclusions

Use algebra tiles to model and solve the equation.

1. $9 + 2x = 1 + 3x$ **8**
2. $3x + 4 = 8 + x$ **2**
3. $5x + 2 = 3x + 14$ **6**
4. **Critical Thinking** In the activity above, would you find the correct solution if you performed Step 3 before Step 2? Explain. **See margin.**
5. ***Writing*** Explain how solving an equation with variables on both sides of the equal sign is different than solving an equation with the variable on one side. **See margin.**

NCTM CURRICULUM STANDARDS
Standard 2: Use models to understand relationships; Use models to represent relationships

LESSON

3.3 Solving Equations *with* Variables *on* Both Sides

Review Vocabulary
equation, p. 85
solution of an equation, p. 85
inverse operations, p. 91

BEFORE	*Now*	WHY?
You solved two-step equations.	You'll solve equations with variables on both sides.	So you can find the price of a DVD, as in Ex. 10.

Spanish Club The Spanish club is arranging a trip to a Mexican restaurant in a nearby city. Those who go must share the $60 cost of using a school bus for the trip. The restaurant's buffet costs $5 per person. How many students must sign up for this trip in order to limit the cost to $10 per student? In Example 2, you will see how to use an equation to answer this question.

Every equation in this lesson has variables on both sides of the equation. You can solve such an equation by getting the variable terms on one side of the equation and the constant terms on the other side.

Study *Strategy*

Another Way To solve the equation in Example 1, you might choose to first subtract $10n$ from each side to obtain the equation $-3n - 5 = 13$. When you solve this equation for n, you get the same solution as in the example, -6.

Example 1 *Solving an Equation with the Variable on Both Sides*

Solve $7n - 5 = 10n + 13$.

$7n - 5 = 10n + 13$	**Write original equation.**
$7n - 5 - 7n = 10n + 13 - 7n$	**Subtract $7n$ from each side.**
$-5 = 3n + 13$	**Simplify.**
$-5 - 13 = 3n + 13 - 13$	**Subtract 13 from each side.**
$-18 = 3n$	**Simplify.**
$\frac{-18}{3} = \frac{3n}{3}$	**Divide each side by 3.**
$-6 = n$	**Simplify.**

Answer The solution is -6.

Checkpoint

Solve the equation. Check your solution.

1. $5n - 2 = 3n + 6$ 4 **2.** $8y + 4 = 11y - 17$ 7 **3.** $m - 1 = 9m + 15$ -2

NCTM CURRICULUM STANDARDS
Standard 1: Understand meanings of operations; Understand how operations are related
Standard 2: Represent situations using algebraic symbols

1 PLAN

Skill Check
Simplify.
1. $5x + 6 + 2x$ $7x + 6$
2. $1 - 3y - 5 + 4y$ $y - 4$
3. $-2(k + 9)$ $-2k - 18$
4. $-3(17 - 2y)$ $-51 + 6y$

Lesson Objective
Solve equations with variables on both sides.

Pacing
Suggested Number of Days
Basic Course: 2 days
Average Course: 2 days
Advanced Course: 2 days
Block: 1 block

Teaching Resources
For a complete list of Teaching Resources, see page 116B.

Transparency
Warm-Up Exercises for this lesson are available on a transparency.

2 TEACH

Motivating the Lesson
Ask students, "If the cost for using the bus is always $60, what happens to the cost per person as the number of students on the trip increases?" **The cost decreases.**

TIPS *for* NEW TEACHERS

Expect some students to be confused by equations with no solution and by equations whose solution is all numbers. See Tips for New Teachers in the *Chapter 3 Resource Book*.

Extra Examples

Example 1 Solve $5k - 8 = 7k + 18$. **−13**

Example 2 A bus tour of celebrities' homes costs $300 for the bus and tour guide plus $8 per person for lunch. How many people does a tour group need to have in it so that the cost per person is $20? **25 people**

Example 3 Solve $4(-2 + 3x) = 12x$. **no solution**

Example 4 Solve $7(2x + 3) = 21 + 14x$. **all numbers**

TEACHING TIP

In Checkpoint Exercises 1–3 on page 131, watch for students who combine steps, moving variable terms and constant terms in a single step. While not incorrect, caution students about performing more than one calculation at a time until they become proficient at the solution process.

VISUALIZE

Have students model Example 3 using algebra tiles to demonstrate to themselves why the given equation has no solution.

ALGEBRAIC REASONING

Have a volunteer continue simplifying the equation in Example 4 on the board until the equation $x = x$ remains. Stress that this statement is true for any value of x.

Flautas are fried tacos, a Mexican specialty.

Example 2 ***Writing and Solving an Equation***

How many students must go on the Spanish club trip to the Mexican restaurant, as described on page 131, in order for the cost per student to be $10?

Solution

Let s represent the number of students. Write a verbal model.

Cost per student	·	Number of students	=	Cost of buffet	·	Number of students	+	Cost of school bus

$10s = 5s + 60$	**Substitute.**
$10s - 5s = 5s - 5s + 60$	**Subtract 5s from each side.**
$5s = 60$	**Simplify.**
$\frac{5s}{5} = \frac{60}{5}$	**Divide each side by 5.**
$s = 12$	**Simplify.**

Answer The club needs 12 students to go on the trip.

Number of Solutions When you solve an equation, you may find that it has no solution or that every number is a solution.

Example 3 ***An Equation with No Solution***

Solve $5(2x + 1) = 10x$.

$5(2x + 1) = 10x$	**Write original equation.**
$10x + 5 = 10x$	**Distributive property**

Notice that $10x + 5 = 10x$ is not true because the number $10x$ cannot be equal to 5 more than itself. The equation has no solution. As a check, you can continue solving the equation.

$10x + 5 - 10x = 10x - 10x$	**Subtract 10x from each side.**
$5 = 0$ ✗	**Simplify.**

The statement $5 = 0$ is not true, so the equation has no solution.

Note *Worthy*

You should summarize what you have learned in Chapter 2 and Chapter 3 about solving equations in your notes.

Example 4 ***Solving an Equation with All Numbers as Solutions***

Solve $6x + 2 = 2(3x + 1)$.

$6x + 2 = 2(3x + 1)$	**Write original equation.**
$6x + 2 = 6x + 2$	**Distributive property**

Notice that for all values of x, the statement $6x + 2 = 6x + 2$ is true. The equation has every number as a solution.

Study *Strategy*

Make sure you understand what you are being asked to find in a problem. In Example 5, you first solve for x, but the problem asks you to find the perimeter of the square.

Example 5 *Solving an Equation to Find a Perimeter*

Geometry Find the perimeter of the square.

(square with sides labeled $x + 4$ and $2x$)

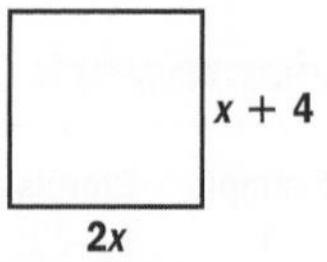

1) A square has four sides of equal length. Write an equation and solve for x.

$2x = x + 4$ **Write equation.**

$2x - x = x + 4 - x$ **Subtract x from each side.**

$x = 4$ **Simplify.**

2) Find the length of one side by substituting 4 for x in either expression.

$2x = 2(4) = 8$ **Substitute 4 for x and multiply.**

3) To find the perimeter, multiply the length of one side by 4.

$4 \cdot 8 = 32$

Answer The perimeter of the square is 32 units.

3.3 Exercises

More Practice, p. 805

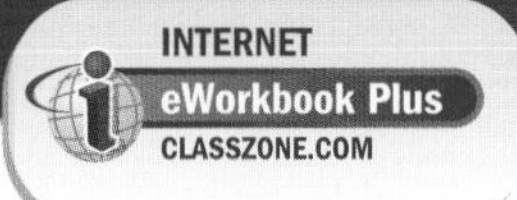

Guided Practice

Vocabulary Check

1. Describe what steps you would take to solve $8x + 5 = 2x - 7$. **See margin.**
2. Explain why the equation $5z + 2 = 5z$ has no solution. ***Sample answer:* Subtracting $5z$ from each side gives $2 = 0$, which is a false statement.**

Skill Check

Solve the equation. Check your solution.

3. $13m - 22 = 9m - 6$ **4**
4. $19c + 26 = 41 + 14c$ **3**
5. $15 - 4x = 42 - 7x$ **9**
6. $14 + 5y = 50 - 4y$ **4**
7. $18w - 2 = 10w + 14$ **2**
8. $-5a + 6 = 6a - 38$ **4**
9. **Error Analysis** Describe and correct the error in solving the equation $4x + 7 = x - 2$.

X

$4x + 7 = x - 2$

$4x + 7 - 4x = x - 2 - 4x$

$7 = 3x - 2$

$7 + 2 = 3x - 2 + 2$

$9 = 3x$

$3 = x$

10. **Shopping** You spend \$60 on clothes and buy 3 DVD movies. Your friend spends nothing on clothes and buys 8 DVD movies. You both spend the same amount of money. All the DVDs cost the same amount. How much does each DVD cost? **\$12**

1. *Sample answer:* First I would get the variable on only one side of the equation by subtracting $2x$ from each side to obtain $6x + 5 = -7$. Then I would subtract 5 from each side to obtain $6x = -12$, and divide each side by 6 to obtain $x = -2$.

9. *Sample answer:* In going from the second to the third statement, the result of subtracting $4x$ from x should have been $-3x$, not $3x$, so the third statement should be $7 = -3x - 2$, followed by $7 + 2 = -3x - 2 + 2$, $9 = -3x$, and $-3 = x$.

Extra Examples

Example 5 Find the perimeter of the square. **16 units**

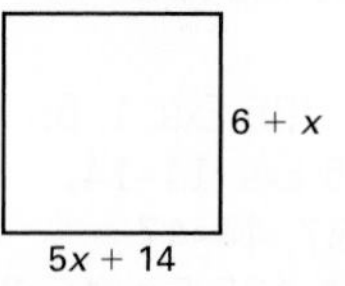

Differentiating Instruction

Alternative Teaching Strategy Invite students to suggest some ways that they could begin to simplify the equation in Example 1. For example, students could subtract $7n$, add 5, subtract $10n$, or subtract 13 from each side. Assign four students to work the example using these four initial steps to show that the correct answer can be found regardless of which first step is used.

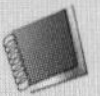

NOTETAKING

As pointed out on page 132, students should summarize what they have learned about solving equations. This summary will prove useful when they begin solving inequalities in the next lesson since the two processes are similar.

Concept Check

How do you solve an equation with variables on both sides? **Use inverse operations to get all the variable terms on one side and all the constant terms on the other side. Then use the division property of equality to find the solution.**

Daily Puzzler

Lauren's age is two thirds of Kyle's age. Twelve years ago, Lauren's age was half of Kyle's age. How old is Lauren now? **24 years old**

3 APPLY

ASSIGNMENT GUIDE

Basic Course

Day 1: SRH p. 785 Exs. 1, 5; pp. 134–135 Exs. 11–14, 23–27, 34–37, 44–47

Day 2: pp. 134–135 Exs. 15–22, 28–30, 48–51

Average Course

Day 1: pp. 134–135 Exs. 11–14, 25–27, 31–35, 44–47

Day 2: pp. 134–135 Exs. 17–22, 28–30, 38–40, 48–51

Advanced Course

Day 1: pp. 134–135 Exs. 11–14, 25–27, 31–33, 39–45*

Day 2: pp. 134–135 Exs. 17–22, 28–30, 36–38, 46–51

Block

pp. 134–135 Exs. 11–14, 17–22, 25–35, 38–40, 44–51

EXTRA PRACTICE

- Student Edition, p. 805
- Chapter 3 Resource Book, pp. 29–31
- Test and Practice Generator

TRANSPARENCY

Even-numbered answers are available on transparencies.

HOMEWORK CHECK

When you review students' homework for this lesson, go over the following exercises to check understanding of key concepts.

Basic: 11, 15, 19, 27, 28
Average: 13, 19, 20, 27, 28
Advanced: 14, 20, 21, 30, 32

Practice and Problem Solving

Homework *Help*

Example	Exercises
1	11-22
2	27, 32
3	11-22
4	11-22
5	28-30

Online Resources
CLASSZONE.COM
- More Examples
- eTutorial Plus

Solve the equation. Check your solution.

A **11.** $25u + 74 = 23u + 92$ **9**

12. $-5k - 19 = 5 - 13k$ **3**

13. $-11y + 32 = 104 - 5y$ **−12**

14. $-15n + 16 = 86 - 29n$ **5**

15. $25t = 5(5t + 1)$ **no solution**

16. $13 - 3p = -5(3 + 2p)$ **−4**

17. $-24s - 53 = 39 - s$ **−4**

18. $14a - 93 = 49 - 57a$ **2**

19. $7(2p + 1) = 14p + 7$ **all numbers**

20. $8v = 2(4v + 2)$ **no solution**

21. $3x + 6 = 3(2 + x)$ **all numbers**

22. $2(-4h - 13) = 37 + 13h$ **−3**

Write the verbal sentence as an equation. Then solve the equation.

23. Nine plus 2 times a number is equal to 2 less than 3 times the number. **$9 + 2n = 3n - 2$; 11**

24. Three less than 11 times a number is equal to 9 plus 5 times the number. **$11n - 3 = 9 + 5n$; 2**

25. Four minus 7 times a number is equal to 12 minus 3 times the number. **$4 - 7n = 12 - 3n$; −2**

26. Twelve less than −9 times a number is equal to 8 minus 4 times the number. **$-9n - 12 = 8 - 4n$; −4**

27. Toll Booth You lose your electronic tag that you use to pay tolls on the highway in your city. It costs you $24 to replace the tag. The cost of one toll when you don't use the tag is $3. The cost of the same toll when you do use the tag is $1.50. How many times will you have to use the tag to pay for the tolls in order for the total cost to be the same as not using the tag? **16 times**

Find the perimeter of the square.

28. 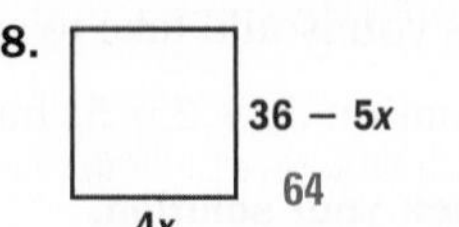

64

29.

288

30. 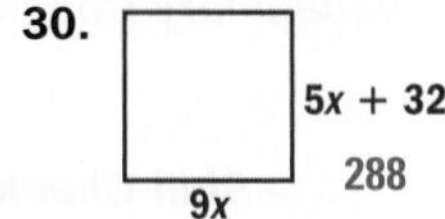

288

31. Driving Your family is driving to Houston, Texas. A sign indicates that you are 700 miles from Houston. Your car's trip odometer indicates that you are 400 miles from home. You are traveling at an average speed of 60 miles per hour.

a. Write an expression for the distance (in miles) you will be from Houston in x hours. **$700 - 60x$**

b. Write an expression for the distance (in miles) you will be from home in x hours. **$400 + 60x$**

c. Use the expressions from parts (a) and (b) to write and solve an equation to find the number of hours you will drive until you are exactly halfway between Houston and your home. **$700 - 60x = 400 + 60x$, 2.5 h**

d. Suppose you travel by local roads instead of the highway. You travel the 700 miles at a speed of 45 miles per hour. How long will you drive before you are exactly halfway between Houston and your home? **$3\frac{1}{3}$ h, or 3 h 20 min**

Houston, Texas

32. **Pasta Machine** A pasta machine costs \$33. The ingredients to make one batch of pasta cost \$.33. The same amount of pasta purchased at a store costs \$.99. How many batches of pasta will you have to make for the cost of the machine and ingredients to equal the cost of buying the same amount of pasta at the store? **50 batches**

33. *Sample answer:* Your brother and sister are saving money for a summer camp. Your brother begins with \$5, and saves \$11 each week. Your sister begins with \$23, and saves \$8 each week. Let x be the number of weeks the two of them have been saving. The solution is 6, and indicates after how many weeks your brother and sister will have saved the same amount.

B 33. ***Writing*** Describe a real-life situation that can be modeled by the equation $11x + 5 = 8x + 23$. Then solve the equation and interpret your solution.

Solve the equation. Check your solution.

34. $3x - 7 = 8 + 6(x + 2)$ **−9**

35. $13y + 19 = 6(9 + y) + 14$ **7**

36. $8(z + 4) = 5(13 + z)$ **11**

37. $8a - 2(a + 5) = 2(a - 1)$ **2**

38. **Geometry** The perimeter of the square is equal to the perimeter of the triangle. The sides of the triangle are equal in length.

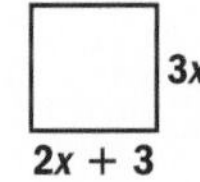

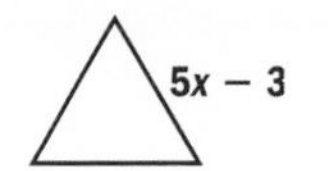

a. **Estimate** Without doing any calculations, estimate which figure has the greater side length. Explain your choice.

b. What is the side length of each figure? **square: 9 units, triangle: 12 units**

c. What is the perimeter of each figure? **36 units**

38a. The triangle. *Sample answer:* The figures have the same perimeter, but the triangle has fewer sides, so each side must be longer.

Use a calculator to solve the equation. Check your solution.

C 39. $0.75m + 14 = 1.87m - 10.3936$ **21.78**

40. $19.5 + 0.5t = 10.6206 - 0.4t$ **−9.866**

41. $-9.39 - 3.4d = -1.1d + 11.08$ **−8.9**

42. $-130.5 - 9b = -55.104 + 3.2b$ **−6.18**

43. **Challenge** Consider the equation $ax + 6 = 2(x + 3)$.

a. For what value(s) of a does the equation have all numbers as a solution? **$a = 2$**

b. For what value(s) of a does the equation have just one solution? **$a \neq 2$**

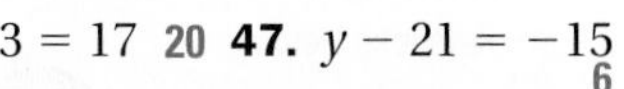

Mixed Review

Algebra Basics Solve the equation. Check your solution. *(Lesson 2.5)*

44. $c - 20 = 14$ **34**

45. $d + 9 = -12$ **−21**

46. $x - 3 = 17$ **20**

47. $y - 21 = -15$ **6**

48. **Gym Membership** To join a gym, your friend pays a one-time fee of \$75 and \$45 per month for the duration of the membership. Your friend has paid a total of \$345. How long has your friend been a member of the gym? *(Lesson 3.1)* **6 mo**

49. The perimeter of the square shown is 32 units. Find the value of x. *(Lesson 3.2)* **5**

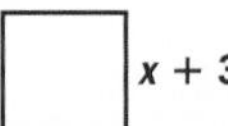

Standardized Test Practice

50. **Multiple Choice** What is the solution of the equation $2(3x + 4) = 6x + 5$? **D**

A. 1 **B.** 3 **C.** All numbers **D.** No solution

51. **Multiple Choice** For which equation is 6 a solution? **F**

F. $-2y - 7 = 11 - 5y$ **G.** $11y - 32 = 7y - 12$

H. $18y - 16 = 13y + 19$ **I.** $-7y - 24 = -8 - 9y$

4 ASSESS

Assessment Resources

For more assessment resources, see:

- Assessment Book
- Test and Practice Generator

Mini-Quiz

Solve the equation.

1. $13x + 9 = 11x + 13$ **2**
2. $-3k - 25 = 5k - 1$ **−3**
3. $6(1 + 5y) = 30y - 2$ **no solution**
4. $-14 + 7m = 7(m - 2)$ **all numbers**
5. **Challenge** For what value(s) of a does the equation $5y + 10 = 5(2 + ay)$ have all numbers as a solution? **1**

5 FOLLOW-UP

Diagnosis/Remediation

- Study Guide in Chapter 3 Resource Book, pp. 32-33
- eTutorial Plus Online
- Extra Practice, p. 805
- Lesson Practice in Chapter 3 Resource Book, pp. 29-31

English Learner Support

- Spanish Study Guide
- Multi-Language Visual Glossary
- Chapter Audio Summaries CDs

Challenge

- Challenge Practice in Chapter 3 Resource Book, p. 34
- Teacher's Edition, p. 116F

1 PLAN

LEARN THE METHOD

- Students will use a table to solve an equation with the variable on both sides.
- Students can use the skill learned in this activity to check their answers to Exercises 11–22 and 34–37 in Lesson 3.3.

GROUPING

Students should work individually.

2 TEACH

TIPS FOR SUCCESS

Point out to students that the difference between the two y-values in the table decreases as you scroll down the table from the line where $x = 0$. Students can use this fact to recognize that they are getting closer to the line in the table where the y-values are equal.

Extra Examples

Example Use a table to solve the equation $12y + 5 = 14y + 11$. -3

3 CLOSE

ASSESSMENT

1. Solve $13k + 6 = 22k + 33$. -3

2. Solve $-12r = -5r + 49$. -7

Technology Activity GRAPHING CALCULATOR

3.3 Solving Equations

Goal Use a table to solve an equation with the variable on both sides.

Example

Use a table to solve $5x - 1 = 4x + 3$.

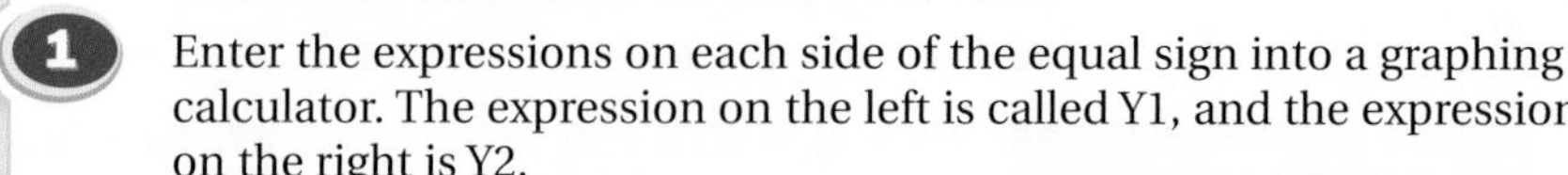

1 Enter the expressions on each side of the equal sign into a graphing calculator. The expression on the left is called Y1, and the expression on the right is Y2.

Keystrokes

[Y=] 5 [x] [−] 1 [ENTER]

4 [x] [+] 3

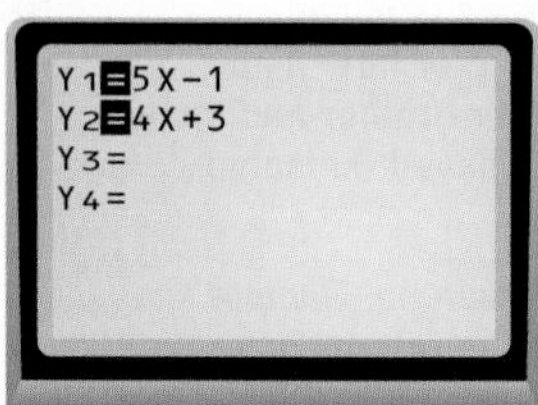

2 Use the calculator's *table* feature to find the value of each expression for different values of x. Press [2nd] **[TBLSET]** and enter the settings shown on the first screen below. (△Tbl represents the increment the calculator uses to go from one x-value to the next in the table.) Then, press [2nd] **[TABLE]** to display the table shown on the second screen.

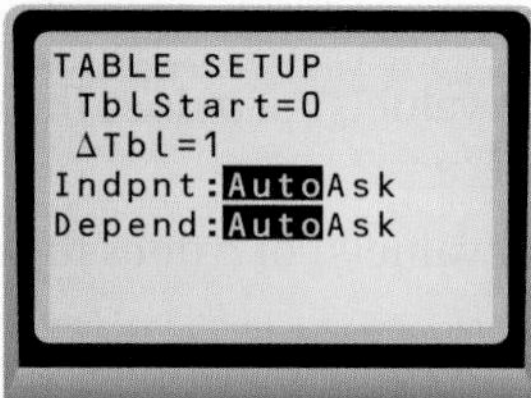

X	Y1	Y2
0	−1	3
1	4	7
2	9	11
3	14	15
4	19	19
5	24	23

X=4

3 Compare the values of the expression in the Y1 column with the values of the expression in the Y2 column. The values are the same when $x = 4$. So, the solution of the equation $5x - 1 = 4x + 3$ is 4.

Tech *Help*

If you do not see the value of x that makes the values of both expressions equal, try using the up or down arrow keys to see additional values of x.

Online Resources CLASSZONE.COM

- Keystroke Help

Draw Conclusions

Use a table to solve the equation.

1. $x - 2 = 2x - 6$ 4 **2.** $3x + 1 = x + 7$ 3 **3.** $12 - x = x - 4$ 8

4. $7x = 16 - x$ 2 **5.** $5x + 2 = 8x - 1$ 1 **6.** $4x - 6 = 2x + 4$ 5

7. Critical Thinking Solve the equation $3x + 6 = 13x + 2$ using paper and a pencil. Explain how you would change the settings in the TABLE SETUP menu so that you could solve the equation using a calculator.

7. $\frac{2}{5}$, or 0.4. *Sample answer:* **If you change the value of △Tbl to .1, you can see that the solution is $x = 0.4$.**

NCTM CURRICULUM STANDARDS

Standard 2: Analyze situations using algebraic symbols

CHAPTER 3 Mid-Chapter Quiz

Write the verbal sentence as an equation. Then solve the equation.

1. Twice a number plus 5 is equal to 27. **$2n + 5 = 27$; 11**
2. Seven times the sum of 4 and a number is -14. **$7(4 + n) = -14$; -6**
3. Three more than 4 times a number is equal to 9 less than twice the number. **$4n + 3 = 2n - 9$; -6**

Solve the equation. Check your solution.

4. $11k + 9 = 42$ **3**
5. $\frac{a}{3} + 11 = -5$ **-48**
6. $\frac{w}{2} - 18 = -7$ **22**
7. $2 + 5t - 3 = 34$ **7**
8. $-3y + 15 - y = 39$ **-6**
9. $5(n + 2) = 10$ **0**
10. $2 - 5(h + 3) = -28$ **3**
11. $5s = 7s + 1 - 2s$ **no solution**
12. $4d - 5 = -d$ **1**
13. $17 - 5m = 50 + 6m$ **-3**
14. $3f - 12 = 3(f - 12)$ **no solution**
15. $8(4p + 1) = 32p + 8$ **all numbers**
16. **Income** Your friend works as a waitress at a local restaurant. Her income consists of an hourly wage plus tips. On Wednesday, your friend earned \$25 in tips over a 5 hour period. On Friday, your friend earned \$30.76 in tips over a 3 hour period. How much is your friend's hourly wage if your friend earned the same amount of money on Wednesday as on Friday? **\$2.88**
17. All three sides of the triangle shown are equal in length. Find the perimeter of the triangle. **39 units**

$2x + 5$ $4x - 3$

Two people are packing equal numbers of small boxes into large boxes. One person has 3 large boxes that are full of smaller boxes and 24 small boxes that are not yet packed. The other person has 5 large boxes that are full of smaller boxes and 10 small boxes that are not yet packed. Each large box holds the same number of small boxes. How many small boxes can each large box hold? What is the total number of small boxes each person will pack? How many large boxes will each person need in order to pack all of his or her small boxes? **7 small boxes; 45 small boxes; 7 large boxes**

ADDITIONAL RESOURCES

The following resources are available to help review the materials in Lessons 3.1–3.3.

Chapter 3 Resource Book
- Lesson Practice
- Study Guide

Assessment Book
- Chapter 3 Quiz 1

Technology
- Test and Practice Generator
- eTutorial CD-ROM

Internet
- Classzone
- eWorkbook Plus Online
- eTutorial Plus Online

ENGLISH LEARNER SUPPORT

- Spanish Study Guide
- Multi-Language Visual Glossary
- Chapter Audio Summaries CDs

1 PLAN

Skill Check

Replace each _?_ with > or <.

1. $2 + 3$ _?_ 4 >
2. 17 _?_ $23 - 5$ <
3. $\frac{1}{2}$ _?_ $\frac{1}{4}$ >
4. -18 _?_ -19 >

LESSON OBJECTIVE

Solve inequalities using addition or subtraction.

PACING

Suggested Number of Days
Basic Course: 2 days
Average Course: 2 days
Advanced Course: 2 days
Block: 1 block

TEACHING RESOURCES

For a complete list of Teaching Resources, see page 116B.

TRANSPARENCY

Warm-Up Exercises for this lesson are available on a transparency.
A support transparency is available for Examples 1–3 and Checkpoint Exercises 1–4.

2 TEACH

MOTIVATING THE LESSON

Ask students for examples of inequality statements they have heard outside of math class that contain phrases such as "at least" or "no more than." Write their inequalities on the board.

LESSON 3.4

Solving Inequalities Using Addition *or* Subtraction

Vocabulary

inequality, p. 138
solution of an inequality, p. 138
equivalent inequalities, p. 139

BEFORE	*Now*	WHY?
You solved one-step equations.	You'll solve inequalities using addition or subtraction.	So you can find the weight a truck can tow, as in Ex. 14.

An **inequality** is a statement formed by placing an inequality symbol between two expressions. For example, $y + 5 \le -6$ is an inequality.

The **solution of an inequality** with a variable is the set of all numbers that produce true statements when substituted for the variable. You can show the solution of an inequality by graphing the inequality on a number line. When you graph an inequality of the form $x > a$ or $x < a$, use an open circle at a. When you graph an inequality of the form $x \ge a$ or $x \le a$, use a closed circle at a.

Inequality	Words	Graph
$x < 3$	All numbers less than 3	−2 −1 0 1 2 3 4 5
$y > 2$	All numbers greater than 2	−2 −1 0 1 2 3 4 5
$z \le 4$	All numbers less than or equal to 4	−2 −1 0 1 2 3 4 5
$n \ge 2$	All numbers greater than or equal to 2	−2 −1 0 1 2 3 4 5

Penguins on a glacier

Example 1 *Writing and Graphing an Inequality*

Science The freezing point of water is 0°C. At temperatures at or below the freezing point, water is a solid (ice). Write an inequality that gives the temperatures at which water is a solid. Then graph the inequality.

Solution

Let t represent the temperature of water. Water is a solid at temperatures less than or equal to 0°C.

Answer The inequality is $t \le 0$. The graph is shown below.

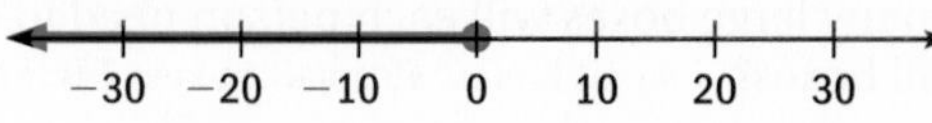

NCTM CURRICULUM STANDARDS

Standard 1: Understand relationships among numbers; Understand how operations are related
Standard 2: Represent situations using algebraic symbols

Solving Inequalities You can use the following properties to find the solutions of inequalities involving addition and subtraction. Using these properties, you can write *equivalent inequalities*. **Equivalent inequalities** are inequalities that have the same solution.

Study *Strategy*

The addition and subtraction properties of inequality are also true for inequalities involving ≤ and ≥.

Addition and Subtraction Properties of Inequality

Words Adding or subtracting the same number on each side of an inequality produces an equivalent inequality.

Algebra If $a < b$, then $a + c < b + c$ and $a - c < b - c$.

If $a > b$, then $a + c > b + c$ and $a - c > b - c$.

Example 2 *Solving an Inequality Using Subtraction*

Solve $m + 5 \geq 10$. Graph and check your solution.

$m + 5 \geq 10$ **Write original inequality.**

$m + 5 - 5 \geq 10 - 5$ **Subtract 5 from each side.**

$m \geq 5$ **Simplify.**

Answer The solution is $m \geq 5$.

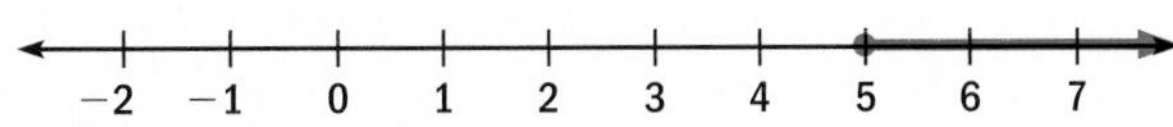

✓ **Check** Choose any number greater than or equal to 5. Substitute the number into the original inequality.

$m + 5 \geq 10$ **Write original inequality.**

$8 + 5 \overset{?}{\geq} 10$ **Substitute 8 for *m*.**

$13 \geq 10$ ✓ **Solution checks.**

Reading *Algebra*

You can read an inequality from left to right as well as from right to left. For instance, the solution of Example 3, read "2 is greater than *x*," can also be read "*x* is less than 2."

Example 3 *Solving an Inequality Using Addition*

Solve $-10 > x - 12$. Graph your solution.

$-10 > x - 12$ **Write original inequality.**

$-10 + 12 > x - 12 + 12$ **Add 12 to each side.**

$2 > x$ **Simplify.**

Answer The solution is $2 > x$, or $x < 2$.

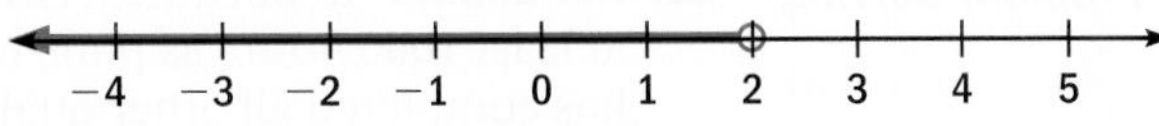

 ***Checkpoint***

Solve the inequality. Graph and check your solution. 1–4. See margin for art.

1. $n + 7 > 3$ $n > -4$
2. $10 \geq y + 4$ $6 \geq y$, or $y \leq 6$
3. $-6 \leq x - 9$ $3 \leq x$, or $x \geq 3$
4. $z - 5 < 1$ $z < 6$

TIPS *for* NEW TEACHERS

Show students how to draw graphs of inequalities so that open circles and closed circles are clear and easy to differentiate. See Tips for New Teachers in the *Chapter 3 Resource Book*.

Extra Examples

Example 1 A cybercafe charges users a minimum fee of $2 for Internet access. Write an inequality to represent the access fee *f*. Then graph the inequality. **$f \geq 2$**

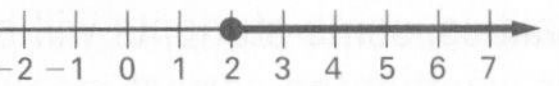

Example 2 Solve $k + 12 \leq -4$. Graph your solution. **$k \leq -16$**

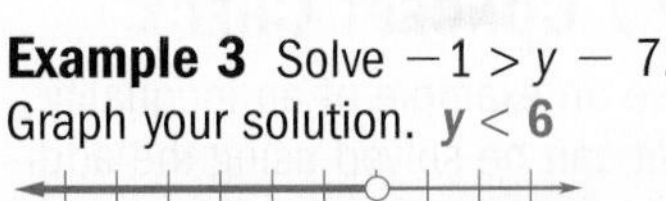

Example 3 Solve $-1 > y - 7$. Graph your solution. **$y < 6$**

Multiple Representations

Inequalities are shown using symbols, in words, and as graphs on page 138. Consider making a large number line on a classroom wall and using a roll of wide ribbon and either a large plastic lid or the outer rim of a plastic lid to model the graphs of inequalities throughout the lesson.

Teaching Tip

Write the addition and subtraction properties of inequality on the board before discussing Examples 2 and 3. After each example, refer to the algebraic representations of the properties and ask students which part(s) of the properties were used in that example.

1–4. See Additional Answers beginning on page AA1.

Extra Examples

Example 4 On the first two tests in math class, Collin had scores of 89 and 95 points. The third math test is tomorrow, and Collin's goal is to have a total score of 279 or higher on the three tests in order to have an A average for this quarter. What possible scores s can he have on the test tommorrow to attain his goal? **$s \geq 95$**

Common Error

In Example 4 and in other real-world inequalities, some students will be unsure whether the correct inequality symbol is $<$ or $\leq$ ($>$ or $\geq$). Ask students how they decide which sign correctly models the situation.

Concept Check

Give an example of an inequality that can be solved using the addition property of inequality, and another that can be solved using the subtraction property of inequality. ***Sample answer:*** **$a - 5 \geq 3$, $-3 < b + 7$**

Daily Puzzler

Tyesha has cats, geese, and snakes as pets. Her animals have a total of 22 legs. If she has more cats than geese and more geese than snakes, how many of each animal does she have? **4 cats, 3 geese, 2 snakes, or 4 cats, 3 geese, 1 snake**

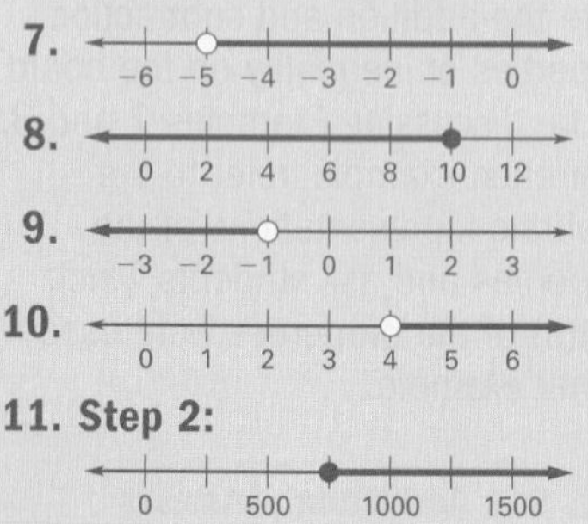

Ironman Triathlon in Roth, Germany

Example 4 *Writing and Solving an Inequality*

Triathlon You are competing in a triathlon, a sports competition with three events. Last year, you finished the triathlon in 85 minutes. The table shows your times for this year's first two events. What possible times can you post in the running event and still beat last year's finishing time?

Triathlon Times	
Event	**Time (min)**
Swimming	17
Biking	45
Running	?

Solution

Let t represent this year's running time. Write a verbal model.

Swimming time + Biking time + Running time < Last year's finishing time

$17 + 45 + t < 85$ **Substitute.**

$62 + t < 85$ **Simplify.**

$62 + t - 62 < 85 - 62$ **Subtract 62 from each side.**

$t < 23$ **Simplify.**

Answer To beat last year's finishing time, you must post a time in the running event that is less than 23 minutes.

3.4 Exercises

More Practice, p. 805

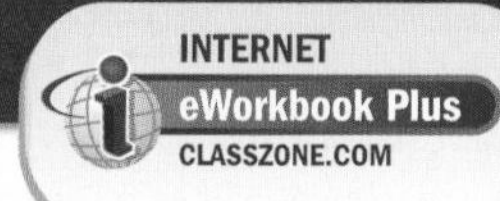

Guided Practice

Vocabulary Check

1. What are equivalent inequalities? **inequalities that have the same solution**
2. Explain how the graph of $x > 5$ is different from the graph of $x \geq 5$. **See margin.**

Skill Check **Tell whether the given number is a solution of $-5 < n$.**

3. 8 **yes**
4. -8 **no**
5. -4 **yes**
6. 4 **yes**

Solve the inequality. Graph and check your solution. **7–10. See margin for art.**

7. $x + 2 > -3$ **$x > -5$**
8. $1 \geq x - 9$ **$10 \geq x$, or $x \leq 10$**
9. $x + 4 < 3$ **$x < -1$**
10. $x + 3 > 7$ **$x > 4$**

Guided Problem Solving

11. **Astronauts** To become a NASA pilot astronaut, a NASA pilot must log at least 1000 hours as pilot-in-command of a jet aircraft. A NASA pilot has completed all other qualifications and has 250 hours logged. How many more hours must the pilot log to become a pilot astronaut?
    1) Write an inequality to represent the situation. **$250 + h \geq 1000$**
    2) Solve the inequality. Then graph and check the solution. **$h \geq 750$; see margin for art.**
    3) Interpret the solution in terms of the real-life situation. **The pilot must log at least 750 additional hours to become a pilot astronaut.**

2. ***Sample answer:*** **The graphs of both inequalities include all points to the right of 5, but the graph of $x > 5$ has an open circle at 5, while the graph of $x \geq 5$ has a closed circle at 5.**

Practice and Problem Solving

Write an inequality to represent the situation.

A **12.** The greatest weight that a forklift can raise is 2500 pounds. **$w \le 2500$**

13. The speed limit is 55 miles per hour. **$s \le 55$**

14. A truck can tow a maximum weight of 7700 pounds. **$w \le 7700$**

15. You must be at least 48 inches tall to ride the roller coaster. **$h \ge 48$**

16. You can save up to \$50 on DVD players this week. **$s \le 50$**

Write an inequality represented by the graph.

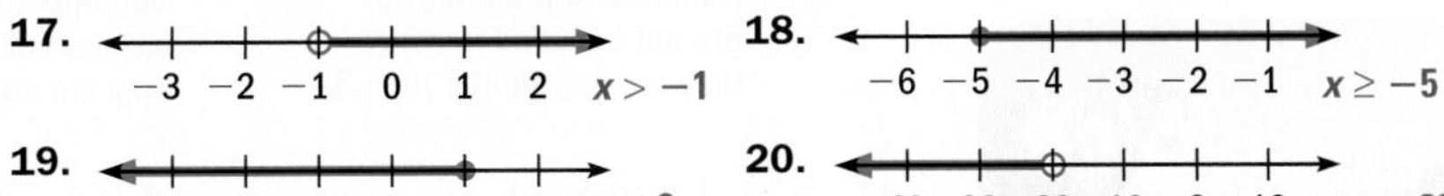

17. (number line −3 to 2) **$x > -1$**

18. (number line −6 to −1) **$x \ge -5$**

19. (number line −2 to 8) **$x \le 6$**

20. (number line −40 to 10) **$x < -20$**

Solve the inequality. Graph your solution. **21–32. See margin for art.**

21. $x + 4 < 5$ **$x < 1$**

22. $m + 8 \ge 12$ **$m \ge 4$**

23. $-11 < y + 5$

24. $-8 \ge d - 7$ **$-1 \ge d$, or $d \le -1$**

25. $-45 > g - 16$

26. $z - 15 > 72$ **$z > 87$**

27. $f + 1 \ge -8$ **$f \ge -9$**

28. $h + 19 \le 15$ **$h \le -4$**

29. $18.1 \le p - 7$

30. $t - 7 < 3.4$ **$t < 10.4$**

31. $b + 2.5 \le 2.5$ **$b \le 0$**

32. $a - 10.2 > 5.3$ **$a > 15.5$**

33. Neon The lowest temperature at which neon is a gas, called its boiling point, is −411°F. Write and graph an inequality to show the temperatures at which neon is a gas. **$t \ge -411$; see margin for art.**

Solve the inequality. Graph your solution. **34–37. See margin for art.**

B **34.** $5 + m + 8 \ge 14$ **$m \ge 1$**

35. $13 + n - 26 < 38$ **$n < 51$**

36. $2.35 + p + 14.9 > 49.25$ **$p > 32$**

37. $q + 4 + 16 \ge 30$ **$q \ge 10$**

38. Bacteria In 1969, Apollo 12 astronauts found a small colony of *Streptococcus* bacteria that had apparently traveled unprotected to the moon on the Surveyor 3 spacecraft's TV camera about three years earlier. The bacteria survived at temperatures as low as −280°F. Write and graph an inequality to show the temperatures at which the bacteria survived. **$t \ge -280$; see margin for art.**

39. *Writing* Is it possible to check *all* the numbers that are solutions of an inequality? Explain. Does checking just *one* number guarantee that a solution is correct? **See margin.**

40. Train Travel You are traveling by train. You are allowed two carryon bags, each with a maximum weight of 50 pounds. You have two bags: one that weighs 14 pounds and one that weighs 21 pounds.

a. Write and solve an inequality that represents the weight w (in pounds) of personal belongings you can add to the first bag without exceeding the weight limit. **$14 + w \le 50$, $w \le 36$**

b. Write and solve an inequality that represents the weight w (in pounds) of personal belongings you can add to the second bag without exceeding the weight limit. **$21 + w \le 50$, $w \le 29$**

Homework *Help*

Example	Exercises
1	12-16, 33, 38
2	21-32, 34-37
3	21-32, 34-37
4	40

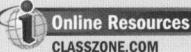

Online Resources CLASSZONE.COM
- More Examples
- eTutorial Plus

23. $-16 < y$, or $y > -16$
25. $-29 > g$, or $g < -29$
29. $25.1 \le p$, or $p \ge 25.1$

In the Real World

Neon Neon is used for signs because it glows when an electric current passes through a glass tube containing the gas. Neon is a liquid if the temperature is between its freezing point and its boiling point. The freezing point of neon is about 5°F lower than its boiling point. Between what temperatures is neon a liquid? **from −416°F to −411°F**

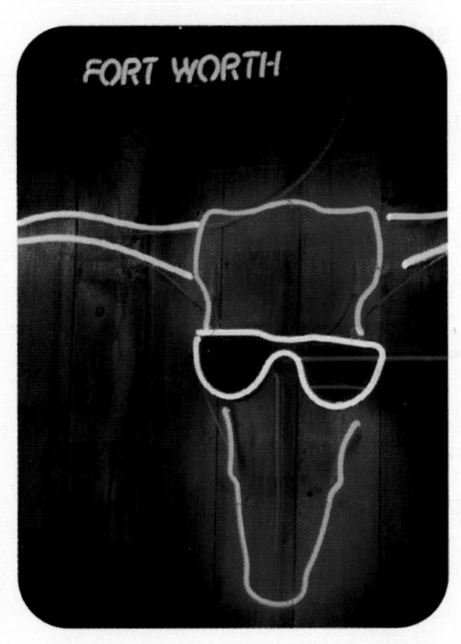

3 APPLY

ASSIGNMENT GUIDE

Basic Course
Day 1: EP p. 803 Exs. 13-15; pp. 141-142 Exs. 12-20, 33, 38, 45-49
Day 2: pp. 141-142 Exs. 21-32, 34-37, 40, 50

Average Course
Day 1: pp. 141-142 Exs. 12-20, 33, 41-43, 45-49
Day 2: pp. 141-142 Exs. 21-32, 34-40, 50

Advanced Course
Day 1: pp. 141-142 Exs. 14-20, 33, 41-48*
Day 2: pp. 141-142 Exs. 25-32, 34-40, 49, 50

Block
pp. 141-142 Exs. 12-43, 45-50

EXTRA PRACTICE
- Student Edition, p. 805
- Chapter 3 Resource Book, pp. 38-40
- Test and Practice Generator

TRANSPARENCY
Even-numbered answers are available on transparencies. A support transparency is available for Exercises 7-11, 21-38, and 41-43.

HOMEWORK CHECK
When you review students' homework for this lesson, go over the following exercises to check understanding of key concepts.
Basic: 12, 21, 32, 33, 40
Average: 13, 22, 32, 38, 40
Advanced: 16, 25, 32, 37, 40

COMMON ERROR
In Exercises 17-38, watch for students who have difficulty differentiating between open and closed circles when writing or graphing inequalities.

21-39. See Additional Answers beginning on page AA1.

4 ASSESS

Assessment Resources

For more assessment resources, see:

- Assessment Book
- Test and Practice Generator

Mini-Quiz

1. A traffic reporter announced that traffic will be delayed at least 15 minutes. Write an inequality to represent this. $t \geq 15$

Solve the inequality. Graph your solution.

2. $17 + a \geq 20$ $a \geq 3$

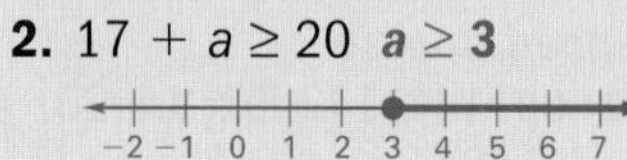

−2 −1 0 1 2 3 4 5 6 7

3. $-5 > s - 1$ $s < -4$

−9 −8 −7 −6 −5 −4 −3 −2 −1 0

4. Challenge Which one of these compound inequalities has a graph that is *not* an empty number line? **A**

A. $x > 3$ and $x > 5$
B. $y < -1$ and $y > 1$
C. $z \geq -5$ and $z \leq -6$

5 FOLLOW-UP

Diagnosis/Remediation

- Study Guide in Chapter 3 Resource Book, pp. 41–42
- Tutor Place, Algebra Cards 14–16
- eTutorial Plus Online
- Extra Practice, p. 805
- Lesson Practice in Chapter 3 Resource Book, pp. 38–40

English Learner Support

- Spanish Study Guide
- Multi-Language Visual Glossary
- Chapter Audio Summaries CDs

Challenge

- Challenge Practice in Chapter 3 Resource Book, p. 44
- Teacher's Edition, p. 116F

41–43. See Additional Answers beginning on page AA1.

In Exercises 41 and 42, graph the *compound inequality.* A compound inequality consists of two inequalities joined by the word *and* or *or.*

Example *Graphing Compound Inequalities*

Graph the compound inequality $x > 3$ *and* $x < 10$.

Include numbers that are both greater than 3 and less than 10.

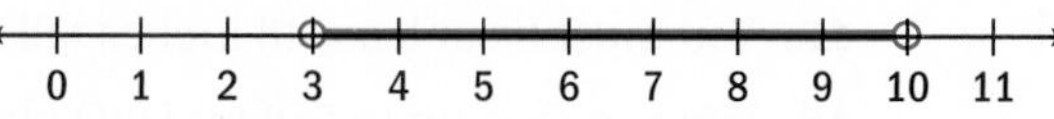

0 1 2 3 4 5 6 7 8 9 10 11
Numbers to the left of 3 are not included because they are not greater than 3.
Numbers to the right of 10 are not included because they are not less than 10.

C **41.** $x \geq -1$ and $x \leq 4$ **42.** $x < 3$ and $x \geq 0$

41–42. See margin.

43. Skiing The ski wax you use keeps your skis performing well at temperatures from −6°C to 15°C. Express the lower limit of the ski wax as an inequality, and express the upper limit as an inequality. Then write the inequalities as a compound inequality and graph it. **$t \geq -6$, $t \leq 15$; $t \geq -6$ and $t \leq 15$; see margin for art.**

44. Challenge Explain how you can graph the compound inequality $x \leq 8$ or $x \geq 10$. How does this graph look different from the graph of $x \geq 8$ and $x \leq 10$? **See margin.**

44. *Sample answer:* **Place a closed circle at 8 and shade the number line to the left. Also, place a closed circle at 10 and shade the number line to the right. This graph consists of two arrows, one heading left and one heading right with a gap in between them, while the graph of $x \geq 8$ *and* $x \leq 10$ is just the portion of the number line between the points 8 and 10 with closed circles at 8 and 10.**

Mixed Review

45. Geometry Find the length of a side of a square with a perimeter of 36.6 meters. *(Lesson 2.7)* **9.15 m**

46. Fundraising A basketball team is raising money for uniforms and equipment. So far, the team has raised $1275. The team plans to spend $450 on equipment and buy as many uniforms as possible. Each uniform costs $55. How many uniforms can the team buy with the money it has raised? *(Lesson 3.1)* **15 uniforms**

Write the verbal sentence as an equation. Then solve the equation. *(Lesson 3.3)*

47. Five plus 4 times a number is equal to the sum of 7 times the number and 11. $5 + 4n = 7n + 11$; -2

48. Eight less than 3 times a number is equal to −3 plus twice the number. $3n - 8 = -3 + 2n$; 5

Standardized Test Practice

49. Multiple Choice Which inequality is represented by the graph shown? **B**

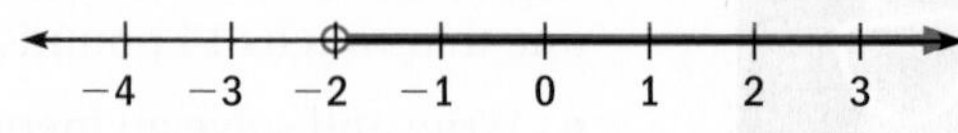

−4 −3 −2 −1 0 1 2 3

A. $y < -2$ **B.** $y > -2$ **C.** $y \leq -2$ **D.** $y \geq -2$

50. Multiple Choice Which number is a solution of the inequality $b + 2 > 2$? **F**

F. 4 **G.** 0 **H.** −1 **I.** −2

Concept *Activity*

3.5 Multiplication and Division Properties of Inequality

Goal
Perform multiplications and divisions on inequality statements.

Materials
- pencil
- paper

Investigate

Determine how multiplication or division affects an inequality.

1 Choose two different integers and insert an inequality symbol between them to make a true statement.

$-2 < 4$

2 Multiply each number in the original inequality by 2. Is the new inequality a true statement?

$2 \cdot (-2) \overset{?}{<} 2 \cdot 4$
$-4 < 8$ ✓
Yes, -4 is less than 8.

3 Multiply each number in the original inequality by -2. Is the new inequality a true statement?

$-2 \cdot (-2) \overset{?}{<} -2 \cdot 4$
$4 < -8$ ✗
No, 4 is not less than -8.

4 Divide each number in the original inequality by 2. Is the new inequality a true statement?

$\frac{-2}{2} \overset{?}{<} \frac{4}{2}$
$-1 < 2$ ✓
Yes, -1 is less than 2.

5 Divide each number in the original inequality by -2. Is the new inequality a true statement?

$\frac{-2}{-2} \overset{?}{<} \frac{4}{-2}$
$1 < -2$ ✗
No, 1 is not less than -2.

Draw Conclusions

1. **Critical Thinking** Repeat the steps above with a new pair of integers. In Steps 3 and 5, what could you do to the inequality symbols to make the statements true? **See margin.**

Given that $a > b$, copy and complete using $<$ or $>$ to make a true statement.

2. $\frac{a}{2} \underline{?} \frac{b}{2}$ $>$ **3.** $\frac{a}{-2} \underline{?} \frac{b}{-2}$ $<$ **4.** $-a \underline{?} -b$ $<$ **5.** $3a \underline{?} 3b$ $>$

NCTM CURRICULUM STANDARDS
Standard 1: Understand relationships among numbers; Understand how operations are related

1 PLAN

Investigate the Concept

- Students perform multiplications and divisions on inequalities.
- This activity leads into solving inequalities by multiplication and division in Lesson 3.5.

Materials

Each student will need pencil and paper.

Recommended Time

Work activity: 10 min
Discuss results: 5 min

Grouping

Students should work individually.

2 TEACH

Tips for Success

Urge students to choose one positive and one negative integer for the Investigate section. Have students use two negative integers when repeating the activity for Exercise 1.

3 CLOSE

Key Discovery

When you multiply or divide each side of an inequality by a negative number, the inequality symbol must be reversed in the resulting inequality.

Assessment

1. Which of these requires the reversal of the symbol in an inequality: *multiplying both sides by* $\frac{1}{2}$ *or dividing both sides by* -2? **dividing both sides by -2**
2. If $x \le y$, then $-x \underline{?} -y$. $\ge$

1. See Additional Answers beginning on page AA1.

1 PLAN

Skill Check

1. $4 \cdot (-4) = \underline{?}$ −16
2. $25 \div (-5) = \underline{?}$ −5
3. $-7 \cdot (-8) = \underline{?}$ 56
4. $-22 \div (-4) = \underline{?}$ 5.5

LESSON OBJECTIVE

Solve inequalities using multiplication or division.

PACING

Suggested Number of Days
Basic Course: 2 days
Average Course: 2 days
Advanced Course: 2 days
Block: 1 block

TEACHING RESOURCES

For a complete list of Teaching Resources, see page 116B.

TRANSPARENCY

Warm-Up Exercises for this lesson are available on a transparency. A support transparency is available for Checkpoint Exercises 1–4.

2 TEACH

MOTIVATING THE LESSON

Share information about other migratory birds with students.

TIPS *for* NEW TEACHERS

Point out that solving inequalities is the same as solving equations except that sometimes you must reverse the inequality symbol. Stress that the symbol is reversed whenever each side is multiplied or divided by a negative number. See Tips for New Teachers in the *Chapter 3 Resource Book*.

LESSON 3.5

Solving Inequalities Using Multiplication *or* Division

Review Vocabulary
inequality, p. 138
equivalent inequalities, p. 139

BEFORE	Now	WHY?
You solved two-step equations.	You'll solve inequalities using multiplication or division.	So you can find how fast you should bike, as in Ex. 38.

Geese Migration Some flocks of Canada geese can fly nonstop for up to 16 hours. In this time, a flock can migrate as far as 848 miles. At what average speeds can such a flock fly during migration? In Example 3, you will see how to answer this question by solving an inequality.

As shown below, when each side of the inequality $2 < 8$ is multiplied by a positive number, the inequality remains true. When each side is multiplied by a negative number, the inequality sign must be reversed.

$2 < 8$	$2 < 8$	
$4 \cdot 2 \overset{?}{<} 4 \cdot 8$	$-4 \cdot 2 \overset{?}{<} -4 \cdot 8$	
$8 < 32$	$-8 > -32$	**Reverse inequality sign.**

These examples suggest the following rules for solving inequalities.

Multiplication Property of Inequality

Words Multiplying each side of an inequality by a *positive* number produces an equivalent inequality.

Multiplying each side of an inequality by a *negative* number and *reversing the direction of the inequality symbol* produces an equivalent inequality.

Algebra If $a < b$ and $c > 0$, then $ac < bc$.

If $a < b$ and $c < 0$, then $ac > bc$.

Example 1 *Solving an Inequality Using Multiplication*

$\frac{m}{-3} > 3$	**Original inequality**
$-3 \cdot \frac{m}{-3} < -3 \cdot 3$	**Multiply each side by −3. Reverse inequality symbol.**
$m < -9$	**Simplify.**

NCTM CURRICULUM STANDARDS
Standard 1: Understand relationships among numbers; Understand how operations are related
Standard 2: Represent situations using algebraic symbols

Division The rules for solving an inequality using division are like the rules for solving an inequality using multiplication.

Study *Strategy*

The multiplication and division properties of inequality are also true for inequalities involving >, ≤, and ≥.

Division Property of Inequality

Words Dividing each side of an inequality by a *positive* number produces an equivalent inequality.

Dividing each side of an inequality by a *negative* number and *reversing the direction of the inequality symbol* produces an equivalent inequality.

Algebra If $a < b$ and $c > 0$, then $\frac{a}{c} < \frac{b}{c}$.

If $a < b$ and $c < 0$, then $\frac{a}{c} > \frac{b}{c}$.

Example 2 *Solving an Inequality Using Division*

$-10t \geq 34$	**Original inequality**
$\frac{-10t}{-10} \leq \frac{34}{-10}$	**Divide each side by −10. Reverse inequality symbol.**
$t \leq -3.4$	**Simplify.**

 ***Checkpoint***

Solve the inequality. Graph your solution. **1–4. See margin for art.**

1. $\frac{n}{6} > 7$ **$n > 42$** **2.** $\frac{t}{-4} \leq 8$ **$t \geq -32$** **3.** $2x > -8$ **$x > -4$** **4.** $-7s \leq 14$ **$s \geq -2$**

In the **Real World**

Geese Migration In North America, not all Canada geese migrate. About 3.6 million "resident" geese live in urban and suburban areas, such as parks, throughout the year. Resident Canada geese outnumber migrating Canada geese. Write an inequality that compares the numbers of migrating geese and resident geese. **$m <$ 3.6 million**

Example 3 *Writing and Solving an Inequality*

Find the average speeds at which the flock of Canada geese described on page 144 can fly during migration.

Solution

Let s represent the average flight speeds. Write a verbal model.

Flight time • Average flight speeds ≤ Maximum flight distance

$16s \leq 848$	**Substitute.**
$\frac{16s}{16} \leq \frac{848}{16}$	**Divide each side by 16.**
$s \leq 53$	**Simplify.**

Answer The flock of Canada geese can fly at average speeds of 53 miles per hour or less during migration.

Extra Examples

Example 1 Solve $\frac{k}{-8} \geq -5$. **$k \leq 40$**

Example 2 Solve $-18y < 72$. **$y > -4$**

Example 3 On average, a customer service representative helps at most 160 customers during an 8-hour workday. Write and solve an inequality to find the average number of customers c she can help each hour during one of her workdays. **$8c \leq 160$, $c \leq 20$; she can help 20 customers or less each hour.**

 **NOTETAKING**

Have students record the multiplication and division properties of inequality using either words or algebra. Then have them record a few examples. Urge students to highlight steps they found confusing and to write a note about how they came to understand these steps.

 **COMMON ERROR**

Expect some students to occasionally forget to reverse the inequality symbol when they multiply or divide an inequality by a negative number.

 **CONCEPT CHECK**

When does the inequality symbol need to be reversed when solving an inequality? **whenever each side of the inequality is multiplied or divided by a negative number**

 **DAILY PUZZLER**

If $a < b$, which is greater, $\frac{a}{b}$ or $\frac{-b}{-a}$? $\frac{-b}{-a}$

1–4. See Additional Answers beginning on page AA1.

3 APPLY

ASSIGNMENT GUIDE

Basic Course

Day 1: pp. 146–148 Exs. 12-19, 30-33, 42-45, 50-54

Day 2: pp. 146–148 Exs. 20-27, 29, 37-41, 55-61

Average Course

Day 1: pp. 146–148 Exs. 16-19, 30-35, 42-44, 50-55

Day 2: pp. 146–148 Exs. 24-29, 36-38, 45-48, 56-61

Advanced Course

Day 1: pp. 146–148 Exs. 16-19, 32-35, 42-46, 54-58

Day 2: pp. 146–148 Exs. 24-29, 36-38, 47-51*, 59-61

Block

pp. 146–148 Exs. 16-19, 24-38, 42-48, 50-61

EXTRA PRACTICE

- Student Edition, p. 805
- Chapter 3 Resource Book, pp. 48-50
- Test and Practice Generator

TRANSPARENCY

Even-numbered answers are available on transparencies. A support transparency is available for Exercises 3-10, 12-27, 39-44, and 55-58.

HOMEWORK CHECK

When you review students' homework for this lesson, go over the following exercises to check understanding of key concepts.

Basic: 12, 14, 22, 26, 29

Average: 17, 19, 24, 27, 29

Advanced: 17, 19, 25, 27, 37

3.5 Exercises

More Practice, p. 805

Guided Practice

Vocabulary Check

1. Which property would you use to solve the inequality $-7y \leq 49$? **division property of inequality**

2. Explain how solving $2x > -14$ is different from solving $-2x > 14$. **See margin.**

Skill Check **Solve the inequality. Graph and check your solution.** **3–10. See margin for art.**

3. $\frac{v}{-2} < -8$ $v > 16$ **4.** $8b > 32$ $b > 4$ **5.** $\frac{u}{6} \geq 3$ $u \geq 18$ **6.** $-6s \leq 54$ $s \geq -9$

7. $5a < -35$ $a < -7$ **8.** $\frac{p}{7} > 6$ $p > 42$ **9.** $3r \geq 21$ $r \geq 7$ **10.** $\frac{t}{4} \leq -9$ $t \leq -36$

Guided Problem Solving

11. Training While training for a marathon, you try to consume at least 2400 Calories each day. For one meal, you like to eat at least 500 Calories. You choose to eat pasta that has 200 Calories per cup. How many cups of pasta should you eat?

1) Let c represent the number of cups of pasta. Write an inequality based on the verbal model given below. $200 \cdot c \geq 500$

Calories per cup • Number of cups ≥ Total calories for meal

2) Solve the inequality. $c \geq 2.5$, or $c \geq 2\frac{1}{2}$

3) Explain what the solution tells you about the situation. *Sample answer:* You must eat at least $2\frac{1}{2}$ cups of pasta at one meal to get the desired number of calories.

2\. *Sample answer:* In $2x > -14$, you divide each side by 2, which is positive, so the direction of the inequality symbol does not change, but in $-2x > 14$, you divide each side by -2, which is negative, so you must reverse the direction of the inequality symbol.

Practice and Problem Solving

Homework Help

Example	Exercises
1	12-27
2	12-27
3	29, 36-38

Online Resources CLASSZONE.COM
- More Examples
- eTutorial Plus

Solve the inequality. Graph your solution. 12–27. See margin for art.

A **12.** $\frac{a}{2} < -9$ $a < -18$ **13.** $\frac{b}{7} > 7$ $b > 49$ **14.** $\frac{c}{8} \geq 3$ $c \geq 24$ **15.** $-16y > 48$ $y < -3$

16. $5z < 65$ $z < 13$ **17.** $\frac{d}{-11} \leq 6$ $d \geq -66$ **18.** $12x \geq -60$ $x \geq -5$ **19.** $4w \leq 68$ $w \leq 17$

20. $\frac{t}{9} < -12$ $t < -108$ **21.** $\frac{h}{-6} \leq 13$ $h \geq -78$ **22.** $-16k \geq 96$ $k \leq -6$ **23.** $6q > -84$ $q > -14$

24. $-7s \geq -84$ $s \leq 12$ **25.** $4m < -60$ $m < -15$ **26.** $\frac{v}{5} > -2$ $v > -10$ **27.** $\frac{n}{-3} \geq -5$ $n \leq 15$

28. Error Analysis Describe and correct the error in solving the inequality $9x > -45$. Since each side was divided by 9, which is positive, the direction of the inequality symbol should not have been reversed in the second statement. It should be $\frac{9x}{9} > \frac{-45}{9}$, followed by $x > -5$.

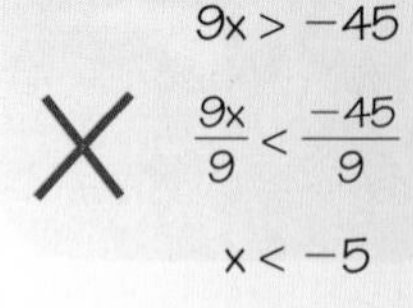

29. **In-Line Skates** You want to use in-line skates. You can either rent in-line skates for \$12 per day or purchase them for \$60. How many times will you have to use the in-line skates in order for the cost of purchasing them to be less than the total cost of renting them? **more than 5 times**

Write the verbal sentence as an inequality. Then solve the inequality.

30. Five times a number is at least 45. $5n \geq 45;\ n \geq 9$
31. A number divided by 4 is at most 8. $\frac{n}{4} \leq 8;\ n \leq 32$
32. A number divided by -3 is less than 6. $\frac{n}{-3} < 6;\ n > -18$
33. Seven times a number is greater than -35. $7n > -35;\ n > -5$
34. A number divided by 2 is no more than 5. $\frac{n}{2} \leq 5;\ n \leq 10$
35. Three times a number is more than -18. $3n > -18;\ n > -6$

36. **Extended Problem Solving** The weight limit for freight loaded onto a freight elevator is 7500 pounds. The elevator is being used to move 50 heavy crates. Each crate weighs 375 pounds.

 a. **Interpret** Write and solve an inequality to determine how many crates you can move in one trip on the elevator. Assume that weight is the only factor affecting how many crates you can move at one time. $375c \leq 7500;\ c \leq 20$ **crates**

 b. **Apply** How many times will you need to load the elevator to move all of the crates? Explain.

36b. 3 times. ***Sample answer:*** **Since 20 crates can be moved in one trip and 50 crates need to be moved, you must divide 50 by 20, which is 2.5. You cannot take half of a trip, so the elevator would have to be loaded 3 times.**

37. **Reading** You need to read at least 105 pages of a book for your English class in the next 7 days. How many pages should you read each day? **at least 15 pages**

38. **Biking** You want to bike at least 45 miles as part of a training program. If you bike for 5 hours, what average speeds will allow you to meet your goal? **at least 9 mi/h**

39–44. See margin for art.

Use a calculator to solve the inequality. Graph your solution.

B 39. $-8.9b \geq 40.94$ $b \leq -4.6$

40. $\frac{x}{2.4} \geq 8.5$ $x \geq 20.4$

41. $\frac{z}{7.2} < -3.4$ $z < -24.48$

42. $6.3a > 10.71$ $a > 1.7$

43. $-3.9c \leq 43.68$ $c \geq -11.2$

44. $\frac{y}{-9.1} \leq 6.5$ $y \geq -59.15$

45. **Water** Filling the bathtub uses 60 gallons of water. Taking a shower uses 2 gallons per minute. How many minutes can you be in the shower and still use less water than you would by filling the bathtub? **less than 30 min**

46. **Caribou** A herd of caribou can migrate as far as 36 miles in 24 hours.

 a. Write and solve an inequality to find the average speeds (in miles per hour) at which caribou can migrate. $24s \leq 36$; **1.5 mi/h or less**

 b. A caribou herd has been moving for three days. On a number line, graph the distances (in miles) the herd could have traveled. **See margin.**

47. **Carpeting** Your parents have decided to install new carpeting in your room, which is rectangular and measures 10 feet by 12 feet. They want to spend at most \$200 on the carpeting. At the flooring store, carpeting is sold by the square foot. How much money will your parents spend per square foot for carpeting? **not more than \$1.66/ft^2**

In the **Real World**

Caribou The caribou in North America are native to Europe, where they are called reindeer. Caribou calves weigh about 13 pounds at birth and may weigh as much as twice that after 10 days. Write an inequality that represents the average weight of a caribou after 10 days. $w \leq 26$

READING STRATEGY

In Exercises 30-35, students should pay particular attention to the words that describe the inequality, since the words indicate whether the proper symbol is <, >, ≤, or ≥. Stress that this is unlike writing verbal sentences as equations where the symbol is always =.

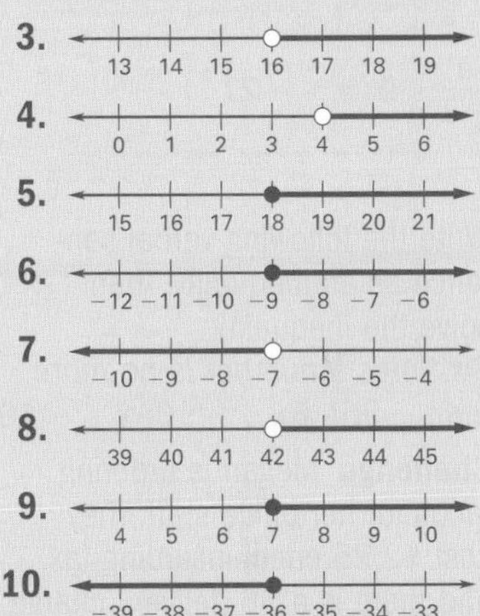

12–27. See Additional Answers beginning on page AA1.

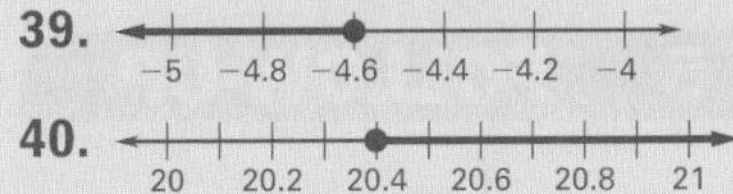

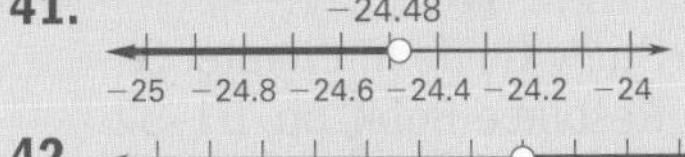

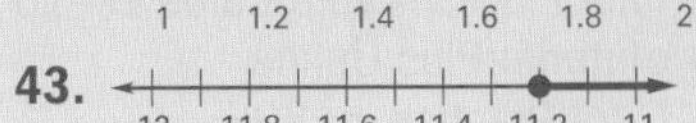

43. −12 −11.8 −11.6 −11.4 −11.2 −11

44. −59.15
−60 −59.8 −59.6 −59.4 −59.2 −59

46b. 104 106 108 110

4 ASSESS

Assessment Resources

For more assessment resources, see:

- Assessment Book
- Test and Practice Generator

Mini-Quiz

Solve. Graph your solution.

1. $14m \geq -56$ **$m \geq -4$**

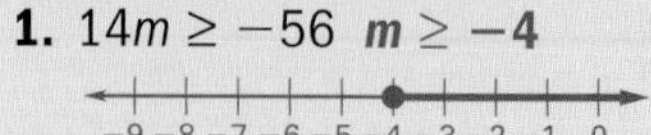

2. $\frac{a}{-3} < 9$ **$a > -27$**

3. Write the following verbal sentence as an inequality. Then solve the inequality.
Six times a number is no more than −96. **$6x \leq -96$; $x \leq -16$**

4. **Challenge** Megan is ordering tacos for her office staff. They cost $2.25 each, including tax, and there is a $6 delivery charge. How many tacos can she buy if she has $42? **at most 16 tacos**

5 FOLLOW-UP

Diagnosis/Remediation

- Study Guide in Chapter 3 Resource Book, pp. 51-52
- Tutor Place, Algebra Cards 14-16
- eTutorial Plus Online
- Extra Practice, p. 805
- Lesson Practice in Chapter 3 Resource Book, pp. 48-50

English Learner Support

- Spanish Study Guide
- Multi-Language Visual Glossary
- Chapter Audio Summaries CDs

Challenge

- Challenge Practice in Chapter 3 Resource Book, p. 53
- Teacher's Edition, p. 116F

55–58. See Additional Answers beginning on page AA1.

C **48. Critical Thinking** The inequalities $2x < 3$ and $4x < 6$ are equivalent inequalities. Write a third inequality equivalent to $2x < 3$ and $4x < 6$. ***Sample answer:* $10x < 15$**

49. Challenge An underwater camera can withstand pressures up to 1500 pounds per square inch. The formula $P = 14.7 + 0.45d$ can be used to find the water pressure P (in pounds per square inch) at depth d (in feet) underwater. Find the depths at which the camera can be used. **at or above $3300\frac{2}{3}$ ft, or 3300 ft 8 in.**

Mixed Review

Algebra Basics Solve the equation. Check your solution. *(Lesson 2.7)*

50. $x + 3.5 = 9.2$ **5.7** **51.** $x - 6.7 = 5.8$ **12.5** **52.** $44.72 = 5.2x$ **8.6** **53.** $\frac{x}{7.6} = 9.5$ **72.2**

54. Find the perimeter of the square. *(Lesson 3.3)* **40 units**

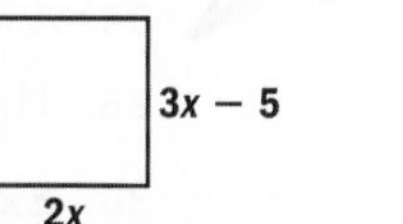

Solve the inequality. Graph your solution. *(Lesson 3.4)* **55–58. See margin for art.**

55. $x + 12 > 96$ **$x > 84$** **56.** $x + 17 \geq 44$ **$x \geq 27$** **57.** $x - 26 \leq 33$ **$x \leq 59$** **58.** $x - 14 < 29$ **$x < 43$**

Standardized Test Practice

59. Multiple Choice Which number is *not* a solution of $\frac{t}{-9} \geq 3$? **D**

A. −35 **B.** −30 **C.** −27 **D.** −25

60. Multiple Choice Which number is a solution of $\frac{x}{-7} < 6$? **I**

F. −100 **G.** −56 **H.** −42 **I.** −14

61. Multiple Choice Which inequality is equivalent to $-18 \leq 3p$? **C**

A. $p \geq -54$ **B.** $-54 \geq p$ **C.** $p \geq -6$ **D.** $-6 \geq p$

Youngest to Oldest

Use the given information to list the six cousins in order from least to greatest age and give their ages. No two cousins are the same age.

Erika is 4 years old.
Charlie's age is greater than 4 times Dawn's age.
All the girls' ages are greater than Anthony's age.
All the cousins' ages are less than or equal to 13.
Matthew is older than exactly three cousins.
Stephanie is 6 years older than Erika.
All the cousins' ages are greater than or equal to 2.
Erika is 1 year older than Dawn.
One boy is 6 years old.

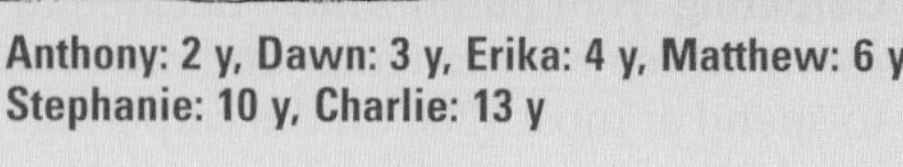

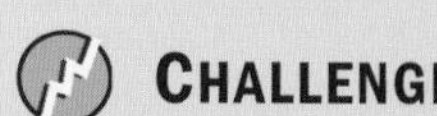

Anthony: 2 y, Dawn: 3 y, Erika: 4 y, Matthew: 6 y, Stephanie: 10 y, Charlie: 13 y

LESSON **3.6**

Solving Multi-Step Inequalities

BEFORE	Now	WHY?
You solved one-step inequalities.	You'll solve multi-step inequalities.	So you can find how long to run a commercial, as in Ex. 23.

Review Vocabulary
inequality, p. 138

Soccer Your school's soccer team is trying to break the school record for goals scored in one season. Your team has already scored 88 goals this season. The record is 138 goals. With 10 games remaining on the schedule, how many goals, on average, does your team need to score per game to break the record?

To solve a multi-step inequality like $2x + 1 > 5$, you should use the properties of inequality from Lessons 3.4 and 3.5 to get the variable terms on one side of the inequality and the constant terms on the other side.

Example 1 *Writing and Solving a Multi-Step Inequality*

Find the average number of goals your team needs to score per game to break the school record, as described above.

Solution

Let g represent the average number of goals scored per game. Write a verbal model.

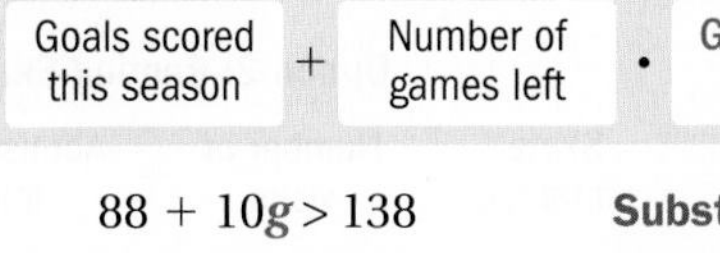

Goals scored this season + Number of games left · Goals scored per game > School record

$88 + 10g > 138$	**Substitute.**
$88 + 10g - 88 > 138 - 88$	**Subtract 88 from each side.**
$10g > 50$	**Simplify.**
$\frac{10g}{10} > \frac{50}{10}$	**Divide each side by 10.**
$g > 5$	**Simplify.**

Answer Your team must score, on average, more than 5 goals per game.

Checkpoint

1. Look back at Example 1. Suppose the season goal record is 124 goals and your team has already scored 52 goals. With 12 games remaining on the schedule, how many goals, on average, does your team need to score per game to break the record? **more than 6 goals per game**

NCTM CURRICULUM STANDARDS
Standard 1: Understand relationships among numbers; Understand how operations are related
Standard 2: Represent situations using algebraic symbols

1 PLAN

Skill Check
Solve.

1. $x - 5 = -4$ **1**
2. $23 = d + 7$ **16**
3. $-2w \geq -4$ **$w \leq 2$**
4. $\frac{a}{-5} < -8$ **$a > 40$**

LESSON OBJECTIVE

Solve multi-step inequalities.

PACING

Suggested Number of Days
Basic Course: 2 days
Average Course: 2 days
Advanced Course: 2 days
Block: 1 block

TEACHING RESOURCES

For a complete list of Teaching Resources, see page 116B.

TRANSPARENCY

Warm-Up Exercises for this lesson are available on a transparency.

2 TEACH

MOTIVATING THE LESSON

Ask volunteers to describe a time when they tried to break a record. Use students' responses to create an example like Example 1.

TIPS *for* NEW TEACHERS

Prior to this lesson you may wish to review writing a verbal model, to restate each of the inequality properties, and to display the solution process for several one-step inequalities. See Tips for New Teachers in the *Chapter 3 Resource Book*.

Extra Examples

Example 1 A city's record rainfall for the month of October is 16.8 inches. So far in October this year, 11.2 inches of rain have fallen. Find the average number of inches of rain that must fall each day to break the record if there are 14 days left in the month. **$n > 0.4$ in.**

Example 2 Solve $-6 \geq \frac{g}{-5} - 2$. **$g \geq 20$**

Example 3 A dance group charges $15 for membership. Members pay $8 for admission to monthly dances, and nonmembers pay $12. How many dances does Dave need to attend for the cost of membership to be less than paying as a nonmember? **at least 4 dances**

Differentiating Instruction

Advanced Students Give students an inequality with a variable on each side. Have students think of a real-world situation that this inequality could model, and then solve the inequality. Encourage students to think of other real-world situations and write their own inequalities.

Concept Check

What must you do with the variables when solving a multi-step inequality that has variables on both sides? **You must get the variables on one side of the inequality and the constant terms on the other side.**

Daily Puzzler

For what value(s) of a do the inequalities $ax - 9 \geq 3$ and $10 \leq \frac{x}{a} + 7$ have the same solution? **$a = -2$**

Note *Worthy*

You may find it helpful to summarize the process used to solve a multi-step inequality in your notes.

Example 2 *Solving a Multi-Step Inequality*

$\frac{x}{-4} - 6 \geq -5$	**Original inequality**
$\frac{x}{-4} - 6 + 6 \geq -5 + 6$	**Add 6 to each side.**
$\frac{x}{-4} \geq 1$	**Simplify.**
$-4 \cdot \frac{x}{-4} \leq -4 \cdot 1$	**Multiply each side by −4. Reverse inequality symbol.**
$x \leq -4$	**Simplify.**

Example 3 *Combining like Terms in a Multi-Step Inequality*

Ice Skating You plan to go ice skating often this winter. The skating rink charges $4 for admission. You can either rent ice skates at the skating rink for $5 per day or buy your own pair for $45. How many times do you have to use the ice skates in order for the cost of buying them to be less than the total cost of renting them?

Solution

You have two options: buying skates or renting skates. Let v represent the number of visits to the skating rink. Write a variable expression for the cost of each option.

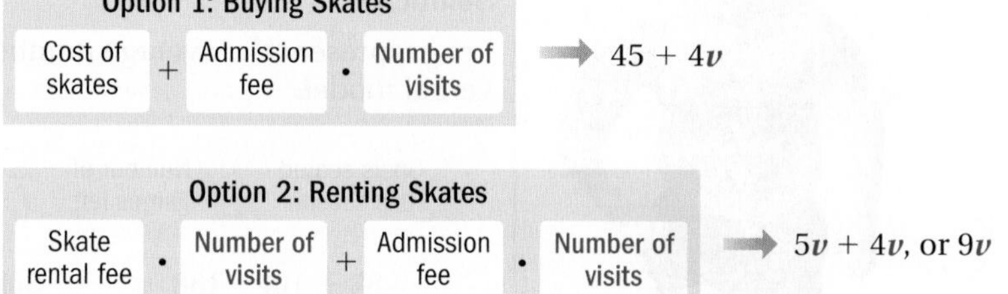

Option 1: Buying Skates
Cost of skates + Admission fee · Number of visits → 45 + 4v
Option 2: Renting Skates
Skate rental fee · Number of visits + Admission fee · Number of visits → 5v + 4v, or 9v

To find the values of v for which the cost of option 1 is less than the cost of option 2, write and solve an inequality.

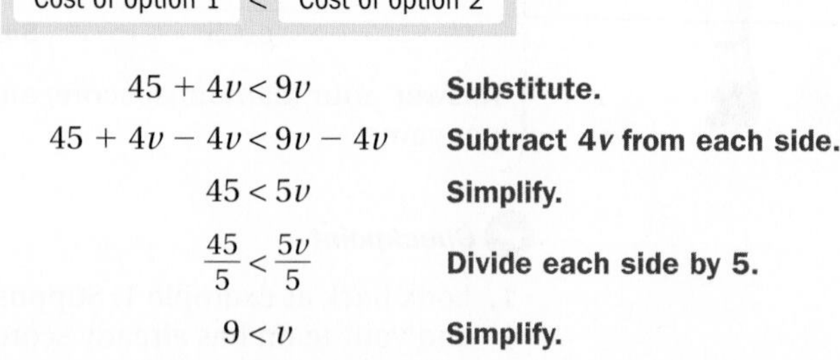

Cost of option 1 < Cost of option 2

$45 + 4v < 9v$	**Substitute.**
$45 + 4v - 4v < 9v - 4v$	**Subtract $4v$ from each side.**
$45 < 5v$	**Simplify.**
$\frac{45}{5} < \frac{5v}{5}$	**Divide each side by 5.**
$9 < v$	**Simplify.**

Answer If you buy skates, the cost will be less after more than 9 visits.

3.6 Exercises

More Practice, p. 805

Guided Practice

Vocabulary Check

1. Write and solve an inequality for the following verbal sentence: Five plus 2 times a number is less than 20. **$5 + 2n < 20$; $n < 7.5$**

2. List the steps you would take to solve the inequality $-5x + 12 < -8$. **See margin.**

Skill Check **Solve the inequality. Graph and check your solution.** **3–8. See margin for art.**

3. $4x + 1 > 1$ **$x > 0$**

4. $7 \geq 5x - 3$ **$2 \geq x$, or $x \leq 2$**

5. $\frac{x}{-2} + 6 < -14$ **$x > 40$**

6. $10 > 6 + \frac{y}{5}$ **$20 > y$, or $y < 20$**

7. $5y + 2 \leq y + 34$ **$y \leq 8$**

8. $6 + y \geq 2y - 3$ **$y \leq 9$**

Guided Problem Solving

9. Amusement Parks You are trying to decide whether to pay $120 for a season pass to an amusement park. If you buy the pass, you get an unlimited number of visits to the park and reduced parking for $8. If you do not buy the pass, you pay $23 admission and $10 for parking each time you visit the park. After how many visits to the park will the cost of the season pass be less than the cost of visiting without the season pass?

1) Write a variable expression for the cost of making v visits to the park if you don't buy a season pass. **$23v + 10v$, or $33v$**

2) Write an inequality in terms of v showing that the cost of visiting the park with a season pass is less than the cost of visiting the park without a season pass. **$120 + 8v < 33v$**

3) Solve the inequality. **$4.8 < v$, or $v > 4.8$. *Sample answer:* You must visit the park at least 5 times for the cost with the season pass to be less.**

2. *Sample answer:* First I would subtract 12 from each side to obtain $-5x < -20$. Then I would divide each side by -5 and reverse the direction of the inequality to obtain $x > 4$.

Practice and Problem Solving

Homework *Help*

Example	Exercises
1	23
2	14-21
3	22, 31

Online Resources
CLASSZONE.COM
- More Examples
- eTutorial Plus

Tell whether the given number is a solution of $5x - 10 > 2x + 4$.

A **10.** 8 **yes** **11.** 5 **yes** **12.** 4 **no** **13.** -2 **no**

Solve the inequality. Graph your solution. **14–21. See margin for art.**

14. $2y + 7 > 11$ **$y > 2$**

15. $6n - 3 \leq -9$ **$n \leq -1$**

16. $11 - 4z < -1$ **$z > 3$**

17. $3m - 8 > -30 + 5m$ **$m < 11$**

18. $19 \geq \frac{x}{90} - 25$ **$3960 \geq x$, or $x \leq 3960$**

19. $3 + \frac{b}{3} < 7$ **$b < 12$**

20. $14p - 5 \geq -3p + 114$ **$p \geq 7$**

21. $-3x - 3 < 2x - 83$ **$x > 16$**

22. Movie Rental At a video store, you have two options for renting movies. You can pay $4 per movie, or you can pay a one-time membership fee of $10 and then pay only $1.50 per movie. After how many movie rentals will the cost of the membership be less than the cost of renting movies without the membership? **after 4 movies**

3 APPLY

ASSIGNMENT GUIDE

Basic Course

Day 1: SRH p. 802 Exs. 1-3; pp. 151-153 Exs. 10-17, 25-30, 47-49

Day 2: pp. 151-153 Exs. 18-23, 31, 35-46

Average Course

Day 1: pp. 151-153 Exs. 10-17, 25-27, 34-43

Day 2: pp. 151-153 Exs. 18-24, 28-32, 44-49

Advanced Course

Day 1: pp. 151-153 Exs. 12-17, 25-27, 39-46

Day 2: pp. 151-153 Exs. 18-24, 28-34*, 47-49

Block

pp. 151-153 Exs. 10-15, 18-32, 34-49

Extra Practice

- Student Edition, p. 805
- Chapter 3 Resource Book, pp. 56-58
- Test and Practice Generator

Transparency

Even-numbered answers are available on transparencies. A support transparency is available for Exercises 3-8, 14-21, 25-30, and 34.

Homework Check

When you review students' homework for this lesson, go over the following exercises to check understanding of key concepts.
Basic: 14, 15, 18, 22, 23
Average: 15, 18, 19, 22, 23
Advanced: 15, 19, 22, 23, 31

3-8, 14-21. See Additional Answers beginning on page AA1.

TEACHING TIP

In Exercises 26 and 28–30, some students may need help to see that the first step of the solution process should be to multiply each side by the denominator of the fractional expression.

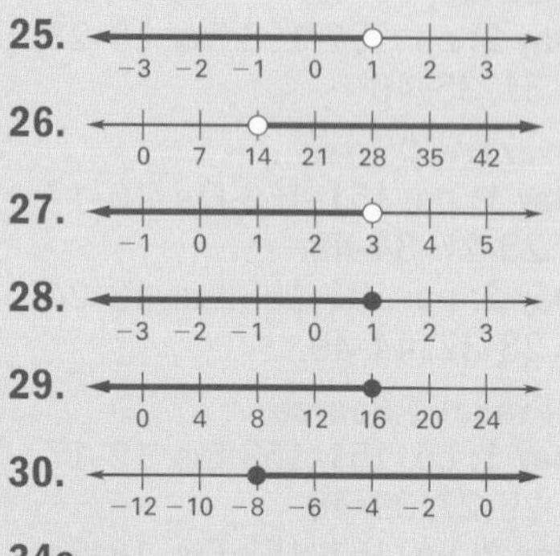

34a.

Months, m	Amount I have paid	Amount friend has paid
1	\$185	\$140
2	\$220	\$180
3	\$255	\$220
4	\$290	\$260
5	\$325	\$300
6	\$360	\$340
7	\$395	\$380
8	\$430	\$420
9	\$465	\$460
10	\$500	\$500
11	\$535	\$540
12	\$570	\$580

34b.

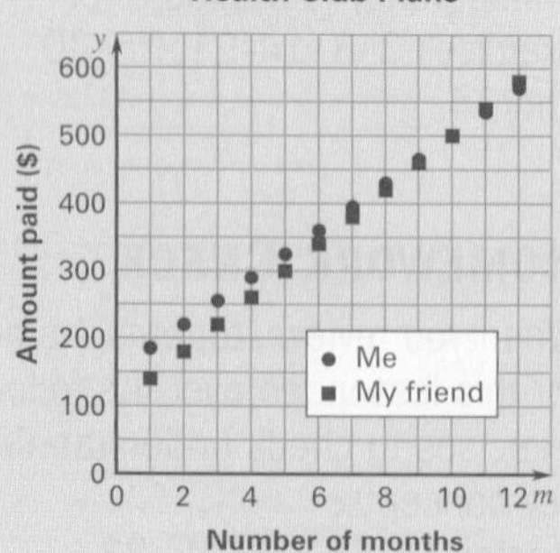

Television crew filming a commercial

23. Advertising A small company has an advertising budget of \$15,000. The company plans to produce and air a television commercial. It will cost \$500 to produce the commercial and an additional \$50 each time the commercial is aired. How many days can the company afford to run the commercial if it is aired once a day? **not more than 290 days**

24. Error Analysis Describe and correct the error in solving the inequality $4x > 6x + 3$. ***Sample answer:* In the fourth statement, the direction of the inequality symbol should have been reversed because each side was divided by a negative number. The statement should have been $\frac{-2x}{-2} < \frac{3}{-2}$, followed by $x < -\frac{3}{2}$.**

$$4x > 6x + 3$$
$$4x - 6x > 6x + 3 - 6x$$
$$-2x > 3$$
$$\frac{-2x}{-2} > \frac{3}{-2}$$
$$x > -\frac{3}{2}$$

Solve the inequality. Graph your solution. **25–30. See margin for art.**

B 25. $4(5 - 3b) > 4b + 4$ **$b < 1$**

26. $\frac{x - 2}{3} > 4$ **$x > 14$**

27. $3y - 5 < 2(17 - 5y)$ **$y < 3$**

28. $\frac{x + 5}{3} \le 2$ **$x \le 1$**

29. $\frac{-5s - 8}{4} \ge -22$ **$s \le 16$**

30. $-3 \le \frac{2x + 4}{4}$ **$-8 \le x$, or $x \ge -8$**

31. Fundraising You are designing greeting cards on your computer to raise money for a charity. You buy card stock at a cost of \$.50 per card and rent a table at the fundraiser for \$20. You will sell the cards in sets of 12 for \$10.20. How many sets of cards do you have to sell in order to make more than what you spend? **at least 5 sets**

32. Long-Distance Calls The table gives information about three long-distance telephone companies. For each company, the table gives the monthly fee and the charge per minute for making long-distance calls.

Long-Distance Rates by Company

Company	Monthly fee	Per-minute charge
A	\$2.00	\$.039
B	No fee	\$.049
C	\$1.95	\$.044

a. After how many minutes of long-distance calls is the cost of using company A for one month less than the cost of using company B for one month? **more than 200 minutes**

b. After how many minutes of long-distance calls is the cost of using company C for one month less than the cost of using company B for one month? **more than 390 minutes**

c. Interpret and Apply If you spend 150 minutes each month making long-distance calls, which company should you use? Explain why.

C 33. Challenge Find all the values of x that make both of the following inequalities true: $2x + 4 < 10$ and $5 - 3x \le 17$. Show how you found your answer.

32c. Company B. *Sample answer:* cost using company A: \$2 + \$.039(150) = \$7.85; cost using company B: \$.049(150) = \$7.35; cost using company C: \$1.95 + \$.044(150) = \$8.55

33. $x \ge -4$ *and* $x < 3$, or all values between −4 and 3, including −4, but not 3. *Sample answer:* I solved $2x + 4 < 10$ to get $x < 3$. Then I solved $5 - 3x \le 17$ to get $x \ge -4$. By graphing $x < 3$ and $x \ge -4$ on number lines, I could see that the values that make both inequalities true are those between −4 and 3, including −4, but not 3.

34. Extended Problem Solving You and a friend join different health clubs. You pay a one-time membership fee of \$150 and a monthly fee of \$35. Your friend pays a one-time membership fee of \$100 and a monthly fee of \$40. **34a–c. See margin.**

a. Analyze Let m be the number of months that you and your friend have been health club members. Make a table with a column for the number m of months, a column for the amount you have paid after m months, and a column for the amount your friend has paid after m months. Complete the table for whole-number values of m from 1 to 12 to represent one year of membership at each health club.

b. Make a scatter plot of the data from part (a). Show months on the x-axis and the amount paid on the y-axis. Plot points representing the amount you have paid in blue and the amount your friend has paid in red.

c. *Writing* Using the scatter plot, determine the number of months you and your friend need to be members of your health clubs before you have paid less than your friend. Explain your reasoning.

d. Check your answer to part (c) by writing and solving an inequality. **$150 + 35m < 100 + 40m$, $m > 10$**

Mixed Review

34c. 11 months. *Sample answer:* After 10 months, the graphs share the same point, which means that the cost is the same. Then after that, the points corresponding to my cost go below those corresponding to my friend's cost, which means that my plan is cheaper.

Give the coordinates of the point. *(Lesson 1.8)*

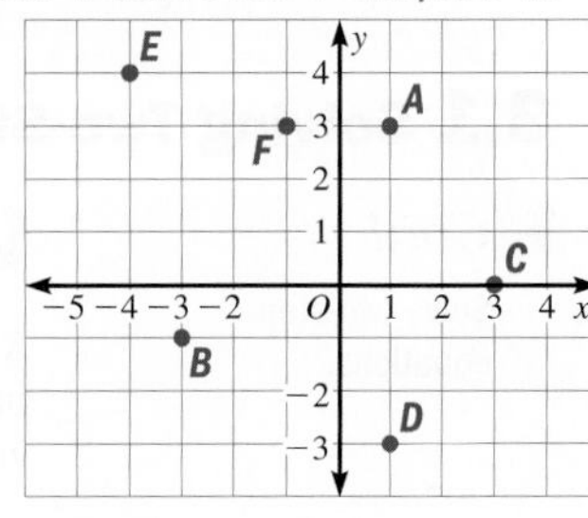

35. A **(1, 3)** **36.** B **(−3, −1)**

37. C **(3, 0)** **38.** D **(1, −3)**

39. E **(−4, 4)** **40.** F **(−1, 3)**

Simplify the expression. *(Lesson 2.3)*

41. $13(2a + 1)$ **$26a + 13$** **42.** $12 + c + 8$ **$c + 20$** **43.** $5a + a$ **$6a$**

Algebra Basics Solve the equation. Check your solution. *(Lesson 3.2)*

44. $3(x + 4) = 9$ **−1** **45.** $4(2d + 1) = 28$ **3** **46.** $-10 = 2(7 - 2x)$ **6**

47. Write and solve an equation for the following verbal sentence: Nine more than 3 times a number is equal to 7 less than twice the number. *(Lesson 3.3)* **$3n + 9 = 2n - 7$, −16**

Standardized Test Practice

48. Multiple Choice Which graph shows the solution of the inequality $7 - 6x \geq 13$? **D**

A. 

B. 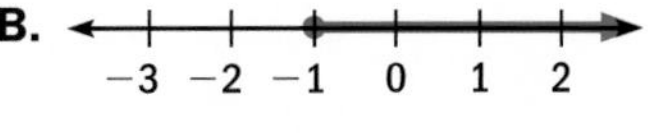

C. −3 −2 −1 0 1 2

D. 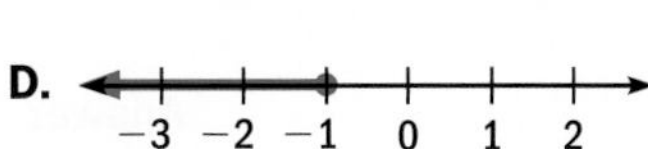

49. Multiple Choice Which number is a solution of the inequality $-7x + 3 < -7.5$? **I**

F. −3 **G.** −1 **H.** 1 **I.** 3

4 ASSESS

Assessment Resources

For more assessment resources, see:
- Assessment Book
- Test and Practice Generator

Mini-Quiz

1. Is −3 a solution of $6 + 4z \geq 7z + 11$? **yes**

Solve the inequality. Graph your solution.

2. $2 + 3k > 35$ **$k > 11$**

9 10 11 12 13 14 15 16 17 18

3. $12 \leq 9 - \frac{m}{3}$ **$m \leq -9$**

−13 −11 −9 −7 −5

4. Challenge Find all the values of x that make both of the following inequalities true: $5 < 4x + 13$ and $8 + 3x \leq 20$. **$-2 < x \leq 4$**

5 FOLLOW-UP

Diagnosis/Remediation

- Study Guide in Chapter 3 Resource Book, pp. 59–60
- eTutorial Plus Online
- Extra Practice, p. 805
- Lesson Practice in Chapter 3 Resource Book, pp. 56–58

English Learner Support

- Spanish Study Guide
- Multi-Language Visual Glossary
- Chapter Audio Summaries CDs

Challenge

- Challenge Practice in Chapter 3 Resource Book, p. 61
- Teacher's Edition, p. 116F

Additional Resources

The following resources are available to help review the materials in Lessons 3.4–3.6.

Chapter 3 Resource Book
- Lesson Practice
- Study Guide

Assessment Book
- Chapter 3 Quiz 2

Technology
- Test and Practice Generator
- eTutorial CD-ROM

Internet
- Classzone
- eWorkbook Plus Online
- eTutorial Plus Online

English Learner Support

- Spanish Study Guide
- Multi-Language Visual Glossary
- Chapter Audio Summaries CDs

4. No. *Sample answer:* The solution of $-2x > 6$ is $x < -3$, or all values less than -3, which is different from $x > -3$, or all values greater than -3.

CHAPTER 3

Chapter Review

Vocabulary Review

inequality, p. 138 | solution of an inequality, p. 138 | equivalent inequalities, p. 139

1. Copy and complete: The value of a variable that, when substituted into an inequality, makes a true statement is a(n) _?_. **solution of an inequality**
2. Give an example of an inequality. ***Sample answer:* $-3x - 2 \geq 6$**
3. Copy and complete: The inequalities $2x < 2$ and $x < 1$ are _?_ inequalities. **equivalent**
4. Are $-2x > 6$ and $x > -3$ equivalent inequalities? Why or why not? **See margin.**

3.1 Solving Two-Step Equations

Examples on pp. 120–122

Goal

Solve two-step equations.

Example **Solve the following problem.**

A one-year membership in a video rental club costs \$10. Members pay \$1.25 per video rental. You spend \$45 in one year. How many videos did you rent?

Solution

Let v represent the number of videos you rented. Write a verbal model.

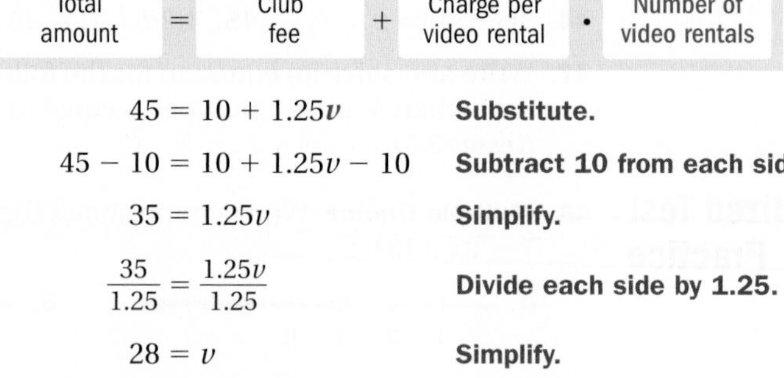

$45 = 10 + 1.25v$ **Substitute.**

$45 - 10 = 10 + 1.25v - 10$ **Subtract 10 from each side.**

$35 = 1.25v$ **Simplify.**

$\frac{35}{1.25} = \frac{1.25v}{1.25}$ **Divide each side by 1.25.**

$28 = v$ **Simplify.**

Answer You rented 28 videos.

5. **Spaghetti** Your friend bought a box of spaghetti for \$1.59 and 2 jars of spaghetti sauce. The total cost was \$6.49. Find the cost of one jar of sauce. **\$2.45**

The following resources are available to help review the materials in this chapter.

Chapter 3 Resource Book
- Chapter Review Games and Activities, p. 62
- Cumulative Practice, Chs. 1-3

English/Spanish Chapter Reviews and Tests

Chapter Audio Summaries CDs

eTutorial CD-ROM

eWorkbook Plus Online

eTutorial Plus Online

3.2 Solving Equations Having Like Terms and Parentheses

Examples on pp. 125–126

Goal

Solve equations having like terms and parentheses.

Example **Solve $2x - x + 1 = 5$ and $4(3r - 9) = 36$.**

a. $2x - x + 1 = 5$ — **Write original equation.**

$x + 1 = 5$ — **Combine like terms.**

$x + 1 - 1 = 5 - 1$ — **Subtract 1 from each side.**

$x = 4$ — **Simplify.**

b. $4(3r - 9) = 36$ — **Write original equation.**

$12r - 36 = 36$ — **Distributive property**

$12r - 36 + 36 = 36 + 36$ — **Add 36 to each side.**

$12r = 72$ — **Simplify.**

$\frac{12r}{12} = \frac{72}{12}$ — **Divide each side by 12.**

$r = 6$ — **Simplify.**

Solve the equation. Check your solution.

6. $17h - 47 + 6h = 160$ 9 **7.** $2(4p + 8) = 128$ 14 **8.** $6(w - 4) + 18 = 30$ 6

3.3 Solving Equations with Variables on Both Sides

Examples on pp. 131–133

Goal

Solve equations with variables on both sides.

Example **Solve $13n - 45 = 36 + 4n$.**

$13n - 45 = 36 + 4n$ — **Write original equation.**

$13n - 45 - 4n = 36 + 4n - 4n$ — **Subtract $4n$ from each side.**

$9n - 45 = 36$ — **Simplify.**

$9n - 45 + 45 = 36 + 45$ — **Add 45 to each side.**

$9n = 81$ — **Simplify.**

$\frac{9n}{9} = \frac{81}{9}$ — **Divide each side by 9.**

$n = 9$ — **Simplify.**

Solve the equation. Check your solution.

9. $11t + 14 = 95 - 16t$ 3 **10.** $9n + 64 = -144 - 17n$ −8

11. $3 + 2x = 2(2 + x)$ no solution **12.** $3(2 + 6b) = 18b$ no solution

13. 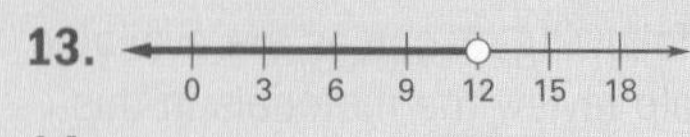

14. 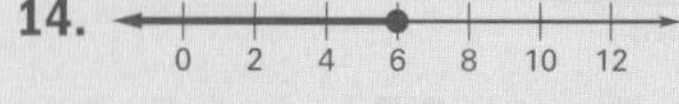

15. 

16. 30 31 32 33 34 35 36

17. −31 −30 −29 −28 −27 −26 −25

18. 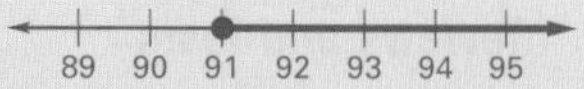 89 90 91 92 93 94 95

19. 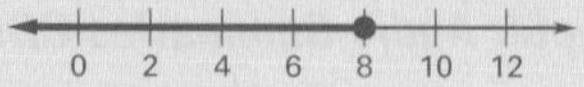 0 2 4 6 8 10 12

20. 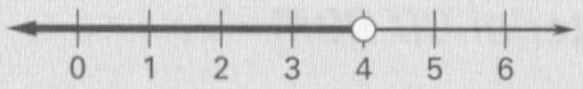 0 1 2 3 4 5 6

21. 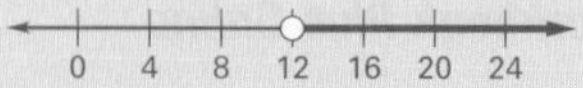 0 4 8 12 16 20 24

22. 11 12 13 14 15 16  17

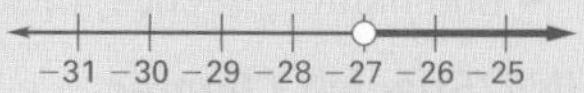

23. 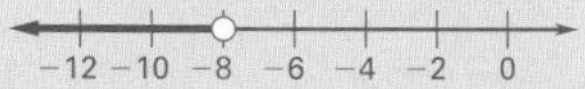 −12 −10 −8 −6 −4 −2 0

24. 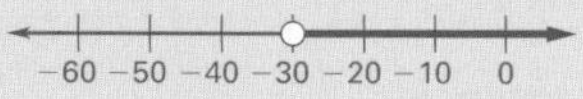 −60 −50 −40 −30 −20 −10 0

3.4 Solving Inequalities Using Addition or Subtraction

Examples on pp. 138–140

Goal

Solve inequalities using addition or subtraction.

Example Solve $x + 13 \le 20$. Graph your solution.

$x + 13 \le 20$	Write original inequality.
$x + 13 - 13 \le 20 - 13$	Subtract 13 from each side.
$x \le 7$	Simplify.

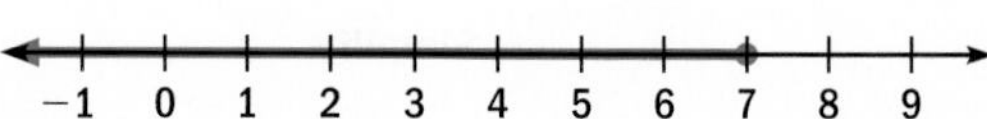

✔ **Solve the inequality. Graph your solution.** 13–16. See margin for art.

13. $y + 11 < 23$ $y < 12$ **14.** $15 \ge z + 9$ $6 \ge z$, or $z \le 6$ **15.** $x - 5 \le 14$ $x \le 19$ **16.** $m - 8 < 26$ $m < 34$

3.5 Solving Inequalities Using Multiplication or Division

Examples on pp. 144–145

Goal

Solve inequalities using multiplication and division.

Example Solve $5x > 30$ and $\frac{t}{-8} \le 5$. Graph your solutions.

a.

$5x > 30$	Write original inequality.
$\frac{5x}{5} > \frac{30}{5}$	Divide each side by 5.
$x > 6$	Simplify.

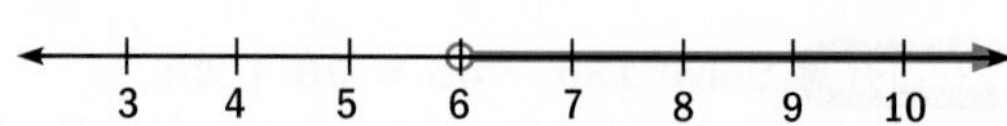

b.

$\frac{t}{-8} \le 5$	Write original inequality.
$-8 \cdot \frac{t}{-8} \ge -8 \cdot 5$	Multiply each side by −8. Reverse inequality symbol.
$t \ge -40$	Simplify.

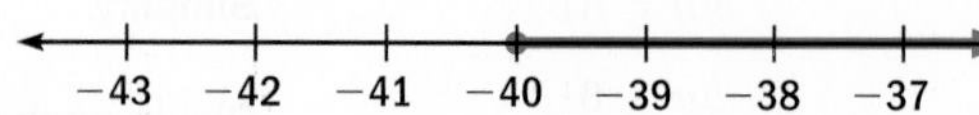

✔ **Solve the inequality. Graph your solution.** 17–24. See margin for art.

17. $3 > \frac{a}{-9}$ $-27 < a$, or $a > -27$ **18.** $\frac{b}{7} \ge 13$ $b \ge 91$ **19.** $12c \le 96$ $c \le 8$ **20.** $-68 < -17d$ $4 > d$, or $d < 4$

21. $-2 > \frac{r}{-6}$ $12 < r$, or $r > 12$ **22.** $196 \le 14z$ $14 \le z$, or $z \ge 14$ **23.** $7h < -56$ $h < -8$ **24.** $\frac{p}{5} > -6$ $p > -30$

3.6 Solving Multi-Step Inequalities

Examples on pp. 149–150

Goal

Solve multi-step inequalities.

Example **Solve $-8y + 5 \le 29$ and $3x - 5 > 6x + 13$. Graph your solutions.**

a.

$-8y + 5 \le 29$	**Write original inequality.**
$-8y + 5 - 5 \le 29 - 5$	**Subtract 5 from each side.**
$-8y \le 24$	**Simplify.**
$\frac{-8y}{-8} \ge \frac{24}{-8}$	**Divide both sides by −8. Reverse inequality symbol.**
$y \ge -3$	**Simplify.**

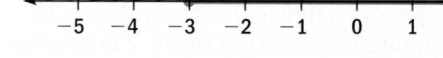

b.

$3x - 5 > 6x + 13$	**Write original inequality.**
$3x - 5 - 3x > 6x + 13 - 3x$	**Subtract 3x from each side.**
$-5 > 3x + 13$	**Simplify.**
$-5 - 13 > 3x + 13 - 13$	**Subtract 13 from each side.**
$-18 > 3x$	**Simplify.**
$\frac{-18}{3} > \frac{3x}{3}$	**Divide each side by 3.**
$-6 > x$	**Simplify.**

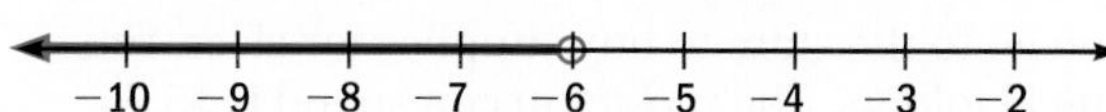

Solve the inequality. Graph your solution.
25–33. See margin for art.

25. $-8m - 6 < 10$ **$m > -2$**

26. $8p + 1 \ge 17$ **$p \ge 2$**

27. $24 \ge 5z - 6$ **$6 \ge z$, or $z \le 6$**

28. $8 > 2 + \frac{b}{3}$ **$18 > b$, or $b < 18$**

29. $\frac{p}{28} + 3 \le 9$ **$p \le 168$**

30. $\frac{n}{3} + 4 > 5$ **$n > 3$**

31. $12 - 4q \ge 6q + 2$ **$q \le 1$**

32. $6x - 5 > 12x + 1$ **$x < -1$**

33. $6(3 - a) \le 8a - 10$ **$a \ge 2$**

34. Snowboarding A ski resort charges $45 for an all-day lift pass and $40 per day for renting boots and a snowboard. At a store, you can buy boots and a snowboard for $360. How many times must you go snowboarding at the ski resort for the cost of buying your own boots and snowboard to be less than renting them? **10 times or more**

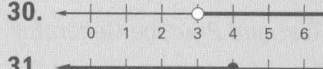

25.–**33.**

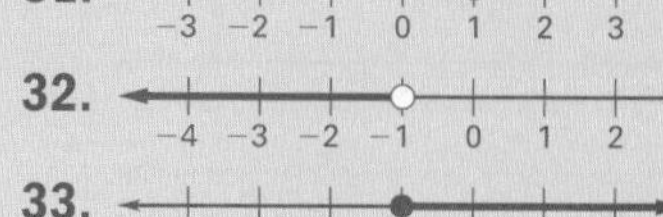

Additional Resources

Assessment Book

- Chapter Test (3 levels), pp. 31–36
- Standardized Chapter Test, p. 37
- Alternative Assessment, pp. 38–39

Test and Practice Generator

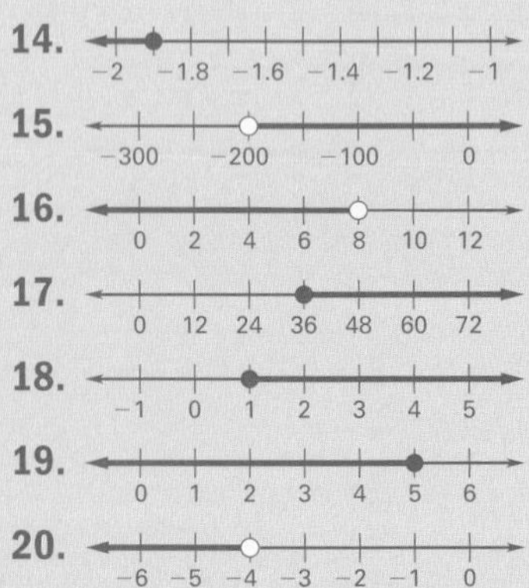

CHAPTER 3

Chapter Test

Solve the equation. Check your solution.

1. $7f + 5 = 68$ 9

2. $14 - 3g = 32$ -6

3. $\frac{h}{3} - 14 = -11$ 9

4. $\frac{z}{-2} + 5 = 7$ -4

5. $12 - 2m + 5 = -1$ 9

6. $-6y + 4 + 11y = -16$ -4

7. $3(8 - a) = 12$ 4

8. $-6(3x + 15) = 18$ -6

9. $5t + 5 = 5t - 4$ no solution

10. $2n - 6 = -8n + 14$ 2

11. $8b + 4 = 4(b - 7)$ -8

12. $16p + 8 = 2(8p + 4)$ all numbers

13. Movie Tickets A family of four goes to a movie theater and spends \$26.50. They buy 2 tickets for children at \$3.50 per ticket, 2 tickets for adults, and 3 boxes of popcorn at \$2.50 per box. What is the cost of one adult movie ticket? \$6

14. Ocean Water The more salt that ocean water contains, the lower the temperature at which it freezes. Some ocean water freezes at temperatures of $-1.9°C$ or less. Write and graph an inequality to show the temperatures at which this ocean water freezes. $t \le -1.9$; See margin for art.

Solve the inequality. Graph your solution. 15–20. See margin for art.

15. $x + 75 > -125$ $x > -200$

16. $w - 18 < -10$ $w < 8$

17. $\frac{t}{12} \ge 3$ $t \ge 36$

18. $-3a - 6 \le -9$ $a \ge 1$

19. $4(2 - d) \ge -12$ $d \le 5$

20. $2c - 5 < -21 - 2c$ $c < -4$

21. School Supplies You go to the store to buy supplies for class. You want to buy 5 identical folders. The most you can spend is \$5.75. What are the individual folder prices that you can afford? \$1.15 or less each

Write the verbal sentence as an inequality. Then solve the inequality.

22. Nine is greater than or equal to 15 minus a number. $9 \ge 15 - n$; $6 \le n$, or $n \ge 6$

23. Eight times the sum of 5 and a number is less than 56. $8(5 + n) < 56$; $n < 2$

24. Fifteen is greater than 3 times the difference of a number and 4. $15 > 3(n - 4)$; $9 > n$, or $n < 9$

25. Seven times a number minus 5 is less than or equal to 16. $7n - 5 \le 16$; $n \le 3$

26. Making Bread A bread-making machine costs \$99. The ingredients to make a one pound loaf of bread cost \$.45. At a store, you pay \$2.19 for the same size loaf of bread. How many whole loaves of bread will you have to make in order for the cost of the machine and ingredients to be less than the cost of buying an equivalent amount of bread at the store? at least 57 loaves

ADDITIONAL RESOURCES

Assessment Book

- Standardized Chapter Test, p. 37

Test and Practice Generator

Chapter Standardized Test

Test-Taking Strategy Start working as soon as the testing time begins and try to stay focused on the test.

1. What is the solution of the equation $\frac{t}{5} - 12 = 10$? D

   A. -14 **B.** 10 **C.** 38 **D.** 110

2. What is the solution of the equation $-4(n + 5) = -32$? H

   F. -13 **G.** -12 **H.** 3 **I.** 13

3. The perimeter of the triangle shown is 15 units. What is the value of x? C

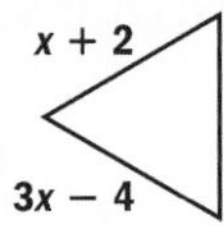

   A. 1 **B.** 2 **C.** 3 **D.** 4

4. Which equation has no solution? I

   F. $4t - 8 = 4(t - 2)$

   G. $3(r - 1) = -2(2 + r)$

   H. $6p + 2 = 9p - 4$

   I. $7(s + 1) = -3 + 7s$

5. Giants Stadium in New Jersey can seat up to 80,242 people. Which inequality represents the number n of people that the stadium can seat? C

   A. $n < 80{,}242$ **B.** $n > 80{,}242$

   C. $n \le 80{,}242$ **D.** $n \ge 80{,}242$

6. What is the solution of the inequality $\frac{z}{-4} + 3 < 15$? G

   F. $z < -48$ **G.** $z > -48$

   H. $z < -3$ **I.** $z > -3$

7. What is the solution of the inequality $-12 > y + 6$? A

   A. $y < -18$ **B.** $y < -6$

   C. $y > -18$ **D.** $y > -6$

8. Which value is *not* a solution of the inequality $-5y - 2 \ge 30.5$? I

   F. -162.5 **G.** -10 **H.** -6.5 **I.** -3

9. **Short Response** Two of your friends go bowling. One friend rents a pair of bowling shoes for \$3 and bowls 3 games. The other friend brings his own bowling shoes, bowls 4 games, and buys a soda for \$.50. Both friends spend the same amount of money. Show how you can write and solve an equation to find the cost of one game. See margin.

10. **Extended Response** The table below shows the cost of renting a moving van for 1 day from two companies. The daily charge and the charge per mile are given.

Company	Daily charge	Charge per mile
A	\$80	\$.35
B	\$75	\$.39

   a. How many miles m will you have to drive before the cost of renting a van for one day from company A is less than the cost of renting a van for one day from company B? Express your answer as an inequality. $m > 125$

   b. Graph your inequality from part (a). See margin.

   c. Which company is less expensive if you drive 100 miles in one day? Explain. See margin.

9. ***Sample answer:*** **Let g represent the cost of one game. An expression for the total amount the first friend spends is $3 + 3g$. An expression for the total amount the second friend spends is $0.5 + 4g$. Equating these expressions gives $3 + 3g = 0.5 + 4g$, which has the solution 2.5. So, one game costs \$2.50.**

10b. 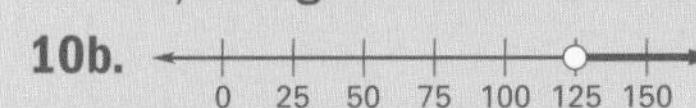

10c. **Company B; since company A is less expensive for $m > 125$, company B is less expensive for $m = 100$ because $100 < 125$.**

TEST-TAKING TIP

Encourage students to quickly examine the answer choices for a multiple-choice question after reading the question. Suggest that this is a good time to eliminate choices that can be readily identified as incorrect, and also to notice answers that are very similar which could lead to inadvertently choosing the wrong one. For example, two answers might differ only in the location of their decimal points, as in 15.63 and 1.563, or they might differ only by the units used, as in 72 in. and 72 ft. Caution students to double-check their answer choice when a mistaken selection could easily be made.

COMMON ERROR

Students will often encounter some questions on a long multiple-choice test that they cannot answer quickly. If students bypass these questions, they may forget to return to some or all of them later after reaching the end of the test. Stress that if students use this test-taking strategy, they must have some method to remind themselves to return to each bypassed question, including where each of them is located.

Unit 1 Chapters 1–3

Building Test-Taking Skills

Strategies for Answering Multiple Choice Questions

You can use the problem solving plan on page 14 to solve a problem. If you have difficulty solving a problem in multiple choice format, you may be able to use one of the strategies below to choose the correct answer. You may also be able to use these strategies and others to check whether your answer to a multiple choice question is reasonable.

Strategy: Use Estimation

Problem 1 You and a friend share the cost of a pizza and a salad. The pizza costs \$8.98. The salad costs \$3.98. How much do each of you pay?

To solve this problem, you need to add the cost of the two items and divide by 2.

A. \$6.48 **B.** \$8.47 **C.** \$10.97 **D.** \$12.96

Estimate: $\frac{9+4}{2} = \frac{13}{2} = 6.5$, so the correct answer is A.

Strategy: Use Visual Clues

Problem 2 The line graph shows the number of people (in millions) who participated in snowboarding in the United States from 1991 to 2001. What was the greatest increase in participation in any two-year period?

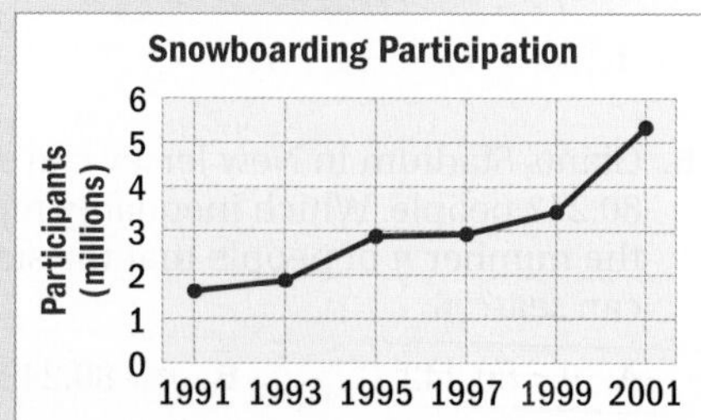

To solve this problem, you need to identify the period with the greatest increase, then find the amount of increase for that period.

F. About 0.5 million

G. About 1 million

H. About 1.5 million

I. About 2 million

The greatest change occurred between 1999 and 2001. The vertical distance between the points for 1999 and 2001 is about 2 units. Each unit represents 1 million people. So, the correct answer is I.

Strategy: Use Number Sense

Problem 3 The temperature in a freezer is $-12°C$. During one 8 minute period, the temperature drops about $0.5°C$ each minute. What is the temperature after those 8 minutes?

To solve this problem, you need to find the total change in temperature and add it to the original temperature.

A. $-16°C$ — The product $-0.5(8)$ is a negative integer. The sum of a negative integer and -12 is a negative integer less than -12. So, the correct answer is A.

B. $-12.5°C$

C. $-11.5°C$

D. $-8°C$

Eliminating Unreasonable Choices The strategies used to find the correct answers for Problems 1–3 can also be used to eliminate answer choices that are unreasonable or obviously incorrect.

Problem 4 The length of a rectangle is 5 meters less than twice the width. The perimeter is 26 meters. What is the width of the rectangle?

To solve this problem, you need to use the perimeter formula $P = 2l + 2w$ and the given information to write and solve an equation.

A. 2 m — *Not* correct; if $w = 2$, then $l = 2(2) - 5 = -1$, but length is never negative.

B. 6 m

C. $10.\overline{3}$ m — *Not* correct; if $w \approx 10$, then $l \approx 2(10) - 5 = 15$, and $P \approx 50$.

D. $42\ m^2$ — *Not* correct; width is *not* measured in square units.

Checkpoint

Explain why the highlighted answer choice is unreasonable. 1–3. See margin.

1. You and 4 friends share the \$29.95 cost of a lunch. How much does each person pay?

A. \$5.99 **B.** \$7.49 **C.** \$24.95 **D.** \$34.95

2. What is the solution of the equation $5x + 3 = -15$?

F. -3.6 **G.** -2.4 **H.** 2.4 **I.** 3.6

3. At 9 P.M., the temperature is 0°F. It drops 3°F each hour for 4 hours. What is the temperature at 1 A.M.?

A. $-12°F$ **B.** $-7°F$ **C.** 7°F **D.** 12°F

Watch *Out*

Some answers may appear correct at first glance, but they may be incorrect answers you would get by making common errors.

1–3. Sample answers are given.

1. This answer choice means that even for only two people the total amount paid would be about \$50, which is way beyond the cost of lunch.

2. After subtracting 3 from each side, the new equation is $5x = -18$. Solving would require dividing a negative number, -18, by a positive number, 5, so the solution must be negative.

3. Since the temperature is dropping each hour, the final temperature must be less than 0°F.

Unit 1 Chapters 1–3

Practicing Test-Taking Skills

Multiple Choice

1. Which variable expression represents the number of inches in y yards? **A**

A. $36y$ **B.** $\frac{y}{36}$ **C.** $\frac{36}{y}$ **D.** $36 - y$

2. What is the value of the expression $15 - 14 \div 2 + 5$? **I**

F. $\frac{1}{7}$ **G.** $5\frac{1}{2}$ **H.** 8 **I.** 13

3. During the month of January, the average high temperature in Montreal, Canada, is $-6°C$, and the average low temperature is $-15°C$. How much greater is the average high temperature than the average low temperature? **C**

A. $-21°C$ **B.** $-9°C$

C. $9°C$ **D.** $21°C$

4. Which point has coordinates $(1, -2)$? **H**

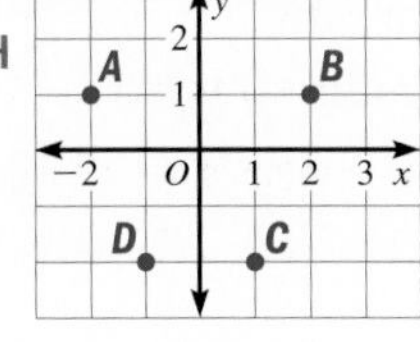

F. A 

G. B

H. C

I. D

5. Which expression is equivalent to $3(0.9 + 7)$? **C**

A. $3(0.9) + 7$ **B.** $0.27 + 21$

C. $3(0.9) + 3(7)$ **D.** $2.7 + 7$

6. Which terms of the expression $4x + 9 + 9x - 4$ are like terms? **H**

F. $4x$ and -4 **G.** $4x$ and 4

H. $4x$ and $9x$ **I.** $9x$ and 9

7. What is the solution of $10 + x = -19$? **A**

A. -29 **B.** -9 **C.** 9 **D.** 29

8. Which expression is equivalent to $8(x + 2) - 5(x - 3)$? **F**

F. $3x + 31$ **G.** $3x + 1$

H. $3x - 1$ **I.** $13x + 31$

9. What is the solution of $3 - 8x = -141$? **D**

A. -18 **B.** -12 **C.** $\frac{1}{18}$ **D.** 18

10. What is the solution of $7(x + 5) - 10 = 2x$? **F**

F. -5 **G.** -1 **H.** 5 **I.** 7

11. Which of the inequalities has the solution whose graph is shown? **B**

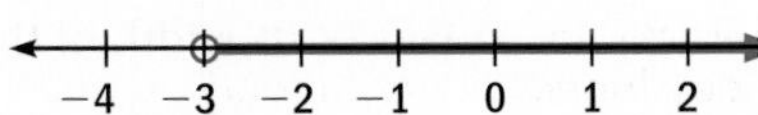

A. $2x + 10 < 16$ **B.** $-4x - 5 < 7$

C. $-3x + 8 < -1$ **D.** $4 - 2x > 10$

12. A soccer goalie has made 175 saves so far this season. The school record is 236 saves in a season. There are 6 games left to play. Which inequality could you solve to find the average number of saves the goalie must make in each of the remaining games to break the school record? **G**

F. $175 + 6x < 236$ **G.** $175 + 6x > 236$

H. $236 + 6x > 175$ **I.** $236 + 6x < 175$

13. What is the solution of the inequality $-3x + 14 > 2x - 11$? **D**

A. $x > -5$ **B.** $x > 5$

C. $x < -5$ **D.** $x < 5$

Short Response

14–17. See margin.

14. Tell whether the statement $|a - b| = |a| - |b|$ is *always, sometimes,* or *never* true for integers a and b. Give examples to explain your reasoning.

15. While waiting in the checkout line at the grocery store, you add the prices of the 3 items you are buying to make sure you have enough money. Explain how to use mental math and the properties of addition to find the total cost if the prices of the 3 items are \$1.85, \$2.74, and \$4.15. Find the total cost.

16. Profit is the difference of income and expenses. The table shows one store's profit for each of its first 4 months. Find the mean profit. Explain your method.

Month	Profit
March	−\$670
April	−\$340
May	\$320
June	\$400

17. You have at most 3 hours to do homework. You spend 45 minutes on math. You want to divide the time remaining equally among 4 other subjects. Write and solve an inequality to find the number of minutes you can spend on each one. Explain your method.

Extended Response

18. You are painting a room that is 16 feet long, 14 feet wide, and 8 feet high. The room has two identical windows and two identical doors. One door leads to a closet 4 feet long, 4 feet wide, and 8 feet high. You do not plan to paint the closet.

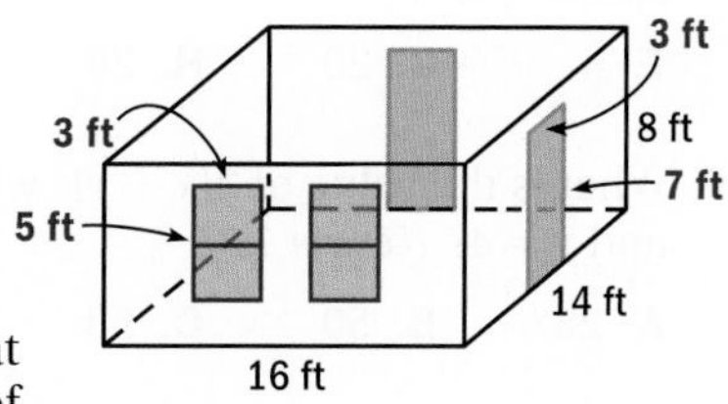

a. The paint you choose is available in both 1 gallon cans that cover about 400 square feet each and 1 quart cans that cover about 100 square feet each. You plan to put 2 coats of paint on each wall, not including the doors or windows. How much paint should you buy? **2 gal and 1 qt**

b. A 1 gallon can of paint costs \$13.90, and a 1 quart can of paint costs \$8.90. How much will it cost to put 2 coats of paint on each wall? **\$36.70**

c. You've budgeted \$40 for paint. Can you afford to paint the inside walls of the closet, excluding the door, with 1 coat of paint? **no**

19. The table shows the annual fee at two gyms and the fee each time members take an aerobics class.

Gym Costs

Gym	Annual fee	Class fee
A	\$540	\$3
B	\$360	\$5

a. In a year's time, which gym is less expensive if you plan to take 4 aerobics classes each month? **gym B**

b. Write and solve an inequality to determine the number of aerobics classes for which the total cost for 1 year at gym A is less than that at gym B. **$540 + 3c < 360 + 5c$, $c > 90$ classes**

c. How many aerobics classes should you average each month so that the total cost for 1 year at gym B is less than that at gym A? **7 or fewer classes per month**

Test-Taking Skills

14. Sometimes. ***Sample answer:*** **For example, if $a = 10$ and $b = 6$, then $|a - b| = |10 - 6| = |4| = 4$ and $|a| - |b| = |10| - |6| = 10 - 6 = 4$, so the statement is true; but if $a = 6$ and $b = 10$, then $|a - b| = |6 - 10| = |-4| = 4$ and $|a| - |b| = |6| - |10| = 6 - 10 = -4$, so the statement is false.**

15. ***Sample answer:*** **Notice that \$1.85 is \$.15 below \$2, and \$4.15 is \$.15 above \$4. This means their sum will be a whole number of dollars. By the commutative and associative properties of addition, you can write the sum as $(1.85 + 4.15) + 2.74$ and then use mental math to simplify this as $6 + 2.74 = 8.74$.**

16. −\$72.50. ***Sample answer:*** **The mean monthly profit for the period is the total profit divided by the number of months:**

$$\frac{-670 + (-340) + 320 + 400}{4} = \frac{-290}{4} = -\$72.50.$$

17. ***Sample answer:*** **Let m be the number of minutes spent on each of the 4 non-math subjects. I can write an inequality for the total time for all the subjects, which must be less than or equal to 3 hours $\cdot \frac{60 \text{ minutes}}{1 \text{ hour}} =$ 180 minutes. Since the total time spent on each of the 4 non-math subjects is $4x$ minutes, an inequality is $4x + 45 \le 180$. Subtracting 45 from each side gives $4x \le 135$, and dividing each side by 4 gives $x \le 33.75$. I can spend no more than 33.75 minutes on each of the 4 subjects beside math.**

ADDITIONAL RESOURCES

The following resources are available to help review the materials in this unit:

Chapter Resource Books

- Chapter 1 CRB, Cumulative Practice, pp. 81–82
- Chapter 2 CRB, Cumulative Practice, pp. 75–76
- Chapter 3 CRB, Cumulative Practice, pp. 69–70

Assessment Book

- Unit Test, pp. 40–41
- Cumulative Test, pp. 42–45

12. deposits: 30, 125, 10, 20, 65; withdrawals: −75, −89, −143, −15, −20; $408

13a. *Sample answer:* Use the x-axis to represent years since 1996 and the y-axis to represent subscribers. Then plot the ordered pairs (years since 1996, subscribers).

13b.

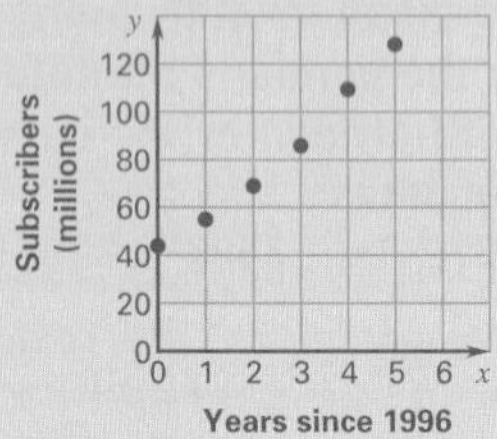

Unit 1 Chapters 1–3 Practicing Test-Taking Skills

Cumulative Practice for Chapters 1–3

Chapter 1

Multiple Choice In Exercises 1–11, choose the letter of the correct answer.

1. What is the value of $9 - x$ when $x = 5$? *(Lesson 1.1)* **B**

A. 1 **B.** 4 **C.** 14 **D.** 45

2. How can you write $7 \times 7 \times 7$ as a power? *(Lesson 1.2)* **H**

F. 7×3 **G.** 3×7 **H.** 7^3 **I.** 3^7

3. What is the value of 6^4? *(Lesson 1.2)* **C**

A. 24 **B.** 216 **C.** 1296 **D.** 4096

4. What is the value of $28 \div 7 + 16$? *(Lesson 1.3)* **G**

F. 4 **G.** 20 **H.** 28 **I.** 212

5. What is the value of $2(x + y)^2$ when $x = 3$ and $y = 4$? *(Lesson 1.3)* **C**

A. 28 **B.** 50 **C.** 98 **D.** 2401

6. Which list of integers is in order from least to greatest? *(Lesson 1.4)* **G**

F. −3, −5, −7, −9 **G.** −5, −3, 0, 4

H. −2, 4, −5, 9 **I.** −8, 7, −6, 3

7. What is the value of $-15 + 9$? *(Lesson 1.5)* **B**

A. −24 **B.** −6 **C.** 6 **D.** 24

8. What is the value of $-27 - x$ when $x = -8$? *(Lesson 1.6)* **G**

F. −35 **G.** −19 **H.** 19 **I.** 35

9. In 24 hours, the temperature went from −8°C to 12°C. What was the change in temperature? *(Lesson 1.6)* **D**

A. −20°C **B.** −4°C **C.** 4°C **D.** 20°C

10. What is the value of $\frac{x^2}{y}$ when $x = -4$ and $y = -2$? *(Lesson 1.7)* **F**

F. −8 **G.** $-\frac{1}{8}$ **H.** $\frac{1}{8}$ **I.** 8

11. In which quadrant is the point (−2, −3) located? *(Lesson 1.8)* **C**

A. Quadrant I **B.** Quadrant II

C. Quadrant III **D.** Quadrant IV

12. Short Response You have $500 in a savings account. You make deposits of $30, $125, $10, $20, and $65, and you make withdrawals of $75, $89, $143, $15, and $20. Write a positive integer to represent each deposit and a negative integer to represent each withdrawal. Find the final balance in your savings account. *(Lessons 1.5, 1.6)* **See margin.**

13. Extended Response The table shows the number of cell phone subscribers (in millions) in the United States from 1996 to 2001. *(Lesson 1.8)*

Years since 1996	Subscribers (millions)
0	44
1	55
2	69
3	86
4	109
5	128

a. Explain how to make a scatter plot of the data. **13a–b. See margin.**

b. Make a scatter plot.

c. Does the scatter plot suggest any relationship between the number of years since 1996 and the number of cell phone subscribers? Explain.

Yes. ***Sample answer:*** **As the number of years since 1996 increases, the number of cell phone subscribers tends to increase quite rapidly.**

Test-Taking Skills

Chapter 2

Multiple Choice In Exercises 14–24, choose the letter of the correct answer.

14. Which property is illustrated by the statement $2x + (y + 1) = (2x + y) + 1$? *(Lesson 2.1)* **C**

A. Identity property of addition

B. Commutative property of addition

C. Associative property of addition

D. Associative property of multiplication

15. Use a conversion factor to convert 1.5 miles to feet. *(Lesson 2.1)* **H**

F. $\frac{1}{7290}$ foot **G.** $\frac{1}{7290}$ mile

H. 7920 feet **I.** 7920 miles

16. Which variable expression is equivalent to $4x - 6$? *(Lesson 2.2)* **D**

A. $2(2x - 6)$ **B.** $4(x - 6)$

C. $2(2x + 3)$ **D.** $2(2x - 3)$

17. What is the value of $x(y - z)$ when $x = -2.5$, $y = 4$, and $z = 0.1$? *(Lesson 2.2)* **G**

F. -10.25 **G.** -9.75

H. 9.75 **I.** 10.25

18. Which terms of the expression $-6k - 6 + 4 + 4k$ are like terms? *(Lesson 2.3)* **B**

A. $-6k$ and -6 **B.** $-6k$ and $4k$

C. $6k$ and $4k$ **D.** 4 and $4k$

19. Which expression is equivalent to $15y - 2(y + 3)$? *(Lesson 2.3)* **F**

F. $13y - 6$ **G.** $13y + 3$

H. $13y + 6$ **I.** $16y + 1$

20. Whippets are among the fastest running dogs. Suppose a whippet can run at a rate of 52 feet per second for a short period of time. How long would it take the whippet to run 156 feet? *(Lesson 2.4)* **C**

A. 1 second **B.** 2 seconds

C. 3 seconds **D.** 4 seconds

21. What is the solution of $x + 11 = 20 - 7$? *(Lesson 2.5)* **F**

F. 2 **G.** 13 **H.** 16 **I.** 24

22. What is the solution of $\frac{z}{-12} = 24$? *(Lesson 2.6)* **A**

A. -288 **B.** -2 **C.** 2 **D.** 288

23. You went shopping with \$42.60 and came home with \$3.33. How much money did you spend? *(Lesson 2.7)* **H**

F. \$3.33 **G.** \$38.70 **H.** \$39.27 **I.** \$45.93

24. What is the solution of $-3y = 14.7$? *(Lesson 2.7)* **B**

A. -44.1 **B.** -4.9 **C.** 4.9 **D.** 17.7

25. Short Response A square has a perimeter of 84 meters. Explain how to write an equation to find the side length of the square. Then find the side length. *(Lesson 2.6)* **See margin.**

26. Extended Response At store A, a wide-screen TV sells for \$1500 after a \$250 mail-in rebate. Store A charges \$50 for delivery and setup. Store B promises to sell any TV for \$75 less than any competitor's original price and to include free delivery and setup. *(Lesson 2.5)*

a. What is the original price of the TV at store A? **\$1750**

b. Which store offers a better deal? Explain your reasoning. **See margin.**

25. ***Sample answer:*** **Let s represent the side length of the square. Because the 4 sides are equal in length, the perimeter is $4s$. So an equation is $4s = 84$, or $s = 21$. The side length is 21 meters.**

26b. Store A. *Sample answer:* The final cost at store A is \$1500 + \$50 = \$1550. At store B, the final cost is \$1750 − \$75 = \$1675, which is more.

37. *Sample answer:* First apply the distributive property on the right side to obtain $15z - 12 = 42 + 9z - 12$ and combine like terms to obtain $15z - 12 = 9z + 30$. Add 12 to both sides to obtain $15z = 9z + 42$. Next, subtract $9z$ from each side, which gives $6z = 42$. Finally, divide both sides by 6, which gives the solution, $z = 7$.

38c. It would decrease the number of tickets that would have to be sold. *Sample answer:* The tickets are more expensive, so you need to sell fewer to have the same income. For part (a), you would start making a profit with 35 tickets sold, and for part (b), you could sell as few as 95 tickets and still make a $300 profit.

Unit 1 Practicing Test-Taking Skills

Chapters 1–3

Cumulative Practice continued

Chapter 3

Multiple Choice In Exercises 27–36, choose the letter of the correct answer.

27. What is the solution of $-2x + 7 = 25$? *(Lesson 3.1)* **B**

A. -16 **B.** -9 **C.** 9 **D.** 16

28. You pay $12.99 for a small pizza and two orders of breadsticks. The pizza costs $7.99. How much does one order of breadsticks cost? *(Lesson 3.1)* **G**

F. $1.99 **G.** $2.50 **H.** $3.00 **I.** $5.00

29. What is the solution of the equation $15 - 2(w + 5) = 11$? *(Lesson 3.2)* **B**

A. -7 **B.** -3 **C.** 8 **D.** 12

30. The area of the rectangle is 28 square units. What is the value of x? *(Lesson 3.2)* **F**

3x + 4

4

F. 1 **G.** 2

H. 7 **I.** 8

31. Which statement about the equation $2(x - 1) = 3x - (x + 2)$ is true? *(Lesson 3.3)* **D**

A. The equation has no solution.

B. The solution is -0.5.

C. The solution is -1.

D. The equation has every number as a solution.

32. At temperatures less than −458°F, helium is a solid. Which inequality describes the temperatures t (in degrees Fahrenheit) at which helium is a solid? *(Lesson 3.4)* **G**

F. $t > -458$ **G.** $t < -458$

H. $t \geq -458$ **I.** $t \leq -458$

33. You and a friend have $25 to pay for your dinners at a restaurant. Your friend's dinner costs $13.35. How much can you spend on your dinner? *(Lesson 3.4)* **C**

A. Less than $11.65 **B.** More than $11.65

C. At most $11.65 **D.** At least $11.65

34. What is the solution of $\frac{h}{-7} \geq 14$? *(Lesson 3.5)* **H**

F. $h \leq -2$ **G.** $h \geq -2$

H. $h \leq -98$ **I.** $h \geq -98$

35. Which number is *not* a solution of $-4s < 42$? *(Lesson 3.5)* **A**

A. -11 **B.** -10 **C.** 10 **D.** 11

36. What is the solution of $4 + 6x \geq -8 + 4x$? *(Lesson 3.6)* **F**

F. $x \geq -6$ **G.** $x \leq -6$

H. $x \geq -1$ **I.** $x \leq -1$

37. Short Response Describe the steps you would take to solve the equation $15z - 12 = 3(14 + 3z) - 12$. Then find the solution. *(Lesson 3.3)* **See margin.**

38. Extended Response Your school is having a fundraising dance. Your costs include $125 for a DJ and $47.50 for decorations. You plan to charge $4.50 for each ticket. *(Lesson 3.6)*

a. How many tickets must you sell before you start making a profit? **at least 39 tickets**

b. How many tickets must you sell to make a profit of at least $300? **at least 105 tickets**

c. How would raising the ticket price to $5.00 affect your answers to parts (a) and (b)? Explain. **See margin.**

UNIT

2

Rational Numbers *and* Proportions

Chapter 4 Factors, Fractions, and Exponents

- Find greatest common factors and least common multiples.
- Identify equivalent fractions and write fractions in simplest form.
- Use rules of exponents and scientific notation.

Chapter 5 Rational Numbers and Equations

- Write fractions as decimals and decimals as fractions.
- Perform operations with fractions and mixed numbers.
- Solve equations and inequalities with rational numbers.

Chapter 6 Ratio, Proportion, and Probability

- Write and compare ratios and rates.
- Write and solve proportions.
- Find theoretical and experimental probabilities.

Chapter 7 Percents

- Find and use equivalent decimals, fractions, and percents.
- Use proportions and the percent equation to solve percent problems.
- Solve problems involving percent of change.

From Chapter 7, p. 338
How many solar cars competed in a race?

Unit Resources

These resources are provided to help you prepare for the unit and to customize review materials:

Chapter Resource Books
- Chapter 4
- Chapter 5
- Chapter 6
- Chapter 7

Assessment Book
- Chapters 4–7, pp. 46–95

Technology
- EasyPlanner CD-ROM
- Test and Practice Generator
- Electronic Lesson Presentations CD-ROM
- eTutorial CD-ROM

Internet
- Classzone
- eEdition Plus Online
- eWorkbook Plus Online
- eTutorial Plus Online
- EasyPlanner Plus Online

English Learner Support

- Spanish Study Guide
- Multi-Language Visual Glossary
- Chapter Audio Summaries CDs
- Teacher's Edition
  Chapter 4, pp. 168E–168F
  Chapter 5, pp. 216E–216F
  Chapter 6, pp. 266E–266F
  Chapter 7, pp. 326E–326F

CHAPTER 4

Pacing and Assignment Guide

REGULAR SCHEDULE

Lesson	Les. Day	BASIC	AVERAGE	ADVANCED
4.1	Day 1	pp. 175-176 Exs. 16-27, 33-41, 50-56, 61-63, 71-82	pp. 175-176 Exs. 22-33, 42-51, 57-67, 77-84	pp. 175-176 Exs. 22-32, 44-49, 56-63, 66-72*, 79-84
4.2	Day 1	pp. 179-181 Exs. 12-23, 28-32, 34-46, 53-65	pp. 179-181 Exs. 16-29, 32-42, 46-50, 55-66	pp. 179-181 Exs. 18-29, 32-39, 43-54*, 59-66
4.3	Day 1	SRH p. 777 Exs. 1-6; pp. 185-186 Exs. 12-23, 28-34, 38-47, 55-64	pp. 185-186 Exs. 16-28, 33-38, 44-53, 57-65	pp. 185-186 Exs. 18-28, 35-39, 44-56*, 60-65
4.4	Day 1	SRH p. 778 Exs. 1-5; pp. 190-191 Exs. 16-23, 28-36, 39-50, 56-66, 71-80	pp. 190-191 Exs. 20-38, 43-57, 64-69, 73-81	pp. 190-191 Exs. 24-38, 43-50, 55-72*, 77-81
4.5	Day 1	pp. 197-198 Exs. 16-29, 36-40, 42-53, 62, 64-77	pp. 197-198 Exs. 20-31, 36-43, 52-62, 66-77	pp. 197-198 Exs. 20-27, 32-41, 50-65*, 70-77
4.6	Day 1	pp. 202-203 Exs. 16-19, 24-27, 41, 51-54, 57, 62-69	pp. 202-203 Exs. 16-29, 51-54, 58-60, 69-72	pp. 202-203 Exs. 18-29, 51-54, 58-61*, 69-72
	Day 2	pp. 202-203 Exs. 20-23, 28-31, 36-40, 43-48, 55, 56, 70-72	pp. 202-203 Exs. 32-42, 47-50, 55-57, 62-68	pp. 202-203 Exs. 36-41, 43-50, 55-57, 63-68
4.7	Day 1	SRH p. 773 Exs. 4-9; pp. 207-208 Exs. 13-25, 31-35, 40-45, 48-51, 55-64	pp. 207-208 Exs. 16-27, 33-41, 46-53, 57-64	pp. 207-208 Exs. 19-24, 28-32, 35-41, 46-55*, 58-64
Review	Day 1	pp. 210-213 Exs. 1-47	pp. 210-213 Exs. 1-47	pp. 210-213 Exs. 1-47
Assess	Day 1	Chapter 4 Test	Chapter 4 Test	Chapter 4 Test

YEARLY PACING Chapter 4 Total – **10 days** Chapters 1–4 Total – **44 days** Remaining – **116 days**

*Challenge Exercises EP = Extra Practice SRH = Skills Review Handbook

BLOCK SCHEDULE

DAY 1	DAY 2	DAY 3	DAY 4	DAY 5
4.1 pp. 175-176 Exs. 22-33, 42-51, 57-67, 77-84 **4.2** pp. 179-181 Exs. 16-29, 32-42, 46-50, 55-66	**4.3** pp. 185-186 Exs. 16-28, 33-38, 44-53, 57-65 **4.4** pp. 190-191 Exs. 20-38, 43-57, 64-69, 73-81	**4.5** pp. 197-198 Exs. 20-31, 36-43, 52-62, 66-77 **4.6** pp. 202-203 Exs. 16-29, 51-54, 58-60, 69-72	**4.6 (cont.)** pp. 202-203 Exs. 32-42, 47-50, 55-57, 62-68 **4.7** pp. 207-208 Exs. 16-27, 33-41, 46-53, 57-64	**Review** pp. 210-213 Exs. 1-47 **Assess** Chapter 4 Test

YEARLY PACING Chapter 4 Total – **5 days** Chapters 1–4 Total – **22 days** Remaining – **58 days**

Support Materials

CHAPTER RESOURCE BOOK

CHAPTER SUPPORT			
Tips for New Teachers	p. 1	Parents as Partners	p. 3

LESSON SUPPORT	4.1	4.2	4.3	4.4	4.5	4.6	4.7
Lesson Plans (regular and block)	p. 5	p. 15	p. 25	p. 33	p. 42	p. 51	p. 60
Technology Activities & Keystrokes		p. 17				p. 53	p. 62
Activity Support Masters	p. 7				p. 44		
Activity Masters				p. 35			
Practice (3 levels)	p. 8	p. 19	p. 27	p. 36	p. 45	p. 54	p. 63
Study Guide	p. 11	p. 22	p. 30	p. 39	p. 48	p. 57	p. 66
Real-World Problem Solving	p. 13						p. 68
Challenge Practice	p. 14	p. 24	p. 32	p. 41	p. 50	p. 59	p. 69

REVIEW			
Chapter Review Games and Activities	p. 70	Extra Credit Project with Rubric	p. 75
Real-Life Project with Rubric	p. 71	Cumulative Practice	p. 77
Cooperative Project with Rubric	p. 73	Resource Book Answers	A1

ASSESSMENT

Quizzes	p. 46	Alternative Assessments with Rubrics	p. 55
Chapter Tests (3 levels)	p. 48	Unit Test	p. 90
Standardized Test	p. 54	Cumulative Test	p. 92

TRANSPARENCIES

	4.1	4.2	4.3	4.4	4.5	4.6	4.7
Warm-Up/Daily Homework Quiz	✔	✔	✔	✔	✔	✔	✔
Notetaking Guide	✔	✔	✔	✔	✔	✔	✔
Teacher Support			✔				
English/Spanish Problem Solving	✔			✔			✔
Answer Transparencies	✔	✔	✔	✔	✔	✔	✔

TECHNOLOGY

- EasyPlanner CD-ROM
- Test and Practice Generator
- Electronic Lesson Presentations
- eTutorial CD-ROM
- Chapter Audio Summaries CDs
- Classzone.com
- eEdition Plus Online
- eWorkbook Plus Online
- eTutorial Plus Online
- EasyPlanner Plus Online

ADDITIONAL RESOURCES

- Worked-Out Solution Key
- Notetaking Guide
- Practice Workbook
- Tutor Place
- Professional Development Book
- Special Activities Book
- Posters
- Spanish Study Guide
- Exercises in Spanish
- English/Spanish Ch. Reviews/Tests
- Multi-Language Visual Glossary

CHAPTER 4

Math Background and Teaching Strategies

Lesson 4.1

MATH BACKGROUND

A **prime number** is a whole number greater than 1 that has only two factors, itself and 1. Whole numbers that have more than two factors are called **composite numbers**. The number 1 is considered to be neither prime nor composite. When you write a composite number as a product of its prime factors, you are writing its **prime factorization**. You can find the prime factorization of a number using a **factor tree**, in which the number is successively divided by factors.

TEACHING STRATEGIES

Write the factor tree for 840 shown at the right on the the board or overhead. Have students use the result to write the prime factorization of 840 as $2^3 \cdot 3 \cdot 5 \cdot 7$. Challenge them to come up with other factor trees for 840. You may want to ask students for the strategies that they used to find factor trees.

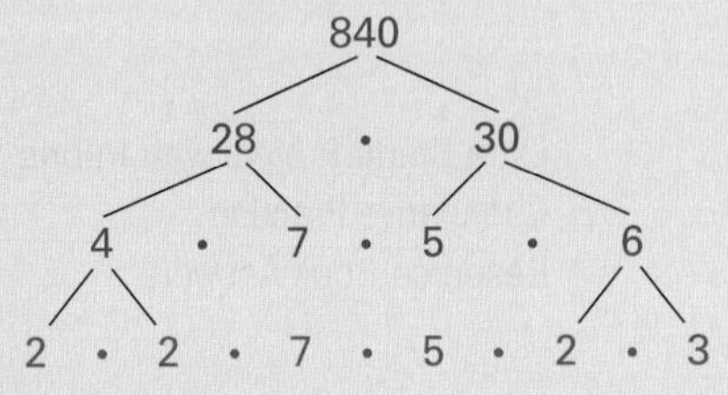

Lesson 4.2

MATH BACKGROUND

The greatest whole number that is a factor of two or more nonzero whole numbers is their **greatest common factor (GCF)**. If two or more numbers share only 1 as a common factor, they are **relatively prime**. To find the GCF of two or more numbers, find the product of the prime factors shared by them. To find the GCF of two or more monomials, multiply the common prime factors and the common variable factors.

TEACHING STRATEGIES

As an additional example of finding the GCF of monomials, have students find the GCF of $9x^2y^2$, $27xy^3$, and $12x^3y^2$.

$$9x^2y^2 = \underline{3} \cdot 3 \cdot \underline{x} \cdot x \cdot \underline{y} \cdot \underline{y}$$
$$27xy^3 = \underline{3} \cdot 3 \cdot 3 \cdot \underline{x} \cdot \underline{y} \cdot \underline{y} \cdot y$$
$$12x^3y^2 = 2 \cdot 2 \cdot \underline{3} \cdot \underline{x} \cdot x \cdot x \cdot \underline{y} \cdot \underline{y}$$

Remind students that the factor(s) must be shared by *all* of the numbers. After students have found the GCF, $3xy^2$, have them compare the exponents of the variables in the GCF and the exponents of the variables in the given monomials. Guide students to realize that the exponent of each variable in the GCF is the least exponent appearing on that variable in the monomials.

Lesson 4.3

MATH BACKGROUND

Equivalent fractions have different numerators and denominators, but they represent the same number. A fraction is in **simplest form** when its numerator and denominator have no common factors other than 1. To write a fraction in simplest form, divide the numerator and denominator by their GCF.

TEACHING STRATEGIES

Write the fraction $\frac{168}{420}$ on the board or overhead. Have students divide out 2 from the numerator and denominator to obtain $\frac{84}{210}$ and then divide out 2 again to obtain $\frac{42}{105}$. Next, have students divide out 3 to obtain $\frac{14}{35}$. Have them divide out 7 to obtain $\frac{2}{5}$. Point out that $\frac{168}{420}$, $\frac{84}{210}$, $\frac{42}{105}$, $\frac{14}{35}$, and $\frac{2}{5}$ are all equivalent fractions. Remind students that if they can find the GCF of the numerator and denominator of the fraction, in this case 84, they will only need to divide once.

Lesson 4.4

MATH BACKGROUND

A **multiple** of a number is the product of the number and any nonzero whole number. Since 6 and 12 are multiples of *both* 2 and 3, they are **common multiples** of 2 and 3. The least of the common multiples of two or more numbers is their **least common multiple (LCM)**. If two numbers have no common factors other than 1, their LCM is their product. The LCM of the denominators of two or more fractions is the **least common denominator (LCD)** of the fractions.

TEACHING STRATEGIES

In the Teaching Strategies note for Lesson 4.2, the GCF of the monomials $9x^2y^2$, $27xy^3$, and $12x^3y^2$ was found to be $3xy^2$. You may want to return to this example to have students compare finding the LCM of the monomials.

$$\begin{aligned} 9x^2y^2 &= 3 \cdot 3 \cdot x \cdot x \cdot y \cdot y \\ 27xy^3 &= \underline{3} \cdot \underline{3} \cdot \underline{3} \cdot x \cdot \underline{y} \cdot \underline{y} \cdot \underline{y} \\ 12x^3y^2 &= \underline{2} \cdot \underline{2} \cdot 3 \cdot \underline{x} \cdot \underline{x} \cdot \underline{x} \cdot y \cdot y \end{aligned}$$

The difference is that the LCM must contain any factor the *greatest* number of times it occurs in *any* of the monomials. After finding the LCM, $108x^3y^3$, have students compare the exponents of the variables in the LCM and the exponents of the variables in each of the given monomials. Help students see that the exponent of each variable in the LCM is the greatest exponent appearing on that variable in any of the monomials. Also point out that any variable appearing in the monomials must appear in the LCM.

Lesson 4.5

MATH BACKGROUND

If two powers have the same base, they can be multiplied using the *product of powers property*, which states that the product of the powers is the power with the same base whose exponent is the sum of the exponents of the powers. For example, $a^7 \cdot a^5 = a^{7+5} = a^{12}$. Powers with the same base can be divided using the *quotient of powers property*, which states that the quotient of the powers is the power with the same base whose exponent is the difference of the exponents of the powers. For example, $\frac{a^7}{a^5} = a^{7-5} = a^2$. The *sum* of powers with the same base but different exponents, such as $a^7 + a^5$, cannot be simplified.

TEACHING STRATEGIES

Many students will have a tendency to want to multiply the exponents when multiplying powers. To counteract this tendency, urge students to have a simple example in mind to use if they get confused. For example, if students face a problem like $m^7 \cdot m^9 \cdot m^5$, and are unsure what to do, they can refer to the example $2^1 \cdot 2^2$. Because students can quickly rewrite $2^1 \cdot 2^2$ as $2 \cdot 2 \cdot 2$, they can see that multiplying the exponents would be an error, since $2^{1 \cdot 2} = 2^2 = 2 \cdot 2$.

Lesson 4.6

MATH BACKGROUND

The zero power of any nonzero number or expression is 1. A negative integer power of any nonzero number or expression is defined as the reciprocal of the corresponding positive power. Also, since $a^{-n} = \frac{1}{a^n}$, then $\frac{1}{a^{-n}} = \frac{1}{\frac{1}{a^n}} = a^n$.

TEACHING STRATEGIES

You can show students examples that validate the definitions of a zero exponent and negative exponents using methods other than the one shown involving the pattern in the powers of 2 on page 199. For example, have students examine the quotient $\frac{3^4}{3^4}$, which is equal to $3^{4-4} = 3^0$ by the quotient of powers property . Students can either factor and cancel to obtain $3^0 = \frac{3^4}{3^4} = \frac{\overset{1}{\cancel{3}} \cdot \overset{1}{\cancel{3}} \cdot \overset{1}{\cancel{3}} \cdot \overset{1}{\cancel{3}}}{\underset{1}{\cancel{3}} \cdot \underset{1}{\cancel{3}} \cdot \underset{1}{\cancel{3}} \cdot \underset{1}{\cancel{3}}} = 1$ or evaluate the powers and divide to obtain $3^0 = \frac{3^4}{3^4} = \frac{81}{81} = 1$.

Lesson 4.7

MATH BACKGROUND

A number in *scientific notation* is written as the product of two factors, the first a number greater than or equal to 1 and less than 10, and the second a power of 10. Scientific notation makes finding products or quotients of very large or very small numbers simpler because the product and quotient of powers properties can be used.

TEACHING STRATEGIES

Make sure students firmly understand that numbers in scientific notation having positive exponents are numbers greater than or equal to 1 (actually, greater than or equal to 10) and those having negative exponents are numbers less than 1. Also, when students find the product of two numbers written in scientific notation, stress that the first number in the scientific notation cannot be greater than or equal to 10. For example, the product of 4×10^5 and 3×10^6 in scientific notation is not 12×10^{11}. Instead, $(4 \times 10^5)(3 \times 10^6) = 12 \times 10^{11} = (1.2 \times 10^1)(1 \times 10^{11}) = 1.2 \times 10^{12}$.

CHAPTER 4

Differentiating Instruction

Strategies for Underachievers

REINFORCE PREREQUISITE SKILLS

Before students attempt to factor numbers in Lesson 4.1 to distinguish between prime and composite numbers, you may want to review with them how to quickly recognize when a number is divisible by 2, 3, 4, 5, 9, or 10.

USE TOOLS AND MANIPULATIVES

EQUIVALENT FRACTIONS In Lesson 4.3, you may wish to have underachievers use manipulatives or drawings to help them gain a visual understanding of equivalent fractions. For example, the fraction strips shown below illustrate through equal area that $\frac{1}{3} = \frac{2}{6}$, and the "pizza model" shows that $\frac{1}{2}$ of a pizza and $\frac{4}{8}$ of a pizza are both the same amount of pizza.

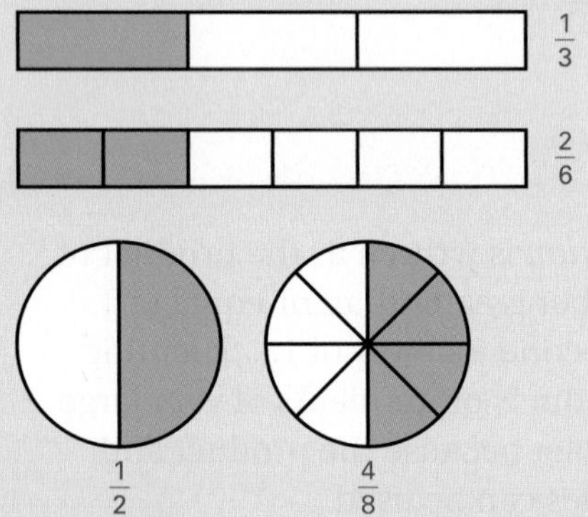

DECREASE DEPTH AND COMPLEXITY

As students find factors, GCFs, and LCMs, you may wish to differentiate your instruction so students are working with numbers that are appropriate to their skill levels. For example, finding the GCF of 36 and 48 might be more appropriate for underachieving students than finding the GCF of 119 and 153.

FOCUS ON VOCABULARY

Students may need a quick daily review of the vocabulary in this chapter, which can easily become confusing for them. Students should firmly understand the progression from the terms *factor* and *multiple* to the expressions *common factor, common multiple,* and *common denominator,* and finally to *greatest common factor, least common multiple,* and *least common denominator.*

PROVIDE EXTRA EXAMPLES

EXPONENTS In Lesson 4.6, some students may have difficulty sorting out the differences among, for example, 5^1, 1^5, 0^5, 5^0, and similar expressions with bases and/or exponents of 0 or 1. You may wish to supply these students with additional examples to make sure they understand the differences. Students can then use these examples as models when they solve exercises.

Strategies for English Learners

REVISE THE ORDER OF THE CHAPTER

Most lessons in this book start with an application designed to get students interested in the material that will be covered in the lesson. This application is followed by examples of new concepts and definitions of new terms. For students who are not reading at or near grade level in English, you may want to begin each lesson with a discussion of the key words and return to the application at the point where the lesson begins a discussion of the mathematics involved in that application. Select key words from the lesson and spend a few minutes discussing them. Keep a cumulative list of key words on chart paper in the room, and pair each key word with an illustration or example. For students with very little English, select the examples so they can be used as a focus, followed by practice problems similar to the given examples. When students encounter the concept again, their language skills should be stronger and they will be able to add to their conceptual understanding at that point.

Strategies for Advanced Learners

INCREASE DEPTH AND COMPLEXITY

PERFECT NUMBERS In Lesson 4.1, you may wish to have some advanced students practice finding factors by determining whether numbers are *deficient*, *abundant*, or *perfect*. For example, 6 is a perfect number because its proper factors (1, 2, and 3) add up to exactly 6; 12 is an abundant number because its proper factors (1, 2, 3, 4, and 6) add up to 16, which is greater than 12; and 10 is a deficient number because its proper factors (1, 2, and 5) add up to 8, which is less than 10. Challenge your students to classify other numbers and to find the only other perfect number that is less than 100. (It is 28; the next perfect number is 496.) Students can also find additional information about these numbers on the Internet. Furthermore, perfect numbers are related to the special prime numbers called Mersenne primes, and some students may wish to do Internet research on these numbers, too.

EMPLOY ALTERNATE APPROACHES

EUCLIDEAN ALGORITHM In Lesson 4.2, you may want to present some students with the use of the Euclidean algorithm to find greatest common factors. This method is especially useful if students have a calculator that can be set to display the result of division with a quotient and remainder instead of a decimal answer. The following is an example, in which the GCF of 234 and 423 is found.

Divide the greater number by the lesser number.

$423 \div 234 = 1$ R189

Divide the previous lesser number by the remainder.

$234 \div 189 = 1$ R45

Continue this process until the remainder equals 0.

$189 \div 45 = 4$ R9

$45 \div 9 = 5$ R0

When the remainder equals zero, the last divisor is the GCF. So, in this example, the GCF is 9.

USE CROSS-CURRICULAR CONNECTIONS

SIEVE OF ERATOSTHENES In Concept Activity 4.1, the method used for determining prime and composite numbers is called the Sieve of Eratosthenes. Eratosthenes was a Greek mathematician who lived from about 276 to 194 B.C. You may wish to work with a history teacher to develop a project for advanced learners that will have students research other mathematical contributions of the ancient Greeks or of other civilizations. Students could do written, visual, or oral presentations of their research. Technologically-savvy students may want to use presentation software to present their results.

In conjunction with Lesson 4.7, you can work with a science or social studies teacher to develop project ideas involving very large and/or very small numbers written in scientific notation. Possible areas of investigation in science include astronomy, sub-atomic particles, and cellular biology, including DNA. Possible areas of investigation in social studies include the national budget and deficit, the gross domestic product of different countries, international trade, resource and energy production and use, and population studies.

The following problem can be used with **Lesson 4.4**:

- **Challenge** A special relationship exists between the GCF and LCM of a pair of numbers and the product of the two numbers. Examine many pairs of numbers to see if you can determine this relationship. The product of two numbers is always equal to the product of their GCF and LCM.

The following problems can be used with **Lesson 4.5**:

- **Challenge** Students who can easily answer Exercise 63 on page 198 can be given the following additional equations to attempt.
  a. $9^n = 3^{n+5}$ 5
  b. $5^{n-6} = 125^{n-4}$ 3
  c. $8^{2n+1} = 32^{n+3}$ 12

CHAPTER 4

Differentiating Instruction: Resource Materials

Differentiating Review, Reteaching, and Remediation

McDougal Littell *Pre-Algebra* offers teachers a wide variety of reteaching and remediation resources. Pictured here are facsimiles of various pages from the *Notetaking Guide*, the Study Guide pages from the *Chapter 4 Resource Book*, and remediation cards from *Tutor Place*.

NOTETAKING GUIDE

The *Notetaking Guide* easily allows students to take notes on and review each lesson in the textbook by using guided examples and Checkpoint exercises. The *Notetaking Guide* is available on transparencies also.

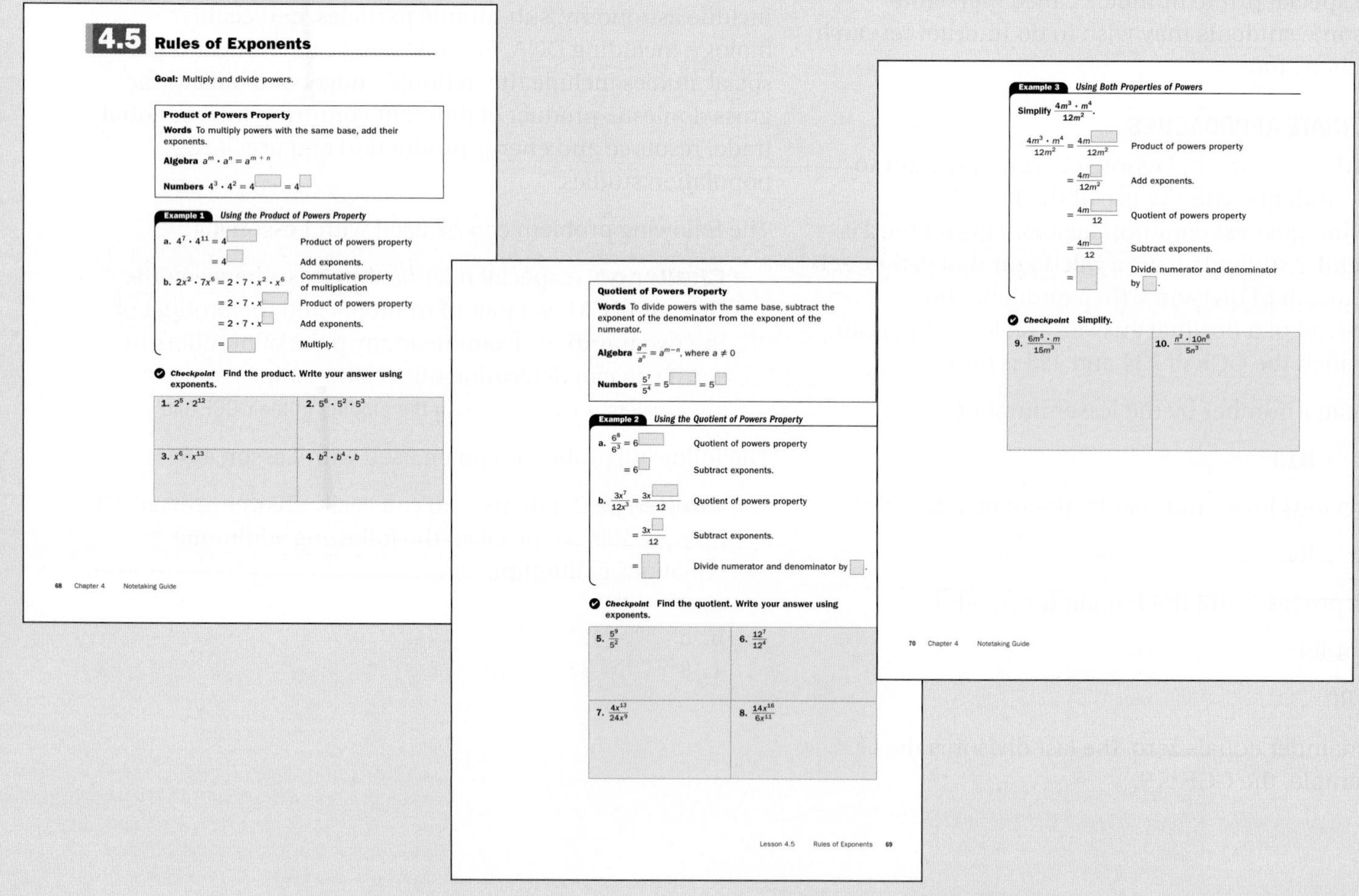

4.5 Rules of Exponents

Goal: Multiply and divide powers.

Product of Powers Property

Words To multiply powers with the same base, add their exponents.

Algebra $a^m \cdot a^n = a^{m+n}$

Numbers $4^3 \cdot 4^2 = 4^{\square} = 4^{\square}$

Example 1 *Using the Product of Powers Property*

a. $4^7 \cdot 4^{11} = 4^{\square}$ Product of powers property

$= 4^{\square}$ Add exponents.

b. $2x^2 \cdot 7x^6 = 2 \cdot 7 \cdot x^2 \cdot x^6$ Commutative property of multiplication

$= 2 \cdot 7 \cdot x^{\square}$ Product of powers property

$= 2 \cdot 7 \cdot x^{\square}$ Add exponents.

$= \square$ Multiply.

Checkpoint **Find the product. Write your answer using exponents.**

1. $2^5 \cdot 2^{12}$	2. $5^6 \cdot 5^2 \cdot 5^3$
3. $x^6 \cdot x^{13}$	4. $b^2 \cdot b^4 \cdot b$

68 Chapter 4 Notetaking Guide

Quotient of Powers Property

Words To divide powers with the same base, subtract the exponent of the denominator from the exponent of the numerator.

Algebra $\frac{a^m}{a^n} = a^{m-n}$, where $a \neq 0$

Numbers $\frac{5^7}{5^4} = 5^{\square} = 5^{\square}$

Example 2 *Using the Quotient of Powers Property*

a. $\frac{6^8}{6^3} = 6^{\square}$ Quotient of powers property

$= 6^{\square}$ Subtract exponents.

b. $\frac{3x^7}{12x^3} = \frac{3x^{\square}}{12}$ Quotient of powers property

$= \frac{3x^{\square}}{12}$ Subtract exponents.

$= \square$ Divide numerator and denominator by $\square$.

Checkpoint **Find the quotient. Write your answer using exponents.**

5. $\frac{5^9}{5^2}$	6. $\frac{12^7}{12^4}$
7. $\frac{4x^{13}}{24x^9}$	8. $\frac{14x^{16}}{6x^{11}}$

Lesson 4.5 Rules of Exponents 69

Example 3 *Using Both Properties of Powers*

Simplify $\frac{4m^3 \cdot m^4}{12m^2}$.

$\frac{4m^3 \cdot m^4}{12m^2} = \frac{4m^{\square}}{12m^2}$ Product of powers property

$= \frac{4m^{\square}}{12m^2}$ Add exponents.

$= \frac{4m^{\square}}{12}$ Quotient of powers property

$= \frac{4m^{\square}}{12}$ Subtract exponents.

$= \square$ Divide numerator and denominator by $\square$.

Checkpoint Simplify.

9. $\frac{6m^5 \cdot m}{15m^3}$	10. $\frac{n^2 \cdot 10n^6}{5n^3}$

70 Chapter 4 Notetaking Guide

RESOURCE BOOK

The *Chapter Resource Books* contain Study Guide pages with reteaching examples and exercises for each lesson in the textbook. (The Study Guide pages are also available in Spanish in the *Spanish Study Guide*.)

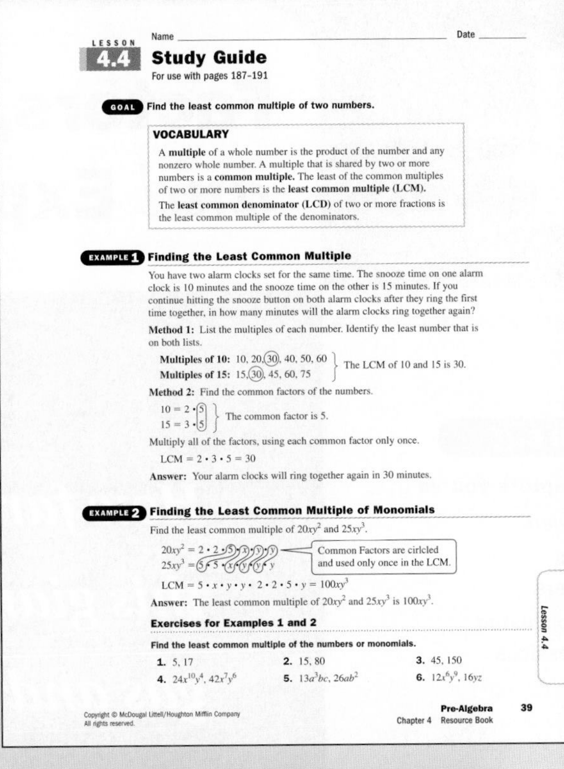

LESSON 4.4 Name ______ Date ______

Study Guide

For use with pages 187–191

GOAL Find the least common multiple of two numbers.

VOCABULARY

A **multiple** of a whole number is the product of the number and any nonzero whole number. A multiple that is shared by two or more numbers is a **common multiple.** The least of the common multiples of two or more numbers is the **least common multiple (LCM).**

The **least common denominator (LCD)** of two or more fractions is the least common multiple of the denominators.

EXAMPLE 1 Finding the Least Common Multiple

You have two alarm clocks set for the same time. The snooze time on one alarm clock is 10 minutes and the snooze time on the other is 15 minutes. If you continue hitting the snooze button on both alarm clocks after they ring the first time together, in how many minutes will the alarm clocks ring together again?

Method 1: List the multiples of each number. Identify the least number that is on both lists.

Multiples of 10: 10, 20, (30), 40, 50, 60
Multiples of 15: 15, (30), 45, 60, 75
The LCM of 10 and 15 is 30.

Method 2: Find the common factors of the numbers.

$10 = 2 \cdot 5$
$15 = 3 \cdot 5$
The common factor is 5.

Multiply all of the factors, using each common factor only once.

$\text{LCM} = 2 \cdot 3 \cdot 5 = 30$

Answer: Your alarm clocks will ring together again in 30 minutes.

EXAMPLE 2 Finding the Least Common Multiple of Monomials

Find the least common multiple of $20xy^2$ and $25xy^3$.

$20xy^2 = 2 \cdot 2 \cdot 5 \cdot x \cdot y \cdot y$
$25xy^3 = 5 \cdot 5 \cdot x \cdot y \cdot y \cdot y$

Common Factors are cirlcled and used only once in the LCM.

$\text{LCM} = 5 \cdot x \cdot y \cdot y \cdot 2 \cdot 2 \cdot 5 \cdot y = 100xy^3$

Answer: The least common multiple of $20xy^2$ and $25xy^3$ is $100xy^3$.

Exercises for Examples 1 and 2

Find the least common multiple of the numbers or monomials.

1. 5, 17 **2.** 15, 80 **3.** 45, 150

4. $24x^{10}y^4, 42x^7y^6$ **5.** $13a^3bc, 26ab^2$ **6.** $12x^6y^9, 16yz$

Lesson 4.4

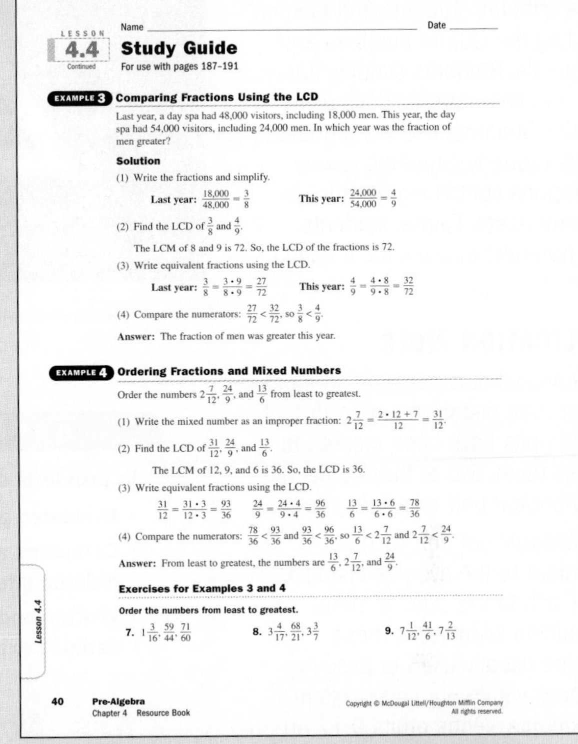

LESSON 4.4 Continued Name ______ Date ______

Study Guide

For use with pages 187–191

EXAMPLE 3 Comparing Fractions Using the LCD

Last year, a day spa had 48,000 visitors, including 18,000 men. This year, the day spa had 54,000 visitors, including 24,000 men. In which year was the fraction of men greater?

Solution

(1) Write the fractions and simplify.

Last year: $\frac{18,000}{48,000} = \frac{3}{8}$ **This year:** $\frac{24,000}{54,000} = \frac{4}{9}$

(2) Find the LCD of $\frac{3}{8}$ and $\frac{4}{9}$.

The LCM of 8 and 9 is 72. So, the LCD of the fractions is 72.

(3) Write equivalent fractions using the LCD.

Last year: $\frac{3}{8} = \frac{3 \cdot 9}{8 \cdot 9} = \frac{27}{72}$ **This year:** $\frac{4}{9} = \frac{4 \cdot 8}{9 \cdot 8} = \frac{32}{72}$

(4) Compare the numerators: $\frac{27}{72} < \frac{32}{72}$, so $\frac{3}{8} < \frac{4}{9}$.

Answer: The fraction of men was greater this year.

EXAMPLE 4 Ordering Fractions and Mixed Numbers

Order the numbers $2\frac{7}{12}, \frac{24}{9}$, and $\frac{13}{6}$ from least to greatest.

(1) Write the mixed number as an improper fraction: $2\frac{7}{12} = \frac{2 \cdot 12 + 7}{12} = \frac{31}{12}$.

(2) Find the LCD of $\frac{31}{12}, \frac{24}{9}$, and $\frac{13}{6}$.

The LCM of 12, 9, and 6 is 36. So, the LCD is 36.

(3) Write equivalent fractions using the LCD.

$\frac{31}{12} = \frac{31 \cdot 3}{12 \cdot 3} = \frac{93}{36}$ $\frac{24}{9} = \frac{24 \cdot 4}{9 \cdot 4} = \frac{96}{36}$ $\frac{13}{6} = \frac{13 \cdot 6}{6 \cdot 6} = \frac{78}{36}$

(4) Compare the numerators: $\frac{78}{36} < \frac{93}{36}$ and $\frac{93}{36} < \frac{96}{36}$, so $\frac{13}{6} < 2\frac{7}{12}$ and $2\frac{7}{12} < \frac{24}{9}$.

Answer: From least to greatest, the numbers are $\frac{13}{6}, 2\frac{7}{12}$, and $\frac{24}{9}$.

Exercises for Examples 3 and 4

Order the numbers from least to greatest.

7. $1\frac{3}{16}, \frac{59}{44}, \frac{71}{60}$ **8.** $3\frac{4}{17}, \frac{68}{21}, 3\frac{3}{7}$ **9.** $7\frac{1}{12}, \frac{41}{6}, 7\frac{2}{13}$

Lesson 4.4

TUTOR PLACE

Tutor Place helps students practice and master essential topics. Instruction is provided by 104 cards containing examples and two sets of practice exercises. Answers are provided in a handy answer key.

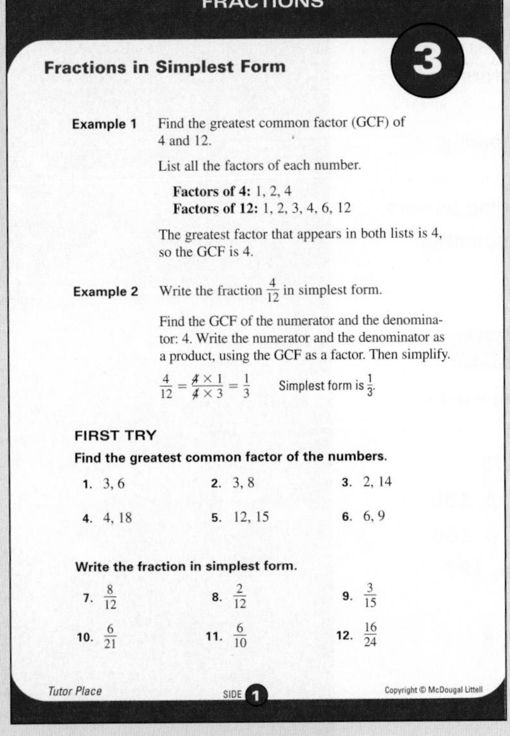

FRACTIONS

Fractions in Simplest Form 3

Example 1 Find the greatest common factor (GCF) of 4 and 12.

List all the factors of each number.

Factors of 4: 1, 2, 4
Factors of 12: 1, 2, 3, 4, 6, 12

The greatest factor that appears in both lists is 4, so the GCF is 4.

Example 2 Write the fraction $\frac{4}{12}$ in simplest form.

Find the GCF of the numerator and the denominator: 4. Write the numerator and the denominator as a product, using the GCF as a factor. Then simplify.

$\frac{4}{12} = \frac{\not{4} \times 1}{\not{4} \times 3} = \frac{1}{3}$ Simplest form is $\frac{1}{3}$.

FIRST TRY

Find the greatest common factor of the numbers.

1. 3, 6 **2.** 3, 8 **3.** 2, 14

4. 4, 18 **5.** 12, 15 **6.** 6, 9

Write the fraction in simplest form.

7. $\frac{8}{12}$ **8.** $\frac{2}{12}$ **9.** $\frac{3}{15}$

10. $\frac{6}{21}$ **11.** $\frac{6}{10}$ **12.** $\frac{16}{24}$

Tutor Place SIDE 1

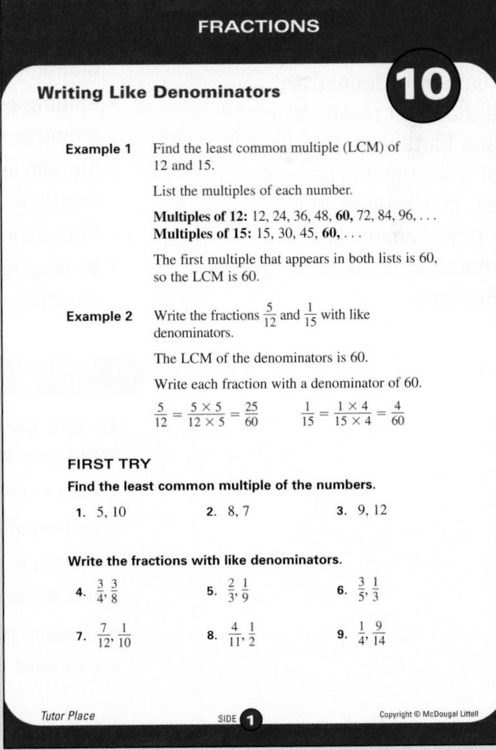

FRACTIONS

Writing Like Denominators 10

Example 1 Find the least common multiple (LCM) of 12 and 15.

List the multiples of each number.

Multiples of 12: 12, 24, 36, 48, **60,** 72, 84, 96, . . .
Multiples of 15: 15, 30, 45, **60,** . . .

The first multiple that appears in both lists is 60, so the LCM is 60.

Example 2 Write the fractions $\frac{5}{12}$ and $\frac{1}{15}$ with like denominators.

The LCM of the denominators is 60.

Write each fraction with a denominator of 60.

$\frac{5}{12} = \frac{5 \times 5}{12 \times 5} = \frac{25}{60}$ $\frac{1}{15} = \frac{1 \times 4}{15 \times 4} = \frac{4}{60}$

FIRST TRY

Find the least common multiple of the numbers.

1. 5, 10 **2.** 8, 7 **3.** 9, 12

Write the fractions with like denominators.

4. $\frac{3}{4}, \frac{3}{8}$ **5.** $\frac{2}{3}, \frac{1}{9}$ **6.** $\frac{3}{5}, \frac{1}{3}$

7. $\frac{7}{12}, \frac{1}{10}$ **8.** $\frac{4}{11}, \frac{1}{2}$ **9.** $\frac{1}{4}, \frac{9}{14}$

Tutor Place SIDE 1

OVERVIEW

Main Ideas

In this chapter, students find factors, including the GCF, of numbers and monomials. Students simplify fractions and compare fractions using the LCD. Students use the product of powers property. Students rewrite expressions containing negative or zero exponents. Finally, students write numbers in scientific notation.

Application Note

Astronomical distances are so much greater than distances on Earth that several units have been created to express them. Two of these units are *astronomical unit* and *light year*.

An *astronomical unit* (AU) is equivalent to the average distance from Earth to the Sun, or about 150 million kilometers. These units are usually used to describe distances within our solar system. For example, Venus orbits 0.72 AU from the Sun, while Pluto orbits an average of 39.5 AU from the Sun.

A *light year* is a distance, not a measure of time. It is defined as the distance that light travels in a vacuum in one Earth year. One light year is about 9.46 trillion kilometers, or about 5.88 trillion miles. The nearest star to our solar system is Proxima Centauri, which is 4.22 light years from the Sun.

CHAPTER 4

Factors, Fractions, *and* Exponents

BEFORE

In previous chapters you've . . .

- Evaluated powers
- Compared and ordered integers
- Written and evaluated variable expressions

Now

In Chapter 4 you'll study . . .

- Factoring numbers and monomials
- Finding common factors and common multiples
- Simplifying and comparing fractions
- Multiplying and dividing powers
- Writing numbers in scientific notation

WHY?

So you can solve real-world problems about . . .

- coin collecting, p. 175
- community gardens, p. 180
- monarch butterflies, p. 186
- the Great Pyramid, p. 197
- geckos, p. 201
- compact discs, p. 208

How far away is this giant cloud of gas and dust?

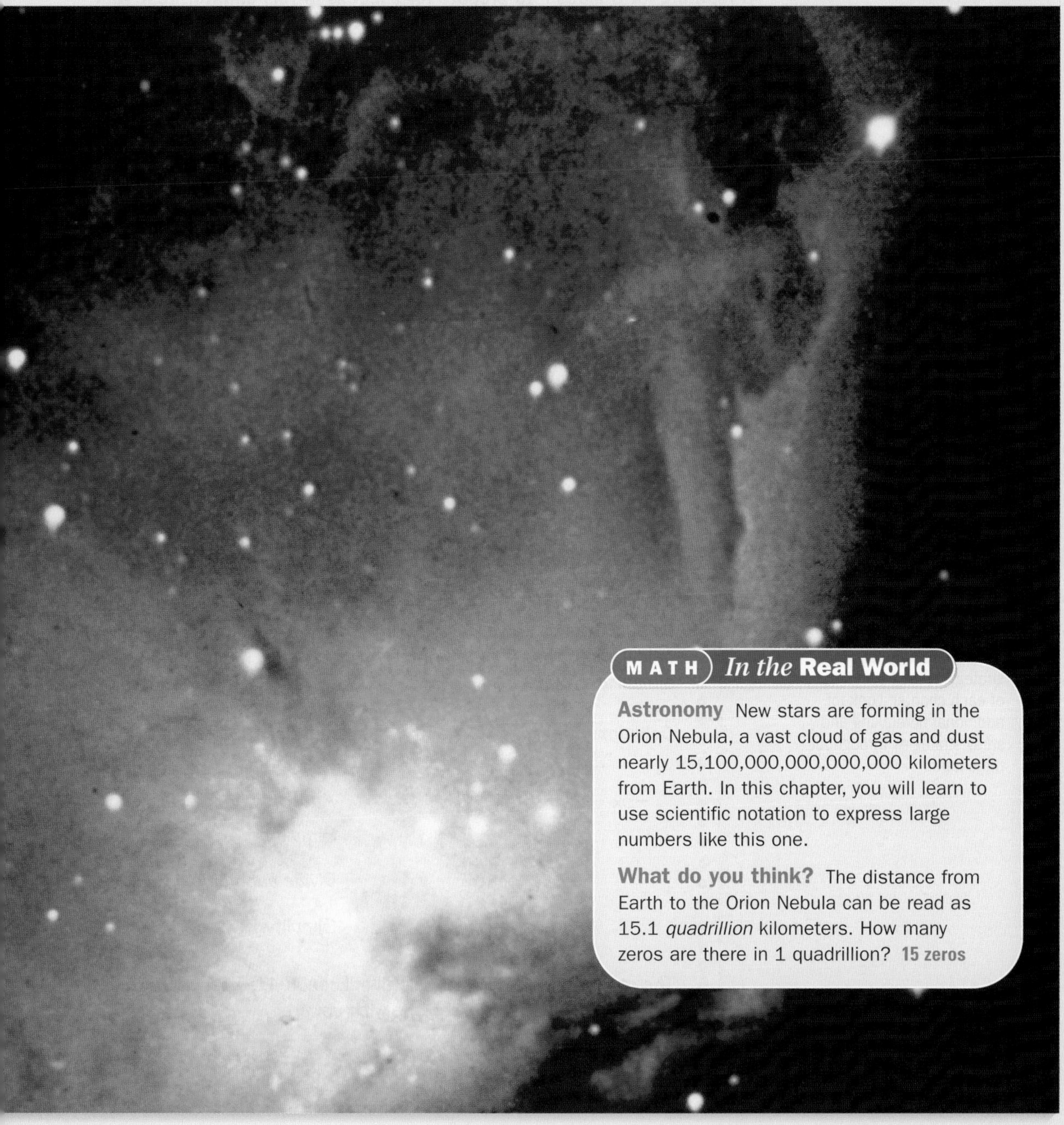

MATH In the Real World

Astronomy New stars are forming in the Orion Nebula, a vast cloud of gas and dust nearly 15,100,000,000,000,000 kilometers from Earth. In this chapter, you will learn to use scientific notation to express large numbers like this one.

What do you think? The distance from Earth to the Orion Nebula can be read as 15.1 *quadrillion* kilometers. How many zeros are there in 1 quadrillion? **15 zeros**

Chapter Resources

These resources are provided to help you prepare for the chapter and to customize review materials:

Chapter 4 Resource Book

- Tips for New Teachers, pp. 1–2
- Lesson Plan, pp. 5, 15, 25, 33, 42, 51, 60
- Lesson Plan for Block Scheduling, pp. 6, 16, 26, 34, 43, 52, 61

Technology

- EasyPlanner CD-ROM
- Test and Practice Generator
- Electronic Lesson Presentations CD-ROM
- eTutorial CD-ROM

Internet

- Classzone
- eEdition Plus Online
- eWorkbook Plus Online
- eTutorial Plus Online
- EasyPlanner Plus Online

English Learner Support

- Spanish Study Guide
- Multi-Language Visual Glossary
- Chapter Audio Summaries CDs
- Teacher's Edition, pp. 168E–168F

PREPARE

DIAGNOSIS/REMEDIATION

Prerequisite Skills Quiz
The Prerequisite Skills Quiz can help you diagnose whether students have the following skills needed in Chapter 4:

- Use vocabulary (Ex. 1)
- Write mixed numbers as improper fractions (Exs. 2–5)
- Find the product of a whole number and a fraction (Exs. 6–9)
- Evaluate powers (Exs. 10–13)

Chapter 4 Resource Book

- Study Guide (Lessons 4.1–4.7)

Tutor Place

NOTETAKING STRATEGIES

As students copy examples into their notebooks, suggest they underline or highlight any calculation steps that they found to be confusing. Further suggestions for keeping a notebook can be found on pages 173, 178, and 195.

For more support on notetaking, see:

- Notetaking Guide Workbook
- Notetaking Transparencies

CHAPTER 4

Chapter Prerequisite Skills

Review Vocabulary
power, p. 10
base, p. 10
exponent, p. 10
positive integer, p. 22
negative integer, p. 22
numerator, p. 777
denominator, p. 777

1. base→9^3←exponent; power ↑ (9^3)

10. 5 to the fourth power; 5 • 5 • 5 • 5; 625

11. 12 to the third power, or 12 cubed; 12 • 12 • 12; 1728

12. 1.3 to the third power, or 1.3 cubed; 1.3 • 1.3 • 1.3; 2.197

13. 0.2 to the second power, or 0.2 squared; 0.2 • 0.2; 0.04

PREREQUISITE SKILLS QUIZ

Preparing for Success **To prepare for success in this chapter, test your knowledge of these concepts and skills. You may want to look at the pages referred to in blue for additional review.**

1. **Vocabulary** Label the power, the base, and the exponent in the expression 9^3.

Write the mixed number as an improper fraction. *(p. 778)*

2. $5\frac{1}{3}$ $\frac{16}{3}$ **3.** $6\frac{2}{5}$ $\frac{32}{5}$ **4.** $3\frac{7}{9}$ $\frac{34}{9}$ **5.** $8\frac{5}{6}$ $\frac{53}{6}$

Find the product. *(p. 780)*

6. $20 \times \frac{3}{5}$ 12 **7.** $32 \times \frac{7}{8}$ 28 **8.** $\frac{2}{3} \times 27$ 18 **9.** $\frac{9}{10} \times 50$ 45

Write the power in words and as a repeated multiplication. Then evaluate the power. *(p. 10)*

10. 5^4 **11.** 12^3 **12.** $(1.3)^3$ **13.** $(0.2)^2$

NOTETAKING STRATEGIES

Note *Worthy*

You will find a notetaking strategy at the beginning of each chapter. Look for additional notetaking and study strategies throughout the chapter.

RECORDING THE PROCESS When copying examples in class, be sure to write a verbal description next to each step in a calculation. Then you can refer to the example when solving similar exercises.

Calculation step:	Verbal description:
$-5x - 8 = -23$	Write original equation.
$-5x - 8 + 8 = -23 + 8$	Add 8 to each side.
$-5x = -15$	Simplify.
$\frac{-5x}{-5} = \frac{-15}{-5}$	Divide each side by −5.
$x = 3$	Simplify.

The strategy above will be helpful in Lesson 4.5 when you are simplifying variable expressions with powers.

Concept *Activity*

4.1 Finding Prime Numbers

Goal
Investigate prime and composite numbers using multiples.

Materials
- pencil
- paper

A *prime number* is a whole number that is greater than 1 and has exactly two whole number factors, 1 and itself. A *composite number* is a whole number that is greater than 1 and has more than two whole number factors. A *multiple* of a number is the product of the number and any nonzero whole number.

Investigate

Use patterns to determine if a number is prime or composite.

1. Write the whole numbers from 2 to 60 in rows of 6 as shown.
2. Start with the number 2. Circle it and cross out every multiple of 2 after 2. (The first few multiples of 2 have been crossed out for you.)
3. Move to the next number that is not crossed out. Circle it and cross out all other multiples of that number.
4. Repeat Step 3 until every number is either crossed out or circled.

	2	3	4	5	6
7	8	9	10	11	12
13	14	15	16	17	18
19	20	21	22	23	24
25	26	27	28	29	30
31	32	33	34	35	36
37	38	39	40	41	42
43	44	45	46	47	48
49	50	51	52	53	54
55	56	57	58	59	60

Draw Conclusions

1–3. See margin.

1. *Writing* What can you say about the numbers that have been crossed out? What can you say about the numbers that have been circled? Use the words *prime* and *composite* in your answers.
2. **Critical Thinking** All the numbers in the sixth column are crossed out because they are all multiples of 6. Explain why all the numbers in the second column (except for 2), in the third column (except for 3), and in the fourth column are crossed out.
3. **Predict** Suppose you repeated the activity but arranged the numbers in rows of 10 instead of 6. Predict which columns would contain only crossed-out numbers. Then check your prediction.

NCTM CURRICULUM STANDARDS
Standard 1: Understand numbers
Standard 2: Understand patterns

1 PLAN

Investigate the Concept

- Students will investigate prime and composite numbers.
- This activity leads into prime factorization in Lesson 4.1.

Materials

Each student will need pencil and paper. See the Activity Support Master in the *Chapter 4 Resource Book*.

Recommended Time

Work activity: 10 min
Discuss results: 10 min

Grouping

Students should work individually.

2 TEACH

Tips for Success

Remind students that the multiples of a number form a pattern; for example, every third number after 3 in the list is a multiple of 3.

3 CLOSE

Key Discovery

Students find the prime numbers from 2 to 60, and they also recognize that composite numbers are multiples of at least one other number.

Assessment

1. Why is the number 2 the only even prime? **Every other even number is a multiple of 2.**
2. Could a prime number be a multiple of another prime? Explain. **No; if a number has a factor other than 1 and itself, then it is not prime.**

1–3. See Additional Answers beginning on page AA1.

1 PLAN

Skill Check

1. $4 \cdot 7 = ?$ 28
2. $39 \div 3 = ?$ 13
3. $720 \div 30 = ?$ 24
4. Write the expression $5 \cdot 5 \cdot 5$ as a power. 5^3

LESSON OBJECTIVE

Write the prime factorization of a number.

PACING

Suggested Number of Days
Basic Course: 1 day
Average Course: 1 day
Advanced Course: 1 day
Block: 0.5 block with 4.2

TEACHING RESOURCES

For a complete list of Teaching Resources, see page 168B.

TRANSPARENCY

Warm-Up Exercises for this lesson are available on a transparency.

2 TEACH

MOTIVATING THE LESSON

Have students work in small groups using 24 note cards or sticky notes (numbered from 1 to 24) to discover the different ways of arranging the 24 photos discussed in the opening paragraph.

TIPS *for* NEW TEACHERS

Be sure students understand that factor trees can only be written for composite numbers. See Tips for New Teachers in the *Chapter 4 Resource Book*.

LESSON 4.1

Factors *and* Prime Factorization

Vocabulary
prime number, p. 173
composite number, p. 173
prime factorization, p. 173
factor tree, p. 173
monomial, p. 174

BEFORE	Now	WHY?
You found the product of two or more numbers.	You'll write the prime factorization of a number.	So you can count ways to display a firefly collection, as in Ex. 56.

Yearbook You are working on your school yearbook. Each page will have 24 student photos. The photos will be arranged in a rectangular display with the same number of photos in each row. How many ways can you arrange the photos so that there are no more than 10 photos in any row or column?

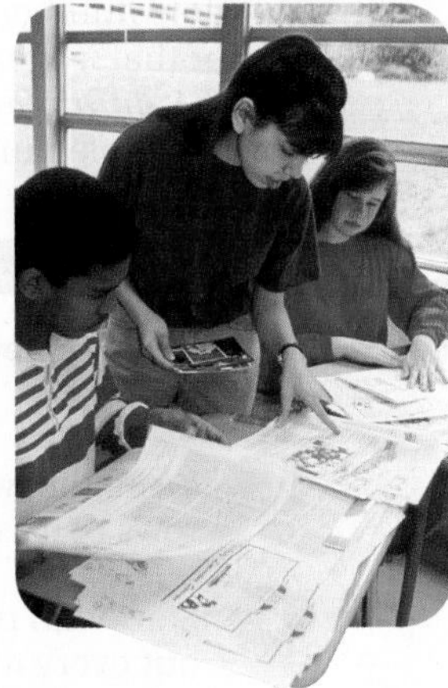

You can use factors to determine the number of possible displays. In this chapter, finding the factors of a given whole number means finding whole numbers that divide the given number without a remainder. For example, two factors of 50 are 5 and 10.

Example 1 *Writing Factors*

For the yearbook described above, each possible display will consist of 24 photos. Because there will be the same number of photos in each row, the number of photos in each row will be a factor of 24.

1) Write 24 as a product of two whole numbers in all possible ways.

$1 \cdot 24$ $2 \cdot 12$ $3 \cdot 8$ $4 \cdot 6$

The factors of 24 are 1, 2, 3, 4, 6, 8, 12, and 24.

2) Use the factors to find all the rectangular displays with no more than 10 photos in any row or column.

3 rows of 8 photos 6 rows of 4 photos
8 rows of 3 photos 4 rows of 6 photos

Answer There are 4 possible displays.

Checkpoint

Write all the factors of the number.

1. 30 1, 2, 3, 5, 6, 10, 15, 30
2. 31 1, 31
3. 45 1, 3, 5, 9, 15, 45
4. 87 1, 3, 29, 87

NCTM CURRICULUM STANDARDS
Standard 1: Understand numbers; Understand meanings of operations; Compute fluently

Prime and Composite Numbers A **prime number** is a whole number that is greater than 1 and has exactly two whole number factors, 1 and itself. A **composite number** is a whole number that is greater than 1 and has more than two whole number factors. The number 1 is neither prime nor composite.

Study *Strategy*

The table lists all the factors of each number. However, to determine whether a number is composite, you need to find only one factor other than the number itself and 1.

Examples of Prime and Composite Numbers		
Number	**Factors**	**Prime or composite?**
24	1, 2, 3, 4, 6, 8, 12, 24	Composite
41	1, 41	Prime
51	1, 3, 17, 51	Composite
89	1, 89	Prime
121	1, 11, 121	Composite

Prime Factorization When you write a number as a product of prime numbers, you are writing its **prime factorization**. You can use a diagram called a **factor tree** to write the prime factorization of a number.

Example 2 *Writing a Prime Factorization*

Write the prime factorization of 630.

One possible factor tree:

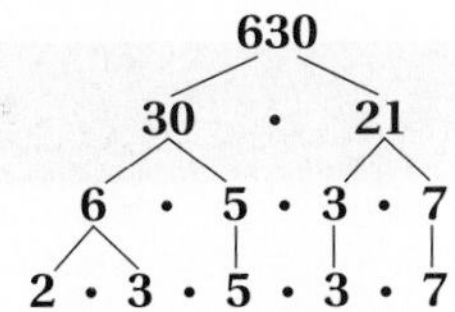

Write original number.

Write 630 as 30 • 21.

Write 30 as 6 • 5. Write 21 as 3 • 7.

Write 6 as 2 • 3.

Another possible factor tree:

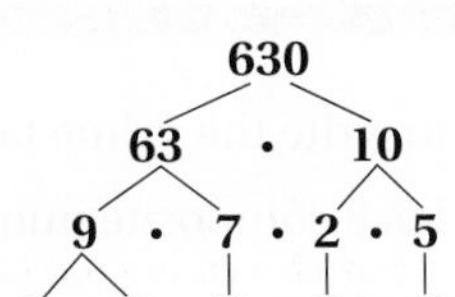

Write original number.

Write 630 as 63 • 10.

Write 63 as 9 • 7. Write 10 as 2 • 5.

Write 9 as 3 • 3.

Both trees give the same result: $630 = 2 \cdot 3 \cdot 3 \cdot 5 \cdot 7 = 2 \cdot 3^2 \cdot 5 \cdot 7$.

Answer The prime factorization of 630 is $2 \cdot 3^2 \cdot 5 \cdot 7$.

Note *Worthy*

It is helpful to include diagrams in your notes. Include a different factor tree for the number 630 in your notes.

 ***Checkpoint***

Tell whether the number is *prime* or *composite*. If it is composite, write its prime factorization.

5. 32 composite; 2^5 **6.** 56 composite; $2^3 \cdot 7$ **7.** 59 prime **8.** 83 prime

9. 101 prime **10.** 175 composite; $5^2 \cdot 7$ **11.** 180 composite; $2^2 \cdot 3^2 \cdot 5$ **12.** 420 composite; $2^2 \cdot 3 \cdot 5 \cdot 7$

Extra Examples

Example 1 There are 36 desks in a large classroom that need to be arranged in rows with the same number of desks in each row. If there are to be no more than 9 desks in a row, how many arrangements are possible? List the arrangements. **3 arrangements; 4 rows of 9 desks, 6 rows of 6 desks, 9 rows of 4 desks**

Example 2 Write the prime factorization of 384. $\mathbf{3 \cdot 2^7}$

Common Error

In Example 1, students see that there are 4 possible displays for 24 items. In Extra Example 1, students may think that there must be more than 4 possible displays because 36 > 24. Point out to students that there are, in fact, less than 4 displays because 36 has fewer factors than 24.

Teaching Tip

Before beginning Example 2, it may be beneficial to provide students with a list of the first ten prime numbers. While discussing Example 2, point out and stress that the two factor trees produce the same result. Make sure students recognize that the order of the factors does not change the prime factorization of a number.

Differentiating Instruction

Advanced Students Encourage students to research mathematicians' attempts to identify the greatest prime number.

Extra Examples

Example 3 Factor the monomial $98g^2h$. **$2 \cdot 7 \cdot 7 \cdot g \cdot g \cdot h$**

CROSS-CURRICULUM

Instrumental Music In marching bands, the instructor must decide how to arrange the band members to a form a grid of musicians that is a visually pleasing arrangement. The use of factors is critical to examining the possible arrangements of the musicians.

TEACHING TIP

One method for ensuring that students do not omit factors is to have them write the factors in order from least to greatest. For example, to find the factors of 32, show students how to begin by writing 1 and 32 on opposite ends of a long line. The next factor pair is 2 and 16, so write those inside 1 and 32. Point out that since there is no whole number between 1 and 2, there cannot be a factor between 16 and 32. The final factor pair to be added is 4 and 8. Writing these two numbers in the middle of the number string produces the list 1, 2, 4, 8, 16, and 32.

CONCEPT CHECK

What is a prime factorization? **the writing of a number as a product of only prime numbers**

DAILY PUZZLER

What is the least odd composite number? **9**

Factoring Monomials A **monomial** is a number, a variable, or the product of a number and one or more variables raised to whole number powers.

Monomials	Not monomials
$7x$	$7 + x$
$25mn^2$	$25m - n^2$
$24y^3z^2$	$24 + y^3 + z^2$

To *factor* a monomial, write the monomial as a product of prime numbers and variables with exponents of 1.

Example 3 *Factoring a Monomial*

Factor the monomial $28xy^3$.

$28xy^3 = 2 \cdot 2 \cdot 7 \cdot x \cdot y^3$ **Write 28 as $2 \cdot 2 \cdot 7$.**

$= 2 \cdot 2 \cdot 7 \cdot x \cdot y \cdot y \cdot y$ **Write y^3 as $y \cdot y \cdot y$.**

Checkpoint

Factor the monomial.

13. $6ab$ **$2 \cdot 3 \cdot a \cdot b$** **14.** $15n^3$ **$3 \cdot 5 \cdot n \cdot n \cdot n$** **15.** $3x^3y^2$ **16.** $36s^4t$

15. $3 \cdot x \cdot x \cdot x \cdot y \cdot y$

16. $2 \cdot 2 \cdot 3 \cdot 3 \cdot s \cdot s \cdot s \cdot s \cdot t$

4.1 Exercises

More Practice, p. 806

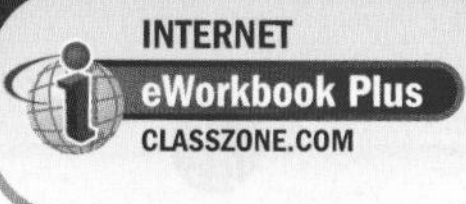

Guided Practice

Vocabulary Check

1. Describe how to write the prime factorization of a number. **See margin.**

2. Explain why 34 is a composite number. ***Sample answer:*** **It has two whole number factors, 2 and 17, that are not equal to 1 or the number itself.**

Skill Check

Write all the factors of the number.

3. 16 **1, 2, 4, 8, 16** **4.** 32 **1, 2, 4, 8, 16, 32** **5.** 29 **1, 29** **6.** 55 **1, 5, 11, 55**

Tell whether the number is *prime* or *composite*.

7. 9 **composite** **8.** 15 **composite** **9.** 17 **prime** **10.** 23 **prime**

Write the prime factorization of the number.

11. 10 **$2 \cdot 5$** **12.** 18 **$2 \cdot 3^2$** **13.** 25 **5^2** **14.** 39 **$3 \cdot 13$**

15. Error Analysis Describe and correct the error in writing the prime factorization of 60. ***Sample answer:*** **The factor 4 is composite, and equals $2 \cdot 2$. The prime factorization is $60 = 2^2 \cdot 3 \cdot 5$.**

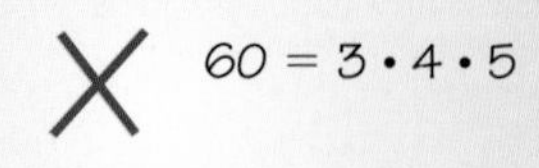

1. ***Sample answer:*** **Write the number as the product of two whole number factors that are not equal to 1 or the number itself. Continue this process with any composite factors until only prime numbers remain. Write the original number as the product of the prime numbers that remain, using exponents for prime factors that repeat.**

Practice and Problem Solving

Homework *Help*

Example	Exercises
1	16-23, 46, 56
2	24-45
3	48-55

CLASSZONE.COM
- More Examples
- eTutorial Plus

47. *Sample answer:* $8x^3y^2$ is a monomial because it is the product only of a number and variables that are raised to whole number powers; $8x^3y^2 + 1$ is not a monomial because it is the sum of two monomials.

Write all the factors of the number.

A **16.** 8 1, 2, 4, 8 **17.** 53 1, 53 **18.** 12 1, 2, 3, 4, 6, 12 **19.** 33 1, 3, 11, 33

20. 36 1, 2, 3, 4, 6, 9, 12, 18, 36 **21.** 60 1, 2, 3, 4, 5, 6, 10, 12, 15, 20, 30, 60 **22.** 71 1, 71 **23.** 144 1, 2, 3, 4, 6, 8, 9, 12, 16, 18, 24, 36, 48, 72, 144

Tell whether the number is *prime* or *composite*.

24. 7 prime **25.** 16 composite **26.** 21 composite **27.** 19 prime

28. 121 composite **29.** 51 composite **30.** 84 composite **31.** 141 composite

Copy and complete the factor tree. Then write the prime factorization of the number.

32. Row 2: 13; Row 3: 4, 13; Row 4: 2; $2^3 \cdot 13$ **33.** Row 2: 20; Row 3: 3, 4; Row 4: 3, 5; $2^2 \cdot 3^2 \cdot 5$

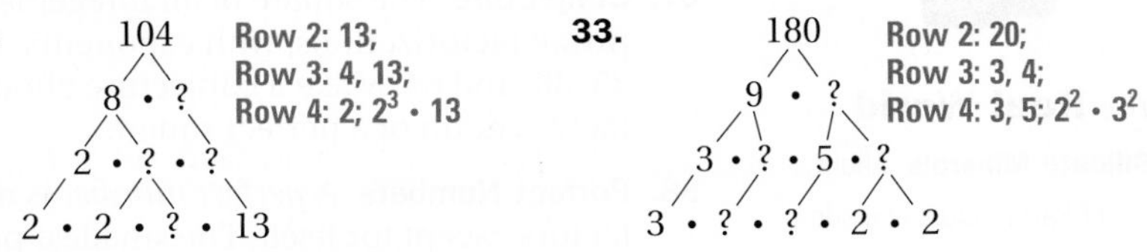

Write the prime factorization of the number.

34. 26 $2 \cdot 13$ **35.** 58 $2 \cdot 29$ **36.** 63 $3^2 \cdot 7$ **37.** 85 $5 \cdot 17$

38. 120 $2^3 \cdot 3 \cdot 5$ **39.** 160 $2^5 \cdot 5$ **40.** 154 $2 \cdot 7 \cdot 11$ **41.** 195 $3 \cdot 5 \cdot 13$

42. 202 $2 \cdot 101$ **43.** 210 $2 \cdot 3 \cdot 5 \cdot 7$ **44.** 217 $7 \cdot 31$ **45.** 225 $3^2 \cdot 5^2$

46. Coin Collecting The U.S. Mint began issuing state quarters in 1999. There will be one state quarter for each of the 50 states. You are collecting the state quarters and want to design a rectangular display with the same number of quarters in each row. How many ways can you arrange your display? 6 ways

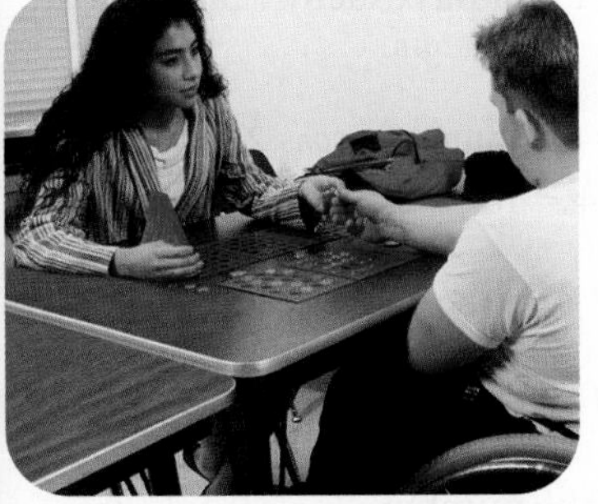

47. *Writing* Give an expression that is a monomial and tell why it is an example of a monomial. Then give an expression that is *not* a monomial and tell why it is not an example of a monomial. See margin.

Factor the monomial.

48. $11cd$ $11 \cdot c \cdot d$ **49.** $19m^3$ $19 \cdot m \cdot m \cdot m$ **50.** $3f^6$ $3 \cdot f \cdot f \cdot f \cdot f \cdot f \cdot f$ **51.** $21ab$ $3 \cdot 7 \cdot a \cdot b$

52. $5xy^2$ $5 \cdot x \cdot y \cdot y$ **53.** $35rs^5$ **54.** $2y^4z^3$ **55.** $40m^2n$

53. $5 \cdot 7 \cdot r \cdot s \cdot s \cdot s \cdot s \cdot s$
54. $2 \cdot y \cdot y \cdot y \cdot y \cdot z \cdot z \cdot z$
55. $2 \cdot 2 \cdot 2 \cdot 5 \cdot m \cdot m \cdot n$

56. Fireflies There are 69 species of flashing fireflies, also known as lightning bugs, in the United States. A museum is designing a rectangular display of these 69 species with the same number of fireflies in each row. How many displays are possible? 4 displays

B **57. Critical Thinking** Explain why all two-digit whole numbers with 5 as the ones' digit are composite. See margin.

Use the prime factorization of the number to list all of its factors. 58–61. See margin.

58. 240 **59.** 335 **60.** 500 **61.** 201

List all the factors of the monomial. 62–65. See margin.

62. $6ab^2$ **63.** $52w$ **64.** $2r^3s$ **65.** $7xyz$

Study *Strategy*

In Exercises 58–61, to list all the factors of a number, first list all the prime factors. Then list all products of two prime factors. Then list all products of three prime factors, and so on.

3 APPLY

ASSIGNMENT GUIDE

Basic Course
Day 1: pp. 175-176 Exs. 16-27, 33-41, 50-56, 61-63, 71-82

Average Course
Day 1: pp. 175-176 Exs. 22-33, 42-51, 57-67, 77-84

Advanced Course
Day 1: pp. 175-176 Exs. 22-32, 44-49, 56-63, 66-72*, 79-84

Block
pp. 175-176 Exs. 22-33, 42-51, 57-67, 77-84 (with 4.2)

EXTRA PRACTICE

- Student Edition, p. 806
- Chapter 4 Resource Book, pp. 8-10
- Test and Practice Generator

TRANSPARENCY

Even-numbered answers are available on transparencies.

HOMEWORK CHECK

When you review students' homework for this lesson, go over the following exercises to check understanding of key concepts.
Basic: 16, 24, 34, 50, 52
Average: 22, 33, 42, 46, 50
Advanced: 22, 32, 44, 49, 56

TEACHING TIP

In Exercises 38–45 and 58–61, encourage students to share tips they have learned about how to find the factors of 3-digit numbers. For example, a number has 3 as a factor if the sum of its digits is a number that is divisible by 3.

57–65. See Additional Answers beginning on page AA1.

4 ASSESS

ASSESSMENT RESOURCES

For more assessment resources, see:
- Assessment Book
- Test and Practice Generator

MINI-QUIZ

1. Write all the factors of 57. **1, 3, 19, 57**
2. Tell whether 91 is *prime* or *composite*. **composite**
3. Write the prime factorization of 100. $2^2 \cdot 5^2$
4. Factor the monomial $45v^2w^3$. $3 \cdot 3 \cdot 5 \cdot v \cdot v \cdot w \cdot w \cdot w$
5. **Challenge** What is the least whole number that has exactly 5 factors, including 1 and itself? Explain your answer. **16. *Sample answer:* Since the number has an odd number of factors, one factor must give the number when multiplied by itself. The possible numbers are 1, 4, 9, 16, 25, ... 16 is the first one with 5 factors: 1, 2, 4, 8, 16.**

5 FOLLOW-UP

DIAGNOSIS/REMEDIATION

- Study Guide in Chapter 4 Resource Book, pp. 11–12
- Tutor Place, Whole Numbers and Decimals Card 14
- eTutorial Plus Online
- Extra Practice, p. 806
- Lesson Practice in Chapter 4 Resource Book, pp. 8–10

ENGLISH LEARNER SUPPORT

- Spanish Study Guide
- Multi-Language Visual Glossary
- Chapter Audio Summaries CDs

CHALLENGE

- Challenge Practice in Chapter 4 Resource Book, p. 14
- Teacher's Edition, p. 168F

In the **Real World**

Silicate Minerals About $\frac{9}{10}$ of Earth's crust is made up of silicate minerals. The mass of the crust is about 30 quintillion tons, which is 30 followed by 18 zeros. What is the approximate mass of the silicate minerals in the crust? **27 quintillion tons**

66. **Extended Problem Solving** A geologist has collected 102 different types of silicate minerals. The geologist has taken a photograph of each mineral and wants to make a display of the photographs.
    a. **Calculate** How many rectangular arrangements of the photographs are possible? **8 arrangements**
    b. The geologist wants no more than 15 photographs in any row or column. How many rectangular arrangements satisfying this requirement are possible? **0 arrangements**
    c. **Analyze** The geologist decreases the number of photographs in the display to 96. How many rectangular arrangements, with no more than 15 photographs in any row or column, are now possible? **2 arrangements**

C 67. **Conjecture** The square of an integer is called a *perfect square*. Write the prime factorizations, with exponents, for these perfect squares: 4, 9, 16, 25, 36, and 64. Make a conjecture about the exponents in the prime factorization of a perfect square. **$2^2, 3^2, 2^4, 5^2, 2^2 \cdot 3^2, 2^6$. *Sample answer:* All exponents in the prime factorization of a perfect square must be even.**

68. **Perfect Numbers** A *perfect number* is a number that is the sum of all its factors except for itself. The smallest perfect number is 6, because $6 = 1 + 2 + 3$. The next perfect number is between 20 and 30. Find the next perfect number. **28**

69. **Critical Thinking** If 18 is a factor of a number, what other numbers must also be factors of that number? Give examples to support your answer. **1, 2, 3, 6, 9. *Sample answer:* 36, 54, and 72 have 18 as a factor, and also have 1, 2, 3, 6, and 9 as factors.**

70. **Challenge** What is the least whole number that has exactly 7 factors, including 1 and itself? Explain your answer. **See margin.**

70. 64. *Sample answer:* The factors are 1, 2, 4, 8, 16, 32, and 64. I looked for a number that is a perfect square, because otherwise the number of factors is even. I also looked for a number that is not the square of a prime number, because such a number has only three factors.

Mixed Review

Algebra Basics Solve the equation. Check your solution. *(Lessons 2.5, 2.6)*

71. $a + 24 = 16$ **−8**
72. $33 + b = 58$ **25**
73. $c - 14 = 18$ **32**
74. $d - 10 = 10$ **20**
75. $6r = 48$ **8**
76. $-10s = 50$ **−5**
77. $\frac{t}{9} = -7$ **−63**
78. $\frac{u}{-2} = -14$ **28**

Write the verbal sentence as an equation. Then solve the equation. *(Lesson 3.3)*

79. Fifteen plus a number is equal to 21 minus the number. **$15 + n = 21 - n$; 3**
80. Two times the sum of 3 and a number is equal to 5 plus the number. **$2(3 + n) = 5 + n$; −1**
81. Eight plus a number is equal to −3 times the number. **$8 + n = -3n$; −2**

Standardized Test Practice

82. **Multiple Choice** For which value of x is the value of the expression $7x + 1$ a prime number? **D**
    A. 0 **B.** 1 **C.** 3 **D.** 4

83. **Multiple Choice** Which expression is the prime factorization of 252? **G**
    F. $2^2 \cdot 3^2 \cdot 7^2$ **G.** $2^2 \cdot 3^2 \cdot 7$ **H.** $2 \cdot 3^2 \cdot 7$ **I.** $2 \cdot 3^2 \cdot 7^2$

84. **Short Response** The area of a rectangle is 54 square inches. The length and width are whole numbers of inches. Find all possible dimensions of the rectangle. Which dimensions result in the rectangle having the greatest perimeter? **1 in. by 54 in., 2 in. by 27 in., 3 in. by 18 in., 6 in. by 9 in.; 1 in. by 54 in.**

LESSON **4.2**

Greatest Common Factor

BEFORE	Now	WHY?
You found all the factors of a whole number.	You'll find the GCF of two or more whole numbers.	So you can organize bands at a music camp, as in Ex. 32.

Vocabulary

common factor, p. 177
greatest common factor (GCF), p. 177
relatively prime, p. 178

Music Choir A choir director wants to divide a choir into smaller groups. The choir has 24 sopranos, 60 altos, and 36 tenors. Each group will have the same number of each type of voice. What is the greatest number of groups that can be formed? How many sopranos, altos, and tenors will be in each group?

A **common factor** is a whole number that is a factor of two or more nonzero whole numbers. The greatest of the common factors is the **greatest common factor (GCF)**.

Example 1 *Finding the Greatest Common Factor*

For the choir described above, the greatest number of groups that can be formed is given by the GCF of 24, 60, and 36. You can use one of two methods to find the GCF.

Method 1 List the factors of each number. Identify the greatest number that is on every list.

Factors of 24: 1, 2, 3, 4, 6, 8, (12), 24
Factors of 60: 1, 2, 3, 4, 5, 6, 10, (12), 15, 20, 30, 60
Factors of 36: 1, 2, 3, 4, 6, 9, (12), 18, 36

The common factors are 1, 2, 3, 4, 6, and 12. The GCF is 12.

Method 2 Write the prime factorization of each number. The GCF is the product of the common prime factors.

$24 = 2 \cdot 2 \cdot 2 \cdot 3$
$60 = 2 \cdot 2 \cdot 3 \cdot 5$
$36 = 2 \cdot 2 \cdot 3 \cdot 3$

The common prime factors are 2, 2, and 3. The GCF is the product $2 \cdot 2 \cdot 3 = 12$.

Answer The greatest number of groups that can be formed is 12. Each group will have $24 \div 12 = 2$ sopranos, $60 \div 12 = 5$ altos, and $36 \div 12 = 3$ tenors.

Watch *Out*

In Method 2 of Example 1, the number 2 appears at least twice in the prime factorization of each number. So, include 2 twice when finding the GCF.

Checkpoint

Find the greatest common factor of the numbers.

1. 12, 30 6 **2.** 21, 42 21 **3.** 16, 32, 40 8 **4.** 27, 45, 90 9

NCTM CURRICULUM STANDARDS
Standard 1: Understand meanings of operations; Compute fluently
Standard 2: Understand patterns

1 PLAN

Skill Check

List the factors of each number or monomial.

1. 22 **1, 2, 11, 22**
2. 34 **1, 2, 17, 34**
3. $8xy$ $2 \cdot 2 \cdot 2 \cdot x \cdot y$
4. $9z^2$ $3 \cdot 3 \cdot z \cdot z$

Lesson Objective

Find the GCF of two or more whole numbers.

Pacing

Suggested Number of Days
Basic Course: 1 day
Average Course: 1 day
Advanced Course: 1 day
Block: 0.5 block with 4.1

Teaching Resources

For a complete list of Teaching Resources, see page 168B.

Transparency

Warm-Up Exercises for this lesson are available on a transparency.

2 TEACH

Motivating the Lesson

Ask a volunteer to explain the terms *soprano*, *alto*, and *tenor*.

TIPS *for* NEW TEACHERS

Students may do better finding the GCF of monomials if they split each monomial into parts. Students can then find the GCFs of the whole number and of each variable, and then combine the results. See Tips for New Teachers in the *Chapter 4 Resource Book*.

Extra Examples

Example 1 Find the GCF of 25, 40, and 55. **5**

Example 2 Find the greatest common factor of the numbers. Then tell whether the numbers are relatively prime.

a. 18, 24 **6; not relatively prime**

b. 39, 56 **1; relatively prime**

Example 3 Find the greatest common factor of $22m^3p$ and $38mp^2$. **$2mp$**

TEACHING TIP

In Example 1, stress that the factors must be written in order from least to greatest.

NOTETAKING

Encourage students to record both methods used in Example 1 and then write a sentence describing which method they prefer and why.

CONCEPT CHECK

How do you find the greatest common factor of two or more numbers? **There are two methods: either list the factors of each number and then identify the greatest factor that appears in each of the lists, or write the prime factorization of each number and then find the product of the common prime factors.**

DAILY PUZZLER

You are trying to find the GCF of six whole numbers. The first two numbers are 18 and 25. What is the GCF? Explain. **1; 18 and 25 are relatively prime.**

Note Worthy

To clarify the meaning of a vocabulary term like *relatively prime*, include both examples and nonexamples of the term in your notebook.

Relatively Prime Two or more numbers are **relatively prime** if their greatest common factor is 1.

Example 2 *Identifying Relatively Prime Numbers*

Find the greatest common factor of the numbers. Then tell whether the numbers are relatively prime.

a. 24, 45 **b.** 35, 54

Solution

a. List the factors of each number. Identify the greatest number that the lists have in common.

Factors of 24: 1, 2, (3), 4, 6, 8, 12, 24

Factors of 45: 1, (3), 5, 9, 15, 45

The GCF is 3. So, the numbers are not relatively prime.

b. Write the prime factorization of each number.

$35 = 5 \cdot 7$ $\quad$ $54 = 2 \cdot 3 \cdot 3 \cdot 3$

There are no common prime factors. However, two numbers always have 1 as a common factor. So, the GCF is 1, and the numbers are relatively prime.

Checkpoint

Find the greatest common factor of the numbers. Then tell whether the numbers are relatively prime.

5. 18, 33 **6.** 39, 50 **7.** 110, 77 **8.** 21, 160

9. Critical Thinking Suppose you divide two numbers by their greatest common factor. What is the relationship between the resulting quotients?

5. 3; not relatively prime
6. 1; relatively prime
7. 11; not relatively prime
8. 1; relatively prime
9. *Sample answer:* They have no remaining common factors except 1, so they are relatively prime.

Monomials and the GCF You can find the greatest common factor of two or more monomials by factoring each monomial.

Example 3 *Finding the GCF of Monomials*

Find the greatest common factor of $18xy^2$ and $28x^2y^2$.

Factor the monomials. The GCF is the product of the common factors.

$$18xy^2 = \boxed{2} \cdot 3 \cdot 3 \cdot \boxed{x} \cdot y \cdot y$$
$$28x^2y^2 = \boxed{2} \cdot 2 \cdot 7 \cdot \boxed{x} \cdot x \cdot y \cdot y$$

Answer The GCF is $2xy^2$.

Checkpoint

Find the greatest common factor of the monomials.

10. $6x$, $15x$ **$3x$** **11.** $20x^2$, $36x$ **$4x$** **12.** $32y^2$, $6x^2y$ **$2y$** **13.** $7xy^3$, $28xy^2$ **$7xy^2$**

4.2 Exercises

More Practice, p. 806

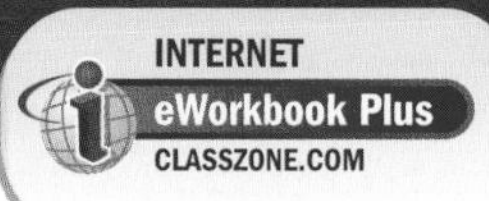

Guided Practice

Vocabulary Check

1. What does it mean for a number to be a common factor of two numbers? ***Sample answer:*** **It is a whole number that is a factor of both numbers.**

2. Find two pairs of relatively prime numbers from 5, 10, 16, and 25. **5 and 16, 16 and 25**

Skill Check

Find the greatest common factor of the numbers. Then tell whether the numbers are relatively prime.

3. 7, 28 **4.** 34, 38 **5.** 11, 51 **6.** 32, 81

3. 7; not relatively prime
4. 2; not relatively prime
5. 1; relatively prime
6. 1; relatively prime

Find the greatest common factor of the monomials.

7. $18c, 4c$ **$2c$** **8.** r, r^4 **r** **9.** $5m, 20m^3$ **$5m$** **10.** $3x^2, 15x^3$ **$3x^2$**

Guided Problem Solving

11. Art Supplies To celebrate a grand opening, the owner of an art supplies store is making free gift bags for customers. The owner has 225 pastel crayons, 75 paintbrushes, and 120 tubes of oil paint. Each gift bag must be identical. What is the greatest number of gift bags the owner can make?

(1) Write the prime factorization of each number. **$225 = 3^2 \cdot 5^2$, $75 = 3 \cdot 5^2$, $120 = 2^3 \cdot 3 \cdot 5$**

(2) What are the common prime factors of the numbers? What is the GCF of the numbers? **3 and 5; 15**

(3) What does the GCF represent in this situation? **the greatest number of gift bags the owner can make, each with 15 pastel crayons, 5 paintbrushes, and 8 tubes of oil paint**

20. 1; relatively prime
21. 11; not relatively prime
22. 3; not relatively prime
23. 1; relatively prime
24. 2; not relatively prime
25. 1; relatively prime
26. 16; not relatively prime
27. 28; not relatively prime

Practice and Problem Solving

Homework *Help*

Example	Exercises
1	12-19, 32-33
2	20-27, 34-36
3	28-31, 37-45

- More Examples
- eTutorial Plus

Find the greatest common factor of the numbers.

A **12.** 28, 42 **14** **13.** 21, 99 **3** **14.** 34, 85 **17** **15.** 12, 36 **12**

16. 32, 55 **1** **17.** 54, 89 **1** **18.** 76, 86 **2** **19.** 120, 960 **120**

Find the greatest common factor of the numbers. Then tell whether the numbers are relatively prime. **20–27. See margin.**

20. 9, 26 **21.** 11, 55 **22.** 12, 33 **23.** 77, 51

24. 58, 60 **25.** 121, 280 **26.** 64, 144 **27.** 28, 84

Find the greatest common factor of the monomials.

28. $16x, 36x$ **$4x$** **29.** $18m^2, 7m$ **m** **30.** $18k, 15k^3$ **$3k$** **31.** $2x, 8x^2, 6x^3$ **$2x$**

3 APPLY

ASSIGNMENT GUIDE

Basic Course

Day 1: pp. 179-181 Exs. 12-23, 28-32, 34-46, 53-65

Average Course

Day 1: pp. 179-181 Exs. 16-29, 32-42, 46-50, 55-66

Advanced Course

Day 1: pp. 179-181 Exs. 18-29, 32-39, 43-54*, 59-66

Block

pp. 179-181 Exs. 16-29, 32-42, 46-50, 55-66 (with 4.1)

EXTRA PRACTICE

- Student Edition, p. 806
- Chapter 4 Resource Book, pp. 19-21
- Test and Practice Generator

TRANSPARENCY

Even-numbered answers are available on transparencies.

HOMEWORK CHECK

When you review students' homework for this lesson, go over the following exercises to check understanding of key concepts.
Basic: 12, 20, 28, 32, 34
Average: 16, 22, 28, 33, 35
Advanced: 18, 24, 29, 35, 37

COMMON ERROR

In Exercises 3-6, 20-27, and 34-36 watch for students who think that the term *relatively prime* applies to a number that has just one or two factors and therefore is "almost prime."

TEACHING TIP

In Exercises 34–36, encourage students to share their techniques for finding the greatest common factor of pairs of greater numbers.

32. Music Camp A summer music camp has 88 participants. The camp has 32 vocalists, 16 drummers, 24 guitarists, and 16 bassists. What is the greatest number of identical bands that can be formed using all the participants? How many vocalists will be in each band? **8 bands; 4 vocalists**

Review Help

For help with reading circle graphs, see p. 783.

33. Flower Bouquets The science club is selling flowers for a fundraiser. The club wants to make bouquets from 4 types of flowers. The circle graph shows how many flowers of each type the club has. What is the greatest number of identical bouquets that can be made? What will each bouquet contain? **7 bouquets; 9 daisies, 8 lilies, 6 irises, 3 freesias**

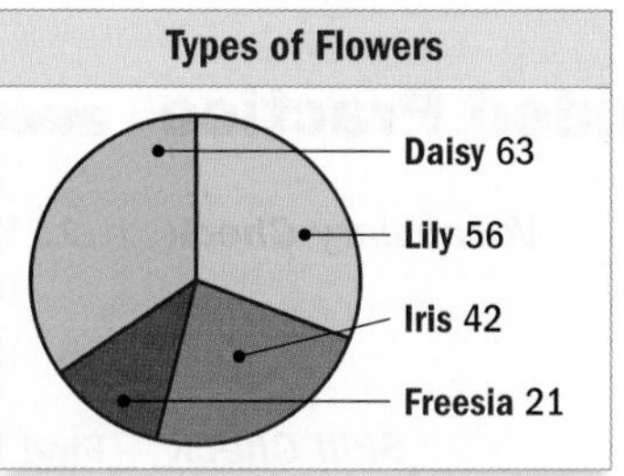

Tell whether the numbers are relatively prime.

B 34. 115, 207 **not relatively prime**

35. 224, 243 **relatively prime**

36. 152, 171 **not relatively prime**

Find the greatest common factor of the monomials.

37. $12m^2n^3$, $70m^3n$ **$2m^2n$**

38. $72a^3b^2$, $86a$ **$2a$**

39. $44m^2n$, $48mn^2$ **$4mn$**

40. a^2b^3, ab^3 **ab^3**

41. $3x$, $7xy^2$ **x**

42. $4rs^2$, $27st^3$ **s**

43. $18wx^2$, $45wx$ **$9wx$**

44. $12y^2$, $15y^3$, $5y$ **y**

45. rs^3, s^3t, r^2st^2 **s**

46. Community Garden You want to cover the walkway of a community garden with square clay tiles. The space you want to cover is a rectangle 42 inches wide by 72 inches long. Assuming you want to cover the space exactly without cutting any tiles, what is the greatest side length you can use for the tiles? **6 in.**

47. Bracelets You want to make woven plastic bracelets. You have 3 pieces of plastic lacing with lengths 45 cm, 75 cm, and 60 cm. You need to cut the lacing into pieces of the same length. What is the greatest possible length each piece can be, without any lacing being wasted? **15 cm**

48. Critical Thinking The greatest common factor of 30 and a number n is 6. Find a possible value for n. Are there other possible values for n? Explain. **See margin.**

48. *Sample answer:* 6; yes; any number that has 6 as a factor but does not have 5 also as a factor will have a greatest common factor of 6 with 30. Some other examples are 18, 24, 36, 54, and 72.

49. Extended Problem Solving In the future, scientists may want to make a unit of time that is convenient for people living on both Earth and Mars. The new unit of time, called the space-hour, should divide evenly into the number of minutes in each planet's day. Under the current Earth definition of minutes, Earth has 1440 minutes per day, and Mars has approximately 1480 minutes per day.

a. Analyze What is the greatest number of minutes that could be in a space-hour? **40 min**

b. Apply How many space-hours would there be each day on Earth? on Mars? **36 space-hours; 37 space-hours**

c. A spacecraft that uses current technology can take 210 days to travel from Earth to Mars. Use a calculator to find how long this trip would be in space-hours. **7560 space-hours**

In the **Real World**

Mars Shown above is an illustration of what a base on Mars might look like. On Mars, there are about 669 solar days in one year. Assuming each day has 1480 minutes, about how many minutes are there in one year on Mars? **990,120 min**

50. a. *Sample answer:* It is given that a is a factor of b. Also, a is the largest factor of itself, so there can be no larger factor of both a and b. Some examples are 6 and 30, with GCF 6; 15 and 45, with GCF 15; and 30 and 180, with GCF 30.

C **50.** ***Writing*** If a and b are nonzero whole numbers and a is a factor of b, what is the GCF of a and b? Explain your thinking and give three numerical examples to support your answer.

51. Critical Thinking If a and b are relatively prime numbers and b and c are relatively prime numbers, are a and c relatively prime numbers? Give examples to support your answer. See margin.

52. Challenge Consider the pattern $2x$, $6x^2$, $18x^3$, $54x^4$, ... What are the next two monomials in the pattern? What is the GCF of all the monomials in the pattern? What is the GCF of all the monomials in the pattern excluding the first monomial? $162x^5$ and $486x^6$; $2x$; $6x^2$

Mixed Review

Find the sum or difference. *(p. 779)*

53. $\frac{2}{9}+\frac{5}{9}$ $\frac{7}{9}$ **54.** $\frac{3}{7}+\frac{3}{7}$ $\frac{6}{7}$ **55.** $\frac{14}{15}-\frac{8}{15}$ $\frac{6}{15}$ **56.** $\frac{11}{20}-\frac{3}{20}$ $\frac{8}{20}$

Find the product. *(p. 780)*

57. $60\times\frac{3}{10}$ 18 **58.** $28\times\frac{1}{4}$ 7 **59.** $\frac{5}{12}\times 36$ 15 **60.** $\frac{3}{7}\times 49$ 21

Write the prime factorization of the number. *(Lesson 4.1)*

61. 125 5^3 **62.** 70 $2\cdot5\cdot7$ **63.** 52 $2^2\cdot13$ **64.** 200 $2^3\cdot5^2$

Standardized Test Practice

65. Multiple Choice Which numbers are *not* relatively prime? C

A. 32, 65 **B.** 34, 69 **C.** 63, 91 **D.** 26, 85

66. Short Response You are making first-aid kits to go camping. You have 48 bandages, 15 squares of gauze, 6 tubes of antibiotic ointment, and 6 ice packs. What is the greatest number of identical first-aid kits that you can make? How many of each item will each first-aid kit contain? 3 kits; 16 bandages, 5 squares of gauze, 2 tubes of antibiotic ointment, and 2 ice packs

Common Factor Commotion

Each number in the third column of the table is the greatest common factor of the numbers in the same row. Each number in the first two columns has exactly one digit that is different from the number above it and exactly one digit that is different from the number below it.

Copy the table and fill in each of the blanks with a number that satisfies the conditions.

First number	Second number	GCF
945	735 ?	105
645 ?	435	15
648	432	? 216
658 ?	532	14

4 ASSESS

Assessment Resources

For more assessment resources, see:
- Assessment Book
- Test and Practice Generator

Mini-Quiz

Find the greatest common factor of the numbers. Then tell whether the numbers are relatively prime.

1. 13, 31 **1; relatively prime**

2. 15, 45 **15; not relatively prime**

Find the greatest common factor of the monomials.

3. $27k^4m$, $36k^3$ $9k^3$

4. $16a^3b^2$, $72a^4b^3$ $8a^3b^2$

5. Challenge What are the next two monomials in the pattern $4a^3$, $12a^4$, $36a^5$? What is the GCF of all five monomials in the pattern? $108a^6$, $324a^7$; $4a^3$

5 FOLLOW-UP

Diagnosis/Remediation

- Study Guide in Chapter 4 Resource Book, pp. 22–23
- Tutor Place, Whole Numbers and Decimals Card 14, Fractions Card 3
- eTutorial Plus Online
- Extra Practice, p. 806
- Lesson Practice in Chapter 4 Resource Book, pp. 19–21

English Learner Support

- Spanish Study Guide
- Multi-Language Visual Glossary
- Chapter Audio Summaries CDs

Challenge

- Challenge Practice in Chapter 4 Resource Book, p. 24
- Teacher's Edition, p. 168F

51. See Additional Answers beginning on page AA1.

1 PLAN

Skill Check

Write the prime factorization of the number.

1. 40 $\quad 2^3 \cdot 5$

2. 42 $\quad 2 \cdot 3 \cdot 7$

Find the GCF of the numbers.

3. 32, 56 $\quad$ 8

4. 23, 46 $\quad$ 23

LESSON OBJECTIVE

Write equivalent fractions.

PACING

Suggested Number of Days

Basic Course: 1 day

Average Course: 1 day

Advanced Course: 1 day

Block: 0.5 block with 4.4

TEACHING RESOURCES

For a complete list of Teaching Resources, see page 168B.

TRANSPARENCY

Warm-Up Exercises for this lesson are available on a transparency.

2 TEACH

MOTIVATING THE LESSON

Have a volunteer look up the word *equivalent* in a dictionary. Use that definition to help students associate this term with the word *interchangeable*. Refer students to the two number lines to the right of the opening paragraph and show that the equivalent fractions are interchangeable.

LESSON

4.3 Equivalent Fractions

BEFORE	Now	WHY?
You wrote fractions and mixed numbers.	You'll write equivalent fractions.	So you can compare the life stages of butterflies, as in Ex. 48.

Vocabulary

equivalent fractions, p. 182

simplest form, p. 183

A *fraction* is a number of the form $\frac{a}{b}$, where a is the *numerator* and b is the *denominator*. The value of b cannot be 0.

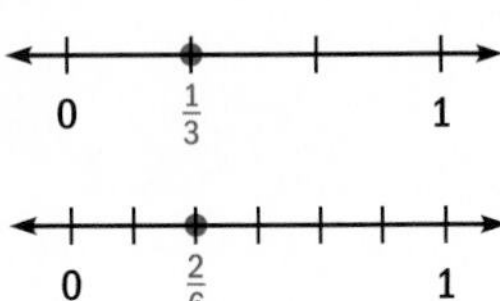

The number lines show the graphs of two fractions, $\frac{1}{3}$ and $\frac{2}{6}$. From the number lines, you can see that these fractions represent the same number. Two fractions that represent the same number are called **equivalent fractions**. You can use the following rule to write equivalent fractions.

Equivalent Fractions

Words To write equivalent fractions, multiply or divide the numerator and the denominator by the same nonzero number.

Algebra For all numbers a, b, and c, where $b \neq 0$ and $c \neq 0$,

$\frac{a}{b} = \frac{a \cdot c}{b \cdot c}$ and $\frac{a}{b} = \frac{a \div c}{b \div c}$.

Numbers $\frac{1}{3} = \frac{1 \cdot 2}{3 \cdot 2} = \frac{2}{6}$ $\qquad$ $\frac{2}{6} = \frac{2 \div 2}{6 \div 2} = \frac{1}{3}$

Example 1 *Writing Equivalent Fractions*

Write two fractions that are equivalent to $\frac{8}{12}$.

Multiply or divide the numerator and the denominator by the same nonzero number.

$\frac{8}{12} = \frac{8 \cdot 3}{12 \cdot 3} = \frac{24}{36}$ $\quad$ **Multiply numerator and denominator by 3.**

$\frac{8}{12} = \frac{8 \div 4}{12 \div 4} = \frac{2}{3}$ $\quad$ **Divide numerator and denominator by 4.**

Answer The fractions $\frac{24}{36}$ and $\frac{2}{3}$ are equivalent to $\frac{8}{12}$.

Study *Strategy*

In Example 1, there are many fractions that are equivalent to $\frac{8}{12}$ because you can multiply the numerator and the denominator by *any* nonzero number.

NCTM CURRICULUM STANDARDS

Standard 1: Understand numbers; Understand relationships among numbers; Compute fluently

Review Help

For help with modeling fractions, see p. 777.

 ***Checkpoint***

1–4. Sample answers are given.

Write two fractions that are equivalent to the given fraction.

1. $\frac{5}{10}$ $\frac{1}{2}, \frac{10}{20}$ **2.** $\frac{6}{9}$ $\frac{2}{3}, \frac{12}{18}$ **3.** $\frac{12}{20}$ $\frac{3}{5}, \frac{6}{10}$ **4.** $\frac{18}{24}$ $\frac{3}{4}, \frac{36}{48}$

Simplest Form A fraction is in **simplest form** when its numerator and its denominator are relatively prime. To write a fraction in simplest form, divide the numerator and the denominator by their GCF.

Example 2 *Writing a Fraction in Simplest Form*

Write $\frac{12}{30}$ in simplest form.

Write the prime factorizations of the numerator and denominator.

$12 = 2^2 \cdot 3$ $\quad$ $30 = 2 \cdot 3 \cdot 5$

The GCF of 12 and 30 is $2 \cdot 3 = 6$.

$\frac{12}{30} = \frac{12 \div 6}{30 \div 6}$ **Divide numerator and denominator by GCF.**

$= \frac{2}{5}$ **Simplify.**

Example 3 *Simplifying a Fraction*

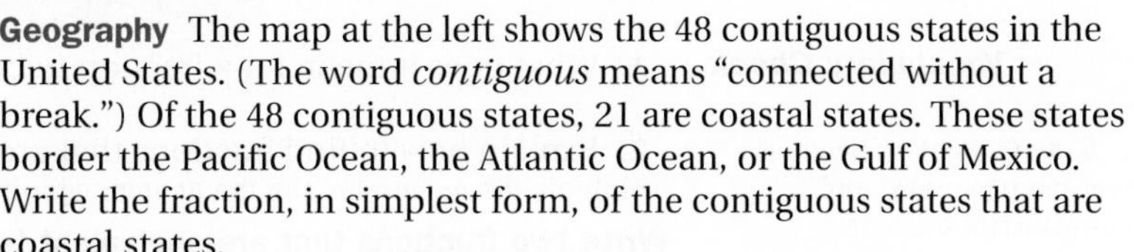

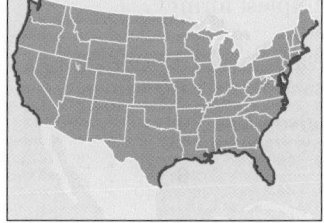

Geography The map at the left shows the 48 contiguous states in the United States. (The word *contiguous* means "connected without a break.") Of the 48 contiguous states, 21 are coastal states. These states border the Pacific Ocean, the Atlantic Ocean, or the Gulf of Mexico. Write the fraction, in simplest form, of the contiguous states that are coastal states.

Solution

$\frac{\text{Number of coastal states}}{\text{Number of contiguous states}} = \frac{21}{48}$ **Write fraction.**

$= \frac{21 \div 3}{48 \div 3}$ **Divide numerator and denominator by GCF, 3.**

$= \frac{7}{16}$ **Simplify.**

Answer Of the contiguous states, $\frac{7}{16}$ are coastal states.

 ***Checkpoint***

Write the fraction in simplest form.

5. $\frac{4}{14}$ $\frac{2}{7}$ **6.** $\frac{8}{36}$ $\frac{2}{9}$ **7.** $\frac{27}{42}$ $\frac{9}{14}$ **8.** $\frac{28}{49}$ $\frac{4}{7}$

TIPS *for* NEW TEACHERS

Be sure to stress the last sentence in the paragraph preceding Example 4 on page 184. Reinforce student's knowledge of this convention periodically as you use the book. See Tips for New Teachers in the *Chapter 4 Resource Book*.

Extra Examples

Example 1 Write two fractions that are equivalent to $\frac{15}{18}$. ***Sample answer:*** $\frac{5}{6}, \frac{30}{36}$

Example 2 Write $\frac{25}{40}$ in simplest form. $\frac{5}{8}$

Example 3 Tanika served 42 customers during the breakfast shift at a diner. Twenty-eight of the customers ordered eggs. Write the fraction, in simplest form, of customers she served who ordered eggs. $\frac{2}{3}$

 **ALGEBRAIC REASONING**

Focus students' attention on the algebraic definition of *equivalent fractions* given on page 182. Ask students to explain why the algebraic form of the definition contains the phrase "where $b \neq 0$ and $c \neq 0$."

MULTIPLE REPRESENTATIONS

On page 182, the definition of *equivalent fractions* is given in three ways: using words, algebra, and numbers. You might also consider using models, such as circles or fraction bars, to show that two fractions are equivalent.

Extra Examples

Example 4 Write $\frac{16bc^3}{24b^2c}$ in simplest form. $\frac{2c^2}{3b}$

COMMON ERROR

Watch for students who think that a fraction has not been rewritten in simplest form until the numerator is 1.

TEACHING TIP

Before discussing Example 4, remind students why the value of the denominator of a fraction cannot be 0.

CONCEPT CHECK

How do you write a fraction in simplest form? **Divide both the numerator and denominator of the fraction by their GCF.**

DAILY PUZZLER

Are the fractions $\frac{36}{64}$ and $\frac{9x}{16x}$ equivalent? Explain. **Yes. *Sample answer:* Both fractions can be simplified as the fraction $\frac{9}{16}$.**

Variable Expressions To simplify fractions that contain variables, factor the numerator and the denominator. Then divide out common factors. In this book, you should assume that any variable in the denominator of a fraction is not equal to zero.

Example 4 *Simplifying a Variable Expression*

Write $\frac{10xy}{15y^2}$ in simplest form.

$\frac{10xy}{15y^2} = \frac{2 \cdot 5 \cdot x \cdot y}{3 \cdot 5 \cdot y \cdot y}$ **Factor numerator and denominator.**

$= \frac{2 \cdot \cancel{5}^1 \cdot x \cdot \cancel{y}^1}{3 \cdot \cancel{5}_1 \cdot \cancel{y}_1 \cdot y}$ **Divide out common factors.**

$= \frac{2x}{3y}$ **Simplify.**

4.3 Exercises

More Practice, p. 806

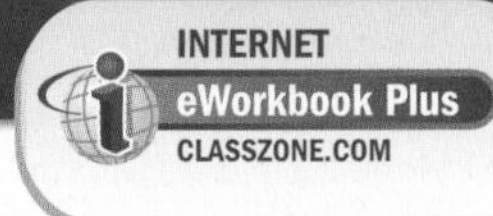

INTERNET eWorkbook Plus CLASSZONE.COM

Guided Practice

Vocabulary Check

1. What does it mean for a fraction to be in simplest form?

1. *Sample answer:* It means that the numerator and denominator have no whole number common factors other than 1.

2. Explain how to find fractions that are equivalent to $\frac{3}{7}$. ***Sample answer:* Multiply the numerator and the denominator by the same nonzero number.**

Write two fractions that are equivalent to the given fraction. **3–6. Sample answers are given.**

3. $\frac{12}{16}$ **$\frac{3}{4}, \frac{24}{32}$**
4. $\frac{15}{18}$ **$\frac{5}{6}, \frac{30}{36}$**
5. $\frac{8}{14}$ **$\frac{4}{7}, \frac{16}{28}$**
6. $\frac{10}{25}$ **$\frac{2}{5}, \frac{20}{50}$**

Write the fraction in simplest form.

7. $\frac{16}{38}$ **$\frac{8}{19}$**
8. $\frac{35}{40}$ **$\frac{7}{8}$**
9. $\frac{21a^3}{11a}$ **$\frac{21a^2}{11}$**
10. $\frac{6b}{24b^2}$ **$\frac{1}{4b}$**

Guided Problem Solving

11. **Film Ratings** The table shows the number of rated films that are owned by a film library. What fraction of the films were rated G?

Rating	G	PG	PG-13
Number of films	30	55	163

1) Find the total number of films owned by the library. **248 films**
2) Write a fraction for the number of films that were rated G. **$\frac{30}{248}$**
3) Simplify the fraction from Step 2. **$\frac{15}{124}$**

Practice and Problem Solving

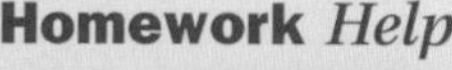

Homework Help

Example	Exercises
1	12-19
2	20-27, 41-46
3	28, 37
4	29-36

Online Resources CLASSZONE.COM
- More Examples
- eTutorial Plus

12–19. Sample answers are given.

Write two fractions that are equivalent to the given fraction.

A **12.** $\frac{6}{12}$ $\frac{1}{2}, \frac{12}{24}$ **13.** $\frac{5}{15}$ $\frac{1}{3}, \frac{10}{30}$ **14.** $\frac{14}{16}$ $\frac{7}{8}, \frac{28}{32}$ **15.** $\frac{18}{21}$ $\frac{6}{7}, \frac{36}{42}$

16. $\frac{16}{20}$ $\frac{4}{5}, \frac{32}{40}$ **17.** $\frac{3}{27}$ $\frac{1}{9}, \frac{6}{54}$ **18.** $\frac{7}{10}$ $\frac{14}{20}, \frac{21}{30}$ **19.** $\frac{5}{8}$ $\frac{10}{16}, \frac{15}{24}$

Write the fraction in simplest form.

20. $\frac{32}{36}$ $\frac{8}{9}$ **21.** $\frac{25}{35}$ $\frac{5}{7}$ **22.** $\frac{46}{72}$ $\frac{23}{36}$ **23.** $\frac{8}{30}$ $\frac{4}{15}$

24. $\frac{54}{60}$ $\frac{9}{10}$ **25.** $\frac{36}{45}$ $\frac{4}{5}$ **26.** $\frac{39}{42}$ $\frac{13}{14}$ **27.** $\frac{48}{76}$ $\frac{12}{19}$

28. Anatomy The human skeleton can be divided into two systems. The axial system has 80 bones. It consists of the skull, spine, and ribs. The appendicular system has 126 bones. It consists of the shoulders, pelvis, and limbs.

a. What fraction of the body's bones are in the axial system? Give your answer in simplest form. $\frac{40}{103}$

b. What fraction of the body's bones are in the appendicular system? Give your answer in simplest form. $\frac{63}{103}$

Write the fraction in simplest form.

29. $\frac{6a}{6a^2}$ $\frac{1}{a}$ **30.** $\frac{4mn^3}{10n^2}$ $\frac{2mn}{5}$ **31.** $\frac{27bcd}{12b}$ $\frac{9cd}{4}$ **32.** $\frac{5s^2t^2}{40st}$ $\frac{st}{8}$

33. $\frac{36w}{60w^2}$ $\frac{3}{5w}$ **34.** $\frac{42r^3}{56r^2}$ $\frac{3r}{4}$ **35.** $\frac{77x^3}{6x}$ $\frac{77x^2}{6}$ **36.** $\frac{49t^2}{7t^3}$ $\frac{7}{t}$

37. Checkers Checkers is a game for two players. A checkerboard has 64 squares. Each player begins with 12 pieces. Players capture each other's pieces.

a. What fraction of the squares hold pieces at the start of the game? $\frac{3}{8}$

b. Later in the game, one player has 5 pieces on the board. The other player has 3 pieces on the board. Now what fraction of the squares hold pieces? $\frac{1}{8}$

Use a number line to determine whether the fractions are equivalent.

38. $\frac{1}{4}, \frac{2}{10}$ no **39.** $\frac{3}{4}, \frac{14}{16}$ no **40.** $\frac{5}{8}, \frac{10}{16}$ yes

Write the fractions in simplest form. Tell whether they are equivalent.

B **41.** $\frac{12}{15}, \frac{26}{30}$ $\frac{4}{5}, \frac{13}{15}$; no **42.** $\frac{18}{20}, \frac{45}{50}$ $\frac{9}{10}, \frac{9}{10}$; yes **43.** $\frac{9}{24}, \frac{15}{48}$ $\frac{3}{8}, \frac{5}{16}$; no

44. $\frac{63}{84}, \frac{45}{60}$ $\frac{3}{4}, \frac{3}{4}$; yes **45.** $\frac{49}{63}, \frac{21}{27}$ $\frac{7}{9}, \frac{7}{9}$; yes **46.** $\frac{30}{36}, \frac{57}{72}$ $\frac{5}{6}, \frac{19}{24}$; no

47. Critical Thinking Consider the fractions $\frac{-12}{27}$, $\frac{25}{-35}$, and $\frac{-33}{-55}$. Explain how to simplify each of the fractions. See margin.

3 APPLY

ASSIGNMENT GUIDE

Basic Course
Day 1: SRH p. 777 Exs. 1-6; pp. 185-186 Exs. 12-23, 28-34, 38-47, 55-64

Average Course
Day 1: pp. 185-186 Exs. 16-28, 33-38, 44-53, 57-65

Advanced Course
Day 1: pp. 185-186 Exs. 18-28, 35-39, 44-56*, 60-65

Block
pp. 185-186 Exs. 16-28, 33-38, 44-53, 57-65 (with 4.4)

EXTRA PRACTICE
- Student Edition, p. 806
- Chapter 4 Resource Book, pp. 27-29
- Test and Practice Generator

TRANSPARENCY

Even-numbered answers are available on transparencies. A support transparency is available for Exercises 38-40.

HOMEWORK CHECK

When you review students' homework for this lesson, go over the following exercises to check understanding of key concepts.
Basic: 12, 20, 28, 29, 41
Average: 16, 21, 28, 33, 44
Advanced: 18, 22, 28, 35, 45

COMMON ERROR

In Exercise 29, watch for students who give the simplest form as $\frac{0}{a}$.

47. See Additional Answers beginning on page AA1.

4 ASSESS

ASSESSMENT RESOURCES

For more assessment resources, see:
- Assessment Book
- Test and Practice Generator

MINI-QUIZ

1. Write two fractions that are equivalent to $\frac{30}{40}$. *Sample:* $\frac{3}{4}, \frac{60}{80}$

Write the fraction in simplest form.

2. $\frac{51}{60}$ **$\frac{17}{20}$**
3. $\frac{63c^3d}{72c^2d^2}$ **$\frac{7c}{8d}$**
4. Write $\frac{15}{35}$ and $\frac{27}{63}$ in simplest form. Are they equivalent? **$\frac{3}{7}, \frac{3}{7}$; yes**
5. **Challenge** If you square the numerator and the denominator of a fraction, is the resulting fraction *sometimes*, *always*, or *never* equivalent to the original fraction? Explain. **Sometimes; the resulting fraction will only be equivalent to the original if the original numerator and denominator are equal.**

5 FOLLOW-UP

DIAGNOSIS/REMEDIATION

- Study Guide in Chapter 4 Resource Book, pp. 30–31
- Tutor Place, Fractions Cards 2, 3
- eTutorial Plus Online
- Extra Practice, p. 806
- Lesson Practice in Chapter 4 Resource Book, pp. 27–29

ENGLISH LEARNER SUPPORT

- Spanish Study Guide
- Multi-Language Visual Glossary
- Chapter Audio Summaries CDs

- Challenge Practice in Chapter 4 Resource Book, p. 32
- Teacher's Edition, p. 168F

53c. See Additional Answers beginning on page AA1.

In the Real World

Monarch Butterflies Some monarchs migrate as far as 2000 miles. If a 2000 mile migration were to last for 3.5 months, what is the average distance the monarchs would fly in 1 day? (Assume there are 30 days in a month.) **about 19 mi**

53a. $\frac{96}{216}, \frac{4}{9}$

53d. (a) $\frac{288}{864}; \frac{1}{3}$ (b) $\frac{4}{3y}; \frac{1}{3}$. *Sample answer:* The results supporting that the second method is easier are even stronger for the new values of *x* and *y*.

48. **Monarch Butterflies** Monarch butterflies go through four stages of life: egg, caterpillar, pupa, and butterfly. A regular monarch lives as a butterfly for about 5 weeks. However, migrating monarchs (born in early fall) live as butterflies for up to 30 weeks.

Length of Monarch's Life Stages in Weeks				
Monarch type	**Egg**	**Caterpillar**	**Pupa**	**Butterfly**
Regular	1	2	1	5
Migrating	1	2	1	30

a. What fraction of a regular monarch's life is spent as a butterfly? **$\frac{5}{9}$**

b. What fraction of a migrating monarch's life is spent as a butterfly? **$\frac{15}{17}$**

Tell what value of *x* makes the fractions equivalent.

49. $\frac{5}{6}, \frac{x}{24}$ **20**
50. $\frac{7}{9}, \frac{28}{x}$ **36**
51. $\frac{x}{12}, \frac{80}{192}$ **5**
52. $\frac{3}{8}, \frac{2+x}{32}$ **10**

C 53. **Critical Thinking** Consider the expression $\frac{8x^2y}{6x^2y^2}$.

a. First evaluate the expression when $x = 2$ and $y = 3$. Then simplify.

b. Now return to the original expression. First simplify the expression. Then evaluate it when $x = 2$ and $y = 3$. **$\frac{4}{3y}; \frac{4}{9}$**

c. **Analyze** Compare your results from parts (a) and (b). Which method requires less work? Explain your answer. **See margin.**

d. **Analyze** Now repeat parts (a) and (b) with the values $x = 3$ and $y = 4$. Compare your results.

54. **Challenge** Does *adding* the same nonzero number to the numerator and denominator of a fraction produce an equivalent fraction? If so, explain why. If not, tell whether it *ever* produces an equivalent fraction. **no; only if the original fraction is equivalent to 1**

Mixed Review

Evaluate the expression when $x = 4$ and $y = -9$. *(Lesson 1.4)*

55. $|x| + |y|$ **13**
56. $|-19| + |y|$ **28**
57. $x + |-14|$ **18**

Identify the property that the statement illustrates. *(Lesson 2.1)*

58. $n + p = p + n$ **commutative property of addition**
59. $1 \cdot \frac{5}{6} = \frac{5}{6}$ **identity property of multiplication**
60. $16 + 0 = 16$ **identity property of addition**

Find the greatest common factor of the monomials. *(Lesson 4.2)*

61. $2x, 8x^2$ **$2x$**
62. $9m^2, 27m^3$ **$9m^2$**
63. $10r, 25r^4$ **$5r$**

Standardized Test Practice

64. **Multiple Choice** Which fraction is *not* equivalent to $\frac{39}{52}$? **D**

A. $\frac{36}{48}$ **B.** $\frac{3}{4}$ **C.** $\frac{78}{104}$ **D.** $\frac{31}{42}$

65. **Multiple Choice** Which fraction is *not* in simplest form? **F**

F. $\frac{13}{65}$ **G.** $\frac{8}{17}$ **H.** $\frac{9}{16}$ **I.** $\frac{15}{37}$

LESSON

4.4 Least Common Multiple

BEFORE	Now	WHY?
You found the GCF of two numbers.	You'll find the least common multiple of two numbers.	So you can design a fitness schedule, as in Ex. 38.

Vocabulary

multiple, p. 187
common multiple, p. 187
least common multiple (LCM), p. 187
least common denominator (LCD), p. 188

Agriculture Crop rotation is a system in which farmers vary the crops they plant in their fields each year. Suppose a farmer grows alfalfa in a certain field every 6 years. In another field, the farmer grows alfalfa every 10 years. This year, the farmer is growing alfalfa in both fields. In how many years will the farmer grow alfalfa in both fields again?

A **multiple** of a whole number is the product of the number and any nonzero whole number. A multiple that is shared by two or more numbers is a **common multiple**. Some of the common multiples of 8 and 12 are shown in blue below.

Multiples of 8: 8, 16, 24, 32, 40, 48, 56, 64, 72, 80, . . .

Multiples of 12: 12, 24, 36, 48, 60, 72, 84, 96, . . .

The least of the common multiples of two or more numbers is the **least common multiple (LCM)**. The LCM of 8 and 12 is 24.

Example 1 *Finding the Least Common Multiple*

For the crop rotation system described above, the number of years until the farmer grows alfalfa in both fields again is given by the LCM of 6 and 10. You can use one of two methods to find the LCM.

Method 1 List the multiples of each number. Identify the least number that is on both lists.

Multiples of 6: 6, 12, 18, 24, (30), 36, 42, 48, 54, 60

Multiples of 10: 10, 20, (30), 40, 50, 60

The LCM of 6 and 10 is 30.

Method 2 Find the common factors of the numbers.

$6 = 2 \cdot 3$

$10 = 2 \cdot 5$

The common factor is 2.

Multiply all of the factors, using each common factor only once.

$\text{LCM} = 2 \cdot 3 \cdot 5 = 30$

Answer The farmer will grow alfalfa in both fields again in 30 years.

Checkpoint

Find the least common multiple of the numbers.

1. 16, 24 48 **2.** 20, 25 100 **3.** 6, 8, 20 120 **4.** 15, 30, 50 150

NCTM CURRICULUM STANDARDS

Standard 1: Understand relationships among numbers; Compute fluently

Standard 2: Understand patterns

1 PLAN

Skill Check

Write the first five multiples of the number.

1. 7 **7, 14, 21, 28, 35**
2. 9 **9, 18, 27, 36, 45**
3. 11 **11, 22, 33, 44, 55**
4. 15 **15, 30, 45, 60, 75**

Lesson Objective

Find the least common multiple of two numbers.

Pacing

Suggested Number of Days
Basic Course: 1 day
Average Course: 1 day
Advanced Course: 1 day
Block: 0.5 block with 4.3

Teaching Resources

For a complete list of Teaching Resources, see page 168B.

Transparency

Warm-Up Exercises for this lesson are available on a transparency.

2 TEACH

Motivating the Lesson

Before they open their textbooks, ask students to choose two numbers less than 20 and then have them write the products of each number and the first 10 whole numbers. Instruct students to count how many of the products in the two lists are the same.

TIPS *for* NEW TEACHERS
Make sure students recognize that the least common multiple of two numbers is either greater than both numbers, or it is the same as the greater of the two numbers. Contrast this with the greatest common factor, which is either less than both numbers or is the same as the lesser number. See Tips for New Teachers in the *Chapter 4 Resource Book*.

Extra Examples

Example 1 One brand of hot dogs is sold in packages of 6. One brand of hot dog buns is sold in packages of 8. What is the least number of hot dogs Kimberly can buy and be able to buy an equal number of hot dog buns? **24 hot dogs (4 packages)**

Example 2 Find the least common multiple of $4g^3h^2$ and $15g^2h^4$. $\mathbf{60g^3h^4}$

Example 3 Last year, a poll of 1200 students found that 300 spoke a first language other than English. This year, a poll of 10,000 students found that 4000 spoke a first language other than English. In which year was the fraction of non-English first language speakers greater? **this year**

COMMON ERROR
Occasionally the least common multiple of two numbers is the product of the numbers, but emphasize to students that this is not always true. Point out that this is only true when the two numbers are relatively prime.

Study *Strategy*

In Example 2, notice that the LCM of the two monomials includes the higher power of each variable, as well as the higher power of each prime number factor.

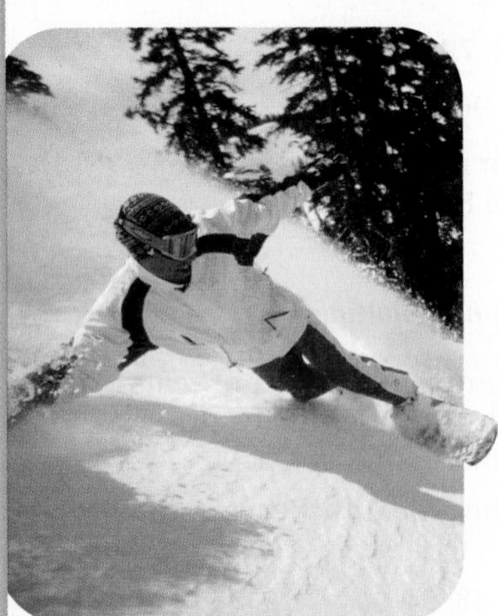

Example 2 ***Finding the Least Common Multiple of Monomials***

Find the least common multiple of $9xy^2$ and $15x^2y$.

$$9xy^2 = 3 \cdot 3 \cdot x \cdot y \cdot y$$
$$15x^2y = 3 \cdot 5 \cdot x \cdot x \cdot y$$
$$\text{LCM} = 3 \cdot x \cdot y \cdot 3 \cdot 5 \cdot x \cdot y = 45x^2y^2$$

Common factors are circled and used only once in the LCM.

Answer The least common multiple of $9xy^2$ and $15x^2y$ is $45x^2y^2$.

Least Common Denominator The **least common denominator (LCD)** of two or more fractions is the least common multiple of the denominators. You can use the LCD to compare and order fractions.

Example 3 ***Comparing Fractions Using the LCD***

Winter Sports Last year, a winter resort had 144,000 visitors, including 45,000 snowboarders. This year, the resort had 160,000 visitors, including 56,000 snowboarders. In which year was the fraction of snowboarders greater?

Solution

1) Write the fractions and simplify.

Last year: $\frac{\text{Number of snowboarders}}{\text{Total number of visitors}} = \frac{45{,}000}{144{,}000} = \frac{5}{16}$

This year: $\frac{\text{Number of snowboarders}}{\text{Total number of visitors}} = \frac{56{,}000}{160{,}000} = \frac{7}{20}$

2) Find the LCD of $\frac{5}{16}$ and $\frac{7}{20}$.

The LCM of 16 and 20 is 80. So, the LCD of the fractions is 80.

3) Write equivalent fractions using the LCD.

Last year: $\frac{5}{16} = \frac{5 \cdot 5}{16 \cdot 5} = \frac{25}{80}$ **This year:** $\frac{7}{20} = \frac{7 \cdot 4}{20 \cdot 4} = \frac{28}{80}$

4) Compare the numerators: $\frac{25}{80} < \frac{28}{80}$, so $\frac{5}{16} < \frac{7}{20}$.

Answer The fraction of snowboarders was greater this year.

Checkpoint

Find the least common multiple of the monomials.

5. $15x^2, 27x$ $\mathbf{135x^2}$ **6.** $6m^2, 10m^3$ $\mathbf{30m^3}$ **7.** $14ab, 21bc$ **42*abc*** **8.** $r^2, 5rst$ $\mathbf{5r^2st}$

Use the LCD to determine which fraction is greater.

9. $\frac{5}{6}, \frac{7}{9}$ $\mathbf{\frac{5}{6}}$ **10.** $\frac{5}{8}, \frac{13}{20}$ $\mathbf{\frac{13}{20}}$ **11.** $\frac{7}{12}, \frac{11}{15}$ $\mathbf{\frac{11}{15}}$ **12.** $\frac{5}{16}, \frac{3}{10}$ $\mathbf{\frac{5}{16}}$

Review *Help*

For help with writing mixed numbers as improper fractions, see p. 778.

Example 4 ***Ordering Fractions and Mixed Numbers***

Order the numbers $3\frac{4}{15}$, $\frac{33}{10}$, and $\frac{19}{6}$ from least to greatest.

1. Write the mixed number as an improper fraction.

$$3\frac{4}{15} = \frac{3 \cdot 15 + 4}{15} = \frac{49}{15}$$

2. Find the LCD of $\frac{49}{15}$, $\frac{33}{10}$, and $\frac{19}{6}$.

The LCM of 15, 10, and 6 is 30. So, the LCD is 30.

3. Write equivalent fractions using the LCD.

$$\frac{49}{15} = \frac{49 \cdot 2}{15 \cdot 2} = \frac{98}{30} \qquad \frac{33}{10} = \frac{33 \cdot 3}{10 \cdot 3} = \frac{99}{30} \qquad \frac{19}{6} = \frac{19 \cdot 5}{6 \cdot 5} = \frac{95}{30}$$

4. Compare the numerators.

$$\frac{95}{30} < \frac{98}{30} \text{ and } \frac{98}{30} < \frac{99}{30}, \text{ so } \frac{19}{6} < \frac{49}{15} \text{ and } \frac{49}{15} < \frac{33}{10}.$$

Answer From least to greatest, the numbers are $\frac{19}{6}$, $3\frac{4}{15}$, and $\frac{33}{10}$.

4.4 Exercises

More Practice, p. 806

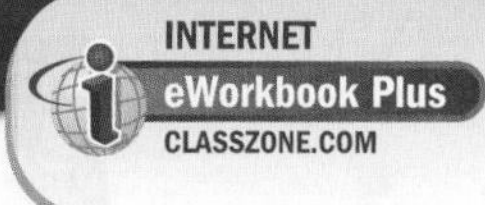

Guided Practice

Vocabulary Check

1. How are the terms *least common multiple* and *least common denominator* related? ***Sample answer:*** **The least common denominator of two or more fractions is the least common multiple of the denominators of the fractions.**
2. Describe how you would use the LCD to compare $\frac{4}{7}$ and $\frac{7}{12}$. **See margin.**

Skill Check

Find the least common multiple of the numbers.

3. 3, 4 **12**
4. 4, 8 **8**
5. 18, 24 **72**
6. 10, 16 **80**

Find the least common multiple of the monomials.

7. $3s, s^2$ **$3s^2$**
8. x^4, x^2 **x^4**
9. $15m^2, 9m$ **$45m^2$**
10. $8b, 20b^2$ **$40b^2$**

Use the LCD to determine which fraction is greater.

11. $\frac{3}{4}, \frac{5}{8}$ **$\frac{3}{4}$**
12. $\frac{2}{3}, \frac{13}{16}$ **$\frac{13}{16}$**
13. $\frac{2}{5}, \frac{3}{8}$ **$\frac{2}{5}$**
14. $\frac{3}{4}, \frac{7}{10}$ **$\frac{3}{4}$**
15. **Error Analysis** Describe and correct the error in finding the LCM of 16 and 30.

X $16 = 2^4$ $\quad 30 = 2 \cdot 3 \cdot 5$

$\text{LCM} = 2^5 \cdot 3 \cdot 5 = 480$

15. ***Sample answer:*** **When you write the product you will compute to find the LCM, you use the power of each prime factor with the greatest exponent that it has in the given numbers. The power of 2 is 2^4, not 2^5; so the LCM is $2^4 \cdot 3 \cdot 5 = 240$.**

Reading Strategy

After students work Example 2, draw their attention to both the Study Strategy to the left of the example and the tip inside the box in Example 2. Discuss these two comments and how the example reflects both of them.

Extra Examples

Example 4 Order the numbers $2\frac{7}{8}$, $2\frac{5}{6}$, and $\frac{23}{10}$ from least to greatest. **$\frac{23}{10}$, $2\frac{5}{6}$, $2\frac{7}{8}$**

Differentiating Instruction

Alternative Teaching Strategy
In Example 4, some students may wish to change the improper fractions to mixed numbers in the first step. Once they determine that the whole number parts of the three mixed numbers are the same, they can proceed to compare just the fractional parts to order the numbers.

Concept Check

How do you find the least common multiple of two numbers? ***Sample answer:*** **Write the prime factorization of both numbers, identify any common factors, and then multiply all of the factors, using each common factor only once.**

Daily Puzzler

What is the least common multiple of three numbers that are relatively prime? **the product of the three numbers**

2. See Additional Answers beginning on page AA1.

3 APPLY

ASSIGNMENT GUIDE

Basic Course

Day 1: SRH p. 778 Exs. 1-5; pp. 190-191 Exs. 16-23, 28-36, 39-50, 56-66, 71-80

Average Course

Day 1: pp. 190-191 Exs. 20-38, 43-57, 64-69, 73-81

Advanced Course

Day 1: pp. 190-191 Exs. 24-38, 43-50, 55-72*, 77-81

Block

pp. 190-191 Exs. 20-38, 43-57, 64-69, 73-81 (with 4.3)

EXTRA PRACTICE

- Student Edition, p. 806
- Chapter 4 Resource Book, pp. 36-38
- Test and Practice Generator

TRANSPARENCY

Even-numbered answers are available on transparencies.

HOMEWORK CHECK

When you review students' homework for this lesson, go over the following exercises to check understanding of key concepts.

Basic: 16, 28, 36, 39, 47

Average: 20, 30, 36, 43, 49

Advanced: 24, 32, 38, 45, 50

TEACHING TIP

In Exercises 18 and 24, remind students that the LCM can be one of the numbers.

47-54. See Additional Answers beginning on page AA1.

Practice and Problem Solving

Homework *Help*

Example	Exercises
1	16-27, 36, 38
2	28-35
3	39-46
4	47-54

Online Resources
CLASSZONE.COM
- More Examples
- eTutorial Plus

37. No. *Sample answer:* You can multiply any common multiple that you can find by a whole number greater than 1 to find an even greater common multiple.

55. 25. *Sample answer:* The prime factorization of 12 is $2^2 \cdot 3$. The only additional factor needed is 5^2 to obtain the product $2^2 \cdot 3 \cdot 5^2$ for the LCM 300. Therefore, 5^2 or 25 is the least number that meets the requirements.

Find the least common multiple of the numbers.

A **16.** 9, 12 **36** **17.** 3, 8 **24** **18.** 4, 16 **16** **19.** 10, 15 **30**

20. 21, 14 **42** **21.** 30, 36 **180** **22.** 55, 15 **165** **23.** 42, 66 **462**

24. 3, 6, 12 **12** **25.** 8, 11, 36 **792** **26.** 10, 12, 14 **420** **27.** 16, 20, 30 **240**

Find the least common multiple of the monomials.

28. $5a^2, 16a^3$ $\mathbf{80a^3}$ **29.** $21w, 9w^2$ $\mathbf{63w^2}$ **30.** $17b^2, 3b^3$ $\mathbf{51b^3}$ **31.** $14x^4, 21x^2$ $\mathbf{42x^4}$

32. $60s^4, 24s^3$ $\mathbf{120s^4}$ **33.** $2n^3, 8n^2$ $\mathbf{8n^3}$ **34.** $25a, 40a^2$ $\mathbf{200a^2}$ **35.** $11s, 33s^2$ $\mathbf{33s^2}$

36. Visual Patterns In the first pattern shown below, the green star repeats every 6 figures. In the second pattern, the green star repeats every 8 figures. How many figures after the first figure will both patterns have a green star? **24 figures**

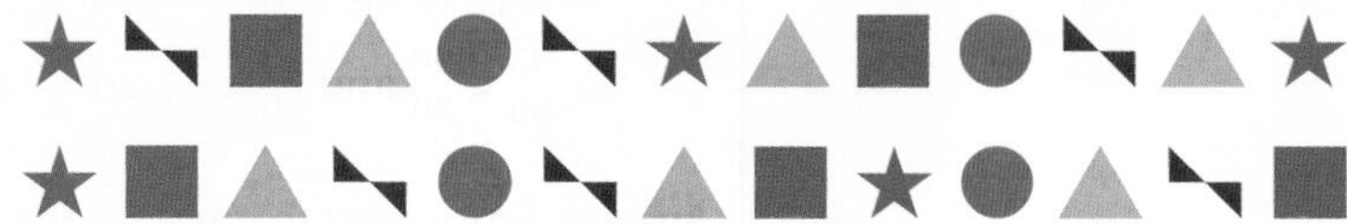

37. *Writing* Could you find the *greatest* common multiple of two numbers? Explain your thinking.

38. Fitness You lift weights every third day and take karate class every Monday. Today you have karate and are lifting weights. In how many days will you next lift weights and have karate on the same day? **21 days**

Use the LCD to determine which fraction is greater.

39. $\frac{1}{4}, \frac{2}{7}$ $\mathbf{\frac{2}{7}}$ **40.** $\frac{2}{3}, \frac{5}{8}$ $\mathbf{\frac{2}{3}}$ **41.** $\frac{7}{10}, \frac{11}{15}$ $\mathbf{\frac{11}{15}}$ **42.** $\frac{3}{5}, \frac{6}{11}$ $\mathbf{\frac{3}{5}}$

43. $\frac{5}{12}, \frac{4}{15}$ $\mathbf{\frac{5}{12}}$ **44.** $\frac{7}{20}, \frac{9}{25}$ $\mathbf{\frac{9}{25}}$ **45.** $\frac{5}{18}, \frac{8}{21}$ $\mathbf{\frac{8}{21}}$ **46.** $\frac{11}{42}, \frac{20}{63}$ $\mathbf{\frac{20}{63}}$

Order the numbers from least to greatest. **47–54. See margin.**

B **47.** $\frac{7}{6}, \frac{11}{9}, 1\frac{1}{3}$ **48.** $\frac{13}{4}, 3\frac{1}{2}, \frac{27}{8}$ **49.** $\frac{8}{15}, \frac{1}{5}, \frac{3}{10}$ **50.** $\frac{5}{11}, \frac{14}{33}, \frac{9}{22}$

51. $\frac{3}{4}, \frac{4}{9}, \frac{7}{15}$ **52.** $\frac{5}{6}, \frac{7}{10}, \frac{11}{15}$ **53.** $\frac{12}{5}, 2\frac{5}{12}, \frac{43}{18}$ **54.** $1\frac{1}{3}, \frac{10}{7}, 1\frac{13}{33}$

55. Critical Thinking What is the least number for which the LCM of the number and 12 is 300? Explain your thinking.

Find the least common multiple of the monomials.

56. $24de^2, 36d^3e$ $\mathbf{72d^3e^2}$ **57.** $x^3y, 15xy^5$ $\mathbf{15x^3y^5}$ **58.** $10a^2b^2, 20ab$ $\mathbf{20a^2b^2}$ **59.** $45gh^3, 33g^4h$ $\mathbf{495g^4h^3}$

60. xyz^3, x^2yz^2 $\mathbf{x^2yz^3}$ **61.** $26ab^2, 28ac^3$ $\mathbf{364ab^2c^3}$ **62.** $11rst, 15r^3t^2$ $\mathbf{165r^3st^2}$ **63.** $30df^2, 40d^3ef$ $\mathbf{120d^3ef^2}$

64. Vice Presidents During the period 1800–1900, 6 out of 23 U.S. Vice Presidents later became U.S. Presidents. During the period 1901–2000, 7 out of 21 Vice Presidents later became Presidents. During which period did a greater fraction of Vice Presidents become Presidents? **1901–2000**

In Exercises 65–68, rewrite the variable expressions with a common denominator.

Example *Rewriting Variable Expressions*

To rewrite $\frac{2a}{5b}$ and $\frac{3}{4ab^2}$ with a common denominator, first find the LCD of the fractions.

The LCM of $5b$ and $4ab^2$ is $20ab^2$. So, the LCD is $20ab^2$.

Then write equivalent fractions using the LCD.

$$\frac{2a}{5b} = \frac{2a \cdot 4ab}{5b \cdot 4ab} = \frac{8a^2b}{20ab^2} \qquad \frac{3}{4ab^2} = \frac{3 \cdot 5}{4ab^2 \cdot 5} = \frac{15}{20ab^2}$$

65. $\frac{x}{3}, \frac{x}{4}$ $\frac{4x}{12}, \frac{3x}{12}$ **66.** $\frac{x}{6y}, \frac{y}{8x}$ $\frac{4x^2}{24xy}, \frac{3y^2}{24xy}$ **67.** $\frac{3x}{4y^2}, \frac{2}{5xy}$ $\frac{15x^2}{20xy^2}, \frac{8y}{20xy^2}$ **68.** $\frac{3x}{2yz}, \frac{5y}{4xz}$ $\frac{6x^2}{4xyz}, \frac{5y^2}{4xyz}$

C **69. Critical Thinking** Let a and b represent nonzero whole numbers. Find a fraction $\frac{a}{b}$ such that $\frac{1}{6} < \frac{a}{b}, \frac{a}{b} < \frac{2}{7}$, and $b < 30$. *Sample answer:* $\frac{1}{4}$

70. Row 1: $2 \cdot 3$, $2 \cdot 3^2$; 18; 6; 108; 108; Row 2: $3 \cdot 5$, $5 \cdot 7$; 105; 5; 525; 525; Row 3: $2 \cdot 3$, $2^2 \cdot 5$; 60; 2; 120; 120; Row 4: $2^2 \cdot 3$, $2^2 \cdot 3 \cdot 5$; 60; 12; 720; 720; the product of the LCM and GCF equals the product of a and b.

70. Challenge Copy and complete the table for the given values of a and b. Describe any relationships you notice between the product of the LCM and the GCF and the product of a and b.

Given numbers	Prime factorizations	LCM	GCF	LCM • GCF	a • b
$a = 6, b = 18$	?	?	?	?	?
$a = 15, b = 35$	?	?	?	?	?
$a = 6, b = 20$	?	?	?	?	?
$a = 12, b = 60$	?	?	?	?	?

Mixed Review

Evaluate the expression when $n = 5$. *(Lesson 1.2)*

71. n^2 25 **72.** n^3 125 **73.** n^4 625 **74.** n^5 3125

Write the prime factorization of the number. *(Lesson 4.1)*

75. 28 $2^2 \cdot 7$ **76.** 39 $3 \cdot 13$ **77.** 81 3^4 **78.** 165 $3 \cdot 5 \cdot 11$

79. Cookies You are making gift boxes filled with cookies to give to friends. You have 64 peanut butter cookies, 80 chocolate chip cookies, and 56 sugar cookies. What is the greatest number of identical gift boxes that you can make? *(Lesson 4.2)* **8 gift boxes**

Standardized Test Practice

80. Multiple Choice Which expression is the least common multiple of the monomials $27w^4z$ and $75w^2z^2$? D

A. $3w^2z$ **B.** $75w^4z^2$ **C.** $675w^2z$ **D.** $675w^4z^2$

81. Multiple Choice Which list shows the fractions in order from least to greatest? H

F. $\frac{2}{9}, \frac{1}{6}, \frac{4}{25}$ **G.** $\frac{3}{7}, \frac{11}{24}, \frac{9}{21}$ **H.** $\frac{7}{20}, \frac{3}{8}, \frac{5}{12}$ **I.** $\frac{2}{5}, \frac{19}{40}, \frac{21}{45}$

4 ASSESS

Assessment Resources

For more assessment resources, see:
- Assessment Book
- Test and Practice Generator

Mini-Quiz

1. Find the least common multiple of 8 and 56. **56**
2. Find the least common multiple of $12x^2y^4$ and $15xy^2$. $60x^2y^4$
3. Use the LCD to determine which fraction is greater, $\frac{3}{5}$ or $\frac{5}{11}$. $\frac{3}{5}$
4. **Challenge** Rewrite the variable expressions $\frac{2s^3}{7r^2t^4}$ and $\frac{5r^2t}{9s^2}$ with a common denominator. $\frac{18s^5}{63r^2s^2t^4}, \frac{35r^4t^5}{63r^2s^2t^4}$

5 FOLLOW-UP

Diagnosis/Remediation

- Study Guide in Chapter 4 Resource Book, pp. 39–40
- Tutor Place, Fractions Cards 2, 4, 10
- eTutorial Plus Online
- Extra Practice, p. 806
- Lesson Practice in Chapter 4 Resource Book, pp. 36–38

English Learner Support

- Spanish Study Guide
- Multi-Language Visual Glossary
- Chapter Audio Summaries CDs

Challenge

- Challenge Practice in Chapter 4 Resource Book, p. 41
- Teacher's Edition, p. 168F

Additional Resources

The following resources are available to help review the materials in Lessons 4.1–4.4.

Chapter 4 Resource Book
- Lesson Practice
- Study Guide

Assessment Book
- Chapter 4 Quiz 1

Technology
- Test and Practice Generator
- eTutorial CD-ROM

Internet
- Classzone
- eWorkbook Plus Online
- eTutorial Plus Online

English Learner Support

- Spanish Study Guide
- Multi-Language Visual Glossary
- Chapter Audio Summaries CDs

Mid-Chapter Quiz

Tell whether the number is *prime* or *composite*. If it is composite, write its prime factorization using exponents.

1. 46 composite; $2 \cdot 23$ **2.** 57 composite; $3 \cdot 19$ **3.** 61 prime **4.** 89 prime

Factor the monomial.

5. $25m^3$ $5 \cdot 5 \cdot m \cdot m \cdot m$ **6.** $14n^4$ $2 \cdot 7 \cdot n \cdot n \cdot n \cdot n$ **7.** $19a^2b$ $19 \cdot a \cdot a \cdot b$ **8.** $64f^2g^2$ $2 \cdot 2 \cdot 2 \cdot 2 \cdot 2 \cdot 2 \cdot f \cdot f \cdot g \cdot g$

Find the greatest common factor of the numbers. Then tell whether the numbers are relatively prime.

9. 9, 16 1; relatively prime **10.** 12, 51 3; not relatively prime **11.** 18, 49 1; relatively prime **12.** 56, 75 1; relatively prime

13. Soccer A soccer league has 180 members. The league consists of 24 eight-year-olds, 96 nine-year-olds, and 60 ten-year-olds. You want to divide the members into teams that have the same number of eight-year-olds, nine-year-olds, and ten-year-olds. What is the greatest number of teams that can be formed? How many ten-year-olds will be on each team? 12 teams; 5 ten-year-olds

Write the fraction in simplest form.

14. $\frac{18}{48}$ $\frac{3}{8}$ **15.** $\frac{42}{81}$ $\frac{14}{27}$ **16.** $\frac{32a}{8a^2}$ $\frac{4}{a}$ **17.** $\frac{15b}{39b^4}$ $\frac{5}{13b^3}$

Find the least common multiple of the numbers.

18. 4, 11 44 **19.** 10, 24 120 **20.** 15, 45 45 **21.** 30, 54 270

Use the LCD to determine which fraction is greater.

22. $\frac{3}{8}, \frac{4}{9}$ $\frac{4}{9}$ **23.** $\frac{7}{10}, \frac{18}{25}$ $\frac{18}{25}$ **24.** $\frac{5}{12}, \frac{9}{20}$ $\frac{9}{20}$ **25.** $\frac{11}{18}, \frac{13}{24}$ $\frac{11}{18}$

Fraction Scramble

Rearrange the numerators and denominators in the five fractions shown to create five new fractions that are all equivalent to each other. Numerators can become denominators and vice versa. The question mark can be any positive integer. $\frac{40}{24}, \frac{25}{15}, \frac{115}{69}, \frac{70}{42}, \frac{55}{33}$

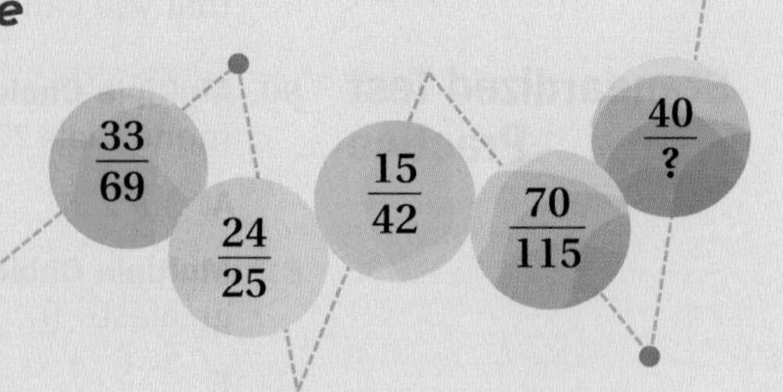

Concept *Activity*

4.5 Finding Rules of Exponents

Goal
Use patterns to discover rules for multiplying and dividing powers.

Materials
- pencil
- paper

Investigate

Use patterns to discover rules for multiplying and dividing powers.

Copy and complete each table.

Products			
Expression	Expression written as repeated multiplication	Number of factors	Product as a power
$2^4 \cdot 2^3$	$(2 \cdot 2 \cdot 2 \cdot 2) \cdot (2 \cdot 2 \cdot 2)$	7	2^7
$3^1 \cdot 3^4$	$(3) \cdot (3 \cdot 3 \cdot 3 \cdot 3)$	? 5	$3^?$ 5
$5^2 \cdot 5^4$	? $(5 \cdot 5) \cdot (5 \cdot 5 \cdot 5 \cdot 5)$	? 6	? 5^6

Quotients				
Expression	Expression written as repeated multiplication	Simplified expression	Number of factors	Quotient as a power
$\frac{2^8}{2^3}$	$\frac{2 \cdot 2 \cdot 2 \cdot 2 \cdot 2 \cdot \cancel{2}^1 \cdot \cancel{2}^1 \cdot \cancel{2}^1}{\cancel{2}_1 \cdot \cancel{2}_1 \cdot \cancel{2}_1}$	$2 \cdot 2 \cdot 2 \cdot 2 \cdot 2$	5	2^5
$\frac{3^5}{3^3}$	?	? $3 \cdot 3$	? 2	$3^?$ 2
$\frac{5^7}{5^6}$	?	? 5	? 1	? 5^1

Row 2: $\frac{3 \cdot 3 \cdot \cancel{3}^1 \cdot \cancel{3}^1 \cdot \cancel{3}^1}{\cancel{3}_1 \cdot \cancel{3}_1 \cdot \cancel{3}_1}$; Row 3: $\frac{5 \cdot \cancel{5}^1 \cdot \cancel{5}^1 \cdot \cancel{5}^1 \cdot \cancel{5}^1 \cdot \cancel{5}^1 \cdot \cancel{5}^1}{\cancel{5}_1 \cdot \cancel{5}_1 \cdot \cancel{5}_1 \cdot \cancel{5}_1 \cdot \cancel{5}_1 \cdot \cancel{5}_1}$

Draw Conclusions

1. **Critical Thinking** In the *Products* table, how are the exponents in the first and last columns related? **The exponents in the last column are the sums of the exponents in the corresponding rows of the first columns.**
2. Use your answer to Exercise 1 to write the product $10^7 \cdot 10^4$ as a power. 10^{11}
3. **Critical Thinking** In the *Quotients* table, how are the exponents in the first and last columns related? **The exponents in the last column are the differences of the exponents in the corresponding rows of the first columns.**
4. Use your answer to Exercise 3 to write the quotient $\frac{6^9}{6^7}$ as a power. 6^2

NCTM CURRICULUM STANDARDS
Standard 1: Understand how operations are related
Standard 2: Understand patterns

1 PLAN

Investigate the Concept

- Students will use patterns to discover rules for multiplying and dividing powers.
- This activity leads into the study of the product of powers and quotient of powers properties in Lesson 4.5.

Materials

Each student will need pencil and paper. See the Activity Support Master in the *Chapter 4 Resource Book*.

Recommended Time

Work activity: 10 min
Discuss results: 5 min

Grouping

Students should work individually.

2 TEACH

Tips for Success

In the second row of both tables, point out the question mark shown as the exponent in the right-hand column. Make sure students do not misread this as the number 7.

3 CLOSE

Key Discovery

The exponent of the product of two like powers is found by adding the exponents of the powers. The exponent of the quotient of two like powers is found by subtracting the exponents of the powers.

Assessment

1. What is $2^5 \cdot 2^3$ as a power? 2^8
2. What is $2^5 \div 2^3$ as a power? 2^2

1 PLAN

Skill Check

1. $6 + 7 = \underline{?}$ 13
2. $14 - 6 = \underline{?}$ 8
3. $6 \cdot 5 = \underline{?}$ 30

Write the fraction in simplest form.

4. $\frac{12}{28}$ $\frac{3}{7}$
5. $\frac{24}{45}$ $\frac{8}{15}$

LESSON OBJECTIVE

Multiply and divide powers.

PACING

Suggested Number of Days
Basic Course: 1 day
Average Course: 1 day
Advanced Course: 1 day
Block: 0.5 block with 4.6

TEACHING RESOURCES

For a complete list of Teaching Resources, see page 168B.

TRANSPARENCY

Warm-Up Exercises for this lesson are available on a transparency.

2 TEACH

MOTIVATING THE LESSON

After discussing the algebraic statement at the beginning of the lesson showing that $a^4 \cdot a^3 = a^7$, encourage students to substitute a few values for a to satisfy themselves that the statement is true.

LESSON **4.5**

Rules *of* Exponents

BEFORE	*Now*	WHY?
You evaluated powers.	You'll multiply and divide powers.	So you can estimate the number of stars, as in Ex. 58.

Review Vocabulary
power, p. 10
exponent, p. 10
base, p. 10

Notice what happens when you multiply two powers with the same base.

$$a^4 \cdot a^3 = \underbrace{(\overbrace{a \cdot a \cdot a \cdot a}^{\text{4 factors}}) \cdot (\overbrace{a \cdot a \cdot a}^{\text{3 factors}})}_{\text{7 factors}} = a^{4+3} = a^7$$

This example suggests a rule for multiplying powers with the same base.

Product of Powers Property

Words To multiply powers with the same base, add their exponents.

Algebra $a^m \cdot a^n = a^{m+n}$ **Numbers** $4^3 \cdot 4^2 = 4^{3+2} = 4^5$

Example 1 *Using the Product of Powers Property*

Lake Powell Lake Powell, the reservoir behind the Glen Canyon Dam in Arizona, can hold about 10^{12} cubic feet of water when full. There are about 10^{27} water molecules in 1 cubic foot of water. About how many water molecules can the reservoir hold?

Solution

Number of water molecules in reservoir	=	Cubic feet of water in reservoir	•	Number of water molecules in a cubic foot

$= 10^{12} \cdot 10^{27}$ **Substitute values.**

$= 10^{12+27}$ **Product of powers property**

$= 10^{39}$ **Add exponents.**

Answer Lake Powell can hold about 10^{39} molecules of water.

Checkpoint

Find the product. Write your answer using exponents.

1. $2^3 \cdot 2^2$ 2^5
2. $8^7 \cdot 8^5$ 8^{12}
3. $5 \cdot 5^2$ 5^3
4. $4^6 \cdot 4^4 \cdot 4^3$ 4^{13}

NCTM CURRICULUM STANDARDS
Standard 1: Understand how operations are related
Standard 2: Understand patterns

Example 2 *Using the Product of Powers Property*

a. $x^6 \cdot x^9 = x^{6+9}$ **Product of powers property**

$= x^{15}$ **Add exponents.**

b. $3x \cdot 5x^5 = 3 \cdot 5 \cdot x^1 \cdot x^5$ **Commutative property of multiplication**

$= 3 \cdot 5 \cdot x^{1+5}$ **Product of powers property**

$= 3 \cdot 5 \cdot x^6$ **Add exponents.**

$= 15x^6$ **Multiply.**

Note *Worthy*

When taking notes about Example 2, be sure to write a verbal description next to each step in the calculation.

Quotients of Powers There is a related rule you can use for dividing powers with the same base. The following example suggests this rule.

$$\frac{a^5}{a^2} = \frac{\overbrace{a \cdot a \cdot a \cdot a \cdot a}^{\text{5 factors}}}{\underbrace{a \cdot a}_{\text{2 factors}}} = \frac{a \cdot a \cdot a \cdot \cancel{a} \cdot \cancel{a}}{\cancel{a} \cdot \cancel{a}} = \underbrace{a \cdot a \cdot a}_{\text{3 factors}} = a^{5-2} = a^3$$

Quotient of Powers Property

Words To divide powers with the same base, subtract the exponent of the denominator from the exponent of the numerator.

Algebra $\frac{a^m}{a^n} = a^{m-n}$, where $a \neq 0$ **Numbers** $\frac{6^8}{6^5} = 6^{8-5} = 6^3$

Example 3 *Using the Quotient of Powers Property*

a. $\frac{7^6}{7^2} = 7^{6-2}$ **Quotient of powers property**

$= 7^4$ **Subtract exponents.**

b. $\frac{4x^8}{10x^2} = \frac{4x^{8-2}}{10}$ **Quotient of powers property**

$= \frac{4x^6}{10}$ **Subtract exponents.**

$= \frac{2x^6}{5}$ **Divide numerator and denominator by 2.**

Checkpoint

Find the product or quotient. Write your answer using exponents.

5. $b^7 \cdot b^2$ b^9 **6.** $a \cdot a^5 \cdot a^2$ a^8 **7.** $2n^{11} \cdot 6n^8$ $12n^{19}$ **8.** $2m^4 \cdot 7m^5$ $14m^9$

9. $\frac{6^9}{6^4}$ 6^5 **10.** $\frac{10^{11}}{10^7}$ 10^4 **11.** $\frac{z^8}{z^3}$ z^5 **12.** $\frac{12n^5}{8n^2}$ $\frac{3n^3}{2}$

TIPS *for* NEW TEACHERS

Review the terms *base*, *power*, and *exponent* with students before beginning the lesson. See Tips for New Teachers in the *Chapter 4 Resource Book*.

Extra Examples

Example 1 Angel Falls in Venezuela is almost 10^3 meters high. It would take about 10^3 dust mites to form a line 1 meter long. About how many dust mites would have to be lined up in order to equal the height of Angel Falls? **about 10^6 dust mites**

Example 2 Use the product of powers property.

a. $b^{10} \cdot b^8$ b^{18}

b. $5m^2 \cdot 6m^4$ $30m^6$

Example 3 Use the quotient of powers property.

a. $\frac{5^8}{5^3}$ 5^5

b. $\frac{7c^9}{21c^3}$ $\frac{c^6}{3}$

Extra Examples

Example 4 Simplify $\frac{5x^4 \cdot x^6}{10x^5}$. $\frac{x^5}{2}$

Teaching Tip

Write the quotient $\frac{k^9}{k^3}$ on the board and point out that the result is k^6, not k^3. Ask students why they think someone would suggest that k^3 is the correct quotient.

Differentiating Instruction

Alternative Teaching Strategy
After discussing Example 3b, write a monomial on the board and have students write a product of powers and a quotient of powers that both result in the monomial you wrote. After discussing Example 4, have students write an expression like the one in this example that simplifies to the monomial you wrote.

Concept Check

How do you multiply two powers with the same base? **Write the base with an exponent that is the sum of the exponents of the two powers.** How do you divide two powers with the same base? **Write the base with an exponent that is the difference of the exponents of the two powers; the exponent of the denominator is subtracted from the exponent of the numerator.**

Daily Puzzler

Simplify the expression $\frac{36m^8 \div 4m^4}{42m^5 \div 14m^3}$. $3m^2$

Example 4 *Using Both Properties of Powers*

Simplify $\frac{3m^5 \cdot m^2}{6m^3}$.

$\frac{3m^5 \cdot m^2}{6m^3} = \frac{3m^{5+2}}{6m^3}$ **Product of powers property**

$= \frac{3m^7}{6m^3}$ **Add exponents.**

$= \frac{3m^{7-3}}{6}$ **Quotient of powers property**

$= \frac{3m^4}{6}$ **Subtract exponents.**

$= \frac{m^4}{2}$ **Divide numerator and denominator by 3.**

Checkpoint

Simplify.

13. $\frac{a^4 \cdot 10a^3}{a^2}$ $10a^5$ **14.** $\frac{13b^4 \cdot b^4}{b}$ $13b^7$ **15.** $\frac{x \cdot 7x^5}{10x^4}$ $\frac{7x^2}{10}$ **16.** $\frac{12y^2 \cdot y^8}{16y^5}$ $\frac{3y^5}{4}$

4.5 Exercises

More Practice, p. 806

Guided Practice

Vocabulary Check

1. Copy and complete: To multiply two powers with the same base, _?_ their exponents. **add**

2. Give an example of an expression you could simplify using the quotient of powers property. ***Sample answer:*** $\frac{14d^8}{16d^5}$

Skill Check **Find the product or quotient. Write your answer using exponents.**

3. $4^2 \cdot 4^9$ 4^{11} **4.** $5^3 \cdot 5^8$ 5^{11} **5.** $6^7 \cdot 6$ 6^8 **6.** $7^3 \cdot 7^4 \cdot 7^2$ 7^9

7. $\frac{2^{12}}{2^7}$ 2^5 **8.** $\frac{5^{14}}{5^2}$ 5^{12} **9.** $\frac{3^5}{3^2}$ 3^3 **10.** $\frac{10^9}{10^7}$ 10^2

Simplify.

11. $m^4 \cdot m^3$ m^7 **12.** $2x^7 \cdot 5x^2$ $10x^9$ **13.** $\frac{x^{10}}{x^4}$ x^6 **14.** $\frac{15y^7}{5y^3}$ $3y^4$

15. Error Analysis Describe and correct the error in simplifying $2x^5 \cdot 2x^4$. **The coefficients of each expression should have been multiplied to obtain $2x^5 \cdot 2x^4 = 2 \cdot 2 \cdot x^{5+4} = 4x^9$.**

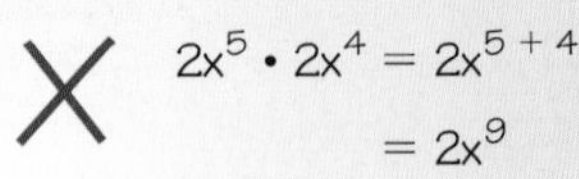

Practice and Problem Solving

Homework Help

Example	Exercises
1	16-19, 36, 37-39
2	24-31, 43-44
3	20-23, 32-35, 40, 42, 45
4	46-57

Online Resources CLASSZONE.COM
- More Examples
- eTutorial Plus

Find the product or quotient. Write your answer using exponents.

A **16.** $10^6 \cdot 10^7$ 10^{13} **17.** $9^2 \cdot 9^3$ 9^5 **18.** $11^4 \cdot 11^4$ 11^8 **19.** $8 \cdot 8^5 \cdot 8^2$ 8^8

20. $\frac{6^3}{6^2}$ 6^1, or 6 **21.** $\frac{8^{12}}{8^6}$ 8^6 **22.** $\frac{7^{20}}{7^4}$ 7^{16} **23.** $\frac{9^{11}}{9}$ 9^{10}

Simplify.

24. $a^4 \cdot a^8$ a^{12} **25.** $b^9 \cdot b^6$ b^{15} **26.** $3w^3 \cdot w^2$ $3w^5$ **27.** $z^7 \cdot 8z^4$ $8z^{11}$

28. $3n^4 \cdot 6n^9$ $18n^{13}$ **29.** $4r^5 \cdot 2r$ $8r^6$ **30.** $x^2 \cdot x^2 \cdot x$ x^5 **31.** $z^5 \cdot z^2 \cdot z^7$ z^{14}

32. $\frac{x^9}{x^4}$ x^5 **33.** $\frac{7y^8}{y^5}$ $7y^3$ **34.** $\frac{24m^{11}}{18m^3}$ $\frac{4m^8}{3}$ **35.** $\frac{28s^{15}}{42s^{12}}$ $\frac{2s^3}{3}$

36. The Great Pyramid The Great Pyramid in Egypt is composed of about 2^{21} limestone and granite blocks. The average mass of one of these blocks is about 2^{11} kilograms. Use the product of powers property to approximate the total mass in kilograms of the Great Pyramid. 2^{32} kg

Copy and complete the statement using <, >, or =.

37. 3^8 _?_ $3^6 \cdot 3^2$ = **38.** 2^7 _?_ $2 \cdot 2^5$ > **39.** 6^5 _?_ $6^2 \cdot 6^2$ >

40. Computers Computer memory is measured in bytes. The table shows related units used to measure computer memory.

Number of bytes	10^3	10^6	10^9	10^{12}	10^{15}
Name of unit	Kilobyte	Megabyte	Gigabyte	Terabyte	Petabyte

a. How many kilobytes are in a megabyte? 10^3, or 1000 kilobytes

b. How many gigabytes are in a petabyte? 10^6, or 1,000,000 gigabytes

c. How many megabytes are in a petabyte? 10^9, or 1,000,000,000 megabytes

41. *Writing* Explain why the product of powers property cannot be used to simplify $a^7 \cdot b^7$. The powers a^7 and b^7 do not have the same base.

Find the missing exponent.

B **42.** $\frac{a^?}{a^3} = a^5$ 8 **43.** $y^5 \cdot y^? = y^7$ 2 **44.** $b^? \cdot b^6 = b^7$ 1 **45.** $\frac{z^7}{z^?} = z^4$ 3

Simplify.

46. $x^2 \cdot y^4 \cdot x^3$ x^5y^4 **47.** $4m^4(n^7m)$ $4m^5n^7$ **48.** $(4ab)(5a^2b^3)$ $20a^3b^4$ **49.** $(p^3q^2)(p^4q^2)$ p^7q^4

50. $\frac{14a^3b^4}{4ab}$ $\frac{7a^2b^3}{2}$ **51.** $\frac{63m^5n^6}{27mn}$ $\frac{7m^4n^5}{3}$ **52.** $\frac{24w^4z^9}{15w^2z^3}$ $\frac{8w^2z^6}{5}$ **53.** $\frac{28c^{10}d^{13}}{24c^6d^8}$ $\frac{7c^4d^5}{6}$

54. $\frac{2x^6 \cdot 4x^3}{24x^5}$ $\frac{x^4}{3}$ **55.** $\frac{3a \cdot 4a^4}{28a^2}$ $\frac{3a^3}{7}$ **56.** $\frac{6z^9 \cdot 8z^3}{27z^2}$ $\frac{16z^{10}}{9}$ **57.** $\frac{2w^6 \cdot 36w^8}{18w^4}$ $4w^{10}$

58. Astronomy There are over 100 billion stars in our galaxy, the Milky Way. Scientists estimate there are about 100 billion galaxies in the universe. Recall that 1 billion = 10^9. If every galaxy has about 100 billion stars, about how many stars are in the universe? 10^{22} stars

In the Real World

Astronomy The galaxy shown below, called M33, is a spiral galaxy like our own Milky Way galaxy. The Milky Way and M33 are about 2.3 million light-years apart. What is this distance in kilometers? Use the fact that 1 light-year is approximately equal to 10 trillion kilometers. 23,000,000,000,000,000,000 km

3 APPLY

ASSIGNMENT GUIDE

Basic Course

Day 1: pp. 197-198 Exs. 16-29, 36-40, 42-53, 62, 64-77

Average Course

Day 1: pp. 197-198 Exs. 20-31, 36-43, 52-62, 66-77

Advanced Course

Day 1: pp. 197-198 Exs. 20-27, 32-41, 50-65*, 70-77

Block

pp. 197-198 Exs. 20-31, 36-43, 52-62, 66-77 (with 4.6)

EXTRA PRACTICE

- Student Edition, p. 806
- Chapter 4 Resource Book, pp. 45-47
- Test and Practice Generator

TRANSPARENCY

Even-numbered answers are available on transparencies.

HOMEWORK CHECK

When you review students' homework for this lesson, go over the following exercises to check understanding of key concepts.
Basic: 16, 20, 24, 36, 46
Average: 20, 25, 37, 40, 54
Advanced: 22, 27, 38, 40, 57

COMMON ERROR

In Exercises 16-35 and 46-57, watch for students who multiply exponents instead of adding them when finding the product of two powers. Also, watch for students who divide exponents instead of subtracting them when finding the quotient of two powers.

4 ASSESS

ASSESSMENT RESOURCES

For more assessment resources, see:

- Assessment Book
- Test and Practice Generator

MINI-QUIZ

Simplify.

1. $b^7 \cdot b^9$ b^{16}
2. $3g^2 \cdot 2g^4$ $6g^6$
3. $\frac{z^{12}}{z^6}$ z^6
4. $\frac{9a^4c^3}{27ac^2}$ $\frac{a^3c}{3}$
5. **Challenge** Find a value of x that makes $5^{x+3} \cdot 5^{x+4} = 5^{23}$ a true statement. Explain how you found your answer. **8. *Sample answer:* Using the product of powers property, the left side of the equation becomes 5^{2x+7}, and therefore $2x + 7$ must equal 23. Solving the equation $2x + 7 = 23$ gives $x = 8$.**

5 FOLLOW-UP

DIAGNOSIS/REMEDIATION

- Study Guide in Chapter 4 Resource Book, pp. 48–49
- eTutorial Plus Online
- Extra Practice, p. 806
- Lesson Practice in Chapter 4 Resource Book, pp. 45–47

ENGLISH LEARNER SUPPORT

- Spanish Study Guide
- Multi-Language Visual Glossary
- Chapter Audio Summaries CDs

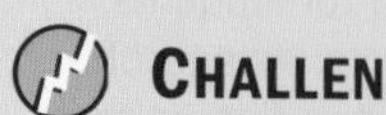

CHALLENGE

- Challenge Practice in Chapter 4 Resource Book, p. 50
- Teacher's Edition, p. 168F

59. Logical Reasoning Consider the equation $\frac{5^m}{5^n} = 5$.

a. Rewrite the left side of the equation using the quotient of powers property. 5^{m-n}

b. Find a pair of integers m and n for which the equation is true. ***Sample answer:* $m = 4$ and $n = 3$**

c. Are there other pairs of integers m and n for which the equation is true? Explain your reasoning. **Yes. *Sample answer:* Any pair of integers m and n such that m is 1 more than n will result in a true equation.**

60. Write $2 \cdot 2^n$ as a power of 2. 2^{n+1}

C **61. Critical Thinking** Write three products of powers that are equal to 2^6. Then write three quotients of powers that are equal to 2^6.

62. Simplify the expression $\frac{a^{m+n}}{a^n}$. a^m

63. Challenge Find a value of n that makes $3^{4n} \cdot 3^{n+4} = 3^{14}$ a true statement. Explain how you found your answer.

61. *Sample answer:* $2^1 \cdot 2^5$, $2^2 \cdot 2^4$, and $2^3 \cdot 2^3$; $\frac{2^7}{2^1}$, $\frac{2^8}{2^2}$, and $\frac{2^9}{2^3}$

63. 2. *Sample answer:* By the product of powers property, I knew that the sum of the exponents $4n$ and $n + 4$ must be 14, so I wrote and solved the equation $4n + (n + 4) = 14$.

Mixed Review

Find the sum or difference. *(Lessons 1.5, 1.6)*

64. $-14 + 98$ **84** **65.** $26 + (-19)$ **7** **66.** $-89 - 23$ **−112** **67.** $78 - (-34)$ **112**

Find the greatest common factor. *(Lesson 4.2)*

68. $44x^3, 24x^2$ **$4x^2$** **69.** $21xy, 25x^2$ **x** **70.** $42x^3y, 70xy^2$ **$14xy$** **71.** $100x^3, 75y^3$ **25**

Find the least common multiple. *(Lesson 4.4)*

72. $6x^2, 12xy^3$ **$12x^2y^3$** **73.** $3y, 5x^2y^2$ **$15x^2y^2$** **74.** $4x^3, 7xy^2$ **$28x^3y^2$** **75.** $9x^2y^3, 8xy$ **$72x^2y^3$**

Standardized Test Practice

76. Multiple Choice Which expression is equivalent to $\frac{24m^{18}}{36m^6}$? **D**

A. $\frac{24m^3}{36}$ **B.** $\frac{2m^6}{3}$ **C.** $\frac{24}{36m^{12}}$ **D.** $\frac{2m^{12}}{3}$

77. Multiple Choice Which expression is equivalent to $36x^3 \cdot 9x^2$? **I**

F. $4x$ **G.** $4x^5$ **H.** $324x$ **I.** $324x^5$

Ones' Digit Wonder

For powers of 3, the digits in the ones' place follow a certain pattern. What is the pattern? What is the digit in the ones' place for 3^{100}?

The ones digits for the first 4 powers of 3 are (in order) 3, 9, 7, 1, and these digits repeat in this same order for succeeding powers of 3; 1.

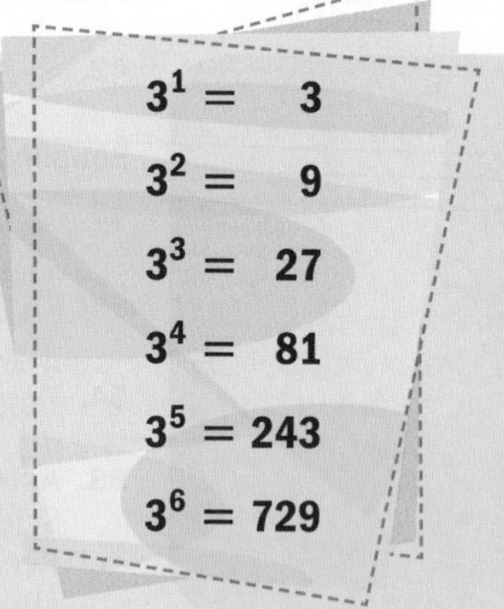

LESSON

4.6 Negative *and* Zero Exponents

BEFORE	Now	WHY?
You worked with positive exponents.	You'll work with negative and zero exponents.	So you can compare nanoseconds to milliseconds, as in Ex. 15.

Review Vocabulary
power, p. 10
exponent, p. 10
base, p. 10

Consider the following pattern of powers of 2.

As exponents decrease by 1 . . . the values of the powers are halved.

$$2^3 = 8$$
$$2^2 = 4$$
$$2^1 = 2$$
$$2^0 = ?$$
$$2^{-1} = ?$$
$$2^{-2} = ?$$

By extending the pattern, you can conclude that $2^0 = 1$, $2^{-1} = \frac{1}{2}$, and $2^{-2} = \frac{1}{4}$. Because $\frac{1}{2} = \frac{1}{2^1}$ and $\frac{1}{4} = \frac{1}{2^2}$, the pattern suggests the following definitions for negative and zero exponents.

Negative and Zero Exponents

For any nonzero number a, $a^0 = 1$.

For any nonzero number a and any integer n, $a^{-n} = \frac{1}{a^n}$.

Reading ***Algebra***

In an expression like $16x^{-6}y$, the exponent is associated only with the variable that comes directly before it, not with the coefficient of the variable.

Example 1 ***Powers with Negative and Zero Exponents***

Write the expression using only positive exponents.

a. $3^{-5} = \frac{1}{3^5}$ **Definition of negative exponent**

b. $m^0n^{-4} = 1 \cdot n^{-4}$ **Definition of zero exponent**

$= \frac{1}{n^4}$ **Definition of negative exponent**

c. $16x^{-6}y = \frac{16y}{x^6}$ **Definition of negative exponent**

 ***Checkpoint***

Write the expression using only positive exponents.

1. 5^{-2} $\frac{1}{5^2}$ **2.** $1{,}000{,}000^0$ 1 **3.** $3y^{-2}$ $\frac{3}{y^2}$ **4.** $a^{-7}b^3$ $\frac{b^3}{a^7}$

NCTM CURRICULUM STANDARDS
Standard 1: Understand meanings of operations; Understand how operations are related
Standard 2: Understand patterns

1 PLAN

Skill Check

1. $8 + (-5) = \underline{?}$ **3**
2. $-6 + 2 = \underline{?}$ **−4**
3. $7 - 9 = \underline{?}$ **−2**
4. $10 - (-3) = \underline{?}$ **13**

Lesson Objective

Work with negative and zero exponents.

Pacing

Suggested Number of Days
Basic Course: 2 days
Average Course: 2 days
Advanced Course: 2 days
Block: 0.5 block with 4.5
0.5 block with 4.7

Teaching Resources

For a complete list of Teaching Resources, see page 168B.

Transparency

Warm-Up Exercises for this lesson are available on a transparency.

2 TEACH

Motivating the Lesson

Ask students to identify any patterns they see in the classroom, such as in the ceiling or floor tiles if your classroom has them. Have volunteers describe the patterns that are found. Then focus students' attention on the numerical pattern in the lesson's first paragraph.

TIPS *for* NEW TEACHERS

Show students how to write a term such as 3^{-5} neatly and carefully so that it will not be confused with the expression $3 - 5$. Stress that writing mathematical expressions clearly becomes increasingly important as the expressions become more complex. See Tips for New Teachers in the *Chapter 4 Resource Book*.

Extra Examples

Example 1 Write the expression using only positive exponents.

a. 7^{-2} $\frac{1}{7^2}$

b. $a^{-5}b^0$ $\frac{1}{a^5}$

c. $4m^{-4}n^3$ $\frac{4n^3}{m^4}$

Example 2 Write the expression without using a fraction bar.

a. $\frac{1}{25}$ 5^{-2}

b. $\frac{x^6}{y^3}$ x^6y^{-3}

Example 3 Find the product or quotient. Write your answer using only positive exponents.

a. $3^8 \cdot 3^{-10}$ $\frac{1}{3^2}$

b. $\frac{10a^4}{a^{-4}}$ $10a^8$

COMMON ERROR

It may be necessary to remind students occasionally that any number raised to the power 0 has a value of 1, not 0.

Rewriting Fractions You can use the prime factorization of a number to write a fraction as an expression involving negative exponents.

Example 2 *Rewriting Fractions*

Write the expression without using a fraction bar.

a. $\frac{1}{16}$ **b.** $\frac{a^2}{c^3}$

Solution

a. $\frac{1}{16} = \frac{1}{2^4}$ **Write prime factorization of 16.**

$= 2^{-4}$ **Definition of negative exponent**

b. $\frac{a^2}{c^3} = a^2c^{-3}$ **Definition of negative exponent**

Products and Quotients of Powers You can use the product of powers property and the quotient of powers property to find products and quotients that involve negative exponents.

Example 3 *Using Powers Properties with Negative Exponents*

Find the product or quotient. Write your answer using only positive exponents.

a. $5^{10} \cdot 5^{-6}$ **b.** $\frac{8n^{-3}}{n^2}$

Solution

a. $5^{10} \cdot 5^{-6} = 5^{10 + (-6)}$ **Product of powers property**

$= 5^4$ **Add exponents.**

b. $\frac{8n^{-3}}{n^2} = 8n^{-3-2}$ **Quotient of powers property**

$= 8n^{-5}$ **Subtract exponents.**

$= \frac{8}{n^5}$ **Definition of negative exponent**

Checkpoint

Write the expression without using a fraction bar.

5. $\frac{1}{25}$ 5^{-2} **6.** $\frac{1}{1000}$ 10^{-3} **7.** $\frac{2}{a^8}$ $2a^{-8}$ **8.** $\frac{x^7}{z^2}$ x^7z^{-2}

Find the product or quotient. Write your answer using only positive exponents.

9. $3^{-7} \cdot 3^{11}$ 3^4 **10.** $5^{-8} \cdot 5^{-7}$ $\frac{1}{5^{15}}$ **11.** $m^{-3} \cdot m^{-1}$ $\frac{1}{m^4}$ **12.** $a^{-2} \cdot a^{10}$ a^8

13. $\frac{2^{-3}}{2^4}$ $\frac{1}{2^7}$ **14.** $\frac{7^2}{7^{-8}}$ 7^{10} **15.** $\frac{5k^3}{k^{-9}}$ $5k^{12}$ **16.** $\frac{b^{-4}}{b^{-6}}$ b^2

Example 4 *Solving Problems Involving Negative Exponents*

Geckos Geckos can easily climb smooth vertical surfaces. Biologists have discovered that tiny hairs are the reason that the feet of a gecko are so sticky. Each hair is about 100 micrometers long. A micrometer is 10^{-6} meter. What is the length of one hair in meters?

Solution

To find the length of one hair in meters, multiply the length of the hair in micrometers by the number of micrometers in one meter.

$100 \cdot 10^{-6} = 10^{2} \cdot 10^{-6}$	**Rewrite 100 as 10^2.**
$= 10^{2+(-6)}$	**Product of powers property**
$= 10^{-4}$	**Add exponents.**
$= \frac{1}{10^4}$	**Definition of negative exponent**
$= \frac{1}{10{,}000}$	**Evaluate power.**

Answer The length of one hair is about $\frac{1}{10{,}000}$ meter.

Extra Examples

Example 4 A meter is equivalent to 1000 millimeters and a kilometer is 1000 meters. What is a millimeter in kilometers? $\frac{1}{10^6}$ km

Teaching Tip

While discussing Example 4, it may be helpful to show students how to write 10^{-6} meter as $\frac{1}{10^6}$, or $\frac{1}{1{,}000{,}000}$ meter.

Concept Check

How is the expression a^{-n} written without using a negative exponent? $\frac{1}{a^n}$

Daily Puzzler

Which is greater, 3^{-4} or 4^{-3}? 4^{-3}

4.6 Exercises

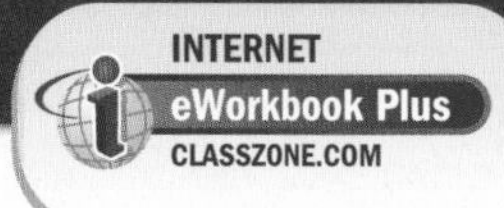

More Practice, p. 806

Guided Practice

Vocabulary Check

1. Write 7^{-2} using a positive exponent. $\frac{1}{7^2}$
2. If a is nonzero, does the value of a^0 depend of the value of a? Explain. No; any nonzero quantity to the zero power equals 1.

Skill Check

Write the expression using only positive exponents.

3. 5^{-3} $\frac{1}{5^3}$ 4. 3^{-5} $\frac{1}{3^5}$ 5. $4a^{-6}$ $\frac{4}{a^6}$ 6. $b^{-3}c^0$ $\frac{1}{b^3}$

Write the expression without using a fraction bar.

7. $\frac{1}{27}$ 3^{-3} 8. $\frac{1}{10^8}$ 10^{-8} 9. $\frac{4}{x^3}$ $4x^{-3}$ 10. $\frac{11}{c^5}$ $11c^{-5}$

Find the product. Write your answer using only positive exponents.

11. $6^{-4} \cdot 6^7$ 6^3 12. $3^{-2} \cdot 3^{-8}$ $\frac{1}{3^{10}}$ 13. $x^{11} \cdot x^{-3}$ x^8 14. $z^{-5} \cdot z^{-1}$ $\frac{1}{z^6}$

Guided Problem Solving

15. How many nanoseconds are in a millisecond?
   1) Write the quotient of the duration of a millisecond and the duration of a nanosecond. $\frac{10^{-3}}{10^{-9}}$
   2) Use the quotient of powers property to simplify the quotient in Step 1. 10^6

Name of unit	Duration
Millisecond	10^{-3} sec
Microsecond	10^{-6} sec
Nanosecond	10^{-9} sec

3 APPLY

ASSIGNMENT GUIDE

Basic Course

Day 1: pp. 202–203 Exs. 16–19, 24–27, 41, 51–54, 57, 62–69

Day 2: pp. 202–203 Exs. 20–23, 28–31, 36–40, 43–48, 55, 56, 70–72

Average Course

Day 1: pp. 202–203 Exs. 16–29, 51–54, 58–60, 69–72

Day 2: pp. 202–203 Exs. 32–42, 47–50, 55–57, 62–68

Advanced Course

Day 1: pp. 202–203 Exs. 18–29, 51–54, 58–61*, 69–72

Day 2: pp. 202–203 Exs. 36–41, 43–50, 55–57, 63–68

Block

pp. 202–203 Exs. 16–29, 51–54, 58–60, 69–72 (with 4.5)

pp. 202–203 Exs. 32–42, 47–50, 55–57, 62–68 (with 4.7)

EXTRA PRACTICE

- Student Edition, p. 806
- Chapter 4 Resource Book, pp. 54–56
- Test and Practice Generator

TRANSPARENCY

Even-numbered answers are available on transparencies.

HOMEWORK CHECK

When you review students' homework for this lesson, go over the following exercises to check understanding of key concepts.

Basic: 16, 24, 36, 40, 43

Average: 16, 26, 36, 40, 47

Advanced: 18, 28, 38, 47, 55

TEACHING TIP

In Exercise 2 on page 201, be sure students understand that $1000^0 = 5^0$, even though $1000 > 5$.

Practice and Problem Solving

Homework Help

Example	Exercises
1	16–23
2	24–31
3	32–39, 43–50
4	40, 55

Online Resources CLASSZONE.COM
- More Examples
- eTutorial Plus

Write the expression using only positive exponents.

A **16.** 13^{-6} $\frac{1}{13^6}$ **17.** 121^0 1 **18.** 8^{-9} $\frac{1}{8^9}$ **19.** 20^{-4} $\frac{1}{20^4}$

20. xy^0 x **21.** $18f^{-1}$ $\frac{18}{f}$ **22.** $6g^{-5}$ $\frac{6}{g^5}$ **23.** c^3d^{-1} $\frac{c^3}{d}$

Write the expression without using a fraction bar.

24. $\frac{1}{25}$ 5^{-2} **25.** $\frac{1}{19}$ 19^{-1} **26.** $\frac{1}{10{,}000}$ 10^{-4} **27.** $\frac{1}{64}$ 2^{-6}

28. $\frac{8}{c^5}$ $8c^{-5}$ **29.** $\frac{4}{d}$ $4d^{-1}$ **30.** $\frac{4y}{x^3}$ $4x^{-3}y$ **31.** $\frac{9a^2}{b^6}$ $9a^2b^{-6}$

Find the product. Write your answer using only positive exponents.

32. $3^4 \cdot 3^{-7}$ $\frac{1}{3^3}$ **33.** $5 \cdot 5^{-5}$ $\frac{1}{5^4}$ **34.** $10^{-2} \cdot 10^{-8}$ $\frac{1}{10^{10}}$ **35.** $13^0 \cdot 13^6$ 13^6

36. $2s^{-5} \cdot s^3$ $\frac{2}{s^2}$ **37.** $5t^{-3} \cdot 3t^{-8}$ $\frac{15}{t^{11}}$ **38.** $4a^0 \cdot 7a^{-4}$ $\frac{28}{a^4}$ **39.** $b^{-5} \cdot b^{-9}$ $\frac{1}{b^{14}}$

40. Historical Documents Scientists have discovered that nanoparticles of a substance called slaked lime can help preserve historical documents. The diameters of these nanoparticles are less than $\frac{1}{100{,}000{,}000{,}000}$ meter. Write this number using a negative exponent. 10^{-11}

41. Critical Thinking Explain how 6^{-2} is different from 6^2.
Sample answer: $6^2 = 6 \cdot 6 = 36$, but $6^{-2} = \frac{1}{6^2} = \frac{1}{36}$.

42. ***Writing*** Explain why the rule $a^{-n} = \frac{1}{a^n}$ does not apply to $a = 0$.
Sample answer: If $a = 0$, you would have $0^{-n} = \frac{1}{0^n} = \frac{1}{0}$, and $\frac{1}{0}$ is not defined.

Find the quotient. Write your answer using only positive exponents.

B **43.** $\frac{2^5}{2^8}$ $\frac{1}{2^3}$ **44.** $\frac{4^{-2}}{4^6}$ $\frac{1}{4^8}$ **45.** $\frac{16^{-9}}{16^{-8}}$ $\frac{1}{16}$ **46.** $\frac{15^3}{15^{-4}}$ 15^7

47. $\frac{17a^3}{a^7}$ $\frac{17}{a^4}$ **48.** $\frac{15b^{-5}}{3b^4}$ $\frac{5}{b^9}$ **49.** $\frac{26w^{-4}}{13w^{-12}}$ $2w^8$ **50.** $\frac{11g^2}{g^{-4}}$ $11g^6$

Use a calculator to evaluate the expression. If necessary, round the result to the nearest thousandth.

51. $(4.5)^{-3}$ 0.011 **52.** $(8.1)^{-2}$ 0.015 **53.** $(3.2)^{-4}$ 0.010 **54.** $(7.5)^{-3}$ 0.002

55. Brittle Stars The brittle star is a type of starfish. A certain species of brittle star has a skeleton that is covered in microscopic crystals. Scientists have discovered that these crystals act as lenses that allow the brittle star to sense light.

a. The surface of each crystal has an area of $\frac{1}{1{,}000{,}000{,}000}$ square meter. Write this number using a negative exponent. 10^{-9} m^2

b. Approximately 10^4 crystals cover the skeleton of a brittle star. What is the total area of all the crystals on a single brittle star? Write your answer using a negative exponent. 10^{-5} m^2

In the **Real World**

Brittle Stars There are over 2000 species of brittle stars. They live anywhere from the shoreline to 6755 feet underwater. How many miles is this distance? about 1.28 mi

Find the quotient. Write your answer using only positive exponents.

C **56.** $\frac{a^6b^4}{a^3b^7}$ $\frac{a^3}{b^3}$ **57.** $\frac{c^2d^{11}}{c^8d^5}$ $\frac{d^6}{c^6}$ **58.** $\frac{m^8n^4}{m^2n^9}$ $\frac{m^6}{n^5}$ **59.** $\frac{x^2y}{x^{10}y^7}$ $\frac{1}{x^8y^6}$

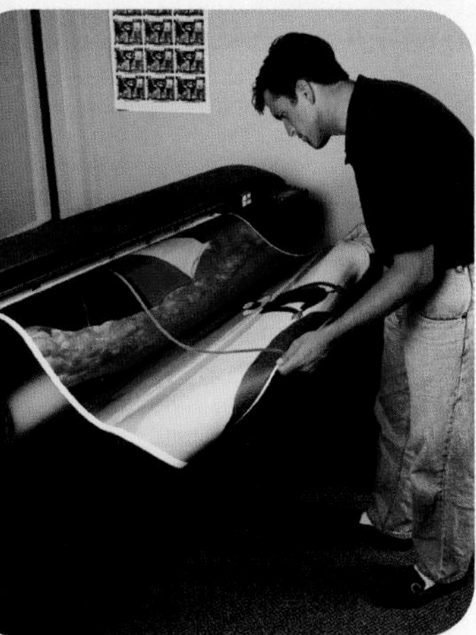

This printer can print pages several feet wide.

60. Extended Problem Solving Inkjet printers spray droplets of ink onto paper. The volume of a single droplet is about 10 picoliters. Some printers spray as many as 10^6 droplets to completely cover a square inch of paper.

a. Find the volume of ink in picoliters needed to completely cover a square inch of paper. 10^7 picoliters

b. There are 10^{12} picoliters in a liter. Find the volume of ink in liters needed to completely cover a square inch of paper. 10^{-5} L

c. Estimate Find the area of a 8.5 inch by 11 inch piece of paper and round this number to the nearest power of 10. Then estimate the volume of ink (in liters) needed to completely cover an entire piece of paper. 10^2 in.^{2}; 10^{-3} L

d. Apply Suppose an inkjet cartridge contains 60 milliliters of ink. About how many pages can this cartridge print if each page is 8.5 inches by 11 inches and is covered completely in ink? 60 pages

61. Challenge One way to develop the definitions of zero and negative exponents is to use the quotient of powers property.

a. Consider $\frac{a^n}{a^n}$. First, simplify using the quotient of powers property.

61a. $\frac{a^n}{a^n} = a^{n-n} = a^0$

b. Then simplify the expression in part (a) in a different way: Write the numerator and denominator as a product of a's and divide out common factors. Which definition of exponents have you developed? See margin.

c. Now consider $\frac{a^0}{a^n}$. First, simplify using the quotient of powers property. $\frac{a^0}{a^n} = a^{0-n} = a^{-n}$

d. Then simplify the expression in part (c) by using the definition of a zero exponent. Which definition of exponents have you developed?

61d. $\frac{a^0}{a^n} = \frac{1}{a^n}$; definition of negative exponents $\left(a^{-n} = \frac{1}{a^n}\right)$

Mixed Review

Algebra Basics Solve the equation using mental math. *(Lesson 2.4)*

62. $9 + x = 17$ 8 **63.** $8 - x = 3$ 5 **64.** $-3x = 36$ -12 **65.** $\frac{x}{-8} = 6$ -48

66. Amusement Parks You must be at least 46 inches tall to ride the bumper cars at an amusement park. Write and graph an inequality to show the heights for which you can ride the bumper cars. *(Lesson 3.4)* $h \geq 46$; see margin for art.

Find the product or quotient. Write your answer using exponents. *(Lesson 4.5)*

67. $3^2 \cdot 3^2$ 3^4 **68.** $5^4 \cdot 5$ 5^5 **69.** $\frac{2^9}{2^4}$ 2^5 **70.** $\frac{10^8}{10^5}$ 10^3

Standardized Test Practice

71. Multiple Choice Which expression is *not* equivalent to $x^2 \cdot x^{-6}$? B

A. x^{-4} **B.** $x^{-2} \cdot x^6$ **C.** $\frac{1}{x^4}$ **D.** $\frac{x^2}{x^6}$

72. Multiple Choice Which expression is equivalent to $\frac{24a^6}{3b^2}$? H

F. $24a^{-6}b^2$ **G.** $24a^6b^{-2}$ **H.** $8a^6b^{-2}$ **I.** $8a^{-6}b^2$

4 ASSESS

Assessment Resources

For more assessment resources, see:

- Assessment Book
- Test and Practice Generator

Mini-Quiz

Write the expression using only positive exponents.

1. 7^{-2} $\frac{1}{7^2}$ **2.** $a^{-3}b^2$ $\frac{b^2}{a^3}$

Find the product or quotient. Write your answer using only positive exponents.

3. $7^{-7} \cdot 7^5$ $\frac{1}{7^2}$ **4.** $\frac{3^2}{3^{-2}}$ 3^4

5. Challenge Which of the following are undefined: $1^1, 1^{-1}, 1^0, 0^1, 0^{-1}$? Explain. 0^{-1}; by the definition of negative exponents, $0^{-1} = \frac{1}{0^1}$ or $\frac{1}{0}$, but division by zero is undefined.

5 FOLLOW-UP

Diagnosis/Remediation

- Study Guide in Chapter 4 Resource Book, pp. 57–58
- eTutorial Plus Online
- Extra Practice, p. 806
- Lesson Practice in Chapter 4 Resource Book, pp. 54–56

English Learner Support

- Spanish Study Guide
- Multi-Language Visual Glossary
- Chapter Audio Summaries CDs

Challenge

- Challenge Practice in Chapter 4 Resource Book, p. 59
- Teacher's Edition, p. 168F

61b, 66. See Additional Answers beginning on page AA1.

1 PLAN

Skill Check

Write each number.

1. one thousand **1000**
2. one hundred thousand **100,000**
3. ten million **10,000,000**
4. one tenth **$\frac{1}{10}$ or 0.1**

LESSON OBJECTIVE

Write numbers using scientific notation.

PACING

Suggested Number of Days
Basic Course: 1 day
Average Course: 1 day
Advanced Course: 1 day
Block: 0.5 block with 4.6

TEACHING RESOURCES

For a complete list of Teaching Resources, see page 168B.

TRANSPARENCY

Warm-Up Exercises for this lesson are available on a transparency.

2 TEACH

MOTIVATING THE LESSON

If possible, have a Biology teacher bring in a model of the human eye and discuss its various parts.

TIPS *for* NEW TEACHERS

Some students will need extra practice writing in scientific notation and may benefit from working with a partner. See Tips for New Teachers in the *Chapter 4 Resource Book*.

LESSON 4.7

Scientific Notation

BEFORE	Now	WHY?
You used properties of exponents.	You'll write numbers using scientific notation.	So you can calculate how much a whale eats, as in Ex. 53.

Vocabulary

scientific notation, p. 204

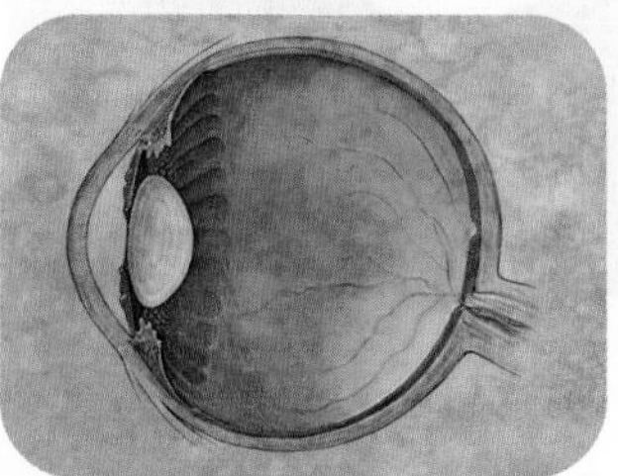

Anatomy The retina is a layer of the eyeball that contains rods and cones. Rods and cones are cells that absorb light and change it to electric signals that are sent to the brain. The human retina is about 0.00012 meter thick and contains about 120,000,000 rods and about 6,000,000 cones.

You can use *scientific notation* to write these numbers. Scientific notation is a shorthand way of writing numbers using powers of 10.

Reading *Algebra*

The inequality $1 \le c < 10$ is read as "1 is less than or equal to *c*, and *c* is less than 10."

Using Scientific Notation

A number is written in **scientific notation** if it has the form $c \times 10^n$ where $1 \le c < 10$ and n is an integer.

Standard form	Product form	Scientific notation
725,000	$7.25 \times 100{,}000$	7.25×10^5
0.006	6×0.001	6×10^{-3}

Example 1 ***Writing Numbers in Scientific Notation***

a. The retina has 120,000,000 rods. Write this number in scientific notation.

Standard form	Product form	Scientific notation
120,000,000	$1.2 \times 100{,}000{,}000$	1.2×10^8
Move decimal point 8 places to the left.		**Exponent is 8.**

b. The thickness of the human retina is 0.00012 meter. Write this number in scientific notation.

Standard form	Product form	Scientific notation
0.00012	1.2×0.0001	1.2×10^{-4}
Move decimal point 4 places to the right.		**Exponent is −4.**

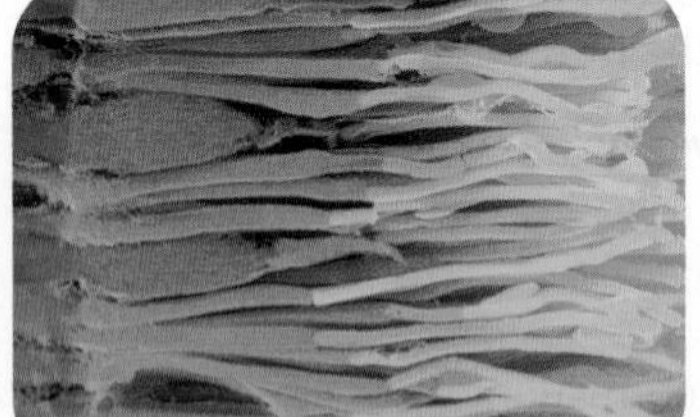

Color-enhanced image of rods and cones in the human retina

NCTM CURRICULUM STANDARDS

Standard 1: Understand ways of representing numbers; Understand relationships among numbers; Compute fluently

Reading *Algebra*

For a positive number written in scientific notation, a positive exponent means the number is greater than 1, and a negative exponent means the number is between 0 and 1.

Example 2 *Writing Numbers in Standard Form*

a. Write 3.2×10^7 in standard form.

Scientific notation	**Product form**	**Standard form**
3.2×10^7	$3.2 \times 10{,}000{,}000$	32,000,000
Exponent is 7.		**Move decimal point 7 places to the right.**

b. Write 8.69×10^{-5} in standard form.

Scientific notation	**Product form**	**Standard form**
8.69×10^{-5}	8.69×0.00001	0.0000869
Exponent is −5.		**Move decimal point 5 places to the left.**

Checkpoint

Write the number in scientific notation.

1. 4100 4.1×10^3 **2.** 0.000067 6.7×10^{-5} **3.** 34,600,000 3.46×10^7 **4.** 0.0000145 1.45×10^{-5}

Write the number in standard form.

5. 7.1×10^4 71,000 **6.** 1.93×10^{-3} 0.00193 **7.** 3.641×10^{-6} 0.000003641 **8.** 5.59×10^8 559,000,000

Comparing Numbers To compare numbers written in scientific notation, first compare the powers of 10, then compare the decimal parts.

Example 3 *Ordering Numbers Using Scientific Notation*

Order 3.9×10^6, 3,800,000, and 4.2×10^5 from least to greatest.

1. Write each number in scientific notation if necessary.
   $3{,}800{,}000 = 3.8 \times 10^6$
2. Order the numbers with different powers of 10.
   Because $10^5 < 10^6$, $4.2 \times 10^5 < 3.9 \times 10^6$ and $4.2 \times 10^5 < 3.8 \times 10^6$.
3. Order the numbers with the same power of 10.
   Because $3.8 < 3.9$, $3.8 \times 10^6 < 3.9 \times 10^6$.
4. Write the original numbers in order from least to greatest.
   4.2×10^5; 3,800,000; 3.9×10^6

Checkpoint

Order the numbers from least to greatest.

9. 2.4×10^5; 3.3×10^4; 49,000 3.3×10^4; 49,000; 2.4×10^5

10. 8.16×10^6; 635,000; 4.08×10^5 4.08×10^5; 635,000; 8.16×10^6

11. 0.00017; 1.9×10^{-4}; 2.8×10^{-3} 0.00017; 1.9×10^{-4}; 2.8×10^{-3}

12. 7.8×10^{-3}; 7.9×10^{-3}; 0.00056 0.00056; 7.8×10^{-3}; 7.9×10^{-3}

Extra Examples

Example 1

a. An earthquake of magnitude 8 on the Richter scale releases the equivalent energy of about 5,643,000 metric tons of explosive. Write this number in scientific notation. **5.643×10^6**

b. A computer chip can be as small as 0.0000005 meter long. Write this number in scientific notation. **5×10^{-7}**

Example 2 Write the number in standard form.

a. 1.85×10^6 **1,850,000**

b. 3.29×10^{-4} **0.000329**

Example 3 Order 9.5×10^4, 9.8×10^3, and 9900 from least to greatest. **9.8×10^3, 9900, 9.5×10^4**

Visualize

To help students see the movement of the decimal points in the two parts of Example 1 more precisely, write the numbers as large as possible across the board and then use two colors of chalk to draw the arcs. Instead of drawing one long arc, show each individual place value movement with individual arcs. Students can then count the arcs to make the connection to the exponent in the scientific notation, and they can use the color of the arcs to help recognize when the exponent should be positive and when it should be negative.

Teaching Tip

In Example 1a, ask students why the decimal point is moved just 8 places to the left and not 9 places. Stress that when a number is written in scientific notation, there is always one nonzero digit to the left of the decimal point.

Extra Examples

Example 4 A nickel has a mass of about 5.2 grams. What would be the mass in grams of $1000 worth of nickels? **1.04×10^5 g**

Differentiating Instruction

Advanced Students Ask students to name something that has a width of approximately 1 meter. Then have them apply powers of 10 first less than 1 meter and then greater than 1 meter, naming objects with these measures. Encourage students to research the sizes of numerous items. Students can find web sites on the Internet that cover similar material by entering "powers of 10" in a search engine.

Concept Check

How are 250,000 and 0.000025 written in scientific notation? **2.5×10^5; 2.5×10^{-5}**

Daily Puzzler

By what value would you multiply 6.2×10^{-2} in order to obtain 6.2×10^2 as the product? **10^4**

This thimble is filled with wolffia plants.

Example 4 *Multiplying Numbers in Scientific Notation*

Plants A wolffia plant is the smallest flowering plant in the world. One wolffia plant has a mass of about 1.5×10^{-4} gram. At least 5×10^3 wolffia plants could fit in a thimble. What is the mass of 5×10^3 wolffia plants?

Solution

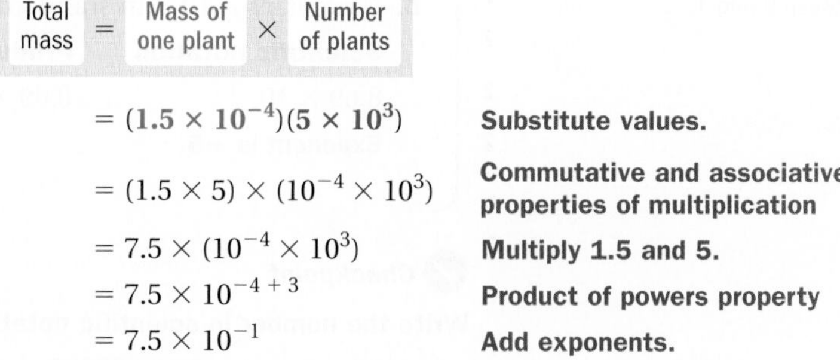

Total mass = Mass of one plant × Number of plants

$= (1.5 \times 10^{-4})(5 \times 10^3)$ **Substitute values.**

$= (1.5 \times 5) \times (10^{-4} \times 10^3)$ **Commutative and associative properties of multiplication**

$= 7.5 \times (10^{-4} \times 10^3)$ **Multiply 1.5 and 5.**

$= 7.5 \times 10^{-4+3}$ **Product of powers property**

$= 7.5 \times 10^{-1}$ **Add exponents.**

Answer The mass of 5×10^3 wolffia plants is 7.5×10^{-1} gram, or 0.75 gram.

4.7 Exercises

More Practice, p. 806

INTERNET eWorkbook Plus CLASSZONE.COM

Guided Practice

Vocabulary Check

1. Give an example of a number that is between 0 and 1 and is written in scientific notation. *Sample answer:* 4.7×10^{-4}
2. Explain why 12.5×10^7 is *not* written in scientific notation. 12.5 is not between 1 and 10.

Skill Check **Write the number in scientific notation.**

3. 9,180,000 9.18×10^6
4. 0.000062 6.2×10^{-5}
5. 723,000 7.23×10^5
6. 0.00000002 2×10^{-8}

Write the number in standard form.

7. 2.78×10^7 27,800,000
8. 5.67×10^{-3} 0.00567
9. 4.15×10^{-5} 0.0000415
10. 1.96×10^5 196,000
11. **Bicycle Chain** Scientists have made a tiny bicycle chain out of silicon links that are thinner than a human hair. The centers of the links are 0.00005 meter apart. Write this distance in scientific notation. 5×10^{-5} m
12. **Error Analysis** Describe and correct the error in comparing 6.5×10^3 and 6.4×10^4. The powers of 10 should have been compared first since they are not the same. Because $10^4 > 10^3$, $6.4 \times 10^4 > 6.5 \times 10^3$.

Practice and Problem Solving

Homework Help

Example	Exercises
1	13-21, 31-33, 39
2	22-30, 34-36
3	40-43, 48-51
4	44-47, 52

Online Resources CLASSZONE.COM
- More Examples
- eTutorial Plus

Write the number in scientific notation.

A **13.** 46,200,000 4.62×10^7 **14.** 9,750,000 9.75×10^6 **15.** 1700 1.7×10^3

16. 8,910,000,000 8.91×10^9 **17.** 104,000 1.04×10^5 **18.** 0.00000062 6.2×10^{-7}

19. 0.000023 2.3×10^{-5} **20.** 0.00095 9.5×10^{-4} **21.** 0.0000106 1.06×10^{-5}

Write the number in standard form.

22. 4.18×10^4 41,800 **23.** 5.617×10^6 5,617,000 **24.** 7.894×10^8 789,400,000

25. 3.8×10^{-9} 0.0000000038 **26.** 9.83×10^{-2} 0.0983 **27.** 6×10^{-7} 0.0000006

28. 1.03×10^{-5} 0.0000103 **29.** 2.28×10^9 2,280,000,000 **30.** 8.391×10^4 83,910

In Exercises 31–33, write the number in scientific notation.

31. Population of Asia in 2001: 3,721,000,000 3.721×10^9 people

32. Distance (in meters) to the star Vega: 239,000,000,000,000,000 2.39×10^{17} m

33. Time (in seconds) required for light to travel 1 meter: 0.00000000334 3.34×10^{-10} sec

In Exercises 34–36, write the number in standard form.

34. Distance (in centimeters) that the North Pacific plate slides along the San Andreas fault in 1 hour: 5.71×10^{-4} 0.000571 cm

35. Diameter (in meters) of a xylem cell in a redwood tree: 3.0×10^{-5} 0.00003 m

36. Cruising speed (in miles per hour) of a supersonic jet: 1.336×10^3 1336 mi/h

37. *Sample answer:* The friend did not compare powers of 10. Because $4 \times 10^3 = 4000$ and $2 \times 10^2 = 200$, 4×10^3 is actually 20 times greater than 2×10^2.

37. Critical Thinking Your friend thinks that 4×10^3 is twice as great as 2×10^2. What error is your friend making? Explain your reasoning.

38. *Writing* When a number between 0 and 1 is written in scientific notation, what can you say about the exponent? When a number greater than 1 is written in scientific notation, what can you say about the exponent? It is negative; it is nonnegative.

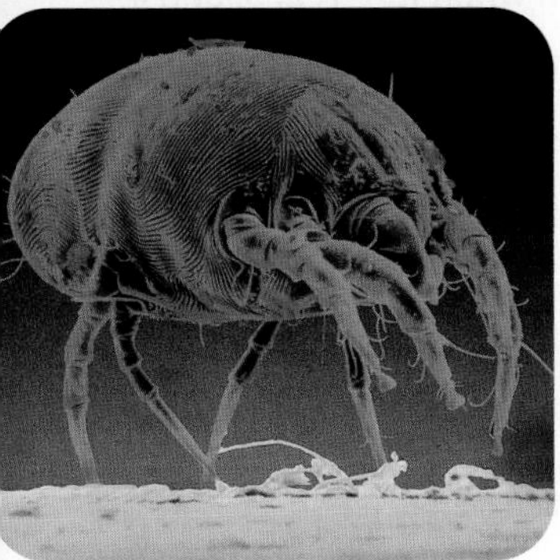

Color-enhanced image of a dust mite

39. Dust Mites Dust mites are microscopic organisms that can be found in most natural and synthetic fibers. Dust mites are 0.00042 meter in length and 0.00028 meter in width. An average mattress contains 2,000,000 dust mites. Write these numbers in scientific notation. 4.2×10^{-4} m, 2.8×10^{-4} m, 2×10^6 dust mites

Copy and complete the statement using $<$, $>$, or $=$.

40. 3.21×10^3 ? 321,000 $<$ **41.** 91,600 ? 9.61×10^4 $<$

42. 2.3×10^{-6} ? 1.3×10^{-2} $<$ **43.** 0.00875 ? 8.75×10^{-4} $>$

Find the product. Write your answer in scientific notation.

B **44.** $(2.5 \times 10^4)(3 \times 10^2)$ 7.5×10^6 **45.** $(6 \times 10^7)(9 \times 10^5)$ 5.4×10^{13}

46. $(5 \times 10^{-3})(7.5 \times 10^8)$ 3.75×10^6 **47.** $(8.5 \times 10^{-2})(7 \times 10^{-7})$ 5.95×10^{-8}

Order the numbers from least to greatest.

48. 2.6×10^4; 3500; 9.2×10^4 3500; 2.6×10^4; 9.2×10^4

49. 8700; 1.97×10^3; 3.98×10^4 1.97×10^3; 8700; 3.98×10^4

50. 9.1×10^{-4}; 5.2×10^{-2}; 0.0013 9.1×10^{-4}; 0.0013; 5.2×10^{-2}

51. 7.61×10^{-3}; 0.00009 ; 8.4×10^{-6} 8.4×10^{-6}; 0.00009; 7.61×10^{-3}

3 APPLY

ASSIGNMENT GUIDE

Basic Course

Day 1: SRH p. 773 Exs. 4-9; pp. 207-208 Exs. 13-25, 31-35, 40-45, 48-51, 55-64

Average Course

Day 1: pp. 207-208 Exs. 16-27, 33-41, 46-53, 57-64

Advanced Course

Day 1: pp. 207-208 Exs. 19-24, 28-32, 35-41, 46-55*, 58-64

Block

pp. 207-208 Exs. 16-27, 33-41, 46-53, 57-64 (with 4.6)

EXTRA PRACTICE

- Student Edition, p. 806
- Chapter 4 Resource Book, pp. 63-65
- Test and Practice Generator

TRANSPARENCY

Even-numbered answers are available on transparencies.

HOMEWORK CHECK

When you review students' homework for this lesson, go over the following exercises to check understanding of key concepts.

Basic: 13, 22, 31, 40, 44
Average: 16, 24, 34, 41, 46
Advanced: 19, 24, 41, 47, 52

COMMON ERROR

In Exercises 25-28, watch for students who think a negative exponent indicates that the number must be negative when it is written in standard form.

4 ASSESS

ASSESSMENT RESOURCES

For more assessment resources, see:
- Assessment Book
- Test and Practice Generator

MINI-QUIZ

Write the number in scientific notation.

1. 76,200 **7.62×10^4**
2. 0.152 **1.52×10^{-1}**

Write the number in standard form.

3. 6.5×10^8 **650,000,000**
4. 3.4×10^{-3} **0.0034**
5. **Challenge** Order the numbers 58.12×10^{-4}, 0.0005812, and 5812×10^{-5} from least to greatest. **0.0005812, 58.12×10^{-4}, 5812×10^{-5}**

5 FOLLOW-UP

DIAGNOSIS/REMEDIATION

- Study Guide in Chapter 4 Resource Book, pp. 66–67
- eTutorial Plus Online
- Extra Practice, p. 806
- Lesson Practice in Chapter 4 Resource Book, pp. 63–65

ENGLISH LEARNER SUPPORT

- Spanish Study Guide
- Multi-Language Visual Glossary
- Chapter Audio Summaries CDs

CHALLENGE

- Challenge Practice in Chapter 4 Resource Book, p. 69
- Teacher's Edition, p. 168F

54a, 61–63. See Additional Answers beginning on page AA1.

Enlarged image of the pits and lands on a compact disc

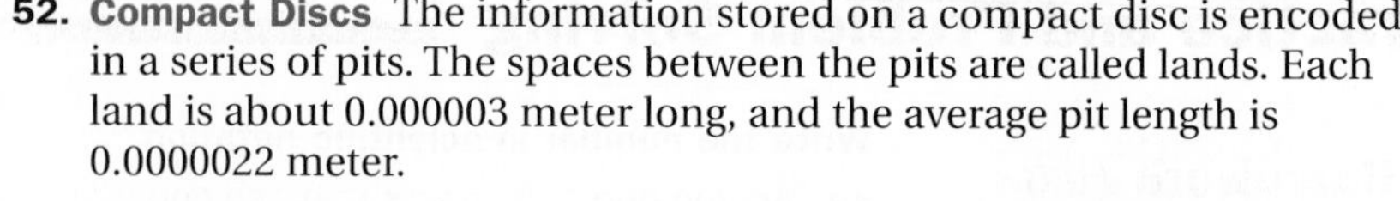

52. **Compact Discs** The information stored on a compact disc is encoded in a series of pits. The spaces between the pits are called lands. Each land is about 0.000003 meter long, and the average pit length is 0.0000022 meter.

 a. Write each of these lengths in scientific notation. Then write the combined length of a pit and a land in scientific notation. **3×10^{-6} m, 2.2×10^{-6} m; 5.2×10^{-6} m**

 b. Suppose a compact disc contains 2,000,000,000 pits and 2,000,000,000 lands. How long would this series of pits and lands be if laid out in a straight line? Give your answer in scientific notation. **1.04×10^4 m**

C 53. **Extended Problem Solving** Plankton are microscopic organisms that drift in water. A right whale feeds by swimming through masses of plankton with its mouth open. Answer the following questions using scientific notation.

 a. Analyze When a right whale feeds, about 2.3 cubic meters of water pass through its mouth each second. Right whales feed in areas with about 9000 plankton per cubic meter. How many plankton does a right whale ingest each second? **2.07×10^4 plankton**

 b. How many plankton does a right whale ingest in 1 hour of feeding? **about 7.45×10^7 plankton**

 c. A right whale may feed for up to 15 hours a day. Use a calculator to find how many plankton a right whale ingests in a day. **about 1.12×10^9 plankton**

 d. Estimate Suppose a right whale consumes 500,000 Calories per day. About how many calories does a single plankton contain? **about 4.47×10^{-4} Cal**

54a. See margin.

54b. Always. *Sample answer:* For any value of n, the exponent in the value of $n \times 10^{n+1}$ is greater than the exponent in the value of $(n + 1) \times 10^n$.

54. **Challenge** Let n be any positive integer. Consider the expressions $n \times 10^{n+1}$ and $(n + 1) \times 10^n$.

 a. Make a table of values for each expression when $n = 1, 2, 3$, and 4.

 b. Is the value of $n \times 10^{n+1}$ *always, sometimes,* or *never* greater than the value of $(n + 1) \times 10^n$? Explain.

Mixed Review

Order the integers from least to greatest. *(Lesson 1.4)*

55. $-16, 13, 11, -17$ **$-17, -16, 11, 13$**
56. $-23, 24, -27, 25$ **$-27, -23, 24, 25$**
57. $-119, 99, -114, -98$ **$-119, -114, -98, 99$**

Algebra Basics Solve the equation. *(Lesson 2.7)*

58. $x + 3.6 = -10.8$ **-14.4**
59. $y - 9.5 = 11.2$ **20.7**
60. $2.5m = -5.1$ **-2.04**

Solve the inequality. Graph and check your solution. *(Lesson 3.6)* **61–63. See margin for art.**

61. $3x - 7 > 8$ **$x > 5$**
62. $-4y + 16 < 36$ **$y > -5$**
63. $2 - 5x > 27$ **$x < -5$**

Standardized Test Practice

64. **Extended Response** The table shows the 2001 populations of several countries.

Country	Population
China	1.273×10^9
Fiji	844,000
Iceland	2.78×10^5
Russia	142,300,000

 a. Which country has the greatest population? **China**

 b. Which country has the least population? **Iceland**

 c. How many times greater is the population of the country in part (a) than the population of the country in part (b)? Explain. **About 5000 times greater. *Sample answer:* Divide China's population by Iceland's population.**

Technology *Activity* CALCULATOR

4.7 Using Scientific Notation

Goal Use a scientific calculator to perform operations on numbers written in scientific notation.

Example

Use a calculator to solve the following problem.

Scientists have discovered over 100 exoplanets (planets outside of our solar system). One of these exoplanets orbits the star Epsilon Eridani. The mass of this exoplanet is about 2.3×10^{27} kilograms. The star and the exoplanet are about 10.5 light-years from the Sun.

How many times more massive is the exoplanet than Earth, which has a mass of 6×10^{24} kilograms? Given that 1 light-year is equal to 9.5×10^{12} kilometers, what is the distance (in kilometers) from the Sun to the exoplanet?

Solution

1 To find how many times more massive the exoplanet is than Earth, divide the mass of the exoplanet by the mass of Earth.

Keystrokes

2.3 [EE] 27 [÷] 6 [EE] 24 [=]

```
2.3E27÷6E24
  383.3333333
```

The exoplanet is about 383 times more massive than Earth.

2 To find the distance (in kilometers) of the exoplanet from the Sun, multiply the distance in light-years by the number of kilometers in a light-year.

Keystrokes

9.5 [EE] 12 [×] 10.5 [=]

```
9.5E12×10.5
  9.975×10^13
```

The exoplanet is about 9.98×10^{13} kilometers from the Sun.

Draw Conclusions

Use a calculator to find the product or quotient.

1. $(6.13 \times 10^{17}) \times (8.92 \times 10^{-11})$ **5.46796×10^{7}**
2. $(4.09 \times 10^{-9}) \div (5.31 \times 10^{23})$ **$7.702448211 \times 10^{-33}$**
3. **Tau Boo** The star Tau Boo has an exoplanet that is about 2.5×10^{3} times as massive as Earth. What is the mass (in kilograms) of the Tau Boo exoplanet? **1.5×10^{28} kilograms**

Tech *Help*

Use the exponent key [EE] on a calculator to enter numbers written in scientific notation.

NCTM CURRICULUM STANDARDS

Standard 1: Understand numbers; Understand ways of representing numbers

1 PLAN

Learn the Method

- Students will use a scientific calculator to perform operations on numbers written in scientific notation.
- Students can use the skills they learn in the activity to rework Exercises 44–47 on page 207 of Lesson 4.7.

2 TEACH

Tips for Success

Students may need to be reminded that a light-year is a measure of distance, not time.

Extra Examples

Example Find $(5.2 \times 10^{6}) \div (1.3 \times 10^{4})$. **$4 \times 10^{2}$**

3 CLOSE

Assessment

1. Find $(3.8 \times 10^{21}) \times (8.2 \times 10^{-10})$. **$3.116 \times 10^{12}$**
2. Find $(1.2 \times 10^{24}) \div (7.5 \times 10^{19})$. **$1.6 \times 10^{4}$**

ADDITIONAL RESOURCES

The following resources are available to help review the materials in Lessons 4.5–4.7.

Chapter 4 Resource Book

- Lesson Practice
- Study Guide

Assessment Book

- Chapter 4 Quiz 2

Technology

- Test and Practice Generator
- eTutorial CD-ROM

Internet

- Classzone
- eWorkbook Plus Online
- eTutorial Plus Online

ENGLISH LEARNER SUPPORT

- Spanish Study Guide
- Multi-Language Visual Glossary
- Chapter Audio Summaries CDs

3. ***Sample answer:*** $\frac{2}{3}$ **and** $\frac{10}{15}$**; they are equivalent because** $\frac{10}{15}$ **in simplest form is** $\frac{10 \div 5}{15 \div 5} = \frac{2}{3}$.

CHAPTER 4

Chapter Review

Vocabulary Review

prime number, p. 173
composite number, p. 173
prime factorization, p. 173
factor tree, p. 173
monomial, p. 174
common factor, p. 177
greatest common factor (GCF), p. 177
relatively prime, p. 178
equivalent fractions, p. 182
simplest form, p. 183
multiple, p. 187
common multiple, p. 187
least common multiple (LCM), p. 187
least common denominator (LCD), p. 188
scientific notation, p. 204

1. Give an example of a prime number and an example of a composite number.
Sample answer: **prime: 23, composite: 120**
2. What does it mean for two nonzero whole numbers to be relatively prime?
Their greatest common factor is 1.
3. Write two equivalent fractions and explain why they are equivalent. **See margin.**
4. Is the number 0.32×10^{-4} written in scientific notation? Why or why not?
No; 0.32 is not between 1 and 10.

4.1 Factors and Prime Factorization

Examples on pp. 172–174

▶ ***Goal***

Factor numbers and monomials.

Example **Write the prime factorization of 240.**

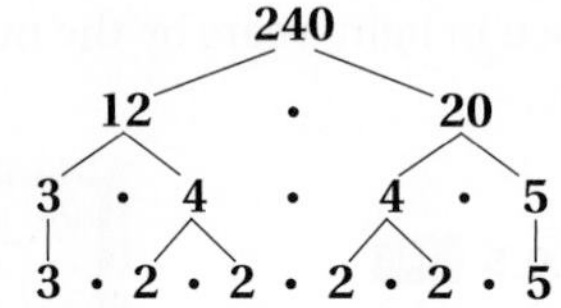

Write original number.
Write 240 as 12 · 20.
Write 12 as 3 · 4 and 20 as 4 · 5.
Write 4 as 2 · 2, twice.

The prime factorization of 240 is $2^4 \cdot 3 \cdot 5$.

Example **Factor the monomial $42x^4y$.**

$42x^4y = 2 \cdot 3 \cdot 7 \cdot x^4 \cdot y$ **Write 42 as 2 · 3 · 7.**

$= 2 \cdot 3 \cdot 7 \cdot x \cdot x \cdot x \cdot x \cdot y$ **Write x^4 as $x \cdot x \cdot x \cdot x$.**

✔ **Write the prime factorization of the number.**

5. 75 $3 \cdot 5^2$ **6.** 104 $2^3 \cdot 13$ **7.** 129 $3 \cdot 43$ **8.** 138 $2 \cdot 3 \cdot 23$

Factor the monomial.

9. $36a^4b^3$ **10.** $98x^3y^2$ **11.** $72w^6z$ **12.** $15r^2s^2$

9. $2 \cdot 2 \cdot 3 \cdot 3 \cdot a \cdot a \cdot a \cdot a \cdot b \cdot b \cdot b$

10. $2 \cdot 7 \cdot 7 \cdot x \cdot x \cdot x \cdot y \cdot y$

11. $2 \cdot 2 \cdot 2 \cdot 3 \cdot 3 \cdot w \cdot w \cdot w \cdot w \cdot w \cdot w \cdot z$

12. $3 \cdot 5 \cdot r \cdot r \cdot s \cdot s$

The following resources are available to help review the materials in this chapter.

Chapter 4 Resource Book

- Chapter Review Games and Activities, p. 70
- Cumulative Practice, Chs. 1–4

English/Spanish Chapter Reviews and Tests

Chapter Audio Summaries CDs

eTutorial CD-ROM

eWorkbook Plus Online

eTutorial Plus Online

4.2 Greatest Common Factor

Examples on pp. 177–178

Goal

Find the GCF of numbers and monomials.

Example **Find the greatest common factor of 45, 18, and 90.**

Write the prime factorization of each number.

$45 = 3 \cdot 3 \cdot 5$

$18 = 2 \cdot 3 \cdot 3$

$90 = 2 \cdot 3 \cdot 3 \cdot 5$

The common prime factors are 3 and 3. The GCF is the product $3 \cdot 3 = 9$.

Find the greatest common factor of the numbers.

13. 26, 74 2 **14.** 32, 64 32 **15.** 12, 40, 68 4 **16.** 15, 42, 63 3

4.3 Equivalent Fractions

Examples on pp. 182–184

Goal

Write fractions in simplest form.

Example **Write $\frac{60}{75}$ in simplest form.**

Write the prime factorization of the numerator and the denominator.

$60 = 2^2 \cdot 3 \cdot 5$ $75 = 3 \cdot 5 \cdot 5$

The GCF of 60 and 75 is $3 \cdot 5 = 15$.

$\frac{60}{75} = \frac{60 \div 15}{75 \div 15}$ **Divide numerator and denominator by GCF.**

$= \frac{4}{5}$ **Simplify.**

Example **Write $\frac{21a^2}{49ab}$ in simplest form.**

$\frac{21a^2}{49ab} = \frac{3 \cdot 7 \cdot a \cdot a}{7 \cdot 7 \cdot a \cdot b}$ **Factor numerator and denominator.**

$= \frac{3 \cdot \overset{1}{\cancel{7}} \cdot \overset{1}{\cancel{a}} \cdot a}{7 \cdot \underset{1}{\cancel{7}} \cdot \underset{1}{\cancel{a}} \cdot b}$ **Divide out common factors.**

$= \frac{3a}{7b}$ **Simplify.**

Write the fraction in simplest form.

17. $\frac{4}{18}$ $\frac{2}{9}$ **18.** $\frac{12}{21}$ $\frac{4}{7}$ **19.** $\frac{17}{68}$ $\frac{1}{4}$ **20.** $\frac{30}{72}$ $\frac{5}{12}$

21. $\frac{6ab}{4b^2}$ $\frac{3a}{2b}$ **22.** $\frac{5cd}{2d}$ $\frac{5c}{2}$ **23.** $\frac{8xy}{2x^2y}$ $\frac{4}{x}$ **24.** $\frac{22m^2n}{11mn^2}$ $\frac{2m}{n}$

4.4 Least Common Multiple

Examples on pp. 187–189

Goal

Use the LCD to compare fractions.

Example Use the LCD to compare $\frac{5}{36}$ and $\frac{17}{90}$.

1) Find the least common multiple of the denominators.

$36 = 2 \cdot 2 \cdot 3 \cdot 3$

$90 = 2 \cdot 3 \cdot 3 \cdot 5$

The common factors are 2, 3, and 3.

Multiply all of the factors, using the common factors only once.

LCM $= 2 \cdot 3 \cdot 3 \cdot 2 \cdot 5 = 180$, so the LCD $= 180$.

2) Write equivalent fractions using the LCD.

$\frac{5}{36} = \frac{5 \cdot 5}{36 \cdot 5} = \frac{25}{180}$ $\qquad \frac{17}{90} = \frac{17 \cdot 2}{90 \cdot 2} = \frac{34}{180}$

3) Compare the numerators: $\frac{25}{180} < \frac{34}{180}$, so $\frac{5}{36} < \frac{17}{90}$.

Use the LCD to determine which fraction is greater.

25. $\frac{1}{12}, \frac{3}{40}$ **$\frac{1}{12}$** **26.** $\frac{4}{15}, \frac{7}{27}$ **$\frac{4}{15}$** **27.** $\frac{7}{30}, \frac{11}{36}$ **$\frac{11}{36}$** **28.** $\frac{4}{45}, \frac{13}{60}$ **$\frac{13}{60}$**

29. Soccer You and your friend are on different soccer teams. This season, your team won 14 out of 20 games. Your friend's team won 18 out of 24 games. Which team won a greater fraction of its games? **the friend's team**

4.5 Rules of Exponents

Examples on pp. 194–196

Goal

Use rules of exponents to simplify products and quotients.

Example Find the product. Write your answer using exponents.

a. $5^8 \cdot 5^6 = 5^{8+6}$ **Product of powers property**

$= 5^{14}$ **Add exponents.**

b. $7a^2 \cdot a^6 = 7 \cdot (a^2 \cdot a^6)$ **Associative property of multiplication**

$= 7 \cdot a^{2+6}$ **Product of powers property**

$= 7a^8$ **Add exponents.**

Find the product. Write your answer using exponents.

30. $2^{11} \cdot 2^3$ **2^{14}** **31.** $3^5 \cdot 3^7$ **3^{12}** **32.** $7^8 \cdot 7^9$ **7^{17}** **33.** $10^4 \cdot 10^4$ **10^8**

34. $16b^4 \cdot b^2$ **$16b^6$** **35.** $c^9 \cdot 8c^2$ **$8c^{11}$** **36.** $5x \cdot 4x^9$ **$20x^{10}$** **37.** $y^4 \cdot y^3 \cdot y^2$ **y^9**

4.6 Negative and Zero Exponents

Examples on pp. 199–201

Goal

Rewrite expressions containing negative or zero exponents.

Example **Write 8^0b^{-5} using only positive exponents.**

$8^0b^{-5} = 1 \cdot b^{-5}$ **Definition of zero exponent**

$= \frac{1}{b^5}$ **Definition of negative exponent**

✔ **Write the expression using only positive exponents.**

38. 12^{-4} $\frac{1}{12^4}$ **39.** 6^0 1 **40.** $7c^{-3}$ $\frac{7}{c^3}$ **41.** $15d^{-9}$ $\frac{15}{d^9}$

4.7 Scientific Notation

Examples on pp. 204–206

Goal

Write numbers in scientific notation.

Example **Write the number in scientific notation.**

	Standard form	Product form	Scientific notation
a.	41,800,000	$4.18 \times 10{,}000{,}000$	4.18×10^7
b.	0.0000037	3.7×0.000001	3.7×10^{-6}

Example **Order 4.7×10^{-5}, 0.000056, and 3.2×10^{-6} from least to greatest.**

1. Write each number in scientific notation if necessary.
   $0.000056 = 5.6 \times 10^{-5}$
2. Order the numbers with different powers of 10.
   Because $10^{-6} < 10^{-5}$, $3.2 \times 10^{-6} < 4.7 \times 10^{-5}$ and $3.2 \times 10^{-6} < 5.6 \times 10^{-5}$.
3. Then order the numbers with the same power of 10.
   Because $4.7 < 5.6$, $4.7 \times 10^{-5} < 5.6 \times 10^{-5}$.
4. Write the original numbers in order from least to greatest.
   3.2×10^{-6}; 4.7×10^{-5}; 0.000056

✔ **Write the number in scientific notation.**

42. 0.000000745 7.45×10^{-7} **43.** 67,000,000 6.7×10^7 **44.** 0.000000881 8.81×10^{-7} **45.** 4,280,000,000 4.28×10^9

Copy and complete the statement using <, >, or =.

46. 4.8×10^{-5} _?_ 4.8×10^{-8} > **47.** 1.08×10^6 _?_ 1.09×10^7 <

ADDITIONAL RESOURCES

Assessment Book

- Chapter Test (3 levels), pp. 48–53
- Standardized Chapter Test, p. 54
- Alternative Assessment, pp. 55–56

Test and Practice Generator

CHAPTER 4

Chapter Test

Write the prime factorization of the number.

1. 27 3^3 **2.** 60 $2^2 \cdot 3 \cdot 5$ **3.** 84 $2^2 \cdot 3 \cdot 7$ **4.** 260 $2^2 \cdot 5 \cdot 13$

Find the greatest common factor of the numbers. Then tell whether they are relatively prime.

5. 25, 75 25; not relatively prime **6.** 30, 49 1; relatively prime **7.** 32, 90 2; not relatively prime **8.** 42, 108 6; not relatively prime

Write the fraction in simplest form.

9. $\frac{27}{90}$ $\frac{3}{10}$ **10.** $\frac{46}{60}$ $\frac{23}{30}$ **11.** $\frac{8xy}{16y}$ $\frac{x}{2}$ **12.** $\frac{12a^2}{2ab}$ $\frac{6a}{b}$

Use the LCD to determine which fraction is greater.

13. $\frac{3}{5}, \frac{8}{15}$ $\frac{3}{5}$ **14.** $\frac{11}{12}, \frac{11}{20}$ $\frac{11}{12}$ **15.** $\frac{3}{35}, \frac{7}{45}$ $\frac{7}{45}$ **16.** $\frac{29}{50}, \frac{61}{100}$ $\frac{61}{100}$

17. Basketball The table shows the points you scored and the total points your team scored for each game in the season playoff.

a. For each game, write the fraction of your team's points that you scored. Give your answers in simplest form. game 1: $\frac{2}{7}$, game 2: $\frac{1}{3}$, game 3: $\frac{3}{13}$, game 4: $\frac{1}{13}$, game 5: $\frac{4}{15}$

b. In which game did you score the greatest fraction of points? game 2

Game	You	Your team
1	12	42
2	19	57
3	15	65
4	4	52
5	16	60

Find the product or quotient. Write your answer using exponents.

18. $13^6 \cdot 13^4$ 13^{10} **19.** $4m^7 \cdot 5m^6$ $20m^{13}$ **20.** $\frac{7^6}{7^9}$ $\frac{1}{7^3}$ or 7^{-3} **21.** $\frac{4w^{15}}{24w^3}$ $\frac{w^{12}}{6}$

Write the expression using only positive exponents.

22. 15^{-4} $\frac{1}{15^4}$ **23.** $16h^{-7}$ $\frac{16}{h^7}$ **24.** $12x^0$ 12 **25.** $m^{-4}n^5$ $\frac{n^5}{m^4}$

Write the number in scientific notation.

26. 5,100,000,000 5.1×10^9 **27.** 6,450,000,000,000 6.45×10^{12} **28.** 0.00000000897 8.97×10^{-9} **29.** 0.00000093 9.3×10^{-7}

Copy and complete the statement using <, >, or =.

30. 9.0×10^{17} ? 5.2×10^{18} $<$ **31.** 7.31×10^{-2} ? 7.31×10^{-3} $>$

32. 1.25×10^{-9} ? 1.05×10^{-9} $>$ **33.** 8.12×10^5 ? 8.18×10^4 $>$

Chapter Standardized Test

Test-Taking Strategy **Be sure to completely read the question and all answer choices before choosing an answer.**

1. Which number is *not* prime? D

   A. 7 **B.** 37 **C.** 53 **D.** 57

2. Which expression is the prime factorization of 168? H

   F. $2^2 \cdot 3^2 \cdot 7$ **G.** $2 \cdot 3 \cdot 7^2$

   H. $2^3 \cdot 3 \cdot 7$ **I.** $2^3 \cdot 3 \cdot 7^2$

3. What is the greatest common factor of $14x^2$ and $38x^3$? B

   A. $2x^3$ **B.** $2x^2$ **C.** $266x^3$ **D.** $532x^2$

4. Which numbers are relatively prime? F

   F. 25, 36 **G.** 12, 20

   H. 24, 28 **I.** 45, 84

5. Which fraction is *not* in simplest form? D

   A. $\frac{1}{2}$ **B.** $\frac{21}{32}$ **C.** $\frac{35}{54}$ **D.** $\frac{54}{72}$

6. In a florist's window, 30 of 36 plants are flowering. Write the fraction of flowering plants in simplest form. F

   F. $\frac{5}{6}$ **G.** $\frac{10}{12}$ **H.** $\frac{15}{18}$ **I.** $\frac{30}{36}$

7. What is the LCM of 16 and 80? B

   A. 8 **B.** 80 **C.** 160 **D.** 320

8. Which fraction is greater than $\frac{17}{60}$? H

   F. $\frac{4}{15}$ **G.** $\frac{7}{30}$ **H.** $\frac{19}{45}$ **I.** $\frac{29}{120}$

9. Which expression is equivalent to $8x^4 \cdot 5x^3$?

   A. $20x^7$ **B.** $40x^7$ **C.** $20x^{12}$ **D.** $40x^{12}$ B

10. Which expression is equivalent to $\frac{15b^9}{25b^3}$? H

    F. $\frac{3b^3}{5}$ **G.** $\frac{3}{5b^3}$ **H.** $\frac{3b^6}{5}$ **I.** $\frac{3}{5b^6}$

11. Which expression is *not* equivalent to $\frac{1}{64}$? B

    A. 2^{-6} **B.** 4^{-4} **C.** 8^{-2} **D.** 64^{-1}

12. Which expression is equivalent to $3^{-4}x^0$? F

    F. $\frac{1}{81}$ **G.** 3^4 **H.** $\frac{1}{81x}$ **I.** $\frac{x}{81}$

13. Which list of numbers is in order from least to greatest? D

    A. 1.4×10^6, 3.28×10^3, 6.3×10^2, 8.2×10^3

    B. 6.3×10^2, 8.2×10^3, 3.28×10^3, 1.4×10^6

    C. 1.4×10^6, 6.3×10^2, 3.28×10^3, 8.2×10^3

    D. 6.3×10^2, 3.28×10^3, 8.2×10^3, 1.4×10^6

14. **Short Response** A certain type of bacteria has been found in lengths 0.000018 meter, 7.5×10^{-6} meter, and 2.5×10^{-6} meter. Order these lengths from least to greatest.
    2.5×10^{-6} m, 7.5×10^{-6} m, 0.000018 m

15. **Extended Response** You have a wooden board that measures 54 centimeters by 90 centimeters. You want to cut the board into identical square pieces with integer side lengths and use all of the wood.

    a. Make a sketch of the board. Find three possible side lengths for the squares.
    See margin for art. *Sample answer:* 2 cm, 3 cm, 6 cm.

    b. What is the largest side length you can choose? Explain.
    18 cm; *Sample answer:* 18 is the GCF of 54 and 90.

    c. How many square pieces will you have?
    15

Additional Resources

Assessment Book
- Standardized Chapter Test, p. 54

Test and Practice Generator

15a.

54 cm

90 cm

CHAPTER 5

Pacing and Assignment Guide

REGULAR SCHEDULE

Lesson	Les. Day	BASIC	AVERAGE	ADVANCED
5.1	Day 1	SRH p. 770 Exs. 9-12; pp. 222-224 Exs. 20-31, 46-48, 62, 66-71	pp. 222-224 Exs. 24-31, 46-48, 61-64, 66-72	pp. 222-224 Exs. 24-31, 46-48, 61-67*, 70-72
	Day 2	SRH p. 778 Exs. 16-20; pp. 222-224 Exs. 32-44, 49-52, 57-60, 72-74	pp. 222-224 Exs. 36-45, 53-60, 73-75	pp. 222-224 Exs. 36-45, 53-60, 73-75
5.2	Day 1	SRH p. 779 Exs. 1-5; pp. 228-229 Exs. 10-21, 27-34, 38-43, 46-48, 54-64	pp. 228-229 Exs. 14-28, 31-37, 41-45, 49-52, 54-65	pp. 228-229 Exs. 15-17, 20-28, 33-37, 41-56*, 61-65
5.3	Day 1	SRH p. 778 Exs. 21-25; pp. 234-235 Exs. 12-23, 53-62	pp. 234-235 Exs. 12-25, 51, 53-62	pp. 234-235 Exs. 16-25, 51-60*
	Day 2	pp. 234-235 Exs. 24-34, 36-39, 45-47, 63	pp. 234-235 Exs. 26-44, 48-50, 63	pp. 234-235 Exs. 26-32, 35-43, 48-50, 61-63
5.4	Day 1	SRH p. 780 Exs. 13-16; pp. 240-241 Exs. 8-17, 20, 23-28, 30-32, 37, 38, 42-52	pp. 240-241 Exs. 11-22, 26-29, 33-40, 42-52	pp. 240-241 Exs. 11, 14-22, 26-29, 33-41*, 44, 47, 50-52
5.5	Day 1	SRH p. 778 Exs. 6-10; pp. 245-246 Exs. 16-19, 30-35, 38-45	pp. 245-246 Exs. 16-19, 29-35, 38-45	pp. 245-246 Exs. 16-23, 29-32, 40-45
	Day 2	pp. 245-246 Exs. 20-29, 46-50	pp. 245-246 Exs. 20-28, 36, 46-50	pp. 245-246 Exs. 24-28, 33-37*, 46-50
5.6	Day 1	EP p. 805 Exs. 1-8; pp. 249-251 Exs. 11-14, 21-26, 35-38	pp. 249-251 Exs. 10-14, 21-26, 35-40	pp. 249-251 Exs. 10, 13-16, 21-26, 37-42
	Day 2	pp. 249-251 Exs. 15-19, 27-31, 39-44	pp. 249-251 Exs. 15-20, 27-33, 41-44	pp. 249-251 Exs. 17-20, 27-34*, 43, 44
5.7	Day 1	EP p. 805 Exs. 57-60; pp. 256-257 Exs. 13-18, 22-27, 41, 43, 47-52	pp. 256-257 Exs. 13-18, 22-27, 40-42, 47-52	pp. 256-257 Exs. 16-21, 25-31, 40-43, 48, 49
	Day 2	pp. 256-257 Exs. 19-21, 28-30, 32-39, 53-57	pp. 256-257 Exs. 19-21, 28-39, 43-45, 53-57	pp. 256-257 Exs. 34-39, 44-46*, 51-57
Review	Day 1	pp. 258-261 Exs. 1-40	pp. 258-261 Exs. 1-40	pp. 258-261 Exs. 1-40
Assess	Day 1	Chapter 5 Test	Chapter 5 Test	Chapter 5 Test

YEARLY PACING Chapter 5 Total – **14 days** Chapters 1–5 Total – **58 days** Remaining – **102 days**

*Challenge Exercises EP = Extra Practice SRH = Skills Review Handbook

BLOCK SCHEDULE

DAY 1	DAY 2	DAY 3	DAY 4	DAY 5	DAY 6	DAY 7
5.1 pp. 222-224 Exs. 24-31, 36-48, 53-64, 66-75	**5.2** pp. 228-229 Exs. 16-28, 31-37, 41-45, 49-52, 54-65 **5.3** pp. 234-235 Exs. 12-25, 51, 53-62	**5.3 (cont.)** pp. 234-235 Exs. 26-44, 48-50, 63 **5.4** pp. 240-241 Exs. 12-22, 26-29, 33-40, 42-52	**5.5** pp. 245-246 Exs. 16-36, 38-50	**5.6** pp. 249-251 Exs. 10-33, 35-44	**5.7** pp. 256-257 Exs. 13-45, 47-57	**Review** pp. 258-261 Exs. 1-40 **Assess** Chapter 5 Test

YEARLY PACING Chapter 5 Total – **7 days** Chapters 1–5 Total – **29 days** Remaining – **51 days**

Support Materials

CHAPTER RESOURCE BOOK

CHAPTER SUPPORT							
Tips for New Teachers	p. 1		Parents as Partners			p. 3	

LESSON SUPPORT	5.1	5.2	5.3	5.4	5.5	5.6	5.7
Lesson Plans (regular and block)	p. 5	p. 14	p. 23	p. 31	p. 41	p. 49	p. 57
Technology Activities & Keystrokes	p. 7			p. 34			
Activity Support Masters							
Activity Masters				p. 33			
Practice (3 levels)	p. 8	p. 16	p. 25	p. 35	p. 43	p. 51	p. 59
Study Guide	p. 11	p. 19	p. 28	p. 38	p. 46	p. 54	p. 62
Real-World Problem Solving		p. 21					p. 64
Challenge Practice	p. 13	p. 22	p. 30	p. 40	p. 48	p. 56	p. 65

REVIEW			
Chapter Review Games and Activities	p. 66	Extra Credit Project with Rubric	p. 71
Real-Life Project with Rubric	p. 67	Cumulative Practice	p. 73
Cooperative Project with Rubric	p. 69	Resource Book Answers	A1

ASSESSMENT

Quizzes	p. 57	Alternative Assessments with Rubrics	p. 66
Chapter Tests (3 levels)	p. 59	Unit Test	p. 90
Standardized Test	p. 65	Cumulative Test	p. 92

TRANSPARENCIES

	5.1	5.2	5.3	5.4	5.5	5.6	5.7
Warm-Up/Daily Homework Quiz	✔	✔	✔	✔	✔	✔	✔
Notetaking Guide	✔	✔	✔	✔	✔	✔	✔
Teacher Support	✔						
English/Spanish Problem Solving	✔		✔		✔		
Answer Transparencies	✔	✔	✔	✔	✔	✔	✔

TECHNOLOGY

- EasyPlanner CD-ROM
- Test and Practice Generator
- Electronic Lesson Presentations
- eTutorial CD-ROM
- Chapter Audio Summaries CDs
- Classzone.com
- eEdition Plus Online
- eWorkbook Plus Online
- eTutorial Plus Online
- EasyPlanner Plus Online

ADDITIONAL RESOURCES

- Worked-Out Solution Key
- Notetaking Guide
- Practice Workbook
- Tutor Place
- Professional Development Book
- Special Activities Book
- Posters
- Spanish Study Guide
- Exercises in Spanish
- English/Spanish Ch. Reviews/Tests
- Multi-Language Visual Glossary

CHAPTER 5

Math Background and Teaching Strategies

Lesson 5.1

MATH BACKGROUND

Any **rational number** can be written as the quotient of two integers, where the divisor is not 0. You can write any rational number in decimal form by carrying out the division. If a remainder of 0 occurs, the decimal *terminates*. Otherwise, the decimal *repeats*, that is, a digit or block of digits repeats without end. A bar is placed over the repeating digit or digits. To write a repeating decimal as a fraction, set it equal to x, multiply this equation by an appropriate power of 10, and then subtract the original equation or its product with a lesser power of 10.

TEACHING STRATEGIES

To give students an idea of when the decimal form of a fraction will terminate and when it will repeat, have them find the decimal forms of $\frac{1}{2}, \frac{3}{4}, \frac{4}{5}, \frac{1}{8}$, and $\frac{7}{20}$. Then have them find the decimal forms of $\frac{1}{3}, \frac{5}{6}, \frac{2}{11}$, and $\frac{4}{15}$. Challenge students to identify what the fractions with terminating decimal forms have in common, which is that their denominators are multiples *only* of 2 and/or 5.

Lesson 5.2

MATH BACKGROUND

To add or subtract fractions that have a common denominator, find the sum or difference of the numerators and keep the common denominator. Then write the result in simplest form if possible. To add or subtract mixed numbers, some students may prefer to first rewrite the mixed numbers as improper fractions, perform the operation, and then convert the result to a mixed number.

TEACHING STRATEGIES

As an additional example that requires students to combine both old and new skills, have students solve the equation $x + \frac{5}{8} = 2\frac{3}{8}$. Solving this equation then requires students to use the subtraction property of equality, to convert from a mixed number to an improper fraction, to subtract fractions with like denominators, and then to convert from an improper fraction to a mixed number.

Lesson 5.3

MATH BACKGROUND

To add or subtract fractions with unlike denominators, a common denominator must first be found. Though the simplest way to find a common denominator is often just to use the product of the denominators, you can avoid having to perform excessive simplification after performing the operation by using the *least* common denominator.

TEACHING STRATEGIES

Have pairs of students roll two number cubes, then write a fraction with the greater number rolled as the denominator and the other as the numerator. (If the numbers are the same, have students roll again.) Challenge students to find the greatest fraction that could be the result of rolling the cubes again if the sum of this fraction and the first fraction must be less than 1. For example, if the fraction is $\frac{2}{5}$, then the answer is $\frac{1}{2}$, and the sum is $\frac{4}{10} + \frac{5}{10} = \frac{9}{10}$.

Lesson 5.4

MATH BACKGROUND

To multiply two fractions, you need only write the product of the numerators as the new numerator and the product of the denominators as the new denominator, and then simplify by dividing out common factors as necessary. It is easiest to multiply mixed numbers by first rewriting the mixed numbers as improper fractions.

TEACHING STRATEGIES

There are some points of confusion to watch for as students begin to multiply fractions. One is that students are used to thinking of multiplication as repeated addition, which is not useful here. Also, students who think "multiplication makes bigger" (at least for positive numbers) may have trouble evaluating the product of fractions for reasonableness. For the product of proper fractions, you can help remedy this misconception by pointing out, for example, that the product of $\frac{3}{4}$ and $\frac{5}{9}$ will be smaller than either factor, since it is a "part of a part." Also, encourage students to estimate products involving fractions before calculating them. For example, $\frac{8}{9} \cdot -\frac{3}{4}$ will be close to $-\frac{3}{4}$ since $\frac{8}{9}$ is close to 1, $\frac{6}{11} \cdot \frac{5}{6}$ will be close to $\frac{1}{2} \cdot 1 = \frac{1}{2}$, and $1\frac{5}{6} \cdot 4\frac{1}{5}$ will be close to $2 \cdot 4 = 8$. Finally, remind students that dividing out common factors before multiplying makes simplification easier.

Lesson 5.5

MATH BACKGROUND

Two numbers whose product is 1, such as 8 and $\frac{1}{8}$ or $-\frac{3}{4}$ and $-\frac{4}{3}$, are **reciprocals**. To divide by a rational number, simply multiply by the reciprocal of the rational number. When performing division involving mixed numbers, first rewrite any mixed numbers as improper fractions.

TEACHING STRATEGIES

It will be helpful to work extra examples of dividing rational numbers. Here is an additional example.

Find the quotient $6\frac{3}{5} \div (-3)$.

$6\frac{3}{5} \div (-3) = \frac{33}{5} \div \left(-\frac{3}{1}\right)$ Write mixed numbers and integers as improper fractions.

$= \frac{33}{5} \cdot \left(-\frac{1}{3}\right)$ Multiply by the reciprocal.

$= \frac{\overset{11}{\cancel{33}} \cdot (-1)}{5 \cdot \underset{1}{\cancel{3}}}$ Use rule for multiplying fractions. Divide out common factors.

$= \frac{-11}{5}$ Multiply.

$= -2\frac{1}{5}$ Write the result as a mixed number.

To emphasize that a quotient may be greater than a dividend, you may also want to have students work a problem such as $6 \div \frac{1}{8}$. Point out that this is like asking how many eighths there are in 6.

Lesson 5.6

MATH BACKGROUND

The product of a number and its **multiplicative inverse**, or reciprocal is 1. All numbers except 0 have a multiplicative inverse. To solve an equation like $\frac{2}{5}x + \frac{2}{3} = 2$, once you have isolated the variable term you can multiply each side by the reciprocal of the coefficient of the variable, which will result in a coefficient of 1.

TEACHING STRATEGIES

In this lesson, since the principle presented is to use multiplicative inverses to solve equations, students should begin by rewriting all fractions with common denominators. Besides giving students practice in this skill, it requires them explicitly to identify multiplicative inverses for rational numbers. In the next lesson, students will learn how to solve similar equations by first clearing fractions.

Lesson 5.7

MATH BACKGROUND

When an equation or inequality contains fractions or decimals, students should first *clear* the fractions or decimals. To do this, they need to multiply each side of the equation or inequality by the LCD of all the fractions or by the power of 10 whose exponent is the greatest number of decimal places present in any of the decimals.

TEACHING STRATEGIES

Since the only new step in this lesson is clearing decimals or fractions, you may want to present students with extra problems for which the only step they must perform is to use the multiplication property of equality (or inequality) and the LCD to write an equivalent equation or inequality that has no decimals or fractions. Remind students that the LCD used is the LCD of *all* denominators in the equation.

CHAPTER

5 Differentiating Instruction

Strategies for Underachievers

USE ACTIVITIES, MANIPULATIVES, AND TOOLS

ORDERING RATIONAL NUMBERS In conjunction with Example 6 of Lesson 5.1, you may wish to use a "human number line" to help students better visualize the relationship of rational numbers and the number line. Give each student a piece of paper with a different rational number written on it. Students should conceal their numbers until called upon. Then call on students one-by-one to reveal their numbers, come to the front, and face the class with their numbers displayed. As each student comes to the front, he or she should take a position in the proper order with the other students to form the human number line. Have students still seated verify that those students at the front are in the proper order.

In conjunction with Concept Activity 5.3, you may wish to have students create their own area models for combining fractions out of strips of paper. Especially for fractions that have denominators of 2, 4, and 8, students can use folding to divide the models instead of, or in addition to, measuring and drawing. In this way, students may not always have to redraw their models as in Step 2, but can create fractions with like denominators by folding.

USE CALCULATORS

REPEATING DECIMALS The method used in Example 5 of Lesson 5.1 for writing a repeating decimal as a fraction may be difficult for many underachievers to grasp. Instead, you may wish to approach repeating decimals in terms of a few basic patterns that students can explore using their calculators. For example, $0.\overline{1} = \frac{1}{9}$, $0.\overline{2} = \frac{2}{9}$, and, in general, if there is a single repeating digit immediately to the right of the decimal point, then the equivalent fraction is that digit over 9. In the case of $0.\overline{3}$ and $0.\overline{6}$, the corresponding fractions $\frac{3}{9}$ and $\frac{6}{9}$ can then be written in simplest form as $\frac{1}{3}$ and $\frac{2}{3}$. Similarly, if there are two repeating digits immediately to the right of the decimal point, then the equivalent fraction is formed by placing those two digits over 99, as in $0.\overline{19} = \frac{19}{99}$, and if there are three repeating digits immediately to the right of the decimal point, then the equivalent fraction is formed by placing those three digits over 999, as in $0.\overline{234} = \frac{234}{999} = \frac{26}{111}$.

FOCUS ON VOCABULARY

This chapter acquaints or re-acquaints students with several important terms that they will need to master. Encourage students to add the terms *rational number, terminating decimal, repeating decimal, reciprocals,* and *multiplicative inverse* to their notebooks or to vocabulary cards. You will also need to make sure that students have already mastered the meanings of the terms *whole number, integer, least common denominator, mixed number, improper fraction, dividend, divisor,* and *quotient* before progressing in this chapter.

USE SCAFFOLDING

In Lesson 5.5, since division of fractions involves several steps, you may wish to provide templates of additional examples with justifications for each step to underachievers so that they can fill in the blanks as they learn the algorithm. Then students can use their completed templates as models when solving exercises.

Strategies for English Learners

DISSECT WORD PROBLEMS

The last sentence of a word problem usually contains a verb that issues a command. It orders the reader to do something. Almost always it is followed by an additional description of what the person is to do, as in "Solve the following equation," with *solve* being the command, and *the following equation* identifying what is to be solved. These command verbs are signals to the student that explain what the student is to do in the word problem. Comprehending these verbs is essential to solving word problems.

COMMAND VERBS The following command verbs were compiled from sample standardized test problems, word problems found in mathematics textbooks, and state standards:

> Apply, approximate, assume, calculate, check, choose, circle, classify, complete, compute, convert, create, decide, demonstrate, describe, design, determine, draw, establish, estimate, explain, examine, extend, find, fit, identify, interpret, investigate, list, make, mark, model, name, order, organize, perform, predict, prove, recognize, read, represent, round, select, show, sketch, solve, state, tell, transform, translate, use, verify, visualize

Ask students to group the words into categories, such as words that tell you to pick from a list, words that tell you to calculate something, and so on. Allow students to make up their own categories. It is important here to let students express and discuss what they think these terms mean. Many of the words would fit into more than one category depending on the context. For example, the term *draw* can be used in the following ways: Draw a picture; Draw a conclusion. These are very different requests, and students need to know both meanings. Through discussion, students can expose the different meanings of words and expand their concepts of what words mean. Watch for the tendency of students to confuse words that sound or look similar, for example *make* and *mark*. Encourage students to write new words in their journals, accompanied by a picture or an explanation in their primary language. Use a dictionary and thesaurus to provide additional meanings of words, as well as synonyms and antonyms.

Strategies for Advanced Learners

INCREASE DEPTH AND COMPLEXITY

REPEATING DECIMALS In conjunction with Example 5 and Exercise 65 of Lesson 5.1, you may wish to have advanced students write fractions for repeating decimals whose repeating digits do not begin immediately after the decimal point. For example, in $0.8\overline{3}$, the 8 does not repeat. Begin by multiplying $x = 0.8\overline{3}$ by the power of 10 whose exponent is the total number of decimal places up to and including the last digit that repeats. In this case, multiply $x = 0.8\overline{3}$ by 100 to obtain $100x = 83.\overline{3}$. Because $0.8\overline{3}$ does not match $83.\overline{3}$ in all of its decimal places, subtract $10x = 8.\overline{3}$ instead of $x = 0.8\overline{3}$.

$$\begin{aligned} 100x &= 83.\overline{3} \\ -\ (10x &= \ \ 8.\overline{3}) \\ \hline 90x &= 75 \\ x &= \frac{75}{90} = \frac{5}{6} \end{aligned}$$

Now look at the steps for writing $0.5\overline{63}$ as a fraction:

$$\begin{aligned} 1000x &= 563.\overline{63} \\ -\ (10x &= \ \ 5.\overline{63}) \\ \hline 990x &= 558 \\ x &= \frac{558}{990} = \frac{31}{55} \end{aligned}$$

Finally, here are the steps for writing $0.33\overline{5}$ as a fraction:

$$\begin{aligned} 1000x &= 335.\overline{5} \\ -\ (100x &= \ \ 33.\overline{5}) \\ \hline 900x &= 302 \\ x &= \frac{302}{900} = \frac{151}{450} \end{aligned}$$

Notice that the two powers of 10 used in each example differ in their numbers of zeros by the number of digits that repeat.

Advanced students may also be interested to know that the number of digits that repeat in the decimal form of a fraction is never more than 1 less than the denominator. For example, when the denominator is 7, there are 6 digits that repeat. Of course, the number of digits that repeat may be much less than the denominator, as in $\frac{2}{15} = 0.1\overline{3}$. Challenge advanced students to find another denominator for which the number of digits in the repeating pattern is only 1 less than that denominator. The next two possibilities after 7 are denominators of 17 and 19.

USE CROSS-CURRICULAR CONNECTIONS

STOCK MARKET You may wish to work with a social studies teacher to have students research the history of the U.S. stock market, including its use of fractions and mixed numbers.

The following problems can be used with **Lesson 5.3**:

- **Challenge** Find a value of x so that the given sum is equal to 1.

  a. $\frac{2}{3x} + \frac{3}{5x}$ $\frac{19}{15}$ **b.** $\frac{3}{x} + \frac{1}{2}$ 6

CHAPTER 5

Differentiating Instruction: Resource Materials

Differentiating Technology

McDougal Littell *Pre-Algebra* offers teachers a wide variety of technology, ranging from calculator activities in the *Chapter Resource Books* to the *Test and Practice Generator CD-ROM* to interactive, online resources and products accessed at Classzone.com.

CLASSZONE.COM

Classzone.com provides helpful online resources for students and teachers, including More Examples, Vocabulary Support, and State Test Practice. Classzone.com is also the access point for the following online products: *eEdition Plus Online*, an interactive, online version of the textbook; *eWorkbook Plus Online*, an interactive practice workbook correlated to the textbook; *eTutorial Plus Online*, an Internet tutorial that makes it easier than ever to help students master skills and concepts; and *EasyPlanner Plus Online*, an online resource with teacher tools and a lesson planner.

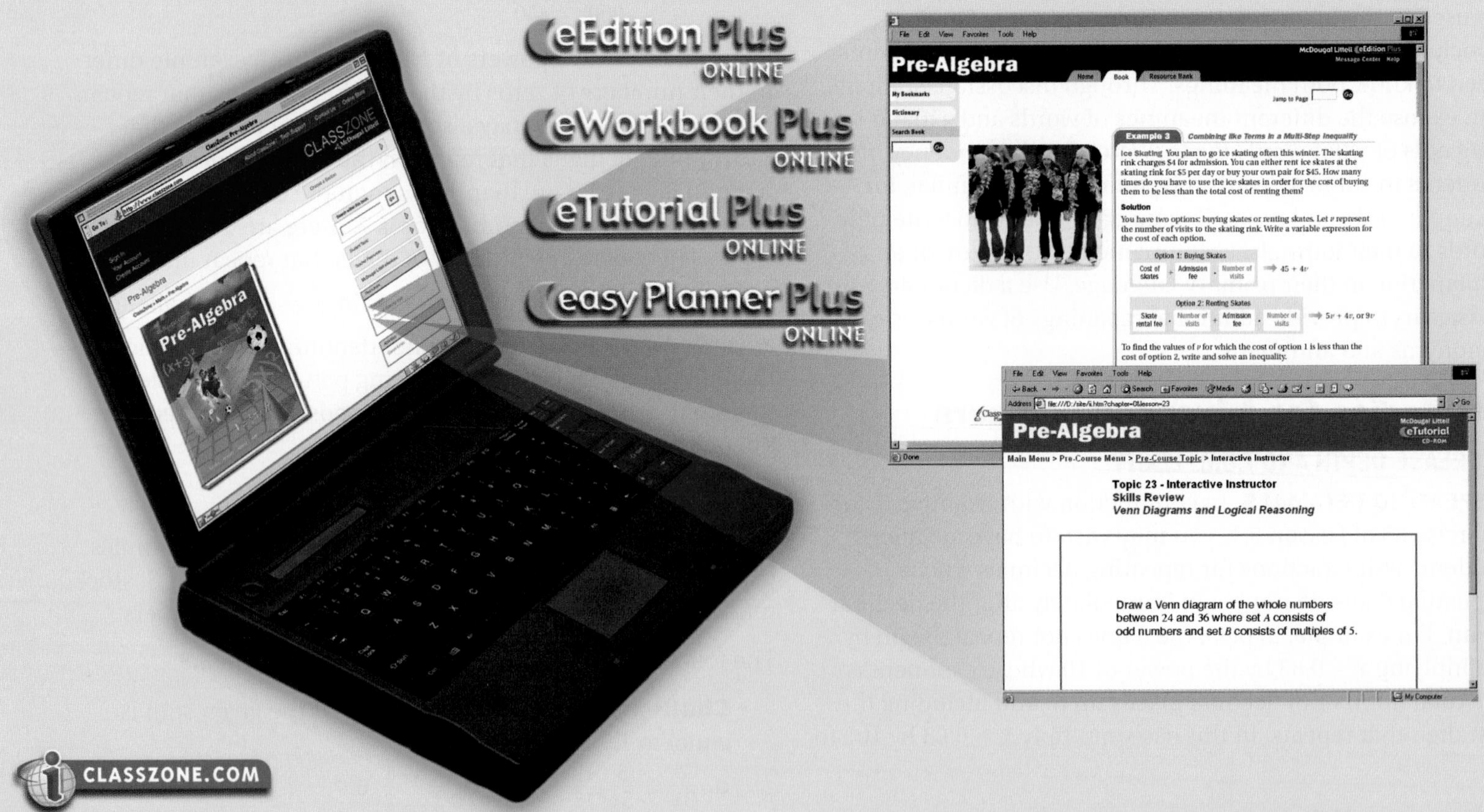

TEST AND PRACTICE GENERATOR CD-ROM

The *Test and Practice Generator* can be used to create numerous practice sheets and quizzes for each lesson and tests for each chapter using both static and algorithmic exercises. Information about creating and editing questions is provided.

Chapter 5 Test **Page 1**

1. Solve the inequality. Then graph its solution.
   $w+\frac{3}{2}<3$

2. Find the quotient. $2\frac{2}{9}\div 3\frac{4}{7}$ [A] $1\frac{5}{16}$ [B] $3\frac{3}{20}$ [C] $\frac{28}{45}$ [D] $1\frac{2}{5}$

3. Solve the equation.
   $k-\frac{2}{3}=\frac{1}{3}$

Find the quotient.

4. $\frac{24}{5}\div\frac{2}{3}$ [A] $3\frac{1}{5}$ [B] $7\frac{1}{5}$ [C] $\frac{5}{36}$ [D] $\frac{5}{16}$

5. $\frac{2}{3}\div\left(-\frac{9}{11}\right)$

6. Evaluate the expression when $a=5$ and $b=8$.
   $\frac{3a}{b}+\frac{7}{12}$

7. Find the quotient.
   $3\frac{1}{2}\div 10$

8. Use mental math to find the quotient. $\frac{1}{4}\div\frac{1}{4}$ [A] $\frac{1}{16}$ [B] 1 [C] 4 [D] 16

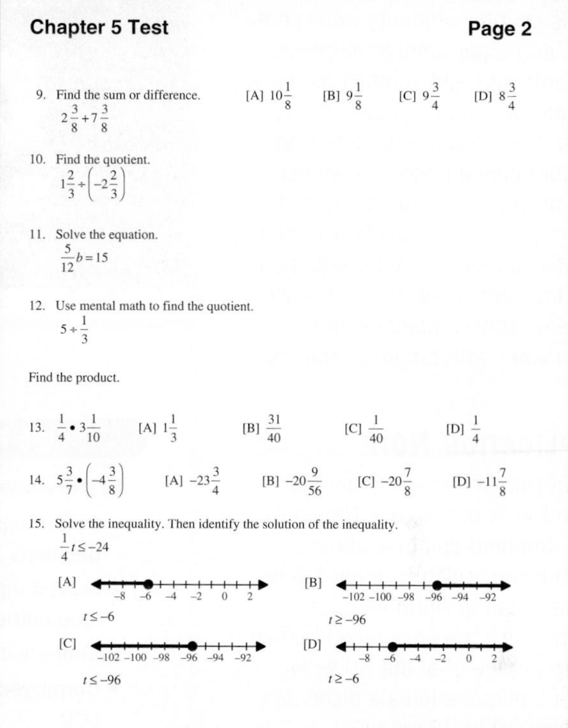

Chapter 5 Test **Page 2**

9. Find the sum or difference. $2\frac{3}{8}+7\frac{3}{8}$ [A] $10\frac{1}{8}$ [B] $9\frac{1}{8}$ [C] $9\frac{3}{4}$ [D] $8\frac{3}{4}$

10. Find the quotient.
    $1\frac{2}{3}\div\left(-2\frac{2}{3}\right)$

11. Solve the equation.
    $\frac{5}{12}b=15$

12. Use mental math to find the quotient.
    $5\div\frac{1}{3}$

Find the product.

13. $\frac{1}{4}\cdot 3\frac{1}{10}$ [A] $1\frac{1}{3}$ [B] $\frac{31}{40}$ [C] $\frac{1}{40}$ [D] $\frac{1}{4}$

14. $5\frac{3}{7}\cdot\left(-4\frac{3}{8}\right)$ [A] $-23\frac{3}{4}$ [B] $-20\frac{9}{56}$ [C] $-20\frac{7}{8}$ [D] $-11\frac{7}{8}$

15. Solve the inequality. Then identify the solution of the inequality.
    $\frac{1}{4}t\le -24$

    [A] number line −8 to 2; $t\le -6$ [B] number line −102 to −92; $t\ge -96$

    [C] number line −102 to −92; $t\le -96$ [D] number line −8 to 2; $t\ge -6$

RESOURCE BOOK

The *Chapter Resource Books* contain technology activities that are different from the activities given in the textbook. Also included, where appropriate, are calculator keystrokes that can be used to do the technology activities and exercises that appear in the textbook and in the *Chapter Resource Books*.

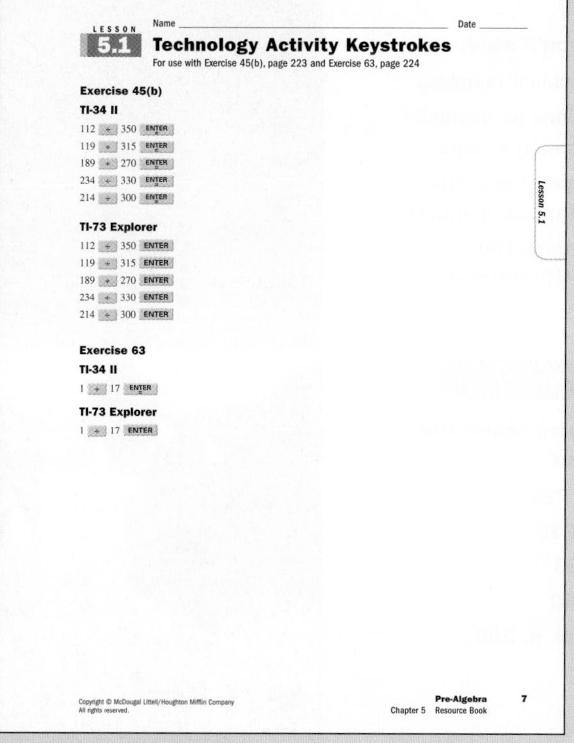

LESSON 5.1 Name ______ Date ______

Technology Activity Keystrokes

For use with Exercise 45(b), page 223 and Exercise 63, page 224

Exercise 45(b)

TI-34 II

112 ÷ 350 ENTER
119 ÷ 315 ENTER
189 ÷ 270 ENTER
234 ÷ 330 ENTER
214 ÷ 300 ENTER

TI-73 Explorer

112 ÷ 350 ENTER
119 ÷ 315 ENTER
189 ÷ 270 ENTER
234 ÷ 330 ENTER
214 ÷ 300 ENTER

Exercise 63

TI-34 II

1 ÷ 17 ENTER

TI-73 Explorer

1 ÷ 17 ENTER

Lesson 5.1

Copyright © McDougal Littell/Houghton Mifflin Company All rights reserved. Pre-Algebra Chapter 5 Resource Book 7

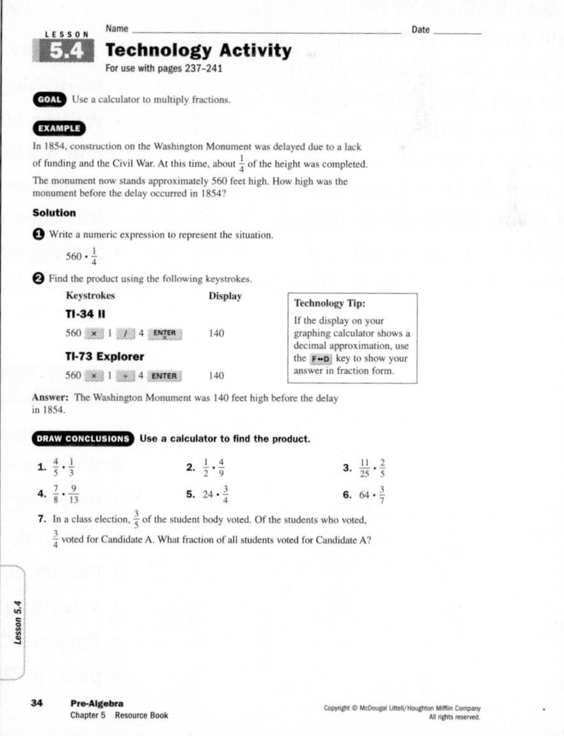

LESSON 5.4 Name ______ Date ______

Technology Activity

For use with pages 237–241

GOAL Use a calculator to multiply fractions.

EXAMPLE

In 1854, construction on the Washington Monument was delayed due to a lack of funding and the Civil War. At this time, about $\frac{1}{4}$ of the height was completed. The monument now stands approximately 560 feet high. How high was the monument before the delay occurred in 1854?

Solution

1. Write a numeric expression to represent the situation.
   $560\cdot\frac{1}{4}$
2. Find the product using the following keystrokes.

Keystrokes	Display
TI-34 II	
560 × 1 / 4 ENTER	140
TI-73 Explorer	
560 × 1 ÷ 4 ENTER	140

Technology Tip: If the display on your graphing calculator shows a decimal approximation, use the F↔D key to show your answer in fraction form.

Answer: The Washington Monument was 140 feet high before the delay in 1854.

DRAW CONCLUSIONS **Use a calculator to find the product.**

1. $\frac{4}{5}\cdot\frac{1}{3}$ 2. $\frac{1}{2}\cdot\frac{4}{9}$ 3. $\frac{11}{25}\cdot\frac{2}{5}$
4. $\frac{7}{8}\cdot\frac{9}{13}$ 5. $24\cdot\frac{3}{4}$ 6. $64\cdot\frac{3}{7}$
7. In a class election, $\frac{3}{5}$ of the student body voted. Of the students who voted, $\frac{3}{4}$ voted for Candidate A. What fraction of all students voted for Candidate A?

Lesson 5.4

34 Pre-Algebra Chapter 5 Resource Book Copyright © McDougal Littell/Houghton Mifflin Company All rights reserved.

OVERVIEW

Main Ideas

In this chapter, students write, compare, and order rational numbers. Students add and subtract fractions and mixed numbers, first with the same denominator and then with different denominators. Students multiply and divide fractions and mixed numbers. Students use multiplicative inverses to solve equations with fractional coefficients. Finally, students solve equations and inequalities with rational numbers.

Application Note

The largest free-roaming herd of bison live in Yellowstone National Park. The herd contains about 3500 bison, which is about 1% of all the bison in North America. Bison, which are also called buffalo, live to an age of about 30 years. In her lifetime, a female bison can produce 20 to 25 calves.

Bison weigh 25 to 35 pounds at birth. Six months after birth, a female calf will weigh around 350 pounds and a male calf will weigh about 425 pounds. A full-grown female weighs about 1100 pounds, while a full-grown male weighs about 2000 pounds. Adult bison are 5 to 6 feet tall at the shoulder. Despite their size, bison can sprint short distances at rates of up to 30 miles per hour.

CHAPTER 5

Rational Numbers *and* Equations

BEFORE

In previous chapters you've . . .

- **Performed operations with decimals**
- **Solved equations and inequalities with integers**
- **Simplified fractions**
- **Compared fractions using the LCD**

Now

In Chapter 5 you'll study . . .

- **Identifying rational numbers**
- **Writing fractions as decimals and decimals as fractions**
- **Performing operations with fractions and mixed numbers**
- **Solving equations and inequalities with rational numbers**

WHY?

So you can solve real-world problems about . . .

- **recycling, p. 223**
- **shot put, p. 228**
- **horses, p. 235**
- **sewing, p. 240**
- **Panama Canal, p. 250**
- **pets, p. 256**

How can you compare bison populations?

- eEdition Plus Online
- eWorkbook Plus Online
- eTutorial Plus Online
- State Test Practice
- More Examples

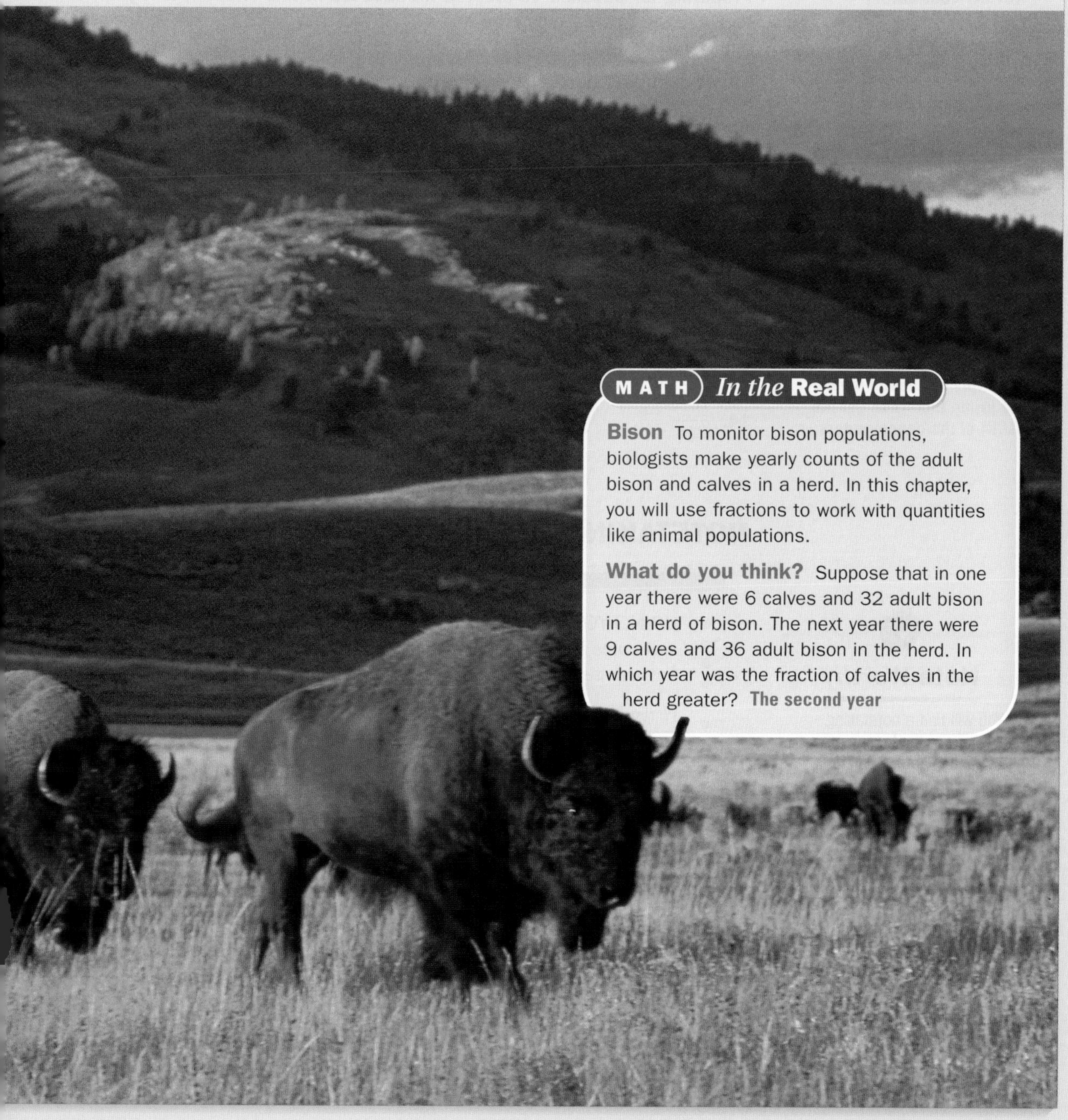

MATH In the Real World

Bison To monitor bison populations, biologists make yearly counts of the adult bison and calves in a herd. In this chapter, you will use fractions to work with quantities like animal populations.

What do you think? Suppose that in one year there were 6 calves and 32 adult bison in a herd of bison. The next year there were 9 calves and 36 adult bison in the herd. In which year was the fraction of calves in the herd greater? **The second year**

CHAPTER RESOURCES

These resources are provided to help you prepare for the chapter and to customize review materials:

Chapter 5 Resource Book

- Tips for New Teachers, pp. 1–2
- Lesson Plan, pp. 5, 14, 23, 31, 41, 49, 57
- Lesson Plan for Block Scheduling, pp. 6, 15, 24, 32, 42, 50, 58

Technology

- EasyPlanner CD-ROM
- Test and Practice Generator
- Electronic Lesson Presentations CD-ROM
- eTutorial CD-ROM

Internet

- Classzone
- eEdition Plus Online
- eWorkbook Plus Online
- eTutorial Plus Online
- EasyPlanner Plus Online

ENGLISH LEARNER SUPPORT

- Spanish Study Guide
- Multi-Language Visual Glossary
- Chapter Audio Summaries CDs
- Teacher's Edition, pp. 216E–216F

PREPARE

DIAGNOSIS/REMEDIATION

Prerequisite Skills Quiz

The Prerequisite Skills Quiz can help you diagnose whether students have the following skills needed in Chapter 5:

- Use vocabulary (Ex. 1)
- Solve equations (Exs. 2–5)
- Solve and graph inequalities (Exs. 6–9)
- Compare fractions (Exs. 10–13)
- Simplify algebraic expressions (Exs. 14–17)

Chapter 5 Resource Book

- Study Guide (Lessons 5.1–5.7)

Tutor Place

NOTETAKING STRATEGIES

Encourage students to record their questions about the exercises and to revisit them as they review the content of the chapter prior to taking the Chapter 5 Test. Students may be able to answer some of their own questions as they work through examples and exercises later in the chapter. In addition, being able to record the answers will help give students a sense that they can solve their own problems and that what seems difficult at first can be mastered with additional effort. Further suggestions for keeping a notebook can be found on pages 221 and 235.

For more support on notetaking, see:

- Notetaking Guide Workbook
- Notetaking Transparencies

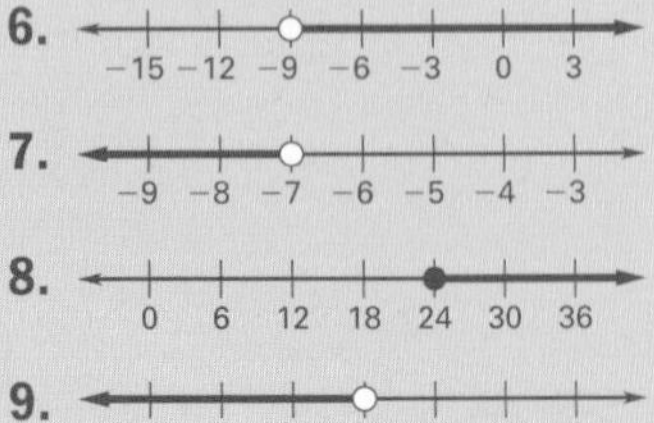

CHAPTER 5

Chapter Prerequisite Skills

Review Vocabulary

equation, p. 85
inequality, p. 138
least common multiple (LCM), p. 187
least common denominator (LCD), p. 188

1. *Sample answer:* Find the least common multiple of the denominators. To find the least common multiple, find the prime factorization of each number. For each prime factor, use the greatest exponent it has in the two numbers, and multiply all these powers of prime factors to get the LCM of the denominators.

PREREQUISITE SKILLS QUIZ

Preparing for Success To prepare for success in this chapter, test your knowledge of these concepts and skills. You may want to look at the pages referred to in blue for additional review.

1. Vocabulary Describe how to find the least common denominator of two fractions.

Solve the equation. Check your solution. *(p. 97)*

2. $4q = 48$ **12** **3.** $-9p = 81$ **−9** **4.** $\frac{n}{4} = 8$ **32** **5.** $\frac{m}{-5} = 3$ **−15**

Solve the inequality. Graph your solution. *(p. 144)* **6–9. See margin for art.**

6. $3s > -27$ $s > -9$ **7.** $-7r > 49$ $r < -7$ **8.** $\frac{x}{-4} \le -6$ $x \ge 24$ **9.** $\frac{y}{3} < -12$ $y < -36$

Use the LCD to determine which fraction is greater. *(p. 187)*

10. $\frac{3}{4}, \frac{7}{9}$ $\frac{7}{9}$ **11.** $\frac{2}{7}, \frac{3}{5}$ $\frac{3}{5}$ **12.** $\frac{7}{8}, \frac{5}{6}$ $\frac{7}{8}$ **13.** $\frac{13}{15}, \frac{11}{18}$ $\frac{13}{15}$

Simplify. *(p. 194)*

14. $\frac{18x^2}{24x}$ $\frac{3x}{4}$ **15.** $\frac{16a^3}{22a}$ $\frac{8a^2}{11}$ **16.** $\frac{15z^3}{63z}$ $\frac{5z^2}{21}$ **17.** $\frac{27m^4}{45m^2}$ $\frac{3m^2}{5}$

NOTETAKING STRATEGIES

Note *Worthy*

You will find a notetaking strategy at the beginning of each chapter. Look for additional notetaking and study strategies throughout the chapter.

USING YOUR HOMEWORK When you are doing your homework and come to an exercise you don't understand, write a question for your teacher. Ask the question the next time you have class.

Write the prime factorization of 324.

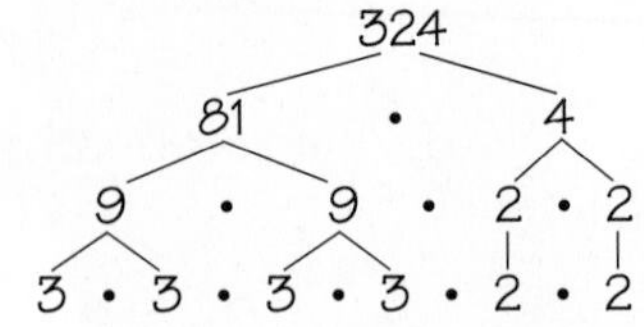

Does it matter in what order I write the factors? Ask in class tomorrow.

The prime factorization is $3^4 \cdot 2^2$.

As you do your homework in Chapter 5, write down questions you have about performing operations on fractions and mixed numbers.

LESSON

5.1 Rational Numbers

BEFORE	Now	WHY?
You wrote decimals and fractions.	You'll write fractions as decimals and vice versa.	So you can assess a recycling plan, as in Ex. 45.

Vocabulary

rational number, p. 219
terminating decimal, p. 219
repeating decimal, p. 219

A **rational number** is a number that can be written as a quotient of two integers. Whole numbers and integers are part of the set of rational numbers, as shown in the Venn diagram.

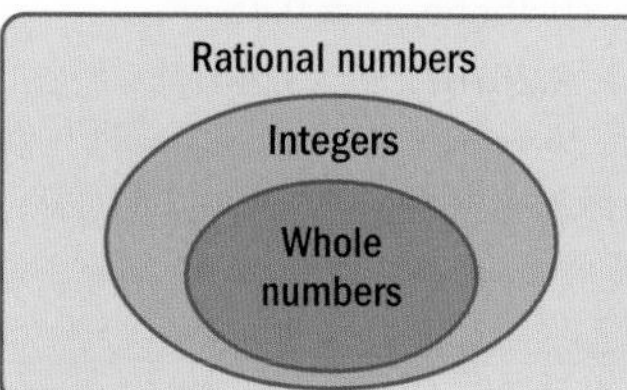

Example 1 Identifying Rational Numbers

Show that the number is rational by writing it as a quotient of two integers.

a. 7 **b.** -10 **c.** $5\frac{3}{4}$ **d.** $-3\frac{1}{2}$

Solution

a. Write the integer 7 as $\frac{7}{1}$.

b. Write the integer -10 as $\frac{-10}{1}$ or $\frac{10}{-1}$. These fractions are equivalent.

c. Write the mixed number $5\frac{3}{4}$ as the improper fraction $\frac{23}{4}$.

d. Think of $-3\frac{1}{2}$ as the opposite of $3\frac{1}{2}$. First write $3\frac{1}{2}$ as $\frac{7}{2}$. Then you can write $-3\frac{1}{2}$ as $-\frac{7}{2}$. To write $-\frac{7}{2}$ as a quotient of two integers, you can assign the negative sign to either the numerator or the denominator. You can write $\frac{-7}{2}$ or $\frac{7}{-2}$.

Review Help

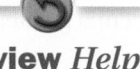

For help with writing mixed numbers as improper fractions, see p. 778.

Terminating and Repeating Decimals If you take a rational number in the form $\frac{a}{b}$ and carry out the division of a by b, the quotient will be either a *terminating decimal* or a *repeating decimal.* In a **terminating decimal**, the division ends because you obtain a final remainder of zero. In a **repeating decimal**, a digit or block of digits in the quotient repeats without end. Example 2 on page 220 shows how to write both a terminating decimal and a repeating decimal.

NCTM CURRICULUM STANDARDS

Standard 1: Understand numbers; Understand ways of representing numbers; Compute fluently

1 PLAN

Skill Check

Write the mixed number as an improper fraction.

1. $5\frac{2}{3}$ **$\frac{17}{3}$** **2.** $8\frac{7}{10}$ **$\frac{87}{10}$**

3. $-2\frac{2}{3}$ **$-\frac{8}{3}$** **4.** $-6\frac{3}{4}$ **$-\frac{27}{4}$**

LESSON OBJECTIVE

Write fractions as decimals and vice versa.

PACING

Suggested Number of Days
Basic Course: 2 days
Average Course: 2 days
Advanced Course: 2 days
Block: 1 block

TEACHING RESOURCES

For a complete list of Teaching Resources, see page 216B.

TRANSPARENCY

Warm-Up Exercises for this lesson are available on a transparency. A support transparency is available for Example 6.

2 TEACH

MOTIVATING THE LESSON

Ask students to explain in their own words what the Venn diagram shows.

TIPS *for* NEW TEACHERS

The number of examples in this lesson may overwhelm students. Stress that the main skills to be mastered are writing fractions as decimals and writing decimals as fractions. See Tips for New Teachers in the *Chapter 5 Resource Book.*

Extra Examples

Example 1 Show that the number is rational by writing it as a quotient of two integers.

a. 22 $\frac{22}{1}$

b. -15 $\frac{-15}{1}$ or $\frac{15}{-1}$

c. $10\frac{1}{2}$ $\frac{21}{2}$

d. $-8\frac{1}{3}$ $\frac{-25}{3}$ or $\frac{25}{-3}$

Example 2 Write the fraction as a decimal.

a. $\frac{7}{12}$ **$0.58\overline{3}$**

b. $\frac{5}{8}$ **0.625**

Example 3 At Mallard Park Townhomes, there are 52 rental units and 13 of them are currently vacant. At Goose Run Apartments, there are 148 rental units and 36 of them are vacant. At which rental property is the vacancy rate greater? **Mallard Park Townhomes**

TEACHING TIP

In Example 2, encourage students to cover up part b while you discuss part a.

READING STRATEGY

Before discussing part b of Example 2, have students read the Reading Algebra feature to the left of the example. After completing your discussion of part b, have students compare the first repeating decimal in the Reading Algebra feature to the repeating decimal found in part b of Example 2. Stress that it is important for students to carefully take notice of the digits that are beneath the bar, and not to read too quickly.

Reading *Algebra*

When you use a bar to show which digit or digits repeat in a decimal, be sure to put the bar over only the repeating digits. For example,

$0.45555\ldots = 0.4\overline{5}$

$3.26767\ldots = 3.2\overline{67}$

Example 2 *Writing Fractions as Decimals*

a. Write $\frac{3}{8}$ as a decimal.

b. Write $\frac{5}{11}$ as a decimal.

a.

$$\begin{array}{r} 0.375 \\ 8\overline{)3.000} \\ \underline{24} \\ 60 \\ \underline{56} \\ 40 \\ \underline{40} \\ 0 \end{array}$$

Answer The remainder is 0, so the decimal is a terminating decimal: $\frac{3}{8} = 0.375$.

b.

$$\begin{array}{r} 0.4545\ldots \\ 11\overline{)5.0000} \\ \underline{44} \\ 60 \\ \underline{55} \\ 50 \\ \underline{44} \\ 60 \\ \underline{55} \end{array}$$

Answer Use a bar to show the repeating digits in the repeating decimal: $\frac{5}{11} = 0.\overline{45}$.

Checkpoint

Write the fraction or mixed number as a decimal.

1. $\frac{3}{10}$ **0.3** **2.** $-\frac{2}{3}$ **$-0.\overline{6}$** **3.** $1\frac{9}{20}$ **1.45** **4.** $\frac{29}{80}$ **0.3625**

In the Real World

Biology The yellow-bellied marmot belongs to the order Rodentia. Yellow-bellied marmots typically live at elevations from 6500 feet to 13,500 feet. Find the difference of these two elevations. **7000 ft**

Example 3 *Using Decimals to Compare Fractions*

Biology Of the 50 mammal species found in Canyonlands National Park, 20 species belong to the order Rodentia. Of the 54 mammal species found in Badlands National Park, 24 belong to Rodentia. In which park is the fraction of mammal species belonging to Rodentia greater?

Solution

1 Write a fraction for each park. Then write each fraction as a decimal by dividing the numerator by the denominator.

Canyonlands National Park $\frac{\text{Rodentia species}}{\text{Mammal species}} = \frac{20}{50}$ **Write fraction.**

$= 0.4$ **Divide.**

Badlands National Park $\frac{\text{Rodentia species}}{\text{Mammal species}} = \frac{24}{54}$ **Write fraction.**

$= 0.444\ldots$ **Divide.**

$= 0.\overline{4}$ **Repeating digit**

2 Compare the decimals. By writing 0.4 as 0.400, you can see that $0.444\ldots$ is greater than 0.400. So $0.\overline{4} > 0.4$, and $\frac{24}{54} > \frac{20}{50}$.

Answer The fraction in Badlands National Park is greater.

Note *Worthy*

In your notebook, you may want to include a list of common fraction-decimal equivalents. You can refer to the list when solving problems, or you may want to memorize the list. Here are some examples you might include:

$\frac{1}{2} = 0.5, \frac{1}{3} = 0.\overline{3},$

$\frac{1}{4} = 0.25, \frac{1}{8} = 0.125$

Writing Decimals as Fractions To write a terminating decimal as a fraction or a mixed number, use the place of the last digit to determine the denominator of the fraction, as shown in Example 4. Example 5 shows a method for writing a repeating decimal as a fraction.

Example 4 *Writing Terminating Decimals as Fractions*

a. $0.7 = \frac{7}{10}$ — **7 is in tenths' place, so denominator is 10.**

b. $-3.05 = -3\frac{5}{100}$ — **5 is in hundredths' place, so denominator is 100.**

$= -3\frac{1}{20}$ — **Simplify fraction.**

Example 5 *Writing a Repeating Decimal as a Fraction*

To write $0.\overline{93}$ as a fraction, let $x = 0.\overline{93}$.

1) Because $0.\overline{93}$ has 2 repeating digits, multiply each side of $x = 0.\overline{93}$ by 10^2, or 100. Then $100x = 93.\overline{93}$.

2) Subtract x from $100x$.

$$\begin{aligned} 100x &= 93.\overline{93} \\ -\ (x &= 0.\overline{93}) \\ \hline 99x &= 93 \end{aligned}$$

3) Solve for x and simplify.

$$\frac{99x}{99} = \frac{93}{99}$$

$$x = \frac{31}{33}$$

Answer The decimal $0.\overline{93}$ is equivalent to the fraction $\frac{31}{33}$.

Checkpoint

5. Critical Thinking Compare writing 0.3 as a fraction with writing $0.\overline{3}$ as a fraction.

5. ***Sample answer:*** **0.3 terminates at the tenths place, so you know that its denominator is 10 when written as a fraction, and the numerator is simply 3. Writing $0.\overline{3}$ as a fraction is much more complicated. First you must multiply $0.\overline{3}$ by $10^1 = 10$ since there is one repeating digit. Then, letting $x = 0.\overline{3}$, you can find that the difference $10x - x = 9x$ is equivalent to 3. Solving the equation $9x = 3$ then gives $x = \frac{1}{3}$, or $0.\overline{3} = \frac{1}{3}$.**

Example 6 *Ordering Rational Numbers*

Order the numbers $-\frac{5}{4}$, −0.2, 4.31, −3, $\frac{5}{2}$, $-\frac{13}{3}$ from least to greatest.

Graph the numbers on a number line. You may want to write improper fractions as mixed numbers.

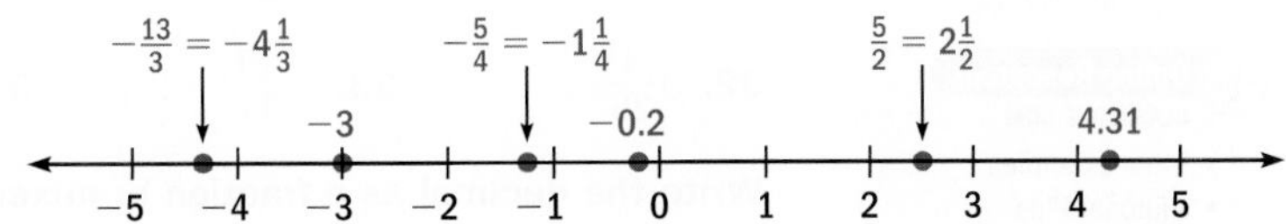

Read the numbers from left to right: $-\frac{13}{3}$, −3, $-\frac{5}{4}$, −0.2, $\frac{5}{2}$, 4.31.

Study *Strategy*

Another Way To order the numbers in Example 6, you can instead write the fractions as decimals. Then order the decimals.

Extra Examples

Example 4 Write the decimal as a fraction or mixed number.

a. 1.6 $1\frac{3}{5}$

b. −9.42 $-9\frac{21}{50}$

Example 5 Write $0.\overline{72}$ as a fraction. $\frac{8}{11}$

Example 6 Order the numbers 2.7, 0.55, −0.9, $\frac{9}{4}$, $-\frac{9}{8}$, $\frac{13}{7}$ from least to greatest.
$-\frac{9}{8}$, **−0.9, 0.55,** $\frac{13}{7}$, $\frac{9}{4}$, **2.7**

Differentiating Instruction

Alternative Teaching Strategy
Have pairs of students work together to practice writing fractions as decimals and vice versa. Ask one student to write a fraction and the other to write a decimal number. Then have them trade papers and rewrite the number they receive in the other form, working together if necessary. Repeat this activity several times.

Concept Check

How do you write a fraction as a decimal? **Divide the denominator into the numerator until the quotient terminates or repeats.** How do you write a repeating decimal as a fraction? ***Sample answer:*** **Let x = the decimal. Multiply both sides of this equality by a power of 10 based on the number of repeating digits in the decimal. Then subtract the original equality from the resulting equation and solve for x.**

Daily Puzzler

Without calculating, is $0.\overline{0011}$ equivalent to $\frac{1}{99}$ or $\frac{1}{909}$? $\frac{1}{909}$

3 APPLY

ASSIGNMENT GUIDE

Basic Course

Day 1: SRH p. 770 Exs. 9-12; pp. 222-224 Exs. 20-31, 46-48, 62, 66-71

Day 2: SRH p. 778 Exs. 16-20; pp. 222-224 Exs. 32-44, 49-52, 57-60, 72-74

Average Course

Day 1: pp. 222-224 Exs. 24-31, 46-48, 61-64, 66-72

Day 2: pp. 222-224 Exs. 36-45, 53-60, 73-75

Advanced Course

Day 1: pp. 222-224 Exs. 24-31, 46-48, 61-67*, 70-72

Day 2: pp. 222-224 Exs. 36-45, 53-60, 73-75

Block

pp. 222-224 Exs. 24-31, 36-48, 53-64, 66-75

Extra Practice

- Student Edition, p. 807
- Chapter 5 Resource Book, pp. 8-10
- Test and Practice Generator

Transparency

Even-numbered answers are available on transparencies. A support transparency is available for Exercises 57-60.

Homework Check

When you review students' homework for this lesson, go over the following exercises to check understanding of key concepts.

Basic: 20, 28, 36, 44, 49
Average: 24, 30, 38, 45, 54
Advanced: 25, 31, 41, 45, 56

5.1 Exercises

More Practice, p. 807

Guided Practice

Vocabulary Check **Tell whether the number is a *terminating decimal* or a *repeating decimal*.** 1–4. See margin.

1. 0.667 **2.** 0.4747... **3.** 35.35 **4.** $2.4\overline{3}$

5. How can you tell whether a number is a rational number? See margin.

1. terminating decimal
2. repeating decimal
3. terminating decimal
4. repeating decimal
5. *Sample answer:* If you can write the number as a quotient of two integers, it is rational. Otherwise, it is not rational.

Skill Check **Show that the number is rational by writing it as a quotient of two integers.**

6. 15 $\frac{15}{1}$ **7.** -2 $\frac{-2}{1}$ or $\frac{2}{-1}$ **8.** $5\frac{4}{7}$ $\frac{39}{7}$ **9.** $-1\frac{1}{3}$ $\frac{-4}{3}$ or $\frac{4}{-3}$

Write the fraction or mixed number as a decimal.

10. $\frac{2}{9}$ $0.\overline{2}$ **11.** $1\frac{4}{5}$ 1.8 **12.** $-\frac{13}{15}$ $-0.8\overline{6}$ **13.** $-9\frac{5}{8}$ -9.625

Write the decimal as a fraction or mixed number.

14. 0.4 $\frac{2}{5}$ **15.** 0.324 $\frac{81}{250}$ **16.** $0.\overline{78}$ $\frac{26}{33}$ **17.** $2.\overline{6}$ $2\frac{2}{3}$

18. Swim Teams Of the 20 students on the girls' swim team, 9 are seniors. Of the 24 students on the boys' swim team, 10 are seniors. On which team is the fraction of students who are seniors greater? the girls' team

19. Error Analysis Describe and correct the error in writing the repeating decimal 5.07878... using a bar. Only the "78" repeats, so these are the only digits that should be under the bar: $5.07878... = 5.0\overline{78}$.

Practice and Problem Solving

Homework Help

Example	Exercises
1	20-27
2	28-35
3	44-45
4	36-43
5	49-56
6	45, 57-60

Online Resources
CLASSZONE.COM
- More Examples
- eTutorial Plus

Show that the number is rational by writing it as a quotient of two integers.

A **20.** 24 $\frac{24}{1}$ **21.** -29 $\frac{-29}{1}$ or $\frac{29}{-1}$ **22.** $5\frac{7}{18}$ $\frac{97}{18}$ **23.** $-\frac{1}{8}$ $\frac{-1}{8}$ or $\frac{1}{-8}$

24. 1 $\frac{1}{1}$ **25.** $-2\frac{3}{7}$ $\frac{-17}{7}$ or $\frac{17}{-7}$ **26.** 0.3 $\frac{3}{10}$ **27.** 0.87 $\frac{87}{100}$

Write the fraction or mixed number as a decimal.

28. $\frac{1}{5}$ 0.2 **29.** $-\frac{7}{8}$ -0.875 **30.** $-\frac{5}{3}$ $-1.\overline{6}$ **31.** $\frac{19}{6}$ $3.1\overline{6}$

32. $3\frac{4}{25}$ 3.16 **33.** $-\frac{13}{11}$ $-1.\overline{18}$ **34.** $8\frac{5}{44}$ $8.11\overline{36}$ **35.** $-13\frac{7}{10}$ -13.7

Write the decimal as a fraction or mixed number.

36. 0.54 $\frac{27}{50}$ **37.** 0.63 $\frac{63}{100}$ **38.** 7.6 $7\frac{3}{5}$ **39.** 2.093 $2\frac{93}{1000}$

40. -0.85 $-\frac{17}{20}$ **41.** 0.019 $\frac{19}{1000}$ **42.** -5.895 $-5\frac{179}{200}$ **43.** -1.102 $-1\frac{51}{500}$

44. Leaves You and a friend are collecting leaves. In your collection of 45 leaves, 4 are oak leaves. In your friend's collection of 36 leaves, 3 are oak leaves. Whose collection has a greater fraction of oak leaves? **my collection**

45. Recycling The table shows monthly amounts of trash and recycled trash at a school.

Month	Total trash (lb)	Recycled trash (lb)
Nov.	350	112
Dec.	315	119
Jan.	270	189
Feb.	330	234
Mar.	300	214

a. For each month, find the fraction of trash that was recycled.

b. **Compare** Use a calculator to write the fractions in part (a) as decimals. Order the decimals from least to greatest. In which month was the fraction of trash that was recycled the greatest?

c. ***Writing*** As of January 1, a new recycling plan was introduced at the school. What effect do you think the plan had on recycling efforts in January and the months that followed? Explain.

Copy and complete the statement using *always*, *sometimes*, or *never*.

46. An integer is _?_ a rational number. **always**

47. A fraction can _?_ be written as a terminating decimal. **sometimes**

48. A repeating decimal is _?_ a rational number. **always**

Write the decimal as a fraction or mixed number.

B 49. $0.\overline{8}$ $\frac{8}{9}$ **50.** $0.\overline{7}$ $\frac{7}{9}$ **51.** $-0.\overline{4}$ $-\frac{4}{9}$ **52.** $-9.\overline{6}$ $-9\frac{2}{3}$

53. $0.\overline{12}$ $\frac{4}{33}$ **54.** $-1.\overline{36}$ $-1\frac{4}{11}$ **55.** $0.\overline{897}$ $\frac{299}{333}$ **56.** $2.\overline{707}$ $2\frac{707}{999}$

Order the numbers from least to greatest.

57. $-2, \frac{7}{8}, 0.8, 2.1, 1\frac{1}{3}$ $-2, 0.8, \frac{7}{8}, 1\frac{1}{3}, 2.1$

58. $0.7, -1, -\frac{5}{4}, \frac{4}{3}, -2.3, -\frac{9}{2}$ $-\frac{9}{2}, -2.3, -\frac{5}{4}, -1, 0.7, \frac{4}{3}$

59. $0.21, 2.3, \frac{8}{3}, -0.1, -\frac{1}{5}, 0.\overline{2}$ $-\frac{1}{5}, -0.1, 0.21, 0.\overline{2}, 2.3, \frac{8}{3}$

60. $0.3, 0.\overline{3}, 0.\overline{30}, -0.3, -0.\overline{3}$ $-0.\overline{3}, -0.3, 0.3, 0.\overline{30}, 0.\overline{3}$

61. Extended Problem Solving The table shows the number of at bats and hits that players on a softball team had in three games.

Player	Game 1		Game 2		Game 3	
Maria	4 at bats	2 hits	5 at bats	2 hits	4 at bats	1 hit
Laura	4 at bats	1 hit	5 at bats	1 hit	4 at bats	1 hit
Jenny	4 at bats	3 hits	4 at bats	2 hits	4 at bats	1 hit

a. Find the total number of at bats and the total number of hits for each player for the three games. **Maria: 13 at bats, 5 hits; Laura: 13 at bats, 3 hits; Jenny: 12 at bats, 6 hits**

b. **Analyze** A player's batting average is the total number of hits divided by the total number of at bats. The batting average is usually expressed as a decimal rounded to the nearest thousandth. Find each player's batting average for the three games. **Maria: 0.385; Laura: 0.231; Jenny: 0.500**

c. **Apply** Rank the players based on batting averages. Explain. **See margin.**

45a. Nov.: $\frac{8}{25}$, Dec.: $\frac{17}{45}$, Jan.: $\frac{7}{10}$, Feb.: $\frac{39}{55}$, Mar.: $\frac{107}{150}$

45b. $0.32, 0.3\overline{7}, 0.7, 0.7\overline{09}, 0.71\overline{3}$; March

45c. *Sample answer:* I think it increased recycling efforts. Before January 1, the portion of trash recycled was less than 0.4. After January 1, the portion recycled was at least 0.7.

61c. *Sample answer:* I would rank Jenny first, followed by Maria, then Laura. I think that the higher a person's batting average is, the better the player is at hitting.

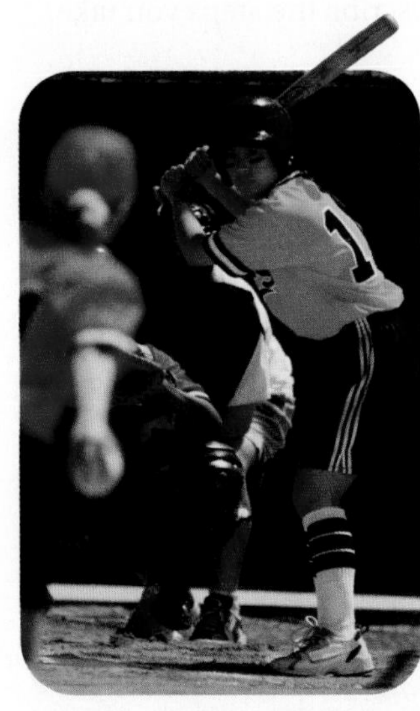

Common Error

In Exercises 51, 52, and 54, watch for students who omit the negative signs or think a different process is required for rewriting negative decimals as fractions.

Teaching Tip

In Exercises 57–60, encourage students to use their mental math skills to make as many comparisons as possible before rewriting any of the fractions as decimals or vice versa. Invite students to share any techniques they use for ordering numbers without rewriting them.

4 ASSESS

Assessment Resources

For more assessment resources, see:

- Assessment Book
- Test and Practice Generator

Mini-Quiz

Write the fraction or mixed number as a decimal.

1. $8\frac{2}{25}$ **8.08**
2. $-\frac{5}{33}$ **$-0.\overline{15}$**

Write the decimal as a fraction or mixed number.

3. -7.125 **$-7\frac{1}{8}$**
4. $0.\overline{18}$ **$\frac{2}{11}$**
5. **Challenge** Write $0.1\overline{58}$ as a fraction. **$\frac{157}{990}$**

5 FOLLOW-UP

Diagnosis/Remediation

- Study Guide in Chapter 5 Resource Book, pp. 11–12
- Tutor Place, Whole Numbers and Decimals Card 4, Fractions Cards 5, 6
- eTutorial Plus Online
- Extra Practice, p. 807
- Lesson Practice in Chapter 5 Resource Book, pp. 8–10

English Learner Support

- Spanish Study Guide
- Multi-Language Visual Glossary
- Chapter Audio Summaries CDs

Challenge

- Challenge Practice in Chapter 5 Resource Book, p. 13
- Teacher's Edition, p. 216F

75. See Additional Answers beginning on page AA1.

---

62. Measurement You have a rope that is $4\frac{1}{3}$ feet long. Your friend has a rope that is $1\frac{1}{2}$ yards long. Who has the longer rope? **my friend**

63. Critical Thinking Try using a calculator to find a decimal value for $\frac{1}{17}$. What do you notice? Then use long division to write $\frac{1}{17}$ as a terminating or repeating decimal. Explain the calculator result you obtained.

63. ***Sample answer:*** **I do not see any repeating pattern of digits or any sign of termination; $0.\overline{0588235294117647}$; the calculator does not show enough decimal places for the repeating pattern to appear, since the pattern has 16 digits.**

64. Critical Thinking Let a and b represent nonzero integers. Find a rational number in the form $\frac{a}{b}$ so that $-1.7 < \frac{a}{b}$ and $\frac{a}{b} < -\frac{5}{3}$. Explain how you found the number. **See margin.**

64. ***Sample answer:*** **$-\frac{42}{25}$; I wrote $-\frac{5}{3}$ as the decimal $-1.\overline{6}$, then chose the decimal -1.68 because it is between -1.7 and $-1.\overline{6}$, and then wrote -1.68 as a fraction.**

C **65. Challenge** Write the decimal $0.3\overline{21}$ as a fraction. **$\frac{53}{165}$**

Mixed Review

Simplify the expression. *(Lesson 2.3)*

66. $k - 9 - (2 + k)$ **-11** **67.** $m + 5 - 2(m + 7)$ **$-m - 9$**

Find the least common multiple of the numbers. *(Lesson 4.4)*

68. 240, 340 **4080** **69.** 18, 60 **180** **70.** 55, 77 **385** **71.** 27, 189 **189**

72. Chemistry A common number used for calculations in chemistry is Avogadro's number, which is approximately equal to 6.02×10^{23}. Write this number in standard form. *(Lesson 4.7)* **602,000,000,000,000,000,000,000**

Standardized Test Practice

73. Multiple Choice Which number is *not* equivalent to $\frac{40}{66}$? **C**

A. $\frac{20}{33}$ **B.** $\frac{60}{99}$ **C.** $0.\overline{6}$ **D.** $0.\overline{60}$

74. Multiple Choice Which number is greater than -1.5? **H**

F. $-1.\overline{5}$ **G.** $-\frac{3}{2}$ **H.** $-1.\overline{45}$ **I.** $-\frac{7}{2}$

75. Short Response Write $0.\overline{475}$ as a fraction. Describe the steps you take to write the fraction. **See margin.**

Rational Number Riddle

What is black when you buy it, red when you use it, and gray when you throw it away?

Order the fractions from least to greatest. The corresponding letters spell out the answer to the riddle.

$\frac{4}{15}, \frac{73}{200}, \frac{11}{30}, \frac{5}{12}, \frac{19}{40}, \frac{17}{25}, \frac{87}{100}, \frac{7}{8}$; CHARCOAL

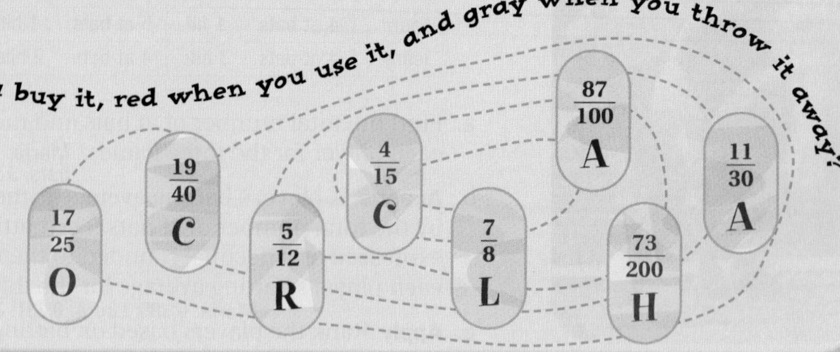

LESSON

5.2 Adding and Subtracting Like Fractions

Review Vocabulary
variable expression, p. 5

BEFORE	*Now*	WHY?
You added and subtracted decimals.	You'll add and subtract like fractions.	So you can analyze a lobster's growth, as in Ex. 52.

Astronomy One night, $\frac{77}{100}$ of the moon's visible surface is illuminated. The next night, an additional $\frac{9}{100}$ is illuminated. What fraction of the moon's visible surface is illuminated on the second night?

Adding and Subtracting Like Fractions

Words To add or subtract fractions with the same denominator, write the sum or difference of the numerators over the denominator.

Numbers $\frac{4}{9}+\frac{1}{9}=\frac{5}{9}$ $\qquad \frac{9}{11}-\frac{2}{11}=\frac{7}{11}$

Algebra $\frac{a}{c}+\frac{b}{c}=\frac{a+b}{c}, c \neq 0$ $\qquad \frac{a}{c}-\frac{b}{c}=\frac{a-b}{c}, c \neq 0$

Review *Help*

For help with adding and subtracting fractions, see p. 779.

Example 1 *Adding Like Fractions*

To find the fraction of the moon's visible surface that is illuminated on the second night, as described above, find the sum of $\frac{77}{100}$ and $\frac{9}{100}$.

$\frac{77}{100}+\frac{9}{100}=\frac{77+9}{100}$ **Write sum of numerators over denominator.**

$=\frac{86}{100}=\frac{43}{50}$ **Add. Then simplify.**

Answer On the second night, $\frac{43}{50}$ of the visible surface is illuminated.

NCTM CURRICULUM STANDARDS
Standard 1: Understand numbers; Understand ways of representing numbers; Compute fluently

1 PLAN

Skill Check
Simplify.

1. $\frac{18}{20}$ $\frac{9}{10}$
2. $-\frac{60}{12}$ -5
3. $\frac{15}{25}$ $\frac{3}{5}$
4. $-\frac{85}{100}$ $-\frac{17}{20}$

LESSON OBJECTIVE
Add and subtract like fractions.

PACING
Suggested Number of Days
Basic Course: 1 day
Average Course: 1 day
Advanced Course: 1 day
Block: 0.5 block with 5.3

TEACHING RESOURCES
For a complete list of Teaching Resources, see page 216B.

TRANSPARENCY
Warm-Up Exercises for this lesson are available on a transparency.

2 TEACH

MOTIVATING THE LESSON
Ask what fraction (with a denominator of 100) of the moon's visible surface is illuminated during a full moon; during a new moon. $\frac{100}{100}$, $\frac{0}{100}$

TIPS *for* NEW TEACHERS
Begin the lesson by reviewing the difference between like and unlike fractions. Stress that the techniques in this lesson apply only to like fractions. See Tips for New Teachers in the *Chapter 5 Resource Book*.

Extra Examples

Example 1 Simone ate $\frac{3}{16}$ of a pizza. Darren ate $\frac{5}{16}$ of the pizza. What fraction of the pizza did they eat altogether? $\frac{1}{2}$

Example 2 Find the difference.

a. $\frac{4}{9} - \frac{7}{9}$ $-\frac{1}{3}$

b. $-\frac{3}{10} - \left(-\frac{9}{10}\right)$ $\frac{3}{5}$

Example 3 Find the sum or difference.

a. $2\frac{11}{12} + 6\frac{7}{12}$ $9\frac{1}{2}$

b. $8\frac{9}{15} - 10\frac{2}{15}$ $-1\frac{8}{15}$

MULTIPLE REPRESENTATIONS

Draw students' attention to the definition box above Example 1. Have students cover up the right side of the box. Explain that the left side shows addition with an example using numbers and with an example using algebra. On the board, show another simple example involving numbers. Then have students cover up the left side and discuss subtracting like fractions in a similar way.

TEACHING TIP

In Example 3, consider working part b using correct math and then working the problem again incorrectly to demonstrate the difficulties that occur when you subtract without first rewriting the mixed numbers as improper fractions.

Study *Strategy*

When you perform operations with negative fractions, be sure to assign a negative sign in front of a fraction to the numerator of the fraction. For instance, in part (a) of Example 2, $-\frac{4}{7}$ is written as $\frac{-4}{7}$.

Example 2 ***Subtracting Like Fractions***

a. $-\frac{4}{7} - \frac{2}{7} = \frac{-4-2}{7}$ **Write difference of numerators over denominator.**

$= \frac{-6}{7} = -\frac{6}{7}$ **Subtract.**

b. $\frac{1}{10} - \left(-\frac{3}{10}\right) = \frac{1}{10} + \frac{3}{10}$ **To subtract $-\frac{3}{10}$, add $\frac{3}{10}$.**

$= \frac{1+3}{10}$ **Write sum of numerators over denominator.**

$= \frac{4}{10} = \frac{2}{5}$ **Add. Then simplify.**

Checkpoint

Find the sum or difference.

1. $\frac{3}{8} + \frac{2}{8}$ $\frac{5}{8}$ **2.** $-\frac{1}{6} + \frac{5}{6}$ $\frac{2}{3}$ **3.** $\frac{2}{15} - \frac{7}{15}$ $-\frac{1}{3}$ **4.** $\frac{1}{12} - \left(-\frac{7}{12}\right)$ $\frac{2}{3}$

Mixed Numbers To add or subtract mixed numbers, you can first write the mixed numbers as improper fractions.

Example 3 ***Adding and Subtracting Mixed Numbers***

a. $5\frac{5}{9} + 2\frac{7}{9} = \frac{50}{9} + \frac{25}{9}$ **Write mixed numbers as improper fractions.**

$= \frac{50+25}{9}$ **Write sum of numerators over denominator.**

$= \frac{75}{9}$ **Add.**

$= \frac{25}{3} = 8\frac{1}{3}$ **Simplify. Then write fraction as a mixed number.**

b. $-10\frac{6}{13} - 6\frac{8}{13} = \frac{-136}{13} - \frac{86}{13}$ **Write mixed numbers as improper fractions.**

$= \frac{-136-86}{13}$ **Write difference of numerators over denominator.**

$= \frac{-222}{13} = -17\frac{1}{13}$ **Subtract. Then write fraction as a mixed number.**

Checkpoint

Find the sum or difference.

5. $2\frac{3}{4} + 1\frac{3}{4}$ $4\frac{1}{2}$ **6.** $-6\frac{2}{3} + 3\frac{1}{3}$ $-3\frac{1}{3}$ **7.** $4\frac{1}{5} - 2\frac{3}{5}$ $1\frac{3}{5}$ **8.** $-3\frac{2}{7} - 6\frac{3}{7}$ $-9\frac{5}{7}$

Example 4 *Simplifying Variable Expressions*

a. $\frac{3a}{20} + \frac{5a}{20} = \frac{3a + 5a}{20}$ **Write sum of numerators over denominator.**

$= \frac{\cancel{8}^{2}a}{\cancel{20}_{5}}$ **Add. Divide out common factor.**

$= \frac{2a}{5}$ **Simplify.**

b. $-\frac{8}{3b} - \left(-\frac{2}{3b}\right) = -\frac{8}{3b} + \frac{2}{3b}$ **To subtract $-\frac{2}{3b}$, add $\frac{2}{3b}$.**

$= \frac{-8 + 2}{3b}$ **Write sum of numerators over denominator.**

$= \frac{\cancel{-6}^{-2}}{{}_{1}\cancel{3}b}$ **Add. Divide out common factor.**

$= \frac{-2}{b} = -\frac{2}{b}$ **Simplify.**

Review *Help*

For help with simplifying fractions that include variables, see p. 184.

Extra Examples

Example 4 Simplify the expression.

a. $\frac{3k}{28} + \frac{9k}{28}$ $\mathbf{\frac{3k}{7}}$

b. $\frac{4}{7y} - \frac{9}{7y}$ $\mathbf{-\frac{5}{7y}}$

Common Error

Throughout the lesson, watch for students who add the denominators as well as the numerators.

Concept Check

What step do you do first when subtracting two mixed numbers? **Write the mixed numbers as improper fractions.**

Daily Puzzler

On Monday, Jessica bought a box of iris bulbs and planted half of them in her garden. On Tuesday, she planted half of the remaining bulbs. On Wednesday, she again planted half of the bulbs that remained from the day before. On Thursday, she planted half of the remaining bulbs. What fraction of the original bulbs was left in the box when she finished her planting on Thursday? $\mathbf{\frac{1}{16}}$

5.2 Exercises

More Practice, p. 807

Guided Practice

Vocabulary Check

1. Copy and complete: To find the sum of two fractions with the same denominator, write the sum of the ___?___ over the denominator. **numerators**

2. Explain how to simplify the expression $\frac{5m}{3} + \left(-\frac{2m}{3}\right)$. **See margin.**

Skill Check **Find the sum or difference.**

3. $\frac{7}{9} + \frac{1}{9}$ $\mathbf{\frac{8}{9}}$

4. $-\frac{2}{7} + \frac{5}{7}$ $\mathbf{\frac{3}{7}}$

5. $\frac{3}{8} - \frac{5}{8}$ $\mathbf{-\frac{1}{4}}$

6. $5\frac{9}{13} + 9\frac{8}{13}$ $\mathbf{15\frac{4}{13}}$

7. $-3\frac{7}{16} - 8\frac{11}{16}$ $\mathbf{-12\frac{1}{8}}$

8. $1\frac{3}{14} - 10\frac{5}{14}$ $\mathbf{-9\frac{1}{7}}$

Guided Problem Solving

9. Crafts You have $5\frac{1}{4}$ feet of ribbon. You want to cut one piece that is $3\frac{3}{4}$ feet long and one that is $1\frac{3}{4}$ feet long. Do you have enough ribbon?

(1) Write $3\frac{3}{4}$ and $1\frac{3}{4}$ as improper fractions. $\mathbf{\frac{15}{4}, \frac{7}{4}}$

(2) Find the sum of the improper fractions. $\mathbf{5\frac{1}{2}}$

(3) Compare the sum in Step 2 with $5\frac{1}{4}$ to determine whether you have enough ribbon.

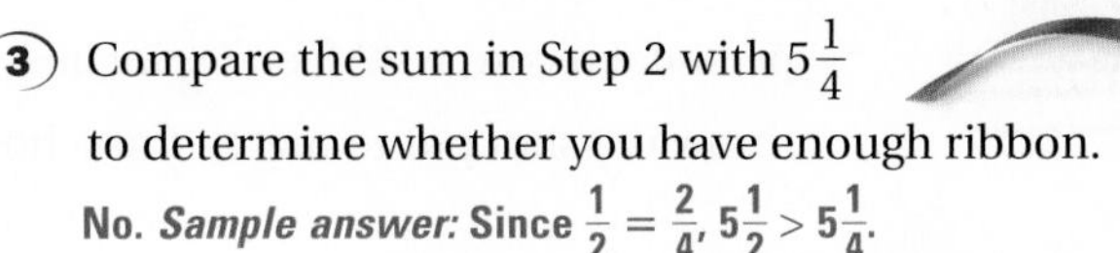

No. *Sample answer:* Since $\frac{1}{2} = \frac{2}{4}$, $5\frac{1}{2} > 5\frac{1}{4}$.

2. *Sample answer:* Write the sum of the numerators over the common denominator, 3. $-\frac{2m}{3}$ is equivalent to $\frac{-2m}{3}$, so this gives $\frac{5m + (-2m)}{3}$, which simplifies to $\frac{3m}{3}$. Now divide out the common factor 3 from the numerator and denominator to obtain the answer *m*.

3 APPLY

ASSIGNMENT GUIDE

Basic Course

Day 1: SRH p. 779 Exs. 1-5; pp. 228-229 Exs. 10-21, 27-34, 38-43, 46-48, 54-64

Average Course

Day 1: pp. 228-229 Exs. 14-28, 31-37, 41-45, 49-52, 54-65

Advanced Course

Day 1: pp. 228-229 Exs. 15-17, 20-28, 33-37, 41-56*, 61-65

Block

pp. 228-229 Exs. 16-28, 31-37, 41-45, 49-52, 54-65 (with 5.3)

EXTRA PRACTICE

- Student Edition, p. 807
- Chapter 5 Resource Book, pp. 16-18
- Test and Practice Generator

TRANSPARENCY

Even-numbered answers are available on transparencies.

HOMEWORK CHECK

When you review students' homework for this lesson, go over the following exercises to check understanding of key concepts.

Basic: 10, 14, 18, 29, 33

Average: 16, 17, 21, 34, 37

Advanced: 15, 17, 22, 35, 37

Practice and Problem Solving

Homework *Help*

Example	Exercises
1	10-17, 27
2	10-17
3	18-25, 28, 37, 44
4	29-36

Online Resources
CLASSZONE.COM
- More Examples
- eTutorial Plus

Find the sum or difference.

A **10.** $\frac{3}{5}+\frac{4}{5}$ $\mathbf{1\frac{2}{5}}$ **11.** $\frac{12}{19}+\frac{8}{19}$ $\mathbf{1\frac{1}{19}}$ **12.** $-\frac{17}{27}-\frac{13}{27}$ $\mathbf{-1\frac{1}{9}}$ **13.** $\frac{3}{7}-\left(-\frac{6}{7}\right)$ $\mathbf{1\frac{2}{7}}$

14. $\frac{13}{15}+\left(-\frac{8}{15}\right)$ $\mathbf{\frac{1}{3}}$ **15.** $-\frac{21}{26}+\frac{15}{26}$ $\mathbf{-\frac{3}{13}}$ **16.** $\frac{9}{22}-\frac{19}{22}$ $\mathbf{-\frac{5}{11}}$ **17.** $-\frac{6}{17}-\frac{12}{17}$ $\mathbf{-1\frac{1}{17}}$

18. $4\frac{1}{4}-5\frac{3}{4}$ $\mathbf{-1\frac{1}{2}}$ **19.** $3\frac{4}{5}+\left(-8\frac{4}{5}\right)$ $\mathbf{-5}$ **20.** $6\frac{3}{10}+7\frac{9}{10}$ $\mathbf{14\frac{1}{5}}$ **21.** $\frac{1}{3}-\left(-2\frac{2}{3}\right)$ **3**

22. $8\frac{9}{11}-3\frac{6}{11}$ $\mathbf{5\frac{3}{11}}$ **23.** $-5\frac{5}{18}-\frac{17}{18}$ $\mathbf{-6\frac{2}{9}}$ **24.** $3\frac{7}{16}-8\frac{11}{16}$ $\mathbf{-5\frac{1}{4}}$ **25.** $2\frac{1}{14}-11\frac{3}{14}$ $\mathbf{-9\frac{1}{7}}$

26. Error Analysis Describe and correct the error in adding $-\frac{3}{7}$ and $\frac{2}{7}$.

$$-\frac{3}{7}+\frac{2}{7}=\frac{-3+2}{7+7}$$
$$=-\frac{1}{14}$$
X

26. ***Sample answer:*** **Only the numerators should be added. The denominator of the sum is the common denominator: $-\frac{3}{7}+\frac{2}{7}=\frac{-3+2}{7}=-\frac{1}{7}$.**

27. Homework One day, you studied math for $\frac{3}{4}$ hour and English for $\frac{3}{4}$ hour. What was the total time that you studied both subjects? $\mathbf{1\frac{1}{2}}$ **h**

28. Baking A blueberry muffin recipe calls for $1\frac{2}{3}$ cups of flour. A banana muffin recipe calls for $2\frac{2}{3}$ cups of flour. How much flour do you need to make both recipes? $\mathbf{4\frac{1}{3}}$ **c**

Simplify the expression.

29. $\frac{5x}{8}+\frac{x}{8}$ $\mathbf{\frac{3x}{4}}$ **30.** $\frac{t}{13}+\frac{12t}{13}$ $\mathbf{t}$ **31.** $-\frac{11}{6p}+\frac{17}{6p}$ $\mathbf{\frac{1}{p}}$ **32.** $\frac{29}{12s}+\frac{19}{12s}$ $\mathbf{\frac{4}{s}}$

33. $\frac{2n}{15}-\frac{7n}{15}$ $\mathbf{-\frac{n}{3}}$ **34.** $\frac{m}{21}-\frac{5m}{21}$ $\mathbf{-\frac{4m}{21}}$ **35.** $-\frac{5}{18a}-\frac{23}{18a}$ $\mathbf{-\frac{14}{9a}}$ **36.** $-\frac{15}{4d}-\frac{21}{4d}$ $\mathbf{-\frac{9}{d}}$

37. Carpentry You are making a shelf from a board that is $12\frac{3}{4}$ inches long. You want to cut the board so that it is $10\frac{1}{4}$ inches long. What length should you cut from the board? $\mathbf{2\frac{1}{2}}$ **in.**

Evaluate the expression.

B **38.** $\frac{3}{9}+\frac{7}{9}+\frac{4}{9}$ $\mathbf{1\frac{5}{9}}$ **39.** $\frac{3}{10}+\frac{5}{10}+\left(-\frac{7}{10}\right)$ $\mathbf{\frac{1}{10}}$ **40.** $-\frac{7}{9}+\frac{2}{9}+\left(-\frac{4}{9}\right)$ $\mathbf{-1}$

41. $\frac{1}{5}-\left(-\frac{3}{5}\right)+\frac{2}{5}$ $\mathbf{1\frac{1}{5}}$ **42.** $-\frac{17}{31}-\frac{21}{31}-\frac{27}{31}$ $\mathbf{-2\frac{3}{31}}$ **43.** $-\frac{13}{14}-\frac{11}{14}-\frac{9}{14}$ $\mathbf{-2\frac{5}{14}}$

44. Shot Put The school record for the shot put is 45 feet, $3\frac{3}{8}$ inches. Your personal record is 42 feet, $6\frac{7}{8}$ inches. How much farther must you throw the shot put to match the school record? **2 ft,** $\mathbf{8\frac{1}{2}}$ **in.**

45. Critical Thinking Find two fractions, one positive and one negative, having the same denominator and a sum of $\frac{1}{2}$. ***Sample answer:*** $-\frac{1}{4}$ **and** $\frac{3}{4}$

Solve the equation. Check your solution.

46. $x + \frac{3}{7} = \frac{5}{7}$ $\frac{2}{7}$ **47.** $y + \frac{8}{11} = \frac{2}{11}$ $-\frac{6}{11}$ **48.** $-\frac{7}{12} + z = -\frac{5}{12}$ $\frac{1}{6}$

49. $m + 2\frac{4}{9} = 5\frac{2}{9}$ $2\frac{7}{9}$ **50.** $7\frac{3}{8} = n + 6\frac{5}{8}$ $\frac{3}{4}$ **51.** $-1\frac{5}{13} + t = 4\frac{10}{13}$ $6\frac{2}{13}$

52. Lobsters A lobster periodically sheds its shell and grows a new shell. During this process, which is called molting, the weight of the lobster increases, as shown in the table.

Lobster Weights (lb)	
Before molting	$1\frac{1}{4}$
After 1 molting	$1\frac{3}{4}$
After 2 moltings	$2\frac{2}{4}$
After 3 moltings	$3\frac{3}{4}$
After 4 moltings	$5\frac{1}{4}$

a. How many pounds did the lobster gain after each molting? **See margin.**

b. How many pounds in all did the lobster gain after four moltings? **4 lb**

c. Suppose the lobster gains $2\frac{1}{4}$ pounds after molting one more time. How much does it weigh then? $7\frac{1}{2}$ **lb**

In the **Real World**

Lobsters Suppose a lobster molts 25 times during the first 7 years of its life. After that, it molts once per year. After 12 years, how many times will it have molted? **30 times**

C **53. Challenge** Solve the equation $\frac{5}{8} + \frac{7x}{3} = \frac{8x}{3}$. Explain how you found the solution. **See margin.**

Mixed Review

54. Watch You buy a watch and a battery for \$57.99. The battery costs \$2.99. Write and solve an equation to find the cost of the watch. *(Lesson 2.5)* $c + 2.99 = 57.99$, **\$55**

Write the fraction in simplest form. *(Lesson 4.3)*

55. $\frac{15s^3}{5s^2}$ $3s$ **56.** $\frac{120t^2}{140t^5}$ $\frac{6}{7t^3}$ **57.** $\frac{65m^4}{80m^2}$ $\frac{13m^2}{16}$ **58.** $\frac{54a^5}{78a^2}$ $\frac{9a^3}{13}$

Find the least common multiple of the monomials. *(Lesson 4.4)*

59. $18m, 3mn$ $18mn$ **60.** $5t, 20s^2t$ $20s^2t$ **61.** $12a^3b, 6a$ $12a^3b$ **62.** $9vw, 36v^2w^2$ $36v^2w^2$

52a. first molting: $\frac{1}{2}$ lb, second molting: $\frac{3}{4}$ lb, third molting: $1\frac{1}{4}$ lb, fourth molting: $1\frac{1}{2}$ lb

Standardized Test Practice

63. Multiple Choice Find the difference $\frac{13}{16} - \left(-\frac{7}{16}\right)$. **D**

A. $-1\frac{1}{4}$ **B.** $-\frac{3}{8}$ **C.** $\frac{3}{8}$ **D.** $1\frac{1}{4}$

64. Multiple Choice Simplify the expression $\frac{16}{3y} - \frac{28}{3y}$. **G**

F. $-\frac{12}{3y}$ **G.** $-\frac{4}{y}$ **H.** 0 **I.** $\frac{44}{3y}$

65. Short Response A rectangular picture frame is made of wooden strips that are $\frac{3}{4}$ inch wide. The outside edge of the frame is $8\frac{1}{4}$ inches long and $6\frac{3}{4}$ inches wide. Can a rectangular picture that is 7 inches long and $5\frac{1}{2}$ inches wide fit inside the frame? Explain your answer.

65. No. ***Sample answer:*** Because the overall length and width of the frame include two $\frac{3}{4}$ inch wooden strips, the space available for a picture has a length of $8\frac{1}{4} - \frac{3}{4} - \frac{3}{4} = 6\frac{3}{4}$ inches and a width of $6\frac{3}{4} - \frac{3}{4} - \frac{3}{4} = 5\frac{1}{4}$ inches, so a picture 7 inches long and $5\frac{1}{2}$ inches wide is both too long and too wide to fit.

4 ASSESS

Assessment Resources

For more assessment resources, see:

- Assessment Book
- Test and Practice Generator

Mini-Quiz

Find the sum or difference.

1. $\frac{11}{12} + \frac{7}{12}$ $1\frac{1}{2}$
2. $5\frac{27}{35} - 3\frac{19}{35}$ $2\frac{8}{35}$
3. $-\frac{9b}{18} + \frac{7b}{18}$ $-\frac{b}{9}$
4. $-\frac{5}{21w} - \frac{16}{21w}$ $-\frac{1}{w}$
5. **Challenge** Solve the equation $\frac{2}{5} + \frac{6k}{9} = \frac{7k}{9}$. $3\frac{3}{5}$

5 FOLLOW-UP

Diagnosis/Remediation

- Study Guide in Chapter 5 Resource Book, pp. 19–20
- Tutor Place, Fractions Cards 7-9, 13
- eTutorial Plus Online
- Extra Practice, p. 807
- Lesson Practice in Chapter 5 Resource Book, pp. 16–18

English Learner Support

- Spanish Study Guide
- Multi-Language Visual Glossary
- Chapter Audio Summaries CDs

Challenge

- Challenge Practice in Chapter 5 Resource Book, p. 22
- Teacher's Edition, p. 216F

53. See Additional Answers beginning on page AA1.

1 PLAN

INVESTIGATE THE CONCEPT

- Students will use area models to add and subtract fractions with different denominators.
- This activity leads into studying how to add and subtract unlike fractions in Lesson 5.3.

MATERIALS

Each student will need paper and colored pencils.

RECOMMENDED TIME

Work activity: 10 min
Discuss results: 10 min

GROUPING

Students should work individually.

2 TEACH

DISCUSSION

As students are working, ask, "How many parts does a model for $\frac{1}{4}$ need to have? Why?" **4; the fraction $\frac{1}{4}$ means the division of 1 whole into 4 parts.** Ask: "How many parts does each model have in the first Step 2? Why?" **12; $4 \cdot 3 = 12$**

3 CLOSE

KEY DISCOVERY

You can use area models to add and subtract unlike fractions.

ASSESSMENT

1. When redrawing the models so they have the same number of parts, how does this number of parts relate to the given fractions? **It equals the product of the two denominators.**

5. See Additional Answers beginning on page AA1.

Concept *Activity*

5.3 Combining Fractions with Different Denominators

Goal
Use area models to add and subtract fractions with different denominators.

Materials
- paper
- colored pencils

Investigate

Use area models to add and subtract fractions.

To model finding the sum $\frac{1}{4} + \frac{2}{3}$, follow the steps below.

Draw area models for $\frac{1}{4}$ and $\frac{2}{3}$, as shown.

Redraw the models so they have the same number of equal parts.

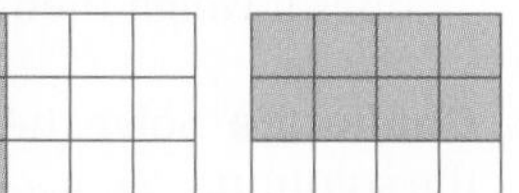

Combine the shaded parts to find the sum.

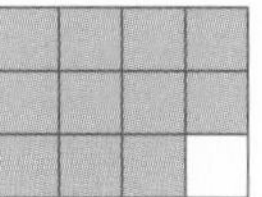

$\frac{1}{4} + \frac{2}{3} = \frac{11}{12}$

To model finding the difference $\frac{3}{5} - \frac{1}{2}$, follow the steps below.

Draw area models for $\frac{3}{5}$ and $\frac{1}{2}$, as shown.

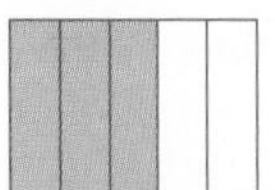

Redraw the models so they have the same number of equal parts.

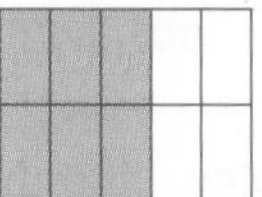

Find the difference of the numbers of shaded parts in the two models.

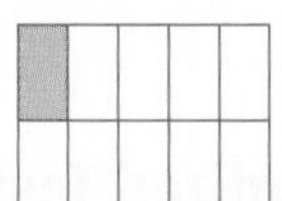

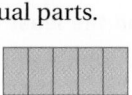

$\frac{3}{5} - \frac{1}{2} = \frac{1}{10}$

Draw Conclusions

Use area models to find the sum or difference.

1. $\frac{3}{4} + \frac{1}{6}$ **$\frac{11}{12}$** **2.** $\frac{1}{2} + \frac{2}{7}$ **$\frac{11}{14}$** **3.** $\frac{2}{3} - \frac{1}{4}$ **$\frac{5}{12}$** **4.** $\frac{5}{6} - \frac{2}{5}$ **$\frac{13}{30}$**

5. Critical Thinking Show how you can use an area model to find the difference $2 - \frac{2}{5}$. **See margin.**

NCTM CURRICULUM STANDARDS
Standard 1: Understand meanings of operations
Standard 10: Use representations to communicate mathematical ideas

LESSON

5.3 Adding *and* Subtracting Unlike Fractions

Review Vocabulary
least common denominator (LCD), p. 188

BEFORE	*Now*	WHY?
You worked with like fractions.	You'll add and subtract unlike fractions.	So you can find the range of salamander lengths, as in Ex. 34.

Hiking You are hiking between two campsites in the Chesapeake and Ohio Canal National Historic Park. The distance between the campsites is $10\frac{1}{5}$ miles. You have already hiked $5\frac{3}{4}$ miles. How many more miles do you have to hike? Example 3 answers this question by finding the difference of two mixed numbers.

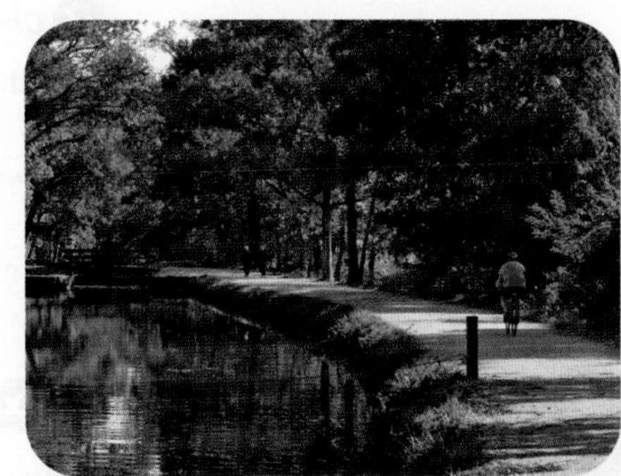

To add or subtract fractions with different denominators, begin by using the LCD of the fractions to write equivalent fractions that have the same denominator.

Review *Help*

For help with finding the least common denominator (LCD) of two or more fractions, see p. 188.

Example 1 ***Adding and Subtracting Fractions***

a. $\frac{5}{12} + \frac{1}{3} = \frac{5}{12} + \frac{4}{12}$ **Write $\frac{1}{3}$ using LCD.**

$= \frac{5+4}{12}$ **Write sum of numerators over denominator.**

$= \frac{9}{12}$ **Add.**

$= \frac{3}{4}$ **Simplify.**

b. $-\frac{5}{6} - \frac{7}{9} = \frac{-15}{18} - \frac{14}{18}$ **Write fractions using LCD.**

$= \frac{-15-14}{18}$ **Write difference of numerators over denominator.**

$= \frac{-29}{18}$ **Subtract.**

$= -1\frac{11}{18}$ **Write fraction as a mixed number.**

NCTM CURRICULUM STANDARDS
Standard 1: Understand numbers; Compute fluently

1 PLAN

Skill Check
Write the mixed number as an improper fraction.

1. $2\frac{1}{3}$ $\frac{7}{3}$ **2.** $-4\frac{5}{8}$ $-\frac{37}{8}$

3. $10\frac{2}{5}$ $\frac{52}{5}$ **4.** $-1\frac{19}{20}$ $-\frac{39}{20}$

Lesson Objective
Add and subtract unlike fractions.

Pacing
Suggested Number of Days
Basic Course: 2 days
Average Course: 2 days
Advanced Course: 2 days
Block: 1 block

Teaching Resources
For a complete list of Teaching Resources, see page 216B.

Transparency
Warm-Up Exercises for this lesson are available on a transparency.

2 TEACH

Motivating the Lesson
Have a student read the opening paragraph. Ask: "Have you hiked more or less than halfway? Explain your answer." Help students understand that since half of 10 is 5 and $\frac{3}{4}$ is more than $\frac{1}{5}$, then $5\frac{3}{4}$ is more than half of $10\frac{1}{5}$.

TIPS *for* NEW TEACHERS
Caution students to verify their work whenever they do a step mentally, such as when they change a mixed number to an improper fraction. Also remind them to write any solutions that are improper fractions as mixed numbers. See Tips for New Teachers in the *Chapter 5 Resource Book*.

Extra Examples

Example 1 Find the sum or difference.

a. $-\frac{3}{8}+\frac{1}{2}$ $\frac{1}{8}$

b. $-\frac{1}{4}-\left(-\frac{2}{3}\right)$ $\frac{5}{12}$

Example 2 Add $3\frac{4}{9}+7\frac{7}{12}$. $11\frac{1}{36}$

Example 3 Tyrone volunteered to work $7\frac{1}{2}$ hours at a weekend fundraiser. On Saturday, he worked for $2\frac{2}{3}$ hours. How many hours will he be working at the fundraiser on Sunday? $4\frac{5}{6}$ h

DIFFERENTIATING INSTRUCTION

Advanced Students After discussing Example 1, have students close their textbooks and then present Examples 2–4 in the following way. Copy the addition or subtraction expression on the board, followed by the descriptive sentences to the right of each step in the example. Ask the students to complete each step of the calculations using the descriptive sentences to guide them.

Study *Strategy*

Reasonableness You can use estimation to check the reasonableness of an answer. In Example 2, you can estimate the result by adding $-4\frac{1}{2}$ and $-2\frac{1}{2}$. Because the sum, -7, is close to $-6\frac{52}{55}$, the answer is reasonable.

Example 2 ***Adding Mixed Numbers***

$-4\frac{2}{5}+\left(-2\frac{6}{11}\right)=\frac{-22}{5}+\left(\frac{-28}{11}\right)$	**Write mixed numbers as improper fractions.**
$=\frac{-242}{55}+\left(\frac{-140}{55}\right)$	**Write fractions using LCD.**
$=\frac{-242+(-140)}{55}$	**Write sum of numerators over denominator.**
$=\frac{-382}{55}=-6\frac{52}{55}$	**Add. Then write fraction as a mixed number.**

Find the sum or difference.

1. $-\frac{2}{3}+\frac{1}{4}$ $-\frac{5}{12}$
2. $\frac{3}{10}-\frac{4}{5}$ $-\frac{1}{2}$
3. $-\frac{4}{15}-\frac{9}{10}$ $-1\frac{1}{6}$
4. $3\frac{5}{9}+2\frac{1}{6}$ $5\frac{13}{18}$
5. $6\frac{7}{10}+\left(-1\frac{1}{5}\right)$ $5\frac{1}{2}$
6. $-2\frac{1}{3}+6\frac{3}{5}$ $4\frac{4}{15}$

Example 3 ***Subtracting Mixed Numbers***

How many more miles do you need to hike before you reach the next campsite in the Chesapeake and Ohio Canal National Historic Park, as described on page 231?

Solution

Your total hiking distance is $10\frac{1}{5}$ miles. You have already hiked $5\frac{3}{4}$ miles. To find the remaining distance, subtract.

$10\frac{1}{5}-5\frac{3}{4}=\frac{51}{5}-\frac{23}{4}$	**Write mixed numbers as improper fractions.**
$=\frac{204}{20}-\frac{115}{20}$	**Write fractions using LCD.**
$=\frac{204-115}{20}$	**Write difference of numerators over denominator.**
$=\frac{89}{20}=4\frac{9}{20}$	**Subtract. Then write fraction as a mixed number.**

Answer You need to hike $4\frac{9}{20}$ miles, or about $4\frac{1}{2}$ miles.

Find the difference.

7. $5\frac{4}{11}-2\frac{2}{3}$ $2\frac{23}{33}$
8. $-1\frac{3}{7}-2\frac{3}{14}$ $-3\frac{9}{14}$
9. $4\frac{3}{8}-\left(-1\frac{2}{3}\right)$ $6\frac{1}{24}$

Example 4 *Simplifying an Expression*

Simplify the expression $\frac{a}{2} - \frac{a}{6}$.

$\frac{a}{2} - \frac{a}{6} = \left(\frac{a}{2} \cdot \frac{3}{3}\right) - \frac{a}{6}$ **Write $\frac{a}{2}$ using LCD.**

$= \frac{3a}{6} - \frac{a}{6}$ **Multiply.**

$= \frac{3a - a}{6}$ **Write difference of numerators over denominator.**

$= \frac{2a}{6}$ **Subtract.**

$= \frac{\overset{1}{\cancel{2}}a}{\cancel{6}_3}$ **Divide out common factor.**

$= \frac{a}{3}$ **Simplify.**

5.3 Exercises

More Practice, p. 807

Guided Practice

Vocabulary Check

1. What is the LCD of $\frac{2}{3}$ and $\frac{1}{2}$? **6**

2. Explain how to add two fractions with different denominators. **See margin.**

Skill Check **Find the sum or difference.**

3. $-\frac{1}{4} + \frac{1}{8}$ $\mathbf{-\frac{1}{8}}$ **4.** $-\frac{3}{4} - \frac{1}{3}$ $\mathbf{-1\frac{1}{12}}$ **5.** $-4\frac{3}{5} + 7\frac{4}{15}$ $\mathbf{2\frac{2}{3}}$ **6.** $2\frac{7}{12} - 9\frac{2}{3}$ $\mathbf{-7\frac{1}{12}}$

Simplify the expression.

7. $\frac{a}{15} + \frac{a}{6}$ $\mathbf{\frac{7a}{30}}$ **8.** $\frac{b}{8} + \frac{b}{12}$ $\mathbf{\frac{5b}{24}}$ **9.** $\frac{5a}{3} - \frac{a}{6}$ $\mathbf{\frac{3a}{2}}$ **10.** $-\frac{d}{5} - \frac{5d}{6}$ $\mathbf{-\frac{31d}{30}}$

2. *Sample answer:* **First find the LCD of the fractions. Use the LCD to write equivalent fractions that have the same denominator. Then use the method for adding like fractions.**

Guided Problem Solving

11. Lumber Newly cut lumber contains a lot of moisture. Before the wood is used for carpentry or construction, it is usually dried. Suppose a freshly cut board weighs $10\frac{1}{2}$ pounds. After drying, the board weighs $4\frac{2}{3}$ pounds. What was the weight of the water that evaporated?

(1) Write $10\frac{1}{2}$ and $4\frac{2}{3}$ as improper fractions. $\mathbf{\frac{21}{2}, \frac{14}{3}}$

(2) Rewrite the improper fractions using the LCD of the fractions. $\mathbf{\frac{63}{6}, \frac{28}{6}}$

(3) Find the difference of the improper fractions from Step 2. $\mathbf{\frac{35}{6}; 5\frac{5}{6}}$ **lb**

Extra Examples

Example 4 Simplify the expression $\frac{m}{5} - \frac{2m}{3}$. $\mathbf{-\frac{7m}{15}}$

ALGEBRAIC REASONING

At the end of Example 4, substitute the numbers 1, 2, and 3 for *a* in the expressions $\frac{a}{2} - \frac{a}{6}$ and $\frac{a}{3}$ to confirm for students that these expressions have the same value for a given value of *a*. Point out that doing this helps check that $\frac{a}{3}$ is the simplified form of $\frac{a}{2} - \frac{a}{6}$.

NOTETAKING

Ask students who express confidence in their knowledge of the lesson content to close their textbooks and work some exercises you have copied from the book onto the board. After presenting the answers, have them record in their notebooks a description of any exercises that challenged them, including a note about how they eventually completed the exercise.

CONCEPT CHECK

What is the first step you should take when subtracting fractions with different denominators? **Find the LCD of the fractions and use it to write equivalent fractions with the same denominator.**

DAILY PUZZLER

What is the value of $\frac{1}{2} - \frac{1}{4} + \frac{1}{6} - \frac{1}{8}$? $\mathbf{\frac{7}{24}}$

3 APPLY

ASSIGNMENT GUIDE

Basic Course

Day 1: SRH p. 778 Exs. 21–25; pp. 234–235 Exs. 12–23, 53–62

Day 2: pp. 234–235 Exs. 24–34, 36–39, 45–47, 63

Average Course

Day 1: pp. 234–235 Exs. 12–25, 51, 53–62

Day 2: pp. 234–235 Exs. 26–44, 48–50, 63

Advanced Course

Day 1: pp. 234–235 Exs. 16–25, 51–60*

Day 2: pp. 234–235 Exs. 26–32, 35–43, 48–50, 61–63

Block

pp. 234–235 Exs. 12–25, 51, 53–62 (with 5.2)

pp. 234–235 Exs. 26–44, 48–50, 63 (with 5.4)

EXTRA PRACTICE

- Student Edition, p. 807
- Chapter 5 Resource Book, pp. 25–27
- Test and Practice Generator

TRANSPARENCY

Even-numbered answers are available on transparencies.

HOMEWORK CHECK

When you review students' homework for this lesson, go over the following exercises to check understanding of key concepts.

Basic: 12, 17, 24, 33, 36

Average: 16, 18, 24, 34, 40

Advanced: 17, 24, 40, 43, 50

35c. See Additional Answers beginning on page AA1.

Practice and Problem Solving

Homework *Help*

Example	Exercises
1	12–23
2	24–33, 45–50
3	24–31, 34, 45–50
4	36–43

- More Examples
- eTutorial Plus

A **Find the sum or difference.**

12. $\frac{1}{12}+\frac{3}{16}$ $\frac{13}{48}$ **13.** $\frac{5}{6}+\left(-\frac{2}{3}\right)$ $\frac{1}{6}$ **14.** $-\frac{7}{10}+\frac{7}{20}$ $-\frac{7}{20}$ **15.** $-\frac{1}{9}-\frac{5}{18}$ $-\frac{7}{18}$

16. $-\frac{4}{15}-\frac{7}{25}$ $-\frac{41}{75}$ **17.** $\frac{5}{8}-\frac{11}{14}$ $-\frac{9}{56}$ **18.** $-\frac{6}{7}+\left(-\frac{16}{21}\right)$ $-1\frac{13}{21}$ **19.** $-\frac{1}{5}-\left(-\frac{2}{11}\right)$ $-\frac{1}{55}$

Evaluate the expression when $m=-\frac{5}{12}$ and $n=\frac{7}{9}$.

20. $m+n$ $\frac{13}{36}$ **21.** $m-n$ $-1\frac{7}{36}$ **22.** $n-m$ $1\frac{7}{36}$ **23.** $-m-n$ $-\frac{13}{36}$

Find the sum or difference.

24. $5\frac{1}{4}+1\frac{2}{5}$ $6\frac{13}{20}$ **25.** $-3\frac{3}{4}+10\frac{7}{8}$ $7\frac{1}{8}$ **26.** $6\frac{7}{18}-8\frac{21}{54}$ -2 **27.** $2\frac{5}{13}-\left(-1\frac{1}{2}\right)$ $3\frac{23}{26}$

28. $-4\frac{7}{10}-9\frac{7}{15}$ $-14\frac{1}{6}$ **29.** $3\frac{1}{2}-\left(-2\frac{1}{3}\right)$ $5\frac{5}{6}$ **30.** $-1\frac{5}{12}+4\frac{5}{14}$ $2\frac{79}{84}$ **31.** $15\frac{1}{6}-7\frac{3}{10}$ $7\frac{13}{15}$

32. Snow On one day it snows $2\frac{1}{2}$ inches. On the next day it snows $2\frac{1}{4}$ inches, and on the third day it snows $4\frac{1}{8}$ inches. What was the total amount of snowfall over the three-day period? **$8\frac{7}{8}$ in.**

33. Geometry The width of a rectangle is $2\frac{3}{8}$ inches. The rectangle is $1\frac{3}{4}$ inches longer than it is wide. Find the length of the rectangle and the perimeter of the rectangle. **length: $4\frac{1}{8}$ in., perimeter: 13 in.**

34. Salamanders Texas blind salamanders have been found in lengths varying from $3\frac{1}{4}$ inches to $5\frac{3}{8}$ inches. Find the range of these lengths. **$2\frac{1}{8}$ in.**

B **35. Extended Problem Solving** A catalog gives the information below about hats. Head size is the distance around a person's head.

Hat size	Small		Medium		Large		Extra Large	
Head size (in.)	$21\frac{1}{8}$	$21\frac{1}{2}$	$21\frac{7}{8}$	$22\frac{1}{4}$	$22\frac{5}{8}$	23	$23\frac{1}{2}$	$23\frac{7}{8}$

a. Analyze For each hat size, find the range in head sizes. **See margin.**

b. Apply The catalog says that if your head size is between two hat sizes, you should buy the larger hat size. You are ordering hats for friends whose head sizes (in inches) are $22\frac{1}{2}$, $21\frac{3}{4}$, $21\frac{5}{8}$, $23\frac{3}{4}$, $22\frac{1}{8}$, and $22\frac{3}{8}$. How many hats of each size should you buy? **3 medium, 2 large, 1 extra large**

c. *Writing* If you assume that customers always measure head size to the nearest $\frac{1}{8}$ inch, how would you revise the table to include all possible head sizes between 21 inches and 24 inches? **See margin.**

35a. small: $\frac{3}{8}$ in., medium: $\frac{3}{8}$ in., large: $\frac{3}{8}$ in., extra large: $\frac{3}{8}$ in.

In the **Real World**

Salamanders The Texas blind salamander inhabits underground streams whose average temperature is about 21°C. Use the formula $F = 1.8C + 32$, where F is the temperature in degrees Fahrenheit, and C is the temperature in degrees Celsius, to convert the average stream temperature to degrees Fahrenheit. **69.8°F**

Simplify the expression.

36. $\frac{d}{6} + \frac{2d}{9}$ **$\frac{7d}{18}$** **37.** $-\frac{y}{5} + \frac{y}{7}$ **$-\frac{2y}{35}$** **38.** $\frac{3a}{2} - \frac{a}{6}$ **$\frac{4a}{3}$** **39.** $-\frac{9r}{11} - \frac{r}{8}$ **$-\frac{83r}{88}$**

40. $\frac{4z}{7} - \frac{7z}{4}$ **$-\frac{33z}{28}$** **41.** $-\frac{x}{8} + \frac{x}{12}$ **$-\frac{x}{24}$** **42.** $-\frac{5c}{3} - \frac{4c}{15}$ **$-\frac{29c}{15}$** **43.** $-\frac{5w}{12} + \frac{7w}{9}$ **$\frac{13w}{36}$**

44. Horses Of the three different types of horses on a ranch, $\frac{1}{4}$ are Arabians, $\frac{2}{5}$ are Thoroughbreds, and the rest are Morgans. What fraction of the horses are Morgans? **$\frac{7}{20}$**

Evaluate the expression.

45. $5\frac{1}{2} + 1\frac{1}{4} + 2\frac{1}{2}$ **$9\frac{1}{4}$** **46.** $-\frac{2}{3} + 1\frac{5}{6} - \frac{3}{4}$ **$\frac{5}{12}$** **47.** $\frac{3}{4} + \frac{11}{12} - 1\frac{3}{8}$ **$\frac{7}{24}$**

48. $1\frac{1}{2} - \frac{3}{8} + 3\frac{4}{5}$ **$4\frac{37}{40}$** **49.** $-\frac{3}{5} - 1\frac{2}{15} - \frac{7}{10}$ **$-2\frac{13}{30}$** **50.** $5\frac{13}{64} - \left(-\frac{3}{16}\right) + 1\frac{1}{8}$ **$6\frac{33}{64}$**

51. Critical Thinking Can you use 48 as a common denominator when you find the sum of $\frac{7}{8}$ and $\frac{5}{12}$? Will you get the same answer that you do if you use the least common denominator of the fractions? Compare the steps you would use to find the sum using each common denominator. **See margin.**

C **52. Challenge** Find a value of x so that the sum $\frac{1}{x} + \frac{3}{2x}$ is equal to 1. Explain how you found your answer.

Note Worthy

You should write down any questions you have about performing operations on fractions in your notebook.

52. $\frac{5}{2}$. *Sample answer:* I rewrote $\frac{1}{x}$ using the LCD as $\frac{2}{2x}$. Then I added $\frac{2}{2x}$ and $\frac{3}{2x}$ to obtain $\frac{5}{2x}$. I set this equal to 1 to obtain the equation $\frac{5}{2x} = 1$, or $\frac{5}{2x} = \frac{1}{1}$, which I rewrote using cross products as $5 \cdot 1 = 2x \cdot 1$ and then solved.

Mixed Review

Find the product. *(p. 780)*

53. $8 \times \frac{3}{4}$ **6** **54.** $\frac{5}{8} \times 16$ **10** **55.** $\frac{6}{7} \times 21$ **18** **56.** $20 \times \frac{3}{5}$ **12**

Find the product or quotient. Write your answer using exponents. *(Lesson 4.5)*

57. $b^3 \cdot b^8$ **b^{11}** **58.** $c^2 \cdot c^5$ **c^7** **59.** $\frac{d^5}{d^7}$ **d^{-2}** **60.** $\frac{3a^6}{a^2}$ **$3a^4$**

61. Track and Field The school record for the javelin throw is 186 feet, $2\frac{1}{4}$ inches. Your personal record for the javelin throw is 172 feet, $\frac{3}{4}$ inch. Suppose you want to match the school record. By how much do you need to increase the distance you can throw the javelin? *(Lesson 5.2)* **14 ft, $1\frac{1}{2}$ in.**

Standardized Test Practice

62. Multiple Choice Find the sum $-6\frac{1}{2} + \frac{5}{8}$. **C**

A. $-7\frac{1}{16}$ **B.** $-7\frac{1}{8}$ **C.** $-5\frac{7}{8}$ **D.** $-5\frac{7}{16}$

63. Multiple Choice Simplify the expression $\frac{x}{4} - \frac{5x}{6}$. **G**

F. $-\frac{4x}{12}$ **G.** $-\frac{7x}{12}$ **H.** $\frac{4x}{12}$ **I.** $\frac{7x}{12}$

4 ASSESS

Assessment Resources

For more assessment resources, see:
- Assessment Book
- Test and Practice Generator

Mini-Quiz

Find the sum or difference.

1. $\frac{7}{8} + \left(-\frac{2}{3}\right)$ **$\frac{5}{24}$**
2. $-\frac{4}{5} - \frac{7}{10}$ **$-1\frac{1}{2}$**
3. $7\frac{1}{2} + 5\frac{5}{6}$ **$13\frac{1}{3}$**
4. $-2\frac{5}{12} - 4\frac{8}{9}$ **$-7\frac{11}{36}$**
5. **Challenge** Find a value of y so that the sum $\frac{8}{3y} + \frac{8}{6y}$ is equal to 2. **2**

5 FOLLOW-UP

Diagnosis/Remediation

- Study Guide in Chapter 5 Resource Book, pp. 28–29
- Tutor Place, Fractions Cards 10–12
- eTutorial Plus Online
- Extra Practice, p. 807
- Lesson Practice in Chapter 5 Resource Book, pp. 25–27

English Learner Support

- Spanish Study Guide
- Multi-Language Visual Glossary
- Chapter Audio Summaries CDs

Challenge

- Challenge Practice in Chapter 5 Resource Book, p. 30
- Teacher's Edition, p. 216F

51. See Additional Answers beginning on page AA1.

Additional Resources

The following resources are available to help review the materials in Lessons 5.1–5.3.

Chapter 5 Resource Book
- Lesson Practice
- Study Guide

Assessment Book
- Chapter 5 Quiz 1

Technology
- Test and Practice Generator
- eTutorial CD-ROM

Internet
- Classzone
- eWorkbook Plus Online
- eTutorial Plus Online

English Learner Support

- Spanish Study Guide
- Multi-Language Visual Glossary
- Chapter Audio Summaries CDs

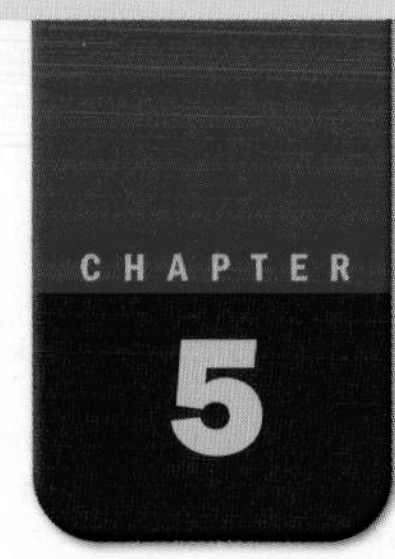

Mid-Chapter Quiz

Write the fraction or mixed number as a decimal.

1. $\frac{1}{12}$ $0.08\overline{3}$ **2.** $-\frac{42}{56}$ -0.75 **3.** $-\frac{7}{4}$ -1.75 **4.** $1\frac{6}{11}$ $1.\overline{54}$

Write the decimal as a fraction or mixed number.

5. 0.55 $\frac{11}{20}$ **6.** -4.22 $-4\frac{11}{50}$ **7.** $0.\overline{8}$ $\frac{8}{9}$ **8.** $0.\overline{54}$ $\frac{6}{11}$

Find the sum or difference.

9. $\frac{2}{15} + \frac{7}{15}$ $\frac{3}{5}$ **10.** $-\frac{1}{6} + \frac{5}{6}$ $\frac{2}{3}$ **11.** $\frac{11}{12} - \frac{7}{12}$ $\frac{1}{3}$ **12.** $-\frac{13}{30} + \frac{17}{30}$ $\frac{2}{15}$

13. $-\frac{1}{4} + \frac{2}{9}$ $-\frac{1}{36}$ **14.** $\frac{2}{3} - \frac{9}{14}$ $\frac{1}{42}$ **15.** $\frac{11}{28} - \frac{25}{42}$ $-\frac{17}{84}$ **16.** $-\frac{3}{4} + \left(-\frac{17}{25}\right)$ $-1\frac{43}{100}$

17. $-4\frac{9}{10} - 2\frac{3}{10}$ $-7\frac{1}{5}$ **18.** $3\frac{1}{4} + 5\frac{3}{4}$ 9 **19.** $-1\frac{1}{4} + \frac{11}{18}$ $-\frac{23}{36}$ **20.** $-10\frac{1}{2} - 14\frac{3}{5}$ $-25\frac{1}{10}$

Simplify the expression.

21. $\frac{9d}{12} - \frac{d}{12}$ $\frac{2d}{3}$ **22.** $\frac{7}{3a} + \frac{5}{3a}$ $\frac{4}{a}$ **23.** $-\frac{7c}{9} + \frac{c}{6}$ $-\frac{11c}{18}$ **24.** $\frac{b}{14} - \frac{b}{22}$ $\frac{2b}{77}$

25. Jogging You are jogging on a trail around a pond. The distance around the pond is $1\frac{5}{16}$ miles. So far, you have jogged $\frac{3}{8}$ mile. How much farther do you need to jog before you have gone exactly once around the pond? $\frac{15}{16}$ mi

Magic Square

Arrange the fractions $\frac{1}{10}, \frac{3}{20}, \frac{1}{5}, \frac{1}{4}, \frac{3}{10}, \frac{7}{20}, \frac{2}{5}$, and $\frac{9}{20}$ in the square so that the sum of the numbers in each row, column, and diagonal is $\frac{3}{4}$.

$\frac{3}{10}$	$\frac{1}{20}$	$\frac{2}{5}$
$\frac{7}{20}$	$\frac{1}{4}$	$\frac{3}{20}$
$\frac{1}{10}$	$\frac{9}{20}$	$\frac{1}{5}$

LESSON

5.4 Multiplying Fractions

BEFORE	Now	WHY?
You added and subtracted fractions.	You'll multiply fractions and mixed numbers.	So you can adjust ingredients in a recipe, as in Ex. 36.

Review Vocabulary
numerator, p. 777
denominator, p. 777

You can use an area model to find the product of two fractions, such as $\frac{3}{5} \cdot \frac{1}{4}$.

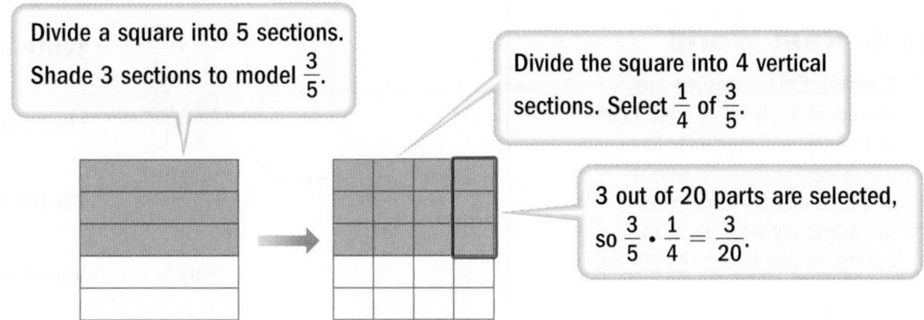

Divide a square into 5 sections. Shade 3 sections to model $\frac{3}{5}$.
Divide the square into 4 vertical sections. Select $\frac{1}{4}$ of $\frac{3}{5}$.
3 out of 20 parts are selected, so $\frac{3}{5} \cdot \frac{1}{4} = \frac{3}{20}$.

The area model suggests the following rule for multiplying fractions.

Multiplying Fractions

Words The product of two or more fractions is equal to the product of the numerators over the product of the denominators.

Numbers $\frac{3}{5} \cdot \frac{4}{7} = \frac{3 \cdot 4}{5 \cdot 7} = \frac{12}{35}$

Algebra $\frac{a}{b} \cdot \frac{c}{d} = \frac{ac}{bd}$, where $b \neq 0$ and $d \neq 0$

Study Strategy

Another Way In Example 1, you can also multiply the fractions without first dividing out common factors. You must simplify the resulting fraction.

$$\frac{7 \cdot (-4)}{10 \cdot 21} = \frac{-28}{210} = -\frac{2}{15}$$

Example 1 *Multiplying Fractions*

$\frac{7}{10} \cdot \left(-\frac{4}{21}\right) = \frac{7}{10} \cdot \left(\frac{-4}{21}\right)$ **Assign negative sign to numerator.**

$= \frac{7 \cdot (-4)}{10 \cdot 21}$ **Use rule for multiplying fractions.**

$= \frac{\overset{1}{\cancel{7}} \cdot (\overset{-2}{\cancel{-4}})}{\underset{5}{\cancel{10}} \cdot \underset{3}{\cancel{21}}}$ **Divide out common factors.**

$= \frac{-2}{15} = -\frac{2}{15}$ **Multiply.**

NCTM CURRICULUM STANDARDS
Standard 1: Understand numbers; Understand how operations are related; Compute fluently

1 PLAN

Skill Check
Simplify.

1. $\frac{28}{40}$ $\frac{7}{10}$
2. $\frac{15}{25}$ $\frac{3}{5}$
3. $\frac{a^4}{a^2}$ a^2
4. $\frac{18m^5}{24m^4}$ $\frac{3m}{4}$

Lesson Objective
Multiply fractions and mixed numbers.

Pacing
Suggested Number of Days
Basic Course: 1 day
Average Course: 1 day
Advanced Course: 1 day
Block: 0.5 block with 5.3

Teaching Resources
For a complete list of Teaching Resources, see page 216B.

Transparency
Warm-Up Exercises for this lesson are available on a transparency.

2 TEACH

Motivating the Lesson
Have students draw several squares on a sheet of paper. Instruct them to use vertical or horizontal lines and shading to model several fractions of their choice.

TIPS *for* NEW TEACHERS

Stress the difference between adding and subtracting fractions, where the denominators must be alike, and multiplying fractions, where the denominators do not need to be alike. See Tips for New Teachers in the *Chapter 5 Resource Book*.

Extra Examples

Example 1 Find the product $-\frac{3}{5} \cdot \frac{11}{12}$. $-\frac{11}{20}$

Example 2 A recipe for one loaf of bread requires $3\frac{1}{4}$ cups of flour. Joe wants to make 15 loaves. How much flour does he need? $48\frac{3}{4}$ c

Example 3 Find the product $7\frac{2}{3} \cdot 2\frac{7}{10}$. $20\frac{7}{10}$

COMMON ERROR

In Example 1, watch for students who cross through the negative sign of the second numerator, −4, when dividing out common factors and then fail to write the negative sign in the next step. Suggest that students mentally determine the sign of the answer before beginning their calculations and use this determination when giving their final solution.

CROSS-CURRICULUM

Art Art offers many opportunities for multiplying fractions. For example, a teacher may wish to calculate how much clay a group of students would need if each student is provided a certain fraction of a container of clay. Or a student calculating the size of an enlarged print might need to multiply mixed number lengths by a scale factor.

In the Real World

Emmys Emmy statues are plated with 18 karat gold. Each of the statues made for the 2002 ceremony cost about \$200 to create. About how much money was spent to create all the statues? **\$12,600**

Example 2 *Multiplying a Mixed Number and an Integer*

Emmys Each year, the Academy of Television Arts and Sciences presents gold-plated Emmy awards for programs and individuals in the television industry. Each Emmy statue weighs $4\frac{3}{4}$ pounds. In 2002, 63 statues were awarded. What was the combined weight of all the statues?

Solution

Combined weight = Statue weight • Number of statues

$= 4\frac{3}{4} \cdot 63$ **Substitute values.**

$= \frac{19}{4} \cdot \frac{63}{1}$ **Write numbers as improper fractions.**

$= \frac{19 \cdot 63}{4 \cdot 1}$ **Use rule for multiplying fractions.**

$= \frac{1197}{4}$ **Multiply.**

$= 299\frac{1}{4}$ **Write fraction as a mixed number.**

Answer The combined weight of the statues was $299\frac{1}{4}$ pounds.

Checkpoint

Find the product.

1. $\frac{2}{3} \cdot \frac{7}{8}$ $\frac{7}{12}$ **2.** $\left(-\frac{5}{12}\right)\left(\frac{3}{10}\right)$ $-\frac{1}{8}$ **3.** $10 \cdot \left(-2\frac{3}{11}\right)$ $-22\frac{8}{11}$ **4.** $\left(\frac{3}{4}\right)(-12)$ -9

Example 3 *Multiplying Mixed Numbers*

$-2\frac{3}{4} \cdot 3\frac{1}{5} = \frac{-11}{4} \cdot \frac{16}{5}$ **Write mixed numbers as improper fractions.**

$= \frac{-11 \cdot \overset{4}{\cancel{16}}}{\underset{1}{\cancel{4}} \cdot 5}$ **Use rule for multiplying fractions. Divide out common factor.**

$= \frac{-44}{5}$ **Multiply.**

$= -8\frac{4}{5}$ **Write fraction as a mixed number.**

Checkpoint

Find the product.

5. $4\frac{7}{8} \cdot 5\frac{2}{3}$ $27\frac{5}{8}$ **6.** $-3\frac{2}{7} \cdot 1\frac{1}{2}$ $-4\frac{13}{14}$ **7.** $-3\frac{3}{5} \cdot \left(-1\frac{5}{9}\right)$ $5\frac{3}{5}$ **8.** $4\frac{1}{8} \cdot \left(-1\frac{2}{3}\right)$ $-6\frac{7}{8}$

Example 4 *Simplifying Expressions*

Simplify the expression.

a. $\frac{m}{3} \cdot \left(-\frac{12}{5}\right)$ **b.** $\frac{n^2}{10} \cdot \frac{5n^3}{9}$

Solution

a. $\frac{m}{3} \cdot \left(-\frac{12}{5}\right) = \frac{m \cdot (-\overset{-4}{\cancel{12}})}{\underset{1}{\cancel{3}} \cdot 5}$ **Use rule for multiplying fractions. Divide out common factor.**

$= \frac{-4m}{5} = -\frac{4m}{5}$ **Multiply.**

b. $\frac{n^2}{10} \cdot \frac{5n^3}{9} = \frac{n^2 \cdot \overset{1}{\cancel{5}}n^3}{\underset{2}{\cancel{10}} \cdot 9}$ **Use rule for multiplying fractions. Divide out common factor.**

$= \frac{n^{2+3}}{18}$ **Product of powers property**

$= \frac{n^5}{18}$ **Add exponents.**

Review *Help*

For help with using the product of powers property, see p. 194.

Checkpoint

Simplify the expression.

9. $\frac{3y}{4} \cdot \frac{y^5}{9}$ $\frac{y^6}{12}$ **10.** $\frac{x^4}{6} \cdot \left(-\frac{16x}{3}\right)$ $-\frac{8x^5}{9}$ **11.** $\frac{3z^5}{25} \cdot \frac{2z^4}{15}$ $\frac{2z^9}{125}$ **12.** $-\frac{4v^2}{21} \cdot \frac{7v^3}{16}$ $-\frac{v^5}{12}$

5.4 Exercises

More Practice, p. 807

Guided Practice

Vocabulary Check

1. Copy and complete: The product of two or more fractions is equal to the product of the _?_ over the product of the _?_. **numerators, denominators**

2. Show how to simplify the expression $\frac{a^2}{7} \cdot \frac{7a}{2}$. **See margin.**

Skill Check **Find the product.**

3. $\frac{3}{4} \cdot \frac{5}{8}$ $\frac{15}{32}$ **4.** $\left(-\frac{7}{12}\right)\left(-\frac{4}{21}\right)$ $\frac{1}{9}$ **5.** $\frac{5}{6} \cdot (-8)$ $-6\frac{2}{3}$ **6.** $-2\frac{1}{2} \cdot 1\frac{3}{4}$ $-4\frac{3}{8}$

7. Error Analysis Describe and correct the error in simplifying the expression $\frac{c^2}{7} \cdot \frac{4c^4}{5}$. ***Sample answer:*** **The product of powers rule was applied incorrectly. To find the product $c^2 \cdot c^4$, you must add the exponents, not multiply them, so the result should be $\frac{4c^6}{35}$.**

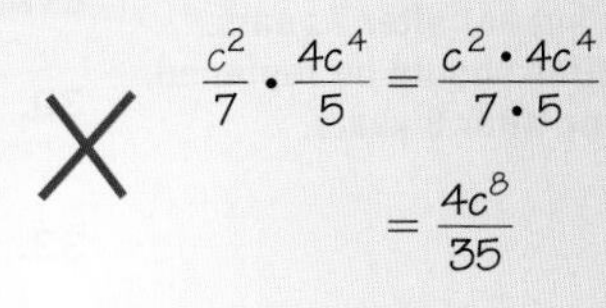

$\frac{c^2}{7} \cdot \frac{4c^4}{5} = \frac{c^2 \cdot 4c^4}{7 \cdot 5}$
$= \frac{4c^8}{35}$

2. *Sample answer:* Use the rule for multiplying fractions to obtain $\frac{a^2 \cdot 7a}{7 \cdot 2}$. Then divide out the common factor 7 from the numerator and denominator to obtain $\frac{a^2 \cdot a}{2}$. Finally, use the product of powers property to multiply a^2 and a, and obtain a final result of $\frac{a^3}{2}$.

Extra Examples

Example 4 Simplify the expression.

a. $\frac{c}{7} \cdot \frac{14}{15}$ $\frac{2c}{15}$

b. $-\frac{2x^3}{9} \cdot \left(-\frac{3x}{4}\right)$ $\frac{x^4}{6}$

Differentiating Instruction

Alternative Teaching Strategy
Give each student two dice of different colors and then have students select a partner. Assign one color of die to represent numerators and the other color die to represent denominators. Each student should roll their two dice and write a fraction using the numbers they roll. Have the partners then work together to find the product of their two fractions.

Concept Check

How do you compute the product of two fractions? **Find the product of the numerators and write this value over the product of the denominators. Simplify the resulting fraction, if necessary.**

Daily Puzzler

When Ruben's friend Jake called and asked him how much of his reading assignment he had finished, Ruben told him that his book was open to two pages whose page numbers have a product of 1056. To which two pages does Ruben have his book open? **pages 32 and 33**

3 APPLY

ASSIGNMENT GUIDE

Basic Course

Day 1: SRH p. 780 Exs. 13–16; pp. 240–241 Exs. 8–17, 20, 23–28, 30–32, 37, 38, 42–52

Average Course

Day 1: pp. 240–241 Exs. 11–22, 26–29, 33–40, 42–52

Advanced Course

Day 1: pp. 240–241 Exs. 11, 14–22, 26–29, 33–41*, 44, 47, 50–52

Block

pp. 240–241 Exs. 12–22, 26–29, 33–40, 42–52 (with 5.3)

EXTRA PRACTICE

- Student Edition, p. 807
- Chapter 5 Resource Book, pp. 35–37
- Test and Practice Generator

TRANSPARENCY

Even-numbered answers are available on transparencies.

HOMEWORK CHECK

When you review students' homework for this lesson, go over the following exercises to check understanding of key concepts.

Basic: 8, 10, 12, 16, 23

Average: 11, 13, 17, 22, 26

Advanced: 11, 14, 18, 26, 28

COMMON ERROR

In Exercise 19, watch for students who incorrectly divide out the common factors of the fractions before rewriting each mixed number as an improper fraction.

29a–b. See Additional Answers beginning on page AA1.

Practice and Problem Solving

Homework *Help*

Example	Exercises
1	8–11
2	12–15, 22
3	16–21
4	23–28

Online Resources
CLASSZONE.COM

- More Examples
- eTutorial Plus

Find the product.

A **8.** $\frac{5}{6} \cdot \frac{3}{8}$ $\frac{5}{16}$ **9.** $\frac{3}{10}\left(-\frac{5}{12}\right)$ $-\frac{1}{8}$ **10.** $-\frac{9}{28} \cdot \frac{49}{54}$ $-\frac{7}{24}$ **11.** $-\frac{35}{38} \cdot \left(-\frac{19}{40}\right)$ $\frac{7}{16}$

12. $32 \cdot \frac{17}{24}$ $22\frac{2}{3}$ **13.** $-18\left(\frac{8}{9}\right)$ -16 **14.** $\frac{5}{16} \cdot (-36)$ $-11\frac{1}{4}$ **15.** $-\frac{25}{28} \cdot (-21)$ $18\frac{3}{4}$

16. $4\frac{14}{15} \cdot 1\frac{7}{38}$ $5\frac{16}{19}$ **17.** $6\frac{1}{14} \cdot 6\frac{37}{51}$ $40\frac{5}{6}$ **18.** $-7\frac{1}{11} \cdot 5\frac{1}{24}$ $-35\frac{3}{4}$ **19.** $-3\frac{3}{20} \cdot \left(-2\frac{14}{23}\right)$ $8\frac{5}{23}$

20. Pineapples About $\frac{4}{5}$ of the weight of a pineapple is water. About how much water would you expect to find in $2\frac{1}{2}$ pounds of pineapple? **2 lb**

21. Painting You want to paint a wall that is $8\frac{3}{4}$ feet high and $11\frac{1}{4}$ feet long. You have a can of paint that will cover 200 square feet with one coat.

a. Find the area of the wall. $98\frac{7}{16}$ ft^2

b. Interpret If you want to apply two coats of paint, do you have enough paint? Explain.

21b. Yes. *Sample answer:* Two coats will take enough paint for $2 \cdot 98\frac{7}{16} = 196\frac{7}{8}$, which is less than the 200 square feet the paint should cover.

22. Sewing You are making 20 fleece jackets for a craft fair. For each jacket, you need $1\frac{7}{8}$ yards of fleece. If fleece costs $9 per yard, how much money will you spend? **$337.50**

Simplify the expression.

23. $\frac{a}{5} \cdot \frac{3a}{11}$ $\frac{3a^2}{55}$ **24.** $\frac{16b}{7} \cdot \frac{35b^3}{4}$ $20b^4$ **25.** $-\frac{11c^2}{6} \cdot \frac{8c^7}{3}$ $-\frac{44c^9}{9}$

26. $-\frac{d^5}{13} \cdot \left(-\frac{3d^7}{4}\right)$ $\frac{3d^{12}}{52}$ **27.** $-\frac{4x}{7} \cdot \left(-\frac{2x}{5}\right)$ $\frac{8x^2}{35}$ **28.** $\frac{ab}{4} \cdot \frac{2a^5b}{9}$ $\frac{a^6b^2}{18}$

B **29. Extended Problem Solving** The tread depth of the tires on your family's new car is $\frac{3}{8}$ inch. You predict that, as a result of driving the car, the change in tire tread depth will be about $-\frac{3}{64}$ inch per year.

a. Analyze Write a variable expression for the tire tread depth after y years of driving. Use your expression to make a table showing the tire tread depth after 1, 2, and 3 years. $\frac{3}{8} - \frac{3}{64}y$; **see margin for table.**

b. Apply Tires should be replaced when the tread depth is $\frac{1}{16}$ inch. Extend your table from part (a) to find the approximate number of years the car can be driven before the tires need to be replaced.

29b. See margin for table. *Sample answer:* Since $\frac{1}{16} = \frac{4}{64}$ and $\frac{3}{32} = \frac{6}{64}$, there is still sufficient tread left after 6 years but not after 7 years, so the tires should be replaced sometime after 6 years.

Evaluate the expression.

30. $\frac{2}{3} \cdot \left(-\frac{9}{10}\right) \cdot \frac{7}{12}$ $-\frac{7}{20}$ **31.** $-\frac{3}{4} \cdot \left(-\frac{8}{15}\right) - \frac{2}{5}$ 0 **32.** $\frac{99}{8} \cdot \frac{2}{17} + \frac{27}{34}$ $2\frac{1}{4}$

33. $3 + \frac{5}{6} \cdot \left(-\frac{3}{20}\right)$ $2\frac{7}{8}$ **34.** $-2 \cdot \frac{7}{8} + \left(-\frac{5}{28}\right)$ $-1\frac{13}{14}$ **35.** $\frac{5}{11} + \frac{5}{22} \cdot \left(-\frac{8}{33}\right)$ $\frac{145}{363}$

36. **Recipe** The recipe shown makes 60 sugar cookies. You want to bake 90 cookies.

a. Write a fraction comparing the number of cookies you want to bake with the number of cookies the recipe makes. $\frac{3}{2}$

b. *Writing* How much of each ingredient will you need to make 90 cookies? Explain how you got your answer.

Ingredients	
$2\frac{1}{2}$ cups flour	1 tsp baking soda
$\frac{1}{2}$ tsp salt	1 cup butter
$\frac{3}{4}$ cup white sugar	$\frac{3}{4}$ cup brown sugar
1 tsp vanilla	2 eggs

36b. $3\frac{3}{4}$ c flour, $1\frac{1}{2}$ tsp baking soda, $\frac{3}{4}$ tsp salt, $1\frac{1}{2}$ c butter, $1\frac{1}{8}$ c white sugar, $1\frac{1}{8}$ c brown sugar, $1\frac{1}{2}$ tsp vanilla, 3 eggs. *Sample answer:* The number of cookies I need is $\frac{3}{2}$ the number that a recipe makes, so I multiplied the amount of each ingredient by $\frac{3}{2}$.

In Exercises 37–40, use the following example to find a quotient of two numbers that are written in scientific notation.

Example ***Finding a Quotient of Numbers in Scientific Notation***

$$\frac{6.6 \times 10^3}{1.5 \times 10^4} = \frac{6.6}{1.5} \times \frac{10^3}{10^4}$$ **Write quotient as a product of two fractions.**

$$= 4.4 \times 10^{3-4}$$ **Divide. Use quotient of powers rule.**

$$= 4.4 \times 10^{-1}$$ **Subtract exponents.**

37. $\frac{7.2 \times 10^5}{3.6 \times 10^3}$ 2.0×10^2

38. $\frac{8.4 \times 10^5}{3.0 \times 10^8}$ 2.8×10^{-3}

39. $\frac{2.4 \times 10^2}{1.2 \times 10^6}$ 2.0×10^{-4}

40. $\frac{5.4 \times 10}{1.2 \times 10^7}$ 4.5×10^{-6}

C 41. **Challenge** Find the next three numbers in the following pattern: $\frac{2}{3}, \frac{2}{5}, \frac{6}{25}, \frac{18}{125}, \ldots$. Explain your reasoning. See margin.

41. $\frac{54}{625}, \frac{162}{3125}, \frac{486}{15,625}$. *Sample answer:* I observed that each term was $\frac{3}{5}$ of the term before it, so I multiplied by $\frac{3}{5}$ three more times to find the next three terms.

Mixed Review

Evaluate the expression. *(Lesson 1.3)*

42. $72 \div [6 - 14 - 1]$ -8

43. $3 \cdot [22 - (16 + 4)]$ 6

44. $5 \cdot [49 \div 7 + 2]$ 45

Solve the equation. Check your solution. *(Lessons 2.6, 2.7)*

45. $-14y = 42$ -3

46. $33w = 39.6$ 1.2

47. $-37.7 = -5.8z$ 6.5

Solve the inequality. Graph your solution. *(Lesson 3.5)* 48–50. See margin for art.

48. $\frac{a}{-10} < -7$ $a > 70$

49. $\frac{b}{2} > -1$ $b > -2$

50. $13 \geq \frac{c}{-7}$ $c \geq -91$

Standardized Test Practice

51. **Multiple Choice** Find the product $2\frac{13}{36} \cdot \left(-1\frac{1}{5}\right)$. A

A. $-2\frac{5}{6}$ **B.** $-2\frac{13}{180}$ **C.** $-1\frac{209}{216}$ **D.** $2\frac{5}{6}$

52. **Multiple Choice** Which product is greater than 1? I

F. $-\frac{4}{5} \cdot 5\frac{2}{3}$ **G.** $-\frac{3}{8} \cdot \left(-\frac{6}{7}\right)$ **H.** $\frac{1}{4} \cdot 2\frac{1}{2}$ **I.** $1\frac{1}{7} \cdot 1\frac{1}{3}$

4 ASSESS

Assessment Resources

For more assessment resources, see:

- Assessment Book
- Test and Practice Generator

Mini-Quiz

Find the product.

1. $-\frac{4}{15} \cdot \frac{5}{8}$ $-\frac{1}{6}$
2. $4\frac{1}{4} \cdot \left(-3\frac{1}{5}\right)$ $-13\frac{3}{5}$
3. Simplify the expression $\frac{25c^3}{12} \cdot \left(-\frac{4c^2}{15}\right)$. $-\frac{5c^5}{9}$
4. Evaluate the expression $\frac{18}{35} \cdot \frac{49}{72} \cdot \frac{16}{63}$. $\frac{4}{45}$
5. **Challenge** Find the next three numbers in the following pattern: $\frac{7}{8}, \frac{7}{12}, \frac{7}{18}, \frac{7}{27}, \ldots$. $\frac{14}{81}, \frac{28}{243}, \frac{56}{729}$

5 FOLLOW-UP

Diagnosis/Remediation

- Study Guide in Chapter 5 Resource Book, pp. 38–39
- Tutor Place, Fractions Cards 15, 18
- eTutorial Plus Online
- Extra Practice, p. 807
- Lesson Practice in Chapter 5 Resource Book, pp. 35–37

English Learner Support

- Spanish Study Guide
- Multi-Language Visual Glossary
- Chapter Audio Summaries CDs

Challenge

- Challenge Practice in Chapter 5 Resource Book, p. 40
- Teacher's Edition, p. 216F

48. 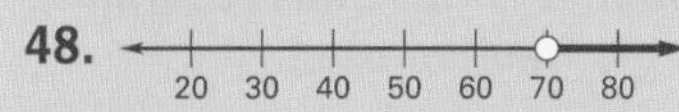

49.
-4 -3 -2 -1 0 1 2

50.
-93 -92 -91 -90 -89 -88 -87

1 PLAN

INVESTIGATE THE CONCEPT

- Students divide rational numbers.
- This activity leads into dividing fractions and mixed numbers in Lesson 5.5.

MATERIALS

Each student will need paper and pencil.

RECOMMENDED TIME

Work activity: 10 min
Discuss results: 10 min

GROUPING

Students should work individually.

2 TEACH

TIPS FOR SUCCCESS

Encourage students to complete the table one row at a time. Urge students to look for patterns between the rows above and the row they are currently completing.

3 CLOSE

KEY DISCOVERY

Students use patterns to discover the use of reciprocals in fraction division, although the term *reciprocal* is not introduced.

ASSESSMENT

1. What pattern do you see in the table for Step 1? ***Sample answer:* Whenever you multiply the dividend and divisor by the same fraction, the resulting quotient is the same regardless of the fraction used.**

10. See Additional Answers beginning on page AA1.

Concept *Activity*

5.5 Dividing Rational Numbers

Goal
Divide rational numbers.

Materials
- paper
- pencil

Investigate

Apply patterns observed in dividing whole numbers to dividing rational numbers.

1 Copy and complete the table. How are the dividend and the divisor of each expression related to the dividend and divisor of the expression 1000 ÷ 8? What do you notice about the quotients? ***Sample answer:* They are the products of a given fraction times the dividend and divisor of 1000 ÷ 8; the quotients are the same.**

Expression	Simplified expression	Quotient
1000 ÷ 8	1000 ÷ 8	? 125
$\frac{1}{2}(1000) \div \frac{1}{2}(8)$	? ÷ ? (500, 4)	? 125
$\frac{1}{4}(1000) \div \frac{1}{4}(8)$	? ÷ ? (250, 2)	? 125
$\frac{1}{8}(1000) \div \frac{1}{8}(8)$	? ÷ ? (125, 1)	? 125

2 Use the pattern you observed in Step 1 to find the quotient $\frac{3}{4} \div \frac{2}{3}$. Copy and complete the table by following the arrow. Begin by finding a fraction to replace the red fraction in the table. That is, find a fraction that makes the following statement true.

Expression	Simplified expression	Quotient
$\frac{3}{4} \div \frac{2}{3}$	$\frac{3}{4} \div \frac{2}{3}$	?
$\frac{?}{?}\left(\frac{3}{4}\right) \div \frac{?}{?}\left(\frac{2}{3}\right)$	$\frac{?}{?} \div 1$	?

$\frac{?}{?} \cdot \frac{2}{3} = 1$ **Row 1: $\frac{9}{8}$; replace the red fraction with $\frac{3}{2}$. Then the expression in row 2 is $\frac{3}{2}\left(\frac{3}{4}\right) \div \frac{3}{2}\left(\frac{2}{3}\right)$, the simplified expression is $\frac{9}{8} \div 1$, and the quotient is $\frac{9}{8}$, or $1\frac{1}{8}$.**

Draw Conclusions

In Exercises 1–8, find the quotient using the method shown above.

1. $\frac{3}{5} \div \frac{1}{2}$ **$1\frac{1}{5}$**
2. $\frac{4}{5} \div \frac{1}{3}$ **$2\frac{2}{5}$**
3. $\frac{7}{9} \div \frac{3}{10}$ **$2\frac{16}{27}$**
4. $\frac{11}{12} \div \frac{5}{6}$ **$1\frac{1}{10}$**
5. $\frac{5}{9} \div \frac{2}{7}$ **$1\frac{17}{18}$**
6. $\frac{4}{13} \div \frac{5}{8}$ **$\frac{32}{65}$**
7. $\frac{6}{11} \div \frac{1}{5}$ **$2\frac{8}{11}$**
8. $\frac{3}{16} \div \frac{2}{5}$ **$\frac{15}{32}$**
9. Copy and complete: For all integers a and all nonzero integers b, c, and d, $\frac{a}{b} \div \frac{c}{d} = \frac{a}{b} \cdot \frac{?}{?}$. **$\frac{d}{c}$**
10. **Critical Thinking** Show how you could find the quotient $2\frac{3}{5} \div \frac{7}{8}$ by multiplying the dividend and the divisor by a number that makes the divisor equal to 1. **See margin.**

NCTM CURRICULUM STANDARDS
Standard 1: Understand how operations are related
Standard 2: Understand patterns

LESSON

5.5 Dividing Fractions

Vocabulary
reciprocals, p. 243

BEFORE	Now	WHY?
You multiplied fractions and mixed numbers.	You'll divide fractions and mixed numbers.	So you can find how many book covers you can print, as in Ex. 36.

Two nonzero numbers whose product is 1 are **reciprocals**. The pairs of numbers below are examples of reciprocals.

Number	Reciprocal	Justification
5	$\frac{1}{5}$	$5 \cdot \frac{1}{5} = 1$
$\frac{2}{7}$	$\frac{7}{2}$	$\frac{2}{7} \cdot \frac{7}{2} = 1$
$-\frac{5}{8}$	$-\frac{8}{5}$	$-\frac{5}{8}\left(-\frac{8}{5}\right) = 1$
0.1	10	$0.1(10) = 1$

Study *Strategy*

To find the reciprocal of a decimal, you can write the decimal as a fraction. For example, because $0.1 = \frac{1}{10}$, the reciprocal of 0.1 is $\frac{10}{1}$, or 10.

As you may have seen in the activity on page 242, you can use reciprocals when dividing rational numbers.

Using Reciprocals to Divide

Words To divide by any nonzero number, multiply by its reciprocal.

Numbers $\frac{2}{9} \div \frac{3}{7} = \frac{2}{9} \cdot \frac{7}{3} = \frac{14}{27}$

Algebra $\frac{a}{b} \div \frac{c}{d} = \frac{a}{b} \cdot \frac{d}{c} = \frac{ad}{bc}$, where $b \neq 0$, $c \neq 0$, and $d \neq 0$

Example 1 *Dividing a Fraction by a Fraction*

$-\frac{2}{5} \div \frac{4}{7} = \frac{-2}{5} \cdot \frac{7}{4}$ **Multiply by reciprocal.**

$= \frac{\overset{-1}{\cancel{-2}} \cdot 7}{5 \cdot \underset{2}{\cancel{4}}}$ **Use rule for multiplying fractions. Divide out common factor.**

$= \frac{-7}{10} = -\frac{7}{10}$ **Multiply.**

✓**Check** To check, multiply the quotient by the divisor:

$-\frac{7}{10} \cdot \frac{4}{7} = -\frac{2}{5}$ ✓ **Solution checks.**

NCTM CURRICULUM STANDARDS
Standard 1: Understand relationships among numbers; Understand how operations are related; Compute fluently

1 PLAN

Skill Check

Write the mixed number as an improper fraction.

1. $2\frac{7}{8}$ $\frac{23}{8}$ **2.** $9\frac{1}{4}$ $\frac{37}{4}$

Find the product.

3. $-\frac{3}{10} \cdot \frac{8}{15}$ $-\frac{4}{25}$

4. $\frac{55}{28} \cdot \left(-\frac{14}{5}\right)$ $-5\frac{1}{2}$

Lesson Objective

Divide fractions and mixed numbers.

Pacing

Suggested Number of Days
Basic Course: 2 days
Average Course: 2 days
Advanced Course: 2 days
Block: 1 block

Teaching Resources

For a complete list of Teaching Resources, see page 216B.

 **Transparency**

Warm-Up Exercises for this lesson are available on a transparency.

2 TEACH

Motivating the Lesson

After defining the term *reciprocal*, ask students to identify the pairs of reciprocals on this page.

TIPS *for* NEW TEACHERS
Students may be confused by the decimal 0.1 in the last row of the table at the beginning of the lesson, thinking that only fractions have reciprocals. Be sure to have these students read the Study Strategy paragraph. See Tips for New Teachers in the *Chapter 5 Resource Book*.

Extra Examples

Example 1 Find the quotient $-\frac{2}{3} \div \left(-\frac{5}{6}\right)$. $\frac{4}{5}$

Example 2 Find the quotient $-6\frac{2}{3} \div 1\frac{5}{9}$. $-4\frac{2}{7}$

Example 3 Carissa mixes 2 gallons (32 cups) of fruit punch for a cookout. If each of the tumblers she plans to serve the punch in holds $2\frac{1}{3}$ cups, how many tumblers can she fill? **13 tumblers**

CONCEPT CHECK
How do you divide one fraction by another fraction? **Multiply the first fraction (the dividend) by the reciprocal of the second fraction (the divisor). Simplify the quotient, if necessary.**

DAILY PUZZLER
Chad, Daryl, and Emily painted a house. Daryl painted twice as much as Chad and Emily painted three times as much as Chad. What fraction of the house did Chad paint? $\frac{1}{6}$

Example 2 Dividing a Mixed Number by a Mixed Number

$4\frac{1}{6} \div \left(-1\frac{2}{3}\right) = \frac{25}{6} \div \left(-\frac{5}{3}\right)$ **Write mixed numbers as improper fractions.**

$= \frac{25}{6} \cdot \left(-\frac{3}{5}\right)$ **Multiply by reciprocal.**

$= \frac{\overset{5}{\cancel{25}} \cdot (\overset{-1}{\cancel{-3}})}{{}_2\cancel{6} \cdot \cancel{5}_1}$ **Use rule for multiplying fractions. Divide out common factors.**

$= \frac{-5}{2} = -2\frac{1}{2}$ **Multiply. Then write fraction as a mixed number.**

Checkpoint

Find the quotient.

1. $\frac{7}{12} \div \frac{2}{3}$ $\frac{7}{8}$ **2.** $-\frac{4}{9} \div \left(-\frac{8}{11}\right)$ $\frac{11}{18}$ **3.** $\frac{3}{8} \div 9\frac{1}{6}$ $\frac{9}{220}$ **4.** $-5\frac{1}{4} \div 2\frac{2}{5}$ $-2\frac{3}{16}$

Example 3 Dividing a Whole Number by a Mixed Number

Woodworking You want to join strips of wood that are 15 inches long and $1\frac{5}{8}$ inches wide to make a cutting board that is at least 12 inches wide. How many strips are needed?

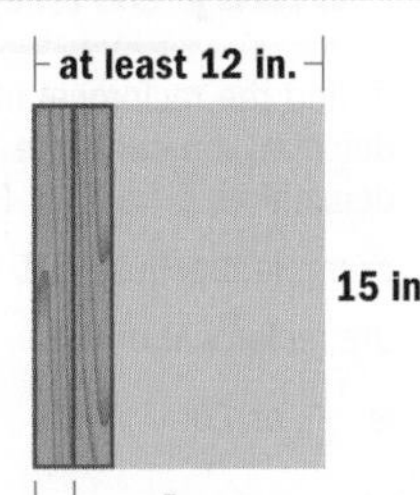

Solution

Divide to find how many strips are needed.

Number of strips = **Cutting board width ÷ Strip width**

$= 12 \div 1\frac{5}{8}$ **Substitute values.**

$= \frac{12}{1} \div \frac{13}{8}$ **Write numbers as improper fractions.**

$= \frac{12}{1} \cdot \frac{8}{13}$ **Multiply by reciprocal.**

$= \frac{12 \cdot 8}{1 \cdot 13}$ **Use rule for multiplying fractions.**

$= \frac{96}{13}$ **Multiply.**

$= 7\frac{5}{13}$ **Write fraction as a mixed number.**

Answer Because a whole number of strips is needed, you should use 8 strips to make sure that the cutting board is at least 12 inches wide.

5.5 Exercises

More Practice, p. 807

Guided Practice

Vocabulary Check

1. Explain why 0.25 and 4 are reciprocals.

1. ***Sample answer:*** **Since 0.25 $= \frac{1}{4}$, $0.25 \cdot 4 = \frac{1}{4} \cdot 4 = 1$.**

2. Describe the steps you would take to find the quotient $\frac{2}{5} \div 1\frac{2}{3}$. **See margin.**

State the reciprocal of the number.

3. 8 $\frac{1}{8}$ **4.** $-\frac{2}{3}$ $-\frac{3}{2}$ **5.** 0.75 $\frac{4}{3}$ **6.** 2.5 $\frac{2}{5}$

Skill Check

2. ***Sample answer:*** **First I would write $1\frac{2}{3}$ as the improper fraction $\frac{5}{3}$. Then I would find the reciprocal of $\frac{5}{3}$, which is $\frac{3}{5}$, and multiply $\frac{2}{5}$ by this reciprocal to obtain $\frac{2}{5} \cdot \frac{3}{5}$. Then I would use the rule for multiplying fractions to multiply the numerators and denominators to obtain $\frac{6}{25}$.**

Find the quotient.

7. $\frac{8}{11} \div \frac{33}{40}$ $\frac{320}{363}$ **8.** $\frac{2}{15} \div \left(-\frac{8}{25}\right)$ $-\frac{5}{12}$ **9.** $-\frac{4}{9} \div \frac{16}{11}$ $-\frac{11}{36}$ **10.** $6\frac{1}{3} \div \left(-3\frac{8}{9}\right)$ $-1\frac{22}{35}$

11. $1\frac{13}{14} \div 13$ $\frac{27}{182}$ **12.** $12 \div \left(-\frac{5}{12}\right)$ $-28\frac{4}{5}$ **13.** $\frac{3}{13} \div 15$ $\frac{1}{65}$ **14.** $7\frac{1}{5} \div \left(-1\frac{3}{10}\right)$ $-5\frac{7}{13}$

15. Error Analysis Describe and correct the error in finding the quotient $6\frac{1}{4} \div \frac{1}{2}$. ***Sample answer:*** **$\frac{25}{4}$ should not have been multiplied by $\frac{1}{2}$, but by its reciprocal, which is 2, to obtain $\frac{25}{4} \cdot \frac{2}{1} = \frac{25}{2} = 12\frac{1}{2}$.**

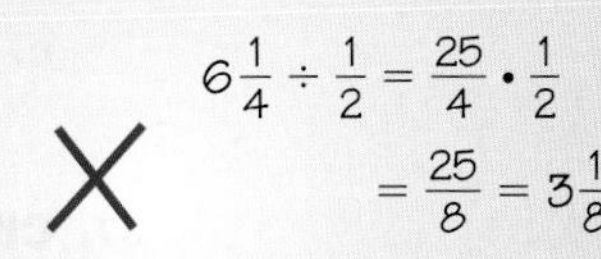

$6\frac{1}{4} \div \frac{1}{2} = \frac{25}{4} \cdot \frac{1}{2}$
$= \frac{25}{8} = 3\frac{1}{8}$

Practice and Problem Solving

Homework Help

Example	Exercises
1	16–19
2	20–23, 29
3	24–28

- More Examples
- eTutorial Plus

Find the quotient.

A 16. $\frac{13}{18} \div \frac{20}{27}$ $\frac{39}{40}$ **17.** $\frac{15}{16} \div \left(-\frac{25}{36}\right)$ $-1\frac{7}{20}$ **18.** $-\frac{32}{45} \div \frac{48}{35}$ $-\frac{14}{27}$ **19.** $-\frac{18}{19} \div \left(-\frac{9}{17}\right)$ $1\frac{15}{19}$

20. $7\frac{7}{9} \div 1\frac{11}{45}$ $6\frac{1}{4}$ **21.** $6\frac{6}{13} \div 2\frac{28}{39}$ $2\frac{20}{53}$ **22.** $8\frac{4}{15} \div \left(-\frac{2}{5}\right)$ $-20\frac{2}{3}$ **23.** $-1\frac{17}{55} \div 1\frac{11}{70}$ $-1\frac{13}{99}$

24. $34 \div \left(-\frac{4}{5}\right)$ $-42\frac{1}{2}$ **25.** $27 \div \left(-\frac{3}{11}\right)$ -99 **26.** $-\frac{40}{77} \div (-44)$ $\frac{10}{847}$ **27.** $-\frac{16}{21} \div 18$ $-\frac{8}{189}$

28. Bookmarks You want to cut bookmarks that are 6 inches long and $2\frac{3}{8}$ inches wide from a sheet of decorative paper that is 13 inches long and 6 inches wide. If you cut the bookmarks as shown, what is the maximum number of bookmarks that you can cut from the paper? **5 bookmarks**

$2\frac{3}{8}$ in.
6 in.
13 in.

ASSIGNMENT GUIDE

Basic Course

Day 1: SRH p. 778 Exs. 6-10; pp. 245-246 Exs. 16-19, 30-35, 38-45

Day 2: pp. 245-246 Exs. 20-29, 46-50

Average Course

Day 1: pp. 245-246 Exs. 16-19, 29-35, 38-45

Day 2: pp. 245-246 Exs. 20-28, 36, 46-50

Advanced Course

Day 1: pp. 245-246 Exs. 16-23, 29-32, 40-45

Day 2: pp. 245-246 Exs. 24-28, 33-37*, 46-50

Block

pp. 245-246 Exs. 16-36, 38-50

EXTRA PRACTICE

- Student Edition, p. 807
- Chapter 5 Resource Book, pp. 43-45
- Test and Practice Generator

TRANSPARENCY

Even-numbered answers are available on transparencies.

HOMEWORK CHECK

When you review students' homework for this lesson, go over the following exercises to check understanding of key concepts.

Basic: 16, 18, 20, 22, 24
Average: 16, 19, 20, 23, 25
Advanced: 17, 19, 21, 23, 27

COMMON ERROR

In Exercises 16-27, watch for students who divide out the common factors of the numerators and denominators before rewriting the division problems as multiplications.

4 ASSESS

Assessment Resources

For more assessment resources, see:
- Assessment Book
- Test and Practice Generator

Mini-Quiz

Find the quotient.

1. $\frac{15}{16} \div \frac{5}{24}$ **$4\frac{1}{2}$**
2. $-\frac{17}{28} \div \frac{8}{35}$ **$-2\frac{21}{32}$**
3. $3\frac{5}{8} \div \left(-2\frac{1}{2}\right)$ **$-1\frac{9}{20}$**
4. Evaluate the expression $\frac{7}{8} \div \left(\frac{4}{5} - \frac{1}{2}\right)$. **$2\frac{11}{12}$**
5. **Challenge** Solve the equation $\frac{7}{20}b = 21$. **60**

5 FOLLOW-UP

Diagnosis/Remediation

- Study Guide in Chapter 5 Resource Book, pp. 46–47
- Tutor Place, Fractions Cards 16–18
- eTutorial Plus Online
- Extra Practice, p. 807
- Lesson Practice in Chapter 5 Resource Book, pp. 43–45

English Learner Support

- Spanish Study Guide
- Multi-Language Visual Glossary
- Chapter Audio Summaries CDs

Challenge

- Challenge Practice in Chapter 5 Resource Book, p. 48
- Teacher's Edition, p. 216F

36a–b, 50b. See Additional Answers beginning on page AA1.

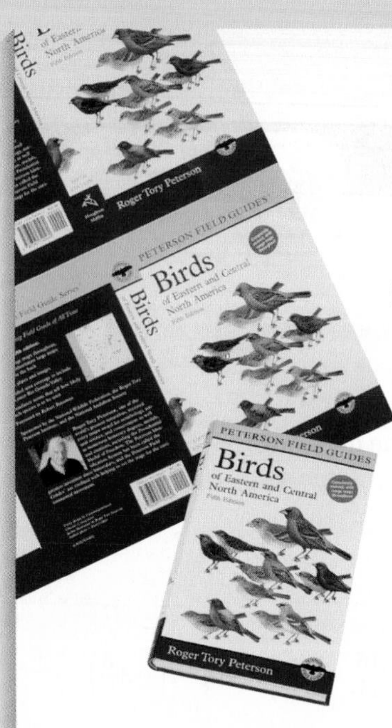

29. **School Fair** At a school fair, the field for a three-legged race is $31\frac{1}{2}$ feet across. Each lane is $5\frac{1}{4}$ feet across. How many lanes are there? **6 lanes**

Evaluate the expression.

B 30. $\frac{6}{7} \div \frac{2}{3} - \frac{3}{7}$ **$\frac{6}{7}$**
31. $\frac{5}{9} \div \left(\frac{4}{9} - \frac{3}{18}\right)$ **2**
32. $-\frac{8}{15} \div \left(\frac{7}{25} + \frac{9}{15}\right)$ **$-\frac{20}{33}$**

33. $5\frac{1}{17} \div 1\frac{9}{34} - \frac{19}{30}$ **$3\frac{11}{30}$**
34. $1\frac{29}{35} \div 1\frac{11}{21} + \frac{7}{15}$ **$1\frac{2}{3}$**
35. $\frac{70}{61} \div \frac{21}{122} - \frac{55}{13}$ **$2\frac{17}{39}$**

36. **Extended Problem Solving** Book covers are printed on large sheets of paper. A cover is printed multiple times on a sheet. In parts (a)–(c), assume that a sheet measures $21\frac{1}{2}$ inches by 36 inches. **36a–b. See margin for art.**

    a. **Analyze** A particular book cover is $7\frac{1}{2}$ inches high and $11\frac{1}{8}$ inches wide. What is the greatest number of covers that can be printed on a sheet? Show how the covers should be arranged. **7 book covers**

    b. **Analyze** Another book cover is 8 inches high and $9\frac{1}{2}$ inches wide. What is the greatest number of these covers that can be printed on a sheet? Show how the covers should be arranged. **8 book covers**

    c. **Apply** Suppose you need to print 12,000 covers of each of the books in parts (a) and (b). How many sheets do you need for each book? **(a) 1715 sheets; (b) 1500 sheets**

C 37. **Challenge** Solve the equation $\frac{6}{11}x = 12$. Explain how you solved it. **See margin.**

37. 22. *Sample answer:* I multiplied each side of the equation by $\frac{11}{6}$ so that the coefficient of x would be 1, and then I divided out the common factor 6 from the numerator and denominator of the right side.

Mixed Review

Solve the equation. Check your solution. *(Lesson 3.1)*

38. $9m + 5 = 4$ **$-\frac{1}{9}$**
39. $1 - n = -5$ **6**
40. $0 = \frac{m}{-5} + 3$ **15**
41. $1 = 2 + \frac{n}{-7}$ **7**

Use the LCD to determine which fraction is greater. *(Lesson 4.4)*

42. $\frac{3}{13}, \frac{1}{4}$ **$\frac{1}{4}$**
43. $\frac{7}{15}, \frac{9}{20}$ **$\frac{7}{15}$**
44. $\frac{9}{17}, \frac{25}{51}$ **$\frac{9}{17}$**
45. $\frac{3}{8}, \frac{29}{84}$ **$\frac{3}{8}$**

Simplify the expression. *(Lessons 5.2, 5.3)*

46. $\frac{a}{13} + \left(-\frac{6a}{65}\right)$ **$-\frac{a}{65}$**
47. $\frac{3b}{22} - \frac{7b}{22}$ **$-\frac{2b}{11}$**
48. $-\frac{c}{11} - \frac{10c}{11}$ **$-c$**
49. $\frac{5d}{18} + \frac{7d}{9}$ **$\frac{19d}{18}$**

Standardized Test Practice

50. **Extended Response** After reading that the average women's shoe size is $8\frac{1}{2}$, a shoe store owner records the sizes of women's shoes sold in one morning. The sizes sold were $6\frac{1}{2}$, $9\frac{1}{2}$, $5\frac{1}{2}$, 10, 11, $8\frac{1}{2}$, 9, and 8.

    a. For each shoe size, find the deviation from the average stated above by subtracting the average from the shoe size. What does a positive deviation from the average indicate? What does a negative deviation from the average indicate?

    b. Find the mean of the deviations from part (a). What might the store owner conclude? Explain your thinking. **See margin.**

50a. −2, +1, −3, $+1\frac{1}{2}$, $+2\frac{1}{2}$, 0, $+\frac{1}{2}$, $-\frac{1}{2}$; a positive deviation indicates a larger than average size; a negative deviation indicates a smaller than average size.

LESSON

5.6 Using Multiplicative Inverses *to* Solve Equations

Vocabulary
multiplicative inverse, p. 247

BEFORE	*Now*	WHY?
You used reciprocals to divide fractions.	You'll use multiplicative inverses to solve equations.	So you can find the width of a U.S. flag, as in Ex. 19.

Caves Stalactites are icicle-shaped stone formations found on cave ceilings. They form from minerals deposited by dripping water. Suppose a stalactite is 10 inches long and is growing at a rate of about $\frac{1}{8}$ inch per decade. How long will it take for the stalactite to reach a length of 1 foot? In Example 3, you'll see how to answer this question by writing and solving an equation.

To solve an equation that has a fractional coefficient, you can multiply each side of the equation by the fraction's *multiplicative inverse*. The **multiplicative inverse** of a nonzero number is the number's reciprocal.

Multiplicative Inverse Property

Words The product of a number and its multiplicative inverse is 1.

Numbers $\frac{3}{5} \cdot \frac{5}{3} = 1$

Algebra $\frac{a}{b} \cdot \frac{b}{a} = 1$, where $a \neq 0, b \neq 0$

Study *Strategy*

When you solve an equation with fractional coefficients, remember to check your solution by substituting the value of the variable in the original equation.

Example 1 ***Solving a One-Step Equation***

$\frac{4}{7}x = -12$	**Original equation**
$\frac{7}{4}\left(\frac{4}{7}\right)x = \frac{7}{4}(-12)$	**Multiply each side by multiplicative inverse of $\frac{4}{7}$.**
$1x = \frac{7}{4}(-12)$	**Multiplicative inverse property**
$x = -21$	**Multiply.**

Answer The solution is −21.

NCTM CURRICULUM STANDARDS
Standard 1: Understand how operations are related; Compute fluently
Standard 2: Represent situations using algebraic symbols

1 PLAN

Skill Check
Solve the equation.
1. $3x = -12$ **−4**
2. $2a + 3 = 13$ **5**
3. $5z + 14 = 4$ **−2**

Lesson Objective
Use multiplicative inverses to solve equations.

Pacing
Suggested Number of Days
Basic Course: 2 days
Average Course: 2 days
Advanced Course: 2 days
Block: 1 block

Teaching Resources
For a complete list of Teaching Resources, see page 216B.

Transparency
Warm-Up Exercises for this lesson are available on a transparency.

2 TEACH

Motivating the Lesson
After reading the growth rate of the stalactite, ask students how many decades it will take for stalactite to grow $\frac{1}{4}$ inch; $\frac{3}{8}$ inch; $\frac{1}{2}$ inch.
2 decades; 3 decades; 4 decades

TIPS *for* NEW TEACHERS
You might wish to review the method for solving two-step equations before discussing Example 2 on page 248. See Tips for New Teachers in the *Chapter 5 Resource Book*.

Extra Examples

Example 1 Solve $-\frac{7}{8}k = 56$. **−64**

Example 2 Solve $\frac{13}{16} = \frac{3}{8}g + \frac{1}{2}$. **$\frac{5}{6}$**

Example 3 There are currently 1680 students at Fairview Middle School. So far this school year, an average of $3\frac{1}{2}$ new students have enrolled at the school each week. The school has a maximum capacity of 1750 students. If this growth rate continues, in how many weeks will the school reach its maximum student capacity? **20 weeks**

TEACHING TIP

Solve the equation in Example 2 a second time, using a different series of steps. First rewrite each term using the LCD, then subtract the constant from each side, and finish by multiplying each side by the multiplicative inverse. Some students may prefer this method.

CONCEPT CHECK

How would you use the multiplicative inverse property to solve the equation $\frac{5}{6}x = 2$? **Multiply each side of the equation by $\frac{6}{5}$, the multiplicative inverse of $\frac{5}{6}$, and simplify.**

DAILY PUZZLER

What is the value of $\dfrac{3}{\frac{1}{2} + \frac{1}{4}}$? **4**

Example 2 *Solving a Two-Step Equation*

$-\frac{11}{15}x + \frac{4}{5} = \frac{1}{3}$	**Original equation**
$-\frac{11}{15}x + \frac{4}{5} - \frac{4}{5} = \frac{1}{3} - \frac{4}{5}$	**Subtract $\frac{4}{5}$ from each side.**
$-\frac{11}{15}x = \frac{1}{3} - \frac{4}{5}$	**Simplify.**
$-\frac{11}{15}x = \frac{5}{15} - \frac{12}{15}$	**Write fractions using LCD.**
$-\frac{11}{15}x = -\frac{7}{15}$	**Subtract.**
$-\frac{15}{11}\left(-\frac{11}{15}\right)x = -\frac{15}{11}\left(-\frac{7}{15}\right)$	**Multiply each side by multiplicative inverse of $-\frac{11}{15}$.**
$x = \frac{7}{11}$	**Multiply.**

Checkpoint

Solve the equation. Check your solution.

1. $\frac{5}{6}m = 20$ **24** **2.** $-16 = \frac{3}{4}n - 20$ **$5\frac{1}{3}$** **3.** $-\frac{2}{3}p + \frac{1}{2} = \frac{5}{6}$ **$-\frac{1}{2}$**

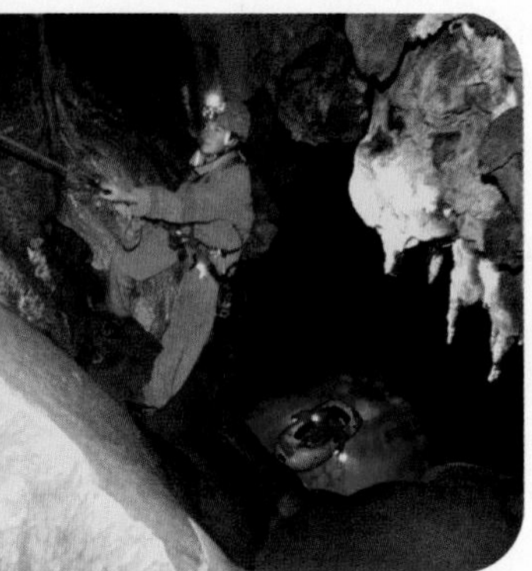

In the **Real World**

Caves The photo above was taken in La Grotte de Gournier, a cave in France. Cave explorers have found that the deepest point in this cave is 680 meters beneath Earth's surface. Give the depth of the cave in kilometers. Then use the fact that 1 km ≈ 0.62 mi to find the depth of the cave in miles. Is the cave more than or less than half a mile deep? **0.68 km; about 0.42 mi; less than**

Example 3 *Writing and Solving a Two-Step Equation*

Find how long it will take the stalactite described on page 247 to reach a length of 1 foot.

Solution

Write a verbal model. Let x represent the number of decades it will take the stalactite to reach a length of 1 foot.

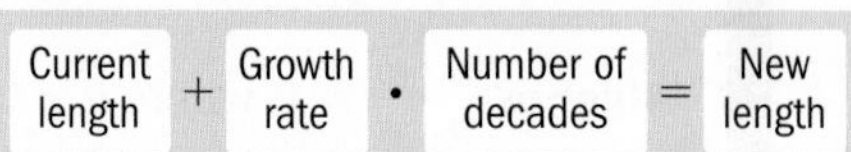

$10 + \frac{1}{8}x = 12$	**Write equation. Write 1 foot as 12 inches.**
$10 + \frac{1}{8}x - \mathbf{10} = 12 - \mathbf{10}$	**Subtract 10 from each side.**
$\frac{1}{8}x = 2$	**Simplify.**
$\mathbf{8}\left(\frac{1}{8}x\right) = \mathbf{8}(2)$	**Multiply each side by multiplicative inverse of $\frac{1}{8}$.**
$x = 16$	**Multiply.**

Answer The stalactite will be 1 foot long after 16 decades, or 160 years.

5.6 Exercises

More Practice, p. 807

Guided Practice

Vocabulary Check

1. What is the multiplicative inverse of a nonzero number? **the number's reciprocal**
2. Describe how to solve the equation $\frac{5}{6}x = \frac{2}{7}$. **See margin.**

Skill Check **Solve the equation. Check your solution.**

3. $\frac{4}{9}x = -16$ **−36**
4. $-\frac{7}{12}x = 28$ **−48**
5. $-\frac{2}{3}x = \frac{6}{7}$ **$-1\frac{2}{7}$**
6. $\frac{1}{3}x + 5 = 11$ **18**
7. $\frac{7}{8}x - 9 = 5$ **16**
8. $-\frac{3}{4}x + \frac{3}{8} = \frac{27}{32}$ **$-\frac{5}{8}$**

Guided Problem Solving

9. **Ants** The diagram shows the distances of two ants from the edge of a picnic table. Ant A travels in a straight line at a speed of $\frac{3}{4}$ inch per second. Ant B travels in a straight line at a speed of $\frac{7}{8}$ inch per second. Which ant will reach the edge first?

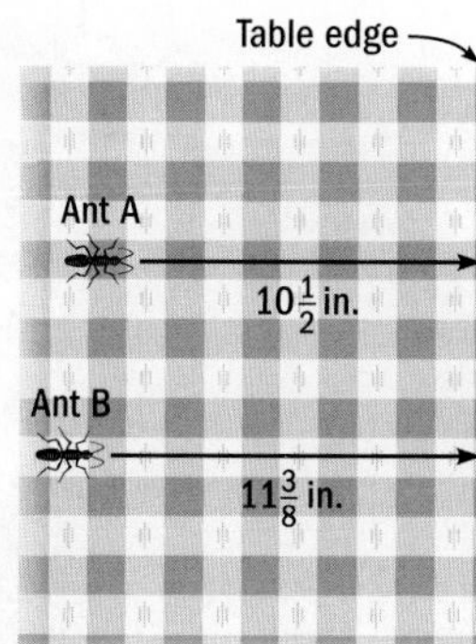

9. Step 1: ant A: $10\frac{1}{2} = \frac{3}{4}t$; ant B: $11\frac{3}{8} = \frac{7}{8}t$

(1) Use the formula *distance* = *rate* × *time* to write an equation for each ant.

(2) Solve each equation from Step 1. **ant A: $t = 14$ sec; ant B: $t = 13$ sec**

(3) Compare your solutions to determine which ant will reach the edge first. **ant B**

Practice and Problem Solving

Homework Help

Example	Exercises
1	11-20
2	21-29
3	30-31

Online Resources
CLASSZONE.COM
- More Examples
- eTutorial Plus

A 10. **Error Analysis** Describe and correct the error in solving the equation $-\frac{1}{6}x = \frac{2}{3}$. **See margin.**

$$-\frac{1}{6}x = \frac{2}{3}$$
$$6\left(-\frac{1}{6}x\right) = 6\left(\frac{2}{3}\right)$$
$$x = 4$$

Solve the equation. Check your solution.

11. $\frac{2}{9}x = 12$ **54**
12. $\frac{3}{8}x = 15$ **40**
13. $-\frac{5}{12}x = 25$ **−60**
14. $-\frac{1}{6}x = 8$ **−48**
15. $\frac{5}{7}x = -\frac{9}{14}$ **$-\frac{9}{10}$**
16. $\frac{2}{5}x = -\frac{8}{15}$ **$-1\frac{1}{3}$**
17. $-\frac{17}{22}x = \frac{4}{11}$ **$-\frac{8}{17}$**
18. $-\frac{10}{21}x = \frac{2}{3}$ **$-1\frac{2}{5}$**

3 APPLY

ASSIGNMENT GUIDE

Basic Course
Day 1: EP p. 805 Exs. 1-8; pp. 249-251 Exs. 11-14, 21-26, 35-38
Day 2: pp. 249-251 Exs. 15-19, 27-31, 39-44

Average Course
Day 1: pp. 249-251 Exs. 10-14, 21-26, 35-40
Day 2: pp. 249-251 Exs. 15-20, 27-33, 41-44

Advanced Course
Day 1: pp. 249-251 Exs. 10, 13-16, 21-26, 37-42
Day 2: pp. 249-251 Exs. 17-20, 27-34*, 43, 44

Block
pp. 249-251 Exs. 10-33, 35-44

Extra Practice

- Student Edition, p. 807
- Chapter 5 Resource Book, pp. 51-53
- Test and Practice Generator

Transparency

Even-numbered answers are available on transparencies.

Homework Check

When you review students' homework for this lesson, go over the following exercises to check understanding of key concepts.
Basic: 11, 15, 21, 25, 30
Average: 12, 16, 23, 25, 30
Advanced: 16, 17, 23, 28, 31

2, 10. See Additional Answers beginning on page AA1.

 **COMMON ERROR**

In Exercises 24–29, watch for students who chose to multiply by the multiplicative inverse of the first fraction in the equation rather than the multiplicative inverse of the fraction that is the coefficient of the variable.

TEACHING TIP

In Exercise 34, clarify for students that "boyhood" and "youth" refer to two distinct (non-overlapping) periods of time.

19. United States Flag The length of the United States flag is $1\frac{9}{10}$ times the width of the flag. A particular U.S. flag is 5 feet long. Write and solve an equation to find the width of the flag. $1\frac{9}{10}w = 5$, $2\frac{12}{19}$ ft

20. *Writing* Solve the equation $\frac{3}{7}x = 5$ by using a multiplicative inverse. Then solve the equation by dividing each side of the equation by $\frac{3}{7}$. Compare these two methods of solving the equation. How are they alike? How are they different?

20. $11\frac{2}{3}$; $11\frac{2}{3}$. *Sample answer:* Since dividing by $\frac{3}{7}$ is equivalent to multiplying by $\frac{7}{3}$, the multiplicative inverse of $\frac{3}{7}$, the methods are the same except that the division method requires the extra step at the beginning of rewriting the division as multiplication.

Solve the equation. Check your solution.

21. $\frac{4}{9}x + 7 = 31$ 54 **22.** $\frac{7}{11}x + (-17) = 4$ 33 **23.** $4 + \left(-\frac{3}{5}\right)x = 16$ -20

24. $\frac{2}{13} = \frac{8}{13}x + \frac{4}{13}$ $-\frac{1}{4}$ **25.** $-\frac{8}{17} = \frac{11}{17} - \frac{5}{17}x$ $3\frac{4}{5}$ **26.** $\frac{13}{15}x - \frac{7}{9} = -\frac{1}{5}$ $\frac{2}{3}$

27. $\frac{5}{14} + \frac{2}{7}x = 1\frac{5}{42}$ $2\frac{2}{3}$ **28.** $\frac{7}{8}x - \frac{9}{10} = -\frac{1}{8}$ $\frac{31}{35}$ **29.** $-\frac{5}{48} = -\frac{5}{6} + \frac{5}{16}x$ $2\frac{1}{3}$

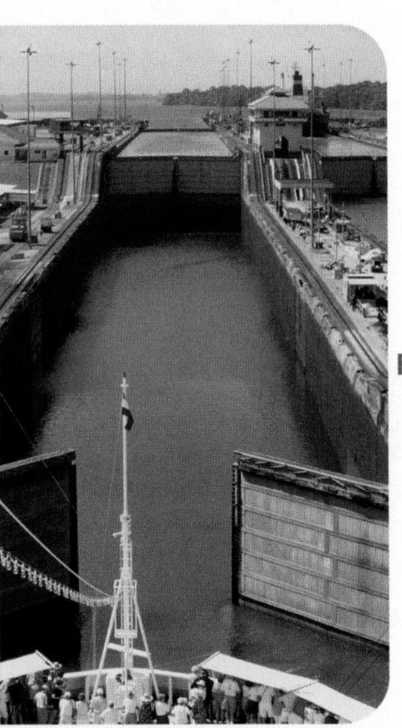

30. Geometry The figure shown is composed of two rectangles. The area of the figure is 1 square inch.

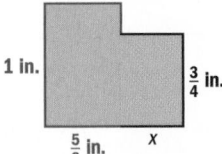

a. Find the area of the red rectangle. $\frac{5}{8}$ in.^{2}

b. Write an expression for the area of the blue rectangle. $\frac{3}{4}x$

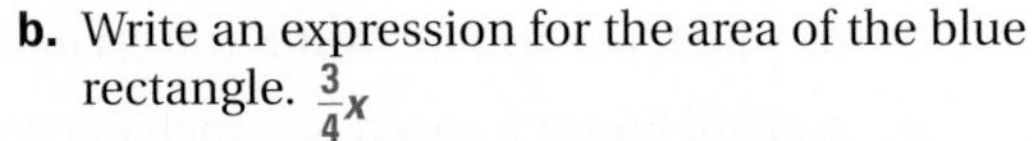

c. Write an equation relating the sum of the areas in parts (a) and (b) to the total area of the figure. Solve the equation to find the value of x. $\frac{5}{8} + \frac{3}{4}x = 1$; $x = \frac{1}{2}$ in.

1 in. $\frac{3}{4}$ in. $\frac{5}{8}$ in. x

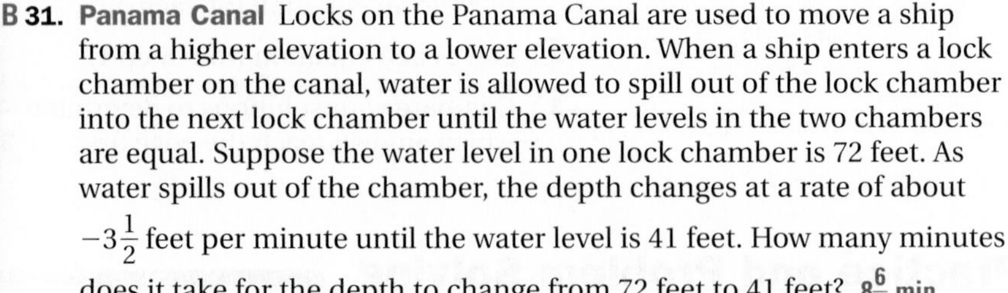

B **31. Panama Canal** Locks on the Panama Canal are used to move a ship from a higher elevation to a lower elevation. When a ship enters a lock chamber on the canal, water is allowed to spill out of the lock chamber into the next lock chamber until the water levels in the two chambers are equal. Suppose the water level in one lock chamber is 72 feet. As water spills out of the chamber, the depth changes at a rate of about $-3\frac{1}{2}$ feet per minute until the water level is 41 feet. How many minutes does it take for the depth to change from 72 feet to 41 feet? $8\frac{6}{7}$ min

32. Baseball Game At a college baseball game, $\frac{4}{5}$ of the spectators are home team fans. The rest of the spectators are opposing team fans. There are 750 opposing team fans.

a. Find the fraction of spectators who are opposing team fans. $\frac{1}{5}$

b. Find the total number of spectators at the game. 3750 spectators

c. One third of the home team fans at the game attend the college. How many home team fans attend the college? 1000 home team fans

33. Critical Thinking Suppose you want to solve the equation $\left(-2\frac{1}{2}\right)x = \frac{8}{15}$ by using the multiplicative inverse of $-2\frac{1}{2}$. What is the multiplicative inverse of $-2\frac{1}{2}$? $-\frac{2}{5}$

In the **Real World**

Panama Canal In the year 2002, 390 general cargo ships traveled through the Panama Canal from the Atlantic Ocean to the Pacific Ocean. The number of general cargo ships was 6 less than 3 times the number of passenger ships. How many passenger ships passed from the Atlantic to the Pacific? **132 passenger ships**

C **34. Challenge** The following is based on a famous problem about Diophantus, a Greek mathematician from the third century.

Let x be the number of years Diophantus lived. Find how long he lived by using the following facts about him to write and solve an equation.

ONE SIXTH OF HIS LIFE WAS SPENT IN BOYHOOD.

ONE TWELFTH OF HIS LIFE WAS SPENT AS A YOUTH.

AFTER $\frac{1}{7}$ MORE OF HIS LIFE PASSED, HE GOT MARRIED.

FIVE YEARS AFTER GETTING MARRIED, HE HAD A SON.

HIS SON LIVED $\frac{1}{2}$ AS LONG AS DIOPHANTUS LIVED.

THE SON DIED FOUR YEARS BEFORE DIOPHANTUS DIED.

$\frac{1}{6}x + \frac{1}{12}x + \frac{1}{7}x + 5 + \frac{1}{2}x + 4 = x$, 84 y

Mixed Review

Algebra Basics Solve the inequality. Graph your solution. *(Lesson 3.6)*
35–37. See margin for art.

35. $-17 + 2y > 11$ $y > 14$ **36.** $5x - 23 < 12$ $x < 7$ **37.** $-6z + 13 \le 31$ $z \ge -3$

38. Commuting Of the 1458 students at school A, 324 students take the bus. Of the 2123 students at school B, 242 take the bus. At which school is the fraction of students who take the bus greater? *(Lesson 5.1)* school A

Find the sum or difference. *(Lesson 5.3)*

39. $-\frac{1}{3} + \frac{3}{4}$ $\frac{5}{12}$ **40.** $\frac{1}{6} + \left(-\frac{5}{8}\right)$ $-\frac{11}{24}$ **41.** $-\frac{4}{9} - \frac{7}{12}$ $-1\frac{1}{36}$ **42.** $\frac{3}{7} - \frac{9}{14}$ $-\frac{3}{14}$

Standardized Test Practice

43. Multiple Choice What is the solution of the equation $\frac{7}{12}x - 5 = -7\frac{1}{3}$? A

A. -4 **B.** $-1\frac{13}{36}$ **C.** $-\frac{1}{4}$ **D.** 4

44. Short Response Two thirds of the lockers at a health club are rented to members at a rate of \$6 per month. The other 48 lockers are available free to members on a first-come, first-serve basis. How much money does the club make from renting lockers each month? \$576

CD Sort

Your friend has a collection of CDs: $\frac{2}{3}$ of the CDs have booklets, $\frac{1}{2}$ of the CDs are singles, and $\frac{1}{4}$ are singles with booklets. All but two of the CDs are either singles or have booklets or both. How many CDs does your friend have? 24 CDs

4 ASSESS

Assessment Resources

For more assessment resources, see:
- Assessment Book
- Test and Practice Generator

Mini-Quiz

Solve the equation.

1. $\frac{7}{8}a = 14$ 16
2. $-\frac{3}{10}d = -\frac{4}{5}$ $2\frac{2}{3}$
3. $12 + \frac{3}{5}d = 39$ 45
4. $-\frac{23}{24} = \frac{11}{12} + \frac{5}{6}g$ $-2\frac{1}{4}$
5. **Challenge** If, on average, a hen and a half can lay an egg and a half in a day and a half, how long will it take 3 hens to lay 12 eggs? 6 days

5 FOLLOW-UP

Diagnosis/Remediation

- Study Guide in Chapter 5 Resource Book, pp. 54-55
- eTutorial Plus Online
- Extra Practice, p. 807
- Lesson Practice in Chapter 5 Resource Book, pp. 51-53

English Learner Support

- Spanish Study Guide
- Multi-Language Visual Glossary
- Chapter Audio Summaries CDs

Challenge

- Challenge Practice in Chapter 5 Resource Book, p. 56
- Teacher's Edition, p. 216F

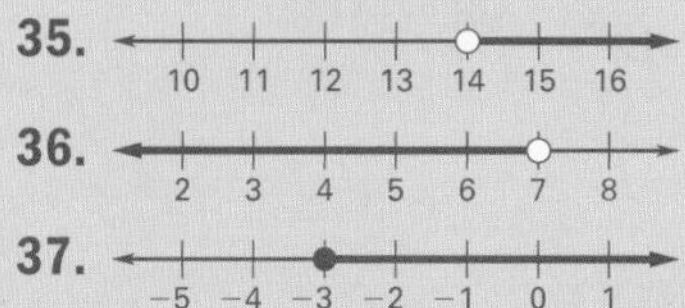

1 PLAN

Learn the Method

- Students will use a calculator to solve an equation with a fractional coefficient.
- Students can rework Exercises 11–14 on page 249 to check their answers and to verify that they are using the calculator correctly.

Grouping

Students should work individually.

2 TEACH

Tips for Success

Urge students to study the keystrokes shown on this page very carefully. Also make sure students understand how the original equation is translated into keystrokes that the calculator will interpret correctly.

Extra Examples

Example Nila runs every morning for a distance of $3\frac{3}{4}$ miles. Her long-term goal is to have run a total of 1000 miles. How many days will she have run when she reaches her goal? **267 days**

3 CLOSE

Assessment

Use a calculator to solve the equation.

1. $\frac{4}{5}x = 52$ **65**
2. $-\frac{7}{12}x = 98$ **−168**

Technology Activity CALCULATOR

5.6 Solving Equations with Fractions

Goal Use a calculator to solve an equation with a fractional coefficient.

Example

Use a calculator to solve the following problem.

Your horses eat about $\frac{2}{3}$ of a bale of hay every day. You have 33 bales of hay. After how many days will you need to buy more hay?

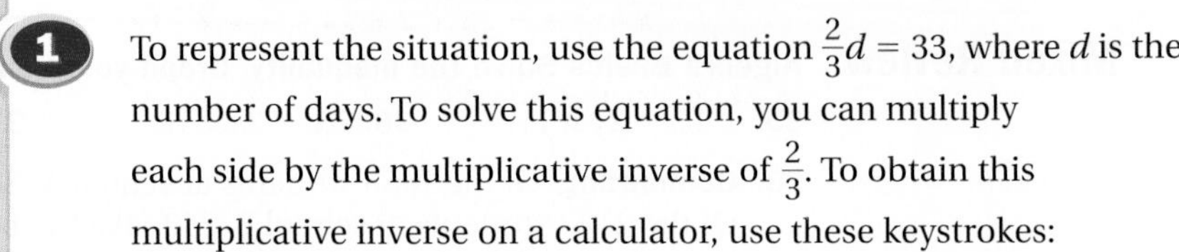

1 To represent the situation, use the equation $\frac{2}{3}d = 33$, where d is the number of days. To solve this equation, you can multiply each side by the multiplicative inverse of $\frac{2}{3}$. To obtain this multiplicative inverse on a calculator, use these keystrokes:

Keystrokes

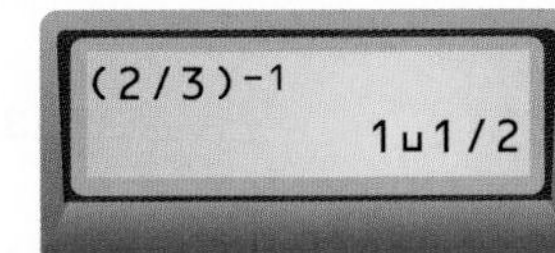

Tech Help

The symbol ⊔ on the calculator display indicates that the number is a mixed number. For example 1⊔1/2 means $1\frac{1}{2}$.

2 Now find the product of the multiplicative inverse and 33.

Keystrokes

× 33 =

Ans refers to the answer, or result, from the previous calculation.

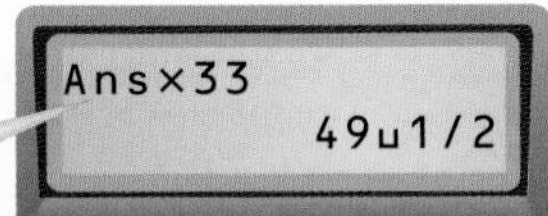

Answer You will run out of hay in $49\frac{1}{2}$ days. To be sure your horses have enough hay, you need to buy more after 49 days.

Draw Conclusions

Use a calculator to solve the equation.

1. $\frac{3}{4}x = 27$ **36**
2. $\frac{5}{16}x = -55$ **−176**
3. $\frac{2}{7}x = -26$ **−91**
4. $-\frac{9}{11}x = 39$ **$-47\frac{2}{3}$**
5. **Sewing** Use a calculator to solve the following problem: The stitches made by a sewing machine are each $\frac{3}{16}$ inch long and lie end to end in a line. How many stitches are there in a line of stitches that is 21 inches long? **112 stitches**

NCTM CURRICULUM STANDARDS

Standard 1: Understand numbers; Understand how operations are related

LESSON

5.7 Equations *and* Inequalities *with* Rational Numbers

Review Vocabulary
inequality, p. 138
solution of an inequality, p. 138

BEFORE	*Now*	WHY?
You used reciprocals to solve equations.	You'll use the LCD to solve equations and inequalities.	So you can find the original price of a sale item, as in Ex. 39.

So far you have followed these steps to solve equations with fractions:

- Undo any addition or subtraction in order to get the variable term alone on one side of the equation.
- Multiply both sides of the equation by the multiplicative inverse of the coefficient of the variable term.

Another way to solve an equation with fractions is to clear fractions by multiplying each side of the equation by the LCD of the fractions. The resulting equation is equivalent to the original equation.

Watch *Out*

In Example 1, notice that each term in the equation is multiplied by the LCD of the fractions in the equation.

Example 1 ***Solving an Equation by Clearing Fractions***

$-\frac{5}{6}x + \frac{1}{2} = \frac{3}{4}$	**Original equation**
$12\left(-\frac{5}{6}x + \frac{1}{2}\right) = 12\left(\frac{3}{4}\right)$	**Multiply each side by LCD of fractions.**
$12\left(-\frac{5}{6}x\right) + 12\left(\frac{1}{2}\right) = 12\left(\frac{3}{4}\right)$	**Use distributive property.**
$-10x + 6 = 9$	**Simplify.**
$-10x + 6 - 6 = 9 - 6$	**Subtract 6 from each side.**
$-10x = 3$	**Simplify.**
$\frac{-10x}{-10} = \frac{3}{-10}$	**Divide each side by −10.**
$x = -\frac{3}{10}$	**Simplify.**

Checkpoint

Solve the equation by first clearing the fractions.

1. $\frac{1}{2}x + \frac{7}{10} = \frac{4}{5}$ $\frac{1}{5}$ **2.** $\frac{3}{8}x - \frac{2}{3} = \frac{7}{12}$ $3\frac{1}{3}$ **3.** $-\frac{2}{9} = \frac{3}{4}x - \frac{1}{6}$ $-\frac{2}{27}$

Solving Equations with Decimals As shown in Example 2 on page 254, you can clear decimals from an equation.

NCTM CURRICULUM STANDARDS
Standard 1: Understand relationships among numbers; Compute fluently
Standard 2: Represent situations using algebraic symbols

1 PLAN

Skill Check
Solve the inequality.
1. $2x + 9 > 13$ $x > 2$
2. $4x - 5 < -17$ $x < -3$
3. $5x - 3 \le 17$ $x \le 4$
4. $-7x + 1 \le -13$ $x \ge 2$

Lesson Objective
Use the LCD to solve equations and inequalities.

Pacing
Suggested Number of Days
Basic Course: 2 days
Average Course: 2 days
Advanced Course: 2 days
Block: 1 block

Teaching Resources
For a complete list of Teaching Resources, see page 216B.

Transparency
Warm-Up Exercises for this lesson are available on a transparency.

2 TEACH

Motivating the Lesson
On the board, write the original equation from Example 1 and the equation $-10x + 6 = 9$. Discuss with students which equation appears easier to solve. Point out that these equations are equivalent.

TIPS *for* NEW TEACHERS

Expect students to need more time to grasp the content of the examples in this lesson. All students may benefit from using a sheet of paper to cover the steps of each example and then uncover one step at a time while you discuss that particular step. See Tips for New Teachers in the *Chapter 5 Resource Book*.

Extra Examples

Example 1 Solve the equation $\frac{7}{16}x - \frac{3}{8} = \frac{3}{4}$. $\mathbf{2\frac{4}{7}}$

Example 2 Solve the equation $2.2b - 3.64 = 8.46$. **5.5**

Example 3 Katie has $50 to spend on tulip bulbs for her new garden. Her husband has given her a gift certificate for $25 for bulbs. For this week only, the garden catalog she orders from is offering $\frac{1}{5}$ off the price of any order, with no shipping charges. What is the total of the original prices of bulbs that Katie can afford to buy? **bulbs whose original prices come to a total of $93.75 or less**

VISUALIZE

Students may benefit from highlighting the variable when they write equations or inequalities that contain fractions. This can be particularly helpful for those students who lose sight of the goal of isolating the variable when they are trying to clear the fractions from the equation or inequality.

Reading *Algebra*

Multiplying each side of the equation in Example 2 by 100 produces an equivalent equation. The new equation, $230 = 514 + 80m$, has the same solution as the equation $2.3 = 5.14 + 0.8m$.

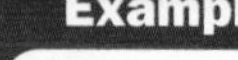

Example 2 *Solving an Equation by Clearing Decimals*

Solve the equation 2.3 = 5.14 + 0.8*m*.

Because the greatest number of decimal places in any of the terms with decimals is 2, multiply each side of the equation by 10^2, or 100.

$2.3 = 5.14 + 0.8m$	**Write original equation.**
$\mathbf{100}(2.3) = \mathbf{100}(5.14 + 0.8m)$	**Multiply each side by 100.**
$230 = 514 + 80m$	**Use distributive property. Simplify.**
$230 - \mathbf{514} = 514 + 80m - \mathbf{514}$	**Subtract 514 from each side.**
$-284 = 80m$	**Simplify.**
$\frac{-284}{\mathbf{80}} = \frac{80m}{\mathbf{80}}$	**Divide each side by 80.**
$-3.55 = m$	**Simplify.**

Solving Inequalities You can use the methods you have learned for solving equations with fractional coefficients to solve inequalities.

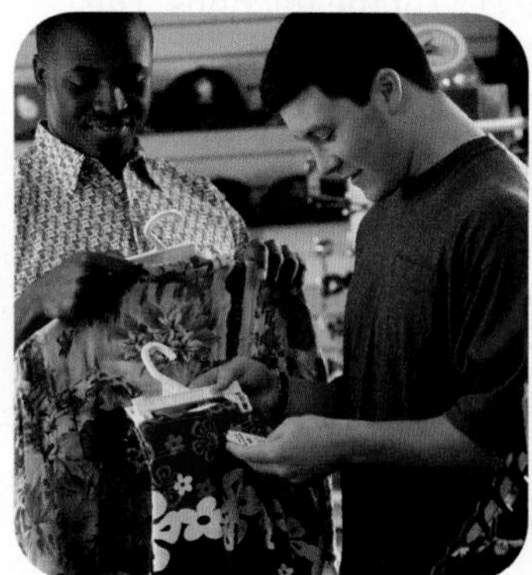

Example 3 *Solving an Inequality with Fractions*

Shopping A sign in a clothing store says to take $\frac{1}{3}$ off the marked price of a shirt. You have $20 in cash and a $5 gift certificate. What are the original prices of the shirts you can afford to buy?

Solution

Write a verbal model. Let x represent the original prices of the shirts you can afford to buy.

Original price − $\frac{1}{3}$ of original price − Gift certificate amount ≤ Cash on hand

$x - \frac{1}{3}x - 5 \le 20$	**Substitute.**
$\left(1 - \frac{1}{3}\right)x - 5 \le 20$	**Combine like terms.**
$\frac{2}{3}x - 5 \le 20$	**Simplify.**
$\frac{2}{3}x - 5 + \mathbf{5} \le 20 + \mathbf{5}$	**Add 5 to each side.**
$\mathbf{\frac{3}{2}}\left(\frac{2}{3}x\right) \le \mathbf{\frac{3}{2}}(25)$	**Multiply each side by multiplicative inverse of $\frac{2}{3}$.**
$x \le 37.50$	**Simplify.**

Answer You can afford a shirt whose original price is $37.50 or less.

Common Error

In Example 2, watch for students who multiply the different decimal terms by different powers of 10 in their attempt to convert the decimals to integers, resulting in an incorrect equation such as $23 = 514 + 8m$.

Teaching Tip

After the solution is found to Example 3, ask students how many of them are surprised by this answer. You may want to demonstrate how a \$37.50 shirt can be bought with \$25 during this sale.

Example 4 *Solving an Inequality by Clearing Fractions*

$-\frac{3}{4}m - \frac{1}{8} \le -\frac{1}{4}$	**Original inequality**
$8\left(-\frac{3}{4}m - \frac{1}{8}\right) \le 8\left(-\frac{1}{4}\right)$	**Multiply each side by LCD of fractions.**
$8\left(-\frac{3}{4}m\right) - 8\left(\frac{1}{8}\right) \le 8\left(-\frac{1}{4}\right)$	**Distributive property**
$-6m - 1 \le -2$	**Simplify.**
$-6m - 1 + 1 \le -2 + 1$	**Add 1 to each side.**
$-6m \le -1$	**Simplify.**
$\frac{-6m}{-6} \ge \frac{-1}{-6}$	**Divide each side by −6. Reverse inequality symbol.**
$m \ge \frac{1}{6}$	**Simplify.**

Extra Examples

Example 4 Solve the inequality $\frac{2}{5} + \frac{3}{5}p \le \frac{1}{3}$. $p \le -\frac{1}{9}$

5.7 Exercises

More Practice, p. 807

Concept Check

How is solving an equation with terms that are fractions different from solving an equation whose terms only involve integers? **You first have to clear the fractions by multiplying each of the terms by the LCD of the fractions.**

Guided Practice

Vocabulary Check

1. Copy and complete: To clear the fractions in an equation, multiply each side of the equation by the _?_ of the fractions. **LCD**
2. To clear the decimals in an equation, how do you determine what power of 10 to multiply each side of the equation by? **See margin.**

Skill Check **Solve the equation by first clearing the fractions or the decimals.**

3. $\frac{2}{3}n + 17 = \frac{5}{6}$ $-24\frac{1}{4}$
4. $\frac{2}{5} = \frac{5}{8}n - 4$ $7\frac{1}{25}$
5. $\frac{3}{4}n - \frac{1}{2} = \frac{7}{4}$ 3
6. $2.3m - 11 = -29.4$ -8
7. $5.3m - 6 = -27.2$ -4
8. $-1.2m + 1.25 = 0.77$ 0.4

Solve the inequality by first clearing the fractions.

9. $\frac{7}{13}x - 1 > \frac{1}{2}$ $x > 2\frac{11}{14}$
10. $\frac{4}{5} \ge \frac{2}{3} - \frac{2}{7}x$ $x \ge -\frac{7}{15}$
11. $\frac{8}{15}x - \frac{17}{30} < \frac{7}{10}$ $x < 2\frac{3}{8}$
12. **Error Analysis** Describe and correct the error in clearing the fractions in the equation $\frac{2}{3}x + 5 = \frac{5}{2}$.

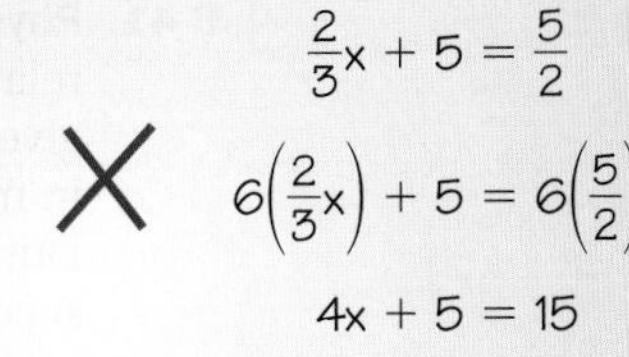

$\frac{2}{3}x + 5 = \frac{5}{2}$
$6\left(\frac{2}{3}x\right) + 5 = 6\left(\frac{5}{2}\right)$
$4x + 5 = 15$

2. *Sample answer:* Multiply by the power of 10 whose exponent is the greatest number of decimal places in any of the terms.

12. *Sample answer:* Only the first term of the left side was multiplied by 6, but the entire left side should have been multiplied by 6 and simplified using the distributive property to give the equation $6\left(\frac{2}{3}x\right) + 6(5) = 6\left(\frac{5}{2}\right)$ and then $4x + 30 = 15$.

Daily Puzzler

You need $\frac{1}{6}$ cup of flour for a recipe but you only have measuring cups for $\frac{1}{2}$ cup and $\frac{1}{3}$ cup. How can you measure out $\frac{1}{6}$ cup of flour? **Fill the $\frac{1}{2}$ cup container with flour. Pour flour from the $\frac{1}{2}$ cup container into the $\frac{1}{3}$ cup container, without spilling any, until the $\frac{1}{3}$ cup container is full. What remains in the $\frac{1}{2}$ cup container is $\frac{1}{6}$ cup of flour.**

3 APPLY

ASSIGNMENT GUIDE

Basic Course

Day 1: EP p. 805 Exs. 57–60; pp. 256–257 Exs. 13–18, 22–27, 41, 43, 47–52

Day 2: pp. 256–257 Exs. 19–21, 28–30, 32–39, 53–57

Average Course

Day 1: pp. 256–257 Exs. 13–18, 22–27, 40–42, 47–52

Day 2: pp. 256–257 Exs. 19–21, 28–39, 43–45, 53–57

Advanced Course

Day 1: pp. 256–257 Exs. 16–21, 25–31, 40–43, 48, 49

Day 2: pp. 256–257 Exs. 34–39, 44–46*, 51–57

Block

pp. 256–257 Exs. 13–45, 47–57

EXTRA PRACTICE

- Student Edition, p. 807
- Chapter 5 Resource Book, pp. 59–61
- Test and Practice Generator

TRANSPARENCY

Even-numbered answers are available on transparencies.

HOMEWORK CHECK

When you review students' homework for this lesson, go over the following exercises to check understanding of key concepts.

Basic: 13, 18, 22, 32, 33
Average: 15, 22, 27, 32, 35
Advanced: 16, 24, 28, 34, 36

COMMON ERROR

In Exercises 13–21, remind students that they have to find the LCD of three terms, and urge them to check that all three denominators are factors of the LCD, not just two of them.

Practice and Problem Solving

Homework *Help*

Example	Exercises
1	13–21, 40
2	22–31, 41
3	32–39
4	32–39

Online Resources CLASSZONE.COM

- More Examples
- eTutorial Plus

Solve the equation by first clearing the fractions.

A **13.** $\frac{1}{2}t + \frac{1}{4} = \frac{5}{16}$ $\frac{1}{8}$ **14.** $\frac{5}{6}s + \frac{2}{9} = -\frac{7}{12}$ $-\frac{29}{30}$ **15.** $\frac{3}{4} = \frac{5}{6}a + \frac{2}{9}$ $\frac{19}{30}$

16. $\frac{5}{8} = \frac{1}{10} + \frac{5}{14}m$ $1\frac{47}{100}$ **17.** $-\frac{41}{60} + \frac{17}{20}p = \frac{29}{30}$ $1\frac{16}{17}$ **18.** $\frac{3}{8} = -\frac{1}{4}x - \frac{3}{5}$ $-3\frac{9}{10}$

19. $-\frac{3}{2}t - \frac{5}{6} = -\frac{4}{9}$ $-\frac{7}{27}$ **20.** $-\frac{3}{5}z - 4 = -\frac{77}{20}$ $-\frac{1}{4}$ **21.** $4w + \frac{2}{7} = -\frac{4}{5}$ $-\frac{19}{70}$

Solve the equation by first clearing the decimals.

22. $6.2x + 3.7 = 22.3$ **3** **23.** $7.8y + 6 = 23.16$ **2.2** **24.** $10.7w + 4 = 47.87$ **4.1**

25. $2 = -6.4z + 10$ **1.25** **26.** $-3.3x + 6.5 = 1.55$ **1.5** **27.** $1.6b - 3 = -9.4$ **−4**

28. $-1.7w - 4 = 2.63$ **−3.9** **29.** $2.875y + 9 = 12.45$ **1.2** **30.** $4.125c + 5 = -9.85$ **−3.6**

31. Saving Money You want to save \$400 for a camping trip. You have \$64.96 in your savings account. Each week you deposit your paycheck from your part-time job. Each paycheck is for \$69.80. How many paychecks must you deposit to reach your goal of \$400? **5 paychecks**

Solve the inequality.

32. $-\frac{4}{11}z - 1 > -\frac{8}{11}$ $z < -\frac{3}{4}$ **33.** $\frac{1}{5}k + 14 \le \frac{2}{9}$ $k \le -68\frac{8}{9}$ **34.** $-\frac{31}{4} < -13 + \frac{7}{8}f$ $f > 6$

35. $\frac{1}{7}r + \frac{53}{56} > \frac{6}{7}$ $r > -\frac{5}{8}$ **36.** $\frac{5}{6}n - \frac{1}{5} < -\frac{8}{15}$ $n < -\frac{2}{5}$ **37.** $\frac{1}{3} + \frac{1}{13}d \ge \frac{17}{39}$ $d \ge 1\frac{1}{3}$

38. Fundraiser Your class is selling gift wrap for a school fundraiser. One fourth of the money collected will be used to pay for the gift wrap. Your class wants to raise at least \$675 after paying for the gift wrap. How much money does your class need to collect? **at least \$900**

39. Sale Price A store displays the sign shown. You want to buy a belt that costs \$8 and a pair of jeans. You have \$18. Write and solve an inequality to find the original prices of the jeans you can afford to buy. **$8 + j - \frac{2}{3}j \le 18$ or $8 + \frac{1}{3}j \le 18$, not more than \$30**

CLEARANCE SALE!
Take $\frac{2}{3}$ off the price of all jeans!

40. Pets Each morning you feed your dog $\frac{3}{4}$ cup of dry dog food. At night you feed him $\frac{1}{3}$ cup of dry dog food. You buy a bag of dog food that contains 40 cups. How many days will the bag last? **36 days (It will run out the night of the 37th day.)**

B **41. Physics** The speed of sound in air depends on temperature. The relationship between the speed of sound and the air temperature is given by the equation $v = 331.4 + 0.6T$, where v is the speed of sound in meters per second and T is the air temperature in degrees Celsius. During a storm, the speed of sound was measured at 343.37 meters per second. What was the air temperature? **19.95°C**

42. *Writing* Compare and contrast the method of using multiplicative inverses with the method of clearing fractions when solving an equation like $\frac{2}{3}x - 1 = \frac{5}{6}$. **See margin.**

43. **Costumes** You buy $12\frac{1}{2}$ yards of material to make costumes for a school play. Each costume consists of a matching hat and cape. You need $1\frac{1}{4}$ feet of the material for each hat. You need $3\frac{1}{2}$ feet of material for each cape. How many costumes can you make? **7 costumes**

44. **Critical Thinking** Can you clear fractions in an equation by multiplying each side of the equation by a common denominator other than the LCD? Give an example to explain your reasoning. **See margin.**

45. **Money** You are visiting Canada. You have \$21.25 in Canadian currency, and the rest of your money is in U.S. currency. You want to exchange your U.S. currency for Canadian currency. For every dollar you have in U.S. currency, you can get \$1.557 in Canadian currency. You want to buy a souvenir that costs \$25.50 in Canadian currency. How much money in U.S. currency do you need to exchange to have enough to buy the souvenir? **\$2.73**

C 46. **Challenge** Solve the equation $\frac{4}{9}\left(\frac{1}{3}x + 6\right) = \frac{5}{18}x + \frac{1}{3}$. Show the steps you take. **See margin.**

Mixed Review

Find the product or quotient. *(Lesson 1.7)*

47. $-3(-40)$ **120** 48. $-5(11)$ **−55** 49. $-180 \div 5$ **−36** 50. $90 \div (-6)$ **−15**

Simplify the expression. *(Lesson 5.3)*

51. $\frac{r}{5} + \frac{7r}{9}$ $\mathbf{\frac{44r}{45}}$ 52. $\frac{s}{7} - \frac{s}{3}$ $\mathbf{-\frac{4s}{21}}$ 53. $\frac{5t}{2} - \frac{t}{6}$ $\mathbf{\frac{7t}{3}}$ 54. $-\frac{3d}{10} - \frac{8d}{15}$ $\mathbf{-\frac{5d}{6}}$

55. **Rain Gauge** The water level in a rain gauge is $2\frac{3}{4}$ inches. A steady rain raises the water level by $\frac{1}{8}$ inch each hour. When the rain stops, the gauge reads 4 inches. How many hours did the rain last? *(Lesson 5.6)* **10 h**

Standardized Test Practice

56. **Multiple Choice** Which graph represents the solution of the inequality $-\frac{3}{8}x > -9$? **A**

A. 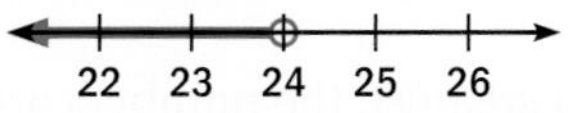

B. 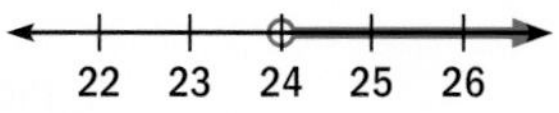

C. 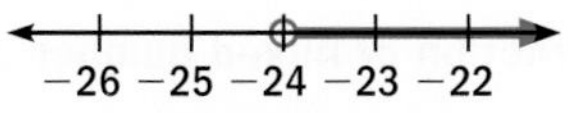

D. 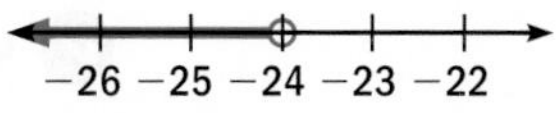

57. **Multiple Choice** Which number is *not* a solution of the inequality $2 - \frac{5}{7}m \geq -3$? **I**

F. −9 **G.** −7 **H.** 7 **I.** 9

4 ASSESS

Assessment Resources

For more assessment resources, see:
- Assessment Book
- Test and Practice Generator

Mini-Quiz

Solve the equation or inequality.

1. $\frac{1}{12}k + \frac{1}{3} = \frac{5}{6}$ **6**
2. $8.6 = 5.8y - 3$ **2**
3. $\frac{7}{8}b + 7 < -\frac{21}{4}$ $\mathbf{b < -14}$
4. $-\frac{17}{20} + \frac{2}{15}m \geq \frac{23}{30}$ $\mathbf{m \geq 12\frac{1}{8}}$
5. **Challenge** Solve the equation $\frac{2}{3}\left(18 + \frac{1}{3}x\right) = \frac{1}{9}x + 5$. **−63**

5 FOLLOW-UP

Diagnosis/Remediation

- Study Guide in Chapter 5 Resource Book, pp. 62–63
- Tutor Place, Fractions Card 10
- eTutorial Plus Online
- Extra Practice, p. 807
- Lesson Practice in Chapter 5 Resource Book, pp. 59–61

English Learner Support

- Spanish Study Guide
- Multi-Language Visual Glossary
- Chapter Audio Summaries CDs

Challenge

- Challenge Practice in Chapter 5 Resource Book, p. 65
- Teacher's Edition, p. 216F

42, 44, 46. See Additional Answers beginning on page AA1.

ADDITIONAL RESOURCES

The following resources are available to help review the materials in Lessons 5.4–5.7.

Chapter 5 Resource Book
- Lesson Practice
- Study Guide

Assessment Book
- Chapter 5 Quiz 2

Technology
- Test and Practice Generator
- eTutorial CD-ROM

Internet
- Classzone
- eWorkbook Plus Online
- eTutorial Plus Online

ENGLISH LEARNER SUPPORT

- Spanish Study Guide
- Multi-Language Visual Glossary
- Chapter Audio Summaries CDs

4. $0.\overline{7}$. ***Sample answer:*** **$0.\overline{7}$ = 0.7777..., which is greater than 0.77 because 0.77 can be thought of as having 0's in the thousandths place and beyond.**

6. ***Sample answer:*** **The multiplicative inverse of a nonzero number is the number's reciprocal.**

CHAPTER 5

Chapter Review

Vocabulary Review

rational number, p. 219
terminating decimal, p. 219
repeating decimal, p. 219
reciprocals, p. 243
multiplicative inverse, p. 247

1–3. Sample answers are given.

1. Give an example of a number that is an integer but not a whole number. **−7**

2. Give an example of a number that is a rational number but not a whole number. $\frac{3}{4}$

3. Give an example of a rational number that is a whole number and an integer. **18**

4. Which number is greater, the repeating decimal $0.\overline{7}$ or the decimal 0.77? Why? **See margin.**

5. Give an example of two numbers that are reciprocals. ***Sample answer:*** $\frac{9}{16}$ **and** $\frac{16}{9}$

6. How is the term *multiplicative inverse* related to the term *reciprocal*? **See margin.**

5.1 Rational Numbers

Examples on pp. 219–221

Goal

Write, compare, and order rational numbers.

Example **Write the fraction as a decimal.**

a. $-\frac{39}{1000} = -0.039$

b. $\frac{3}{11} = 0.272727\ldots = 0.\overline{27}$

Example **Order $1\frac{19}{20}$, −3.06, −0.8, $\frac{9}{20}$, and $-\frac{54}{25}$ from least to greatest.**

Graph the numbers on a number line. Write improper fractions as mixed numbers.

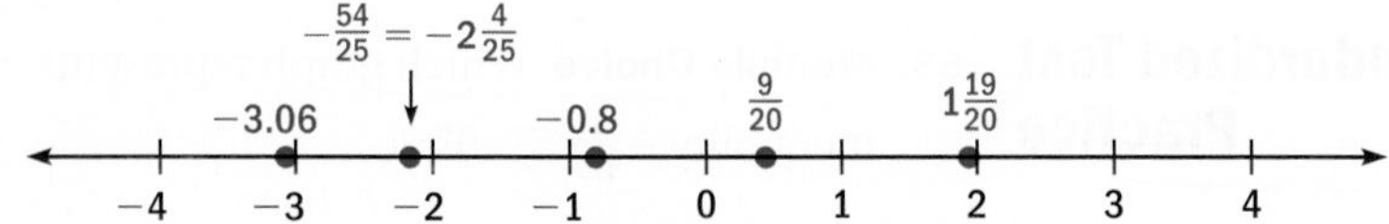

From least to greatest, the numbers are −3.06, $-\frac{54}{25}$, −0.8, $\frac{9}{20}$, $1\frac{19}{20}$.

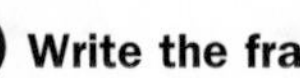

Write the fraction or mixed number as a decimal.

7. $\frac{7}{11}$ **$0.\overline{63}$**

8. $-\frac{7}{80}$ **−0.0875**

9. $-2\frac{3}{5}$ **−2.6**

10. $4\frac{2}{90}$ **$4.0\overline{2}$**

11. Order −5.24, $5.\overline{3}$, $\frac{134}{25}$, $-\frac{263}{25}$, and $5\frac{9}{20}$ from least to greatest. **$-\frac{263}{25}$, −5.24, $5.\overline{3}$, $\frac{134}{25}$, $5\frac{9}{20}$**

The following resources are available to help review the materials in this chapter.

Chapter 5 Resource Book
- Chapter Review Games and Activities, p. 66
- Cumulative Practice, Chs. 1–5

English/Spanish Chapter Reviews and Tests

Chapter Audio Summaries CDs

eTutorial CD-ROM

eWorkbook Plus Online

eTutorial Plus Online

5.2 Adding and Subtracting Like Fractions

Examples on pp. 225–227

Goal

Add and subtract fractions and mixed numbers with the same denominator.

Example Find the sum $-6\frac{5}{8} + \left(-4\frac{1}{8}\right)$.

$-6\frac{5}{8} + \left(-4\frac{1}{8}\right) = \frac{-53}{8} + \left(\frac{-33}{8}\right)$ — Write mixed numbers as improper fractions.

$= \frac{-53 + (-33)}{8}$ — Write sum of numerators over denominator.

$= \frac{-86}{8}$ — Add.

$= \frac{-43}{4} = -10\frac{3}{4}$ — Simplify. Then write improper fraction as a mixed number.

Find the sum or difference.

12. $\frac{1}{12} + \left(-\frac{5}{12}\right)$ $-\frac{1}{3}$ **13.** $-\frac{4}{7} - \frac{5}{7}$ $-1\frac{2}{7}$ **14.** $7\frac{2}{9} - 3\frac{8}{9}$ $3\frac{1}{3}$ **15.** $9\frac{7}{10} + 5\frac{3}{10}$ 15

5.3 Adding and Subtracting Unlike Fractions

Examples on pp. 231–233

Goal

Add and subtract fractions and mixed numbers with different denominators.

Example Find the difference $4\frac{5}{18} - 6\frac{8}{9}$.

$4\frac{5}{18} - 6\frac{8}{9} = \frac{77}{18} - \frac{62}{9}$ — Write mixed numbers as improper fractions.

$= \frac{77}{18} - \frac{124}{18}$ — Write $\frac{62}{9}$ using LCD.

$= \frac{77 - 124}{18}$ — Write difference of numerators over denominator.

$= \frac{-47}{18}$ — Subtract.

$= -2\frac{11}{18}$ — Write improper fraction as a mixed number.

Find the sum or difference.

16. $\frac{7}{12} - \frac{5}{24}$ $\frac{3}{8}$ **17.** $-\frac{8}{21} + \frac{9}{14}$ $\frac{11}{42}$ **18.** $\frac{3}{17} - \frac{15}{34}$ $-\frac{9}{34}$

19. $2\frac{3}{4} + 2\frac{5}{6}$ $5\frac{7}{12}$ **20.** $-13\frac{9}{14} + 21\frac{17}{28}$ $7\frac{27}{28}$ **21.** $9\frac{14}{15} - 18\frac{5}{21}$ $-8\frac{32}{105}$

5.4 Multiplying Fractions

Examples on pp. 237–239

Goal

Multiply fractions and mixed numbers.

Example Find the product $-\frac{4}{5}\left(\frac{25}{42}\right)$.

$$-\frac{4}{5}\left(\frac{25}{42}\right) = \frac{\overset{-2}{\cancel{-4}} \cdot \overset{5}{\cancel{25}}}{\underset{1}{\cancel{5}} \cdot \underset{21}{\cancel{42}}}$$ Use rule for multiplying fractions. Divide out common factors.

$$= -\frac{10}{21}$$ Multiply.

Example Simplify the expression.

$$\frac{m^3}{8} \cdot \frac{2m}{5} = \frac{m^3 \cdot \overset{1}{\cancel{2}}m}{\underset{4}{\cancel{8}} \cdot 5}$$ Use rule for multiplying fractions. Divide out common factor.

$$= \frac{m^{3+1}}{20}$$ Product of powers property

$$= \frac{m^4}{20}$$ Add exponents.

Find the product.

22. $\frac{18}{19}\left(-\frac{38}{27}\right)$ $\mathbf{-1\frac{1}{3}}$ **23.** $-\frac{2}{15} \cdot \frac{5}{8}$ $\mathbf{-\frac{1}{12}}$ **24.** $-3\frac{1}{17} \cdot \left(-\frac{3}{4}\right)$ $\mathbf{2\frac{5}{17}}$ **25.** $6\frac{3}{4} \cdot \left(-7\frac{1}{9}\right)$ $\mathbf{-48}$

Simplify the expression.

26. $\frac{a^3}{2} \cdot \frac{2a}{9}$ $\mathbf{\frac{a^4}{9}}$ **27.** $\frac{3b^2}{4} \cdot \frac{16b}{21}$ $\mathbf{\frac{4b^3}{7}}$ **28.** $-\frac{12n^3}{5} \cdot \frac{n^4}{3}$ $\mathbf{\frac{-4n^7}{5}}$ **29.** $-\frac{5s}{4} \cdot \frac{12s^4}{25}$ $\mathbf{\frac{-3s^5}{5}}$

5.5 Dividing Fractions

Examples on pp. 243–244

Goal

Divide fractions and mixed numbers.

Example Find the quotient $\frac{2}{3} \div \left(-\frac{6}{7}\right)$.

$$\frac{2}{3} \div \left(-\frac{6}{7}\right) = \frac{2}{3} \cdot \left(-\frac{7}{6}\right)$$ Multiply by reciprocal.

$$= \frac{\overset{1}{\cancel{2}} \cdot (-7)}{3 \cdot \underset{3}{\cancel{6}}}$$ Use rule for multiplying fractions. Divide out common factor.

$$= -\frac{7}{9}$$ Multiply.

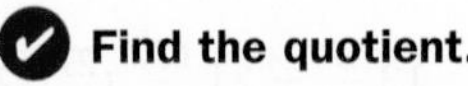

Find the quotient.

30. $-\frac{6}{7} \div \frac{36}{77}$ $\mathbf{-1\frac{5}{6}}$ **31.** $-\frac{21}{58} \div \frac{3}{16}$ $\mathbf{-1\frac{27}{29}}$ **32.** $16\frac{2}{3} \div 2$ $\mathbf{8\frac{1}{3}}$ **33.** $-3\frac{3}{11} \div 1\frac{17}{55}$ $\mathbf{-2\frac{1}{2}}$

5.6 Using Multiplicative Inverses to Solve Equations

Examples on pp. 247–248

Goal

Use multiplicative inverses to solve equations with fractional coefficients.

Example Solve the equation $\frac{4}{5}t = -\frac{8}{11}$.

$\frac{4}{5}t = -\frac{8}{11}$ Write original equation.

$\frac{5}{4}\left(\frac{4}{5}t\right) = \frac{5}{4}\left(-\frac{8}{11}\right)$ Multiply each side by multiplicative inverse of $\frac{4}{5}$.

$1t = \frac{5}{4}\left(-\frac{8}{11}\right)$ Multiplicative inverse property

$t = -\frac{10}{11}$ Multiply.

Solve the equation.

34. $\frac{14}{27}x = -\frac{7}{12}$ $-1\frac{1}{8}$ **35.** $-\frac{5}{8}x = \frac{10}{17}$ $-\frac{16}{17}$ **36.** $1\frac{3}{8} = \frac{3}{4}x + 1$ $\frac{1}{2}$ **37.** $\frac{5}{6}x - \frac{1}{4} = -\frac{11}{24}$ $-\frac{1}{4}$

5.7 Equations and Inequalities with Rational Numbers

Examples on pp. 253–255

Goal

Solve equations and inequalities with rational numbers.

Example Solve the equation $-\frac{8}{9}x + \frac{1}{6} = \frac{49}{54}$ by first clearing the fractions.

$-\frac{8}{9}x + \frac{1}{6} = \frac{49}{54}$ Write original equation.

$54\left(-\frac{8}{9}x + \frac{1}{6}\right) = 54\left(\frac{49}{54}\right)$ Multiply each side by LCD of fractions.

$54\left(-\frac{8}{9}x\right) + 54\left(\frac{1}{6}\right) = 54\left(\frac{49}{54}\right)$ Distributive property

$-48x + 9 = 49$ Simplify.

$-48x + 9 - 9 = 49 - 9$ Subtract 9 from each side.

$-48x = 40$ Simplify.

$\frac{-48x}{-48} = \frac{40}{-48}$ Divide each side by -48.

$x = -\frac{5}{6}$ Simplify.

Solve the equation by first clearing the fractions.

38. $\frac{3}{7}x + \frac{5}{14} = \frac{19}{42}$ $\frac{2}{9}$ **39.** $\frac{5}{16} = -\frac{3}{32} + \frac{7}{8}n$ $\frac{13}{28}$ **40.** $-\frac{3}{4}x - \frac{5}{8} = -\frac{1}{56}$ $-\frac{17}{21}$

ADDITIONAL RESOURCES

Assessment Book

- Chapter Test (3 levels), pp. 59–64
- Standardized Chapter Test, p. 65
- Alternative Assessment, pp. 66–67

Test and Practice Generator

CHAPTER 5

Chapter Test

Write the fraction or mixed number as a decimal.

1. $-\frac{7}{125}$ **−0.056**
2. $10\frac{4}{9}$ **$10.\overline{4}$**
3. $-\frac{2}{27}$ **$-0.\overline{074}$**
4. $\frac{37}{10{,}000}$ **0.0037**

Write the decimal as a fraction or mixed number.

5. 11.85 **$11\frac{17}{20}$**
6. −7.52 **$-7\frac{13}{25}$**
7. $0.\overline{7}$ **$\frac{7}{9}$**
8. $0.\overline{63}$ **$\frac{7}{11}$**

Find the sum or difference.

9. $-\frac{15}{24} + \frac{19}{24}$ **$\frac{1}{6}$**
10. $-4\frac{1}{3} - 8\frac{1}{3}$ **$-12\frac{2}{3}$**
11. $\frac{4}{5} - \frac{11}{15}$ **$\frac{1}{15}$**
12. $-3\frac{5}{7} + 1\frac{2}{9}$ **$-2\frac{31}{63}$**

13. **Birds** The Northern junco, a bird found in Alaska and Canada, varies in length from $5\frac{1}{2}$ inches to $6\frac{3}{4}$ inches. Find the range of the lengths of the Northern junco. **$1\frac{1}{4}$ in.**

Simplify the expression.

14. $\frac{4m}{21} + \frac{17m}{21}$ **m**
15. $-\frac{3t}{22} - \frac{5t}{44}$ **$-\frac{t}{4}$**
16. $-\frac{7n}{18} - \frac{11n}{30}$ **$-\frac{34n}{45}$**
17. $-\frac{4z}{35} - \frac{8z}{25}$ **$-\frac{76z}{175}$**

18. **Geometry** The side lengths of a triangle are $3\frac{5}{8}$ inches, $4\frac{5}{16}$ inches, and 2 inches. What is the perimeter of the triangle? **$9\frac{15}{16}$ in.**

Find the product or quotient.

19. $\frac{8}{9} \cdot \left(-\frac{3}{10}\right)$ **$-\frac{4}{15}$**
20. $4 \div \left(-2\frac{4}{15}\right)$ **$-1\frac{13}{17}$**
21. $-\frac{9}{20} \cdot 2\frac{2}{3}$ **$-1\frac{1}{5}$**
22. $14\frac{5}{6} \div 2\frac{1}{8}$ **$6\frac{50}{51}$**

Simplify the expression.

23. $\frac{4r^3}{15} \cdot \frac{5r^3}{12}$ **$\frac{r^6}{9}$**
24. $-\frac{7n^2}{12} \cdot \left(-\frac{18n}{49}\right)$ **$\frac{3n^3}{14}$**
25. $-\frac{9t^2}{13} \cdot \frac{t}{12}$ **$-\frac{3t^3}{52}$**
26. $-\frac{25w^3}{42} \cdot \left(-\frac{3w}{10}\right)$ **$\frac{5w^4}{28}$**

27. **Encyclopedia** An encyclopedia has 30 volumes. The total weight of these volumes is $71\frac{1}{4}$ pounds. Find the average weight of a volume. **$2\frac{3}{8}$ lb**

Solve the equation. Check your solution.

28. $\frac{7}{8}m = -8$ **$-9\frac{1}{7}$**
29. $\frac{9}{25} = \frac{3}{5}t$ **$\frac{3}{5}$**
30. $-\frac{13}{20} = \frac{1}{4} + \frac{3}{5}t$ **$-1\frac{1}{2}$**
31. $\frac{1}{7}g + 8 = 2$ **−42**

Solve the equation or inequality by first clearing the fractions or decimals.

32. $9.2m + 1.4 = 12.9$ **1.25**
33. $10 = 8.22w - 3.152$ **1.6**
34. $\frac{2}{15}b - \frac{4}{5} < \frac{2}{3}$ **$b < 11$**
35. $\frac{1}{3}m - \frac{7}{18} = \frac{4}{9}$ **$2\frac{1}{2}$**

Chapter Standardized Test

Test-Taking Strategy Mark test questions that you can't answer on the first try. Move on to new questions and return later to the marked questions.

1. Which fraction is equivalent to $0.\overline{52}$? **C**

A. $\frac{4}{9}$ **B.** $\frac{51}{99}$ **C.** $\frac{52}{99}$ **D.** $\frac{5}{9}$

2. Which list of numbers is in order from least to greatest? **F**

F. $-\frac{33}{10}, -3.2, \frac{7}{8}, 0.9, 0.\overline{9}$

G. $-3.2, -\frac{33}{10}, \frac{7}{8}, 0.9, 0.\overline{9}$

H. $-3.2, -\frac{33}{10}, \frac{7}{8}, 0.\overline{9}, 0.9$

I. $-\frac{33}{10}, -3.2, 0.\overline{9}, 0.9, \frac{7}{8}$

3. Simplify the expression $-\frac{12n}{35} - \frac{13n}{35}$. **B**

A. $-\frac{25n}{35}$ **B.** $-\frac{5n}{7}$ **C.** $-\frac{n}{35}$ **D.** $\frac{25n}{35}$

4. Find the sum $3\frac{1}{4} + \left(-2\frac{3}{8}\right)$. **H**

F. $-5\frac{5}{8}$ **G.** $-\frac{7}{8}$ **H.** $\frac{7}{8}$ **I.** $5\frac{5}{8}$

5. Find the product $-2\frac{5}{8} \cdot \left(-5\frac{3}{7}\right)$. **D**

A. $-14\frac{1}{4}$ **B.** $-2\frac{19}{28}$ **C.** $2\frac{19}{28}$ **D.** $14\frac{1}{4}$

6. Find the quotient $1\frac{1}{12} \div 2\frac{7}{16}$. **G**

F. $\frac{2}{21}$ **G.** $\frac{4}{9}$ **H.** $2\frac{7}{192}$ **I.** $2\frac{41}{64}$

7. What is the solution of the equation $\frac{4}{5} - 12 = \frac{3}{10}x$? **A**

A. $-37\frac{1}{3}$ **B.** $-9\frac{1}{3}$ **C.** $9\frac{1}{3}$ **D.** $37\frac{1}{3}$

8. Half the books you own are mysteries. One third are historical fiction. The other four books are science fiction. How many of your books are mysteries? **H**

F. 4 **G.** 8 **H.** 12 **I.** 24

9. Which number is *not* a solution of $\frac{2}{3}x + \frac{1}{6} \geq 1\frac{17}{18}$? **A**

A. 2 **B.** 3 **C.** 4 **D.** 5

10. **Short Response** You have a length of cloth that is $2\frac{3}{4}$ yards long and $1\frac{1}{4}$ yards wide. You want to cut the cloth into 20 squares that are $1\frac{1}{4}$ feet long on each side. Do you have enough cloth to cut all the squares? Explain why or why not. **See margin.**

11. **Extended Response** A recipe for making 24 pretzels calls for using $1\frac{1}{2}$ cups of milk. A baker wants to use the recipe to make pretzels to sell. He wants to buy enough milk to make 100 pretzels each day over the next 5 days.

a. How many cups of milk does the baker need for all the pretzels? **$31\frac{1}{4}$ c**

b. How many gallons of milk should he buy? Use the fact that 1 gallon = 16 cups. Explain your answer. **See margin.**

ADDITIONAL RESOURCES

Assessment Book
- Standardized Chapter Test, p. 65

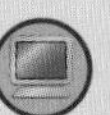
Test and Practice Generator

10. No. ***Sample answer:*** **$2\frac{3}{4}$ yards = $8\frac{1}{4}$ feet and $1\frac{1}{4}$ yards = $3\frac{3}{4}$ feet, so you can fit $3\frac{3}{4} \div 1\frac{1}{4} = 3$ squares along the width of the cloth. Because $8\frac{1}{4} \div 1\frac{1}{4} = 6\frac{3}{5}$, you can fit 6 squares along the length of the cloth. So, you can fit a total of $3 \cdot 6 = 18$ squares.**

11b. 2 gal. ***Sample answer:*** **He needs $31\frac{1}{4}$ cups of milk, and 1 gallon is only 16 cups. He will need to buy an additional gallon to have enough milk.**

1 PLAN

BACKGROUND FOCUS

When students solve word problems, they should recognize that there is often more than one strategy they can use. Students who are used to comparing their work with that of their classmates may be disconcerted to find that different methods have been used. In this activity, different strategies for solving the same problem will be described.

2 TEACH

GUIDING STUDENTS' WORK

Some students may need help understanding that the painting time when working together is less than either individual's time. Students may simply add 3 hours and 6 hours, or they may try to solve the problem by adding $\frac{1}{3}$ and $\frac{1}{6}$.

Extra Examples

Example Three gardeners needed 8 hours to remove all the weeds in Don's garden. The gardening company wants to spend no more than 2 hours in Don's garden next year. How many gardeners should be assigned to the job next year if all of the company's gardeners work at the same pace and the amount of weeding needed next year is expected to be the same as was done this year? **12 gardeners**

Unit 2 *Focus On* Problem Solving

Making *a* Plan

Using Multiple Strategies

When you make a plan to solve a problem, be aware that there is often more than one strategy you can use to find the solution.

Problem You and your younger brother have volunteered to paint a wall of a community center as part of a community service project. You could paint the wall by yourself in 3 hours. Your brother (who has less experience painting) could paint the wall by himself in 6 hours. How long will it take to paint the wall if you and your brother work together?

1 Use estimation.

An upper limit on the time you and your brother take to paint the wall is the time it would take the faster painter to do the job working alone. Because you are the faster painter and can do the job in 3 hours, you can estimate that you and your brother will paint the wall in less than 3 hours.

2 Draw a diagram.

Your work rate when painting is $\frac{1}{3}$ of the wall per hour. Your brother's work rate is $\frac{1}{6}$ of the wall per hour. Use these rates to draw a diagram showing how much of the wall is painted after each hour. The diagram below shows that you and your brother will take 2 hours to paint the wall.

After 1 hour:

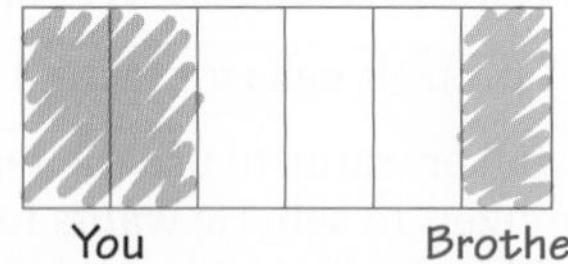

After 2 hours:

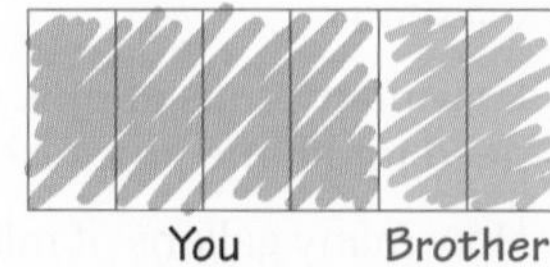

3 Solve an equation.

A third way to solve the problem is to use an equation. Let t represent the time (in hours) that you and your brother take to paint the wall. Make a table to find how much work each person does in t hours.

	Work rate	× Time	= Work done
You	$\frac{1}{3}$	t	$\frac{t}{3}$
Brother	$\frac{1}{6}$	t	$\frac{t}{6}$

The sum of your work and your brother's work equals 1 whole wall painted. Use this fact to write and solve an equation.

$$\frac{t}{3} + \frac{t}{6} = 1$$

$$6\left(\frac{t}{3} + \frac{t}{6}\right) = 6(1)$$

$$6\left(\frac{t}{3}\right) + 6\left(\frac{t}{6}\right) = 6$$

$$2t + t = 6$$

$$3t = 6$$

$$t = 2$$

So, you and your brother will take 2 hours to paint the wall.

Problem Solving Practice

1. **Wallpapering** You and your sister are wallpapering a wall of your family's living room. The diagram below shows how much of the wall each of you finished in 1 hour. What is the total time you and your sister spend wallpapering the wall? **4 h**

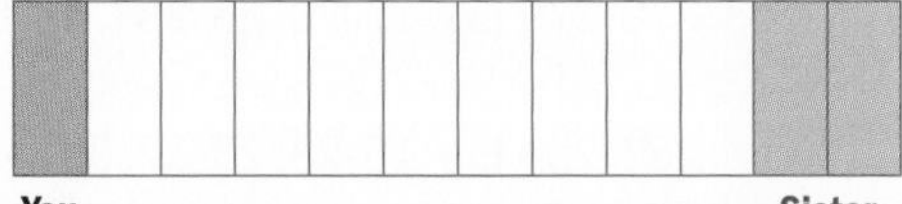

In Exercises 2–5, use at least two strategies to solve the problem.

2. **Shingling a Roof** A contractor estimates that either she or her assistant could shingle the roof of a certain building in 8 days working alone. How long would the contractor and her assistant take to shingle the roof if they work together? **4 days**

3. **Splitting Wood** Paul can split a cord of wood in 12 hours. His father can split a cord of wood in 4 hours. How long do Paul and his father take to split a cord of wood if they work together? **3 h**

4. **Shoveling Snow** Sara can shovel the snow off her family's driveway in 30 minutes. Her sister can shovel the driveway in 20 minutes. How long do Sara and her sister take to shovel the driveway if they work together? **12 min**

5. **Mowing a Lawn** You and a friend run a lawn mowing service. You can mow your next-door neighbor's lawn in 45 minutes. Your friend can mow the lawn in 1 hour. How long do you and your friend take to mow the lawn when working together? **about 26 min**

6. **Filling a Sink** The faucet of a sink can fill the sink with water in 2 minutes. The drain can empty the sink in 3 minutes. If the faucet is turned on and the drain is left open, does the sink ever fill up with water? Justify your answer in two different ways. **See margin.**

7. **Painting** Look back at the painting problem on page 264. Suppose your sister helps you and your brother paint the wall. She can paint the wall by herself in 2 hours. Use a diagram and an equation to find how long the three of you take to paint the wall when working together. **1 h**

8. **Biking** Heidi is riding her bike from her house to a park. After Heidi has traveled 400 feet, her brother Josh leaves the house on his bike to catch up to her. Heidi's speed is 22 feet per second, while Josh's speed is 27 feet per second. In parts (a) and (b), use the specified strategy to find how long Josh takes to catch up to Heidi.

   a. Copy and complete the table below. Continue adding rows to the table until you know the solution to the problem. **See margin.**

Time (sec)	Heidi's distance traveled (ft)	Josh's distance traveled (ft)
0	400	0
10	?	?
20	?	?

   b. Write and solve an equation. **Let t represent the time that Josh rides; $400 + 22t = 27t$; 80 sec.**

9. **Car Wash** A science club holds a car wash to raise money. Two groups of students wash the cars. One group can wash 6 cars per hour. The other group can wash 4 cars per hour. How long do both groups take to wash a total of 30 cars? Use a diagram and an equation to find the answer. **3 h**

3 APPLY

TRANSPARENCY

Even-numbered answers are available on transparencies.

TEACHING TIP

In Exercises 2-9, have students confirm their answer using a different strategy than they used to solve the problem.

SUGGESTED STRATEGIES

You may wish to suggest the following strategies for the problems in the Problem Solving Practice:

- Exercise 1: Draw a Diagram
- Exercise 2: Draw a Diagram; Solve an Equation
- Exercise 3: Draw a Diagram; Solve an Equation
- Exercise 4: Draw a Diagram; Solve an Equation
- Exercise 5: Draw a Diagram; Solve an Equation
- Exercise 6: Draw a Diagram; Solve an Equation
- Exercise 7: Draw a Diagram; Solve an Equation
- Exercise 8: Make a Table; Look for a Pattern; Solve an Equation
- Exercise 9: Draw a Diagram; Solve an Equation

6, 8a. See Additional Answers beginning on page AA1.

CHAPTER 6

Pacing and Assignment Guide

REGULAR SCHEDULE

Lesson	Les. Day	BASIC	AVERAGE	ADVANCED
6.1	Day 1	EP p. 806 Exs. 17-20; pp. 272-274 Exs. 10-15, 22-27, 40-42, 48-52	pp. 272-274 Exs. 10-15, 26-29, 40-43, 48-52	pp. 272-274 Exs. 12-15, 26-29, 40-44, 50-54
	Day 2	pp. 272-274 Exs. 16-21, 30-38, 43-45, 53-55	pp. 272-274 Exs. 16-21, 33-39, 44-46, 53-56	pp. 272-274 Exs. 16-19, 33-39, 45-47*, 55, 56
6.2	Day 1	SRH p. 780 Exs. 1-4; pp. 278-279 Exs. 9-20, 25-27, 32-34, 37-49	pp. 278-279 Exs. 13-16, 21-35, 37-50	pp. 278-279 Exs. 15-20, 25-38*, 43-50
6.3	Day 1	pp. 283-284 Exs. 12-27, 33-35, 37-40, 45-55	pp. 283-284 Exs. 16-23, 28-36, 39-43, 46-55	pp. 283-284 Exs. 16-23, 28-32, 35-44*, 49-55
6.4	Day 1	pp. 291-292 Exs. 7-10, 16-18, 24-28	pp. 291-292 Exs. 7-10, 16-19, 24-27	pp. 291-292 Exs. 7-10, 16-20, 26-29
	Day 2	pp. 291-292 Exs. 11-15, 19-21, 29-31	pp. 291-292 Exs. 11-15, 20-22, 28-31	pp. 291-292 Exs. 11-15, 21-25*, 30, 31
6.5	Day 1	pp. 295-297 Exs. 6-12, 14, 15, 18-25	pp. 295-297 Exs. 8-16, 18-25	pp. 295-297 Exs. 8-17*, 20-25
6.6	Day 1	SRH p. 788 Exs. 1-4; pp. 302-304 Exs. 12-23, 28-37, 40-42, 45, 47-51	pp. 302-304 Exs. 16-27, 32-39, 42-45, 47-51	pp. 302-304 Exs. 16-19, 24-31, 38, 39, 42-51*
6.7	Day 1	pp. 309-311 Exs. 7-13, 17-19, 23-31	pp. 309-311 Exs. 7-12, 14-20, 23-32	pp. 309-311 Exs. 9-11, 14-22*, 27-32
6.8	Day 1	SRH p. 799 Exs. 1-3; pp. 315-317 Exs. 7, 8, 11-15, 17, 20-30	pp. 315-317 Exs. 7-10, 13-17, 19-30	pp. 315-317 Exs. 9-21*, 26-30
Review	Day 1	pp. 318-321 Exs. 1-35	pp. 318-321 Exs. 1-35	pp. 318-321 Exs. 1-35
Assess	Day 1	Chapter 6 Test	Chapter 6 Test	Chapter 6 Test

YEARLY PACING Chapter 6 Total – **12 days** Chapters 1–6 Total – **70 days** Remaining – **90 days**

*Challenge Exercises EP = Extra Practice SRH = Skills Review Handbook

BLOCK SCHEDULE

DAY 1	DAY 2	DAY 3	DAY 4	DAY 5	DAY 6
6.1 pp. 272-274 Exs. 10-21, 26-29, 33-46, 48-56	**6.2** pp. 278-279 Exs. 13-16, 21-35, 37-50 **6.3** pp. 283-284 Exs. 16-23, 28-36, 39-43, 46-55	**6.4** pp. 291-292 Exs. 7-22, 24-31	**6.5** pp. 295-297 Exs. 8-16, 18-25 **6.6** pp. 302-304 Exs. 16-27, 32-39, 42-45, 47-51	**6.7** pp. 309-311 Exs. 7-12, 14-20, 23-32 **6.8** pp. 315-317 Exs. 7-10, 13-17, 19-30	**Review** pp. 318-321 Exs. 1-35 **Assess** Chapter 6 Test

YEARLY PACING Chapter 6 Total – **6 days** Chapters 1–6 Total – **35 days** Remaining – **45 days**

Support Materials

CHAPTER RESOURCE BOOK

CHAPTER SUPPORT			
Tips for New Teachers	p. 1	Parents as Partners	p. 3

LESSON SUPPORT	6.1	6.2	6.3	6.4	6.5	6.6	6.7	6.8
Lesson Plans (regular and block)	p. 5	p. 16	p. 24	p. 33	p. 41	p. 50	p. 59	p. 68
Technology Activities & Keystrokes	p. 7						p. 61	
Activity Support Masters								
Activity Masters								p. 70
Practice (3 levels)	p. 10	p. 18	p. 26	p. 35	p. 43	p. 52	p. 62	p. 71
Study Guide	p. 13	p. 21	p. 29	p. 38	p. 46	p. 55	p. 65	p. 74
Real-World Problem Solving			p. 31			p. 57		
Challenge Practice	p. 15	p. 23	p. 32	p. 40	p. 48	p. 58	p. 67	p. 76

REVIEW			
Games Support Masters	p. 49	Cooperative Project with Rubric	p. 80
Chapter Review Games and Activities	p. 77	Extra Credit Project with Rubric	p. 82
Real-Life Project with Rubric	p. 78	Cumulative Practice	p. 84
		Resource Book Answers	A1

ASSESSMENT

Quizzes	p. 68	Alternative Assessments with Rubrics	p. 77
Chapter Tests (3 levels)	p. 70	Unit Test	p. 90
Standardized Test	p. 76	Cumulative Test	p. 92

TRANSPARENCIES

	6.1	6.2	6.3	6.4	6.5	6.6	6.7	6.8
Warm-Up/Daily Homework Quiz	✔	✔	✔	✔	✔	✔	✔	✔
Notetaking Guide	✔	✔	✔	✔	✔	✔	✔	✔
Teacher Support								
English/Spanish Problem Solving	✔			✔		✔		
Answer Transparencies	✔	✔	✔	✔	✔	✔	✔	✔

TECHNOLOGY

- EasyPlanner CD-ROM
- Test and Practice Generator
- Electronic Lesson Presentations
- eTutorial CD-ROM
- Chapter Audio Summaries CDs
- Classzone.com
- eEdition Plus Online
- eWorkbook Plus Online
- eTutorial Plus Online
- EasyPlanner Plus Online

ADDITIONAL RESOURCES

- Worked-Out Solution Key
- Notetaking Guide
- Practice Workbook
- Tutor Place
- Professional Development Book
- Special Activities Book
- Posters
- Spanish Study Guide
- Exercises in Spanish
- English/Spanish Ch. Reviews/Tests
- Multi-Language Visual Glossary

CHAPTER

6 Math Background and Teaching Strategies

Lesson 6.1

MATH BACKGROUND

A **ratio** compares quantities using division, and may be written in fraction form, using the word "to," as in "3 to 2," or using a colon, as in "3 : 2." A **rate** is a special ratio in which the quantities are measured in different units. In a ratio, any units of measurement "cancel," and the ratio can be represented as a simple rational number. In a rate, the units of measurement are integral. You can write a rate as a **unit rate** by writing an equivalent rate that has a denominator of 1.

TEACHING STRATEGIES

One difficulty for students in dealing with rates lies in working with the units of measurement, especially with conversion factors. Students may have trouble deciding which value should be the numerator and which the denominator in a conversion factor. Emphasize that they should choose the orientation that will result in canceling any units of measure that are not to be in the final answer.

Lesson 6.2

MATH BACKGROUND

A mathematical sentence stating that one ratio is equal to another is called a **proportion**. A proportion containing a variable may be solved in several ways. In some cases, especially when the numerator (denominator) of one ratio is a multiple of the other, you may be able to find an equivalent ratio using mental math. You can also use the multiplication property of equality. A third method, using *cross products*, is introduced in Lesson 6.3.

TEACHING STRATEGIES

You may want to tell students that no new equation-solving skills are needed for this lesson. You will want to focus your instruction on writing proportions to represent word problems. Here the main concern is to help students realize that the numerators of the two ratios and the denominators of the two ratios must compare corresponding quantities, as in $\frac{5 \text{ apples}}{8 \text{ oranges}} = \frac{x \text{ apples}}{40 \text{ oranges}}$. It may help some students set up proportions if you suggest that they use the phrase "__ is to __ as __ is to __." For example, "3 pounds of peaches is to 4 dollars as x pounds of peaches is to 12 dollars."

Lesson 6.3

MATH BACKGROUND

For any proportion $\frac{a}{b} = \frac{c}{d}$ ($b \neq 0$, $d \neq 0$), the **cross products** are $a \cdot d$ and $b \cdot c$. The cross products of any true proportion are equal. Conversely, if the cross products of two ratios are equal, then the ratios form a proportion. You can use the cross products property to solve a proportion.

TEACHING STRATEGIES

Make sure students understand the justification for the cross products property given at the top of page 281 so they realize it follows from the multiplication property of equality. Also, make sure students realize that the cross products property is useful only for solving proportions. So, for example, they can use it to solve $\frac{d}{5} = \frac{11}{8}$, but not $\frac{d}{5} + \frac{1}{2} = \frac{11}{8}$.

Lesson 6.4

MATH BACKGROUND

Similar figures have the same shape, though not necessarily the same size. For similar polygons, corresponding angles are congruent and corresponding sides are proportional, that is, they have the same ratio. **Congruent figures** have the same shape *and* the same size. For congruent polygons, corresponding angles are congruent and corresponding sides are congruent.

TEACHING STRATEGIES

Use cutouts of similar and congruent polygons and an overhead projector to help students learn to identify corresponding sides and angles of similar and congruent polygons. You can place a few polygons on the overhead in various orientations, and then let a student come up and physically manipulate the cutouts to identify which ones are similar and which are congruent.

Lesson 6.5

MATH BACKGROUND

Since the ratios of corresponding sides of similar polygons are equal, if you know that two polygons are similar you can write a proportion comparing two pairs of corresponding sides. If the length of one of these sides is unknown, you can solve the proportion to find the missing length, a process called *indirect* measurement.

TEACHING STRATEGIES

You can continue using the cutouts of polygons from the Teaching Strategies for Lesson 6.4 in this lesson by having some measures shown and some missing on the polygons. Have students use the cutouts to write appropriate proportions and then solve them to find the missing lengths.

Lesson 6.6

MATH BACKGROUND

Scale drawings and **scale models** allow you to represent larger distances or objects in a convenient way. The **scale** of the drawing or model gives the relationship between the dimensions on the drawing or model and the actual dimensions. The scale is frequently written with a colon, as in "1 in. : 400 ft," which is read "1 inch to 400 feet." Because a scale model or drawing is similar to what it represents, you can write and solve proportions to find unknown lengths.

TEACHING STRATEGIES

Here is an additional example that you can use with students: A souvenir replica of the Statue of Liberty is 8.5 inches tall, including the statue's base and pedestal. If the scale of the model is 1 in. : 430 in., how tall is the statue?

Write a proportion using the scale.

$\frac{1}{430} = \frac{8.5}{x}$ ← Dimension of souvenir / ← Dimension of statue

$1x = 430 \cdot 8.5$ Cross products property

$x = 3655$ Multiply.

The actual height of the Statue of Liberty is about 3655 inches, or $3655 \div 12 \approx 305$ feet.

Another approach that you can use is to bring, or have students bring, some road maps to class, and have students use the scale of the map and a ruler to find actual distances.

Lesson 6.7

MATH BACKGROUND

An experiment has different possible results, or **outcomes**. An **event** is an outcome or a collection of outcomes. **Probability** expresses the likelihood of an event as the ratio of favorable outcomes to total outcomes, **odds in favor** is the ratio of favorable outcomes to unfavorable outcomes, and **odds against** is the ratio of unfavorable outcomes to favorable outcomes. If you know all the equally likely outcomes of an experiment, you can determine a **theoretical probability**. Alternatively, you can repeat an experiment many times to determine an **experimental probability**.

TEACHING STRATEGIES

Here is an example to emphasize the difference between odds and probability: A spinner has 1 blue, 1 green, 1 yellow, and 1 red section, and is equally likely to land in each of the sections. For the event "the spinner lands on red," there is 1 favorable outcome and 3 unfavorable outcomes.

$P(\text{red}) = \frac{1}{4}$ Odds in favor $= \frac{1}{3}$ Odds against $= \frac{3}{1}$

Point out that the odds in favor and odds against a particular event are reciprocals.

Lesson 6.8

MATH BACKGROUND

The **counting principle** states that if one event can occur in a ways and a second event can occur in b ways, then the two events can occur together in $a \cdot b$ ways. You can draw a **tree diagram** to count possibilities if the number is not great.

TEACHING STRATEGIES

Present students with the situation of drawing 2 marbles, one at a time, from a bag containing 5 red marbles, 3 blue marbles, and 1 yellow marble without replacing the first marble. There are 9 possibilities for the first draw and 8 possibilities for the second, so there are $9 \cdot 8 = 72$ possible outcomes. There are 5 possibilities for the first marble to be red, but only 4 for the second selection, so the number of favorable outcomes for drawing two red marbles is $5 \cdot 4 = 20$. Therefore, the probability of drawing two red marbles, one after the other, is $\frac{20}{72} = \frac{5}{18}$.

CHAPTER

6 Differentiating Instruction

Strategies for Underachievers

FOCUS ON VOCABULARY

There are many new terms in this chapter that students should add to their notebooks or write on note cards. As students make entries, encourage them to draw diagrams or give examples to illustrate the terms.

By now, students will have accumulated many definitions, and may need help organizing them. You might suggest that they group terms by general concept. Students can color code note cards related to the same concept. For example, one color group might contain terms related to ratio and proportion, another might contain terms related to basic geometric concepts, and a third might contain terms related to probability. Terms that relate to more than one concept would have more than one color code.

USE SCAFFOLDING

CONVERSION FACTORS In Lesson 6.1, problems that involve using conversion factors to write equivalent rates, such as those in Examples 4 and 5 on page 271, will be difficult for many students. It may be helpful for underachievers to review fraction multiplication and simplification at this point. Make sure students understand that a conversion factor is just another way to write the number 1. They must also understand how to choose each conversion factor. You may want to provide students with partially-completed templates of extra examples of measurement conversion for them to fill in.

USE MANIPULATIVES AND TOOLS

The Teaching Strategies notes for Lessons 6.4 and 6.5 spoke of using cutouts of polygons to help students understand the idea of similarity. You may wish to give underachieving students their own cutouts that they can manipulate as needed. It will help if they can also see correctly written and solved proportions involving the cutouts.

EXPERIMENTAL PROBABILITY As students are introduced to probability and counting in Lessons 6.7 and 6.8, they should have access to calculators. Use an experimental approach with students whenever possible. For example, you may wish to give small groups or pairs of students number cubes and have them perform the experiment in Example 1 on page 306 a large number of times to compare the theoretical and experimental probabilities. Students can then combine their results to compare the experimental probabilities found in the small groups with the experimental probability for the class as a whole. You can also perform other experiments with students by spinning spinners, dropping cups, flipping coins, drawing cards from a deck, and so on. This should help students make a better connection between the theoretical concepts and the real world.

USE A CO-TEACHING MODEL

SCALE DRAWINGS You may wish to co-teach Concept Activity 6.6 with a Special Educator who can help students read and interpret situations involving scales and scale drawings, which can be confusing for students. Also, students who have difficulty with the fine motor skills needed for this activity may need extra attention. Finally, a Special Educator can help students with strategies for organization, which is critical in an activity such as this that requires many steps. For additional practice, you may want to have students make scale drawings of actual objects in your classroom. This will help students develop an intuitive understanding for the relationship between a scale drawing and the actual object that it represents.

Strategies for English Learners

BUILD ON WHAT STUDENTS KNOW

English learners who have arrived recently from other countries may have had adequate or excellent prior schooling in mathematics. They may be familiar with algorithms that are not commonly used in this country. Encourage recent immigrants to share alternate forms of describing mathematical concepts or algorithms and provide an opportunity for the whole class to understand and discuss these alternative methods. Such a discussion not only promotes respect for cultural diversity and gives the teacher a glimpse into the student's thinking, but it also allows all students an opportunity to build a deeper understanding of mathematics.

USE A PICTURE OR MODEL

Students who are not yet fluent in English can investigate the concepts of similarity and congruence by cutting up shapes. Have students do the following: Take a sheet of $8\frac{1}{2}$-by-11 inch paper. Draw a line between one pair of opposite corners and cut the sheet into two right triangles along this line. Then have students rotate and flip the shapes until the two triangles can be placed one on top of the other. This illustrates the concept of congruence. Now have the students take one of the two triangles and divide it into two smaller right triangles by folding the large triangle on the altitude to the hypotenuse and cutting along this fold.

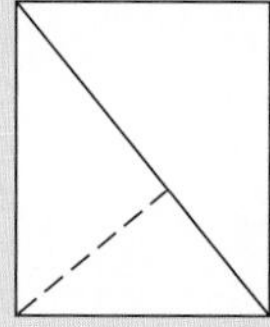

They will then have three right triangles that are similar, but not congruent. You can also illustrate the concept of proportion by having students measure the lengths of the sides of the triangles and compare them.

Strategies for Advanced Learners

INCREASE DEPTH AND COMPLEXITY

In Lesson 6.8, you can have advanced students use tree diagrams to investigate experiments for which all outcomes are not equally likely. Present the experiment of flipping a coin and spinning a spinner divided into four equal regions, one red, one blue, and two white. Have students create a tree diagram displaying all of the possible outcomes, and then have them find the probabilities of each outcome, such as *tails and white*. Because each region of the spinner is equally likely, students can draw the tree diagram to represent each region and then find the corresponding outcome afterward. For example, 2 of the 8 branches will indicate the outcome *tails and white*, so this probability is $\frac{1}{4}$, while the probability of *tails and red* is $\frac{1}{8}$.

COUNTING Lesson 6.8 introduces the counting principle. Ask advanced students how many different medium pizzas can be ordered if the pizza can have a thin crust, a thick crust, or a regular crust, and the pizza can be topped with one of the ingredients cheese, pepperoni, sausage, or mushrooms. Then have them extend this concept to how many different 2-, 3-, and 4-topping pizzas can be ordered. Though this exploration leads into the idea of combinations, it can be completed easily using only listing techniques. You may also want to have students investigate local pizzerias to explore the actual possibilities of type of crust, size, and toppings. They may be surprised at how many possibilities exist. For example, if there are 3 sizes, 3 types of crust, and 12 different toppings, then there are $3 \cdot 3 \cdot 12 = 108$ different 1-topping pizzas (and 11,880 3-topping pizzas!).

USE CROSS-CURRICULAR CONNECTIONS

Concept Activity 6.6 and Lesson 6.6 offer several possibilities for cross-curricular connections. You may wish to work with an art teacher to have students investigate the use of scale in art. You may wish to work with an industrial arts teacher to have students investigate the role of scale drawings and models in building and architecture. You may also wish to work with a social studies teacher to have students use maps to investigate historical or archaeological sites.

CHAPTER

6 Differentiating Instruction: Resource Materials

Differentiating Enrichment and Activities

McDougal Littell *Pre-Algebra* offers teachers enrichment for all levels of students. Pictured on these pages are facsimiles of the Real-World Problem Solving pages, Chapter Review Games, and Chapter Projects from the *Chapter 6 Resource Book* and a number of activities from the *Special Activities Book*. Also available is the *Poster Package* containing large, full-color posters, one for each unit.

RESOURCE BOOK

The *Chapter Resource Books* contain Real-World Problem Solving activities for various lessons, Chapter Review Games for a motivating review of each chapter, and Chapter Projects with rubrics that apply the mathematics of the chapter.

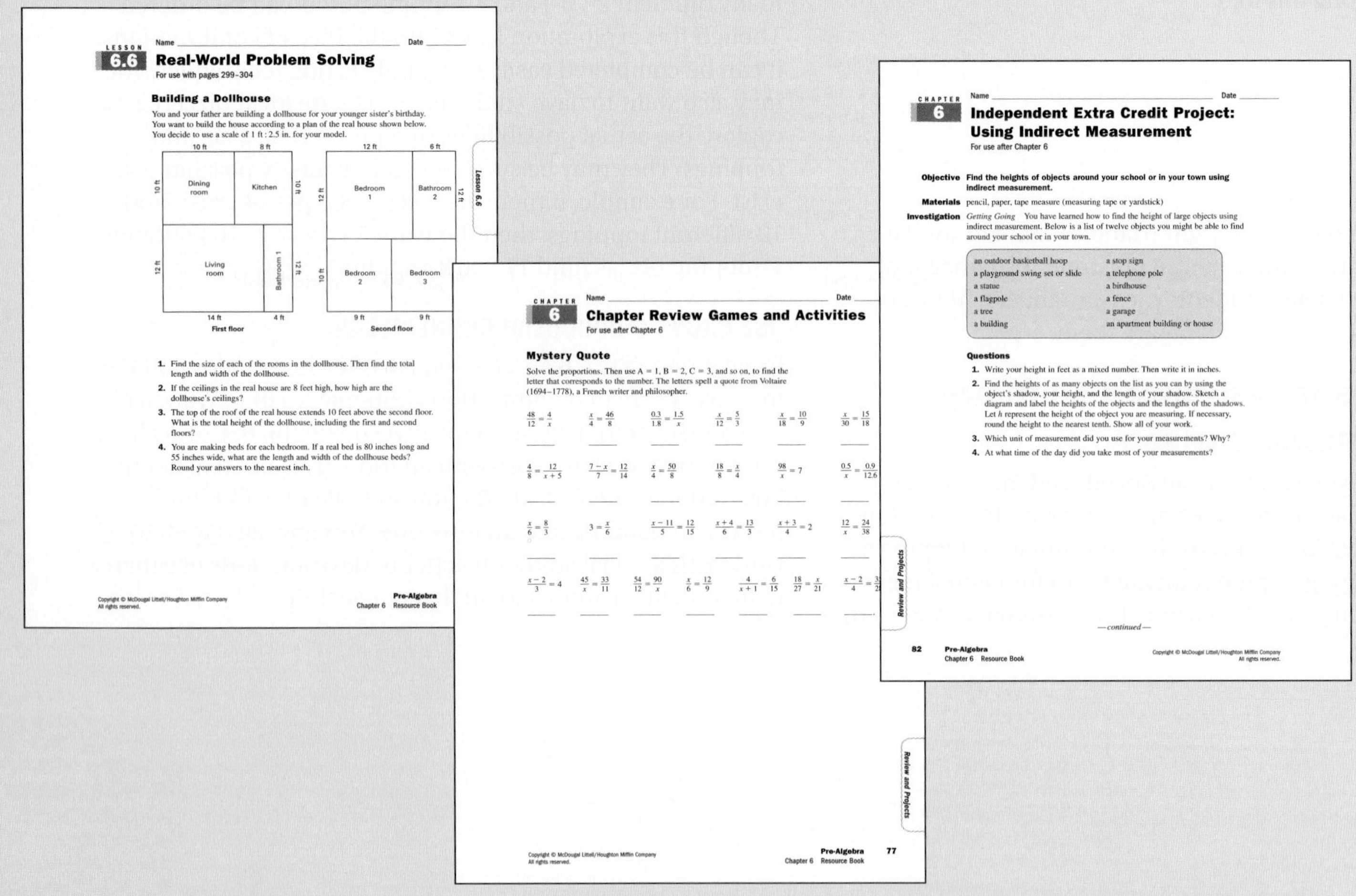

LESSON 6.6

Name ______ Date ______

Real-World Problem Solving

For use with pages 299–304

Building a Dollhouse

You and your father are building a dollhouse for your younger sister's birthday. You want to build the house according to a plan of the real house shown below. You decide to use a scale of 1 ft : 2.5 in. for your model.

1. Find the size of each of the rooms in the dollhouse. Then find the total length and width of the dollhouse.
2. If the ceilings in the real house are 8 feet high, how high are the dollhouse's ceilings?
3. The top of the roof of the real house extends 10 feet above the second floor. What is the total height of the dollhouse, including the first and second floors?
4. You are making beds for each bedroom. If a real bed is 80 inches long and 55 inches wide, what are the length and width of the dollhouse beds? Round your answers to the nearest inch.

CHAPTER 6

Name ______ Date ______

Chapter Review Games and Activities

For use after Chapter 6

Mystery Quote

Solve the proportions. Then use A = 1, B = 2, C = 3, and so on, to find the letter that corresponds to the number. The letters spell a quote from Voltaire (1694–1778), a French writer and philosopher.

$\frac{48}{12} = \frac{4}{x}$ ____ $\frac{x}{4} = \frac{46}{8}$ ____ $\frac{0.3}{1.8} = \frac{1.5}{x}$ ____ $\frac{x}{12} = \frac{5}{3}$ ____ $\frac{x}{18} = \frac{10}{9}$ ____ $\frac{x}{30} = \frac{15}{18}$ ____

$\frac{4}{8} = \frac{12}{x+5}$ ____ $\frac{7-x}{7} = \frac{12}{14}$ ____ $\frac{x}{4} = \frac{50}{8}$ ____ $\frac{18}{8} = \frac{x}{4}$ ____ $\frac{98}{x} = 7$ ____ $\frac{0.5}{x} = \frac{0.9}{12.6}$ ____

$\frac{x}{6} = \frac{8}{3}$ ____ $3 = \frac{x}{6}$ ____ $\frac{x-11}{5} = \frac{12}{15}$ ____ $\frac{x+4}{6} = \frac{13}{3}$ ____ $\frac{x+3}{4} = 2$ ____ $\frac{12}{x} = \frac{24}{38}$ ____

$\frac{x-2}{3} = 4$ ____ $\frac{45}{x} = \frac{33}{11}$ ____ $\frac{54}{12} = \frac{90}{x}$ ____ $\frac{x}{6} = \frac{12}{9}$ ____ $\frac{4}{x+1} = \frac{6}{15}$ ____ $\frac{18}{27} = \frac{x}{21}$ ____ $\frac{x-2}{4} =$ ____.

Review and Projects

CHAPTER 6

Name ______ Date ______

Independent Extra Credit Project: Using Indirect Measurement

For use after Chapter 6

Objective **Find the heights of objects around your school or in your town using indirect measurement.**

Materials pencil, paper, tape measure (measuring tape or yardstick)

Investigation *Getting Going* You have learned how to find the height of large objects using indirect measurement. Below is a list of twelve objects you might be able to find around your school or in your town.

an outdoor basketball hoop	a stop sign
a playground swing set or slide	a telephone pole
a statue	a birdhouse
a flagpole	a fence
a tree	a garage
a building	an apartment building or house

Questions

1. Write your height in feet as a mixed number. Then write it in inches.
2. Find the heights of as many objects on the list as you can by using the object's shadow, your height, and the length of your shadow. Sketch a diagram and label the heights of the objects and the lengths of the shadows. Let *h* represent the height of the object you are measuring. If necessary, round the height to the nearest tenth. Show all of your work.
3. Which unit of measurement did you use for your measurements? Why?
4. At what time of the day did you take most of your measurements?

—continued—

Review and Projects

SPECIAL ACTIVITIES BOOK

The *Special Activities Book* contains numerous activities including activities for the start of school, activities for substitute teachers, activities for use before holiday breaks, and short change-of-pace activities.

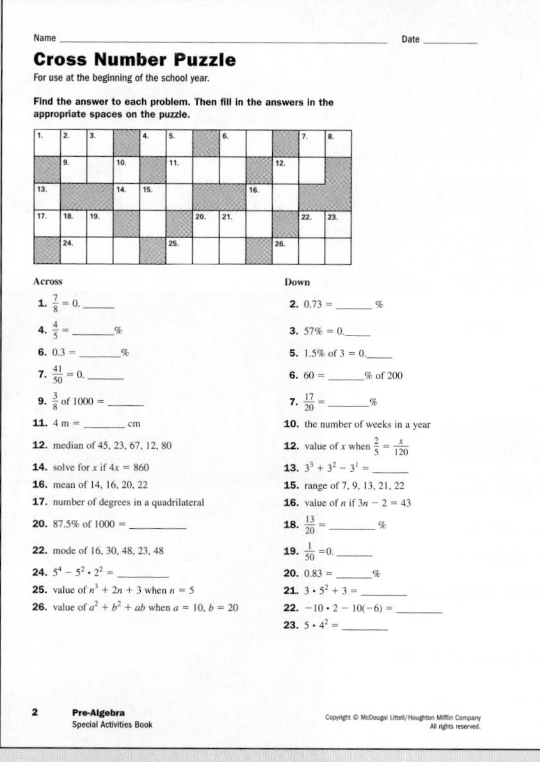

Name ______ Date ______

Cross Number Puzzle

For use at the beginning of the school year.

Find the answer to each problem. Then fill in the answers in the appropriate spaces on the puzzle.

Across

1. $\frac{7}{8} = 0.$____
4. $\frac{4}{5} =$ ____%
6. $0.3 =$ ____%
7. $\frac{41}{50} = 0.$____
9. $\frac{3}{8}$ of $1000 =$ ____
11. 4 m = ____ cm
12. median of 45, 23, 67, 12, 80
14. solve for x if $4x = 860$
16. mean of 14, 16, 20, 22
17. number of degrees in a quadrilateral
20. 87.5% of 1000 = ____
22. mode of 16, 30, 48, 23, 48
24. $5^4 - 5^2 \cdot 2^2 =$ ____
25. value of $n^3 + 2n + 3$ when $n = 5$
26. value of $a^2 + b^2 + ab$ when $a = 10$, $b = 20$

Down

2. $0.73 =$ ____%
3. $57\% = 0.$____
5. 1.5% of $3 = 0.$____
6. $60 =$ ____% of 200
7. $\frac{17}{20} =$ ____%
10. the number of weeks in a year
12. value of x when $\frac{2}{5} = \frac{x}{120}$
13. $3^3 + 3^2 - 3^1 =$ ____
15. range of 7, 9, 13, 21, 22
16. value of n if $3n - 2 = 43$
18. $\frac{13}{20} =$ ____%
19. $\frac{1}{50} = 0.$____
20. $0.83 =$ ____%
21. $3 \cdot 5^2 + 3 =$ ____
22. $-10 \cdot 2 - 10(-6) =$ ____
23. $5 \cdot 4^2 =$ ____

2 Pre-Algebra Special Activities Book

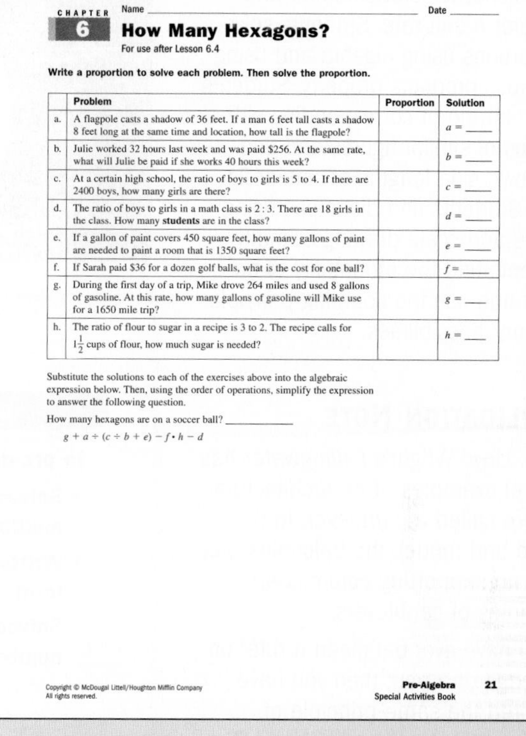

CHAPTER 6 Name ______ Date ______

How Many Hexagons?

For use after Lesson 6.4

Write a proportion to solve each problem. Then solve the proportion.

	Problem	Proportion	Solution
a.	A flagpole casts a shadow of 36 feet. If a man 6 feet tall casts a shadow 8 feet long at the same time and location, how tall is the flagpole?		$a =$ ____
b.	Julie worked 32 hours last week and was paid \$256. At the same rate, what will Julie be paid if she works 40 hours this week?		$b =$ ____
c.	At a certain high school, the ratio of boys to girls is 5 to 4. If there are 2400 boys, how many girls are there?		$c =$ ____
d.	The ratio of boys to girls in a math class is 2 : 3. There are 18 girls in the class. How many **students** are in the class?		$d =$ ____
e.	If a gallon of paint covers 450 square feet, how many gallons of paint are needed to paint a room that is 1350 square feet?		$e =$ ____
f.	If Sarah paid \$36 for a dozen golf balls, what is the cost for one ball?		$f =$ ____
g.	During the first day of a trip, Mike drove 264 miles and used 8 gallons of gasoline. At this rate, how many gallons of gasoline will Mike use for a 1650 mile trip?		$g =$ ____
h.	The ratio of flour to sugar in a recipe is 3 to 2. The recipe calls for $1\frac{1}{2}$ cups of flour, how much sugar is needed?		$h =$ ____

Substitute the solutions to each of the exercises above into the algebraic expression below. Then, using the order of operations, simplify the expression to answer the following question.

How many hexagons are on a soccer ball? ______

$g + a \div (c \div b + e) - f \cdot h - d$

Pre-Algebra Special Activities Book 21

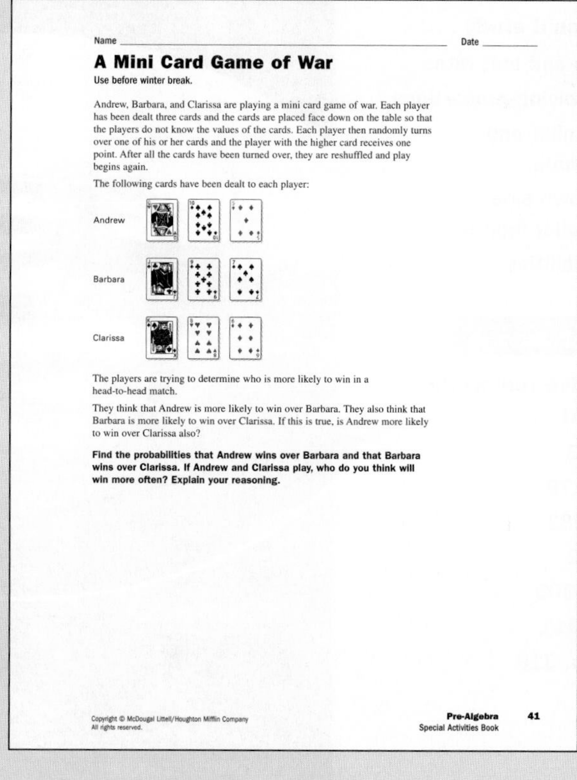

Name ______ Date ______

A Mini Card Game of War

Use before winter break.

Andrew, Barbara, and Clarissa are playing a mini card game of war. Each player has been dealt three cards and the cards are placed face down on the table so that the players do not know the values of the cards. Each player then randomly turns over one of his or her cards and the player with the higher card receives one point. After all the cards have been turned over, they are reshuffled and play begins again.

The following cards have been dealt to each player:

Andrew

Barbara

Clarissa

The players are trying to determine who is more likely to win in a head-to-head match.

They think that Andrew is more likely to win over Barbara. They also think that Barbara is more likely to win over Clarissa. If this is true, is Andrew more likely to win over Clarissa also?

Find the probabilities that Andrew wins over Barbara and that Barbara wins over Clarissa. If Andrew and Clarissa play, who do you think will win more often? Explain your reasoning.

Pre-Algebra Special Activities Book 41

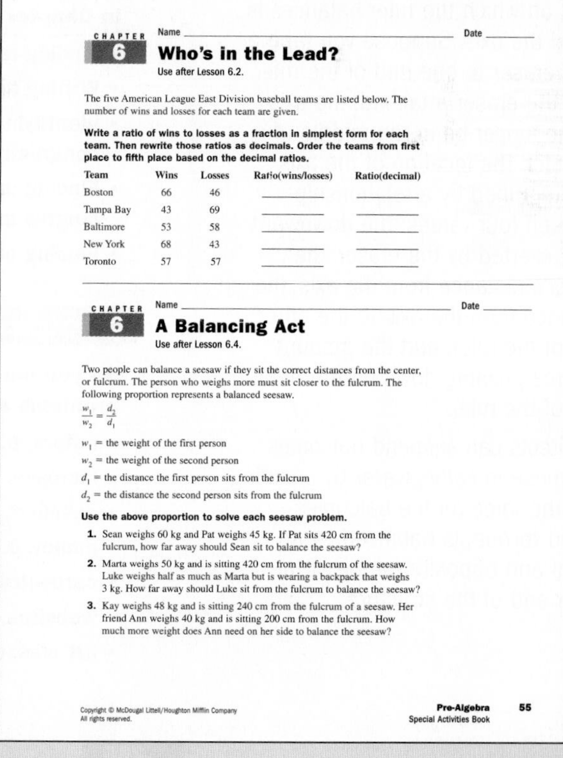

CHAPTER 6 Name ______ Date ______

Who's in the Lead?

Use after Lesson 6.2.

The five American League East Division baseball teams are listed below. The number of wins and losses for each team are given.

Write a ratio of wins to losses as a fraction in simplest form for each team. Then rewrite those ratios as decimals. Order the teams from first place to fifth place based on the decimal ratios.

Team	Wins	Losses	Ratio(wins/losses)	Ratio(decimal)
Boston	66	46	____	____
Tampa Bay	43	69	____	____
Baltimore	53	58	____	____
New York	68	43	____	____
Toronto	57	57	____	____

CHAPTER 6 Name ______ Date ______

A Balancing Act

Use after Lesson 6.4.

Two people can balance a seesaw if they sit the correct distances from the center, or fulcrum. The person who weighs more must sit closer to the fulcrum. The following proportion represents a balanced seesaw.

$\frac{w_1}{w_2} = \frac{d_2}{d_1}$

w_1 = the weight of the first person

w_2 = the weight of the second person

d_1 = the distance the first person sits from the fulcrum

d_2 = the distance the second person sits from the fulcrum

Use the above proportion to solve each seesaw problem.

1. Sean weighs 60 kg and Pat weighs 45 kg. If Pat sits 420 cm from the fulcrum, how far away should Sean sit to balance the seesaw?
2. Marta weighs 50 kg and is sitting 420 cm from the fulcrum of the seesaw. Luke weighs half as much as Marta but is wearing a backpack that weighs 3 kg. How far away should Luke sit from the fulcrum to balance the seesaw?
3. Kay weighs 48 kg and is sitting 240 cm from the fulcrum of a seesaw. Her friend Ann weighs 40 kg and is sitting 200 cm from the fulcrum. How much more weight does Ann need on her side to balance the seesaw?

Pre-Algebra Special Activities Book 55

OVERVIEW

MAIN IDEAS

In this chapter, students find and interpret a unit rate. Students solve proportions using algebra and using the cross products property. Students find the ratio of corresponding side lengths of similar figures and find unknown side lengths of similar figures. Students find distances using scales and scale drawings. Finally, students find the probability of an event and use the counting principle to count possibilities.

APPLICATION NOTE

Frank Lloyd Wright's *Fallingwater* has several examples of an architectural feature called a *cantilever*. In the photo and model, the balconies that have no supporting columns are examples of cantilevers.

If you have ever balanced a ruler on the edge of a pen, then you have explored the same principle of physics that governs cantilevers. The point on which the ruler balances is called the axis. Suppose you tape a large eraser to one end of the ruler. With the eraser attached, the axis will no longer be in the middle of the ruler. The location of the axis is determined by a relationship between four values: the downward force exerted by the eraser, the eraser's distance from the axis, the distance from the axis to the other end of the ruler, and the amount of force pushing down on the other end of the ruler.

Architects can suspend balconies like those in *Fallingwater* by ensuring that the force on the balconies, called *torque*, is balanced by an equal and opposite torque at the other end of the structure.

CHAPTER

6 Ratio, Proportion, *and* Probability

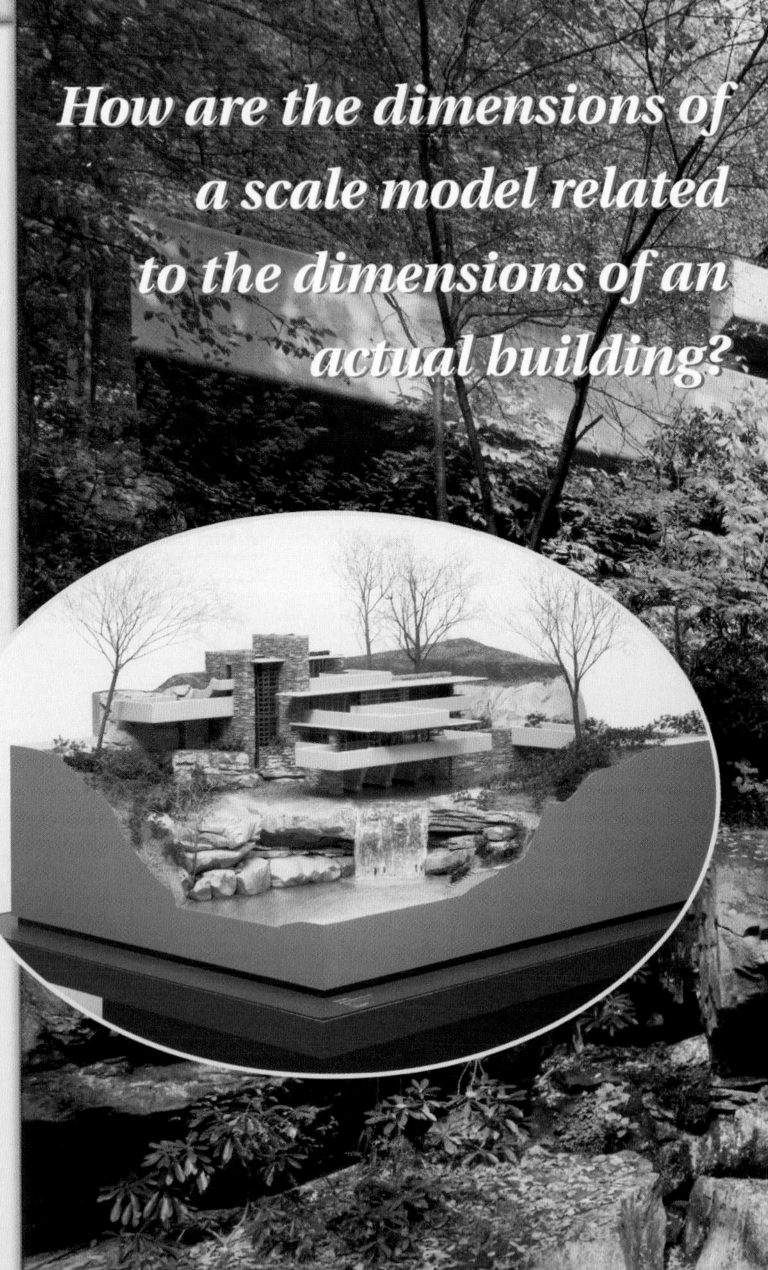

How are the dimensions of a scale model related to the dimensions of an actual building?

BEFORE

In previous chapters you've . . .

- **Solved equations using multiplication or division**
- **Written fractions in simplest form**
- **Solved equations with rational numbers**

Now

In Chapter 6 you'll study . . .

- **Finding ratios and unit rates**
- **Writing and solving proportions**
- **Identifying similar and congruent figures**
- **Finding unknown side lengths of similar figures**
- **Finding probabilities**

WHY?

So you can solve real-world problems about . . .

- **nature, p. 273**
- **lacrosse, p. 278**
- **gasoline, p. 283**
- **money, p. 292**
- **carpentry, p. 303**
- **websites, p. 311**
- **art classes, p. 316**

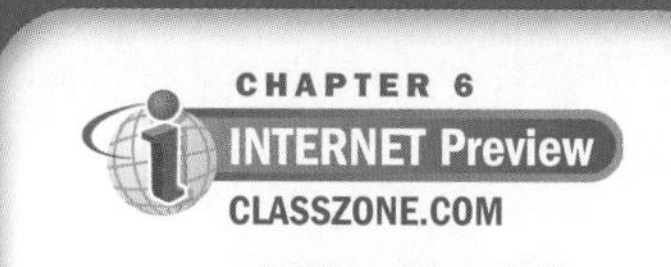

- eEdition Plus Online
- eWorkbook Plus Online
- eTutorial Plus Online
- State Test Practice
- More Examples

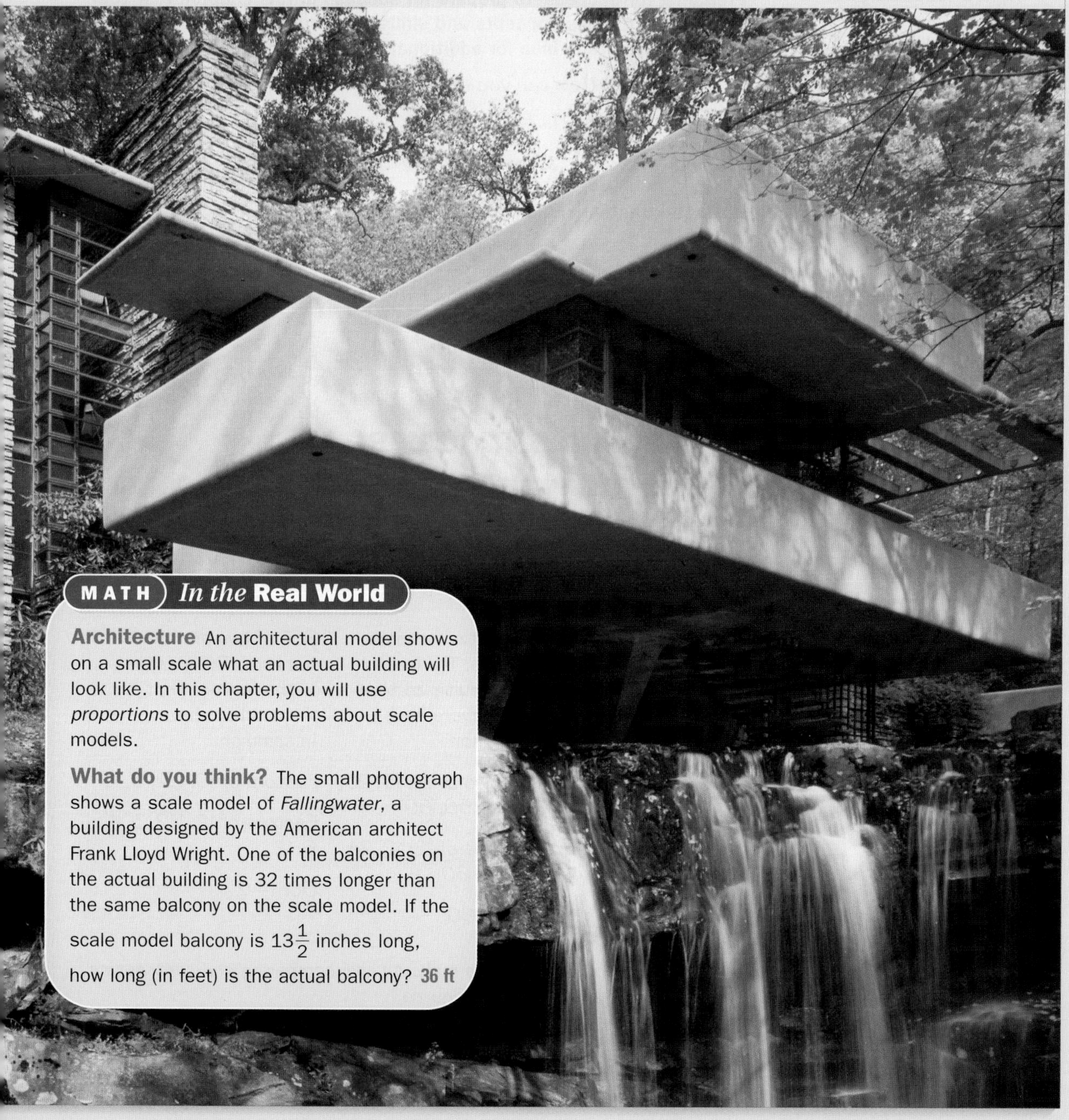

MATH *In the* **Real World**

Architecture An architectural model shows on a small scale what an actual building will look like. In this chapter, you will use *proportions* to solve problems about scale models.

What do you think? The small photograph shows a scale model of *Fallingwater*, a building designed by the American architect Frank Lloyd Wright. One of the balconies on the actual building is 32 times longer than the same balcony on the scale model. If the scale model balcony is $13\frac{1}{2}$ inches long, how long (in feet) is the actual balcony? 36 ft

Chapter Resources

These resources are provided to help you prepare for the chapter and to customize review materials:

Chapter 6 Resource Book

- Tips for New Teachers, pp. 1–2
- Lesson Plan, pp. 5, 16, 24, 33, 41, 50, 59, 68
- Lesson Plan for Block Scheduling, pp. 6, 17, 25, 34, 42, 51, 60, 69

Technology

- EasyPlanner CD-ROM
- Test and Practice Generator
- Electronic Lesson Presentations CD-ROM
- eTutorial CD-ROM

Internet

- Classzone
- eEdition Plus Online
- eWorkbook Plus Online
- eTutorial Plus Online
- EasyPlanner Plus Online

English Learner Support

- Spanish Study Guide
- Multi-Language Visual Glossary
- Chapter Audio Summaries CDs
- Teacher's Edition, pp. 266E–266F

PREPARE

Diagnosis/Remediation

Prerequisite Skills Quiz
The Prerequisite Skills Quiz can help you diagnose whether students have the following skills needed in Chapter 6:
- Describe equivalent fractions (Ex. 1)
- Solve one-step equations (Exs. 2–5)
- Simplify fractions (Exs. 6–9)
- Use multiplicative inverses to solve equations (Exs. 10–13)

Chapter 6 Resource Book
- Study Guide (Lessons 6.1–6.8)

Tutor Place

Notetaking Strategies

Students may wish to use a table similar to the one shown for recording the definitions of terms that they confuse, along with a tip or mnemonic to help them differentiate between the terms. Further suggestions for keeping a notebook can be found on pages 282 and 290.

For more support on notetaking, see:
- Notetaking Guide Workbook
- Notetaking Transparencies

CHAPTER 6

Chapter Prerequisite Skills

Review Vocabulary
rate, p. 76
unit rate, p. 76
equation, p. 85
equivalent fractions, p. 182

1. *Sample answer:* If two fractions are equivalent, they will be the same when written in simplest form, that is, when for each fraction the numerator and denominator are divided by their greatest common factor.

PREREQUISITE SKILLS QUIZ

Preparing for Success **To prepare for success in this chapter, test your knowledge of these concepts and skills. You may want to look at the pages referred to in blue for additional review.**

1. Vocabulary How can you tell whether two fractions are equivalent?

Solve the equation. *(p. 97)*

2. $-45 = 5x$ -9 3. $4y = -32$ -8 4. $-12 = \frac{n}{4}$ -48 5. $\frac{x}{6} = 7$ 42

Write the fraction in simplest form. *(p. 182)*

6. $\frac{24}{40}$ $\frac{3}{5}$ 7. $\frac{42}{144}$ $\frac{7}{24}$ 8. $\frac{14x^2y^3}{35xy^2}$ $\frac{2xy}{5}$ 9. $\frac{a^3b^2c^2}{bc^2}$ a^3b

Solve the equation. *(p. 247)*

10. $\frac{2}{9}x + \frac{5}{9} = 3$ 11 11. $-\frac{3}{8}x - 5 = 7$ -32 12. $\frac{1}{4}x - \frac{3}{8} = 9$ $37\frac{1}{2}$ 13. $\frac{3}{5}x - \frac{2}{5} = 2$ 4

NOTETAKING STRATEGIES

COMPARING AND CONTRASTING When you learn related vocabulary words or ideas, it may be helpful to make a table comparing and contrasting the ideas.

Definition	LCM of two or more numbers: The least of the multiples that the numbers have in common	GCF of two or more numbers: The greatest of the factors that the numbers have in common
Example	Multiples of 10: 10, 20, 30, 40, 50, (60) Multiples of 12: 12, 24, 36, 48, (60) LCM = 60	Factors of 10: 1, (2), 5, 10 Factors of 12: 1, (2), 3, 4, 6, 12 GCF = 2

In Lesson 6.4, you can make a table comparing and contrasting similar and congruent figures.

Note Worthy

You will find a notetaking strategy at the beginning of each chapter. Look for additional notetaking and study strategies throughout the chapter.

LESSON

6.1 Ratios *and* Rates

BEFORE	Now	WHY?
You wrote equivalent fractions.	You'll find ratios and unit rates.	So you can see if you'll have enough for a guitar, as in Ex. 38.

Vocabulary
ratio, p. 269
equivalent ratios, p. 270

Archery An archer shoots 60 arrows at a target, with 44 arrows hitting the scoring area and 16 missing the scoring area. How can you evaluate the archer's performance? You can compare the archer's number of hits to the archer's number of misses using a *ratio*. A **ratio** uses division to compare two quantities.

Writing Ratios

You can write the ratio of two quantities, a and b, where b is not equal to 0, in three ways.

a to b $\qquad a:b \qquad \frac{a}{b}$

Each ratio is read "the ratio of a to b." You should write the ratio in simplest form, as shown in Example 1 below.

Example 1 *Writing Ratios*

Use the archery information given above. Write the ratio in three ways.

a. The number of hits to the number of misses

b. The number of hits to the number of shots

Solution

a. $\frac{\text{Number of hits}}{\text{Number of misses}} = \frac{44}{16} = \frac{11}{4}$

Three ways to write the ratio are $\frac{11}{4}$, 11 to 4, and 11 : 4.

b. $\frac{\text{Number of hits}}{\text{Number of shots}} = \frac{44}{60} = \frac{11}{15}$

Three ways to write the ratio are $\frac{11}{15}$, 11 to 15, and 11 : 15.

Review Help

For help with simplifying fractions, see p. 182.

Checkpoint

1. Using the archery information above, compare the number of misses to the number of shots using a ratio. Write the ratio in three ways.

$\frac{4}{15}$, 4 to 15, 4 : 15

NCTM CURRICULUM STANDARDS
Standard 1: Understand ways of representing numbers
Standard 4: Understand the units of measurement
Standard 6: Solve problems in math and other contexts

1 PLAN

Skill Check

Simplify.

1. $\frac{750}{1000}$ **$\frac{3}{4}$**
2. $\frac{210}{315}$ **$\frac{2}{3}$**
3. $\frac{94}{188}$ **$\frac{1}{2}$**
4. $\frac{156}{416}$ **$\frac{3}{8}$**

Lesson Objective

Find ratios and unit rates.

Pacing

Suggested Number of Days
Basic Course: 2 days
Average Course: 2 days
Advanced Course: 2 days
Block: 1 block

Teaching Resources

For a complete list of Teaching Resources, see page 266B.

Transparency

Warm-Up Exercises for this lesson are available on a transparency.

2 TEACH

Motivating the Lesson

Ask students to name sports in which an athlete's success is described in terms of his or her number of successes at some task. Invite students to bring data to class that can be used to find ratios.

TIPS *for* NEW TEACHERS

It may be necessary to refresh students' knowledge of unit analysis before discussing Example 5, where common units are canceled. See Tips for New Teachers in the *Chapter 6 Resource Book*.

Extra Examples

Example 1 Carmen tosses a foam ball at her wastebasket. Out of 40 tosses, she hits the basket 22 times and misses it 18 times. Write the ratio in three ways.

a. The number of hits to the number of misses $\frac{11}{9}$, **11 to 9, 11 : 9**

b. The number of misses to the number of tosses $\frac{9}{20}$, **9 to 20, 9 : 20**

Example 2 The table shows the amount and years of growth of three snakes at a zoo. Order the snakes in the table from the greatest growth per year to the least. **Topaz, Sylvia, Louise**

Snake	Growth (ft)	Years of growth
Louise	4	12
Sylvia	2.5	5
Topaz	2.5	3

Example 3 In one hour, 4 club members assemble 320 newsletters. What is their assembly rate per person? **80 newsletters per person**

Differentiating Instruction

Advanced Students Invite students to create rate problems on subjects that interest them. For example, students who listen to the radio could write a rate problem about the ratio of songs to commercials on their favorite station. Have students exchange problems and solve them, or post some of them on a bulletin board for all students to solve.

Comparing Ratios To compare two ratios, you can write both ratios as fractions or as decimals. Two ratios are called **equivalent ratios** when they have the same value.

Example 2 *Comparing and Ordering Ratios*

Biology The ratio comparing the length of a bird's wings to the average width of the bird's wings is the bird's *aspect ratio*. Order the birds in the table from the greatest aspect ratio to the least.

Bird	Wing length (cm)	Average wing width (cm)
White-tailed eagle	209	30
European jay	47	12
Black-headed gull	83	8

Solution

Write each ratio as a fraction. Then use a calculator to write each fraction as a decimal. Round to the nearest hundredth and compare the decimals.

White-tailed eagle: $\frac{\text{Wing length}}{\text{Wing width}} = \frac{209}{30} \approx 6.97$

European jay: $\frac{\text{Wing length}}{\text{Wing width}} = \frac{47}{12} \approx 3.92$

Black-headed gull: $\frac{\text{Wing length}}{\text{Wing width}} = \frac{83}{8} \approx 10.38$

Answer The gull's aspect ratio of 10.38 is the greatest. The eagle's aspect ratio of 6.97 is the next greatest. The jay's aspect ratio of 3.92 is the least.

In the **Real World**

Biology Birds with high aspect ratios are better suited for gliding over long distances, while birds with low aspect ratios have adapted for rapid takeoffs and maneuverability. Which bird in Example 2 is best suited for gliding over long distances? **black-headed gull**

Rates A rate is a ratio of two quantities measured in different units. A *unit rate* is a rate that has a denominator of 1 when expressed in fraction form. Unit rates are often expressed using the word *per*, which means "for every."

Example 3 *Finding a Unit Rate*

Party You host a party for 12 people. The food and drinks for the party cost $66. What is the cost per person?

Solution

First, write a rate comparing the total cost of the party to the number of people at the party. Then rewrite the rate so the denominator is 1.

$\frac{\$66}{12\text{ people}} = \frac{\$66 \div 12}{12\text{ people} \div 12}$ **Divide numerator and denominator by 12.**

$= \frac{\$5.50}{1\text{ person}}$ **Simplify.**

Answer The cost of food and drinks is $5.50 per person.

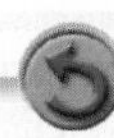

Review *Help*

For help with using conversion factors, see p. 65.

Example 4 *Writing an Equivalent Rate*

Jet A jet flies 540 miles per hour. Write its rate in miles per minute.

Solution

To convert from miles per hour to miles per minute, multiply the rate by a conversion factor. There are 60 minutes in 1 hour, so $\frac{1\text{ h}}{60\text{ min}} = 1$.

$\frac{540\text{ mi}}{1\text{ h}} = \frac{540\text{ mi}}{1\text{ h}} \cdot \frac{1\text{ h}}{60\text{ min}}$ **Multiply rate by conversion factor.**

$= \frac{\overset{9}{\cancel{540}}\text{ mi}}{1\cancel{\text{h}}} \cdot \frac{1\cancel{\text{h}}}{\underset{1}{\cancel{60}}\text{ min}}$ **Divide out common factor and unit.**

$= \frac{9\text{ mi}}{1\text{ min}}$ **Simplify.**

Answer The jet travels at a rate of 9 miles per minute.

Example 5 *Using Equivalent Rates*

Robots Engineers designed a miniature robot that can crawl through pipes and vents that humans can't access. The robot travels 1 inch in 3 seconds. How many feet does the robot travel in 4 minutes?

Solution

1 Express the robot's rate in inches per minute.

$\frac{1\text{ in.}}{3\text{ sec}} = \frac{1\text{ in.}}{\underset{1}{\cancel{3}}\cancel{\text{sec}}} \cdot \frac{\overset{20}{\cancel{60}}\cancel{\text{sec}}}{1\text{ min}}$ **Multiply by conversion factor. Divide out common factor and unit.**

$= \frac{20\text{ in.}}{\text{min}}$ **Simplify.**

2 Find the distance (in feet) that the robot can travel in 4 minutes.

Distance = Rate • Time **Write formula for distance.**

$= \frac{20\text{ in.}}{\cancel{\text{min}}} \cdot 4\cancel{\text{ min}}$ **Substitute values. Divide out common unit.**

$= 80\text{ in.}$ **Multiply.**

$= \overset{20}{\cancel{80}}\cancel{\text{ in.}} \cdot \frac{1\text{ ft}}{\underset{3}{\cancel{12}}\cancel{\text{ in.}}}$ **Multiply by conversion factor. Divide out common factor and unit.**

$= 6\frac{2}{3}\text{ ft}$ **Simplify.**

Answer The robot travels $6\frac{2}{3}$ feet in 4 minutes.

The miniature robot is 0.25 cubic inch in volume and weighs less than 1 ounce.

 ***Checkpoint***

Write the equivalent rate.

2. $\frac{5\text{ cm}}{1\text{ min}} = \frac{?\text{ cm}}{1\text{ h}}$ **300** **3.** $\frac{5\text{ m}}{1\text{ sec}} = \frac{?\text{ m}}{1\text{ h}}$ **18,000** **4.** $\frac{3\text{ lb}}{\$1} = \frac{?\text{ oz}}{\$1}$ **48**

Extra Examples

Example 4 A car is traveling at 60 miles per hour. Write its rate in feet per second. **88 ft/sec**

Example 5 An insect crawls 1 foot in 10 seconds. At this rate, how far will it crawl in 5 minutes? **30 ft**

VISUALIZE

Have students refer to a ruler as you discuss Example 5. Have them mark one inch on the ruler with a finger to represent 3 seconds. Then have them slide the finger to 2 inches as you tell them this is the distance covered in 6 seconds. Students could even count off each 3-second interval to act out the speed of the robot. Then ask students questions such as "How far does the robot travel in 30 seconds? in 60 seconds? in 2 minutes? in 4 minutes?"

COMMON ERROR

In Examples 4 and 5, watch for students who swap distance and time and write the rate incorrectly. Encourage students to write the formula $rate = \frac{distance}{time}$ in their notebooks.

CONCEPT CHECK

One adult chaperone is required to accompany every six students on a museum tour. How would you write this ratio of students to adults?

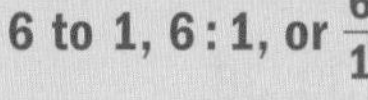

6 to 1, 6 : 1, or $\frac{6}{1}$

DAILY PUZZLER

A rope ladder is hanging over the side of a boat so that half of the ladder is under water. The tide is rising at a rate of 8 inches per hour. In how many hours will the entire ladder be under water? Explain. **Never; the boat rises with the tide.**

3 APPLY

ASSIGNMENT GUIDE

Basic Course

Day 1: EP p. 806 Exs. 17–20; pp. 272–274 Exs. 10–15, 22–27, 40–42, 48–52

Day 2: pp. 272–274 Exs. 16–21, 30–38, 43–45, 53–55

Average Course

Day 1: pp. 272–274 Exs. 10–15, 26–29, 40–43, 48–52

Day 2: pp. 272–274 Exs. 16–21, 33–39, 44–46, 53–56

Advanced Course

Day 1: pp. 272–274 Exs. 12–15, 26–29, 40–44, 50–54

Day 2: pp. 272–274 Exs. 16–19, 33–39, 45–47*, 55, 56

Block

pp. 272–274 Exs. 10–21, 26–29, 33–46, 48–56

EXTRA PRACTICE

- Student Edition, p. 808
- Chapter 6 Resource Book, pp. 10–12
- Test and Practice Generator

TRANSPARENCY

Even-numbered answers are available on transparencies.

HOMEWORK CHECK

When you review students' homework for this lesson, go over the following exercises to check understanding of key concepts.

Basic: 10, 18, 22, 30, 38

Average: 14, 20, 26, 33, 39

Advanced: 15, 19, 28, 34, 46

6.1 Exercises

More Practice, p. 808

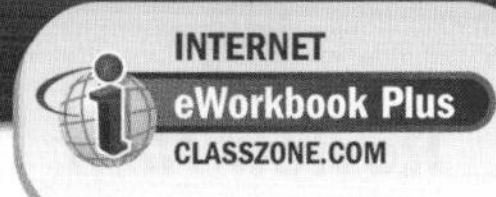

Guided Practice

Vocabulary Check

1. What is a unit rate? Give an example. See margin.
2. Write the ratio 8 to 5 in two other ways. $\frac{8}{5}$, 8 : 5

Skill Check

Tell whether the ratio is in simplest form. If not, write it in simplest form. Then write the ratio in two other ways.

3. 8 to 6 — no; 4 to 3; $\frac{4}{3}$, 4 : 3
4. 7 to 26 — yes; $\frac{7}{26}$, 7 : 26
5. 39 : 13 — no; 3 : 1; $\frac{3}{1}$, 3 to 1
6. 120 : 64 — no; 15 : 8; $\frac{15}{8}$, 15 to 8

Order the ratios from least to greatest. 7–8. See margin.

7. 2 to 9, 1 : 7, $\frac{7}{28}$, 2 to 6, $\frac{3}{10}$
8. 1 to 3, $\frac{2}{8}$, 5 : 18, 7 to 20, $\frac{9}{25}$

Guided Problem Solving

9. **Roses** Three decorators purchased bouquets of roses. Decorator A paid $120 for 5 bouquets that contained 25 roses each. Decorator B paid $204 for 20 bouquets that contained 12 roses each. Decorator C paid $180 for 40 bouquets that contained 6 roses each. Which decorator paid the least amount per rose?
   1. Find the total number of roses each decorator bought. decorator A: 125 roses, decorator B: 240 roses, decorator C: 240 roses
   2. Find the price per rose for each decorator. decorator A: $.96, decorator B: $.85, decorator C: $.75
   3. Compare the unit prices to determine which decorator paid the least per rose. decorator C

1. *Sample answer:* A unit rate is a ratio of two quantities that have different units for which the denominator is 1 when expressed in fraction form; $\frac{\$5.20}{1 \text{ lb}}$.

7. 1 : 7, 2 to 9, $\frac{7}{28}$, $\frac{3}{10}$, 2 to 6

8. $\frac{2}{8}$, 5 : 18, 1 to 3, 7 to 20, $\frac{9}{25}$

22. $\frac{35 \text{ words}}{1 \text{ min}}$

23. $\frac{\$23}{1 \text{ share}}$

24. $\frac{32 \text{ oz}}{1 \text{ serving}}$

25. $\frac{14 \text{ mi}}{1 \text{ h}}$

26. $\frac{\$80}{1 \text{ person}}$

Practice and Problem Solving

Homework Help

Example	Exercises
1	10–17, 36, 41
2	18–21, 40
3	22–29, 37, 39, 45
4	30–35, 45
5	38, 39, 46

Online Resources CLASSZONE.COM
- More Examples
- eTutorial Plus

Tell whether the ratio is in simplest form. If not, write it in simplest form. Then write the ratio in two other ways.

A

10. 9 to 12 — no; 3 to 4; $\frac{3}{4}$, 3 : 4
11. 4 : 5 — yes; $\frac{4}{5}$, 4 to 5
12. $\frac{15}{3}$ — no; $\frac{5}{1}$; 5 to 1, 5 : 1
13. $\frac{50}{6}$ — no; $\frac{25}{3}$; 25 to 3, 25 : 3
14. 63 : 18 — no; 7 : 2; $\frac{7}{2}$, 7 to 2
15. 24 : 8 — no; 3:1; $\frac{3}{1}$, 3 to 1
16. 64 to 3 — yes; $\frac{64}{3}$, 64 : 3
17. 28 to 10 — no; 14 to 5; $\frac{14}{5}$, 14 : 5

Order the ratios from least to greatest.

18. $\frac{4}{2}$, 11 to 2, 22 : 3, $\frac{30}{4}$, 36 : 5 — $\frac{4}{2}$, 11 to 2, 36 : 5, 22 : 3, $\frac{30}{4}$
19. $\frac{15}{4}$, 19 to 5, $\frac{53}{15}$, 4 : 1, 18 to 6 — 18 to 6, $\frac{53}{15}$, $\frac{15}{4}$, 19 to 5, 4 : 1
20. 7 : 11, 8 : 12, 6 : 10, $\frac{1}{2}$, 7 : 4 — $\frac{1}{2}$, 6 : 10, 7 : 11, 8 : 12, 7 : 4
21. $\frac{22}{4}$, 65 : 12, 9 : 2, $\frac{100}{19}$, 5 : 1 — 9 : 2, 5 : 1, $\frac{100}{19}$, 65 : 12, $\frac{22}{4}$

Find the unit rate. 22–29. See margin.

22. $\frac{140 \text{ words}}{4 \text{ min}}$
23. $\frac{\$161}{7 \text{ shares}}$
24. $\frac{80 \text{ oz}}{2.5 \text{ servings}}$
25. $\frac{70 \text{ mi}}{5 \text{ h}}$
26. $\frac{\$320}{4 \text{ people}}$
27. $\frac{26 \text{ points}}{3 \text{ quarters}}$
28. $\frac{24 \text{ muffins}}{\$15}$
29. $\frac{25 \text{ wins}}{40 \text{ games}}$

Write the equivalent rate.

30. $\frac{15 \text{ mi}}{1 \text{ h}} = \frac{? \text{ ft}}{1 \text{ h}}$ **79,200** **31.** $\frac{300 \text{ mi}}{20 \text{ sec}} = \frac{? \text{ mi}}{1 \text{ min}}$ **900** **32.** $\frac{390 \text{ m}}{1 \text{ min}} = \frac{? \text{ m}}{1 \text{ h}}$ **23,400**

33. $\frac{\$33{,}000}{1 \text{ year}} = \frac{? \text{ dollars}}{1 \text{ month}}$ **2750** **34.** $\frac{\$43}{1 \text{ day}} = \frac{? \text{ dollars}}{1 \text{ week}}$ **301** **35.** $\frac{45 \text{ min}}{2 \text{ mi}} = \frac{? \text{ h}}{1 \text{ mi}}$ **0.375, or $\frac{3}{8}$**

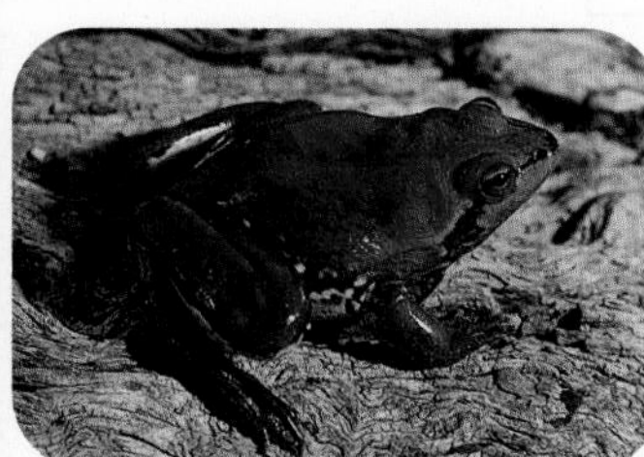

36. Nature As a tadpole, the paradoxical frog is 24 centimeters long. As an adult, the frog is 6 centimeters long.

a. Write the ratio of the tadpole's length to the adult frog's length. $\frac{4}{1}$

b. Something is called *paradoxical* if it seems impossible. What is paradoxical about the frog? Explain using your answer to part (a). **See margin.**

37. Estimate A store sells 16 cookies for \$11.88. Estimate the cost per cookie. Explain how you made your estimate. **See margin.**

38. Guitar You want to save all the money you earn to buy a guitar that costs \$400. You earn \$9 per hour and plan to work 15 hours each week for the next 3 weeks. Will you earn enough money in that time to buy the guitar? **yes**

39. Extended Problem Solving Your family used two full tanks of gasoline on a road trip. Your car drives about 25 miles per gallon, and the tank holds 12 gallons of gasoline.

a. Find the approximate number of gallons of gasoline used on the trip. **24 gal**

b. Find the approximate number of miles you drove on the trip. **600 mi**

c. Calculate Assume gasoline costs \$1.50 per gallon. How much did you spend per mile on gasoline? **\$.06**

d. Apply You have \$20 to spend on gasoline for another trip. The trip is 350 miles. You spend the same amount per mile on gasoline as on the first trip. Do you have enough money for gasoline? Explain.

40. Drinks A restaurant sells drinks in 3 sizes of cups: small, medium, and large. The small cup costs \$.89 and holds 9 ounces. The medium cup costs \$1.29 and holds 12 ounces. The large cup costs \$1.59 and holds 15 ounces. Which size cup costs the least per ounce? **the small cup**

B **41. Aquarium** An aquarium has twice as many angelfish as goldfish. The aquarium contains only angelfish and goldfish. Write a ratio for the number of goldfish to the total number of fish. $\frac{1}{3}$

42. Geometry For each rectangle below, the measure of the longer side is the length, and the measure of the shorter side is the width.

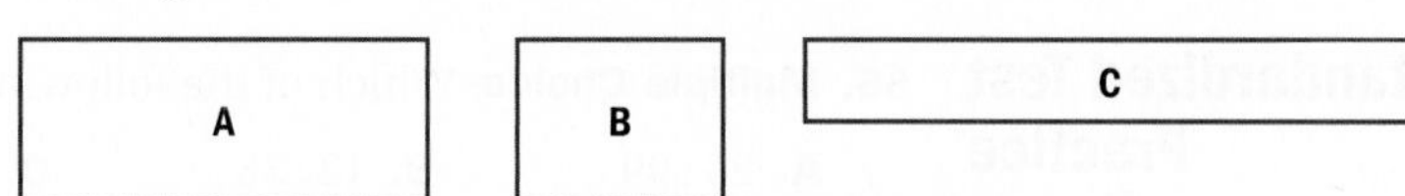

a. Which rectangle has the greatest ratio of length to width? **rectangle C**

b. For which rectangle is the ratio of length to width closest to 1 : 1? **rectangle B**

c. Critical Thinking The ratio of another rectangle's length to its width is 1 : 1. What type of rectangle is it? **a square**

36b. ***Sample answer:*** **That the adult frog is smaller than the tadpole; since the ratio is $\frac{4}{1}$, it means the tadpole is 4 times as big as the adult frog, which seems impossible.**

37. ***Sample answer:*** **About \$.75 per cookie; I rounded \$11.88 to \$12 and \$12 divided by 16 cookies is \$0.75.**

39d. No. ***Sample answer:*** **At a rate of \$.06 per mile, gasoline for 350 miles will cost $350 \text{ mi} \cdot \frac{\$.06}{1 \text{ mi}} = \$21$.**

Teaching Tip

In Exercises 30–35, stress that the first step is to identify the change in measurement from the ratio on the left to the ratio on the right. In Exercise 39c, some students may need help seeing that the answers to parts a and b can be used to find the number of gallons of gas used per mile, and that when this rate is multiplied by the cost per gallon for the gas the result is the cost per mile.

27. $\frac{8\frac{2}{3} \text{ points}}{1 \text{ quarter}}$

28. $\frac{1\frac{3}{5} \text{ muffins}}{\$1}$

29. $\frac{\frac{5}{8} \text{ win}}{1 \text{ game}}$

4 ASSESS

ASSESSMENT RESOURCES

For more assessment resources, see:
- Assessment Book
- Test and Practice Generator

MINI-QUIZ

1. Order the ratios $\frac{26}{5}$, 17:3, 30 to 8, $\frac{50}{12}$, and 4 : 1 from least to greatest. **30 to 8, 4 : 1, $\frac{50}{12}$, $\frac{26}{5}$, 17 : 3**
2. Donald feeds his dog 35 dog treats in 7 days. Find the unit rate. **$\frac{5 \text{ treats}}{1 \text{ day}}$**

Write the equivalent rate.

3. $\frac{\$20}{1 \text{ h}} = \frac{? \text{ dollars}}{42 \text{ h}}$ **840**
4. $\frac{475 \text{ m}}{5 \text{ sec}} = \frac{? \text{ m}}{1 \text{ sec}}$ **95**
5. **Challenge** If you travel at 30 miles per hour, how many seconds will it take you to travel 1 mile? **120 sec**

5 FOLLOW-UP

DIAGNOSIS/REMEDIATION

- Study Guide in Chapter 6 Resource Book, pp. 13–14
- Tutor Place, Ratio, Proportion, and Percent Cards 1, 2
- eTutorial Plus Online
- Extra Practice, p. 808
- Lesson Practice in Chapter 6 Resource Book, pp. 10–12

ENGLISH LEARNER SUPPORT

- Spanish Study Guide
- Multi-Language Visual Glossary
- Chapter Audio Summaries CDs

CHALLENGE

- Challenge Practice in Chapter 6 Resource Book, p. 15
- Teacher's Edition, p. 266F

Find the ratio of the area of the shaded region to the area of the unshaded region. The figures are composed of squares and triangles.

43. $\frac{1}{1}$

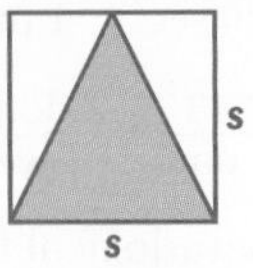

44. $\frac{1}{3}$

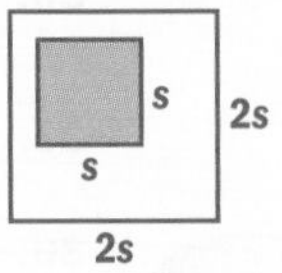

45. Running In 2002, Khalid Khannouchi set the world record for a marathon when he ran 26.2 miles in 2 hours, 5 minutes, and 38 seconds. Round your answers to the nearest tenth.

a. Find Khannouchi's rate in miles per hour. **12.5 mi/h**

b. Find Khannouchi's rate in miles per minute. **0.2 mi/min**

c. Find Khannouchi's rate in feet per minute. **1101.1 ft/min**

46. Earth Science Due to the movement of Earth's landmasses, Los Angeles and other portions of coastal Southern California are moving northwest toward San Francisco at an average rate of 46 millimeters per year.

a. How many meters per year does Los Angeles move? **0.046 m/y**

b. How many meters per century does Los Angeles move? **4.6 m/century**

c. In 2000, San Francisco was 554,000 meters from Los Angeles. In about how many years will Los Angeles be where San Francisco was in 2000? **about 12,043,500 y**

C **47. Challenge** If you travel 55 miles per hour, how many minutes will it take you to travel 1 mile? **$1\frac{1}{11}$ min, or about 1 min, 5.5 sec**

Mixed Review

Find the product. *(Lesson 5.4)*

48. $\frac{3}{8} \cdot \left(\frac{6}{15}\right)$ **$\frac{3}{20}$**

49. $-\frac{6}{21} \cdot \left(\frac{14}{54}\right)$ **$-\frac{2}{27}$**

50. $-2\frac{3}{4} \cdot \left(-3\frac{5}{9}\right)$ **$9\frac{7}{9}$**

51. Stamps You have 15 stamps from Canada in your stamp collection. These stamps make up $\frac{3}{11}$ of your entire collection. The rest of the stamps are from the U.S. How many stamps are in your collection? How many stamps from the U.S. do you have? *(Lesson 5.6)* **55 stamps; 40 stamps**

Solve the inequality. *(Lesson 5.7)*

52. $\frac{2}{3}x + 9 \le \frac{17}{2}$ **$x \le -\frac{3}{4}$**

53. $\frac{1}{5}y + 14 \le \frac{13}{5}$ **$y \le -57$**

54. $-\frac{5}{9}x + 1 > \frac{22}{27}$ **$x < \frac{1}{3}$**

Standardized Test Practice

55. Multiple Choice Which of the following ratios is greater than 5 : 12? **C**

A. 25 : 99 **B.** 12 : 36 **C.** 4 : 8 **D.** 5 : 13

56. Short Response One afternoon, you read 24 pages of a novel in 30 minutes. Another afternoon, you read 33 pages in 45 minutes. How can you decide whether you read at the same rate or at different rates on the two afternoons? On which afternoon did you read at a faster rate? Explain. **See margin.**

56. *Sample answer:* Write a rate for each day as a fraction, and then write the fractions in decimal form and compare them; the first afternoon. The rate for the first afternoon is $\frac{24 \text{ pages}}{30 \text{ minutes}}$ = 0.8 pages per minute. The rate for the second afternoon is $\frac{33 \text{ pages}}{45 \text{ minutes}} \approx$ 0.73 pages per minute. Since 0.8 > 0.73, the first afternoon had the faster rate.

LESSON

6.2 Writing *and* Solving Proportions

BEFORE	Now	WHY?
You wrote and compared ratios.	You'll write and solve proportions.	So you can find the salinity of saltwater, as in Ex. 31.

Vocabulary
proportion, p. 275

Elephants Each day, an elephant eats 5 pounds of food for every 100 pounds of its body weight. How much does a 9300 pound elephant eat per day?

In Example 3, you'll see how to use a *proportion* to answer this question.

Reading *Algebra*

The proportion $\frac{2}{3} = \frac{8}{12}$ is read "2 is to 3 as 8 is to 12."

Proportions

Words A **proportion** is an equation that states that two ratios are equal.

Numbers $\frac{2}{3} = \frac{8}{12}$

Algebra $\frac{a}{b} = \frac{c}{d}$, where $b \neq 0$ and $d \neq 0$

Equivalent Ratios If one of the numbers in a proportion is unknown, you can solve the proportion to find the unknown number. One way to solve a proportion is to use mental math to find an equivalent ratio.

Example 1 *Solving a Proportion Using Equivalent Ratios*

Solve the proportion $\frac{5}{6} = \frac{x}{18}$.

1) Compare denominators.

$\frac{5}{6} \xrightarrow{\times 3} \frac{x}{18}$

2) Find x.

$\frac{5}{6} \xrightarrow{\times 3} \frac{x}{18}$

Answer Because $5 \times 3 = 15$, $x = 15$.

Use equivalent ratios to solve the proportion.

1. $\frac{2}{7} = \frac{x}{21}$ 6
2. $\frac{3}{8} = \frac{x}{32}$ 12
3. $\frac{x}{2} = \frac{20}{10}$ 4
4. $\frac{x}{48} = \frac{6}{12}$ 24

NCTM CURRICULUM STANDARDS

Standard 2: Represent situations using algebraic symbols; Analyze situations using algebraic symbols

Standard 6: Solve problems in math and other contexts

1 PLAN

Skill Check

Simplify.

1. $\frac{18}{20}$ $\frac{9}{10}$
2. $\frac{66}{110}$ $\frac{3}{5}$
3. $\frac{182}{273}$ $\frac{2}{3}$
4. $\frac{350}{630}$ $\frac{5}{9}$

LESSON OBJECTIVE

Write and solve proportions.

PACING

Suggested Number of Days
Basic Course: 1 day
Average Course: 1 day
Advanced Course: 1 day
Block: 0.5 block with 6.3

TEACHING RESOURCES

For a complete list of Teaching Resources, see page 266B.

TRANSPARENCY

Warm-Up Exercises for this lesson are available on a transparency.

2 TEACH

MOTIVATING THE LESSON

Ask: "How is the ratio 5 to 100 written as a fraction in simplest form?" $\frac{1}{20}$ Ask: "How is this written as a decimal? as a percent?" **0.05; 5%**

TIPS *for* NEW TEACHERS

Expect some students to need additional assistance setting up proportions correctly. See Tips for New Teachers in the *Chapter 6 Resource Book*.

Extra Examples

Example 1 Solve the proportion $\frac{5}{8} = \frac{x}{72}$. **45**

Example 2 Solve the proportion $\frac{x}{98} = \frac{3}{7}$. Check your answer. **42**

COMMON ERROR

In Example 2, watch for students who examine the denominators 12 and 8 and decide that each side should be multiplied by 24, the LCM of these two numbers. Point out that multiplying each side by 12 is all that is required to isolate the variable *x*.

MULTIPLE REPRESENTATIONS

Focus students' attention on the definition of *proportions* on page 275. Point out that proportions are shown in words, numbers, and algebra. Invite students to suggest problems from different subject areas or from their lives that could be solved using proportions. Encourage students to record the different representations in their notebooks and illustrate them with some real-world examples.

Using Algebra You can use the same methods you used to solve equations to solve proportions that have a variable in the numerator.

Example 2 *Solving a Proportion Using Algebra*

Solve the proportion $\frac{x}{12} = \frac{2}{8}$. Check your answer.

$\frac{x}{12} = \frac{2}{8}$	**Write original proportion.**
$12 \cdot \frac{x}{12} = 12 \cdot \frac{2}{8}$	**Multiply each side by 12.**
$x = \frac{24}{8}$	**Simplify.**
$x = 3$	**Divide.**
✓Check $\frac{x}{12} = \frac{2}{8}$	**Write original proportion.**
$\frac{3}{12} \stackrel{?}{=} \frac{2}{8}$	**Substitute 3 for *x*.**
$\frac{1}{4} = \frac{1}{4}$ ✓	**Simplify. Solution checks.**

Checkpoint

Use algebra to solve the proportion.

5. $\frac{2}{5} = \frac{x}{25}$ 10 **6.** $\frac{3}{10} = \frac{x}{100}$ 30 **7.** $\frac{x}{9} = \frac{42}{54}$ 7 **8.** $\frac{x}{4} = \frac{13}{2}$ 26

Setting up a Proportion There are different ways to set up a proportion. Consider the following problem.

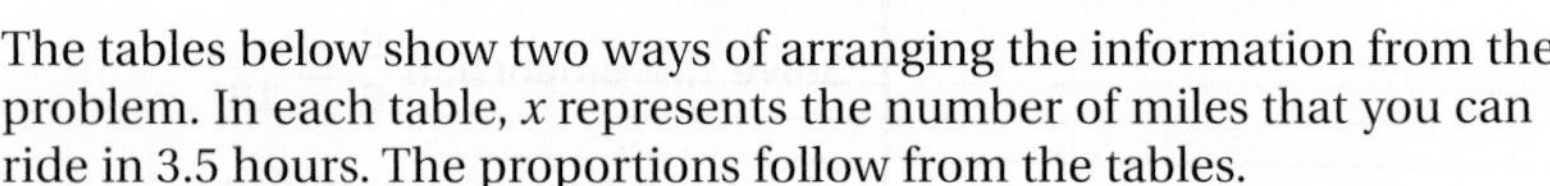

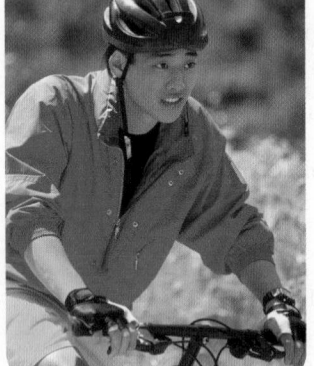

Yesterday you rode your bike 18 miles in 2.5 hours. Today you plan to ride for 3.5 hours. If you ride at the same rate as yesterday, how far will you ride?

The tables below show two ways of arranging the information from the problem. In each table, *x* represents the number of miles that you can ride in 3.5 hours. The proportions follow from the tables.

	Today	Yesterday
Miles	*x*	18
Hours	3.5	2.5

Proportion: $\frac{x}{3.5} = \frac{18}{2.5}$

	Miles	Hours
Today	*x*	3.5
Yesterday	18	2.5

Proportion: $\frac{x}{18} = \frac{3.5}{2.5}$

When writing a proportion, make sure you use comparable ratios. For example, you cannot write a proportion to compare $\frac{\text{miles}}{\text{hours}}$ and $\frac{\text{hours}}{\text{miles}}$.

Example 3 *Writing and Solving a Proportion*

Use the information on page 275 to write and solve a proportion to determine how much food an elephant that weighs 9300 pounds eats per day.

Solution

First, write a proportion involving two ratios that compare the weight of the food with the weight of the elephant.

$$\frac{5}{100} = \frac{x}{9300} \quad \begin{matrix} \leftarrow \text{Weight of food} \\ \leftarrow \text{Weight of elephant} \end{matrix}$$

Then, solve the proportion.

$$9300 \cdot \frac{5}{100} = 9300 \cdot \frac{x}{9300} \quad \textbf{Multiply each side by 9300.}$$

$$\frac{46{,}500}{100} = x \quad \textbf{Simplify.}$$

$$465 = x \quad \textbf{Divide.}$$

Answer A 9300 pound elephant eats about 465 pounds of food per day.

Checkpoint

9. Use the information given on page 275 to determine how much food a 12,500 pound elephant eats per day. **about 625 lb**

6.2 Exercises

More Practice, p. 808

Guided Practice

Vocabulary Check

1. Give an example of a proportion that uses the numbers 2, 3, 4, and 6. **See margin.**
2. Explain how to use equivalent ratios to solve the proportion $\frac{3}{2} = \frac{x}{12}$. **See margin.**

Skill Check **Solve the proportion.**

3. $\frac{1}{2} = \frac{x}{50}$ 25
4. $\frac{3}{4} = \frac{y}{24}$ 18
5. $\frac{a}{9} = \frac{21}{27}$ 7
6. $\frac{b}{5} = \frac{28}{35}$ 4

7. **Error Analysis** Describe and correct the error in writing a proportion to find the cost of 30 pencils if 12 pencils cost \$2.00. **See margin.**

   X $\frac{12}{2.00} = \frac{x}{30}$

8. **Pizza** You know that 3 pizzas are enough to feed 12 people. Write and solve a proportion to find the number of pizzas that will feed 28 people. ***Sample answer:*** $\frac{3}{12} = \frac{x}{28}$; **7 pizzas**

1. ***Sample answer:*** $\frac{2}{3} = \frac{4}{6}$, **or** $\frac{2}{4} = \frac{3}{6}$

2. ***Sample answer:*** **Compare denominators. Notice that the denominator of the fraction on the right is 6 times that of the fraction on the left. So, multiply the numerator of the fraction on the left by 6 to obtain** $x = 18$.

Teaching Tip

Before presenting Example 3, point out that there are several ways to set up a proportion which will result in the same answer. After discussing the given solution, consider solving Example 3 again using a different proportion.

Extra Examples

Example 3 During an outbreak of influenza, 2 students in Mr. Hendrick's 3rd period class were absent. There are 30 students taking this class. If the same absentee rate is valid for the entire student population of 1200 students, write and solve a proportion to determine how many students were absent from school during the outbreak. ***Sample answer:*** $\frac{2}{30} = \frac{x}{1200}$; **80 students**

Concept Check

An Internet store charges \$8 to ship a \$100 book order. How do you set up a proportion that can be used to find the shipping charge on a \$500 book order? ***Sample answer:*** $\frac{8}{100} = \frac{x}{500}$

Daily Puzzler

Write an expression whose value is 5, using each of the digits 1, 2, 3, and 4 just once. ***Sample answer:*** **1(4 + 3 − 2)**

7. ***Sample answer:*** **A proportion must use comparable ratios. Because the fraction on the left compares pencils to cost, the fraction on the right must do likewise, so it should be** $\frac{30}{x}$, **not** $\frac{x}{30}$.

3 APPLY

ASSIGNMENT GUIDE

Basic Course

Day 1: SRH p. 780 Exs. 1–4; pp. 278–279 Exs. 9–20, 25–27, 32–34, 37–49

Average Course

Day 1: pp. 278–279 Exs. 13–16, 21–35, 37–50

Advanced Course

Day 1: pp. 278–279 Exs. 15–20, 25–38*, 43–50

Block

pp. 278–279 Exs. 13–16, 21–35, 37–50 (with 6.3)

EXTRA PRACTICE

- Student Edition, p. 808
- Chapter 6 Resource Book, pp. 18–20
- Test and Practice Generator

TRANSPARENCY

Even-numbered answers are available on transparencies.

HOMEWORK CHECK

When you review students' homework for this lesson, go over the following exercises to check understanding of key concepts.

Basic: 9, 15, 17, 20, 25

Average: 14, 21, 22, 25, 32

Advanced: 15, 18, 20, 26, 33

29. ***Sample answer:*** $\frac{15}{18} = \frac{5}{6}$; **8 ways; there are 2 ways to arrange the proportion with 15 as the numerator of the first fraction,** $\frac{15}{18} = \frac{5}{6}$ **or** $\frac{15}{5} = \frac{18}{6}$. **15 is 1 of 4 numbers that could be the numerator of the first fraction, so there are 4 × 2 or 8 ways to rearrange the 4 numbers.**

Practice and Problem Solving

Homework *Help*

Example	Exercises
1	9–16
2	17–24
3	25–28, 30–34

Online Resources CLASSZONE.COM

- More Examples
- eTutorial Plus

Use equivalent ratios to solve the proportion.

A **9.** $\frac{5}{6} = \frac{x}{30}$ **25** **10.** $\frac{6}{7} = \frac{y}{49}$ **42** **11.** $\frac{a}{12} = \frac{33}{36}$ **11** **12.** $\frac{b}{14} = \frac{27}{42}$ **9**

13. $\frac{14}{3} = \frac{a}{15}$ **70** **14.** $\frac{11}{9} = \frac{y}{81}$ **99** **15.** $\frac{x}{5} = \frac{200}{25}$ **40** **16.** $\frac{b}{15} = \frac{26}{30}$ **13**

Use algebra to solve the proportion.

17. $\frac{x}{8} = \frac{35}{56}$ **5** **18.** $\frac{y}{4} = \frac{42}{28}$ **6** **19.** $\frac{a}{32} = \frac{9}{16}$ **18** **20.** $\frac{b}{45} = \frac{8}{9}$ **40**

21. $\frac{25}{60} = \frac{c}{12}$ **5** **22.** $\frac{39}{54} = \frac{d}{18}$ **13** **23.** $\frac{17}{26} = \frac{w}{52}$ **34** **24.** $\frac{3}{7} = \frac{z}{63}$ **27**

25. School Supplies At a store, 5 erasers cost $2.50. How many erasers can you buy for $7.50? **15 erasers**

26. Driving You are driving 2760 miles across the country. During the first 3 days of your trip, you drive 1380 miles. If you continue to drive at the same rate each day, how many days will the entire trip take? **6 days**

27. Lacrosse Last season, a lacrosse player scored 41 goals in 15 games. So far this season, the player has scored 24 goals in 9 games.

a. Does the player have a greater number of goals per game this season compared with last season? **no**

b. Suppose the player plays in as many games this season as last season and continues to score at this season's rate. Write and solve a proportion to find the number of goals the player will score this season. ***Sample proportion:*** $\frac{24}{9} = \frac{x}{15}$; **40 goals**

28. Exchange Rates In 2003, the exchange rate between the United States and Canada was about 3 Canadian dollars to 2 U.S. dollars. Cindy had 78 U.S. dollars to exchange when she visited Canada. How many Canadian dollars could she get in exchange? **117 Canadian dollars**

29. *Writing* Write a proportion without using any variables. In how many different ways can you rearrange the four numbers so that ratios are still equivalent? Explain your answer. **See margin.**

B **30. Population Density** A region's population density is the number of people per square mile. The tiny country of Monaco has the highest population density in the world, with 33,000 people living in an area of 0.75 square mile. The state of New York has a population of about 19,000,000 people living in an area of about 47,000 square miles. Use a calculator to complete the following. Round your answers to the nearest whole number.

a. Write and solve a proportion to find how many people would live in Monaco if Monaco had the population density of New York.

b. Write and solve a proportion to find how many people would live in New York if New York had the population density of Monaco. ***Sample proportion:*** $\frac{33,000}{0.75} = \frac{x}{47,000}$; **2,068,000,000 people**

30a. ***Sample proportion:*** $\frac{19,000,000}{47,000} = \frac{x}{0.75}$; **303 people**

31. **Saltwater** The salinity of saltwater is the ratio of the mass of the salt in the water to the mass of the salt and fresh water mixed together.

  a. A sample of saltwater is made by mixing 3 grams of salt with 75 grams of water. Find the salinity of the sample. **1 : 26**

  b. A sample of saltwater has a salinity of 3 : 45. The sample has a mass of 30 kilograms. How much salt is in the sample? **2 kg**

32. **Jewel Cases** Store A sells 10 CD jewel cases for \$9. Store B sells 15 CD jewel cases for \$12. How much money will you save if you buy 30 CD jewel cases at the store with the lower unit price? **\$3**

33. **Knitting** You are knitting an afghan with red, green, and blue stripes. There are equal numbers of red and blue stripes. There are twice as many green stripes as there are red stripes. The afghan has 20 stripes.

  a. Find the ratio of the number of red stripes to the total number of stripes on the afghan. $\frac{1}{4}$

  b. How many red stripes are there on the afghan? **5 red stripes**

34. **Election** In an election, the winning candidate received 3 votes for every vote the opponent received. Altogether, 1000 votes were cast. How many votes did the winner receive? **750 votes**

C 35. **Critical Thinking** In the proportion $\frac{10}{x} = \frac{y}{6}$, how does the value of y change as the value of x increases? **It decreases.**

36. **Challenge** A painter is making a specific shade of green that requires 3 parts of yellow paint for every 4 parts of blue paint. To make the mixture, the painter uses 9 ounces of yellow paint and 2 tubes of blue paint. How many ounces are in each tube of blue paint? **6 oz**

Mixed Review

Simplify the expression. *(Lesson 4.5)*

37. $\frac{8m^3 \cdot 9m^4}{3m^5}$ **$24m^2$** 38. $\frac{7n^3 \cdot n^2}{n^4}$ **$7n$** 39. $\frac{5a^2 \cdot 2a^2}{10a^4}$ **1** 40. $\frac{2x^4 \cdot x^3}{6x^6}$ **$\frac{x}{3}$**

Find the quotient. *(Lesson 5.5)*

41. $-\frac{3}{20} \div \frac{4}{5}$ **$-\frac{3}{16}$** 42. $\frac{15}{16} \div \left(-\frac{5}{8}\right)$ **$-1\frac{1}{2}$** 43. $\frac{11}{42} \div \frac{4}{7}$ **$\frac{11}{24}$** 44. $\frac{25}{36} \div \frac{8}{9}$ **$\frac{25}{32}$**

Solve the inequality. *(Lesson 5.7)*

45. $\frac{3}{8}z - \frac{4}{5} > \frac{9}{10}$ **$z > 4\frac{8}{15}$** 46. $\frac{1}{3} < \frac{6}{7}y - \frac{7}{15}$ **$y > \frac{14}{15}$** 47. $\frac{1}{3} \geq \frac{7}{12}x - \frac{11}{15}$ **$x \leq 1\frac{29}{35}$** 48. $-\frac{2}{5}x + \frac{6}{5} \geq \frac{1}{10}$ **$x \leq 2\frac{3}{4}$**

Standardized Test Practice

49. **Multiple Choice** Solve the proportion $\frac{48}{28} = \frac{x}{63}$. **C**

  A. $5\frac{1}{3}$ **B.** 96 **C.** 108 **D.** 432

50. **Short Response** A 12 ounce box of pasta costs \$.99. A 2 pound box costs \$2.09. Which box has the lower price per ounce? You buy 6 pounds of pasta. How much money do you save if you buy pasta in the box with the lower price per ounce? Explain.

50. The 2 pound box; \$1.65. ***Sample answer:*** **The 12 ounce box costs \$0.0825 per ounce, while the 2 pound box costs \$0.0653125 per ounce. Six pounds is 96 ounces, so you save 96(0.0825 − 0.0653125) = \$1.65.**

4 ASSESS

Assessment Resources

For more assessment resources, see:
- Assessment Book
- Test and Practice Generator

Mini-Quiz

Use equivalent ratios to solve the proportion.

1. $\frac{7}{8} = \frac{a}{40}$ **35** 2. $\frac{3}{4} = \frac{d}{88}$ **66**

Use algebra to solve the proportion.

3. $\frac{40}{72} = \frac{f}{18}$ **10** 4. $\frac{g}{15} = \frac{78}{90}$ **13**

5. **Challenge** Tanika is making syrup for the hummingbird feeders at a bird sanctuary. The recipe in her bird book calls for $\frac{1}{4}$ cup of sugar for each cup of water. She has 5 cups of sugar. How much water should she add to the sugar? **20 c**

5 FOLLOW-UP

Diagnosis/Remediation

- Study Guide in Chapter 6 Resource Book, pp. 21–22
- Tutor Place, Ratio, Proportion, and Percent Card 3, Algebra Card 10
- eTutorial Plus Online
- Extra Practice, p. 808
- Lesson Practice in Chapter 6 Resource Book, pp. 18–20

English Learner Support

- Spanish Study Guide
- Multi-Language Visual Glossary
- Chapter Audio Summaries CDs

Challenge

- Challenge Practice in Chapter 6 Resource Book, p. 23
- Teacher's Edition, p. 266F

1 PLAN

Skill Check

1. $36 \cdot 7 = \underline{?}$ 252
2. $61 \cdot 4 = \underline{?}$ 244
3. $83 \cdot 5 = \underline{?}$ 415
4. $47 \cdot 6 = \underline{?}$ 282

Lesson Objective

Solve proportions using cross products.

Pacing

Suggested Number of Days
Basic Course: 1 day
Average Course: 1 day
Advanced Course: 1 day
Block: 0.5 block with 6.2

Teaching Resources

For a complete list of Teaching Resources, see page 266B.

Transparency

Warm-Up Exercises for this lesson are available on a transparency.

2 TEACH

Motivating the Lesson

Write the proportion $\frac{2}{5} = \frac{8}{20}$ on the board and then superimpose a large X over it in a different color to reinforce the definition of a cross product. Emphasize this visual connection to the word "cross" in the term *cross product*.

LESSON **6.3**

Solving Proportions Using Cross Products

Vocabulary
cross product, p. 280

BEFORE You solved simple proportions.

Now You'll solve proportions using cross products.

WHY? So you can find the mass of gold in a ring, as in Ex. 35.

Every pair of ratios has two *cross products*. A **cross product** of two ratios is the product of the numerator of one ratio and the denominator of the other ratio.

Ratios: $\frac{3}{5}, \frac{6}{10}$ $\frac{2}{3}, \frac{6}{11}$

Cross products: $3 \cdot 10$ $5 \cdot 6$ $2 \cdot 11$ $3 \cdot 6$

Notice that for the ratios $\frac{3}{5}$ and $\frac{6}{10}$, the ratios are equal and their cross products are also equal. For the ratios $\frac{2}{3}$ and $\frac{6}{11}$, the ratios are not equal, and neither are their cross products.

You can use cross products to tell whether two ratios form a proportion. If the cross products are equal, then the ratios form a proportion.

Example 1 Determining if Ratios Form a Proportion

Tell whether the ratios form a proportion.

a. $\frac{9}{51}, \frac{6}{34}$ **b.** $\frac{12}{20}, \frac{32}{50}$

Solution

a.

$\frac{9}{51} \stackrel{?}{=} \frac{6}{34}$	**Write proportion.**
$9 \cdot 34 \stackrel{?}{=} 51 \cdot 6$	**Form cross products.**
$306 = 306$	**Multiply.**

Answer The ratios form a proportion.

b.

$\frac{12}{20} \stackrel{?}{=} \frac{32}{50}$	**Write proportion.**
$12 \cdot 50 \stackrel{?}{=} 20 \cdot 32$	**Form cross products.**
$600 \neq 640$	**Multiply.**

Answer The ratios do not form a proportion.

NCTM CURRICULUM STANDARDS
Standard 2: Represent situations using algebraic symbols; Analyze situations using algebraic symbols
Standard 6: Solve problems in math and other contexts

Checkpoint

Tell whether the ratios form a proportion.

1. $\frac{6}{14}, \frac{3}{7}$ yes
2. $\frac{14}{35}, \frac{8}{20}$ yes
3. $\frac{6}{11}, \frac{9}{16}$ no
4. $\frac{15}{24}, \frac{10}{16}$ yes

Reading *Algebra*

The sequence of steps shown at the right constitutes a *proof*, or convincing argument, for the cross products property. The process of starting with one or more given facts, such as $\frac{a}{b} = \frac{c}{d}$, and using rules, definitions, or properties to reach a conclusion, such as $ad = cb$, is called *deductive reasoning*.

You can use the multiplication property of equality to demonstrate an important property about the cross products of a proportion.

$\frac{a}{b} = \frac{c}{d}$	**Given**
$\frac{a}{\not b_1} \cdot \frac{{}^1\not b d}{1} = \frac{c}{\not d_1} \cdot \frac{b \not d^1}{1}$	**Multiply each side by *bd*. Divide out common factors.**
$ad = cb$	**Simplify.**

This result proves the following property.

Cross Products Property

Words The cross products of a proportion are equal.

Numbers Given that $\frac{2}{5} = \frac{6}{15}$, you know that $2 \cdot 15 = 5 \cdot 6$.

Algebra If $\frac{a}{b} = \frac{c}{d}$, where $b \neq 0$ and $d \neq 0$, then $ad = bc$.

You can use the cross products property to solve proportions.

In the Real World

Hair The average adult human head has an area of about 120 square inches and contains about 100,000 hairs. How many hairs per square inch does the average adult human have? **about 830 hairs**

Example 2 *Writing and Solving a Proportion*

Hair Growth Human hair grows about 0.7 centimeter in 2 weeks. How long does hair take to grow 14 centimeters?

Solution

$\frac{0.7}{2} = \frac{14}{x}$	← **Length of hair grown** / ← **Number of weeks**
$0.7 \cdot x = 2 \cdot 14$	**Cross products property**
$0.7x = 28$	**Multiply.**
$\frac{0.7x}{0.7} = \frac{28}{0.7}$	**Divide each side by 0.7.**
$x = 40$	**Simplify.**

Answer Hair takes about 40 weeks to grow 14 centimeters.

Checkpoint

Use the cross products property to solve the proportion.

5. $\frac{18}{42} = \frac{3}{t}$ 7
6. $\frac{16}{p} = \frac{10}{45}$ 72
7. $\frac{9}{b} = \frac{1.5}{7}$ 42
8. $\frac{0.4}{6} = \frac{18}{z}$ 270

TIPS *for* NEW TEACHERS

While discussing the algebraic form of the cross products property stated on page 281, ask students why *b* and *d* cannot be zero. See Tips for New Teachers in the *Chapter 6 Resource Book*.

Extra Examples

Example 1 Tell whether the ratios form a proportion.

a. $\frac{11}{12}, \frac{67}{72}$ **no**

b. $\frac{10}{75}, \frac{2}{15}$ **yes**

Example 2 The worms in Janet's compost bin can break down about 0.25 pound of food scraps per day. How long would it take the worms to break down 8 pounds of food scraps? **32 days**

Differentiating Instruction

Alternative Teaching Strategy
In Example 1, show students how simplifying the ratios before multiplying can make the multiplication easier and reduce the chance of making an error. In part b for instance, instead of multiplying $12 \cdot 50$ and $32 \cdot 20$, the ratios can be reduced to $\frac{3}{5}$ and $\frac{16}{25}$ which yield the cross products $3 \cdot 25$ and $16 \cdot 5$.

Teaching Tip

Before presenting Example 2, solve a proportion using the method shown in the previous lesson. Then solve the proportion using the cross products property to demonstrate the difference between the two methods.

NOTETAKING

Have students copy the summary on this page into their notebooks. As they are doing this, point out that the same proportion is being solved using each method. Ask students which method they prefer, or which method they would use for proportions containing values that are more difficult to multiply and divide mentally.

CONCEPT CHECK

How do you determine that two ratios do *not* form a proportion? **If the cross products of the ratios are not equal, they do not form a proportion.**

DAILY PUZZLER

Calvin has 10 coins in his hand worth \$1.19, but he cannot make change for a nickel, a dime, a quarter, a half dollar, or a dollar. What coins does he have in his hand? **4 pennies, 4 dimes, 1 quarter, and 1 half dollar**

Note Worthy

The main ideas from Lessons 6.2 and 6.3 are summarized at the right. You may want to include a summary like this one in your notes.

SUMMARY Methods for Solving a Proportion

To solve the proportion $\frac{5}{12} = \frac{x}{36}$, use one of the following:

Equivalent ratios

$\frac{5}{12} \xrightarrow{\times 3} \frac{x}{36}$ $\qquad$ $\frac{5}{12} \xrightarrow{\times 3} \frac{15}{36}$

Algebra

$36 \cdot \frac{5}{12} = 36 \cdot \frac{x}{36}$ **Multiply each side by 36.**

$15 = x$ **Simplify.**

Cross products

$5 \cdot 36 = 12x$ **Cross products property**

$15 = x$ **Divide each side by 12.**

6.3 Exercises

More Practice, p. 808

INTERNET eWorkbook Plus CLASSZONE.COM

Guided Practice

Vocabulary Check

1. Find the cross products of the proportion $\frac{3}{4} = \frac{9}{12}$. **3 • 12 and 4 • 9**

2. Explain how to use cross products to determine if two ratios are equal. **See margin.**

2. *Sample answer:* **Find the cross products. If the cross products are equal, the ratios are equal.**

Skill Check **Tell whether the ratios form a proportion.**

3. $\frac{5}{8}, \frac{10}{16}$ **yes**   **4.** $\frac{9}{32}, \frac{3}{8}$ **no**   **5.** $\frac{40}{125}, \frac{8}{25}$ **yes**   **6.** $\frac{6}{9}, \frac{12}{16}$ **no**

Use the cross products property to solve the proportion.

7. $\frac{24}{36} = \frac{2}{x}$ **3**   **8.** $\frac{60}{15} = \frac{12}{y}$ **3**   **9.** $\frac{0.8}{a} = \frac{3.2}{8}$ **2**   **10.** $\frac{1.6}{b} = \frac{8}{25}$ **5**

Guided Problem Solving

11. Long Distance You made a 12 minute phone call using a calling card. The call cost \$.66. There is \$1.21 left on your calling card. The cost per minute of long distance calls is constant. How many more minutes can you talk long distance using your calling card?

1) Write a ratio of the form $\frac{\text{Cost of phone call}}{\text{Minutes of phone call}}$ for the phone call. **$\frac{\$.66}{12 \text{ min}}$**

2) Let m represent the number of minutes you can talk for \$1.21. Write a ratio of the same form as the one in Step 1. **$\frac{\$1.21}{m \text{ min}}$**

3) Use the two ratios to write a proportion. Solve the proportion. **$\frac{\$.66}{12 \text{ min}} = \frac{\$1.21}{m \text{ min}}$; 22 min**

Practice and Problem Solving

Homework Help

Example	Exercises
1	12–19, 32
2	20–31, 33–35, 42

Online Resources CLASSZONE.COM
- More Examples
- eTutorial Plus

Tell whether the ratios form a proportion.

A **12.** $\frac{12}{30}, \frac{18}{45}$ yes **13.** $\frac{42}{20}, \frac{63}{60}$ no **14.** $\frac{28}{8}, \frac{42}{6}$ no **15.** $\frac{45}{35}, \frac{9}{21}$ no

16. $\frac{40}{210}, \frac{60}{630}$ no **17.** $\frac{588}{105}, \frac{84}{20}$ no **18.** $\frac{70}{147}, \frac{50}{105}$ yes **19.** $\frac{75}{40}, \frac{15}{8}$ yes

Solve the proportion.

20. $\frac{16}{36} = \frac{4}{d}$ 9 **21.** $\frac{3}{21} = \frac{c}{35}$ 5 **22.** $\frac{30}{w} = \frac{24}{12}$ 15 **23.** $\frac{35}{z} = \frac{7}{5}$ 25

24. $\frac{144}{40} = \frac{x}{5}$ 18 **25.** $\frac{9}{105} = \frac{15}{y}$ 175 **26.** $\frac{t}{12} = \frac{20}{8}$ 30 **27.** $\frac{s}{21} = \frac{16}{12}$ 28

28. $\frac{7}{m} = \frac{0.6}{3}$ 35 **29.** $\frac{26}{p} = \frac{13}{0.4}$ 0.8 **30.** $\frac{51}{3.4} = \frac{n}{4}$ 60 **31.** $\frac{1.4}{1.05} = \frac{4}{r}$ 3

32. Drink Mix A store is selling powdered drink mix in two different sizes. You can buy 10 ounces for \$2.25, or you can buy 35 ounces for \$7. Are the two rates equivalent? Explain.

32. No. *Sample answer:* The rates $\frac{\$2.25}{10\text{ oz}}$ and $\frac{\$7}{35\text{ ounces}}$ do not form a proportion because the cross products of the ratios $\frac{2.25}{10}$ and $\frac{7}{35}$ are not equal: $2.25 \cdot 35 \neq 10 \cdot 7$.

33. Gasoline You paid \$5 at a gas station for 3 gallons of gasoline.

a. How much would 12 gallons of gasoline cost? \$20

b. How much gasoline can you buy for \$30? 18 gal

34. Biking You travel 24 miles in 2 hours while biking.

a. At this rate, how far can you bike in 5 hours? 60 mi

b. At this rate, how long will it take to bike 30 miles? Write your answer in hours and minutes. 2 h 30 min

35. Gold Jewelers often mix gold with other metals. A *karat* is a unit of measure that compares the mass of the gold in an object with the mass of the object. Karats are expressed as a number that is understood to be the numerator of a ratio whose denominator is 24. For example, 24 karat gold means an object is pure gold, and 18 karat gold means that $\frac{18}{24}$, or $\frac{3}{4}$, of the object's mass is gold.

a. A 15 karat gold ring has a mass of 200 grams. How much gold is in the ring? 125 g

b. An 18 karat gold bracelet contains 27 grams of gold. What is the mass of the bracelet? 36 g

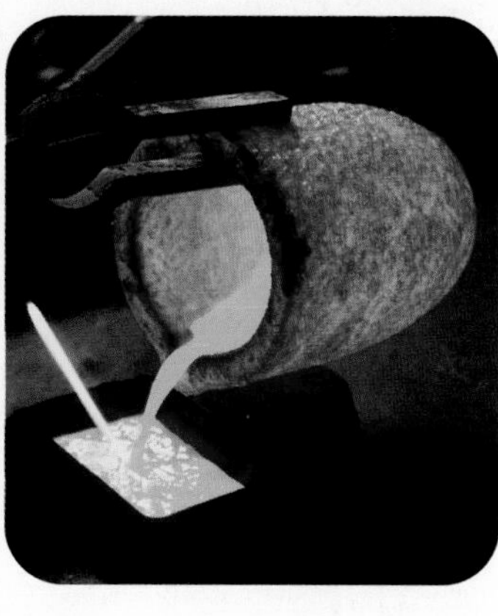

In the **Real World**

Gold Gold is heated in a crucible and poured into a mold to form gold bars. Suppose a gold bar weighs 400 ounces and the price of gold on a given day is \$322 per ounce. How much is the bar of gold worth? \$128,800

36. *Writing* Describe three ways you could solve the proportion $\frac{6}{10} = \frac{x}{40}$. See margin.

Find the value of *x*.

B **37.** $\frac{36}{54} = \frac{18}{x+5}$ 22 **38.** $\frac{39}{x+7} = \frac{21}{7}$ 6 **39.** $\frac{15-x}{45} = \frac{15}{75}$ 6 **40.** $\frac{28}{16} = \frac{x-8}{20}$ 43

41. Critical Thinking Use the cross products property to show that if $\frac{a}{b} = \frac{c}{d}$, then $\frac{d}{c} = \frac{b}{a}$. See margin.

3 APPLY

ASSIGNMENT GUIDE

Basic Course
Day 1: pp. 283–284 Exs. 12–27, 33–35, 37–40, 45–55

Average Course
Day 1: pp. 283–284 Exs. 16–23, 28–36, 39–43, 46–55

Advanced Course
Day 1: pp. 283–284 Exs. 16–23, 28–32, 35–44*, 49–55

Block
pp. 283–284 Exs. 16–23, 28–36, 39–43, 46–55 (with 6.2)

EXTRA PRACTICE
- Student Edition, p. 808
- Chapter 6 Resource Book, pp. 26–28
- Test and Practice Generator

TRANSPARENCY

Even-numbered answers are available on transparencies.

HOMEWORK CHECK

When you review students' homework for this lesson, go over the following exercises to check understanding of key concepts.
Basic: 12, 17, 20, 26, 33
Average: 16, 18, 20, 30, 34
Advanced: 18, 20, 23, 32, 35

TEACHING TIP

In Exercises 12–19, some students may be confused by ratios whose numerator is greater than the denominator. Stress that the cross products property still applies.

36, 41. See Additional Answers beginning on page AA1.

4 ASSESS

Assessment Resources

For more assessment resources, see:

- Assessment Book
- Test and Practice Generator

Mini-Quiz

Tell whether the ratios form a proportion.

1. $\frac{3}{14}, \frac{9}{42}$ yes
2. $\frac{19}{24}, \frac{75}{96}$ no

Solve the proportion.

3. $\frac{3}{b} = \frac{36}{60}$ 5
4. $\frac{81}{63} = \frac{f}{14}$ 18
5. **Challenge** For what whole number values of a less than 25 will the value of x in the proportion $\frac{a}{x} = \frac{x}{2}$ be an integer? $a = 2, 8, 18$

5 FOLLOW-UP

Diagnosis/Remediation

- Study Guide in Chapter 6 Resource Book, pp. 29–30
- Tutor Place, Ratio, Proportion, and Percent Cards 4, 5
- eTutorial Plus Online
- Extra Practice, p. 808
- Lesson Practice in Chapter 6 Resource Book, pp. 26–28

English Learner Support

- Spanish Study Guide
- Multi-Language Visual Glossary
- Chapter Audio Summaries CDs

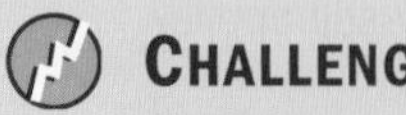

Challenge

- Challenge Practice in Chapter 6 Resource Book, p. 32
- Teacher's Edition, p. 266F

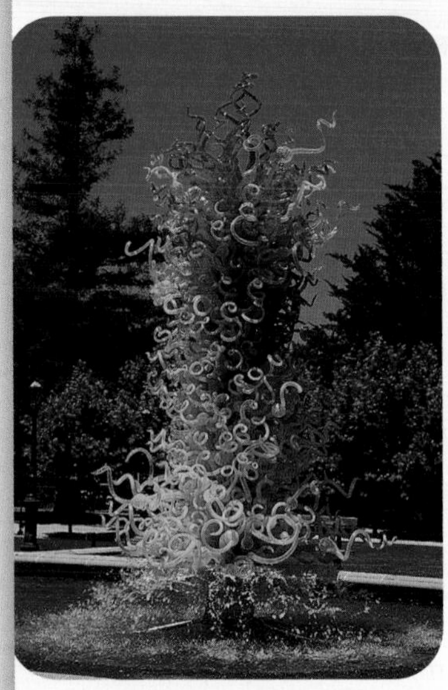

***Saffron and Red Tower* is a glass sculpture by Dale Chihuly.**

42c. The yellow glass. *Sample answer:* To find the amount of sand in the red glass, solve the proportion $\frac{100}{50} = \frac{200}{x}$ to get $x = 100$. To find the amount of sand in the yellow glass, solve the proportion $\frac{1}{65} = \frac{4}{x}$ to get $x = 260$. $260 > 100$, so the yellow glass has more sand.

42. **Extended Problem Solving** The tables show ingredients needed to make colored glass. Use the numbers in the *Parts* columns to form ratios comparing the masses of ingredients. For example, if you use 65 grams of sand to make yellow glass, you need 3 grams of chalk.

Red Glass	
Ingredients	**Parts**
Sand	50
Red lead	100
Copper oxide	3
Ferric oxide	3

Yellow Glass	
Ingredients	**Parts**
Sand	65
Soda ash	25
Chalk	3
Wood charcoal	1

a. **Calculate** A piece of red glass contains 60 grams of sand. How much ferric oxide does it contain? 3.6 g

b. **Calculate** A piece of yellow glass contains 31 kilograms of soda ash. How much chalk does it contain? 3.72 kg

c. **Compare** Which has more sand: red glass with 200 grams of red lead, or yellow glass with 4 grams of wood charcoal? Explain.

C 43. **Critical Thinking** The ratio $\frac{a}{b}$ is equivalent to $\frac{3}{4}$. The ratio $\frac{b}{c}$ is equivalent to $\frac{4}{5}$. What is the ratio $\frac{a}{c}$ equivalent to? Explain. See margin.

44. **Challenge** For a half circle like the one shown below, if you know lengths a and b, then length x can be found by solving $\frac{a}{x} = \frac{x}{b}$.

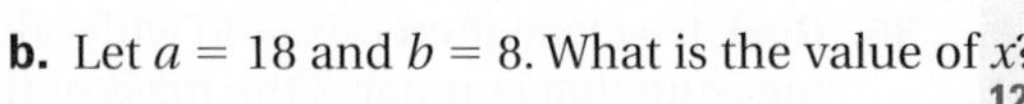

a. Let $a = 9$ and $b = 4$. What is the value of x? 6

b. Let $a = 18$ and $b = 8$. What is the value of x? 12

c. In terms of x, what does ab equal? x^2

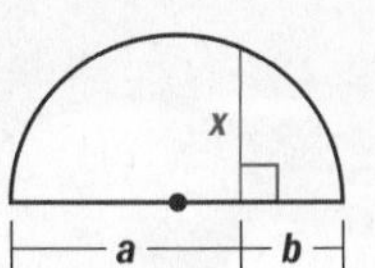

Mixed Review

43. $\frac{3}{5}$. *Sample answer:* Forming cross products gives $4a = 3b$ and $4c = 5b$. I noticed that because $\frac{a}{c} = \frac{4a}{4c}$, I could substitute $3b$ for $4a$ and $5b$ for $4c$ and write $\frac{a}{c} = \frac{3b}{5b} = \frac{3}{5}$.

Use a ruler to draw a segment with the given length. *(p. 787)* 45–47. Check student's work.

45. 1.2 centimeters
46. 3.5 centimeters
47. 0.2 centimeters

Write the number in scientific notation. *(Lesson 4.7)*

48. 34,000,000,000 3.4×10^{10}
49. 5,001,000 5.001×10^{6}
50. 0.000000000672 6.72×10^{-10}

Write the ratio in simplest form. *(Lesson 6.1)*

51. 8 to 18 4 to 9
52. 6 : 22 3 : 11
53. $\frac{14}{24}$ $\frac{7}{12}$

Standardized Test Practice

54. **Multiple Choice** Solve the proportion $\frac{90}{y} = \frac{27}{12}$. B

A. 3.6 **B.** 40 **C.** 90 **D.** 1080

55. **Multiple Choice** Last week you saved $24. At this rate, how many weeks will it take you to save $600? H

F. 24 days **G.** 14,400 weeks **H.** 25 weeks **I.** 15 weeks

Student Reference

Basic Geometry Concepts

▶ **Review** these topics in preparation for solving problems that involve basic geometry concepts in Lessons 6.4 and 6.5.

Points, Lines, and Planes

Word	Notation	Diagram
point	point A	• A
line	$\overleftrightarrow{BC}$	line through points B and C
plane	M	plane M

Example Use the diagram to name three points, two lines, and a plane.

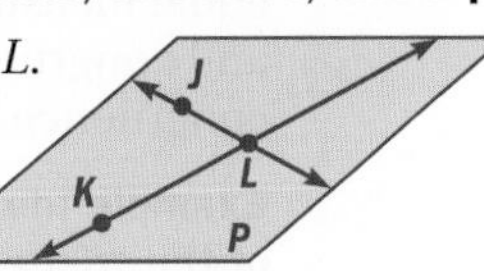

Three points are point J, point K, and point L.

Two lines are $\overleftrightarrow{KL}$ and $\overleftrightarrow{JL}$.

The plane is plane P.

Segments, Rays, and Angles

Word	Notation	Diagram
line segment, or segment length of a line segment	$\overline{AB}$ AB	endpoints, A, B
ray	$\overrightarrow{CD}$	endpoint, C, D
angle measure of an angle	$\angle EFG$ or $\angle F$ $m\angle EFG$ or $m\angle F$	E, F, G, 23°, vertex

Example Use the diagram to name two segments and their lengths, two rays, and an angle and its measure.

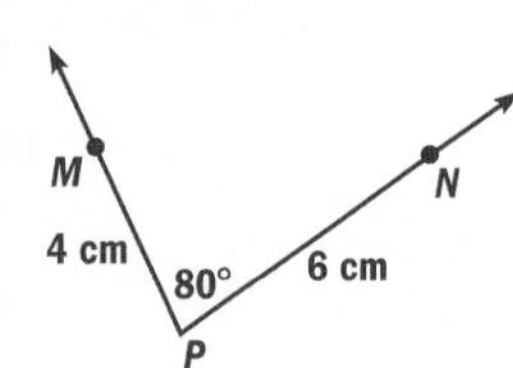

A segment is $\overline{MP}$, and $MP = 4$ centimeters.

Another segment is $\overline{NP}$, and $NP = 6$ centimeters.

Two rays are $\overrightarrow{PM}$ and $\overrightarrow{PN}$.

An angle is $\angle P$, and $m\angle P = 80°$.

Continued

NCTM CURRICULUM STANDARDS

Standard 3: Analyze properties of 2-D shapes

Standard 10: Use representations to communicate mathematical ideas

1 PLAN

Skill Check

Name a shape with the given number of sides.

1. 3 **triangle**

2. 4 ***Sample answer:* square**

3. 0 ***Sample answer:* circle**

Lesson Objective

Prepare for solving problems that involve basic geometry concepts.

2 TEACH

Common Error

When writing the names of lines and segments, many students initially confuse the symbols for segment and line, or omit them. Students also confuse $\overline{AB}$ and AB, thinking that the rule over the letters represents "the measure of."

Teaching Tip

When you discuss the naming of rays, point out that $\overrightarrow{PM}$ means that the ray begins at point P and continues through and beyond point M. Emphasize that a ray extends in only one direction.

Extra Examples

Example 1 Use the diagram to name three points, two lines, and a plane.

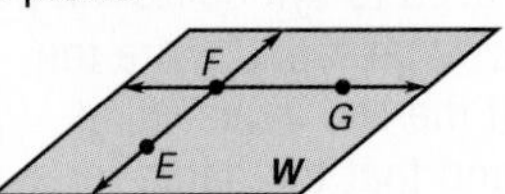

points: E, F, G; lines: $\overleftrightarrow{EF}$, $\overleftrightarrow{FG}$; plane: W

Extra Examples

Example 2 Use the diagram to name two segments and their lengths, two rays, and an angle and its measure.

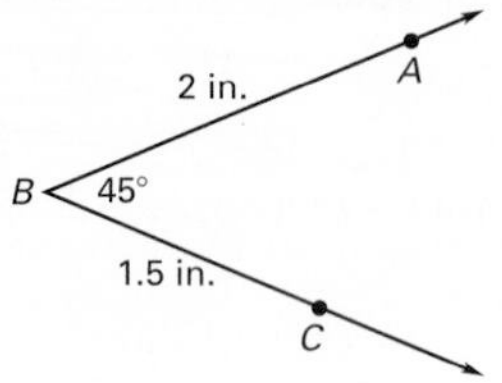

segments: $\overline{BA}$ ($BA = 2$ in.), $\overline{BC}$ ($BC = 1.5$ in.); rays: $\overrightarrow{BA}$, $\overrightarrow{BC}$; angle: $\angle B$ ($m\angle B = 45°$)

Example 3 Identify the angles, sides, congruent angles, and congruent sides of the parallelogram.

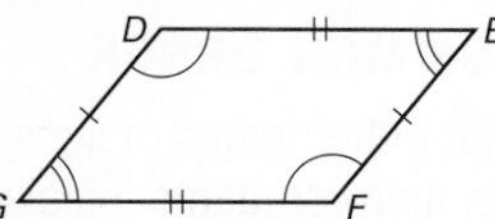

angles: $\angle D$, $\angle E$, $\angle F$, $\angle G$; sides: $\overline{DE}$, $\overline{EF}$, $\overline{FG}$, $\overline{GD}$; congruent angles: $\angle D \cong \angle F$, $\angle E \cong \angle G$; congruent sides: $\overline{DE} \cong \overline{FG}$, $\overline{GD} \cong \overline{EF}$

3 APPLY

TRANSPARENCY

Even-numbered answers are available on transparencies.

COMMON ERROR

In Exercise 1, students may name *Y* or *Z* as points. Stress that the label for a point will always be near a dot, which is used to symbolize the point. Emphasize that *Y* and *Z* are the names of the two intersecting planes, and that the name for a plane will be shown in a corner of the parallelogram that represents the plane.

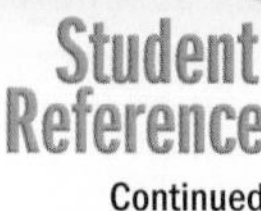

Triangles, Quadrilaterals, and Congruent Parts

Word	Notation	Diagram
triangle	$\triangle ABC$	A ← vertex, B, C
A **quadrilateral** is made of four segments that intersect only at their endpoints.	quadrilateral *PQRS*	P, Q, R, S

Congruent segments have equal lengths, and **congruent angles** have equal measures. Congruent sides of a figure are marked using tick marks, and congruent angles of a figure are marked using arcs. The symbol for congruence is ≅.

Example Identify the angles, sides, congruent angles, and congruent sides of the triangle.

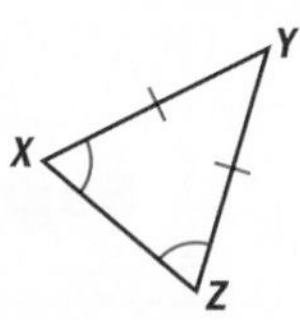

The angles of the triangle are $\angle X$, $\angle Y$, and $\angle Z$.

The sides of the triangle are $\overline{XY}$, $\overline{YZ}$, and $\overline{XZ}$.

Congruent angles: $\angle X \cong \angle Z$

Congruent sides: $\overline{XY} \cong \overline{YZ}$

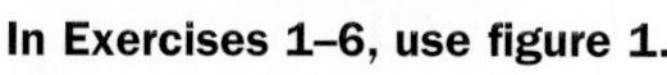

Checkpoint

▶ **Test** your knowledge of basic geometry concepts by solving these problems.

In Exercises 1–6, use figure 1.

1. Name three points. **any three of *M, N, P, R, S***
2. Name two lines. **$\overleftrightarrow{MN}$ and $\overleftrightarrow{RS}$**
3. Name two planes. **plane *Y* and plane *Z***
4. Name two rays.
5. Name a segment.
6. Name an angle and give its measure. **$\angle N$ (or $\angle MNP$), $m\angle N = 85°$**

4. any two of $\overrightarrow{NM}$, $\overrightarrow{NP}$, $\overrightarrow{RS}$, $\overrightarrow{SR}$

5. any one of $\overline{RS}$, $\overline{MN}$, $\overline{NP}$

Figure 1

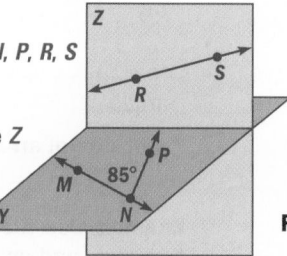

In Exercises 7–10, use figure 2.

7. Name the quadrilateral. ***Sample answer:* Quadrilateral *DEFG***
8. Name the sides. **$\overline{DE}$, $\overline{EF}$, $\overline{FG}$, $\overline{DG}$**
9. Name the angles. **$\angle D$, $\angle E$, $\angle F$, $\angle G$**
10. Identify the congruent angles and congruent sides. **$\angle D \cong \angle F$, $\angle E \cong \angle G$, $\overline{DE} \cong \overline{FG}$, $\overline{EF} \cong \overline{DG}$**

Figure 2

Concept *Activity*

6.4 Investigating Similar Figures

Goal
Investigate corresponding sides and angles of similar figures.

Materials
- graph paper
- metric ruler
- protractor

Two figures are *similar* if they have the same shape but not necessarily the same size. For example, when a figure is enlarged, the enlarged figure is similar to the original figure.

Investigate

Compare corresponding parts of a figure and its enlargement.

Draw $\triangle ABC$ so that $m\angle A = 90°$, $AB = 1.5$ cm, and $AC = 2$ cm. Find BC to the nearest 0.1 cm.

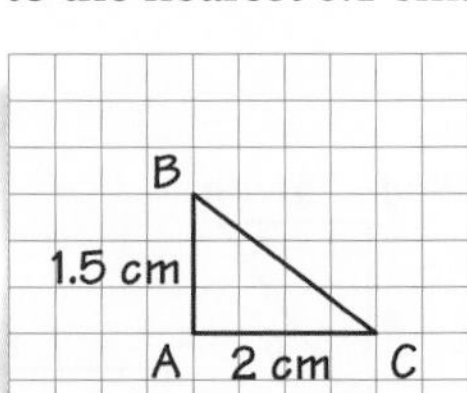

Draw $\triangle DEF$ so that $m\angle D = 90°$, $DE = 2 \cdot AB$, and $DF = 2 \cdot AC$. Find the side lengths of $\triangle DEF$.

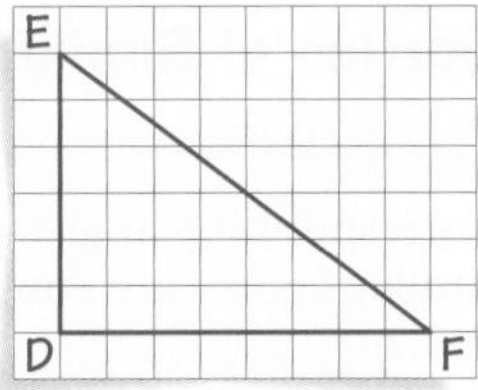

Use a protractor to find the measures of the angles of both triangles to the nearest degree.

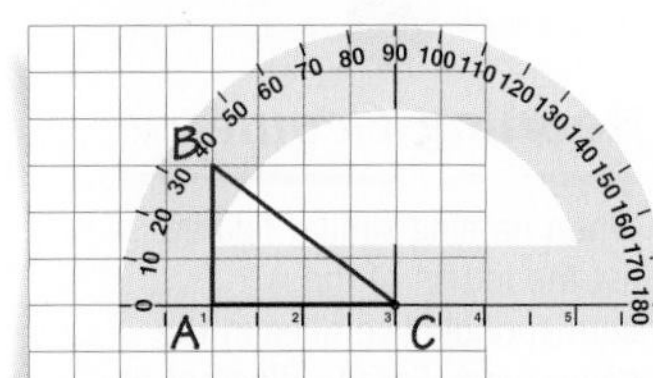

Draw Conclusions

1. Copy and complete the tables.

Side of $\triangle ABC$	Corresponding side of $\triangle DEF$
$AB = 1.5$ cm	$DE = ?$ **3 cm**
$AC = 2$ cm	$DF = ?$ **4 cm**
$BC = ?$ **2.5 cm**	$EF = ?$ **5 cm**

Angle of $\triangle ABC$	Corresponding angle of $\triangle DEF$
$m\angle A = 90°$	$m\angle D = 90°$
$m\angle B = ?$ **53°**	$m\angle E = ?$ **53°**
$m\angle C = ?$ **37°**	$m\angle F = ?$ **37°**

2. For each pair of corresponding sides, find the ratio of the length of a side of $\triangle ABC$ to the length of the corresponding side of $\triangle DEF$. What do you notice about these ratios? **$\frac{1}{2}$; they are the same.**
3. What do you notice about the measures of the corresponding angles? **They are the same.**
4. **Conjecture** Use your answers to Exercises 2 and 3 to write two conjectures about similar figures. ***Sample answer:* In similar figures, (1) the ratios of the lengths of corresponding sides are the same, and (2) corresponding angles are congruent.**

NCTM CURRICULUM STANDARDS
Standard 3: Analyze properties of 2-D shapes
Standard 8: Organize thinking through communication

1 PLAN

Investigate the Concept

- Students investigate corresponding sides and angles of similar figures.
- This activity leads into using and determining similar figures in Lesson 6.4.

Materials

Each student will need graph paper, a metric ruler, and a protractor. Support transparencies are available for this activity.

Recommended Time

Work activity: 10 min
Discuss results: 5 min

Grouping

Students should work individually.

2 TEACH

Tips for Success

Urge students to read each step thoroughly before beginning.

3 CLOSE

Key Discovery

Corresponding angles of similar figures are congruent, and corresponding sides have lengths that form the same ratio for each pair of sides.

Assessment

1. What happens to the angle measures when a figure is doubled in size? **They are unchanged.**
2. What happens to the side lengths of a figure that is enlarged by a given percent? **They all increase by the same percent.**

1 PLAN

Skill Check

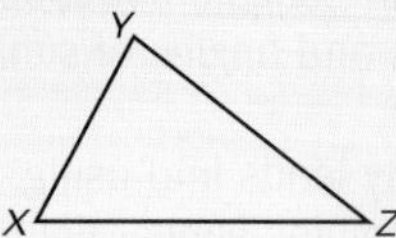

1. Name the triangle.
   Sample answer: $\triangle XYZ$

Name the parts.

2. The angles $\angle X, \angle Y, \angle Z$
3. The sides $\overline{XY}, \overline{YZ}, \overline{XZ}$

LESSON OBJECTIVE

Identify similar and congruent figures.

PACING

Suggested Number of Days
Basic Course: 2 days
Average Course: 2 days
Advanced Course: 2 days
Block: 1 block

TEACHING RESOURCES

For a complete list of Teaching Resources, see page 266B.

TRANSPARENCY

Warm-Up Exercises for this lesson are available on a transparency.

2 TEACH

MOTIVATING THE LESSON

Point out shapes in the classroom that are similar and dissimilar. Ask students to identify others.

TIPS *for* NEW TEACHERS

Stress that the term *similar* is a mathematical term with a specific meaning, not to be confused with its casual English usage. See Tips for New Teachers in the *Chapter 6 Resource Book.*

LESSON 6.4

Similar *and* Congruent Figures

BEFORE	Now	WHY?
You worked with basic geometric figures.	You'll identify similar and congruent figures.	So you can compare TV screens to computer screens, as in Ex. 20.

Vocabulary

similar figures, p. 288
corresponding parts, p. 288
congruent figures, p. 290

Two figures are **similar figures** if they have the same shape but not necessarily the same size. The symbol ~ indicates that two figures are similar. When working with similar figures, you should identify the *corresponding parts* of the figures. **Corresponding parts** of figures are sides or angles that have the same relative position.

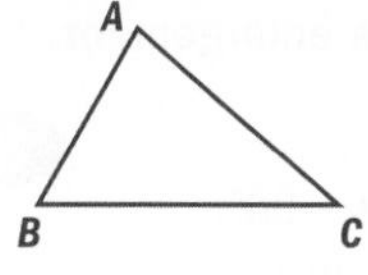

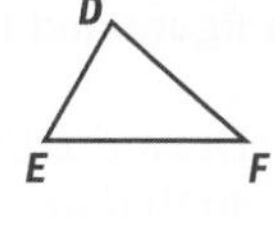

$\triangle ABC \sim \triangle DEF$

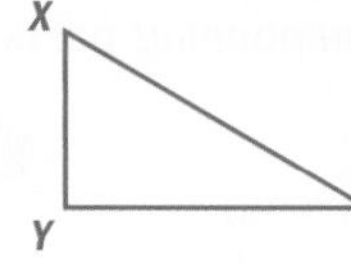

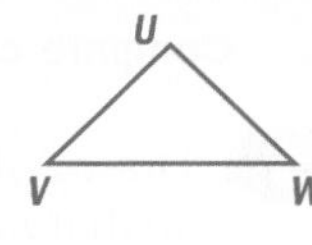

$\triangle XYZ$ is not similar to $\triangle UVW$

Reading *Geometry*

When naming similar figures, list the letters of the corresponding vertices in the same order. For the diagram at the right, it is *not* correct to say $\triangle CBA \sim \triangle EFD$, because $\angle C$ and $\angle E$ are not corresponding angles.

Properties of Similar Figures

$\triangle ABC \sim \triangle DEF$

1. Corresponding angles of similar figures are congruent.
   $\angle A \cong \angle D, \angle B \cong \angle E, \angle C \cong \angle F$
2. The ratios of the lengths of corresponding sides of similar figures are equal.
   $\frac{AB}{DE} = \frac{BC}{EF} = \frac{AC}{DF} = \frac{1}{2}$

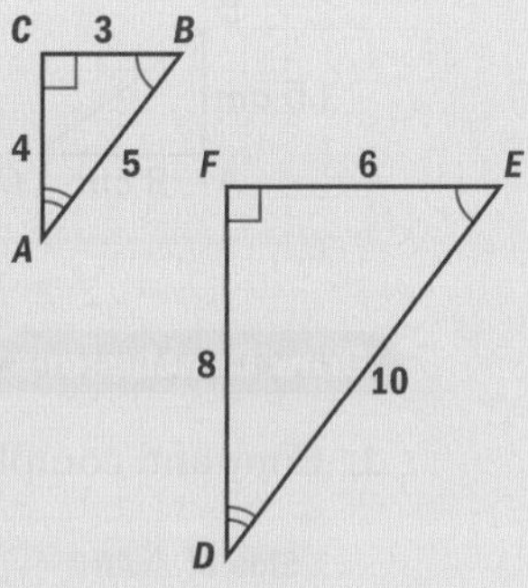

Example 1 ***Identifying Corresponding Parts of Similar Figures***

Given $\triangle LMN \sim \triangle PQR$, name the corresponding angles and the corresponding sides.

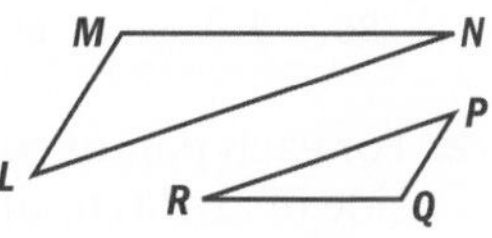

Solution

Corresponding angles: $\angle L$ and $\angle P$, $\angle M$ and $\angle Q$, $\angle N$ and $\angle R$

Corresponding sides: $\overline{LM}$ and $\overline{PQ}$, $\overline{MN}$ and $\overline{QR}$, $\overline{LN}$ and $\overline{PR}$

NCTM CURRICULUM STANDARDS
Standard 2: Use models to understand relationships
Standard 3: Analyze properties of 2-D shapes
Standard 6: Solve problems in math and other contexts

1. corresponding angles: $\angle A$ and $\angle W$, $\angle B$ and $\angle X$, $\angle C$ and $\angle Y$, $\angle D$ and $\angle Z$; corresponding sides: $\overline{AB}$ and $\overline{WX}$, $\overline{BC}$ and $\overline{XY}$, $\overline{CD}$ and $\overline{YZ}$, $\overline{AD}$ and $\overline{WZ}$

Study *Strategy*

Because all the ratios of the lengths of corresponding sides of the figures in Example 2 are equal, you can use any pair of lengths of corresponding sides to write the ratio. To check the solution, choose another pair of lengths of corresponding sides.

Checkpoint

1. Given $ABCD \sim WXYZ$, name the corresponding angles and the corresponding sides.

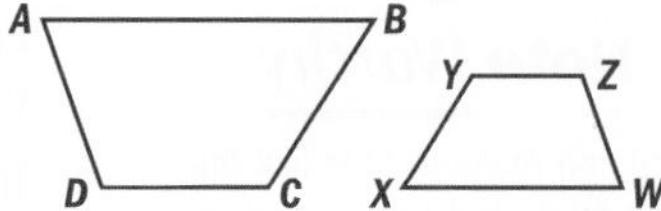

Example 2 *Finding the Ratio of Corresponding Side Lengths*

Given $ABCD \sim JKLM$, find the ratio of the lengths of corresponding sides of $ABCD$ to $JKLM$.

Write a ratio comparing the lengths of a pair of corresponding sides. Then substitute the lengths of the sides and simplify.

$$\frac{AB}{JK} = \frac{8}{12} = \frac{2}{3}$$

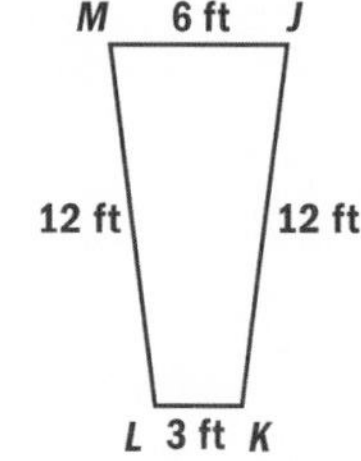

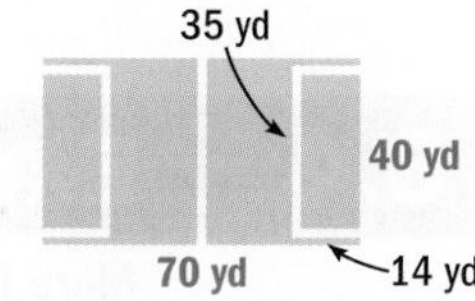

Answer The ratio of the lengths of the corresponding sides is $\frac{2}{3}$.

Example 3 *Checking for Similarity*

Soccer A soccer field is a rectangle that is 70 yards long and 40 yards wide. The penalty area of the soccer field is a rectangle that is 35 yards long and 14 yards wide. Is the penalty area similar to the field?

35 yd
40 yd
70 yd
14 yd

Solution

Because all rectangles have four right angles, the corresponding angles are congruent. To decide if the rectangles are similar, determine whether the ratios of the lengths of corresponding sides are equal.

$\frac{\text{Length of field}}{\text{Length of penalty area}} \stackrel{?}{=} \frac{\text{Width of field}}{\text{Width of penalty area}}$	**Write proportion.**
$\frac{70}{35} \stackrel{?}{=} \frac{40}{14}$	**Substitute values.**
$70 \cdot 14 \stackrel{?}{=} 35 \cdot 40$	**Form cross products.**
$980 \neq 1400$	**Multiply.**

Answer The ratios of the lengths of corresponding sides are not equal, so the penalty area is not similar to the field.

Checkpoint

2. Inside the penalty area of the soccer field in Example 3 is a smaller rectangle known as the goal area. The goal area of a soccer field is 19 yards long and 6 yards wide. Is the goal area similar to the penalty area? Explain. **No; the ratios of the lengths of corresponding sides are not equal.**

Extra Examples

Example 1 Given $\triangle STU \sim \triangle VWX$, name the corresponding angles and the corresponding sides.

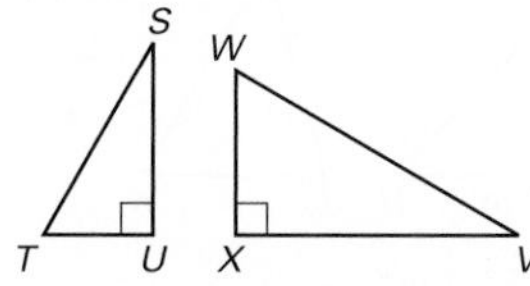

corresponding angles: $\angle S$ and $\angle V$, $\angle T$ and $\angle W$, $\angle U$ and $\angle X$; corresponding sides: $\overline{ST}$ and $\overline{VW}$, $\overline{TU}$ and $\overline{WX}$, $\overline{SU}$ and $\overline{VX}$

Example 2 Given $FGHJ \sim KLMN$, find the ratio of the lengths of the corresponding sides of $FGHJ$ to $KLMN$. $\frac{4}{3}$

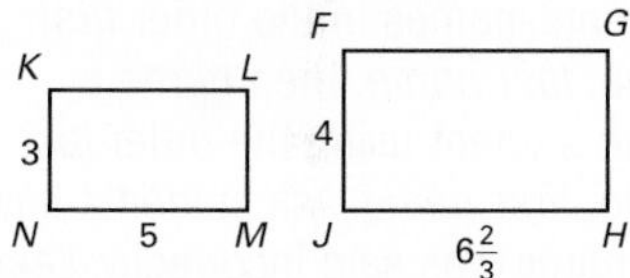

Example 3 The top of Selena's rectangular dining room table measures 60 inches by 108 inches. She has a matching rectangular coffee table whose top measures 18 inches by 48 inches. Are the two tables similar? **The ratios of the lengths of the corresponding sides $\left(\frac{18}{60}\text{ and }\frac{48}{108}\right)$ are not equal, so the two tables are not similar.**

READING STRATEGY

Show students how to read similarity statements, like the one given in Example 1, while tracing the parts of the similar figures using a finger, following the order of the vertices in the similarity statement.

Extra Examples

Example 4 Given $\triangle FGH \cong \triangle JKL$, find the indicated measure.

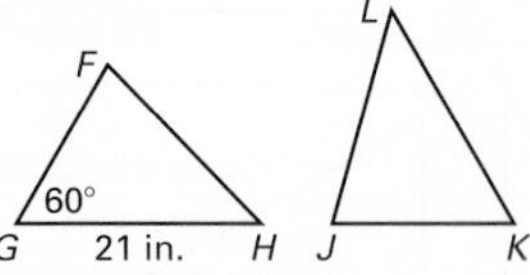

a. KL **21 in.**
b. $m\angle K$ **60°**

COMMON ERROR

Some students may not understand why it is important to name similar and congruent figures using the corresponding vertices in the same order. Consider calling out three students' names in the order *first name, last name*. Then name a fourth student using the order *last name, first name*. Ask students how this name was said incorrectly. Lead students to recognize the inconsistency and relate this to the naming of similar and congruent figures.

TEACHING TIP

After discussing the definition of *congruent* prior to Example 4, inform students that all congruent figures are also similar figures, but not all similar figures are congruent.

CONCEPT CHECK

How are similar figures and congruent figures different? ***Sample answer:*** **Congruent figures are the same shape and the same size, while similar figures are the same shape, but not necessarily the same size.**

DAILY PUZZLER

If you double the length of the sides of a square, does the perimeter double or quadruple? **It doubles.**

Note *Worthy*

You can make a table like the one on p. 268 to compare and contrast similar and congruent figures.

Congruent Figures Two figures are **congruent** if they have the same shape *and* the same size. If two figures are congruent, then the corresponding angles are congruent and the corresponding sides are congruent. Congruent figures are also similar.

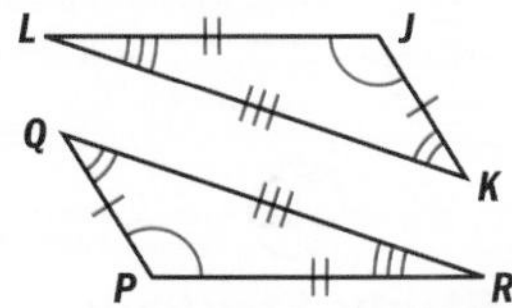

In the diagram, $\triangle JKL \cong \triangle PQR$ because:

1. $\angle J \cong \angle P$, $\angle K \cong \angle Q$, and $\angle L \cong \angle R$.
2. $\overline{JK} \cong \overline{PQ}$, $\overline{KL} \cong \overline{QR}$, and $\overline{JL} \cong \overline{PR}$.

Example 4 *Finding Measures of Congruent Figures*

Given $ABCD \cong WXYZ$, find the indicated measure.

a. WZ **b.** $m\angle W$

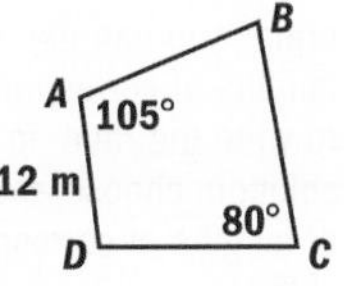

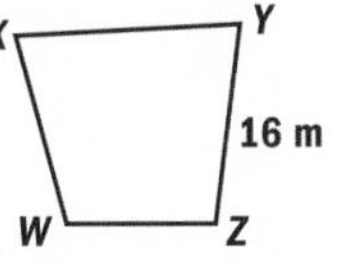

Solution

Because the quadrilaterals are congruent, the corresponding angles are congruent and the corresponding sides are congruent.

a. $\overline{WZ} \cong \overline{AD}$. So, $WZ = AD = 12$ m.

b. $\angle W \cong \angle A$. So, $m\angle W = m\angle A = 105°$.

6.4 Exercises

More Practice, p. 808

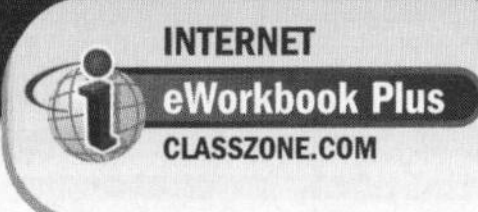

Guided Practice

Vocabulary Check

1. What do you know about the corresponding angles and corresponding sides of two figures that are congruent? **Corresponding angles are congruent and corresponding sides are congruent.**
2. Given $\triangle JKL \sim \triangle PQR$, identify all pairs of corresponding sides and corresponding angles.

2. corresponding sides: $\overline{JK}$ and $\overline{PQ}$, $\overline{KL}$ and $\overline{QR}$, $\overline{JL}$ and $\overline{PR}$; corresponding angles: $\angle J$ and $\angle P$, $\angle K$ and $\angle Q$, $\angle L$ and $\angle R$

Skill Check

In Exercises 3–6, $\triangle ABC \sim \triangle DEF$.

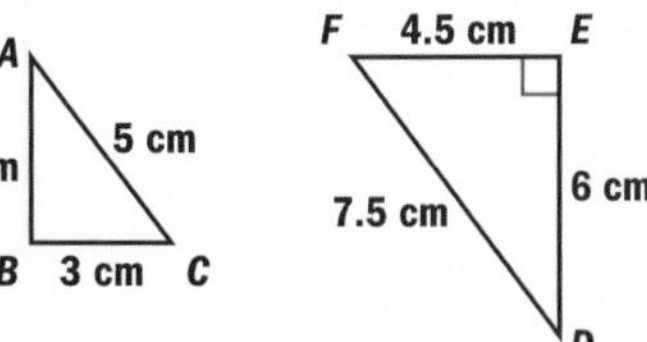

3. Identify all corresponding sides and corresponding angles.
4. Find the ratio of the lengths of corresponding sides of $\triangle ABC$ to $\triangle DEF$. $\frac{2}{3}$
5. Find $m\angle B$. **90°**
6. **Error Analysis** Describe and correct the error in writing another similarity statement for the triangles.

X $\triangle BAC \sim \triangle EFD$

3. corresponding sides: $\overline{AB}$ and $\overline{DE}$, $\overline{BC}$ and $\overline{EF}$, $\overline{AC}$ and $\overline{DF}$; corresponding angles: $\angle A$ and $\angle D$, $\angle B$ and $\angle E$, $\angle C$ and $\angle F$

6. *Sample answer:* The order in which the triangles are written does not match up corresponding parts. For example, $\angle A$ and $\angle F$ are not corresponding angles. A correct statement is $\triangle BAC \sim \triangle EDF$.

Practice and Problem Solving

Homework Help

Example	Exercises
1	7, 8
2	9-12
3	9-12, 20
4	13-15

Online Resources CLASSZONE.COM
- More Examples
- eTutorial Plus

7. corresponding angles: $\angle A$ and $\angle D$, $\angle B$ and $\angle E$, $\angle C$ and $\angle F$; corresponding sides: $\overline{AB}$ and $\overline{DE}$, $\overline{BC}$ and $\overline{EF}$, $\overline{AC}$ and $\overline{DF}$

8. corresponding angles: $\angle J$ and $\angle X$, $\angle K$ and $\angle W$, $\angle L$ and $\angle V$, $\angle M$ and $\angle Z$, $\angle N$ and $\angle Y$; corresponding sides: $\overline{JK}$ and $\overline{XW}$, $\overline{KL}$ and $\overline{WV}$, $\overline{LM}$ and $\overline{VZ}$, $\overline{MN}$ and $\overline{ZY}$, $\overline{JN}$ and $\overline{XY}$

16. Always. *Sample answer:* Corresponding angles of congruent figures are congruent, and the ratios of the lengths of corresponding sides are equal, so they have the same ratio, $\frac{1}{1}$.

Giant TV screen at the Olympic Stadium in Barcelona, Spain

Name the corresponding angles and the corresponding sides. 7–8. See margin.

A **7.** $\triangle ABC \sim \triangle DEF$ **8.** $JKLMN \cong XWVZY$

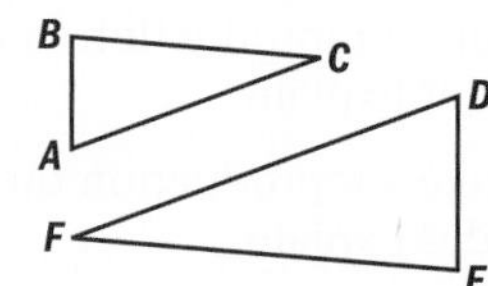

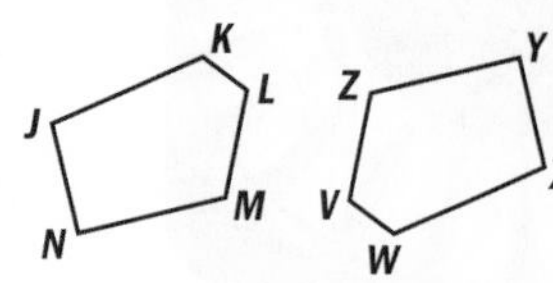

The figures are similar. Find the ratio of the lengths of corresponding sides of figure A to figure B.

9. $\frac{10}{13}$ **10.** $\frac{1}{1}$

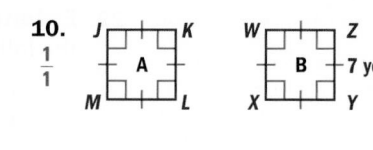

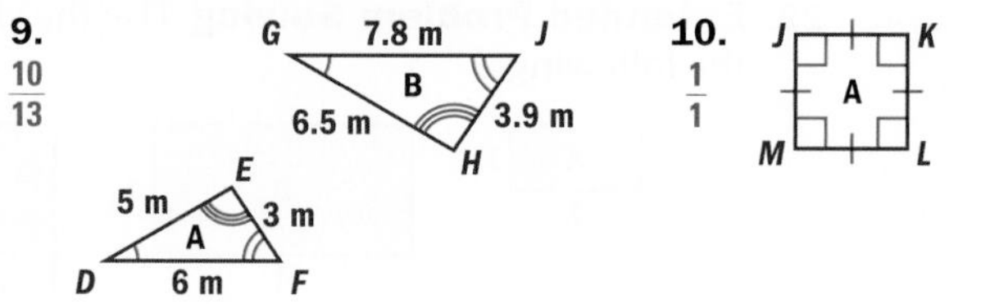

11. $\frac{2}{3}$ **12.** $\frac{3}{2}$

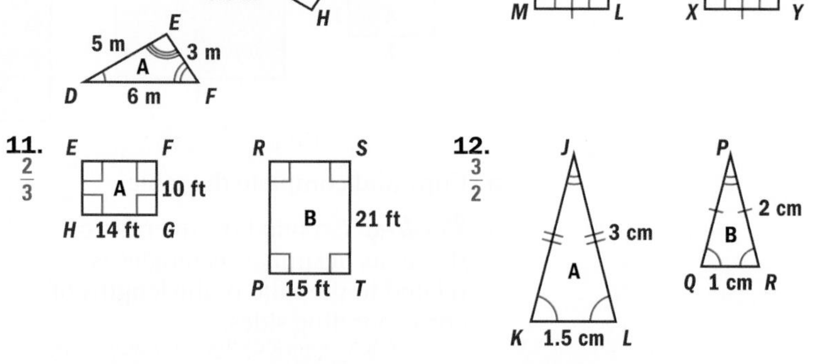

Given $RSTU \cong ABCD$, find the indicated measure.

13. $m\angle R$ 128°

14. $m\angle B$ 110°

15. AB 18 in.

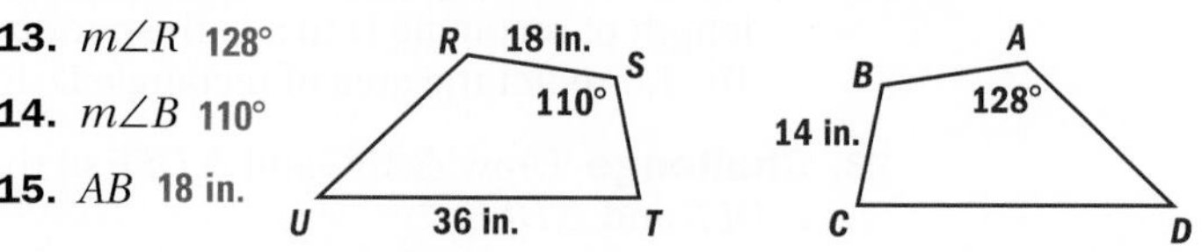

Critical Thinking Copy and complete the statement using *always*, *sometimes*, or *never*. Explain your answer. 16–19. See margin.

16. Congruent figures are ? similar. **17.** Similar figures are ? congruent.

18. Two squares are ? similar. **19.** Two rectangles are ? congruent.

20. Screens The table shows the heights and widths of various rectangular viewing screens. Use the table to complete the following.

a. Are the two computer screens similar? Explain. 20a–20b. See margin.

b. Is the television screen similar to either computer screen? Explain.

c. Compare Compare the height to width ratios of the high definition TV and movie screen. They are the same, $\frac{16}{9}$.

Item	Height	Width
Television	18 in.	24 in.
Computer 1	9 in.	12 in.
Computer 2	12 in.	15 in.
High definition TV	48 in.	27 in.
Movie screen	32 ft	18 ft

3 APPLY

ASSIGNMENT GUIDE

Basic Course
Day 1: pp. 291-292 Exs. 7-10, 16-18, 24-28
Day 2: pp. 291-292 Exs. 11-15, 19-21, 29-31

Average Course
Day 1: pp. 291-292 Exs. 7-10, 16-19, 24-27
Day 2: pp. 291-292 Exs. 11-15, 20-22, 28-31

Advanced Course
Day 1: pp. 291-292 Exs. 7-10, 16-20, 26-29
Day 2: pp. 291-292 Exs. 11-15, 21-25*, 30, 31

Block
pp. 291-292 Exs. 7-22, 24-31

EXTRA PRACTICE
- Student Edition, p. 808
- Chapter 6 Resource Book, pp. 35-37
- Test and Practice Generator

TRANSPARENCY

Even-numbered answers are available on transparencies.

HOMEWORK CHECK

When you review students' homework for this lesson, go over the following exercises to check understanding of key concepts.
Basic: 7, 10, 11, 12, 13
Average: 8, 10, 12, 14, 20
Advanced: 8, 10, 12, 15, 20

17-19, 20a-b. See Additional Answers beginning on page AA1.

4 ASSESS

ASSESSMENT RESOURCES

For more assessment resources, see:

- Assessment Book
- Test and Practice Generator

MINI-QUIZ

Given $CDEF \cong GHJK$, find the indicated measure.

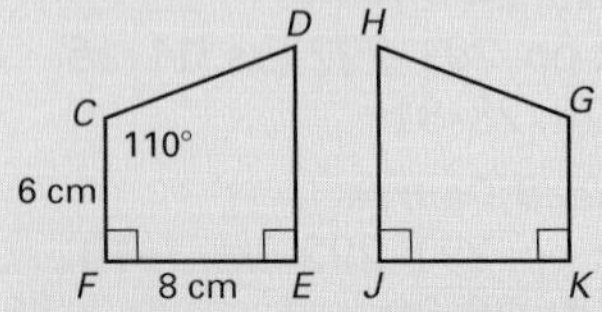

1. $m\angle G$ **110°**
2. GK **6 cm**
3. JK **8 cm**
4. **Challenge** Describe $\triangle EFG$ and $\triangle HIJ$ if $\triangle EFG$ is congruent to $\triangle HIJ$, $\triangle IJH$, and $\triangle JHI$. **The two triangles are congruent and equilateral.**

5 FOLLOW-UP

DIAGNOSIS/REMEDIATION

- Study Guide in Chapter 6 Resource Book, pp. 38–39
- Tutor Place, Geometry Card 17
- eTutorial Plus Online
- Extra Practice, p. 808
- Lesson Practice in Chapter 6 Resource Book, pp. 35–37

ENGLISH LEARNER SUPPORT

- Spanish Study Guide
- Multi-Language Visual Glossary
- Chapter Audio Summaries CDs

CHALLENGE

- Challenge Practice in Chapter 6 Resource Book, p. 40
- Teacher's Edition, p. 266F

23. See Additional Answers beginning on page AA1.

21a. Yes. ***Sample answer:*** **The ratio of the lengths is $\frac{9.41}{6.14} \approx$ 1.53, and the ratio of the widths is $\frac{4.00}{2.61} \approx 1.53$, so both ratios are greater than $1\frac{1}{2}$, or 1.5.**

21b. Yes. ***Sample answer:*** **The ratio of the lengths is $\frac{4.00}{6.14} \approx$ 0.65, and the ratio of the widths is $\frac{1.70}{2.61} \approx 0.65$, so both ratios are less than $\frac{3}{4}$, or 0.75.**

22c. 200 square units. ***Sample answer:*** **The area of rectangle D will be $10^2 = 100$ times greater than the area of rectangle A.**

B **21. Money** It is illegal to reproduce a genuine U.S. bill except according to the following rule: Every side length of the reproduction must be less than $\frac{3}{4}$ times, or greater than $1\frac{1}{2}$ times, the corresponding side length of a genuine bill. Genuine bills are 6.14 inches long and 2.61 inches wide.

a. Is it legal to make a reproduction that is 9.41 inches long and 4.00 inches wide? Explain.

b. Is it legal to make a reproduction that is 4.00 inches long and 1.70 inches wide? Explain.

c. If a reproduction is 2 feet long and 9 inches wide, is it similar to a genuine U.S. bill? **no**

22. Extended Problem Solving Use the similar rectangles to complete the following.

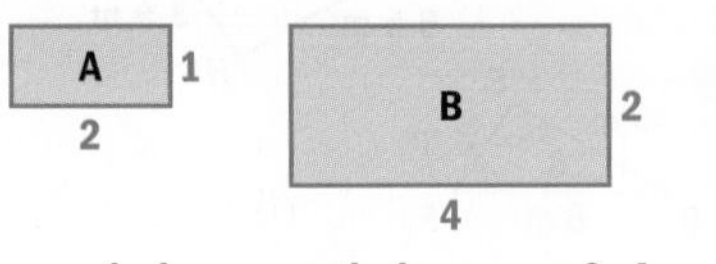

Row 1: $\frac{1}{2}, \frac{1}{4}$; Row 2: $\frac{1}{3}, \frac{1}{9}$; Row 3: $\frac{2}{3}, \frac{4}{9}$

a. Copy and complete the table.

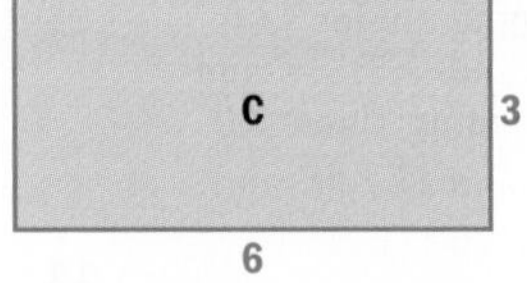

Figures	Ratio of side lengths	Ratio of areas
A to B	?	?
A to C	?	?
B to C	?	?

b. *Writing* Explain how the ratio of the areas of similar rectangles is related to the ratio of the lengths of corresponding sides. **The ratio of the areas is the square of the ratio of the side lengths.**

c. Predict Rectangle D is similar to rectangle A. The ratio of a side length of rectangle D to a corresponding side length of rectangle A is 10 : 1. Predict the area of rectangle D. Explain your thinking.

C **23. Challenge** Draw $\triangle ABC$ and $\triangle DEF$ so that $\triangle ABC$ is congruent to both $\triangle DEF$ and $\triangle DFE$. **See margin.**

Mixed Review

31. No. ***Sample answer:*** **The dimensions of the tablecloth are 7 feet by 5 feet. So, the ratio of the lengths of the table and tablecloth is $\frac{5}{7}$, but the ratio of the widths is $\frac{3}{5}$, and $\frac{5}{7} \neq \frac{3}{5}$.**

Write the fraction in simplest form. *(Lesson 4.3)*

24. $\frac{48}{64}$ **$\frac{3}{4}$** **25.** $\frac{90}{108}$ **$\frac{5}{6}$** **26.** $\frac{7ab^5}{21a^2}$ **$\frac{b^5}{3a}$** **27.** $\frac{24x}{60x^2y^3}$ **$\frac{2}{5xy^3}$**

28. A bird flies 266 miles in 19 hours. Find the bird's speed in miles per hour. *(Lesson 6.1)* **14 mi/h**

29. You can hike 6.5 miles in 2 hours. At this rate, how long will it take you to hike 19.5 miles? *(Lesson 6.3)* **6 h**

Standardized Test Practice

30. Multiple Choice If quadrilateral $ABCD \cong$ quadrilateral $GHEF$, which angle must be congruent to $\angle C$? **A**

A. $\angle E$ **B.** $\angle F$ **C.** $\angle G$ **D.** $\angle H$

31. Short Response A tablecloth is spread over a 5 foot by 3 foot rectangular table. The tablecloth extends 1 foot beyond the table's surface on each side. Is the tablecloth similar to the surface of the table? Explain. **See margin.**

LESSON

6.5 Similarity *and* Measurement

BEFORE	*Now*	WHY?
You identified similar figures.	You'll find unknown side lengths of similar figures.	So you can find the height of a palm tree, as in Ex. 5.

Review Vocabulary
ratio, p. 269
proportion, p. 275
similar figures, p. 288

Cactus A man who is 6 feet tall is standing near a saguaro cactus. The length of the man's shadow is 2 feet. The cactus casts a shadow 5 feet long. How tall is the cactus?

In Example 2, you will see how to use similar triangles to measure the cactus's height indirectly.

Example 1 *Finding an Unknown Side Length in Similar Figures*

Given $ABCD \sim EFGH$, find EH.

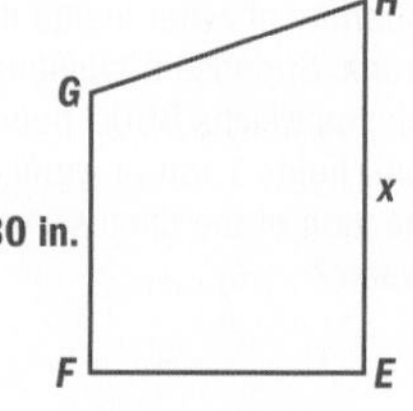

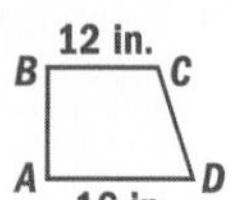

Solution

Use the ratios of the lengths of corresponding sides to write a proportion involving the unknown length, EH.

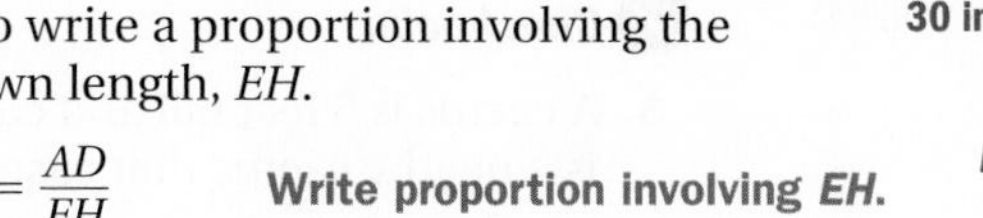

$\frac{BC}{FG} = \frac{AD}{EH}$ **Write proportion involving *EH*.**

$\frac{12}{30} = \frac{16}{x}$ **Substitute.**

$12x = 30 \cdot 16$ **Cross products property**

$12x = 480$ **Multiply.**

$x = 40$ **Divide each side by 12.**

Answer The length of $\overline{EH}$ is 40 inches.

Checkpoint

1. Given $\triangle STU \sim \triangle DEF$, find DF.

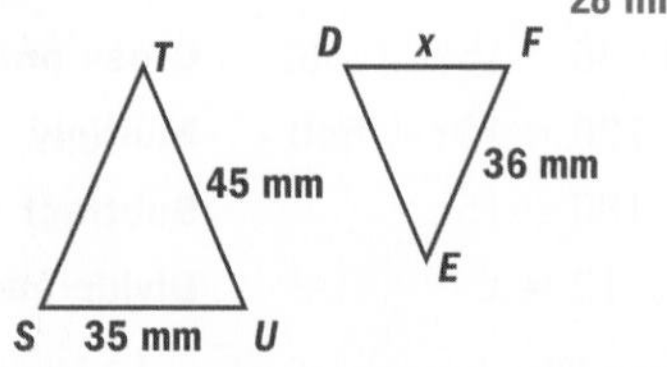

2. Given $JKLM \sim PQRS$, find PQ.

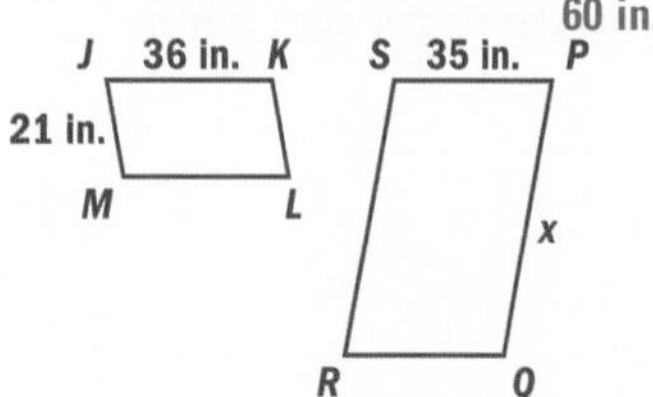

NCTM CURRICULUM STANDARDS
Standard 2: Represent situations using algebraic symbols
Standard 3: Analyze properties of 2-D shapes
Standard 6: Solve problems in math and other contexts

1 PLAN

Skill Check

Solve the proportion.

1. $\frac{a}{8} = \frac{21}{56}$ 3
2. $\frac{6}{18} = \frac{b}{48}$ 16
3. $\frac{8}{c} = \frac{64}{104}$ 13
4. $\frac{x}{3} = \frac{12 + x}{12}$ 4

LESSON OBJECTIVE

Find unknown side lengths of similar figures.

PACING

Suggested Number of Days
Basic Course: 1 day
Average Course: 1 day
Advanced Course: 1 day
Block: 0.5 block with 6.6

TEACHING RESOURCES

For a complete list of Teaching Resources, see page 266B.

TRANSPARENCY

Warm-Up Exercises for this lesson are available on a transparency.

2 TEACH

MOTIVATING THE LESSON

Ask students if they have noticed that taller objects cast longer shadows on a sunny day. Then ask them if they have ever used the lengths of the shadows to attempt to determine the height of an object that was too tall to measure.

TIPS *for* NEW TEACHERS
Urge students to always write their proportion using symbols first, to verify they have it written correctly, and then to substitute values into the proportion. See Tips for New Teachers in the *Chapter 6 Resource Book*.

Extra Examples

Example 1 Given $KLMN \sim PQRS$, find SR. **4.5 cm**

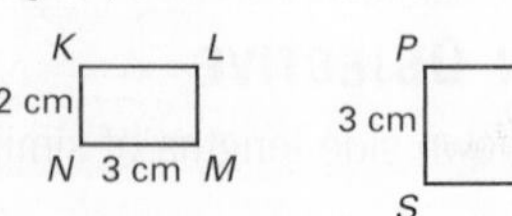

Example 2 The shadow cast by a 4-foot tall female ostrich is 10 feet long. A male ostrich standing nearby casts a shadow that is 15 feet long. How tall is the male ostrich? **6 ft tall**

Example 3 Given $\triangle GHJ \sim \triangle GKL$, find GH. **10 cm**

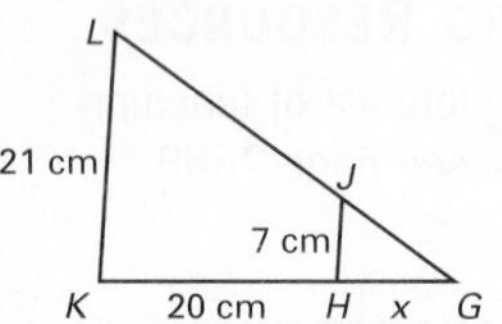

CONCEPT CHECK
Give an example of a situation in which you would use a proportion to find an indirect measurement. ***Sample answer:* To determine the height of a flagpole, you could use your own height, the length of your shadow, and the length of the flagpole's shadow to write and solve a proportion.**

DAILY PUZZLER
If you triple the length of the sides of a square, what happens to its area? **It is multiplied by 9.**

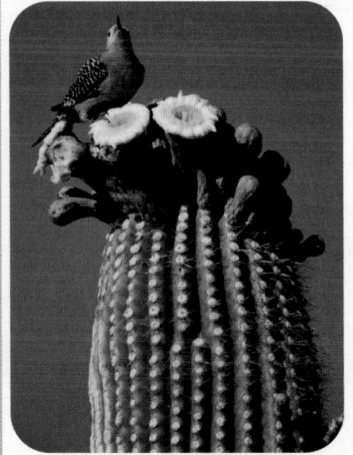

In the **Real World**

Cactus To live in the desert, a cactus contains an enormous quantity of water inside its trunk. Suppose a saguaro cactus weighs 8000 pounds and holds 1 ton of water. What fraction of the cactus's weight is water? $\frac{1}{4}$ **water**

Study *Strategy*

To solve a problem like the one in Example 3, you may find it helpful to redraw the two triangles so they don't overlap.

Indirect Measurement You can use similar figures to find lengths that are difficult to measure directly.

Example 2 *Using Indirect Measurement*

Use indirect measurement to find the height of the cactus described on page 293. The cactus and the man are perpendicular to the ground. The sun's rays strike the cactus and the man at the same angle, forming two similar triangles.

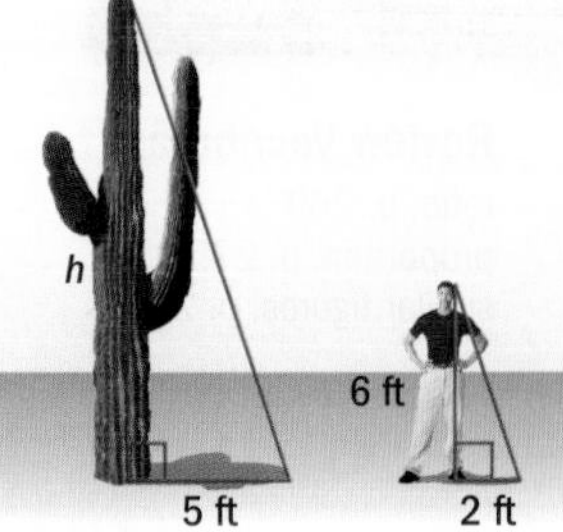

Solution

Write and solve a proportion to find the height h (in feet) of the cactus.

$$\frac{\text{Height of cactus}}{\text{Height of man}} = \frac{\text{Length of cactus's shadow}}{\text{Length of man's shadow}}$$

$\frac{h}{6} = \frac{5}{2}$ **Substitute.**

$2h = 6 \cdot 5$ **Cross products property**

$2h = 30$ **Multiply.**

$h = 15$ **Divide each side by 2.**

Answer The cactus has a height of 15 feet.

Checkpoint

3. A cactus is 5 feet tall and casts a shadow that is 1.5 feet long. How tall is a nearby cactus that casts a shadow that is 8 feet long?
$26\frac{2}{3}$ **ft, or 26 ft 8 in.**

Example 3 *Using Algebra and Similar Triangles*

Given $\triangle ABC \sim \triangle DEC$, find BE.

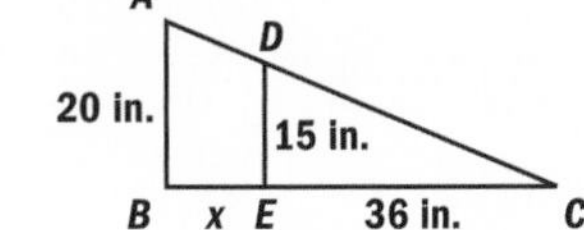

To find BE, write and solve a proportion.

$\frac{AB}{DE} = \frac{BC}{EC}$ **Write proportion.**

$\frac{AB}{DE} = \frac{BE + EC}{EC}$ **Use the fact that $BC = BE + EC$.**

$\frac{20}{15} = \frac{x + 36}{36}$ **Substitute.**

$20 \cdot 36 = 15(x + 36)$ **Cross products property**

$720 = 15x + 540$ **Multiply.**

$180 = 15x$ **Subtract 540 from each side.**

$12 = x$ **Divide each side by 15.**

Answer The length of $\overline{BE}$ is 12 inches.

6.5 Exercises

More Practice, p. 808

Guided Practice

Vocabulary Check

1. $EFGH \sim JKLM$. Which side of $EFGH$ corresponds with $\overline{JM}$? $\overline{EH}$
2. Describe how similar triangles are useful for indirect measurement. See margin.

In Exercises 3 and 4, $\triangle ABC \sim \triangle DEF$.

Skill Check

3. Find EF. 4 m
4. Find FD. 8.5 m

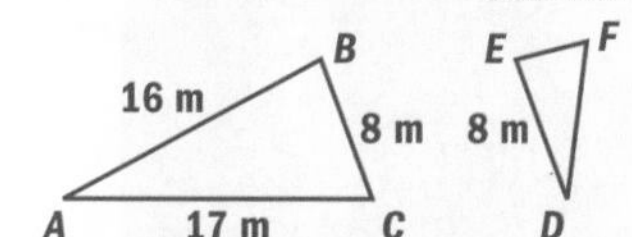

Guided Problem Solving

5. **Palm Tree** A man who is 74 inches tall stands beside a palm tree. The length of the man's shadow is 26 inches. The palm tree's shadow is 80 inches long. How tall is the palm tree?

   ① The rays of the sun create similar triangles for the man and the palm tree. Write a proportion using the triangles.

   ② Find the height of the palm tree to the nearest inch. 228 in.

x
74 in.
80 in.
26 in.

2. ***Sample answer:*** If you know the lengths of two corresponding sides of similar triangles, you can find their ratio. Then if you know the length of a second side of one of the triangles, you can find the length of the corresponding side of the other triangle without having to measure it by writing a proportion using the ratio you have found and the given length.

5. Step 1: *Sample answer:* $\frac{x}{74} = \frac{80}{26}$

Practice and Problem Solving

Homework Help

Example	Exercises
1	6–9, 13
2	12, 14
3	10, 11, 15

Online Resources
CLASSZONE.COM
- More Examples
- eTutorial Plus

A 6. Given $\triangle ABC \sim \triangle LMN$, find LN. 24 in.

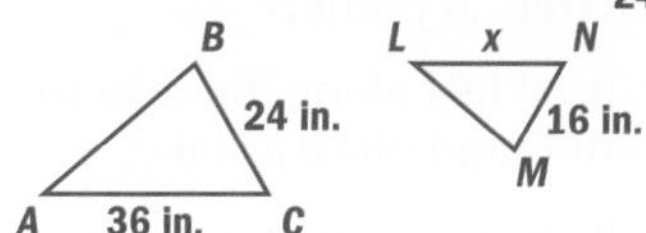

7. Given $LMNP \sim QRST$, find RS. 15 mm

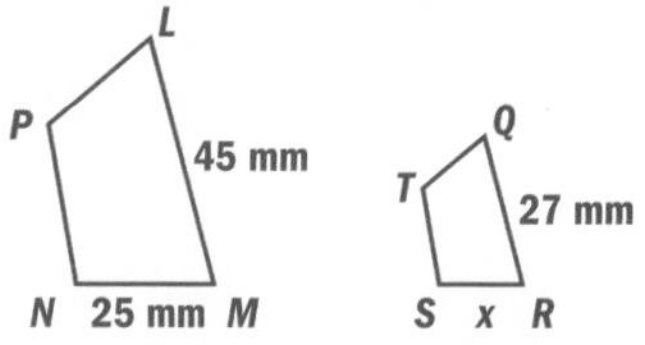

8. Given $ABCD \sim KLMJ$, find KL. 9 cm

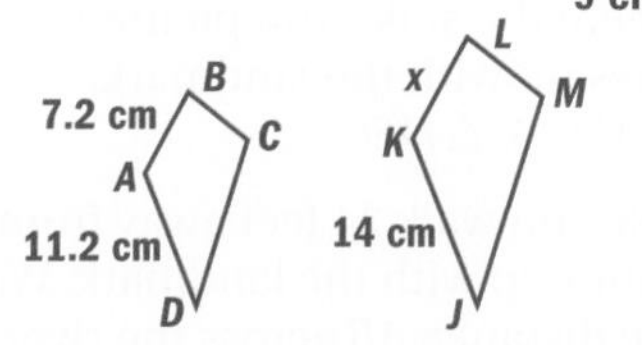

9. Given $ABCD \sim RSTU$, find UR. 12.5 yd

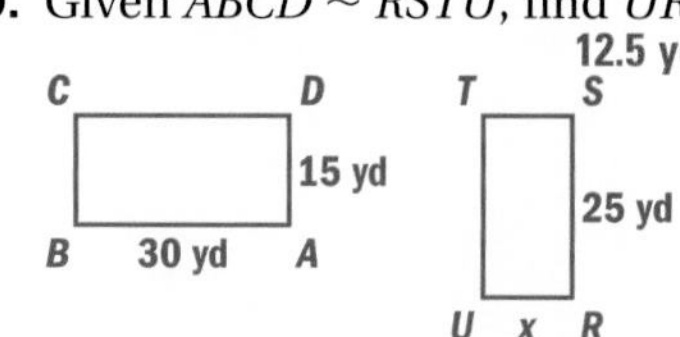

3 APPLY

ASSIGNMENT GUIDE

Basic Course
Day 1: pp. 295–297 Exs. 6–12, 14, 15, 18–25

Average Course
Day 1: pp. 295–297 Exs. 8–16, 18–25

Advanced Course
Day 1: pp. 295–297 Exs. 8–17*, 20–25

Block
pp. 295–297 Exs. 8–16, 18–25 (with 6.6)

Extra Practice

- Student Edition, p. 808
- Chapter 6 Resource Book, pp. 43–45
- Test and Practice Generator

Transparency

Even-numbered answers are available on transparencies.

Homework Check

When you review students' homework for this lesson, go over the following exercises to check understanding of key concepts.
Basic: 6, 8, 10, 11, 12
Average: 8, 10, 11, 12, 13
Advanced: 8, 10, 12, 14, 15

Common Error

In Exercise 6, watch for students who do not correctly identify the corresponding vertices due to the fact that this exercise requires them to visualize flipping one triangle over to make the corresponding vertices have the same orientation.

TEACHING TIP

In Exercise 10, make sure students understand why the proportion used to find DE must include the sum of AE and EC. For many students, it may be helpful to sketch the two triangles, $\triangle ABC$ and $\triangle ADE$, separately in order to correctly identify the known lengths.

Brain Game.

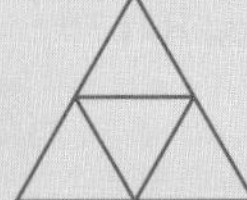

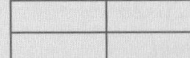

Find the length of $\overline{DE}$.

10. $\triangle ABC \sim \triangle ADE$ **6 ft**

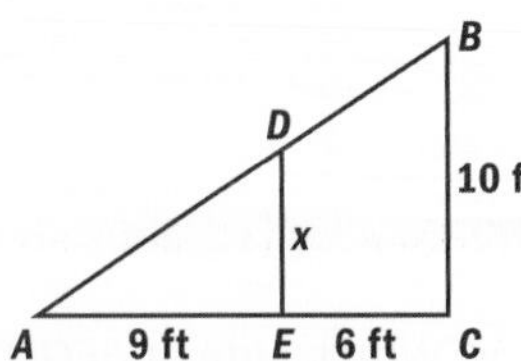

11. $ABCD \sim AGFE$ **9 m**

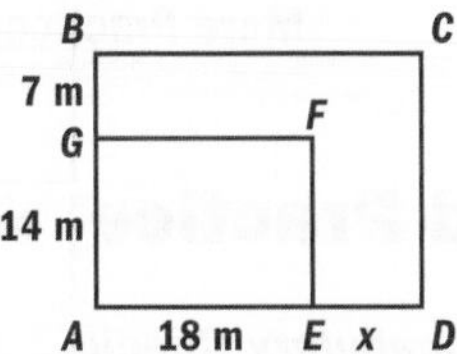

12. Bryce Canyon Bryce Canyon National Park in Utah is known for its unusual rock formations. One rock casts a shadow 21 feet long. A girl standing near this rock is 5 feet 3 inches tall and casts a shadow 7 feet long.

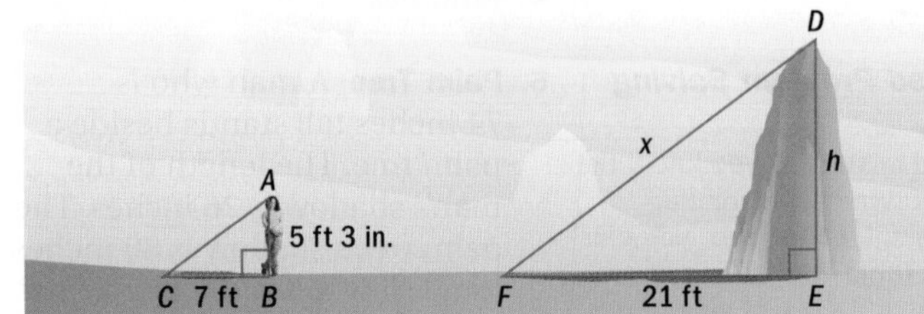

a. Convert Write the girl's height in inches. **63 in.**

b. Write and solve a proportion to find the height of the rock in feet and inches. ***Sample answer:*** $\frac{h}{5.25} = \frac{21}{7}$, **15.75 ft, or 15 ft 9 in.**

Hikers in Bryce Canyon National Park, Utah

Review *Help*

You may find it helpful to draw a diagram when solving problems about similar figures. For help with drawing a diagram, see p. 795.

13. Poster You are enlarging a photograph to make a poster. The poster will be similar to the original photograph. The photograph is 6 inches tall and 4 inches wide. The poster will be 2.5 feet wide. How tall will the poster be? Find the poster's perimeter. **3.75 ft; 12.5 ft**

14. Surveying You can use indirect measurement to find the distance across a river by following these steps.

1) Start at a point A directly across the river from a landmark, such as a tree, at point B.
2) Walk 30 feet along the river to point C and place a stake.
3) Walk 20 feet farther along the river to point D.
4) Turn and walk directly away from the river. Stop at point E, where the stake you planted lines up with the landmark. $\triangle ABC \sim \triangle DEC$.

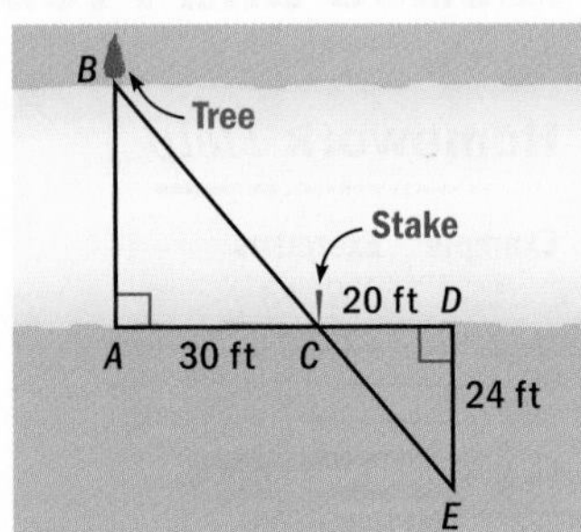

Suppose you walk 24 feet away from the river along $\overline{DE}$ before the stake lines up with the landmark. Write and solve a proportion to find the distance AB across the river.

Sample answer: $\frac{24}{AB} = \frac{20}{30}$, **36 ft**

B 15. In the figure, $\triangle ABC$, $\triangle ADE$, and $\triangle AFG$ are all similar.

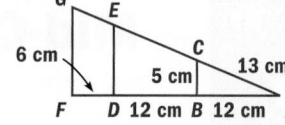

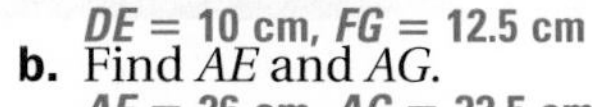

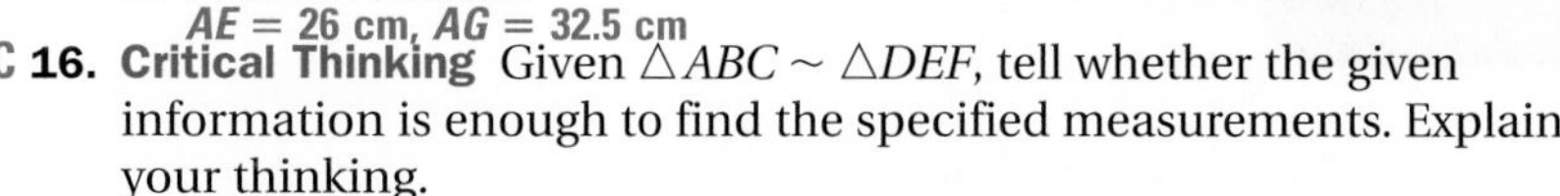

a. Find DE and FG.
$DE = 10$ cm, $FG = 12.5$ cm

b. Find AE and AG.
$AE = 26$ cm, $AG = 32.5$ cm

C 16. Critical Thinking Given $\triangle ABC \sim \triangle DEF$, tell whether the given information is enough to find the specified measurements. Explain your thinking.

a. You know AB, BC, CA, and DE. You want to find EF and FD.

b. You know AB, BC, and FD. You want to find CA. **See margin.**

c. You know $m\angle B$. You want to find $m\angle E$.
Yes. *Sample answer:* $\angle B$ and $\angle E$ are corresponding angles, so $m\angle E = m\angle B$.

16a. Yes. *Sample answer:* AB and DE are lengths of corresponding sides, so you can find the ratio of the lengths of corresponding sides of the triangles. The known length BC corresponds to the unknown length EF and the known length CA corresponds to the unknown length FD, so you can write a proportion involving the ratio for which only one quantity is unknown.

17. Challenge A rectangular box has a length of 3 inches, a width of 2 inches, and a height of 4 inches. Find the dimensions of three similar boxes: one that has a length of 6 inches, one that has a width of 6 inches, and one that has a height of 6 inches. **first box: 6 in. by 4 in. by 8 in.; second box: 9 in. by 6 in. by 12 in.; third box: 4.5 in. by 3 in. by 6 in.**

Mixed Review

16b. No. *Sample answer:* You do not know the lengths of any pair of corresponding sides, so you cannot find the ratio of the lengths of corresponding sides of the triangles.

Solve the equation. *(Lesson 5.6)*

18. $\frac{5}{7}x = 16$ $22\frac{2}{5}$ **19.** $-\frac{4}{9}x = 12$ -27 **20.** $\frac{3}{4}x + \frac{5}{8} = 1$ $\frac{1}{2}$ **21.** $-\frac{1}{2}x + 6 = 5\frac{4}{5}$ $\frac{2}{5}$

Order the ratios from least to greatest. *(Lesson 6.1)*

22. $5:3, 6:4, \frac{11}{3}$, 3 to 1, $33:100$
$33:100, 6:4, 5:3$, 3 to 1, $\frac{11}{3}$

23. 15 to 9, $35:25, \frac{44}{33}, \frac{22}{20}, 8:3$
$\frac{22}{20}, \frac{44}{33}, 35:25$, 15 to 9, $8:3$

Standardized Test Practice

In Exercises 24 and 25, $\triangle RST \sim \triangle VUT$.

S
9 yd
U
5 yd
R 8 yd V 4 yd T

24. Multiple Choice Find UV. **A**

A. 3 yards **B.** 4 yards
C. 4.5 yards **D.** 5 yards

25. Multiple Choice Find ST. **I**

F. 8 yards **G.** 10 yards **H.** 12 yards **I.** 15 yards

Putting the Pieces Together

Arrange the four congruent triangles to create a larger similar triangle. Arrange the four congruent rectangles to create a larger similar rectangle. Sketch your answers.

Can you arrange the four congruent quadrilaterals in the bottom row to create a larger similar quadrilateral?
See margin for art; no.

4 ASSESS

Assessment Resources

For more assessment resources, see:
- Assessment Book
- Test and Practice Generator

Mini-Quiz

1. Given $\triangle KLM \sim \triangle NPQ$, find PQ.

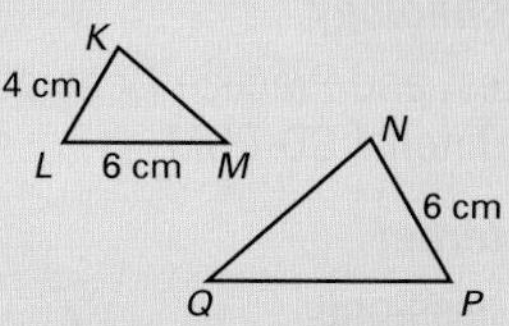

9 cm

2. Challenge A rectangular box has a length of 10 inches, a width of 5 inches, and a height of 3 inches. Find the dimensions of three similar boxes: one that has a length of 15 inches, one that has a width of 15 inches, and one that has a height of 15 inches. **15 in. by 7.5 in. by 4.5 in.; 30 in. by 15 in. by 9 in.; 50 in. by 25 in. by 15 in.**

5 FOLLOW-UP

Diagnosis/Remediation

- Study Guide in Chapter 6 Resource Book, pp. 46–47
- eTutorial Plus Online
- Extra Practice, p. 808
- Lesson Practice in Chapter 6 Resource Book, pp. 43–45

English Learner Support

- Spanish Study Guide
- Multi-Language Visual Glossary
- Chapter Audio Summaries CDs

Challenge

- Challenge Practice in Chapter 6 Resource Book, p. 48
- Teacher's Edition, p. 266F

ADDITIONAL RESOURCES

The following resources are available to help review the materials in Lessons 6.1–6.5.

Chapter 6 Resource Book
- Lesson Practice
- Study Guide

Assessment Book
- Chapter 6 Quiz 1

Technology
- Test and Practice Generator
- eTutorial CD-ROM

Internet
- Classzone
- eWorkbook Plus Online
- eTutorial Plus Online

ENGLISH LEARNER SUPPORT

- Spanish Study Guide
- Multi-Language Visual Glossary
- Chapter Audio Summaries CDs

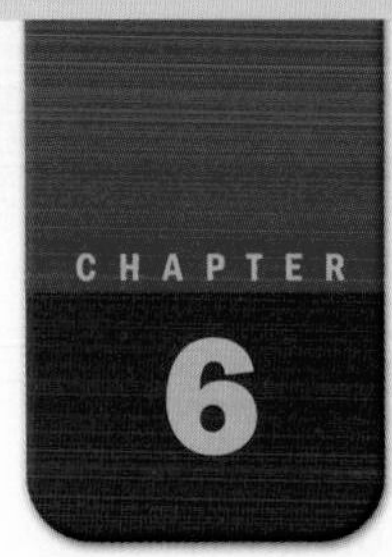

Mid-Chapter Quiz

1. Activities The table gives the number of hours Chad spends doing various activities on a school day. Write the following ratios in simplest form.

a. The hours he is at school or traveling to and from school to the hours in a day $\frac{1}{3}$

b. The hours he is asleep to the hours in a day $\frac{3}{8}$

c. The hours he is awake to the hours he is asleep $\frac{5}{3}$

Daily activities	Time
School	7 hours
Relaxing or doing homework at home	5 hours
Football practice	2 hours
Traveling to and from school	1 hour
Sleeping	9 hours

2. Car A car travels at a speed of 44 feet per second. What is this speed in miles per hour? **30 mi/h**

Solve the proportion.

3. $\frac{w}{7} = \frac{36}{42}$ 6 **4.** $\frac{x}{10} = \frac{35}{50}$ 7 **5.** $\frac{3}{4} = \frac{y}{52}$ 39 **6.** $\frac{7}{12} = \frac{z}{105}$ 61.25

7. $\frac{5}{8} = \frac{25}{a}$ 40 **8.** $\frac{8}{b} = \frac{60}{75}$ 10 **9.** $\frac{0.4}{c} = \frac{1.2}{21}$ 7 **10.** $\frac{5.2}{3} = \frac{78}{d}$ 45

Tell whether the ratios form a proportion.

11. $\frac{25}{36}, \frac{5}{6}$ no **12.** $\frac{8}{9}, \frac{36}{32}$ no **13.** $\frac{8}{18}, \frac{12}{27}$ yes **14.** $\frac{6}{31.2}, \frac{2.5}{13}$ yes

15. American Flag The blue portion of the American flag is known as the union. Using the measurements in the diagram, determine if the rectangle enclosing the union is similar to the rectangle enclosing the entire flag. **no**

18.24 in.
13 in.
2 ft
3.8 ft

16. Given $\triangle ABC \sim \triangle FGH$, find FG. **9 m**

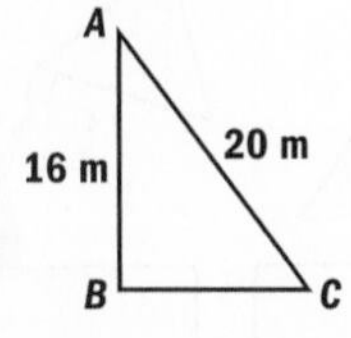

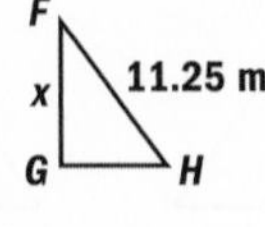

17. Given $PQRS \sim JKLM$, find KL. **1.8 ft**

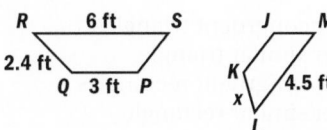

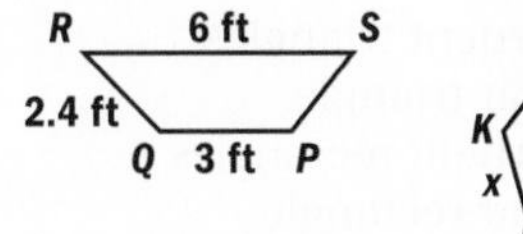

Concept *Activity*

6.6 Making a Scale Drawing

Goal
Make a scale drawing of an object.

Materials
- metric ruler

A *scale drawing* is a drawing that is similar to the object it represents. You are making a scale drawing of a rectangular stage so that you can plan the arrangement of props for a school play. The stage is 12 meters long and 9 meters wide. In your drawing, 1 centimeter represents 3 meters on the stage. What dimensions should you use for the stage in the drawing?

Investigate

Use proportions to make a scale drawing.

Use a proportion to find the length l (in centimeters) of the stage in the drawing.

$$\frac{1 \text{ cm}}{3 \text{ m}} = \frac{l}{12 \text{ m}}$$

$$1 \cdot 12 = 3 \cdot l$$

$$4 = l$$

Use a proportion to find the width w (in centimeters) of the stage in the drawing.

$$\frac{1 \text{ cm}}{3 \text{ m}} = \frac{w}{9 \text{ m}}$$

$$1 \cdot 9 = 3 \cdot w$$

$$3 = w$$

Use a ruler to draw a 4 cm by 3 cm rectangle. This rectangle represents the stage.

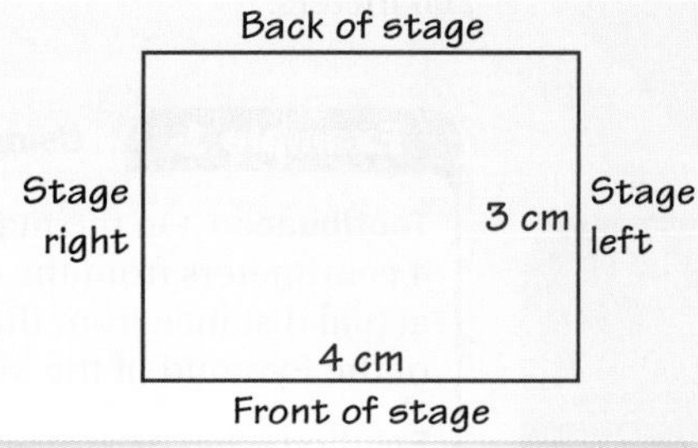

Draw Conclusions

1. The table shows the dimensions of rectangular pieces of furniture to be placed on the stage. Find the length and width you should use for each piece of furniture in the scale drawing. **sofa: 0.6 cm, 0.3 cm; table: 0.4 cm, 0.3 cm; piano: 0.5 cm, 0.2 cm**

Item	Length	Width
Sofa	1.8 m	0.9 m
Table	1.2 m	0.9 m
Upright piano	1.5 m	0.6 m

2. Make a scale drawing of the stage. Include scale drawings of the sofa, the table, and the piano so that the sofa is near the back of the stage, the table is stage left near the front, and the piano is stage right near the front. **See margin.**

NCTM CURRICULUM STANDARDS
Standard 10: Create representations to communicate mathematical ideas; Use representations to solve problems

1 PLAN

INVESTIGATE THE CONCEPT

- Students make a scale drawing of an object.
- This activity leads into using scale drawings to find actual distances in Lesson 6.6.

MATERIALS

Each student will need a metric ruler.

RECOMMENDED TIME

Work activity: 10 min
Discuss results: 5 min

GROUPING

Students should work individually.

2 TEACH

ALTERNATIVE STRATEGY

Clear a large space in the classroom. Have all students collectively create a scale model using a 30-cm metric ruler to represent each meter of the stage. They will need 12 rulers to model the front and back of the stage and 9 rulers to model both of the sides of the stage.

3 CLOSE

KEY DISCOVERY

You can use scale drawings to find measures indirectly.

ASSESSMENT

1. When you make a sketch of a figure, how is the sketch like a scale drawing? **It is a smaller representation of a figure with side measures in proportion to the real figure.**

2. See Additional Answers beginning on page AA1.

1 PLAN

Skill Check

Convert.

1. 2 meters to centimeters **200 cm**
2. 6 feet to inches **72 in.**
3. 60 inches to feet **5 ft**
4. 350 centimeters to meters **3.5 m**

Lesson Objective

Use proportions with scale drawings.

Pacing

Suggested Number of Days
Basic Course: 1 day
Average Course: 1 day
Advanced Course: 1 day
Block: 0.5 block with 6.5

Teaching Resources

For a complete list of Teaching Resources, see page 266B.

Transparency

Warm-Up Exercises for this lesson are available on a transparency.

2 TEACH

Motivating the Lesson

Invite students to describe where they have seen or used a scale model or scale drawing. Students may have seen or built models, or they may have seen scale drawings in museum displays or elsewhere.

LESSON 6.6

Scale Drawings

BEFORE	Now	WHY?
You solved proportions.	You'll use proportions with scale drawings.	So you can find the height of a roller coaster, as in Ex. 40.

Vocabulary
scale drawing, p. 300
scale model, p. 300
scale, p. 300

Scale Drawings The map shows a portion of Teotihuacan, a large city built over 2000 years ago. The ruins of the city still exist in central Mexico.

The map is an example of a *scale drawing*. A **scale drawing** is a two-dimensional drawing that is similar to the object it represents. A **scale model** is a three-dimensional model that is similar to the object it represents.

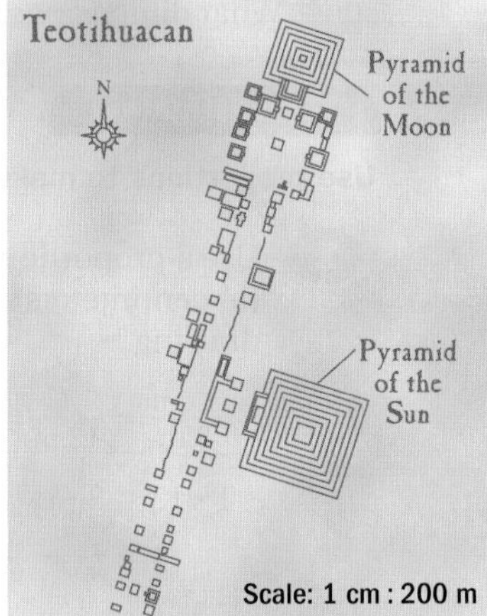

The **scale** of a scale drawing or scale model gives the relationship between the drawing or model's dimensions and the actual dimensions. For example, in the map shown, the scale 1 cm : 200 m means that 1 centimeter in the scale drawing represents an actual distance of 200 meters.

Reading *Algebra*

In this course, all scales are written as
scale measure : actual measure.

Example 1 *Using a Scale Drawing*

Teotihuacan On the map, the center of the Pyramid of the Sun is 4 centimeters from the center of the Pyramid of the Moon. What is the actual distance from the center of the Pyramid of the Sun to the center of the Pyramid of the Moon?

Solution

Let x represent the actual distance (in meters) between the two pyramids. The ratio of the map distance between the two pyramids to the actual distance x is equal to the scale of the map. Write and solve a proportion using this relationship.

$$\frac{1 \text{ cm}}{200 \text{ m}} = \frac{4 \text{ cm}}{x \text{ m}}$$ ← **Map distance** / ← **Actual distance**

$1x = 200 \cdot 4$ **Cross products property**

$x = 800$ **Multiply.**

Answer The actual distance is 800 meters.

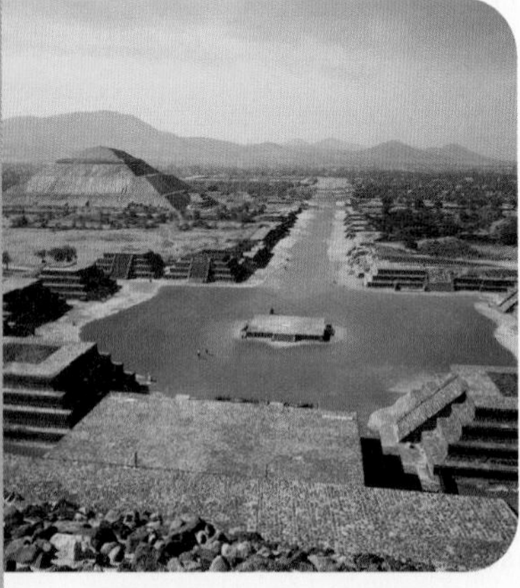

View of the Pyramid of the Sun from the Pyramid of the Moon

NCTM CURRICULUM STANDARDS
Standard 2: Represent situations using algebraic symbols
Standard 10: Use representations to solve problems

 *Checkpoint*

1. On the map on page 300, the Pyramid of the Sun has a length and a width of 1.1 centimeters. Find the actual dimensions of the Pyramid of the Sun. **220 m by 220 m**

The floral carpet in 2002 was made of 800,000 begonias.

Example 2 *Finding the Scale of a Drawing*

Floral Carpet Every few years, the Grand Place in Brussels, Belgium, is decorated with a large floral carpet made of begonias. Before making the carpet, designers make detailed scale drawings. Suppose the floral carpet is to be 40 meters wide. A designer creates a scale drawing of the carpet that is 20 centimeters wide. Find the drawing's scale.

Solution

Write a ratio using corresponding side lengths of the scale drawing and the actual carpet. Then simplify the ratio so that the numerator is 1.

$\frac{20 \text{ cm}}{40 \text{ m}}$ ← **Width of scale drawing** / ← **Width of carpet**

$\frac{20 \text{ cm}}{40 \text{ m}} = \frac{1 \text{ cm}}{2 \text{ m}}$ **Simplify.**

Answer The drawing's scale is 1 cm : 2 m.

The scale of a scale drawing or scale model can be written without units if the measurements have the same unit. To write the scale from Example 2 without units, write 2 meters as 200 centimeters, as shown.

Scale with units → **Scale without units**

1 cm : 2 m → $\frac{1 \text{ cm}}{2 \text{ m}}$ → $\frac{1 \text{ cm}}{200 \text{ cm}}$ → 1 : 200

Example 3 *Finding a Dimension of a Scale Model*

Space Shuttle A model of a space shuttle has a scale of 1 : 52. The space shuttle has a wingspan of 78 feet. Find the model's wingspan.

Solution

Write a proportion using the scale.

$\frac{1}{52} = \frac{x}{78}$ ← **Dimension of model** / ← **Dimension of space shuttle**

$78 = 52x$ **Cross products property**

$1.5 = x$ **Divide each side by 52.**

Answer The wingspan of the model is 1.5 ft.

Checkpoint

2. The length of a space shuttle is a 122 feet. Find the length of the scale model in Example 3 to the nearest tenth of a foot. **2.3 ft**

TIPS *for* NEW TEACHERS

Students must understand precisely what the scale is on each problem they encounter. Urge students to write the scale for each problem, even if it is provided to them. See Tips for New Teachers in the *Chapter 6 Resource Book*.

Extra Examples

Example 1 A map uses a scale of 1 inch = 5 miles. Two towns on the map are 4.5 inches apart. How far apart are the actual towns? **22.5 mi**

Example 2 Mike's map shows a bicycle route that is 112 miles long. On his map, this distance is 14 inches. What is the scale of the map? **1 in. = 8 mi**

Example 3 A model of a sailboat has a scale of 1 : 20. The actual sailboat is 32 feet long. How long is the model? **1.6 ft**

CONCEPT CHECK

What does a scale of 1 : 50 mean? ***Sample answer:* 1 unit on the drawing represents 50 units on the real object. For example, a length of 1 centimeter on the drawing would represent a length of 50 centimeters on the actual object.**

DAILY PUZZLER

Our solar system has a radius of about 5,900,000,000 kilometers. What scale could you use to make a model that would fit in a school gymnasium? ***Sample answer:* 1 m : 1 × 10^9 km**

3 APPLY

ASSIGNMENT GUIDE

Basic Course

Day 1: SRH p. 788 Exs. 1-4; pp. 302-304 Exs. 12-23, 28-37, 40-42, 45, 47-51

Average Course

Day 1: pp. 302-304 Exs. 16-27, 32-39, 42-45, 47-51

Advanced Course

Day 1: pp. 302-304 Exs. 16-19, 24-31, 38, 39, 42-51*

Block

pp. 302-304 Exs. 16-27, 32-39, 42-45, 47-51 (with 6.5)

EXTRA PRACTICE

- Student Edition, p. 808
- Chapter 6 Resource Book, pp. 52-54
- Test and Practice Generator

TRANSPARENCY

Even-numbered answers are available on transparencies.

HOMEWORK CHECK

When you review students' homework for this lesson, go over the following exercises to check understanding of key concepts.

Basic: 12, 20, 23, 36, 40
Average: 16, 22, 25, 37, 40
Advanced: 16, 25, 36, 37, 41

6.6 Exercises

More Practice, p. 808

Guided Practice

Vocabulary Check

1. What is a scale drawing?
A two-dimensional drawing that is similar to the object it represents.
2. Write the scale 1 inch : 1 foot without units. 1 : 12

Skill Check

A map has a scale of 1 inch : 40 miles. Use the given map distance to find the actual distance.

3. 5 inches 200 mi
4. 12 inches 480 mi
5. 32 inches 1280 mi
6. 1 foot 480 mi

Write the scale without units.

7. 1 in. : 28 yd 1 : 1008
8. 1 in. : 4 ft 1 : 48
9. 1 cm : 12 m 1 : 1200
10. 1 mm : 2 m 1 : 2000

Guided Problem Solving

11. **Bedroom** Shown below is a scale drawing of a student's bedroom. Use the scale drawing to determine the dimensions of the student's desk.

(1) The student's bed is 2 meters long. In the scale drawing, the bed is 2.5 centimeters long. Find the scale of the drawing. 1 cm : 0.8 m

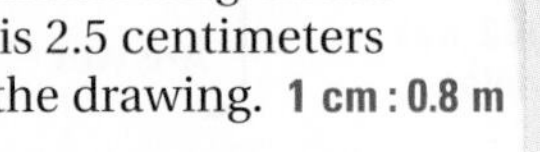

(2) Write the scale from Step 1 without units. 1 : 80

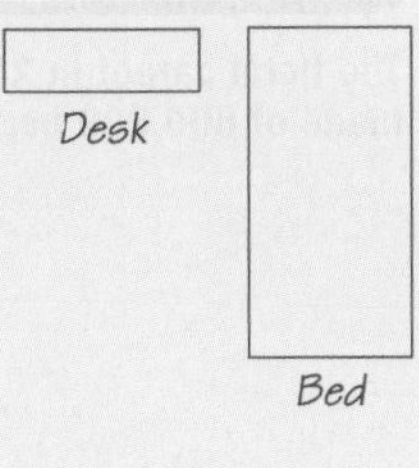

(3) In the drawing, the desk is 1.5 centimeters long and 0.5 centimeter wide. Write and solve a proportion to find the dimensions of the student's actual desk.
Sample answer: $\frac{1}{80} = \frac{1.5}{l}$, $l = 120$ cm, or 1.2 m; $\frac{1}{80} = \frac{0.5}{w}$, $w = 40$ cm, or 0.4 m

Practice and Problem Solving

Homework *Help*

Example	Exercises
1	12-27, 38, 41,
2	36, 37
3	38-41

Online Resources
CLASSZONE.COM
- More Examples
- eTutorial Plus

A map has a scale of 1 centimeter : 5 kilometers. Use the given map distance to find the actual distance.

A
12. 6 cm 30 km
13. 11 cm 55 km
14. 26 cm 130 km
15. 37 cm 185 km
16. 0.6 cm 3 km
17. 1.5 cm 7.5 km
18. 20 cm 100 km
19. 9 cm 45 km

A map has a scale of 1 inch : 3 kilometers. Use the given actual distance to find the distance on the map.

20. 18 km 6 in.
21. 90 km 30 in.
22. 76 km $25\frac{1}{3}$ in.
23. 14 km $4\frac{2}{3}$ in.
24. 0.9 km 0.3 in.
25. 1.5 km 0.5 in.
26. 0.3 km 0.1 in.
27. 0.5 km $\frac{1}{6}$ in.

Write the scale without units.

28. 1 in. : 10 yd 1 : 360
29. 1 in. : 20 ft 1 : 240
30. 1 cm : 1 m 1 : 100
31. 1 mm : 36 cm 1 : 360
32. 1 cm : 3 km 1 : 300,000
33. 1 cm : 5 km 1 : 500,000
34. 1 cm : 2 m 1 : 200
35. 1 mm : 34 cm 1 : 340

Teaching Tip

In Exercise 16, ask students whether 0.6 centimeters is more or less than 1 centimeter. Then ask whether the actual distance should be more or less than 5 kilometers. Prior to assigning Exercises 28–35, you might wish to review converting among the units listed in these exercises: inches, feet, and yards; millimeters, centimeters, meters, and kilometers.

36. Architecture In a scale drawing, a wall is 8 centimeters long. The actual wall is 20 meters long. Find the scale of the drawing. **1 : 250**

37. Interior Design A sofa is 8 feet long. In a scale drawing, the sofa is 3 inches long. Find the scale of the drawing. **1 : 32**

38. Basketball Court A scale drawing of a basketball court has a scale of 1 inch : 9 feet.

a. The basketball court is 94 feet by 50 feet. Find the dimensions of the court in the drawing. **$10\frac{4}{9}$ in. by $5\frac{5}{9}$ in.**

b. The free throw line is 15 feet from the backboard. How far is the free throw line from the backboard in the drawing? **$1\frac{2}{3}$ in.**

39. Carpentry A carpenter is building a house from an architect's blueprint. The blueprint has a scale of 1 : 42.

a. Find the actual length of a wall that is 3 inches long in the blueprint. **126 in., or 10 ft 6 in.**

b. A door on the blueprint is 2 inches high. Find the height of the actual door. **84 in., or 7 ft**

c. A window on the house is drawn as a rectangle that is $\frac{1}{2}$ inch by $\frac{3}{4}$ inch. Find the actual dimensions of the window. **21 in. by $31\frac{1}{2}$ in.**

40. Model Roller Coaster You are building a model of the Viper roller coaster in California using a scale of 1 : 47. The model is 4 feet high. How many feet high is the Viper? **188 ft**

41. Banner You want to make a banner that says WELCOME HOME. You want the letters to be 2 feet high. You make a sketch in which the letters are 2 inches high. The entire phrase in your sketch is 20 inches long. What length of paper should you buy? **20 ft**

B **42. Lincoln** A mask of Abraham Lincoln's head was made when he was alive. The mask has a height of $9\frac{3}{4}$ inches.

a. The profile of Lincoln's head on a penny has a height of $\frac{11}{32}$ inch. Write the scale of the penny to the mask without units. **11 : 312, or about 1 : 28.4**

b. The carving of Lincoln's face on Mount Rushmore is 60 feet high. Write the scale of the mask to the carving without units. **13 : 960, or about 1 : 73.8**

c. Write the scale of the penny to the carving without units. **11 : 23,040, or about 1 : 2094.5**

d. Lincoln's nose on the penny is about $\frac{1}{16}$ inch long. Find the length of Lincoln's nose on the carving and on the mask. Round your answers to the nearest inch. **carving: 131 in., mask: 2 in.**

43. Critical Thinking The ratio of the length of an object to its width is 3 : 2. A scale drawing of the object has a scale of 1 inch : 3 feet. In the scale drawing, what is the ratio of the object's length to its width? **3 : 2**

44. Critical Thinking Write a scale for a scale model whose dimensions are 20 times the dimensions of the actual object. Explain your reasoning. **See margin.**

44. 20 : 1. *Sample answer:* The scale is the relationship between the length of the model and the corresponding length of the actual object, so it has to be 20 : 1, which means the model is larger than the actual object.

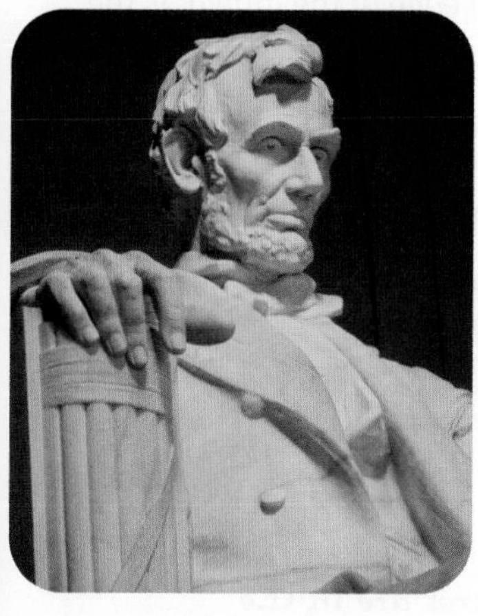

In the Real World

Lincoln The statue of Abraham Lincoln in the Lincoln Memorial in Washington, D.C., was created by Daniel Chester French over a period of 9 years. To plan his creation, French made a scale model of the statue that was 7 inches tall. The final statue was 19 feet tall. How many times taller than the scale model was the statue? **$32\frac{4}{7}$ times taller**

4 ASSESS

ASSESSMENT RESOURCES

For more assessment resources, see:
- Assessment Book
- Test and Practice Generator

MINI-QUIZ

A map has a scale of 1 in. : 80 mi. Use the given map distance to find the actual distance.

1. 3 in. **240 mi**
2. 0.75 in. **60 mi**
3. Write the scale 1 in. : 2 ft without units. **1 : 24**
4. **Challenge** You are making a scale model of Earth and the moon. The Earth's diameter is about 1.3×10^4 km. In the model, Earth's diameter is 50 cm. The Earth and the moon are about 382,500 km apart. To the nearest centimeter, how far apart should your models of Earth and the moon be? **1471 cm**

5 FOLLOW-UP

DIAGNOSIS/REMEDIATION

- Study Guide in Chapter 6 Resource Book, pp. 55–56
- Tutor Place, Ratio, Proportion, and Percent Card 6
- eTutorial Plus Online
- Extra Practice, p. 808
- Lesson Practice in Chapter 6 Resource Book, pp. 52–54

ENGLISH LEARNER SUPPORT

- Spanish Study Guide
- Multi-Language Visual Glossary
- Chapter Audio Summaries CDs

CHALLENGE

- Challenge Practice in Chapter 6 Resource Book, p. 58
- Teacher's Edition, p. 266F

51b. See Additional Answers beginning on page AA1.

Review Help

For help with using a ruler to measure lengths, see p. 788.

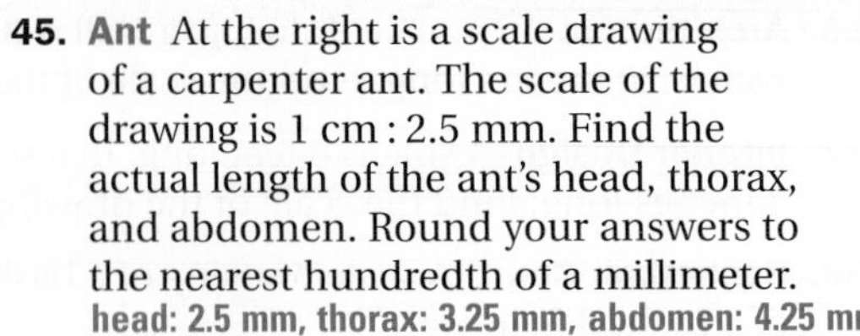

45. Ant At the right is a scale drawing of a carpenter ant. The scale of the drawing is 1 cm : 2.5 mm. Find the actual length of the ant's head, thorax, and abdomen. Round your answers to the nearest hundredth of a millimeter. **head: 2.5 mm, thorax: 3.25 mm, abdomen: 4.25 mm**

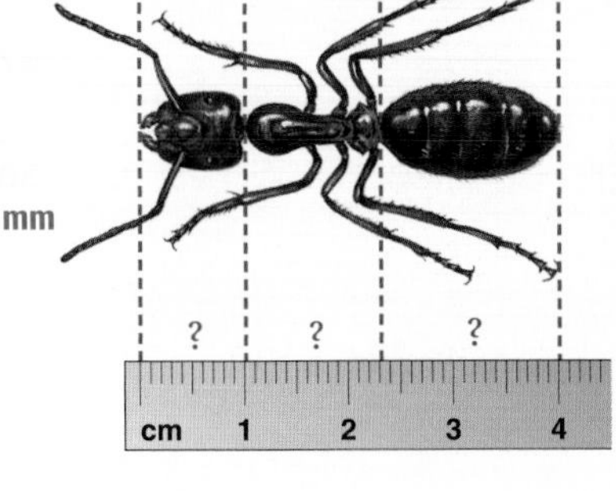

C **46. Challenge** You made a scale model of Earth and the moon. The Earth's diameter is about 1.3×10^4 kilometers. In the model, Earth's diameter is 50 centimeters. The moon's diameter is about 3.5×10^3 kilometers. Find the diameter of the moon in your model. Round your answer to the nearest tenth of a centimeter. **13.5 cm**

Mixed Review

Find the sum or difference. *(Lesson 5.2)*

47. $9\frac{8}{11} + 7\frac{6}{11}$ **$17\frac{3}{11}$**　**48.** $7\frac{5}{6} - 1\frac{5}{6}$ **6**　**49.** $-6\frac{7}{12} - 8\frac{11}{12}$ **$-15\frac{1}{2}$**

50. Baseball A square tarp is spread over a 90 foot by 90 foot baseball infield. The tarp extends 15 feet beyond each edge of the infield. Is the tarp similar to the infield? *(Lesson 6.4)* **yes**

Standardized Test Practice

51. Extended Response An architect builds a scale model of a house. The model has a scale of 1 inch : 1 yard.

a. The scale model is 1 foot high. How high is the actual house? **12 yd, or 36 ft**

b. The house's deck is a 15 foot by 12 foot rectangle. Explain how to find the area of the deck in the model. **See margin.**

Brain Game: 64 white squares; 3 : 1, or 1 to $\frac{1}{3}$. *Sample answer:* With each stage, a side of the white square is $\frac{1}{3}$ the length of a side in the previous stage.

Brain GAME

Rolling out the Carpet

Sierpinski's carpet is a pattern that involves repeatedly dividing a square into 9 smaller squares of equal size and removing the center square. The first and second stages of this pattern are shown below.

How many new white squares are in the third stage?

Write a ratio that compares the side lengths of the white square in the first stage to one small white square in the second stage. Explain how you found this ratio.

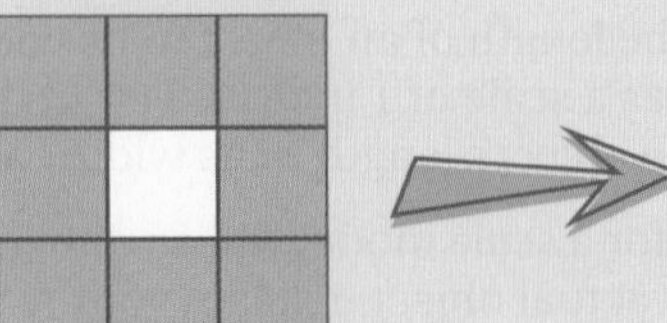

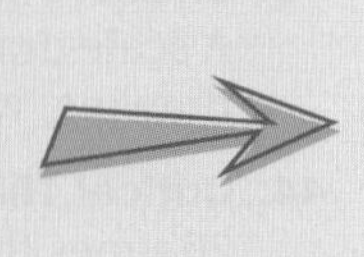

Concept *Activity*

6.7 Performing an Experiment

Goal
Use an experiment to estimate the likelihood that an event will occur.

Materials
- paper cup

Investigate

Perform an experiment to find the position in which a tossed paper cup will land most often.

 Toss a small paper cup 30 times. Note whether the cup lands on its side, lands rim side up, or lands bottom side up.

 For each toss, record the result in the *Tally* column of a frequency table like the one shown below. After 30 tosses, record the frequencies.

Position of cup	Tally	Frequency
On its side	卌 I	?
Rim side up	I	?
Bottom side up	I	?

1–5. Sample answers are given for an experiment in which the cup lands on its side 25 times, rim side up 2 times, and bottom side up 3 times, and for which after being cut in half the cup lands on its side 14 times, rim side up 15 times, and bottom side up 1 time.

Draw Conclusions

1. **Analyze** For what fraction of the tosses did the cup land on its side? rim side up? bottom side up? $\frac{5}{6}, \frac{1}{15}, \frac{1}{10}$
2. **Critical Thinking** In which position do you think the paper cup is most likely to land on your next toss? Explain your choice. **On its side.** ***Sample answer:*** **The most likely result on the next toss is the result that has been most likely in the experiment.**
3. **Predict** Find the ratio of the number of times the cup landed on its side to the total number of times the cup was tossed. Use the ratio to predict the number of times the cup will land on its side if it is tossed 1000 times. $\frac{5}{6}$**, or 5 : 6; about 833 times**
4. **Compare** Cut the paper cup so that it is only half as tall. Repeat the experiment. Then compare your results with the results of the first experiment. **See margin.**
5. **Predict** Use the results from Exercise 4 to predict the number of times the cut cup will land on its side if it is tossed 1000 times. **about 467 times**

NCTM CURRICULUM STANDARDS
Standard 5: Collect, organize, and display data; Develop inferences that are based on data
Standard 7: Make mathematical conjectures

1 PLAN

Investigate the Concept

- Students use an experiment to estimate the likelihood that an event will occur.
- This activity leads into studying odds and probability in Lesson 6.7.

Materials

Each student will need a paper cup.

Recommended Time

Work activity: 15 min
Discuss results: 5 min

Grouping

Students should work individually.

2 TEACH

Tips for Success

Before students begin, stress that the goal is not to try to get the cup to land in a specific way.

3 CLOSE

Key Discovery

You can use the results of an experiment to predict the outcomes of a larger number of trials.

Assessment

1. Which position is least likely to occur? **rim side up**
2. If you increase the number of tosses, do you expect this to change the fraction of tosses that result in the cup landing rim side up? **No, the fraction should remain about the same.**

4. See Additional Answers beginning on page AA1.

1 PLAN

Skill Check

Write the fraction as a decimal.

1. $\frac{16}{50}$ **0.32** 2. $\frac{7}{10}$ **0.7**
3. $\frac{19}{20}$ **0.95** 4. $\frac{7}{8}$ **0.875**

LESSON OBJECTIVE

Find probabilities.

PACING

Suggested Number of Days
Basic Course: 1 day
Average Course: 1 day
Advanced Course: 1 day
Block: 0.5 block with 6.8

TEACHING RESOURCES

For a complete list of Teaching Resources, see page 266B.

TRANSPARENCY

Warm-Up Exercises for this lesson are available on a transparency.

2 TEACH

MOTIVATING THE LESSON

Display a number cube and ask students questions such as "What even numbers can you roll? odd numbers? prime numbers?"

TIPS *for* NEW TEACHERS

Stress the difference between the terms *probability* and *odds*. Be sure students understand how to calculate the odds for an event when they are given the probability, and vice versa. See Tips for New Teachers in the *Chapter 6 Resource Book.*

LESSON 6.7

Probability *and* Odds

BEFORE	Now	WHY?
You wrote ratios.	You'll find probabilities.	So you can describe the accuracy of a weather forecast, as in Ex. 6.

Vocabulary

outcomes, p. 306
event, p. 306
favorable outcomes, p. 306
probability, p. 306
theoretical probability, p. 307
experimental probability, p. 307
odds in favor, p. 308
odds against, p. 308

You are rolling a number cube and want to know how likely you are to roll a certain number. Each time you roll the number cube there are six possible results.

Rolling a number cube is an example of an experiment. The possible results of an experiment are **outcomes**. When you roll a number cube, there are 6 possible outcomes: rolling a 1, 2, 3, 4, 5, or 6. An **event** is an outcome or a collection of outcomes, such as rolling a 1 or rolling an odd number. Once you specify an event, the outcomes for that event are called **favorable outcomes**. The favorable outcomes for rolling an odd number are rolling a 1, rolling a 3, and rolling a 5.

The **probability** that an event occurs is a measure of the likelihood that the event will occur.

Reading *Algebra*

Vocabulary The set of all possible outcomes for an experiment is sometimes called the *sample space.*

Probability of an Event

The probability of an event when all the outcomes are equally likely is:

$$P(\text{event}) = \frac{\text{Number of favorable outcomes}}{\text{Number of possible outcomes}}$$

Example 1 ***Finding a Probability***

Suppose you roll a number cube. What is the probability that you roll an even number?

Solution

Rolls of 2, 4, and 6 are even, so there are 3 favorable outcomes. There are 6 possible outcomes.

$$P(\text{rolling an even number}) = \frac{\text{Number of favorable outcomes}}{\text{Number of possible outcomes}}$$

$$= \frac{3}{6} = \frac{1}{2}$$

Answer The probability that you roll an even number is $\frac{1}{2}$.

NCTM CURRICULUM STANDARDS

Standard 5: Understand basic concepts of probability; Apply basic concepts of probability
Standard 7: Make mathematical conjectures

Checkpoint

1. Suppose you roll a number cube. What is the probability that you roll a number greater than 1? **$\frac{5}{6}$**

Experimental Probability The probability found in Example 1 is an example of a *theoretical probability*. A **theoretical probability** is based on knowing all of the equally likely outcomes of an experiment. A probability that is based on repeated *trials* of an experiment is called an **experimental probability**. Each trial in which the event occurs is a *success*.

Experimental Probability

The experimental probability of an event is:

$$P(\text{event}) = \frac{\text{Number of successes}}{\text{Number of trials}}$$

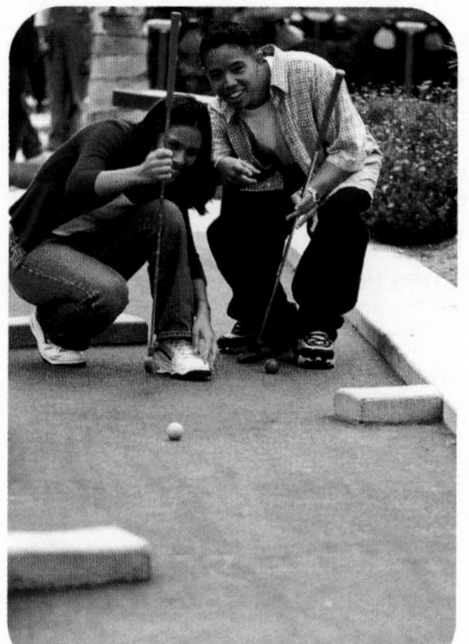

Example 2 *Finding Experimental Probability*

Miniature Golf A miniature golf course offers a free game to golfers who make a hole-in-one on the last hole. Last week, 44 out of 256 golfers made a hole-in-one on the last hole. Find the experimental probability that a golfer makes a hole-in-one on the last hole.

Solution

$$P(\text{hole-in-one}) = \frac{44}{256} \quad \begin{matrix}\leftarrow \textbf{Number of successes} \\ \leftarrow \textbf{Number of trials}\end{matrix}$$

$$= \frac{11}{64} \qquad \textbf{Simplify.}$$

Answer The experimental probability that a golfer makes a hole-in-one on the last hole is $\frac{11}{64}$, or about 0.17.

Checkpoint

2. You interviewed 45 randomly chosen students for the newspaper. Of the students you interviewed, 15 play sports. Find the experimental probability that the next randomly chosen student will play sports. **$\frac{1}{3}$, or about 0.33**

Interpreting Probabilities Probabilities can range from 0 to 1. The closer the probability of an event is to 1, the more likely the event will occur.

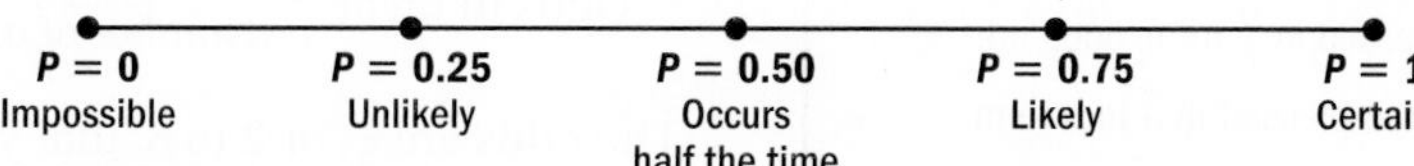

You can use probabilities to make predictions about uncertain occurrences.

Study *Strategy*

Probabilities can be written as fractions or decimals.

Extra Examples

Example 1 Suppose you roll a number cube. What is the probability that you roll either a 4 or a 5? **$\frac{1}{3}$**

Example 2 Of the first 70 visitors through the turnstiles at a theme park, 18 visitors agreed to participate in a survey being conducted by park employees. Find the experimental probability that a theme park visitor will participate in the survey. **$\frac{9}{35}$, or about 0.26**

Teaching Tip

Explain the difference between *theoretical probability* and *experimental probability*, and discuss when you would use each of the two types.

Differentiating Instruction

Alternative Teaching Strategy
Ask students the theoretical probability of rolling a 2 when a number cube is rolled. **$\frac{1}{6}$** Then provide pairs of students with a number cube and have them roll it 30 times, recording the number of times they rolled a 2. Have students compare the experimental and theoretical probabilities of rolling a 2 on a number cube.

Extra Examples

Example 3 Last year, Alexia planted 12 tulip bulbs, but only 10 of them bloomed. This year she intends to plant 60 tulip bulbs. Use experimental probability to predict how many bulbs will bloom. **50 bulbs**

Example 4 Suppose you randomly choose one letter from A through J.

a. What are the odds in favor of choosing a vowel? $\frac{3}{7}$

b. What are the odds against choosing a vowel? $\frac{7}{3}$

ALGEBRAIC REASONING

Lead students to recognize that probability is calculated using the *total number of possible outcomes.* Stress that odds are calculated using *favorable* and *unfavorable outcomes*. Help students reason that in order to find the probability of an event given its odds of occurring, they must add the favorable and unfavorable outcomes to find the total number of possible outcomes.

CONCEPT CHECK

How are the odds of an event different from the probability of the event? ***Sample answer:* Odds are the ratio of the number of favorable outcomes to the number of unfavorable outcomes, while the probability is the ratio of favorable outcomes to the total number of possible outcomes.**

DAILY PUZZLER

Using a fair coin, are you more likely to flip four heads in a row or heads, tails, heads, tails? **Both are equally likely.**

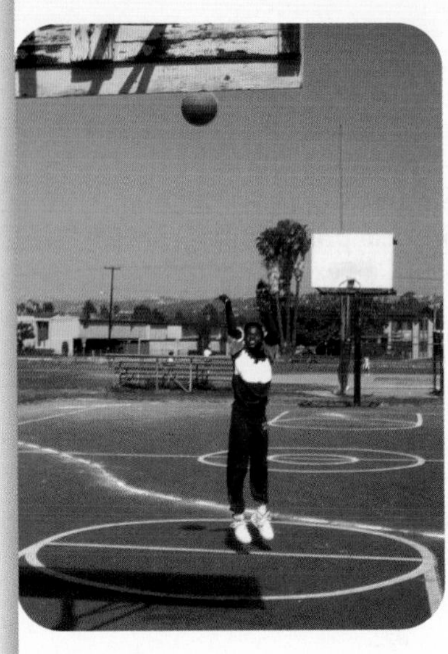

Example 3 *Using Probability to Make a Prediction*

Basketball Today, you attempted 50 free throws and made 32 of them. Use experimental probability to predict how many free throws you will make tomorrow if you attempt 75 free throws.

Solution

1. Find the experimental probability that you make a free throw.

$$P(\text{make a free throw}) = \frac{32}{50} = 0.64$$

2. Multiply the experimental probability by the number of free throws you will attempt tomorrow.

$$0.64 \cdot 75 = 48$$

Answer If you continue to make free throws at the same rate, you will make 48 free throws in 75 attempts tomorrow.

Checkpoint

3. Use the information in Example 3 to predict how many free throws you would make if you attempt 150 free throws. **96 free throws**

Odds When all outcomes are equally likely, the ratio of the number of favorable outcomes to the number of unfavorable outcomes is called the **odds in favor** of an event. The ratio of the number of unfavorable outcomes to the number of favorable outcomes is called the **odds against** an event.

$$\text{Odds in favor} = \frac{\text{Number of favorable outcomes}}{\text{Number of unfavorable outcomes}}$$

$$\text{Odds against} = \frac{\text{Number of unfavorable outcomes}}{\text{Number of favorable outcomes}}$$

Example 4 *Finding the Odds*

Suppose you randomly choose a number between 1 and 20.

a. What are the odds in favor of choosing a prime number?

b. What are the odds against choosing a prime number?

Solution

a. There are 8 favorable outcomes (2, 3, 5, 7, 11, 13, 17, and 19) and $20 - 8 = 12$ unfavorable outcomes.

$$\text{Odds in favor} = \frac{\text{Number of favorable outcomes}}{\text{Number of unfavorable outcomes}} = \frac{8}{12} = \frac{2}{3}$$

The odds are $\frac{2}{3}$, or 2 to 3, that you choose a prime number.

b. The odds against choosing a prime number are $\frac{3}{2}$, or 3 to 2.

Reading *Algebra*

While probabilities are often expressed in $\frac{a}{b}$ form, odds are often expressed in *a* to *b* form.

6.7 Exercises

More Practice, p. 808

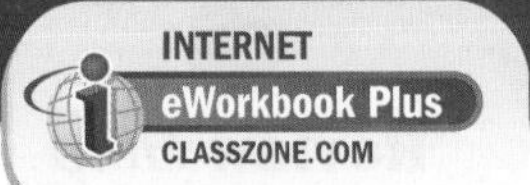

Guided Practice

Vocabulary Check

1. Copy and complete: When a coin is flipped 20 times and lands heads up 11 times, the _?_ probability that the coin lands heads up is $\frac{11}{20}$. **experimental**

2. The odds in favor of event A are 2 to 1. The odds against event B are 2 to 1. Which event is more likely to occur, event A or event B? **event A**

Skill Check

In Exercises 3–5, suppose you roll a number cube. Find the probability of the event.

3. A prime number $\frac{1}{2}$ **4.** A multiple of 2 $\frac{1}{2}$ **5.** A number less than 5 $\frac{2}{3}$

Guided Problem Solving

6. Forecast Over the course of a month, you keep track of how many times the next day's weather forecast is accurate. The forecast is correct 22 times in a month of 30 days. Predict how many days over the course of a year the forecast will be correct.

1) Find the experimental probability that the forecast is correct. $\frac{11}{15}$

2) Multiply your answer from Step 1 by 365 to predict how many days the forecast will be correct over the course of a year. **about 268 days**

Practice and Problem Solving

Homework *Help*

Example	Exercises
1	7, 11-12
2	12, 14
3	10, 13, 14, 19
4	8-9, 11

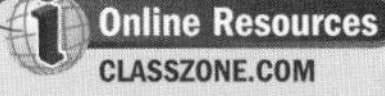

CLASSZONE.COM
- More Examples
- eTutorial Plus

In Exercises 7–10, use the spinner to find the probability. The spinner is divided into equal parts.

A **7.** What is the probability that the spinner stops on a multiple of 3? $\frac{1}{4}$

8. What are the odds in favor of stopping on a multiple of 4? **1 to 3**

9. What are the odds against stopping on a 1 or a 2? **3 to 1**

10. If you spin the spinner 100 times, how many times do you expect it to stop on 8? **about 12 or 13 times**

11. Each letter in the word THEORETICAL is written on a separate slip of paper and placed in a hat. A letter is chosen at random from the hat.

a. What is the probability that the letter chosen is an E? $\frac{2}{11}$

b. What is the probability that the letter chosen is a vowel? $\frac{5}{11}$

c. What are the odds in favor of choosing a consonant? **6 to 5**

d. Critical Thinking Find a word for which the probability that you choose an R when you randomly choose a letter from the word is $\frac{2}{5}$. ***Sample answer:* RIVER**

3 APPLY

ASSIGNMENT GUIDE

Basic Course
Day 1: pp. 309–311 Exs. 7-13, 17-19, 23-31

Average Course
Day 1: pp. 309–311 Exs. 7-12, 14-20, 23-32

Advanced Course
Day 1: pp. 309–311 Exs. 9-11, 14-22*, 27-32

Block
pp. 309-311 Exs. 7-12, 14-20, 23-32 (with 6.8)

EXTRA PRACTICE

- Student Edition, p. 808
- Chapter 6 Resource Book, pp. 62–64
- Test and Practice Generator

TRANSPARENCY

Even-numbered answers are available on transparencies.

HOMEWORK CHECK

When you review students' homework for this lesson, go over the following exercises to check understanding of key concepts.
Basic: 7, 8, 10, 12, 13
Average: 9, 10, 11, 12, 14
Advanced: 9, 10, 11, 14, 19

TEACHING TIP

In Exercises 7–10, instruct students to read carefully to determine whether probability or odds are to be found.

Common Error

In Exercise 21, point out that the probability of rolling any other number from 2 through 6 is also $\frac{1}{6}$. Stress that there is no connection between the number 6 and the 6 in the denominator of the probability $\frac{1}{6}$, but rather that the connection is to the number of sides on the number cube.

16. ***Sample answer:*** **I would use experimental probability if I was watching a baseball game and wanted to predict the number of strikes a pitcher would throw in the next inning. I would use theoretical probability if I were playing a card game and wanted to predict if the next card drawn from the deck was the card I needed to win.**

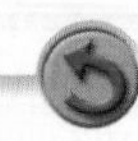

Review *Help*

When finding an experimental probability, you may find it helpful to use the *act it out* strategy for problem solving. For help with this strategy, see p. 798.

12c. ***Sample answer:*** **The experimental probability is close to the theoretical probability; I think that if I flipped the coin 100 times the experimental probability would be very close to the theoretical probability because it seems just as likely that there are times in the experiment that tails seem to come up more than might be expected as there are times that heads seem to come up more than might be expected, so the difference from the theoretical probability should tend to "even out" with more tosses.**

14c. ***t:*** **$\frac{5}{68}$, or about 0.074,** ***s:*** **$\frac{2}{17}$, or about 0.118.** ***Sample answer:*** **The experimental probability for the letter *t* is only about half the theoretical probability, and the experimental probability for the letter *s* is nearly twice the theoretical probability.**

15. ***Sample answer:*** **Write the probability as a ratio. For the odds in favor, write a ratio whose numerator is the numerator of the probability ratio, and whose denominator is the difference in the denominator and numerator of the probability ratio. The odds against are just the reciprocal of the odds in favor.**

12. Experiment Use a coin to complete the following.

a. What is the theoretical probability that the coin lands heads up when tossed? $\frac{1}{2}$

b. Flip the coin 20 times. Record whether it lands heads up or tails up for each flip. Then find the experimental probability that the coin lands heads up when tossed. **Check work. About 74% of responses will be from 0.4 to 0.6, and about 96% from 0.3 to 0.7.**

c. ***Writing*** Compare the theoretical probability with the experimental probability. What do you think would happen if you tossed the coin 100 times? Explain.

13. Flowers You plant 30 African violet seeds and 9 of them sprout. Use an experimental probability to predict how many African violet seeds will sprout if you plant 20 more seeds. **15 seeds**

14. Extended Problem Solving In normal English texts, letters appear with regular frequency. The table gives the probability that a letter, chosen at random from a page of English text, will be a certain letter.

Letter	Probability
e	0.131
t	0.104
a	0.081
s	0.061
x	0.002
z	0.001

a. Predict A page contains 300 letters. Predict how many *e*'s are on the page and how many *a*'s. **about 39 *e*'s, about 24 *a*'s**

b. Predict An essay contains 1000 letters. How many *z*'s would you predict are in the essay? How many *x*'s? **about 1 *z*; about 2 *x*'s**

c. Compare The three sentences in part (b) contain 68 letters. Find the experimental probability that a letter randomly chosen from these sentences is a *t* and the probability that it is an *s*. How do these probabilities compare with the probabilities given in the table?

15. Critical Thinking If you know the probability of an event, explain how to find the odds in favor of and the odds against the event.

16. ***Writing*** Describe a situation where you would use experimental probability and a situation where you would use theoretical probability. **See margin.**

In Exercises 17 and 18, use *geometric probability* to solve the problem. If a point in a region is chosen at random, the geometric probability that the point is located in a specified part of the region is given by

$$P(\text{point in part}) = \frac{\text{Area of specified part}}{\text{Area of entire region}}$$

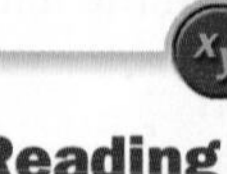

Reading *Algebra*

The probability of an event is often called the *chance* that the event will occur.

B **17. Ring** You lost a ring in a rectangular field that is 110 yards by 65 yards. You search a rectangular section of the field that is 25 yards by 32 yards. What is the probability that the ring is in the section you search? **$\frac{16}{143}$, or about 0.1119**

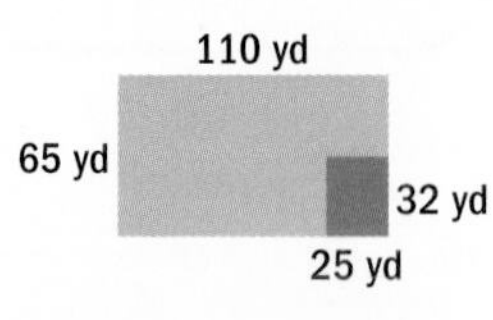

18. Treasure Chest A treasure chest is buried somewhere in a rectangular field. The field is 100 feet by 60 feet. You search 25 square feet of the field. What is the chance that the chest is in the region you search? **$\frac{1}{240}$, or about 0.0042**

19. Websites Many websites have ads whose appearance is based on probability. Advertisers pay the website based on the number of times the ad appears.

a. The probability that an ad appears when a particular website is loaded is 0.2. The website gets 2000 hits a day. About how many times does the ad appear? **about 400 times**

b. The probability that an ad appears when a particular website is loaded is 0.05. About how many hits must the website have for the ad to appear 1000 times? **about 20,000 hits**

20. Critical Thinking An event has *even odds* when the odds in favor of (or against) the event are 1 : 1. What is the probability of an event with even odds? $\frac{1}{2}$

C 21. Critical Thinking The probability of rolling a 1 on a number cube is $\frac{1}{6}$. What is the probability of *not* rolling a 1? In general, if the probability of an event is $\frac{1}{n}$, what is the probability that the event does *not* occur? Explain your thinking.

21. $\frac{5}{6}$; $1 - \frac{1}{n}$. ***Sample answer:*** **In a probability experiment, it is certain that a given event must either occur or not occur. The probability of something that is certain is 1. So, the sum of the probabilities of an event occurring and not occurring is 1. If the probability of an event is $\frac{1}{n}$, then $P(\text{not event}) + \frac{1}{n} = 1$, and $P(\text{not event}) = 1 - \frac{1}{n}$.**

22. Challenge A train runs every 15 minutes. You arrive at the train station without consulting the train's time schedule. What is the probability that you will wait more than 10 minutes for the train? $\frac{1}{3}$

Mixed Review

Algebra Basics Evaluate the expression when $x = 3$, $y = -3$, and $z = 4$. *(Lesson 1.7)*

23. $2xy$ **−18** **24.** $5yz$ **−60** **25.** $7xyz$ **−252** **26.** $6xz$ **72**

Order the numbers from least to greatest. *(Lesson 5.1)*

27. $1\frac{5}{9}, -\frac{3}{5}, \frac{13}{5}, -1.5, -2.7$ **28.** $-0.625, -\frac{3}{8}, 1\frac{5}{8}, \frac{21}{8}, -1.6$

27. $-2.7, -1.5, -\frac{3}{5}, 1\frac{5}{9}, \frac{13}{5}$

28. $-1.6, -0.625, -\frac{3}{8}, 1\frac{5}{8}, \frac{21}{8}$

29. Given $ABCD \sim EFGH$, find EH. *(Lesson 6.5)* **7 m**

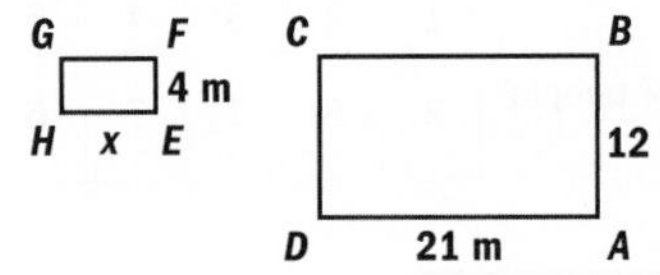

30. Given $\triangle LMN \sim \triangle PQR$, find LN. *(Lesson 6.5)* **8 in.**

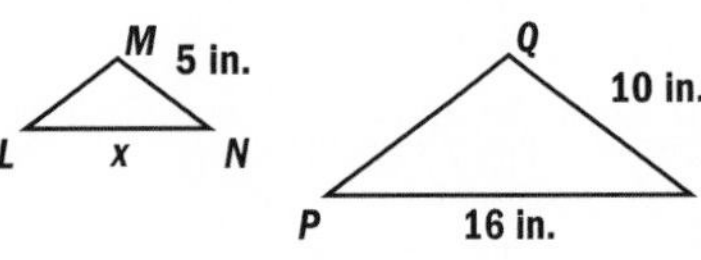

Standardized Test Practice

31. Multiple Choice You have a bag filled with 12 red marbles, 9 blue marbles, and 14 green marbles. You randomly select a marble from the bag. What is the probability that you select a blue marble? **C**

A. $\frac{1}{9}$ **B.** $\frac{1}{35}$ **C.** $\frac{9}{35}$ **D.** $\frac{9}{26}$

32. Short Response A traffic light is green for 17 seconds, yellow for 3 seconds, and red for 20 seconds. Suppose your approach to the light is not affected by traffic or other factors. What is the probability that the light will be green when you first see the light? Explain.

32. $\frac{17}{40}$, **or 0.425.** ***Sample answer:*** **A complete cycle of the lights lasts 40 seconds, and then repeats. I am equally likely to notice the light at any point of a cycle, and 17 seconds of each cycle the light is green, so the probability is $\frac{17}{40}$.**

4 ASSESS

Assessment Resources

For more assessment resources, see:

- Assessment Book
- Test and Practice Generator

Mini-Quiz

Suppose you roll a number cube.

1. What is the probability of rolling a 3 or a 4? $\frac{1}{3}$
2. What are the odds in favor of rolling a 3 or a 4? **1 to 2**
3. What are the odds against rolling an even number? **1 to 1**
4. If you roll a number cube 30 times, how many times would you expect to roll a multiple of 3? **10 times**
5. **Challenge** A bus arrives and leaves from a bus stop every 20 minutes. If you arrive at the bus stop at random, what is the probability that you will have to wait more than 5 minutes for the bus? $\frac{3}{4}$

5 FOLLOW-UP

Diagnosis/Remediation

- Study Guide in Chapter 6 Resource Book, pp. 65–66
- Tutor Place, Fractions Card 19
- eTutorial Plus Online
- Extra Practice, p. 808
- Lesson Practice in Chapter 6 Resource Book, pp. 62–64

English Learner Support

- Spanish Study Guide
- Multi-Language Visual Glossary
- Chapter Audio Summaries CDs

Challenge

- Challenge Practice in Chapter 6 Resource Book, p. 67
- Teacher's Edition, p. 266F

1 PLAN

LEARN THE METHOD

- Students will use a calculator to generate random integers.
- The experiment in Exercise 12 on page 310 of Lesson 6.7 can be conducted without a coin by using random integers of 0 and 1 to represent heads and tails, respectively.

GROUPING

Students should work individually.

2 TEACH

TIPS FOR SUCCESS

Instruct students to keep a written record of the random numbers generated by the calculator, since the numbers will scroll off the screen.

Extra Examples

Example Use a calculator to find how many people, on average, you need to assemble in a group for two members of the group to have a birthday falling on the same day of the week this year. **Answers may vary; check students' work.**

3 CLOSE

ASSESSMENT

1. What is the least number of people you would need in a group so that two of them might share something in common? **2 people**
2. Is a number generator truly random if some numbers are repeating more often than others? Explain. **Yes; the previously generated numbers do not influence the next random number that is generated.**

Technology Activity CALCULATOR

6.7 Generating Random Numbers

Goal Use a calculator to generate random integers.

Example Steps 1–3. Check work.

Use a calculator to solve the following problem.

On average, how many people do you need to assemble in a group for two members of the group to have the same birth month?

Although months have different numbers of days, you can make a good prediction by assuming that the 12 months of the year are equally likely to be a person's birth month. Assign the integers 1 through 12 to the months of the year and use a calculator's random number generator to generate numbers as described below.

1 To generate a random integer from 1 through 12, use the random integer generator on a calculator. Note that your calculator may generate a different number than the one in the display below.

Keystrokes

RANDI(1,12)
2

Tech Help

To tell the calculator that you want random integers from 1 to 12, you should enter 1 and 12 after RANDI(.

Online Resources CLASSZONE.COM
- Keystroke Help

2 Continue to generate random numbers until one of the numbers repeats. A repeated number means that two members of the group have the same birth month. Record how many random numbers you generate until a number repeats.

3 Perform the experiment described in Steps 1 and 2 a total of 10 times. Keep a tally of your results in a table like the one below.

Trial	1	2	3	4	5	6	7	8	9	10
Number of people in group	3	6	7	7	6	6	5	5	5	4

Draw Conclusions

1. **Analyze** The number of random numbers generated in each trial represents the size of the group you need to assemble for two people to have the same birth month. What is the average (mean) size of such a group?
2. **Left-handed** About 10% of people are left-handed. Choose a number from 1 to 10 to represent a left-handed person. Then use your calculator to perform an experiment to determine how many people you need to assemble before 2 of them are left-handed. Perform the experiment 10 times and find the average (mean) of your results.

1. Check work. Note that there is a 43% chance that the experiment will require 4 or fewer trials and a 62% chance that it will require 5 or fewer trials. A typical mean might be between 4 and 5.

2. Check work. Note that there is a 48.5% chance that the experiment will require 16 or fewer trials and a 51.8% chance that it will require 17 or fewer trials, but means may vary a fair amount from these values.

NCTM CURRICULUM STANDARDS
Standard 5: Understand basic concepts of probability; Apply basic concepts of probability
Standard 7: Make mathematical conjectures

LESSON

6.8 The Counting Principle

BEFORE	*Now*	WHY?
You counted outcomes to find probabilities.	You'll use the counting principle to find probabilities.	So you can count possible NBA finals matchups, as in Ex. 9.

Vocabulary
tree diagram, p. 313
counting principle, p. 314

Eyeglasses You are buying new eyeglasses and must choose the frame material and shape. The frame material can be plastic or metal. The frame shape can be rectangular, oval, cat's eye, or round. How many different frames are possible?

One way to count the number of possibilities is to use a **tree diagram**. A tree diagram uses branching to list choices.

Example 1 *Making a Tree Diagram*

To count the number of possible choices for frames, as described above, make a tree diagram.

List the frame materials.	List the frame shapes for each frame material.	List the possibilities.
plastic	rectangular	plastic rectangular
	oval	plastic oval
	cat's eye	plastic cat's eye
	round	plastic round
metal	rectangular	metal rectangular
	oval	metal oval
	cat's eye	metal cat's eye
	round	metal round

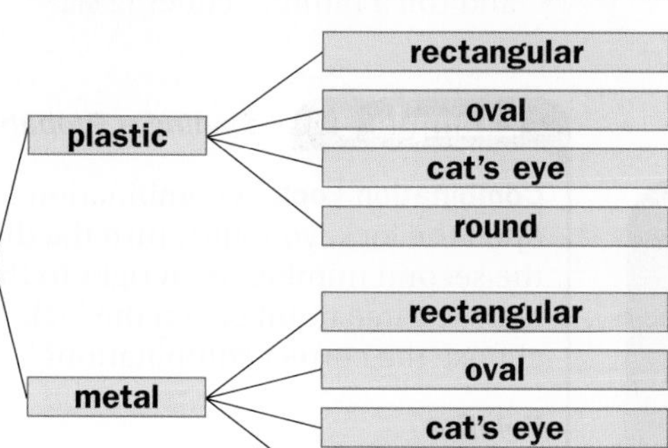

Answer Eight different frames are possible.

 ***Checkpoint***

1. See margin for art; 16 choices.

1. Suppose each of the different eyeglasses in Example 1 also comes in two colors, black and red. Copy the tree diagram above and add the new choices. How many possible choices for frames are there?

NCTM CURRICULUM STANDARDS
Standard 6: Solve problems in math and other contexts
Standard 10: Create representations to communicate math ideas; Use representations to solve problems

1 PLAN

Skill Check
1. $26 \cdot 26 = \underline{?}$ 676
2. $8 \cdot 8 \cdot 8 = \underline{?}$ 512
3. $6 \cdot 6 \cdot 6 \cdot 6 = \underline{?}$ 1296

Lesson Objective
Use the counting principle to find probabilities.

Pacing
Suggested Number of Days
Basic Course: 1 day
Average Course: 1 day
Advanced Course: 1 day
Block: 0.5 block with 6.7

Teaching Resources
For a complete list of Teaching Resources, see page 266B.

 **Transparency**
Warm-Up Exercises for this lesson are available on a transparency.

2 TEACH

Motivating the Lesson
When discussing the opening paragraph, ask students to suggest other choices customers have when they purchase eyeglasses. Use their suggestions to create another tree diagram after presenting Example 1.

TIPS *for* NEW TEACHERS
Make sure students understand that a tree diagram is a way to visualize the counting principle. See Tips for New Teachers in the *Chapter 6 Resource Book*.

1. See Additional Answers beginning on page AA1.

Extra Examples

Example 1 A sandwich shop makes egg salad, tuna salad, or tomato salad sandwiches using either wheat or rye bread. Make a tree diagram to count the number of possible sandwich choices.

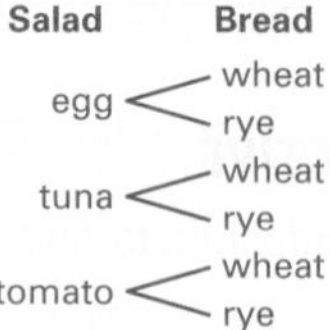

6 different sandwiches are possible.

Example 2 A yogurt shop offers 18 flavors of yogurt, as well as 3 types of cones, and 12 different toppings. Assuming a frozen yogurt is a combination of one cone, one yogurt flavor, and one topping, how many choices are possible? **648 choices**

Example 3 As part of its 20th anniversary celebration, a museum is offering $20 off an art print to each 20th visitor to the museum. You visit the museum on Thursday and again on Friday. What is the probability that you receive the $20-off coupon on both days? $\frac{1}{400}$

Concept Check

How are tree diagrams useful? What is their disadvantage? ***Sample answer:*** **They help you see all the possible choices. They take too long to draw when there are a large number of choices.**

Daily Puzzler

What sum are you most likely to roll with two number cubes, each numbering 1 through 6? **7**

Counting Principle A quick way to count the number of possibilities displayed in a tree diagram is to use the *counting principle.* The **counting principle** uses multiplication to find the number of possible ways two or more events can occur.

The Counting Principle

If one event can occur in m ways, and for each of these ways a second event can occur in n ways, then the number of ways that the two events can occur together is $m \cdot n$.

The counting principle can be extended to three or more events.

Study *Strategy*

Another Way In Example 2, you can make a table to list the 36 possible outcomes. The beginning of such a table is shown below.

	1	2	3
1	1, 1	1, 2	1, 3
2	2, 1	2, 2	2, 3
3	3, 1	3, 2	3, 3

Example 2 ***Using the Counting Principle***

You roll a blue and a red number cube. Use the counting principle to find the number of different outcomes that are possible.

Number of outcomes for the red cube		Number of outcomes for the blue cube		Total number of possible outcomes
6	$\cdot$	6	=	36

Answer There are 36 different possible outcomes.

Checkpoint

2. How many different outcomes are possible when you flip a coin and roll a number cube? **12 outcomes**

Example 3 ***Finding a Probability***

Combination Lock A combination lock has 40 numbers on its dial. To open the lock, you must turn the dial right to the first number, left to the second number, then right to the third number. You randomly choose three numbers on the lock. What is the probability that you choose the correct combination?

Solution

First find the number of different combinations.

$40 \cdot 40 \cdot 40 = 64{,}000$ **Use the counting principle.**

Then find the probability that you choose the correct combination.

$P(\text{correct combination}) = \frac{1}{64{,}000}$ ← **There is only one correct combination.**

Answer The probability that you choose the correct combination is $\frac{1}{64{,}000}$.

6.8 Exercises

More Practice, p. 808

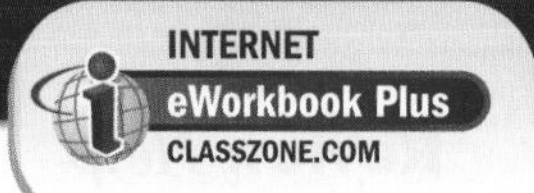

Guided Practice

Vocabulary Check

1. Draw a tree diagram to show the possible outcomes when you flip two coins. **See margin.**
2. Explain how to use the counting principle to determine how many outcomes are possible if you roll 3 number cubes. **See margin.**

2. *Sample answer:* **With each of the three rolls, there are six possible outcomes, so the total number of possible outcomes by the counting principle is 6 • 6 • 6 = 216.**

Skill Check

In Exercises 3–5, use the counting principle to determine the number of possible outfits that can be made using 1 of each type of item from the articles of clothing listed.

3. 4 shirts and 3 pairs of pants **12 outfits**
4. 5 shirts, 3 pairs of pants, and 5 pairs of socks **75 outfits**
5. 8 shirts, 4 pairs of pants, 4 pairs of socks, and 2 belts **256 outfits**

Guided Problem Solving

6. **Coins** You flip three coins. What is the probability that all three coins show heads or all three coins show tails?
   1) Make a tree diagram to show all the different possible outcomes. **See margin.**
   2) How many different possible outcomes are there? **8 outcomes**
   3) How many favorable outcomes are there? **2 favorable outcomes**
   4) Find the probability that all three coins show heads or all three coins show tails. $\frac{1}{4}$

Practice and Problem Solving

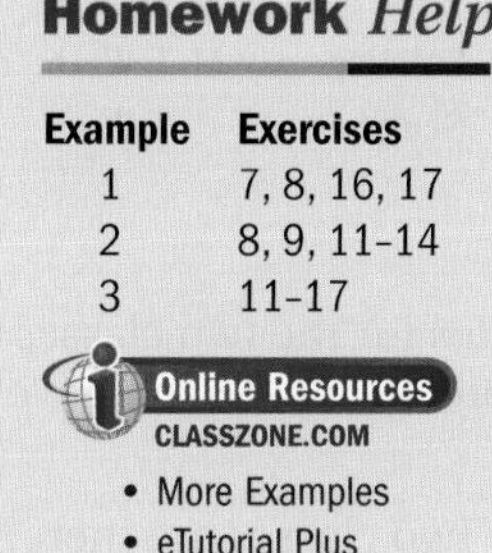

Homework Help
Example Exercises
1 7, 8, 16, 17
2 8, 9, 11–14
3 11–17
Online Resources
CLASSZONE.COM
• More Examples
• eTutorial Plus

A 7. **Computers** You are ordering a computer and must choose a multimedia drive, a hard drive, and a monitor. Using the choices listed in the tables, make a tree diagram of the different computers you can order. How many different computers can you order? **See margin for art; 12 computers.**

Multimedia Drive
CD-ROM
DVD-ROM
CD-RW

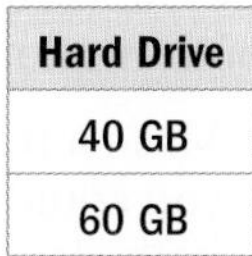

Hard Drive
40 GB
60 GB

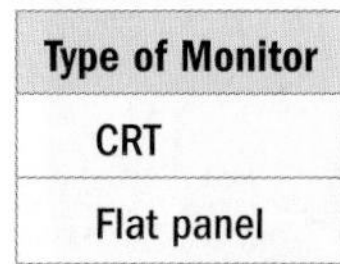

Type of Monitor
CRT
Flat panel

8. **Music Store** A music store manager wants to arrange the store's merchandise into different sections. The manager wants to put CDs, tapes, and singles in different sections. Each section will be divided into different genres: rock, R & B, rap, classical, international music, and country. How many different divisions will the store have? **18 divisions**

3 APPLY

ASSIGNMENT GUIDE

Basic Course
Day 1: SRH p. 799 Exs. 1–3; pp. 315–317 Exs. 7, 8, 11–15, 17, 20–30

Average Course
Day 1: pp. 315–317 Exs. 7–10, 13–17, 19–30

Advanced Course
Day 1: pp. 315–317 Exs. 9–21*, 26–30

Block
pp. 315–317 Exs. 7–10, 13–17, 19–30 (with 6.7)

EXTRA PRACTICE

- Student Edition, p. 808
- Chapter 6 Resource Book, pp. 71–73
- Test and Practice Generator

TRANSPARENCY

Even-numbered answers are available on transparencies.

HOMEWORK CHECK

When you review students' homework for this lesson, go over the following exercises to check understanding of key concepts.
Basic: 7, 8, 11, 12, 17
Average: 7, 9, 13, 14, 16
Advanced: 9, 13, 14, 16, 17

1.

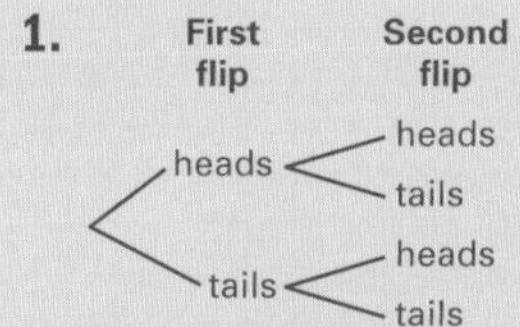

6 (Step 1), 7. See Additional Answers beginning on page AA1.

TEACHING TIP

In Exercise 13, students may want to sketch a tree diagram to help them visualize that there are 4 ways out of 20 possibilities in which both spinners can stop on the same number.

16a.

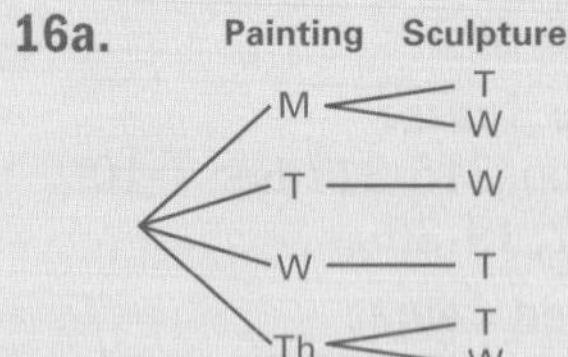

17a.

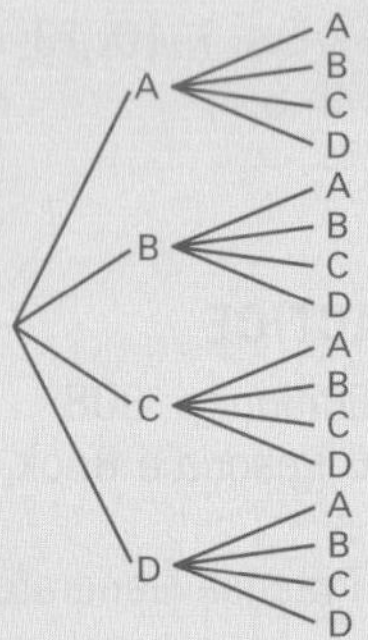

Review *Help*

Sometimes solving a simpler problem can help you to solve a problem that seems complicated. For help with this strategy, see p. 800.

9c. No. ***Sample answer:*** **Part (b) only considers possible matchups. The probability of two teams reaching the finals is not random, but depends at least partially on how good the teams are.**

10. ***Sample answer:*** **By the counting principle, the student should multiply the possibilities, not add them, so the possible number of outfits is $3 \cdot 3 = 9$.**

14. 400 possible outcomes; $\frac{1}{100}$

16d. ***Sample answer:*** **Some of the "possibilities" that the counting principle produces are not allowed in this case because you cannot have the classes on the same day.**

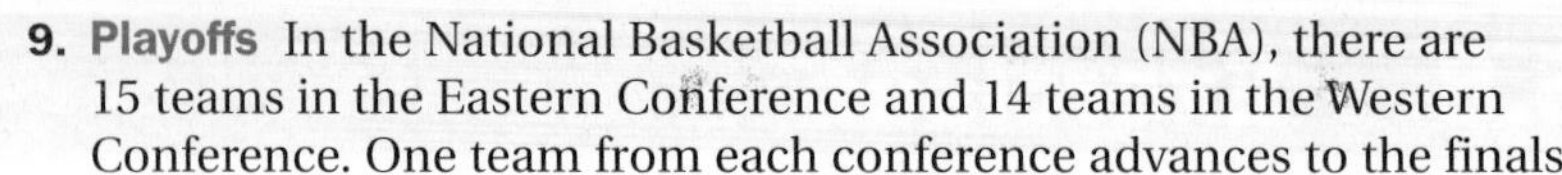

9. Playoffs In the National Basketball Association (NBA), there are 15 teams in the Eastern Conference and 14 teams in the Western Conference. One team from each conference advances to the finals.

a. How many different team matchups could there be in the finals? **210 matchups**

b. Eight teams from the Eastern Conference and eight teams from the Western Conference make the NBA playoffs. How many different matchups of the playoff teams could meet in the finals? **64 matchups**

c. *Writing* Can you use the result from part (b) to determine the probability that two teams in the NBA playoffs meet in the finals? Explain why or why not.

10. Critical Thinking A student claims that because he has 3 sweaters and 3 pairs of pants, he has 6 different possible combinations of sweaters and pants. Describe and correct the student's error.

In Exercises 11–14, use the counting principle to find the total number of possible outcomes. Then determine the probability of the specified event. Each spinner is divided into equal parts.

11. You spin spinner A two times. Find the probability that the spinner stops on 1, then 2. **25 possible outcomes; $\frac{1}{25}$**

12. You spin spinner B two times. Find the probability that the spinner stops on 1, then 2. **16 possible outcomes; $\frac{1}{16}$**

13. You spin each spinner once. Find the probability that both spinners stop on the same number. **20 possible outcomes; $\frac{1}{5}$**

14. You spin spinners A and B two times each. Find the probability that the spinner stops on the same number in all four spins. **See margin.**

A

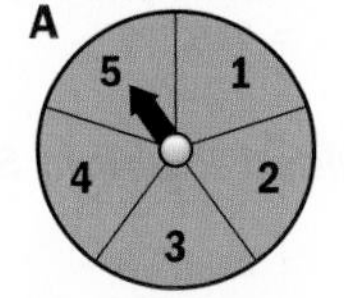

B

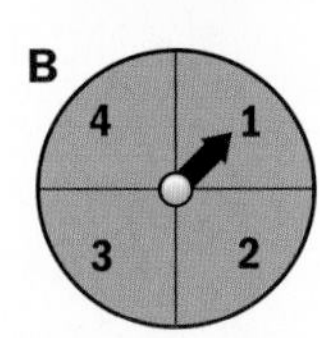

15. **Password** Your computer password has 4 capital letters followed by 4 digits. Your friend randomly chooses 4 capital letters and 4 digits. Use a calculator to find the probability that your friend chooses your password. **$\frac{1}{4{,}569{,}760{,}000}$**

B 16. Art Classes You want to take two art classes after school. You may take only one painting and one sculpture class per week. The table gives the days that the classes are offered. The classes are offered at 3:00 each day, so you cannot take both classes on the same day.

Class	Days offered
Painting	M, T, W, Th
Sculpture	T, W

a. Make a tree diagram of all the possible schedules for the two classes you could take. Be sure to eliminate the possibilities where you have both classes on the same day. **See margin.**

b. How many different possible schedules for the two classes are there? **6 schedules**

c. You sign up for the two classes and are randomly assigned a schedule. What is the probability that your sculpture class is on Tuesday? **$\frac{1}{2}$**

d. *Writing* Explain why, for a situation like this one, it is better to make a tree diagram than to use the counting principle. **See margin.**

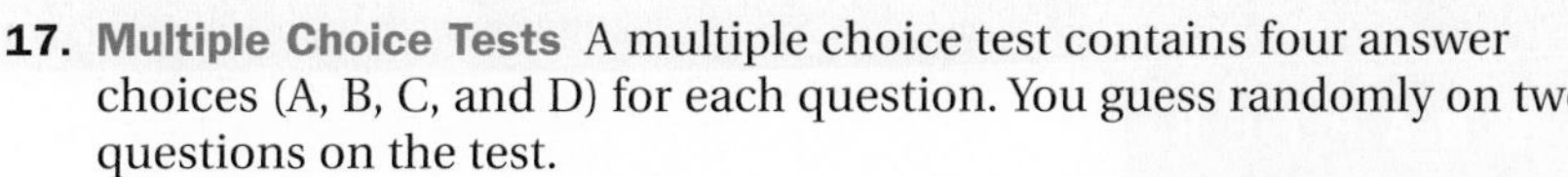

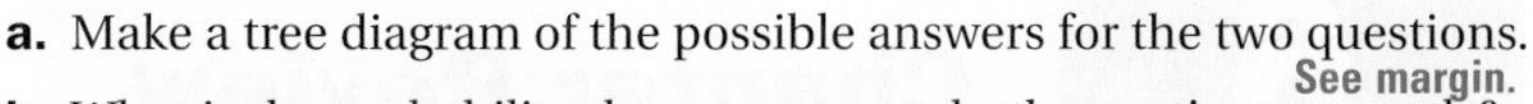

17. **Multiple Choice Tests** A multiple choice test contains four answer choices (A, B, C, and D) for each question. You guess randomly on two questions on the test.
    a. Make a tree diagram of the possible answers for the two questions. **See margin.**
    b. What is the probability that you answer both questions correctly? $\frac{1}{16}$
    c. **Analyze** Suppose the answer to both questions is A. Use the tree diagram to count how many outcomes there are in which you answer at least one of the two questions correctly. What is the probability that you answer at least one question correctly? **7 outcomes;** $\frac{7}{16}$

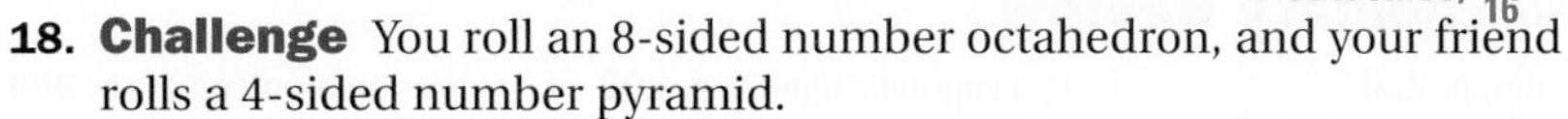

18. **Challenge** You roll an 8-sided number octahedron, and your friend rolls a 4-sided number pyramid.
    a. How many different possible outcomes are there for the pairs of numbers rolled? **32 outcomes**
    b. Find the probability that you and your friend roll the same number. $\frac{1}{8}$
    c. Find the odds in favor of rolling a number greater than the number your friend rolls. **11 to 5**

C 19. **Phone Numbers** You remember part of your friend's 7-digit phone number, but you cannot remember the rest.
    a. Your friend's number begins with 79 and ends with five other digits. How many different phone numbers can begin with 79? **100,000 phone numbers**
    b. You remember that the next digit after 79 is 8. How many possible phone numbers can begin with 798? **10,000 phone numbers**
    c. How many digits of a 7-digit phone number do you have to know before the probability that you randomly guess the number correctly on the first try is $\frac{1}{100}$? **5 digits**

Mixed Review

Find the quotient. *(Lesson 5.5)*

20. $-\frac{4}{9} \div \frac{2}{3}$ $-\frac{2}{3}$ 21. $\frac{5}{6} \div \left(-\frac{2}{3}\right)$ $-1\frac{1}{4}$ 22. $\frac{11}{24} \div \frac{3}{8}$ $1\frac{2}{9}$ 23. $\frac{25}{63} \div \frac{8}{9}$ $\frac{25}{56}$

Solve the proportion. *(Lesson 6.3)*

24. $\frac{y}{20} = \frac{15}{4}$ 75 25. $\frac{15}{6} = \frac{p}{8}$ 20 26. $\frac{5}{g} = \frac{2}{14}$ 35 27. $\frac{8}{9} = \frac{12}{b}$ 13.5

28. **Cash** You have four \$1 bills, two \$5 bills, and one \$20 bill in your wallet. You choose one of the bills at random. Find the odds in favor of and the odds against choosing a bill greater than \$1. *(Lesson 6.7)* **odds in favor of: 3 to 4, odds against: 4 to 3**

Standardized Test Practice

29. **Multiple Choice** A car comes in two different styles. Each style comes in four colors. How many different versions of the car are available? **D**

    A. 2 **B.** 4 **C.** 6 **D.** 8

30. **Multiple Choice** A hot dog stand sells 2 sizes of hot dog, 6 kinds of soda, and 3 sizes of soda. How many different combinations of a hot dog and soda could you order? **H**

    F. 12 **G.** 24 **H.** 36 **I.** 11

4 ASSESS

Assessment Resources

For more assessment resources, see:
- Assessment Book
- Test and Practice Generator

Mini-Quiz

A spinner is divided into 10 equal parts numbered 1 through 10.

1. How many possible outcomes result from spinning this spinner twice? **100 outcomes**
2. What is the probability of spinning a 9, then spinning an even number? $\frac{1}{20}$

Challenge Suppose you roll two number cubes, one numbered 1 through 6, and the second numbered 7 through 12.

3. Find the probability of rolling a pair of numbers whose sum is 13. $\frac{1}{6}$
4. What is the probability of rolling a pair of numbers whose sum is at least 15? $\frac{5}{18}$

5 FOLLOW-UP

Diagnosis/Remediation

- Study Guide in Chapter 6 Resource Book, pp. 74–75
- Tutor Place, Fractions Cards 19, 20
- eTutorial Plus Online
- Extra Practice, p. 808
- Lesson Practice in Chapter 6 Resource Book, pp. 71–73

English Learner Support

- Spanish Study Guide
- Multi-Language Visual Glossary
- Chapter Audio Summaries CDs

Challenge

- Challenge Practice in Chapter 6 Resource Book, p. 76
- Teacher's Edition, p. 266F

ADDITIONAL RESOURCES

The following resources are available to help review the materials in Lessons 6.6–6.8.

Chapter 6 Resource Book
- Lesson Practice
- Study Guide

Assessment Book
- Chapter 6 Quiz 2

Technology
- Test and Practice Generator
- eTutorial CD-ROM

Internet
- Classzone
- eWorkbook Plus Online
- eTutorial Plus Online

ENGLISH LEARNER SUPPORT

- Spanish Study Guide
- Multi-Language Visual Glossary
- Chapter Audio Summaries CDs

1. ***Sample answer:*** **You can write the ratios in simplest form or as decimals. If they have the same simplest form or decimal form, they are equivalent. Another way is to find the cross products of the ratios. If the cross products are equal, then the ratios form a proportion, and are equivalent.**
2. **An equation that states that two ratios are equivalent**
3. ***Sample answer:*** **Congruent figures have the same size and shape. Similar figures have the same shape, but are not necessarily the same size. The lengths of corresponding sides of similar figures have the same ratio, but that ratio is not necessarily 1, as it is for congruent figures.**
4. ***Sample answer:*** **An outcome is any possible result of an experiment, while a favorable outcome is an outcome that corresponds to an event that you have specified.**

7. $\frac{55 \text{ mi}}{1 \text{ h}}$

8. $\frac{15 \text{ min}}{1 \text{ game}}$

9. $\frac{\frac{1}{4} \text{ lap}}{1 \text{ min}}$, or $\frac{0.25 \text{ lap}}{1 \text{ min}}$

10. $\frac{6 \text{ oz}}{1 \text{ serving}}$

CHAPTER 6

Chapter Review

Vocabulary Review

ratio, p. 269	congruent figures, p. 290	favorable outcomes, p. 306	odds against, p. 308
equivalent ratios, p. 270	scale drawing, p. 300	probability, p. 306	tree diagram, p. 313
proportion, p. 275	scale model, p. 300	theoretical probability, p. 307	counting principle, p. 314
cross product, p. 280	scale, p. 300	experimental probability, p. 307	
similar figures, p. 288	outcomes, p. 306	odds in favor, p. 308	
corresponding parts, p. 288	event, p. 306		

1–6. See margin.

1. Explain how to tell if two ratios are equivalent.
2. What is a proportion?
3. How are similar figures different from congruent figures?
4. What is the difference between an outcome and a favorable outcome?
5. Describe the difference between the probability that an event occurs and the odds in favor of an event.
6. What is the counting principle?

6.1 Ratios and Rates

Examples on pp. 269–271

Goal

Find and interpret a unit rate.

Example **You worked 15 hours and earned \$195. How much did you earn per hour?**

$\frac{\$195}{15 \text{ hours}} = \frac{\$195 \div 15}{15 \text{ hours} \div 15}$ **Divide numerator and denominator by 15.**

$= \frac{\$13}{1 \text{ hour}}$ **Simplify.**

Answer You earned \$13 per hour.

 **Find the unit rate.**

7. $\frac{330 \text{ miles}}{6 \text{ hours}}$ **8.** $\frac{60 \text{ minutes}}{4 \text{ games}}$ **9.** $\frac{5 \text{ laps}}{20 \text{ minutes}}$ **10.** $\frac{24 \text{ ounces}}{4 \text{ servings}}$

11. Tickets The drama club pays \$144.50 to buy 17 movie tickets. What is the cost per ticket? **\$8.50 per ticket**

12. Cereal One brand of cereal contains 18 ounces and costs \$3.20. Another brand contains 1 pound and costs \$3.00. Which brand has a lower price per ounce? **the one that contains 18 oz**

6.2 Writing and Solving Proportions

Examples on pp. 275–277

Goal

Solve proportions using algebra.

Example **Solve the proportion $\frac{x}{9} = \frac{15}{27}$.**

$\frac{x}{9} = \frac{15}{27}$ **Write original proportion.**

$9 \cdot \frac{x}{9} = 9 \cdot \frac{15}{27}$ **Multiply each side by 9.**

$x = \frac{15}{3}$ **Simplify.**

$x = 5$ **Divide.**

Use algebra to solve the proportion.

13. $\frac{10}{25} = \frac{a}{5}$ 2 **14.** $\frac{18}{24} = \frac{x}{4}$ 3 **15.** $\frac{z}{6} = \frac{35}{42}$ 5 **16.** $\frac{b}{54} = \frac{8}{9}$ 48

17. Lions Lions sleep 5 out of every 6 hours. Write and solve a proportion to find how many hours per day lions sleep. ***Sample answer:*** $\frac{5}{6} = \frac{s}{24}$, **20 h**

6.3 Solving Proportions Using Cross Products

Examples on pp. 280–282

Goal

Solve proportions using the cross products property.

Example **Solve the proportion $\frac{8}{20} = \frac{38}{y}$ using the cross products property.**

$\frac{8}{20} = \frac{38}{y}$ **Write original proportion.**

$8 \cdot y = 20 \cdot 38$ **Cross products property**

$8y = 760$ **Multiply.**

$\frac{8y}{8} = \frac{760}{8}$ **Divide each side by 8.**

$y = 95$ **Simplify.**

Use the cross products property to solve the proportion.

18. $\frac{6}{2.7} = \frac{40}{z}$ 18 **19.** $\frac{6}{17} = \frac{3}{x}$ 8.5 **20.** $\frac{17}{c} = \frac{34}{46}$ 23 **21.** $\frac{50}{a} = \frac{25}{7}$ 14

22. Field Trip Your school is going on a field trip. It takes 2 buses to carry 64 people. Write and solve a proportion to find the number of buses needed to carry 150 people. ***Sample answer:*** $\frac{2}{64} = \frac{b}{150}$, **5 buses**

The following resources are available to help review the materials in this chapter.

Chapter 6 Resource Book

- Chapter Review Games and Activities, p. 77
- Cumulative Practice, Chs. 1–6

English/Spanish Chapter Reviews and Tests

Chapter Audio Summaries CDs

eTutorial CD-ROM

eWorkbook Plus Online

eTutorial Plus Online

5. ***Sample answer:*** **The probability of an event is the ratio of the number of favorable outcomes to the number of possible outcomes, while the odds in favor of an event is the ratio of the number of favorable outcomes to the number of unfavorable outcomes.**

6. ***Sample answer:*** **The counting principle is a method to find in how many ways two or more events can occur together when for each of any number of ways one event can occur, another event can occur in a given number of ways. In this case, the counting principle says to multiply the number of ways each event can occur to find the number of ways they can occur together.**

6.4 Similar and Congruent Figures

Examples on pp. 288–290

Goal

Find the ratio of corresponding side lengths of similar figures.

Example **Given $\triangle ABC \sim \triangle MNP$, find the ratio of the lengths of corresponding sides of $\triangle ABC$ to $\triangle MNP$.**

Two corresponding sides are $\overline{AB}$ and $\overline{MN}$.

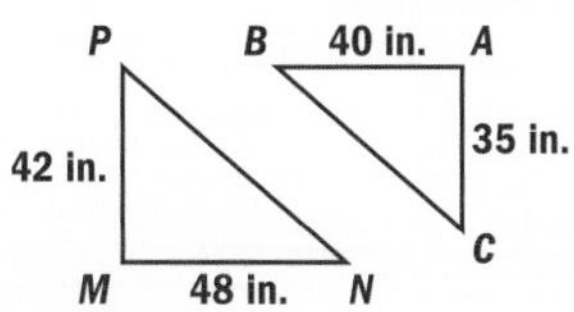

The ratio of the length of these sides is $\frac{AB}{MN}$.

Substitute the lengths of the sides and simplify.

$$\frac{AB}{MN} = \frac{40}{48} = \frac{5}{6}$$

Answer The ratio of the lengths of the corresponding sides is $\frac{5}{6}$.

Find the ratio of the lengths of corresponding sides of figure A to figure B.

23. *GHJK* ~ *PQRS* $\frac{9}{5}$

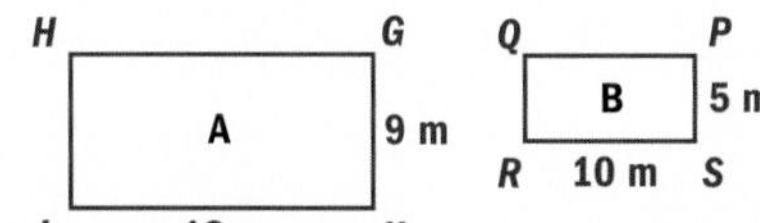

24. *KLMN* ~ *WXYZ* $\frac{2}{3}$

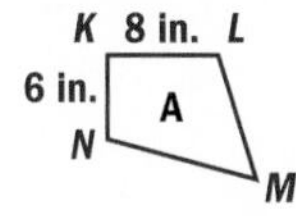

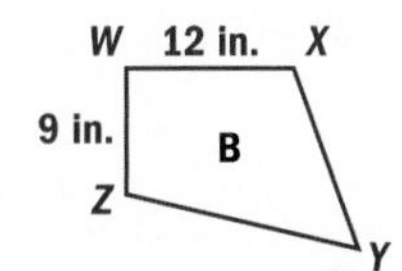

6.5 Similarity and Measurement

Examples on pp. 293–294

Goal

Find unknown side lengths of similar figures.

Example **Given *DEFG* ~ *JKLM*, find *KL*.**

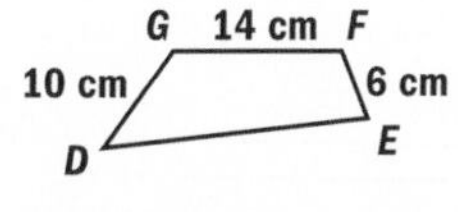

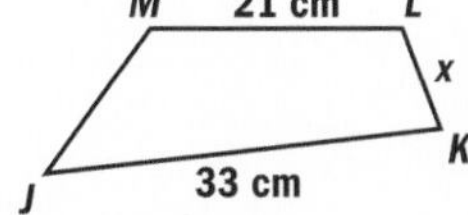

$\frac{EF}{KL} = \frac{FG}{LM}$ **Write proportion involving *KL*.**

$\frac{6}{x} = \frac{14}{21}$ **Substitute.**

$6 \cdot 21 = 14x$ **Cross products property**

$126 = 14x$ **Multiply.**

$9 = x$ **Divide each side by 14.**

Answer The length of $\overline{KL}$ is 9 centimeters.

In Exercises 25 and 26, use the similar figures above.

25. Find *JM*. 15 cm

26. Find *DE*. 22 cm

6.6 Scale Drawings

Examples on pp. 300–301

Goal

Find distances using scales and scale drawings.

Example **The distance between two cities on a map is 7 centimeters. The map has a scale of 1 cm : 20 km. Find the actual distance between the two cities.**

$\frac{1 \text{ cm}}{20 \text{ km}} = \frac{7 \text{ cm}}{x \text{ km}}$ **Write proportion.**

$1x = 20 \cdot 7$ **Cross products property**

$x = 140$ **Multiply.**

Answer The actual distance is 140 kilometers.

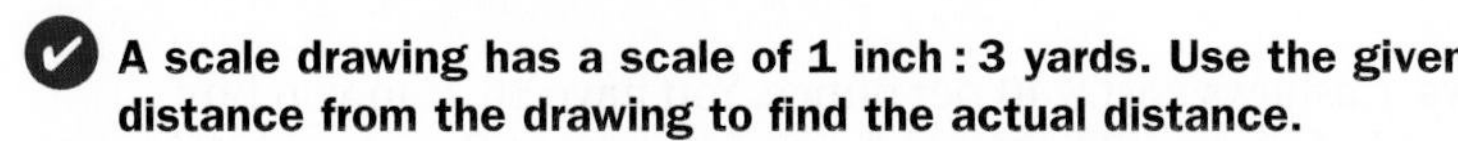

✔ **A scale drawing has a scale of 1 inch : 3 yards. Use the given distance from the drawing to find the actual distance.**

27. 7 inches 21 yd **28.** 14 inches 42 yd **29.** 18 inches 54 yd **30.** 22 inches 66 yd

6.7 Probability and Odds

Examples on pp. 306–308

Goal

Find the probability of an event.

Example **The spinner shown is divided into equal parts. Find the probability that the spinner stops on a 5.**

$$P(\text{stopping on a } 5) = \frac{\text{Number of favorable outcomes}}{\text{Number of outcomes}} = \frac{3}{8}$$

✔ **Find the probability that the spinner above stops on the number.**

31. 4 $\frac{1}{4}$ **32.** 3 $\frac{1}{8}$ **33.** 2 $\frac{1}{8}$ **34.** 1 $\frac{1}{8}$

6.8 The Counting Principle

Examples on pp. 313–314

Goal

Use the counting principle to count possibilities.

Example **In a game, you are to choose a 2 letter code from the 26 capital letters of the alphabet. Find the number of possible codes.**

Number of possibilities for first letter		Number of possibilities for second letter		Total number of possibilities
26	•	26	=	676

✔ **35. Clothing** You have 6 shirts and 3 pairs of pants. How many outfits are possible using one of each item? 18 outfits

ADDITIONAL RESOURCES

Assessment Book

- Chapter Test (3 levels), pp. 70–75
- Standardized Chapter Test, p. 76
- Alternative Assessment, pp. 77–78

Test and Practice Generator

CHAPTER 6

Chapter Test

Order the ratios from least to greatest.

1. 51 to 25, $\frac{5}{4}$, 13 : 10, $\frac{33}{20}$, 17 to 20
   17 to 20, $\frac{5}{4}$, 13 : 10, $\frac{33}{20}$, 51 to 25

2. $\frac{64}{25}$, 9 to 40, 59 : 20, $\frac{53}{25}$, 37 : 20
   9 to 40, 37 : 20, $\frac{53}{25}$, $\frac{64}{25}$, 59 : 20

Write the equivalent rate.

3. $\frac{18\text{ ft}}{1\text{ sec}} = \frac{?\text{ ft}}{1\text{ min}}$ **1080**

4. $\frac{\$5.60}{1\text{ lb}} = \frac{?}{1\text{ oz}}$ **$.35**

5. $\frac{1296\text{ cars}}{1\text{ day}} = \frac{?\text{ cars}}{1\text{ hour}}$ **54**

6. $\frac{8.5\text{ km}}{1\text{ h}} = \frac{?\text{ m}}{1\text{ h}}$ **8500**

7. **Cashews** Cashews cost $.40 per ounce. You have $6. Can you buy one pound of cashews? Explain. **No. *Sample answer:* One pound is 16 ounces, and 16 ounces of cashews cost 16 • $.40 = $6.40.**

Solve the proportion.

8. $\frac{5}{12} = \frac{x}{36}$ **15**

9. $\frac{4}{7} = \frac{a}{35}$ **20**

10. $\frac{b}{54} = \frac{12}{18}$ **36**

11. $\frac{7}{8} = \frac{z}{12}$ **10.5**

12. $\frac{9}{t} = \frac{3}{8}$ **24**

13. $\frac{21}{7} = \frac{9}{p}$ **3**

14. $\frac{6}{14} = \frac{15}{c}$ **35**

15. $\frac{8}{w} = \frac{1.2}{3}$ **20**

16. Given $\triangle ABC \cong \triangle EFG$, name the corresponding angles and the corresponding side lengths. Then find the unknown side lengths.

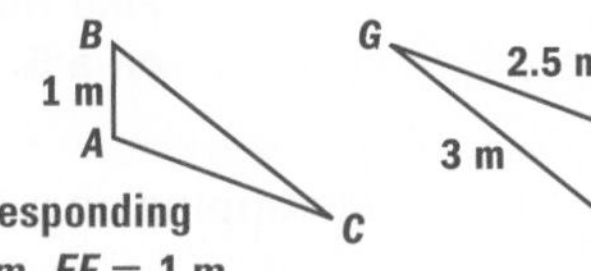

corresponding angles: $\angle A$ and $\angle E$, $\angle B$ and $\angle F$, $\angle C$ and $\angle G$; corresponding sides: $\overline{AB}$ and $\overline{EF}$, $\overline{BC}$ and $\overline{FG}$, $\overline{AC}$ and $\overline{EG}$; AC = 2.5 m, BC = 3 m, EF = 1 m

17. **Football** The shadow of a goalpost on a football field is 20 feet long. A football player who is 6 feet tall stands next to the goalpost and casts a shadow 32 inches long. How tall is the goalpost? **540 in., or 45 ft**

A scale drawing has a scale of 1 inch : 10 feet. Use the given actual length to find the length of the object in the scale drawing.

18. 8 feet **0.8 in., or $\frac{4}{5}$ in.**

19. 7 feet **0.7 in., or $\frac{7}{10}$ in.**

20. 6 feet **0.6 in., or $\frac{3}{5}$ in.**

21. 4 feet **0.4 in., or $\frac{2}{5}$ in.**

22. **Marbles** A bag contains 8 blue marbles, 6 red marbles, 15 green marbles, and 16 orange marbles. A marble is chosen at random from the bag. What is the probability that the marble is red? What are the odds in favor of choosing a green marble? **$\frac{2}{15}$; 15 to 30**

23. **Wildlife** A wildlife preserve identifies each animal in the preserve with a one-digit number and a capital letter. How many animals can the preserve identify? How many animals can the preserve identify using a two-digit number and a capital letter? **260 animals; 2600 animals**

Chapter Standardized Test

Test-Taking Strategy Work at a comfortable pace. Do not pay attention to how fast other students are working.

1. Which rate is equivalent to $\frac{15 \text{ mi}}{1 \text{ h}}$? **B**

A. $\frac{22 \text{ ft}}{1 \text{ min}}$ **B.** $\frac{1320 \text{ ft}}{1 \text{ min}}$

C. $\frac{79{,}200 \text{ ft}}{1 \text{ min}}$ **D.** $\frac{4{,}752{,}000 \text{ ft}}{1 \text{ min}}$

2. What is the solution of the proportion $\frac{x}{5} = \frac{16}{20}$? **G**

F. 2 **G.** 4 **H.** 6 **I.** 8

3. What is the solution of the proportion $\frac{2.4}{4} = \frac{3}{y}$? **D**

A. 0.2 **B.** 0.5 **C.** 2 **D.** 5

4. Which statement is *not* necessarily true? **G**

F. Corresponding angles of similar figures are congruent.

G. Corresponding sides of similar figures are congruent.

H. Two squares with different side lengths are similar figures.

I. Corresponding sides of congruent figures are congruent.

5. A woman is standing next to a tree. She is 64 inches tall and casts a shadow 24 inches long. The tree's shadow is 67.5 inches long. How tall is the tree? **B**

A. 10 feet **B.** 15 feet

C. 22.75 feet **D.** 180 feet

6. A bag holds 8 slips of paper numbered 1 through 8. You randomly choose one slip of paper. What is the probability that the number on the slip of paper is greater than 5? **G**

F. $\frac{1}{8}$ **G.** $\frac{3}{8}$ **H.** $\frac{1}{2}$ **I.** $\frac{5}{8}$

7. An identification system assigns each item a code using 3 capital letters. How many different codes are possible? **D**

A. 78 **B.** 7800

C. 15,600 **D.** 17,576

8. Short Response You make a pattern by drawing three similar rectangles. The width of the smallest rectangle is $\frac{4}{5}$ of the width of the medium-sized rectangle. The width of the medium-sized rectangle is $\frac{4}{5}$ of the width of the largest rectangle. The largest rectangle is 12 inches long and 8 inches wide. Find the dimensions of the smallest rectangle. Explain your reasoning. **See margin.**

9. Extended Response You are making a scale drawing of a room using a scale of 1 inch : 4 feet.

a. The room is 14 feet by 18 feet. Find its dimensions in the drawing. **3.5 in. by 4.5 in.**

b. A sofa in the room has a length of 6 feet. Find the length of the sofa in the drawing. **1.5 in.**

c. You want to enlarge the scale drawing. How would you change the scale to double the dimensions of the drawing? Explain. **See margin.**

ADDITIONAL RESOURCES

Assessment Book

- Standardized Chapter Test, p. 76

Test and Practice Generator

8. $7\frac{17}{25}$ **in. by** $5\frac{3}{25}$ **in., or 7.68 in. by 5.12 in.** ***Sample answer:*** **The rectangles are similar, so the ratio that applies to the widths also applies to the lengths. I found the dimensions of the medium-sized rectangle by multiplying the dimensions of the largest rectangle by** $\frac{4}{5}$**, then I found the dimensions of the smallest rectangle by multiplying the dimensions of the medium-sized rectangle by** $\frac{4}{5}$**.**

9c. ***Sample answer:*** **To double the dimensions in the drawing means that it will take twice the current distance in the drawing to equal the same actual distance, so the new scale will be 2 inches : 4 feet, which is equivalent to 1 inch : 2 feet.**

OVERVIEW

Mathematical Goals

In this project, students will write and solve proportions. They will sketch models. Students will relate proportions to real-world situations.

Managing the Project

Classroom Management
Students can work individually or in groups of two. In groups, students can each solve Step 1 and compare their answers. One group member can solve Step 2 while the other solves Step 3. They should then work Step 4 together. The partners should work together to choose prices for the ads and to create the poster.

Guiding Students' Work
Be sure students notice that \$1800 is to be collected from 10 pages of ads, not just 1 page. For students who mentally calculate in Step 2 that a 1-section ad costs \$20, urge them to write a proportion for finding the price of a 4-section ad, even if they can find this price mentally.

Concluding the Project
Students should present their poster, showing each ad size and its price. The poster should explain how the prices meet the financial goal. You can use questions like the following for class discussion:

- Suppose you offer a discounted price for full-page ads. Based on the 1-section price of \$20, how can you still meet the \$1800 goal?
- An advertiser wants an ad to cover two facing pages. What is a reasonable charge for this ad? Justify your answer.

Chapter 6 **Project**

Making a Business Decision

Goal
Decide what the prices of ads in the school yearbook will be.

Key Skill
Solving proportions

Materials
- graph paper

To help pay for the cost of publishing a school yearbook, some yearbook staffs sell ads in the yearbook. Suppose you want to raise \$1800 for your school's yearbook. What prices should you set for the ads in order to reach your goal?

Here are the guidelines:

- You have 10 pages of ads to sell.
- The ad pages are divided into 9 sections.
- A single ad can cover 1, 2, 4, or 9 sections, as shown.

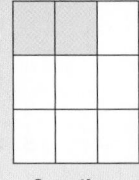

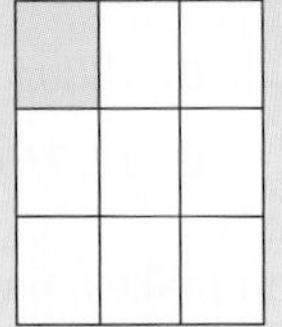
1 section

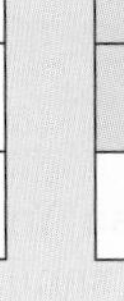
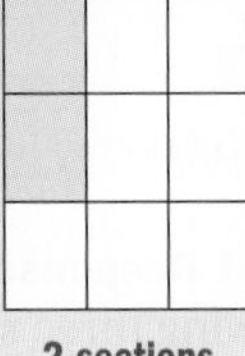
2 sections

2 sections

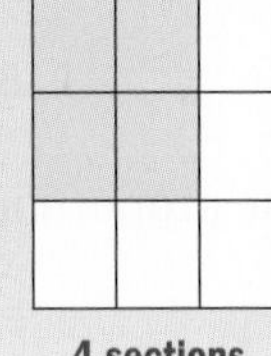
4 sections

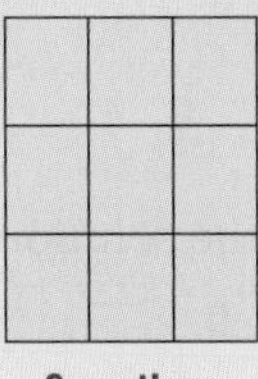
9 sections

A reasonable way to set the prices for ads of different sizes is to let the price of an ad be proportional to its area.

2–3. Sample proportions are given.

2. $\frac{\$180}{9 \text{ sections}} = \frac{x}{4 \text{ sections}}$; $x = \$80$

3. $\frac{\$180}{9 \text{ sections}} = \frac{x}{2 \text{ sections}}$; $x = \$40$;

$\frac{\$180}{9 \text{ sections}} = \frac{x}{1 \text{ section}} = \$20$

Investigate

1. In order to raise \$1800, how much must you raise from each page of ads? **\$180**
2. Let the amount you calculated in Step 1 be the cost of a 9-section (full-page) ad. Write and solve a proportion to calculate the cost of a 4-section ad.
3. Write and solve proportions to calculate the cost of a 2-section ad and a 1-section ad.
4. On graph paper, sketch a few different ways that an ad page can be filled with the ad sizes shown above. **See margin.**

Consider and Decide

Decide on the prices for the ads. Consider the following:

- When designing the layout of a page with ads, you may have some ads that include photos and text and others that include only text. You may want to charge more for ads that include photos.
- You may want to slightly discount the price of larger ads in order to encourage customers to buy larger ads. For example, you may want to make the price of a 4-section ad slightly less than 4 times the cost of a 1-section ad.

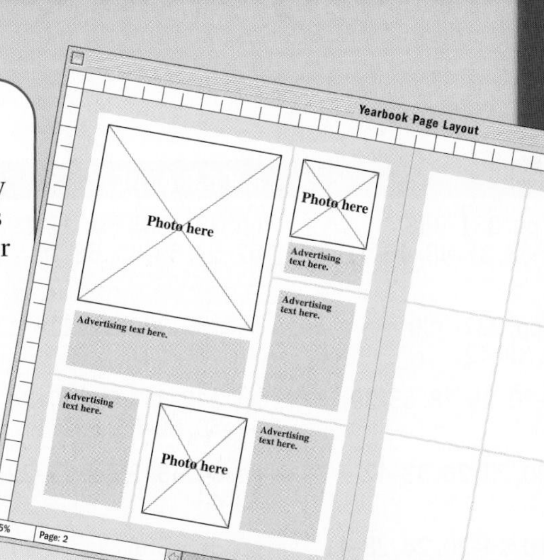

Present Your Results

Make a poster that shows the sizes of the yearbook ads and the prices that you chose. Explain how the prices you chose will help you meet the financial goal for the yearbook.

Using Proportions: **\$70, \$140.** ***Sample answer:*** **To find the prices, I solved the proportions** $\frac{\$210}{9 \text{ sections}} = \frac{x}{3 \text{ sections}}$ **and** $\frac{\$210}{9 \text{ sections}} = \frac{x}{6 \text{ sections}}$.

Project Extensions

Using Proportions Suppose you decide also to allow 3-section and 6-section ads, as shown. What prices should you set for these ads if price is proportional to area and the price of a 9-section ad is \$210? Explain your answers.

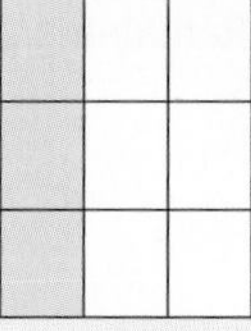
3 sections

3 sections

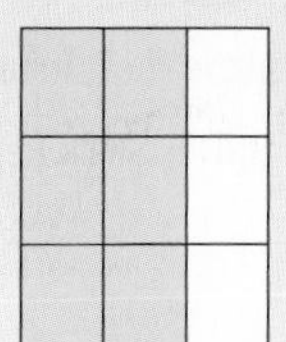
6 sections

6 sections

Ad prices for newspapers and magazines are sometimes listed on rate cards. Use the Internet to find rate cards for several different newspapers or magazines. Are ad prices for sections of a page proportional to ad prices for a full page? Explain how you found your answer. **Check students' work.**

Career Most magazines and newspapers are at least partially funded by advertising sales. Find out more about careers in selling advertising space and careers in designing print ads.

Explore Find several yearbooks, magazines, or newspapers. How do these publications divide pages into sections for ads? Describe your findings. **Check students' work.**

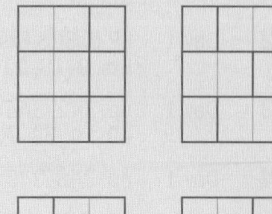

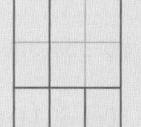

Grading the Project

A well-written project will have the following characteristics:

- The results of Steps 1–4 are complete and reasonable.
- All possible ad sizes and their prices are listed.
- An explanation of how the price structure of the ads will achieve the financial goal for the yearbook is clear and reasonable.

4. ***Sample:***

CHAPTER 7

Pacing and Assignment Guide

REGULAR SCHEDULE

Lesson	Les. Day	BASIC	AVERAGE	ADVANCED
7.1	Day 1	SRH p. 780 Exs. 5-8; pp. 331-333 Exs. 8-11, 20-25, 28-33, 37-43, 46-51, 60-69	pp. 331-333 Exs. 12-19, 26-36, 43-46, 52-57, 59-65, 68-70	pp. 331-333 Exs. 14-19, 26-28, 37-48, 52-61*, 66-70
7.2	Day 1	EP p. 808 Exs. 9-12; pp. 337-339 Exs. 9-18, 21, 26-28, 32-42	pp. 337-339 Exs. 11-21, 23-30, 34-42	pp. 337-339 Exs. 13-17, 20-31*, 34-42
7.3	Day 1	pp. 342-344 Exs. 13-20, 25-28, 33-39, 49-54, 63-70	pp. 342-344 Exs. 17-24, 29-33, 40-44, 47-50, 55-59, 62-71	pp. 342-344 Exs. 17-20, 31-37, 44-50, 55-62*, 66-71
7.4	Day 1	pp. 348-349 Exs. 8-20, 23-26, 33-42	pp. 348-349 Exs. 12-22, 25-28, 31, 33-43	pp. 348-349 Exs. 14-21, 25-33*, 38-43
7.5	Day 1	pp. 355-356 Exs. 7-10, 14-20, 24, 28-41	pp. 355-356 Exs. 10-17, 20-25, 27-33, 38-41	pp. 355-356 Exs. 11-15, 18-27*, 30-33, 38-41
7.6	Day 1	EP p. 804 Exs. 56-59; pp. 360-361 Exs. 8-13, 24-26, 35-40	pp. 360-361 Exs. 8-13, 24-26, 35-40	pp. 360-361 Exs. 9-13, 24-26, 35-40
	Day 2	pp. 360-361 Exs. 14-23, 29-34, 41	pp. 360-361 Exs. 14-23, 27, 29-34, 41	pp. 360-361 Exs. 15-23, 27-32*, 41
7.7	Day 1	pp. 365-366 Exs. 8-16, 18-22, 29-37	pp. 365-366 Exs. 10-19, 22-27, 29-37	pp. 365-366 Exs. 12-17, 20-30*, 33-37
Review	Day 1	pp. 368-371 Exs. 1-49	pp. 368-371 Exs. 1-49	pp. 368-371 Exs. 1-49
Assess	Day 1	Chapter 7 Test	Chapter 7 Test	Chapter 7 Test

YEARLY PACING Chapter 7 Total – **10 days** Chapters 1–7 Total – **80 days** Remaining – **80 days**

*Challenge Exercises EP = Extra Practice SRH = Skills Review Handbook

BLOCK SCHEDULE

DAY 1	DAY 2	DAY 3	DAY 4	DAY 5
7.1 pp. 331-333 Exs. 12-19, 26-36, 43-46, 52-57, 59-65, 68-70 **7.2** pp. 337-339 Exs. 11-21, 23-30, 34-42	**7.3** pp. 342-344 Exs. 17-24, 29-33, 40-44, 47-50, 55-59, 62-71 **7.4** pp. 348-349 Exs. 12-22, 25-28, 31, 33-43	**7.5** pp. 355-356 Exs. 10-17, 20-25, 27-33, 38-41 **7.6** pp. 360-361 Exs. 8-13, 24-26, 35-41	**7.6 (cont.)** pp. 360-361 Exs. 14-23, 27, 29-34 **7.7** pp. 365-366 Exs. 10-19, 22-27, 29-37	**Review** pp. 368-371 Exs. 1-49 **Assess** Chapter 7 Test

YEARLY PACING Chapter 7 Total – **5 days** Chapters 1–7 Total – **40 days** Remaining – **40 days**

Support Materials

CHAPTER RESOURCE BOOK

CHAPTER SUPPORT			
Tips for New Teachers	p. 1	Parents as Partners	p. 3

LESSON SUPPORT	7.1	7.2	7.3	7.4	7.5	7.6	7.7
Lesson Plans (regular and block)	p. 5	p. 13	p. 21	p. 31	p. 41	p. 50	p. 59
Technology Activities & Keystrokes			p. 24	p. 33	p. 43		p. 61
Activity Support Masters							
Activity Masters			p. 23				
Practice (3 levels)	p. 7	p. 15	p. 25	p. 35	p. 44	p. 52	p. 62
Study Guide	p. 10	p. 18	p. 28	p. 38	p. 47	p. 55	p. 65
Real-World Problem Solving						p. 57	p. 67
Challenge Practice	p. 12	p. 20	p. 30	p. 40	p. 49	p. 58	p. 68

REVIEW			
Chapter Review Games and Activities	p. 69	Extra Credit Project with Rubric	p. 74
Real-Life Project with Rubric	p. 70	Cumulative Practice	p. 76
Cooperative Project with Rubric	p. 72	Resource Book Answers	A1

ASSESSMENT

Quizzes	p. 79	Alternative Assessments with Rubrics	p. 88
Chapter Tests (3 levels)	p. 81	Unit Test	p. 90
Standardized Test	p. 87	Cumulative Test	p. 92

TRANSPARENCIES

	7.1	7.2	7.3	7.4	7.5	7.6	7.7
Warm-Up/Daily Homework Quiz	✔	✔	✔	✔	✔	✔	✔
Notetaking Guide	✔	✔	✔	✔	✔	✔	✔
Teacher Support	✔		✔				✔
English/Spanish Problem Solving		✔	✔		✔		
Answer Transparencies	✔	✔	✔	✔	✔	✔	✔

TECHNOLOGY

- EasyPlanner CD-ROM
- Test and Practice Generator
- Electronic Lesson Presentations
- eTutorial CD-ROM
- Chapter Audio Summaries CDs
- Classzone.com
- eEdition Plus Online
- eWorkbook Plus Online
- eTutorial Plus Online
- EasyPlanner Plus Online

ADDITIONAL RESOURCES

- Worked-Out Solution Key
- Notetaking Guide
- Practice Workbook
- Tutor Place
- Professional Development Book
- Special Activities Book
- Posters
- Spanish Study Guide
- Exercises in Spanish
- English/Spanish Ch. Reviews/Tests
- Multi-Language Visual Glossary

CHAPTER 7

Math Background and Teaching Strategies

Lesson 7.1

MATH BACKGROUND

A **percent** is a ratio whose denominator is 100. Because 1 dollar equals 100 cents, parts of a dollar make a useful model for percent. To write a fraction as a percent, create an equivalent fraction with a denominator of 100. For example, $\frac{4}{5} = \frac{4}{5} \cdot \frac{20}{20} = \frac{80}{100} = 80\%$. To write a percent as a fraction, write the percent as the numerator of a fraction whose denominator is 100 and simplify as necessary.

TEACHING STRATEGIES

You can use 10-by-10 grids with students as on page 329 to help them model percents as fractions and vice versa. It is also useful to have students create a chart or poster in the style of the table on page 330 to provide a quick reference to the relationship between common percents and fractions.

Lesson 7.2

MATH BACKGROUND

One way to solve percent problems is to use the proportion $\frac{a}{b} = \frac{p}{100}$. In this proportion, a is part of a base b and p is the percent. This proportion states that the number a is the same part of the base b as the percent p is part of 100. You can solve the proportion to find a missing base, part of the base, or percent.

TEACHING STRATEGIES

Students often have difficulty setting up percent problems correctly. One advantage of using the percent proportion is that it can be used to solve for a, b, or p, but students may have trouble deciding what value goes in each position in the proportion. Help them see that the words "What percent..." indicate they will be solving for p. If they see a number with a percent sign, they should substitute it for p. Point out that in Examples 2 and 3 on page 336 and in the box at the bottom of that page, the word "of" precedes the base. Encourage students always to check that their answers are reasonable in the original situation.

Lesson 7.3

MATH BACKGROUND

Writing a decimal as a percent requires only moving the decimal point two places to the right and adding a percent sign. Conversely, writing a percent as a decimal requires only removing the percent sign and moving the decimal point two places to the left. To write a fraction as a percent, you can first write the fraction as a decimal.

TEACHING STRATEGIES

Expand the chart mentioned in the Teaching Strategies for Lesson 7.1 to include fractions, decimals, and percents. The chart should include fractions that have repeating decimal equivalents, such as $\frac{2}{3} = 0.\overline{6} = 66\frac{2}{3}\%$, as well as those that have terminating decimal equivalents, such as $\frac{5}{8} = 0.625 = 62.5\%$. You may also want to include equivalents for values less than 1% and for whole numbers.

Lesson 7.4

MATH BACKGROUND

The percent equation $a = p\% \cdot b$ is just the percent proportion $\frac{a}{b} = \frac{p}{100}$ solved for a, but it offers an alternative approach to solving percent problems. You can read the percent equation as "a is p percent of b," where a is the part and b is the whole.

TEACHING STRATEGIES

You will need to ensure that students are dealing with the form of percents correctly. For example, students may not have too much trouble solving $a = 70\% \cdot 40$ for a and $28 = 70\% \cdot b$, but when they solve $28 = p\% \cdot 40$ for p, students may be confused as to whether the answer is 0.7% or 70%. Remind them that $p\%$ means $\frac{p}{100}$, so $\frac{28}{40} = p\%$ is equivalent to $\frac{28}{40} = \frac{p}{100}$. So, $p = 70$, and the answer to the question "What percent of 40 is 28?" is 70%.

Lesson 7.5

MATH BACKGROUND

A **percent of change** gives the ratio of an amount of change relative to an original amount, written as a percent. A positive percent of change is a **percent of increase**, and a negative percent of change is a **percent of decrease**, but by using the terms "increase" and "decrease," you can avoid having to worry about positive and negative signs.

TEACHING STRATEGIES

Make sure that students always use the original amount for comparison when they compute percents of change. Students may find it easier to find a percent of change than to use a percent of change to find a new amount. An example of finding a new amount follows.

During one month, the price of gas increases 25% from an original price of $1.52 per gallon. What is the new price?

Students must realize that the new price is the original price plus 25% of the original price. This can be found in two ways:

$$\begin{aligned} \$1.52 + 25\% \cdot \$1.52 &= \$1.52 + 0.25 \cdot \$1.52 \\ &= \$1.52 + \$.38 = \$1.90 \end{aligned}$$

$$\begin{aligned} \$1.52 \cdot (100\% + 25\%) &= \$1.52 \cdot 125\% \\ &= \$1.52 \cdot 1.25 = \$1.90 \end{aligned}$$

Lesson 7.6

MATH BACKGROUND

Two commonly used percents of change are **markup**, a percent of increase added to a wholesale price to form a retail price, and **discount**, a percent of decrease subtracted from an original price to form a sale price. You can use the formulas for markup and discount to find a wholesale or sale price, or you can solve the equations to find an original amount. Sales taxes and tips are two other percents of increase.

TEACHING STRATEGIES

As students gain experience working percent problems, you may want to have them explore applications that will give them a better sense of what is reasonable. Here are examples.

A markup of 100% means a doubling of the wholesale price: A wholesale price of $80 with a markup of 100% gives a retail price of $160.

A discount of 50% means the item is half price: A 50% discount on $124 gives a sale price of $62.

A markup followed by a discount by the same percent does not result in the original price: $100 marked up 50% gives $150, but $150 discounted 50% gives $75.

Multiple discount percents cannot be added: If a $100 item is discounted 50% and then the new price is discounted 20%, the final price is $40, not $30, which is a 70% discount.

Lesson 7.7

MATH BACKGROUND

When you borrow money for a house, a car, or when making a purchase with a credit card, you must pay the lender **interest**. When you place money in a bank account or buy a certificate of deposit, the institution must pay you interest, since they are borrowing your money. The **simple interest** on a principal P at an annual interest rate r (written as a decimal) for a time t in years is given by the formula $I = Prt$, and the balance A of an account earning simple interest is $A = P(1 + rt)$. Today, you will usually encounter only **compound interest**, in which you also earn interest on previously-earned interest. If the interest is **compounded** yearly, then the balance for an account earning compound interest is $A = P(1 + r)^t$. If the interest is compounded n times per year, the formula becomes $A = P\left(1 + \frac{r}{n}\right)^{nt}$.

TEACHING STRATEGIES

Make sure that students work Exercise 25 on page 366, or work a similar problem with your students so that they can see how an account that earns compound interest grows more rapidly over time than an account earning simple interest. You may also want to explore Exercise 27 with students, in which they find that an account earning 10% simple interest takes 10 years to double. You can extend this exercise by having students choose a sample principal and use their calculators to see that if the interest is compounded annually, the principal nearly doubles in 7 years, and more than doubles in 8 years.

CHAPTER 7

Differentiating Instruction

Strategies for Underachievers

USE SCAFFOLDING

For Lessons 7.1 and 7.3, students may need to review changing fractions to decimals and then to percents. The Teaching Strategies for these lessons mention using tables or charts to help students learn common fraction/decimal/percent conversions. Tables are shown below for tenths/fifths, eighths/fourths, and sixths/thirds, which all occur frequently. Make sure students recognize the equivalence $\frac{5}{10} = \frac{4}{8} = \frac{3}{6} = \frac{1}{2}$ between the tables. After students have become comfortable with these tables, encourage them to combine the tables so that only fractions in lowest terms are given, and with the fractions listed in order from least to greatest.

Fraction	Decimal	Percent
$\frac{1}{10}$	0.1	10%
$\frac{2}{10} = \frac{1}{5}$	0.2	20%
$\frac{3}{10}$	0.3	30%
⋮	⋮	⋮
$\frac{9}{10}$	0.9	90%

Fraction	Decimal	Percent
$\frac{1}{8}$	0.125	12.5%
$\frac{2}{8} = \frac{1}{4}$	0.25	25%
$\frac{3}{8}$	0.375	37.5%
⋮	⋮	⋮
$\frac{7}{8}$	0.875	87.5%

Fraction	Decimal	Percent
$\frac{1}{6}$	$0.1\overline{6}$	$16.\overline{6}\%$
$\frac{2}{6} = \frac{1}{3}$	$0.\overline{3}$	$33.\overline{3}\%$
$\frac{3}{6} = \frac{1}{2}$	0.5	50%
$\frac{4}{6} = \frac{2}{3}$	$0.\overline{6}$	$66.\overline{6}\%$
$\frac{5}{6}$	$0.8\overline{3}$	$83.\overline{3}\%$

EMPHASIZE NOTETAKING STRATEGIES

PERCENTS OF CHANGE In Lesson 7.5, you may want to have students model finding a new amount after an increase and after a decrease on note cards for reference. Students should recognize that there are two methods they can use in each case: find an original amount and then add/subtract the change, or multiply the original amount by the quantity 100% plus or minus the percent change.

USE A CO-TEACHING MODEL

For Lessons 7.2 and 7.4, which may be difficult even for students achieving at or above grade level, you may wish to consider co-teaching with a Special Educator who can help students with language-based disabilities develop strategies to help them differentiate among the three types of percent problems and help them identify verbal cues in application problems that will help them use the models correctly. You may want to continue working with the Special Educator to help students with the many problem situations involving percents of increase and decrease in Lessons 7.5 and 7.6.

Strategies for English Learners

USE PICTURES

RATIOS Simple problems involving ratios can often be expressed with pictures rather than words. Here is an example.

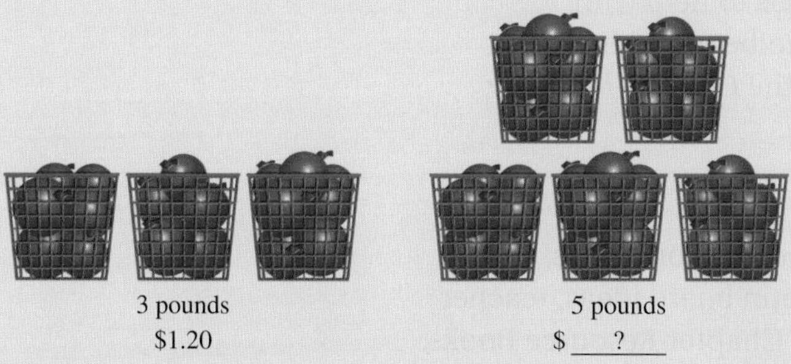

For students at the beginning and intermediate levels of English fluency, beginning the lesson with picture problems instead of word problems can help focus on the mathematical concepts. Students can then use their understanding of the mathematical concept to understand what is asked for in the word problems. Another pictorial way to represent problems involving rates and ratios is with the following type of picture:

758 is what percent of 976?

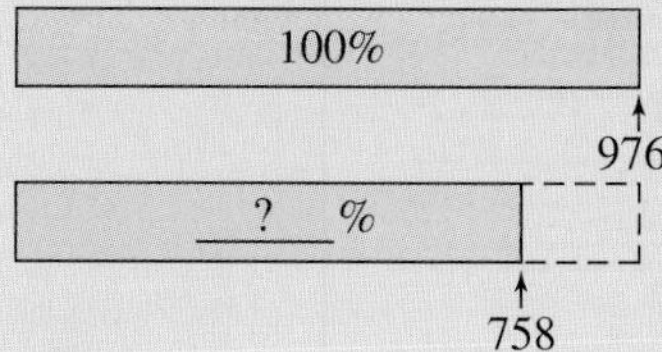

Strategies for Advanced Learners

INCREASE DEPTH AND COMPLEXITY

TAXES In Lesson 7.6, in conjunction with Example 3 on page 358, you may wish to present some advanced learners with the following scenario. Most U.S. states levy a sales tax, with typical rates between 5% and 8%. Usually, the tax is rounded to the nearest cent. For example, at a sales tax rate of 5%, a taxable item costing $2.09 would be charged $.10 in tax, while an item costing $2.10 would be charged $.11. Some states, however, use a "round up always" system to calculate sales tax. In this case, an item costing $2.01 would be charged $.11 in sales tax. Though the result is very minor on an individual purchase, you might want to encourage students to investigate the total cost to consumers on a statewide basis. You will likely need to point out that the key is not the dollar *amount* of taxable sales transactions, but the *number* of taxable sales transactions, since the total effect on the sales tax on any single transaction can only be to add a penny. Students should also note that the "penny penalty" will only be assessed on half the transactions. Students can use the Internet to research taxable revenues and transactions for their state and use the data to predict what they think the economic impact of a round up method would be.

USE CROSS-CURRICULAR CONNECTIONS

In Lesson 7.6, you may wish to collaborate with a social studies teacher to research the sales tax structures of the various states, including whether they have a sales tax (almost all do), and what items incur sales taxes (for example, states vary on which grocery items are taxed). Students can also explore city and county sales taxes, and the federal taxes that are paid on items such as gasoline. One other pertinent area of research is property taxes, which often provide a significant portion of the revenues for schools. For property taxes, students may need to learn about the *mill rate assessment*, which is based on thousandths of a dollar.

COMPOUND INTEREST In Technology Activity 7.7, students will explore the effects of compounding interest at different intervals. Make sure that advanced students complete Exercise 4. You may also want to have them find the result of daily compounding, which is used by many financial institutions, in the setting of this exercise. Encourage students to investigate the difference between a *nominal* interest rate and an *effective* interest rate. You can also have students explain what compounding interval they would prefer on an account on which they *earn* interest and what compounding interval they would prefer for an account, such as a credit card account, for which they must *pay* interest.

CHAPTER 7

Differentiating Instruction: Resource Materials

Differentiating Teacher Materials

McDougal Littell *Pre-Algebra* offers a wide variety of materials to help with professional development and teaching. These resources can be found in this *Teacher's Edition*, in the *Professional Development Book*, in the *Chapter Resource Books*, and in the multi-language resources.

PROFESSIONAL DEVELOPMENT BOOK

The *Professional Development Book* contains ideas for in-service workshops, professional articles, mathematical background notes, bulletin board ideas, teacher tips, and a reprint of the Parents as Partners pages from the Chapter Resource Books. (Parents as Partners is also available in Spanish in the *Spanish Study Guide*.)

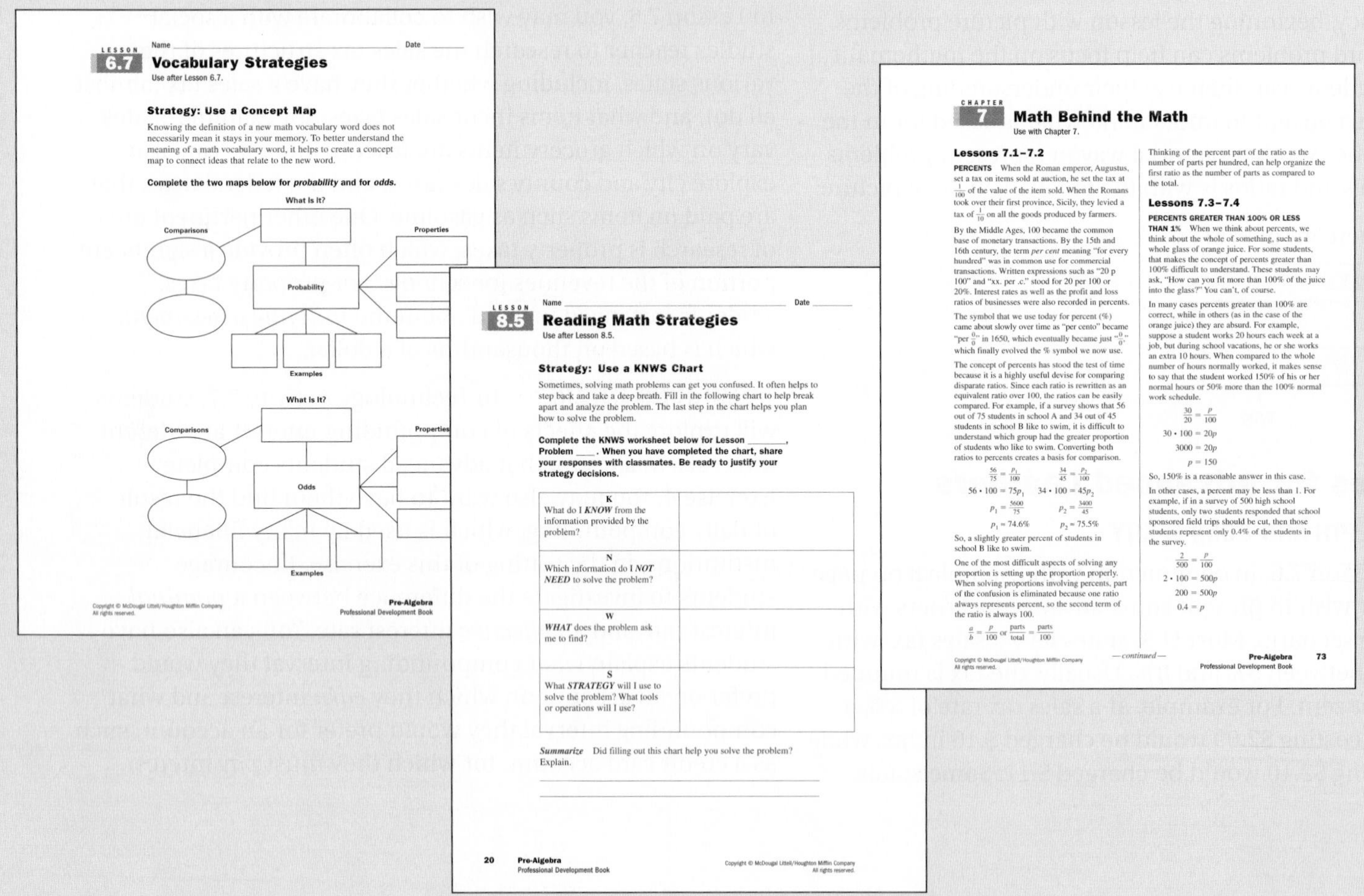

LESSON 6.7 Name ______ Date ______

Vocabulary Strategies

Use after Lesson 6.7.

Strategy: Use a Concept Map

Knowing the definition of a new math vocabulary word does not necessarily mean it stays in your memory. To better understand the meaning of a math vocabulary word, it helps to create a concept map to connect ideas that relate to the new word.

Complete the two maps below for *probability* and for *odds*.

Pre-Algebra
Professional Development Book

LESSON 8.5 Name ______ Date ______

Reading Math Strategies

Use after Lesson 8.5.

Strategy: Use a KNWS Chart

Sometimes, solving math problems can get you confused. It often helps to step back and take a deep breath. Fill in the following chart to help break apart and analyze the problem. The last step in the chart helps you plan how to solve the problem.

Complete the KNWS worksheet below for Lesson ________, Problem ____. When you have completed the chart, share your responses with classmates. Be ready to justify your strategy decisions.

K What do I ***KNOW*** from the information provided by the problem?	
N Which information do I ***NOT NEED*** to solve the problem?	
W ***WHAT*** does the problem ask me to find?	
S What ***STRATEGY*** will I use to solve the problem? What tools or operations will I use?	

Summarize Did filling out this chart help you solve the problem? Explain.

____

____

20 Pre-Algebra
Professional Development Book

CHAPTER 7

Math Behind the Math

Use with Chapter 7.

Lessons 7.1–7.2

PERCENTS When the Roman emperor, Augustus, set a tax on items sold at auction, he set the tax at $\frac{1}{100}$ of the value of the item sold. When the Romans took over their first province, Sicily, they levied a tax of $\frac{1}{10}$ on all the goods produced by farmers.

By the Middle Ages, 100 became the common base of monetary transactions. By the 15th and 16th century, the term *per cent* meaning "for every hundred" was in common use for commercial transactions. Written expressions such as "20 p 100" and "xx. per .c." stood for 20 per 100 or 20%. Interest rates as well as the profit and loss ratios of businesses were also recorded in percents.

The symbol that we use today for percent (%) came about slowly over time as "per cento" became "per $\frac{0}{0}$" in 1650, which eventually became just "$\frac{0}{0}$" which finally evolved the % symbol we now use.

The concept of percents has stood the test of time because it is a highly useful devise for comparing disparate ratios. Since each ratio is rewritten as an equivalent ratio over 100, the ratios can be easily compared. For example, if a survey shows that 56 out of 75 students in school A and 34 out of 45 students in school B like to swim, it is difficult to understand which group had the greater proportion of students who like to swim. Converting both ratios to percents creates a basis for comparison.

$$\frac{56}{75} = \frac{p_1}{100} \qquad \frac{34}{45} = \frac{p_2}{100}$$
$$56 \cdot 100 = 75p_1 \qquad 34 \cdot 100 = 45p_2$$
$$p_1 = \frac{5600}{75} \qquad p_2 = \frac{3400}{45}$$
$$p_1 \approx 74.6\% \qquad p_2 \approx 75.5\%$$

So, a slightly greater percent of students in school B like to swim.

One of the most difficult aspects of solving any proportion is setting up the proportion properly. When solving proportions involving percents, part of the confusion is eliminated because one ratio always represents percent, so the second term of the ratio is always 100.

$$\frac{a}{b} = \frac{p}{100} \text{ or } \frac{\text{parts}}{\text{total}} = \frac{\text{parts}}{100}$$

Thinking of the percent part of the ratio as the number of parts per hundred, can help organize the first ratio as the number of parts as compared to the total.

Lessons 7.3–7.4

PERCENTS GREATER THAN 100% OR LESS THAN 1% When we think about percents, we think about the whole of something, such as a whole glass of orange juice. For some students, that makes the concept of percents greater than 100% difficult to understand. These students may ask, "How can you fit more than 100% of the juice into the glass?" You can't, of course.

In many cases percents greater than 100% are correct, while in others (as in the case of the orange juice) they are absurd. For example, suppose a student works 20 hours each week at a job, but during school vacations, he or she works an extra 10 hours. When compared to the whole number of hours normally worked, it makes sense to say that the student worked 150% of his or her normal hours or 50% more than the 100% normal work schedule.

$$\frac{30}{20} = \frac{p}{100}$$
$$30 \cdot 100 = 20p$$
$$3000 = 20p$$
$$p = 150$$

So, 150% is a reasonable answer in this case.

In other cases, a percent may be less than 1. For example, if in a survey of 500 high school students, only two students responded that school sponsored field trips should be cut, then those students represent only 0.4% of the students in the survey.

$$\frac{2}{500} = \frac{p}{100}$$
$$2 \cdot 100 = 500p$$
$$200 = 500p$$
$$0.4 = p$$

—*continued*—

Pre-Algebra
Professional Development Book 73

RESOURCE BOOK

Each *Chapter Resource Book* contains a section of tips for new teachers and a section on parental involvement. There is also a lesson plan page for both a regular schedule course and a block schedule course for each lesson in the textbook.

CHAPTER 7

Tips for New Teachers

For use with Chapter 7

Chapter Support

Lesson 7.1

INCLUSION Help students make the connection of *percent* meaning *per hundred* by reminding them of the meanings of words that have cent- as a prefix. Use words such as century, centipede, and centimeter. Also, you may wish to remind students how many cents are in a dollar.

TEACHING TIP In Example 3 on page 330, point out to students that the word *of* can be replaced with a multiplication symbol. Remind students that they must first change the percent to a fraction before they multiply.

TEACHING TIP Memorizing common percents as fractions, such as the ones given on the top of page 330, will save students a great deal of time in the long run. You may want to start by having students memorize percents that are multiples of 10, such as $10\% = \frac{1}{10}$, $20\% = \frac{2}{10}$ or $\frac{1}{5}$, and so on.

Lesson 7.2

TEACHING TIP As an alternative method in Example 1 on page 335, you may wish to have students solve this proportion by using cross products.

TEACHING TIP As mentioned in the Teaching Tip for Lesson 6.3, students might be helped by using a general template for proportions, such as

$$\frac{\text{part}}{\text{whole}} = \frac{\text{part}}{\text{whole}}.$$

Similarly, they might be helped by using a general template for proportions used to solve percent problems, such as

$$\frac{\text{part}}{\text{whole}} = \frac{\%}{100}.$$

Lesson 7.3

COMMON ERROR Students tend to make various errors in converting decimals and percents. If you teach the "two decimal place" method, be sure to supply examples such as 0.8 = 80%, 0.08 = 8%, 0.008 = 0.8%, 8 = 800%, and so on.

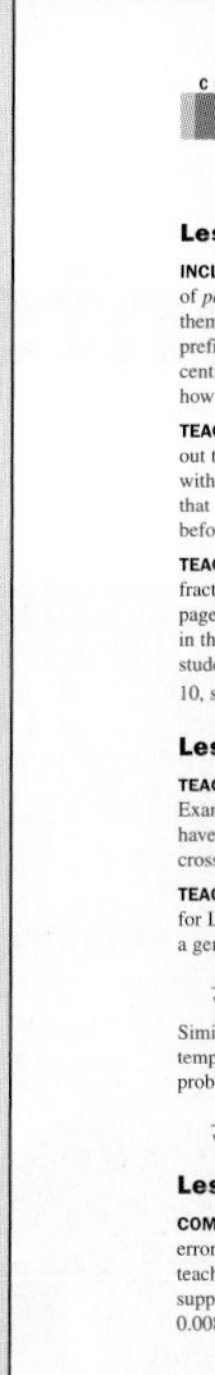

TEACHING TIP In Example 3, remind students that to convert a fraction to a decimal (before eventually converting to a percent), they should read the decimal number using place value. For example, 0.375 is three hundred seventy five thousandths, which is 37.5%.

Lesson 7.4

COMMON ERROR In Example 2 on page 346, some students may write 6.5% as 0.65. Remind them of the "two place rule" and that when 6.5% is written as a decimal number, it is 0.065.

TEACHING TIP Point out to students that in Example 3 on page 346 the part is greater than the whole and, therefore, the per cent is greater than 100%.

TEACHING TIP Take the time to review the Summary of Methods for Solving a Percent Problem on page 347 before proceeding to Lesson 7.5.

Lesson 7.5

TEACHING TIP Students might be helped by using a general template for percent of change problems, such as

$$\frac{\text{amount of change}}{\text{original amount}} = \frac{\%}{100}.$$

COMMON ERROR When calculating two or more percent changes, remind students that if the number of items increases and then decreases by the same percent, it will not end up being equal to the original amount. For example, a store buys a television for $400 and marks it up by 25%, then puts it on sale for 25% off the retail price. Show students that the sale price will not be $400 by using the following reasoning: The store buys the television and marks it up 25%. 125% of $400 is $500. If the store then sells the television for 25% off the retail price, 25% of $500 is $125, so the sale price would be $375, not $400. (Note that 25% of the larger number is more than 25% of the smaller number).

—continued—

CHAPTER 7 Name ______________ Date ______

Parents as Partners

For use with Chapter 7

Chapter Support

Chapter Overview One way you can help your student succeed in Chapter 7 is by discussing the lesson goals in the chart below. When a lesson is completed, ask your student the following questions. "What were the goals of the lesson? What new words and formulas did you learn? How can you apply the ideas of the lesson to your life?"

Lesson Title	*Lesson Goals*	*Key Applications*
7.1: Percents and Fractions	Use a fraction to find the percent of a number.	• Music • Tortoises • Tennis • Chess
7.2: Percents and Proportions	Use proportions to solve percent problems.	• Heptathlon • Cats • Tanana River • Solar Cars
7.3: Percents and Decimals	Use decimals to solve percent problems.	• Pygmy Hippos • Winds • Roller Coasters • Ships
7.4: The Percent Equation	Use equations to solve percent problems.	• Astronomy • Community Service • Bake Sale • Election
7.5: Percent of Change	Find a percent of change in a quantity.	• Balloons • Action Sports • Hot Dogs • Wetlands
7.6: Percent Applications	Find markups, discounts, sales tax, and tips.	• Jewelry • Electronics • Bicycles • In-line Skates
7.7: Simple and Compound Interest	Calculate interest earned and account balances.	• Bonds • Summer Job • Loan

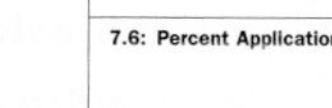

Notetaking Strategies

Concept grid is the strategy featured in Chapter 7 (see page 328). Encourage your student to put concept grids in his/her notebook. These grids can be broken up into sections that include a definition, characteristics, examples, and nonexamples.

—continued—

MULTI-LANGUAGE RESOURCES

A number of resources are available to help students acquiring English. These include a *Spanish Study Guide, Exercises in Spanish, English/Spanish Chapter Reviews and Tests, English-Spanish Problem Solving Transparencies, Chapter Audio Summaries,* and a *Multi-Language Visual Glossary.*

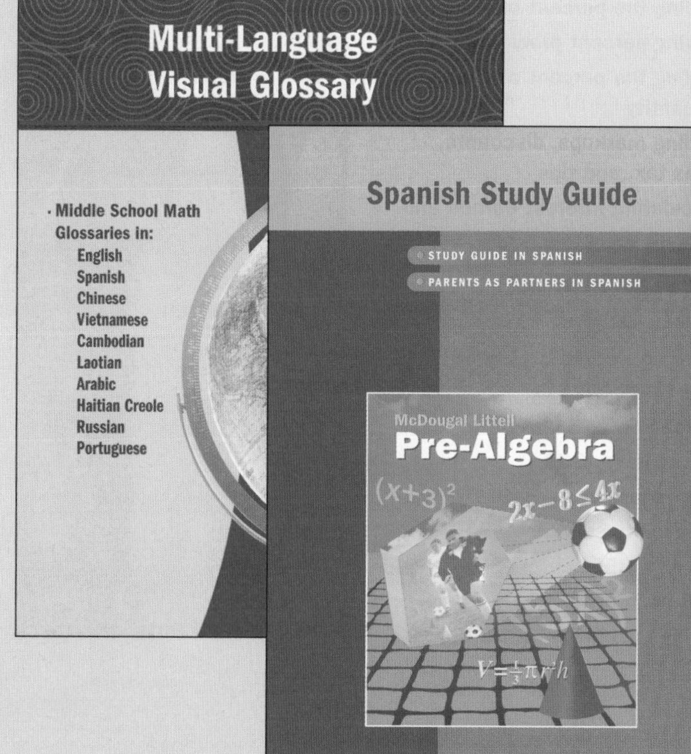

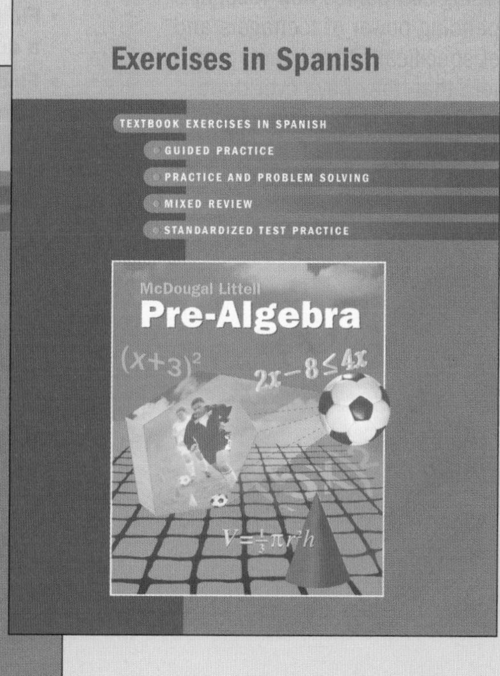

OVERVIEW

MAIN IDEAS

In this chapter, students use fractions and decimals to find the percent of a number. Students use proportions and equations to solve percent problems. Students solve problems involving percent of change, find markups, discounts, sales tax, and tips. Finally, students calculate the interest earned on an account, as well as the account balance.

APPLICATION NOTE

Between 1997 and 2002, spending by teenagers in the United States increased by more than half the amount they spent in 1997. There are several reasons for this.

There are currently more teenagers in the United States than at any other time in history. Many of those teenagers do not receive a set amount of money each week (an allowance), but instead receive money in smaller amounts as they request it.

Advertising companies now recognize the spending power of teenagers and market specifically to the teen market more than they have ever done before. By one estimate, teenagers are exposed to 3000 advertisements every day.

CHAPTER 7

Percents

BEFORE

In previous chapters you've . . .

- Written ratios
- Solved equations with decimals
- Written fractions as decimals
- Solved proportions

Now

In Chapter 7 you'll study . . .

- Finding the percent of a number
- Solving percent problems
- Finding the percent of change in a quantity
- Finding markups, discounts, sales tax, and tips
- Calculating interest earned and account balances

WHY?

So you can solve real-world problems about . . .

- astronomy, p. 332
- solar cars, p. 338
- roller coasters, p. 343
- community service, p. 348
- lakes, p. 355
- laptops, p. 360
- savings accounts, p. 364

How can you find the sale price of an item?

326

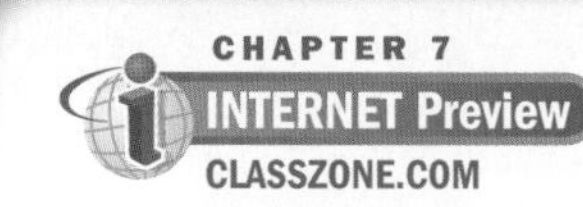

- eEdition Plus Online
- eWorkbook Plus Online
- eTutorial Plus Online
- State Test Practice
- More Examples

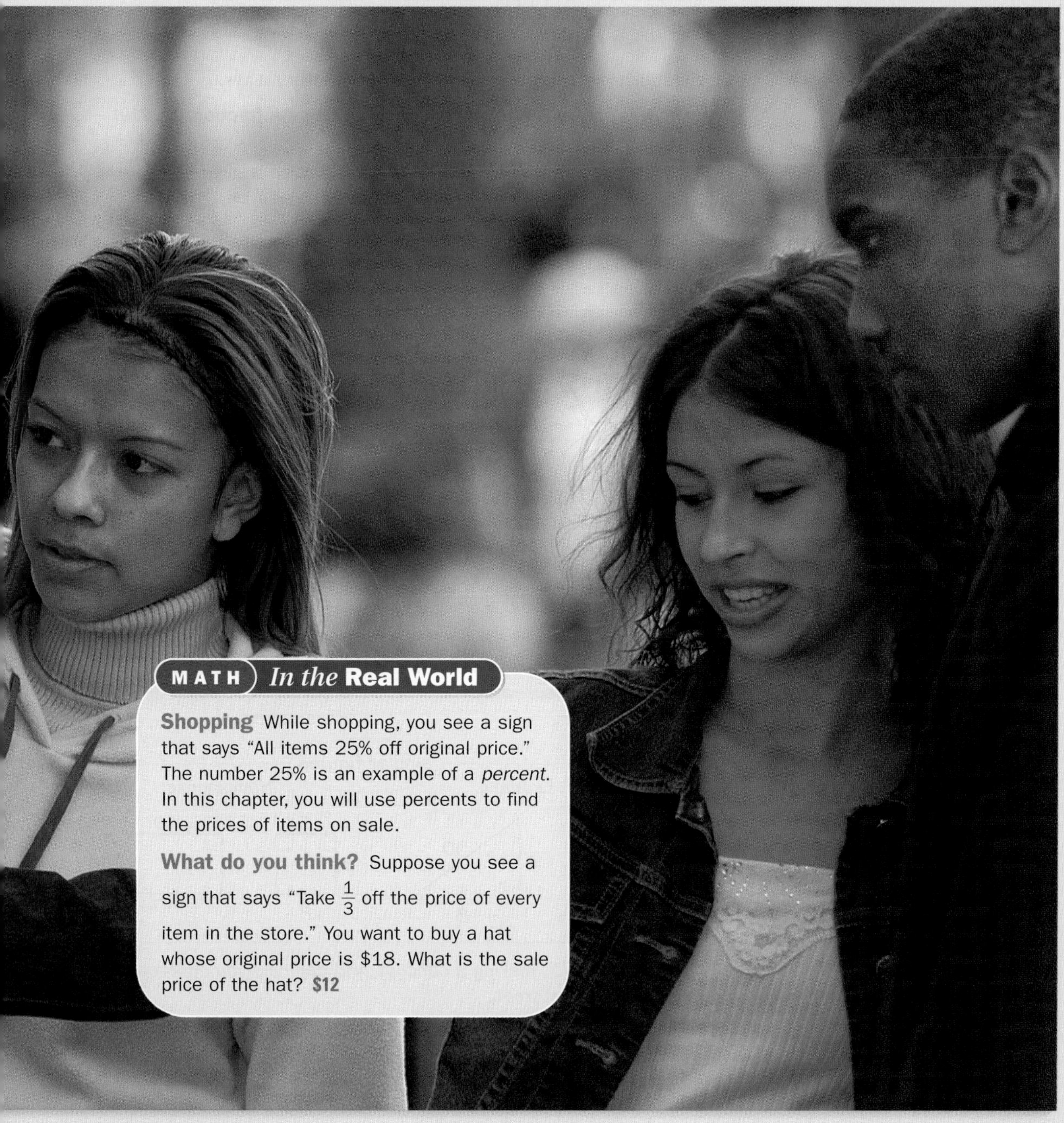

MATH *In the* **Real World**

Shopping While shopping, you see a sign that says "All items 25% off original price." The number 25% is an example of a *percent*. In this chapter, you will use percents to find the prices of items on sale.

What do you think? Suppose you see a sign that says "Take $\frac{1}{3}$ off the price of every item in the store." You want to buy a hat whose original price is $18. What is the sale price of the hat? **$12**

CHAPTER RESOURCES

These resources are provided to help you prepare for the chapter and to customize review materials:

Chapter 7 Resource Book

- Tips for New Teachers, pp. 1–2
- Lesson Plan, pp. 5, 13, 21, 31, 41, 50, 59
- Lesson Plan for Block Scheduling, pp. 6, 14, 22, 32, 42, 51, 60

Technology

- EasyPlanner CD-ROM
- Test and Practice Generator
- Electronic Lesson Presentations CD-ROM
- eTutorial CD-ROM

Internet

- Classzone
- eEdition Plus Online
- eWorkbook Plus Online
- eTutorial Plus Online
- EasyPlanner Plus Online

ENGLISH LEARNER SUPPORT

- Spanish Study Guide
- Multi-Language Visual Glossary
- Chapter Audio Summaries CDs
- Teacher's Edition, pp. 326E–326F

PREPARE

DIAGNOSIS/REMEDIATION

Prerequisite Skills Quiz
The Prerequisite Skills Quiz can help you diagnose whether students have the following skills needed in Chapter 7:

- Write ratios (Ex. 1)
- Write fractions as decimals or decimals as fractions (Exs. 2–5)
- Solve proportions (Exs. 6–9)

Chapter 7 Resource Book

- Study Guide (Lessons 7.1–7.7)

Tutor Place

NOTETAKING STRATEGIES

Whenever students include a non-example in their notes, encourage them to write down why the non-example is incorrect. You might also consider having them write a few sentences about how to change the nonexample into an example. Further suggestions for keeping a notebook can be found on pages 338, 347, and 364.

For more support on notetaking, see:

- Notetaking Guide Workbook
- Notetaking Transparencies

CHAPTER 7

Chapter Prerequisite Skills

Review Vocabulary
ratio, p. 269
proportion, p. 275
decimal, p. 770
fraction, p. 777

PREREQUISITE SKILLS QUIZ

Preparing for Success **To prepare for success in this chapter, test your knowledge of these concepts and skills. You may want to look at the pages referred to in blue for additional review.**

1. **Vocabulary** Write the ratio 4 to 12 in two other ways. $\frac{4}{12}$, 4 : 12

Write the fraction as a decimal or the decimal as a fraction. *(p. 219)*

2. $\frac{5}{8}$ 0.625 **3.** $\frac{3}{25}$ 0.12 **4.** 0.35 $\frac{7}{20}$ **5.** 0.175 $\frac{7}{40}$

Solve the proportion. *(pp. 275, 280)*

6. $\frac{3}{4} = \frac{y}{16}$ 12 **7.** $\frac{30}{48} = \frac{10}{h}$ 16 **8.** $\frac{7.5}{x} = \frac{5}{8}$ 12 **9.** $\frac{r}{6} = \frac{10.5}{9}$ 7

NOTETAKING STRATEGIES

CONCEPT GRID You can use a concept grid to take notes. A concept grid usually includes a definition, characteristics, examples, and nonexamples.

Definition:	Characteristics:
Two figures are similar if they have the same shape but not necessarily the same size.	Corresponding angles are congruent. The ratios of lengths of corresponding sides are equal.
similar figures	
Example:	Nonexample:

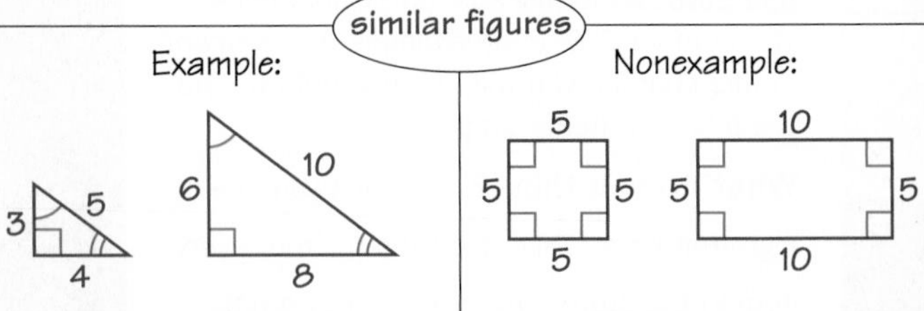

In Lesson 7.7, making a concept grid can help you understand compound interest.

Note Worthy

You will find a notetaking strategy at the beginning of each chapter. Look for additional notetaking and study strategies throughout the chapter.

LESSON

7.1 Percents *and* Fractions

BEFORE You multiplied fractions and whole numbers.

Now You'll use a fraction to find the percent of a number.

WHY? So you can compare tennis players' serves, as in Ex. 7.

Vocabulary
percent, p. 329

Music In marching band competitions, each band is judged on its musical performance, marching, and visual effect. At many competitions, a marching band is rated on a 100 point scale. A band that earns 85 points has earned *85 percent* of the total possible points.

The word *percent* means "per hundred." A **percent** is a ratio whose denominator is 100. The symbol for percent is %.

Writing Percents

Words In the area model shown, 85 of the 100 squares are shaded. You can say that 85 percent of the squares are shaded.

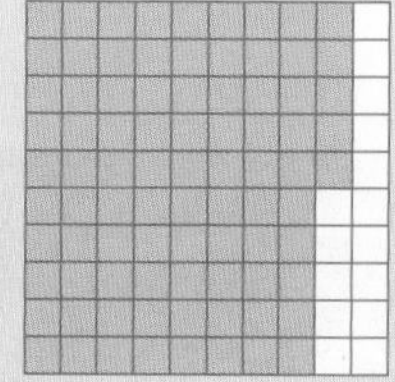

Numbers $\frac{85}{100} = 85\%$ **Algebra** $\frac{p}{100} = p\%$

Example 1 *Writing Percents as Fractions, Fractions as Percents*

Write 29% and 45% as fractions in simplest form.

a. $29\% = \frac{29}{100}$

b. $45\% = \frac{45}{100} = \frac{9}{20}$

Write $\frac{7}{10}$ and $\frac{3}{5}$ as percents.

a. $\frac{7}{10} = \frac{7 \cdot 10}{10 \cdot 10} = \frac{70}{100} = 70\%$

b. $\frac{3}{5} = \frac{3 \cdot 20}{5 \cdot 20} = \frac{60}{100} = 60\%$

Review *Help*

For help with writing equivalent fractions, see p. 182.

Checkpoint

Write the percent as a fraction in simplest form, or write the fraction as a percent.

1. 51% $\frac{51}{100}$ **2.** 25% $\frac{1}{4}$ **3.** $\frac{11}{20}$ 55% **4.** $\frac{4}{25}$ 16%

NCTM CURRICULUM STANDARDS
Standard 1: Understand numbers; Understand ways of representing numbers
Standard 6: Solve problems in math and other contexts

1 PLAN

Skill Check

1. $\frac{1}{5} \cdot 20 = \underline{?}$ 4

2. $\frac{3}{4} \cdot 10 = \underline{?}$ $7\frac{1}{2}$

3. $\frac{1}{2} \cdot 5 = \underline{?}$ $2\frac{1}{2}$

Lesson Objective

Use a fraction to find the percent of a number.

Pacing

Suggested Number of Days
Basic Course: 1 day
Average Course: 1 day
Advanced Course: 1 day
Block: 0.5 block with 7.2

Teaching Resources

For a complete list of Teaching Resources, see page 326B.

Transparency

Warm-Up Exercises for this lesson are available on a transparency.

2 TEACH

Motivating the Lesson

Ask students about competitions they have participated in that use scoring systems involving percents.

TIPS *for* NEW TEACHERS
When you discuss the common percent-fraction equivalents on page 330, have students use hundredths grids and colored pencils to make a bulletin board display. See Tips for New Teachers in the *Chapter 7 Resource Book*.

Extra Examples

Example 1 Write the percent as a fraction in simplest form.

a. 80% $\frac{4}{5}$ **b.** 61% $\frac{61}{100}$

Write the fraction as a percent.

a. $\frac{27}{50}$ **54%** **b.** $\frac{13}{25}$ **52%**

Example 2 An airport security screener searches the luggage brought to the ticket counter by 3 of every 10 passengers. If you are one of the persons in a group of 10 passengers, what is the probability that you will be chosen to have your luggage searched? Write your answer as a percent. **30%**

Example 3 Ninety percent of the flights that left a certain airport yesterday departed on time. If there were 150 flights from the airport yesterday, how many of them departed on time? **135 flights**

TEACHING TIP

If students are having difficulty memorizing the table of common percents, remind them that they can write the percent as a fraction with a denominator of 100 and then simplify it. For example, 75% = $\frac{75}{100} = \frac{3}{4}$.

CONCEPT CHECK

How do you write $\frac{3}{4}$ as a percent?

Rewrite $\frac{3}{4}$ by multiplying both the numerator and the denominator by 25 to get $\frac{75}{100}$, and then write this fraction as 75%.

DAILY PUZZLER

What is 25% of 60% of a number? **15% of the number**

Here are some common percent-fraction equivalents that may be useful to memorize.

Common Percents					
10% = $\frac{1}{10}$	20% = $\frac{1}{5}$	25% = $\frac{1}{4}$	30% = $\frac{3}{10}$	40% = $\frac{2}{5}$	50% = $\frac{1}{2}$
60% = $\frac{3}{5}$	70% = $\frac{7}{10}$	75% = $\frac{3}{4}$	80% = $\frac{4}{5}$	90% = $\frac{9}{10}$	100% = 1

Study *Strategy*

Probabilities can be written as percents between 0% (for an impossible event) and 100% (for an event that is certain to occur).

Example 2 *Writing a Probability as a Percent*

Prizes A radio station randomly selects 1 of 5 finalists for a prize. You are one of the finalists. What is the probability that you will win? Write your answer as a percent.

Solution

There are 5 possible outcomes, and 1 outcome is favorable.

$P(\text{you win}) = \frac{1}{5}$ **Write probability as a fraction.**

$= 20\%$ **Write fraction as a percent.**

Answer The probability that you will win is 20%.

Example 3 *Finding a Percent of a Number*

Tortoises A desert tortoise can go a year or more without drinking water. When it does drink, its body weight can increase by 40%. Suppose a desert tortoise weighs 15 pounds after a long period without water. How many pounds can the tortoise gain when it drinks?

Solution

To find 40% of 15 pounds, use the fact that 40% = $\frac{2}{5}$. Then multiply.

40% of 15 = $\frac{2}{5} \cdot 15$ **Write percent as a fraction.**

$= \frac{30}{5}$ **Multiply.**

$= 6$ **Simplify.**

Answer The desert tortoise can gain 6 pounds when it drinks.

In the **Real World**

Tortoises A desert tortoise spends about 95% of its life in underground burrows. About what fraction of a desert tortoise's life is spent underground? $\frac{19}{20}$

Checkpoint

5. In Example 2, suppose that there are 10 finalists. What is the probability that you will win? Write your answer as a percent. **10%**

Find the percent of the number.

6. 25% of 36 **9**
7. 70% of 70 **49**
8. 50% of 14 **7**
9. 75% of 80 **60**

7.1 Exercises

More Practice, p. 809

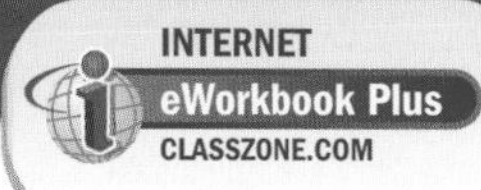

Guided Practice

Vocabulary Check

1. Copy and complete: A percent is a ratio whose denominator is _?_. 100

2. Explain how you would rewrite $\frac{13}{25}$ as a percent. See margin.

Skill Check

Write the percent as a fraction in simplest form, or write the fraction as a percent.

3. 65% $\frac{13}{20}$ 4. 98% $\frac{49}{50}$ 5. $\frac{12}{25}$ 48% 6. $\frac{9}{10}$ 90%

Guided Problem Solving

2. *Sample answer:* Write $\frac{13}{25}$ as a fraction with a denominator of 100 by multiplying the numerator and denominator by 4, then write the numerator of the resulting fraction with a percent symbol: $\frac{13}{25} = \frac{13 \cdot 4}{25 \cdot 4} = \frac{52}{100} = 52\%$.

7. **Tennis** In tennis, you can serve the ball a second time if your first serve is not successful. The table shows the first serves by you and your opponent in a match. How many more successful first serves did you have than did your opponent?

Player	Total first serves	Percent successful
You	152	75%
Your opponent	125	60%

1) Find the number of successful first serves you had. 114 serves
2) Find the number of successful first serves your opponent had. 75 serves
3) Find the difference of the numbers in Steps 1 and 2. 39 serves

Practice and Problem Solving

Homework Help

Example	Exercises
1	8-27, 45
2	28-34
3	35-44

Online Resources
CLASSZONE.COM
- More Examples
- eTutorial Plus

Write the percent as a fraction.

A 8. 34% $\frac{17}{50}$ 9. 40% $\frac{2}{5}$ 10. 71% $\frac{71}{100}$ 11. 27% $\frac{27}{100}$

12. 55% $\frac{11}{20}$ 13. 18% $\frac{9}{50}$ 14. 90% $\frac{9}{10}$ 15. 85% $\frac{17}{20}$

Write the fraction as a percent.

16. $\frac{4}{5}$ 80% 17. $\frac{3}{25}$ 12% 18. $\frac{9}{20}$ 45% 19. $\frac{7}{10}$ 70%

20. $\frac{33}{50}$ 66% 21. $\frac{1}{4}$ 25% 22. $\frac{18}{25}$ 72% 23. $\frac{17}{20}$ 85%

24. **Food** You buy ice cream that contains 10% milk fat. What fraction of the ice cream is milk fat? $\frac{1}{10}$

25. **Currency** The composition of a U.S. dollar bill is $\frac{3}{4}$ cotton and $\frac{1}{4}$ linen. What percent of a dollar bill is cotton? 75%

26. **Football** A football player completes 19 of his 25 passes during the season. What percent of his passes did the player complete? 76%

3 APPLY

ASSIGNMENT GUIDE

Basic Course

Day 1: SRH p. 780 Exs. 5-8; pp. 331-333 Exs. 8-11, 20-25, 28-33, 37-43, 46-51, 60-69

Average Course

Day 1: pp. 331-333 Exs. 12-19, 26-36, 43-46, 52-57, 59-65, 68-70

Advanced Course

Day 1: pp. 331-333 Exs. 14-19, 26-28, 37-48, 52-61*, 66-70

Block

pp. 331-333 Exs. 12-19, 26-36, 43-46, 52-57, 59-65, 68-70 (with 7.2)

Extra Practice

- Student Edition, p. 809
- Chapter 7 Resource Book, pp. 7-9
- Test and Practice Generator

Transparency

Even-numbered answers are available on transparencies. A support transparency is available for Exercises 46-48.

Homework Check

When you review students' homework for this lesson, go over the following exercises to check understanding of key concepts.
Basic: 8, 20, 28, 30, 37
Average: 12, 16, 29, 32, 43
Advanced: 14, 18, 28, 37, 44

Common Error

In Exercises 8-15, watch for students who reduce percents to fractions incorrectly because they do not factor the numerator and denominator correctly. Give these students extra practice in simplifying fractions.

TEACHING TIP

In Exercises 35–42, point out that a quick way for students to mentally check the reasonableness of their answers is to compare the given percent to 50%. If the given percent is greater than 50%, then their answer should be greater than half the given number. If the given percent is less than 50%, then their answer should be less than half the given number.

55a.

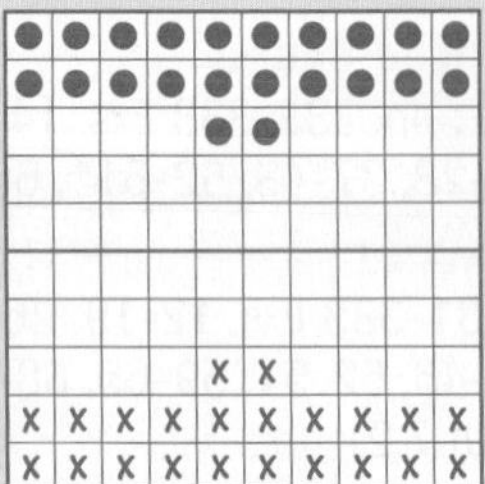

45. *Sample answer:* Because $p\% = \frac{p}{100}$, $100\% = \frac{100}{100}$. Simplifying $\frac{100}{100}$ gives 1, so $100\% = 1$.

46. $\frac{7}{10}$, $\frac{4}{5}$, 0.83, 89%

47. $\frac{9}{20}$, 54%, 0.62, $\frac{16}{25}$

55c. 19 pieces. *Sample answer:* To start the game, there are 44 total pieces on the board. 75% of 44 is 33, so there are 33 pieces remaining. If 14 of these 33 belong to you, then 33 − 14 or 19 pieces belong to the opponent.

In the **Real World**

Chess A modern chess board is 8 squares by 8 squares. How many more squares does the board described in Exercise 55 have than a modern chess board? **36 more squares**

27. Art The bristles on a Chinese writing brush are 70% rabbit hair and 30% goat hair. What fraction of the bristles is goat hair? $\frac{3}{10}$

A computer randomly generates an integer from 1 to 10. Find the probability of the given event. Write your answer as a percent.

28. $P(5)$ **10%** **29.** $P(4)$ **10%** **30.** P(odd number) **50%**

31. P(even number) **50%** **32.** P(factor of 20) **50%** **33.** P(prime number) **40%**

34. Tests A multiple choice question on a test has 4 answer choices. You guess at the answer. What is the probability that you will select the correct choice? Write your answer as a percent. **25%**

Find the percent of the number.

35. 75% of 12 **9** **36.** 20% of 95 **19** **37.** 30% of 50 **15** **38.** 70% of 90 **63**

39. 50% of 94 **47** **40.** 10% of 130 **13** **41.** 40% of 175 **70** **42.** 25% of 500 **125**

43. Plants Alfalfa plants can take up metals from the ground and store them in their roots and stems. In 2002, a scientist claimed that an alfalfa plant could produce 20% of its weight in gold by taking up tiny gold particles left behind from rock mining. How many pounds of gold could be produced from 3000 pounds of alfalfa plants? **600 lb**

44. Astronomy The International Space Station orbits Earth about every 90 minutes. About 40% of the time, Earth prevents the space station from receiving direct sunlight. About how many minutes per orbit does the space station *not* receive sunlight? **36 min**

45. *Writing* Use the definition of percent to explain why 100% = 1. **See margin.**

Use a number line to order the numbers from least to greatest.

B **46.** 89%, $\frac{4}{5}$, $\frac{7}{10}$, 0.83 **47.** 54%, $\frac{9}{20}$, 0.62, $\frac{16}{25}$ **48.** $\frac{9}{25}$, 17%, 0.22, $\frac{9}{50}$ **17%, $\frac{9}{50}$, 0.22, $\frac{9}{25}$**

46–47. See margin.

Algebra Evaluate the expression when $k = 20$.

49. $k\%$ of 90 **18** **50.** 40% of k **8** **51.** $(80 - k)\%$ of 30 **18**

52. 25% of $(k + 8)$ **7** **53.** $(k + 10)\%$ of 200 **60** **54.** $(k - 10)\%$ of 350 **35**

55. Extended Problem Solving An 18th century Indian version of chess uses a 10 square by 10 square board. On the board shown, the dots represent your opponent's chess pieces at the start of the game.

a. Illustrate Copy the board shown. Mark X's on your side of the board to represent your chess pieces in an arrangement that matches your opponent's. **See margin.**

b. What percent of the squares are occupied at the start of a game? **44%**

c. Explain During one game, 75% of the pieces are still on the board. Of these pieces, 14 belong to you. How many pieces belong to your opponent? Explain. **See margin.**

Opponent's side

Your side

58. No. *Sample answer:* Because $40\% = \frac{2}{5}$, the area of rectangle A is $\frac{2}{5} \cdot \frac{2}{5} = \frac{4}{25}$, or 16%, of the area of rectangle B. For example, if rectangle B has length 10 units and width 5 units, then rectangle A has length 4 units and width 2 units. So the area of rectangle B is $10 \cdot 5 = 50$ square units, and the area of rectangle A is $4 \cdot 2 = 8$ square units, or 16% of the area of rectangle B.

59a. No. *Sample answer:* 40% of x is $0.4x$, and 60% of y is $0.6y$, so their sum is $0.4x + 0.6y$, which is not the same as 100% of $x + y$, which is just $x + y$.

59b. No. *Sample answer:* The average of 40% of x and 60% of y is $\frac{1}{2}(0.4x + 0.6y)$, but 50%, or $\frac{1}{2}$, of the sum of x and y is $\frac{1}{2}(x + y)$.

56. Phone Numbers You forgot the last two digits of your friend's phone number. You know that the next-to-last digit is 4 or 5, and the last digit is an odd number. If you guess the phone number, what is the probability that you will be correct? Write your answer as a percent. 10%

57. Estimation The circle graph shows the results of a class survey that asked 800 students where they make most of their music purchases.
Estimates may vary. Sample estimates are given.

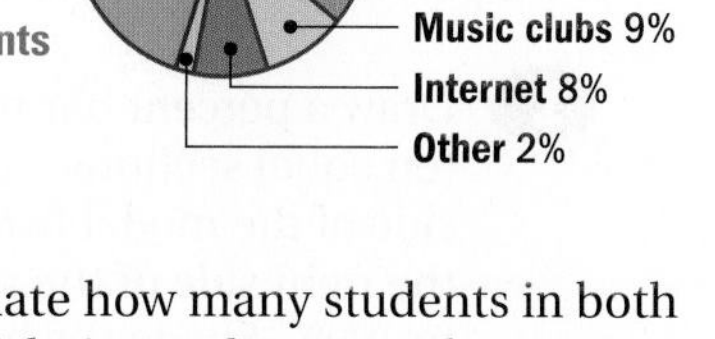

a. Estimate how many students chose either record stores or other stores. about 640 students

b. Estimate how many more students chose record stores than music clubs. about 320 students

c. The class surveyed 100 other students and found that 9% of them make most of their purchases on the Internet. Estimate how many students in both surveys combined make most of their purchases on the Internet. about 90 students

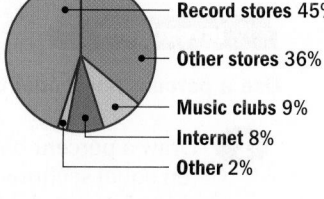

C **58. Challenge** Suppose the length and width of rectangle A are each 40% of the length and width of rectangle B. Is the area of rectangle A 40% of the area of rectangle B? Justify your answer. See margin.

59. Critical Thinking Let x and y represent two different whole numbers.

a. Suppose you add 40% of x to 60% of y. Is this sum equal to 100% of the sum $x + y$? Justify your answer.

b. Suppose you find the average of 40% of x and 60% of y. Is this average equal to 50% of the sum $x + y$? Justify your answer.

Mixed Review

Find the product or quotient. *(Lessons 5.4, 5.5)*

60. $-8 \cdot 3\frac{3}{4}$ -30 **61.** $-\frac{11}{25} \cdot \frac{10}{11}$ $-\frac{2}{5}$ **62.** $\frac{5}{12} \div \left(-\frac{5}{6}\right)$ $-\frac{1}{2}$ **63.** $3\frac{3}{14} \div \frac{3}{7}$ $7\frac{1}{2}$

Use equivalent ratios to solve the proportion. *(Lesson 6.2)*

64. $\frac{a}{3} = \frac{14}{21}$ 2 **65.** $\frac{b}{18} = \frac{5}{9}$ 10 **66.** $\frac{11}{13} = \frac{x}{26}$ 22 **67.** $\frac{5}{30} = \frac{y}{6}$ 1

68. Groceries A grocery store charges \$3 for 4 mangoes. How many mangoes can you buy with \$6.75? *(Lesson 6.3)* 9 mangoes

Standardized Test Practice

69. Multiple Choice The table shows how many of the 50 states entered the Union in each century. What percent of the states entered the Union after the 18th century? D

Century	States
18th century	16
19th century	29
20th century	5

A. 16% **B.** 29%

C. 34% **D.** 68%

70. Short Response In a survey of 300 adults, 32% said they read the daily newspaper, and 56% said they read only the Sunday newspaper. Estimate how many more adults surveyed read only the Sunday newspaper than the daily newspaper. Explain your reasoning.

70. Estimates may vary. About 90 more. *Sample answer:* 60% of 300 is 180, and 30% of 300 is 90, so about $180 - 90 = 90$ more people read only the Sunday paper than read the daily paper.

4 ASSESS

Assessment Resources

For more assessment resources, see:
- Assessment Book
- Test and Practice Generator

Mini-Quiz

Write the percent as a fraction.

1. 22% $\frac{11}{50}$ **2.** 92% $\frac{23}{25}$

Write the fraction as a percent.

3. $\frac{13}{20}$ 65% **4.** $\frac{21}{25}$ 84%

5. Challenge Suppose the base and height of triangle A are each 60% of the base and height of triangle B. Is the area of triangle A 60% of the area of triangle B? Justify your answer. No. *Sample answer:* Since $60\% = \frac{3}{5}$, the area of triangle A is $\frac{3}{5} \cdot \frac{3}{5} = \frac{9}{25}$, or 36% of the area of triangle B.

5 FOLLOW-UP

Diagnosis/Remediation

- Study Guide in Chapter 7 Resource Book, pp. 10–11
- Tutor Place, Ratio, Proportion, and Percent Cards 7, 9, 10, 16
- eTutorial Plus Online
- Extra Practice, p. 809
- Lesson Practice in Chapter 7 Resource Book, pp. 7–9

English Learner Support

- Spanish Study Guide
- Multi-Language Visual Glossary
- Chapter Audio Summaries CDs

Challenge

- Challenge Practice in Chapter 7 Resource Book, p. 12
- Teacher's Edition, p. 326F

1 PLAN

INVESTIGATE THE CONCEPT

- Students use a percent bar model to find the percent of a number.
- This activity leads into using proportions to solve percent problems.

MATERIALS

Each student will need paper and pencil.

RECOMMENDED TIME

Work activity: 10 min
Discuss results: 5 min

GROUPING

Students should work individually.

2 TEACH

ALTERNATIVE STRATEGY

Explain that the word "of" in a percent problem can be replaced by a multiplication symbol. So 24% of 75 is rewritten as 24% • 75. Students can then evaluate $\frac{24}{100} \cdot \frac{75}{1}$.

3 CLOSE

KEY DISCOVERY

The percent of a number can be found using a proportion.

ASSESSMENT

1. How do you solve a proportion written from a percent bar model? **Multiply both sides by the denominator of the ratio having the variable as its numerator.**

7, 8. See Additional Answers beginning on page AA1.

Concept *Activity*

7.2 Using Percent Bar Models

Goal
Use a percent bar model to find the percent of a number.

Materials
- paper
- pencil

Investigate

Use a percent bar model to find 24% of 75.

Draw a percent bar model that has ten equal sections. Label the left side of the model from 0 to 75. Label the right side of the model from 0% to 100%. Shade the bar to the 24% mark. Let x represent the number that you need to find.

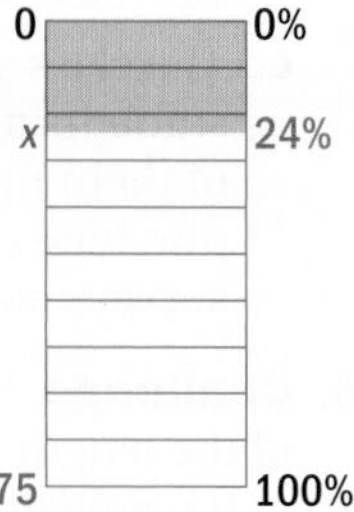

Write a proportion using the arrangement of the numbers in the percent bar model. Then solve the proportion to find 24% of 75.

$$\frac{x}{75} = \frac{24}{100}$$

$$75 \cdot \frac{x}{75} = 75 \cdot \frac{24}{100}$$

$$x = 18$$

Draw Conclusions

Use a percent bar model to find the percent of the number.

1. 18% of 30 **5.4**
2. 65% of 140 **91**
3. 36% of 225 **81**
4. 7% of 400 **28**
5. 22% of 600 **132**
6. 85% of 780 **663**
7. **Critical Thinking** Suppose that 40% of a number b is 28. You want to find b. Explain how you would use a percent bar model to illustrate the problem. Then write and solve a proportion to find b. **See margin.**
8. **Critical Thinking** You want to find what percent of 150 is 102. Draw a percent bar model that has ten equal sections. Explain how you would decide what part of the bar that you should shade. Then write and solve a proportion to find the percent. **See margin.**

NCTM CURRICULUM STANDARDS

Standard 2: Analyze situations using algebraic symbols; Use models to understand relationships

LESSON **7.2**

Percents *and* Proportions

BEFORE	*Now*	WHY?
You found a percent of a number.	You'll use proportions to solve percent problems.	So you can find how much food adult cats eat daily, as in Ex. 16.

Review Vocabulary
proportion, p. 275
percent, p. 329

A percent bar model compares a *part* to a *base*. In the model shown, 35 is the base, and 14 is a part of the base. The percent bar model shows that 14 is 40% of 35 or, equivalently, that $\frac{14}{35} = \frac{40}{100}$.

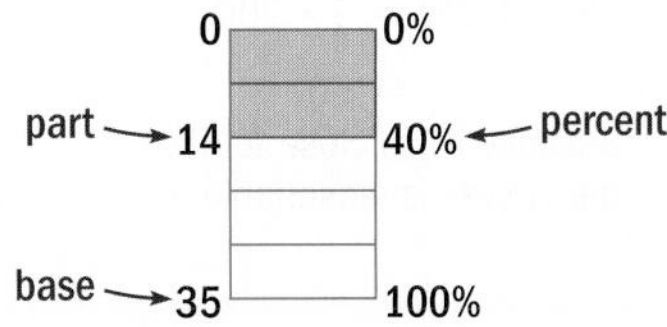

Solving Percent Problems

You can represent "*a* is *p* percent of *b*" using the proportion

$$\frac{a}{b} = \frac{p}{100}$$

where *a* is a part of the base *b* and *p*%, or $\frac{p}{100}$, is the percent.

Study *Strategy*

Notice in Example 1 that $\frac{4}{7}$ can be written as $57\frac{1}{7}\%$. This example suggests that you can use a proportion to write a fraction as a percent.

Example 1 *Finding a Percent*

What percent of 7 is 4?

$\frac{a}{b} = \frac{p}{100}$	**Write proportion.**
$\frac{4}{7} = \frac{p}{100}$	**Substitute 4 for *a* and 7 for *b*.**
$100 \cdot \frac{4}{7} = 100 \cdot \frac{p}{100}$	**Multiply each side by 100.**
$57\frac{1}{7} = p$	**Simplify.**

Answer 4 is $57\frac{1}{7}\%$ of 7.

Checkpoint

Use a proportion to answer the question.

1. What percent of 72 is 54? **75%**
2. What percent of 60 is 25? **$41\frac{2}{3}\%$**
3. What percent of 90 is 40? **$44\frac{4}{9}\%$**
4. What percent of 35 is 7? **20%**

NCTM CURRICULUM STANDARDS
Standard 2: Represent situations using algebraic symbols; Analyze situations using algebraic symbols
Standard 6: Solve problems in math and other contexts

1 PLAN

Skill Check

1. $200 \cdot 28 = \underline{?}$ **5600**
2. $400 \cdot 42 = \underline{?}$ **16,800**
3. $300 \cdot \frac{16}{100} = \underline{?}$ **48**
4. $200 \cdot \frac{72}{100} = \underline{?}$ **144**

LESSON OBJECTIVE

Use proportions to solve percent problems.

PACING

Suggested Number of Days
Basic Course: 1 day
Average Course: 1 day
Advanced Course: 1 day
Block: 0.5 block with 7.1

TEACHING RESOURCES

For a complete list of Teaching Resources, see page 326B.

TRANSPARENCY

Warm-Up Exercises for this lesson are available on a transparency.

2 TEACH

MOTIVATING THE LESSON

Have students model the fraction $\frac{1}{4}$ anyway they wish. Write the fraction on the board and relate the terms *part* and *base* to the fraction and also to several student models.

TIPS *for* NEW TEACHERS

Some students will have more difficulty than others setting up proportions. In Examples 1, 2, and 3, guide students slowly through the process of deciding where the values should appear in the proportions. See Tips for New Teachers in the *Chapter 7 Resource Book*.

Extra Examples

Example 1 What percent of 15 is 2? **$13\frac{1}{3}$%**

Example 2 What number is 45% of 400? **180**

Example 3 A python consumes a meal that weighs 3 pounds. This weight is 5% of the python's weight before the meal. How much did the python weigh before eating the meal? **60 lb**

TEACHING TIP

While finishing the discussion of Example 1, point out that the percent in the answer is a mixed number. Stress that students do not always need to write a non-whole-number percent as a decimal.

CONCEPT CHECK

How do you write a proportion to solve a percent problem of the following type: "What percent of *b* is *a*?" ***Sample answer:* Write a proportion of the form $\frac{a}{b} = \frac{p}{100}$, where *p* is the percent.**

DAILY PUZZLER

The number 0.001 is 1% of what number? **0.1**

Study *Strategy*

Reasonableness You can use common percents to check that an answer is reasonable. In Example 2, you know that 25% is close to 24%. Find 25% of 200.

$$25\% \text{ of } 200 = \frac{1}{4} \cdot 200 = 50$$

Because 50 is close to 48, the answer is reasonable.

Example 2 *Finding a Part of a Base*

What number is 24% of 200?

$\frac{a}{b} = \frac{p}{100}$ **Write proportion.**

$\frac{a}{200} = \frac{24}{100}$ **Substitute 200 for *b* and 24 for *p*.**

$200 \cdot \frac{a}{200} = 200 \cdot \frac{24}{100}$ **Multiply each side by 200.**

$a = 48$ **Simplify.**

Answer 48 is 24% of 200.

Example 3 *Finding a Base*

Heptathlon In a heptathlon, an athlete earns points in seven track-and-field events. Suppose an athlete earns 836 points in the 100 meter hurdles. This score makes up 16% of the total score. What is the total score?

Solution

In this situation, 836 is a part of the total score, which is the base.

$\frac{a}{b} = \frac{p}{100}$ **Write proportion.**

$\frac{836}{b} = \frac{16}{100}$ **Substitute 836 for *a* and 16 for *p*.**

$836 \cdot 100 = 16 \cdot b$ **Cross products property**

$83{,}600 = 16b$ **Multiply.**

$5225 = b$ **Divide each side by 16.**

Answer The athlete's total score is 5225 points.

Checkpoint

Use a proportion to answer the question.

5. What number is 18% of 50? **9**
6. 105 is 84% of what number? **125**

You may find it useful to group percent problems into three types.

Percent problem	Example	Proportion
Find a percent.	What percent of 48 is 12?	$\frac{12}{48} = \frac{p}{100}$
Find a part of a base.	What number is 15% of 80?	$\frac{a}{80} = \frac{15}{100}$
Find a base.	20 is 30% of what number?	$\frac{20}{b} = \frac{30}{100}$

7.2 Exercises

More Practice, p. 809

Guided Practice

Vocabulary Check

1. Choose the proportion you can use to represent this statement: 15 is 30% of 50. **B**

   A. $\frac{30}{15} = \frac{50}{100}$ **B.** $\frac{15}{50} = \frac{30}{100}$ **C.** $\frac{30}{50} = \frac{15}{100}$

2. Tell whether the answer to the following question represents *the base, the part of the base,* or *the percent*: 30 is 85% of what number? **the base**

Skill Check

Use a proportion to answer the question.

3. What number is 65% of 120? **78**
4. What percent of 24 is 4? **$16\frac{2}{3}$%**
5. What percent of 30 is 27? **90%**
6. 18 is 45% of what number? **40**
7. **Error Analysis** Describe and correct the error in finding what percent of 30 is 20.

$$\frac{a}{30} = \frac{20}{100}$$
$$100 \cdot a = 30 \cdot 20$$
$$100a = 600$$
$$a = 6$$

X

7. *Sample answer:* The proportion shown is to find part of a base, not a percent, which is what is being sought. The unknown is the percent, p%, so the proportion should be $\frac{20}{30} = \frac{p}{100}$, which gives $100 \cdot \frac{20}{30} = 100 \cdot \frac{p}{100}$, and $p = 66\frac{2}{3}$%.

8. **Soccer** In the 2002 World Cup, 5 of the 32 soccer teams that competed were from South America. What percent of the teams were from South America? **$15\frac{5}{8}$%**

Practice and Problem Solving

Homework *Help*

Example	Exercises
1	9-14, 18-20
2	9-16, 20
3	9-14, 17, 20

Online Resources
CLASSZONE.COM
- More Examples
- eTutorial Plus

Use a proportion to answer the question.

A
9. What percent of 56 is 14? **25%**
10. What percent of 125 is 98? **$78\frac{2}{5}$%**
11. What number is 55% of 80? **44**
12. What number is 30% of 130? **39**
13. 11 is 22% of what number? **50**
14. 48 is 75% of what number? **64**
15. **Basketball** Of the 325 teams in NCAA Division 1 Women's Basketball, 4% are in the Mid-American Conference. How many teams are in the Mid-American Conference? **13 teams**
16. **Cats** An adult cat has a body mass of 3500 grams. It can eat up to 8% of its body mass in food each day. How many grams of food can the cat eat each day? Use estimation to justify that your answer is reasonable.
17. **Paintings** An artist's collection of paintings includes 22 portraits. The portraits make up 40% of the collection. How many paintings are in the collection? **55 paintings**

16. 280 g. *Sample answer:* 8% is close to 10%, and 10% of 3500 is $\frac{1}{10}$ of 3500, or 350. Because 8% is a little less than 10%, and 280 is a little less than 350, this is reasonable.

3 APPLY

ASSIGNMENT GUIDE

Basic Course
Day 1: EP p. 808 Exs. 9-12; pp. 337-339 Exs. 9-18, 21, 26-28, 32-42

Average Course
Day 1: pp. 337-339 Exs. 11-21, 23-30, 34-42

Advanced Course
Day 1: pp. 337-339 Exs. 13-17, 20-31*, 34-42

Block
pp. 337-339 Exs. 11-21, 23-30, 34-42 (with 7.1)

EXTRA PRACTICE

- Student Edition, p. 809
- Chapter 7 Resource Book, pp. 15-17
- Test and Practice Generator

TRANSPARENCY

Even-numbered answers are available on transparencies.

HOMEWORK CHECK

When you review students' homework for this lesson, go over the following exercises to check understanding of key concepts.
Basic: 9, 11, 13, 17, 18
Average: 11, 13, 15, 17, 20
Advanced: 13, 14, 16, 17, 20

COMMON ERROR

In Exercises 9-14, expect some students to have difficulty setting up the proportions. Invite students to explain how they set up their proportions for the different problem types.

TEACHING TIP

In Exercise 31, stress that the art director is going to add more color photos to the exhibit, and not replace some of the black-and-white photos with color photos.

22c. About 234 students. *Sample answer:* Of the 360 students in the original survey, 108 prefer spring. I solved the proportion $\frac{108}{360} = \frac{p}{100}$ to find that this is 30% of the students surveyed. Then I assumed that 30% of all students in the school would prefer spring, and I solved the proportion $\frac{a}{780} = \frac{30}{100}$ to find that this is 234 students.

In the **Real World**

Solar Cars A solar car collects sunlight in its solar panels, which then convert the light to electricity. In the 2001 American Solar Challenge, the smallest panel area on a car was 7.2 square meters, and the largest panel area was 8 square meters. What percent of the largest area was the smallest area? **90%**

21. *Sample answer:* Biologists have tagged 40% of a herd of elk. If they have tagged 30 elk in the herd, what is the total number of elk in the herd? Solving the proportion gives $x = 75$, so there are 75 elk in the herd.

Note *Worthy*

In your notes, you can create a table of percent-fraction equivalents like the one in Exercise 23. Include in your table other fractions whose percents may be useful to memorize.

18. Tanana River When a certain section of the ice breaks on the Tanana River in Nenana, Alaska, the townspeople consider spring to have started. During the period 1917–2001, the ice broke 34 times on or between May 4 and May 10. What percent of those 85 years were years in which the ice broke on or between May 4 and May 10? **40%**

19. Talent Show You are performing in a talent show. To decide who performs first, the names of all 15 participants are written on slips of paper and put in a hat. One name is drawn from the hat. What is the probability that you go first? Write your answer as a percent. **$6\frac{2}{3}\%$**

20. Solar Cars The 2001 American Solar Challenge was a race among solar-powered cars traveling from Chicago, Illinois, to Claremont, California.

a. Three of the cars in the race weighed less than 600 pounds. These cars made up 10% of all the cars. How many cars were in the race? **30 cars**

b. There were 16 three-wheeled cars in the race. What percent of the cars were three-wheeled? **$53\frac{1}{3}\%$**

c. The course was 2247.39 miles long, and it was completed by 40% of the cars. How many cars completed the course? **12 cars**

B 21. *Writing* Write a real-world percent problem that can be solved by using the proportion $\frac{30}{x} = \frac{40}{100}$. Then find the value of x and solve the problem. **See margin.**

22. Extended Problem Solving You conduct a survey asking middle school students in which season they would prefer to hold their school trip. The bar graph shows the results of your survey.

a. What percent of the students surveyed prefer summer? fall? **50%; $12\frac{1}{2}\%$**

b. Calculate Of the students who prefer spring, 75% are 8th graders. How many 8th graders prefer spring? **81 8th graders**

c. Predict You are using the results of the survey to predict the preferences of all 780 students in the school. How many students do you predict would prefer a school trip in the spring? Explain your reasoning. **See margin.**

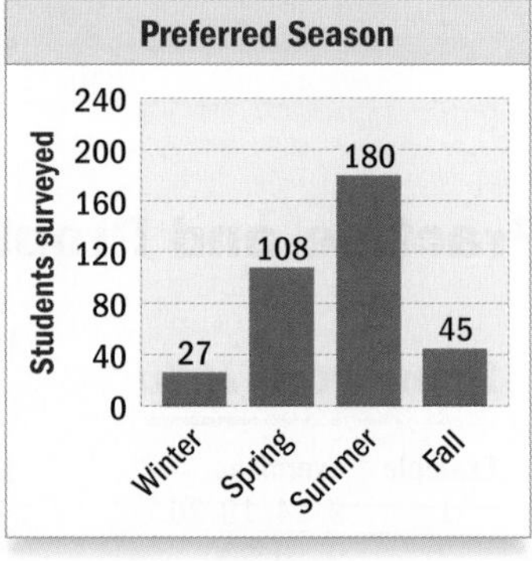

23. The table below shows several fractions whose percents may be useful to know. Use a proportion to find the equivalent percent for each fraction. Then copy and complete the table with the equivalent percents.

Fraction	$\frac{1}{8}$	$\frac{1}{3}$	$\frac{3}{8}$	$\frac{5}{8}$	$\frac{2}{3}$	$\frac{7}{8}$
Percent	?	?	?	?	?	?

$12\frac{1}{2}\%$, $33\frac{1}{3}\%$, $37\frac{1}{2}\%$, $62\frac{1}{2}\%$, $66\frac{2}{3}\%$, $87\frac{1}{2}\%$

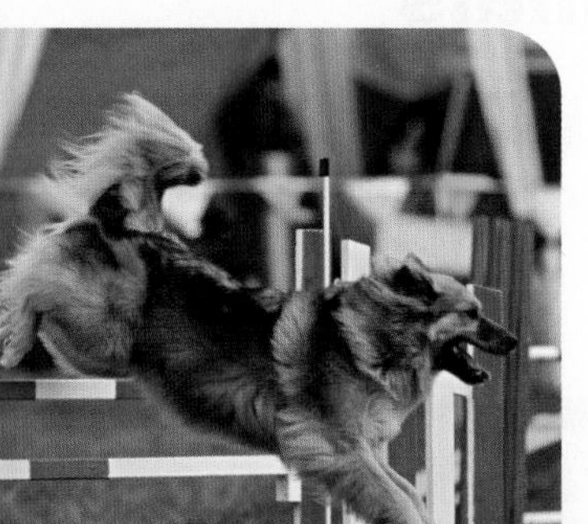

24. Baseball A baseball player makes 152 hits in 570 times at bat in one season and 180 hits in 580 times at bat in the next season. For both seasons combined, what percent of the times at bat were hits? $28\frac{20}{23}\%$

25. Dogs In a dog agility competition, dogs are tested in their ability to get past obstacles. The table shows the number of dogs from each breed that competed in a dog agility competition.

a. What percent of the dogs that competed were spaniels? sheepdogs? 20%; $62\frac{1}{2}\%$

b. In the competition, 70% of the dogs that finished in the top half were sheepdogs. What percent of the sheepdogs finished in the top half? 56%

Dog breed	Number that competed
Sheepdog	75
Spaniel	24
Terrier	14
Other	7

26. Algebra Solve for x in the following equation: $x\% = \frac{2x + 1}{300}$. 1

Use a proportion to answer the question in terms of *y*.

C **27.** What number is 40% of $10y$? $4y$ **28.** What number is 75% of $8y$? $6y$

29. $3y$ is 60% of what number? $5y$ **30.** $11y$ is 25% of what number? $44y$

31. Challenge An art director has 75 photos to display in an art exhibit. Of these, 9 are color photos and 66 are black-and-white photos. The director wants to add more color photos so that they represent 25% of the photos at the exhibit. Write and solve a proportion to find the number of color photos to be added. Then find the total number of photos in the exhibit. $\frac{9 + x}{75 + x} = \frac{25}{100}$, 13 photos; 88 photos

Mixed Review

Find the product. *(p. 775)*

32. 0.2×7 1.4 **33.** 0.75×1.3 0.975 **34.** 0.7×2.4 1.68 **35.** 0.003×0.5 0.0015

36. Personal Finance You use an ATM to withdraw \$20 from your checking account. The ATM receipt shows a balance of \$168 after the withdrawal. Write and solve an equation to find the balance before the withdrawal. *(Lesson 2.5)* $x - 20 = 168$, \$188

Write the fraction or mixed number as a decimal. *(Lesson 5.1)*

37. $-\frac{1}{3}$ $-0.\overline{3}$ **38.** $\frac{7}{10}$ 0.7 **39.** $-1\frac{3}{5}$ -1.6 **40.** $\frac{11}{25}$ 0.44

Standardized Test Practice

41. Multiple Choice Of the 32 teams in the National Football League, 4 teams are in the AFC East division. What percent of the teams are in the AFC East division? C

A. 4% **B.** 8% **C.** $12\frac{1}{2}\%$ **D.** 28%

42. Multiple Choice A camel that weighs 1500 pounds can drink up to about 20% of its weight in water at one time. About how many pounds of water can a camel that weighs 1500 pounds drink at one time? H

F. 10 pounds **G.** 75 pounds **H.** 300 pounds **I.** 30,000 pounds

4 ASSESS

Assessment Resources

For more assessment resources, see:

- Assessment Book
- Test and Practice Generator

Mini-Quiz

1. What percent of 900 is 36? 4%
2. What number is 8% of 2600? 208
3. 81 is 27% of what number? 300
4. **Challenge** At a deli, there are breads, quiches, and cakes in a display case. Of the 30 items in the case, 14 are breads and quiches, and the rest are cakes. The deli owner wants to add more cakes so that the cakes represent 60% of the items in the display case. Write and solve a proportion to find the number of cakes that need to be added. Then find the total number of items in the display case. $\frac{16 + x}{30 + x} = \frac{60}{100}$, 5 cakes; 35 items

5 FOLLOW-UP

Diagnosis/Remediation

- Study Guide in Chapter 7 Resource Book, pp. 18–19
- Tutor Place, Ratio, Proportion, and Percent Cards 11–13, 15
- eTutorial Plus Online
- Extra Practice, p. 809
- Lesson Practice in Chapter 7 Resource Book, pp. 15–17

English Learner Support

- Spanish Study Guide
- Multi-Language Visual Glossary
- Chapter Audio Summaries CDs

Challenge

- Challenge Practice in Chapter 7 Resource Book, p. 20
- Teacher's Edition, p. 326F

1 PLAN

Skill Check

Write the fraction as a decimal.

1. $\frac{1}{4}$ 0.25
2. $\frac{1}{5}$ 0.2
3. $\frac{7}{8}$ 0.875
4. $\frac{7}{4}$ 1.75

LESSON OBJECTIVE

Use decimals to solve percent problems.

PACING

Suggested Number of Days

Basic Course: 1 day

Average Course: 1 day

Advanced Course: 1 day

Block: 0.5 block with 7.4

TEACHING RESOURCES

For a complete list of Teaching Resources, see page 326B.

TRANSPARENCY

Warm-Up Exercises for this lesson are available on a transparency.

2 TEACH

MOTIVATING THE LESSON

Point out that students can estimate the adult pygmy hippo's weight by finding 10% of 5600 pounds. Ask students to explain how to find 10% of a number mentally.

TIPS *for* NEW TEACHERS

Some students may need extra practice with percents less than 1% as well as those greater than 100%. See Tips for New Teachers in the *Chapter 7 Resource Book*.

LESSON **7.3**

Percents *and* Decimals

BEFORE	Now	WHY?
You used fractions to solve percent problems.	You'll use decimals to solve percent problems.	So you can find the wind speed in a tornado, as in Ex. 45.

Review Vocabulary

percent, p. 329

decimal, p. 770

Pygmy Hippos The African pygmy hippo is the smallest species of hippopotamus. Suppose a common adult hippo weighs 5600 pounds, and an adult pygmy hippo's weight is 10.5% of the common adult hippo's weight. How much does the adult pygmy hippo weigh? You will find the answer in Example 4.

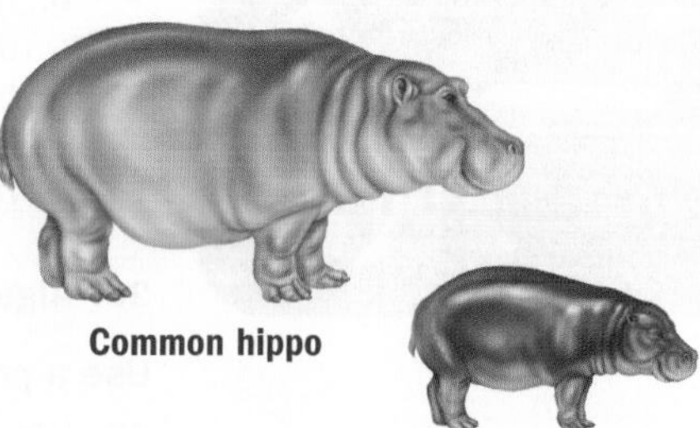

Because $0.25 = \frac{25}{100}$ and $\frac{25}{100} = 25\%$, you can say that $0.25 = 25\%$.

This relationship suggests the following rules for writing decimals as percents and percents as decimals.

Percents and Decimals

- To write a decimal as a percent, move the decimal point two places to the right and write a percent sign.
- To write a percent as a decimal, move the decimal point two places to the left and remove the percent sign.

Study *Strategy*

Percents greater than 100% are written as numbers greater than 1. Percents less than 1% are written as numbers less than 0.01. To write such percents as decimals, follow the same steps as you would for percents between 1% and 100%.

Example 1 ***Writing Decimals as Percents***

Write 0.62, 1, and 2.3 as percents.

a. $0.62 = 0.62$
$= 62\%$

b. $1 = 1.00$
$= 100\%$

c. $2.3 = 2.30$
$= 230\%$

Example 2 ***Writing Percents as Decimals***

Write 75%, 0.4%, and 168% as decimals.

a. $75\% = 75\%$
$= 0.75$

b. $0.4\% = 00.4\%$
$= 0.004$

c. $168\% = 168\%$
$= 1.68$

NCTM CURRICULUM STANDARDS

Standard 1: Understand numbers; Understand ways of representing numbers; Understand relationships among numbers

 **Checkpoint**

Write the decimal as a percent or the percent as a decimal.

1. 0.461 46.1% **2.** 5 500% **3.** 1.9 190% **4.** 0.007 0.7%

5. 27% 0.27 **6.** 184% 1.84 **7.** 3% 0.03 **8.** 0.55% 0.0055

Fractions, Decimals, and Percents A fraction, a decimal, and a percent can all represent the same number. You can write a fraction as a percent by first writing the fraction as a decimal.

Review *Help*

For help with writing fractions as decimals, see p. 219.

Example 3 ***Writing Fractions as Percents***

Write $\frac{3}{8}$ and $\frac{5}{3}$ as percents.

a. $\frac{3}{8} = 0.375$ **Write fraction as a decimal.**

$= 37.5\%$ **Write decimal as a percent.**

b. $\frac{5}{3} = 1.666\ldots$ **Write fraction as a decimal.**

$= 166.\overline{6}\%$ **Write decimal as a percent.**

 **Checkpoint**

Write the fraction as a percent.

9. $\frac{7}{8}$ 87.5% **10.** $\frac{5}{12}$ $41.\overline{6}\%$ **11.** $\frac{11}{6}$ $183.\overline{3}\%$ **12.** $\frac{5}{4}$ 125%

***In the* Real World**

Pygmy Hippos Pygmy hippos weigh about 8 pounds at birth. How many times heavier than a newborn pygmy hippo is the adult pygmy hippo described in Example 4? **73.5 times**

Example 4 ***Finding a Percent of a Number***

Find the weight of the pygmy hippo described on page 340.

Solution

Find 10.5% of 5600.

10.5% of $5600 = 0.105 \cdot 5600$ **Write percent as a decimal.**

$= 588$ **Multiply.**

Answer The adult pygmy hippo weighs about 588 pounds.

✓ **Check** You can use estimation to check the reasonableness of the result. Because 10% of 5600 is 560, the answer is reasonable.

 **Checkpoint**

In Exercises 13–16, find the percent of the number.

13. 20% of 85 17 **14.** 3.8% of 45 1.71 **15.** 125% of 64 80 **16.** 0.5% of 600 3

17. In a survey of 1100 adults, 2% chose cooking as their favorite leisure activity. How many adults chose cooking? 22 adults

Extra Examples

Example 1 Write the decimal as a percent.
a. 0.021 **2.1%**
b. 1.55 **155%**
c. 6 **600%**

Example 2 Write the percent as a decimal.
a. 54% **0.54**
b. 0.95% **0.0095**
c. 220% **2.2**

Example 3 Write the fraction as a percent.
a. $\frac{1}{6}$ $\mathbf{16.\overline{6}\%}$
b. $\frac{9}{5}$ **180%**

Example 4 About 5.2% of the 8460 visitors to a tropical resort last month registered to try parasailing. Approximately how many visitors registered for parasailing? **about 440 visitors**

Reading Strategy

Be certain students read and understand the Study Strategy on page 340 before doing Examples 1–3. This should help students better understand parts b and c of Examples 1 and 2 and part b of Example 3.

Concept Check

Explain the procedure for writing 14% as a decimal. **Move the decimal point in the number 14 two places to the left and remove the percent sign. The result is 0.14.**

Daily Puzzler

Which is greater: 0.4% of 10,000 or 4.04% of 1000? **4.04% of 1000**

3 APPLY

ASSIGNMENT GUIDE

Basic Course

Day 1: pp. 342–344 Exs. 13–20, 25–28, 33–39, 49–54, 63–70

Average Course

Day 1: pp. 342–344 Exs. 17–24, 29–33, 40–44, 47–50, 55–59, 62–71

Advanced Course

Day 1: pp. 342–344 Exs. 17–20, 31–37, 44–50, 55–62*, 66–71

Block

pp. 342–344 Exs. 17–24, 29–33, 40–44, 47–50, 55–59, 62–71 (with 7.4)

EXTRA PRACTICE

- Student Edition, p. 809
- Chapter 7 Resource Book, pp. 25–27
- Test and Practice Generator

TRANSPARENCY

Even-numbered answers are available on transparencies. A support transparency is available for Exercises 49 and 50.

HOMEWORK CHECK

When you review students' homework for this lesson, go over the following exercises to check understanding of key concepts.

Basic: 13, 19, 25, 33, 36
Average: 17, 19, 29, 33, 40
Advanced: 17, 20, 31, 35, 48

COMMON ERROR

In Exercises 13–24, remind students that only numbers followed by a percent sign are percents. Students may fall into the habit of thinking that every number is a percent to be rewritten as a decimal.

7.3 Exercises

More Practice, p. 809

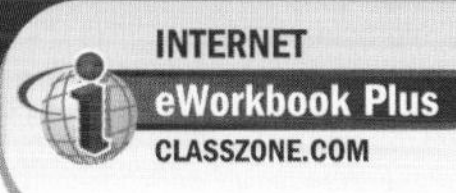

Guided Practice

Vocabulary Check

1. When you write a decimal as a percent, do you move the decimal point two places to the left or to the right? **to the right**

2. Is 0.5 *less than*, *greater than*, or *equal to* 0.5%? Explain. **Greater than. *Sample answer:* 0.5 = 50%, which is greater than 0.5%.**

Skill Check

Write the decimal as a percent or the percent as a decimal.

3. 0.13 **13%** 4. 6.27 **627%** 5. 5% **0.05** 6. 0.98% **0.0098**

Write the fraction as a percent.

7. $\frac{1}{2}$ **50%** 8. $\frac{2}{3}$ **$66.\overline{6}$%** 9. $\frac{7}{6}$ **$116.\overline{6}$%** 10. $\frac{11}{4}$ **275%**

11. **Error Analysis** Describe and correct the error in writing 1.5 as a percent.

X 1.5 = .01.5 = 0.015%

11. The decimal point should have been moved two places to the right instead of to the left: 1.5 = 1.50 = 150%.

12. **Geography** The area of Earth's dry land is about 58 million square miles. The land area of North America is about 16% of Earth's land area. What is the approximate land area of North America? **about 9.3 million square miles**

Practice and Problem Solving

Homework *Help*

Example	Exercises
1	13–18, 33
2	19–24, 34
3	25–32, 35
4	36–48

Online Resources
CLASSZONE.COM
- More Examples
- eTutorial Plus

Write the decimal as a percent or the percent as a decimal.

A 13. 0.28 **28%** 14. 0.1 **10%** 15. 2 **200%** 16. 5.46 **546%**

17. 0.087 **8.7%** 18. 0.00205 **0.205%** 19. 8% **0.08** 20. 19% **0.19**

21. 108% **1.08** 22. 104.2% **1.042** 23. 0.302% **0.00302** 24. 0.051% **0.00051**

Write the fraction as a percent.

25. $\frac{3}{20}$ **15%** 26. $\frac{1}{8}$ **12.5%** 27. $\frac{2}{15}$ **$13.\overline{3}$%** 28. $\frac{1}{9}$ **$11.\overline{1}$%**

29. $\frac{7}{2}$ **350%** 30. $\frac{9}{4}$ **225%** 31. $\frac{4}{3}$ **$133.\overline{3}$%** 32. $\frac{6}{5}$ **120%**

33. **Electricity** Wind power generates about 0.0015 of the world's electricity. What percent of the world's electricity does wind power generate? **0.15%**

34. **Water** About 0.3% of the water on Earth is usable by humans. Write 0.3% as a decimal. **0.003**

35. **Music** Of a radio station's 40 most popular songs for the week, $\frac{5}{8}$ were sung by female soloists. What percent of the songs were sung by female soloists? **62.5%**

Teaching Tip

In Exercises 29–32, point out that when the numerator of a fraction is greater than the denominator, then the equivalent percent is greater than 100%. In Exercise 59, encourage students to create a table to organize the information into three categories: "sales from \$0 to \$45 million," "sales from \$45 to \$500 million," and "sales over \$500 million." In parts b and c, suggest they begin by determining how much of the sales fall into each category before applying the appropriate percent to these sales.

Find the percent of the number.

36. 12% of 150 **18** **37.** 80% of 340 **272** **38.** 18.2% of 90 **16.38** **39.** 60.1% of 70 **42.07**

40. 225% of 80 **180** **41.** 120% of 400 **480** **42.** 0.4% of 260 **1.04** **43.** 0.35% of 50 **0.175**

44. Raffle A total of 600 tickets were sold for a raffle. The probability that your friend will win the prize is 7%. How many of the raffle tickets did your friend buy? **42 raffle tickets**

45. Winds The winds on Neptune are the strongest on any planet in our solar system and can reach a speed of about 1500 miles per hour. The winds of a tornado near Bridge Creek, Oklahoma, in 1999 were about 21.2% as fast as the winds on Neptune. What was the wind speed in the tornado? **about 318 mi/h**

46. Internet Sales A company made \$350 million in retail sales last year. About 0.9% of those sales were over the Internet. About how much money did the company make in sales over the Internet? **about \$3.15 million**

47. Roller Coasters There were 1429 operating roller coasters in the world in 2001. Copy the table. Then use a calculator to complete the table with the number of roller coasters in each region. Be sure to round answers to the nearest whole number.

Region	North America	South America	Central America	Europe	Asia and Australia	Middle East and Africa
Roller coasters	? 606	? 39	? 6	? 383	? 365	? 30
Percent of total	42.4%	2.74%	0.42%	26.8%	25.54%	2.1%

49. $\frac{3}{4}$, 100%, 150%, $\frac{5}{3}$, 2

50. 4%, $\frac{2}{5}$, 42%, 0.45, 0.5

In the Real World

Ships The *Sussex* may have resembled the 17th century ship shown above. The *Sussex* was about 154 feet long. If a car is 15.5 feet long, about how many car lengths equal the length of the *Sussex*? **about 10 car lengths**

48. Number Sense Find 5% of 185. Use the result to find 15% of 185. **9.25, 27.75**

Use a number line to order the numbers from least to greatest. **49–50. See margin.**

B **49.** 150%, 2, $\frac{5}{3}$, 100%, $\frac{3}{4}$ **50.** 0.45, 42%, $\frac{2}{5}$, 4%, 0.5

Algebra Evaluate the expression when $k = 10$.

51. k% of 67 **6.7** **52.** 25% of k **2.5** **53.** 120% of k **12** **54.** k% of 400 **40**

55. 7.9% of $3k$ **2.37** **56.** 0.8% of $2k$ **0.16** **57.** $(k - 9)$% of 9 **0.09** **58.** $\left(\frac{k}{4}\right)$% of 20 **0.5**

59. Ships In 1694, the English ship *Sussex* sank in the Mediterranean Sea while on its way to Spain. In 2002, a U.S. salvage company and Great Britain agreed to share any money made from the sale of gold and silver coins recovered from the wreckage of the ship.

a. The company will get 80% of the first \$45 million of the sales. If sales total \$45 million, how much money will the company get? **\$36 million**

b. The company will get 50% of any sales between \$45 million and \$500 million. If sales total \$500 million, how much money will the company get? **\$263.5 million**

c. The company will get 40% of any sales above \$500 million. If sales total \$650 million, how much money will the company get? **\$323.5 million**

4 ASSESS

ASSESSMENT RESOURCES

For more assessment resources, see:

- Assessment Book
- Test and Practice Generator

MINI-QUIZ

Write the decimal as a percent or the percent as a decimal.

1. 2.9 **290%**
2. 0.085 **8.5%**
3. 525% **5.25**
4. 11.5% **0.115**

Write the fraction as a percent.

5. $\frac{7}{20}$ **35%**
6. $\frac{11}{12}$ **$91.\overline{6}\%$**
7. **Challenge** Suppose k is 20% of m. What percent of k is m? **500%**

5 FOLLOW-UP

DIAGNOSIS/REMEDIATION

- Study Guide in Chapter 7 Resource Book, pp. 28–29
- Tutor Place, Ratio, Proportion, and Percent Cards 8–10, 14
- eTutorial Plus Online
- Extra Practice, p. 809
- Lesson Practice in Chapter 7 Resource Book, pp. 25–27

ENGLISH LEARNER SUPPORT

- Spanish Study Guide
- Multi-Language Visual Glossary
- Chapter Audio Summaries CDs

CHALLENGE

- Challenge Practice in Chapter 7 Resource Book, p. 30
- Teacher's Edition, p. 326F

Brain Game. See Additional Answers beginning on page AA1.

60. Extended Problem Solving The circle graph shows the results of a survey asking 500 students their main reason for using the Internet.

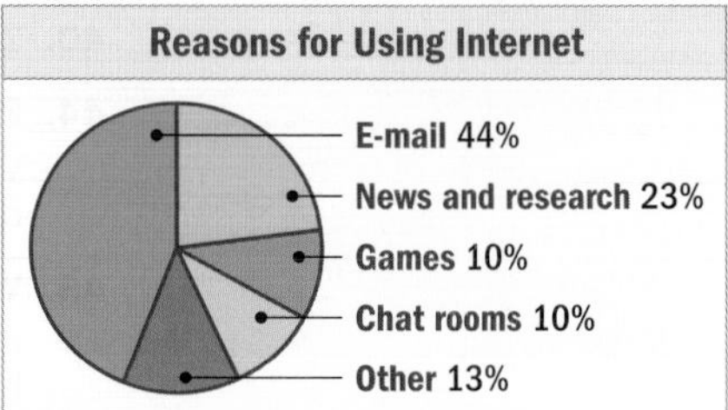

a. How many students chose either games or chat rooms? **100 students**

b. **Compare** How many more students chose e-mail than news and research? **105 more students**

c. **Apply** Suppose 300 other students were surveyed, and 14% of them chose games. What percent of all 800 students chose games? **11.5%**

C **61. Challenge** Suppose x is 200% of y. What percent of x is y? **50%**

62. Geometry The area of square A is 400 square centimeters. The side length of square B is 65% of the side length of square A. Is the area of square B 65% of the area of square A? Explain your reasoning.

62. No. ***Sample answer:*** **Because $20^2 = 400$, the side length of square A must be 20 centimeters, so the side length of square B is $0.65 \cdot 20 = 13$ centimeters, and its area is $13^2 = 169$ centimeters. This is $\frac{169}{400} = 0.4225 = 42.25\%$ of the area of square A.**

Mixed Review

Algebra Basics Solve the equation. *(Lesson 2.7)*

63. $0.3 = 5x$ **0.06** **64.** $8 = 3.5 + x$ **4.5** **65.** $7.6 = x - 8.3$ **15.9** **66.** $1.2 = \frac{x}{6}$ **7.2**

67. The odds in favor of your winning a prize are 3 to 7. What is the probability that you will win the prize? *(Lesson 6.7)* **$\frac{3}{10}$**

Use a proportion to answer the question. *(Lesson 7.2)*

68. What number is 10% of 60? **6** **69.** 93 is 124% of what number? **75**

Standardized Test Practice

70. Multiple Choice You made 82.5% of your 160 attempted free throws in a basketball season. How many free throws did you make? **C**

A. 28 **B.** 78 **C.** 132 **D.** 140

71. Short Response In a survey of 3000 music buyers, 5% of them preferred cassettes and 89% preferred CDs. How many more music buyers preferred CDs than cassettes? Explain your reasoning. **2520 more music buyers.** ***Sample answer:*** **$0.89 \cdot 3000 = 2670$ buyers preferred CDs and $0.05 \cdot 3000 = 150$ preferred cassettes, so $2670 - 150 = 2520$ more preferred CDs than cassettes.**

Percents in the Squares

Describe the pattern. Then draw the grid that represents the fifth figure. **See margin.**

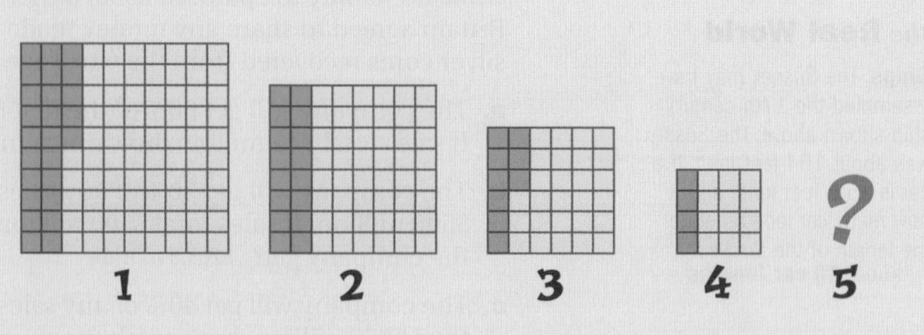

LESSON

7.4 The Percent Equation

BEFORE	Now	WHY?
You used proportions to solve percent problems.	You'll use equations to solve percent problems.	So you can analyze the results of an election, as in Ex. 29.

Review Vocabulary
percent, p. 329

Astronomy On June 14, 2002, the distance between Earth and the moon was about 375,000 kilometers. On that day, a traveling asteroid missed Earth by about 32% of that distance. How far away from Earth was the asteroid at that time?

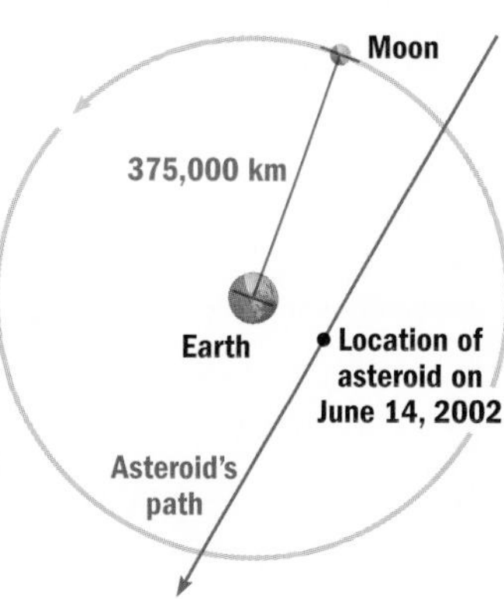

You have used the proportion $\frac{a}{b} = \frac{p}{100}$ to solve percent problems. When you solve this proportion for a and write $\frac{p}{100}$ as $p\%$, you get the equation $a = p\% \cdot b$.

The Percent Equation

You can represent "a is p percent of b" using the equation

$$a = p\% \cdot b$$

where a is a part of the base b and $p\%$ is the percent.

Reading *Algebra*

Certain words can represent mathematical symbols. In the statement "*a* is *p*% of *b*," the word *is* corresponds to the equal sign, =, and the word *of* corresponds to the multiplication symbol, •.

Example 1 *Finding a Part of a Base*

To find how far away from Earth the asteroid was, as described above, use the percent equation.

$a = p\% \cdot b$	**Write percent equation.**
$= 32\% \cdot 375{,}000$	**Substitute 32 for *p* and 375,000 for *b*.**
$= 0.32 \cdot 375{,}000$	**Write percent as a decimal.**
$= 120{,}000$	**Multiply.**

Answer The asteroid was about 120,000 kilometers away from Earth.

Checkpoint

Use the percent equation to answer the question.

1. What number is 16% of 75? 12
2. What number is 89% of 110? 97.9

NCTM CURRICULUM STANDARDS
Standard 1: Compute fluently
Standard 2: Represent situations using algebraic symbols
Standard 6: Solve problems in math and other contexts

1 PLAN

Skill Check

1. 50% of 10 = ? 5
2. 40% of 50 = ? 20
3. 20% of 1250 = ? 250
4. 300% of 16 = ? 48

Lesson Objective

Use equations to solve percent problems.

Pacing

Suggested Number of Days
Basic Course: 1 day
Average Course: 1 day
Advanced Course: 1 day
Block: 0.5 block with 7.3

Teaching Resources

For a complete list of Teaching Resources, see page 326B.

Transparency

Warm-Up Exercises for this lesson are available on a transparency.

2 TEACH

Motivating the Lesson

As the moon travels around Earth, its orbit is an oval. The distance from Earth to the moon varies from 356,410 kilometers to 406,697 kilometers. Ask a student to compare 375,000 kilometers to these values.

TIPS *for* NEW TEACHERS

The Reading Algebra tip to the left of Example 1 will be helpful to students having difficulty writing a percent equation. See Tips for New Teachers in the *Chapter 7 Resource Book*.

Extra Examples

Example 1 What number is 65% of 84? **54.6**

Example 2 A hotel charges a couple $1500 to hold a small wedding ceremony in their garden. The couple must pay the hotel 12.5% of the charge as a deposit. How much is the deposit? **$187.50**

Example 3 What percent of 70 is 245? **350%**

Example 4 A tourist dining at an outdoor restaurant in the Caribbean counts 6 iguanas in cages on the restaurant's patio. A waitress informs the tourist that these 6 iguanas represent 30% of the iguanas living on the restaurant's property. How many iguanas are there at the restaurant? **20 iguanas**

Common Error

Watch for students who substitute values into the percent equation too quickly and fail to check that their solution is reasonable. In Checkpoint Exercise 2, for example, students should first estimate 89% of 110 as 90% of 110, or about 99.

Teaching Tip

In Example 3, explain to students that since 60 is greater than 25, the percent will be greater than 100%. To get an idea of how much greater than 100%, point out to students that 200% is twice a number, so 200% of 25 would be 50. And 300% would be three times 25, or 75. Stress that since 60 is between 50 and 75, the percent that 25 is of 60 must be between 200% and 300%.

Example 2 *Finding a Commission*

Commission A car salesperson earns a 6.5% commission on every car sold. The salesperson sells a car for $21,800. What is the commission?

Solution

$a = p\% \cdot b$	**Write percent equation.**
$= 6.5\% \cdot 21{,}800$	**Substitute 6.5 for *p* and 21,800 for *b*.**
$= 0.065 \cdot 21{,}800$	**Write percent as a decimal.**
$= 1417$	**Multiply.**

Answer The salesperson's commission is $1417.

Checkpoint

3. In Example 2, find the commission if a car is sold for $23,000. **$1495**

Example 3 *Finding a Percent*

What percent of 25 is 60?

$a = p\% \cdot b$	**Write percent equation.**
$60 = p\% \cdot 25$	**Substitute 60 for *a* and 25 for *b*.**
$2.4 = p\%$	**Divide each side by 25.**
$240\% = p\%$	**Write decimal as a percent.**

Answer 60 is 240% of 25.

In the **Real World**

Movies In 2000, a person who went to a movie theater in the United States spent an average of $6.92. The average ticket price was $5.39. To the nearest whole percent, what percent of the average amount spent at a movie theater was for a movie ticket? **about 78%**

Example 4 *Finding a Base*

Movies Your friend paid $9 for a movie ticket. This amount was 72% of the total amount your friend spent at the theater. How much money did your friend spend?

Solution

$a = p\% \cdot b$	**Write percent equation.**
$9 = 72\% \cdot b$	**Substitute 9 for *a* and 72 for *p*.**
$9 = 0.72 \cdot b$	**Write percent as a decimal.**
$12.5 = b$	**Divide each side by 0.72.**

Answer Your friend spent $12.50 at the theater.

Checkpoint

Use the percent equation to answer the question.

4. What percent of 48 is 45? **93.75%**
5. 27 is 7.5% of what number? **360**

Note Worthy

In your notes, you should include examples of percent problems and their solutions. You can use these notes to help you decide which method to use when solving a percent problem.

SUMMARY Methods for Solving a Percent Problem

To find the percent of a number:

- **Write the percent as a fraction.**

  Example:

  $20\% \text{ of } 35 = \frac{1}{5} \cdot 35 = 7$

- **Write the percent as a decimal.**

  Example:

  $5\% \text{ of } 16 = 0.05 \cdot 16 = 0.8$

To find the percent p%, the base b, or a part a of the base:

- **Use the proportion $\frac{a}{b} = \frac{p}{100}$.**

  Example:

  21 is 35% of what number?

  $$\frac{21}{b} = \frac{35}{100}$$

  $$60 = b$$

- **Use the percent equation $a = p\% \cdot b$.**

  Example:

  What percent of 250 is 40?

  $$40 = p\% \cdot 250$$

  $$16\% = p\%$$

7.4 Exercises

More Practice, p. 809

Guided Practice

Vocabulary Check

1. Identify the percent, the base, and the part of the base in the following statement: 32 is 40% of 80. **percent: 40%, base: 80, part of the base: 32**

2. Tell whether the answer to the following question represents *the base*, *the part of the base*, or *the percent*: What number is 20% of 65? **the part of the base**

Skill Check **Use the percent equation to answer the question.**

3. What number is 60% of 25? **15**

4. What percent of 25 is 24? **96%**

5. 18 is 36% of what number? **50**

6. What percent of 48 is 36? **75%**

Guided Problem Solving

7. Income You earn a weekly salary of \$200 plus a 3% commission on the total value of the sales made in the week. This week, your sales total \$2000. What are your total earnings for the week?

1) Identify the percent, the base, and the part of the base. **percent: 3%, base: \$2000, part of the base: amount of commission**
2) Write and solve a percent equation to find the commission. **$a = 3\% \cdot \$2000$, \$60**
3) Add the commission to the weekly salary to find the total earnings. **\$260**

ALGEBRAIC REASONING

Write the proportion $\frac{a}{b} = \frac{p}{100}$ on the board. Then have three volunteers come to the board and solve the equation three different ways, once for each of the variables a, b, and p.

VISUALIZE

Have students write the percent equation in their notebooks using a different colored pencil for each of the variables a, b, and p. Then, in the corresponding color, have students write a note summarizing what the variable represents.

NOTETAKING

Have students record in their notebooks the two methods summarized at the bottom of the box shown at the top of this page. Have students use both methods to find a percent greater than 100 and a percent less than 100. Then have them write a sentence explaining which of the two methods they prefer to use.

CONCEPT CHECK

How would you set up the percent equation to solve the following percent problem: "12 is 0.1% of what number?" **$12 = 0.1\% \cdot b$**

DAILY PUZZLER

Is 40% of 20 *greater than*, *less than*, or *equal to* 20% of 40? **equal to**

3 APPLY

ASSIGNMENT GUIDE

Basic Course
Day 1: pp. 348–349 Exs. 8–20, 23–26, 33–42

Average Course
Day 1: pp. 348–349 Exs. 12–22, 25–28, 31, 33–43

Advanced Course
Day 1: pp. 348–349 Exs. 14–21, 25–33*, 38–43

Block
pp. 348–349 Exs. 12–22, 25–28, 31, 33–43 (with 7.3)

EXTRA PRACTICE

- Student Edition, p. 809
- Chapter 7 Resource Book, pp. 35–37
- Test and Practice Generator

TRANSPARENCY

Even-numbered answers are available on transparencies.

HOMEWORK CHECK

When you review students' homework for this lesson, go over the following exercises to check understanding of key concepts.
Basic: 8, 12, 16, 17, 20
Average: 12, 16, 19, 20, 22
Advanced: 14, 16, 19, 20, 21

TEACHING TIP

In Exercise 22, suggest that students make a table to organize the numbers and costs of the items sold.

Practice and Problem Solving

Homework *Help*

Example	Exercises
1	8-19
2	20
3	8-17, 22
4	8-17, 21

Online Resources
CLASSZONE.COM
- More Examples
- eTutorial Plus

Use the percent equation to answer the question.

A **8.** What number is 20% of 45? **9**

9. What number is 10% of 56? **5.6**

10. What percent of 500 is 25? **5%**

11. What percent of 200 is 1? **0.5%**

12. 9 is 0.03% of what number? **30,000**

13. 10.5 is 30% of what number? **35**

14. 90 is 120% of what number? **75**

15. What percent of 90 is 72? **80%**

16. What percent of 80 is 212? **265%**

17. What number is 150% of 96? **144**

18. Music A music collector has 1200 CDs, and 65% of them were produced after 1990. How many of the CDs were produced after 1990? **780 CDs**

19. Community Service Your class surveyed 560 students and asked what kind of community service activity they prefer. Of the students surveyed, 25% chose recycling. How many students chose recycling? **140 students**

20. Televisions A salesperson earns a 4% commission on the sales of televisions. If the salesperson's television sales total $7000, how much is the commission? **$280**

21. Survey A school newspaper says that 3 students, or 6% of the students surveyed, can wiggle their ears. How many students were surveyed? **50 students**

22. Bake Sale At a club bake sale, cookies cost $.40 each and cupcakes cost $.65 each. The club sells 65 cookies and 60 cupcakes.

a. How much money was made from selling cookies? cupcakes? **$26; $39**

b. What percent of the money made came from sales of cookies? **40%**

c. Critical Thinking What percent of the baked goods sold were cookies? Why is this percent not the same as the percent you found in part (b)? **52%. *Sample answer:* The prices of cookies and cupcakes are not the same.**

Use the percent equation to answer the question when $k = 20$.

23. What is $(k - 15)$% of 90? **4.5**

24. What percent of 70 is $(k + 36)$? **80%**

B **25.** $(2k)$ is 8% of what number? **500**

26. What is $(3k)$% of 130? **78**

27. *Writing* Would you change the percent to *a fraction* or to *a decimal* in order to find 75% of 120? 31% of 120? Explain your choices.

27. ***Sample answer:*** **A fraction; a decimal; I would convert 75% to the fraction $\frac{3}{4}$ because 120 is evenly divisible by 4, but because 120 is not evenly divisible by 100, there is no clear advantage to changing 31% to a fraction.**

Football stadium at Houston, Texas

28. Sports The table shows a breakdown of the seats in a football stadium at Houston, Texas. Use a calculator to answer the following questions.

Type of seat	Seats
Main level seats	25,739
Middle level seats	14,446
Upper level seats	24,968
Seats in suites	4,185

a. About what percent of the seats are either main level seats or middle level seats? **about 58%**

b. Suppose that 75% of the upper level seats and 50% of the middle level seats are occupied. How many seats in these two sections together are occupied? **25,949 seats**

29b. Popular votes. *Sample answer:* The difference in the popular votes was about 49.0% − 40.6%, or about 8%, while the difference in the electoral votes was about 70.4% − 29.6%, or about 41%.

29. **Extended Problem Solving** In a presidential election, the candidate who receives the most popular votes in a state usually receives that state's electoral votes. In the 1996 election, about 96 million popular votes were cast, and 538 electoral votes were cast. The table shows the voting results for the election.

Candidate	Electoral votes	Popular votes (estimated)
Clinton	379	47 million
Dole	159	39 million
Other	0	10 million

a. **Compare** For which candidate, Clinton or Dole, was the percent of popular votes greater than the percent of electoral votes? **Dole**

b. **Interpret** Was this election closer with respect to popular votes or to electoral votes? Explain.

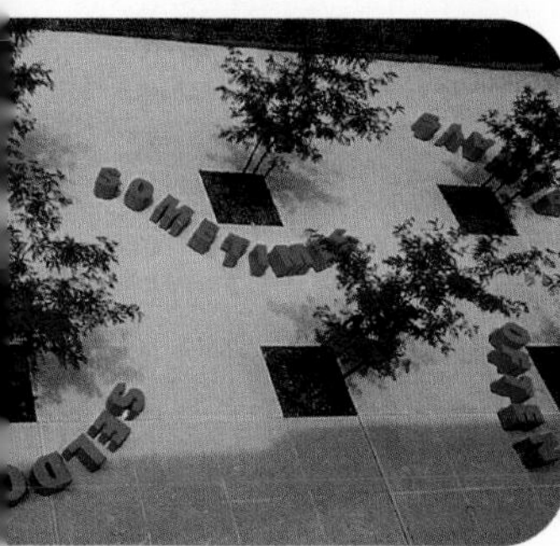

In the Real World

Art Programs The artwork shown above was financed by New York City's Percent for Art Program. Titled *Multiple Choice*, it shows five benches that spell out the words ALWAYS, NEVER, OFTEN, SELDOM, and SOMETIMES. About what percent of the 31 letters used for the benches are E's? **about 19.4%**

30. **Computers** A salesperson earns a 4% commission on every computer sold. The salesperson wants to earn $1000 in commissions in the next 4 days. What is the average amount of computer sales that the salesperson needs to make per day to reach the goal? **$6250**

C 31. **Art Programs** In New York City's Percent for Art Program, money is set aside for creating artwork at public building sites. The program requires that 1% of the first $20,000,000 of the cost of a building project and 0.5% of the remaining cost be spent on the artwork.

a. How much money must be spent on artwork if a project is expected to cost $30,000,000? **$250,000**

b. For each project, no more than $400,000 can be spent on artwork. The maximum amount that can be spent on artwork per year on all projects in the city is $1,500,000. Suppose that in one year the city has a project that costs $50,000,000 and another project that costs $62,000,000. What percent of the yearly maximum amount for artwork is used by the two projects? **50%**

32. **Challenge** The base b of a triangle is 60% of the height h. Write a formula for the area of the triangle in terms of h only. $A = 0.3h^2$

Mixed Review

Find the difference. *(p. 774)*

33. 892.1 − 420.5 **471.6** 34. 73.98 − 5.16 **68.82** 35. 18.9 − 6.72 **12.18**

Solve the equation. Check your solution. *(Lesson 2.6)*

36. $6x = 12$ **2** 37. $7x = -42$ **−6** 38. $-9x = -36$ **4**

Write the fraction as a percent. *(Lesson 7.3)*

39. $\frac{1}{8}$ **12.5%** 40. $\frac{11}{20}$ **55%** 41. $\frac{12}{9}$ **$133.\overline{3}$%**

Standardized Test Practice

42. **Multiple Choice** In a class of 35 students, 28 take the bus to school. What percent of the students take the bus to school? **C**

A. 7% B. 63% C. 80% D. 125%

43. **Short Response** There are 20 marbles in a bag, and 35% of them are blue. You put 6 more blue marbles in the bag. What percent of the marbles in the bag are now blue? Explain how you got your answer. **See margin.**

4 ASSESS

Assessment Resources

For more assessment resources, see:
- Assessment Book
- Test and Practice Generator

Mini-Quiz

1. What number is 3% of 700? **21**
2. What percent of 220 is 44? **20%**
3. 81 is 18% of what number? **450**
4. 63 is what percent of 36? **175%**
5. **Challenge** The length l of a rectangle is 180% of its width w. Write a formula for the perimeter P of the rectangle in terms of w only. $P = 5.6w$

5 FOLLOW-UP

Diagnosis/Remediation

- Study Guide in Chapter 7 Resource Book, pp. 38-39
- Tutor Place, Ratio, Proportion, and Percent Cards 14, 15
- eTutorial Plus Online
- Extra Practice, p. 809
- Lesson Practice in Chapter 7 Resource Book, pp. 35-37

English Learner Support

- Spanish Study Guide
- Multi-Language Visual Glossary
- Chapter Audio Summaries CDs

Challenge

- Challenge Practice in Chapter 7 Resource Book, p. 40
- Teacher's Edition, p. 326F

43. See Additional Answers beginning on page AA1.

Additional Resources

The following resources are available to help review the materials in Lessons 7.1–7.4.

Chapter 7 Resource Book
- Lesson Practice
- Study Guide

Assessment Book
- Chapter 7 Quiz 1

Technology
- Test and Practice Generator
- eTutorial CD-ROM

Internet
- Classzone
- eWorkbook Plus Online
- eTutorial Plus Online

English Learner Support

- Spanish Study Guide
- Multi-Language Visual Glossary
- Chapter Audio Summaries CDs

Brain Game. Row A: 75, 100, 75, 75, or 100, 75, 75, 75; Row B: 40, 64, 25.6, 25.6, or 64, 40, 25.6, 25.6; Row C: 28, 35, 9.8, 9.8, or 35, 28, 9.8, 9.8; 110.4

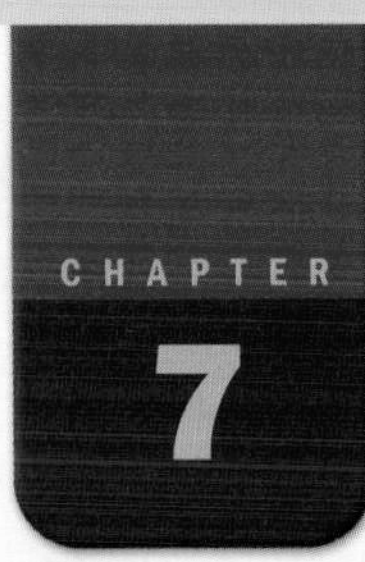

Mid-Chapter Quiz

Write the fraction as a percent.

1. $\frac{17}{25}$ **68%** **2.** $\frac{1}{5}$ **20%** **3.** $\frac{5}{6}$ **$83\frac{1}{3}$%** **4.** $\frac{11}{16}$ **$68\frac{3}{4}$%**

Write the decimal as a percent.

5. 0.87 **87%** **6.** 0.728 **72.8%** **7.** 2 **200%** **8.** 0.0061 **0.61%**

Find the percent of the number.

9. 75% of 64 **48** **10.** 20% of 18 **3.6** **11.** 30% of 300 **90** **12.** 25% of 980 **245**

13. 35% of 90 **31.5** **14.** 22.5% of 200 **45** **15.** 140% of 500 **700** **16.** 0.6% of 600 **3.6**

17. Flowers A bouquet of 40 flowers is made up of roses, carnations, and daisies. The bouquet is 45% roses and 15% carnations. How many of the flowers are roses? carnations? **18 roses; 6 carnations**

Use a proportion or the percent equation to answer the question.

18. What number is 95% of 80? **76**

19. What percent of 40 is 4? **10%**

20. What percent of 400 is 190? **47.5%**

21. 6 is 7.5% of what number? **80**

22. Furniture A furniture salesperson earns a 4.5% commission on every piece of furniture sold. The salesperson sells a sofa for $1000 and a chair for $200. What commission does the salesperson earn? **$54**

The Greatest Sum

Fill in the blue boxes with the numbers shown. Use each number only once. Find the percent of the number in parts (a), (b), and (c). Then add the results. What is the greatest sum that you can make? **See margin.**

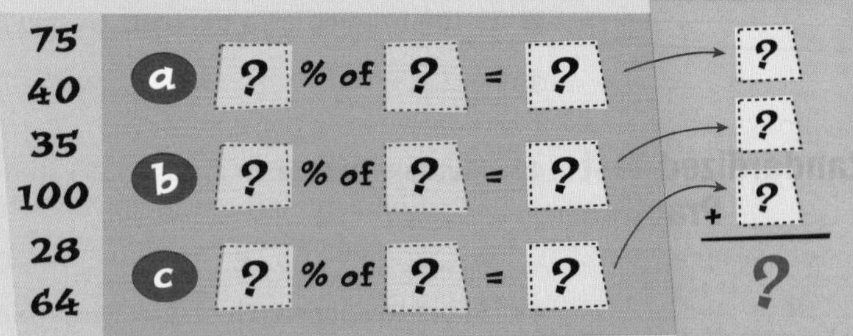

Concept *Activity*

7.5 Modeling Percent of Change

Goal
Model the percent of change in a quantity.

Materials
- graph paper
- colored pencils

Investigate

A figure has an area of 10 square units. You increase its area to 15 square units. By what percent does the area of the figure change?

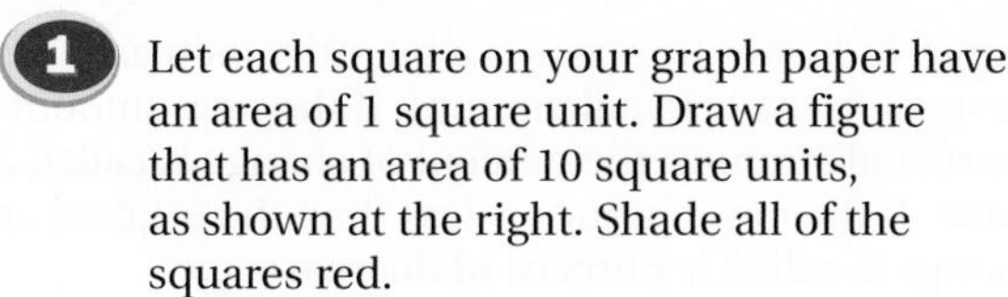

1 Let each square on your graph paper have an area of 1 square unit. Draw a figure that has an area of 10 square units, as shown at the right. Shade all of the squares red.

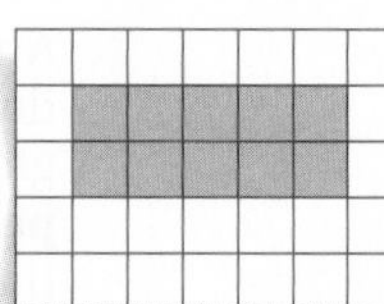

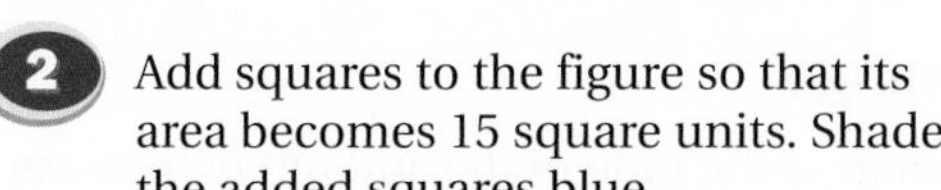

2 Add squares to the figure so that its area becomes 15 square units. Shade the added squares blue.

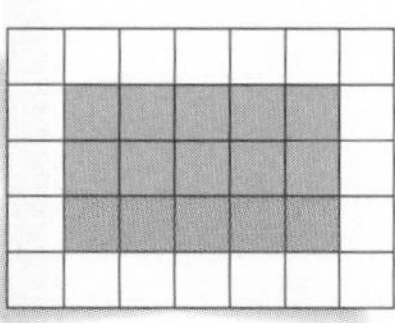

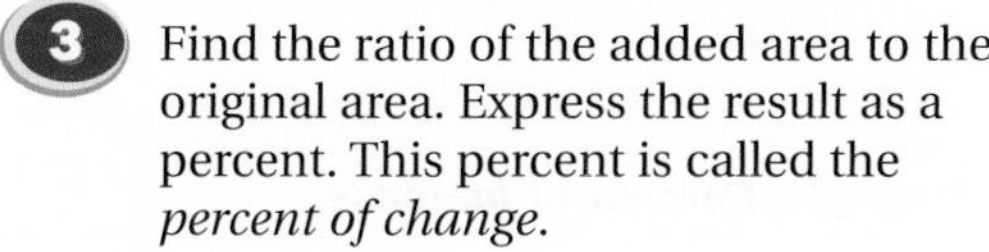

3 Find the ratio of the added area to the original area. Express the result as a percent. This percent is called the *percent of change.*

$$\frac{\text{Added area}}{\text{Original area}} = \frac{5 \text{ square units}}{10 \text{ square units}} = 50\%$$

Draw Conclusions

Use a model to find the percent of change in the area of the figure.

1. Original area: 5 square units **40%**
   New area: 7 square units
2. Original area: 4 square units **25%**
   New area: 5 square units
3. Original area: 3 square units **100%**
   New area: 6 square units
4. Original area: 5 square units **140%**
   New area: 12 square units
5. **Critical Thinking** A figure has an area of 16 square units, and you increase its area to 20 square units. What percent of the original area is the new area? How is this percent related to the percent of change in the area? **125%; it is the sum of 100% and the percent of change.**

NCTM CURRICULUM STANDARDS
Standard 2: Use models to understand relationships; Use models to represent relationships

1 PLAN

Investigate the Concept

- Students model the percent of change in a quantity.
- This activity leads into calculating percents of increase and decrease, finding discounts and markups, and calculating simple and compound interest.

Materials

Each student will need graph paper and colored pencils. A support transparency is available for this activity.

Recommended Time

Work activity: 10 min
Discuss results: 5 min

Grouping

Students should work individually.

2 TEACH

Discussion

In step 3, lead students to recognize that the 50% increase means that the *original area* increased by 50%. Stress that the added area is $\frac{1}{3}$ of the final shaded area.

3 CLOSE

Key Discovery

The percent of change in a quantity is found by comparing the new quantity to the original quantity.

Assessment

1. An original area of 10 square units is increased 100%. What is the new area? **20 square units**
2. An original area of 10 square units is increased 10%. What is the new area? **11 square units**

1 PLAN

Skill Check

Simplify the expression.

1. $\frac{24 - 14}{14}$ $\frac{5}{7}$
2. $\frac{600 - 135}{600}$ $\frac{31}{40}$
3. $\frac{150 - 132}{132}$ $\frac{3}{22}$

LESSON OBJECTIVE

Find a percent of change in a quantity.

PACING

Suggested Number of Days
Basic Course: 1 day
Average Course: 1 day
Advanced Course: 1 day
Block: 0.5 block with 7.6

TEACHING RESOURCES

For a complete list of Teaching Resources, see page 326B.

 **TRANSPARENCY**

Warm-Up Exercises for this lesson are available on a transparency.

2 TEACH

MOTIVATING THE LESSON

Have students determine the percent of the class members who have either ridden in a hot-air balloon, seen one in person, or who want to ride in one.

LESSON 7.5

Percent *of* Change

Vocabulary
percent of change, p. 352
percent of increase, p. 352
percent of decrease, p. 352

BEFORE	Now	WHY?
You found a percent of a number.	You'll find a percent of change in a quantity.	So you can analyze data about wetlands, as in Ex. 22.

Balloons The International Balloon Fiesta takes place every year in Albuquerque, New Mexico. In 1999, 903 balloons participated. In 2000, 1019 balloons participated. By about what percent did the number of balloons increase from 1999 to 2000?

A **percent of change** indicates how much a quantity increases or decreases with respect to the original amount. If the new amount is greater than the original amount, the percent of change is called a **percent of increase**. If the new amount is less than the original amount, the percent of change is called a **percent of decrease**.

Percent of Change

The percent of change is the ratio of the amount of increase or decrease to the original amount.

$$\text{Percent of change, } p\% = \frac{\text{Amount of increase or decrease}}{\text{Original amount}}$$

Example 1 *Finding a Percent of Increase*

To answer the question stated above, find the percent of increase in the number of balloons from 1999 to 2000.

$p\% = \frac{\text{Amount of increase}}{\text{Original amount}}$ **Write formula for percent of increase.**

$= \frac{1019 - 903}{903}$ **Substitute.**

$= \frac{116}{903}$ **Subtract.**

$\approx 0.128 = 12.8\%$ **Divide. Then write decimal as a percent.**

Answer The number of balloons increased by about 12.8%.

 ***Checkpoint***

Find the percent of increase.

1. Original: 20 New: 25 **25%**
2. Original: 150 New: 189 **26%**
3. Original: 55 New: 143 **160%**

NCTM CURRICULUM STANDARDS
Standard 1: Understand numbers; Compute fluently
Standard 6: Solve problems in math and other contexts

Study *Strategy*

Reasonableness In Example 2, a decrease from 512 to 320 is about the same as a decrease from 500 to 300. Because $\frac{500 - 300}{500} = \frac{200}{500} = 40\%$, 37.5% is a reasonable answer.

Example 2 *Finding a Percent of Decrease*

Find the percent of decrease from 512 to 320.

$p\% = \frac{\text{Amount of decrease}}{\text{Original amount}}$ — **Write formula for percent of decrease.**

$= \frac{512 - 320}{512}$ — **Substitute.**

$= \frac{192}{512}$ — **Subtract.**

$= \frac{3}{8} = 37.5\%$ — **Simplify fraction. Then write as a percent.**

Answer The percent of decrease is 37.5%.

 ***Checkpoint***

Find the percent of decrease.

4. Original: 20 **25%** New: 15

5. Original: 75 **$53.\overline{3}\%$** New: 35

6. Original: 102 **50%** New: 51

Finding a New Amount If you know the original amount and the percent of change, you can find the new amount. First multiply the percent of change by the original amount to find the amount of change. Then increase or decrease the original amount by the amount of change.

Example 3 *Using a Percent of Increase*

Action Sports There were about 198,000 spectators at an action sports event in 1995. The number of spectators increased by about 12% from 1995 to 2002. About how many spectators were there in 2002?

Solution

To find the number of spectators in 2002, you need to increase the number of spectators in 1995 by 12%.

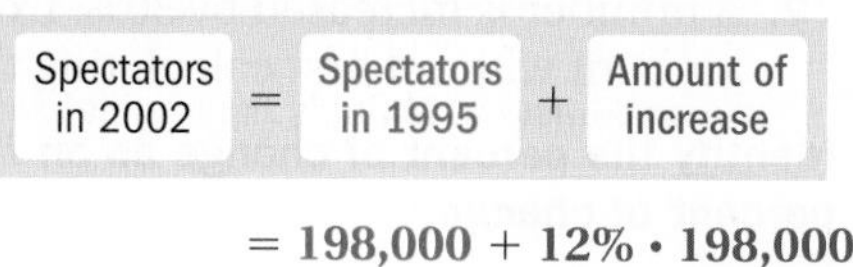

$= 198{,}000 + 12\% \cdot 198{,}000$ — **Substitute.**

$= 198{,}000 + 0.12 \cdot 198{,}000$ — **Write percent as a decimal.**

$= 221{,}760$ — **Evaluate.**

Answer There were about 221,760 spectators in 2002.

Athlete in a motocross competition

 ***Checkpoint***

Find the new amount.

7. Increase 45 by 20%. **54**

8. Decrease 85 by 28%. **61.2**

TIPS *for* NEW TEACHERS

Ask students to provide examples from their own lives of quantities that have increased or decreased, such as hours worked or money saved. Use their examples to find the percent of change. See Tips for New Teachers in the *Chapter 7 Resource Book*.

Extra Examples

Example 1 At its first visit to a veterinarian, a puppy weighed 28 pounds. Three months later, the puppy weighed 46 pounds. Find the percent of increase in its weight. **about 64.3%**

Example 2 Find the percent of decrease from 250 to 145. **42%**

Example 3 An annual concert was attended by 4212 people last year. This year, the number attending increased by about 14% over last year. How many people attended the concert this year? **about 4802 people**

TEACHING TIP

When discussing Example 3, stress that the increase is added to the original amount. It may be helpful to suggest that students think of this as having 100% of the original amount and then adding the increase. Some students may recognize that the new amount in Example 3 can be calculated in one step by finding 112% (100% + 12%) of the original amount.

COMMON ERROR

Watch for students who use the new amount instead of the original amount in the denominator of the ratio when finding the percent of change.

Extra Examples

Example 4 Last month, a restaurant charged $12.95 for a seafood pasta dinner. This month, the owner had new menus printed, with all dinner prices increased by 12%. What is the new price for a seafood pasta dinner? **$14.50**

CROSS-CURRICULUM

Social Studies Social Studies courses offer numerous opportunities to find percents of change; for example, changes in population statistics, per capita income, and so on.

CONCEPT CHECK

How do you find the percent of change in a quantity? **Divide the amount of the change by the original quantity and write the result as a percent. Identify the change as an increase if the new quantity is greater than the original quantity, or as a decrease if the new quantity is less than the original quantity.**

DAILY PUZZLER

The percent of change in a quantity is 10%. The new amount and the original amount are either 90 and 100, respectively, or 100 and 90, respectively. Which amount is which? How do you know? **The original amount is 100 and the new amount is 90. *Sample answer:* The difference of the two amounts is 10. Since 10% of 90 is 9 and not 10, the original amount must be 100. So, the change is a 10% decrease from 100 to 90.**

Another Way In Example 3, you can find the new amount by evaluating 100% • 198,000 + 12% • 198,000, or 198,000 • (100% + 12%). This result suggests another way to find a new amount.

- For a $p\%$ increase, multiply the original amount by (100% + $p\%$).
- For a $p\%$ decrease, multiply the original amount by (100% − $p\%$).

Example 4 *Finding a New Amount*

Music In 1983, the average price of an audio CD was $21.50. By 2000, the average price had decreased by 34.8%. What was the average price of a CD in 2000?

Solution

Price in 2000 = **Price in 1983** • (100% − $p\%$)

= **21.5** • (100% − **34.8%**) **Substitute.**

= 21.5 • 65.2% **Subtract percents.**

= 21.5 • 0.652 **Write percent as a decimal.**

= 14.018 **Multiply.**

Answer The average price of a CD in 2000 was about $14.02.

7.5 Exercises

More Practice, p. 809

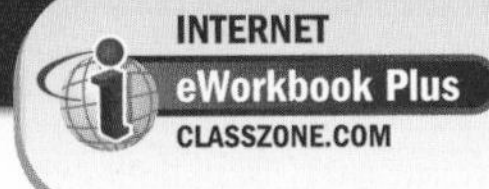

Guided Practice

Vocabulary Check

1. Is the percent of change from 79 to 56 *a percent of increase* or *a percent of decrease*? **a percent of decrease**
2. A number is increased by 30%. Explain how you can find the new amount without first calculating the amount of increase. ***Sample answer:* Multiply the original amount by 100% + 30% = 130%.**

Skill Check **Identify the percent of change as an *increase* or a *decrease*. Then find the percent of change.**

3. Original: 30 New: 45 **increase; 50%**
4. Original: 65 New: 117 **increase; 80%**
5. Original: 28 New: 7 **decrease; 75%**

Guided Problem Solving

6. **Reptiles** In 1981, there were 25 endangered and threatened species of reptiles in the U.S. In 2001, there were 36 species. By what percent did the number of these reptile species change from 1981 to 2001?
   1) Tell whether the amount of change is *an increase* or *a decrease*. **an increase**
   2) Find the amount of change from 1981 to 2001. **11 species**
   3) Divide the amount of change by the original amount. Write the quotient as a percent. **44% increase**

Practice and Problem Solving

Homework Help

Example	Exercises
1	7-14
2	7-13, 15
3	16-19, 21
4	16-20

Online Resources
CLASSZONE.COM
- More Examples
- eTutorial Plus

Identify the percent of change as an *increase* or a *decrease*. Then find the percent of change.

A **7.** Original: 28
New: 35
increase; 25%

8. Original: 45
New: 72
increase; 60%

9. Original: 70
New: 42
decrease; 40%

10. Original: 40
New: 9
decrease; 77.5%

11. Original: 140
New: 189
increase; 35%

12. Original: 350
New: 196
decrease; 44%

13. Error Analysis Describe and correct the error in finding the percent of change from 90 to 50. **See margin.**

X $p\% = \frac{90 - 50}{50} = \frac{40}{50} = 0.8 = 80\%$

13. In the formula for percent of change, the denominator is the original amount, not the new amount, so the denominator should be 90: $p = \frac{90 - 50}{90} = \frac{40}{90} = \frac{4}{9} = 44.\bar{4}\%$.

14. Hot Dogs In 1991, the price of a hot dog at a Texas baseball stadium was $1.25. In 2001, the price of a hot dog at the stadium was $2.25. By what percent did the price change from 1991 to 2001? **80% increase**

15. Lakes Lake Chad in Africa had a surface area of about 10,000 square miles in 1963. Because of climate changes and increased water usage by humans, the surface area decreased to about 850 square miles in 2001. By what percent did the surface area change from 1963 to 2001? **91.5% decrease**

23. Yes. *Sample answer:* A 100% increase represents only a doubling, so if a quantity is more than doubled, the increase is greater than 100%.

Find the new amount.

16. Increase 25 by 24%. **31**

17. Increase 120 by 75%. **210**

18. Decrease 35 by 60%. **14**

19. Decrease 72 by 65%. **25.2**

20. Computers In 1992, one gigabyte of information stored in computers cost $3000. In 2002, one gigabyte of stored information cost 99.9% less. How much did one gigabyte of stored information cost in 2002? **$3**

21. Auctions A sweater is being sold at an online auction. The minimum bid is $9. At the end of the auction, the sweater is sold for 75% above the minimum bid. What is the selling price of the sweater? **$15.75**

B **22.**  **Wetlands** A wetland is a region where water is usually present near or on the soil. The states in the table below had the greatest acreage of wetlands in the United States in the 1980s. The table shows the surface area of wetlands in these states in the 1780s and in the 1980s.

a. Compare In which state was the percent of change in the area of wetlands from the 1780s to the 1980s the least? the greatest? **Alaska; Florida**

b. Analyze For the four states combined, by about what percent did the area of wetlands change from the 1780s to the 1980s? **about 10.5% decrease**

Area of Wetlands (millions of acres)		
State	**1780s**	**1980s**
Alaska	170.2	170.0
Florida	20.3	11.0
Louisiana	16.2	8.8
Minnesota	15.1	8.7

23. *Writing* Can you increase an amount by more than 100%? Explain. **See margin.**

In the Real World

Wetlands The wetland shown above is located in Ocean City, Maryland. The land that makes up the United States had about 391 million acres of wetlands in the 1780s and about 274 million acres in the 1980s. By about what percent did the area of wetlands in the United States change from the 1780s to the 1980s? **about 29.9% decrease**

3 APPLY

ASSIGNMENT GUIDE

Basic Course
Day 1: pp. 355–356 Exs. 7-10, 14-20, 24, 28-41

Average Course
Day 1: pp. 355-356 Exs. 10-17, 20-25, 27-33, 38-41

Advanced Course
Day 1: pp. 355-356 Exs. 11-15, 18-27*, 30-33, 38-41

Block
pp. 355-356 Exs. 10-17, 20-25, 27-33, 38-41 (with 7.6)

EXTRA PRACTICE
- Student Edition, p. 809
- Chapter 7 Resource Book, pp. 44-46
- Test and Practice Generator

TRANSPARENCY
Even-numbered answers are available on transparencies.

HOMEWORK CHECK
When you review students' homework for this lesson, go over the following exercises to check understanding of key concepts.
Basic: 7, 10, 15, 16, 18
Average: 10, 13, 15, 20, 21
Advanced: 11, 14, 18, 20, 21

TEACHING TIP
In Exercises 7-12, some students may have better success if the values have a real-world context. Invite students to suggest a real-world change that the given values could represent.

4 ASSESS

ASSESSMENT RESOURCES

For more assessment resources, see:
- Assessment Book
- Test and Practice Generator

MINI-QUIZ

Identify the percent of change as an *increase* or a *decrease*. Then find the percent of change.

1. original: 210, new: 315 **increase; 50%**
2. original: 135, new: 54 **decrease; 60%**

Find the new amount. Round to the nearest whole number.

3. Increase 540 by 22%. **659**
4. Decrease 380 by 77%. **87**
5. **Challenge** After a road surface test, the number of potholes in a one-mile stretch of test pavement increased 259% to 43. How many potholes were there before the test? **about 12 potholes**

5 FOLLOW-UP

DIAGNOSIS/REMEDIATION

- Study Guide in Chapter 7 Resource Book, pp. 47–48
- eTutorial Plus Online
- Extra Practice, p. 809
- Lesson Practice in Chapter 7 Resource Book, pp. 44–46

ENGLISH LEARNER SUPPORT

- Spanish Study Guide
- Multi-Language Visual Glossary
- Chapter Audio Summaries CDs

CHALLENGE

- Challenge Practice in Chapter 7 Resource Book, p. 49
- Teacher's Edition, p. 326F

24. **Investing** An investor buys 500 shares of a stock at a price of \$24 per share. Three years later the value of each share has increased by 15%. What is the total value of the 500 shares of the stock? **\$13,800**

25. **Extended Problem Solving** The bar graph shows the number of pairs of footwear that were manufactured in the U.S. for 5 years. You may want to use a calculator to answer the following questions.

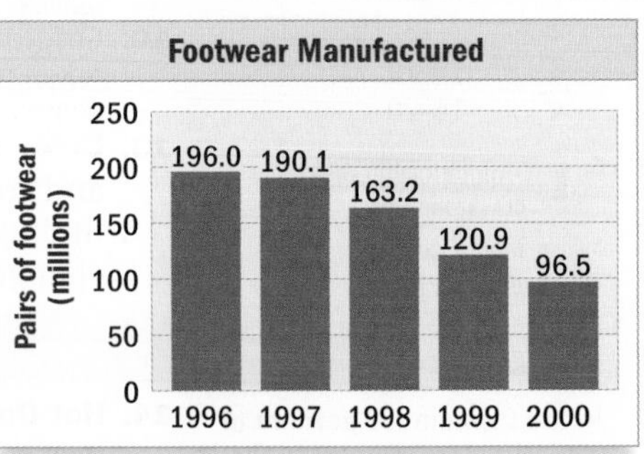

a. By about what percent did the number of pairs of footwear change from 1996 to 2000? **about 50.8% decrease**

b. **Compare** In which year did the number of pairs of footwear decrease the most from the previous year? What was the approximate percent of change? **1999; about 25.9%**

c. **Interpret and Apply** Can you conclude from the graph that footwear manufacturers have been making less money every year from 1996 to 2000? Explain.

25c. No. *Sample answer:* The graph does not indicate the amount that is made per pair of shoes. Also, it is possible that the decrease might be because the manufacturers are having the shoes made for them outside of the United States.

C 26. **Challenge** The number of people between the ages of 2 and 18 who accessed streaming media on the Internet in November 1999 increased by 65% to about 7 million in November 2000. About how many people in this age group accessed streaming media in November 1999? **about 4.2 million people**

27. **Critical Thinking** Suppose an original amount decreases by 75%. By what percent must the new amount increase in order to return to the original amount? Justify your answer. **See margin.**

27. 300%. *Sample answer:* A decrease of 75% is the same as 100% − 75% = 25%, or $\frac{1}{4}$, of the original amount. So to return to the original amount requires adding back $\frac{3}{4}$ of the original amount, and $\frac{3}{4}$ is 300% of $\frac{1}{4}$.

Mixed Review

Find the sum or difference. *(p. 774)*

28. 5.98 + 3.72 **9.7**
29. 9 + 4.55 **13.55**
30. 3.4 − 1.9 **1.5**
31. 8.04 − 2.6 **5.44**

Algebra Basics Solve the equation. Check your solution. *(Lesson 3.1)*

32. $9 = 5n + 4$ **1**
33. $6y + 1 = 19$ **3**
34. $14 = 4w - 2$ **4**
35. $9x - 7 = 20$ **3**

Use the percent equation to answer the question. *(Lesson 7.4)*

36. What number is 60% of 135? **81**
37. What percent of 120 is 78? **65%**
38. What percent of 96 is 84? **87.5%**
39. 36 is 48% of what number? **75**

Standardized Test Practice

40. **Multiple Choice** A homebuilder orders 10% more floor tiles than the original estimate of 170 tiles in case some tiles break while they are being installed. How many tiles does the homebuilder order? **C**

A. 153 tiles **B.** 180 tiles **C.** 187 tiles **D.** 1700 tiles

41. **Multiple Choice** There were about 23,000 movie screens in the U.S. in 1990. The number of screens increased to about 34,500 by 2001. By what percent did the number of screens change from 1990 to 2001? **H**

F. 25% **G.** 33% **H.** 50% **I.** 250%

LESSON

7.6 Percent Applications

BEFORE	Now	WHY?
You found percents of change.	You'll find markups, discounts, sales tax, and tips.	So you can find the cost of in-line skates, as in Ex. 25.

Vocabulary
markup, p. 357
discount, p. 358

Jewelry A street vendor buys bracelets from a manufacturer for $7 each. The vendor marks up the price by 150%. What is the retail price?

A retailer buys items from manufacturers at *wholesale prices*. The retailer then sells those items to customers at *retail prices*. An increase from the wholesale price of an item to the retail price is a **markup**. The markup is calculated using a percent of the wholesale price.

Example 1 *Finding a Retail Price*

Find the retail price of a bracelet, as described above.

Solution

Method 1 Add the markup to the wholesale price.

Retail price = Wholesale price + Markup

$= 7 + 150\% \cdot 7$ **Substitute.**

$= 7 + 1.5 \cdot 7$ **Write 150% as a decimal.**

$= 7 + 10.5$ **Multiply.**

$= 17.5$ **Add.**

Method 2 Multiply the wholesale price by (100% + Markup percent).

Retail price = Wholesale price • (100% + Markup percent)

$= 7 \cdot (100\% + 150\%)$ **Substitute.**

$= 7 \cdot 250\%$ **Add percents.**

$= 7 \cdot 2.5$ **Write 250% as a decimal.**

$= 17.5$ **Multiply.**

Answer The retail price of a bracelet is $17.50.

Checkpoint

1. In Example 1, what is the retail price of a bracelet if the markup percent is 120%? $15.40

NCTM CURRICULUM STANDARDS
Standard 1: Understand numbers; Compute fluently
Standard 6: Solve problems in math and other contexts

1 PLAN

Skill Check

1. 1.5 • 8 = ? 12
2. 2.5 • 6 = ? 15
3. 0.75(5) = ? 3.75
4. 0.85(9) = ? 7.65

Lesson Objective

Find markups, discounts, sales tax, and tips.

Pacing

Suggested Number of Days
Basic Course: 2 days
Average Course: 2 days
Advanced Course: 2 days
Block: 0.5 block with 7.5
0.5 block with 7.7

Teaching Resources

For a complete list of Teaching Resources, see page 326B.

Transparency

Warm-Up Exercises for this lesson are available on a transparency.

2 TEACH

Motivating the Lesson

Ask students about store advertisements they have seen where prices have been "marked down drastically." Ask them what they think the term *markup* means.

TIPS *for* NEW TEACHERS
Students may initially think their correct answers are wrong because they do not believe that markups of more than 100% are reasonable. Also, stress that markups are *added on* to the cost and not a percent of change from the cost. See Tips for New Teachers in the *Chapter 7 Resource Book*.

Extra Examples

Example 1 Find the retail price of a collectible figurine with a wholesale cost of $12 that is marked up 75%. **$21**

Example 2 Mason buys a suit that is on sale for 20% off the original price of $180. What is the sale price? **$144**

Example 3 The bill for a family's meal at a restaurant is $68. They leave a 15% tip. The sale tax is 6%. What is the total cost of their meal? **$82.28**

READING STRATEGY

Before discussing Example 3, draw students' attention to the "Watch Out" comment in the margin. While discussing Example 3, make sure students notice that the sales tax and the tip are calculated separately using the cost of the meal, and then the amounts are totaled.

COMMON ERROR
In Checkpoint Exercise 3, watch for students who calculate the tip after adding the sales tax to the bill.

Discounts A decrease from the original price of an item to the sale price is a **discount**. The discount is calculated using a percent of the original price.

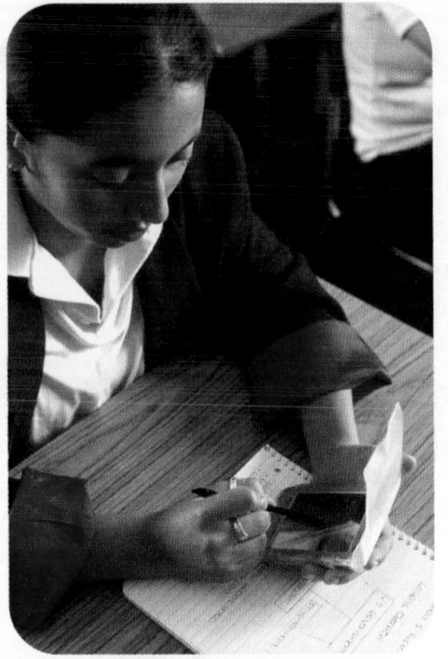

Example 2 ***Finding a Sale Price***

Electronics You buy an electronic organizer that is on sale for 15% off the original price of $25. What is the sale price?

Solution

Method 1 Subtract the discount from the original price.

Sale price = **Original price** − **Discount**	
= **25** − **15%** • **25**	**Substitute.**
= 25 − 0.15 • 25	**Write 15% as a decimal.**
= 25 − 3.75	**Multiply.**
= 21.25	**Subtract.**

Method 2 Multiply the original price by (100% − Discount percent).

Sale price = **Original price** • (100% − **Discount percent**)	
= **25** • (100% − **15%**)	**Substitute.**
= 25 • 85%	**Subtract percents.**
= 25 • 0.85	**Write 85% as a decimal.**
= 21.25	**Multiply.**

Answer The sale price of the electronic organizer is $21.25.

Watch *Out*

The tip at a restaurant is based on the food bill only. Do not include the sales tax when finding a tip.

Example 3 ***Using Sales Tax and Tips***

Restaurants The bill for your restaurant meal is $22. You leave a 15% tip. The sales tax is 6%. What is the total cost of your meal?

Solution

Sales tax and tips are calculated using a percent of the purchase price. These amounts are then added to the purchase price.

Total = **Food bill** + **Sales tax** + **Tip**	
= **22** + **6%** • **22** + **15%** • **22**	**Substitute.**
= 22 + 0.06 • 22 + 0.15 • 22	**Write 6% and 15% as decimals.**
= 22 + 1.32 + 3.3	**Multiply.**
= 26.62	**Add.**

Answer The total cost of the meal is $26.62.

Checkpoint

2. A pair of jeans that originally costs $42 is 25% off. Find the sale price. **$31.50**
3. In Example 3, find the total cost of the meal if the sales tax is 5%. **$26.40**

Study *Strategy*

Another Way In Example 4, you can use the verbal model

$$\text{Retail price} = \text{Wholesale price} + \text{Markup}$$

to find the wholesale price. When you substitute variables and values, you get the equation $35 = x + 0.8x$, where x is the wholesale price.

Example 4 *Finding an Original Amount*

Lamps A furniture store marks up the wholesale price of a desk lamp by 80%. The retail price is \$35. What is the wholesale price?

Solution

Let x represent the wholesale price.

Retail price = **Wholesale price** • (100% + **Markup percent**)

$35 = x \cdot (100\% + 80\%)$	**Substitute.**
$35 = x \cdot 180\%$	**Add percents.**
$35 = x \cdot 1.8$	**Write 180% as a decimal.**
$19.44 \approx x$	**Divide each side by 1.8.**

Answer The wholesale price of the lamp is about \$19.44.

 ***Checkpoint***

4. A store marks up the wholesale price of a printer by 80%. The retail price is \$120. What is the wholesale price of the printer? **about \$66.67**

7.6 Exercises

More Practice, p. 809

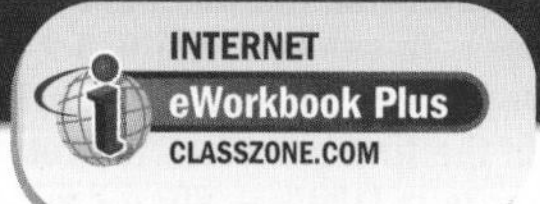

Guided Practice

Vocabulary Check

1. Copy and complete: The retail price of an item for sale is the sum of the wholesale price and the _?_. **markup**

2. Describe two methods for finding the sale price of an item if you know the original price and the discount percent. **See margin.**

Skill Check **In Exercises 3–6, use the given information to find the new amount.**

3. Wholesale price: \$13 **\$27.30**
Markup percent: 110%

4. Original price: \$60 **\$48**
Discount percent: 20%

5. Food bill: \$15 **\$15.75**
Sales tax: 5%

6. Taxi fare: \$22 **\$24.20**
Tip: 10%

Guided Problem Solving

7. Headsets When you use a coupon for 15% off the original price of a headset, you pay \$27. What is the original price of the headset?

1. Identify the discount price and the discount percent. **discount price: \$27, discount percent: 15%**
2. Let x represent the original price. Write an equation that you can use to find the original price. **$27 = x - 15\% \cdot x$ or $27 = x \cdot (100\% - 15\%)$**
3. Solve the equation to find the original price of the headset. **about \$31.76**

2. ***Sample answer:*** **(1) Use the discount percent to calculate the discount, then subtract the discount from the original price. (2) Multiply the original price by (100% − discount percent).**

NOTETAKING

Have students record the meanings of the terms *retail*, *wholesale*, *markup*, and *discount* in their notebooks.

Extra Examples

Example 4 A dress shop marks up the wholesale price of a prom dress by 115%. The retail price is \$180. What is the wholesale price of the dress? **\$83.72**

DIFFERENTIATING INSTRUCTION

Alternate Teaching Strategy
Bring in sale advertisements from the newspaper or mailbox fliers and create a variety of discount problems for students to solve.

CONCEPT CHECK

How do you find a sale price if you know the original price and the discount percent? **Multiply the original price by the percent to find the discount, and then subtract this amount from the original price to find the sale price.**

DAILY PUZZLER

A group of diners left their waiter a 15% tip in the amount of \$10.25. What was the cost of their meal? **\$68.33**

3 APPLY

ASSIGNMENT GUIDE

Basic Course

Day 1: EP p. 804 Exs. 56–59; pp. 360–361 Exs. 8–13, 24–26, 35–40

Day 2: pp. 360–361 Exs. 14–23, 29–34, 41

Average Course

Day 1: pp. 360–361 Exs. 8–13, 24–26, 35–40

Day 2: pp. 360–361 Exs. 14–23, 27, 29–34, 41

Advanced Course

Day 1: pp. 360–361 Exs. 9–13, 24–26, 35–40

Day 2: pp. 360–361 Exs. 15–23, 27–32*, 41

Block

pp. 360–361 Exs. 8–13, 24–26, 35–41 (with 7.5)

pp. 360–361 Exs. 14–23, 27, 29–34 (with 7.7)

EXTRA PRACTICE

- Student Edition, p. 809
- Chapter 7 Resource Book, pp. 52–54
- Test and Practice Generator

TRANSPARENCY

Even-numbered answers are available on transparencies.

HOMEWORK CHECK

When you review students' homework for this lesson, go over the following exercises to check understanding of key concepts.

Basic: 8, 10, 13, 14, 19

Average: 9, 11, 13, 16, 20

Advanced: 9, 11, 17, 22, 23

COMMON ERROR

In Exercises 8–11, watch for students who multiply the given price by the given percent and then think this amount is the new price.

Practice and Problem Solving

Homework *Help*

Example	Exercises
1	8–12
2	8–11, 13
3	14–18
4	19–23

Online Resources CLASSZONE.COM
- More Examples
- eTutorial Plus

In Exercises 8–11, use the given information to find the new price.

A **8.** Wholesale price: \$34 **\$76.50**
Markup percent: 125%

9. Wholesale price: \$125 **\$187.50**
Markup percent: 50%

10. Original price: \$37 **\$27.75**
Discount percent: 25%

11. Original price: \$54 **\$32.40**
Discount percent: 40%

12. Outdoor Speakers A music store buys a set of outdoor speakers for \$90. The store marks up the wholesale price by 110%. What is the retail price of the speakers? **\$189**

13. Zoo Trips For a child, the regular admission price to a zoo is \$13. With a special pass, the admission price is discounted 20%. What is the admission price when the pass is used? **\$10.40**

In Exercises 14–17, use the given information to find the total cost.

14. Original price: \$42 **\$44.10**
Sales tax: 5%

15. Original price: \$78 **\$82.68**
Sales tax: 6%

16. Food bill: \$25 **\$30.25**
Sales tax: 6%
Tip: 15%

17. Food bill: \$18 **\$22.50**
Sales tax: 5%
Tip: 20%

18. Walking Dogs A dog owner pays you \$20 plus a 10% tip for walking a dog. What is the total amount of money that the dog owner pays you? **\$22**

In Exercises 19–22, use the given information to find the original price.

19. Retail price: \$50 **about \$26.32**
Markup percent: 90%

20. Retail price: \$24 **about \$11.16**
Markup percent: 115%

21. Sale price: \$150 **\$200**
Discount percent: 25%

22. Sale price: \$210 **\$300**
Discount percent: 30%

23. Bicycles A store marks up the wholesale price of a bicycle by 120%. The retail price is \$215. What is the wholesale price of the bicycle? **about \$97.73**

B **24. Laptops** A laptop computer is on sale for 10% off the original price of \$1500. When it doesn't sell, the laptop goes on sale for 15% off the sale price. What is the new sale price of the laptop? **\$1147.50**

25. In-line Skates A sports store is having a sale on in-line skates. You want to buy a pair of in-line skates that originally costs \$135. The sales tax is 5.5%, and it will be applied to the sale price of the skates. What is the total cost of the skates? **\$113.94**

SALE!
20% OFF
every pair of
in-line skates

26. Critical Thinking Which situation results in a greater final amount, an 80% markup of the wholesale price followed by a 30% discount of the retail price, or a 30% markup of the wholesale price followed by an 80% discount of the retail price? Justify your answer. **See margin.**

26. An 80% markup of the wholesale price followed by a 30% discount of the retail price. *Sample answer:* The markup is greater and the discount is less. To see the results, let x represent the wholesale price. In the first situation, the retail price is $(100\% + 80\%) \cdot x = 1.8x$, and the sale price is then $1.8x \cdot (100\% - 30\%) = 1.26x$. In the second situation, the retail price is $(100\% + 30\%) \cdot x = 1.3x$, and the sale price is then $1.3x \cdot (100\% - 80\%) = 0.26x$, which is less than $1.26x$.

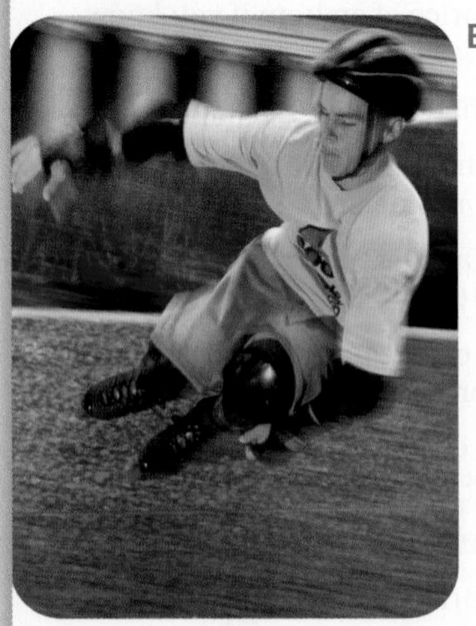

27. **Extended Problem Solving** The pizzas you order for home delivery cost $19. The sales tax is 4.9%, and you plan to give a 15% tip.

a. **Estimate** Estimate the amount of the sales tax. about $1

b. **Estimate** Use mental math to estimate a 15% tip. Explain the method of estimation you use.

c. **Interpret** Estimate the total cost of the order. Is your estimate a *high estimate* or a *low estimate* of the total cost? Explain.

d. Find the exact total cost of the order. How close was your estimate? $22.78. *Sample answer:* My estimate was $1.22 high.

27b. *Sample answer:* About $3; first I rounded the price up to $20. Then because 10% of $20 is $2, and 5% of $20 is half of 10% of $20, I estimated the tip as $2 + $1 = $3.

27c. *Sample answer:* About $24; a high estimate; I rounded the price up to $20 and the tax up to 5%, and also calculated the tip based on the $20 price, so I overestimated both the tax and the tip.

C 28. **Challenge** A store marks up the wholesale price of an item by 60%. A month later the store puts the item on sale. If the store doesn't want to lose money on the item, what is the maximum discount percent the store can use? 37.5%

Mixed Review

Give the place and value of the red digit. Then round the number to that place. (p. 770) 29–32. See margin.

29. 93.21 30. 341.073 31. 1595.962 32. 17,024.981

Evaluate the expression when $x = 5$, $y = 7$, and $z = 10$. (Lesson 1.3)

33. xyz 350 34. $x(3z + y)$ 185 35. $x(5 + yz)$ 375 36. $xz - xy$ 15

Write the percent as a decimal. (Lesson 7.3)

37. 45% 0.45 38. 8.6% 0.086 39. 102% 1.02 40. 0.4% 0.004

41b. $2.34; about 21.3%. *Sample answer:* I wrote and solved $11 + 0.06(11) + t = 14$ to find the tip t, which is $2.34. To find what percent of the food bill $2.34 is, I solved the equation $2.34 = p\% \cdot 11$ to get about 21.3%.

Standardized Test Practice

41. **Extended Response** Your bill for a meal at a diner is $11. The sales tax is 6%, and you plan to give a 15% tip.

a. What is the total cost of the meal? $13.31

b. If you have $14, what is the maximum amount you can give for a tip and still cover the food bill and sales tax? About what percent of the food bill would this tip be? Explain your thinking. See margin.

Going $hopping

You have $500 to spend on items from the list shown. Spend as much of the money as you can using the following conditions:

- Buy no more than 1 of each item.
- Use a coupon for 15% off the original prices of your purchases.
- Add a sales tax of 5% of the sale prices of your purchases.

Hiking backpack .. $47
Digital camera $179
DVD player $90
Skateboard $79
Video game console .. $197
Electric guitar ... $125
Bicycle $130
Television $110
Stereo system ... $250
Music keyboard . $149
Telescope $50

Which items did you buy, and how much money did you spend? Buying the hiking backpack, the digital camera, the skateboard, the electric guitar, and the bicycle results in a total cost of $499.80.

4 ASSESS

Assessment Resources

For more assessment resources, see:
- Assessment Book
- Test and Practice Generator

Mini-Quiz

Find the new price.

1. Wholesale price: $75; Markup percent: 150% $187.50
2. Original price: $80; Discount percent: 20% $64

Find the total cost.

3. Original price: $95; Sales tax: 5% $99.75
4. Food bill: $28; Sales tax: 6%; Tip: 15% $33.88
5. **Challenge** A vendor marks up the wholesale price of his ornaments by 100%. When sales are slow, he puts the ornaments on sale by changing the markup to 80%. By what percent is he going to discount the retail price of the ornaments to reflect the change to an 80% markup? 10%

5 FOLLOW-UP

Diagnosis/Remediation

- Study Guide in Chapter 7 Resource Book, pp. 55–56
- Tutor Place, Ratio, Proportion, and Percent Card 15
- eTutorial Plus Online
- Extra Practice, p. 809
- Lesson Practice in Chapter 7 Resource Book, pp. 52–54

English Learner Support

- Spanish Study Guide
- Multi-Language Visual Glossary
- Chapter Audio Summaries CDs

Challenge

- Challenge Practice in Chapter 7 Resource Book, p. 58
- Teacher's Edition, p. 326F

29–32. See Additional Answers beginning on page AA1.

1 PLAN

Skill Check

Evaluate the expression.

1. 1200 • 0.03 • 5 **180**
2. 15,000 • 0.01 • 4 **600**
3. $1000(1 + 0.01)^2$ **1020.1**
4. Find $2500(1 + 0.025)^3$ to the nearest hundredth. **2692.23**

Lesson Objective

Calculate interest earned and account balances.

Pacing

Suggested Number of Days

Basic Course: 1 day

Average Course: 1 day

Advanced Course: 1 day

Block: 0.5 block with 7.6

Teaching Resources

For a complete list of Teaching Resources, see page 326B.

Transparency

Warm-Up Exercises for this lesson are available on a transparency.

2 TEACH

Motivating the Lesson

Have students brainstorm to create a list of things you can pay to rent, such as videos. Link this discussion to the idea of earning interest from banks by "lending" them money when you make a deposit into a savings account.

LESSON 7.7

Simple *and* Compound Interest

BEFORE	Now	WHY?
You solved percent problems.	You'll calculate interest earned and account balances.	So you can find the amount of a loan with interest, as in Ex. 14.

Vocabulary

interest, p. 362
principal, p. 362
simple interest, p. 362
annual interest rate, p. 362
balance, p. 363
compound interest, p. 363

Bonds People buy bonds as a way to earn money. If a \$1500 bond earns 4% *simple interest* per year on its purchase price, how much will it earn in interest after 2 years?

The amount earned or paid for the use of money is called **interest**. The amount of money deposited or borrowed is the **principal**. Interest that is earned or paid only on the principal is called **simple interest**. The percent of the principal earned or paid per year is the **annual interest rate**.

For example, if you deposit \$3000 into an account that earns simple interest, at an annual rate of 4.5%, then after one year the interest yielded would be \$3000(0.045) = \$135. The interest is only earned on the principal \$3000, so another \$135 would be earned in the second year. During the first three years, the total interest earned would be \$3000(0.045) + \$3000(0.045) + \$3000(0.045) = \$3000(0.045)(3) = \$405. This suggests a formula for finding the amount of simple interest earned over time.

Simple Interest Formula

Simple interest I is given by the formula $I = Prt$ where P is the principal, r is the annual interest rate (written as a decimal), and t is the time in years.

Example 1 *Finding Simple Interest*

Find the interest earned after 2 years for the bond described above.

Solution

$I = Prt$	**Write simple interest formula.**
$= (1500)(0.04)(2)$	**Substitute 1500 for *P*, 0.04 for *r*, and 2 for *t*.**
$= 120$	**Multiply.**

Answer The bond will earn \$120 in interest after 2 years.

Checkpoint

1. A \$1000 bond earns 6% simple annual interest. What is the interest earned after 4 years? **\$240**

NCTM CURRICULUM STANDARDS

Standard 1: Compute fluently

Standard 2: Represent situations using algebraic symbols

Standard 6: Solve problems in math and other contexts

Balance When an account earns interest, the interest is added to the money in the account. The **balance** A of an account that earns simple annual interest is the sum of the principal P and the interest Prt.

$$A = P + Prt \quad \text{or} \quad A = P(1 + rt)$$

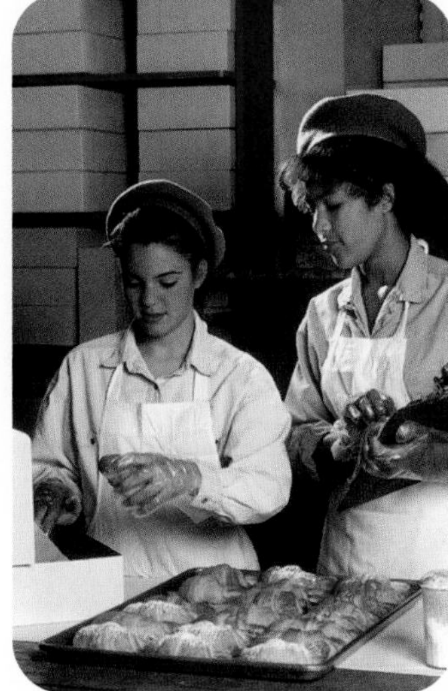

Example 2 *Finding an Interest Rate*

Summer Job You get a summer job at a bakery. Suppose you save \$1400 of your pay and deposit it into an account that earns simple annual interest. After 9 months, the balance is \$1421. Find the annual interest rate.

Solution

Because t in the formula $A = P(1 + rt)$ is the time in years, write 9 months as $\frac{9}{12}$, or $\frac{3}{4}$ year. Then solve for r after substituting values for A, P, and t in $A = P(1 + rt)$.

$A = P(1 + rt)$	**Write formula for finding balance.**
$1421 = 1400\left[1 + r\left(\frac{3}{4}\right)\right]$	**Substitute.**
$1421 = 1400 + 1050r$	**Distributive property**
$21 = 1050r$	**Subtract 1400 from each side.**
$0.02 = r$	**Divide each side by 1050.**

Answer The annual interest rate is 2%.

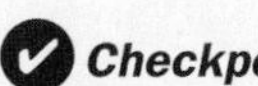

Checkpoint

Find the unknown quantity for an account that earns simple annual interest.

2. $A = \underline{?}$, $P = \$1000$, $r = 2.5\%$, $t = 2$ years **\$1050**

3. $A = \$1424.50$, $P = \underline{?}$, $r = 3.5\%$, $t = 6$ months **\$1400**

Compound Interest **Compound interest** is interest that is earned on both the principal and any interest that has been earned previously. Suppose you deposit \$50 into a savings account that earns 2% interest compounded annually. The table below shows the balance of your account after each of 3 years.

Year	Principal at start of year	Balance at end of year
1	50	$50(1 + 0.02) = 50(1 + 0.02)^1$
2	$50(1 + 0.02)^1$	$50(1 + 0.02)^1 \cdot (1 + 0.02) = 50(1 + 0.02)^2$
3	$50(1 + 0.02)^2$	$50(1 + 0.02)^2 \cdot (1 + 0.02) = 50(1 + 0.02)^3$

The table above suggests a formula, shown on the next page, for finding the balance of an account that earns interest compounded annually.

Reading *Algebra*

When you read the table, notice that the balances at the end of years 2 and 3 are found by adding exponents using the product of powers property.

TIPS *for* NEW TEACHERS

Students may be overwhelmed by the amount of vocabulary in this lesson. Encourage students to talk about the terms and use them correctly as you discuss the examples during class. See Tips for New Teachers in the *Chapter 7 Resource Book*.

Extra Examples

Example 1 Find the simple interest earned on \$500 after 5 years in a money market account paying 5%. **\$125**

Example 2 Jose deposits \$2000 of his tax refund into an account that earns simple annual interest. After 6 months, the balance is \$2040. Find the annual interest rate. **4%**

VISUALIZE

You might consider using play money to help some students visualize the principal and its growth over time as interest is earned.

DIFFERENTIATING INSTRUCTION

Advanced Learners Have students research five different corporate or government bonds to discover how much they paid in interest last year. Have students calculate what they would have earned if they had invested \$1000 in each of the bonds 1 year ago.

Multiple Representations

The calculations in the table at the bottom of page 363 show one way to find compound interest for the first 3 years on an investment. The formula at the top of this page summarizes the method. Show how the formula produces the same year-end balances as the method on page 363, and then continue using the formula to find the balance at the end of the 4th, 5th, and 6th years. Help students visualize how the formula relates to the calculations in the table.

Extra Examples

Example 3 You deposit \$1200 into an account that earns 3.8% interest compounded annually. Find the balance after 5 years. **\$1446**

Common Error

Before discussing Example 3, review the order of operations and discuss how to evaluate the compound interest formula correctly. In particular, watch for students who multiply the quantity $1 + r$ by the principal P before applying the power t to the quantity.

Concept Check

What formula do you use to find the balance in an account 5 years after \$1000 was deposited if the account pays 3% interest compounded annually? $A = 1000(1 + 0.03)^5$

Daily Puzzler

How many years would it take to double the balance in an account receiving 5% interest compounded annually? Hint: Use the *guess, check,* and *revise* strategy. 15 y

Note *Worthy*

In your notes, you can make a concept grid that includes a definition, characteristics, an example, and a nonexample of compound interest. Your concept grid should have the formula for calculating compound interest.

Compound Interest Formula

When an account earns interest compounded annually, the balance A is given by the formula

$$A = P(1 + r)^t$$

where P is the principal, r is the annual interest rate (written as a decimal), and t is the time in years.

Example 3 *Calculating Compound Interest*

You deposit \$1500 into an account that earns 2.4% interest compounded annually. Find the balance after 6 years.

Solution

$A = P(1 + r)^t$ **Write formula.**

$= 1500(1 + 0.024)^6$ **Substitute.**

≈ 1729.38 **Use a calculator.**

Answer The balance of the account after 6 years is about \$1729.38.

7.7 Exercises

More Practice, p. 809

INTERNET eWorkbook Plus CLASSZONE.COM

Guided Practice

Vocabulary Check

1. In the simple interest formula $I = Prt$, what does P represent? **the principal, or the amount deposited or borrowed**
2. How is compound interest different from simple interest? **See margin.**

2. Sample answer: In simple interest, interest is earned only on the original principal, while in compound interest, interest is earned both on the principal and any previously-earned interest.

Skill Check

For an account that earns simple annual interest, find the interest and the balance of the account.

3. $P = \$500$, $r = 7\%$, $t = 4$ years **\$140, \$640**
4. $P = \$2500$, $r = 3\%$, $t = 9$ months **\$56.25, \$2556.25**

Find the unknown quantity for an account that earns simple annual interest.

5. $A = \$563$, $P = \$500$, $r = \underline{?}$, $t = 7$ years **1.8%**
6. $A = \$1670$, $P = \$1600$, $r = 3.5\%$, $t = \underline{?}$ **1.25 y, or 15 mo**
7. **Savings Account** You deposit \$700 into a savings account that earns 2% interest compounded annually. Find the balance of the account after 4 years. Round your answer to the nearest cent. **\$757.70**

Practice and Problem Solving

Homework Help

Example	Exercises
1	8-13, 17
2	8-16
3	18-21

Online Resources
CLASSZONE.COM
- More Examples
- eTutorial Plus

In the following exercises, you may find it helpful to use a calculator for compound interest.

For an account that earns simple annual interest, find the interest and the balance of the account.

A **8.** $P = \$1250$, $r = 4\%$, $t = 10$ years $500, $1750

9. $P = \$325$, $r = 7\%$, $t = 8$ years $182, $507

10. $P = \$600$, $r = 2.7\%$, $t = 4.5$ years $72.90, $672.90

11. $P = \$3200$, $r = 3.5\%$, $t = 3.5$ years $392, $3592

12. $P = \$100$, $r = 8\%$, $t = 6$ months $4, $104

13. $P = \$495$, $r = 5\%$, $t = 21$ months $43.31, $538.31

14. Loan You loan your brother $300 and charge him 2% simple annual interest. He promises to repay you one year later. How much will your brother have to pay you? $306

15. The table shows three accounts that earn simple annual interest. Copy and complete the table by finding the unknown quantity.

Balance	Principal	Interest rate	Time
$5,000	$4,000	5%	? 5 y
$11,160	? $9000	8%	36 months
$3,207	$3,000	? 4.6%	18 months

16. Suppose you deposit $800 into an account that earns simple annual interest. After 2 years, the account balance is $900. Find the annual interest rate. 6.25%

17. Error Analysis A $200 bond earns 5.5% simple annual interest. Describe and correct the error in finding the total interest earned after 6 months.

$I = Prt$
$= (200)(0.055)(6)$
$= 66$

17. In the formula, t represents the time in years. Because 6 months = 0.5 year, 0.5 should have been substituted for t: $I = Prt = (200)(0.055)(0.5) = 5.5$. The interest earned is $5.50.

For an account that earns interest compounded annually, find the balance of the account. Round your answer to the nearest cent.

18. $P = \$800$, $r = 5\%$, $t = 3$ years $926.10

19. $P = \$2200$, $r = 7\%$, $t = 8$ years $3780.01

20. $P = \$1750$, $r = 2.3\%$, $t = 4$ years $1916.64

21. $P = \$680$, $r = 6.2\%$, $t = 10$ years $1240.95

B **22. Bonds** A certain bond pays simple annual interest directly to the investor every 6 months. Suppose an investor purchases this bond for $5000 at a 4.5% annual interest rate. What is the total amount of interest paid after 6 months? 18 months? 30 months? $112.50; $337.50; $562.50

23. Compare The accounts below earn interest compounded annually. Which account will have the greater balance in the given time? account A

Account A
Principal: $150
Interest rate: 3.25%
Time: 20 years

Account B
Principal: $150
Interest rate: 6.5%
Time: 10 years

24. ***Writing*** Does the amount of interest earned each year *increase*, *decrease*, or *stay the same* in a simple interest account? in a compound interest account? Explain your answers. See margin.

In the Real World

Bonds To pay for the 1933 construction of the Golden Gate Bridge, the state of California raised $35 million by selling bonds. The state had paid about $39 million in interest by the time the last of the bonds were repaid in 1971. What percent of the $35 million raised in 1933 is the $39 million paid in interest? about 111.4%

3 APPLY

ASSIGNMENT GUIDE

Basic Course
Day 1: pp. 365-366 Exs. 8-16, 18-22, 29-37

Average Course
Day 1: pp. 365-366 Exs. 10-19, 22-27, 29-37

Advanced Course
Day 1: pp. 365-366 Exs. 12-17, 20-30*, 33-37

Block
pp. 365-366 Exs. 10-19, 22-27, 29-37 (with 7.6)

EXTRA PRACTICE

- Student Edition, p. 809
- Chapter 7 Resource Book, pp. 62-64
- Test and Practice Generator

TRANSPARENCY

Even-numbered answers are available on transparencies. A support transparency is available for Exercise 25.

HOMEWORK CHECK

When you review students' homework for this lesson, go over the following exercises to check understanding of key concepts.
Basic: 8, 10, 11, 16, 18
Average: 10, 13, 16, 17, 19
Advanced: 12, 13, 16, 17, 21

COMMON ERROR

In Exercise 12, watch for students who calculate interest for 6 years instead of 6 months, which should be calculated using $t = \frac{1}{2}$. Similarly, check these students' calculations in Exercise 13 where $t = 1\frac{3}{4}$.

24. See Additional Answers beginning on page AA1.

4 ASSESS

ASSESSMENT RESOURCES

For more assessment resources, see:
- Assessment Book
- Test and Practice Generator

MINI-QUIZ

Find the simple interest and the balance of the account.

1. $P = \$500$, $r = 3\%$, $t = 10$ years **\$150, \$650**
2. $P = \$220$, $r = 2.5\%$, $t = 5$ years **\$27.50, \$247.50**
3. A deposit of \$650 is made into an account that earns interest compounded annually. If the interest rate is 3%, what is the balance after 4 years? **\$731.58**
4. **Challenge** At the start of every year, Val deposits \$2000 into an account that earns 5% interest compounded annually. What is the balance at the end of the third year? **\$6620.25**

5 FOLLOW-UP

DIAGNOSIS/REMEDIATION

- Study Guide in Chapter 7 Resource Book, pp. 65–66
- eTutorial Plus Online
- Extra Practice, p. 809
- Lesson Practice in Chapter 7 Resource Book, pp. 62–64

ENGLISH LEARNER SUPPORT

- Spanish Study Guide
- Multi-Language Visual Glossary
- Chapter Audio Summaries CDs

CHALLENGE

- Challenge Practice in Chapter 7 Resource Book, p. 68
- Teacher's Edition, p. 326F

25b. See Additional Answers beginning on page AA1.

25c. ***Sample answer:*** **The points on the simple interest graph lie along a straight line, while the points on the compound interest graph lie on a curve that keeps rising more and more steeply.**

27. 10 y. ***Sample answer:*** **The account will double when the interest earned equals the principal. The interest earned is $P(0.1)t$, so I reasoned that this quantity will equal P when $0.1t = 1$, or when $t = 10$.**

28b. Yes. ***Sample answer:*** **You will have \$18,459.87. I found this quantity by calculating the sum $3000(1 + 0.07)^5 + 3000(1 + 0.07)^4 + 3000(1 + 0.07)^3 + 3000(1 + 0.07)^2 + 3000(1 + 0.07)^1$. This represents the first \$3000 earning compound interest for 5 years, the second \$3000 earning compound interest for 4 years, and so on.**

25. Extended Problem Solving You deposit \$1000 into an account that earns 5% simple annual interest, and your friend deposits \$1000 into an account that earns 5% interest compounded annually.

a. Calculate Copy and complete the table.

Years	Simple interest account balance	Compound interest account balance
1	? \$1050	? \$1050
2	? \$1100	? \$1102.50
5	? \$1250	? \$1276.28
10	? \$1500	? \$1628.89
20	? \$2000	? \$2653.30

b. Graph Make a scatter plot of the data. Show the time in years on the x-axis and the account balance on the y-axis. Plot points representing the simple interest account balance in blue and the compound interest account balance in red. **See margin.**

c. Compare Describe how the graph of the simple interest balance is different from the graph of the compound interest balance.

26. You deposit \$1400 into an account that earns 4% interest compounded annually. You check the balance of the account after 5 years. By about what percent did the balance of the account change over those 5 years? **about 21.7%**

C **27. Critical Thinking** How long will it take you to double your principal when you deposit it into an account that earns 10% simple annual interest? Explain how you found your answer. **See margin.**

28. Challenge At the start of every year, you deposit \$3000 into an account that earns 7% interest compounded annually.

a. What is the balance at the end of the second year? third year? **\$6644.70; \$10,319.83**

b. Will you have enough money at the end of the fifth year to buy a car that costs \$18,000? Explain your reasoning. **See margin.**

Mixed Review

Solve the equation. Check your solution. *(Lesson 3.3)*

29. $5x + 9 = 2x + 6$ **−1** **30.** $-5y - 13 = 7 - 15y$ **2**

Find the least common multiple of the numbers. *(Lesson 4.4)*

31. 3, 7 **21** **32.** 9, 45 **45** **33.** 12, 18 **36** **34.** 40, 50 **200**

35. Video Game You buy a video game that is on sale for 15% off the original price of \$35. Find the sale price. *(Lesson 7.6)* **\$29.75**

Standardized Test Practice

36. Multiple Choice A \$1200 bond earns 8.5% simple annual interest. What is the interest earned after 15 months? **B**

A. \$15.30 **B.** \$127.50 **C.** \$1275 **D.** \$1530

37. Multiple Choice You deposit \$3500 into an account that earns 10% interest compounded annually. What is the balance after 2 years? **H**

F. \$700 **G.** \$4200 **H.** \$4235 **I.** \$7000

7.7 Computing Compound Interest

Goal Use a calculator to compute compound interest.

In many investment accounts, the interest is compounded several times a year. The balance A of an account that earns interest compounded n times a year is given by the formula

$$A = P\left(1 + \frac{r}{n}\right)^{nt}$$

where P is the principal, r is the annual interest rate (written as a decimal), and t is the time in years.

Example

You deposit \$1000 into an account that earns 6% interest compounded semiannually. What is the balance after 4 years?

When interest is compounded semiannually, or twice a year, $n = 2$.

1 Use the compound interest formula given above.

$$A = P\left(1 + \frac{r}{n}\right)^{nt} \quad \textbf{Write compound interest formula.}$$

$$= 1000\left(1 + \frac{0.06}{2}\right)^{2 \cdot 4} \quad \textbf{Substitute.}$$

2 Enter the expression $1000\left(1 + \frac{0.06}{2}\right)^{2 \cdot 4}$ into your calculator.

Keystrokes

1000 [( ] **1** [+] **.06** [÷] **2** [ )] [^] [( ] **2** [×] **4** [ )] [=]

```
1000(1+.06÷2)→
   1266.770081
```

Answer The balance of the account after 4 years is about \$1266.77.

Draw Conclusions

For an account that earns compound interest, find the balance of the account when interest is compounded as specified.

1. $P = \$200$, $r = 5\%$, $t = 9$ years; compounded semiannually **\$311.93**
2. $P = \$3000$, $r = 6.2\%$, $t = 7$ years; compounded quarterly **\$4614.87**
3. $P = \$500$, $r = 4\%$, $t = 8$ years; compounded monthly **\$688.20**
4. **Critical Thinking** In the example above, would the account have the greatest balance if the interest were compounded annually, semiannually, quarterly, or monthly? Justify your answer. **See margin.**

In Step 2 of the example, you can simplify the expression to $1000(1.03)^8$ before you enter it into your calculator.

4. Monthly. ***Sample answer:*** **Annual compounding gives a balance of $1000(1 + 0.06)^4 \approx \$1262.48$, semiannual compounding gives a balance of \$1266.77 as shown in the example, quarterly compounding gives a balance of $1000\left(1 + \frac{0.06}{4}\right)^{4 \cdot 4} \approx \$1268.99$, monthly compounding gives a balance of $1000\left(1 + \frac{0.06}{12}\right)^{12 \cdot 4} \approx \$1270.49$.**

NCTM CURRICULUM STANDARDS

Standard 2: Represent situations using algebraic symbols; Analyze situations using algebraic symbols

1 PLAN

Learn the Method

- Students will use a calculator to compute compound interest.
- Students can check their answers to Exercises 18–21 on page 365.

Grouping

Students should work individually.

2 TEACH

Discussion

Point out the Tech Help note. Ask students whether they think fewer mistakes would occur by simplifying the equation first or by keystroking the expression without simplifying.

Extra Examples

Example You deposit \$800 into an account that earns 5% interest compounded quarterly. What is the balance after 5 years? **\$1025.63**

3 CLOSE

Assessment

1. In the Example, why is the exponent given as 2 • 4? **Compounding semiannually means twice per year, so $n = 2$; t is the number of years the account is earning interest, so $t = 4$. Therefore, $nt = 2 \cdot 4$.**
2. Would the balance found in the Example be the same if the account earned interest compounded annually for 8 years? Explain. **No; this amount would be found using $A = 1000(1 + 0.06)^{1 \cdot 8}$ which gives $A = \$1593.85$.**

Additional Resources

The following resources are available to help review the materials in Lessons 7.5–7.7.

Chapter 7 Resource Book
- Lesson Practice
- Study Guide

Assessment Book
- Chapter 7 Quiz 2

Technology
- Test and Practice Generator
- eTutorial CD-ROM

Internet
- Classzone
- eWorkbook Plus Online
- eTutorial Plus Online

English Learner Support
- Spanish Study Guide
- Multi-Language Visual Glossary
- Chapter Audio Summaries CDs

CHAPTER 7

Chapter Review

Vocabulary Review

percent, p. 329	percent of decrease, p. 352	interest, p. 362	annual interest rate, p. 362
percent of change, p. 352	markup, p. 357	principal, p. 362	balance, p. 363
percent of increase, p. 352	discount, p. 358	simple interest, p. 362	compound interest, p. 363

Copy and complete the statement.

1. A(n) _?_ is a ratio whose denominator is 100. **percent**
2. A(n) _?_ is an increase from the wholesale price of an item to the retail price. **markup**
3. Is the percent of change from 85 to 34 a *percent of increase* or a *percent of decrease*? **percent of decrease**
4. You open an account with \$500. After 1 year, the account has \$510. Identify the principal, interest earned, and balance. **principal: \$500, interest earned: \$10, balance: \$510**

7.1 Percents and Fractions

Examples on pp. 329–330

Goal

Use fractions to find the percent of a number.

Example Write 44% as a fraction and $\frac{4}{5}$ as a percent.

a. $44\% = \frac{44}{100} = \frac{11}{25}$

b. $\frac{4}{5} = \frac{4 \cdot 20}{5 \cdot 20} = \frac{80}{100} = 80\%$

Example Find 75% of 32.

$75\% \text{ of } 32 = \frac{3}{4} \cdot 32$ **Write percent as a fraction.**

$= \frac{96}{4}$ **Multiply.**

$= 24$ **Simplify.**

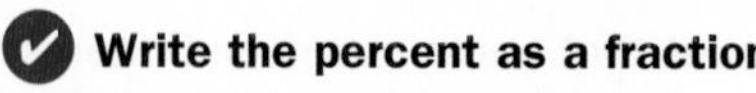

Write the percent as a fraction.

5. 53% $\frac{53}{100}$
6. 85% $\frac{17}{20}$
7. 60% $\frac{3}{5}$
8. 28% $\frac{7}{25}$

Write the fraction as a percent.

9. $\frac{31}{100}$ 31%
10. $\frac{7}{20}$ 35%
11. $\frac{31}{50}$ 62%
12. $\frac{24}{25}$ 96%

Find the percent of the number.

13. 25% of 76 **19**
14. 60% of 50 **30**
15. 20% of 25 **5**
16. 90% of 70 **63**

The following resources are available to help review the materials in this chapter.

 ***Chapter 7 Resource Book***

- Chapter Review Games and Activities, p. 69
- Cumulative Practice, Chs. 1–7

English/Spanish Chapter Reviews and Tests

Chapter Audio Summaries CDs

eTutorial CD-ROM

eWorkbook Plus Online

eTutorial Plus Online

7.2 Percents and Proportions

Examples on pp. 335–336

Goal

Use proportions to solve percent problems.

Example **117 is 65% of what number?**

$\frac{a}{b} = \frac{p}{100}$ **Write proportion.**

$\frac{117}{b} = \frac{65}{100}$ **Substitute 117 for *a* and 65 for *p*.**

$117 \cdot 100 = 65 \cdot b$ **Cross products property**

$11{,}700 = 65b$ **Multiply.**

$180 = b$ **Divide each side by 65.**

Use a proportion to answer the question.

17. 36 is 24% of what number? 150 **18.** What number is 92% of 75? 69

19. What percent of 85 is 34? 40% **20.** 51 is 60% of what number? 85

21. What number is 22% of 150? 33 **22.** What percent of 120 is 108? 90%

7.3 Percents and Decimals

Examples on pp. 340–341

Goal

Use decimals to find the percent of a number.

Example **Write 0.6 and $\frac{5}{8}$ as percents.**

a. $0.6 = 0.60 = 60\%$ **b.** $\frac{5}{8} = 0.625 = 62.5\%$

Example **Find 21.5% of 80.**

21.5% of $80 = 0.215 \cdot 80$ **Write percent as a decimal.**

$= 17.2$ **Multiply.**

Write the decimal as a percent.

23. 0.589 58.9% **24.** 1.3 130% **25.** 0.48 48% **26.** 3 300%

Write the fraction as a percent.

27. $\frac{3}{8}$ 37.5% **28.** $\frac{9}{16}$ 56.25% **29.** $\frac{2}{3}$ $66.\overline{6}\%$ **30.** $\frac{6}{5}$ 120%

Find the percent of the number.

31. 45% of 75 33.75 **32.** 30.2% of 130 39.26 **33.** 105% of 450 472.5 **34.** 0.8% of 675 5.4

35. Shopping Last year you spent \$210 on clothes. You spent 37.5% of this amount on school clothes. How much money did you spend last year on school clothes? \$78.75

7.4 The Percent Equation

Examples on pp. 345–347

Goal

Use an equation to solve percent problems.

Example **What percent of 70 is 31.5?**

$a = p\% \cdot b$	**Write percent equation.**
$31.5 = p\% \cdot 70$	**Substitute 31.5 for *a* and 70 for *b*.**
$0.45 = p\%$	**Divide each side by 70.**
$45\% = p\%$	**Write decimal as a percent.**

Use the percent equation to answer the question.

36. What number is 40% of 26? **10.4**

37. What percent of 130 is 104? **80%**

38. What percent of 80 is 72? **90%**

39. 2.56 is 8% of what number? **32**

7.5 Percent of Change

Examples on pp. 352–354

Goal

Solve problems involving percent of change.

Example **Find the percent of decrease from 55 to 33.**

$$p\% = \frac{\text{Amount of decrease}}{\text{Original amount}}$$ **Write formula for percent of decrease.**

$$= \frac{55 - 33}{55}$$ **Substitute.**

$$= \frac{22}{55} = 40\%$$ **Subtract. Then write as a percent.**

Example **Find the new amount when you increase 90 by 24%.**

New amount = **Original amount** • (100% + p%)

$= 90 \cdot (100\% + 24\%)$	**Substitute.**
$= 90 \cdot 124\%$	**Add percents.**
$= 90 \cdot 1.24 = 111.6$	**Write as a decimal. Multiply.**

Identify the percent of change as an *increase* or a *decrease*. Then find the percent of change.

40. Original: 50
New: 90
increase; 80%

41. Original: 40
New: 42
increase; 5%

42. Original: 25
New: 24
decrease; 4%

43. Original: 96
New: 36
decrease; 62.5%

Find the new amount.

44. Increase 38 by 10%. **41.8**

45. Decrease 670 by 42%. **388.6**

7.6 Percent Applications

Examples on pp. 357–359

Goal

Find markups, discounts, sales tax, and tips.

Example **You buy a cell phone that is 20% off the original price of $129. Find the sale price.**

Sale price = **Original price** • (100% − **Discount percent**)	
= **129** • (100% − **20%**)	**Substitute.**
= 129 • 80%	**Subtract percents.**
= 129 • 0.8	**Write 80% as a decimal.**
= 103.2	**Multiply. The sale price is $103.20.**

Use the given information to find the new price.

46. Wholesale price: $95
Markup percent: 120% **$209**

47. Original price: $330
Discount percent: 15% **$280.50**

7.7 Simple and Compound Interest

Examples on pp. 362–364

Goal

Calculate interest earned and account balances.

Example **Suppose you deposit $400 into an account that earns 5% simple annual interest. Find the balance of the account after 3 years.**

$A = P(1 + rt)$	**Write formula for finding balance.**
$= 400(1 + 0.05 \cdot 3)$	**Substitute 400 for *P*, 0.05 for *r*, and 3 for *t*.**
$= 460$	**Evaluate. The balance is $460.**

Example **You deposit $500 into an account that earns 4.5% interest compounded annually. Find the balance of the account after 6 years.**

$A = P(1 + r)^t$	**Write formula for finding balance.**
$= 500(1 + 0.045)^6$	**Substitute 500 for *P*, 0.045 for *r*, and 6 for *t*.**
≈ 651.13	**Evaluate. The balance is about $651.13.**

48. Suppose you deposit $900 into an account that earns 4% simple annual interest. Find the balance of the account after 6 months. **$918**

49. You deposit $6000 into an account that earns 3.8% interest compounded annually. Find the balance of the account after 7 years. **$7789.92**

ADDITIONAL RESOURCES

Assessment Book

- Chapter Test (3 levels), pp. 81–86
- Standardized Chapter Test, p. 87
- Alternative Assessment, pp. 88–89

Test and Practice Generator

CHAPTER 7

Chapter Test

Write the percent as a fraction or the fraction as a percent.

1. 33% $\frac{33}{100}$ **2.** 65% $\frac{13}{20}$ **3.** $\frac{6}{25}$ 24% **4.** $\frac{7}{50}$ 14%

Write the percent as a decimal or the decimal as a percent.

5. 68% 0.68 **6.** 42.5% 0.425 **7.** 0.9 90% **8.** 1.47 147%

Find the percent of the number.

9. 75% of 68 51 **10.** 40% of 180 72 **11.** 27.5% of 300 82.5 **12.** 0.6% of 980 5.88

13. Baseball A baseball team won 55% of its 160 games during a season. How many games did the team win during the season? 88 games

Use a proportion or the percent equation to answer the question.

14. What number is 24% of 95? 22.8

15. What number is 78% of 370? 288.6

16. What percent of 90 is 60? $66.\overline{6}\%$

17. What percent of 70 is 31.5? 45%

18. 4.5 is 0.9% of what number? 500

19. 80 is 125% of what number? 64

20. Stamps Your friend has 480 stamps in a collection. Of these, 156 stamps depict historical events. What percent of the stamps in the collection depict historical events? $32\frac{1}{2}\%$

Identify the percent of change as an *increase* or a *decrease*. Then find the percent of change.

21. Original: 30 New: 21 decrease; 30%

22. Original: 50 New: 55 increase; 10%

23. Original: 128 New: 176 increase; 37.5%

24. Original: 380 New: 323 decrease; 15%

25. Teen Spending In 2000, about $155 billion was spent by teenagers in the United States. In 2001, the amount spent by teenagers increased by about 11%. About how much money did teenagers spend in 2001? about $172 billion

Use the given information to find the new amount.

26. Wholesale price: $400 Markup percent: 110% $840

27. Original price: $650 Discount percent: 20% $520

28. Food bill: $30 Sales tax: 6.5% $31.95

29. Bonds A $500 bond earns 6% simple annual interest. Find the total interest earned after 5 years. $150

30. Savings Account You deposit $1800 into a savings account that earns 2% interest compounded annually. Find the balance after 2 years. $1872.72

Chapter Standardized Test

Test-Taking Strategy If you are having trouble with a question, skip it and return to it after you have answered the other questions on the test.

1. What is 45% as a fraction? B

A. $\frac{1}{45}$ **B.** $\frac{9}{20}$ **C.** $\frac{9}{10}$ **D.** $\frac{20}{9}$

2. What number is 40% of 20? G

F. 0.8 **G.** 8 **H.** 80 **I.** 800

3. What is $\frac{19}{50}$ as a percent? C

A. 19% **B.** 31% **C.** 38% **D.** 260%

4. What percent of 140 is 56? F

F. 40% **G.** 56% **H.** 84% **I.** 250%

5. In a survey of 380 people, 25% said that they enjoy reading before going to sleep. How many of the people surveyed enjoy reading before going to sleep? C

A. 25 people **B.** 76 people
C. 95 people **D.** 355 people

6. Which situation represents the greatest percent of increase? I

F. Original: 60 New: 75
G. Original: 900 New: 1000
H. Original: 140 New: 200
I. Original: 30 New: 60

7. What is the new amount when you increase 40 by 25%? A

A. 50 **B.** 65 **C.** 70 **D.** 100

8. A hat costs $28 after a 30% discount is applied. What was the hat's original price? H

F. $8.40 **G.** $36.40 **H.** $40.00 **I.** $58.00

9. The food bill for a meal at a restaurant is $12. The sales tax is 6.5%, and you leave a 15% tip. What is the total cost of the meal? D

A. $12.22 **B.** $12.96 **C.** $14.15 **D.** $14.58

10. A retail store buys a DVD player from a manufacturer for $140. The store then marks up the price by 115%. What is the retail price of the DVD player? H

F. $161 **G.** $255 **H.** $301 **I.** $1610

11. An $800 bond earns 4% simple annual interest. How much will the bond earn in interest after 6 years? C

A. $16 **B.** $32 **C.** $192 **D.** $1920

12. Short Response A backpack is on sale for 15% off the original price of $40. Another backpack is on sale for 40% off the original price of $55. Which backpack costs less after the discounts are applied? How much less? Explain how you got your answers. See margin.

13. Extended Response Suppose you deposit $500 into an account that earns 5% simple annual interest, and your friend deposits $350 into an account that earns 5.5% interest compounded annually.

a. Find the balance of each account after 10 years. your account: $750, friend's account: $597.85

b. For each account, find the total interest earned after 10 years. your account: $250, friend's account: $247.85

c. Which account balance will have the greater amount of change after 10 years? Will this account balance also have the greater percent of change after 10 years? Explain your reasoning. See margin.

Additional Resources

Assessment Book
- Standardized Chapter Test, p. 87

Test and Practice Generator

12. The second backpack; $1. *Sample answer:* The sale price of the first backpack is $40 \cdot (100\% - 15\%) = \$34$, while the sale price of the second backpack is $55 \cdot (100\% - 40\%) = \$33$, which is $1 less.

13c. Your account; no. *Sample answer:* The percent of change for your account is $\frac{250}{500} = 50\%$, while the percent of change for the friend's account is $\frac{247.85}{350} \approx 71\%$. This is a greater percent of change because, while the amount of change is about the same, the original amount is much lower.

USING RUBRICS

The rubric given on the pupil page is a sample of a three-level rubric. Other rubrics may contain four, five, or six levels. For more information on rubrics, see the Professional Development Book.

TEST-TAKING TIP

Caution students, especially advanced students, to show all of the steps they perform when solving a short response question. Some students may do part of their calculations mentally and then neglect to write down enough information to receive full credit. Encourage students to "think like a reviewer" who is scoring their work, asking themselves if they have shown all of the important information.

 COMMON ERROR

Students can become so focused on doing all of the necessary computations and getting a solution for a short response question that they fail to answer the question posed. Remind students to quickly read the problem again after completing their computations. Stress that the result of their calculations is not always the answer to the question.

VISUALIZE

Suggest that students draw percent bar models, like those they used in Concept Activity 7.2, to find the retail prices of the CD player at the store and on the Internet.

Building Test-Taking Skills

Strategies for Answering Short Response Questions

Scoring Rubric

Full Credit
- answer is correct, *and*
- work or reasoning is included

Partial Credit
- answer is correct, but reasoning is incorrect, *or*
- answer is incorrect, but reasoning is correct

No Credit
- no answer is given, *or*
- answer makes no sense

Problem A CD player is on sale at a store for 25% off the retail price of \$120. If you buy the CD player at the store, you pay a 5% sales tax on the sale price. An identical CD player is on sale at an Internet site for 30% off the retail price of \$120. If you buy the CD player online, you pay a \$20 shipping cost. Which is less, the total cost at the store or the total cost online?

Full credit solution

The total cost at the store is the sum of the sale price and a 5% sales tax on the sale price.

The steps of the solution are clearly written.

Sale price = Retail price − Discount
= 120 − 25% • 120 = 120 − 0.25 • 120 = 90

The correct calculations are performed to find the total cost at the store and the total cost online.

Total cost at store = Sale price + Sales tax
= 90 + 5% • 90 = 90 + 0.05 • 90 = 94.50

The total cost online is the sum of the sale price and the shipping cost.

Sale price = Retail price − Discount
= 120 − 30% • 120 = 120 − 0.3 • 120 = 84

Total cost online = Sale price + Shipping cost
= 84 + 20 = 104

The question asked is answered correctly.

The total cost at the store, \$94.50, is less than the total cost online, \$104.

Partial credit solution

The total cost at the store and the total cost online are correct.

Total cost at store = \$90 + \$4.50 = \$94.50

Total cost online = \$84 + \$20 = \$104

There are no explanations to support the student's calculations.

Because \$94.50 is less than \$104, the total cost at the store is less than the total cost online.

Partial credit solution

The sales tax should be calculated using a percent of the sale price, not of the original price.

Sale price at store = $120 - 0.25 \cdot 120 = 90$
Sales tax = $0.05 \cdot 120 = 6$
Total cost at store = $90 + 6 = 96$
Sale price online = $120 - 0.3 \cdot 120 = 84$
Shipping cost = 20
Total cost online = $84 + 20 = 104$
The total cost is less at the store than online.

The total cost online is correct.

No credit solution

The student wrongly interpreted a 25% discount as a \$25 discount and a 5% sales tax as a \$5 sales tax.

Total cost at store = Retail price − Discount + Sales tax
$= 120 - 25 + 5 = 100$

Total cost online = Retail price − Discount + Shipping
$= 120 - 30 + 20 = 110$

The CD player costs \$100 at the store and \$110 online.

The total cost at the store and the total cost online are incorrect, and the question isn't answered.

Checkpoint

Score each solution to the short response question below as *full credit*, *partial credit*, or *no credit*. Explain your reasoning.

Problem The speed of light is about 3×10^8 meters per second in space. In 2 hours, how many meters does light travel? Write your answer in scientific notation.

1. $(3 \times 10^8) \div 2 = 1.5 \times 10^8$. In 2 h, light travels 1.5×10^8 m.

2. Because $\frac{60 \text{ sec}}{1 \text{ min}} \times \frac{60 \text{ min}}{1 \text{ h}} \times 2 \text{ h} = 7200$ sec, there are 7200 seconds in 2 hours. In 2 hours, light travels $7200 \times (3 \times 10^8) = 21{,}600 \times 10^8 = 2.16 \times 10^{12}$ meters.

1–3. See margin.

3. Because 60 sec = 1 min and 60 min = 1 h, there are 3600 seconds in 1 hour. So, light travels $3600 \times (3 \times 10^8) = 1.08 \times 10^{12}$ meters.

Watch Out

When solving a problem that involves measurements, convert between units if necessary.

Test-Taking Skills

1. **No credit. *Sample answer:* The approach shown is incorrect, since the distance is found by multiplying rate times time, not by dividing. Also, there is no explanation of the work, and the necessary measurement conversions are not carried out.**
2. **Full credit. *Sample answer:* The answer is correct, the appropriate steps are described and carried out, and the measurement conversions are carried out correctly.**
3. **Partial credit. *Sample answer:* The measurement conversions are carried out correctly, and multiplication is applied and carried out correctly, but the question is not answered correctly because the solution represents the distance traveled in 1 hour, not 2 hours.**

2. 149,600,000 km, 778,400,000 km, 227,900,000 km, 57,900,000 km, 4,498,200,000 km, 1,426,700,000 km, 2,870,900,000 km, 108,200,000 km; Mercury, Venus, Earth, Mars, Jupiter, Saturn, Uranus, Neptune

11. Your friend. *Sample answer:* Your odds of winning are 1 to 49 = 3 to 147, which is less than your friend's odds of 3 to 140.

Unit 2 Practicing Test-Taking Skills

Chapters 4–7

Short Response

1. You are arranging 48 tables for a science fair. You want each row to have the same number of tables. You can have at most 6 tables per row and at most 20 rows. How many different arrangements are possible? **3 arrangements**

2. The table shows the mean distance of each planet from the Sun. Write the mean distances in standard notation. Then list the planets in order from the least to the greatest mean distance from the Sun. **See margin.**

Planet	Distance from Sun (km)
Earth	1.496×10^8
Jupiter	7.784×10^8
Mars	2.279×10^8
Mercury	5.79×10^7
Neptune	4.4982×10^9
Saturn	1.4267×10^9
Uranus	2.8709×10^9
Venus	1.082×10^8

3. A recipe calls for $\frac{2}{3}$ cup of milk, $\frac{1}{2}$ cup of sugar, and $2\frac{1}{4}$ cups of flour. You need to reduce the recipe by half. How much of each ingredient do you need? **$\frac{1}{3}$ c milk, $\frac{1}{4}$ c sugar, $1\frac{1}{8}$ c flour**

4. A model train is $5\frac{1}{4}$ inches long. The scale used for the model is 1 inch : 160 inches. What is the length of the actual train? **840 in. or 70 ft**

5. A store sells hot dogs in packages of 10 and hot dog buns in packages of 6. You want to buy an equal number of hot dogs and hot dog buns. What is the least number of packages of hot dogs and hot dog buns you can buy? **3 packages of hot dogs and 5 packages of buns**

6. For 5 days a week, you walk from home to school and back home. It takes you 14 minutes to walk each way. How many hours per week do you spend walking from home to school and back home? Write your answer as a mixed number. **$2\frac{1}{3}$ h**

7. You are ordering dinner at a restaurant. For the pasta, you can choose spaghetti, ziti, or shells. For a pasta topping, you can choose meatballs, veal, chicken, or eggplant. For the sauce, you can choose tomato sauce or cheese sauce. How many dinner combinations are possible? **24 dinner combinations**

8. You enlarge a 4 inch by 6 inch photo so that the shorter side is 8.5 inches long. What is the length of the longer side? **12.75 in.**

9. The original price of a hat is \$28. You can buy it online for \$17, or you can buy it at the store and use a coupon for a 30% discount. Does the hat cost less if you buy it online or at the store? **online**

10. The circle graph shows the results of a survey asking 800 students what they prefer to receive as a gift. Of the students surveyed, how many more chose clothes than sports equipment? **64 students**

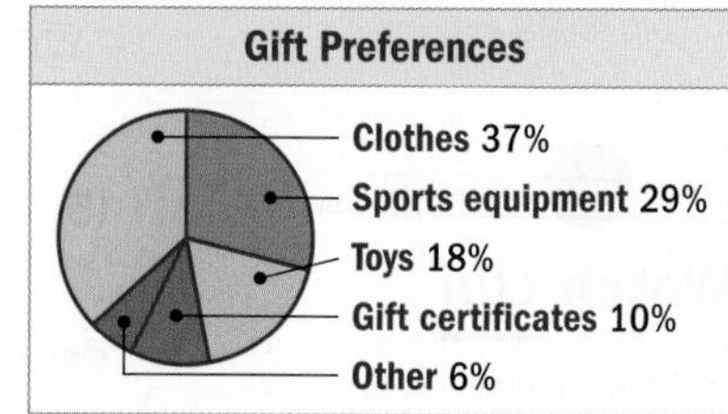

11. The odds in favor of your winning a raffle are 1 to 49. The odds in favor of your friend's winning are 3 to 140. Who has the greater chance of winning the raffle, you or your friend? Explain your reasoning. **See margin.**

Multiple Choice

12. What is the prime factorization of 620? C

A. $2 \cdot 3^2 \cdot 5 \cdot 7$ B. $2 \cdot 5 \cdot 61$
C. $2^2 \cdot 5 \cdot 31$ D. $2^7 \cdot 5$

13. What is the greatest common factor of $15x^3y^5$ and $6xy^2$? G

F. $30x^3y^5$ G. $3xy^2$ H. $3x^3y^5$ I. $30xy^2$

14. Suppose you deposit $400 into an account that earns 3% simple annual interest. What is the account balance after 9 months? C

A. $9 B. $108 C. $409 D. $508

15. Given $\triangle ABC \sim \triangle DEF$, what is the length of $\overline{DE}$? G

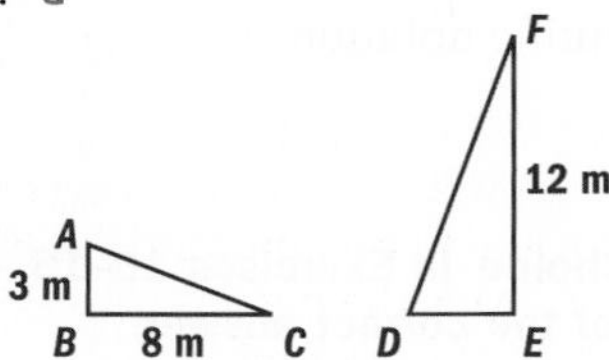

F. 2 m G. 4.5 m H. 24 m I. 32 m

16. You toss a coin 15 times, and the coin lands heads up 9 times. What is the experimental probability that the coin lands heads up? C

A. 0.4 B. 0.5 C. 0.6 D. 0.9

17. What is the solution of the equation $1.6x - 5.2 = 9.28$? H

F. 1.48 G. 2.55 H. 9.05 I. 11

18. Simplify the expression $\frac{4r^3}{5} \cdot \frac{15r^2}{14}$. A

A. $\frac{6r^5}{7}$ B. $\frac{6r^6}{7}$ C. $\frac{64r^5}{75}$ D. $\frac{64r^6}{75}$

19. What is the percent of change from 76 to 190? H

F. 60% G. 114% H. 150% I. 350%

20. A map has a scale of 1 cm : 150 m. If a map distance is 2.5 centimeters, what is the actual distance? D

A. 151.5 meters B. 225 meters
C. 300 meters D. 375 meters

Extended Response

21. The table shows the population of Washington, D.C., every 10 years from 1950 to 2000.

Year	Population
1950	802,000
1960	764,000
1970	757,000
1980	638,000
1990	607,000
2000	572,000

a. Make a data display that shows the population for those years. **See margin.**

b. In which year did the population decrease the most from 10 years earlier, and what was the approximate percent of change? **1980; about 15.7% decrease**

c. Can you conclude from the table that the population of Washington, D.C., has decreased every year since 1950? Explain your reasoning. **See margin.**

22. A store sells granola bars in boxes of 8 and 20. A box of 8 bars costs $3.12, and a box of 20 bars costs $7.00.

a. List all the possible ways that you can buy exactly 80 granola bars. **4 boxes of 20 bars, 5 boxes of 8 bars and 2 boxes of 20 bars, or 10 boxes of 8 bars**

b. How should you buy exactly 80 granola bars if you want to spend the least amount of money? Explain your reasoning. **See margin.**

21a.

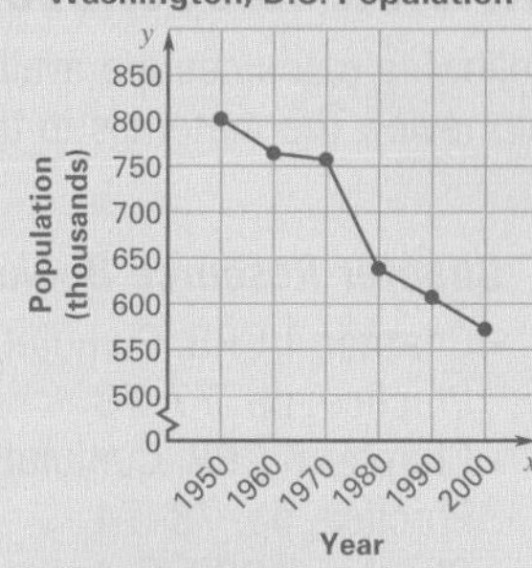

21c. No. *Sample answer:* We do not have data for each year. It is possible that the population could have increased briefly at some point before continuing its decline.

22b. 4 boxes of 20 bars. *Sample answer:* The cost per bar in a box of 8 bars is $.39, and the cost per bar in a box of 20 bars is $.35, so you should buy all the bars in boxes of 20.

ADDITIONAL RESOURCES

The following resources are available to help review the materials in this unit:

Chapter Resource Books

- Chapter 4 CRB, Cumulative Practice, pp. 77–78
- Chapter 5 CRB, Cumulative Practice, pp. 73–74
- Chapter 6 CRB, Cumulative Practice, pp. 84-85
- Chapter 7 CRB, Cumulative Practice, pp. 76–77

Assessment Book

- Unit Test, pp. 90-91
- Cumulative Test, pp. 92–95

Unit 2 Chapters 4–7 Practicing Test-Taking Skills

Cumulative Practice for Chapters 4–7

Chapter 4

Multiple Choice In Exercises 1–7, choose the letter of the correct answer.

1. Which expression is equivalent to $x \cdot x \cdot y \cdot y \cdot y$? *(Lesson 4.1)* **B**

A. $6xy$ **B.** x^2y^3 **C.** $2xy^3$ **D.** $3x^2y$

2. What is the greatest common factor of $6mn$ and $27m^3$? *(Lesson 4.2)* **F**

F. $3m$ **G.** $3m^3n$ **H.** $6m$ **I.** $54m^3n$

3. Which expression is equivalent to $\frac{18a^6}{3a^2}$? *(Lesson 4.3)* **B**

A. $6a^3$ **B.** $6a^4$ **C.** $15a^3$ **D.** $15a^4$

4. What is the LCM of 32 and 48? *(Lesson 4.4)*

F. 6 **G.** 48 **H.** 96 **I.** 144 **H**

5. Which expression is equivalent to $-2x^2 \cdot 3x^3y$? *(Lesson 4.5)* **A**

A. $-6x^5y$ **B.** $-6x^2y$ **C.** $-6x^6y$ **D.** x^2

6. Which list of numbers is ordered from least to greatest? *(Lesson 4.6)* **I**

F. $3^{-2}, 5^0, 2^{-3}, -7$ **G.** $2^{-3}, 3^{-2}, -7, 5^0$

H. $-7, 3^{-2}, 5^0, 2^{-3}$ **I.** $-7, 3^{-2}, 2^{-3}, 5^0$

7. Which number is equivalent to 8×10^{-3}? *(Lesson 4.7)* **D**

A. 8000 **B.** 800 **C.** 0.08 **D.** 0.008

8. Short Response You are arranging 60 pictures on a poster board. The board can fit up to 4 rows of pictures, and each row can have up to 20 pictures. You want each row to have the same number of pictures. How many different ways can you arrange the pictures? *(Lesson 4.1)* **2 ways**

9. Extended Response The table shows the typical lengths of four species of roundworm. *(Lesson 4.7)*

Roundworm	Length (m)
Monochus	3.4×10^{-3}
Cephalobus	6×10^{-4}
Placentonema gigantissima	7.9×10^0
Syphacia peromysci	9.1×10^{-4}

a. Order the lengths from least to greatest. **6×10^{-4}, 9.1×10^{-4}, 3.4×10^{-3}, 7.9×10^0**

b. How many meters less is the length of the shortest roundworm than the length of the next shortest roundworm? Write your answer in standard form and in scientific notation. **0.00031 m, 3.1×10^{-4} m**

Chapter 5

Multiple Choice In Exercises 10–16, choose the letter of the correct answer.

10. Which fraction is equivalent to 0.8? *(Lesson 5.1)* **D**

A. $\frac{9}{10}$ **B.** $\frac{8}{9}$ **C.** $\frac{6}{7}$ **D.** $\frac{4}{5}$

11. Your pants have a length of 30 inches. A tailor cuts off $2\frac{1}{3}$ inches from the length so that the pants fit you. How long are the pants now? *(Lesson 5.2)* **G**

F. $27\frac{1}{3}$ inches **G.** $27\frac{2}{3}$ inches

H. $28\frac{1}{3}$ inches **I.** $28\frac{2}{3}$ inches

12. Simplify the expression $\frac{a}{3} + \frac{3a}{4}$. *(Lesson 5.3)* **B**

A. $\frac{4a}{7}$ **B.** $\frac{13a}{12}$ **C.** $\frac{a}{3}$ **D.** $\frac{7a}{12}$

17. **$6.** ***Sample answer:*** **There are four $\frac{1}{4}$ miles in one mile, so you donate 4 • $.10 = $.40 for each mile. Your friend ran 15 miles, so you donate 15 • $.40 = $6.**

Test-Taking Skills

13. Simplify the expression $\frac{6r}{5} \cdot \frac{15r}{2}$. *(Lesson 5.4)* **G**

F. $9r$ **G.** $9r^2$ **H.** $\frac{4r}{25}$ **I.** $\frac{4r^2}{25}$

14. Find the quotient $\frac{3}{4} \div 1\frac{7}{8}$. *(Lesson 5.5)* **B**

A. $\frac{1}{3}$ **B.** $\frac{2}{5}$ **C.** $\frac{2}{3}$ **D.** $1\frac{1}{14}$

15. Your friend buys a skateboard that is on sale for one third off the original price. Your friend spent $36 less than the original price. What was the original price of the skateboard? *(Lesson 5.6)* **H**

F. $12 **G.** $72 **H.** $108 **I.** $144

16. Which number is *not* a solution of the inequality $-\frac{3}{4}x - \frac{1}{4} \le 3$? *(Lesson 5.7)* **A**

A. $-4\frac{2}{3}$ **B.** $-3\frac{1}{3}$ **C.** $3\frac{1}{3}$ **D.** $4\frac{2}{3}$

17. **Short Response** You agree to donate $.10 for every $\frac{1}{4}$ mile that your friend runs in a race for charity. If your friend runs 15 miles, how much money will you donate? Explain your reasoning. *(Lesson 5.6)* **See margin.**

18. **Extended Response** You have $1275.25 to buy stock in a company. Your stockbroker charges a brokerage fee of $12.75 for each transaction. Each share is currently worth $25.75. *(Lesson 5.7)*

a. How many shares can you buy in one transaction? **49 shares**

b. You save $800 to buy more stock. Each share is now worth $31.49. How many shares can you buy in one transaction of $800? **25 shares**

c. Suppose that the shares in parts (a) and (b) are now worth $28.36 each. What is the total value of the shares? Explain your reasoning. **$2098.64.** ***Sample answer:*** **You have 74 shares in all, and 74 • $28.36 = $2098.64.**

Chapter 6

Multiple Choice In Exercises 19–25, choose the letter of the correct answer.

19. Which rate is equivalent to $\frac{40\text{ m}}{1\text{ sec}}$? **C** *(Lesson 6.1)*

A. $\frac{2.4\text{ km}}{1\text{ h}}$ **B.** $\frac{24\text{ km}}{1\text{ h}}$

C. $\frac{144\text{ km}}{1\text{ h}}$ **D.** $\frac{1440\text{ km}}{1\text{ h}}$

20. You can buy 3 pens for $2. How much money will you spend if you buy 15 pens? *(Lesson 6.2)* **F**

F. $10 **G.** $15 **H.** $30 **I.** $60

21. What is the solution of the proportion $\frac{8}{y} = \frac{5}{7}$? *(Lesson 6.3)* **D**

A. 5.4 **B.** 5.7 **C.** 6 **D.** 11.2

22. Given $\triangle ABC \sim \triangle DEF$, which statement is *not* necessarily true? *(Lesson 6.4)* **G**

F. $\angle A \cong \angle D$ **G.** $\overline{AC} \cong \overline{DF}$

H. $\frac{AB}{DE} = \frac{AC}{DF}$ **I.** $\frac{AB}{DE} = \frac{BC}{EF}$

23. Rectangle $ABCD$ is similar to rectangle $EFGH$. What is the length of $\overline{EF}$? *(Lesson 6.5)* **D**

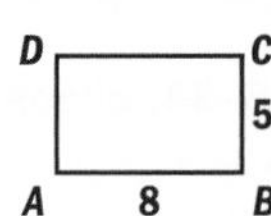

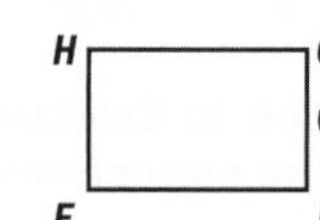

A. 6.3 **B.** 7.5 **C.** 9 **D.** 9.6

24. An airplane is 38.75 feet tall. A model of the airplane is 7.75 inches tall. What is the scale used for the model? *(Lesson 6.6)* **G**

F. 1 in. : 0.2 ft **G.** 1 in. : 5 ft

H. 5 in. : 1 ft **I.** 7 in. : 38 ft

26. 22 sit-ups. *Sample answer:* The total number of sit-ups each of us can do in 4.5 minutes is 4.5 times the number we can do in 1 minute, so I multiplied to find that I can do $45 \cdot 4.5 = 202.5$ sit-ups and my friend can do $40 \cdot 4.5 = 180$ sit-ups. Since a half sit-up doesn't count, I rounded my number down to 202 sit-ups. Then I subtracted to find that I can do $202 - 180 = 22$ more sit-ups than my friend.

27c. Increase. *Sample answer:* Now there are $4 \cdot 3 =$ 12 possible outcomes. The outcomes are the original ones plus (3, 4), (3, 5), and (3, 9). The outcomes (3, 5) and (3, 9) correspond to the event that the sum is even, so there are $4 + 2 = 6$ outcomes in all corresponding to an even sum, and the new probability is $\frac{6}{12} = \frac{1}{2}$, which is greater than $\frac{4}{9}$.

35. $639. *Sample answer:* The discount is 25% of $800, or $0.25 \cdot \$800 = \$200$. The sale price is then $\$800 - \$200 = \$600$. The tax is 6.5% of $\$600 = 0.065 \cdot \$600 = \$39$. So the price with tax is $\$600 + \$39 = \$639$.

36b. 20 y. *Sample answer:* I earn $15 per year, and my friend earns $20 per year. After x years, my balance is $(500 + 15x)$ dollars and my friend's balance is $(400 + 20x)$ dollars. The balances are equal when $500 + 15x = 400 + 20x$, or when $100 + 15x = 20x$, $100 = 5x$, and $x = 20$.

Unit 2 Chapters 4–7 Practicing Test-Taking Skills

Cumulative Practice continued

25. You roll a number cube. What are the odds in favor of rolling a number less than 3? *(Lesson 6.7)* B

A. 1 to 3 **B.** 1 to 2 **C.** 3 to 7 **D.** 3 to 5

26. Short Response You can do 45 sit-ups in a minute. Your friend can do 40 sit-ups in a minute. At these rates, how many more sit-ups can you do than your friend in 4.5 minutes? Explain your steps. *(Lesson 6.1)* See margin.

27. Extended Response Six numbers are written on slips of paper and placed in one of two hats, as shown. You randomly choose a number from each hat. *(Lesson 6.8)*

First hat 2 6 7  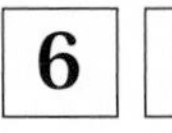

Second hat 4 5 9  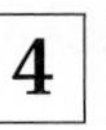

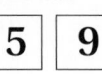

a. Use a tree diagram to list all the possible outcomes of choosing two numbers. 2, 4; 2, 5; 2, 9; 6, 4; 6, 5; 6, 9; 7, 4; 7, 5; 7, 9

b. What is the probability that the sum of the two numbers you choose is even? $\frac{4}{9}$

c. The number 3 is written on a slip of paper and placed in the first hat. Does the probability of choosing two numbers whose sum is even *increase, decrease,* or *stay the same*? Explain. See margin.

Chapter 7

Multiple Choice In Exercises 28–34, choose the letter of the correct answer.

28. What is 40% of 2100? *(Lesson 7.1)* C

A. 84 **B.** 525 **C.** 840 **D.** 2060

29. 6 is what percent of 16? *(Lesson 7.2)* G

F. $2\frac{2}{3}\%$ **G.** $37\frac{1}{2}\%$ **H.** 96% **I.** 267%

30. What is 3.4% of 8700? *(Lesson 7.3)* B

A. 29.58 **B.** 295.8 **C.** 2958 **D.** 29,580

31. 27 is 18% of what number? *(Lesson 7.4)* I

F. 4.86 **G.** 45 **H.** 48.6 **I.** 150

32. What is the new amount when 70 is increased by 30%? *(Lesson 7.5)* B

A. 73 **B.** 91 **C.** 100 **D.** 2100

33. You are ordering pizzas for home delivery. The pizzas cost $18. The sales tax is 6%, and you plan to give a 15% tip. What is the total cost of the order? *(Lesson 7.6)* H

F. $18.21 **G.** $20.10 **H.** $21.78 **I.** $37.80

34. You deposit $1000 into an account that earns 10% interest compounded annually. What is the balance of the account after 2 years? *(Lesson 7.7)* B

A. $1200 **B.** $1210 **C.** $1800 **D.** $3528

35. Short Response A computer is on sale for 25% off the original price of $800. You must pay a sales tax of 6.5% of the sale price. How much money do you spend for the computer? Explain your steps. *(Lesson 7.6)* See margin.

36. Extended Response Suppose you deposit $500 into an account that earns 3% simple annual interest, and your friend deposits $400 into an account that earns 5% simple annual interest. *(Lesson 7.7)*

a. Copy and complete the table.

Years	Your account balance	Your friend's account balance
1	? $515	? $420
3	? $545	? $460
5	? $575	? $500
10	? $650	? $600

b. After how many years will the balance in your friend's account equal the balance in your account? Explain your reasoning. See margin.

UNIT 3

Functions, Geometry, *and* Measurement

Chapter 8 Linear Functions

- Represent and interpret relations and functions.
- Write and graph linear equations in two variables.
- Write and graph linear systems and linear inequalities.

Chapter 9 Real Numbers and Right Triangles

- Use square roots and the Pythagorean theorem to solve problems.
- Identify rational and irrational numbers.
- Use special right triangles and trigonometric ratios to solve problems.

Chapter 10 Measurement, Area, and Volume

- Find angle measures and side lengths of triangles and quadrilaterals.
- Find the areas of parallelograms, trapezoids, and circles.
- Find the surface areas and volumes of prisms, cylinders, pyramids, and cones.

From Chapter 10, p. 544
What is the surface area of a pyramid?

UNIT RESOURCES

These resources are provided to help you prepare for the unit and to customize review materials:

Chapter Resource Books
- Chapter 8
- Chapter 9
- Chapter 10

Assessment Book
- Chapters 8–10, pp. 96–134

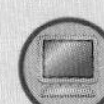

Technology
- EasyPlanner CD-ROM
- Test and Practice Generator
- Electronic Lesson Presentations CD-ROM
- eTutorial CD-ROM

Internet
- Classzone
- eEdition Plus Online
- eWorkbook Plus Online
- eTutorial Plus Online
- EasyPlanner Plus Online

ENGLISH LEARNER SUPPORT

- Spanish Study Guide
- Multi-Language Visual Glossary
- Chapter Audio Summaries CDs
- Teacher's Edition
  Chapter 8, pp. 382E–382F
  Chapter 9, pp. 450E–450F
  Chapter 10, pp. 508E–508F

CHAPTER

8

Pacing and Assignment Guide

REGULAR SCHEDULE

Lesson	Les. Day	BASIC	AVERAGE	ADVANCED
8.1	Day 1	EP p. 803 Exs. 38-41; pp. 388-390 Exs. 8-16, 18-21, 27-37	pp. 388-390 Exs. 10-17, 20-24, 26-37	pp. 388-390 Exs. 10-18, 21-28*, 33-37
8.2	Day 1	SRH p. 780 Exs. 9-12; pp. 394-396 Exs. 12-15, 32-38, 43-50	pp. 394-396 Exs. 12-15, 32-38, 43-50	pp. 394-396 Exs. 12-15, 32-34, 37, 38, 45-48
	Day 2	pp. 394-396 Exs. 16-27, 51-56	pp. 394-396 Exs. 20-31, 39-41, 51-56	pp. 394-396 Exs. 20-27, 39-44*, 53-56
8.3	Day 1	SRH p. 785 Exs. 1, 4, 5, 7; pp. 400-402 Exs. 10-19, 22-25, 30, 34-47	pp. 400-402 Exs. 13-24, 27-32, 36-39, 42-48	pp. 400-402 Exs. 15-20, 23-35*, 40-48
8.4	Day 1	pp. 407-409 Exs. 8-16, 18-27, 35, 41-53	pp. 407-409 Exs. 8-24, 28-38, 41-53	pp. 407-409 Exs. 11-21, 28-42*, 47-53
8.5	Day 1	pp. 415-417 Exs. 10-20, 22-30, 34-46	pp. 415-417 Exs. 10-13, 17-24, 28-32, 34-47	pp. 415-417 Exs. 10-13, 17-21, 25-35*, 38-47
8.6	Day 1	pp. 422-424 Exs. 8-11, 18-23, 27-30, 35-42	pp. 422-424 Exs. 8-11, 18-23, 27-30, 35-42	pp. 422-424 Exs. 10, 11, 18-23, 29-31, 40-44
	Day 2	pp. 422-424 Exs. 12-17, 24-26, 43-48	pp. 422-424 Exs. 12-17, 24-26, 31-33, 43-48	pp. 422-424 Exs. 13-17, 24-26, 32-36*, 45-48
8.7	Day 1	pp. 429-430 Exs. 11-22, 26-28, 32-43	pp. 429-430 Exs. 14-25, 28-30, 32-44	pp. 429-430 Exs. 14-16, 20-33*, 34-37, 40-44
8.8	Day 1	pp. 434-435 Exs. 7-18, 22-24, 30-41	pp. 434-435 Exs. 7-12, 16-28, 32-41	pp. 434-435 Exs. 7-12, 16-18, 22-31*, 34-41
8.9	Day 1	pp. 439-441 Exs. 12-14, 20-27, 38-43	pp. 439-441 Exs. 12-15, 24-27, 38-43	pp. 439-441 Exs. 12-15, 24-27, 40-46
	Day 2	pp. 439-441 Exs. 16-19, 28-33, 44-48	pp. 439-441 Exs. 16-23, 28-34, 44-48	pp. 439-441 Exs. 18-23, 30-37*, 47, 48
Review	Day 1	pp. 442-445 Exs. 1-29	pp. 442-445 Exs. 1-29	pp. 442-445 Exs. 1-29
Assess	Day 1	Chapter 8 Test	Chapter 8 Test	Chapter 8 Test

YEARLY PACING Chapter 8 Total – **14 days** Chapters 1–8 Total – **94 days** Remaining – **66 days**

*Challenge Exercises EP = Extra Practice SRH = Skills Review Handbook

BLOCK SCHEDULE

DAY 1	DAY 2	DAY 3	DAY 4	DAY 5	DAY 6	DAY 7
8.1 pp. 388-390 Exs. 10-17, 20-24, 26-37 **8.2** pp. 394-396 Exs. 12-15, 32-38, 43-50	**8.2 (cont.)** pp. 394-396 Exs. 20-31, 39-41, 51-56 **8.3** pp. 400-402 Exs. 13-24, 27-32, 36-48	**8.4** pp. 407-409 Exs. 8-24, 28-38, 43-53 **8.5** pp. 415-417 Exs. 10-13, 17-24, 28-32, 34-47	**8.6** pp. 422-424 Exs. 8-33, 35-48	**8.7** pp. 429-430 Exs. 14-25, 28-30, 32-44 **8.8** pp. 434-435 Exs. 7-12, 16-28, 32-41	**8.9** pp. 439-441 Exs. 12-34, 38-48	**Review** pp. 442-445 Exs. 1-29 **Assess** Chapter 8 Test

YEARLY PACING Chapter 8 Total – **7 days** Chapters 1–8 Total – **47 days** Remaining – **33 days**

Support Materials

CHAPTER RESOURCE BOOK

CHAPTER SUPPORT			
Tips for New Teachers	p. 1	Parents as Partners	p. 3

LESSON SUPPORT	8.1	8.2	8.3	8.4	8.5	8.6	8.7	8.8	8.9
Lesson Plans (regular and block)	p. 5	p. 13	p. 21	p. 29	p. 37	p. 48	p. 56	p. 65	p. 74
Technology Activities & Keystrokes					p. 40		p. 58	p. 67	p. 76
Activity Support Masters									
Activity Masters					p. 39				
Practice (3 levels)	p. 7	p. 15	p. 23	p. 31	p. 41	p. 50	p. 59	p. 68	p. 77
Study Guide	p. 10	p. 18	p. 26	p. 34	p. 44	p. 53	p. 62	p. 71	p. 80
Real-World Problem Solving					p. 46				p. 82
Challenge Practice	p. 12	p. 20	p. 28	p. 36	p. 47	p. 55	p. 64	p. 73	p. 83

REVIEW			
Chapter Review Games and Activities	p. 84	Extra Credit Project with Rubric	p. 89
Real-Life Project with Rubric	p. 85	Cumulative Practice	p. 91
Cooperative Project with Rubric	p. 87	Resource Book Answers	A1

ASSESSMENT

Quizzes	p. 96	Alternative Assessments with Rubrics	p. 105
Chapter Tests (3 levels)	p. 98	Unit Test	p. 129
Standardized Test	p. 104	Cumulative Test	p. 131

TRANSPARENCIES

TRANSPARENCIES	8.1	8.2	8.3	8.4	8.5	8.6	8.7	8.8	8.9
Warm-Up/Daily Homework Quiz	✔	✔	✔	✔	✔	✔	✔	✔	✔
Notetaking Guide	✔	✔	✔	✔	✔	✔	✔	✔	✔
Teacher Support	✔	✔	✔	✔	✔	✔	✔	✔	✔
English/Spanish Problem Solving		✔	✔		✔				✔
Answer Transparencies	✔	✔	✔	✔	✔	✔	✔	✔	✔

TECHNOLOGY

- EasyPlanner CD-ROM
- Test and Practice Generator
- Electronic Lesson Presentations
- eTutorial CD-ROM
- Chapter Audio Summaries CDs
- Classzone.com
- eEdition Plus Online
- eWorkbook Plus Online
- eTutorial Plus Online
- EasyPlanner Plus Online

ADDITIONAL RESOURCES

- Worked-Out Solution Key
- Notetaking Guide
- Practice Workbook
- Tutor Place
- Professional Development Book
- Special Activities Book
- Posters
- Spanish Study Guide
- Exercises in Spanish
- English/Spanish Ch. Reviews/Tests
- Multi-Language Visual Glossary

CHAPTER 8

Math Background and Teaching Strategies

Lesson 8.1

MATH BACKGROUND

A set of ordered pairs of numbers forms a **relation**. A relation pairs numbers in one set, the **domain**, with numbers in a second set, the **range**. Each domain element serves as an **input**, and is represented by an x-coordinate of an ordered pair. Each range element serves as an **output**, and is represented by a y-coordinate. A **function** is a relation in which each domain value is paired with only one range value.

TEACHING STRATEGIES

Provide students with a list of 5-10 ordered pairs. Have them find the domain and range of the relation formed by the ordered pairs. Then ask them if the relation is a function. You may need to remind them that more than one input can be mapped to the same output, but that no input can be mapped to more than one output.

Lesson 8.2

MATH BACKGROUND

An **equation in two variables**, such as $y = 3x + 2$, has infinitely many solutions: any ordered pair (x, y) that makes the equation true. The **graph** of an equation in two variables represents all points corresponding to these ordered pairs in a coordinate plane. Since all the points lie along a line, $y = 3x + 2$ is a **linear** equation.

TEACHING STRATEGIES

By encouraging students to use the function form of an equation, you can emphasize that a function describes a rule which allows them to find an output value for any input value. Students may need to review the addition and subtraction properties of equality.

Lesson 8.3

MATH BACKGROUND

Because two points determine a line, a quick way to graph a line that does not pass through the origin $(y = ax)$, is not horizontal $(y = b)$, and is not vertical $(x = a)$, is to find the ***x*-intercept** and the ***y*-intercept** of the graph. These values can be found, respectively, by letting $y = 0$ and solving for x, and by letting $x = 0$ and solving for y.

TEACHING STRATEGIES

Students often confuse which intercept has been found after substituting 0 for one of the variables. Stress that the most important thing is just to substitute 0 for each variable in turn, as shown below in finding the intercepts of $4x + 7y = -28$.

Let $x = 0$: $4(0) + 7y = -28 \rightarrow 7y = -28$
So, $y = -4$ and $(0, -4)$ is on the graph.

Let $y = 0$: $4x + 7(0) = -28 \rightarrow 4x = -28$
So, $x = -7$ and $(-7, 0)$ is on the graph.

Plotting the points on a coordinate plane will reinforce that $(0, -4)$ is the y-intercept and $(-7, 0)$ is the x-intercept.

Lesson 8.4

MATH BACKGROUND

The **slope** of a line is the *rate of change* of the dependent variable with respect to the independent variable. To find the slope of the line through two points (x_1, y_1) and (x_2, y_2), calculate the ratio of the change in the y-coordinates, $y_2 - y_1$, to the change in the x-coordinates, $x_2 - x_1$. A positive slope indicates a line that rises from left to right, and a negative slope indicates a line that falls from left to right. A horizontal line has zero slope, and a vertical line has undefined slope.

TEACHING STRATEGIES

Students may get confused with the meaning of the word "rise" in the slope algorithm, since some lines rise to the right and some fall. You may want to work examples with students, one for a line with positive slope and one for a line with negative slope, in which students use each of two points as (x_1, y_1) in turn. This way, they can see that as long as one point supplies both x_1 and y_1 and the other supplies both x_2 and y_2, the order in which points are chosen does not matter.

Lesson 8.5

MATH BACKGROUND

The equation $y = mx + b$ is known as the *slope-intercept* form of a line, since you can readily identify the slope m and y-intercept b. This form aids graphing, since you can plot the point $(0, b)$ and identify a second point by applying the rise and run indicated by the slope.

TEACHING STRATEGIES

Using the rise and run to find a second point on a line can confuse some students, especially when a line has negative slope. You can extend Example 2 on page 413 to show that students do not have to approach this in a single way. Show students that in Example 2, counting 2 units down and then 3 to the right also gives a second point of (3, 2).

Lesson 8.6

MATH BACKGROUND

If you know the slope and y-intercept of a line, its equation can be found by substituting these values in the slope-intercept form. If you can identify the y-intercept and one other point on a line, you can use the slope-intercept form to find the slope. If the points on a scatter plot seem to lie roughly on a line, you can approximate the data by drawing a **best-fitting line**.

TEACHING STRATEGIES

Make sure students are proficient at finding slope from two points and that they can identify the y-intercept from an ordered pair if the x-coordinate is 0. For practice finding a best-fitting line, plot data points for which you have already used technology to find the best-fitting line. Have a few students draw the line they think is "best." Draw the actual best-fitting line so students can compare it to theirs.

Lesson 8.7

MATH BACKGROUND

Function notation allows you to identify the independent and dependent variables in a function. In the function $d(t) = 60t$, the independent variable is t (time), and the dependent variable is d (distance). Function notation is also useful for finding the value of a function for a specific input.

TEACHING STRATEGIES

Be sure students understand how function notation is used, by discussing the following situations with them.

- For the ordered pair (0, 3), if f is a function of x, then $f(0) = 3$.
- If $g(5) = 6$ for the function g, then (5, 6) is on the graph of g.

Lesson 8.8

MATH BACKGROUND

Two lines in a plane with different slopes must intersect in a point. The coordinates of this point satisfy the equations of both lines and the ordered pair is the solution of the **system of two linear equations**. Two lines with the same slope are parallel and do not intersect, so the system of two equations has no solution. If two equations represent the same line, then the system of equations has infinitely many solutions.

TEACHING STRATEGIES

Since students solve linear systems only by graphing in this lesson, make sure that they understand the information presented in Examples 2 and 3. Namely, if they write the equations in slope-intercept form, they can quickly identify systems that have no solution (the slopes are the same, but the y-intercepts are not), and systems that have infinitely many solutions (the slope-intercept forms of the lines are the same). Otherwise, students should realize that they are looking for a single point of intersection.

Lesson 8.9

MATH BACKGROUND

A **linear inequality** in two variables expresses an order relation, using one of the symbols $>$, $<$, $\geq$, or $\leq$. The solution is a **half-plane** whose boundary line is the graph of the related equation. For inequalities involving $\geq$ or $\leq$, the boundary line is solid, while for those involving $>$ or $<$, it is dashed.

TEACHING STRATEGIES

In Example 4, make sure that students realize that while the solutions of the inequality $5x + 2y \leq 100$ do form a half-plane, the graph is only shown in the first quadrant because the other solutions do not make sense in the real-world context of the problem. Students should always be encouraged to use a test point to determine the half-plane to be shaded.

CHAPTER

8 Differentiating Instruction

Strategies for Underachievers

USE MANIPULATIVES AND TOOLS

Throughout Chapter 8, you may wish to provide students with templates for mapping diagrams, 2-column or 2-row tables, and coordinate grids to help them complete their work efficiently. Depending on the level of students, you may choose to make only generic templates or templates that are specific to problems or groups of problems. Students should be required to label the axes on coordinate grids.

You can have students use straws or uncooked linguine to perform a vertical line test in Lesson 8.1, and with coordinate grids to model changes in slope or y-intercept as well as points of intersection, the latter of which will be useful as students work with systems of equations in Lesson 8.8.

FOCUS ON VOCABULARY

RELATIONS AND FUNCTIONS In Lesson 8.1, students must thoroughly understand the terms *relation, domain, range, input, output,* and *function.* You may wish to have underachieving students create note cards showing the definition of each term along with examples that illustrate the term. For instance, the card for *function* should include examples of relations that *are* functions as well as relations that are *not* functions. In addition, this card should compare relations that match two or more inputs with the same output (a function) to relations that match two or more outputs with the same input (not a function). Be sure students understand that *relation* and *function* are not opposites, but that all functions are also relations, while only some relations are functions and some are not functions. Having students include a Venn diagram, like the one below, may be helpful.

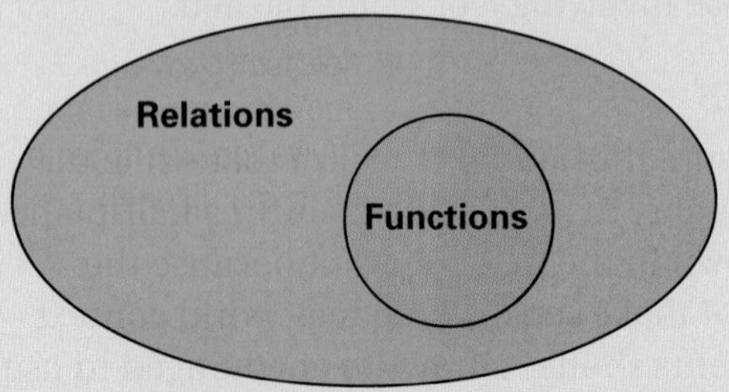

USE SCAFFOLDING

GRAPHING LINES In Lesson 8.3, you may wish to provide students with (or have them create) note cards that illustrate the step-by-step process of graphing a line using intercepts. These cards should contain several examples that illustrate all the possible sign combinations for the coefficients of x and y.

In Lesson 8.4, you may wish to have underachievers make a set of reference note cards for the four situations involving slope shown at the top of page 405. Additionally, you may wish to have students choose two points on each of the lines and use the coordinates of the ordered pairs to calculate the slope for each example. Have students pay particular attention to the case involving a vertical line, where attempts at calculating slope will result in division by zero, which students should be able to interpret as meaning that the slope cannot be determined.

In Lesson 8.5, students will be faced with solving linear equations for y before graphing them. It may help underachieving students if you provide a reference sheet that gives examples of solving equations for y. The sheet should include worked-out examples for situations involving linear equations in standard form, both with positive coefficients for y, as in Example 4 on page 414, and with negative coefficients for y, as in Exercises 18 and 19 on page 416. You may also want to include examples of other situations, such as an equation that is solved for x, as in Exercise 27 on page 416. Students can use the reference-sheet examples as templates as they complete the exercises.

Strategies for English Learners

ELIMINATE UNNECESSARY INFORMATION

This chapter has many word problems, so it may be more difficult for English learners to read. You can minimize the amount of reading required and focus on the mathematics by making sure that students know key phrases and by presenting problems in a predictable format. For example, the following phrase occurs in Exercises 29 and 30 on page 401:

Write an equation describing ...

In several places in this chapter, the questions are organized so that the basic sentence structure remains consistent, and the student must come up with the same type of answer each time even though the particular facts of the problem change. For example, in Lesson 8.6, Exercises 26a and 33a use the same format: "Make a scatter plot of the data pairs (x, y)." Presenting questions to students in this way helps them focus on the mathematics because the English only has to be understood once. You can use this technique of repetitive English with any type of mathematics problem.

Furthermore, it would be helpful for English learners to cross out all but the most essential words (think telegram), as a way of demonstrating that it's not always necessary to know every word. For example, English learners don't need to spend a lot of time decoding a proper noun that appears to be someone's name, but instead can substitute a familiar name with the same result.

Also, make sure that English learners are attending to the beginning and end of sentences (not all languages use punctuation and capitals). This would be preliminary to identifying the predictable format of word problems. (How many sentences? Look at first sentence. Where is the question mark? and so on.)

Strategies for Advanced Learners

ADD REAL-WORLD APPLICATIONS

SLOPE In Lesson 8.4 many real-world examples involving slope are given, but you may wish to challenge some advanced students to consider and report on other applications of slope in the real world. One possibility would be to explore the importance of slope in both the form and function of stairs in architecture. Another is how slope is involved in the building codes for appropriate handicapped-access ramps. A third possibility might be to research the significance of slope in the difficulty ratings of trails at ski and snowboard resorts, which can be extended to include researching what degree of steepness on mountain slopes makes avalanche danger the highest. In their research, students are likely to need to compare other measures of steepness, such as *percent grade* and *pitch* (in regard to roofs), to the mathematical definition of slope.

USE TECHNOLOGY

Students who have access to graphing calculators or mathematics software programs can benefit greatly from technology in this chapter. Students can explore the graphs of lines, including how changing one parameter at a time, such as the y-intercept or slope, affects the graph of a line. Students can also graph systems of linear equations to find their solutions, can create tables of values for functions, and can even graph linear inequalities.

USE CROSS-CURRICULAR CONNECTIONS

In Lesson 8.4, you may wish to work with an industrial arts teacher, graphic arts teacher, physical education teacher, or an appropriate coach or club sponsor to develop activities that will investigate the use of slope in various real-world applications such as those listed previously under "Add Real-World Applications." Especially for applications of slope in areas such as building and architecture, you may even want to make arrangements for interested students to meet a professional who uses computer-aided design (CAD). This might include field trip possibilities.

The following problems can be used with **Lesson 8.6**:

- **Challenge** Plot each set of points. Draw the line that contains these points. Examine the slope and y-intercept of each line and try to write an equation of the line. Then substitute the values of x and y from each point into your equation to see if it is correct. If it is not, modify your equation and check again. Check students' graphs.

  a. (0, 4), (1, 6), (2, 8) $y = 2x + 4$

  b. (−4, 4), (0, 1), (4, −2) $y = -\frac{3}{4}x + 1$

  c. (1, −2), (2, 1), (3, 4) $y = 3x - 5$

  d. (−2, −2), (1, −2), (5, −2) $y = -2$

CHAPTER 8

Differentiating Instruction: Resource Materials

Differentiating Practice

McDougal Littell *Pre-Algebra* offers teachers a wide variety of practice for all levels of students. Pictured on these pages are facsimiles of the Level A, Level C, and Challenge Practice pages from the *Chapter 8 Resource Book*, pages from the *Practice Workbook*, and the *Test and Practice Generator*.

RESOURCE BOOK

The *Chapter Resource Books* contain three levels of practice, A (Basic), B (Average), and C (Advanced), for each lesson in the textbook. Also, included is a page of Challenge practice for each lesson for your most advanced students.

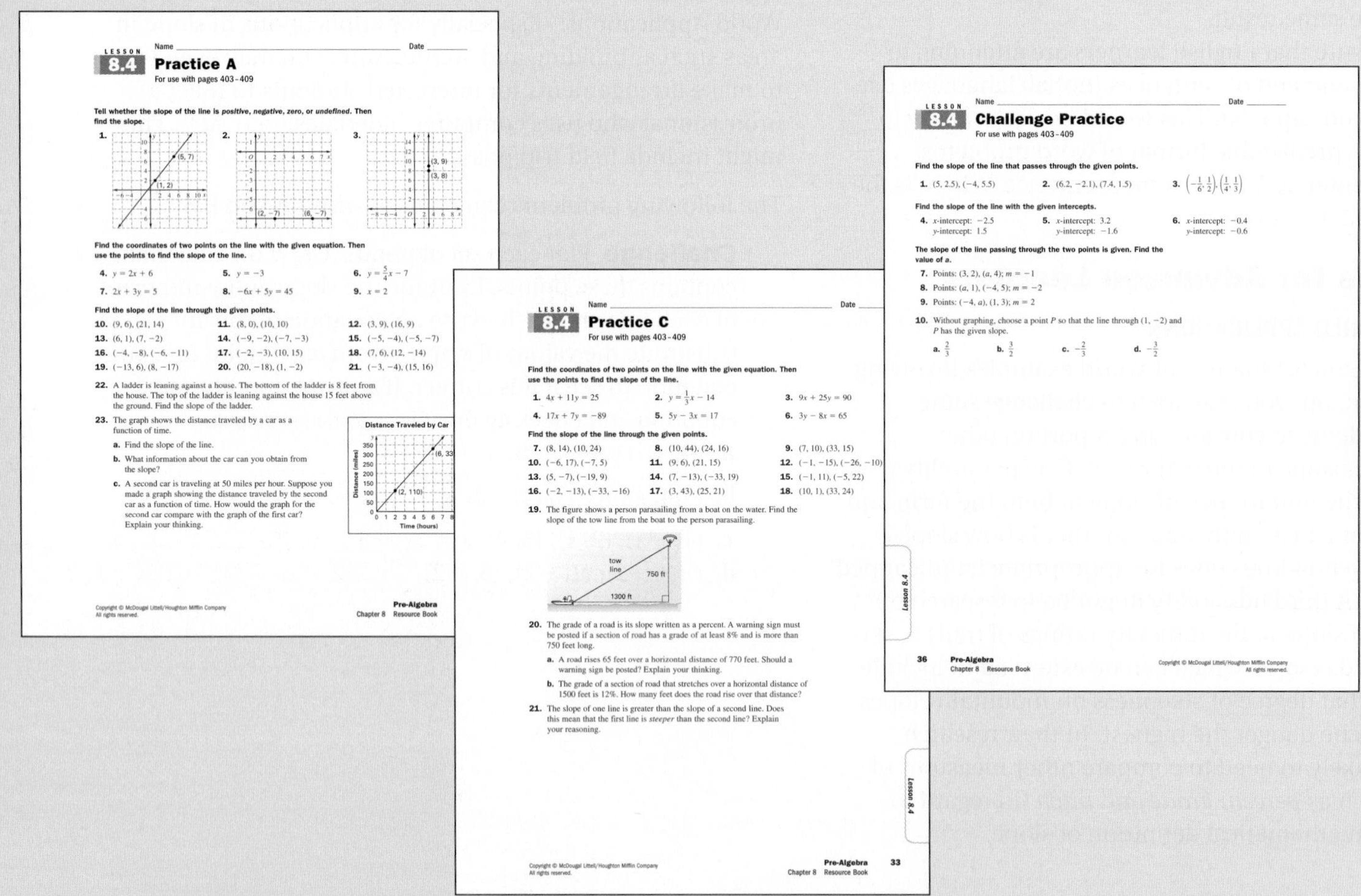

PRACTICE WORKBOOK

The *Practice Workbook* contains the average B-level practice for each lesson reformatted in workbook form to allow students to show their work for each exercise.

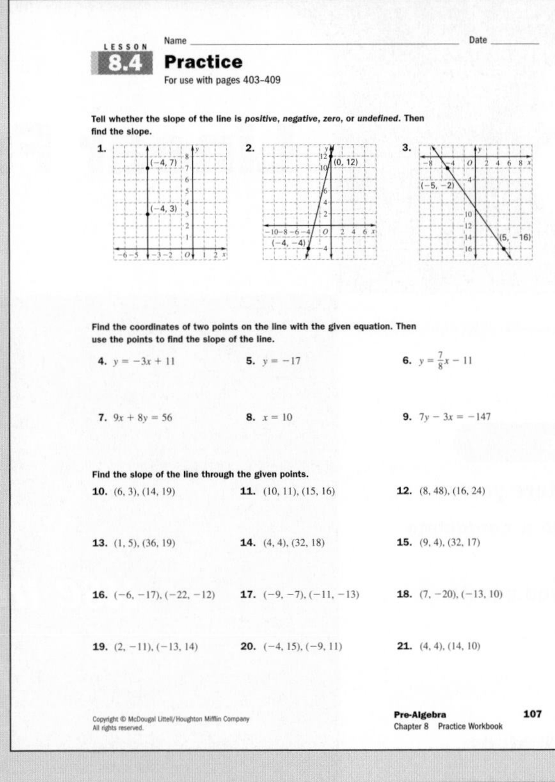

LESSON 8.4 Name ______ Date ______

Practice

For use with pages 403–409

Tell whether the slope of the line is *positive, negative, zero,* or *undefined.* Then find the slope.

1. (−4, 7), (−4, 3) **2.** (0, 12), (−4, −4) **3.** (−5, −2), (5, −16)

Find the coordinates of two points on the line with the given equation. Then use the points to find the slope of the line.

4. $y = -3x + 11$ **5.** $y = -17$ **6.** $y = \frac{7}{8}x - 11$

7. $9x + 8y = 56$ **8.** $x = 10$ **9.** $7y - 3x = -147$

Find the slope of the line through the given points.

10. (6, 3), (14, 19) **11.** (10, 11), (15, 16) **12.** (8, 48), (16, 24)

13. (1, 5), (36, 19) **14.** (4, 4), (32, 18) **15.** (9, 4), (32, 17)

16. (−6, −17), (−22, −12) **17.** (−9, −7), (−11, −13) **18.** (7, −20), (−13, 10)

19. (2, −11), (−13, 14) **20.** (−4, 15), (−9, 11) **21.** (4, 4), (14, 10)

Copyright © McDougal Littell/Houghton Mifflin Company All rights reserved. **Pre-Algebra** Chapter 8 Practice Workbook **107**

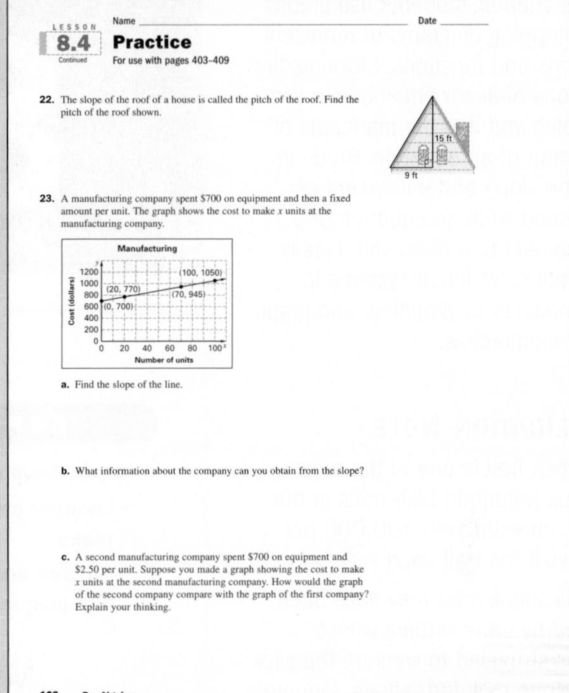

LESSON 8.4 Continued Name ______ Date ______

Practice

For use with pages 403–409

22. The slope of the roof of a house is called the pitch of the roof. Find the pitch of the roof shown.

23. A manufacturing company spent $700 on equipment and then a fixed amount per unit. The graph shows the cost to make x units at the manufacturing company.

a. Find the slope of the line.

b. What information about the company can you obtain from the slope?

c. A second manufacturing company spent $700 on equipment and $2.50 per unit. Suppose you made a graph showing the cost to make x units at the second manufacturing company. How would the graph of the second company compare with the graph of the first company? Explain your thinking.

108 **Pre-Algebra** Chapter 8 Practice Workbook Copyright © McDougal Littell/Houghton Mifflin Company All rights reserved.

TEST AND PRACTICE GENERATOR CD-ROM

The *Test and Practice Generator* allows you to create practice worksheets for each lesson using both static and algorithmic exercises.

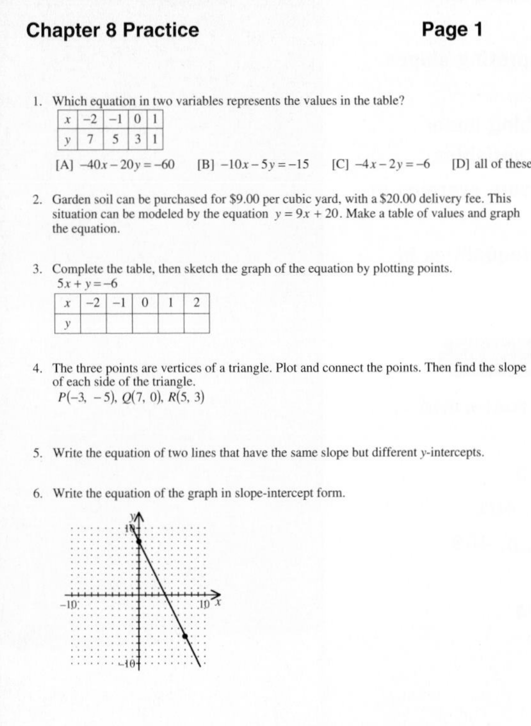

Chapter 8 Practice **Page 1**

1. Which equation in two variables represents the values in the table?

x	−2	−1	0	1
y	7	5	3	1

[A] $-40x - 20y = -60$ [B] $-10x - 5y = -15$ [C] $-4x - 2y = -6$ [D] all of these

2. Garden soil can be purchased for $9.00 per cubic yard, with a $20.00 delivery fee. This situation can be modeled by the equation $y = 9x + 20$. Make a table of values and graph the equation.

3. Complete the table, then sketch the graph of the equation by plotting points.
$5x + y = -6$

x	−2	−1	0	1	2
y					

4. The three points are vertices of a triangle. Plot and connect the points. Then find the slope of each side of the triangle.
$P(-3, -5)$, $Q(7, 0)$, $R(5, 3)$

5. Write the equation of two lines that have the same slope but different y-intercepts.

6. Write the equation of the graph in slope-intercept form.

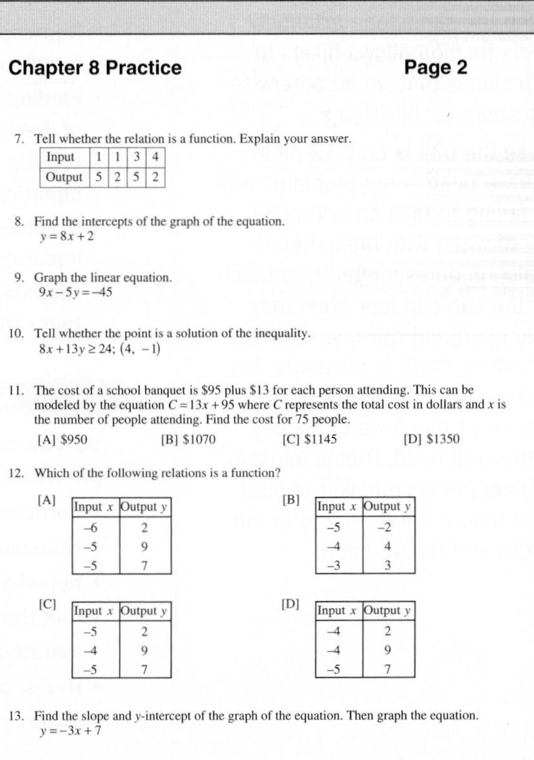

Chapter 8 Practice **Page 2**

7. Tell whether the relation is a function. Explain your answer.

Input	1	1	3	4
Output	5	2	5	2

8. Find the intercepts of the graph of the equation.
$y = 8x + 2$

9. Graph the linear equation.
$9x - 5y = -45$

10. Tell whether the point is a solution of the inequality.
$8x + 13y \geq 24$; $(4, -1)$

11. The cost of a school banquet is $95 plus $13 for each person attending. This can be modeled by the equation $C = 13x + 95$ where C represents the total cost in dollars and x is the number of people attending. Find the cost for 75 people.
[A] $950 [B] $1070 [C] $1145 [D] $1350

12. Which of the following relations is a function?

[A]

Input x	Output y
−6	2
−5	9
−5	7

[B]

Input x	Output y
−5	−2
−4	4
−3	3

[C]

Input x	Output y
−5	2
−4	9
−5	7

[D]

Input x	Output y
−4	2
−4	9
−5	7

13. Find the slope and y-intercept of the graph of the equation. Then graph the equation.
$y = -3x + 7$

OVERVIEW

Main Ideas

In this chapter, students use graphs and mapping diagrams to represent relations and functions. Students find solutions of linear equations in two variables and find the intercepts of the graph of an equation. Students find the slope and y-intercept of a line and write an equation of a line parallel to a given line. Finally, students solve linear systems in two variables by graphing, and graph linear inequalities.

Application Note

Slickrock Trail is one of the most famous mountain bike trails in the world. An estimated 100,000 persons visit the trail each year.

The Slickrock area may have been named by early settlers whose horses struggled to walk on the slick sandstone rock formations. Mountain bikers, however, find that their bike tires grip the sandstone extremely well. This traction allows bikers to ride up slopes that would otherwise be too steep for bicycling.

Because the trail is only 12 miles, there have been some problems with riders failing to take an adequate supply of water with them. Riders have also underestimated how much hotter the sun can feel when they are biking up and down sandstone slopes where there is no shade. For safety reasons, riders are urged to take twice as much water as they think they will need. During midsummer, riders are encouraged to start the trail before 7 A.M. and to be off the rocks well before noon.

CHAPTER 8

Linear Functions

BEFORE

In previous chapters you've . . .

- **Located points in a coordinate plane**
- **Written and solved equations and inequalities**

Now

In Chapter 8 you'll study . . .

- **Representing relations and functions**
- **Finding and interpreting slopes of lines**
- **Writing and graphing linear equations in two variables**
- **Graphing and solving systems of linear equations**
- **Graphing linear inequalities in two variables**

WHY?

So you can solve real-world problems about . . .

- **hurricanes, p. 389**
- **transportation, p. 401**
- **horseback riding, p. 409**
- **robotics, p. 416**
- **marathons, p. 424**
- **rivers, p. 430**
- **video, p. 440**

How can you use math to describe the steepness of a bike trail?

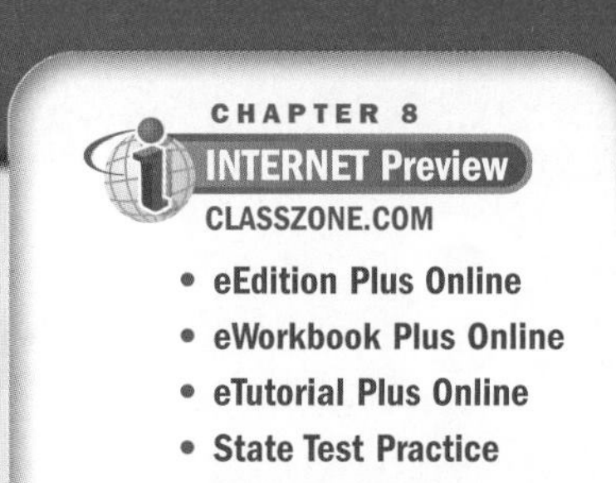

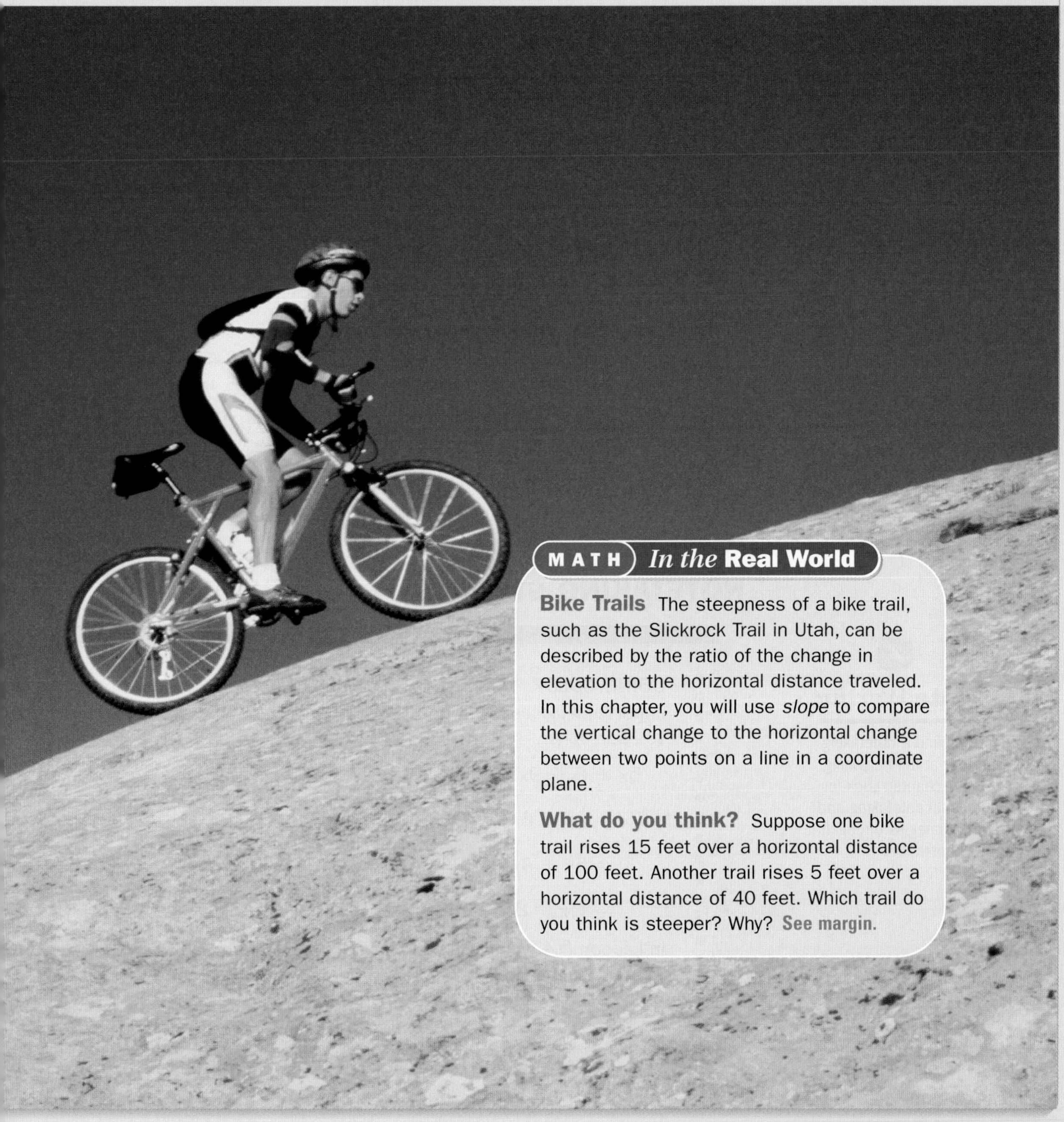

MATH In the Real World

Bike Trails The steepness of a bike trail, such as the Slickrock Trail in Utah, can be described by the ratio of the change in elevation to the horizontal distance traveled. In this chapter, you will use *slope* to compare the vertical change to the horizontal change between two points on a line in a coordinate plane.

What do you think? Suppose one bike trail rises 15 feet over a horizontal distance of 100 feet. Another trail rises 5 feet over a horizontal distance of 40 feet. Which trail do you think is steeper? Why? See margin.

Chapter Resources

These resources are provided to help you prepare for the chapter and to customize review materials:

Chapter 8 Resource Book
- Tips for New Teachers, pp. 1–2
- Lesson Plan, pp. 5, 13, 21, 29, 37, 48, 56, 65, 74
- Lesson Plan for Block Scheduling, pp. 6, 14, 22, 30, 38, 49, 57, 66, 75

Technology
- EasyPlanner CD-ROM
- Test and Practice Generator
- Electronic Lesson Presentations CD-ROM
- eTutorial CD-ROM

Internet
- Classzone
- eEdition Plus Online
- eWorkbook Plus Online
- eTutorial Plus Online
- EasyPlanner Plus Online

English Learner Support

- Spanish Study Guide
- Multi-Language Visual Glossary
- Chapter Audio Summaries CDs
- Teacher's Edition, pp. 382E–382F

The first trail. *Sample answer:* The ratio of the change in elevation to the horizontal distance traveled for this trail is $\frac{15}{100} = 0.15$. The ratio of the change in elevation to the horizontal distance traveled for the second trail is $\frac{5}{40} = 0.125$. Because $0.15 > 0.125$, the first trail is steeper.

PREPARE

DIAGNOSIS/REMEDIATION

Prerequisite Skills Quiz

The Prerequisite Skills Quiz can help you diagnose whether students have the following skills needed in Chapter 8:

- Use vocabulary (Ex. 1)
- Solve a real-world problem (Ex. 2)
- Solve an equation (Exs. 3–6)
- Write an inequality given its graph (Exs. 7–8)
- Solve an inequality and graph its solution (Exs. 9–12)

 ***Chapter 8 Resource Book***

- Study Guide (Lessons 8.1–8.9)

 ***Tutor Place***

NOTETAKING STRATEGIES

When students write equations in slope-intercept form in Lesson 8.5, they may want to choose two highlighter colors that they use consistently to identify the slope and the *y*-intercept as they write examples in their notebooks. Further suggestions for keeping a notebook can be found on pages 404 and 432.

For more support on notetaking, see:

- Notetaking Guide Workbook
- Notetaking Transparencies

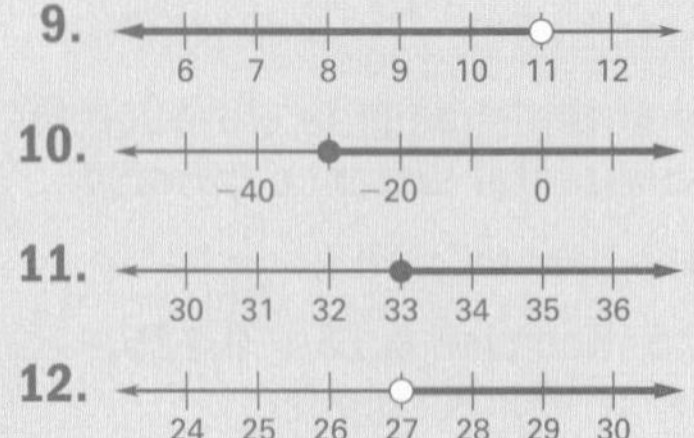

CHAPTER 8

Chapter Prerequisite Skills

Review Vocabulary

equation, p. 85
solving an equation, p. 86
inequality, p. 138

1. ***Sample answer:*** **An equation is a mathematical sentence formed by placing an equal sign between two expressions, while an inequality is a mathematical sentence formed by placing an inequality symbol (>, <, ≥, or ≤) between two expressions. While a solution of an equation like $5x + 1 = 6$ is a single number, the solution of an inequality like $5x + 1 > 6$, $5x + 1 < 6$, $5x + 1 \geq 6$, or $5x + 1 \leq 6$ is all numbers greater or less than a number, and may or may not include the number itself.**

PREREQUISITE SKILLS QUIZ

Preparing for Success **To prepare for success in this chapter, test your knowledge of these concepts and skills. You may want to look at the pages referred to in blue for additional review.**

1. **Vocabulary** Describe the difference between an equation and an inequality.
2. **School Trip** You are saving money for a school trip. You have saved \$156. This is \$62 less than the trip costs. How much money does the trip cost? *(p. 91)* **\$218**

Solve the equation. Check your solution. *(p. 125)*

3. $4(7 - 2t) = 4$ **3**

4. $-18 = 3(w - 1)$ **−5**

5. $11y + 9 - 5y = -15$ **−4**

6. $29 + 4(f + 2) = -7$ **−11**

Write an inequality represented by the graph. *(p. 138)*

7. −3 −2 −1 0 1 2 3 **$x < 1$**

8. 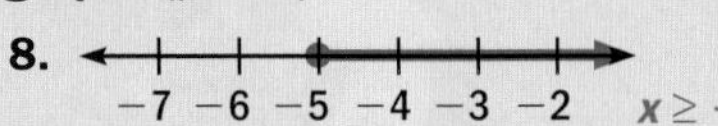

$x \geq -5$

Solve the inequality. Graph your solution. *(pp. 138, 144)* **9–12. See margin for art.**

9. $x + 14 < 25$ **$x < 11$**

10. $-5y \leq 150$ **$y \geq -30$**

11. $\frac{n}{3} \geq 11$ **$n \geq 33$**

12. $m - 6 > 21$ **$m > 27$**

NOTETAKING STRATEGIES

USING COLOR You may find it helpful to use color to identify important pieces of information and show how they are related to each other.

$5x + 6 + 9x + 2$

$= 5x + 6 + 9x + 2$ Use color to identify like terms.

$= 5x + 9x + 6 + 2$ Group like terms.

$= 14x + 8$ Combine like terms.

In Lesson 8.4, you can use color when finding slopes of lines.

Note *Worthy*

You will find a notetaking strategy at the beginning of each chapter. Look for additional notetaking and study strategies throughout the chapter.

LESSON

8.1 Relations *and* Functions

BEFORE	*Now*	WHY?
You graphed ordered pairs.	You'll use graphs to represent relations and functions.	So you can show the growth of a bird over time, as in Ex. 26.

Vocabulary

relation, p. 385
domain, p. 385
range, p. 385
input, p. 385
output, p. 385
function, p. 386
vertical line test, p. 387

Alligators The table below shows the ages and lengths of five alligators.

Age (years), x	2	4	5	5	7
Length (in.), y	32	59	65	69	96

You can represent the relationship between age and length using the ordered pairs (x, y):

(2, 32), (4, 59), (5, 65), (5, 69), (7, 96)

The ordered pairs form a *relation*. A **relation** is a pairing of numbers in one set, called the **domain**, with numbers in another set, called the **range**. Each number in the domain is an **input**. Each number in the range is an **output**. For a relation represented by ordered pairs, the inputs are the x-coordinates and the outputs are the y-coordinates.

Example 1 *Identifying the Domain and Range*

a. Identify the domain and range of the relation given above.

b. Identify the domain and range of the relation represented by the table below, which shows one alligator's length at different ages.

Age (years), x	1	2	3	4	5
Length (in.), y	23	36	47	61	73

Solution

a. The domain of the relation is the set of all inputs, or x-coordinates. The range is the set of all outputs, or y-coordinates.

Domain: 2, 4, 5, 7 **Range:** 32, 59, 65, 69, 96

b. The relation consists of the ordered pairs (1, 23), (2, 36), (3, 47), (4, 61), and (5, 73). The domain and range are shown below.

Domain: 1, 2, 3, 4, 5 **Range:** 23, 36, 47, 61, 73

Study *Strategy*

When you specify a domain or range, you should list each repeated value only once. In part (a) of Example 1, for instance, the domain is 2, 4, 5, 7, not 2, 4, 5, 5, 7.

Checkpoint

Identify the domain and range of the relation.

1. (0, 1), (2, 4), (3, 7), (5, 4) **2.** $(-1, 2), (-3, -1), (6, 0), (-1, 4)$

1. domain: 0, 2, 3, 5; range: 1, 4, 7

2. domain: $-3, -1, 6$; range: $-1, 0, 2, 4$

NCTM CURRICULUM STANDARDS

Standard 2: Understand relations; Understand functions

Standard 10: Create representations to communicate mathematical ideas

1 PLAN

Skill Check

Graph the ordered pairs in the same coordinate plane.

1. (0, 2) **2.** $(-2, 1)$
3. (1, 1) **4.** $(-3, -2)$

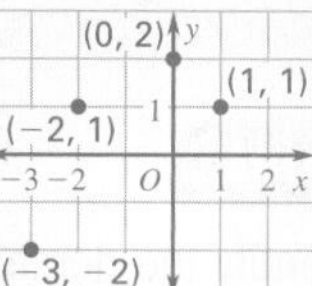

LESSON OBJECTIVE

Use graphs to represent relations and functions.

PACING

Suggested Number of Days
Basic Course: 1 day
Average Course: 1 day
Advanced Course: 1 day
Block: 0.5 block with 8.2

TEACHING RESOURCES

For a complete list of Teaching Resources, see page 382B.

TRANSPARENCY

Warm-Up Exercises for this lesson are available on a transparency. A support transparency is available for Examples 2 and 4, and Checkpoint Exercises 3 and 4.

2 TEACH

MOTIVATING THE LESSON

Have students read aloud the pairs of values in each column of the table as you write the corresponding ordered pairs on the board. Be sure students understand the connection between the cells of the table and the ordered pairs.

TIPS *for* NEW TEACHERS

After discussing the definition of *function*, immediately refer students back to Example 2 and have students determine that the given relation is *not* a function. See Tips for New Teachers in the *Chapter 8 Resource Book*.

Extra Examples

Example 1 Identify the domain and range of the relation represented by the table below, which shows the number of miles traveled after different numbers of hours driving.

Hours	1	2	3	4	5
Miles	60	100	160	210	270

Domain: 1, 2, 3, 4, 5;
Range: 60, 100, 160, 210, 270

Example 2 Represent the relation (2, 0), (1, −1), (2, 2), (0, 0), (−1, 1) as indicated.

a. A graph

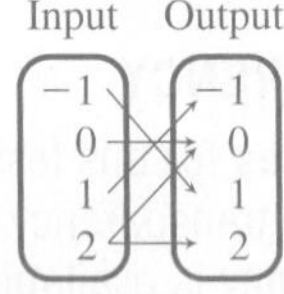

b. A mapping diagram

Input Output

Input	Output
−1	−1
0	0
1	1
2	2

Example 3 Tell whether the relation is a function. Explain your reasoning.

a. (1, 60), (2, 100), (3, 160), (4, 210), (5, 270) **Yes; every input is paired with exactly one output.**

b. (2, 0), (1, 1), (2, 2), (0, 0), (-1, 1) **No; the input 2 is paired with two outputs, 0 and 2.**

3, 4. See Additional Answers beginning on page AA1.

Representing Relations In addition to using ordered pairs or a table to represent a relation, you can also use a graph or a *mapping diagram.*

Example 2 *Representing a Relation*

Represent the relation (−1, 1), (2, 0), (3, 1), (3, 2), (4, 5) as indicated.

a. A graph

b. A mapping diagram

Solution

a. Graph the ordered pairs as points in a coordinate plane.

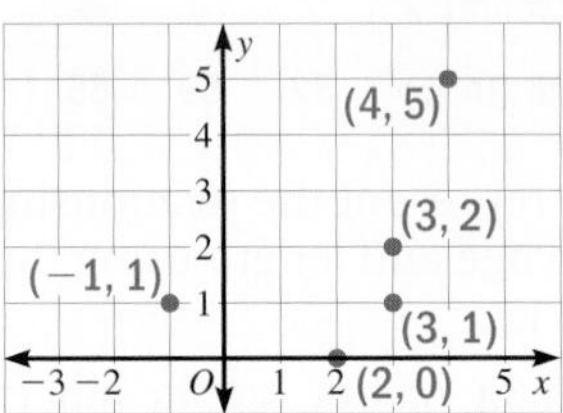

b. List the inputs and the outputs in order. Draw arrows from the inputs to their outputs.

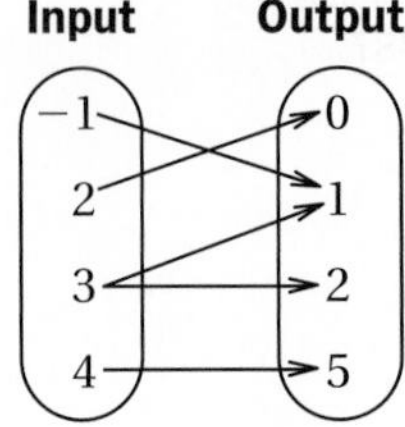

Functions A relation is a **function** if for each input there is *exactly one* output. In this case, the output *is a function of* the input.

Example 3 *Identifying Functions*

Tell whether the relation is a function.

a. The relation at the top of page 385, consisting of the ordered pairs (age, length) for five different alligators:

(2, 32), (4, 59), (5, 65), (5, 69), (7, 96)

b. The relation in part (b) of Example 1, consisting of the ordered pairs (age, length) for one alligator at different times:

(1, 23), (2, 36), (3, 47), (4, 61), (5, 73)

Solution

a. The relation *is not* a function because the input 5 is paired with two outputs, 65 and 69. This makes sense, as two alligators of the same age do not necessarily have the same length.

b. The relation *is* a function because every input is paired with exactly one output. This makes sense, as a single alligator can have only one length at a given point in time.

In the **Real World**

Alligators A newborn alligator is about 8 to 10 inches long. If the alligator is well fed, it will grow roughly 1 foot per year until it reaches a length of about 11 feet. What is the approximate length, in inches, of a 6-year-old alligator? **about 80–82 in.**

 ***Checkpoint***

Represent the relation as a graph and as a mapping diagram. Then tell whether the relation is a function. Explain your reasoning.

3–4. See margin for art.

3. (0, 3), (1, 2), (2, −1), (4, 4), (5, 4) **Yes; every input is paired with exactly one output.**

4. (−2, −1), (0, 2), (2, 3), (−2, −4) **No; the input −2 is paired with two outputs, −1 and −4.**

Vertical Line Test When a relation is represented by a graph, you can use the *vertical line test* to tell whether the relation is a function. The **vertical line test** says that if you can find a vertical line passing through more than one point of the graph, then the relation *is not* a function. Otherwise, the relation *is* a function.

Study *Strategy*

In part (b) of Example 4, notice why the vertical line test works. Because the vertical line at $x = 3$ intersects the graph twice, the input 3 must be paired with two outputs, 1 and -2. So, the graph does not represent a function.

Example 4 *Using the Vertical Line Test*

a. In the graph below, no vertical line passes through more than one point. So, the relation represented by the graph *is* a function.

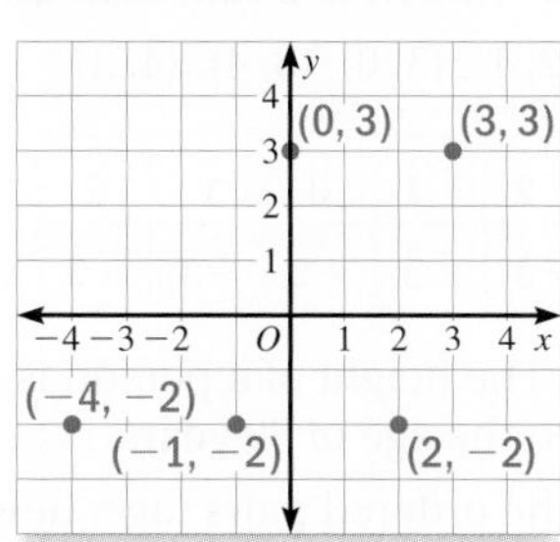

b. In the graph below, the vertical line shown passes through two points. So, the relation represented by the graph *is not* a function.

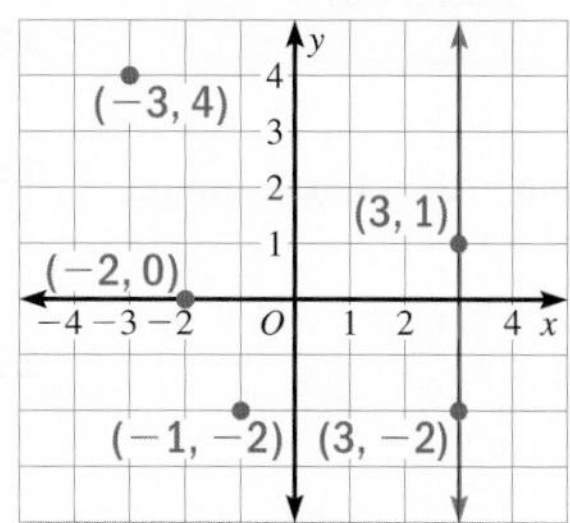

8.1 Exercises

More Practice, p. 810

Guided Practice

Vocabulary Check

1. Copy and complete: A relation is a(n) _?_ if for each input there is exactly one output. **function**

2. Draw a mapping diagram that represents a relation with domain $-1, 0, 2$ and range $1, 4$. Is only one answer possible? Explain. **See margin.**

Skill Check

Identify the domain and range of the relation.

3. (0, 0), (1, 2), (2, 4), (3, 6), (4, 8)
domain: 0, 1, 2, 3, 4; range: 0, 2, 4, 6, 8

4. (2, 5), (−5, 2), (1, 5), (2, −3), (7, 5)
domain: −5, 1, 2, 7; range: −3, 2, 5

Represent the relation as a graph and as a mapping diagram. Then tell whether the relation is a function. Explain your reasoning.

5. (1, 2), (1, 5), (2, 4), (3, 3), (4, 1)

6. (−4, 2), (2, 3), (4, 8), (0, 3), (−2, 2)

7. Error Analysis Describe and correct the error in the given statement. **See margin.**

The relation (1, −5), (2, −5), (3, 6), (4, 11) is not a function because the inputs 1 and 2 are both paired with the output −5.

2. See margin for art; no. *Sample answer:* Each element of the domain can be paired with either or both of the elements of the range.

5–6. See margin for art.

5. No; the input 1 is paired with two outputs, 2 and 5.

6. Yes; every input is paired with exactly one output.

Extra Examples

Example 4 Tell whether the relation represented by the graph is a function.

a.

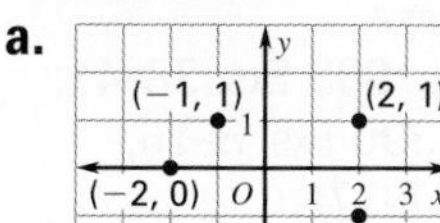

No; a vertical line would pass through (2, 1) and (2, −1).

b.

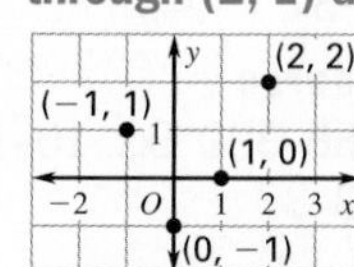

Yes; no vertical line passes through more than one point.

Multiple Representations

In their notebooks, have students record an example of each different representation of a relation (ordered pairs, table, graph, mapping diagram).

Visualize

Encourage students to draw their own examples of mapping diagrams and graphs representing relations that are *not* functions. Doing this should help students reinforce their understanding of a function.

Concept Check

How can you tell from the graph of a relation that it is a function? ***Sample answer:*** **Use the vertical line test. If no vertical line will pass through more than one point on the graph, the relation is a function.**

Daily Puzzler

Angie and Dave began running laps at the same time. Angie ran 4 laps in the same time it took Dave to run 3 laps. What is the ratio of Dave's speed to Angie's speed? **3 to 4**

2, 5–7. See Additional Answers beginning on page AA1.

3 APPLY

ASSIGNMENT GUIDE

Basic Course

Day 1: EP p. 803 Exs. 38–41; pp. 388–390 Exs. 8–16, 18–21, 27–37

Average Course

Day 1: pp. 388–390 Exs. 10–17, 20–24, 26–37

Advanced Course

Day 1: pp. 388–390 Exs. 10–18, 21–28*, 33–37

Block

pp. 388–390 Exs. 10–17, 20–24, 26–37 (with 8.2)

EXTRA PRACTICE

- Student Edition, p. 810
- Chapter 8 Resource Book, pp. 7–9
- Test and Practice Generator

TRANSPARENCY

Even-numbered answers are available on transparencies. A support transparency is available for Exercises 5, 6, 13–16, and 26.

HOMEWORK CHECK

When you review students' homework for this lesson, go over the following exercises to check understanding of key concepts.
Basic: 8, 13, 16, 18, 21
Average: 10, 14, 17, 21, 22
Advanced: 10, 15, 17, 21, 24

13–16. See Additional Answers beginning on page AA1.

21b.

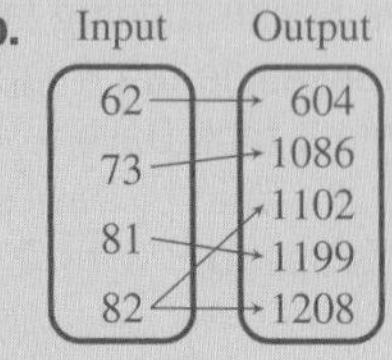

Practice and Problem Solving

Homework *Help*

Example	Exercises
1	8–11, 21, 24
2	13–16, 21
3	13–17, 21
4	18–20, 22, 24

Online Resources
CLASSZONE.COM
- More Examples
- eTutorial Plus

Identify the domain and range of the relation. 8–11. See margin.

A **8.** $(-2, 5), (-1, 2), (0, 4), (1, -9)$

9. $(7, 3), (7, 6), (7, 9), (3, 3), (3, 6)$

10.

x	4	2	−3	4	−4
y	0	−1	0	−1	0

11.

x	1.5	1.5	2.8	2.8	6.5
y	4.3	6.5	4.3	3.9	0.2

12. Copy and complete using *always, sometimes,* or *never*: A relation is _?_ a function. sometimes

Represent the relation as a graph and as a mapping diagram. Then tell whether the relation is a function. Explain your reasoning. 13–16. See margin.

13. $(1, 2), (2, 1), (3, 0), (3, 4), (4, 3)$

14. $(0, 4), (2, 0), (6, -4), (-4, 2), (8, 0)$

15.

x	−2	−1	0	1	2
y	−3	−3	−3	−3	−3

16.

x	0	−5	−10	5	−10
y	15	−10	−5	−15	20

17. Height The height of a person is measured every year from the age of 1 year to the age of 50 years. 17a–b. See margin.

a. Do the ordered pairs (age, height) represent a function? Explain.

b. Critical Thinking Would you expect the ordered pairs (height, age) to represent a function? Why or why not?

Tell whether the relation represented by the graph is a function.

18. no

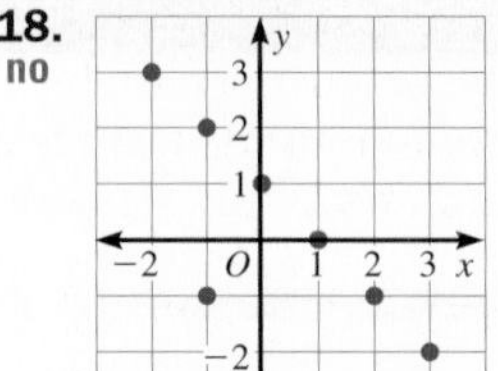

19. yes

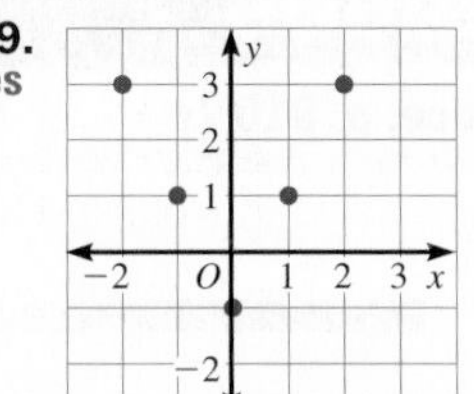

20. no

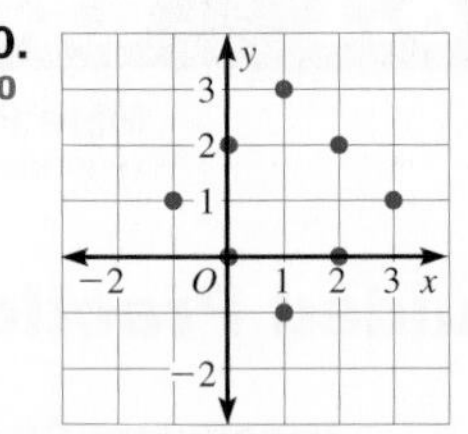

21. Basketball The table shows the numbers of games played and points scored by each starting player on the New Jersey Nets basketball team during the team's 2001–2002 regular season.

Player	Games played, *x*	Points scored, *y*
Todd MacCulloch	62	604
Kenyon Martin	73	1086
Keith Van Horn	81	1199
Kerry Kittles	82	1102
Jason Kidd	82	1208

a. Identify the domain and range of the relation given by the ordered pairs (x, y). domain: 62, 73, 81, 82; range: 604, 1086, 1102, 1199, 1208

b. Draw a mapping diagram for the relation. See margin.

c. Is the relation a function? Explain. No; the input 82 is paired with two outputs, 1102 and 1208.

8. domain: −2, −1, 0, 1; range: −9, 2, 4, 5

9. domain: 3, 7; range: 3, 6, 9

10. domain: −4, −3, 2, 4; range: −1, 0

11. domain: 1.5, 2.8, 6.5; range: 0.2, 3.9, 4.3, 6.5

13–16. See margin for art.

13. No; the input 3 is paired with two outputs, 0 and 4.

14. Yes; every input is paired with exactly one output.

15. Yes; every input is paired with exactly one output.

16. No; the input −10 is paired with two outputs, −5 and 20.

17a. Yes. *Sample answer:* A person can have only one height (output) for any given age (input).

17b. No. *Sample answer:* A person can have more than one age (outputs) for a given height (input) because the height of an adult remains the same for many years.

Teaching Tip

In Exercises 8–11, to help students remember that the domain of a relation is the set of all x-coordinates and the range is the set of all y-coordinates, point out that *domain* comes before *range* alphabetically just as x comes before y in the alphabet.

Common Error

Students may believe that if a relation is a function, then its inverse is also a function. They will first encounter the idea of the inverse of a function in Exercise 17 and then discuss inverses explicitly in Exercise 25.

23. Mapping diagram. *Sample answer:* A mapping diagram allows you to just look at the mapping and see if there is an input that has more than one arrow going from it, whereas with ordered pairs, you need to compare x and y values.

24b. *Sample answer:* The domain represents the altitude in feet of the skydiver during the jump, and includes the values from 0 to 12,000. The range represents the air pressure the skydiver experiences during the jump in pounds per square foot, and includes the values from about 1350 to 2125.

Computer-enhanced satellite image of a hurricane

22a. Yes. *Sample answer:* The advisories are issued at different times, so for any advisory number (input), the hurricane can have only one wind speed (output). This shows on the graph, because it passes the vertical line test.

24c. Yes. *Sample answer:* For any altitude (input), there is exactly one air pressure (output). The graph passes the vertical line test.

Reading *Algebra*

In the graph for Exercise 24, the symbol ⏚ on the vertical axis indicates a break in the scale. The interval between the first two tick marks represents 1200 lb/ft^2, while the interval between other consecutive tick marks represents only 200 lb/ft^2.

22. Hurricanes In 1995, a total of 32 regular weather advisories were issued during the storm that became Hurricane Opal. The graph shows the wind speed inside Opal at the time of each advisory.

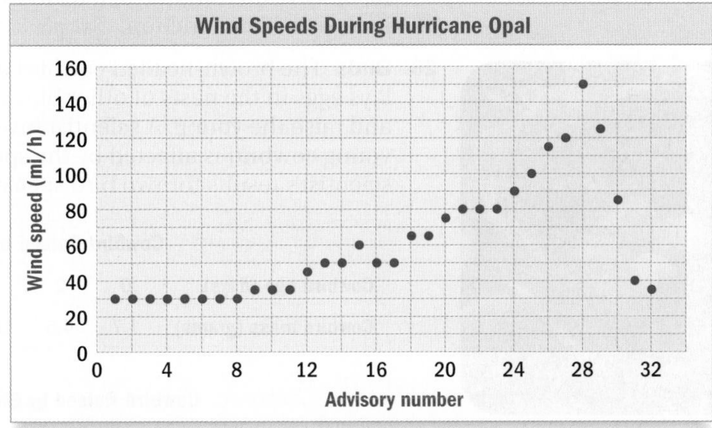

a. Is wind speed a function of advisory number? Explain.

b. Estimation An ocean storm is considered a hurricane if its wind speed is at least 74 miles per hour. For which advisories did Opal qualify as a hurricane? **advisories 20–30**

B **23.** ***Writing*** Suppose a relation is represented as a set of ordered pairs and as a mapping diagram. Which representation more clearly shows whether or not the relation is a function? Explain. **See margin.**

24. Extended Problem Solving A skydiver uses an altimeter to track altitude so that he or she knows when to open the parachute. The altimeter determines altitude by measuring changes in atmospheric pressure. The graph below shows how pressure varies with altitude as a skydiver falls from 12,000 feet to ground level. (The elevation of the ground is assumed to be 0 feet with respect to sea level.)

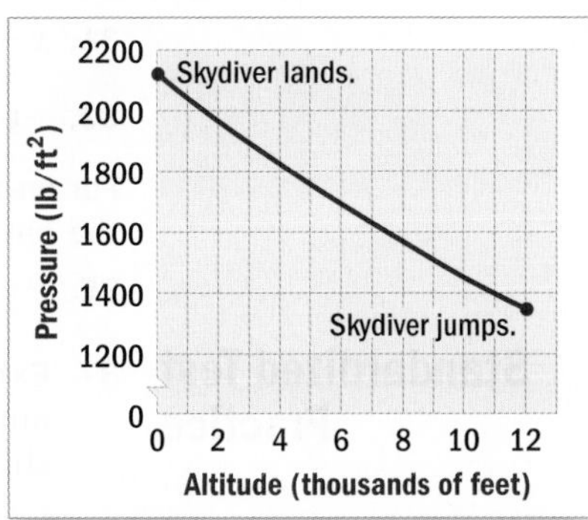

a. As a skydiver falls, does the atmospheric pressure increase or decrease? Does the reading on the skydiver's altimeter increase or decrease? **increase; decrease**

b. ***Writing*** Describe the domain and range of the relation represented by the graph. **See margin.**

c. Is the relation a function? Explain. **See margin.**

d. Interpret and Apply Some altimeters can sound an alarm warning a skydiver to open the parachute when the altitude falls to a certain level. If the alarm is set to go off at an altitude of 3000 feet, approximately what atmospheric pressure will trigger the alarm? **about 1900 lb/ft^2**

4 ASSESS

ASSESSMENT RESOURCES

For more assessment resources, see:
- Assessment Book
- Test and Practice Generator

MINI-QUIZ

Use the relation $(-2, 2)$, $(-1, 0)$, $(-1, 1)$, $(1, 2)$, and $(2, 1)$.

1. Identify the domain and range. **−2, −1, 1, 2; 0, 1, 2**
2. Represent the relation as a graph.

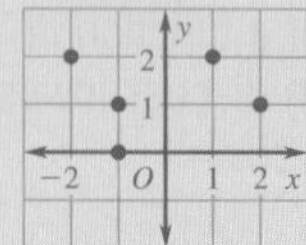

3. Tell whether the relation is a function. Explain your reasoning. **No; the input −1 is paired with two outputs, 0 and 1.**
4. **Challenge** Give an example of a relation that is *not* a function, but whose inverse is a function. ***Sample answer:*** **(2, 1), (2, 2), (2, 3), (2, 4)**

5 FOLLOW-UP

DIAGNOSIS/REMEDIATION

- Study Guide in Chapter 8 Resource Book, pp. 10–11
- eTutorial Plus Online
- Extra Practice, p. 810
- Lesson Practice in Chapter 8 Resource Book, pp. 7–9

ENGLISH LEARNER SUPPORT

- Spanish Study Guide
- Multi-Language Visual Glossary
- Chapter Audio Summaries CDs

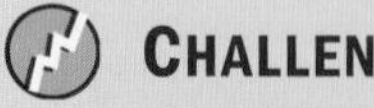

CHALLENGE

- Challenge Practice in Chapter 8 Resource Book, p. 12
- Teacher's Edition, p. 382F

26a–b. See Additional Answers beginning on page AA1.

C **25. Challenge** To form the *inverse* of a relation represented by a set of ordered pairs, you switch the coordinates of each ordered pair. For example, the inverse of the relation (1, 2), (3, 4), (5, 6) is (2, 1), (4, 3), (6, 5). Give an example of a relation that is a function, but whose inverse is *not* a function. ***Sample answer:*** **(2, 3), (5, 8), (9, 3)**

Nest with three wood thrush eggs and one cowbird egg

26. Birds The brown-headed cowbird does not raise its own offspring. It lays eggs in the nests of other bird species, which then hatch the eggs and raise the young. A scientist investigated whether the growth of a young cowbird is affected by the species of bird that raises it. The scientist's results for two bird species are shown below.

Cowbird Raised by Red-Eyed Vireo								
Cowbird age (days)	0	2	4	6	8	10	12	14
Cowbird mass (grams)	1.7	4.5	10.7	20.0	28.3	33.0	35.0	35.7

Cowbird Raised by Blue-Gray Gnatcatcher								
Cowbird age (days)	0	2	4	6	8	10	12	14
Cowbird mass (grams)	2.2	5.2	10.1	15.5	19.3	21.2	22.0	22.3

26a–b. See margin.

a. For each table, draw a graph for the relation given by the ordered pairs (age, mass). Draw both graphs in the same coordinate plane, and use a different color for each graph.

b. Interpret Compare the graphs from part (a). How is a cowbird's growth when raised by a red-eyed vireo like its growth when raised by a blue-gray gnatcatcher? How is its growth different?

Mixed Review

Evaluate the expression when $x = -5$ and $y = -7$. *(Lessons 1.5–1.7)*

27. $x + y$ **−12** **28.** $y - x + 10$ **8** **29.** $2x^2y$ **−350** **30.** $3x - 4y$ **13**

Tell whether the given value of the variable is a solution of the equation. *(Lesson 2.4)*

31. $x + 11 = 3;\ x = -8$ **yes** **32.** $-17 - a = -23;\ a = -6$ **no**

33. $-6m = -84;\ m = 13$ **no** **34.** $\frac{-144}{u} = 12;\ u = -12$ **yes**

For an account that earns simple annual interest, find the interest and the balance of the account. *(Lesson 7.7)*

35. $P = \$850$, $r = 3\%$, $t = 6$ years **\$153, \$1003** **36.** $P = \$4200$, $r = 5\%$, $t = 7.5$ years **\$1575, \$5775**

Standardized Test Practice

37. Extended Response The table shows the amount charged for standard ground shipping by an online electronics store.

Total cost of merchandise	Shipping cost
\$.01–\$25.00	\$5.95
\$25.01–\$50.00	\$7.95
\$50.01–\$75.00	\$9.95
\$75.01–\$100.00	\$11.95
Over \$100.00	\$13.95

a. Is shipping cost a function of merchandise cost? Explain.

b. Is merchandise cost a function of shipping cost? Explain. **No. *Sample answer:* Each shipping cost (input) corresponds to many different merchandise costs (outputs).**

37a. Yes. *Sample answer:* For any merchandise cost (input), there is exactly one shipping cost (output).

LESSON

8.2 Linear Equations *in* Two Variables

Vocabulary

equation in two variables, p. 391
solution of an equation in two variables, p. 391
graph of an equation in two variables, p. 392
linear equation, p. 392
function form, p. 393

BEFORE You solved equations in one variable.

Now You'll find solutions of equations in two variables.

WHY? So you can find the speed of a platypus, as in Ex. 41.

Volcanoes The Hawaiian volcano Mauna Loa has erupted many times. In 1859, lava from the volcano traveled 32 miles to the Pacific Ocean at an average speed of 4 miles per hour. In Example 2, you'll see how to use an *equation in two variables* to describe the flow of the lava toward the ocean.

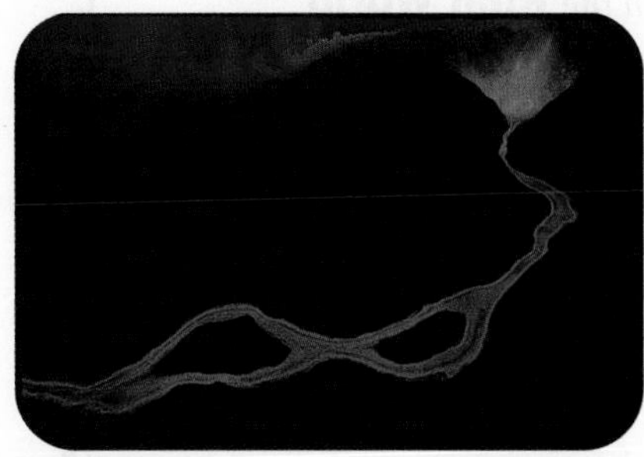

An example of an **equation in two variables** is $2x - y = 5$. A **solution** of an equation in x and y is an ordered pair (x, y) that produces a true statement when the values of x and y are substituted into the equation.

Example 1 *Checking Solutions*

Tell whether the ordered pair is a solution of $2x - y = 5$.

a. $(1, -3)$ **b.** $(4, 7)$

Solution

a.

$2x - y = 5$	**Write original equation.**
$2(1) - (-3) \stackrel{?}{=} 5$	**Substitute 1 for x and -3 for y.**
$5 = 5$ ✓	**Simplify.**

Answer $(1, -3)$ is a solution of $2x - y = 5$.

b.

$2x - y = 5$	**Write original equation.**
$2(4) - 7 \stackrel{?}{=} 5$	**Substitute 4 for x and 7 for y.**
$1 \neq 5$	**Simplify.**

Answer $(4, 7)$ is not a solution of $2x - y = 5$.

 ***Checkpoint***

Tell whether the ordered pair is a solution of $3x + 2y = -8$.

1. $(0, 4)$ no **2.** $(-2, -1)$ yes **3.** $(4, -12)$ no **4.** $(10, -19)$ yes

NCTM CURRICULUM STANDARDS

Standard 2: Analyze situations using algebraic symbols; Use models to understand relationships

Standard 10: Use representations to communicate ideas

1 PLAN

Skill Check

Find the value of the expression if $x = 2$ and $y = -1$.

1. $2x - 3y$ 7
2. $y - 2x$ −5
3. $x + y$ 1
4. $4y - x$ −6

LESSON OBJECTIVE

Find solutions of equations in two variables.

PACING

Suggested Number of Days
Basic Course: 2 days
Average Course: 2 days
Advanced Course: 2 days
Block: 0.5 block with 8.1
0.5 block with 8.3

TEACHING RESOURCES

For a complete list of Teaching Resources, see page 382B.

TRANSPARENCY

Warm-Up Exercises for this lesson are available on a transparency. A support transparency is available for Examples 3–5 and Checkpoint Exercises 5–10.

2 TEACH

MOTIVATING THE LESSON

Ask students how far a car would travel in 1 hour, 2 hours, and 3 hours if it travels at an average speed of 55 miles per hour. Ask for the distances again if the car had traveled at 65 miles per hour.

TIPS *for* NEW TEACHERS
Be sure students understand that equations in two variables do not have just one correct answer, but rather an infinite number of solutions. See Tips for New Teachers in the *Chapter 8 Resource Book*.

Extra Examples

Example 1 Tell whether the ordered pair is a solution of $x - 3y = -1$.
a. (4, 2) **no** **b.** (2, 1) **yes**

Example 2 The number of pages p that Donald has left to write for his 30-page research paper depends on how many days d he writes 5 pages per day. This situation can be modeled by the equation $p = 30 - 5d$.
a. Make a table of solutions for the equation. ***Sample:***

d	0	1	2
p	30	25	20

b. How many days does he need to finish his paper? **6 days**

Example 3 Graph $y = \frac{1}{2}x - 1$.

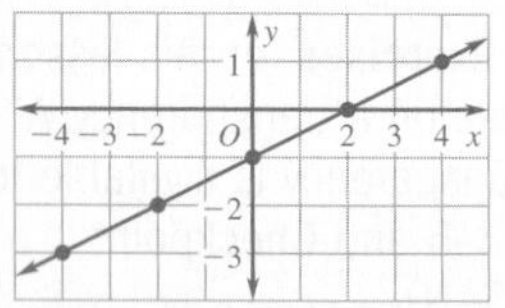

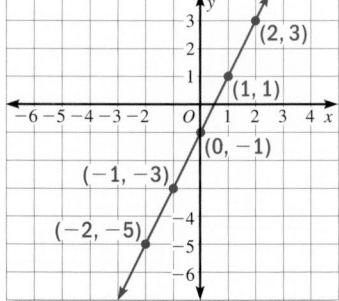

NOTETAKING
Point out to students that each example in the text has a subhead beside the Example title that summarizes the skill covered. Students should make sure their notes include all the skills.

5–10. See Additional Answers beginning on page AA1.

In the **Real World**

Volcanoes The temperature of lava from a Hawaiian volcano is about 1160°C. You can use the equation $F = 1.8C + 32$ to convert a Celsius temperature C to a Fahrenheit temperature F. What is the lava's temperature in degrees Fahrenheit? **2120°F**

Example 2 *Finding Solutions*

For the 1859 Mauna Loa eruption described on page 391, the lava's distance d (in miles) from the ocean t hours after it left the volcano can be approximated by the equation $d = 32 - 4t$.

a. Make a table of solutions for the equation.

b. How long did it take the lava to reach the ocean?

Solution

a. Substitute values of t into the equation $d = 32 - 4t$, and find values of d. The table shows that the following ordered pairs are solutions of the equation:

(0, 32), (1, 28), (2, 24)

t	Substitution	d
0	$d = 32 - 4(0)$	32
1	$d = 32 - 4(1)$	28
2	$d = 32 - 4(2)$	24

b. Find the value of t when $d = 0$.

$0 = 32 - 4t$ **Substitute 0 for d in the equation $d = 32 - 4t$.**

$-32 = -4t$ **Subtract 32 from each side.**

$8 = t$ **Divide each side by −4.**

Answer It took the lava about 8 hours to reach the ocean.

Graphs The **graph** of an equation in two variables is the set of points in a coordinate plane that represent all the solutions of the equation. An equation whose graph is a line is called a **linear equation**.

Example 3 *Graphing a Linear Equation*

Graph $y = 2x - 1$.

1 Make a table of solutions.

x	−2	−1	0	1	2
y	−5	−3	−1	1	3

2 List the solutions as ordered pairs.

(−2, −5), (−1, −3), (0, −1), (1, 1), (2, 3)

3 Graph the ordered pairs, and note that the points lie on a line. Draw the line, which is the graph of $y = 2x - 1$.

Study *Strategy*

In Example 3, *every* point on the line shown represents a solution of $y = 2x - 1$, not just the points from the table. For instance, you can verify that the point (0.5, 0) on the line is a solution:

$y = 2x - 1$
$0 \stackrel{?}{=} 2(0.5) - 1$
$0 = 0$ ✓

Checkpoint

Graph the equation. **5–8. See margin.**

5. $y = 2x$ **6.** $y = -x + 3$ **7.** $y = 3x - 4$ **8.** $y = \frac{1}{2}x + 1$

Horizontal and Vertical Lines The graph of the equation $y = b$ is the horizontal line through $(0, b)$. The graph of the equation $x = a$ is the vertical line through $(a, 0)$.

Study *Strategy*

In Example 4, notice that the graph of $y = 3$ consists of all points with a y-coordinate of 3. Similarly, the graph of $x = -2$ consists of all points with an x-coordinate of -2.

Example 4 *Graphing Horizontal and Vertical Lines*

Graph $y = 3$ and $x = -2$.

a. The graph of the equation $y = 3$ is the horizontal line through $(0, 3)$.

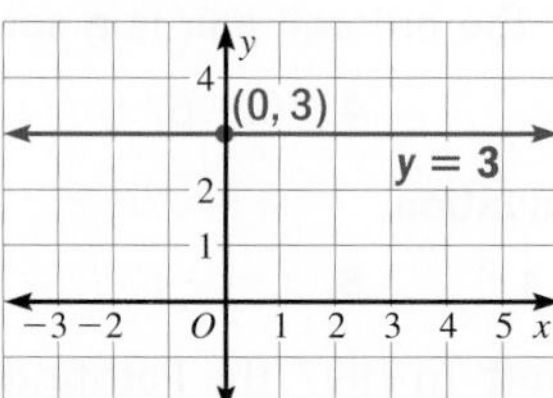

b. The graph of the equation $x = -2$ is the vertical line through $(-2, 0)$.

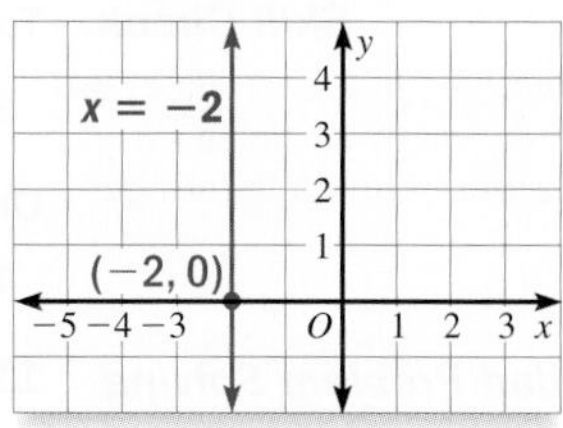

Equations as Functions In Examples 3 and 4, the vertical line test shows that $y = 2x - 1$ and $y = 3$ are functions, while $x = -2$ is not a function. In general, a linear equation is a function *unless* its graph is a vertical line. An equation that is solved for y is in **function form**. You may find it helpful to write an equation in function form before graphing it.

Not function form: $3x + y = 7$ **Function form:** $y = -3x + 7$

Example 5 *Writing an Equation in Function Form*

Write $x + 2y = 6$ in function form. Then graph the equation.

To write the equation in function form, solve for y.

$x + 2y = 6$ **Write original equation.**

$2y = -x + 6$ **Subtract x from each side.**

$y = -\frac{1}{2}x + 3$ **Multiply each side by $\frac{1}{2}$.**

Study *Strategy*

In the table for Example 5, only even x-values are used so that all the y-values are integers. This makes the ordered pairs (x, y) easy to graph. Be sure to choose convenient x-values when you graph an equation that involves a fraction.

To graph the equation, use its function form to make a table of solutions. Graph the ordered pairs (x, y) from the table, and draw a line through the points.

x	−4	−2	0	2	4
y	5	4	3	2	1

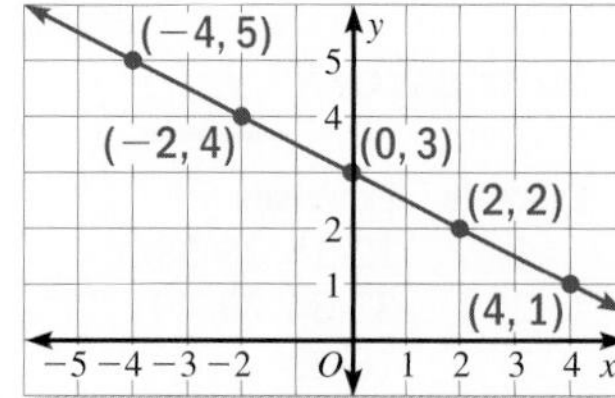

Checkpoint

9–10. See margin for art.

9. Graph $y = -1$ and $x = 4$. Tell whether each equation is a function. **$y = -1$ is a function; $x = 4$ is not a function.**

$y = \frac{2}{3}x - 1$ **10.** Write $2x - 3y = 3$ in function form. Then graph the equation.

Extra Examples

Example 4 Graph the equation.

a. $x = 1$

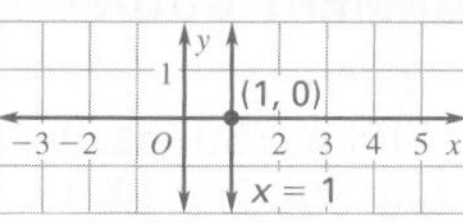

b. $y = -4$

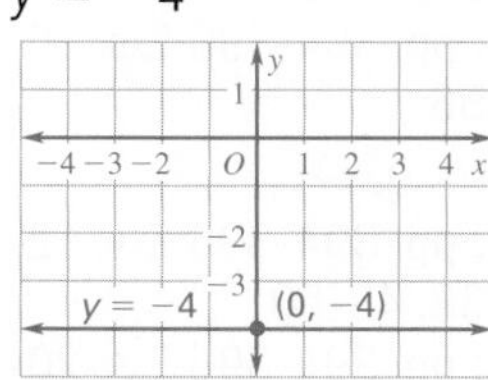

Example 5 Write $x + 3y = 3$ in function form. Then graph the equation. $\mathbf{y = -\frac{1}{3}x + 1}$

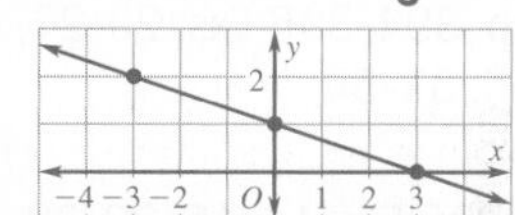

DIFFERENTIATING INSTRUCTION

Alternative Teaching Strategy
Assign each student a different integer value of x. Using the equation in Example 5, have students find their corresponding y-value. Draw a large coordinate grid on the board and have the students graph their ordered pairs. Draw a line through the points.

CONCEPT CHECK

How would you graph $y = 4x + 1$? ***Sample answer:*** **Choose at least three values for x and then use the equation to find corresponding values of y. Plot the ordered pairs (x, y) on a coordinate grid and then draw a line through them.**

DAILY PUZZLER

Andre raises ducks and dogs. In all, his animals have 25 heads and 66 legs. How many of each animal does Andre have? **17 ducks, 8 dogs**

3 APPLY

ASSIGNMENT GUIDE

Basic Course

Day 1: SRH p. 780 Exs. 9-12; pp. 394-396 Exs. 12-15, 32-38, 43-50

Day 2: pp. 394-396 Exs. 16-27, 51-56

Average Course

Day 1: pp. 394-396 Exs. 12-15, 32-38, 43-50

Day 2: pp. 394-396 Exs. 20-31, 39-41, 51-56

Advanced Course

Day 1: pp. 394-396 Exs. 12-15, 32-34, 37, 38, 45-48

Day 2: pp. 394-396 Exs. 20-27, 39-44*, 53-56

Block

pp. 394-396 Exs. 12-15, 32-38, 43-50 (with 8.1)

pp. 394-396 Exs. 20-31, 39-41, 51-56 (with 8.3)

EXTRA PRACTICE

- Student Edition, p. 810
- Chapter 8 Resource Book, pp. 15-17
- Test and Practice Generator

TRANSPARENCY

Even-numbered answers are available on transparencies. A support transparency is available for Exercises 7-11, 16-31, and 42.

HOMEWORK CHECK

When you review students' homework for this lesson, go over the following exercises to check understanding of key concepts.

Basic: 12, 16, 20, 24, 32

Average: 13, 20, 22, 26, 34

Advanced: 15, 20, 21, 27, 39

8.2 Exercises

More Practice, p. 810

Guided Practice

Vocabulary Check

1. Copy and complete: An equation whose graph is a line is called a(n) _?_. **linear equation**

2. Is the equation $x = 4y + 3$ in function form? Explain. **See margin.**

2. No. *Sample answer:* In function form, an equation is solved for *y*. The equation in function form is $y = \frac{1}{4}x - \frac{3}{4}$.

Skill Check **Tell whether the ordered pair is a solution of $y = 5x - 7$.**

3. (2, 3) **yes** **4.** (0, −6) **no** **5.** (4, 14) **no** **6.** (−3, −22) **yes**

Graph the equation. **7–10. See margin.**

7. $y = x - 4$ **8.** $x = -1$ **9.** $y = 2$ **10.** $3x + 2y = -2$

Guided Problem Solving

11. Spacecraft In 1997, the Pathfinder spacecraft landed on Mars. It contained a robotic vehicle named Sojourner that could roam up to 500 meters from the lander. The distance *d* (in meters) that Sojourner could travel in *t* hours is given by $d = 24t$. How long would it take Sojourner to reach its maximum distance from the lander?

1) Copy and complete the table using the given equation.

t	0	5	10	15	20	25	30
d	?	?	?	?	?	?	?
	0	120	240	360	480	600	720

2) Use your completed table to graph $d = 24t$. **See margin.**

3) Find the point on the graph whose *d*-coordinate is 500, and estimate the *t*-coordinate of this point. How much time would it take Sojourner to reach its maximum distance from the lander? **about 21; about 21 h**

Practice and Problem Solving

Homework Help

Example	Exercises
1	12-15, 35-38
2	32-34, 39, 40
3	16-23
4	16-23
5	24-31

Online Resources CLASSZONE.COM
- More Examples
- eTutorial Plus

Tell whether the ordered pair is a solution of the equation.

A **12.** $y = x - 3$; (1, −4) **no** **13.** $y = -4x + 9$; (3, −3) **yes**

14. $x - 2y = 8$; (−6, −7) **yes** **15.** $3x - 5y = -1$; (9, 5) **no**

Graph the equation. Tell whether the equation is a function. **16–23. See margin for art.**

16. $y = -x$ **yes** **17.** $y = 2x - 3$ **yes** **18.** $y = 1$ **yes** **19.** $x = -4$ **no**

20. $y = \frac{3}{2}x + 1$ **yes** **21.** $y = -5$ **yes** **22.** $x = 3$ **no** **23.** $y = -5x + 2$ **yes**

Write the equation in function form. Then graph the equation. **24–31. See margin for art.**

24. $y - x = -1$ $y = x - 1$ **25.** $2x + y = 1$ $y = -2x + 1$ **26.** $3x - y = 5$ $y = 3x - 5$ **27.** $8x + 2y = -4$ $y = -4x - 2$

28. $x - 3y = -9$ $y = \frac{1}{3}x + 3$ **29.** $3x + 4y = 0$ $y = -\frac{3}{4}x$ **30.** $5x - 2y = 6$ $y = \frac{5}{2}x - 3$ **31.** $2x + 3y = 12$ $y = -\frac{2}{3}x + 4$

32. Converting Weights The formula $y = 2000x$ converts a weight x in tons to a weight y in pounds. The largest known blue whale weighed 195 tons. Find the weight of the whale in pounds. **390,000 lb**

33. Converting Units of Capacity The formula $y = 0.001x$ converts a capacity x in milliliters to a capacity y in liters. A juice can has a capacity of 355 milliliters. Find the capacity of the can in liters. **0.355 L**

34. Converting Areas The formula $y \approx 2.59x$ converts an area x in square miles to an approximate area y in square kilometers. The state of Iowa has an area of 56,276 square miles. Find this area in square kilometers. Round your answer to the nearest thousand square kilometers. **146,000 km²**

Find the value of *a* that makes the ordered pair a solution of the equation.

B **35.** $y = 2x + 5$; $(-1, a)$ **3**

36. $y = -3x - 1$; $(a, 5)$ **−2**

37. $4x - 7y = 19$; $(-4, a)$ **−5**

38. $6x + 5y = 21$; $(a + 2, -3)$ **4**

39. Extended Problem Solving The fork length of a shark is the distance from the tip of the shark's snout to the fork of its tail, as shown.

The table lists equations giving the fork length f as a function of the total length t for three species of sharks, where both f and t are measured in centimeters.

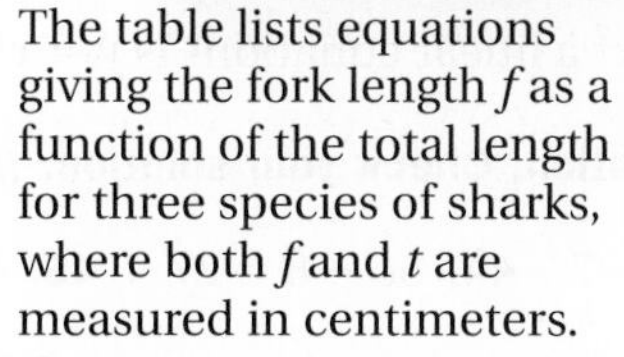

Species	Equation
Bigeye thresher	$f = 0.560t + 17.7$
Scalloped hammerhead	$f = 0.776t - 0.313$
White shark	$f = 0.944t - 5.74$

a. To the nearest centimeter, approximate the fork length of each given species of shark if the shark's total length is 250 centimeters.
bigeye thresher: 158 cm, scalloped hammerhead: 194 cm, white shark: 230 cm

b. Interpret For each species of shark, what percent of the total length does the fork length represent if the shark is 250 centimeters long? Round your answers to the nearest percent.
bigeye thresher: 63%, scalloped hammerhead: 78%, white shark: 92%

c. *Writing* Which species of shark do you think has the longest tail relative to its body size? Explain your reasoning.

39c. Bigeye thresher. *Sample answer:* The bigeye thresher has the shortest body relative to its total length, so it must have the longest tail relative to its body length.

40. Volcanoes The Hawaiian-Emperor chain of volcanoes is shown at the left. The age a (in millions of years) of a volcano in the chain can be approximated by $a = 0.0129d - 2.25$, where d is the volcano's distance (in kilometers) from Kilauea, measured along the chain.

a. Suiko is 4794 kilometers from Kilauea, measured along the chain. Approximate the age of Suiko to the nearest tenth of a million years. **59.6 million years**

b. Midway is about 27.7 million years old. Approximate Midway's distance along the chain from Kilauea to the nearest ten kilometers. **2320 km**

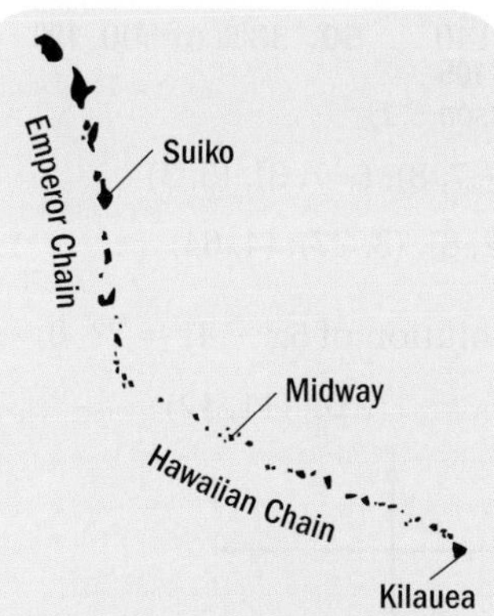

Some of the volcanoes on the map are extinct, and some are underwater.

COMMON ERROR

In Exercises 18 and 21, students may think that since the y-axis is vertical, the graphs of $y = 1$ and $y = -5$ are also vertical so they graph $x = 1$ and $x = -5$ instead. Similarly, in Exercises 19 and 22, students may think that since the x-axis is horizontal, the graphs of $x = -4$ and $x = 3$ are also horizontal so they graph $y = -4$ and $y = 3$ instead.

TEACHING TIP

In Exercises 35–38, point out that the result of substituting the given ordered pair into the equation will be an equation in one variable.

7.

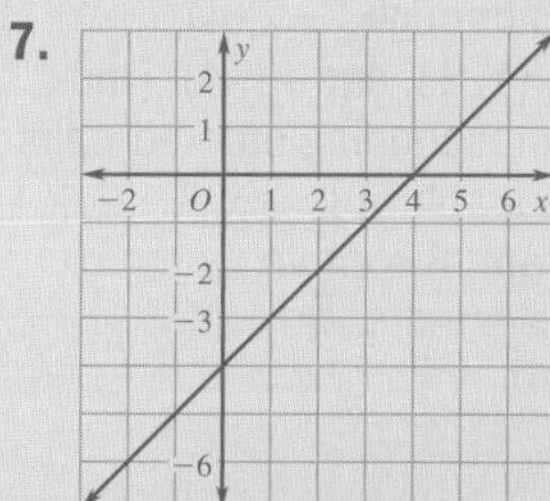

8.

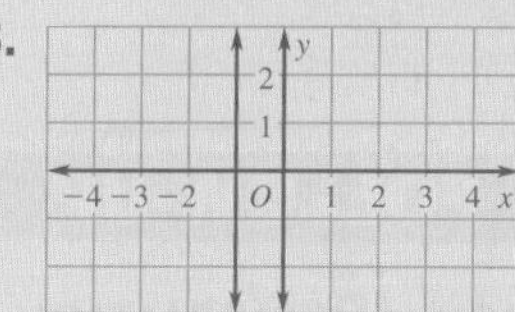

9.

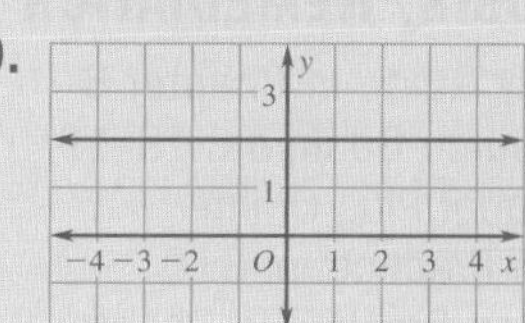

10.

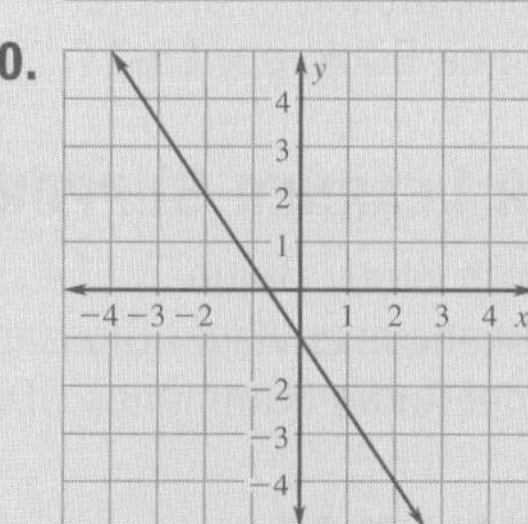

11 (Step 2), 16–31. See Additional Answers beginning on page AA1.

4 ASSESS

ASSESSMENT RESOURCES

For more assessment resources, see:
- Assessment Book
- Test and Practice Generator

MINI-QUIZ

1. Is (2, −3) a solution of the equation $2x + y = 1$? **yes**
2. Write $2x + y = 1$ in function form. **$y = -2x + 1$**
3. Graph $x + 2y = 4$.

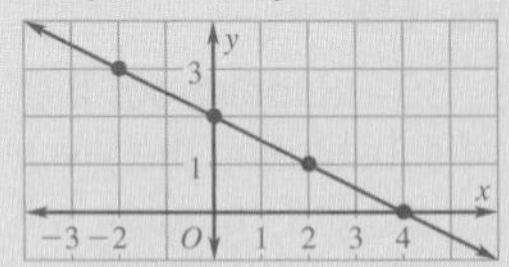

4. **Challenge** The graph of $y = x^2$ passes through (−2, 4), (−1, 1), (0, 0), (1, 1), and (2, 4). Find five corresponding ordered pairs for the graph of $y = x^2 - 2$ and graph the curve.

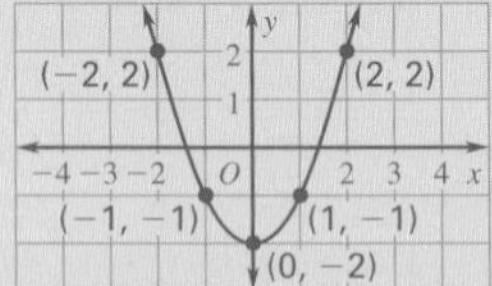

5 FOLLOW-UP

DIAGNOSIS/REMEDIATION

- Study Guide in Chapter 8 Resource Book, pp. 18–19
- eTutorial Plus Online
- Extra Practice, p. 810
- Lesson Practice in Chapter 8 Resource Book, pp. 15–17

ENGLISH LEARNER SUPPORT

- Spanish Study Guide
- Multi-Language Visual Glossary
- Chapter Audio Summaries CDs

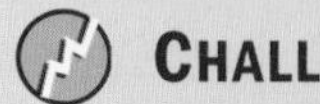

CHALLENGE

- Challenge Practice in Chapter 8 Resource Book, p. 20
- Teacher's Edition, p. 382F

42b. See Additional Answers beginning on page AA1.

C **41. Platypuses** The platypus is an animal with a broad flat tail, webbed feet, and a snout like a duck's bill. Although a platypus spends much of its time in the water, it can also walk on land. The diagram below shows one complete stride of a walking platypus.

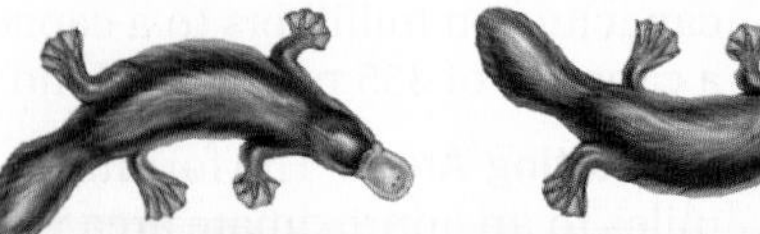  

The stride frequency f is the number of strides per second the platypus takes. It can be approximated by the equation $f = 2.13s + 1.19$, where s is the speed of the platypus in meters per second.

a. Solve the given equation for s to obtain an equation that gives speed as a function of stride frequency. $s = \frac{f - 1.19}{2.13}$, or $s \approx \frac{f}{2.13} - 0.56$

b. Apply Use the equation from part (a) to approximate the speed of a platypus that takes 3 strides per second. Round your answer to the nearest tenth of a meter per second. **0.8 m/sec**

42. Challenge In this exercise, you will investigate the graph of $y = x^2$.

a. Copy and complete the table of solutions for $y = x^2$.

x	−3	−2	−1	0	1	2	3
y	?	?	?	?	?	?	?
	9	4	1	0	1	4	9

b. Graph $y = x^2$ by plotting the points from the table and drawing a smooth curve that passes through all the points. **See margin.**

c. Is $y = x^2$ a linear equation? Is $y = x^2$ a function? Explain.

42c. No; yes. ***Sample answer:*** It is not linear because its graph is a curve, not a straight line. It is a function because its graph passes the vertical line test.

Mixed Review

Solve the equation. Check your solution. *(Lesson 3.1)*

43. $2x + 5 = -7$ **−6** **44.** $5c - 8 = 27$ **7** **45.** $4 - 3w = 16$ **−4** **46.** $\frac{n}{6} + 2 = 9$ **42**

Find the percent of the number. *(Lesson 7.1)*

47. 25% of 12 **3** **48.** 90% of 80 **72** **49.** 75% of 140 **105** **50.** 38% of 500 **190**

Identify the domain and range of the relation. *(Lesson 8.1)*

51. (−2, 1), (0, 2), (2, 3), (4, 4) **52.** (5, 0), (−7, 8), (−7, 3), (5, 3)

53. (6, 4), (6, −2), (6, 9), (6, 1) **54.** (1, 1), (2, 8), (3, 27), (4, 64)

51. domain: −2, 0, 2, 4; range: 1, 2, 3, 4

52. domain: −7, 5; range: 0, 3, 8

53. domain: 6; range: −2, 1, 4, 9

54. domain: 1, 2, 3, 4; range: 1, 8, 27, 64

Standardized Test Practice

55. Multiple Choice Which ordered pair is *not* a solution of $5x - 4y = 7$? **B**

A. (−9, −13) **B.** (−5, −9) **C.** (7, 7) **D.** (11, 12)

56. Multiple Choice The graph of which equation is shown? **I**

F. $x = -2$ **G.** $y = -2$

H. $x = 2$ **I.** $y = 2$

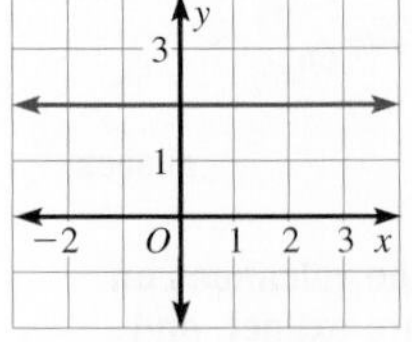

8.2 Graphing Linear Equations

Goal Use a graphing calculator to graph linear equations.

Example

Use a graphing calculator to solve the following problem.

A pool charges \$6 for a summer membership, plus \$1.25 per visit. The equation $C = 6 + 1.25v$ gives your cost C if you visit v times. How many times can you visit if you have \$30 to spend on swimming?

1 Rewrite the equation using x and y.

$C = 6 + 1.25v$ **Write original equation.**

$y = 6 + 1.25x$ **Substitute x for v and y for C.**

2 Enter the equation.

Keystrokes  **6**  **1.25** [x]

3 Press [WINDOW] to set the borders of the graph. Set the cursor increment to 1 unit: ΔX = 1.

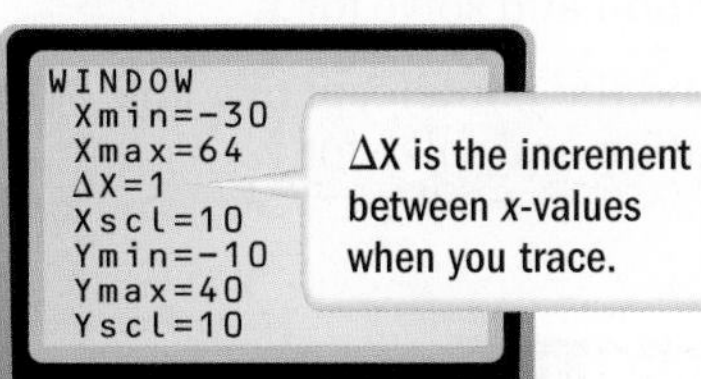

Press [GRAPH] to graph the equation. Press [TRACE] and move the cursor along the graph using [◄] and [►].

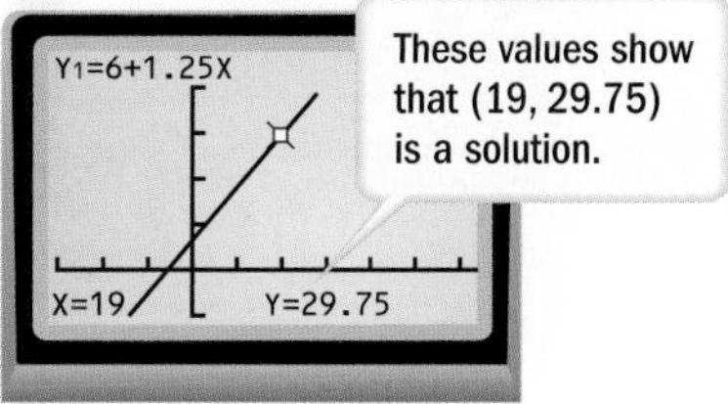

Answer The graph shows that you can visit 19 times for \$29.75.

Tech Help

If the cursor moves out of view as you trace, press [ENTER] to redraw the screen with the cursor in the center.

Online Resources
CLASSZONE.COM
- Keystroke Help

Draw Conclusions

Use a graphing calculator to graph the equation. Find the unknown value in the ordered pair. (Use ΔX = 0.1.) 1–4. See margin for art.

1. $y = 5 - x$; (1.8, ?) 3.2
2. $y = x - 5$; (?, −2.2) 2.8
3. $y = -2.5x + 6$; (3.2, ?) −2
4. $y = -0.5x + 4$; (?, 5.2) −2.4
5. **Video Games** A video game store has a \$15 membership fee and rents games for \$3.25 each. Use a graphing calculator to graph $C = 15 + 3.25g$, which gives your cost C if you rent g games. How many games can you rent if you have \$45 to spend? See margin for art; 9 games.

NCTM CURRICULUM STANDARDS
Standard 6: Solve problems in math and other contexts
Standard 10: Create representations to communicate mathematical ideas

1 PLAN

Learn the Method

- Students will use a graphing calculator to graph linear equations.
- Students can check their work on Exercises 24–31 in Lesson 8.2.

Grouping

Students should work individually.

2 TEACH

Discussion

As students are working, ask: "Why are negative values of x irrelevant in this problem?" **There cannot be a negative number of pool visits.**

Extra Examples

Example Use a graphing calculator to graph the equation $y = 4 + 0.5x$. Find the unknown value in the ordered pair (2.2, ?). (Use ΔX = 0.1.) 5.1

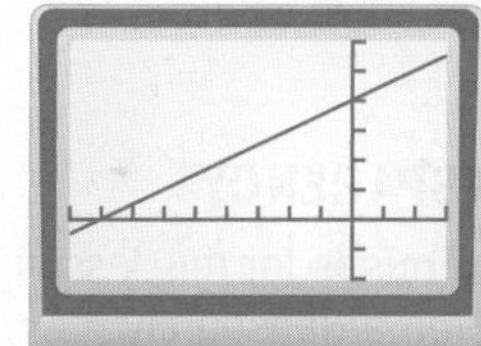

3 CLOSE

Assessment

1. Use a graphing calculator to graph the equation $y = 0.5 + x$. Find the unknown value in the ordered pair (?, −1.7). (Use ΔX = 0.1.) **−2.2**

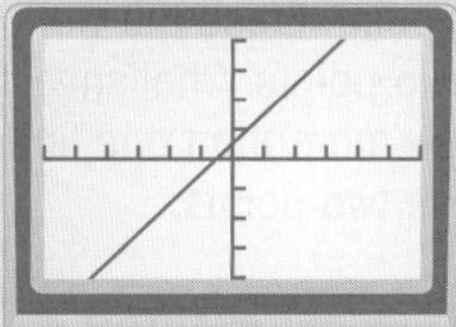

1–5. See Additional Answers beginning on page AA1.

1 PLAN

Skill Check

Solve the equation.

1. $2y = 12$ **6**
2. $3x = -9$ **−3**
3. $-8y = 8$ **−1**
4. $-4x = -32$ **8**

Lesson Objective

Use *x*- and *y*-intercepts to graph linear equations.

Pacing

Suggested Number of Days
Basic Course: 1 day
Average Course: 1 day
Advanced Course: 1 day
Block: 0.5 block with 8.2

Teaching Resources

For a complete list of Teaching Resources, see page 382B.

Transparency

Warm-Up Exercises for this lesson are available on a transparency. A support transparency is available for Examples 2 and 3, and Checkpoint Exercises 1–3.

2 TEACH

Motivating the Lesson

On the board, graph a single point on a coordinate grid. Have three students each draw a different line through the point. Erase the work and graph two points. Challenge students to draw more than one line through these two points.

1–3. See Additional Answers beginning on page AA1.

LESSON **8.3**

Using Intercepts

BEFORE	*Now*	WHY?
You graphed using tables of solutions.	You'll use *x*- and *y*-intercepts to graph linear equations.	So you can find how much food to buy for a barbecue, as in Ex. 9.

Vocabulary
x-intercept, p. 398
y-intercept, p. 398

You can graph a linear equation quickly by recognizing that only two points are needed to draw a line. It is often convenient to choose points where the line crosses the axes.

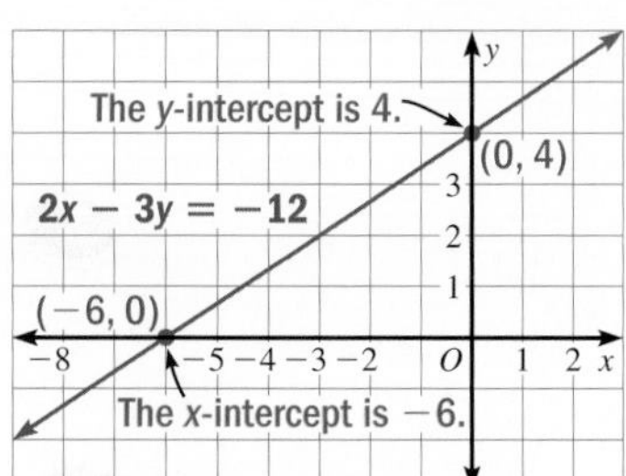

The *x*-coordinate of a point where a graph crosses the *x*-axis is an **x-intercept**. The *y*-coordinate of a point where a graph crosses the *y*-axis is a **y-intercept**. The graph shown has an *x*-intercept of −6 and a *y*-intercept of 4.

Finding Intercepts

To find the *x*-intercept of a line, substitute 0 for *y* in the line's equation and solve for *x*.

To find the *y*-intercept of a line, substitute 0 for *x* in the line's equation and solve for *y*.

Example 1 ***Finding Intercepts of a Graph***

Find the intercepts of the graph of $3x - 2y = 6$.

To find the *x*-intercept, let $y = 0$ and solve for *x*.

$3x - 2y = 6$ **Write original equation.**

$3x - 2(0) = 6$ **Substitute 0 for *y*.**

$3x = 6$ **Simplify.**

$x = 2$ **Divide each side by 3.**

To find the *y*-intercept, let $x = 0$ and solve for *y*.

$3x - 2y = 6$ **Write original equation.**

$3(0) - 2y = 6$ **Substitute 0 for *x*.**

$-2y = 6$ **Simplify.**

$y = -3$ **Divide each side by −2.**

Answer The *x*-intercept is 2, and the *y*-intercept is −3.

Watch *Out*

The intercepts of a graph are numbers, not ordered pairs. In Example 1, for instance, the *x*-intercept is 2, not (2, 0). Similarly, the *y*-intercept is −3, not (0, −3).

NCTM CURRICULUM STANDARDS
Standard 2: Understand functions; Use models to understand relationships
Standard 6: Solve problems in math and other contexts

Example 2 *Using Intercepts to Graph a Linear Equation*

Graph the equation $3x - 2y = 6$ from Example 1.

The x-intercept is 2, so plot the point (2, 0). The y-intercept is -3, so plot the point $(0, -3)$.

Draw a line through the two points.

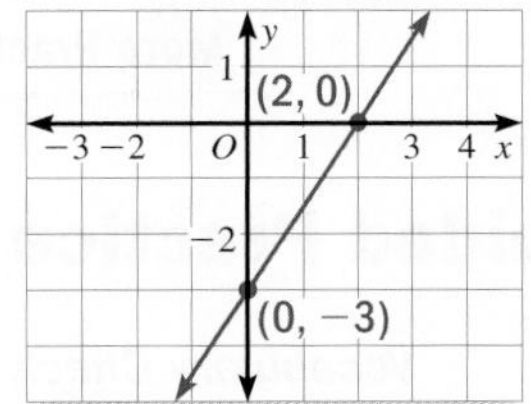

1. x-intercept: -2; y-intercept: 1
2. x-intercept: 3; y-intercept: 4
3. x-intercept: -4; y-intercept: -8

Checkpoint

Find the intercepts of the equation's graph. Then graph the equation. **1–3. See margin for art.**

1. $x - 2y = -2$ **2.** $4x + 3y = 12$ **3.** $y = -2x - 8$

Example 3 *Writing and Graphing an Equation*

Canoeing You are canoeing along a 12 mile stretch of river. You travel 4 miles per hour when paddling and 2 miles per hour when drifting. Write and graph an equation describing your possible paddling and drifting times for the trip. Give three possible combinations of paddling and drifting times.

Solution

1) To write an equation, let x be the paddling time and let y be the drifting time (both in hours). First write a verbal model.

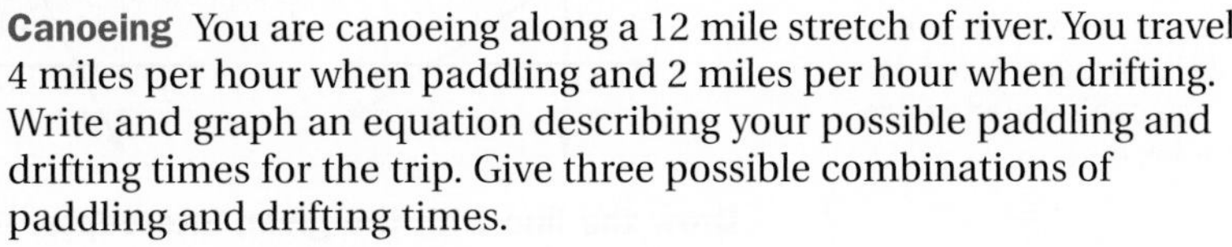

Then use the verbal model to write the equation.

$$4x + 2y = 12$$

2) To graph the equation, find and use the intercepts.

Find x-intercept: $4x + 2y = 12$
$4x + 2(\mathbf{0}) = 12$
$4x = 12$
$x = 3$

Find y-intercept: $4x + 2y = 12$
$4(\mathbf{0}) + 2y = 12$
$2y = 12$
$y = 6$

Drifting time (h) / Paddling time (h): graph of $4x + 2y = 12$ through (0, 6) and (3, 0).

3) Three points on the graph are (0, 6), (2, 2), and (3, 0). So, you can either not paddle at all and drift for 6 hours, or paddle for 2 hours and drift for 2 hours, or paddle for 3 hours and not drift at all.

Study *Strategy*

In Example 3, the graph lies entirely in the first quadrant because the paddling time x and the drifting time y must be nonnegative.

TIPS *for* NEW TEACHERS

Stress that the x-intercept of a graph has a y-coordinate of 0 and that the y-intercept of a graph has an x-coordinate of 0. See Tips for New Teachers in the *Chapter 8 Resource Book*.

Extra Examples

Example 1 Find the intercepts of the graph of $2y = x + 2$. **x-intercept: -2, y-intercept: 1**

Example 2 Graph the equation $2y = x + 2$.

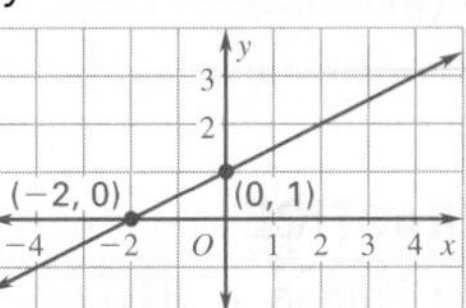

Example 3 While at the beach, you can rent a boogie board for \$1 per hour or a surfboard for \$2 per hour. You have \$10 to spend. Write and graph an equation describing the possible combinations of hours x renting a boogie board and hours y renting a surfboard that you can afford. **$x + 2y = 10$**

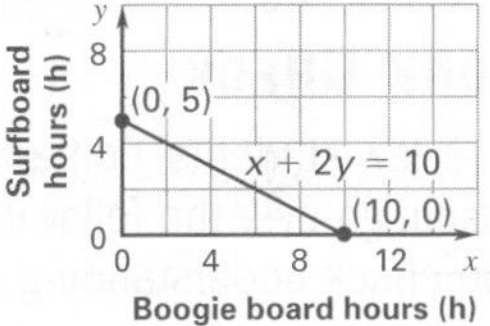

Concept Check

How do you find the y-intercept of a line from the equation of the line? **Substitute 0 for x and solve the resulting equation for y.**

Daily Puzzler

Draw a horizontal line with more than one y-intercept or explain why the line is not possible? **This is not possible since a horizontal line can only cross the y-axis once.**

3 APPLY

ASSIGNMENT GUIDE

Basic Course

Day 1: SRH p. 785 Exs. 1, 4, 5, 7; pp. 400–402 Exs. 10–19, 22–25, 30, 34–47

Average Course

Day 1: pp. 400–402 Exs. 13–24, 27–32, 36–39, 42–48

Advanced Course

Day 1: pp. 400–402 Exs. 15–20, 23–35*, 40–48

Block

pp. 400–402 Exs. 13–24, 27–32, 36–48 (with 8.2)

Extra Practice

- Student Edition, p. 810
- Chapter 8 Resource Book, pp. 23–25
- Test and Practice Generator

Transparency

Even-numbered answers are available on transparencies. A support transparency is available for Exercises 6–26, 29, and 30.

Homework Check

When you review students' homework for this lesson, go over the following exercises to check understanding of key concepts.

Basic: 10, 16, 19, 22, 24

Average: 13, 17, 19, 21, 30

Advanced: 16, 18, 20, 24, 29

6–18, 19b. See Additional Answers beginning on page AA1.

8.3 Exercises

More Practice, p. 810

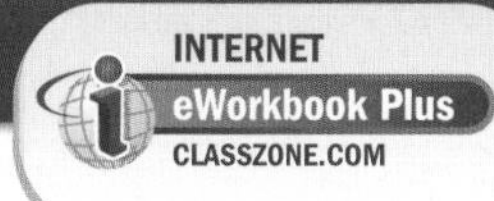

Guided Practice

Vocabulary Check

1. Copy and complete: For the line that passes through the points $(0, -7)$ and $(3, 0)$, the _?_ is -7 and the _?_ is 3. **y-intercept, x-intercept**

2. Describe how you can find the x- and y-intercepts of a line by using the line's equation. **See margin.**

Skill Check **Identify the x-intercept and the y-intercept of the line.**

3.

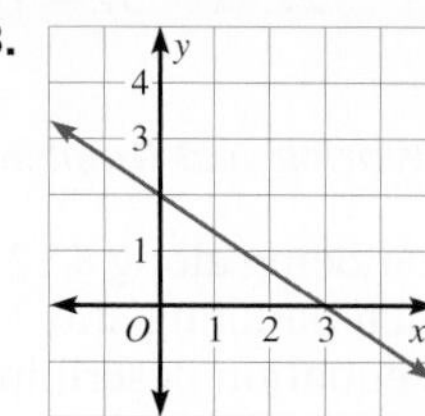

4.

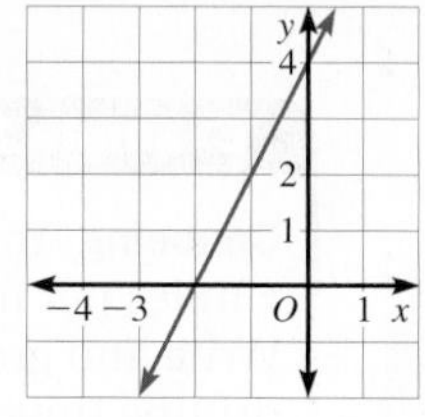

5.

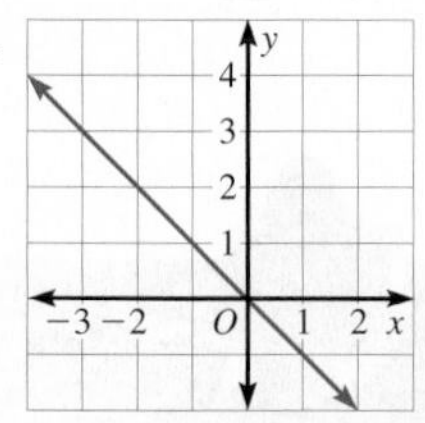

2. ***Sample answer:*** **To find the x-intercept, substitute 0 for y in the line's equation and solve for x. To find the y-intercept, substitute 0 for x in the line's equation and solve for y.**

3. x-intercept: 3; y-intercept: 2

4. x-intercept: -2; y-intercept: 4

5. x-intercept: 0; y-intercept: 0

Draw the line with the given intercepts. **6–8. See margin.**

6. x-intercept: 4
y-intercept: 5

7. x-intercept: -6
y-intercept: 3

8. x-intercept: -1
y-intercept: -2

9. Shopping You are in charge of buying food for a barbecue. You have budgeted \$30 for ground beef and chicken. Ground beef costs \$3 per pound, and chicken costs \$5 per pound. Write an equation describing the possible amounts of ground beef and chicken that you can buy. Use intercepts to graph the equation.
Let x be the amount of ground beef and y be the amount of chicken (both in pounds). Then $3x + 5y = 30$; see margin for art.

Practice and Problem Solving

Homework ***Help***

Example	Exercises
1	10–18, 21–26
2	10–18, 21–26
3	19, 20, 29, 30

- More Examples
- eTutorial Plus

Find the intercepts of the equation's graph. Then graph the equation. **10–18. See margin.**

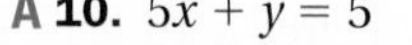

A **10.** $5x + y = 5$ **11.** $x - 2y = 4$ **12.** $3x - 2y = -6$

13. $4x + 5y = -20$ **14.** $4x + 3y = 24$ **15.** $2x - 3y = -18$

16. $y = 2x - 4$ **17.** $y = -x + 7$ **18.** $y = 3x + 9$

19. Animal Nutrition Your beagle is allowed to eat 800 Calories of food each day. You buy canned food containing 40 Calories per ounce and dry food containing 100 Calories per ounce.

a. Write an equation describing the possible amounts of canned and dry food that you can feed your beagle each day.

b. Use intercepts to graph the equation from part (a). **See margin.**

c. Apply Give three possible combinations of canned and dry food that you can feed your beagle each day.
Sample answer: **0 oz canned and 8 oz dry, 10 oz canned and 4 oz dry, 20 oz canned and 0 oz dry**

19a. Let x be the amount of canned food and y be the amount of dry food (both in ounces). Then $40x + 100y = 800$.

20. **Transportation** At the start of a trip, you fill up your car's fuel tank with gas. After you drive for x hours, the amount y (in gallons) of gas remaining is given by the equation $y = 18 - 2x$.

  a. Find the x-intercept and the y-intercept of the given equation's graph. Use the intercepts to graph the equation. **x-intercept: 9; y-intercept: 18; see margin for art.**

  b. Interpret What real-life quantities do the x- and y-intercepts represent in this situation?

  c. After how many hours of driving do you have only $\frac{1}{4}$ tank of gas left? **$6\frac{3}{4}$ h**

Find the intercepts of the equation's graph. Then graph the equation. **21–26. See margin.**

B 21. $1.9x - 1.9y = 3.8$ 22. $2.1x + 3.5y = 10.5$ 23. $y = 1.5x + 6$

24. $y = -\frac{2}{7}x - 2$ 25. $\frac{1}{2}x + \frac{1}{4}y = \frac{3}{2}$ 26. $y = \frac{7}{3}x - \frac{7}{2}$

27. **Critical Thinking** Write an equation of a line that has no x-intercept and an equation of a line that has no y-intercept. Describe the graph of each equation.

28. **Visual Thinking** For a certain line, the x-intercept is negative and the y-intercept is positive. Does the line slant *upward* or *downward* from left to right? Sketch a graph to justify your answer. **Upward; see margin for art.**

29. **Extended Problem Solving** At a flight school, pilots-in-training can rent single-engine airplanes for \$60 per hour and twin-engine airplanes for \$180 per hour. The flight school's goal is to take in \$9000 in rental fees each month.

  a. Write an equation describing the number of hours per month each type of plane should be rented if the flight school is to meet its goal.

  b. Use intercepts to graph the equation from part (a). **See margin.**

  c. Estimation During one month, the twin-engine planes are rented for 30 hours. Use your graph to estimate how many hours the single-engine planes must be rented if the flight school is to meet its goal. **about 60 h**

  d. Reasonableness Check your answer to part (c) by writing and solving an equation. **$60x + 180(30) = 9000$, $x = 60$ h**

30. **Geometry** The rectangle shown has a perimeter of 16 inches.

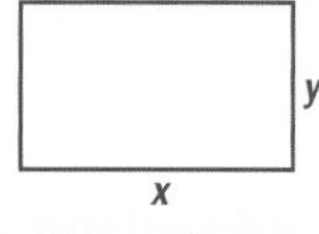

  a. Write an equation describing the possible values of x and y. **$2x + 2y = 16$**

  b. Use intercepts to graph the equation from part (a). **See margin.**

  c. Give three pairs of whole-number values of x and y that could represent side lengths of the rectangle.

  d. Critical Thinking Does either the x-intercept or the y-intercept represent a possible side length of the rectangle? Explain.

31. **Number Sense** Consider the equation $4x + 6y = c$. Find three values of c for which both the x-intercept and the y-intercept are integers. How are your values of c related to the coefficients of x and y in the given equation? ***Sample answer:* 12, 24, and 36; they are common multiples of the coefficients.**

20b. ***Sample answer:*** **The x-intercept represents how many hours it will take you to run out of gas. The y-intercept represents how much gas is in a full tank.**

27. ***Sample answer:*** **$y = 3$, $x = 4$; the graph of $y = 3$ is the horizontal line with y-intercept 3, and the graph of $x = 4$ is the vertical line with x-intercept 4.**

29a. Let x be the time the single-engine plane is rented and y be the time the twin-engine plane is rented (both in hours). Then $60x + 180y = 9000$.

In the **Real World**

Pilot's License To get a private pilot's license, a pilot-in-training must have 40 hours of flight time in a single-engine plane. What is the total cost of this much flight time at the flight school in Exercise 29? **\$2400**

30c. ***Sample answer:*** **$x = 3$ and $y = 5$, $x = 4$ and $y = 4$, $x = 7$ and $y = 1$**

30d. No. ***Sample answer:*** **For the x-intercept, $y = 0$, and for the y-intercept, $x = 0$, and neither the length nor the width of a rectangle can be 0.**

TEACHING TIP

In Exercise 21, point out that since the two coefficients are opposites, then the two intercepts will be opposites.

20a.

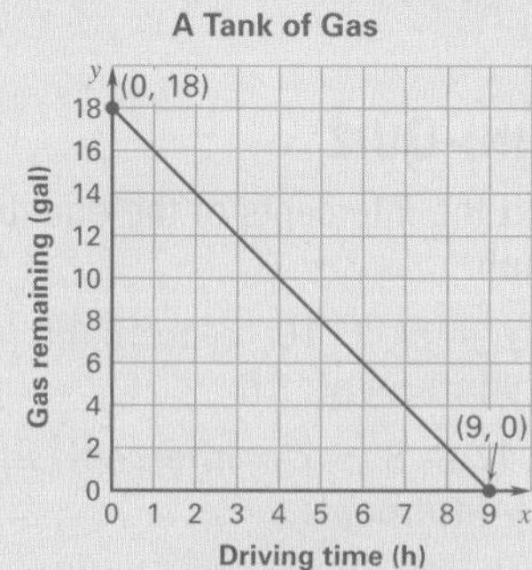

21–26. See Additional Answers beginning on page AA1.

28.

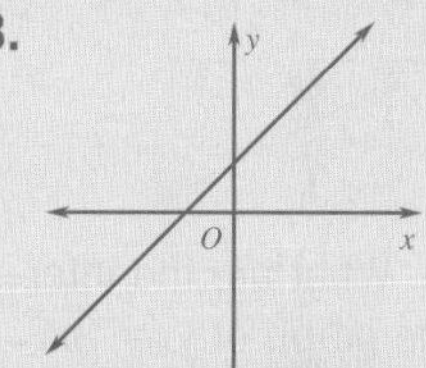

29b.

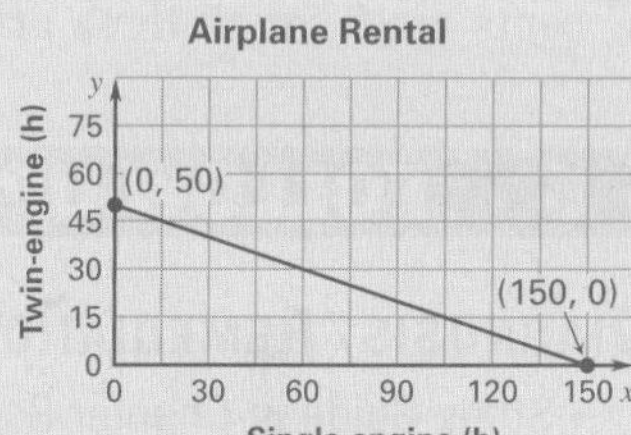

30b.

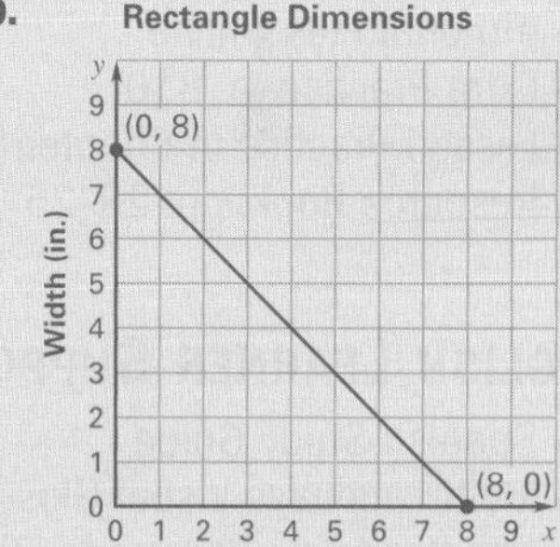

4 ASSESS

ASSESSMENT RESOURCES

For more assessment resources, see:
- Assessment Book
- Test and Practice Generator

MINI-QUIZ

Find the intercepts of the equation's graph.

1. $y = 5x + 10$ **x-intercept: −2; y-intercept: 10**
2. $4y = 8 - x$ **x-intercept: 8; y-intercept: 2**
3. Use intercepts to graph the equation $x + 2y = -1$.

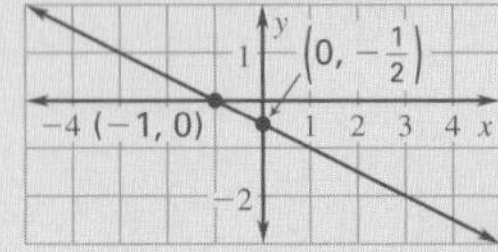

4. **Challenge** What are the intercepts of the graph of $y = 3x$? $y = 4x$? $y = kx$? **Both intercepts are 0 for all three graphs.**

5 FOLLOW-UP

DIAGNOSIS/REMEDIATION

- Study Guide in Chapter 8 Resource Book, pp. 26–27
- eTutorial Plus Online
- Extra Practice, p. 810
- Lesson Practice in Chapter 8 Resource Book, pp. 23–25

ENGLISH LEARNER SUPPORT

- Spanish Study Guide
- Multi-Language Visual Glossary
- Chapter Audio Summaries CDs

CHALLENGE

- Challenge Practice in Chapter 8 Resource Book, p. 28
- Teacher's Edition, p. 382F

32a, 33, 48. See Additional Answers beginning on page AA1.

32b. ***Sample answer:*** **The y-intercept stays the same, but the x-intercept moves closer to the origin, resulting in the graph getting steeper.**

32c. ***Sample answer:*** **The x-intercept stays the same, but the y-intercept moves closer to the origin, resulting in the graph getting less steep.**

32d. ***Sample answer:*** **Both the x- and y-intercepts move farther from the origin together in such a way that the steepness of the line does not change for different distances.**

C **32. Fitness** You use a combination of running and walking to complete a race d miles long. Your running speed is r miles per hour and your walking speed is w miles per hour. Let x be your running time and let y be your walking time (both in hours). Then $rx + wy = d$.

a. The table below shows equations of the form $rx + wy = d$. In each column, one of the values r, w, or d increases while the other two values stay the same. Draw a coordinate plane for each column, and graph the equations in the column on that plane. **See margin.**

r increases.	*w* increases.	*d* increases.
$3x + 2y = 18$	$9x + 2y = 18$	$6x + 2y = 12$
$6x + 2y = 18$	$9x + 3y = 18$	$6x + 2y = 18$
$9x + 2y = 18$	$9x + 6y = 18$	$6x + 2y = 24$

b. What happens to the graph of $rx + wy = d$ when running speed increases while walking speed and racing distance stay the same?

c. What happens to the graph of $rx + wy = d$ when walking speed increases while running speed and racing distance stay the same?

d. What happens to the graph of $rx + wy = d$ when racing distance increases while running speed and walking speed stay the same?

33. Challenge For the graph of $y = ax + b$ where $a \neq 0$, show that the x-intercept is $-\frac{b}{a}$ and the y-intercept is b. Use these results to find the intercepts of the graph of $y = 3x + 12$. **See margin.**

Mixed Review

Evaluate the expression. *(Lessons 1.6, 1.7)*

34. $\frac{8-(-1)}{4-1}$ **3** **35.** $\frac{-3-(-5)}{6-8}$ **−1** **36.** $\frac{4-24}{9-5}$ **−5** **37.** $\frac{-7-11}{-12-(-3)}$ **2**

Identify the percent of change as an *increase* or *decrease*. Then find the percent of change. *(Lesson 7.5)*

38. Original: 40, New: 52 **30% increase**
39. Original: 60, New: 111 **85% increase**
40. Original: 78, New: 39 **50% decrease**
41. Original: 250, New: 195 **22% decrease**

Tell whether the ordered pair is a solution of the equation. *(Lesson 8.2)*

42. $y = -2x + 7$; $(8, -9)$ **yes**
43. $y = 10x - 4$; $(0, 10)$ **no**
44. $5x + y = 15$; $(-6, 15)$ **no**
45. $3x - 8y = 12$; $(-4, -3)$ **yes**

Standardized Test Practice

46. Multiple Choice What is the x-intercept of the graph of $y = 4x + 32$? **B**

A. −32 **B.** −8 **C.** 8 **D.** 32

47. Multiple Choice What is the y-intercept of the graph of $5x + 2y = 30$? **I**

F. −15 **G.** −6 **H.** 6 **I.** 15

48. Short Response A car wash charges $8 for a basic wash and $12 for a deluxe wash that includes a wax. On a certain day, sales at the car wash total $960. Write and graph an equation describing the possible numbers of basic and deluxe washes that could have been done. Give three possible combinations of basic and deluxe washes.

48. Let x be the number of basic washes and y be the number of deluxe washes. Then $8x + 12y = 960$; see margin for art. ***Sample answer:*** **0 basic and 80 deluxe, 90 basic and 20 deluxe, 120 basic and 0 deluxe**

Concept *Activity*

8.4 Investigating Slope

Goal
Use slope to describe the steepness of a ramp.

Materials
- 5 books
- 2 rulers

A ramp's steepness is described by its *slope*, the ratio of the vertical rise to the horizontal run.

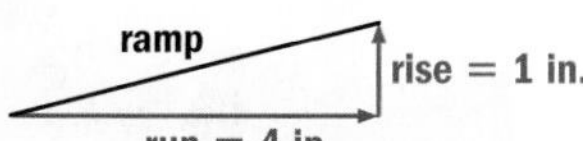

$\text{slope} = \frac{\text{rise}}{\text{run}} = \frac{1}{4}$

Investigate Steps 1–3. Check work.

Use slope to describe the steepness of a ramp.

1 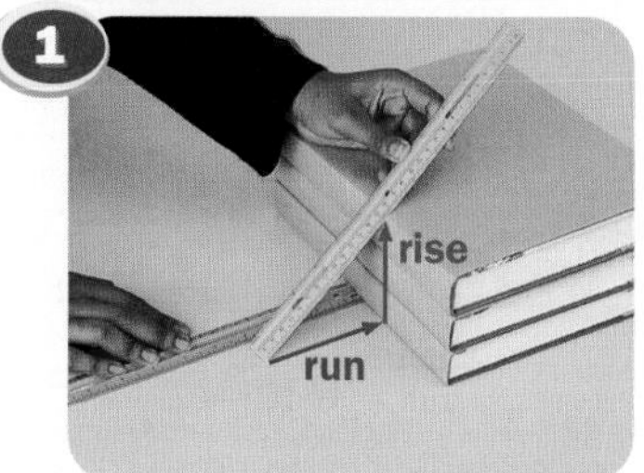

Make a stack of books. Use one ruler as a ramp. Using the other ruler, measure and record the rise and the run of the ramp. Calculate and record the slope of the ramp.

2 

Create ramps with the same rise but three different runs by moving the lower end of the ruler. Measure and record the rise and the run of each ramp. Calculate and record each slope.

3 

Create ramps with the same run but three different rises. Keep the lower end of the ruler in one spot. Add or subtract books to change the rise. Record the rise, the run, and the slope of each ramp.

Draw Conclusions

1. ***Writing*** If one ramp is steeper than a second ramp, what is true about the slopes of the two ramps? **The slope of the steeper ramp is greater.**
2. **Describe** What is the relationship between the rise and the run of a ramp when the slope is 1? Explain. **See margin.**
3. **Critical Thinking** What happens to the slope of a ramp when the rise increases and the run stays the same? **It increases.**

NCTM CURRICULUM STANDARDS
Standard 2: Use models to understand relationships
Standard 10: Create representations to communicate mathematical ideas

1 PLAN

Investigate the Concept
- Students use slope to describe the steepness of a ramp.
- This activity leads into calculating the slope of a line in a coordinate plane in Lesson 8.4.

Materials
Each student will need 5 books and 2 rulers.

Recommended Time
Work activity: 10 min
Discuss results: 5 min

Grouping
Students should work individually.

2 TEACH

Tips for Success
Urge students to be sure the ruler acting as a ramp does not shift as they are measuring its rise and run.

3 CLOSE

Key Discovery
Slope can be described as the ratio of rise over run.

Assessment
1. If the slope of a ramp is $\frac{2}{1}$, what is the slope of a ramp that is twice as steep? $\frac{4}{1}$
2. How could you reduce the slope of a ramp by half without changing the distance the ramp rises? **Double the run.**

2. See Additional Answers beginning on page AA1.

1 PLAN

Skill Check

Simplify.

1. $\frac{8-5}{6-2}$ $\frac{3}{4}$
2. $\frac{3-(-1)}{4-5}$ -4
3. $\frac{7-7}{0-(-4)}$ 0

Lesson Objective

Find and interpret slopes of lines.

Pacing

Suggested Number of Days
Basic Course: 1 day
Average Course: 1 day
Advanced Course: 1 day
Block: 0.5 block with 8.5

Teaching Resources

For a complete list of Teaching Resources, see page 382B.

Transparency

Warm-Up Exercises for this lesson are available on a transparency. A support transparency is available for Examples 2–4.

2 TEACH

Motivating the Lesson

Ask students how they could compare two slopes and describe how the slopes were different.

TIPS *for* NEW TEACHERS

Emphasize that slope is a ratio of two values, not just a single value. Make sure students understand that changing either value in the ratio changes the slope. See Tips for New Teachers in the *Chapter 8 Resource Book*.

LESSON 8.4

The Slope *of a* Line

BEFORE	Now	WHY?
You graphed lines in a coordinate plane.	You'll find and interpret slopes of lines.	So you can compare animal speeds, as in Ex. 17.

Vocabulary
slope, p. 404
rise, p. 404
run, p. 404

Wakeboarding How steep is a wakeboard ramp like the one shown? To find out, you can calculate the ramp's *slope*. The **slope** of a line is the ratio of the line's vertical change, called the **rise**, to its horizontal change, called the **run**.

Example 1 *Finding Slope*

A wakeboard ramp has a rise of 6 feet and a run of 10 feet. Find its slope.

$$\text{slope} = \frac{\text{rise}}{\text{run}} = \frac{6}{10} = \frac{3}{5}$$

Answer The wakeboard ramp has a slope of $\frac{3}{5}$.

To determine the slope of a line in a coordinate plane, you can find the ratio of the vertical change between two points on the line and the horizontal change between the points.

Note *Worthy*

You may find it helpful to use colors when you include examples in your notebook. In the notebook shown, notice how colors are used to associate the rise and run in the slope formula with the rise and run in the graph.

Slope of a Line

Given two points on a nonvertical line, you can find the slope m of the line using this formula:

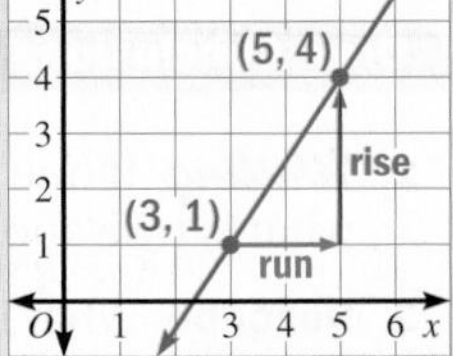

$$m = \frac{\text{rise}}{\text{run}}$$

$$= \frac{\text{difference of } y\text{-coordinates}}{\text{difference of } x\text{-coordinates}}$$

Example $m = \frac{4-1}{5-3} = \frac{3}{2}$

NCTM CURRICULUM STANDARDS
Standard 2: Use models to understand relationships
Standard 10: Create/use representations to communicate mathematical ideas

Comparing Slopes You can use the diagrams below to compare the slopes of different lines. Imagine that you are walking *to the right.*

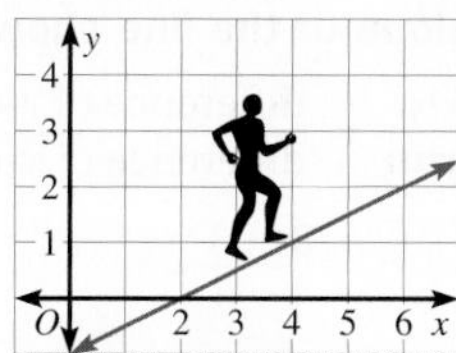

Positive slope
If the line rises, the slope is *positive.*

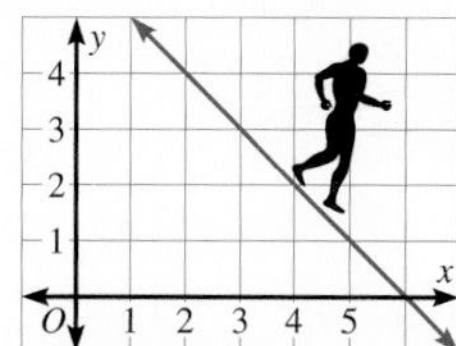

Negative slope
If the line falls, the slope is *negative.*

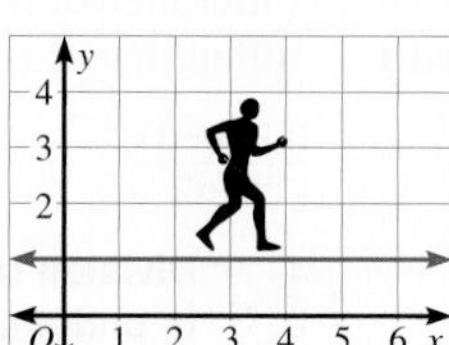

Zero slope
If the line is horizontal, the slope is *zero.*

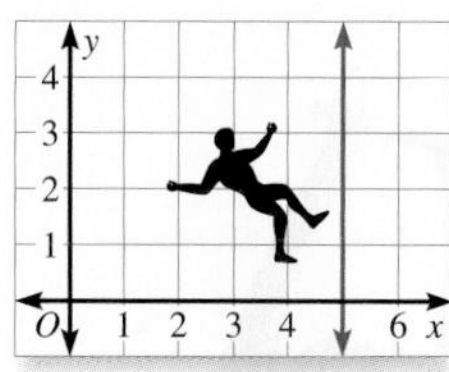

Undefined slope
If the line is vertical, the slope is *undefined.*

Example 2 *Finding Positive and Negative Slope*

Find the slope of the line shown.

a. $m = \frac{\text{rise}}{\text{run}} = \frac{\text{difference of } y\text{-coordinates}}{\text{difference of } x\text{-coordinates}}$

$= \frac{5-2}{4-1}$

$= \frac{3}{3} = 1$

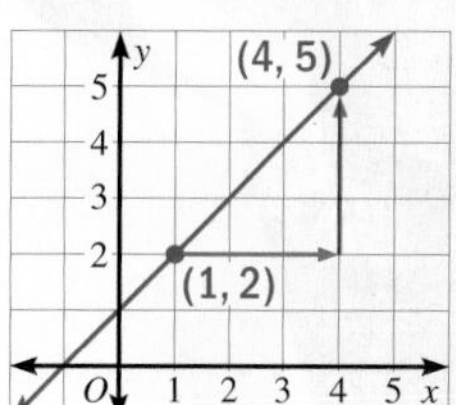

Answer The slope is 1.

b. $m = \frac{\text{rise}}{\text{run}} = \frac{\text{difference of } y\text{-coordinates}}{\text{difference of } x\text{-coordinates}}$

$= \frac{-3-1}{3-0}$

$= \frac{-4}{3} = -\frac{4}{3}$

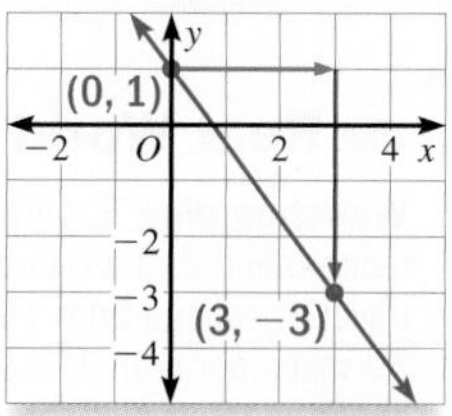

Answer The slope is $-\frac{4}{3}$.

Checkpoint

Find the slope of the line through the given points.

1. (1, 2), (4, 7) $\frac{5}{3}$ **2.** (−2, 5), (6, 1) $-\frac{1}{2}$ **3.** (0, 0), (3, −9) −3 **4.** (5, 0), (7, 8) 4

Watch Out

When you calculate a slope, be sure to use the *x*- and *y*-coordinates of the two points in the same order. In part (a) of Example 2, for instance, the following expression for the slope would be incorrect:

$m = \frac{5-2}{1-4}$ ✗

Extra Examples

Example 1 A ramp has a rise of 3 feet and a run of 18 feet. Find its slope. $\frac{1}{6}$

Example 2 Find the slope of the line shown.

a. $-\frac{1}{3}$

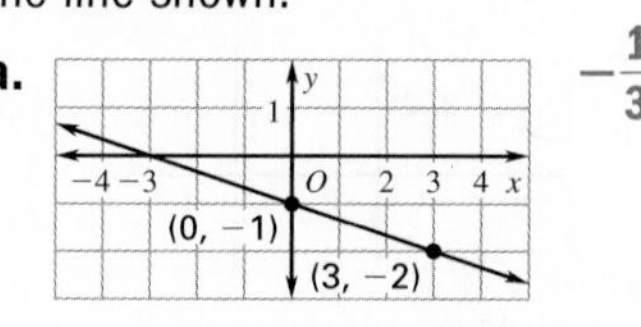

b. $\frac{3}{2}$

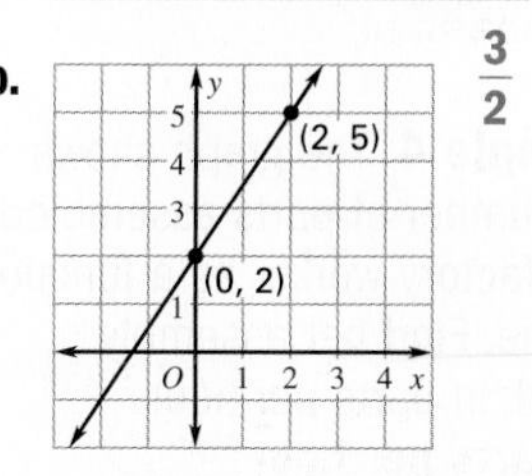

READING STRATEGY

Have students read the Watch Out feature on this page before discussing Example 2.

DIFFERENTIATING INSTRUCTION

Alternative Teaching Strategy Draw a large coordinate grid on the board. Show that a slope of 1, written $\frac{1}{1}$, means that the line goes up 1 unit for every unit it goes to the right. Then revisit part b of Example 2 and show that the slope of $-\frac{4}{3}$ means the line goes down 4 units for every 3 units it goes to the right.

CROSS-CURRICULUM

Physical Education Encourage students to brainstorm for a list of sports that use slopes. Discuss how slope is involved in each of them. For example, whenever a ball is thrown, the slope of its initial flight impacts how far it will travel.

Extra Examples

Example 3 Find the slope of the line shown.

a. 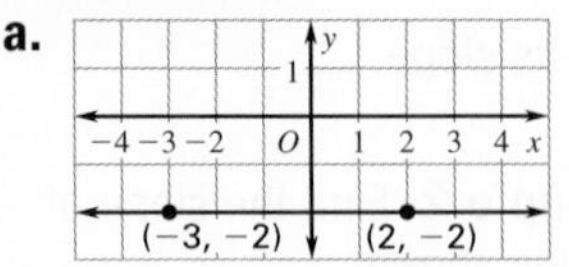 **0**

b. 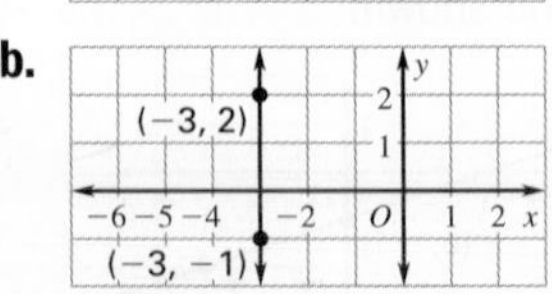

undefined

Example 4 The graph shows the number of parts assembled by a factory worker as a function of time. Find her assembly speed, in parts per hour.
32 parts per hour

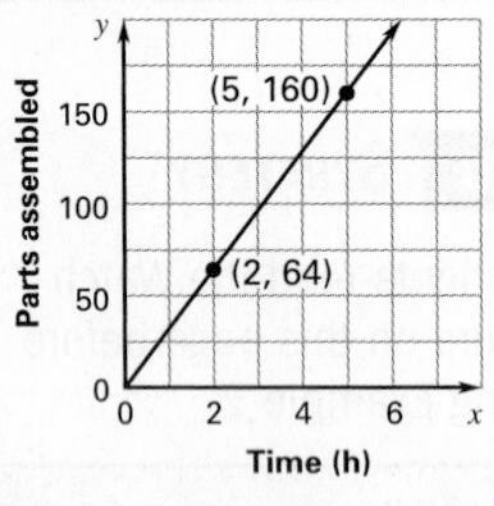

 **CONCEPT CHECK**

How do you find the slope of a line? **Calculate the value of the ratio $\frac{\text{rise}}{\text{run}}$.**

 **DAILY PUZZLER**

Chip and Phil hiked up a steep trail at a rate of 2 miles per hour to the top of a peak and descended back down the same trail at a rate of 4 miles per hour. Their hike took 6 hours. How long was the trail to the top of the peak? **8 mi**

In the Real World

Wakeboarding Experts recommend that wakeboarders travel at speeds from 16 to 19 miles per hour. Is the speed of the wakeboarder in Example 4 within this interval? Explain.
Yes. *Sample answer:* $\frac{26 \text{ ft}}{1 \text{ sec}} \cdot \frac{1 \text{ mi}}{5280 \text{ ft}} \cdot \frac{60 \text{ sec}}{1 \text{ min}} \cdot \frac{60 \text{ min}}{1 \text{ h}} \approx$ 17.7 mi/h

Example 3 *Zero and Undefined Slope*

Find the slope of the line shown.

a. $m = \frac{\text{rise}}{\text{run}} = \frac{\text{difference of } y\text{-coordinates}}{\text{difference of } x\text{-coordinates}}$

$= \frac{3 - 3}{4 - 1}$

$= \frac{0}{3} = 0$

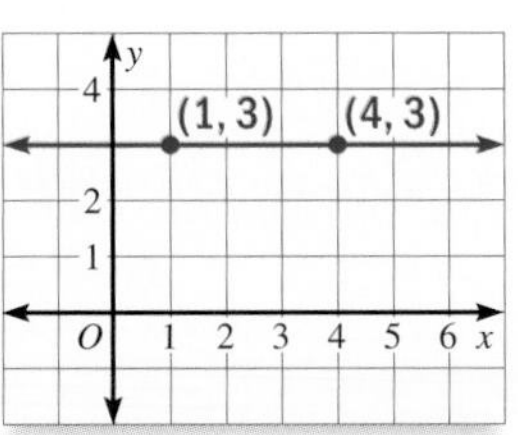

Answer The slope is 0.

b. $m = \frac{\text{rise}}{\text{run}} = \frac{\text{difference of } y\text{-coordinates}}{\text{difference of } x\text{-coordinates}}$

$= \frac{3 - (-1)}{2 - 2}$

$= \frac{4}{0}$ **Division by zero is undefined.**

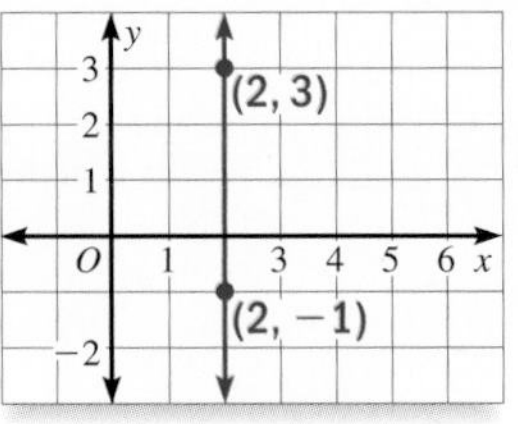

Answer The slope is undefined.

✔ *Checkpoint*

Find the slope of the line through the given points. Tell whether the slope is *positive, negative, zero,* or *undefined.*

5. (2, 3), (4, 5) **1; positive**

6. (6, 3), (6, −1) **undefined**

7. (−7, 4), (5, 4) **0; zero**

8. (1, 5), (4, 1) **$-\frac{4}{3}$; negative**

Example 4 *Interpreting Slope as a Rate of Change*

The graph shows the distance traveled by a wakeboarder as a function of time. The slope of the line gives the wakeboarder's speed, which is the *rate of change* in distance traveled with respect to time. Find the wakeboarder's speed.

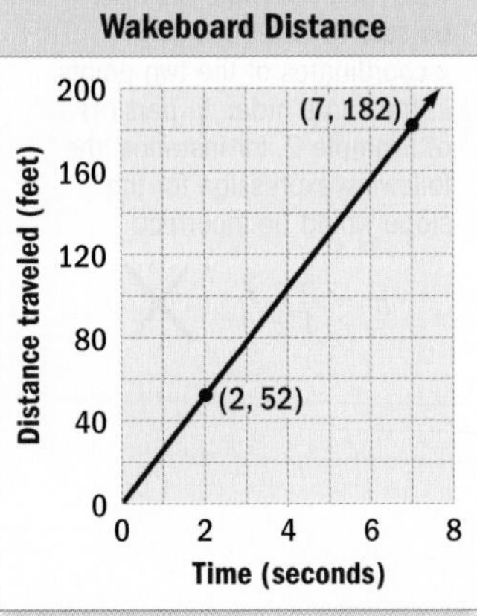

Solution

Use the points (2, 52) and (7, 182) to find the slope of the line.

$m = \frac{\text{difference of } y\text{-coordinates}}{\text{difference of } x\text{-coordinates}}$

$= \frac{182 \text{ ft} - 52 \text{ ft}}{7 \text{ sec} - 2 \text{ sec}}$

$= \frac{130 \text{ ft}}{5 \text{ sec}}$

$= 26 \text{ ft/sec}$

Answer The wakeboarder's speed is 26 feet per second.

8.4 Exercises

More Practice, p. 810

Guided Practice

Vocabulary Check

1. Copy and complete: The vertical change between two points on a line is called the _?_, and the horizontal change is called the _?_. **rise, run**

2. Why is the slope of a vertical line undefined? **See margin.**

Skill Check

3. **Error Analysis** Describe and correct the error in calculating the slope of the line through the points (5, 4) and (0, 2). **See margin.**

$m = \frac{2-4}{5-0} = -\frac{2}{5}$

Tell whether the slope of the line is *positive, negative, zero,* or *undefined.* Then find the slope.

4. 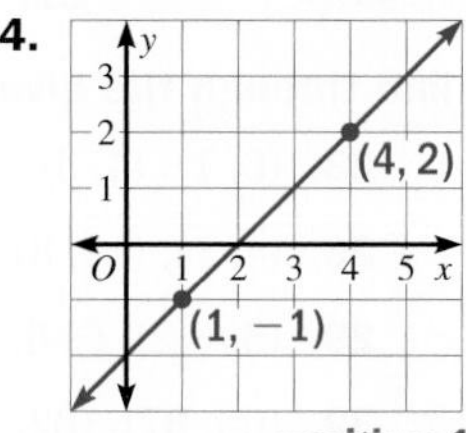

positive; 1

5. 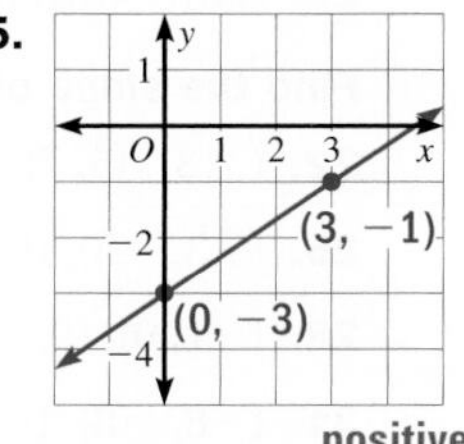

positive; $\frac{2}{3}$

6. 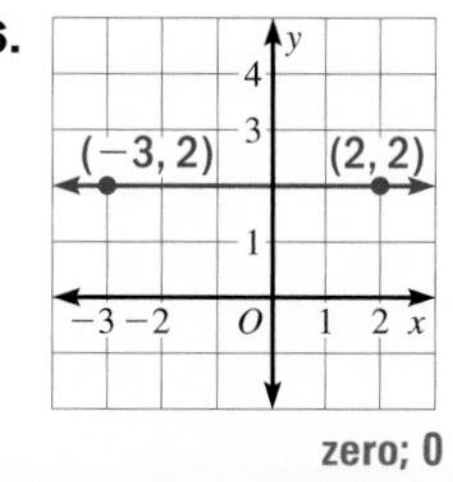

zero; 0

7. *Writing* A wakeboard ramp has a rise of 5 feet and a run of 12 feet. Find the slope of the ramp. Compare this slope with the slope of the ramp in Example 1. **$\frac{5}{12}$. *Sample answer:* $\frac{5}{12} = 0.41\overline{6}$ and $\frac{3}{5} = 0.6$, so the slope of the ramp in Example 1 is greater.**

2. ***Sample answer:*** **The denominator of the slope ratio for a vertical line is always 0 because the *x*-coordinate of every point on a vertical line is the same, and division by 0 is undefined.**

3. ***Sample answer:*** **The *x*- and *y*-coordinates of the two points are not used in the same order. If you subtract the second *x*-coordinate from the first *x*-coordinate to obtain the denominator 5 − 0, then you should subtract the second *y*-coordinate from the first *y*-coordinate to obtain the numerator 4 − 2. So, $m = \frac{4-2}{5-0} = \frac{2}{5}$.**

Practice and Problem Solving

Homework *Help*

Example	Exercises
1	35-38
2	8-16, 18-33
3	8-16, 18-33
4	17

Online Resources
CLASSZONE.COM
- More Examples
- eTutorial Plus

Tell whether the slope of the line is *positive, negative, zero,* or *undefined.* Then find the slope.

A 8. 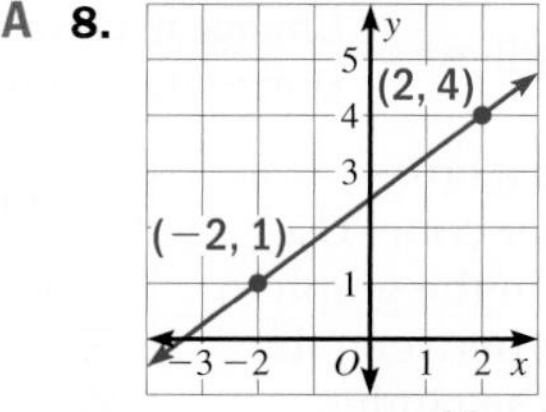

positive; $\frac{3}{4}$

9. 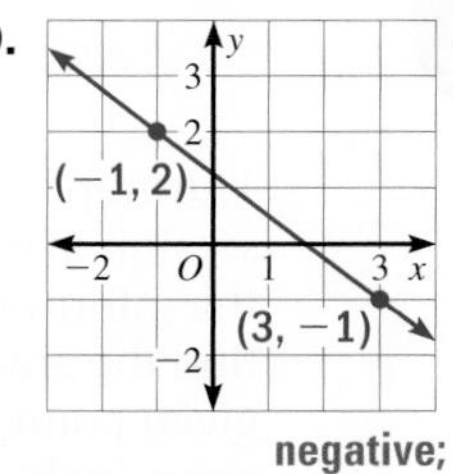

negative; $-\frac{3}{4}$

10. 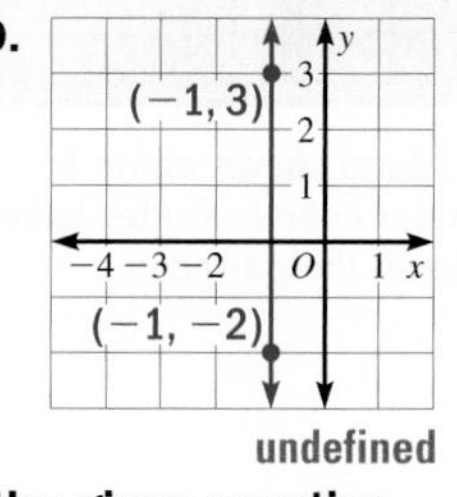

undefined

Find the coordinates of two points on the line with the given equation. Then use the points to find the slope of the line.
11–16. Sample coordinates are given.

11. $y = 2x + 4$ **(−2, 0) and (0, 4); 2**
12. $y = -1$ **(0, −1) and (4, −1); 0**
13. $y = \frac{3}{2}x - 5$ **(0, −5) and (4, 1); $\frac{3}{2}$**
14. $x + 2y = 6$ **(6, 0) and (0, 3); $-\frac{1}{2}$**
15. $4x - 3y = 12$ **(3, 0) and (0, −4); $\frac{4}{3}$**
16. $x = 3$ **(3, 0) and (3, 5); undefined**

3 APPLY

ASSIGNMENT GUIDE

Basic Course
Day 1: pp. 407-409 Exs. 8-16, 18-27, 35, 41-53

Average Course
Day 1: pp. 407-409 Exs. 8-24, 28-38, 41-53

Advanced Course
Day 1: pp. 407-409 Exs. 11-21, 28-42*, 47-53

Block
pp. 407-409 Exs. 8-24, 28-38, 43-53 (with 8.5)

EXTRA PRACTICE

- Student Edition, p. 810
- Chapter 8 Resource Book, pp. 31-33
- Test and Practice Generator

TRANSPARENCY

Even-numbered answers are available on transparencies. A support transparency is available for Exercises 18-21 and 49-51.

HOMEWORK CHECK

When you review students' homework for this lesson, go over the following exercises to check understanding of key concepts.
Basic: 8, 13, 17, 18, 35
Average: 8, 13, 17, 20, 36
Advanced: 14, 17, 24, 28, 37

TEACHING TIP

Before assigning Exercises 11-16, review how to find two points on a line whose equation is given.

COMMON ERROR

In Exercises 22–33, watch for students who inadvertently subtract the *x*-coordinates in the opposite order than they subtracted the *y*-coordinates.

18–21. Sample answers are given.

18.

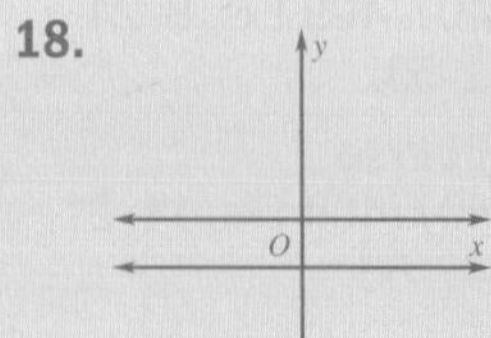

19.

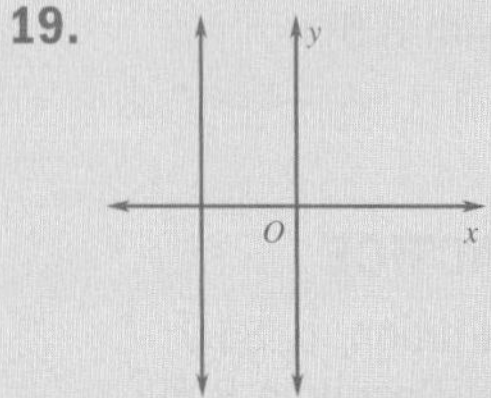

20.

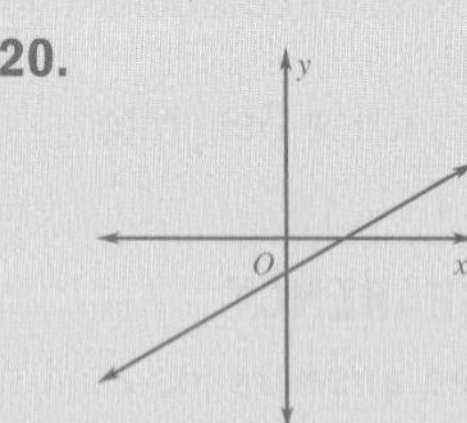

21.

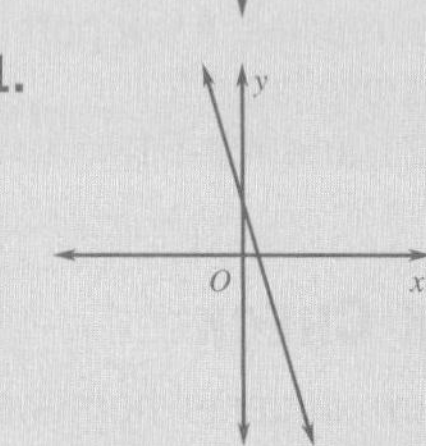

38. Trail A. *Sample answer:* Trail A has a slope of $\frac{15}{50} = \frac{3}{10} =$ 0.3, which is less steep than trail B's slope of $\frac{30}{75} = \frac{2}{5} =$ 0.4.

49–51. See Additional Answers beginning on page AA1.

17c. *Sample answer:* It would also start at the origin, but rise less steeply because the gazelle's speed of 22 meters per second is less than the cheetah's speed of 27 meters per second, and the speed is indicated by the slope.

34. A line with zero slope is a horizontal line, while a line with an undefined slope is a vertical line.

The island shown above is a cinder cone in Crater Lake National Park, Oregon.

17. Extended Problem Solving The graph shows the distance run by a cheetah as a function of time.

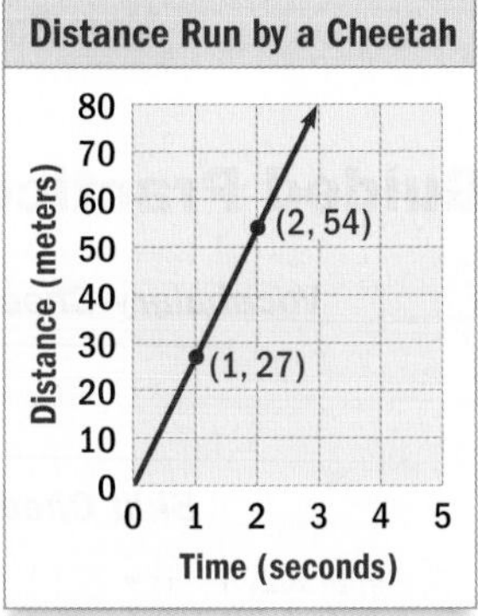

a. Find the slope of the line. 27

b. Interpret What information about the cheetah can you obtain from the slope? its speed in meters per second

c. Compare and Contrast A gazelle's top speed is about 22 meters per second. Suppose you made a graph showing the distance run by a gazelle as a function of time. How would the graph for the gazelle compare with the graph for the cheetah? Explain your thinking.

Sketch an example of the type of line described. 18–21. See margin.

18. A line with zero slope
19. A line with undefined slope
20. A line with positive slope
21. A line with negative slope

Find the slope of the line through the given points.

22. (3, 3), (5, 7) 2
23. (6, 1), (4, 3) −1
24. (7, 3), (7, 2) undefined
25. (−3, −5), (6, −11) $-\frac{2}{3}$
26. (4, 1), (12, 8) $\frac{7}{8}$
27. (5, −7), (0, −7) 0
28. (−1, 0), (0, −5) −5
29. (3, −2), (−8, −2) 0
30. (−2, −6), (−2, 6) undefined
31. (−8, −8), (−2, −6) $\frac{1}{3}$
32. (65, 87), (82, 16) $-\frac{71}{17}$
33. (−10, 10), (−10, 0) undefined

B **34.** *Writing* Describe the difference between a line with zero slope and a line with undefined slope.

35. Wheelchair Ramp You are building a wheelchair ramp that leads to a doorway 22 inches above the ground. The slope of the ramp must be $\frac{1}{12}$. Find the length of ground (in feet) that the ramp covers. 22 ft

36. Cinder Cones A cinder cone is a type of volcano. To describe the steepness of a cinder cone from one point on the cone to another, you can find the *gradient* between the two points.

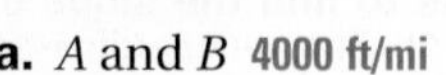

$$\text{Gradient} = \frac{\text{Change in elevation (in feet)}}{\text{Horizontal change (in miles)}}$$

The graph shows a cross section of a cinder cone. Use the information in the graph to find the gradient between the given points on the cinder cone. Include units in your answers.

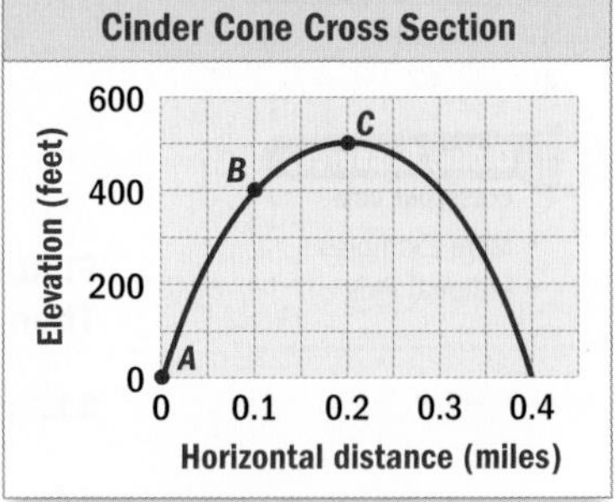

a. *A* and *B* 4000 ft/mi

b. *B* and *C* 1000 ft/mi

c. *A* and *C* 2500 ft/mi

37a. No. *Sample answer:* The grade is $\frac{63}{840} = 0.075 = 7.5\%$, which is less than 8%.

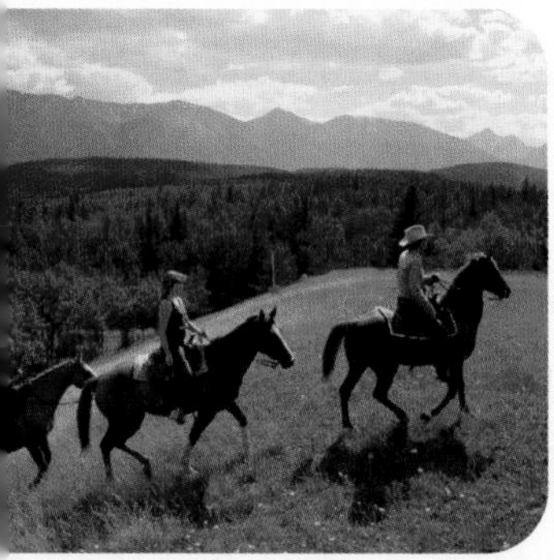

39a. For any pair of points, the slope is $\frac{1}{2}$; the slope does not depend on which two different points are chosen.

39b. For any pair of points, the slope is $-\frac{2}{3}$; the slope does not depend on which two different points are chosen.

37. Roads The *grade* of a road is its slope written as a percent. A warning sign must be posted if a section of road has a grade of at least 8% and is more than 750 feet long.

a. Interpret and Apply A road rises 63 feet over a horizontal distance of 840 feet. Should a warning sign be posted? Explain your thinking.

b. Critical Thinking The grade of a section of road that stretches over a horizontal distance of 1000 feet is 9%. How many feet does the road rise over that distance? 90 ft

38. Horseback Riding A riding instructor takes students on mountain trails. The instructor wants to avoid steep trails. On the steepest part of trail A, the path rises 15 feet over a horizontal distance of 50 feet. On the steepest part of trail B, the path rises 30 feet over a horizontal distance of 75 feet. Which trail should the instructor take? Explain. See margin.

C **39. Logical Reasoning** Choose three different pairs of points on the given line, and find the slope of the line using each pair. What conclusion can you draw from your results?

a.

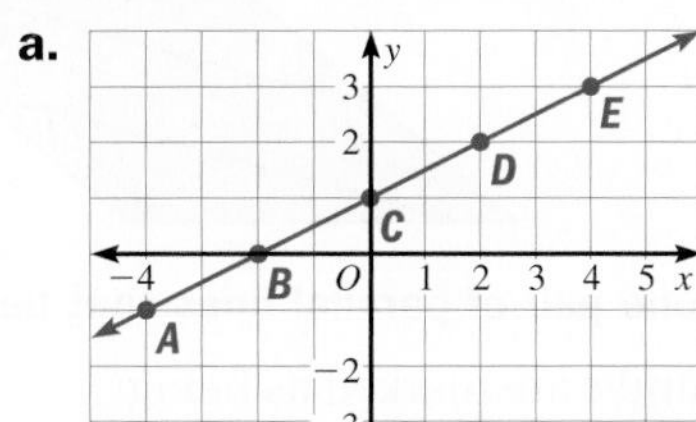

b.

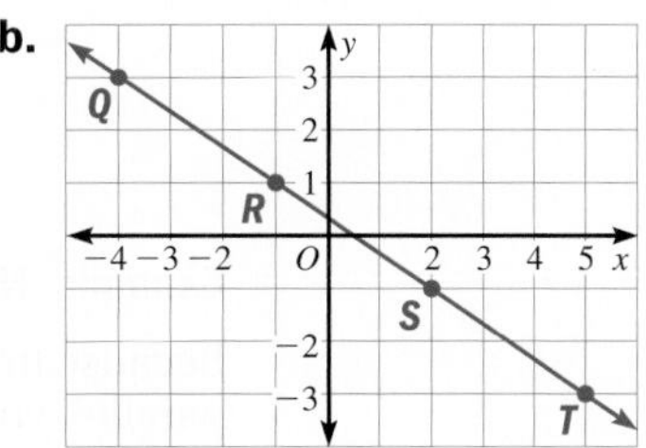

40. Challenge Without graphing, choose a point P so that the slope of the line through $(-1, 1)$ and P is $\frac{1}{9}$. *Sample answer: P*(8, 2)

Mixed Review

Solve the equation. Check your solution. *(Lessons 2.5, 2.6)*

41. $x + 7 = -5$ -12 **42.** $x - 3 = 21$ 24 **43.** $-3y = 33$ -11 **44.** $\frac{m}{-5} = 10$ -50

Find the greatest common factor of the numbers. *(Lesson 4.2)*

45. 15, 48 3 **46.** 64, 56 8 **47.** 105, 125 5 **48.** 121, 132 11

Find the intercepts of the equation's graph. Then graph the equation. *(Lesson 8.3)*

49. $2x - y = 2$ **50.** $9x + 2y = 18$ **51.** $3x + 4y = -24$

49–51. See margin for art.

49. x-intercept: 1; y-intercept: -2

50. x-intercept: 2; y-intercept: 9

51. x-intercept: -8; y-intercept: -6

Standardized Test Practice

52. Multiple Choice What is the slope of the line that passes through the points $(-1, -14)$ and $(5, 4)$? D

A. -3 **B.** $-\frac{1}{3}$ **C.** $\frac{1}{3}$ **D.** 3

53. Multiple Choice The slope of a line through the point (0, 0) is 2. Which point is also on the line? G

F. $(-4, 2)$ **G.** $(2, 4)$ **H.** $(-2, 4)$ **I.** $(2, -4)$

4 ASSESS

Assessment Resources

For more assessment resources, see:

- Assessment Book
- Test and Practice Generator

Mini-Quiz

Tell whether the slope of the line is *positive*, *negative*, *zero*, or *undefined*. Then find the slope if it is defined.

1.

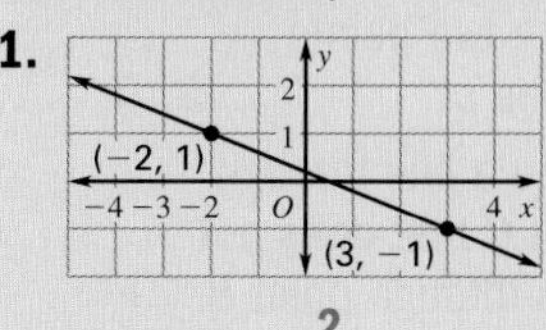

negative, $-\frac{2}{5}$

2. line through (0, 10) and (1, 6) negative, -4

3. line through (0, 6) and (2, 6) zero, 0

4. Challenge Without graphing, choose a point A so that the slope of the line through (2, 1) and A is $\frac{4}{3}$. *Sample answer:* (5, 5)

5 FOLLOW-UP

Diagnosis/Remediation

- Study Guide in Chapter 8 Resource Book, pp. 34–35
- eTutorial Plus Online
- Extra Practice, p. 810
- Lesson Practice in Chapter 8 Resource Book, pp. 31-33

English Learner Support

- Spanish Study Guide
- Multi-Language Visual Glossary
- Chapter Audio Summaries CDs

Challenge

- Challenge Practice in Chapter 8 Resource Book, p. 36
- Teacher's Edition, p. 382F

1 PLAN

Skill Check

Use the figure.

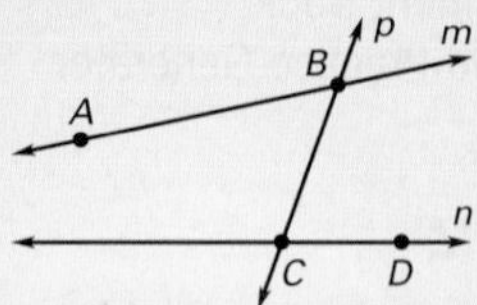

1. Name a line that passes through point *A*. ***m***
2. Name two points on line *p*. ***B, C***
3. Name a line through point *C* that does not pass through point *B*. ***n***

Lesson Objective

Prepare for solving problems in Lesson 8.5 that involve parallel and perpendicular lines.

2 TEACH

Common Error

Stress that two lines which appear to be parallel cannot be assumed to be parallel unless they are marked with the parallel line symbols (matching solid triangles on the lines).

Extra Examples

Example 1 Name one pair of parallel lines that lie in plane *Q*. ***g* and *h***

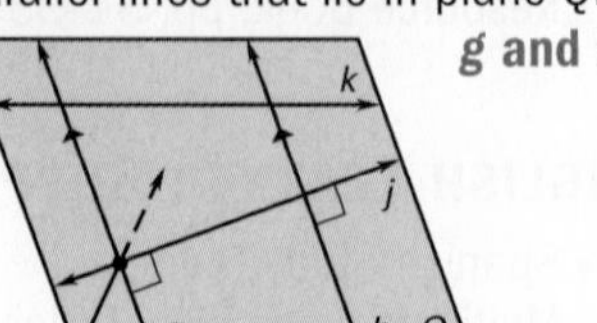

Example 2 In the figure for Extra Example 1, name two lines that are perpendicular to line *j*. ***g, h***

Student Reference

Parallel, Perpendicular, and Skew Lines

▶ **Review** these topics in preparation for solving problems that involve parallel and perpendicular lines in Lesson 8.5.

Parallel Lines

Two lines are **parallel lines** if they lie in the same plane and do not intersect. The symbol ∥ is used to state that two lines are parallel. Triangles (▶) are used in a diagram to indicate that lines are parallel. In the diagram below, lines *t* and *v* are parallel.

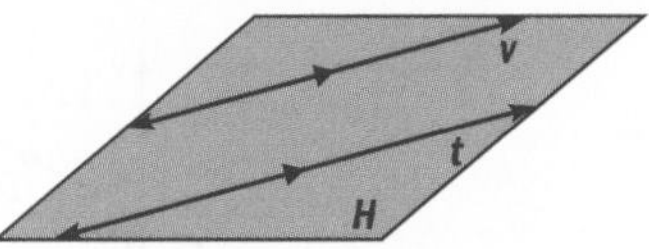

Example Name one pair of parallel lines that lie in plane *P*.

Because lines *a* and *c* are marked as being parallel, you know that $a \parallel c$.

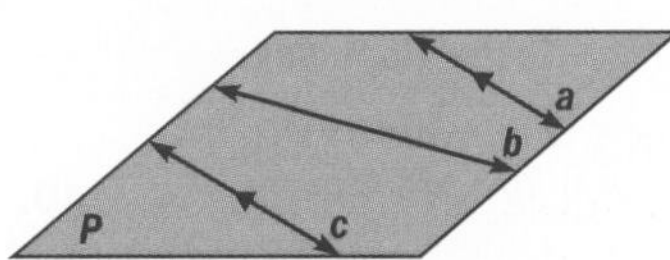

Perpendicular Lines

Two lines are **perpendicular lines** if they intersect to form a right angle. The symbol ⊥ is used to state that two lines are perpendicular. In the diagram, lines *m* and *n* are perpendicular.

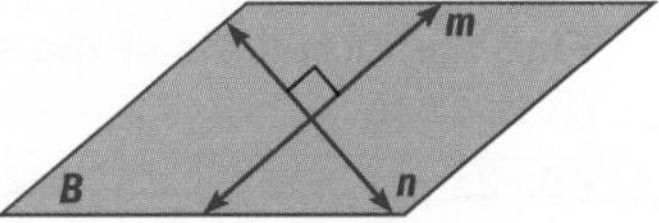

Example Name two lines that are perpendicular to line *f*.

Because lines *g* and *j* intersect line *f* at right angles, you know that $g \perp f$ and $j \perp f$.

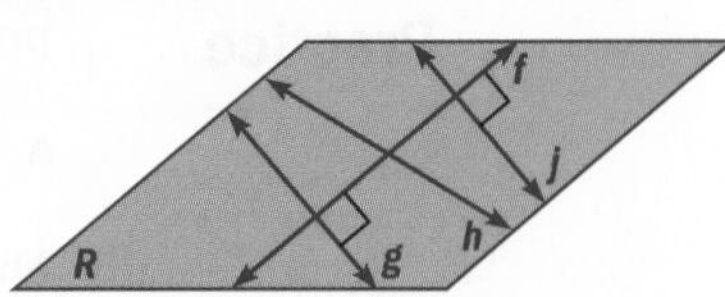

NCTM CURRICULUM STANDARDS

Standard 3: Analyze properties of 2-D shapes; Analyze properties of 3-D shapes

Skew Lines

Two lines are **skew lines** if they do not lie in the same plane and do not intersect. In the diagram, lines r and s are skew lines.

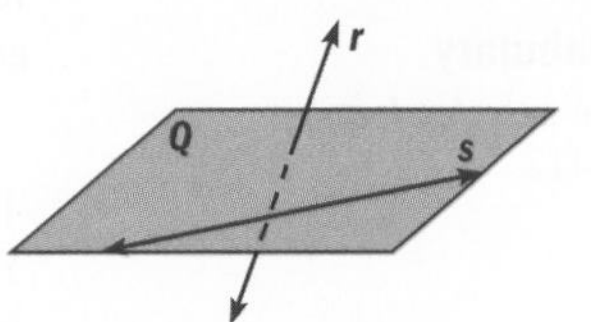

Example Name two lines that are skew.

Lines u and w are skew. Note that lines u and v are not skew because they intersect.

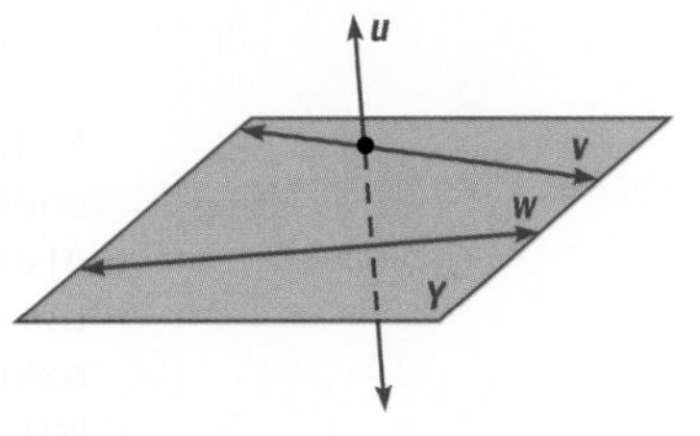

✔ Checkpoint

▶ **Test** your knowledge of parallel, perpendicular, and skew lines by solving these problems.

Tell whether the lines are *parallel* or *perpendicular*.

1. Lines a and b **parallel**

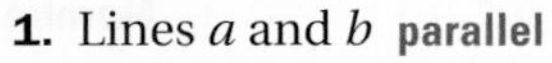

2. Lines a and c **perpendicular**

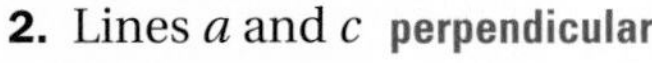

3. Lines d and b **perpendicular**

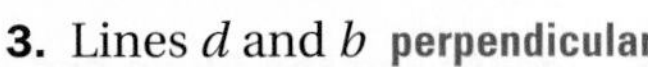

4. Lines c and d **parallel**

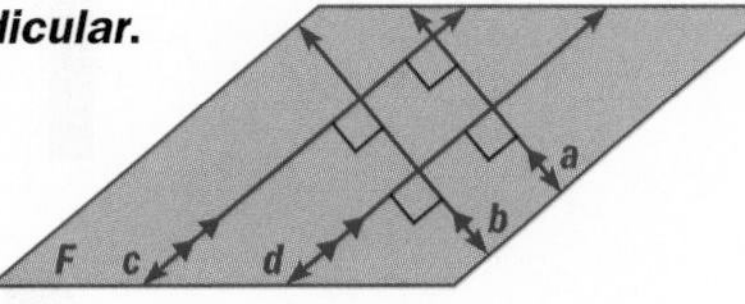

Tell whether the lines are skew. Explain.

5. Lines k and m **No; they lie in the same plane.**
6. Lines k and j **No; they intersect.**
7. Lines j and m
   Yes; they do not lie in the same plane and do not intersect.

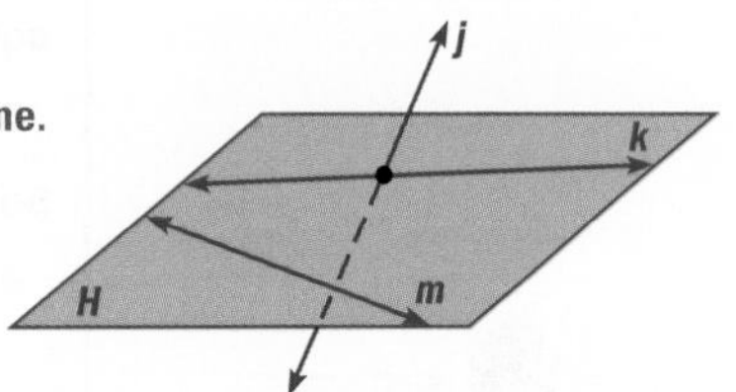

In Exercises 8–10, use the radio shown. The radio has the shape of a box with rectangular sides. Consider the antenna and each edge of the radio as part of a line.

8–10. Sample answers are given.

8. Name three lines perpendicular to $\overleftrightarrow{GE}$.
9. Name two lines parallel to $\overleftrightarrow{AC}$. $\overleftrightarrow{BD}, \overleftrightarrow{EG}$
10. Name two lines that are skew to $\overleftrightarrow{CD}$. $\overleftrightarrow{HJ}, \overleftrightarrow{EG}$

8. $\overleftrightarrow{AG}, \overleftrightarrow{CE}, \overleftrightarrow{EF}$

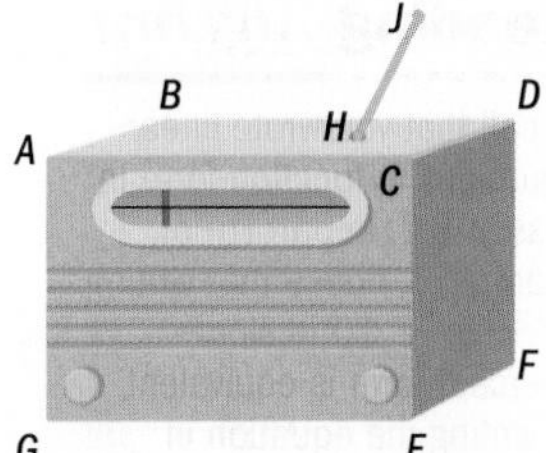

Extra Examples

Example 3 Refer to the figure for Extra Example 1. Name two lines that are skew. ***Sample answer: f and k***

Teaching Tip

Explain the geometric meaning of the word *skew* and differentiate this meaning from the non-mathematical use of the term. Stress that skew has a precise meaning and does not refer to a line that looks crooked.

3 APPLY

Transparency

Even-numbered answers are available on transparencies.

Teaching Tip

In Checkpoint Exercises 1–4, draw students' attention to the double parallel symbols on lines c and d. Explain what these symbols mean and why they are used in figures with multiple pairs of parallel lines.

1 PLAN

Skill Check

Name the reciprocal of the number.

1. -2 $\quad -\frac{1}{2}$ **2.** $\frac{3}{4}$ $\quad \frac{4}{3}$

3. $-\frac{1}{10}$ $\quad -10$ **4.** 5 $\quad \frac{1}{5}$

Lesson Objective

Graph linear equations in slope-intercept form.

Pacing

Suggested Number of Days
Basic Course: 1 day
Average Course: 1 day
Advanced Course: 1 day
Block: 0.5 block with 8.4

Teaching Resources

For a complete list of Teaching Resources, see page 382B.

Transparency

Warm-Up Exercises for this lesson are available on a transparency. A support transparency is available for Example 2 and Checkpoint Exercises 1–3.

2 TEACH

Motivating the Lesson

While referring to the graph of $y = 2x + 3$ shown at the top of this page, ask students for the value of y when $x = 0$ and when $x = 1$. **3, 5** Ask students to describe how the line changes between the x-values 0 and 1, and how this relates to the equation of the graph.

LESSON 8.5

Slope-Intercept Form

BEFORE	Now	WHY?
You used intercepts to graph linear equations.	You'll graph linear equations in slope-intercept form.	So you can find how long it will take to knit a scarf, as in Ex. 9.

Vocabulary
slope-intercept form, p. 412

The graph of $y = 2x + 3$ is shown. You can see that the line's y-intercept is 3, and the line's slope m is 2:

$$m = \frac{\text{rise}}{\text{run}} = \frac{2}{1} = 2$$

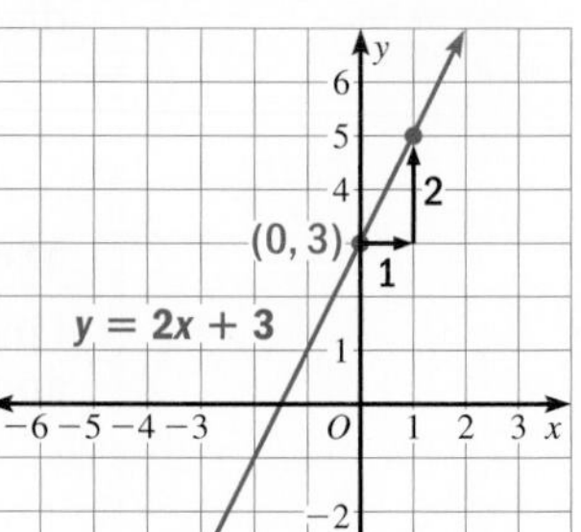

Notice that the slope is equal to the coefficient of x in the equation $y = 2x + 3$. Also notice that the y-intercept is equal to the constant term in the equation. These results are always true for an equation written in *slope-intercept form.*

Slope-Intercept Form

Words A linear equation of the form $y = mx + b$ is said to be in **slope-intercept form**. The slope is m and the y-intercept is b.

Algebra $y = mx + b$ **Numbers** $y = 2x + 3$

Example 1 *Identifying the Slope and y-Intercept*

Identify the slope and y-intercept of the line with the given equation.

a. $y = x - 4$ **b.** $3x + 5y = 10$

Solution

a. Write the equation $y = x - 4$ as $y = 1x + (-4)$.

Answer The line has a slope of 1 and a y-intercept of -4.

b. Write the equation $3x + 5y = 10$ in slope-intercept form by solving for y.

$3x + 5y = 10$ **Write original equation.**

$5y = -3x + 10$ **Subtract 3x from each side.**

$y = -\frac{3}{5}x + 2$ **Multiply each side by $\frac{1}{5}$.**

Answer The line has a slope of $-\frac{3}{5}$ and a y-intercept of 2.

Reading Algebra

Recall that you wrote linear equations in function form in Lesson 8.2. In part (b) of Example 1, notice that writing $3x + 5y = 10$ in slope-intercept form is equivalent to writing the equation in function form.

NCTM CURRICULUM STANDARDS

Standard 2: Understand functions; Use models to understand relationships

Standard 6: Solve problems in math and other contexts

Study *Strategy*

Reasonableness To check the line drawn in Example 2, substitute the coordinates of the second plotted point, (3, 2), into the equation $y = -\frac{2}{3}x + 4$. You should get a true statement.

Example 2 *Graphing an Equation in Slope-Intercept Form*

Graph the equation $y = -\frac{2}{3}x + 4$.

1. The y-intercept is 4, so plot the point (0, 4).
2. The slope is $-\frac{2}{3} = \frac{-2}{3}$.

   Starting at (0, 4), plot another point by moving right 3 units and down 2 units.
3. Draw a line through the two points.

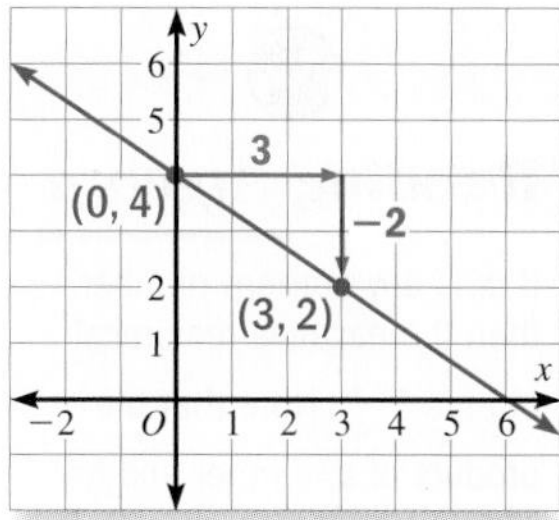

Checkpoint

Identify the slope and y-intercept of the line with the given equation. Use the slope and y-intercept to graph the equation.

1. $y = -x + 1$ **2.** $3x - 2y = 6$ **3.** $y = 4x$

1–3. See margin for art.

1. slope: −1; y-intercept: 1

2. slope: $\frac{3}{2}$; y-intercept: −3

3. slope: 4; y-intercept: 0

Real-Life Situations In a real-life problem involving a linear equation, the y-intercept is often an initial value, and the slope is a rate of change.

Example 3 *Using Slope and y-Intercept in Real Life*

Earth Science The temperature at Earth's surface averages about 20°C. In the crust below the surface, the temperature rises by about 25°C per kilometer of depth.

a. Write an equation that approximates the temperature below Earth's surface as a function of depth.

b. Underground bacteria exist that can survive temperatures of up to 110°C. Find the maximum depth at which these bacteria can live.

Solution

a. Let x be the depth (in kilometers) below Earth's surface, and let y be the temperature (in degrees Celsius) at that depth. Write a verbal model. Then use the verbal model to write an equation.

Temperature below surface	=	Temperature at surface	+	Rate of change in temperature	•	Depth below surface

$$y = 20 + 25x$$

b. Graph $y = 20 + 25x$ on a graphing calculator. Trace along the graph until the cursor is on a point where $y \approx 110$. For this point, $x \approx 3.6$. So, the maximum depth at which the bacteria can live is about 3.6 kilometers.

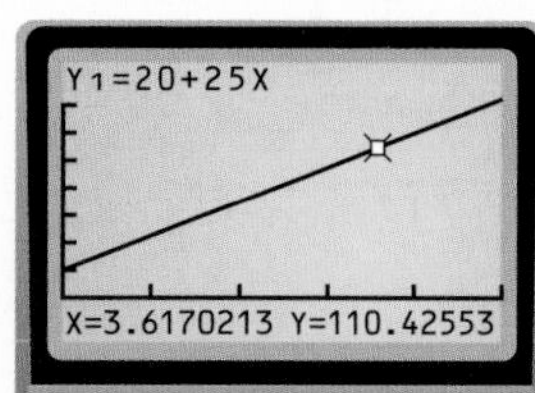

Scientists use airtight enclosures like the one shown to preserve bacteria found in Earth's crust.

TIPS *for* NEW TEACHERS

Students may embrace the new concepts in this lesson more readily once they discover that the slope-intercept form of an equation allows them to graph the equation without having to create a table of values. See Tips for New Teachers in the *Chapter 8 Resource Book*.

Extra Examples

Example 1 Identify the slope and y-intercept of the line with the given equation.

a. $y = 5x - 12$ **slope: 5, y-intercept: −12**

b. $8x - 3y = 2$ **slope: $\frac{8}{3}$, y-intercept: $-\frac{2}{3}$**

Example 2 Graph the equation $y = -\frac{1}{2}x - 1$.

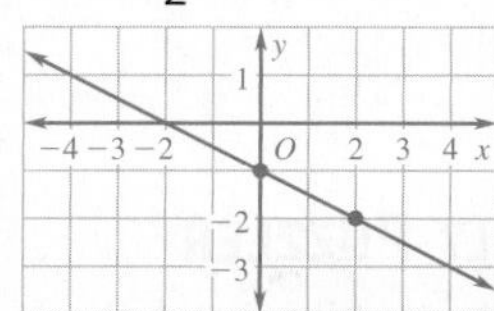

Example 3 Stephon has $42 in his bank account and each week he deposits another $3. Write an equation that models his account balance after x weeks. Use the equation to determine when he will have $120.

$y = 42 + 3x$; in 26 weeks

COMMON ERROR

Make sure students recognize that the slope is the coefficient of the x term and not simply the first coefficient in an equation.

1–3. See Additional Answers beginning on page AA1.

Extra Examples

Example 4 Find the slope of a line that has the given relationship to the line with equation $3y - x = 6$.

a. parallel to the line $\frac{1}{3}$

b. perpendicular to the line -3

Teaching Tip

In Example 4, stress that students cannot find the slope of a line by inspection until they have rewritten the equation in slope-intercept form.

Concept Check

What is the slope-intercept form of an equation, and why is it called by this name? **An equation in the form $y = mx + b$; it has this name because m is the slope and b is the y-intercept, and you can identify both values quickly from the equation when it is written in this form.**

Daily Puzzler

On a coordinate grid, sketch the graph of $y = mx + m$ for three different values of m. What point do all three graphs have in common? **$(-1, 0)$**

Parallel and Perpendicular Lines There is an important relationship between the slopes of two nonvertical lines that are parallel and between the slopes of two nonvertical lines that are perpendicular.

Reading *Algebra*

If m is any nonzero number, then the negative reciprocal of m is $-\frac{1}{m}$. Note that the product of a number and its negative reciprocal is -1:

$$m\left(-\frac{1}{m}\right) = -1$$

Slopes of Parallel and Perpendicular Lines

Two nonvertical parallel lines have the same slope. For example, the parallel lines a and b below both have a slope of 2.

Two nonvertical perpendicular lines, such as lines a and c below, have slopes that are negative reciprocals of each other.

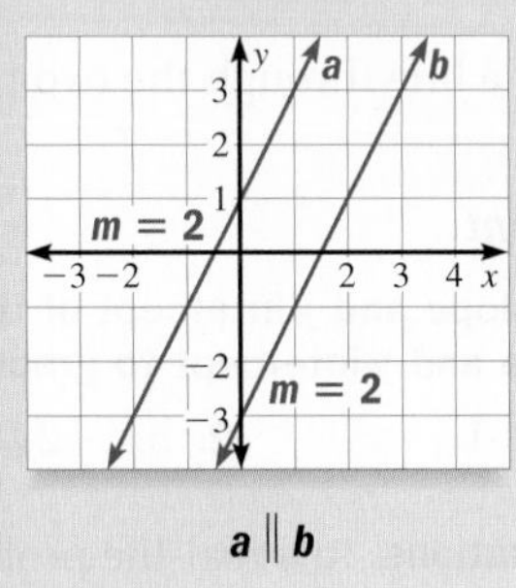

a ∥ b

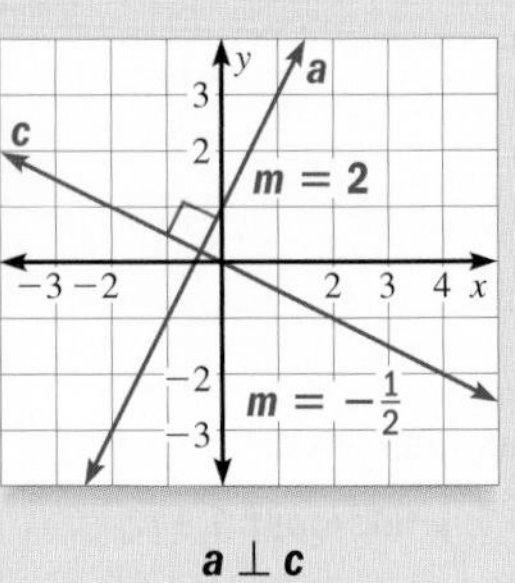

a ⊥ c

4. **parallel: -3; perpendicular: $\frac{1}{3}$**

5. **parallel: 4; perpendicular: $-\frac{1}{4}$**

6. **parallel: $\frac{2}{5}$; perpendicular: $-\frac{5}{2}$**

Example 4 *Finding Slopes of Parallel and Perpendicular Lines*

Find the slope of a line that has the given relationship to the line with equation $4x + 3y = -18$.

a. Parallel to the line

b. Perpendicular to the line

Solution

a. First write the given equation in slope-intercept form.

$4x + 3y = -18$	**Write original equation.**
$3y = -4x - 18$	**Subtract $4x$ from each side.**
$y = -\frac{4}{3}x - 6$	**Multiply each side by $\frac{1}{3}$.**

The slope of the given line is $-\frac{4}{3}$. Because parallel lines have the same slope, the slope of a parallel line is also $-\frac{4}{3}$.

b. From part (a), the slope of the given line is $-\frac{4}{3}$. The slope of a perpendicular line is the negative reciprocal of $-\frac{4}{3}$, or $\frac{3}{4}$.

Study *Strategy*

Reasonableness In part (b) of Example 4, you can verify that the two slopes are negative reciprocals by checking that their product is -1:

$$-\frac{4}{3} \cdot \frac{3}{4} = -1 \checkmark$$

Checkpoint

For the line with the given equation, find the slope of a parallel line and the slope of a perpendicular line. 4–6. See margin.

4. $y = -3x$ **5.** $y = 4x + 10$ **6.** $2x - 5y = 15$

8.5 Exercises

More Practice, p. 810

Guided Practice

Vocabulary Check

1. Copy and complete: An equation of the form $y = mx + b$ is written in _?_ form. **slope-intercept**

2. Without graphing, tell whether the lines with equations $y = 7x - 1$ and $y = 7x + 3$ are *parallel, perpendicular,* or *neither*. Explain. **See margin.**

Skill Check

2. Parallel. *Sample answer:* Lines with the same slope and different *y*-intercepts are parallel. Both of these lines have slopes of 7 and they have different *y*-intercepts.

Identify the slope and *y*-intercept of the line with the given equation. Use the slope and *y*-intercept to graph the equation. 3–5. See margin for art.

3. $y = 2x$ slope: 2; *y*-intercept: 0
4. $y = -3x + 4$ slope: −3; *y*-intercept: 4
5. $x - 2y = 2$ slope: $\frac{1}{2}$; *y*-intercept: −1

For the line with the given equation, find the slope of a parallel line and the slope of a perpendicular line.

6. $y = x$ parallel: 1; perpendicular: −1
7. $y = -6x + 9$
8. $3x + 2y = 16$

7–8. See margin.

7. parallel: −6; perpendicular: $\frac{1}{6}$

8. parallel: $-\frac{3}{2}$; perpendicular: $\frac{2}{3}$

Guided Problem Solving

9. **Knitting** You and a friend are knitting a scarf that will be 72 inches long. Your friend knits the first 24 inches and then gives you the scarf to finish. You expect to knit at a rate of 8 inches per day. After how many days will you finish the scarf?

   1) Use the verbal model to write an equation giving the length *y* of the scarf (in inches) after you have been knitting for *x* days. $y = 24 + 8x$

Length of scarf	=	Length knitted by your friend	+	Knitting rate	•	Knitting time

   2) Identify the slope and *y*-intercept of the line with the equation from Step 1. Then graph the equation. **Slope: 8; *y*-intercept: 24; see margin for art.**

   3) Use the graph to estimate how long you will take to finish the scarf. **about 6 days**

Practice and Problem Solving

Homework *Help*

Example	Exercises
1	10-12, 14-19
2	10-12, 14-19
3	20, 21, 31
4	13, 22-31

Online Resources
CLASSZONE.COM
- More Examples
- eTutorial Plus

Match the equation with its graph.

A 10. $y = x + 2$ **C**
11. $y = -x + 2$ **A**
12. $y = x - 2$ **B**

A. 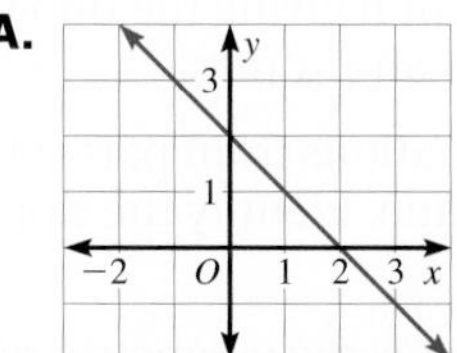

B. 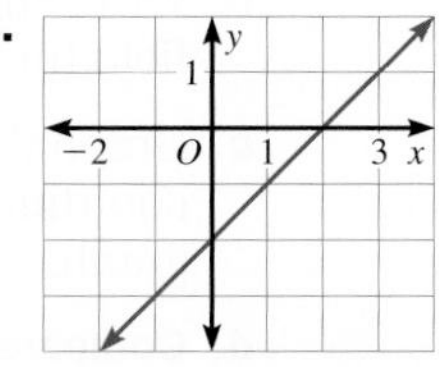

C. 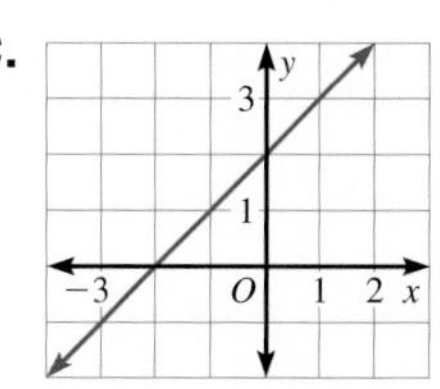

13. **Critical Thinking** Give the equations of three lines that are parallel to the line with equation $y = 3x + 2$.
Sample answer: $y = 3x$, $y = 3x + 8$, $y = 3x - 1.1$

3 APPLY

ASSIGNMENT GUIDE

Basic Course
Day 1: pp. 415-417 Exs. 10-20, 22-30, 34-46

Average Course
Day 1: pp. 415-417 Exs. 10-13, 17-24, 28-32, 34-47

Advanced Course
Day 1: pp. 415-417 Exs. 10-13, 17-21, 25-35*, 38-47

Block
pp. 415-417 Exs. 10-13, 17-24, 28-32, 34-47 (with 8.4)

Extra Practice

- Student Edition, p. 810
- Chapter 8 Resource Book, pp. 41-43
- Test and Practice Generator

Transparency

Even-numbered answers are available on transparencies. A support transparency is available for Exercises 3-5, 9, 14-20, and 31.

Homework Check

When you review students' homework for this lesson, go over the following exercises to check understanding of key concepts.
Basic: 10, 13, 14, 18, 20
Average: 11, 13, 17, 19, 21
Advanced: 12, 13, 18, 21, 25

Teaching Tip

Use Exercises 10-12 to discuss with students the similarities and differences among the graphs and among the equations.

3-5, 9 (Step 2). See Additional Answers beginning on page AA1.

Common Error

Students who are confused by Exercise 16 may need to add the term $0x$ to the right side of the equation in order to help them recognize it as the slope-intercept form of an equation for a horizontal line.

14–19. See Additional Answers beginning on page AA1.

20.

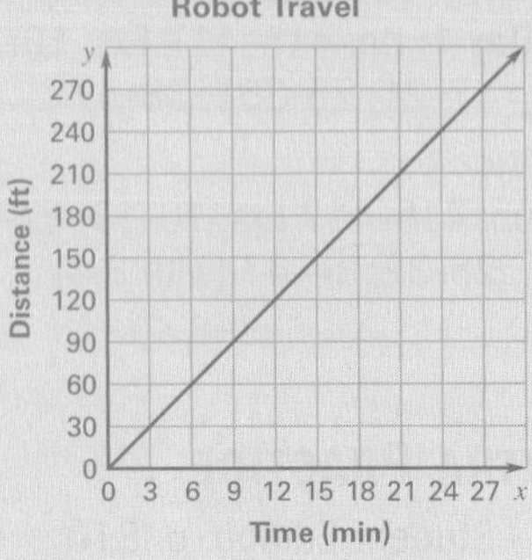

21a.

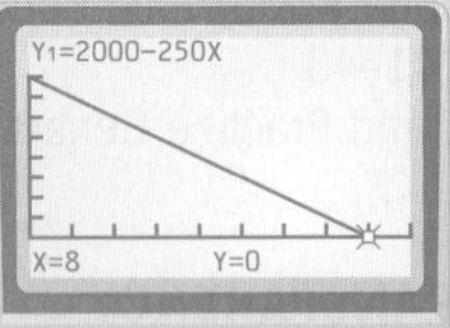

31c.

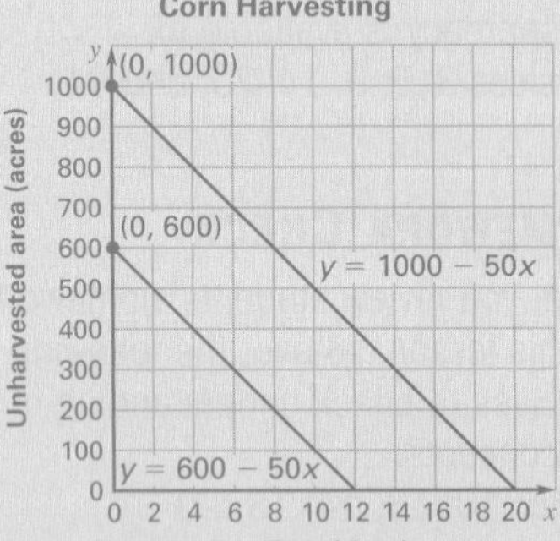

For $y = 1000 - 50x$, the slope is -50 and the y-intercept is 1000. For $y = 600 - 50x$, the slope is -50 and the y-intercept is 600.

14–19. See margin for art.
14. slope: -2; y-intercept: 3
15. slope: $\frac{1}{4}$; y-intercept: 1
16. slope: 0; y-intercept: -2
17. slope: -3; y-intercept: -1
18. slope: $\frac{2}{3}$; y-intercept: 0
19. slope: $\frac{5}{2}$; y-intercept: 2

Identify the slope and y-intercept of the line with the given equation. Use the slope and y-intercept to graph the equation.

14. $y = -2x + 3$ **15.** $y = \frac{1}{4}x + 1$ **16.** $y = -2$

17. $3x + y = -1$ **18.** $2x - 3y = 0$ **19.** $5x - 2y = -4$

20. Robotics In 2002, a robot explored a tunnel 210 feet long inside the Great Pyramid in Egypt. The robot could travel about 10 feet per minute. Write and graph an equation giving the distance y (in feet) that the robot could travel in x minutes. Use the graph to estimate how quickly the robot could reach the end of the tunnel. **$y = 10x$; see margin for art; about 21 min.**

21. Paramotoring A paramotor is a parachute propelled by a fan-like motor. Suppose that x minutes after beginning a descent, a paramotorist has an altitude y (in feet) given by $y = 2000 - 250x$.

a. Graph the given equation on a graphing calculator. Use the *trace* feature to find how long it takes the paramotorist to reach the ground. **See margin for art; 8 min.**

b. Interpret Identify the slope and y-intercept of the graph. What real-life quantities do the slope and y-intercept represent? **See margin.**

Paramotor

For the line with the given equation, find the slope of a parallel line and the slope of a perpendicular line. 22–27. See margin.

22. $y = 8x + 5$ **23.** $y = -x - 9$ **24.** $y = -7x + 4$

25. $4x - 5y = 30$ **26.** $11x + 6y = 18$ **27.** $x = 3y - 7$

Find the slope of a line parallel to the given line and the slope of a line perpendicular to the given line. 28–30. See margin.

B **28.**

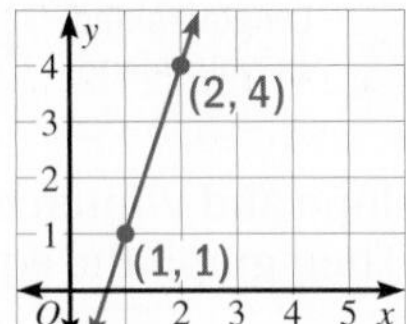

29.

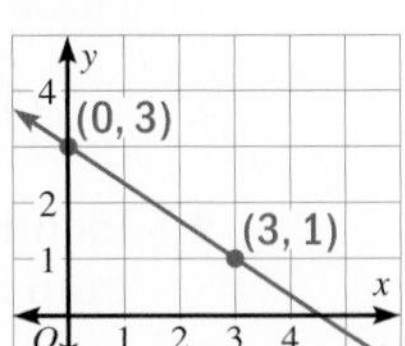

30.

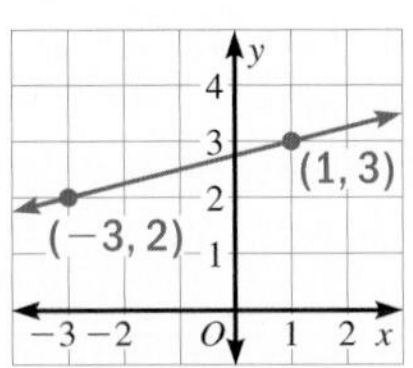

31. Extended Problem Solving Two farmers each harvest 50 acres of corn per day from their fields. The area of one farmer's field is 1000 acres, and the area of the other farmer's field is 600 acres.

a. Write an equation giving the unharvested area y of the larger field (in acres) after x days. **$y = 1000 - 50x$**

b. Write an equation giving the unharvested area y of the smaller field (in acres) after x days. **$y = 600 - 50x$**

c. Graph the equations from parts (a) and (b) in the same coordinate plane. Identify the slope and y-intercept of each graph. **See margin.**

d. Compare What is the geometric relationship between the graphs from part (c)? How do you know? **They are parallel; they have the same slope, -50, and different y-intercepts.**

e. Interpret and Apply How long does it take to harvest the corn in the larger field? in the smaller field? **20 days; 12 days**

21b. Slope: -250; y-intercept: 2000; the slope represents the rate of descent in feet per minute, and the y-intercept represents the beginning altitude in feet.

22. parallel: 8; perpendicular: $-\frac{1}{8}$
23. parallel: -1; perpendicular: 1
24. parallel: -7; perpendicular: $\frac{1}{7}$
25. parallel: $\frac{4}{5}$; perpendicular: $-\frac{5}{4}$
26. parallel: $-\frac{11}{6}$; perpendicular: $\frac{6}{11}$
27. parallel: $\frac{1}{3}$; perpendicular: -3
28. parallel: 3; perpendicular: $-\frac{1}{3}$
29. parallel: $-\frac{2}{3}$; perpendicular: $\frac{3}{2}$
30. parallel: $\frac{1}{4}$; perpendicular: -4

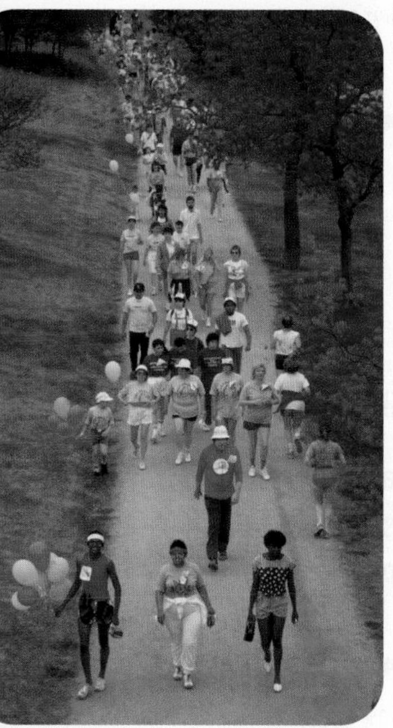

C **32. Walk-a-thon** You are participating in a walk-a-thon. Donors can pledge a certain amount of money for each mile that you walk, or a fixed amount that doesn't depend on how far you walk, or both. The table gives the amounts pledged by four donors on your street.

Donor	Amount per mile	Fixed amount	Equation
Janette	None	\$35	?
Ben	\$2	\$20	?
Salil	\$5	None	?
Mary	\$3	\$15	?

a. Copy the table. For each person, write an equation giving the amount of money y the person will donate if you walk x miles. **Janette: $y = 35$, Ben: $y = 2x + 20$, Salil: $y = 5x$, Mary: $y = 3x + 15$**

b. Write an equation giving the *total* amount of money y you will raise from the donors on your street if you walk x miles. **$y = 35 + (2x + 20) + 5x + (3x + 15)$, or $y = 10x + 70$**

c. *Writing* Consider the equations from part (a) and the equation from part (b). Which equation has the graph with the greatest slope? Explain why this is so.

32c. The equation from part (b). ***Sample answer:*** **Because the slope represents how much money is earned per mile, and the amount earned per mile in part (b) is the sum of the amounts earned per mile for Ben, Salil, and Mary in part (a), the slope is greater for the equation in part (b).**

33. Challenge Complete the following steps to show that the slope of the line $y = mx + b$ is m.

a. Show that two points on the graph of $y = mx + b$ are $(0, b)$ and $(1, m + b)$. (*Hint*: Find y when $x = 0$ and when $x = 1$.) **See margin.**

b. For the points $(0, b)$ and $(1, m + b)$, what is the difference of the second y-coordinate and the first y-coordinate? What is the difference of the second x-coordinate and the first x-coordinate? **m; 1**

c. Use your results from part (b) to write an expression for the slope of the line $y = mx + b$. Show that the slope is equal to m. **slope $= \frac{m}{1} = m$**

Mixed Review

Solve the equation. Check your solution. *(Lesson 3.2)*

34. $2(x - 4) = 16$ **12**

35. $-20 = 4(7 - 3z)$ **4**

36. $-6 + 5a + 13 = -8$ **−3**

37. $14c + 33 - 10c = 5$ **−7**

Use the percent equation to answer the question. *(Lesson 7.4)*

38. What number is 20% of 50? **10**

39. What number is 125% of 80? **100**

40. 45 is 75% of what number? **60**

41. What percent of 140 is 56? **40%**

Find the slope of the line through the given points. *(Lesson 8.4)*

42. $(0, 0), (2, 8)$ **4**

43. $(1, 5), (4, -1)$ **−2**

44. $(2, 6), (5, 4)$ **$-\frac{2}{3}$**

45. $(-3, 7), (1, 17)$ **$\frac{5}{2}$**

Standardized Test Practice

46. Multiple Choice Which equation's graph has the greatest slope? **D**

A. $y = 3x$ **B.** $y = x + 12$ **C.** $y = 5x - 1$ **D.** $y = 8x + 4$

47. Short Response You buy a prepaid phone card that has 500 minutes of calling time. You use about 25 minutes of calling time per week. Write and graph an equation that approximates your remaining calling time y (in minutes) after x weeks. **$y = 500 - 25x$; see margin for art.**

4 ASSESS

Assessment Resources

For more assessment resources, see:
- Assessment Book
- Test and Practice Generator

Mini-Quiz

Identify the slope and y-intercept of the line with the given equation.

1. $y = -6x$ **slope: −6, y-intercept: 0**
2. $2x + y = 3$ **slope: −2, y-intercept: 3**
3. For the line with equation $y = \frac{1}{4}x + 1$, find the slope of a parallel line and the slope of a perpendicular line. **$\frac{1}{4}$, −4**
4. **Challenge** For the line with equation $y - ax = b$, find the slope of a parallel line and the slope of a perpendicular line. **$a, -\frac{1}{a}$**

5 FOLLOW-UP

Diagnosis/Remediation

- Study Guide in Chapter 8 Resource Book, pp. 44–45
- eTutorial Plus Online
- Extra Practice, p. 810
- Lesson Practice in Chapter 8 Resource Book, pp. 41–43

English Learner Support

- Spanish Study Guide
- Multi-Language Visual Glossary
- Chapter Audio Summaries CDs

Challenge

- Challenge Practice in Chapter 8 Resource Book, p. 47
- Teacher's Edition, p. 382F

33a, 47. See Additional Answers beginning on page AA1.

ADDITIONAL RESOURCES

The following resources are available to help review the materials in Lessons 8.1–8.5.

Chapter 8 Resource Book

- Lesson Practice
- Study Guide

Assessment Book

- Chapter 8 Quiz 1

Technology

- Test and Practice Generator
- eTutorial CD-ROM

Internet

- Classzone
- eWorkbook Plus Online
- eTutorial Plus Online

ENGLISH LEARNER SUPPORT

- Spanish Study Guide
- Multi-Language Visual Glossary
- Chapter Audio Summaries CDs

1–9. See Additional Answers beginning on page AA1.

10.

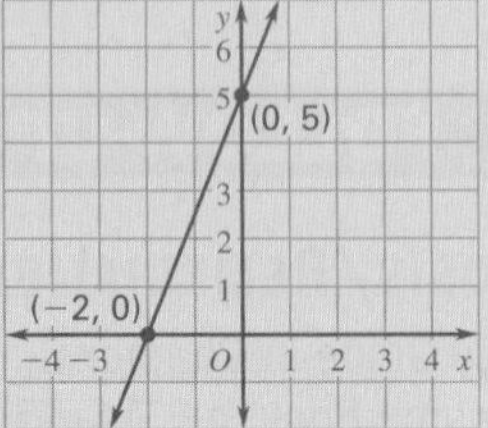

15.

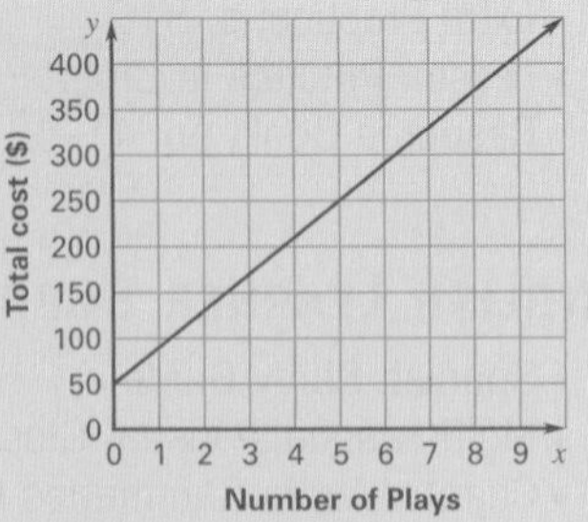

Brain Game.

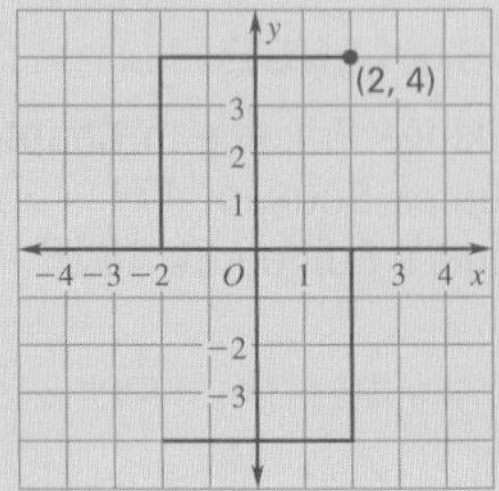

Mid-Chapter Quiz

Represent the relation as a graph and as a mapping diagram. Then tell whether the relation is a function. Explain your reasoning. 1–2. See margin for art.

1. (2, 1), (2, 2), (2, 3), (2, 4)
No; the input 2 is paired with four outputs, 1, 2, 3, and 4.

2. (8, −1), (6, 0), (4, 0), (2, −1)
Yes; every input is paired with exactly one output.

Graph the equation. Tell whether the equation is a function. 3–6. See margin for art.

3. $y = -x + 7$ yes **4.** $x = 5$ no **5.** $y = -1$ yes **6.** $x + 4y = 32$ yes

Find the intercepts of the equation's graph. Then graph the equation. 7–10. See margin for art.

7. $6x + 3y = 12$ x-intercept: 2; y-intercept: 4

8. $4x - y = 8$ x-intercept: 2; y-intercept: −8

9. $y = 2x - 6$ x-intercept: 3; y-intercept: −6

10. $-5x + 2y = 10$ x-intercept: −2; y-intercept: 5

Find the slope of the line through the given points.

11. (1, 2), (2, 8) 6 **12.** (0, 4), (4, 4) 0 **13.** (−6, 10), (1, 2) $-\frac{8}{7}$ **14.** (−1, 2), (−1, 6) undefined

15. Drama Club The drama club pays a registration fee of \$50 to take part in a festival of one-act plays and \$40 for each play the club enters. Write and graph an equation giving the total cost y (in dollars) of entering x plays. $y = 40x + 50$; see margin for art.

Quarter Count

The U.S. Mint began issuing special state quarters in 1999. Using a coordinate plane, follow the steps below to find out how many states had quarters issued each year. For each step after the first, start at the point in the plane where you ended in the previous step. All segments you draw should be 4 units long. See margin for art; 5 states.

1. Start at (2, 4) and draw a segment that has a slope of 0 and an endpoint in Quadrant II.
2. Draw a segment on the line $x = -2$ with an endpoint on the x-axis.
3. Draw a segment on the line $y = 0$ that has a positive x-coordinate.
4. Draw a segment that has an undefined slope and an endpoint in Quadrant IV.
5. Draw a segment on the line $y = -4$ that has an endpoint in Quadrant III.

LESSON **8.6**

Writing Linear Equations

BEFORE	Now	WHY?
You graphed linear equations.	You'll write linear equations.	So you can describe the area of glaciers, as in Ex. 26.

Vocabulary

best-fitting line, p. 421

Bamboo Bamboo is one of the fastest-growing plants on Earth. It can grow up to 4 feet in one day! In Example 4, you'll see how to write a linear equation that describes the growth of a bamboo plant.

You can write a linear equation in slope-intercept form, $y = mx + b$, if you know the slope m and the y-intercept b of the equation's graph.

Example 1 *Writing an Equation Given the Slope and y-Intercept*

Write an equation of the line with a slope of 3 and a *y*-intercept of −7.

$y = mx + b$ **Write general slope-intercept equation.**

$y = 3x + (-7)$ **Substitute 3 for *m* and −7 for *b*.**

$y = 3x - 7$ **Simplify.**

Example 2 *Writing an Equation of a Graph*

Write an equation of the line shown.

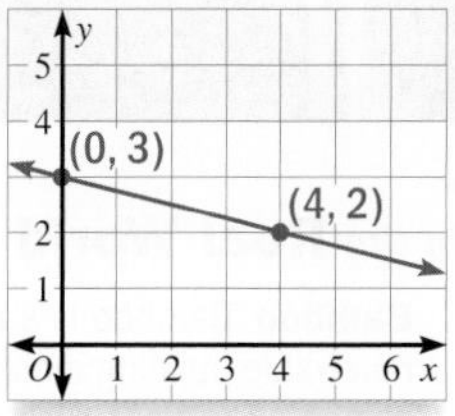

1. Find the slope m using the labeled points.

$$m = \frac{2-3}{4-0} = \frac{-1}{4} = -\frac{1}{4}$$

2. Find the y-intercept b. The line crosses the y-axis at (0, 3), so $b = 3$.

3. Write an equation of the form $y = mx + b$.

$$y = -\frac{1}{4}x + 3$$

✔ *Checkpoint*

1. Write an equation of the line with a slope of 1 and a y-intercept of 5. $y = x + 5$
2. Write an equation of the line through the points (−2, 6) and (0, −4).

2. $y = -5x - 4$

NCTM CURRICULUM STANDARDS

Standard 2: Represent situations using algebraic symbols; Use models to understand relationships

Standard 5: Use proper statistical methods to analyze data

1 PLAN

Skill Check

Find the slope of the line through the pair of points.

1. (3, 1) and (5, 2) $\frac{1}{2}$
2. (−1, 4) and (1, 8) 2
3. (8, 3) and (3, 5) $-\frac{2}{5}$

Lesson Objective

Write linear equations.

Pacing

Suggested Number of Days

Basic Course: 2 days

Average Course: 2 days

Advanced Course: 2 days

Block: 1 block

Teaching Resources

For a complete list of Teaching Resources, see page 382B.

Transparency

Warm-Up Exercises for this lesson are available on a transparency. A support transparency is available for Examples 4 and 5.

2 TEACH

Motivating the Lesson

Ask students how many feet per hour the bamboo is growing. **$\frac{1}{6}$ ft** Ask: "How many inches per hour is it growing?" **2 in.**

TIPS *for* NEW TEACHERS
Reassure students who feel overwhelmed by this chapter that the material in this lesson is not new. Instead of graphing a line given its equation, they will be finding the equation of a line given its graph. See Tips for New Teachers in the *Chapter 8 Resource Book.*

Extra Examples

Example 1 Write an equation of the line with a slope of -5 and a y-intercept of 12.
$y = -5x + 12$

Example 2 Write an equation of the line shown. **$y = x - 1$**

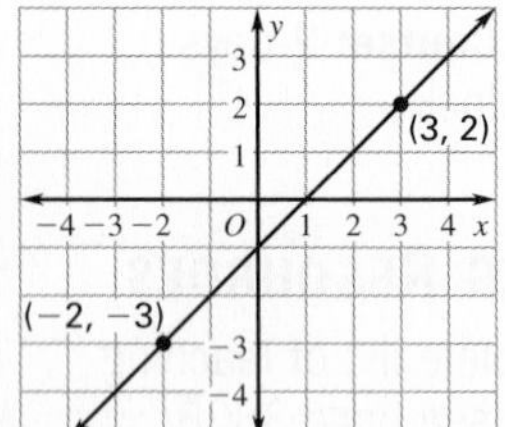

Example 3
a. Write an equation of the line that is parallel to the line $y = -2x + 5$ and passes through the point (0, 3).
$y = -2x + 3$
b. Write an equation of the line that is perpendicular to the line $y = \frac{1}{4}x + 12$ and passes through the point $(0, -4)$. **$y = -4x - 4$**

Example 4 The table below shows the amount of cash in dollars left from $25 after x loads of laundry have been done at a laundromat. Write an equation for the function.

Loads, x	0	1	2	3
Cash left ($), y	25	23	21	19

$y = 25 - 2x$

3. A graph. ***Sample answer:*** **A table shows several discrete input and output values, while a graph can show those values and intermediate values. A graph also makes it easier to see whether the points all lie along a line, whereas you cannot tell immediately if a function is linear when looking at a table of values.**

In the **Real World**

Bamboo Bamboo is a rapidly renewable building material compared to trees such as oak. Bamboo takes about 5 years to grow, while oak takes about 120 years. How many bamboo forests can be grown and harvested in the time it takes to grow one oak forest?
24 bamboo forests

Example 3 *Writing Equations of Parallel or Perpendicular Lines*

a. Write an equation of the line that is parallel to the line $y = 4x - 8$ and passes through the point (0, 2).

b. Write an equation of the line that is perpendicular to the line $y = -5x + 1$ and passes through the point $(0, -9)$.

Solution

a. The slope of the given line is 4, so the slope of the parallel line is also 4. The parallel line passes through (0, 2), so its y-intercept is 2.

Answer An equation of the line is $y = 4x + 2$.

b. Because the slope of the given line is -5, the slope of the perpendicular line is the negative reciprocal of -5, or $\frac{1}{5}$. The perpendicular line passes through $(0, -9)$, so its y-intercept is -9.

Answer An equation of the line is $y = \frac{1}{5}x + (-9)$, or $y = \frac{1}{5}x - 9$.

Example 4 *Writing an Equation from a Table*

The table shows a bamboo plant's growth over 8 hours. Show that the table represents a linear function. Write an equation for the function.

Time (h), x	0	2	4	6	8
Height (in.), y	6	10	14	18	22

Solution

1) Make a scatter plot. The points lie on a nonvertical line, so the table represents a linear function.

2) Find the slope m using any two points on the line, such as (0, 6) and (2, 10).

$$m = \frac{10 - 6}{2 - 0} = \frac{4}{2} = 2$$

3) Find the y-intercept b. The line intersects the y-axis at (0, 6), so $b = 6$.

4) Write the equation $y = mx + b$.

$$y = 2x + 6$$

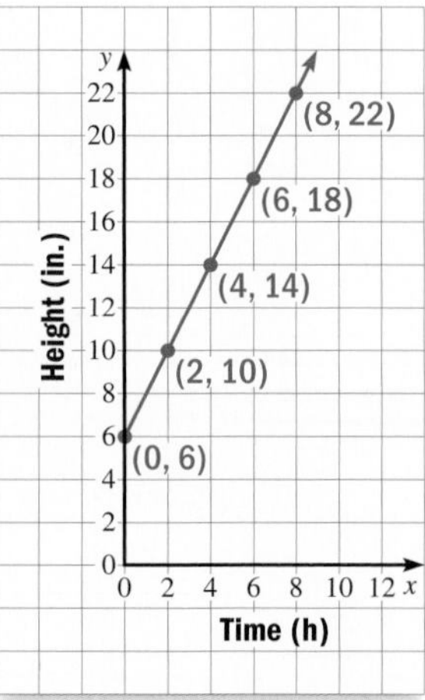

Checkpoint

3. Which representation of a function more clearly shows whether or not the function is linear: a table of values or a graph? Explain.
See margin.

Best-Fitting Lines In Example 4, the points in the scatter plot lie *exactly* on a line. Often, however, there is no single line that passes through all the points in a data set. In such cases, you can find the **best-fitting line**, which is the line that lies as close as possible to the data points.

The following example uses a graphical method to approximate the equation of a best-fitting line. In the activity on page 425, you'll use a graphing calculator to find a better approximation of this line.

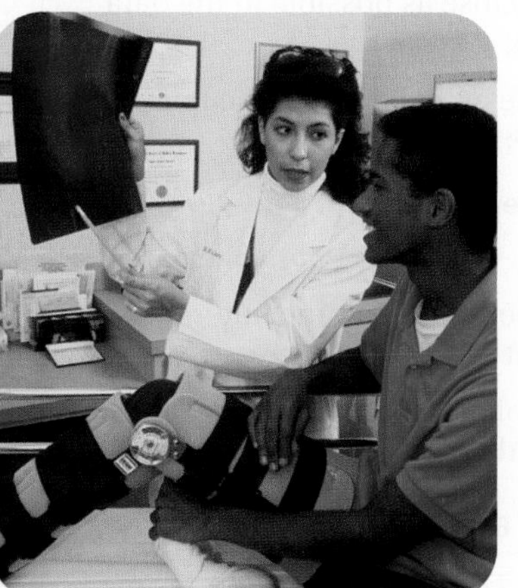

Example 5 *Approximating a Best-Fitting Line*

Medicine The table shows the number of female physicians in the United States for the years 1992–1999.

Years since 1992, x	0	1	2	3	4	5	6	7
Female physicians (in thousands), y	110	117	125	140	148	158	168	177

a. Approximate the equation of the best-fitting line for the data.

b. Predict the number of female physicians in 2005.

Solution

a. *First,* make a scatter plot of the data pairs.

Next, draw the line that appears to best fit the data points. There should be about the same number of points above the line as below it. The line does not have to pass through any of the data points.

Finally, write an equation of the line. To find the slope, estimate the coordinates of two points on the line, such as (0, 108) and (7, 177).

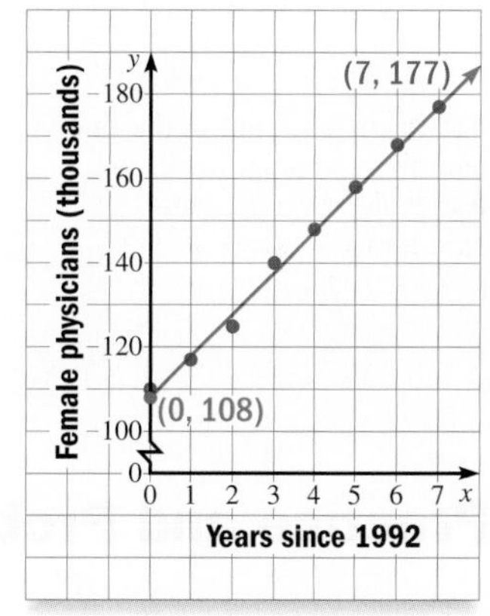

$$m = \frac{177 - 108}{7 - 0} = \frac{69}{7} \approx 9.86$$

The line intersects the y-axis at (0, 108), so the y-intercept is 108.

Answer An approximate equation of the best-fitting line is $y = 9.86x + 108$.

b. Note that $2005 - 1992 = 13$, so 2005 is 13 years after 1992. Calculate y when $x = 13$ using the equation from part (a).

$y = 9.86x + 108$	**Write equation of best-fitting line.**
$y = 9.86(13) + 108$	**Substitute 13 for x.**
$y \approx 236$	**Simplify.**

Answer In 2005, there will be about 236,000 female physicians in the United States.

Watch *Out*

In the table for Example 5, each year's number y of female physicians is given in thousands. So in part (b), a y-value of 236 means that the number of female physicians in 2005 will be about 236 *thousand*, not 236.

Extra Examples

Example 5 The table below shows the number of miles driven after x hours of driving.

Hours, x	0	1	2	3	4
Miles, y	0	50	105	147	198

a. Approximate the equation of the best-fitting line for the data. **$y = 50x$**

b. Predict the number of miles driven after 8 hours. **about 400 mi**

Common Error

In Example 5, stress that students should not connect the points one to another. Stress that the best-fitting line does not need to pass through or even near all the points.

Algebraic Reasoning

Have a student graph a line with slope 1 on the board. Show students how a line with a slope greater than 1 compares to a line with a slope of 1. Repeat this with a line whose slope is less than 1. Urge students to always compare the graph of an equation to a line with a slope of 1 to assess its steepness.

Concept Check

How do you write an equation given its slope and y-intercept? **Write the slope-intercept form $y = mx + b$, substituting the slope for m and the y-intercept for b.**

Daily Puzzler

Shelby spent half her cash buying furniture at a yard sale. She noticed that her amount of cents after the purchase equaled her amount of dollars before the purchase, and her amount of dollars after the purchase equaled half her amount of cents before the purchase. How much cash did Shelby take to the yard sale? **$99.98**

3 APPLY

ASSIGNMENT GUIDE

Basic Course

Day 1: pp. 422–424 Exs. 8–11, 18–23, 27–30, 35–42

Day 2: pp. 422–424 Exs. 12–17, 24–26, 43–48

Average Course

Day 1: pp. 422–424 Exs. 8–11, 18–23, 27–30, 35–42

Day 2: pp. 422–424 Exs. 12–17, 24–26, 31–33, 43–48

Advanced Course

Day 1: pp. 422–424 Exs. 10, 11, 18–23, 29–31, 40–44

Day 2: pp. 422–424 Exs. 13–17, 24–26, 32–36*, 45–48

Block

pp. 422–424 Exs. 8–33, 35–48

EXTRA PRACTICE

- Student Edition, p. 810
- Chapter 8 Resource Book, pp. 50–52
- Test and Practice Generator

TRANSPARENCY

Even-numbered answers are available on transparencies. A support transparency is available for Exercises 7, 26, 33, and 43–46.

HOMEWORK CHECK

When you review students' homework for this lesson, go over the following exercises to check understanding of key concepts.

Basic: 8, 12, 18, 24, 26
Average: 10, 14, 19, 25, 26
Advanced: 11, 16, 21, 25, 33

8.6 Exercises

More Practice, p. 810

Guided Practice

Vocabulary Check

1. Copy and complete: The line that lies as close as possible to the data points in a scatter plot is called the _?_. **best-fitting line**

2. Describe the steps you would use to write an equation of the line through the points $(-2, 3)$ and $(0, 9)$. **See margin.**

Skill Check

Write an equation of the line through the given points.

3. $(0, 8), (1, 9)$ **$y = x + 8$**
4. $(-2, 13), (0, 1)$ **$y = -6x + 1$**
5. $(0, -5), (3, -3)$ **$y = \frac{2}{3}x - 5$**

6. Write an equation of the line that is perpendicular to the line $y = 2x - 11$ and passes through the point $(0, -7)$. **$y = -\frac{1}{2}x - 7$**

Guided Problem Solving

7. **Clams** The table shows the dimensions of seven butter clams. What is the approximate length of a butter clam that is 85 millimeters wide?

Width (mm), x	13	21	30	39	50	60	71
Length (mm), y	17	28	40	52	62	77	91

1) Make a scatter plot of the data pairs. Draw the line that appears to best fit the data points. **See margin for art; best-fitting lines may vary.**

2) Write an equation of your line. ***Sample answer:*** **Using (10, 14) and (60, 77): $y = 1.26x + 1.4$**

3) Use your equation to predict, to the nearest millimeter, the length of a butter clam that is 85 millimeters wide. **109 mm**

2\. ***Sample answer:*** **First use the points to find the slope: $m = \frac{9-3}{0-(-2)} = \frac{6}{2} = 3$. Then find the y-intercept b: the line contains the point (0, 9), so $b = 9$. Finally, write the equation $y = mx + b$: $y = 3x + 9$.**

Practice and Problem Solving

Homework *Help*

Example	Exercises
1	8–11
2	12–17
3	18–23
4	24, 25, 32
5	26, 33

Online Resources
CLASSZONE.COM
- More Examples
- eTutorial Plus

Write an equation of the line with the given slope and *y*-intercept.

A
8. slope $= -3$; y-intercept $= 5$ **$y = -3x + 5$**
9. slope $= 4$; y-intercept $= 10$ **$y = 4x + 10$**
10. slope $= 13$; y-intercept $= -8$ **$y = 13x - 8$**
11. slope $= -1$; y-intercept $= -20$ **$y = -x - 20$**

Write an equation of the line.

12. (1, 4), (0, 1) **$y = 3x + 1$**

13. **$y = \frac{2}{3}x - 2$**

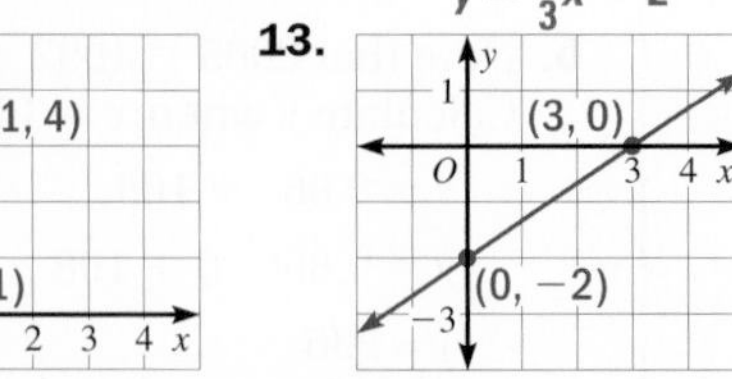

14. **$y = -2x + 3$**

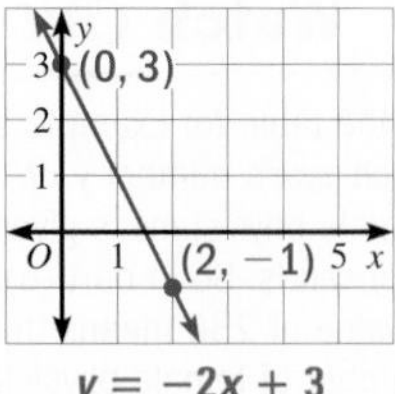

Write an equation of the line through the given points.

15. $(0, 9), (3, 15)$ **$y = 2x + 9$**
16. $(0, -6), (8, -16)$ **$y = -\frac{5}{4}x - 6$**
17. $(-2, -11), (0, -11)$ **$y = -11$**

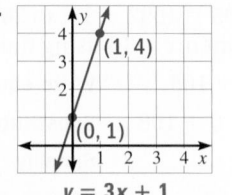

Write an equation of the line that is parallel to the given line and passes through the given point.

18. $y = 2x + 1$; (0, 4) $y = 2x + 4$ **19.** $y = -x - 3$; (0, 7) $y = -x + 7$ **20.** $y = -8x + 9$; (0, −2) $y = -8x - 2$

Write an equation of the line that is perpendicular to the given line and passes through the given point.

21. $y = 3x + 4$; (0, 6) $y = -\frac{1}{3}x + 6$ **22.** $y = x - 7$; (0, −5) $y = -x - 5$ **23.** $y = -\frac{1}{4}x + 3$; (0, 1) $y = 4x + 1$

Show that the table represents a linear function. Then write an equation for the function.

24.

x	−2	−1	0	1	2
y	−5	−2	1	4	7

25.

x	0	2	4	6	8
y	−3	−2	−1	0	1

B **26.** **Extended Problem Solving** Since 1912, scientists have created five maps of the glaciers on top of Mount Kilimanjaro in Africa. The maps indicate that the glaciers are shrinking, as shown by the table.

Map number	1	2	3	4	5
Year map was made	1912	1953	1976	1989	2000
Area of glaciers (km^2)	12.1	6.7	4.2	3.3	2.2

a. Graph Let x be the number of years since 1912. Let y be the area of the glaciers (in square kilometers). Make a scatter plot of the data pairs (x, y). Draw the line that appears to best fit the data points. See margin for art; best-fitting lines may vary.

b. Represent Write an equation of your line. *Sample answer:* Using (20, 9.5) and (60, 5): $y = -0.1125x + 11.75$

c. Predict Estimate the year when the glaciers will disappear. about 2016

Glacier on Mount Kilimanjaro

Two variables x and y show ***direct variation*** if $y = kx$ for some nonzero number k. In Exercises 27–30, write a direct variation equation that has the given ordered pair as a solution.

Example *Writing a Direct Variation Equation*

Write a direct variation equation that has (4, 20) as a solution.

$y = kx$ Write general equation for direct variation.

$20 = k(4)$ Substitute 4 for x and 20 for y.

$5 = k$ Divide each side by 4.

Answer A direct variation equation is $y = 5x$.

27. (5, 15) $y = 3x$ **28.** (−3, 21) $y = -7x$ **29.** (−8, −4) $y = \frac{1}{2}x$ **30.** (12, −16) $y = -\frac{4}{3}x$

31. **Sales** Lisa and John work in different department stores. Lisa earns a salary of $18,000 per year plus a 2% commission on her sales. John receives no salary but earns a 6% commission on his sales. For each person, tell whether annual sales and annual earnings show direct variation. Justify your answers mathematically.

24. See margin for art; the points lie on a nonvertical line, so the table represents a linear function; $y = 3x + 1$.

25. See margin for art; the points lie on a nonvertical line, so the table represents a linear function; $y = \frac{1}{2}x - 3$.

31. Lisa: no; John: yes. *Sample answer:* Let x represent annual sales and y represent annual earnings. Lisa's earnings would then be $y = 0.02x + 18,000$ which does not model the direct variation equation $y = kx$. John's earnings would be $y = 0.06x$ which does model the direct variation equation.

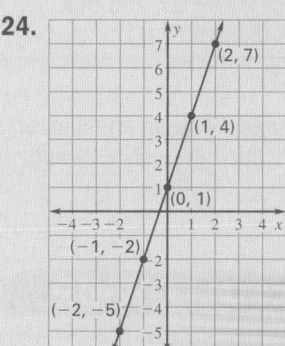

Teaching Tip

Be sure to discuss the example shown above Exercises 27–30 before assigning them.

7. Step 1:

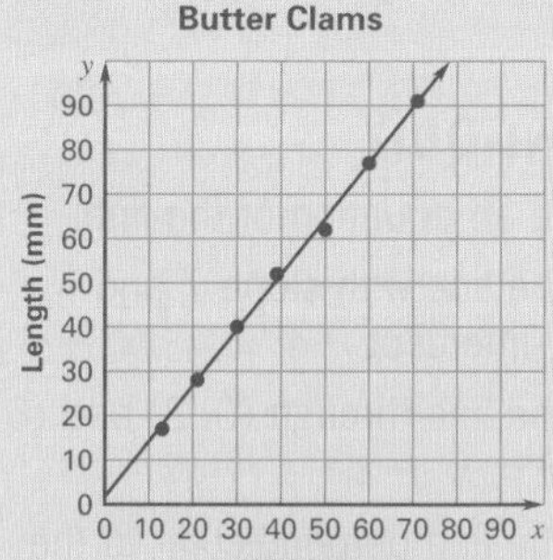

24.

(2, 7)
(1, 4)
(0, 1)
(−1, −2)
(−2, −5)

25.

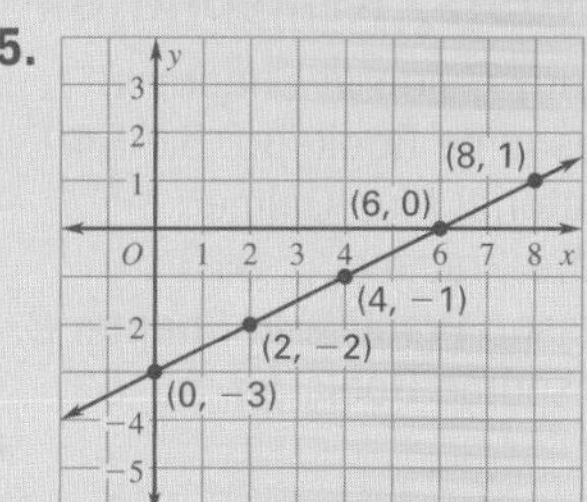

26a.

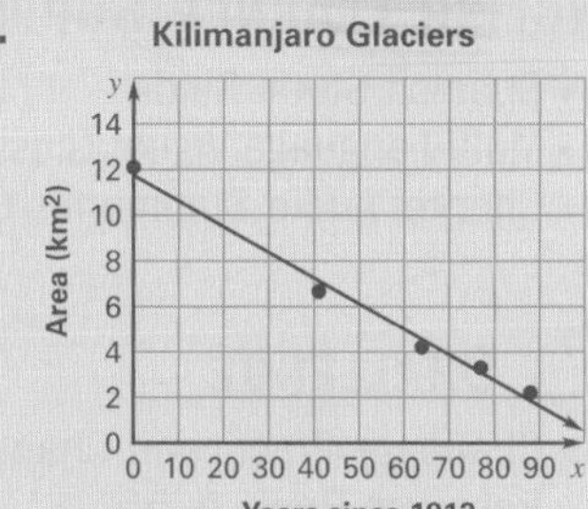

4 ASSESS

Assessment Resources

For more assessment resources, see:

- Assessment Book
- Test and Practice Generator

Mini-Quiz

Write an equation of the line.

1. the line with slope 7 and y-intercept -4 $y = 7x - 4$
2. the line through (0, 2) and (6, 8) $y = x + 2$
3. the line perpendicular to the graph of $y = -2x + 5$ that passes through (1, 1) $y = \frac{1}{2}x + \frac{1}{2}$
4. **Challenge** Write an equation of the line through $(-3, -2)$ and (5, 8). $y = \frac{5}{4}x + \frac{7}{4}$

5 FOLLOW-UP

Diagnosis/Remediation

- Study Guide in Chapter 8 Resource Book, pp. 53–54
- eTutorial Plus Online
- Extra Practice, p. 810
- Lesson Practice in Chapter 8 Resource Book, pp. 50–52

English Learner Support

- Spanish Study Guide
- Multi-Language Visual Glossary
- Chapter Audio Summaries CDs

Challenge

- Challenge Practice in Chapter 8 Resource Book, p. 55
- Teacher's Edition, p. 382F

32a, 33a, 34, 43–46. See Additional Answers beginning on page AA1.

32a. See margin for art; the points lie on a nonvertical line, so the table represents a linear function.

33b. *Sample answer:* Using (0, 160) and (90, 130): $y = -\frac{1}{3}x + 160$

32. Physics The table below gives the length of a spring when different masses are suspended from it.

Mass (g), x	0	50	100	150	200
Length (mm), y	80	110	140	170	200

length y

mass x

a. Show that the table represents a linear function.

b. Write an equation for the function. $y = \frac{3}{5}x + 80$

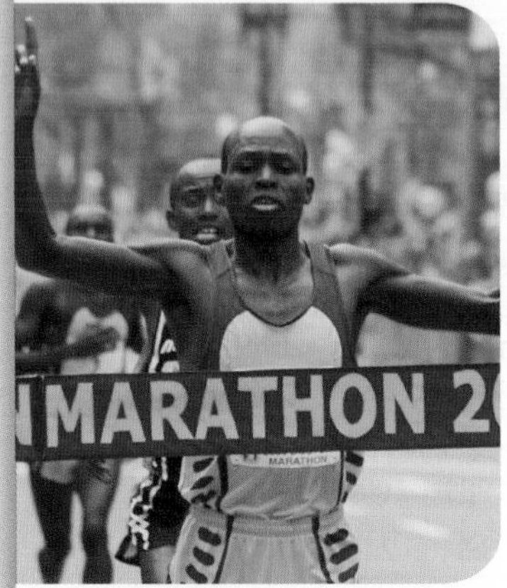

Elijah Lagat, winner of the men's Boston Marathon in 2000

C **33. Marathons** The table below shows the men's winning times in the Boston Marathon for every tenth year from 1900 to 2000. In the table, x represents the number of years since 1900, and y represents the corresponding winning time (to the nearest minute).

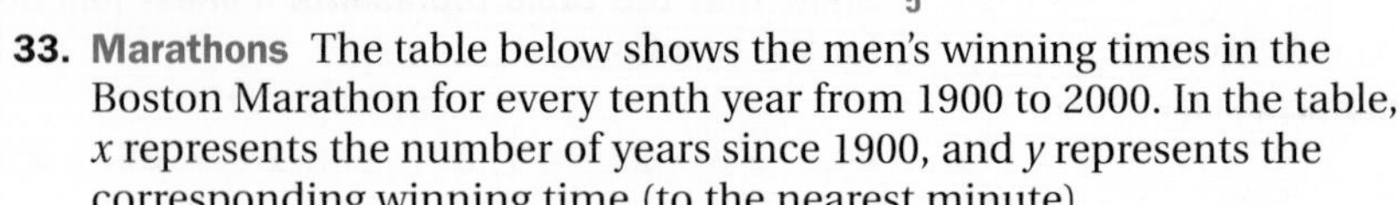

x	0	10	20	30	40	50	60	70	80	90	100
y	160	149	150	155	148	153	141	131	132	128	130

a. Make a scatter plot of the data pairs (x, y). Draw the line that appears to best fit the data points. See margin for art; best-fitting lines may vary.

b. Write an equation of your line. See margin.

c. **Predict** Use your equation to predict, to the nearest minute, the men's winning time in the Boston Marathon for the year 2010. about 123 min

d. *Writing* Do you think your equation will accurately predict winning times far into the future? Explain your reasoning. See margin.

34. Challenge Write an equation of the line through $(2, -1)$ and (6, 5). Describe the method you used to determine the equation. See margin.

Mixed Review

33d. No. *Sample answer:* The equation predicts a winning time of 0 minutes eventually, which is impossible. I would expect the winning times eventually to level off and decrease very little, if any.

Solve the equation. Check your solution. *(Lesson 3.3)*

35. $8x - 5 = 5x + 7$ 4

36. $-7y + 4 = -y + 22$ -3

37. $4(m - 4) = 2m$ 8

38. $6(1 - n) = -6n + 1$ no solution

Write the fraction as a percent. *(Lesson 7.3)*

39. $\frac{7}{10}$ 70% **40.** $\frac{3}{8}$ 37.5% **41.** $\frac{5}{2}$ 250% **42.** $\frac{9}{5}$ 180%

Identify the slope and y-intercept of the line with the given equation. Use the slope and y-intercept to graph the equation. *(Lesson 8.5)* 43–46. See margin.

43. $y = 3x - 2$ **44.** $y = -x + 5$ **45.** $3x + 2y = 0$ **46.** $x - 2y = -2$

Standardized Test Practice

43–46. See margin for art.

43. slope: 3; y-intercept: -2

44. slope: -1; y-intercept: 5

45. slope: $-\frac{3}{2}$; y-intercept: 0

46. slope: $\frac{1}{2}$; y-intercept: 1

47. Multiple Choice What is an equation of the line through the points (0, 8) and (2, 0)? D

A. $y = 4x + 2$ **B.** $y = 4x + 8$ **C.** $y = -4x + 2$ **D.** $y = -4x + 8$

48. Multiple Choice What is an equation of the line that is parallel to the line $y = 5x + 3$ and passes through the point $(0, -1)$? F

F. $y = 5x - 1$ **G.** $y = -5x - 1$ **H.** $y = \frac{1}{5}x - 1$ **I.** $y = -\frac{1}{5}x - 1$

8.6 Finding Best-Fitting Lines

Goal Use a graphing calculator to find the best-fitting line for a scatter plot.

Example

Use a graphing calculator to make a scatter plot of the female physician data on page 421 and find the best-fitting line.

1 Press LIST and enter the data into two lists, L1 and L2. Use the arrow keys to navigate.

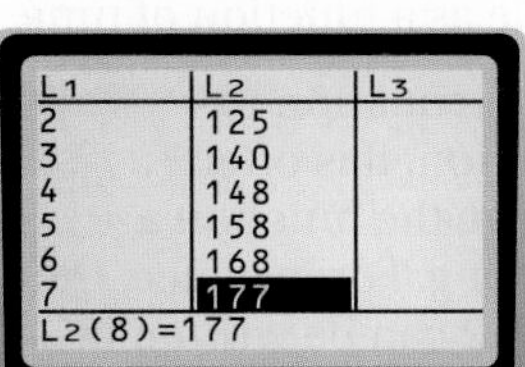

2 Press 2nd **[PLOT]**, select Plot1, turn it from Off to On, and select the scatter plot icon. Then press GRAPH.

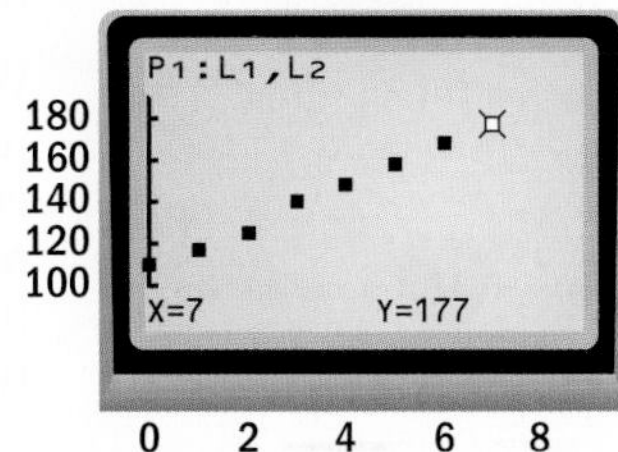

3 Press 2nd **[STAT]**, select CALC, and select LinReg(ax+b). Then press ENTER.

4 The best-fitting line has slope a and y-intercept b. Enter the equation of the line and graph it.

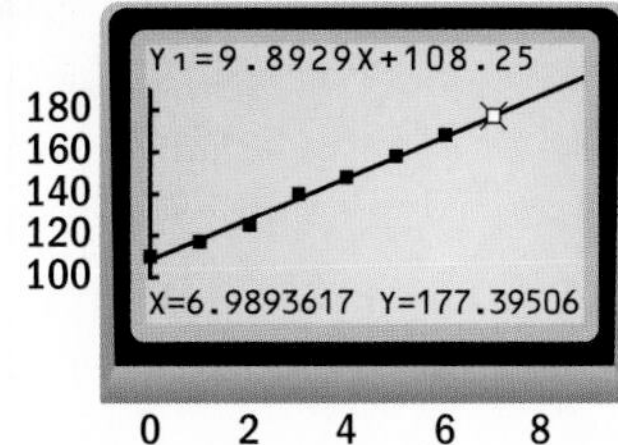

Tech Help

Press ZOOM and select ZoomStat to set a viewing window that will show all points in the scatter plot.

Press TRACE to move among the data points in the scatter plot or along the best-fitting line.

Draw Conclusions

1. **Predict** Use the best-fitting line from the example above to predict the number of female physicians in 2005. **about 237,000 physicians**
2. **Dentistry** The table shows the average amount each person in the U.S. spent on dental services for the years 1992–1999. Use a graphing calculator to find the best-fitting line for the data. $y = 8.93x + 139$

Years since 1992, x	0	1	2	3	4	5	6	7
Amount (dollars), y	140	148	156	166	173	184	193	202

NCTM CURRICULUM STANDARDS
Standard 5: Use proper statistical methods to analyze data; Develop inferences that are based on data

1 PLAN

Learn the Method

- Students will use a graphing calculator to find the best-fitting line for a scatter plot.
- Students can use the skill learned here to check their work on Exercises 26 and 33 in Lesson 8.6.

Grouping

Students should work individually.

2 TEACH

Tips for Success

Urge students to check their keystrokes carefully. Point out that mistyping just one ordered pair can cause the best-fitting line to be altered significantly.

Extra Examples

Example The table shows the number of miles y driven after x hours of driving. Use a graphing calculator to find the best-fitting line for the data. $y = 52x + 2.6$

Hours, x	0	1	2	3	4
Miles, y	0	52	111	168	202

3 CLOSE

Assessment

1. How does a best-fitting line help you make a prediction? **The line extends beyond the points you graphed so you can make predictions about the future.**
2. How would you know if your best-fitting line was incorrectly calculated? ***Sample answer:* If significantly more points were on one side of the line than on the other, then the line is incorrect.**

1 PLAN

Skill Check

Find the value of x when $y = 5$.

1. $y = -x + 4$ **-1**
2. $y = \frac{1}{2}x - 10$ **30**
3. $y = -20x$ **$-\frac{1}{4}$**
4. $y = 3x$ **$\frac{5}{3}$**

Lesson Objective

Use function notation.

Pacing

Suggested Number of Days
Basic Course: 1 day
Average Course: 1 day
Advanced Course: 1 day
Block: 0.5 block with 8.8

Teaching Resources

For a complete list of Teaching Resources, see page 382B.

 **Transparency**

Warm-Up Exercises for this lesson are available on a transparency. A support transparency is available for Example 2 and Checkpoint Exercises 4–6.

2 TEACH

Motivating the Lesson

Ask students what they think it means for one variable to be a function of another variable. Use the responses to lead into a discussion of function notation.

LESSON **8.7**

Function Notation

BEFORE	*Now*	WHY?
You wrote equations in function form.	You'll use function notation.	So you can find the mass of a squid, as in Ex. 28.

Vocabulary
function notation, p. 426

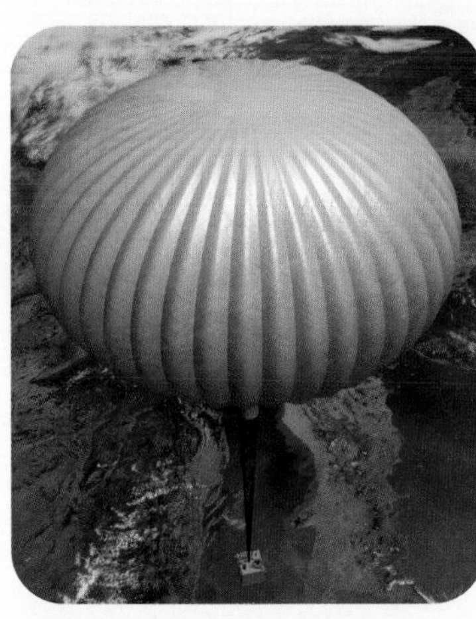

Science In 2001, a scientific balloon like the one shown was launched near McMurdo Station in Antarctica. In Example 4, you'll see how *function notation* can be used to describe the balloon's altitude as a function of time.

When you use an equation to represent a function, it is often convenient to give the function a name, such as f or g. For instance, the function $y = x + 2$ can be written in **function notation** as follows:

$$f(x) = x + 2$$

The symbol $f(x)$, which replaces y, is read "f of x" and represents the value of the function f at x. For instance, $f(3)$ is the value of f when $x = 3$.

Watch *Out*

Don't confuse the parentheses in $f(x)$ with parentheses used to indicate multiplication. The symbol $f(x)$ does *not* mean "f times x."

Example 1 *Working with Function Notation*

Let $f(x) = -3x + 8$. Find $f(x)$ when $x = 5$, and find x when $f(x) = -22$.

a. $f(x) = -3x + 8$ **Write function.**
$f(5) = -3(5) + 8$ **Substitute 5 for x.**
$= -7$ **Simplify.**

Answer When $x = 5$, $f(x) = -7$.

b. $f(x) = -3x + 8$ **Write function.**
$-22 = -3x + 8$ **Substitute -22 for $f(x)$.**
$-30 = -3x$ **Subtract 8 from each side.**
$10 = x$ **Divide each side by -3.**

Answer When $f(x) = -22$, $x = 10$.

 ***Checkpoint***

Let $g(x) = 4x - 5$. Find the indicated value.

1. $g(x)$ when $x = 2$ **3**
2. $g(-10)$ **-45**
3. x when $g(x) = 19$ **6**

NCTM CURRICULUM STANDARDS
Standard 2: Understand functions; Use models to understand relationships
Standard 6: Solve problems in math and other contexts

Graphing Functions To graph a function written in function notation, you may find it helpful to first rewrite the function in terms of x and y.

Example 2 *Graphing a Function*

Graph the function $f(x) = \frac{3}{4}x + 1$.

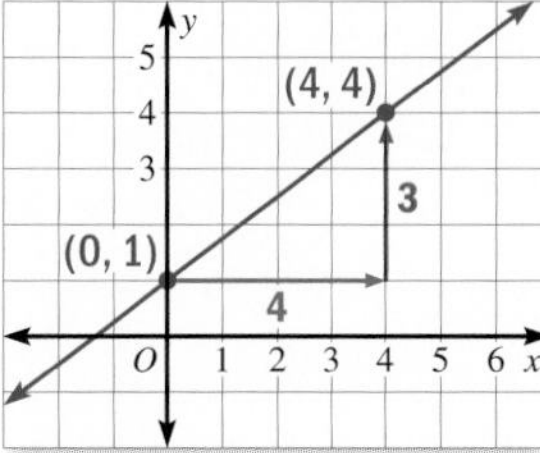

1) Rewrite the function as $y = \frac{3}{4}x + 1$.

2) The y-intercept is 1, so plot the point (0, 1).

3) The slope is $\frac{3}{4}$. Starting at (0, 1), plot another point by moving right 4 units and up 3 units.

4) Draw a line through the two points.

Checkpoint

Graph the function. 4–6. See margin.

4. $f(x) = 2x - 4$ 5. $g(x) = -\frac{3}{2}x + 3$ 6. $h(x) = -1$

If $f(c) = d$ for a function f, then you can conclude that the graph of f passes through the point (c, d).

Example 3 *Writing a Function*

Write a linear function g given that $g(0) = 9$ and $g(3) = -6$.

1) Find the slope m of the function's graph. From the values of $g(0)$ and $g(3)$, you know that the graph of g passes through the points (0, 9) and (3, −6). Use these points to calculate the slope.

$$m = \frac{-6 - 9}{3 - 0} = \frac{-15}{3} = -5$$

2) Find the y-intercept b of the function's graph. The graph passes through (0, 9), so $b = 9$.

3) Write an equation of the form $g(x) = mx + b$.

$$g(x) = -5x + 9$$

Checkpoint

Write a linear function that satisfies the given conditions.

7. $f(0) = 1, f(2) = 9$ **$f(x) = 4x + 1$**
8. $f(0) = -7, f(6) = 5$ **$f(x) = 2x - 7$**
9. $g(-6) = 16, g(0) = -5$ **$g(x) = -\frac{7}{2}x - 5$**
10. $r(-7) = 3, r(0) = 3$ **$r(x) = 3$**

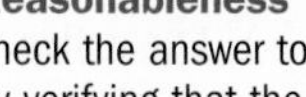

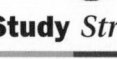

Study *Strategy*

Reasonableness You can check the answer to Example 3 by verifying that the function g gives the desired values for $g(0)$ and $g(3)$:

$g(0) = -5(0) + 9 = 9$ ✓
$g(3) = -5(3) + 9 = -6$ ✓

TIPS *for* NEW TEACHERS

Make sure students read the Watch Out feature on page 426. Also point out that f, g, and h are the letters used most often in function notation. See Tips for New Teachers in the *Chapter 8 Resource Book*.

Extra Examples

Example 1 Let $f(x) = 10x - 8$.
a. Find $f(x)$ when $x = 3$. **22**
b. Find x when $f(x) = -18$. **−1**

Example 2 Graph the function $f(x) = -\frac{1}{2}x - 2$.

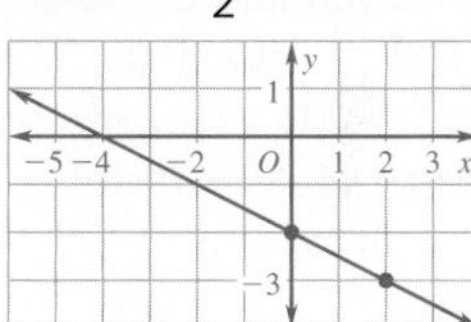

Example 3 Write a linear function h given that $h(0) = 10$ and $h(4) = -18$. **$h(x) = -7x + 10$**

COMMON ERROR

In Example 1b, watch for students who substitute the given value for x rather than for $f(x)$.

***READING* STRATEGY**

In Example 1, point out the use of different colors for the substituted values in the two parts of the example. This should help students see that the substitution is for x in part a, but that the substitution is for $f(x)$ in part b.

4–6. See Additional Answers beginning on page AA1.

Extra Examples

Example 4 A new book is selling at a rate of 8 copies per second during its first week of release.

a. Use function notation to write an equation giving the number of copies sold as a function of time in hours. **$c(h) = 28{,}800h$**

b. How many hours will it take to sell one million copies? **about 34.7 h**

CONCEPT CHECK

What does the notation $f(-2)$ mean? How do you find the value of $f(-2)$ if $f(x) = -6x + 1$. **The value of the function $f(x)$ when x has the value -2; substitute -2 for x in the expression $-6x + 1$ and evaluate.**

DAILY PUZZLER

Katrina was 8 when her mother turned 31. Today Katrina is half the age of her mother. How old is Katrina now? **23 years old**

6.

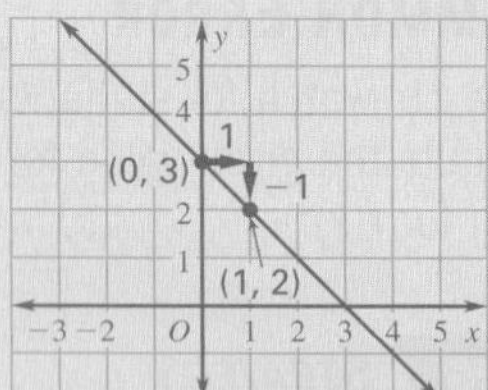

7.

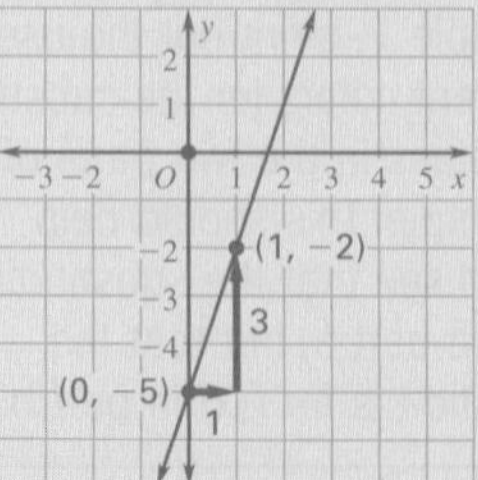

8.

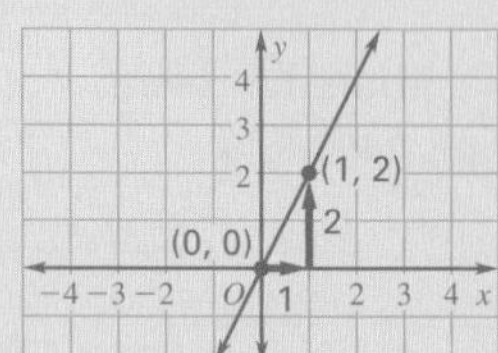

Example 4 *Using Function Notation in Real Life*

After the balloon described on page 426 was launched, it rose at a rate of about 500 feet per minute to a final altitude of 120,000 feet.

a. Use function notation to write an equation giving the altitude of the balloon as a function of time.

b. How long did it take the balloon to reach its final altitude?

Solution

a. Let t be the elapsed time (in minutes) since the balloon was launched, and let $a(t)$ be the altitude (in feet) at that time. Write a verbal model. Then use the verbal model to write an equation.

Altitude = Rate of climb • Time since launch

$a(t) = 500t$

b. Find the value of t for which $a(t) = 120{,}000$.

$a(t) = 500t$ **Write function for altitude.**

$120{,}000 = 500t$ **Substitute 120,000 for $a(t)$.**

$240 = t$ **Divide each side by 500.**

Answer It took the balloon about 240 minutes (or about 4 hours) to reach its final altitude.

8.7 Exercises

More Practice, p. 810

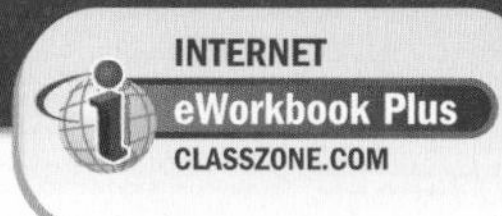

Guided Practice

Vocabulary Check

1. Write the equation $y = 4x - 3$ using function notation. **$f(x) = 4x - 3$**

2. Suppose f is a linear function with $f(2) = 5$ and $f(6) = -1$. Describe how you can find the slope of the graph of f. **See margin.**

2. *Sample answer:* **The given values of $f(x)$ mean that the graph of f passes through (2, 5) and (6, −1). Use these points to calculate the slope: $m = \frac{-1-5}{6-2} = \frac{-6}{4} = -\frac{3}{2}$.**

Skill Check

Let $f(x) = 7x + 4$. Find the indicated value.

3. $f(x)$ when $x = -8$ **−52**

4. $f(3)$ **25**

5. x when $f(x) = 67$ **9**

Graph the function. **6–8. See margin.**

6. $f(x) = -x + 3$

7. $g(x) = 3x - 5$

8. $h(x) = 2x$

9. Write a linear function f given that $f(-4) = 12$ and $f(0) = 8$. **$f(x) = -x + 8$**

10. Cable TV The average monthly cost of basic cable TV was \$9.73 in 1985 and has increased by about \$1.35 each year since then. Let t be the number of years since 1985. Use function notation to write an equation giving the monthly cost of basic cable TV as a function of t. **$f(t) = 1.35t + 9.73$**

Practice and Problem Solving

Homework Help

Example	Exercises
1	11-16
2	17-22
3	24-27
4	28-30

- More Examples
- eTutorial Plus

Let $f(x) = -3x + 1$ and $g(x) = 10x - 4$. Find the indicated value.

A **11.** $f(x)$ when $x = -1$ 4 **12.** $g(x)$ when $x = 5$ 46 **13.** x when $f(x) = -17$ 6

14. x when $g(x) = 31$ $3\frac{1}{2}$ **15.** $f(-20)$ 61 **16.** $f(4) + g(-3)$ −45

Match the function with its graph.

17. $f(x) = 2x - 1$ C **18.** $g(x) = x - 1$ A **19.** $h(x) = 2x + 1$ B

A.

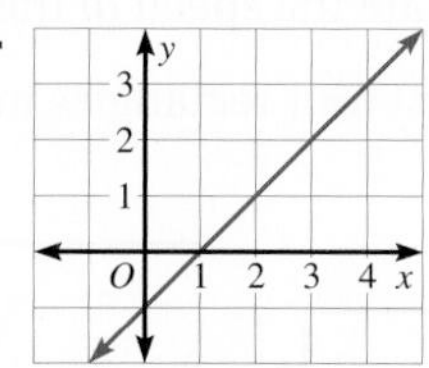

B.

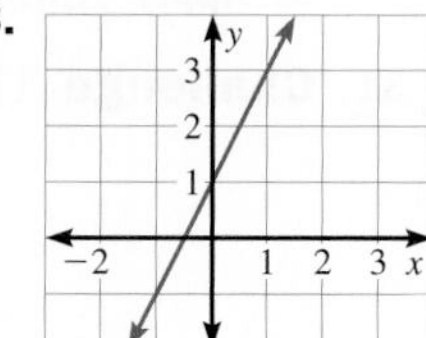

C.

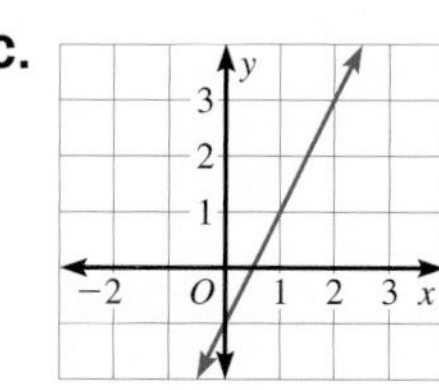

Graph the function. 20–22. See margin.

20. $f(x) = -2x$ **21.** $g(x) = 4x - 4$ **22.** $h(x) = -\frac{2}{3}x + 5$

23. Critical Thinking Write a linear function g whose graph passes through the origin and is parallel to the graph of $f(x) = -8x - 2$. $g(x) = -8x$

Write a linear function that satisfies the given conditions.

24. $f(0) = 4, f(1) = 7$ $f(x) = 3x + 4$ **25.** $g(-2) = 10, g(0) = 0$ $g(x) = -5x$

26. $h(0) = 13, h(3) = 1$ $h(x) = -4x + 13$ **27.** $r(-9) = -7, r(0) = -1$ $r(x) = \frac{2}{3}x - 1$

28. Squid An arrow squid has a beak used for eating. Given the length b (in millimeters) of an arrow squid's lower beak, you can approximate the squid's mass (in grams) using the function $m(b) = 236b - 513$.

a. The beak of an arrow squid washes ashore on a beach, where it is found and measured by a biologist. The lower beak has a length of 5 millimeters. Approximate the mass of the squid. about 667 g

b. To the nearest tenth of a millimeter, about how long is the lower beak of an arrow squid with a mass of 1100 grams? 6.8 mm

Arrow squid

B **29. Extended Problem Solving** You make and sell birdhouses. Your fixed costs for your tools and workspace are \$3000. The cost of wood and other materials needed to make a birdhouse is \$10. You sell each birdhouse for \$50. Let x represent the number of birdhouses you make and sell.

a. Write a function for your total costs, $c(x)$. $c(x) = 10x + 3000$

b. Write a function for your income, $i(x)$. $i(x) = 50x$

c. Analyze Your profit is the difference of your income and total costs. Write a function for your profit, $p(x)$. $p(x) = 40x - 3000$

d. What is your profit when you make and sell 100 birdhouses? \$1000

e. Interpret and Apply You are said to "break even" when your profit is \$0. How many birdhouses do you need to make and sell in order to break even? 75 birdhouses

3 APPLY

ASSIGNMENT GUIDE

Basic Course

Day 1: pp. 429-430 Exs. 11-22, 26-28, 32-43

Average Course

Day 1: pp. 429-430 Exs. 14-25, 28-30, 32-44

Advanced Course

Day 1: pp. 429-430 Exs. 14-16, 20-33*, 34-37, 40-44

Block

pp. 429-430 Exs. 14-25, 28-30, 32-44 (with 8.8)

EXTRA PRACTICE

- Student Edition, p. 810
- Chapter 8 Resource Book, pp. 59-61
- Test and Practice Generator

TRANSPARENCY

Even-numbered answers are available on transparencies. A support transparency is available for Exercises 6-8 and 20-22.

HOMEWORK CHECK

When you review students' homework for this lesson, go over the following exercises to check understanding of key concepts.

Basic: 11, 17, 20, 26, 28
Average: 14, 18, 21, 24, 29
Advanced: 16, 19, 22, 25, 30

TEACHING TIP

In Exercise 16, explain that students should find $f(4)$ and $g(-3)$ and then find the sum of these two values.

20-22. See Additional Answers beginning on page AA1.

4 ASSESS

ASSESSMENT RESOURCES

For more assessment resources, see:
- Assessment Book
- Test and Practice Generator

MINI-QUIZ

Let $f(x) = -9x + 2$.

1. Find $f(2)$. **-16**
2. Find x when $f(x) = 29$. **-3**
3. Write a linear function f given that $f(-4) = 37$ and $f(3) = -19$. **$f(x) = -8x + 5$**
4. **Challenge** The base and height of the first three triangles in a pattern are shown in the table.

Triangle	1	2	3
Base	2	4	6
Height	1	2	3

a. For the nth triangle in the pattern, what are the dimensions in terms of n? **$2n, n$**

b. Write a function for the area $A(n)$ of the nth triangle. **$A(n) = n^2$**

5 FOLLOW-UP

DIAGNOSIS/REMEDIATION

- Study Guide in Chapter 8 Resource Book, pp. 62–63
- eTutorial Plus Online
- Extra Practice, p. 810
- Lesson Practice in Chapter 8 Resource Book, pp. 59–61

ENGLISH LEARNER SUPPORT

- Spanish Study Guide
- Multi-Language Visual Glossary
- Chapter Audio Summaries CDs

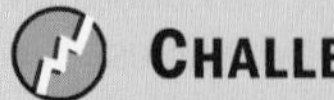

CHALLENGE

- Challenge Practice in Chapter 8 Resource Book, p. 64
- Teacher's Edition, p. 382F

30a. See Additional Answers beginning on page AA1.

30. Rivers Surveyors measured the speed of the current below a dam on the Columbia River in Washington. Based on their data, the speed (in feet per second) can be approximated by $s(d) = -0.117d + 1.68$, where d is the depth (in feet) below the river's surface.

a. Graph the given function on a graphing calculator. Remember to replace d with x and $s(d)$ with y. **See margin.**

b. *Writing* Describe what happens to the speed of the current as you go deeper below the river's surface. **It decreases.**

c. **Apply** Approximate the speed of the current at a depth of 9 feet. **0.627 ft/sec**

C **31. Challenge** The first four rectangles in a pattern are shown below.

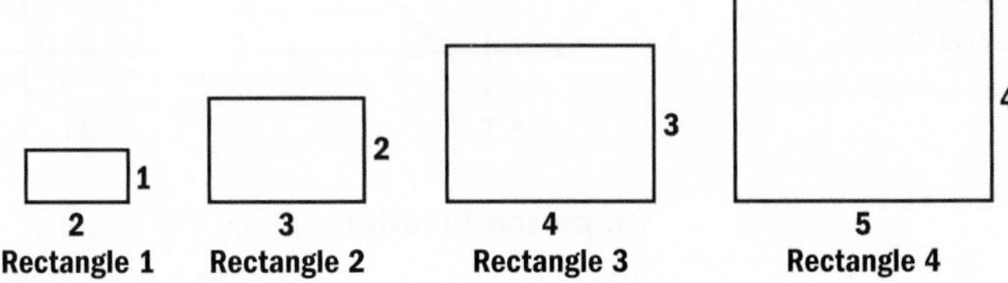

a. For the nth rectangle in the pattern, what are the dimensions in terms of n? **$(n + 1)$ by n**

b. Write a function for the area $A(n)$ of the nth rectangle. **$A(n) = n(n + 1)$, or $A(n) = n^2 + n$**

c. Write a function for the perimeter $P(n)$ of the nth rectangle. **$P(n) = 2(n + 1) + 2n$, or $P(n) = 4n + 2$**

d. Find the area and the perimeter of the 50th rectangle in the pattern. **area: 2550 units^2; perimeter: 202 units**

Mixed Review

Simplify. *(Lesson 4.5)*

32. $x^3 \cdot x^5$ **x^8** **33.** $2n^7 \cdot 5n^4$ **$10n^{11}$** **34.** $\frac{a^{12}}{a^8}$ **a^4** **35.** $\frac{30c^9}{12c^2}$ **$\frac{5c^7}{2}$**

Write the percent as a fraction in simplest form. *(Lesson 7.1)*

36. 40% **$\frac{2}{5}$** **37.** 64% **$\frac{16}{25}$** **38.** 99% **$\frac{99}{100}$** **39.** 150% **$\frac{3}{2}$**

Write an equation of the line that is perpendicular to the given line and passes through the given point. *(Lesson 8.6)*

40. $y = 6x + 10$; $(0, -4)$ **$y = -\frac{1}{6}x - 4$** **41.** $y = -\frac{5}{9}x - 1$; $(0, 3)$ **$y = \frac{9}{5}x + 3$**

Standardized Test Practice

42. Multiple Choice Let $f(x) = -7x - 11$. What is the value of $f(-4)$? **D**

A. -39 **B.** -22 **C.** 0 **D.** 17

43. Multiple Choice Suppose g is a linear function with $g(-3) = 28$ and $g(0) = 4$. What is the slope of the graph of g? **F**

F. -8 **G.** $-\frac{1}{8}$ **H.** $\frac{1}{8}$ **I.** 8

44. Short Response For Oregon counties with population p, the function $w(p) = 0.878p - 4764$ approximates the amount of solid waste (in tons) that was disposed of during 1998. The population of Marion County, Oregon, was 271,750 in 1998. To the nearest thousand tons, about how much solid waste was disposed of in Marion County during 1998? **234,000 tons**

LESSON

8.8 Systems *of* Linear Equations

BEFORE	Now	WHY?
You graphed linear equations.	You'll graph and solve systems of linear equations.	So you can decide which of two printers to buy, as in Ex. 25.

Vocabulary

system of linear equations, p. 431

solution of a linear system, p. 431

Internet Some providers of high-speed Internet service offer a choice of two plans. With plan A, you buy the modem and pay a monthly fee for Internet service. With plan B, the modem is free, but you pay a higher monthly fee than for plan A.

When is plan A a better deal than plan B? In Example 4, you'll see how to answer this question by solving a *system of linear equations*.

A **system of linear equations**, or simply a *linear system*, consists of two or more linear equations with the same variables. Below is an example.

$y = 2x - 4$ **Equation 1**

$y = -3x + 1$ **Equation 2**

A **solution of a linear system** in two variables is an ordered pair that is a solution of each equation in the system. A linear system has a solution at each point where the graphs of the equations in the system intersect.

Example 1 *Solving a System of Linear Equations*

Solve the linear system: $y = 2x - 4$ **Equation 1**

$y = -3x + 1$ **Equation 2**

1. Graph the equations.
2. Identify the apparent intersection point, $(1, -2)$.
3. Verify that $(1, -2)$ is the solution of the system by substituting 1 for x and -2 for y in each equation.

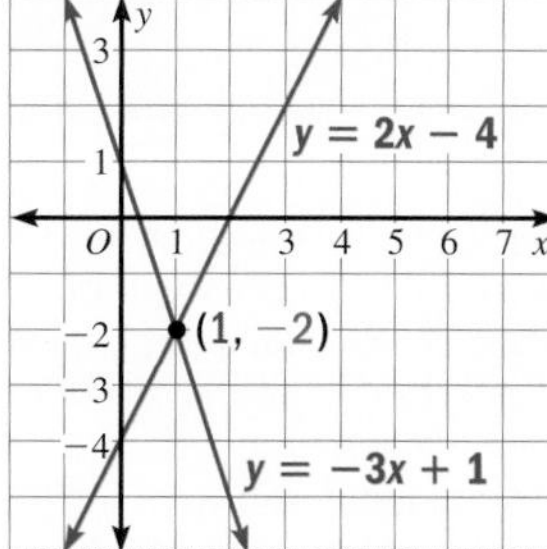

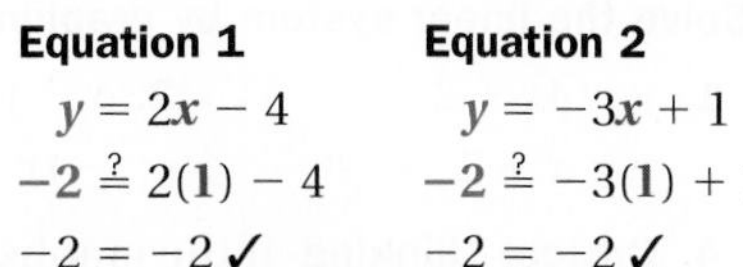

Equation 1	**Equation 2**
$y = 2x - 4$	$y = -3x + 1$
$-2 \stackrel{?}{=} 2(1) - 4$	$-2 \stackrel{?}{=} -3(1) + 1$
$-2 = -2$ ✓	$-2 = -2$ ✓

Answer The solution is $(1, -2)$.

NCTM CURRICULUM STANDARDS

Standard 2: Represent situations using algebraic symbols; Analyze situations using algebraic symbols

Standard 6: Solve problems in math and other contexts

1 PLAN

Skill Check

Write the equation in slope-intercept form.

1. $2x - y = 10$
   $y = 2x - 10$
2. $2y - 14 = -x$
   $y = -\frac{1}{2}x + 7$
3. $3y = 4x - 27$
   $y = \frac{4}{3}x - 9$
4. $16y + 10x = 16$
   $y = -\frac{5}{8}x + 1$

LESSON OBJECTIVE

Graph and solve systems of linear equations.

PACING

Suggested Number of Days

Basic Course: 1 day

Average Course: 1 day

Advanced Course: 1 day

Block: 0.5 block with 8.7

TEACHING RESOURCES

For a complete list of Teaching Resources, see page 382B.

TRANSPARENCY

Warm-Up Exercises for this lesson are available on a transparency. A support transparency is available for Examples 1-3 and Checkpoint Exercises 1-3.

2 TEACH

MOTIVATING THE LESSON

Encourage students to research rate plans of local Internet service providers and bring the data to class. Try to incorporate their data into in-class examples.

TIPS *for* NEW TEACHERS

Throughout the lesson, stress that a system of two linear equations can have no solutions, one solution, or an infinite number of solutions. See Tips for New Teachers in the *Chapter 8 Resource Book*.

Extra Examples

Example 1 Solve the linear system:
$y = x + 1$
$y = -\frac{1}{2}x - \frac{1}{2}$ **(−1, 0)**

Example 2 Solve the linear system:
$-x = 1 - 3y$
$3y = x - 3$ **no solution**

Example 3 Solve the linear system:
$4y = x + 1$
$2x = 8y - 2$
infinitely many solutions—any point on the line $y = \frac{1}{4}x + \frac{1}{4}$

Common Error

Make sure students do not confuse the term *intersect* with the term *intercept*, leading them to think that the solution of a system of equations is always on one of the two axes.

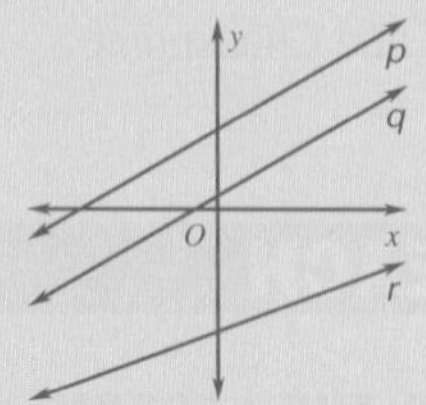

Numbers of Solutions As you saw in Example 1, when the graphs of two linear equations have exactly one point of intersection, the related system has exactly one solution. It is also possible for a linear system to have no solution or infinitely many solutions.

Example 2 *Solving a Linear System with No Solution*

Solve the linear system: $y = -2x + 1$ **Equation 1**
$y = -2x + 5$ **Equation 2**

Graph the equations. The graphs appear to be parallel lines. You can confirm that the lines are parallel by observing from their equations that they have the same slope, −2, but different *y*-intercepts, 1 and 5.

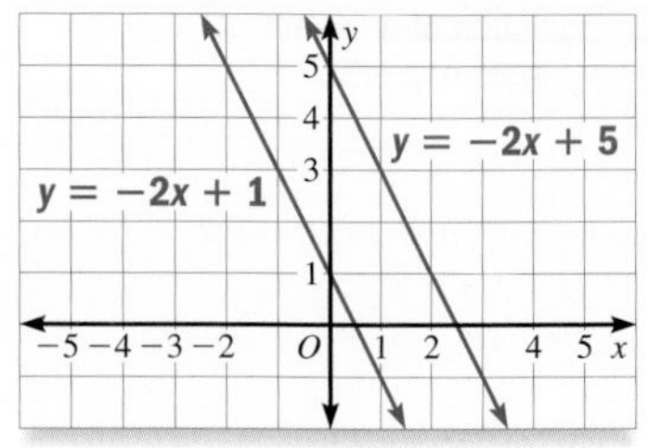

Answer Because parallel lines do not intersect, the linear system has no solution.

Example 3 *Solving a Linear System with Many Solutions*

Solve the linear system: $2x - y = -3$ **Equation 1**
$-4x + 2y = 6$ **Equation 2**

Write each equation in slope-intercept form.

Equation 1	**Equation 2**
$2x - y = -3$	$-4x + 2y = 6$
$-y = -2x - 3$	$2y = 4x + 6$
$y = 2x + 3$	$y = 2x + 3$

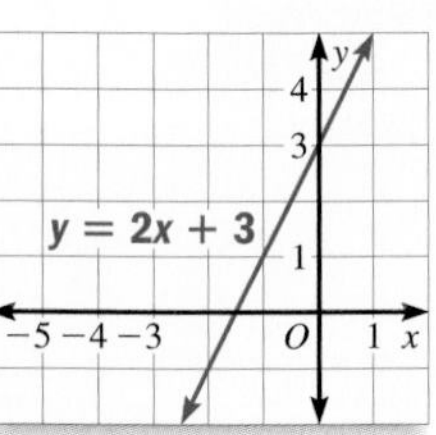

The slope-intercept forms of equations 1 and 2 are identical, so the graphs of the equations are the same line (shown at the right).

Answer Because the graphs have infinitely many points of intersection, the system has infinitely many solutions. Any point on the line $y = 2x + 3$ represents a solution.

Note Worthy

In your notebook, draw diagrams showing the possible ways in which the graphs of two equations in a linear system can intersect. For each diagram, indicate the number of solutions the system has.

Checkpoint

Solve the linear system by graphing.

1. $y = 4x + 2$
   $y = x + 2$ **(0, 2)**
2. $x - y = -3$
   $-4x + 4y = 12$
3. $-3x + y = -1$
   $y = 3x + 4$ **no solution**
4. **Critical Thinking** If the graphs of two linear equations have different slopes, how many solutions does the related system have? Give a verbal and a graphical justification for your answer.

2. infinitely many solutions—any point on the line $y = x + 3$

4. One. *Sample answer:* If two lines in a plane are not parallel (and are not the same line), they must intersect in one point. Two lines in a plane with different slopes are not parallel, so they must intersect in one point. See margin for art; in the drawing, lines *p* and *q* are parallel and will never intersect. Line *r* has a different slope from either *p* or *q*, and will clearly intersect each in a single point.

Example 4 *Writing and Solving a Linear System*

A company offers two plans for high-speed Internet service, as described on page 431.

Plan A: You pay $200 for the modem and $30 per month for service.

Plan B: The modem is free and you pay $40 per month for service.

a. After how many months are the total costs of the plans the same?

b. When is plan A a better deal? When is plan B a better deal?

Solution

a. Let y be the cost of each plan after x months. Write a linear system.

Plan A: $y = 200 + 30x$

Plan B: $y = 40x$

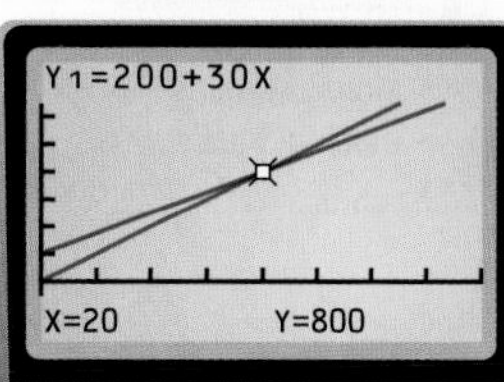

Use a graphing calculator to graph the equations. Trace along one of the graphs until the cursor is on the point of intersection. This point is (20, 800).

Answer The total costs of the plans are the same after 20 months, when each plan costs $800.

b. The graph for plan A lies below the graph for plan B when $x > 20$, so plan A costs less if you have service for more than 20 months.

The graph for plan B lies below the graph for plan A when $x < 20$, so plan B costs less if you have service for less than 20 months.

Tech *Help*

In Example 4, you can get a closer look at the point where the graphs intersect by using the calculator's *zoom* feature to zoom in on the intersection point.

8.8 Exercises

More Practice, p. 810

Guided Practice

Vocabulary Check

1. What is a solution of a system of linear equations in two variables? **an ordered pair that is a solution of each equation in the system**
2. If the graphs of the two equations in a system are parallel lines, what can you say about the solution(s) of the system? **There are no solutions.**

Skill Check **Solve the linear system by graphing.**

3. $y = 3x - 8$
   $y = 2x - 5$ **(3, 1)**
4. $x + y = 3$
   $x - y = -5$ **(−1, 4)**
5. $y = -4x + 1$
   $y = 5 - 4x$ **no solution**
6. **Shoes** One wall of a shoe store is used to display court shoes and running shoes. There is enough room on the wall for 120 styles of shoes. Based on past sales, the store manager wants to display twice as many running shoes as court shoes. Write and solve a linear system to find the number of each type of shoe to display.

6. Let x be the number of types of court shoes and y be the number of types of running shoes.
$x + y = 120$
$y = 2x$
40 types of court shoes and 80 types of running shoes

TEACHING TIP

Emphasize that a system of two linear equations cannot have two solutions because two lines that intersect either intersect at one point or they intersect entirely (that is, they are the same line).

Extra Examples

Example 4 Kate has $600 in her bank account and she deposits an additional $30 into the account each week. Jim has $440 in his bank account and he deposits an additional $50 into the account each week.

a. After how many weeks will Jim and Kate have the same amount in their accounts? **8 weeks**

b. When does Kate have more money in her account than Jim has in his account? When does Jim have more than Kate? **during the first 7 weeks; after 8 weeks**

CONCEPT CHECK

For an ordered pair to be a solution of a linear system of equations, what must be true? **The ordered pair must be a solution of both equations in the system.**

DAILY PUZZLER

Using just addition symbols and the digits 1 through 9, you can write an expression that has a value of 99 like this: 9 + 8 + 7 + 6 + 5 + 43 + 21. Find another expression with a value of 99. **9 + 8 + 7 + 65 + 4 + 3 + 2 + 1**

3 APPLY

ASSIGNMENT GUIDE

Basic Course

Day 1: pp. 434–435 Exs. 7–18, 22–24, 30–41

Average Course

Day 1: pp. 434–435 Exs. 7–12, 16–28, 32–41

Advanced Course

Day 1: pp. 434–435 Exs. 7–12, 16–18, 22–31*, 34–41

Block

pp. 434–435 Exs. 7–12, 16–28, 32–41 (with 8.7)

EXTRA PRACTICE

- Student Edition, p. 810
- Chapter 8 Resource Book, pp. 68–70
- Test and Practice Generator

TRANSPARENCY

Even-numbered answers are available on transparencies. A support transparency is available for Exercises 3–6, 13–24, and 30–33.

HOMEWORK CHECK

When you review students' homework for this lesson, go over the following exercises to check understanding of key concepts.

Basic: 7, 11, 13, 17, 22

Average: 8, 11, 16, 17, 23

Advanced: 9, 12, 17, 18, 25

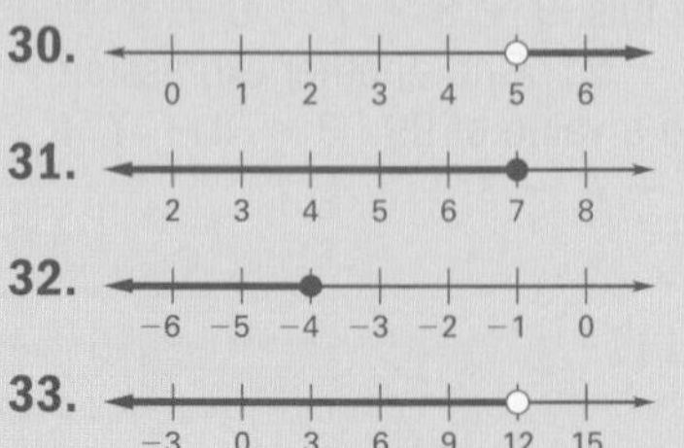

Practice and Problem Solving

Homework *Help*

Example	Exercises
1	7–21
2	13–21
3	13–21
4	22, 23, 25

Online Resources CLASSZONE.COM

- More Examples
- eTutorial Plus

Tell whether the ordered pair is a solution of the linear system.

A **7.** $(0, -2)$; **no**
$3x - 2y = 4$
$-2x - y = -2$

8. $(4, 2)$; **yes**
$y = -5x + 22$
$y = 8x - 30$

9. $(-24, -10)$; **yes**
$x - 4y = 16$
$-2x + 6y = -12$

Use the graph to identify the solution of the related linear system.

10. **(2, 2)**

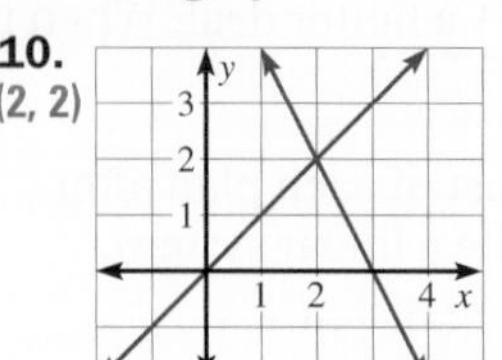

11. **(0, 3)**

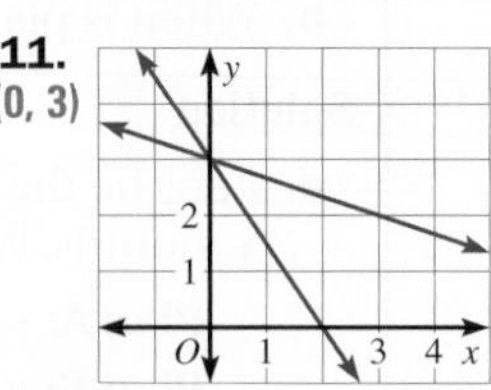

12. **(−2, −1)**

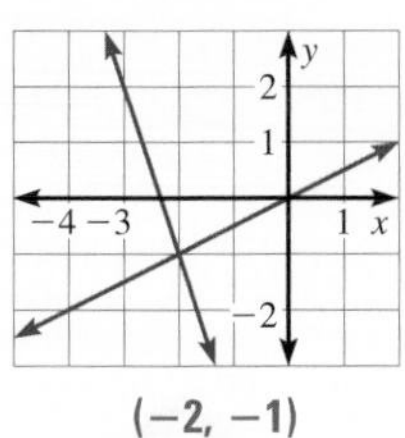

Solve the linear system by graphing.

13. $y = -3x + 2$ **(1, −1)**
$y = x - 2$

14. $y = 2x - 1$ **(2, 3)**
$y = 4x - 5$

15. $2x + 4y = 8$
$3x + 6y = 12$

15. infinitely many solutions—any point on the line $y = -\frac{1}{2}x + 2$

16. $2x + y = -8$ **(−4, 0)**
$-x + y = 4$

17. $y = 5x - 3$
$y = 5x + 2$
no solution

18. $x + y = -7$ **(−5, −2)**
$y = x + 3$

19. $x - 3y = -6$ **(−3, 1)**
$2x + 3y = -3$

20. $3x + 2y = 8$
$4y = 16 - 6x$

20. infinitely many solutions—any point on the line $y = -\frac{3}{2}x + 4$

21. $4x + y = 5$ **(0, 5)**
$3x + 5y = 25$

22. Vacation Rentals A business rents in-line skates and bicycles to tourists on vacation. A pair of skates rents for \$15 per day. A bicycle rents for \$20 per day. On a certain day, the owner of the business has 25 rentals and takes in \$450. Using the verbal model below, write and solve a system of equations to find the number of each item rented.

Let x be the number of pairs of skates and y be the number of bicycles.

Pairs of skates + Number of bicycles = Total rentals

Rent per pair of skates • Pairs of skates + Rent per bicycle • Number of bicycles = Total income

$x + y = 25$
$15x + 20y = 450$
10 pairs of skates and 15 bicycles

B **23. Advertising** You own a business that advertises in a local newspaper and over the radio. A newspaper ad costs \$600. A radio ad costs \$300. You have a monthly advertising budget of \$24,000 and want to run 50 ads each month. Write and solve a system of equations to find how many newspaper ads and radio ads you should run each month.

23. Let x be the number of newspaper ads and y be the number of radio ads.
$x + y = 50$
$600x + 300y = 24{,}000$
30 newspaper ads and 20 radio ads

24. Geometry The graphs of the three equations below form a triangle. Find the coordinates of the triangle's vertices. **(3, 2), (0, −4), (−3, 6)**

$2x - y = 4$
$2x + 3y = 12$
$10x + 3y = -12$

25. **Extended Problem Solving** You are trying to decide whether to buy an inkjet printer for \$100 or a laser printer for \$400. The operating costs are estimated to be \$.15 per page for the inkjet printer and \$.03 per page for the laser printer.

a. Write a system of equations describing the total cost of buying and operating each printer.

b. Use a graphing calculator to solve the system of equations. After how many pages are the total costs of the printers equal? **2500 pages**

c. Interpret When does the inkjet printer have the lower total cost? When does the laser printer have the lower total cost? **when fewer than 2500 pages are printed; when more than 2500 pages are printed**

d. Apply You plan to own the printer you buy for 3 years. Which printer offers the lower total cost if you print an average of 2 pages per day? if you print an average of 4 pages per day? Explain.

Visual Thinking In Exercises 26–28, find values of *m* and *b* for which the system below has the given number of solutions. Justify your answers. **26–28. See margin.**

$$y = 3x - 2$$
$$y = mx + b$$

C **26.** Exactly one **27.** None **28.** Infinitely many

29. Challenge You are designing a reflecting pool for a park. The design specifications say that the area of the pool should be 450 square feet. You want the pool to be rectangular and have a length that is twice the width. Let l be the pool's length, and let w be its width.

a. Write a system of two equations for this situation. Each equation should be solved for l. **See margin.**

b. Enter the equations from part (a) into a graphing calculator. Use the *table* feature to make a table of solutions for each equation. What ordered pair (w, l) has positive coordinates and satisfies both equations? What should the dimensions of the reflecting pool be? **(15, 30); 15 ft by 30 ft**

Mixed Review

Solve the inequality. Graph your solution. *(Lessons 3.4, 3.5)* **30–33. See margin for art.**

30. $x + 4 > 9$ **$x > 5$** **31.** $y - 5 \le 2$ **$y \le 7$** **32.** $-3t \ge 12$ **$t \le -4$** **33.** $\frac{n}{2} < 6$ **$n < 12$**

Write the number in scientific notation. *(Lesson 4.7)*

34. 1200 **1.2×10^3** **35.** 309,000 **3.09×10^5** **36.** 0.0005 **5×10^{-4}** **37.** 0.00000748 **7.48×10^{-6}**

Write a linear function that satisfies the given conditions. *(Lesson 8.7)*

38. $f(0) = 8, f(3) = 10$ **$f(x) = \frac{2}{3}x + 8$** **39.** $h(-4) = -7, h(0) = -27$ **$h(x) = -5x - 27$**

Standardized Test Practice

40. Multiple Choice Which ordered pair is the solution of the linear system $y = 2x + 16$ and $y = -x + 1$? **C**

A. (0, 16) **B.** (2, −1) **C.** (−5, 6) **D.** (−8, 9)

41. Multiple Choice Which ordered pair is *not* a solution of the linear system $x - 3y = -12$ and $-3x + 9y = 36$? **F**

F. (−3, 2) **G.** (0, 4) **H.** (3, 5) **I.** (6, 6)

25a. Let x be the number of pages and y be the total cost. inkjet: $y = 0.15x + 100$ laser: $y = 0.03x + 400$

Tech *Help*

In Exercise 25, you may need to adjust the calculator's viewing window to see the intersection point for the graph of the system of equations.

25d. The inkjet printer; the laser printer. *Sample answer:* For 3 years, 2 pages per day is $2 \cdot 365 \cdot 3 = 2190$ pages, which is less than 2500, and 4 pages per day is $4 \cdot 365 \cdot 3 = 4380$ pages, which is more than 2500.

26. *Sample answer:* $m = 4$, $b = 0$; for there to be one solution, the lines should have different slopes.

27. *Sample answer:* $m = 3$, $b = 5$; for there to be no solution, the lines should be parallel, which means that they must have the same slope but not be the same line.

28. $m = 3$, $b = -2$. *Sample answer:* For there to be infinitely many solutions, the lines must be the same.

29a. $l = \frac{450}{w}$
$l = 2w$

4 ASSESS

Assessment Resources

For more assessment resources, see:
- Assessment Book
- Test and Practice Generator

Mini-Quiz

1. Tell whether (0, 9) is a solution of the linear system.
$y = -5x + 9$
$6x - y = 11$ **no**

2. Solve the system by graphing.
$y = -x + 1$
$y = \frac{1}{2}x + 1$ **(0, 1)**

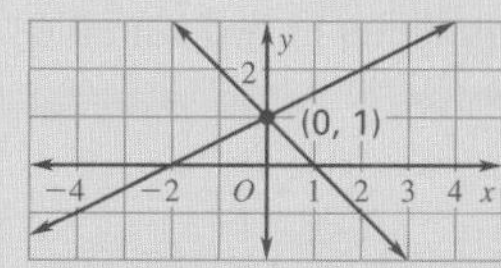

3. Challenge A carpet has a perimeter of 120 meters. The length l is twice the width w.

a. Write a system of two equations for this situation. Each equation should be solved for l. **$l = 2w, l = -w + 60$**

b. Solve the system to find the dimensions of the carpet. **width: 20 m, length: 40 m**

5 FOLLOW-UP

Diagnosis/Remediation

- Study Guide in Chapter 8 Resource Book, pp. 71–72
- eTutorial Plus Online
- Extra Practice, p. 810
- Lesson Practice in Chapter 8 Resource Book, pp. 68–70

English Learner Support

- Spanish Study Guide
- Multi-Language Visual Glossary
- Chapter Audio Summaries CDs

Challenge

- Challenge Practice in Chapter 8 Resource Book, p. 73
- Teacher's Edition, p. 382F

1 PLAN

Skill Check

Identify the slope and y-intercept of the equation.

1. $y = 5x - 2$ **slope: 5, y-intercept: −2**
2. $y = 5 - 8x$ **slope: −8, y-intercept: 5**
3. $4y = 5x - 4$ **slope: $\frac{5}{4}$, y-intercept: −1**

Lesson Objective

Graph inequalities in two variables.

Pacing

Suggested Number of Days
Basic Course: 2 days
Average Course: 2 days
Advanced Course: 2 days
Block: 1 block

Teaching Resources

For a complete list of Teaching Resources, see page 382B.

Transparency

Warm-Up Exercises for this lesson are available on a transparency. A support transparency is available for Examples 2–4 and Checkpoint Exercises 1–4.

2 TEACH

Motivating the Lesson

Present students with this problem: *You have \$1. Gumballs cost 5¢ each and chocolate mints cost 25¢ each. What combination of the two items could you afford to buy?* Encourage students to list all of the possible combinations.

LESSON **8.9**

Graphs *of* Linear Inequalities

BEFORE
You solved inequalities in one variable.

Now
You'll graph inequalities in two variables.

WHY?
So you can find how many kites to make from paper, as in Ex. 34.

Vocabulary
linear inequality in two variables, p. 436
solution of a linear inequality in two variables, p. 436
graph of a linear inequality in two variables, p. 436
half-plane, p. 436

Pottery How many bowls and vases can you make from a fixed amount of clay? In Example 4, you'll see how a *linear inequality* can be used to answer this question.

A **linear inequality** in two variables, such as $2x - 3y < 6$, is the result of replacing the equal sign in a linear equation with $<$, $\leq$, $>$, or $\geq$.

An ordered pair (x, y) is a **solution of a linear inequality** if substituting the values of x and y into the inequality produces a true statement.

Example 1 Checking Solutions of a Linear Inequality

Tell whether the ordered pair is a solution of $2x - 3y < 6$.

a. (0, 1) **b.** (4, −2)

Solution

a. Substitute 0 for x and 1 for y.

$$2x - 3y < 6$$
$$2(\mathbf{0}) - 3(\mathbf{1}) \overset{?}{<} 6$$
$$-3 < 6 \checkmark$$

(0, 1) is a solution.

b. Substitute 4 for x and −2 for y.

$$2x - 3y < 6$$
$$2(\mathbf{4}) - 3(\mathbf{-2}) \overset{?}{<} 6$$
$$14 \nless 6$$

(4, −2) is not a solution.

Graphs The **graph of a linear inequality** in two variables is the set of points in a coordinate plane that represent all the inequality's solutions.

Reading *Algebra*

In the graph shown, a dashed boundary line is used to indicate that points on the line are *not* solutions of $2x - 3y < 6$. A solid boundary line would indicate that points on the line *are* solutions.

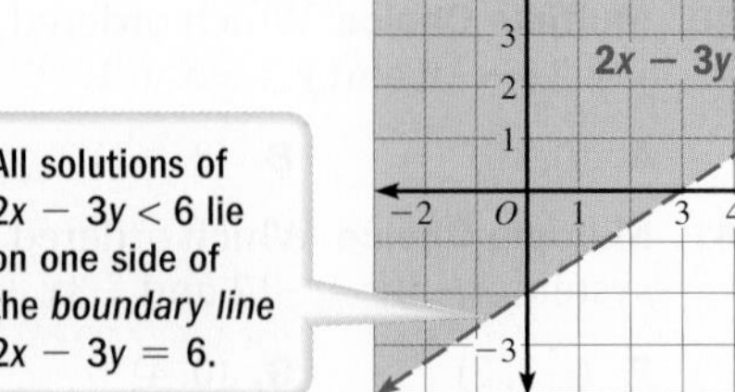

The boundary line divides the plane into two **half-planes**. The shaded half-plane is the graph of $2x - 3y < 6$.

NCTM CURRICULUM STANDARDS
Standard 2: Analyze situations using algebraic symbols; Use models to understand relationships
Standard 6: Solve problems in math and other contexts

Graphing Linear Inequalities

1. Find the equation of the boundary line by replacing the inequality symbol with =. Graph this equation. Use a dashed line for < or >. Use a solid line for ≤ or ≥.
2. Test a point in one of the half-planes to determine whether it is a solution of the inequality.
3. If the test point is a solution, shade the half-plane that contains the point. If not, shade the other half-plane.

Example 2 *Graphing a Linear Inequality*

Graph $y \geq 2x + 4$.

1) Draw the boundary line $y = 2x + 4$. The inequality symbol is ≥, so use a solid line.

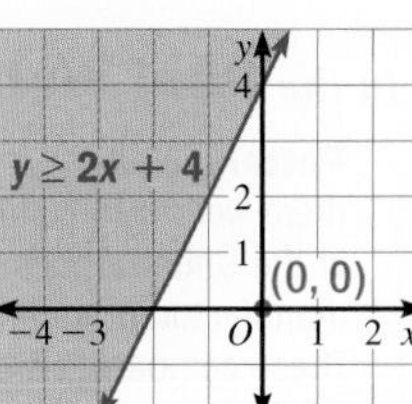

2) Test the point (0, 0) in the inequality.

$$y \geq 2x + 4$$
$$0 \overset{?}{\geq} 2(0) + 4$$
$$0 \ngeq 4$$

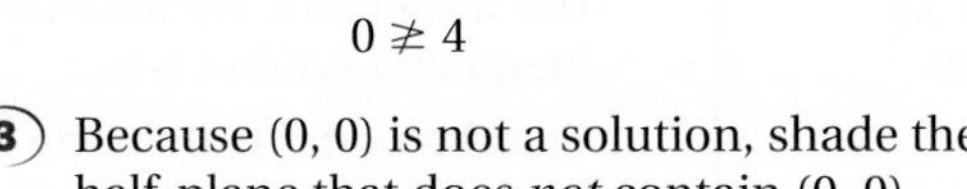

3) Because (0, 0) is not a solution, shade the half-plane that does *not* contain (0, 0).

Study Strategy

You can use any point not on the boundary line as a test point. Using (0, 0) is convenient because it is easy to evaluate expressions when 0 is substituted for each variable.

Example 3 *Graphing Inequalities with One Variable*

Graph $x < 3$ and $y \geq -2$ in a coordinate plane.

a. Graph $x = 3$ using a dashed line. Use (0, 0) as a test point.

$$x < 3$$
$$0 < 3 \checkmark$$

Shade the half-plane that contains (0, 0).

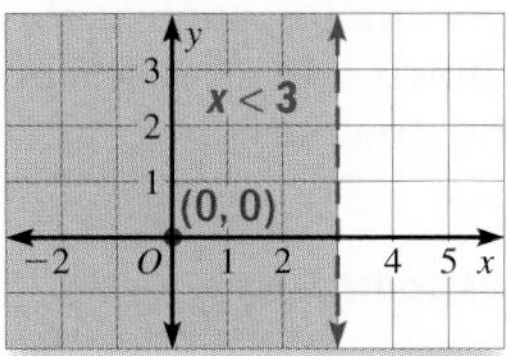

b. Graph $y = -2$ using a solid line. Use (0, 0) as a test point.

$$y \geq -2$$
$$0 \geq -2 \checkmark$$

Shade the half-plane that contains (0, 0).

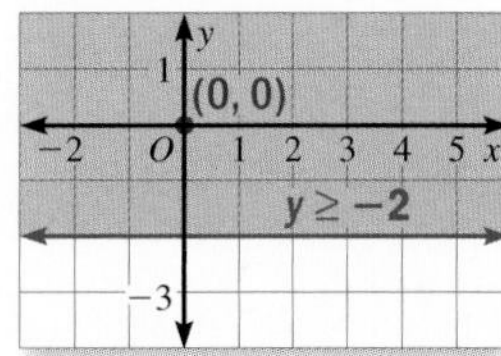

Checkpoint

Graph the inequality in a coordinate plane. 1–3. See margin.

1. $x + 2y > 6$
2. $x \geq -1$
3. $y < 3$

TIPS *for* NEW TEACHERS

Be sure students understand that the shaded region in a graph in this lesson means all the points in the region are solutions, not just the ordered pairs with integer coordinates. See Tips for New Teachers in the *Chapter 8 Resource Book.*

Extra Examples

Example 1 Tell whether the ordered pair is a solution of $3x + 4y > 10$.

a. (−3, 4) **no**

b. (5, −1) **yes**

Example 2 Graph $y \leq x - 1$.

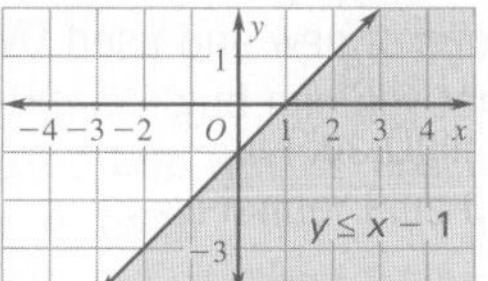

Example 3

a. Graph $x \geq -2$.

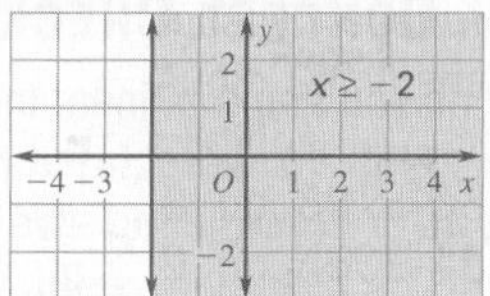

b. Graph $y < -1$.

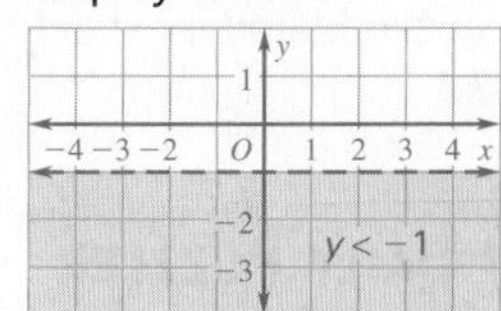

TEACHING TIP

Ask students to name numbers less than 8. Lead students to recognize that there are an infinite number of correct possible answers. Stress that linear inequalities are no different in that each has an infinite number of correct possible answers, indicated by shading part of the coordinate plane.

1–3. See Additional Answers beginning on page AA1.

Extra Examples

Example 4 You have a $150 gift certificate to spend on DVDs at a store selling both new and used DVDs. New DVDs cost $15 each and used DVDs cost $9 each.

a. Write an inequality describing the possible numbers of new and used DVDs that you can buy. **$15x + 9y \le 150$**

b. Graph the inequality from part (a).

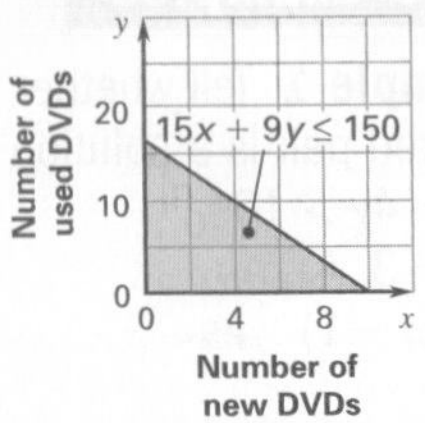

c. Give three possible combinations of new and used DVDs that you can buy. ***Sample answer:*** **5 new and 5 used, 10 new and 0 used, 4 new and 10 used**

 **CONCEPT CHECK**

How do you graph a linear inequality? **First graph the associated boundary line, after determining whether it should be dashed or solid. Then use a test point to determine which side of the boundary should be shaded.**

 **DAILY PUZZLER**

Using addition symbols and the digits 1 through 7, you can write an expression whose value is 100 in two ways. What are they? **1 + 2 + 34 + 56 + 7 and 1 + 23 + 4 + 5 + 67**

4. See Additional Answers beginning on page AA1.

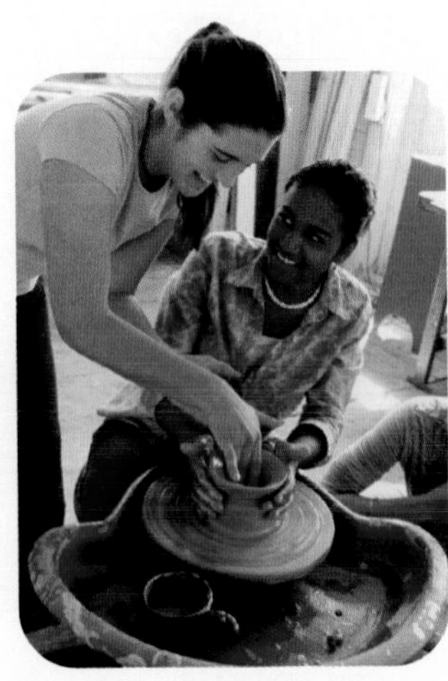

In the Real World

Pottery In the year 2000, there were 904 companies in the United States that manufactured pottery products. These companies employed 20,054 people. What was the mean number of employees per company? **about 22 employees**

Example 4 *Writing and Graphing a Linear Inequality*

You have 100 pounds of clay to use for making bowls and vases. You need 5 pounds of clay for each bowl and 2 pounds for each vase.

a. Write an inequality describing the possible numbers of bowls and vases that you can make.

b. Graph the inequality from part (a).

c. Give three possible combinations of bowls and vases that you can make.

Solution

a. Let x be the number of bowls you make. Let y be the number of vases you make. Write a verbal model. Then use the verbal model to write an inequality.

$$5x + 2y \le 100$$

b. To graph the inequality, first draw the boundary line $5x + 2y = 100$. Use a solid line because the inequality symbol is $\le$.

Test the point (0, 0) in the inequality.

$$5x + 2y \le 100$$

$$5(0) + 2(0) \overset{?}{\le} 100$$

$$0 \le 100 \checkmark$$

Because (0, 0) is a solution, all solutions of $5x + 2y \le 100$ lie in the half-plane containing (0, 0). Shade the portion of this half-plane that lies in the first quadrant, as the numbers of bowls and vases made must be nonnegative.

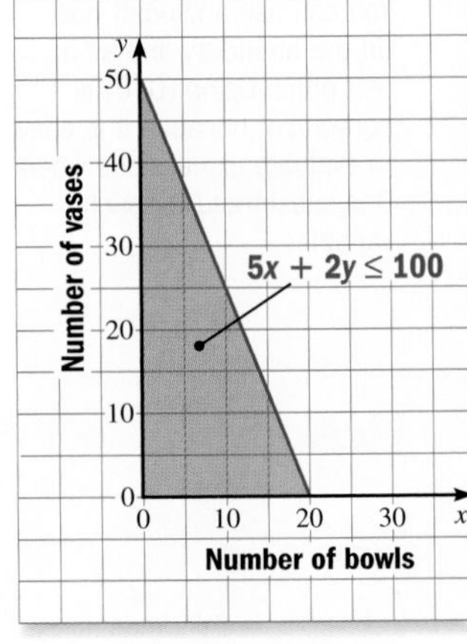

c. Choose three points on the graph with whole-number coordinates, such as (5, 20), (10, 10), and (20, 0). You can make 5 bowls and 20 vases, or 10 bowls and 10 vases, or 20 bowls and no vases.

Checkpoint

4. It is recommended that you get at least 60 milligrams of vitamin C each day. One fluid ounce of orange juice contains about 15 milligrams of vitamin C, and one fluid ounce of grapefruit juice contains about 12 milligrams. Write and graph an inequality describing the possible amounts of orange juice and grapefruit juice you can drink to meet your daily requirement for vitamin C.

4. Let x be the amount of orange juice and y be the amount of grapefruit juice (both in fluid ounces). Then $15x + 12y \ge 60$; see margin for art.

8.9 Exercises

More Practice, p. 810

Guided Practice

Vocabulary Check

1. Copy and complete: The graph of a linear inequality in two variables is called a(n) ? . **half-plane**

2. When graphing a linear inequality in two variables, explain how to determine which side of the boundary line to shade. **See margin.**

Skill Check **Tell whether the ordered pair is a solution of $4x + y > -1$.**

3. $(-2, 5)$ **no** **4.** $(0, 0)$ **yes** **5.** $(4, -4)$ **yes** **6.** $(-1, 3)$ **no**

Graph the inequality in a coordinate plane. **7–10. See margin.**

7. $y < 3x + 1$ **8.** $4x - 5y \leq 20$ **9.** $x > -2$ **10.** $y \geq 1$

Guided Problem Solving

11. Movies You have a gift certificate for $40 to use at a movie theater. Matinees cost $5 and evening shows cost $8. What are some possible combinations of matinees and evening shows that you can see?

(1) Write an inequality for this situation. **Let x be the number of matinee tickets and y be the number of evening tickets. Then $5x + 8y \leq 40$.**

(2) Graph the inequality from Step 1. **See margin.**

(3) Give three possible combinations of matinees and evening shows that you can see. ***Sample answer:*** **0 matinees and 5 evening shows, 3 matinees and 3 evening shows, 6 matinees and 1 evening show**

2. *Sample answer:* Test a point in one of the half-planes (not on the boundary) to see whether it is a solution. If it is, shade the half-plane containing the point. If it is not, shade the half-plane not containing the point.

Practice and Problem Solving

Homework *Help*

Example	Exercises
1	16-19
2	12, 13, 20-27
3	28-31
4	32-34

Online Resources
CLASSZONE.COM
- More Examples
- eTutorial Plus

Error Analysis **Describe and correct the error in the graph of the given inequality.**

A **12.** $y > x - 1$ **The inequality is >, so the boundary line should be dashed, not solid.**

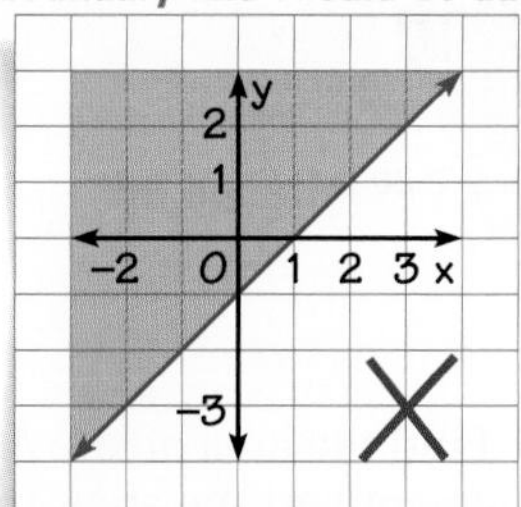

13. $y \leq 2x + 2$ **The wrong half-plane is shaded. The half-plane to the right and below the boundary should be shaded.**

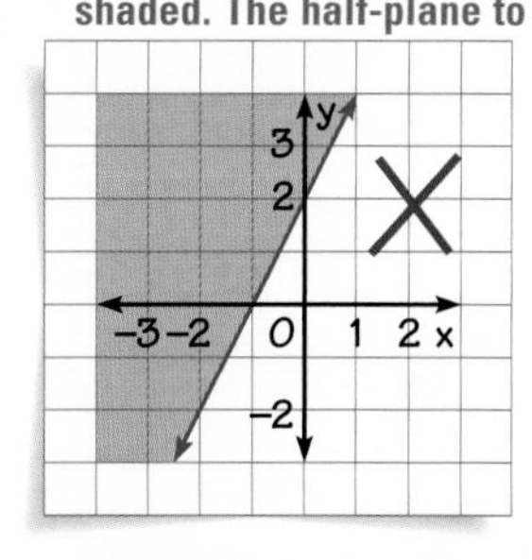

14. Critical Thinking When graphing the inequality $y \geq 2x$, can you use (0, 0) as a test point to determine which side of the boundary line to shade? Explain.

14. No. *Sample answer:* The point (0, 0) is on the line $y = 2x$. Whether or not a point on the boundary line is a solution of an inequality has no bearing on which half-plane is shaded.

15. Logical Reasoning Find an ordered pair that is a solution of $y \leq x + 5$ but is *not* a solution of $y < x + 5$.
Sample answer: **$(-2, 3)$, or any other point on the line $y = x + 5$**

ASSIGNMENT GUIDE

Basic Course
Day 1: pp. 439-441 Exs. 12-14, 20-27, 38-43
Day 2: pp. 439-441 Exs. 16-19, 28-33, 44-48

Average Course
Day 1: pp. 439-441 Exs. 12-15, 24-27, 38-43
Day 2: pp. 439-441 Exs. 16-23, 28-34, 44-48

Advanced Course
Day 1: pp. 439-441 Exs. 12-15, 24-27, 40-46
Day 2: pp. 439-441 Exs. 18-23, 30-37*, 47, 48

Block
pp. 439-441 Exs. 12-34, 38-48

EXTRA PRACTICE

- Student Edition, p. 810
- Chapter 8 Resource Book, pp. 77-79
- Test and Practice Generator

TRANSPARENCY

Even-numbered answers are available on transparencies. A support transparency is available for Exercises 7-11, 20-34, 36, and 44-46.

HOMEWORK CHECK

When you review students' homework for this lesson, go over the following exercises to check understanding of key concepts.
Basic: 12, 16, 18, 28, 32
Average: 13, 18, 29, 31, 33
Advanced: 13, 19, 30, 31, 34

7-10, 11 (Step 2). See Additional Answers beginning on page AA1.

TEACHING TIP

In Exercise 18, students may need help deciding whether or not (8, −9) is a solution. Encourage students to sketch the inequality $x \le 6$ and then ask them about the characteristics of points that are solutions.

COMMON ERROR

In Exercises 20–31, watch for students who shade on the wrong side of the boundary line. Remind them to check their work by substituting the coordinates of an ordered pair for a point located in the shaded area into the original inequality and seeing if a true statement results.

20–31. See Additional Answers beginning on page AA1.

32b.

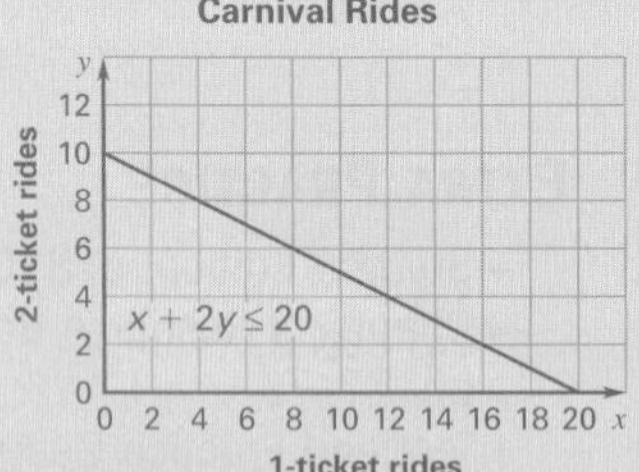

33a.

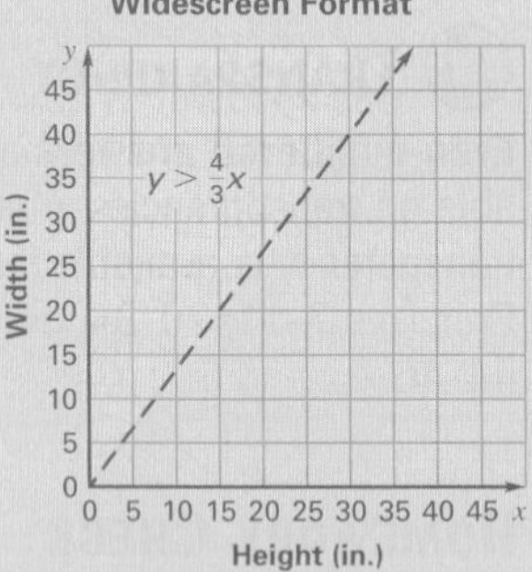

34b.

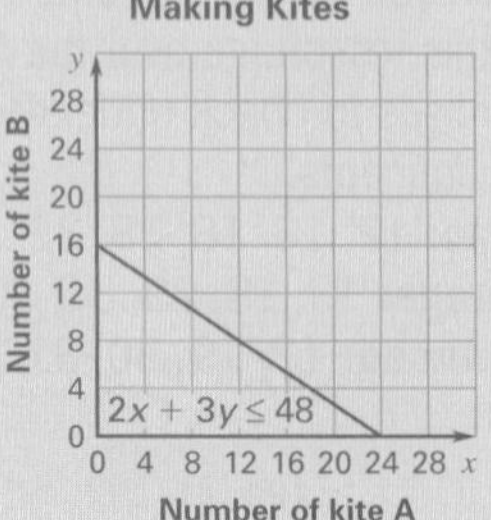

36. See Additional Answers beginning on page AA1.

Tell whether the ordered pair is a solution of the inequality.

16. $y \ge -7x + 9$; (1, 4) **yes**

17. $y < 10x - 1$; (−1, −11) **no**

18. $x \le 6$; (8, −9) **no**

19. $5x - 8y \ge 2$; (0, −3) **yes**

Graph the inequality in a coordinate plane. **20–31. See margin.**

20. $y < x + 4$ **21.** $y > -3x$ **22.** $y \ge \frac{2}{3}x - 5$ **23.** $y \le -2x - 3$

24. $x + y \ge -2$ **25.** $-x + 2y \le 6$ **26.** $3x - 2y > 2$ **27.** $4x + 3y < -12$

28. $y > -3$ **29.** $x \ge 1$ **30.** $x < -4$ **31.** $y \le -1$

32. Entertainment At a county fair, you buy 20 tickets that you can use for carnival rides and other attractions. Some rides require 1 ticket while others require 2 tickets.

a. Write an inequality describing the possible numbers of 1-ticket rides and 2-ticket rides that you can go on.

b. Graph the inequality from part (a). **See margin.**

c. Interpret and Apply Give three possible combinations of 1-ticket rides and 2-ticket rides that you can go on.

32a. Let x be the number of 1-ticket rides you go on and y be the number of 2-ticket rides you go on. Then $x + 2y \le 20$.

32c. *Sample answer:* four 1-ticket and eight 2-ticket rides, ten 1-ticket and five 2-ticket rides, fourteen 1-ticket and three 2-ticket rides

B **33. Video** A widescreen format for a movie or TV show is one in which the image's height x and width y satisfy the inequality $y > \frac{4}{3}x$.

a. Graph the given inequality. **See margin.**

b. *Writing* Suppose the height of a widescreen image is 18 inches. Describe the possible widths of the image. **any width greater than 24 inches**

34. Extended Problem Solving You have 48 square feet of paper to use for making kites. You want to make the two types of kites shown below. Assume that the amount of paper needed for each kite is the area of the kite.

Kite A

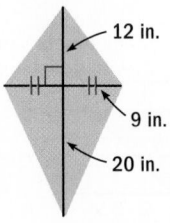

12 in.
9 in.
20 in.

Kite B

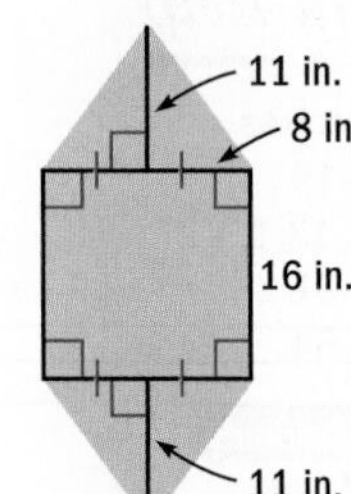

a. Calculate Find the area of kite A and the area of kite B in square inches. Then convert the areas to square feet. **kite A: 288 in.^{2}, or 2 ft^2; kite B: 432 in.^{2}, or 3 ft^2**

b. Graph Write and graph an inequality describing how many of kite A and kite B you can make. **Let x be the number of kite A and y be the number of kite B. Then $2x + 3y \le 48$; see margin for art.**

c. Analyze What property is shared by points that represent solutions where you use up all your paper? What property is shared by points that represent solutions where you have paper left over? **They lie on the boundary line; they lie in the shaded half-plane, but not on the boundary line.**

Challenge In Exercises 35–37, use the *system* of linear inequalities shown below. A *solution* of the system is an ordered pair that is a solution of each inequality.

$$y < x + 3$$
$$y \geq -2x - 3$$

C **35.** Tell whether each ordered pair is a solution of the system.

a. $(0, -4)$ no **b.** $(1, 3)$ yes **c.** $(-2, 1)$ no

36. Graph the inequalities in the system. Draw both graphs in the same coordinate plane, and use a different color for each graph. See margin.

37. *Writing* Describe the region of the plane that contains the solutions of the system.

37. *Sample answer:* It is the intersection of two half-planes, and consists of all points that are below and to the right of the line $y = x + 3$ *and* that are also on or above and to the right of the line $y = -2x - 3$.

Mixed Review

Write the product using an exponent. *(Lesson 1.2)*

38. $8 \cdot 8 \cdot 8 \cdot 8 \cdot 8$ 8^5 **39.** $(1.2)(1.2)(1.2)$ 1.2^3 **40.** $x \cdot x \cdot x \cdot x \cdot x \cdot x \cdot x$ x^7

Write the expression using only positive exponents. *(Lesson 4.6)*

41. $5x^{-2}$ $\frac{5}{x^2}$ **42.** $2a^{-3}b^8$ $\frac{2b^8}{a^3}$ **43.** $9m^{-5}n^{-4}$ $\frac{9}{m^5n^4}$

Solve the linear system by graphing. *(Lesson 8.8)*

44. $y = 2x - 3$, $y = x + 1$ $(4, 5)$ **45.** $y = -3x - 6$, $y = 2x + 4$ $(-2, 0)$ **46.** $x + y = -2$, $2x + y = 0$ $(2, -4)$

Standardized Test Practice

47. Multiple Choice Which ordered pair is *not* a solution of $y \geq -9x + 1$? D

A. $(1, -5)$ **B.** $(2, 1)$ **C.** $(-1, 10)$ **D.** $(-3, -1)$

48. Multiple Choice Which inequality has no solutions in the first quadrant of a coordinate plane? I

F. $x < 1$ **G.** $y \leq -2x + 6$ **H.** $x + y \leq 5$ **I.** $-3x - y > 6$

Brain GAME — Right to the Point

A list of ordered pairs is shown below.

(−3, −6) (4, −4) (−6, 9) (2, −3) (5, 2)

Only one of the ordered pairs is a solution of *all* of the following inequalities. Which ordered pair is it? (2, −3)

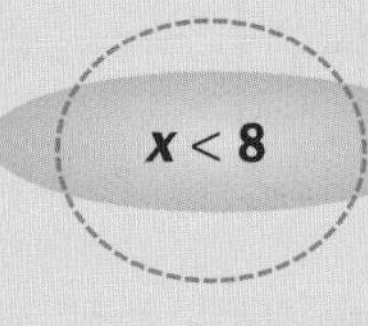
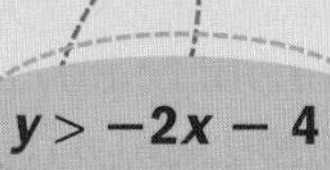
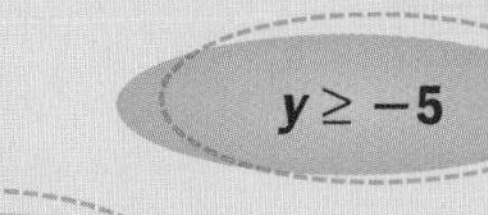

$x < 8$ $y > -2x - 4$ $y \geq -5$ $x + y < 3$ $3x - y \leq 9$

4 ASSESS

Assessment Resources

For more assessment resources, see:
- Assessment Book
- Test and Practice Generator

Mini-Quiz

Tell whether the ordered pair is a solution of the inequality.

1. $y \leq 6x - 5$; $(0, -1)$ no
2. $3x - 2y \geq 7$; $(-1, -4)$ no
3. $x > 5$; $(8, -3)$ yes
4. **Challenge** Use the system of inequalities shown below.
$y > 2x$
$y \leq -x + 2$
Draw both graphs in the same coordinate plane, and use a different color for each graph. Is the ordered pair $(-1, 3)$ a solution of the system? yes

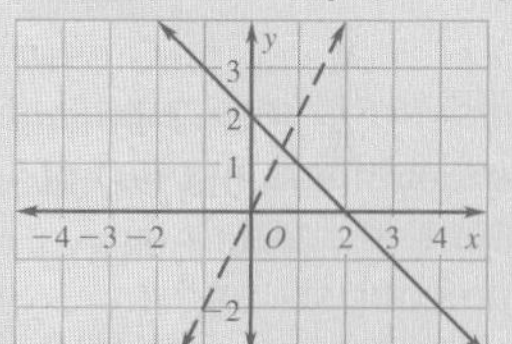

5 FOLLOW-UP

Diagnosis/Remediation

- Study Guide in Chapter 8 Resource Book, pp. 80–81
- eTutorial Plus Online
- Extra Practice, p. 810
- Lesson Practice in Chapter 8 Resource Book, pp. 77–79

English Learner Support

- Spanish Study Guide
- Multi-Language Visual Glossary
- Chapter Audio Summaries CDs

Challenge

- Challenge Practice in Chapter 8 Resource Book, p. 83
- Teacher's Edition, p. 382F

ADDITIONAL RESOURCES

The following resources are available to help review the materials in Lessons 8.6–8.9.

Chapter 8 Resource Book
- Lesson Practice
- Study Guide

Assessment Book
- Chapter 8 Quiz 2

Technology
- Test and Practice Generator
- eTutorial CD-ROM

Internet
- Classzone
- eWorkbook Plus Online
- eTutorial Plus Online

ENGLISH LEARNER SUPPORT

- Spanish Study Guide
- Multi-Language Visual Glossary
- Chapter Audio Summaries CDs

1. ***Sample answer:*** **In a relation, which pairs numbers in one set with numbers in another set, the domain consists of the inputs and the range consists of the outputs. In a relation represented by ordered pairs (x, y), the domain consists of the x-coordinates and the range consists of the y-coordinates.**

CHAPTER 8

Chapter Review

Vocabulary Review

relation, p. 385
domain, p. 385
range, p. 385
input, p. 385
output, p. 385
function, p. 386
vertical line test, p. 387
equation in two variables, p. 391
solution of an equation in two variables, p. 391
graph of an equation in two variables, p. 392
linear equation, p. 392
function form, p. 393
x-intercept, p. 398
y-intercept, p. 398
slope, p. 404
rise, p. 404
run, p. 404
slope-intercept form, p. 412
best-fitting line, p. 421
function notation, p. 426
system of linear equations, p. 431
solution of a linear system, p. 431
linear inequality in two variables, p. 436
solution of a linear inequality in two variables, p. 436
graph of a linear inequality in two variables, p. 436
half-plane, p. 436

1. What is the difference between the domain and the range of a relation? **See margin.**

2. Write a linear equation in slope-intercept form. Identify the slope and y-intercept.
Sample answer: $y = \frac{2}{3}x - 4$; slope: $\frac{2}{3}$, y-intercept: -4

3. How are the rise and run between two points on a line related to the line's slope?
Sample answer: **The slope is the ratio of the rise to the run.**

4. Write the equation $y = -5x + 2$ using function notation. $f(x) = -5x + 2$

8.1 Relations and Functions

Examples on pp. 385–387

Goal

Use graphs and mapping diagrams to represent relations.

Represent the relation (−2, −2), (−1, 3), (0, 4), (3, 0) as a graph and as a mapping diagram.

a. Graph the ordered pairs as points in a coordinate plane.

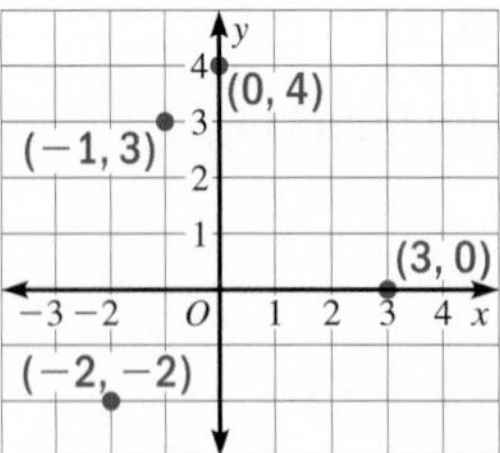

b. List the inputs and the outputs in order. Draw arrows from the inputs to their outputs.

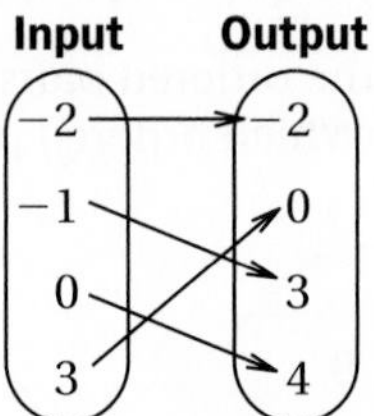

Represent the relation as a graph and as a mapping diagram. **5–6. See margin.**

5. (−5, 6), (−4, 3), (0, 0), (4, −3)

6. (7, −2), (6, 5), (2, 3), (2, −8), (3, 0)

The following resources are available to help review the materials in this chapter.

Chapter 8 Resource Book
- Chapter Review Games and Activities, p. 84
- Cumulative Practice, Chs. 1-8

English/Spanish Chapter Reviews and Tests

Chapter Audio Summaries CDs

eTutorial CD-ROM

eWorkbook Plus Online

eTutorial Plus Online

8.2 Linear Equations in Two Variables

Examples on pp. 391–393

Goal

Find solutions of linear equations in two variables.

Example **Tell whether (−4, −6) or (2, 8) is a solution of −3x + y = 6.**

a. $-3x + y = 6$ **Write original equation.**

$-3(-4) + (-6) \stackrel{?}{=} 6$ **Substitute −4 for x and −6 for y.**

$6 = 6$ ✓ **Simplify.**

Answer $(-4, -6)$ is a solution of $-3x + y = 6$.

b. $-3x + y = 6$ **Write original equation.**

$-3(2) + 8 \stackrel{?}{=} 6$ **Substitute 2 for x and 8 for y.**

$2 \neq 6$ **Simplify.**

Answer $(2, 8)$ is not a solution of $-3x + y = 6$.

✓ **Tell whether the ordered pair is a solution of the equation.**

7. $y = -8x - 2$; $(-1, 6)$ yes **8.** $14x + 2y = -22$; $(-2, -3)$ no

8.3 Using Intercepts

Examples on pp. 398–399

Goal

Find the intercepts of the graph of an equation.

Example **Find the intercepts of the graph of 9x + 3y = 27.**

To find the x-intercept, let $y = 0$ and solve for x.

$9x + 3y = 27$ **Write original equation.**

$9x + 3(0) = 27$ **Substitute 0 for y.**

$9x = 27$ **Simplify.**

$x = 3$ **Divide each side by 9.**

To find the y-intercept, let $x = 0$ and solve for y.

$9x + 3y = 27$ **Write original equation.**

$9(0) + 3y = 27$ **Substitute 0 for x.**

$3y = 27$ **Simplify.**

$y = 9$ **Divide each side by 3.**

Answer The x-intercept is 3, and the y-intercept is 9.

✓ **Find the intercepts of the equation's graph.**

9. $3x - 12y = 24$ **10.** $y = 2x - 10$ **11.** $20x + 4y = -20$

9. x-intercept: 8; y-intercept: −2

10. x-intercept: 5; y-intercept: −10

11. x-intercept: −1; y-intercept: −5

5.

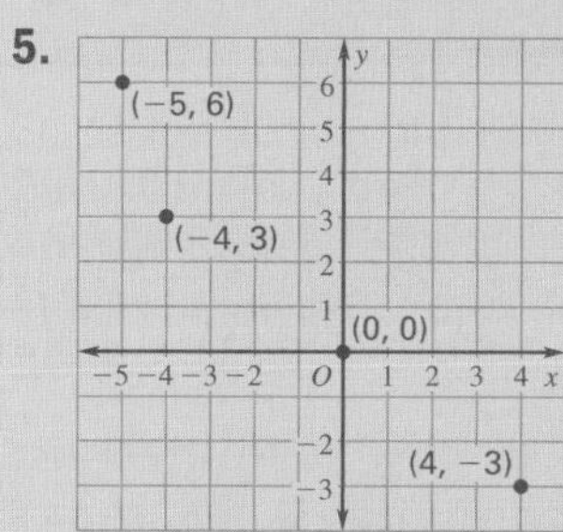

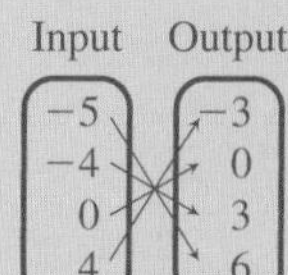

6.

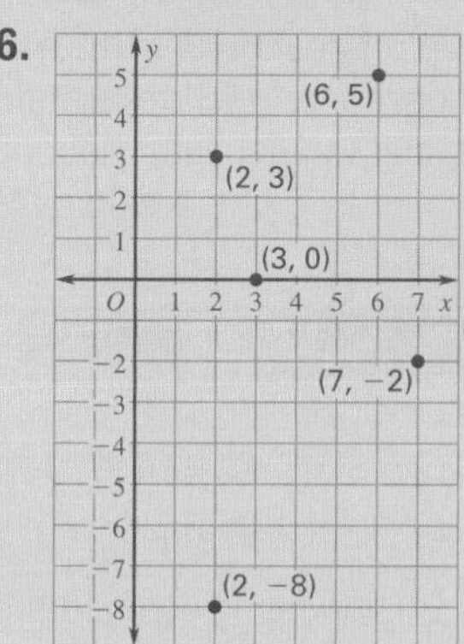

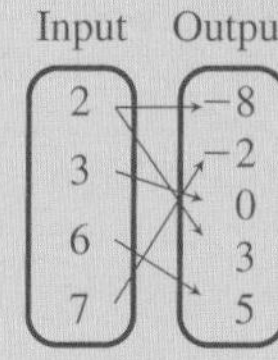

8.4 The Slope of a Line

Examples on pp. 404–406

Goal

Find the slope of a line.

Example **Find the slope of the line through the points (−3, 6) and (−1, 2).**

$$m = \frac{\text{rise}}{\text{run}} = \frac{\text{difference of } y\text{-coordinates}}{\text{difference of } x\text{-coordinates}}$$

$$= \frac{2 - 6}{-1 - (-3)} = \frac{-4}{2} = -2$$

Find the slope of the line through the given points.

12. (4, −7), (−2, −10) $\frac{1}{2}$ **13.** (6, 9), (−3, 9) 0 **14.** (3, 4), (7, −12) −4

8.5 Slope-Intercept Form

Examples on pp. 412–414

Goal

Find the slope and *y*-intercept of a line.

Example **Identify the slope and *y*-intercept of the line 24*x* + 4*y* = 80.**

$24x + 4y = 80$ **Write original equation.**

$4y = -24x + 80$ **Subtract 24*x* from each side.**

$y = -6x + 20$ **Multiply each side by $\frac{1}{4}$.**

Answer The line has a slope of −6 and a *y*-intercept of 20.

Identify the slope and *y*-intercept of the line with the given equation.

15. $y = -3x + 2$ slope: −3; *y*-intercept: 2

16. $2x + 3y = -6$ slope: $-\frac{2}{3}$; *y*-intercept: −2

17. $-36x + 9y = 18$ slope: 4; *y*-intercept: 2

8.6 Writing Linear Equations

Examples on pp. 419–421

Goal

Write an equation of a line parallel to a given line.

Example **Write an equation of the line that is parallel to the line *y* = −3*x* + 4 and passes through (0, 7).**

Because the slope of the given line is −3, the slope of the parallel line is also −3. The parallel line passes through (0, 7), so its *y*-intercept is 7.

Answer An equation of the line is $y = -3x + 7$.

Write an equation of the line that is parallel to the given line and passes through the given point.

18. $y = 3x - 8$; (0, 2) $y = 3x + 2$

19. $y = -x$; (0, −6) $y = -x - 6$

20. $y = -9x + 1$; (0, 5) $y = -9x + 5$

8.7 Function Notation

Examples on pp. 426–428

Goal

Use function notation.

Example **Let $f(x) = 4x - 5$. Find $f(x)$ when $x = -3$.**

$f(x) = 4x - 5$ **Write function.**

$f(-3) = 4(-3) - 5 = -17$ **Substitute −3 for x and simplify.**

✔ **Let $g(x) = -2x + 6$. Find the indicated value.**

21. $g(x)$ when $x = 4$ **−2**

22. x when $g(x) = 14$ **−4**

23. $g(-2)$ **10**

8.8 Systems of Linear Equations

Examples on pp. 431–433

Goal

Solve linear systems in two variables by graphing.

Example **Solve the linear system: $y = -x + 4$**
$y = 2x + 1$

1. Graph the equations.
2. Identify the apparent intersection point, (1, 3).
3. Verify that (1, 3) is the solution of the system by substituting 1 for x and 3 for y in each equation.

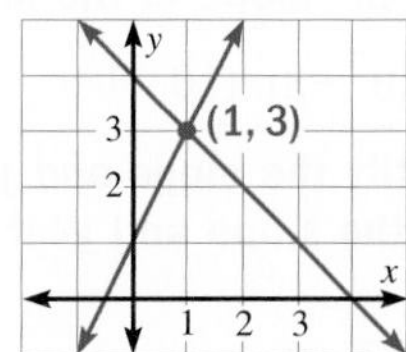

✔ **Solve the linear system by graphing.**

24. $y = -2x - 12$
$y = x - 3$
(−3, −6)

25. $y = -2x + 5$
$y = 4x - 1$
(1, 3)

26. $2x + y = 1$
$4x - 2y = 22$
(3, −5)

8.9 Graphs of Linear Inequalities

Examples on pp. 436–438

Goal

Graph linear inequalities in two variables.

Example **Graph $y > x - 3$.**

1. Graph the boundary line $y = x - 3$. Use a dashed line.
2. Use (0, 0) as a test point.

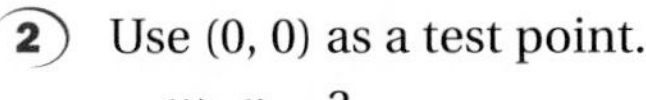

$y > x - 3$

$0 > 0 - 3 = -3$ ✔

3. Shade the half-plane that contains (0, 0).

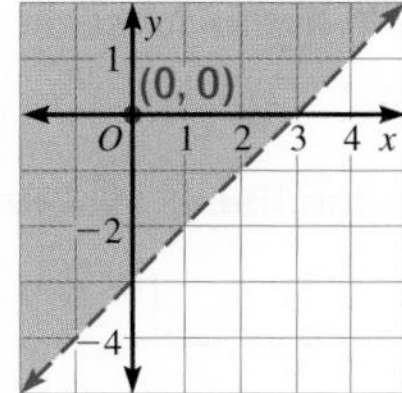

✔ **Graph the inequality in a coordinate plane.** **27–29. See margin.**

27. $y \le 2x + 3$

28. $y \ge -4$

29. $3x + y > -6$

27.

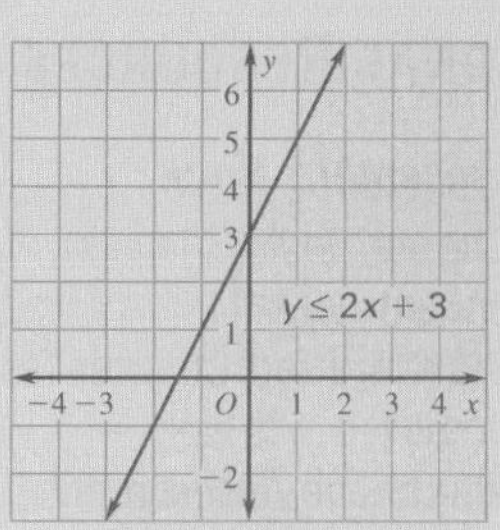

$y \le 2x + 3$

28.

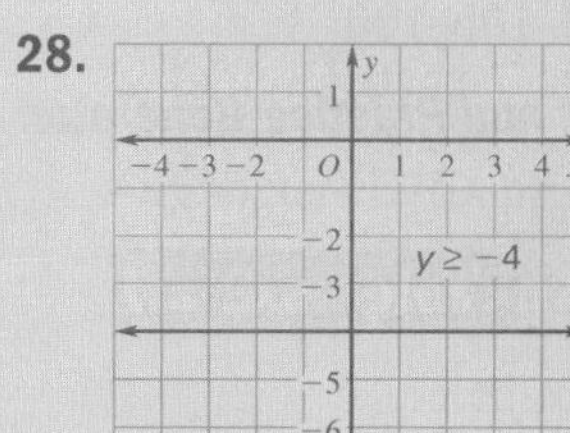

29.

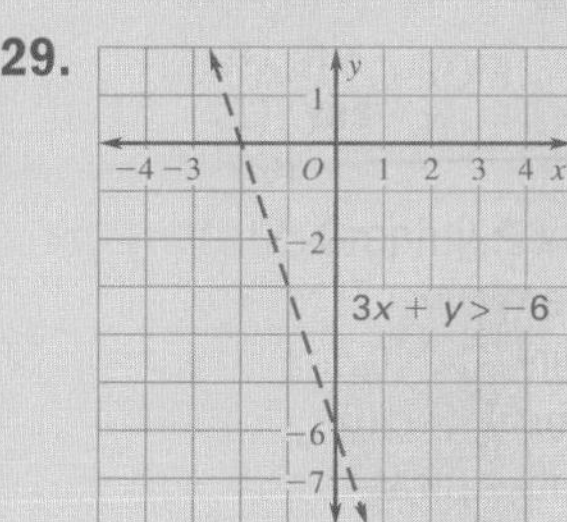

Additional Resources

Assessment Book

- Chapter Test (3 levels), pp. 98–103
- Standardized Chapter Test, p. 104
- Alternative Assessment, pp. 105–106

Test and Practice Generator

1–2. See Additional Answers beginning on page AA1.

5.

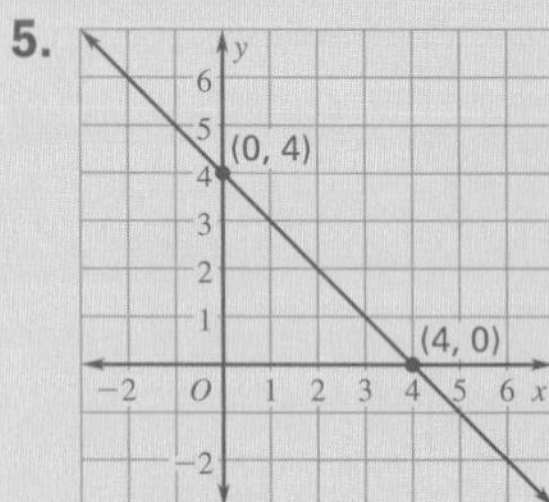

6.

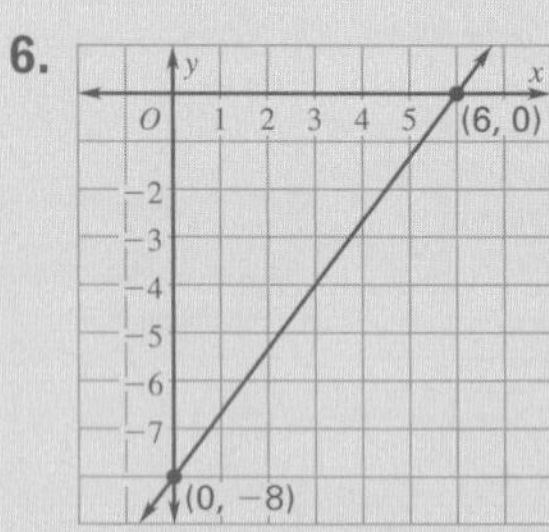

7.

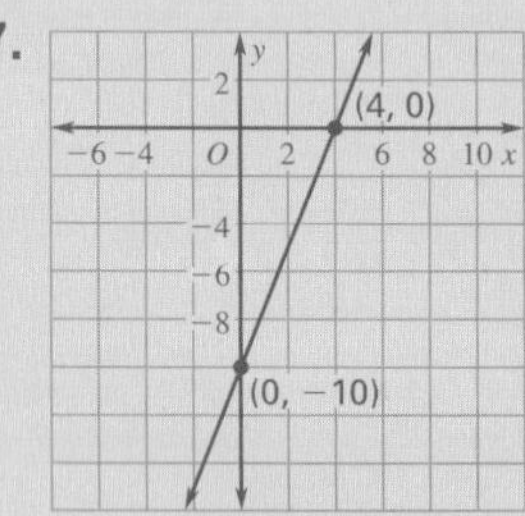

8.

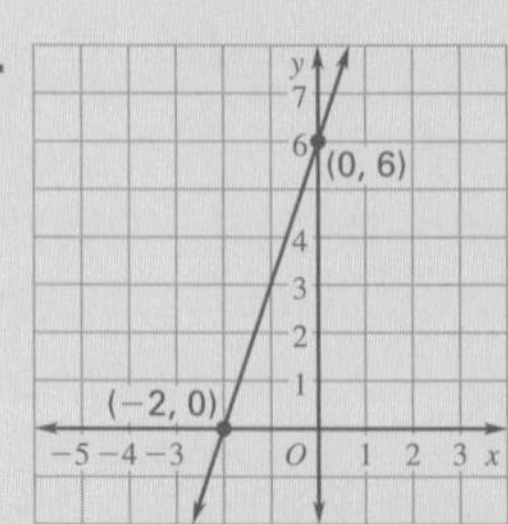

13–16, 17a, 24–26. See Additional Answers beginning on page AA1.

CHAPTER 8

Chapter Test

Represent the relation as a graph and as a mapping diagram. Then tell whether the relation is a function. Explain your reasoning. 1–2. See margin.

1. $(0, -2), (0, -1), (0, 0), (0, 1), (0, 2)$

2. $(3, 5), (6, 7)\ (9, 9), (8, 1)$

Tell whether each ordered pair is a solution of the equation.

3. $y = 7 - 2x$; $(5, 1), (6, -5), (2, 3)$ no, yes, yes

4. $y = -3x - 4$; $(-1, -1), (0, -4), (10, 34)$ yes, yes, no

Find the intercepts of the equation's graph. Then graph the equation. 5–8. See margin for art.

5. $x + y = 4$ x-intercept: 4; y-intercept: 4

6. $4x - 3y = 24$ x-intercept: 6; y-intercept: −8

7. $y = \frac{5}{2}x - 10$ x-intercept: 4; y-intercept: −10

8. $y = 3x + 6$ x-intercept: −2; y-intercept: 6

Find the slope of the line through the given points.

9. $(8, -3), (10, 7)$ 5

10. $(4, 2), (0, 3)$ $-\frac{1}{4}$

11. $(-2, 0), (-2, 5)$ undefined

12. $(4, 7), (10, 7)$ 0

Identify the slope and *y*-intercept of the line with the given equation. Use the slope and *y*-intercept to graph the equation. 13–16. See margin for art.

13. $y = \frac{4}{3}x - 7$ slope: $\frac{4}{3}$; y-intercept: −7

14. $y = 5x + 1$ slope: 5; y-intercept: 1

15. $-6x + y = -2$ slope: 6; y-intercept: −2

16. $6x - 5y = 10$ slope: $\frac{6}{5}$; y-intercept: −2

17. Televisions The table shows the number of televisions sold each month at a retail store.

Month, *x*	Televisions, *y*
1	360
2	375
3	380
4	389
5	402

a. Make a scatter plot of the data pairs. Draw the line that appears to best fit the data points. See margin for art; best-fitting lines may vary.

b. Write an equation of your line in slope-intercept form. *Sample answer:* Using (0, 352) and (5, 401): $y = 9.8x + 352$

c. Predict the number of televisions sold at the store during the 7th month. about 421 televisions

Write a linear function that satisfies the given conditions.

18. $f(0) = 3, f(4) = 9$ $f(x) = \frac{3}{2}x + 3$

19. $g(0) = -6, g(15) = -9$ $g(x) = -\frac{1}{5}x - 6$

20. $h(-4) = -5, h(0) = 10$ $h(x) = \frac{15}{4}x + 10$

Solve the linear system by graphing.

21. $x + 5y = -10$, $x + 5y = 5$ no solution

22. $3x - y = -7$, $-3x + y = 7$ infinitely many solutions—any point on the line $y = 3x + 7$

23. $2x - y = 5$, $x + 2y = -10$ (0, −5)

Graph the inequality in a coordinate plane. 24–26. See margin.

24. $x < 7$

25. $y \leq 3x - 5$

26. $x + 2y > 6$

Chapter Standardized Test

Test-Taking Strategy **You should use your answer sheet only for writing answers, but you can use your test booklet to write notes or draw sketches.**

1. What is the domain of the relation (8, 2), (6, 4), (4, 2), (2, 4)? **B**

A. 2, 4 **B.** 2, 4, 6, 8
C. 6, 8 **D.** 2, 4, 8

2. Which equation is *not* a function? **H**

F. $x + y = 5$ **G.** $2x - y = 3$
H. $x = 4$ **I.** $y = -1$

3. What is the x-intercept of the graph of $y = \frac{1}{4}x - 6$? **D**

A. -6 **B.** $\frac{1}{4}$ **C.** 6 **D.** 24

4. What is the slope of the line through the points (2, 2) and (4, 6)? **I**

F. $\frac{1}{2}$ **G.** $\frac{3}{4}$ **H.** $\frac{4}{3}$ **I.** 2

5. What is the y-intercept of the graph of $-x + 4y = -24$? **A**

A. -6 **B.** 4 **C.** 6 **D.** 24

6. What is the slope of the line with equation $-x + 4y = -24$? **G**

F. -6 **G.** $\frac{1}{4}$ **H.** 6 **I.** 24

7. What is the slope of a line perpendicular to the line with equation $y = 4x - 5$? **B**

A. -4 **B.** $-\frac{1}{4}$ **C.** $\frac{1}{5}$ **D.** 5

8. Given that $f(x) = -2x + 1$, what is $f(5)$? **G**

F. -11 **G.** -9 **H.** -2 **I.** 2

9. How many solutions does the system of equations $4x + 2y = 6$ and $y = -2x + 6$ have? **A**

A. 0 **B.** 1
C. 2 **D.** Infinitely many

10. What is the solution of the system of equations $3x + y = -11$ and $y = 2x + 9$? **I**

F. $(1, -4)$ **G.** $(-1, 4)$
H. $(4, -1)$ **I.** $(-4, 1)$

11. The graph of which inequality is shown? **C**

A. $y < \frac{3}{2}x - 1$
B. $2x + \frac{1}{3}y \geq -2$
C. $3x + 2y > -2$
D. $3x + 2y < -2$

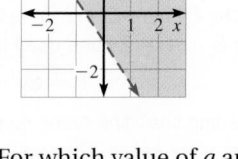

12. **Short Response** For which value of a are the lines $y = ax + 6$ and $x + 2y = 4$ parallel? For which value of a are the lines $y = ax + 6$ and $x + 2y = 4$ perpendicular? Explain. **See margin.**

13. **Extended Response** You have a \$100 gift card to a store that rents movies and video games. The rental fee for a movie is \$4, and the rental fee for a video game is \$5. **13a–c. See margin.**

a. Write an equation describing the possible numbers of movies and video games you can rent.

b. Use intercepts to graph the equation from part (a).

c. Give three possible combinations of movies and video games you can rent.

Additional Resources

Assessment Book
- Standardized Chapter Test, p. 104

Test and Practice Generator

12. $-\frac{1}{2}$**; 2.** ***Sample answer:*** **Since** $x + 2y = 4$ **in slope-intercept form is** $y = -\frac{1}{2}x + 2$**, the slope is** $-\frac{1}{2}$**. Any line parallel to this line must also have slope** $-\frac{1}{2}$**. The slope of any line perpendicular to this line must be the negative reciprocal of** $-\frac{1}{2}$**, which is 2.**

13a. Let x be the number of movie rentals and y be the number of video game rentals. Then $4x + 5y = 100$**.**

13b.

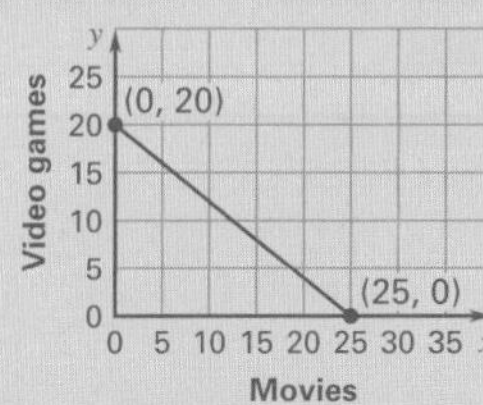

13c. ***Sample answer:*** **25 movies and 0 video games, 15 movies and 8 video games, 5 movies and 16 video games**

1 PLAN

Background Focus

While solving word problems, students may come across problems that have more than one correct solution, or problems that have no solution. Students should become familiar with these types of problems so they do not assume they made an error when they find no solution or multiple solutions.

2 TEACH

Guiding Students' Work

Have students draw diagrams modeling combinations of packages of hot dogs and packages of buns for the given situation. Have students relate their models to the ordered pairs labeled on the graph in Step 2.

Extra Examples

Example While standing at his bus stop, David notices that at 6:20 A.M. a bus leaves northbound from his side of the street at the same time that another bus leaves southbound from the bus stop across the street. He knows that a northbound bus leaves every 7 minutes and a southbound bus leaves every 12 minutes. In the next 24 hours, how often and how many times will two buses leave from these bus stops simultaneously? Assume the buses run 24 hours every day. **every 84 minutes; 17 times**

Unit 3 *Focus On* Problem Solving

Solving *the* Problem

Problems with No Solution or Many Solutions

Not all problems have a single solution. Instead, a problem may have no solution or many solutions.

Problem At your class picnic, you volunteer to grill hot dogs. The hot dogs come in packages of 8, and the hot dog buns come in packages of 6. After everyone is finished eating, you have an open package of hot dogs that contains 2 hot dogs and an open package of hot dog buns that contains 4 buns. How many hot dogs were eaten?

1 Write an equation.

Let x be the number of complete packages of hot dogs used. The total number d of hot dogs eaten is the sum of the 8x hot dogs in the complete packages used and the $8 - 2 = 6$ hot dogs used in the last package.

$$d = 8x + 6$$

Let y be the number of complete packages of buns used. The total number b of buns eaten is the sum of the 6y buns in the complete packages used and the $6 - 4 = 2$ buns used in the last package.

$$b = 6y + 2$$

Assume that the same number of buns and hot dogs were eaten. Then you can write an equation giving y as a function of x.

$$b = d$$
$$6y + 2 = 8x + 6$$
$$6y = 8x + 4$$
$$y = \frac{8}{6}x + \frac{4}{6}$$
$$y = \frac{4}{3}x + \frac{2}{3}$$

The possible numbers of complete hot dog and bun packages used are given by the solutions (x, y) of $y = \frac{4}{3}x + \frac{2}{3}$, where x and y are whole numbers.

2 Make a graph.

Graph $y = \frac{4}{3}x + \frac{2}{3}$. Label the points on the graph that have whole-number coordinates.

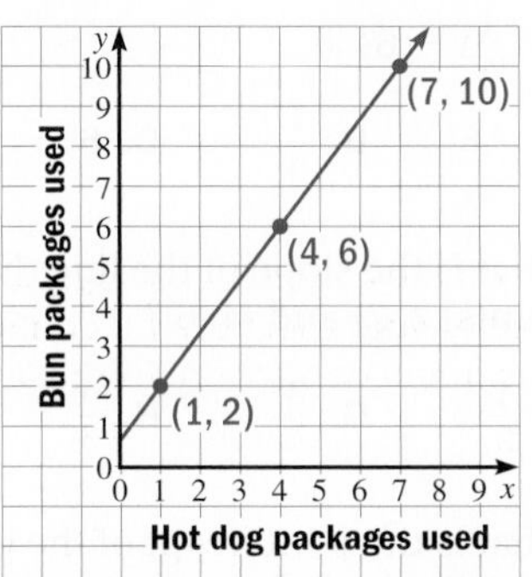

3 Solve the problem.

Make a table of values for $d = 8x + 6$ using the x-coordinates of the labeled points on the graph.

x	Substitution	d
1	$d = 8(1) + 6$	14
4	$d = 8(4) + 6$	38
7	$d = 8(7) + 6$	62

Answer Some possible numbers of hot dogs eaten are 14, 38, and 62.

3 APPLY

TRANSPARENCY

Even-numbered answers are available on transparencies.

COMMON ERROR

In Exercise 9, clarify that parts a and b are to be done separately. Students should not be seeking one pair of numbers with a sum of 20 *and* a product of 20. Also make sure students remember the meaning of the term *consecutive*.

SUGGESTED STRATEGIES

You may wish to suggest the following strategies for the problems in the Problem Solving Practice:

- Exercise 1: Guess, Check, and Revise
- Exercise 2: Draw a Graph; Make a Table
- Exercise 3: Act It Out; Use Number Sense
- Exercise 4: Guess, Check, and Revise
- Exercise 5: Use Number Sense; Guess, Check, and Revise
- Exercise 6: Draw a Graph; Make a Table
- Exercise 7: Draw a Diagram; Make a Table
- Exercise 8: Solve a Simpler Problem; Act It Out
- Exercise 9: Guess, Check, and Revise; Make a List

2. No solution. *Sample answer:* The second refrigerator costs more initially and more each year to operate, so the total costs will keep getting farther apart with time.

4–8, 9a. See Additional Answers beginning on page AA1.

Problem Solving Practice

Solve the given problem. If the problem has no solution, say so and explain why.

1. **Number Sense** Write three expressions such that each expression is equal to 1 and contains four 4's (but no other numbers). The following is an example: ***Sample answer:*** $\frac{4 \cdot 4}{4 \cdot 4}$, $\frac{4 \div 4}{4 \div 4}$, $4^4 \div 4^4$

$$\frac{4+4}{4+4}$$

2. **Refrigerators** Refrigerator A has a price of \$600 and costs \$35 per year in electricity to operate. Refrigerator B has a price of \$800 and costs \$40 per year in electricity to operate. After how many years are the total costs of the two refrigerators the same? **See margin.**

3. **Coins** Your uncle gives you and your sister a jar of coins from around the world. You divide them equally and have 1 coin left over. Then your mother tells you to share the coins with your cousin as well. After you divide the coins equally among the three of you, there are no coins left over. How many coins were in the jar? **Some possible numbers of coins are 9, 15, and 21.**

4. **Magic Squares** A 3-by-3 *magic square* contains 9 consecutive integers arranged so that the sum of the numbers in each row, column, or diagonal is the same. Below is a 3-by-3 magic square that uses the integers 1 through 9. Make a 3-by-3 magic square that uses a different set of consecutive integers. **See margin.**

4	9	2
3	5	7
8	1	6

5. **Baking** You have 12 cups of fresh pumpkin to use for baking. You need $1\frac{1}{2}$ cups to make a pumpkin pie and 1 cup to make a loaf of pumpkin bread. Find three possible combinations of pies and loaves of bread you can make that use up all the pumpkin. **See margin.**

6. **Class Picnic** You are in charge of grilling hamburgers at your class picnic. The hamburger patties come in packages of 12, and the hamburger buns come in packages of 8. After everyone is finished eating, you have an open package of hamburger patties that contains 5 patties and an open package of hamburger buns that contains 5 buns. How many hamburgers were eaten? **See margin.**

7. **Swimming Pool** A municipal swimming pool is rectangular and covers an area of 15,000 square feet. What are the length and the width of the pool? **See margin.**

8. **Checkerboard** A standard checkerboard has 32 red squares and 32 black squares. Shown below is a checkerboard with two black squares removed from its upper left and lower right corners. Can you cover this checkerboard with dominoes, where each domino covers two adjacent squares in the same row or column? Explain. **See margin.**

9. **Logical Reasoning** Find two consecutive integers that have the given property.
   - **a.** The sum of the integers is 20. **See margin.**
   - **b.** The product of the integers is 20. **4 and 5 or −4 and −5**

CHAPTER 9

Pacing and Assignment Guide

REGULAR SCHEDULE

Lesson	Les. Day	BASIC	AVERAGE	ADVANCED
9.1	Day 1	EP p. 803 Exs. 1-8; pp. 456-457 Exs. 16-24, 33-38, 54-57, 60-62, 70-73	pp. 456-457 Exs. 18-24, 33-40, 54-57, 70-77	pp. 456-457 Exs. 20-24, 37-40, 54-57, 72-75
	Day 2	pp. 456-457 Exs. 25-30, 41-50, 63-65, 74-83	pp. 456-457 Exs. 27-32, 41-53, 58-62, 66-68, 78-83	pp. 456-457 Exs. 29-32, 43-53, 58, 59, 63-69*, 78-83
9.2	Day 1	pp. 460-461 Exs. 9-14, 31, 34-41	pp. 460-461 Exs. 9-14, 29-32, 34-41	pp. 460-461 Exs. 11-14, 28-33*, 44-46
	Day 2	pp. 460-461 Exs. 15-26, 42-47	pp. 460-461 Exs. 15-28, 42-47	pp. 460-461 Exs. 15-27, 36-43, 47
9.3	Day 1	pp. 467-469 Exs. 7-16, 19, 23, 25-27, 31, 37-43	pp. 467-469 Exs. 9-12, 16-24, 28-34, 37-44	pp. 467-469 Exs. 9-12, 16-21, 24, 28-38*, 41-44
9.4	Day 1	SRH p. 773 Exs. 10-12, p. 784 Exs. 1-4; pp. 473-474 Exs. 12-21, 26-31, 33, 34, 36-39, 44-53	pp. 473-474 Exs. 16-25, 28-37, 40-42, 44-53	pp. 473-474 Exs. 18-25, 28-35, 38-44*, 47-53
9.5	Day 1	EP p. 830 Exs. 9-12, 32-37; pp. 479-481 Exs. 7-14, 19-24, 27-38, 40, 43-46, 55-62	pp. 479-481 Exs. 9-18, 21-26, 30-35, 39-44, 47-53, 55-63	pp. 479-481 Exs. 9-14, 21-29, 36-44, 47-56*, 60-63
9.6	Day 1	pp. 486-487 Exs. 7-12, 22-26	pp. 486-487 Exs. 7-12, 22-27	pp. 486-487 Exs. 7-12, 24-29
	Day 2	pp. 486-487 Exs. 13, 15-19, 27-31	pp. 486-487 Exs. 13-20, 28-32	pp. 486-487 Exs. 13-21*, 30-32
9.7	Day 1	pp. 491-493 Exs. 7-13, 18-21, 23-26, 28, 31-38	pp. 491-493 Exs. 7-9, 14-29, 31-38	pp. 491-493 Exs. 7-9, 14-19, 21-31*, 34-38
9.8	Day 1	pp. 497-498 Exs. 5-15, 30-35	pp. 497-498 Exs. 5-15, 30-36	pp. 497-498 Exs. 5-15, 31-35
	Day 2	pp. 497-498 Exs. 16-22, 24-26, 36-39	pp. 497-498 Exs. 16-28, 37-39	pp. 497-498 Exs. 18-29*, 38, 39
Review	Day 1	pp. 500-503 Exs. 1-33	pp. 500-503 Exs. 1-33	pp. 500-503 Exs. 1-33
Assess	Day 1	Chapter 9 Test	Chapter 9 Test	Chapter 9 Test

YEARLY PACING — Chapter 9 Total – **14 days** — Chapters 1–9 Total – **108 days** — Remaining – **52 days**

*Challenge Exercises EP = Extra Practice SRH = Skills Review Handbook

BLOCK SCHEDULE

DAY 1	DAY 2	DAY 3	DAY 4	DAY 5	DAY 6	DAY 7
9.1 pp. 456-457 Exs. 18-24, 27-62, 66-68, 70-83	**9.2** pp. 460-461 Exs. 9-32, 34-47	**9.3** pp. 467-469 Exs. 9-12, 16-24, 28-34, 37-44 **9.4** pp. 473-474 Exs. 16-25, 28-37, 40-42, 44-53	**9.5** pp. 479-481 Exs. 9-18, 21-26, 30-35, 39-44, 47-53, 55-63 **9.6** pp. 486-487 Exs. 7-12, 22-27	**9.6 (cont.)** pp. 486-487 Exs. 13-20, 28-32 **9.7** pp. 491-493 Exs. 7-9, 14-29, 31-38	**9.8** pp. 497-498 Exs. 5-28, 30-39	**Review** pp. 500-503 Exs. 1-33 **Assess** Chapter 9 Test

YEARLY PACING — Chapter 9 Total – **7 days** — Chapters 1–9 Total – **54 days** — Remaining – **26 days**

Support Materials

CHAPTER RESOURCE BOOK

CHAPTER SUPPORT			
Tips for New Teachers	p. 1	Parents as Partners	p. 3

LESSON SUPPORT	9.1	9.2	9.3	9.4	9.5	9.6	9.7	9.8
Lesson Plans (regular and block)	p. 5	p. 14	p. 22	p. 30	p. 38	p. 48	p. 56	p. 65
Technology Activities & Keystrokes	p. 7							
Activity Support Masters								
Activity Masters					p. 40			
Practice (3 levels)	p. 8	p. 16	p. 24	p. 32	p. 41	p. 50	p. 58	p. 67
Study Guide	p. 11	p. 19	p. 27	p. 35	p. 44	p. 53	p. 61	p. 70
Real-World Problem Solving					p. 46		p. 63	
Challenge Practice	p. 13	p. 21	p. 29	p. 37	p. 47	p. 55	p. 64	p. 72

REVIEW			
Chapter Review Games and Activities	p. 73	Extra Credit Project with Rubric	p. 78
Real-Life Project with Rubric	p. 74	Cumulative Practice	p. 80
Cooperative Project with Rubric	p. 76	Resource Book Answers	A1

ASSESSMENT

Quizzes	p. 107	Alternative Assessments with Rubrics	p. 116
Chapter Tests (3 levels)	p. 109	Unit Test	p. 129
Standardized Test	p. 115	Cumulative Test	p. 131

TRANSPARENCIES

	9.1	9.2	9.3	9.4	9.5	9.6	9.7	9.8
Warm-Up/Daily Homework Quiz	✔	✔	✔	✔	✔	✔	✔	✔
Notetaking Guide	✔	✔	✔	✔	✔	✔	✔	✔
Teacher Support	✔			✔				
English/Spanish Problem Solving	✔		✔					
Answer Transparencies	✔	✔	✔	✔	✔	✔	✔	✔

TECHNOLOGY

- EasyPlanner CD-ROM
- Test and Practice Generator
- Electronic Lesson Presentations
- eTutorial CD-ROM
- Chapter Audio Summaries CDs
- Classzone.com
- eEdition Plus Online
- eWorkbook Plus Online
- eTutorial Plus Online
- EasyPlanner Plus Online

ADDITIONAL RESOURCES

- Worked-Out Solution Key
- Notetaking Guide
- Practice Workbook
- Tutor Place
- Professional Development Book
- Special Activities Book
- Posters
- Spanish Study Guide
- Exercises in Spanish
- English/Spanish Ch. Reviews/Tests
- Multi-Language Visual Glossary

CHAPTER 9

Math Background and Teaching Strategies

Lesson 9.1

MATH BACKGROUND

For two numbers x and y, if $x^2 = y$, then x is a **square root** of y. Every positive number y has two square roots, one positive and one negative. The positive square root of y is indicated by $\sqrt{y}$, and the negative square root by $-\sqrt{y}$. A **perfect square** has integer square roots. To solve the equation $x^2 = c$, you can use the definition of square root to obtain $x = \pm\sqrt{c}$.

TEACHING STRATEGIES

In situations like Example 5 on page 455, where students solve an equation by taking square roots, they will learn when they see a variable term squared alone on one side of an equation to identify the solutions as "plus or minus the square root" of the other side of the equation, but they may not fully understand what they are doing. You may want to take some extra time with students to work through this step.

Lesson 9.2

MATH BACKGROUND

The *product property of square roots* states that for two nonnegative numbers, the square root of the product is the product of the square roots of the numbers. The *quotient property of square roots* states that the square root of the quotient of a nonnegative number and a positive number is the quotient of the square roots of the two numbers.

TEACHING STRATEGIES

It will take students some practice to become proficient at factoring using the greatest perfect square factor. You may want to review finding the prime factorization of a number, and apply this to identifying perfect square factors. For example, for $\sqrt{288}$, students can use a factor tree or other method to determine that $288 = 2^5 \cdot 3^2$. Since even exponents indicate squares, this can be rewritten using the product property of exponents as $2 \cdot 2^4 \cdot 3^2$. Because 2^4 and 3^2 are perfect squares, so is $2^4 \cdot 3^2 = 144$, which has the square root $2^2 \cdot 3^1 = 12$. So, $\sqrt{288} = \sqrt{144} \cdot \sqrt{2} = 12\sqrt{2}$.

Lesson 9.3

MATH BACKGROUND

The **Pythagorean theorem** states that the sum of the squares of the lengths of the legs of a right triangle is equal to the square of the hypotenuse of the triangle. This fact can be used to find a missing leg or hypotenuse length in a right triangle. By the *converse* of the Pythagorean theorem, if the sum of the squares of two sides of a triangle equals the square of the third side, the triangle is a right triangle.

TEACHING STRATEGIES

Sketch the diagram at the right and ask students to find the area of the square. To do so, they will first have to use the Pythagorean theorem to find the length of the hypotenuse of the right triangle.

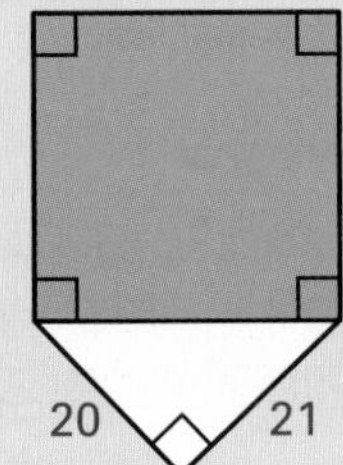

Lesson 9.4

MATH BACKGROUND

While all rational numbers can be represented by a ratio of two integers, an **irrational number** cannot. Though the decimal form of an irrational number can display a pattern, such as 2.303303330333330..., it never terminates and never contains a block of digits that repeat. If a positive number is not the square of a rational number, then its square root is irrational. The rational and irrational numbers form the **real numbers**.

TEACHING STRATEGIES

Have students predict which is greater, 0.4 or $\sqrt{0.4}$. Many will think that 0.4 is greater, since for whole numbers greater than 1, the principal square root is less than the number. Also, some students may think that $\sqrt{0.4} = 0.2$, and conclude that 0.4 is greater. Point out that if you multiply a number between 0 and 1 by itself, you are in effect finding "part of a part," so the product will be less than the number that is squared, that is, less than its square root.

Lesson 9.5

MATH BACKGROUND

The **distance formula** for the distance d between two points (x_1, y_1) and (x_2, y_2) is $d = \sqrt{(x_2 - x_1)^2 + (y_2 - y_1)^2}$. The midpoint M of a segment is the point whose x- and y-coordinates are the averages of the x- and y-coordinates, respectively, of the endpoints of the segment: $M = \left(\frac{x_1 + x_2}{2}, \frac{y_1 + y_2}{2}\right)$.

TEACHING STRATEGIES

The distance formula is more complex when compared to formulas students have encountered so far. Encourage them to show their work at each step. It is also a good time to make sure students understand how the order of operations works with the distance formula: find each difference, square each difference, add the squares, and then find the square root of the result. Fortunately, the distance formula is "forgiving" in one sense: if students use one point for the first point when finding the x-differences and the other point for the first point when finding the y-differences, the process of squaring prevents the result from being incorrect.

Lesson 9.6

MATH BACKGROUND

In a 45°-45°-90° triangle, the lengths of the legs are the same, and the hypotenuse is $\sqrt{2}$ times the leg length. In a 30°-60°-90° triangle, the hypotenuse is twice the length of the leg opposite the 30° angle, and the length of the leg opposite the 60° angle is $\sqrt{3}$ times the length of the leg opposite the 30° angle.

TEACHING STRATEGIES

Here is an additional example you can work with students:

A kite string that is 100 feet long makes an angle with the ground of 60°. The roll of string is being held 4 feet above the ground. About how high is the kite?

The kite string forms the hypotenuse of a 30°-60°-90° triangle whose vertices are the roll of string, the kite, and a point 4 feet above the ground directly under the kite. The horizontal leg is the shorter leg, and its length is 100 ÷ 2, or 50 feet. The length of the vertical leg is $50\sqrt{3} \approx 86.6$ feet. The height of the kite is about 4 feet + 86.6 feet = 90.6 feet.

Lesson 9.7

MATH BACKGROUND

A **trigonometric ratio** is a ratio of the lengths of two sides of a right triangle. Because all right triangles with a given acute angle are similar, the ratio of two sides in one right triangle with a given acute angle will be the same as the ratio of the two corresponding sides in any right triangle with the same acute angle. The **tangent** of an acute angle of a right triangle is the ratio of the length of the leg opposite that angle to the length of the leg adjacent to that angle.

TEACHING STRATEGIES

Have students plot the points (1, 1), (5, −2), and (4, 5) on a coordinate grid and connect the points to form a right triangle. Then ask students how they can find the tangent of each of the acute angles. Students should realize that they can use the distance formula to find the lengths of the legs, and then use the results to find the tangent ratios. Have students find and compare the tangent ratios, which are both equal to 1. When students realize that they are the same (with prompting as necessary), they should be able to deduce that the triangle is a 45°-45°-90° triangle. They can also verify that the hypotenuse is $\sqrt{2}$ times the leg length.

Lesson 9.8

MATH BACKGROUND

The **sine** and **cosine** ratios express relationships involving the hypotenuse of a right triangle. The sine ratio is the ratio of the side opposite an acute angle to the hypotenuse, and the cosine ratio is the ratio of the side adjacent an acute angle to the hypotenuse. Together with the tangent, the sine and cosine form the three principal trigonometric ratios.

TEACHING STRATEGIES

Students often confuse the sine and cosine ratios. Encourage them to create and share mnemonic devices to help them remember. These could be as basic as SOCA, for "Sine Opposite; Cosine Adjacent," or more colorful. Also, as they write trigonometric ratios, help students make the connection that the sine of one acute angle in a right triangle is the cosine of the other acute angle, and vice versa.

CHAPTER

9 Differentiating Instruction

Strategies for Underachievers

USE TOOLS AND MANIPULATIVES

In conjunction with Lesson 9.1, you may wish to have a large number line posted in the classroom that matches whole numbers with radical expressions involving perfect squares. For example, the number line could have the labels 1, 2, 3, 4, … below the tick marks, and the labels $\sqrt{1}$, $\sqrt{4}$, $\sqrt{9}$, $\sqrt{16}$, … above the tick marks. This will help students when approximating square roots.

PERFECT SQUARES In conjunction with Lesson 9.2, you may wish to create or have students create a chart of perfect squares through $20^2 = 400$, or perhaps even $25^2 = 625$, so that they will be more likely to recognize perfect squares. Also, encourage students to make note cards or flash cards of perfect squares. They can also make lists or cards containing some of the multiples of the lesser perfect squares, such as $16 \cdot 2 = 32$, $16 \cdot 3 = 48$, $16 \cdot 5 = 80$, and so on. You may wish to allow students to use calculators when working with factors of greater numbers, but if so, make sure students show all their work in simplifying radical expressions so that they do not rely only on the calculator to find square roots. You may also want to allow students to use calculators when working with the distance formula in Lesson 9.5. If you do so, you may need to give students instructions for using the calculator, especially in working with squares and square roots, and in entering the keystrokes correctly to ensure that the order of operations is followed when evaluating results.

EMPHASIZE NOTETAKING STRATEGIES

In Lesson 9.5, you may wish to have students create note cards detailing the distance and midpoint formulas. The cards should contain worked-out examples to serve as templates. You may wish for students to have access to these cards throughout the remainder of the chapter.

SPECIAL RIGHT TRIANGLES In Lesson 9.6, it will again be helpful for students to have note cards for quick reference, this time in regard to the special right triangles. Students can picture the relationships without variable expressions by drawing and labeling a 45°-45°-90° triangle with legs 1 unit long and a hypotenuse $\sqrt{2}$ units long, and a 30°-60°-90° triangle with legs 1 unit and $\sqrt{3}$ units long and a hypotenuse 2 units long. These values make the relationships clear without variables, and also make it easy to use the Pythagorean theorem to show that the triangles are indeed right triangles.

In Lessons 9.7 and 9.8, have students add drawings and examples that illustrate the use of the sine, cosine, and tangent ratios to their note cards.

PROVIDE MNEMONIC DEVICES

TRIGONOMETRIC RATIOS The Teaching Strategies note for Lesson 9.8 gave some suggestions for mnemonic devices to distinguish the sine and cosine ratios. You may also want to challenge students to come up with mnemonics that incorporate all three trigonometric ratios. For example, using the scheme S = sine, A = adjacent, and so on, some possibilities include the following:

(1) SOHCAHTOA
(2) Sally's Orange Hen Caught Another Hen Taking Oats Away
(3) Summer Offers Heat; Cares Aren't Heavy; Time Off Algebra

Strategies for English Learners

VOCABULARY STUDY OF ROOTS

Many mathematical terms stem from a common root word, usually of Latin origins. Recognizing the Latin prefixes and roots can help students comprehend sophisticated mathematics vocabulary. Consider the roots and words in the table shown.

Latin Root	Mathematical Terms
aequus (even)	equal, equality, equate, equation, unequal, inequality
ex (out) and premere (to press)	express, expression

Latin Root	Mathematical Terms
numerus (number)	number, numeral, numeration, numerical, numerator
radicare (to root)	radical, radicand
ratus (to think) and ration (to reason)	ratio, rational, irrational
simplex (simple)	simple, simplify, simple interest
solvere (solve, loosen, dissolve)	solve, solution, soluble, solvable, solubility
value	value, evaluate
variare (various, diverse)	vary, variance, variable, variation

Encourage students to look at the similarity between new words and known words. Recognizing, for example, that *irrational* has the word *ratio* in it, plus the prefix *ir-*, which generally means *not*, will help students remember that an irrational number is one that cannot be expressed as the ratio of two integers. You may want to have students keep an ongoing list in their notebooks.

Strategies for Advanced Learners

INCREASE DEPTH AND COMPLEXITY

In Lesson 9.1, you may wish to have some advanced students write an explanation of the use of the order of operations in Example 4 on page 454. Though students will not know yet that a square root sign is equivalent to an exponent of $\frac{1}{2}$, and so has the same rank in the order of operations as an exponent, they should be able to perceive that the square root symbol in a radical expression serves as a grouping symbol similar to that of a fraction bar.

In Lesson 9.2, you may wish to have some advanced students examine the following equations. Challenge them to explain when and why absolute value bars are needed. They should observe that the absolute value symbols are used only when the square root has an odd exponent. This is because if the exponent is even, then the square root is already positive, and no absolute value bars are needed.

$$\sqrt{y^2} = |y| \qquad \sqrt{y^4} = y^2$$
$$\sqrt{y^6} = |y^3| \qquad \sqrt{y^8} = y^4$$

PYTHAGOREAN TRIPLES In Lesson 9.3, Exercise 21 on page 468 deals with Pythagorean triples. You may want to ask advanced students whether they think every multiple of a Pythagorean triple is also a Pythagorean triple. Though they will not be ready to deduce this algebraically [if $a^2 + b^2 = c^2$, then $(ka)^2 + (kb)^2 = k^2a^2 + k^2b^2 = k^2(a^2 + b^2) = k^2c^2 = (kc)^2$], students should be able to use several numerical examples to convince themselves that this is true.

In conjunction with Concept Activity 9.3 and Lesson 9.3, it can be a great help to students to explore the Pythagorean theorem using geometric drawing software. These software packages usually include instructions for using the software to complete relevant activities.

USE CO-CURRICULAR ACTIVITIES

In conjunction with Lesson 9.3, you may wish to work with a social studies teacher to develop a unit revolving around the Pythagorean theorem. The content of this theorem has a rich history through many different cultures, and the theorem has been proven in many different eras in many different ways. Some proofs have been by people not usually associated with mathematics, including former United States President James A. Garfield. The problem of finding square roots and how to make sense of what we now know as irrational numbers also reach back into antiquity and span across many cultures, and therefore also offer possibilities for co-curricular instruction.

The following problems can be used with **Lesson 9.2**:

- **Challenge** Given that if $a^3 = c$, then $a = \sqrt[3]{c}$ (for example, $\sqrt[3]{8} = 2$), simplify each expression.
  a. $\sqrt[3]{16}$ $2\sqrt[3]{2}$
  b. $\sqrt[3]{24}$ $2\sqrt[3]{3}$
  c. $\sqrt[3]{500}$ $5\sqrt[3]{4}$
  d. $\sqrt[4]{48}$ $2\sqrt[4]{3}$

CHAPTER 9

Differentiating Instruction: Resource Materials

Differentiating Assessment

McDougal Littell *Pre-Algebra* offers a wide variety of assessment. This includes Level A, Level B, and Level C Chapter Tests, Standardized Tests, Cumulative Tests, and Quizzes from the *Assessment Book*, Daily Homework Quizzes from the *Warm-Up Transparencies*, and the *Test and Practice Generator*.

ASSESSMENT BOOK

The *Assessment Book* contains two quizzes, three levels of chapter tests, A (Basic), B (Average), and C (Advanced), and a standardized test for each chapter in the textbook. Also included are cumulative tests and unit tests.

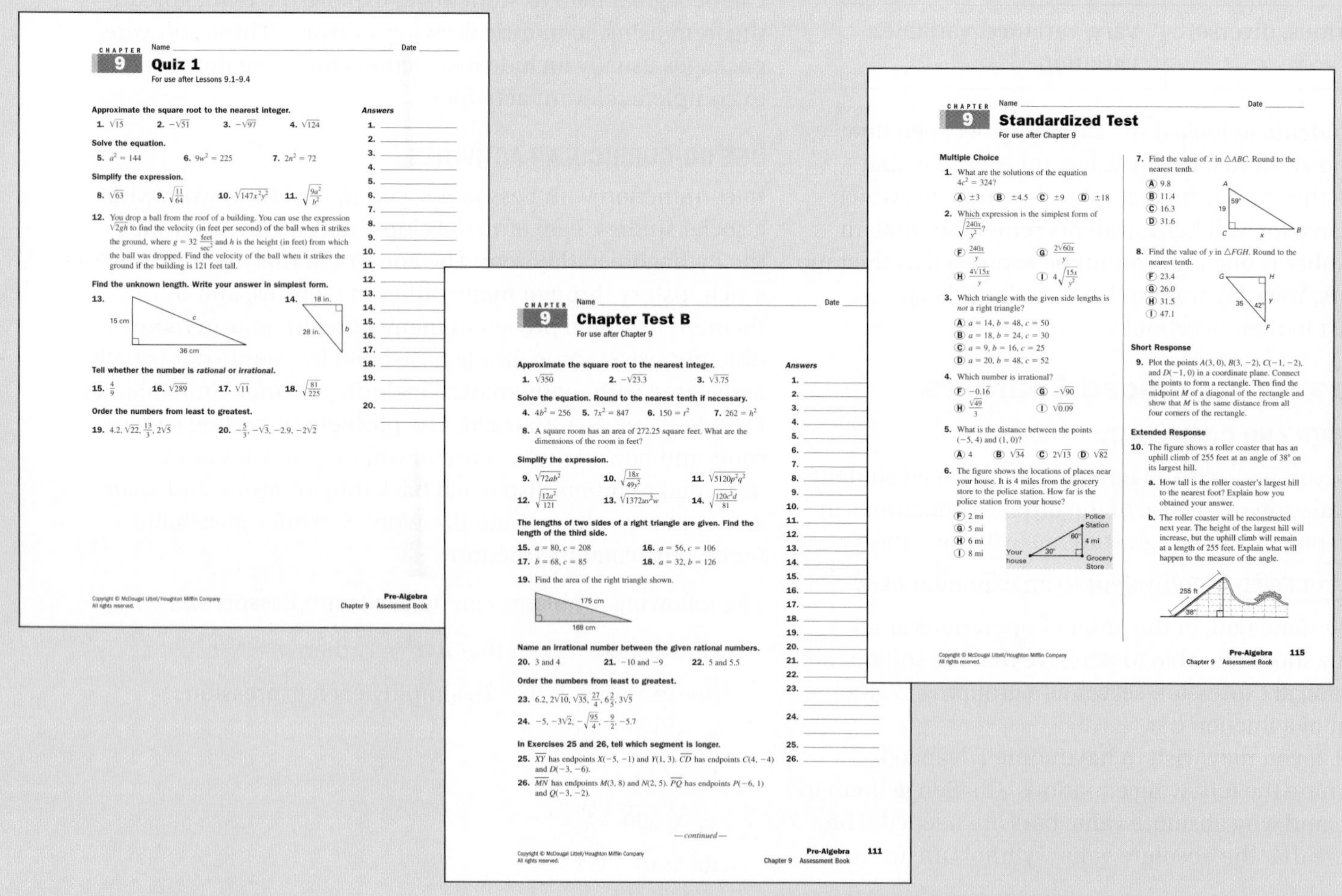

CHAPTER 9 Name ______ Date ______

Quiz 1

For use after Lessons 9.1-9.4

Approximate the square root to the nearest integer.

1. $\sqrt{15}$ 2. $-\sqrt{51}$ 3. $-\sqrt{97}$ 4. $\sqrt{124}$

Solve the equation.

5. $a^2 = 144$ 6. $9w^2 = 225$ 7. $2n^2 = 72$

Simplify the expression.

8. $\sqrt{63}$ 9. $\sqrt{\frac{11}{64}}$ 10. $\sqrt{147x^2y^2}$ 11. $\sqrt{\frac{9a^2}{b^2}}$

12. You drop a ball from the roof of a building. You can use the expression $\sqrt{2gh}$ to find the velocity (in feet per second) of the ball when it strikes the ground, where $g = 32 \frac{\text{feet}}{\text{sec}^2}$ and h is the height (in feet) from which the ball was dropped. Find the velocity of the ball when it strikes the ground if the building is 121 feet tall.

Find the unknown length. Write your answer in simplest form.

13. 14.

Tell whether the number is *rational* or *irrational*.

15. $\frac{4}{9}$ 16. $\sqrt{289}$ 17. $\sqrt{11}$ 18. $\sqrt{\frac{81}{225}}$

Order the numbers from least to greatest.

19. $4.2, \sqrt{22}, \frac{13}{3}, 2\sqrt{5}$ 20. $-\frac{5}{3}, -\sqrt{3}, -2.9, -2\sqrt{2}$

Answers

1. ______ 2. ______ 3. ______ 4. ______ 5. ______ 6. ______ 7. ______ 8. ______ 9. ______ 10. ______ 11. ______ 12. ______ 13. ______ 14. ______ 15. ______ 16. ______ 17. ______ 18. ______ 19. ______ 20. ______

Pre-Algebra
Chapter 9 Assessment Book

CHAPTER 9 Name ______ Date ______

Chapter Test B

For use after Chapter 9

Approximate the square root to the nearest integer.

1. $\sqrt{350}$ 2. $-\sqrt{23.3}$ 3. $\sqrt{3.75}$

Solve the equation. Round to the nearest tenth if necessary.

4. $4b^2 = 256$ 5. $7x^2 = 847$ 6. $150 = t^2$ 7. $262 = h^2$

8. A square room has an area of 272.25 square feet. What are the dimensions of the room in feet?

Simplify the expression.

9. $\sqrt{72ab^2}$ 10. $\sqrt{\frac{18x}{49y^2}}$ 11. $\sqrt{5120p^2q^2}$

12. $\sqrt{\frac{12a^2}{121}}$ 13. $\sqrt{1372uv^2w}$ 14. $\sqrt{\frac{120c^2d}{81}}$

The lengths of two sides of a right triangle are given. Find the length of the third side.

15. $a = 80, c = 208$ 16. $a = 56, c = 106$

17. $b = 68, c = 85$ 18. $a = 32, b = 126$

19. Find the area of the right triangle shown.

Name an irrational number between the given rational numbers.

20. 3 and 4 21. −10 and −9 22. 5 and 5.5

Order the numbers from least to greatest.

23. $6.2, 2\sqrt{10}, \sqrt{35}, \frac{27}{4}, 6\frac{2}{5}, 3\sqrt{5}$

24. $-5, -3\sqrt{2}, -\sqrt{\frac{95}{4}}, -\frac{9}{2}, -5.7$

In Exercises 25 and 26, tell which segment is longer.

25. $\overline{XY}$ has endpoints $X(-5, -1)$ and $Y(1, 3)$. $\overline{CD}$ has endpoints $C(4, -4)$ and $D(-3, -6)$.

26. $\overline{MN}$ has endpoints $M(3, 8)$ and $N(2, 5)$. $\overline{PQ}$ has endpoints $P(-6, 1)$ and $Q(-3, -2)$.

Answers

1. ______ 2. ______ 3. ______ 4. ______ 5. ______ 6. ______ 7. ______ 8. ______ 9. ______ 10. ______ 11. ______ 12. ______ 13. ______ 14. ______ 15. ______ 16. ______ 17. ______ 18. ______ 19. ______ 20. ______ 21. ______ 22. ______ 23. ______ 24. ______ 25. ______ 26. ______

—*continued*—

Pre-Algebra 111
Chapter 9 Assessment Book

CHAPTER 9 Name ______ Date ______

Standardized Test

For use after Chapter 9

Multiple Choice

1. What are the solutions of the equation $4c^2 = 324$?
   (A) ±3 (B) ±4.5 (C) ±9 (D) ±18

2. Which expression is the simplest form of $\sqrt{\frac{240x}{y^2}}$?
   (F) $\frac{240x}{y}$ (G) $\frac{2\sqrt{60x}}{y}$
   (H) $\frac{4\sqrt{15x}}{y}$ (I) $4\sqrt{\frac{15x}{y^2}}$

3. Which triangle with the given side lengths is *not* a right triangle?
   (A) $a = 14, b = 48, c = 50$
   (B) $a = 18, b = 24, c = 30$
   (C) $a = 9, b = 16, c = 25$
   (D) $a = 20, b = 48, c = 52$

4. Which number is irrational?
   (F) $-0.1\overline{6}$ (G) $-\sqrt{90}$
   (H) $\frac{\sqrt{49}}{3}$ (I) $\sqrt{0.09}$

5. What is the distance between the points $(-5, 4)$ and $(1, 0)$?
   (A) 4 (B) $\sqrt{34}$ (C) $2\sqrt{13}$ (D) $\sqrt{82}$

6. The figure shows the locations of places near your house. It is 4 miles from the grocery store to the police station. How far is the police station from your house?
   (F) 2 mi
   (G) 5 mi
   (H) 6 mi
   (I) 8 mi

7. Find the value of x in $\triangle ABC$. Round to the nearest tenth.
   (A) 9.8
   (B) 11.4
   (C) 16.3
   (D) 31.6

8. Find the value of y in $\triangle FGH$. Round to the nearest tenth.
   (F) 23.4
   (G) 26.0
   (H) 31.5
   (I) 47.1

Short Response

9. Plot the points $A(3, 0)$, $B(3, -2)$, $C(-1, -2)$, and $D(-1, 0)$ in a coordinate plane. Connect the points to form a rectangle. Then find the midpoint M of a diagonal of the rectangle and show that M is the same distance from all four corners of the rectangle.

Extended Response

10. The figure shows a roller coaster that has an uphill climb of 255 feet at an angle of 38° on its largest hill.
    a. How tall is the roller coaster's largest hill to the nearest foot? Explain how you obtained your answer.
    b. The roller coaster will be reconstructed next year. The height of the largest hill will increase, but the uphill climb will remain at a length of 255 feet. Explain what will happen to the measure of the angle.

Pre-Algebra 115
Chapter 9 Assessment Book

WARM-UP TRANSPARENCIES WITH DAILY HOMEWORK QUIZ

The *Warm-Up Transparencies with Daily Homework Quiz* contains a daily homework quiz for each lesson in the textbook. Each quiz appears with a set of warm-up exercises.

LESSON 9.4 Warm-Up Exercises

For use before Lesson 9.4, pages 470–474

Write the fraction as a decimal.

1. $\frac{7}{10}$ **2.** $\frac{3}{5}$ **3.** $\frac{1}{5}$

4. $\frac{1}{8}$ **5.** $\frac{7}{8}$ **6.** $\frac{9}{20}$

Daily Homework Quiz

For use after Lesson 9.3, pages 464–469

Determine whether the triangle with the given side lengths is a right triangle.

1. 10, 24, 26 **2.** 15, 36, 38

The lengths of two sides of a right triangle are given. Find the length of the third side.

3. $a = 11, b = 60$ **4.** $a = 16, c = 34$

5. Challenge Find each unknown length in simplest form.

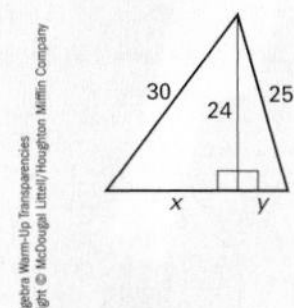

ANSWERS

Warm-Ups: 1. 0.7 **2.** 0.6 **3.** 0.2 **4.** 0.125 **5.** 0.875 **6.** 0.45

Daily Homework Quiz: 1. yes **2.** no **3.** 61 **4.** 30
5. $x = 18, y = 7$

63

LESSON 9.7 Warm-Up Exercises

For use before Lesson 9.7, pages 488–493

Solve.

1. $42 = \frac{x}{6}$ **2.** $9 = \frac{63}{x}$ **3.** $18 = \frac{x}{4}$

Find the value of each variable.

4. **5.** **6.**

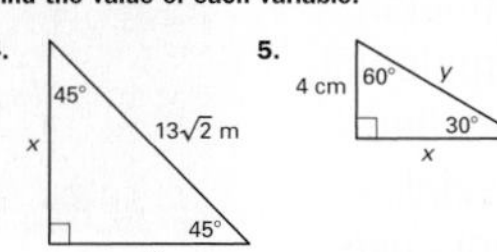

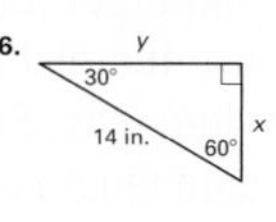

Daily Homework Quiz

For use after Lesson 9.6, pages 482–487

Use the figure to find the unknown lengths. Write your answers in simplest form.

1. a
2. b
3. c
4. d

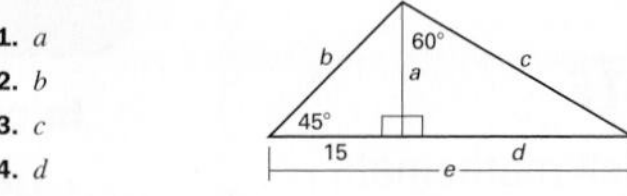

5. Challenge Find the value of e in the figure above.

ANSWERS

Warm-Ups: 1. 252 **2.** 7 **3.** 72 **4.** 13 m
5. $x = 4\sqrt{3}$ cm; $y = 8$ cm **6.** $x = 7$ in.; $y = 7\sqrt{3}$ in.

Daily Homework Quiz: 1. 15 **2.** $15\sqrt{2}$ **3.** 30 **4.** $15\sqrt{3}$
5. $15 + 15\sqrt{3}$

66

TEST AND PRACTICE GENERATOR CD-ROM

The *Test and Practice Generator* can be used to create numerous quizzes and tests for each lesson and for each chapter using both static and algorithmic exercises.

Chapter 9 Test — Page 1

1. Find the unknown length. Round to the nearest hundredth, if necessary.

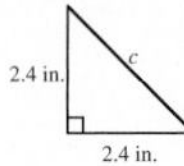

[A] 2.19 in. [B] 2.86 in. [C] 3.39 in. [D] 4.80 in.

Let a and b represent the lengths of the legs of a right triangle, and let c represent the length of the hypotenuse. Find the unknown length. Then find the area and perimeter.

2. $a = 10$ ft, $b = ?$ ft, $c = 14.5$ ft
   [A] 4.5 ft, 52.5 ft^2, 29 ft [B] 10.5 ft, 52.5 ft^2, 32.9 ft
   [C] 10.5 ft, 52.5 ft^2, 35 ft [D] 17.6 ft, 52.5 ft^2, 42.1 ft

3. $a = ?, b = 20$ m, $c = 20.5$ m

4. Let a and b represent the lengths of the legs of a right triangle, and let c represent the length of the hypotenuse. Find the unknown length.
   $a = ?, b = 4, c = \sqrt{17}$

5. Use a calculator to approximate the given expression. Round your answer to four decimal places.
   tan 33°

6. Find the perimeter of the right triangle given its area and the length of one leg.
   $a = 10$ ft
   Area = 120 ft^2

7. Find the square root.
   $-\sqrt{144}$

Chapter 9 Test — Page 2

8. Let a and b represent the lengths of the legs of a right triangle, and let c represent the length of the hypotenuse. Find the unknown length.
   $a = 4, b = ?, c = 8.5$
   [A] 5.5 [B] 7.5 [C] 10.3 [D] 13.5

9. Which set(s) of numbers below forms a Pythagorean triple?
   (27, 36, 45), (20, 20, 29), (9, 40, 40), (2, 4, 5)

10. Find the square root. [A] 260 [B] 2.6 [C] 26 [D] 676
    $\sqrt{676}$

11. Find the value of each variable. Give exact answers.

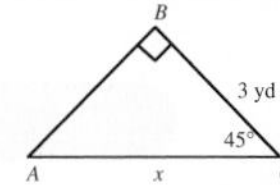

12. Approximate the square root to the nearest whole number.
    $\sqrt{218}$

13. Find the sine, cosine, and tangent ratios for $\angle T$.

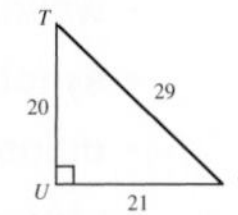

[A] $\sin T = \frac{21}{29}; \cos T = \frac{20}{29}; \tan T = \frac{20}{21}$ [B] $\sin T = \frac{20}{21}; \cos T = \frac{20}{29}; \tan T = \frac{21}{29}$

[C] $\sin T = \frac{29}{21}; \cos T = \frac{21}{20}; \tan T = \frac{29}{20}$ [D] $\sin T = \frac{21}{29}; \cos T = \frac{20}{29}; \tan T = \frac{21}{20}$

OVERVIEW

MAIN IDEAS

In this chapter, students use square roots and simplify radical expressions. Students use the Pythagorean theorem to find unknown side lengths of right triangles. Students compare and order real numbers. Students use the distance, midpoint, and slope formulas. Students find unknown side lengths in special right triangles. Finally, students use the tangent, sine, and cosine ratios to find unknown lengths in right triangles.

APPLICATION NOTE

Pythagoras was a Greek mathematician who lived about 2500 years ago. He developed interests in mathematics and astronomy as a teenager. He continued exploring mathematics as an adult and also studied philosophy and religion in Babylon.

Pythagoras founded his own philosophical and religious school in southern Italy based on his beliefs. Pythagoras believed and taught that symbols had mystical significance. Both men and women were admitted as students. Many important advances in philosophy, mathematics, and even music theory were developed in the school.

The theorem we call the Pythagorean theorem today was known for at least 1000 years before Pythagoras, but Pythagoras was the first to formally prove it.

CHAPTER

9 Real Numbers *and* Right Triangles

BEFORE

In previous chapters you've . . .

- **Used ratios and proportions**
- **Solved problems using similar triangles**
- **Found the slope of a line through two points**

Now

In Chapter 9 you'll study . . .

- **Using square roots**
- **Solving problems using the Pythagorean theorem**
- **Comparing and ordering real numbers**
- **Using the distance, midpoint, and slope formulas**
- **Applying the tangent, sine, and cosine ratios**

WHY?

So you can solve real-world problems about . . .

- **photography, p. 456**
- **walking speed, p. 460**
- **synchronized swimming, p. 468**
- **maps, p. 480**
- **stereo speakers, p. 486**
- **forestry, p. 492**

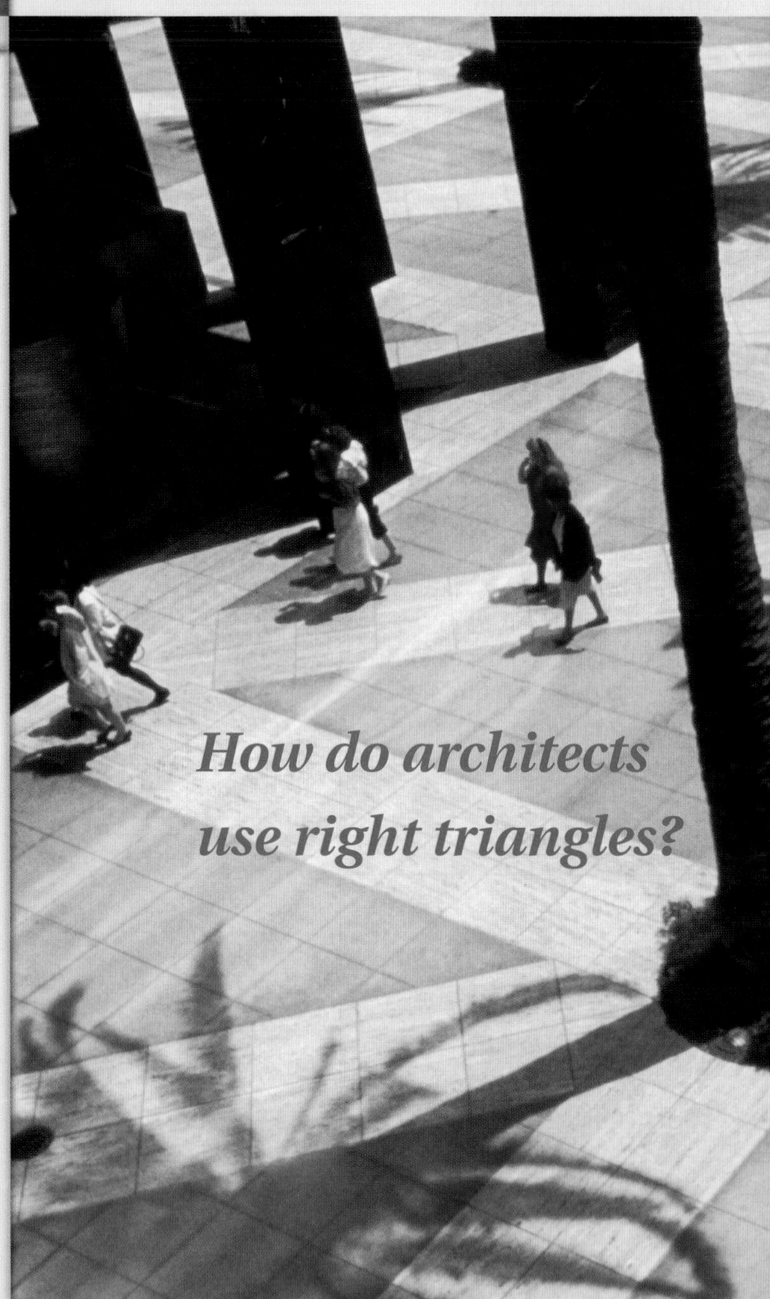

How do architects use right triangles?

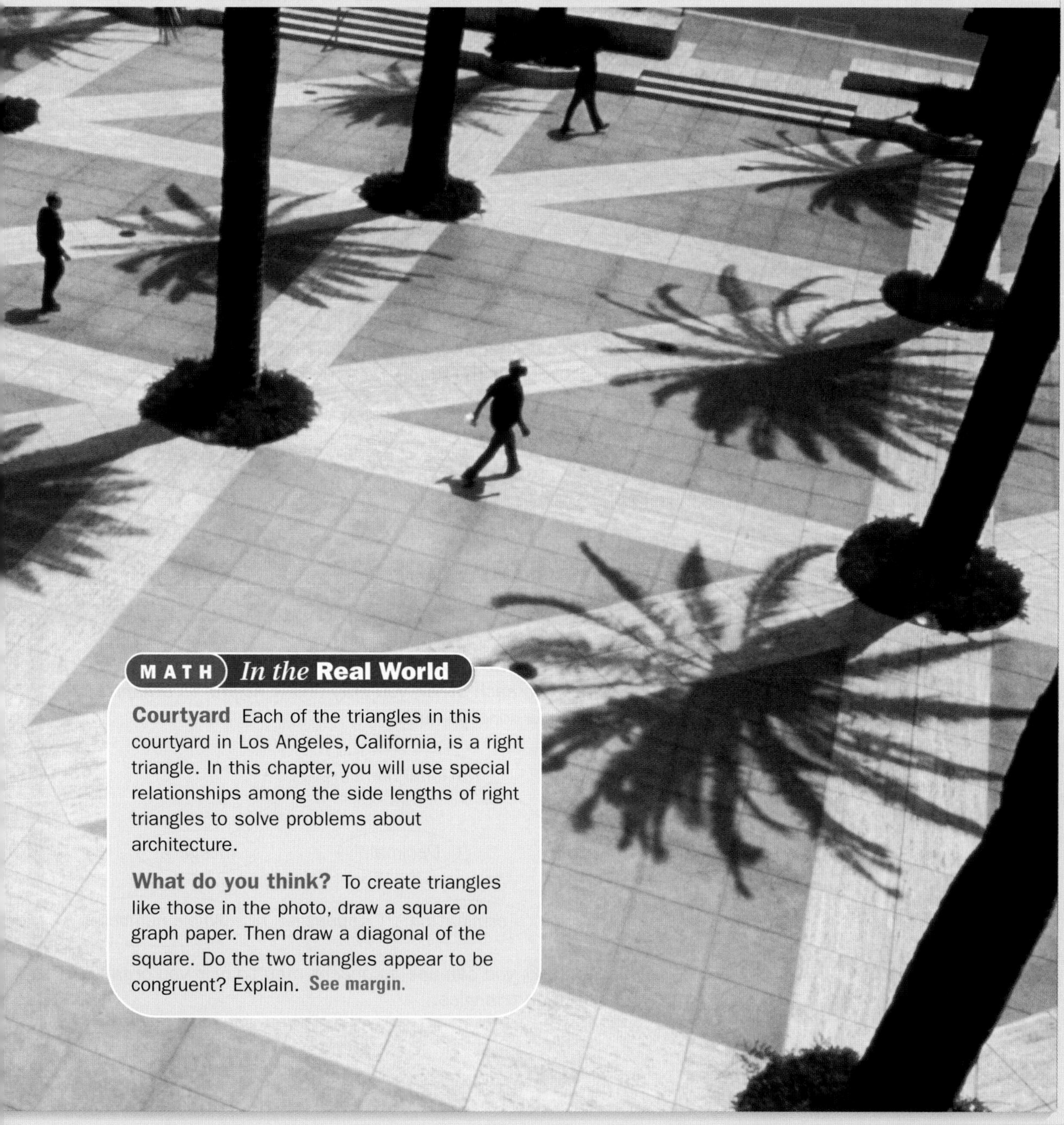

- eEdition Plus Online
- eWorkbook Plus Online
- eTutorial Plus Online
- State Test Practice
- More Examples

MATH In the Real World

Courtyard Each of the triangles in this courtyard in Los Angeles, California, is a right triangle. In this chapter, you will use special relationships among the side lengths of right triangles to solve problems about architecture.

What do you think? To create triangles like those in the photo, draw a square on graph paper. Then draw a diagonal of the square. Do the two triangles appear to be congruent? Explain. **See margin.**

CHAPTER RESOURCES

These resources are provided to help you prepare for the chapter and to customize review materials:

Chapter 9 Resource Book

- Tips for New Teachers, pp. 1–2
- Lesson Plan, pp. 5, 14, 22, 30, 38, 48, 56, 65
- Lesson Plan for Block Scheduling, pp. 6, 15, 23, 31, 39, 49, 57, 66

Technology

- EasyPlanner CD-ROM
- Test and Practice Generator
- Electronic Lesson Presentations CD-ROM
- eTutorial CD-ROM

Internet

- Classzone
- eEdition Plus Online
- eWorkbook Plus Online
- eTutorial Plus Online
- EasyPlanner Plus Online

ENGLISH LEARNER SUPPORT

- Spanish Study Guide
- Multi-Language Visual Glossary
- Chapter Audio Summaries CDs
- Teacher's Edition, pp. 450E–450F

Yes; the diagonal forms the longest sides of both triangles, so those sides are congruent. The other sides of both triangles are sides of the square, so they are congruent. One angle of each triangle is a right angle. You can use a protractor to measure the other angles and see that they are also congruent. Since corresponding parts of the triangles are congruent, the triangles are congruent.

PREPARE

DIAGNOSIS/REMEDIATION

Prerequisite Skills Quiz

The Prerequisite Skills Quiz can help you diagnose whether students have the following skills needed in Chapter 9:

- Use vocabulary (Ex. 1)
- Order rational numbers (Ex. 2)
- Simplify ratios (Exs. 3–6)
- Use a proportion (Ex. 7)
- Find the slope of a line (Exs. 8–10)

Chapter 9 Resource Book

- Study Guide (Lessons 9.1–9.8)

Tutor Place

NOTETAKING STRATEGIES

A concept map might be most useful as a summary device when students are reviewing an entire chapter. With an understanding of the content in the entire chapter, students will be better prepared to see how the lessons are related. Students can also use concept maps to link the concepts found in several chapters. Further suggestions for keeping a notebook can be found on pages 454 and 484.

For more support on notetaking, see:

- Notetaking Guide Workbook
- Notetaking Transparencies

CHAPTER 9

Chapter Prerequisite Skills

Review Vocabulary

rational number, p. 219
terminating decimal, p. 220
repeating decimal, p. 220
ratio, p. 269
similar figures, p. 288
slope, p. 404

PREREQUISITE SKILLS QUIZ

Preparing for Success **To prepare for success in this chapter, test your knowledge of these concepts and skills. You may want to look at the pages referred to in blue for additional review.**

1. **Vocabulary** Is the number −3 a rational number? an integer? a whole number? **yes; yes; no**
2. Order the numbers $-\frac{17}{9}$, −2, $\frac{16}{3}$, and −3.7 from least to greatest. *(p. 219)* **−3.7, −2, $-\frac{17}{9}$, $\frac{16}{3}$**

Tell whether the ratio is in simplest form. If it is not, write it in simplest form. *(p. 269)*

3. 3 to 6 **no; 1 to 2**
4. $\frac{34}{51}$ **no; $\frac{2}{3}$**
5. $\frac{23}{3}$ **yes**
6. 76 : 38 **no; 2 : 1**

7. **Shadows** A student who is 5 feet tall is standing next to a fence post. The student casts a shadow 15 feet long. The fence post casts a shadow 18 feet long. How tall is the fence post? *(p. 293)* **6 ft**

Find the slope of the line through the given points. *(p. 404)*

8. (−2, −8), (7, 3) **$\frac{11}{9}$**
9. (4, 5), (4, 2) **undefined**
10. (−5, 3), (−10, 13) **−2**

NOTETAKING STRATEGIES

USING A CONCEPT MAP When you learn new concepts that are related to each other, you may find it helpful to organize the ideas in a concept map.

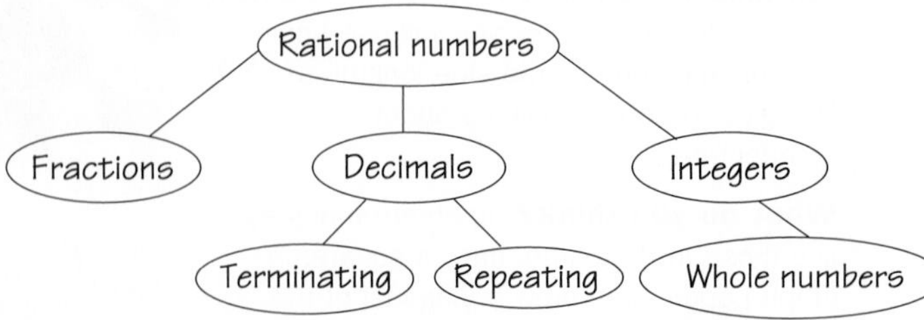

In Lesson 9.6, you can use a concept map to help you organize your notes on triangles.

Note *Worthy*

You will find a notetaking strategy at the beginning of each chapter. Look for additional notetaking and study strategies throughout the chapter.

LESSON

9.1 Square Roots

BEFORE You found squares of numbers.

Now You'll find and approximate square roots of numbers.

WHY? So you can find a person's running speed, as in Ex. 59.

Vocabulary
square root, p. 453
perfect square, p. 454
radical expression, p. 454

Human Chess In September of every even-numbered year, people in Marostica, Italy, play an unusual chess game. Each chess piece is portrayed by a person. The people portraying the knights are even on horseback!

The chessboard is a square with an area of 324 square meters. What is the length of each side of the board? To answer this question, you need to find the *square root* of 324.

A **square root** of a number n is a number m such that $m^2 = n$. Every positive number has two square roots. One square root is positive and the other is negative. The radical sign, $\sqrt{\ }$, represents a nonnegative square root. The symbol $\pm$, read "plus or minus," refers to both square roots of a positive number. For example:

$\sqrt{100} = 10$ **Positive square root of 100**

$-\sqrt{100} = -10$ **Negative square root of 100**

$\pm\sqrt{100} = \pm 10$ **Positive or negative square root of 100**

Zero has only one square root, itself.

Study *Strategy*

In Example 1, it doesn't make sense to find the negative square root of 324, because length cannot be negative.

Example 1 *Finding a Square Root*

The chessboard described above is a square with an area of 324 square meters, so the length of each side of the chessboard is the positive square root of 324.

$\sqrt{324} = 18$ because $18^2 = 324$.

Answer The length of each side of the chessboard is 18 meters.

Checkpoint

Find the square roots of the number.

1. 16 ± 4 **2.** 64 ± 8 **3.** 144 ± 12 **4.** 256 ± 16

NCTM CURRICULUM STANDARDS
Standard 1: Understand number systems; Make reasonable estimates

1 PLAN

Skill Check

1. $10 \cdot 10 = \underline{?}$ **100**
2. $12 \cdot 12 = \underline{?}$ **144**
3. $14 \cdot 14 = \underline{?}$ **196**
4. $17 \cdot 17 = \underline{?}$ **289**

Lesson Objective

Find and approximate square roots of numbers.

Pacing

Suggested Number of Days
Basic Course: 2 days
Average Course: 2 days
Advanced Course: 2 days
Block: 1 block

Teaching Resources

For a complete list of Teaching Resources, see page 450B.

Transparency

Warm-Up Exercises for this lesson are available on a transparency.

2 TEACH

Motivating the Lesson

Ask: "How many squares are on a chess board?" **64** "How many squares wide is the chess board?" **8** "How many human chess pieces would be needed for a game?" **32**

TIPS *for* NEW TEACHERS

Throughout the lesson, remind students that a positive number has two square roots, one positive and one negative. See Tips for New Teachers in the *Chapter 9 Resource Book*.

Extra Examples

Example 1 A square courtyard has an area of 400 square yards. Find the length of one side of the courtyard. **20 yd**

Example 2 Approximate $\sqrt{67}$ to the nearest integer. **8**

Example 3 Use a calculator to approximate $\sqrt{632}$. Round to the nearest tenth. **25.1**

Example 4 Evaluate $\sqrt{g(h + 2)}$ when $g = 5$ and $h = 3$. **5**

Common Error

In Example 4 and Checkpoint Exercises 6–8, watch for students who think two terms added within a radical can be simplified as the sum of two radicals, for example $\sqrt{a + b} = \sqrt{a} + \sqrt{b}$. Stress that this is not true.

Teaching Tip

Stress that it is important for students to write radicals carefully so it is clear to other readers what numbers and variables are under the radical symbol.

Note *Worthy*

You may find it helpful to make a list of the first 20 perfect squares and their square roots in your notebook and memorize them. You can find a table of squares and square roots on p. 822.

Approximating Square Roots A **perfect square** is a number that is the square of an integer. For example, 1, 4, and 9 are perfect squares.

$$1 = 1^2,\ 4 = 2^2, \text{ and } 9 = 3^2$$

You can use perfect squares to approximate a square root of a number.

Example 2 *Approximating a Square Root*

Approximate $\sqrt{51}$ to the nearest integer.

The perfect square closest to, but less than, 51 is 49. The perfect square closest to, but greater than, 51 is 64. So, 51 is between 49 and 64. This statement can be expressed by the *compound inequality* $49 < 51 < 64$.

$49 < 51 < 64$	**Identify perfect squares closest to 51.**
$\sqrt{49} < \sqrt{51} < \sqrt{64}$	**Take positive square root of each number.**
$7 < \sqrt{51} < 8$	**Evaluate square root of each perfect square.**

Answer Because 51 is closer to 49 than to 64, $\sqrt{51}$ is closer to 7 than to 8. So, to the nearest integer, $\sqrt{51} \approx 7$.

Checkpoint

5. Approximate $\sqrt{125}$ to the nearest whole number. **11**

Tech *Help*

When you enter a square root on the calculator, you should also enter a right parenthesis to close the left parenthesis that the calculator enters. Although the calculator shows 8 digits for the decimal part of the square root in Example 3, the decimal actually continues without end.

Example 3 *Using a Calculator*

Use a calculator to approximate $\sqrt{515}$. Round to the nearest tenth.

Keystrokes

2nd [√] **515**) =

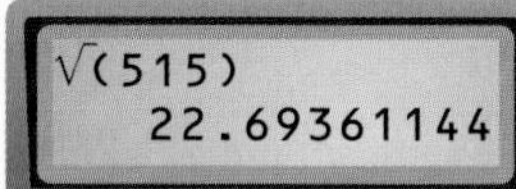

Answer

$\sqrt{515} \approx 22.7$

Radical Expressions A **radical expression** is an expression that involves a radical sign. The horizontal bar in a radical sign is a grouping symbol. When you evaluate a radical expression, evaluate the expression inside the radical symbol before finding the square root.

Example 4 *Evaluating a Radical Expression*

Evaluate $2\sqrt{a + b^2}$ when $a = 11$ and $b = 5$.

$2\sqrt{a + b^2} = 2\sqrt{11 + 5^2}$	**Substitute 11 for *a* and 5 for *b*.**
$= 2\sqrt{36}$	**Evaluate expression inside radical symbol.**
$= 2 \cdot 6 = 12$	**Evaluate square root. Multiply.**

Checkpoint

Evaluate the expression when $a = 12$ and $b = 4$.

6. $\sqrt{a+b}$ 4 7. $\sqrt{b^2 - a}$ 2 8. $3\sqrt{ab+1}$ 21

Example 5 *Solving an Equation Using Square Roots*

Physics An amusement park ride includes a free fall drop of 272 feet. You can use the equation $d = 16t^2$ to determine the time t in seconds that it takes a dropped object to fall a distance of d feet. How long does the free fall part of the ride take?

Solution

$d = 16t^2$	Write original equation.
$272 = 16t^2$	Substitute 272 for d.
$17 = t^2$	Divide each side by 16.
$\pm\sqrt{17} = t$	Use definition of square root.
$\pm 4.1 \approx t$	Use a calculator to approximate square root.

Answer Because only the positive solution makes sense in this situation, the free fall part of the ride takes about 4.1 seconds.

9.1 Exercises

More Practice, p. 811

Guided Practice

Vocabulary Check

1. Describe and give an example of a perfect square. See margin.
2. You know that one square root of a number x is -9. What is the other square root? What is the value of x? 9; 81

1. *Sample answer:* A perfect square is the square of an integer. An example is 169, since $13^2 = 169$.

Skill Check **Find the square roots of the number.**

3. 4 ± 2 4. 36 ± 6 5. 121 ± 11 6. 225 ± 15

Approximate the square root to the nearest integer.

7. $\sqrt{10}$ 3 8. $-\sqrt{84}$ -9 9. $\sqrt{151}$ 12 10. $-\sqrt{200}$ -14

Solve the equation.

11. $a^2 = 9$ ± 3 12. $n^2 = 25$ ± 5 13. $361 = x^2$ ± 19 14. $400 = y^2$ ± 20

Guided Problem Solving

15. **Eiffel Tower** The base of the Eiffel Tower is a square with an area of 15,625 square feet. What is the length of a side of the base?
 (1) Write an equation that relates base area A and side length s. $A = s^2$
 (2) Substitute 15,625 for A in the equation in Step 1 and solve for s. $15{,}625 = s^2$, 125 ft

Extra Examples

Example 5 A construction worker building a skyscraper accidentally drops a bolt from a height of 500 feet. Use the equation $d = 16t^2$ to determine the time t, in seconds, that it takes the bolt to fall to the ground below. **about 5.6 sec**

Cross-Curriculum

Science As in Example 5, students will learn in science how square roots can be used to predict the speed and acceleration of a falling object or an object that is launched into the air.

Concept Check

How do you approximate $\sqrt{149}$ to the nearest integer without using a calculator? **Identify the two perfect squares closest to 149, one less than 149 and one greater than 149. Then choose the one that is closer to 149 and find its square root.**

Daily Puzzler

Find $\sqrt{4\sqrt{16}}$. **4**

3 APPLY

ASSIGNMENT GUIDE

Basic Course

Day 1: EP p. 803 Exs. 1-8; pp. 456-457 Exs. 16-24, 33-38, 54-57, 60-62, 70-73

Day 2: pp. 456-457 Exs. 25-30, 41-50, 63-65, 74-83

Average Course

Day 1: pp. 456-457 Exs. 18-24, 33-40, 54-57, 70-77

Day 2: pp. 456-457 Exs. 27-32, 41-53, 58-62, 66-68, 78-83

Advanced Course

Day 1: pp. 456-457 Exs. 20-24, 37-40, 54-57, 72-75

Day 2: pp. 456-457 Exs. 29-32, 43-53, 58, 59, 63-69*, 78-83

Block

pp. 456-457 Exs. 18-24, 27-62, 66-68, 70-83

EXTRA PRACTICE

- Student Edition, p. 811
- Chapter 9 Resource Book, pp. 8-10
- Test and Practice Generator

TRANSPARENCY

Even-numbered answers are available on transparencies. A support transparency is available for Exercise 66.

HOMEWORK CHECK

When you review students' homework for this lesson, go over the following exercises to check understanding of key concepts.

Basic: 16, 25, 33, 41, 45

Average: 18, 27, 34, 42, 47

Advanced: 20, 29, 35, 43, 52

66a–b. See Additional Answers beginning on page AA1.

Practice and Problem Solving

Homework *Help*

Example	Exercises
1	16-24
2	25-32, 54-57
3	33-40
4	41-44
5	45-53, 58-59

Online Resources
CLASSZONE.COM
- More Examples
- eTutorial Plus

In the following exercises, you may find it helpful to use a calculator for approximating square roots.

Find the square roots of the number.

A **16.** 25 ± 5 **17.** 169 ± 13 **18.** 81 ± 9 **19.** 289 ± 17

20. 1024 ± 32 **21.** 484 ± 22 **22.** 1600 ± 40 **23.** 900 ± 30

24. Geometry The area of a square is 49 square feet. Find the side length. 7 ft

Approximate the square root to the nearest integer.

25. $\sqrt{38}$ 6 **26.** $-\sqrt{120}$ -11 **27.** $-\sqrt{148}$ -12 **28.** $\sqrt{17}$ 4

29. $-\sqrt{78}$ -9 **30.** $\sqrt{250}$ 16 **31.** $\sqrt{15.3}$ 4 **32.** $-\sqrt{7.4}$ -3

Use a calculator to approximate the square root. Round to the nearest tenth.

33. $\sqrt{3}$ 1.7 **34.** $-\sqrt{10}$ -3.2 **35.** $\sqrt{86}$ 9.3 **36.** $\sqrt{110}$ 10.5

37. $-\sqrt{33}$ -5.7 **38.** $\sqrt{1325}$ 36.4 **39.** $\sqrt{19.5}$ 4.4 **40.** $\sqrt{6.92}$ 2.6

Evaluate the expression when $a = 48$ and $b = 12$.

41. $\sqrt{a-b}$ 6 **42.** $\sqrt{a+b+4}$ 8 **43.** $-3\sqrt{ab}$ -72 **44.** $\sqrt{b^2-(a+15)}$ 9

Solve the equation. Round to the nearest tenth if necessary.

45. $x^2 = 49$ ± 7 **46.** $y^2 = 676$ ± 26 **47.** $441 = t^2$ ± 21 **48.** $n^2 = 576$ ± 24

49. $20 = m^2$ ± 4.5 **50.** $c^2 = 125$ ± 11.2 **51.** $5y^2 = 110$ ± 4.7 **52.** $200 = 16t^2$ ± 3.5

53. Critical Thinking Write an equation that has exactly two solutions, 1.5 and -1.5. *Sample answer:* $x^2 = 2.25$

In Exercises 54–57, match the number with a point on the number line.

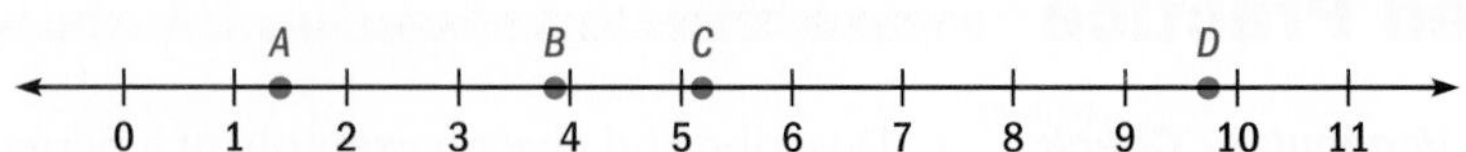

54. $\sqrt{15}$ B **55.** $\sqrt{2}$ A **56.** $\sqrt{95}$ D **57.** $\sqrt{27}$ C

58. Photography You can use the following rule of thumb when photographing fireworks: The f-stop, a number that describes the size of the opening of the camera lens, should be the number closest to the square root of the film speed. You have a camera with f-stop numbers 2.8, 4, 5.6, 8, 11, 16, and 22. Which f-stop should you use to photograph fireworks if you are using a film speed of 64? of 100? 8; 11

59. Running You can use the formula $l = 0.0625s^2$ to approximate the maximum running speed s (in meters per second) that a person with leg length l (in meters) can sustain. Find the maximum running speed for a person with a leg length of 0.64 meter. 3.2 m/sec

Fireworks near the Space Needle in Seattle, Washington

Solve the equation. Round to the nearest hundredth if necessary.

B **60.** $15 = 2h^2 - 3$ ± 3 **61.** $162 = 0.5t^2$ ± 18 **62.** $1400 = 10z^2 + 2$ ± 11.82

63. $3x^2 + 5 = 30$ ± 2.89 **64.** $1.5n^2 + 7 = 20$ ± 2.94 **65.** $2a^2 + 1 = 98$ ± 6.96

66. Consider the function $y = \sqrt{x}$. **66a–b. See margin.**

a. Make a table of ordered pairs (x, y) for $x = 0, 1, 4, 9, 16$, and 25.

b. Plot the ordered pairs from part (a) on a coordinate plane.

c. ***Writing*** Is $y = \sqrt{x}$ a linear function? Explain. **No. *Sample answer:* The points do not all lie along a straight line.**

In the **Real World**

Tsunamis An earthquake occurred off the coast of Chile in 1960, generating a tsunami. The tsunami reached Japan, about 10,000 miles away, 22 hours later. To the nearest mile per hour, how fast did the tsunami travel? **455 mi/h**

67. **Extended Problem Solving** A *tsunami* is an ocean wave that moves very fast in deep water, but slows as it reaches shallow water. As the wave slows, it rises to great heights, often causing enormous destruction on land. A tsunami's speed s (in feet per second) and the depth d of the water (in feet) are related by the equation $s^2 = 32d$. Suppose an earthquake at sea produces a tsunami in water 15,000 feet deep.

a. **Calculate** Find the original speed of the wave to the nearest mile per hour. **472 mi/h**

b. **Apply** The wave enters a harbor 45 feet deep. Find the change in the wave's speed from the original speed. Give your answer to the nearest mile per hour. **446 mi/h slower**

C 68. The *cube root* of a number n is the number m such that $m^3 = n$. For example, because $2^3 = 8$, the cube root of 8 is 2. You write this as $\sqrt[3]{8} = 2$. The table shows some whole numbers and their cube roots.

a	$\sqrt[3]{a}$
0	0
1	1
8	2
27	3
64	4

a. Use the table to approximate each cube root to the nearest integer: $\sqrt[3]{3}$, $\sqrt[3]{55}$, $\sqrt[3]{22}$. **1, 4, 3**

b. **Critical Thinking** Do negative numbers have cube roots? Explain.

c. Solve the equation $x^3 = 125$. **5**

68b. Yes. *Sample answer:* A negative number has a negative cube root, since a negative number times a negative number times a negative number is a negative number. For example, the cube root of −1000 is −10 because (−10)(−10)(−10) = −1000.

69. **Challenge** Solve $(x - 2)^2 + 1 = 37$. Describe the steps you use. **See margin.**

Mixed Review

69. −4, 8. *Sample answer:* First I subtracted 1 from each side to obtain $(x - 2)^2 = 36$. Then I used the definition of square root to write $x - 2 = \pm\sqrt{36}$, which I simplified to $x - 2 = \pm 6$. I wrote this as two equations, $x - 2 = -6$ and $x - 2 = 6$. Finally, I solved each equation by adding 2 to each side to obtain $x = -4$ and $x = 8$.

Write the prime factorization of the number. *(Lesson 4.1)*

70. 45 **$3^2 \cdot 5$** 71. 98 **$2 \cdot 7^2$** 72. 484 **$2^2 \cdot 11^2$** 73. 700 **$2^2 \cdot 5^2 \cdot 7$**

Write the fraction in simplest form. *(Lesson 4.3)*

74. $\frac{21}{48}$ **$\frac{7}{16}$** 75. $\frac{13}{52}$ **$\frac{1}{4}$** 76. $\frac{30}{125}$ **$\frac{6}{25}$** 77. $\frac{30}{162}$ **$\frac{5}{27}$**

Use the percent equation to answer the question. *(Lesson 7.4)*

78. What percent of 240 is 42? **17.5%** 79. What number is 80% of 60? **48**

80. 7 is 3.5% of what number? **200** 81. What percent of 20 is 1.3? **6.5%**

Standardized Test Practice

82. **Multiple Choice** What is $\sqrt{500}$ to the nearest integer? **C**

A. 20 B. 21 C. 22 D. 23

83. **Multiple Choice** What is the value of the expression $\sqrt{mn^2}$ when $m = 4$ and $n = 5$? **F**

F. 10 G. 20 H. 80 I. 100

4 ASSESS

Assessment Resources

For more assessment resources, see:
- Assessment Book
- Test and Practice Generator

Mini-Quiz

Find the square roots of the number.

1. 2500 **±50**
2. 225 **±15**

Use a calculator to approximate the square root. Round to the nearest tenth.

3. $\sqrt{98}$ **9.9**
4. $-\sqrt{220}$ **−14.8**
5. **Challenge** Solve $(x + 3)^2 + 5 = 105$. **−13, 7**

5 FOLLOW-UP

Diagnosis/Remediation

- Study Guide in Chapter 9 Resource Book, pp. 11–12
- eTutorial Plus Online
- Extra Practice, p. 811
- Lesson Practice in Chapter 9 Resource Book, pp. 8–10

English Learner Support

- Spanish Study Guide
- Multi-Language Visual Glossary
- Chapter Audio Summaries CDs

Challenge

- Challenge Practice in Chapter 9 Resource Book, p. 13
- Teacher's Edition, p. 450F

1 PLAN

Skill Check

Find the square root of each number.

1. 169 **13** **2.** 324 **18**
3. 484 **22** **4.** 625 **25**

LESSON OBJECTIVE

Simplify radical expressions.

PACING

Suggested Number of Days
Basic Course: 2 days
Average Course: 2 days
Advanced Course: 2 days
Block: 1 block

TEACHING RESOURCES

For a complete list of Teaching Resources, see page 450B.

TRANSPARENCY

Warm-Up Exercises for this lesson are available on a transparency.

2 TEACH

MOTIVATING THE LESSON

Ask students the following series of questions and record their answers on the board. "What is $\sqrt{9}$?" **3** "What is $\sqrt{25}$?" **5** "What is 9 • 25?" **225** "What is $\sqrt{225}$?" **15** "What is 3 • 5?" **15** "What do you notice?" ***Sample answer:*** $\sqrt{9} \cdot \sqrt{25} = \sqrt{225}$

TIPS *for* NEW TEACHERS

Have students write a list of the first fifteen perfect squares and their square roots for use during this lesson. See Tips for New Teachers in the *Chapter 9 Resource Book.*

LESSON **9.2**

Simplifying Square Roots

BEFORE	*Now*	WHY?
You found square roots.	You'll simplify radical expressions.	So you can find the distance to the horizon, as in Ex. 27.

Vocabulary

simplest form of a radical expression, p. 458

Compare the following pair of products:

$$\sqrt{4} \cdot \sqrt{16} = 2 \cdot 4 = 8 \qquad \sqrt{4 \cdot 16} = \sqrt{64} = 8$$

Notice that $\sqrt{4} \cdot \sqrt{16} = \sqrt{4 \cdot 16}$. This result suggests the product property of square roots.

Product Property of Square Roots

Algebra

$\sqrt{ab} = \sqrt{a} \cdot \sqrt{b}$, where $a \geq 0$ and $b \geq 0$

Numbers

$\sqrt{9 \cdot 7} = \sqrt{9} \cdot \sqrt{7} = 3\sqrt{7}$

You can use the product property of square roots to simplify radical expressions. A radical expression is in **simplest form** when:

- No factor of the expression under the radical sign has any perfect square factor other than 1.
- There are no fractions under the radical sign, and no radical sign in the denominator of any fraction.

In this book, all variables in radical expressions represent nonnegative numbers.

Example 1 ***Simplifying a Radical Expression***

$\sqrt{180} = \sqrt{36 \cdot 5}$	**Factor using greatest perfect square factor.**
$= \sqrt{36} \cdot \sqrt{5}$	**Product property of square roots**
$= 6\sqrt{5}$	**Simplify.**

Example 2 ***Simplifying a Variable Expression***

$\sqrt{24s^2} = \sqrt{4 \cdot 6 \cdot s^2}$	**Factor using greatest perfect square factor.**
$= \sqrt{4} \cdot \sqrt{6} \cdot \sqrt{s^2}$	**Product property of square roots**
$= 2 \cdot \sqrt{6} \cdot s$	**Simplify.**
$= 2s\sqrt{6}$	**Commutative property**

Reading *Algebra*

The final variable expression in Example 2 is written as $2s\sqrt{6}$ rather than as $2\sqrt{6}s$ to make it clear than the variable is *not* under the radical sign.

NCTM CURRICULUM STANDARDS

Standard 1: Understand numbers; Understand ways of representing numbers; Understand how operations are related

Quotients Notice that $\sqrt{\frac{100}{4}} = \sqrt{25} = 5$, and $\frac{\sqrt{100}}{\sqrt{4}} = \frac{10}{2} = 5$. This result suggests the quotient property of square roots, which you can also use to simplify radical expressions.

Quotient Property of Square Roots

Algebra

$\sqrt{\frac{a}{b}} = \frac{\sqrt{a}}{\sqrt{b}}$, where $a \geq 0$ and $b > 0$

Numbers

$\sqrt{\frac{11}{4}} = \frac{\sqrt{11}}{\sqrt{4}} = \frac{\sqrt{11}}{2}$

Example 3 *Simplifying a Radical Expression*

$\sqrt{\frac{13}{36}} = \frac{\sqrt{13}}{\sqrt{36}}$ **Quotient property of square roots**

$= \frac{\sqrt{13}}{6}$ **Simplify.**

Checkpoint

Simplify the expression.

1. $\sqrt{63}$ $3\sqrt{7}$ **2.** $\sqrt{54t^2}$ $3t\sqrt{6}$ **3.** $\sqrt{\frac{15}{16}}$ $\frac{\sqrt{15}}{4}$ **4.** $\sqrt{\frac{32}{n^2}}$ $\frac{4\sqrt{2}}{n}$

Example 4 *Using Radical Expressions*

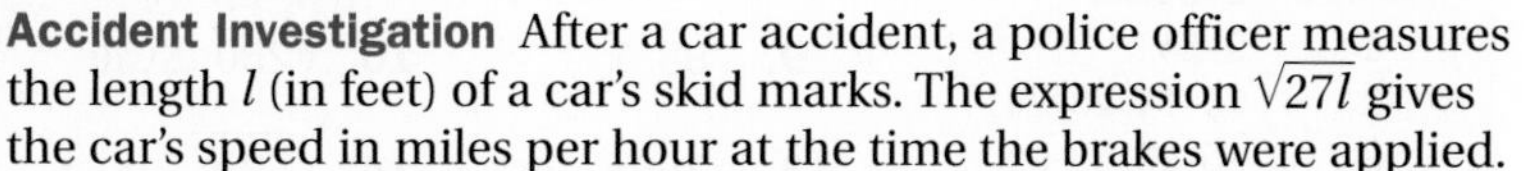

Accident Investigation After a car accident, a police officer measures the length l (in feet) of a car's skid marks. The expression $\sqrt{27l}$ gives the car's speed in miles per hour at the time the brakes were applied.

a. Write the expression in simplest form.

b. The skid marks are 125 feet long. Use the simplified expression to approximate the car's speed when the brakes were applied.

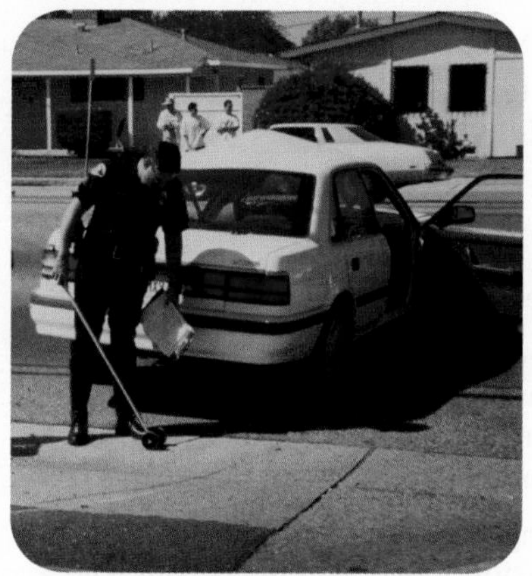

Solution

a. $\sqrt{27l} = \sqrt{9 \cdot 3 \cdot l}$ **Factor using greatest perfect square factor.**

$= \sqrt{9} \cdot \sqrt{3l}$ **Product property of square roots**

$= 3\sqrt{3l}$ **Simplify.**

Answer In simplest form, $\sqrt{27l} = 3\sqrt{3l}$.

b. $3\sqrt{3l} = 3\sqrt{3 \cdot 125}$ **Substitute 125 for l.**

$= 3\sqrt{375}$ **Multiply.**

≈ 58 **Approximate using a calculator.**

Answer The car's speed was about 58 miles per hour.

Extra Examples

Example 1 Simplify the expression $\sqrt{675}$. $\mathbf{15\sqrt{3}}$

Example 2 Simplify the expression $\sqrt{176a^2}$. $\mathbf{4a\sqrt{11}}$

Example 3 Simplify the expression $\sqrt{\frac{49}{121x^2}}$. $\mathbf{\frac{7}{11x}}$

Example 4 The expression $\sqrt{\frac{16x}{9}}$ gives the maximum speed (in nautical miles per hour) that certain boats can travel, where x is the boat's water line length in feet.

a. Write the expression in simplest form. $\mathbf{\frac{4}{3}\sqrt{x}}$

b. A boat's water line length is 30 feet. Use the simplified expression to approximate the boat's maximum speed. **about 7.3 nautical miles per hour**

NOTETAKING

Instruct students to record the product and quotient properties of square roots in their notebooks, along with an example of both properties.

CONCEPT CHECK

How do you simplify the expression $\sqrt{\frac{9}{4}}$? **Using the quotient property, write $\sqrt{\frac{9}{4}} = \frac{\sqrt{9}}{\sqrt{4}}$, which equals $\frac{3}{2}$.**

DAILY PUZZLER

Simplify $\dfrac{\sqrt{9}}{\frac{\sqrt{16}}{\sqrt{64}}}$. **6**

3 APPLY

ASSIGNMENT GUIDE

Basic Course

Day 1: pp. 460–461 Exs. 9–14, 31, 34–41

Day 2: pp. 460–461 Exs. 15–26, 42–47

Average Course

Day 1: pp. 460–461 Exs. 9–14, 29–32, 34–41

Day 2: pp. 460–461 Exs. 15–28, 42–47

Advanced Course

Day 1: pp. 460–461 Exs. 11–14, 28–33*, 44–46

Day 2: pp. 460–461 Exs. 15–27, 36–43, 47

Block

pp. 460–461 Exs. 9–32, 34–47

EXTRA PRACTICE

- Student Edition, p. 811
- Chapter 9 Resource Book, pp. 16–18
- Test and Practice Generator

TRANSPARENCY

Even-numbered answers are available on transparencies.

HOMEWORK CHECK

When you review students' homework for this lesson, go over the following exercises to check understanding of key concepts.

Basic: 9, 13, 15, 21, 23
Average: 10, 13, 16, 22, 24
Advanced: 11, 14, 18, 22, 26

COMMON ERROR

In Exercises 9–20, watch for students who correctly remove a perfect square factor from within a radical but then write the square rather than the square root outside the radical.

2. See Additional Answers beginning on page AA1.

9.2 Exercises

More Practice, p. 811

Guided Practice

Vocabulary Check

1. Tell whether the expression $3\sqrt{5}$ is in simplest form. Explain. **See margin.**
2. Explain how to use the product property of square roots to simplify the expression $\sqrt{700}$. **See margin.**

Skill Check **In Exercises 3–6, simplify the expression.**

3. $\sqrt{12}$ $2\sqrt{3}$
4. $\sqrt{48}$ $4\sqrt{3}$
5. $\sqrt{\frac{81}{4}}$ $\frac{9}{2}$
6. $\sqrt{\frac{7}{25}}$ $\frac{\sqrt{7}}{5}$
7. A square has an area of 300 square units. Find the length of a side of the square as a radical expression in simplest form. $10\sqrt{3}$ **units**
8. **Error Analysis** Describe and correct the error in writing $\sqrt{72}$ in simplest form.

$$\sqrt{72} = \sqrt{4 \cdot 18} = \sqrt{4} \cdot \sqrt{18} = 2\sqrt{18}$$

1. Yes. *Sample answer:* The only perfect square factor of 5 is 1, so it is in simplest form.

8. *Sample answer:* 18 has a perfect square factor, 9, that is greater than 1. The greatest perfect square factor of 72 is 36: $\sqrt{72} = \sqrt{36 \cdot 2} = \sqrt{36} \cdot \sqrt{2} = 6\sqrt{2}$.

Practice and Problem Solving

Homework Help

Example	Exercises
1	9–14
2	13–14, 23–26
3	15–20, 23–26
4	21–22

Online Resources
CLASSZONE.COM
- More Examples
- eTutorial Plus

In the following exercises, you may find it helpful to use a calculator for approximating square roots.

Simplify the expression.

A 9. $\sqrt{98}$ $7\sqrt{2}$
10. $\sqrt{250}$ $5\sqrt{10}$
11. $\sqrt{288}$ $12\sqrt{2}$
12. $\sqrt{243}$ $9\sqrt{3}$
13. $\sqrt{300x}$ $10\sqrt{3x}$
14. $\sqrt{63b^2}$ $3b\sqrt{7}$
15. $\sqrt{\frac{11}{36}}$ $\frac{\sqrt{11}}{6}$
16. $\sqrt{\frac{35}{144}}$ $\frac{\sqrt{35}}{12}$
17. $\sqrt{\frac{80}{81}}$ $\frac{4\sqrt{5}}{9}$
18. $\sqrt{\frac{105}{121}}$ $\frac{\sqrt{105}}{11}$
19. $\sqrt{\frac{z}{64}}$ $\frac{\sqrt{z}}{8}$
20. $\sqrt{\frac{28f^2}{9}}$ $\frac{2f\sqrt{7}}{3}$
21. **Dropped Object** You can use the expression $\sqrt{\frac{h}{16}}$ to find the time in seconds that it takes an object dropped from a height of h feet to hit the ground. You drop an object from a height of 63 feet. Write an expression in simplest form for the time it takes the object to hit the ground. Then approximate the time to the nearest second.
22. **Walking Speed** Your maximum walking speed in inches per second can be approximated using the expression $\sqrt{384l}$, where l is your leg length in inches. Suppose your leg length is 28 inches. Write an expression in simplest form for your maximum walking speed. Then approximate the speed to the nearest inch per second. $16\sqrt{42}$ **; 104 in./sec**

21. $\frac{3\sqrt{7}}{4}$; 2 sec

Simplify the expression.

B 23. $\sqrt{75x^2y}$ $5x\sqrt{3y}$
24. $\sqrt{\frac{500n}{4y^2}}$ $\frac{5\sqrt{5n}}{y}$
25. $\sqrt{7200m^2n^2}$ $60mn\sqrt{2}$
26. $\sqrt{\frac{5b^2}{125}}$ $\frac{b}{5}$

27a. yours: 4 nautical miles, your friend's: $4\sqrt{13}$ nautical miles

27b. *Sample answer:* For you and your friend on top of the lighthouse to see each other, you must first come close enough to be able to see to the same spot on the ocean. The first moment this happens is at the visual horizon both for you and your friend, so your distance from each other is the sum of your visual horizon and your friend's.

27. **Extended Problem Solving** The visual horizon is the distance you can see before your line of sight is blocked by Earth's surface. If you are in a boat on the ocean, the visual horizon in nautical miles can be approximated by the expression $\sqrt{4h}$, where h is the vertical distance in meters from your eye to the water's surface. Suppose your boat is approaching a lighthouse from which your friend is observing you. **27a–b. See margin.**
    a. **Calculate** Your eyes are 4 meters above the water's surface. Your friend's eyes are 52 meters above the water's surface. Find your visual horizon and your friend's visual horizon in simplest form.
    b. **Critical Thinking** You will be able to see the lighthouse when your distance from it is the sum of your visual horizon and your friend's. Use the diagram to explain why this is true.

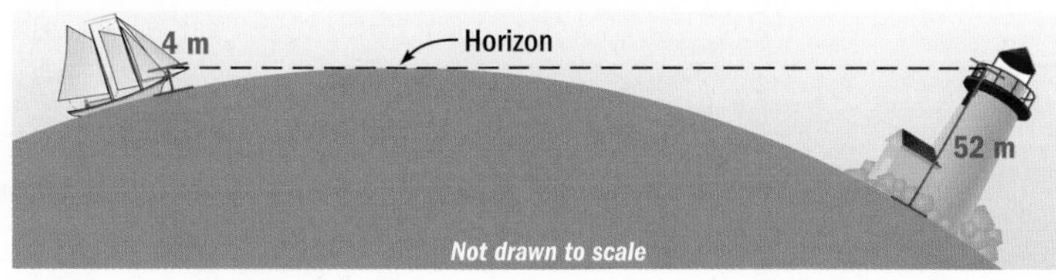

    c. **Interpret and Apply** Find the value of each expression in part (a) to the nearest nautical mile. Use the results to determine how far you will be from the lighthouse when you first see it. **4, about 14; 18 nautical miles**

28. ***Writing*** Describe how you could use the prime factorization of 450 to write $\sqrt{450}$ in simplest form. **See margin.**

Write the expression in simplest form.

C 29. $\sqrt{y^3}$ $y\sqrt{y}$ 30. $\sqrt{n^5}$ $n^2\sqrt{n}$ 31. $\sqrt{a^8}$ a^4 32. $\sqrt{n^9}$ $n^4\sqrt{n}$

33. **Challenge** Predict the next three numbers in the pattern: $\sqrt{2}, 2, \sqrt{6}, 2\sqrt{2}, \sqrt{10}, 2\sqrt{3}, \sqrt{14}, 4, \ldots$ $3\sqrt{2}, 2\sqrt{5}, \sqrt{22}$

Mixed Review

Evaluate the expression when $x = 6$, $y = 10$, and $z = 12$. *(Lesson 1.3)*

34. $x^2 + y^2$ 136 35. $x^2 + z^2$ 180 36. $z^2 - x^2$ 108 37. $y^2 - x^2$ 64

Write the fraction in simplest form. *(Lesson 4.3)*

38. $\frac{28x}{x^2}$ $\frac{28}{x}$ 39. $\frac{6y^3}{9y^2}$ $\frac{2y}{3}$ 40. $\frac{21n}{6n^3}$ $\frac{7}{2n^2}$ 41. $\frac{8cd}{40c^2}$ $\frac{d}{5c}$

Approximate the square root to the nearest integer. *(Lesson 9.1)*

42. $\sqrt{27}$ 5 43. $\sqrt{47}$ 7 44. $\sqrt{79}$ 9 45. $\sqrt{103}$ 10

Standardized Test Practice

46. **Multiple Choice** Which expression is *not* equivalent to $\sqrt{48}$? **B**
    A. $\sqrt{3 \cdot 16}$ B. $16\sqrt{3}$ C. $\sqrt{4^2 \cdot 3}$ D. $4\sqrt{3}$

47. **Multiple Choice** Which expression represents $\sqrt{\frac{9x}{y^2}}$ in simplest form? **I**
    F. $\frac{3x}{y}$ G. $\frac{\sqrt{3x}}{y}$ H. $\frac{\sqrt{9x}}{y}$ I. $\frac{3\sqrt{x}}{y}$

4 ASSESS

ASSESSMENT RESOURCES

For more assessment resources, see:
- Assessment Book
- Test and Practice Generator

MINI-QUIZ

Simplify the expression.

1. $\sqrt{192}$ $8\sqrt{3}$
2. $\sqrt{\frac{71}{81}}$ $\frac{\sqrt{71}}{9}$
3. $\sqrt{200j^2g}$ $10j\sqrt{2g}$
4. $\sqrt{\frac{400k}{625c^2}}$ $\frac{4\sqrt{k}}{5c}$
5. **Challenge** Predict the next three numbers in the pattern: $\frac{\sqrt{3}}{2}, \sqrt{3}, 1, 2, \frac{\sqrt{5}}{2}, \sqrt{5}, \frac{\sqrt{6}}{2}, \sqrt{6}, \ldots$. $\frac{\sqrt{7}}{2}, \sqrt{7}, \sqrt{2}$

5 FOLLOW-UP

DIAGNOSIS/REMEDIATION

- Study Guide in Chapter 9 Resource Book, pp. 19–20
- eTutorial Plus Online
- Extra Practice, p. 811
- Lesson Practice in Chapter 9 Resource Book, pp. 16–18

ENGLISH LEARNER SUPPORT

- Spanish Study Guide
- Multi-Language Visual Glossary
- Chapter Audio Summaries CDs

CHALLENGE

- Challenge Practice in Chapter 9 Resource Book, p. 21
- Teacher's Edition, p. 450F

28. See Additional Answers beginning on page AA1.

1 PLAN

Skill Check

Solve for x.

1. $32 + 48 + x = 180$ **100**
2. $90 + 54 + x = 180$ **36**
3. $15 + x + 85 = 180$ **80**
4. $x + 60 + 75 = 180$ **45**

LESSON OBJECTIVE

Prepare for solving problems that involve triangles.

2 TEACH

COMMON ERROR

Some students may be surprised that the angle measures of a triangle have a sum of 180°, instead of a number such as 150°, 175°, or 200°. Some students may have difficulty remembering this value. Suggest they memorize the fact that an equiangular triangle has three 60° angles to help them remember that the sum is 180°.

TEACHING TIP

Ask students to recall the definitions of *obtuse*, *right*, and *acute* angles.

Extra Examples

Example 1 Find the value of x.

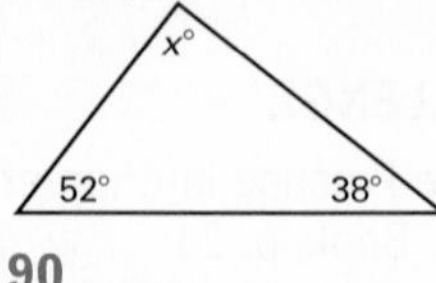

90

Example 2 Classify the triangle shown in Extra Example 1 by its angle measures. **right**

Student Reference

Triangles

▶ **Review** these topics in preparation for solving problems that involve triangles in Lessons 9.3, 9.6–9.8, and 10.1.

Sum of Angle Measures in a Triangle

The sum of the angle measures in any triangle is 180°, as the diagram below suggests. You can use this fact to find unknown measures in triangles.

Example **Find the value of *x*.**

$90° + 48° + x° = 180°$ **Sum of angle measures is 180°.**

$138 + x = 180$ **Add.**

$x = 42$ **Subtract 138 from each side.**

Answer The value of x is 42.

Classifying Triangles by Angle Measures

Triangles can be classified by the measures of their angles.

Acute triangle	**Right triangle**	**Obtuse triangle**	**Equiangular triangle**
3 acute angles	1 right angle	1 obtuse angle	3 congruent angles
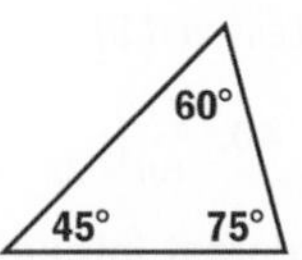	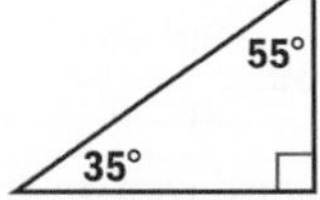	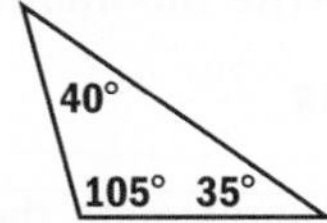	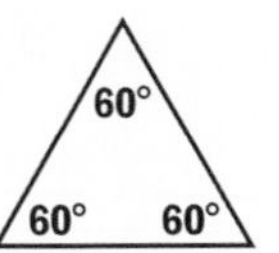

Example **Classify the triangle by its angle measures.**

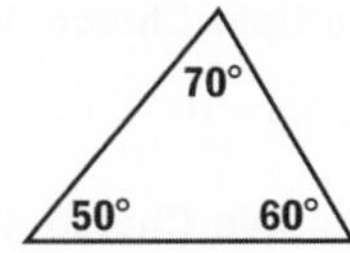

The triangle has 3 acute angles, so it is an acute triangle.

NCTM CURRICULUM STANDARDS

Standard 3: Analyze properties of 2-D shapes

Standard 4: Understand measurable attributes of objects

Classifying Triangles by Side Lengths

Triangles can be classified by the lengths of their sides.

Equilateral triangle
3 congruent sides

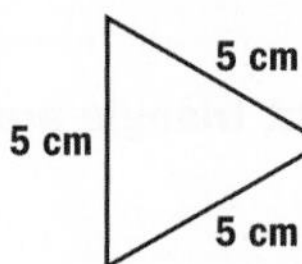

Isosceles triangle
At least 2 congruent sides

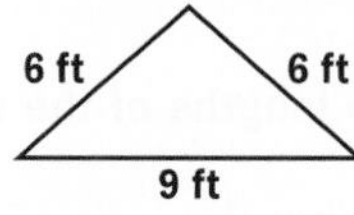

Scalene triangle
No congruent sides

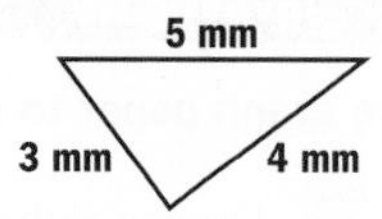

An equilateral triangle is isosceles and is also equiangular.

Example **Classify the triangle by its side lengths.**

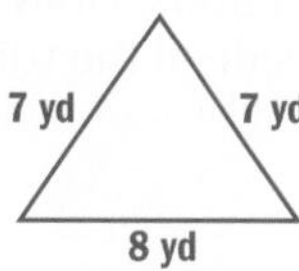

The triangle has two congruent sides, so it is an isosceles triangle.

Checkpoint

▶ **Test** your knowledge of triangles by solving these problems.

Find the value of *x*.

1. 45

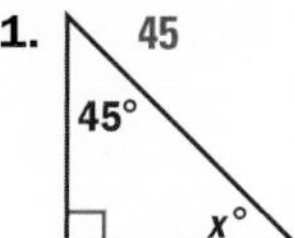

2. 120

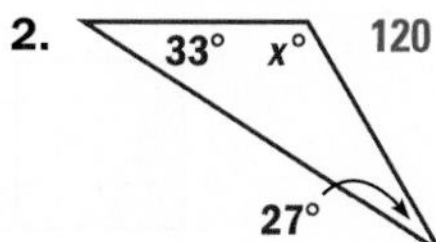

3. 85

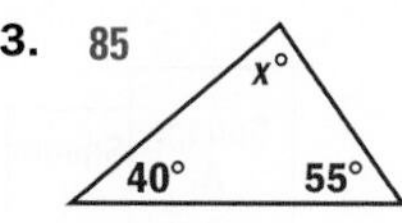

4. Pennants The angles at the wide end of the pennant have measures of 80° and 75°. Find the measure of the angle at the narrow end of the pennant. 25°

Classify the triangle by its angle measures.

5. 82°, 60°, 38° acute

6.

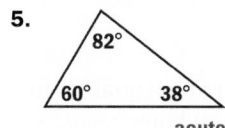

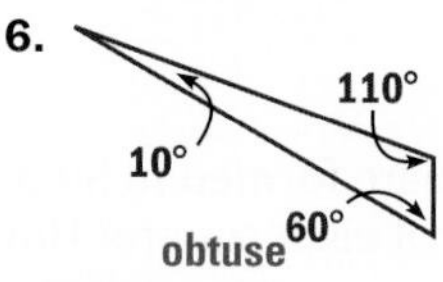

obtuse

7.

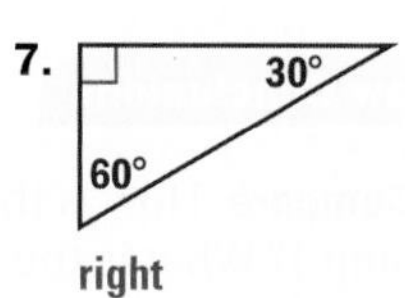

right

Classify the triangle by its side lengths.

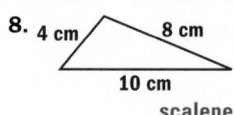

8. 4 cm, 8 cm, 10 cm scalene

9.

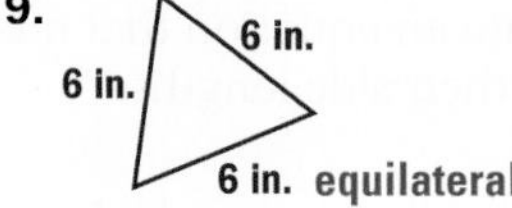

equilateral

10.

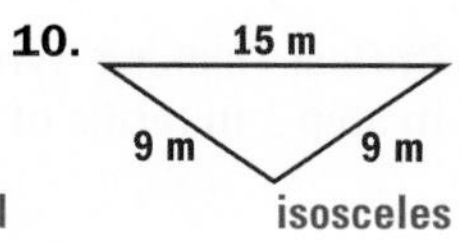

isosceles

Extra Examples

Example 3 Classify the triangle by its side lengths. **scalene**

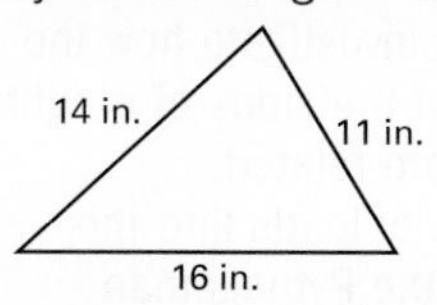

3 APPLY

Transparency

Even-numbered answers are available on transparencies.

Teaching Tip

In Exercise 9, some students may point out that this triangle meets the definitions of both an isosceles triangle and an equilateral triangle. Confirm that this is indeed true.

1 PLAN

INVESTIGATE THE CONCEPT

- Students investigate how the lengths of the sides of a right triangle are related.
- This activity leads into the study of the Pythagorean theorem in Lesson 9.3.

MATERIALS

Each student will need graph paper, pencil, scissors, and tape.

RECOMMENDED TIME

Work activity: 15 min
Discuss results: 10 min

GROUPING

Students should work individually.

2 TEACH

ALTERNATIVE STRATEGY

If you have square floor tiles in the classroom or cement paving stones on the school grounds, students can use string, masking tape, or chalk to model the shapes in steps 1 through 4 rather than cutting them out of graph paper.

3 CLOSE

KEY DISCOVERY

Students discover the Pythagorean theorem.

ASSESSMENT

1. How is the area of square C related to the areas of squares A and B? **The area of square C is equal to the sum of the areas of squares A and B.**

1–2. See Additional Answers beginning on page AA1.

Concept *Activity*

9.3 Investigating Right Triangles

Goal
Investigate how the lengths of the sides of a right triangle are related.

Materials
- graph paper
- pencil
- scissors
- tape

Investigate

Use graph paper to see how the lengths of the sides of a right triangle are related.

Draw a right triangle so that the sides that form the right angle have lengths of 3 units and 4 units. Draw a square on each side of the triangle.
Steps 1–4. Check work.

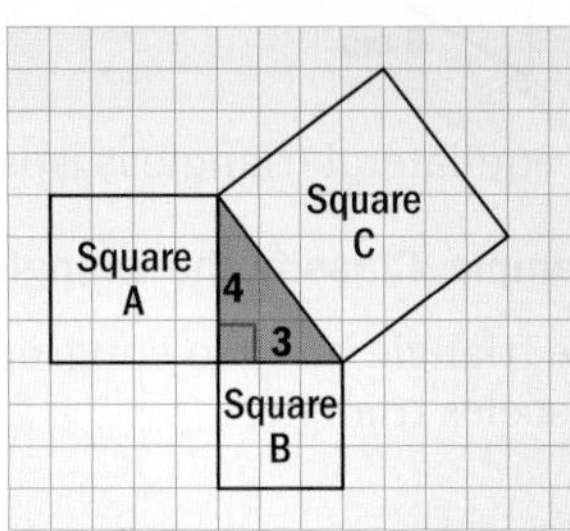

2. Cut out square A and square B. Arrange them side by side as shown.

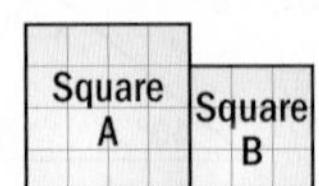

Draw two copies of the right triangle in Step 1 on the squares as shown.

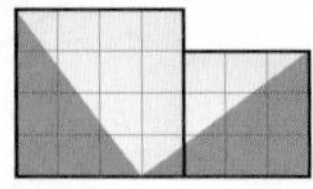

Cut along the longest side of the right triangles. Then reposition and tape the pieces as shown.

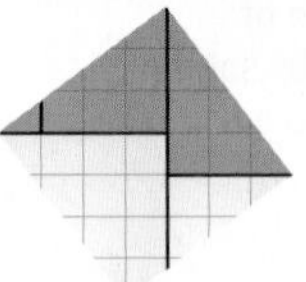

Position the square from Step 4 on the longest side of the triangle in Step 1. What do you notice? **It matches square C.**

Draw Conclusions

1. **Compare** How is the square formed in Step 4 related to square C in Step 1? What is the area of each square? How do you know? **See margin.**
2. *Writing* What is the length of a side of the square in Step 4? Explain. **See margin.**
3. **Critical Thinking** Write an equation that relates the areas of the squares in Step 1 in terms of their side lengths. $3^2 + 4^2 = 5^2$

NCTM CURRICULUM STANDARDS
Standard 3: Analyze properties of 2-D shapes
Standard 9: Grasp connections among math ideas

LESSON

9.3 The Pythagorean Theorem

BEFORE	Now	WHY?
You used square roots.	You'll use the Pythagorean theorem to solve problems.	So you can find the length of a side of a TV screen, as in Ex. 19.

Vocabulary

hypotenuse, p. 465
leg, p. 465
Pythagorean theorem, p. 465

Bridges The William H. Harsha Bridge is a cable-stayed bridge that spans the Ohio River between Maysville, Kentucky, and Aberdeen, Ohio. About how long is the cable shown in red?

In a right triangle, the **hypotenuse** is the side opposite the right angle. The **legs** are the sides that form the right angle. The lengths of the legs and the length of the hypotenuse of a right triangle are related by the **Pythagorean theorem**.

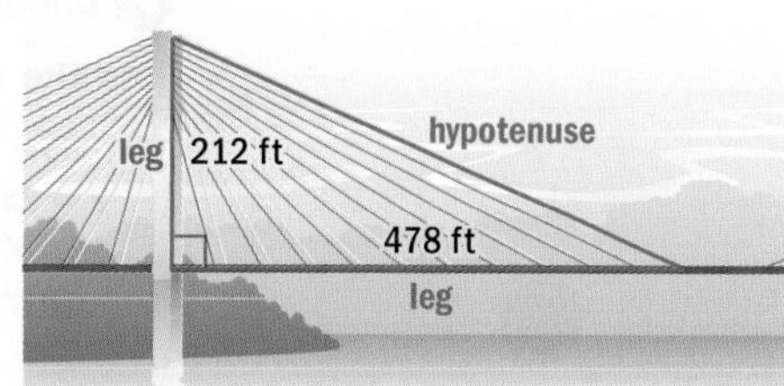

Pythagorean Theorem

Words For any right triangle, the sum of the squares of the lengths of the legs equals the square of the length of the hypotenuse.

Algebra $a^2 + b^2 = c^2$

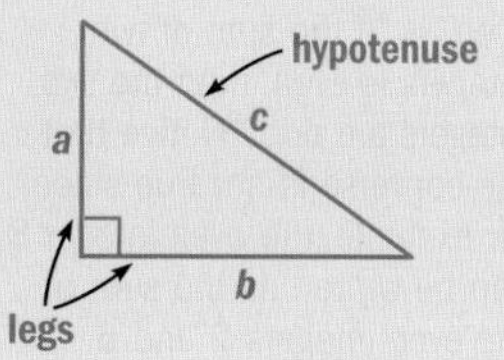

Example 1 *Finding the Length of a Hypotenuse*

To find the length (to the nearest foot) of the cable shown above, use the right triangle formed by the tower, the bridge surface, and the cable.

$a^2 + b^2 = c^2$	Pythagorean theorem
$212^2 + 478^2 = c^2$	Substitute 212 for a and 478 for b.
$44{,}944 + 228{,}484 = c^2$	Evaluate powers.
$273{,}428 = c^2$	Add.
$\sqrt{273{,}428} = c$	Take positive square root of each side.
$523 \approx c$	Use a calculator. Round to nearest whole number.

Answer The length of the cable is about 523 feet.

NCTM CURRICULUM STANDARDS
Standard 2: Represent situations using algebraic symbols
Standard 3: Analyze properties of 2-D shapes
Standard 9: Grasp connections among math ideas

1 PLAN

Skill Check
Simplify.

1. $\sqrt{2^2 + 3^2}$ — $\sqrt{13}$
2. $\sqrt{9^2 - 4^2}$ — $\sqrt{65}$
3. $\sqrt{5^2 + 8^2}$ — $\sqrt{89}$
4. $\sqrt{11^2 - 7^2}$ — $6\sqrt{2}$

Lesson Objective

Use the Pythagorean theorem to solve problems.

Pacing

Suggested Number of Days
Basic Course: 1 day
Average Course: 1 day
Advanced Course: 1 day
Block: 0.5 block with 9.4

Teaching Resources

For a complete list of Teaching Resources, see page 450B.

Transparency

Warm-Up Exercises for this lesson are available on a transparency.

2 TEACH

Motivating the Lesson

Ask students to give other real-world examples of right triangles.

TIPS *for* NEW TEACHERS

Use an equilateral triangle and an isosceles triangle to demonstrate that the Pythagorean theorem applies only to right triangles. See Tips for New Teachers in the *Chapter 9 Resource Book*.

Extra Examples

Example 1 Kyle is building a triangular model of a mountain for the scenery for a play. Find the length of the base of the model, to the nearest foot. **14 ft**

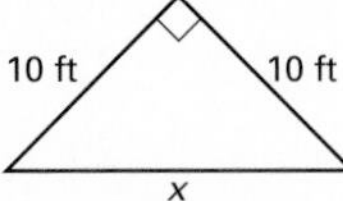

Example 2 Find the unknown length b in simplest form. **24**

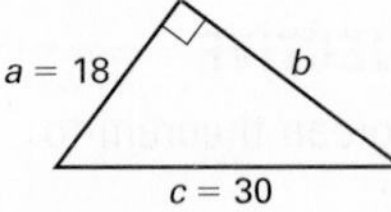

Example 3 Determine whether the triangle with the given side lengths is a right triangle.

a. 2, 4, 5 **no**

b. 9, 40, 41 **yes**

DIFFERENTIATING INSTRUCTION

Alternative Teaching Strategy
Have students use rods of different lengths to form right triangles of different sizes. They can then measure the sides to confirm that the Pythagorean theorem applies to all right triangles.

CONCEPT CHECK

How do you find the length of the hypotenuse of a right triangle if the lengths of the other two sides are known? **Find the sum of the squares of the other two side lengths and take the square root of the sum.**

DAILY PUZZLER

The sides of a triangle have lengths $4x$, $5x$, and $7x$. Is the triangle a right triangle? Explain. **No. *Sample answer:* The ratio of the lengths is 4 : 5 : 7, but $4^2 + 5^2 \neq 7^2$.**

Example 2 *Finding the Length of a Leg*

Find the unknown length *a* in simplest form.

$a^2 + b^2 = c^2$	**Pythagorean theorem**
$a^2 + 10^2 = 12^2$	**Substitute.**
$a^2 + 100 = 144$	**Evaluate powers.**
$a^2 = 44$	**Subtract 100 from each side.**
$a = \sqrt{44}$	**Take positive square root of each side.**
$a = 2\sqrt{11}$	**Simplify.**

b = 10, c = 12, a

Answer The unknown length a is $2\sqrt{11}$ units.

Checkpoint

Find the unknown length. Write your answer in simplest form.

1. 15 (c = 25, a = 20, b)

2. 26 (a = 10, b = 24, c)

3. $2\sqrt{13}$ (b = 12, c = 14, a)

Reading *Algebra*

The converse of the theorem "If two integers are odd, then the sum of the integers is even" is "If the sum of two integers is even, then the two integers are odd." Notice that the converse is *not* true since, for example, the even integer 8 can be written as the sum of the even integers 2 and 6.

Converse of the Pythagorean Theorem The Pythagorean theorem can be written in "if-then" form.

Theorem: If **a triangle is a right triangle**, then $a^2 + b^2 = c^2$.

If you reverse the two parts of the statement, the new statement is called the *converse* of the Pythagorean theorem.

Converse: If $a^2 + b^2 = c^2$, then **the triangle is a right triangle**.

Although not all converses of true statements are true, the converse of the Pythagorean theorem is true. You can use it to determine whether a triangle is a right triangle.

Study *Strategy*

When determining whether three given lengths a, b, and c satisfy the equation $a^2 + b^2 = c^2$, always let c be the greatest length.

Example 3 *Identifying Right Triangles*

Determine whether the triangle with the given side lengths is a right triangle.

a. $a = 3, b = 5, c = 7$

b. $a = 15, b = 8, c = 17$

Solution

a.
$a^2 + b^2 = c^2$
$3^2 + 5^2 \stackrel{?}{=} 7^2$
$9 + 25 \stackrel{?}{=} 49$
$34 \neq 49$

Answer Not a right triangle

b.
$a^2 + b^2 = c^2$
$15^2 + 8^2 \stackrel{?}{=} 17^2$
$225 + 64 \stackrel{?}{=} 289$
$289 = 289$ ✓

Answer A right triangle

9.3 Exercises

More Practice, p. 811

Guided Practice

Vocabulary Check

1. Copy and complete: The side opposite the right angle of a right triangle is called the _?_. **hypotenuse**

2. The lengths of the sides of a triangle are 6, 8, and 10. Explain how you can determine whether the triangle is a right triangle. **See margin.**

Skill Check

In Exercises 3–5, find the unknown length.

3. 39 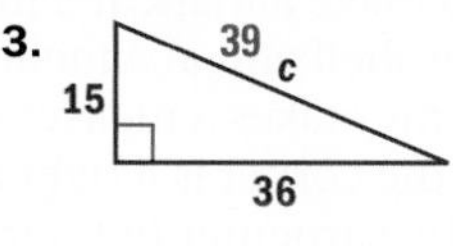

4. 24 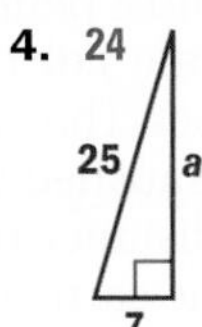

5. 12 9 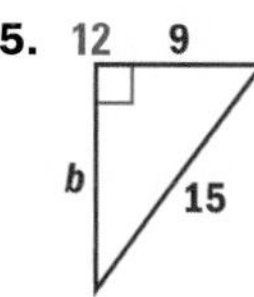

Guided Problem Solving

6. **Ladders** A ladder that is 15 feet long is placed against a wall. The bottom of the ladder is 5 feet from the wall. To the nearest foot, how far up the wall does the ladder reach?

   1) Copy the diagram. Label the known lengths. Label the unknown length x. **See margin.**
   2) Use the Pythagorean theorem to write an equation you can use to find the value of x. $5^2 + x^2 = 15^2$
   3) Solve the equation in Step 2 for x. $x = \sqrt{200} = 10\sqrt{2}$
   4) Round your answer from Step 3 to the nearest whole number. **14 ft**

2. ***Sample answer:*** **Find the sum of the squares of the smaller numbers, 6 and 8. If this sum equals the square of the larger number, 10, then the triangle is a right triangle. In this case, $6^2 + 8^2 = 36 + 64 = 100 = 10^2$, so the triangle is a right triangle.**

Practice and Problem Solving

Homework *Help*

Example	Exercises
1	7–9, 20, 22–24, 29–30
2	10–12, 19, 25–28
3	13–18, 20–21

- More Examples
- eTutorial Plus

Find the unknown length. Write your answer in simplest form.

A 7. 29 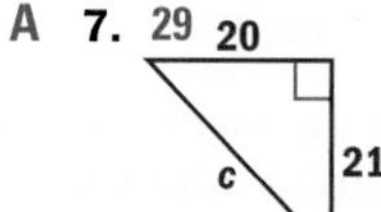

8. 13 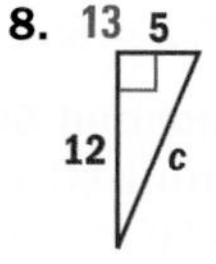

9. $\sqrt{34}$ 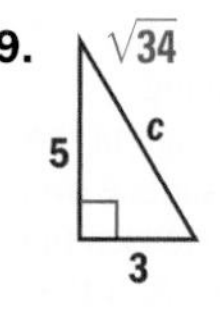

10. 24 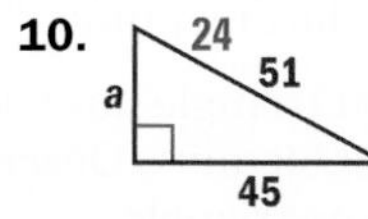

11. $2\sqrt{31}$ 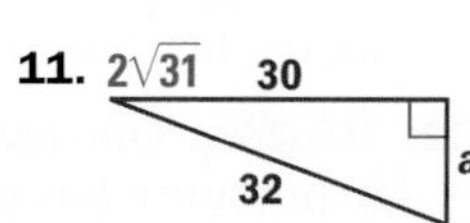

12. $\sqrt{871}$ 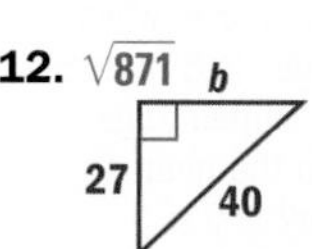

3 APPLY

ASSIGNMENT GUIDE

Basic Course

Day 1: pp. 467–469 Exs. 7–16, 19, 23, 25–27, 31, 37–43

Average Course

Day 1: pp. 467–469 Exs. 9–12, 16–24, 28–34, 37–44

Advanced Course

Day 1: pp. 467–469 Exs. 9–12, 16–21, 24, 28–38*, 41–44

Block

pp. 467–469 Exs. 9–12, 16–24, 28–34, 37–44 (with 9.4)

Extra Practice

- Student Edition, p. 811
- Chapter 9 Resource Book, pp. 24–26
- Test and Practice Generator

Transparency

Even-numbered answers are available on transparencies.

Homework Check

When you review students' homework for this lesson, go over the following exercises to check understanding of key concepts.

Basic: 7, 10, 13, 19, 26

Average: 9, 11, 16, 20, 22

Advanced: 9, 12, 17, 21, 24

Common Error

In Exercises 10–12, watch for students who find the sum of the squares of the two known side lengths even though one of them is the hypotenuse of the triangle.

6. Step 1:

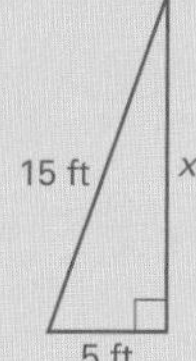

22–24. Sample answers are given.

22. Calculator; the squares of 87 and 136 are not easily calculated mentally or on paper.

23. Mental math; the squares of 1 and 2 can be calculated quickly mentally.

24. Paper and pencil; the squares of 15 and 20 can be calculated easily with paper and pencil.

32. *Sample answer:* Use the Pythagorean theorem to find the length x of the other leg: $32^2 + x^2 = 68^2$, $x^2 = \sqrt{3600}$, $x = 60$ units. The legs represent the base and height of the triangle. Assign one as the base and one as the height (it does not matter which is which) in the area formula $A = \frac{1}{2}bh$: $A = \frac{1}{2}(60)(32) = 960$, so the area is 960 square units.

20. 5 in. *Sample answer:* By the converse of the Pythagorean theorem, a triangle with sides of length 3, 4, and 5 is a right triangle, with right angle opposite the longest side, because $3^2 + 4^2 = 5^2$.

21a. *Sample answer:* Let $n = 5$. Then $2n = 2(5) = 10$, $n^2 - 1 = 5^2 - 1 = 24$, and $n^2 + 1 = 5^2 + 1 = 26$.

21b. *Sample answer:* $10^2 + 24^2 = 100 + 576 = 676 = 26^2$

Determine whether the triangle with the given side lengths is a right triangle.

13. 2, 3, 4 **no** **14.** 12, 35, 37 **yes** **15.** 5, 12, 13 **yes**

16. 8, 16, 18 **no** **17.** 11, 60, 61 **yes** **18.** 8, 9, 12 **no**

19. Television Screen A television screen is a rectangle, and its size is indicated by the length of a diagonal. A 42 inch television screen is about 21 inches high. How wide is the screen to the nearest inch? **36 in.**

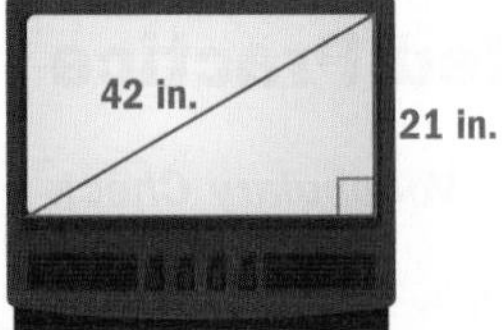

20. Carpentry To determine whether the corner of a shelf is actually a right angle, a carpenter uses a ruler and a pencil to make a mark at 3 inches along one side of the shelf and at 4 inches along the other. The carpenter takes a measurement and is satisfied that the corner is a right angle. What distance did the carpenter measure? Why does the carpenter's method work?

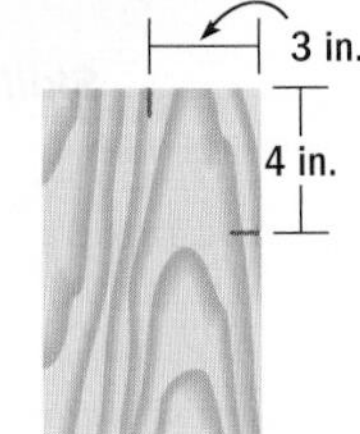

21. Pythagorean Triples A *Pythagorean triple* is a set of three positive integers a, b, and c such that $a^2 + b^2 = c^2$. That is, the integers a, b, and c are a Pythagorean triple if a triangle with side lengths a, b, and c is a right triangle. You can generate a Pythagorean triple by substituting an integer greater than 1 into each of these expressions: $2n$, $n^2 - 1$, and $n^2 + 1$. For example, the integers 3, 4, and 5 form a Pythagorean triple that is generated by the given expressions when $n = 2$.

a. Choose an integer value of n greater than 2 and substitute the given value into each of the given expressions.

b. Verify that the numbers you generated form a Pythagorean triple.

The lengths of the legs of a right triangle are given. Tell whether you would use *mental math, paper and pencil,* or a *calculator* to find the length of the hypotenuse. Explain your answers. **22–24. See margin.**

22. $a = 87$, $b = 136$ **23.** $a = 1$, $b = 2$ **24.** $a = 15$, $b = 20$

The lengths of two sides of a right triangle are given. Find the length of the third side.

B **25.** $a = 28$, $c = 53$ **45** **26.** $a = 48$, $c = 73$ **55** **27.** $b = 24$, $c = 26$ **10**

28. $b = 77$, $c = 85$ **36** **29.** $a = 84$, $b = 80$ **116** **30.** $a = 48$, $b = 189$ **195**

31. Synchronized Swimming At the beginning of a performance, two synchronized swimmers start at opposite corners of a rectangular pool that is 50 meters long and 25 meters wide. They swim toward each other along a diagonal and meet halfway. To the nearest tenth of a meter, how far from their starting points do the swimmers meet? **28.0 m**

32. *Writing* One leg of a right triangle has a length of 32 units. The hypotenuse has a length of 68 units. Describe how you would go about finding the area of the triangle. **See margin.**

In the **Real World**

Synchronized Swimming In a pool that meets minimum standards for an Olympic synchronized swimming competition, the bottom of the pool has a sloped surface over which the depth decreases from 3 meters to 2.5 meters. If the horizontal distance over which the depth changes is 8 meters, how long is the sloped edge of the bottom to the nearest tenth of a meter? **8.0 m**

34b. 1.1 m. *Sample answer:* After subtracting the extra 10 centimeters for each of the 6 attachment points, you have $4.2 - 0.6 = 3.6$ meters of wire. Each diagonal can be $3.6 \div 3 = 1.2$ meters long. By the Pythagorean theorem, if h is the greatest height at which you can attach the wires, $0.5^2 + h^2 = 1.2^2$. Solving gives $h^2 = 1.19$, so $h \approx 1.1$ m.

33. Soccer In a college soccer league, the smallest field allowed is a rectangle 65 yards wide and 110 yards long. The largest field allowed is a rectangle 80 yards wide and 120 yards long. To the nearest yard, how much longer is the diagonal of the largest field than the diagonal of the smallest field? **16 yd**

34. Extended Problem Solving You plan to support a young tree by attaching three wires to the tree. Your plan is to attach one end of each wire to the tree at a point 1.2 meters above the ground, and the other end of each wire to a stake in the ground at a point 0.5 meter from the tree.

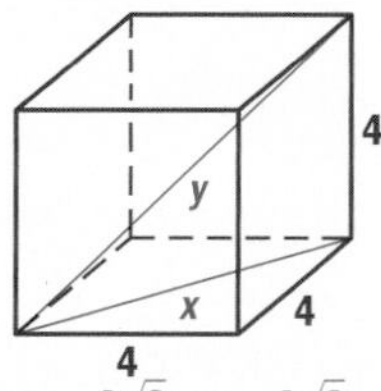

a. Calculate Find the total amount of wire you need. Include an extra 10 centimeters of wire at each attachment point. **4.5 m**

b. Interpret and Apply You have only 4.2 meters of wire and plan to attach each wire 0.5 meter out from the tree, allowing extra wire as described in part (a). To the nearest tenth of a meter, how far up the tree can you attach each wire? Explain.

Challenge Find each unknown length in simplest form. In Exercise 36, use the fact that the edges of a cube meet at right angles.

C **35.**

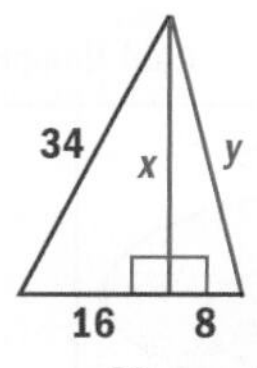

$x = 30$, $y = 2\sqrt{241}$

36.

$x = 4\sqrt{2}$, $y = 4\sqrt{3}$

Mixed Review

Write the decimal as a fraction or mixed number. *(Lesson 5.1)*

37. 0.16 $\frac{4}{25}$ **38.** −0.45 $-\frac{9}{20}$ **39.** 1.075 $1\frac{3}{40}$ **40.** −3.875 $-3\frac{7}{8}$

41. Tree House You are building a tree house. In a scale drawing of the tree house, the length of one wall is 6 inches. The length of the actual wall is 5 feet. Find the scale of the drawing. *(Lesson 6.6)* **1 : 10**

42. Eating Out At a restaurant, you choose a first course, a main dish, and a vegetable for dinner. You can choose fruit cup or soup for the first course. For the main course, you can choose steak, chicken, fish, or lasagna. For a vegetable, you can choose beans, broccoli, or carrots. Find the number of possible meals you can choose. *(Lesson 6.8)* **24 meals**

Standardized Test Practice

43. Multiple Choice Which lengths are *not* side lengths of a right triangle? **C**

A. 9, 12, 15 **B.** 13, 84, 85 **C.** 8, 14, 18 **D.** 24, 70, 74

44. Short Response A ship travels 7 miles due north, then 20 miles due east. The ship then sails directly back to its starting point. Explain how you would find the total distance of the trip. Then find the distance to the nearest mile.

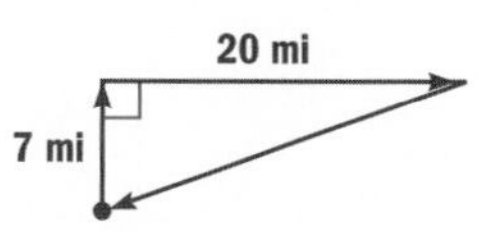

44. *Sample answer:* First find the distance d directly back using the Pythagorean theorem: $7^2 + 20^2 = d^2$, $449 = d^2$, $d = \sqrt{449} \approx 21$. Now add the distances to find the total distance: $7 + 20 + 21 = 48$. The ship sailed about 48 miles.

4 ASSESS

Assessment Resources

For more assessment resources, see:
- Assessment Book
- Test and Practice Generator

Mini-Quiz

Determine whether the triangle with the given side lengths is a right triangle.

1. 10, 24, 26 **yes**

2. 15, 36, 38 **no**

The lengths of two sides of a right triangle are given. Find the length of the third side.

3. $a = 11$, $b = 60$ **61**

4. $a = 16$, $c = 34$ **30**

5. Challenge Find each unknown length in simplest form.

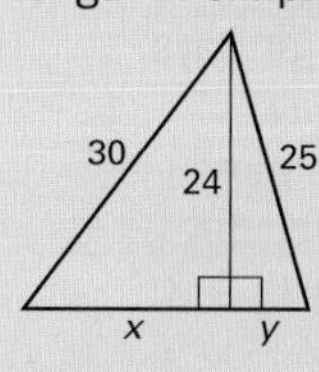

$x = 18$, $y = 7$

5 FOLLOW-UP

Diagnosis/Remediation

- Study Guide in Chapter 9 Resource Book, pp. 27–28
- eTutorial Plus Online
- Extra Practice, p. 811
- Lesson Practice in Chapter 9 Resource Book, pp. 24–26

English Learner Support

- Spanish Study Guide
- Multi-Language Visual Glossary
- Chapter Audio Summaries CDs

Challenge

- Challenge Practice in Chapter 9 Resource Book, p. 29
- Teacher's Edition, p. 450F

1 PLAN

Skill Check

Write the fraction or mixed number as a decimal.

1. $\frac{3}{8}$ 0.375
2. $\frac{11}{16}$ 0.6875
3. $4\frac{1}{2}$ 4.5
4. $6\frac{1}{3}$ $6.\overline{3}$
5. Simplify $\sqrt{49}$. 7

Lesson Objective

Compare and order real numbers.

Pacing

Suggested Number of Days

Basic Course: 1 day
Average Course: 1 day
Advanced Course: 1 day
Block: 0.5 block with 9.3

Teaching Resources

For a complete list of Teaching Resources, see page 450B.

Transparency

Warm-Up Exercises for this lesson are available on a transparency. A support transparency is available for Examples 2 and 3, and Checkpoint Exercises 6–11.

2 TEACH

Motivating the Lesson

Ask students what rational numbers are, and have them provide several examples.

LESSON 9.4

Real Numbers

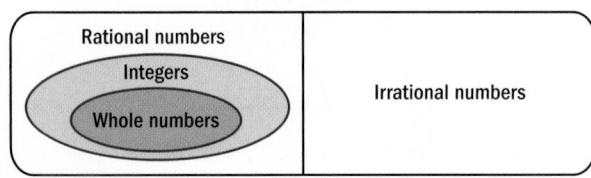

BEFORE	Now	WHY?
You ordered rational numbers.	You'll compare and order real numbers.	So you can compare the periods of two pendulums, as in Ex. 34.

Vocabulary

irrational number, p. 470
real number, p. 470

In Lesson 5.1, you learned that a rational number is a number that can be written as a quotient of two integers. All rational numbers have decimal forms that terminate or repeat.

An **irrational number** is a number that cannot be written as a quotient of two integers. The decimal form of an irrational number neither terminates nor repeats. For example, in the irrational number below, the pattern of ones separated by an increasing number of zeros continues without end. The decimal neither terminates nor repeats.

$$0.101001000100001000001000000 1...$$

The **real numbers** consist of all rational and irrational numbers. The Venn diagram shows the relationships among the real numbers.

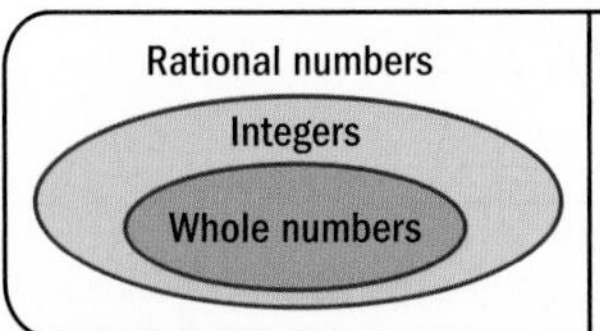

Study Strategy

Notice in part (c) of Example 1 that $\sqrt{19}$ is irrational. The square root of any whole number that is not a perfect square is irrational.

Example 1 Classifying Real Numbers

	Number	Decimal Form	Decimal Type	Type
a.	$\frac{5}{8}$	$\frac{5}{8} = 0.625$	Terminating	Rational
b.	$\frac{5}{6}$	$\frac{5}{6} = 0.83333... = 0.8\overline{3}$	Repeating	Rational
c.	$\sqrt{19}$	$\sqrt{19} = 4.35889894...$	Nonterminating, nonrepeating	Irrational

Checkpoint

Tell whether the number is *rational* or *irrational*.

1. $\frac{2}{3}$ rational
2. $\sqrt{100}$ rational
3. $\sqrt{6}$ irrational
4. $\sqrt{\frac{16}{25}}$ rational
5. **Critical Thinking** Consider the positive square roots of the whole numbers from 1 to 10. What percent of these numbers are irrational?

5. 70%

NCTM CURRICULUM STANDARDS

Standard 1: Understand relationships among numbers; Understand number systems

Review *Help*

For help with using a compass, see p. 794.

Graphing Irrational Numbers You can graph an irrational number on a number line. For instance, to graph $\sqrt{2}$, draw a right triangle with one leg on the number line and each leg with a length of 1 unit, as shown. By the Pythagorean theorem, the length of the hypotenuse is $\sqrt{1^2 + 1^2} = \sqrt{2}$.

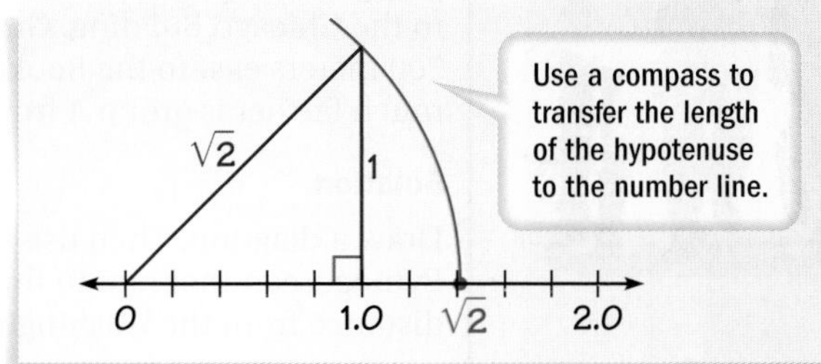

Notice that the graph of $\sqrt{2}$ is close to the graph of 1.4. So, $\sqrt{2} \approx 1.4$, which agrees with the decimal form of $\sqrt{2}$, which is 1.41421356. . . .

Example 2 *Comparing Real Numbers*

Copy and complete $\sqrt{2}$? $\frac{9}{5}$ using <, >, or =.

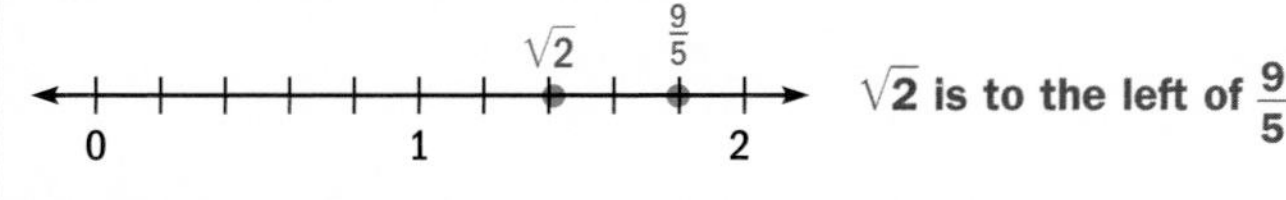

$\sqrt{2}$ is to the left of $\frac{9}{5}$.

Answer $\sqrt{2} < \frac{9}{5}$

Example 3 *Ordering Real Numbers*

Use a number line to order the numbers $\frac{4}{3}$, −2.8, $\sqrt{3}$, and $-\sqrt{5}$ from least to greatest.

Graph the numbers on a number line and read them from left to right.

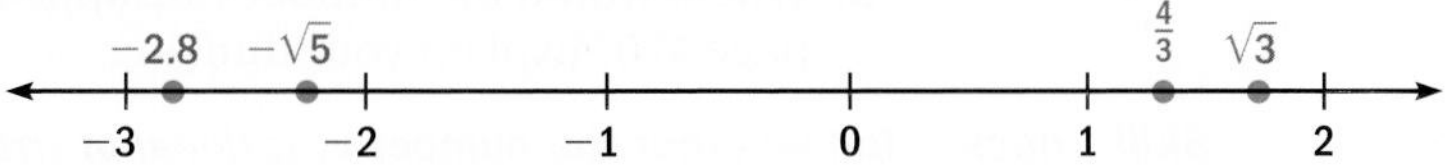

Answer From least to greatest, the numbers are −2.8, $-\sqrt{5}$, $\frac{4}{3}$, and $\sqrt{3}$.

Study *Strategy*

Another Way You can compare and order real numbers by using a calculator to find decimal forms of the numbers, then comparing and ordering the decimals.

Checkpoint

Copy and complete the statement using <, >, or =.

6. $\sqrt{7}$? $\frac{8}{3}$ < **7.** $-\frac{3}{2}$? $-\sqrt{2}$ < **8.** $-3\sqrt{2}$? -4.2 < **9.** $\frac{15}{4}$? $\sqrt{15}$ <

Use a number line to order the numbers from least to greatest.

10. 2.9, $\sqrt{10}$, $\frac{7}{3}$, $2\sqrt{2}$ $\frac{7}{3}$, $2\sqrt{2}$, 2.9, $\sqrt{10}$

11. $-\frac{16}{3}$, $-\sqrt{22}$, $-3\sqrt{2}$, −4.6 $-\frac{16}{3}$, $-\sqrt{22}$, −4.6, $-3\sqrt{2}$

TIPS *for* NEW TEACHERS

When students are asked to compare numbers that are represented in different ways, urge them to rewrite the numbers in the same form before comparing them. See Tips for New Teachers in the *Chapter 9 Resource Book*.

Extra Examples

Example 1 Tell whether the number is *rational* or *irrational*.

a. $\frac{1}{5}$ **rational**

b. $\frac{1}{9}$ **rational**

c. $\sqrt{22}$ **irrational**

Example 2 Copy and complete $\sqrt{5}$? $\frac{11}{4}$ using <, >, or =. <

Example 3 Use a number line to order the numbers $-\sqrt{3}$, $\sqrt{7}$, $\frac{21}{8}$, $-\frac{9}{5}$ from least to greatest.
$-\frac{9}{5}$, $-\sqrt{3}$, $\frac{21}{8}$, $\sqrt{7}$

NOTETAKING

After presenting Example 1, discuss how you can tell whether a number is rational or irrational. Encourage students to write a summary of the method in their notebooks.

DIFFERENTIATING INSTRUCTION

Alternative Teaching Strategy
Create a group of notecards with a rational or irrational number written on each one. Give each student one of the cards and then have groups of students work together to arrange their numbers in order from least to greatest.

Extra Examples

Example 4 Starting at their campsite, Alaina and Bob walk two separate paths that are each 500 feet long. Alaina walks 400 feet east and then 100 feet south. Bob walks 200 feet south and then 300 feet east. Who is farther from the campsite and by how many feet? **Alaina; about 52 ft**

CONCEPT CHECK

Which rational numbers have square roots that are irrational? **those positive rational numbers having either a numerator or denominator (or both) that is not a perfect square when the rational number is written in simplest form**

DAILY PUZZLER

True or *false*: Every nonrepeating decimal number is a terminating decimal number, and therefore is rational. Justify your answer. **False. *Sample answer:* Numbers such as $\sqrt{2}$ are nonrepeating decimal numbers that are irrational.**

Example 4 *Using Irrational Numbers*

Landmark Buildings Your class is visiting historical landmarks in Chicago. Outside the Washington Block, you break up into two groups. Group A walks about 800 meters east and 200 meters south to the Chicago Building. Group B walks about 600 meters south and 200 meters east to the Rookery Building. To the nearest 10 meters, how much farther is group A from the Washington Block than group B is?

Solution

Draw a diagram. Then use the Pythagorean theorem to find each distance from the Washington Block.

Group A: $\sqrt{800^2 + 200^2} = \sqrt{680{,}000} \approx \mathbf{825}$

Group B: $\sqrt{600^2 + 200^2} = \sqrt{400{,}000} \approx \mathbf{632}$

Difference in distances: 825 − 632 = 193

Answer To the nearest 10 meters, group A is about 190 meters farther from the Washington Block than group B is.

9.4 Exercises

More Practice, p. 811

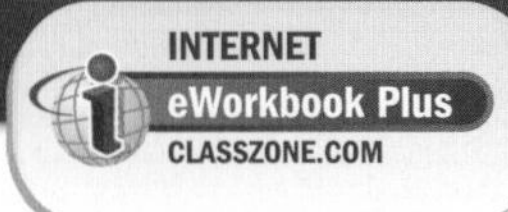

Guided Practice

Vocabulary Check

1. Explain what an irrational number is. Give an example. **See margin.**
2. Where would the number $7.\overline{52}$ appear in the Venn diagram on page 470? Explain your thinking. **See margin.**

Skill Check **Tell whether the number is *rational* or *irrational*.**

3. $\frac{2}{7}$ **rational** 4. $\sqrt{49}$ **rational** 5. $-\sqrt{71}$ **irrational** 6. $8.\overline{34}$ **rational**

Copy and complete the statement using <, >, or =.

7. $-\sqrt{7}$? -2 **<** 8. $\sqrt{11}$? $\sqrt{9}$ **>** 9. $\sqrt{16}$? $\frac{8}{3}$ **>** 10. $\frac{5}{3}$? $\sqrt{2}$ **>**

11. **Fences** A wire fence with wooden posts and rails has the dimensions shown. Each section of fence has a diagonal support brace as shown. Is the exact length of the brace a *rational* or an *irrational* number of feet? **irrational**

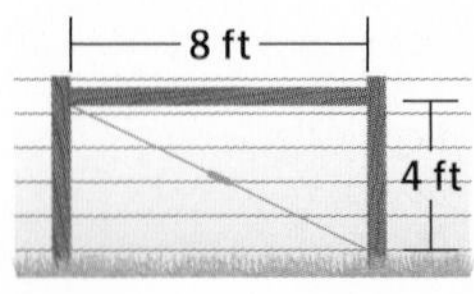

1. A number that cannot be written as the quotient of two integers. *Sample answer:* $\sqrt{11}$

2. Inside the region for the rational numbers but outside the oval for the integers. *Sample answer:* $7.\overline{52} = 7\frac{52}{99} = \frac{745}{99}$, so it is a quotient of integers, though not an integer itself.

Practice and Problem Solving

Homework *Help*

Example	Exercises
1	12-19, 28-32
2	20-23
3	24-27
4	33-35

Online Resources
CLASSZONE.COM

- More Examples
- eTutorial Plus

Tell whether the number is *rational* or *irrational*.

A **12.** $\frac{3}{4}$ rational **13.** $\sqrt{8}$ irrational **14.** $-\sqrt{81}$ rational **15.** $\frac{\sqrt{16}}{5}$ rational

16. $\sqrt{\frac{16}{5}}$ irrational **17.** $-\sqrt{14.4}$ irrational **18.** $17.\overline{65}$ rational **19.** $\sqrt{10.\overline{1}}$ irrational

Copy and complete the statement using <, >, or =.

20. $\frac{5}{2}$ _?_ $\sqrt{6.25}$ = **21.** $4\sqrt{3}$ _?_ $\frac{27}{4}$ > **22.** $\sqrt{32}$ _?_ 5.6 > **23.** $\sqrt{0.5}$ _?_ 0.5 >

Use a number line to order the numbers from least to greatest.

24. 3.5, $2\sqrt{3}$, $\sqrt{13}$, $\frac{19}{5}$, $3\frac{1}{4}$, $\sqrt{8}$ **25.** $\sqrt{4}$, $-\sqrt{5}$, 0, $\frac{9}{5}$, -2, $\sqrt{3}$

26. $\frac{17}{2}$, 8.6, $\sqrt{64}$, $3\sqrt{6}$, $7\frac{3}{4}$, $\sqrt{50}$ **27.** -4, $-\sqrt{18}$, $-\sqrt{\frac{67}{4}}$, $-\frac{25}{6}$

24. $\sqrt{8}$, $3\frac{1}{4}$, $2\sqrt{3}$, 3.5, $\sqrt{13}$, $\frac{19}{5}$

25. $-\sqrt{5}$, -2, 0, $\sqrt{3}$, $\frac{9}{5}$, $\sqrt{4}$

26. $\sqrt{50}$, $3\sqrt{6}$, $7\frac{3}{4}$, $\sqrt{64}$, $\frac{17}{2}$, 8.6

27. $-\sqrt{18}$, $-\frac{25}{6}$, $-\sqrt{\frac{67}{4}}$, -4

Copy and complete the statement using *always*, *sometimes*, or *never*. Explain your reasoning.

28. A negative integer is _?_ a whole number.

29. A square root of a positive number is _?_ an irrational number.

30. A real number is _?_ a rational number. **30–31. See margin.**

31. A whole number is _?_ an irrational number.

32. *Writing* The area of a square is 7 square meters. Is the perimeter of the square a *rational* or an *irrational* number of meters? Explain. **See margin.**

33. Geometry A rectangle is twice as long as it is wide, and it has an area of 20 square meters.

a. Let w represent the width of the rectangle. Write a variable expression in terms of w for the length of the rectangle. $2w$

b. Use the formula for the area of a rectangle to write an equation for the area of the given rectangle. $20 = (2w)(w)$, or $20 = 2w^2$

c. Find the width of the rectangle to the nearest tenth of a meter. 3.2 m

d. Find the length of the rectangle to the nearest tenth of a meter. 6.3 m

34. Pendulums The period of a pendulum is the time that it takes the pendulum to swing from one side to the other and back. A pendulum's period P (in seconds) and its length l (in feet) are related by the equation $P = 1.1\sqrt{l}$.

The giant pendulum in the Science Museum of Virginia in Richmond is about 96 feet long. The giant pendulum in the New Detroit Science Center in Detroit is 40 feet long. How much longer, to the nearest second, is the period of the pendulum in Richmond than the period of the pendulum in Detroit? **4 sec**

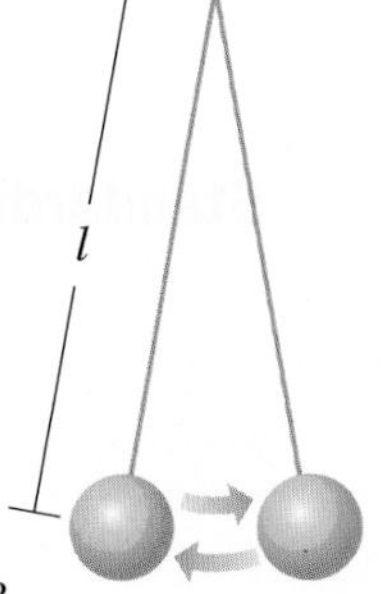

28. Never. *Sample answer:* The whole numbers consist only of 0 and the positive integers.

29. Sometimes. *Sample answer:* For example, $\sqrt{\frac{4}{9}} = \frac{2}{3}$ is rational, but $\sqrt{20}$ is irrational.

Pendulum in the Museum of Science in Boston, Massachusetts

3 APPLY

ASSIGNMENT GUIDE

Basic Course

Day 1: SRH p. 773 Exs. 10-12, p. 784 Exs. 1-4; pp. 473-474 Exs. 12-21, 26-31, 33, 34, 36-39, 44-53

Average Course

Day 1: pp. 473-474 Exs. 16-25, 28-37, 40-42, 44-53

Advanced Course

Day 1: pp. 473-474 Exs. 18-25, 28-35, 38-44*, 47-53

Block

pp. 473-474 Exs. 16-25, 28-37, 40-42, 44-53 (with 9.3)

EXTRA PRACTICE

- Student Edition, p. 811
- Chapter 9 Resource Book, pp. 32-34
- Test and Practice Generator

TRANSPARENCY

Even-numbered answers are available on transparencies. A support transparency is available for Exercises 7-10, 20-27, and 43.

HOMEWORK CHECK

When you review students' homework for this lesson, go over the following exercises to check understanding of key concepts.
Basic: 12, 20, 26, 28, 33
Average: 16, 21, 24, 30, 34
Advanced: 18, 22, 25, 32, 35

30. Sometimes. *Sample answer:* The real numbers consist of the rational numbers and the irrational numbers, which do not overlap.

31–32. See Additional Answers beginning on page AA1.

4 ASSESS

Assessment Resources

For more assessment resources, see:

- Assessment Book
- Test and Practice Generator

Mini-Quiz

Tell whether the number is *rational* or *irrational*.

1. $\frac{1}{3}$ **rational** 2. $\sqrt{21}$ **irrational**

3. Use a number line to order the numbers $-\sqrt{9}$, $\sqrt{\frac{121}{4}}$, $\frac{21}{4}$, $4\sqrt{3}$, from least to greatest. **$-\sqrt{9}$, $\frac{21}{4}$, $\sqrt{\frac{121}{4}}$, $4\sqrt{3}$**

4. **Challenge** Graph $\sqrt{41}$ on a number line using a right triangle.

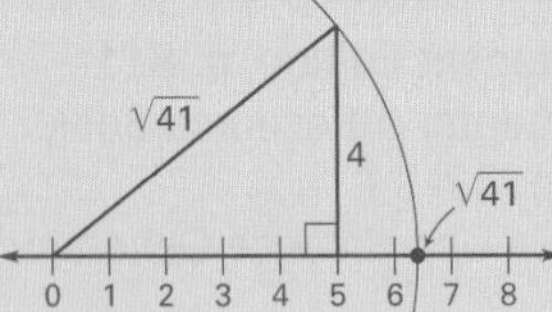

5 FOLLOW-UP

Diagnosis/Remediation

- Study Guide in Chapter 9 Resource Book, pp. 35–36
- eTutorial Plus Online
- Extra Practice, p. 811
- Lesson Practice in Chapter 9 Resource Book, pp. 32–34

English Learner Support

- Spanish Study Guide
- Multi-Language Visual Glossary
- Chapter Audio Summaries CDs

Challenge

- Challenge Practice in Chapter 9 Resource Book, p. 37
- Teacher's Edition, p. 450F

42a–b, 43, 53a. See Additional Answers beginning on page AA1.

35. Sailing The maximum speed at which a boat can travel is called its hull speed. The hull speed h (in nautical miles per hour) of some boats is given by the equation $h = \sqrt{1.8l}$, where l is the length in feet of the boat at the water line. One boat is 40 feet long at the water line. A second boat is 60 feet long at the water line. Which boat has a faster hull speed? How much faster? Give your answer to the nearest nautical mile per hour. **the longer boat; 2 nautical miles per hour**

Name an irrational number between the given rational numbers.
36–39. Sample answers are given.

B **36.** 1 and 2 **$\sqrt{3}$** **37.** -4 and -3 **$-\sqrt{10}$** **38.** 15 and $15\frac{1}{2}$ **15.40440444044440...** **39.** -10.1 and -10 **$-\sqrt{101}$**

40. Error Analysis Your friend says that $\sqrt{2}$ is rational because $\sqrt{2}$ can be written as the fraction $\frac{2\sqrt{2}}{2}$. Explain your friend's error.

41. Critical Thinking Is the product of two irrational numbers *always*, *sometimes*, or *never* irrational? Give examples to support your answer.

40. ***Sample answer:*** **If a number is rational, it can be written as a fraction in which the numerator and denominator are both integers. The numerator of the fraction $\frac{2\sqrt{2}}{2}$ is not an integer.**

41. Sometimes. ***Sample answer:*** **$\sqrt{2} \cdot \sqrt{2} = 2$, which is rational, but $\sqrt{2} \cdot \sqrt{3} = \sqrt{6}$, which is irrational.**

C **42. Extended Problem Solving** Use the following method to draw the *Wheel of Theodorus*. The first three triangles in the wheel are shown.
42a–b. See margin.

a. **Draw a Diagram** Start near the center of a large sheet of paper. Draw a right triangle with legs 1 unit long. Draw the next right triangle using the hypotenuse of the previous triangle as one leg, and a length of 1 unit for the second leg. Repeat this process to draw at least six triangles.

b. **Calculate** Beginning with the first triangle you drew, find the length of the hypotenuse of each triangle in simplest form. Label the length of each hypotenuse on your drawing.

c. **Critical Thinking** Make a list of the hypotenuse lengths in your drawing. Describe the numbers in the list.

This quilt is entitled *Wheel of Theodorus*.

42c. $\sqrt{2}$, $\sqrt{3}$, 2, $\sqrt{5}$, $\sqrt{6}$, $\sqrt{7}$. ***Sample answer:*** **They are the square roots of the successive whole numbers beginning with 2.**

43. Challenge Show how to graph $\sqrt{34}$ on a number line using a right triangle. Explain your method. **See margin.**

Mixed Review

Evaluate the expression when $a = 1.5$. *(Lesson 1.2)*

44. a^2 **2.25** **45.** a^3 **3.375** **46.** a^4 **5.0625**

Find the slope of the line through the given points. *(Lesson 8.4)*

47. $(-5, 2), (4, 3)$ **$\frac{1}{9}$** **48.** $(3, 7), (-1, -5)$ **3** **49.** $(-6, 2), (4, 8)$ **$\frac{3}{5}$**

Evaluate the expression when $a = 26$ and $b = 10$. *(Lesson 9.1)*

50. $\sqrt{a - b}$ **4** **51.** $\sqrt{a + b}$ **6** **52.** $\sqrt{b^2 - (a + 10)}$ **8**

Standardized Test Practice

53. Extended Response You are building four corner shelves, each in the shape of a right triangle. Each leg of each triangle is 14 inches long. You plan to cover the longest edge of each shelf with a strip of decorative trim that can be purchased only by the foot.

a. Explain how to estimate the number of feet of trim you need to purchase for all four shelves. **See margin.**

b. Find the exact amount of trim you need to use for all the shelves. **$\frac{14\sqrt{2}}{3}$ ft**

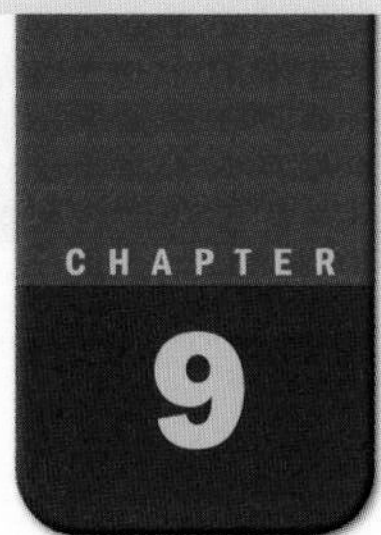

Mid-Chapter Quiz

Find the square roots of the number.

1. 1 ± 1 **2.** 36 ± 6 **3.** 169 ± 13 **4.** 196 ± 14

5. NASA Scientists at NASA drop objects from tall towers to study weightlessness. An object is dropped from a tower that is 24.1 meters high. Use the equation $d = 4.9t^2$ where d is the distance in meters that an object falls in t seconds to find (to the nearest tenth of a second) the time it takes the object to reach the ground. 2.2 sec

Simplify the expression.

6. $\sqrt{108}$ $6\sqrt{3}$ **7.** $\sqrt{\frac{9}{49}}$ $\frac{3}{7}$ **8.** $\sqrt{\frac{200}{x^2}}$ $\frac{10\sqrt{2}}{x}$ **9.** $\sqrt{12b^2d}$ $2b\sqrt{3d}$

Find the unknown length. Write your answer in simplest form.

10. 33 (legs: 44, a; hypotenuse: 55)

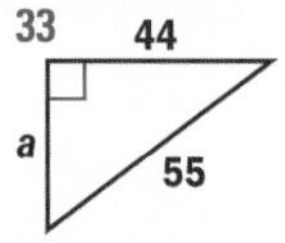

11. 35 (legs: 12, b; hypotenuse: 37)

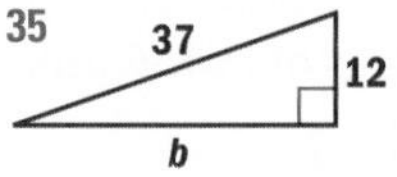

12. $\sqrt{34}$ (legs: 3, 5; hypotenuse: c)

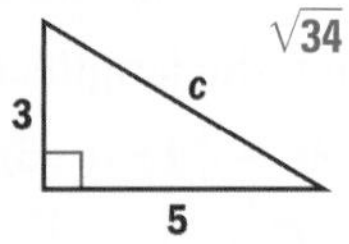

13. $8\sqrt{6}$ (legs: b, 10; hypotenuse: 22)

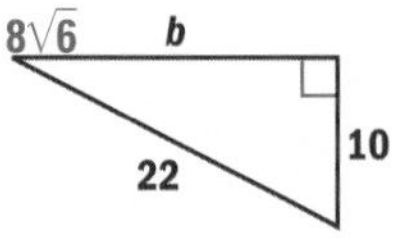

Tell whether the number is *rational* or *irrational*.

14. $\frac{7}{3}$ rational **15.** $\sqrt{12}$ irrational **16.** $-\sqrt{64}$ rational **17.** $\frac{\sqrt{9}}{2}$ rational

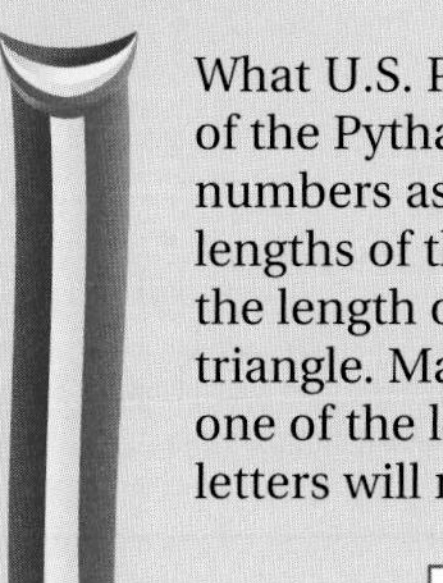

★★★ Presidential Proof ★★★

What U.S. President came up with a proof of the Pythagorean theorem? The pair of numbers associated with each letter are the lengths of the legs of a right triangle. Find the length of the hypotenuse of the triangle. Match the corresponding letter to one of the lengths shown below. Some letters will not be used. GARFIELD

R: $\sqrt{7}$, 11 N: 7, $\sqrt{11}$ I: $\sqrt{19}$, 9
E: 10, 24 D: 2, 3 F: 5, 12
O: 1, 2 A: 2, $\sqrt{3}$ T: 5, 8
S: $\sqrt{10}$, $\sqrt{12}$ L: 15, 20 G: 3, 4

Additional Resources

The following resources are available to help review the materials in Lessons 9.1–9.4.

Chapter 9 Resource Book
- Lesson Practice
- Study Guide

Assessment Book
- Chapter 9 Quiz 1

Technology
- Test and Practice Generator
- eTutorial CD-ROM

Internet
- Classzone
- eWorkbook Plus Online
- eTutorial Plus Online

English Learner Support

- Spanish Study Guide
- Multi-Language Visual Glossary
- Chapter Audio Summaries CDs

1 PLAN

Skill Check

Simplify.

1. $\sqrt{6^2 + 8^2}$ **10**
2. $\sqrt{9^2 + 9^2}$ **$9\sqrt{2}$**
3. $\sqrt{5^2 + 10^2}$ **$5\sqrt{5}$**
4. $\sqrt{9^2 + 40^2}$ **41**

Lesson Objective

Use the distance, midpoint, and slope formulas.

Pacing

Suggested Number of Days
Basic Course: 1 day
Average Course: 1 day
Advanced Course: 1 day
Block: 0.5 block with 9.6

Teaching Resources

For a complete list of Teaching Resources, see page 450B.

Transparency

Warm-Up Exercises for this lesson are available on a transparency.

2 TEACH

Motivating the Lesson

While referring to the figure at the top of this page, ask students to determine the distance from A to C, and from B to C. Then ask them how they could use the Pythagorean theorem to find the distance from A to B.

LESSON 9.5

The Distance *and* Midpoint Formulas

Vocabulary
midpoint, p. 478

BEFORE	Now	WHY?
You used the Pythagorean theorem.	You'll use the distance, midpoint, and slope formulas.	So you can compare points of interest on a map, as in Ex. 39.

To find the distance between points A and B, draw a right triangle as shown. Points A and C lie on a horizontal line. The distance between points A and C is the absolute value of the difference of their x-coordinates. Points B and C lie on a vertical line. The distance between points B and C is the absolute value of the difference of their y-coordinates.

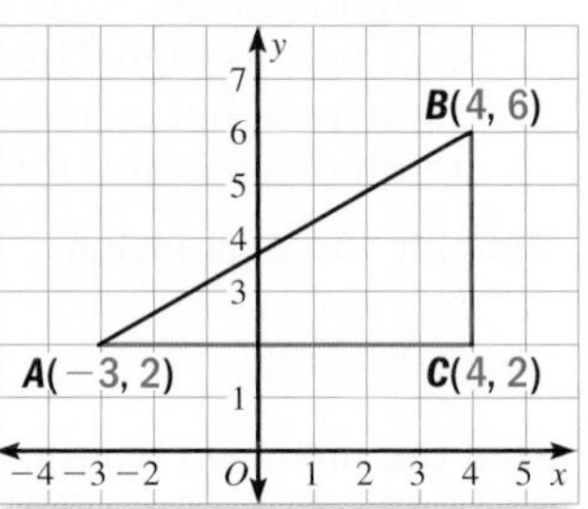

Then the lengths of the legs of $\triangle ABC$ are:

$AC = |4 - (-3)| = |7| = 7$

$BC = |6 - 2| = |4| = 4$

Because AB is the length of the hypotenuse of the triangle, use the Pythagorean theorem to find AB.

$(AB)^2 = (AC)^2 + (BC)^2$	**Pythagorean theorem**
$AB = \sqrt{(AC)^2 + (BC)^2}$	**Take positive square root of each side.**
$= \sqrt{7^2 + 4^2}$	**Substitute 7 for *AC* and 4 for *BC*.**
$= \sqrt{65}$	**Simplify.**

The example above suggests the following formula for finding the distance between any two points in a plane.

Reading Algebra

The ordered pairs (x_1, y_1) and (x_2, y_2) are read as "x sub one, y sub one" and "x sub two, y sub two," respectively. The subscripts 1 and 2 are used to distinguish the two x-coordinates and the two y-coordinates.

The Distance Formula

Words The distance between two points in a coordinate plane is equal to the square root of the sum of the horizontal change squared and the vertical change squared.

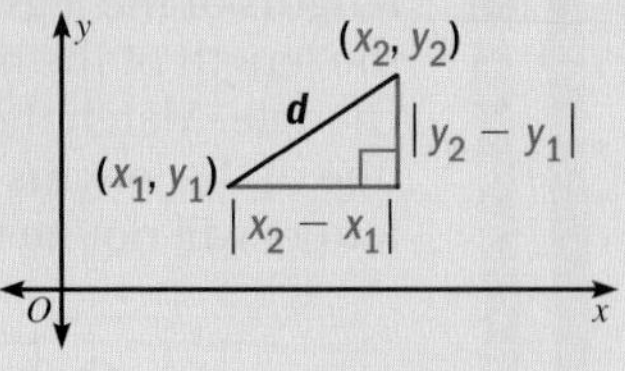

Algebra $d = \sqrt{(x_2 - x_1)^2 + (y_2 - y_1)^2}$

NCTM CURRICULUM STANDARDS
Standard 3: Specify locations using coordinate geometry; Describe spatial relationships using coordinate geometry; Use geometric modeling to solve problems

Study *Strategy*

Because the distance formula involves squaring the difference in the *x*-coordinates and the difference in the *y*-coordinates, you don't need to find the absolute value of either difference before squaring.

Example 1 *Finding the Distance Between Two Points*

Find the distance between the points *M*(6, 3) and *N*(5, 7).

$d = \sqrt{(x_2 - x_1)^2 + (y_2 - y_1)^2}$ — **Distance formula**

$= \sqrt{(5 - 6)^2 + (7 - 3)^2}$ — **Substitute 5 for x_2, 6 for x_1, 7 for y_2, and 3 for y_1.**

$= \sqrt{(-1)^2 + 4^2}$ — **Subtract.**

$= \sqrt{1 + 16}$ — **Evaluate powers.**

$= \sqrt{17}$ — **Add.**

Answer The distance between the points *M*(6, 3) and *N*(5, 7) is $\sqrt{17}$ units.

Checkpoint

Find the distance between the points.

1. (11, −2), (7, −5) **5 units**

2. (−1, 3), (5, −2) **$\sqrt{61}$ units**

3. (0, −1), (10, −5) **$2\sqrt{29}$ units**

Example 2 *Using the Distance Formula*

Bird Watching A bird watcher uses a grid to photograph and record the locations of birds feeding on the ground. The grid is made of fishing net with strands that are 1 foot apart. In the grid shown, each point represents the location of a bird. How far apart are the birds at points *A* and *B*?

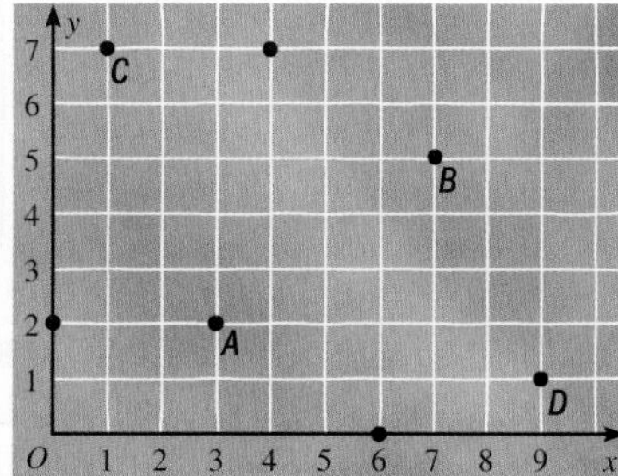

Solution

The coordinates of point *A* are (3, 2). The coordinates of point *B* are (7, 5).

$d = \sqrt{(x_2 - x_1)^2 + (y_2 - y_1)^2}$ — **Distance formula**

$= \sqrt{(7 - 3)^2 + (5 - 2)^2}$ — **Substitute 7 for x_2, 3 for x_1, 5 for y_2, and 2 for y_1.**

$= \sqrt{4^2 + 3^2}$ — **Subtract.**

$= \sqrt{16 + 9}$ — **Evaluate powers.**

$= \sqrt{25}$ — **Add.**

$= 5$ — **Simplify.**

Answer The birds at points *A* and *B* are 5 feet apart.

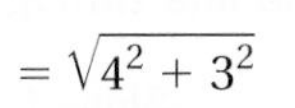

Checkpoint

4. In Example 2, how far apart are the birds at points *C* and *D*? **10 ft**

TIPS *for* NEW TEACHERS

Stress that the choice of which point to use as (x_1, y_1) and which to use as (x_2, y_2) in the distance, midpoint, and slope formulas does not matter, as long as students subtract or add the coordinates in the proper order. See Tips for New Teachers in the *Chapter 9 Resource Book*.

Extra Examples

Example 1 Find the distance between the points *A*(−2, −3) and *B*(4, 2). **$\sqrt{61}$ units**

Example 2 On a gridded map, Clive's hometown is shown at the point (5, 17). His cousin's hometown is shown at the point (10, 14). A straight road connects the two towns. If one unit on the map represents 10 kilometers, how far apart are these two towns? **$10\sqrt{34}$ km**

VISUALIZE

Sketch a figure like the one shown on page 465 of Lesson 9.3 to illustrate the Pythagorean theorem. Write the formula $a^2 + b^2 = c^2$ beneath the figure. Then label the vertices of the hypotenuse of the triangle with the ordered pairs (x_1, y_1) and (x_2, y_2). Lead students to connect what they already know about the Pythagorean theorem with the distance formula.

READING STRATEGY

Point out the use of blue and red ink in this lesson to distinguish the *x*-coordinates from the *y*-coordinates in the ordered pairs.

Extra Examples

Example 3 Find the midpoint of the segment with endpoints (10, −2) and (14, −10). **(12, −6)**

Example 4 Find the slope of the line through (−2, 3) and (7, −3). $-\frac{2}{3}$

Concept Check

How is finding the midpoint of a segment whose two endpoints are given different from finding the distance between the two endpoints? ***Sample answer:*** **The distance formula uses the square of the difference between the *x*-coordinates and the square of the difference between the *y*-coordinates, while the midpoint formula uses the average of the *x*-coordinates and the average of the *y*-coordinates.**

Daily Puzzler

The midpoint of $\overline{AB}$ is the origin. If the coordinates of point *A* are (x_1, y_1), what are the coordinates of point *B*? $(-x_1, -y_1)$

Midpoint The **midpoint** of a segment is the point on the segment that is equally distant from the endpoints.

The Midpoint Formula

Words The coordinates of the midpoint of a segment are the average of the endpoints' *x*-coordinates and the average of the endpoints' *y*-coordinates.

Algebra $M = \left(\frac{x_1 + x_2}{2}, \frac{y_1 + y_2}{2}\right)$

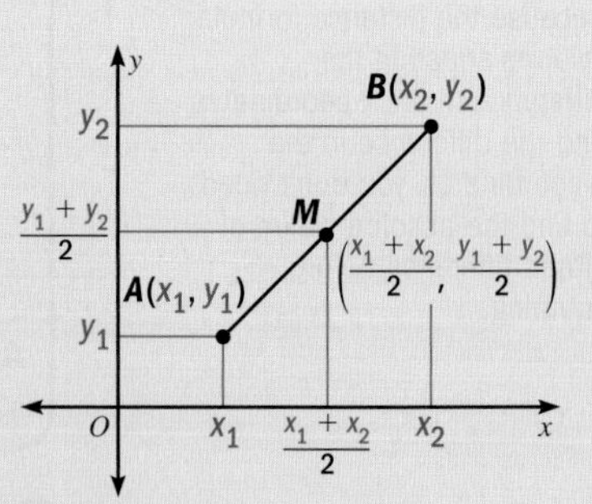

Example 3 *Finding a Midpoint*

Find the midpoint *M* of the segment with endpoints (3, 8) and (−9, −4).

$M = \left(\frac{x_1 + x_2}{2}, \frac{y_1 + y_2}{2}\right)$ **Midpoint formula**

$= \left(\frac{3 + (-9)}{2}, \frac{8 + (-4)}{2}\right)$ **Substitute 3 for x_1, −9 for x_2, 8 for y_1, and −4 for y_2.**

$= (-3, 2)$ **Simplify.**

Review Help

For help with slope, see p. 404.

Slope If points $A(x_1, y_1)$ and $B(x_2, y_2)$ do not lie on a vertical line, you can use coordinate notation to write a formula for the slope of the line through *A* and *B*.

$$\text{slope} = \frac{\text{difference of } y\text{-coordinates}}{\text{difference of } x\text{-coordinates}} = \frac{y_2 - y_1}{x_2 - x_1}$$

Example 4 *Finding Slope*

Find the slope of the line through (3, 7) and (8, −3).

$\text{slope} = \frac{y_2 - y_1}{x_2 - x_1}$ **Slope formula**

$= \frac{-3 - 7}{8 - 3}$ **Substitute −3 for y_2, 7 for y_1, 8 for x_2, and 3 for x_1.**

$= \frac{-10}{5} = -2$ **Simplify.**

Checkpoint

5. Find the midpoint *M* of the segment with endpoints (−7, 1) and (5, 11). ***M*(−1, 6)**
6. Find the slope of the line through (2, 7) and (−3, 5). $\frac{2}{5}$

9.5 Exercises

More Practice, p. 811

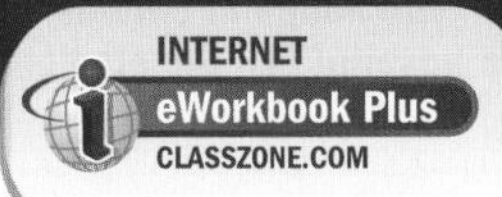

Guided Practice

Vocabulary Check

1. Copy and complete: To find the length of a segment in a coordinate plane, you can use the _?_ formula. **distance**
2. Point M is the midpoint of $\overline{AB}$. How are AM and MB related? **They are equal.**

Skill Check **In Exercises 3–5, use the coordinate grid shown.**

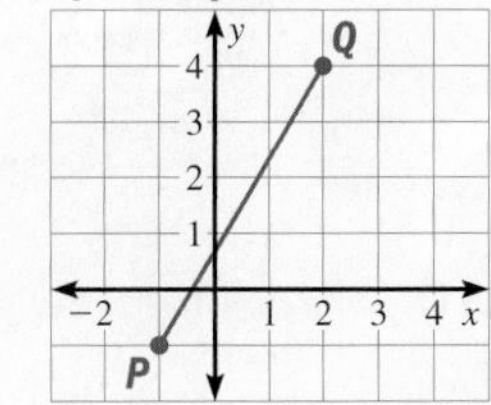

3. Find the length of $\overline{PQ}$. $\sqrt{34}$ **units**
4. Find the midpoint of $\overline{PQ}$. $\left(\frac{1}{2}, \frac{3}{2}\right)$
5. Find the slope of the line though P and Q. $\frac{5}{3}$
6. **Error Analysis** Describe and correct the error in finding the midpoint of the segment with endpoints (1, 8) and (7, 2).

$$M = \left(\frac{7-1}{2}, \frac{2-8}{2}\right) = (3, -3)$$

In the midpoint formula, the x- and y-coordinates are added, not subtracted. So, $M = \left(\frac{1+7}{2}, \frac{8+2}{2}\right) = (4, 5)$.

Practice and Problem Solving

Homework Help

Example	Exercises
1	7-18, 39-42
2	39-40, 42
3	19-22, 27-32, 39-40, 42
4	23-26, 33-38

Online Resources
CLASSZONE.COM
- More Examples
- eTutorial Plus

Find the distance between the points. Write your answer in simplest form.

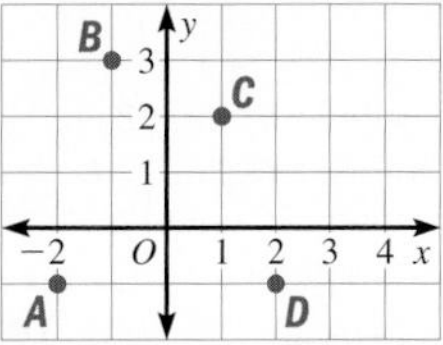

A 7. A and B $\sqrt{17}$ **units** 8. B and C $\sqrt{5}$ **units**

9. C and D $\sqrt{10}$ **units** 10. A and C $3\sqrt{2}$ **units**

11–14. See margin.

Find the distance between the points. Write your answer in simplest form.

11. (1, 3), (5, 8) 12. (−9, 0), (0, 7) 13. (12, 8), (0, 2) 14. (−4, 2), (5, −1)

15. (1.5, 4), (3, 6) **2.5 units** 16. (−8, 6), (1, 7) $\sqrt{82}$ **units** 17. (1, 5), (−2, 2) $3\sqrt{2}$ **units** 18. (1.2, 2), (8.7, 6) **8.5 units**

Find the midpoint of the segment.

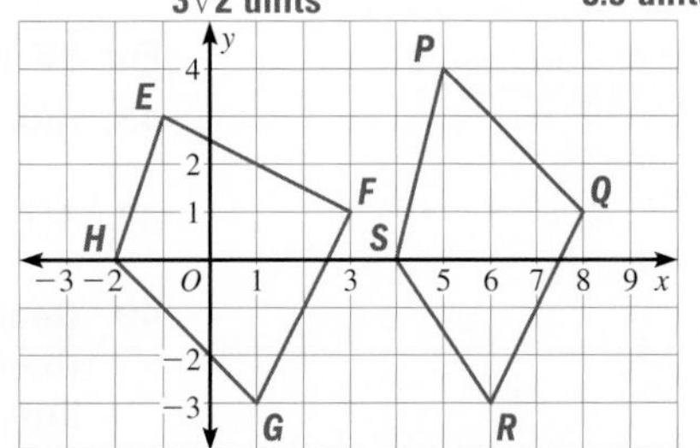

19. $\overline{EF}$ **(1, 2)** 20. $\overline{FG}$ **(2, −1)**

21. $\overline{GH}$ $\left(-\frac{1}{2}, -\frac{3}{2}\right)$ 22. $\overline{EH}$ $\left(-\frac{3}{2}, \frac{3}{2}\right)$

Find the slope of the line through the given points.

23. P and Q **−1** 24. Q and R **2**

25. R and S $-\frac{3}{2}$ 26. P and S **4**

11. $\sqrt{41}$ **units**
12. $\sqrt{130}$ **units**
13. $6\sqrt{5}$ **units**
14. $3\sqrt{10}$ **units**

3 APPLY

ASSIGNMENT GUIDE

Basic Course
Day 1: EP p. 803 Exs. 9-12, 32-37; pp. 479-481 Exs. 7-14, 19-24, 27-38, 40, 43-46, 55-62

Average Course
Day 1: pp. 479-481 Exs. 9-18, 21-26, 30-35, 39-44, 47-53, 55-63

Advanced Course
Day 1: pp. 479-481 Exs. 9-14, 21-29, 36-44, 47-56*, 60-63

Block
pp. 479-481 Exs. 9-18, 21-26, 30-35, 39-44, 47-53, 55-63 (with 9.6)

EXTRA PRACTICE

- Student Edition, p. 811
- Chapter 9 Resource Book, pp. 41-43
- Test and Practice Generator

TRANSPARENCY

Even-numbered answers are available on transparencies.

HOMEWORK CHECK

When you review students' homework for this lesson, go over the following exercises to check understanding of key concepts.
Basic: 7, 19, 23, 27, 40
Average: 9, 21, 24, 31, 39
Advanced: 9, 22, 26, 29, 42

COMMON ERROR

In Exercises 19-22 and 27-32, watch for students who confuse the midpoint and distance formulas and find the midpoint by subtracting pairs of coordinates instead of finding the averages.

TEACHING TIP

In Exercises 45–48, suggest that students use the midpoint formula to write an equality with x_1 and y_1 as the unknowns.

42a. 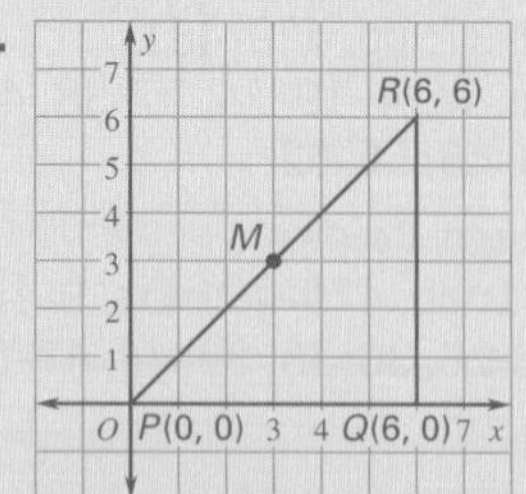

49. No. *Sample answer:* The line through (−3, 9) and (1, 1) has slope −2, the line through (−3, 9) and (4, −4) has slope $-\frac{13}{7}$, and the line through (1, 1) and (4, −4) has slope $-\frac{5}{3}$. Since the lines have different slopes, the three points do not lie on the same line.

50. 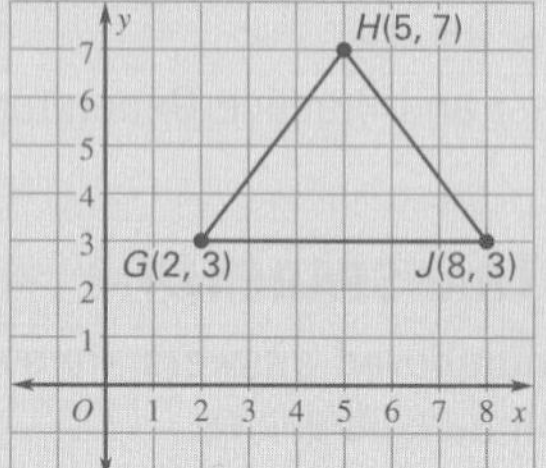

51. 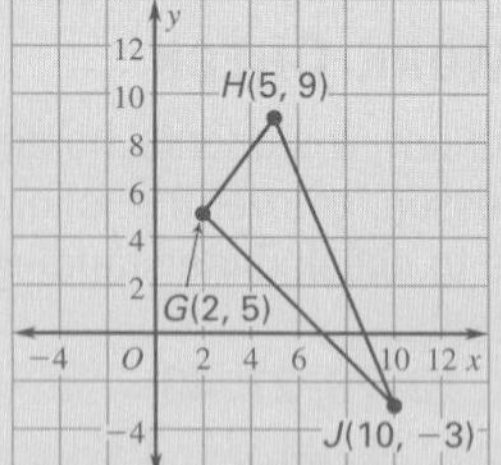

54, 63. See Additional Answers beginning on page AA1.

39a. The midpoint between the hospital and the stadium is $\left(\frac{1+9}{2}, \frac{2+6}{2}\right) = (5, 4)$, which matches the coordinates of the Civic Center.

39b. the hospital and the State House

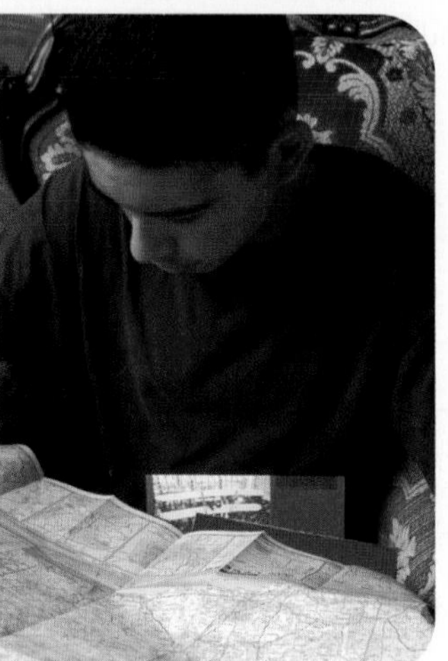

40. (−4, 6); distance from (−4, 6) to (−6, 8): $d = \sqrt{(-6-(-4))^2 + (8-6)^2} = \sqrt{8} = 2\sqrt{2}$; distance from (−4, 6) to (−2, 4): $d = \sqrt{(-2-(-4))^2 + (4-6)^2} = \sqrt{8} = 2\sqrt{2}$; the distances are the same, so the midpoint is equally distant from the endpoints.

41. No. *Sample answer:* Since the differences between the *x*-coordinates and between the *y*-coordinates are squared in the distance formula, the results are the same. For example, $(2-3)^2 = (-1)^2 = 1$, and $(3-2)^2 = (1)^2 = 1$.

42c. $MP = \sqrt{(3-0)^2 + (3-0)^2} = \sqrt{18} = 3\sqrt{2}$

$MQ = \sqrt{(6-3)^2 + (0-3)^2} = \sqrt{18} = 3\sqrt{2}$

$MR = \sqrt{(6-3)^2 + (6-3)^2} = \sqrt{18} = 3\sqrt{2}$

Find the midpoint of the segment with the given endpoints.

27. (8, −6), (2, 12) **(5, 3)**
28. (−10, 7), (4, 5) **(−3, 6)**
29. (6, −1), (9, 5) $\left(7\frac{1}{2}, 2\right)$

30. (3.8, 4), (6, 0.2) **(4.9, 2.1)**
31. (3, −2), $\left(5\frac{1}{2}, 7\right)$ $\left(4\frac{1}{4}, 2\frac{1}{2}\right)$
32. (17.4, 9.1), (3, 1.3) **(10.2, 5.2)**

Find the slope of the line through the given points.

33. (1, 2), (5, 6) **1**
34. (4, 3), (−2, 8) $-\frac{5}{6}$
35. (6, 1), (0, −7) $\frac{4}{3}$

36. (−4.2, 4), (8.6, 7.2) $\frac{1}{4}$
37. $\left(7\frac{3}{4}, -1\right)$, $\left(6\frac{1}{4}, -5\right)$ $\frac{8}{3}$
38. (−1.5, 0), (−6, 9) **−2**

39. Maps A grid is superimposed on the map of a town to locate points of interest, as shown.

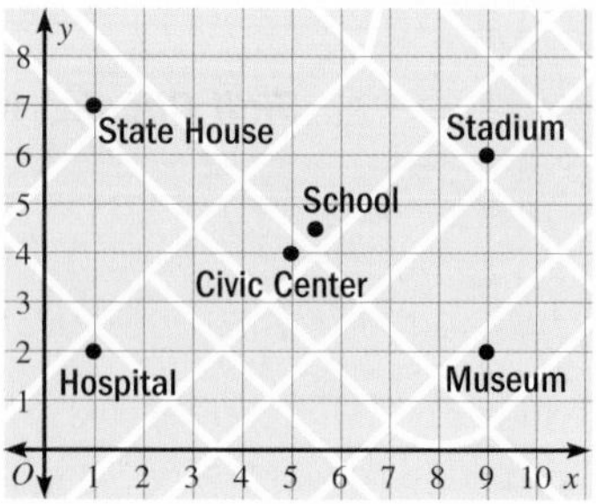

a. Show that the Civic Center is halfway between the hospital and the stadium. **a–b. See margin.**

b. Compare Which buildings are farther apart, the Civic Center and the stadium or the hospital and the State House?

40. Geometry Find the midpoint of the segment with endpoints (−6, 8) and (−2, 4). Use the distance formula to verify that the midpoint you found is equally distant from the endpoints. **See margin.**

41. Critical Thinking Does it matter which point you call (x_1, y_1) and which point you call (x_2, y_2) when you use the distance formula to find the distance between two points? Explain. **See margin.**

42. Geometry The points *P*(0, 0), *Q*(6, 0), and *R*(6, 6) are the vertices of a right triangle in a coordinate plane.

a. Draw the triangle in a coordinate plane. **See margin.**

b. Find the coordinates of the midpoint *M* of the hypotenuse of △*PQR*. ***M*(3, 3)**

c. Analyze Show that *M* is equally distant from *P*, *Q*, and *R*.

Tell which segment is longer.

B 43. $\overline{AB}$ has endpoints *A*(−1, −2) and *B*(6, 1). $\overline{PQ}$ has endpoints *P*(1, 1) and *Q*(6, 7). $\overline{PQ}$

44. $\overline{MN}$ has endpoints *M*(−3, 2) and *N*(5, 0). $\overline{JK}$ has endpoints *J*(−3, 1) and *K*(3, −5). $\overline{JK}$

For $\overline{AB}$ with midpoint *M*, determine the coordinates of point *B*.

45. *A*(0, 6); *M* = (−4, 3) **B(−8, 0)**
46. *A*(15, 25); *M* = (6.5, 16.5) **B(−2, 8)**

47. *A*(7, 6); *M* = (12, 9) **B(17, 12)**
48. *A*(−2, 2); $M = \left(1, 1\frac{1}{2}\right)$ **B(4, 1)**

49. Geometry Three points *A*, *B*, and *C* are on the same line if the slopes of the following three lines are equal: the line through points *A* and *B*, the line through points *A* and *C*, and the line through points *B* and *C*. Are the points (−3, 9), (1, 1), and (4, −4) on the same line? Explain. **See margin.**

Plot the points G, H, and J in a coordinate plane and draw triangle GHJ. Determine whether the triangle is a right triangle. 50–51. See margin for art.

50. $G(2, 3)$, $H(5, 7)$, $J(8, 3)$ no **51.** $G(2, 5)$, $H(5, 9)$, $J(10, -3)$ no

52. Extended Problem Solving An urban forester uses a grid to record information about trees in a city park. Each unit on the grid represents 10 meters.

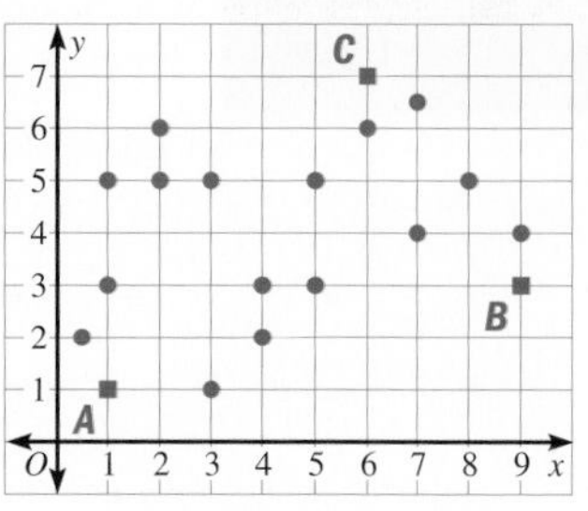

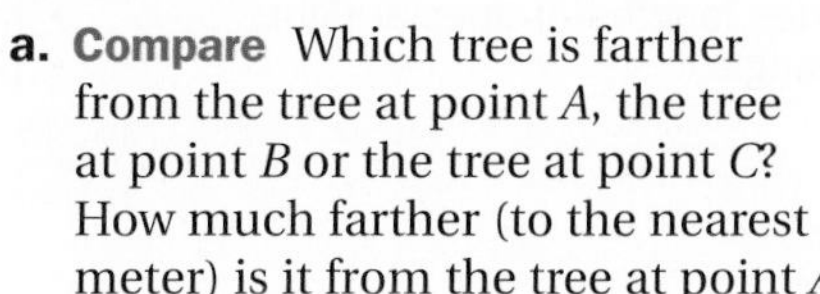

a. Compare Which tree is farther from the tree at point A, the tree at point B or the tree at point C? How much farther (to the nearest meter) is it from the tree at point A? **the tree at point B; 4 m**

b. Apply The trees at points A, B, and C are to be cut down. Two trees will be planted, one at the midpoint of the segment with endpoints A and B, the other at the midpoint of the segment with endpoints B and C. To the nearest meter, how far apart will the new trees be? **39 m**

In the Real World

Urban Forest The area of Central Park in New York City is 843 acres, of which 136 acres are woodlands. There are approximately 26,000 trees, of which 1700 are American elms. To the nearest tenth of a percent, what percent of the trees are American elms? **6.5%**

C **53. Geometry** The *center* of a circle is equally distant from all points on the circle. Consider a circle with center C and a segment that has endpoints $A(-2, -1)$ and $B(6, 5)$ on the circle. The segment passes through point C. Find the coordinates of point C. **$C(2, 2)$**

54. Challenge Plot the point $A(1, 3)$ in a coordinate plane. Find and plot at least 6 points that are 5 units from A. Explain how you found the points. **See margin.**

Mixed Review

55. Sewing You are making curtains. The fabric costs \$2.49 per yard. You have \$15. Do you have enough money to buy 5 yards of fabric? *(Lesson 6.1)* **yes**

Write the decimal as a percent. *(Lesson 7.3)*

56. 0.206 **20.6%** **57.** 1.31 **131%** **58.** 0.004 **0.4%**

Copy and complete the statement using <, >, or =. *(Lesson 9.4)*

59. $\sqrt{15}$? $\frac{11}{3}$ **>** **60.** $\sqrt{\frac{1}{2}}$? $-\frac{5}{7}$ **>** **61.** 7.25 ? $3\sqrt{6}$ **<**

Standardized Test Practice

62. Multiple Choice What is the distance between points A and B? **D**

A. $\sqrt{17}$ units

B. 5 units

C. $\sqrt{41}$ units

D. $5\sqrt{2}$ units

63. Short Response Let M be the midpoint of the segment with endpoints $A(1, 2)$ and $B(9, 6)$. Use the distance formula to show that $AB = 2 \cdot AM$ and $AB = 2 \cdot MB$. **See margin.**

4 ASSESS

Assessment Resources

For more assessment resources, see:

- Assessment Book
- Test and Practice Generator

Mini-Quiz

Find the distance between the given points, and the midpoint and slope of the segment connecting them.

1. (5, 10), (8, 6) **5, $\left(6\frac{1}{2}, 8\right)$, $-\frac{4}{3}$**

2. (−4, 1), (8, −7) **$4\sqrt{13}$, (2, −3), $-\frac{2}{3}$**

3. Challenge Plot the point $X(2, 0)$ in a coordinate plane. Find and plot at least 6 points that are 3 units from X. ***Sample:***

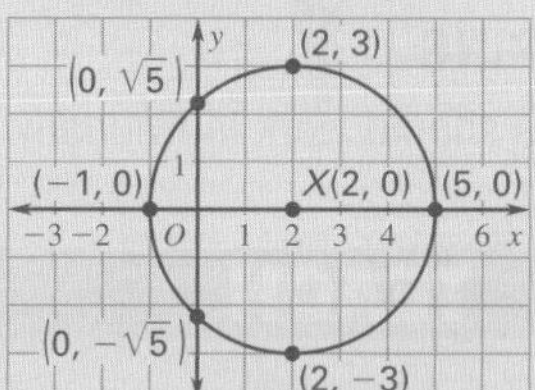

5 FOLLOW-UP

Diagnosis/Remediation

- Study Guide in Chapter 9 Resource Book, pp. 44–45
- eTutorial Plus Online
- Extra Practice, p. 811
- Lesson Practice in Chapter 9 Resource Book, pp. 41–43

English Learner Support

- Spanish Study Guide
- Multi-Language Visual Glossary
- Chapter Audio Summaries CDs

Challenge

- Challenge Practice in Chapter 9 Resource Book, p. 47
- Teacher's Edition, p. 450F

1 PLAN

Investigate the Concept

- Students investigate the relationships among side lengths of special right triangles.
- This activity leads to the use of the ratios in 30°-60°-90° and 45°-45°-90° triangles in Lesson 9.6.

Materials

Each student will need graph paper, a metric ruler, and a protractor.

Recommended Time

Work activity: 15 min
Discuss results: 10 min

Grouping

Students should work individually.

2 TEACH

Tips for Success

Stress that the metric rulers are only to be used for drawing the given side lengths and not for measuring the unknown lengths. The lengths found using the Pythagorean theorem should be written in simplest radical form so the ratios can be easily seen.

3 CLOSE

Key Discovery

In both of the two types of special right triangles, the ratios of the side lengths are always the same.

Assessment

1. Which special triangle has side lengths in the ratio $1 : 1 : \sqrt{2}$? $1 : \sqrt{3} : 2$? **45°-45°-90° triangle; 30°-60°-90° triangle**

Concept *Activity*

9.6 Investigating Special Right Triangles

Goal
Investigate the relationships among sides lengths of special right triangles.

Materials
- graph paper
- metric ruler
- protractor

In this activity, you will investigate two special right triangles. One is a 45°-45°-90° triangle. The legs of such a triangle are congruent.

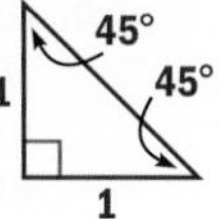

Another special right triangle is a 30°-60°-90° triangle. The hypotenuse of a 30°-60°-90° triangle is twice as long as the shorter leg.

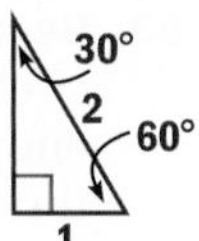

Investigate

Use the Pythagorean theorem to establish relationships among the side lengths of special right triangles.

1 Draw 3 different 45°-45°-90° triangles using the leg lengths given in the table. Find the length (in centimeters) of the hypotenuse for each triangle. Write your answers in simplest form. **Check students' drawings.**

Length of leg	Length of hypotenuse	
1 cm	?	$\sqrt{2}$ cm
2 cm	?	$2\sqrt{2}$ cm
3 cm	?	$3\sqrt{2}$ cm

2 Draw 3 different 30°-60°-90° triangles using the side lengths given in the table. Find the length (in centimeters) of the longer leg for each triangle. Write your answers in simplest form. **Check students' drawings.**

Length of hypotenuse	Length of shorter leg	Length of longer leg	
2 cm	1 cm	?	$\sqrt{3}$ cm
4 cm	2 cm	?	$2\sqrt{3}$ cm
6 cm	3 cm	?	$3\sqrt{3}$ cm

Draw Conclusions

1. **Critical Thinking** Identify any pattern you see in the table for Step 1. Use the pattern to find the length of the hypotenuse of a 45°-45°-90° triangle with legs that are each n units long. **1. The length of the hypotenuse is $\sqrt{2}$ times the length of a leg; $n\sqrt{2}$.**
2. *Writing* Describe the relationship between the length of the longer leg of a 30°-60°-90° triangle and the length of the shorter leg. **The length of the longer leg is $\sqrt{3}$ times the length of the shorter leg.**

NCTM CURRICULUM STANDARDS
Standard 3: Analyze properties of 2-D shapes

LESSON

9.6 Special Right Triangles

BEFORE You found side lengths of right triangles.

Now You'll use special right triangles to solve problems.

WHY? So you can find the distance a softball is thrown, as in Ex. 15.

Review Vocabulary
hypotenuse, p. 465
leg, p. 465

A diagonal of a square divides it into two 45°-45°-90° triangles. In such a triangle, the lengths of the legs are equal. Let a represent the length of each leg, and let c represent the length of the hypotenuse. By the Pythagorean theorem, $c^2 = a^2 + a^2 = 2a^2$, so $c = \sqrt{2a^2} = a\sqrt{2}$.

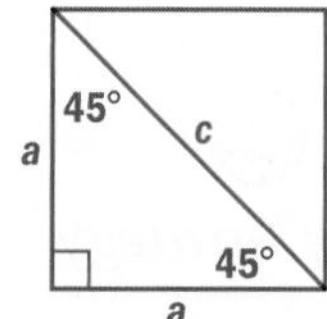

45°-45°-90° Triangle

Words In a 45°-45°-90° triangle, the length of the hypotenuse is the product of the length of a leg and $\sqrt{2}$.

Algebra hypotenuse = leg • $\sqrt{2}$

$= a\sqrt{2}$

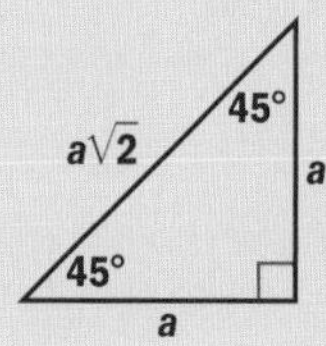

Example 1 *Using a 45°-45°-90° Triangle*

Gymnastics The mat used for floor exercises at a gymnastics competition is a square with a side length of 12 meters. A gymnast starts at one corner of the mat and does a tumbling routine along the diagonal to the opposite corner. To the nearest meter, how long is the gymnast's path?

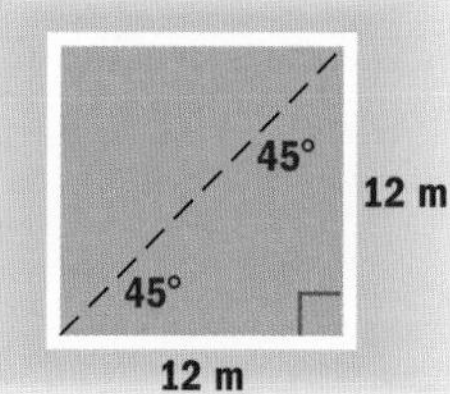

Solution

The diagonal divides the mat into two 45°-45°-90° triangles. The diagonal is the hypotenuse of each of the triangles.

hypotenuse = leg • $\sqrt{2}$	**Rule for 45°-45°-90° triangle**
$= 12 \cdot \sqrt{2}$	**Substitute.**
≈ 17	**Use a calculator.**

Answer The gymnast's path is about 17 meters long.

NCTM CURRICULUM STANDARDS
Standard 2: Represent situations using algebraic symbols
Standard 3: Analyze properties of 2-D shapes

1 PLAN

Skill Check
Simplify.

1. $\sqrt{32}$	$4\sqrt{2}$
2. $\sqrt{27}$	$3\sqrt{3}$
3. $5\sqrt{18}$	$15\sqrt{2}$
4. $8\sqrt{50}$	$40\sqrt{2}$

Lesson Objective
Use special right triangles to solve problems.

Pacing
Suggested Number of Days
Basic Course: 2 days
Average Course: 2 days
Advanced Course: 2 days
Block: 0.5 block with 9.5
0.5 block with 9.7

Teaching Resources
For a complete list of Teaching Resources, see page 450B.

Transparency
Warm-Up Exercises for this lesson are available on a transparency.

2 TEACH

Motivating the Lesson
Give each student a square sheet of paper. Have them fold it in half along the diagonal and measure the acute angles with a protractor to see that the angles have measures of 45°.

TIPS *for* NEW TEACHERS

Show students how to make quick sketches of the two special right triangles for solving problems. Stress that students should not expect to recall all of the angles and length ratios without first making a sketch. See Tips for New Teachers in the *Chapter 9 Resource Book*.

Extra Examples

Example 1 Mrs. Gregory is buying paving stones to lay along a diagonal path across her square lawn, which is 17 feet on each side. To the nearest tenth of a foot, what is the length of the path? **24.0 ft**

Example 2 Find the length x of the hypotenuse and the length y of the longer leg of the triangle.

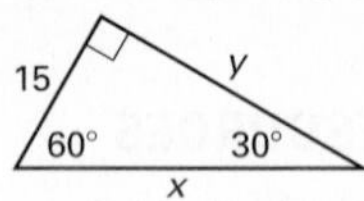

$x = 30$ units, $y = 15\sqrt{3}$ units

COMMON ERROR

Watch for students who believe $\sqrt{3} > 2$ and therefore think that the hypotenuse is $\sqrt{3}$ times the length of the shortest leg in a 30°-60°-90° triangle.

ALGEBRAIC REASONING

Encourage students to record the figure at the top of this page in their notebooks. The three equilateral sides can help students remember that the hypotenuse is twice the length of the shorter leg in the 30°-60°-90° triangle.

Note *Worthy*

You can organize information about right triangles in your notebook using a concept map like the one on p. 452.

Study *Strategy*

In a 30°-60°-90° triangle, the shorter leg is opposite the 30° angle, and the longer leg is opposite the 60° angle.

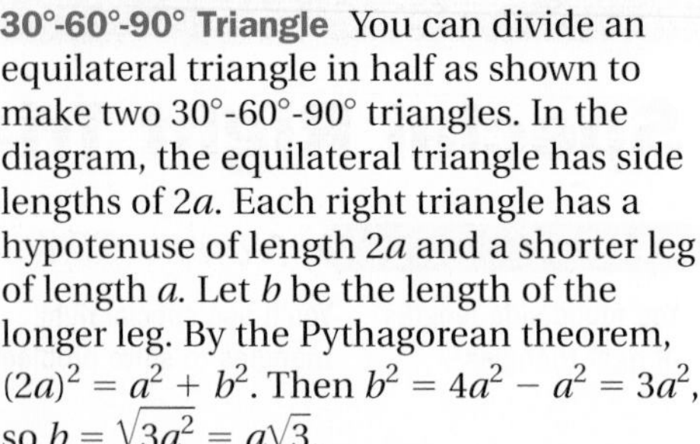

30°-60°-90° Triangle You can divide an equilateral triangle in half as shown to make two 30°-60°-90° triangles. In the diagram, the equilateral triangle has side lengths of $2a$. Each right triangle has a hypotenuse of length $2a$ and a shorter leg of length a. Let b be the length of the longer leg. By the Pythagorean theorem, $(2a)^2 = a^2 + b^2$. Then $b^2 = 4a^2 - a^2 = 3a^2$, so $b = \sqrt{3a^2} = a\sqrt{3}$.

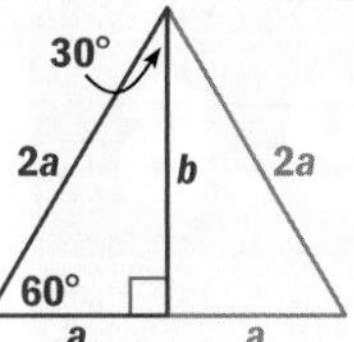

30°-60°-90° Triangle

Words In a 30°-60°-90° triangle, the length of the hypotenuse is twice the length of the shorter leg. The length of the longer leg is the product of the length of the shorter leg and $\sqrt{3}$.

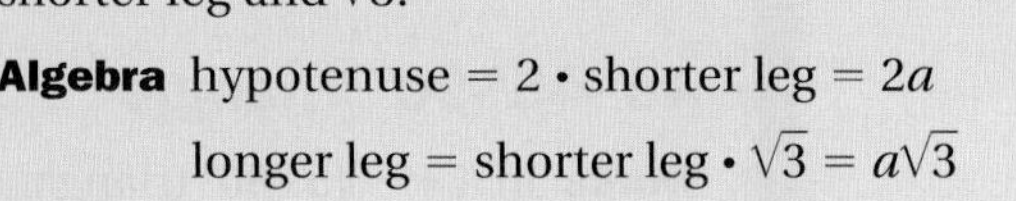

Algebra hypotenuse $= 2 \cdot$ shorter leg $= 2a$

longer leg $=$ shorter leg $\cdot \sqrt{3} = a\sqrt{3}$

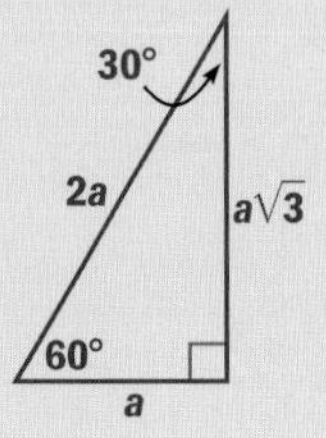

Example 2 ***Using a 30°-60°-90° Triangle***

Find the length x of the hypotenuse and the length y of the longer leg of the triangle.

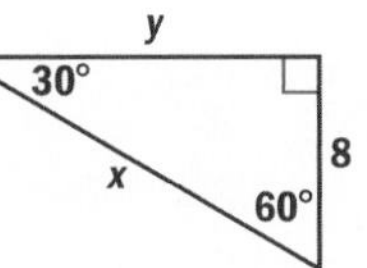

The triangle is a 30°-60°-90° triangle. The length of the shorter leg is 8 units.

a. hypotenuse $= 2 \cdot$ shorter leg

$x = 2 \cdot 8$

$= 16$

Answer The length x of the hypotenuse is 16 units.

b. longer leg $=$ shorter leg $\cdot \sqrt{3}$

$y = 8\sqrt{3}$

Answer The length y of the longer leg is $8\sqrt{3}$ units.

Checkpoint

Find the unknown lengths. Write your answer in simplest form.

1.

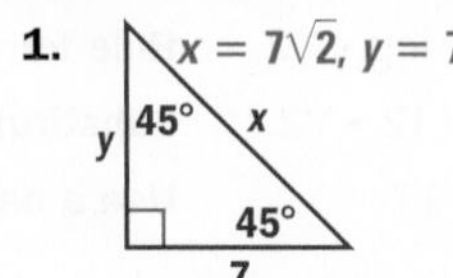

$x = 7\sqrt{2}$, $y = 7$

2.

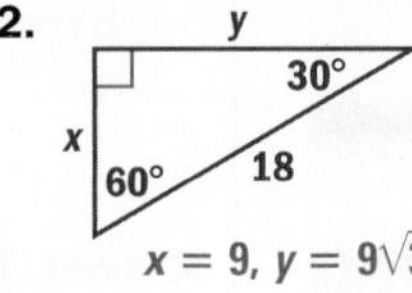

$x = 9$, $y = 9\sqrt{3}$

3.

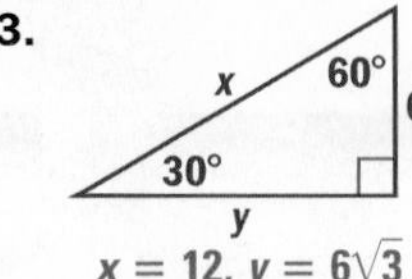

$x = 12$, $y = 6\sqrt{3}$

Example 3 *Using a Special Right Triangle*

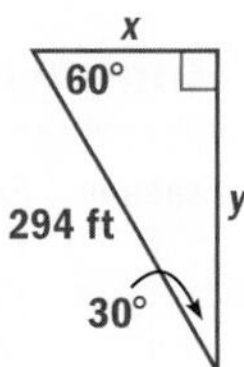

Architecture The base of the Massachusetts Institute of Technology's Building 66, an engineering laboratory, is approximately a 30°-60°-90° triangle. The length of the hypotenuse of the triangle is about 294 feet. Find, to the nearest foot, the lengths of the legs of the triangle.

Solution

You need to find the length of the shorter leg first.

1. Find the length x of the shorter leg.

hypotenuse = 2 • shorter leg	**Rule for 30°-60°-90° triangle**
$294 = 2x$	**Substitute.**
$147 = x$	**Divide each side by 2.**

2. Find the length y of the longer leg.

longer leg = shorter leg • $\sqrt{3}$	**Rule for 30°-60°-90° triangle**
$y = 147\sqrt{3}$	**Substitute.**
≈ 255	**Use a calculator.**

Answer The length of the shorter leg of the triangle is 147 feet. The length of the longer leg is about 255 feet.

9.6 Exercises

More Practice, p. 811

Guided Practice

Vocabulary Check

1. Each leg of a 45°-45°-90° triangle has a length of 15 units. What is the length of the hypotenuse? **$15\sqrt{2}$ units**
2. How is the length of the longer leg of a 30°-60°-90° triangle related to the length of the shorter leg? **It is the product of the length of the shorter leg and $\sqrt{3}$.**

Skill Check **Find the unknown length. Write your answer in simplest form.**

3. **$6\sqrt{2}$**

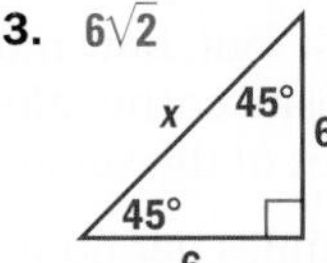

4. **$18\sqrt{3}$**

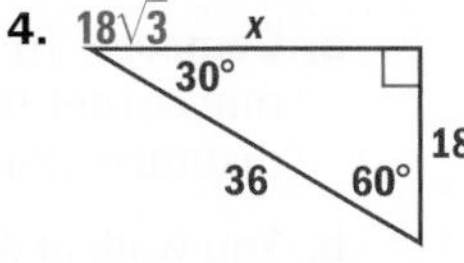

5. **$5\sqrt{3}$**

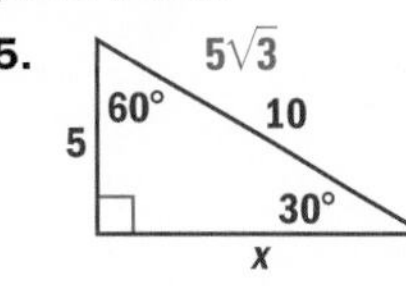

6. **Graphic Arts** A graphic artist's tools include a 30°-60°-90° triangle. The hypotenuse of the triangle has a length of 10 inches. To the nearest inch, how long are the legs of the triangle? **5 in. and 9 in.**

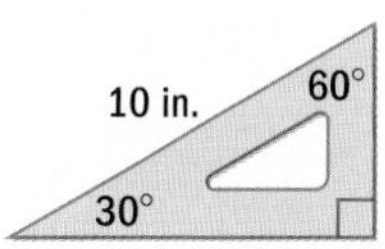

Extra Examples

Example 3 The corner shelf in Darryl's bathroom is a 45°-45°-90° triangle. The longest edge of the shelf is about 17 inches long. Find the lengths of the two shorter sides. **about 12 in.**

Teaching Tip

Encourage students to share any mnemonic devices they have developed to help recall the measures of the two special right triangles.

Differentiating Instruction

Advanced Students Ask students to write a summary of the minimum information needed about a special right triangle in order to be able to find every angle and side measure. Encourage students to list all the possible combinations of minimum information they might be given and how they would use this information to find the other measures.

Concept Check

How do you find the other two side lengths in a 30°-60°-90° triangle if you are given only the length of the shorter leg? **The length of the hypotenuse is twice the length of the shorter leg and the longer leg is $\sqrt{3}$ times the length of the shorter leg.**

Daily Puzzler

What do you know about the lengths of the sides of an equilateral right triangle? **No such triangle exists.**

3 APPLY

ASSIGNMENT GUIDE

Basic Course

Day 1: pp. 486–487 Exs. 7–12, 22–26

Day 2: pp. 486–487 Exs. 13, 15–19, 27–31

Average Course

Day 1: pp. 486–487 Exs. 7–12, 22–27

Day 2: pp. 486–487 Exs. 13–20, 28–32

Advanced Course

Day 1: pp. 486–487 Exs. 7–12, 24–29

Day 2: pp. 486–487 Exs. 13–21*, 30–32

Block

pp. 486–487 Exs. 7–12, 22–27 (with 9.5)

pp. 486–487 Exs. 13–20, 28–32 (with 9.7)

EXTRA PRACTICE

- Student Edition, p. 811
- Chapter 9 Resource Book, pp. 50–52
- Test and Practice Generator

TRANSPARENCY

Even-numbered answers are available on transparencies.

HOMEWORK CHECK

When you review students' homework for this lesson, go over the following exercises to check understanding of key concepts.

Basic: 7, 10, 13, 15, 16

Average: 8, 11, 13, 14, 16

Advanced: 9, 12, 13, 15, 18

14. See Additional Answers beginning on page AA1.

Practice and Problem Solving

Homework *Help*

Example	Exercises
1	7–9, 14, 16–18
2	10–12, 16–18
3	13, 15

Online Resources CLASSZONE.COM

- More Examples
- eTutorial Plus

Find the unknown lengths. Write your answers in simplest form.

A **7.** $x = 11$, $y = 11\sqrt{2}$

8. 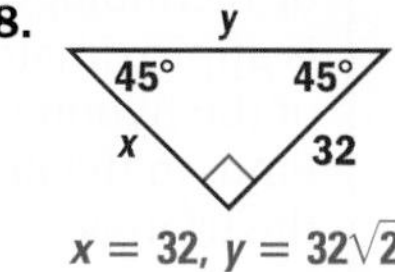

$x = 32$, $y = 32\sqrt{2}$

9. 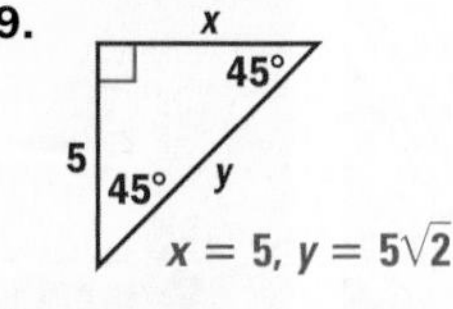

$x = 5$, $y = 5\sqrt{2}$

10. $x = 9\sqrt{3}$, $y = 18$

11. 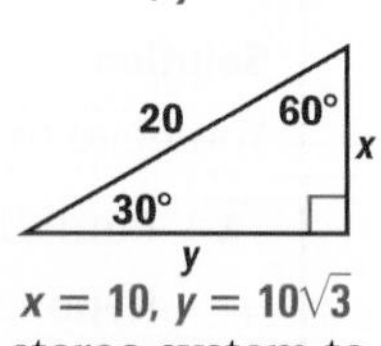

$x = 10$, $y = 10\sqrt{3}$

12. 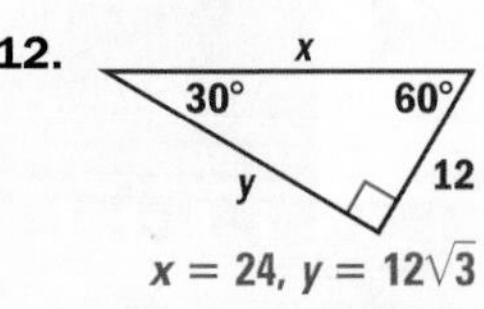

$x = 24$, $y = 12\sqrt{3}$

13. Speakers You connect a stereo system to your television set. The directions say that the speakers should be in line with your television and 12 feet apart as shown.

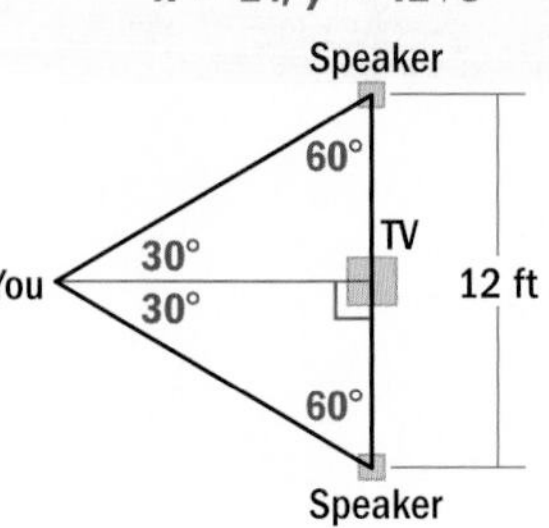

a. Find the distance between you and the television set to the nearest foot. **10 ft**

b. Find the distance between you and each speaker to the nearest foot. **12 ft**

14. *Writing* Explain why any two 45°-45°-90° triangles are similar. **See margin.**

15. Softball The bases on a softball field form a square with a side length of 60 feet. You throw a softball from first base to third base. How far do you throw the softball? Round your answer to the nearest foot. **85 ft**

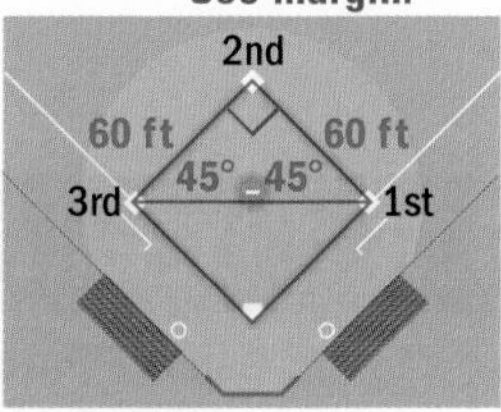

Find the unknown lengths. Write your answers in simplest form.

B **16.** 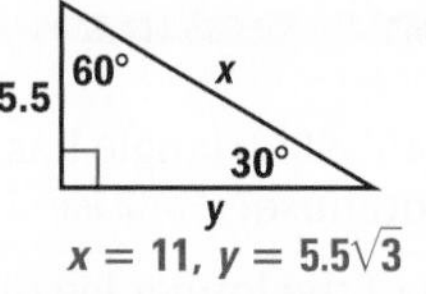

$x = 11$, $y = 5.5\sqrt{3}$

17. 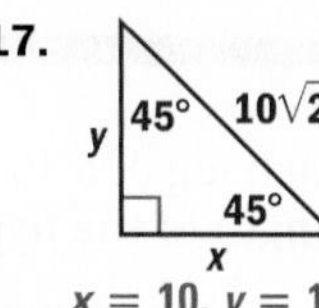

$x = 10$, $y = 10$

18. 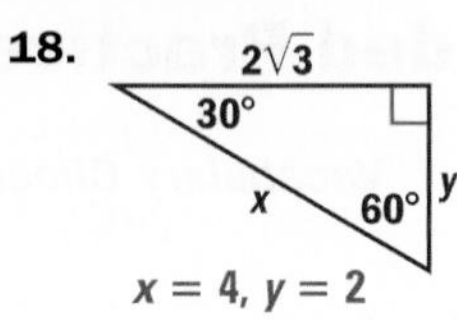

$x = 4$, $y = 2$

19. Extended Problem Solving There is a park in your town that is a square with a side length of 800 feet. You plan to walk from one corner of the square to the opposite corner.

a. Compare To the nearest foot, how much shorter is the distance from one corner to the opposite corner along the diagonal than the distance along two sides of the square? **469 ft**

b. You walk at a rate of 3 miles per hour. Find your rate in feet per second. **4.4 ft/sec**

c. Interpret To the nearest second, how much time would you save by walking along the diagonal rather than walking along two sides of the square? **107 sec, or 1 min, 47 sec**

C **20. Wrenches** You must choose the right size wrench to tighten a nut. Each edge of the nut has a length of $\frac{1}{4}$ inch. You should choose a wrench size that is close to the distance across the nut from one edge to the opposite edge. Which wrench size should you use, $\frac{3}{8}$ inch, $\frac{7}{16}$ inch, or $\frac{1}{2}$ inch? $\frac{7}{16}$ in.

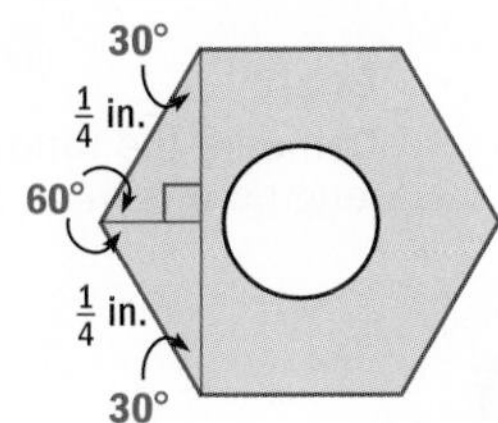

21. Challenge Find the value of x. Give your answer as a radical in simplest form. $15\sqrt{2}$

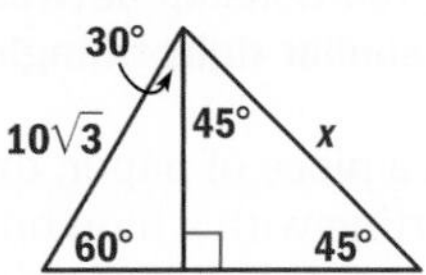

Mixed Review

Solve the proportion. *(Lesson 6.2)*

22. $\frac{w}{7} = \frac{36}{42}$ 6 **23.** $\frac{x}{10} = \frac{35}{50}$ 7 **24.** $\frac{3}{4} = \frac{y}{52}$ 39 **25.** $\frac{7}{12} = \frac{z}{105}$ 61.25

26. Submarines A sailor on a submarine uses a periscope to view the surface of the ocean. The periscope's height h (in feet) above the surface and the distance d (in miles) that the sailor can see are related by the formula $h = \frac{d^2}{1.4}$. Suppose the periscope is at a height of 3 feet. To the nearest mile, how far can the sailor see? *(Lesson 9.1)* 2 mi

Find the midpoint of the segment with the given endpoints. *(Lesson 9.5)*

27. $(-3, 4), (-1, 6)$ $(-2, 5)$ **28.** $(8, -3), (-2, 7)$ $(3, 2)$ **29.** $(4, -1.1), (-2.4, -1.7)$ $(0.8, -1.4)$

Standardized Test Practice

30. Multiple Choice What is the value of x? C

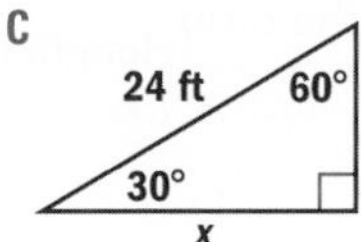

A. $\frac{12}{\sqrt{3}}$ ft **B.** 12 ft

C. $12\sqrt{3}$ ft **D.** $24\sqrt{3}$ ft

31. Multiple Choice Each leg of a 45°-45°-90° triangle has a length of 15 units. What is the length of the hypotenuse? I

F. 7.5 units **G.** $\frac{15}{\sqrt{2}}$ units **H.** 15 units **I.** $15\sqrt{2}$ units

32. Short Response Explain how to find the area of the equilateral triangle shown.

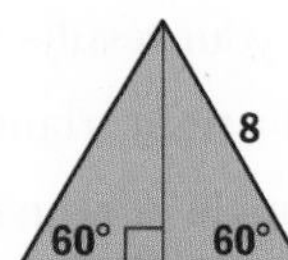

32. *Sample answer:* The triangle is equilateral, so its base is 8, and half the base is 4. By the rule for a 30°-60°-90° triangle, the height of the equilateral triangle is then $4\sqrt{3}$. Then by the area formula for a triangle, the area is $\frac{1}{2}(8)(4\sqrt{3}) = 16\sqrt{3}$ square units.

4 ASSESS

Assessment Resources

For more assessment resources, see:
- Assessment Book
- Test and Practice Generator

Mini-Quiz

Use the figure to find the unknown lengths. Write your answers in simplest form.

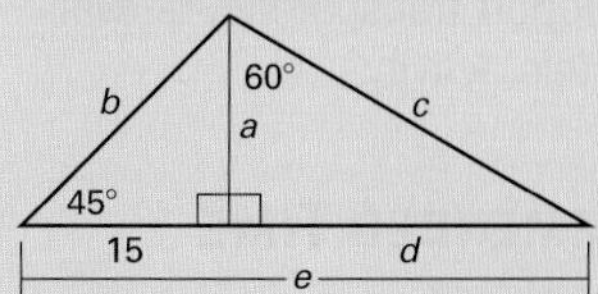

1. a 15
2. b $15\sqrt{2}$
3. c 30
4. d $15\sqrt{3}$
5. **Challenge** Find the value of e in the figure above. $15 + 15\sqrt{3}$

5 FOLLOW-UP

Diagnosis/Remediation

- Study Guide in Chapter 9 Resource Book, pp. 53-54
- eTutorial Plus Online
- Extra Practice, p. 811
- Lesson Practice in Chapter 9 Resource Book, pp. 50-52

English Learner Support

- Spanish Study Guide
- Multi-Language Visual Glossary
- Chapter Audio Summaries CDs

Challenge

- Challenge Practice in Chapter 9 Resource Book, p. 55
- Teacher's Edition, p. 450F

1 PLAN

INVESTIGATE THE CONCEPT

- Students compare ratios of leg lengths of similar right triangles.
- This activity leads to using the tangent ratio in Lesson 9.7.

MATERIALS

Each student will need a metric ruler, a protractor, and colored pencils. A support transparency is available for this activity.

RECOMMENDED TIME

Work activity: 15 min
Discuss results: 10 min

GROUPING

Students should work individually.

2 TEACH

DISCUSSION

As students are working, ask: "As the blue side of each triangle gets longer, what happens to the red side?" **It gets longer.** "When the length of the blue side doubles, does the length of the red side double?" **yes**

3 CLOSE

KEY DISCOVERY

The tangent ratio for a given acute angle in a right triangle does not depend on the size of the triangle.

ASSESSMENT

1. If you continued to draw vertical segments in step 2, what would happen to the ratio $\frac{\text{opposite}}{\text{adjacent}}$? **It would remain constant.**

2. See Additional Answers beginning on page AA1.

Concept *Activity*

9.7 Ratios of Leg Lengths of Similar Right Triangles

Goal
Compare the ratios of the leg lengths of similar right triangles.

Materials
- metric ruler
- protractor
- colored pencils

Investigate

Describe a relationship between the ratios of the leg lengths of similar right triangles. **Steps 1–2. Check work.**

1 On a piece of paper, draw a 35° angle, starting with a blue horizontal ray as shown. Label the angle *A*.

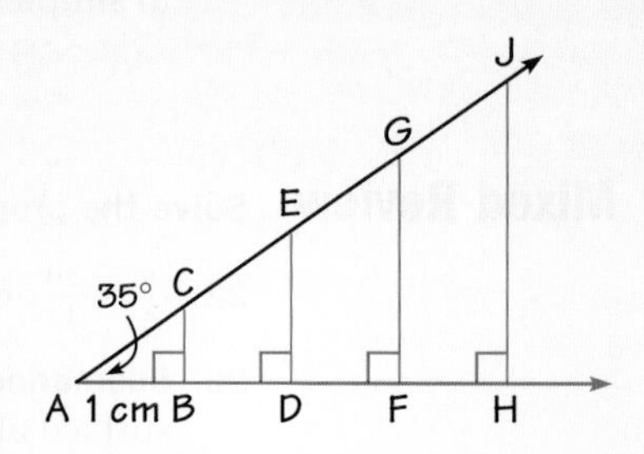

2 At intervals of 1 centimeter along the horizontal ray, draw vertical red segments to form at least four right triangles as shown. In each triangle, the leg shown in red is *opposite* $\angle A$. The leg shown in blue is *adjacent* to $\angle A$.

3 Copy and complete the table. For each triangle, measure (to the nearest tenth of a centimeter) the length of the leg opposite $\angle A$. Then calculate (to the nearest tenth) the ratio $\frac{\text{length of opposite leg}}{\text{length of adjacent leg}}$.
Row 1: 0.7 cm, 0.7; Row 2: 1.4 cm, 0.7; Row 3: 2.1 cm, 0.7; Row 4: 2.8 cm, 0.7

Triangle	Leg opposite $\angle A$	Leg adjacent to $\angle A$	$\frac{\text{opposite}}{\text{adjacent}}$
$\triangle ABC$	$BC = ?$	1 cm	?
$\triangle ADE$	$DE = ?$	2 cm	?
$\triangle AFG$	$FG = ?$	3 cm	?
$\triangle AHJ$	$HJ = ?$	4 cm	?

Draw Conclusions

1. **Critical Thinking** What do you notice about the ratios of the leg lengths in the fourth column of your table? **They are the same.**
2. *Writing* Use your results to answer the following question: For an acute angle of a right triangle, does the ratio $\frac{\text{opposite}}{\text{adjacent}}$ depend on the size of the triangle, on the measure of the angle, or on both? Explain. **See margin.**

NCTM CURRICULUM STANDARDS
Standard 3: Analyze properties of 2-D shapes
Standard 9: Grasp connections among math ideas

LESSON **9.7**

The Tangent Ratio

BEFORE	Now	WHY?
You found side lengths of special right triangles.	You'll use tangent to find side lengths of right triangles.	So you can find the distance across a pond, as in Ex. 23.

Vocabulary

trigonometric ratio, p. 489
tangent, p. 489

Lunar Formations Scientists can use the measure of the angle at which the sun's rays strike the moon's surface to determine the height or depth of a lunar formation. In Example 3, you will see how you can use a *trigonometric ratio* to estimate the depth of a lunar crater.

A **trigonometric ratio** is a ratio of the lengths of two sides of a right triangle. One basic trigonometric ratio is *tangent*, abbreviated *tan*.

The Tangent Ratio

The **tangent** of an acute angle of a right triangle is the ratio of the length of the side opposite the angle to the length of the side adjacent to the angle.

$$\tan A = \frac{\text{side opposite } \angle A}{\text{side adjacent to } \angle A} = \frac{a}{b}$$

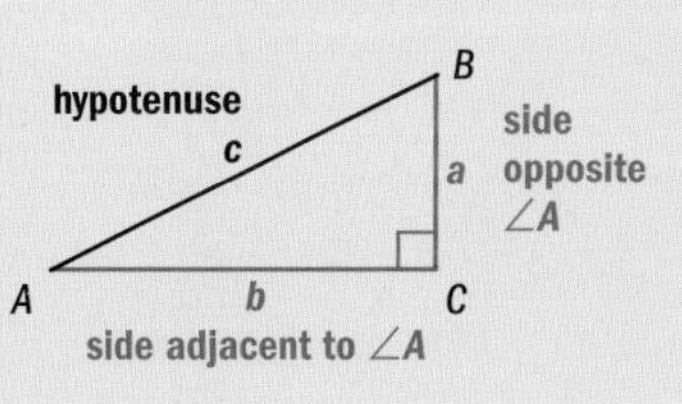

As the activity on page 488 suggests, the value of the tangent of an acute angle of a right triangle depends only on the measure of the angle, not on the size of the triangle.

Reading *Geometry*

The leg *adjacent* to an acute angle of a right triangle is also a side of the angle. The leg *opposite* the angle is not a side of the angle.

Example 1 *Finding a Tangent Ratio*

For △*PQR*, find the tangent of ∠*P*.

$$\tan P = \frac{\text{opposite}}{\text{adjacent}} = \frac{77}{36}$$

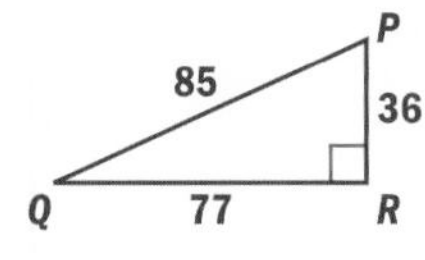

Checkpoint

1. For △*PQR* in Example 1, find tan *Q*. $\frac{36}{77}$

NCTM CURRICULUM STANDARDS

Standard 3: Analyze properties of 2-D shapes
Standard 6: Solve problems in math and other contexts
Standard 9: Grasp connections among math ideas

1 PLAN

Skill Check

Use the triangle.

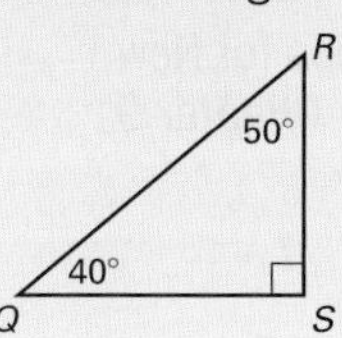

1. Which side is adjacent to ∠*R*? $\overline{RS}$

2. Which side is opposite ∠*R*? $\overline{QS}$

3. Which angle has the least measure? ∠*Q*

4. Which side is the hypotenuse? $\overline{QR}$

Lesson Objective

Use tangent to find side lengths of right triangles.

Pacing

Suggested Number of Days
Basic Course: 1 day
Average Course: 1 day
Advanced Course: 1 day
Block: 0.5 block with 9.6

Teaching Resources

For a complete list of Teaching Resources, see page 450B.

Transparency

Warm-Up Exercises for this lesson are available on a transparency.

2 TEACH

Motivating the Lesson

After reading the first paragraph of the lesson, invite students to suggest how the angle of the sun's rays could be used to find a height or depth.

TIPS *for* NEW TEACHERS

Use the diagram in the middle of page 489 to show students that $\tan B = \frac{b}{a}$, the reciprocal of tan *A*. See Tips for New Teachers in the *Chapter 9 Resource Book*.

Extra Examples

Example 1 For $\triangle TUV$, find the tangent of $\angle T$. $\frac{15}{8}$

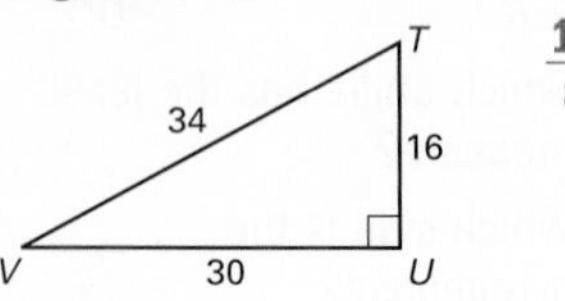

Example 2 Use a calculator to approximate the tangent value to four decimal places.

a. tan 27° **0.5095**

b. tan 66° **2.2460**

Example 3 When the sun's rays strike the Earth's surface at an angle of 32°, a tree casts a shadow that is 54 feet long. What is the height of the tree to the nearest foot? **34 ft**

CONCEPT CHECK

What is the tangent of one of the acute angles in a 45°-45°-90° triangle? Explain. **1. *Sample answer:* The legs of a 45°-45°-90° triangle have the same length, so their ratio is 1.**

DAILY PUZZLER

The tangent of one acute angle in a right triangle is 0.75. What is the tangent of this same angle after each side of the triangle is tripled in length? **0.75**

Tech *Help*

When using a calculator to find a trigonometric ratio, make sure the calculator is in degree mode. You do not need to enter a degree symbol, but you should enter a right parenthesis to close the left parenthesis that the calculator enters. Round the result to four decimal places if necessary.

Tangents of Angles You can use a calculator or the table of trigonometric ratios on page 823 to find tangents of angles. In this book, trigonometric ratios are rounded to four decimal places.

Example 2 ***Using a Calculator***

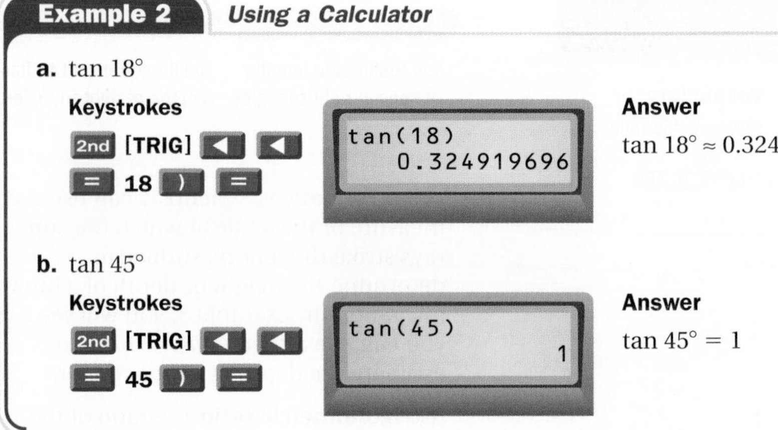

a. tan 18°

Keystrokes

2nd [TRIG] ◀ ◀ = 18) =

Answer

tan 18° ≈ 0.3249

b. tan 45°

Keystrokes

2nd [TRIG] ◀ ◀ = 45) =

Answer

tan 45° = 1

Checkpoint

2. Use a calculator to approximate tan 10° and tan 75° to four decimal places. **0.1763, 3.7321**

Example 3 ***Using a Tangent Ratio***

When the sun's rays strike the moon's surface at an angle of 6°, the edge of a lunar crater casts a shadow that has a length of about 4700 meters. What is the depth *d* (in meters) of the crater to the nearest 10 meters?

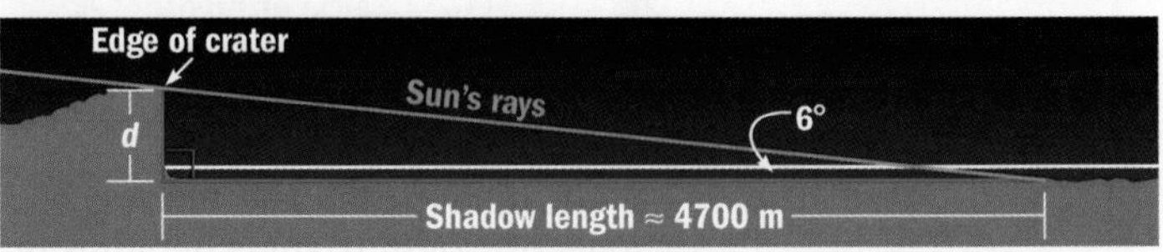

Solution

Use the tangent ratio. In the diagram, the length of the leg opposite the 6° angle is *d*. The length of the adjacent leg is about 4700 m.

$\tan 6° = \frac{\text{opposite}}{\text{adjacent}}$ **Definition of tangent ratio**

$\tan 6° = \frac{d}{4700}$ **Substitute.**

$0.1051 \approx \frac{d}{4700}$ **Use a calculator to approximate tan 6°.**

$494 \approx d$ **Multiply each side by 4700.**

Answer The depth of the crater is about 490 meters.

9.7 Exercises

More Practice, p. 811

Guided Practice

Vocabulary Check **In Exercises 1 and 2, use $\triangle ABC$ shown.**

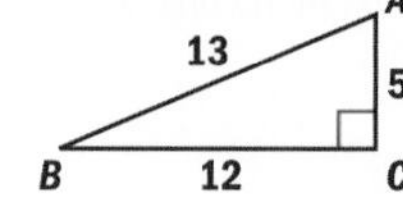

1. **a.** Identify the leg opposite $\angle A$. $\overline{BC}$

   b. Identify the leg adjacent to $\angle A$. $\overline{AC}$

2. Which angle of $\triangle ABC$ has a tangent of $\frac{12}{5}$? $\angle A$

Skill Check **Find tan *A*.**

3. $\frac{7}{24}$ 4. $\frac{15}{8}$ 5. $\frac{4}{3}$

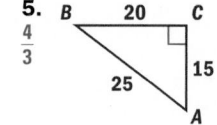

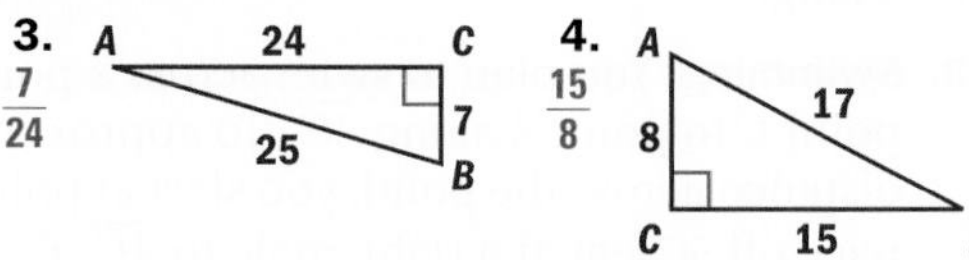

6. **Roofs** Use a calculator to find, to the nearest foot, the height h of the roof shown in the diagram. 9 ft

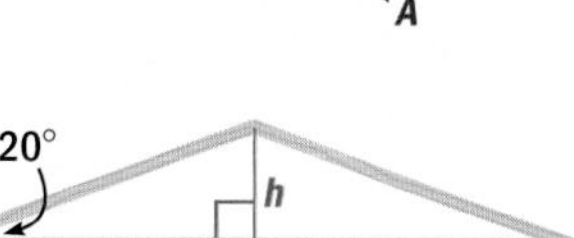

Practice and Problem Solving

Homework *Help*

Example	Exercises
1	7-9
2	10-17
3	18-23

Online Resources
CLASSZONE.COM
- More Examples
- eTutorial Plus

In the following exercises, you may find it helpful to use a calculator for approximating tangent values.

Find the tangent of each acute angle. Write your answers as fractions in simplest form. 7–9. See margin.

A 7. 8. 9.

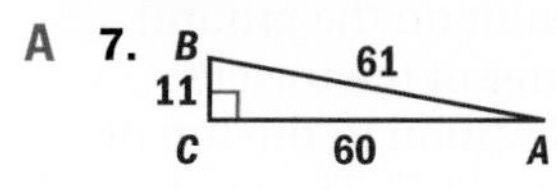

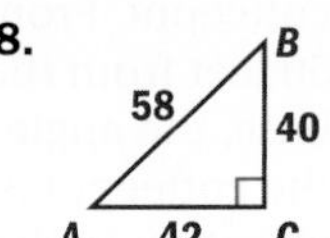

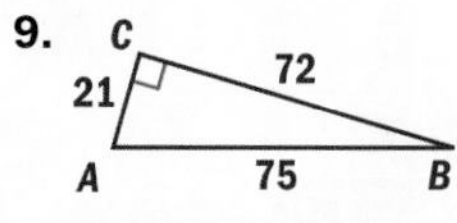

Approximate the tangent value to four decimal places.

10. tan 52° 1.2799 11. tan 66° 2.2460 12. tan 9° 0.1584 13. tan 15° 0.2679

14. tan 30° 0.5774 15. tan 33° 0.6494 16. tan 70° 2.7475 17. tan 89° 57.2900

Find the value of *x*. Round to the nearest tenth.

18. 30.7 19. 19.6 20. 9.4

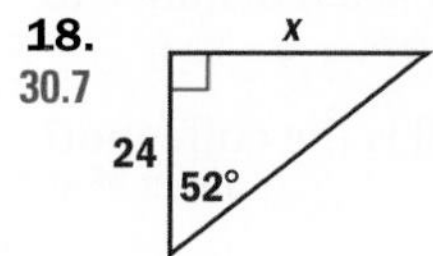

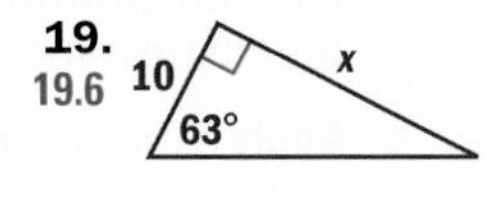

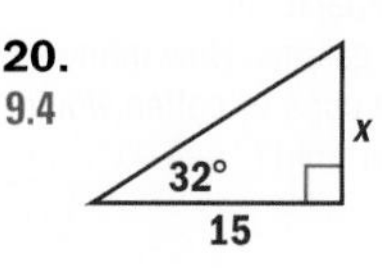

7. $\tan A = \frac{11}{60}$, $\tan B = \frac{60}{11}$

8. $\tan A = \frac{20}{21}$, $\tan B = \frac{21}{20}$

9. $\tan A = \frac{24}{7}$, $\tan B = \frac{7}{24}$

3 APPLY

ASSIGNMENT GUIDE

Basic Course
Day 1: pp. 491–493 Exs. 7–13, 18–21, 23–26, 28, 31–38

Average Course
Day 1: pp. 491–493 Exs. 7–9, 14–29, 31–38

Advanced Course
Day 1: pp. 491–493 Exs. 7–9, 14–19, 21–31*, 34–38

Block
pp. 491–493 Exs. 7–9, 14–29, 31–38 (with 9.6)

Extra Practice

- Student Edition, p. 811
- Chapter 9 Resource Book, pp. 58–60
- Test and Practice Generator

Transparency

Even-numbered answers are available on transparencies.

Homework Check

When you review students' homework for this lesson, go over the following exercises to check understanding of key concepts.
Basic: 7, 9, 10, 13, 18
Average: 8, 9, 15, 18, 21
Advanced: 8, 9, 17, 18, 23

Common Error

In Exercises 10–17, watch for students who are confused when their calculator gives a tangent value greater than 1.

Teaching Tip

In Exercise 14, ask students to sketch a 30°-60°-90° triangle with its relative side lengths labeled and use it to verify that $\tan 30° = \frac{1}{\sqrt{3}} \approx 0.5774$.

22. 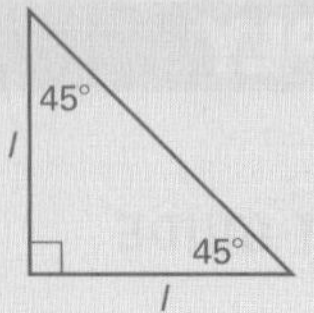

27. *Sample:*

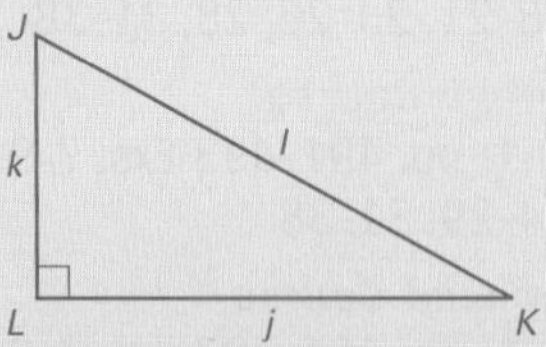

They are reciprocals. *Sample answer:* The side opposite each of the acute angles is the side adjacent to the other. From the drawing, $\tan J = \frac{j}{k}$ and $\tan K = \frac{k}{j}$, and $\frac{j}{k}$ and $\frac{k}{j}$ are reciprocals since $\frac{j}{k} \cdot \frac{k}{j} = 1$.

Reading *Algebra*

Vocabulary The angle that your line of sight to an object above your line of sight makes with a horizontal line from your eyes is called the *angle of elevation* of the object.

22. See margin for art. *Sample answer:* The legs of a 45°-45°-90° triangle are the same length. Since the lengths of the opposite and adjacent sides in the tangent ratio for each of the acute angles will always be leg lengths, if ℓ is a leg length, the tangent of each acute angle will be $\frac{\ell}{\ell} = 1$.

In the Real World

World's Largest Coffeepot The water tower in the photo has a capacity of 40,000 gallons. How many 8 ounce cups of coffee would the tower hold? **640,000 cups**

21. Forestry A forester stands 50 meters from the trunk of a tree and uses an instrument called a clinometer to measure the angle of elevation from eye level to the top of the tree. The distance from the forester's eye level to the ground is 1.5 meters.

Not drawn to scale

a. Let *d* represent the distance from the forester's eye level to the top of the tree. Write an expression for the height of the tree in terms of *d*. **$d + 1.5$**

b. Find *d* to the nearest tenth of a meter. **64.0 m**

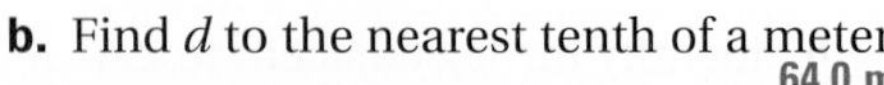

c. Find the height of the tree to the nearest tenth of a meter. **65.5 m**

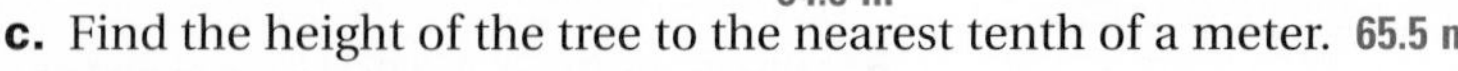

22. *Writing* Draw a 45°-45°-90° triangle. Explain how you know what the tangent of each acute angle is without measuring the sides of the triangle.

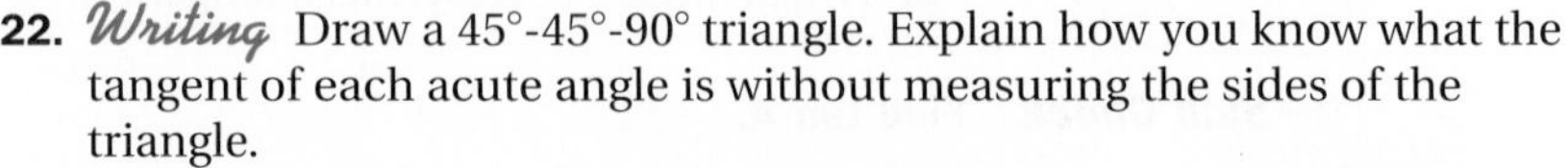

23. Swimming You plan to swim across a pond from point *C* to point *A* along $\overline{AC}$. To approximate the distance across the pond, you start at point *C* and pace off 50 feet at a right angle to $\overline{AC}$ as shown, stopping at point *B*. You estimate that the measure of $\angle B$ is about 70°. To the nearest foot, how far do you have to swim? **137 ft**

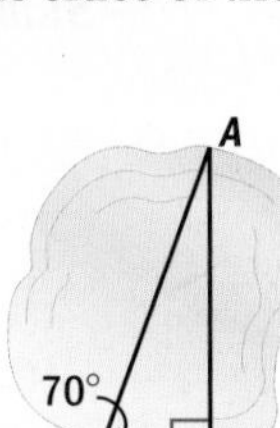

B Find the area of the triangle. Round your answer to the nearest tenth.

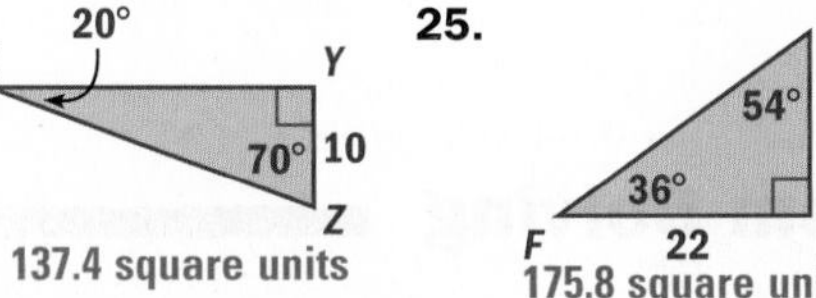

24. **137.4 square units**

25. **175.8 square units**

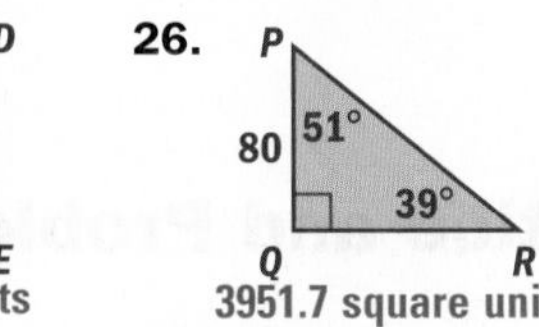

26. **3951.7 square units**

27. *Writing* Draw $\triangle JKL$ with a right angle at *L*. Describe the relationship between $\tan J$ and $\tan K$. Use your drawing to justify your reasoning. **See margin.**

28. World's Largest Coffeepot A water tower in Stanton, Iowa, is the world's largest coffeepot. From a point on the ground 50 feet from the center of the tower's base, the angle of elevation to the top of the coffeepot is about 68.2°. The angle of elevation to the bottom of the coffeepot is about 60.7°.

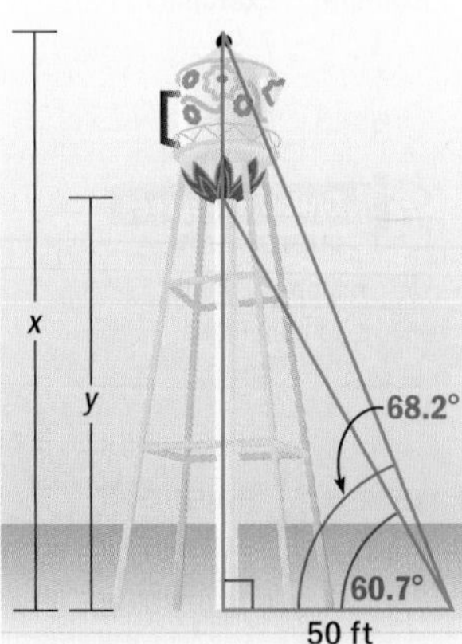

a. Calculate Find the distance *x* between the top of the coffeepot and the ground, and find the distance *y* between the bottom of the coffeepot and the ground. Give each distance to the nearest foot. **$x \approx 125$ ft, $y \approx 89$ ft**

b. Apply About how tall is the coffeepot? **about 36 ft**

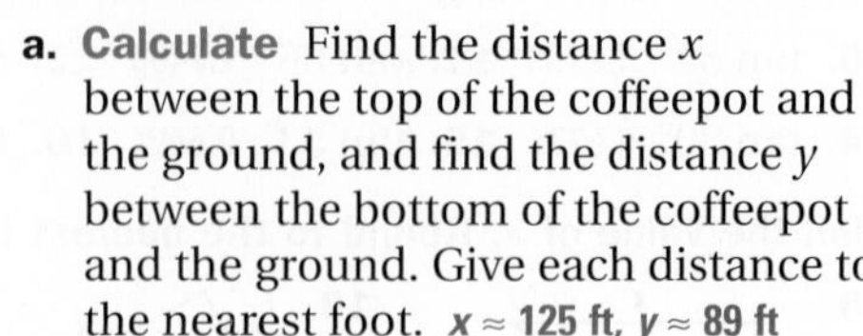

29a. About 4400 ft. *Sample answer:* Since $d = rt$, $d = 1100 \cdot 4 = 4400$ feet.

29b. *Sample answer:* Use the fact that triangles *ABD* and *CBD* are right triangles with an acute angle with measure $\frac{x°}{2}$ at your eye. Then you can use the tangent ratio: $\tan \frac{x°}{2} = \frac{s}{d}$.

C **29. Extended Problem Solving** You can estimate the size of a fireworks star. As shown, let *AC* be the distance across the star, let *d* be the distance in feet from your eye to the star, and let $x°$ be the measure of the angle determined by point *A*, your eye, and point *C*.

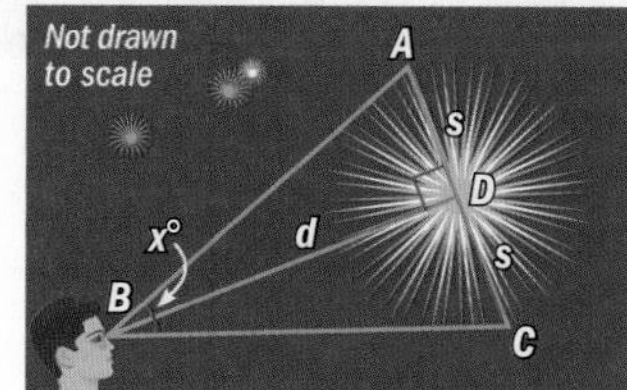

a. Explain You see the light from the explosion almost instantly, but its sound travels at about 1100 feet per second. Suppose you count *n* seconds from the time you see the explosion until you hear it. Find *d* when $n = 4$. Explain your reasoning.

b. Critical Thinking In the diagram, $\triangle ABD \cong \triangle CBD$. How you can use one of the triangles to find *s* if you know the values of *x* and *d*?

c. Interpret and Apply Suppose $x = 5$. Use your answer from part (a) to estimate the distance across the fireworks star to the nearest foot. 384 ft

30. Challenge Find the value of *x* to the nearest tenth of a centimeter. 17.6 cm

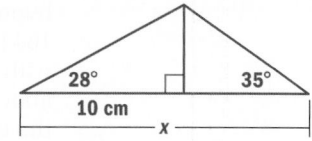

28°, 35°, 10 cm, x

Mixed Review

31. You pay \$1.17 for 3 cans of cat food. How much would you pay for 8 cans? *(Lesson 6.1)* \$3.12

In Exercises 32–35, simplify the expression. *(Lesson 9.2)*

32. $\sqrt{25x^2}$ $5x$ **33.** $\sqrt{36b}$ $6\sqrt{b}$ **34.** $\sqrt{18a^2b}$ $3a\sqrt{2b}$ **35.** $\sqrt{162f^2g^2}$ $9fg\sqrt{2}$

36. Find the distance between the points $(-9, 1)$ and $(6, 9)$. *(Lesson 9.5)* 17 units

Standardized Test Practice

37. Multiple Choice In $\triangle XYZ$, which ratio is equal to $\tan Y$? B

A. $\frac{x}{y}$ **B.** $\frac{y}{x}$ **C.** $\frac{x}{z}$ **D.** $\frac{y}{z}$

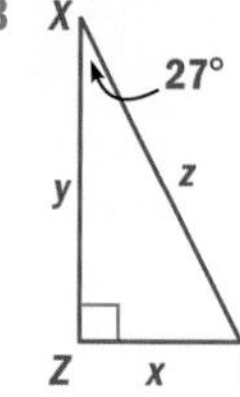

38. Multiple Choice In $\triangle XYZ$, let $y = 10$. Given that $\tan 27° \approx 0.5095$, what is the approximate value of *x*? G

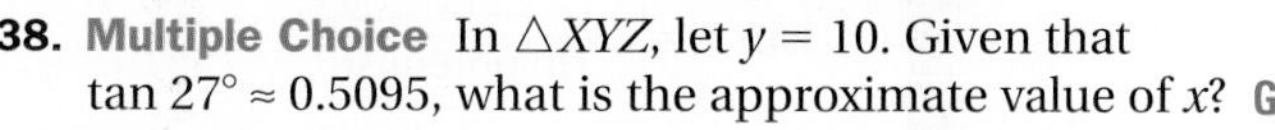

F. 0.05 **G.** 5 **H.** 10.5 **I.** 20

To a "T"

List the angle measures so that the tangents of the angles are in order from least to greatest. Write the letters for the first 6 angles in your list. TPATOE

60°	80°	11°	71°	31°	52°	23°	45°	68°
E	N	T	R	A	O	P	T	G

Unscramble the letters to answer the riddle.

What begins with T, ends with T, and has T in it?

TEAPOT

4 ASSESS

Assessment Resources

For more assessment resources, see:

- Assessment Book
- Test and Practice Generator

Mini-Quiz

Find the tangent of each acute angle in a triangle with the given side lengths. Write your answers as fractions in simplest form.

1. 24, 70, 74 $\frac{12}{35}, \frac{35}{12}$

2. 15, 36, 39 $\frac{5}{12}, \frac{12}{5}$

3. Use a calculator to approximate tan 20° and tan 86° to four decimal places. **0.3640, 14.3007**

4. Challenge Find the value of *x* to the nearest tenth of a centimeter.

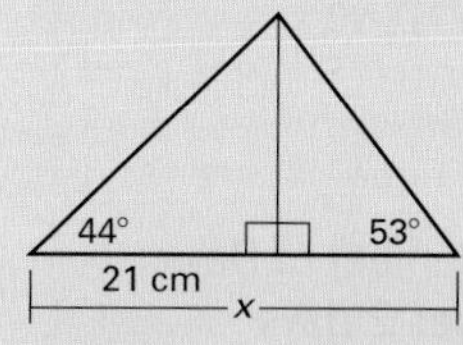

36.3 cm

5 FOLLOW-UP

Diagnosis/Remediation

- Study Guide in Chapter 9 Resource Book, pp. 61–62
- eTutorial Plus Online
- Extra Practice, p. 811
- Lesson Practice in Chapter 9 Resource Book, pp. 58–60

English Learner Support

- Spanish Study Guide
- Multi-Language Visual Glossary
- Chapter Audio Summaries CDs

Challenge

- Challenge Practice in Chapter 9 Resource Book, p. 64
- Teacher's Edition, p. 450F

1 PLAN

Skill Check
Use the triangle to name the side.

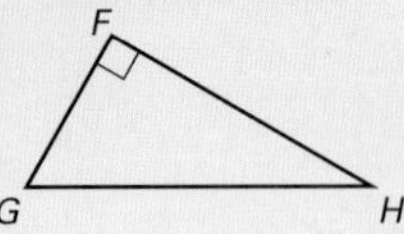

1. The side opposite $\angle H$ $\overline{FG}$
2. The side adjacent to $\angle G$ $\overline{FG}$
3. The hypotenuse $\overline{GH}$
4. The side adjacent to $\angle H$ $\overline{FH}$

LESSON OBJECTIVE
Use sine and cosine to find triangle side lengths.

PACING
Suggested Number of Days
Basic Course: 2 days
Average Course: 2 days
Advanced Course: 2 days
Block: 1 block

TEACHING RESOURCES
For a complete list of Teaching Resources, see page 450B.

TRANSPARENCY
Warm-Up Exercises for this lesson are available on a transparency.

2 TEACH

MOTIVATING THE LESSON
After reading the introduction, ask: "Why can't the Pythagorean theorem be used to find the height?" **Only one of the side lengths is known.** "Why can't the tangent ratio be used? **Only the length of the hypotenuse is given.**

494

LESSON 9.8

The Sine *and* Cosine Ratios

BEFORE	Now	WHY?
You used tangent to find triangle side lengths.	You'll use sine and cosine to find triangle side lengths.	So you can determine how to position a ladder, as in Ex. 22.

Vocabulary
sine, p. 494
cosine, p. 494

Ancient Sundial The structure shown is a sundial, built on a sunken platform in Jaipur, India, in the eighteenth century. The part of the structure above ground level is a right triangle. Its hypotenuse has a length of about 164 feet and makes an angle of 27° with the horizontal. About how far above ground level is the top of the triangle? In Example 4, you will see how to use a *sine* ratio to answer this question. Sine, abbreviated sin, *cosine*, abbreviated cos, and tangent are the three basic trigonometric ratios.

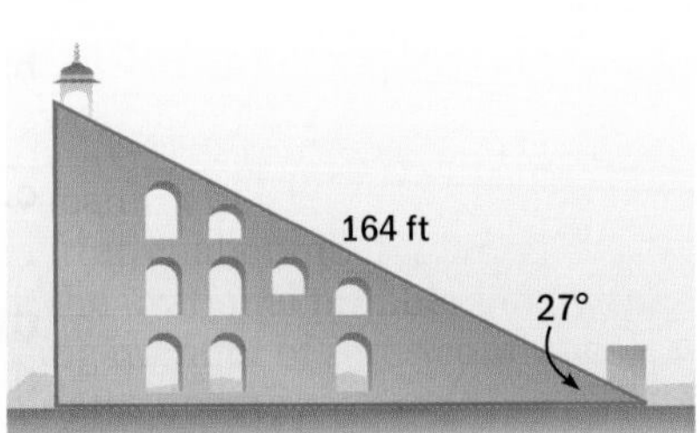

The Sine and Cosine Ratios

The **sine** of an acute angle of a right triangle is the ratio of the length of the side opposite the angle to the length of the hypotenuse.

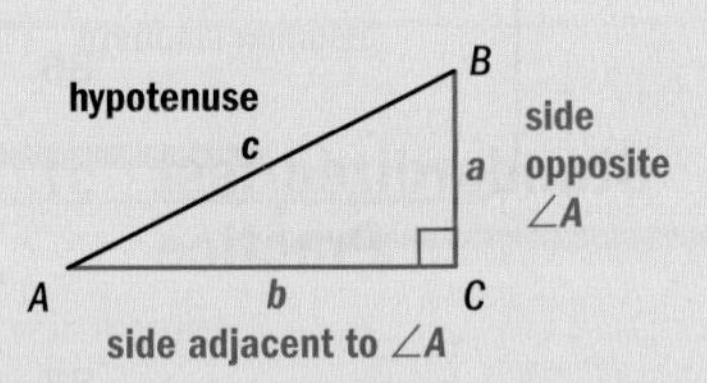

$$\sin A = \frac{\text{side opposite } \angle A}{\text{hypotenuse}} = \frac{a}{c}$$

The **cosine** of an acute angle of a right triangle is the ratio of the length of the angle's adjacent side to the length of the hypotenuse.

$$\cos A = \frac{\text{side adjacent to } \angle A}{\text{hypotenuse}} = \frac{b}{c}$$

Example 1 *Finding Sine and Cosine Ratios*

For $\triangle JKL$, find the sine and cosine of $\angle L$.

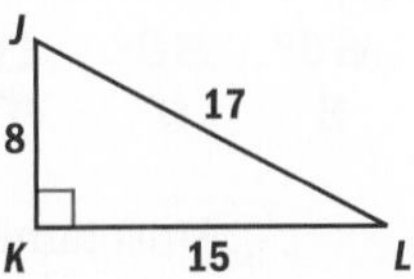

$$\sin L = \frac{\text{opposite}}{\text{hypotenuse}} = \frac{8}{17}$$

$$\cos L = \frac{\text{adjacent}}{\text{hypotenuse}} = \frac{15}{17}$$

NCTM CURRICULUM STANDARDS
Standard 3: Analyze properties of 2-D shapes
Standard 6: Solve problems in math and other contexts
Standard 9: Grasp connections among math ideas

Example 2 *Using a Calculator*

a. sin 38°

Keystrokes 2nd [TRIG] = 38) =

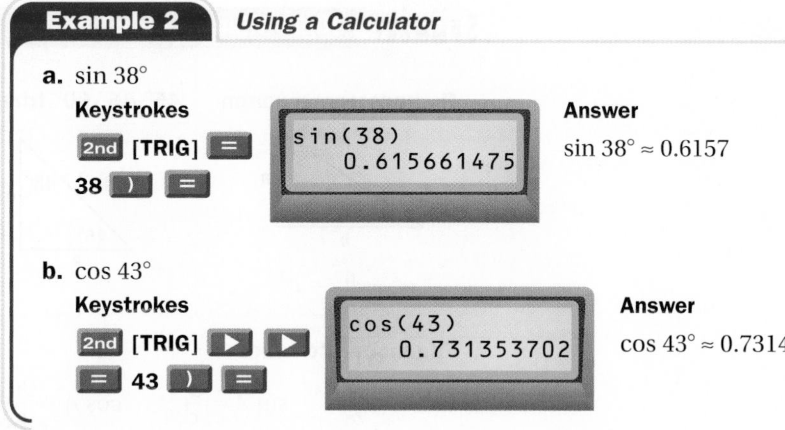

Answer sin 38° ≈ 0.6157

b. cos 43°

Keystrokes 2nd [TRIG] ▶ ▶ = 43) =

Answer cos 43° ≈ 0.7314

Checkpoint

1. Use a calculator to approximate sin 74° and cos 12° to four decimal places. **0.9613, 0.9781**

Example 3 *Using a Cosine Ratio*

In △*DEF* shown, $\overline{DE}$ is adjacent to ∠*D*. You know the length of the hypotenuse. To find the value of *x*, use cos *D*.

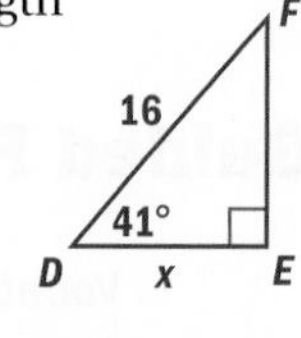

$\cos D = \frac{\text{adjacent}}{\text{hypotenuse}}$ **Definition of cosine ratio**

$\cos 41° = \frac{x}{16}$ **Substitute.**

$0.7547 \approx \frac{x}{16}$ **Use a calculator to approximate cos 41°.**

$12.1 \approx x$ **Multiply each side by 16.**

Example 4 *Using a Sine Ratio*

To find the height above ground level of the top of the triangle on page 494, find the length of the side opposite the 27° angle. Because you know the length of the hypotenuse, use sin 27°.

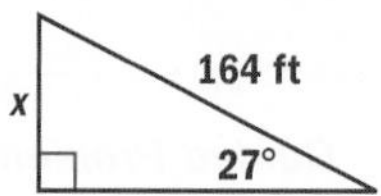

$\sin 27° = \frac{\text{opposite}}{\text{hypotenuse}}$ **Definition of sine ratio**

$\sin 27° = \frac{x}{164}$ **Substitute.**

$0.4540 \approx \frac{x}{164}$ **Use a calculator to approximate sin 27°.**

$74.456 \approx x$ **Multiply each side by 164.**

Answer The top of the triangle is about 74 feet above ground level.

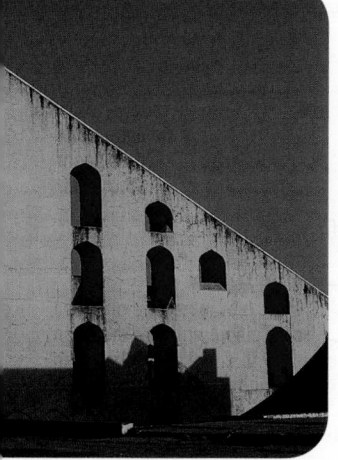

In the **Real World**

Ancient Sundial The sunken platform on which the ancient sundial described on page 494 stands is a rectangle approximately 134 feet wide and 146 feet long. What is the area of the platform? **about 19,564 ft²**

TIPS *for* NEW TEACHERS

Encourage students to write out the definitions of all three trigonometric ratios they have now learned and create a mnemonic to remember them. One such mnemonic is SOH-CAH-TOA [read as "sō-kŭ-tō-ă"] (**S**ine: **O**pposite over **H**ypotenuse; **C**osine: **A**djacent over **H**ypotenuse; **T**angent: **O**pposite over **A**djacent). See Tips for New Teachers in the *Chapter 9 Resource Book.*

Extra Examples

Example 1 For △*KLM*, find the sine and cosine of ∠*M*.

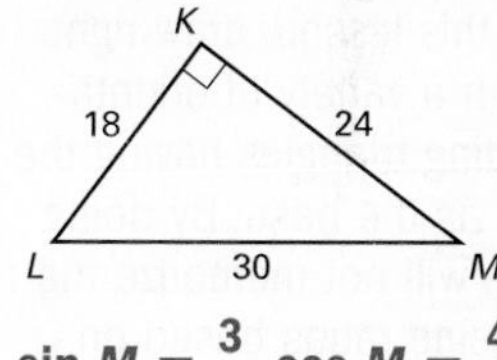

$\sin M = \frac{3}{5}, \cos M = \frac{4}{5}$

Example 2 Use a calculator to approximate the sine or cosine value to four decimal places.

a. sin 18° **0.3090**

b. cos 52° **0.6157**

Example 3 Use cos *R* to find the value of *x* to the nearest tenth. **17.7**

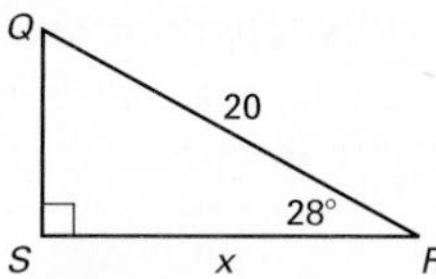

Example 4 Use sin *U* to find the value of *x* to the nearest tenth. **65.6**

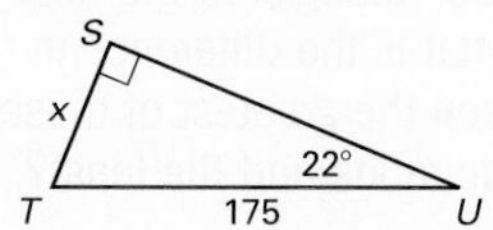

MULTIPLE REPRESENTATIONS

The summary of the right triangle relationships on this page utilizes both diagrams and symbols. Encourage students to verbally explain each diagram.

COMMON ERROR

Watch for students who incorrectly memorize the sine and cosine ratios in terms of the lengths of the sides. For example, they might incorrectly think of the sine ratio as the short side length divided by the length of the hypotenuse because this is true in the particular triangle they are viewing.

TEACHING TIP

Throughout this lesson, draw right triangles with a variety of orientations, including triangles having the hypotenuse as the base. By doing so, students will not memorize the sine and cosine ratios based on one particular orientation of a right triangle.

CONCEPT CHECK

How is the cosine ratio useful for finding an unknown side length in a triangle? *Sample answer:* **Whenever you know the measure of one acute angle in a right triangle and either the length of the hypotenuse or the length of one of the other two sides, you can find the unknown side length.**

DAILY PUZZLER

Sarah finds the sine, cosine, and tangent of the smaller acute angle in a 30°-60°-90° triangle. To the nearest tenth, what is the difference in value between the greatest of these trigonometric ratios and the least? **0.4**

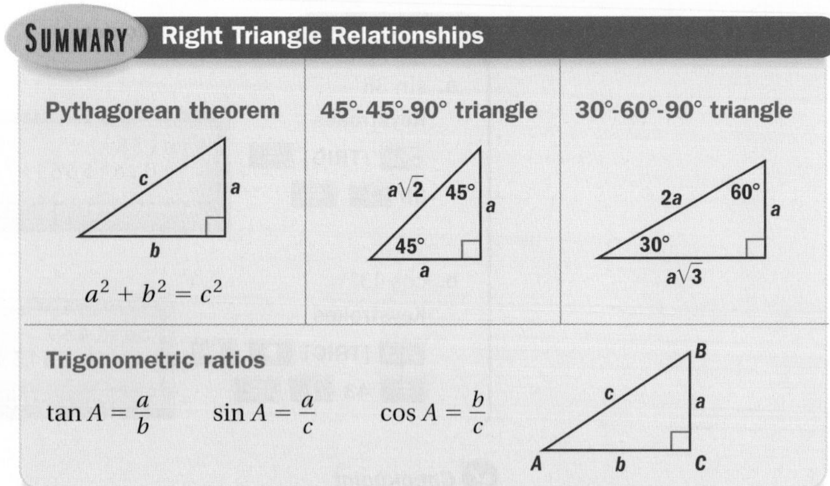

9.8 Exercises

More Practice, p. 811

Guided Practice

Vocabulary Check **In Exercises 1 and 2, use $\triangle DEF$.**

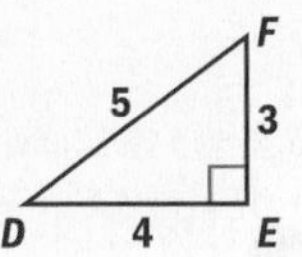

1. Which ratio is equal to sin F? **C**

   A. $\frac{3}{5}$ **B.** $\frac{3}{4}$ **C.** $\frac{4}{5}$

2. Which side lengths do you need to know to find sin D? $\overline{EF}$ **and** $\overline{DF}$

Skill Check

3. Write the sine and cosine ratio for each acute angle of $\triangle JKL$.

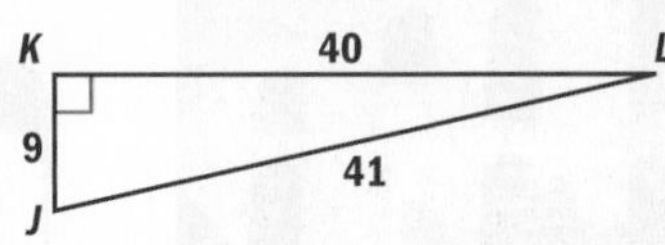

3. $\sin J = \frac{40}{41}$, $\cos J = \frac{9}{41}$, $\sin L = \frac{9}{41}$, $\cos L = \frac{40}{41}$

Guided Problem Solving

4. **Radio Tower** A support wire 225 feet long is fastened to the top of a radio tower. The wire makes an angle of 70° with the ground. How tall is the tower to the nearest foot?

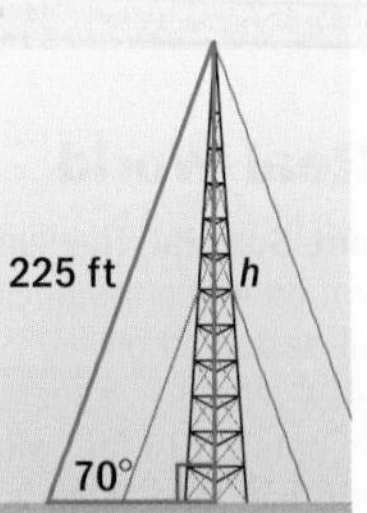

   (1) Determine which trigonometric ratio you can use to find the height h of the tower. Write an equation you can use to find h. **sine; $\sin 70° = \frac{h}{225}$**

   (2) Use a calculator to find the height of the tower to the nearest foot. **211 ft**

Practice and Problem Solving

Homework Help

Example	Exercises
1	5-7
2	8-15
3	16-25
4	16-25

Online Resources
CLASSZONE.COM
- More Examples
- eTutorial Plus

5. $\sin P = \frac{3}{5}$, $\cos P = \frac{4}{5}$, $\sin Q = \frac{4}{5}$, $\cos Q = \frac{3}{5}$

6. $\sin J = \frac{15}{17}$, $\cos J = \frac{8}{17}$, $\sin L = \frac{8}{17}$, $\cos L = \frac{15}{17}$

7. $\sin A = \frac{12}{13}$, $\cos A = \frac{5}{13}$, $\sin B = \frac{5}{13}$, $\cos B = \frac{12}{13}$

23. See margin for art; the side opposite each of the acute angles is the side adjacent to the other, so the sine of one acute angle is equal to the cosine of the other acute angle. From the drawing, $\sin D = \frac{d}{e} = \cos F$, and $\sin F = \frac{f}{e} = \cos D$.

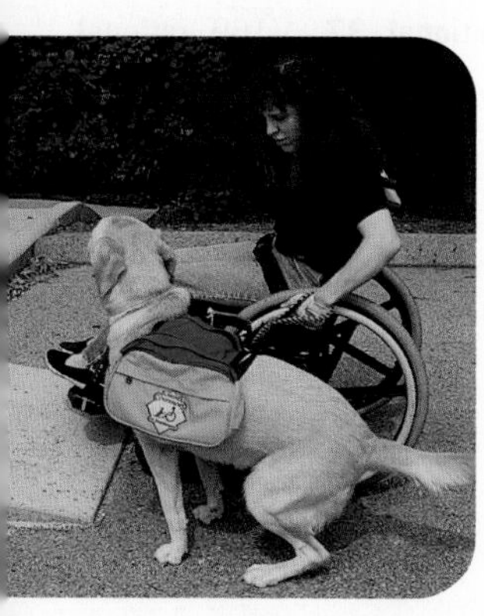

In the following exercises, you may find it helpful to use a calculator for approximating sine and cosine values.

Find the sine and cosine of each acute angle. Write your answers as fractions in simplest form. 5–7. See margin.

A **5.**

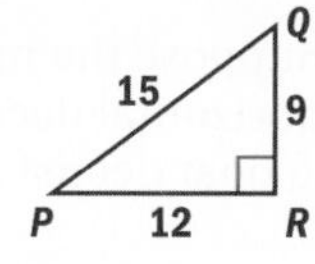

6.

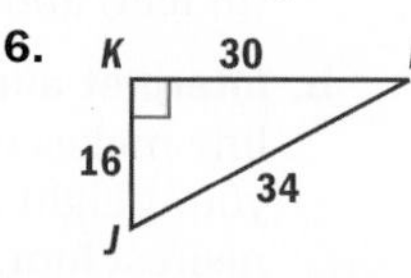

7.

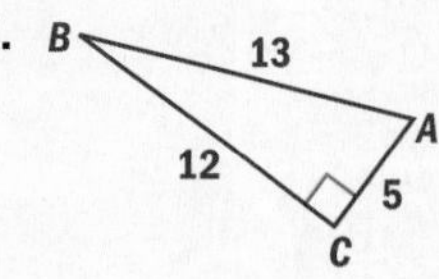

Approximate the sine or cosine value to four decimal places.

8. sin 60° 0.8660 **9.** cos 22° 0.9272 **10.** cos 34° 0.8290 **11.** sin 72° 0.9511

12. cos 15° 0.9659 **13.** sin 65° 0.9063 **14.** sin 23° 0.3907 **15.** cos 1° 0.9998

Find the value of x to the nearest tenth.

16.

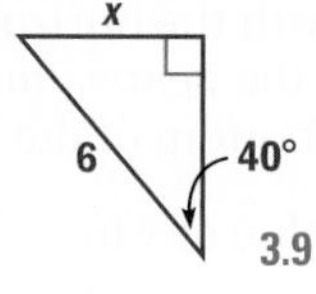

3.9

17.

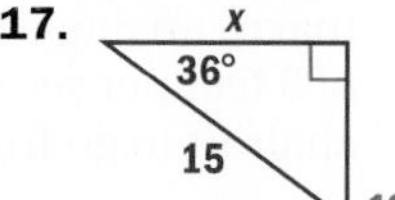

12.1

18.

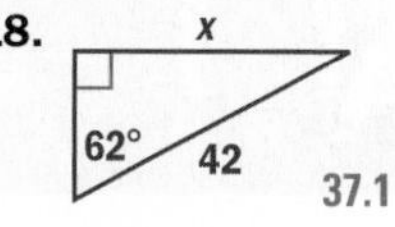

37.1

19. 58°, 104, x 88.2

20.

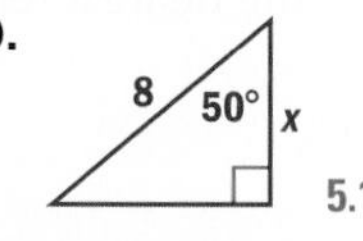

5.1

21.

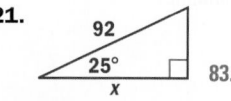

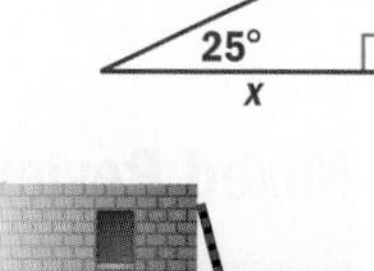

83.4

22. Ladders You set a 24 foot ladder against a building. For safety reasons, the angle that the ladder makes with the ground should be about 75°. To the nearest foot, how far from the building should you place the bottom of the ladder? 6 ft

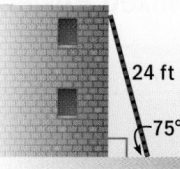

(24 ft, 75°)

23. *Writing* Draw $\triangle DEF$ with a right angle at E. Use your drawing to describe the relationship between the sine of one acute angle of a right triangle and the cosine of the other acute angle.

24. Pyramids A diagram of a cross section of the pyramid of Amenemhet III at Hawara, Egypt, is shown. Find the height h of the pyramid to the nearest meter. 58 m

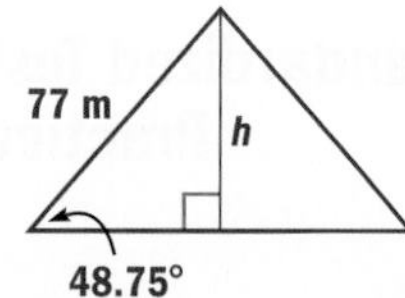

25. Ramps An access ramp that is 4 meters long makes an angle of 4.8° with the ground, as shown. What horizontal distance d does the ramp cover? Round your answer to the nearest tenth of a meter. 4.0 m

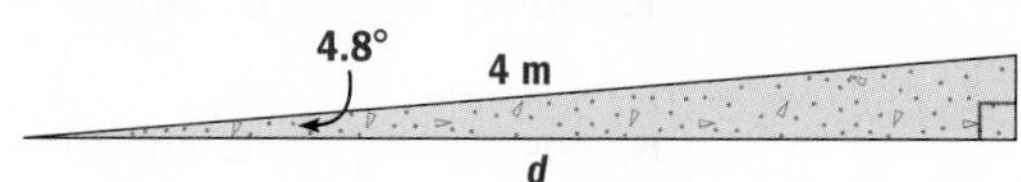

3 APPLY

ASSIGNMENT GUIDE

Basic Course

Day 1: pp. 497–498 Exs. 5-15, 30-35

Day 2: pp. 497–498 Exs. 16-22, 24-26, 36-39

Average Course

Day 1: pp. 497–498 Exs. 5-15, 30-36

Day 2: pp. 497–498 Exs. 16-28, 37-39

Advanced Course

Day 1: pp. 497–498 Exs. 5-15, 31-35

Day 2: pp. 497–498 Exs. 18-29*, 38, 39

Block

pp. 497–498 Exs. 5-28, 30-39

Extra Practice

- Student Edition, p. 811
- Chapter 9 Resource Book, pp. 67-69
- Test and Practice Generator

Transparency

Even-numbered answers are available on transparencies.

Homework Check

When you review students' homework for this lesson, go over the following exercises to check understanding of key concepts.

Basic: 5, 8, 10, 16, 20
Average: 6, 11, 15, 18, 21
Advanced: 7, 12, 14, 19, 22

23. ***Sample:***

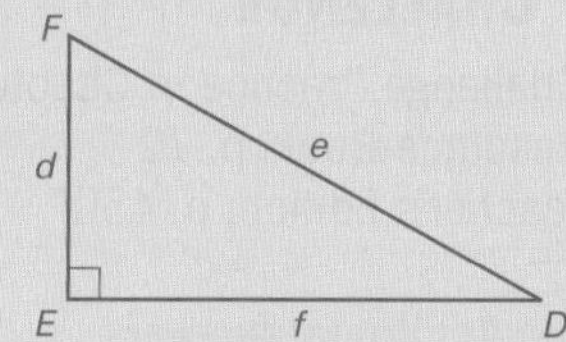

4 ASSESS

Assessment Resources

For more assessment resources, see:

- Assessment Book
- Test and Practice Generator

Mini-Quiz

Find the sine and cosine of each acute angle in a triangle with these side lengths. Write your answers as fractions in simplest form.

1. 12, 35, 37 $\frac{12}{37}, \frac{35}{37}$
2. 7, 24, 25 $\frac{7}{25}, \frac{24}{25}$
3. Use a calculator to approximate cos 21° and sin 48° to four decimal places. **0.9336, 0.7431**
4. **Challenge** Find the value of x to the nearest tenth. **39.3**

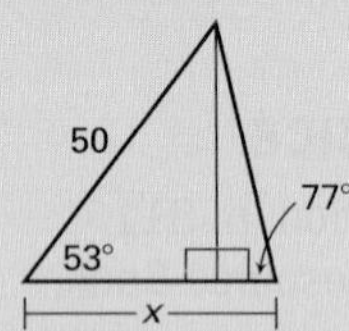

5 FOLLOW-UP

Diagnosis/Remediation

- Study Guide in Chapter 9 Resource Book, pp. 70–71
- eTutorial Plus Online
- Extra Practice, p. 811
- Lesson Practice in Chapter 9 Resource Book, pp. 67–69

English Learner Support

- Spanish Study Guide
- Multi-Language Visual Glossary
- Chapter Audio Summaries CDs

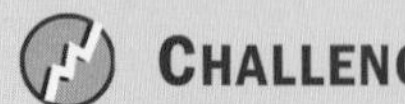

Challenge

- Challenge Practice in Chapter 9 Resource Book, p. 72
- Teacher's Edition, p. 450F

27. See Additional Answers beginning on page AA1.

B **26. Extended Problem Solving** You are wearing a parachute and being pulled through the air by a tow line attached to a boat. The tow line is 600 feet long and makes an angle of 30° with the horizontal.

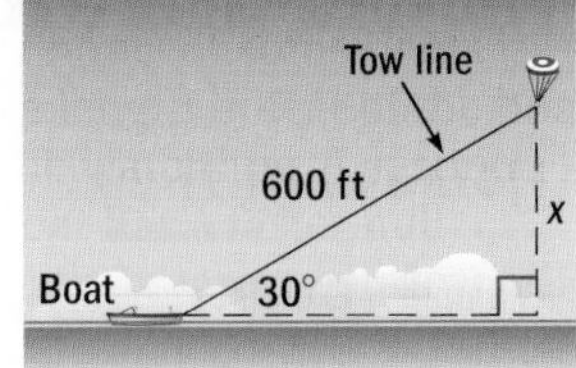

a. **Calculate** What is your height x (in feet) above the boat? **300 ft**

b. **Interpret and Apply** Suppose the measure of the angle that the tow line makes with the horizontal decreases by 3°. By how much does your height above the boat decrease? Give your answer to the nearest foot. **28 ft**

27. Critical Thinking In $\triangle ABC$, the measure of $\angle B$ is about 37°. Describe four methods you could use to find the value of b. **See margin.**

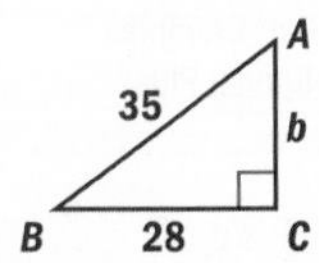

C **28. Chairlift** A chairlift at a ski resort has a vertical climb of 440 feet and makes an angle of 11° with the horizontal. The chairlift travels at a rate of 9 feet per second. To the nearest minute, how long does it take the chairlift to go from the bottom of the hill to the top? **4 min**

Bicyclists using a chairlift in summer

29. Challenge Find the value of x to the nearest tenth. **24.4**

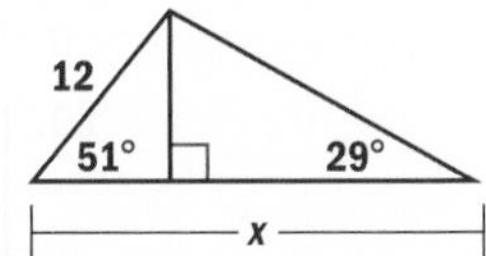

Mixed Review

Determine whether the triangle with the given side lengths is a right triangle. *(Lesson 9.3)*

30. 2.5, 6, 6.5 **yes** **31.** 10, 12, 16 **no** **32.** 20, 22, 30 **no**

33. In the figure, $\triangle ABC \sim \triangle DEF$. Name the corresponding parts of the figures. *(Lesson 6.4)* **$\angle A$ and $\angle D$, $\angle B$ and $\angle E$, $\angle C$ and $\angle F$, $\overline{AB}$ and $\overline{DE}$, $\overline{BC}$ and $\overline{EF}$, $\overline{AC}$ and $\overline{DF}$**

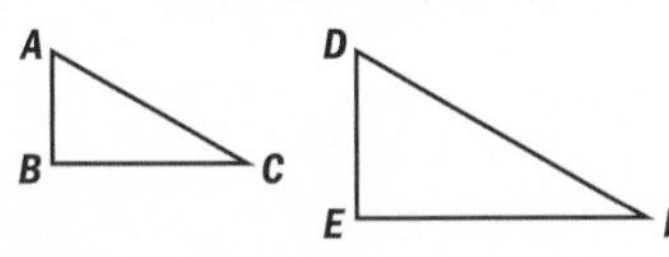

Tell whether the number is *rational* or *irrational*. *(Lesson 9.4)*

34. $\sqrt{900}$ **rational** **35.** $\sqrt{32}$ **irrational** **36.** $\sqrt{8.5}$ **irrational** **37.** $\sqrt{169}$ **rational**

Standardized Test Practice

In Exercises 38 and 39, use $\triangle PQR$.

38. Multiple Choice Which ratio is equal to sin P? **C**

A. $\frac{p}{r}$ **B.** $\frac{r}{q}$ **C.** $\frac{p}{q}$ **D.** $\frac{q}{p}$

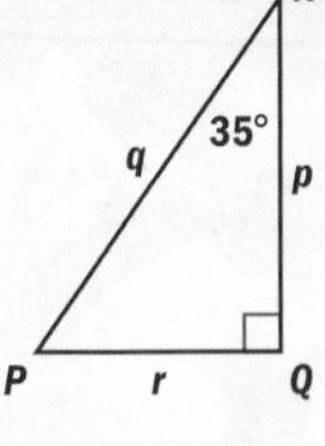

39. Multiple Choice If $q = 45$, which equation can you use to find r? **F**

F. $\sin 35° = \frac{r}{45}$ **G.** $\sin 35° = \frac{45}{r}$

H. $\cos 35° = \frac{r}{45}$ **I.** $\cos 35° = \frac{45}{r}$

9.8 Inverse Sine, Cosine, and Tangent

Goal Use a calculator to find angles using inverse trigonometric functions.

For right triangles, the sine, cosine, and tangent are functions that accept angle measures as inputs and give ratios of side lengths as outputs. The *inverse* sine, cosine, and tangent functions (written as $\sin^{-1}$, $\cos^{-1}$, and $\tan^{-1}$) accept ratios of side lengths as inputs and give angle measures as outputs. For instance:

$$\text{If } \sin x° = \frac{a}{b}, \text{ then } \sin^{-1}\left(\frac{a}{b}\right) = x°.$$

Example

A moving truck has a loading ramp that is 10 feet long. The deck of the truck is 3 feet above the ground. Use a calculator to find the angle the ramp makes with the ground.

When the loading ramp is extended from the back of the truck, a right triangle is formed.

$$\sin A = \frac{\text{opposite}}{\text{hypotenuse}} = \frac{3}{10}$$

$$m\angle A = \sin^{-1}\left(\frac{3}{10}\right)$$

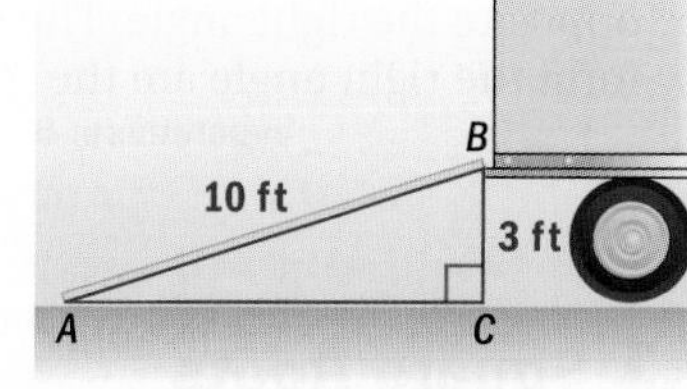

Keystrokes

2nd [TRIG] ▶ = 3 / 10) =

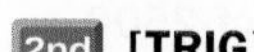

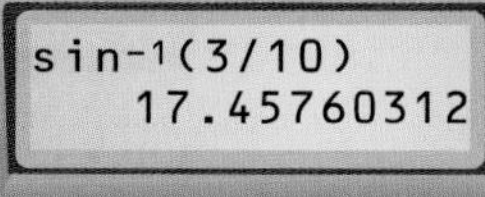

Answer The ramp makes an angle of about 17.5° with the ground.

Tech Help

You use / to enter a ratio as a fraction, but you can also use ÷ to enter the ratio as a decimal.

Draw Conclusions

Use a calculator to evaluate the expression. Round to the nearest tenth of a degree.

1. $\sin^{-1}\left(\frac{3}{5}\right)$ 36.9°
2. $\sin^{-1}\left(\frac{1}{2}\right)$ 30°
3. $\cos^{-1}\left(\frac{12}{13}\right)$ 22.6°
4. $\cos^{-1}\left(\frac{2}{3}\right)$ 48.2°
5. $\tan^{-1}\left(\frac{4}{3}\right)$ 53.1°
6. $\tan^{-1}\left(\frac{1}{10}\right)$ 5.7°
7. **Moving Truck** The deck of another moving truck is only 2 feet above the ground. If a ramp is 10 feet long, what angle does it make with the ground? 11.5°

NCTM CURRICULUM STANDARDS

Standard 6: Solve problems in math and other contexts
Standard 9: Grasp connections among math ideas

1 PLAN

Learn the Method

- Students will use a calculator to find angles using inverse trigonometric functions.
- Students can use this method to find the measures of the acute angles in Exercises 5–7 on page 497.

Grouping

Students should work individually.

2 TEACH

Tips for Success

Have students look back through the examples in the two previous lessons and make a list of sine, cosine, and tangent values they know are correct. Have them use these values to test that the inverse functions they try on the calculator produce the correct angles.

Extra Examples

Example A remote-control airplane leaves a level runway and steadily climbs to a height of 8 feet in the time it takes to fly 40 feet along the runway. Use a calculator to find the takeoff angle that the plane's path makes with the ground? **about 11.3°**

3 CLOSE

Assessment

Use a calculator to evaluate the expression. Round to the nearest tenth of a degree.

1. $\sin^{-1}\left(\frac{3}{4}\right)$ **48.6°**
2. $\cos^{-1}\left(\frac{1}{3}\right)$ **70.5°**

ADDITIONAL RESOURCES

The following resources are available to help review the materials in Lessons 9.5–9.8.

Chapter 9 Resource Book
- Lesson Practice
- Study Guide

Assessment Book
- Chapter 9 Quiz 2

Technology
- Test and Practice Generator
- eTutorial CD-ROM

Internet
- Classzone
- eWorkbook Plus Online
- eTutorial Plus Online

ENGLISH LEARNER SUPPORT

- Spanish Study Guide
- Multi-Language Visual Glossary
- Chapter Audio Summaries CDs

3. the point on the segment that is equally distant from the endpoints

CHAPTER 9

Chapter Review

Vocabulary Review

square root, p. 453	simplest form of a radical expression, p. 458	Pythagorean theorem, p. 465	trigonometric ratio, p. 489
perfect square, p. 454	hypotenuse, p. 465	irrational number, p. 470	tangent, p. 489
radical expression, p. 454	leg, p. 465	real number, p. 470	sine, p. 494
		midpoint, p. 478	cosine, p. 494

In Exercises 1 and 2, copy and complete the statement.

1. A(n) _?_ of a number n is a number m such that $m^2 = n$. **square root**

2. In a right triangle, the _?_ is the side opposite the right angle. The sides that form the right angle are the _?_. **hypotenuse; legs**

3. What is the midpoint of a segment? **See margin.**

4. For $\triangle DEF$ below, write sin D, cos D, and tan D in terms of d, e, and f. $\sin D = \frac{d}{f}$, $\cos D = \frac{e}{f}$, $\tan D = \frac{d}{e}$

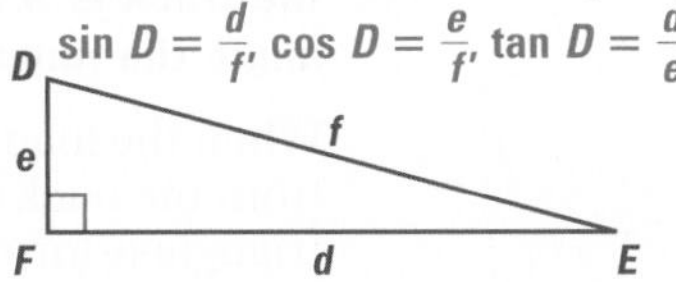

9.1 Square Roots

Examples on pp. 453–455

Goal

Find and approximate square roots.

Example **Find the square roots of 2500.**

You know that $50^2 = 2500$ and $(-50)^2 = 2500$. Therefore, the square roots of 2500 are 50 and -50.

Example **Approximate $\sqrt{78}$ to the nearest integer.**

$64 < 78 < 81$	Identify perfect squares closest to 78.
$\sqrt{64} < \sqrt{78} < \sqrt{81}$	Take positive square root of each number.
$8 < \sqrt{78} < 9$	Evaluate square root of each perfect square.

Answer Because 78 is closer to 81 than 64, $\sqrt{78}$ is closer to 9 than to 8. So, to the nearest integer, $\sqrt{78} \approx 9$.

 **5.** Find the square roots of 625 and the square roots of 8100. **±25, ±90**

Approximate the square root to the nearest integer.

6. $\sqrt{18}$ **4** **7.** $-\sqrt{28}$ **−5** **8.** $-\sqrt{39}$ **−6** **9.** $\sqrt{60}$ **8**

9.2 Simplifying Square Roots

Examples on pp. 458–459

Goal

Simplify radical expressions.

Example Simplify $\sqrt{112}$ and $\sqrt{\frac{33b}{25}}$.

a. $\sqrt{112} = \sqrt{16 \cdot 7}$ Factor using greatest perfect square factor.

$= \sqrt{16} \cdot \sqrt{7}$ Product property of square roots

$= 4\sqrt{7}$ Simplify.

b. $\sqrt{\frac{33b}{25}} = \frac{\sqrt{33b}}{\sqrt{25}}$ Quotient property of square roots

$= \frac{\sqrt{33b}}{5}$ Simplify.

Simplify the expression.

10. $\sqrt{350}$ $5\sqrt{14}$ **11.** $\sqrt{72}$ $6\sqrt{2}$ **12.** $\sqrt{\frac{48}{49}}$ $\frac{4\sqrt{3}}{7}$ **13.** $\sqrt{\frac{29a}{100}}$ $\frac{\sqrt{29a}}{10}$

14. $\sqrt{\frac{8}{n^2}}$ $\frac{2\sqrt{2}}{n}$ **15.** $\sqrt{18z^2}$ $3z\sqrt{2}$ **16.** $\sqrt{75m}$ $5\sqrt{3m}$ **17.** $\sqrt{\frac{2a^2}{49}}$ $\frac{a\sqrt{2}}{7}$

9.3 The Pythagorean Theorem

Examples on pp. 465–466

Goal

Use the Pythagorean theorem to find unknown side lengths of right triangles.

Example Find the unknown length c in simplest form.

$a^2 + b^2 = c^2$ Pythagorean theorem

$8^2 + 14^2 = c^2$ Substitute 8 for a and 14 for b.

$64 + 196 = c^2$ Evaluate powers.

$260 = c^2$ Add.

$\sqrt{260} = c$ Take positive square root of each side.

$2\sqrt{65} = c$ Simplify.

8, c, 14

Answer The length c of the hypotenuse of the triangle is $2\sqrt{65}$ units.

Find the unknown length. Write your answer in simplest form.

18.

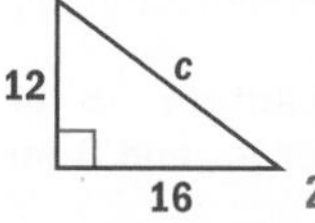

20

19.

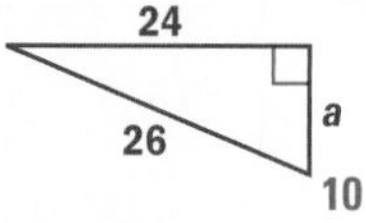

10

20.

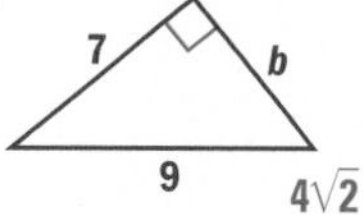

$4\sqrt{2}$

21. Find the length x of the diagonal of the rectangle. Write your answer in simplest form. $\sqrt{58}$

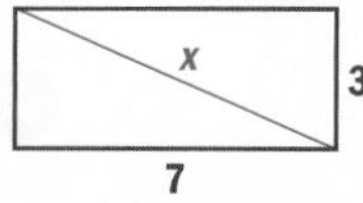

The following resources are available to help review the materials in this chapter.

Chapter 9 Resource Book
- Chapter Review Games and Activities, p. 73
- Cumulative Practice, Chs. 1-9

English/Spanish Chapter Reviews and Tests

Chapter Audio Summaries CDs

eTutorial CD-ROM

eWorkbook Plus Online

eTutorial Plus Online

9.4 Real Numbers

Examples on pp. 470–472

Goal

Compare and order real numbers.

Example **Use a number line to order the numbers -2.5, $\sqrt{6}$, $\frac{17}{8}$, 1.8, and $-\sqrt{2}$ from least to greatest.**

Graph the numbers on a number line and read them from left to right.

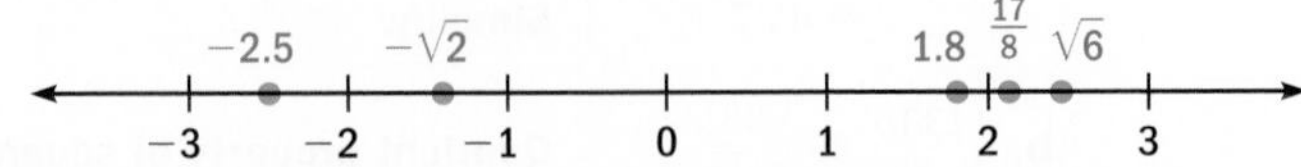

From least to greatest, the numbers are -2.5, $-\sqrt{2}$, 1.8, $\frac{17}{8}$, and $\sqrt{6}$.

Copy and complete the statement using <, >, or =.

22. $\sqrt{10}$? 2.1 >
23. $\sqrt{15}$? $2\frac{1}{3}$ >
24. $\sqrt{1.44}$? 1.2 =
25. $5\frac{1}{2}$? $\sqrt{48}$ <

Use a number line to order the numbers from least to greatest.

26. $\sqrt{30}$, -3.5, $\frac{17}{5}$, $-\sqrt{12}$
-3.5, $-\sqrt{12}$, $\frac{17}{5}$, $\sqrt{30}$

27. $\frac{19}{6}$, $-\sqrt{18}$, $\sqrt{20}$, -5.01
-5.01, $-\sqrt{18}$, $\frac{19}{6}$, $\sqrt{20}$

9.5 The Distance and Midpoint Formulas

Examples on pp. 476–478

Goal

Use the distance and midpoint formulas.

Example **Given points $A(-5, 6)$ and $B(3, 8)$, find the distance d between the points, and find the midpoint M of $\overline{AB}$.**

a. $d = \sqrt{(x_2 - x_1)^2 + (y_2 - y_1)^2}$ — **Distance formula**

$= \sqrt{(3 - (-5))^2 + (8 - 6)^2}$ — **Substitute 3 for x_2, −5 for x_1, 8 for y_2, and 6 for y_1.**

$= \sqrt{(8)^2 + (2)^2}$ — **Subtract.**

$= \sqrt{64 + 4}$ — **Evaluate powers.**

$= \sqrt{68}$ — **Add.**

$= 2\sqrt{17}$ — **Simplify.**

b. $M = \left(\frac{x_1 + x_2}{2}, \frac{y_1 + y_2}{2}\right)$ — **Midpoint formula**

$= \left(\frac{-5 + 3}{2}, \frac{6 + 8}{2}\right)$ — **Substitute −5 for x_1, 3 for x_2, 6 for y_1, and 8 for y_2.**

$= (-1, 7)$ — **Simplify.**

28. Find the distance between points $A(9, 10)$ and $B(6, 6)$, and find the midpoint M of $\overline{AB}$. 5, $M\left(7\frac{1}{2}, 8\right)$

9.6 Special Right Triangles

Examples on pp. 483–485

▶ Goal

Find unknown side lengths in special right triangles.

Example **Find the value of x.**

The triangle is a 45°-45°-90° triangle. The value of x, which is the length of the hypotenuse, is the product of the length of a leg and $\sqrt{2}$.

$x = \text{leg} \cdot \sqrt{2} = 6\sqrt{2}$

✔ **Find the values of x and y. Write your answers in simplest form.**

29.

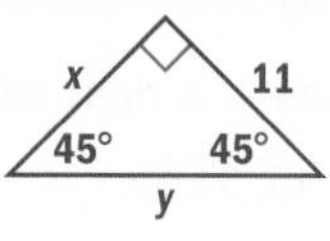

$x = 11,\ y = 11\sqrt{2}$

30.

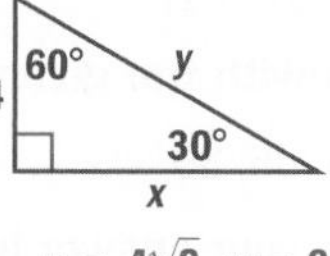

$x = 4\sqrt{3},\ y = 8$

31.

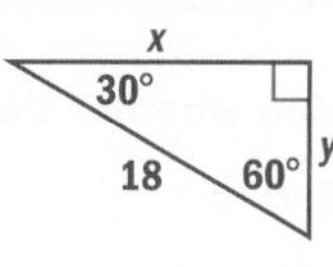

$x = 9\sqrt{3},\ y = 9$

9.7 The Tangent Ratio

Examples on pp. 489–490

▶ Goal

Use the tangent ratio to find an unknown length in a right triangle.

Example **Find the value of m. Round to the nearest tenth.**

$\tan 20° = \frac{m}{48}$ — **Definition of tangent ratio**

$0.3640 \approx \frac{m}{48}$ — **Use a calculator to approximate tan 20°.**

$17.5 \approx m$ — **Multiply each side by 48. Round.**

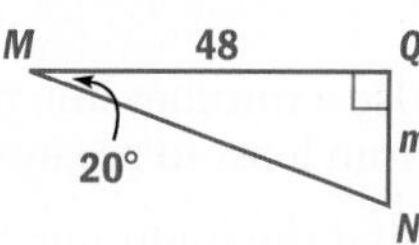

✔ **32.** In $\triangle PQR$ with right angle at R, $\angle P$ has a measure of 72°. The leg adjacent to $\angle P$ has a length of 8 units. Find the length of the leg opposite $\angle P$ to the nearest tenth. **24.6 units**

9.8 The Sine and Cosine Ratios

Examples on pp. 494–495

▶ Goal

Use the sine and cosine ratios to find unknown lengths in a right triangle.

Example **Find the value of a. Round to the nearest tenth.**

$\sin 40° = \frac{a}{15}$ — **Definition of sine ratio**

$0.6428 \approx \frac{a}{15}$ — **Use a calculator to approximate sin 40°.**

$9.6 \approx a$ — **Multiply each side by 15. Round.**

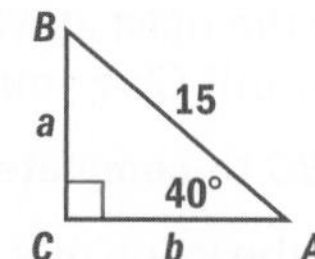

✔ **33.** Find the value of b in $\triangle ABC$. Round to the nearest tenth. **11.5**

ADDITIONAL RESOURCES

Assessment Book
- Chapter Test (3 levels), pp. 109–114
- Standardized Chapter Test, p. 115
- Alternative Assessment, pp. 116–117

Test and Practice Generator

CHAPTER 9

Chapter Test

Solve the equation. Round to the nearest tenth if necessary.

1. $x^2 = 25$ ±5 **2.** $225 = t^2$ ±15 **3.** $216 = 2z^2$ ±10.4 **4.** $3y^2 = 147$ ±7

Simplify the expression.

5. $\sqrt{162}$ $9\sqrt{2}$ **6.** $\sqrt{\frac{20}{121}}$ $\frac{2\sqrt{5}}{11}$ **7.** $\sqrt{\frac{x}{400}}$ $\frac{\sqrt{x}}{20}$ **8.** $\sqrt{50a^2}$ $5a\sqrt{2}$

Determine whether the triangle with the given side lengths is a right triangle.

9. 4, 5, 6 no **10.** 15, 36, 39 yes **11.** 24, 45, 51 yes **12.** 5, 13, 15 no

Find the unknown length. Write your answer in simplest form.

13. 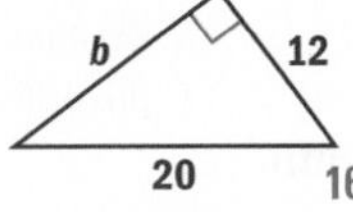

16

14. 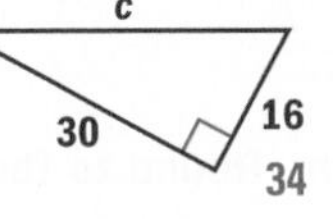

34

15. 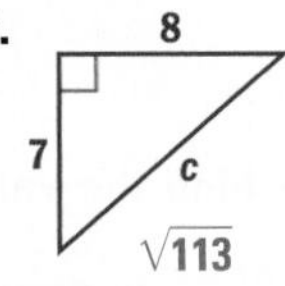

$\sqrt{113}$

16. 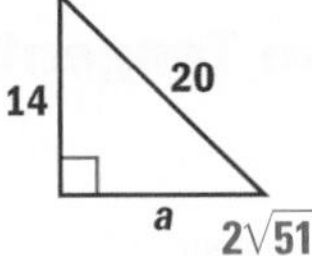

$2\sqrt{51}$

17. Use a number line to order the numbers $2\sqrt{5}$, 4.5, $\sqrt{19}$, $\frac{19}{4}$, and $3\sqrt{2}$ from least to greatest. $3\sqrt{2}$, $\sqrt{19}$, $2\sqrt{5}$, 4.5, $\frac{19}{4}$

18. Find the midpoint M of the segment with endpoints $A(-2, 3)$ and $B(4, 6)$. $M\left(1, 4\frac{1}{2}\right)$

19. Find the distance between the points $P(-6, -2)$ and $Q(-2, 1)$. 5 units

20. **Lightning Protection** Many boats have a lightning protection system that includes a mast or other metal pole extending above the vessel. The pole and all the larger metal parts of the boat are connected to form a path along which electricity can be conducted to the water. The system forms a "cone of protection" extending 60° around the tip of the pole. How far does the cone extend from the mast at water level (distance DC in the diagram)? Give your answer to the nearest foot. 61 ft

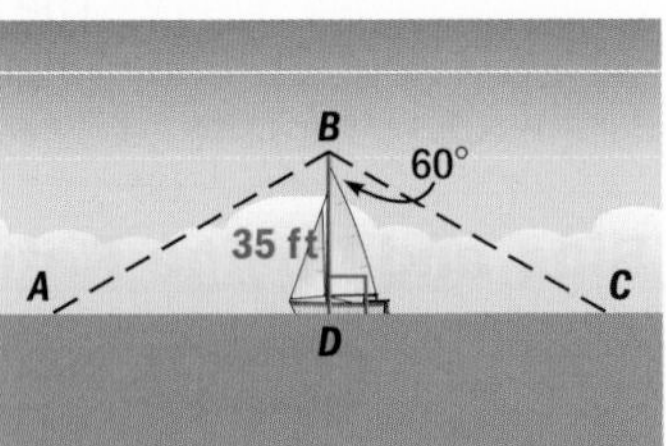

Use $\triangle ABC$ to complete Exercises 21 and 22.

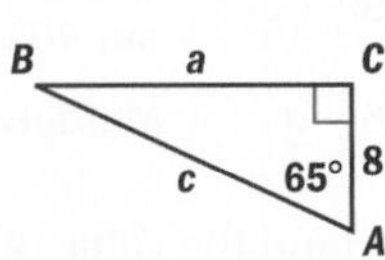

21. Find the value of a to the nearest tenth. 17.2

22. Find the value of c to the nearest tenth. 18.9

Chapter Standardized Test

Test-Taking Strategy Make sure that you are answering the question that is asked. Some questions have several steps.

1. Evaluate $\sqrt{x+y}$ when $x = 16$ and $y = 9$. **B**

A. $\sqrt{7}$ **B.** 5 **C.** 7 **D.** 25

2. Which expression is the simplest form of $\sqrt{\frac{320}{x^2}}$? **H**

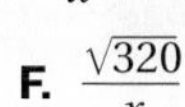

F. $\frac{\sqrt{320}}{x}$ **G.** $\frac{4\sqrt{20}}{x}$ **H.** $\frac{8\sqrt{5}}{x}$ **I.** $8\sqrt{\frac{5}{x^2}}$

3. In 432 B.C., part of the Greek city of Olynthus was divided into rectangular city blocks measuring 120 feet by 300 feet. To the nearest foot, what is the diagonal distance across each city block? **B**

A. 275 feet **B.** 323 feet

C. 420 feet **D.** 104,400 feet

4. Which number is irrational? **G**

F. $-\sqrt{49}$ **G.** $\sqrt{\frac{16}{2}}$ **H.** $\frac{\sqrt{25}}{6}$ **I.** $\sqrt{\frac{8}{2}}$

5. What is the distance between the points $(-8, 8)$ and $(4, 6)$? **B**

A. 12 **B.** $2\sqrt{37}$ **C.** $4\sqrt{53}$ **D.** $4\sqrt{85}$

6. What is the midpoint of the segment with endpoints $(-8, 8)$ and $(4, 6)$? **F**

F. $(-2, 7)$ **G.** $(-1, 6)$ **H.** $(0, 5)$ **I.** $(6, -1)$

7. The length of a leg in a 45°-45°-90° triangle is 13 yards. What is the length of the hypotenuse? **C**

A. 6.5 yards **B.** 13 yards

C. $13\sqrt{2}$ yards **D.** $13\sqrt{3}$ yards

8. Find the value of r in $\triangle PQR$. Round to the nearest tenth. **F**

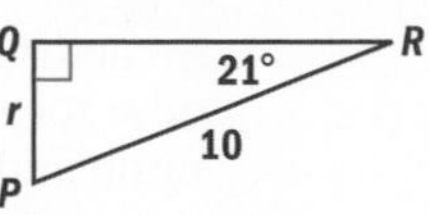

F. 3.6 **G.** 3.8 **H.** 9.3 **I.** 9.6

9. Find the value of b in $\triangle ABC$. Round to the nearest tenth. **A**

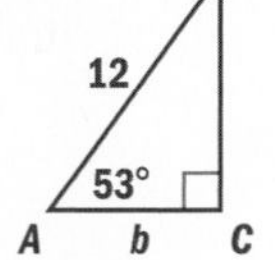

A. 7.2 **B.** 9.6

C. 11.2 **D.** 11.4

10. **Short Response** Plot the points $D(7, 3)$, $E(4, 7)$, $F(-4, 1)$, and $G(-1, -3)$ in a coordinate plane. Connect the points to form a rectangle. Explain how to find the perimeter and the area of the rectangle. Then find the perimeter and the area. See margin.

11. **Extended Response** You are in a high-rise building and look out a window. You see another building 100 feet away. The angle formed by the top of the building, your eye, and the horizontal is 65°. The angle formed by the horizontal, your eye, and the bottom of the building is 55°.

a. Find the value of a to the nearest foot. **214 ft**

b. Find the value of b to the nearest foot. **143 ft**

c. How tall is the building you see? **about 357 ft**

d. Explain how you decided which trigonometric ratio(s) to use to solve parts (a) and (b). See margin.

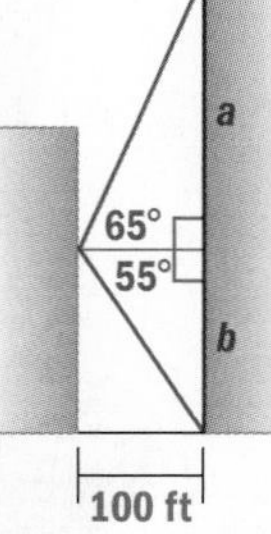

ADDITIONAL RESOURCES

Assessment Book
- Standardized Chapter Test, p. 115

Test and Practice Generator

10.

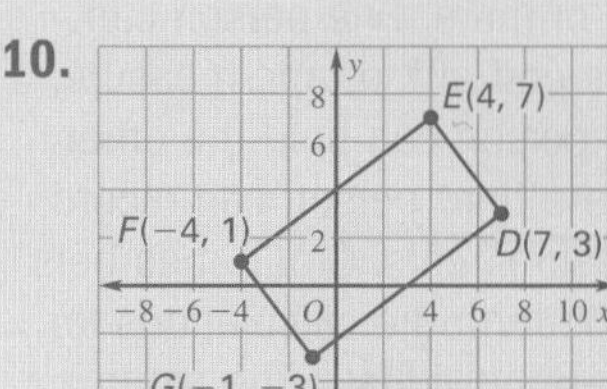

Sample answer: **You can use the distance formula to find the lengths of the sides (and to verify that the lengths of opposite sides are equal): $FG = \sqrt{(-4-(-1))^2 + (1-(-3))^2} = \sqrt{25} = 5$; $DE = \sqrt{(4-7)^2 + (7-3)^2} = \sqrt{25} = 5$; $GD = \sqrt{(7-(-1))^2 + (3-(-3))^2} = \sqrt{100} = 10$; $EF = \sqrt{(4-(-4))^2 + (7-1)^2} = \sqrt{100} = 10$. So, the length of the rectangle is 10 units and its width is 5 units. Now you can use the formulas for the perimeter P and area A of a rectangle: $P = 2l + 2w = 2(10) + 2(5) = 30$ units; $A = lw = 10(5) = 50$ square units.**

11d. ***Sample answer:*** **In parts (a) and (b), I knew the side adjacent to the given angle and was looking for the side opposite this angle, so I used the tangent ratio, which involves the sides opposite and adjacent to an angle.**

OVERVIEW

Mathematical Goals

In this project, students will explore the rise and run of a ramp using the Pythagorean theorem. They will calculate the slope of the ramp. Students will create a scale drawing of a ramp.

Managing the Project

Classroom Management

Students should work in groups of three or more. One person can hold one end of the tape measure, another person can hold the other end, and a third person can record the measurements. Group members should perform the calculations for Steps 4–6 individually. The group should work together to choose the best design, and to create the scale drawing of this design.

Guiding Students' Work

Students should begin their work by considering a few different locations for their ramp. Also ask them to consider the other factors that are involved when actually constructing the ramp, such as acquiring the appropriate tools and fasteners, fastening the ramp in place, ensuring that its surface is not slippery, and possibly making it moveable.

Concluding the Project

Students should present their scale drawing, explaining their calculations and their design choice. You can use questions like the following for class discussion:

- What factors might require a ramp that is not very steep?
- What benefits might a shorter ramp provide?

Chapter 9 Project

Designing a Ramp

Goal
Design a ramp for your school auditorium.

Key Skill
Using the Pythagorean theorem

Materials
- calculator
- measuring tape

An actor dashes through the audience and up onto the stage. Band members walk down a ramp and surround the audience with music. Exciting stage entrances and exits can be made on a ramp that connects the stage and the seating area. To design a ramp for your school's auditorium, you must first choose its dimensions and its slope.

Investigate

1–6. Answers will vary.

1. Measure the distance (in inches) between the floor of the auditorium and the stage. This distance is a.
2. Choose a point on the floor of the auditorium where the ramp can end. The distance from this point to the base of the stage should be greater than or equal to $3a$. Call this distance b.
3. Measure the distance b. Then choose two other points for the ramp's end and measure the distances from these points to the base of the stage. You will use these three values of b to design 3 different ramps.
4. Use the Pythagorean theorem to find the length of the walkway for each ramp design. Round to the nearest inch.
5. Find the slope of each ramp design.
6. Suppose the ramp must be 4 feet wide. What is the area of the walkway for each ramp design?

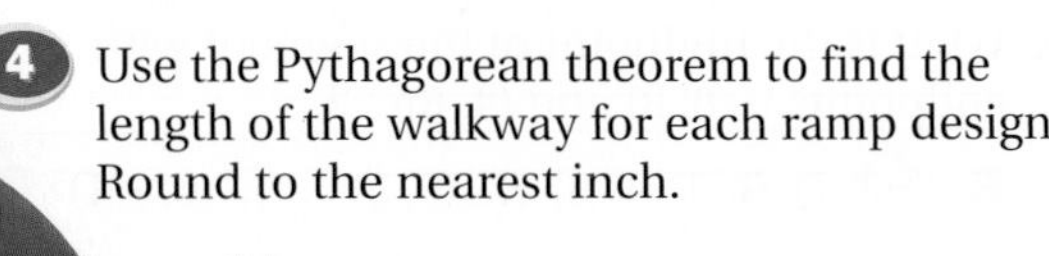

RESOURCE BOOK

The *Chapter Resource Books* contain three different projects for each chapter: Real Life, Cooperative, and Independent Extra Credit. Each project is accompanied by a scoring rubric. A complete discussion of rubrics is available in the *Professional Development Book*.

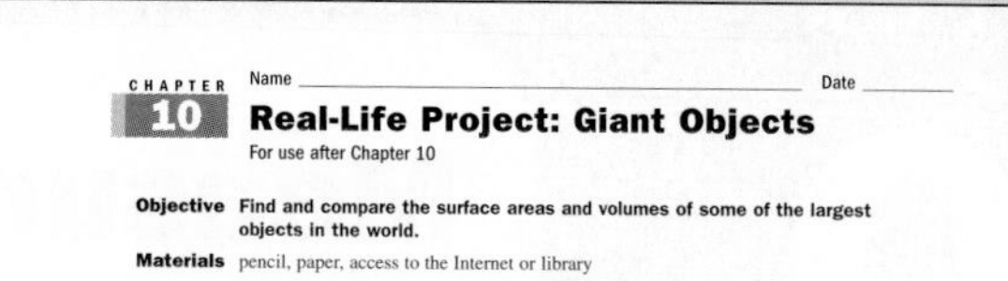

CHAPTER 10 Name ______________________ Date ________

Real-Life Project: Giant Objects

For use after Chapter 10

Objective **Find and compare the surface areas and volumes of some of the largest objects in the world.**

Materials pencil, paper, access to the Internet or library

Investigation *Getting Going* A standard hockey puck has a diameter of 7.6 centimeters and a thickness of 2.5 centimeters as shown. Arguably, the largest hockey puck in the world is located in British Columbia, Canada at the Cowichan Community Center. The giant puck has a thickness of about 100 centimeters and a diameter of about 304 centimeters.

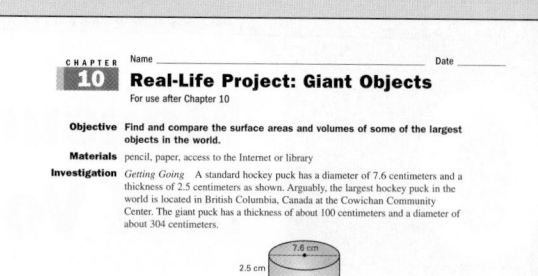

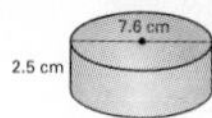

Questions

1. Find the radius of each puck.
2. Complete the table for each puck. Use a calculator. If necessary, round your answers to the nearest hundredth.

	Base area	Surface area	Volume
Standard puck			
Giant puck			

3. Find the approximate ratio of the surface area of the giant puck to the surface area of the standard puck.
4. Find the approximate ratio of the volume of the giant puck to the volume of the standard puck.
5. There are several objects around the world that are larger replicas of the regular size objects they represent. Use the Internet or a library to research the dimensions of some of these objects. If possible, compare their dimensions to their regular size counterpart. Then compare their volumes and surface areas. Below are some examples of objects you can research.

- largest aluminum can
- largest cardboard box
- largest jar of jellybeans
- largest stick of candy
- tallest paper cup
- largest ball of twine

Review and Projects

CHAPTER 10 Continued

Teacher's Notes for Giant Objects

For use after Chapter 10

Project Goals
- Find the surface area of certain solids.
- Find the volume of certain solids.
- Compare the surface areas and volumes of solids.

Managing the Project *Guiding Students' Work* The Guinness World Records book is an excellent source for looking up information on some of the world's largest objects. For some objects, students will be unable to compare them to regular size objects because they do not exist. For example, there is no standard object for the world's largest ball of twine.

Some of the calculations may contain very large numbers, so encourage students to use calculators.

Rubric for Project **The following rubric can be used to assess student work.**

4 The student finds the radius of each puck. The table is completed correctly. The ratios in Questions 3 and 4 are correct. The student researches information on several objects. The surface areas and volumes are correctly calculated and compared to the standard objects. All of the calculations are correct. The student's work is neat.

3 The student finds the radius of each puck. The table is completed with one or two minor errors. The ratios in Questions 3 and 4 are found with little difficulty. The student researches information on several objects. The surface areas and volumes are calculated and compared to the standard objects. Most of the calculations are correct. The student's work is neat.

2 The student finds the radius of each puck. The table is completed with one or two errors. The student has some difficulty finding the ratios in Questions 3 and 4. The student researches information on a few objects. The surface areas and volumes are calculated and compared to the standard objects, but there are some errors. Some of the calculations are incorrect. The student's work is a little sloppy.

1 The student finds the radius of each puck. The table is incomplete. The student cannot find the ratios in Questions 3 and 4. The student cannot find information on any objects or no attempt is made. Most of the calculations are incorrect. The student's work is incomplete or sloppy.

Review and Projects

CHAPTER 10 Name ______________________ Date ________

Cooperative Project: Identifying Objects

For use after Chapter 10

Objective **Identify real-life examples of solids or combinations of solids.**

Materials paper, pencil, graph paper, colored pencils, markers, binder

Investigation *Getting Going* This project is for two students. The purpose of this project is for each student to find real-life examples of solids, describe each solid, and see if his/her partner can identify the solids using the given information.

1. Find real-life examples of each of the solids or combination of solids.
   a. prism with either a square, rectangular, or triangular base
   b. cylinder
   c. pyramid with a square or triangular base
   d. cone
   e. sphere
   f. a combination of two different solids from above
   g. a combination of three different solids from above
2. Use graph paper to draw a net of each solid.
3. Label each solid's dimensions. If dimensions for a particular object cannot be found, you can estimate.
4. Give the location of where each solid was found.

Exchange work with your partner.

5. Identify the shape of the base, if possible, of each of your partner's solids.
6. Sketch each of your partner's solids so that they appear to be three-dimensional and label all dimensions.
7. Count the number of faces, edges, and vertices of each of your partner's solids.
8. Identify each of your partner's solids.
9. If possible, find the surface area and volume of each of your partner's solids.
10. Name the object that each solid represents.

Organize all of your work and present it neatly in a binder.

Review and Projects

—*continued*—

CHAPTER 10 Name ______________________ Date ________

Independent Extra Credit Project: Ice Cream Cones

For use after Chapter 10

Objective **Find and compare the surface areas and volumes of various sizes of ice cream cones.**

Materials pencil, paper

Investigation *Getting Going* Manufacturers use ice cream cone baking machines to produce different sizes of ice cream cones. The machine has many different molds that are used to vary the diameter and height of a cone.

The table below shows the sizes of seven different types of ice cream cones that can be produced by a manufacturer. Copy and complete the table. Use a calculator and round your answers to the nearest tenth.

Cone	Diameter	Height	Slant Height	Surface Area	Volume
1	56 mm	120 mm			
2	45 mm	118 mm			
3	35 mm	116 mm			
4	36 mm	104 mm			
5	30 mm	96 mm			
6	30 mm	72 mm			
7	28 mm	70 mm			

Questions

1. What is the relationship between the lateral area and the surface area of each cone?
2. The manufacturer wants all of the cones to have either the same diameter and different heights, or the same height and different diameters. Discuss how changing the diameters and heights of an ice cream cone affect its surface area. Give examples to support your answer.
3. Discuss how changing the diameters and heights of an ice cream cone affect its volume. Give examples to support your answer.
4. The figure shows a cone with a scoop of ice cream. Use a calculator to find the surface area of the cone with ice cream. Round your answer to the nearest tenth.

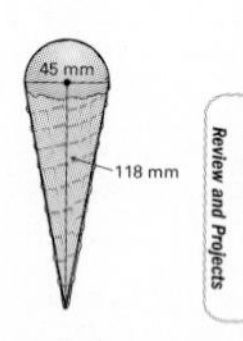

Review and Projects

—*continued*—

OVERVIEW

Main Ideas

In this chapter, students find unknown angle measures and classify triangles, polygons, and quadrilaterals. Students find the areas of parallelograms and trapezoids. Students find the circumferences and areas of circles. Finally, students find the surface areas and volumes of prisms, cylinders, pyramids, and cones.

Application Note

Drums have been used for musical, communications, and religious purposes for over 8000 years.

The typical drum consists of several parts. The body is most often a hollow cylinder. Drum bodies can be made of many different materials, including plastic, wood, metal, or ceramic. The membrane of either animal skin or, more recently, synthetic material is stretched across one end of the cylinder. Pegs allow controlled stretching of the membrane to tune the instrument. Finally, one or more strikers must be used to beat the drum. A striker can be a bare or padded wooden stick, fingers or palms, or other objects.

Most drums do not play a definite pitch; however, some do. For example, kettle drums or timpani are precisely tuned for orchestral performances. Others, such as congas and bongos, are tuned to fairly specific ranges.

CHAPTER

10 Measurement, Area, *and* Volume

BEFORE

In previous chapters you've . . .

- **Written and solved proportions**
- **Solved problems involving similar figures**
- **Used the Pythagorean theorem**

Now

In Chapter 10 you'll study . . .

- **Classifying triangles and polygons**
- **Finding areas of parallelograms and trapezoids**
- **Finding circumferences and areas of circles**
- **Finding surface areas and volumes of solids**

WHY?

So you can solve real-world problems about . . .

- **box kites, p. 515**
- **picnic tables, p. 520**
- **aircraft wings, p. 525**
- **wrestling, p. 531**
- **marimba pipes, p. 542**
- **ant lions, p. 548**
- **salsa, p. 556**
- **grain silos, p. 559**

How does the size of a drum affect its sound?

CHAPTER 10

INTERNET Preview

CLASSZONE.COM

- eEdition Plus Online
- eWorkbook Plus Online
- eTutorial Plus Online
- State Test Practice
- More Examples

MATH *In the* **Real World**

Drums When you strike a drum, it vibrates, producing sound. One reason a large drum sounds lower in pitch than a small drum is that the large drum vibrates more slowly. In this chapter, you will find the surface area and volume of objects like drums.

What do you think? The drums in the photo are cylinders. What shape do the top and bottom of a cylinder have? If you were to cut a cylinder's curved side straight down from top to bottom and flatten it, what shape would you see? **A circle; a rectangle**

CHAPTER RESOURCES

These resources are provided to help you prepare for the chapter and to customize review materials:

Chapter 10 Resource Book

- Tips for New Teachers, pp. 1–2
- Lesson Plan, pp. 5, 13, 22, 31, 39, 47, 56, 66
- Lesson Plan for Block Scheduling, pp. 6, 14, 23, 32, 40, 48, 57, 67

Technology

- EasyPlanner CD-ROM
- Test and Practice Generator
- Electronic Lesson Presentations CD-ROM
- eTutorial CD-ROM

Internet

- Classzone
- eEdition Plus Online
- eWorkbook Plus Online
- eTutorial Plus Online
- EasyPlanner Plus Online

ENGLISH LEARNER SUPPORT

- Spanish Study Guide
- Multi-Language Visual Glossary
- Chapter Audio Summaries CDs
- Teacher's Edition, pp. 508E–508F

PREPARE

DIAGNOSIS/REMEDIATION

Prerequisite Skills Quiz

The Prerequisite Skills Quiz can help you diagnose whether students have the following skills needed in Chapter 10:

- Use vocabulary (Ex. 1)
- Solve two-step equations (Exs. 2–5)
- Solve proportions (Exs. 6–9)
- Use a scale drawing (Ex. 10)
- Determine whether a triangle is a right triangle (Ex. 11)

Chapter 10 Resource Book

- Study Guide (Lessons 10.1–10.8)

Tutor Place

NOTETAKING STRATEGIES

Suggest that students use colored pens or highlighters in their notebooks to mark formulas they should memorize or to identify material they found confusing. Further suggestions for keeping a notebook can be found on page 560.

For more support on notetaking, see:

- Notetaking Guide Workbook
- Notetaking Transparencies

1.

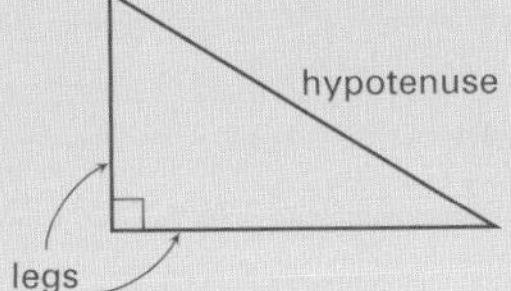

CHAPTER 10

Chapter Prerequisite Skills

Review Vocabulary

scale drawing, p. 300
scale, p. 300
hypotenuse, p. 465
leg, p. 465
Pythagorean theorem, p. 465

8. $\frac{217}{3}$, or $72\frac{1}{3}$

PREREQUISITE SKILLS QUIZ

Preparing for Success **To prepare for success in this chapter, test your knowledge of these concepts and skills. You may want to look at the pages referred to in blue for additional review.**

1. Vocabulary Draw a right triangle. Label the hypotenuse and legs. **See margin.**

Solve the equation. *(p. 120)*

2. $15 = 2x - 7$ **11** **3.** $8 - 3n = 50$ **−14** **4.** $-9 - 4y = 19$ **−7** **5.** $78 = 2p + 12$ **33**

Solve the proportion. *(pp. 275, 280)*

6. $\frac{a}{16} = \frac{5}{4}$ **20** **7.** $\frac{90}{15} = \frac{t}{34}$ **204** **8.** $\frac{3}{7} = \frac{31}{z}$ **9.** $\frac{2}{74} = \frac{96}{m}$ **3552**

10. Architecture A scale drawing of a rectangular wall is 8 inches long and 14 inches high. The drawing has a scale of 1 inch : 3 feet. Find the wall's dimensions. *(p. 300)* **24 ft by 42 ft**

11. Determine whether a triangle with side lengths 20, 37.5, and 42.5 is a right triangle. *(p. 465)* **yes**

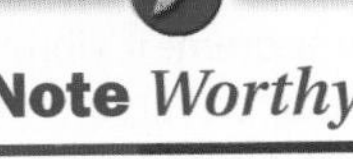

Note *Worthy*

You will find a notetaking strategy at the beginning of each chapter. Look for additional notetaking and study strategies throughout the chapter.

NOTETAKING STRATEGIES

MAIN IDEA WEB When you learn a new concept, you may want to make a web of details surrounding the concept in your notebook.

$\tan A = \frac{\text{side opposite } \angle A}{\text{side adjacent to } \angle A} = \frac{a}{b}$

Main idea: A trigonometric ratio is a ratio of the lengths of two sides of a right triangle.

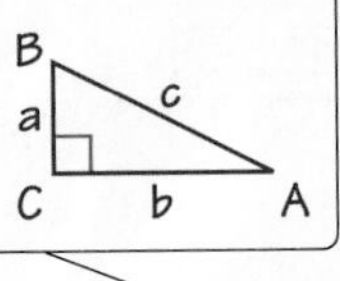

$\sin A = \frac{\text{side opposite } \angle A}{\text{hypotenuse}} = \frac{a}{c}$

$\cos A = \frac{\text{side adjacent to } \angle A}{\text{hypotenuse}} = \frac{b}{c}$

A main idea web will help you in Lesson 10.8.

LESSON

10.1 Triangles

BEFORE	Now	WHY?
You solved problems using right triangles.	You'll solve problems involving triangles.	So you can find measurements of nested tables, as in Ex. 23.

Review Vocabulary
acute triangle, p. 462
right triangle, p. 462
obtuse triangle, p. 462
equiangular triangle, p. 462
equilateral triangle, p. 463
isosceles triangle, p. 463
scalene triangle, p. 463

Construction Homes are often built with sloped roofs so that they can shed rain. Such roofs are built using a series of triangular roof trusses. The trusses may include braces that help the roof bear weight, such as the weight of snow.

Recall that you can classify a triangle by its angle measures or by its side lengths. When classified by angle measures, triangles are acute, right, obtuse, or equiangular. When classified by side lengths, triangles are equilateral, isosceles, or scalene.

Review *Help*

For help with classifying triangles, see pp. 462–463.

Example 1 *Classifying a Triangle by Angle Measures*

In the diagram, $m\angle DBE = 64°$ and $m\angle BDE = m\angle BED$. Find $m\angle BDE$ and $m\angle BED$. Then classify $\triangle BDE$ by its angle measures.

A C E G J L M B D F H K

Solution

Let $x°$ represent $m\angle BDE$ and $m\angle BED$.

$m\angle BDE + m\angle BED + m\angle DBE = 180°$	**Sum of angle measures is 180°.**
$x° + x° + 64° = 180°$	**Substitute values.**
$2x + 64 = 180$	**Combine like terms.**
$2x = 116$	**Subtract 64 from each side.**
$x = 58$	**Divide each side by 2.**

Answer $m\angle BDE = m\angle BED = 58°$. Because $\angle BDE$, $\angle DBE$, and $\angle BED$ are acute angles, $\triangle BDE$ is an acute triangle.

Checkpoint

1. Use the diagram in Example 1. Given that $m\angle EDG = 38°$ and the measure of $\angle DEG$ is 38° more than $m\angle DGE$, find $m\angle DGE$ and $m\angle DEG$. Then classify $\triangle DEG$ by its angle measures.

$m\angle DGE = 52°$, $m\angle DEG = 90°$; because $\angle DEG$ is a right angle, $\triangle DEG$ is a right triangle.

NCTM CURRICULUM STANDARDS
Standard 2: Represent situations using algebraic symbols
Standard 3: Analyze properties of 2-D shapes
Standard 6: Solve problems in math and other contexts

1 PLAN

Skill Check
Classify the triangle.
1. A triangle with two sides the same length **isosceles**
2. A triangle with no sides the same length **scalene**
3. A triangle with one angle that measures 90° **right**

LESSON OBJECTIVE
Solve problems involving triangles.

PACING
Suggested Number of Days
Basic Course: 1 day
Average Course: 1 day
Advanced Course: 1 day
Block: 0.5 block with 10.2

TEACHING RESOURCES
For a complete list of Teaching Resources, see page 508B.

TRANSPARENCY
Warm-Up Exercises for this lesson are available on a transparency.

2 TEACH

MOTIVATING THE LESSON
Have students describe each type of triangle listed in the Review Vocabulary.

TIPS *for* NEW TEACHERS
Emphasize the Study Strategy on page 512. Using ratios to write an equation is a skill that many students have difficulty with initially. See Tips for New Teachers in the *Chapter 10 Resource Book*.

Extra Examples

Example 1 In the diagram, $m\angle U = 23°$ and $m\angle S = m\angle U$. Find $m\angle S$ and $m\angle T$. Then classify $\triangle STU$ by its angle measures. **23°, 134°; obtuse**

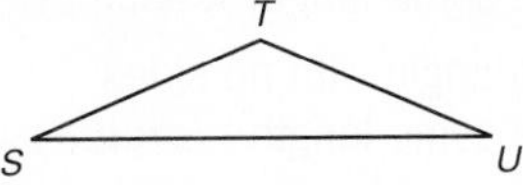

Example 2 The perimeter of an isosceles triangle is 35 inches. The length of the shortest side is 4 inches less than the length of each of the other two sides. Find the lengths of all three sides of the triangle. **9 in., 13 in., 13 in.**

Example 3 The ratio of the angle measures of a triangle is 7 : 9 : 20. Find the angle measures. Then classify the triangle by its angle measures. **35°, 45°, 100°; obtuse**

Concept Check

If you know the measure of just one angle in a triangle, what information do you need in order to find the measures of the other angles? **either the relationship between the two unknown angle measures, or the relationship between the known measure and one of the two unknown measures**

Daily Puzzler

Dan draws a triangle and concludes that the side lengths have the ratio 1 : 1 : 3. How do you know he made a mistake? ***Sample answer:* A triangle with side lengths in this ratio is not possible. For example, if the sides lengths are 1 inch, 1 inch, and 3 inches, the two shorter sides together are not as long as the longer side.**

Example 2 *Finding Unknown Side Lengths*

The perimeter of a scalene triangle is 65 centimeters. The length of the first side is twice the length of the second side. The length of the third side is 20 centimeters. Find the lengths of the other two sides.

Solution

Draw the triangle. Let x and $2x$ represent the unknown side lengths. Write an equation for the perimeter P. Then solve for x.

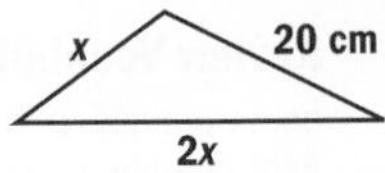

$P = 2x + x + 20$	**Formula for perimeter**
$65 = 2x + x + 20$	**Substitute 65 for *P*.**
$65 = 3x + 20$	**Combine like terms.**
$45 = 3x$	**Subtract 20 from each side.**
$15 = x$	**Divide each side by 3.**

Answer The length of the second side is 15 centimeters, and the length of the first side is $2(15) = 30$ centimeters.

Checkpoint

2. The perimeter of an equilateral triangle is 42 meters. Find the length of each side. **14 m**

Study *Strategy*

For a triangle whose angles measure 50°, 60°, and 70°, you can say that the ratio of the angle measures is 50 : 60 : 70, or 5 : 6 : 7. Therefore, if you know that the ratio of the angle measures is 5 : 6 : 7, you can say that the angle measures are $5x°$, $6x°$, and $7x°$ for some value of x.

Example 3 *Finding Angle Measures Using a Ratio*

The ratio of the angle measures of a triangle is 1 : 3 : 5. Find the angle measures. Then classify the triangle by its angle measures.

Solution

1) Let $x°$, $3x°$, and $5x°$ represent the angle measures. Write an equation for the sum of the angle measures.

$x° + 3x° + 5x° = 180°$	**Sum of angle measures is 180°.**
$9x = 180$	**Combine like terms.**
$x = 20$	**Divide each side by 9.**

2) Substitute 20 for x in the expression for each angle measure.

$(20)° = 20°$ $(3 \cdot 20)° = 60°$ $(5 \cdot 20)° = 100°$

Answer The angle measures of the triangle are 20°, 60°, and 100°. So, the triangle is an obtuse triangle.

Checkpoint

3. The ratio of the angle measures of a triangle is 3 : 5 : 12. Find the angle measures. Then classify the triangle by its angle measures. **27°, 45°, and 108°; obtuse**

10.1 Exercises

More Practice, p. 812

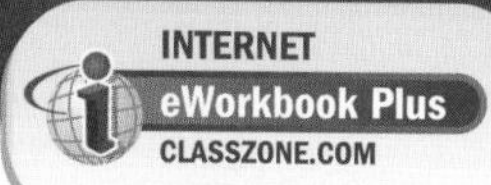

Guided Practice

Vocabulary Check

1. The ratio of the angle measures of a triangle is 1 : 1 : 1. Find the angle measures. Then classify the triangle by its angle measures. **60°, 60°, and 60°; acute or equiangular**

Skill Check **Find the value of *x*. Then classify the triangle by its angle measures.**

2. 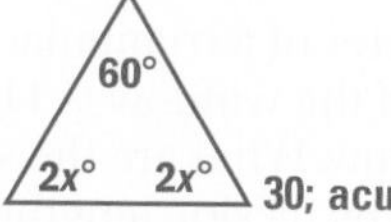

30; acute or equiangular

3. 80°, 4x°, x° **20; acute**

4. 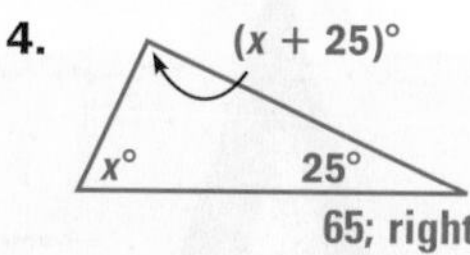

65; right

5. The perimeter of an isosceles triangle is 14 meters. The length of one side is 4 meters. The lengths of the other two sides are equal. Find the lengths of the other two sides. **5 m**

6. The ratio of the angle measures in a triangle is 6 : 5 : 4. Find the angle measures. Then classify the triangle by its angle measures. **72°, 60°, and 48°; acute**

7. **Error Analysis** Describe and correct the error in finding the value of x for the triangle shown below.

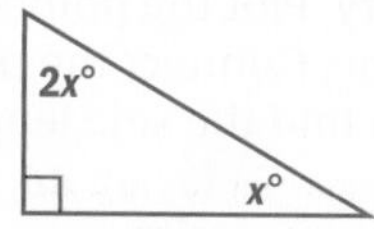

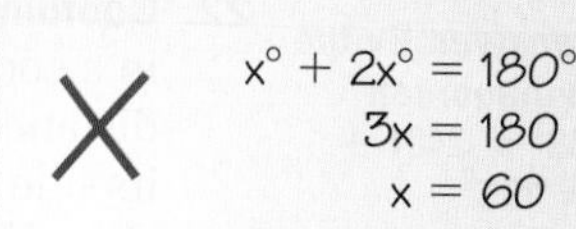

Sample answer: **The measure of the right angle was omitted. The correct equation and solution are $x° + 2x° + 90° = 180°$, $3x = 90$, and $x = 30$.**

Practice and Problem Solving

Homework Help

Example	Exercises
1	8-13
2	15-18
3	19-21

Online Resources
CLASSZONE.COM
- More Examples
- eTutorial Plus

Find the value of *x*. Then classify the triangle by its angle measures.

A 8. 42°, 2x°, x° **46; obtuse**

9. 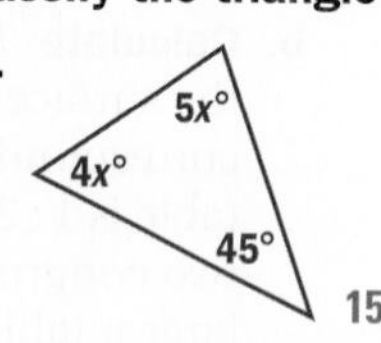

15; acute

10. 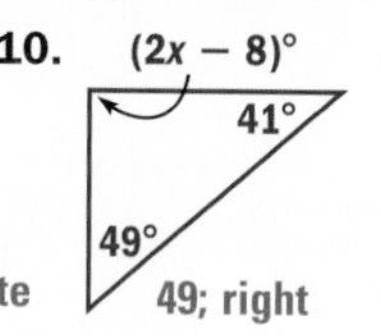

49; right

11. 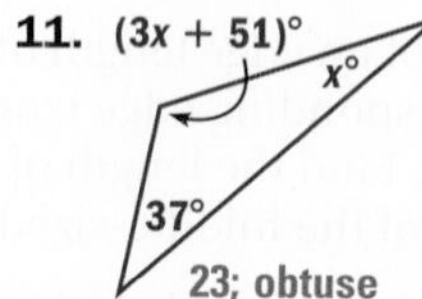

23; obtuse

12. 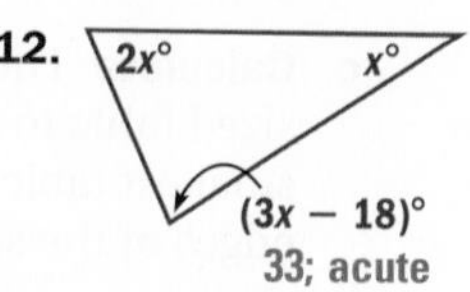

33; acute

13. 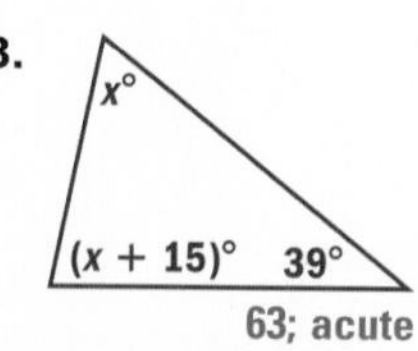

63; acute

14. *Writing* Explain why the sum of the measures of the acute angles of a right triangle is 90°. ***Sample answer:*** **The right angle has a measure of 90°. So if the acute angles measure $x°$ and $y°$, then $x° + y° + 90° = 180°$, and $x° + y° = 90°$.**

3 APPLY

ASSIGNMENT GUIDE

Basic Course

Day 1: SRH p. 793 Exs. 1-3; pp. 513-515 Exs. 8-13, 15-21, 26, 29-32

Average Course

Day 1: pp. 513-515 Exs. 11-26, 28-32

Advanced Course

Day 1: pp. 513-515 Exs. 11-14, 17-28*, 30-32

Block

pp. 513-515 Exs. 11-26, 28-32 (with 10.2)

Extra Practice

- Student Edition, p. 812
- Chapter 10 Resource Book, pp. 7-9
- Test and Practice Generator

Transparency

Even-numbered answers are available on transparencies.

Homework Check

When you review students' homework for this lesson, go over the following exercises to check understanding of key concepts.
Basic: 8, 10, 15, 17, 19
Average: 11, 12, 15, 18, 20
Advanced: 12, 13, 17, 19, 21

Common Error

In Exercises 8-13, stress that students must find the measure of each angle before classifying the triangle. Also caution students about making any assumptions about the classification of the triangle based on its appearance.

TEACHING TIP

Before assigning Exercises 16 and 17, you might wish to have students describe the process they will use to find the side lengths before classifying the triangles.

19.

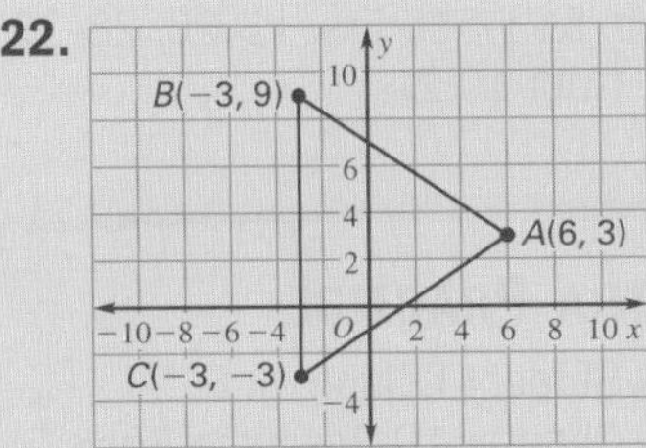

22.

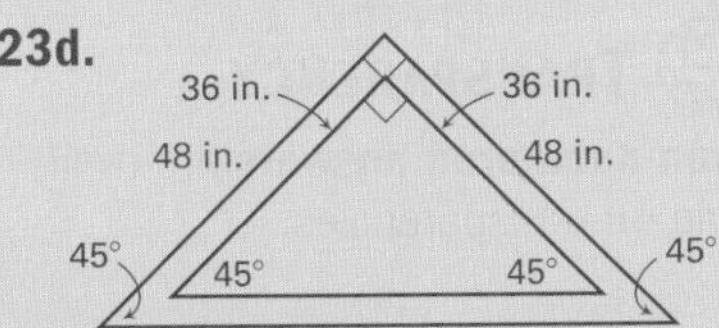

23a.

24 in. 24 in. 45° 45°

23d.

36 in. 36 in. 48 in. 48 in. 45° 45° 45° 45°

24b, 25. See Additional Answers beginning on page AA1.

26a. These lengths do not form a triangle, because 4 + 5 < 10.

26b. These lengths do not form a triangle, because 4 + 5 = 9.

26c. These lengths do form a triangle, because 4 + 5 > 7, 4 + 7 > 5, and 5 + 7 > 4.

27. See Additional Answers beginning on page AA1.

Find the unknown side length of the triangle given the perimeter *P*. Then classify the triangle by its side lengths.

15. $P = 49$ in.

18 in. 12 in. x

19 in.; scalene

16. $P = 22.5$ yd

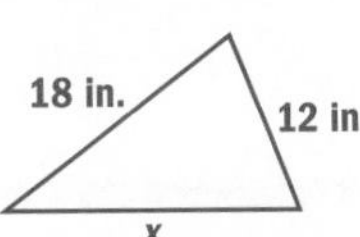

8.1 yd; isosceles

17. $P = 84.3$ cm

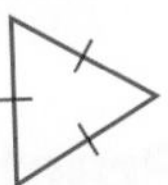

28.1 cm; equilateral

18. The perimeter of a triangle is 29 millimeters. The length of the first side is twice the length of the second side. The length of the third side is 5 more than the length of the second side. Find the side lengths of the triangle. Then classify the triangle by its side lengths. **12 mm, 6 mm, 11 mm; scalene**

21b. Yes. ***Sample answer:*** **By the converse of the Pythagorean theorem: $49^2 + 168^2 = 2401 + 28{,}224 = 30{,}625 = 175^2$.**

19. Window The perimeter of a triangular window is 141 inches. The ratio of the side lengths of the window is 11 : 18 : 18. Draw and label a diagram of the window. What are the side lengths of the window? Classify the window by its side lengths. **See margin for art; 33 in., 54 in., and 54 in.; isosceles.**

20. The ratio of the angle measures of a triangle is 7 : 16 : 22. Find the angle measures. Then classify the triangle by its angle measures. **28°, 64°, and 88°; acute**

B 21. The ratio of the side lengths of a triangle is 7 : 24 : 25. The perimeter of the triangle is 392 inches.

a. Find the side lengths. Then classify the triangle by its side lengths. **49 in., 168 in., 175 in.; scalene**

b. Analyze Is the triangle a right triangle? How do you know?

22. Coordinate Geometry Plot the points $A(6, 3)$, $B(-3, 9)$, and $C(-3, -3)$ in a coordinate plane. Connect the points to form a triangle. Use the distance formula to find the side lengths. Then classify the triangle by its side lengths. **See margin for art; $AB = 3\sqrt{13} \approx 10.8$ units, $BC = 12$ units, $AC = 3\sqrt{13} \approx 10.8$ units; isosceles.**

23. Extended Problem Solving You are building a set of nested tables. The surfaces of the tables will be 45°-45°-90° triangles.

a. Visual Thinking Each of the two congruent edges of the surface of the smallest table has a length of 24 inches. Make and label a scale drawing of the surface of the smallest table. **See margin.**

b. Calculate The ratio of an edge length of the surface of the smallest table to a corresponding edge length of the largest table is 1 : 2. Find the length of each of the two congruent edges of the surface of the largest table. **48 in.**

c. Calculate The ratio of an edge length of the surface of the middle-sized table to a corresponding edge length of the surface of the smallest table is 3 : 2. Find the length of each of the two congruent edges of the surface of the middle-sized table. **36 in.**

d. For each table surface, find the length of the third edge to the nearest inch. Make and label scale drawings of the surfaces of the two larger tables. **34 in., 51 in., 68 in.; see margin for art.**

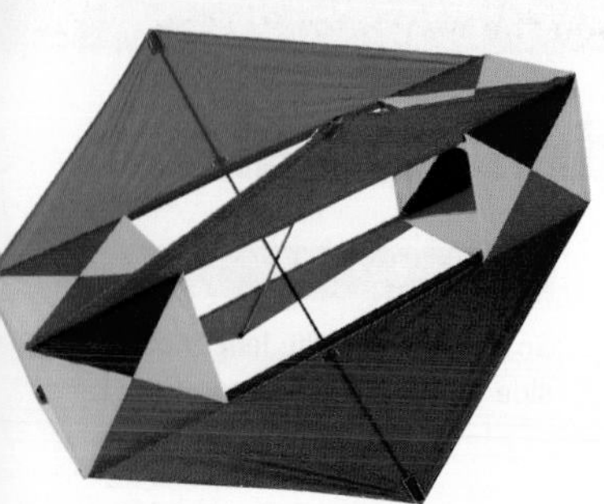

In the Real World

Winged Box Kite Using lightweight materials makes a kite easier to fly. Suppose you are choosing between two types of wooden dowels, each 50 inches long. The dowel made of balsa wood weighs 0.003 ounce per inch. The dowel made of pine weighs 0.017 ounce per inch. How much less does the dowel made of balsa wood weigh than the dowel made of pine? **0.7 oz**

24. Winged Box Kite The design for a winged box kite uses four triangular pieces of cloth. To cut out one of these pieces, you fold a piece of cloth in half and pin a pattern on the cloth, as shown. You cut along $\overline{AB}$ and $\overline{BC}$. Then you remove the pattern and unfold the cloth.

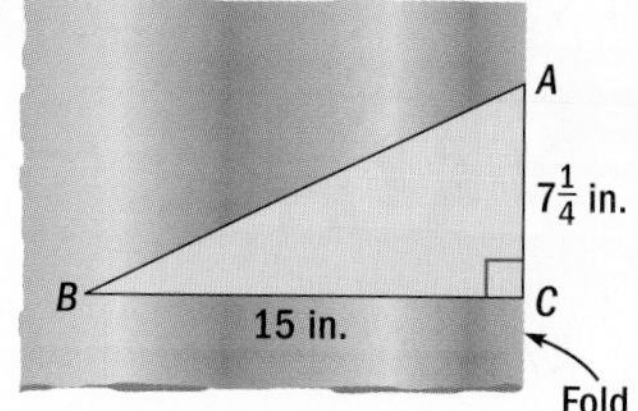

a. How many square inches of cloth do you need for each unfolded triangle? Round your answer to the nearest square inch. **109 in.^{2}**

b. Apply You need to attach wooden dowels to the congruent shorter sides of each of the 4 unfolded triangles. You can buy dowels that are 50 inches long. How many do you need to buy? Explain. **See margin.**

C **25. Critical Thinking** The perimeter of an isosceles triangle is 17 centimeters. The length of one side is 5 centimeters. Your friend claims that there is not enough information to find the other two side lengths of the triangle. Is your friend correct? Explain your reasoning. Include diagrams in your answer. **See margin.**

26. Triangle Inequality The triangle inequality theorem states that the sum of the lengths of any two sides of a triangle is greater than the length of the third side. Using this theorem, determine if the given side lengths form a triangle. Explain your reasoning. **See margin.**

a. 4, 5, 10 **b.** 4, 5, 9 **c.** 4, 5, 7

27. Challenge The triangle shown is an equilateral triangle. Make 6 copies of the triangle. Put the 6 equilateral triangles together so that they all share a vertex and do not overlap. The figure formed is a *regular hexagon*. Find the sum of the measures of the angles of the regular hexagon. Explain your reasoning. **See margin.**

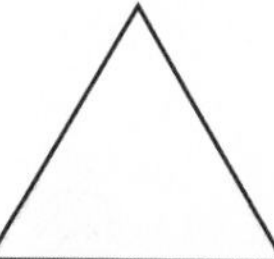

28. *Writing* Is it possible to have a triangle whose angle measures are in the ratio 3 : 4 : 5 and whose side lengths are in the same ratio? Explain. **See margin.**

28. No. ***Sample answer:*** **If the angle measures are in the ratio 3 : 4 : 5, then $3x + 4x + 5x = 180$, and $x = 15$, so the angles measure 45°, 60°, and 75°, and the triangle is an acute triangle. If the sides are in the ratio 3 : 4 : 5, then the triangle must be a right triangle, because $3^2 + 4^2 = 25 = 5^2$.**

Mixed Review

Write the sine and cosine ratios for both acute angles of the triangle. *(Lesson 9.8)*

29.

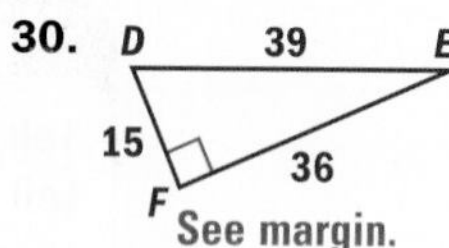

30. D 39 E; 15; 36; F **See margin.**

29. $\sin B = \frac{3}{5}$, $\sin C = \frac{4}{5}$, $\cos B = \frac{4}{5}$, $\cos C = \frac{3}{5}$

Standardized Test Practice

31. Multiple Choice The ratio of the side lengths of a triangle is 3 : 3 : 4. Classify the triangle by its side lengths. **C**

A. Scalene **B.** Equilateral **C.** Isosceles **D.** Acute

32. Multiple Choice The ratio of the angle measures of a triangle is 1 : 2 : 3. Classify the triangle by its angle measures. **H**

F. Acute **G.** Obtuse **H.** Right **I.** Equiangular

30. $\sin D = \frac{12}{13}$, $\sin E = \frac{5}{13}$, $\cos D = \frac{5}{13}$, $\cos E = \frac{12}{13}$

4 ASSESS

Assessment Resources

For more assessment resources, see:
- Assessment Book
- Test and Practice Generator

Mini-Quiz

1. Find the side lengths and classify the triangle by its side lengths. **23 in., 23 in., 23 in.; equilateral**

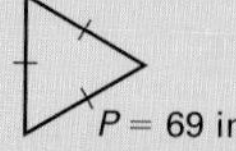

2. The ratio of the angle measures of a triangle is 14 : 31 : 45. Find the angle measures. Then classify the triangle by its angle measures. **28°, 62°, 90°; right**

3. Challenge Draw a triangle with angles measuring 54°, 54°, and 72°. Label the angles with their measure. Make 5 copies of the triangle. Put the triangles together so they all share the 72° vertex and do not overlap. The figure formed is a *regular pentagon*. Find the sum of the measures of the angles in the regular pentagon. **540°**

5 FOLLOW-UP

Diagnosis/Remediation

- Study Guide in Chapter 10 Resource Book, pp. 10–11
- Tutor Place, Geometry Cards 3, 7, 8, 10
- eTutorial Plus Online
- Extra Practice, p. 812
- Lesson Practice in Chapter 10 Resource Book, pp. 7–9

English Learner Support

- Spanish Study Guide
- Multi-Language Visual Glossary
- Chapter Audio Summaries CDs

Challenge

- Challenge Practice in Chapter 10 Resource Book, p. 12
- Teacher's Edition, p. 508F

1 PLAN

Skill Check

Find the value of x.

1. $22 + x + 10 = 65$ **33**
2. $5x + 125 = 360$ **47**
3. $180 = 55 + x$ **125**
4. $x + 2x = 30$ **10**

LESSON OBJECTIVE

Classify polygons and quadrilaterals.

PACING

Suggested Number of Days

Basic Course: 1 day

Average Course: 1 day

Advanced Course: 1 day

Block: 0.5 block with 10.1

TEACHING RESOURCES

For a complete list of Teaching Resources, see page 508B.

TRANSPARENCY

Warm-Up Exercises for this lesson are available on a transparency.

2 TEACH

MOTIVATING THE LESSON

Point out several polygons found in the classroom. Ask students to find other examples. Then point out some figures that are not polygons and invite students to suggest others.

TIPS *for* NEW TEACHERS

Some lessons later in this book make use of the vocabulary introduced in this lesson. Urge students to record all of the terms in their notebooks and to memorize their meanings. See Tips for New Teachers in the *Chapter 10 Resource Book*.

LESSON 10.2

Polygons *and* Quadrilaterals

BEFORE You classified triangles.

Now You'll classify polygons and quadrilaterals.

WHY? So you can find the length of a side of a clock face, as in Ex. 21.

Vocabulary

polygon, p. 516
regular polygon, p. 516
convex, p. 516
concave, p. 516
pentagon, p. 516
hexagon, p. 516
heptagon, p. 516
octagon, p. 516
trapezoid, p. 517
parallelogram, p. 517
rhombus, p. 517
diagonal of a polygon, p. 518

A **polygon** is a closed plane figure whose sides are segments that intersect only at their endpoints. In a **regular polygon**, all the sides have the same length and all the angles have the same measure.

Polygons	Regular polygons	Not polygons

A polygon is **convex** if a segment joining any two interior points lies completely within the polygon. A polygon that is not convex is called **concave**.

convex

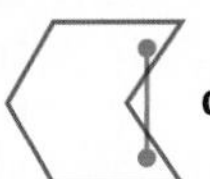

concave

Reading *Geometry*

The name n-gon refers to a polygon that has n sides. For example, a 15-gon is a polygon that has 15 sides.

You already know that a 3-sided polygon is a triangle and a 4-sided polygon is a quadrilateral. Below are names of other polygons.

Polygons	Pentagon	Hexagon	Heptagon	Octagon	n-gon
Number of sides	5	6	7	8	n

Example 1 *Identifying and Classifying Polygons*

Tell whether the figure is a polygon. If it is a polygon, classify it and tell whether it is *convex* or *concave*. If not, explain why.

a.

The keyhole is not a polygon because the top part of the keyhole is round.

b.

The stop sign is an 8-sided polygon. So it is an octagon. It is convex and regular.

NCTM CURRICULUM STANDARDS

Standard 2: Represent situations using algebraic symbols

Standard 3: Analyze properties of 2-D shapes; Develop geometric arguments

 *Checkpoint*

Tell whether the figure is a polygon. If it is a polygon, classify it and tell whether it is *convex* or *concave*. If not, explain why.

1. 

No; it has curved sides.

2. 

yes; pentagon, convex

3. 

yes; heptagon, concave

Quadrilaterals Some quadrilaterals have special names based on whether they have parallel or congruent sides and whether they have right angles.

Quadrilaterals	Diagram
Trapezoid A **trapezoid** is a quadrilateral with exactly 1 pair of parallel sides.	
Parallelogram A **parallelogram** is a quadrilateral with both pairs of opposite sides parallel.	
Rhombus A **rhombus** is a parallelogram with 4 congruent sides.	
Rectangle A *rectangle* is a parallelogram with 4 right angles.	
Square A *square* is a parallelogram with 4 right angles and 4 congruent sides.	

Example 2 *Classifying Quadrilaterals*

Classify the quadrilateral.

a. 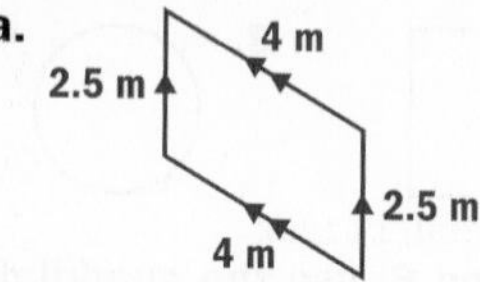

The quadrilateral is a parallelogram because both pairs of opposite sides are parallel.

b.

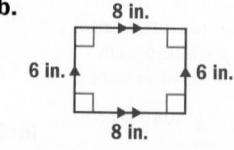

8 in.
6 in.
6 in.
8 in.

The quadrilateral is a parallelogram with 4 right angles. So, it is a rectangle.

Review *Help*

For help with identifying parallel lines, see pp. 410–411.

Watch *Out*

You cannot conclude that the quadrilateral in part (a) of Example 2 is a rectangle because no information is given about its angles.

Extra Examples

Example 1 Tell whether the figure is a polygon. If it is a polygon, classify it and tell whether it is *convex* or *concave*. If not, explain why.

a. 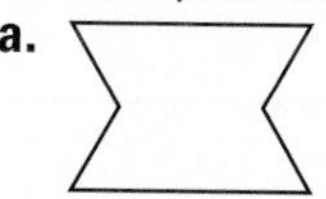

yes; hexagon, concave

b. 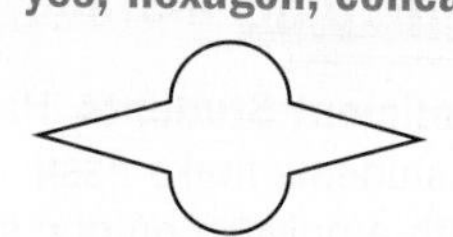

No; it has curved sides.

Example 2 Classify the quadrilateral.

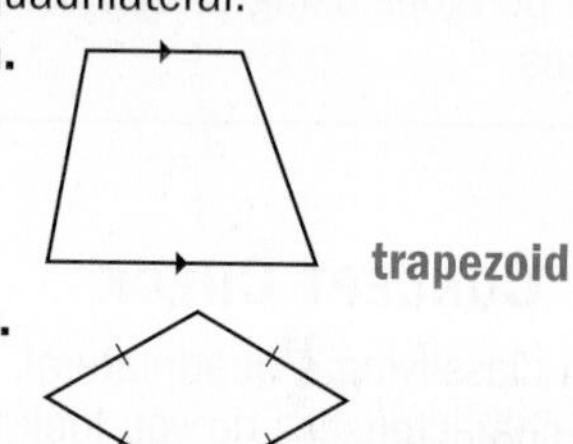

a. **trapezoid**

b. **rhombus**

 **COMMON ERROR**

In Checkpoint Exercise 3, watch for students who assume that a figure must be regular in order to be classified as a polygon.

TEACHING TIP

As you discuss the various quadrilaterals shown above Example 2, be sure students understand the meaning of the symbols indicating congruent sides and parallel sides.

CROSS-CURRICULUM

World Language In language classes, students can explore the use of prefixes such as *penta-*, *octa-*, and *hexa-* in languages such as French and Spanish.

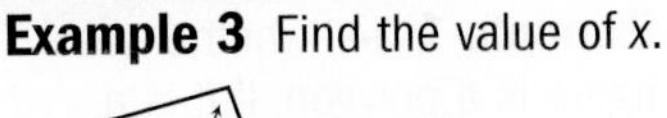

Extra Examples

Example 3 Find the value of x.

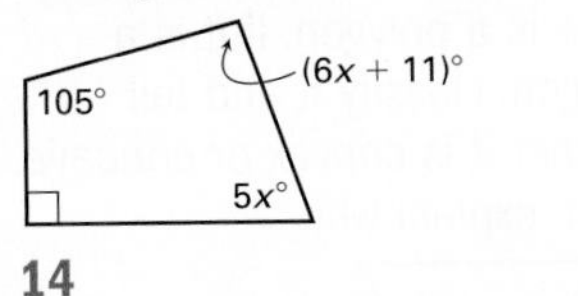

14

DIFFERENTIATING INSTRUCTION

Less Proficient Students Have pairs of students make flash cards with a polygon on one side and its name and attributes on the other. The partners can then test each other's knowledge of the polygons using these flash cards.

CONCEPT CHECK

When classifying a quadrilateral, what characteristics do you look for? **parallel sides, congruent sides, right angles**

DAILY PUZZLER

The sides of a given square are each 8 inches long. The two diagonals of the square are drawn, dividing the square into four congruent triangles. What is the height of each triangle if the 8-inch side is the base, and what kind of triangles are they, classified by their angles? **4 in.; right triangles**

Reading *Geometry*

Segments that connect adjacent vertices of a polygon are the *sides* of the polygon. These segments are *not* considered to be diagonals.

Angle Measures in Quadrilaterals A **diagonal of a polygon** is a segment that joins two vertices that are not adjacent. You can use a diagonal of a quadrilateral to show that the sum of the angle measures in a quadrilateral is 360°.

1. Draw diagonal $\overline{FH}$, which divides quadrilateral $FGHI$ into two triangles.
2. The sum of the angle measures in each triangle is 180°.
3. The sum of the angle measures in a quadrilateral is 180° + 180° = 360°.

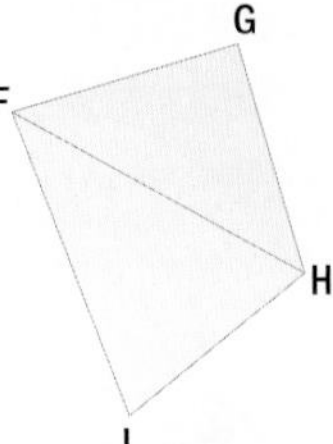

Example 3 *Finding an Unknown Angle Measure*

Find the value of x.

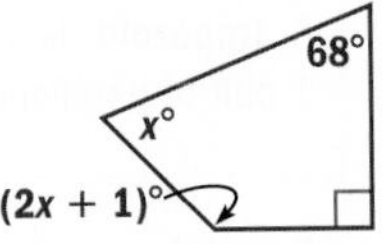

$x° + (2x + 1)° + 90° + 68° = 360°$	**Sum of angle measures in quadrilateral is 360°.**
$3x + 159 = 360$	**Combine like terms.**
$3x = 201$	**Subtract 159 from each side.**
$x = 67$	**Divide each side by 3.**

10.2 Exercises

More Practice, p. 812

INTERNET eWorkbook Plus CLASSZONE.COM

Guided Practice

Vocabulary Check **1.** How are a trapezoid and a parallelogram different from each other? **See margin.**

Skill Check **Tell whether the figure is a polygon. If it is a polygon, classify it and tell whether it is *convex* or *concave*. If not, explain why.**

2. [rectangle] **yes; quadrilateral, convex**

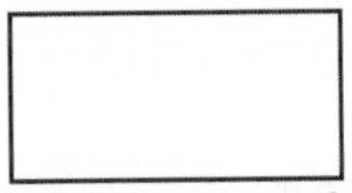

3. [circle]

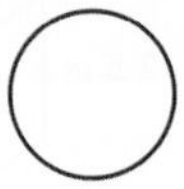

4. [figure] **yes; pentagon, concave**

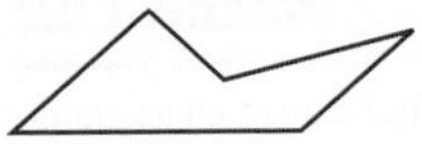

In Exercises 5 and 6, use the quadrilateral shown.

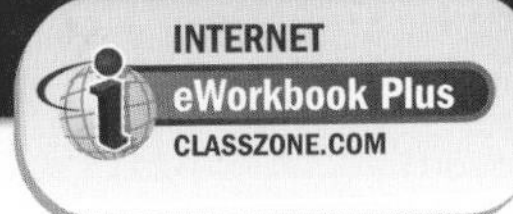

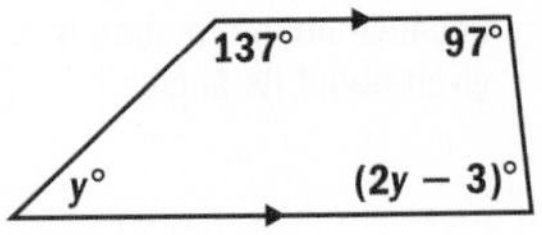

5. Classify the quadrilateral. **trapezoid**

6. Find the value of y. **43**

1. *Sample answer:* **A trapezoid has exactly one pair of parallel sides, while a parallelogram has two pairs of parallel sides.**

3. **No; it is a circle, which is curved.**

3 APPLY

Practice and Problem Solving

Homework Help

Example	Exercises
1	7-9
2	11-17
3	18-20

Online Resources CLASSZONE.COM
- More Examples
- eTutorial Plus

Tell whether the figure is a polygon. If it is a polygon, classify it and tell whether it is *convex* or *concave*. If not, explain why.

A **7.**  yes; 16-gon, concave

8. 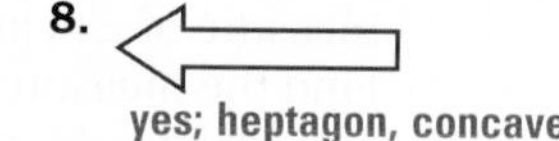 yes; heptagon, concave

9.  See margin.

10. Error Analysis Describe and correct the error in solving the following problem.

A quadrilateral has 4 congruent sides, and the opposite sides of the quadrilateral are parallel. Sketch and classify the quadrilateral.

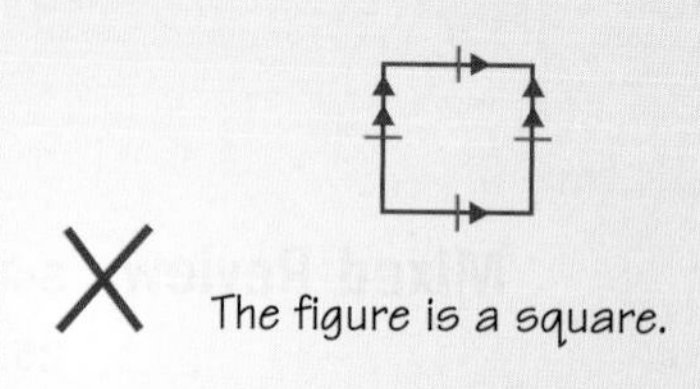

Classify the quadrilateral.

11. 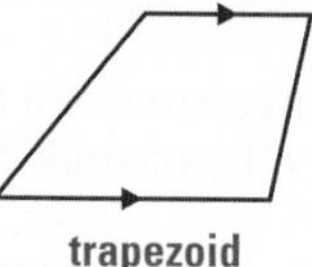 trapezoid

12. 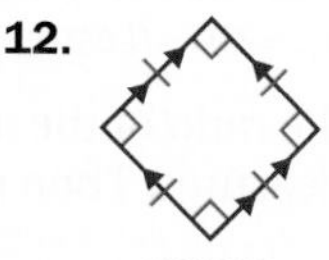 square

13.  parallelogram

Copy and complete the statement using *always*, *sometimes*, or *never*.

14. A square is _?_ a rectangle. always

15. A square is _?_ a rhombus. always

16. A rhombus is _?_ a square. sometimes

17. A trapezoid is _?_ a parallelogram. never

Find the value of x.

18. 76 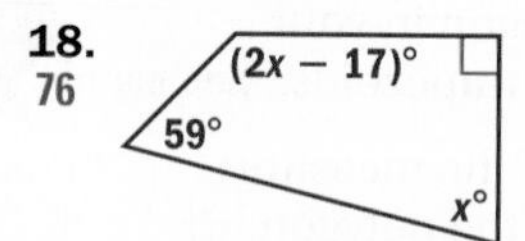

19. 90 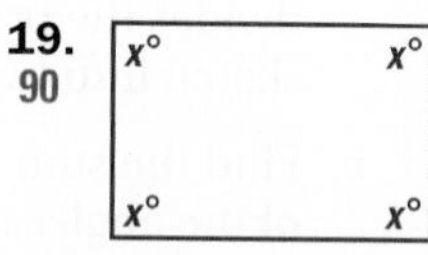

20. 54 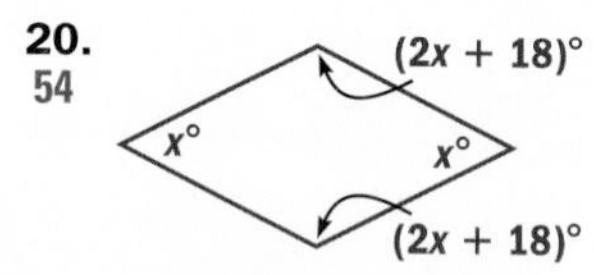

B **21. Extended Problem Solving** The Allen-Bradley Clock Tower in Milwaukee, Wisconsin, has four faces. Each face is a regular octagon. The perimeter of one octagonal face is approximately 133 feet.

a. Calculate Find the length of one side of one of the octagonal faces.

b. Visual Thinking Your friend says that you can find the area of one of the clocks by dividing one of the octagons into 8 congruent triangles. Sketch a regular octagon and show how to divide it into 8 congruent triangles. See margin.

c. Critical Thinking What additional information would you need in part (b) to find the area of the clock face? Assume that you had this information. What would your next steps be?

22. For the trapezoid shown, the ratio $m\angle A : m\angle C$ is $2:1$. Write and solve an equation to find the value of x.
$x + 2x + 2x + x = 360$, $x = 60$

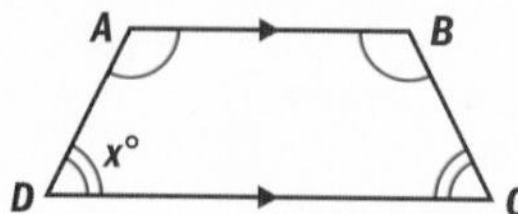

9. No; the top of the figure is curved.

10. *Sample answer:* Since no information is given about the angles, we can conclude only that the figure is a rhombus.

21a. about $16\frac{5}{8}$ ft, or 16 ft 7.5 in.

21c. *Sample answer:* You would need to know the height of each triangle. Then you could use the area formula for a triangle, $A = \frac{1}{2}bh$, to find the area of one of the triangles, and multiply the result by 8 to find the area of the octagon.

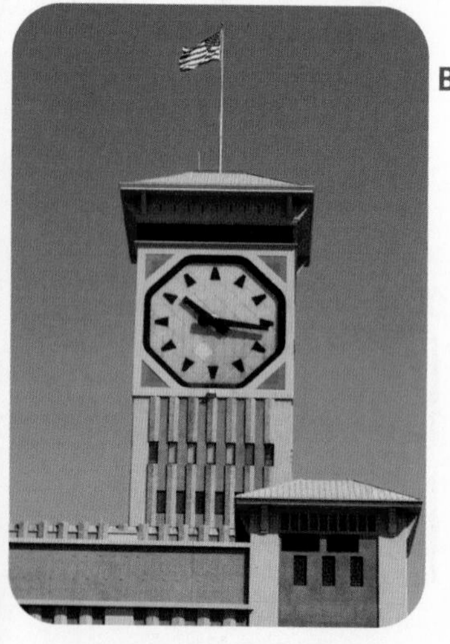
Allen-Bradley Clock Tower

ASSIGNMENT GUIDE

Basic Course
Day 1: EP p. 805 Exs. 9-11; pp. 519-520 Exs. 7-9, 11-20, 22, 23, 25-30

Average Course
Day 1: pp. 519-520 Exs. 7-23, 25-30

Advanced Course
Day 1: pp. 519-520 Exs. 8-12, 14-18, 20-25*, 27-30

Block
pp. 519-520 Exs. 8-12, 14-17, 19-23, 25-30 (with 10.1)

EXTRA PRACTICE
- Student Edition, p. 812
- Chapter 10 Resource Book, pp. 16-18
- Test and Practice Generator

TRANSPARENCY
Even-numbered answers are available on transparencies. A support transparency is available for Exercises 25-27.

HOMEWORK CHECK
When you review students' homework for this lesson, go over the following exercises to check understanding of key concepts.
Basic: 7, 9, 11, 14, 18
Average: 8, 12, 15, 19, 20
Advanced: 9, 14, 16, 18, 20

21b. 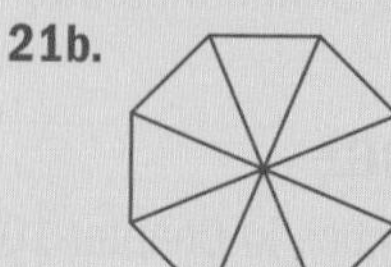

4 ASSESS

ASSESSMENT RESOURCES

For more assessment resources, see:
- Assessment Book
- Test and Practice Generator

MINI-QUIZ

1. What type of quadrilateral has exactly one pair of parallel sides? **trapezoid**

Copy and complete the statement using *always*, *sometimes*, or *never*.

2. A rhombus is _?_ a parallelogram. **always**
3. A square is _?_ a trapezoid. **never**
4. **Challenge** Find $m\angle 1$. **50°**

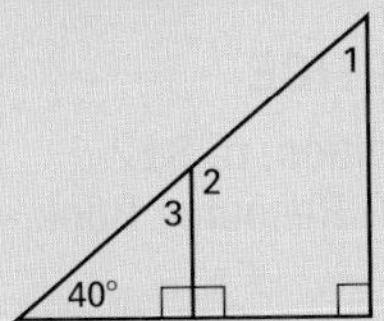

5 FOLLOW-UP

DIAGNOSIS/REMEDIATION

- Study Guide in Chapter 10 Resource Book, pp. 19–20
- Tutor Place, Geometry Cards 3, 7, 8, 10
- eTutorial Plus Online
- Extra Practice, p. 812
- Lesson Practice in Chapter 10 Resource Book, pp. 16–18

ENGLISH LEARNER SUPPORT

- Spanish Study Guide
- Multi-Language Visual Glossary
- Chapter Audio Summaries CDs

CHALLENGE

- Challenge Practice in Chapter 10 Resource Book, p. 21
- Teacher's Edition, p. 508F

24, 30a–b, Brain Game. See Additional Answers beginning on page AA1.

23. In mathematics, a *kite* is a special type of quadrilateral. Two pairs of sides are congruent, but opposite sides are not congruent. Exactly one pair of opposite angles are congruent. In kite *ABCD* shown, the measure of $\angle A$ is twice the measure of $\angle C$, and $\angle B$ has a measure of 114°. Find the measures of $\angle A$, $\angle C$, and $\angle D$.
$m\angle A = 88°$, $m\angle C = 44°$, $m\angle D = 114°$

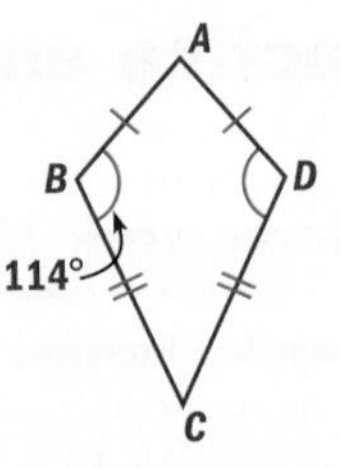

C **24. Challenge** Use the figure shown to find $m\angle WXY$ and $m\angle XYZ$. Explain your reasoning. **See margin.**

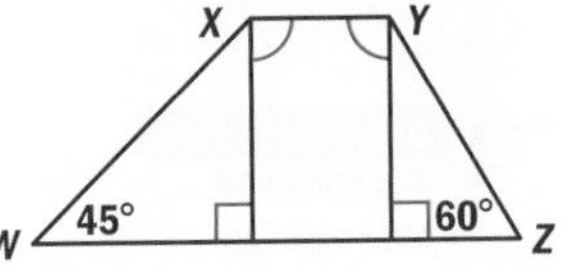

Mixed Review

Solve the linear system by graphing. *(Lesson 8.8)*

25. $y = x - 5$
$y = 2x + 1$ **(−6, −11)**

26. $y = -3x + 7$
$y = 3x + 4$ **(0.5, 5.5)**

27. $x + y = 6$
$2x - 8y = -11$ **(3.7, 2.3)**

28. Find the midpoint of the segment with endpoints $(-7, 5)$ and $(4, -20)$. *(Lesson 9.5)* **(−1.5, −7.5)**

29. The ratio of the angle measures of a triangle is 2 : 3 : 7. Find the angle measures. Then classify the triangle by its angle measures. *(Lesson 10.1)* **30°, 45°, 105°; obtuse**

Standardized Test Practice

30. Extended Response The top of the picnic table shown has the shape of a regular polygon.

a. Sketch and classify the polygon. Is it convex or concave? **See art in part b; regular hexagon; convex.**

b. Draw a single segment that divides the polygon in your sketch into two trapezoids. **See margin.**

c. Find the sum of the measures of the angles of the polygon. **720°**

Toothpick Task

Move exactly two toothpicks in the figure at the right to make 4 congruent squares instead of 5. Each toothpick must be used as a side of a square. **See margin.**

LESSON

10.3 Areas *of* Parallelograms *and* Trapezoids

Vocabulary

base of a parallelogram, p. 521

height of a parallelogram, p. 521

bases of a trapezoid, p. 522

height of a trapezoid, p. 522

BEFORE	Now	WHY?
You classified polygons.	You'll find the areas of parallelograms and trapezoids.	So you can compare the areas of two parking lots, as in Ex. 26.

The **base of a parallelogram** is the length of any one of its sides. The **height of a parallelogram** is the perpendicular distance between the side whose length is the base and the opposite side. The diagrams below show how to change a parallelogram into a rectangle with the same base, height, and area as the parallelogram.

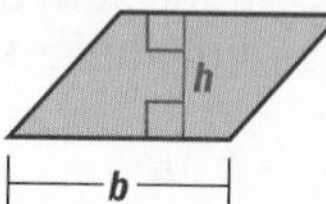

1) Start with any parallelogram.

2) Cut to form a right triangle and a trapezoid.

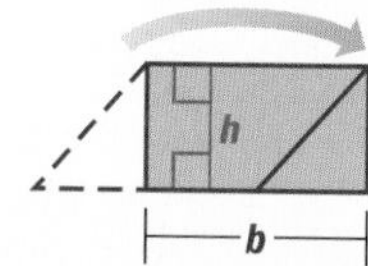

3) Move the triangle to form a rectangle.

Notice that the area of the rectangle above is the product of the base b and the height h. The diagram suggests the formula below.

Area of a Parallelogram

Words The area A of a parallelogram is the product of the base b and the height h.

Algebra $A = bh$ **Numbers** $A = 8 \cdot 6 = 48 \text{ m}^2$

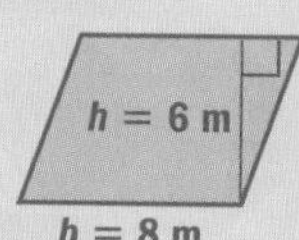

Example 1 *Finding the Area of a Parallelogram*

The base of a parallelogram is 5 inches. The height is twice the base. Find the area of the parallelogram.

1) Find the height.

$$h = 2b = 2(5) = 10 \text{ in.}$$

2) Find the area.

$$A = bh = 5(10) = 50 \text{ in.}^2$$

Answer The parallelogram has an area of 50 square inches.

NCTM CURRICULUM STANDARDS

Standard 3: Analyze properties of 2-D shapes

Standard 4: Apply proper formulas to find measures

Standard 6: Solve problems in math and other contexts

1 PLAN

Skill Check

Solve for *x*.

1. $12x = 96$ **8**
2. $9x = 99$ **11**
3. $\frac{1}{2}(x + 12) = 11$ **10**
4. $\frac{1}{2}(x + 8)28 = 280$ **12**

Lesson Objective

Find the areas of parallelograms and trapezoids.

Pacing

Suggested Number of Days

Basic Course: 2 days

Average Course: 2 days

Advanced Course: 2 days

Block: 1 block

Teaching Resources

For a complete list of Teaching Resources, see page 508B.

Transparency

Warm-Up Exercises for this lesson are available on a transparency.

2 TEACH

Motivating the Lesson

Show the class a side view of a large stack of index cards. Then push the upper part of the stack sideways so the rectangular side view becomes a parallelogram, and lead students to recognize that the area of this side of the stack did not change even though its shape changed.

TIPS *for* NEW TEACHERS

You might want to show students how to use the formula for the area of a triangle to derive the area formula for a trapezoid. Draw a trapezoid and one of its diagonals to begin the derivation. See Tips for New Teachers in the *Chapter 10 Resource Book*.

Extra Examples

Example 1 The height of a parallelogram is 12 inches. The base is two thirds of the height. Find the area of the parallelogram. **96 in.^{2}**

Example 2 Find the area of the trapezoid. **33 in.^{2}**

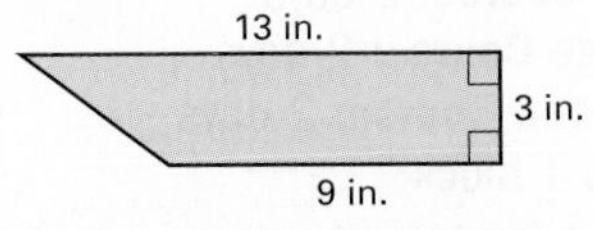

ALGEBRAIC REASONING

Lead students to recognize that the formula for the area of a trapezoid can be thought of as the average of the base lengths multiplied by the height. This recognition will allow some students to be able to mentally compute the area of some trapezoids.

COMMON ERROR

Watch for students who find one half of the sum of the bases but then forget to multiply by the height when finding the area of a trapezoid.

Trapezoids The **bases of a trapezoid** are the lengths of its parallel sides. The **height of a trapezoid** is the perpendicular distance between the sides whose lengths are the bases. The diagram below shows how two congruent trapezoids with height h and bases b_1 and b_2 can be put together to form a parallelogram with base $b_1 + b_2$ and height h.

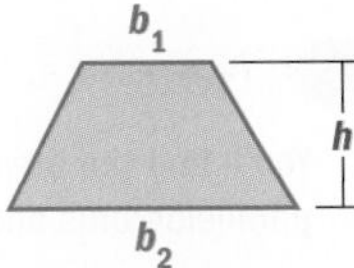

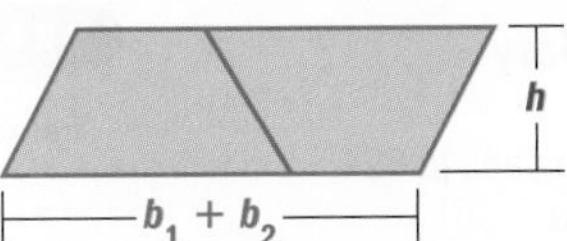

Notice the area of the parallelogram is twice the area of either trapezoid. This result suggests the formula below.

Area of a Trapezoid

Words The area A of a trapezoid is one half of the product of the sum of the bases, b_1 and b_2, and the height, h.

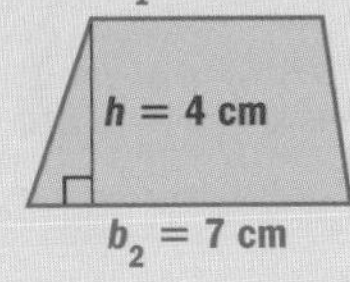

Algebra $A = \frac{1}{2}(b_1 + b_2)h$

Numbers $A = \frac{1}{2}(5 + 7)4 = 24 \text{ cm}^2$

Example 2 ***Finding the Area of a Trapezoid***

Quilts The diagram shows one of the trapezoids in a quilt design. Find the area of the trapezoid.

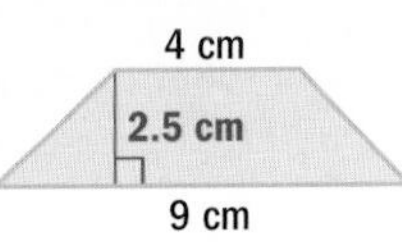

Solution

$A = \frac{1}{2}(b_1 + b_2)h$ **Write formula for area of a trapezoid.**

$= \frac{1}{2}(4 + 9)2.5$ **Substitute 4 for b_1, 9 for b_2, and 2.5 for h.**

$= 16.25$ **Simplify.**

Answer The trapezoid has an area of 16.25 square centimeters.

Checkpoint

Find the area of the parallelogram or trapezoid.

1. **30 ft^2**

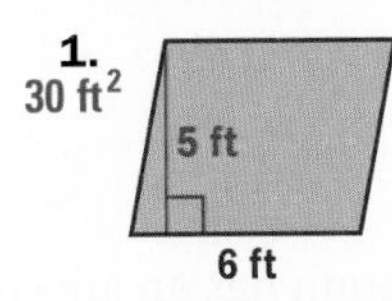

2. **51 m^2**

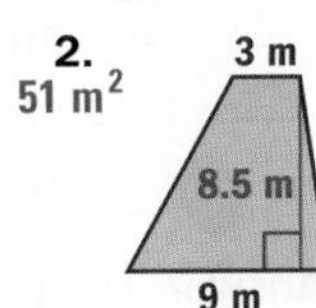

3. **280 in.^{2}**

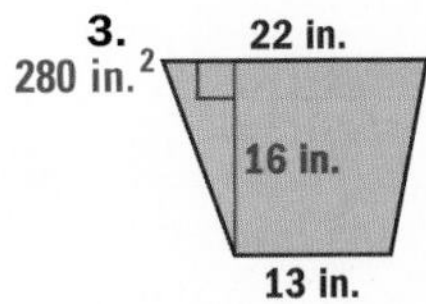

Example 3 *Finding an Unknown Length*

The height of a trapezoid is 6 meters. One of its bases is 8 meters. The area of the trapezoid is 54 square meters. Find the other base.

$A = \frac{1}{2}(b_1 + b_2)h$	**Write formula for area of a trapezoid.**
$54 = \frac{1}{2}(8 + b_2)6$	**Substitute 54 for *A*, 8 for b_1, and 6 for *h*.**
$54 = 3(8 + b_2)$	**Multiply.**
$54 = 24 + 3b_2$	**Distributive property**
$30 = 3b_2$	**Subtract 24 from each side.**
$10 = b_2$	**Divide each side by 3.**

Answer The other base is 10 meters.

Study *Strategy*

Another Way You can divide the desktop in Example 4 in other ways. For instance, you can have an 8 ft by 3 ft rectangle and a trapezoid with bases 4 ft and 6 ft and height 3 ft.

Example 4 *Using Area of Trapezoids*

Desk You are building an L-shaped desk for your room. The dimensions of the desktop are shown. Find the area of the desktop.

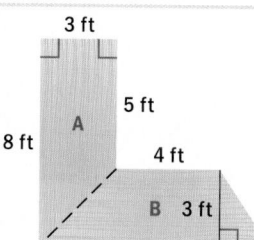

Solution

1. Divide the desktop into two trapezoids, A and B, as shown.
2. Find the sum of the areas of trapezoids A and B.

Area of trapezoid A $= \frac{1}{2}(b_1 + b_2)h$	**Formula for area of a trapezoid**
$= \frac{1}{2}(5 + 8)3 = \frac{39}{2} = 19\frac{1}{2}$	**Substitute. Then simplify.**
Area of trapezoid B $= \frac{1}{2}(b_1 + b_2)h$	**Formula for area of a trapezoid**
$= \frac{1}{2}(4 + 9)3 = \frac{39}{2} = 19\frac{1}{2}$	**Substitute. Then simplify.**

3. Add the areas.

Area of trapezoid A + Area of trapezoid B $= 19\frac{1}{2} + 19\frac{1}{2} = 39$

Answer The total area of the desktop is 39 square feet.

Checkpoint

4. One base of a trapezoid is 9 feet, and the height is 4 feet. The area of the trapezoid is 28 square feet. Find the other base. **5 ft**

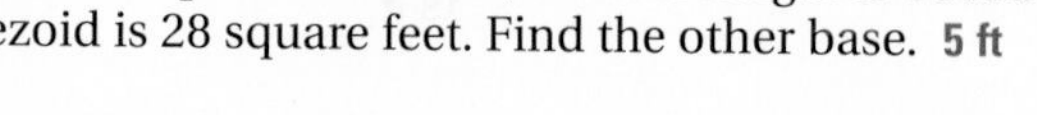

Extra Examples

Example 3 The bases of a trapezoid are 11 inches and 17 inches. The area of the trapezoid is 56 square inches. Find the height. **4 in.**

Example 4 A banner is made of two congruent trapezoids. Find the area of the banner. **28 ft^2**

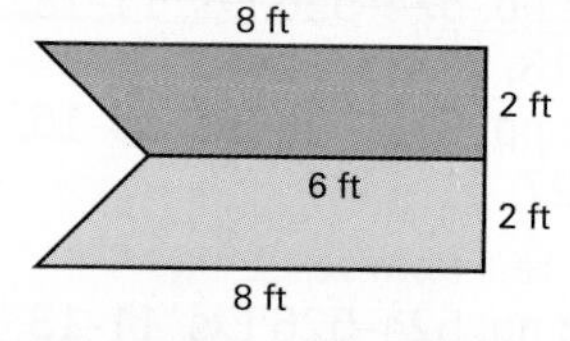

VISUALIZE

While presenting Example 4, you might wish to discuss other ways that the desktop could have been divided in Step 1. For example, the dashed line could have been drawn straight down from the 5-foot side to meet the bottom of the figure where it would divide the 9-foot measure into pieces measuring 3 feet and 6 feet. Point out that part A of the resulting figure would then be a rectangle while part B would again be a trapezoid.

CONCEPT CHECK

How do you find the area of a trapezoid? **Multiply $\frac{1}{2}$ times the sum of the bases and then multiply this product by the height.**

DAILY PUZZLER

Six equilateral triangles are arranged to form a regular hexagon. If each triangle has a perimeter of 6 centimeters, what is the perimeter of the regular hexagon? **12 cm**

3 APPLY

ASSIGNMENT GUIDE

Basic Course

Day 1: pp. 524–526 Exs. 11–13, 18, 28, 30–32, 35–40

Day 2: pp. 524–526 Exs. 14–17, 19–25, 41–43

Average Course

Day 1: pp. 524–526 Exs. 11–13, 17, 18, 28–33, 35–40

Day 2: pp. 524–526 Exs. 14–16, 19–27, 41–43

Advanced Course

Day 1: pp. 524–526 Exs. 11–13, 17, 18, 27–35*

Day 2: pp. 524–526 Exs. 14–16, 19–26, 39–43

Block

pp. 524–526 Exs. 11–33, 35–43

EXTRA PRACTICE

- Student Edition, p. 812
- Chapter 10 Resource Book, pp. 24–26
- Test and Practice Generator

TRANSPARENCY

Even-numbered answers are available on transparencies. A support transparency is available for Exercises 27 and 28.

HOMEWORK CHECK

When you review students' homework for this lesson, go over the following exercises to check understanding of key concepts.

Basic: 11, 14, 17, 19, 25
Average: 12, 15, 17, 20, 26
Advanced: 13, 16, 18, 23, 26

1. *Sample:*

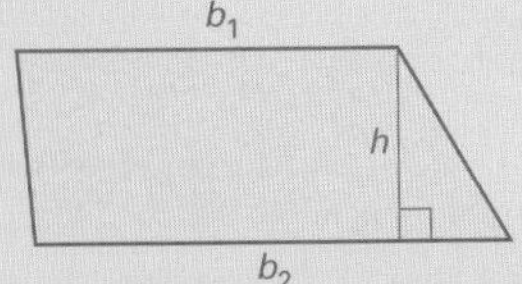

10.3 Exercises

More Practice, p. 812

Guided Practice

Vocabulary Check

1. Sketch a trapezoid and label its bases and height. State the formula for finding its area. **See margin for art; $A = \frac{1}{2}(b_1 + b_2)h$.**

2. The height of a parallelogram is 22 inches. The base is one half of the height. Find the area of the parallelogram. **242 in.^{2}**

Skill Check **Find the area of the trapezoid.**

3. 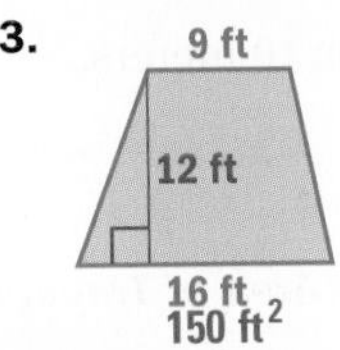

150 ft^2

4. 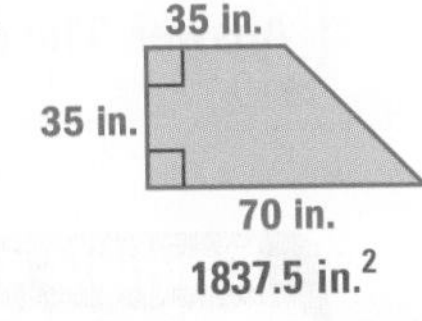

1837.5 in.^{2}

5. 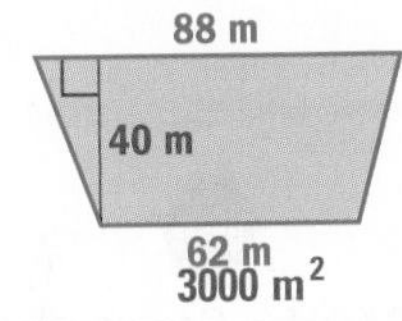

3000 m^2

Find the unknown base or height of the parallelogram.

6. $A = 40 \text{ in.}^2$, $b = 25$ in., $h = \underline{?}$ **1.6 in.**

7. $A = 300 \text{ m}^2$, $b = \underline{?}$, $h = 20$ m **15 m**

Find the unknown base or height of the trapezoid.

8. $A = 12 \text{ ft}^2$, $b_1 = 2$ ft, $b_2 = \underline{?}$, $h = 3$ ft **6 ft**

9. $A = 240 \text{ m}^2$, $b_1 = 16$ m, $b_2 = 8$ m, $h = \underline{?}$ **20 m**

10. **Track Uniform** You are sewing a red stripe on the front of a track uniform. As shown, the stripe is a parallelogram. What is the area of the stripe? **60 in.^{2}**

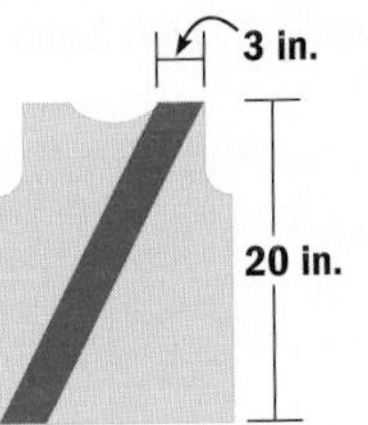

Practice and Problem Solving

Homework *Help*

Example	Exercises
1	11–13, 17
2	14–16, 18
3	19–24
4	25, 26

Online Resources
CLASSZONE.COM
- More Examples
- eTutorial Plus

Find the area of the parallelogram.

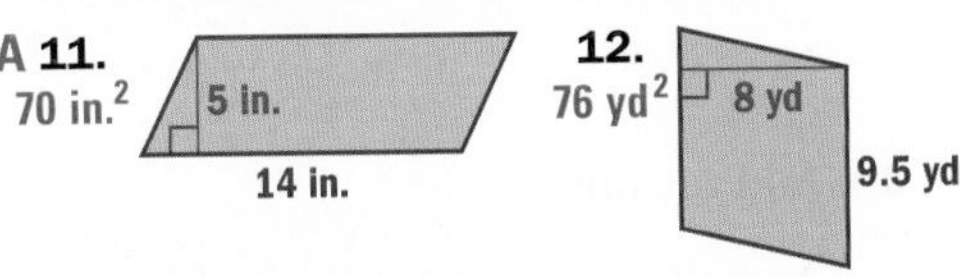

13. 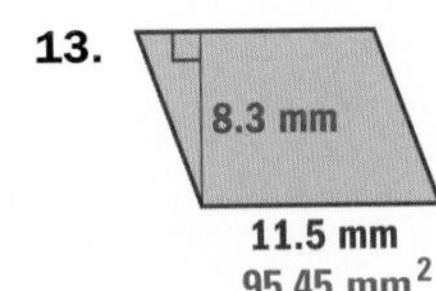

95.45 mm^2

Find the area of the trapezoid.

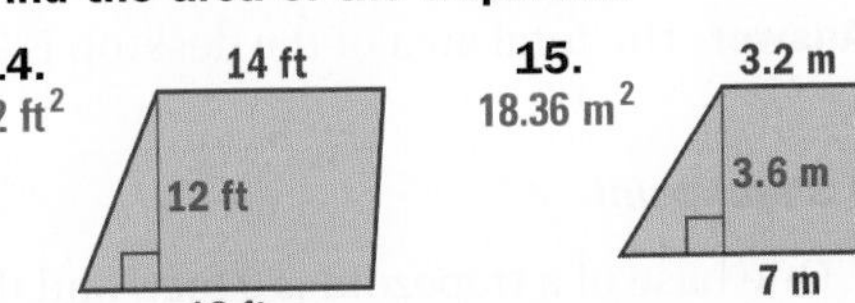

16. **135.15 cm^2**

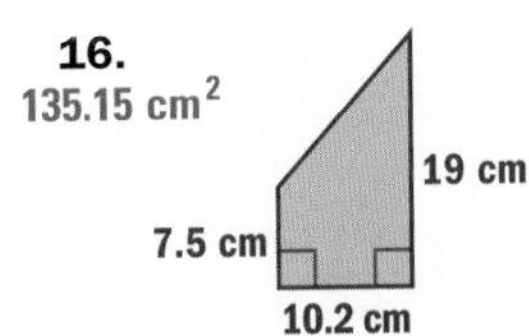

17. The base of a parallelogram is 10 meters. The height is one fourth of the base. Find the area of the parallelogram. **25 m^2**

18. The height of a trapezoid is 2 feet. One of the bases is three times the height, and the other base is four times the height. Find the area of the trapezoid. **14 ft^2**

Find the unknown measure of the parallelogram.

19. $A = 2025\ m^2$ **45 m**

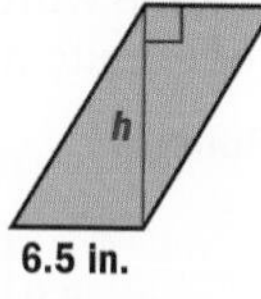

20. $A = 71.5\ in.^2$ **11 in.**

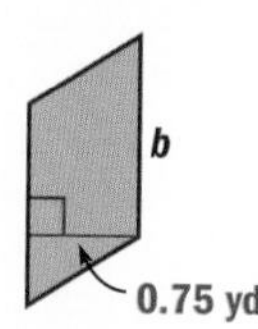

21. $A = 1\ yd^2$ **$1\frac{1}{3}$ yd**

Find the unknown measure of the trapezoid.

22. $A = 192.5\ cm^2$ **10 cm**

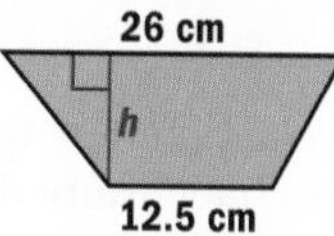

23. $A = 1800\ ft^2$ **25 ft**

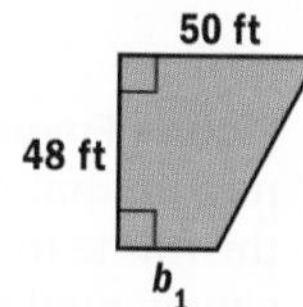

24. $A = 16.555\ mm^2$ **5.6 mm**

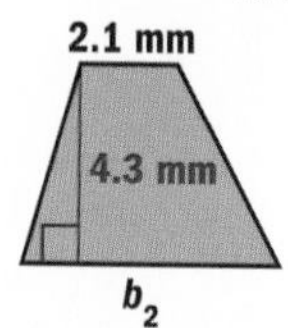

B 25. **Aircraft Wings** A wing of each aircraft described has the shape of a trapezoid. Find the area of the wing.

a. An F-18 wing has bases of 6 feet and 15 feet and height of 13 feet. **136.5 ft^2**

b. A Boeing 747 wing has bases of 13.3 feet and 54.3 feet and height of 81.3 feet. **2747.94 ft^2**

26. **Parking Lot** Two parking lots each have space for 5 cars, as shown in the diagrams below.

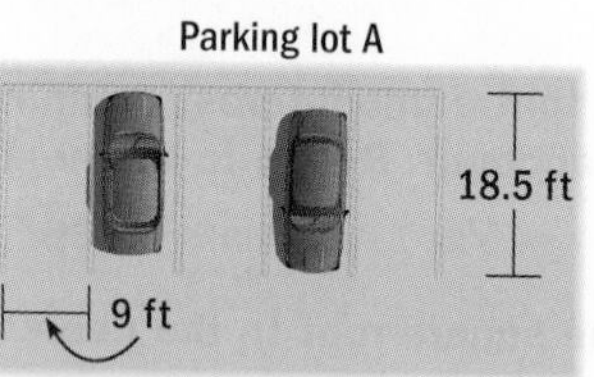

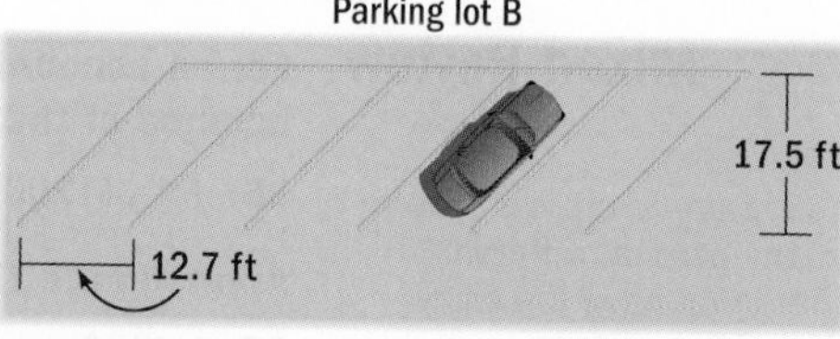

a. Find the base of each figure formed by the 5 parking spaces. **A: 45 ft, B: 63.5 ft**

b. Find the area of each figure formed by the 5 parking spaces. **A: 832.5 ft^2, B: 1111.25 ft^2**

c. Compare Which parking lot covers less area to park 5 cars? **Parking lot A**

Coordinate Geometry In Exercises 27 and 28, plot the points in a coordinate plane. Connect the points so that they form a polygon. Identify the polygon and find its area. **27–28. See margin for art.**

27. $(-2, -3), (-2, 0), (2, 3), (2, -4)$ **trapezoid, 20 square units**

28. $(-1, 3), (4, 3), (2, -1), (-3, -1)$ **parallelogram, 20 square units**

29. *Writing* What happens to the area of a trapezoid if you double its height? if you double both its bases? if you double the height and both bases? **It doubles; it doubles; it quadruples.**

In the Real World

Aircraft Wings The F-18 is a military plane used by the U.S. Blue Angels Demonstration Squad. The Boeing 747 shown above is a commercial plane. The wingspan of an F-18 is 40 feet 5 inches. The wingspan of a Boeing 747 is 211 feet 5 inches. The wingspan of a Boeing 747 is about how many times greater than the wingspan of an F-18? **about 5.23 times**

TEACHING TIP

Before assigning Exercise 14, discuss with students why the figure is a trapezoid and not a parallelogram. Exercise 16 provides an opportunity to show students that the bases of a trapezoid are not always the "top" and "bottom" of the figure.

27.

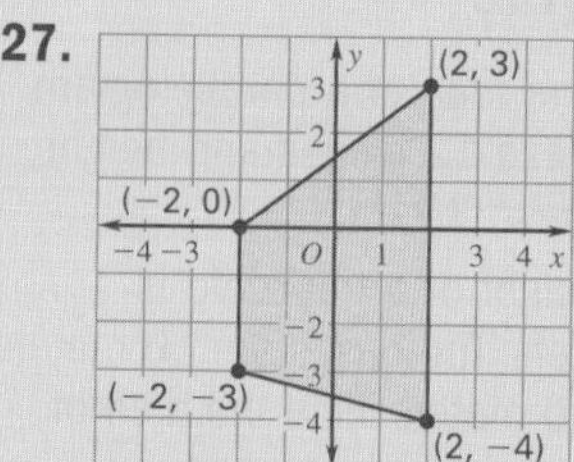

28.

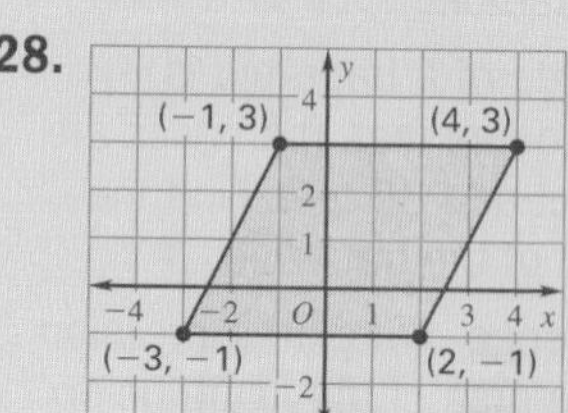

4 ASSESS

ASSESSMENT RESOURCES

For more assessment resources, see:

- Assessment Book
- Test and Practice Generator

MINI-QUIZ

1. Find the area of a parallelogram with base 12 inches and height 3 inches. **36 in.^{2}**
2. The height of a trapezoid is 7 meters. The bases are 16 meters and 20 meters. Find the area of the trapezoid. **126 m^2**
3. The area of a trapezoid is 132 square feet. The bases are 30 feet and 36 feet. Find the height of the trapezoid. **4 ft**
4. **Challenge** Write an expression for the area of the figure below in terms of n. **$4n^2\sqrt{3}$**

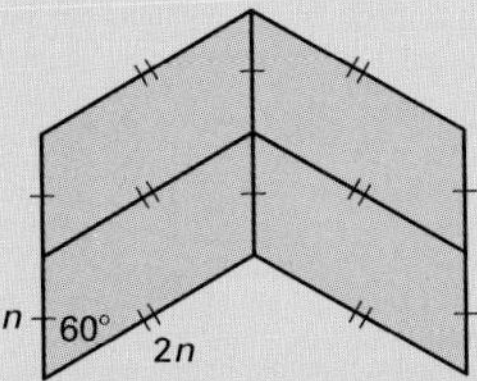

5 FOLLOW-UP

DIAGNOSIS/REMEDIATION

- Study Guide in Chapter 10 Resource Book, pp. 27–28
- eTutorial Plus Online
- Extra Practice, p. 812
- Lesson Practice in Chapter 10 Resource Book, pp. 24–26

ENGLISH LEARNER SUPPORT

- Spanish Study Guide
- Multi-Language Visual Glossary
- Chapter Audio Summaries CDs

CHALLENGE

- Challenge Practice in Chapter 10 Resource Book, p. 30
- Teacher's Edition, p. 508F

Find the area of the figure.

30. **49 m^2**

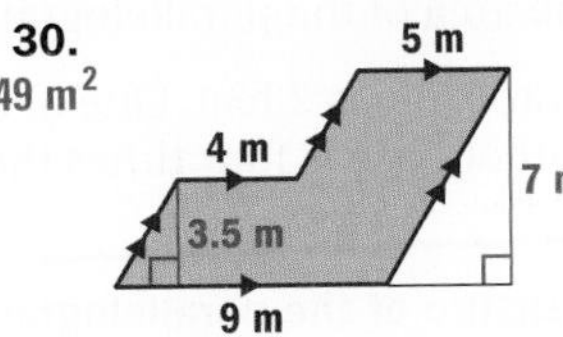

31. **156 cm^2**

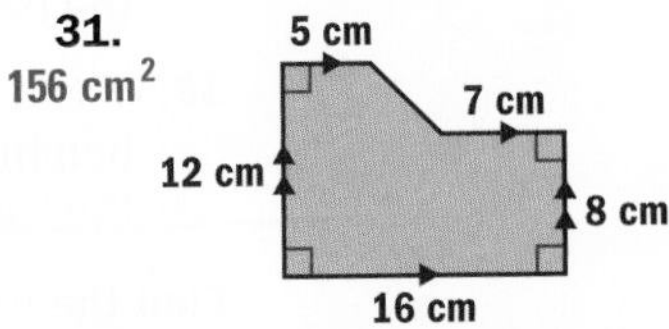

32. **Summer Camp** This summer at camp, you can stay in room A or room B with one roommate. Which room will give you and your roommate more space? **room B**

Room A

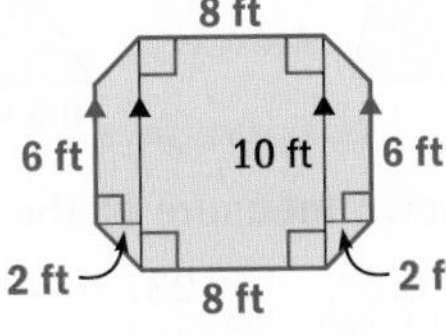

Room B

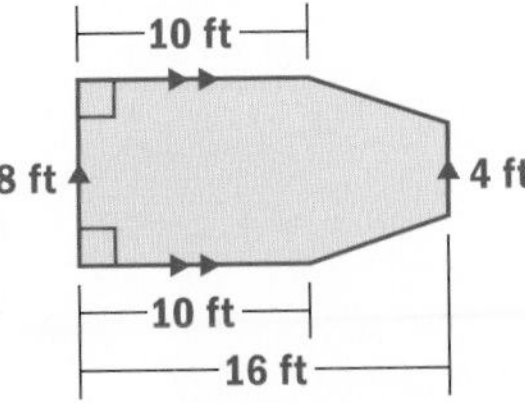

33. **Picture Frame** You have a 4 inch by 6 inch picture that you want to have framed. You want the frame to be 2 inches wide. A wooden frame can be made from four trapezoids, as shown. Find the areas of the bottom and side trapezoids. Then find the ratio of the area of the bottom trapezoid to the area of the side trapezoid. **16 in.^{2}, 12 in.^{2}; $\frac{4}{3}$**

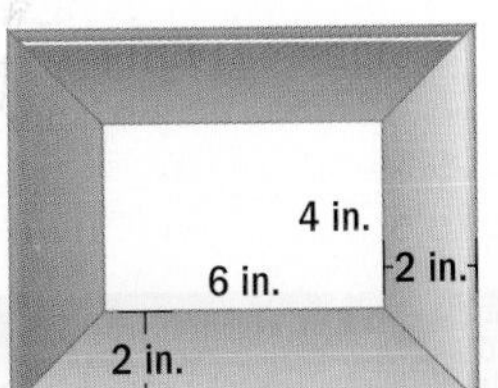

C 34. **Challenge** You form a rhombus by putting two equilateral triangles with side length $2n$ together, as shown. Write an expression for the area of the rhombus in terms of n. Explain your reasoning.

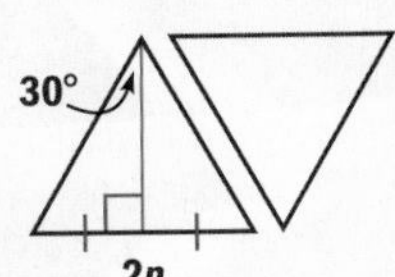

34. $A = 2n^2\sqrt{3}$. *Sample answer:* The area of a rhombus is $A = bh$. In this case, $b = 2n$. To find h, note that the height segment forms the longer leg of a 30°-60°-90° right triangle in which the shorter leg has a length of n. So, $h = n\sqrt{3}$, and the area is $A = 2n(n\sqrt{3}) = 2n^2\sqrt{3}$.

Mixed Review

For an account that earns interest compounded annually, find the balance of the account. Round to the nearest cent. *(Lesson 7.7)*

35. $P = \$1200$, $r = 5\%$, $t = 3$ years **\$1389.15**

36. $P = \$8550$, $r = 3.5\%$, $t = 20$ years **\$17,012.69**

Approximate the square root to the nearest integer. *(Lesson 9.1)*

37. $\sqrt{40}$ **6**

38. $\sqrt{587}$ **24**

39. $\sqrt{10.2}$ **3**

40. $\sqrt{0.725}$ **1**

41. Find the value of x in the quadrilateral shown. *(Lesson 10.2)* **107**

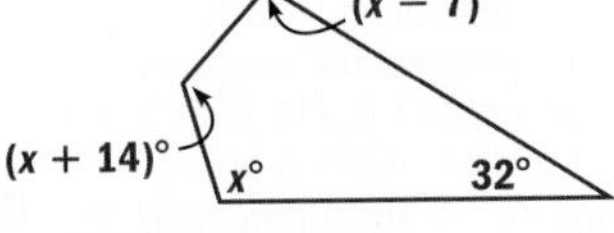

Standardized Test Practice

42. **Multiple Choice** The height of a parallelogram is 13.5 feet. The base is four times the height. What is the area of the parallelogram? **D**

A. 45.5625 ft^2 **B.** 54 ft^2 **C.** 182.25 ft^2 **D.** 729 ft^2

43. **Short Response** Is it possible for two parallelograms to have the same area but not be congruent? Explain why or why not. **See margin.**

43. Yes. *Sample answer:* There are many pairs of different numbers that have the same product. For example, parallelograms with $b = 24$ and $h = 2$, with $b = 16$ and $h = 3$, and with $b = 8$ and $h = 6$ all have areas of 48 square units, but are not congruent.

Concept *Activity*

10.4 Investigating Circles

Goal
Compare the circumferences and the diameters of circles.

Materials
- compass
- metric ruler
- paper and pencil
- string

The *diameter* of a circle is the distance across the circle through its center. The *circumference* of a circle is the distance around the circle.

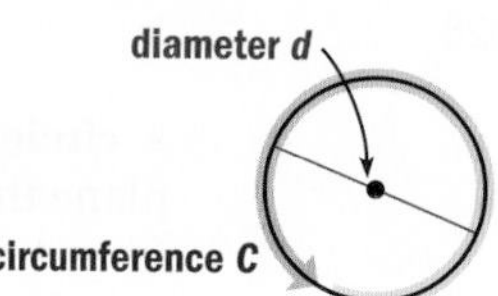

Investigate

Find the ratio of circumference to diameter of a circle.
Steps 1–4. Check students' work. Ratios should be close to 3.14.

 Draw a circle of any size using a compass.

 Lay a string around the circle. Mark the point where the string completes the circle. Straighten the string, and measure its length with a ruler.

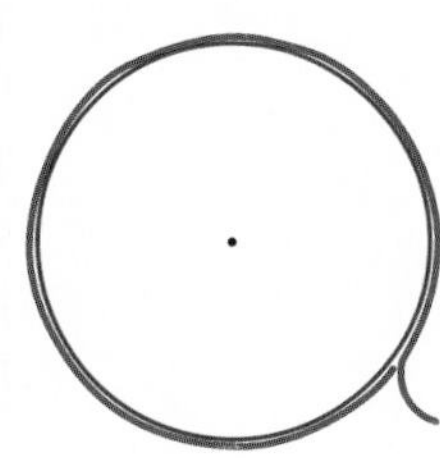

The circumference is about 9.4 centimeters.

3 Measure the diameter of the circle with a ruler. Make sure the ruler goes through the center of the circle.

 Write the ratio of the circumference to the diameter for the circle. Write the ratio as a decimal.

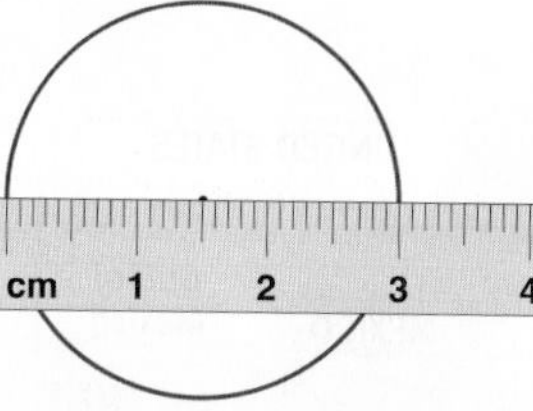

$$\frac{\text{circumference}}{\text{diameter}} \approx \frac{9.4}{3} \approx 3.13$$

The diameter is 3 centimeters.

Draw Conclusions

1. **Conjecture** Repeat Steps 1–4 of the activity for two circles of different diameters. What do you notice about the ratios in Step 4? **They seem to be the same.**

Predict the circumference of a circle with the given diameter *d*. **2–5. Answers may vary.**

2. $d = 4$ feet **12.6 ft** 3. $d = 2$ meters **6.3 m** 4. $d = 0.75$ inch **2.4 in.** 5. $d = 12$ feet **37.7 ft**

NCTM CURRICULUM STANDARDS
Standard 4: Understand the processes of measurement; Apply proper techniques to find measures

1 PLAN

Investigate the Concept

- Students compare the circumferences and the diameters of circles.
- This activity leads into finding circumferences and areas of circles in Lesson 10.4.

Materials

Each student will need a compass, a metric ruler, paper and pencil, and string. A support transparency is available for this activity.

Recommended Time

Work activity: 10 min
Discuss results: 5 min

Grouping

Students should work individually.

2 TEACH

Tips for Success

Stress that a circle of any size will work. Point out that students should not be expecting the circumference of their circle to be 9.4 centimeters; the example shown is just one possibility.

3 CLOSE

Key Discovery

The ratio of circumference to diameter is the same for all circles.

Assessment

1. How can you predict the circumference of a circle if you know its diameter? **Multiply the diameter by 3.13 (or 3.14).**

1 PLAN

Skill Check

1. $6^2 = ?$ 36
2. $8 \cdot 2^2 = ?$ 32
3. $12 \cdot 5^2 = ?$ 300
4. $33^2 = ?$ 1089

Lesson Objective

Find circumferences and areas of circles.

Pacing

Suggested Number of Days
Basic Course: 2 days
Average Course: 2 days
Advanced Course: 2 days
Block: 1 block

Teaching Resources

For a complete list of Teaching Resources, see page 508B.

Transparency

Warm-Up Exercises for this lesson are available on a transparency.

2 TEACH

Motivating the Lesson

Use a bicycle wheel to point out the features of a circle and describe how they are related.

TIPS *for* NEW TEACHERS

Remind students that area is measured in square units. To help students avoid confusing the formulas for area and circumference, stress that the area formula involves r^2 while the circumference formula does not. See Tips for New Teachers in the *Chapter 10 Resource Book*.

LESSON 10.4

Circumference *and* Area *of a* Circle

Vocabulary
circle, p. 528
center, p. 528
radius, p. 528
diameter, p. 528
circumference, p. 528

BEFORE	Now	WHY?
You found perimeters and areas of polygons.	You'll find the circumferences and areas of circles.	So you can find the diameter of a circular floor, as in Ex. 28.

A **circle** consists of all points in a plane that are the same distance from a fixed point called the **center**. The distance between the center and any point on the circle is the **radius**. The distance across the circle through the center is the **diameter**.

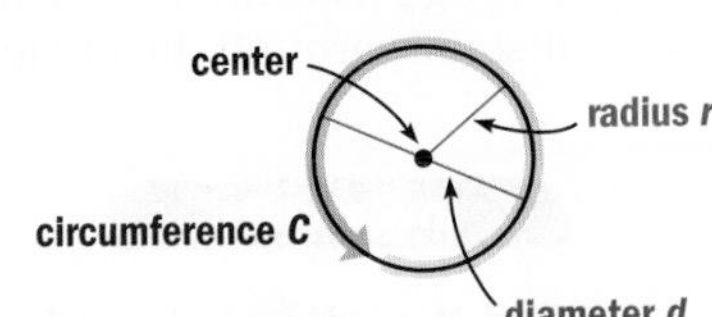

The **circumference** of a circle is the distance around the circle. For any circle, the ratio of its circumference to its diameter is an irrational number that is approximately equal to 3.14 or $\frac{22}{7}$. The Greek letter π (pi) is used to represent this ratio.

Circumference of a Circle

Words The circumference C of a circle is the product of π and the diameter d, or twice the product of π and the radius r.

Algebra $C = \pi d$ $C = 2\pi r$

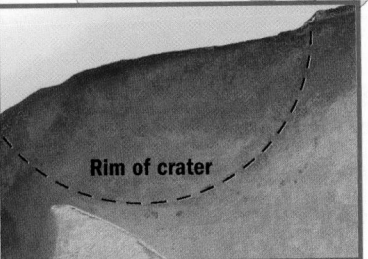

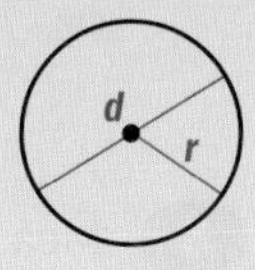

Example 1 *Finding the Circumference of a Circle*

Meteor Crater Scientists have identified the faint outline of part of an ancient meteor crater on the coast of Mexico. The rest of the approximately circular crater lies underwater. The crater's diameter is about 170 kilometers. Approximate the distance around the crater to the nearest kilometer.

Solution

$C = \pi d$	**Write formula for circumference of a circle.**
$\approx 3.14(170)$	**Substitute 3.14 for π and 170 for d.**
$= 533.8$	**Multiply.**

Answer The distance around the crater is about 534 kilometers.

NCTM CURRICULUM STANDARDS
Standard 3: Analyze properties of 2-D shapes
Standard 4: Apply proper formulas to find measures
Standard 6: Solve problems in math and other contexts

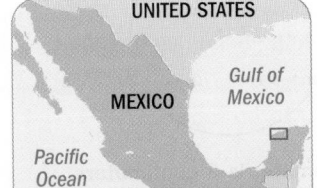

Example 2 *Finding the Radius of a Circle*

The circumference of a circle is 70 inches. Find the radius of the circle to the nearest inch.

$C = 2\pi r$	**Write formula for circumference of a circle.**
$70 \approx 2(3.14)r$	**Substitute 70 for *C* and 3.14 for π.**
$70 \approx 6.28r$	**Multiply.**
$11.1 \approx r$	**Divide each side by 6.28. Use a calculator.**

Answer The radius of the circle is about 11 inches.

Study *Strategy*

When the radius or diameter of a circle is divisible by 7, use $\frac{22}{7}$ to approximate π. Otherwise, use 3.14 to approximate π.

Checkpoint

1. The diameter of a circle is 28 feet. Find the circumference of the circle to the nearest foot. **88 ft**
2. The circumference of a circle is 186 centimeters. Find the radius of the circle to the nearest centimeter. **30 cm**

Area of a Circle

Words The area A of a circle is the product of π and the square of the radius r.

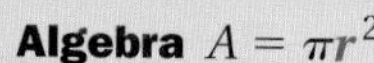

Algebra $A = \pi r^2$

Example 3 *Finding the Area of a Circle*

Find the area of the circle to the nearest square foot.

26 ft

1) Find the radius.

$$r = \frac{d}{2} = \frac{26}{2} = 13$$

2) Find the area.

$A = \pi r^2$	**Write formula for area of a circle.**
$\approx 3.14(13)^2$	**Substitute 3.14 for π and 13 for *r*.**
≈ 530.7	**Simplify.**

Answer The area of the circle is about 531 square feet.

Checkpoint

3. The diameter of a circle is 14 inches. Find the area of the circle to the nearest square inch. **154 in.^{2}**
4. **Critical Thinking** One circle has a diameter of 12 centimeters. Another circle has a radius of 7 centimeters. Which circle has a greater area? Explain your reasoning.

4. Circle with radius 7 cm. *Sample answer:* The circle with diameter 12 centimeters has a radius of $12 \div 2 = 6$ centimeters, so it is smaller than the other circle.

Extra Examples

Example 1 The supercollider ring of the physics research facility CERN in Switzerland is a circle with a radius of about 4.25 kilometers. Find the circumference of the ring to the nearest kilometer. **27 km**

Example 2 The circumference of a circle is 500 feet. Find the radius of the circle to the nearest foot. **80 ft**

Example 3 The diameter of a circle is 54 centimeters. Find the area of the circle to the nearest square centimeter. **2289 cm^2**

COMMON ERROR

Watch for students who confuse the terms *radius* and *diameter*. Point out that the word "radius" is shorter than the word "diameter." Suggest that students use this fact to remember that a radius of a circle is shorter than a diameter of the circle.

Extra Examples

Example 4 The area of a circle is 250 square inches. Find the radius of the circle to the nearest inch. **9 in.**

Example 5 Find the area of the figure to the nearest square centimeter. **164 cm^2**

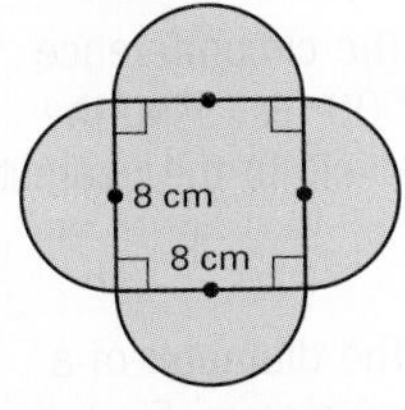

TEACHING TIP

In Example 5, point out that all of the rectangular panes of glass are the same size. This will help students understand the statement in Step 2, which says the radius of the half circle is half of the width of the window.

CONCEPT CHECK

What information do you need to know in order to find either the area or the circumference of a circle? **either the radius or the diameter of the circle**

DAILY PUZZLER

In 1998, a group of community college students in Michigan designed a tricycle with a front wheel that had a diameter of 15.3 feet and whose back wheels had diameters of 7.3 feet. To the nearest foot, how much greater was the circumference of the front wheel than the circumference of each back wheel? **25 ft**

8. *Sample answer:* When finding the diameter of a circle for a given area, you must double the result found using the area formula because it involves the radius.

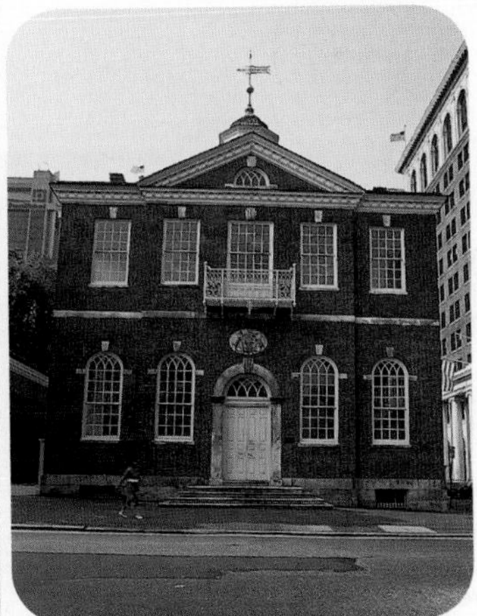

In the Real World

Norman Windows
Philadelphia was the capital of the United States from 1790 to 1800. During that time, the United States Congress met in Congress Hall. Congress Hall has 19 Norman windows of the same size. To the nearest square foot, what is the total area of the 19 windows? **746 ft^2**

Example 4 *Finding the Radius of a Circle*

The area of a circle is 72 square millimeters. Find the radius of the circle to the nearest millimeter.

$A = \pi r^2$	Write formula for area of a circle.
$72 \approx (3.14)r^2$	Substitute 72 for *A* and 3.14 for π.
$22.9 \approx r^2$	Divide each side by 3.14.
$\sqrt{22.9} \approx r$	Take positive square root of each side.
$4.8 \approx r$	Use a calculator to approximate square root.

Answer To the nearest millimeter, the radius is 5 millimeters.

Checkpoint

Find the unknown measure. Round to the nearest whole number.

5. $A = 1567 \text{ in.}^2$ $r = \underline{?}$ **22 in.**

6. $A = 59 \text{ ft}^2$ $d = \underline{?}$ **9 ft**

7. $A = 197 \text{ cm}^2$ $d = \underline{?}$ **16 cm**

8. Critical Thinking How is finding the diameter of a circle when given its area different from finding the radius when given its area?

Example 5 *Finding the Area of a Figure*

Norman Windows A Norman window from Congress Hall in Philadelphia consists of a rectangle and a half circle, as shown. Find the area of the window to the nearest square foot.

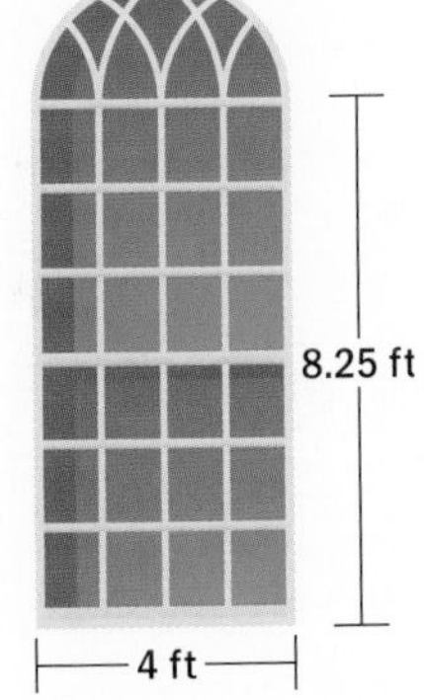

Solution

1) Find the area of the rectangle.

$A = lw = 8.25(4) = 33$

2) For the window shown, the radius of the half circle is half the width of the window, or 2 feet.

$A = \frac{1}{2}\pi r^2$	Write formula for area of a half circle.
$\approx \frac{1}{2}(3.14)(2)^2$	Substitute 3.14 for π and 2 for *r*.
$= 6.28$	Simplify.

3) Find the total area.

Total area $\approx 33 + 6.28 = 39.28$

Answer The area of the Norman window is about 39 square feet.

10.4 Exercises

More Practice, p. 812

Guided Practice

Vocabulary Check

1. The diameter of a circle is 5 centimeters. What is the radius? **2.5 cm**

2. Copy and complete: The ratio of the _?_ of a circle to its diameter is equal to π. **circumference**

Skill Check

3. Find the circumference and area of the circle shown. Use $\frac{22}{7}$ for π. Round your answers to the nearest whole number. **88 cm, 616 cm²**

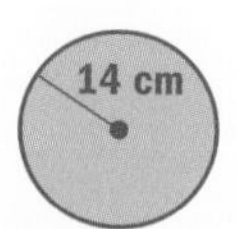

4. The circumference of a circle is 22 meters. Find the radius of the circle to the nearest tenth of a meter. **3.5 m**

5. The area of a circle is 87 square feet. Find the diameter of the circle to the nearest foot. **11 ft**

Guided Problem Solving

6. **Wrestling** Use the diagram of the square wrestling mat shown. The circle is the part of the mat used for competition. What is the area of the part that is *not* used for competition?

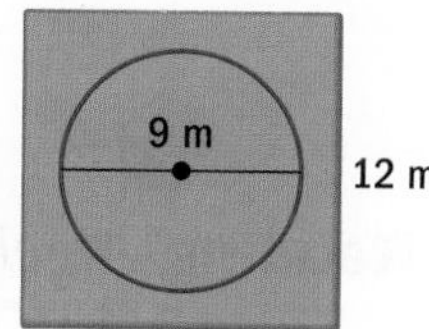

(1) Find the area of the entire mat. **144 m²**

(2) Find the area of the circle used for competition to the nearest square meter. **64 m²**

(3) Subtract the area of the circle from the area of the mat. **80 m²**

Practice and Problem Solving

Homework Help

Example	Exercises
1	7-12
2	13-15
3	17-22, 26, 27
4	23-25, 28
5	30

Online Resources
CLASSZONE.COM
- More Examples
- eTutorial Plus

Find the circumference of the circle. Use 3.14 or $\frac{22}{7}$ for π. Round to the nearest whole number.

A **7.**

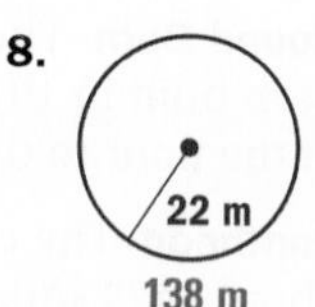

113 in.

8.

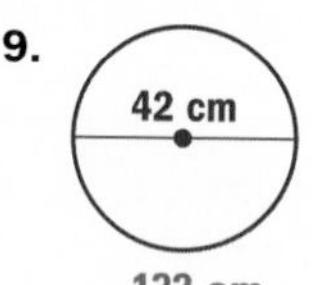

138 m

9. 42 cm

132 cm

10.

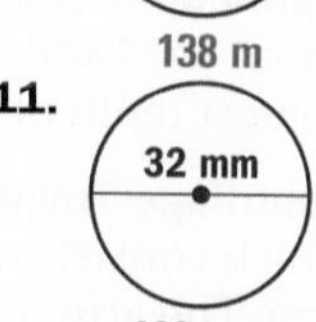

220 yd

11.

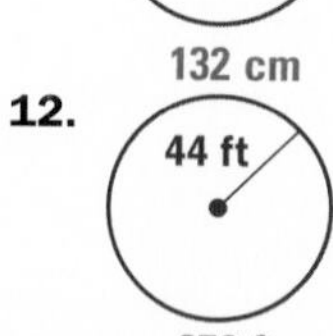

100 mm

12. 44 ft

276 ft

For a circle with the given circumference C, find the radius and diameter of the circle. Round to the nearest whole number.

13. $C = 37$ m **6 m, 12 m**
14. $C = 25$ cm **4 cm, 8 cm**
15. $C = 51$ in. **8 in., 16 in.**

3 APPLY

ASSIGNMENT GUIDE

Basic Course

Day 1: EP p. 811 Exs. 5-8; pp. 531-533 Exs. 7-12, 17-19, 27, 35-40

Day 2: pp. 531-533 Exs. 13-16, 20-25, 28-30, 41-44

Average Course

Day 1: pp. 531-533 Exs. 10-12, 17-19, 26, 27, 34-40

Day 2: pp. 531-533 Exs. 13-16, 20-25, 28-32, 41-45

Advanced Course

Day 1: pp. 531-533 Exs. 10-12, 19-22, 26, 37-41

Day 2: pp. 531-533 Exs. 13-16, 23-25, 28-34*, 43-45

Block

pp. 531-533 Exs. 10-32, 34-45

Extra Practice

- Student Edition, p. 812
- Chapter 10 Resource Book, pp. 33-35
- Test and Practice Generator

Transparency

Even-numbered answers are available on transparencies.

Homework Check

When you review students' homework for this lesson, go over the following exercises to check understanding of key concepts.

Basic: 7, 13, 17, 23, 30
Average: 10, 14, 17, 25, 30
Advanced: 12, 15, 19, 28, 30

ALGEBRAIC REASONING

Some students may be uncomfortable expressing answers in terms of π in Exercise 26. Usually, these students have trouble recognizing π as a number; they see π as a variable. Stress to students that π represents a number just like 8, 4.7, and $\frac{3}{4}$ do. Also, make sure students read the Reading Algebra note to the left of Exercise 26.

30.

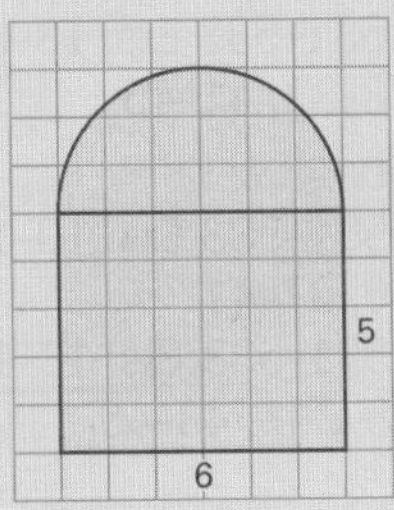

16. Error Analysis Describe and correct the error in finding the approximate area of a circle with a diameter of 20 feet. ***Sample answer:*** **The diameter was used instead of the radius. If the diameter is 20 feet, then the radius is 10 feet, so** $A = \pi r^2 \approx 3.14(10)^2 = 314$ **square feet.**

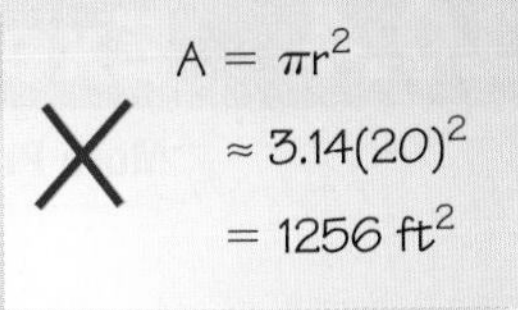

Find the area of the circle. Use 3.14 or $\frac{22}{7}$ for π. Round to the nearest whole number.

17. 8 in. **201 in.^{2}**

18. 14 ft **154 ft^2**

19. 28 cm **2464 cm^2**

20. 46 mm **1661 mm^2**

21. 33 m **855 m^2**

22. 52 yd **8491 yd^2**

For a circle with the given area *A*, find the radius and diameter of the circle. Round to the nearest whole number.

23. $A = 254 \text{ m}^2$ **9 m, 18 m**
24. $A = 615 \text{ cm}^2$ **14 cm, 28 cm**
25. $A = 1109 \text{ in.}^2$ **19 in., 38 in.**

Reading *Algebra*

In parts (a) and (b) of Exercise 26, expressing an answer in terms of π means *not* substituting an approximation for π. For instance, a circle with a radius of 2 units has an area of 4π square units when the area is expressed in terms of π.

26. Extended Problem Solving A signal from a walkie-talkie can be received up to 1 mile away. A signal from a CB radio can be received up to 5 miles away.

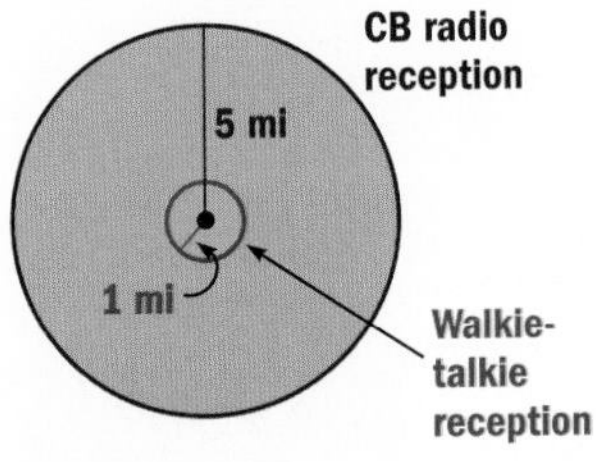

a. Calculate Over how great an area can a walkie-talkie transmit a signal? Express your answer in terms of π. **π mi^2**

b. Calculate Over how great an area can a CB radio transmit a signal? Express your answer in terms of π. **25π mi^2**

c. Compare Write a ratio to compare the area of CB radio reception to the area of walkie-talkie reception. $\frac{25}{1}$

27. Round Barn The Ryan barn in Annawan Township, Illinois, is a round barn built in 1910. The floor has a diameter of 85 feet. What is the area of the floor to the nearest square foot? **5672 ft^2**

28. Pantheon The circular floor in the Pantheon in Rome has an area of about 1473 square meters. What is the diameter of the floor to the nearest tenth of a meter? **43.3 m**

B 29. Centrifuge Training Astronauts train for space flight in a centrifuge, which consists of a rotating arm with a cab at the outer end of the arm. The arm, which has a length of 58 feet, is revolved about the center of the centrifuge. An astronaut sits in the cab, which is then rotated 50 times per minute. To the nearest hundred feet, how far does the astronaut travel in one minute? **18,200 ft**

30. Draw a rectangle that is 6 units by 5 units on graph paper. Use a compass to draw a half circle with a radius of 3 units on a longer side of the rectangle. Find the area of the figure to the nearest whole number. **See margin for art; 44 square units.**

31. **Predict** You double the radius of a circle. Predict what will happen to the circle's circumference and what will happen to its area. Test your prediction for a few circles. Use a different radius for each circle. Then predict how doubling a circle's diameter will affect its circumference and area. Test your prediction for a few circles with different diameters.

C 32. In the diagram, the diameter of the large circle is 18 meters. All four small circles are the same size. Find the area of one small circle and the area of the large circle in terms of π. Then find the ratio of the area of a small circle to the area of the large circle. **20.25π square meters, 81π square meters; $\frac{1}{4}$**

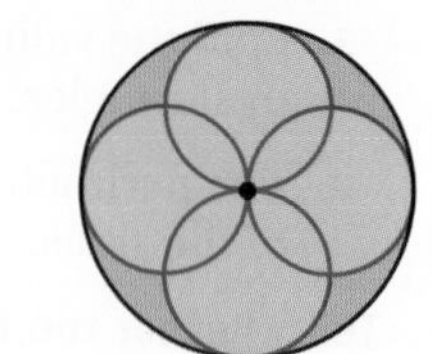

33. **Challenge** An air traffic control radar screen is a circle with a diameter of 24 inches.

a. What is the area of the screen to the nearest square inch? **452 in.^{2}**

b. The radar screen is set to have a scale of 6 inches : 25 nautical miles. To the nearest square nautical mile, what is the area of the circular region covered by the radar? **7850 square nautical miles**

34. *Writing* A half circle is drawn on each side of a right triangle as shown. What is the relationship among the areas of the 3 half circles? Explain your reasoning. **See margin.**

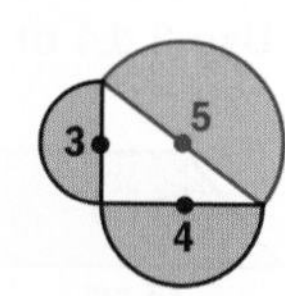

Mixed Review

Evaluate the expression. *(Lesson 1.3)*

35. $64 \div 16 + 6 \div 2$ **7**

36. $3 \cdot 14 + 8$ **50**

37. $7 \cdot 5 + 3 \cdot 9 \cdot 5$ **170**

Find the slope of the line through the given points. *(Lesson 8.4)*

38. (6, 1), (3, 4) **−1**

39. (−5, −3), (−5, 6) **undefined**

40. (3, −6), (−1, −6) **0**

Find the area of the parallelogram or trapezoid. *(Lesson 10.3)*

41. **35 cm^2**

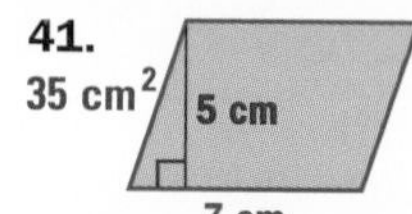

42. **30 m^2**

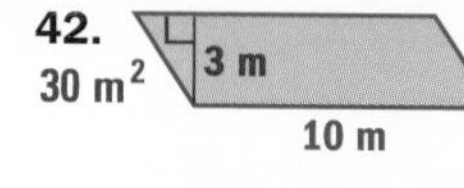

43. **37.5 in.^{2}**

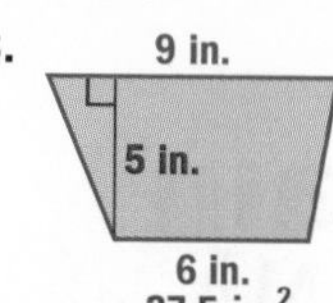

Standardized Test Practice

44. **Multiple Choice** The diameter of a circle is 22 meters. What is the approximate area? **C**

A. 35 m^2 B. 69 m^2 C. 380 m^2 D. 1520 m^2

45. **Short Response** The base of the sundial shown is a square with a circle inside it. To the nearest square inch, what is the area of the part of the base that is *not* within the circle? Explain your answer.

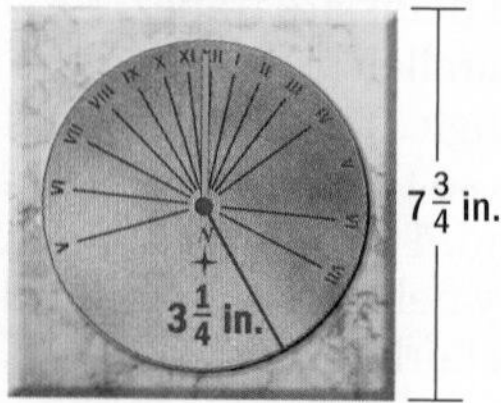

31. Doubling the radius will double the circumference and quadruple the area. *Sample answer:* For example, if the radius is 7, then the circumference is about 44 units and the area is about 154 square units. If the radius is 14, the circumference is about 88 units and the area is about 616 square units. Doubling the diameter will also double the circumference and quadruple the area. For example, if the diameter is 2, then the circumference is about 6.28 units and the area is about 3.14 square units. If the diameter is 4, the circumference is about 12.56 units and the area is about 12.56 square units.

34. The sum of the areas of the half circles on the legs equals the area of the half circle on the hypotenuse. *Sample answer:* The radii of the half circles are 1.5, 2, and 2.5. Their areas are $0.5\pi(1.5)^2 = 1.125\pi$, $0.5\pi(2)^2 = 2\pi$, and $0.5\pi(2.5)^2 = 3.125\pi$, respectively, and $1.125\pi + 2\pi = 3.125\pi$.

45. 27 in^2. *Sample answer:* The area of the base is $7.75^2 = 60.0625$ square inches. The area of the circle is $\pi(3.25^2) \approx 33.17$ square inches. The area of the base outside the circle is the difference in these two areas: $60.0625 - 33.17 \approx 27$ square inches.

4 ASSESS

Assessment Resources

For more assessment resources, see:

- Assessment Book
- Test and Practice Generator

Mini-Quiz

A circle has a radius of 16 inches. Use 3.14 for π.

1. Find the circumference. Round to the nearest inch. **100 in.**
2. Find the area. Round to the nearest square inch. **804 in.^{2}**
3. Find the radius and diameter of a circle whose area is 1662 square feet. Round to the nearest foot. **23 ft, 46 ft**
4. **Challenge** The rim of Meteor Crater in Arizona is a circle with a diameter of about 1.2 kilometers. A map of the state has a scale of 10 cm : 1 km. What is the area of the crater represented on the map? **about 113 cm^2**

5 FOLLOW-UP

Diagnosis/Remediation

- Study Guide in Chapter 10 Resource Book, pp. 36-37
- Tutor Place, Geometry Cards 15, 16
- eTutorial Plus Online
- Extra Practice, p. 812
- Lesson Practice in Chapter 10 Resource Book, pp. 33-35

English Learner Support

- Spanish Study Guide
- Multi-Language Visual Glossary
- Chapter Audio Summaries CDs

Challenge

- Challenge Practice in Chapter 10 Resource Book, p. 38
- Teacher's Edition, p. 508F

Additional Resources

The following resources are available to help review the materials in Lessons 10.1–10.4.

Chapter 10 Resource Book

- Lesson Practice
- Study Guide

Assessment Book

- Chapter 10 Quiz 1

Technology

- Test and Practice Generator
- eTutorial CD-ROM

Internet

- Classzone
- eWorkbook Plus Online
- eTutorial Plus Online

English Learner Support

- Spanish Study Guide
- Multi-Language Visual Glossary
- Chapter Audio Summaries CDs

CHAPTER 10

Mid-Chapter Quiz

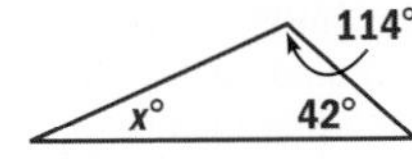

1. Find the value of x for the triangle shown. Then classify the triangle by its angles. **24; obtuse**

2. The perimeter of an equilateral triangle is 219 feet. Find the lengths of the sides. **73 ft**

Tell whether the figure is a polygon. If it is a polygon, classify it and tell whether it is *convex* or *concave*. If not, explain why.

3.  **yes; octagon, concave**

4. 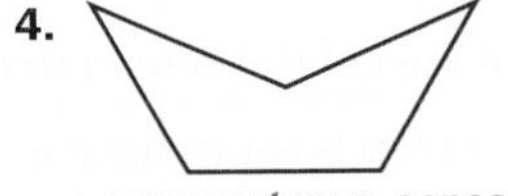 **yes; pentagon, concave**

5. **No; it has a curved side.**

Find the area of the parallelogram, trapezoid, or circle to the nearest square unit. Use 3.14 or $\frac{22}{7}$ for π.

6. 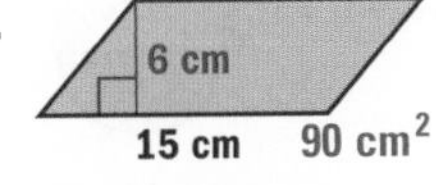

90 cm²

7. **875 in.²**
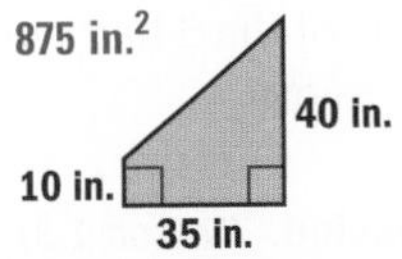

8. **122 ft²**
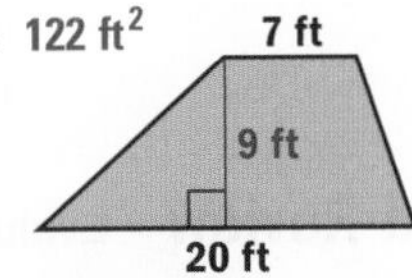

9. 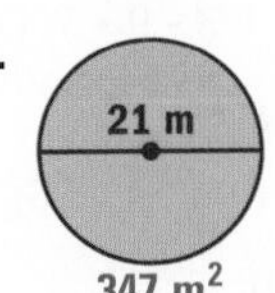

347 m²

10. 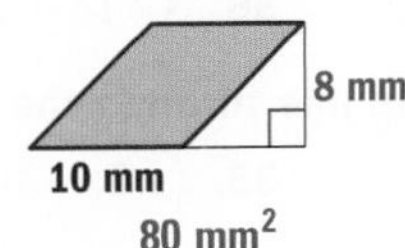

80 mm²

11. 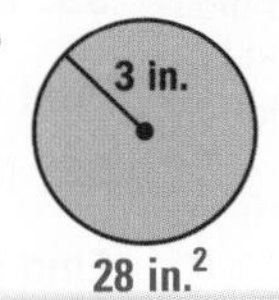

28 in.²

Three farmers inherit farmland that is divided into six fields. In the drawing, the green fields are trapezoids, the yellow fields are parallelograms, and the blue field is a rectangle. The farmers want to divide up the fields so that each farmer has the same area of land. They don't want to change the shape of any field. How can they distribute the fields fairly? **A and F, B and C, D and E**

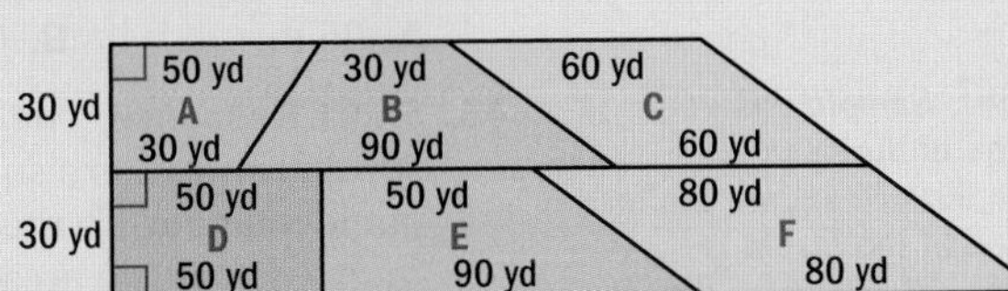

Student Reference

Solids

▶ **Review** this topic in preparation for solving problems that involve solids in Lessons 10.5–10.8.

Classifying Solids

A **solid** is a three-dimensional figure that encloses a part of space. The polygons that form the sides of a solid are called **faces**.

Four Types of Solids

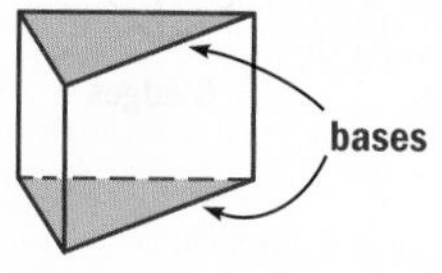 A **prism** is a solid formed by polygons. Prisms have two congruent bases that lie in parallel planes. The other faces are rectangles.	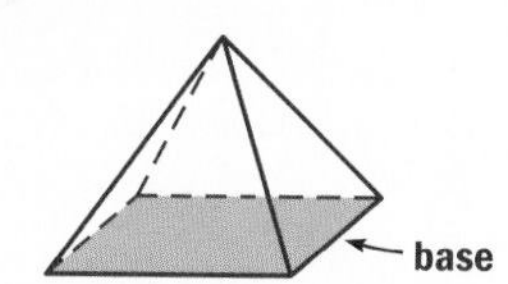 A **pyramid** is a solid formed by polygons. The base can be any polygon, and the other faces are triangles.
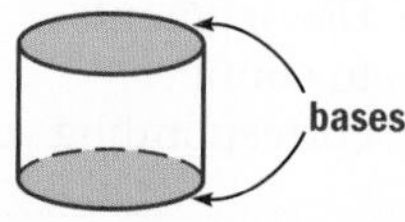 A **cylinder** is a solid with two congruent circular bases that lie in parallel planes.	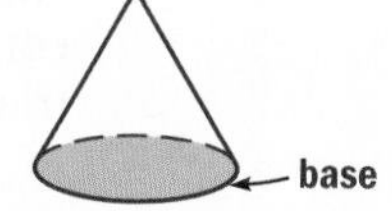 A **cone** is a solid with one circular base.

Example Classify the solid as a *prism, pyramid, cylinder,* or *cone*.

a. 

b. 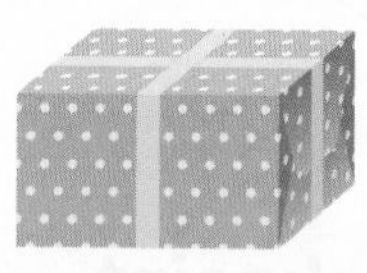

c. 

Solution

a. The soup can has two congruent circular bases. It is a cylinder.

b. All sides of the gift box are rectangles. Any two opposite sides can be considered bases. The gift box is a rectangular prism.

c. The ice cream novelty has one circular base. It is a cone.

Continued

NCTM CURRICULUM STANDARDS

Standard 3: Analyze properties of 3-D shapes

Standard 10: Create representations to communicate mathematical ideas

1 PLAN

Skill Check

State the number of sides in the given polygon.

1. triangle 3
2. square 4
3. rectangle 4
4. pentagon 5

LESSON OBJECTIVE

Prepare for solving problems that involve solids.

2 TEACH

COMMON ERROR

Some students may need help differentiating between a triangular prism and a square pyramid, as well as some of the other solids. If possible, bring solids to class for students to examine to help them understand the difference.

Extra Examples

Example 1 Classify the solid as a *prism*, *pyramid*, *cylinder*, or *cone*.

a. 

cylinder

b. 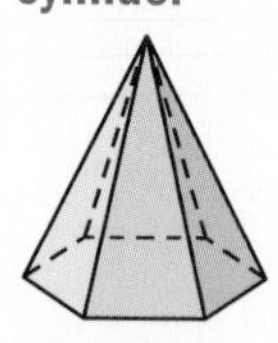

pyramid

Extra Examples

Example 2 Count the number of faces, edges, and vertices in a square pyramid. **5 faces, 8 edges, 5 vertices**

Example 3 Sketch a rectangular pyramid.

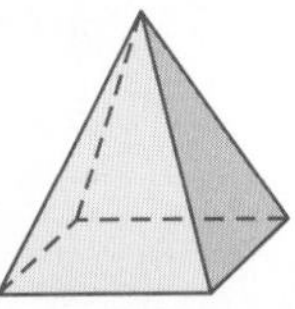

3 APPLY

TRANSPARENCY

Even-numbered answers are available on transparencies.

TEACHING TIP

In Exercises 1–3, stress that the faces, edges, and vertices are only counted if the solid is a prism or pyramid.

4–6. Samples answers are given.

4.

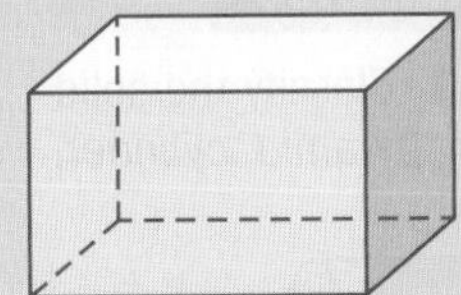

5.

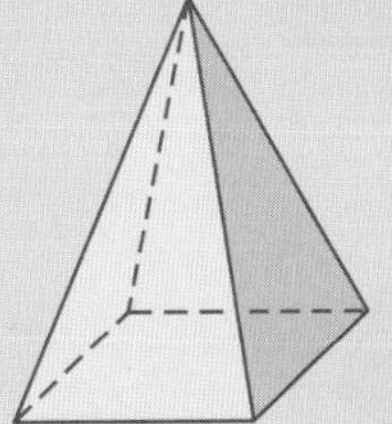

6.

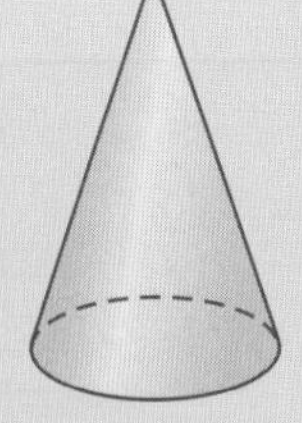

Counting Faces, Edges, and Vertices

The faces of a prism or a pyramid meet in segments called **edges**. Edges meet at points called **vertices**. (The singular form of *vertices* is *vertex*.)

Example **Count the number of faces, edges, and vertices in a triangular pyramid.**

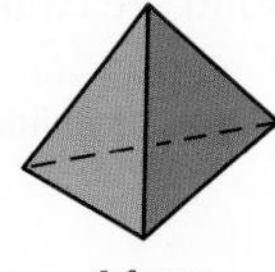

4 faces

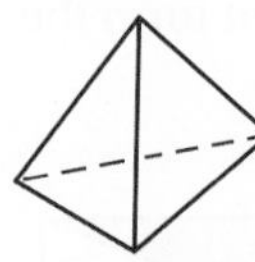

6 edges

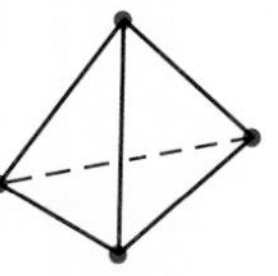

4 vertices

Sketching a Solid

You can sketch a solid so that it appears to be three-dimensional.

Example **Sketch a triangular prism.**

1) Sketch two congruent triangles.

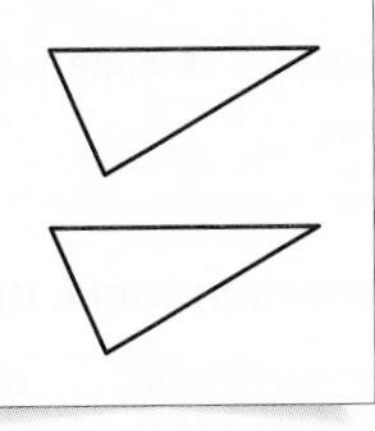

2) Use segments to connect corresponding vertices.

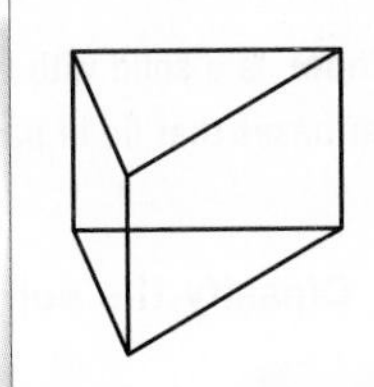

3) Make any "hidden" lines dashed.

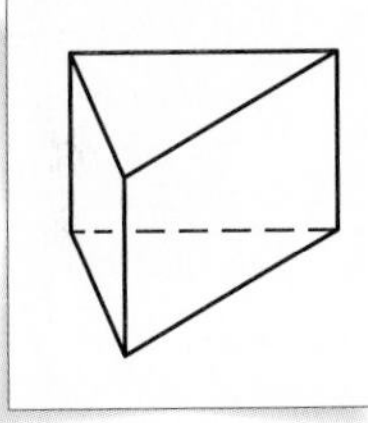

Checkpoint

▶ **Test** your knowledge of solids by solving these problems.

2. pyramid; 6 faces, 10 edges, 6 vertices

Classify each solid as a *prism, pyramid, cylinder,* or *cone*. If the solid is a prism or a pyramid, count the number of faces, edges, and vertices.

1.

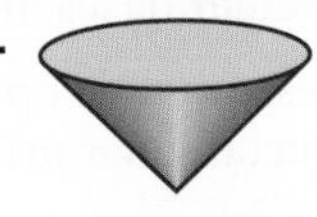

cone

2.

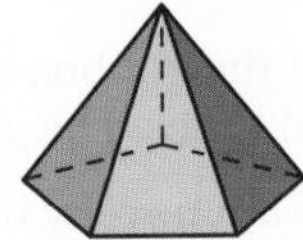

3.

cylinder

Sketch the solid. **4–6. See margin.**

4. Rectangular prism **5.** Square pyramid **6.** Cone

Concept *Activity*

10.5 Nets and Surface Area

Goal
Use the net of a rectangular prism to find the prism's surface area.

Materials
- cereal box
- ruler
- scissors

The *surface area* of a solid is the sum of the areas of all of its surfaces.

Investigate

Find the surface area of a cereal box. **Steps 1–2. Answers will vary.**

1 Cut along the edges of the box until you can flatten it as shown below. The resulting shape is called a *net*. Measure the length of each edge of the net using a ruler.

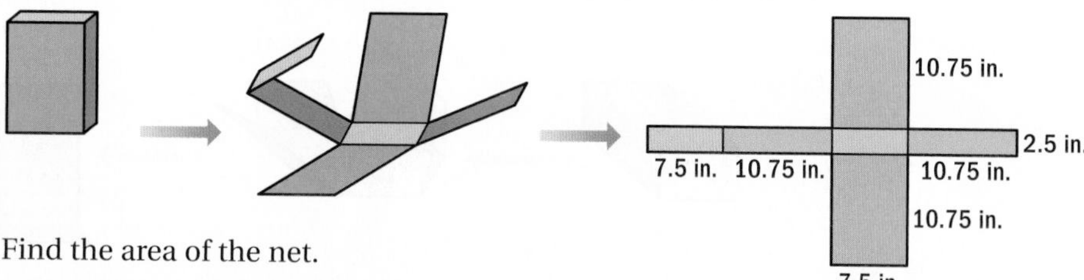

2 Find the area of the net.

First find the area of each face.

Area of front or back: $(7.5)(10.75) = 80.625 \text{ in.}^2$
Area of top or bottom: $(7.5)(2.5) = 18.75 \text{ in.}^2$
Area of each side: $(2.5)(10.75) = 26.875 \text{ in.}^2$

Then find the sum of the areas of the faces.

$$80.625 + 80.625 + 18.75 + 18.75 + 26.875 + 26.875 = 252.5 \text{ in.}^2$$

The surface area of the cereal box shown is 252.5 square inches.

Draw Conclusions **1–2. See margin.**

1. **Critical Thinking** How can you find the surface area of a box without making a net? Explain.
2. ***Writing*** Describe the net of the cylindrical oatmeal container shown. Make a sketch of the net. Find the surface area of the container and explain your reasoning.

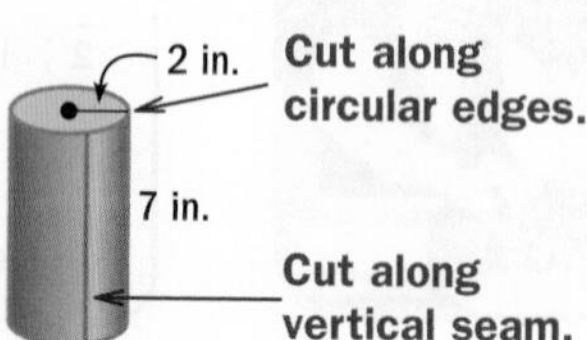

NCTM CURRICULUM STANDARDS
Standard 4: Understand measurable attributes of objects
Standard 10: Create representations to communicate mathematical ideas

1 PLAN

Investigate the Concept

- Students use the net of a rectangular prism to find the prism's surface area.
- This activity leads into finding the surface areas of prisms, cylinders, cones, and pyramids.

Materials

Each student will need a cereal box, a ruler, and scissors. See also the Activity Support Master in the *Chapter 10 Resource Book*.

Recommended Time

Work activity: 10 min
Discuss results: 5 min

Grouping

Students should work individually.

2 TEACH

Alternative Strategy

Perform the activity for the class using a cereal box covered in white paper. Label each face of the box and discuss which faces have the same dimensions. On the board, record the dimensions of each face, noting which faces are congruent.

3 CLOSE

Key Discovery

The surface area of a solid is the sum of the areas of all its surfaces.

Assessment

1. Can more than one net be drawn for a given solid? If so, are the areas different? **yes; no**

1–2. See Additional Answers beginning on page AA1.

1 PLAN

Skill Check

Find the area of a rectangle having the given length and width.

1. length: 4 inches, width: 7 inches **28 in.^{2}**
2. length: 12 inches, width: 20 inches **240 in.^{2}**
3. length: 30 inches, width: 40 inches **1200 in.^{2}**
4. length: 2.5 inches, width: 5.5 inches **13.75 in.^{2}**

LESSON OBJECTIVE

Find the surface areas of prisms and cylinders.

PACING

Suggested Number of Days
Basic Course: 1 day
Average Course: 1 day
Advanced Course: 1 day
Block: 0.5 block with 10.6

TEACHING RESOURCES

For a complete list of Teaching Resources, see page 508B.

TRANSPARENCY

Warm-Up Exercises for this lesson are available on a transparency.

2 TEACH

MOTIVATING THE LESSON

Bring a clean pizza box or a similar box to class for students to open, fold flat, and examine as you discuss nets and surface area.

LESSON 10.5

Surface Areas of Prisms *and* Cylinders

Vocabulary
surface area, p. 538
net, p. 538
lateral face of a prism, p. 539
lateral area of a prism, p. 539
lateral surface of a cylinder, p. 540
lateral area of a cylinder, p. 540

BEFORE	Now	WHY?
You found the areas of triangles and rectangles.	You'll find the surface areas of prisms and cylinders.	So you can find the area you need to paint, as in Ex. 14.

Pizza Box The **surface area** of a solid is the sum of the areas of its faces. The pizza box shown has the shape of a rectangular prism. What is its surface area?

In Example 1, a *net* is used to find the surface area of the pizza box. A **net** is a two-dimensional representation of a solid. The surface area of a solid is equal to the area of its net.

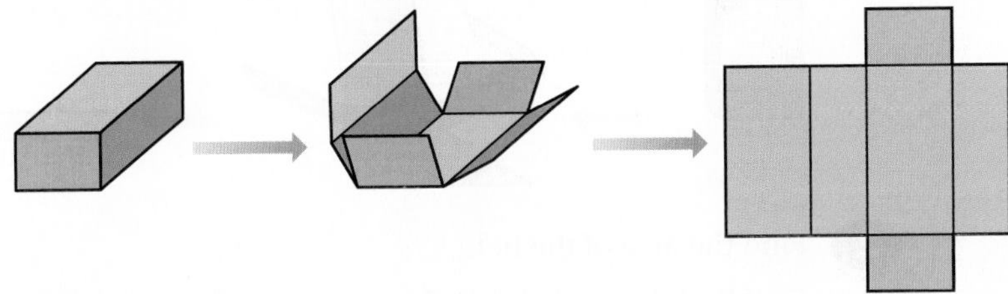

Example 1 Using a Net to Find Surface Area

The net at the right represents the pizza box shown above. (Any flaps or foldovers to hold the box together have been ignored.) Use the net to find the surface area of the pizza box.

16 in.
2 in.
16 in.

Solution

1. Find the area of each face.

Area of top or bottom: $16 \cdot 16 = 256$ in.^{2}

Area of each side: $16 \cdot 2 = 32$ in.^{2}

2. Find the sum of the areas of the faces.

$256 + 256 + 32 + 32 + 32 + 32 = 640$ in.^{2}

Answer The surface area of the pizza box is 640 square inches.

NCTM CURRICULUM STANDARDS
Standard 3: Analyze properties of 3-D shapes
Standard 4: Apply proper formulas to find measures
Standard 6: Solve problems in math and other contexts

Study *Strategy*

In this book, every prism is a *right prism*, which means that the edges connecting the bases are perpendicular to the bases.

Surface Areas of Prisms The **lateral faces** of a prism are the faces that are not bases. The **lateral area** of a prism is the sum of the areas of the lateral faces. The surface area of a prism is the sum of the areas of the bases and the lateral area. In the diagram, P is the base perimeter.

Surface area	=	**2 • Base area**	+	**Lateral area**
	=	$2B$	+	Ph

Study *Strategy*

The formula given in the notebook applies to any prism. When finding the surface area of a rectangular prism, you can substitute lw for B and $2l + 2w$ for P. So, the formula becomes $S = 2lw + (2l + 2w)h$.

Surface Area of a Prism

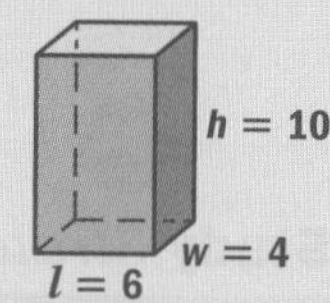

Words The surface area S of a prism is the sum of twice the base area B and the product of the base perimeter P and the height h.

Algebra $S = 2B + Ph$

Numbers $S = 2(6 \cdot 4) + [2(6) + 2(4)]10 = 248$ square units

Example 2 *Using a Formula to Find Surface Area*

Find the surface area of the prism.

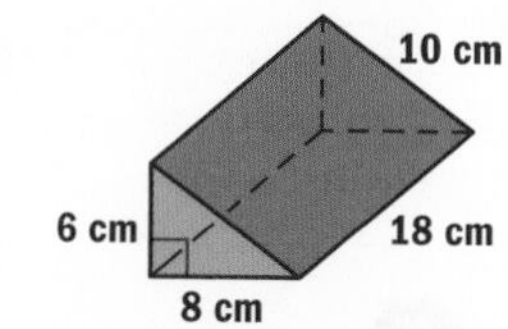

The bases of the prism are right triangles.

$S = 2B + Ph$ **Write formula for surface area.**

$= 2\left(\frac{1}{2} \cdot 6 \cdot 8\right) + (6 + 8 + 10)(18)$ **Substitute.**

$= 480$ **Simplify.**

Answer The surface area of the prism is 480 square centimeters.

Checkpoint

Find the surface area of the prism.

1.

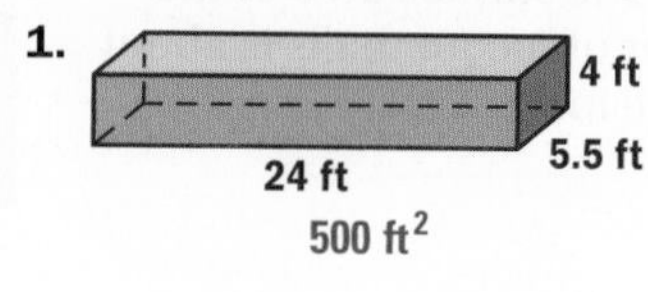

500 ft^2

2.

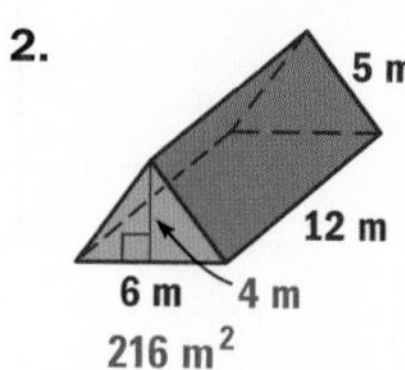

216 m^2

TIPS *for* NEW TEACHERS

Stress the similarities between the formulas for the surface area of a prism and the surface area of a cylinder. See Tips for New Teachers in the *Chapter 10 Resource Book*.

Extra Examples

Example 1 Use the net to find the surface area of the prism.

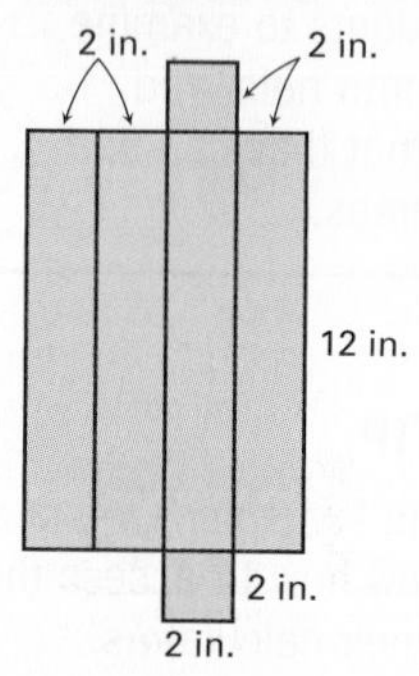

104 in.^{2}

Example 2 Find the surface area of the prism. **202 cm^2**

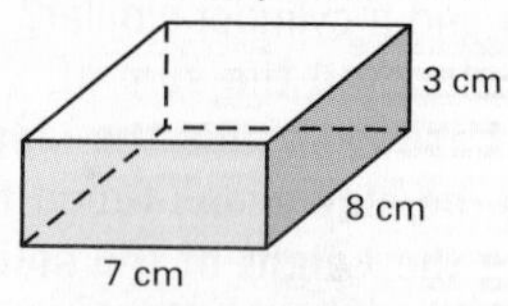

MULTIPLE REPRESENTATIONS

The surface area formulas for prisms and for cylinders are presented on this page and page 540 using words, algebra, and numbers. You can also demonstrate the formula using models on which you could write labels for the faces.

COMMON ERROR

Watch for students who include the area of only one base instead of two bases when they calculate surface areas of both prisms and cylinders.

Extra Examples

Example 3 Find the surface area of a fluorescent light tube that is 36 inches long and has a diameter of 1.5 inches. Round to the nearest square inch.
173 in.^{2}

Differentiating Instruction

Less Proficient Students Bring to class a variety of boxes and tubes for students to examine, write on, cut into nets, and measure so that they can find the surface areas.

Teaching Tip

While discussing Example 3, be sure all students know how to access the value of π on their calculators.

Concept Check

How are the surface area formulas for a prism and a cylinder similar? **Both formulas find the sum of twice the base area plus the side area, with the side areas found by multiplying the height of the solid by the distance around the base (the perimeter or circumference).**

Daily Puzzler

The perimeter of a square is p inches and the area of the square is q square inches. If $p = q$, what is the value of these variables?
$p = q = 16$

Study *Strategy*

In this book, all cylinders are *right cylinders*, which means that the segment connecting the centers of the bases is perpendicular to the bases.

Surface Areas of Cylinders The curved surface of a cylinder is called the **lateral surface**. The **lateral area** of a cylinder is the area of the lateral suface. The surface area of a cylinder is the sum of the areas of the bases and the product of the base circumference and the height. In the diagram below, C represents the base circumference.

Surface area	=	2 • Base area	+	Lateral area
	=	$2B$	+	Ch

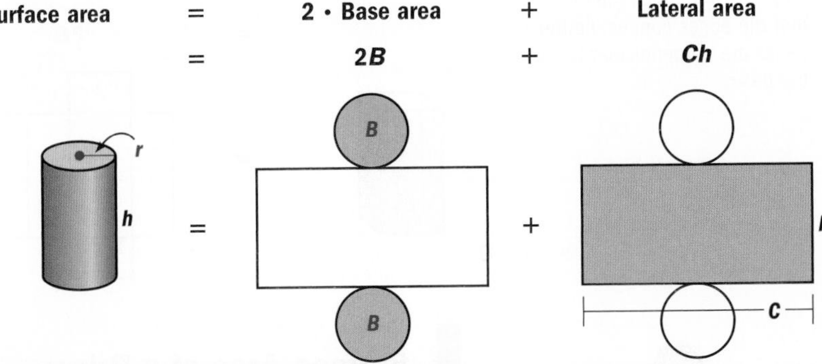

Study *Strategy*

The formula for the surface area of a cylinder is obtained by substituting πr^2 for B and $2\pi r$ for C. So, the formula $S = 2B + Ch$ becomes $S = 2\pi r^2 + 2\pi rh$.

Surface Area of a Cylinder

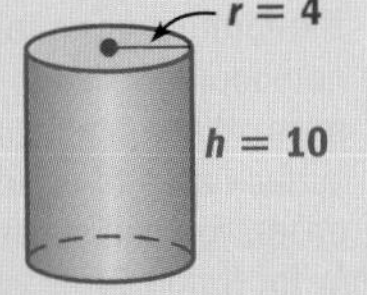

Words The surface area S of a cylinder is the sum of twice the base area B and the product of the base circumference C and the height h.

Algebra $S = 2B + Ch = 2\pi r^2 + 2\pi rh$

Numbers $S = 2\pi(4)^2 + 2\pi(4)(10) \approx 352$ square units

Tech *Help*

Although you used 3.14 as an approximation for π previously, you can obtain a more accurate approximation by using the π key on a calculator.

Example 3 *Using a Formula to Find Surface Area*

Racquetball Find the surface area of the container of racquetballs. Round to the nearest square inch.

Solution

The radius is one half of the diameter, so $r = 1.25$ inches.

$S = 2\pi \mathbf{r}^2 + 2\pi \mathbf{r}\mathbf{h}$	**Write formula for surface area of a cylinder.**
$= 2\pi(\mathbf{1.25})^2 + 2\pi(\mathbf{1.25})(\mathbf{5})$	**Substitute.**
$= 15.625\pi$	**Simplify.**
≈ 49.1	**Evaluate. Use a calculator.**

Answer The surface area of the container of racquetballs is about 49 square inches.

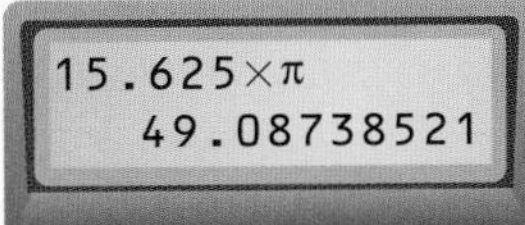

10.5 Exercises

More Practice, p. 812

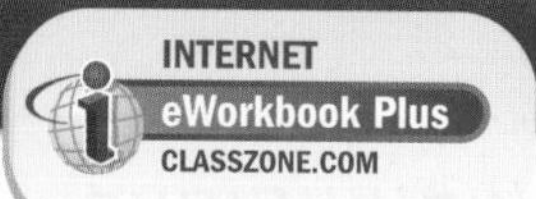

Guided Practice

Vocabulary Check

1. What formula would you use to find the surface area of a triangular prism? $S = 2B + Ph$

2. How do you find the area of the bases of a cylinder? How do you find the lateral area of a cylinder? See margin.

Skill Check

Draw a net for the solid. Then find the surface area. 3–4. See margin for art.

3.

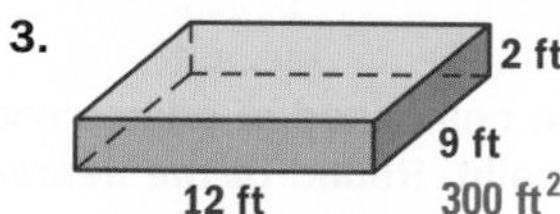

4.

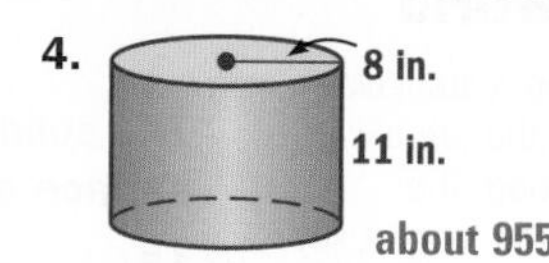

5. Error Analysis Describe and correct the error in finding the surface area of the prism.

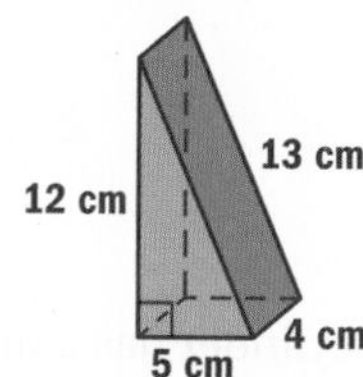

$S = 2B + Ph$
$= 2(5 \cdot 4) + (5 + 12 + 13)(4)$
$= 160$ square centimeters

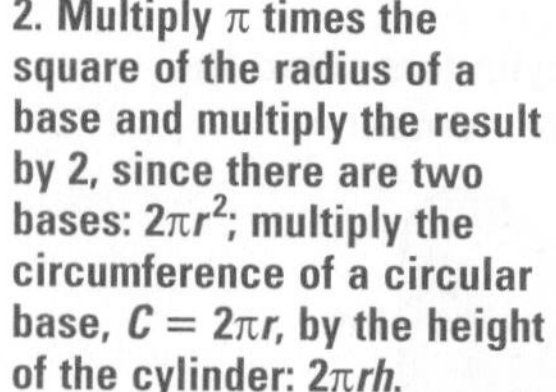

2. Multiply π times the square of the radius of a base and multiply the result by 2, since there are two bases: $2\pi r^2$; multiply the circumference of a circular base, $C = 2\pi r$, by the height of the cylinder: $2\pi rh$.

5. *Sample answer:* In this case, the base is not the surface on which the prism is resting, but a triangle with sides 5, 12, and 13: $S = 2B + Ph = 2(0.5 \cdot 5 \cdot 12) + (5 + 12 + 13)(4) = 180$ square centimeters.

Practice and Problem Solving

Homework *Help*

Example	Exercises
1	6-9, 14
2	6-9, 14
3	10-12, 13

Online Resources
CLASSZONE.COM
- More Examples
- eTutorial Plus

Draw a net for the solid. Then find the surface area. Round to the nearest whole number. 6–11. See margin for art.

A **6.** **7.** **8.** **9.** **10.** **11.**

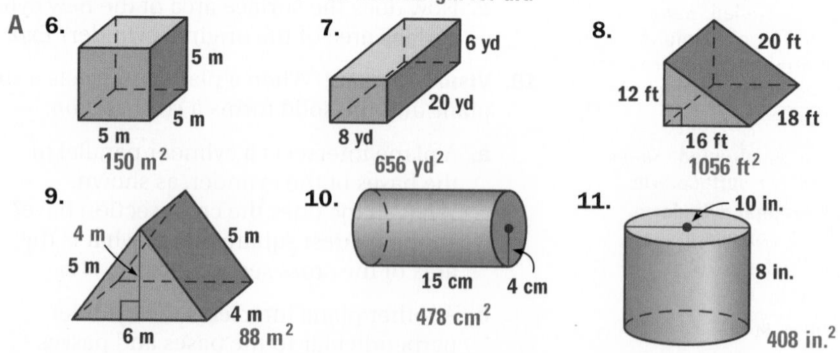

12. Cans A can of vegetables is in the shape of a cylinder. The diameter of the can is 7 centimeters, and the height is 11 centimeters. Find the surface area of the can. Round to the nearest square centimeter. 319 cm²

3 APPLY

ASSIGNMENT GUIDE

Basic Course
Day 1: pp. 541-543 Exs. 6-16, 20, 23-31

Average Course
Day 1: pp. 541-543 Exs. 8-21, 23-31

Advanced Course
Day 1: pp. 541-543 Exs. 9-24*, 28-31

Block
pp. 541-543 Exs. 9-21, 23-31 (with 10.6)

Extra Practice

- Student Edition, p. 812
- Chapter 10 Resource Book, pp. 41-43
- Test and Practice Generator

Transparency

Even-numbered answers are available on transparencies.

Homework Check

When you review students' homework for this lesson, go over the following exercises to check understanding of key concepts.
Basic: 6, 8, 10, 12, 14
Average: 8, 10, 11, 12, 14
Advanced: 9, 10, 12, 13, 14

3. ***Sample:***

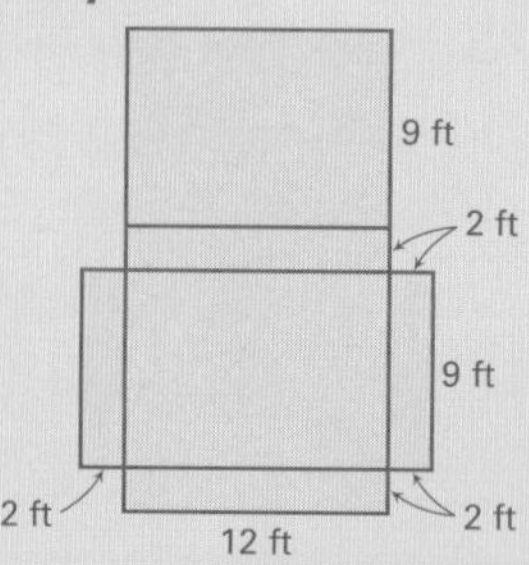

4, 6-11. See Additional Answers beginning on page AA1.

22.

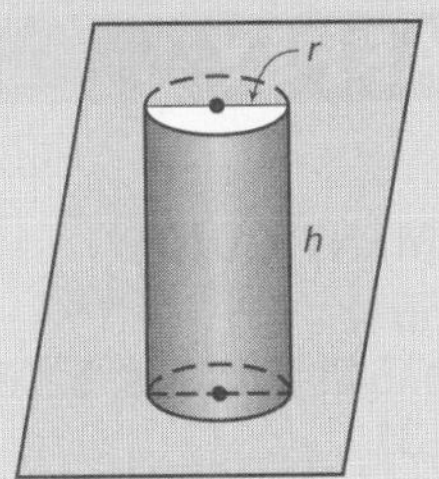

In the **Real World**

Marimbas The rectangular keys of a marimba are always made of rosewood. The dimensions of the longest key are $20\frac{1}{4}$ in. by $3\frac{1}{4}$ in. The dimensions of the shortest key are $7\frac{5}{8}$ in. by $1\frac{5}{8}$ in. What is the ratio of the area of the longest key to the area of the shortest key?

$\frac{324}{61}$, or about 5.3 : 1

13. Marimba Pipes Find the lateral area of the marimba pipe. Round to the nearest square inch. **126 in.^{2}**

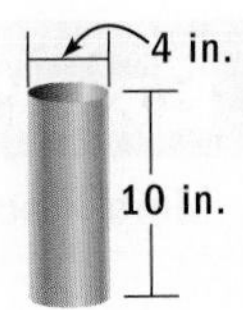

14. Painting You are going to paint the platforms shown below for your school's theater production. All sides of each platform must be painted yellow. What total area must the paint cover? **136 ft^2**

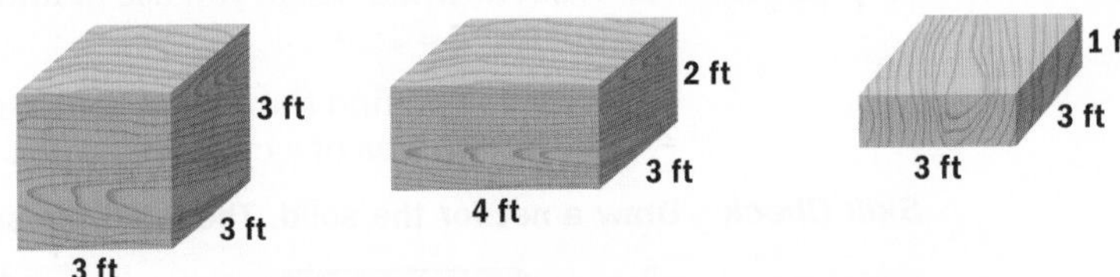

The solids shown are composed of prisms and half cylinders. Find the surface area of the solid. Round to the nearest whole number.

B **15.** **384 ft^2**

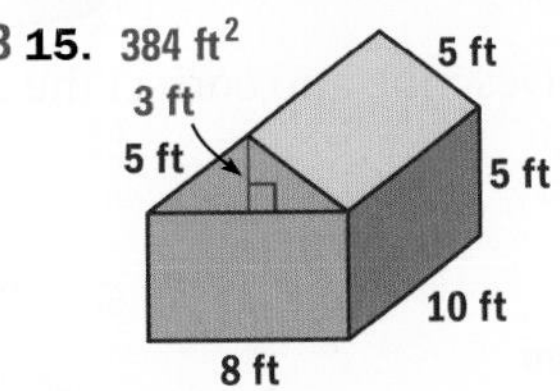

16. **715 m^2**

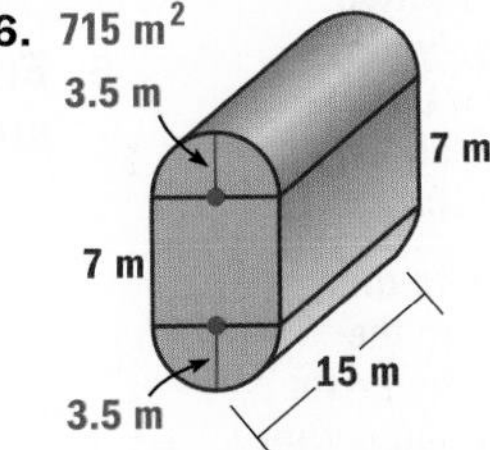

17. Critical Thinking A cylinder has a radius of r inches and a height of h inches. Suppose the radius and height of the cylinder are both doubled.

a. How does the area of the base of the new cylinder compare with the area of the base of the original cylinder? Explain.

b. How does the circumference of the new cylinder compare with the circumference of the original cylinder? Explain.

c. How does the surface area of the new cylinder compare with the surface area of the original cylinder? Explain.

17a. It is quadrupled. *Sample answer:* The area of a base of the original cylinder is πr^2, and of the new cylinder is $\pi(2r)^2 = 4\pi r^2$.

17b. It is doubled. *Sample answer:* The circumference of the original cylinder is $2\pi r$, and of the new cylinder is $2\pi(2r) = 4\pi r$.

17c. It is quadrupled. *Sample answer:* The surface area of the original cylinder is $2\pi r^2 + 2\pi rh$, and of the new cylinder is $2(4\pi r^2) + (4\pi r)(2h) = 4(2\pi r^2) + 4(2\pi rh) = 4(2\pi r^2 + 2\pi rh)$.

18. Visual Thinking When a plane intersects a solid, the intersection of the plane and the solid forms a *cross section.*

a. A plane intersects a cylinder parallel to the bases of the cylinder, as shown. What shape does the cross section have? To the nearest square meter, what is the area of the cross section? **circle; 13 m^2**

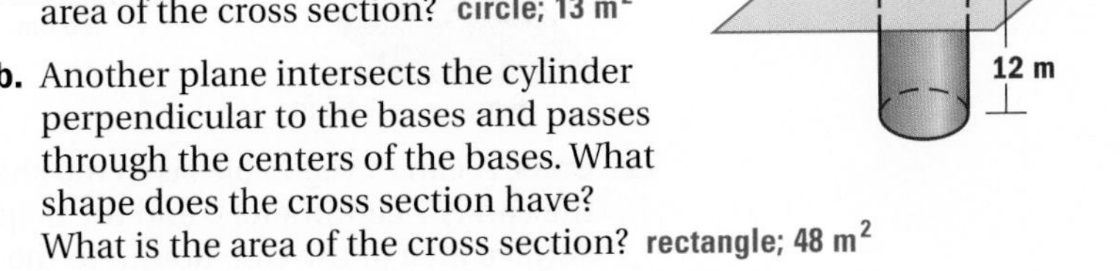

b. Another plane intersects the cylinder perpendicular to the bases and passes through the centers of the bases. What shape does the cross section have? What is the area of the cross section? **rectangle; 48 m^2**

Snowboarder on a mailbox slider

19. **Mailbox Sliders** Some snowboarding parks have a feature shaped like an elongated mailbox and called a mailbox slider. Snowboarders use their boards to jump onto the mailbox slider and slide along its top surface. A mailbox slider is composed of a half cylinder and a rectangular prism. Find the surface area of the mailbox slider shown. Round your answer to the nearest square inch. **6760 in.^{2}**

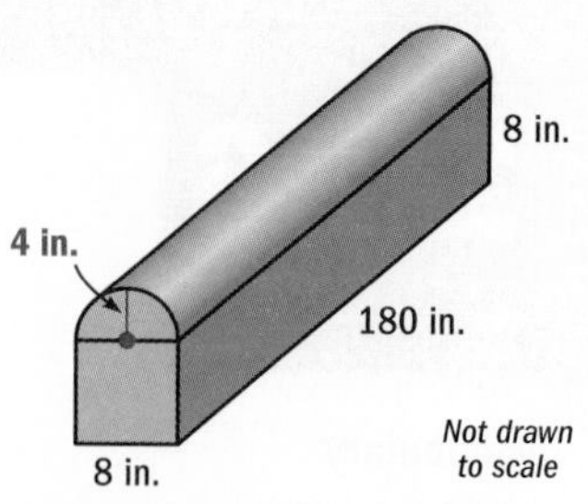

20. **Measurement** Find an object that is shaped like a cylinder. Measure its radius and height, then find its surface area. Describe the procedure you used. **Answers will vary.**

21. The diameter of a base of a cylinder is twice the height of the cylinder.
    a. Write a formula in terms of h for the surface area of the cylinder. **$S = 4\pi h^2$**
    b. The surface area of the cylinder is 64π square units. Find the radius and height of the cylinder. **4 units; 4 units**

C 22. **Challenge** Draw a cylinder and label the radius r and the height h. Assume a plane slices the cylinder in half by passing through the center of each base. Write a formula for the surface area of a half cylinder, including the region where the plane intersects the cylinder. **See margin for art; $S = \pi r^2 + \pi rh + 2rh$.**

Mixed Review

23. The perimeter of a triangle is 37 feet. The length of the first side is 4 more than the length of the second side. The length of the third side is equal to the length of the second side. Find the length of each side. Then classify the triangle by its side lengths. *(Lesson 10.1)* **15 ft, 11 ft, 11 ft; isosceles**

Find the area of the parallelogram or trapezoid. *(Lesson 10.3)*

24. 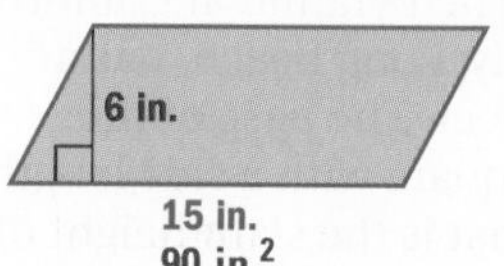

90 in.^{2}

25. 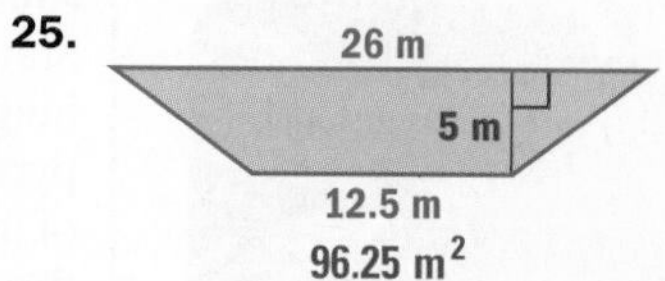

96.25 m^2

Find the circumference of the circle given the diameter d or the radius r. Use 3.14 or $\frac{22}{7}$ for π. Round to the nearest whole number. *(Lesson 10.4)*

26. $d = 30$ m **94 m**
27. $d = 84$ in. **264 in.**
28. $r = 78$ ft **490 ft**
29. $r = 102$ cm **641 cm**

Standardized Test Practice

30. **Multiple Choice** What is the approximate surface area of the cylinder shown? **D**

(2 yd, 4.4 yd)

A. 35 yd^2 B. 57 yd^2
C. 68 yd^2 D. 80 yd^2

31. **Short Response** The length of a base of a rectangular prism is twice the width of the base. The height of the prism is 3 times the width of a base. The surface area is 792 square centimeters. What are the dimensions of the prism? **width = 6 cm, length = 12 cm, height = 18 cm**

4 ASSESS

Assessment Resources

For more assessment resources, see:
- Assessment Book
- Test and Practice Generator

Mini-Quiz

Find the surface area of the solid. Round to the nearest whole number.

1. a rectangular prism with a height of 16 inches and a base of length 3 inches and width 4 inches **248 in.^{2}**
2. a cylinder with radius 2 meters and height 14 meters **201 m^2**
3. Find the lateral area of a pipe with diameter 6 feet and length 60 feet. Round to the nearest square foot. **1131 ft^2**
4. **Challenge** You have a cylindrical rod that has a radius of 1 inch and is 12 inches long. If you cut the rod into three pieces of the same size, by how much would the total surface area increase? **about 12.6 in.^{2}**

5 FOLLOW-UP

Diagnosis/Remediation

- Study Guide in Chapter 10 Resource Book, pp. 44–45
- Tutor Place, Geometry Card 21
- eTutorial Plus Online
- Extra Practice, p. 812
- Lesson Practice in Chapter 10 Resource Book, pp. 41–43

English Learner Support

- Spanish Study Guide
- Multi-Language Visual Glossary
- Chapter Audio Summaries CDs

Challenge

- Challenge Practice in Chapter 10 Resource Book, p. 46
- Teacher's Edition, p. 508F

1 PLAN

Skill Check

Find the area of the circle whose radius is given. Round to the nearest square inch.

1. 4 inches — 50 in.^{2}
2. 10 inches — 314 in.^{2}
3. 15 inches — 707 in.^{2}
4. 20 inches — 1257 in.^{2}

LESSON OBJECTIVE

Find the surface areas of pyramids and cones.

PACING

Suggested Number of Days
Basic Course: 1 day
Average Course: 1 day
Advanced Course: 1 day
Block: 0.5 block with 10.5

TEACHING RESOURCES

For a complete list of Teaching Resources, see page 508B.

TRANSPARENCY

Warm-Up Exercises for this lesson are available on a transparency.

2 TEACH

MOTIVATING THE LESSON

Invite students to draw a variety of regular polygons on the board. Use the polygons to draw pyramids.

TIPS *for* NEW TEACHERS

You may need to review the Pythagorean theorem before presenting Example 1. See Tips for New Teachers in the *Chapter 10 Resource Book.*

LESSON 10.6 Surface Areas *of* Pyramids *and* Cones

Vocabulary

BEFORE	*Now*	WHY?
You found surface areas of prisms and cylinders.	You'll find the surface areas of pyramids and cones.	So you can find the surface area of an ant lion cone, as in Ex. 20.

Recall that the base of a pyramid is a polygon, and the lateral faces of the pyramid are triangles with a common vertex. The **height of a pyramid** is the perpendicular distance between the base and this common vertex.

In this lesson, all pyramids are *regular pyramids.* In a **regular pyramid**, the base is a regular polygon and all of the lateral faces of the pyramid are congruent isosceles triangles. The **slant height of a pyramid** is the height of any of these triangular lateral faces.

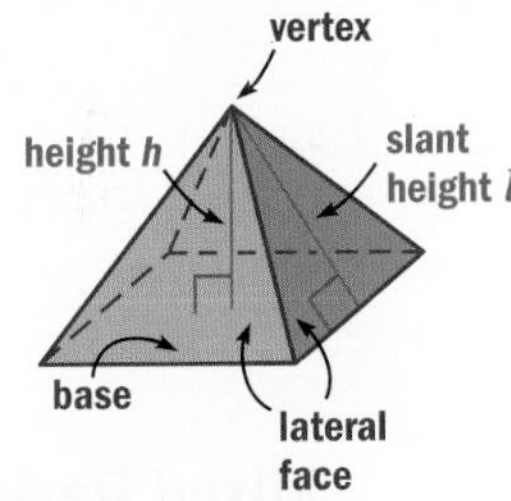

In this lesson, the variable h represents the height of the pyramid, and the variable l represents the slant height.

Example 1 Finding the Slant Height of a Pyramid

The Pyramid at California State University, Long Beach

Architecture The Pyramid at California State University, Long Beach, has a height of 192 feet. The base of the pyramid is a square with a side length of 345 feet. What is the slant height of the pyramid to the nearest foot?

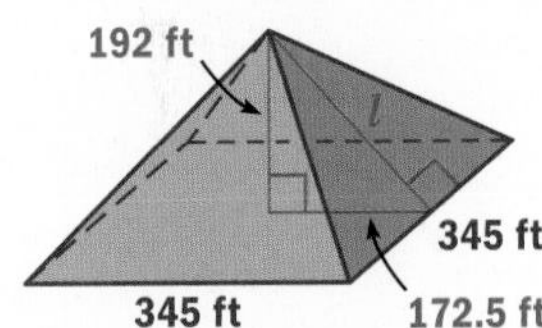

Solution

Notice that the slant height l of the pyramid is the hypotenuse of a right triangle. The length of one leg of this triangle is 192 feet. The length of the other leg is $\frac{345}{2} = 172.5$ feet. Use the Pythagorean theorem to find the slant height.

$192^2 + (172.5)^2 = l^2$ — **Pythagorean theorem**

$66{,}620.25 = l^2$ — **Simplify. Use a calculator.**

$\sqrt{66{,}620.25} = l$ — **Take positive square root of each side.**

$258.1 \approx l$ — **Approximate using a calculator.**

Answer The slant height of the Pyramid is about 258 feet.

NCTM CURRICULUM STANDARDS

Standard 3: Analyze properties of 3-D shapes
Standard 4: Apply proper formulas to find measures
Standard 6: Solve problems in math and other contexts

Surface Areas of Regular Pyramids You can use a net of a pyramid with a square base to find a formula for its surface area. Let l be the slant height of the pyramid, and let s be the side length of the square base. The lateral area of the pyramid is the sum of the areas of the 4 triangular faces. In the diagram below, the area of 1 triangular face is $\frac{1}{2}sl$, and P is the perimeter of the square base.

Surface area	=	**Base area**	+	**Lateral area**
	=	B	+	$4\left(\frac{1}{2}sl\right)$
	=	B	+	$\frac{1}{2}(4sl)$
	=	B	+	$\frac{1}{2}Pl$

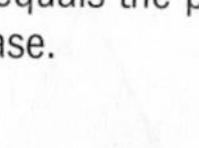

Study *Strategy*

In simplifying the expression for the lateral area of a regular pyramid, you can substitute P for $4s$ because the product of the number of triangular faces and the side length of the base equals the perimeter of the base.

Study *Strategy*

The formula $S = B + \frac{1}{2}Pl$ can be used to find the surface area of *any* regular pyramid, not just a square pyramid.

Surface Area of a Regular Pyramid

Words The surface area S of a regular pyramid is the sum of the base area B and one half of the product of the base perimeter P and the slant height l.

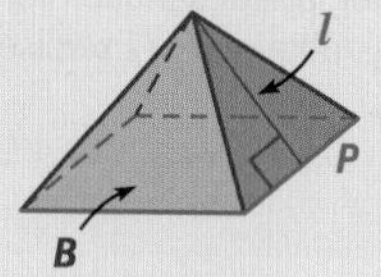

Algebra $S = B + \frac{1}{2}Pl$

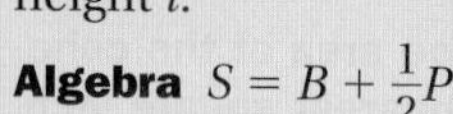

Example 2 *Finding the Surface Area of a Regular Pyramid*

Find the surface area of the regular pyramid.

1. Find the perimeter and area of the base.

   $P = 4(10) = 40$ cm

   $B = 10^2 = 100\text{ cm}^2$

2. Find the surface area.

$S = B + \frac{1}{2}Pl$	**Write formula for surface area of a pyramid.**
$= 100 + \frac{1}{2}(40)(13)$	**Substitute 100 for *B*, 40 for *P*, and 13 for *l*.**
$= 360$	**Simplify.**

Answer The surface area of the pyramid is 360 square centimeters.

Extra Examples

Example 1 What is the slant height of the pyramid to the nearest inch? **13 in.**

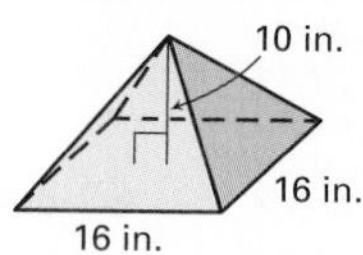

Example 2 Find the surface area of the regular pyramid.

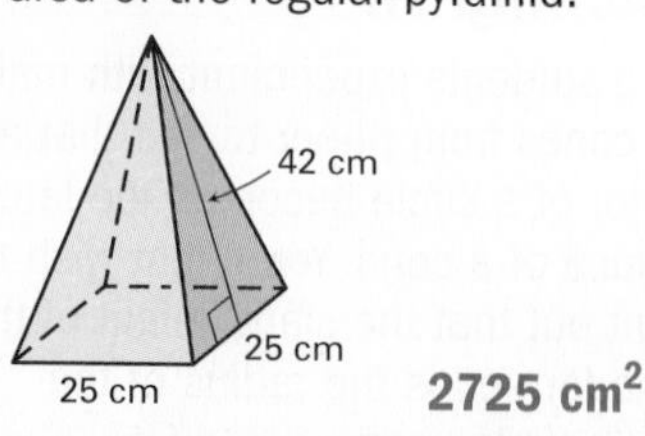

2725 cm²

Common Error

Some students may not be convinced that the height and slant height of a pyramid are different. On the board, sketch a pyramid with a very wide base and a short height so students can see it has a slant height that is much greater than its height.

Visualize

Using the net of a pyramid shown on this page, help students recognize that the slant height of a pyramid is the height of each triangular face of the pyramid.

Extra Examples

Example 3 Find the surface area of the cone. Round to the nearest square centimeter.

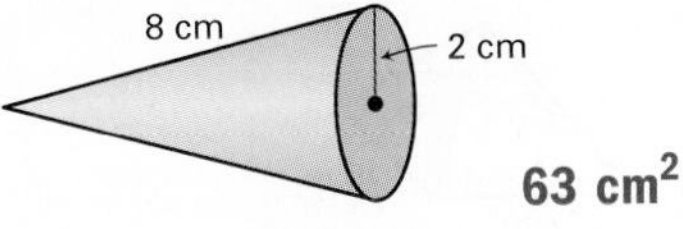

63 cm²

TEACHING TIP

Have students experiment with making cones from paper to see that a sector of a circle becomes the lateral surface of a cone. You might wish to point out that the slant height of the cone formed is the radius of the paper circle used.

DIFFERENTIATING INSTRUCTION

Advanced Students Refer students to the net of the cone at the top of this page. Have them consider the various cones that would be formed as the lateral surface ranges from one quarter of a circle to one half of a circle.

CONCEPT CHECK

How do you find the surface area of a cone given the area of the base and the slant height? **From the area of the base, you can find the radius by dividing this area by π and finding the square root of the result. The surface area of the cone is the area of the base plus π times the product of the slant height and the computed radius.**

DAILY PUZZLER

A square pyramid has a slant height of 10 feet and a base with sides that are 8 feet long. Your job is to paint the visible surfaces of the pyramid. Since you do not need to paint the base, what percent of the total surface area needs to be painted? **about 71%**

Study *Strategy*

In this book, all cones are *right cones*, which means that the segment connecting the center of the circular base to the vertex is perpendicular to the base.

Surface Areas of Cones The point on a cone directly above the center of its base is called the *vertex* of the cone. The distance between the vertex and center of the base is the **height of the cone**. The **slant height of the cone** is the distance between the vertex and any point on the edge of the base. To find the surface area of a cone, you need to know the radius r of the circular base and the slant height l.

Surface area	=	Base area	+	Lateral area
	=	B	+	πrl

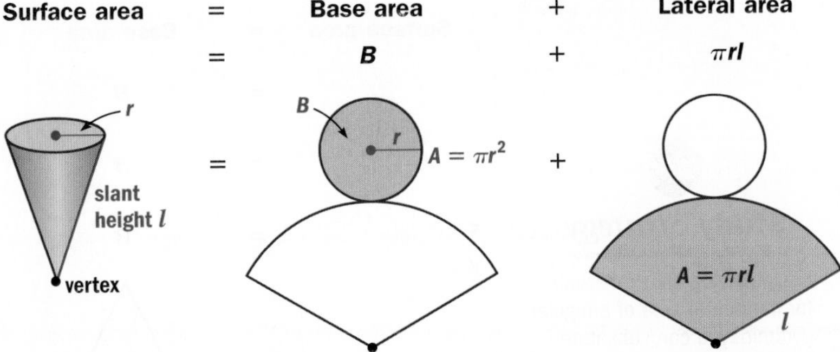

Study *Strategy*

The formula given in the notebook applies to any cone. You will see how the formula for lateral surface area, πrl, is obtained in Exercise 30 on p. 549.

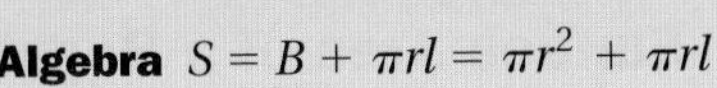

Surface Area of a Cone

Words The surface area S of a cone is the sum of the base area B and the product of π, the base radius r, and the slant height l.

Algebra $S = B + \pi rl = \pi r^2 + \pi rl$

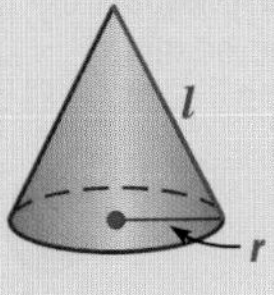

Example 3 *Finding the Surface Area of a Cone*

Find the surface area of the cone. Round to the nearest square inch.

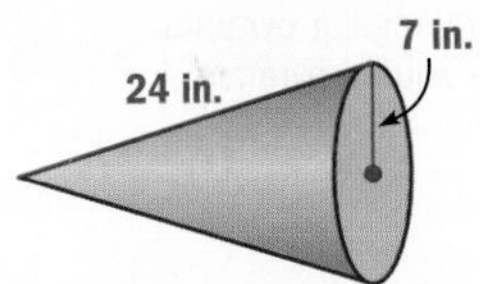

$S = \pi r^2 + \pi rl$	**Write formula for surface area of a cone.**
$= \pi(7)^2 + \pi(7)(24)$	**Substitute 7 for r and 24 for l.**
$= 217\pi \approx 681.7$	**Simplify. Then evaluate using a calculator.**

Answer The surface area of the cone is about 682 square inches.

Checkpoint

Find the surface area of the pyramid or cone. Round to the nearest whole number.

1. 22 m²

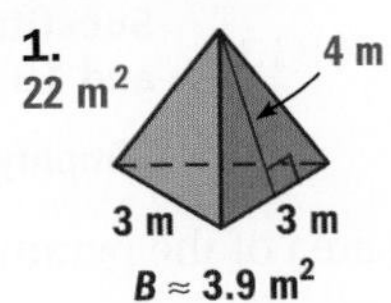

2.

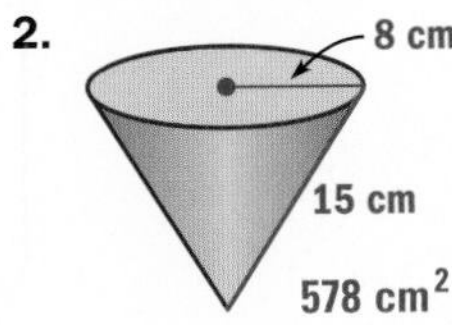

578 cm²

10.6 Exercises

More Practice, p. 812

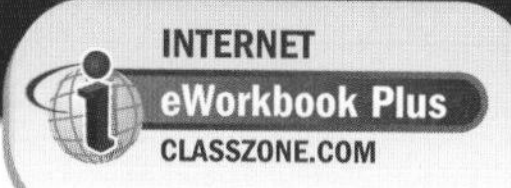

Guided Practice

Vocabulary Check

1. Explain the difference between the height and the slant height of a pyramid. **See margin.**

2. What part of the formula $S = \pi r^2 + \pi rl$ gives you the base area of a cone? Which part gives you the lateral area? πr^2; πrl

Skill Check **Find the surface area of the pyramid or cone. Round to the nearest whole number.**

1. *Sample answer:* The height is the perpendicular distance between the base and the vertex that is not on the base, while the slant height is the height of a lateral face.

3. 736 in.^{2}

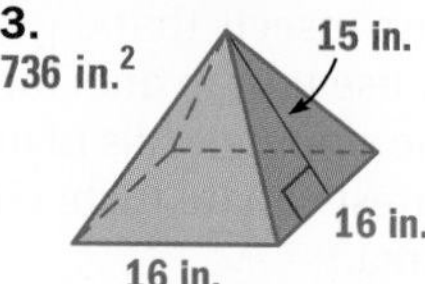

4. 37 ft^2

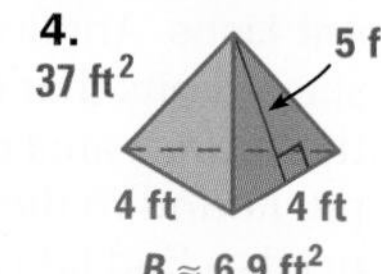

5. 352 ft^2

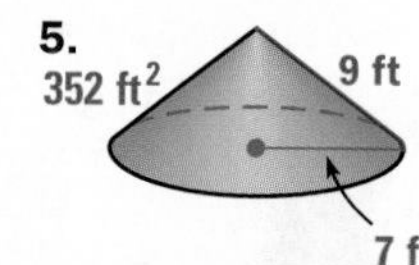

Guided Problem Solving

6. What is the surface area of the cone? Round to the nearest square centimeter.

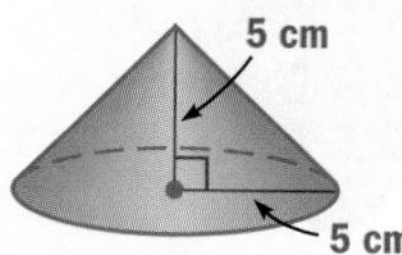

(1) Find the slant height of the cone. $5\sqrt{2} \approx 7.07$ cm

(2) Find the surface area of the cone to the nearest square centimeter. 190 cm^2

Practice and Problem Solving

Homework Help

Example	Exercises
1	7-9
2	10, 12, 14-16, 21
3	9, 11, 17-19, 22, 23

- More Examples
- eTutorial Plus

Find the slant height of the pyramid or cone. Round to the nearest whole number.

A **7.** 29 yd

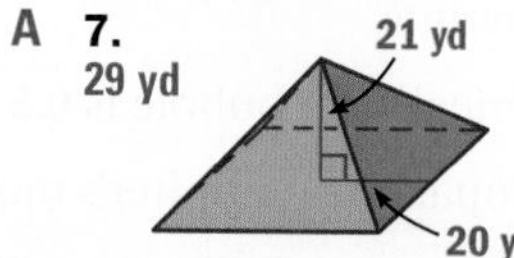

8. 52 cm

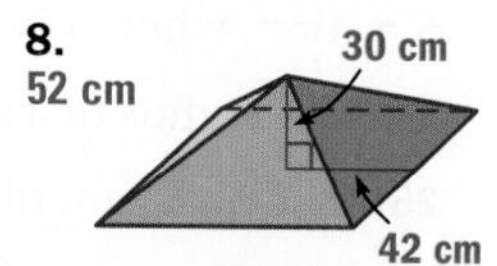

9. 39 m

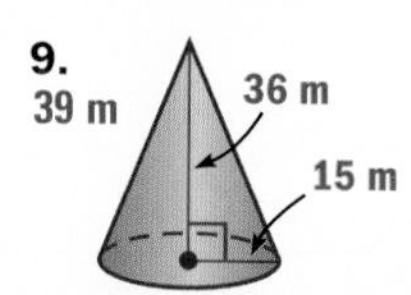

Use the net to sketch the solid and find its surface area. Round to the nearest whole number. 10–12. See margin for art.

10. 140 in.^{2} **11.** 641 ft^2

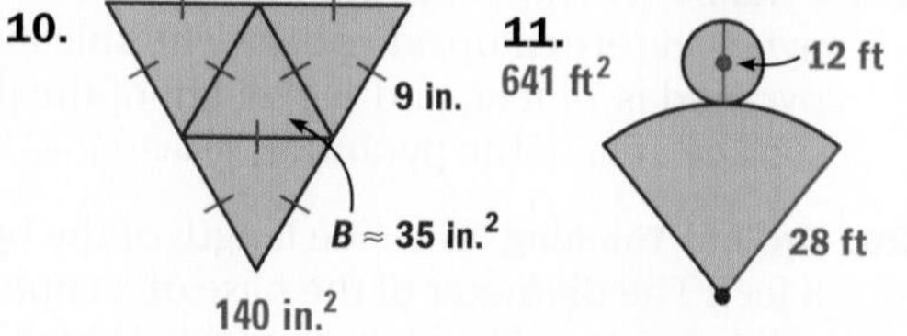

12. 903 m^2

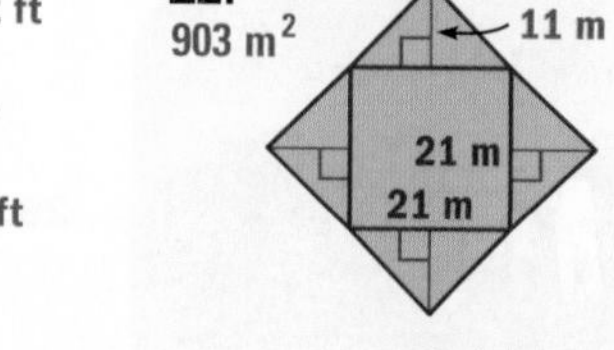

13. *Writing* Which is greater, a pyramid's height or its slant height? Explain your reasoning. **See margin.**

3 APPLY

ASSIGNMENT GUIDE

Basic Course
Day 1: EP p. 811 Exs. 13-16; pp. 547-549 Exs. 7-12, 14-19, 21-25, 28, 34-40

Average Course
Day 1: pp. 547-549 Exs. 8-15, 18-22, 26-31, 34-41

Advanced Course
Day 1: pp. 547-549 Exs. 9-11, 13-15, 19-22, 26-33*, 36-41

Block
pp. 547-549 Exs. 8-15, 18-22, 26-31, 34-41 (with 10.5)

EXTRA PRACTICE

- Student Edition, p. 812
- Chapter 10 Resource Book, pp. 50-52
- Test and Practice Generator

TRANSPARENCY

Even-numbered answers are available on transparencies.

HOMEWORK CHECK

When you review students' homework for this lesson, go over the following exercises to check understanding of key concepts.
Basic: 7, 9, 10, 12, 17
Average: 8, 10, 11, 14, 18
Advanced: 9, 10, 14, 19, 22

10-13. See Additional Answers beginning on page AA1.

TEACHING TIP

In Exercise 14, students may not notice that the pyramid has a triangular base. Point out that the base is an equilateral triangle since the pyramid is regular.

29.

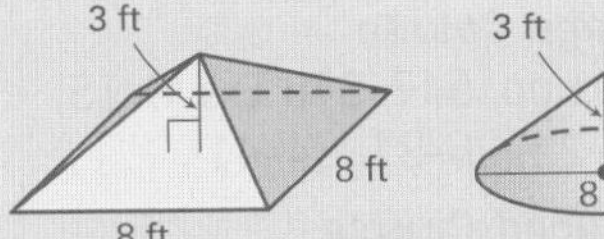

Find the surface area of the regular pyramid.

14. about 85.8 ft²

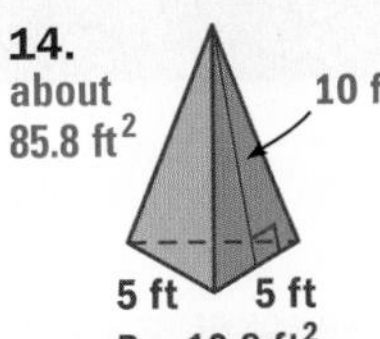

15. 7812 mm²

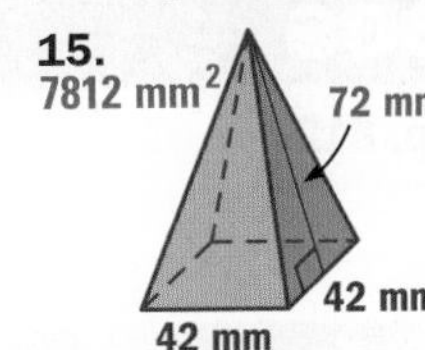

16. 838.55 cm²

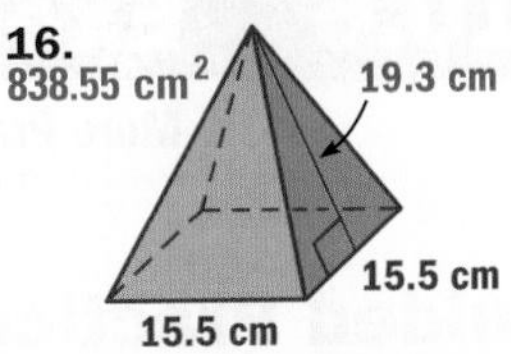

Find the surface area of the cone. Round to the nearest whole number.

17. 120 m²

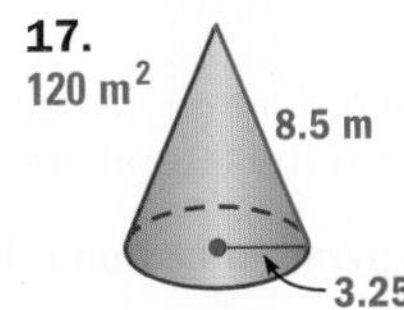

18. 594 ft²

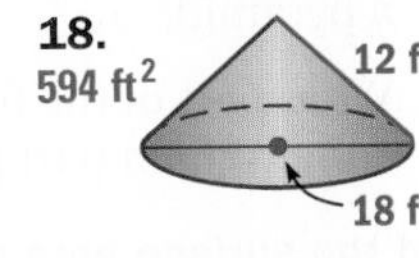

19.

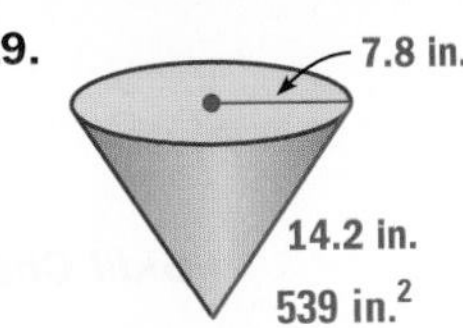

539 in.²

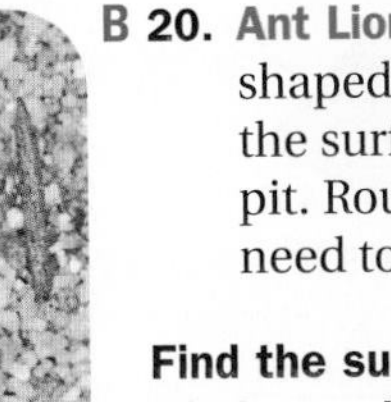

Ant lion

B **20. Ant Lions** Ant lions are insects that dig cone-shaped pits that they use to trap ants for food. Find the surface area of the sloping walls of an ant lion pit. Round to the nearest square inch. (*Hint:* You need to find lateral area.) 7 in.²

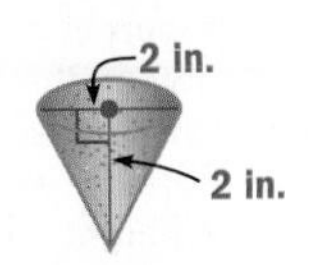

Find the surface area of the pyramid or cone. Round to the nearest whole number.

21. 2649 in.²

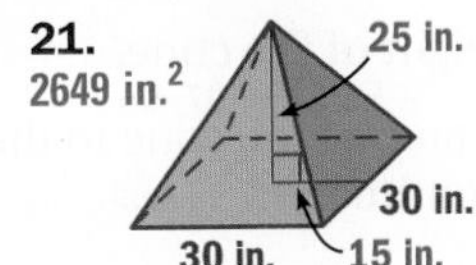

22.

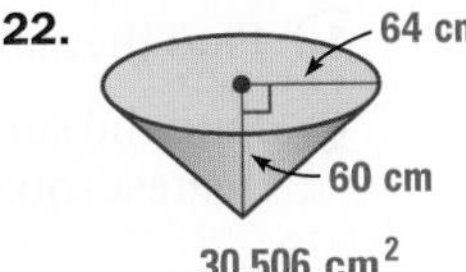

30,506 cm²

23. 72 yd²

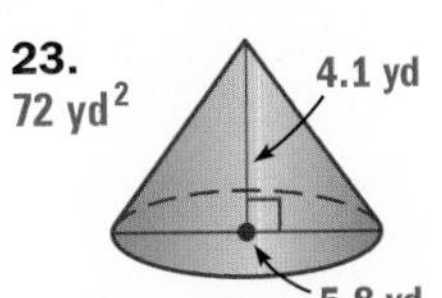

Spheres In Exercises 24–27, use the following information to find the surface area of the specified objects. Round to the nearest square unit.

A *sphere* is a solid formed by all points in space that are the same distance from a fixed point (the center). The formula for the surface area of a sphere is $S = 4\pi r^2$, where r is the radius.

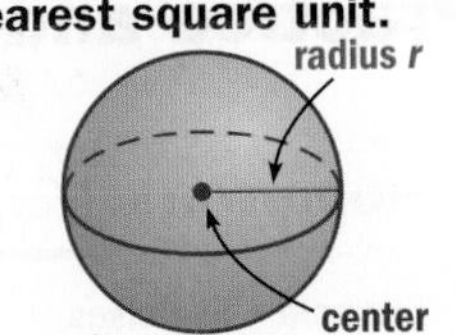

24. The radius of a spherical soap bubble is 0.5 inch. 3 in.²

25. The diameter of Europa, one of Jupiter's moons, is about 1950 miles. 11,945,906 mi²

26. The diameter of a table tennis ball is 40 millimeters. 5027 mm²

27. The diameter of a large exercise ball is 2.5 feet. 20 ft²

28. Pyramid The unusual building shown in the photo includes a square pyramid turned upside down. The side length of the base of the pyramid is 74 feet, and the height of the pyramid is 48 feet. What is the surface area of the pyramid? about 14,446 ft²

29. Critical Thinking The side length of the base of a square pyramid is 8 feet. The diameter of the base of a cone is 8 feet. The height of both solids is 3 feet. Sketch both solids. Which one has the greater surface area? See margin for art; the square pyramid.

30b. Area $= \pi rl$. *Sample answer:* This is the part of the formula for the surface area of a cone that gives the lateral surface area.

41. No. *Sample answer:* Let l represent the slant height of the first pyramid. Then $3l$ is the slant height of the second pyramid. Because B and P are the same for the two pyramids, the surface area of the first pyramid is $B + \frac{1}{2}Pl$, and of the second pyramid is $B + \frac{1}{2}P(3l) = B + \frac{3}{2}Pl$, and $B + \frac{1}{2}Pl \neq \frac{1}{3}\left(B + \frac{3}{2}Pl\right)$.

30. **Visual Thinking** You can cut the lateral surface of a cone into congruent wedges. You can rearrange these wedges to form a figure that resembles a parallelogram as shown. The more wedges you cut, the more closely the shape will resemble a parallelogram.

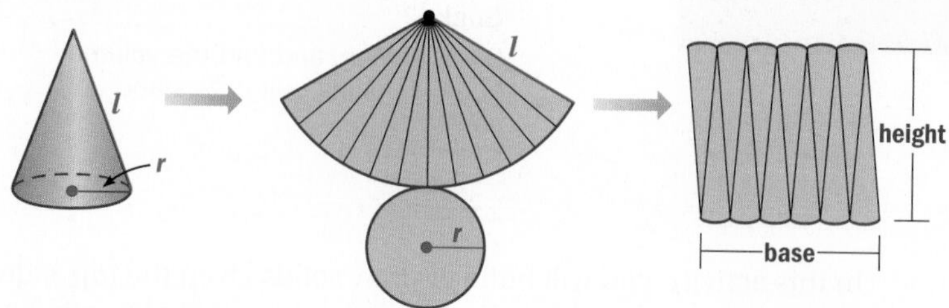

a. Write expressions for the height and the base of the parallelogram in terms of r and l. **height: l, base: $\frac{1}{2}(2\pi r)$, or πr**

b. Use the expressions from part (a) to write a formula for the area of the parallelogram in terms of r and l. How is this formula related to the formula for the surface area of a cone?

The solids shown are composed of cones, cylinders, and pyramids. Find the surface area of the solid. Round to the nearest whole number.

C 31. **220 m²**

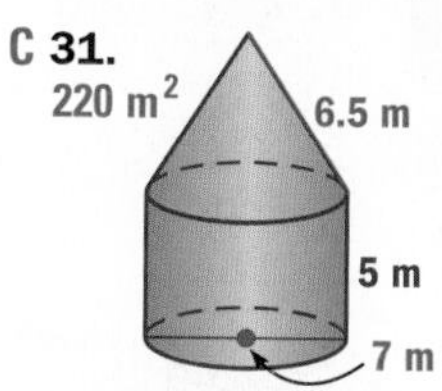

32. **7200 ft²**

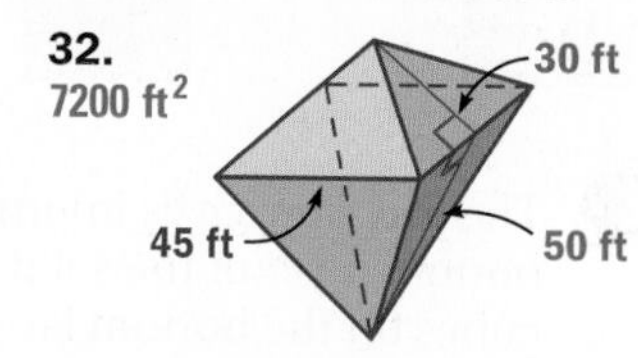

33. **Challenge** The surface area of a cone is 90π square inches. The base radius of the cone is 5 inches. Find the slant height of the cone. **13 in.**

Mixed Review

Simplify the expression *(Lesson 9.2)*

34. $\sqrt{48}$ **$4\sqrt{3}$** 35. $\sqrt{288}$ **$12\sqrt{2}$** 36. $\sqrt{\frac{40}{9}}$ **$\frac{2\sqrt{10}}{3}$** 37. $\sqrt{\frac{24}{121}}$ **$\frac{2\sqrt{6}}{11}$**

38. Find the unknown side lengths of the triangle. Give exact answers. *(Lesson 9.6)* **$x = 26\sqrt{3}$ m, $y = 52$ m**

26 m, 60°, y, 30°, x

39. The base radius of a cylinder is 5 centimeters, and the height is 12 centimeters. Find the surface area of the cylinder. Round your answer to the nearest square centimeter. *(Lesson 10.5)* **534 cm²**

Standardized Test Practice

40. **Multiple Choice** What is the approximate surface area of a cone that has a height of 14.5 meters and base diameter of 10 meters? **C**

A. 140 m² **B.** 306 m² **C.** 319 m² **D.** 795 m²

41. **Short Response** Two pyramids have congruent bases. The slant height of the first pyramid is one third of the slant height of the second pyramid. Is the surface area of the first pyramid one third of the surface area of the second pyramid? Explain your reasoning. **See margin.**

4 ASSESS

Assessment Resources

For more assessment resources, see:
- Assessment Book
- Test and Practice Generator

Mini-Quiz

1. Find the slant height of the cone.

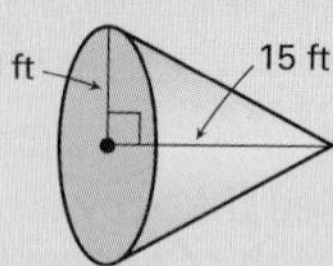

17 ft

2. The height of a square pyramid is 22 inches and its base has sides 14 inches long. Find the surface area to the nearest square inch. **842 in.²**
3. Find the surface area of a cone with radius 7 meters and slant height 35 meters. Round to the nearest square meter. **924 m²**
4. **Challenge** The surface area of a cone is 36π square inches. The slant height of the cone is 16 inches. Find the radius. **2 in.**

5 FOLLOW-UP

Diagnosis/Remediation

- Study Guide in Chapter 10 Resource Book, pp. 53–54
- Tutor Place, Geometry Card 20
- eTutorial Plus Online
- Extra Practice, p. 812
- Lesson Practice in Chapter 10 Resource Book, pp. 50–52

English Learner Support

- Spanish Study Guide
- Multi-Language Visual Glossary
- Chapter Audio Summaries CDs

Challenge

- Challenge Practice in Chapter 10 Resource Book, p. 55
- Teacher's Edition, p. 508F

1 PLAN

Investigate the Concept

- Students build, sketch, and find the volume of solids using unit cubes and dot paper.
- This activity leads into calculating the volume of prisms in Lesson 10.7.

Materials

Each student will need unit cubes and dot paper. See the Activity Support Master in the *Chapter 10 Resource Book*. A support transparency is also available.

Recommended Time

Work activity: 15 min
Discuss results: 10 min

Grouping

Students should work individually.

2 TEACH

Tips for Success

After completing Step 3, point out that the U-shaped solid still matches the top and side views. Some students may need help understanding why the top view is still correct when the top layer is missing some cubes.

1a.

1b.

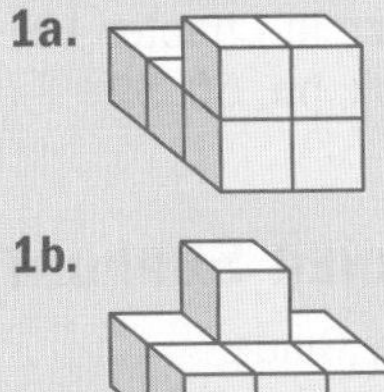

Concept *Activity*

10.7 Building and Sketching Solids

Goal
Build, sketch, and find the volume of solids using unit cubes and dot paper.

Materials
- unit cubes
- dot paper

In this activity, you will build or draw solids given the top, side, and front views. Assume that there are no missing blocks in views that are not shown.

Investigate

Use the three views of a solid to build the solid using unit cubes. Find the volume of the solid.

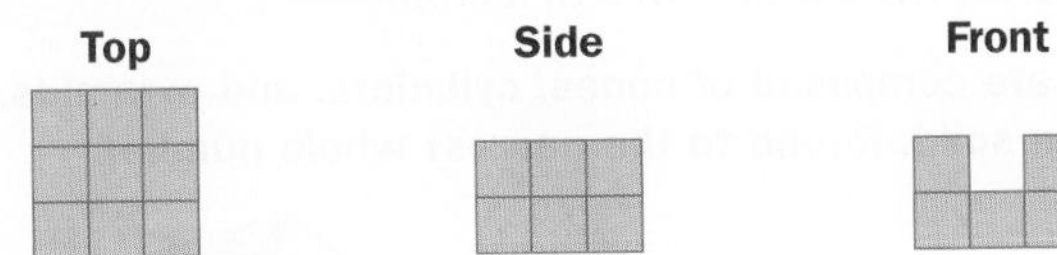

1 The top view gives information about the bottom layer of the solid. There are 9 unit cubes on the bottom layer.

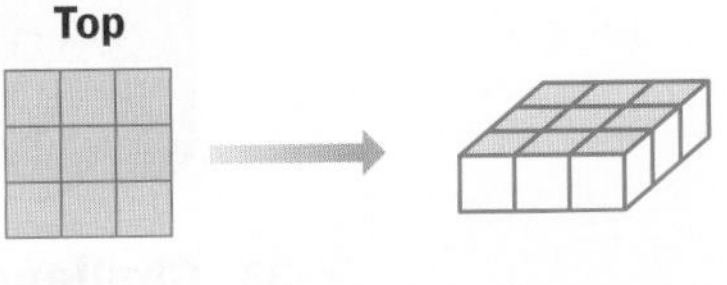

2 The side view shows that there are two layers in the solid.

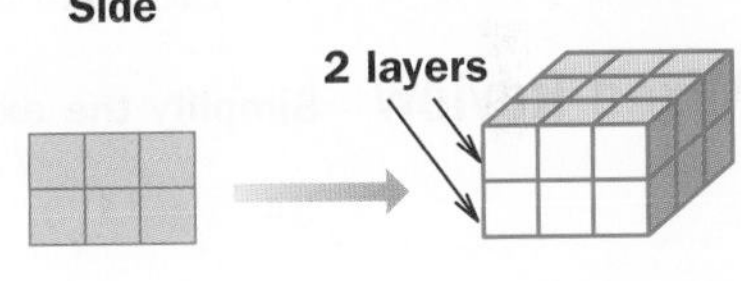

3 The front view shows you how to form the two layers of cubes. The middle row of cubes is missing from the top layer. The volume of the solid is 15 cubic units.

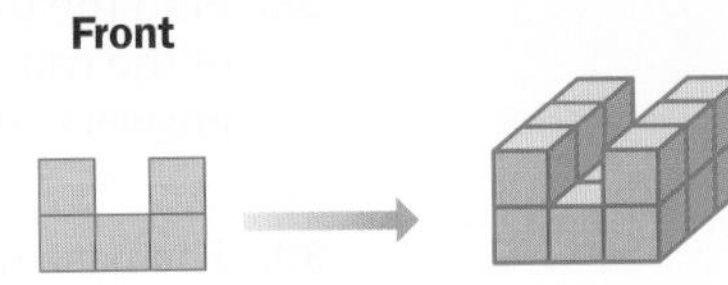

Draw Conclusions

1. Use the three views of a solid to build the solid using unit cubes. Which solid has a greater volume? **1a–b. See margin for art; the solid in (b).**

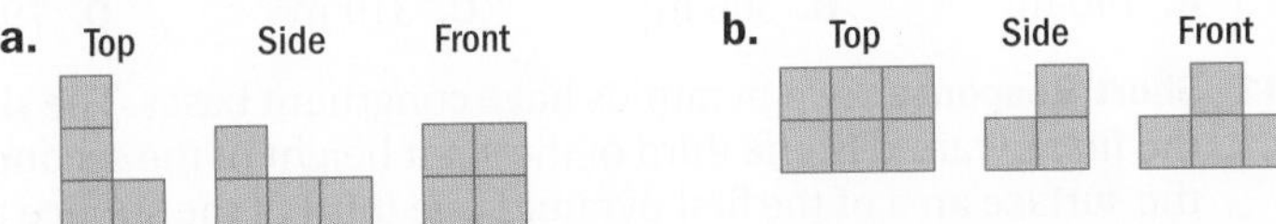

NCTM CURRICULUM STANDARDS
Standard 3: Analyze properties of 3-D shapes
Standard 10: Create representations to communicate mathematical ideas

Investigate

Use the three views of a solid to draw the solid using dot paper. Find the volume of the solid.

Top  Side  Front 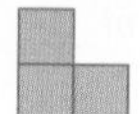

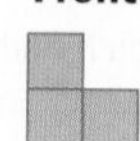

1 On dot paper, draw a set of three axes that form 120° angles.

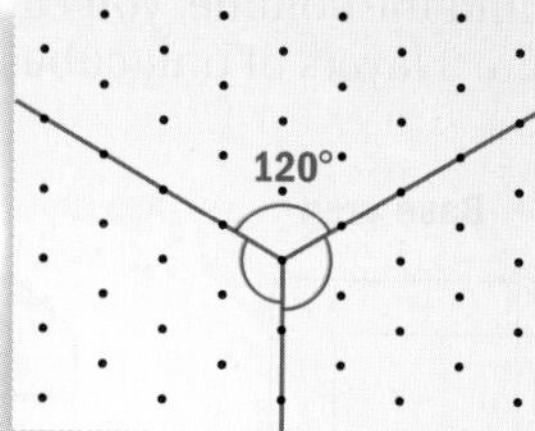

2 Draw a unit cube where the three axes intersect.

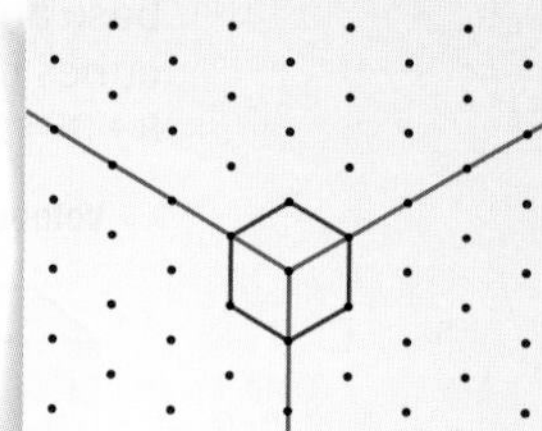

3 Draw the cubes you can see from the front.

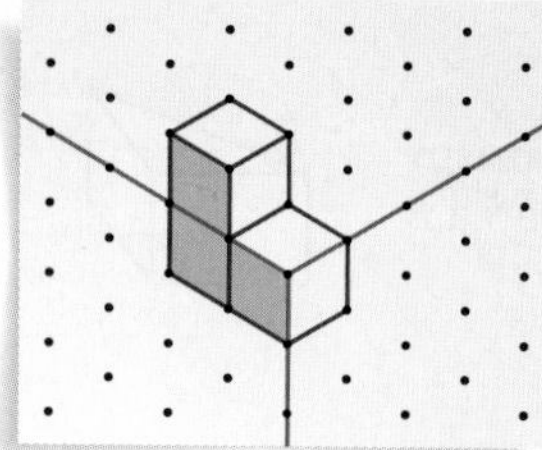

4 Draw the cubes you can see from the side.

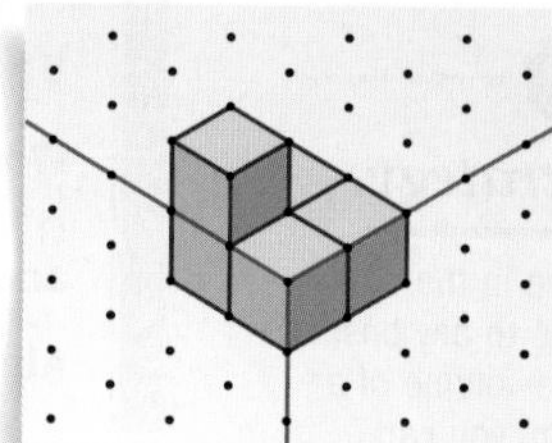

5 Check that the top view matches what you have drawn. The solid has a volume of 5 cubic units.

Draw Conclusions

2. Use the three views of each solid to draw the solids using dot paper. Which solid has a greater volume? **2a–b. See margin for art; the solid in (b).**

a. Top Side Front

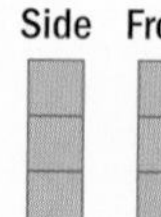

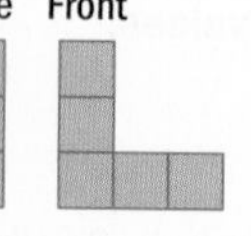

b. Top Side Front

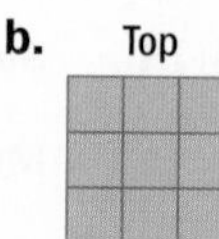

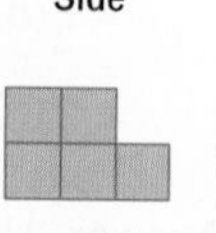

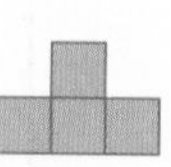

Tips for Success

In Step 3, point out that the shaded surface indicates that the front of the solid is the view seen from the bottom left corner of the dot paper. In Step 4, point out that the green surfaces indicate that the side of the solid is the view seen from the bottom right corner of the dot paper. Stress that this orientation is to be used for Exercise 2 also.

3 CLOSE

Key Discovery

Students can build or sketch models of solids based on top, side, and front views, and can use these models to find their volumes.

Assessment

1. Can the three views of a solid (front, side, top) all be different? Give an example. **Yes. *Sample answer:* The solid in the Investigate on page 550 is an example.**
2. Can the three views of a solid all be the same? Give an example. **Yes. *Sample answer:* Any cube is an example.**

2a.

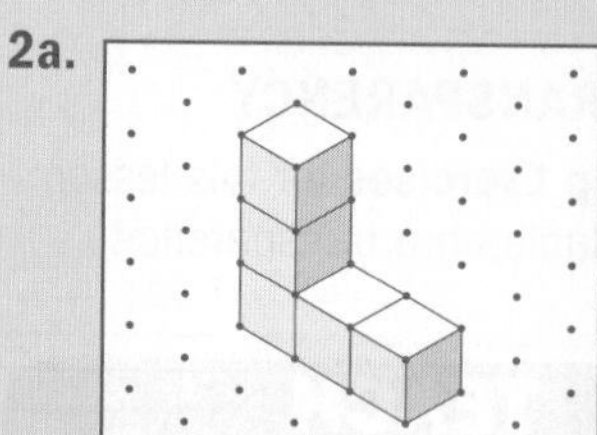

2b.

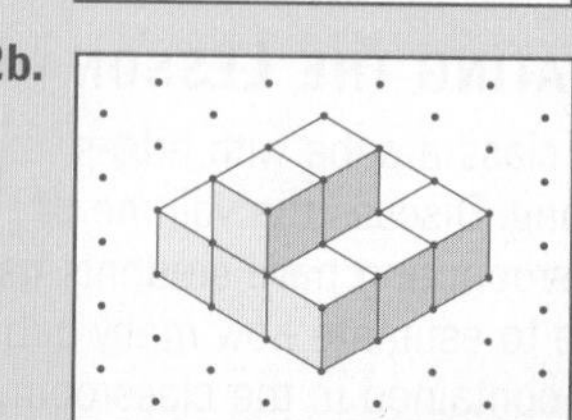

1 PLAN

Skill Check

Find the area of the figure to the nearest whole number.

1. a circle with a radius of 3 centimeters **28 cm^2**
2. a triangle with a base of 4 feet and a height of 7 feet **14 ft^2**
3. a rectangle 8 inches wide and 1.5 inches high **12 in.^{2}**

LESSON OBJECTIVE

Find the volumes of prisms and cylinders.

PACING

Suggested Number of Days
Basic Course: 1 day
Average Course: 1 day
Advanced Course: 1 day
Block: 0.5 block with 10.8

TEACHING RESOURCES

For a complete list of Teaching Resources, see page 508B.

TRANSPARENCY

Warm-Up Exercises for this lesson are available on a transparency.

2 TEACH

MOTIVATING THE LESSON

Bring to class a cube with edges 1 foot long. Discuss the volume of the classroom and have students use the cube to estimate how many cubic feet are contained in the classroom.

LESSON **10.7**

Volumes *of* Prisms *and* Cylinders

Review Vocabulary
volume, p. 789

BEFORE	*Now*	WHY?
You found surface areas of prisms and cylinders.	You'll find the volumes of prisms and cylinders.	So you can compare the volumes of two suitcases, as in Ex. 14.

Recall that the volume of a solid is the amount of space the solid occupies. Volume is measured in cubic units. For the prism below, the base area is 8 square units. To find the volume, you can imagine unit cubes filling the prism. There are 3 layers of unit cubes, so the volume is $8 \cdot 3 = 24$ cubic units.

Volume of a prism = **Base area** × **Height**

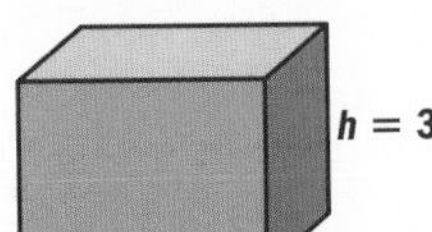

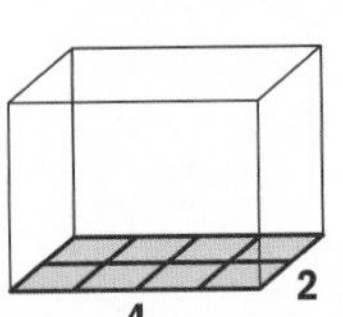

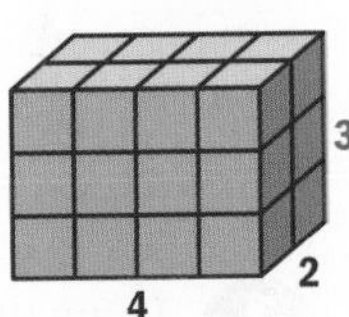

Study *Strategy*

The formula given in the notebook applies to any prism. When finding the volume of a rectangular prism, you can substitute *lw* for *B*. So, the formula $V = Bh$ becomes $V = lwh$.

Volume of a Prism

Words The volume V of a prism is the product of the base area B and the height h.

Algebra $V = Bh$

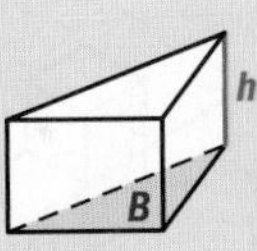

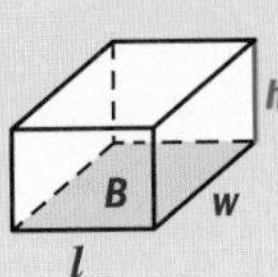

Example 1 ***Finding the Volume of a Prism***

Find the volume of the prism shown.

The bases of the prism are triangles, so use the formula for the area of a triangle to find B.

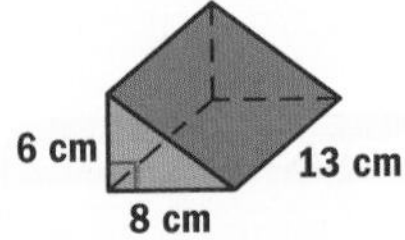

$V = Bh$ **Write formula for volume of a prism.**

$= \frac{1}{2}(8)(6)(13)$ **Substitute values.**

$= 312$ **Multiply.**

Answer The volume of the prism is 312 cubic centimeters.

NCTM CURRICULUM STANDARDS
Standard 3: Analyze properties of 3-D shapes
Standard 4: Apply proper formulas to find measures
Standard 6: Solve problems in math and other contexts

Cylinders The formula for the volume of a cylinder is like the formula for the volume of a prism.

Volume of a cylinder = **Base area** × **Height**

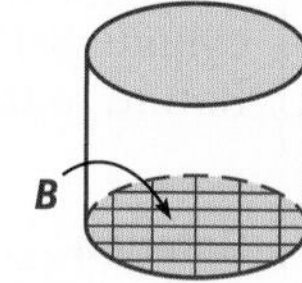

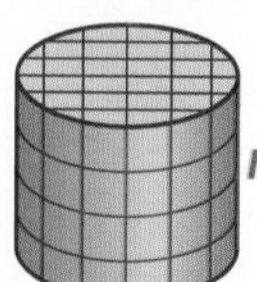

Volume of a Cylinder

Words The volume V of a cylinder is the product of the base area B and the height h.

Algebra $V = Bh = \pi r^2 h$

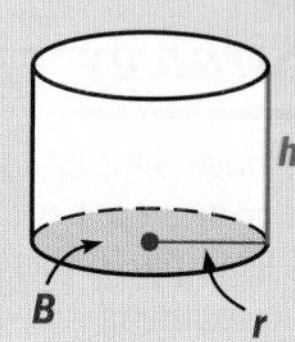

Example 2 *Finding the Volume of a Cylinder*

Swimming Pool Find the capacity (in gallons) of the swimming pool shown. Round to the nearest whole number. (Use the fact that 1 ft³ ≈ 7.481 gal.)

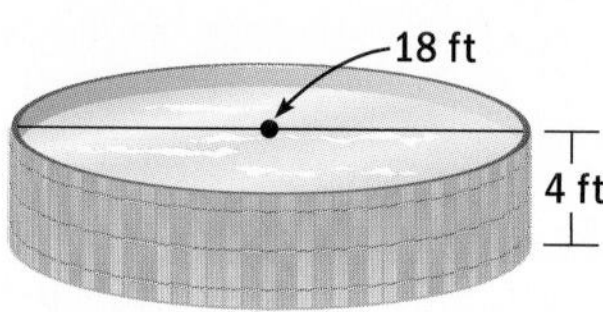

Solution

1) The radius is one half of the diameter. So, $r = 9$.

$V = \pi r^2 h$	**Write formula for volume of a cylinder.**
$= \pi(9)^2(4)$	**Substitute 9 for *r* and 4 for *h*.**
$= 324\pi$	**Simplify.**

2) Use a conversion factor that converts cubic feet to gallons.

$$324\pi \cancel{\text{ft}^3} \cdot \frac{7.481 \text{ gal}}{1 \cancel{\text{ft}^3}} \approx 7614.7 \text{ gal}$$ **Evaluate. Use a calculator.**

Answer The capacity of the swimming pool is about 7615 gallons.

Checkpoint

Find the volume of the prism or cylinder.

1.

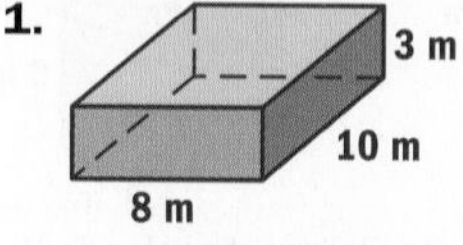

240 m³

2.

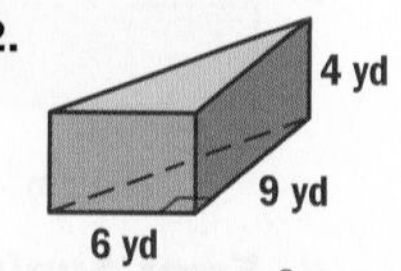

108 yd³

3.

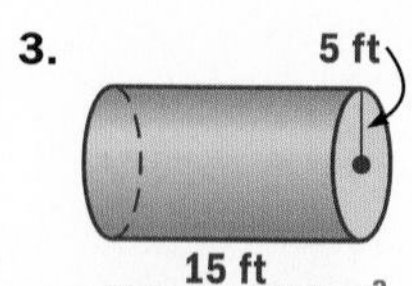

$375\pi \approx 1178$ ft³

4. **Critical Thinking** Which solid has a greater volume, a prism with bases that are squares with side length 8 units and a height of 11 units or a cylinder with a diameter of 11 units and a height of 8 units? Which solid has the greater surface area? **cylinder; prism**

Study *Strategy*

The formula for the volume of a cylinder is obtained by substituting πr^2 for B. So, the formula $V = Bh$ becomes $V = \pi r^2 h$.

TIPS *for* NEW TEACHERS

Help students distinguish between surface area and volume. Ask them to describe the surface area of a box and then the volume of the box. See Tips for New Teachers in the *Chapter 10 Resource Book*.

Extra Examples

Example 1 Find the volume of the prism shown. **300 in.³**

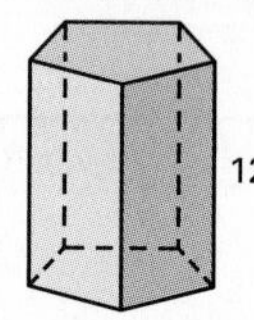

Example 2 At a state fair, a vendor sells cashew nuts in a plastic cylinder that is 36 inches long and has a diameter of 2 inches. Find the volume of the cylinder. Round to the nearest whole number. **113 in.³**

COMMON ERROR

In Example 1, watch for students who assume the base is the 8 centimeter by 13 centimeter face instead of the triangular faces.

NOTETAKING

As students make sketches of solids in their notebooks, encourage them to color or shade the bases. Also encourage them to draw solids oriented in different ways to remind themselves that the bases are not always the surfaces that are at the "top" and "bottom" of the figure.

Extra Examples

Example 3 The hot tub shown below is comprised of a square prism that is 4 feet deep with sides 6 feet wide and four identical half cylinders that are each 3 feet deep. Find the volume of the hot tub to the nearest cubic foot. **314 ft^3**

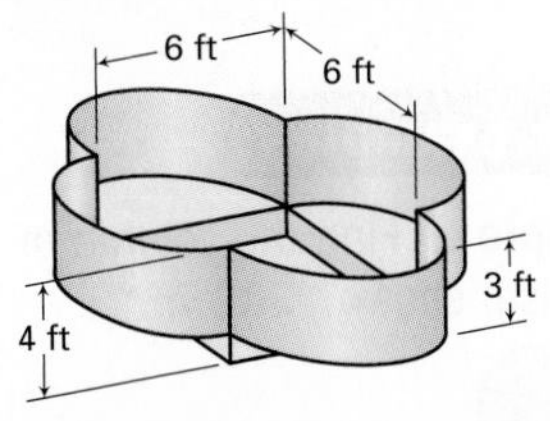

Teaching Tip

In Example 3, discuss how the total volume of the solid could also be found by calculating the volume of the prism and the volume of each half cylinder separately and then adding these volumes together.

Concept Check

How is the formula for the volume of a cylinder similar to the formula for a prism? **Both formulas are the product of the height and the area of a base.**

Daily Puzzler

A cylinder has radius 10 inches and height 20 inches. If you increase the radius by 1 inch, what must you do to the height in order to keep the volume the same? **Reduce the height to about 16.5 inches.**

Study *Strategy*

Notice that the base area is left in terms of π in Step 1 of the solution of Example 3. This is done to avoid rounding twice, once when calculating B and again when calculating V. When possible, you should avoid rounding until the *end* of a calculation.

Example 3 *Finding the Volume of a Solid*

The solid shown is composed of a rectangular prism and two half cylinders. Find the volume of the solid. Round to the nearest cubic foot.

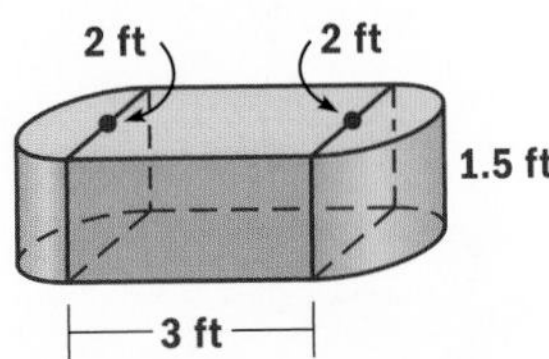

Solution

1. Find the area of a base. Each end of a base is a half circle with a radius of 1 foot. Together, the ends form a complete circle.

B = Area of rectangle + Area of circle

$= lw + \pi r^2$ **Use formulas for area of a rectangle and area of a circle.**

$= 3(2) + \pi(1)^2$ **Substitute 3 for *l*, 2 for *w*, and 1 for *r*.**

$= 6 + \pi$ **Simplify. Leave in terms of π.**

2. $V = Bh$ **Write formula for volume of a prism.**

$= (6 + \pi)1.5$ **Substitute 6 + π for *B* and 1.5 for *h*.**

$= 9 + 1.5\pi$ **Use distributive property.**

≈ 13.71 **Evaluate. Use a calculator.**

Answer The volume of the solid shown is about 14 cubic feet.

10.7 Exercises

More Practice, p. 812

Guided Practice

Vocabulary Check

1. Copy and complete: The volume of a solid is measured in _?_ units. **cubic**
2. Explain how to find the volume of any prism. **Multiply the area of a base by the height.**

Skill Check **Find the volume of the prism or cylinder. Round to the nearest whole number.**

3. 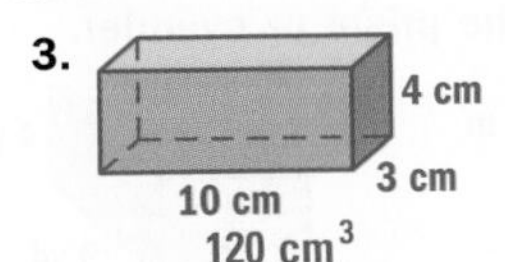

120 cm^3

4. 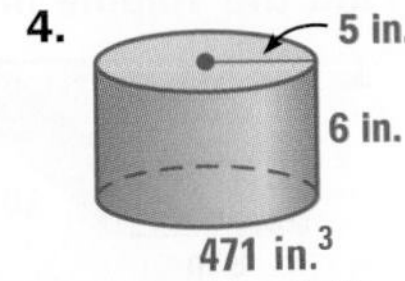

471 in.^{3}

5. 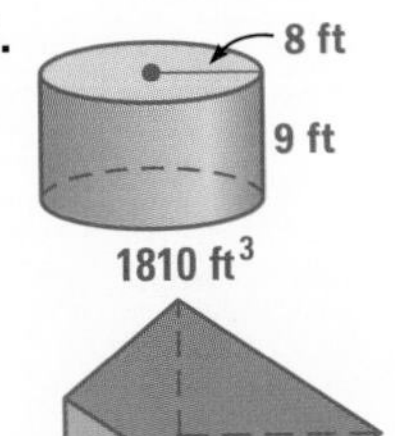

1810 ft^3

6. **Error Analysis** Explain why the following calculation would not give the correct volume for the prism: $V = Bh = 6 \cdot 9 \cdot 10$. **Because the base is a triangle, not a rectangle, its area is $0.5 \cdot 9 \cdot 6$, so $V = Bh = 0.5 \cdot 9 \cdot 6 \cdot 10$.**

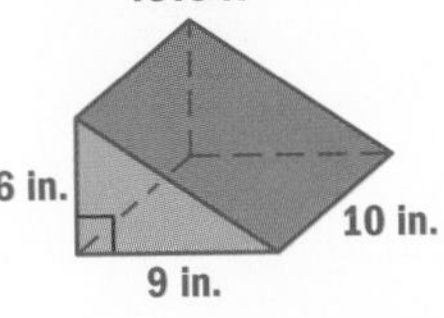

Practice and Problem Solving

Homework *Help*

Example	Exercises
1	7-9, 13-14
2	10-12, 15
3	19-20

- More Examples
- eTutorial Plus

Find the volume of the prism or cylinder. Round to the nearest whole number.

A **7.** 88 m^3 **8.** 216 ft^3 **9.** 3168 cm^3

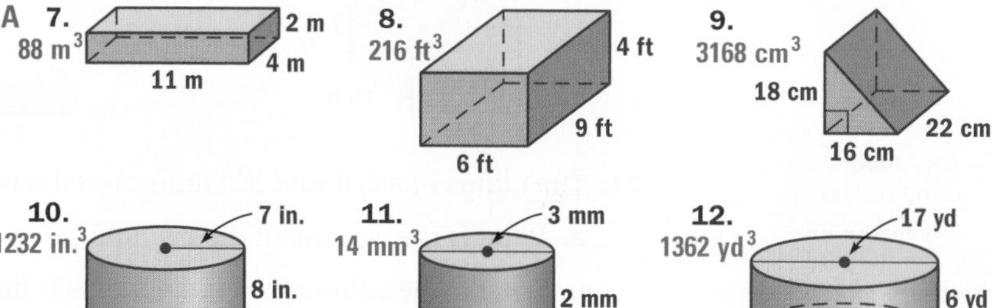

10. 1232 in.^{3} **11.** 14 mm^3 **12.** 1362 yd^3

7 in.
8 in.
3 mm
2 mm
17 yd
6 yd

13. Mailing You are mailing a gift box that is 17 inches by 14 inches by 10 inches. You want to put it in a larger box and surround it with foam packing. The larger box is 20 inches by 17 inches by 13 inches. How many cubic inches of foam packing do you need? **2040 in.^{3}**

14. Suitcases Tell which suitcase holds more. **suitcase B**

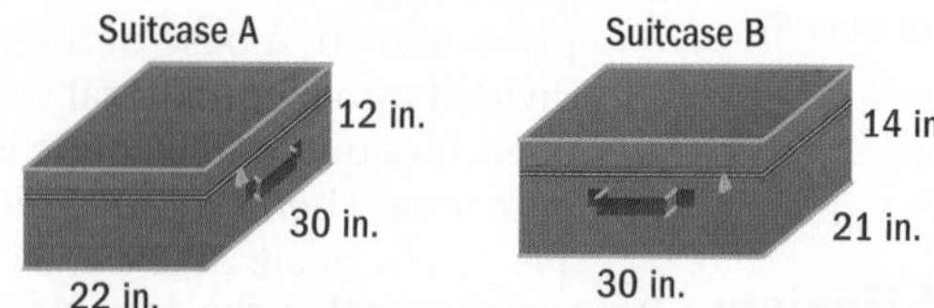

15. Candles The red candle costs \$7.05, the blue candle costs \$7.80, and the green candle costs \$10.55.

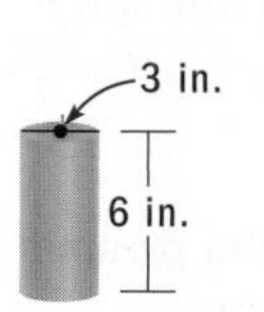

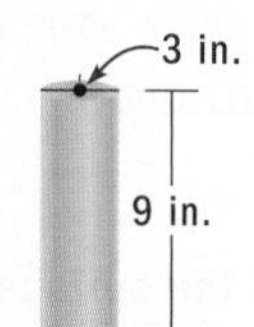

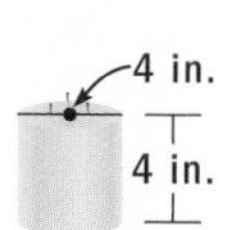

a. How much wax is used in each candle? Round to the nearest cubic inch. **red: 42 in.^{3}, blue: 64 in.^{3}, green: 50 in.^{3}**

b. Find the ratio of the cost of a candle to the volume of wax used in the candle. **red: about \$.168/in.^{3}, blue: about \$.122/in.^{3}, green: \$.211/in.^{3}**

c. Interpret and Apply Which candle is the best buy? Explain. **The blue candle. *Sample answer:* It has the lowest price per cubic inch of wax.**

Find the unknown dimension. Round to the nearest whole number.

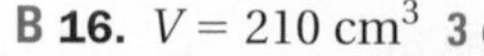

B **16.** $V = 210$ cm^3 **3 cm** **17.** $V = 301$ in.^{3} **8 in.** **18.** $V = 254$ m^3 **1 m**

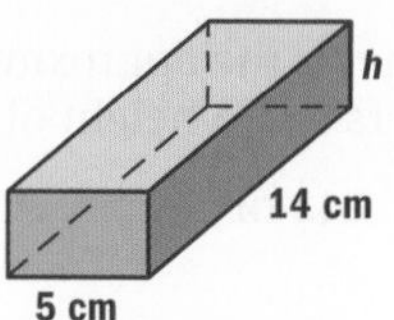

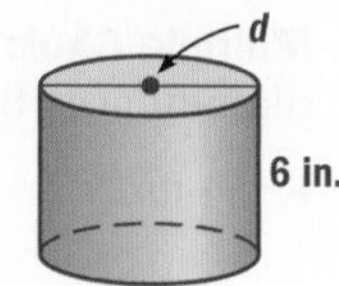

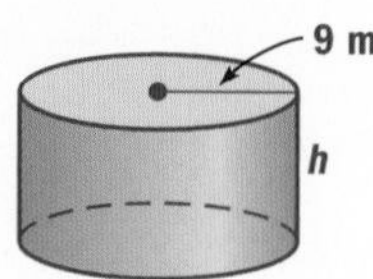

3 APPLY

ASSIGNMENT GUIDE

Basic Course

Day 1: SRH p. 791 Exs. 2-5; pp. 555-556 Exs. 7-14, 16-20, 24-32

Average Course

Day 1: pp. 555-556 Exs. 8-11, 13-22, 24-32

Advanced Course

Day 1: pp. 555-556 Exs. 8-10, 12-16, 18-24*, 27-32

Block

pp. 555-556 Exs. 8-11, 13-22, 24-32 (with 10.8)

Extra Practice

- Student Edition, p. 812
- Chapter 10 Resource Book, pp. 59-61
- Test and Practice Generator

Transparency

Even-numbered answers are available on transparencies.

Homework Check

When you review students' homework for this lesson, go over the following exercises to check understanding of key concepts.
Basic: 7, 10, 11, 13, 19
Average: 8, 11, 13, 15, 19
Advanced: 9, 12, 14, 19, 20

4 ASSESS

ASSESSMENT RESOURCES

For more assessment resources, see:

- Assessment Book
- Test and Practice Generator

MINI-QUIZ

Find the volume of the prism or cylinder. Round to the nearest whole number.

1. triangular prism with height 14 meters and bases that are right triangles with base 3 meters and height 4 meters **84 m^3**
2. cylinder with diameter 24 inches and height 20 inches **9048 $in.^3$**
3. **Challenge** The base of a regular pentagonal prism can be divided into five isosceles triangles, each with a base of 4 inches and a height of about 2.75 inches. Find the volume of the prism if it is 10 inches long. **about 275 $in.^3$**

5 FOLLOW-UP

DIAGNOSIS/REMEDIATION

- Study Guide in Chapter 10 Resource Book, pp. 62–63
- Tutor Place, Geometry Card 21
- eTutorial Plus Online
- Extra Practice, p. 812
- Lesson Practice in Chapter 10 Resource Book, pp. 59–61

ENGLISH LEARNER SUPPORT

- Spanish Study Guide
- Multi-Language Visual Glossary
- Chapter Audio Summaries CDs

CHALLENGE

- Challenge Practice in Chapter 10 Resource Book, p. 65
- Teacher's Edition, p. 508F

23. See Additional Answers beginning on page AA1.

The solids shown are composed of prisms, cylinders, and half cylinders. Find the volume of the solid. Round to the nearest whole number.

19. 948 ft^3

4.5 ft, 7 ft, 10 ft, 9 ft

20. 286 $in.^3$

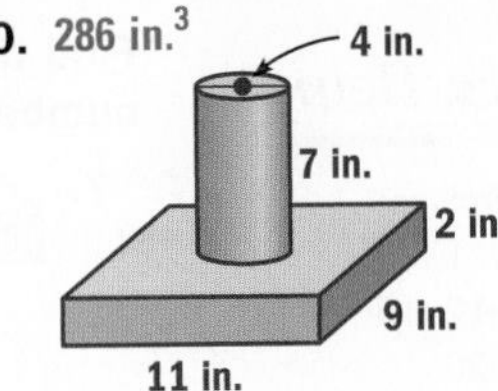

21c. ***Sample answer:*** **Doubling the radius quadruples the volume. Doubling the height doubles the volume. Doubling both the radius and the height multiplies the volume by a factor of 8.**

21. The radius of a cylinder is 3 units, and the height is 4 units.

a. What is the volume of the cylinder? **36π cubic units**

b. What is the volume when the radius is doubled? when the height is doubled? when both the radius and height are doubled? **144π cubic units, 72π cubic units, 288π cubic units**

c. Compare For each cylinder in part (b), compare its volume to the volume of the cylinder in part (a). What do you notice in each case?

22. Salsa You made 10 quarts of salsa. You are putting the salsa in jars with a diameter of 3 inches and a height of 5.5 inches. How many full jars of salsa will you have? (Use the fact that 1 $in.^3 \approx 0.017$ qt.) **15 jars**

Review *Help*

For help with units of capacity, see p. 791.

C **23. Challenge** Copy the regular hexagonal prism shown. A base of the prism can be divided into 6 equilateral triangles. The height of each equilateral triangle is $2\sqrt{3}$. Find the base area. Then find the volume of the prism.

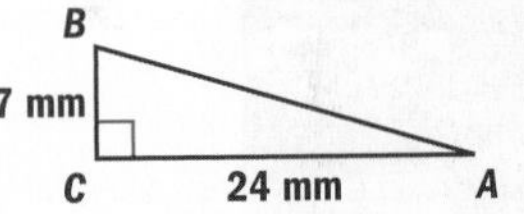

See margin for art; $24\sqrt{3} \approx 41.6$ square units; $288\sqrt{3} \approx 498.8$ cubic units.

Mixed Review

Determine whether the triangle with the given side lengths is a right triangle. *(Lesson 9.3)*

24. 8, 11, 14 **no**

25. 8, 15, 17 **yes**

26. 2, 4.8, 5.2 **yes**

27. For $\triangle ABC$, find tan A and tan B. *(Lesson 9.7)* **$\tan A = \frac{7}{24}$, $\tan B = \frac{24}{7}$**

B, 7 mm, C, 24 mm, A

Find the surface area of the pyramid or cone. Round to the nearest whole number. *(Lesson 10.6)*

28. 225 m^2

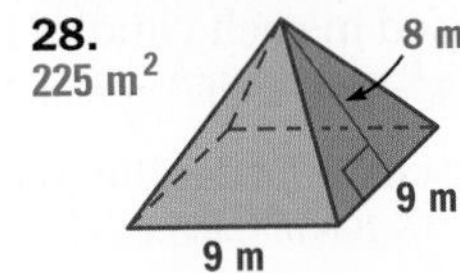

29. 144 $in.^2$

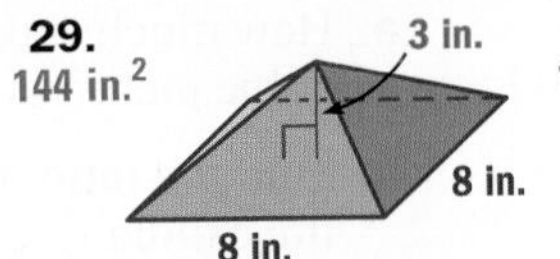

30. 163 $in.^2$

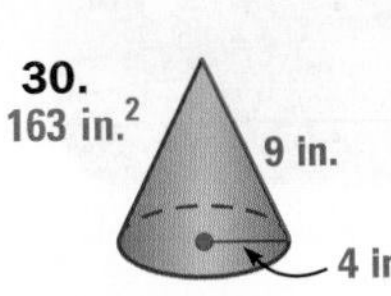

Standardized Test Practice

31. Multiple Choice What is the volume of a rectangular prism with a length of 16 inches, a height of 4 inches, and a width of 12 inches? **B**

A. 48 $in.^3$ **B.** 768 $in.^3$ **C.** 1810 $in.^3$ **D.** 2413 $in.^3$

32. Multiple Choice What is the approximate volume of a cylinder with a diameter of 18 meters and a height of 3 meters? **H**

F. 54 m^3 **G.** 243 m^3 **H.** 763 m^3 **I.** 3054 m^3

10.7 Surface Area and Volume

Goal Use a spreadsheet to compare the surface areas and volumes of solids.

Example

Efficient packaging uses the least amount of material for the greatest volume. Compare the ratios of volume to surface area of the rectangular prisms below. Which prism is a more efficient package?

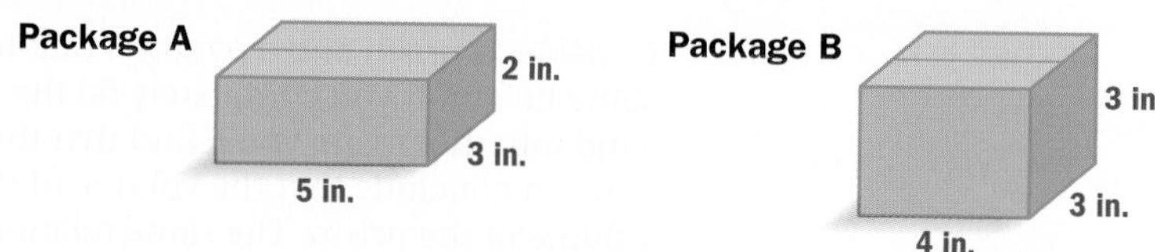

Use a spreadsheet to compare the ratios of volume to surface area. The prism with the greater ratio is the more efficient package.

1 Label columns for length, width, height, surface area, volume, and ratio in row 1. Enter the dimensions of package A and the formulas for surface area, volume, and ratio in row 2 as shown.

	A	B	C	D	E	F
1	*l*	*w*	*h*	Surface area	Volume	Ratio
2	5	3	2	=2*A2*B2+2*A2*C2+2*B2*C2	=A2*B2*C2	=E2/D2

Tech Help

Each cell in a spreadsheet is referred to by its column letter and row number. A2 refers to the cell in column A, row 2.

2 Enter the dimensions of package B in row 3. Use the *Fill down* feature to calculate the surface area, volume, and ratio of the second prism.

	A	B	C	D	E	F
1	*l*	*w*	*h*	Surface area	Volume	Ratio
2	5	3	2	62	30	0.48
3	4	3	3	66	36	0.55

Because 0.55 > 0.48, package B is more efficient than package A.

Draw Conclusions

1. **Compare** Find the ratio of volume to surface area for a cube that is 5 inches long, 5 inches wide, and 5 inches high. Is the cube more efficient or less efficient than the packages in the example above? **about 0.83; more efficient**
2. **Critical Thinking** A product is packaged in cylinders. Package A has a radius of 2 inches and a height of 6 inches. Package B has a radius of 3 inches and a height of 4 inches. Which package is more efficient? **package B**

NCTM CURRICULUM STANDARDS
Standard 2: Analyze situations using algebraic symbols
Standard 6: Build knowledge through problem solving

1 PLAN

Learn the Method

- Students will use a spreadsheet to compare the surface areas and volumes of solids.
- Students can use the spreadsheet to confirm their calculations in the examples and exercises in Lesson 10.7.

Grouping

Students should work individually.

2 TEACH

Discussion

As students are working, you may wish to ask them: "What does A2 × B2 represent?" **the area of the base** "How can you verify that the spreadsheet is correct?" ***Sample answer:* Enter some dimensions for a prism whose surface area and volume you had already calculated, and check to see if the results match.**

Extra Examples

Example The dimensions of package C are length 6 inches, width 2.5 inches, and height 2.5 inches. How does its packaging efficiency relate to those of packages A and B? **With a ratio of 0.52, package C is not as efficient as package B, but it is more efficient than package A.**

3 CLOSE

Assessment

1. Which cylinder is more efficient: cylinder A with radius 1 and height 8 or cylinder B with radius 2 and height 4? **cylinder B**

1 PLAN

Skill Check

Find the area of the circle with the given radius. Round to the nearest whole number.

1. 2 m — 13 m^2

2. 8 m — 201 m^2

Find the area of the rectangle with the given dimensions.

3. width: 3 ft, length: 4 ft — 12 ft^2

4. width: 10 ft, length: 12 ft — 120 ft^2

Lesson Objective

Find the volumes of pyramids and cones.

Pacing

Suggested Number of Days

Basic Course: 1 day

Average Course: 1 day

Advanced Course: 1 day

Block: 0.5 block with 10.7

Teaching Resources

For a complete list of Teaching Resources, see page 508B.

Transparency

Warm-Up Exercises for this lesson are available on a transparency.

2 TEACH

Motivating the Lesson

Bring modeling clay to class and have students make two identical cubes from the clay. Then have them remove clay from one cube to leave a pyramid. Students can then reshape the removed clay into a prism with the same base area as the cube but with two thirds of its height.

LESSON **10.8**

Volumes *of* Pyramids *and* Cones

Review Vocabulary
volume, p. 789

BEFORE	*Now*	WHY?
You found the volumes of prisms and cylinders.	You'll find the volumes of pyramids and cones.	So you can find the volume of a composter, as in Ex. 15.

Consider a prism and a pyramid that have the same base area and the same height. If you completely fill the pyramid with sand and pour the sand into the prism, you'll find that the sand fills one third of the prism. You can conclude that the volume of the pyramid is one third of the volume of the prism. The same relationship holds for a cylinder and a cone with the same base area and the same height.

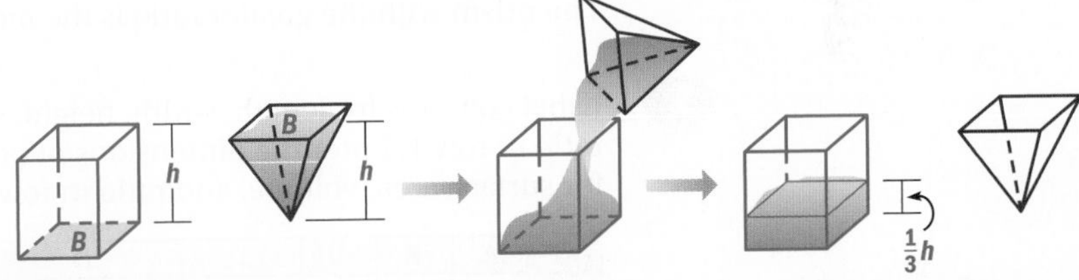

Study *Strategy*

Unlike the formula for the surface area of a pyramid, the formula for the volume of a pyramid can also be used for pyramids whose bases are not regular.

Volume of a Pyramid or a Cone

Words The volume V of a pyramid or a cone is one third of the product of the base area B and the height h.

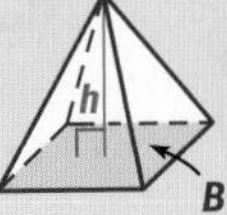

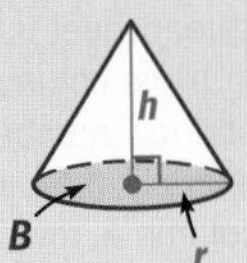

Algebra 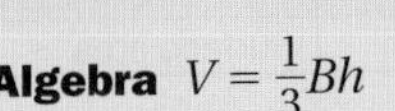 $V = \frac{1}{3}Bh$

Example 1 ***Finding the Volume of a Pyramid***

The base of a pyramid is a square. The side length of the square is 24 feet. The height of the pyramid is 9 feet. Find the volume of the pyramid.

$V = \frac{1}{3}Bh$ — **Write formula for volume of a pyramid.**

$= \frac{1}{3}(24^2)(9)$ — **Substitute 24^2 for B and 9 for h.**

$= 1728$ — **Simplify.**

Answer The volume of the pyramid is 1728 cubic feet.

NCTM CURRICULUM STANDARDS

Standard 3: Analyze properties of 3-D shapes

Standard 4: Apply proper formulas to find measures

Standard 6: Solve problems in math and other contexts

Example 2 *Finding the Volume of a Cone*

Find the volume of the cone shown. Round to the nearest cubic millimeter.

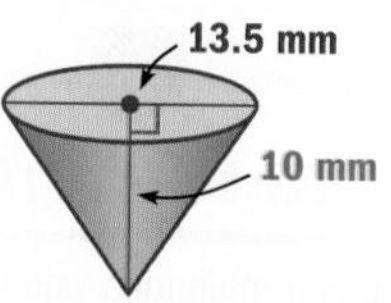

The radius is one half of the diameter, so $r = 6.75$.

$V = \frac{1}{3}\pi r^2 h$	**Write formula for volume of a cone.**
$= \frac{1}{3}\pi(6.75)^2(10)$	**Substitute 6.75 for *r* and 10 for *h*.**
≈ 477.1	**Evaluate. Use a calculator.**

Answer The volume of the cone is about 477 cubic millimeters.

Example 3 *Finding the Volume of a Solid*

Silos The grain silo shown is composed of a cylinder and a cone. Find the volume of the silo to the nearest cubic foot.

Solution

1) Find the volume of the cylindrical section. The radius is one half of the diameter, so $r = 9$.

$V = \pi r^2 h$	**Write formula for volume of a cylinder.**
$= \pi(9)^2(29) = 2349\pi$	**Substitute values. Then simplify.**

2) Find the volume of the conical section.

$V = \frac{1}{3}\pi r^2 h$	**Write formula for volume of a cone.**
$= \frac{1}{3}\pi(9)^2(7) = 189\pi$	**Substitute 9 for *r* and 7 for *h*. Then simplify.**

3) Find the sum of the volumes.

$2349\pi + 189\pi = 2538\pi \approx 7973.4$

Answer The volume of the silo is about 7973 cubic feet.

In the Real World

Silos Suppose you have planted 360 acres of corn on your family farm and expect to produce about 140 bushels of shelled corn per acre. A bushel is a unit of volume equal to about 1.25 cubic feet. How many silos, each the size of the one in Example 3, would it take to store your entire crop? **8 silos**

✔ *Checkpoint*

Find the volume of the pyramid or cone. Round to the nearest whole number.

1. 653 cm^3

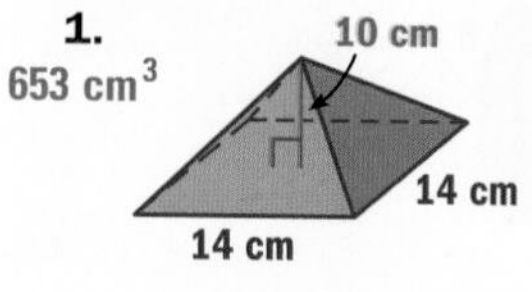

2. 115 m^3

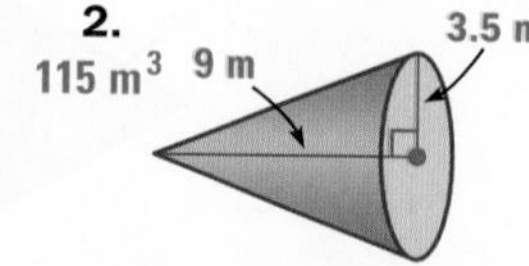

3. 480 ft^3

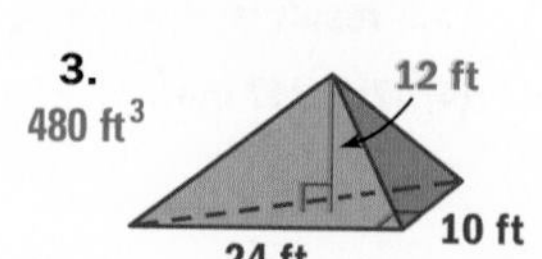

TIPS *for* NEW TEACHERS

Students may be overwhelmed by the number of formulas in this chapter. Encourage them to keep their notebooks up to date and to organize the formulas in an orderly fashion. On page 560, a summary chart is provided which can be used to verify that they have included all of the formulas. See Tips for New Teachers in the *Chapter 10 Resource Book*.

Extra Examples

Example 1 The base of a pyramid is a square. The side length of the square is 12 inches. The height of the pyramid is 5 inches. Find the volume of the pyramid. **240 in.^{3}**

Example 2 Find the volume of a cone with radius 5 centimeters and height 15 centimeters. Round to the nearest cubic centimeter. **393 cm^3**

Example 3 Find the volume of the solid. **2640 in.^{3}**

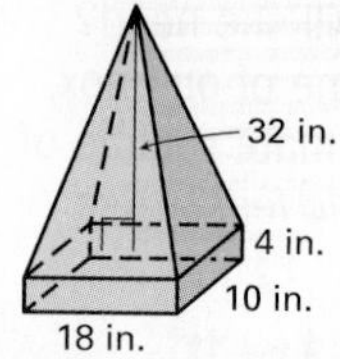

Common Error

In Checkpoint Exercise 3, watch for students who either fail to notice that the base is not a square, or who are unable to find the volume of the pyramid because it has a triangular base.

Reading Strategy

As students review the summary chart, suggest that they focus on one solid at a time while covering the other three formulas with their hand.

Concept Check

How do you find the volume of a pyramid with a base area of 30 square inches and a height of 10 inches? **Multiply $\frac{1}{3}$ times the base area times the height, or $\frac{1}{3} \cdot 30 \cdot 10$, which is 100 cubic inches.**

Daily Puzzler

Dakota is building a store display for a boxed set of DVDs. Each box is a cube 8 inches on a side. Dakota plans to build a pyramid with 1 box on the top layer, 4 boxes on the second layer, 9 boxes on the third layer, 16 boxes on the fourth layer, and so on. She wants to make the pyramid 8 feet high. How many layers will there be in her pyramid? How many boxes will she need? Based on the volume of one box, what is the approximate volume of the pyramid in *cubic feet*? (Use $1 \text{ ft}^3 = 1728 \text{ in.}^3$) **12 layers; 650 boxes; about 193 ft^3**

Note Worthy

Use a main idea web like the one on p. 510 to summarize the concepts of surface area and volume in your notes.

Summary: Surface Areas and Volumes of Solids

Prism

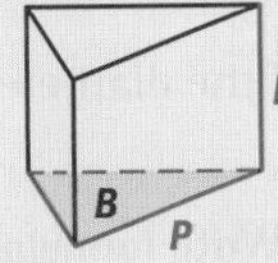

Surface Area
$S = 2B + Ph$

Volume
$V = Bh$

Cylinder

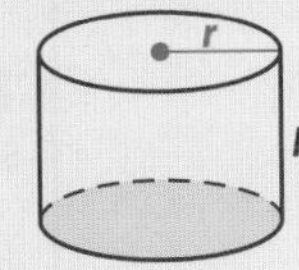

Surface Area
$S = 2\pi r^2 + 2\pi rh$

Volume
$V = \pi r^2 h$

Pyramid

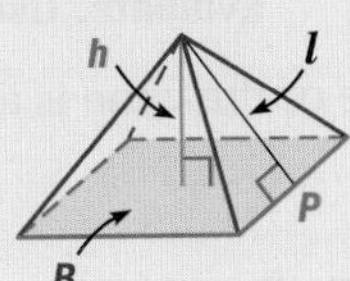

Surface Area
$S = B + \frac{1}{2}Pl$

Volume
$V = \frac{1}{3}Bh$

Cone

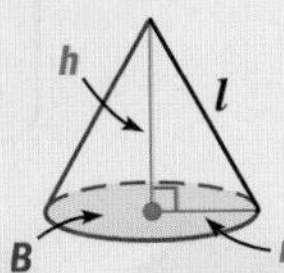

Surface Area
$S = \pi r^2 + \pi rl$

Volume
$V = \frac{1}{3}\pi r^2 h$

10.8 Exercises

More Practice, p. 812

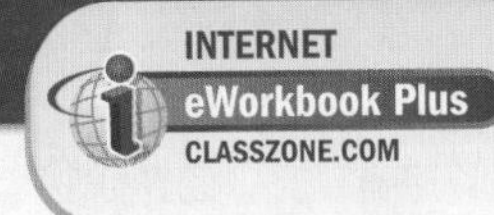

Guided Practice

Vocabulary Check

1. What formula can you use to find the volume of a pyramid? **$V = \frac{1}{3}Bh$**
2. How is the formula for the volume of a cone related to the formula for the volume of a cylinder? **The volume of a cone is one third the volume of a cylinder with the same radius and height.**

Skill Check **Find the volume of the pyramid or cone. Round to the nearest whole number.**

3. **20 in.^{3}**

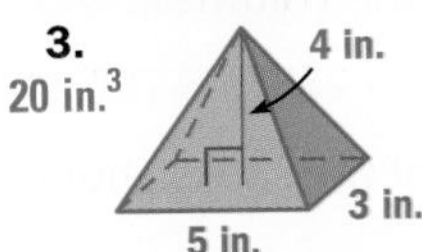

4. **1885 in.^{3}**

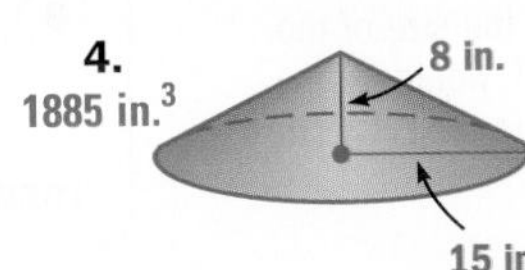

5. **Error Analysis** Describe and correct the error in finding the volume of the solid shown.

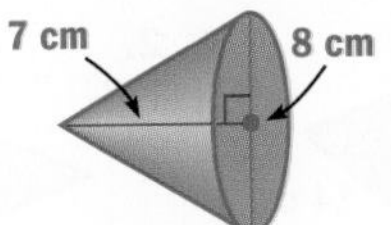

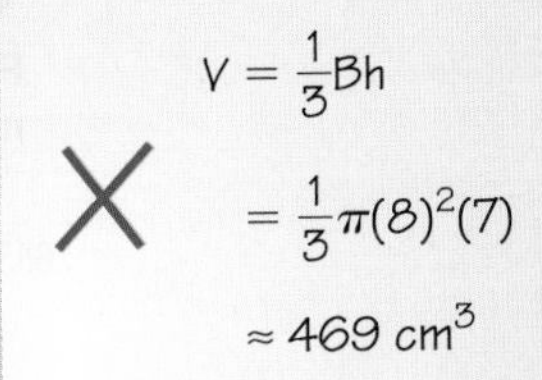

5. In finding the area of the base, the diameter was used instead of the radius. The correct result is $\frac{1}{3}\pi(4)^2(7) \approx 117 \text{ cm}^3$.

Practice and Problem Solving

Homework Help

Example	Exercises
1	6–8
2	9–12, 16
3	13–15

Online Resources
CLASSZONE.COM
- More Examples
- eTutorial Plus

Find the volume of the pyramid or cone. Round to the nearest whole number.

A **6.** 60 cm^3 **7.** 24 yd^3 **8.** 12 in.^3

9. 564 yd^3 **10.** $10{,}472\text{ m}^3$ **11.** 268 ft^3

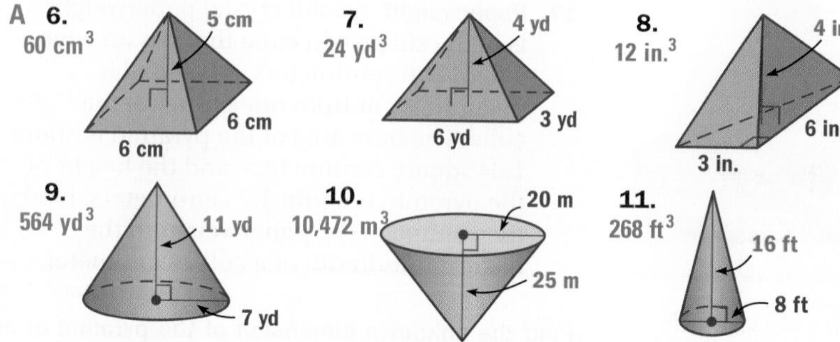

12. The diameter of a cone-shaped paper cup is 8 centimeters, and the height is 10 centimeters. The radius of another cone-shaped paper cup is 3 centimeters, and the height is 11 centimeters.

a. Predict Which cup do you predict will hold more water? Explain your prediction. The first cup. *Sample answer:* I think the radius is more important to the volume than the height.

b. Compare Find the volume of each paper cup to the nearest tenth of a cubic centimeter. Which cup holds more water? 167.6 cm^3; 103.7 cm^3; the first cup

The solid in Exercise 13 is composed of a cylinder and a cone. The solid in Exercise 14 is a cube with a cone-shaped hole in it. Find the volume of the solid. Round your answer to the nearest whole number.

13. 283 cm^3

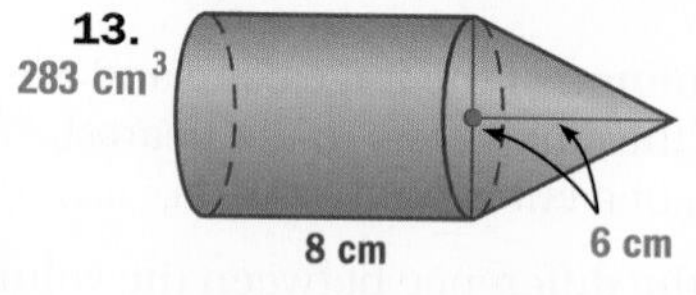

14. 670 yd^3

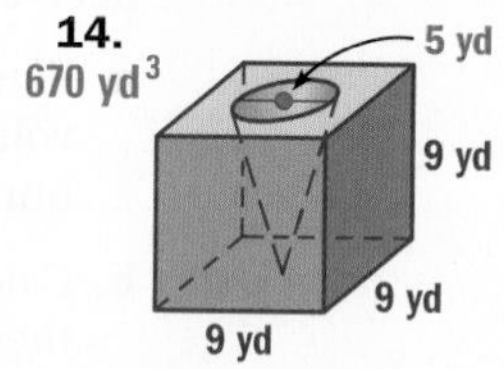

15d. Radius. *Sample answer:* In the volume formulas for cylinders and cones, the radius is squared, but the height is not.

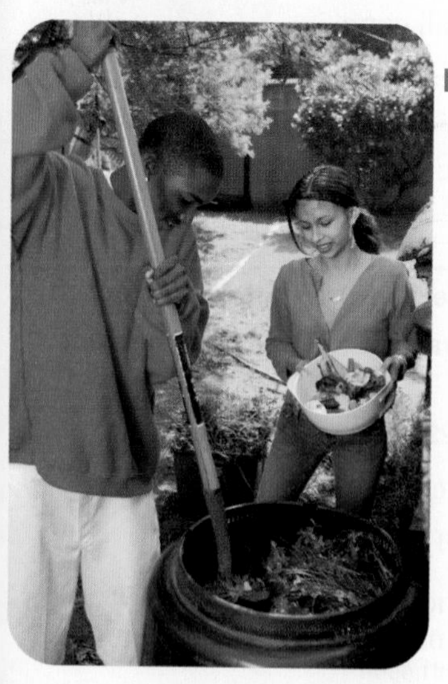

B **15. Extended Problem Solving** The composter shown turns biodegradable materials like leaves and grass into fertilizer.

a. Find the volume of the cylindrical portion of the composter in terms of π. $15{,}200\pi\text{ in.}^3$

b. Find the volume of the top cone and the volume of the bottom cone in terms of π. top: $1333\frac{1}{3}\pi\text{ in.}^3$, bottom: $1066\frac{2}{3}\pi\text{ in.}^3$

c. Apply Find the total volume of the composter to the nearest cubic inch. $48{,}590\text{ in.}^3$

d. *Writing* When assembling the composter, you can adjust the height and the radius. Which has the greater effect on the volume of the composter, changing the *height* or changing the *radius*? Explain. See margin.

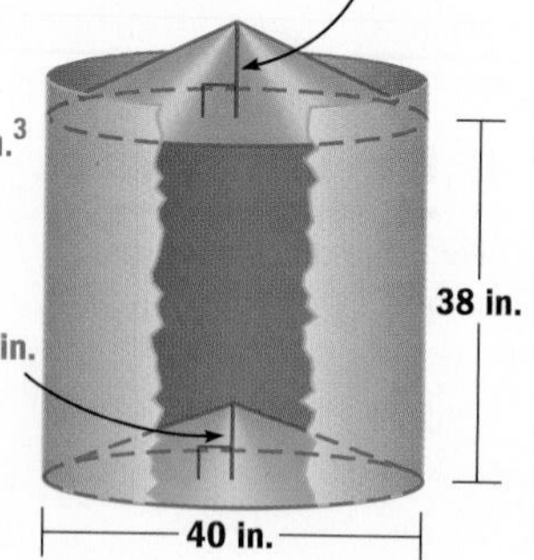

3 APPLY

ASSIGNMENT GUIDE

Basic Course
Day 1: pp. 561–563 Exs. 6–14, 18, 19, 21–23, 25–33

Average Course
Day 1: pp. 561–563 Exs. 7–10, 12–23, 25–34

Advanced Course
Day 1: pp. 561–563 Exs. 7–9, 12–25*, 28–34

Block
pp. 561–563 Exs. 8–10, 12–23, 25–34 (with 10.7)

EXTRA PRACTICE
- Student Edition, p. 812
- Chapter 10 Resource Book, pp. 68–70
- Test and Practice Generator

TRANSPARENCY

Even-numbered answers are available on transparencies.

HOMEWORK CHECK

When you review students' homework for this lesson, go over the following exercises to check understanding of key concepts.
Basic: 6, 8, 9, 12, 13
Average: 7, 10, 12, 13, 14
Advanced: 8, 12, 13, 14, 16

COMMON ERROR

In Exercise 11, watch for students who fail to notice that the 8-foot dimension is the diameter of the base and use it as the radius in the volume formula.

TEACHING TIP

In Exercise 20, students may feel overwhelmed by the amount of work needed to solve this problem. You might wish to assign this exercise as a group exercise so students can either work together or split up the work.

16. **Compare** The radius of cone A is 3 inches, and its height is 7 inches. The radius of cone B is 4 inches, and its height is 6 inches. Create a spreadsheet to compare the volumes and surface areas of the cones. Which cone has a greater ratio of volume to surface area? **See margin.**

17. **Paperweight** A solid crystal paperweight is in the shape of a cube that has an edge length of 6 centimeters. A triangular pyramid is cut from one corner of the cube. The base area of the pyramid is about 7.64 square centimeters, and the height of the pyramid is about 1.7 centimeters. Find the volume of the paperweight to the nearest hundredth of a cubic centimeter. **211.67 cm^3**

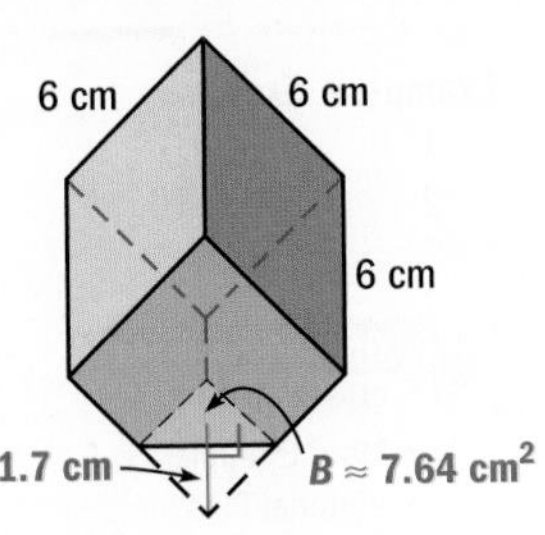

16. cone A: $S \approx 100.05$ in.^{2}, $V \approx 65.97$ in.^{3}; cone B: $S \approx 140.88$ in.^{2}, $V \approx 100.53$ in.^{3}; cone B

Find the unknown dimension of the pyramid or cone. Round to the nearest whole number.

18. $V = 12.4\pi$ ft^3 **7 ft**

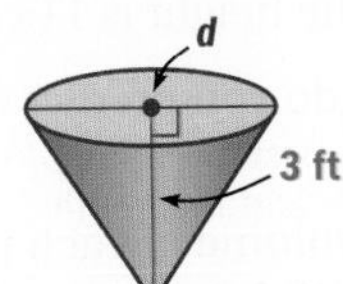

19. $V = 1452$ mm^3 **36 mm**

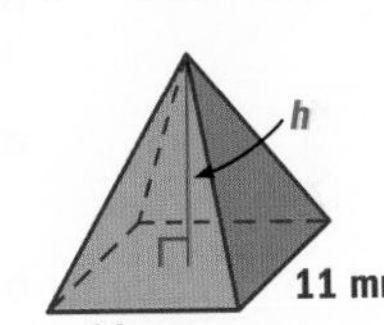

20. **Funnel** Most funnels consist of a cone whose tip is removed. The cone is then attached to a narrow cylinder. In the diagram below, the small cone inside the cylinder shows the portion of the large cone that has been cut off.

a. Find the volume of the large cone and the volume of the small cone to the nearest hundredth of a cubic inch. **20.94 in.^{3}, 0.17 in.^{3}**

b. Calculate the difference between the volume of the large cone and the volume of the small cone. **about 20.77 in.^{3}**

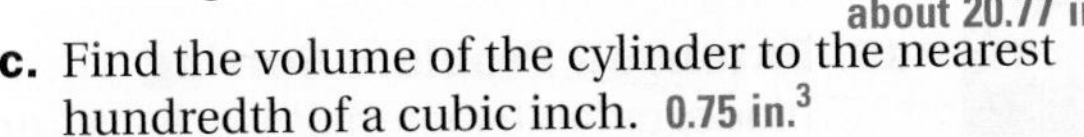

c. Find the volume of the cylinder to the nearest hundredth of a cubic inch. **0.75 in.^{3}**

d. Use your results from part (b) and part (c) to find the total volume of the funnel to the nearest tenth of a cubic inch. **21.5 in.^{3}**

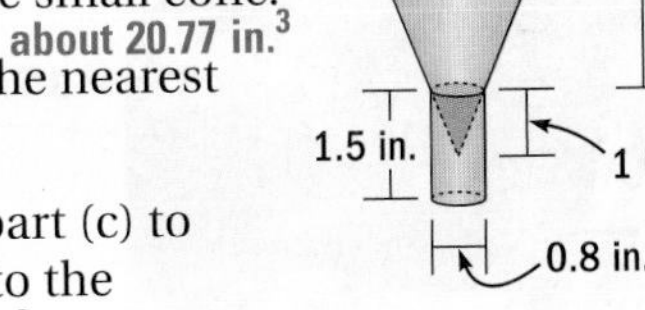

Spheres In Exercises 21–23, find the volume V of the spherical object using the formula $V = \frac{4}{3}\pi r^3$, where r is the radius. Round to the nearest cubic unit.

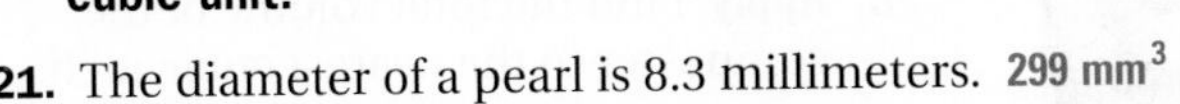

Review *Help*

For help with spheres, see p. 548.

21. The diameter of a pearl is 8.3 millimeters. **299 mm^3**

22. The radius of a women's basketball is 4.5 inches. **382 in.^{3}**

23. The diameter of an inflatable beach ball is 3 feet. **14 ft^3**

C **24.** **Challenge** Find the volume of the cone shown. Round to the nearest hundredth of a cubic meter. **601.48 m^3**

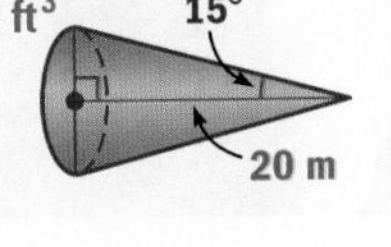

Mixed Review

25. Given that $\triangle ABC \sim \triangle ADE$, find DE. *(Lesson 6.5)* **4 ft**

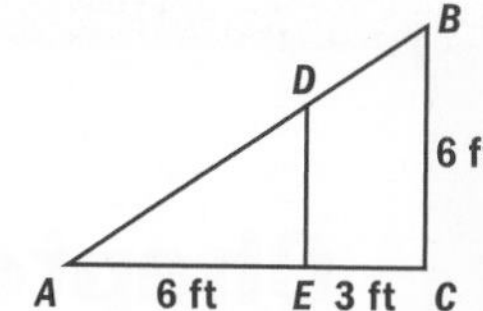

26. slope: −5, *y*-intercept: 2
27. slope: $\frac{3}{2}$, *y*-intercept: −1
28. slope: 0, *y*-intercept: 13
29. slope: 0, *y*-intercept: $\frac{9}{2}$, or $4\frac{1}{2}$

Algebra Basics Identify the slope and *y*-intercept of the line. *(Lesson 8.5)*

26. $y = -5x + 2$
27. $y = \frac{3}{2}x - 1$
28. $y = 13$
29. $2y = 9$

30. What is the volume of the cylinder shown? Round to the nearest cubic inch. *(Lesson 10.7)* **1728 in.^{3}**

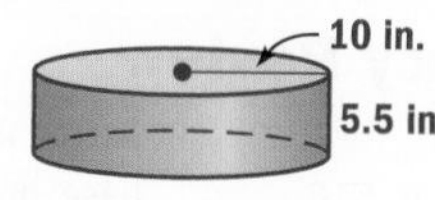

31. What is the volume of a rectangular prism with a length of 8 inches, a width of 4 inches, and a height of 4 inches? *(Lesson 10.7)* **128 in.^{3}**

Standardized Test Practice

32. **Multiple Choice** A cone has a height of 3 feet. The radius of the base is 4 feet. What is the approximate volume of the cone? **C**

 A. 12.6 ft^3 **B.** 37.7 ft^3 **C.** 50.3 ft^3 **D.** 150.8 ft^3

33. **Multiple Choice** The base area of a triangular pyramid is 12 square centimeters. The height of the pyramid is 5 centimeters. What is the volume of the pyramid? **F**

 F. 20 cm^3 **G.** 30 cm^3 **H.** 60 cm^3 **I.** 120 cm^3

34. **Short Response** A marble monument is in the shape of a square pyramid. The side length of the base is 5 feet. The height of the pyramid is 5 feet. Find the volume of the pyramid. Use the fact that 1 cubic foot of marble weighs about 170 pounds. To the nearest pound, how much does the monument weigh? Explain your reasoning.

 $41\frac{2}{3}$ ft^3; 7083 lb. *Sample answer:* The weight is $41\frac{2}{3}$ ft^3 • $\frac{170 \text{ lb}}{\text{ft}^3}$ = 7083 pounds.

Thinking About Sculptures

Each sculpture below is a prism, a cylinder, a cone, or a pyramid. Find the volume of each sculpture in terms of *a* and *b*. Then compare the coefficients of the five volume expressions to order the volumes from least to greatest. The letters associated with the sculptures will spell out the last name of the artist who created a famous statue called *The Thinker.* **RODIN**

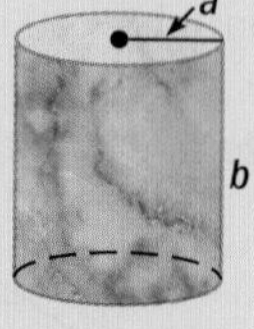

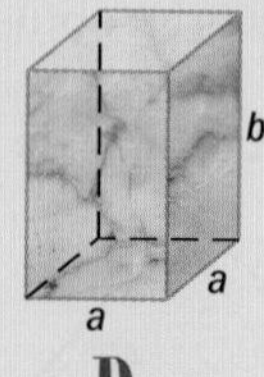

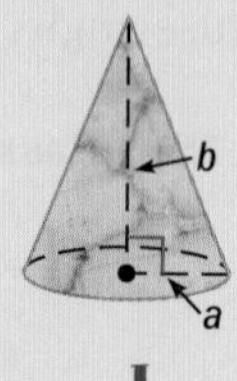

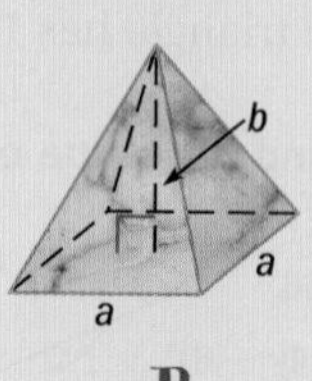

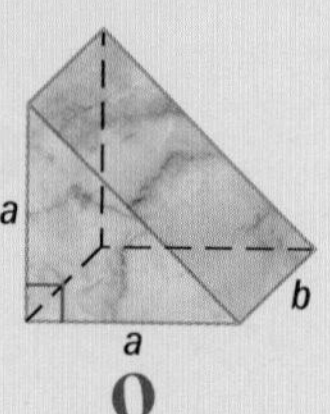

4 ASSESS

Assessment Resources

For more assessment resources, see:
- Assessment Book
- Test and Practice Generator

Mini-Quiz

1. Find the volume of a pyramid with height 8 meters and a rectangular base that is 3 meters wide and 4 meters long. **32 m^3**
2. Find the volume of a cone with radius 9 yards and height 12 yards. Round to the nearest cubic yard. **1018 yd^3**
3. **Challenge** If you could reshape the volume within your classroom and make it into a pyramid with the same base area as the room, what would be the height of your pyramid? **3 times the height of the room**

5 FOLLOW-UP

Diagnosis/Remediation

- Study Guide in Chapter 10 Resource Book, pp. 71-72
- eTutorial Plus Online
- Extra Practice, p. 812
- Lesson Practice in Chapter 10 Resource Book, pp. 68-70

English Learner Support

- Spanish Study Guide
- Multi-Language Visual Glossary
- Chapter Audio Summaries CDs

Challenge

- Challenge Practice in Chapter 10 Resource Book, p. 73
- Teacher's Edition, p. 508F

Additional Resources

The following resources are available to help review the materials in Lessons 10.5–10.8.

Chapter 10 Resource Book

- Lesson Practice
- Study Guide

Assessment Book

- Chapter 10 Quiz 2

Technology

- Test and Practice Generator
- eTutorial CD-ROM

Internet

- Classzone
- eWorkbook Plus Online
- eTutorial Plus Online

English Learner Support

- Spanish Study Guide
- Multi-Language Visual Glossary
- Chapter Audio Summaries CDs

2. ***Sample answer:*** **In a convex polygon, any segment you can draw with endpoints inside the polygon lies entirely inside the polygon, while in a concave polygon this is not true. A concave polygon has at least two sides that appear to "cave in," or for which the angle formed by the sides points into the interior of the polygon. In a convex polygon, all the angles formed by adjacent sides point away from the polygon's interior.**
3. ***Sample answer:*** **Form a net by imagining cutting along the edges of the prism so that you can flatten it out. Then find the area of the polygons in the net, which represent the faces of the prism, and add the areas.**

CHAPTER 10

Chapter Review

Vocabulary Review

polygon, p. 516
regular polygon, p. 516
convex, concave p. 516
polygons: pentagon, hexagon, heptagon, octagon, p. 516
quadrilaterals: trapezoid, parallelogram, rhombus, p. 517
diagonal of a polygon, p. 518
base, height of a parallelogram, p. 521
bases, height of a trapezoid, p. 522
circles: center, radius, diameter, p. 528
circumference, p. 528
surface area, p. 538
net, p. 538
lateral face of a prism, p. 539
lateral area of a prism, p. 539
lateral surface of a cylinder, p. 540
lateral area of a cylinder, p. 540
height, slant height of a pyramid, p. 544
regular pyramid, p. 544
height, slant height of a cone, p. 546

1. When finding the area of a trapezoid, what lengths do you need to know? **the lengths of the bases and the height**
2. Describe convex and concave polygons. Tell how they are alike and how they are different. **See margin.**
3. Describe how to find the surface area of a prism using a net. **See margin.**
4. Tell how the slant height of a cone is different from the height of the cone. **See margin.**

10.1 Triangles

Examples on pp. 511–512

▶ ***Goal***

Find unknown angle measures and classify triangles.

Example **Find the value of *y*. Then classify the triangle by its angle measures.**

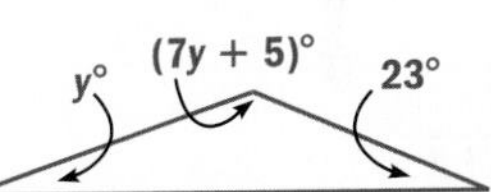

$23° + (7y + 5)° + y° = 180°$	**Sum of angle measures is 180°.**
$8y + 28 = 180$	**Combine like terms.**
$8y = 152$	**Subtract 28 from each side.**
$y = 19$	**Divide each side by 8.**
$7y + 5 = 7(19) + 5 = 138$	**Find unknown angle measure.**

The triangle has 1 obtuse angle, so it is an obtuse triangle.

 **Find the value of *y*. Then classify the triangle by its angle measures.**

5. 66°, $(4y - 6)°$, $y°$ **24; right**
6. $(\frac{1}{2}y - 3)°$, $y°$, 48° **90; right**
7. 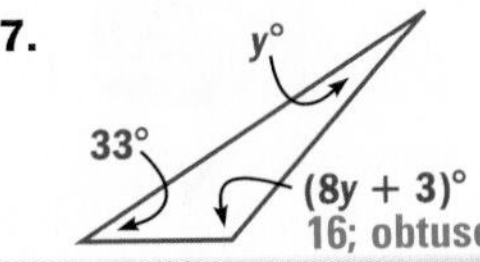

16; obtuse

The following resources are available to help review the materials in this chapter.

Chapter 10 Resource Book
- Chapter Review Games and Activities, p. 74
- Cumulative Practice, Chs. 1–10

English/Spanish Chapter Reviews and Tests

Chapter Audio Summaries CDs

eTutorial CD-ROM

eWorkbook Plus Online

eTutorial Plus Online

4. ***Sample answer:*** **The height of a cone is the distance between its vertex and the center of its base, while the slant height is the distance from the vertex to any point on the edge of the base.**

10.2 Polygons and Quadrilaterals

Examples on pp. 516–518

Goal

Classify polygons and quadrilaterals.

Example **Tell whether the figure is a polygon. If it is, classify it. If not, explain why.**

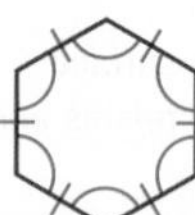

The figure is a 6-sided polygon. So, it is a hexagon. It is convex and regular.

✓ Tell whether the figure is a polygon. If it is, classify it. If not, explain why.

8.

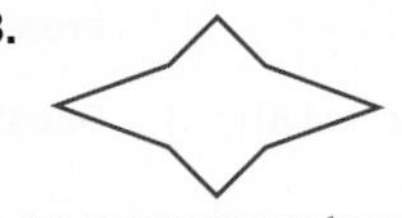

yes; concave octagon

9.

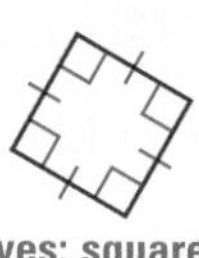

yes; square

10.

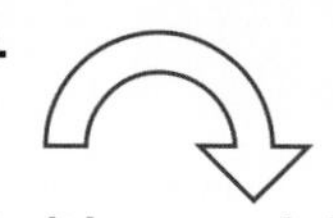

No; it has curved sides.

10.3 Areas of Parallelograms and Trapezoids

Examples on pp. 521–523

Goal

Find the areas of parallelograms and trapezoids.

Example **Find the area of the trapezoid.**

$A = \frac{1}{2}(b_1 + b_2)h$ **Write formula for area of a trapezoid.**

$= \frac{1}{2}(3 + 7)(1.5)$ **Substitute 3 for b_1, 7 for b_2, and 1.5 for h.**

$= 7.5 \text{ cm}^2$ **Simplify.**

✓ Find the area of the parallelogram or trapezoid.

11. 6 in.^2

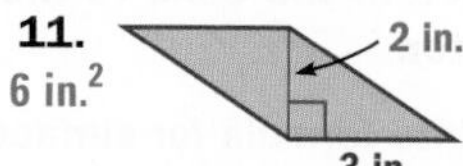

12. 250 ft^2

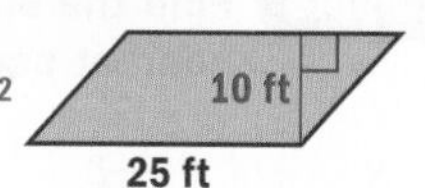

13. 10 m^2

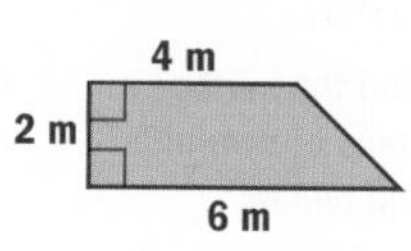

10.4 Circumference and Area of a Circle

Examples on pp. 528–530

Goal

Find circumferences and areas of circles.

Example **Find the area of the circle to the nearest square inch. Use 3.14 for π.**

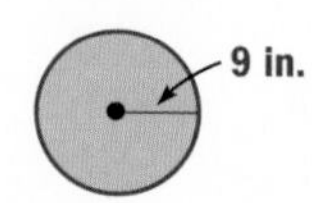

$A = \pi r^2$ **Write the area of a circle.**

$\approx 3.14(9)^2$ **Substitute 3.14 for π and 9 for r.**

$\approx 254 \text{ in.}^2$ **Simplify.**

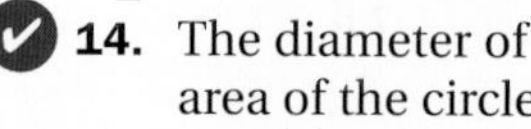

✓ 14. The diameter of a circle is 16 inches. Find the circumference and area of the circle. Round your answers to the nearest whole number. 50 in., 201 in.^2

10.5 Surface Areas of Prisms and Cylinders

Examples on pp. 538–540

Goal

Find the surface areas of prisms and cylinders.

Example **Find the surface area of the prism.**

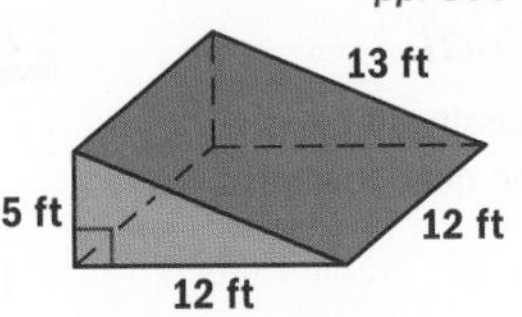

The bases of the prism are right triangles.

$S = 2B + Ph$	**Write formula for surface area of a prism.**
$= 2\left(\frac{1}{2} \cdot 5 \cdot 12\right) + (5 + 12 + 13)(12)$	**Substitute values.**
$= 420 \text{ ft}^2$	**Simplify.**

Find the surface area of the prism or cylinder to the nearest square inch.

15.

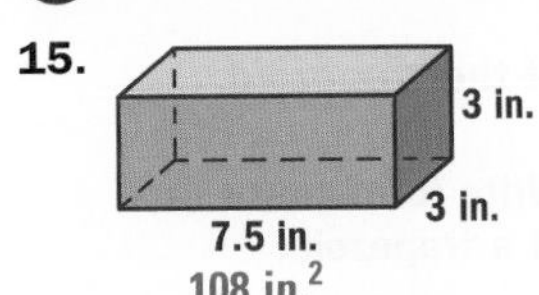

108 in.^2

16. 4 in., 5 in., 5 in., 4 in., 6 in.

88 in.^2

17.

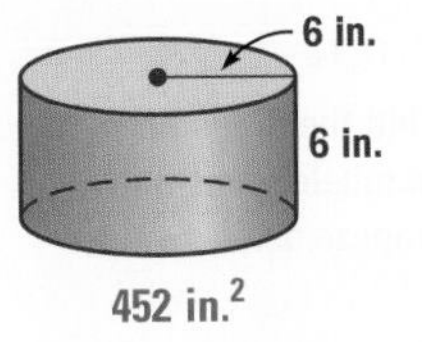

452 in.^2

10.6 Surface Areas of Pyramids and Cones

Examples on pp. 544–546

Goal

Find the surface areas of pyramids and cones.

Example **Find the surface area of the cone to the nearest square meter.**

$S = \pi r^2 + \pi rl$	**Write formula for surface area of a cone.**
$= \pi(9)^2 + \pi(9)(41)$	**Substitute 9 for r and 41 for l.**
$\approx 1414 \text{ m}^2$	**Evaluate. Use a calculator.**

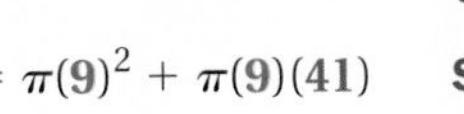

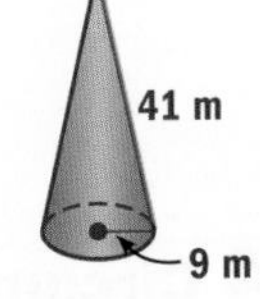

Find the surface area of the regular pyramid or cone to the nearest square foot.

18. 163 ft^2

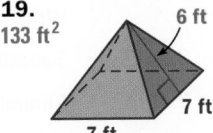

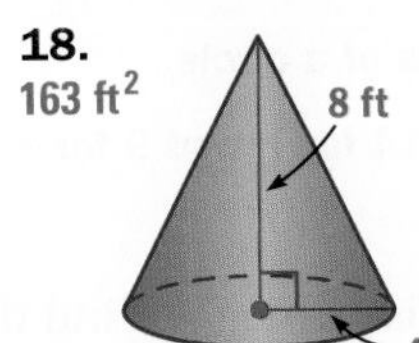

19. 133 ft^2

6 ft, 7 ft, 7 ft

20. 115 ft^2

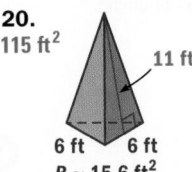

11 ft, 6 ft, 6 ft, $B \approx 15.6 \text{ ft}^2$

10.7 Volumes of Prisms and Cylinders

Examples on pp. 552–554

Goal

Find the volumes of prisms and cylinders.

Example **Find the volume of the cylinder to the nearest cubic centimeter.**

The radius is one half of the diameter, so $r = 10$.

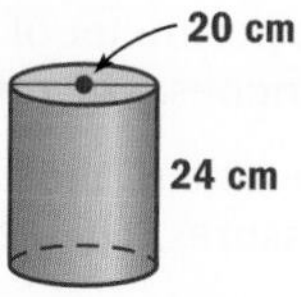

20 cm

24 cm

$V = \pi r^2 h$	**Write formula for volume of a cylinder.**
$= \pi(10)^2(24)$	**Substitute 10 for *r* and 24 for *h*.**
$= 2400\pi$	**Simplify.**
≈ 7539.8	**Evaluate. Use a calculator.**

The volume of the cylinder is about 7540 cubic centimeters.

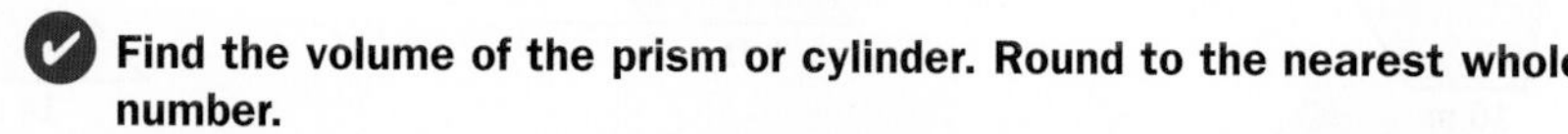

Find the volume of the prism or cylinder. Round to the nearest whole number.

21.

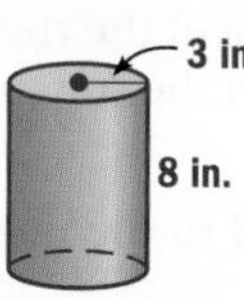

$226\ \text{in.}^3$

22.

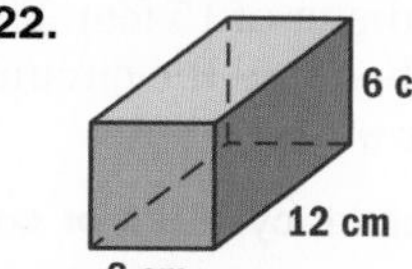

$432\ \text{cm}^3$

23.

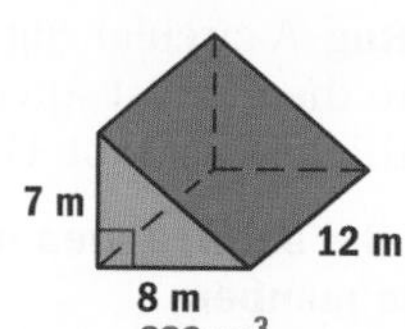

$336\ \text{m}^3$

10.8 Volumes of Pyramids and Cones

Examples on pp. 558–559

Goal

Find the volumes of pyramids and cones.

Example **Find the volume of the pyramid.**

$V = \frac{1}{3}Bh$	**Write formula for volume of a pyramid.**
$= \frac{1}{3}(5^2)(3)$	**Substitute 5^2 for *B* (because the base is a square) and 3 for *h*.**
$= 25$	**Simplify.**

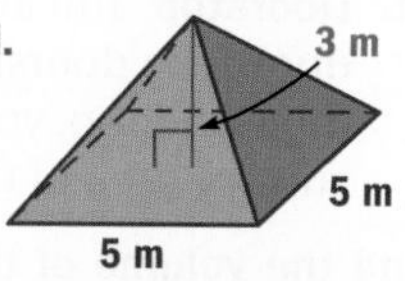

The volume of the pyramid is 25 cubic meters.

Find the volume of the pyramid or cone. Round to the nearest whole number.

24. $96\ \text{ft}^3$

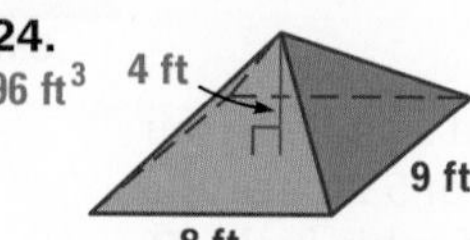

25.

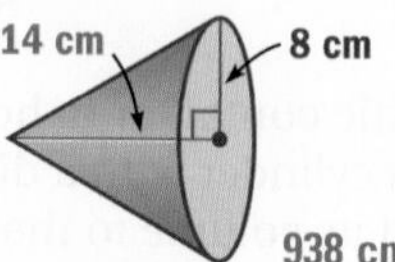

$938\ \text{cm}^3$

26.

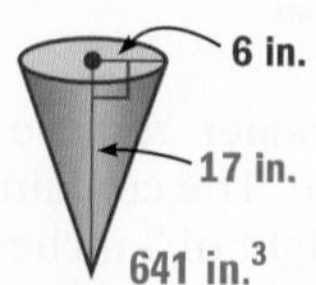

$641\ \text{in.}^3$

ADDITIONAL RESOURCES

Assessment Book

- Chapter Test (3 levels), pp. 120–125
- Standardized Chapter Test, p. 126
- Alternative Assessment, pp. 127–128

Test and Practice Generator

CHAPTER 10

Chapter Test

1. The perimeter of a triangle is 53 inches. The length of one side is 15 inches. The other two sides are congruent. Find their lengths. 19 in.

2. The ratio of the angle measures of a triangle is 1 : 3 : 8. Find the angle measures. Then classify the triangle by its angle measures. 15°, 45°, 120°; obtuse

3. Tell whether the figure shown is a polygon. If it is, classify it. If not, explain why. yes; rhombus

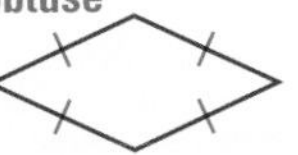

Find the area of the parallelogram or trapezoid.

4. 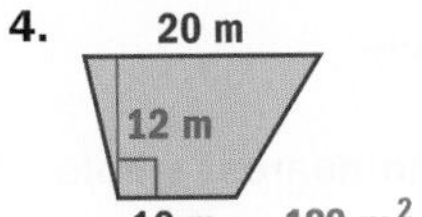

180 m^2

5. 40 ft^2 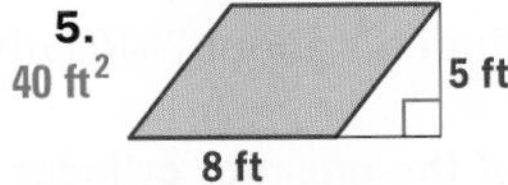

6. 72 m^2 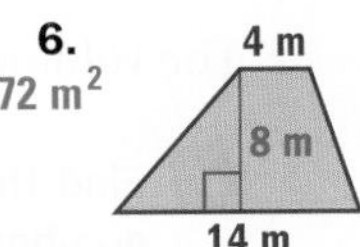

7. **Rug** A circular rug has a diameter of 15 feet. Find the area of the rug to the nearest square foot. Then find the circumference of the rug to the nearest foot. Use 3.14 for π. 177 ft^2; 47 ft

Find the surface area of the pyramid, cylinder, or cone. Round to the nearest whole number.

8. 1307 mm^2 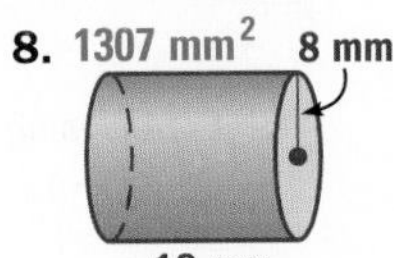

9. 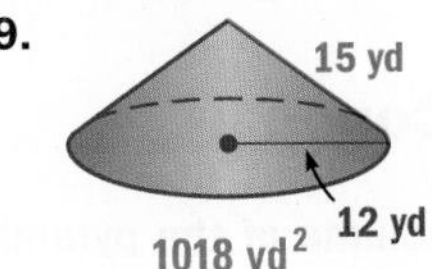

1018 yd^2

10. 340 ft^2 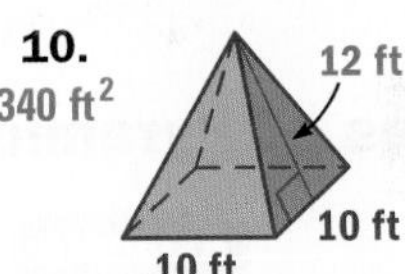

11. **Doorstop** You are decorating a doorstop to use for your bedroom door. The doorstop is a triangular prism. In order to buy paint for the doorstop, you need to know its surface area. What is the surface area of the doorstop? 180 cm^2

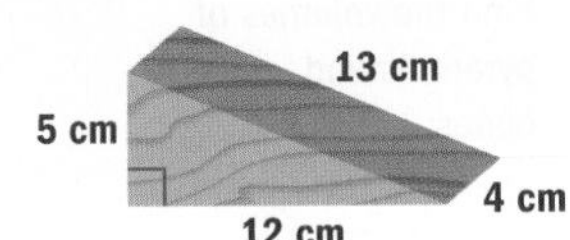

Find the volume of the prism, pyramid, or cone. Round to the nearest whole number.

12. 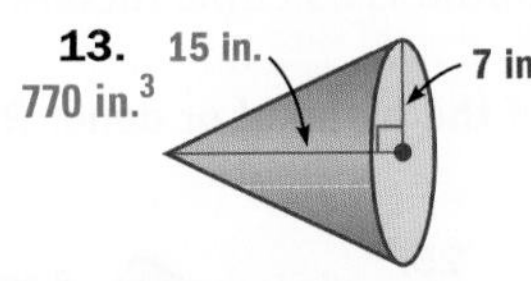

45 cm^3

13. 770 in.^3

14. 128 ft^3 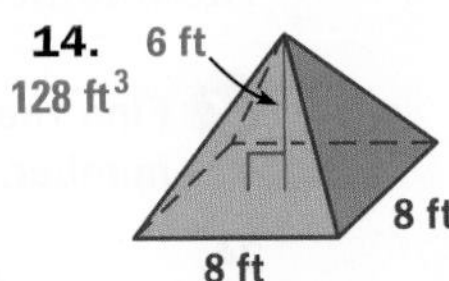

15. **Container** You use a plastic container to hold pasta salad for your lunch. The container is a cylinder with a diameter of 5 inches and a height of 3 inches. Find its volume to the nearest cubic inch. 59 in.^3

Additional Resources

Assessment Book

- Standardized Chapter Test, p. 126

Test and Practice Generator

Chapter Standardized Test

Test-Taking Strategy If you finish the test and have time, look over your work and check as many of your answers as possible.

1. The perimeter of a triangle is 20 feet. The length of a side is 4 feet. The lengths of the other two sides are equal. What are the lengths of the other two sides? B

A. 4 ft **B.** 8 ft **C.** 10 ft **D.** 16 ft

2. What is the value of x in the quadrilateral shown? G

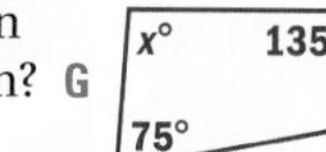

F. 11 **G.** 94

H. 105 **I.** 285

3. The height of a parallelogram is 20 meters. The base is one fifth of the height. What is the area of the parallelogram? C

A. 4 m^2 **B.** 40 m^2 **C.** 80 m^2 **D.** 100 m^2

4. What is the approximate circumference of the circle? H

3.9 ft

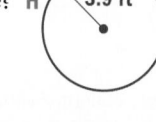

F. 6 ft **G.** 12 ft

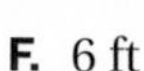

H. 24 ft **I.** 48 ft

5. The area of a circle is 64 square inches. What is its approximate diameter? B

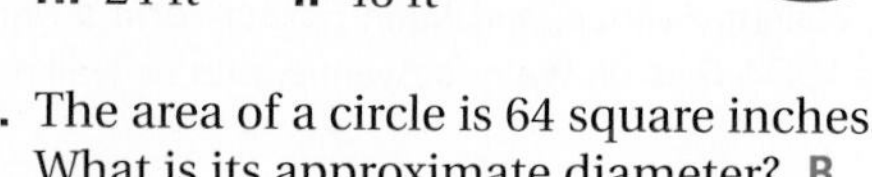

A. 5 in. **B.** 9 in. **C.** 10 in. **D.** 20 in.

6. What is the surface area of the rectangular prism? I

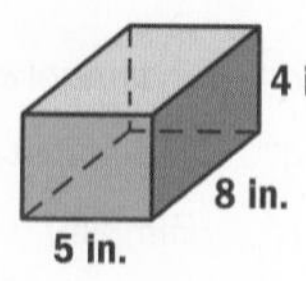

F. 92 in.^{2} **G.** 104 in.^{2}

H. 160 in.^{2} **I.** 184 in.^{2}

7. What is the volume of the prism in Exercise 6? C

A. 92 in.^{3} **B.** 104 in.^{3}

C. 160 in.^{3} **D.** 184 in.^{3}

8. The height of a cylinder is 10 inches, and the diameter of the base is 6 inches. What is the approximate volume of the cylinder? G

F. 117 in.^{3} **G.** 283 in.^{3}

H. 360 in.^{3} **I.** 1130 in.^{3}

9. What is the approximate volume of the cone? B

A. 9.42 mm^3

B. 18.84 mm^3

C. 28.26 mm^3

D. 56.52 mm^3

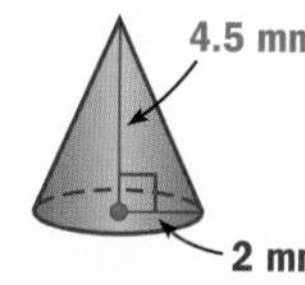

10. Short Response A base of a trapezoid is 16 feet, and the height is 3 feet. The area of the trapezoid is 36 square feet. Find the length of the other base. 8 ft

11. Extended Response The lampshade shown below can be described as part of a cone.

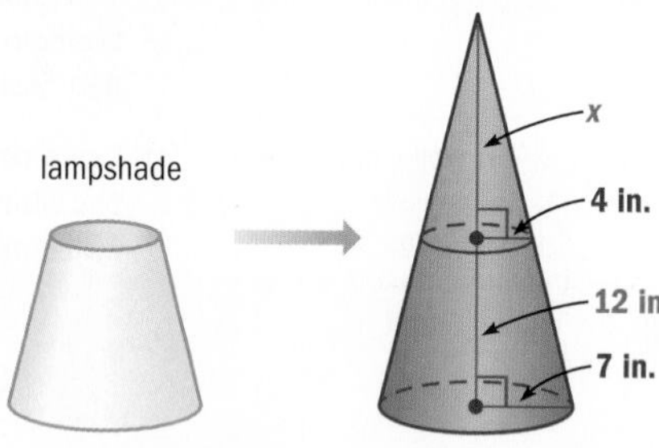

a. The right triangles shown with the cone are similar. Find the value of x. Explain how you found your answer. See margin.

b. Find the lateral areas of the large and small cones to the nearest square inch. 635 in.^{2}, 207 in.^{2}

c. Find the lateral area of the lampshade. 428 in.^{2}

11a. 16. *Sample answer:* Since the right triangles are similar, I wrote the proportion $\frac{x}{4} = \frac{x + 12}{7}$. Solving for x gives $x = 16$.

TEST-TAKING TIP

Encourage students to read the questions thoroughly. Remind them that some information in context-based questions may not be needed when solving the problem.

COMMON ERROR

Students will sometimes make assumptions based on the appearance of a figure that is provided with a question. Emphasize that properties of a figure, such as having a right angle or the congruence of two angles, must be specifically indicated on a figure.

Unit 3 Chapters 8–10 Building Test-Taking Skills

Strategies for Answering Context-Based Multiple Choice Questions

Some of the information you need to solve a context-based multiple choice question may appear in a table, a diagram, or a graph.

Problem 1 Tim and Karen leave school at different times but agree to meet each other at the theater. Tim takes the path in blue, while Karen takes the path in red. How much farther does Tim walk than Karen?

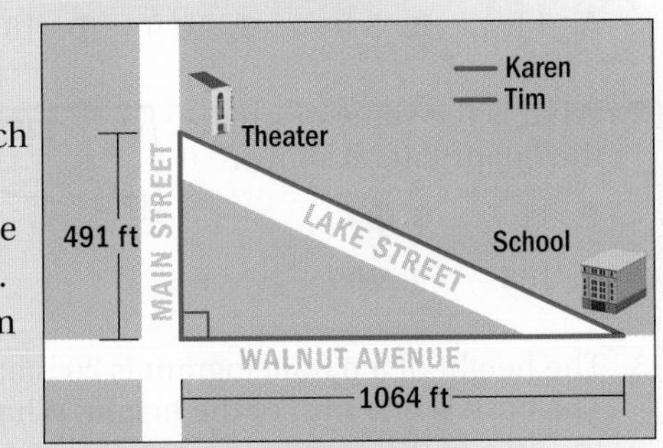

A. 108 ft **B.** 383 ft

C. 681 ft **D.** 1172 ft

Solution

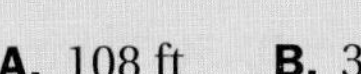

Read the problem carefully. Decide what information you are given and how you can use it to solve the problem.

1) You know that Lake Street, Walnut Avenue, and Main Street form a right triangle. You know Tim walks 1064 feet on Walnut Avenue, and he walks 491 feet on Main Street.

The path that Tim walks and the path that Karen walks form a right triangle. You can use the Pythagorean theorem to find the distance that Karen walks.

2) Let a represent the distance Tim walks on Walnut Avenue. Let b represent the distance Tim walks on Main Street. Let c represent the distance Karen walks on Lake Street.

$a^2 + b^2 = c^2$ Pythagorean theorem

$1064^2 + 491^2 = c^2$ Substitute for a and b.

$1{,}373{,}177 = c^2$ Simplify.

$1172 \approx c$ Take positive square root of each side.

Subtract to find how much farther Tim walks than Karen.

3) Distance Tim walks − Distance Karen walks $\approx (1064 + 491) - 1172 = 383$

Tim walks about 383 feet farther than Karen.

The correct answer is B.

Problem 2 The graph of which equation is perpendicular to the line shown?

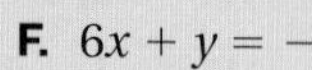

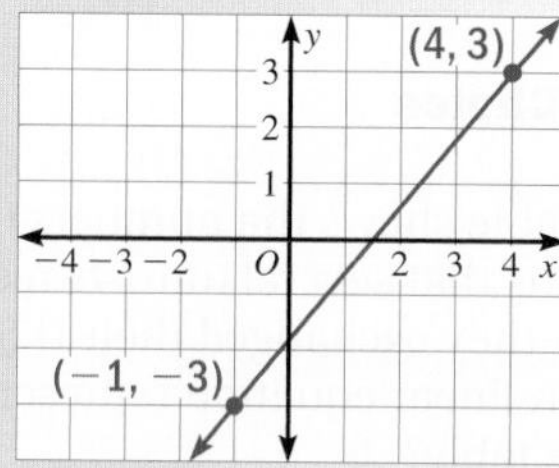

F. $6x + y = -7$

G. $y = \frac{6}{5}x + 4$

H. $5x + 6y = 24$

I. $6x - 5y = -15$

Solution

Use the given points to find the slope of the line.

1) Use the graph to find the slope of the line.

$$m = \frac{\text{rise}}{\text{run}} = \frac{\text{difference of y-coordinates}}{\text{difference of x-coordinates}} = \frac{3 - (-3)}{4 - (-1)} = \frac{6}{5}$$

Find the slope of a line perpendicular to the given line.

2) A line perpendicular to the line shown would have a slope that is the negative reciprocal of the slope found in Step 1. The negative reciprocal of $\frac{6}{5}$ is $-\frac{5}{6}$.

Eliminate answer choices that have the incorrect slope.

3) Find the answer choice with a slope of $-\frac{5}{6}$ by writing each equation in slope-intercept form.

F. $6x + y = -7$ → $y = -6x - 7$ ✗

G. $y = \frac{6}{5}x + 4$ ✗

H. $5x + 6y = 24$ → $y = -\frac{5}{6}x + 4$ ✓

The equation $5x + 6y = 24$ has a slope of $-\frac{5}{6}$.

The correct answer is H.

Checkpoint

Watch Out

Be sure that you know what question you are asked to answer. Some answers may be intended to distract you.

1. What is the surface area of the prism shown? C

A. 190 cm^2 **B.** 305 cm^2
C. 330 cm^2 **D.** 350 cm^2

2. What is the volume of the prism in Exercise 1? I

F. 190 cm^3 **G.** 305 cm^3 **H.** 330 cm^3 **I.** 350 cm^3

10. Let p represent the number of packages of wrapping paper sold and c represent the number of boxes of greeting cards sold; $5p + 2c = 1546$. *Sample answer:* 100 packages of wrapping paper and 523 boxes of cards, 150 packages of wrapping paper and 398 boxes of cards, 200 packages of wrapping paper and 273 boxes of cards

Unit 3 Chapters 8–10 Practicing Test-Taking Skills

Multiple Choice

1. The table shows the numbers of British pounds that several tourists received when they exchanged their U.S. dollars. Which linear equation represents the data in the table? C

Dollars, x	25	75	90	130
Pounds, y	15	45	54	78

A. $y = \frac{3}{5}x - 15$ B. $y = -\frac{5}{3}x$

C. $y = \frac{3}{5}x$ D. $y = \frac{5}{3}x$

2. The graph of which equation is shown? F

F. $y = -\frac{3}{2}x + 3$

G. $y = -\frac{2}{3}x + 2$

H. $y = \frac{3}{2}x - 3$

I. $y = \frac{2}{3}x + 3$

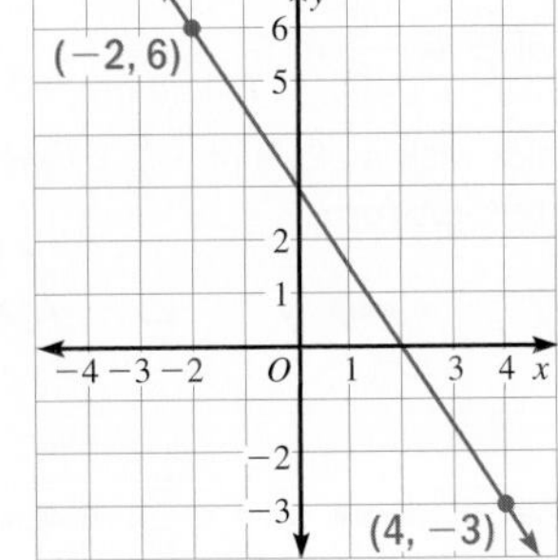

3. What is the distance between points C and D? C

A. $2\sqrt{2}$

B. 4

C. 10

D. 14

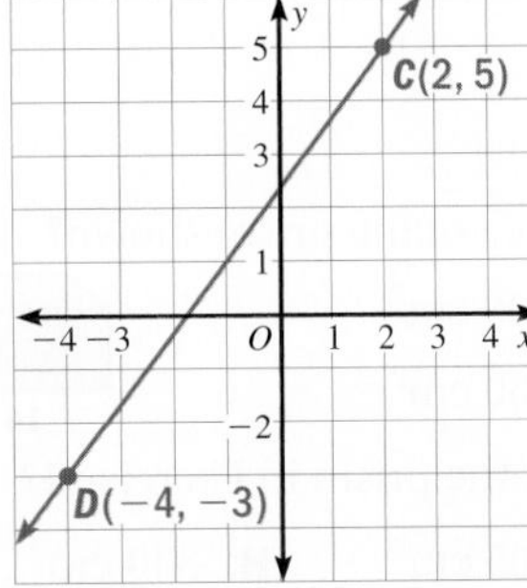

4. What is the midpoint of $\overline{CD}$ in Exercise 3? G

F. $(-2, -4)$ G. $(-1, 1)$

H. $(-1, -1)$ I. $(2, 4)$

5. What is the value of x? B

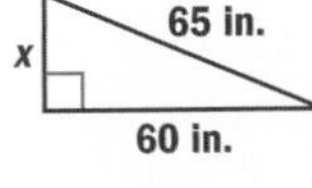

A. 5 in. B. 25 in.

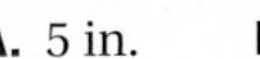

C. 88.5 in. D. 625 in.

6. The bases of a baseball diamond form a square. What is the distance between second base and home plate? H

F. $\sqrt{19}$ ft

G. $6\sqrt{5}$ ft

H. $90\sqrt{2}$ ft

I. $90\sqrt{3}$ ft

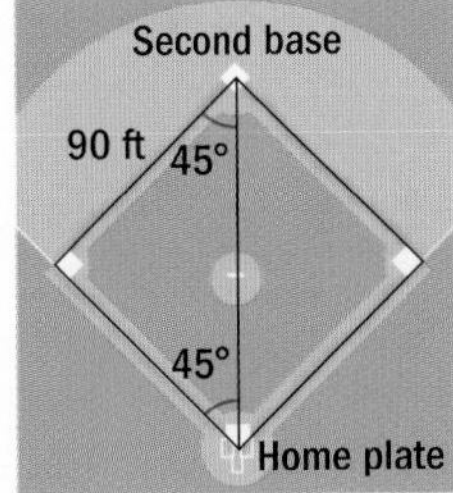

7. What is the approximate circumference of the circular pizza stone shown? A

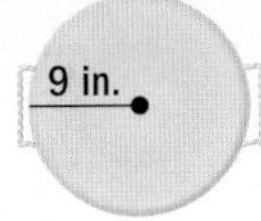

A. 57 in. B. 113 in.

C. 254 in. D. 1018 in.

8. What is the approximate area of the pizza stone in Exercise 7? H

F. 57 in.^{2} G. 113 in.^{2}

H. 254 in.^{2} I. 1018 in.^{2}

9. The tent shown has the shape of a triangular prism. What is the surface area of the tent? C

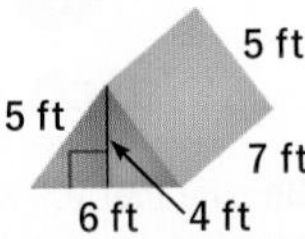

A. 28 ft^2 B. 140 ft^2

C. 136 ft^2 D. 160 ft^2

Short Response 10–12. See margin.

10. As a fundraiser, your class sells packages of wrapping paper for \$5 and boxes of greeting cards for \$2. Total sales from the fundraiser are \$1546. Write an equation describing the possible numbers of packages of wrapping paper and boxes of greeting cards that could have been sold. Then give three possible combinations of packages of wrapping paper and boxes of greeting cards that could have been sold.

11. A stained glass light fixture is in the shape of a square pyramid. Describe how you would find the area of the 4 triangular faces of the pyramid. Then find the combined area of these faces.

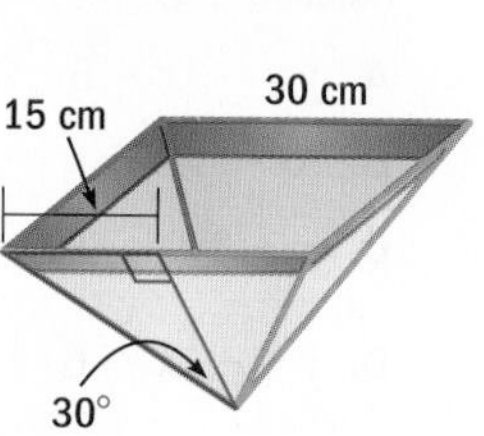

12. Plot the points $A(-2, 1)$, $B(-5, -3)$, $C(5, -3)$, and $D(2, 1)$ in a coordinate plane. Connect the points to form a trapezoid. Explain how you would find the perimeter and area of the trapezoid. Then find the perimeter and area.

13. Graph the linear inequality $y \le 2x + 3$. Name three ordered pairs that are solutions of the inequality. **See margin for art.** ***Sample answer:*** **(0, 3), (2, 0), (−3, −4)**

14. An enter sign is composed of a triangle, a rectangle, and two congruent parallelograms. Find the area of the sign. **104 in.^{2}**

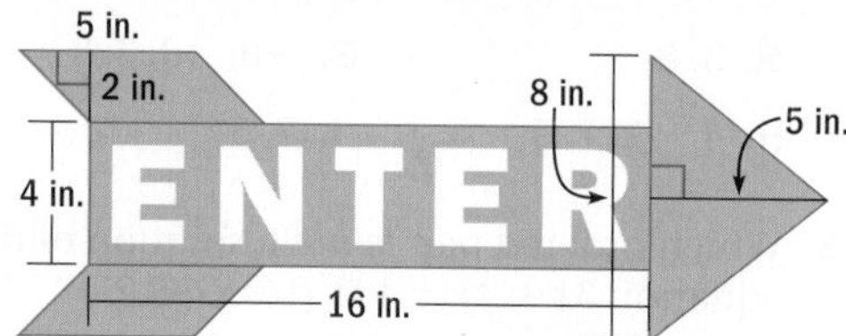

Extended Response

15. a. Write an equation of the line shown. $y = -\frac{3}{4}x + \frac{7}{4}$

b. Write an equation of a line that is parallel to the line shown and passes through the point $(-7, -6)$. $y = -\frac{3}{4}x - \frac{45}{4}$

c. Write an equation of a line that is perpendicular to the line shown and passes through the point $(-3, 4)$. $y = \frac{4}{3}x + 8$

d. Write an equation of a line that is perpendicular to the line shown and passes through the point $(5, -2)$. $y = \frac{4}{3}x - \frac{26}{3}$

e. Graph the lines in parts (a)–(d) in the same coordinate plane. Identify the polygon formed. Explain your reasoning. **See margin for art; rectangle.** ***Sample answer:*** **The lines forming adjacent sides are perpendicular, so each angle is a right angle.**

16. The diagram shows an escalator in the Louisville International Airport in Kentucky.

a. What is the measure of $\angle A$? **60°**

b. Use the sine ratio to find the length of $\overline{AC}$. **27.5 ft**

c. Use the cosine ratio to find the length of $\overline{BC}$. **about 47.6 ft**

d. Use the tangent ratio to verify the lengths of $\overline{AC}$ and $\overline{BC}$.

$\tan B = \frac{AC}{BC}$, so $\tan B \approx \frac{27.5}{47.6}$, or about 0.58; $\tan 30° \approx 0.58$, so the lengths are verified.

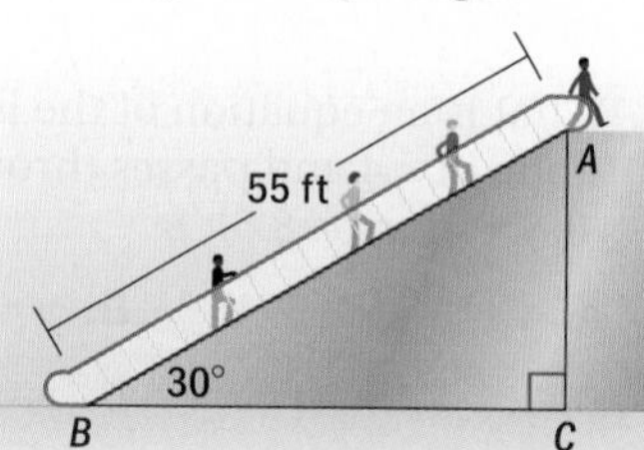

11. ***Sample answer:*** **In a 30°-60°-90° right triangle, the longer leg is $\sqrt{3}$ times the length of the shorter leg, so the longer leg, or the slant height, is $15\sqrt{3}$ centimeters. So the area of each face is $\frac{1}{2}(30)(15\sqrt{3}) = 225\sqrt{3}$ square centimeters, and the total area of the four faces is $4(225\sqrt{3}) = 900\sqrt{3}$ square centimeters.**

12.

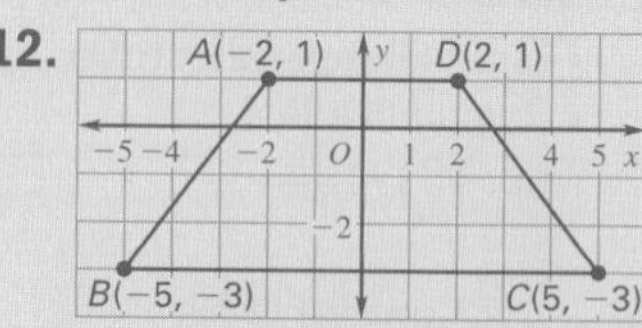

Sample answer: **To find the perimeter, first find the length of each side using the distance formula. The perimeter is 5 + 10 + 5 + 4 = 24 units. To find the area, recognize that the height of the trapezoid is the distance between the two bases or 4 units, so the area is $\frac{1}{2}(4)(4 + 10) = 28$ square units.**

13.

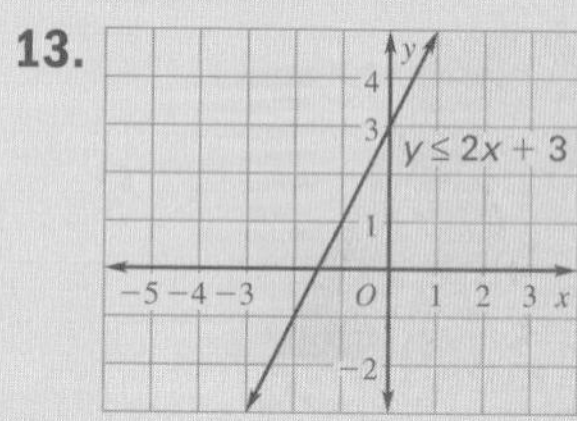

15e.

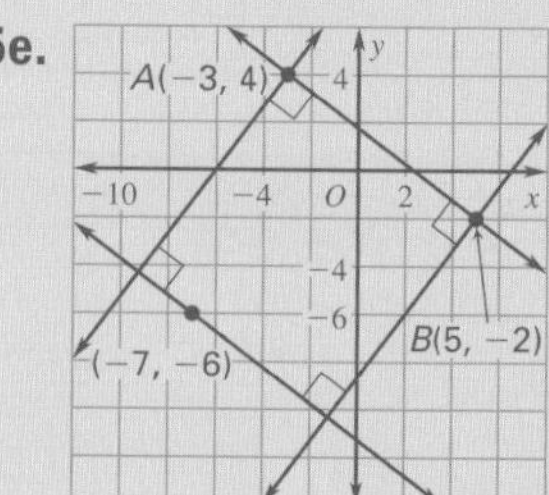

ADDITIONAL RESOURCES

The following resources are available to help review the materials in this unit:

Chapter Resource Books

- Chapter 8 CRB, Cumulative Practice, pp. 91–92
- Chapter 9 CRB, Cumulative Practice, pp. 80–81
- Chapter 10 CRB, Cumulative Practice, pp. 81–82

Assessment Book

- Unit Test, pp. 129–130
- Cumulative Test, pp. 131–134

11a.

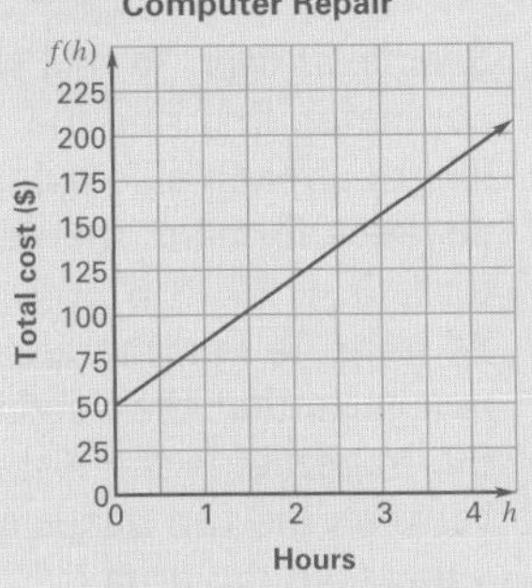

Unit 3 Practicing Test-Taking Skills

Chapters 8–10

Cumulative Practice for Chapters 8–10

Chapter 8

Multiple Choice In Exercises 1–9, choose the letter of the correct answer.

1. What is the domain of the relation $(-9, 4)$, $(-3, -2)$, $(3, 7)$, $(8, 5)$? *(Lesson 8.1)* **B**

A. 3, 8 **B.** $-9, -3, 3, 8$

C. $4, -2, 7, 5$ **D.** 7, 5

2. What is the range of the relation in Exercise 1? *(Lesson 8.1)* **H**

F. 3, 8 **G.** $-9, -3, 3, 8$

H. $4, -2, 7, 5$ **I.** 7, 5

3. Which ordered pair is *not* a solution of the equation $3x + 4y = 14$? *(Lesson 8.2)* **C**

A. $(-10, 11)$ **B.** $(2, 2)$

C. $(6, 8)$ **D.** $(10, -4)$

4. What is the y-intercept of the graph of $-6x - 3y = 18$? *(Lesson 8.3)* **F**

F. -6 **G.** -3 **H.** 3 **I.** 6

5. What is the x-intercept of the graph of the equation in Exercise 4? *(Lesson 8.3)* **B**

A. -6 **B.** -3 **C.** 3 **D.** 6

6. What is the slope of the line through the points $(6, -4)$ and $(9, 3)$? *(Lesson 8.4)* **I**

F. $-\frac{7}{3}$ **G.** $-\frac{3}{7}$ **H.** $\frac{3}{7}$ **I.** $\frac{7}{3}$

7. What is an equation of the line that has a slope of -4 and passes through the point $(0, 7)$? *(Lesson 8.6)* **B**

A. $y = -4x - 7$ **B.** $y = -4x + 7$

C. $y = 7x - 4$ **D.** $y = 7x + 4$

8. Which ordered pair is a solution of the linear system $x + 4y = 18$ and $-3x + 2y = 16$? *(Lesson 8.8)* **G**

F. $(-2, -5)$ **G.** $(-2, 5)$

H. $(2, 5)$ **I.** $(2, -5)$

9. The graph of which inequality is shown? *(Lesson 8.9)* **C**

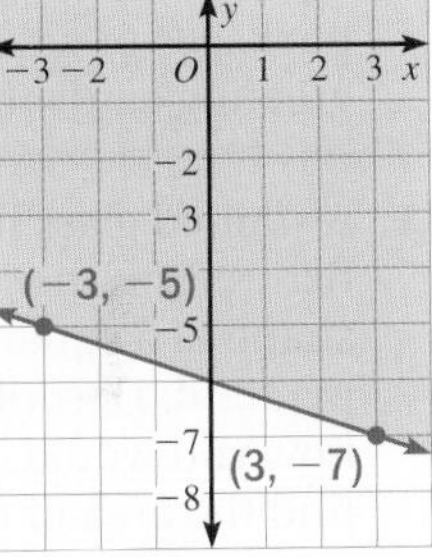

A. $y > -3x - 6$

B. $3x - y < 6$

C. $x + 3y \geq -18$

D. $y \leq -\frac{1}{3}x - 6$

10. Short Response Find the slope of a line perpendicular to the line $-5x + 2y = 16$. Then find an equation of a line that is perpendicular to the line $-5x + 2y = 16$ and passes through the point $(5, 7)$. *(Lesson 8.5)* $-\frac{2}{5}$; $y = -\frac{2}{5}x + 9$

11. Extended Response A computer repair shop charges a flat rate of \$50 plus \$35 per hour spent repairing each computer. *(Lesson 8.7)*

a. Let h be the number of hours spent repairing a computer. Use function notation to write an equation that gives the total charges for repairing a computer as a function of h. Graph the function. $f(h) = 35h + 50$; see margin for art.

b. How much will the repair shop charge if the shop does 2.5 hours of work? **\$137.50**

c. The repair shop charges \$172.50 to repair a computer. How many hours did the shop work on the computer? **3.5 h**

CHAPTER 10

Differentiating Instruction: Resource Materials

Differentiating Alternative Assessment

McDougal Littell *Pre-Algebra* offers teachers a wide variety of alternative assessment for all levels of students. Pictured here are facsimiles of the alternative assessment pages from the *Assessment Book*, and the various types of chapter projects available in the *Chapter 10 Resource Book.*

ASSESSMENT BOOK

The *Assessment Book* contains two pages of alternative assessment for each chapter in the textbook.

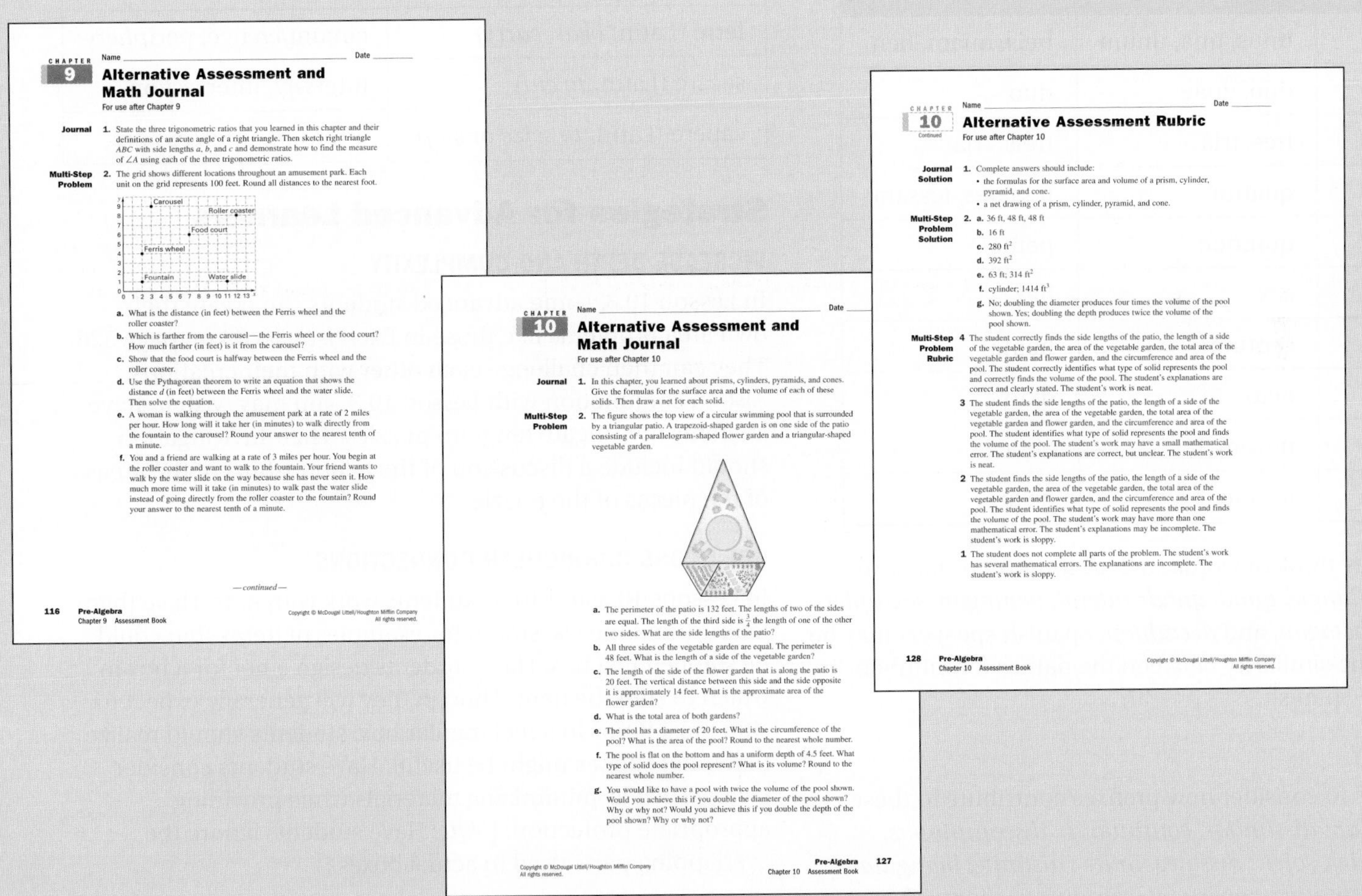

CHAPTER 9 Name ______ Date ______

Alternative Assessment and Math Journal

For use after Chapter 9

Journal 1. State the three trigonometric ratios that you learned in this chapter and their definitions of an acute angle of a right triangle. Then sketch right triangle ABC with side lengths a, b, and c and demonstrate how to find the measure of $\angle A$ using each of the three trigonometric ratios.

Multi-Step Problem 2. The grid shows different locations throughout an amusement park. Each unit on the grid represents 100 feet. Round all distances to the nearest foot.

a. What is the distance (in feet) between the Ferris wheel and the roller coaster?

b. Which is farther from the carousel—the Ferris wheel or the food court? How much farther (in feet) is it from the carousel?

c. Show that the food court is halfway between the Ferris wheel and the roller coaster.

d. Use the Pythagorean theorem to write an equation that shows the distance d (in feet) between the Ferris wheel and the water slide. Then solve the equation.

e. A woman is walking through the amusement park at a rate of 2 miles per hour. How long will it take her (in minutes) to walk directly from the fountain to the carousel? Round your answer to the nearest tenth of a minute.

f. You and a friend are walking at a rate of 3 miles per hour. You begin at the roller coaster and want to walk to the fountain. Your friend wants to walk by the water slide on the way because she has never seen it. How much more time will it take (in minutes) to walk past the water slide instead of going directly from the roller coaster to the fountain? Round your answer to the nearest tenth of a minute.

—continued—

116 **Pre-Algebra** Chapter 9 Assessment Book

Copyright © McDougal Littell/Houghton Mifflin Company All rights reserved.

CHAPTER 10 Name ______ Date ______

Alternative Assessment and Math Journal

For use after Chapter 10

Journal 1. In this chapter, you learned about prisms, cylinders, pyramids, and cones. Give the formulas for the surface area and the volume of each of these solids. Then draw a net for each solid.

Multi-Step Problem 2. The figure shows the top view of a circular swimming pool that is surrounded by a triangular patio. A trapezoid-shaped garden is on one side of the patio consisting of a parallelogram-shaped flower garden and a triangular-shaped vegetable garden.

a. The perimeter of the patio is 132 feet. The lengths of two of the sides are equal. The length of the third side is $\frac{3}{4}$ the length of one of the other two sides. What are the side lengths of the patio?

b. All three sides of the vegetable garden are equal. The perimeter is 48 feet. What is the length of a side of the vegetable garden?

c. The length of the side of the flower garden that is along the patio is 20 feet. The vertical distance between this side and the side opposite it is approximately 14 feet. What is the approximate area of the flower garden?

d. What is the total area of both gardens?

e. The pool has a diameter of 20 feet. What is the circumference of the pool? What is the area of the pool? Round to the nearest whole number.

f. The pool is flat on the bottom and has a uniform depth of 4.5 feet. What type of solid does the pool represent? What is its volume? Round to the nearest whole number.

g. You would like to have a pool with twice the volume of the pool shown. Would you achieve this if you double the diameter of the pool shown? Why or why not? Would you achieve this if you double the depth of the pool shown? Why or why not?

Copyright © McDougal Littell/Houghton Mifflin Company All rights reserved.

Pre-Algebra 127 Chapter 10 Assessment Book

CHAPTER 10 Continued Name ______ Date ______

Alternative Assessment Rubric

For use after Chapter 10

Journal Solution 1. Complete answers should include:

- the formulas for the surface area and volume of a prism, cylinder, pyramid, and cone.
- a net drawing of a prism, cylinder, pyramid, and cone.

Multi-Step Problem Solution 2. a. 36 ft, 48 ft, 48 ft

b. 16 ft

c. 280 ft^2

d. 392 ft^2

e. 63 ft; 314 ft^2

f. cylinder; 1414 ft^3

g. No; doubling the diameter produces four times the volume of the pool shown. Yes; doubling the depth produces twice the volume of the pool shown.

Multi-Step Problem Rubric

4 The student correctly finds the side lengths of the patio, the length of a side of the vegetable garden, the area of the vegetable garden, the total area of the vegetable garden and flower garden, and the circumference and area of the pool. The student correctly identifies what type of solid represents the pool and correctly finds the volume of the pool. The student's explanations are correct and clearly stated. The student's work is neat.

3 The student finds the side lengths of the patio, the length of a side of the vegetable garden, the area of the vegetable garden, the total area of the vegetable garden and flower garden, and the circumference and area of the pool. The student identifies what type of solid represents the pool and finds the volume of the pool. The student's work may have a small mathematical error. The student's explanations are correct, but unclear. The student's work is neat.

2 The student finds the side lengths of the patio, the length of a side of the vegetable garden, the area of the vegetable garden, the total area of the vegetable garden and flower garden, and the circumference and area of the pool. The student identifies what type of solid represents the pool and finds the volume of the pool. The student's work may have more than one mathematical error. The student's explanations may be incomplete. The student's work is sloppy.

1 The student does not complete all parts of the problem. The student's work has several mathematical errors. The explanations are incomplete. The student's work is sloppy.

128 **Pre-Algebra** Chapter 10 Assessment Book

Copyright © McDougal Littell/Houghton Mifflin Company All rights reserved.

Strategies for English Learners

STUDY OF ROOTS

The analysis of Greek and Latin roots in mathematical terms and common English words is a good activity for all students because it helps them figure out the meanings of new words. Students who speak a language in addition to English may find words in other languages that are derived from Greek and Latin roots. This word study could be covered in a few minutes each week during math class or in a more extended way during the language arts period.

Put these Latin and Greek words for cardinal numbers on the board and ask students to think of words that use these:

English	Cardinal Numbers in Latin	Cardinal Numbers in Greek
one	unus, una, unum	heis, miam, hen
two	duo, duae	duo
three	tres, tria	treis, tria
four	quattor	tessares, tessara
five	quinque	pente
six	sex	hex
seven	septum	hepta
eight	octo	okto
nine	novem	ennea
ten	decem	deka

Students may think of words such as *uniform* or *unicorn, duo, duet, triangle, quad, quadrilateral, pentagon, sextuplet, hexagonal, octagon,* and *decathlon*. Spanish speakers may be amazed at the similarity between the names for numbers in Latin and in Spanish.

VOCABULARY

Ask students to consider how prefixes contribute to these words: *similar* : *dissimilar, continuous* : *discontinuous, order* : *disorder, solve* : *dissolve, unite* : *disunite, biangular, bisect, commutative, congruent, coordinate, diagram, diameter, distance, distribute, isosceles, monomial, multiple, multiply, parabola, parallax, parallelogram, parallel, parameter, percent, polynomial, quadrant* and *subtract*. Students will be amazed to see how many words in English start from the prefixes *poly-* or *multi-*.

Greek or Latin Root	Mathematical Terms
congruere (Latin, *to agree*)	*congru*ent, *congru*ence, *congru*ity, *congru*ous
polys (Greek, *many*)	*poly*gon, *poly*hedron
hedra (Greek, *surface*)	poly*hedr*on, octa*hedr*al
circum (Latin, *around*)	*circum*ference
circulus (Latin, *circle* or *ring*)	*circ*le, *circul*ar
ferre (Latin, *bear, carry*)	circum*fer*ence, peri*pher*y
secare (Latin, *to cut*)	inter*sect*, inter*sect*ion
capere (Latin, *to seize* or *stop*)	inter*cept*, inter*cept*ion

Strategies for Advanced Learners

INCREASE DEPTH AND COMPLEXITY

In Lesson 10.3, some advanced students can create their own area problems like those in Exercises 30–33 on page 526. They can then challenge each other with their creations. Also in conjunction with Lesson 10.3, you may wish to have students investigate tangram puzzles. Their investigation should include a discussion of the relationships of the areas of the pieces of the puzzle.

USE CROSS-CURRICULAR CONNECTIONS

In Lessons 10.5 and 10.6, students work with nets. Have them look around the classroom for examples of items that could be shipped in a box. Have students design a net for a box in which to ship the item. Though they will generally expect to ship most items in a rectangular box, students should realize that other shapes might be useful. Have students consider factors such as minimizing materials while providing appropriate protection. [*Note:* Have students ignore the overlapping parts used in actual boxes.]

CHAPTER

10 Differentiating Instruction

Strategies for Underachievers

EMPHASIZE NOTETAKING STRATEGIES

Throughout this chapter, as students encounter new formulas for area, surface area, and volume, encourage them to create note cards or a list containing all the formulas. Each formula should contain a labeled diagram, along with a worked-out example that students can use as a template for problems of a similar type.

USE MODELS AND MANIPULATIVES

CIRCLES In Lesson 10.4, you can have students explore the area of a circle. Give each of three groups of students a circle with a radius of about 4 inches. Have different groups cut their circles into 4, 8, and 16 equal-sized wedges. Then have each group use their pieces to form an "almost parallelogram" by alternating the pieces point up and point down. Have the groups compare their results. Students should see that the more sections that are used, the closer the figure approximates a parallelogram. Help students see that in each case the height of the "parallelogram" is the radius of the circle, and the length of the base approximates half the distance around the circle, πr, as the number of pieces increases. So, it appears that the area of this "parallelogram," which actually models the area of a circle, is $\pi r \cdot r = \pi r^2$.

SOLIDS AND NETS In conjunction with the Student Reference feature on pages 535–536, Concept Activity 10.5, and Lesson 10.5, it will be helpful to have samples of various prisms, pyramids, cylinders, and cones that students can examine. These may be actual models created for this purpose, but it will be especially useful for underachieving students if you have them bring in various examples from home, such as cereal boxes, cans, tissue boxes, and so on. Allow students to examine the models so that they can compare and contrast the features of the different solids. For example, have students use the models to help them describe the ways that prisms and cylinders are alike and ways that they are different. Note that students can also use models of solids to help them understand how solids and their nets are related. For example, to draw the net of a pyramid, students can first outline the base, then tilt the pyramid onto one of its faces, outline that face, and tilt the pyramid back to its base. By repeating this process for each side, students can draw a net. You may also wish to have available solids with pre-made nets that students can fold onto the solids and then unfold.

CONES In Lesson 10.6, you can have students further explore cones by first dividing the students into small groups. Pass out pieces of construction paper or oak tag. Have students use a compass to draw a circle with a 4-inch radius. Then have the different groups cut out wedges with different central angles from the circles. Have students in each group fold and tape the wedge they have removed into a cone, and fold and tape the remainder of the original circle into another cone. Have students in each group see if they can determine what their two cones have in common (they have the same slant height). Then have groups compare their cones to examine how the cones change as the wedge that is removed gets larger (the cone gets shorter and wider).

VOLUME As students explore the concept of volume in Lessons 10.7 and 10.8, they may at times have trouble keeping the distinction between volume and surface area clear in their minds. To help them clarify the distinction, have them take two pieces of $8\frac{1}{2}$ inch by 11 inch paper. Have them roll one piece the short way to make a cylinder by connecting the 11 inch sides, then have them roll the other piece the long way to make a cylinder by connecting the $8\frac{1}{2}$ inch sides. Ask students if they think the volume of the two cylinders will be about the same. Students may be surprised that even though the surface areas of the cylinders are nearly the same, the volume of the shorter cylinder, about 81.8 cubic inches, is almost one third more than that of the taller cylinder, which is about 63.2 cubic inches. (If you want students to estimate these volumes themselves, you will need to help them). [*Note:* The actual surface area of the shorter cylinder is about 7% more than for the taller cylinder, but this is much less than the volume difference.] This activity can lead into a discussion of why products are packaged as they are.

Lesson 10.5

MATH BACKGROUND

The **surface area** of a solid is the total area of all its faces. A **net** is a two-dimensional representation of a solid. Prisms and cylinders have two congruent bases, so their total surface areas will include twice the base area B. The total surface areas will also include the area of the side(s), or the **lateral area** of the solid. For a prism, this is the base perimeter P times the height h. For a cylinder, this is the base circumference C times the height h.

TEACHING STRATEGIES

Have students cut a label from a soup or vegetable can and flatten it to help them see that the length of the rectangle formed is the same as the circumference of the can. They can also cut circles for the top and bottom of the can and use these to form the remainder of the net for the can. For a prism, students can cut an empty cereal or cracker box and flatten it, paying special attention to how the net formed relates to the perimeter of a base of the box.

Lesson 10.6

MATH BACKGROUND

For a **regular pyramid**, the base is a polygon and the lateral faces are congruent triangles that share a common vertex. The surface area of a pyramid is the sum of the base area and the lateral area. The lateral faces are triangles, so their total area is *half* the perimeter times the height of each triangle, which is the **slant height** l of the pyramid. A **cone** has a circular base with area πr^2 and its lateral area is πrl.

TEACHING STRATEGIES

Help students understand the connections among the various surface area formulas. For example, in the formula for the surface area of a cone, $S = \pi r^2 + \pi rl$, the quantity πr^2 corresponds to B in the formula for the surface area of a pyramid, $S = B + \frac{1}{2}Pl$. Also, you can point out that in the formula for a pyramid, $\frac{1}{2}P$ is half the perimeter of the base. Because the "perimeter" of a circle is its circumference, half of the circumference of the base of a cone is half of $2\pi r$, or πr. So, $\frac{1}{2}Pl$ corresponds to πrl.

Lesson 10.7

MATH BACKGROUND

For both prisms and cylinders, the volume V can be found by multiplying the area of the base times the height: $V = Bh$. For a cylinder, which has base area πr^2, this translates to $V = \pi r^2 h$. For a solid composed of a combination of cylinders, prisms, or other solids, the volume is the sum of the volumes of the individual solids.

TEACHING STRATEGIES

The relationships between measures of length and capacity in the metric system make it is easy to investigate the volume of a cylinder. Divide students into small groups. Give each group an empty can, a centimeter ruler, and a metric measuring cup. Inform students that 1 milliliter of water exactly fills a cube that has an edge length of 1 centimeter. That is, 1 mL = 1 cm^3. Have each group measure the diameter and height of their can and calculate the radius. Then have students use the volume formula $V = \pi r^2 h$ to find the volume of the can in cubic centimeters. Students can then measure out the same number of milliliters of water, which should exactly fill the can.

Lesson 10.8

MATH BACKGROUND

The volumes of pyramids and cones are, respectively, one third the volumes of the prism and cylinder with the same base and height: $V = \frac{1}{3}Bh$ for a pyramid and $V = \frac{1}{3}\pi r^2 h$ for a cone. Although the formulas for the surface areas of pyramids and cones use the slant heights of the lateral surfaces, the formulas for volume use the heights of the solids.

TEACHING STRATEGIES

Perhaps because the formula for the surface area of a pyramid has the fraction $\frac{1}{2}$ in it, students may expect the volume of a pyramid or cone to be one half the volume of the prism or cylinder with the same height and base, so you will need to to stress that the fraction $\frac{1}{3}$ appears in the volume formula, not $\frac{1}{2}$.

CHAPTER

10 Math Background and Teaching Strategies

Lesson 10.1

MATH BACKGROUND

The sum of the measures of the angles of a triangle is 180°. This allows you to find missing angle measures when you know the measures of two angles or one angle measure and some other relevant information, such as that the other two angles have the same measure. If you know the ratio of the angle measures, you can write and solve an equation to find the angle measures.

TEACHING STRATEGIES

Students may have difficulty with Example 3. Before students attempt to use the ratio of angle measures to write and solve an equation, you may wish to give them some sets of angle measures for different triangles and have them find the ratio of the angle measures. For example, present students with a triangle with angle measures of 30°, 45°, and 105°. Then have them find the ratio of the angle measures by dividing out the GCF of the measures.

Lesson 10.2

MATH BACKGROUND

A **polygon** is a closed figure in a plane whose sides are line segments intersecting only at their endpoints. If all angles of a polygon have equal measure and all sides have equal length, it is **regular**. The set of **quadrilaterals** includes *trapezoids*, *parallelograms*, *rhombuses*, *rectangles*, and *squares*.

TEACHING STRATEGIES

While discussing the table of quadrilaterals on page 517, ask students which categories include others (e.g. *parallelogram* includes *rhombus*), which categories overlap (e.g. *rhombus* and *rectangle* overlap in *square*), and which category is exclusive of the others (*trapezoid* excludes all the others). You may also want to extend the exploration of the sum of the angle measures in a quadrilateral on page 518 to finding the sum of the angle measures in polygons with more than 4 sides.

Lesson 10.3

MATH BACKGROUND

Either diagonal of a parallelogram divides it into two congruent triangles, each with base and height equal to that of the parallelogram. Since the area of each triangle is half the base times the height, the area of the parallelogram is base times height. The area of a trapezoid is half the sum of its bases times its height.

TEACHING STRATEGIES

Have students draw two parallelograms with the same base and same height, but with obviously different slants. Then have them cut each parallelogram, rearrange the pieces to form rectangles as shown on page 521, and tape the pieces together. Have students place one rectangle on top of the other to show that the two parallelograms have the same area. You can also have students perform a similar activity with two trapezoids that have the same bases and height, rearranging the pieces to form parallelograms, as shown for the trapezoid at the top of page 522.

Lesson 10.4

MATH BACKGROUND

Because the ratio of the **circumference** C of any circle to the diameter d of the circle is the irrational number π, the circumference of a circle is given by $C = \pi d$, or $C = 2\pi r$, where r is the radius of the circle. The area of a circle is given by the formula $A = \pi r^2$.

TEACHING STRATEGIES

To reinforce students' understanding of the area of a circle, have pairs of students use compasses to draw three circles on grid paper. Then have students use the grid to measure the diameter/radius of each circle, and have them count the grid squares and partial squares inside each circle to estimate the area of each circle. Students can then compute the areas using the formula and compare the results.

Support Materials

CHAPTER RESOURCE BOOK

CHAPTER SUPPORT			
Tips for New Teachers	p. 1	Parents as Partners	p. 3

LESSON SUPPORT	10.1	10.2	10.3	10.4	10.5	10.6	10.7	10.8
Lesson Plans (regular and block)	p. 5	p. 13	p. 22	p. 31	p. 39	p. 47	p. 56	p. 66
Technology Activities & Keystrokes						p. 49		
Activity Support Masters							p. 58	
Activity Masters		p. 15						
Practice (3 levels)	p. 7	p. 16	p. 24	p. 33	p. 41	p. 50	p. 59	p. 68
Study Guide	p. 10	p. 19	p. 27	p. 36	p. 44	p. 53	p. 62	p. 71
Real-World Problem Solving			p. 29				p. 64	
Challenge Practice	p. 12	p. 21	p. 30	p. 38	p. 46	p. 55	p. 65	p. 73

REVIEW			
Chapter Review Games and Activities	p. 74	Extra Credit Project with Rubric	p. 79
Real-Life Project with Rubric	p. 75	Cumulative Practice	p. 81
Cooperative Project with Rubric	p. 77	Resource Book Answers	A1

ASSESSMENT

Quizzes	p. 118	Alternative Assessments with Rubrics	p. 127
Chapter Tests (3 levels)	p. 120	Unit Test	p. 129
Standardized Test	p. 126	Cumulative Test	p. 131

TRANSPARENCIES

	10.1	10.2	10.3	10.4	10.5	10.6	10.7	10.8
Warm-Up/Daily Homework Quiz	✔	✔	✔	✔	✔	✔	✔	✔
Notetaking Guide	✔	✔	✔	✔	✔	✔	✔	✔
Teacher Support		✔	✔					
English/Spanish Problem Solving		✔	✔	✔	✔			✔
Answer Transparencies	✔	✔	✔	✔	✔	✔	✔	✔

TECHNOLOGY

- EasyPlanner CD-ROM
- Test and Practice Generator
- Electronic Lesson Presentations
- eTutorial CD-ROM
- Chapter Audio Summaries CDs
- Classzone.com
- eEdition Plus Online
- eWorkbook Plus Online
- eTutorial Plus Online
- EasyPlanner Plus Online

ADDITIONAL RESOURCES

- Worked-Out Solution Key
- Notetaking Guide
- Practice Workbook
- Tutor Place
- Professional Development Book
- Special Activities Book
- Posters
- Spanish Study Guide
- Exercises in Spanish
- English/Spanish Ch. Reviews/Tests
- Multi-Language Visual Glossary

CHAPTER 10

Pacing and Assignment Guide

REGULAR SCHEDULE

Lesson	Les. Day	BASIC	AVERAGE	ADVANCED
10.1	Day 1	SRH p. 793 Exs. 1-3; pp. 513-515 Exs. 8-13, 15-21, 26, 29-32	pp. 513-515 Exs. 11-26, 28-32	pp. 513-515 Exs. 11-14, 17-28*, 30-32
10.2	Day 1	EP p. 805 Exs. 9-11; pp. 519-520 Exs. 7-9, 11-20, 22, 23, 25-30	pp. 519-520 Exs. 7-23, 25-30	pp. 519-520 Exs. 8-12, 14-18, 20-25*, 27-30
10.3	Day 1	pp. 524-526 Exs. 11-13, 18, 28, 30-32, 35-40	pp. 524-526 Exs. 11-13, 17, 18, 28-33, 35-40	pp. 524-526 Exs. 11-13, 17, 18, 27-35*
	Day 2	pp. 524-526 Exs. 14-17, 19-25, 41-43	pp. 524-526 Exs. 14-16, 19-27, 41-43	pp. 524-526 Exs. 14-16, 19-26, 39-43
10.4	Day 1	EP p. 811 Exs. 5-8; pp. 531-533 Exs. 7-12, 17-19, 27, 35-40	pp. 531-533 Exs. 10-12, 17-19, 26, 27, 34-40	pp. 531-533 Exs. 10-12, 19-22, 26, 37-41
	Day 2	pp. 531-533 Exs. 13-16, 20-25, 28-30, 41-44	pp. 531-533 Exs. 13-16, 20-25, 28-32, 41-45	pp. 531-533 Exs. 13-16, 23-25, 28-34*, 43-45
10.5	Day 1	pp. 541-543 Exs. 6-16, 20, 23-31	pp. 541-543 Exs. 8-21, 23-31	pp. 541-543 Exs. 9-24*, 28-31
10.6	Day 1	EP p. 811 Exs. 13-16; pp. 547-549 Exs. 7-12, 14-19, 21-25, 28, 34-40	pp. 547-549 Exs. 8-15, 18-22, 26-31, 34-41	pp. 547-549 Exs. 9-11, 13-15, 19-22, 26-33*, 36-41
10.7	Day 1	SRH p. 791 Exs. 2-5; pp. 555-556 Exs. 7-14, 16-20, 24-32	pp. 555-556 Exs. 8-11, 13-22, 24-32	pp. 555-556 Exs. 8-10, 12-16, 18-24*, 27-32
10.8	Day 1	pp. 561-563 Exs. 6-14, 18, 19, 21-23, 25-33	pp. 561-563 Exs. 7-10, 12-23, 25-34	pp. 561-563 Exs. 7-9, 12-25*, 28-34
Review	Day 1	pp. 564-567 Exs. 1-26	pp. 564-567 Exs. 1-26	pp. 564-567 Exs. 1-26
Assess	Day 1	Chapter 10 Test	Chapter 10 Test	Chapter 10 Test

YEARLY PACING Chapter 10 Total – **12 days** Chapters 1–10 Total – **120 days** Remaining – **40 days**

*Challenge Exercises EP = Extra Practice SRH = Skills Review Handbook

BLOCK SCHEDULE

DAY 1	DAY 2	DAY 3	DAY 4	DAY 5	DAY 6
10.1 pp. 513-515 Exs. 11-26, 28-32 **10.2** pp. 519-520 Exs. 8-12, 14-17, 19-23, 25-30	**10.3** pp. 524-526 Exs. 11-33, 35-43	**10.4** pp. 531-533 Exs. 10-32, 34-45	**10.5** pp. 541-543 Exs. 9-21, 23-31 **10.6** pp. 547-549 Exs. 8-15, 18-22, 26-31, 34-41	**10.7** pp. 555-556 Exs. 8-11, 13-22, 24-32 **10.8** pp. 561-563 Exs. 8-10, 12-23, 25-34	**Review** pp. 564-567 Exs. 1-26 **Assess** Chapter 10 Test

YEARLY PACING Chapter 10 Total – **6 days** Chapters 1–10 Total – **60 days** Remaining – **20 days**

Consider and Decide

Choose the best ramp design for your auditorium. Consider the following:

- Which ramp is the steepest? Which is the least steep? Which ramp will be easiest to walk up or down? Why?
- Plywood is sold in sheets that are 4 feet by 8 feet. Which ramp design requires the fewest sheets of plywood?

Present Your Design

Make a scale drawing of the ramp design that works best for your auditorium. Include all the dimensions of the ramp and its slope. Explain why you chose this design.

2.5 ft

8 ft

Project Extensions

Using Trigonometry Suppose the measure of the angle formed by the ramp and the floor of the auditorium must be less than 15°. What should the length of the ramp be? Show your work.

Using Trigonometry:
Answers will vary, but students should use the relationship $\tan 15° = \frac{a}{b}$ and conclude that $b > \frac{a}{\tan 15°}$, or $b > 3.73a$. Students can then use the Pythagorean theorem to find the length of the ramp.

Explore Measure the rise and run of a ramp at your school or another building. What are the length of the walkway and the slope of the ramp? What is the purpose of the ramp? Compare the dimensions of this ramp with the dimensions of the one that you designed.
Check students' work.

Career Many people are involved in the production of a play, including set designers, costume designers, and lighting designers. Find out more about one of these careers. Present your findings.

Research CLASSZONE.COM Use the Internet to learn about other uses of ramps, such as for skateboards, bikes, or wheelchairs. How are these ramps constructed? What slopes are commonly used for each type of ramp? Present your research.
Check students' work.

Grading the Project

A well-written project will have the following characteristics:

- The results of Steps 1–6 are complete and reasonable.
- A scale drawing of at least one feasible ramp is included, noting dimensions and slope.
- Two or more good reasons are given as to why the recommended design was chosen.
- The Pythagorean theorem is used correctly, and correct conclusions are drawn from its use.

Chapter 9

Multiple Choice In Exercises 12–22, choose the letter of the correct answer.

12. What is the value of $\sqrt{y^2 - z}$ when $y = -6$ and $z = 3$? *(Lesson 9.1)* **B**

A. $\sqrt{15}$ **B.** $\sqrt{33}$ **C.** 15 **D.** 33

13. Which expression is *not* equivalent to $\sqrt{32}$? *(Lesson 9.2)* **H**

F. $4\sqrt{2}$ **G.** $\sqrt{2 \cdot 4^2}$ **H.** $16\sqrt{2}$ **I.** $\sqrt{2 \cdot 16}$

14. The length of the hypotenuse of a right triangle is 32.5 centimeters, and the length of one leg is 12.5 centimeters. What is the length of the other leg? *(Lesson 9.3)* **B**

A. 25 cm **B.** 30 cm **C.** 35 cm **D.** 900 cm

15. Which list of numbers is in order from least to greatest? *(Lesson 9.4)* **H**

F. $-2.4, -\sqrt{6}, \sqrt{5}, \frac{7}{3}$ **G.** $-2.4, -\sqrt{6}, \frac{7}{3}, \sqrt{5}$

H. $-\sqrt{6}, -2.4, \sqrt{5}, \frac{7}{3}$ **I.** $-\sqrt{6}, -2.4, \frac{7}{3}, \sqrt{5}$

16. What is the midpoint of the segment with endpoints $(-3, 4)$ and $(6, -2)$? *(Lesson 9.5)* **A**

A. $(1\frac{1}{2}, 1)$ **B.** $(-1\frac{1}{2}, 1)$

C. $(4\frac{1}{2}, 3)$ **D.** $(-4\frac{1}{2}, 3)$

17. The length of each leg of a 45°-45°-90° triangle is 7 meters. What is the length of the hypotenuse? *(Lesson 9.6)* **I**

F. 2.6 m **G.** 4.9 m **H.** 7 m **I.** $7\sqrt{2}$ m

18. The length of the hypotenuse of a 30°-60°-90° triangle is 11 inches. What is the length of the shorter leg? *(Lesson 9.6)* **A**

A. 5.5 in. **B.** $\frac{11\sqrt{3}}{2}$ in.

C. $11\sqrt{3}$ in. **D.** 22 in.

19. Which ratio is equal to tan A? *(Lesson 9.7)* **I**

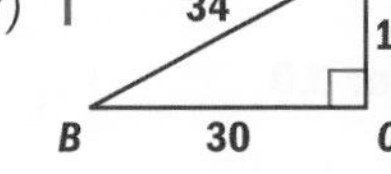

F. $\frac{16}{34}$ **G.** $\frac{16}{30}$

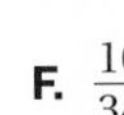

H. $\frac{30}{34}$ **I.** $\frac{30}{16}$

20. Which ratio is equal to tan B for the triangle in Exercise 19? *(Lesson 9.7)* **B**

A. $\frac{16}{34}$ **B.** $\frac{16}{30}$ **C.** $\frac{30}{34}$ **D.** $\frac{30}{16}$

21. Which ratio is equal to sin B for the triangle in Exercise 19? *(Lesson 9.8)* **F**

F. $\frac{16}{34}$ **G.** $\frac{16}{30}$ **H.** $\frac{30}{34}$ **I.** $\frac{30}{16}$

22. Which ratio is equal to sin A for the triangle in Exercise 19? *(Lesson 9.8)* **C**

A. $\frac{16}{34}$ **B.** $\frac{16}{30}$ **C.** $\frac{30}{34}$ **D.** $\frac{30}{16}$

23. Short Response The time t (in seconds) that it takes a dropped object to fall a distance d (in feet) is given by the formula $d = 16t^2$. Two balls are dropped from the tops of two buildings. The heights of the two buildings are 150 feet and 600 feet. How much longer does it take the ball dropped from the taller building to hit the ground? Show your work. *(Lesson 9.2)* **See margin.**

24. Extended Response The vertices of an isosceles triangle are $P(6, 5)$, $Q(-4, 3)$, and $R(2, -1)$. *(Lessons 9.3, 9.5)*

a. Graph the triangle. **24a–b. See margin.**

b. Find the lengths of $\overline{PQ}$, $\overline{QR}$, and $\overline{RP}$.

c. Find the midpoint M of $\overline{PQ}$. **$M(1, 4)$**

d. Find the distance between points M and R. **$\sqrt{26}$ units**

e. Use the converse of the Pythagorean theorem to show that $\triangle MQR$ and $\triangle PMR$ are right triangles. **See margin.**

Test-Taking Skills

23. About 3.1 sec. *Sample answer:* Solve the two equations $150 = 16t^2$ and $600 = 16t^2$ for t, then subtract the two values of t. The two values are $t \approx 3.06$ and $t \approx 6.12$, which gives a difference of about 3.1 seconds.

24a.

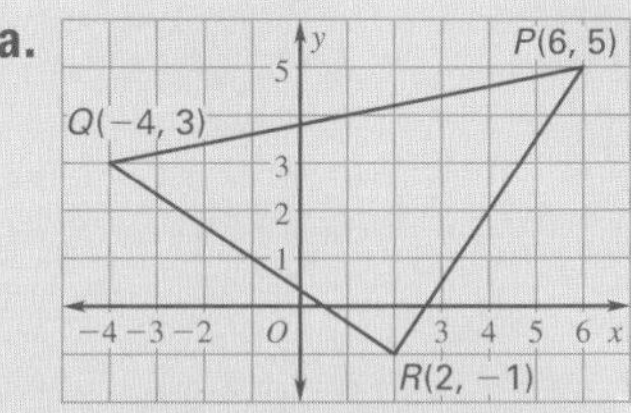

24b. $PQ = 2\sqrt{26}$ units, $QR = 2\sqrt{13}$ units, $RP = 2\sqrt{13}$ units

24e. $(MQ)^2 + (MR)^2 = (\sqrt{26})^2 + (\sqrt{26})^2 = 52$, and $(QR)^2 = (2\sqrt{13})^2 = 52$, so $\triangle MQR$ is a right triangle; $(MP)^2 + (MR)^2 = (\sqrt{26})^2 + (\sqrt{26})^2 = 52$, and $(RP)^2 = (2\sqrt{13})^2 = 52$, so $\triangle PMR$ is a right triangle.

Unit 3 Chapters 8–10 Practicing Test-Taking Skills

Cumulative Practice continued

Chapter 10

Multiple Choice In Exercises 25–32, choose the letter of the correct answer.

25. What is the value of x? *(Lesson 10.1)* **B**

A. 10.5 **B.** 21

C. 24 **D.** 42

26. Classify the triangle in Exercise 25 by its angle measures. *(Lesson 10.1)* **H**

F. Acute **G.** Isosceles

H. Obtuse **I.** Right

27. What is the value of z? *(Lesson 10.2)* **A**

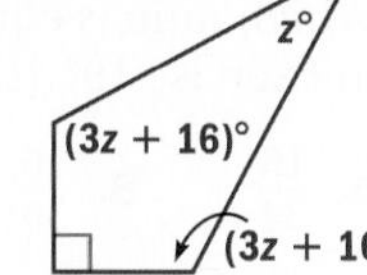

A. 34 **B.** 90

C. 118 **D.** 208

28. Your garden is in the shape of a parallelogram. The height of the parallelogram is 18 feet. The base is $1\frac{1}{2}$ times the height. What is the area of the garden? *(Lesson 10.3)* **I**

F. 18 ft^2 **G.** 40.5 ft^2

H. 216 ft^2 **I.** 486 ft^2

29. The area of a circle is 94.2 square centimeters. What is the approximate radius of the circle? *(Lesson 10.4)* **B**

A. 3.9 cm **B.** 5.5 cm **C.** 15 cm **D.** 30 cm

30. A box has the shape of a rectangular prism that is 15 centimeters long, 4.5 centimeters wide, and 22 centimeters high. What is the surface area of the prism? *(Lesson 10.5)* **H**

F. 41.5 cm **G.** 496.5 cm^2

H. 993 cm^2 **I.** 1485 cm^3

31. What is the surface area of the square pyramid shown? *(Lesson 10.6)* **C**

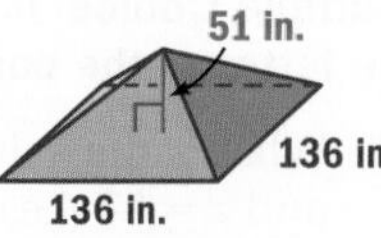

A. 23,256 in.^{2} **B.** 32,368 in.^{2}

C. 41,616 in.^{2} **D.** 314,432 in.^{2}

32. A mailbox is composed of a prism and a half cylinder. What is the approximate volume of the mailbox? *(Lessons 10.7, 10.8)* **I**

F. 1148 in.^{3}

G. 1778 in.^{3}

H. 2036 in.^{3}

I. 2746 in.^{3}

33. Short Response The area of a trapezoid is 225 square meters. The height of the trapezoid is 25 meters. One of the bases is twice the other base. Do you have enough information to find each of the bases? If so, find the bases. If not, explain why not. *(Lesson 10.3)* **yes; 12 m and 6 m**

34. Extended Response A cylindrical display tank at an aquarium has a cylindrical viewing chamber inside it. Water fills the space between the two glass cylinders, as shown. *(Lesson 10.7)*

a. What is the volume of the water in the tank to the nearest cubic inch? **97,691 in.^{3}**

b. How many gallons of water are needed to fill the tank? Use the fact that 1 cubic inch of water is approximately equal to 0.00433 gallon. **about 423 gal**

UNIT 4

Data Analysis, Polynomials, *and* Transformations

Chapter 11 Data Analysis and Probability

- Make and interpret data displays.
- Conduct surveys and analyze survey results.
- Calculate probabilities of events.

Chapter 12 Polynomials and Nonlinear Functions

- Add, subtract, and multiply polynomials.
- Evaluate powers of products, quotients, and powers.
- Graph quadratic and exponential functions.

Chapter 13 Angle Relationships and Transformations

- Identify special pairs of angles and find their measures.
- Find the measures of interior and exterior angles of polygons.
- Translate, reflect, rotate, and dilate geometric figures.

From Chapter 12, p. 651
What is the height of the volleyball?

Unit Resources

These resources are provided to help you prepare for the unit and to customize review materials:

 ***Chapter Resource Books***
- Chapter 11
- Chapter 12
- Chapter 13

 ***Assessment Book***
- Chapters 11–13, pp. 135–173

 ***Technology***
- EasyPlanner CD-ROM
- Test and Practice Generator
- Electronic Lesson Presentations CD-ROM
- eTutorial CD-ROM

 ***Internet***
- Classzone
- eEdition Plus Online
- eWorkbook Plus Online
- eTutorial Plus Online
- EasyPlanner Plus Online

English Learner Support

- Spanish Study Guide
- Multi-Language Visual Glossary
- Chapter Audio Summaries CDs
- Teacher's Edition
  Chapter 11, pp. 578E–578F
  Chapter 12, pp. 648E–648F
  Chapter 13, pp. 706E–706F

CHAPTER 11

Pacing and Assignment Guide

REGULAR SCHEDULE

Lesson	Les. Day	BASIC	AVERAGE	ADVANCED
11.1	Day 1	SRH p. 781 Exs. 4–7; pp. 584–586 Exs. 6–9, 14, 16, 23–26	pp. 584–586 Exs. 6–9, 14, 16, 17, 23–26	pp. 584–586 Exs. 7–9, 14, 16, 22–26*
	Day 2	pp. 584–586 Exs. 10–13, 15, 18, 19, 27–30	pp. 584–586 Exs. 10–13, 15, 18–21, 27–30	pp. 584–586 Exs. 11–13, 15, 17–21, 27–30
11.2	Day 1	pp. 591–592 Exs. 6–11, 14–23	pp. 591–592 Exs. 6–12, 14–23	pp. 591–592 Exs. 7–13*, 16–23
11.3	Day 1	SRH p. 782 Exs. 4–7; pp. 599–600 Exs. 6–15, 19–25	pp. 599–600 Exs. 6–17, 19–26	pp. 599–600 Exs. 6–18*, 21–26
11.4	Day 1	pp. 604–605 Exs. 5–10, 12–15, 19–26	pp. 604–605 Exs. 5–17, 19–27	pp. 604–605 Exs. 7–18*, 21, 24–27
11.5	Day 1	EP p. 809 Exs. 5–8; pp. 612–613 Exs. 5–9, 13, 14, 16–26	pp. 612–613 Exs. 6–14, 16–26	pp. 612–613 Exs. 7–15*, 18–21, 24–26
11.6	Day 1	SRH p. 798 Exs. 1–3; pp. 618–619 Exs. 10–21, 26–30, 33–36, 38, 44–50	pp. 618–619 Exs. 12–17, 20–25, 28–34, 37–42, 44–50	pp. 618–619 Exs. 14–17, 22–25, 29–32, 35–44*, 47–50
11.7	Day 1	pp. 623–625 Exs. 9–18, 23–28, 32, 36–41	pp. 623–625 Exs. 9, 10, 17–34, 36–41	pp. 623–625 Exs. 9–14, 23–25, 28–37*, 39–41
11.8	Day 1	SRH p. 779 Exs. 6–10; pp. 631–632 Exs. 12–15, 30–38	pp. 631–632 Exs. 12–15, 23, 27, 28, 30–34	pp. 631–632 Exs. 12–15, 26–28, 32–35
	Day 2	pp. 631–632 Exs. 8–11, 16–23, 25, 39	pp. 631–632 Exs. 8–11, 16–22, 24–26, 35–40	pp. 631–632 Exs. 10, 11, 17–19, 22–25, 29*, 38–40
11.9	Day 1	pp. 637–639 Exs. 6–8, 14, 17, 20–22	pp. 637–639 Exs. 6–8, 15–17, 19–22	pp. 637–639 Exs. 6–8, 15–19*
	Day 2	pp. 637–639 Exs. 9–13, 23–25	pp. 637–639 Exs. 9–14, 23–26	pp. 637–639 Exs. 9–14, 22–26
Review	Day 1	pp. 640–643 Exs. 1–15	pp. 640–643 Exs. 1–15	pp. 640–643 Exs. 1–15
Assess	Day 1	Chapter 11 Test	Chapter 11 Test	Chapter 11 Test

YEARLY PACING Chapter 11 Total – **14 days** Chapters 1–11 Total – **134 days** Remaining – **26 days**

*Challenge Exercises EP = Extra Practice SRH = Skills Review Handbook

BLOCK SCHEDULE

DAY 1	DAY 2	DAY 3	DAY 4	DAY 5	DAY 6	DAY 7
11.1 pp. 584–586 Exs. 6–21, 23–30	**11.2** pp. 591–592 Exs. 6–12, 14–23 **11.3** pp. 599–600 Exs. 6–17, 19–26	**11.4** pp. 604–605 Exs. 5–17, 19–27 **11.5** pp. 612–613 Exs. 6–14, 16–26	**11.6** pp. 618–619 Exs. 12–17, 20–25, 28–34, 37–42, 44–50 **11.7** pp. 623–625 Exs. 9, 10, 17–34, 36–41	**11.8** pp. 631–632 Exs. 8–28, 30–40	**11.9** pp. 637–639 Exs. 6–17, 19–26	**Review** pp. 640–643 Exs. 1–15 **Assess** Chapter 11 Test

YEARLY PACING Chapter 11 Total – **7 days** Chapters 1–11 Total – **67 days** Remaining – **13 days**

Support Materials

CHAPTER RESOURCE BOOK

CHAPTER SUPPORT			
Tips for New Teachers	p. 1	Parents as Partners	p. 3

LESSON SUPPORT	11.1	11.2	11.3	11.4	11.5	11.6	11.7	11.8	11.9
Lesson Plans (regular and block)	p. 5	p. 14	p. 24	p. 32	p. 41	p. 49	p. 58	p. 69	p. 78
Technology Activities & Keystrokes	p. 7	p. 16		p. 34			p. 60		
Activity Support Masters								p. 71	
Activity Masters						p. 51			
Practice (3 levels)	p. 8	p. 17	p. 26	p. 35	p. 43	p. 52	p. 62	p. 72	p. 80
Study Guide	p. 11	p. 20	p. 29	p. 38	p. 46	p. 55	p. 65	p. 75	p. 83
Real-World Problem Solving		p. 22					p. 67		
Challenge Practice	p. 13	p. 23	p. 31	p. 40	p. 48	p. 57	p. 68	p. 77	p. 85

REVIEW			
Chapter Review Games and Activities	p. 86	Extra Credit Project with Rubric	p. 91
Real-Life Project with Rubric	p. 87	Cumulative Practice	p. 93
Cooperative Project with Rubric	p. 89	Resource Book Answers	A1

ASSESSMENT

Quizzes	p. 135	Alternative Assessments with Rubrics	p. 144
Chapter Tests (3 levels)	p. 137	Unit Test	p. 168
Standardized Test	p. 143	Cumulative Test	p. 170

TRANSPARENCIES

	11.1	11.2	11.3	11.4	11.5	11.6	11.7	11.8	11.9
Warm-Up/Daily Homework Quiz	✔	✔	✔	✔	✔	✔	✔	✔	✔
Notetaking Guide	✔	✔	✔	✔	✔	✔	✔	✔	✔
Teacher Support		✔					✔		
English/Spanish Problem Solving	✔	✔							
Answer Transparencies	✔	✔	✔	✔	✔	✔	✔	✔	✔

TECHNOLOGY

- EasyPlanner CD-ROM
- Test and Practice Generator
- Electronic Lesson Presentations
- eTutorial CD-ROM
- Chapter Audio Summaries CDs
- Classzone.com
- eEdition Plus Online
- eWorkbook Plus Online
- eTutorial Plus Online
- EasyPlanner Plus Online

ADDITIONAL RESOURCES

- Worked-Out Solution Key
- Notetaking Guide
- Practice Workbook
- Tutor Place
- Professional Development Book
- Special Activities Book
- Posters
- Spanish Study Guide
- Exercises in Spanish
- English/Spanish Ch. Reviews/Tests
- Multi-Language Visual Glossary

CHAPTER 11

Math Background and Teaching Strategies

Lesson 11.1

MATH BACKGROUND

A **stem-and-leaf plot** is a visual way of listing all the values of a set of data in order. The data are grouped by separating each value into a *stem* made up of the leading digit(s), and a *leaf*, made up of the last digit. A **histogram** displays data using bars whose lengths correspond to the frequency of the data values in intervals of equal size that have no gaps between intervals. Unlike a bar graph, the bars of a histogram have no gaps between them.

TEACHING STRATEGIES

As an additional example, you can present the following situation to students: In July, a student did odd jobs for people, and earned the amounts of money shown below.

$12, $9, $15, $17, $20, $12, $9, $6, $13, $15,
$11, $17, $18, $14, $15, $20, $25, $13, $12, $15

Have students make a stem-and-leaf plot of the data. Have them use the stem-and-leaf plot to find the mean, median, and mode. Then have them make histograms of the data.

Lesson 11.2

MATH BACKGROUND

A **box-and-whisker plot** shows several important statistics: the **lower extreme**, the **lower quartile**, the **median**, the **upper quartile**, and the **upper extreme**. From the extremes, you can also find the *range* of the data, and from the quartiles, you can find the **interquartile range**.

TEACHING STRATEGIES

Make sure students understand the following things about box-and-whisker plots. For an odd number of data values, the median is the middle value and it is *excluded* when finding the lower and upper quartiles. For an even number of data values, the median is the average of the two middle values. The box represents the middle half of the data values. Each whisker represents one fourth of the data values.

Lesson 11.3

MATH BACKGROUND

Bar and circle graphs are best for representing **categorical** (nonnumerical) data, while line graphs, scatter plots, stem-and-leaf plots, histograms, and box-and-whisker plots are used to represent various types of **numerical** data. It is very important to look at a data display with a critical eye in order to determine if it is misleading.

TEACHING STRATEGIES

Bring a misleading graph to class. The graph can be one found in a newspaper, magazine, or from some other source. Point out the misleading aspects of the graph and ask students to suggest how to change the graph in order to avoid each one. Then redraw the graph using their suggestions and discuss how the "new" graph is a better representation of the information.

Lesson 11.4

MATH BACKGROUND

If you need data about a large group, or **population**, you can collect data about a small number, or **sample**, of the population. In a **random sample**, each population member has an equal chance of being selected. Some methods, such as **self-selected sampling**, in which members of a population can select themselves, may result in an unrepresentative, or **biased**, sample.

TEACHING STRATEGIES

On commercials, students are likely to hear claims like "3 out of 4 doctors recommend Cure-All for …". Present this situation to students and ask them if they think this means that Cure-All must be the best medicine for the job, or if they need more information before they draw any conclusions. Some things students might like to know include how the doctors were chosen, how many doctors were sampled, and how *exactly* the doctors were asked about their preferences.

Lesson 11.5

MATH BACKGROUND

For a sample that is representative of a population, the sample proportion gives an estimate of the population proportion, and this fact can be used to make a prediction about a population.

TEACHING STRATEGIES

Though students will not yet be faced with the formula for determining the margin of error of a sample, you can tell them that it is based on size, and that the larger the size of the sample, the smaller the margin of error. However, stress the content of the Watch Out on page 610 which points out that the margin of error is designed to account *only* for chance variations and *not* to problems with biased sampling.

Lesson 11.6

MATH BACKGROUND

An arrangement of objects in which the order of the objects is important is called a **permutation**. The formula for the number of permutations of a set of n objects taken r at a time is $_nP_r = \frac{n!}{(n-r)!}$, where $n!$ (read "***n* factorial**") is given by $n! = n \cdot (n-1) \cdot (n-2) \cdot \ldots \cdot 1$.

TEACHING STRATEGIES

To help students better understand the permutation formula, point out that the effect of the formula is to find the first r factors of $n!$. For example, $_8P_3$ indicates finding the first 3 factors of 8!, or $8 \cdot 7 \cdot 6$. Suppose you want to place any 3 of 5 books on a shelf, then you must stop after $r = 3$ choices.

Lesson 11.7

MATH BACKGROUND

An arrangement of objects in which the order of the objects is *not* important is called a **combination**. To find the number of combinations of n objects taken r at a time, divide the corresponding number of permutations by $r!$: $_nC_r = \frac{_nP_r}{r!}$.

TEACHING STRATEGIES

Return to the discussion in the Teaching Strategies note for Lesson 11.6. Suppose the five books are *Robinson Crusoe* (R), *Tom Sawyer* (T), *The Hobbit* (H), *The Martian Chronicles* (M), and *Harry Potter and the Sorcerer's Stone* (P). For any 3 books you choose, there are 6 permutations; for example, for the first 3 books these are RTH, RHT, TRH, THR, HRT, HTR. Since it does not matter in which order you pick the books, you can divide the number of permutations of 3 books chosen from the group of 5 by 6 = 3! to find the number of combinations.

Lesson 11.8

MATH BACKGROUND

Two events that have no outcomes in common are **disjoint**. To find the probability of two disjoint events, you need only add the probabilities of the events: $P(A \text{ or } B) = P(A) + P(B)$. If two events overlap, such as rolling an odd number and rolling a 5 on a number cube, then you must subtract the probability of the events both happening: $P(A \text{ or } B) = P(A) + P(B) - P(A \text{ and } B)$. If two events are **complementary**, then the two events encompass all outcomes of an experiment.

TEACHING STRATEGIES

Give students another opportunity to use a Venn diagram to model disjoint events. Suppose each letter in VERMONT is placed in a hat and one letter is drawn. What is the probability that the letter is a vowel or is in the first half of the alphabet (A–M)? Students should show that the first event consists of the outcomes E and O and the second consists of the outcomes E and M. Students' diagrams should illustrate that 3 different outcomes correspond to the event, giving a probability of $\frac{3}{7}$. The formula yields $\frac{2}{7} + \frac{2}{7} - \frac{1}{7} = \frac{3}{7}$.

Lesson 11.9

MATH BACKGROUND

If two events are **independent**, then the occurrence of one event has no effect on the probability that the second event occurs. For **dependent** events, the occurrence of one event *does* affect the probability of the other.

TEACHING STRATEGIES

Help students identify as many events as possible as independent or dependent. Drawing objects with or without replacement provides one example of the distinction. For example, experiments with playing cards drawn without replacement make good examples of dependent events.

CHAPTER

11 Differentiating Instruction

Strategies for Underachievers

FOCUS ON VOCABULARY

BOX-AND-WHISKER PLOTS To help with the vocabulary terms *median, lower extreme, upper extreme, lower quartile, upper quartile,* and *interquartile range* in Lesson 11.2, encourage students to draw a generic box-and-whisker plot in their notebooks or on a note card, with each of the terms placed appropriately on the plot. Students can write very brief definitions beside each term, such as "greatest value" for the upper extreme, "upper quartile minus lower quartile" for the interquartile range, and so on. Students can also label each whisker and each half of the box with "25%" to remind them that the plot separates the data into fourths.

ADJUST PACING

DATA DISPLAYS In Lesson 11.1, three types of data displays are presented: stem-and-leaf plots, frequency tables, and histograms. Although these three are closely related, you may need to slow the pacing a bit to make sure that underachieving students master each type of display before moving on to the next. After students are comfortable with each type of display, you can then bring the information together by stressing the connections, such as that a stem-and-leaf plot is like a horizontal histogram with the stems corresponding to the intervals and the rows of leaves corresponding to the bars.

USE TOOLS AND MANIPULATIVES

TECHNOLOGY In Lesson 11.2, you may wish to have students work with computer software to draw box-and-whisker plots. This will help students create plots quickly so they can concentrate on the relevant information, or this can provide students with a means for checking their own plots.

In Lesson 11.9, it is helpful to have students use an experimental approach with physical objects such as cards, coins, number cubes, and spinners whenever possible to explore probabilities and to check that theoretically-derived probabilities are reasonable. You can also concentrate on performing simulations to find experimental probabilities, as in Concept Activity 11.9.

USE SCAFFOLDING

DATA DISPLAYS In Lesson 11.1, you may wish to provide underachievers with templates for stem-and-leaf plots, frequency tables, and histograms. Students can then fill in the relevant information without spending too much time getting started making a display. In Lesson 11.2, you may wish to provide pre-drawn number lines to give students a starting point for their box-and-whisker plots. You can also have students start working from ordered lists of data or from data displayed in stem-and-leaf plots to make their box-and-whisker plots before progressing to using unordered lists. Starting out with a stem-and-leaf plot also emphasizes the relationship of the two kinds of plots.

Strategies for English Learners

DISSECT WORD PROBLEMS

Throughout this chapter, students will be asked to express their thinking in words as well as in mathematical symbols. For example, at the end of a word problem they may be told, "Explain;" "Give an example;" "Explain your thinking;" "Justify your reasoning;" or "Explain why or why not." Some word problems will be open-ended, where students are expected not just to solve the problem and produce the right answer but to discuss how they solved the problem, show their steps, and explain their thinking.

OPEN-ENDED PROBLEMS Open-ended word problems present three challenges for English learners:
(1) understanding what is being asked; (2) being able to develop a solution and perform the computations; and (3) finding the right English to explain their thinking. Reassure students that they are not required to write English perfectly. As a general rule, mathematics tests are not scored in terms of English grammar. Furthermore, many open-ended word problems can be explained by showing the mathematical steps that led you to a logical conclusion. Use of the English language can be minimal. Drawing a picture, in many cases, really can be worth a thousand words.

MORE PRACTICE Have students practice reading open-ended prompts (such as the ones below) and discussing what is asked for. Then have them respond by using pictures or standard phrases to express their thinking. If students are asked to label their steps, make sure they do so with numerals or using words such as *first, second, third,* or *finally.* Words that are useful to show conclusions are *thus,* and *so, in conclusion,* and the Latin abbreviation QED (*quod erat demonstrandum*), which is put at the end of a proof.

Here is a sample of word problems that ask students to do more than find a right answer:

Page 585, Exercise 15. . . . How does Shanghai compare with the data given for North America and Europe? Explain.

Page 612, Exercise 11. . . . Can you use this information to predict how many people in your town have the flu? Explain why or why not.

Have students work in small groups to brainstorm how these questions could be answered using mathematical explanations and a minimum of English.

Strategies for Advanced Learners

USE REAL-WORLD CONNECTIONS

QUADRILATERALS Lotteries provide an excellent opportunity for students to explore combinations and probability. A lottery has been defined by some as "a tax on people who are bad at math." A typical lottery game may require players to choose six numbers correctly from a field of 49 numbers. Students—and adults—often have misconceptions about the reality of winning such a lottery. In conjunction with Lesson 11.7, you may wish to have each student write down 10 possible 6-number "picks," corresponding to buying 10 lottery tickets. Collect these, photocopy them for your reference, and return them to the students. Then write the numbers 1 through 49 on slips of paper or balls, place them in a container, and mix them up. Draw six numbers, and write them on the board or overhead. Have students circle any numbers on their lists of numbers that match the numbers you have drawn. Have students report the greatest number of matches in any of their lists. Students will likely be surprised that even the highest numbers of matches on their lists are very low—it will be very rare for any list to contain even two matching numbers—and that most lists will contain no matching numbers. Then point out that the number of combinations of six winning numbers chosen from 49 numbers is almost 14 million, so the chance that any ticket is a winner is only about 1 in 14 million!

USE CROSS-CURRICULAR CONNECTIONS

SURVEYS This chapter affords an opportunity to work with other teachers to develop a project that involves a survey. For example, you can work with a social studies teacher on a project in which students conduct a survey about some sort of student demographic or a survey that relates to a topic currently being covered in a social studies class. You can work with an English teacher to help students learn to write clear, unambiguous, unbiased survey questions. You can then help students, possibly in conjunction with a computer sciences teacher, to use their mathematical skills to organize their results and present their conclusions.

Also in this chapter, you may wish to have students look for graphs in newspapers, magazines, or on the Internet that they think are misleading. Students can then bring these graphs to class, explain why they think a particular graph is misleading, and then make a conjecture as to why the graph was used the way that it was. You may want to encourage students to look for graphs that match topics in other classes, such as a social studies or science class. You can expand this project not only to having students find misleading displays, but when a display is given along with the survey questions that were asked, students can also look for biased questions. Have students also watch for and bring in survey results that give a margin of error.

The following problems can be used with **Lesson 11.2**:

- **Challenge** In addition to Exercise 13 on page 592, you may wish to have some advanced students try to write a data set that meets the conditions described for the following problems. Answers will vary.
  a. The whiskers are both the same length as the box portion of the plot.
  b. The part of the box from the median to the upper quartile is three times as long as the part of the box from the lower quartile to the median.
  c. There is no left whisker.

CHAPTER 11

Differentiating Instruction: Resource Materials

Differentiating Review, Reteaching, and Remediation

McDougal Littell *Pre-Algebra* offers teachers a wide variety of reteaching and remediation resources. Pictured here are facsimiles of various pages from the *Notetaking Guide*, the Study Guide pages from the *Chapter 11 Resource Book*, and remediation cards from *Tutor Place*.

NOTETAKING GUIDE

The *Notetaking Guide* easily allows students to take notes on and review each lesson in the textbook by using guided examples and Checkpoint exercises. The *Notetaking Guide* is available on transparencies also.

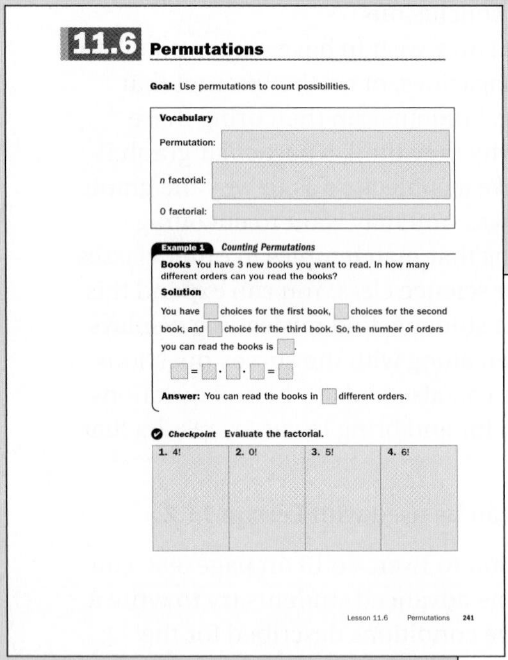

11.6 Permutations

Goal: Use permutations to count possibilities.

Vocabulary

Permutation: ______

n factorial: ______

0 factorial: ______

Example 1 *Counting Permutations*

Books You have 3 new books you want to read. In how many different orders can you read the books?

Solution

You have ☐ choices for the first book, ☐ choices for the second book, and ☐ choice for the third book. So, the number of orders you can read the books is ☐.

☐ = ☐ · ☐ · ☐ = ☐

Answer: You can read the books in ☐ different orders.

Checkpoint **Evaluate the factorial.**

1. 4!	2. 0!	3. 5!	4. 6!

Lesson 11.6 Permutations 241

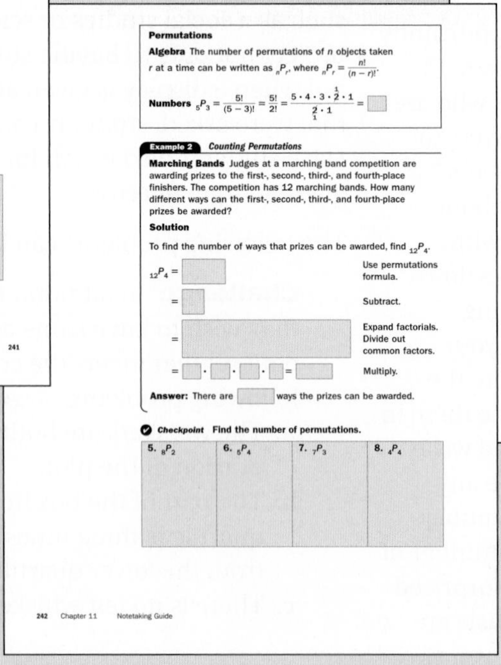

Permutations

Algebra The number of permutations of n objects taken r at a time can be written as $_nP_r$, where $_nP_r = \frac{n!}{(n-r)!}$.

Numbers $_5P_3 = \frac{5!}{(5-3)!} = \frac{5!}{2!} = \frac{5 \cdot 4 \cdot 3 \cdot 2 \cdot 1}{2 \cdot 1} =$ ☐

Example 2 *Counting Permutations*

Marching Bands Judges at a marching band competition are awarding prizes to the first-, second-, third-, and fourth-place finishers. The competition has 12 marching bands. How many different ways can the first-, second-, third-, and fourth-place prizes be awarded?

Solution

To find the number of ways that prizes can be awarded, find $_{12}P_4$.

$_{12}P_4 =$ ☐ Use permutations formula.

= ☐ Subtract.

= ☐ Expand factorials. Divide out common factors.

= ☐ · ☐ · ☐ · ☐ = ☐ Multiply.

Answer: There are ☐ ways the prizes can be awarded.

Checkpoint **Find the number of permutations.**

5. $_8P_2$	6. $_5P_4$	7. $_7P_3$	8. $_4P_4$

242 Chapter 11 Notetaking Guide

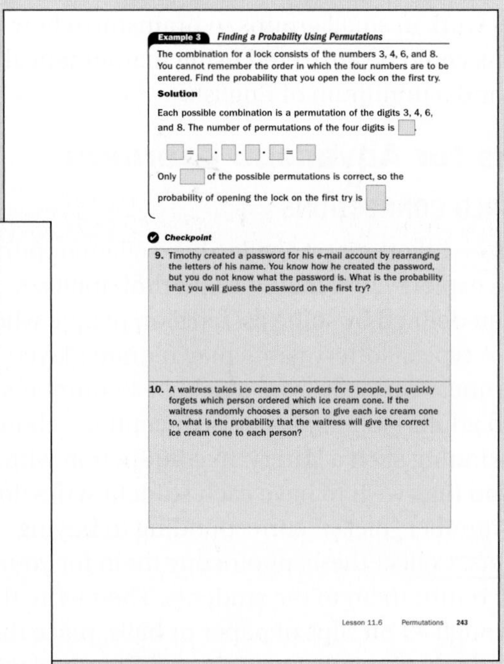

Example 3 *Finding a Probability Using Permutations*

The combination for a lock consists of the numbers 3, 4, 6, and 8. You cannot remember the order in which the four numbers are to be entered. Find the probability that you open the lock on the first try.

Solution

Each possible combination is a permutation of the digits 3, 4, 6, and 8. The number of permutations of the four digits is ☐.

☐ = ☐ · ☐ · ☐ · ☐ = ☐

Only ☐ of the possible permutations is correct, so the probability of opening the lock on the first try is ☐.

Checkpoint

9. Timothy created a password for his e-mail account by rearranging the letters of his name. You know how he created the password, but you do not know what the password is. What is the probability that you will guess the password on the first try?

10. A waitress takes ice cream cone orders for 5 people, but quickly forgets which person ordered which ice cream cone. If the waitress randomly chooses a person to give each ice cream cone to, what is the probability that the waitress will give the correct ice cream cone to each person?

Lesson 11.6 Permutations 243

RESOURCE BOOK

The *Chapter Resource Books* contain Study Guide pages with reteaching examples and exercises for each lesson in the textbook. (The Study Guide pages are also available in Spanish in the *Spanish Study Guide*.)

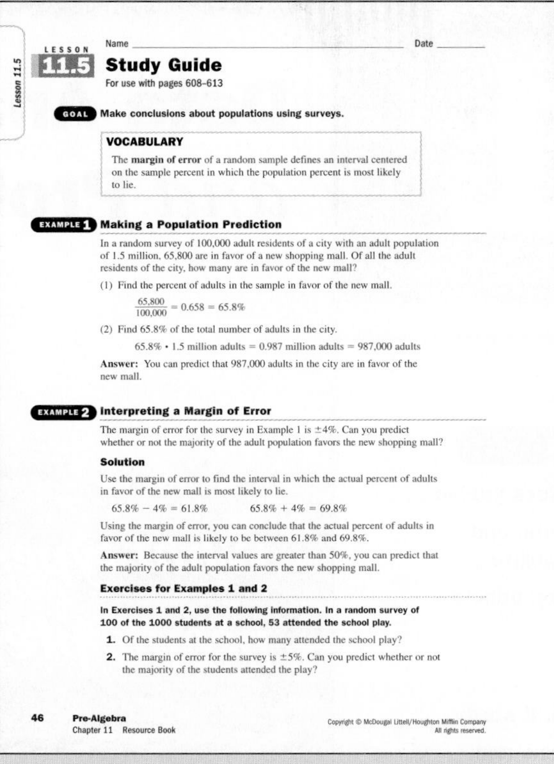

LESSON 11.5 Name ______ Date ______

Study Guide

For use with pages 608–613

GOAL Make conclusions about populations using surveys.

VOCABULARY

The **margin of error** of a random sample defines an interval centered on the sample percent in which the population percent is most likely to lie.

EXAMPLE 1 **Making a Population Prediction**

In a random survey of 100,000 adult residents of a city with an adult population of 1.5 million, 65,800 are in favor of a new shopping mall. Of all the adult residents of the city, how many are in favor of the new mall?

(1) Find the percent of adults in the sample in favor of the new mall.

$\frac{65,800}{100,000} = 0.658 = 65.8\%$

(2) Find 65.8% of the total number of adults in the city.

$65.8\% \cdot 1.5$ million adults $= 0.987$ million adults $= 987,000$ adults

Answer: You can predict that 987,000 adults in the city are in favor of the new mall.

EXAMPLE 2 **Interpreting a Margin of Error**

The margin of error for the survey in Example 1 is ±4%. Can you predict whether or not the majority of the adult population favors the new shopping mall?

Solution

Use the margin of error to find the interval in which the actual percent of adults in favor of the new mall is most likely to lie.

$65.8\% - 4\% = 61.8\%$ $\quad 65.8\% + 4\% = 69.8\%$

Using the margin of error, you can conclude that the actual percent of adults in favor of the new mall is likely to be between 61.8% and 69.8%.

Answer: Because the interval values are greater than 50%, you can predict that the majority of the adult population favors the new shopping mall.

Exercises for Examples 1 and 2

In Exercises 1 and 2, use the following information. In a random survey of 100 of the 1000 students at a school, 53 attended the school play.

1. Of the students at the school, how many attended the school play?
2. The margin of error for the survey is ±5%. Can you predict whether or not the majority of the students attended the play?

46 Pre-Algebra Chapter 11 Resource Book

Copyright © McDougal Littell/Houghton Mifflin Company All rights reserved.

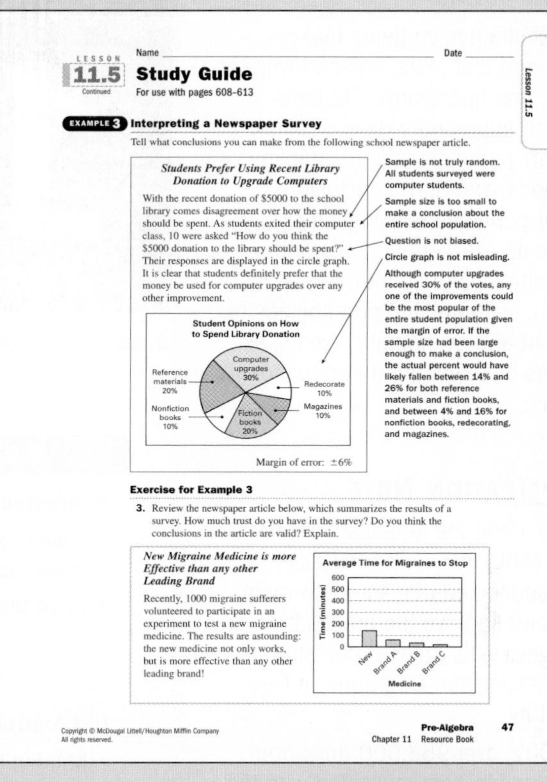

LESSON 11.5 Continued Name ______ Date ______

Study Guide

For use with pages 608–613

EXAMPLE 3 **Interpreting a Newspaper Survey**

Tell what conclusions you can make from the following school newspaper article.

Students Prefer Using Recent Library Donation to Upgrade Computers

With the recent donation of $5000 to the school library comes disagreement over how the money should be spent. As students exited their computer class, 10 were asked "How do you think the $5000 donation to the library should be spent?" Their responses are displayed in the circle graph. It is clear that students definitely prefer that the money be used for computer upgrades over any other improvement.

Sample is not truly random. All students surveyed were computer students.

Sample size is too small to make a conclusion about the entire school population.

Question is not biased.

Circle graph is not misleading.

Although computer upgrades received 30% of the votes, any one of the improvements could be the most popular of the entire student population given the margin of error. If the sample size had been large enough to make a conclusion, the actual percent would have likely fallen between 14% and 26% for both reference materials and fiction books, and between 4% and 16% for nonfiction books, redecorating, and magazines.

Exercise for Example 3

3. Review the newspaper article below, which summarizes the results of a survey. How much trust do you have in the survey? Do you think the conclusions in the article are valid? Explain.

New Migraine Medicine is more Effective than any other Leading Brand

Recently, 1000 migraine sufferers volunteered to participate in an experiment to test a new migraine medicine. The results are astounding: the new medicine not only works, but is more effective than any other leading brand!

Copyright © McDougal Littell/Houghton Mifflin Company All rights reserved.

Pre-Algebra Chapter 11 Resource Book 47

TUTOR PLACE

Tutor Place helps students practice and master essential topics. Instruction is provided by 104 cards containing examples and two sets of practice exercises. Answers are provided in a handy answer key.

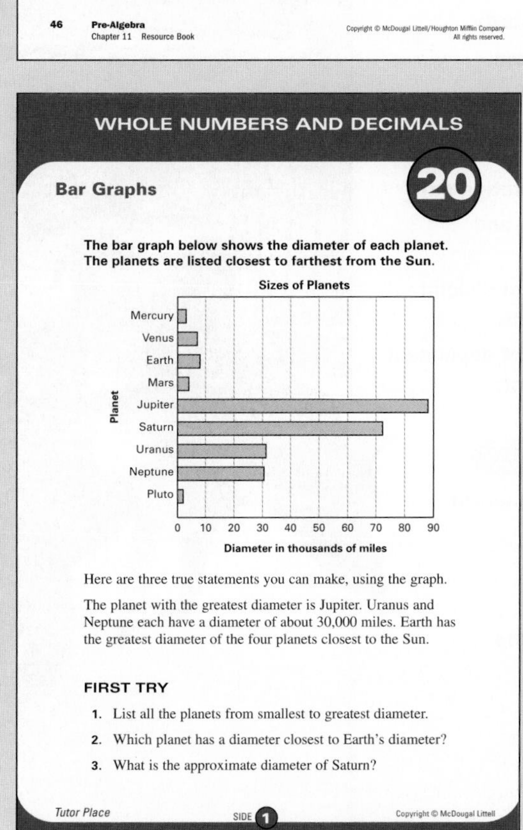

WHOLE NUMBERS AND DECIMALS

Bar Graphs 20

The bar graph below shows the diameter of each planet. The planets are listed closest to farthest from the Sun.

Here are three true statements you can make, using the graph.

The planet with the greatest diameter is Jupiter. Uranus and Neptune each have a diameter of about 30,000 miles. Earth has the greatest diameter of the four planets closest to the Sun.

FIRST TRY

1. List all the planets from smallest to greatest diameter.
2. Which planet has a diameter closest to Earth's diameter?
3. What is the approximate diameter of Saturn?

Tutor Place SIDE 1 Copyright © McDougal Littell

RATIO, PROPORTION, AND PERCENT

Circle Graphs 17

Example The surface of Earth is 29% land and 71% water. Use a circle graph to show these data.

Draw a circle and divide it into two parts, called **sectors.** One sector is 29% of the circle, and the other sector is 71%. Write and solve a proportion to find the angle measure of the sector for 29%.

$\frac{29}{100} = \frac{a}{360}$ ← The angle measure for the whole circle is 360°.

$100 \times a = 29 \times 360$

$100a = 10,440$

$\frac{100a}{100} = \frac{10,440}{100}$

$a = 104.4$ → Round to 104°.

Draw a 104° angle, using the center of the circle as the vertex. This forms the sector for 29% of the circle. The rest is 71% of the circle. Label the circle graph.

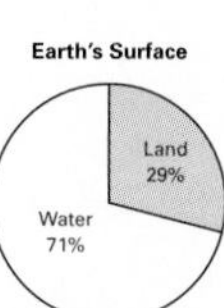

FIRST TRY

1. For the problem above, write and solve a proportion to find the angle measure of the sector for 71% of the circle. Measure the angle in the circle to check your answer.

Tutor Place SIDE  Copyright © McDougal Littell

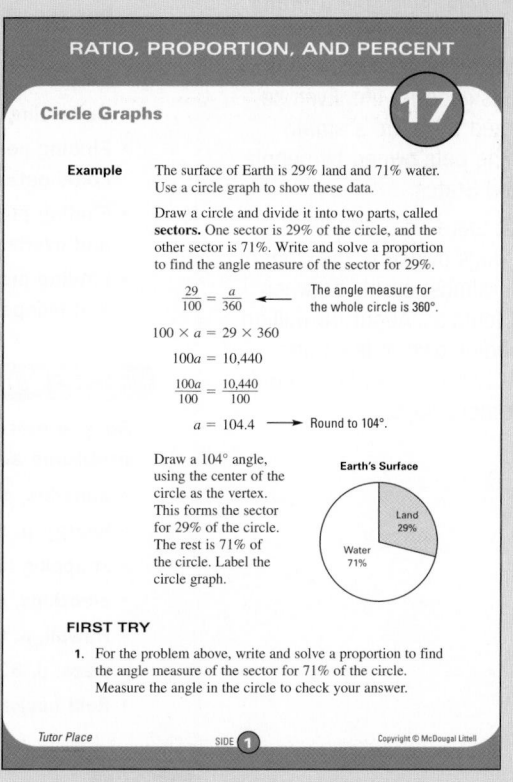

OVERVIEW

Main Ideas

In this chapter, students make stem-and-leaf plots, box-and-whisker plots, and histograms. Students choose appropriate data displays, identify populations and sampling methods, and draw conclusions about populations using surveys. Students use permutations and combinations to count possibilities. Finally, students find probabilities of disjoint and overlapping events, as well as independent and dependent events.

Application Note

Since 1884 the American Kennel Club (AKC) has registered dogs and sponsored dog shows to maintain and improve the breeds it recognizes. Its premier dog show is the Westminster Dog Show in New York City.

In 2002, over 958,000 dogs from 150 breeds were registered with the AKC. This is just a small proportion of the registered dogs, since a dog's registration is good for life. Even so, AKC-registered dogs are a small fraction of the pets owned by people in the United States.

As of 2002, there were about 68 million dogs owned in the United States, split almost evenly between males and females. About 40 million U.S. households own at least one dog. About 37% of these households own two or more dogs.

CHAPTER 11

Data Analysis *and* Probability

What types of dogs do people prefer as pets?

BEFORE

In previous chapters you've . . .

- **Found experimental and theoretical probabilities**
- **Used the counting principle**

Now

In Chapter 11 you'll study . . .

- **Making histograms and box-and-whisker plots**
- **Choosing appropriate displays for data**
- **Collecting and interpreting data**
- **Finding permutations and combinations**
- **Finding probabilities of disjoint and overlapping events**
- **Finding probabilities of dependent and independent events**

WHY?

So you can solve real-world problems about . . .

- **canaries, p. 585**
- **energy, p. 599**
- **snapping turtles, p. 604**
- **elections, p. 612**
- **Hawaii, p. 618**
- **pizza, p. 624**
- **field hockey, p. 639**

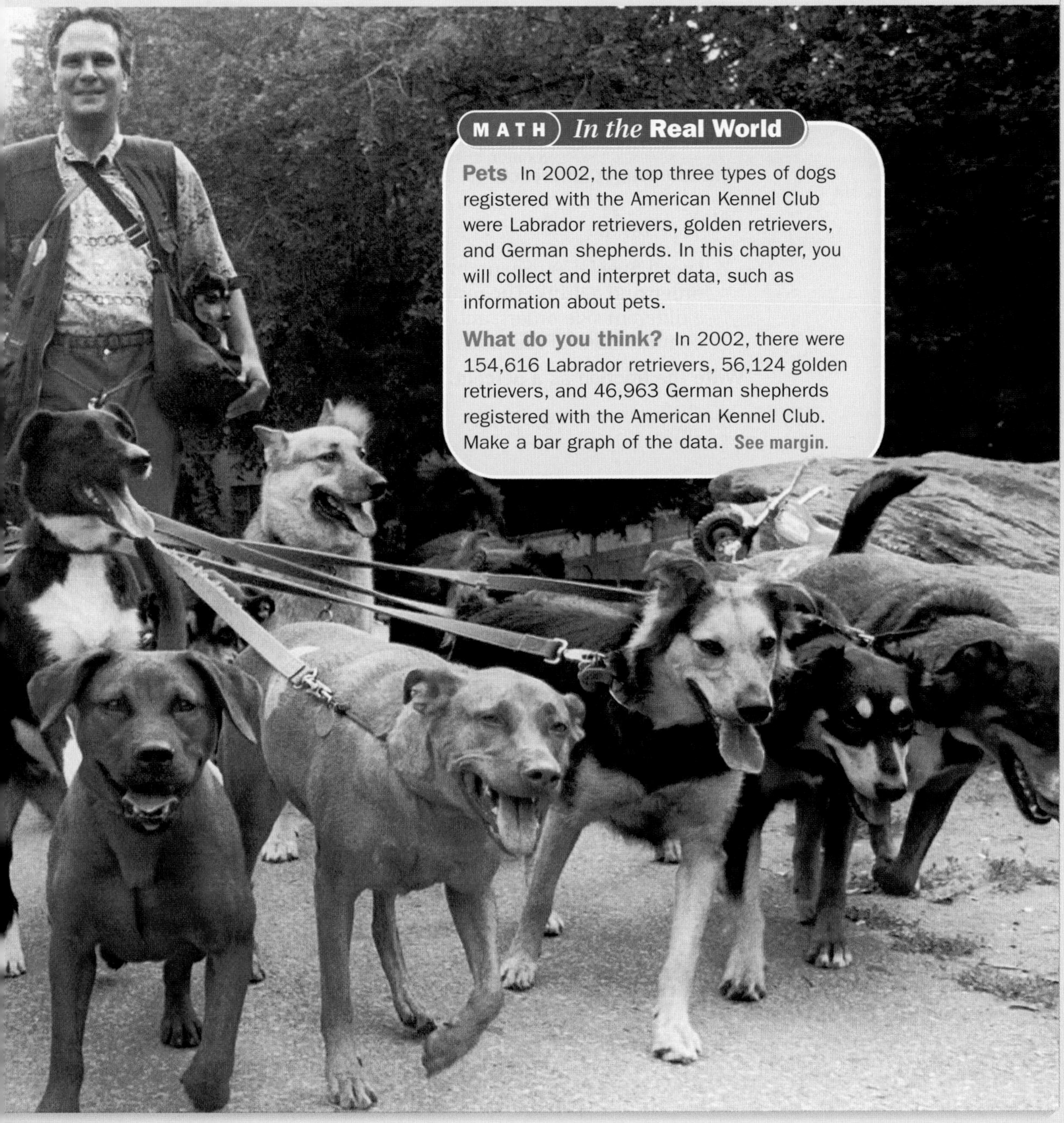

MATH *In the* **Real World**

Pets In 2002, the top three types of dogs registered with the American Kennel Club were Labrador retrievers, golden retrievers, and German shepherds. In this chapter, you will collect and interpret data, such as information about pets.

What do you think? In 2002, there were 154,616 Labrador retrievers, 56,124 golden retrievers, and 46,963 German shepherds registered with the American Kennel Club. Make a bar graph of the data. **See margin.**

CHAPTER RESOURCES

These resources are provided to help you prepare for the chapter and to customize review materials:

Chapter 11 Resource Book

- Tips for New Teachers, pp. 1–2
- Lesson Plan, pp. 5, 14, 24, 32, 41, 49, 58, 69, 78
- Lesson Plan for Block Scheduling, pp. 6, 15, 25, 33, 42, 50, 59, 70, 79

Technology

- EasyPlanner CD-ROM
- Test and Practice Generator
- Electronic Lesson Presentations CD-ROM
- eTutorial CD-ROM

Internet

- Classzone
- eEdition Plus Online
- eWorkbook Plus Online
- eTutorial Plus Online
- EasyPlanner Plus Online

ENGLISH LEARNER SUPPORT

- Spanish Study Guide
- Multi-Language Visual Glossary
- Chapter Audio Summaries CDs
- Teacher's Edition, pp. 578E–578F

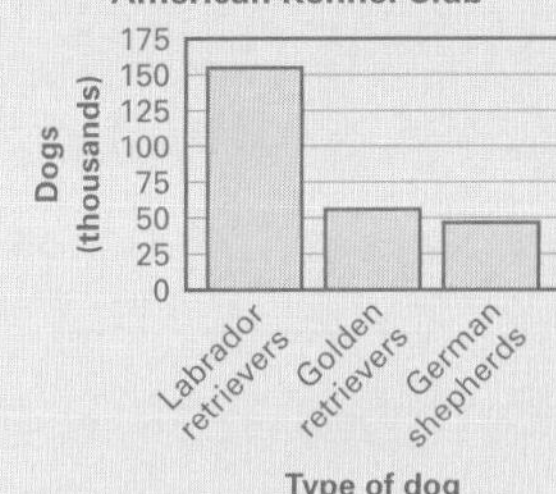

PREPARE

DIAGNOSIS/REMEDIATION

Prerequisite Skills Quiz
The Prerequisite Skills Quiz can help you diagnose whether students have the following skills needed in Chapter 11:

- Use vocabulary (Exs. 1–2)
- Add and subtract fractions (Exs. 3–6)
- Use the counting principle (Ex. 7)
- Write a fraction as a percent (Exs. 8–11)

 ***Chapter 11 Resource Book***

- Study Guide (Lessons 11.1–11.9)

 ***Tutor Place***

NOTETAKING STRATEGIES

Suggest that students use colored pens or pencils so the Example, Details, and Definition portions of each word triangle are shown in different colors. Further suggestions for keeping a notebook can be found on pages 596 and 615.

For more support on notetaking, see:

- Notetaking Guide Workbook
- Notetaking Transparencies

CHAPTER 11

Chapter Prerequisite Skills

Review Vocabulary
reciprocal, p. 243
outcomes, p. 306
event, p. 306
favorable outcomes, p. 306
probability, p. 306
odds in favor, p. 308
odds against, p. 308
tree diagram, p. 313
counting principle, p. 314

PREREQUISITE SKILLS QUIZ

Preparing for Success **To prepare for success in this chapter, test your knowledge of these concepts and skills. You may want to look at the pages referred to in blue for additional review.**

1. **Vocabulary** Copy and complete: The _?_ of an event is never greater than 1 and never less than 0. **probability**
2. **Vocabulary** Give an example of an event involving a number cube. ***Sample answer:*** **the number cube shows an even number**

Find the sum or difference. *(p. 225)*

3. $\frac{15}{16} + \frac{3}{16}$ $1\frac{1}{8}$
4. $-\frac{5}{7} + \frac{2}{7}$ $-\frac{3}{7}$
5. $-\frac{4}{5} - \frac{2}{5}$ $-1\frac{1}{5}$
6. $\frac{8}{9} - \frac{1}{9}$ $\frac{7}{9}$

7. **Lunch Special** A restaurant's lunch special includes a sandwich, a side order, and a drink. The restaurant's menu has 5 different sandwiches, 3 different side orders, and 4 different drinks. How many different combinations of the lunch special are possible? *(p. 313)* **60 combinations**

Write the fraction as a percent. *(p. 329)*

8. $\frac{3}{20}$ 15%
9. $\frac{5}{4}$ 125%
10. $\frac{5}{8}$ 62.5%
11. $\frac{1}{500}$ 0.2%

NOTETAKING STRATEGIES

WORD TRIANGLE When you learn a new vocabulary word or formula, write it in your notes with details and examples in a word triangle like the one shown.

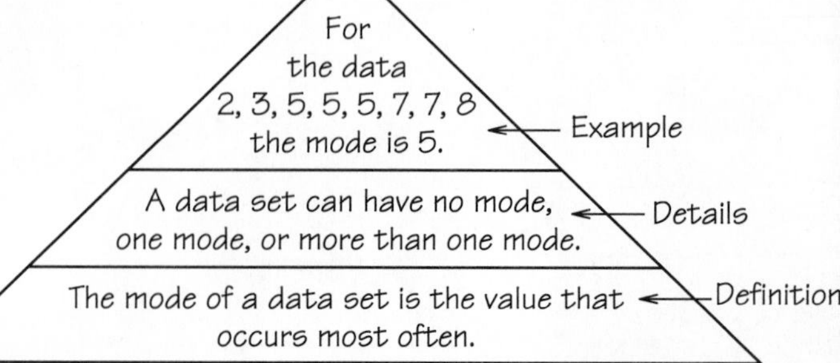

For the data 2, 3, 5, 5, 5, 7, 7, 8 the mode is 5.
Example
A data set can have no mode, one mode, or more than one mode.
Details
The mode of a data set is the value that occurs most often.
Definition

In Lesson 11.6, you can use a word triangle to take notes about permutations.

Note *Worthy*

You will find a notetaking strategy at the beginning of each chapter. Look for additional notetaking and study strategies throughout the chapter.

LESSON **11.1**

Stem-and-Leaf Plots *and* Histograms

Vocabulary
stem-and-leaf plot, p. 581
frequency, p. 582
frequency table, p. 582
histogram, p. 583

BEFORE	Now	WHY?
You found the median of a data set.	You'll make stem-and-leaf plots and histograms.	So you can compare marathon times, as in Ex. 16.

Track The distances (in centimeters) of 11 jumps from the final round of a women's long jump competition are listed below. How can you display the data to show the distribution of the distances?

669, 702, 644, 701, 684, 686,
676, 673, 688, 670, 662

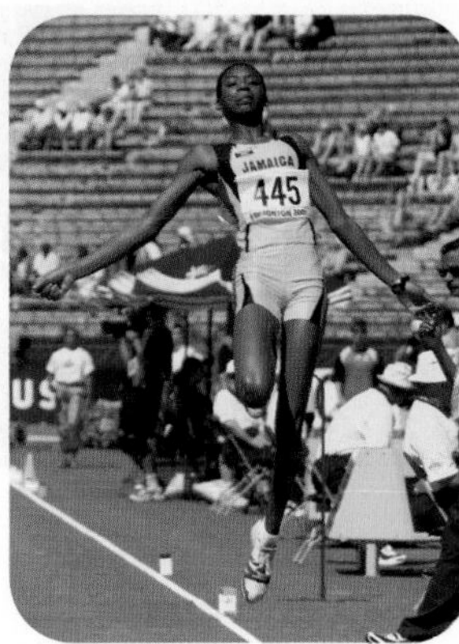

A **stem-and-leaf plot** is a data display that organizes data based on their digits. Each data value is separated into a *stem* (the leading digits) and a *leaf* (the last digit).

Example 1 *Making a Stem-and-Leaf Plot*

You can use a stem-and-leaf plot to display the distances listed above.

1) The least data value is 644 and the greatest is 702. Let the **stems** be the hundreds' and tens' digits of the data values (from 64 to 70). Let the **leaves** be the ones' digits.

2) Write the stems first. Then record each distance by writing its ones' digit on the same line as its corresponding stem.

3) Make an ordered plot. Give it a key and a title.

Women's Long Jump

Unordered Plot

Stem	Leaves
64	4
65	
66	9 2
67	6 3 0
68	4 6 8
69	
70	2 1

Key: 64 | 4 = 644 cm

Ordered Plot

Stem	Leaves
64	4
65	
66	2 9
67	0 3 6
68	4 6 8
69	
70	1 2

Key: 64 | 4 = 644 cm

In an ordered stem-and-leaf plot, list the leaves for each stem in order from least to greatest.

A stem-and-leaf plot's key tells what numbers the stems and leaves represent.

Reading *Algebra*

Each stem in a stem-and-leaf plot determines an interval. For the stem-and-leaf plot in Example 1, for instance, the stem 64 determines the interval 640–649. There is only one data value, 644, that falls in this interval.

NCTM CURRICULUM STANDARDS
Standard 5: Collect, organize, and display data; Use proper statistical methods to analyze data; Develop inferences that are based on data

1 PLAN

Skill Check
Order from least to greatest.

1. 15, 25, 17, 11 **11, 15, 17, 25**
2. 84, 77, 91, 83 **77, 83, 84, 91**
3. 270, 258, 273, 266 **258, 266, 270, 273**

Lesson Objective
Make stem-and-leaf plots and histograms.

Pacing
Suggested Number of Days
Basic Course: 2 days
Average Course: 2 days
Advanced Course: 2 days
Block: 1 block

Teaching Resources
For a complete list of Teaching Resources, see page 578B.

Transparency
Warm-Up Exercises for this lesson are available on a transparency.

2 TEACH

Motivating the Lesson
Have students identify the greatest distance from the list and ask a volunteer to measure that distance across the classroom.

TIPS *for* NEW TEACHERS
Stress that the intervals of a histogram must have equal size and that there is no space between the bars. See Tips for New Teachers in the *Chapter 11 Resource Book*.

Extra Examples

Example 1 The number of passengers on each of 10 city buses is given below. Display the data in a stem-and-leaf plot.
12, 35, 17, 39, 25, 23, 20, 20, 35, 14

Bus Passengers

1	2 4 7
2	0 0 3 5
3	5 5 9

Key: 1 | 2 = 12

Example 2 The stem-and-leaf plots show the grades on a history test for two classes. What can you conclude about the grades?

Class A

7	2 2 5 7 8
8	1 1 3 3
9	0 0 1

Class B

7	1 5 6
8	5 7 9
9	0 1 2 2 3 4

Key: 7 | 1 = 71

***Sample answer:* Class A has a median score of 81 while Class B has a median score of 89.5. Class B has twice as many scores in the 90s as does Class A.**

Example 3 Madison asked 20 classmates how many CDs they own. The numbers are listed below. Make a frequency table of the data, using intervals of 5.
12, 12, 12, 2, 6, 7, 18, 19, 7, 4, 13, 13, 7, 8, 9, 4, 10, 14, 14, 14

CDs	Tally	Frequency
1–5	|||	3
6–10	𝍸 ||	7
11–15	𝍸 |||	8
16–20	||	2

Teaching Tip

Prior to discussing Example 2, you may wish to review how to find the mean, median, and mode.

Review *Help*

For help with finding the mean, median, mode, or range of a data set, see p. 39.

Data Distributions A stem-and-leaf plot shows how data are distributed. From a stem-and-leaf plot you can draw conclusions about the data. For example, you can see if data values are grouped together or tell whether most of the data are above or below the mean.

Example 2 *Interpreting Stem-and-Leaf Plots*

Sneakers The stem-and-leaf plots show the prices (in dollars) of pairs of sneakers at two shoe stores. What can you conclude about the prices at the two stores?

Store A

3	0 2 5 6 9
4	1 1 5 5 9
5	0 3 4 5 8
6	0 0 2 5

Store B

3	0 0 5 5 9
4	0 0 2 3 3 5 5 5
5	4 4 5 8
6	5 9

Key: 3 | 0 = $30

Solution

- Store A has a median price of $49. Store B has a median price of $43.
- Store B has more sneakers priced under $50 than Store A.
- More than half of the sneakers at Store B have prices in the $30–$39 and $40–$49 intervals. The sneaker prices at Store A are more evenly distributed over all intervals.

Frequency Tables A stem-and-leaf plot shows the *frequency* of each interval in the display. The **frequency** of an interval is the number of data values in that interval. A **frequency table** is another type of display that groups data into intervals to show frequencies.

Study *Strategy*

To choose the interval size for a frequency table, divide the range of the data by the number of intervals you want the table to have. Use the quotient as an approximate interval size.

Example 3 *Making a Frequency Table*

Hurricanes In the United States, hurricane season starts June 1 and lasts about 26 weeks. Meteorologists record the number of weeks into the season each hurricane occurs. The number of weeks into the hurricane season in which Atlantic hurricanes occurred from 1997 to 2000 are listed below. Make a frequency table of the data.

6, 7, 14, 12, 13, 14, 16, 16, 17, 17, 19, 21, 26, 12, 12,
13, 15, 15, 20, 20, 24, 10, 12, 15, 16, 17, 17, 18, 20

Solution

1. Choose intervals of equal size for the data.
2. Use a tally mark to record the interval in which each data value falls.
3. Write the frequency for each interval by counting the number of tally marks for the interval.

Weeks	Tally	Frequency
6–8	||	2
9–11			1
12–14	𝍸 |||	8
15–17	𝍸 𝍸	10
18–20	𝍸	5
21–23			1
24–26	||	2

Histograms A **histogram** displays data from a frequency table. A histogram has one bar for each interval. The length of a bar indicates the frequency of the interval. There is no space between bars because there are no gaps between intervals. Because the intervals of a histogram have equal size, the bars have equal width.

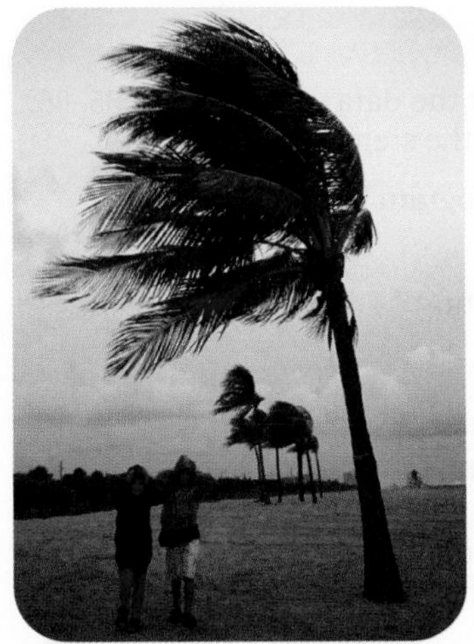

Example 4 *Making a Histogram*

Make a histogram using the frequency table in Example 3.

1) Show the intervals from the frequency table on the horizontal axis, and show the frequencies on the vertical axis.

2) Draw a bar to represent the frequency for each interval.

3) Give the histogram a title.

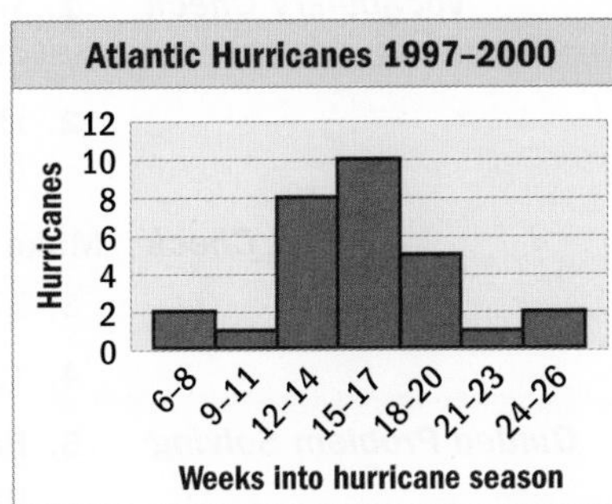

Example 5 *Interpreting a Histogram*

Internet The histogram shows the number of minutes that 100 students spent on the Internet in one day. Make several conclusions about the data.

Student Internet Use on One Day

Students: 0, 10, 20, 30, 40, 50

0–14, 15–29, 30–44, 45–59, 60–74, 75–89

Minutes

Solution

- Almost half of the students spent less than 15 minutes on the Internet.
- Of the students who spent more than 15 minutes on the Internet, the majority spent from 30 to 59 minutes on the Internet.
- Few of the students spent 60 minutes or more on the Internet.

Checkpoint

1. Your bowling scores in your last 15 games are as follows: 125, 158, 143, 177, 135, 117, 101, 158, 160, 144, 199, 129, 122, 131, 116.
   a. Make a frequency table and histogram for your bowling scores. **See margin.**
   b. Interpret the histogram. What scores do you usually bowl? Are your scores distributed evenly over all intervals? How unusual is it for you to bowl a game over 150?

1b. ***Sample answer:*** **I bowl in the 120's more frequently than in any other interval, with the majority of my scores fairly evenly spread out between 110 and 159. Above that, there are a few scores widely spread out. I bowl over 150 one third of the time.**

Extra Examples

Example 4 Make a histogram using the frequency table in Extra Example 3.

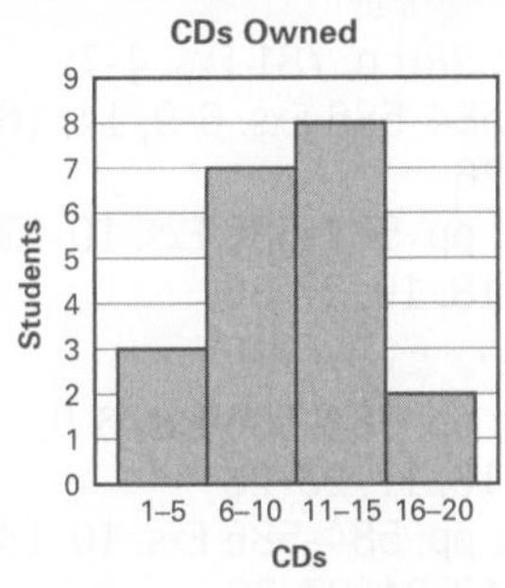

Example 5 The histogram shows the ages of customers in a diner. Make conclusions about the data.

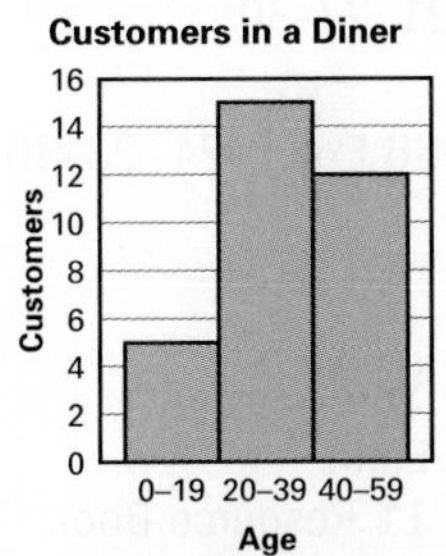

Sample answer: **Amost half of the customers are in the 20–39 age range. There are three times as many people in the 20–39 age range as are in the 0–19 age range.**

Concept Check

How is a stem-and-leaf plot similar to a histogram? **You can see which intervals have the fewest and the most data values.**

Daily Puzzler

Name a set of five numbers that have the same mean, median, mode, and range. ***Sample answer:*** **2, 4, 4, 4, 6**

1a. See Additional Answers beginning on page AA1.

3 APPLY

ASSIGNMENT GUIDE

Basic Course

Day 1: SRH p. 781 Exs. 4-7; pp. 584-586 Exs. 6-9, 14, 16, 23-26

Day 2: pp. 584-586 Exs. 10-13, 15, 18, 19, 27-30

Average Course

Day 1: pp. 584-586 Exs. 6-9, 14, 16, 17, 23-26

Day 2: pp. 584-586 Exs. 10-13, 15, 18-21, 27-30

Advanced Course

Day 1: pp. 584-586 Exs. 7-9, 14, 16, 22-26*

Day 2: pp. 584-586 Exs. 11-13, 15, 17-21, 27-30

Block

pp. 584-586 Exs. 6-21, 23-30

EXTRA PRACTICE

- Student Edition, p. 813
- Chapter 11 Resource Book, pp. 8-10
- Test and Practice Generator

TRANSPARENCY

Even-numbered answers are available on transparencies.

HOMEWORK CHECK

When you review students' homework for this lesson, go over the following exercises to check understanding of key concepts.

Basic: 6, 10, 14, 15, 18

Average: 8, 12, 14, 15, 19

Advanced: 9, 13, 16, 19, 21

COMMON ERROR

In Exercises 10-13, watch for students who do not draw their tick marks carefully and then miscount them, resulting in an incorrect frequency table and histogram.

11.1 Exercises

More Practice, p. 813

Guided Practice

Vocabulary Check

1. You want to make a stem-and-leaf plot of the data values 90, 93, 85, 86, and 74. What numbers would you use as the stems? 7, 8, and 9
2. How can you tell which interval on a histogram has the greatest frequency? It has the tallest bar.

Skill Check

Make an ordered stem-and-leaf plot of the data. 3–4. See margin.

3. 27, 56, 40, 29, 44, 40, 60, 58, 62, 21, 56, 31, 33, 46, 41
4. 12, 50, 72, 67, 33, 98, 44, 16, 91, 47, 42, 53, 33, 11, 60, 77, 35, 79

Guided Problem Solving

5. **Earthquakes** For the period 1980–1998, the table below shows the number of earthquakes with magnitudes greater than 7.0 on the Richter scale. In 1999 there were 11 earthquakes greater than 7.0 on the Richter scale. How did 1999 compare with the preceding years?

   1) Make a frequency table of the data.
   2) Use your frequency table to make a histogram. Steps 1–2. See margin.
   3) Into which interval does the number of earthquakes in 1999 fall? How does the frequency of this interval compare with the frequencies of the other intervals? *Sample answer:* 9–12; it is the third most frequent interval, after 13–16 and 5–8. Nearly two thirds of the annual numbers of earthquakes, however, are above the interval in which 11 lies.

High-Magnitude Earthquakes Per Year
18, 14, 10, 15, 8, 15, 6, 11, 8, 7, 13, 10, 23, 16, 15, 25, 22, 20, 16

3.

Stem	Leaves
2	1 7 9
3	1 3
4	0 0 1 4 6
5	6 6 8
6	0 2

Key: 2 | 1 = 21

Practice and Problem Solving

Homework *Help*

Example	Exercises
1	6-9, 14
2	14, 16
3	10-13, 21
4	10-13, 18, 19, 21
5	15, 21

Online Resources CLASSZONE.COM
- More Examples
- eTutorial Plus

Make an ordered stem-and-leaf plot of the data. 6–9. See margin.

A 6. 350, 314, 378, 391, 395, 300, 357, 309, 312, 343, 389, 350, 306, 387, 381

7. 62, 77, 50, 6, 44, 61, 70, 9, 62, 71, 65, 41, 54, 63, 58, 64, 70
8. 3.23, 3.01, 2.68, 3.16, 2.88, 3.11, 2.55, 3.19, 2.56, 3.21, 2.66, 3.50, 2.66
9. 13.5, 15.7, 15.0, 12.6, 14.2, 15.1, 18.0, 13.9, 15.2, 14.1, 12.5, 12.1, 13.4

Use the data to make a frequency table and a histogram. 10–13. See margin.

10. 9, 15, 2, 4, 9, 11, 10, 1, 18, 4, 9, 2, 8, 7, 4, 11, 10, 9, 16, 5
11. 137, 182, 145, 109, 118, 200, 120, 136, 191, 133, 122, 184, 127, 140
12. 1300, 2800, 9100, 7600, 3100, 2200, 1300, 2500, 4200, 1800, 1100, 6000
13. 66, 78, 91, 42, 45, 88, 69, 73, 76, 80, 50, 63, 57, 54, 71, 66

14a. Canary Weights

0	9 9
1	1 2 5 7 7 9
2	0 0 1 2 5

Key: 1 | 1 = 11 grams

15c. *Sample answer:* The vacation days in Shanghai are fewer than for most cities in North America and Europe. At least two thirds of the cities in Europe and North America have more vacation days.

16d. *Sample answer:* It is just 3 minutes slower than the median of the men's time, so it would rank about in the middle of the men's times.

17. *Sample answer:* 4.6 and 46; in 4.6, the stem 4 represents the ones place and 6 represents the tenths place; in 46, the stem 4 represents the tens place and 6 represents the ones place.

In the **Real World**

Marathon A marathon is about 1,660,000 inches long. Suppose a wheelchair has a rear wheel with a diameter of 18 inches. If the wheelchair travels the entire marathon route, about how many revolutions does the wheel make? **about 29,355 revolutions**

14. Canaries The weights (in grams) of 13 canaries at a pet shop are as follows: 15, 17, 9, 22, 19, 21, 20, 25, 11, 12, 9, 20, 17.

a. Make an ordered stem-and-leaf plot of the data.

b. Find the median and the range of the data. **median: 17, range: 16**

c. Compare Another canary weighs 18 grams. How does this canary compare with the others? ***Sample answer:* It is very close, only slightly above, the median weight of the others.**

15. Extended Problem Solving The histogram shows the average number of vacation days that working citizens in 30 major cities in Europe and North America have each year.

a. What interval has the greatest frequency? **25–29**

b. Interpret In what percent of the cities surveyed do working citizens have fewer than 20 vacation days per year? $33\frac{1}{3}\%$

c. Critical Thinking Citizens of Shanghai, China, average 16 vacation days per year. How does Shanghai compare with the data given for North America and Europe? Explain.

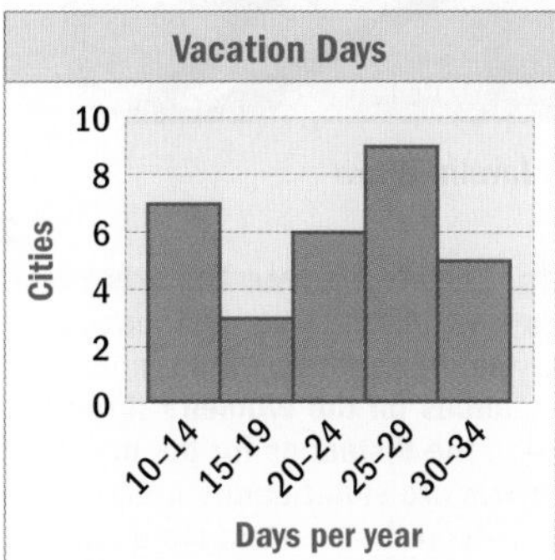

16. Marathon The stem-and-leaf plot shows the times (in minutes) for 30 men who completed the 2002 Boston Marathon using a wheelchair.

a. What was the fastest time? **83 min**

b. Find the median of the times. **103 min**

c. What percent of the participants finished the race in less than 2 hours? **80%**

d. The fastest female wheelchair time in the marathon was 1 hour 46 minutes. How does this time compare with the times of the 30 male participants? **See margin.**

Wheelchair Marathon Times

8	3 6
9	0 3 3 5 6
10	0 0 1 3 3 3 3 3 3 3 6 9
11	1 2 3 9 9
12	1 2 4 9 9
13	3

Key: 8 | 3 = 83 minutes

17. Critical Thinking A stem-and-leaf plot has a stem of 4 and a leaf of 6, but the plot has no key. Give two possible values that the stem and leaf could represent. Explain your thinking. **See margin.**

Make a histogram from the stem-and-leaf plot. Do not use the same intervals in your histogram as are used in the stem-and-leaf plot. **18–19. See margin.**

B **18.**

36	4
37	0 0 5
38	2 2 3 7 7 7 7 8 9
39	0 1 4 6 7

Key: 36 | 4 = 364

19.

9	1 3 5 7 8 8 9
10	2 2 2 2 3 7 7 8 9
11	3 5 7
12	1 2 5 6 6 7 8 8 8 8

Key: 9 | 1 = 9.1

4, 5. See Additional Answers beginning on page AA1.

6.

30	0 6 9
31	2 4
32	
33	
34	3
35	0 0 7
36	
37	8
38	1 7 9
39	1 5

Key: 30 | 0 = 300

7.

0	6 9
1	
2	
3	
4	1 4
5	0 4 8
6	1 2 2 3 4 5
7	0 0 1 7

Key: 0 | 6 = 6

8.

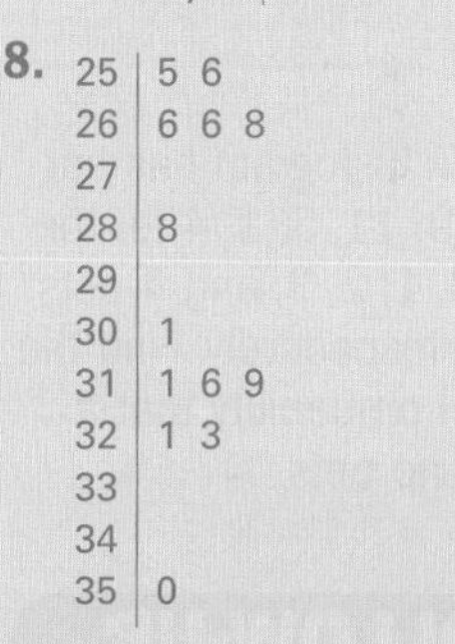

25	5 6
26	6 6 8
27	
28	8
29	
30	1
31	1 6 9
32	1 3
33	
34	
35	0

Key: 25 | 5 = 2.55

9.

12	1 5 6
13	4 5 9
14	1 2
15	0 1 2 7
16	
17	
18	0

Key: 12 | 1 = 12.1

10–13, 18, 19. See Additional Answers beginning on page AA1.

4 ASSESS

ASSESSMENT RESOURCES

For more assessment resources, see:
- Assessment Book
- Test and Practice Generator

MINI-QUIZ

Use this data: 82, 61, 84, 75, 61, 87, 88, 79, 64, 66.

1. Make an ordered stem-and-leaf plot of the data.

6	1 1 4 6
7	5 9
8	2 4 7 8

Key: 6 | 1 = 61

2. Use the data to make a histogram. *Sample:*

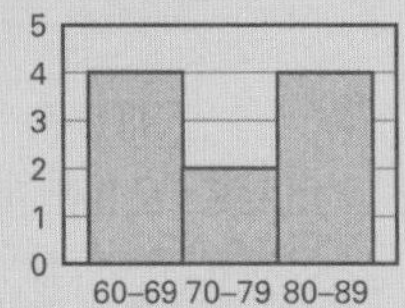

3. **Challenge** A histogram has bar heights of 19, 11, 5, 1, 4 for the categories 0, 1, 2, 3, and 4 pets per student, respectively. Find the experimental probability that a student has no pets. **47.5%**

5 FOLLOW-UP

DIAGNOSIS/REMEDIATION

- Study Guide in Chapter 11 Resource Book, pp. 11–12
- eTutorial Plus Online
- Extra Practice, p. 813
- Lesson Practice in Chapter 11 Resource Book, pp. 8–10

ENGLISH LEARNER SUPPORT

- Spanish Study Guide
- Multi-Language Visual Glossary
- Chapter Audio Summaries CDs

CHALLENGE

- Challenge Practice in Chapter 11 Resource Book, p. 13
- Teacher's Edition, p. 578F

20, 21a–b. See Additional Answers beginning on page AA1.

586

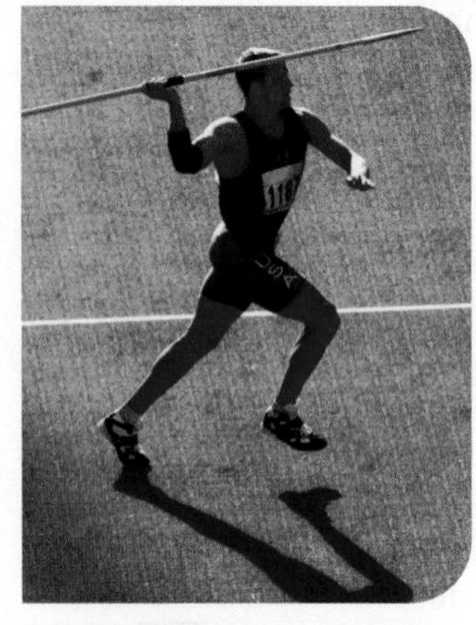

Javelin throw

21c. *Sample answer:* There is more variation in the distances for the men's throws than in the distances for the women's throws. All of the distances for the men's throws are significantly greater than even the greatest distances for the women's throws.

20. *Writing* Compare stem-and-leaf plots and histograms. How are they alike? What advantages do stem-and-leaf plots have over histograms? What advantages do histograms have over stem-and-leaf plots? **See margin.**

21. Javelin The results of the top ten distances (in meters) for men and women in a javelin competition are listed below.

Men: 87.00, 92.80, 85.52, 89.95, 86.46, 83.64, 91.31, 81.80, 80.56, 82.82

Women: 63.11, 61.01, 65.78, 58.45, 69.53, 61.60, 62.08, 64.69, 61.94, 60.91

a. Make frequency tables for both the men's and women's distances. **21a–b. See margin.**

b. Use the frequency tables you made in part (a) to make histograms for the two sets of data.

c. Analyze What conclusions can you make from the distributions of the data?

C **22. Challenge** The histogram shows the results of a survey that asked 40 students at one school how many pets they owned. Use the histogram to find the experimental probability that a student at the school has 2 or more pets. **25%**

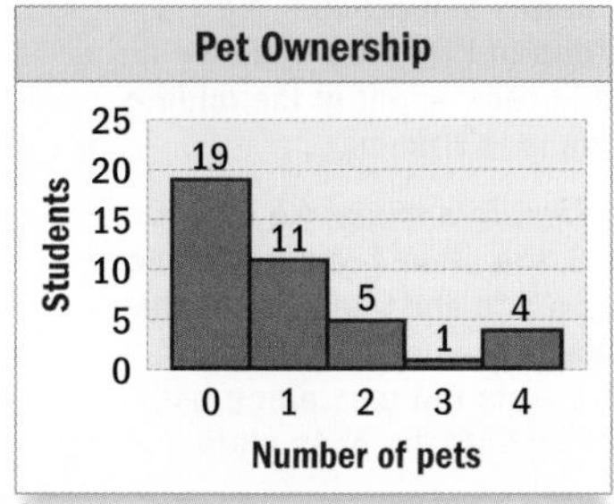

Mixed Review

23. Sweater You buy a sweater that is on sale for 15% off the original price of \$40. What is the sale price of the sweater? *(Lesson 7.6)* **\$34**

Find the slope of the line through the given points. *(Lesson 8.4)*

24. (4, 2), (3, 8) **−6** **25.** (−3, −5), (−6, 7) **−4** **26.** (3, −6), (−2, 2) $-\frac{8}{5}$

Find the midpoint of the segment with the given endpoints. *(Lesson 9.5)*

27. (2, 6), (−10, −2) **(−4, 2)** **28.** (−16, −5), (5, 5) **(−5.5, 0)** **29.** (−3, 4), (4, −2) **(0.5, 1)**

Standardized Test Practice

30b. 30–39. *Sample answer:* There were 35 people in the survey, so the median age is the eighteenth ordered data value. The interval 30–39 contains the thirteenth through the twenty-sixth ordered data values.

30c. *Sample answer:* One that younger adults like; almost 75% of the people surveyed were younger than 40, so it appears that younger adults may be more interested in the performances.

30. Extended Response A theater group handed out cards at its last performance to gather information about the ages of people who attend the group's performances. The histogram shows the results of the survey.

a. What percent of people who attended the show were under 30 years old? Round your answer to the nearest percent. **34%**

b. In which age group does the median age fall? Explain.

c. The theater group advertises its performances on the radio. Should the group advertise on a station that younger adults like or one that older adults like? Explain.

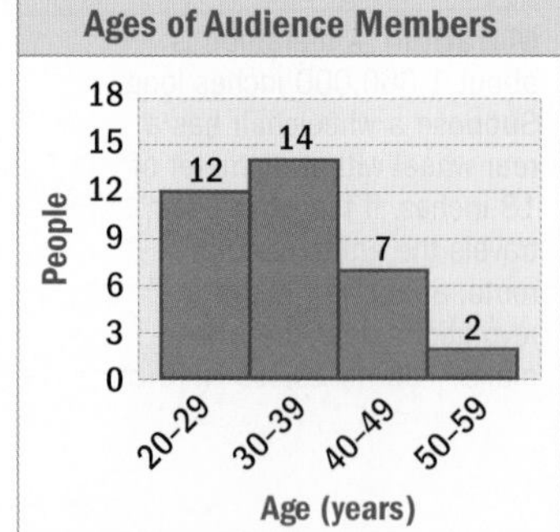

11.1 Making a Histogram

Goal Use a graphing calculator to make a histogram.

Example

Use a graphing calculator to make a histogram of the following data.

The average precipitation (in inches) for each month in Juneau, Alaska, is given below.

4.54, 3.75, 3.28, 2.77, 3.42, 3.15, 4.16, 5.32, 6.73, 7.84, 4.91, 4.44

1 Press LIST. Enter the data into list L1.

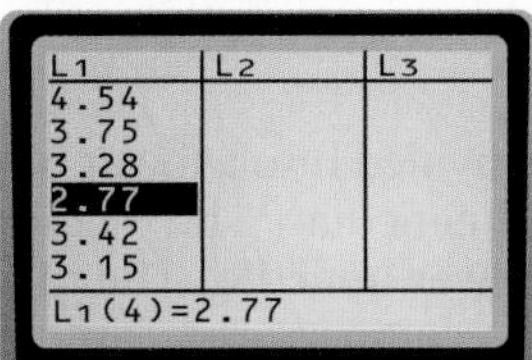

2 Press 2nd **[PLOT]**. Select Plot1 and choose the histogram from the menu. Set the value for Xlist to L1.

3 Press WINDOW. Set Xmin and Xmax to include all the data values. Use Xscl to set the width of the bars. Set Ymin and Ymax so that the tops and bottoms of the bars can be viewed.

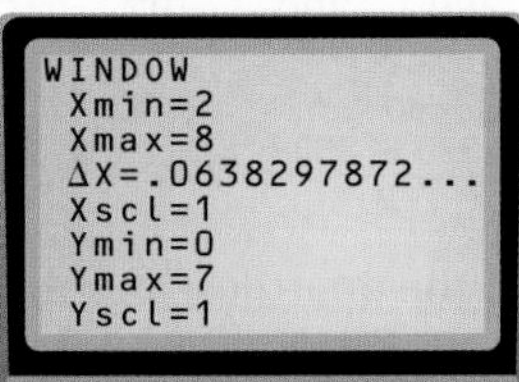

4 Press GRAPH to graph the data. Press TRACE and the left and right arrow keys to move from bar to bar and examine the histogram.

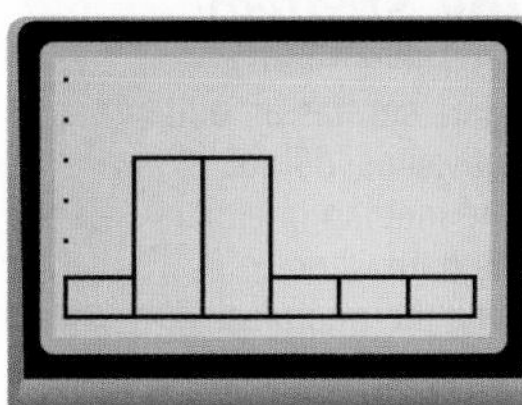

Draw Conclusions

1. Use a graphing calculator to make a histogram of the following test scores: 67, 68, 75, 73, 82, 96, 71, 73, 89, 84, 82, 91, 85, 88, 94. **See margin.**
2. **Analyze** Interpret the histogram in the example above. Are the data bunched together or spread out? Would you say that the average monthly precipitation is less than or greater than 5 inches? Explain.

Tech *Help*

You do not need to change the value of ΔX in the WINDOW settings.

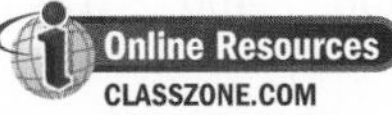

- Keystroke Help

2. *Sample answer:* The data are bunched together, with two thirds of the data values between 3 and 5 inches. The average monthly precipitation appears to be below 5 inches, since the precipitation in three fourths of the months is less than 5 inches

NCTM CURRICULUM STANDARDS

Standard 5: Collect, organize, and display data; Use proper statistical methods to analyze data

1 PLAN

Learn the Method

- Students will use a graphing calculator to make a histogram.
- This activity can be used to check Exercises 10–13 in Lesson 11.1.

Grouping

Students should work individually.

2 TEACH

Discussion

As students are working, ask: "How do you choose the values for Xmin and Xmax?" **Answers may vary.**

Extra Examples

Example The ages, in years, of 8 children in a pediatrician's waiting room are given below. Use a graphing calculator to make a histogram of the data.

$\frac{1}{2}, \frac{1}{2}, 1, 2, 3, 1\frac{1}{2}, 1\frac{1}{4}, 2$

Sample:

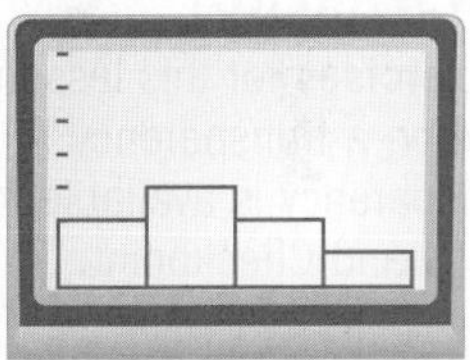

3 CLOSE

Assessment

1. When graphing a histogram on a graphing calculator, what is represented along the *y*-axis? **The number of values in each interval**
2. When setting the viewing window for a histogram, to what value should Ymin always be set? **0**

1. See Additional Answers beginning on page AA1.

1 PLAN

Skill Check

Find the median of the data.

1. 7, 3, 5, 7, 2 — 5
2. 24, 15, 10, 25, 22 — 22
3. 27, 28, 17, 27 — 27
4. 90, 89, 86, 91 — 89.5

LESSON OBJECTIVE

Make and interpret box-and-whisker plots.

PACING

Suggested Number of Days
Basic Course: 1 day
Average Course: 1 day
Advanced Course: 1 day
Block: 0.5 block with 11.3

TEACHING RESOURCES

For a complete list of Teaching Resources, see page 578B.

TRANSPARENCY

Warm-Up Exercises for this lesson are available on a transparency. A support transparency is available for Examples 1–3 and Checkpoint Exercise 1.

2 TEACH

MOTIVATING THE LESSON

On the board, sketch a cat's head with long whiskers out to the sides. Point out that the whiskers are the widest part of the cat. Lead students to recognize that the whiskers of a box-and-whisker plot represent the extremes of a data set.

LESSON **11.2**

Box-and-Whisker Plots

BEFORE	Now	WHY?
You made stem-and-leaf plots and histograms.	You'll make and interpret box-and-whisker plots.	So you can compare clothing prices, as in Ex. 12.

Vocabulary

box-and-whisker plot, p. 588
lower quartile, p. 588
upper quartile, p. 588
lower extreme, p. 588
upper extreme, p. 588
interquartile range, p. 590

Agriculture A farmer recorded the number of oranges that an orange tree produced for each of the last 9 years. The data are given below.

572, 452, 457, 460, 360, 407, 380, 458, 264

A useful way to display the data is with a *box-and-whisker plot*. A **box-and-whisker plot** is a data display that organizes data values into four groups.

Ordered data are divided into a lower half and an upper half by the median. The median of the lower half is the **lower quartile**. The median of the upper half is the **upper quartile**. The **lower extreme** is the least data value, and the **upper extreme** is the greatest data value.

Study Strategy

When a data set has an odd number of values, do not include the median in either half of the data when determining the quartiles.

Example 1 *Making a Box-and-Whisker Plot*

To display the data given above in a box-and-whisker plot, first order the data to find the median, the quartiles, and the extremes.

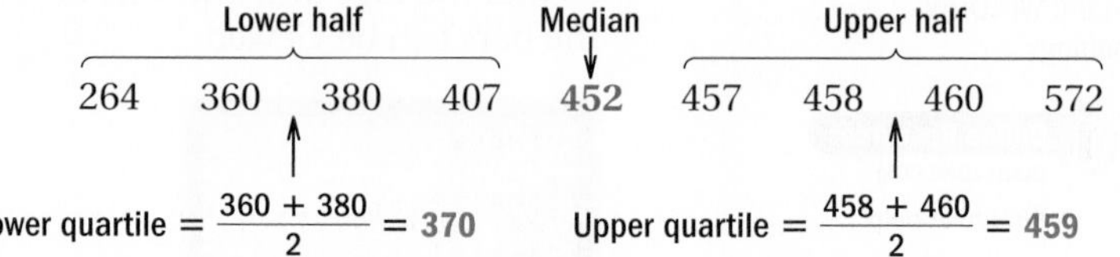

Lower quartile $= \frac{360 + 380}{2} = 370$ Upper quartile $= \frac{458 + 460}{2} = 459$

Plot the median, the quartiles, and the extremes below a number line.

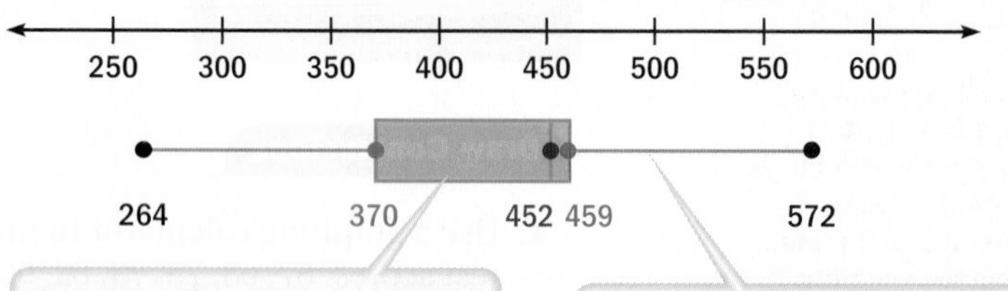

NCTM CURRICULUM STANDARDS

Standard 5: Collect, organize, and display data; Use proper statistical methods to analyze data; Develop inferences that are based on data

Interpreting a Box-and-Whisker Plot A box-and-whisker plot separates data into four sections: the two parts of the box and two whiskers. All four sections contain approximately the same number of data values.

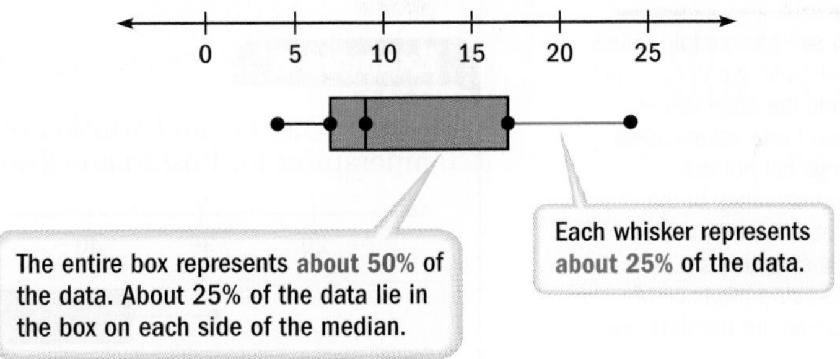

0
5
10
15
20
25
The entire box represents about 50% of the data. About 25% of the data lie in the box on each side of the median.
Each whisker represents about 25% of the data.

The lengths of sections tell you how spread out the data are. For instance, the data in Example 1 are more spread out between the lower quartile and the median than they are between the median and the upper quartile.

Example 2 *Interpreting a Box-and-Whisker Plot*

State Parks The box-and-whisker plot below displays the number of visitors (in millions) to the state parks in each of the 50 states in 2000.

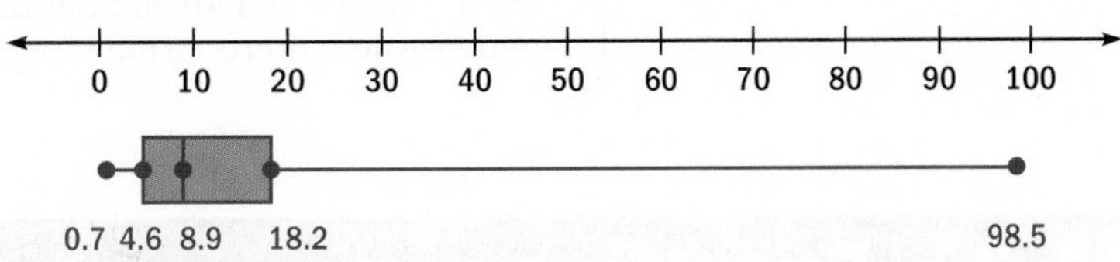

a. About how many states had fewer than 18.2 million visitors to their state parks?

b. West Virginia had 8.0 million visitors to its state parks. How does West Virginia compare with the rest of the states?

Solution

a. The upper quartile is 18.2. Each whisker and each part of the box represents about 25% of the states. So, about 75% of the 50 states, or 37 states, had fewer than 18.2 million visitors.

b. West Virginia's number of visitors is greater than the lower quartile ($8.0 > 4.6$), so West Virginia had more visitors than about 25% of the states. West Virginia's number of visitors is also less than the median ($8.0 < 8.9$), so West Virginia had fewer visitors than about 50% of the states.

Checkpoint

1. The prices (in dollars) of several CD players are as follows: 35, 65, 90, 30, 120, 100, 80, 49, 60, 30, 55, 72, 108. Make a box-and-whisker plot of the data. Is the $72 CD player more expensive than 50% of the CD players? Explain. **See margin.**

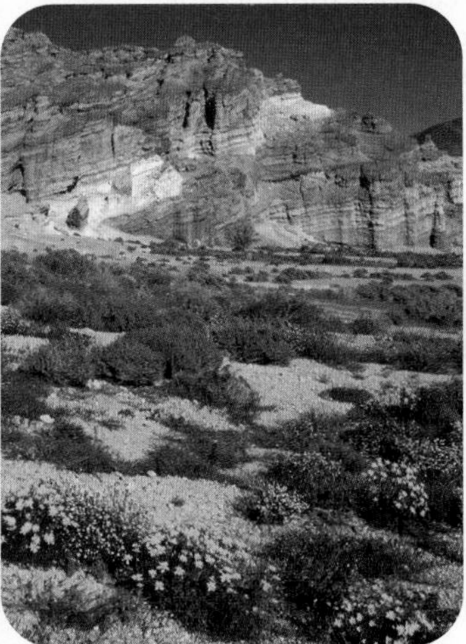

In the **Real World**

State Parks Approximately 750 million people visit state parks in the United States each year, with the state of California having the most visitors. Based on the data in Example 2, about what percent of the total visitors to U.S. state parks visit California state parks? **about 13%**

TIPS *for* NEW TEACHERS

Use information from your students, such as the length of time it takes them to get home from school, to create data sets for additional box-and-whisker plots. See Tips for New Teachers in the *Chapter 11 Resource Book*.

Extra Examples

Example 1 The ages of nine people at a birthday party are given below. Make a box-and-whisker plot of the data.
15, 37, 45, 62, 14, 12, 17, 10, 11

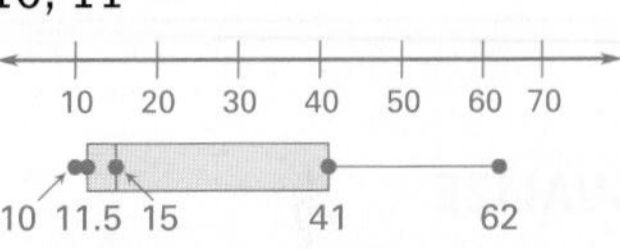

Example 2 The box-and-whisker plot below displays the cost, in dollars, of a wetsuit sold by several online diving stores.

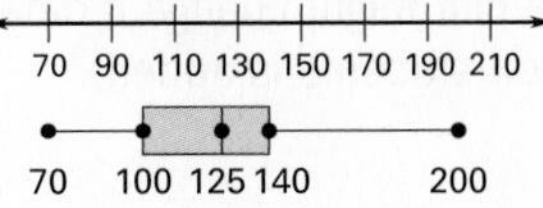

a. What is the median price for the wetsuit? **$125**

b. What is the range of the prices? **$130**

TEACHING TIP

In Example 1, stress that the median and the quartiles do not necessarily have to be values in the data set.

1.

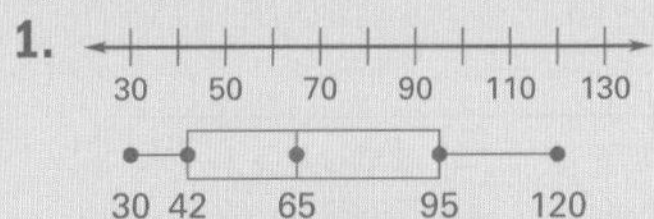

Yes. *Sample answer:* The box-and-whisker plot shows a median value of 65 and 72 > 65, so the $72 CD player is more expensive than 50% of the CD players whose prices are given.

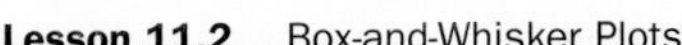

Extra Examples

Example 3 The box-and-whisker plots below show Nicole's and Barry's scores on their math tests. What conclusions can you make?

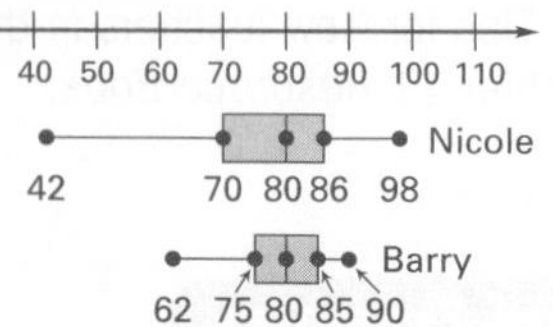

***Sample answer:* Their median scores are identical and their upper quartile scores are nearly the same. Nicole's scores have a greater range than Barry's.**

VISUALIZE

Collect data about the number of school activities your students are participating in this year. On the board, draw a box-and-whisker plot for the data. Ask students to explain how the plot might change if data for three new students is added.

CONCEPT CHECK

What do the four sections of a box-and-whisker plot have in common? **They each contain about the same number of data values.**

DAILY PUZZLER

Give a set of data values whose box-and-whisker plot has key values that are whole numbers that differ by 1. ***Sample answer:* 1, 2, 2, 3, 4, 4, 5**

3.–4.

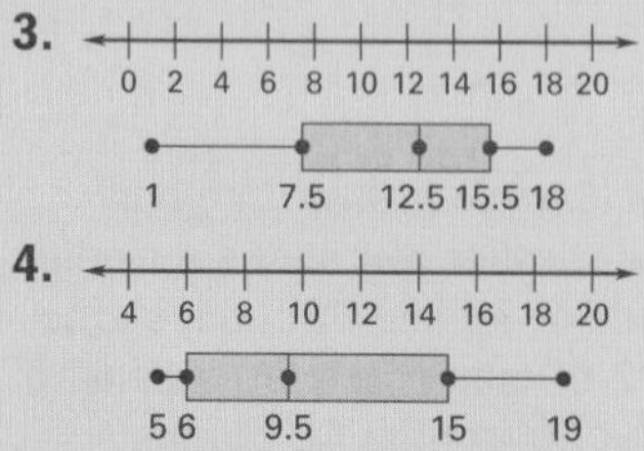

5. See Additional Answers beginning on page AA1.

Study *Strategy*

A data set may contain values that are much greater or much less than the other values. Because these values affect the range but not the interquartile range of the data set, the interquartile range is sometimes a more representative measure of how spread out the data are.

Interquartile Range The range of a set of data is the difference of the greatest and least values. The **interquartile range** of a data set is the difference of the upper quartile and the lower quartile.

Example 3 *Comparing Box-and-Whisker Plots*

Weather The box-and-whisker plots below show the average monthly temperatures for Boston and Seattle. What conclusions can you make?

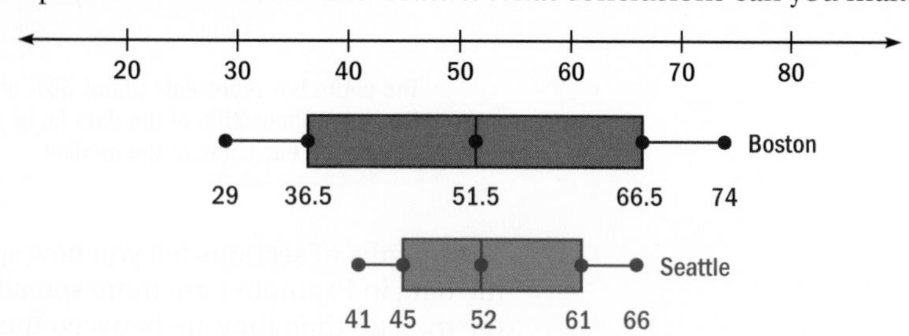

Solution

- Boston and Seattle have nearly identical median temperatures.
- Boston's temperatures are much more spread out than Seattle's. Both Boston's range $(74 - 29 = 45)$ and Boston's interquartile range $(66.5 - 36.5 = 30)$ are greater than Seattle's range $(66 - 41 = 25)$ and Seattle's interquartile range $(61 - 45 = 16)$, respectively.

11.2 Exercises

More Practice, p. 813

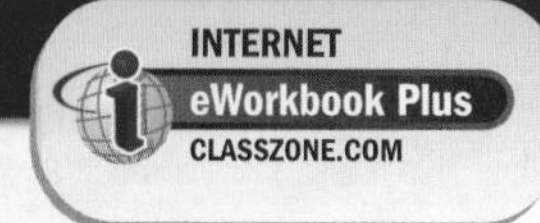

Guided Practice

Vocabulary Check

1. Which value is the upper extreme for the data 12, 6, 23, 10? **23**
2. Explain how to determine the interquartile range for a data set. **See margin.**

Skill Check **Make a box-and-whisker plot of the data.** **3–4. See margin.**

3. 14, 6, 13, 17, 1, 12, 9, 18
4. 7, 19, 6, 12, 5, 17, 6, 13

Guided Problem Solving

5. **Archery** On 6 different days, two archers record the number of bull's-eyes they score out of 10 tries. Which archer is more consistent?

Day	1	2	3	4	5	6
Archer 1	3	5	8	4	9	1
Archer 2	4	7	6	5	8	6

(1) Make a box-and-whisker plot for each archer. **See margin.**

(2) Find the range and interquartile range for each archer. **Archer 1: 8, 5; Archer 2: 4, 2**

(3) For which archer is the range of the scores less? **Archer 2**

2. ***Sample answer:* First find the upper and lower quartiles. Then subtract the lower quartile from the upper quartile.**

Practice and Problem Solving

Homework Help

Example	Exercises
1	6-9, 11, 12
2	11
3	9, 10, 12

Online Resources
CLASSZONE.COM
- More Examples
- eTutorial Plus

In Exercises 6–8, make a box-and-whisker plot of the data. **6–8. See margin.**

A **6.** Students' heights (in inches): 50, 61, 55, 54, 53, 60, 65, 66, 57, 68

7. Sweater prices (in dollars): 15, 20, 19, 18, 17, 26, 22, 25, 20, 23, 18

8. Number of CDs in collections: 25, 32, 16, 40, 68, 52, 45, 95, 60, 41

9. Test Scores The data below are a class's test scores for two tests.

Test 1: 50, 93, 81, 75, 70, 66, 68, 59, 60, 58, 71, 62, 84, 88, 65, 85

Test 2: 65, 73, 84, 92, 87, 83, 80, 77, 67, 74, 75, 81, 90, 88, 78, 85

a. Make a box-and-whisker plot for each data set. Draw both box-and-whisker plots using the same number line. **See margin.**

b. Compare the range and the interquartile range for the two tests.

c. Interpret On test 1 you scored 71. On test 2 you scored 74. On which test did you do better compared with the rest of the class? Explain. **See margin.**

9b. ***Sample answer:*** **On test 1, the range was 43, and the interquartile range was 21.5. These are considerably greater than the range of 27 and interquartile range of 11.5 for test 2.**

10. Baseball The box-and-whisker plots below show the ages of the players on the New York Yankees and the Texas Rangers baseball teams during the 2002 season.

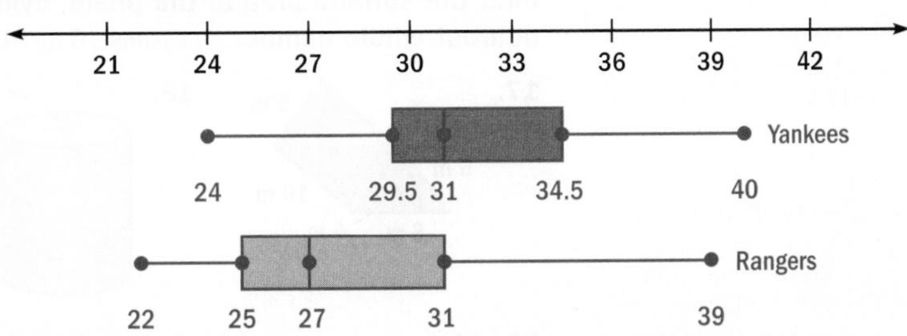

The Ballpark at Arlington, Texas

a. Compare Compare the median, range, and interquartile range for the two teams.

b. Analyze About what percent of the Yankees are less than 31 years old? About what percent of the Rangers are less than 31 years old? **about 50%; about 75%**

c. *Writing* Which team would you say is the "older" team? Explain. **See margin.**

10a. ***Sample answer:*** **The median for the Yankees is higher than the median for the Rangers. The ranges are almost the same: 16 for the Yankees and 17 for the Rangers. The interquartile ranges are also close to the same: 5 for the Yankees and 6 for the Rangers.**

10c. The Yankees. ***Sample answer:*** **At every corresponding measure on the box-and-whisker plots, the ages for the Yankees are older than the ages for the Rangers.**

B **11. Extended Problem Solving** An *outlier* is a data value whose distance from the upper or lower quartile is more than 1.5 times the interquartile range.

a. Make a box-and-whisker plot for the following data: 109, 113, 119, 121, 124, 125, 128, 134, 134, 136, 198. **See margin.**

b. Calculate Determine if there are any outliers in the data set. **198**

c. Make a box-and-whisker plot for the data, excluding any outliers. **See margin.**

d. *Writing* Explain how removing an outlier changes the appearance of the box-and-whisker plot. What conclusion can you make from the plot in part (c) that you would not make from the plot in part (a)? **See margin.**

3 APPLY

ASSIGNMENT GUIDE

Basic Course
Day 1: pp. 591-592 Exs. 6-11, 14-23

Average Course
Day 1: pp. 591-592 Exs. 6-12, 14-23

Advanced Course
Day 1: pp. 591-592 Exs. 7-13*, 16-23

Block
pp. 591-592 Exs. 6-12, 14-23 (with 11.3)

EXTRA PRACTICE

- Student Edition, p. 813
- Chapter 11 Resource Book, pp. 17-19
- Test and Practice Generator

TRANSPARENCY

Even-numbered answers are available on transparencies. A support transparency is available for Exercises 3-9, 11, 12, and 14-16.

HOMEWORK CHECK

When you review students' homework for this lesson, go over the following exercises to check understanding of key concepts.
Basic: 6, 7, 9, 10, 11
Average: 7, 9, 10, 11, 12
Advanced: 8, 9, 10, 11, 12

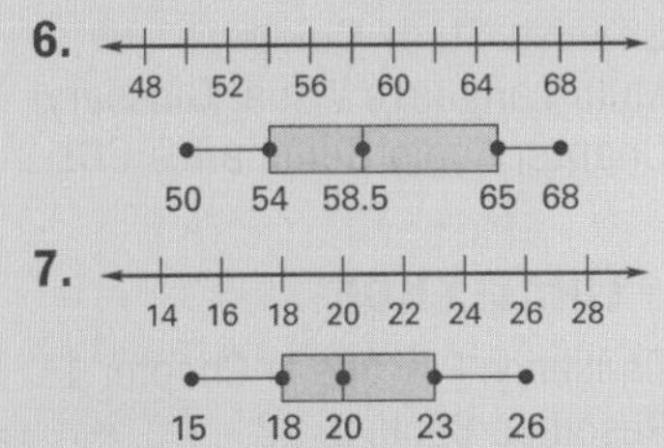

8, 9a, 9c, 11a, 11c, 11d. See Additional Answers beginning on page AA1.

4 ASSESS

ASSESSMENT RESOURCES

For more assessment resources, see:
- Assessment Book
- Test and Practice Generator

MINI-QUIZ

A: 10, 13, 12, 12, 11, 9, 8, 18
B: 15, 15, 14, 14, 14, 13, 16, 12

1. Make a box-and-whisker plot for each data set.

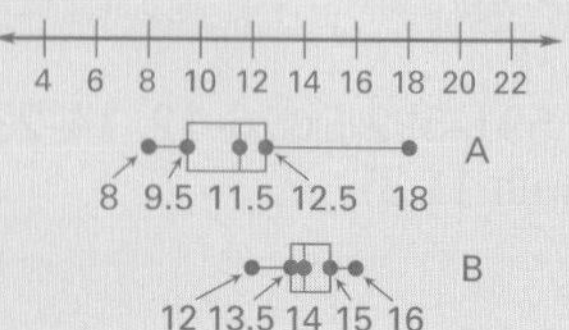

2. Compare the range and the interquartile range of the two sets. **For A, the range is 10 and the interquartile range is 3. These are greater than B's range of 4 and interquartile range of 1.5.**
3. **Challenge** Write a set of data whose range is 3 times its interquartile range. ***Sample answer:* 8, 10, 10, 11, 12, 12, 12, 14**

5 FOLLOW-UP

DIAGNOSIS/REMEDIATION

- Study Guide in Chapter 11 Resource Book, pp. 20–21
- eTutorial Plus Online
- Extra Practice, p. 813
- Lesson Practice in Chapter 11 Resource Book, pp. 17–19

ENGLISH LEARNER SUPPORT

- Spanish Study Guide
- Multi-Language Visual Glossary
- Chapter Audio Summaries CDs

CHALLENGE

- Challenge Practice in Chapter 11 Resource Book, p. 23
- Teacher's Edition, p. 578F

12a, 14–16. See Additional Answers beginning on page AA1.

12. **Clothing Prices** The table lists the prices of a set of comparable items of women's and men's clothing in 9 different cities. **12a–c. See margin.**

City	Women's	Men's
New York	\$690	\$1190
Los Angeles	\$450	\$620
Chicago	\$590	\$1100
Houston	\$440	\$900
Paris	\$430	\$700
London	\$350	\$660
Toronto	\$310	\$850
Tokyo	\$760	\$1050
Mexico City	\$380	\$620

   a. Make box-and-whisker plots for the women's and men's data.

   b. How do the prices in Houston compare with the rest of the cities for both women's and men's clothing? Explain your reasoning.

   c. **Interpret** Would you say women's clothing prices or men's clothing prices vary more in the cities in the survey? Explain your reasoning.

C 13. **Challenge** Write a set of data values for which the extremes, quartiles, and median are all equally spaced. Explain how you chose the values. **See margin.**

12b. ***Sample answer:*** **They are fairly typical. The Houston median for women equals the overall median for women, and the Houston median for men is just a little higher (\$50 higher) than the overall median for men.**

12c. **Men's clothing. *Sample answer:* The range of \$570 for men's clothing is greater than the range of \$450 for women's clothing, and the interquartile range of \$435 for men's clothing is greater than the interquartile range of \$275 for women's clothing.**

13. ***Sample answer:* 6, 7, 9, 9, 10, 12, 13, 14, 15, 17, 18; I picked a number of data values, 11, for which each of the plot measures is a data value. Then I wrote each of the extremes and quartiles in the appropriate positions and filled in other data values between them.**

20.

0	8 9
1	1 1 3 4 5 6 6 7 7 8
2	0 1 1 2 3 4 5
3	5 7

Key: 0 | 8 = 8

Mixed Review

Graph the inequality in a coordinate plane. *(Lesson 8.9)* **14–16. See margin.**

14. $y < -2x + 3$ 15. $y > 3x - 5$ 16. $y > 0.5x + 1.5$

Find the surface area of the prism, cylinder, or pyramid. Round to the nearest whole number. *(Lessons 10.5, 10.6)*

17. 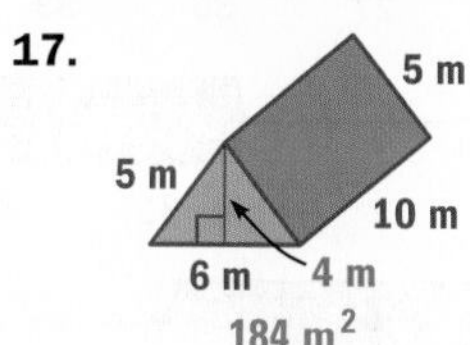

184 m²

18. 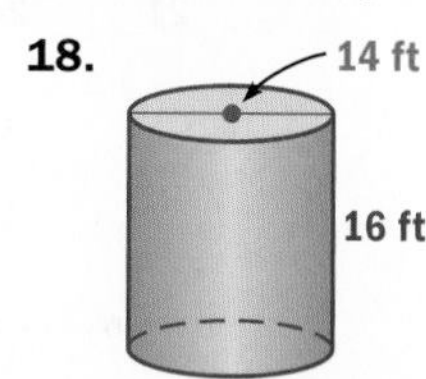

1012 ft²

19. 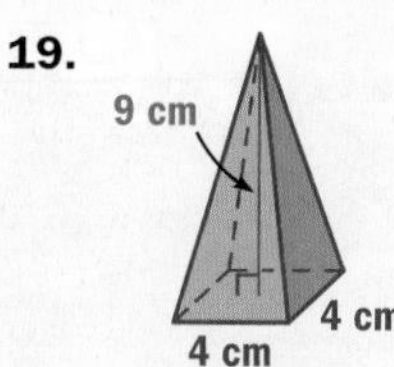

90 cm²

20. Make a stem-and-leaf plot of the following data: 8, 11, 23, 24, 13, 35, 14, 11, 16, 17, 18, 9, 16, 17, 15, 21, 25, 20, 21, 37, 22. *(Lesson 11.1)* **See margin.**

Standardized Test Practice

In Exercises 21–23, use the box-and-whisker plot below.

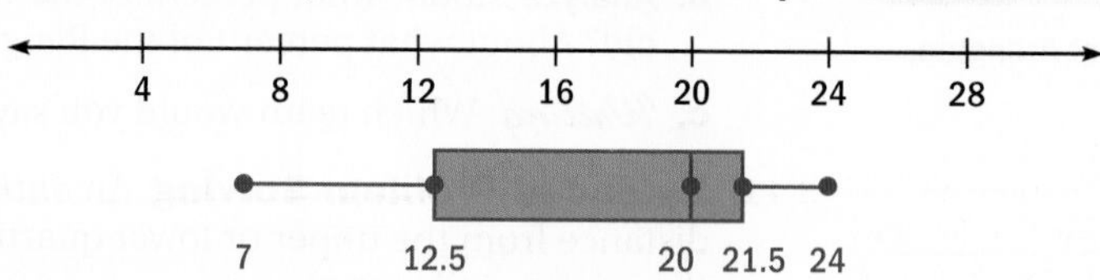

21. **Multiple Choice** What is the interquartile range of the data in the box-and-whisker plot? **A**

   A. 9 **B.** 12.5 **C.** 20 **D.** 21.5

22. **Multiple Choice** About what percent of data values are less than 21? **I**

   F. 12.5% **G.** 25% **H.** 50% **I.** 75%

23. **Short Response** The data set consisted of 12 whole numbers. How many of the numbers are less than 12.5? Explain. **3. *Sample answer:* For 12 data values, the lower quartile is the average of the third and fourth data values. Because the lower quartile is not a whole number, the three lowest data values must be less than the lower quartile.**

Technology *Activity* GRAPHING CALCULATOR

11.2 Making a Box-and-Whisker Plot

Goal Use a graphing calculator to make a box-and-whisker plot.

Example

Use a graphing calculator to make a box-and-whisker plot of the following data.

In the 2002–2003 season, the roster for the NBA's Boston Celtics listed 13 players, and the roster for the Houston Rockets listed 14 players. The heights (in inches) of the players are given below.

Celtics: 83, 84, 74, 79, 81, 74, 81, 82, 78, 86, 81, 80, 74

Rockets: 74, 83, 84, 75, 82, 79, 76, 75, 89, 81, 81, 80, 80, 81

1 Press LIST. Enter the data into two lists, L1 and L2.

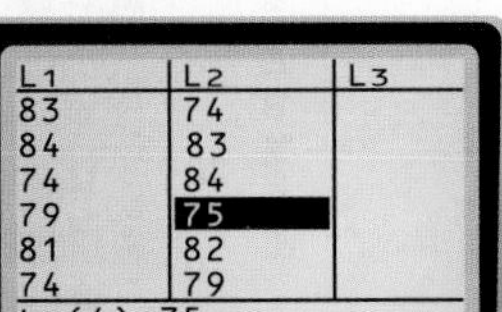

2 Press 2nd **[PLOT]**. Select Plot1 and choose the box-and-whisker plot from the menu. Set the value for Xlist to L1.

3 Press 2nd **[PLOT]**. Select Plot2 and choose the box-and-whisker plot from the menu. Set the value for Xlist to L2.

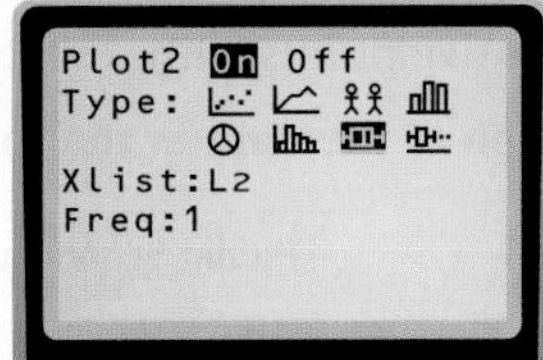

4 To graph the plots, press ZOOM **7**. Press TRACE and the left and right arrow keys to examine the plots.

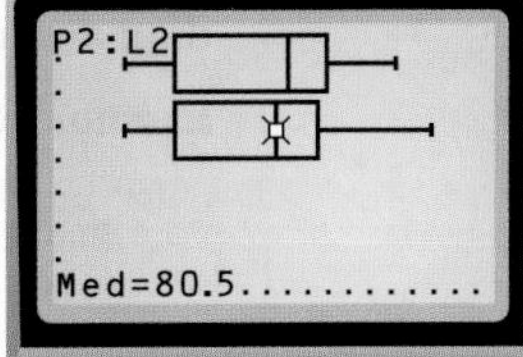

Draw Conclusions

1. Use a graphing calculator to make a box-and-whisker plot of the following data: 8, 11, 12, 7, 11, 14, 13, 4, 11, 9, 9, 17. **See margin.**
2. **Analyze** Compare the median heights of the two teams in the example above. Also compare the ranges of the heights of the two teams. What conclusions can you make?

Tech *Help*

You do not need to set the values on the WINDOW screen. ZOOM **7** will set these automatically.

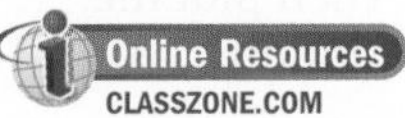

- Keystroke Help

2. *Sample answer:* The median height for the Celtics of 81 inches is 0.5 inch greater than the median height for the Rockets. The range for the Rockets is greater, however: 15 inches versus 12 inches. Overall, the heights of the Celtics seem to be a little greater and more tightly grouped than for the Rockets, though the Rockets have the tallest player.

NCTM CURRICULUM STANDARDS

Standard 5: Collect, organize, and display data; Develop inferences that are based on data

1 PLAN

Learn the Method

- Students will use a graphing calculator to make a box-and-whisker plot.
- This activity can be used to check Exercises 6–9, 11, and 12 in Lesson 11.2.

Grouping

Students should work individually.

2 TEACH

Discussion

As students are working, ask: "What does 'Med' stand for on the calculator display in Step 4?" **median** "How do you know which plot the median applies to?" **by noting which plot the cursor is on**

Extra Examples

Example Make a box-and-whisker plot of the data. 95, 99, 91, 88, 80, 83, 88, 86, 87, 86, 85, 88

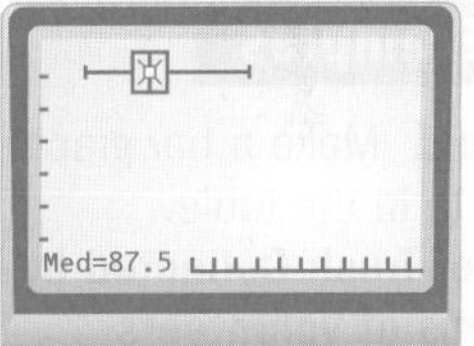

3 CLOSE

Assessment

1. In Step 4 of the Example, the box parts of the two plots are nearly the same. What does this tell you about the two teams? **The heights of half the players on both teams have nearly the same quartile values.**

1. See Additional Answers beginning on page AA1.

1 PLAN

Skill Check

Find the percent of 360°.

1. 10% **36°**
2. 25% **90°**
3. 45% **162°**
4. 75% **270°**

LESSON OBJECTIVE

Prepare for using bar graphs, line graphs, and circle graphs.

TRANSPARENCY

A support transparency is available for this Student Reference.

2 TEACH

TEACHING TIP

In Example 1, discuss how to choose a vertical scale for the bar graph. In Example 2, discuss how to choose the scales for both axes.

Extra Examples

Example 1 Make a bar graph of the data in the table.

Pounds of Trash Collected by Five Teams of Volunteers

Team	Pounds
A	82
B	55
C	125
D	95
E	108

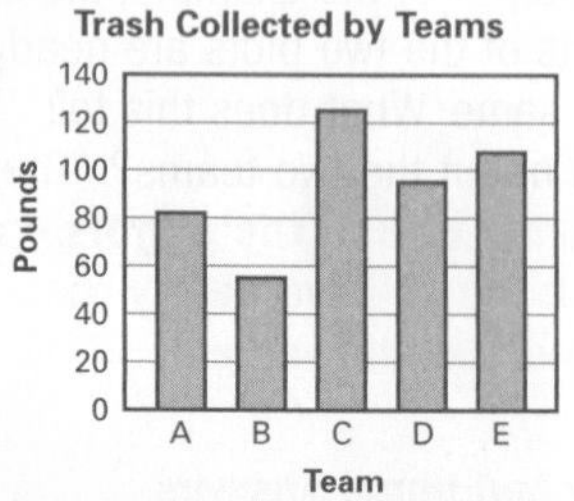

Student Reference

Making Data Displays

▶ **Review** these topics in preparation for using bar graphs, line graphs, and circle graphs in Lesson 11.3.

Making a Bar Graph

In a **bar graph**, the lengths of the bars are used to represent and compare data. The bars can be vertical or horizontal. To make a bar graph, first choose a scale. Then draw and label the graph.

Example **Make a bar graph of the data in the table.**

Households with Computers in 2001	
State	**Percent**
Alaska	68.7%
Texas	67.7%
Georgia	63.1%
Florida	52.4%

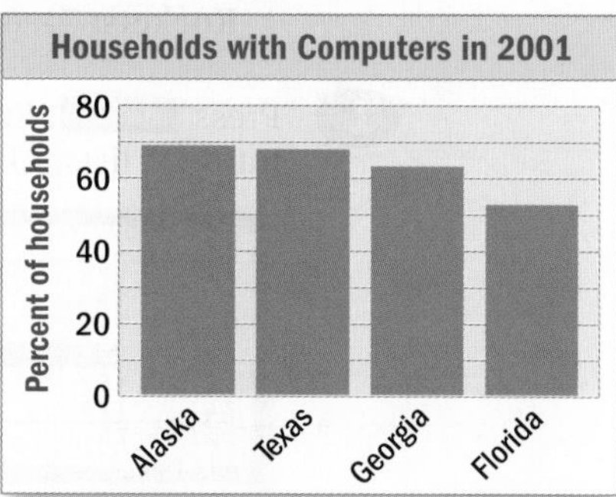

Making a Line Graph

In a **line graph**, points that represent data values are connected using segments. Line graphs often show a change in data over time. To make a line graph, first choose scales for the horizontal and vertical axes. Then plot the data and connect consecutive points with segments. Label the graph.

Example **Make a line graph of the data in the table.**

Public Schools with Internet Access	
Year	**Percent**
1996	65%
1997	78%
1998	89%
1999	95%
2000	98%
2001	99%

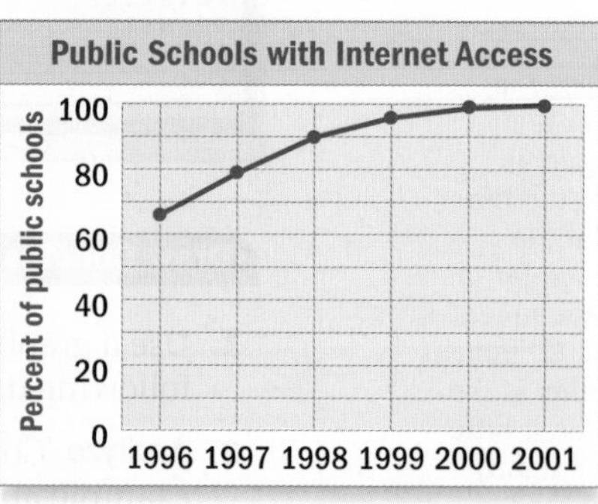

NCTM CURRICULUM STANDARDS

Standard 5: Collect, organize, and display data

Standard 10: Create representations to communicate ideas

Making a Circle Graph

A **circle graph** displays data as sections of a circle. The entire circle represents all the data. To make a circle graph, first find the angle measure for each section by finding the product of the percent for that section and 360°, the number of degrees in a circle. Then use a compass to draw a circle. Finally, use a protractor to measure and draw an angle for each section.

Example Make a circle graph of the data in the table.

Percent of Internet Users by Age	
Age	**Percent**
18–34	39%
35–54	47%
55 and over	14%

Internet Users by Age

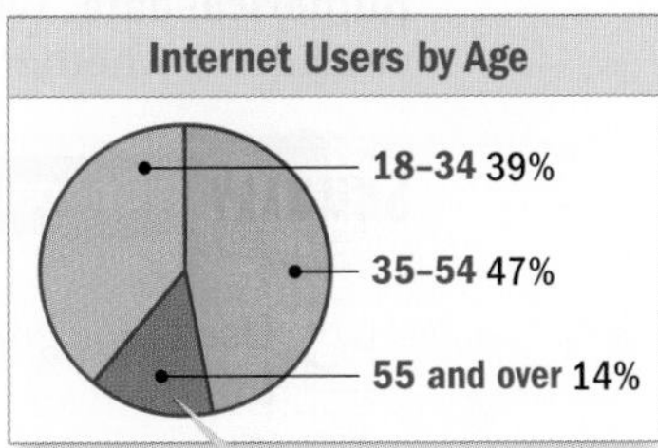

The angle measure for this section is $0.14 \times 360° \approx 50°$.

The angle for this section measures 50°.

✔ Checkpoint 1–3. See margin.

▶ **Test** your knowledge of bar graphs, line graphs, and circle graphs by solving these problems.

1. Make a bar graph showing the percent of people surveyed who enjoy each kind of entertainment.

Activities People Choose for Entertainment			
Activity	Movies	Sporting events	Amusement park
Percent	66%	41%	57%

2. Make a line graph showing the percent of single women who worked in the U.S. from 1970 to 2000.

U.S. Single Women Who Work				
Year	1970	1980	1990	2000
Percent	53%	62%	66%	69%

3. Make a circle graph showing the percent of U.S. curbside recycling programs in 2000 that existed in each region.

U.S. Curbside Recycling Programs by Region in 2000				
Region	Northeast	South	Midwest	West
Percent	37.41%	15.43%	38.74%	8.42%

4. Explain why you cannot use a circle graph to display the data in Exercise 1. **It is possible for people surveyed to choose more than one activity. The sum of the percents shown in the table is greater than 100%, so the data cannot be used to make a circle graph.**

Extra Examples

Example 2 Make a line graph.
William's Books

Year	Books
1998	8
1999	18
2000	32
2001	54
2002	75

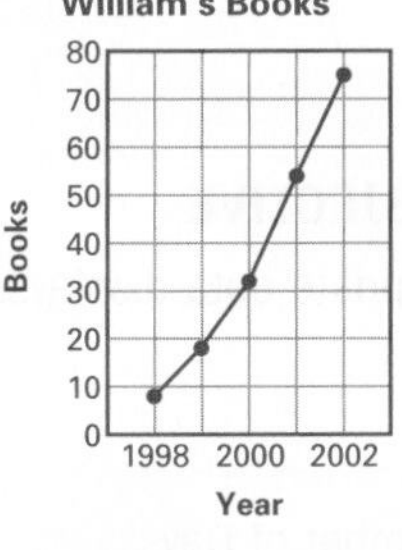

Example 3 Make a circle graph.
Ages of Dogs Taken to a Veterinarian's Office

Age(years)	Percent
0–4	42%
5–8	32%
9–12	18%
13 and over	8%

Ages of Dogs Taken to a Veterinarian's Office

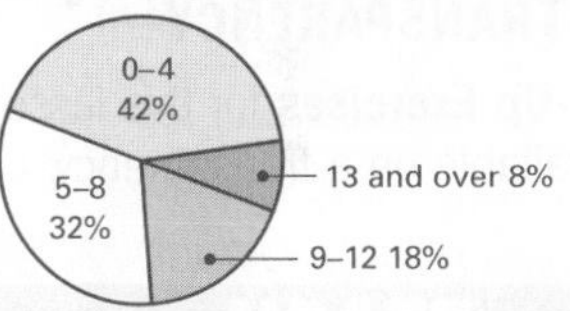

3 APPLY

TRANSPARENCY

Even-numbered answers are available on transparencies.

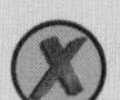

COMMON ERROR

In Exercise 3, watch for students who use the given percents as degree measures when drawing the graph.

1–3. See Additional Answers beginning on page AA1.

1 PLAN

Skill Check

Find the median, quartiles, and extremes of the data.

1. 5, 8, 6, 10, 3, 8, 8, 5
7, 5 and 8, 3 and 10
2. 65, 42, 47, 34, 24, 51, 30
42, 30 and 51, 24 and 65

LESSON OBJECTIVE

Choose appropriate data displays.

PACING

Suggested Number of Days
Basic Course: 1 day
Average Course: 1 day
Advanced Course: 1 day
Block: 0.5 block with 11.2

TEACHING RESOURCES

For a complete list of Teaching Resources, see page 578B.

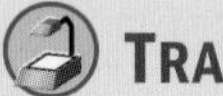

TRANSPARENCY

Warm-Up Exercises for this lesson are available on a transparency.

2 TEACH

MOTIVATING THE LESSON

As you discuss each type of data display, ask students for examples of class data that could be graphed using that display.

TIPS *for* NEW TEACHERS

Plan to spend extra time giving students a variety of data sets and having them choose whether they are categorical or numerical. See Tips for New Teachers in the *Chapter 11 Resource Book*.

LESSON 11.3

Using Data Displays

BEFORE	Now	WHY?
You interpreted data displays.	You'll choose appropriate displays for data sets.	So you can interpret data about winter sports, as in Ex. 16.

Vocabulary
categorical data, p. 596
numerical data, p. 596

Data that consist of names, labels, or other nonnumerical values, such as types of animals or colors of hair, are **categorical data**. Data that consist of numbers, such as weights of animals or lengths of hair, are **numerical data**. When you choose a data display, one factor you should consider is whether the data are categorical or numerical.

SUMMARY Choosing Appropriate Data Displays

- Use a *line graph* to display numerical data that change over time.
- Use a *scatter plot* to see trends in paired numerical data.
- Use a *bar graph* to compare categorical data.
- Use a *circle graph* to represent categorical data as parts of a whole.
- Use a *stem-and-leaf plot* to organize numerical data based on their digits.
- Use a *histogram* to compare the frequencies of numerical data that fall in equal intervals.
- Use a *box-and-whisker plot* to organize numerical data into four groups of approximately equal size.

Note *Worthy*

You may want to include an example of each type of data display in your notes.

Example 1 *Choosing an Appropriate Data Display*

The table shows the results of a survey that asked students to name their favorite type of movie. Which display(s) can you use to display the data?

Favorite Type of Movie	
Type	**Percent**
Drama	17%
Comedy	44%
Action	28%
Sci-Fi	9%
Other	2%

Solution

The responses to the survey consist of movie types, which are categorical data. Notice that the sum of the percents is 100%. So, the best choice is to use a circle graph. A bar graph could also be used.

NCTM CURRICULUM STANDARDS
Standard 5: Collect, organize, and display data
Standard 8: Communicate thinking clearly to others
Standard 10: Create representations to communicate ideas

Example 2 *Comparing Data Displays*

Test Scores A teacher uses a histogram and a box-and-whisker plot to display the test scores of the students in a math class. What are the advantages of each display?

a.

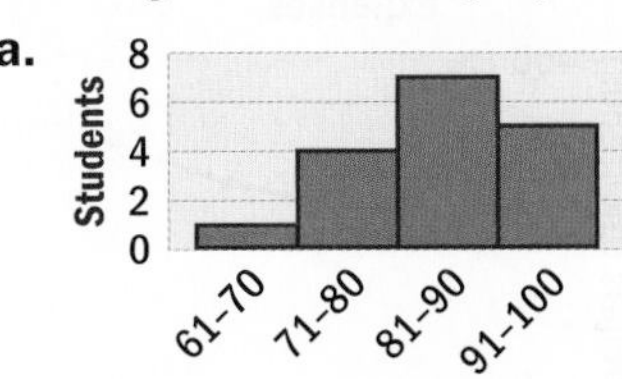

b.

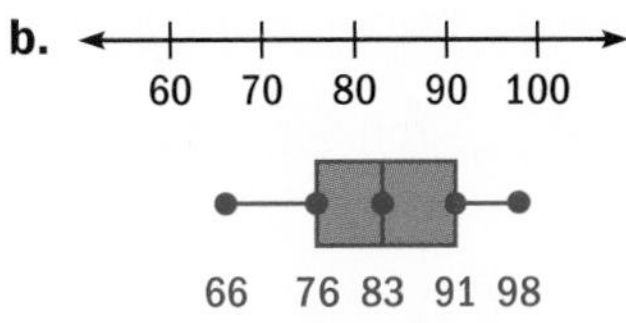

Solution

a. Using the histogram, the teacher can quickly compare the number of students in each of the intervals. For example, the teacher can see that 7 students scored from 81 to 90, while only 4 students scored from 71 to 80.

b. Using the box-and-whisker plot, the teacher can easily divide the scores into low, low-middle, high-middle, and high groups of approximately equal size. For example, the teacher can conclude that about 25% of the class scored 91 or better, and that about 50% of the class scored from 76 to 91.

Checkpoint

1. In Example 2, the teacher wants to display the test scores so that the display shows all the individual scores. What type of display should the teacher use? **stem-and-leaf plot**

Misleading Data Displays The way a data display is drawn can lead people to make incorrect conclusions. Three examples of potentially misleading data displays are shown below.

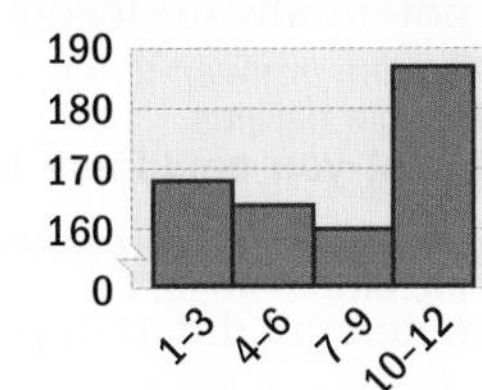

Broken Vertical Axis
The broken vertical axis exaggerates the differences in the bar lengths.

2000
1500
1000
500
0
0 5 10 15 20 25 30

Large Increments
The large increments on the vertical axis minimize the changes in the data.

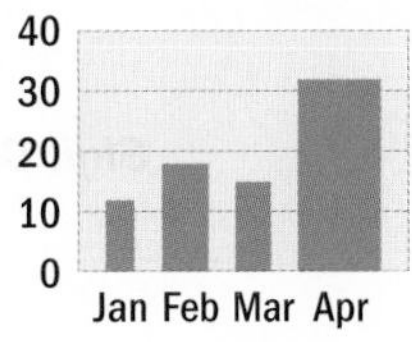

Different Widths
The different bar widths suggest a comparison of areas, not lengths.

Checkpoint

2. The rightmost bar of the histogram above appears to be twice as long as any of the other bars. Is the frequency of the 10–12 interval twice as great as the frequency of any other interval? Explain.

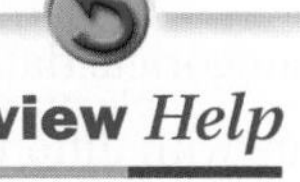

Review *Help*

For help with reading line graphs, see p. 782.

2. No. *Sample answer:* The frequency of the 10–12 interval appears to be about 187, while the frequency of the shortest bar appears to be about 160. So, the frequency of the 10–12 interval is only about 17% greater than the interval with the lowest frequency.

Extra Examples

Example 1 A student group solicited pledges for the number of kilometers they walked during a fundraiser. Ashley created a table listing the students who participated, their age, and the number of kilometers each student walked. Which display(s) could Ashley use to display the data? ***Sample answer:* scatter plot, histogram, box-and-whisker plot**

Example 2 A scuba instructor uses a stem-and-leaf plot and a circle graph to display the ages of students in her class. What are the advantages of each display?

Ages of Scuba Diving Class Members

Stem	Leaves
2	6 8
3	3 7 8
4	2 3 5 6 8
5	1 1 2 4 6 7
6	2 3 3 4

Key: 2 | 8 = 28

Ages of Scuba Diving Class Members

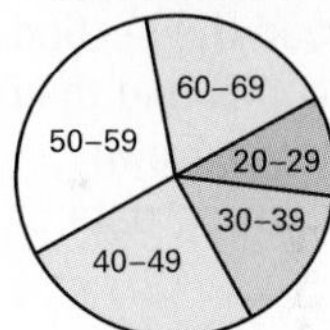

With the stem-and-leaf plot, the instructor can see every student's age. With the circle graph, she can quickly see what part of the entire class falls into each age range.

NOTETAKING

Encourage students to copy the summary on page 596 into their notebooks. For each type of display, have students sketch an example and note the advantages and disadvantages.

Extra Examples

Example 3 The histogram shows the ages of people who requested a brochure at a home show. What is misleading about the display?

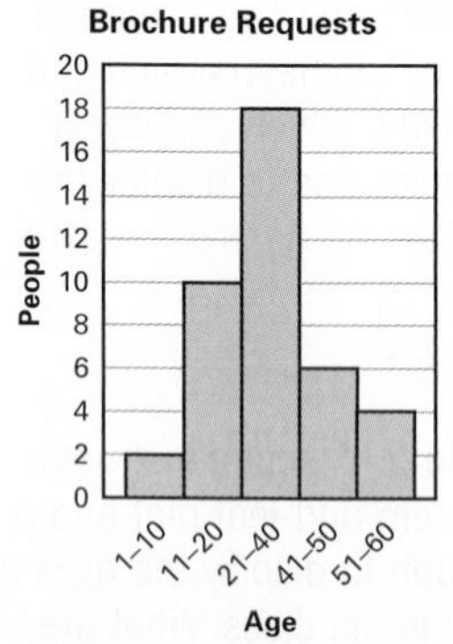

The bar for 21–40 appears taller because it represents a range of 20 years rather than the 10-year range represented by the other bars.

DIFFERENTIATING INSTRUCTION

Alternative Teaching Strategy Have students read the section on misleading graphs and then have them create their own misleading graph using data of their choosing.

 **COMMON ERROR**

Histograms and bar graphs are frequently confused because they are very similar. Help students understand how they differ.

 **CONCEPT CHECK**

What is the first thing to decide when choosing a data display to use? **whether the data are categorical or numerical**

 **DAILY PUZZLER**

If $0 < a < b < 1$, which is greater, $\frac{1}{a}$ or $\frac{1}{b}$? $\frac{1}{a}$

Example 3 *Identifying Misleading Data Displays*

Business The line graphs display a company's expenses and profits for each year from 2000 to 2003. What is misleading about each display?

a.

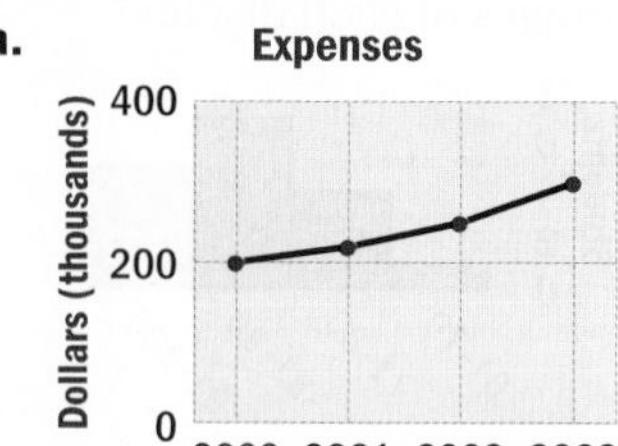

b.

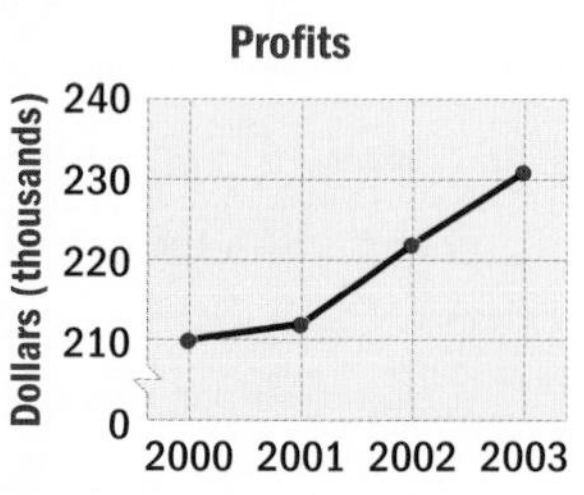

Solution

a. The increments on the vertical axis are too large. It appears that the company's expenses have increased only slightly from 2000 to 2003, when they have actually increased by 50%.

b. The vertical axis is broken. It appears that profits have risen dramatically from 2000 to 2003, when they have risen only 10%.

11.3 Exercises

More Practice, p. 813

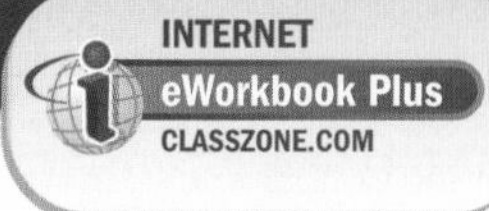

Guided Practice

Vocabulary Check

1. Name two data displays that can be used with categorical data. **bar graph, circle graph**
2. How could it be potentially misleading to use bars with different widths in a bar graph? ***Sample answer:*** **It can mislead people into comparing the areas of the bars rather than the heights.**

Skill Check

Tell which data display(s) you could use to display the data. Explain why.

3. The responses to a survey question with a choice of yes, no, or maybe **Bar graph, circle graph. *Sample answer:* These are categorical data.**
4. The heights (in meters) of different palm trees **See margin.**

Guided Problem Solving

5. **Bikes** The bar graph shows the number of bikes shipped in the U.S. over four years. Is the graph potentially misleading?

   1) Compare the lengths of the bars for 1997 and 2000. About how many times longer is the bar for 2000 than the bar for 1997? **about 4 times**
   2) How many times more bikes were shipped in 2000 than 1997? **about 1.4 times more bikes**
   3) Do you think the bar graph is misleading? Explain. **See margin.**

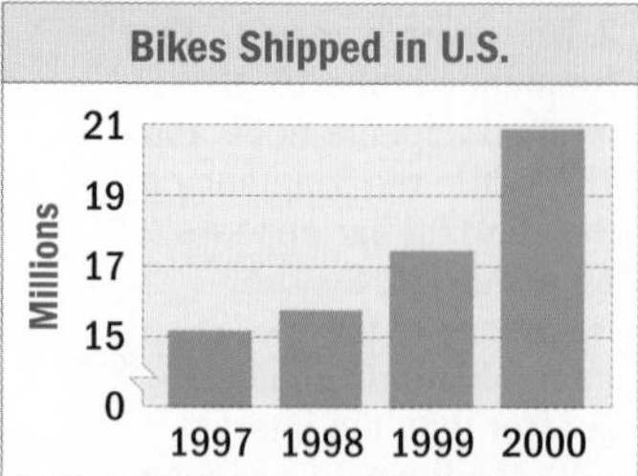

4. Stem-and-leaf plot, histogram, box-and-whisker plot. *Sample answer:* These are numerical data that can be listed individually or divided into equal intervals. You can also calculate quartiles and extremes from the ordered data.

Practice and Problem Solving

Homework Help

Example	Exercises
1	6-12
2	13, 15
3	14, 16, 17

Online Resources
CLASSZONE.COM
- More Examples
- eTutorial Plus

6. Numerical. ***Sample answer:*** **If the data values are few, I might use a stem-and-leaf plot so that I can view all the values. If there are many data values, I might use a histogram, since I can divide the data into equal intervals, or a box-and-whisker plot, since I can calculate the extremes and the quartiles for the data. Either of these displays would provide a convenient pictorial representation.**

In the **Real World**

Winter Sports In 1978, the Rocky Mountains had 15.8 million skiers and snowboarders. In 2000, the Rocky Mountains had 19.3 million skiers and snowboarders. Did the Rocky Mountains or the entire U.S. have a greater percent of increase in the number of skiers and snowboarders from 1978 to 2000? **Rocky Mountains**

In Exercises 6–8, tell whether the data are *numerical* or *categorical*. Then tell which data display(s) you would use to display the data. Explain your reasoning. 6–8. See margin.

A **6. Bald Eagles** A study was done to find the wingspans (in centimeters) of captured bald eagles.

7. Hockey A coach recorded the number of goals scored by each member of a hockey team.

8. Energy A study determined the amount of energy that was produced by different means, such as electric, solar, wind, and natural gas.

In Exercises 9–12, tell which data display(s) allow you to identify the specified information.

9. The median of the data set

10. The greatest value of the data set

9–10. See margin.

11. The mode of the data set **stem-and-leaf plot**

12. The frequency of an interval **histogram**

13. Critical Thinking What information can you get from a box-and-whisker plot that you cannot get from a histogram? What information can you get from a histogram that you cannot get from a box-and-whisker plot? Explain. **See margin.**

14. Exercising Twenty people were asked to state the number of hours per week that they exercise. The frequency table shows the results. **14a–b. See margin.**

a. Is the frequency table misleading? Explain.

b. Interpret What conclusions can you make from the frequency table?

Exercise Per Week (hours)		
Interval	**Tally**	**Frequency**
0-2 hours	II	2
2-4 hours	卌	5
4-8 hours	卌 I	6
8-16 hours	卌 II	7

15. Club A club president records the ages of the members in a club and wants to group the data in intervals of 2 years. Should the president use a stem-and-leaf plot or a histogram? Explain. **Histogram.** ***Sample answer:*** **There are no stems that correspond to 2 year intervals.**

B **16. Extended Problem Solving** The table shows the number of visitors (in millions) to ski areas in the United States in 10 different years.

a. Interpret Make a line graph using every 5th year, starting with 1980. What trend does the graph show? **16a–c. See margin.**

b. Interpret Make a new line graph using all the years given in the table. What trend does it show?

c. Critical Thinking Which line graph represents the data more accurately, the one in part (a) or the one in part (b)? Explain.

U.S. Skier/Snowboarder Visits			
Year	**Visitors**	**Year**	**Visitors**
1978	50.2	1990	46.7
1980	39.7	1993	54.6
1983	50.6	1995	54.0
1985	51.9	1998	52.1
1988	53.3	2000	57.3

3 APPLY

ASSIGNMENT GUIDE

Day 1: SRH p. 782 Exs. 4-7; pp. 599-600 Exs. 6-15, 19-25

Average Course
Day 1: pp. 599-600 Exs. 6-17, 19-26

Advanced Course
Day 1: pp. 599-600 Exs. 6-18*, 21-26

Block
pp. 599-600 Exs. 6-17, 19-26 (with 11.2)

EXTRA PRACTICE

- Student Edition, p. 813
- Chapter 11 Resource Book, pp. 26-28
- Test and Practice Generator

TRANSPARENCY

Even-numbered answers are available on transparencies.

HOMEWORK CHECK

When you review students' homework for this lesson, go over the following exercises to check understanding of key concepts.
Basic: 6, 9, 13, 14, 15
Average: 7, 10, 13, 14, 15
Advanced: 8, 12, 13, 16, 17

5. Step 3: Yes. ***Sample answer:*** **The break in the vertical axis exaggerates the differences in the bar heights.**

7. Categorical. ***Sample answer:*** **I would use a bar graph, because it would allow the most direct visual comparison between players' numbers of goals.**

8-10, 13, 14a-b, 16a-c. See Additional Answers beginning on page AA1.

4 ASSESS

ASSESSMENT RESOURCES

For more assessment resources, see:
- Assessment Book
- Test and Practice Generator

MINI-QUIZ

Are the data *numerical* or *categorical*? Which data display(s) would you use to display the data?

1. A survey was done to find what percents of students walk, bicycle, take public transportation, or ride a school bus to school. **categorical; circle graph**
2. A mail-order company records the sales of DVDs over the last 5 years. **numerical; line graph**
3. **Challenge** How could you make a box-and-whisker plot misleading? ***Sample answer:* Break the number line somewhere between the quartiles.**

5 FOLLOW-UP

DIAGNOSIS/REMEDIATION

- Study Guide in Chapter 11 Resource Book, pp. 29–30
- Tutor Place, Whole Numbers and Decimals Card 20, Ratio, Proportion, and Percent Card 17
- eTutorial Plus Online
- Extra Practice, p. 813
- Lesson Practice in Chapter 11 Resource Book, pp. 26–28

ENGLISH LEARNER SUPPORT

- Spanish Study Guide
- Multi-Language Visual Glossary
- Chapter Audio Summaries CDs

CHALLENGE

- Challenge Practice in Chapter 11 Resource Book, p. 31
- Teacher's Edition, p. 578F

24. See Additional Answers beginning on page AA1.

17. *Sample answer:* You might mistakenly conclude that volleyball is more popular than water skiing, though the numbers are the same. This is because the view at an angle makes the distance along the circle greater for the "Volleyball" section than for the "Water skiing" section.

C **17. Critical Thinking** The circle graph shows the results of a survey that asked students what their favorite beach activity is. In what way is this graph misleading? Explain.

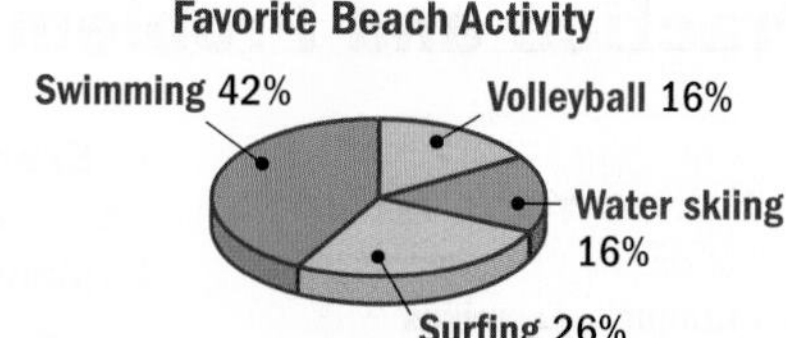

18. Challenge Find and copy a data display from a newspaper or magazine.

a. Are the data in the display numerical or categorical?

18a–b. Answers may vary.

b. *Writing* Do you think the display is potentially misleading? Explain.

Mixed Review

Find the sum or difference. *(Lessons 5.2, 5.3)*

19. $\frac{3}{7} + \left(-\frac{2}{7}\right)$ $\frac{1}{7}$ **20.** $-\frac{7}{18} - \frac{5}{18}$ $-\frac{2}{3}$ **21.** $\frac{4}{5} - \frac{7}{15}$ $\frac{1}{3}$ **22.** $-\frac{3}{4} + \frac{1}{12}$ $-\frac{2}{3}$

23. Geometry A trapezoid has an area of 140 square centimeters and bases of 15 centimeters and 20 centimeters. What is the height of the trapezoid? *(Lesson 10.3)* **8 cm**

24. Make a box-and-whisker plot of the following data: 255, 287, 299, 224, 200, 360, 231, 388, 318, 364, 381. *(Lesson 11.2)* **See margin.**

Standardized Test Practice

25. Multiple Choice Which would be an appropriate display for the data? **B**

Candidate	Percent of vote
A	43%
B	28%
C	29%

A. Line graph **B.** Circle graph

C. Scatter plot **D.** Histogram

26. Short Response A meteorologist has measured the amount of precipitation each month in a certain area. The meteorologist wants to use a data display that shows patterns in monthly precipitation changes. What type of display should the meteorologist use? Explain.

Line graph. *Sample answer:* A line graph shows changes over time.

Double Data

Two of the displays shown represent the same data. Which one doesn't?

the stem-and-leaf plot

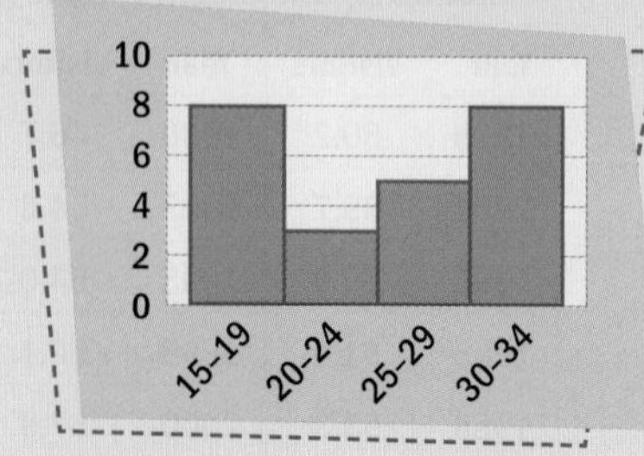

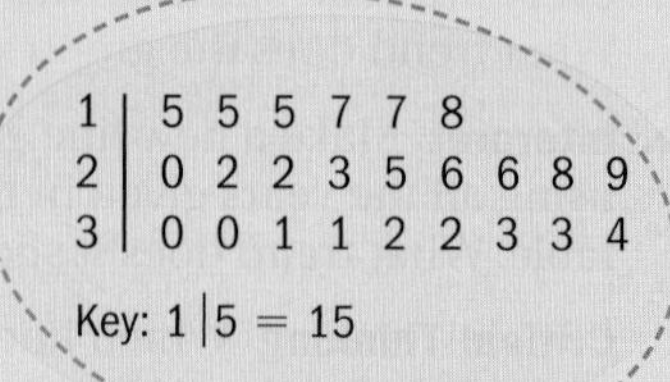

1	5 5 5 7 7 8
2	0 2 2 3 5 6 6 8 9
3	0 0 1 1 2 2 3 3 4

Key: 1 | 5 = 15

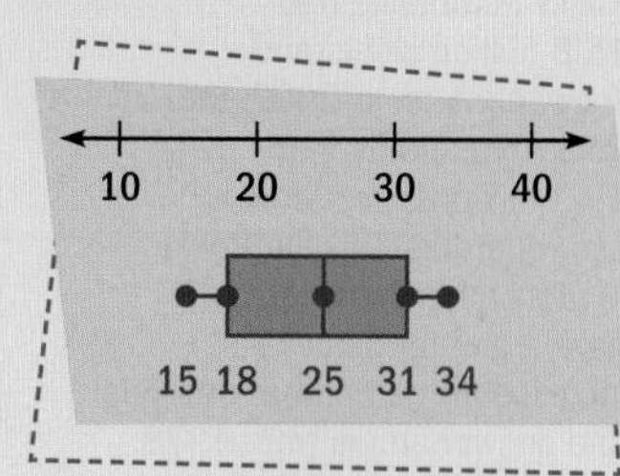

LESSON

11.4 Collecting Data

BEFORE You interpreted data displays.

Now You'll identify populations and sampling methods.

WHY? So you can predict if students will join a club, as in Ex. 16.

Vocabulary

population, p. 601
sample, p. 601
samples: random, systematic, stratified, convenience, self-selected, p. 601
biased sample, p. 602
biased question, p. 603

One way to collect data about a group is to conduct a survey. The entire group that you want information about is called a **population**. It is usually difficult to survey every member of a population. Instead, you can survey a **sample**, which is a part of the population. Five sampling methods are described below.

Sampling Methods

In a **random sample**, every member of the population has an equal chance of being selected.

In a **systematic sample**, a rule is used to select members of the population.

In a **stratified sample**, the population is divided into distinct groups. Members are selected from each group.

In a **convenience sample**, only members of the population who are easily accessible are selected.

In a **self-selected sample**, members of the population can select themselves by volunteering.

Example 1 *Identifying Populations and Sampling Methods*

For each survey, describe the population and the sampling method.

a. A school newspaper reporter asks every fifth student entering a school building whether a new gymnasium should be built.

b. A manager at a television station randomly telephones 75 residents under 30 years old and 75 residents 30 years old and over to determine the station's most watched programs.

Solution

a. The population consists of all the students at the school. Because the reporter uses the rule "interview every fifth person," the sample is a systematic sample.

b. The population consists of the television station's entire viewing audience. Because the manager divides the population into two groups and chooses members from each group, the sample is a stratified sample.

NCTM CURRICULUM STANDARDS

Standard 5: Collect, organize, and display data; Select proper statistical methods to analyze data

Standard 8: Use the language of math to express ideas

1 PLAN

Skill Check

1. $\frac{4}{9} \div \frac{2}{3} = \underline{?}$ $\frac{2}{3}$
2. $\frac{10}{13} \div \frac{5}{6} = \underline{?}$ $\frac{12}{13}$
3. $\frac{17}{18} \div \frac{5}{12} = \underline{?}$ $2\frac{4}{15}$

LESSON OBJECTIVE

Identify populations and sampling methods.

PACING

Suggested Number of Days
Basic Course: 1 day
Average Course: 1 day
Advanced Course: 1 day
Block: 0.5 block with 11.5

TEACHING RESOURCES

For a complete list of Teaching Resources, see page 578B.

TRANSPARENCY

Warm-Up Exercises for this lesson are available on a transparency.

2 TEACH

MOTIVATING THE LESSON

Ask students if they have ever participated in a survey or if they have conducted an informal survey of their own by asking friends their opinions on an issue.

TIPS *for* NEW TEACHERS

Consider introducing each sampling method by acting it out using a group of students as the population. See Tips for New Teachers in the *Chapter 11 Resource Book*.

Extra Examples

Example 1 For each survey, describe the population and the sampling method.

a. During an airplane flight, a newspaper reporter surveys ten passengers seated near him about airport security. **The population consists of all passengers on the reporter's flight; convenience.**

b. A magazine invites its readers to mail in their answers to a questionnaire. **The population consists of all the subscribers to the magazine; self-selected.**

Example 2 The board of trustees for a city library is considering extending the library's hours and wants to survey some of the city's residents regarding their proposed changes. Tell whether the survey method could result in a biased sample. Explain.

a. Survey all library patrons who visit the library on one particular evening. **This method could result in a biased sample because evening patrons might be more likely to favor extending library hours.**

b. Survey people at a city park each morning for one week. **This method is less likely to result in a biased sample because a wide range of people will be surveyed. However, this method is not a true random sample, so it may be biased.**

NOTETAKING

Give students time to record in their notebooks all the vocabulary in this lesson, along with examples that illustrate the various terms.

Watch *Out*

A random sample does not guarantee that the sample is representative, but it removes the potential for bias that other sampling methods have.

Samples When conducting a survey, you want a sample that is *representative* of the population. A sample that is not representative is a **biased sample**.

The sampling method can affect how representative a sample is. The most reliable way to have a representative sample is to use random sampling. However, non-random sampling is often used because it usually takes less time, money, and effort to perform.

Example 2 *Identifying Potentially Biased Samples*

Government A city council wants residents to help choose a new building project. Residents can choose one of the three ideas listed at the right.

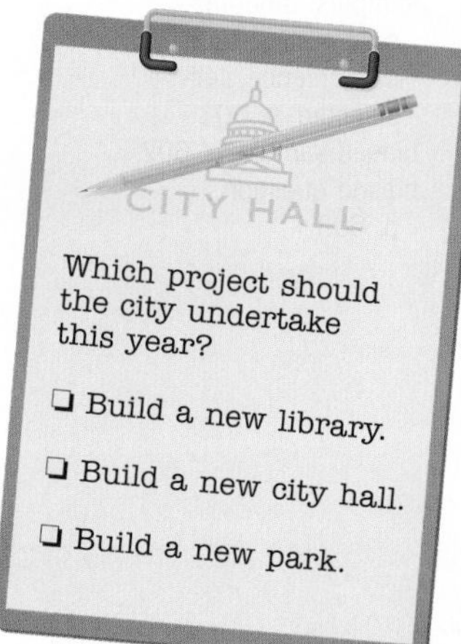

CITY HALL
Which project should the city undertake this year?
❑ Build a new library.
❑ Build a new city hall.
❑ Build a new park.

Because the council cannot survey every resident, it decides to survey a sample. Tell whether the survey method could result in a biased sample. Explain.

a. Survey the city council members and their families.

b. Survey parents at the city's recreation center.

c. Survey shoppers at the local mall.

Solution

a. This method could result in a biased sample because the city council members and their families have an interest in city government. They may favor building a new city hall.

b. This method could result in a biased sample because the parents at the recreation center have an interest in recreation. They may favor building a new park.

c. This method is less likely to result in a biased sample because a wide range of people will be surveyed. This method is not a true random sample because people who are not at the mall have no chance of being selected. As a result, the sample may be biased.

Checkpoint

1. The manager of an apartment building wants to know if noise is a problem in the building. The manager asks one person on each floor if the person thinks noise is a problem.

a. Describe the survey's population and sampling method.

b. Do you think the survey could result in a biased sample? Explain.

c. Describe another sampling method the manager could use. Could this method result in a biased sample? Explain.

1a. population: all the tenants in the apartment building; sampling method: stratified sample

1b. Yes. *Sample answer:* The noise level might, for example, be different for those who live on middle floors as opposed to the top and bottom floors.

1c. Self-selected sample. *Sample answer:* The manager could send surveys to every person asking about the noise. This could result in a biased sample, because every person might not respond.

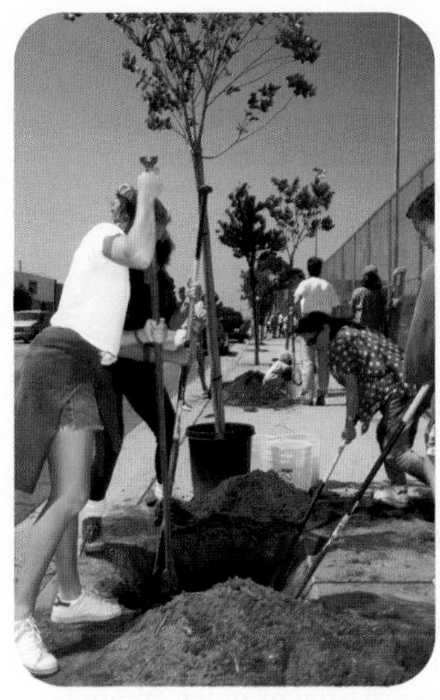

Biased Questions Questions that encourage particular responses are **biased questions**. When creating a survey, you should phrase questions to avoid bias.

Example 3 *Identifying Potentially Biased Questions*

Tell whether the question is potentially biased. Explain your answer. If the question is biased, rewrite it so that it is not.

a. Don't you agree that planting more shade trees will make our beautiful downtown area even better?

b. Are you willing to pay higher taxes so that the city can build a new stadium, even though we already have a stadium?

Solution

a. This question is biased because it suggests that planting shade trees is a good thing to do. An unbiased question is "Are you in favor of the plan to plant new shade trees in the downtown area?"

b. This question is biased because it suggests that another stadium is not necessary and will be expensive. An unbiased question is "Do you support the plan to build a new stadium?"

11.4 Exercises

More Practice, p. 813

Guided Practice

Vocabulary Check

1. Copy and complete: A sample in which every member of the population has an equal chance of being selected is a(n) __?__. **random sample**

2. Give an example of a non-random sampling method. **See margin.**

Skill Check

3. You ask the first 30 people coming out of a movie theater what type of movie they prefer. Is your sample likely to represent the population of all moviegoers? Explain. **See margin.**

Guided Problem Solving

4. **Camping** A survey was conducted to find the percent of Americans who enjoy camping. The surveyor randomly selected 20 individuals from each of the 50 states and asked, "Do you enjoy, greatly enjoy, or not enjoy camping in the woods, where the air is fresh and clean?" How much should you trust the results of this survey?

   (1) Identify the sampling method and population. **sampling method: stratified sample; population: all Americans**

   (2) Do you think the sample chosen was representative of the population? Explain. **Steps 2–3. See margin.**

   (3) Do you think the question is biased? If so, explain how it would affect the results of the survey.

2. *Sample answer:* **Ask everyone at a large table in the student cafeteria what they think about an issue that affects students.**

3. No. *Sample answer:* **Since the movies usually end at different times, it is possible that all the people you interview have gone to the same movie, so they may be inclined to like the same kind of movie.**

Extra Examples

Example 3 Tell whether the question is potentially biased. Explain your answer. If it is biased, rewrite it so it is not. *How many times per month do you use the city's new library?* **No; the question is straightforward and can be answered with a simple numerical response.**

Differentiating Instruction

Advanced Students Ask students to rate how much they like carrots on a scale of 1 to 10. After a few seconds, ask students if the rating is easier if the scale is only 1 to 5. Encourage interested students to research different rating scales and share their findings.

Teaching Tip

Some students may have difficulty identifying the bias identified in both parts of Example 3. Have small groups of students discuss who might have written the two given questions, and what that person might be expecting as the results of the survey. Point out that sometimes it is easier to spot the bias in a question if you know something about the person or group who is conducting the survey.

Concept Check

What are some things to consider when you are planning to conduct a survey? ***Sample answer:* Whom you want to sample; how you want to phrase your questions**

Daily Puzzler

If $x = 3^2$, what is the value of x^2? **81**

4 (Steps 2–3). See Additional Answers beginning on page AA1.

3 APPLY

ASSIGNMENT GUIDE

Basic Course

Day 1: pp. 604–605 Exs. 5–10, 12–15, 19–26

Average Course

Day 1: pp. 604–605 Exs. 5–17, 19–27

Advanced Course

Day 1: pp. 604–605 Exs. 7–18*, 21, 24–27

Block

pp. 604–605 Exs. 5–17, 19–27 (with 11.5)

EXTRA PRACTICE

- Student Edition, p. 813
- Chapter 11 Resource Book, pp. 35–37
- Test and Practice Generator

TRANSPARENCY

Even-numbered answers are available on transparencies.

HOMEWORK CHECK

When you review students' homework for this lesson, go over the following exercises to check understanding of key concepts.

Basic: 5, 7, 9, 10, 12
Average: 7, 8, 9, 11, 12
Advanced: 8, 9, 11, 12, 14

15. The sample from several ponds. *Sample answer:* The turtles from a single pond are likely to be more genetically similar, and are all subject to the availability of food in just that single pond.

Practice and Problem Solving

Homework *Help*

Example	Exercises
1	5–11
2	9–11
3	12–14

Online Resources
CLASSZONE.COM
- More Examples
- eTutorial Plus

A school newspaper is conducting a survey to predict who will win the next school election. Tell whether the sampling method is *random*, *systematic*, *stratified*, *convenience*, or *self-selected*.

A **5.** Set up a booth where students can come to give their opinions. **self-selected**

6. Get the ID numbers of every student in the school and have a computer randomly choose which students will be surveyed. **random**

7. Interview every third student as students leave the school. **systematic**

8. Interview 20 students from each grade. **stratified**

In Exercises 9 and 10, describe the population and tell what type of sampling method is used. Then tell whether the sample is likely to represent the population. Explain your answer.

9. A writer for a magazine wants to determine the most popular flavor of ice cream among residents in a town. The writer asks each customer at several local ice cream shops what their favorite flavor of ice cream is.

10. A researcher wants to know the opinions that people in a state have about filling out surveys. The researcher asks the first 30 people who volunteer to take a survey, "Do you think surveys are a useful tool for gathering information?"

11. Museum The director of a museum wants to know which exhibits museum visitors enjoy the most. The director places the questionnaire shown near the exit for people to fill out as they leave the museum.

a. Describe the population and the sampling method.

b. Critical Thinking Is the questionnaire likely to represent the population? Explain why or why not.

Which exhibits did you see today?
Which exhibit was your favorite?
Which exhibit was your least favorite?

9. Population: residents of the town; sampling method: convenience sample. No. *Sample answer:* The customers of the ice cream shops are likely more enthusiastic about ice cream than the general population, and may have different preferences.

10. Population: the people in the state; sampling method: self-selected. No. *Sample answer:* People who volunteer to participate in a survey are probably very likely to think that surveys are useful.

11a. Population: museum visitors; sampling method: self-selected

11b. No. *Sample answer:* The people who decide to fill out the survey are likely those with strong opinions, and as such may not represent the views of most museum visitors.

12. Yes; it suggests that one should not support a team that is doing poorly. An alternative question is "Do you support the school football team?"

14. Yes; it suggests that cats are better pets than dogs. An alternative question is "Do you think cats or dogs make better pets?"

In Exercises 12–14, tell whether the question is potentially biased. Explain your answer. If the question is biased, rewrite it so that it is not. **12–14. Sample answers are given.**

12. Do you still support the school football team, even though the team is having its worst season in 10 years?

13. How many times per week do you eat cereal? **No; the question is straightforward and can be answered with a simple numerical fact.**

14. Don't you think that cats are better pets than dogs?

15. Snapping Turtles Two scientists are attempting to gather data in order to find the average weight of snapping turtles. The first scientist weighs all of the snapping turtles that live in a certain pond. The second scientist weighs a number of snapping turtles from several ponds. Which sample do you think will give a more accurate estimate of the average weight of snapping turtles? Explain. **See margin.**

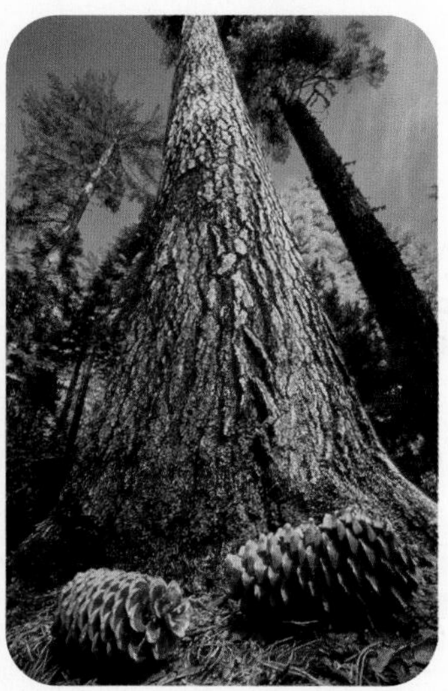

B 16. **Photography Club** You want to find out if the students in your school would be interested in joining a new photography club.

a. *Writing* Describe a method for choosing a representative sample of the student population. ***Sample answer:*** **Get an alphabetical list of all students and survey every twentieth student.**

b. Write an unbiased question that you could ask to find out if students are interested in joining the club. ***Sample answer:*** **If there were a photography club at school, would you want to be a member?**

17. **Pine Trees** Scientists conducted a study to determine the average height of pine trees in a large forest. They did so by measuring 200 trees from the forest. Tell whether the following statements, if true, would lower your confidence in the results of the study. Explain your answers. **17a–d. Sample answers are given.**

a. The scientists chose the trees in their sample randomly. **No; a random sample should be representative.**

b. The scientists selected trees only from the western portion of the forest. **Yes; trees in one portion might be genetically more similar, as well as subject to local environmental influences.**

c. Some of the trees measured in the study were much taller than others. **Yes; if some trees were unusually tall, they would make the average height taller than might be "typical" for the forest.**

d. The scientists measured only a small fraction of the total number of pine trees in the forest they studied. **See margin.**

C 18. **Challenge** Find the results of a survey in a newspaper or magazine. Identify the population and the sampling method used and tell whether any of the questions asked are likely to be biased. How much confidence do you have in the results of the survey? Explain. **Answers may vary.**

Mixed Review

17d. No; it is the function of a sample to represent a larger population. If the sample is representative, and not biased in any way, the results should reflect those in the forest as a whole.

Solve the equation. Check your solution. *(Lesson 3.3)*

19. $5x - 12 = 2x + 6$ **6**
20. $10 - 3x = -x - 8$ **9**
21. $4x + 7 = 6 - 3(x + 1)$ $-\frac{4}{7}$

A map has a scale of 1 centimeter : 25 kilometers. Use the given map distance to find the actual distance. *(Lesson 6.6)*

22. 11 cm **275 km**
23. 6 cm **150 km**
24. 5 mm **12.5 km**

25. Find the value of x to the nearest tenth. *(Lesson 9.8)* **26.4**

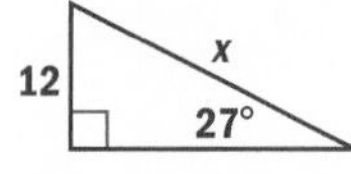

Standardized Test Practice

26. **Multiple Choice** Which question is *not* biased? **B**

A. Don't you think that renovating the old town hall would be a mistake?

B. Do you support the governor's proposal to reduce state taxes?

C. Are you willing to deal with heavy increases in traffic where you live just so another mall can be built?

D. Do you think we should elect a new mayor in the next election, or re-elect the leader who has served this town for so many years?

27. **Short Response** You ask 10 students in your math class a survey question. Which population is better represented by the responses you get, the 30 students in your math class or the 1000 students in your school? Explain.

27. The 30 students in your math class. *Sample answer:* Students do not all take the same math classes. Also, the students in a class may all be in the same grade, or at least mostly in the same grade.

4 ASSESS

Assessment Resources

For more assessment resources, see:
- Assessment Book
- Test and Practice Generator

Mini-Quiz

A veterinarian conducts a survey to find out how many bird owners might use his services. Tell whether the sampling method is *random*, *systematic*, *stratified*, *convenience*, or *self-selected*.

1. A booth is set up in a bird store and all customers are asked. **convenience**
2. A newspaper advertisement asks bird owners to call and vote. **self-selected**
3. Phone numbers of bird owners are collected from pet stores and the owners are called and polled. **systematic**
4. **Challenge** Think of an advertisement you have seen that claims to report on a survey. How could this survey be biased? **Answers may vary.**

5 FOLLOW-UP

Diagnosis/Remediation

- Study Guide in Chapter 11 Resource Book, pp. 38–39
- eTutorial Plus Online
- Extra Practice, p. 813
- Lesson Practice in Chapter 11 Resource Book, pp. 35–37

English Learner Support

- Spanish Study Guide
- Multi-Language Visual Glossary
- Chapter Audio Summaries CDs

Challenge

- Challenge Practice in Chapter 11 Resource Book, p. 40
- Teacher's Edition, p. 578F

1 PLAN

LEARN THE METHOD

- Students will use an Internet search engine to find data, and use a spreadsheet to make data displays.
- This activity builds on the ideas of collecting data in Lesson 11.4 and displaying data in Lesson 11.3, and gives students an opportunity to compare different data displays they have collected.

GROUPING

Students should work individually if possible. If there is an insufficient number of computers with Internet access for all students, divide the class into groups of 3 or 4 students, making sure students understand that each member of the group should have an opportunity to use the computer.

2 TEACH

ALTERNATIVE STRATEGY

To save time, you may wish to demonstrate Example 1 using a projector system so your Internet search is visible to the whole class. Alternatively, demonstrate the search to small groups of students, inviting them to suggest keywords that will narrow the search.

Extra Examples

Example 1 Use an Internet search engine to find the number of moons currently known for four planets in our solar system. Enter the data in a spreadsheet. **Answers may vary.**

11.4 Searching for Data

Goal Use an Internet search engine to find data. Use a spreadsheet to make data displays.

Example 1

Use an Internet search engine to find the record of wins, losses, ties, and overtime losses of a National Hockey League (NHL) team.

1. Choose a search engine. Type keywords that cover the topic you would like to search. Then select Search.

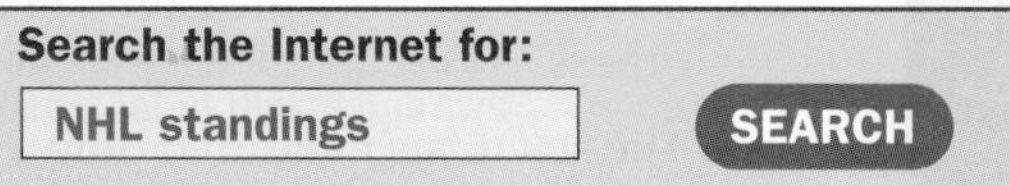

2. Of the results the search engine finds, choose a website that is likely to have the information you need.

3. Select a team. Enter the data in the first two columns of a spreadsheet, as shown for the Philadelphia Flyers' 2001–2002 record.

	A	B
1	Result of game	Number
2	Win	42
3	Loss	27
4	Tie	10
5	Overtime loss	3

Tech *Help*

When searching for data on the Internet, if the first keywords you try do not give you the results you want, try other keywords.

- Keystroke Help

Draw Conclusions

Use the Internet and spreadsheet software to complete the following exercises. **1–3. Answers may vary.**

1. Search the Internet for the record of wins, losses, ties, and overtime losses for two NHL teams. Enter the data into a spreadsheet.
2. **Analyze** Compare the records of the two teams. Which team has the better record? Explain.
3. **Compare** Find the records of wins, losses, and ties for two Major League Soccer (MLS) teams. Use the phrase "MLS standings" to search for the data. Then enter the data into a spreadsheet. Use the spreadsheet to compare the team records.

NCTM CURRICULUM STANDARDS

Standard 5: Collect, organize, and display data; Select proper statistical methods to analyze data

Example 2

Use a spreadsheet to display the data from Example 1.

Each cell on a spreadsheet is labeled using a letter to indicate the column and a number to indicate the row. Highlight the data in cells A2:B5. The expression A2:B5 refers to the rectangular array of cells with A2 and B5 at the corners.

1 Use the *insert* menu to insert a graph. Select a vertical bar graph, or column chart, as the type of graph. Then choose options for your graph, such as a title and labels for the horizontal and vertical axes.

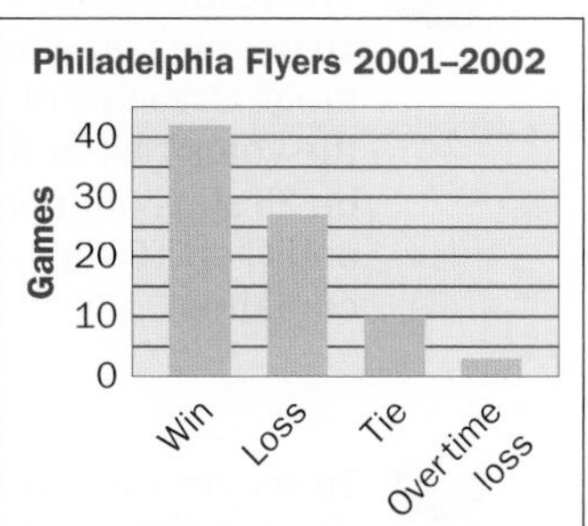

2 To change other features of your graph after it has been created, double click on the part of the graph that you wish to change and adjust the formatting.

3 To obtain a different data display, such as a circle graph, repeat Steps 1 and 2, but this time select a circle graph.

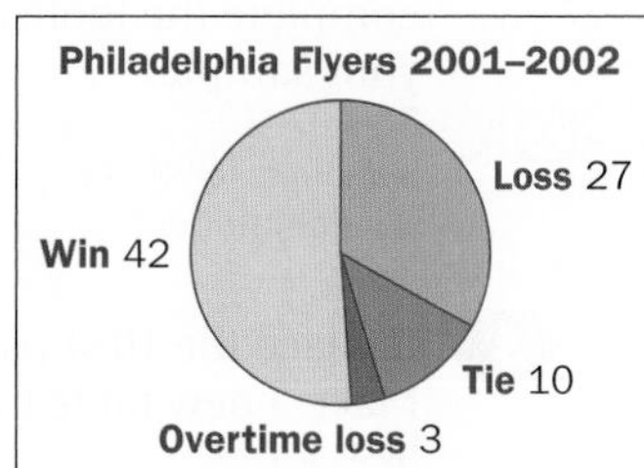

Tech *Help*

The spreadsheet sets the scale for the bar graph automatically.

• Keystroke Help

Draw Conclusions

Use spreadsheet software to complete the following exercises. **4–6. Answers may vary.**

4. Use the data from Exercise 1 on page 606 to make a bar graph and a circle graph for each team.
5. **Analyze** Use the circle graphs from Exercise 4 to compare the records of the two teams. Which team has a greater percent of games won?
6. **Compare** Use the data from Exercise 3 on page 606 to make a circle graph and a bar graph for each team. Which team has the better record? Explain.

Tips for Success

Because students choose different teams for their work in Exercises 1 and 3, they will not be able to compare their bar graphs. Remind students to check that every row of the spreadsheet table is represented on the graph. Also remind them to check their keystroking, as scores mistyped from the Internet will be graphed as if correct.

Extra Examples

Example 2 Use a spreadsheet to display your moon data from Example 1 as a vertical bar graph. **Answers may vary.**

3 CLOSE

Assessment

1. Which graph in Example 2 do you think is better for comparing the team's wins and losses? Explain your answer. **The bar graph. *Sample answer:* It is easier to compare the heights of the two bars.**
2. Which graph in Example 2 makes it easier to estimate the percent of all games won by the Philadelphia Flyers during the 2001–2002 season? Explain your answer. **The circle graph. *Sample answer:* You can compare the size of the "Win" sector to the whole circle.**

1 PLAN

INVESTIGATE THE CONCEPT

- Students determine how well a random sample represents a population.
- This activity leads into drawing conclusions about populations from surveys in Lesson 11.5.

MATERIALS

Each student will need 50 slips of paper, a container, and a pencil.

RECOMMENDED TIME

Work activity: 15 min
Discuss results: 10 min

GROUPING

Students should work individually.

2 TEACH

ALTERNATIVE STRATEGY

To save time, prepare one set of the slips of paper prior to class. Then have 10 volunteers each choose a slip of paper and an 11th volunteer tally the results on the board. Discuss the differences between the sample and the population before repeating the activity in Step 3.

3 CLOSE

KEY DISCOVERY

A small sample does not represent a population well. A larger sample represents a population better.

ASSESSMENT

1. What happens to the accuracy of a prediction based on a sample as the size of that sample increases? **The accuracy increases.**

1. See Additional Answers beginning on page AA1.

608

Concept *Activity*

11.5 Investigating Random Samples

Goal

Determine how well a random sample represents a population.

Materials

- 50 slips of paper
- container
- pencil

Investigate

Use slips of paper to see how well a random sample represents the population from which it was taken.

The results of an election in which 50 people voted are given in the table. Use slips of paper to represent the votes cast in the election. Write A on 25 slips of paper, B on 15 slips, and C on 10 slips. Put the slips in a container.

Candidate	Number of votes	Percent of population's votes
A	25	50%
B	15	30%
C	10	20%
Total	50	100%

To see how well a sample represents the population of voters in an election, randomly select 10 slips of paper from the container. Copy and complete the table at the right using your sample.
Steps 2–3. Sample answers are given based on random numbers generated by a calculator.

Candidate	Number of votes	Percent of sample's votes
A	? 3	? 30%
B	? 6	? 60%
C	? 1	? 10%
Total	10	100%

Replace the 10 slips of paper and repeat Step 2 three more times. Make a new table for each new sample. **second trial: Row 2: 5, 50%; Row 3: 4, 40%; Row 4: 1, 10%; third trial: Row 2: 4, 40%; Row 3: 3, 30%; Row 4: 3, 30%**

Draw Conclusions

1. **Compare** For each sample, compare each candidate's percent of the sample's votes with the candidate's percent of the population's votes. Are the values the same for any candidate? How well does each sample represent the population? Explain your thinking. **See margin.**
2. **Critical Thinking** Find the mean of the results for each candidate from the random samples drawn by the entire class. How well do the means of these samples represent the population? **Check work.**

NCTM CURRICULUM STANDARDS

Standard 5: Collect, organize, and display data; Evaluate predictions that are based on data

Standard 8: Communicate thinking clearly to others

LESSON

11.5 Interpreting Data

BEFORE	Now	WHY?
You identified biased surveys.	You'll make conclusions about populations using surveys.	So you can interpret a survey about pets, as in Ex. 9.

Vocabulary
margin of error, p. 610

Television Television networks rely on surveys to determine how many people watch their programs. In a survey of 5000 randomly selected American households, 780 of the households watched a certain program. Of all American households, how many watched the program?

You can use a sample to make a prediction about a population. If $p\%$ of a sample gives a particular response and the sample is representative of the population, then:

Predicted number of people in population giving the response	=	$p\%$	•	Number of people in population

Example 1 *Making a Population Prediction*

There are about 105 million households in the United States. To estimate the number of households that watched the program described above, follow these steps:

1. Find the percent of households in the sample that watched the program.

$$\frac{780}{5000} = 0.156 = 15.6\%$$

2. Find 15.6% of the total number of households in the United States.

$$15.6\% \cdot 105 \text{ million households} \approx 16.4 \text{ million households}$$

Answer About 16.4 million households in the United States watched the program.

Checkpoint

1. In a survey of 5000 randomly selected American households, 460 households watched a certain program. Of all American households, about how many watched the program?

1. about 9.7 million households

NCTM CURRICULUM STANDARDS

Standard 5: Use proper statistical methods to analyze data; Develop inferences that are based on data
Standard 8: Use the language of math to express ideas

1 PLAN

Skill Check

Write the fraction as a percent.

1. $\frac{46}{100}$ **46%** 2. $\frac{32}{200}$ **16%**
3. $\frac{45}{500}$ **9%** 4. $\frac{35}{700}$ **5%**

LESSON OBJECTIVE

Make conclusions about populations using surveys.

PACING

Suggested Number of Days
Basic Course: 1 day
Average Course: 1 day
Advanced Course: 1 day
Block: 0.5 block with 11.4

TEACHING RESOURCES

For a complete list of Teaching Resources, see page 578B.

TRANSPARENCY

Warm-Up Exercises for this lesson are available on a transparency.

2 TEACH

MOTIVATING THE LESSON

Ask: "If you knew that 15% of the students in your math class supported a field trip, how could you relate this information to the number of students in the entire school who might support the trip?"

TIPS *for* NEW TEACHERS

Point out that a small survey might be easier and less expensive than a larger survey, but a larger survey is more accurate. See Tips for New Teachers in the *Chapter 11 Resource Book*.

Extra Examples

Example 1 One student out of a class of 20 was absent with a cold. What percent of the class was absent and how many students out of a school of 1600 would you estimate to be absent based on this percent? **5%; 80 students**

Example 2 The mayor of a city is running for re-election. A survey of some city residents predicts that the mayor will receive 58% of the votes from likely voters and her challenger will receive 42% of the votes. The margin of error for the survey is ±5%. Can you predict who will win the election? Explain. **Yes. The mayor will likely receive between 53% and 63% of the votes and the challenger will likely receive between 37% and 47%. Since the intervals do not overlap, the mayor will probably win the election.**

Cross-Curriculum

Language Arts In language arts class, students may wish to explore ways that language is used to create bias. Some subjects to explore might include the use of provocative wording, propaganda techniques, and advertising methods.

Teaching Tip

Students may benefit from learning that the margin of error is found using the number of people surveyed. The exact calculation is not important but students might appreciate learning that the larger the number of people surveyed, the smaller the margin of error.

Watch Out

A margin of error accounts only for errors due to the nature of random sampling. It does not account for errors that result from biased questions or biased sampling.

Margin of Error When a survey samples only a portion of a population, different surveys of the same population may have different results. For example, one survey might find that 32% of the population uses a cell phone. Another might find that 36% does. The actual percent might be 33%.

Due to such variation, a survey should include a *margin of error*. The **margin of error** of a random sample defines an interval centered on the sample percent in which the population percent is most likely to lie. For example, a sample percent of 32% with a margin of error of ±5% means that the population percent is most likely between 27% and 37%.

The population percent most likely lies between 27% and 37%.

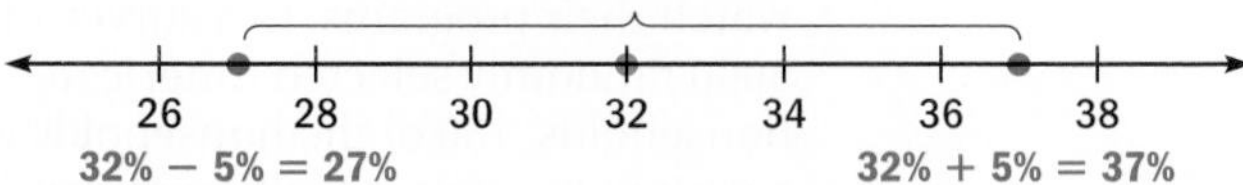

Example 2 Interpreting a Margin of Error

Election A survey of a random sample of voters predicts that candidate A will receive 52% of the votes and that candidate B will receive 48% of the votes. The margin of error is ±3%. Can you predict who will win the election?

Solution

Use the margin of error to find intervals in which each candidate's actual percent is most likely to lie.

Candidate A: 52% − 3% = 49%   52% + 3% = 55%

Candidate B: 48% − 3% = 45%   48% + 3% = 51%

Using the margin of error, you can conclude that candidate A is likely to receive between 49% and 55% of the votes. Candidate B is likely to receive between 45% and 51% of the votes.

Answer Because the intervals overlap for the two candidates, you cannot predict which candidate will win the election.

Summary — Summary of Data Analysis

When reading the results of a survey, consider the following.

- Identify the population and the sampling method.
- Determine whether the sample represents the population.
- Determine whether the survey questions are biased.
- Identify the margin of error.
- Determine whether any data displays are potentially misleading.
- Decide if the conclusions are supported by the data.

Example 3 *Interpreting a Newspaper Survey*

Tell what conclusions you can make from the following newspaper article.

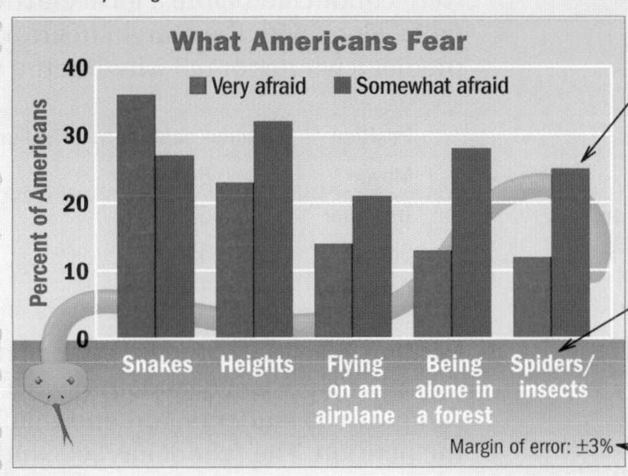

Snakes Are Americans' Number One Fear!

Recently, researchers surveyed about 1000 Americans by telephone and asked them if they were "very afraid," "somewhat afraid," or "not afraid" of a number of things. From the results shown below, only one conclusion is possible: Americans fear snakes more than anything else!

Sample is not truly random. Not everyone participates in phone surveys.

Question is not biased, but respondents may have different interpretations of what "very afraid" means.

Bar graph doesn't appear misleading. There is no break in the frequency axis, and all the bars have the same width.

List of fearful things is limited. Something not on this list might be the number one fear.

Margin of error is given.

Extra Examples

Example 3 Tell what conclusions you can make from the following report.
Recently, researchers surveyed 1000 patrons of a local shopping mall and asked them if they were "strongly for", "mildly for", or "against" the city's plans to buy some residents' houses and demolish them to make room for an new upscale mall. Most residents—780 out of 1000—were for having the new mall.
Sample answer: **The sample is not random since mall patrons would be more likely to favor another mall than persons chosen at random from throughout the city. Of the three response choices, two of them are positive, and this also biases the results. Finally, there is no information given in the report about which neighborhood would be affected, and this information could lead people to change their opinion.**

11.5 Exercises

More Practice, p. 813

INTERNET
eWorkbook Plus
CLASSZONE.COM

Guided Practice

Vocabulary Check

1. Explain what is meant by a margin of error for a survey. **See margin.**
2. List several things to check when you read the results of a survey. **See margin.**

Skill Check

3. **Dog Food** A survey of 200 randomly selected dog owners finds that 130 dog owners prefer brand A dog food. Predict how many owners in a town of 1500 dog owners prefer brand A dog food. **about 975 dog owners**

Guided Problem Solving

4. **Polls** A newspaper surveys a random sample of 200 voters with a margin of error of ±7%. Of these voters, 88 plan to vote for candidate A, and 112 plan to vote for candidate B. Can you predict the winner?
   1) Find the percent of voters who plan to vote for each candidate. **candidate A: 44%, candidate B: 56%**
   2) Find the interval in which the percent of votes for each candidate is most likely to lie. **candidate A: 37% to 51%; candidate B: 49% to 63%**
   3) Does the survey tell you who will win the election? Explain. **No. Sample answer: The intervals overlap.**

Concept Check

What does a ±2% margin of error mean? **It means that each percentage given as a result of the survey may be incorrect by as much as 2% in either direction (higher or lower).**

Daily Puzzler

What is 11 − 22 + 33 − 44 + 55 − 66 + 77 − 88? **−44**

1. ***Sample answer:*** **It is an amount added and subtracted to a sample percent to determine the upper and lower boundaries for an interval in which the population percent is most likely to lie.**

2. See Additional Answers beginning on page AA1.

3 APPLY

ASSIGNMENT GUIDE

Basic Course

Day 1: EP p. 809 Exs. 5–8; pp. 612–613 Exs. 5–9, 13, 14, 16–26

Average Course

Day 1: pp. 612–613 Exs. 6–14, 16–26

Advanced Course

Day 1: pp. 612–613 Exs. 7–15*, 18–21, 24–26

Block

pp. 612–613 Exs. 6–14, 16–26 (with 11.4)

EXTRA PRACTICE

- Student Edition, p. 813
- Chapter 11 Resource Book, pp. 43–45
- Test and Practice Generator

TRANSPARENCY

Even-numbered answers are available on transparencies.

HOMEWORK CHECK

When you review students' homework for this lesson, go over the following exercises to check understanding of key concepts.

Basic: 5, 6, 7, 9, 13
Average: 6, 8, 9, 12, 13
Advanced: 7, 8, 9, 12, 13

TEACHING TIP

In Exercise 5, point out that the problem can also be solved using the proportion $\frac{35}{200} = \frac{x}{6000}$.

9. See Additional Answers beginning on page AA1.

Practice and Problem Solving

Homework Help

Example	Exercises
1	5, 6, 8, 12
2	7, 13
3	9

Online Resources CLASSZONE.COM
- More Examples
- eTutorial Plus

7. mayor: leading candidate; treasurer: too close to call; sheriff: leading candidate; controller: too close to call

8. Yes. *Sample answer:* The sample percent is 74%. If the population percent is the same, then 74% of 900, or about 666 students, should sign the petition.

11. No. *Sample answer:* The sample is not random, and represents only a few people of a certain age. Also, because all the students in the classroom are close together, they may be likely to transmit the flu among each other.

A **5. DVD Player** A survey finds that 35 families in a random sample of 200 families in a town own a DVD player. The town has 6000 families. Predict how many families in the town own a DVD player. about 1050 families

6. Favorite Subject You interview a random sample of 100 students in a school. Thirty students say that math is their favorite subject. There are 1200 students in the school. Predict how many students in the school would say that math is their favorite subject. about 360 students

7. Election Four surveys based on random samples of registered voters were conducted before a local election. The results are shown in the table, along with the margin of error for each survey. For each election, predict a winner or tell whether the election is too close to call.

Position	Leading candidate	Trailing candidate	Margin of error
Mayor	56%	44%	±3.5%
Treasurer	53%	47%	±4%
Sheriff	55%	45%	±4%
Controller	54%	46%	±6%

8. Petition A school's student council has said that it would change the school's colors if 600 students sign a petition. You interview a random sample of 50 students. You find that 37 students say they would sign the petition. The school has 900 students. Do you think enough students will sign the petition? Justify your reasoning.

9. Pet Survey Review the newspaper article below, which summarizes the results of a survey. How much trust do you have in the survey? Do you think the conclusions in the article are valid? Explain. See margin.

Reptiles and Birds Becoming Common Pets!

A recent survey of 200 people at the local mall found that more people in town own reptiles or birds than own traditional mammals, such as cats and dogs. The survey was conducted by Reba's Reptiles, a store in the local mall that sells unusual pets.

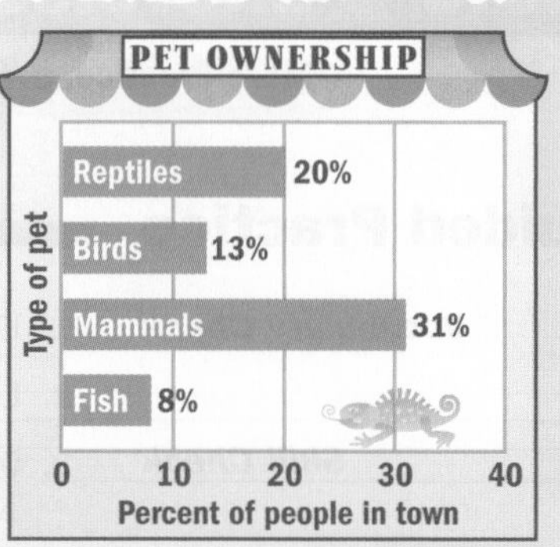

10. Critical Thinking A survey claims that a population percent is very likely to be between 35% and 45%. What is the margin of error for the survey? What percent did the survey obtain from its sample? ±5%; 40%

B **11. Critical Thinking** Suppose there are 20 students in your math class. Four of the students have the flu. Can you use this information to predict how many people in your town have the flu? Explain why or why not.

12c. Part (a). *Sample answer:* The survey was nationwide, and thus likely more representative of the population. The sample in the math class is just too small to draw any conclusions, especially considering that only 2 of the students played the saxophone, and it is even possible that there could be some kind of relationship between those who study math and music.

15b. Increase. *Sample answer:* If n increases, then the denominator of $\frac{100}{\sqrt{n}}$ increases, which means that the fraction, and thus the margin of error, decreases.

21. 118.125, or $118\frac{1}{8}$

12. Extended Problem Solving A nationwide survey of a random sample of teenagers asked whether or not they play the saxophone.

a. Predict The survey concluded that 4% of teenagers play the saxophone. Use this information to predict how many students in a school with 1000 teenage students play the saxophone. **about 40 students**

b. Predict Suppose 2 of the 29 people in a math class play the saxophone. Use this information to predict how many of the 1000 students in the school play the saxophone. **about 69 students**

c. *Writing* Do you think the prediction from part (a) or the prediction from part (b) is more accurate? Explain your answer.

13. Part-time Jobs A school has 1200 students. A survey of a random sample of 250 students found that 65 students have part-time jobs. The survey has a margin of error of ±6%. Find the interval in which the total number of students who have part-time jobs is likely to lie. **240 students to 384 students**

14. Hair Color A town has 5000 residents. A survey finds that 81 residents out of a random sample of 625 residents have red hair. The margin of error for the survey is ±4%. Find the interval in which the total number of residents with red hair is most likely to lie. **448 people to 848 people**

C **15. Challenge** When a random sample of size n is taken from a large population, the sample has a margin of error of about $\pm\frac{100}{\sqrt{n}}\%$.

a. How many people need to be surveyed for a sample to have a margin of error of about ±3%? Round to the nearest whole number. **1111 people**

b. To have a margin of error of ±2%, should you increase or decrease the sample size in part (a)? Explain. **See margin.**

Mixed Review

Simplify. *(Lesson 4.5)*

16. $\frac{2x^2 \cdot 34x}{17x}$ **$4x^2$** **17.** $\frac{3m^4 \cdot 16m^2}{6m^2}$ **$8m^4$** **18.** $\frac{5a \cdot 2a}{a^2}$ **10** **19.** $\frac{15c \cdot 4c}{6c^2}$ **10**

Solve the proportion. *(Lesson 6.3)*

20. $\frac{12}{x} = \frac{4}{10}$ **30** **21.** $\frac{400}{525} = \frac{90}{y}$ **See margin.** **22.** $\frac{16}{z} = \frac{20}{30}$ **24** **23.** $\frac{15}{24} = \frac{10}{w}$ **16**

24. Survey A researcher interviews 75 men and 75 women in a town. Describe the sampling method used by the researcher. *(Lesson 11.4)* **stratified sample**

Standardized Test Practice

25. Multiple Choice A survey with a margin of error of ±2% finds that history is the favorite subject of 39% of a random sample of students. In which interval is the population percent most likely to lie? **B**

A. Between 36% and 42% **B.** Between 37% and 41%

C. Between 37% and 39% **D.** Between 39% and 41%

26. Multiple Choice A school has 800 students. A survey of a random sample of 80 students finds that 48 students enjoy swimming. Predict the total number of students in the school who enjoy swimming. **H**

F. 48 **G.** 384 **H.** 480 **I.** 3840

4 ASSESS

Assessment Resources

For more assessment resources, see:
- Assessment Book
- Test and Practice Generator

Mini-Quiz

1. In a random survey, it is found that 15 out of 300 households in a town have a piano. Predict how many households in the town of 18,000 households would have a piano. **900 households**
2. A survey claims that between 41% and 53% of voters are likely to vote against a new proposition. What is the margin of error for the survey? **±6%**
3. **Challenge** A random sample of size n taken from a large population has a margin of error of $\pm\frac{100}{\sqrt{n}}\%$. How many people need to be surveyed for the sample to have a margin of error of ±1%? **10,000 people**

5 FOLLOW-UP

Diagnosis/Remediation

- Study Guide in Chapter 11 Resource Book, pp. 46–47
- eTutorial Plus Online
- Extra Practice, p. 813
- Lesson Practice in Chapter 11 Resource Book, pp. 43–45

English Learner Support

- Spanish Study Guide
- Multi-Language Visual Glossary
- Chapter Audio Summaries CDs

Challenge

- Challenge Practice in Chapter 11 Resource Book, p. 48
- Teacher's Edition, p. 578F

Additional Resources

The following resources are available to help review the materials in Lessons 11.1–11.5.

Chapter 11 Resource Book
- Lesson Practice
- Study Guide

Assessment Book
- Chapter 11 Quiz 1

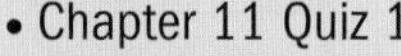

Technology
- Test and Practice Generator
- eTutorial CD-ROM

Internet
- Classzone
- eWorkbook Plus Online
- eTutorial Plus Online

English Learner Support

- Spanish Study Guide
- Multi-Language Visual Glossary
- Chapter Audio Summaries CDs

1. ***Sample:***

Temperature (°F)	Tally	Frequency
7–12	I	1
13–18	III	3
19–24		0
25–30	~~IIII~~	5
31–36	I	1

Low Temperatures in Chicago

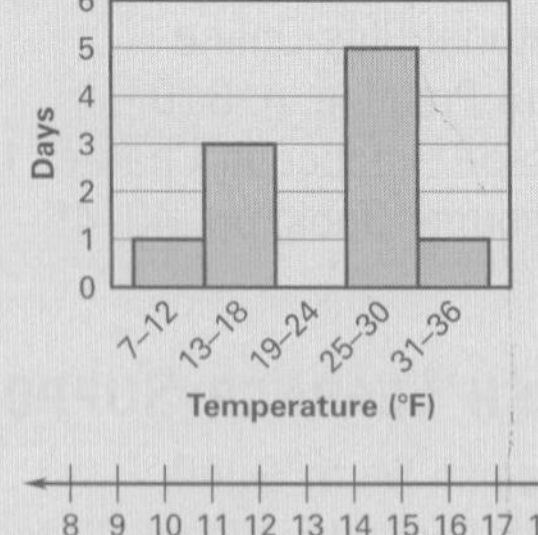

2. 8 9 10 11 12 13 14 15 16 17 18

9 11 13 15 17

3–6. See Additional Answers beginning on page AA1.

Mid-Chapter Quiz

1. Temperature Make a frequency table and a histogram of the following low temperatures (in degrees Fahrenheit) that were recorded over a 10 day period in Chicago, Illinois: 28, 14, 8, 26, 18, 15, 30, 31, 30, 28. **See margin.**

2. CD Prices Make a box-and-whisker plot of the following prices (in dollars) of CDs you bought: 9, 16, 17, 13, 14, 12, 9, 11, 14, 16, 13, 11. **See margin.**

In Exercises 3 and 4, tell whether the data are *numerical* or *categorical*. Then tell which data display(s) you would use to display the data. Explain your reasoning. **3–4. See margin.**

3. The number of games won by each team in a softball league

4. The ways people travel to school, such as car, bus, and walking

In Exercises 5 and 6, describe the population and tell what type of sampling method is used. Then tell whether the sampling method is likely to represent the population. Explain your answer. **5–6. See margin.**

5. A writer for the school newspaper wants to find out students' favorite lunch. She asks 20 students who work on the newspaper to name their favorite lunch.

6. The director at an amusement park wants to determine which rides visitors enjoy the most. The director asks every tenth person who leaves the park to list his or her three favorite rides.

7. Cell Phones A survey found that 35 families out of a random sample of 150 families in a town own at least one cell phone. The town has 7500 families. How many families would you predict own at least one cell phone? **about 1750 families**

Musical Chairs

In a survey about music, 30 people liked rock, 31 people liked hip-hop, and 32 people liked pop. Of the people who liked rock, 6 also liked hip-hop, and 10 also liked pop. Of the people who liked pop, 12 also liked hip-hop. Five people liked all three types of music, and 5 people didn't like any of the three.

How many people were surveyed? **75 people**

LESSON **11.6**

Permutations

BEFORE	Now	WHY?
You used the counting principle.	You'll use permutations to count possibilities.	So you can count possible TV lineups, as in Ex. 26.

Vocabulary
permutation, p. 615
n factorial, p. 615

A **permutation** is an arrangement of objects in which order is important. For example, the six permutations of the letters A, B, and C are shown.

ABC ACB BAC BCA CAB CBA

You can use the counting principle to count permutations. Each time you choose a letter to make a permutation of the letters A, B, and C, the number of remaining letters that can be chosen decreases by 1.

Number of permutations = Choices for first letter • Choices for second letter • Choices for third letter

$= 3 \cdot 2 \cdot 1$

$= 6$

The expression $3 \cdot 2 \cdot 1$ can be written as 3!, which is read as "3 *factorial*." For any positive integer n, the product of the integers from 1 to n is called ***n* factorial** and is written $n!$.

$n! = n \cdot (n-1) \cdot (n-2) \cdot \ldots \cdot 1$

The value of 0! is defined to be 1.

Note Worthy
You can make a word triangle, like the one on page 580, to take notes about factorials.

Example 1 *Counting Permutations*

Posters You have four posters to hang in your room. You want to put one poster on each wall. How many ways can you arrange the posters?

Solution

You have 4 choices for the first wall, 3 for the second wall, 2 for the third wall, and 1 for the fourth wall. So, the number of ways you can arrange the posters is 4!.

$4! = 4 \cdot 3 \cdot 2 \cdot 1 = 24$

Answer There are 24 ways you can arrange the posters.

Checkpoint

Evaluate the factorial.

1. 2! 2 **2.** 5! 120 **3.** 6! 720 **4.** 7! 5040

NCTM CURRICULUM STANDARDS
Standard 2: Understand patterns; Represent situations using algebraic symbols
Standard 6: Solve problems in math and other contexts

1 PLAN

Skill Check

1. $8 \cdot 7 = \underline{?}$ 56
2. $7 \cdot 6 \cdot 5 = \underline{?}$ 210
3. $6 \cdot 5 \cdot 4 \cdot 3 = \underline{?}$ 360
4. $10 \cdot 9 \cdot 8 \cdot 7 = \underline{?}$ 5040
5. $5 \cdot 4 \cdot 3 \cdot 2 \cdot 1 = \underline{?}$ 120

Lesson Objective
Use permutations to count possibilities.

Pacing
Suggested Number of Days
Basic Course: 1 day
Average Course: 1 day
Advanced Course: 1 day
Block: 0.5 block with 11.7

Teaching Resources
For a complete list of Teaching Resources, see page 578B.

Transparency
Warm-Up Exercises for this lesson are available on a transparency.

2 TEACH

Motivating the Lesson
Have pairs of students count ways to arrange 2 items, 3 items, and 4 items. One student can arrange the items while their partner records the arrangements. Students should use 4 items that are different, such as a ruler, eraser, pen, and pencil.

TIPS *for* NEW TEACHERS

Expect some students to question the use of an exclamation mark as a math symbol. Stress that in mathematics this is the factorial symbol. See Tips for New Teachers in the *Chapter 11 Resource Book*.

Extra Examples

Example 1 You have six different fountain pens and six bottles of ink of different colors. How many ways can you fill the six pens each with a different color of ink? **720 ways**

Example 2 At a high school, each grade chooses a class president and vice president in a general election where each student casts votes for their two favorite candidates in their grade. The person with the most votes becomes the class president and the person who receives the second highest vote total is named vice president. How many ways are there to choose a class president and a class vice president if there are 20 candidates? **380 ways**

COMMON ERROR

In Example 1, watch for students who think the answer is 4 • 4 • 4 • 4. Students may want to make a poster showing the 24 possible arrangements of 4 items to convince themselves that 4! is the correct number of arrangements.

Suppose in Example 1 you had 7 posters and wanted to choose 1 poster for each wall. As in Example 1, you can use the counting principle to count the number of possible arrangements of the posters.

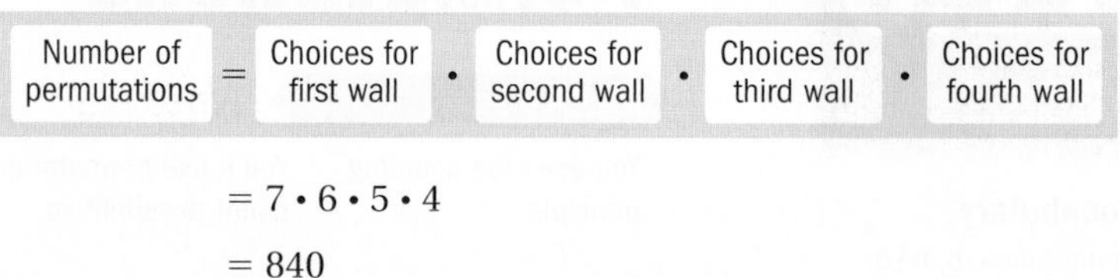

Number of permutations = Choices for first wall • Choices for second wall • Choices for third wall • Choices for fourth wall

$= 7 \cdot 6 \cdot 5 \cdot 4$

$= 840$

This situation is an example of finding the number of permutations of 7 objects taken 4 at a time. Notice that $7 \cdot 6 \cdot 5 \cdot 4$ can be written as $\frac{7 \cdot 6 \cdot 5 \cdot 4 \cdot 3 \cdot 2 \cdot 1}{3 \cdot 2 \cdot 1} = \frac{7!}{3!}$. This example suggests the following rule.

Reading *Algebra*

${}_nP_r$ is read "permutations of n choose r."

Permutations

Algebra The number of permutations of n objects taken r at a time can be written as ${}_nP_r$, where ${}_nP_r = \frac{n!}{(n-r)!}$.

Numbers ${}_5P_3 = \frac{5!}{(5-3)!} = \frac{5!}{2!} = \frac{5 \cdot 4 \cdot 3 \cdot \cancel{2}^1 \cdot 1}{\cancel{2}_1 \cdot 1} = 60$

Example 2 ***Counting Permutations***

Science Fair Judges at a science fair are awarding prizes to the first-, second-, and third-place finishers. The science fair has 10 contestants. How many different ways can the first-, second-, and third-place prizes be awarded?

Solution

To find the number of ways that prizes can be awarded, find ${}_{10}P_3$.

$${}_{10}P_3 = \frac{10!}{(10-3)!}$$ **Use permutations formula.**

$$= \frac{10!}{7!}$$ **Subtract.**

$$= \frac{10 \cdot 9 \cdot 8 \cdot \cancel{7} \cdot \cancel{6} \cdot \cancel{5} \cdot \cancel{4} \cdot \cancel{3} \cdot \cancel{2} \cdot 1}{\cancel{7} \cdot \cancel{6} \cdot \cancel{5} \cdot \cancel{4} \cdot \cancel{3} \cdot \cancel{2} \cdot 1}$$ **Expand factorials. Divide out common factors.**

$$= 10 \cdot 9 \cdot 8 = 720$$ **Multiply.**

Answer There are 720 ways the prizes can be awarded.

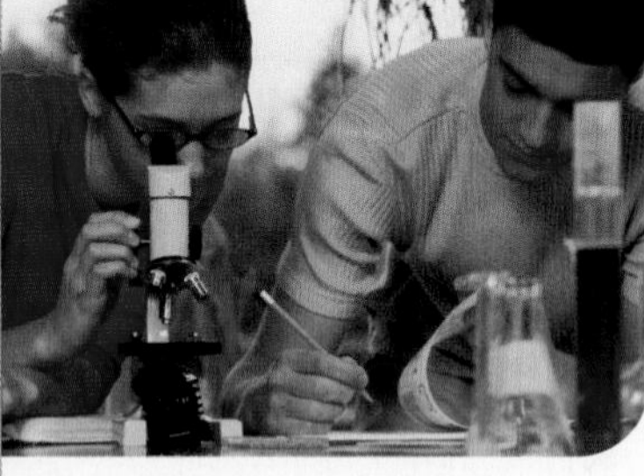

Checkpoint

Find the number of permutations.

5. ${}_6P_2$ **30** **6.** ${}_8P_3$ **336** **7.** ${}_5P_5$ **120** **8.** ${}_{70}P_2$ **4830**

Tech *Help*

To evaluate a factorial or use permutation notation with your calculator, press PRB and choose from the list of commands.

Using a Calculator You may want to use a calculator to find factorials and permutations that involve multiplying large numbers. Many calculators have commands that allow you to evaluate factorials and use the permutation notation $_nP_r$. The solutions to Examples 1 and 2 are shown.

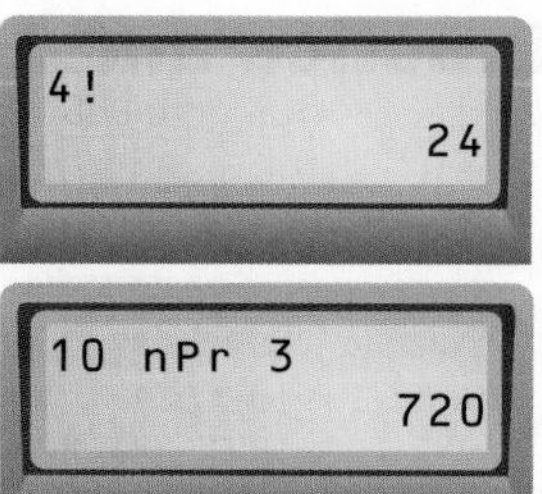

Example 3 ***Finding a Probability Using Permutations***

Garage Door Your garage has a keypad that can be used to open the garage door. The code has five digits. You remember that the five digits are 1, 3, 5, 7, and 9, but you cannot remember the sequence. What is the probability that you open the garage on the first try?

Solution

Each possible code is a permutation of the digits 1, 3, 5, 7, and 9. The number of permutations of the five digits is 5!.

$5! = 5 \cdot 4 \cdot 3 \cdot 2 \cdot 1 = 120$

Only one of the possible permutations is correct, so the probability of opening the garage door on the first try is $\frac{1}{120}$.

11.6 Exercises

More Practice, p. 813

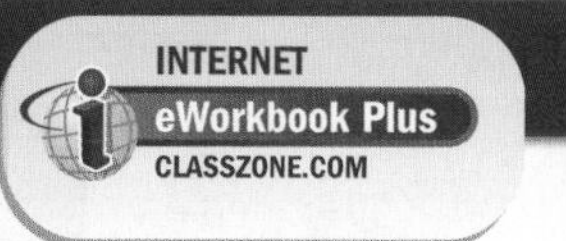

Guided Practice

Vocabulary Check

1. Write and evaluate an expression for 6 factorial. $6! = 720$
2. List all the permutations of the letters A, B, C, and D. **See margin.**

Skill Check **Find the number of permutations.**

3. $_5P_3$ 60
4. $_4P_1$ 4
5. $_2P_2$ 2
6. $_6P_0$ 1
7. **Books** You have 6 books, but there is enough space on your bookshelf for only 4 of them. How many different arrangements of the books are possible on your bookshelf? **360 arrangements**
8. **Lock** The combination for a lock consists of the numbers 4, 22, and 8. You don't remember the order in which the three numbers are to be entered. Find the probability that you open the lock on the first try. $\frac{1}{6}$
9. **Error Analysis** Describe and correct the error in finding the number of permutations of 4 objects taken 3 at a time.

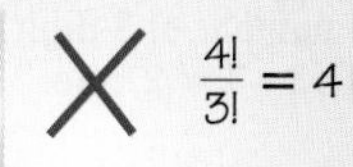

2. ABCD, ABDC, ACBD, ACDB, ADBC, ADCB, BACD, BADC, BCAD, BCDA, BDAC, BDCA, CABD, CADB, CBAD, CBDA, CDAB, CDBA, DABC, DACB, DBAC, DBCA, DCAB, DCBA

9. *Sample answer:* In this situation, $n = 4$ and $r = 3$. The formula is $_nP_r = \frac{n!}{(n-r)!}$, but the quantity shown is $\frac{n!}{r!}$. The correct solution is $\frac{4!}{(4-3)!} = 4! = 24$.

Teaching Tip

Help students confirm the result in Example 2 by pointing out that there are 10 persons who can be chosen as the first-place prizewinner, leaving 9 persons who can be awarded the second-place prize, and then just 8 persons who can win the third-place prize. Stress that this result is shown in the last computation line of the example.

Extra Examples

Example 3 Don buys four science fiction books and puts them on his bookshelf side-by-side in random order. What is the probability that they are in alphabetical order by title from left to right? $\frac{1}{24}$

Concept Check

What formula would you use to find the number of ways a chairperson and an assistant chairperson can be chosen from 5 nominees? How many ways are there?
$_5P_2 = \frac{5!}{(5-2)!}$; **20 ways**

Daily Puzzler

For any value of n, what is the value of $_nP_0$? **1**

3 APPLY

ASSIGNMENT GUIDE

Basic Course

Day 1: SRH p. 798 Exs. 1-3; pp. 618-619 Exs. 10-21, 26-30, 33-36, 38, 44-50

Average Course

Day 1: pp. 618-619 Exs. 12-17, 20-25, 28-34, 37-42, 44-50

Advanced Course

Day 1: pp. 618-619 Exs. 14-17, 22-25, 29-32, 35-44*, 47-50

Block

pp. 618-619 Exs. 12-17, 20-25, 28-34, 37-42, 44-50 (with 11.7)

EXTRA PRACTICE

- Student Edition, p. 813
- Chapter 11 Resource Book, pp. 52-54
- Test and Practice Generator

TRANSPARENCY

Even-numbered answers are available on transparencies.

HOMEWORK CHECK

When you review students' homework for this lesson, go over the following exercises to check understanding of key concepts.
Basic: 10, 15, 18, 28, 29
Average: 14, 22, 28, 29, 30
Advanced: 15, 24, 31, 38, 40

TEACHING TIP

After completing Exercises 18-25, ask students to suggest a real-world situation that could be modeled by one of the expressions. For example, the expression in Exercise 19 would model the number of ways to choose one of the starting players from a baseball team to deliver the lineup card to the umpire.

Practice and Problem Solving

Homework *Help*

Example	Exercises
1	10-17, 30
2	18-27, 29, 40
3	28, 31, 38

Online Resources
CLASSZONE.COM
- More Examples
- eTutorial Plus

Evaluate the factorial.

A **10.** 3! 6 **11.** 0! 1 **12.** 1! 1 **13.** 10! 3,628,800

14. 8! 40,320 **15.** 11! 39,916,800 **16.** 9! 362,880 **17.** 12! 479,001,600

Find the number of permutations.

18. ${}_5P_4$ 120 **19.** ${}_9P_1$ 9 **20.** ${}_7P_2$ 42 **21.** ${}_8P_5$ 6720

22. ${}_6P_6$ 720 **23.** ${}_{11}P_0$ 1 **24.** ${}_{25}P_2$ 600 **25.** ${}_{18}P_6$ 13,366,080

26. TV Lineups A TV network has 15 comedy shows that it plans to air. It wants to choose 4 of them for a special Monday night lineup. How many different possible lineups are there for Monday night? 32,760 lineups

27. Shirts You have 8 shirts and plan to wear a different one each day from Monday through Friday. How many possible arrangements of shirts are possible for those 5 days? 6720 arrangements

28. Password Sonia created a password for her computer by rearranging the letters of her name. You know how she created the password, but you do not know what the password is. What is the probability that you will guess the password on the first try? $\frac{1}{120}$

29. Restaurant A restaurant has 12 identical tables. One evening, the restaurant accepts reservations for 6 of the tables. How many choices does the restaurant have for seating the 6 groups? 665,280 choices

30. Hawaii You are visiting Hawaii and plan to stay for 3 days. You want to go to the beach, see Mauna Loa, and shop in Honolulu. How many ways can you arrange your schedule for the 3 days so that you do 1 activity each day? 6 ways

31. Waiter A waiter takes lunch orders for 5 people, but quickly forgets which person ordered which meal. If the waiter randomly chooses a person to give each meal to, what is the probability that the waiter will serve the correct meal to each person? $\frac{1}{120}$

32. *Writing* You have 5 objects. Are there more ways to arrange 4 of the objects or more ways to arrange 5 of the objects? Explain. See margin.

32. Neither, the number of ways is the same. *Sample answer:* Once I have chosen 4 of the 5 objects, there is no choice left for the last object—its place is already decided.

Write the expression using factorials.

B **33.** $30 \cdot 29$ $\frac{30!}{28!}$ **34.** $20 \cdot 19 \cdot 18 \cdot 17$ $\frac{20!}{16!}$

35. $12 \cdot 11 \cdot 10 \cdot 9 \cdot 8 \cdot 7 \cdot 6$ $\frac{12!}{5!}$ **36.** 60 $\frac{60!}{59!}$

37. Critical Thinking For each of the following situations, tell how you found your answer. Then tell whether the situation involves permutations.

a. How many 3-digit numbers can you make using each of the digits 1, 2, and 3 exactly once?

b. How many 3-digit numbers can you make using only the digits 1, 2, or 3 if you are able to use each digit more than once?

37a. *Sample answer:* This is the number of permutations of 3 digits taken 3 at a time: ${}_3P_3 = 6$; yes.

37b. *Sample answer:* For each of the 3 places, you have the same number of choices, 3. The number of 3-digit numbers is $3 \cdot 3 \cdot 3 = 27$; no.

40. 5, 20, 60, 120, 120. *Sample answer:* The second term is 4 times the first, the third is 3 times the second, the fourth is 2 times the third, and the fifth is 1 times the fourth. This is because with each successive choice for an arrangement from 5 objects, the number of objects you have to choose from decreases by 1.

41. n times. *Sample answer:* $n! = n \cdot (n-1) \cdot (n-2) \cdot \ldots \cdot 1 = n \cdot [(n-1) \cdot (n-2) \cdot \ldots \cdot 1] = n \cdot (n-1)!$

42. *Sample answer:* When $n = r$, $\frac{n!}{(n-r)!} = \frac{n!}{(n-n)!} = \frac{n!}{0!} = \frac{n!}{1} = n!$

43b. Less than. *Sample answer:* In each arrangement you cannot tell which of the two L's is which, so there are only half as many arrangements as if there were 4 different letters.

48. Ages at the Reunion

0	2 3 5 5 8 9
1	3 5 7 8
2	1 5 8
3	7 9
	4 6 9
?	
	8

)| 2 = 2 years

38. Anagrams An anagram is a rearrangement of the letters in a word to form another word. For example, an anagram of STOP is POST.

a. How many arrangements of the letters R, A, and T are there? **6 arrangements**

b. What is the probability that a random arrangement of the letters in the word RAT will be an anagram of RAT? $\frac{1}{3}$

39. Seating At a party, 2 men and 2 women are to be seated on one side of a table so that no man is sitting next to another man and no woman is sitting next to another woman.

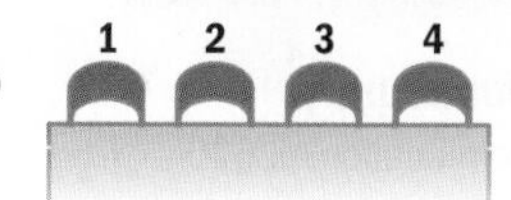

a. How many possible seating arrangements are there if a man sits in the first seat? **4 arrangements**

b. How many possible seating arrangements are there if a woman sits in the first seat? **4 arrangements**

c. How many possible seating arrangements are there altogether? **8 arrangements**

40. *Writing* Find ${}_5P_1$, ${}_5P_2$, ${}_5P_3$, ${}_5P_4$, and ${}_5P_5$. What pattern do you notice? Explain why this pattern occurs.

C **41. Critical Thinking** How many times greater is $n!$ than $(n-1)!$? Explain.

42. Critical Thinking Explain why ${}_nP_r = n!$ when $n = r$.

43. Challenge The letters of the word BALL are written on cards and placed in a hat. The two cards with L on them are identical.

a. Three cards are randomly drawn from the hat, one at a time. Write all the different permutations of 3 letters that could result. **ABL, ALB, ALL, BAL, BLA, BLL, LAB, LAL, LBA, LBL, LLA, LLB**

b. Is your answer to part (a) greater than or less than ${}_4P_3$? Explain.

Mixed Review

44. You roll two number cubes. Find the probability that you roll two even numbers. *(Lesson 6.8)* $\frac{1}{4}$

Find the unknown length. Write your answer in simplest form. *(Lesson 9.3)*

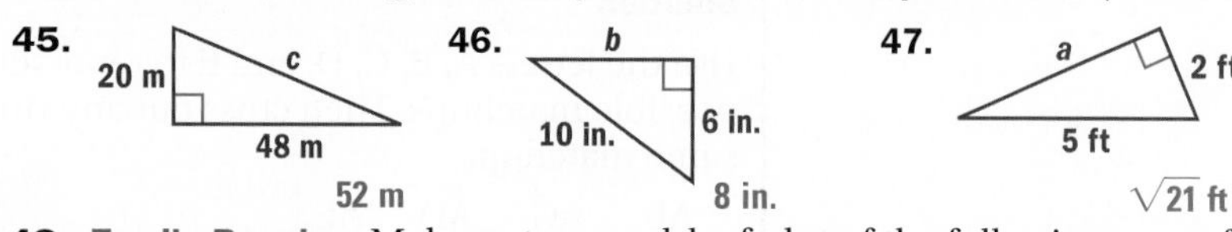

48. Family Reunion Make a stem-and-leaf plot of the following ages of people at a family reunion: 46, 66, 3, 5, 18, 49, 28, 2, 21, 44, 9, 13, 17, 8, 52, 25, 39, 68, 73, 37, 5, 15. *(Lesson 11.1)*

[St]andardized Test Practice

49. Multiple Choice You have 12 CDs and choose 4 of them to play one afternoon. Which expression gives the number of possible orders for playing the 4 CDs? **C**

A. $\frac{4!}{12!}$ B. $\frac{8!}{12!}$ C. $\frac{12!}{8!}$ D. $\frac{12!}{4!}$

50. Multiple Choice Eight horses are running in a race. In how many ways can the horses finish in first, second, and third place? **G**

F. 6 G. 336 H. 6720 I. 40,320

4 ASSESS

Assessment Resources

For more assessment resources, see:
- Assessment Book
- Test and Practice Generator

Mini-Quiz

1. Evaluate 5!. **120**
2. Find the value of ${}_{11}P_3$. **990**
3. Kelly has 18 scarves and plans to wear one on Monday and a different one on Tuesday. How many different arrangements of scarves are possible for those 2 days? **306 arrangements**
4. Write the expression 15 • 14 • 13 • 12 using factorials. $\frac{15!}{11!}$
5. **Challenge** How many different permutations of the letters in ELF are possible? of the letters in EEL? of the letters in EEE? **6 permutations; 3 permutations; 1 permutation**

5 FOLLOW-UP

Diagnosis/Remediation

- Study Guide in Chapter 11 Resource Book, pp. 55–56
- eTutorial Plus Online
- Extra Practice, p. 813
- Lesson Practice in Chapter 11 Resource Book, pp. 52–54

English Learner Support

- Spanish Study Guide
- Multi-Language Visual Glossary
- Chapter Audio Summaries CDs

Challenge

- Challenge Practice in Chapter 11 Resource Book, p. 57
- Teacher's Edition, p. 578F

1 PLAN

Skill Check

1. $\frac{9 \cdot 8 \cdot 7 \cdot 6}{4 \cdot 3 \cdot 2} = \underline{?}$ 126
2. $\frac{14 \cdot 13 \cdot 12}{3 \cdot 2} = \underline{?}$ 364

LESSON OBJECTIVE

Use combinations to count possibilities.

PACING

Suggested Number of Days
Basic Course: 1 day
Average Course: 1 day
Advanced Course: 1 day
Block: 0.5 block with 11.6

TEACHING RESOURCES

For a complete list of Teaching Resources, see page 578B.

TRANSPARENCY

Warm-Up Exercises for this lesson are available on a transparency.

2 TEACH

MOTIVATING THE LESSON

Have five students arrange themselves into as many different pairs as possible, while the other students record all the arrangements. Stress that the order of the persons in each pair is not important.

TIPS *for* NEW TEACHERS

All students will benefit from a large number of examples of permutations and combinations in order to learn how to differentiate between them. See Tips for New Teachers in the *Chapter 11 Resource Book*.

LESSON **11.7**

Combinations

Vocabulary
combination, p. 620

BEFORE	*Now*	WHY?
You used permutations to count possibilities.	You'll use combinations to count possibilities.	So you can count possible yearbook designs, as in Ex. 9.

Basketball A basketball league has 5 teams. Two of the teams are chosen to play one another. How many different possible matchups are there?

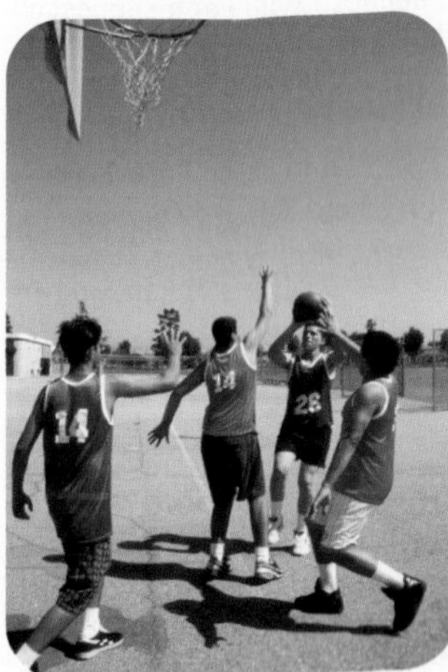

In Lesson 11.6, you learned that a permutation is an arrangement in which order is important. A **combination** is a selection of objects where the order in which the objects are chosen is not important. In the problem above, suppose team A and team B are the two teams selected to play one another. It does not matter if team A is chosen first or if team B is chosen first. The same game will be played.

Example 1 *Listing Combinations*

List and count the different possible matchups of the basketball teams described above.

Solution

Use the letters A, B, C, D, and E to represent the five teams. List all possible matchups. Then cross out any duplicates that represent the same matchup.

AB	AC	AD	AE
~~BA~~	BC	BD	BE
~~CA~~	~~CB~~	CD	CE
~~DA~~	~~DB~~	~~DC~~	DE
~~EA~~	~~EB~~	~~EC~~	~~ED~~

DE and ED are duplicates, because they represent the same matchup.

Answer There are 10 different matchups.

Checkpoint

1. You want to buy 4 different CDs. You can afford to buy on[...] them. How many combinations of CDs can you buy? 4 c[...]

NCTM CURRICULUM STANDARDS
Standard 2: Understand patterns; Repres[...]uations using algebraic symbols
Standard 6: Solve problems in math an[...]ther contexts

Study *Strategy*

For every combination of 2 teams, there are 2!, or 2, permutations of the chosen teams. So, ${}_5P_2 = 2! \cdot {}_5C_2$, or ${}_5C_2 = \frac{{}_5P_2}{2!}$.

Relating Combinations and Permutations Before matchups are crossed out, the list in Example 1 shows the permutations of 5 teams chosen 2 at a time, or ${}_5P_2$. After the duplicate matchups are crossed out, the list shows the number of combinations of 5 teams chosen 2 at a time. This is written as ${}_5C_2$. Notice that in this situation ${}_5C_2 = \frac{{}_5P_2}{2!}$, which suggests the following result.

Combinations

Words To find the number of combinations of n objects taken r at a time, divide the number of permutations of n objects taken r at a time by $r!$.

Numbers ${}_9C_5 = \frac{{}_9P_5}{5!}$ **Algebra** ${}_nC_r = \frac{{}_nP_r}{r!}$

Example 2 *Counting Combinations*

Book Reports You need to write 4 book reports for your English class. Your teacher gives the class a list of 7 books from which to choose. How many different groups of 4 books can you choose from the list?

Solution

The order in which you choose the books is not important. So, to find the number of different ways to choose 4 books from 7, find ${}_7C_4$.

${}_7C_4 = \frac{{}_7P_4}{4!}$	**Use combinations formula.**
$= \frac{7 \cdot 6 \cdot 5 \cdot 4}{4 \cdot 3 \cdot 2 \cdot 1}$	**Write ${}_7P_4$ and 4! as products.**
$= \frac{7 \cdot \cancel{6}^{1} \cdot 5 \cdot \cancel{4}^{1}}{\cancel{4}_1 \cdot \cancel{3}_1 \cdot \cancel{2}_1 \cdot 1}$	**Divide out common factors.**
$= 35$	**Simplify.**

Answer There are 35 different combinations of books.

Find the number of combinations.

2. ${}_6C_3$ **20** **3.** ${}_8C_5$ **56** **4.** ${}_{10}C_2$ **45** **5.** ${}_4C_4$ **1**

Using a Calculator Many calculators can evaluate combinations. The solution for Example 2 is shown. You may find it helpful to use a calculator when evaluating combinations that involve large numbers.

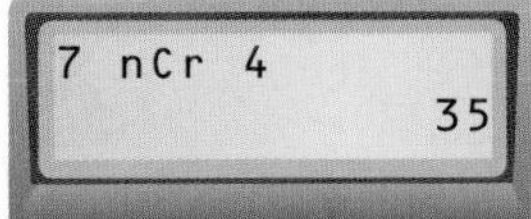

Extra Examples

Example 1 You and 6 friends are going to lunch. You can only take two people with you in your car. How many different combinations of friends could ride with you? **15 combinations**

Example 2 A credit card company offers its users 3 free magazine subscriptions from a selection of 30 magazines. How many different combinations of 3 magazines can you choose? **4060 combinations**

Teaching Tip

In Example 1, draw students' attention to the way the matchups are organized. Stress that students should avoid recording combinations at random as they think of them and that they should find an organized way to record the combinations instead. This will assure them that they have included every possibility.

Common Error

In Example 2, students may assume the question is asking how many ways to arrange the 4 books. Help students understand that the problem involves choosing 4 books from 7 books and also that the order in which the books are read does not matter.

Multiple Representations

In Example 1, students represent the team combinations using letters. Immediately afterward, they learn the formula for ${}_5C_2$. After students are formally introduced to the combinations formula, revisit these different representations and make sure students understand that they are both representations of the same situation.

Extra Examples

Example 3 Tell whether the possibilities can be counted using *permutations* or *combinations*.

a. There are 50 sculptures being exhibited at an art show. A Best-in-Show prize and a runner-up prize are awarded to the top two sculptors. How many different pairs of sculptors can receive the prizes? **permutations**

b. There are 50 students in the Speech Club. Three of these students will be chosen to represent the school at a regional competition. How many different groups of three students can be chosen? **combinations**

Example 4 Kaitlin, Jessica, and six other girls put their names into a hat. Two names are drawn at random. Find the probability that Kaitlin's name and Jessica's name are the two names drawn. $\frac{1}{28}$

CONCEPT CHECK

How do you decide whether the possibilities in a problem should be counted using a permutation or a combination? **Determine whether or not the order of the choices is important. If order is important, use a permutation. If not, use a combination.**

DAILY PUZZLER

Ashley, Collin, Penny, and Anton are different heights. Collin is taller than Anton, Penny is shorter than Ashley, and Anton's height is between those of Ashley and Penny. List the friends in order from tallest to shortest. **Collin, Ashley, Anton, Penny**

You can determine whether a problem requires permutations or combinations by deciding if order is important.

Example 3 *Choosing Between Permutations and Combinations*

Tell whether the possibilities can be counted using *permutations* or *combinations*.

a. There are 30 dogs in a dog show. Blue ribbons are awarded to the top 3 dogs. How many different groups of dogs can receive blue ribbons?

b. There are 30 runners in a cross country race. How many different groups of runners can finish first, second, and third?

Solution

a. The order in which the 3 blue ribbons are awarded does not matter. So, the possibilities can be counted using combinations.

b. Because the runners can finish first, second, or third, order is important. So, the possibilities can be counted using permutations.

Example 4 *Finding a Probability Using Combinations*

Marbles You have 10 marbles in a bag. Each marble is a different color, including red, blue, and green. You draw 3 marbles at random. Find the probability that you draw a red, a blue, and a green marble.

Solution

The order in which the marbles are drawn is not important. Find ${}_{10}C_3$.

$${}_{10}C_3 = \frac{{}_{10}P_3}{3!}$$ **Use combinations formula.**

$$= \frac{10 \cdot 9 \cdot 8}{3 \cdot 2 \cdot 1}$$ **Write ${}_{10}P_3$ and 3! as products.**

$$= \frac{10 \cdot \overset{3}{\cancel{9}} \cdot \overset{4}{\cancel{8}}}{\underset{1}{\cancel{3}} \cdot \underset{1}{\cancel{2}} \cdot 1}$$ **Divide out common factors.**

$$= 120$$ **Simplify.**

Answer There are 120 different combinations of 3 marbles you can draw. Only one of the combinations includes a red, a blue, and a green marble. So, the probability is $\frac{1}{120}$.

Checkpoint

6. You are choosing 10 of 30 friends to invite to a party. Can you count the possibilities using *permutations* or *combinations*? **combinations**
7. You have 12 marbles in a bag. Each marble is a different color, including red and blue. You draw 2 marbles at random. What is the probability that you draw a red marble and a blue marble? $\frac{1}{66}$

11.7 Exercises

More Practice, p. 813

Guided Practice

Vocabulary Check

1. Copy and complete: You can write the number of combinations of 12 objects taken 3 at a time as _?_. $_{12}C_3$

2. Explain when to use a permutation and when to use a combination when choosing r objects from n objects.

2. *Sample answer:* Use a permutation when the order of the r objects is important, and a combination when the order is not important.

Skill Check

Find the number of combinations.

3. $_2C_1$ 2 **4.** $_5C_4$ 5 **5.** $_3C_3$ 1 **6.** $_6C_4$ 15

7. Track and Field A gym coach selects a team of 4 athletes from 14 athletes to represent the school at a track and field meet. Tell whether the number of teams the coach can select can be counted using permutations or combinations. Then find the number of teams. combinations; 1001 teams

Guided Problem Solving

8. Concert A radio station takes the names of the first 20 listeners who call in after hearing a certain song. The station will randomly select 3 of the callers to win tickets to a concert. If 3 friends are among the first 20 callers, what is the probability that the 3 friends will win tickets?

1) How many possible combinations of 3 callers can be selected to win tickets? 1140 combinations

2) How many possible combinations of 3 ticket winners include all 3 of the friends? 1 combination

3) Find the probability that the 3 friends win tickets. $\frac{1}{1140}$

9. 4 sets; winter, spring, and summer; winter, spring, and fall; winter, summer, and fall; spring, summer, and fall

10. 10 schedules; MTuW, MTuTh, MTuF, MWTh, MWF, MThF, TuWTh, TuWF, TuThF, WThF

Practice and Problem Solving

Homework *Help*

Example	Exercises
1	9, 10
2	11-22
3	23-26, 28
4	27, 31

Online Resources
CLASSZONE.COM
- More Examples
- eTutorial Plus

A **9. Yearbook** The school yearbook photographer took one photo of the school during each of the 4 seasons and wants to choose 3 of the photos for the cover. How many sets of 3 photos are there? Make a list of all the possible combinations. See margin.

10. Club Meetings A club is scheduling a week of meetings to plan for its annual fundraiser. The club wants to meet on 3 of the evenings next week, from Monday through Friday. How many different schedules can the club choose? Make a list of all the possible combinations. See margin.

Find the number of combinations.

11. $_3C_2$ 3 **12.** $_4C_1$ 4 **13.** $_7C_3$ 35 **14.** $_6C_5$ 6

15. $_4C_3$ 4 **16.** $_9C_8$ 9 **17.** $_8C_3$ 56 **18.** $_{11}C_7$ 330

19. $_{12}C_3$ 220 **20.** $_{15}C_6$ 5005 **21.** $_7C_7$ 1 **22.** $_{10}C_0$ 1

3 APPLY

ASSIGNMENT GUIDE

Basic Course
Day 1: pp. 623-625 Exs. 9-18, 23-28, 32, 36-41

Average Course
Day 1: pp. 623-625 Exs. 9, 10, 17-34, 36-41

Advanced Course
Day 1: pp. 623-625 Exs. 9-14, 23-25, 28-37*, 39-41

Block
pp. 623-625 Exs. 9, 10, 17-34, 36-41 (with 11.6)

EXTRA PRACTICE

- Student Edition, p. 813
- Chapter 11 Resource Book, pp. 62-64
- Test and Practice Generator

TRANSPARENCY

Even-numbered answers are available on transparencies. A support transparency is available for Exercises 37 and 38.

HOMEWORK CHECK

When you review students' homework for this lesson, go over the following exercises to check understanding of key concepts.
Basic: 9, 11, 18, 23, 27
Average: 9, 19, 22, 26, 27
Advanced: 10, 13, 23, 28, 31

TEACHING TIP

In Exercise 9, you might suggest that another way to think of the situation is in terms of what is *not* chosen. There are 4 ways to ignore 1 photograph from a group of 4 photographs.

COMMON ERROR

In Exercise 33, watch for students who find $_5C_3$ and think they are through with the exercise. Make sure they understand that several of the 10 possible arrangements will not fit the conditions of the problem.

33. 9 ways. ***Sample answer:*** **If 8 is the only number greater than 6 that is chosen, then there are $_3C_2 = 3$ ways. If 9 is the only number greater than 6 that is chosen, then there are $_3C_2 = 3$ ways. If 8 and 9 are both chosen, then there are $_3C_1 = 3$ ways. There are $3 + 3 + 3 = 9$ ways total.**

37.–38.

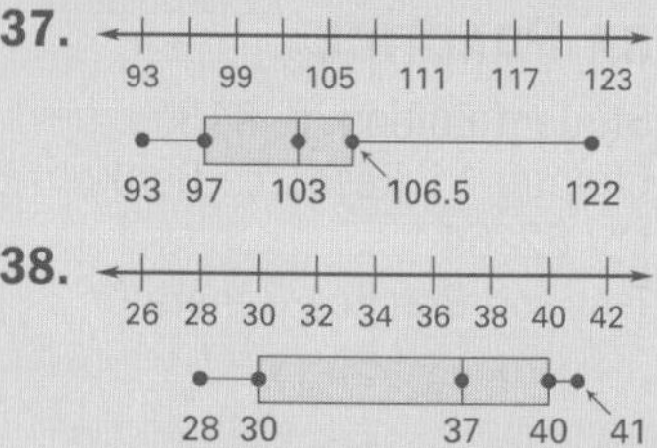

29. ***Sample answer:*** **If you choose 4 objects from a group of 5, then for each group of 4 objects chosen, there is 1 object not chosen. Likewise, each time you choose 1 object from 5, there is a group of 4 objects not chosen. Because each group has exactly 1 matching group, there are the same number in each group. Another example is $_7C_3 = {_7C_4} = 35$.**

30. $_4P_2$. ***Sample answer:*** **For each combination of 2 objects from a group of 4, there are 2 different orders, or permutations.**

31b. No. ***Sample answer:*** **It multiplies it by 6. If you have 4 of the tickets, then you have $_4C_2 = 6$ of the combinations of two tickets in your hand, so the probability that you are holding both winning tickets is $\frac{6}{1225}$.**

In Exercises 23–25, tell whether the possibilities can be counted using *permutations* or *combinations*. Then answer the question.

23. A survey asks people to rank basketball, baseball, tennis, soccer, and football according to how much they enjoy watching each sport. How many possible responses are there? **permutations; 120 responses**

24. A history test lists the names of 5 presidents, and each student is to choose two of them to compare in an essay. How many different pairings are possible? **combinations; 10 pairings**

25. A subway car has 8 empty seats. At one stop, 5 people enter the car and no one gets off. How many ways can the 5 people arrange themselves in the 8 empty seats if each person takes one seat? **permutations; 6720 ways**

26. Talent Show At an upcoming talent show, you plan to play 3 songs on the piano. There are 6 songs you know well enough to perform.

a. How many different groups of 3 songs can you choose to play? **20 groups**

b. Once you have chosen 3 songs, in how many ways can you play them at the talent show? **6 ways**

27. Chocolates A box of chocolates contains 10 pieces of chocolate, and 4 of the pieces have cream in the center. Suppose you randomly select 4 pieces of chocolate. Find the probability that you select all 4 of the pieces that have cream in the center. $\frac{1}{210}$

28. Tiles A designer is making a sample design that will use 3 different kinds of tiles. The designer has 9 different kinds of tiles from which to choose.

a. How many possible combinations of tiles can the designer choose? **84 combinations**

b. The designer will create a sample design by placing 3 tiles side by side. How many different sample designs can the designer make from the 3 chosen tiles? **6 designs**

29. *Writing* Explain why $_5C_4 = {_5C_1}$. Find another example of two different combinations that are equal. **See margin.**

30. Critical Thinking Which is greater, $_4C_2$ or $_4P_2$? Explain why.

B 31. Raffle In a raffle, 2 of 50 tickets are randomly selected to be the winning tickets.

a. You have 2 raffle tickets. Find the probability that you are holding both winning tickets. $\frac{1}{1225}$

b. Does buying twice as many tickets double the probability that you are holding both winning tickets? Explain.

32. Pizza You and your friends are choosing toppings for a pizza. There are 4 meat toppings and 6 vegetable toppings from which to choose.

a. How many pizzas having 1 meat topping and 2 different vegetable toppings can you choose? **60 pizzas**

b. How many pizzas having 2 different meat toppings and 1 vegetable topping can you choose? **36 pizzas**

c. How many pizzas having 3 different toppings can you choose? **120 pizzas**

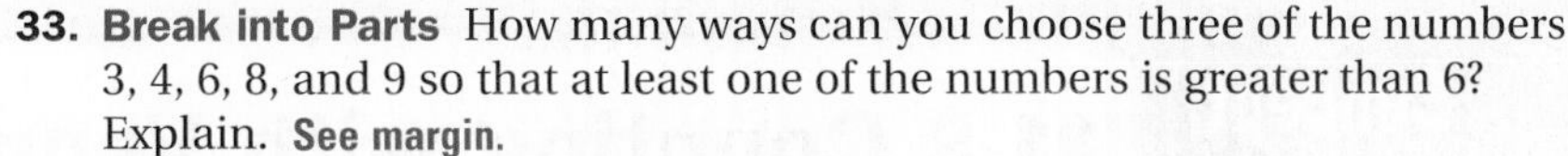

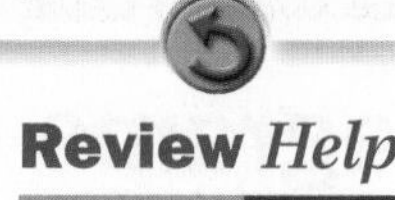

Review *Help*

To review the strategy *break into parts*, see p. 802.

33. **Break into Parts** How many ways can you choose three of the numbers 3, 4, 6, 8, and 9 so that at least one of the numbers is greater than 6? Explain. **See margin.**

C 34. **Critical Thinking** You have 100 different coins. Are there more combinations of 99 of the coins than there are of 100 coins? Explain. **See margin.**

35. **Challenge** The numbers 1 through 5 are written on separate slips of paper and placed in a hat, and 3 of the slips are drawn randomly. What is the probability that one of the slips that are drawn shows a 4? $\frac{3}{5}$

34. Yes. *Sample answer:* There is only 1 combination of all 100 of the coins—the whole set of coins—but 100 combinations of 99 of the coins, since you can exclude 1 of the 100 coins at a time to form combinations of 99 of the coins

Mixed Review

36. **Roads** There are 3 roads from town A to town B. There are 4 roads from town B to town C. How many different ways are there to get from town A to town B to town C? *(Lesson 6.8)* **12 ways**

In Exercises 37 and 38, make a box-and-whisker plot of the data. *(Lesson 11.2)* **37–38. See margin.**

37. Basketball game scores: 98, 104, 93, 96, 122, 106, 102, 107

38. Temperatures (in degrees Fahrenheit): 30, 35, 38, 28, 41, 30, 40, 37, 40, 36, 38

39. **Movies** You rent 6 movies. In how many different ways can you watch all 6 of the movies? *(Lesson 11.6)* **720 ways**

Standardized Test Practice

40. **Multiple Choice** What is the value of ${}_8C_4$? **B**

A. 56 **B.** 70 **C.** 1680 **D.** 40,296

41. **Multiple Choice** Two cars are available for 7 students to take to a high school football game. Car A holds 4 students, and car B holds 3 students. How many different groups of 3 students can be formed to ride in car B? **H**

F. 4 **G.** 24 **H.** 35 **I.** 210

Playoff Series

In many playoff series, the team that wins a majority of the games is the winner. In a best-of-five series, the first team to win 3 games is the winner of the series. One way to win a best-of-five series is to win the first 3 games. Another way is to lose the first 2 games, then win the next 3.

How many different ways are there to win a best-of-three series? a best-of-five series? a best-of-seven series? **3 ways; 10 ways; 35 ways**

4 ASSESS

Assessment Resources

For more assessment resources, see:

- Assessment Book
- Test and Practice Generator

Mini-Quiz

Find the number of combinations.

1. ${}_6C_4$ **15** **2.** ${}_8C_5$ **56**

3. Alex has two dogs to take to the veterinarian but he must take them separately on different days. Appointments are available on weekdays only. How many possible combinations of days are there for Alex to take the dogs to the vet? **10 combinations**

4. Challenge The letters A through D are written on separate slips of paper, placed in a hat, and two of the slips are drawn randomly. What is the probability that at least one of the slips drawn has B or C on it? $\frac{5}{6}$

5 FOLLOW-UP

Diagnosis/Remediation

- Study Guide in Chapter 11 Resource Book, pp. 65–66
- eTutorial Plus Online
- Extra Practice, p. 813
- Lesson Practice in Chapter 11 Resource Book, pp. 62–64

English Learner Support

- Spanish Study Guide
- Multi-Language Visual Glossary
- Chapter Audio Summaries CDs

Challenge

- Challenge Practice in Chapter 11 Resource Book, p. 68
- Teacher's Edition, p. 578F

1 PLAN

INVESTIGATE THE CONCEPT

- Students count outcomes using Venn diagrams.
- This activity leads into a discussion of overlapping and disjoint events in Lesson 11.8 so their probabilities can be calculated.

MATERIALS

Each student will need paper and pencil. See the Activity Support Master in the *Chapter 11 Resource Book*.

RECOMMENDED TIME

Work activity: 15 min
Discuss results: 5 min

GROUPING

Students should work individually.

2 TEACH

ALTERNATIVE STRATEGY

Instead of having students collect the data, collect it yourself during the previous class day and create a chart that lists each student, whether he or she plays an instrument, and whether he or she plays on a school sports team.

3 CLOSE

KEY DISCOVERY

Venn diagrams provide a better visual representation of overlapping data than a table of the same data does.

ASSESSMENT

1. In the Venn diagram, what data does the overlapping region represent? **Those data values that belong to both categories.**

Concept *Activity*

11.8 Counting with Venn Diagrams

Goal
Count outcomes using Venn diagrams.

Materials
- paper
- pencil

Investigate

Use a Venn diagram to count the number of students in your math class who participate in two activities.

Copy the Venn diagram shown. Ask the members of your math class if they play a musical instrument, play on a school sports team, do both, or do neither. Write their names in the appropriate part of the Venn diagram. **Steps 1–2. Check work.**

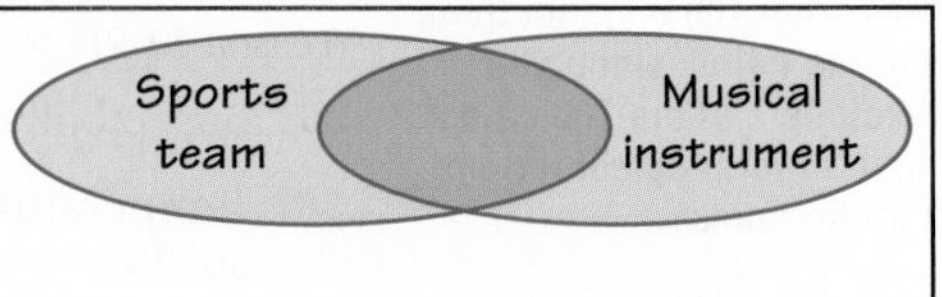

Copy and complete the frequency table. When determining the frequency for a category, be sure to include all the students in your math class who are in the category.

Description	Number of students
Play a musical instrument	?
Play on a school sports team	?
Play a musical instrument *and* play on a school sports team	?
Play a musical instrument *or* play on a school sports team	?
Do *not* play an instrument and do *not* play on a school sports team	?

Draw Conclusions

1. **Critical Thinking** Your friend uses the following verbal model to find the number of students in your class who play on a school sports team *or* play a musical instrument.

   Number of students who play on a school sports team + Number of students who play a musical instrument = Number of students who play on a school sports team *or* play a musical instrument

   Do you agree with your friend's reasoning? Explain why or why not. If not, correct the left side of the verbal model.

2. **Probability** A student from your class is chosen at random. Find the probability of each event. Explain how you found the probability. **2a–b. Check work.**

   a. Choosing a student who plays a musical instrument

   b. Choosing a student who plays a musical instrument *and* plays on a school sports team

1. No. *Sample answer:* The model counts students who play on a school sports team *and* who play an instrument twice. The new term "the number of students who play on a school sports team and who play an instrument" should be subtracted from the left side of the verbal model.

NCTM CURRICULUM STANDARDS
Standard 10: Create representations to communicate mathematical ideas; Use representations to communicate mathematical ideas

LESSON

11.8 Probabilities *of* Disjoint *and* Overlapping Events

Vocabulary

disjoint events, p. 627
mutually exclusive events, p. 627
overlapping events, p. 627
complementary events, p. 630

BEFORE	*Now*	WHY?
You found the probability of an event.	You'll find the probability that event A *or* event B occurs.	So you can analyze data about blood types, as in Ex. 23.

In this lesson, you will find the probability that an event A *or* an event B occurs. To find the probability, first determine whether the events are *disjoint* or *overlapping*. **Disjoint events**, or **mutually exclusive events**, are events that have no outcomes in common. **Overlapping events** are events that have one or more outcomes in common.

For example, suppose you roll a number cube. The Venn diagrams below illustrate examples of disjoint events and overlapping events.

Review *Help*

For help with using Venn diagrams, see p. 784.

Disjoint Events

Event A: Roll a 2.

Event B: Roll an odd number.

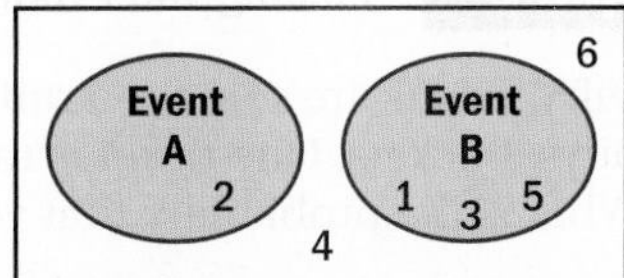

Overlapping Events

Event A: Roll an even number.

Event B: Roll a prime number.

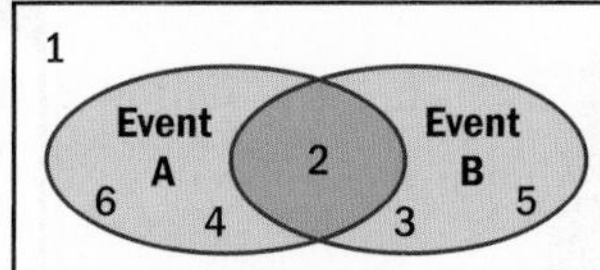

Example 1 *Identifying Disjoint and Overlapping Events*

Tell whether the events are *disjoint* or *overlapping*.

a. Roll a number cube.

Event A: Roll a number less than 4.

Event B: Roll a 5.

b. Randomly select a student.

Event A: Select a 7th grader.

Event B: Select a boy.

Solution

a. The outcomes for event A are 1, 2, and 3. The outcome for event B is 5. There are no outcomes in common.

Answer The events are disjoint.

b. Because some 7th graders are boys, the events have outcomes in common.

Answer The events are overlapping.

Checkpoint

1. Suppose you choose a book to read. Are the events "choosing a hard cover book" and "choosing a fiction book" disjoint or overlapping?

1. overlapping

NCTM CURRICULUM STANDARDS

Standard 5: Understand basic concepts of probability; Apply basic concepts of probability

Standard 10: Create representations to communicate ideas

1 PLAN

Skill Check

Simplify.

1. $\frac{6}{20} + \frac{5}{20} - \frac{3}{20}$ **$\frac{2}{5}$**

2. $\frac{2}{10} + \frac{4}{10} - \frac{1}{10}$ **$\frac{1}{2}$**

3. $\frac{7}{25} + \frac{13}{25} - \frac{2}{25}$ **$\frac{18}{25}$**

LESSON OBJECTIVE

Find the probability that event A *or* event B occurs.

PACING

Suggested Number of Days
Basic Course: 2 days
Average Course: 2 days
Advanced Course: 2 days
Block: 1 block

TEACHING RESOURCES

For a complete list of Teaching Resources, see page 578B.

TRANSPARENCY

Warm-Up Exercises for this lesson are available on a transparency.

2 TEACH

MOTIVATING THE LESSON

After reading the introduction, invite students to suggest other examples of disjoint or overlapping events resulting from two rolls of the number cube.

TIPS *for* NEW TEACHERS

Be sure that students not only understand the difference between disjoint events and overlapping events, but that they can identify which category an event belongs to when reading a description of the event. See Tips for New Teachers in the *Chapter 11 Resource Book*.

Extra Examples

Example 1 Tell whether the two events are *disjoint* or *overlapping*.

a. Roll a number cube.
Event A: Roll an odd number.
Event B: Roll a 5 or 6.
overlapping

b. Randomly select a letter of the alphabet.
Event A: Select a vowel.
Event B: Select a consonant.
disjoint

Example 2 Ten people are in line to buy theme park tickets. When buying their tickets, three pay with a credit card and four pay with a debit card. At the turnstiles, a survey taker randomly selects one of these ten people. What is the probability that the chosen person paid with a credit card or a debit card? $\frac{7}{10}$

READING STRATEGY

After having a volunteer read the first paragraph about the probability of disjoint events at the top of this page, discuss with students how the Venn diagram relates to the descriptions of Event A and Event B. Then have students reread the paragraph silently to assure themselves that they understand how the Venn diagram models the two events.

Probability of Disjoint Events The Venn diagram shows two disjoint events that involve rolling a number cube.

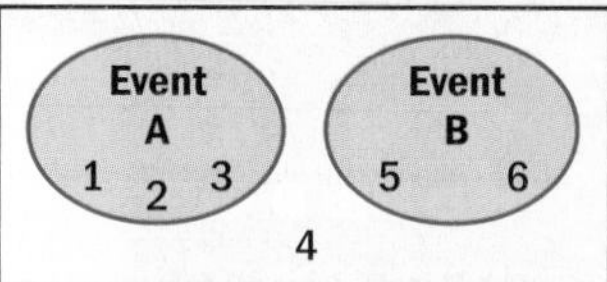

Event A: Roll a number less than 4.

Event B: Roll a number greater than 4.

There are 6 possible outcomes. There are 5 favorable outcomes for the event A *or* B. So, $P(\text{A or B}) = \frac{5}{6}$. You can also find $P(\text{A or B})$ by finding the sum of the probability of event A and the probability of event B.

$$P(\text{A or B}) = P(\text{A}) + P(\text{B}) = \frac{3}{6} + \frac{2}{6} = \frac{5}{6}$$

This result suggests the following rule.

Probability of Disjoint Events

Words For two disjoint events, the probability that either of the events occurs is the sum of the probabilities of the events.

Algebra If A and B are disjoint events, then $P(\text{A or B}) = P(\text{A}) + P(\text{B})$.

Example 2 *Finding the Probability of Disjoint Events*

Raffle Fifty tickets are sold for a raffle. You buy 2 tickets, and your friend buys 3 tickets. One ticket is randomly chosen as the winning ticket. What is the probability that you or your friend wins the raffle?

Solution

The events are disjoint because you and your friend cannot both win.

Event A: You win the raffle.

Event B: Your friend wins the raffle.

$P(\text{A or B}) = P(\text{A}) + P(\text{B})$ **Probability of disjoint events**

$= \frac{2}{50} + \frac{3}{50}$ **Substitute probabilities.**

$= \frac{5}{50} = \frac{1}{10}$ **Add. Then simplify.**

Answer The probability that you or your friend wins the raffle is $\frac{1}{10}$.

Checkpoint

2. In an election, candidate A received 35% of the vote, candidate B received 22% of the vote, and candidate C received 43% of the vote. If you randomly select a person from all who voted, what is the probability that the person voted for either candidate A *or* candidate B? **57%**

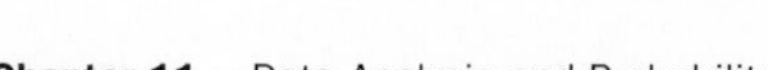

Probability of Overlapping Events The Venn diagram shows two overlapping events that involve rolling a number cube.

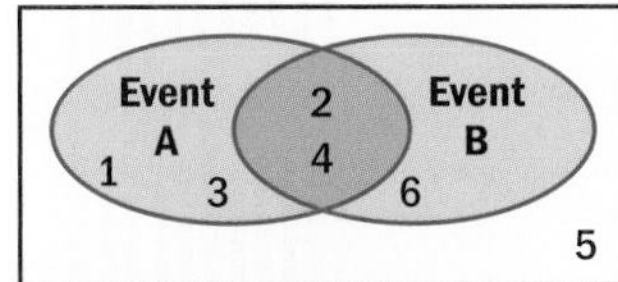

Event A: Roll a number less than 5.

Event B: Roll an even number.

There are 6 possible outcomes. There are 5 favorable outcomes for the event A *or* B. So, $P(\text{A or B}) = \frac{5}{6}$. There are 2 favorable outcomes for the event A *and* B. So, $P(\text{A and B}) = \frac{2}{6}$. These outcomes are counted twice when you find the sum of $P(\text{A})$ and $P(\text{B})$. In order to find $P(\text{A or B})$ using the sum of $P(\text{A})$ and $P(\text{B})$, you must subtract $P(\text{A and B})$ *once*.

$$P(\text{A or B}) = P(\text{A}) + P(\text{B}) - P(\text{A and B}) = \frac{4}{6} + \frac{3}{6} - \frac{2}{6} = \frac{5}{6}$$

Probability of Overlapping Events

Words For two overlapping events, the probability that either of the events occurs is the sum of the probabilities of the events minus the probability of both events.

Algebra If A and B are overlapping events, then $P(\text{A or B}) = P(\text{A}) + P(\text{B}) - P(\text{A and B})$.

Example 3 *Finding the Probability of Overlapping Events*

You roll two number cubes, one red and one blue. What is the probability that you roll a 4 on at least one of the number cubes?

Solution

The table lists all the possible outcomes of rolling the two number cubes.

Event A: The red number cube shows 4.

Event B: The blue number cube shows 4.

1, 1	2, 1	3, 1	4, 1	5, 1	6, 1
1, 2	2, 2	3, 2	4, 2	5, 2	6, 2
1, 3	2, 3	3, 3	4, 3	5, 3	6, 3
1, 4	2, 4	3, 4	4, 4	5, 4	6, 4
1, 5	2, 5	3, 5	4, 5	5, 5	6, 5
1, 6	2, 6	3, 6	4, 6	5, 6	6, 6

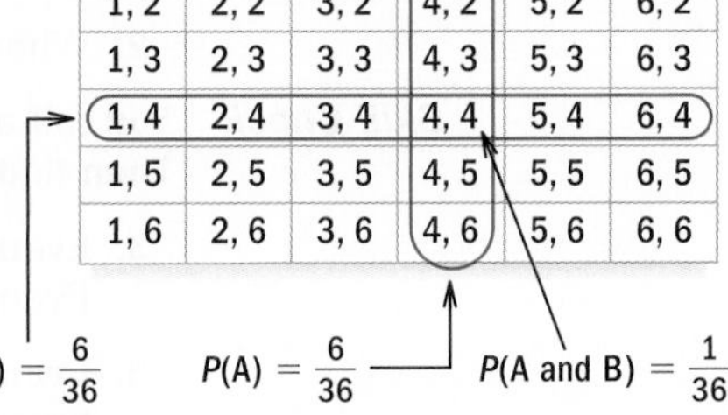

$P(\text{B}) = \frac{6}{36}$ $P(\text{A}) = \frac{6}{36}$ $P(\text{A and B}) = \frac{1}{36}$

$P(\text{A or B}) = P(\text{A}) + P(\text{B}) - P(\text{A and B})$ **Probability of overlapping events**

$= \frac{6}{36} + \frac{6}{36} - \frac{1}{36}$ **Substitute probabilities.**

$= \frac{11}{36}$ **Simplify.**

Answer The probability that you roll a 4 is $\frac{11}{36}$.

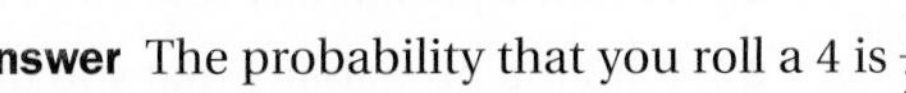

Review *Help*

In Example 2, a table is used to display all the possible outcomes. For help with making tables, see p. 799.

Extra Examples

Example 3 You roll two number cubes, one red and one blue. What is the probability that you roll a 5 or a 6 on at least one of the number cubes? $\frac{5}{9}$

DIFFERENTIATING INSTRUCTION

Alternative Teaching Strategy
To help students understand why it is necessary to subtract P(A and B) in the rule for the probability of overlapping events (that is, subtracting the probability of the overlapping events both occurring), do the following activity. Have all of the girls in the class stand up. Count the number of girls and write this number on the board. After having the girls sit back down, have all the students who ride the bus stand up. Again, count the students who are standing and record the number on the board. Ask the students who stood up both times to raise their hand. Count the number of raised hands and write this number on the board also. Now ask every student who either rides the bus or is a girl to raise his or her hand. Again, count the number of raised hands and write the number on the board. Lead students to realize that this number divided by the total number of students in class is the probability that a randomly selected student either rides the bus or is a girl. Now ask students to use the other three numbers on the board to arrive at the same probability. Students will find that they must subtract the number of bus-riding girls from the sum of the other two numbers in order to arrive at the correct probability.

VISUALIZE

Show students two sheets of paper and then overlap them slightly. Make sure students understand that for events to be overlapping, they do not have to be completely identical; only a subset needs to be common to both events.

Extra Examples

Example 4 A surgical group knows that statistics show a certain surgical procedure has an 80% success rate. What is the probability that any given surgery of this type will not be a success? **20%**

CONCEPT CHECK

How do you decide whether two events are overlapping or disjoint? **If two events have no outcomes in common, they are disjoint. If they have at least one outcome in common, the events are overlapping.**

DAILY PUZZLER

Events A and B are disjoint events. Find P(A and B). **0**

Complementary Events Two events are **complementary events** if they are disjoint events and one event or the other must occur. The sum of the probabilities of complementary events is always 1. If you know the probability of an event A, then the probability of the complementary event, *not* A, is given by the following rule.

$$P(\text{not A}) = 1 - P(\text{A})$$

Example 4 *Finding the Probability of Complementary Events*

Weather The forecast claims that there is a 40% probability of snow tomorrow. What is the probability that it will *not* snow tomorrow?

Solution

The events snow and no snow are complementary events because one or the other must occur.

$P(\text{no snow}) = 1 - P(\text{snow})$	**Probability of complementary events**
$= 1 - 0.4$	**Substitute 40%, or 0.4, for P(snow).**
$= 0.6$	**Subtract.**

Answer The probability that it will not snow tomorrow is 0.6, or 60%.

11.8 Exercises

More Practice, p. 813

Guided Practice

Vocabulary Check

1. Explain what it means for two events to be disjoint. **They have no outcomes in common.**
2. What is the complement of rolling an odd number on a number cube? **rolling an even number**

Skill Check **You roll a number cube. Tell whether the events are *disjoint* or *overlapping*. Then find P(A or B).**

3. **Event A:** Roll an even number. **Event B:** Roll a 3. **disjoint; $\frac{2}{3}$**
4. **Event A:** Roll a number less than 2. **Event B:** Roll an odd number. **overlapping; $\frac{1}{2}$**
5. **Event A:** Roll a multiple of 3. **Event B:** Roll a 5. **disjoint; $\frac{1}{2}$**
6. **Event A:** Roll an odd number. **Event B:** Roll a 1. **overlapping; $\frac{1}{2}$**

Guided Problem Solving

7. **Marbles** A bag contains 3 red marbles, 4 black marbles, 4 blue marbles, and 3 yellow marbles. You randomly draw a marble from the bag. What is the probability that you draw a red or a blue marble?
   1) Are the events disjoint or overlapping? **disjoint**
   2) Find the probability that you draw a red marble. $\frac{3}{14}$
   3) Find the probability that you draw a blue marble. $\frac{2}{7}$
   4) Find the probability that you draw a red or a blue marble. $\frac{1}{2}$

3 APPLY

Practice and Problem Solving

Homework Help

Example	Exercises
1	8-11,
2	8-15, 23
3	8-11,16-18, 24
4	19-23, 25

Online Resources
CLASSZONE.COM

- More Examples
- eTutorial Plus

The spinner is divided into equal parts. For the specified events A and B, tell whether the events are *disjoint* or *overlapping*. Then find *P*(A or B).

A **8.** **Event A:** Stops on an even number.
Event B: Stops on green. overlapping; $\frac{2}{3}$

9. **Event A:** Stops on an odd number.
Event B: Stops on a multiple of 3. overlapping; $\frac{2}{3}$

10. **Event A:** Stops on red.
Event B: Stops on blue. disjoint; $\frac{2}{3}$

11. **Event A:** Stops on blue.
Event B: Stops on a multiple of 3. overlapping; $\frac{1}{2}$

Events A and B are disjoint. Find *P*(A or B).

12. $P(A) = \frac{4}{25}, P(B) = \frac{17}{25}$ $\frac{21}{25}$

13. $P(A) = \frac{7}{15}, P(B) = \frac{2}{15}$ $\frac{3}{5}$

14. $P(A) = \frac{7}{20}, P(B) = \frac{3}{20}$ $\frac{1}{2}$

15. $P(A) = \frac{13}{50}, P(B) = \frac{22}{50}$ $\frac{7}{10}$

Events A and B are overlapping. Find *P*(A or B).

16. $P(A) = \frac{7}{10}, P(B) = \frac{3}{10}, P(A \text{ and } B) = \frac{1}{10}$ $\frac{9}{10}$

17. $P(A) = \frac{13}{25}, P(B) = \frac{8}{25}, P(A \text{ and } B) = \frac{3}{25}$ $\frac{18}{25}$

18. $P(A) = \frac{1}{6}, P(B) = \frac{1}{9}, P(A \text{ and } B) = \frac{3}{36}$ $\frac{7}{36}$

Given *P*(A), find *P*(not A).

19. $P(A) = 45\%$ 55%

20. $P(A) = 82\%$ 18%

21. $P(A) = \frac{11}{23}$ $\frac{12}{23}$

22. $P(A) = \frac{16}{33}$ $\frac{17}{33}$

23. Blood Types A city surveyed its population to find the blood types of its residents. Each resident has only one type of blood. The results of the survey are given in the circle graph.

Blood Types in a City

O 45%
A 40%
B 11%
AB 4%

a. Individuals with type A blood can accept type A or type O blood in a blood transfusion. Find the probability that blood from a randomly selected resident will be either type A or type O. 85%

b. Individuals with type B blood can accept type B or type O blood in a blood transfusion. Find the probability that blood from a randomly selected resident will be either type B or type O. 56%

c. What is the probability that a randomly selected resident does not have type O blood? 55%

d. What is the probability that a randomly selected resident does not have type A or type B blood? 49%

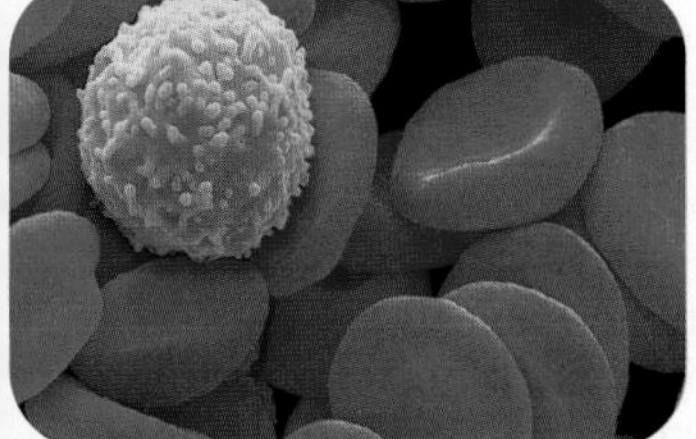

In the **Real World**

Blood Cells The color-enhanced photo of red and white blood cells above was taken through a microscope. Red blood cells have a diameter of about 7×10^{-6} m. White blood cells have a diameter as large as 1.2×10^{-5} m. How many times wider are white blood cells than red blood cells? about 1.7 times

ASSIGNMENT GUIDE

Basic Course
Day 1: SRH p. 779 Exs. 6-10; pp. 631-632 Exs. 12-15, 30-38
Day 2: pp. 631-632 Exs. 8-11, 16-23, 25, 39

Average Course
Day 1: pp. 631-632 Exs. 12-15, 23, 27, 28, 30-34
Day 2: pp. 631-632 Exs. 8-11, 16-22, 24-26, 35-40

Advanced Course
Day 1: pp. 631-632 Exs. 12-15, 26-28, 32-35
Day 2: pp. 631-632 Exs. 10, 11, 17-19, 22-25, 29*, 38-40

Block
pp. 631-632 Exs. 8-28, 30-40

EXTRA PRACTICE

- Student Edition, p. 813
- Chapter 11 Resource Book, pp. 72-74
- Test and Practice Generator

TRANSPARENCY

Even-numbered answers are available on transparencies.

HOMEWORK CHECK

When you review students' homework for this lesson, go over the following exercises to check understanding of key concepts.
Basic: 8, 10, 12, 16, 19
Average: 8, 12, 17, 19, 23
Advanced: 10, 13, 18, 23, 25

4 ASSESS

ASSESSMENT RESOURCES

For more assessment resources, see:

- Assessment Book
- Test and Practice Generator

MINI-QUIZ

1. You have an equally-divided spinner numbered 1 to 8. Are the events *disjoint* or *overlapping*? Find *P*(A or B).

   Event A: Spin a prime number.
   Event B: Spin a 4, 6, or 8.
   disjoint; $\frac{7}{8}$

2. A and B are overlapping. Find $P(\text{A or B})$ if $P(\text{A}) = \frac{7}{20}$, $P(\text{B}) = \frac{9}{20}$, and $P(\text{A and B}) = \frac{3}{20}$. **$\frac{13}{20}$**

3. **Challenge** Suppose events A and B are disjoint, and events B and C are disjoint. Are events A and C disjoint? Explain. **Not necessarily; events A and C could have some common outcomes, but they might not.**

5 FOLLOW-UP

DIAGNOSIS/REMEDIATION

- Study Guide in Chapter 11 Resource Book, pp. 75–76
- eTutorial Plus Online
- Extra Practice, p. 813
- Lesson Practice in Chapter 11 Resource Book, pp. 72–74

ENGLISH LEARNER SUPPORT

- Spanish Study Guide
- Multi-Language Visual Glossary
- Chapter Audio Summaries CDs

CHALLENGE

- Challenge Practice in Chapter 11 Resource Book, p. 77
- Teacher's Edition, p. 578F

29a. See Additional Answers beginning on page AA1.

26. ***Sample answer:*** **This calculation counts the probability that both coins show heads, which is 0.25, twice. So the probability of at least one heads is 0.5 + 0.5 − 0.25 = 0.75.**

27. They are disjoint. ***Sample answer:*** ***P*(A and B) = 0 means that A and B will not happen at the same time, therefore events A and B are disjoint.**

24. Pets A survey found that in a city, 19% of the population owned dogs, 14% of the population owned cats, and 6% of the population owned both a cat and a dog. Find the probability that a randomly chosen member of the population owns a cat or a dog. **27%**

B **25. Speech** You and your friend are among 12 students who will give speeches in front of the class. The teacher will randomly choose one of the 12 students to give the first speech. Each student has an equal probability of being chosen. Find the probability that *neither* you *nor* your friend will be chosen to give the first speech. **$\frac{5}{6}$**

26. *Writing* The probability that a coin shows heads when you flip it is 0.5. Explain why, when you flip two coins at the same time, the probability that at least one coin shows heads is *not* 0.5 + 0.5 = 1.0.

27. Critical Thinking You know that *P*(A and B) = 0. What can you conclude about event A and event B? Explain.

28. Critical Thinking You roll a number cube. What is the probability that the number cube shows a number that is not even *or* that is not a multiple of 3? **$\frac{5}{6}$**

C **29. Challenge** The numbers 1 through 20 are written on separate slips of paper and placed in a hat. One of the slips is randomly drawn.

a. Draw a Venn diagram that shows the possible outcomes for three events: the number drawn is less than 5, the number drawn is prime, and the number drawn is a multiple of 3. **See margin.**

b. Find the probability that the number drawn is less than 5 *or* a prime number *or* a multiple of 3. **$\frac{3}{4}$**

c. Write a general rule for finding *P*(A or B or C) for overlapping events A, B, and C. ***P*(A or B or C) = *P*(A) + *P*(B) + *P*(C) − *P*(A and B) − *P*(A and C) − *P*(B and C) + *P*(A and B and C)**

Mixed Review

Find the product. *(Lesson 5.4)*

30. $-\frac{4}{7} \cdot \frac{5}{9}$ **$-\frac{20}{63}$** **31.** $-\frac{5}{8} \cdot \left(-\frac{3}{4}\right)$ **$\frac{15}{32}$** **32.** $-\frac{9}{10} \cdot \frac{5}{12}$ **$-\frac{3}{8}$** **33.** $\frac{13}{18} \cdot \left(-\frac{15}{48}\right)$ **$-\frac{65}{288}$**

34. Map A cartographer is creating a map of 5 states. Each state is to be a different color. The cartographer will use red, green, blue, brown, and yellow. How many different ways can the cartographer color the map? *(Lesson 11.6)* **120 ways**

Find the number of combinations. *(Lesson 11.7)*

35. ${}_{11}C_5$ **462** **36.** ${}_{9}C_4$ **126** **37.** ${}_{10}C_6$ **210** **38.** ${}_{15}C_8$ **6435**

Standardized Test Practice

39. Multiple Choice A meteorologist forecasts that there is a 30% probability of rain tomorrow. What is the probability that it will *not* rain tomorrow? **C**

A. 30% **B.** 60% **C.** 70% **D.** 100%

40. Short Response The numbers 1 through 10 are written on separate slips of paper and placed in a hat. One of the slips is randomly drawn. Find the probability that the slip shows a number that is *neither* odd *nor* greater than 5. Explain your reasoning.

40. $\frac{1}{5}$. ***Sample answer:*** **The only numbers that satisfy both conditions are 2 and 4. So the probability is $\frac{2}{10}$, or $\frac{1}{5}$.**

Concept *Activity*

11.9 Performing a Simulation

Goal
Use a simulation to find an experimental probability.

Materials
- number cube
- paper
- pencil

A *simulation* is an experiment that you can use to represent a real-world situation and make predictions.

Investigate

Each box of a brand of cereal contains 1 of 6 different prizes. Use a simulation to predict the number of boxes you must buy before you have all 6 prizes.

1 Assume that the probability that a box contains a particular prize is $\frac{1}{6}$. Because there are 6 equally likely outcomes for each box you buy, you can use each of the 6 numbers on a number cube to represent one of the 6 prizes.

2 Roll the number cube one time for each box of cereal you buy. Record the results of the rolls in a table like the one shown.

Roll	1	2	3	4	5	6	. . .
Prize number	?	?	?	?	?	?	. . .

Steps 2–4. Answers will vary. Check students' work.

3 Keep rolling until you have rolled all six numbers at least once. Circle the first occurrence of each number. How many rolls did it take before you rolled all 6 numbers?

4 Repeat the simulation 4 more times. Based on your 5 simulations, what is the average (mean) number of boxes you have to buy before you have all 6 prizes? Round to the nearest whole number.

Draw Conclusions

1. **Critical Thinking** Another brand of cereal is offering 1 of 3 different prizes in each box. Assume that the probability that a box contains a particular prize is $\frac{1}{3}$. You want to collect all 3 prizes. Explain how you could use a number cube simulation to determine how many boxes, on average, you have to buy before you have all 3 prizes. **See margin.**
2. *Writing* Compare performing the simulation above to carrying out an experiment that involves buying actual cereal boxes. What are the advantages of the simulation? ***Sample answer:*** **The simulation is very quick, and you don't have to spend any money for cereal.**

NCTM CURRICULUM STANDARDS
Standard 5: Collect, organize, and display data; Select proper statistical methods to analyze data

1 PLAN

Investigate the Concept

- Students use a simulation to find an experimental probability.
- This activity leads into finding the probabilities of independent and dependent events in Lesson 11.9.

Materials

Each student will need a number cube, paper, and a pencil.

Recommended Time

Work activity: 15 min
Discuss results: 5 min

Grouping

Students should work individually.

2 TEACH

Discussion

Before students begin their work, ask: "Will buying 6 boxes of the cereal be enough to guarantee all 6 prizes? What about 12 boxes? 24 boxes?" Invite students' discussion about how many boxes they think they would need to purchase.

3 CLOSE

Key Discovery

An experiment can be performed to simulate a situation that is difficult to define mathematically.

Assessment

1. If someone bought 6 boxes of cereal and got all 6 prizes, would you be surprised? Explain. **Yes; this outcome is very unlikely.**

1. See Additional Answers beginning on page AA1.

1 PLAN

Skill Check

1. $\frac{3}{4} \cdot \frac{2}{3} = ?$ $\frac{1}{2}$
2. $\frac{2}{5} \cdot \frac{1}{3} = ?$ $\frac{2}{15}$
3. $\frac{1}{2} \cdot \frac{4}{10} = ?$ $\frac{1}{5}$
4. $\frac{4}{8} \cdot \frac{2}{3} = ?$ $\frac{1}{3}$

Lesson Objective

Find the probability that event A *and* event B occur.

Pacing

Suggested Number of Days
Basic Course: 2 days
Average Course: 2 days
Advanced Course: 2 days
Block: 1 block

Teaching Resources

For a complete list of Teaching Resources, see page 578B.

Transparency

Warm-Up Exercises for this lesson are available on a transparency.

2 TEACH

Motivating the Lesson

Tell students that you have six U.S. state quarters in your pocket, of which three are the newest state quarter to be released. Before selecting one from your pocket, ask students for the probability that it will be one of the newest quarters. Show students the quarter and then ask them for the probability that the next quarter you select will be one of the newest quarters. Discuss why this probability depends on the result of the first selection.

LESSON **11.9**

Independent *and* Dependent Events

Vocabulary
independent events, p. 634
dependent events, p. 634

BEFORE	*Now*	WHY?
You found P(A or B).	You'll find the probability that event A *and* event B occur.	So you can predict field hockey goals, as in Ex. 16.

Jelly Beans A jar of jelly beans contains 50 red jelly beans, 45 yellow jelly beans, and 30 green jelly beans. You reach into the jar and randomly select a jelly bean, then select another without putting the first jelly bean back. What is the probability that you draw two red jelly beans? Example 3 shows how to find this probability.

To find the probability that one event *and* another event occur, first decide if the events are *independent* or *dependent*. Two events are **independent events** if the occurrence of one event does *not* affect the probability of the occurrence of the other event. Two events are **dependent events** if the occurrence of one event *does* affect the probability of the occurrence of the other event.

Example 1 *Identifying Independent and Dependent Events*

Tell whether the events are *independent* or *dependent*.

a. You toss a coin and it shows heads. You toss the coin again and it shows tails.

b. You randomly draw a name from a hat. Then, without putting the first name back, you randomly draw a second name.

Solution

a. The result of the first coin toss does not affect the result of the second coin toss. So, the events are independent.

b. Because you do not replace the first name, there is one fewer name in the hat for the second draw. This affects the results of the second draw. So, the events are dependent.

 ***Checkpoint***

Tell whether the events are *independent* or *dependent*.

1. You roll a 5 on a number cube, then you roll a 6. **independent**
2. You randomly draw a marble from a bag. Then you put it back in the bag and randomly draw another marble from the bag. **independent**

NCTM CURRICULUM STANDARDS
Standard 5: Understand basic concepts of probability; Apply basic concepts of probability
Standard 6: Solve problems in math and other contexts

Independent Events You roll a number cube and toss a coin. These events are independent because rolling the number cube does not affect the result of the coin toss. From the table, you can see that there are 12 possible outcomes. The probability of rolling an odd number *and* getting heads is $\frac{3}{12}$, or $\frac{1}{4}$.

Possible Outcomes	
(1, H)	1, T
2, H	2, T
(3, H)	3, T
4, H	4, T
(5, H)	5, T
6, H	6, T

You can also find the probability of rolling an odd number and getting heads by multiplying.

$$P(\text{odd number and heads}) = P(\text{odd number}) \cdot P(\text{heads})$$

$$= \frac{3}{6} \cdot \frac{1}{2} = \frac{3}{12} = \frac{1}{4}$$

This result suggests the following rule.

Study *Strategy*

You can extend the formula for the probability of independent events to include more than two events. For example, the probability that independent events A, B, and C occur is the product $P(A) \cdot P(B) \cdot P(C)$.

Probability of Independent Events

Words For two independent events, the probability that both events occur is the product of the probabilities of the events.

Algebra If A and B are independent events, then $P(\text{A and B}) = P(\text{A}) \cdot P(\text{B})$.

Example 2 *Finding the Probability of Independent Events*

Passwords A computer randomly generates 4-digit passwords. Each digit can be used more than once. What is the probability that the first two digits in your password are both 1?

Solution

Each digit can be used more than once, so generating a digit and generating another digit are independent events. Because there are 10 digits, the probability of randomly generating a 1 is $\frac{1}{10}$.

$P(1 \text{ and } 1) = P(1) \cdot P(1)$ **Probability of independent events**

$= \frac{1}{10} \cdot \frac{1}{10}$ **Substitute probabilities.**

$= \frac{1}{100}$ **Multiply.**

Answer The probability that the first two digits are both 1 is $\frac{1}{100}$.

Checkpoint

3. Refer to Example 2. What is the probability that all four digits are 1? $\frac{1}{10{,}000}$

4. **Critical Thinking** In Example 2, if each digit can be used only once, are the events still independent? Explain.

4. No. *Sample answer:* If each digit can be used only once, when you generate a digit, there is one digit less remaining to be generated for the next digit, which affects the results of the second, third and fourth digit. So, the events are dependent.

TIPS *for* NEW TEACHERS

The mathematics of calculating probabilities is not difficult; the tricky part is deciding whether events are dependent or independent. Make sure all students are able to make this determination correctly. See Tips for New Teachers in the *Chapter 11 Resource Book*.

Extra Examples

Example 1 Tell whether the events are *independent* or *dependent*.

a. You roll a 3 on a number cube, then you roll another 3. **independent**

b. You randomly draw a marble from a bag. Then you draw a second marble without returning the first one. **dependent**

Example 2 What is the probability of rolling a 5 on each of three different number cubes? $\mathbf{\frac{1}{216}}$

TEACHING TIP

During your discussion of Example 1, bring up the mistaken belief that after tossing a string of heads with a coin, the likelihood of the next toss being a tail is somehow greater than $\frac{1}{2}$.

Extra Examples

Example 3 A group of students consists of 6 girls and 7 boys. Two students are chosen at random one at a time. What is the probability that both students who are selected are girls?
$\frac{5}{26}$, or about 19%

 **COMMON ERROR**

In Example 3, watch for students who forget that the denominator of the second fraction is 1 less than the denominator of the first fraction.

 **CONCEPT CHECK**

What are dependent events?
Two events are dependent if the occurrence of one event affects the probability of the occurrence of the other event.

 **DAILY PUZZLER**

Donald has white, blue, and black socks in a drawer. In the dark, he reaches into the drawer for two socks, hoping they will be the same color. How many socks must he take in order to be sure he has one matching pair of socks of any color?
4 socks

Dependent Events A bag contains 5 red marbles and 5 blue marbles. You randomly draw a marble, then you randomly draw a second marble without replacing the first marble. Because you don't replace the first marble, the probability that the second marble is a certain color is affected by the color of the first marble that you draw. These two events are dependent.

The probability that you draw a blue marble after drawing a red marble is written as P(blue given red). You can find the probability of drawing a red marble and then drawing a blue marble as shown.

$P(\text{red}) = \frac{5}{10} = \frac{1}{2}$ $\quad$ $P(\text{blue given red}) = \frac{5}{9}$

$$P(\text{red and then blue}) = P(\text{red}) \cdot P(\text{blue given red}) = \frac{1}{2} \cdot \frac{5}{9} = \frac{5}{18}$$

Probability of Dependent Events

Words For two dependent events, the probability that both events occur is the product of the probability that the first event occurs and the probability that the second event occurs given that the first event has occurred.

Algebra If A and B are dependent events, then
$P(\text{A and B}) = P(\text{A}) \cdot P(\text{B given A})$.

Example 3 *Finding the Probability of Dependent Events*

Find the probability that both the first and second jelly bean drawn from the jar described on page 634 are red.

Solution

Because you don't replace the first jelly bean, the events are dependent. So, $P(\text{red and then red}) = P(\text{red}) \cdot P(\text{red given red})$.

$P(\text{red}) = \frac{50}{125}$ — **There are 50 red jelly beans and 125 total jelly beans.**

$P(\text{red given red}) = \frac{49}{124}$ — **There are 49 red jelly beans remaining and 124 total jelly beans remaining.**

$P(\text{red and then red}) = \frac{50}{125} \cdot \frac{49}{124}$ — **Substitute probabilities.**

$= \frac{2,450}{15,500} \approx 0.16$ — **Multiply. Write as a decimal.**

Answer The probability that you draw two red jelly beans is about 16%.

11.9 Exercises

More Practice, p. 813

Guided Practice

Vocabulary Check

1. Tell what it means for two events to be independent. See margin.
2. Give an example of dependent events. *Sample answer:* You draw a card from a deck, then you draw another card without replacing the first.

1. *Sample answer:* Whether or not one of the events occurs does not affect whether or not the other occurs.

Skill Check **Tell whether the events are *independent* or *dependent*.**

3. **Event A:** You roll an odd number on a number cube.
Event B: You roll the number cube again and roll an even number. independent
4. **Event A:** You choose a member of a baseball team to be the pitcher.
Event B: You choose a different member of the team to be the catcher. dependent

Guided Problem Solving

5. **Raffle** You and your friend each purchased a ticket in a raffle in which 30 tickets were sold. The owner of the first ticket drawn wins the grand prize and is removed from the drawing. The owner of the second ticket drawn wins the runner-up prize. What is the probability that you win the grand prize and your friend wins the runner-up prize?
   1) Decide whether your winning the grand prize and your friend's winning the runner-up prize are independent or dependent events. dependent
   2) What is the probability that you win the grand prize? $\frac{1}{30}$
   3) If you win the grand prize, what is the probability that your friend wins the runner-up prize? $\frac{1}{29}$
   4) Find the probability that you win the grand prize and your friend wins the runner-up prize. $\frac{1}{870}$

Practice and Problem Solving

Homework *Help*

Example	Exercises
1	6-8, 10
2	12, 14, 16, 17
3	9, 11, 13

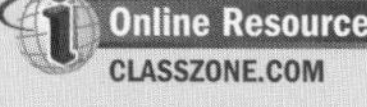

- More Examples
- eTutorial Plus

In Exercises 6–8, tell whether the events are *independent* or *dependent*.

A 6. A teacher is randomly assigning you, your friend, and 4 other students to 6 different seats.
Event A: You are assigned the first seat.
Event B: Your friend is assigned the second seat. dependent

7. A computer randomly chooses a digit from 1 to 100. A digit can be chosen more than once.
Event A: The digit is prime.
Event B: The digit is odd. independent

8. You randomly choose a utensil from a drawer with 12 spoons, 8 forks, and 6 knives. Without replacing the first item, you draw another.
Event A: You draw a spoon first.
Event B: You draw a fork second. dependent

3 APPLY

ASSIGNMENT GUIDE

Basic Course
Day 1: pp. 637-639 Exs. 6-8, 14, 17, 20-22
Day 2: pp. 637-639 Exs. 9-13, 23-25

Average Course
Day 1: pp. 637-639 Exs. 6-8, 15-17, 19-22
Day 2: pp. 637-639 Exs. 9-14, 23-26

Advanced Course
Day 1: pp. 637-639 Exs. 6-8, 15-19*
Day 2: pp. 637-639 Exs. 9-14, 22-26

Block
pp. 637-639 Exs. 6-17, 19-26

Extra Practice

- Student Edition, p. 813
- Chapter 11 Resource Book, pp. 80-82
- Test and Practice Generator

Transparency

Even-numbered answers are available on transparencies.

Homework Check

When you review students' homework for this lesson, go over the following exercises to check understanding of key concepts.
Basic: 6, 9, 10, 12, 14
Average: 8, 10, 11, 14, 16
Advanced: 8, 9, 13, 14, 17

TEACHING TIP

In Exercise 10, clarify that the CD player does keep track of which songs have been played when the shuffle setting is used.

15. If you do replace it. *Sample answer:* The probability if you replace the red marble is $\frac{1}{2} \cdot \frac{1}{2} = \frac{1}{4} = 0.25$, and the probability if you do not replace it is $\frac{1}{2} \cdot \frac{19}{39} = \frac{19}{78} \approx 0.244$.

In the **Real World**

Seeds A package of seeds must be labeled according to state regulations. A package of snapdragon seeds claims that the probability that a seed sprouts under optimal conditions is 55%. Suppose you plant 35 snapdragon seeds. How many seeds do you expect will sprout? **about 19 seeds**

9. Art Class An art class consists of 8 boys and 10 girls. The teacher randomly chooses 3 students to present their work. Find the probability that all 3 of the students chosen are girls. $\frac{5}{34}$

10. CD Player A CD player has two settings, random and shuffle. The shuffle setting plays all the songs on the CD only once in random order. The random setting selects songs randomly from the CD, but does not keep track of which songs have already been played.

a. You play a CD using the random setting. Are the selections of the first two songs that are played independent or dependent events? **independent**

b. You play a CD that has 11 songs using the random setting. Find the probability that the CD player plays song 3 first and then song 5. $\frac{1}{121}$

c. You play a CD using the shuffle setting. Are the selections of the first two songs that are played independent or dependent events? **dependent**

d. You play a CD with 11 songs using the shuffle setting. Find the probability that the CD player plays song 3 first and then song 5. $\frac{1}{110}$

11. Candy A gumball machine has 21 red gumballs, 24 yellow gumballs, and 15 blue gumballs. The gumballs are randomly mixed.

a. What is the probability that the gumball machine dispenses 2 red gumballs in a row? $\frac{7}{59}$

b. What is the probability that the gumball machine dispenses a red gumball, then a yellow gumball? $\frac{42}{295}$

c. What is the probability that the gumball machine dispenses a red gumball, then a blue gumball? $\frac{21}{236}$

12. Seeds A package of daisy seeds claims that the probability that each seed in the package sprouts under optimal conditions is 55%. Suppose you plant two daisy seeds under optimal conditions.

a. What is the probability that both seeds sprout? **30.25%**

b. What is the probability that neither of the seeds sprouts? **20.25%**

13. Socks A drawer contains 4 blue socks, 6 gray socks, and 8 black socks. You randomly choose one sock, then another from the drawer.

a. Find the probability that you choose 2 blue socks. $\frac{2}{51}$

b. Find the probability that you choose 2 gray socks. $\frac{5}{51}$

c. Find the probability that you choose 2 black socks. $\frac{28}{153}$

d. Find the probability that you choose 2 socks that match. $\frac{49}{153}$

14. Batteries A company has determined that 1% of the batteries it sells are defective. You recently bought 2 batteries from the company. What is the probability that they are both defective? $\frac{1}{10,000}$

15. *Writing* A bag contains 20 red marbles and 20 blue marbles. You randomly draw a marble from the bag, then randomly draw another marble. Do you have a greater probability of drawing 2 red marbles if you replace the first marble after you draw it, or if you do not replace the first marble? Explain. **See margin.**

16c. *Sample answer:* Yes; though there might be psychological or other factors, there doesn't seem to be any particular reason why one shot would influence the next unless proven otherwise.

18. $\left(\frac{1}{2}\right)^n$, or $\frac{1}{2^n}$

19c. $\frac{5}{9} \approx 56\%$. *Sample answer:* Since the complement of catching at least one rainbow trout is catching no rainbow trout, I subtracted the probability for BB from 1.

B **16. Extended Problem Solving** Suppose that a field hockey player scores a goal in 17% of her goal attempts. Assume that each attempt is independent of the previous one.

a. Calculate Find the probability that the player will score on her next two attempts. **about 2.9%**

b. Calculate Find the probability that the player will score on her next three attempts. **about 0.5%**

c. *Writing* Do you think it is reasonable to assume that each attempt is independent of the previous one? Explain your answer.

17. Contest The probability of winning \$1000 in a contest is advertised to be 1 in 10^5. The probability that one entry wins is independent of whether or not the other entries win. What is the probability that two friends who enter the contest both win \$1000? **1 in 10^{10}, or $\frac{1}{10{,}000{,}000{,}000}$**

C **18. Challenge** Write a general rule for the probability that a coin shows heads each time when it is flipped n times in a row.

19. Fishing You are fishing in a small pond that is stocked with 10 rainbow trout and 20 brook trout. There are no other types of fish in the pond. You keep any rainbow trout that you catch. You throw any brook trout back into the pond as soon as you catch them.

a. Suppose you catch exactly 2 fish. Make a list of all the possible arrangements of 2 fish that you could catch. **BR, RB, RR, BB**

b. Suppose each fish has an equal chance of being caught. Find the probability of each arrangement in part (a). Round your answers to the nearest percent. **BR: $\frac{2}{9} \approx 22\%$, RB: $\frac{20}{87} \approx 23\%$, RR: $\frac{3}{29} \approx 10\%$, BB: $\frac{4}{9} \approx 44\%$**

c. Find the probability that at least one of the two fish you catch is a rainbow trout. Explain how you found your answer.

Mixed Review

Simplify the expression. *(Lesson 2.3)*

20. $7x + 3 - 2x$ **$5x + 3$** **21.** $-3 + 4s^2 + 1 - 7s^2$ **$-3s^2 - 2$** **22.** $2a^2 + 6a + 3a + 11a^2$ **$13a^2 + 9a$**

23. Term Project A group of 5 students is to be chosen from a class of 20 students to work on a term project. How many different groups of students can be chosen from the class? *(Lesson 11.7)* **15,504 groups**

24. Sports A soccer goalie has a save percentage of 95%. What is the probability that the goalie will *not* make the next save? *(Lesson 11.8)* **5%**

Standardized Test Practice

26. 40%. *Sample answer:* For dependent events A and B, $P(\text{A and B}) = P(\text{A}) \cdot P(\text{B given A})$. Substituting the given values gives $0.08 = 0.2 \cdot P(\text{B given A})$. Dividing each side by 0.2 gives $0.4 = P(\text{B given A})$.

25. Multiple Choice If a digit can be used more than once, what is the probability that the last two digits of a randomly generated 5-digit number are both 4? **A**

A. $\frac{1}{100}$ **B.** $\frac{1}{90}$ **C.** $\frac{1}{81}$ **D.** $\frac{1}{10}$

26. Short Response Events A and B are dependent events. The probability that event A occurs is 20%. The probability that events A and B both occur is 8%. What is the probability that event B occurs given that event A occurs? Explain how you found your answer.

4 ASSESS

ASSESSMENT RESOURCES

For more assessment resources, see:
- Assessment Book
- Test and Practice Generator

MINI-QUIZ

1. Tell whether the events are *independent* or *dependent*.
Event A: You choose a member of a volleyball team to be the captain.
Event B: You choose another member of the team to be the co-captain. **dependent**

2. There are 6 blue CD covers, 8 green CD covers, and 2 red CD covers in a bag. Dave reaches into the bag without looking and selects two covers. What is the probability that both covers are red? $\frac{1}{120}$

3. Challenge Write a general rule for the probability that you roll a 3 on a number cube n times in a row. $\frac{1}{6^n}$

5 FOLLOW-UP

DIAGNOSIS/REMEDIATION

- Study Guide in Chapter 11 Resource Book, pp. 83–84
- eTutorial Plus Online
- Extra Practice, p. 813
- Lesson Practice in Chapter 11 Resource Book, pp. 80–82

ENGLISH LEARNER SUPPORT

- Spanish Study Guide
- Multi-Language Visual Glossary
- Chapter Audio Summaries CDs

CHALLENGE

- Challenge Practice in Chapter 11 Resource Book, p. 85
- Teacher's Edition, p. 578F

Additional Resources

The following resources are available to help review the materials in Lessons 11.6–11.9.

Chapter 11 Resource Book

- Lesson Practice
- Study Guide

Assessment Book

- Chapter 11 Quiz 2

Technology

- Test and Practice Generator
- eTutorial CD-ROM

Internet

- Classzone
- eWorkbook Plus Online
- eTutorial Plus Online

English Learner Support

- Spanish Study Guide
- Multi-Language Visual Glossary
- Chapter Audio Summaries CDs

3. *Sample:*

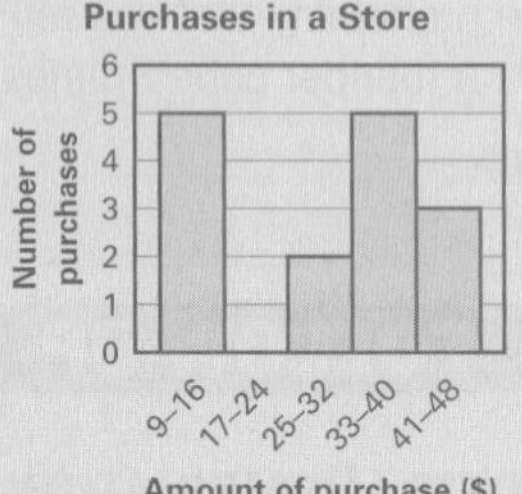

4. *Sample:*

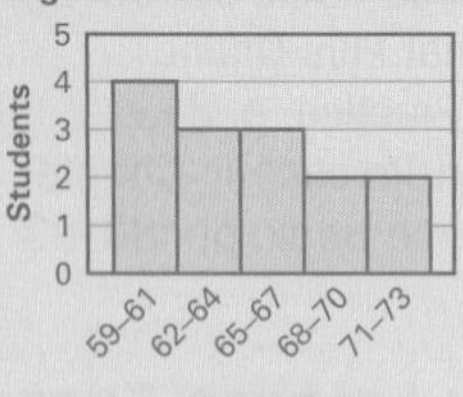

CHAPTER 11

Chapter Review

Vocabulary Review

- stem-and-leaf plot, p. 581
- frequency, p. 582
- frequency table, p. 582
- histogram, p. 583
- box-and-whisker plot, p. 588
- lower quartile, p. 588
- upper quartile, p. 588
- lower extreme, p. 588
- upper extreme, p. 588
- interquartile range, p. 590
- categorical data, p. 596
- numerical data, p. 596
- population, p. 601
- sample, p. 601
- samples: random, systematic, stratified, convenience, self-selected, p. 601
- biased sample, p. 602
- biased question, p. 603
- margin of error, p. 610
- permutation, p. 615
- *n* factorial, p. 615
- combination, p. 620
- events: disjoint, mutually exclusive, overlapping, p. 627
- complementary events, p. 630
- independent events, p. 634
- dependent events, p. 634

Copy and complete the statement.

1. The _?_ of a random sample provides an interval around a sample percent in which the population percent most likely occurs. **margin of error**

2. Two events are _?_ if the occurrence of one event does *not* affect the probability of the occurrence of the other event. **independent**

11.1 Stem-and-Leaf Plots and Histograms

Examples on pp. 581–583

Goal

Make stem-and-leaf plots and histograms.

 **Make a stem-and-leaf plot and a histogram of the following ages (in years) of customers in a store.**

27, 11, 39, 21, 45, 23, 42, 28, 30, 16, 31, 42, 35, 38, 17, 40, 35, 31

Ages of Customers

Stem	Leaves
1	1 6 7
2	1 3 7 8
3	0 1 1 5 5 8 9
4	0 2 2 5

Key: 3 | 8 = 38 years

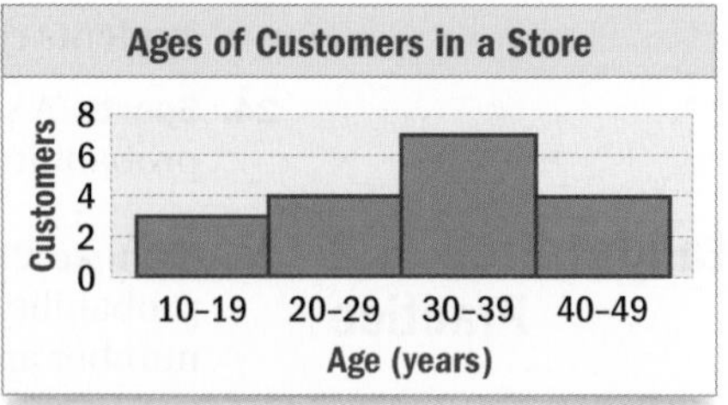

 3. Make a stem-and-leaf plot and a histogram of the following amounts (in dollars) spent on purchases in a store: 16, 15, 35, 10, 16, 34, 45, 33, 32, 36, 12, 44, 48, 32, 34.

3. Amount of Purchases

Stem	Leaves
1	0 2 5 6 6
2	
3	2 2 3 4 4 5 6
4	4 5 8

Key: 1 | 0 = $10

See margin for art.

4. Make a histogram of the following heights (in inches) of students in a club: 59, 60, 62, 72, 70, 67, 71, 61, 62, 63, 68, 67, 66, 61. **See margin.**

The following resources are available to help review the materials in this chapter.

Chapter 11 Resource Book
- Chapter Review Games and Activities, p. 86
- Cumulative Practice, Chs. 1–11

English/Spanish Chapter Reviews and Tests

Chapter Audio Summaries CDs

eTutorial CD-ROM

eWorkbook Plus Online

eTutorial Plus Online

5.

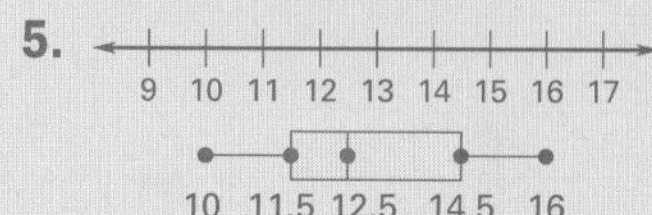

11.2 Box-and-Whisker Plots

Examples on pp. 588–590

Goal

Make box-and-whisker plots.

Example **Make a box-and-whisker plot of the following costs (in dollars) of 11 different computer desks.**

98.85, 88.64, 109.97, 95.99, 129.75, 100.50, 87.95, 99.99, 110.54, 105.61, 96.84

Order the data to find the median, the quartiles, and the extremes.

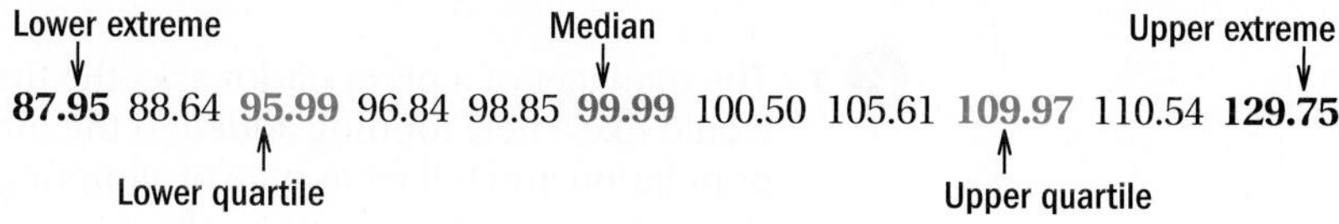

Draw a box-and-whisker plot using these values.

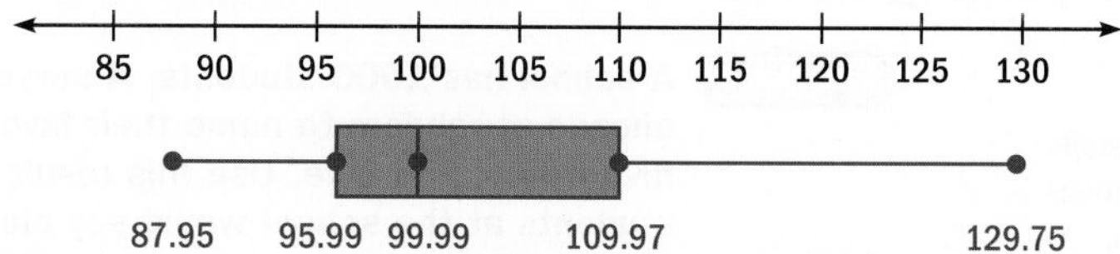

5. Make a box-and-whisker plot of the following ages (in years) of people performing in a play: 15, 12, 11, 16, 10, 14, 13, 12. **See margin.**

11.3 Using Data Displays

Examples on pp. 596–598

Goal

Choose appropriate displays for data sets.

 **The data below are the numbers of points scored by a girls' high school basketball team in the last 15 games. What data display(s) can you use to display the data?**

49, 84, 65, 71, 53, 54, 52, 64, 66, 63, 61, 70, 81, 78, 55

You can use a stem-and-leaf plot to display the data in numerical order. You can use a histogram to compare the numbers of scores that fall into intervals of equal size. You can also use a box-and-whisker plot to show the data divided into four groups of approximately equal size.

6. Line graph. ***Sample answer:*** **A line graph is appropriate for numerical data that change over time. A scatter plot could also be used.**

 **6.** The table shows the average yearly food cost (in dollars) in the United States. What data display(s) can you use to display the data? Explain your reasoning.

Year	1994	1995	1996	1997	1998	1999	2000
Cost (dollars)	4411	4505	4698	4801	4810	5031	5158

11.4 Collecting Data

Examples on pp. 601–603

Goal

Identify populations and sampling methods.

Example **A website operator posts the question "Should the background color on this page be blue?" on a website along with a link to a page where anyone can post a reply. Describe the population and tell what type of sampling method is used.**

The population consists of all visitors to the website. Because visitors have the choice of answering or not, the sample is self-selected.

7. The manager of a pizza parlor asks the first 10 customers if they would like a new topping added to the menu. Describe the population and tell what type of sampling method is used. **population: customers of a pizza parlor; sampling method: systematic sample**

11.5 Interpreting Data

Examples on pp. 609–611

Goal

Make conclusions about populations using surveys.

Example **A school has 1000 students. A survey asks 375 students chosen at random to name their favorite color. Thirty say their favorite color is blue. Use this result to predict how many students at the school would say blue is their favorite color.**

1) Find the sample percent: $\frac{30}{375} = 0.08 = 8\%$

2) Find 8% of 1000: $8\% \cdot 1000$ students $= 80$ students

8. In a survey of a random sample of 400 students at the school in the example above, 70 students said they prefer to exercise before school. Predict how many students at the school would prefer to exercise before school. **about 175 students**

11.6 Permutations

Examples on pp. 615–617

Goal

Use permutations to count possibilities.

Example **Find ${}_7P_3$.**

$${}_7P_3 = \frac{7!}{(7-3)!} = \frac{7!}{4!}$$ **Use permutations formula. Subtract.**

$$= \frac{7 \cdot 6 \cdot 5 \cdot \cancel{4} \cdot \cancel{3} \cdot \cancel{2} \cdot 1}{\cancel{4} \cdot \cancel{3} \cdot \cancel{2} \cdot 1}$$ **Expand factorials. Divide out common factors.**

$$= 7 \cdot 6 \cdot 5 = 210$$ **Multiply.**

Find the number of permutations.

9. ${}_9P_2$ **72** **10.** ${}_{11}P_3$ **990** **11.** ${}_8P_6$ **20,160** **12.** ${}_{36}P_2$ **1260**

11.7 Combinations

Examples on pp. 620–622

Goal

Use combinations to count possibilities.

Example **Find $_{12}C_4$.**

$$_{12}C_4 = \frac{_{12}P_4}{4!} = \frac{12 \cdot 11 \cdot 10 \cdot 9}{4 \cdot 3 \cdot 2 \cdot 1}$$ **Use combinations formula. Write $_{12}P_4$ and 4! as products.**

$$= \frac{\overset{1}{\cancel{\overset{3}{\cancel{12}}}} \cdot 11 \cdot \overset{5}{\cancel{10}} \cdot 9}{\underset{1}{\cancel{4}} \cdot \underset{1}{\cancel{3}} \cdot \underset{1}{\cancel{2}} \cdot 1} = 495$$ **Divide out common factors. Multiply.**

✔ **13.** Find $_5C_2$ and $_{12}C_5$. **10; 792**

11.8 Probabilities of Disjoint and Overlapping Events

Examples on pp. 627–630

Goal

Find probabilities of disjoint and overlapping events.

Example **You roll a number cube. What is the probability that you roll a multiple of 3 (event A) or an even number (event B)?**

$P(\text{A}) = \frac{2}{6}$ $\quad P(\text{B}) = \frac{3}{6}$ $\quad P(\text{A and B}) = \frac{1}{6}$

$P(\text{A or B}) = P(\text{A}) + P(\text{B}) - P(\text{A and B})$ **Probability of overlapping events**

$= \frac{2}{6} + \frac{3}{6} - \frac{1}{6} = \frac{4}{6} = \frac{2}{3}$ **Substitute probabilities. Simplify.**

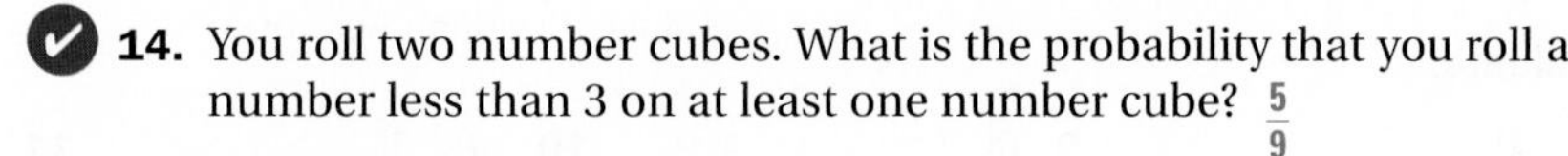

✔ **14.** You roll two number cubes. What is the probability that you roll a number less than 3 on at least one number cube? $\frac{5}{9}$

11.9 Independent and Dependent Events

Examples on pp. 634–636

Goal

Find probabilities of independent and dependent events.

Example **A bag has 5 green, 6 red, and 9 blue marbles. You randomly draw one marble, then you randomly draw a second without replacing the first. What is the probability that you draw a red and then a green marble?**

$P(\text{red}) = \frac{6}{20}$ $\quad P(\text{green given red}) = \frac{5}{19}$ **← 5 green marbles still in bag ← 19 marbles left after 1 is drawn**

$P(\text{red and green}) = P(\text{red}) \cdot P(\text{green given red})$

$= \frac{6}{20} \cdot \frac{5}{19} = \frac{3}{38} \approx 0.079$ **Substitute probabilities. Multiply.**

✔ **15.** Refer to the bag of marbles described above. What is the probability that you draw a blue marble then another blue marble without replacing the first marble? $\frac{18}{95}$

ADDITIONAL RESOURCES

Assessment Book

- Chapter Test (3 levels), pp. 137–142
- Standardized Chapter Test, p. 143
- Alternative Assessment, pp. 144–145

Test and Practice Generator

1. Grade Point Averages

1	8
2	4 5 8
3	0 2 2 2 5 8 9 9

Key: 1 | 8 = 1.8

Sample:

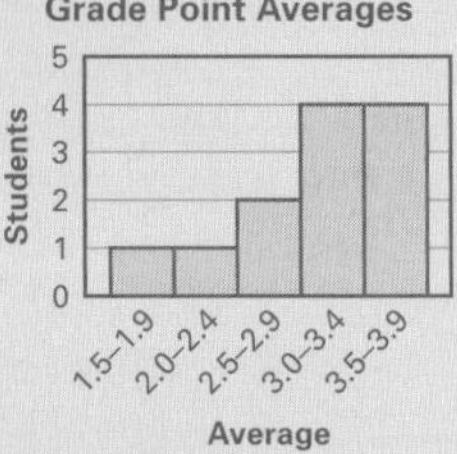

2. Video Game Scores

52	2 9
53	1 1 8
54	0 2 8
55	
56	2 4 6

Key: 52 | 2 = 522

Sample:

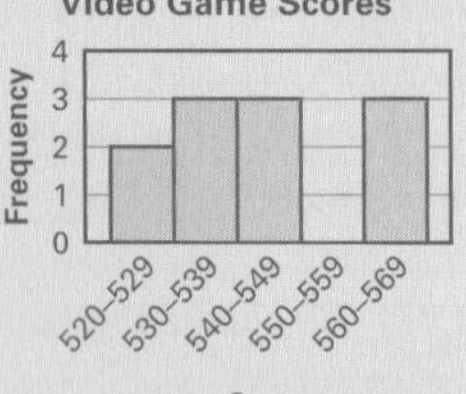

3. 8 10 12 14 16 18 20 22 24 26 28

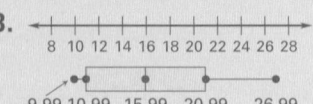

9.99 10.99 15.99 20.99 26.99

CHAPTER 11

Chapter Test

In Exercises 1 and 2, make a stem-and-leaf plot and a histogram of the data. 1–2. See margin.

1. Grade point averages: 3.2, 2.5, 3.9, 3.0, 3.2, 2.4, 3.2, 3.5, 3.8, 1.8, 3.9, 2.8
2. Video game scores: 542, 529, 564, 531, 566, 538, 562, 540, 522, 548, 531
3. **DVDs** Make a box-and-whisker plot of the following prices (in dollars) of some DVDs:
   10.99, 12.99, 15.99, 10.99, 26.99, 14.99, 19.99, 19.99, 9.99, 21.99, 20.99
   See margin.
4. Give two examples of categorical data. Which data display(s) can be used to display categorical data? *Sample answer:* T-shirt sizes (S, M, L, XL, XXL, XXXL) and types of fish in an aquarium; bar graphs and circle graphs

In Exercises 5 and 6, tell whether the question is potentially biased. Explain your answer. If the question is biased, rewrite it so that it is not.

5. Would you prefer to take a long, difficult essay test or a quick, simple multiple choice test? 5. Yes. *Sample answer:* The question indicates that essay tests are hard and multiple choice tests are easy. An alternative is "Do you prefer to take essay tests or multiple-choice tests?"
6. Which team do you think will win the race? No. *Sample answer:* The question doesn't indicate a preference for any team.
7. **Surveys** The U.S. population is about 290 million. In a survey of a random sample of 2000 Americans, 600 said that they enjoy watching plays. Predict about how many Americans enjoy watching plays. about 87 million Americans

Evaluate.

8. 4! 24	**9.** 6! 720	**10.** $_5P_2$ 20	**11.** $_8P_4$ 1680
12. $_9P_4$ 3024	**13.** $_3C_1$ 3	**14.** $_6C_6$ 1	**15.** $_5C_0$ 1

In Exercises 16 and 17, tell whether the possibilities can be counted using *permutations* or *combinations*. Then answer the question.

16. You and five friends are posing for a photograph. In how many ways can you pose in a line for the photograph? permutations; 720 ways
17. You are setting up a display for a store. There are 12 different types of sweaters. In how many ways can you display 4 different types of sweaters? combinations; 495 ways
18. **Projects** The 25 students in your class will present projects. Your teacher randomly selects a student to give the first presentation. Find the probability that you are *not* selected first. $\frac{24}{25}$, or 96%
19. **Jobs** Of the 400 students at a school, 35% have part-time jobs. Find the probability that two students selected at random have part-time jobs. $\frac{139}{1140}$, or about 12%

Chapter Standardized Test

Test-Taking Strategy **To check an answer, solve the problem using a method different from the one you originally used. Then compare your answers.**

1. Which statement about the stem-and-leaf plot shown is *not* true? **C**

5	1 6 7
6	0 2 5
7	4 6 7 7 9

Key: 5 | 1 = 51

A. The greatest data value is 79.

B. The range is 28.

C. The median is 67.

D. The mode is 77.

2. Which of the following could produce a misleading histogram? **H**

F. There is no space between bars.

G. Intervals are of equal size.

H. Vertical axis is broken.

I. Bar heights are different.

3. Your teacher asks every third student if he or she would rather have homework or a quiz. What is this method of sampling called? **D**

A. Convenience **B.** Self-selected

C. Stratified **D.** Systematic

4. A town's population is 3400. In a random sample of 400 townspeople, 24 said they are in favor of a new tax. Predict how many townspeople would be in favor of the tax. **I**

F. 9 **G.** 17 **H.** 142 **I.** 204

5. Which expression is equivalent to ${}_{20}P_{14}$? **C**

A. $\frac{14!}{20!}$ **B.** $\frac{6!}{20!}$ **C.** $\frac{20!}{6!}$ **D.** $\frac{20!}{14!}$

6. A club has 10 members. How many different combinations of 4 members can be chosen? **G**

F. 40 **G.** 210 **H.** 5040 **I.** 151,200

7. You roll a number cube. What is the probability that you roll a 3 *or* a 5? **D**

A. $\frac{1}{36}$ **B.** $\frac{1}{12}$ **C.** $\frac{1}{6}$ **D.** $\frac{1}{3}$

8. Your friend made 12 vanilla, 12 chocolate, and 16 strawberry cupcakes. You randomly choose a cupcake for yourself, then you randomly choose one for a friend. Find the probability that you choose 2 vanilla ones. **F**

F. $\frac{11}{130}$ **G.** $\frac{9}{100}$ **H.** $\frac{227}{390}$ **I.** $\frac{3}{5}$

9. **Short Response** The data in the histogram are for the year 2001. Make at least three conclusions about the data. **See margin.**

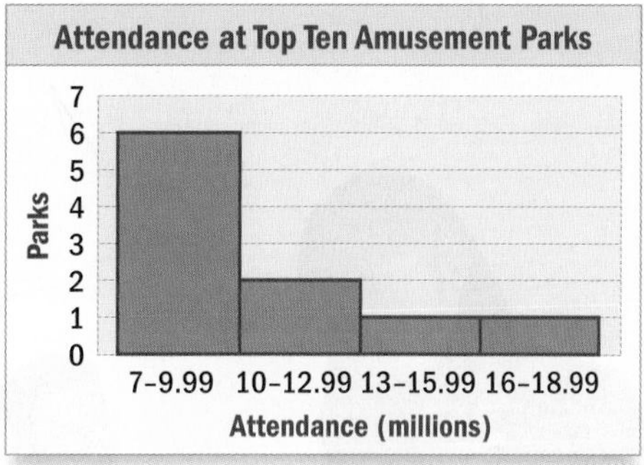

10. **Extended Response** The data below are the 60 meter dash times (in seconds) of two runners on 6 different days.

Rachel: 9.82, 10.35, 9.75, 9.91, 10.04, 9.87

Vivian: 9.79, 10.24, 10.08, 9.73, 9.81, 9.85

a. Make a box-and-whisker plot of each set of data. **10a–c. See margin.**

b. Compare the medians and ranges for the two runners.

c. Which runner is faster? Explain.

Additional Resources

Assessment Book

- Standardized Chapter Test, p. 143

Test and Practice Generator

9. ***Sample answer:*** **In 60% of the parks, attendance was between 7 and 10 million. In only one of the parks was attendance greater than 16 million. Three times as many parks had an attendance between 7 and 10 million as had an attendance between 10 and 13 million.**

10a.

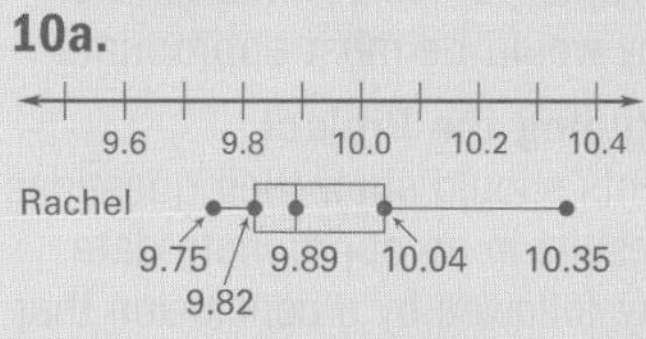

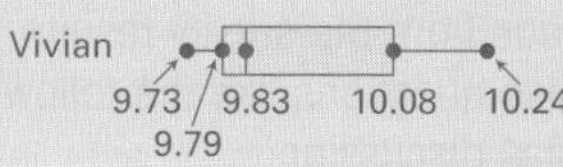

10b. **For Vivian, the median time of 9.83 seconds was 0.06 seconds faster than Rachel's median time of 9.89 seconds. Rachel's range of 0.6 seconds was greater than Vivian's range of 0.51 seconds.**

10c. **Vivian.** ***Sample answer:*** **Vivian's time is faster than Rachel's time on 4 of the 5 corresponding measures shown on the plots (all but the upper quartile.)**

OVERVIEW

Mathematical Goals

In this project, students will write unbiased survey questions, choose a sample, and conduct the survey. Students will choose and make a data display for their results.

Managing the Project

Classroom Management
Students should work in groups of 3–5 students. Students should work Steps 1 and 2 together. One or two of the group members should conduct the survey. The remaining students should analyze the data. A student who conducts the survey should still contribute to the group discussion and help to make the poster.

Guiding Students' Work
Stress that students should avoid writing open-ended questions. As they are writing their questions, urge them to begin thinking about how they will display the results. Suggest students list the possible answers to each survey question and then use this list to decide what kind of display would be most appropriate.

Concluding the Project
Students should show their questions and results in an appropriate data display, followed by a conclusion that clearly leads from the survey results. You can use questions like the following for class discussion:

- Why do surveys usually consist of yes/no questions or questions with numerical responses, such as a rating from 1 to 5?
- Is there something wrong with your survey if the numbers of respondents for and against the issue are about equal?

Chapter 11 Project

Conducting a Survey

Goal
Decide whether students in your school are in favor of a longer or shorter lunch period.

Key Skill
Collecting data

Materials
- calculator

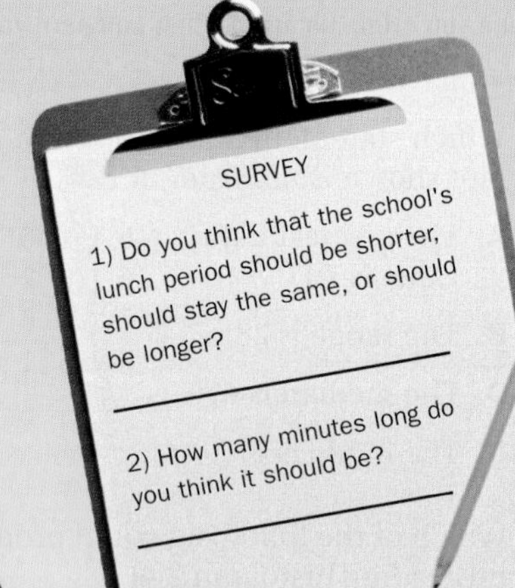

SURVEY
1) Do you think that the school's lunch period should be shorter, should stay the same, or should be longer?
2) How many minutes long do you think it should be?

Do you think students at your school want a longer lunch period, even if this means extending the school day? If so, how much longer? Do you think students at your school want a shorter lunch period if it means a shortened school day? If so, how much shorter?

To answer these questions, you will work in a group. Instead of asking every student in the school, your group will survey a sample of students at your school. Then you will analyze the results and create data displays to decide what the answers to these questions are.

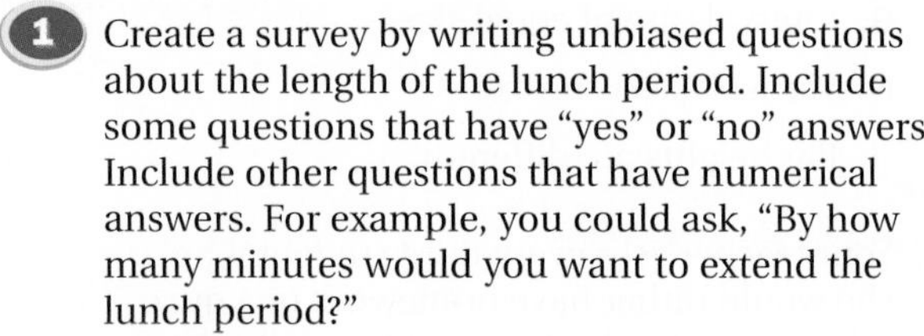

Investigate

1–3. Answers will vary.

1. Create a survey by writing unbiased questions about the length of the lunch period. Include some questions that have "yes" or "no" answers. Include other questions that have numerical answers. For example, you could ask, "By how many minutes would you want to extend the lunch period?"
2. Decide how to choose a sample of students at your school.
3. Decide which group members will conduct the survey. Then ask the students in your sample the questions in your survey.

Consider and Decide

Analyze the data that you collected. Consider the following:

- Do you have a clear answer to the questions asked in your survey, or are your data inconclusive? Explain. How could you improve your questions?
- Which type of data displays are most appropriate for your data? Make data displays for your data.
- Do students in your school want a longer lunch period or a shorter lunch period? How do your data support your answer?

Present Your Results

Make a poster that shows your survey results. Include your survey questions, your data displays, and your conclusions. Explain how you decided what length of lunch period students at your school prefer.

Project Extensions

Using Proportions Use the results of your survey to estimate the total number of students at your school who want a longer lunch period. **Check students' work.**

Writing Write an article for your school newspaper or website about how students feel about the length of the lunch period. Include your survey results and data displays. **Check students' work.**

Research CLASSZONE.COM Use the Internet to find a report of the results of a public opinion poll. Investigate how the poll was conducted and what the poll questions were. Do you think that the report accurately reflects the poll results? Present your research. **Check students' work.**

Career Many people conduct or analyze surveys as part of their jobs, including population analysts, market researchers, and public opinion pollsters. Find out more about one of these careers.

GRADING THE PROJECT

A well-written project will have the following characteristics:

- The results of Steps 1–3 are complete and reasonable.
- The survey questions are unbiased and quantifiable.
- The chosen data display is appropriate for the data.
- The students' conclusions about the length of the lunch period lead logically from their survey results.

CHAPTER

12 Pacing and Assignment Guide

REGULAR SCHEDULE

Lesson	Les. Day	BASIC	AVERAGE	ADVANCED
12.1	Day 1	EP p. 804 Exs. 9-12, 24-27; pp. 654-655 Exs. 19-27, 33-36, 39-42, 47-58, 60, 64-72	pp. 654-655 Exs. 22-32, 36-49, 53-62, 64-72	pp. 654-655 Exs. 22-32, 37-49, 53-65*, 68-72
12.2	Day 1	pp. 660-661 Exs. 12-17, 20-25, 29-34, 41-52	pp. 660-661 Exs. 14-19, 22-28, 31-39, 41-52	pp. 660-661 Exs. 16-19, 24-30, 35-42*, 47-52
12.3	Day 1	EP p. 806 Exs. 21-24; pp. 664-666 Exs. 10-18, 22-33, 36-41, 49-56	pp. 664-666 Exs. 13-21, 25-35, 39-47, 49-56	pp. 664-666 Exs. 16-21, 25-38, 42-50*, 53-56
12.4	Day 1	EP p. 806 Exs. 37, 38, p. 812 Exs. 9-12; pp. 670-672 Exs. 13-18, 25-30, 49-56	pp. 670-672 Exs. 13-18, 26-29, 39-43, 49-56	pp. 670-672 Exs. 16-20, 26-29, 42-44, 51-54
	Day 2	pp. 670-672 Exs. 19-24, 33-41, 44, 57-62	pp. 670-672 Exs. 19-24, 31-38, 44-46, 57-62	pp. 670-672 Exs. 21-24, 31-34, 37-40, 45-48*, 59-62
12.5	Day 1	EP p. 806 Exs. 45-48; pp. 677-678 Exs. 13-24, 27-31, 35-41, 44-46, 53-65	pp. 677-678 Exs. 17-28, 32-37, 40-43, 46-51, 53-65	pp. 677-678 Exs. 19-28, 32-35, 38-43, 47-55*, 59-65
12.6	Day 1	EP p. 810 Exs. 31-34; pp. 682-684 Exs. 13-21, 25-30, 50-55	pp. 682-684 Exs. 13-21, 25-30, 50-58	pp. 682-684 Exs. 18-24, 27-30, 50-58
	Day 2	pp. 682-684 Exs. 22-24, 31-36, 38-43, 56-59	pp. 682-684 Exs. 22-24, 34-48, 59, 60	pp. 682-684 Exs. 34-37, 41-49*, 59, 60
12.7	Day 1	pp. 689-691 Exs. 8-19, 29-31, 37-43	pp. 689-691 Exs. 10-19, 29-31, 37-43	pp. 689-691 Exs. 10-19, 29-31, 38-41
	Day 2	pp. 689-691 Exs. 20-27, 32, 33, 44-49	pp. 689-691 Exs. 20-28, 32-35, 44-50	pp. 689-691 Exs. 20-28, 32-36*, 45-50
12.8	Day 1	SRH p. 796 Exs. 1-3; pp. 695-697 Exs. 10-18, 32-34, 41-47	pp. 695-697 Exs. 13-21, 32-34, 41-47	pp. 695-697 Exs. 16-21, 32-34, 41-47
	Day 2	pp. 695-697 Exs. 22-27, 35-37, 48, 49	pp. 695-697 Exs. 25-31, 35-39, 48, 49	pp. 695-697 Exs. 25-31, 35-40*, 48, 49
Review	Day 1	pp. 698-701 Exs. 1-43	pp. 698-701 Exs. 1-43	pp. 698-701 Exs. 1-43
Assess	Day 1	Chapter 12 Test	Chapter 12 Test	Chapter 12 Test

YEARLY PACING Chapter 12 Total – **14 days** Chapters 1–12 Total – **148 days** Remaining – **12 days**

*Challenge Exercises EP = Extra Practice SRH = Skills Review Handbook

BLOCK SCHEDULE

DAY 1	DAY 2	DAY 3	DAY 4	DAY 5	DAY 6	DAY 7
12.1 pp. 654-655 Exs. 22-32, 36-49, 53-62, 64-72 **12.2** pp. 660-661 Exs. 14-19, 22-28, 31-39, 41-52	**12.3** pp. 664-666 Exs. 16-21, 25-35, 39-47, 49-56 **12.4** pp. 670-672 Exs. 13-18, 26-29, 39-43, 49-56	**12.4 (cont.)** pp. 670-672 Exs. 19-24, 31-38, 44-46, 57-62 **12.5** pp. 677-678 Exs. 17-28, 32-37, 40-43, 46-51, 53-65	**12.6** pp. 682-684 Exs. 13-30, 34-48, 50-60	**12.7** pp. 689-691 Exs. 10-35, 37-50	**12.8** pp. 695-697 Exs. 13-21, 25-39, 41-49	**Review** pp. 698-701 Exs. 1-43 **Assess** Chapter 12 Test

YEARLY PACING Chapter 12 Total – **7 days** Chapters 1–12 Total – **74 days** Remaining – **6 days**

Support Materials

CHAPTER RESOURCE BOOK

CHAPTER SUPPORT

Tips for New Teachers	p. 1	Parents as Partners	p. 3

LESSON SUPPORT	12.1	12.2	12.3	12.4	12.5	12.6	12.7	12.8
Lesson Plans (regular and block)	p. 5	p. 13	p. 23	p. 32	p. 42	p. 51	p. 61	p. 71
Technology Activities & Keystrokes				p. 35		p. 53	p. 63	p. 73
Activity Support Masters		p. 15		p. 34				
Activity Masters					p. 44			
Practice (3 levels)	p. 7	p. 17	p. 25	p. 36	p. 45	p. 54	p. 65	p. 74
Study Guide	p. 10	p. 20	p. 28	p. 39	p. 48	p. 57	p. 68	p. 77
Real-World Problem Solving			p. 30			p. 59		
Challenge Practice	p. 12	p. 22	p. 31	p. 41	p. 50	p. 60	p. 70	p. 79

REVIEW

Chapter Review Games and Activities	p. 80	Extra Credit Project with Rubric	p. 85
Real-Life Project with Rubric	p. 81	Cumulative Practice	p. 87
Cooperative Project with Rubric	p. 83	Resource Book Answers	A1

ASSESSMENT

Quizzes	p. 146	Alternative Assessments with Rubrics	p. 155
Chapter Tests (3 levels)	p. 148	Unit Test	p. 168
Standardized Test	p. 154	Cumulative Test	p. 170

TRANSPARENCIES

TRANSPARENCIES	12.1	12.2	12.3	12.4	12.5	12.6	12.7	12.8
Warm-Up/Daily Homework Quiz	✔	✔	✔	✔	✔	✔	✔	✔
Notetaking Guide	✔	✔	✔	✔	✔	✔	✔	✔
Teacher Support					✔	✔	✔	✔
English/Spanish Problem Solving		✔		✔		✔		
Answer Transparencies	✔	✔	✔	✔	✔	✔	✔	✔

TECHNOLOGY

- EasyPlanner CD-ROM
- Test and Practice Generator
- Electronic Lesson Presentations
- eTutorial CD-ROM
- Chapter Audio Summaries CDs
- Classzone.com
- eEdition Plus Online
- eWorkbook Plus Online
- eTutorial Plus Online
- EasyPlanner Plus Online

ADDITIONAL RESOURCES

- Worked-Out Solution Key
- Notetaking Guide
- Practice Workbook
- Tutor Place
- Professional Development Book
- Special Activities Book
- Posters
- Spanish Study Guide
- Exercises in Spanish
- English/Spanish Ch. Reviews/Tests
- Multi-Language Visual Glossary

CHAPTER 12

Math Background and Teaching Strategies

Lesson 12.1

MATH BACKGROUND

A *monomial* is a constant, a variable with nonnegative exponent, or the product of a constant and one or more variables with nonnegative exponents. A **polynomial** is the sum of two or more monomials. Each monomial in a polynomial is a **term** of the polynomial. A **binomial** is a polynomial with two terms, and a **trinomial** is a polynomial with three terms. To find the **degree of a term**, add the exponents of its variables. The **degree of a polynomial** is just the greatest degree of any of its terms. A polynomial is written in **standard form** if it is simplified and the terms are written so that the degree of each term decreases or stays the same from left to right.

TEACHING STRATEGIES

Students will need to simplify polynomials before writing them in standard form, so you may want to review the distributive property, especially when negative numbers and subtraction are involved. Remind students that when evaluating a power in a polynomial for a negative value of a variable they must include the negative sign in the exponentiation.

Lesson 12.2

MATH BACKGROUND

Two polynomials can be added using a horizontal format or a vertical format. Only like terms can be added. To subtract polynomials, change the subtraction to addition of the opposite by first using the distributive property to find the opposite of each term of the subtrahend.

TEACHING STRATEGIES

Concept Activity 12.2, which introduces Lesson 12.2, shows an example of using algebra tiles to model polynomial addition. You may also want to work examples with students of using algebra tiles to model polynomial subtraction. First have students model the original polynomials. Then they can replace each tile in the model for the subtrahend with its opposite and add using tiles as before.

Lesson 12.3

MATH BACKGROUND

To multiply a monomial and a polynomial, you must first use the distributive property to rewrite the product before you can simplify by multiplying the monomial factors. To divide two polynomials, you apply the quotient of powers property to simplify powers. To divide a polynomial by a monomial, divide each term in the polynomial by the monomial and then simplify using the quotient of powers property.

TEACHING STRATEGIES

Work additional examples with students. For multiplication, use examples both with the monomial on the left side and on the right side of the polynomial, use polynomials with different numbers of terms, and use various combinations of signs. For division, have students follow the multi-step approach of Example 3.

Lesson 12.4

MATH BACKGROUND

Finding the binomial product $(ax + b)(cx + d)$ requires using the distributive property in two stages: $(ax + b)(cx + d) = ax(cx + d) + b(cx + d) = acx^2 + adx + bcx + bd$. Notice that these four products are the products of the First $\left(ax \cdot cx = acx^2\right)$, Outer $(ax \cdot d = adx)$, Inner $(b \cdot cx = bcx)$, and Last $(b \cdot d = bd)$ terms in the original product $(ax + b)(cx + d)$.

TEACHING STRATEGIES

In Concept Activity 12.4, students use algebra tiles to model binomial multiplication. You can also have students use algebra tiles to model multiplying binomials one or both of which include a negative constant term, though this will require that students understand zero pairs. Finally, point out that the FOIL and table methods are just different ways of organizing the work of applying the distributive property.

Lesson 12.5

MATH BACKGROUND

The *power of a product property* states that a power of a product is the product of the powers of the factors. The *power of a quotient property* states that a power of a quotient is the quotient of the powers of the factors. Because a number in scientific notation is written as a product, the power of a product property can be used to find a power of a number written in scientific notation.

TEACHING STRATEGIES

Students will likely confuse the names of the various properties of exponents. The most important thing is for them to be able to recognize when to perform what operation with the exponents. Conduct a review of the definition of a power in terms of repeated multiplication to help students work through the different scenarios.

Lesson 12.6

MATH BACKGROUND

Unlike a linear function, a **quadratic function** has a second degree term. A quadratic function can be written in the form $y = ax^2 + bx + c$, where $a \neq 0$. Because the graph of a quadratic function is a U-shaped curve (a **parabola**), it has a **minimum value** (when $a > 0$, for which the parabola opens upward) or a **maximum value** (when $a < 0$, for which the parabola opens downward). So, the range of a quadratic function is not all real numbers.

TEACHING STRATEGIES

Students will not learn at this level that the x-coordinate of the vertex of a parabola is $x = -\frac{b}{2a}$. Because of this, they may have some difficulty finding the best x-values to use in their tables of values. You may want to let students know that if they notice two x-values that have the same y-value, then the vertex of the parabola will have an x-value halfway between the x-values of these two y-values. For example, if students notice that substituting both $x = 0$ and $x = 4$ in the quadratic function $y = 2x^2 - 8x + 5$ results in a y-value of 5, they can conclude that the vertex has an x-coordinate of 2.

Lesson 12.7

MATH BACKGROUND

While a linear function models a constant *amount* of growth (or decrease) over a given time interval, an **exponential function** models a constant *rate* of growth over a given time interval. For the general exponential function $y = ab^x$, with $a > 0$, $b > 0$, and $b \neq 1$, a value of b greater than 1 indicates **exponential growth**, while a value of b between 0 and 1 indicates **exponential decay**.

TEACHING STRATEGIES

It will be very helpful for students to be able to use a graphing calculator to examine graphs of exponential functions $y = ab^x$ for many values of b, and also for different values of a. This may also help students start to observe patterns, such as if $a = 1$, then the y-intercept of the graph remains (0, 1) even as b changes. Have students also use the Table feature of their graphing calculators so they can more easily see that the growth (or decay) is proportional.

Lesson 12.8

MATH BACKGROUND

A **sequence** is an ordered list of numbers, each of which is called a **term**. You can represent a sequence as a function whose domain is a set of consecutive integers (typically 1, 2, 3, …) and whose range is the values in the sequence. In an **arithmetic sequence**, successive terms differ by the same *amount*, called the **common difference**. In a **geometric sequence**, successive terms differ by the same *ratio*, called the **common ratio**. For positive values of the common difference or ratio, you can think of an arithmetic function as showing *linear* growth and a geometric sequence as showing *exponential* growth.

TEACHING STRATEGIES

You may want to have students explore a few sequences that are not arithmetic or linear to give them practice in identifying patterns. You can include the Fibonnacci sequence 1, 1, 2, 3, 5, 8, 13, … to give them exposure to a sequence in which a term is found by considering the *two* previous terms. You can also have students represent functions such as $y = 2x + 1$ or $y = x^2$ as sequences for natural number values of x.

CHAPTER

12 Differentiating Instruction

Strategies for Underachievers

FOCUS ON VOCABULARY

POLYNOMIALS In Lesson 12.1, be sure students understand that terms are connected by addition or subtraction symbols. For example, x^3y^3 has only one term, but $x^3 - y^3$ has two terms. Relate the prefixes of the words monomial, binomial, trinomial, and polynomial to words such as *monorail, monopoly, bicycle, binary, triangle, tricycle, polygon,* and *polygraph.* Have students brainstorm to think of other examples and explain how the prefix of each word relates to its meaning.

In Lesson 12.6, some students may relate the prefix *quad-* in *quadratic* to the number 4, as in *quadruplets,* and may wonder why this word is used for functions of degree two. You may want to point out that the word comes from a word meaning "to make square," which fits in with the use of the exponent 2 to mean "squared."

USE TOOLS AND MANIPULATIVES

ALGEBRA TILES Plan on allotting plenty of time to complete Concept Activity 12.2 with students. It is best if each student has her or his own set of algebra tiles. If you have access to a translucent set of tiles for an overhead projector, you can provide extra guidance for students. If necessary, you can start by having students add only 1-tiles, then only x-tiles, and then only x^2-tiles. Then you can progress to adding polynomials using tiles. Allow students to use algebra tiles until they are comfortable with the polynomial operations modeled. Students will naturally move to algebraic methods when they are ready to break from manipulatives.

You will also need to allow plenty of time for Concept Activity 12.4 where students model binomial multiplication. Make sure students understand the area model that algebra tiles are based on: a 1-tile is a square whose dimensions are 1 by 1, an x-tile is a rectangle whose dimensions are 1 by x, and an x^2-tile is a square whose dimensions are x by x. Also, point out that a tile length of x has no relationship to the width of a 1-tile, and was purposely chosen not to be a whole-number length in order to help keep students from making a false connection. The relative sizes of the tiles were chosen so they would be convenient to manipulate.

QUADRATIC FUNCTIONS In Lesson 12.7, you may wish to make a large wall chart of the Summary of Linear and Nonlinear Functions found on page 688. Alternately, you may want to have students create note cards containing this information.

USE SCAFFOLDING

FOIL METHOD In Lesson 12.4, you may wish to guide students in creating notecards showing step-by-step examples of the use of the FOIL method. Students' cards should include several examples, and should use various sign combinations in the binomials.

In Lesson 12.6, as graphing quadratic functions can be time-consuming for underachievers, you may wish to supply students with pre-made coordinate grids for them to use. You may also wish to create blank templates of tables of values. For some students, you may even want to suggest appropriate choices for values of x to use in tables for various quadratic functions.

Strategies for English Learners

FOCUS ON MATHEMATICAL SYMBOLS

In spite of the fact that the English used in the text is becoming increasingly abstract, part of students' developing competence in mathematics is being able to learn the language of the discipline. Some of the new phrases are:

Power of a Product Property (p. 674)
Power of a Quotient Property (p. 674)
Power of a Power Property (p. 675)

For English learners, however, you may want to express the concepts in mathematical symbols first and follow with a discussion of the verbal description. For example, when teaching the power of a product property, teachers may want to start by writing this expression from page 674 on the board:

$$(ab)^m = a^m b^m$$

Next, substitute numbers for variables, so that students can see that the rule works. Then discuss the explanation in English on that same page.

Students should be reassured that even though they are working with mathematical expressions and equations that are more complex, logical mathematical reasoning underlies all of mathematics. Everything can be explained, although some explanations have to be taken at face value at this point, because students are still learning the mathematics they need to be able to understand the proofs. The same basic rules, including the associative property, the distributive property, and the commutative property, still apply. The same basic strategies for evaluating polynomials, such as combining like terms and removing factors of one, still apply.

Strategies for Advanced Learners

INCREASE DEPTH AND COMPLEXITY

In Lesson 12.3, Example 3 on page 663 shows how to divide a polynomial by a monomial. You may wish to challenge some of your advanced students to write an explanation of how this process is related to the distributive property. You may also wish to have them rewrite this quotient as the related multiplication problem, and have them explain how to use multiplication to check the result.

NONLINEAR FUNCTIONS In conjunction with Lesson 12.6, you may wish to have advanced learners explore graphs of other types of nonlinear functions, such as cubic functions and quartic functions. Since it may be difficult for students to understand how the tables of values of some functions relate to their graphs, especially for odd-numbered powers, encourage students to use graphing calculators or graphing software in their exploration.

Also in conjunction with Lesson 12.6, you may wish to have advanced students explore quadratic functions written in vertex form, such as $y - 6 = 2(x + 3)^2$, and in factored form, such as $y = (x - 4)(x + 2)$. Again, encourage students to use technology in their explorations, and to look for any patterns they can find between the appearance of the equation of a function and the appearance of its graph.

In conjunction with exponential functions and their graphs in Lesson 12.7, you may wish to have advanced students explore the concept of an *asymptote*.

USE CO-CURRICULAR ACTIVITIES

In conjunction with Exercise 30 on page 696 of Lesson 12.8, you may wish to work with a technology or computer sciences teacher to develop a unit expanding the exploration of Sierpinski's triangle into a more general exploration of fractals and self-similarity. There are many excellent software tools for such an exploration.

The following problem can be used with **Lesson 12.4**:

- **Challenge** Have students find the following products. Then have them make generalizations based upon any patterns they observe.
  a. $(x + 1)^2$ $x^2 + 2x + 1$
  b. $(x + 2)^2$ $x^2 + 4x + 4$
  c. $(x + 3)^2$ $x^2 + 6x + 9$
  d. $(x - 1)^2$ $x^2 - 2x + 1$
  e. $(x - 2)^2$ $x^2 - 4x + 4$
  f. $(x - 3)^2$ $x^2 - 6x + 9$
  Sample answer: To find the square of a binomial that is some number added to a variable, square the variable term, add twice the product of the variable term and the number, and add the square of the number. To find the square of a binomial that is some number subtracted from a variable, square the variable term, subtract twice the product of the variable term and the number, and add the square of the number.

CHAPTER 12

Differentiating Instruction: Resource Materials

Differentiating Technology

McDougal Littell *Pre-Algebra* offers teachers a wide variety of technology, ranging from calculator activities in the *Chapter Resource Books* to the *Test and Practice Generator CD-ROM* to interactive, online resources and products accessed at Classzone.com.

CLASSZONE.COM

Classzone.com provides helpful online resources for students and teachers, including More Examples, Vocabulary Support, and State Test Practice. Classzone.com is also the access point for the following online products: *eEdition Plus Online*, an interactive, online version of the textbook; *eWorkbook Plus Online*, an interactive practice workbook correlated to the textbook; *eTutorial Plus Online*, an Internet tutorial that makes it easier than ever to help students master skills and concepts; and *EasyPlanner Plus Online*, an online resource with teacher tools and a lesson planner.

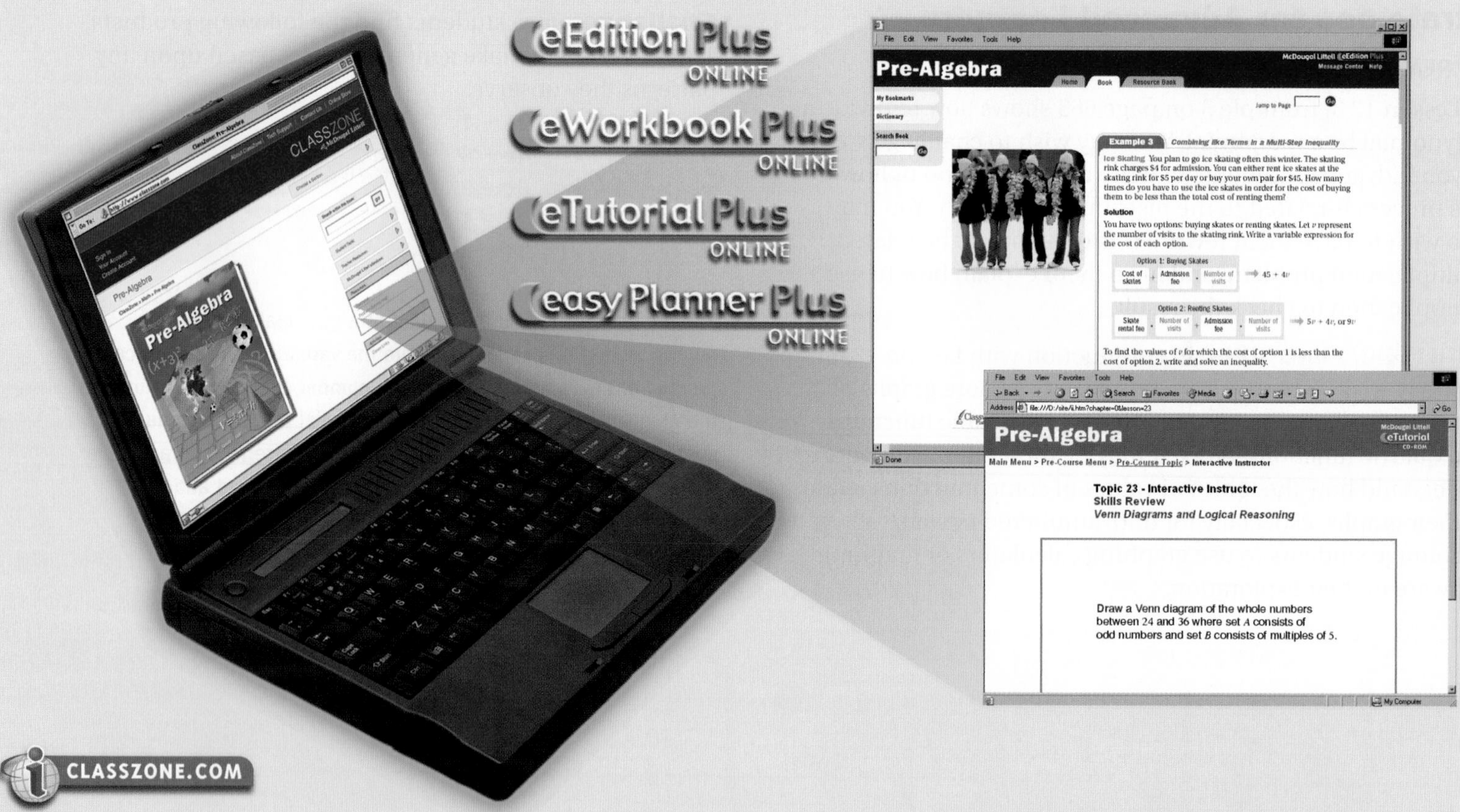

CLASSZONE.COM

TEST AND PRACTICE GENERATOR CD-ROM

The *Test and Practice Generator* can be used to create numerous practice sheets and quizzes for each lesson and tests for each chapter using both static and algorithmic exercises. Information about creating and editing questions is provided.

Chapter 12 Test — Page 1

Find the product and simplify.

1. $(m^2+4)(m^2-3)$
   [A] $2m^2-12$ [B] m^4-m^2-12 [C] m^4+m^2+1 [D] m^4+m^2-12

2. $(x-6)(x+9)$

3. Simplify the polynomial.
   $3w+(w+6)-4(3w-9)$

4. Rewrite $y=-2x^2+x-3$ using function notation.

5. Find the product and simplify.
   $(x+3)(2x^2-3x+4)$

6. Perform the indicated operations.
   $3(6y-3)-2(y^2-7y-5)$

7. Find the product and simplify.
   $(8x-3)(8x+3)$

8. Graph the function.
   $f(x)=x^2+1$

9. Evaluate the function $f(x)=2x^2+4x-7$ for $x=-3$.

10. Simplify the polynomial and write it in standard form.
    $4x+6(3x^2-x+7)$

11. Perform the indicated operations.
    $(-7x^2+3)+(4x^2+2x-1)$

Chapter 12 Test — Page 2

12. Evaluate the function $f(x)=3x^2+3x+6$ for $x=-2$.
    [A] 24 [B] 18 [C] 12 [D] −6

13. A rocket is launched from atop a 78-foot cliff with an initial velocity of 128 feet per second. The height of the rocket, in feet, is found with the function $f(x)=-16x^2+128x+78$, where x is the number of seconds after the rocket is launched. Graph this function to estimate how many seconds will pass before the rocket hits the ground.
    [A] 8.6 seconds [B] 10.0 seconds [C] 3.0 seconds [D] 0.6 seconds

14. Identify the function that produces the graph below.

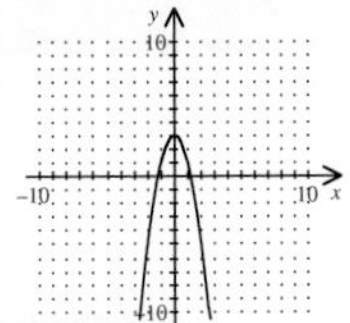

    [A] $f(x)=-2x^2+3$ [B] $f(x)=-x^2+3$ [C] $f(x)=2x^2-3$ [D] $f(x)=3x^2+2$

15. Simplify the polynomial and write it in standard form.
    $-12(x+2x^2-2-3x)+26x^2-9$
    [A] $2x^2+24x+15$ [B] $-2x^2+12x+15$ [C] $2x^2-10x+15$ [D] $2x^2+50x-15$

16. Find the difference.
    $(4x^2-3x)-(6x-3-7x^2)$
    [A] $-10x^2+3x-3$ [B] $-3x^2+9x+3$ [C] $-2x^2-10x-3$ [D] $11x^2-9x+3$

17. Simplify the polynomial and write it in standard form. Then state whether it is a *monomial*, a *binomial*, or a *trinomial*.
    $7+2x^2+8x-3-6x^2-1$

RESOURCE BOOK

The *Chapter Resource Books* contain technology activities that are different from the activities given in the textbook. Also included, where appropriate, are calculator keystrokes that can be used to do the technology activities and exercises that appear in the textbook and in the *Chapter Resource Books*.

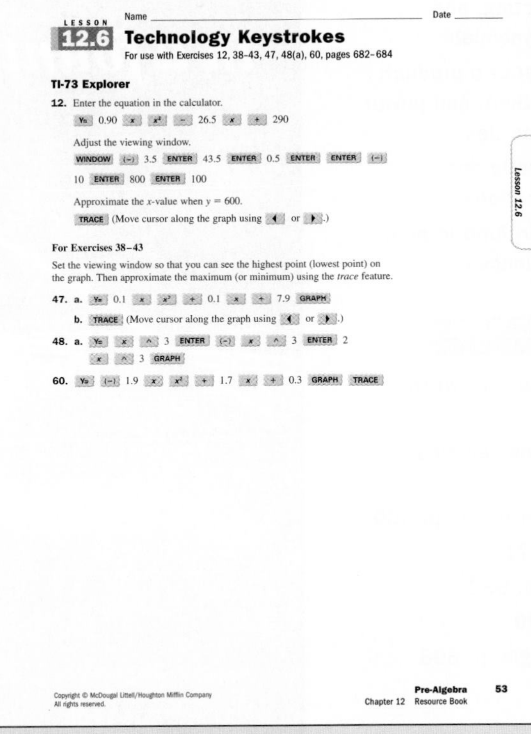

LESSON 12.6 Name ______ Date ______

Technology Keystrokes

For use with Exercises 12, 38–43, 47, 48(a), 60, pages 682–684

TI-73 Explorer

12. Enter the equation in the calculator.

Y= 0.90 x x² − 26.5 x + 290

Adjust the viewing window.

WINDOW (−) 3.5 ENTER 43.5 ENTER 0.5 ENTER ENTER (−) 10 ENTER 800 ENTER 100

Approximate the x-value when $y = 600$.

TRACE (Move cursor along the graph using ◀ or ▶.)

For Exercises 38–43

Set the viewing window so that you can see the highest point (lowest point) on the graph. Then approximate the maximum (or minimum) using the *trace* feature.

47. a. Y= 0.1 x x² + 0.1 x + 7.9 GRAPH

b. TRACE (Move cursor along the graph using ◀ or ▶.)

48. a. Y= x ^ 3 ENTER (−) x ^ 3 ENTER 2 x ^ 3 GRAPH

60. Y= (−) 1.9 x x² + 1.7 x + 0.3 GRAPH TRACE

Lesson 12.6

Copyright © McDougal Littell/Houghton Mifflin Company All rights reserved.

Pre-Algebra Chapter 12 Resource Book 53

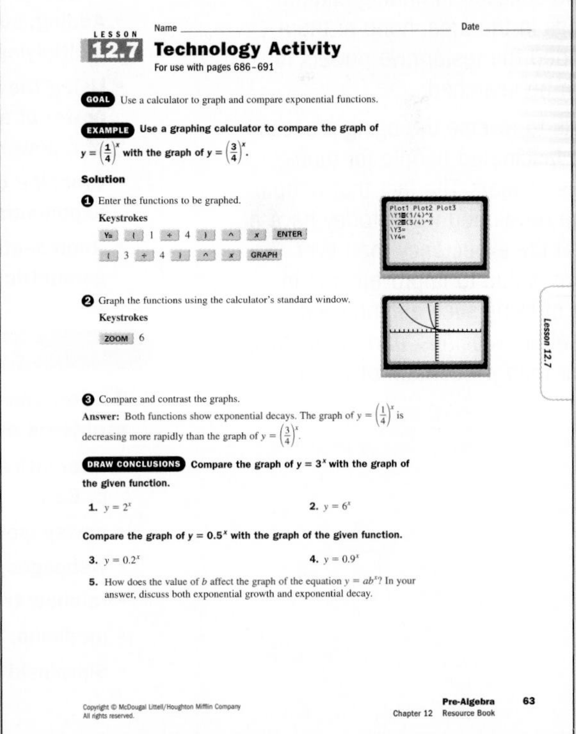

LESSON 12.7 Name ______ Date ______

Technology Activity

For use with pages 686–691

GOAL Use a calculator to graph and compare exponential functions.

EXAMPLE **Use a graphing calculator to compare the graph of $y=\left(\frac{1}{4}\right)^x$ with the graph of $y=\left(\frac{3}{4}\right)^x$.**

Solution

❶ Enter the functions to be graphed.

Keystrokes

Y= (1 ÷ 4) ^ x ENTER (3 ÷ 4) ^ x GRAPH

Plot1 Plot2 Plot3
\Y1=(1/4)^X
\Y2=(3/4)^X
\Y3=
\Y4=

❷ Graph the functions using the calculator's standard window.

Keystrokes

ZOOM 6

❸ Compare and contrast the graphs.

Answer: Both functions show exponential decays. The graph of $y=\left(\frac{1}{4}\right)^x$ is decreasing more rapidly than the graph of $y=\left(\frac{3}{4}\right)^x$.

DRAW CONCLUSIONS **Compare the graph of $y = 3^x$ with the graph of the given function.**

1. $y=2^x$ **2.** $y=6^x$

Compare the graph of $y=0.5^x$ with the graph of the given function.

3. $y=0.2^x$ **4.** $y=0.9^x$

5. How does the value of b affect the graph of the equation $y=ab^x$? In your answer, discuss both exponential growth and exponential decay.

Lesson 12.7

Copyright © McDougal Littell/Houghton Mifflin Company All rights reserved.

Pre-Algebra Chapter 12 Resource Book 63

OVERVIEW

Main Ideas

In this chapter, students identify polynomials and write them in standard form. Students add and subtract polynomials, multiply binomials, and multiply a monomial and a polynomial. Students simplify powers of products and quotients. Students graph quadratic and exponential functions. Students solve problems involving exponential growth. Finally, students extend arithmetic and geometric sequences.

Application Note

Fountains have fascinated people for many years. Ponce de Leon, a Spanish explorer during the early 1500's, was fascinated by the legend of a fountain whose waters were reputed to reverse the aging process. While searching for the fountain, Ponce de Leon landed in the area of St. Augustine, Florida, claiming the area for Spain. While he did succeed in finding mineral springs in the area, none of them provided the restorative powers for which he searched.

Efforts to reverse the aging process have fascinated people for thousands of years. The fact that people in the developed world today have a higher life expectancy than ever before is due to improvements in style of living such as improved sanitation, vaccines, and antibiotics, rather than a "fountain of youth."

CHAPTER 12

Polynomials *and* Nonlinear Functions

BEFORE

In previous chapters you've . . .

- **Used the product of powers and quotient of powers properties**
- **Represented linear functions**

Now

In Chapter 12 you'll study . . .

- **Classifying and simplifying polynomials**
- **Adding, subtracting, and multiplying polynomials**
- **Using the power of a product, power of a quotient, and power of a power properties**
- **Graphing quadratic and exponential functions**
- **Representing arithmetic and geometric sequences**

WHY?

So you can solve real-world problems about . . .

- **alternative-fueled vehicles, p. 654**
- **newspaper advertising, p. 660**
- **webpages, p. 671**
- **rainbow trout, p. 682**
- **medicine, p. 690**
- **Sierpinski triangle, p. 696**

How can you use math to describe the path of a stream of water in a fountain?

CHAPTER 12

INTERNET Preview

CLASSZONE.COM

- eEdition Plus Online
- eWorkbook Plus Online
- eTutorial Plus Online
- State Test Practice
- More Examples

MATH In the Real World

Fountains Gravity pulls down on the drops of water in the stream from a fountain, causing them to fall back to the fountain's basin. In this chapter, you will use *quadratic functions* to describe the motion of objects affected by gravity.

What do you think? The equation $y = x^2$ is a quadratic function. Make a table of values for this function. Use the table to write and graph at least seven ordered pairs. Can you connect the points with a straight line? Explain. **See margin.**

CHAPTER RESOURCES

These resources are provided to help you prepare for the chapter and to customize review materials:

Chapter 12 Resource Book

- Tips for New Teachers, pp. 1–2
- Lesson Plan, pp. 5, 13, 23, 32, 42, 51, 61, 71
- Lesson Plan for Block Scheduling, pp. 6, 14, 24, 33, 43, 52, 62, 72

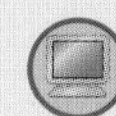

Technology

- EasyPlanner CD-ROM
- Test and Practice Generator
- Electronic Lesson Presentations CD-ROM
- eTutorial CD-ROM

Internet

- Classzone
- eEdition Plus Online
- eWorkbook Plus Online
- eTutorial Plus Online
- EasyPlanner Plus Online

ENGLISH LEARNER SUPPORT

- Spanish Study Guide
- Multi-Language Visual Glossary
- Chapter Audio Summaries CDs
- Teacher's Edition, pp. 648E–648F

Sample answer:

x	−3	−2	−1	0	1	2	3
y	9	4	1	0	1	4	9

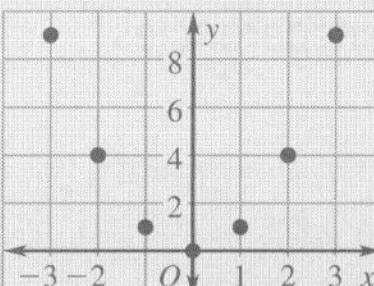

You cannot connect the points with a straight line. No three consecutive points lie on the same line. You can draw a smooth curve to connect the points.

PREPARE

DIAGNOSIS/REMEDIATION

Prerequisite Skills Quiz

The Prerequisite Skills Quiz can help you diagnose whether students have the following skills needed in Chapter 12:

- Use vocabulary (Ex. 1)
- Simplify expressions involving exponents (Exs. 2–5)
- Write expressions using positive exponents (Exs. 6–9)
- Graph linear equations (Exs. 10–13)

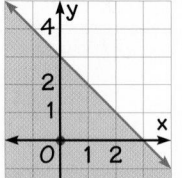 ***Chapter 12 Resource Book***

- Study Guide (Lessons 12.1–12.8)

 ***Tutor Place***

NOTETAKING STRATEGIES

When taking notes, students often omit key details that they are certain they will remember later. Encourage students to imagine they are taking notes for a classmate who is out sick and record extra detail even if students are sure they will remember the information later. In addition, the act of writing notes will help students reinforce the facts they are recording. Further suggestions for keeping a notebook can be found on pages 669 and 687.

For more support on notetaking, see:

- Notetaking Guide Workbook
- Notetaking Transparencies

10–13. See Additional Answers beginning on page AA1.

CHAPTER 12

Chapter Prerequisite Skills

Review Vocabulary

monomial, p. 174
function, p. 386
graph of an equation in two variables, p. 392
function form, p. 393

PREREQUISITE SKILLS QUIZ

Preparing for Success **To prepare for success in this chapter, test your knowledge of these concepts and skills. You may want to look at the pages referred to in blue for additional review.**

1. Vocabulary When is a relation a function?
when every input is paired with exactly one output

Simplify. *(p. 194)*

2. $6^8 \cdot 6^5$ 6^{13} **3.** $a^4 \cdot a^{11}$ a^{15} **4.** $\frac{7^9}{7^7}$ 7^2 **5.** $\frac{3z \cdot 8z^{12}}{6z^6}$ $4z^7$

Write the expression using only positive exponents. *(p. 199)*

6. 7^{-4} $\frac{1}{7^4}$ **7.** 120^{-2} $\frac{1}{120^2}$ **8.** $5x^{-6}$ $\frac{5}{x^6}$ **9.** $m^{-3}n^5$ $\frac{n^5}{m^3}$

Graph the equation. *(p. 391)* **10–13. See margin.**

10. $y = x + 5$ **11.** $y = -3x - 6$ **12.** $y = -\frac{1}{2}x$ **13.** $y = \frac{1}{4}x - 2$

Note *Worthy*

You will find a notetaking strategy at the beginning of each chapter. Look for additional notetaking and study strategies throughout the chapter.

NOTETAKING STRATEGIES

TAKING NOTES IN CLASS Leave space after examples that your teacher writes on the board. Use the space to write down any questions asked by you or other students. Record the teacher's answer.

Example: Graph $y \le -x + 3$.

Step 1: Graph $y = -x + 3$. Use a solid line.

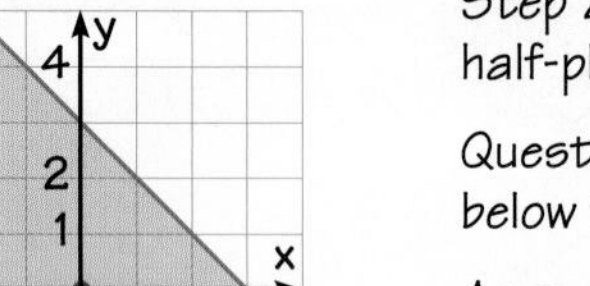

Step 2: Shade the appropriate half-plane.

Question: Do I shade above or below the line?

Answer: To determine which half-plane to shade, test the coordinates of a point in the inequality.

In Lesson 12.7, write down any questions you have about exponential functions, as well as your teacher's answers.

LESSON

12.1 Polynomials

BEFORE	Now	WHY?
You simplified expressions.	You'll classify and write polynomials in standard form.	So you can find the braking distance of a train, as in Ex. 59.

Vocabulary

polynomial, p. 651
term, p. 651
binomial, p. 651
trinomial, p. 651
degree of a term, p. 652
degree of a polynomial, p. 652
standard form, p. 652

Volleyball A volleyball is hit upward from a height of 1.2 meters. You can use the expression $-4.9t^2 + 8.1t + 1.2$ to find the height (in meters) of the volleyball t seconds after it is hit. What is the height of the volleyball after 1 second? In Example 4, you'll see how to answer this question by evaluating the expression.

Recall that expressions such as $-4.9t^2$, $8.1t$, and 1.2 are called monomials. A **polynomial** is a sum of monomials. Each monomial in a polynomial is called a **term**. A polynomial like $3x^2 + (-5x) + (-2)$ is usually written as $3x^2 - 5x - 2$. Some polynomials can be classified by the number of their terms.

Monomial (1 term)	Binomial (2 terms)	Trinomial (3 terms)
$-3xyz$	$5x + 1$	$-4b^2 + 6b - 3$
8	$-p^3 - 2p^2$	$2 + 11t - 7t^3$

Example 1 *Identifying and Classifying Polynomials*

Tell whether the expression is a polynomial. If it is a polynomial, list its terms and classify it.

a. $7m^{-2} + 4$ **b.** $-b$ **c.** $3x^2 + 8xy - 1$

Solution

a. This expression is not a polynomial. The variable m has an exponent that is not a whole number.

b. This expression is a polynomial. The only term is $-b$. Because it has one term, it is a monomial.

c. This expression is a polynomial. The terms are $3x^2$, $8xy$, and -1. Because it has three terms, it is a trinomial.

Study *Strategy*

To identify the terms of the expression in part (c) of Example 1, write the expression $3x^2 + 8xy - 1$ as $3x^2 + 8xy + (-1)$.

Checkpoint

Tell whether the expression is a polynomial. If it is a polynomial, list its terms and classify it.

1. $6x^4 - 5x^3$ **2.** $m^3 - m^{-1} - 1$ no **3.** $-3a + 7ab^2 + 2$

1. yes; $6x^4$ and $-5x^3$; binomial

3. yes; $-3a$, $7ab^2$, and 2; trinomial

NCTM CURRICULUM STANDARDS

Standard 2: Represent situations using algebraic symbols; Analyze situations using algebraic symbols

Standard 6: Solve problems in math and other contexts

1 PLAN

Skill Check

Simplify the expression.

1. $8x - 7x$ x

2. $15k - 17k$ $-2k$

3. $-5y + 12y$ $7y$

4. $-4a + 2a - 5a$ $-7a$

Lesson Objective

Classify and write polynomials in standard form.

Pacing

Suggested Number of Days
Basic Course: 1 day
Average Course: 1 day
Advanced Course: 1 day
Block: 0.5 block with 12.2

Teaching Resources

For a complete list of Teaching Resources, see page 648B.

Transparency

Warm-Up Exercises for this lesson are available on a transparency.

2 TEACH

Motivating the Lesson

Have a student draw a line on the board that is 1.2 meters above the floor. You might also want to have a volunteer explain the rules about hitting a volleyball to the class.

TIPS *for* NEW TEACHERS

This lesson contains many new terms. Urge students to keep their notebooks available so they can record the terms and their definitions. See Tips for New Teachers in the *Chapter 12 Resource Book.*

Extra Examples

Example 1 Tell whether the expression is a polynomial. If it is a polynomial, list its terms and classify it.

a. x^2 **yes; x^2; monomial**

b. $2s^{-1} - s$ **no**

c. $k^2 - k^3 + \frac{k}{4}$ **yes; k^2, $-k^3$, and $\frac{k}{4}$; trinomial**

Example 2 Find the degree of the polynomial.

a. $6c^2 + 5c + 3$ **2**

b. $2a^3 + 5a^4b + 3b^6$ **6**

Example 3 Write $3(k^3 + 2k^2) - k^4 - 2k^3$ as a polynomial in standard form. $\mathbf{-k^4 + k^3 + 6k^2}$

Teaching Tip

Before discussing Example 3, review like and unlike terms.

Common Error

In Example 3, watch for students who write polynomials in the order of the coefficients of the terms rather than the order of the degree of each term.

Degree The **degree of a term** is the sum of the exponents of its variables. The **degree of a polynomial** is the greatest degree of its terms. The degree of a nonzero constant is 0. The constant 0 has no degree.

Watch *Out*

Don't confuse the number of terms in a polynomial with the degree of the polynomial. For example, $x^2 + 5x + 4$ has 3 terms, and its degree is 2.

Example 2 *Finding the Degree of a Polynomial*

Find the degree of the polynomial.

a. Polynomial: $5x^3 + 8x - 9$

Degree of term: 3 1 0

The greatest degree of the terms is 3. So, the degree of $5x^3 + 8x - 9$ is 3.

b. Polynomial: $p - p^3q^2 + q^4$

Degree of term: 1 $3 + 2 = 5$ 4

The greatest degree of the terms is 5. So, the degree of $p - p^3q^2 + q^4$ is 5.

Checkpoint

Find the degree of the polynomial.

4. $8x^4 - x + 1$ **4**

5. $2 + 6z^3 - 5z$ **3**

6. $-y^4 + y^5 - 8$ **5**

7. $a^2 - b^3$ **3**

8. $7cd + 4c^2d^2$ **4**

9. $mn^3 - 3n^4$ **4**

Standard Form To simplify a polynomial, combine like terms. Remember that like terms are terms with identical variable parts, such as $8ab^2$ and $3ab^2$. A polynomial is written in **standard form** if it is simplified and the terms are arranged so the degree of each term decreases or stays the same from left to right.

Reading *Algebra*

In Example 3, the term $-m^2$ is equivalent to $-1m^2$. It is *not* equivalent to $(-m)^2$.

Example 3 *Writing a Polynomial in Standard Form*

Write $-m^2 + 5 + 2(4m + m^2)$ as a polynomial in standard form.

$-m^2 + 5 + 2(4m + m^2)$

$= -m^2 + 5 + 8m + 2m^2$ **Distributive property**

$= -1m^2 + 5 + 8m + 2m^2$ **Write $-m^2$ as $-1m^2$.**

$= \mathbf{-1m^2 + 2m^2} + 5 + 8m$ **Group like terms.**

$= m^2 + 5 + 8m$ **Combine like terms.**

$= m^2 + 8m + 5$ **Standard form**

Checkpoint

Write the expression as a polynomial in standard form.

10. $3x - 4x^2 + 8$ $\mathbf{-4x^2 + 3x + 8}$

11. $7t^3 + 2 + t^3 - 5$ $\mathbf{8t^3 - 3}$

12. $9y^2 + 8y^4 - y^2$ $\mathbf{8y^4 + 8y^2}$

13. $4a - 5(a^3 + a) - 3$ $\mathbf{-5a^3 - a - 3}$

14. $3(4b + b^2) - b^2$ $\mathbf{2b^2 + 12b}$

15. $c^2 + 8c^3 - 2(c - 5)$ $\mathbf{8c^3 + c^2 - 2c + 10}$

Example 4 *Evaluating a Polynomial*

Find the height of the volleyball 1 second after it is hit, as described on page 651.

Solution

Evaluate the polynomial $-4.9t^2 + 8.1t + 1.2$ when $t = 1$.

$-4.9t^2 + 8.1t + 1.2 = -4.9(1)^2 + 8.1(1) + 1.2$	**Substitute 1 for t.**
$= -4.9(1) + 8.1(1) + 1.2$	**Evaluate power.**
$= -4.9 + 8.1 + 1.2$	**Multiply.**
$= 4.4$	**Add.**

Answer The volleyball's height after 1 second is 4.4 meters.

 ***Checkpoint***

Evaluate the polynomial when $x = 3$ and $y = -2$.

16. $x^2 - 4x + 4$ **1** **17.** $2y^2 + 5y - 1$ **−3** **18.** $x + 3y$ **−3**

19. $xy - 7x - 2$ **−29** **20.** $-2x^2 + y^3 + 1$ **−25** **21.** $x^2y^2 + xy$ **30**

12.1 Exercises

More Practice, p. 814

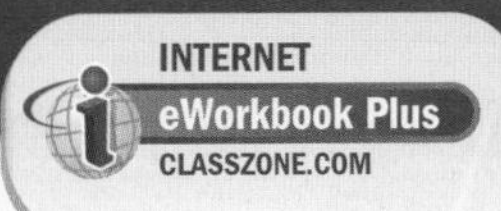

Guided Practice

Vocabulary Check

1. Copy and complete: The polynomial $4x^2 + 3x + 5$ has a(n) __?__ of 2. **degree**

2. Give an example of a polynomial of degree 3 that is written in standard form. ***Sample answer:*** $7x^2y + 4x - 6$

Skill Check

Tell whether the expression is a polynomial. If it is a polynomial, list its terms and classify it.

3. $5x^3$ **yes; $5x^3$; monomial** **4.** $2a + 9$ **yes; $2a$ and 9; binomial** **5.** $p^3 + p^2 + 3p^{-1}$ **no**

Find the degree of the polynomial.

6. $-6x^2 + x - 5$ **2** **7.** $10 - y$ **1** **8.** $b^3 - 7b^2 + b$ **3**

Write the expression as a polynomial in standard form.

9. $2x + 7 + 5 + 4x$ **$6x + 12$** **10.** $4g^2 + 9 - g^2 + 3g$ **$3g^2 + 3g + 9$** **11.** $3z + 8 + 6z - z^2 + z$ **$-z^2 + 10z + 8$**

12. $a^2 - 1 - 3(6a + 7)$ **$a^2 - 18a - 22$** **13.** $5(x^2 + 2x) - 3x^2$ **$2x^2 + 10x$** **14.** $11y + 2(7 - 3y^2) + 9$ **$-6y^2 + 11y + 23$**

Evaluate the polynomial when $x = 4$.

15. $5x - 3$ **17** **16.** $2x^2 + x - 7$ **29** **17.** $x^3 + x^2 - 6x - 8$ **48**

18. Error Analysis Your friend says that the degree of the polynomial $x^2 + xy^2$ is 2. Describe and correct your friend's error.

18. ***Sample answer:*** **The degree of the term xy^2 is $1 + 2 = 3$ because the exponent on x is 1. Therefore the degree of the polynomial is 3, not 2.**

Extra Examples

Example 4 Evaluate the polynomial $-4.9t^2 + 8.1t + 1.2$ when $t = 1.5$ to find the height in meters of a volleyball 1.5 seconds after it is hit. **2.325 m**

NOTETAKING

Have students draw a large 3 by 3 grid with the columns labeled "Degree 1," "Degree 2," and "Degree 3" and the rows labeled "1 Term," "2 Terms," and "3 Terms." Then ask them to write an expression in each cell of the grid that has the degree and number of terms indicated.

DIFFERENTIATING INSTRUCTION

Alternative Teaching Strategy
Have pairs of students work together to write four different polynomial expressions that simplify to $m^2 + 8m - 5$ when written in standard form.

CONCEPT CHECK

How do you write a polynomial in standard form? **First simplify the polynomial as much as possible, and then arrange the terms so the degree of each term decreases or stays the same from left to right.**

DAILY PUZZLER

A skydiver's altitude in feet after falling from a plane for t seconds can be found using the polynomial $-16t^2 + 12{,}000$. To the nearest tenth of a second, how long does it take the skydiver to reach an altitude of 8000 feet? **15.8 sec**

3 APPLY

ASSIGNMENT GUIDE

Basic Course

Day 1: EP p. 804 Exs. 9-12, 24-27; pp. 654-655 Exs. 19-27, 33-36, 39-42, 47-58, 60, 64-72

Average Course

Day 1: pp. 654-655 Exs. 22-32, 36-49, 53-62, 64-72

Advanced Course

Day 1: pp. 654-655 Exs. 22-32, 37-49, 53-65*, 68-72

Block

pp. 654-655 Exs. 22-32, 36-49, 53-62, 64-72 (with 12.2)

EXTRA PRACTICE

- Student Edition, p. 814
- Chapter 12 Resource Book, pp. 7-9
- Test and Practice Generator

TRANSPARENCY

Even-numbered answers are available on transparencies.

HOMEWORK CHECK

When you review students' homework for this lesson, go over the following exercises to check understanding of key concepts.

Basic: 19, 25, 27, 33, 39
Average: 22, 27, 31, 37, 39
Advanced: 24, 30, 37, 39, 42

TEACHING TIP

In Exercises 48 and 49, make sure students understand why there are two types of tick marks.

Practice and Problem Solving

Homework *Help*

Example	Exercises
1	19-24
2	25-30, 32
3	31, 33-38, 47-49
4	39-46

Online Resources
CLASSZONE.COM
- More Examples
- eTutorial Plus

31. No. *Sample answer:* In standard form, the degree of each term decreases or stays the same from left to right. The degree of the term $5x^2y$ is 3, so the polynomial in standard form is $5x^2y + 3x^2 + 7$.

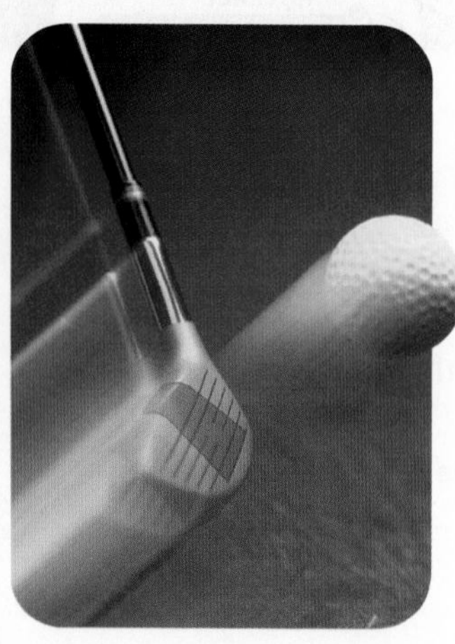

Tell whether the expression is a polynomial. If it is a polynomial, list its terms and classify it.

A **19.** $8a^2$ yes; $8a^2$; monomial
20. $3b^{-1} + 6b$ no
21. $3c^3 - 2c^2 - 7$ yes; $3c^3$, $-2c^2$, and -7; trinomial
22. $\frac{x}{y} + 29$ no
23. $\frac{x^2+2}{x}$ no
24. $\frac{x^2}{7} - 4x - 3$ yes; $\frac{x^2}{7}$, $-4x$, and -3; trinomial

Find the degree of the polynomial.

25. $4m^2 + 5m - 2$ 2
26. 7 0
27. $-2x^3 - 6x^2 + 3x - 4$ 3
28. $x^2 + 3x^4 - 7$ 4
29. $-3n + 5$ 1
30. $24a^3 + 24a^5$ 5

31. *Writing* Is the polynomial $3x^2 + 5x^2y + 7$ written in standard form? Explain your reasoning.

32. Critical Thinking Give an example of a term that has degree 6 but that contains no variable with an exponent greater than 2. Explain your answer.
Sample answer: $6x^2y^2z^2$; the degree is the sum of the exponents: $2 + 2 + 2 = 6$.

Write the expression as a polynomial in standard form.

33. $9x + 4 - 2 - 3x$ $6x + 2$
34. $-7x^2 - 3 - 3x^2$ $-10x^2 - 3$
35. $8 + 5y + 5 - y - 6$ $4y + 7$
36. $-3y^2 - y - 8(2y^2 + 7)$ $-19y^2 - y - 56$
37. $10z^2 + 3(z^2 - 6z) - 4z$ $13z^2 - 22z$
38. $2z^2 + 4(1 - 5z) + 11$ $2z^2 - 20z + 15$

39. Golf The height (in feet) of a golf ball t seconds after it is hit is given by the polynomial $-16t^2 + 100t$. What is the height of the golf ball 3 seconds after it is hit? 5 seconds after it is hit? 156 ft; 100 ft

Evaluate the polynomial when $a = 2$.

40. $5a^2 + 3a + 1$ 27
41. $a^4 + 7a^2$ 44
42. $a^2 - 2a^2 - 6$ -10
43. $-9a^2 + a^2 - 20$ -52
44. $3a^3 - 10a + 1$ 5
45. $-a^2 + 2a + 7$ 7

46. Alternative-Fueled Vehicles For the period 1993–2001, the number (in thousands) of alternative-fueled vehicles in the United States can be approximated by the polynomial $2.1t^2 + 4.6t + 320$, where t is the number of years since 1993.

a. What is the degree of the polynomial? 2

b. Evaluate the polynomial when $t = 0$ to find the approximate number (in thousands) of alternative-fueled vehicles in 1993. about 320 thousand vehicles

c. Evaluate the polynomial when $t = 8$ to find the approximate number (in thousands) of alternative-fueled vehicles in 2001. about 491 thousand vehicles

Write a polynomial expression for the perimeter of the figure. Give your answer in standard form.

B **47.**
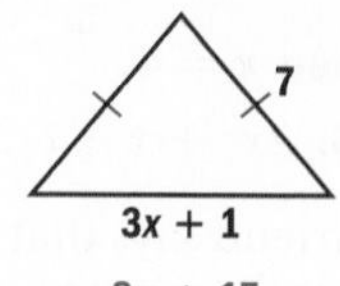

$3x + 15$

48.
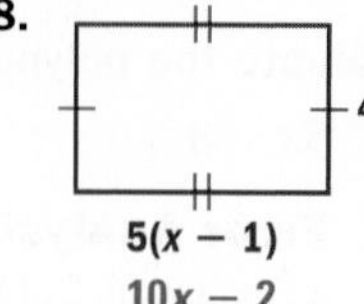

$10x - 2$

49.
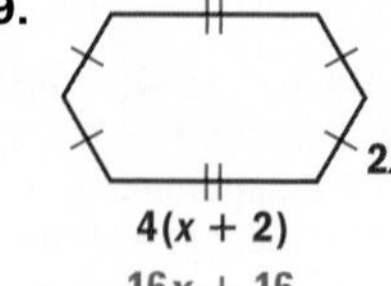

$16x + 16$

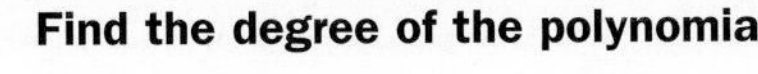

Find the degree of the polynomial.

50. $a + b + c + d$ 1 **51.** $25abc$ 3 **52.** $ab + cd + ac$ 2

53. $ab + a^2b^2$ 4 **54.** $-a^2b^3c^2 + 5$ 7 **55.** $a^3 - a^2b^2 + b^2$ 4

Evaluate the polynomial when $x = -1$ and $y = 2$.

56. $4x^2 + 3y^3$ 28 **57.** $x^4 - x^2y$ −1 **58.** $-2x^2 + x^2y^3$ 6

59. Extended Problem Solving The polynomials below give the approximate braking distance (in feet) needed to stop a car or train. In each polynomial, v is the vehicle's speed in miles per hour and r is the reaction time (in seconds) of the car's driver or the train's engineer. For the questions below, use $r = 0.5$ second.

Car: $1.47vr + 0.05v^2$ **Train**: $1.47vr + 0.5v^2$

a. Calculate What is the braking distance (to the nearest foot) of a car traveling 30 miles per hour? 55 miles per hour? 67 ft; 192 ft

b. Calculate What is the braking distance (to the nearest foot) of a train traveling 80 miles per hour? 125 miles per hour? 3259 ft; 7904 ft

c. Compare How much greater is the braking distance of a train than the braking distance of a car if both vehicles are traveling at 55 miles per hour? about 1361 ft

In the **Real World**

Vehicles A typical midsize car weighs about 3000 pounds. A train (consisting of a locomotive and 3 boxcars) weighs about 385,000 pounds. About how many times greater is the weight of the train than the weight of the car? **about 128 times**

C **Find the degree of the polynomial. Write your answer in terms of n.**

60. $x^n + x^{n-1} + x^{n-2}$ n **61.** $x^ny^4 + 5x^3y^n$ $n + 4$ **62.** $6x^ny^n + x^2y^{2n}$ $2n + 2$

63. Challenge If possible, give an example of the polynomial described. If it is not possible to give an example, explain why not.

a. A simplified binomial of degree 0 See margin.

b. A simplified trinomial of degree 1 *Sample answer:* $7x - 3y + 4$

63a. Not possible. ***Sample answer:*** **Any term of degree 0 must be a constant. In a simplified binomial, there can be only one constant term, so there must also be a variable term, which means that the degree of a simplified binomial must be at least 1.**

Mixed Review

State the opposite of the number. *(Lesson 1.4)*

64. −12 12 **65.** 27 −27 **66.** 61 −61 **67.** −135 135

Find the area of the parallelogram or trapezoid. *(Lesson 10.3)*

68.

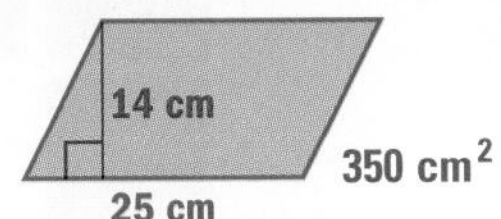

69.

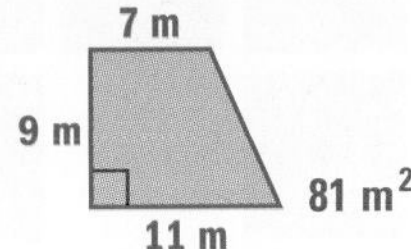

70. Each letter in the word POLYNOMIAL is written on a separate card and placed in a stack. You randomly select a card from the stack. Then you randomly select a second card without putting the first card back. Find the probability of selecting O, then M. *(Lesson 11.9)* $\frac{1}{45}$

Standardized Test Practice

71. Multiple Choice Which expression is *not* a polynomial? B

A. $-12b$ **B.** $x^2 + x^{-1}$ **C.** $y^2 - 2y + 7$ **D.** -50

72. Multiple Choice What is the degree of $x^2 - x^3 + 4$? H

F. 1 **G.** 2 **H.** 3 **I.** 4

4 ASSESS

Assessment Resources

For more assessment resources, see:

- Assessment Book
- Test and Practice Generator

Mini-Quiz

Find the degree of the polynomial.

1. $8 + 4m^2 - m^3$ **3**

2. $10a^3b^4 - 6ab^5$ **7**

Write the expression as a polynomial in standard form.

3. $7x + 2 - 3x - 4$ $\mathbf{4x - 2}$

4. $y(y + y^3) - y^2 + 6$ $\mathbf{y^4 + 6}$

5. Challenge If possible, give an example of the polynomial described. If it is not possible to give an example, explain why not.

a. A simplified monomial of degree 0, containing a variable **Not possible.** ***Sample answer:*** **Any term containing a variable must have at least degree 1.**

b. A simplified trinomial of degree 2 that contains four variables ***Sample answer:*** $\mathbf{ab + c + d}$

5 FOLLOW-UP

Diagnosis/Remediation

- Study Guide in Chapter 12 Resource Book, pp. 10–11
- eTutorial Plus Online
- Extra Practice, p. 814
- Lesson Practice in Chapter 12 Resource Book, pp. 7–9

English Learner Support

- Spanish Study Guide
- Multi-Language Visual Glossary
- Chapter Audio Summaries CDs

Challenge

- Challenge Practice in Chapter 12 Resource Book, p. 12
- Teacher's Edition, p. 648F

1 PLAN

INVESTIGATE THE CONCEPT

- Students model polynomial addition using algebra tiles.
- This activity leads into adding and subtracting polynomials in Lesson 12.2.

MATERIALS

Each student will need algebra tiles. See the Activity Support Masters in the *Chapter 12 Resource Book*. A support transparency is also available.

RECOMMENDED TIME

Work activity: 10 min
Discuss results: 5 min

GROUPING

Students should work individually.

2 TEACH

DISCUSSION

Ask students: "Are the polynomials in standard form? How do you know?" **Yes; the degree of each term decreases from left to right.**

3 CLOSE

KEY DISCOVERY

Polynomials can be added by combining like terms.

ASSESSMENT

1. What is a *zero pair*? **a tile and its opposite**
2. Why are there no $-x^2$ tiles in this activity? **There are no $-x^2$ terms in the polynomials.**

3. See Additional Answers beginning on page AA1.

Concept *Activity*

12.2 Modeling Polynomial Addition

Goal
Model polynomial addition using algebra tiles.

Materials
- algebra tiles

You can use algebra tiles to model polynomials.

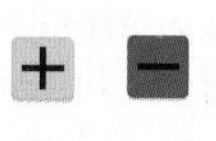

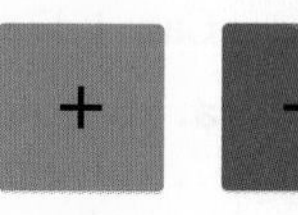

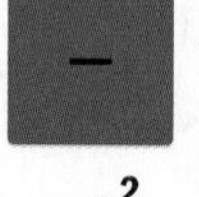

Each of these x-by-x square tiles has an area of x^2 square units.

Investigate

Find the sum of $2x^2 + 3x - 4$ and $x^2 + 2x + 5$ using algebra tiles.

1 Use algebra tiles to model $2x^2 + 3x - 4$ and $x^2 + 2x + 5$.

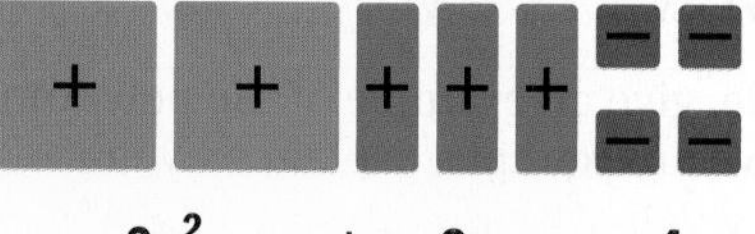

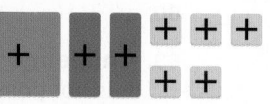

2 To add the polynomials, combine like terms. Group the x^2-tiles, the x-tiles, and the 1-tiles.

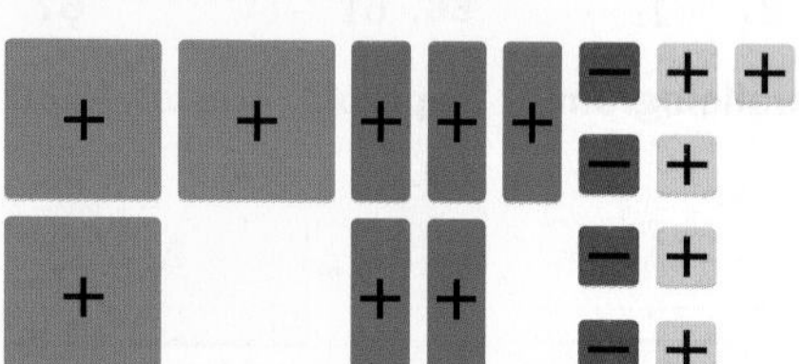

3 A tile and its opposite form a *zero pair*. Remove the zero pairs. The sum is $3x^2 + 5x + 1$.

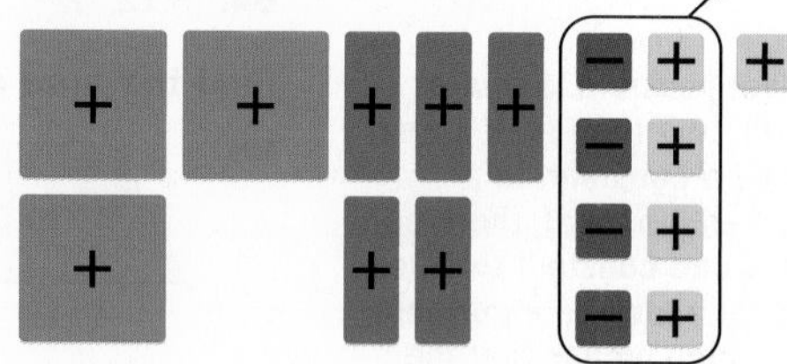

Draw Conclusions

Use algebra tiles to find the sum.

1. $(x^2 + 5x + 2) + (3x^2 + x + 2)$ **$4x^2 + 6x + 4$**
2. $(x^2 - x + 5) + (-3x^2 + x + 5)$ **$-2x^2 + 10$**
3. **Critical Thinking** You can also use algebra tiles to model polynomial subtraction. Use algebra tiles to find the difference of $2x^2 + 5x + 2$ and $x^2 + 3x + 1$. Include drawings of the tiles to illustrate your steps. **See margin.**

NCTM CURRICULUM STANDARDS
Standard 10: Create representations to communicate mathematical ideas; Use representations to communicate mathematical ideas

LESSON

12.2 Adding *and* Subtracting Polynomials

Review Vocabulary
opposite, p. 23
like terms, p. 78

BEFORE	*Now*	WHY?
You classified and simplified polynomials.	You'll add and subtract polynomials.	So you can compare spending on newspaper ads, as in Ex. 39.

Money You are saving for a trip to Costa Rica. You deposit \$500 into a bank account that earns interest compounded annually. One year later, you deposit an additional \$600 into the account. Let r be the annual interest rate. What is the balance A of the account 2 years after the initial deposit? In Example 2, you will see how to solve this problem by adding polynomials.

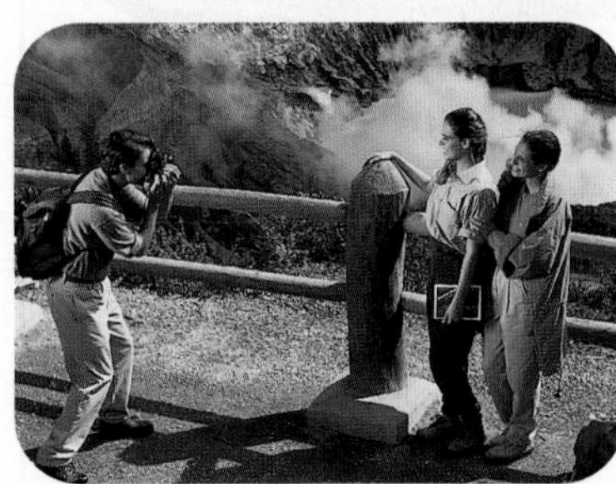

You add polynomials by combining like terms. One way to add polynomials is to align like terms in columns. If one of the polynomials is missing a term, you can either leave a space in that term's column, or write the term with a coefficient of 0.

Example 1 *Adding Polynomials Vertically*

Find the sum.

a. $(-8x^3 + 4x^2 + x + 1) + (3x^3 - 2x^2 + 7)$

b. $(2x^4 + 6x^3 - 5x^2 + x - 7) + (x^3 - 3x^2 + 2x + 1)$

Solution

a.
$$\begin{array}{r} -8x^3 + 4x^2 + x + 1 \\ +\ \ 3x^3 - 2x^2 \qquad + 7 \\ \hline -5x^3 + 2x^2 + x + 8 \end{array}$$
Arrange like terms in columns.
Add like terms.

b.
$$\begin{array}{r} 2x^4 + 6x^3 - 5x^2 + x - 7 \\ + \qquad x^3 - 3x^2 + 2x + 1 \\ \hline 2x^4 + 7x^3 - 8x^2 + 3x - 6 \end{array}$$
Arrange like terms in columns.
Add like terms.

 *Checkpoint*

Find the sum using a vertical format.

1. $(5p^2 + 3p - 7) + (2p^2 - 8p + 4)$ $7p^2 - 5p - 3$
2. $(-4z + 7) + (3z^2 - 3z - 8)$ $3z^2 - 7z - 1$
3. $(4x^2 - 6x + 3) + (8x + 1)$
4. $(-w^3 + w + 2) + (w^2 - 5)$

3. $4x^2 + 2x + 4$
4. $-w^3 + w^2 + w - 3$

NCTM CURRICULUM STANDARDS
Standard 2: Understand patterns; Analyze situations using algebraic symbols
Standard 6: Solve problems in math and other contexts

1 PLAN

Skill Check

Simplify the expression.

1. $4x + (-6x)$ **$-2x$**
2. $-8y^2 + 8y^2$ **0**
3. $a^3 + (-7a^3)$ **$-6a^3$**
4. $2c + 8c$ **$10c$**

Lesson Objective

Add and subtract polynomials.

Pacing

Suggested Number of Days
Basic Course: 1 day
Average Course: 1 day
Advanced Course: 1 day
Block: 0.5 block with 12.1

Teaching Resources

For a complete list of Teaching Resources, see page 648B.

 **Transparency**

Warm-Up Exercises for this lesson are available on a transparency.

2 TEACH

Motivating the Lesson

Have students explain the meaning of the banking terms *interest*, *compounded*, *annual*, and *deposit*.

TIPS *for* NEW TEACHERS

When students add or subtract polynomials with multiple terms, point out that they should not expect the result to be an expression that can be simplified to a single term. Stress that their answers will usually include two or more unlike terms. See Tips for New Teachers in the *Chapter 12 Resource Book*.

Extra Examples

Example 1 Find the sum.

a. $(3y^3 + 8y - 12) + (y^3 - 6y^2 + 3y - 4)$ **$4y^3 - 6y^2 + 11y - 16$**

b. $(9b^4 - b^3 + 7b^2 - 17) + (12b^3 - 4b^2 + 3b - 1)$ **$9b^4 + 11b^3 + 3b^2 + 3b - 18$**

Example 2 The number of passengers waiting in Terminal A of an airport h hours after the first scheduled flight of the day is given by the polynomial $350 + 80h$. The number of passengers waiting in Terminal B is given by the polynomial $220 + 75h$.

a. Find the total number of passengers T waiting in both terminals after h hours. **$T = 570 + 155h$**

b. Find the total number of passengers waiting in both terminals 4 hours after the first scheduled flight of the day. **1190 passengers**

Example 3 Find the difference $(5y^2 - 9y - 3) - (y^2 - 2y + 6)$. **$4y^2 - 7y - 9$**

TEACHING TIP

In Example 3, show students how to write the opposite of every term in a polynomial and how to add the resulting polynomials.

In the **Real World**

Money The unit of currency in Costa Rica is the *colon*. One dollar is worth about 385 *colones*. What is the approximate value in dollars of 50,000 colones? **about \$130**

Example 2 *Adding Polynomials Horizontally*

For the savings account described on page 657, the balance from the first deposit is given by the polynomial $500 + 1000r + 500r^2$. After 1 year, the balance from the second deposit is given by $600 + 600r$. In both polynomials, r is expressed as a decimal.

a. Find the balance A in terms of r after 2 years.

b. Find the balance after 2 years when $r = 0.02$.

Solution

a. To find the total balance A, add the balances from each deposit.

$A = (500 + 1000r + 500r^2) + (600 + 600r)$	**Add balances.**
$= 500 + 600 + 1000r + 600r + 500r^2$	**Group like terms.**
$= 1100 + 1600r + 500r^2$	**Combine like terms.**

Answer After 2 years, the balance is $1100 + 1600r + 500r^2$.

b. Evaluate the polynomial when $r = 0.02$.

$1100 + 1600r + 500r^2$	**Write polynomial.**
$= 1100 + 1600(0.02) + 500(0.02)^2$	**Substitute 0.02 for *r*.**
$= 1100 + 1600(0.02) + 500(0.0004)$	**Evaluate power.**
$= 1100 + 32 + 0.2$	**Multiply.**
$= 1132.2$	**Add.**

Answer The balance after 2 years when $r = 0.02$ is \$1132.20.

Checkpoint

Find the sum using a horizontal format.

5. $(2x^2 + x + 10) + (3x^2 - 7x - 2)$ **$5x^2 - 6x + 8$**

6. $(-5y^3 + 6y^2 - 2y) + (2y^3 - y)$ **$-3y^3 + 6y^2 - 3y$**

Subtracting Polynomials You can subtract a polynomial by adding its opposite. To find the opposite of a polynomial, multiply each of its terms by -1. You can subtract polynomials vertically or horizontally.

Example 3 *Subtracting Polynomials Vertically*

Find the difference $(6x^2 + 4x - 7) - (2x^2 - x + 8)$.

$$\begin{array}{r} 6x^2 + 4x - 7 \\ \underline{-\,(2x^2 - x + 8)} \end{array}$$

$$\begin{array}{r} 6x^2 + 4x - 7 \\ \underline{+\,(-2x^2 + x - 8)} \\ 4x^2 + 5x - 15 \end{array}$$

Write opposite.
Add like terms.

Checkpoint

Find the difference using a vertical format.

7. $(6x^2 + 4x + 7) - (5x^2 + x - 9)$ **$x^2 + 3x + 16$**

8. $(14b^2 - 12b) - (9b^2 - 5b + 1)$ **$5b^2 - 7b - 1$**

Example 4 *Subtracting Polynomials Horizontally*

Find the difference $(x^2 + 4x - 9) - (4x^2 - 5x + 11)$.

$(x^2 + 4x - 9) - (4x^2 - 5x + 11)$	**Write difference.**
$= x^2 + 4x - 9 + (-4x^2 + 5x - 11)$	**Write opposite of second polynomial.**
$= x^2 - 4x^2 + 4x + 5x - 9 - 11$	**Group like terms.**
$= -3x^2 + 9x - 20$	**Combine like terms.**

Checkpoint

Find the difference using a horizontal format.

9. $(10y^2 - y + 6) - (7y^2 + 3y - 5)$ **$3y^2 - 4y + 11$**

10. $(c^2 + 4c - 13) - (8c^2 - 2c + 7)$ **$-7c^2 + 6c - 20$**

11. $(3t^3 + 7t) - (3t^3 + 2t^2 - t + 4)$ **$-2t^2 + 8t - 4$**

12. $(5n^3 - n + 2) - (n^3 - 6n^2 - 9)$ **$4n^3 + 6n^2 - n + 11$**

12.2 Exercises

More Practice, p. 814

Guided Practice

Vocabulary Check

1. Copy and complete: To add polynomials, you combine _?_. **like terms**

2. Finding the difference of $x^2 - 4x + 1$ and $x^2 - x + 3$ is the same as finding the sum of what two polynomials? **$x^2 - 4x + 1$ and $-x^2 + x - 3$**

Skill Check **Find the sum using a vertical format.**

3. $(x + 4) + (2x + 7)$ **$3x + 11$**

4. $(z^2 + 3z + 9) + (-2z^2 + 5)$ **$-z^2 + 3z + 14$**

Find the sum using a horizontal format.

5. $(3a^2 + 1) + (a^2 - 5)$ **$4a^2 - 4$**

6. $(9a - 7) + (a^2 - 2a + 8)$ **$a^2 + 7a + 1$**

Find the difference using a vertical format.

7. $(10z - 1) - (z + 4)$ **$9z - 5$**

8. $(x^2 + 7x - 3) - (x^2 + 1)$ **$7x - 4$**

Find the difference using a horizontal format.

9. $(b^2 + 9) - (3b^2 + b + 2)$ **$-2b^2 - b + 7$**

10. $(5b^2 + 6b + 7) - (b^2 + 4b - 6)$ **$4b^2 + 2b + 13$**

11. **Error Analysis** Describe and correct the error in finding the difference of $x^2 + 3x - 1$ and $x^2 + x + 2$.

$$
\begin{aligned}
(x^2 + 3x - 1) - (x^2 + x + 2) &= x^2 + 3x - 1 - x^2 + x + 2 \\
&= x^2 - x^2 + 3x + x - 1 + 2 \\
&= 4x + 1
\end{aligned}
$$

11. *Sample answer:* When subtracting the second polynomial, the opposite should have been found for each term, not just the first term. So, $(x^2 + 3x - 1) - (x^2 + x + 2) = x^2 + 3x - 1 - x^2 - x - 2 = x^2 - x^2 + 3x - x - 1 - 2 = 2x - 3$.

Extra Examples

Example 4 Find the difference $(7g^2 - 2g - 5) - (g^2 - 6g + 1)$. **$6g^2 + 4g - 6$**

Common Error

In Example 4, be sure students understand that they must write the opposite of every term in the subtracted polynomial and not just the opposite of the first term.

Visualize

Suggest students use colored pencils or highlighters to "color code" the like terms in the polynomials they are adding or subtracting. This technique will help students visually identify like terms and separate this identification stage from the computation stage of their work.

Differentiating Instruction

Advanced Students Challenge students to write two polynomials whose difference is a polynomial with four unlike terms, each with a coefficient of 4. Additionally, the two polynomials should not share or repeat any coefficients. ***Sample answer:*** **$(9x^4 + 8x^3 + 7x^2 + 6x) - (5x^4 + 4x^3 + 3x^2 + 2x)$**

Concept Check

How do you add two polynomials? ***Sample answer:*** **Write the two polynomials horizontally, group the like terms, and then combine the like terms.**

Daily Puzzler

Write two trinomials whose sum is a monomial. ***Sample answer:*** **$3x^2 + x + 7, -3x^2 + 2x - 7$**

3 APPLY

ASSIGNMENT GUIDE

Basic Course

Day 1: pp. 660–661 Exs. 12–17, 20–25, 29–34, 41–52

Average Course

Day 1: pp. 660–661 Exs. 14–19, 22–28, 31–39, 41–52

Advanced Course

Day 1: pp. 660–661 Exs. 16–19, 24–30, 35–42*, 47–52

Block

pp. 660–661 Exs. 14–19, 22–28, 31–39, 41–52 (with 12.1)

EXTRA PRACTICE

- Student Edition, p. 814
- Chapter 12 Resource Book, pp. 17–19
- Test and Practice Generator

TRANSPARENCY

Even-numbered answers are available on transparencies.

HOMEWORK CHECK

When you review students' homework for this lesson, go over the following exercises to check understanding of key concepts.

Basic: 12, 20, 23, 29, 33
Average: 16, 24, 28, 29, 33
Advanced: 18, 25, 28, 30, 35

COMMON ERROR

In Exercises 14, 17, 20, 24, and 25, caution students about examining the exponents carefully to be sure they are not combining unlike terms.

28d.

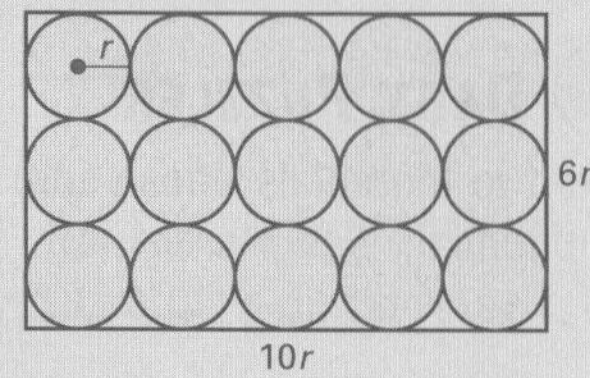

Practice and Problem Solving

Homework Help

Example	Exercises
1	12–19, 29–32
2	12–19, 29–32, 39
3	20–27, 28, 33–36
4	20–27, 28, 33–36

Online Resources CLASSZONE.COM
- More Examples
- eTutorial Plus

Find the sum.

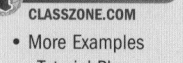

A **12.** $(x^2 + x + 15) + (x^2 + x + 6)$ **$2x^2 + 2x + 21$**

13. $(-x^2 - 9x) + (x^2 + 3x - 8)$ **$-6x - 8$**

14. $(y^2 - 2y + 1) + (4y^3 - y - 5)$ **$4y^3 + y^2 - 3y - 4$**

15. $(y^4 - 5y^2) + (y^4 + 2y^2 - 9)$ **$2y^4 - 3y^2 - 9$**

16. $(-12z^2 - z + 3) + (2z^2 + 6z - 1)$ **$-10z^2 + 5z + 2$**

17. $(-4z^3 + 6z - 8) + (z^2 - 3z + 5)$ **$-4z^3 + z^2 + 3z - 3$**

18. $(13m^3 + 12m) + (4m^2 - 8m + 5)$ **$13m^3 + 4m^2 + 4m + 5$**

19. $(3m^2 + 1) + (m^2 - 4m)$ **$4m^2 - 4m + 1$**

Find the difference.

20. $(5a + 2) - (3a^2 + 1)$ **$-3a^2 + 5a + 1$**

21. $(8a^2 + 7a + 2) - (5a^2 + 4)$ **$3a^2 + 7a - 2$**

22. $(4b^2 + 3b + 5) - (6b^2 + 7)$ **$-2b^2 + 3b - 2$**

23. $(b^3 - 5b^2 + b) - (-2b^3 - b^2 - b)$ **$3b^3 - 4b^2 + 2b$**

24. $(4c^3 - 7c - 2) - (c^2 + 6c - 5)$ **$4c^3 - c^2 - 13c + 3$**

25. $(c^2 - c + 6) - (-3c^3 + c - 6)$ **$3c^3 + c^2 - 2c + 12$**

26. $(8d^4 + 5) - (7d^4 - 1)$ **$d^4 + 6$**

27. $(d^2 + 5d + 2) - (3d^2 + d + 2)$ **$-2d^2 + 4d$**

28. Extended Problem Solving You want to cut 12 circles from a rectangular sheet of leather that measures $6r$ inches by $10r$ inches. Each circle has a radius of r inches.

a. Write a polynomial expression for the area of the rectangular sheet. **$60r^2$**

b. Analyze Write a polynomial expression for the combined area of the 12 circles. Use 3.14 for π. **$37.68r^2$**

c. Apply What area of the rectangular sheet is unused? **$22.32r^2$**

d. Visual Thinking Could you cut *more* than 12 circles from the rectangular sheet? Draw a diagram and explain your answer. **See margin.**

A machine cuts circles of leather.

28d. Yes; see margin for art. *Sample answer:* You could cut 15 circles. Since the diameter of each circle is $2r$, you can fit $10r \div 2r = 5$ circles across on a sheet and $6r \div 2r = 3$ circles top to bottom as shown in the diagram.

38. Not necessarily. *Sample answer:* The polynomials $x^2 + 4x - 6$ and $x^2 + x + 11$ have degree 2 and their sum, $2x^2 + 5x + 5$, has degree 2, but the polynomials $2x^2 + 14x + 9$ and $-2x^2 - 14x + 3$ have degree 2 while their sum, 12, has degree 0.

Find the sum or difference.

B **29.** $(13x - 4y) + (2x + 5y)$ **$15x + y$**

30. $(-2r + 3s + 17t) + (15r - 7t)$ **$13r + 3s + 10t$**

31. $(3cd + 2) + (-9cd - 4)$ **$-6cd - 2$**

32. $(8a^2b - 7a) + (2a^2b - 9b)$ **$10a^2b - 7a - 9b$**

33. $(m - 8n) - (-3m + 9n)$ **$4m - 17n$**

34. $(6a + 7b) - (11a + 5b + 14c)$ **$-5a + 2b - 14c$**

35. $(2rs + 4r - 3s) - (13rs + 2r)$ **$-11rs + 2r - 3s$**

36. $(2x^2 + 7y^2) - (x^2 - y^2 - 18)$ **$x^2 + 8y^2 + 18$**

37. Critical Thinking What polynomial do you add to $x^2 + 5x + 1$ to get a sum of $4x^2 - 3$? **$3x^2 - 5x - 4$**

38. ***Writing*** Suppose two polynomials have the same degree. Will their sum have this degree also? Give an example to support your answer.

C **39. Newspaper Advertising** The polynomials below approximate the amounts (in millions of dollars) spent on advertising in national and local newspapers for each year during the period 1990–2000. In each polynomial, x represents the number of years since 1990.

National: $59x^2 - 262x + 3888$

Local: $-33x^3 + 611x^2 - 1433x + 28{,}060$

Write a polynomial that gives the *combined* amount spent each year on national and local newspaper advertising. **$-33x^3 + 670x^2 - 1695x + 31{,}948$**

40. Challenge The solid shown is composed of two cylinders. Write a polynomial expression for the entire surface area of the solid. Give your answer in standard form. $18\pi r^2 + 44\pi r$

Mixed Review

Use the distributive property to write an equivalent variable expression. *(Lesson 2.2)*

41. $7(3 + a)$ $21 + 7a$ **42.** $-3(z - 14)$ $-3z + 42$ **43.** $(-3t + 15)4$ $-12t + 60$ **44.** $(8 - w)(-2)$ $-16 + 2w$

Find the product. Write your answer using exponents. *(Lesson 4.5)*

45. $3^4 \cdot 3^2$ 3^6 **46.** $11^2 \cdot 11^5$ 11^7 **47.** $m^4 \cdot m^9$ m^{13} **48.** $3b^6 \cdot 5b^2$ $15b^8$

Tell whether the expression is a polynomial. *(Lesson 12.1)*

49. $y^5 - y^3 + y - 8$ yes **50.** $4y^{-2} + 2y^{-1} - 1$ no

Standardized Test Practice

51. Multiple Choice What is the sum of $(4x^2 + 5x - 8)$ and $(3x^2 - 6x + 1)$? B

A. $7x^2 + x - 7$ **B.** $7x^2 - x - 7$ **C.** $7x^2 + x + 7$ **D.** $7x^2 - x + 7$

52. Multiple Choice Which expression is equivalent to $3x^2 + 4x - 1$? H

F. $(x^2 + 3x - 1) - (2x^2 + x)$ **G.** $(3x^2 - 8) + (4x^2 + 7)$

H. $(2x^2 + 4x + 1) - (-x^2 + 2)$ **I.** $(2x^2 + 4x + 1) + (-x^2 + 2)$

Puzzling Polynomials

Four of the sums below equal four of the differences. Match the sums and the differences that are equal. Then unscramble the corresponding letters to answer the riddle. Do not use the letters of sums or differences without a match. AE, RY, BO, KD

What has keys that don't open locks, has space but no rooms, and you can enter but not go into?

KEYBOARD

A $(-9x^4 - 3x^3 - 7x) + (8x^4 - 5x^2 + 6x + 4)$

N $(3x^2 - 7x + 1) + (2x^3 + 4x^2 + 3x)$

R $(5x^4 + 3x^2 + 5) + (-5x^4 - 5x^2 - 2x + 7)$

B $(4x^3 - 3x^2 - 5x - 1) + (x^3 - 2x - 4)$

T $(-8x^3 + 4x^2 - 5x) + (-7x^4 - x^3 + 2x)$

K $(x^2 + 5x - 4) + (-3x^3 - x^2 + 2)$

D $(2x^3 + 9x - 8) - (5x^3 + 4x - 6)$

S $(2x^3 - 8x^2 - 5) - (-15x^2 - 3x + 6)$

I $(-11x^3 + 2x^2 - 4x) - (7x^4 - 2x^3 - x)$

Y $(7x^3 - 2x^2 + x) - (7x^3 + 3x - 12)$

E $(-x^3 - 5x^2 - 3) - (x^4 + 2x^3 + x - 7)$

O $(x^2 - 7x - 12) - (-5x^3 + 4x^2 - 7)$

4 ASSESS

Assessment Resources

For more assessment resources, see:
- Assessment Book
- Test and Practice Generator

Mini-Quiz

Find the sum or difference.

1. $(2n^2 - n + 3) + (n^2 + 5n - 8)$ $3n^2 + 4n - 5$
2. $(14k - 7m) + (2k + 6m)$ $16k - m$
3. $(9xy + 6x) - (4xy + 6x)$ $5xy$
4. $(7ab + a - 12) - (7ab - b - 8)$ $a + b - 4$
5. **Challenge** The solid shown is composed of three cylinders. Write a polynomial expression for the entire surface area of the solid. Give your answer in standard form. $50\pi r^2 + 82\pi r$

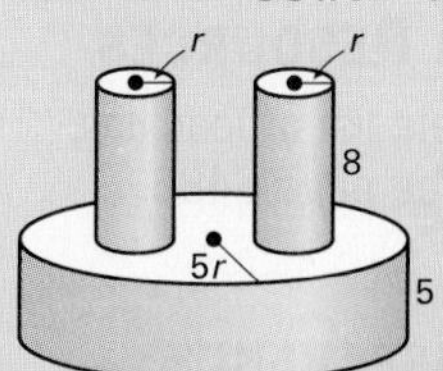

5 FOLLOW-UP

Diagnosis/Remediation

- Study Guide in Chapter 12 Resource Book, pp. 20–21
- eTutorial Plus Online
- Extra Practice, p. 814
- Lesson Practice in Chapter 12 Resource Book, pp. 17–19

English Learner Support

- Spanish Study Guide
- Multi-Language Visual Glossary
- Chapter Audio Summaries CDs

Challenge

- Challenge Practice in Chapter 12 Resource Book, p. 22
- Teacher's Edition, p. 648F

1 PLAN

Skill Check

Find the product or quotient.

1. $x^2 \cdot x^3$ x^5
2. $x^5 \cdot x^4$ x^9
3. $a^3 \div a$ a^2
4. $a^6 \div a^6$ 1

Lesson Objective

Multiply polynomials and monomials.

Pacing

Suggested Number of Days

Basic Course: 1 day

Average Course: 1 day

Advanced Course: 1 day

Block: 0.5 block with 12.4

Teaching Resources

For a complete list of Teaching Resources, see page 648B.

Transparency

Warm-Up Exercises for this lesson are available on a transparency.

2 TEACH

Motivating the Lesson

Have students propose different possible values of *l* and *w* for the horse corral fencing, given the constraint that the total amount of fencing available is 200 feet.

TIPS *for* NEW TEACHERS

Review the product of powers property and the quotient of powers property with students before discussing Examples 2 and 3. See Tips for New Teachers in the *Chapter 12 Resource Book*.

LESSON **12.3**

Multiplying Monomials *and* Polynomials

Review Vocabulary
monomial, p. 174
binomial, p. 651
trinomial, p. 651

BEFORE	Now	WHY?
You added and subtracted polynomials.	You'll multiply polynomials and monomials.	So you can write a polynomial for the area of a rug, as in Ex. 35.

Horse Corral You are enclosing a rectangular horse corral that will be connected to a barn as shown. You have 200 feet of fencing. Let l represent the length of the corral. What is a polynomial expression in terms of l that represents the area of the corral?

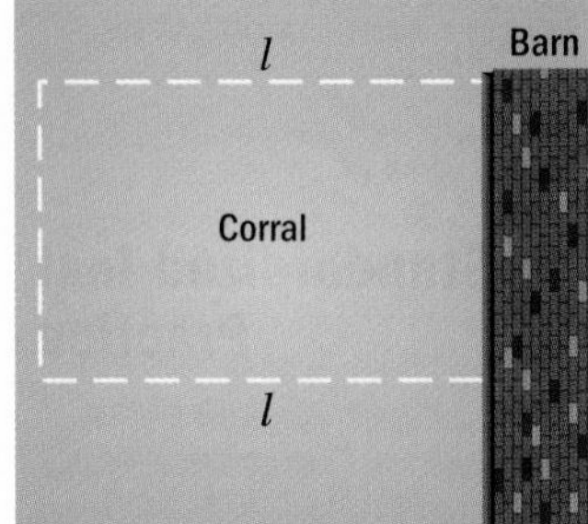

To find the area of the corral, you need to find the product of a monomial and a binomial.

Example 1 *Multiplying a Monomial and a Binomial*

To find a polynomial expression in terms of l for the corral's area as described above, follow the steps below.

1) You are enclosing only three sides of the corral, so you can write the equation $F = 2l + w$, where F is the total length of the fencing and w is the width of the corral. Solve this equation for w after substituting 200 for F.

$F = 2l + w$ **Write equation.**

$200 = 2l + w$ **Substitute 200 for *F*.**

$200 - 2l = w$ **Subtract 2*l* from each side.**

2) Find the area in terms of l.

$A = lw$ **Formula for area of a rectangle**

$= l(200 - 2l)$ **Substitute 200 − 2*l* for *w*.**

$= l(200) - l(2l)$ **Distributive property**

$= 200l - 2l^2$ **Product of powers property**

Answer The area can be represented by the polynomial $200l - 2l^2$.

Checkpoint

Find the product.

1. $3x(5x + 6)$ **2.** $(-7z + 1)2z$ **3.** $(t - 4)(-5t^2)$ **4.** $a^2(a^2 - 7a)$

1. $15x^2 + 18x$
2. $-14z^2 + 2z$
3. $-5t^3 + 20t^2$
4. $a^4 - 7a^3$

NCTM CURRICULUM STANDARDS

Standard 2: Represent situations using algebraic symbols; Analyze situations using algebraic symbols; Use models to understand relationships

Review *Help*

To review the product of powers property, see p. 194.

Example 2 ***Multiplying a Monomial and a Trinomial***

Find the product.

a. $(x^3 - 3x + 7)2x^3$ **b.** $-ab(2ab - a + 4b)$

Solution

a. $(x^3 - 3x + 7)2x^3$ **Write product.**

$= x^3(2x^3) - 3x(2x^3) + 7(2x^3)$ **Distributive property**

$= 2x^6 - 6x^4 + 14x^3$ **Product of powers property**

b. $-ab(2ab - a + 4b)$ **Write product.**

$= (-ab)2ab - (-ab)a + (-ab)4b$ **Distributive property**

$= -2a^2b^2 + a^2b - 4ab^2$ **Product of powers property**

Checkpoint

Find the product.

5. $3x(4x^2 - x + 2)$ $12x^3 - 3x^2 + 6x$

6. $(w^2 + w - 3)(-7w)$ $-7w^3 - 7w^2 + 21w$

7. $-8y(2y^2 + 3y - 5)$ $-16y^3 - 24y^2 + 40y$

8. $x^2(xy + x - 8y)$ $x^3y + x^3 - 8x^2y$

9. $(ab + 3b^2 - b)a^2$ $a^3b + 3a^2b^2 - a^2b$

10. $2cd(d^2 - 7cd - 1)$ $2cd^3 - 14c^2d^2 - 2cd$

Dividing by a Monomial To divide a polynomial by a monomial, divide each term in the polynomial by the monomial, then use the quotient of powers property.

Review *Help*

To review the quotient of powers property, see p. 195.

Example 3 ***Dividing a Polynomial by a Monomial***

Find the quotient $\dfrac{6x^6 - 10x^4 + 2x^2}{-2x^2}$.

$\dfrac{6x^6 - 10x^4 + 2x^2}{-2x^2} = \dfrac{6x^6}{-2x^2} + \dfrac{-10x^4}{-2x^2} + \dfrac{2x^2}{-2x^2}$ **Rewrite quotient.**

$= \dfrac{-3x^6}{x^2} + \dfrac{5x^4}{x^2} + \dfrac{-x^2}{x^2}$ **Divide numerators and denominators by −2.**

$= -3x^{6-2} + 5x^{4-2} - x^{2-2}$ **Quotient of powers property**

$= -3x^4 + 5x^2 - x^0$ **Simplify exponents.**

$= -3x^4 + 5x^2 - 1$ **Definition of zero exponent**

Checkpoint

Find the quotient.

11. $\dfrac{9x^2 - 15x + 6}{-3}$ $-3x^2 + 5x - 2$

12. $\dfrac{35x^3 + 5x^2 - 25x}{5x}$ $7x^2 + x - 5$

13. $\dfrac{2x^4 + 8x^3 - 6x^2}{-2x^2}$ $-x^2 - 4x + 3$

Extra Examples

Example 1 Nan is creating a dog pen attached to her house using 25 feet of fencing. Write a polynomial expression in terms of l for the area of the dog pen.

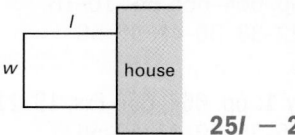

$25l - 2l^2$

Example 2 Find the product.

a. $(y^4 - 7y^3 + 2y^2)(-3y)$ $-3y^5 + 21y^4 - 6y^3$

b. $y^2z(z^2 + 3yz - 2y^2)$ $y^2z^3 + 3y^3z^2 - 2y^4z$

Example 3 Find the quotient $\dfrac{15z^4 - 9z^3 - 3z^2}{3z^2}$. $5z^2 - 3z - 1$

CROSS-CURRICULUM

Art When deciding the size of a final canvas, an artist might measure the length of the available framing material he wants to use. The length of the material would then dictate the possible dimensions of the art.

COMMON ERROR

In Example 3, students may overlook the negative sign in the denominator. Remind students that this negative sign must be applied to each term as the quotient is being determined.

CONCEPT CHECK

How do you divide $x^3 - 2x^2 + 5x$ by x? **Divide each of the terms (x^3, $-2x^2$, and $5x$) by x to get $x^2 - 2x + 5$.**

DAILY PUZZLER

Suppose x represents an integer. If the word name for the integer has x letters, what is x? 4

3 APPLY

ASSIGNMENT GUIDE

Basic Course

Day 1: EP p. 806 Exs. 21–24; pp. 664–666 Exs. 10–18, 22–33, 36–41, 49–56

Average Course

Day 1: pp. 664–666 Exs. 13–21, 25–35, 39–47, 49–56

Advanced Course

Day 1: pp. 664–666 Exs. 16–21, 25–38, 42–50*, 53–56

Block

pp. 664–666 Exs. 16–21, 25–35, 39–47, 49–56 (with 12.4)

EXTRA PRACTICE

- Student Edition, p. 814
- Chapter 12 Resource Book, pp. 25–27
- Test and Practice Generator

TRANSPARENCY

Even-numbered answers are available on transparencies.

HOMEWORK CHECK

When you review students' homework for this lesson, go over the following exercises to check understanding of key concepts.

Basic: 10, 22, 28, 29, 36

Average: 15, 21, 28, 29, 33

Advanced: 16, 26, 28, 30, 35

28.

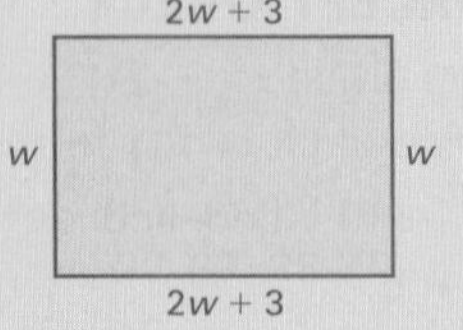

12.3 Exercises

More Practice, p. 814

Guided Practice

Vocabulary Check

1. Copy and complete: To find the product of x and $y + 3$, use the _?_ property. **distributive**

2. Describe how to use the product of powers property when finding the product of y^3 and $y^2 + 7y - 3$. **See margin.**

Skill Check **Find the product.**

3. $-2x(3x^2 + x)$ $\;$ $-6x^3 - 2x^2$

4. $(6y - 1)4y^2$ $\;$ $24y^3 - 4y^2$

5. $(8z + 3)z^2$ $\;$ $8z^3 + 3z^2$

6. $-3a^2(3a^2 + a + 2)$ $\;$ $-9a^4 - 3a^3 - 6a^2$

7. $10b(3b^2 + 7b + 4)$ $\;$ $30b^3 + 70b^2 + 40b$

8. $(d^2 + 9d - 2)(-7d)$ $\;$ $-7d^3 - 63d^2 + 14d$

Guided Problem Solving

9. Rabbits You have 50 feet of wire fencing that you want to use to make a rectangular pen for rabbits. Let l be the length of the pen. What is a polynomial expression in terms of l for the area of the pen?

1) Write the formula for the perimeter of a rectangle. Substitute 50 for the perimeter. $50 = 2l + 2w$

2) Solve the equation from Step 1 for w to obtain a polynomial expression in terms of l for the width. $w = 25 - l$

3) Multiply the expression from Step 2 by l to obtain a polynomial expression in terms of l for the area of the pen. $25l - l^2$

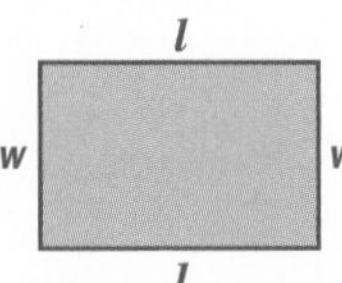

Perimeter = 50 ft

2. *Sample answer:* First use the distributive property to write the product of y^3 with each term of $y^2 + 7y - 3$: $y^3(y^2 + 7y - 3) = y^3(y^2) + y^3(7y) + y^3(-3)$. Then you can use the product of powers property to simplify the first two terms by adding the exponents: $y^3(y^2) = y^{3+2} = y^5$ and $y^3(7y) = 7 \cdot y^{3+1} = 7y^4$. So $y^3(y^2 + 7y - 3) = y^5 + 7y^4 - 3y^3$.

Practice and Problem Solving

Homework *Help*

Example	Exercises
1	10–15, 28, 33, 35
2	16–21, 29–32, 34, 36–44
3	22–27, 29–32

Online Resources
CLASSZONE.COM
- More Examples
- eTutorial Plus

Find the product.

A **10.** $(3g + 10)12g$ $\;$ $36g^2 + 120g$

11. $5x(x^2 - 2x)$ $\;$ $5x^3 - 10x^2$

12. $-8t^2(4 + t^2)$ $\;$ $-32t^2 - 8t^4$

13. $(4f^2 - 1)3f$ $\;$ $12f^3 - 3f$

14. $-4n^2(n^2 + 2n)$ $\;$ $-4n^4 - 8n^3$

15. $-g^2(g^2 - 6g)$ $\;$ $-g^4 + 6g^3$

16. $2(3x^2 + x + 2)$ $\;$ $6x^2 + 2x + 4$

17. $5d^2(d^2 - 7d + 1)$ $\;$ $5d^4 - 35d^3 + 5d^2$

18. $-r(-r^2 + 2r - 1)$ $\;$ $r^3 - 2r^2 + r$

19. $-7y(3y^2 + 4y - 2)$ $\;$ $-21y^3 - 28y^2 + 14y$

20. $(m^3 + 9m^2 + 1)3m^2$ $\;$ $3m^5 + 27m^4 + 3m^2$

21. $(w^3 - 6w^2 + w)6w$ $\;$ $6w^4 - 36w^3 + 6w^2$

Find the quotient.

22. $\dfrac{24p^2 + 16p}{-4p}$ $\;$ $-6p - 4$

23. $\dfrac{-10z^2 - 25z}{5z}$ $\;$ $-2z - 5$

24. $\dfrac{-6h^4 + h^3 + 10h^2}{2h^2}$ $\;$ $-3h^2 + \frac{h}{2} + 5$

25. $\dfrac{11m^8 - m^6 - 2m^4}{m^2}$ $\;$ $11m^6 - m^4 - 2m^2$

26. $\dfrac{2t^6 + t^4 - 3t^3}{-t^2}$ $\;$ $-2t^4 - t^2 + 3t$

27. $\dfrac{-3n^3 + n^2 - 2n}{-2n}$ $\;$ $\frac{3n^2}{2} - \frac{n}{2} + 1$

28. Geometry A rectangle has a length that is 3 units more than twice the width w. Sketch the rectangle. Write a polynomial expression in terms of w for the area of the rectangle. Give your answer in standard form. **See margin for art; $2w^2 + 3w$.**

In Exercises 29–32, match the product or quotient with the equivalent polynomial.

29. $-3x(2x^2 - x - 7)$ **B**   A. $21 - 3x + 6x^2$

30. $\dfrac{-12x^2 + 6x^3 - 42x^4}{-2x^2}$ **C**   B. $21x + 3x^2 - 6x^3$

31. $(-7 + x + 2x^2)3x^2$ **D**   C. $21x^2 - 3x + 6$

32. $\dfrac{-21x + 3x^2 - 6x^3}{-x}$ **A**   D. $-21x^2 + 3x^3 + 6x^4$

33. **Geometry** Write a polynomial expression for the area of the figure. Give your answer in standard form. **$3x^2 + x$**

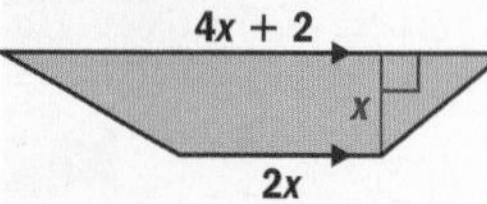

34. *Writing* Your friend says that the product of x^2 and $x^3 + 5x^2 + 1$ is $x^6 + 5x^4 + x^2$. Do you agree with your friend? If not, explain your reasoning. **No. *Sample answer:* The product of x^2 and x^3 is x^5, not x^6.**

35. **Rugs** The length of a rug is three times the width. There are 2 inches of fringe on each end of the rug, as shown. Write a polynomial expression for the area of the rug, including the fringe. Give your answer in standard form. **$3x^2 + 4x$**

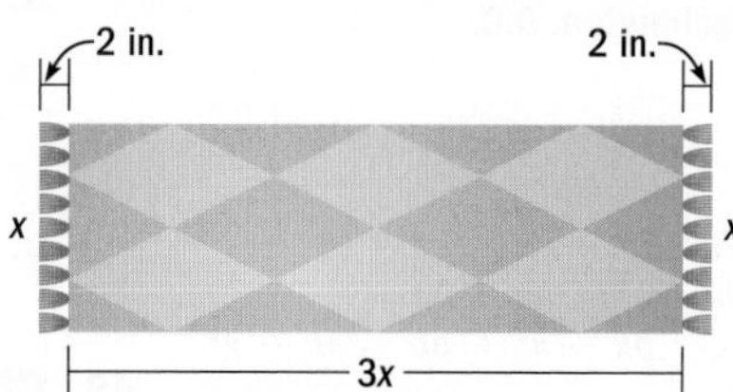

Find the product.

B 36. $a(3a + 4b - c)$ **$3a^2 + 4ab - ac$**

37. $(9m + n - 4)2n$ **$18mn + 2n^2 - 8n$**

38. $(g + 11h + gh)(-4g)$ **$-4g^2 - 44gh - 4g^2h$**

39. $(5x + 6y + 8)xy$ **$5x^2y + 6xy^2 + 8xy$**

40. $-2x(x + xy + 3y)$ **$-2x^2 - 2x^2y - 6xy$**

41. $-3n^2(m + n^2 + 2)$ **$-3mn^2 - 3n^4 - 6n^2$**

42. $(5rs - 2r - s^2)(-rs)$ **$-5r^2s^2 + 2r^2s + rs^3$**

43. $-5c(-c^2 + 7d^2 - d)$ **$5c^3 - 35cd^2 + 5cd$**

44. $(2ab - a^2 + 4b)ab$ **$2a^2b^2 - a^3b + 4ab^2$**

45. **Extended Problem Solving** You are designing a poster for a student government election. The poster includes text and an enlarged photo. The original photo was 10 inches long and 8 inches wide. The dimensions of the enlarged photo are x times the dimensions of the original photo. As shown, you want space for 5 inches of text at the top and bottom of the poster, along the shorter sides of the photo.

a. Write polynomial expressions in terms of x for the length and width of the poster. **length: $10x + 10$, width: $8x$**

b. **Apply** Write a polynomial expression in terms of x for the area of the poster. What is the area of the poster when $x = 5$? **$80x^2 + 80x$; 2400 in.^{2}**

c. **Compare** Compare the area of the poster when $x = 10$ to the area of the poster when $x = 5$.
Sample answer: **When $x = 10$, the area is 8800 in.^{2}, which is $3\frac{2}{3}$ times the area when $x = 5$.**

COMMON ERROR

In Exercise 25, watch for students who divide powers instead of subtracting them when the exponent in the denominator is a factor of each exponent in the numerator.

TEACHING TIP

You may wish to review the area formula for a trapezoid before assigning Exercise 33.

4 ASSESS

ASSESSMENT RESOURCES

For more assessment resources, see:
- Assessment Book
- Test and Practice Generator

MINI-QUIZ

Find the product or quotient.

1. $8g(2g^2 - 6g)$ $16g^3 - 48g^2$
2. $(-h^3 + 4h)3h^2$ $-3h^5 + 12h^3$
3. $\dfrac{9a^4 - 6a^2 + 3a}{-3a}$ $-3a^3 + 2a - 1$
4. **Challenge** You are dividing a trinomial by a monomial. How is the degree of the quotient related to the degree of the trinomial and the degree of the monomial? **The degree of the quotient trinomial is the difference between the degree of the monomial and the degree of the term with the greatest degree in the original trinomial.**

5 FOLLOW-UP

DIAGNOSIS/REMEDIATION

- Study Guide in Chapter 12 Resource Book, pp. 28–29
- eTutorial Plus Online
- Extra Practice, p. 814
- Lesson Practice in Chapter 12 Resource Book, pp. 25–27

ENGLISH LEARNER SUPPORT

- Spanish Study Guide
- Multi-Language Visual Glossary
- Chapter Audio Summaries CDs

CHALLENGE

- Challenge Practice in Chapter 12 Resource Book, p. 31
- Teacher's Edition, p. 648F

48, 56a. See Additional Answers beginning on page AA1.

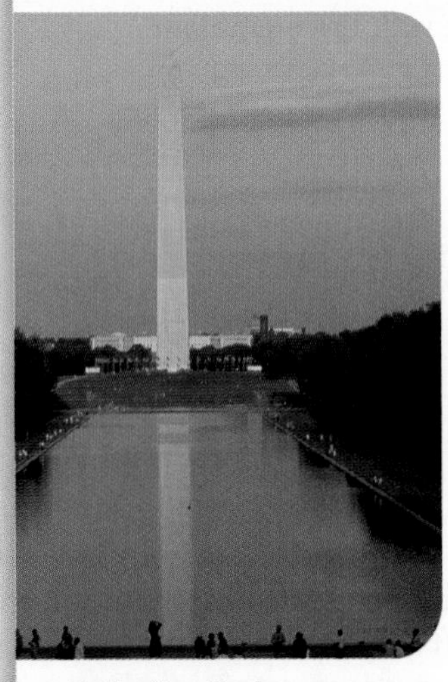

Reflecting Pool, Washington, D.C.

46. Reflecting Pool The rectangular Reflecting Pool near the Washington Monument in Washington, D.C., has a length that is 50 feet more than 15 times the width. The pool has a depth that is $\frac{1}{50}$ of the width. Let w represent the width of the pool. **length: $15w + 50$, depth: $\frac{w}{50}$; $\frac{3w^3}{10} + w^2$**

a. Write polynomial expressions in terms of w for the length and depth of the pool. Write a polynomial expression in terms of w for the volume of the pool. Give your answers in standard form.

b. The depth of the pool is 3 feet. What is the volume of the pool? **1,035,000 ft^3**

C **47. Geometry** To form the figure shown, start with a rectangle measuring a units by b units, and remove a square measuring x units on a side. Use the figure to complete the following.

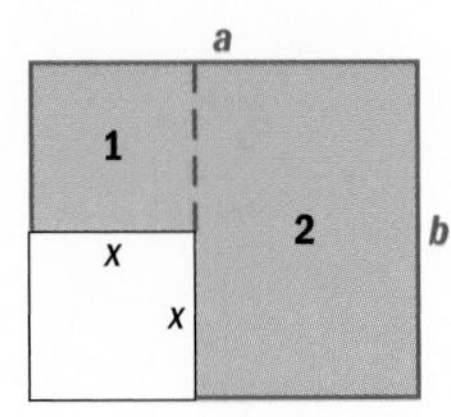

a. Find a polynomial expression for the area of the shaded figure by adding the areas of rectangle 1 and rectangle 2. **$x(b - x) + b(a - x)$**

b. Find a polynomial expression for the area of the shaded figure by subtracting the area of the square from the area of the rectangle that includes the shaded figure and the square. **$ab - x^2$**

c. Critical Thinking Show that the polynomial expressions from parts (a) and (b) are equivalent.

47c. $x(b - x) + b(a - x) =$
$xb - x^2 + ba - bx =$
$bx - bx - x^2 + ab = ab - x^2$

48. Challenge You are finding the product of a monomial and a binomial. How is the degree of the product related to the degree of the monomial and the degree of the binomial? Give examples and explain your reasoning. **See margin.**

Mixed Review

Identify the domain and range of the relation. *(Lesson 8.1)*

49. (5, 0), (0, 5), (3, 3), (−4, −4)

50. (2, 7), (3, 8), (2, 8), (3, 7), (4, 9)

51. (9, 9), (7, −8), (6, 10), (8, −8)

52. (0, 2), (5, 7), (8, 10), (0, −2)

49. domain: −4, 0, 3, 5; range: −4, 0, 3, 5

50. domain: 2, 3, 4; range: 7, 8, 9

51. domain: 6, 7, 8, 9; range: −8, 9, 10

52. domain: 0, 5, 8; range: −2, 2, 7, 10

53. Skateboard Ramp A skateboard ramp is 12 feet long. The ramp makes an angle of 30° with the ground. Find the distance d along the bottom of the ramp. Round to the nearest tenth of a foot. *(Lesson 9.6)* **10.4 ft**

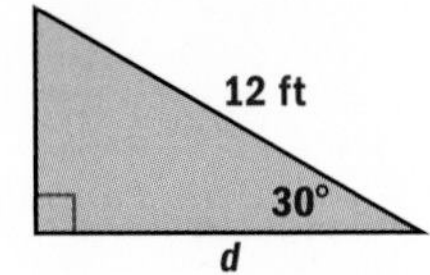

Find the sum or difference. *(Lesson 12.2)*

54. $(7x^3 - 2x^2 + x) + (-2x^2 - 1)$ **$7x^3 - 4x^2 + x - 1$**

55. $(-2x^2 + 5x + 4) - (x^2 + 7x - 6)$ **$-3x^2 - 2x + 10$**

Standardized Test Practice

56. Extended Response You have 24 feet of fencing that you want to use to make a rectangular dog pen. Let l represent the length of the pen.

a. Draw a diagram of the pen. **See margin.**

b. Write a polynomial for the width in terms of l. Write a polynomial for the area in terms of l. **$12 - l$; $12l - l^2$**

c. What is the area of the pen if $l = 4$? if $l = 10$? **32 ft^2; 20 ft^2**

Concept *Activity*

12.4 Modeling Binomial Multiplication

Goal
Model binomial multiplication using algebra tiles.

Materials
- algebra tiles

Investigate

Find the product $(3x + 1)(x + 4)$ using algebra tiles.

Represent each binomial using algebra tiles. Arrange the first binomial vertically and the second binomial horizontally, as shown.

The binomials define a rectangular region with length $(3x + 1)$ units and width $(x + 4)$ units. Fill in the region with the appropriate tiles.

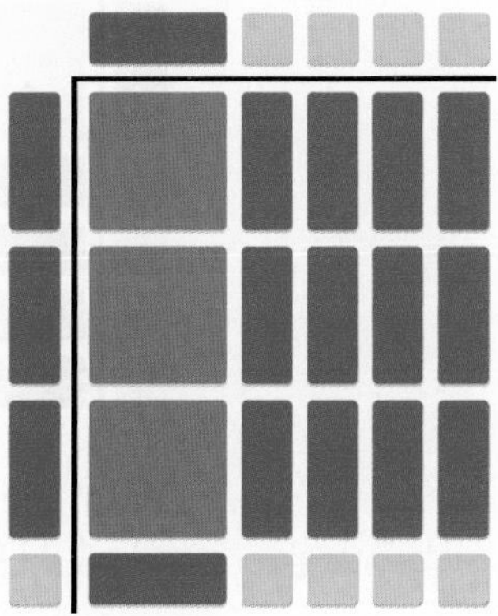

The tiles covering the rectangular region represent $3x^2 + 13x + 4$. This expression is the product of the binomials.

Draw Conclusions

Use algebra tiles to find the product. Draw your model. **1–6. See margin for art.**

1. $(x + 3)(x + 3)$ **$x^2 + 6x + 9$**
2. $(2x + 1)(x + 3)$ **$2x^2 + 7x + 3$**
3. $(5x + 1)(x + 2)$ **$5x^2 + 11x + 2$**
4. $(3x + 4)(2x + 1)$ **$6x^2 + 11x + 4$**
5. $(4x + 2)(3x + 1)$ **$12x^2 + 10x + 2$**
6. $(x + 5)(6x + 2)$ **$6x^2 + 32x + 10$**
7. *Writing* Describe how you can use algebra tiles to find the product $2x(x + 3)$. Do you get the same result using the distributive property, as in Lesson 12.3? Explain. **See margin.**
8. **Critical Thinking** You can also use the distributive property to multiply binomials. Describe how you could use the distributive property to find the product $(3x + 1)(x + 4)$. Begin by distributing $x + 4$ to each term of $3x + 1$. **See margin.**

NCTM CURRICULUM STANDARDS
Standard 10: Create representations to communicate mathematical ideas; Use representations to communicate mathematical ideas

1 PLAN

Investigate the Concept

- Students model binomial multiplication using algebra tiles.
- This activity leads into using the FOIL method to multiply binomials in Lesson 12.4.

Materials

Each student will need algebra tiles. See the Activity Support Masters in the *Chapter 12 Resource Book*. A support transparency is also available.

Recommended Time

Work activity: 10 min
Discuss results: 5 min

Grouping

Students should work individually.

2 TEACH

Teaching Tip

Urge students to arrange the tiles for the binomial factors as shown in the example. While not mandatory, point out that this arrangement makes it easy to determine the modeled product.

3 CLOSE

Key Discovery

Binomial multiplication using algebra tiles is related to the use of the distributive property.

Assessment

1. In the example, where did the term $3x^2$ in the trinomial product come from? **It is the result of multiplying $3x$ and x, the first terms of the binomials.**

1–8. See Additional Answers beginning on page AA1.

1 PLAN

Skill Check

Find the product.

1. $-7x \cdot 3$ — $-21x$
2. $4 \cdot 8c^2$ — $32c^2$
3. $c^3(c - 1)$ — $c^4 - c^3$
4. $-3r(r^2 + 3)$ — $-3r^3 - 9r$

LESSON OBJECTIVE

Multiply binomials.

PACING

Suggested Number of Days
Basic Course: 2 days
Average Course: 2 days
Advanced Course: 2 days
Block: 0.5 block with 12.3
0.5 block with 12.5

TEACHING RESOURCES

For a complete list of Teaching Resources, see page 648B.

TRANSPARENCY

Warm-Up Exercises for this lesson are available on a transparency.

2 TEACH

MOTIVATING THE LESSON

Have a volunteer point out which algebra tiles correspond to each term of the polynomial.

TIPS *for* NEW TEACHERS

Students may have difficulty applying the distributive property to binomial products. Urge them to think of one of the binomials as a single item. This should help make a connection to their previous use of the property. See Tips for New Teachers in the *Chapter 12 Resource Book*.

LESSON

12.4 Multiplying Binomials

BEFORE	Now	WHY?
You multiplied monomials and polynomials.	You'll multiply binomials.	So you can find the area of a garden and walkway, as in Ex. 32.

Review Vocabulary
binomial, p. 651

In the activity on page 667, you learned how to model binomial multiplication using algebra tiles. You can also use a table to multiply two binomials. The model and table below show the product $(x + 4)(2x + 3)$. Notice how using a table is similar to using algebra tiles.

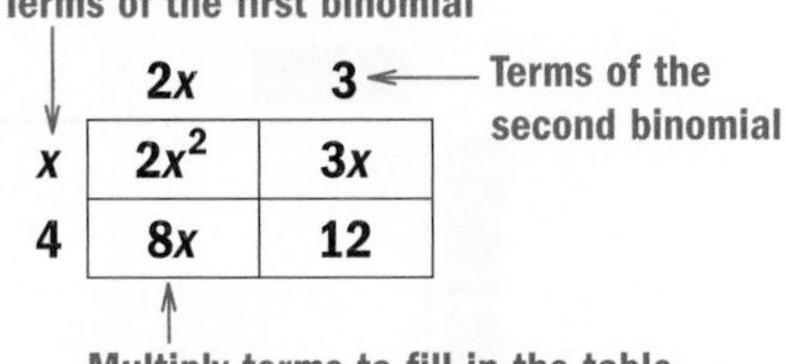
Terms of the first binomial
Terms of the second binomial
Multiply terms to fill in the table. For example, 4 • 2x = 8x.

	$2x$	3
x	$2x^2$	$3x$
4	$8x$	12

From the table, you can see that $(x + 4)(2x + 3)$ is $2x^2 + 3x + 8x + 12$, or $2x^2 + 11x + 12$.

Example 1 Multiplying Binomials Using a Table

Find the product $(-2x + 5)(3x - 1)$.

Write any subtractions in the binomials as additions.

$(-2x + 5)(3x - 1) = (-2x + 5)[3x + (-1)]$

First binomial → ; Second binomial ←

	$3x$	-1
$-2x$	$-6x^2$	$2x$
5	$15x$	-5

The product is $-6x^2 + 2x + 15x - 5$, or $-6x^2 + 17x - 5$.

Checkpoint

Use a table to find the product.

1. $(4x + 1)(2x + 3)$ — $8x^2 + 14x + 3$
2. $(-m + 2)(5m + 2)$ — $-5m^2 + 8m + 4$
3. $(2a - 3)(5a - 6)$ — $10a^2 - 27a + 18$
4. $(-n + 7)(11n + 1)$
5. $(6s - 9)(-2s + 5)$
6. $(-6b - 4)(-b + 3)$

4. $-11n^2 + 76n + 7$
5. $-12s^2 + 48s - 45$
6. $6b^2 - 14b - 12$

NCTM CURRICULUM STANDARDS

Standard 2: Analyze situations using algebraic symbols
Standard 10: Create/use representations to communicate mathematical ideas

Distributive Property Another way to multiply binomials is to use the distributive property.

Example 2 *Using the Distributive Property*

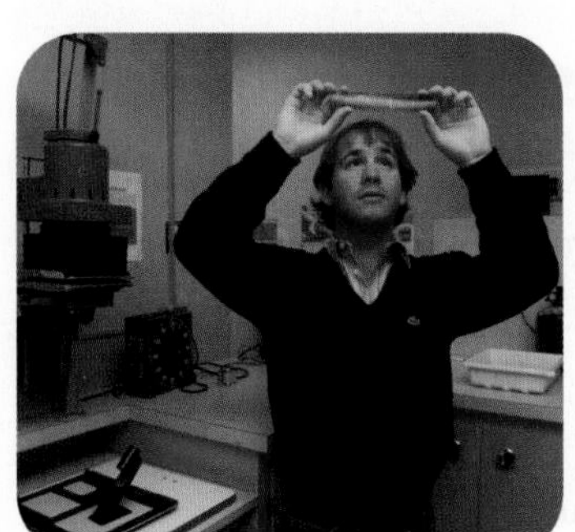

Photograph You are enlarging a photo that is 7 inches long and 5 inches wide. The length and width of the enlargement are x times the length and width of the original photo. The enlargement will have a 2 inch mat. Write a polynomial expression for the combined area of the enlargement and mat.

Solution

The total length of the enlargement and mat is $(7x + 4)$ inches. The total width is $(5x + 4)$ inches. To find the area, multiply.

$(7x + 4)(5x + 4) = 7x(5x + 4) + 4(5x + 4)$ **Distribute $5x + 4$.**

$= 35x^2 + 28x + 20x + 16$ **Distribute $7x$ and 4.**

$= 35x^2 + 48x + 16$ **Combine like terms.**

Answer The area is $(35x^2 + 48x + 16)$ square inches.

FOIL Method Notice that using the distributive property to multiply binomials produces four products that are then added. These four products are the products of the *first* terms, the *outer* terms, the *inner* terms, and the *last* terms of the binomials. You can use the shorthand **FOIL** to remind you of the words **F**irst, **O**uter, **I**nner, and **L**ast.

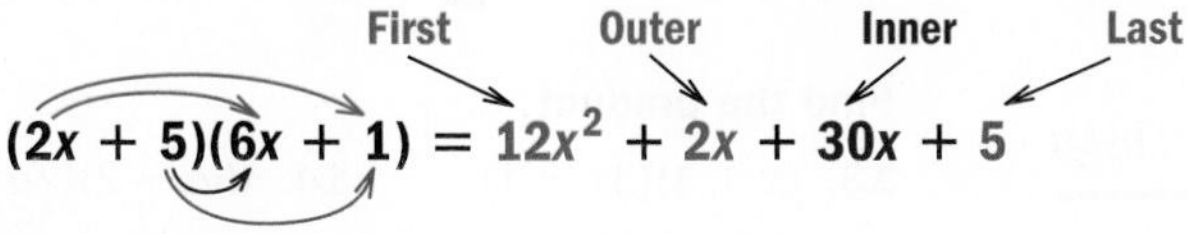

Note *Worthy*

In this lesson you have learned three methods for multiplying binomials. Record and compare these methods in your notebook.

Example 3 *Using the FOIL Method*

Find the product $(4x + 3)(5x - 2)$.

First	+ Outer	+ Inner	+ Last	
$(4x)(5x)$	$+ (4x)(-2)$	$+ (3)(5x)$	$+ (3)(-2)$	**Write products of terms.**
$20x^2$	$+ (-8x)$	$+ 15x$	$+ (-6)$	**Multiply.**
$20x^2 + 7x - 6$				**Combine like terms.**

Checkpoint

Find the product.

7. $(x + 5)(x - 9)$ $x^2 - 4x - 45$

8. $(8k - 1)(-3k - 5)$ $-24k^2 - 37k + 5$

9. $(-z + 6)(10z + 2)$ $-10z^2 + 58z + 12$

10. $(b + 4)(b + 9)$ $b^2 + 13b + 36$

11. $(m - 3)(m - 2)$ $m^2 - 5m + 6$

12. $(5t - 1)(2t + 7)$ $10t^2 + 33t - 7$

Extra Examples

Example 1 Find the product $(c - 3)(-4c + 1)$.
$-4c^2 + 13c - 3$

Example 2 A rectangular pool has a length that is three times its width. You plan to build a deck around the pool that is 3 feet wide. Write a polynomial expression for the combined area of the pool's surface and the deck around it.
$(3x^2 + 24x + 36)$ ft^2

Example 3 Find the product $(7a - 3)(2a + 9)$.
$14a^2 + 57a - 27$

Teaching Tip

While discussing Example 3, point out that after multiplying two binomials students will usually be able to combine like terms. However, inform them that some binomial products will not have any like terms. You might wish to show the product $(a + b)(c + d)$ as an example of this fact.

Concept Check

Why does the product of two binomials result in four terms? **Both of the terms in one binomial are multiplied by the two terms in the other binomial, resulting in four terms. There may be like terms that can be combined in order to give a final product.**

Daily Puzzler

Find k if $(kx + 4)(kx + 3) = 9x^2 + 21x + 12$. **3**

3 APPLY

ASSIGNMENT GUIDE

Basic Course

Day 1: EP p. 806 Exs. 37, 38, p. 812 Exs. 9–12; pp. 670–672 Exs. 13–18, 25–30, 49–56

Day 2: pp. 670–672 Exs. 19–24, 33–41, 44, 57–62

Average Course

Day 1: pp. 670–672 Exs. 13–18, 26–29, 39–43, 49–56

Day 2: pp. 670–672 Exs. 19–24, 31–38, 44–46, 57–62

Advanced Course

Day 1: pp. 670–672 Exs. 16–20, 26–29, 42–44, 51–54

Day 2: pp. 670–672 Exs. 21–24, 31–34, 37–40, 45–48*, 59–62

Block

pp. 670–672 Exs. 13–18, 26–29, 39–43, 49–56 (with 12.3)

pp. 670–672 Exs. 19–24, 31–38, 44–46, 57–62 (with 12.5)

EXTRA PRACTICE

- Student Edition, p. 814
- Chapter 12 Resource Book, pp. 36–38
- Test and Practice Generator

TRANSPARENCY

Even-numbered answers are available on transparencies.

HOMEWORK CHECK

When you review students' homework for this lesson, go over the following exercises to check understanding of key concepts.

Basic: 13, 20, 25, 33, 35

Average: 15, 21, 26, 35, 39

Advanced: 17, 21, 27, 33, 40

12.4 Exercises

More Practice, p. 814

Guided Practice

Vocabulary Check

1. What does each letter in FOIL represent? **F: First, O: Outer, I: Inner, L: Last**
2. Describe how you can use the distributive property to find the product of two binomials. **See margin.**

Skill Check **Use a table to find the product.**

3. $(a + 2)(4a + 3)$ $\quad 4a^2 + 11a + 6$
4. $(3b - 7)(3b + 2)$ $\quad 9b^2 - 15b - 14$
5. $(-4c + 5)(2c - 4)$ $\quad -8c^2 + 26c - 20$

Use the distributive property to find the product.

6. $(2x + 1)(3x + 8)$ $\quad 6x^2 + 19x + 8$
7. $(8y + 2)(y - 2)$ $\quad 8y^2 - 14y - 4$
8. $(-5z - 3)(4z + 6)$ $\quad -20z^2 - 42z - 18$

Use the FOIL method to find the product.

9. $(a + 7)(3a + 1)$ $\quad 3a^2 + 22a + 7$
10. $(-2b + 5)(3b + 6)$ $\quad -6b^2 + 3b + 30$
11. $(10c - 4)(5c - 1)$ $\quad 50c^2 - 30c + 4$
12. **Error Analysis** Describe and correct the error in finding the product $(x - 3)(4x + 2)$.

$$(x - 3)(4x + 2) = x(4x + 2) + (-3)(4x + 2)$$
$$= 4x^2 + 2x - 12x + 6$$
$$= 4x^2 - 10x + 6$$

2. ***Sample answer:*** **Apply the distributive property twice. First distribute the second binomial over the terms of the first binomial. Then distribute each of the terms of the first binomial over the terms of the second binomial.**

12. ***Sample answer:*** **In the second line, −3 was not correctly distributed over the second term of $4x + 2$, since $-3(2) = -6$, not 6. The second line should be $4x^2 + 2x - 12x - 6$, followed by $4x^2 - 10x - 6$.**

Practice and Problem Solving

Homework *Help*

Example	Exercises
1	13-30, 32-41
2	13-27, 32-41
3	13-27, 32-41

- More Examples
- eTutorial Plus

Find the product.

A 13. $(x + 4)(3x + 1)$ $\quad 3x^2 + 13x + 4$

14. $(5a + 2)(2a + 3)$ $\quad 10a^2 + 19a + 6$
15. $(4t - 8)(3t + 2)$ $\quad 12t^2 - 16t - 16$
16. $(b + 12)(b - 10)$ $\quad b^2 + 2b - 120$
17. $(7p - 4)(6p - 2)$ $\quad 42p^2 - 38p + 8$
18. $(9n - 6)(2n - 5)$ $\quad 18n^2 - 57n + 30$
19. $(-3w + 8)(8w + 1)$ $\quad -24w^2 + 61w + 8$
20. $(10s - 4)^2$ $\quad 100s^2 - 80s + 16$
21. $(-4m + 7)^2$ $\quad 16m^2 - 56m + 49$
22. $(-8r + 9)(-3r - 2)$ $\quad 24r^2 - 11r - 18$
23. $(11v - 6)(-v - 6)$ $\quad -11v^2 - 60v + 36$
24. $(-2y - 11)(-12y - 3)$ $\quad 24y^2 + 138y + 33$

Geometry **Write a polynomial expression for the area of the figure. Give your answer in standard form.**

25.

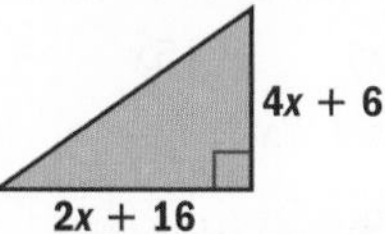

$4x^2 + 38x + 48$

26.

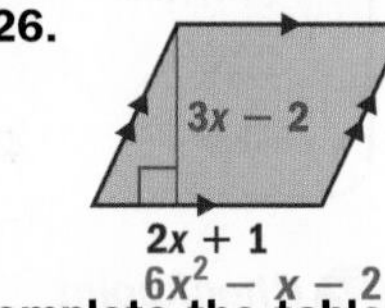

$6x^2 - x - 2$

27. $3x^2 + 32x + 20$

2x + 5

x + 10

4x − 1

Mental Math **Copy and complete the table.**

28.

	$-5x$	2
x	$-5x^2$	? $2x$
-1	? $5x$	-2

29.

	? $2x$	4
$-3x$	$-6x^2$	$-12x$
7	$14x$	? 28

30.

	$2x$	? 5
$4x$?	$8x^2$	$20x$
-3	$-6x$	-15

31. *Sample answer:* It is similar because you can use the distributive property. It is different because when you multiply two binomials you have to apply the distributive property twice instead of once and because you may also have to combine like terms to simplify the product.

36. $\frac{1}{2}k^2 - \frac{44}{7}k + \frac{24}{7}$

37. $36h^2 + \frac{129}{8}h + \frac{15}{32}$

38. $6u^2 - \frac{112}{3}u + 8$

45. The distributive property. *Sample answer:* First I would use the FOIL method to multiply two of the binomials, but then I would use the distributive property to multiply the result by the third binomial because the result will likely have too many terms for the FOIL method to work, and because algebra tiles and tables would be burdensome with the extra computation.

In the Real World

Mozzarella Wisconsin produces more cheese than any other state. It produces about 700,000 pounds of mozzarella each year. About how much mozzarella does Wisconsin produce each day? **about 1918 lb**

31. *Writing* How is finding the product of two binomials like finding the product of a monomial and a polynomial? How is it different?

32. **Garden** The length of a rectangular garden is three times the width. A stone walkway 4 feet wide surrounds the garden. Write a polynomial expression for the area of the garden and walkway. Give your answer in standard form. $3x^2 + 32x + 64$

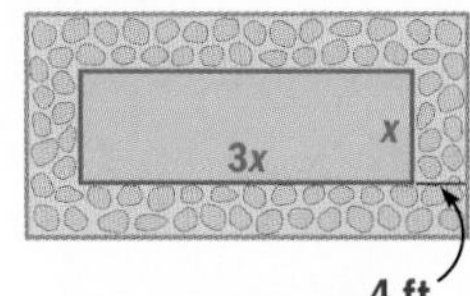

Find the product.

B 33. $(-x + 1.2)(2x + 5)$ $-2x^2 - 2.6x + 6$

34. $(4t + 0.6)(t - 1)$ $4t^2 - 3.4t - 0.6$

35. $(5g - 4)(0.2g + 3.5)$ $g^2 + 16.7g - 14$

36. $\left(\frac{1}{2}k - 6\right)\left(k - \frac{4}{7}\right)$

37. $\left(12h + \frac{3}{8}\right)\left(3h + \frac{5}{4}\right)$

38. $\left(\frac{4}{3}u - 8\right)\left(\frac{9}{2}u - 1\right)$

39. $(11a - b)(2a + 8b)$ $22a^2 + 86ab - 8b^2$

40. $(7c + 2d)(-c + d)$ $-7c^2 + 5cd + 2d^2$

41. $(-3x + 2y)(4x - y)$ $-12x^2 + 11xy - 2y^2$

42. **Webpages** You are designing a webpage. At the top is a banner ad that is 1.5 inches high. On the left side is an index that is 2 inches wide. The width and height of the page depend on the user's browser. Use the diagram to find a polynomial expression for the area of the webpage, excluding the banner ad and index. Give your answer in standard form. $1.4x^2 - 4.1x + 3$

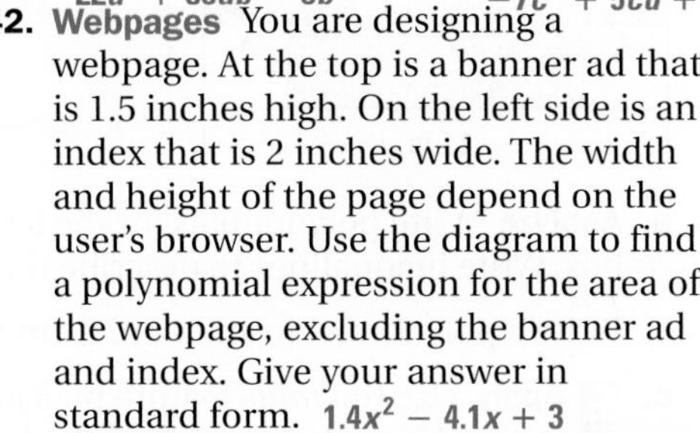

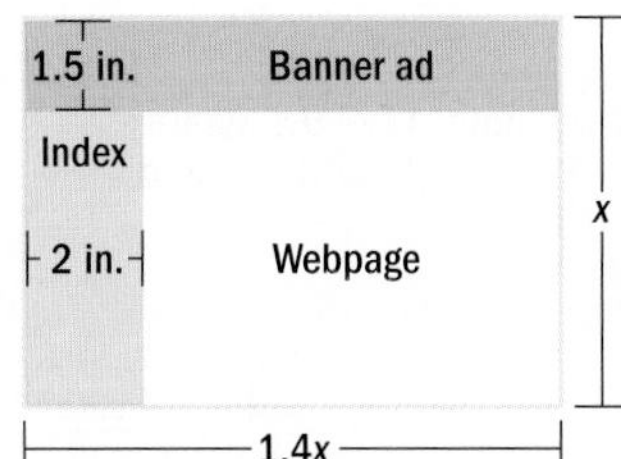

43. **Mozzarella** For the period 1990–1999, the amount of mozzarella (in pounds) consumed each year by a typical person in the U.S. can be approximated by the first polynomial below. For the same period, the U.S. population (in millions) can be approximated by the second polynomial below. In both polynomials, x represents the number of years since 1990.

Mozzarella consumption: $0.2x + 7$ **U.S. population:** $2.6x + 250$

a. Write a polynomial, in terms of x, that approximates the *total* amount of mozzarella (in millions of pounds) consumed in the U.S. $0.52x^2 + 68.2x + 1750$

b. Evaluate the polynomial from part (a) when $x = 0$ to find the approximate total consumption of mozzarella in the U.S. in 1990. **1750 million pounds**

c. Evaluate the polynomial from part (a) when $x = 9$ to find the approximate total consumption of mozzarella in the U.S. in 1999. Round your answer to the nearest million pounds. **2406 million pounds**

44. **Geometry** The figure shown is composed of a triangle and a rectangle. Write a polynomial expression for the area of the figure. Give your answer in standard form. $25x^2 - 40x + 12$

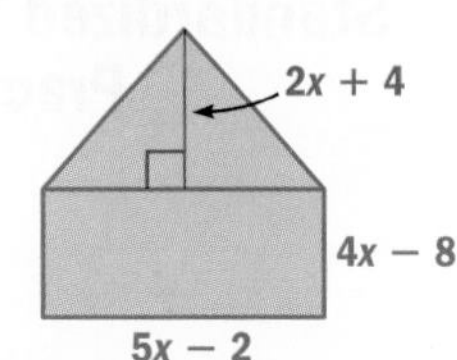

45. **Critical Thinking** You want to find the product of three binomials. Which method would you use—algebra tiles, a table, the distributive property, or the FOIL method? Explain your reasoning. See margin.

Teaching Tip

In Exercises 20 and 21, suggest that students rewrite the product as two binomials. Students may make mistakes if they try to apply the FOIL method without first rewriting the given expression.

Common Error

In Exercise 25, watch for students who multiply both the base and the height by $\frac{1}{2}$ when applying the area formula. Encourage students to write out all steps, starting with area $= \frac{1}{2}bh$ and then substituting the binomial expressions for b and h before multiplying. In Exercise 32, point out that twice the width of the walkway must be used in the overall width and overall length of the figure.

4 ASSESS

ASSESSMENT RESOURCES

For more assessment resources, see:
- Assessment Book
- Test and Practice Generator

MINI-QUIZ

Find the product.

1. $(y-3)(y+4)$ y^2+y-12
2. $(-4k+2)(-k+5)$
$4k^2-22k+10$
3. $(3w+1.5)(w-0.8)$
$3w^2-0.9w-1.2$
4. **Challenge** Find the products below. What pattern do you notice? Make and test a conjecture based on your observations. $(x+1)^2$; $(x+2)^2$; $(x+3)^2$; $(x+4)^2$ x^2+2x+1; x^2+4x+4; x^2+6x+9; $x^2+8x+16$. *Sample answer:* It appears that the square of a binomial is the square of the first term plus 2 times the product of the two terms plus the square of the second term: $(x+a)^2=x^2+2ax+a^2$.

5 FOLLOW-UP

DIAGNOSIS/REMEDIATION

- Study Guide in Chapter 12 Resource Book, pp. 39–40
- eTutorial Plus Online
- Extra Practice, p. 814
- Lesson Practice in Chapter 12 Resource Book, pp. 36–38

ENGLISH LEARNER SUPPORT

- Spanish Study Guide
- Multi-Language Visual Glossary
- Chapter Audio Summaries CDs

CHALLENGE

- Challenge Practice in Chapter 12 Resource Book, p. 41
- Teacher's Edition, p. 648F

C **46.** Write polynomial expressions for the surface area and volume of the rectangular prism shown. Give your answers in standard form. surface area: $10x^2-18x-30$, volume: $2x^3-7x^2-15x$

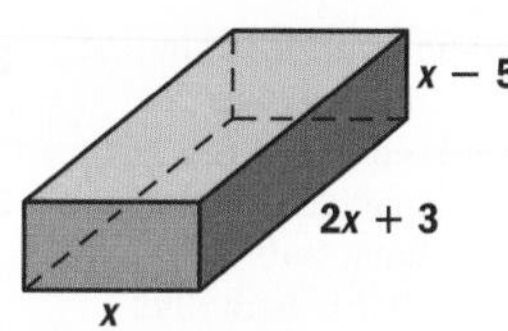

47. Extended Problem Solving You want to make a box with no lid for storing small items. You have an 11 inch by 7 inch piece of stiff cardboard. You cut out squares of side length x inches from each corner. Then you fold the sides up and tape them together as shown.

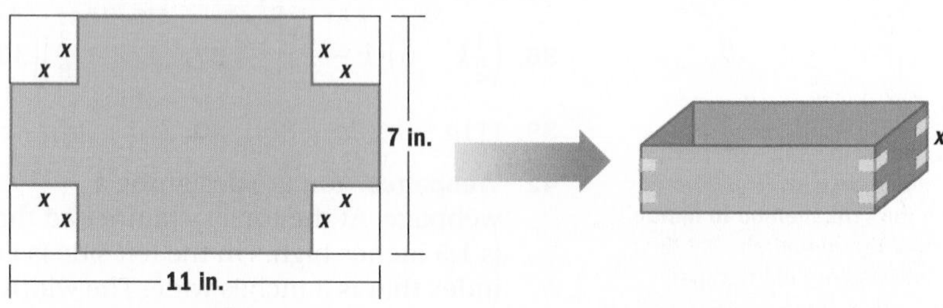

a. Analyze Write polynomials for the length, width, and height of the box. Write inequalities to describe the possible values of x.

b. Write a polynomial in standard form for the volume of the box. $4x^3-36x^2+77x$

c. Apply Use the *table* feature on a graphing calculator to find the value of x, to the nearest tenth of an inch, that gives the greatest volume. 1.4 in.

48. Challenge Find the products below. What pattern do you notice? Make and test a conjecture based on your observations.

$(x+1)(x-1)$ $(x+2)(x-2)$ $(x+3)(x-3)$ $(x+4)(x-4)$

47a. length: $11-2x$, width: $7-2x$, height: x; $x>0$ and $x<3.5$

48. x^2-1, x^2-4, x^2-9, x^2-16. *Sample answer:* It appears that the product of two binomials that are the sum and difference of the same two terms is just the square of the first term minus the square of the second term. For example, $(2x+5)(2x-5)$ should be $(2x)^2-(5)^2=4x^2-25$, which checks by the FOIL method.

Mixed Review

Find the product. Write your answer using only positive exponents. *(Lesson 4.6)*

49. $(5^{-4})(5^7)$ 5^3 **50.** $(11^{-2})(11^{-4})$ $\frac{1}{11^6}$ **51.** $(x^{-12})(x^5)$ $\frac{1}{x^7}$ **52.** $(m^{-9})(m^{-4})$ $\frac{1}{m^{13}}$

Approximate the square root to the nearest integer. *(Lesson 9.1)*

53. $-\sqrt{10}$ -3 **54.** $\sqrt{68}$ 8 **55.** $\sqrt{145}$ 12 **56.** $-\sqrt{232}$ -15

Find the product. *(Lesson 12.3)*

57. $7x(3x-4)$ $21x^2-28x$ **58.** $12z(5z+1)$ $60z^2+12z$ **59.** $4s^2(-s-10)$ $-4s^3-40s^2$ **60.** $-2y^2(7y^2+8y)$ $-14y^4-16y^3$

Standardized Test Practice

61. Multiple Choice A rectangular painting is twice as long as it is wide. The painting has a 3 inch wide frame. Let x represent the painting's width. Which product gives the area of the painting and frame? D

A. $(2x)(x)$ **B.** $(2x+3)(x+3)$

C. $(2x+3)(x+6)$ **D.** $(2x+6)(x+6)$

62. Multiple Choice Which product equals $6x^2-7x+2$? I

F. $(6x+1)(x-7)$ **G.** $(-6x+1)(-x+7)$

H. $(2x-1)(3x+2)$ **I.** $(-2x+1)(-3x+2)$

Mid-Chapter Quiz

Find the degree of the polynomial.

1. $5x^3 - x + 2$ **3**

2. $-1 + 3z^4 - 7z$ **4**

3. $5y^3 - 3xy + 7x^2$ **3**

Write the expression as a polynomial in standard form.

4. $y + 2y^2 - 9 + 5y$ **$2y^2 + 6y - 9$**

5. $-14 + 5b^2 - 7b(b + 1)$ **$-2b^2 - 7b - 14$**

6. $3k^2(2 - k) + 18k^4$ **$18k^4 - 3k^3 + 6k^2$**

Find the sum or difference.

7. $(8x^2 + 3x) + (7x^2 - 15x)$ **$15x^2 - 12x$**

8. $(-x^3 + 5x) + (3x^2 - 7x)$ **$-x^3 + 3x^2 - 2x$**

9. $(x^3 - x^2 + 7x) - (2x^3 + x + 1)$ **$-x^3 - x^2 + 6x - 1$**

10. Photography You have a photograph that is 5 inches long and 3 inches wide. You want to surround the photo with a mat that will be x inches wide on all sides, as shown.

a. Write a polynomial expression for the total width of the photo and the mat. **$2x + 3$**

b. Write a polynomial expression for the total length of the photo and the mat. **$2x + 5$**

c. Write a polynomial expression for the combined area of the photo and mat. **$4x^2 + 16x + 15$**

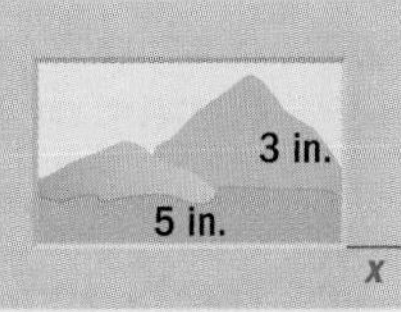

Find the product.

11. $(3b + 4)(b - 7)$ **$3b^2 - 17b - 28$**

12. $(9p - 1)^2$ **$81p^2 - 18p + 1$**

13. $(n - 8)(3n - 5)$ **$3n^2 - 29n + 40$**

Missing Monomials

Find the missing terms in the equations below. Locate these terms in the table. Then unscramble the letters below the terms to answer the following riddle.

How many letters are there in the alphabet? ELEVEN

$(2a + 5)(3a - 8) = 6a^2 + \underline{?} - 40$

$(b - 6)(2b + \underline{?}) = 2b^2 - 8b - 24$

$(4c + \underline{?})(\underline{?} - 1) = 4c^2 - 7c + 3$

$(3d + 7)(\underline{?} + \underline{?}) = 12d^2 + 34d + 14$

Term	$-a$	b	c	$-d$	$2a$	$3b$	$-2c$	$4d$	-8	-3	1	2	4
Letter	E	D	L	R	T	W	I	E	H	E	O	V	N

Additional Resources

The following resources are available to help review the materials in Lessons 12.1–12.4.

Chapter 12 Resource Book
- Lesson Practice
- Study Guide

Assessment Book
- Chapter 12 Quiz 1

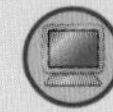

Technology
- Test and Practice Generator
- eTutorial CD-ROM

Internet
- Classzone
- eWorkbook Plus Online
- eTutorial Plus Online

English Learner Support

- Spanish Study Guide
- Multi-Language Visual Glossary
- Chapter Audio Summaries CDs

1 PLAN

Skill Check

Simplify the expression.

1. $(-5)^3$ −125
2. 6^2 36
3. $(-3)^4$ 81
4. 2^5 32

LESSON OBJECTIVE

Simplify powers of products and quotients.

PACING

Suggested Number of Days
Basic Course: 1 day
Average Course: 1 day
Advanced Course: 1 day
Block: 0.5 block with 12.4

TEACHING RESOURCES

For a complete list of Teaching Resources, see page 648B.

TRANSPARENCY

Warm-Up Exercises for this lesson are available on a transparency.

2 TEACH

MOTIVATING THE LESSON

Have students evaluate each of the expressions 2^3, 3^3, $27 \cdot 8$, and 6^3 on the board. Then ask students how 6^3 is related to the product of 27 and 8. $6^3 = 27 \cdot 8$ Ask students to draw a conclusion from this result.

LESSON **12.5**

Other Rules *of* Exponents

Review Vocabulary
power, p. 10
exponent, p. 10

BEFORE	Now	WHY?
You simplified products and quotients of powers.	You'll simplify powers of products and quotients.	So you can find the area of a transistor, as in Ex. 11.

Notice what happens when you raise a product or a quotient to a power.

$$(ab)^3 = (ab)(ab)(ab) = (a \cdot a \cdot a)(b \cdot b \cdot b) = a^3b^3$$

$$\left(\frac{a}{b}\right)^3 = \left(\frac{a}{b}\right)\left(\frac{a}{b}\right)\left(\frac{a}{b}\right) = \frac{a \cdot a \cdot a}{b \cdot b \cdot b} = \frac{a^3}{b^3}$$

Rules of Exponents

Power of a Product Property

Words To find the power of a product, find the power of each factor and multiply.

Algebra $(ab)^m = a^mb^m$ **Numbers** $(3 \cdot 4)^2 = 3^2 \cdot 4^2$

Power of a Quotient Property

Words To find the power of a quotient, find the power of the numerator and the power of the denominator and divide.

Algebra $\left(\frac{a}{b}\right)^m = \frac{a^m}{b^m}$, where $b \neq 0$ **Numbers** $\left(\frac{4}{7}\right)^5 = \frac{4^5}{7^5}$

Example 1 ***Finding Powers of Products***

a. $(2x)^3 = 2^3 \cdot x^3$ **Power of a product property**
$= 8x^3$ **Evaluate power.**

b. $(-5y)^2 = (-5)^2 \cdot y^2$ **Power of a product property**
$= 25y^2$ **Evaluate power.**

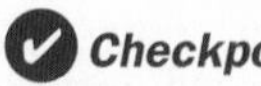

Checkpoint

Simplify the expression.

1. $(4y)^3$ $64y^3$
2. $(3x)^4$ $81x^4$
3. $(-5m)^3$ $-125m^3$
4. $(-7b)^2$ $49b^2$

NCTM CURRICULUM STANDARDS
Standard 1: Understand ways of representing numbers
Standard 2: Represent situations using algebraic symbols; Analyze situations using algebraic symbols

Example 2 *Finding Powers of Quotients*

Simplify the expression.

a. $\left(\frac{m}{n}\right)^7 = \frac{m^7}{n^7}$ **Power of a quotient property**

b. $\left(\frac{-3}{k}\right)^5 = \frac{(-3)^5}{k^5}$ **Power of a quotient property**

$= \frac{-243}{k^5}$ **Evaluate power.**

Checkpoint

Simplify the expression.

5. $\left(\frac{a}{6}\right)^2$ $\frac{a^2}{36}$ **6.** $\left(\frac{b}{c}\right)^3$ $\frac{b^3}{c^3}$ **7.** $\left(\frac{x}{-9}\right)^2$ $\frac{x^2}{81}$ **8.** $\left(\frac{-2}{n}\right)^5$ $-\frac{32}{n^5}$

Power of a Power Property Another rule of exponents is the power of a power property. The example below suggests the general rule.

$$(a^2)^4 = (a^2)(a^2)(a^2)(a^2)$$
$$= (a \cdot a)(a \cdot a)(a \cdot a)(a \cdot a)$$
$$= a^8$$

Rules of Exponents

Power of a Power Property

Words To find the power of a power, multiply the exponents.

Algebra $(a^m)^n = a^{mn}$ **Numbers** $(7^2)^3 = 7^{2 \times 3} = 7^6$

Watch *Out*

When you multiply exponents to apply the power of a power property, don't forget to consider the signs of the exponents.

Example 3 *Finding a Power of a Power*

Simplify the expression. Use positive exponents.

a. $(10^3)^3 = 10^9$ **Power of a power property**

b. $(p^{-4})^5 = p^{-20}$ **Power of a power property**

$= \frac{1}{p^{20}}$ **Definition of negative exponent**

Checkpoint

Simplify the expression. Write your answer using positive exponents.

9. $(2^3)^4$ 2^{12} **10.** $(5^2)^{-2}$ $\frac{1}{5^4}$ **11.** $(k^6)^3$ k^{18} **12.** $(a^{-2})^5$ $\frac{1}{a^{10}}$

13. $(4^{-1})^3$ $\frac{1}{4^3}$ **14.** $(3^{-4})^2$ $\frac{1}{3^8}$ **15.** $(b^7)^4$ b^{28} **16.** $(x^{-3})^{-2}$ x^6

TIPS *for* NEW TEACHERS

Expect students to find the power of a power property confusing since it involves multiplying exponents rather than adding them. Invite students to suggest mnemonics to help them decide when exponents should be multiplied and when they should be added. See Tips for New Teachers in the *Chapter 12 Resource Book*.

Extra Examples

Example 1 Simplify the expression.
a. $(5y)^4$ $625y^4$
b. $(-10g)^3$ $-1000g^3$

Example 2 Simplify the expression.
a. $\left(\frac{x}{2y}\right)^2$ $\frac{x^2}{4y^2}$
b. $\left(\frac{-5}{3b}\right)^3$ $-\frac{125}{27b^3}$

Example 3 Simplify the expression. Use positive exponents.
a. $(c^5)^4$ c^{20}
b. $(d^{-3})^{-1}$ d^3

Common Error

In Example 2b, point out the negative sign in the numerator of the result. Review the rules for when a product of negative numbers results in a positive value and when it results in a negative value. Lead students to recognize that a negative number with an odd exponent will have a negative value, while a negative number with an even exponent will have a positive value.

Extra Examples

Example 4 A city park is 1.4×10^3 meters on each side. What is the approximate area of this park? **1.96×10^6 m²**

ALGEBRAIC REASONING

Before discussing Example 4, write the statement $a(a \cdot a) = a^2 \cdot a^2 = a^4$ on the board. Ask students to identify the mistake in the statement. Make sure students understand that the use of the distributive property is inappropriate here because $a \cdot a = a^2$ and $a(a^2) = a^3$.

TEACHING TIP

In Checkpoint Exercise 20, review with students the correct form for scientific notation, reminding them that the first term should be greater than or equal to 1 but less than 10.

CONCEPT CHECK

Is $(x^3)^4$ equal to x^7 or x^{12}? Explain. **x^{12}. *Sample answer:* $(x^3)^4 = (x^3)(x^3)(x^3)(x^3) = (x \cdot x \cdot x) \cdot (x \cdot x \cdot x)(x \cdot x \cdot x)(x \cdot x \cdot x) = x^{12}$**

DAILY PUZZLER

Find $((x^3)^4)^5$. **x^{60}**

Example 4 ***Using Properties of Exponents***

World's Tiniest Book The square pages of the world's tiniest book are about 2.5×10^{-3} meter on each side. What is the approximate area of one page of this book?

Solution

To find the area of one page, use the formula for the area of a square.

$A = s^2$	**Formula for area of a square**
$= (2.5 \times 10^{-3})^2$	**Substitute 2.5×10^{-3} for s.**
$= (2.5)^2 \times (10^{-3})^2$	**Power of a product property**
$= (2.5)^2 \times 10^{-6}$	**Power of a power property**
$= 6.25 \times 10^{-6}$	**Evaluate power.**

Answer Each page has an area of about 6.25×10^{-6} square meter.

1. ***Sample answer:*** **The power of a quotient property states that the power of a quotient is the power of the numerator divided by the power of the denominator. For example, $\left(\frac{2x}{y}\right)^3 = \frac{(2x)^3}{y^3} = \frac{8x^3}{y^3}$.**

Checkpoint

Simplify the expression. Write your answer in scientific notation.

17. $(3.1 \times 10^8)^2$ **9.61×10^{16}**
18. $(2.1 \times 10^{-5})^2$ **4.41×10^{-10}**
19. $(1.7 \times 10^{-9})^3$ **4.913×10^{-27}**
20. $(4.5 \times 10^7)^3$ **9.1125×10^{22}**

12.5 Exercises

More Practice, p. 814

Guided Practice

Vocabulary Check

1. Describe the power of a quotient property and give an example. **See margin.**

2. Tell what property or properties of exponents you could use to simplify the expression. **2a–d. See margin.**

a. $(x^3)^4$ **b.** $(mn)^5$ **c.** $\left(\frac{p}{q}\right)^3$ **d.** $(a^2b)^6$

2a. power of a power property
2b. power of a product property
2c. power of a quotient property
2d. power of a product property, power of a power property

Skill Check **Simplify the expression. Write your answer using positive exponents.**

3. $(-6x)^3$ **$-216x^3$** **4.** $(5y)^4$ **$625y^4$** **5.** $\left(\frac{n}{-7}\right)^2$ **$\frac{n^2}{49}$** **6.** $\left(\frac{2}{m}\right)^5$ **$\frac{32}{m^5}$**

7. $(7^{-1})^{-6}$ **7^6** **8.** $(3^2)^{-5}$ **$\frac{1}{3^{10}}$** **9.** $(y^3)^2$ **y^6** **10.** $(a^{-1})^4$ **$\frac{1}{a^4}$**

11. Computers Some transistors used in computers are squares with a side length of 1.3×10^{-7} meter. What is the area of one of these transistors? **1.69×10^{-14} m²**

12. Error Analysis Describe and correct the error in simplifying $(3x)^4$.

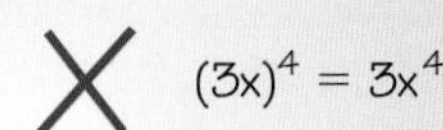

12. ***Sample answer:*** **By the power of a product property, the exponent should have been applied also to the 3 to give $(3x)^4 = 3^4x^4 = 81x^4$.**

Practice and Problem Solving

Homework *Help*

Example	Exercises
1	13-20, 36-39
2	21-24, 40-43
3	25-28, 36-43
4	29-35

CLASSZONE.COM

- More Examples
- eTutorial Plus

Simplify the expression. Write your answer using positive exponents.

A **13.** $(yz)^6$ y^6z^6 **14.** $(pr)^7$ p^7r^7 **15.** $(3t)^4$ $81t^4$ **16.** $(5c)^2$ $25c^2$

17. $(-3y)^8$ $6561y^8$ **18.** $(-7x)^3$ $-343x^3$ **19.** $(ab)^3$ a^3b^3 **20.** $(pq)^8$ p^8q^8

21. $\left(\frac{p}{10}\right)^5$ $\frac{p^5}{100{,}000}$ **22.** $\left(\frac{w}{12}\right)^2$ $\frac{w^2}{144}$ **23.** $\left(\frac{-3}{x}\right)^4$ $\frac{81}{x^4}$ **24.** $\left(\frac{m}{-2}\right)^6$ $\frac{m^6}{64}$

25. $(5^2)^4$ 5^8 **26.** $(4^{-3})^2$ $\frac{1}{4^6}$ **27.** $(a^4)^{-2}$ $\frac{1}{a^8}$ **28.** $(x^{-1})^{-6}$ x^6

Simplify the expression. Write your answer in scientific notation. Round the decimal part of your answer to the nearest hundredth.

29. $(1.8 \times 10^6)^3$ 5.83×10^{18} **30.** $(2.4 \times 10^{-8})^2$ 5.76×10^{-16} **31.** $(2.2 \times 10^{12})^2$ 4.84×10^{24}

32. $(6.1 \times 10^2)^5$ 8.45×10^{13} **33.** $(3.5 \times 10^{-10})^3$ 4.29×10^{-29} **34.** $(9.6 \times 10^{-1})^4$ 8.49×10^{-1}

35. Hoag's Object Hoag's Object is a galaxy composed of a blue ring around a yellow center. The diameter of the blue ring is about 1.2×10^5 light-years. Find the area of the circle formed by the blue ring. Use 3.14 for π. Write your answer in scientific notation, rounding the decimal part to the nearest hundredth. 1.13×10^{10} square light-years

Hoag's Object

Simplify the expression. Write your answer using positive exponents.

B **36.** $(ab^2)^3$ a^3b^6 **37.** $(x^2y)^4$ x^8y^4 **38.** $(m^2n)^5$ $m^{10}n^5$ **39.** $(d^3e^4)^2$ d^6e^8

40. $\left(\frac{x^5}{y^4}\right)^6$ $\frac{x^{30}}{y^{24}}$ **41.** $\left(\frac{w^3}{v^5}\right)^5$ $\frac{w^{15}}{v^{25}}$ **42.** $\left(\frac{p^3}{t^2}\right)^2$ $\frac{p^6}{t^4}$ **43.** $\left(\frac{-r}{s^4}\right)^3$ $-\frac{r^3}{s^{12}}$

In Exercises 44–49, copy and complete the statement.

Example *Converting Units For Area or Volume*

Copy and complete: 3 ft³ = ? in.³

Cube the conversion factor for converting feet to inches.

$$3\text{ ft}^3 = 3\text{ ft}^3 \times \left(\frac{12\text{ in.}}{1\text{ ft}}\right)^3$$ **Multiply by cube of conversion factor.**

$$= 3\text{ ft}^3 \times \frac{(12\text{ in.})^3}{(1\text{ ft})^3}$$ **Power of a quotient property**

$$= 3\text{ ft}^3 \times \frac{1728\text{ in.}^3}{1\text{ ft}^3}$$ **Evaluate powers. Divide out common unit.**

$$= 5184\text{ in.}^3$$ **Simplify.**

44. $5\text{ ft}^2 = \underline{?}\text{ in.}^2$ 720 **45.** $45\text{ m}^2 = \underline{?}\text{ km}^2$ 0.000045 **46.** $1\text{ yd}^2 = \underline{?}\text{ ft}^2$ 9

47. $6\text{ m}^3 = \underline{?}\text{ cm}^3$ 6,000,000 **48.** $3\text{ mm}^3 = \underline{?}\text{ cm}^3$ 0.003 **49.** $2\text{ mi}^2 = \underline{?}\text{ ft}^2$ 55,756,800

50. *Writing* Compare the power of a product property from this lesson with the product of powers property on page 194. Write an expression to which *both* properties can be applied, then apply the properties.

50. ***Sample answer:*** **The power of a product property states that to find a power of a product, find the power of each factor in the product and multiply the powers. The product of powers property states that to find the product of powers that have the same base, keep the base and add the exponents. For example, to simplify $x^2(xy)^3$, first use the power of a product property to obtain $x^2(x^3y^3)$. Then use the product of powers property to obtain x^5y^3.**

3 APPLY

ASSIGNMENT GUIDE

Basic Course

Day 1: EP p. 806 Exs. 45-48; pp. 677-678 Exs. 13-24, 27-31, 35-41, 44-46, 53-65

Average Course

Day 1: pp. 677-678 Exs. 17-28, 32-37, 40-43, 46-51, 53-65

Advanced Course

Day 1: pp. 677-678 Exs. 19-28, 32-35, 38-43, 47-55*, 59-65

Block

pp. 677-678 Exs. 17-28, 32-37, 40-43, 46-51, 53-65 (with 12.4)

EXTRA PRACTICE

- Student Edition, p. 814
- Chapter 12 Resource Book, pp. 45-47
- Test and Practice Generator

TRANSPARENCY

Even-numbered answers are available on transparencies. A support transparency is available for Exercises 57-60.

HOMEWORK CHECK

When you review students' homework for this lesson, go over the following exercises to check understanding of key concepts.

Basic: 13, 21, 27, 29, 36
Average: 17, 22, 26, 32, 40
Advanced: 19, 24, 28, 34, 42

4 ASSESS

Assessment Resources

For more assessment resources, see:
- Assessment Book
- Test and Practice Generator

Mini-Quiz

Simplify the expression. Write your answer using positive exponents.

1. $(2m)^3$ **$8m^3$**
2. $(a^2b)^4$ **a^8b^4**
3. $\left(-\frac{2x}{y^2}\right)^3$ **$-\frac{8x^3}{y^6}$**
4. $(n^{-3})^5$ **$\frac{1}{n^{15}}$**
5. **Challenge** The formula for the surface area of a sphere is $S = 4\pi r^2$. Use this formula to find the surface area of a nanosphere with a radius of 4.5×10^{-8} meter. Use 3.14 for π. Write your answer in scientific notation, rounding the decimal part to the nearest hundredth. **2.54×10^{-14} m^2**

5 FOLLOW-UP

Diagnosis/Remediation

- Study Guide in Chapter 12 Resource Book, pp. 48–49
- eTutorial Plus Online
- Extra Practice, p. 814
- Lesson Practice in Chapter 12 Resource Book, pp. 45–47

English Learner Support

- Spanish Study Guide
- Multi-Language Visual Glossary
- Chapter Audio Summaries CDs

Challenge

- Challenge Practice in Chapter 12 Resource Book, p. 50
- Teacher's Edition, p. 648F

53–60. See Additional Answers beginning on page AA1.

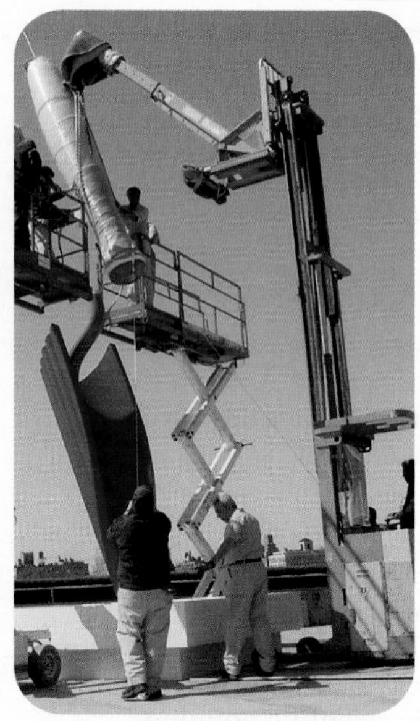

This hydraulic crane is being used to assemble a sculpture.

C **51. Extended Problem Solving** The pistons in a hydraulic system are cylinders containing fluid. When one piston is pushed down, another piston is pushed up by an equal volume of fluid. Use the information in the diagram to answer the following questions.

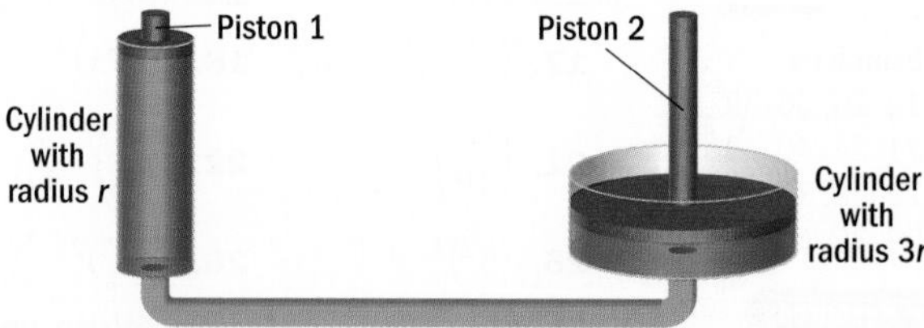

a. Piston 1 is pushed down 7 inches. What volume of fluid is displaced from piston 1? Use 3.14 for π. **about $21.98r^2$ in.^{3}**

b. Interpret and Apply How many inches will the volume you calculated in part (a) push up piston 2? Explain. **See margin.**

c. Critical Thinking Suppose piston 2 is pushed down a distance d (in inches). How far (in terms of d) is piston 1 pushed up? **$9d$ in.**

52. Challenge Scientists have developed microscopic spheres called nanospheres that circulate in the bloodstream and deliver medicine for several hours. A nanosphere's radius can be as small as 4.5×10^{-8} m. The formula for the volume of a sphere is $V = \frac{4}{3}\pi r^3$. Use this formula to find the volume of a nanosphere. Use 3.14 for π. Write your answer in scientific notation, rounding the decimal part to the nearest hundredth. **3.82×10^{-22} m^3**

Mixed Review

51b. $\frac{7}{9}$ **in.** ***Sample answer:*** **The volumes of oil in each cylinder must be equal. The volume in the cylinder with radius $3r$ is about $3.14(3r)^2h$, so $3.14(3r)^2h = 21.98r^2$. Solving for h gives $h = \frac{7}{9}$ inch.**

Algebra Basics Graph the equation. Tell whether the equation is a function. *(Lesson 8.2)* **53–56. See margin for art.**

53. $y = -\frac{1}{3}x + 6$ **yes** **54.** $y = 4x - 3$ **yes** **55.** $x = 30$ **no** **56.** $24x + 4y = 16$ **yes**

Algebra Basics Graph the inequality in a coordinate plane. *(Lesson 8.9)* **57–60. See margin.**

57. $y > 2x - 7$ **58.** $y \geq -\frac{5}{6}x - 3$ **59.** $8x + 48 \leq 12y$ **60.** $-8x + 3y < 21$

Write a polynomial expression for the area of the rectangle, triangle, or parallelogram. Give your answer in standard form. *(Lesson 12.4)*

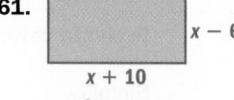

61. Rectangle with sides $x - 6$ and $x + 10$. **$x^2 + 4x - 60$**

62. Right triangle with legs $4x - 5$ and $2x + 8$. **$4x^2 + 11x - 20$**

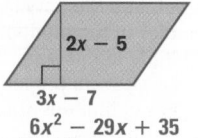

63. Parallelogram with height $2x - 5$ and base $3x - 7$. **$6x^2 - 29x + 35$**

Standardized Test Practice

64. Multiple Choice Which expression is equivalent to $\left(\frac{-4}{x^2}\right)^3$? **B**

A. $\frac{64}{x^6}$ **B.** $\frac{-64}{x^6}$ **C.** $\frac{64}{x^3}$ **D.** $\frac{-64}{x^3}$

65. Multiple Choice Which expression is equivalent to $-a^8b^6$? **F**

F. $-(a^4b^3)^2$ **G.** $(-a^4b^3)^2$ **H.** $(-a)^8(b^3)^2$ **I.** $-(a^4)(b^3)^2$

LESSON **12.6**

Quadratic Functions

BEFORE	Now	WHY?
You graphed linear functions.	You'll graph quadratic functions.	So you can estimate wave heights, as in Ex. 37.

Vocabulary

quadratic function, p. 679
parabola, p. 680
nonlinear function, p. 680
minimum value, p. 681
maximum value, p. 681

Acrobats An acrobat is launched into the air from a teeterboard. The acrobat's height from the ground (in feet) is given by the function

$$h = -16t^2 + 33t + 3,$$

where t is the time in seconds after the launch. What is the greatest height that the acrobat reaches? You will see how to answer this question in Example 4.

The function $h = -16t^2 + 33t + 3$ is a *quadratic function*. A **quadratic function** is an equation in two variables that can be written in the form $y = ax^2 + bx + c$, where a, b, and c are constants and $a \neq 0$.

Example 1 *Evaluating a Quadratic Function*

To make a table of values for the quadratic function $y = 2x^2 + 3x + 1$, substitute several values of x into the equation. Then simplify to find the corresponding values for y.

x	Substitution	y
−2	$y = 2(-2)^2 + 3(-2) + 1$ $= 8 + (-6) + 1$ $= 3$	3
−1	$y = 2(-1)^2 + 3(-1) + 1$	0
0	$y = 2(0)^2 + 3(0) + 1$	1
1	$y = 2(1)^2 + 3(1) + 1$	6
2	$y = 2(2)^2 + 3(2) + 1$	15

For $x = -2$, the process of substituting and simplifying is shown.

For $x = -1, 0, 1,$ and 2, only the substitution is shown.

Checkpoint

Make a table of values for the given function.

1. $y = -x^2 + 2x + 1$
2. $y = x^2 - 4x + 7$
3. $y = 3x^2 + 6x - 9$

1–3. Sample tables are given.

1.

x	−1	0	1	2	3
y	−2	1	2	1	−2

2.

x	0	1	2	3	4
y	7	4	3	4	7

3.

x	−3	−2	−1	0	1
y	0	−9	−12	−9	0

NCTM CURRICULUM STANDARDS

Standard 2: Understand functions; Analyze situations using algebraic symbols; Use models to understand relationships

1 PLAN

Skill Check

Find value of the expression when $x = -2$.

1. $2x - 4$ **−8**
2. $x^2 - x + 1$ **7**
3. $-2x^2 - 3x - 4$ **−6**
4. $-5x + 12$ **22**

Lesson Objective

Graph quadratic functions.

Pacing

Suggested Number of Days
Basic Course: 2 days
Average Course: 2 days
Advanced Course: 2 days
Block: 1 block

Teaching Resources

For a complete list of Teaching Resources, see page 648B.

Transparency

Warm-Up Exercises for this lesson are available on a transparency. A support transparency is available for Examples 1–3 and Checkpoint Exercises 1–9.

2 TEACH

Motivating the Lesson

After reading the introduction, have students find the acrobat's height at 0, 1, and 2 seconds. **3 ft, 20 ft, 5 ft**

TIPS *for* NEW TEACHERS

Show students a quadratic curve. Stress that this curve does not have a slope in the same way that the graph of a line does. See Tips for New Teachers in the *Chapter 12 Resource Book*.

Extra Examples

Example 1 Make a table of values for the quadratic function $y = x^2 + 4x - 2$, using the integers from -2 to 2 as the values of x.

x	y
−2	−6
−1	−5
0	−2
1	3
2	10

Example 2 Graph the function $y = \frac{1}{4}x^2 + 1$.

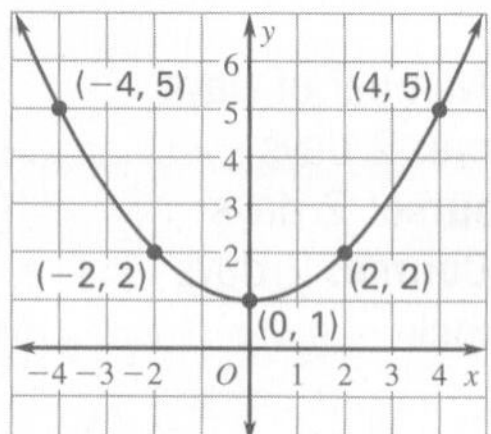

Example 3 Graph the function $y = -\frac{1}{2}x^2 + 4x - 3$.

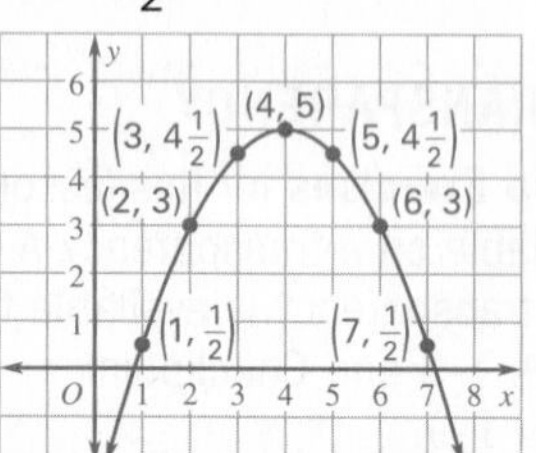

Differentiating Instruction

Less Proficient Students Have pairs of students work together to make a table of values for a quadratic function. Check students' tables before they graph the points to assure them that they are correct or tell them which points are incorrect.

4–6. See Additional Answers beginning on page AA1.

Study Strategy

If you are having difficulty seeing the curve of a graph, plot additional points.

Graphing Quadratic Functions The graph of a quadratic function is a U-shaped curve called a **parabola**. A quadratic function is an example of a *nonlinear function*. A **nonlinear function** is any function whose graph is not a line.

Example 2 *Graphing a Quadratic Function*

Graph the function $y = \frac{1}{2}x^2 + 1$.

1) Make a table of values. Choose several x-values and find the corresponding y-values.

x	−4	−2	0	2	4
y	9	3	1	3	9

2) Use the table to make a list of ordered pairs.

(−4, 9), (−2, 3), (0, 1), (2, 3), (4, 9)

3) Graph the ordered pairs. Then draw a smooth curve through the points.

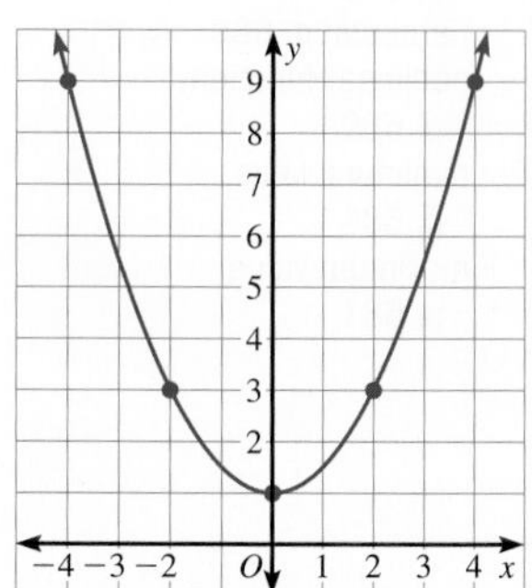

Checkpoint

4–6. See margin.

Make a table of values for the given function. Then graph the function.

4. $y = 2x^2 + 5$ **5.** $y = x^2 - 8x - 2$ **6.** $y = x^2 + 4x$

Example 3 *Graphing a Quadratic Function*

Graph the function $y = -x^2 + 2x - 1$.

1) Make a table of values. Choose several x-values and find the corresponding y-values.

x	−2	−1	0	1	2	3
y	−9	−4	−1	0	−1	−4

2) Use the table to make a list of ordered pairs.

(−2, −9), (−1, −4), (0, −1), (1, 0), (2, −1), (3, −4)

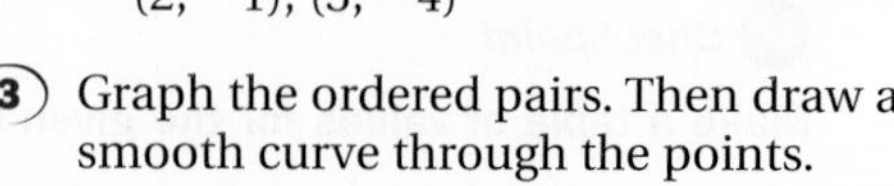

3) Graph the ordered pairs. Then draw a smooth curve through the points.

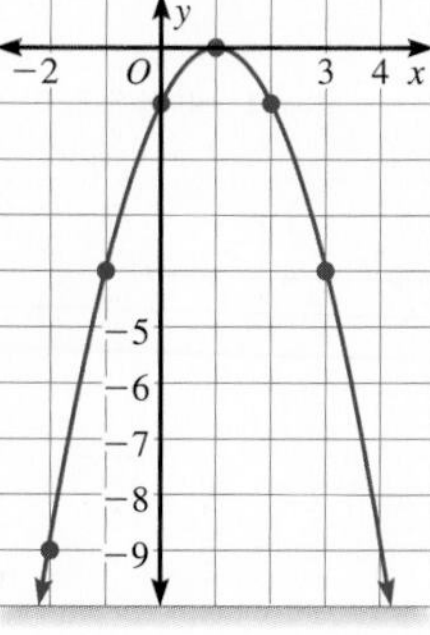

7–9. See margin.

Make a table of values for the given function. Then graph the function.

7. $y = -x^2 - 3$ **8.** $y = -2x^2 + 4x$ **9.** $y = -x^2 + 6x + 1$

Maximum and Minimum Values In the quadratic function $y = ax^2 + bx + c$, the value of a indicates whether the graph opens upward or downward.

When $a > 0$, as in Example 2, the graph of the function opens upward. In this case, the function has a **minimum value**, which is the y-coordinate of the lowest point on the graph.

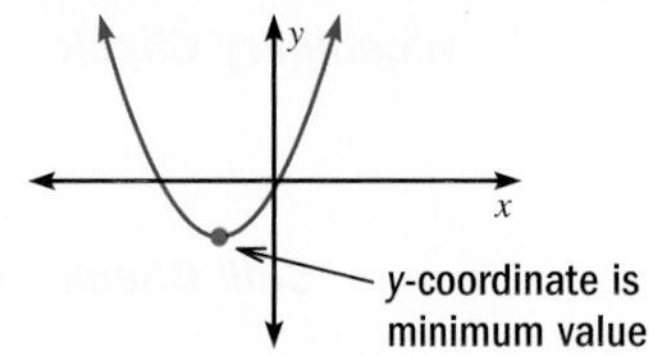

When $a < 0$, as in Example 3, the graph of the function opens downward. In this case, the function has a **maximum value**, which is the y-coordinate of the highest point on the graph.

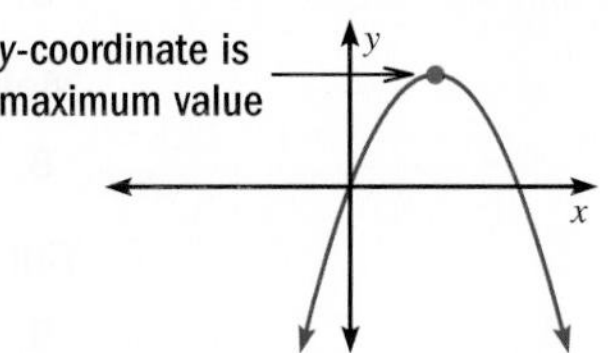

Study *Strategy*

The function in Example 2 has a minimum value of 1 at $x = 0$. The function in Example 3 has a maximum value of 0 at $x = 1$.

Example 4 *Using a Calculator to Find a Maximum Value*

Find the greatest height reached by the acrobat described on page 679.

Solution

Use a graphing calculator to graph $h = -16t^2 + 33t + 3$. Set the viewing window so that you can see the highest point on the graph. Using the calculator's *trace* feature, you can determine that the highest point on the graph is about (1.02, 20.01). So, the maximum value is about 20.

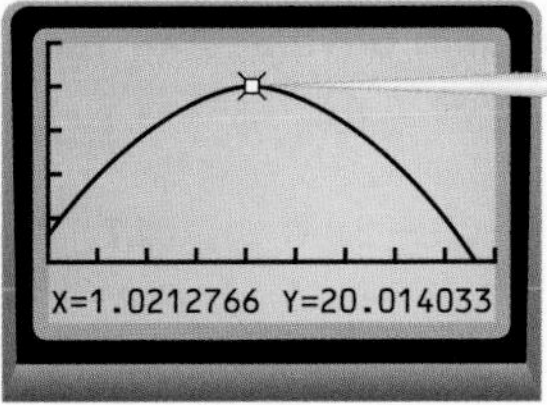

The coordinates of this point are about (1.02, 20.01).

Answer The greatest height reached by the acrobat is about 20 feet.

Checkpoint

Tell whether the function has a *maximum* or *minimum* value.

10. $y = 4.5x^2 - 9x$ minimum **11.** $y = x^2 - 17$ minimum **12.** $y = -3x^2 - 6x + 3$ maximum

Tell whether the function has a *maximum* or *minimum* value. Then graph the function using a graphing calculator and approximate the maximum or minimum value. 13–15. See margin for art.

13. $y = -x^2 + 6x + 5$ maximum; 14 **14.** $y = -x^2 + 9x + 1$ maximum; 21.25 **15.** $y = 5x^2 - 10x + 13$ minimum; 8

Common Error

Students will not be able to graph quadratic functions correctly if they make errors while creating the table of values. Stress that the plotted points should be easy to connect with a curve. If the points do not lie along a smooth curve, students should check their work.

Reading Strategy

Have students read the paragraphs on Maximum and Minimum Values aloud in class, one sentence at a time. After each sentence, have students repeat to themselves what they just read while referring to the figures.

Extra Examples

Example 4 Tell whether the function $y = -2x^2 + 5x - 3$ has a *maximum* or *minimum* value. Then find this value using a graphing calculator. **maximum; 0.125**

Concept Check

In a quadratic function, what does the coefficient of the squared term tell you about the graph of the function? **The sign of this coefficient determines whether the graph opens upward (positive) or downward (negative).**

Daily Puzzler

For $a < b$, which has a greater value, a^2 or b^2? Explain. ***Sample answer:* Either expression could have the greater value; for example, if $a = 1$ and $b = 2$, then $b^2 > a^2$, but if $a = -5$ and $b = 1$, then $a^2 > b^2$.**

7–9, 13–15. See Additional Answers beginning on page AA1.

3 APPLY

ASSIGNMENT GUIDE

Basic Course

Day 1: EP p. 810 Exs. 31–34; pp. 682–684 Exs. 13–21, 25–30, 50–55

Day 2: pp. 682–684 Exs. 22–24, 31–36, 38–43, 56–59

Average Course

Day 1: pp. 682–684 Exs. 13–21, 25–30, 50–58

Day 2: pp. 682–684 Exs. 22–24, 34–48, 59, 60

Advanced Course

Day 1: pp. 682–684 Exs. 18–24, 27–30, 50–58

Day 2: pp. 682–684 Exs. 34–37, 41–49*, 59, 60

Block

pp. 682–684 Exs. 13–30, 34–48, 50–60

EXTRA PRACTICE

- Student Edition, p. 814
- Chapter 12 Resource Book, pp. 54–56
- Test and Practice Generator

TRANSPARENCY

Even-numbered answers are available on transparencies. A support transparency is available for Exercises 3–8, 13–21, 25–30, 44, 46, 49, and 53–55.

HOMEWORK CHECK

When you review students' homework for this lesson, go over the following exercises to check understanding of key concepts.

Basic: 13, 22, 25, 31, 38

Average: 16, 23, 27, 34, 41

Advanced: 19, 24, 29, 35, 43

1, 6–8, 12 (Step 1), 13–21. See Additional Answers beginning on page AA1.

12.6 Exercises

More Practice, p. 814

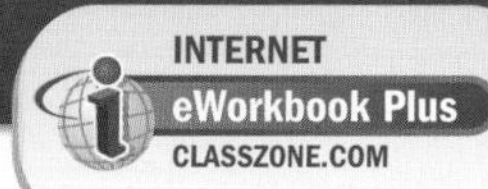

Guided Practice

Vocabulary Check

1. Describe the shape of the graph of a quadratic function. **See margin.**

2. Copy and complete: The graph of a quadratic function with a maximum value opens $\underline{?}$. **downward**

Skill Check

Make a table of values for the given function.

3. $y = -x^2 + 17$ **4.** $y = -4x^2 - 5$ **5.** $y = 3x^2 + 12x$

Make a table of values for the given function. Then graph the function. 6–8. See margin.

6. $y = -x^2$ **7.** $y = x^2 + 1$ **8.** $y = -2x^2 - 1$

Tell whether the function has a *maximum* or *minimum* value.

9. $y = -14x^2 + 9x$ **maximum** **10.** $y = 3x^2 - 17$ **minimum** **11.** $y = -6x^2 - 6x + 5$ **maximum**

3–5. Sample tables are given.

3.

x	−2	−1	0	1	2
y	13	16	17	16	13

4.

x	−2	−1	0	1	2
y	−21	−9	−5	−9	−21

5.

x	−4	−3	−2	−1	0
y	0	−9	−12	−9	0

Guided Problem Solving

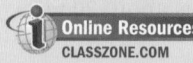

12. **Rainbow Trout** The lengths and masses of rainbow trout taken from the Spokane River in Washington are related by the quadratic function $y = 0.90x^2 - 26.5x + 290$, where x is the length (in centimeters) of a rainbow trout and y is its mass (in grams). What is the approximate length of a rainbow trout with a mass of 600 grams?

(1) Use a graphing calculator to graph the function. **See margin.**

(2) Use trace to find the approximate x-value when $y = 600$. **about 38.5 cm**

Practice and Problem Solving

Homework Help

Example	Exercises
1	13-21
2	22-30
3	22-30
4	31-36, 38-43

Online Resources CLASSZONE.COM
- More Examples
- eTutorial Plus

Make a table of values for the given function. 13–21. See margin.

A **13.** $y = -x^2 - 6x$ **14.** $y = 3x^2 + 4$ **15.** $y = 5x^2 - 20x$

16. $y = \frac{1}{4}x^2 - 2x$ **17.** $y = x^2 - 4x + 5$ **18.** $y = -x^2 + 6x + 4$

19. $y = \frac{1}{2}x^2 + x + 4$ **20.** $y = 4x^2 + 8x - 3$ **21.** $y = -\frac{1}{2}x^2 + 4x - 6$

Matching **Match the function with its graph.**

22. B

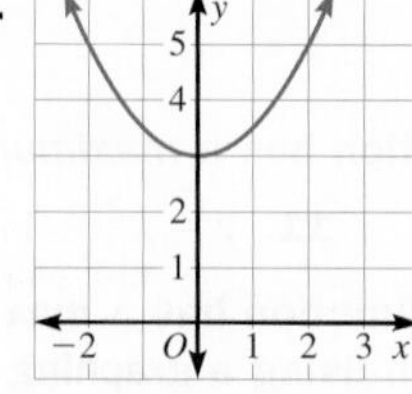

23. C

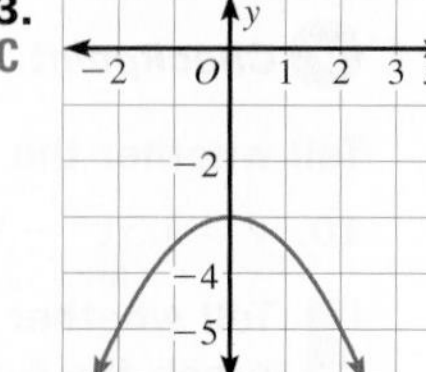

24. A

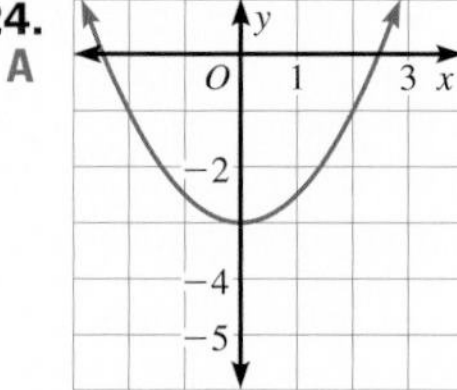

A. $y = \frac{1}{2}x^2 - 3$ **B.** $y = \frac{1}{2}x^2 + 3$ **C.** $y = -\frac{1}{2}x^2 - 3$

Make a table of values for the given function. Then graph the function.

25–30. See margin.

25. $y = -x^2 + 5$ **26.** $y = \frac{1}{2}x^2 + 2x$ **27.** $y = x^2 + 9$

28. $y = \frac{1}{2}x^2 - 3x + 2$ **29.** $y = \frac{1}{6}x^2 - 3x$ **30.** $y = \frac{1}{4}x^2 + \frac{1}{2}x$

Tell whether the function has a *maximum* or *minimum* value.

31. $y = -20x^2 - 9x$ maximum **32.** $y = 5x^2 - 20x + 3$ minimum **33.** $y = 2x^2 - 4x + 5$ minimum

34. $y = -x^2 + 9x + 2$ maximum **35.** $y = -x^2 - 9x + 17$ maximum **36.** $y = 3.5x^2 - 1.5x - 2$ minimum

37. Wind and Waves For certain bodies of water, the height of the waves and the speed of the wind can be related by the quadratic function $h = 0.007s^2 + 0.15s - 0.15$, where s is the wind speed in meters per second and h is the wave height in meters. Use the graph below to answer the following questions.

a. The ideal wave height for sailing is between 3 meters and 7 meters. What wind speeds correspond to these wave heights?
about 13 m/sec to 23 m/sec

b. Wave heights greater than 11 meters are considered dangerous when sailing. What wind speeds correspond to wave heights greater than 11 meters?
above about 31 m/sec

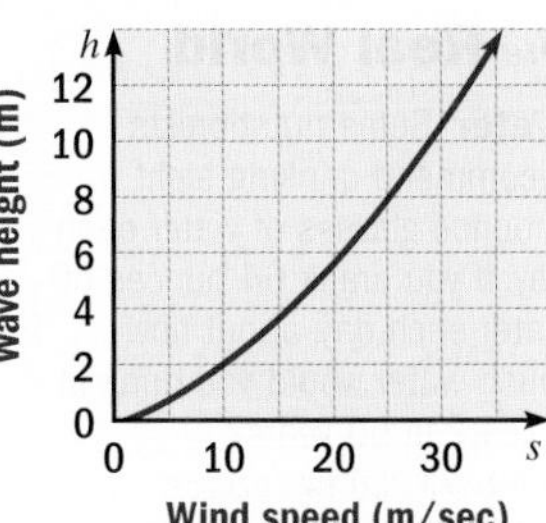

Tell whether the function has a *maximum* or *minimum* value. Then graph the function using a graphing calculator and approximate the maximum or minimum value. 38–43. See margin for art.

B 38. $y = -x^2 + 11x + 5$ maximum; 35.25 **39.** $y = -8x^2 + 9x + 1$ maximum; about 3.53 **40.** $y = 5x^2 - 9x + 13$ minimum; 8.95

41. $y = -16x^2 + 192x$ maximum; 576 **42.** $y = x^2 - 25x - 100$ minimum; −256.25 **43.** $y = 3x^2 + x - 42$ minimum; −42

44. *Writing* Graph the functions $y = x^2$, $y = x^2 - 1$, and $y = x^2 + 1$ in the same coordinate plane. Describe how the graphs are related. Predict what the graph of $y = x^2 - 2$ looks like. Then test your prediction.

44. See margin for art. *Sample answer:* The 3 graphs all have the same shape. The last 2 graphs are the first graph shifted up or down. The graph of $y = x^2 - 1$ is the graph of $y = x^2$ shifted down 1 unit and the graph of $y = x^2 + 1$ is the graph of $y = x^2$ shifted up 1 unit. The graph of $y = x^2 - 2$ should be the graph of $y = x^2$ shifted down 2 units. This prediction checks, as shown in the graph.

45. Critical Thinking Describe how to find the y-intercept of the graph of a quadratic function *without* graphing the function.
Sample answer: Substitute $x = 0$ in the equation of the function and solve for y.

46. Geometry Recall that the formula for the volume V of a cylinder is $V = \pi r^2 h$, where r is the radius and h is the height. Use 3.14 for π.
46a–b. See margin.

a. A cylinder has a fixed height of 4 units. The radius can vary. Write a formula for the volume of this cylinder as a function of its radius. Make a table of values for zero and whole number values of r. Graph the function.

b. A cylinder has a fixed radius of 3 units. The height can vary. Write a formula for the volume of this cylinder as a function of its height. Make a table of values for zero and whole number values of h. Graph the function.

c. Compare Compare the functions from parts (a) and (b). Which of the functions is linear and which is nonlinear?
$V = 9\pi h$ is linear; $V = 4\pi r^2$ is nonlinear.

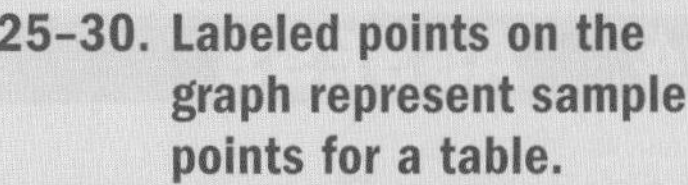

25–30. Labeled points on the graph represent sample points for a table.

25.

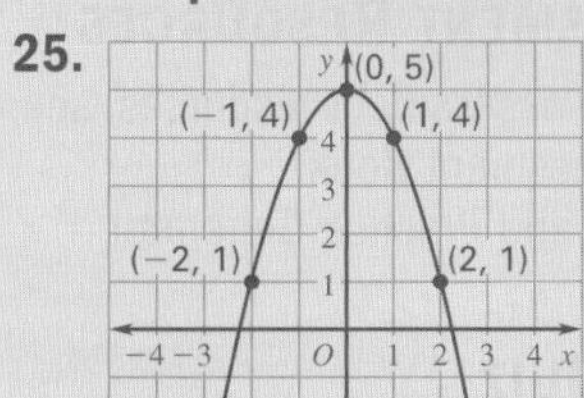

26.

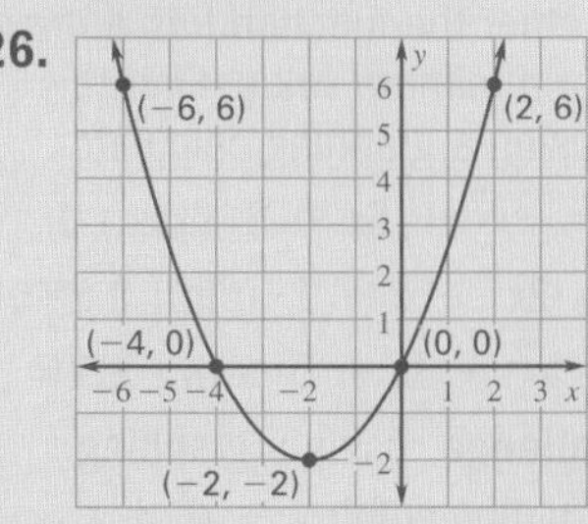

27.

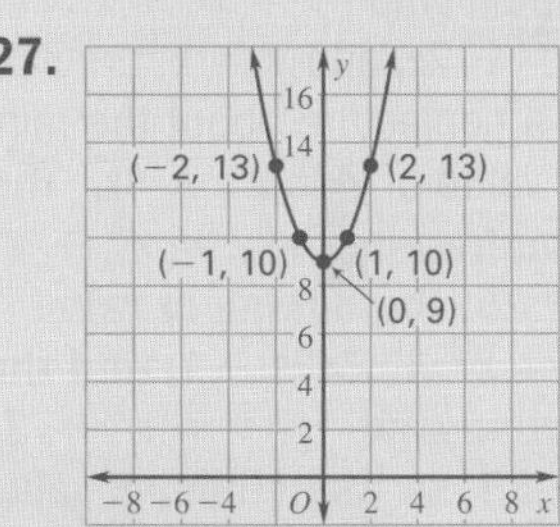

28.

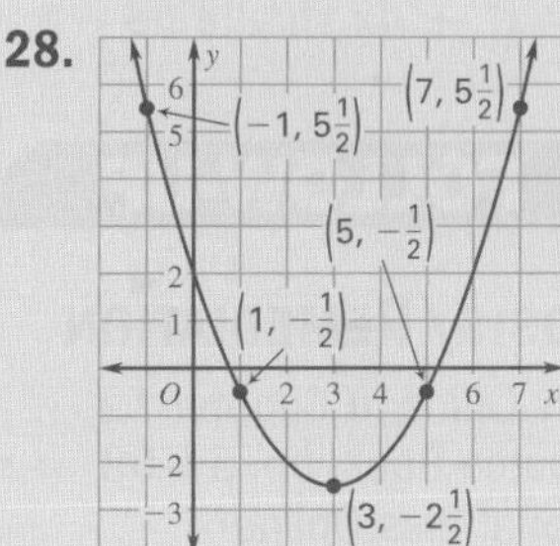

29.

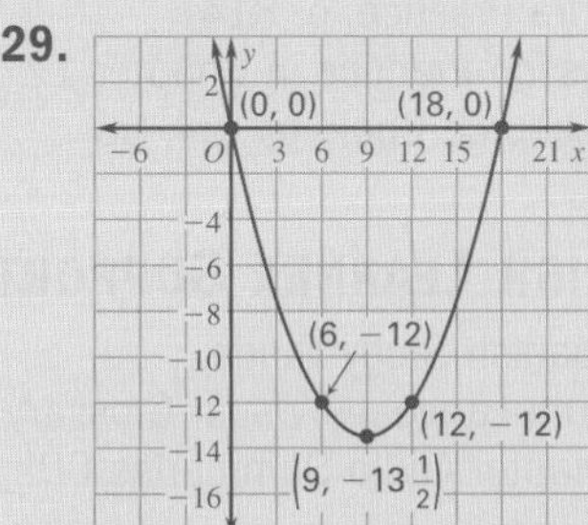

30.

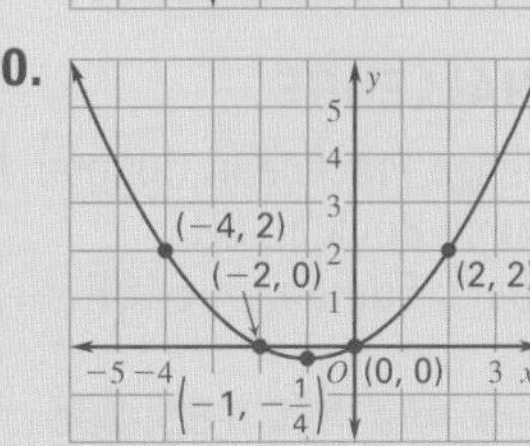

38–44, 46a–b. See Additional Answers beginning on page AA1.

4 ASSESS

ASSESSMENT RESOURCES

For more assessment resources, see:
- Assessment Book
- Test and Practice Generator

MINI-QUIZ

Tell whether the function has a *maximum* or *minimum* value. Find this value using a graphing calculator.

1. $y = -x^2 + 6x - 3$ **max.; 6**
2. $y = 2x^2 + x + 1$ **min.; 0.875**
3. $y = x^2 + 3x + 5$ **min.; 2.75**
4. **Challenge** Using a graphing calculator, graph $y = x^2 + x$, $y = x^2 + 2x$, and $y = x^2 + 3x$. Make a conjecture about the minimum value of $y = x^2 + 4x$. **The minimum value for $y = x^2 + x$ is -0.25, the minimum value for $y = x^2 + 2x$ is -1, and the minimum value for $y = x^2 + 3x$ is -2.25, so the minimum value of $y = x^2 + 4x$ should be -4.**

5 FOLLOW-UP

DIAGNOSIS/REMEDIATION

- Study Guide in Chapter 12 Resource Book, pp. 57-58
- eTutorial Plus Online
- Extra Practice, p. 814
- Lesson Practice in Chapter 12 Resource Book, pp. 54-56

ENGLISH LEARNER SUPPORT

- Spanish Study Guide
- Multi-Language Visual Glossary
- Chapter Audio Summaries CDs

CHALLENGE

- Challenge Practice in Chapter 12 Resource Book, p. 60
- Teacher's Edition, p. 648F

47a, 48a–b, 49a–b, 53–55. See Additional Answers beginning on page AA1.

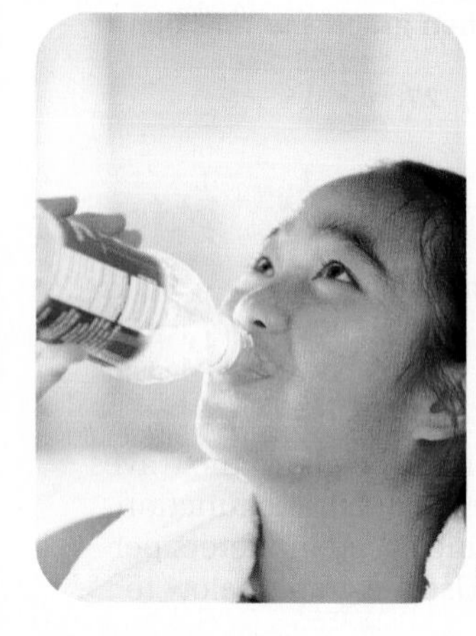

In the **Real World**

Water Some nutritionists recommend drinking eight 8 ounce glasses of water each day. If you drank 64 ounces of water each day, about how much water would you drink in a year? in 50 years? **about 23,360 oz; about 1,168,000 oz**

47c. 1999. *Sample answer:* The graph gets steeper as the year increases, which means that the amount of increase in water consumption gets larger as the year increases.

47. **Extended Problem Solving** For the period 1990–1999, the amount of bottled water consumed annually by a typical person in the United States can be approximated by $y = 0.1x^2 + 0.1x + 7.9$, where y is the amount of water (in gallons) and x is the number of years since 1990.
   a. Use a graphing calculator to graph the function. **See margin.**
   b. **Analyze** What was the first year that a typical person in the United States consumed more than 9 gallons of bottled water annually? **1993**
   c. **Interpret and Apply** In which year did annual bottled water consumption increase the most from the previous year? Explain how you can use the graph to answer this question. **See margin.**

C 48. **Cubic Functions** A *cubic function* is an equation in two variables that can be written in the form $y = ax^3 + bx^2 + cx + d$, where a, b, c, and d are constants and $a \neq 0$. **48a–b. See margin.**
   a. Use a graphing calculator to graph the functions $y = x^3$, $y = -x^3$, and $y = 2x^3$.
   b. **Compare** Describe the shapes of the graphs. How are the graphs alike? How are they different?

49. **Challenge** Consider the functions $y = -4x + 3$ and $y = -2x^2 + 6x + 4$.
   a. For each function, make a table of values for $x = 0, 1, 2, 3, 4, 5, 6$. Then graph each function. **49a–b. See margin.**
   b. For each function, find the slope between each consecutive pair of points you plotted in part (a).
   c. **Interpret** What can you say about the slopes you calculated for the linear function? What can you say about the slopes you calculated for the quadratic function? ***Sample answer:* They are the same for each pair of points; they are different for each pair of points.**

Mixed Review

Write the expression using only positive exponents. *(Lesson 4.6)*

50. 7^{-3} $\frac{1}{7^3}$
51. $5b^{-7}$ $\frac{5}{b^7}$
52. $m^{-9}n^2$ $\frac{n^2}{m^9}$

Graph the function. *(Lesson 8.7)* **53–55. See margin.**

53. $f(x) = 4x + 3$
54. $f(x) = -0.5x + 9$
55. $g(x) = -x - 10$

Simplify. Write your answer using positive exponents. *(Lesson 12.5)*

56. $(-3y)^3$ $-27y^3$
57. $\left(\frac{5}{n}\right)^2$ $\frac{25}{n^2}$
58. $(m^8)^{-11}$ $\frac{1}{m^{88}}$

Standardized Test Practice

59. **Multiple Choice** At what point does the minimum value of the function $y = 3x^2 - 8$ occur? **B**

   A. (0, 8) **B.** (0, −8) **C.** (8, 0) **D.** (−8, 0)

60. **Short Response** Scientists have studied how protein consumption affects the growth of pigs. The average growth of the pigs can be approximated by $y = -1.9x^2 + 1.7x + 0.3$, where y is the average daily growth in kilograms and x is the daily protein consumption in kilograms. Use a graphing calculator to approximate the maximum daily growth and the daily protein consumption needed to achieve that growth. **about 0.68 kilogram growth for about 0.45 kilogram of protein consumption**

Technology *Activity*
GRAPHING CALCULATOR

12.6 Graphing Quadratic Functions

Goal Use a graphing calculator to investigate the graph of $y = ax^2$.

Investigate

Use a graphing calculator to compare the graph of $y = x^2$ with the graph of $y = \frac{1}{2}x^2$.

Enter the functions to be graphed. (Note: Your calculator will not show any colors. Red is used here to distinguish the two functions.)

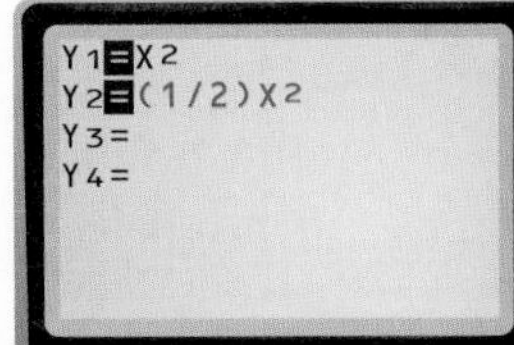

Keystrokes

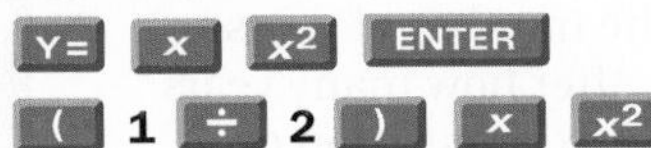

Graph the functions using the calculator's standard window.

Keystrokes

ZOOM 6

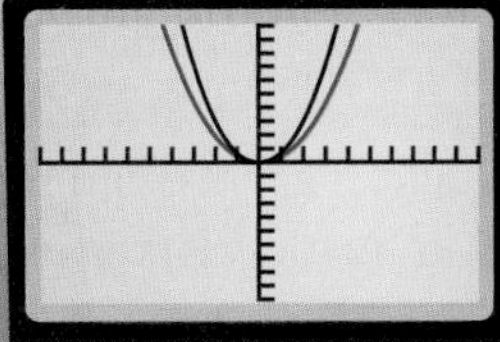

3 Compare and contrast the graphs.

Both parabolas open up, and both pass through the origin. But the graph of $y = \frac{1}{2}x^2$ is wider than the graph of $y = x^2$.

Draw Conclusions

Compare the graph of $y = x^2$ with the graph of the given function. **1–5. See margin.**

1. $y = 4x^2$

2. $y = -3x^2$

3. $y = -0.5x^2$

4. $y = 0.2x^2$

5. Analyze How does the value of a affect the shape of the graph of the equation $y = ax^2$? In your answer, discuss both positive and negative values of a.

1–4. Sample answers are given.

1. Both open up and pass through the origin, but the graph of $y = 4x^2$ is narrower than the graph of $y = x^2$.

2. Both pass through the origin, but the graph of $y = -3x^2$ opens downward and is narrower than the graph of $y = x^2$.

3. Both pass through the origin, but the graph of $y = -0.5x^2$ opens downward and is wider than the graph of $y = x^2$.

4. Both open up and pass through the origin, but the graph of $y = 0.2x^2$ is wider than the graph of $y = x^2$.

5. *Sample answer:* If a is positive, the graph opens upward. If a is negative, the graph opens downward. Also, the greater the absolute value of a, the narrower the graph.

Tech *Help*

You can press ^ 2 instead of x^2 to raise a number or a variable to the second power.

Online Resources
CLASSZONE.COM

- Keystroke Help

NCTM CURRICULUM STANDARDS

Standard 2: Understand functions; Use models to represent relationships

1 PLAN

Learn the Method

- Students will use a graphing calculator to investigate the graph of $y = ax^2$.
- Students can use what they learn in this activity to re-examine their answer to Exercise 44 on page 683.

Grouping

Students should work individually.

2 TEACH

Discussion

Ask students: "How would substituting 2 for x in both equations help you determine in step 3 which graph is which?" **You would know that the graph of $y = x^2$ contains the point (2, 4) and the graph of $y = \frac{1}{2}x^2$ contains the point (2, 2), so you could determine that the wider graph is that of $y = \frac{1}{2}x^2$.**

Extra Examples

Example Use a graphing calculator to compare the graph of $y = -\frac{1}{2}x^2$ with the graph of $y = -\frac{1}{4}x^2$. **Both parabolas open down, and both pass through the origin. The graph of $y = -\frac{1}{4}x^2$ is wider than the graph of $y = -\frac{1}{2}x^2$.**

3 CLOSE

Assessment

1. How do the graphs of $y = x^2$ and $y = -x^2$ differ? ***Sample answer:* The graphs are reflections of each other in the x-axis.**

1 PLAN

Skill Check

Evaluate the function $y = \frac{1}{2}(10)^x$ for the given value of x.

1. -1 $\frac{1}{20}$ **2.** 0 $\frac{1}{2}$

3. 1 5 **4.** 2 50

Lesson Objective

Graph exponential functions.

Pacing

Suggested Number of Days

Basic Course: 2 days

Average Course: 2 days

Advanced Course: 2 days

Block: 1 block

Teaching Resources

For a complete list of Teaching Resources, see page 648B.

Transparency

Warm-Up Exercises for this lesson are available on a transparency. A support transparency is available for Examples 1–3 and Checkpoint Exercises 1–4.

2 TEACH

Motivating the Lesson

Ask students what a value of 0 for the variable t means in the given situation. **the year 1937** Have students evaluate the function for $t = 1$ and for $t = 2$. **42.9, 47.19**

TIPS *for* NEW TEACHERS

Stress that the graph of an exponential function is not symmetrical like the graph of a quadratic function. See Tips for New Teachers in the *Chapter 12 Resource Book.*

LESSON 12.7

Exponential Growth *and* Decay

BEFORE	Now	WHY?
You graphed quadratic functions.	You'll graph exponential functions.	So you can calculate rounds in a tournament, as in Ex. 32.

Vocabulary

exponential function, p. 686

exponential growth, p. 687

exponential decay, p. 687

Muskoxen In 1937, there were 39 muskoxen on Nunivak Island, Alaska. For the period 1937–1948, the muskox population on the island can be approximated by

$$P = 39(1.1)^t,$$

where t is the number of years since 1937. After how many years did the muskox population on Nunivak Island double? Example 4 shows how to use a graphing calculator to answer this question.

The function $P = 39(1.1)^t$ is an example of an *exponential function.* An **exponential function** is an equation in two variables that can be written in the form $y = ab^x$, where $a \neq 0$, $b > 0$, and $b \neq 1$.

Study *Strategy*

Exponential functions are nonlinear functions because their graphs are not lines.

Example 1 ***Graphing an Exponential Function***

Graph the exponential function $y = 4(2)^x$.

1) Make a table of values. Choose several x-values and find the corresponding y-values.

x	−3	−2	−1	0	1	2
y	$\frac{1}{2}$	1	2	4	8	16

2) Use the table to make a list of ordered pairs.

$\left(-3, \frac{1}{2}\right)$, $(-2, 1)$, $(-1, 2)$, $(0, 4)$, $(1, 8)$, $(2, 16)$

3) Graph the ordered pairs. Draw a smooth curve through the points as shown.

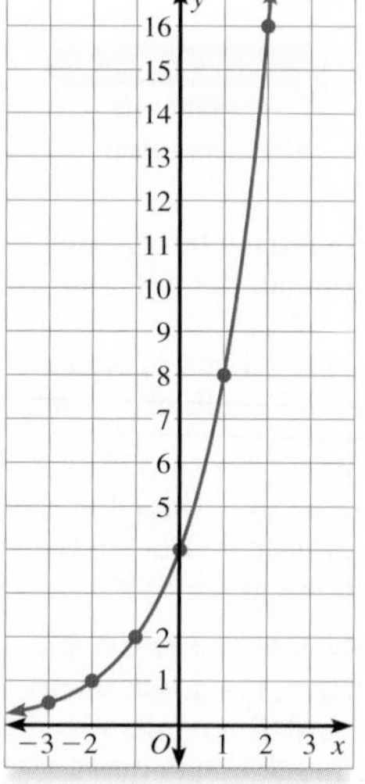

NCTM CURRICULUM STANDARDS

Standard 2: Analyze situations using algebraic symbols; Use models to understand relationships; Use models to represent relationships

Reading *Algebra*

The expression 3^{-x} means "3 raised to the opposite of x." When evaluating $y = 3^{-x}$ in Step 2 of Example 2, don't forget to take the opposite of x. For instance, when $x = -2$, $y = 3^{-(-2)} = 3^2 = 9$.

Example 2 *Graphing an Exponential Function*

Graph the exponential function $y = \left(\frac{1}{3}\right)^x$.

1. Rewrite the function. Because $\left(\frac{1}{3}\right)^x = (3^{-1})^x = 3^{-x}$, the given function is equivalent to the function $y = 3^{-x}$.

2. Make a table of values. Choose x-values and find the corresponding y-values.

x	−2	−1	0	1	2
y	9	3	1	$\frac{1}{3}$	$\frac{1}{9}$

3. Make a list of ordered pairs.

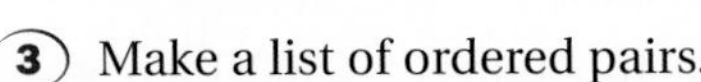

$(-2, 9), (-1, 3), (0, 1), \left(1, \frac{1}{3}\right), \left(2, \frac{1}{9}\right)$

4. Graph the ordered pairs. Draw a smooth curve through the points as shown.

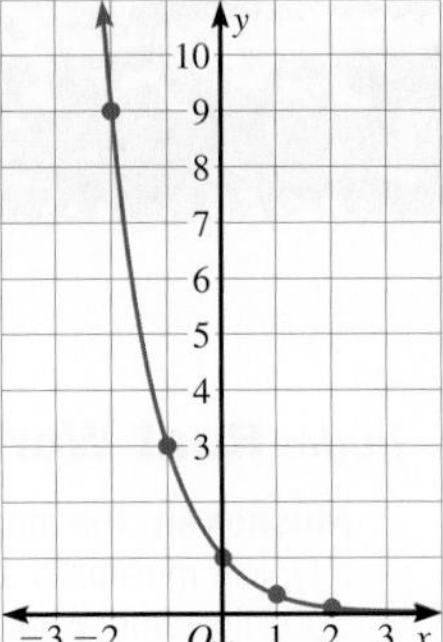

Checkpoint

1–4. See margin.

Make a table of values for the given function. Then graph the function.

1. $y = 3^x$ **2.** $y = 5^x$ **3.** $y = \left(\frac{1}{4}\right)^x$ **4.** $y = 4\left(\frac{1}{2}\right)^x$

Growth and Decay A quantity that increases shows **exponential growth** if it can be described by an exponential function of the form $y = ab^x$, where $a > 0$ and $b > 1$. A quantity that decreases shows **exponential decay** if it can be described by an exponential function of the form $y = ab^x$, where $a > 0$ and $0 < b < 1$.

Note *Worthy*

When taking notes on Example 3, be sure to leave space to write down questions asked by you or other students. Record your teacher's answers.

Example 3 *Solving Problems Involving Exponential Decay*

Cars The value of a car decreases over time. Suppose your parents buy a car for \$10,000. The car's value t years after purchase can be approximated by the function $V = 10{,}000(0.9)^t$. After how many years will the value of the car be less than \$7000?

Solution

Make a table of values for the function.

t	0	1	2	3	4
V	10,000	9,000	8,100	7,290	6,561

Notice that when $t = 4$, $V < 7000$.

Answer After four years the car will be worth less than \$7000.

Extra Examples

Example 1 Graph the exponential function $y = 2(3)^x$.

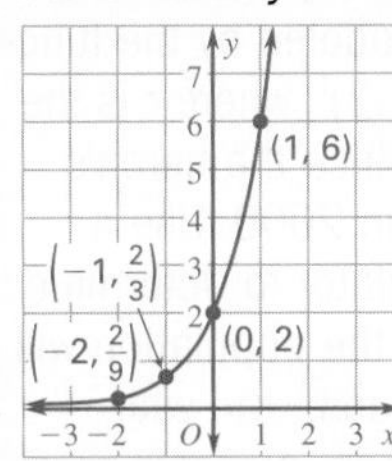

Example 2 Graph the exponential function $y = \left(\frac{2}{3}\right)^x$.

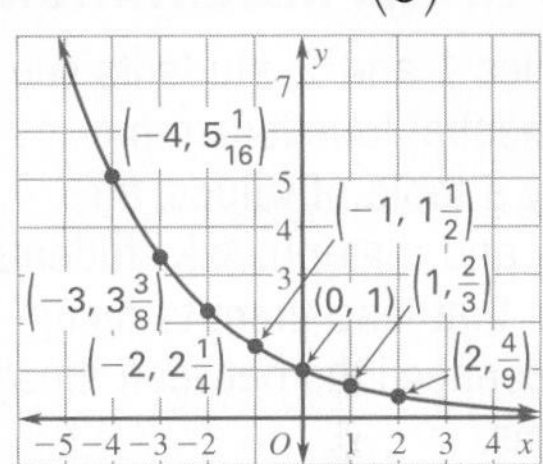

Example 3 A test tube contains 15,000 bacteria that are dying at a rate modeled by the function $B = 15{,}000(0.4)^t$, where t is the number of hours since the bacteria were exposed to a chemical solution. After how many hours will there be less than 200 bacteria alive in the test tube? **after 5 h**

Teaching Tip

In Example 1, stress that the curve gets increasingly closer to the x-axis as the value of x decreases, but never actually touches the axis.

Common Error

In Example 3, remind students that the exponent is applied to the base 0.9 before multiplying by 10,000. You might wish to provide a review of the order of operations.

1–4. See Additional Answers beginning on page AA1.

Extra Examples

Example 4 A population of herons are multiplying at a rate that can be modeled by the function $P = 16(1.2)^t$, where t is the time in years since the heron's were counted in 2000. Use a graphing calculator to determine the year when the population will reach 100 herons. **the year 2011**

Multiple Representations

In Examples 1 and 2, students see the exponential functions represented by a table of values, an equation, and a graph. Ask students questions that lead them to recognize the connections between these three forms.

Concept Check

What is an exponential function? **an equation in two variables that can be written in the form $y = ab^x$, where $a \neq 0$, $b > 0$, and $b \neq 1$**

Describe the graph of an exponential function. ***Sample answer:* The graph is a curve that either rises or falls steeply as the value of x increases; the graph approaches the x-axis but never actually reaches it.**

Daily Puzzler

Latisha invested \$200 in an account that has increased in value 8% every other year. How much money was in the account 10 years after she made the investment? **\$293.87**

In the **Real World**

Muskoxen The mass of a typical muskox is about 300 kilograms. What is the approximate mass of a herd of 78 muskoxen?

about 23,400 kg

Example 4 *Solving Problems Involving Exponential Growth*

Find when the muskox population described on page 686 doubled.

Solution

Use a graphing calculator to graph the exponential function $P = 39(1.1)^t$. To estimate the value of t when $P = 2 \cdot 39 = 78$, use the calculator's *trace* feature. You can determine that when $P = 78$, $t \approx 7.3$.

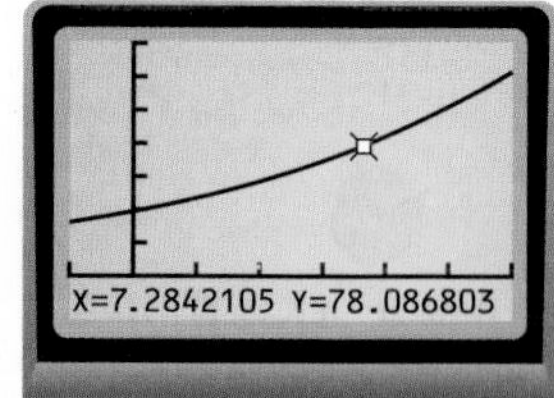

Answer The muskox population doubled after about 7.3 years.

Checkpoint

5. The function $A = 2500(1.05)^t$ gives the balance (in dollars) of a savings account t years after it is opened. Tell whether this function is an example of exponential growth or decay. Explain your answer.
Exponential growth. *Sample answer:* It is of the form $y = ab^x$ where $a = 2500 > 0$ and $b = 1.05 > 1$.

Summary Linear and Nonlinear Functions

Linear Functions

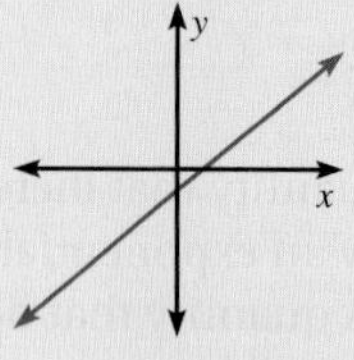

$y = mx + b$
$m > 0$

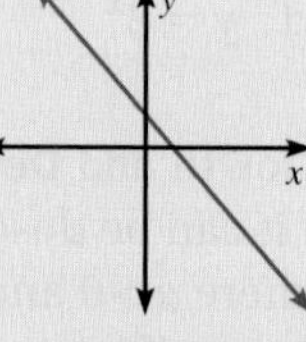

$y = mx + b$
$m < 0$

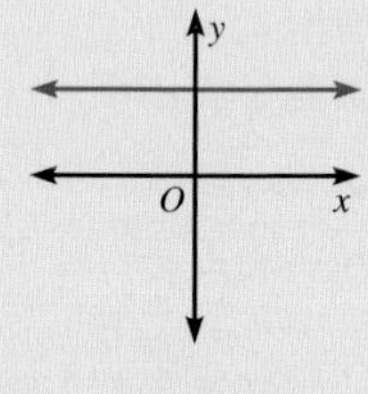

$y = b$
$m = 0$

Nonlinear Functions

Quadratic Functions

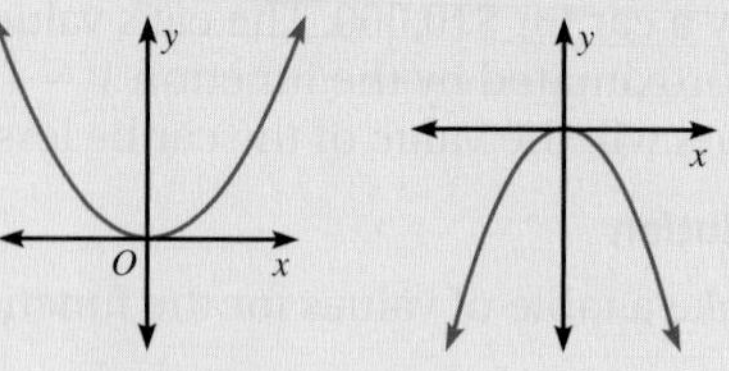

$y = ax^2 + bx + c$
$a > 0$

$y = ax^2 + bx + c$
$a < 0$

Exponential Functions

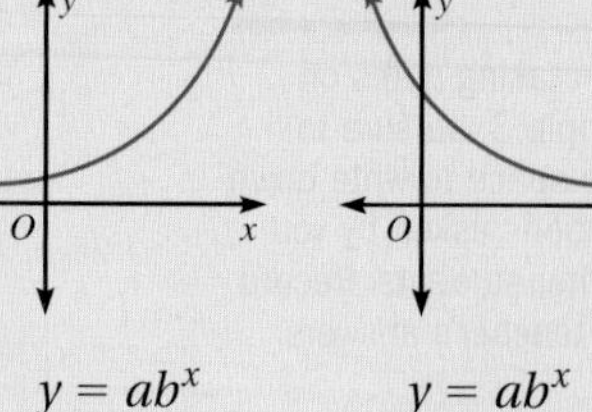

$y = ab^x$
$a > 0, b > 1$
Exponential growth

$y = ab^x$
$a > 0, 0 < b < 1$
Exponential decay

12.7 Exercises

More Practice, p. 814

Guided Practice

Vocabulary Check

1. Tell whether the function $y = 5(0.5)^x$ is an example of *exponential growth* or *exponential decay*. **exponential decay**

2. Give an example of an exponential function whose graph rises from left to right. ***Sample answer:*** $y = 2.5^x$

Skill Check

Make a table of values for the given function. Then graph the function. **3–6. See margin.**

3. $y = 4^x$ **4.** $y = 5(2)^x$ **5.** $y = 3\left(\frac{1}{2}\right)^x$ **6.** $y = 2\left(\frac{1}{3}\right)^x$

Guided Problem Solving

7. Paper Cutting You have a 10 centimeter by 10 centimeter piece of paper. You cut the paper in half repeatedly. After each cut you discard one half. After how many cuts is the area of the remaining paper less than 6 square centimeters?

1 Copy and complete the table.

Number of cuts	0	1	2	3	4	5
Area (in square centimeters)	100	50	?	?	?	?
			25	12.5	6.25	3.125

2 After how many cuts is the area of the paper less than 6 square centimeters? **5 cuts**

28. ***Sample answer:*** **Both graphs pass through (0, 8). They appear to be mirror images of each other about the *y*-axis. The graph of $y = 8(2)^x$ rises from left to right (exponential growth), while the graph of $y = 8\left(\frac{1}{2}\right)^x$ falls from left to right (exponential decay).**

Practice and Problem Solving

Homework *Help*

Example	Exercises
1	8-23, 29-31
2	8-23, 29-31
3	32
4	24-27, 34

- More Examples
- eTutorial Plus

Make a table of values for the given function. **8–15. See margin.**

A **8.** $y = 5(4)^x$ **9.** $y = 2(3)^x$ **10.** $y = 12(2)^x$ **11.** $y = \frac{1}{2}(6)^x$

12. $y = 2\left(\frac{1}{2}\right)^x$ **13.** $y = 9\left(\frac{1}{3}\right)^x$ **14.** $y = 3\left(\frac{1}{4}\right)^x$ **15.** $y = 10\left(\frac{1}{2}\right)^x$

Graph the function. **16–23. See margin.**

16. $y = 2(3)^x$ **17.** $y = 3(6)^x$ **18.** $y = 6^x$ **19.** $y = 3(5)^x$

20. $y = 2\left(\frac{1}{2}\right)^x$ **21.** $y = 3\left(\frac{1}{3}\right)^x$ **22.** $y = 8\left(\frac{1}{4}\right)^x$ **23.** $y = 3\left(\frac{1}{2}\right)^x$

Use a graphing calculator to graph the function. Then tell whether the function is an example of *exponential growth* or *exponential decay*. **24–27. See margin for art.**

24. $y = (0.2)^x$ **exponential decay** **25.** $y = 6(0.4)^x$ **exponential decay** **26.** $y = (3.5)^x$ **exponential growth** **27.** $y = 4(1.5)^x$ **exponential growth**

28. ***Writing*** Compare the graphs of the functions $y = 8(2)^x$ and $y = 8\left(\frac{1}{2}\right)^x$. **See margin.**

3 APPLY

ASSIGNMENT GUIDE

Basic Course

Day 1: pp. 689-691 Exs. 8-19, 29-31, 37-43

Day 2: pp. 689-691 Exs. 20-27, 32, 33, 44-49

Average Course

Day 1: pp. 689-691 Exs. 10-19, 29-31, 37-43

Day 2: pp. 689-691 Exs. 20-28, 32-35, 44-50

Advanced Course

Day 1: pp. 689-691 Exs. 10-19, 29-31, 38-41

Day 2: pp. 689-691 Exs. 20-28, 32-36*, 45-50

Block

pp. 689-691 Exs. 10-35, 37-50

Extra Practice

- Student Edition, p. 814
- Chapter 12 Resource Book, pp. 65-67
- Test and Practice Generator

Transparency

Even-numbered answers are available on transparencies. A support transparency is available for Exercises 3-23, 32, 36, and 44-47.

Homework Check

When you review students' homework for this lesson, go over the following exercises to check understanding of key concepts.

Basic: 8, 16, 24, 29, 32

Average: 10, 20, 24, 30, 32

Advanced: 12, 22, 25, 31, 32

3-6, 8-27. See Additional Answers beginning on page AA1.

Common Error

In Exercise 36, stress that the price is not reduced by $9 each week. Clarify that the 20% reduction is taken on the price at the end of each successive week and therefore will be a different amount each week.

34c.

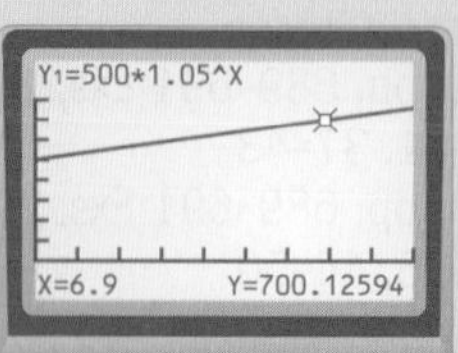

35b.

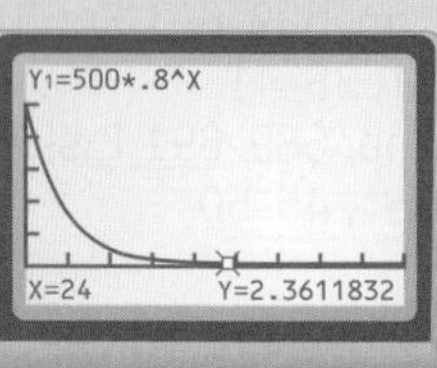

36b. Labeled points on the graph represent sample points for a table.

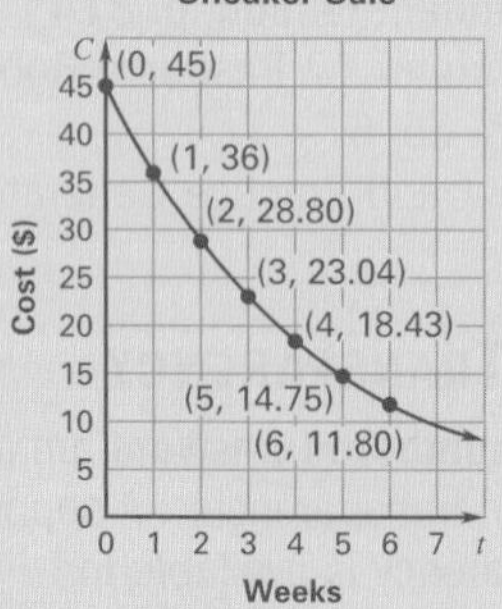

50.

X	Y1
1	1284
2	1373.9
3	1470.1
4	1573
5	1683.1
6	1800.9

Y1=1200*1.07^X

32a.

x	0	1	2	3	4	5	6	7
y	128	64	32	16	8	4	2	1

33. $y = 2(3)^x$. *Sample answer:* Since $y = 2(3)^x$ is increasing by powers of 3, it increases faster than $y = 3(2)^x$, which is increasing by powers of 2.

Match the function with its graph.

29. $y = \frac{1}{4}(3)^x$ **B** **30.** $y = 3\left(\frac{1}{4}\right)^x$ **C** **31.** $y = \frac{1}{3}(4)^x$ **A**

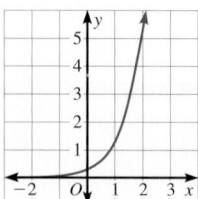

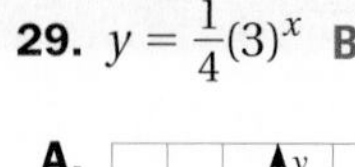

A. **B.** **C.**

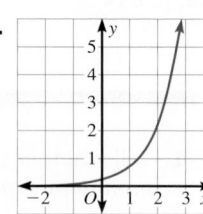

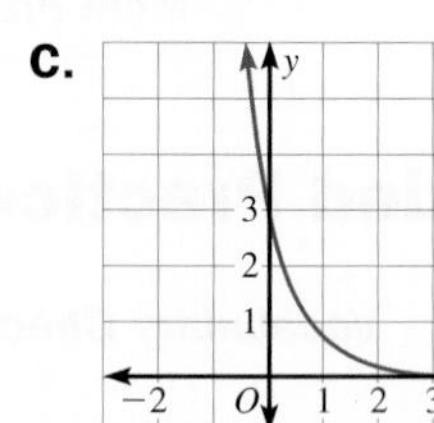

32. Extended Problem Solving A citywide youth tennis tournament has 128 players at the start. After each round, half the players are eliminated. The number of players remaining at the end of each round is given by the function $y = 128\left(\frac{1}{2}\right)^x$ where x is the number of rounds played.

a. Make a table of values for the function. **See margin.**

b. **Analyze** After how many rounds do only 2 players remain? After how many rounds does only 1 player remain? **6 rounds; 7 rounds**

c. **Critical Thinking** Suppose the tournament started with 512 players instead of 128. After how many rounds would only 1 player remain? **9 rounds**

B **33.** **Predict** Consider the functions $y = 2(3)^x$ and $y = 3(2)^x$. Suppose you were to graph each function and find the value of x when $y = 100$. Predict which function would have a lesser x-value. Explain your prediction. Then use a graphing calculator to check your prediction. **See margin.**

34. Compound Interest Recall that the balance A of an account earning interest compounded annually is given by the equation $A = P(1 + r)^t$, where P is the principal, r is the annual interest rate (expressed as a decimal), and t is the number of years.

a. **Critical Thinking** For any given values of P and r, is the equation $A = P(1 + r)^t$ an example of exponential growth or exponential decay? Explain your answer.

b. You deposit $500 into an account earning 5% interest compounded annually. Write a function that gives the balance after t years. **$A = 500(1.05)^t$**

c. Use a graphing calculator to graph the function from part (b). After how many years will the balance be greater than $700? **See margin for art; 7 y.**

C **35. Medicine** You take 500 milligrams of aspirin. The amount of aspirin (in milligrams) in your bloodstream after t hours is given by the function $y = 500(0.8)^t$.

a. **Critical Thinking** Is this function an example of exponential growth or exponential decay? Explain your answer.

b. Use a graphing calculator to graph the function. How much aspirin is left in your bloodstream after 24 hours? **See margin for art; about 2.36 mg.**

c. **Interpret and Apply** When will the amount of aspirin in your bloodstream be less than 132 milligrams? less than 22 milligrams? **after about 6 h; after about 14 h**

Review *Help*

For help with compound interest, see p. 364.

34a. Exponential growth. *Sample answer:* It is of the form $y = ab^x$ where $a = P$ and $b = (1 + r)$. Because r is positive, $(1 + r)$ must be greater than 1, which indicates exponential growth.

35a. Exponential decay. *Sample answer:* It is of the form $y = ab^x$ where $a = 500$ and $b = 0.8$. Since $0 < b < 1$, the function represents exponential decay.

36. **Challenge** A pair of sneakers costs \$45. The price of the sneakers will be reduced by 20% at the end of each week until the sneakers are sold.

a. Write an exponential function that gives the cost of the sneakers after t weeks. **$C = 45(0.8)^t$**

b. Make a table of values and graph the function from part (a). **See margin.**

c. After how many weeks will the sneakers cost less than \$20? **4 wk**

37. $\sin A = \frac{4}{5}$, $\cos A = \frac{3}{5}$, $\sin B = \frac{3}{5}$, $\cos B = \frac{4}{5}$

38. $\sin E = \frac{9}{41}$, $\cos E = \frac{40}{41}$, $\sin F = \frac{40}{41}$, $\cos F = \frac{9}{41}$

39. $\sin J = \frac{5}{13}$, $\cos J = \frac{12}{13}$, $\sin K = \frac{12}{13}$, $\cos K = \frac{5}{13}$

Mixed Review

Find the sine and cosine of each acute angle. Write your answers as fractions in simplest form. *(Lesson 9.8)*

37. 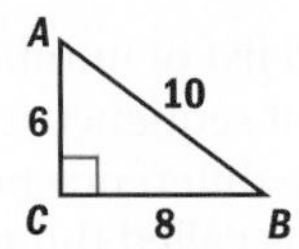

38. 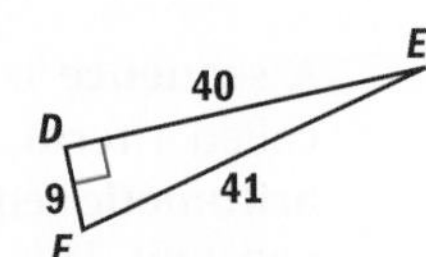

39. 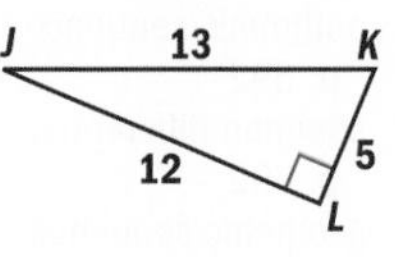

Find the number of combinations. *(Lesson 11.7)*

40. ${}_9C_4$ **126** 41. ${}_8C_7$ **8** 42. ${}_6C_4$ **15** 43. ${}_5C_5$ **1**

Make a table of values for the given function. *(Lesson 12.6)*

44. $y = -x^2 + 4$ 45. $y = 2x^2 + 1$ 46. $y = x^2 - 5$ 47. $y = 3x^2 - 9$

44–47. Sample tables are given.

44.

x	−2	−1	0	1	2
y	0	3	4	3	0

45.

x	−2	−1	0	1	2
y	9	3	1	3	9

46.

x	−2	−1	0	1	2
y	−1	−4	−5	−4	−1

47.

x	−2	−1	0	1	2
y	3	−6	−9	−6	3

Standardized Test Practice

48. **Multiple Choice** For the function $y = 2(5)^x$, what is the value of y when $x = 4$? **C**

A. $\frac{1}{1250}$ **B.** $\frac{1}{625}$ **C.** 1250 **D.** 3125

49. **Multiple Choice** Which function is an example of exponential decay? **G**

F. $y = 0.5(3)^x$ **G.** $y = 3(0.5)^x$ **H.** $y = 0.2(2)^x$ **I.** $y = 3(5)^x$

50. **Short Response** You deposit \$1200 into an account that earns 7% interest compounded annually. The balance A after t years is given by the function $A = 1200(1.07)^t$. Use a calculator to make a table of values for the function. After how many years will the balance be greater than \$1700? **See margin for art; 6 y.**

Payday Puzzle

You are hired for a job that lasts 20 days. You have a choice of how you will be paid. You can either be paid \$300 per day or \$.01 on the first day, \$.02 on the second day, \$.04 on the third day, and so on, with the amount you're paid doubling each day. Which offer should you accept? Explain your reasoning.

The second offer. *Sample answer:* The amount you earn on the *n*th day will be $0.01(2)^{n-1}$ dollars. So on the 19th and 20th days alone you will earn $0.01(2)^{18} + 0.01(2)^{19} = 2621.44 + 5242.88 =$ \$7864.32, which is more than the total of 20(300) = \$6000 you would earn from the first offer.

4 ASSESS

Assessment Resources

For more assessment resources, see:
- Assessment Book
- Test and Practice Generator

Mini-Quiz

1. Make a table of values for the function $y = \frac{1}{4}(2)^x$. ***Sample:***

x	−1	0	1	2	3
y	$\frac{1}{8}$	$\frac{1}{4}$	$\frac{1}{2}$	1	2

2. Is the function $y = 6\left(\frac{2}{5}\right)^x$ an example of *exponential growth* or *exponential decay*? **exp. decay**

3. **Challenge** A group of vacuums priced at \$200 are reduced by 10% each Friday. Write an exponential function for the cost of the vacuums t weeks after the reductions began. Make a table of values. After how many weeks will they sell for less than \$100? **$C = 200(0.9)^t$; 7 weeks;**

t	1	2	3	4
C	180	162	145.80	131.22

5 FOLLOW-UP

Diagnosis/Remediation
- Study Guide in Chapter 12 Resource Book, pp. 68–69
- eTutorial Plus Online
- Extra Practice, p. 814
- Lesson Practice in Chapter 12 Resource Book, pp. 65–67

English Learner Support
- Spanish Study Guide
- Multi-Language Visual Glossary
- Chapter Audio Summaries CDs

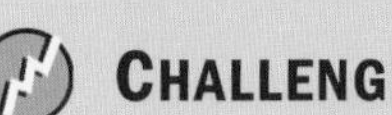

Challenge
- Challenge Practice in Chapter 12 Resource Book, p. 70
- Teacher's Edition, p. 648F

1 PLAN

Skill Check

Solve using mental math.

1. $x - 6 = 6$ **12**
2. $2x = 30$ **15**
3. $\frac{1}{2}x = 48$ **96**
4. $10 + x = 26$ **16**

LESSON OBJECTIVE

Extend and graph sequences.

PACING

Suggested Number of Days
Basic Course: 2 days
Average Course: 2 days
Advanced Course: 2 days
Block: 1 block

TEACHING RESOURCES

For a complete list of Teaching Resources, see page 648B.

TRANSPARENCY

Warm-Up Exercises for this lesson are available on a transparency. A support transparency is available for Examples 3 and 4, and Checkpoint Exercises 4–6.

2 TEACH

MOTIVATING THE LESSON

Ask students to suggest sequences of numbers that follow a set rule, like the even numbers. Look for arithmetic or geometric sequences that you can use to illustrate the content of the lesson.

LESSON 12.8

Sequences

BEFORE	Now	WHY?
You wrote rules for and graphed functions.	You'll extend and graph sequences.	So you can find the height of a bouncing ball, as in Ex. 31.

Vocabulary
sequence, p. 692
term, p. 692
arithmetic sequence, p. 692
common difference, p. 692
geometric sequence, p. 692
common ratio, p. 692

A **sequence** is an ordered list of numbers. Each number in a sequence is called a **term**. One type of sequence is an *arithmetic sequence.* In an **arithmetic sequence**, the difference between consecutive terms is constant. This difference is called the **common difference**.

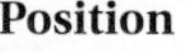

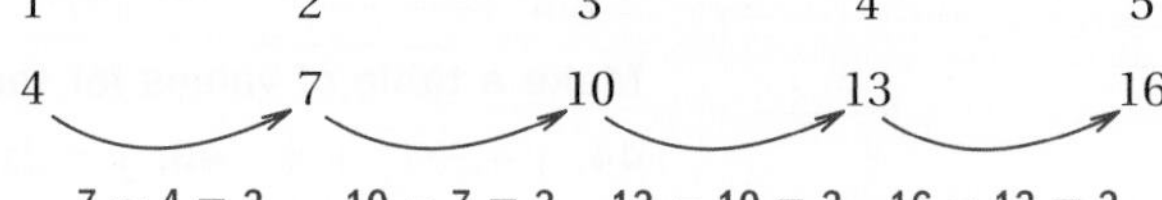

Position number:	1	2	3	4	5 . . .
Term:	4	7	10	13	16 . . .

$7 - 4 = 3$ $\quad 10 - 7 = 3$ $\quad 13 - 10 = 3$ $\quad 16 - 13 = 3$

The common difference is 3.

Example 1 ***Extending Arithmetic Sequences***

Find the common difference for the arithmetic sequence. Then find the next three terms.

a. 12, 17, 22, 27, 32, . . .

b. 5, 3, 1, −1, −3, . . .

Solution

a. 12, 17, 22, 27, 32, . . .

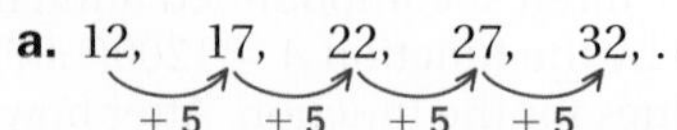

+5 +5 +5 +5

The common difference is 5. The next three terms in the sequence are 37, 42, and 47.

b. 5, 3, 1, −1, −3, . . .

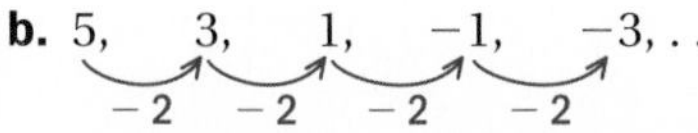

−2 −2 −2 −2

The common difference is −2. The next three terms in the sequence are −5, −7, and −9.

Watch *Out*

In part (b) of Example 1, each term is 2 *less* than the previous term, so the common difference is −2, not 2.

Geometric Sequences Another type of sequence is a *geometric sequence.* In a **geometric sequence**, the ratio of any term to the previous term is constant. This ratio is called the **common ratio**.

Position number:	1	2	3	4	5 . . .
Term:	3	6	12	24	48 . . .

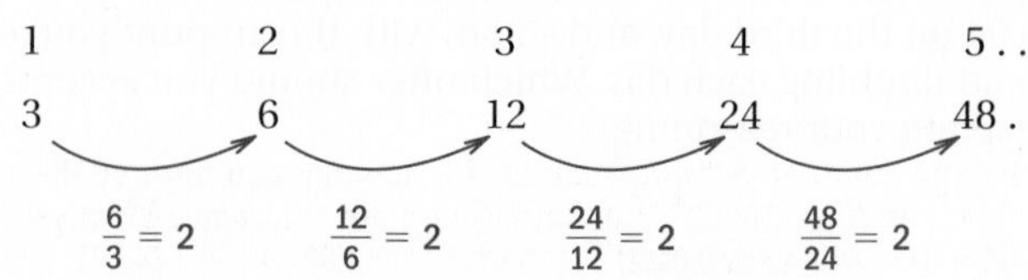

$\frac{6}{3} = 2$ $\quad \frac{12}{6} = 2$ $\quad \frac{24}{12} = 2$ $\quad \frac{48}{24} = 2$

The common ratio is 2.

NCTM CURRICULUM STANDARDS
Standard 2: Understand patterns; Analyze situations using algebraic symbols
Standard 6: Solve problems in math and other contexts

Study *Strategy*

In Example 2, notice that the common ratio is the number you can multiply one term by to get the next term in the sequence.

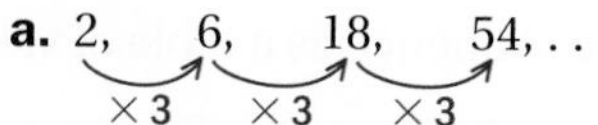

Example 2 *Extending Geometric Sequences*

Find the common ratio for the geometric sequence. Then find the next three terms.

a. 2, 6, 18, 54, . . .　　**b.** 160, 80, 40, 20, . . .

Solution

a. 2, 6, 18, 54, . . . ($\times 3$, $\times 3$, $\times 3$)

The common ratio is 3. The next three terms in the sequence are 162, 486, and 1458.

b. 160, 80, 40, 20, . . . ($\times \frac{1}{2}$, $\times \frac{1}{2}$, $\times \frac{1}{2}$)

The common ratio is $\frac{1}{2}$. The next three terms in the sequence are 10, 5, and 2.5.

Checkpoint

Tell whether the sequence is *arithmetic* or *geometric*. Then find the common difference or common ratio, and write the next three terms.

1. $-4, 2, 8, 14, \ldots$　**2.** $3, -4, -11, -18, \ldots$　**3.** $100, 10, 1, 0.1, \ldots$

1. arithmetic; common difference: 6; 20, 26, 32

2. arithmetic; common difference: −7; −25, −32, −39

3. geometric; common ratio: 0.1; 0.01, 0.001, 0.0001

Example 3 *Using Sequences*

Mountain Bike You start saving for a $360 mountain bike in January when you receive $200 in cash for your birthday. In February and each month after, you save $20 from doing chores. After how many months of saving will you have enough for the bike?

Solution

1 Use a table to write a sequence for your savings after each month.

Month number	1	2	3	4	. . .
Savings	200	200 + 20(1)	200 + 20(2)	200 + 20(3)	. . .
Sequence	200	220	240	260	. . .

2 Notice that the sequence is arithmetic. Your savings from chores is the product of $20 and 1 less than the month number. Your total savings is the sum of $200 and your savings from chores.

Savings after n months $= 200 + 20(n - 1)$

3 Write and solve an equation to find how many months will pass before you have the $360 you need for the mountain bike.

$360 = 200 + 20(n - 1)$　**Write equation.**

$160 = 20(n - 1)$　**Subtract 200 from each side.**

$8 = n - 1$　**Divide each side by 20.**

$9 = n$　**Add 1 to each side.**

Answer You will have saved enough for the bike after 9 months.

TIPS *for* NEW TEACHERS

Watch for students who struggle during this lesson because their mental math skills are weak. Urge these students to do extra practice at home with flash cards to build their mental math skills. See Tips for New Teachers in the *Chapter 12 Resource Book*.

Extra Examples

Example 1 Find the common difference for the arithmetic sequence. Then find the next three terms.

a. 32, 39, 46, 53, 60, ... **7; 67, 74, 81**

b. 88, 83, 78, 73, 68, ... **−5; 63, 58, 53**

Example 2 Find the common ratio for the geometric sequence. Then find the next three terms.

a. 24, 48, 96, 192, ... **2; 384, 768, 1536**

b. 625, 125, 25, 5, ... **$\frac{1}{5}$; 1, 0.2, 0.04**

Example 3 You are saving for an $1100 laptop. In August, you save $380 from a summer job. Starting in September, you save $120 per month from a part-time job. After how many months of saving will you have enough money for the laptop?
7 months

Teaching Tip

In Example 2, discuss how students can tell that the sequences are *not* arithmetic by checking for a common difference.

Extra Examples

Example 4 Graph the arithmetic sequence 25, 21, 17, 13, 9, ...

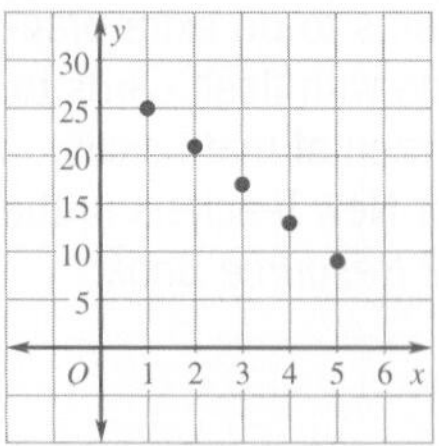

Example 5 Write the next three terms of the sequence 20, 30, 45, 67.5, 101.25, ... Then graph the sequence. **151.875, 227.8125, 341.71875**

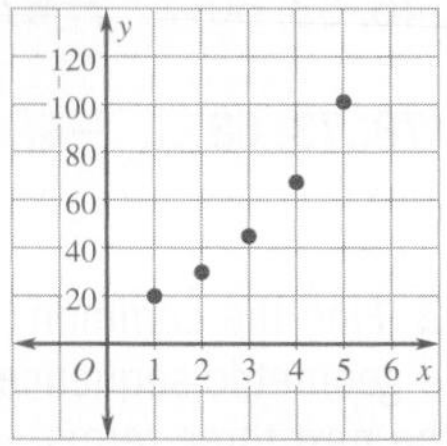

Concept Check

How is a common ratio for a sequence different from a common difference? **The common ratio is the ratio of two consecutive terms in a geometric sequence, while a common difference is the difference between two consecutive terms in an arithmetic sequence.**

Daily Puzzler

When you fold a sheet of paper in half once, there are 2 layers of paper. After folding the sheet of paper in half 6 more times, how many layers of paper are there? **128 layers**

4–6. See Additional Answers beginning on page AA1.

Graphing Sequences To graph a sequence, let the position numbers of the terms in the sequence be the x-coordinates and let the terms be the y-coordinates. Each term corresponds to a point on the graph.

Study *Strategy*

Notice that for the arithmetic sequence in Example 4, the points of the graph lie on a line. This is true for *any* arithmetic sequence.

Example 4 *Graphing an Arithmetic Sequence*

Graph the arithmetic sequence 5, 10, 15, 20, 25, ...

Write the sequence as a table of values.

Position number, x	1	2	3	4	5
Term, y	5	10	15	20	25

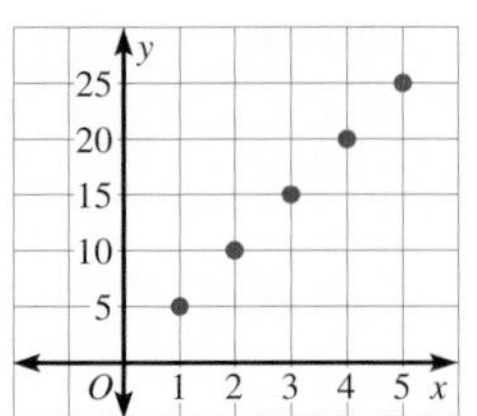

Then plot the points (1, 5), (2, 10), (3, 15), (4, 20), (5, 25), ...

Example 5 *Graphing a Geometric Sequence*

Fractal Tree To construct what is known as a *fractal tree,* begin with a single segment (the trunk) and add two shorter segments to form the first pair of branches, as shown in Step 1. Then continue adding pairs of shorter branches to each existing branch.

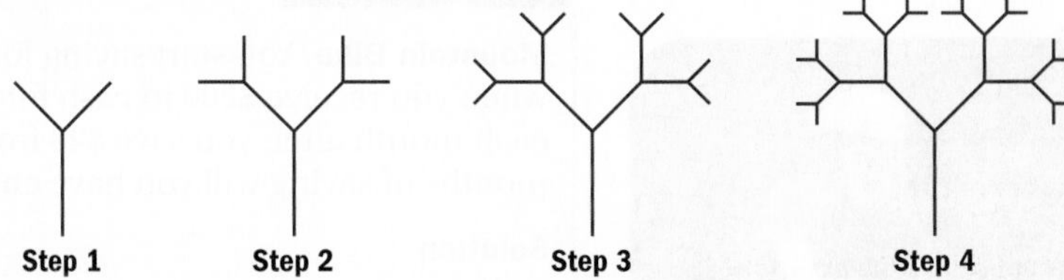

Write and graph a sequence for the number of new branches at each step of constructing the fractal tree.

Solution

The sequence 2, 4, 8, 16, . . . gives the number of new branches at each step. Because each term is 2 times the previous term, the sequence is geometric.

To graph the sequence, write the sequence as a table of values.

Position number, x	1	2	3	4	5
Term, y	2	4	8	16	32

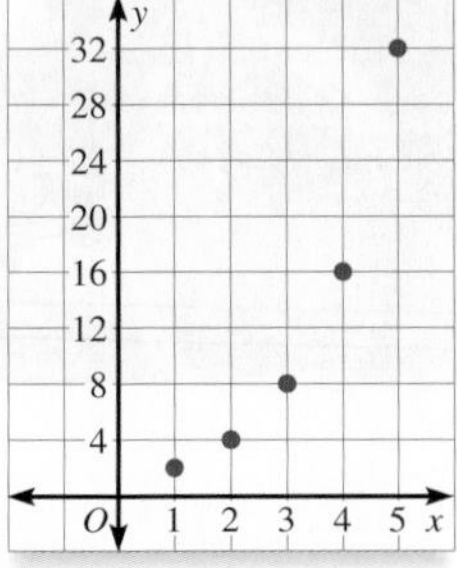

Then plot the points (1, 2), (2, 4), (3, 8), (4,16), (5, 32), ...

Study *Strategy*

Notice that for the geometric sequence in Example 5, the points lie on an exponential curve. This is true for *any* geometric sequence with a positive common ratio.

Checkpoint

Write the next three terms of the sequence. Then graph the sequence. **4–6. See margin for art.**

4. 1, 2, 4, 8, . . . **16, 32, 64**

5. 16, 13, 10, 7, . . . **4, 1, −2**

6. 11, 17, 23, 29, . . . **35, 41, 47**

12.8 Exercises

More Practice, p. 814

Guided Practice

Vocabulary Check

1. Copy and complete: In a geometric sequence, the ratio of any term to the previous term is the _?_. **common ratio**

2. Tell whether the following sequence is *arithmetic* or *geometric*: $-4, 8, 20, 32, \ldots$. **arithmetic**

Skill Check

Find the common difference for the arithmetic sequence. Then write the next three terms.

3. $3, 8, 13, 18, \ldots$ **5; 23, 28, 33**

4. $14, 12, 10, 8, \ldots$ **−2; 6, 4, 2**

5. $-16, -8, 0, 8, \ldots$ **8; 16, 24, 32**

Find the common ratio for the geometric sequence. Then write the next three terms.

6. $1, 5, 25, 125, \ldots$ **5; 625, 3125, 15,625**

7. $-2, -6, -18, \ldots$ **3; −54, −162, −486**

8. $96, 48, 24, 12, \ldots$ **$\frac{1}{2}$; 6, 3, $\frac{3}{2}$**

9. Error Analysis Describe and correct the error in graphing the sequence $3, 5, 7, 9, \ldots$.

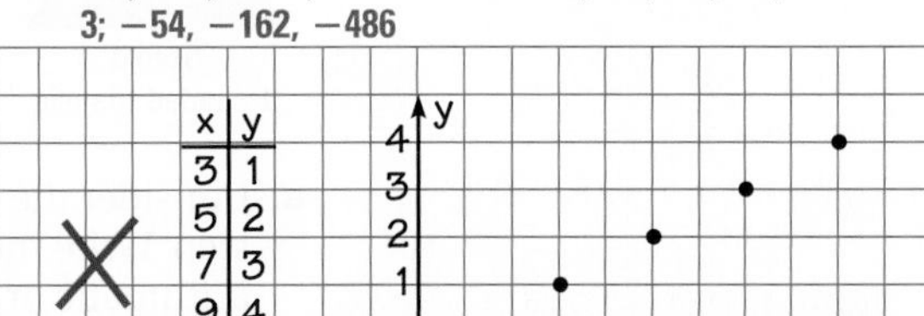

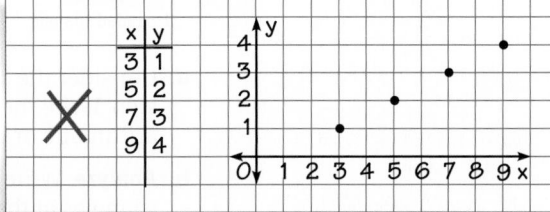

Sample answer: **The coordinates in the table are not in the correct columns. The first term is 3, so 1 should go under the *x* and 3 under the *y*. The second term is 5, so 2 goes under *x* and 5 under *y*, and so on. The points plotted should be (1, 3), (2, 5), (3, 7), and (4, 9).**

13. arithmetic; common difference: 15; 64, 79, 94

14. geometric; common ratio: $\frac{1}{4}$; 16, 4, 1

15. geometric; common ratio: 4; 128, 512, 2048

16. arithmetic; common difference: 9; 88, 97, 106

17. geometric; common ratio: $\frac{1}{5}$; $\frac{4}{5}$, $\frac{4}{25}$, $\frac{4}{125}$

18. geometric; common ratio: −2; 16, −32, 64

19. arithmetic; common difference: 18; 90, 108, 126

20. geometric; common ratio: $\frac{3}{2}$; 81, $121\frac{1}{2}$, $182\frac{1}{4}$

21. geometric; common ratio: $\frac{2}{3}$; 48, 32, $21\frac{1}{3}$

Practice and Problem Solving

Homework Help

Example	Exercises
1	10-21
2	10-21
3	29-37
4	22-27
5	22-27

Online Resources
CLASSZONE.COM
- More Examples
- eTutorial Plus

Tell whether the sequence is *arithmetic* or *geometric*. Then find the common difference or the common ratio, and write the next three terms.

A **10.** $15, 11, 7, 3, \ldots$ **arithmetic; common difference: −4; −1, −5, −9**

11. $-2, 4, -8, 16, \ldots$ **geometric; common ratio: −2; −32, 64, −128**

12. $-7, -1, 5, 11, \ldots$ **arithmetic; common difference: 6; 17, 23, 29**

13. $4, 19, 34, 49, \ldots$ **13–21. See margin.**

14. $1024, 256, 64, \ldots$

15. $\frac{1}{2}, 2, 8, 32, \ldots$

16. $52, 61, 70, 79, \ldots$

17. $500, 100, 20, 4, \ldots$

18. $1, -2, 4, -8, \ldots$

19. $18, 36, 54, 72, \ldots$

20. $16, 24, 36, 54, \ldots$

21. $243, 162, 108, 72, \ldots$

Tell whether the sequence is *arithmetic* or *geometric*. Write the next three terms of the sequence. Then graph the sequence. **22–27. See margin for art.**

22. $16, 8, 4, 2, \ldots$ **geometric; 1, $\frac{1}{2}$, $\frac{1}{4}$**

23. $-18, -4, 10, \ldots$ **arithmetic; 24, 38, 52**

24. $-2, -5, -8, -11, \ldots$ **arithmetic; −14, −17, −20**

25. $15, 25, 35, 45, \ldots$ **arithmetic; 55, 65, 75**

26. $20, 10, 5, 2.5, \ldots$ **geometric; 1.25, 0.625, 0.3125**

27. $4, 12, 36, 108, \ldots$ **geometric; 324, 972, 2916**

28. *Writing* The first two terms of a sequence are 3 and 6. Can you tell whether this sequence is arithmetic or geometric? To justify your answer, give examples of sequences that begin with these two terms.

28. No. *Sample answer:* The sequence 3, 6, 9, 12, . . . is arithmetic, but the sequence 3, 6, 12, 24, . . . is geometric.

3 APPLY

ASSIGNMENT GUIDE

Basic Course

Day 1: SRH p. 796 Exs. 1-3; pp. 695-697 Exs. 10-18, 32-34, 41-47

Day 2: pp. 695-697 Exs. 22-27, 35-37, 48, 49

Average Course

Day 1: pp. 695-697 Exs. 13-21, 32-34, 41-47

Day 2: pp. 695-697 Exs. 25-31, 35-39, 48, 49

Advanced Course

Day 1: pp. 695-697 Exs. 16-21, 32-34, 41-47

Day 2: pp. 695-697 Exs. 25-31, 35-40*, 48, 49

Block

pp. 695-697 Exs. 13-21, 25-39, 41-49

Extra Practice

- Student Edition, p. 814
- Chapter 12 Resource Book, pp. 74-76
- Test and Practice Generator

Transparency

Even-numbered answers are available on transparencies. A support transparency is available for Exercises 22-27, 39, and 45-47.

Homework Check

When you review students' homework for this lesson, go over the following exercises to check understanding of key concepts.

Basic: 10, 17, 22, 25, 32

Average: 13, 18, 25, 27, 33

Advanced: 16, 20, 25, 26, 35

22-27. See Additional Answers beginning on page AA1.

39c.

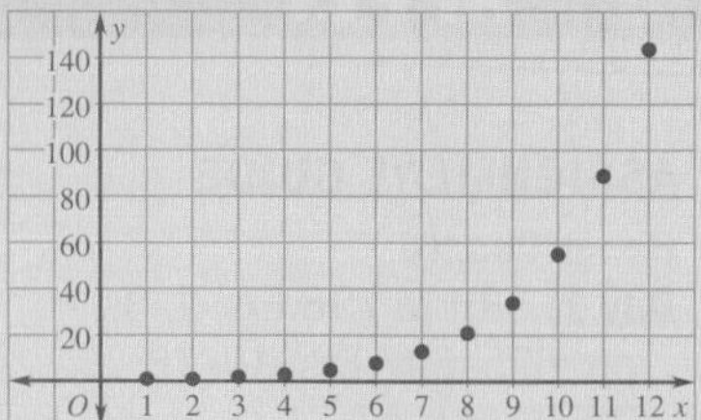

40a.

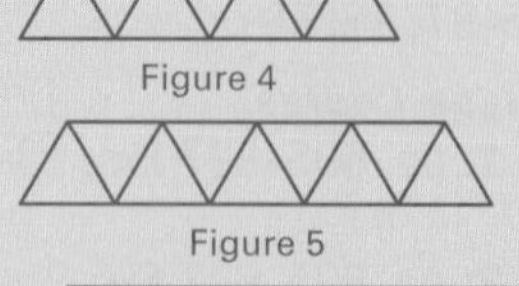

Figure 4

Figure 5

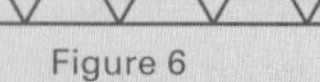

Figure 6

45.

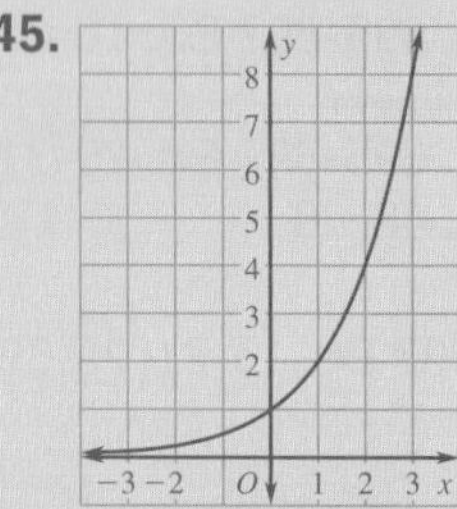

46.

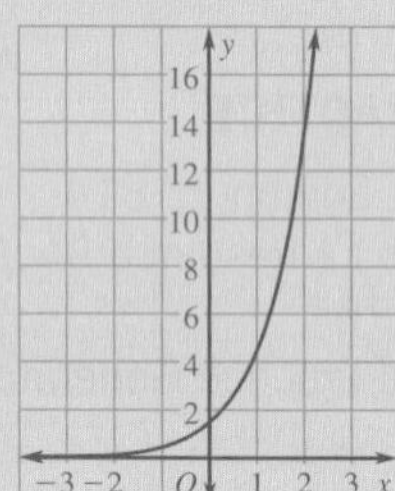

47.

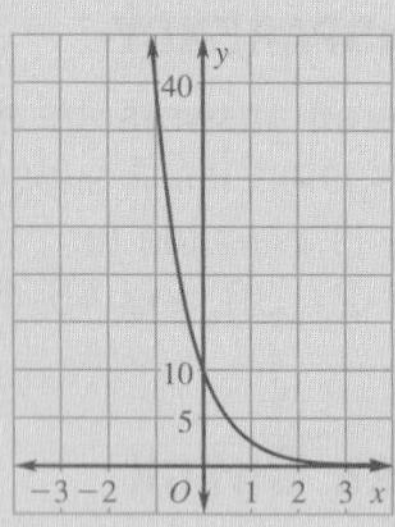

29. **Extended Problem Solving** A supermarket stores shopping carts by nesting them. Each shopping cart is 36 inches long. The first cart contributes its entire length to the line. Each additional cart adds 9 inches to the line. Consider the sequence that gives the length of a line of carts, starting with 1 cart, then 2 carts, then 3 carts, and so on.

   a. Write the first 6 terms of the sequence. Is the sequence arithmetic or geometric? **36, 45, 54, 63, 72, 81; arithmetic**

   b. **Analyze** Write a variable expression for the length of a line of n carts. **$9n + 27$**

   c. **Apply** The supermarket has a space that is 240 inches long to store the carts. How many nested carts can fit in this space? **23 carts**

B 30. **Sierpinski Triangle** To create the *Sierpinski triangle,* begin with a shaded triangle. Replace the middle of the shaded triangle with a smaller white triangle, as shown. Then, for every shaded triangle that is formed, replace its middle with a smaller white triangle.

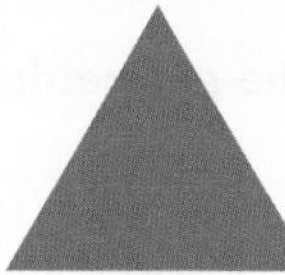

Step 1
1 shaded triangle

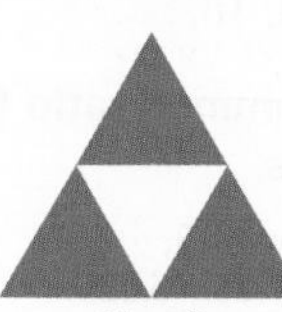

Step 2
3 shaded triangles

Step 3
9 shaded triangles

Step 4
27 shaded triangles

   a. Consider the sequence for the number of shaded triangles at each step. Write the first 6 terms of the sequence. Is the sequence arithmetic or geometric? **1, 3, 9, 27, 81, 243; geometric**

   b. **Analyze** Write a variable expression for the number of shaded triangles at the nth step. **3^{n-1}**

   c. Use a calculator to find the number of shaded triangles at the 15th step. **4,782,969 shaded triangles**

31. **Bounce Height** When you drop a ball, the height to which the ball rises, called its bounce height, decreases on each successive bounce. For a certain ball, the bounce height of each bounce is 40% of the previous bounce height. You drop the ball from a height of 30 feet.

   a. Consider the sequence that gives the bounce height at each bounce. Is this sequence arithmetic or geometric? **geometric**

   b. Use a calculator to find the first 7 terms of this sequence. After how many bounces is the bounce height less than 0.25 foot? **12, 4.8, 1.92, 0.768, 0.3072, 0.12288, 0.049152; after 6 bounces**

Write the next three terms of the arithmetic sequence. Then write a variable expression for the nth term and evaluate it for $n = 12$. **32–34. See margin.**

32. 52, 41, 30, 19, . . . **33.** −3, −1.5, 0, 1.5, . . . **34.** 7, 23, 39, 55, . . .

Write the next three terms of the geometric sequence. Then write a variable expression for the nth term and evaluate it for $n = 9$. **35–37. See margin.**

35. 1, 11, 121, 1331, . . . **36.** 800, 80, 8, 0.8, . . . **37.** 128, 64, 32, 16, . . .

38. **Critical Thinking** The first term of an arithmetic sequence is 15. The fourth term is 39. What is the second term of this sequence? Explain.

32. 8, −3, −14; $52 - 11(n - 1)$, or $-11n + 63$; −69

33. 3, 4.5, 6; $-3 + 1.5(n - 1)$, or $1.5n - 4.5$; 13.5

34. 71, 87, 103; $7 + 16(n - 1)$, or $16n - 9$; 183

35. 14,641; 161,051; 1,771,561; 11^{n-1}; 214,358,881

36. 0.08, 0.008, 0.0008; $800(0.1)^{n-1}$; 0.000008

37. 8, 4, 2; $128\left(\frac{1}{2}\right)^{n-1}$; $\frac{1}{2}$

38. 23. *Sample answer:* To form the second, third, and fourth terms, a common difference must be added each time. So, it takes 3 common differences to get from 15 to 39. This means that the common difference must be $\frac{1}{3}$ the difference of 39 and 15, which is 24. So, the common difference is $\frac{1}{3} \cdot 24 = 8$, and the second term then must be $15 + 8 = 23$.

The number of clockwise and counterclockwise spirals formed by a pine cone's scales are numbers in the Fibonacci sequence. This pine cone has 8 clockwise spirals and 13 counterclockwise spirals.

39a. Neither. *Sample answer:* **The difference between consecutive terms varies, as does the ratio between consecutive terms.**

C **39. Fibonacci Sequence** The *Fibonacci sequence* is a sequence in which each term is the sum of the two terms before it. The sequence begins as shown.

1,	1,	2,	3,	5,	8,	13,	...
first term	second term	1 + 1	1 + 2	2 + 3	3 + 5	5 + 8	

a. Is the Fibonacci sequence arithmetic, geometric, or neither? Explain. **See margin.**

b. Write the next 5 terms of the Fibonnaci sequence. **21, 34, 55, 89, 144**

c. Graph the sequence. Is the graph linear? **See margin for art; no.**

40. Challenge Consider the figures made of toothpicks below.

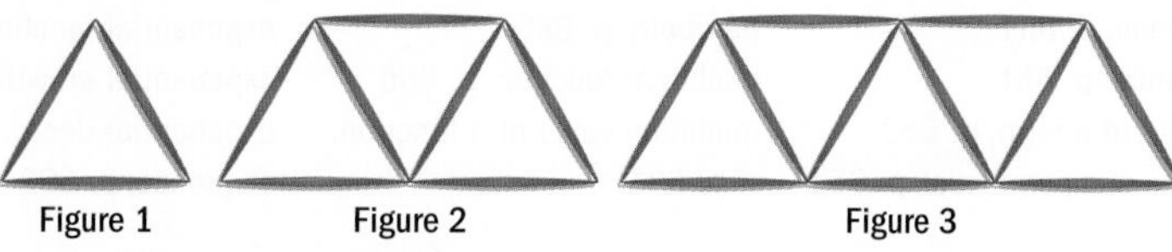

a. Draw the next three figures in the pattern. **See margin.**

b. Analyze How is the number of triangles in each figure related to the figure number? Write a sequence that gives the number of triangles in each figure. **It is 1 less than twice the figure number; $y = 2x - 1$.**

c. Analyze How is the number of toothpicks in each figure related to the figure number? Write a formula for the sequence that gives the number of toothpicks in each figure. **It is 1 less than 4 times the figure number; $y = 4x - 1$.**

d. Apply Suppose you have 100 toothpicks. What is the greatest number of triangles you can construct using the given pattern? **49 triangles**

Mixed Review

41. The perimeter of an isosceles triangle is 16 meters. The length of a side is 4 meters. The lengths of the other two sides are equal. Find the lengths of the other two sides. *(Lesson 10.1)* **6 m**

Find the degree of the polynomial. *(Lesson 12.1)*

42. $5x^6 - 8x + 2$ **6** **43.** $12 - 9t^2 - 4t$ **2** **44.** $-c^3 + c^3d + dc^2$ **4**

Graph the function. *(Lesson 12.7)* **45–47. See margin.**

45. $y = 2^x$ **46.** $y = 1.5(3)^x$ **47.** $y = 10(0.25)^x$

Standardized Test Practice

48. Multiple Choice What is the next term in the sequence 12, 8, 4, 0, . . . ? **D**

A. 2 **B.** 1 **C.** 0 **D.** −4

49. Multiple Choice The cost of a taxicab ride is $1.50 for the first quarter-mile and $.25 for each additional quarter-mile. Which sequence gives the cost of a taxicab ride, starting with a ride that is 1 quarter-mile, then 2 quarter-miles, then 3 quarter-miles, and so on? **H**

F. 0.25, 1.75, 3.25, 4.75, . . . **G.** 0.25, 1.50, 2.75, 4.25, . . .

H. 1.50, 1.75, 2.00, 2.25, . . . **I.** 1.75, 2.00, 2.25, 2.50, . . .

4 ASSESS

Assessment Resources

For more assessment resources, see:
- Assessment Book
- Test and Practice Generator

Mini-Quiz

Tell whether the sequence is *arithmetic* or *geometric*. Then find the common difference or the common ratio, and write the next three terms.

1. 1, −3, −7, −11, ... **arithmetic; −4; −15, −19, −23**

2. 1000, 200, 40, 8, ... **geometric; $\frac{1}{5}$; $\frac{8}{5}$, $\frac{8}{25}$, $\frac{8}{125}$**

3. $\frac{1}{16}, \frac{1}{8}, \frac{1}{4}, \frac{1}{2}, \ldots$ **geometric; 2; 1, 2, 4**

4. Challenge Study the figures.

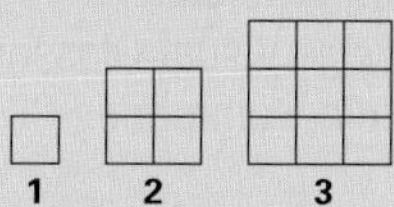

Suppose the pattern continues. Write a sequence that gives the number of squares in each figure. How many squares will be in figure 12? **1, 4, 9, 16, 25, 36, ...; 144 squares**

5 FOLLOW-UP

Diagnosis/Remediation

- Study Guide in Chapter 12 Resource Book, pp. 77–78
- eTutorial Plus Online
- Extra Practice, p. 814
- Lesson Practice in Chapter 12 Resource Book, pp. 74–76

English Learner Support

- Spanish Study Guide
- Multi-Language Visual Glossary
- Chapter Audio Summaries CDs

Challenge

- Challenge Practice in Chapter 12 Resource Book, p. 79
- Teacher's Edition, p. 648F

ADDITIONAL RESOURCES

The following resources are available to help review the materials in Lessons 12.5–12.8.

Chapter 12 Resource Book
- Lesson Practice
- Study Guide

Assessment Book
- Chapter 12 Quiz 2

Technology
- Test and Practice Generator
- eTutorial CD-ROM

Internet
- Classzone
- eWorkbook Plus Online
- eTutorial Plus Online

ENGLISH LEARNER SUPPORT

- Spanish Study Guide
- Multi-Language Visual Glossary
- Chapter Audio Summaries CDs

5. ***Sample answer:*** **First find the degree of each term by finding the sum of the exponents of its variables. The degree of the polynomial is the greatest degree of its terms.**

8. ***Sample answer:*** **It is a curve that falls from left to right. The farther to the left, the more quickly the graph is falling. To the right, the curve falls less and less quickly so that it appears to flatten out barely above the x-axis.**

CHAPTER 12 Chapter Review

Vocabulary Review

polynomial, p. 651
term of a polynomial, p. 651
binomial, p. 651
trinomial, p. 651
degree of a term, p. 652
degree of a polynomial, p. 652
standard form, p. 652
quadratic function, p. 679
parabola, p. 680
nonlinear function, p. 680
minimum value of a function, p. 681
maximum value of a function, p. 681
exponential function, p. 686
exponential growth, p. 687
exponential decay, p. 687
sequence, p. 692
term of a sequence, p. 692
arithmetic sequence, p. 692
common difference, p. 692
geometric sequence, p. 692
common ratio, p. 692

Copy and complete.

1. A(n) _?_ is any function whose graph is not a line. **nonlinear function**
2. The graph of a quadratic function is a U-shaped curve called a(n) _?_. **parabola**
3. In a(n) _?_, the difference between consecutive terms is constant. **arithmetic sequence**
4. In a(n) _?_, the ratio of any term to the previous term is constant. **geometric sequence**
5. Describe how to find the degree of a polynomial. **See margin.**
6. Give an example of a trinomial in standard form. ***Sample answer:*** $5x^2 + 4x - 6$
7. Describe the graph of a quadratic function that has a maximum value. ***Sample answer:*** **It is a U-shaped curve that opens downward.**
8. Describe the graph of a function that shows exponential decay. **See margin.**

12.1 Polynomials

Examples on pp. 651–653

Goal

Identify polynomials and write them in standard form.

Write $-5x - 4x^2 + 3(2x^2 + 3x)$ as a polynomial in standard form.

$$-5x - 4x^2 + 3(2x^2 + 3x)$$
$$= -5x - 4x^2 + 6x^2 + 9x \quad \text{Distributive property}$$
$$= -5x + 9x + (-4x^2) + 6x^2 \quad \text{Group like terms.}$$
$$= 4x + 2x^2 \quad \text{Combine like terms.}$$
$$= 2x^2 + 4x \quad \text{Standard form}$$

Write the expression as a polynomial in standard form.

9. $3x - 7 + 2x^2 - 3$ $\mathbf{2x^2 + 3x - 10}$
10. $10x + 4x^3 - 9 + 7x - 3x^3$ $\mathbf{x^3 + 17x - 9}$
11. $-6x - 5 + 4(2x^2 + x + 3)$ $\mathbf{8x^2 - 2x + 7}$
12. $15x^2 - 4x + 6(3 - 8x^2 - 2x)$ $\mathbf{-33x^2 - 16x + 18}$

The following resources are available to help review the materials in this chapter.

Chapter 12 Resource Book
- Chapter Review Games and Activities, p. 80
- Cumulative Practice, Chs. 1–12

English/Spanish Chapter Reviews and Tests

Chapter Audio Summaries CDs

eTutorial CD-ROM

eWorkbook Plus Online

eTutorial Plus Online

12.2 Adding and Subtracting Polynomials

Examples on pp. 657–659

Goal

Add and subtract polynomials.

Example **Find the difference $(y^2 - 6y + 3) - (5y^2 + 8y)$.**

$(y^2 - 6y + 3) - (5y^2 + 8y)$	**Write difference.**
$= y^2 - 6y + 3 + (-5y^2 - 8y)$	**Write opposite of second polynomial.**
$= y^2 - 5y^2 - 6y - 8y + 3$	**Group like terms.**
$= -4y^2 - 14y + 3$	**Combine like terms.**

Find the sum or difference.

13. $(m^2 + 2m - 3) - (5m + 7)$ **$m^2 - 3m - 10$**

14. $(8d^2 + 4d + 4) + (9d - 15)$ **$8d^2 + 13d - 11$**

15. $(4a^3 - 6a^2 + 3) + (7a^2 + a + 7)$ **$4a^3 + a^2 + a + 10$**

16. $(6y^3 - 4y + 1) - (7y^3 + 2y^2 - 3)$ **$-y^3 - 2y^2 - 4y + 4$**

12.3 Multiplying Monomials and Polynomials

Examples on pp. 662–663

Goal

Multiply a monomial and a polynomial.

Example **Find the product $x(5x^2 + 3x + 2)$.**

$x(5x^2 + 3x + 2) = x(5x^2) + x(3x) + x(2)$	**Distributive property**
$= 5x^3 + 3x^2 + 2x$	**Product of powers property**

Find the product.

17. $-7z(z^3 - 6z)$ **$-7z^4 + 42z^2$**

18. $(-c^2 + 3)4c^2$ **$-4c^4 + 12c^2$**

19. $(p^2 + 8p + 3)(-9p)$ **$-9p^3 - 72p^2 - 27p$**

20. $6a^2(a^2 - 4a + 1)$ **$6a^4 - 24a^3 + 6a^2$**

21. $-5n^2(5 - 3n)$ **$-25n^2 + 15n^3$**

22. $(6s^2 - 7)8s$ **$48s^3 - 56s$**

12.4 Multiplying Binomials

Examples on pp. 668–669

Goal

Multiply binomials.

Example **Find the product $(5x + 4)(2x - 7)$.**

First	+	Outer	+	Inner	+	Last	
$5x \cdot 2x$	+	$5x(-7)$	+	$4 \cdot 2x$	+	$4(-7)$	**Write products of terms.**
$10x^2$	+	$(-35x)$	+	$8x$	+	(-28)	**Multiply.**
		$10x^2 - 27x - 28$					**Combine like terms.**

Find the product.

23. $(b + 7)(b + 2)$ **$b^2 + 9b + 14$**

24. $(x + 3)(x + 9)$ **$x^2 + 12x + 27$**

25. $(z - 5)(z - 4)$ **$z^2 - 9z + 20$**

26. $(y - 8)(y + 11)$ **$y^2 + 3y - 88$**

27. $(3c + 1)(c - 6)$ **$3c^2 - 17c - 6$**

28. $(8a + 7)(2a + 9)$ **$16a^2 + 86a + 63$**

37–39. **Labeled points on the graph represent sample points for a table.**

37.

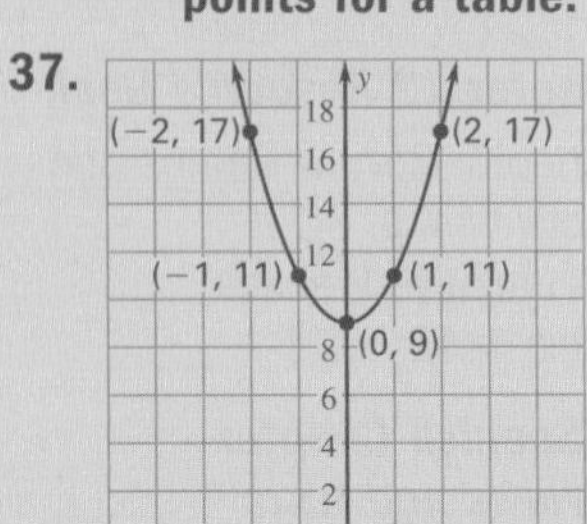

38.

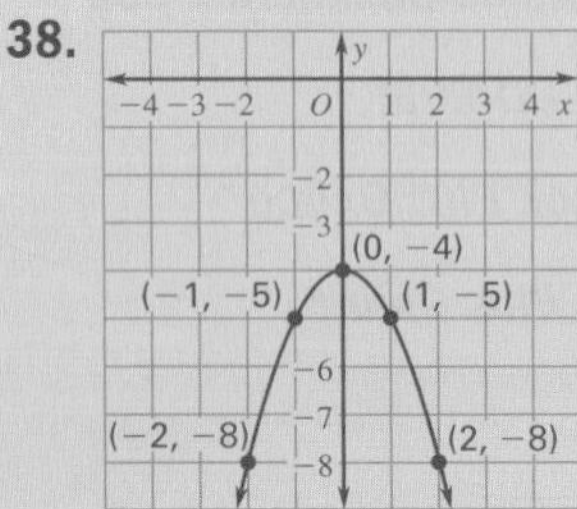

39.

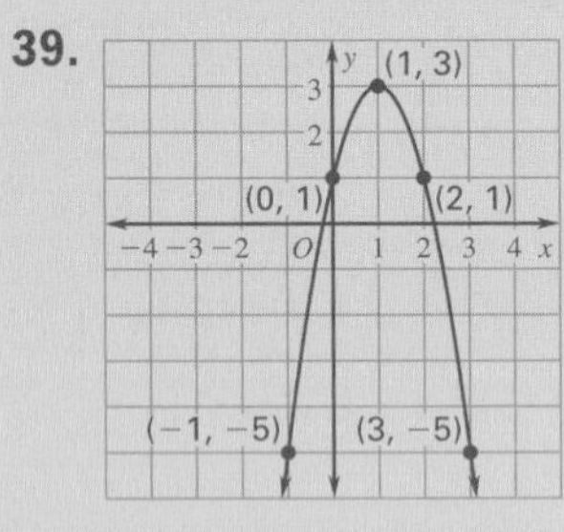

12.5 Other Rules of Exponents

Examples on pp. 674–676

▶ *Goal*

Simplify powers of products and quotients.

Example **Simplify the expressions $(3y)^3$, $\left(\frac{7}{k}\right)^2$, and $(-2m^4)^3$.**

a. $(3y)^3 = 3^3 \cdot y^3$ **Power of a product property**

$= 27y^3$ **Evaluate power.**

b. $\left(\frac{7}{k}\right)^2 = \frac{7^2}{k^2}$ **Power of a quotient property**

$= \frac{49}{k^2}$ **Evaluate power.**

c. $(-2m^4)^3 = (-2)^3 \cdot (m^4)^3$ **Power of a product property**

$= (-2)^3 \cdot m^{12}$ **Power of a power property**

$= -8m^{12}$ **Evaluate power.**

✔ **Simplify the expression. Write your answer using positive exponents.**

29. $(yz)^6$ y^6z^6 **30.** $(h^7)^{-2}$ $\frac{1}{h^{14}}$ **31.** $\left(\frac{x}{2}\right)^4$ $\frac{x^4}{16}$ **32.** $\left(\frac{w}{-9}\right)^3$ $-\frac{w^3}{729}$

33. $(5k)^4$ $625k^4$ **34.** $(abc)^3$ $a^3b^3c^3$ **35.** $(z^{-3})^{-4}$ z^{12} **36.** $(3b^2)^7$ $2187b^{14}$

12.6 Quadratic Functions

Examples on pp. 679–681

▶ *Goal*

Graph quadratic functions.

Example **Graph the function $y = x^2 - 2x - 1$.**

1) Make a table of values. Choose several x-values and find the corresponding y-values.

x	−1	0	1	2	3
y	2	−1	−2	−1	2

2) Use the table to make a list of ordered pairs.

(−1, 2), (0, −1), (1, −2), (2, −1), (3, 2)

3) Graph the ordered pairs. Then draw a smooth curve through the points.

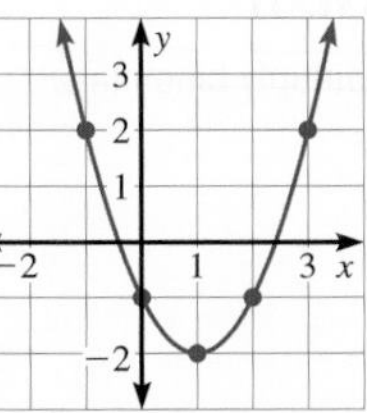

✔ **Make a table of values for the given function. Then graph the function.**

37–39. See margin.

37. $y = 2x^2 + 9$ **38.** $y = -x^2 - 4$ **39.** $y = -2x^2 + 4x + 1$

12.7 Exponential Growth and Decay

Examples on pp. 686–688

Goal

Solve problems involving exponential growth.

Example **This year 10,000 people attended a benefit concert. The concert's organizers want to make it an annual event. They predict the attendance A in t years using the function $A = 10{,}000(1.05)^t$. When will the attendance exceed 12,000?**

Make a table of values for the function.

t	0	1	2	3	4
A	10,000	10,500	11,025	11,576	12,155

From the table, you can see that when $t = 4$, $A > 12{,}000$.

Answer The attendance at the benefit concert will exceed 12,000 after 4 years.

40. You deposit $450 into an account earning 4% interest compounded annually. The balance A of the account is given by the function $A = 450(1.04)^t$, where t is the number of years after the deposit. After how many years will the account have a balance greater than $500? **after 3 y**

12.8 Sequences

Examples on pp. 692–694

Goal

Extend sequences.

Example **Tell whether the sequence is *arithmetic* or *geometric.* Then find the common difference or common ratio, and write the next three terms.**

a. 6, 10, 14, 18, . . .

Each term after the first is 4 more than the previous term. So, the sequence is arithmetic. The common difference is 4. The next three terms in the sequence are 22, 26, and 30.

b. 13, 65, 325, 1625, . . .

Each term after the first is 5 times the previous term. So, the sequence is geometric. The common ratio is 5. The next three terms in the sequence are 8125, 40,625, and 203,125.

Tell whether the sequence is *arithmetic* or *geometric.* Then find the common difference or common ratio, and write the next three terms.

41. −1, 4, 9, 14, . . . **42.** 448, 112, 28, 7, . . . **43.** 3, 21, 147, 1029, . . .

41. arithmetic; common difference: 5; 19, 24, 29

42. geometric; common ratio: $\frac{1}{4}$; $\frac{7}{4}$, $\frac{7}{16}$, $\frac{7}{64}$

43. geometric; common ratio: 7; 7203; 50,421; 352,947

Additional Resources

Assessment Book

- Chapter Test (3 levels), pp. 148–153
- Standardized Chapter Test, p. 154
- Alternative Assessment, pp. 155–156

Test and Practice Generator

18–21. Labeled points on the graph represent sample points for a table.

18.

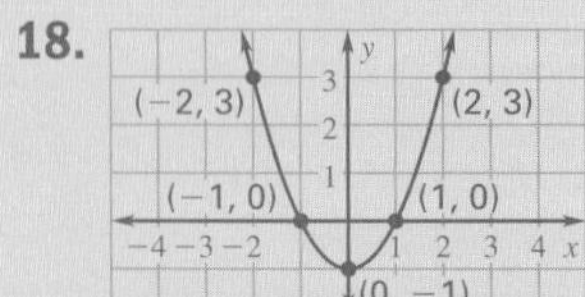

19.

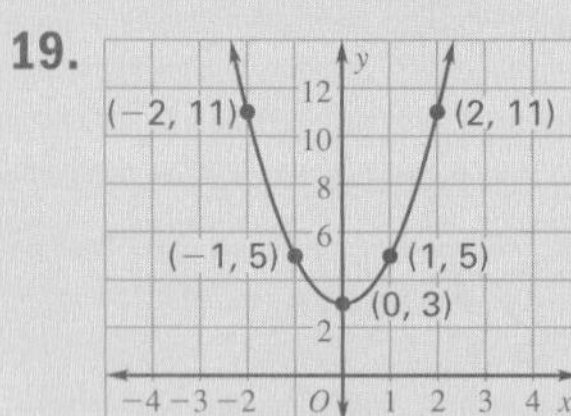

20.

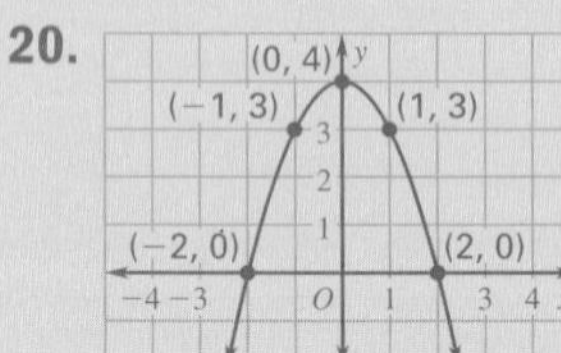

21.

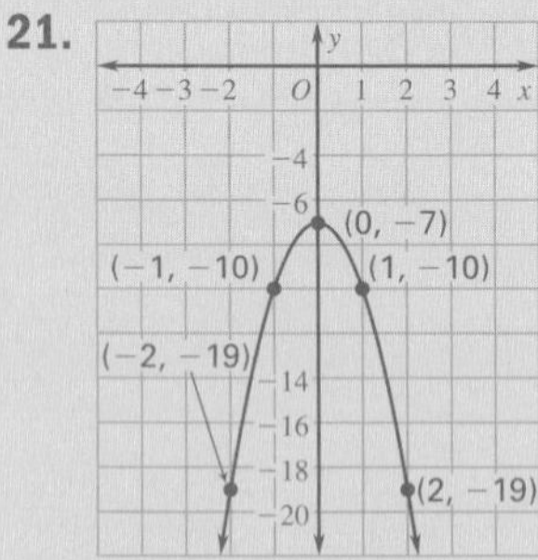

22–26. See Additional Answers beginning on page AA1.

27. geometric; common ratio: −3; 243, −729, 2187

28. geometric; common ratio: 3; 972, 2916, 8748

29. arithmetic; common difference: −15; 5, −10, −25

30. arithmetic; common difference: 11; 61, 72, 83

CHAPTER 12

Chapter Test

Find the degree of the polynomial.

1. $-4h$ **1** **2.** 0 **no degree** **3.** $x - 3x^2y^3 - 2y^4$ **5** **4.** $9z^2$ **2**

5. Write the expression $-9 + 5y^2 + y(2 - 3y)$ as a polynomial in standard form. $\mathbf{2y^2 + 2y - 9}$

Find the sum or difference.

6. $(7x^2 - 3x + 4) + (-3x^2 + 3x + 2)$ $\mathbf{4x^2 + 6}$

7. $(4x^3 + 10x) + (5x^2 - 3x + 1)$ $\mathbf{4x^3 + 5x^2 + 7x + 1}$

8. $(6d^2 + 1) - (-7 + 11d^2)$ $\mathbf{-5d^2 + 8}$

9. $(2y^2 - y + 7) - (-8y^2 + y - 15)$ $\mathbf{10y^2 - 2y + 22}$

Find the product.

10. $3m(m^4 - 2m^2)$ $\mathbf{3m^5 - 6m^3}$

11. $(b^2 + 4)2b$ $\mathbf{2b^3 + 8b}$

12. $(x + 9)(2x + 5)$ $\mathbf{2x^2 + 23x + 45}$

13. $(3h - 8)(2h - 5)$ $\mathbf{6h^2 - 31h + 40}$

Simplify the expression. Write your answer using positive exponents.

14. $(-ab)^5$ $\mathbf{-a^5b^5}$ **15.** $(3m^4)^2$ $\mathbf{9m^8}$ **16.** $\left(\frac{15}{t}\right)^2$ $\mathbf{\frac{225}{t^2}}$ **17.** $\left(\frac{7}{c}\right)^3$ $\mathbf{\frac{343}{c^3}}$

Make a table of values for the given function. Then graph the function. **18–21. See margin.**

18. $y = x^2 - 1$ **19.** $y = 2x^2 + 3$ **20.** $y = -x^2 + 4$ **21.** $y = -3x^2 - 7$

22. **Baseball** You are throwing a baseball up in the air. The baseball's height (in feet) is given by the function $h = -16t^2 + 40t + 4$, where t is the time in seconds after the ball leaves your hand. Use a graphing calculator to graph the function. Then find the greatest height the baseball reaches. **See margin for art; 29 ft.**

Graph the function. **23–26. See margin.**

23. $y = 4^x$ **24.** $y = 3(4)^x$ **25.** $y = 5\left(\frac{1}{4}\right)^x$ **26.** $y = (0.3)^x$

Tell whether the sequence is *arithmetic* or *geometric*. Then find the common difference or the common ratio, and write the next three terms. **27–30. See margin.**

27. 3, −9, 27, −81, . . . **28.** 12, 36, 108, 324, . . . **29.** 65, 50, 35, 20, . . . **30.** 17, 28, 39, 50, . . .

31. **Plants** You run a business that takes care of people's plants while they are out of town. You charge \$5 for the first day and \$4 for each additional day that you water plants.

a. Write the first 6 terms of the sequence. Is the sequence *arithmetic* or *geometric*? **5, 9, 13, 17, 21, 25; arithmetic**

b. Write a variable expression for how much you are paid for n days. $\mathbf{4n + 1}$

Chapter Standardized Test

Test-Taking Strategy **Before you take a test, know what topics the test will cover and what types of questions will be asked.**

1. Which of the following is a trinomial? **C**

A. $9x^3$ **B.** $3x^4 - 4x$

C. $x^5 - x^2 + 1$ **D.** $x^3 - x^2 - x + 9$

2. What is the degree of the polynomial $9 - 3x + 4y - x^2$? **G**

F. 1 **G.** 2 **H.** 3 **I.** 4

3. Find the sum $(4z^2 - 5z) + (2z^3 - z^2 + 3z)$. **D**

A. $6z^3 - 6z$ **B.** $2z^3 + 3z^2 - 8z$

C. $6z^3 - z^2 - 2z$ **D.** $2z^3 + 3z^2 - 2z$

4. You are painting a rectangular tabletop. The length of the tabletop is 6 inches less than 3 times the width. Let w represent the width. Which expression represents the area you are painting? **F**

F. $3w^2 - 6w$ **G.** $6w - 3w^2$

H. $8w - 12$ **I.** $4w - 6$

5. Find the product $(3x + 4)(x - 9)$. **B**

A. $3x^2 - 23x + 36$ **B.** $3x^2 - 23x - 36$

C. $3x^2 - 31x + 36$ **D.** $3x^2 - 31x - 36$

6. A square painting has sides of length s inches. The frame for the painting is 5 inches wide all around. Which expression represents the combined area (in square inches) of the painting and the frame? **I**

F. $s^2 + 25$

G. $s^2 + 10s + 25$

H. $s^2 + 15s + 50$

I. $s^2 + 20s + 100$

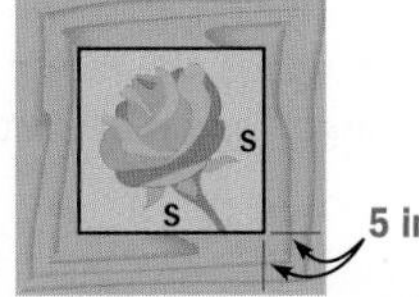

7. Which expression is equivalent to $\left(\frac{3a^{-3}}{4b}\right)^2$? **D**

A. $\frac{3}{4ab^2}$ **B.** $\frac{3}{4a^6b^2}$ **C.** $\frac{9}{16ab^2}$ **D.** $\frac{9}{16a^6b^2}$

8. Which function has a minimum value? **I**

F. $y = -4x^2 + 3$ **G.** $y = -4x^2 - 3$

H. $y = -4x^2$ **I.** $y = 4x^2 + 3$

9. What is the common ratio of the geometric sequence $54, -18, 6, -2, \ldots$? **C**

A. -3 **B.** 3 **C.** $-\frac{1}{3}$ **D.** $\frac{1}{3}$

10. What is the next term in the sequence $-3, -6, -9, -12, \ldots$? **F**

F. -15 **G.** -3 **H.** 3 **I.** 15

11. Short Response Describe how to determine if the exponential function $y = ab^x$ shows exponential growth or decay. ***Sample answer:*** **If $a > 0$ and $b > 1$, it shows exponential growth. If $a > 0$ and $0 < b < 1$, it shows exponential decay.**

12. Extended Response Use the trapezoid.

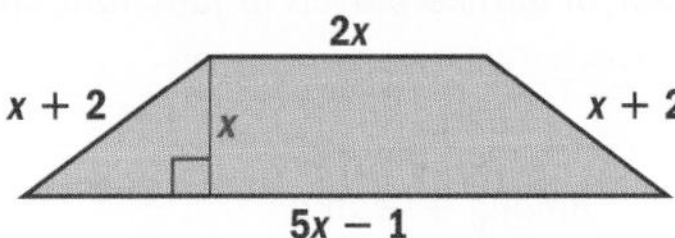

a. Write a polynomial expression in standard form for the perimeter of the figure. **$9x + 3$**

b. Write a polynomial expression in standard form for the area of the figure. **$\frac{7}{2}x^2 - \frac{1}{2}x$**

c. Are the degrees of the polynomials in parts (a) and (b) the same or different? Explain. **See margin.**

ADDITIONAL RESOURCES

Assessment Book

- Standardized Chapter Test, p. 154

Test and Practice Generator

12c. Different. *Sample answer:* Perimeter is measured in linear units and area is measured in square units, so the polynomial in part (a) has a degree of 1, and the polynomial in part (b) has a degree of 2.

1 PLAN

BACKGROUND FOCUS

For some types of word problems, students may see a pattern and be able to extend the solution to other related problems. Using variables, students may be able to write a formula that can be used to find the solution for all similar situations.

2 TEACH

GUIDING STUDENTS' WORK

The formula for the number of segments drawn may not be obvious to students. Have them make a table showing the number of games for 2 teams, then 3 teams, 4 teams, 5 teams, and finally n teams.

Extra Examples

Example Write the numbers 1 to 100 sequentially in a 10-by-10 grid.

a. Draw a square around the four numbers 2, 3, 12, and 13. Find and compare the products of the diagonal numbers. **$2 \cdot 13 = 26$, $3 \cdot 12 = 36$; 36 is 10 more than 26.**

b. Repeat part a for the numbers 5, 6, 15, and 16. **$5 \cdot 16 = 80$, $6 \cdot 15 = 90$; 90 is 10 more than 80.**

c. Use your results from parts a and b to write variable expressions for the diagonal products of any square containing four numbers in the grid. **Letting the four numbers be n, $n + 1$, $n + 10$, and $n + 11$, the diagonal products are $n(n + 11) = n^2 + 11n$ and $(n + 1)(n + 10) = n^2 + 11n + 10$.**

d. What do you notice about the difference between each pair of products? **The difference is always 10.**

Unit 4 Focus On Problem Solving

Looking Back

Generalizing and Extending a Solution

Once you solve a problem, you may be able to generalize or extend the solution to solve other problems.

Problem In a soccer tournament, each team plays every other team exactly once. Find the number of games played if there are 4 teams and if there are n teams. Then extend the solutions of these problems to find a formula for the number of diagonals of an n-gon.

1 Solve a specific problem.

For the specific case where there are 4 teams, represent the teams as 4 points on a circle. When one team plays another team, let the game be represented by a segment connecting the teams. Draw a segment from each team to every other team. From any of the 4 teams, there are 3 possible segments that you can draw. So, the total number of segments is $4 \cdot 3 = 12$.

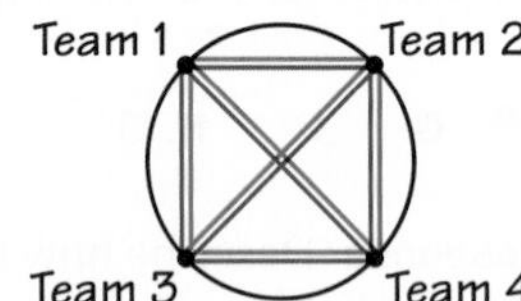

However, the procedure described above causes each pair of teams to be connected twice even though they play each other only once. Therefore, the number of games played is just half the number of segments.

$$\text{Games played among 4 teams} = \frac{12}{2} = 6$$

You can represent the games played using 6 segments (rather than 12), as shown below.

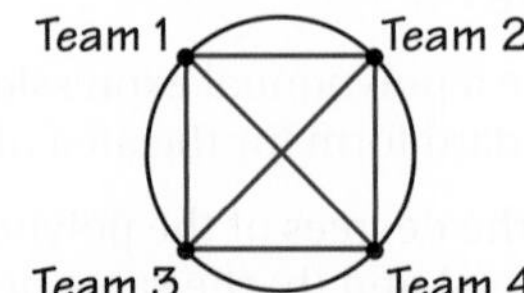

2 Generalize the solution.

To find the number of games played when there are n teams, generalize the solution in Step 1. Represent the teams as n points on a circle, and draw a segment from each team to every other team. The number of segments drawn is $n(n - 1) = n^2 - n$. The number of games played is half the number of segments.

$$\text{Games played among n teams} = \frac{n^2 - n}{2} = \frac{1}{2}n^2 - \frac{1}{2}n$$

3 Extend the solution.

You can extend the solutions in Steps 1 and 2 to find a formula for the number of diagonals $d(n)$ of an n-gon. First look at the second diagram in Step 1. The segments connecting the 4 points on the circle form a 4-gon and the diagonals of the 4-gon. Therefore:

$$d(4) = \text{Number of ways to connect 4 points} - \text{Number of sides of 4-gon}$$

You can generalize this result to the case where there are n points connected by segments.

$$d(n) = \text{Number of ways to connect n points} - \text{Number of sides of n-gon}$$

Now use the result in Step 2 and the fact that an n-gon has n sides to find a formula for $d(n)$.

$$d(n) = \left(\frac{1}{2}n^2 - \frac{1}{2}n\right) - n = \frac{1}{2}n^2 - \frac{3}{2}n$$

Problem Solving Practice

1. **Geometry** A circle inside a square just touches each side, as shown.

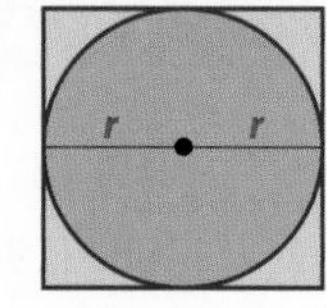

   a. Copy and complete the table. What do you notice about the ratios? **See margin.**

Value of r	1	2	3	4
Area of circle	?	?	?	?
Area of square	?	?	?	?
Ratio of circle's area to square's area	?	?	?	?

   b. Generalize your results from part (a) by first writing expressions in terms of r for the area of the circle and the area of the square. Then write and simplify an expression for the ratio of the circle's area to the square's area. Compare your answer with the results from part (a). **See margin.**

2. **Video Games** Of the video game consoles made by a company, 2% are defective. What is the probability that a console is not defective? that neither of 2 consoles is defective? that there are no defective consoles in a shipment of n consoles? **98%; 96.04%; 98^n%**

3. **Finance** You invest \$500 from a summer job in shares of a company's stock.

   a. Suppose the value of your shares increases by 10% the first year and then decreases by 10% the second year. What is the value of your shares after 2 years? Did you have an overall gain or loss? **\$495; loss**

   b. Consider a more general case in which the value of your shares has a percent of increase p the first year and a percent of decrease p the second year (where p is written as a decimal). Write a polynomial in terms of p for the value of your shares after 2 years. Did you have an overall gain or loss? Explain. **See margin.**

4. **Soccer** You need 4 teams to hold an elimination soccer tournament with 2 rounds, as shown below.

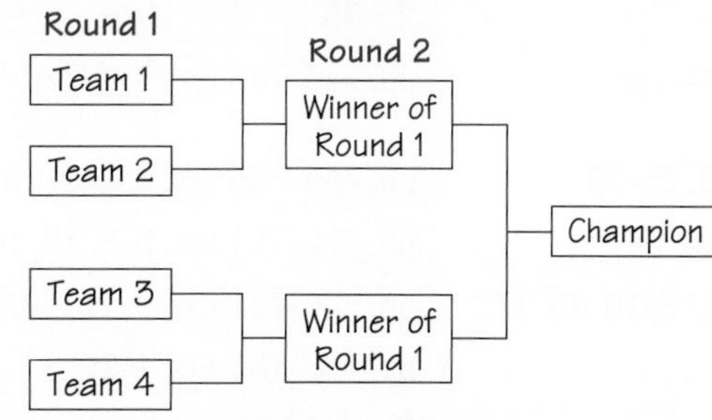

   a. How many teams do you need for an elimination tournament with 3 rounds? **8 teams**

   b. Write a formula for the number of teams $t(n)$ that you need for an elimination tournament with n rounds. $t(n) = 2^n$

   c. A men's tournament and a women's tournament each have n rounds. Write and simplify an expression for the total number of teams in both tournaments. $2 \cdot 2^n = 2^{n+1}$

5. **Patterns** Consider the following sequence:

$$\frac{1}{2}, \left(\frac{1}{2}\right)^2, \left(\frac{1}{2}\right)^3, \left(\frac{1}{2}\right)^4, \ldots$$

Let $S(n)$ represent the sum of the first n terms in the sequence.

   a. Find $S(1)$, $S(2)$, $S(3)$, and $S(4)$. Write your answers as fractions in simplest form. **See margin.**

   b. Based on the pattern from part (a), write a formula for $S(n)$ in terms of n. $S(n) = 1 - \left(\frac{1}{2}\right)^n$

3 APPLY

TRANSPARENCY

Even-numbered answers are available on transparencies.

COMMON ERROR

In Exercise 3, watch for students who, without calculating, assume that the increase and decrease are equal dollar values.

SUGGESTED STRATEGIES

You may wish to suggest the following strategies for the problems in the Problem Solving Practice:

- Exercise 1: Make a Table; Look for a Pattern
- Exercise 2: Look for a Pattern
- Exercise 3: Make a Table; Look for a Pattern
- Exercise 4: Draw a Diagram; Look for a Pattern
- Exercise 5: Look for a Pattern

1a. Row 2: $\pi, 4\pi, 9\pi, 16\pi$; Row 3: 4, 16, 36, 64; Row 4: $\frac{\pi}{4}, \frac{\pi}{4}, \frac{\pi}{4}, \frac{\pi}{4}$; the ratios are the same.

1b. Circle: πr^2; square: $(2r)^2 = 4r^2$; ratio: $\frac{\pi r^2}{4r^2} = \frac{\pi}{4}$; the results are the same.

3b. $500 - 500p^2$; loss. *Sample answer:* p^2 is positive, so $500p^2$ is positive. You are subtracting a positive number from 500, so the result is less than 500.

5a. $S(1) = \frac{1}{2}$, $S(2) = \frac{3}{4}$, $S(3) = \frac{7}{8}$, $S(4) = \frac{15}{16}$

CHAPTER

13 Pacing and Assignment Guide

REGULAR SCHEDULE

Lesson	Les. Day	BASIC	AVERAGE	ADVANCED
13.1	Day 1	pp. 711–713 Exs. 9–23, 26–30, 36–46	pp. 711–713 Exs. 9–13, 17–24, 26–34, 36–46	pp. 711–713 Exs. 9, 10, 14–26, 30–36*, 40–46
13.2	Day 1	pp. 719–720 Exs. 9–14, 17–20, 23, 25–32	pp. 719–720 Exs. 11–23, 25–33	pp. 719–720 Exs. 11–24*, 27–29, 32, 33
13.3	Day 1	pp. 725–727 Exs. 8–11, 22, 24–26, 37–44	pp. 725–727 Exs. 8–11, 22–26, 32–35, 37–44	pp. 725–727 Exs. 9–11, 22–24, 31–36*, 39–41
	Day 2	pp. 725–727 Exs. 12–20, 28–30, 45–48	pp. 725–727 Exs. 15–21, 27–31, 45–49	pp. 725–727 Exs. 15–21, 26–30, 44–49
13.4	Day 1	pp. 732–733 Exs. 6–10, 12–15, 17, 22–30	pp. 732–733 Exs. 6–8, 10–20, 22–30	pp. 732–733 Exs. 7, 10–13, 15–22*, 27–30
13.5	Day 1	pp. 736–738 Exs. 8–16, 18, 19, 22, 25–34	pp. 736–738 Exs. 9–12, 14–18, 20–23, 25–35	pp. 736–738 Exs. 10–13, 15–17, 19–26*, 31–35
13.6	Day 1	SRH p. 792 Exs. 1–4; pp. 744–746 Exs. 8–12, 20–22	pp. 744–746 Exs. 8–12, 20–22, 25–28	pp. 744–746 Exs. 8–12, 20–22, 27–29
	Day 2	pp. 744–746 Exs. 13–18, 23, 25–30	pp. 744–746 Exs. 13–19, 23, 29, 30	pp. 744–746 Exs. 13–19, 23, 24*, 30
13.7	Day 1	pp. 750–751 Exs. 5–8, 14, 19–24	pp. 750–751 Exs. 5–8, 12–16, 19–24	pp. 750–751 Exs. 6–8, 12–16, 19, 22–24
	Day 2	pp. 750–751 Exs. 9–11, 13, 15, 16, 25–27	pp. 750–751 Exs. 9–11, 18, 25–27	pp. 750–751 Exs. 9–11, 17*, 18, 25–27
Review	Day 1	pp. 752–755 Exs. 1–29	pp. 752–755 Exs. 1–29	pp. 752–755 Exs. 1–29
Assess	Day 1	Chapter 13 Test	Chapter 13 Test	Chapter 13 Test

YEARLY PACING Chapter 13 Total – **12 days** Chapters 1–13 Total – **160 days** Remaining – **0 days**

*Challenge Exercises EP = Extra Practice SRH = Skills Review Handbook

BLOCK SCHEDULE

DAY 1	DAY 2	DAY 3	DAY 4	DAY 5	DAY 6
13.1 pp. 711–713 Exs. 9–13, 17–24, 26–34, 36–46 **13.2** pp. 719–720 Exs. 11–23, 25–33	**13.3** pp. 725–727 Exs. 8–11, 15–35, 37–49	**13.4** pp. 732–733 Exs. 6–8, 10–20, 22–30 **13.5** pp. 736–738 Exs. 9–12, 14–18, 20–23, 25–35	**13.6** pp. 744–746 Exs. 8–23, 25–30	**13.7** pp. 750–751 Exs. 5–16, 18–27	**Review** pp. 752–755 Exs. 1–29 **Assess** Chapter 13 Test

YEARLY PACING Chapter 13 Total – **6 days** Chapters 1–13 Total – **80 days** Remaining – **0 days**

Support Materials

CHAPTER RESOURCE BOOK

CHAPTER SUPPORT

Tips for New Teachers	p. 1	Parents as Partners	p. 3

LESSON SUPPORT	13.1	13.2	13.3	13.4	13.5	13.6	13.7
Lesson Plans (regular and block)	p. 5	p. 13	p. 22	p. 30	p. 39	p. 47	p. 56
Technology Activities & Keystrokes				p. 32			
Activity Support Masters							
Activity Masters		p. 15					
Practice (3 levels)	p. 7	p. 16	p. 24	p. 33	p. 41	p. 49	p. 58
Study Guide	p. 10	p. 19	p. 27	p. 36	p. 44	p. 52	p. 61
Real-World Problem Solving						p. 54	p. 63
Challenge Practice	p. 12	p. 21	p. 29	p. 38	p. 46	p. 55	p. 64

REVIEW

Chapter Review Games and Activities	p. 65	Extra Credit Project with Rubric	p. 70
Real-Life Project with Rubric	p. 66	Cumulative Practice	p. 72
Cooperative Project with Rubric	p. 68	Resource Book Answers	A1

ASSESSMENT

Quizzes	p. 157	Alternative Assessments with Rubrics	p. 166
Chapter Tests (3 levels)	p. 159	Unit Test	p. 168
Standardized Test	p. 165	Cumulative Test	p. 170

TRANSPARENCIES

	13.1	13.2	13.3	13.4	13.5	13.6	13.7
Warm-Up/Daily Homework Quiz	✔	✔	✔	✔	✔	✔	✔
Notetaking Guide	✔	✔	✔	✔	✔	✔	✔
Teacher Support			✔	✔	✔	✔	✔
English/Spanish Problem Solving					✔		
Answer Transparencies	✔	✔	✔	✔	✔	✔	✔

TECHNOLOGY

- EasyPlanner CD-ROM
- Test and Practice Generator
- Electronic Lesson Presentations
- eTutorial CD-ROM
- Chapter Audio Summaries CDs
- Classzone.com
- eEdition Plus Online
- eWorkbook Plus Online
- eTutorial Plus Online
- EasyPlanner Plus Online

ADDITIONAL RESOURCES

- Worked-Out Solution Key
- Notetaking Guide
- Practice Workbook
- Tutor Place
- Professional Development Book
- Special Activities Book
- Posters
- Spanish Study Guide
- Exercises in Spanish
- English/Spanish Ch. Reviews/Tests
- Multi-Language Visual Glossary

CHAPTER 13

Math Background and Teaching Strategies

Lesson 13.1

MATH BACKGROUND

If the sum of the measures of two angles is 90°, the angles are **complementary angles**. If the sum of the measures of two angles is 180°, the angles are **supplementary angles**. When two different lines intersect, the pairs of opposite angles are **vertical angles**. Vertical angles have the same measure.

TEACHING STRATEGIES

To help students distinguish between *complementary* and *supplementary*, suggest they associate "complement" with "corner," as in the corner of a room, which forms a right angle, and "supplement" with "straight," as in a straight angle. Have students look around the classroom to find examples of complementary and supplementary angles.

Lesson 13.2

MATH BACKGROUND

A **transversal** is a line that intersects two or more lines at separate points. If an angle formed by the transversal and one of the other two lines lies in the *corresponding* position of an angle formed by the transversal and the other line, then the two angles are **corresponding angles**. **Alternate interior angles** lie on opposite sides of the transversal between the other two lines, and **alternate exterior angles** lie on opposite sides of the transversal outside the other two lines. If a transversal intersects two parallel lines, then any two corresponding, alternate interior, or alternate exterior angles are congruent. Conversely, if any two corresponding, alternate interior, or alternate exterior angles are congruent, the two lines intersected by the transversal are parallel.

TEACHING STRATEGIES

It will help students to work with various orientations of lines intersected by a transversal. One way is to sketch two pairs of intersecting lines, as shown in the following figure. In this case, any of the four lines can be considered as a transversal for two of the others. Have students identify pairs of corresponding angles, alternate interior angles, and alternate exterior angles. As they do so, they should identify the line that they are considering as the transversal. For example, $\angle 1$ and $\angle 5$ are corresponding angles of transversal q, and $\angle 1$ and $\angle 9$ are corresponding angles of transversal s.

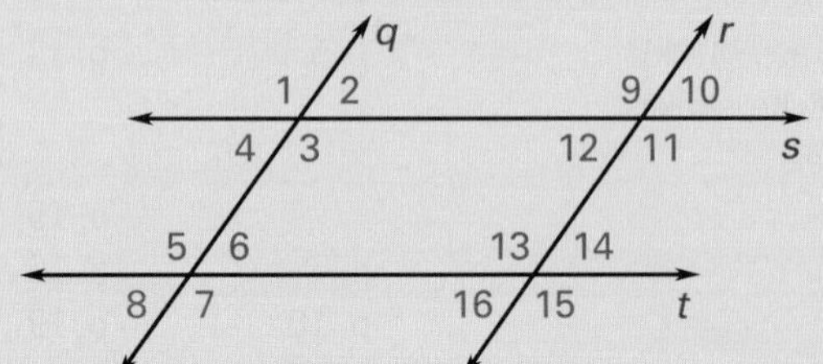

Lesson 13.3

MATH BACKGROUND

Any two adjacent sides of a polygon form an **interior angle** of the polygon. If you extend either of these two sides beyond the vertex, the angle formed that is adjacent to the interior angle is an **exterior angle**. Either exterior angle at a given vertex of a polygon forms a straight angle with the interior angle at that vertex. You can draw diagonals from any vertex of any n-sided convex polygon that divide it into $n - 2$ non-overlapping triangles, so the sum of the interior angle measures in any convex polygon is $(n - 2) \cdot 180°$. If a polygon is *regular*, then the measure of each interior angle is this quantity divided by n. The sum of the measures of the exterior angles (one at each vertex) of any convex polygon is 360°.

TEACHING STRATEGIES

Make sure that students internalize the process used in the Concept Activity for this lesson of dividing the interior of a polygon into triangles to find the sum of the interior angles. In the lesson, students may get confused by exterior angles, since two can be drawn at any vertex. Make sure that when they draw exterior angles, students get in the practice of working their way in one direction only—either clockwise or counterclockwise—around the polygon. Point out that *which* direction they choose is unimportant, because the two exterior angles at each vertex are congruent since each forms a straight angle with the interior angle at that vertex.

Lesson 13.4

MATH BACKGROUND

A **transformation** of a figure changes its location, size, orientation, or some combination of these. The result of performing a transformation on a figure is the **image** of the figure. A transformation called a **translation** "slides" a figure in the coordinate plane. The image of a translation is congruent to the original figure, and has the same orientation. Translations can be used to create *tessellations*.

TEACHING STRATEGIES

Draw a triangle or quadrilateral on a coordinate grid on the board or overhead so that no vertex of the figure lies at the origin. Then have students choose a vertex of the figure and write the coordinate notation for the translation for which the image of that vertex would lie at the origin. You can have students repeat this exercise with each vertex.

Lesson 13.5

MATH BACKGROUND

A **reflection** of a figure about a line is a transformation in which the figure is reflected, or flipped, over the line. Reflection in a line reverses the orientation of a figure. If the vertices of a figure are labeled clockwise, its image after a reflection will have the corresponding vertices labeled counterclockwise. A **line of symmetry** is a line of reflection that divides a figure into two parts that are mirror images. A figure can have no lines of symmetry (e.g., a scalene triangle), one line of symmetry (e.g., an isosceles, non-equilateral triangle), two lines of symmetry (e.g., a non-square rectangle), three lines of symmetry (e.g., an equilateral triangle), or many lines of symmetry.

TEACHING STRATEGIES

Have pairs of students fold a piece of tracing paper in half. Then have them unfold the paper and label the halves I and II. On half I, have students draw a scalene triangle *ABC*, refold the paper, and then trace the triangle on the back of half II. Now have students unfold the paper and trace this triangle onto the front of half II, labeling the vertices of this triangle A', B', and C' to correspond to the vertices of triangle *ABC*. Have students compare the distances of each pair of corresponding vertices from the fold. Also, have them describe whether the vertices of each triangle are labeled in a clockwise or counterclockwise direction.

Lesson 13.6

MATH BACKGROUND

A **rotation** of a figure is a transformation in which the figure is turned about a fixed point, the **center of rotation**. The angle with vertex at the center of rotation through which the figure turns is called the **angle of rotation**. If rotating a figure 180° or less about its center in either direction maps the figure onto itself, it has **rotational symmetry**.

TEACHING STRATEGIES

Physically performing rotations will help students better understand them. To explore rotational symmetry, you can have students cut out a figure that they want to test for symmetry, trace the outline of the figure on a piece of paper, and then, placing the point of a pencil at the center of the figure, rotate the figure until it matches the outline. For rotation about the origin, you can have students attach figures to a toothpick or popsicle stick, and then, keeping one end at the origin of a coordinate grid, perform the rotation.

Lesson 13.7

MATH BACKGROUND

A geometric figure is stretched or shrunk under the transformation called a **dilation**. The **scale factor** of a dilation is the ratio of the corresponding side lengths of a figure and its image under the dilation. The image of a dilation is *not* necessarily congruent to the original figure, but it *is* similar. In the coordinate plane, the image of a point with coordinates (x, y) after a dilation by a scale factor of k has coordinates (kx, ky).

TEACHING STRATEGIES

You can use a copy machine that enlarges and reduces to make copies of a polygon using different scale factors. Use a simple outline of a polygon with unmarked axes and without a grid, since this would also be enlarged or reduced. Then mark scales on the axes, and let students examine these dilations. Since copy machines usually perform dilations in terms of percent, you can have students translate the scale factor to decimal numbers or fractions.

CHAPTER

13 Differentiating Instruction

Strategies for Underachievers

FOCUS ON VOCABULARY

Students will need to learn many new vocabulary terms to be successful in this chapter. Encourage students to add each new term to their notebooks, or to make a notecard for each term. The terms should have a well-labeled, accurate diagram illustrating the term whenever appropriate. You may want to suggest that if students use notecards, they should color code any cards related to the same topic. For example, one color group might contain vocabulary terms related to general angles, such as *obtuse angle*, *supplementary angles*, *vertical angles*, and so on, while another color group might contain terms related to angles associated specifically with transversals, such as *corresponding angles* and *alternate interior angles*. Another color group could contain terms related to transformations, and so on. If students think that a vocabulary term belongs in more than one color group—for example, *vertical angles* could be considered appropriate in either of the first two groups mentioned above—have them place a card for the term in each group.

Throughout this chapter, try to help students connect vocabulary terms with the everyday uses of words that they contain. For example, if students *alternate* using their left and right hands when drumming, it means that they change from one hand to the other. In a similar way, alternate interior angles "alternate" from one side of a transversal to the other.

In Lesson 13.4, the terms *transformation* and *translation* look similar, so make sure students read these words carefully and do not confuse them. Because the word *transform* has the same meaning as the word *change*, a transformation is a more general description than a translation—a translation is just one of the types of transformations that change a figure.

In Lessons 13.5 and 13.6, make sure students understand the differences between the terms *line symmetry* and *rotational symmetry*, and that a figure can exhibit neither, either, or both of these types of symmetry.

USE MODELS AND MANIPULATIVES

You can have students use pieces of uncooked linguine to help them model lines. Students can model vertical angles with two pieces of linguine by "opening" and "closing" the pieces of linguine as they would a pair of scissors. This makes it obvious which pairs of angles remain congruent. Using three pieces of linguine, students can model two parallel lines and a transversal. If students need to, suggest they use a piece of tape to secure their "parallel lines" while they manipulate the transversal to observe which pairs of angles are congruent. Students can also model a transversal with two lines that are not parallel so that they can see that the relationships observed for parallel lines no longer hold.

CONSTRUCTIONS In the Student Reference on pages 714 and 715, students use a compass and straightedge to perform constructions. You may wish to supply some underachievers, especially those who have difficulty with fine motor skills, with higher quality compasses with wheels. These are much easier to use, since they do not collapse or flop open. You may also wish to supply students with *non-ruled* straightedges to prohibit them from trying to circumvent the construction process by using measurements.

If you have a large coordinate grid for the classroom, you can attach cutouts of various figures to a piece of dowel rod and physically perform rotations about the origin of the coordinate grid. Also in conjunction with this lesson, you may wish to use an analog clock to help students visualize angles of rotation.

USE SCAFFOLDING

ANGLE MEASURES For Exercises 26–28 on page 712 of Lesson 13.1 and for similar exercises later, you may wish to provide students with templates that they can complete to help them set up and solve equations to find missing angle measures. This scaffolding method may also be useful for situations like the one shown in Example 3 on page 718.

TRANSFORMATIONS In Lessons 13.4 through 13.7, it can be difficult for some students to keep track of the coordinate notation for the different types of transformation. Have them create a series of notecards containing the information in the Summary of Transformations in a Coordinate Plane at the top of page 749. Students should include illustrations of the various transformations performed on figures in the coordinate plane.

Strategies for English Learners

VOCABULARY STUDY

If students seem comfortable with opposites, introduce the idea of analogies. An analogy expresses a similarity between otherwise dissimilar things. In other words, it points to the similarity of two things that are not identical. Write this simple analogy on the board and ask students to think of others, using terms used in geometry.

Complementary is to 90 degrees as supplementary is to ___?___.

This can be written in different ways, for example, complementary: 90° as supplementary : 180°.

Other possible examples include:

Line of reflection is to reflection as center of rotation is to rotation.

Angle of rotation is to rotation as scale factor is to dilation.

Have students make up their own analogies using mathematical terms and concepts that they know. Note that these analogies, since they are focusing on the relationships between concepts, can be translated into any language and the concepts stay the same.

Students can also try analogies with shapes that are rotated or reflected, such as:

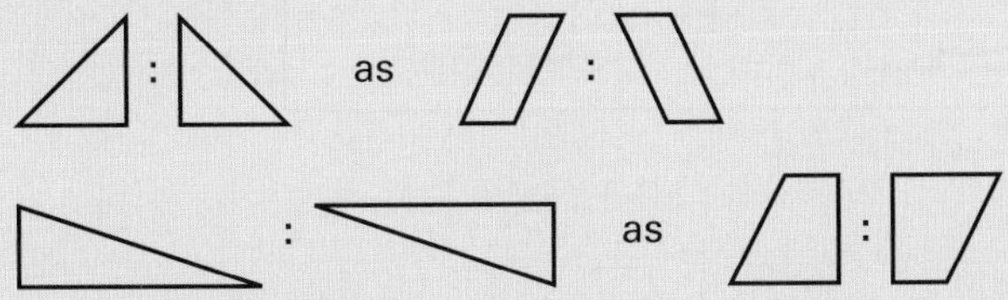

Strategies for Advanced Learners

INCREASE DEPTH AND COMPLEXITY

In the Student Reference on pages 714–715, students learn how to bisect an angle using a compass and a straightedge. Some students may wonder about dividing an angle into a greater number of parts. You might wish to point out that through the ages many people tried to trisect an angle using a construction. However, this has since been proven to be impossible. You may wish to have advanced students investigate and report on one of the famous incorrect construction attempts.

In Lesson 13.3, you may also wish to challenge advanced students to find the measures of the interior and exterior angles of regular polygons with large numbers of sides. Have them consider what happens as the number of sides becomes increasingly greater. Have them make a conjecture about what would happen to the measures of the interior and exterior angles of regular polygons as the number of sides increases without bound.

In conjunction with Lesson 13.5, you may wish to challenge advanced learners to make generalizations about reflections in the lines $y = x$ and $y = -x$.

After completing Exercise 24 on page 746, you may wish to have a group of advanced students create their own problems similar to this exercise. They should be able to solve their own problems first, and then they can challenge others with their problems.

In Lesson 13.7, you may wish to have advanced students explore using centers of dilation other than the origin.

USE CROSS-CURRICULAR ACTIVITIES

You may wish to work with an art teacher, home economics teacher, or other teacher to develop a project that explores tessellations. Quilting, tiling, and other creative projects regularly make great use of tessellated figures. Many students will enjoy investigating the complex tessellations created by M.C. Escher. Alternately, you may wish to work with a technology teacher to engage students with software that will help them create their own tessellations. Projects can also include studying tessellating patterns in nature, such as in the honeycomb of bees, and studying why some fundamental regions will tessellate and others will not.

CHAPTER 13

Differentiating Instruction: Resource Materials

Differentiating Enrichment and Activities

McDougal Littell *Pre-Algebra* offers teachers enrichment for all levels of students. Pictured on these pages are facsimiles of the Real-World Problem Solving pages, Chapter Review Games, and Chapter Projects from the *Chapter 13 Resource Book* and a number of activities from the *Special Activities Book*. Also available is the *Poster Package* containing large, full-color posters, one for each unit.

RESOURCE BOOK

The *Chapter Resource Books* contain Real-World Problem Solving activities for various lessons, Chapter Review Games for a motivating review of each chapter, and Chapter Projects with rubrics that apply the mathematics of the chapter.

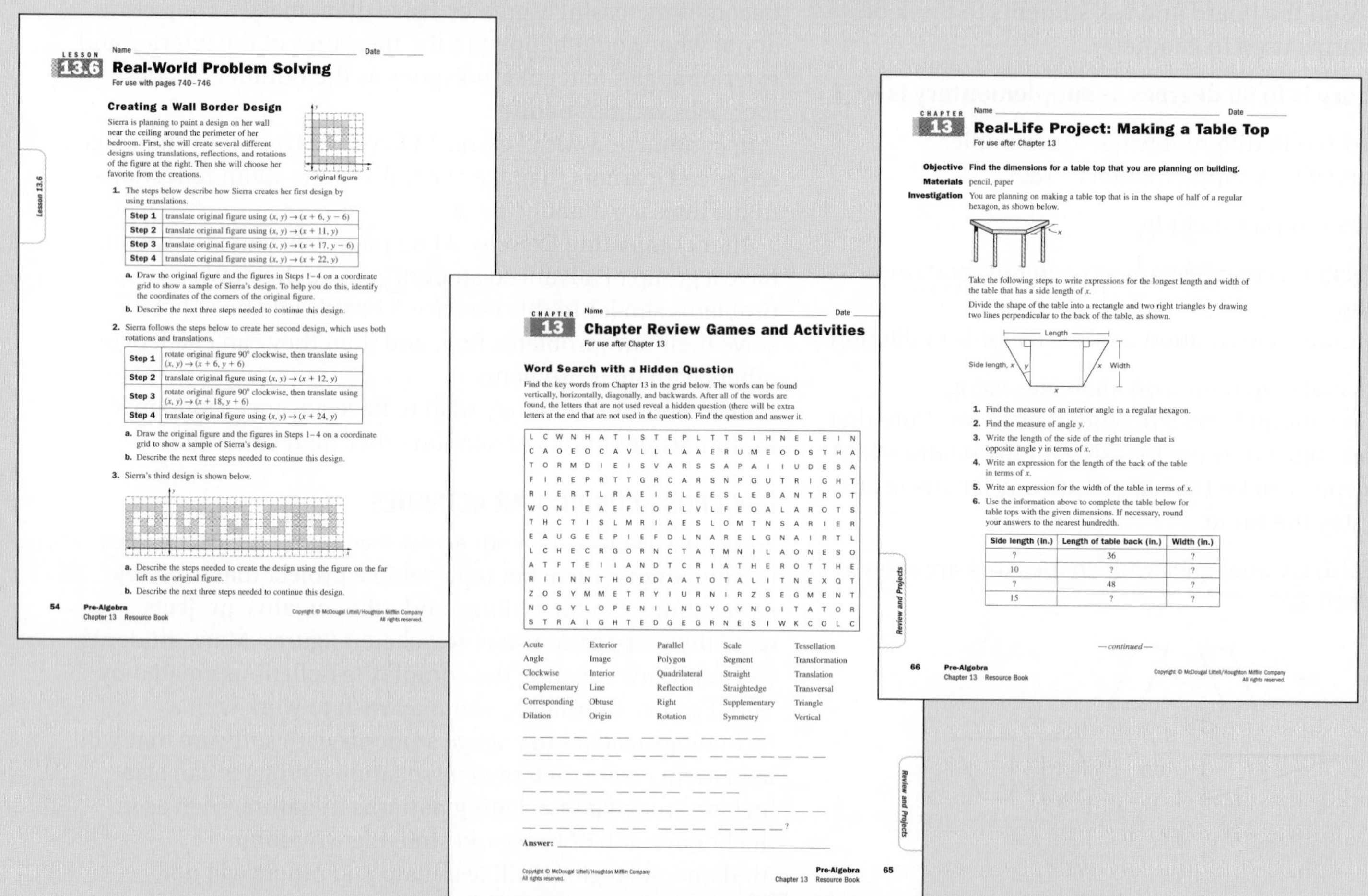

LESSON 13.6 Name ______ Date ______

Real-World Problem Solving

For use with pages 740–746

Creating a Wall Border Design

Sierra is planning to paint a design on her wall near the ceiling around the perimeter of her bedroom. First, she will create several different designs using translations, reflections, and rotations of the figure at the right. Then she will choose her favorite from the creations.

original figure

1. The steps below describe how Sierra creates her first design by using translations.

Step 1	translate original figure using $(x, y) \to (x + 6, y - 6)$
Step 2	translate original figure using $(x, y) \to (x + 11, y)$
Step 3	translate original figure using $(x, y) \to (x + 17, y - 6)$
Step 4	translate original figure using $(x, y) \to (x + 22, y)$

a. Draw the original figure and the figures in Steps 1–4 on a coordinate grid to show a sample of Sierra's design. To help you do this, identify the coordinates of the corners of the original figure.

b. Describe the next three steps needed to continue this design.

2. Sierra follows the steps below to create her second design, which uses both rotations and translations.

Step 1	rotate original figure 90° clockwise, then translate using $(x, y) \to (x + 6, y + 6)$
Step 2	translate original figure using $(x, y) \to (x + 12, y)$
Step 3	rotate original figure 90° clockwise, then translate using $(x, y) \to (x + 18, y + 6)$
Step 4	translate original figure using $(x, y) \to (x + 24, y)$

a. Draw the original figure and the figures in Steps 1–4 on a coordinate grid to show a sample of Sierra's design.

b. Describe the next three steps needed to continue this design.

3. Sierra's third design is shown below.

a. Describe the steps needed to create the design using the figure on the far left as the original figure.

b. Describe the next three steps needed to continue this design.

54 **Pre-Algebra** Chapter 13 Resource Book

Lesson 13.6

CHAPTER 13 Name ______ Date ______

Chapter Review Games and Activities

For use after Chapter 13

Word Search with a Hidden Question

Find the key words from Chapter 13 in the grid below. The words can be found vertically, horizontally, diagonally, and backwards. After all of the words are found, the letters that are not used reveal a hidden question (there will be extra letters at the end that are not used in the question). Find the question and answer it.

L C W N H A T I S T E P L T T S I H N E L E I N
C A O E O C A V L L L A A E R U M E O D S T H A
T O R M D I E I S V A R S S A P A I I U D E S A
F I R E P R T T G R C A R S N P G U T R I G H T
R I E R T L R A E I S L E E S L E B A N T R O T
W O N I E A E F L O P L V L F E O A L A R O T S
T H C T I S L M R I A E S L O M T N S A R I E R
E A U G E E P I E F D L N A R E L G N A I R T L
L C H E C R G O R N C T A T M N I L A O N E S O
A T F T E I I A N D T C R I A T H E R O T T H E
R I I N N T H O E D A A T O T A L I T N E X Q T
Z O S Y M M E T R Y I U R N I R Z S E G M E N T
N O G Y L O P E N I L N Q Y O Y N O I T A T O R
S T R A I G H T E D G E G R N E S I W K C O L C

Acute	Exterior	Parallel	Scale	Tessellation
Angle	Image	Polygon	Segment	Transformation
Clockwise	Interior	Quadrilateral	Straight	Translation
Complementary	Line	Reflection	Straightedge	Transversal
Corresponding	Obtuse	Right	Supplementary	Triangle
Dilation	Origin	Rotation	Symmetry	Vertical

_ _ _ _ _ _ _ _ _ _ _ _ _

_ _ _ _ _ _ _ _ _ _ _ _ _ _ _ _ _

_ _ _ _ _ _ _ _ _ _ _ _ _ _

_ _ _ _ _ _ _ _ _ _ _ _

_ _ _ _ _ _ _ _ _ _ _ _ _ _ _ _ _

_ _ _ _ _ _ _ _ _ _ _ _ _ _?

Answer: ______

Pre-Algebra Chapter 13 Resource Book 65

Review and Projects

CHAPTER 13 Name ______ Date ______

Real-Life Project: Making a Table Top

For use after Chapter 13

Objective **Find the dimensions for a table top that you are planning on building.**

Materials pencil, paper

Investigation You are planning on making a table top that is in the shape of half of a regular hexagon, as shown below.

Take the following steps to write expressions for the longest length and width of the table that has a side length of x.

Divide the shape of the table into a rectangle and two right triangles by drawing two lines perpendicular to the back of the table, as shown.

1. Find the measure of an interior angle in a regular hexagon.
2. Find the measure of angle y.
3. Write the length of the side of the right triangle that is opposite angle y in terms of x.
4. Write an expression for the length of the back of the table in terms of x.
5. Write an expression for the width of the table in terms of x.
6. Use the information above to complete the table below for table tops with the given dimensions. If necessary, round your answers to the nearest hundredth.

Side length (in.)	Length of table back (in.)	Width (in.)
?	36	?
10	?	?
?	48	?
15	?	?

—continued—

66 **Pre-Algebra** Chapter 13 Resource Book

Review and Projects

SPECIAL ACTIVITIES BOOK

The *Special Activities* Book contains numerous activities including activities for the start of school, activities for substitute teachers, activities for use before holiday breaks, and short change-of-pace activities.

Name ______________________ Date ________

Diagonally Speaking

For use at the beginning of the school year.

The diagonal of a convex polygon connects two nonconsecutive vertices.

1. Use the triangle, quadrilateral, pentagon and hexagon below. Draw in diagonals from ONE vertex.

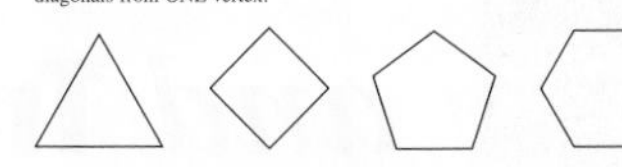

How many diagonals can you draw from ONE vertex?

________ ________ ________ ________

2. Now draw in all of the diagonals for each of the figures given above and record your results in the table below.

Figure	Number of sides	Number of diagonals from ONE vertex	Total number of diagonals
Triangle			
Quadrilateral			
Pentagon			
Hexagon			

3. Extend the table given above to find the number of diagonals in a polygon with n sides. ________________

4. Look back at the first question. When the diagonals from ONE vertex of a polygon with four or more sides are drawn, the polygon is divided into triangles. Fill in the table below, which states the number of triangles the polygon is divided into when the diagonals from ONE vertex are drawn.

Figure	Number of sides	Number of diagonals from ONE vertex	Total number of triangles
Quadrilateral			
Pentagon			
Hexagon			
Heptagon			
n-gon			

5. What is the sum of the measures of the interior angles of a triangle? ________
Use the chart above to predict the sum of the measures of the interior angles of an n-gon. ________________

CHAPTER 13 Name ______________________ Date ________

Transformations

For use after Lesson 13.7

1. On a coordinate grid, draw $\triangle ABC$ with vertices $A(2, 5)$, $B(2, 1)$, and $C(8, 3)$.
2. Find the area of $\triangle ABC$.
3. Find the perimeter of $\triangle ABC$.
4. Find the image of $\triangle ABC$ after the transformation $(x, y) \rightarrow (x, -y)$. Label the image $\triangle DEF$.
5. What type of transformation did you perform in Exercise 4? Be specific.
6. Find the area of $\triangle DEF$.
7. Find the perimeter of $\triangle DEF$.
8. Find the image of $\triangle DEF$ after the transformation $(x, y) \rightarrow (x - 9, y - 1)$. Label the image $\triangle GHI$.
9. What type of transformation did you perform in Exercise 8? Be specific.
10. Find the area of $\triangle GHI$.
11. Find the perimeter of $\triangle GHI$.
12. Find the image of $\triangle GHI$ after the transformation $(x, y) \rightarrow (y, -x)$. Label the image $\triangle JKL$.
13. What type of transformation did you perform in Exercise 12? Be specific.
14. Find the area of $\triangle JKL$.
15. Find the perimeter of $\triangle JKL$.
16. Find the image of $\triangle JKL$ after the transformation $(x, y) \rightarrow (3x, 3y)$. Label the image $\triangle MNO$.
17. What type of transformation did you perform in Exercise 16? Be specific.
18. Find the area of $\triangle MNO$.
19. Find the perimeter of $\triangle MNO$.
20. Explain the similarities and differences in your answers to Exercises 2, 6, 10, 14, and 18.
21. Explain the similarities and differences in your answers to Exercises 3, 7, 11, 15, and 19.

Name ______________________ Date ________

Let's have a Pizza Party!

Use before spring break. (Work may be done in small groups.)

The student council is planning a pizza party to welcome the incoming freshman class. They are on a budget and decide to research the local pizza parlors to find out which pizza will be the most economical to purchase. When they contacted the local pizza parlors, they asked them what the diameters of their pizzas are and what the costs are for cheese and for one topping pizzas. The results are given in the table below.

1. Use the table below to determine which pizzeria has the best prices.

Pizza Parlor	Diameter of small pizza	Cost of small cheese pizza	Cost of small one topping pizza	Diameter of large pizza	Cost of large cheese pizza	Cost of large one topping pizza
Brother's Pizza	9 in.	\$4.25	\$4.75	14 in.	\$6.75	\$7.50
Brickhouse Pizza	10 in.	\$4.50	\$5.50	15 in.	\$7.25	\$7.95
House of Pizza	10 in.	\$4.75	\$5.35	16 in.	\$7.85	\$8.45

Fill in the table below showing the area of each pizza and cost per square inch. (Round cost to the nearest thousandth of a dollar.)

Pizza Parlor	Area of small pizza	Cost per square inch cheese	Cost per square inch one topping	Area of large pizza	Cost per square inch cheese	Cost per square inch one topping
Brother's Pizza						
Brickhouse Pizza						
House of Pizza						

2. The student council is expecting to purchase pizza for 240 incoming freshmen. They have a budget of \$500. They know that, on average, a student will eat two large slices or three small slices of pizza. They decide to buy half of the pizzas needed with just cheese and half with one topping from the pizzeria. Small pizzas are cut into 6 pieces and large pizzas are cut into 8 pieces. Determine the minimum cost of the pizza for the pizza party. Does the student council have enough money for the pizza party?

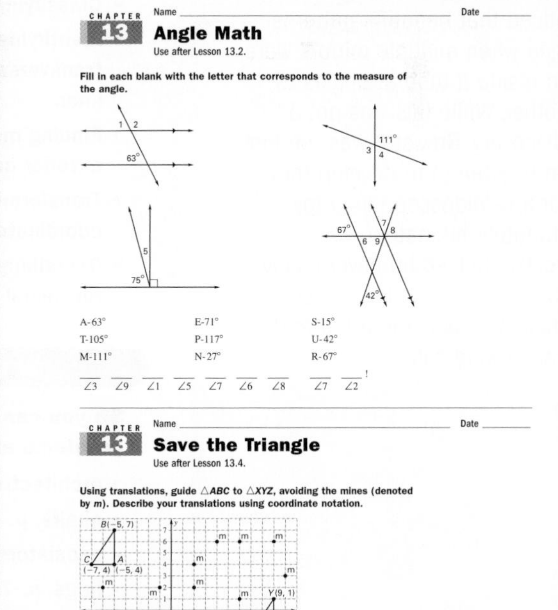

CHAPTER 13 Name ______________________ Date ________

Angle Math

Use after Lesson 13.2.

Fill in each blank with the letter that corresponds to the measure of the angle.

A-63° E-71° S-15°
T-105° P-117° U-42°
M-111° N-27° R-67°

___ ___ ___ ___ ___ ___ ___   ___ ___ !
∠3 ∠9 ∠1 ∠5 ∠7 ∠6 ∠8   ∠7 ∠2

CHAPTER 13 Name ______________________ Date ________

Save the Triangle

Use after Lesson 13.4.

Using translations, guide $\triangle ABC$ to $\triangle XYZ$, avoiding the mines (denoted by m). Describe your translations using coordinate notation.

OVERVIEW

MAIN IDEAS

In this chapter, students identify and find measures of complementary, supplementary, and vertical angles. Students identify angles formed when a transversal intersects two lines. Students find measures of interior and exterior angles of convex polygons. Finally, students translate, rotate, dilate, and reflect figures in a coordinate plane.

APPLICATION NOTE

A kaleidoscope is a tube containing 2 or more flat mirrors that run the length of the tube. An ever-changing arrangement of colored pieces of plastic or glass at one end of the tube is reflected by the mirrors into a myriad of designs. The number of reflections is determined by the number of mirrors used, as well as the angle between the mirrors.

Sir David Brewster was a Scottish scientist who lived from 1781 to 1868. While experimenting with light, he noticed that beautiful patterns emerged when multiple mirrors were placed inside a tube at angles to each other. While this was not a new discovery, Brewster was the first person to attempt to develop the idea of a kaleidoscope as a toy. Unfortunately, his patent was incorrectly filed, so he never received any money for his idea when kaleidoscopes became a fad and thousands were sold.

CHAPTER 13

Angle Relationships *and* Transformations

What kind of patterns do kaleidoscopes produce?

BEFORE

In previous chapters you've . . .

- **Used scale drawings**
- **Graphed lines in a coordinate plane**
- **Classified triangles and polygons**

Now

In Chapter 13 you'll study . . .

- **Classifying special angle pairs**
- **Identifying angles formed by a transversal intersecting two lines**
- **Finding measures of interior and exterior angles of polygons**
- **Transforming figures in a coordinate plane**
- **Describing line symmetry and rotational symmetry**

WHY?

So you can solve real-world problems about . . .

- **architecture, p. 712**
- **chairs, p. 719**
- **escalators, p. 733**
- **flags, p. 735**
- **family crests, p. 743**
- **nesting dolls, p. 750**

CHAPTER 13

INTERNET Preview

CLASSZONE.COM

- eEdition Plus Online
- eWorkbook Plus Online
- eTutorial Plus Online
- State Test Practice
- More Examples

MATH *In the* **Real World**

Kaleidoscopes Each of the images on this page was produced by a kaleidoscope, an instrument that uses mirrors to create a pattern with rotational symmetry. In this chapter, you will identify figures that have rotational symmetry.

What do you think? Lay the edge of a small mirror through the center of the image shown in the circular inset photograph. Hold the mirror perpendicular to the image. What do you notice? What happens if you turn the mirror so that it lies along a different diameter of the circle? **See margin.**

CHAPTER RESOURCES

These resources are provided to help you prepare for the chapter and to customize review materials:

Chapter 13 Resource Book

- Tips for New Teachers, pp. 1–2
- Lesson Plan, pp. 5, 13, 22, 30, 39, 47, 56
- Lesson Plan for Block Scheduling, pp. 6, 14, 23, 31, 40, 48, 57

Technology

- EasyPlanner CD-ROM
- Test and Practice Generator
- Electronic Lesson Presentations CD-ROM
- eTutorial CD-ROM

Internet

- Classzone
- eEdition Plus Online
- eWorkbook Plus Online
- eTutorial Plus Online
- EasyPlanner Plus Online

ENGLISH LEARNER SUPPORT

- Spanish Study Guide
- Multi-Language Visual Glossary
- Chapter Audio Summaries CDs
- Teacher's Edition, pp. 706E–706F

Sample answer: **Yes; if the mirror's edge passes through the center and through two vertices on the outside of the star-shaped polygon, the actual image and its reflection will have the same shape.**

PREPARE

DIAGNOSIS/REMEDIATION

Prerequisite Skills Quiz
The Prerequisite Skills Quiz can help you diagnose whether students have the following skills needed in Chapter 13:

- Classify angles (Exs. 1–4)
- Use map scales to find distances (Exs. 5–8)
- Write and solve equations based on the interior angle measures of polygons (Exs. 9–10)

 ***Chapter 13 Resource Book***

- Study Guide (Lessons 13.1–13.7)

 ***Tutor Place***

NOTETAKING STRATEGIES

Urge students to look back over their notes after each lesson to find ideas that are related and can be linked together. Further suggestions for keeping a notebook can be found on pages 717 and 749.

For more support on notetaking, see:

- Notetaking Guide Workbook
- Notetaking Transparencies

CHAPTER 13

Chapter Prerequisite Skills

Review Vocabulary
quadrilateral, p. 286
scale, p. 300
triangle, p. 785
acute angle, p. 793
right angle, p. 793
obtuse angle, p. 793
straight angle, p. 793

PREREQUISITE SKILLS QUIZ

Preparing for Success **To prepare for success in this chapter, test your knowledge of these concepts and skills. You may want to look at the pages referred to in blue for additional review.**

Vocabulary **Classify the angle with the given measure as *acute*, *right*, *obtuse*, or *straight*.** *(p. 793)*

1. $74°$ acute **2.** $180°$ straight **3.** $90°$ right **4.** $31°$ acute

A map has a scale of 1 inch : 24 miles. Use the map distance to find the actual distance. *(p. 300)*

5. 3 inches 72 mi **6.** 8 inches 192 mi **7.** 2.5 inches 60 mi **8.** $\frac{1}{4}$ inch 6 mi

Find the value of *x* or *y*. *(pp. 511, 516)*

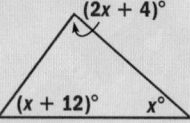

9. 41
(triangle with angles $(2x + 4)°$, $(x + 12)°$, $x°$)

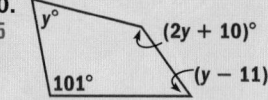

10. 65
(quadrilateral with angles $y°$, $(2y + 10)°$, $(y - 11)°$, $101°$)

Note *Worthy*

You will find a notetaking strategy at the beginning of each chapter. Look for additional notetaking and study strategies throughout the chapter.

NOTETAKING STRATEGIES

SUMMARIZING MATERIAL In your notes, you should write a summary of key ideas that are related to one another. Include examples in your summary.

Ways to Represent a Function

Equation: $y = 2x + 1$

Table:

x	−2	−1	0	1	2
y	−3	−1	1	3	5

Graph:

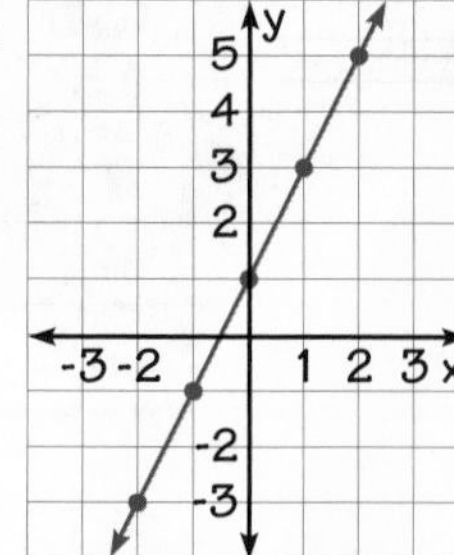

In Lesson 13.7, you can summarize key ideas about transformations in a coordinate plane.

LESSON **13.1**

Angle Relationships

BEFORE You classified angles and triangles.

Now You'll classify special pairs of angles.

WHY? So you can find the height of a sculpture, as in Ex. 32.

Vocabulary

Two angles are **complementary angles** if the sum of their measures is 90°. Two angles are **supplementary angles** if the sum of their measures is 180°.

Complementary angles

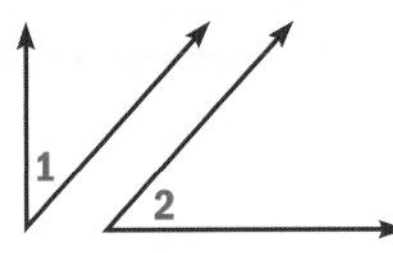

$m\angle 1 = 42°$, $m\angle 2 = 48°$
$m\angle 1 + m\angle 2 = 90°$

Supplementary angles

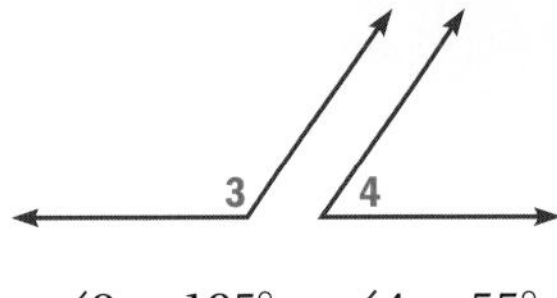

$m\angle 3 = 125°$, $m\angle 4 = 55°$
$m\angle 3 + m\angle 4 = 180°$

Adjacent angles that form a right angle are complementary. Adjacent angles that form a straight angle are supplementary. In the diagram at the right, $\angle BEC$ and $\angle CED$ are complementary angles, and $\angle AEC$ and $\angle CED$ are supplementary angles.

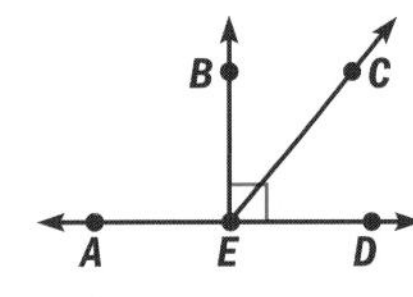

Review Help

For help with classifying angles, see p. 793.

Example 1 *Identifying Complementary, Supplementary Angles*

In quadrilateral $ABCD$, identify all pairs of complementary angles and supplementary angles.

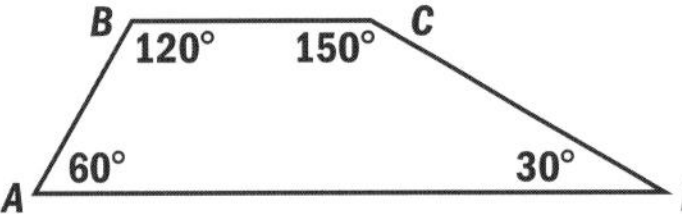

Solution

a. Because $m\angle A + m\angle D = 60° + 30° = 90°$, $\angle A$ and $\angle D$ are complementary angles.

b. Because $m\angle A + m\angle B = 60° + 120° = 180°$, $\angle A$ and $\angle B$ are supplementary angles.

Because $m\angle C + m\angle D = 150° + 30° = 180°$, $\angle C$ and $\angle D$ are supplementary angles.

 ***Checkpoint***

Tell whether the angles are *complementary, supplementary,* or *neither.*

1. $m\angle 1 = 63°$, $m\angle 2 = 27°$

2. $m\angle 3 = 146°$, $m\angle 4 = 44°$

3. $m\angle 5 = 95°$, $m\angle 6 = 85°$

1. complementary
2. neither
3. supplementary

NCTM CURRICULUM STANDARDS
Standard 2: Represent situations using algebraic symbols
Standard 3: Analyze properties of 2-D shapes
Standard 6: Solve problems in math and other contexts

1 PLAN

Skill Check

1. 180 − 42 = ?		**138**
2. 56 + 34 = ?		**90**
3. 90 − 72 = ?		**18**
4. 62 + 118 = ?		**180**

LESSON OBJECTIVE

Classify special pairs of angles.

PACING

Suggested Number of Days
Basic Course: 1 day
Average Course: 1 day
Advanced Course: 1 day
Block: 0.5 block with 13.2

TEACHING RESOURCES

For a complete list of Teaching Resources, see page 706B.

TRANSPARENCY

Warm-Up Exercises for this lesson are available on a transparency.

2 TEACH

MOTIVATING THE LESSON

Have students name objects in the classroom that appear to contain pairs of complementary or supplementary angles.

TIPS *for* NEW TEACHERS

To help students distinguish between the terms *complementary angles* and *supplementary angles*, point out that alphabetically *complementary* comes before *supplementary*, while numerically 90° comes before 180°. See Tips for New Teachers in the *Chapter 13 Resource Book*.

Extra Examples

Example 1 Tell whether the angles are *complementary*, *supplementary*, or *neither*.

a. $m\angle 1 = 155°, m\angle 2 = 35°$ **neither**

b. $m\angle 3 = 54°, m\angle 4 = 36°$ **complementary**

Example 2 In the figure, $\angle 3$ and $\angle 4$ are supplementary. If $m\angle 3 = 127°$, find $m\angle 4$.

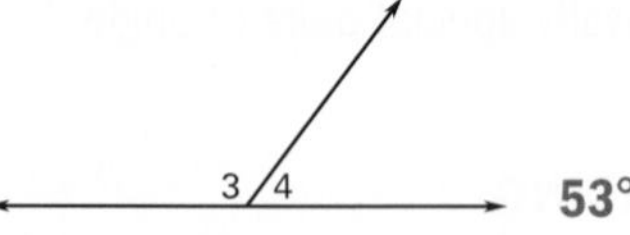

53°

Example 3 In the figure below, suppose $m\angle 5 = 25°$. Find $m\angle 6$, $m\angle 7$, and $m\angle 8$.

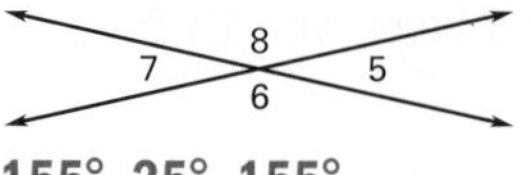

155°, 25°, 155°

Cross-Curriculum

Art In art class, students will learn about using perspective correctly when drawing. Their understanding of perspective will depend on their knowledge of angle relationships.

Common Error

Watch for students who do their work mentally and make mistakes such as getting a sum of 90 when adding 55 and 45.

Concept Check

If two angles are both vertical and complementary, what are their angle measures? **45°, 45°**

Daily Puzzler

Lines *c* and *d* intersect. Each angle that is formed is supplementary to the other three angles. What is the relationship between the lines? **They are perpendicular.**

Example 2 *Finding an Angle Measure*

Stage Monitors Stage monitors are speakers that performers use so that they can clearly hear the sounds they make on a stage. For the stage monitor shown, $\angle 1$ and $\angle 2$ are complementary angles, and $m\angle 1 = 35°$. Find $m\angle 2$.

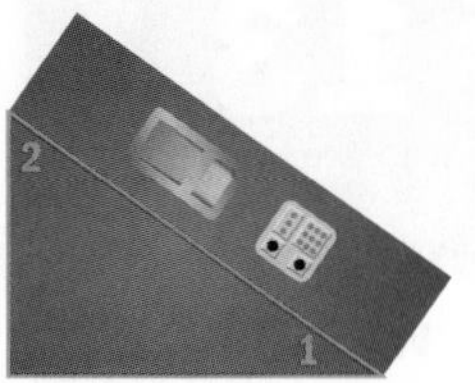

Solution

$m\angle 1 + m\angle 2 = 90°$ **Definition of complementary angles**

$35° + m\angle 2 = 90°$ **Substitute 35° for $m\angle 1$.**

$m\angle 2 = 55°$ **Subtract 35° from each side.**

Vertical Angles When two lines intersect at one point, the angles that are opposite each other are **vertical angles**. Vertical angles have the same measure, as you will see in Exercise 31.

Vertical angles

$\angle 1$ and $\angle 3$

$\angle 2$ and $\angle 4$

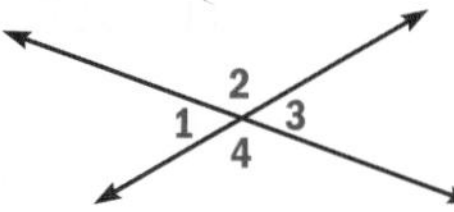

Example 3 *Using Supplementary and Vertical Angles*

Television Trays For the television tray shown, $m\angle 1 = 110°$. Find $m\angle 2$, $m\angle 3$, and $m\angle 4$.

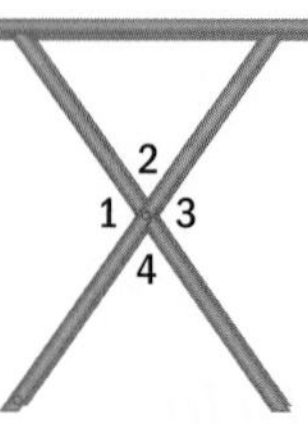

Solution

a. $m\angle 1 + m\angle 2 = 180°$ **$\angle 1$ and $\angle 2$ are supplementary.**

$110° + m\angle 2 = 180°$ **Substitute 110° for $m\angle 1$.**

$m\angle 2 = 70°$ **Subtract 110° from each side.**

b. $m\angle 3 = m\angle 1$ **Vertical angles have same measure.**

$m\angle 3 = 110°$ **Substitute 110° for $m\angle 1$.**

c. $m\angle 4 = m\angle 2$ **Vertical angles have same measure.**

$m\angle 4 = 70°$ **Substitute 70° for $m\angle 2$.**

Checkpoint

4. $\angle 1$ and $\angle 2$ are supplementary angles, and $m\angle 1 = 118°$. Find $m\angle 2$. **62°**
5. $\angle 3$ and $\angle 4$ are complementary angles, and $m\angle 3 = 24°$. Find $m\angle 4$. **66°**
6. In Example 3, suppose that $m\angle 1 = 135°$. Find $m\angle 2$, $m\angle 3$, and $m\angle 4$.

6. $m\angle 2 = 45°$, $m\angle 3 = 135°$, $m\angle 4 = 45°$

13.1 Exercises

More Practice, p. 815

Guided Practice

Vocabulary Check

1. Copy and complete: The sum of the measures of two _?_ angles is 90°. **complementary**
2. What can you say about the measures of two vertical angles? **They are the same.**

Skill Check **Tell whether the angles are *complementary*, *supplementary*, or *neither*.**

3. $m\angle 1 = 10°$, $m\angle 2 = 70°$ **neither**
4. $m\angle 3 = 108°$, $m\angle 4 = 72°$ **supplementary**
5. $m\angle 5 = 58°$, $m\angle 6 = 32°$ **complementary**

In Exercises 6 and 7, use the given information to find $m\angle 2$.

6. $\angle 1$ and $\angle 2$ are complementary angles, and $m\angle 1 = 45°$. **45°**
7. $\angle 1$ and $\angle 2$ are supplementary angles, and $m\angle 1 = 160°$. **20°**

Guided Problem Solving

8. In the diagram shown, $m\angle 1 = 35°$ and $m\angle 3 = 110°$. What is $m\angle 5$?

(1) Tell how $\angle 1$ and $\angle 2$ are related. Then find $m\angle 2$. **They are vertical angles; 35°.**

(2) Tell how $\angle 3$ and $\angle 4$ are related. Then find $m\angle 4$. **They are supplementary; 70°.**

(3) Use what you know about the sum of the measures of the angles of a triangle to find $m\angle 5$. **75°**

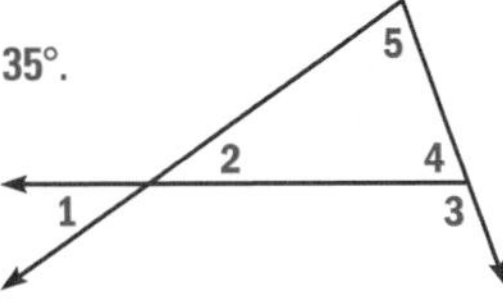

Practice and Problem Solving

Homework Help

Example	Exercises
1	9-16
2	17, 22-24
3	18-21, 24-25

Online Resources
CLASSZONE.COM
- More Examples
- eTutorial Plus

Use the diagram shown. Identify all pairs of the specified angles.

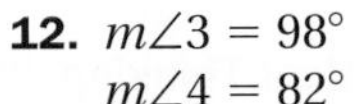

A 9. Complementary angles **$\angle A$ and $\angle D$**

10. Supplementary angles **$\angle A$ and $\angle C$, $\angle B$ and $\angle D$**

Tell whether the angles are *complementary*, *supplementary*, or *neither*.

11. $m\angle 1 = 22°$, $m\angle 2 = 58°$ **neither**
12. $m\angle 3 = 98°$, $m\angle 4 = 82°$ **supplementary**
13. $m\angle 5 = 37°$, $m\angle 6 = 53°$ **complementary**
14. $m\angle 1 = 71°$, $m\angle 2 = 19°$ **complementary**
15. $m\angle 3 = 64°$, $m\angle 4 = 116°$ **supplementary**
16. $m\angle 5 = 98°$, $m\angle 6 = 72°$ **neither**

Find $m\angle 1$.

17. **62°**

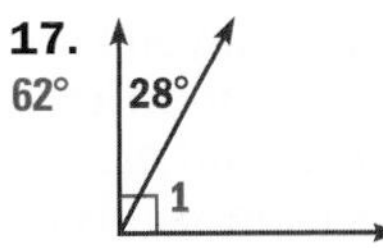

18. **56°**

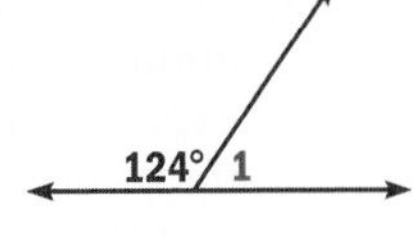

19. **65°**

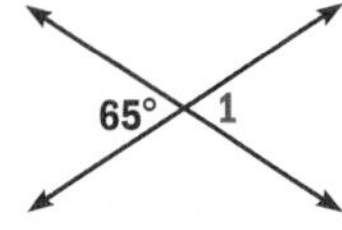

3 APPLY

ASSIGNMENT GUIDE

Basic Course
Day 1: pp. 711-713 Exs. 9-23, 26-30, 36-46

Average Course
Day 1: pp. 711-713 Exs. 9-13, 17-24, 26-34, 36-46

Advanced Course
Day 1: pp. 711-713 Exs. 9, 10, 14-26, 30-36*, 40-46

Block
pp. 711-713 Exs. 9-13, 17-24, 26-34, 36-46 (with 13.2)

Extra Practice

- Student Edition, p. 815
- Chapter 13 Resource Book, pp. 7-9
- Test and Practice Generator

Transparency

Even-numbered answers are available on transparencies.

Homework Check

When you review students' homework for this lesson, go over the following exercises to check understanding of key concepts.
Basic: 9, 11, 17, 18, 22
Average: 10, 13, 17, 18, 24
Advanced: 10, 14, 22, 24, 25

Teaching Tip

Before assigning Exercises 11–16, ask students when the answer would be *neither* for these exercises.

Common Error

In Exercise 31, watch for students who think angles are only vertical if one is located above the other. These students will fail to indicate that $\angle 1$ and $\angle 3$ have the same measure.

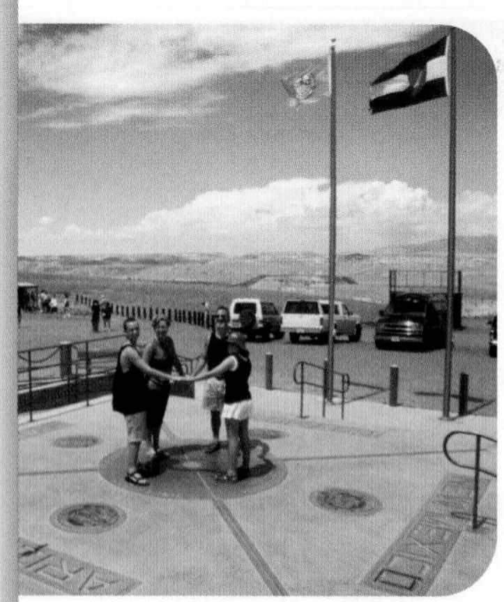

20. Geography The intersection of the borders of Utah, Colorado, New Mexico, and Arizona is called Four Corners. On the map, $m\angle 1 = 90°$. Find $m\angle 2$, $m\angle 3$, and $m\angle 4$. **$m\angle 2 = m\angle 3 = m\angle 4 = 90°$**

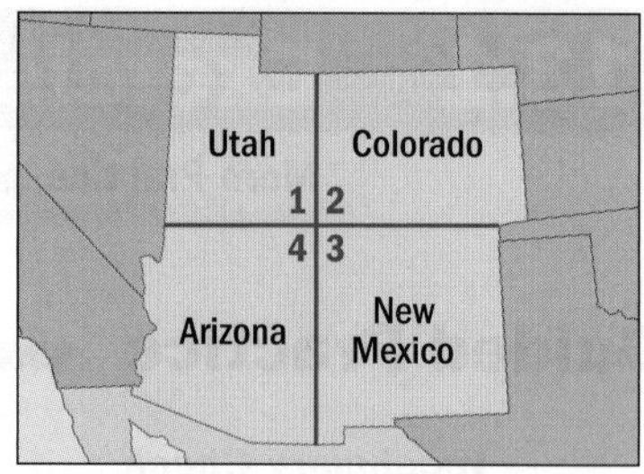

In the Real World

Geography The Four Corners Monument is the only place in the United States where you can stand in four states at one time. How many pairs of supplementary angles are formed by the borders of the four states? **6 pairs**

Use the given information to find $m\angle 2$.

21. $\angle 1$ and $\angle 2$ are vertical angles, and $m\angle 1 = 140°$. **140°**

22. $\angle 1$ and $\angle 2$ are supplementary angles, and $m\angle 1 = 137°$. **43°**

23. $\angle 1$ and $\angle 2$ are complementary angles, and $m\angle 1 = 81°$. **9°**

24. Architecture As shown in the diagram, the two structures of the *Puerta de Europa* (Door of Europe) in Madrid, Spain, lean toward each other at an angle of 15° from the vertical.

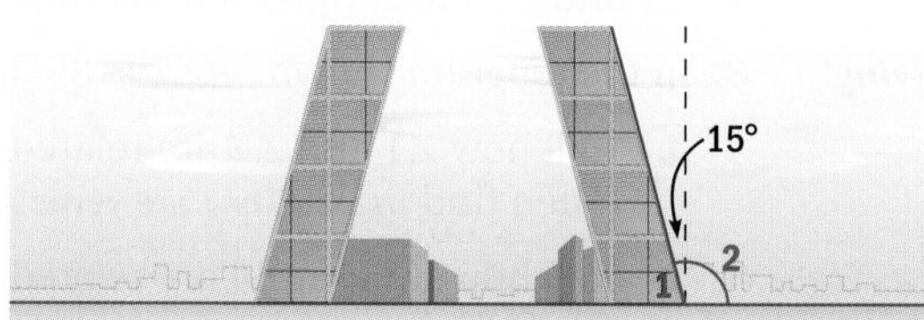

a. In the diagram, $\angle 1$ and the angle that measures 15° are complementary angles. Find $m\angle 1$. **75°**

b. Tell whether $\angle 1$ and $\angle 2$ are *complementary* or *supplementary* angles. Then use your answer to part (a) to find $m\angle 2$. **supplementary; 105°**

25. *Writing* When two lines intersect at one point, how many pairs of vertical angles are formed? Explain your answer.

Algebra Find the value of x in the figure. Then find the unknown angle measures.

B **26.**

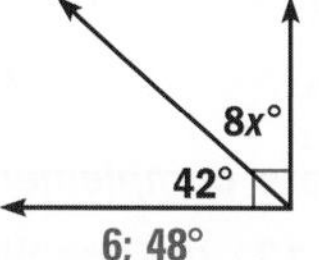

6; 48°

27.

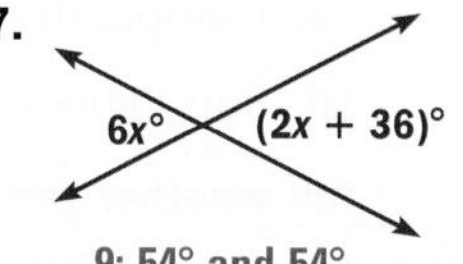

9; 54° and 54°

28.

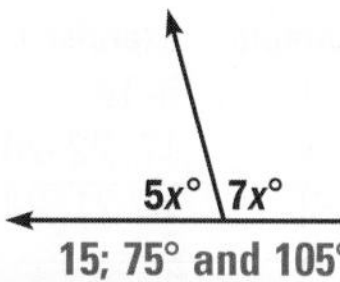

15; 75° and 105°

Critical Thinking In Exercises 29 and 30, tell whether a triangle exists for the given description. If so, classify the triangle by its angles. If not, explain why not.

29. Two of the angles are complementary. **yes; right**

30. Two of the angles are supplementary.

31. In the diagram, use only what you know about supplementary angles to write expressions for $m\angle 1$, $m\angle 2$, and $m\angle 3$ in terms of x. Then use the expressions to show that the vertical angles have equal measures.

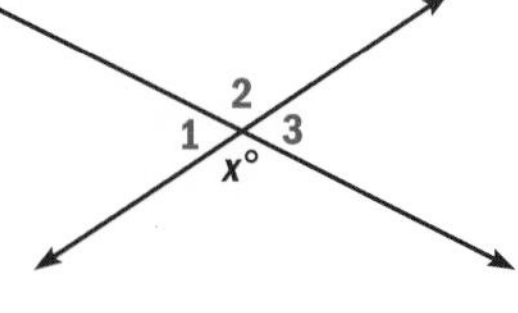

25. 2 pairs. ***Sample answer:*** **Vertical angles are opposite each other, and meet only at one point. There are only two pairs of angles in this situation for which this is true. Any other pair of angles share a side.**

30. No. ***Sample answer:*** **If two of the angles are supplementary, the sum of their measures is 180°. Since the sum of the measures of the angles of a triangle is 180°, this means that the third angle would have a measure of 0°, which is not possible.**

31. $m\angle 1 = 180° - x°$, $m\angle 2 = x°$, $m\angle 3 = 180° - x°$; $m\angle 1 = m\angle 3 = 180° - x°$, m(angle labeled $x°$) $= m\angle 2 = x°$

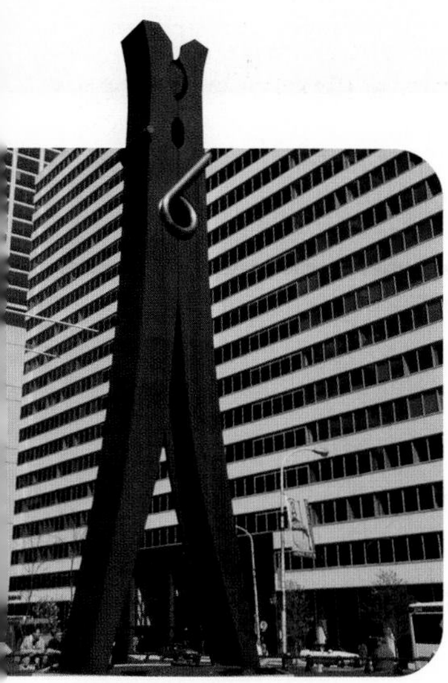

***Clothespin* by Claes Oldenburg**

32. Sculptures The diagram shows the sculpture *Clothespin* casting a shadow. In the diagram, $\angle 2$ is the angle of the sun above the horizon.

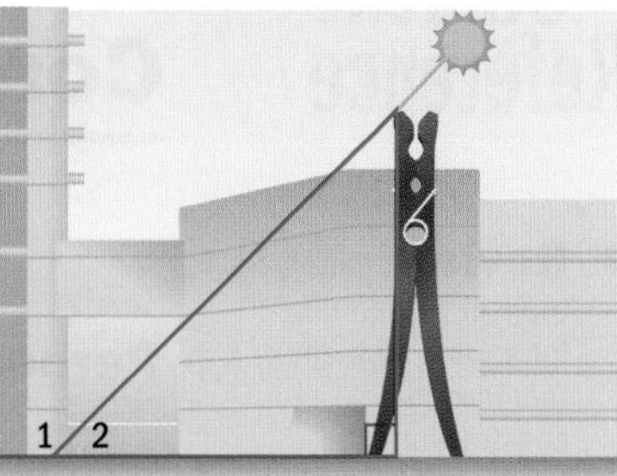

a. At a certain time of the day, $m\angle 1 = 148°$, and the shadow has a length of 72 feet. Use a calculator to find the height of the sculpture. Round to the nearest tenth. **45.0 ft**

b. At a certain time of the day, $m\angle 1 = 135°$. How is the length of the shadow related to the height of the sculpture? Explain your reasoning.

33. Critical Thinking Let $\angle 1$ and $\angle 2$ be vertical angles. What are their measures if they are complementary angles? supplementary angles? **45°; 90°**

34. Geometry Use the diagram shown.

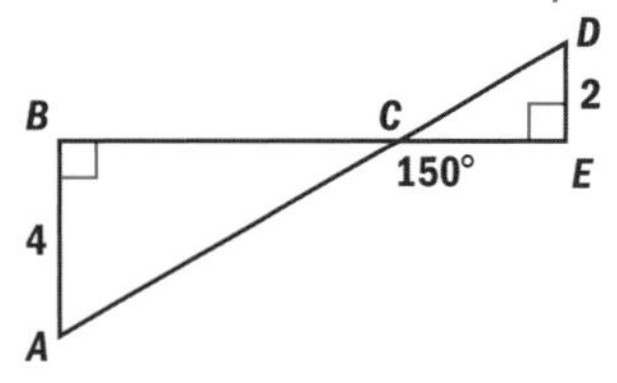

a. For $\triangle ABC$ and $\triangle DEC$, find the measure of each angle and the length of each side. **34a–b. See margin.**

b. Compare How are $\triangle ABC$ and $\triangle DEC$ related? Explain your reasoning.

C **35. Challenge** Let $\angle 1$ and $\angle 2$ be complementary angles, and let $\angle 2$ and $\angle 3$ be supplementary angles. If $m\angle 1 = x°$ and $m\angle 2 = 2x°$, find x. Then find $m\angle 1$, $m\angle 2$, and $m\angle 3$. **30; $m\angle 1 = 30°$, $m\angle 2 = 60°$, $m\angle 3 = 120°$**

Mixed Review

Use a compass and a straightedge to draw a segment whose length is the sum of the lengths of the given segments. *(p. 794)* **36–38. Check students' work.**

36. ______ ______ **37.** ______ ______ **38.** ______ ______

Solve the equation. Check your solution. *(Lesson 3.1)*

39. $5x - 12 = 38$ **10** **40.** $10 - 3x = 37$ **−9** **41.** $4x + 7 = -113$ **−30**

Tell whether the sequence is *arithmetic* or *geometric*. *(Lesson 12.8)*

42. 1, 5, 25, 125, . . . **geometric** **43.** 3, 11, 19, 27, . . . **arithmetic** **44.** 80, 40, 20, 10, . . . **geometric**

Standardized Test Practice

45. Multiple Choice If $\angle 1$ and $\angle 2$ are complementary angles, what could their measures be? **B**

A. $m\angle 1 = 36°$, $m\angle 2 = 24°$ **B.** $m\angle 1 = 52°$, $m\angle 2 = 38°$ **C.** $m\angle 1 = 61°$, $m\angle 2 = 61°$ **D.** $m\angle 1 = 89°$, $m\angle 2 = 91°$

46. Multiple Choice In the diagram shown, $m\angle 3 = 72°$. What is $m\angle 4$? **H**

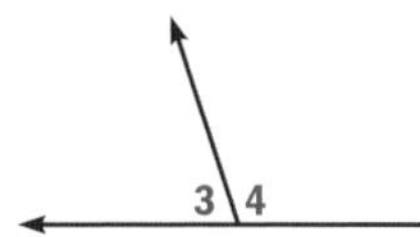

F. 18° **G.** 36° **H.** 108° **I.** 144°

32b. They are the same. ***Sample answer:*** **If h represents the height of the sculpture and s represents the length of the shadow, then because $m\angle 2 = 180° - 135° = 45°$, $\tan 45° = \frac{h}{s}$. $\tan 45° = 1$, $1 = \frac{h}{s}$, so $s = h$.**

34a. $\triangle ABC$: $m\angle A = 60°$, $m\angle B = 90°$, $m\angle BCA = 30°$, $AB = 4$, $BC = 4\sqrt{3}$, $AC = 8$; $\triangle DEC$: $m\angle D = 60°$, $m\angle E = 90°$, $m\angle DCE = 30°$, $DE = 2$, $EC = 2\sqrt{3}$, $DC = 4$

34b. They are similar. ***Sample answer:*** **Corresponding angles are congruent, and corresponding sides have the same ratio, 2 : 1.**

4 ASSESS

Assessment Resources

For more assessment resources, see:
- Assessment Book
- Test and Practice Generator

Mini-Quiz

Use the given information to find $m\angle 2$.

1. $\angle 1$ and $\angle 2$ are vertical angles, and $m\angle 1 = 35°$. **35°**
2. $\angle 1$ and $\angle 2$ are supplementary angles, and $m\angle 1 = 102°$. **78°**
3. $\angle 1$ and $\angle 2$ are complementary angles, and $m\angle 1 = 29°$. **61°**
4. **Challenge** Let $\angle 1$ and $\angle 2$ be supplementary angles, and let $\angle 1$ and $\angle 3$ be complementary angles. If $m\angle 1 = x°$ and $m\angle 2 = 3x°$, find x. Then find $m\angle 1$, $m\angle 2$, and $m\angle 3$. **45; $m\angle 1 = 45°$, $m\angle 2 = 135°$, $m\angle 3 = 45°$**

5 FOLLOW-UP

Diagnosis/Remediation

- Study Guide in Chapter 13 Resource Book, pp. 10–11
- Tutor Place, Geometry and Measurement Card 4
- eTutorial Plus Online
- Extra Practice, p. 815
- Lesson Practice in Chapter 13 Resource Book, pp. 7–9

English Learner Support

- Spanish Study Guide
- Multi-Language Visual Glossary
- Chapter Audio Summaries CDs

Challenge

- Challenge Practice in Chapter 13 Resource Book, p. 12
- Teacher's Edition, p. 706F

1 PLAN

Skill Check

Identify the given part of the figure as a ray, segment, or line.

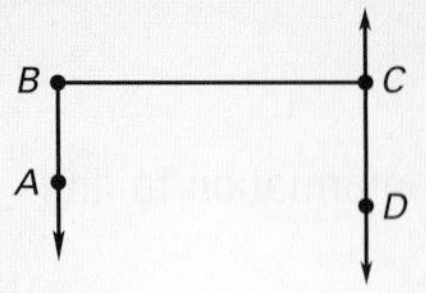

1. $\overrightarrow{BA}$ **ray**
2. $\overline{BC}$ **segment**
3. $\overleftrightarrow{CD}$ **line**

LESSON OBJECTIVE

Prepare for solving problems that involve constructions.

2 TEACH

 **COMMON ERROR**

Students should make sure the pivot of their compass is tight, so the compass setting does not change as they are using it.

Extra Examples

Example 1 Use a compass and a straightedge to construct a perpendicular bisector of a vertical segment with endpoints *P* and *Q*.

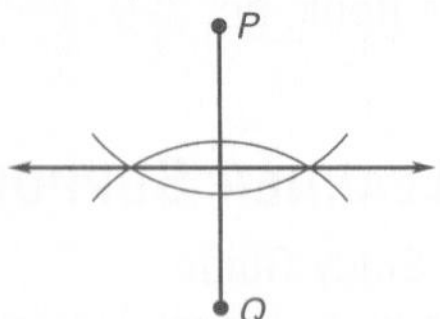

Example 2 Use a compass and a straightedge to copy an obtuse angle.

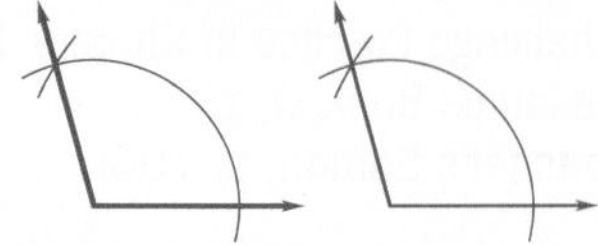

Student Reference

Constructions

▶ **Review** this topic in preparation for solving problems that involve constructions in Lesson 13.2. For a review of using a compass and a straightedge, see p. 794.

Perpendicular Bisectors

A **perpendicular bisector** of $\overline{AB}$ is a line, ray, or segment that is perpendicular to $\overline{AB}$ at its midpoint.

Example Use a compass and a straightedge to construct a perpendicular bisector of a segment.

1. Draw $\overline{KL}$. Using a compass setting greater than half the length of $\overline{KL}$, draw an arc with center *K*. Using the same compass setting, draw an arc with center *L*.

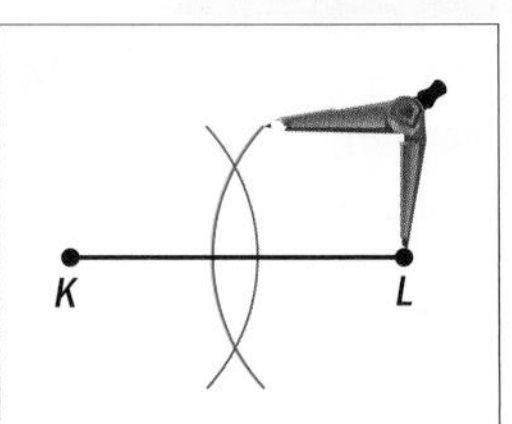

2. Label *M* and *N* as shown. Then draw $\overleftrightarrow{MN}$, the perpendicular bisector of $\overline{KL}$.

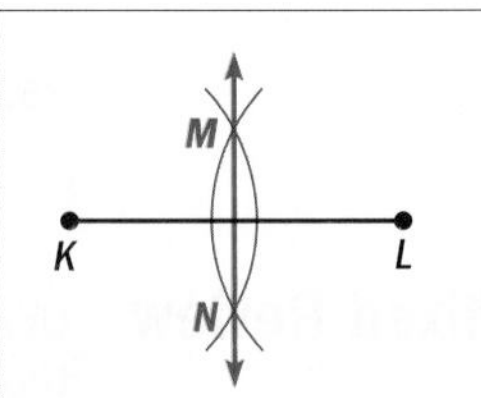

Copying an Angle

Example Use a compass and a straightedge to copy an angle.

1. Draw $\angle E$ and a ray with endpoint *H*. Then draw an arc with center *E*. Label *F* and *G* as shown. Using the same compass setting, draw an arc with center *H*. Label *J* as shown.

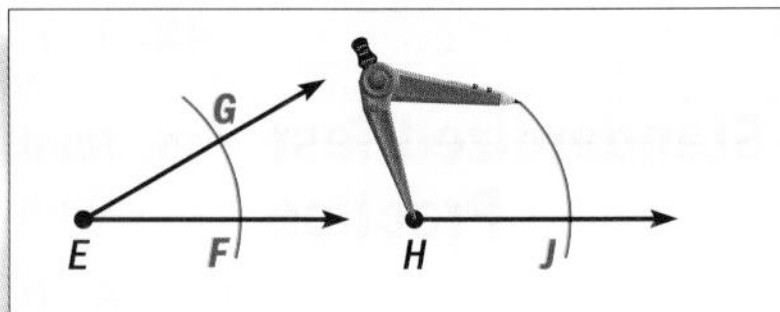

2. Draw an arc with center *F* that intersects *G*. Using the same compass setting, draw an arc with center *J*. Label *K* as shown. Then draw $\overrightarrow{HK}$.

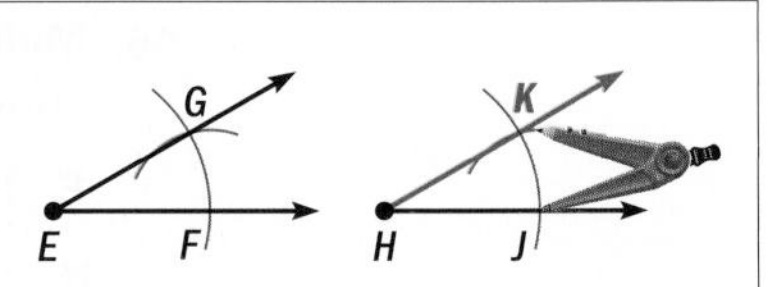

NCTM CURRICULUM STANDARDS

Standard 3: Analyze properties of 2-D shapes; Use symmetry to analyze math situations

Angle Bisectors

An **angle bisector** is a ray that divides an angle into two adjacent, congruent angles.

Example Use a compass and a straightedge to construct the bisector of an angle.

1. Draw $\angle P$. Then draw an arc with center P. Label Q and R as shown.

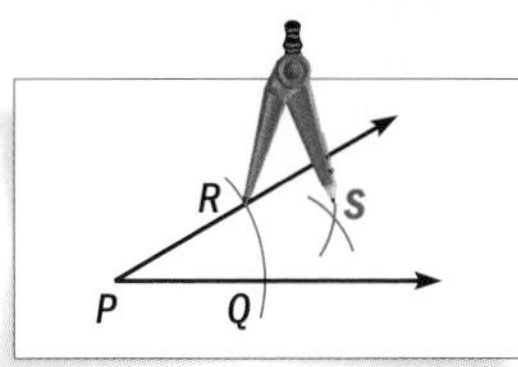

2. Draw an arc with center Q. Then, using the same compass setting, draw an arc with center R. Label S as shown.
3. Draw $\overrightarrow{PS}$, the bisector of $\angle RPQ$.

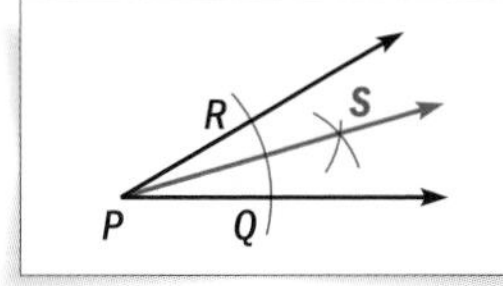

Checkpoint

▶ **Test** your knowledge of constructions by solving these problems.

Draw two segments like the ones shown. Then use a compass and a straightedge to perform the construction. 1–3. See margin.

1. Copy $\overline{AB}$. Then construct the perpendicular bisector of $\overline{AB}$.
2. Copy $\overline{CD}$. Then construct the perpendicular bisector of $\overline{CD}$.
3. Construct a segment whose length is $\frac{1}{4}$ of the length of $\overline{CD}$. Describe the steps you take.

In Exercises 4–6, draw two angles like the ones shown. Then use a compass and a straightedge to perform the construction. 4–6. See margin.

4. Copy $\angle F$ and $\angle J$. Then construct the bisectors of $\angle F$ and $\angle J$.
5. Construct an angle whose measure is twice the measure of $\angle J$.
6. Construct an angle whose measure is the sum of the measures of $\angle F$ and $\angle J$. Then construct the bisector of that angle.
7. **Apply** Construct a 45° angle using what you know about constructing perpendicular bisectors and angle bisectors. Describe the steps you take. See margin.

Extra Examples

Example 3 Use a compass and a straightedge to construct the bisector of an obtuse angle.

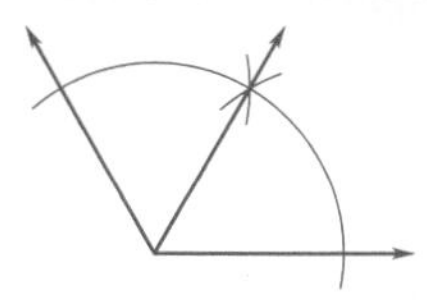

Teaching Tip

In Extra Example 3, students may need to use a slightly larger compass setting to be sure that the arcs drawn in Step 2 will intersect.

3 APPLY

Transparency

Even-numbered answers are available on transparencies.

Teaching Tip

In preparation for Exercises 4–6, students can either trace the two angles or measure the angles using a protractor in order to be sure they are copying the angles correctly.

1–6. See Additional Answers beginning on page AA1.

7.

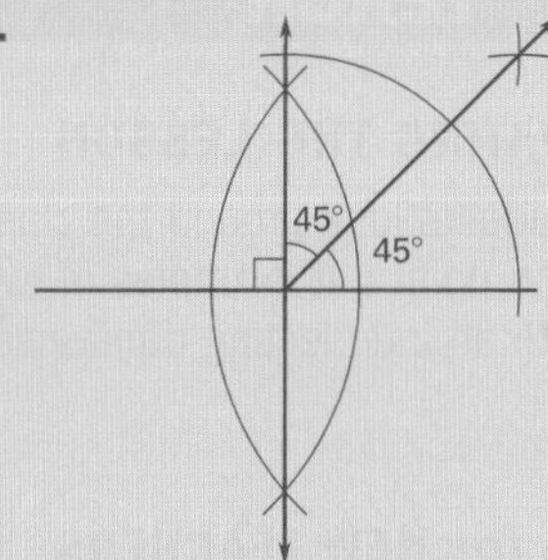

Sample answer: **First I drew a segment and constructed its perpendicular bisector, forming four right angles. Then I constructed the angle bisector of one of the right angles to create two 45° angles.**

1 PLAN

Skill Check

Solve the equation.

1. $5x = 75$ 15
2. $3y + 20 = 68$ 16
3. $4k + 3 = 59$ 14
4. $6(g + 11) = 96$ 5

LESSON OBJECTIVE

Identify angles when a transversal intersects lines.

PACING

Suggested Number of Days
Basic Course: 1 day
Average Course: 1 day
Advanced Course: 1 day
Block: 0.5 block with 13.1

TEACHING RESOURCES

For a complete list of Teaching Resources, see page 706B.

TRANSPARENCY

Warm-Up Exercises for this lesson are available on a transparency.

2 TEACH

MOTIVATING THE LESSON

Have students look around the classroom and point out examples of two lines with an intersecting transversal.

TIPS *for* NEW TEACHERS

Throughout the lesson, continually stress that the special angle pairs exist regardless of whether the lines intersected by the transversal are parallel or not. See Tips for New Teachers in the *Chapter 13 Resource Book*.

LESSON 13.2

Angles *and* Parallel Lines

BEFORE	*Now*	WHY?
You classified special pairs of angles.	You'll identify angles when a transversal intersects lines.	So you can analyze the shape of a chair, as in Ex. 16.

Vocabulary

transversal, p. 716
corresponding angles, p. 716
alternate interior angles, p. 716
alternate exterior angles, p. 716

1. alternate interior
2. alternate exterior
3. corresponding

A line that intersects two or more lines at different points is a **transversal**. When a transversal intersects two lines, several pairs of angles are formed. Two angles that occupy corresponding positions are **corresponding angles**. Two angles that lie between the two lines on opposite sides of the transversal are **alternate interior angles**. Two angles that lie outside the two lines on opposite sides of the transversal are **alternate exterior angles**.

Corresponding angles
$\angle 1$ and $\angle 5$, $\angle 2$ and $\angle 6$, $\angle 3$ and $\angle 7$, $\angle 4$ and $\angle 8$

Alternate interior angles
$\angle 3$ and $\angle 6$, $\angle 4$ and $\angle 5$

Alternate exterior angles
$\angle 1$ and $\angle 8$, $\angle 2$ and $\angle 7$

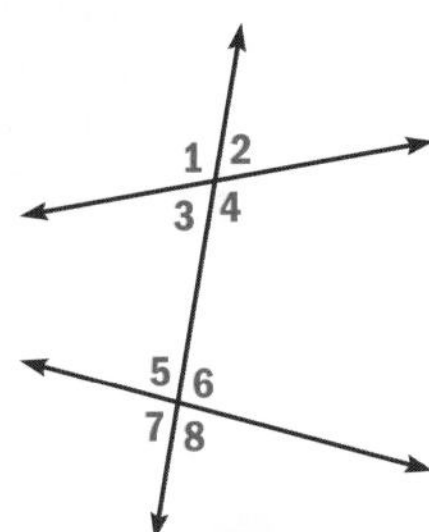

John Hancock Center

Example 1 *Identifying Angles*

Skyscrapers In the diagram of the John Hancock Center in Chicago, line t is a transversal. Tell whether the angles are corresponding, alternate interior, or alternate exterior angles.

a. $\angle 1$ and $\angle 8$

b. $\angle 2$ and $\angle 6$

c. $\angle 4$ and $\angle 5$

Solution

a. $\angle 1$ and $\angle 8$ are alternate exterior angles.

b. $\angle 2$ and $\angle 6$ are corresponding angles.

c. $\angle 4$ and $\angle 5$ are alternate interior angles.

Checkpoint

In Example 1, tell whether the angles are *corresponding*, *alternate interior*, or *alternate exterior* angles. 1–3. See margin.

1. $\angle 2$ and $\angle 7$ **2.** $\angle 3$ and $\angle 6$ **3.** $\angle 4$ and $\angle 8$

NCTM CURRICULUM STANDARDS

Standard 3: Analyze properties of 2-D shapes; Use spatial reasoning to solve problems

Transversals and Parallel Lines When a transversal intersects two parallel lines, certain pairs of angles that are formed have equal measures.

Angles and Parallel Lines

In the diagram, transversal t intersects parallel lines m and n.

Corresponding angles

$m\angle 1 = m\angle 5$ $\quad m\angle 2 = m\angle 6$

$m\angle 3 = m\angle 7$ $\quad m\angle 4 = m\angle 8$

Alternate interior angles

$m\angle 3 = m\angle 6$ $\quad m\angle 4 = m\angle 5$

Alternate exterior angles

$m\angle 1 = m\angle 8$ $\quad m\angle 2 = m\angle 7$

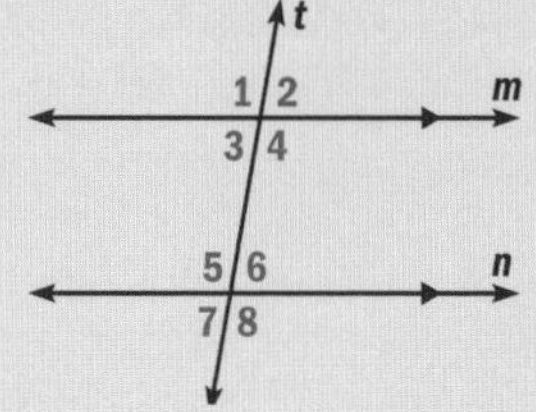

Example 2 *Finding Angle Measures*

In the diagram, transversal t intersects parallel lines m and n. If $m\angle 1 = 75°$, find the measures of the other numbered angles.

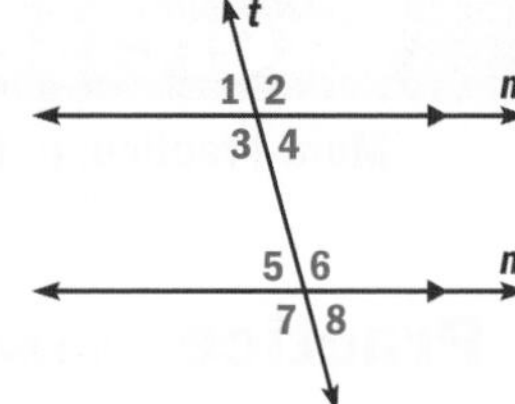

Solution

$m\angle 5 = 75°$, because $\angle 1$ and $\angle 5$ are corresponding angles.

$m\angle 4 = 75°$, because $\angle 4$ and $\angle 5$ are alternate interior angles.

$m\angle 8 = 75°$, because $\angle 1$ and $\angle 8$ are alternate exterior angles.

$m\angle 2 = 105°$, because $\angle 1$ and $\angle 2$ are supplementary angles.

$m\angle 6 = 105°$, because $\angle 2$ and $\angle 6$ are corresponding angles.

$m\angle 3 = 105°$, because $\angle 3$ and $\angle 6$ are alternate interior angles.

$m\angle 7 = 105°$, because $\angle 2$ and $\angle 7$ are alternate exterior angles.

Checkpoint

Find the measures of the numbered angles in the diagram. 4–5. See margin.

4. 80° 1 2 3 4 5 6 7

5.

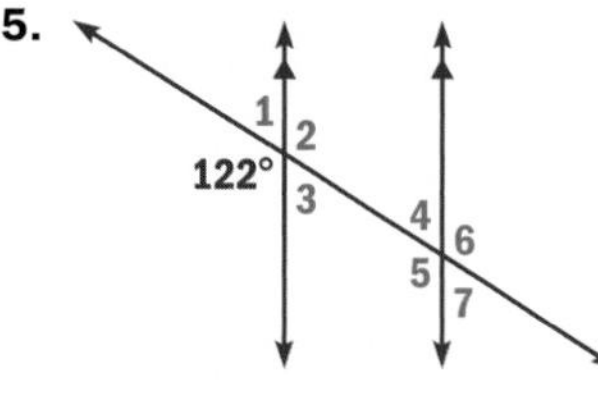

6. **Critical Thinking** In Example 2, if you know only $m\angle 6$, can you find the measures of the other numbered angles? Explain.

Note *Worthy*

In your notebook, include a diagram similar to the one at the right. On your diagram, mark the angles that have the same measure as $\angle 1$ with one arc, and mark the angles that have the same measure as $\angle 2$ with two arcs.

4. $m\angle 1 = 100°$, $m\angle 2 = 100°$, $m\angle 3 = 80°$, $m\angle 4 = 80°$, $m\angle 5 = 100°$, $m\angle 6 = 100°$, $m\angle 7 = 80°$

5. $m\angle 1 = 58°$, $m\angle 2 = 122°$, $m\angle 3 = 58°$, $m\angle 4 = 58°$, $m\angle 5 = 122°$, $m\angle 6 = 122°$, $m\angle 7 = 58°$

Study *Strategy*

Another Way In the diagram for Example 2, you can find $m\angle 2$, $m\angle 3$, and $m\angle 4$ by using what you know about supplementary and vertical angles. Then you can find $m\angle 5$, $m\angle 6$, $m\angle 7$, and $m\angle 8$ using what you know about corresponding angles.

6. Yes. *Sample answer:* $m\angle 6 = m\angle 7$ because they are vertical angles. $m\angle 6 = m\angle 2$ because they are corresponding angles. Since $\angle 2$ and $\angle 3$ are vertical angles, they are congruent, so $m\angle 6 = m\angle 3$. Supplementary angles are formed by $\angle 1$ and $\angle 2$, $\angle 3$ and $\angle 4$, $\angle 5$ and $\angle 6$, and $\angle 7$ and $\angle 8$. So $m\angle 1 = m\angle 4 = m\angle 5 = m\angle 8 = 180 - m\angle 6$.

Extra Examples

Example 1 Tell whether the angles are *corresponding*, *alternate interior*, or *alternate exterior* angles.

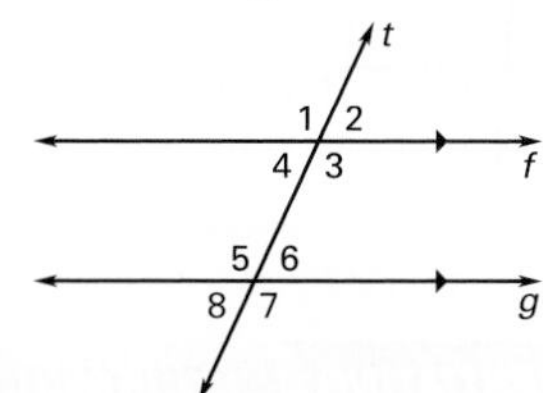

a. $\angle 3$ and $\angle 7$ **corresponding**

b. $\angle 2$ and $\angle 8$ **alternate exterior**

c. $\angle 4$ and $\angle 6$ **alternate interior**

Example 2 In the diagram, transversal t intersects parallel lines a and b. If $m\angle 1 = 125°$, find the measures of the other numbered angles.

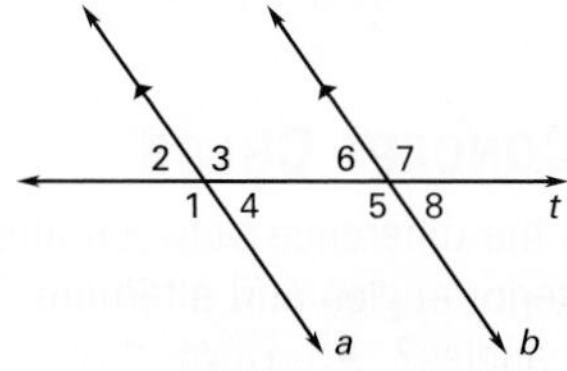

$m\angle 2 = 55°$, $m\angle 3 = 125°$, $m\angle 4 = 55°$, $m\angle 5 = 125°$, $m\angle 6 = 55°$, $m\angle 7 = 125°$, $m\angle 8 = 55°$

Teaching Tip

In Checkpoint Exercises 4 and 5, make sure students can justify each angle measure they give. Stress that they should not be choosing measures based on the appearance of the angles in the figure.

Common Error

In many of the examples and exercises in this lesson, the transversal is nearly vertical. You might wish to provide additional practice identifying angles when the transversal is a horizontal line.

Extra Examples

Example 3 Find the value of x that makes lines c and d parallel. **12**

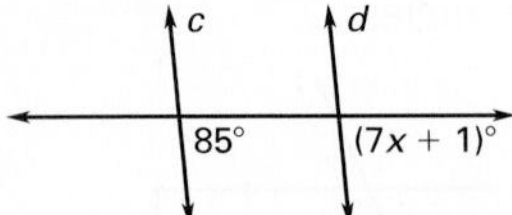

Differentiating Instruction

Less Proficient Students Have students work in groups of three. Provide each group with masking tape or string to model two parallel lines and a transversal on the floor. As one student in the group names a special type of angle pair, the other two students stand at each pair of angles in the model that fit that type.

Concept Check

What is the difference between alternate interior angles and alternate exterior angles? **Alternate interior angles are a pair of angles between the parallel lines and on opposite sides of the transversal, while alternate exterior angles are outside of the parallel lines and on opposite sides of the transversal.**

Daily Puzzler

What is the maximum number of right angles in a pentagon? in a trapezoid? in a triangle? **3, 2, 1**

1. ***Sample:***

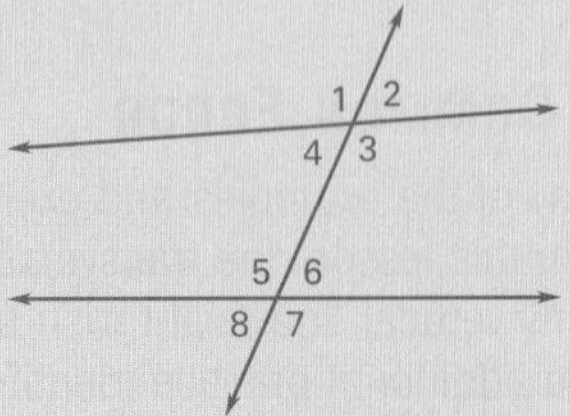

∠4 and ∠6, ∠3 and ∠5

Corresponding Angles If a transversal intersects two lines so that the corresponding angles have the same measure, then the lines are parallel.

Example 3 *Finding the Value of a Variable*

Find the value of x that makes lines m and n parallel.

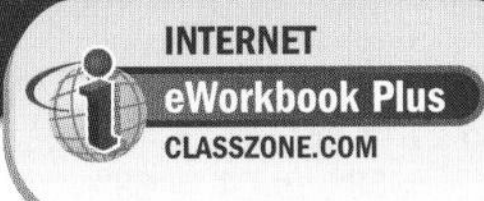

Solution

The labeled angles in the diagram are corresponding angles. Lines m and n are parallel when the measures are equal.

$(5x + 18)° = 63°$ **Set measures equal.**

$5x = 45$ **Subtract 18 from each side.**

$x = 9$ **Divide each side by 5.**

13.2 Exercises

More Practice, p. 815

INTERNET eWorkbook Plus CLASSZONE.COM

Guided Practice

Vocabulary Check

1. Draw two lines and a transversal intersecting both lines. Then number the angles and identify both pairs of alternate interior angles. **See margin.**

2. A transversal intersects lines m and n. If the corresponding angles are congruent, what can you conclude about lines m and n? **They are parallel.**

Skill Check **In Exercises 3–6, tell whether the angles in the diagram are *corresponding, alternate interior,* or *alternate exterior* angles.**

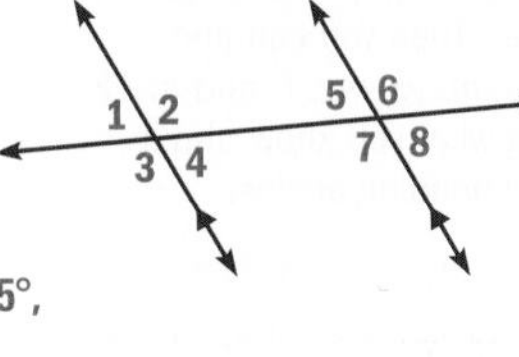

3. ∠2 and ∠6 **corresponding**

4. ∠4 and ∠8 **corresponding**

5. ∠3 and ∠6 **alternate exterior**

6. ∠2 and ∠7 **alternate interior**

7. If $m\angle 1 = 65°$, find the measures of the other numbered angles in the diagram. **$m\angle 2 = 115°$, $m\angle 3 = 115°$, $m\angle 4 = 65°$, $m\angle 5 = 65°$, $m\angle 6 = 115°$, $m\angle 7 = 115°$, $m\angle 8 = 65°$**

Guided Problem Solving

8. Use the diagram. For lines m and n to be parallel, what must the value of x be?

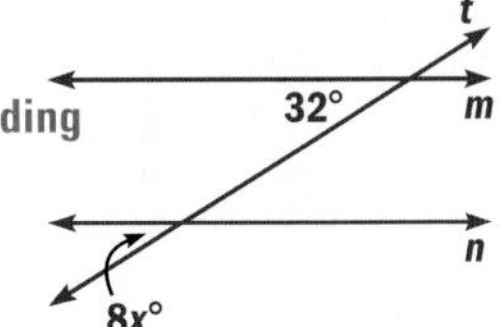

1) Tell whether the labeled angles are *corresponding, alternate interior,* or *alternate exterior* angles. **corresponding**

2) Write an equation that relates the angle measures. **$8x° = 32°$**

3) Solve the equation for x. **4**

Practice and Problem Solving

Homework *Help*

Example	Exercises
1	9-12, 15-16
2	13-16
3	17-18

Online Resources
CLASSZONE.COM
- More Examples
- eTutorial Plus

15b. Yes. *Sample answer:* Since *m* and *n* are parallel, alternate interior angles have the same measure.

In Exercises 9–12, tell whether the angles in the diagram are *corresponding, alternate interior,* or *alternate exterior* angles.

A **9.** $\angle 1$ and $\angle 8$ alternate exterior **10.** $\angle 4$ and $\angle 5$ alternate interior

11. $\angle 1$ and $\angle 5$ corresponding **12.** $\angle 3$ and $\angle 7$ corresponding

13. Which angles have the same measure as $\angle 1$ in the diagram? $\angle 4$, $\angle 5$, $\angle 8$

14. If $m\angle 1 = 43°$, find the measures of the other numbered angles in the diagram. $m\angle 2 = 137°$, $m\angle 3 = 137°$, $m\angle 4 = 43°$, $m\angle 5 = 43°$, $m\angle 6 = 137°$, $m\angle 7 = 137°$, $m\angle 8 = 43°$

15. Extended Problem Solving In the bicycle frame shown, $\angle 1$ is called the head angle, and $\angle 2$ is called the seat angle. Lines *m* and *n* are parallel.

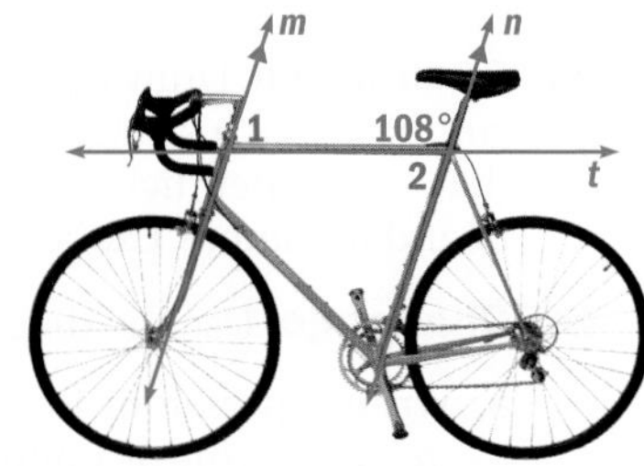

a. Identify Are $\angle 1$ and $\angle 2$ *corresponding, alternate interior,* or *alternate exterior* angles? alternate interior

b. Explain Do $\angle 1$ and $\angle 2$ have the same measure? Explain.

c. Calculate Find $m\angle 1$ and $m\angle 2$. Explain how you got your answers. See margin.

16. Chairs The diagram shown is a side view of a chair designed in the 1930s. In the diagram, $m\angle 1 = 95°$ and $m\angle 3 = 45°$. Tell whether the statement is *true* or *false*. Explain your reasoning.

a. $\angle 2$ and $\angle 3$ are corresponding angles. 16a–d. See margin.

b. $\angle 2$ and $\angle 3$ have equal measures.

c. $\angle 2$ and $\angle 3$ are complementary angles.

d. The sum of the measures of $\angle 1$, $\angle 2$, and $\angle 3$ is 180°.

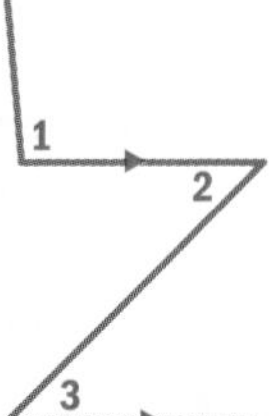

Algebra Find the value of *x* that makes lines *m* and *n* parallel.

17. 5

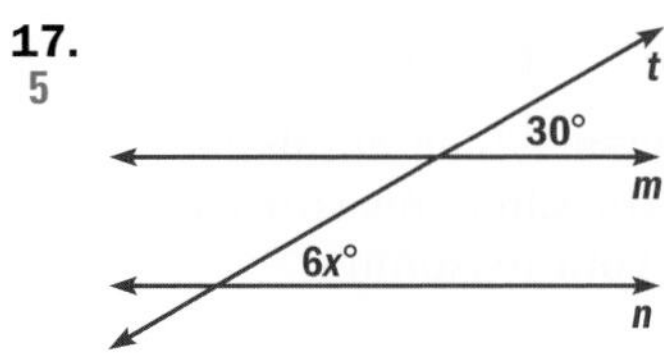

18. $20\frac{2}{3}$

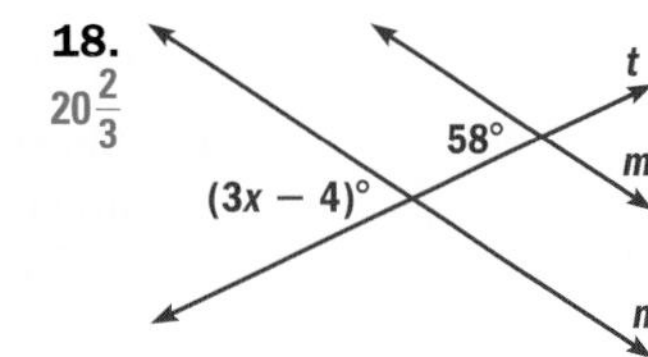

In the **Real World**

Chairs The chair shown is called a zig-zag chair. In 1934, Gerrit Rietveld built a zig-zag chair that was 74 centimeters high, 45 centimeters long, and 37.5 centimeters wide. If the chair is enclosed in a box with these dimensions, what is the volume of the box?
124,875 cm^3, or 0.124875 m^3

3 APPLY

ASSIGNMENT GUIDE

Basic Course

Day 1: pp. 719-720 Exs. 9-14, 17-20, 23, 25-32

Average Course

Day 1: pp. 719-720 Exs. 11-23, 25-33

Advanced Course

Day 1: pp. 719-720 Exs. 11-24*, 27-29, 32, 33

Block

pp. 719-720 Exs. 11-23, 25-33 (with 13.1)

EXTRA PRACTICE

- Student Edition, p. 815
- Chapter 13 Resource Book, pp. 16-18
- Test and Practice Generator

TRANSPARENCY

Even-numbered answers are available on transparencies.

HOMEWORK CHECK

When you review students' homework for this lesson, go over the following exercises to check understanding of key concepts.
Basic: 9, 12, 13, 14, 17
Average: 11, 12, 13, 16, 17
Advanced: 12, 13, 15, 17, 18

TEACHING TIP

In Exercise 16, have students copy the diagram and extend the parallel segments if they are having difficulty visualizing the angle relationships.

15c. $m\angle 1 = m\angle 2 = 72°$. ***Sample answer:*** $\angle 2$ and the angle with measure 108° are supplementary, so $m\angle 2 = 180° - 108° = 72°$. Also, $m\angle 1 = m\angle 2$ as noted.

16a–d. See Additional Answers beginning on page AA1.

4 ASSESS

ASSESSMENT RESOURCES

For more assessment resources, see:

- Assessment Book
- Test and Practice Generator

MINI-QUIZ

Tell whether the angles in the diagram are *corresponding*, *alternate interior*, or *alternate exterior* angles.

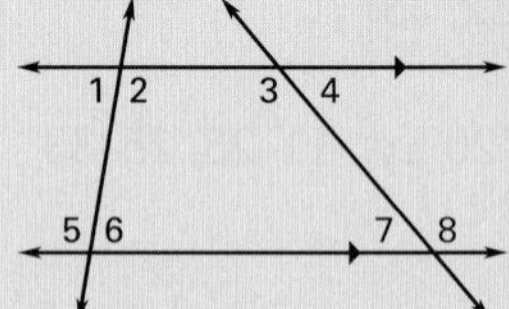

1. $\angle 2$ and $\angle 4$ **corresponding**
2. $\angle 1$ and $\angle 6$ **alternate interior**
3. $\angle 5$ and $\angle 7$ **corresponding**
4. **Challenge** Use the figure above. If $m\angle 4 = 50°$ and $m\angle 2 = 100°$, find $m\angle 6$. **80°**

5 FOLLOW-UP

DIAGNOSIS/REMEDIATION

- Study Guide in Chapter 13 Resource Book, pp. 19–20
- eTutorial Plus Online
- Extra Practice, p. 815
- Lesson Practice in Chapter 13 Resource Book, pp. 16–18

ENGLISH LEARNER SUPPORT

- Spanish Study Guide
- Multi-Language Visual Glossary
- Chapter Audio Summaries CDs

CHALLENGE

- Challenge Practice in Chapter 13 Resource Book, p. 21
- Teacher's Edition, p. 706F

21, 23. See Additional Answers beginning on page AA1.

Geometry **Find the measures of the numbered angles in the diagram.**

B **19.**

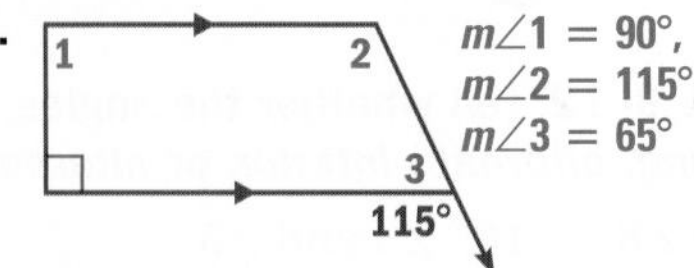

$m\angle 1 = 90°$, $m\angle 2 = 115°$, $m\angle 3 = 65°$

20.

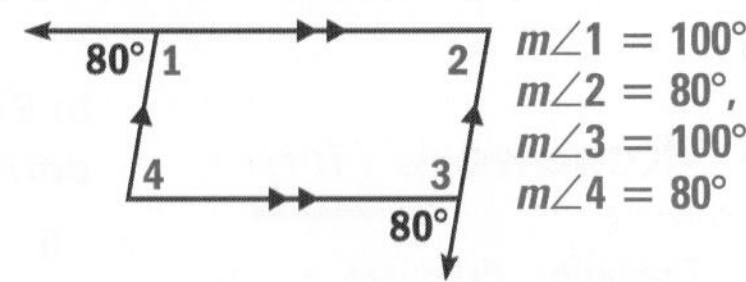

$m\angle 1 = 100°$, $m\angle 2 = 80°$, $m\angle 3 = 100°$, $m\angle 4 = 80°$

21. Visual Thinking A transversal intersects two parallel lines, forming alternate interior angles $\angle 1$ and $\angle 2$ and vertical angles $\angle 1$ and $\angle 3$. Illustrate the situation. How are $m\angle 2$ and $m\angle 3$ related? Explain.

21. See margin for art; they are the same; they are the measures of corresponding angles formed by a transversal intersecting two parallel lines: $m\angle 1 = m\angle 2$, and $m\angle 1 = m\angle 3$, so $m\angle 2 = m\angle 3$.

22. *Writing* The drawing is a Hering illusion, in which intersecting transversals make two parallel lines appear to be curved. Describe a way you can use a protractor to verify that the two lines are parallel.

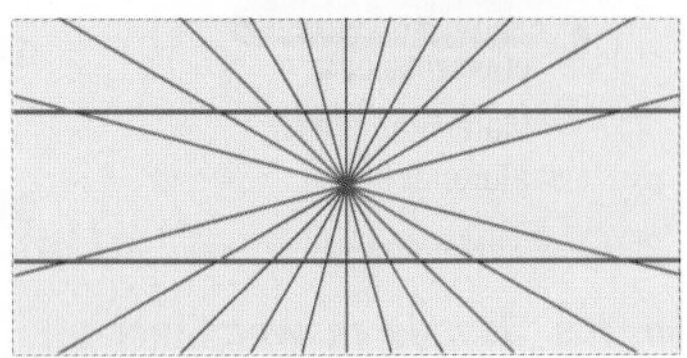

Review Help

For help with using a protractor, see p. 792.

22. *Sample answer:* Measure two corresponding angles formed by one of the transversals intersecting the two red lines. If the angles have the same measure, the red lines are parallel.

C **23. Construction** Draw a line t using a straightedge. Then use a compass and a straightedge to construct two lines m and n that are perpendicular to t at two different points. How are m and n related? Explain your reasoning.

23. See margin for art; they are parallel. *Sample answer:* Line t is a transversal of lines m and n. Since m and n intersect t in right angles, the corresponding angles have the same measure, so m and n must be parallel.

24. Challenge Use the diagram.

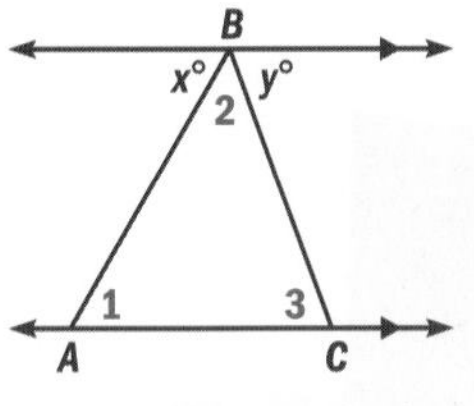

a. Write expressions for $m\angle 1$, $m\angle 2$, and $m\angle 3$ in terms of x and y. Explain your reasoning. **24a–b. See margin.**

b. Use the expressions you wrote in part (a) to show that the sum of the measures of the angles in $\triangle ABC$ is 180°.

Mixed Review

24a. *Sample answer:* $m\angle 1 = x°$ because the angles are alternate interior angles; $m\angle 2 = 180° - (x + y)°$ because the three angles together form a straight angle; $m\angle 3 = y°$ because the angles are alternate interior angles.

24b. $m\angle 1 + m\angle 2 + m\angle 3 = x° + 180° - (x + y)° + y° = x° + 180° - x° - y° + y° = 180°$

Solve the equation by first clearing the fractions. *(Lesson 5.7)*

25. $\frac{1}{2}x + \frac{3}{4} = \frac{5}{6}$ **$\frac{1}{6}$**

26. $\frac{7}{10}x - \frac{1}{5} = \frac{3}{8}$ **$\frac{23}{28}$**

27. $-\frac{1}{12} = \frac{1}{2}x - \frac{4}{9}$ **$\frac{13}{18}$**

28. A quadrilateral has angle measures of $(2x + 1)°$, $(x - 3)°$, 100°, and $(3x - 2)°$. Find the value of x. *(Lesson 10.2)* **44**

Tell whether the angles are *complementary*, *supplementary*, or *neither*. *(Lesson 13.1)*

29. $m\angle 1 = 140°$, $m\angle 2 = 40°$ **supplementary**

30. $m\angle 3 = 118°$, $m\angle 4 = 72°$ **neither**

31. $m\angle 5 = 24°$, $m\angle 6 = 66°$ **complementary**

Standardized Test Practice

In Exercises 32 and 33, use the diagram.

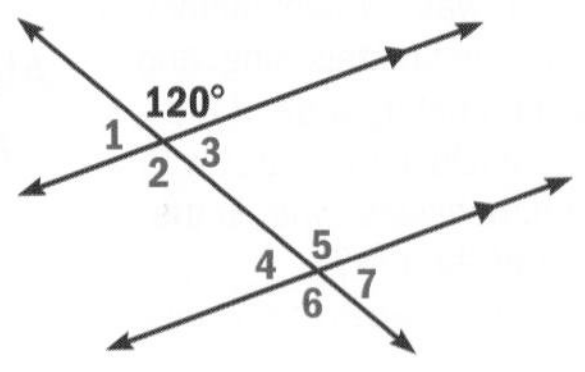

32. Multiple Choice What is $m\angle 6$? **D**

A. 30° **B.** 60°

C. 90° **D.** 120°

33. Short Response Which numbered angles have the same measure as $\angle 1$? Explain your reasoning.

33. $\angle 3$, $\angle 4$, and $\angle 7$. *Sample answer:* $\angle 1$ and $\angle 4$ are corresponding angles, $\angle 3$ and $\angle 4$ are alternate interior angles, and $\angle 3$ and $\angle 7$ are corresponding angles.

Concept *Activity*

13.3 Finding Sums of Angle Measures

Goal
Find the sum of the measures of the angles of a convex polygon.

Materials
- paper
- pencil

Investigate

Find the sum of the measures of the angles of a convex polygon.

Steps 1–2. Check students' work.

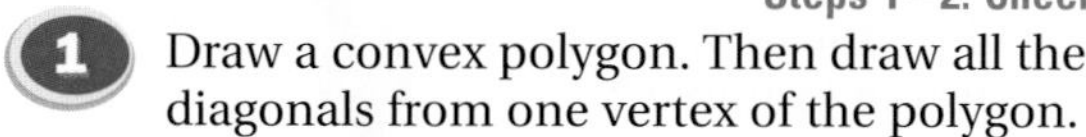

1 Draw a convex polygon. Then draw all the diagonals from one vertex of the polygon.

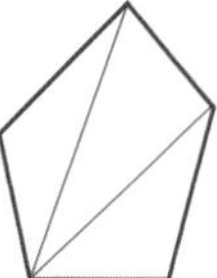

2 Multiply the number of triangles formed in Step 1 by 180°. The product is the sum of the measures of the angles of the polygon.

$3 \cdot 180° = 540°$

3 Copy and complete the table.

Convex polygon	Quadrilateral	Pentagon	Hexagon	Heptagon	Octagon
Sides	? 4	5	? 6	? 7	? 8
Triangles formed	? 2	3	? 4	? 5	? 6
Sum of angle measures	?	$3 \cdot 180° = 540°$	?	?	?

$2 \cdot 180° = 360°$ $4 \cdot 180° = 720°$ $6 \cdot 180° = 1080°$
$5 \cdot 180° = 900°$

Draw Conclusions

1. **Critical Thinking** In Step 2, why do you multiply the number of triangles formed by 180°? **The sum of the angle measures in any triangle is 180°.**
2. **Compare** How is the number of triangles formed by drawing diagonals from one vertex related to the number of sides of a convex polygon? How many triangles would be formed using a convex polygon with n sides? **It is 2 less than the number of sides; $n - 2$.**
3. **Analyze** Write a formula for the sum of the measures of the angles of a convex polygon with n sides. $180° \cdot (n - 2)$
4. **Apply** Use the formula you wrote in Exercise 3 to find the sum of the measures of the angles of a convex polygon with 9 sides. 1260°

NCTM CURRICULUM STANDARDS
Standard 2: Use models to understand relationships
Standard 3: Analyze properties of 2-D shapes

1 PLAN

Investigate the Concept
- Students will find the sum of the measures of the angles of a convex polygon.
- This activity leads into solving problems using the sums of the measures of the interior or exterior angles of polygons in Lesson 13.3.

Materials
Each student will need paper and pencil.

Recommended Time
Work activity: 10 min
Discuss results: 5 min

Grouping
Students should work individually.

2 TEACH

Alternative Strategy
On the board, reproduce the last three rows of the table. Then divide the class into five groups and assign each group one of the polygons. Each group completes the column they are assigned, filling in their results on the board.

3 CLOSE

Key Discovery
The sum of the measures of the interior angles of a convex n-gon is given by the formula $180° \cdot (n - 2)$.

Assessment
1. As the number of sides of a convex polygon increases by 1, by how many degrees does the sum of the interior angle measures increase? 180°

1 PLAN

Skill Check

Simplify.

1. $180 \cdot (18 - 2)$ 2880
2. $\frac{(10 - 2) \cdot 180}{10}$ 144
3. $\frac{(8 - 2) \cdot 180}{8}$ 135

LESSON OBJECTIVE

Find measures of interior and exterior angles.

PACING

Suggested Number of Days
Basic Course: 2 days
Average Course: 2 days
Advanced Course: 2 days
Block: 1 block

TEACHING RESOURCES

For a complete list of Teaching Resources, see page 706B.

 **TRANSPARENCY**

Warm-Up Exercises for this lesson are available on a transparency.

2 TEACH

MOTIVATING THE LESSON

Bring in real-world examples of convex polygons. Have students measure the interior angles of a polygon and find the sum of the measures.

TIPS *for* NEW TEACHERS

Stress the fact that the formula for the sum of the measures of the interior angles of a polygon is only for convex polygons. See Tips for New Teachers in the *Chapter 13 Resource Book*.

LESSON **13.3**

Angles *and* Polygons

BEFORE	*Now*	WHY?
You found angle measures of triangles.	You'll find measures of interior and exterior angles.	So you can analyze a street map, as in Ex. 22.

Vocabulary

interior angle, p. 722
exterior angle, p. 723

Tambourines The frame of the tambourine shown is a regular heptagon. What is the measure of each angle of the heptagon? You will find the answer in Example 2.

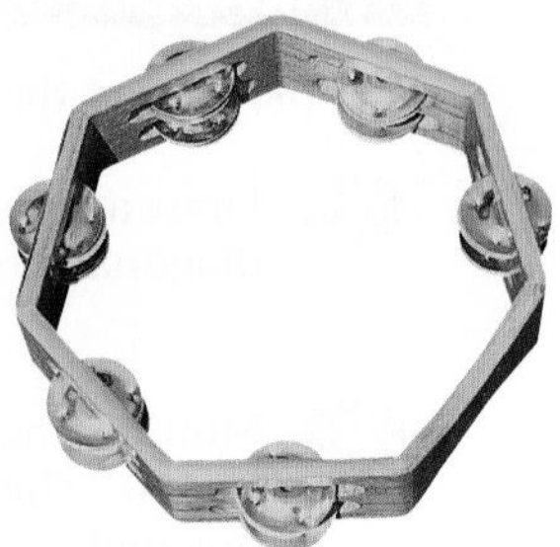

An **interior angle** of a polygon is an angle inside the polygon. In the activity on page 721, you used triangles to find the sum of the measures of the interior angles of a convex polygon. You can find the measure of an interior angle of a regular polygon by dividing the sum of the measures of the interior angles by the number of sides.

 **Review *Help***

For help with convex polygons and regular polygons, see p. 516.

Measures of Interior Angles of a Convex Polygon

The sum of the measures of the interior angles of a convex n-gon is given by the formula $(n - 2) \cdot 180°$.

The measure of an interior angle of a regular n-gon is given by the formula $\frac{(n - 2) \cdot 180°}{n}$.

Example 1 *Finding the Sum of a Polygon's Interior Angles*

Find the sum of the measures of the interior angles of the polygon.

a. 

b. 

Solution

a. For a convex pentagon, $n = 5$.

$(n - 2) \cdot 180° = (5 - 2) \cdot 180°$
$= 3 \cdot 180°$
$= 540°$

b. For a convex octagon, $n = 8$.

$(n - 2) \cdot 180° = (8 - 2) \cdot 180°$
$= 6 \cdot 180°$
$= 1080°$

NCTM CURRICULUM STANDARDS

Standard 2: Analyze situations using algebraic symbols
Standard 3: Analyze properties of 2-D shapes; Use spatial reasoning to solve problems

Watch *Out*

The formula $\frac{(n-2) \cdot 180°}{n}$ is valid only for a regular polygon. You cannot use this formula to find the measure of an interior angle of a convex polygon that is not regular.

Example 2 *Finding the Measure of an Interior Angle*

Find the measure of an interior angle of the frame of the tambourine shown on page 722.

Solution

Because the tambourine is a regular heptagon, $n = 7$.

Measure of an interior angle	$= \frac{(n-2) \cdot 180°}{n}$	**Write formula.**
	$= \frac{(7-2) \cdot 180°}{7}$	**Substitute 7 for *n*.**
	$\approx 128.6°$	**Evaluate. Use a calculator.**

Answer The measure of an interior angle of the frame of the tambourine is about 128.6°.

Checkpoint

1. Find the sum of the measures of the interior angles of a convex 10-gon. 1440°
2. Find the measure of an interior angle of a regular 12-gon. 150°

Exterior Angles When you extend a side of a polygon, the angle that is adjacent to the interior angle is an **exterior angle**. In the diagram, ∠1 and ∠2 are exterior angles. An interior angle and an exterior angle at the same vertex form a straight angle.

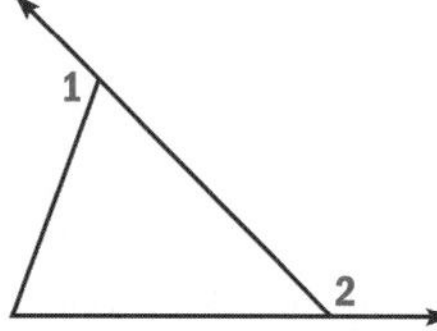

Example 3 *Finding the Measure of an Exterior Angle*

Find $m\angle 1$ in the diagram.

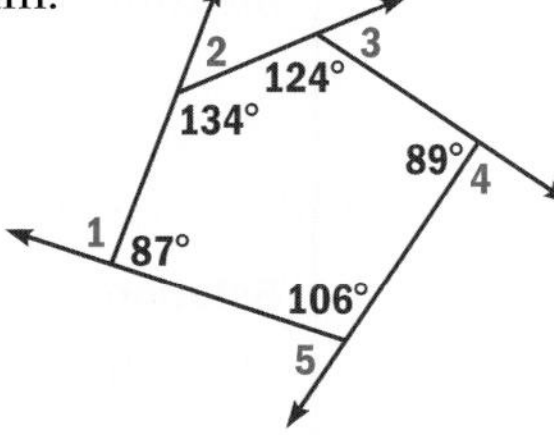

Solution

The angle that measures 87° forms a straight angle with ∠1, which is the exterior angle at the same vertex.

$m\angle 1 + 87° = 180°$	**Angles are supplementary.**
$m\angle 1 = 93°$	**Subtract 87° from each side.**

Checkpoint

3. In Example 3, find $m\angle 2$, $m\angle 3$, $m\angle 4$, and $m\angle 5$.
$m\angle 2 = 46°$, $m\angle 3 = 56°$, $m\angle 4 = 91°$, $m\angle 5 = 74°$

Extra Examples

Example 1 Find the sum of the measures of the interior angles of a convex polygon with the given number of sides.
a. 9 **1260°**
b. 11 **1620°**

Example 2 Find the measure of an interior angle of a regular 11-gon. **about 147.3°**

Example 3 Find $m\angle 1$ in the diagram. **155°**

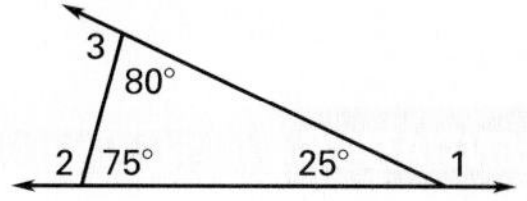

NOTETAKING

In their notebooks, suggest that students illustrate both of the formulas given on page 722 with examples in different colors for a triangle, a quadrilateral, and a pentagon.

COMMON ERROR

Watch for students who apply the formula for the measure of an interior angle of a regular *n*-gon to polygons that are not regular. Although this may yield a correct result in some cases, such as for a rectangle, it will not do so in all cases and is therefore not a valid formula unless the polygon is regular.

Extra Examples

Example 4 Find the measure of an exterior angle of a regular 12-gon. **30°**

Example 5 Find the unknown angle measure in the diagram.

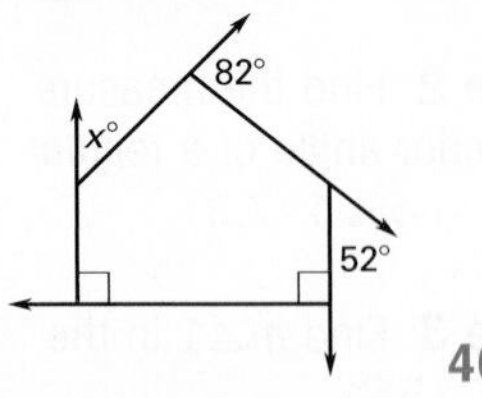

46°

DIFFERENTIATING INSTRUCTION

Alternative Teaching Strategy Have students draw four different non-regular pentagons. Then have them measure the interior angles of each pentagon. Ask students to find the sum of these measures for each pentagon. Finally, have them summarize the results by writing the formula for the sum of the measures of the interior angles of a convex polygon, having convinced themselves that the formulas work for all pentagons.

TEACHING TIP

Be sure students understand that the sum of the measures of the exterior angles of every convex polygon is 360°.

CONCEPT CHECK

Explain how to find the measure of each interior angle of a regular polygon. **Subtract 2 from the number of sides and multiply this difference by 180°. Then divide this product by the number of sides.**

DAILY PUZZLER

What is the measure of an exterior angle of a regular 10-gon? **36°**

Example 4 *An Exterior Angle Measure of a Regular Polygon*

Teapots The diagram shows a teapot in the shape of a regular hexagon. Find $m\angle 2$.

Solution

The measure of an interior angle of a regular hexagon is $\frac{(6-2) \cdot 180^\circ}{6}$.

$m\angle 1 + m\angle 2 = 180^\circ$	**Angles are supplementary.**
$\frac{(6-2) \cdot 180^\circ}{6} + m\angle 2 = 180^\circ$	**Substitute formula for $m\angle 1$.**
$120^\circ + m\angle 2 = 180^\circ$	**Simplify.**
$m\angle 2 = 60^\circ$	**Subtract 120° from each side.**

Sum of Exterior Angle Measures Each vertex of a convex polygon has two exterior angles. If you draw one exterior angle at each vertex, then the sum of the measures of these angles is 360°. The calculations below show that this is true for a triangle.

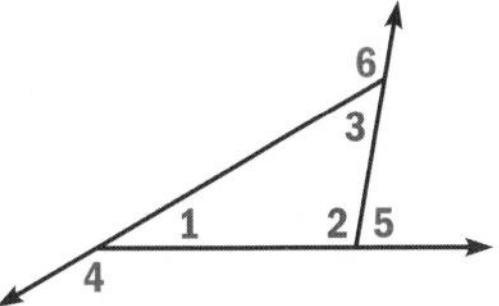

$$\begin{aligned} m\angle 4 + m\angle 5 + m\angle 6 &= (180^\circ - m\angle 1) + (180^\circ - m\angle 2) + (180^\circ - m\angle 3) \\ &= (180^\circ + 180^\circ + 180^\circ) - (m\angle 1 + m\angle 2 + m\angle 3) \\ &= 540^\circ - 180^\circ = 360^\circ \end{aligned}$$

Example 5 *Using the Sum of Measures of Exterior Angles*

Find the unknown angle measure in the diagram.

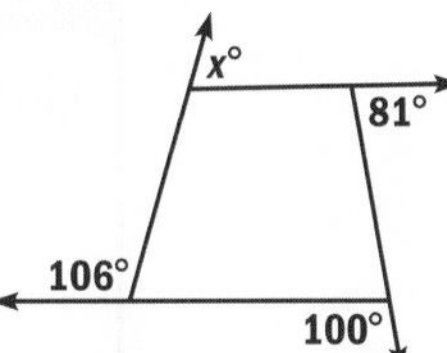

Solution

$x^\circ + 81^\circ + 100^\circ + 106^\circ = 360^\circ$	**Sum of measures of exterior angles of convex polygon is 360°.**
$x + 287 = 360$	**Add.**
$x = 73$	**Subtract 287 from each side.**

Answer The angle measure is 73°.

Checkpoint

4. Find the measure of an exterior angle of a regular pentagon. **72°**
5. Four exterior angles of a convex pentagon have measures 14°, 87°, 56°, and 30°. Find the measure of the fifth exterior angle. **173°**

13.3 Exercises

More Practice, p. 815

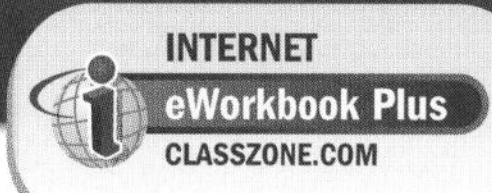

Guided Practice

Vocabulary Check

1. Draw a convex polygon that has exactly 8 interior angles. See margin.

2. Draw a quadrilateral and show one exterior angle at each vertex. See margin.

Skill Check **In Exercises 3–6, match the description with the correct value.**

3. Sum of measures of interior angles of a convex heptagon C — **A.** 360°

4. Measure of an interior angle of a regular hexagon D — **B.** 45°

5. Measure of an exterior angle of a regular octagon B — **C.** 900°

6. Sum of measures of exterior angles of a convex 12-gon A — **D.** 120°

Guided Problem Solving

7. In the diagram shown, what is $m\angle 2$?

1) Find the sum of the measures of the interior angles of the polygon. 360°

2) Find $m\angle 1$. 69°

3) Subtract your answer to Step 2 from 180°. 111°

107° 120° 64° 1 2

Practice and Problem Solving

Homework *Help*

Example	Exercises
1	8-11
2	12-17, 22-23
3	18, 22
4	12-17, 21
5	19-20

Online Resources
CLASSZONE.COM
- More Examples
- eTutorial Plus

Find the sum of the measures of the interior angles of the polygon.

A **8.** 540°

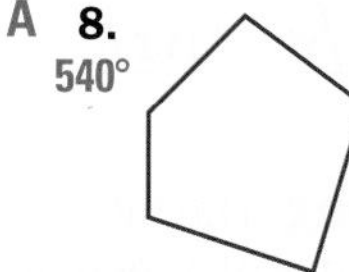

9. 900°

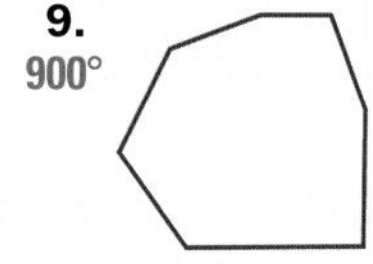

10. 720°

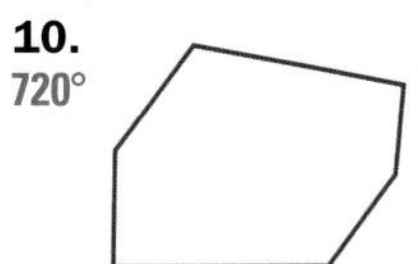

11. *Writing* Is the formula for the sum of the interior angles of a polygon valid for a triangle? Explain your reasoning. Yes. *Sample answer:* For a triangle, $n = 3$, so $(n - 2) \cdot 180^\circ = (3 - 2) \cdot 180^\circ = 180^\circ$, as expected.

In Exercises 12–17, find the measure of an interior angle and the measure of an exterior angle for the regular polygon.

12. Triangle **13.** Quadrilateral **14.** Octagon

15. Pentagon **16.** 10-gon **17.** 15-gon

18. For the triangle shown, what is the measure of an exterior angle at vertex A? at vertex B? at vertex C? 148°; 79°; 133°

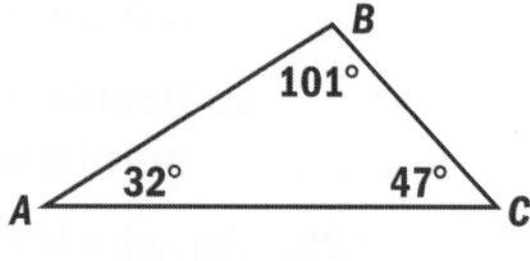

12. interior: 60°, exterior: 120°
13. interior: 90°, exterior: 90°
14. interior: 135°, exterior: 45°
15. interior: 108°, exterior: 72°
16. interior: 144°, exterior: 36°
17. interior: 156°, exterior: 24°

3 APPLY

ASSIGNMENT GUIDE

Basic Course

Day 1: pp. 725–727 Exs. 8–11, 22, 24–26, 37–44

Day 2: pp. 725–727 Exs. 12–20, 28–30, 45–48

Average Course

Day 1: pp. 725–727 Exs. 8–11, 22–26, 32–35, 37–44

Day 2: pp. 725–727 Exs. 15–21, 27–31, 45–49

Advanced Course

Day 1: pp. 725–727 Exs. 9–11, 22–24, 31–36*, 39–41

Day 2: pp. 725–727 Exs. 15–21, 26–30, 44–49

Block

pp. 725–727 Exs. 8–11, 15–35, 37–49

EXTRA PRACTICE

- Student Edition, p. 815
- Chapter 13 Resource Book, pp. 24–26
- Test and Practice Generator

TRANSPARENCY

Even-numbered answers are available on transparencies. A support transparency is available for Exercises 27 and 41–44.

HOMEWORK CHECK

When you review students' homework for this lesson, go over the following exercises to check understanding of key concepts.

Basic: 8, 12, 18, 19, 22

Average: 9, 15, 18, 19, 21

Advanced: 10, 16, 18, 20, 21

1, 2. See Additional Answers beginning on page AA1.

27a.

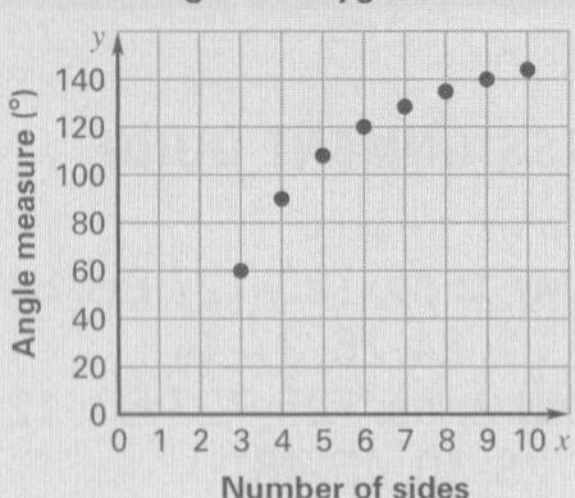

31. ***Sample:***

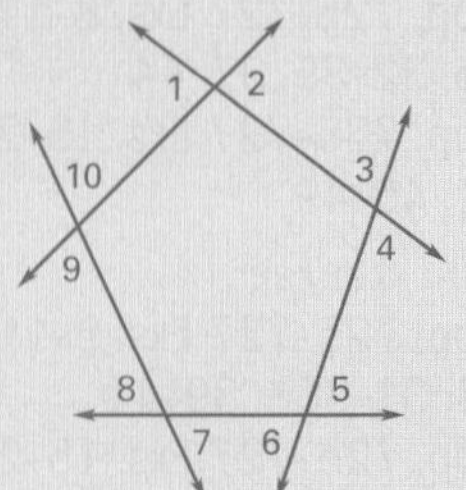

36. ***Sample answer:*** **Since each exterior angle forms a straight angle with an interior angle, the measures of the exterior angles are $(180 - w)°$, $(180 - x)°$, $(180 - y)°$, and $(180 - z)°$. The sum of the measures of the exterior angles is $(180 - w)° + (180 - x)° + (180 - y)° + (180 - z)° = (180 + 180 + 180 + 180)° - (w + x + y + z)°$. The sum of the measures of the interior angles is 360°, so this simplifies to $720° - 360° = 360°$.**

41.

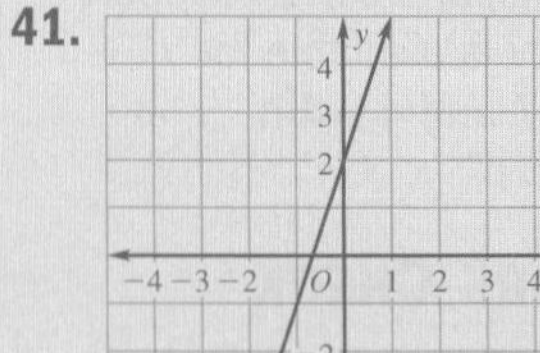

42.

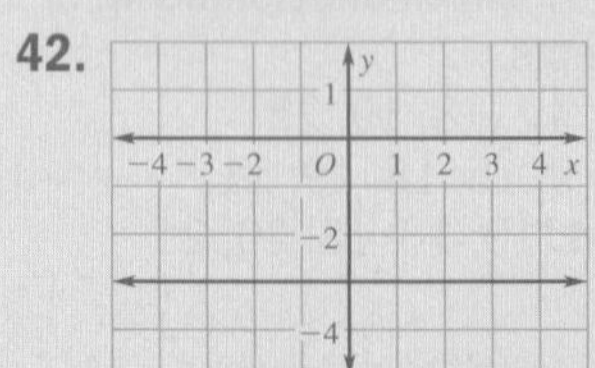

43, 44. See Additional Answers beginning on page AA1.

In Exercises 19 and 20, find the unknown angle measure.

19.

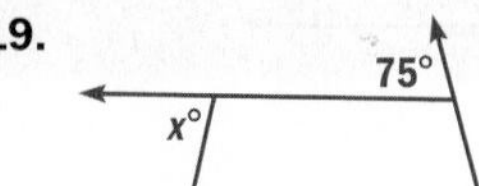

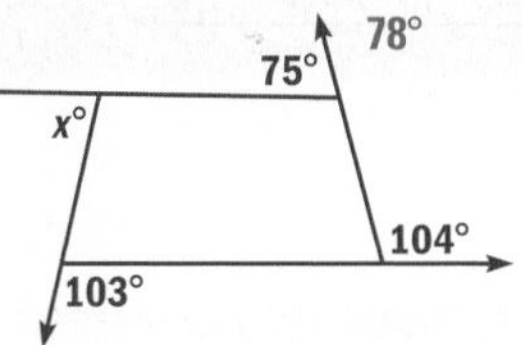

20.

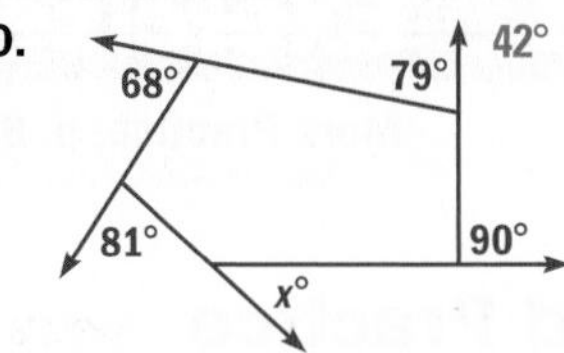

21. *Writing* Suppose you know only the number of sides of a regular polygon. Describe the steps you would take to find the measure of an exterior angle of the polygon. **See margin.**

22. Cotati Hub The map shows a section of Cotati, California. This area is called the Cotati Hub. It is made up of six streets that form a regular hexagon.

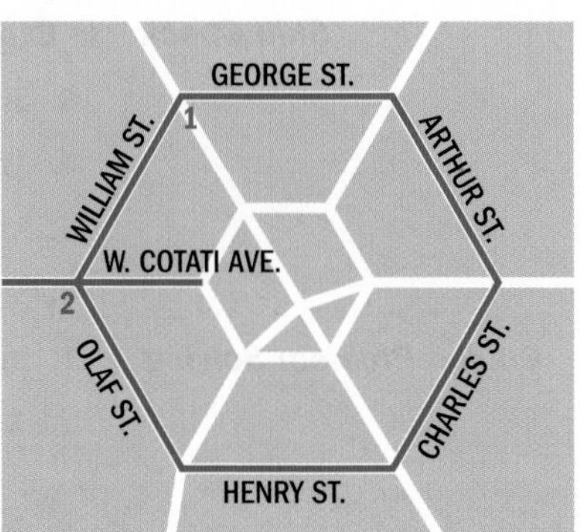

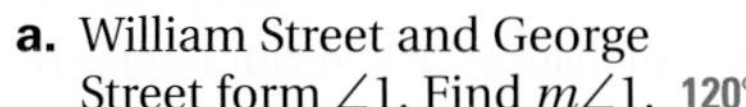

a. William Street and George Street form ∠1. Find $m\angle 1$. **120°**

b. West Cotati Avenue bisects the interior angle formed by William Street and Olaf Street. Find $m\angle 2$. **120°**

23. Critical Thinking Suppose you know only the sum of the measures of the interior angles of a pentagon. Can you always find the measure of one of the interior angles? Explain your reasoning. **See margin.**

Algebra Find the values of *x* and *y*.

B 24.

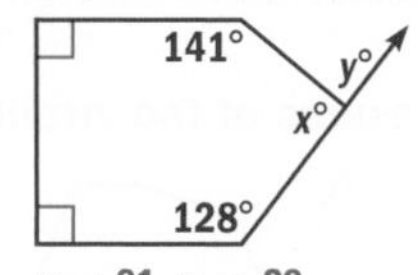

$x = 91$, $y = 89$

25.

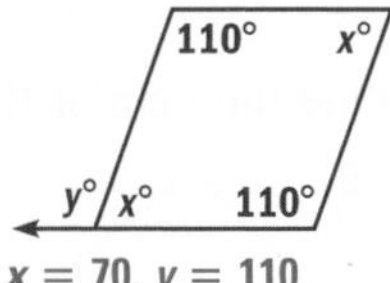

$x = 70$, $y = 110$

26.

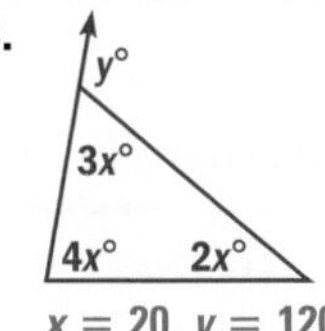

$x = 20$, $y = 120$

27. Extended Problem Solving The table shows the relationship between *x*, the number of sides of a regular polygon, and *y*, the measure of an interior angle.

x	3	4	5	6	7	8	9	10
y	60°	?	?	?	?	?	?	?

90° 108° 120° 128.6° 135° 140° 144°

a. Graph Copy and complete the table. Round to the nearest tenth, if necessary. Then plot the ordered pairs (x, y) in a coordinate plane. **See margin for art.**

b. Analyze As the number of sides increases, does the change in the measure of an interior angle *increase, decrease,* or *stay the same*? **decrease**

c. Decide Your friend says that $y = 148°$ when $x = 11$. Based on the numbers in the table, do you agree? Explain your reasoning.

28. For which regular polygon is the ratio of an exterior angle measure to an interior angle measure 1 to 1? 2 to 1? 2 to 3?

In the **Real World**

Cotati Hub In the photo of Cotati, California, shown, suppose that each of the 6 streets that form the larger hexagon is about 760 feet long. What is the perimeter of the hexagon? **about 4560 ft**

21. ***Sample answer:*** **First use the formula for the measure of an interior angle of a regular *n*-gon. Then use the fact that the sum of the measures of an interior angle and an exterior angle at each vertex is 180°.**

23. No. ***Sample answer:*** **You can only apply the formula for the measure of an interior angle if the pentagon is regular.**

27c. No. ***Sample answer:*** **The numbers in the second row of the table are increasing by a smaller amount each time. The last increment was 4, so this increment will be less than 4, which would make $y < 148°$.**

28. regular quadrilateral; regular triangle; regular pentagon

29. **Baseball** In baseball, home plate is in the shape of a pentagon, as shown. Find the value of x. **135**

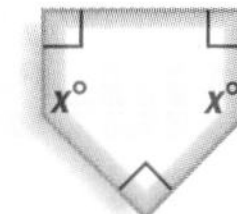

30. **Interpret** Generate a sequence by evaluating the expression $180 \cdot (n - 2)$ for $n = 3, 4, 5, 6$, and 7. Then tell whether the sequence is *arithmetic* or *geometric*. **180, 360, 540, 720, 900; arithmetic**

31. **Critical Thinking** Draw a convex polygon and show two exterior angles at each vertex. Why do the two exterior angles at one vertex of the polygon have the same measure?

31. See margin for art. *Sample answer:* Each combines with the same interior angle to form a straight angle.

32. The measures of the exterior angles of a triangle are $5x°$, $(x + 47)°$, and $(6x - 35)°$. Classify the triangle by its angles. Explain your reasoning.

32. Obtuse triangle. *Sample answer:* The measures of the exterior angles are 145°, 76°, and 139°. The interior angles measure 35°, 104°, and 41°, respectively. Since one of the angles is obtuse, the triangle is obtuse.

In Exercises 33–35, the sum of the measures of the interior angles of a convex polygon is given. Classify the polygon.

C 33. 1620° **11-gon** 34. 2160° **14-gon** 35. 2700° **17-gon**

36. **Challenge** Let $w°$, $x°$, $y°$, and $z°$ represent the measures of the interior angles of a quadrilateral. Show that the sum of the exterior angles, one exterior angle at each vertex, is 360°. **See margin.**

Mixed Review

Find the sum. *(Lesson 1.5)*

37. $8 + (-3)$ **5** 38. $-17 + 8$ **−9** 39. $-9 + (-5)$ **−14** 40. $-10 + (-12)$ **−22**

Graph the equation. Tell whether the equation is a function. *(Lesson 8.2)* **41–44. See margin for art.**

41. $y = 3x + 2$ **yes** 42. $y = -3$ **yes** 43. $y = x - 4$ **yes** 44. $x = 6$ **no**

Find the value of *x* that makes lines *m* and *n* parallel. *(Lesson 13.2)*

45. **15**

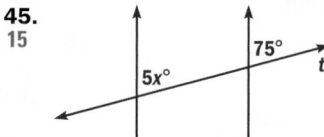

46. **8**

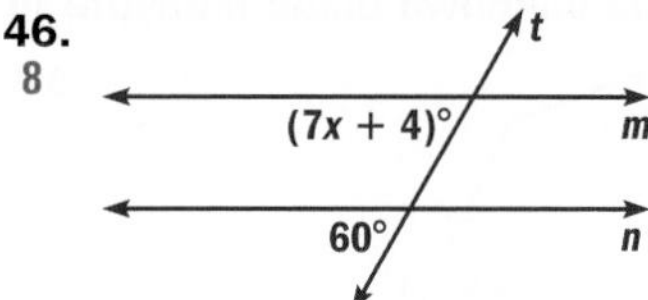

Standardized Test Practice

47. **Multiple Choice** The base of a gazebo is in the shape of a hexagon. What is the sum of the measures of the interior angles of the base? **C**

A. 360° **B.** 540° **C.** 720° **D.** 900°

48. **Multiple Choice** The shape of a traffic sign usually indicates the sign's meaning. The shape of a stop sign is always a regular octagon. What is the measure of an interior angle of a stop sign? **H**

F. 90° **G.** 108° **H.** 135° **I.** 144°

49. **Short Response** The 20 cent Euro coin has 7 indentations. If you connect the indentations with segments, you obtain a regular polygon, as shown. What is the measure of an exterior angle of the polygon? Explain your reasoning.

49. About 51.4°. *Sample answer:* For a regular polygon with 7 sides, an interior angle measures $\frac{(7-2) \cdot 180°}{7} \approx 128.6°$. The sum of the measures of an interior angle and an exterior angle at each vertex is 180°, so an exterior angle has a measure of about $180° - 128.6° = 51.4°$.

4 ASSESS

ASSESSMENT RESOURCES

For more assessment resources, see:

- Assessment Book
- Test and Practice Generator

MINI-QUIZ

Find the measure of an interior angle and the measure of an exterior angle for the regular polygon.

1. 16-gon **157.5°; 22.5°**
2. 20-gon **162°; 18°**
3. Find the unknown angle measure.

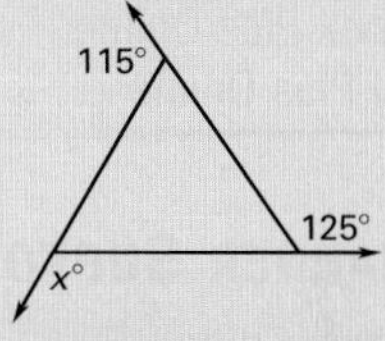

120°

4. **Challenge** In a regular polygon, the measure of each interior angle is $x°$ and the measure of each exterior angle is $2x°$. Find the value of x. **60**

5 FOLLOW-UP

DIAGNOSIS/REMEDIATION

- Study Guide in Chapter 13 Resource Book, pp. 27–28
- eTutorial Plus Online
- Extra Practice, p. 815
- Lesson Practice in Chapter 13 Resource Book, pp. 24–26

ENGLISH LEARNER SUPPORT

- Spanish Study Guide
- Multi-Language Visual Glossary
- Chapter Audio Summaries CDs

CHALLENGE

- Challenge Practice in Chapter 13 Resource Book, p. 29
- Teacher's Edition, p. 706F

ADDITIONAL RESOURCES

The following resources are available to help review the materials in Lessons 13.1–13.3.

Chapter 13 Resource Book
- Lesson Practice
- Study Guide

Assessment Book
- Chapter 13 Quiz 1

Technology
- Test and Practice Generator
- eTutorial CD-ROM

Internet
- Classzone
- eWorkbook Plus Online
- eTutorial Plus Online

ENGLISH LEARNER SUPPORT

- Spanish Study Guide
- Multi-Language Visual Glossary
- Chapter Audio Summaries CDs

Mid-Chapter Quiz

Tell whether the angles are *complementary*, *supplementary*, or *neither*.

1. $m\angle 1 = 54°$
$m\angle 2 = 126°$
supplementary

2. $m\angle 3 = 18°$
$m\angle 4 = 18°$
neither

3. $m\angle 5 = 37°$
$m\angle 6 = 53°$
complementary

Find $m\angle 1$.

4. 113°

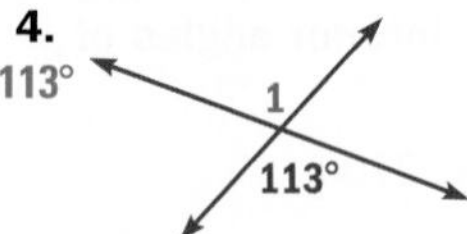

5. 48°

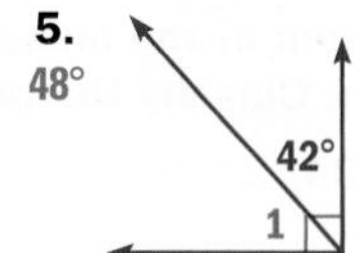

6. 45°

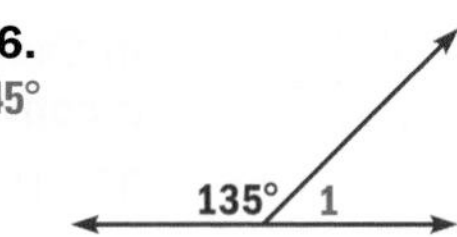

In Exercises 7–10, tell whether the angles in the diagram are *corresponding*, *alternate interior*, or *alternate exterior* angles.

7. $\angle 1$ and $\angle 8$
alternate exterior

8. $\angle 3$ and $\angle 6$
alternate exterior

9. $\angle 2$ and $\angle 7$
alternate interior

10. $\angle 2$ and $\angle 6$
corresponding

11. If $m\angle 6 = 112°$, find the measures of the other numbered angles in the diagram.
$m\angle 1 = 68°$, $m\angle 2 = 112°$, $m\angle 3 = 112°$, $m\angle 4 = 68°$, $m\angle 5 = 68°$, $m\angle 7 = 112°$, $m\angle 8 = 68°$

12. Find the measure of an interior angle of a regular pentagon. 108°

Find the unknown angle measure in the diagram.

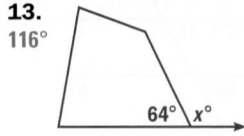

13. 116°

14. 122°

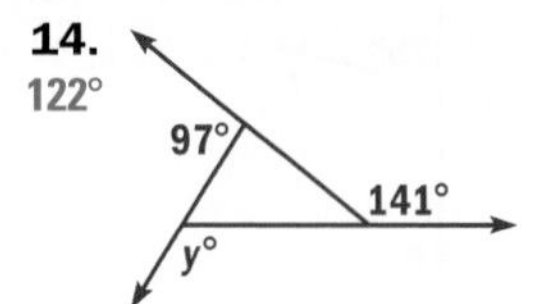

15. 94°

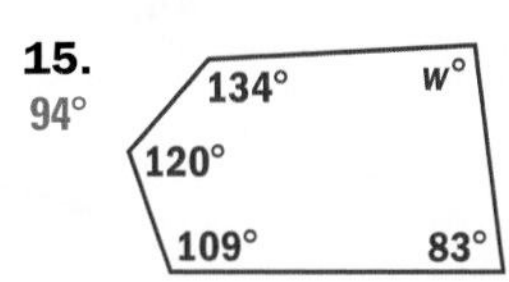

A Perfect Fit

In the figure shown, point X is the common vertex of an equilateral triangle, two squares, and a fourth regular polygon. Two of the sides of the fourth polygon are $\overline{XZ}$ and $\overline{XY}$. How many sides does the fourth polygon have? Explain your reasoning. 6 sides. *Sample answer:* The sum of the measures of the angles at the shared vertex is 360°. The sum of the measures of the angles from the two squares and the equilateral triangle is $90° + 90° + 60° = 240°$, so the measure of $\angle YXZ$ is 120°. Using the formula for the measure of each interior angle of a regular polygon when the angle measure is 120° gives $n = 6$.

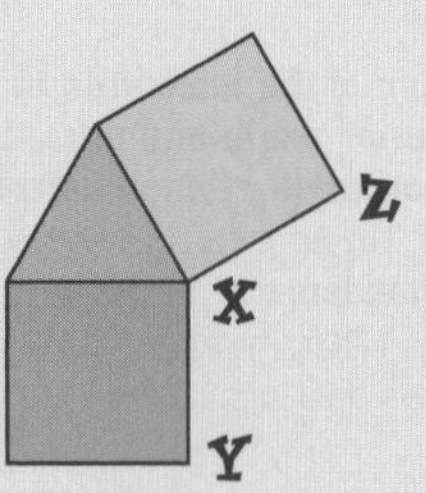

LESSON **13.4**

Translations

BEFORE	Now	WHY?
You plotted points in a coordinate plane.	You'll translate figures in a coordinate plane.	So you can create a design for a blanket, as in Ex. 12.

Vocabulary

transformation, p. 729
image, p. 729
translation, p. 729
tessellation, p. 730

Snow Tubing Snow tubing involves sliding down a snow-covered hill on an inflated tube. As you will see in Example 1, you can use a *translation* to describe a change in the position of a person sliding down a hill.

A **transformation** is a change made to the location or to the size of a figure. The new figure formed by a transformation is called an **image**. In this book, the original figure is blue, and the image is red. *Prime notation* is used to identify the image of point A. You read A' as "A prime."

A **translation** is a transformation in which each point of a figure moves the same distance in the same direction. In a translation, a figure and its image are congruent.

Example 1 *Describing a Translation*

For the diagram shown, describe the translation in words.

Solution

Think of moving horizontally and vertically from a point on the original figure to the corresponding point on the new figure. For instance, you move 200 feet to the right and 40 feet down from $A(0, 100)$ to reach $A'(200, 60)$.

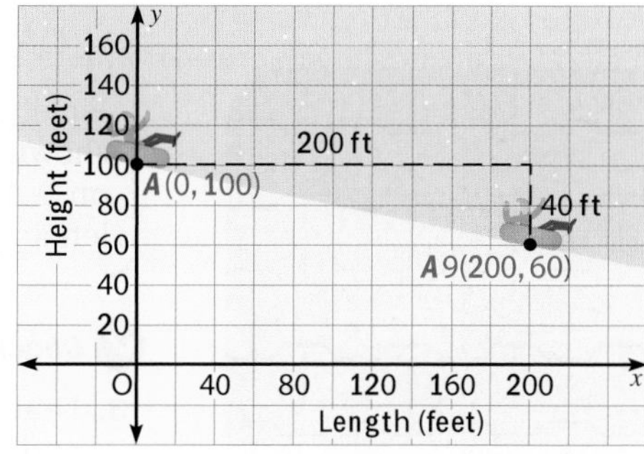

Checkpoint

Describe the translation in words.

1.

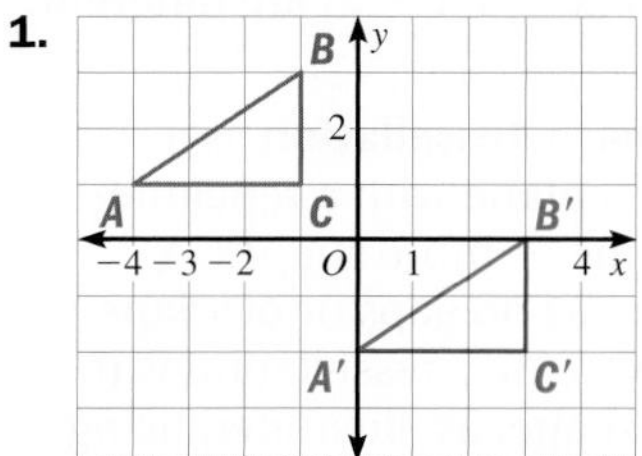

2.

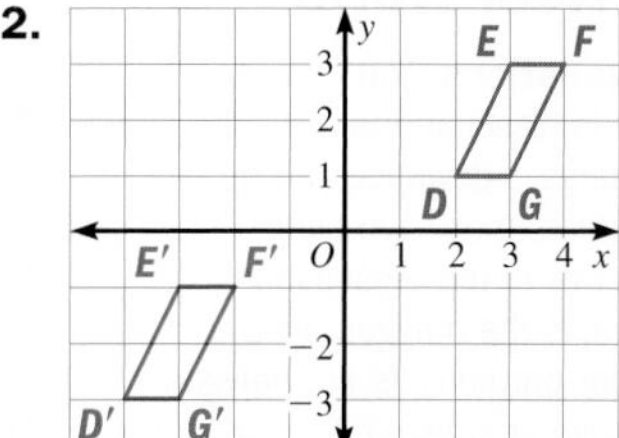

1. 4 units right and 3 units down
2. 6 units left and 4 units down

NCTM CURRICULUM STANDARDS

Standard 3: Analyze properties of 2-D shapes; Apply transformations to math situations; Use visualization to solve problems

1 PLAN

Skill Check

Name the point whose ordered pair is given.

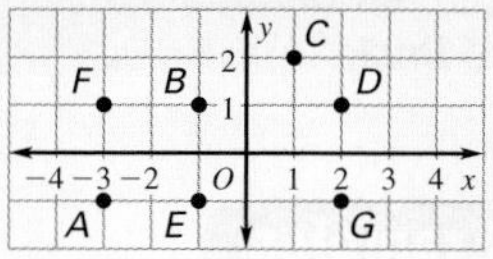

1. $(-1, 1)$ **B**
2. $(1, 2)$ **C**
3. $(-3, 1)$ **F**
4. $(2, -1)$ **G**

LESSON OBJECTIVE

Translate figures in a coordinate plane.

PACING

Suggested Number of Days
Basic Course: 1 day
Average Course: 1 day
Advanced Course: 1 day
Block: 0.5 block with 13.5

TEACHING RESOURCES

For a complete list of Teaching Resources, see page 706B.

TRANSPARENCY

Warm-Up Exercises for this lesson are available on a transparency. A support transparency is available for Example 2 and Checkpoint Exercise 3.

2 TEACH

MOTIVATING THE LESSON

Connect the words *translation* and *slide* by physically sliding a model of a polygon across the board.

TIPS *for* NEW TEACHERS

Encourage students to explore tessellations using library books and web sites that link mathematics to art. See Tips for New Teachers in the *Chapter 13 Resource Book*.

Extra Examples

Example 1 Describe the translation in words.

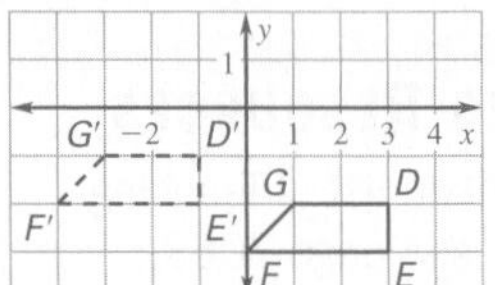

4 units right and 1 unit down

Example 2 Draw quadrilateral *DEFG* with vertices *D*(3, −2), *E*(3, −3), *F*(0, −3), and *G*(1, −2). Then find the coordinates of the vertices of the image after the translation $(x, y) \rightarrow (x - 4, y + 1)$, and draw the image. **D′(−1, −1), E′(−1, −2), F′(−4, −2), G′(−3, −1)**

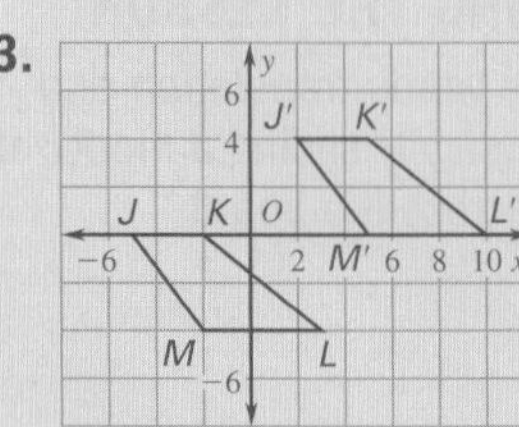

MULTIPLE REPRESENTATIONS

Coordinate notation is a way to describe translations algebraically. Students who have learned a dance routine or those in marching band might be able to help explain how coordinate notation works and provide a demonstration using the classroom floor as a large grid.

3.

Reading *Algebra*

In the translation $(x, y) \rightarrow (x + 4, y - 1)$, the expression $y - 1$ can be written as $y + (-1)$ to indicate that each point (x, y) of a figure moves 1 unit down.

Coordinate Notation You can describe a translation of each point (x, y) of a figure using the coordinate notation

$$(x, y) \rightarrow (x + a, y + b)$$

where *a* indicates how many units a point moves horizontally, and *b* indicates how many units a point moves vertically. Move the point (x, y) to the right if *a* is positive and to the left if *a* is negative. Move the point up if *b* is positive and down if *b* is negative.

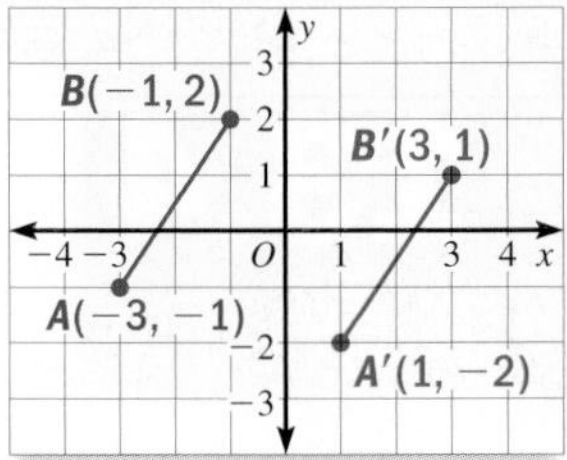

$(x, y) \rightarrow (x + 4, y - 1)$

Example 2 *Translating a Figure*

Draw $\triangle ABC$ with vertices *A*(3, −4), *B*(3, 0), and *C*(5, 2). Then find the coordinates of the vertices of the image after the translation $(x, y) \rightarrow (x - 6, y + 2)$, and draw the image.

Solution

First draw $\triangle ABC$. Then, to translate $\triangle ABC$, subtract 6 from the *x*-coordinate and add 2 to the *y*-coordinate of each vertex.

Original		Image
(x, y)	→	$(x - 6, y + 2)$
A(3, −4)	→	*A′*(−3, −2)
B(3, 0)	→	*B′*(−3, 2)
C(5, 2)	→	*C′*(−1, 4)

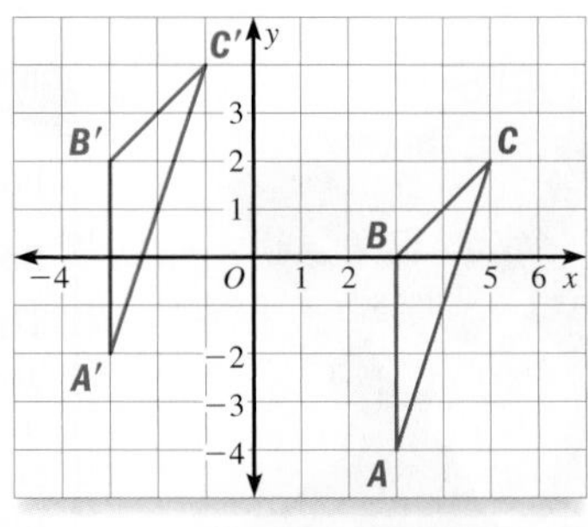

Finally, draw $\triangle A'B'C'$, as shown. Notice that each point on $\triangle ABC$ moves 6 units to the left and 2 units up.

Checkpoint

3. Draw quadrilateral *JKLM* with vertices *J*(−5, 0), *K*(−2, 0), *L*(3, −4), and *M*(−2, −4). Then find the coordinates of the vertices of the image after the translation $(x, y) \rightarrow (x + 7, y + 4)$, and draw the image. **See margin for art; J′(2, 4), K′(5, 4), L′(10, 0), M′(5, 0).**

4. **Compare** Describe how the translations $(x, y) \rightarrow (x + 3, y + 2)$ and $(x, y) \rightarrow (x - 3, y + 2)$ are different. ***Sample answer:* In the first, the translation is 3 units right and 2 units up, while in the second, the translation is 3 units left and 2 units up.**

In the **Real World**

Tessellations You can see various tessellations on buildings, sidewalks, and other structures that have tiling patterns. In the tessellation above, is the polygon used a regular polygon? Is the polygon *concave* or *convex*? **No; concave.**

Tessellations A **tessellation** is a covering of a plane with a repeating pattern of one or more shapes. A tessellation has no gaps or overlaps. One way to create a tessellation is to translate a shape, as illustrated using a parallelogram.

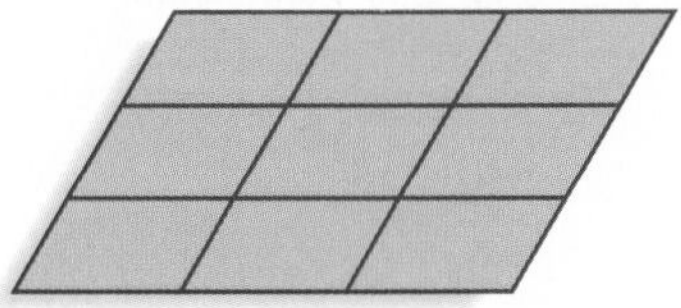

Example 3 *Creating Tessellations*

Tell whether you can create a tessellation using only translations of the given polygon. If you can, create a tessellation. If not, explain why not.

a. 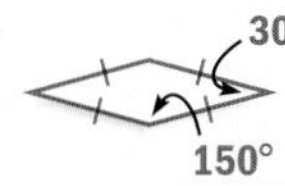

b. 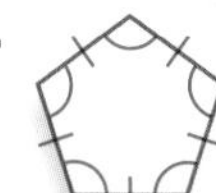

Solution

a. You can translate the rhombus to create a tessellation. Notice in the design that there are no gaps or overlaps.

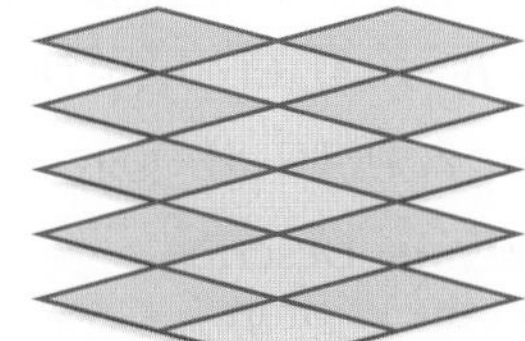

b. You can't translate a regular pentagon to create a tessellation. As shown below, there will be gaps or overlaps.

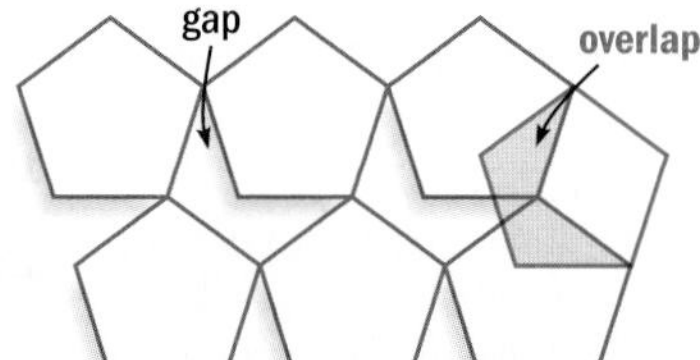

Study *Strategy*

Notice in part (a) of Example 3 that the two 30° angles and the two 150° angles at each vertex in the tessellation have a total measure of 360°.

13.4 Exercises

More Practice, p. 815

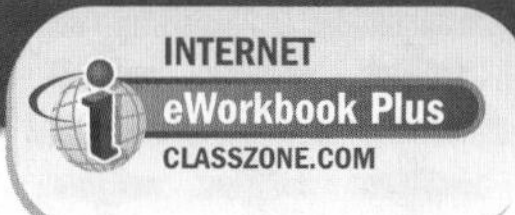

Guided Practice

Vocabulary Check

1. Copy and complete: The figure formed by a translation of a figure is the _?_ of the figure. **image**

2. Describe the translation $(x, y) \rightarrow (x + 3, y - 7)$ in words.
3 units right and 7 units down

Skill Check **Describe the translation in words.**

3. 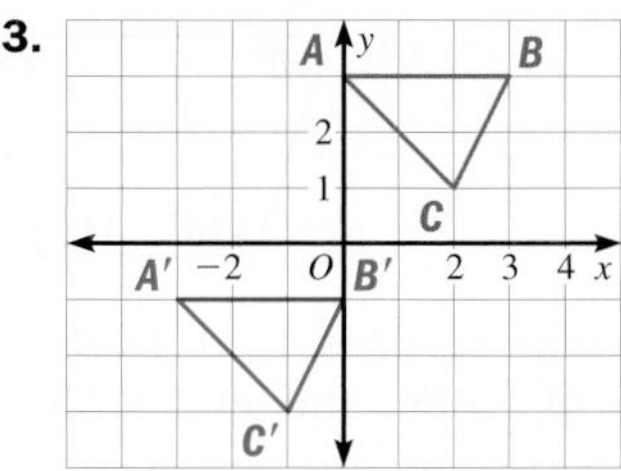

3 units left and 4 units down

4. 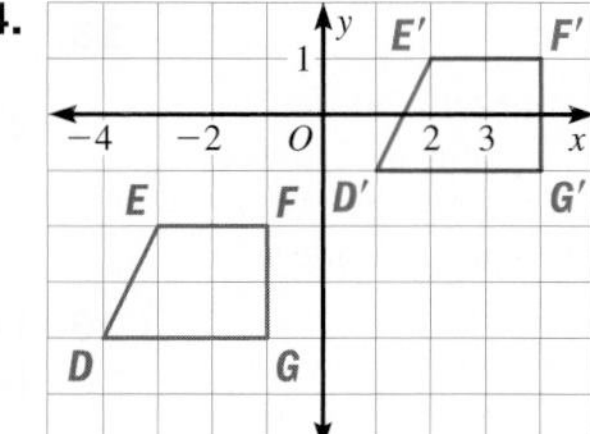

5 units right and 3 units up

5. Draw $\triangle DEF$ with vertices $D(-1, -6)$, $E(-2, 4)$, and $F(3, -2)$. Then find the coordinates of the vertices of the image after the translation $(x, y) \rightarrow (x - 2, y - 1)$, and draw the image.
See margin for art; $D'(-3, -7)$, $E'(-4, 3)$, $F'(1, -3)$.

Extra Examples

Example 3 Tell whether you can create a tessellation using only translations of the given polygon. If not, explain why not.

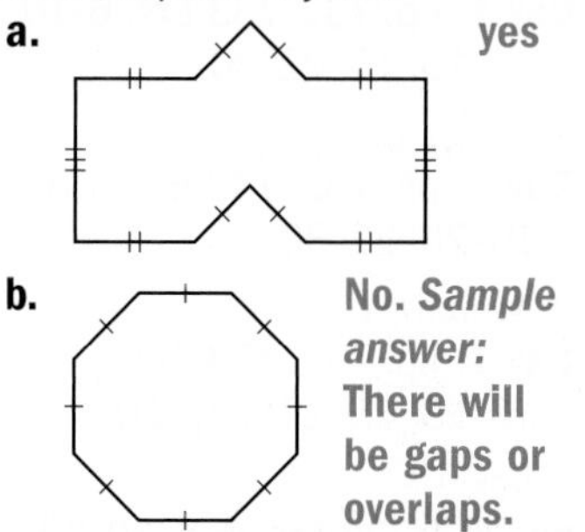

a. **yes**

b. **No. *Sample answer:* There will be gaps or overlaps.**

Differentiating Instruction

Advanced Students Challenge students to discover which regular polygons can tessellate a plane (triangle, square, hexagon). Ask them to determine or research how the interior angle measures of these polygons indicate this trait.

Common Error

In Example 3, watch for students who rotate the polygons to try to make them tessellate. Stress that rotations are not translations.

Concept Check

What are the coordinates of the point $F(-3, 5)$ after the translation $(x, y) \rightarrow (x - 2, y - 10)$?
$F'(-5, -5)$

Daily Puzzler

The area of $\triangle DEF$ is exactly five times the area of $\triangle ABC$, which has angle measures of 90°, 40°, and 50°. What is the sum of the angle measures of $\triangle DEF$? **180°**

5. See Additional Answers beginning on page AA1.

3 APPLY

ASSIGNMENT GUIDE

Basic Course

Day 1: pp. 732–733 Exs. 6–10, 12–15, 17, 22–30

Average Course

Day 1: pp. 732–733 Exs. 6–8, 10–20, 22–30

Advanced Course

Day 1: pp. 732–733 Exs. 7, 10–13, 15–22*, 27–30

Block

pp. 732–733 Exs. 6–8, 10–20, 22–30 (with 13.5)

EXTRA PRACTICE

- Student Edition, p. 815
- Chapter 13 Resource Book, pp. 33–35
- Test and Practice Generator

TRANSPARENCY

Even-numbered answers are available on transparencies. A support transparency is available for Exercises 5, 8–10, 12, and 16.

HOMEWORK CHECK

When you review students' homework for this lesson, go over the following exercises to check understanding of key concepts.

Basic: 6, 8, 10, 13, 15
Average: 6, 8, 12, 14, 15
Advanced: 7, 10, 13, 15, 16

8–10. See Additional Answers beginning on page AA1.

12c. (graph)

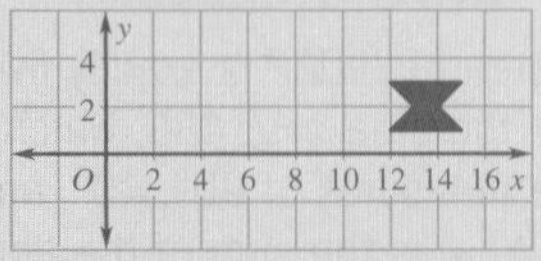

13, 15, 16a–b, 17. See Additional Answers beginning on page AA1.

Practice and Problem Solving

Homework *Help*

Example	Exercises
1	6-7, 16
2	8-12, 16
3	13-15

Online Resources CLASSZONE.COM
- More Examples
- eTutorial Plus

Describe the translation in words.

A **6.**

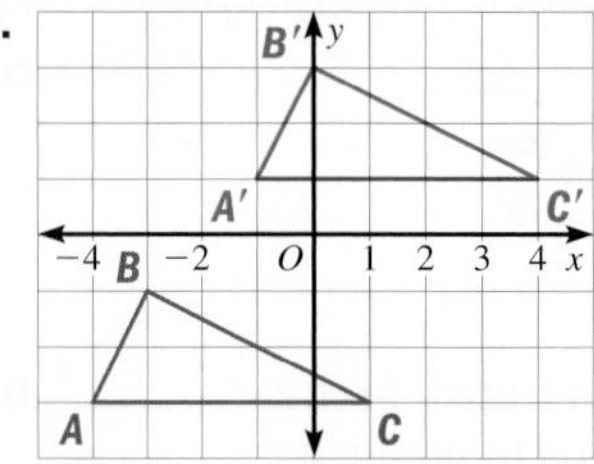

3 units right and 4 units up

7. (graph)

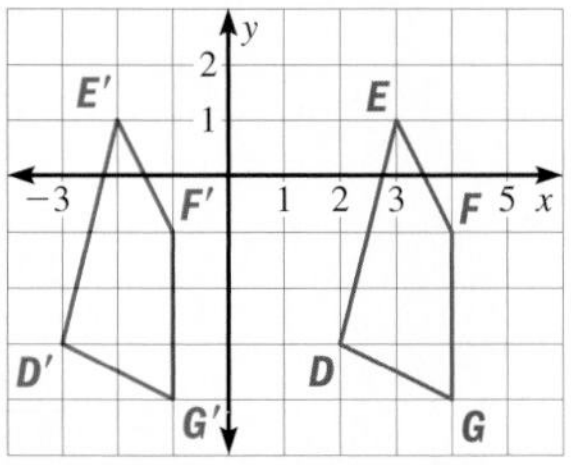

5 units left

The vertices of a polygon are given. Draw the polygon. Then find the coordinates of the vertices of the image after the specified translation, and draw the image. 8–10. See margin for art.

8. $P(-5, 4)$, $Q(1, 4)$, $R(1, 1)$; $(x, y) \to (x + 1, y - 6)$
$P'(-4, -2)$, $Q'(2, -2)$, $R'(2, -5)$

9. $A(-2, -1)$, $B(-3, 4)$, $C(-1, 3)$, $D(-1, -1)$; $(x, y) \to (x - 4, y - 2)$

10. $J(-3, 2)$, $K(-2, 1)$, $L(1, 1)$, $M(1, -2)$, $N(0, -4)$; $(x, y) \to (x - 3, y)$

9. $A'(-6, -3)$, $B'(-7, 2)$, $C'(-5, 1)$, $D'(-5, -3)$

10. $J'(-6, 2)$, $K'(-5, 1)$, $L'(-2, 1)$, $M'(-2, -2)$, $N'(-3, -4)$

11. Error Analysis Describe and correct the error in finding the coordinates of the endpoints of the image of $\overline{AB}$ after the translation $(x, y) \to (x + 3, y - 4)$.

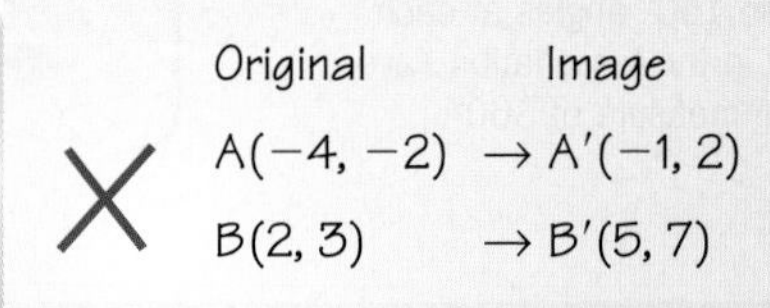

11. *Sample answer:* For the *y*-coordinates, the translation is $y - 4$, which means that 4 should be subtracted from the original *y*-coordinates instead of added. The correct image points are $A'(-1, -6)$ and $B'(5, -1)$.

12. Blankets You can create designs for a blanket using translations.

a. Use coordinate notation to describe the translation from figure 1 to figure 2. $(x, y) \to (x + 4, y)$

b. Use coordinate notation to describe the translation from figure 2 to figure 3. $(x, y) \to (x + 4, y)$

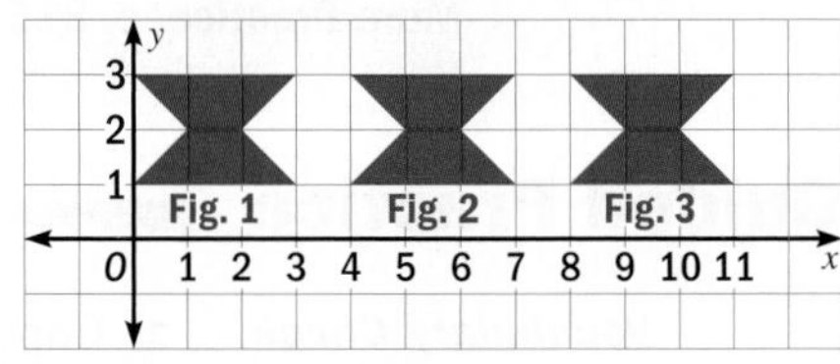

c. Use your answers to parts (a) and (b) to draw figure 4. See margin.

Tell whether you can create a tessellation using only translations of the given polygon. If you can, create a tessellation. If not, explain why not.

13.

Yes; see margin for art.

14. (trapezoid with angles 70°, 70°, 110°, 110°)

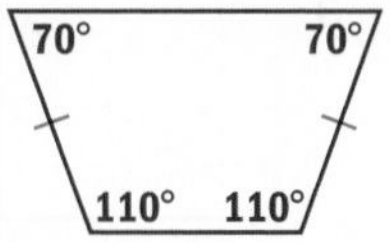

14. No. *Sample answer:* A tessellation cannot be created from the given shape without flipping or turning the figure.

15. (hexagon)

Yes; see margin for art.

B **16.** Draw $\triangle ABC$ with vertices $A(-4, 1)$, $B(1, 2)$, and $C(1, -3)$. Let $\triangle A'B'C'$ be the image of $\triangle ABC$, and let $\triangle A''B''C''$ be the image of $\triangle A'B'C'$.

a. Draw $\triangle A'B'C'$ using the translation $(x, y) \to (x + 2, y - 5)$.

b. Draw $\triangle A''B''C''$ using the translation $(x, y) \to (x - 4, y - 3)$.
16a–b. See margin for art.

c. How could you move $\triangle ABC$ to $\triangle A''B''C''$ using only one translation?
Translate $\triangle ABC$ 2 units left and 8 units down.

18. $(x, y) \to (x + 3, y - 5)$. *Sample answer:* To translate from the image to the original figure, you must "undo" the original translation. Since the original move was 3 units left, the new move is 3 units right. Since the original move was 5 units up, the new move is 5 units down.

19. Yes. *Sample answer:* Begin with $(2, -7)$. Applying $(x, y) \to (x - 3, y - 4)$ gives $(-1, -11)$. Then applying $(x, y) \to (x + 2, y - 6)$ to $(-1, -11)$ gives $(1, -17)$. If instead you first apply $(x, y) \to (x + 2, y - 6)$ to $(2, -7)$, you get $(4, -13)$. Then applying $(x, y) \to (x - 3, y - 4)$ to $(4, -13)$ gives $(1, -17)$, which is the same result.

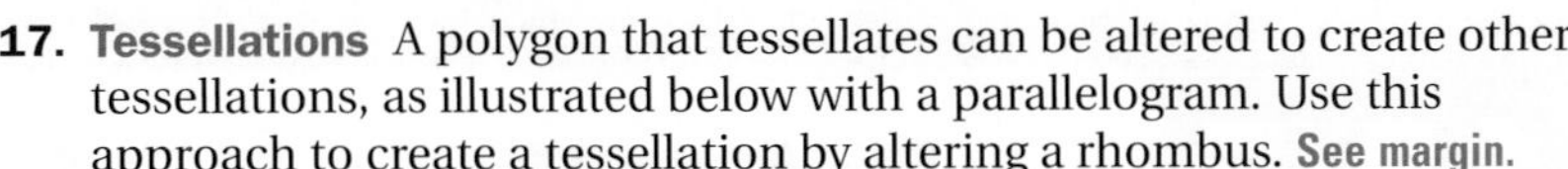

17. Tessellations A polygon that tessellates can be altered to create other tessellations, as illustrated below with a parallelogram. Use this approach to create a tessellation by altering a rhombus. **See margin.**

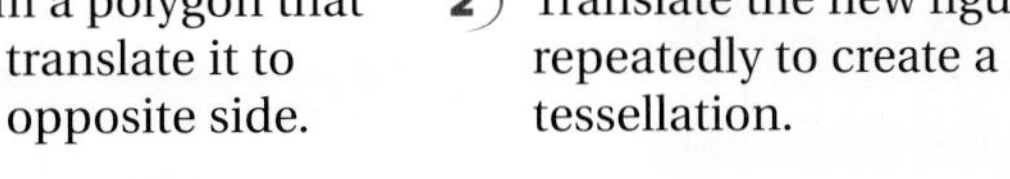

(1) Cut a piece from a polygon that tessellates and translate it to any part of the opposite side.

(2) Translate the new figure repeatedly to create a tessellation.

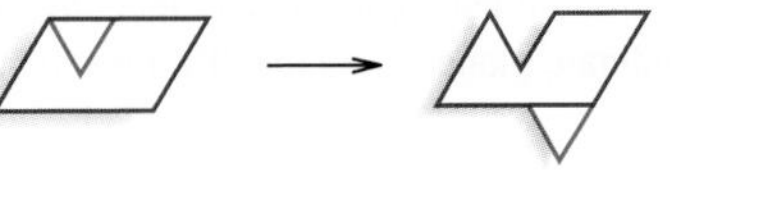

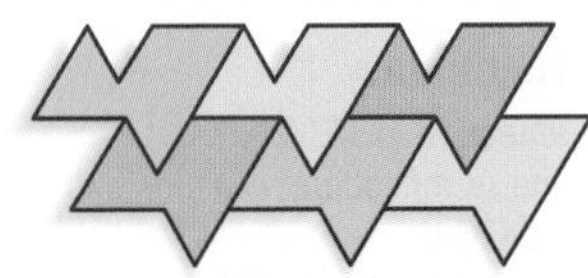

18. ***Writing*** You translate a figure using $(x, y) \to (x - 3, y + 5)$. Use coordinate notation to describe the translation from the image to the original figure. Explain your reasoning.

19. Critical Thinking You translate a figure using $(x, y) \to (x - 3, y - 4)$. You then translate its image using $(x, y) \to (x + 2, y - 6)$. If you switch the order of the translations, is the final image the same? Justify your answer with an example.

C **20. Escalators** Use the diagram of the escalator shown.

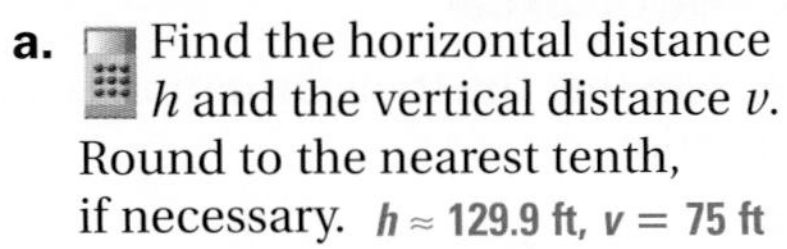

a. Find the horizontal distance h and the vertical distance v. Round to the nearest tenth, if necessary. **$h \approx 129.9$ ft, $v = 75$ ft**

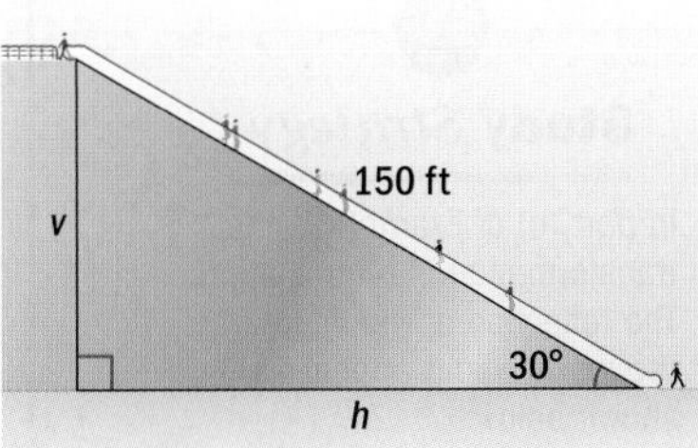

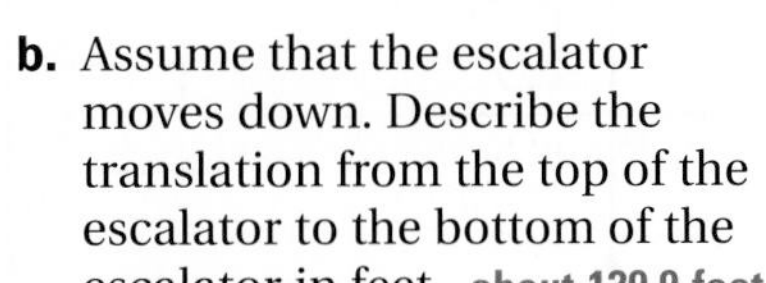

b. Assume that the escalator moves down. Describe the translation from the top of the escalator to the bottom of the escalator in feet. **about 129.9 feet right and 75 feet down**

21. Challenge Given points $A(-6, -4)$ and $B(5, 5)$, use coordinate notation to describe a translation from A to the midpoint of $\overline{AB}$. **$(x, y) \to (x + 5.5, y + 4.5)$**

Mixed Review

Find the product. *(Lesson 1.7)*

22. $-8 \cdot (-3)$ **24** **23.** $-12 \cdot 5$ **−60** **24.** $9 \cdot (-4)$ **−36**

Find the distance between the points. *(Lesson 9.5)*

25. $(3, -2), (3, 2)$ **4 units** **26.** $(5, 9), (-2, 4)$ **$\sqrt{74}$ units** **27.** $(3, -1), (-2, -5)$ **$\sqrt{41}$ units**

28. Find the measure of an interior angle of a regular 9-gon. *(Lesson 13.3)* **140°**

Standardized Test Practice

In Exercises 29 and 30, $\triangle ABC$ has vertices $A(1, 2)$, $B(5, 3)$, and $C(4, 1)$. Let $\triangle A'B'C'$ be the image of $\triangle ABC$ after the translation $(x, y) \to (x - 3, y + 2)$.

29. Multiple Choice What are the coordinates of B'? **D**

A. $(-3, 2)$ **B.** $(-2, 4)$ **C.** $(-1, 3)$ **D.** $(2, 5)$

30. Multiple Choice In which quadrant does A' lie? **G**

F. Quadrant I **G.** Quadrant II **H.** Quadrant III **I.** Quadrant IV

4 ASSESS

Assessment Resources

For more assessment resources, see:
- Assessment Book
- Test and Practice Generator

Mini-Quiz

The vertices of a polygon are given. Find the coordinates of the vertices of the image after the specified translation.

1. $Q(-3, -2)$, $R(-1, 3)$, $S(1, 4)$; $(x, y) \to (x - 2, y + 3)$ **$Q'(-5, 1)$, $R'(-3, 6)$, $S'(-1, 7)$**
2. $D(-1, 1)$, $E(3, 2)$, $F(2, -2)$, $G(-2, -3)$; $(x, y) \to (x + 1, y - 5)$ **$D'(0, -4)$, $E'(4, -3)$, $F'(3, -7)$, $G'(-1, -8)$**
3. **Challenge** Given points $A(5, -1)$, $B(-3, -4)$, and $C(3, -12)$, use coordinate notation to describe a translation from A to the midpoint of $\overline{BC}$. **$(x, y) \to (x - 5, y - 7)$**

5 FOLLOW-UP

Diagnosis/Remediation

- Study Guide in Chapter 13 Resource Book, pp. 36–37
- Tutor Place, Geometry and Measurement Card 19
- eTutorial Plus Online
- Extra Practice, p. 815
- Lesson Practice in Chapter 13 Resource Book, pp. 33–35

English Learner Support

- Spanish Study Guide
- Multi-Language Visual Glossary
- Chapter Audio Summaries CDs

Challenge

- Challenge Practice in Chapter 13 Resource Book, p. 38
- Teacher's Edition, p. 706F

1 PLAN

Skill Check

State the opposite.

1. −8 8 **2.** 3.5 −3.5

3. 0 0 **4.** $-\frac{1}{2}$ $\frac{1}{2}$

LESSON OBJECTIVE

Reflect figures and identify lines of symmetry.

PACING

Suggested Number of Days

Basic Course: 1 day
Average Course: 1 day
Advanced Course: 1 day
Block: 0.5 block with 13.4

TEACHING RESOURCES

For a complete list of Teaching Resources, see page 706B.

TRANSPARENCY

Warm-Up Exercises for this lesson are available on a transparency. A support transparency is available for Example 2 and Checkpoint Exercise 1.

2 TEACH

MOTIVATING THE LESSON

Challenge students to write their name so its reflection will appear correct when viewed in a mirror.

TIPS *for* NEW TEACHERS

Expect some students to have difficulty visualizing reflections and understanding how a reflection relates to a coordinate change. See Tips for New Teachers in the *Chapter 13 Resource Book*.

LESSON 13.5 Reflections *and* Symmetry

BEFORE	Now	WHY?
You translated figures in a coordinate plane.	You'll reflect figures and identify lines of symmetry.	So you can analyze the symmetry of flags, as in Example 3.

Vocabulary

reflection, p. 734
line of reflection, p. 734
line symmetry, p. 735
line of symmetry, p. 735

Birds In the photo, a bird is reflected in a pool of water to produce a mirror image. A **reflection** is a transformation in which a figure is reflected, or flipped, in a line, called the **line of reflection**. In the photo, the red line is a line of reflection.

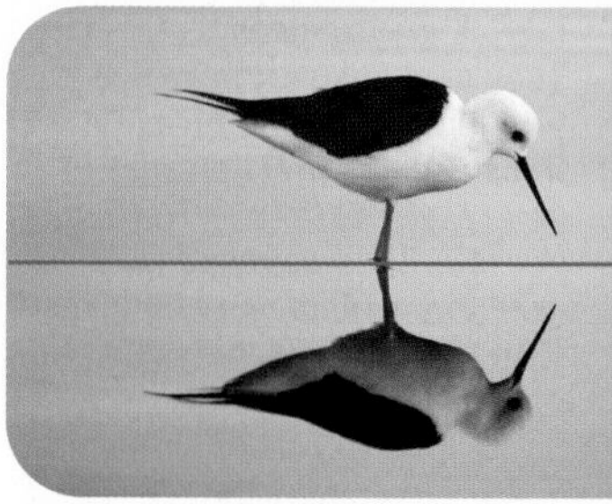

Example 1 *Identifying Reflections*

Tell whether the transformation is a reflection. If so, identify the line of reflection.

a.

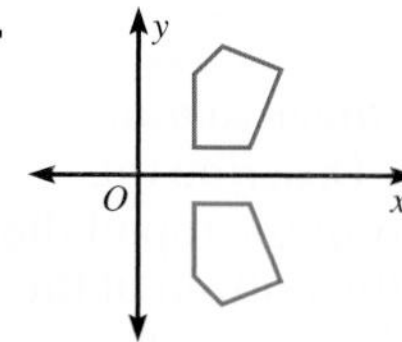

b.

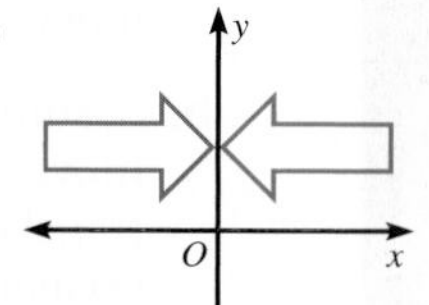

c.

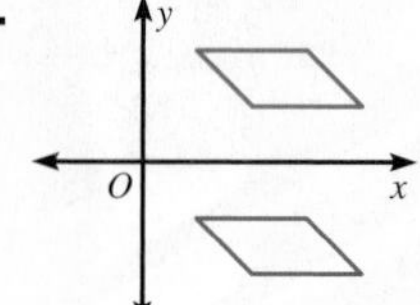

Solution

a. Reflection in x-axis **b.** Reflection in y-axis **c.** Not a reflection

Study *Strategy*

In part (c) of Example 1, the transformation is a translation. The reflection of the figure in the x-axis would appear as shown below:

Coordinate Notation You can use coordinate notation to describe the images of figures after reflections in the axes of a coordinate plane.

Reflection in the x-axis

A(−2, 3), B(4, 1), A′(−2, −3), B′(4, −1)

Multiply the y-coordinate by −1.
$(x, y) \rightarrow (x, -y)$

Reflection in the y-axis

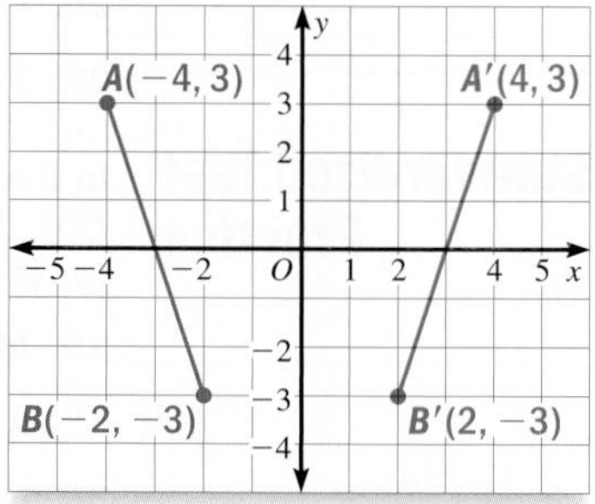

Multiply the x-coordinate by −1.
$(x, y) \rightarrow (-x, y)$

NCTM CURRICULUM STANDARDS

Standard 3: Describe spatial relationships using coordinate geometry; Apply transformations to math situations; Use symmetry to analyze math situations

Study *Strategy*

In a reflection, a point and its image are the same distance from the line of reflection. Notice that in Example 2, B and B' are both 3 units from the y-axis, which is the line of reflection.

Example 2 *Reflecting a Triangle*

Draw $\triangle ABC$ with vertices $A(1, -1)$, $B(3, 2)$, and $C(4, -3)$. Then find the coordinates of the vertices of the image after a reflection in the y-axis, and draw the image.

Solution

First draw $\triangle ABC$. Then, to reflect $\triangle ABC$ in the y-axis, multiply the x-coordinate of each vertex by -1.

Original		Image
(x, y)	$\to$	$(-x, y)$
$A(1, -1)$	$\to$	$A'(-1, -1)$
$B(3, 2)$	$\to$	$B'(-3, 2)$
$C(4, -3)$	$\to$	$C'(-4, -3)$

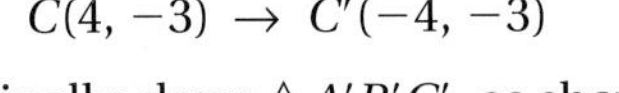

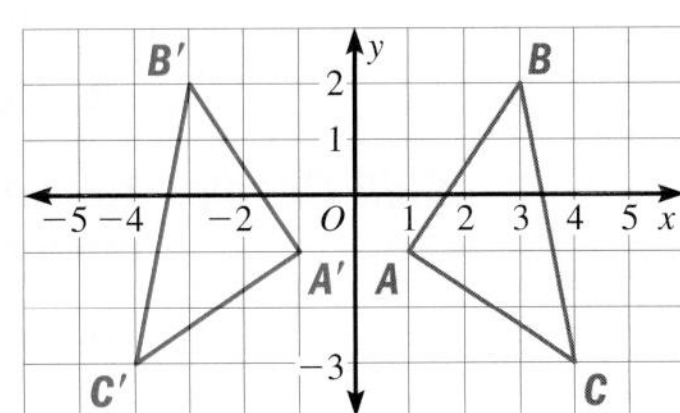

Finally, draw $\triangle A'B'C'$, as shown.

Checkpoint

1. Draw $\triangle ABC$ with vertices $A(-1, 3)$, $B(2, 4)$, and $C(4, 1)$. Then find the coordinates of the vertices of the image of $\triangle ABC$ after a reflection in the x-axis, and draw the image.
$A'(-1, -3)$, $B'(2, -4)$, $C'(4, -1)$; see margin for art.

Line Symmetry A figure has **line symmetry** if a line, called the **line of symmetry**, divides the figure into two parts that are reflections of each other in the line. A figure may have more than one line of symmetry.

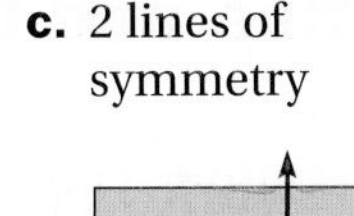

Example 3 *Identifying Lines of Symmetry*

Flags **Tell how many lines of symmetry the flag has.**

a. 1 line of symmetry

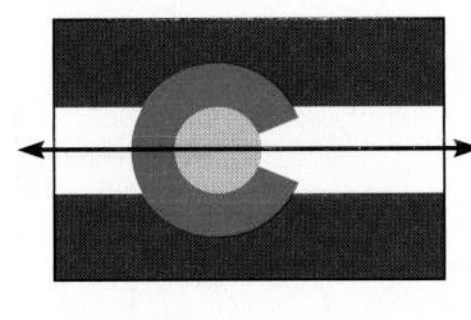

Colorado

b. No lines of symmetry

Puerto Rico

c. 2 lines of symmetry

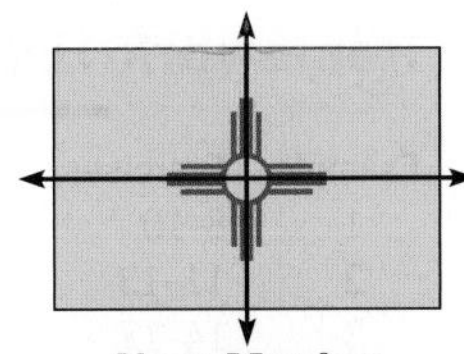

New Mexico

Checkpoint

Tell how many lines of symmetry the figure has.

2.

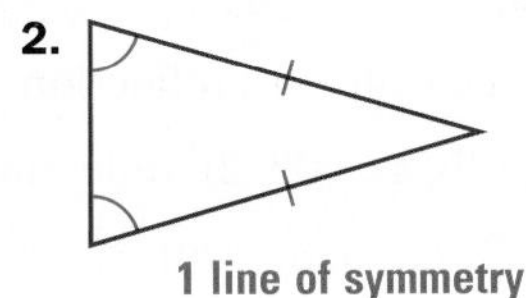

1 line of symmetry

3.

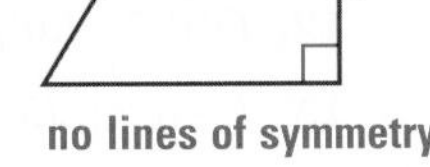

no lines of symmetry

4.

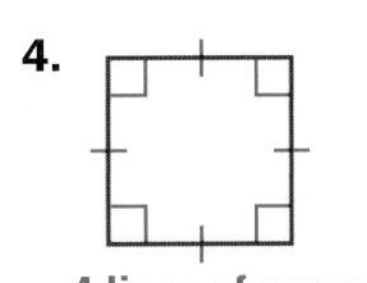

4 lines of symmetry

Extra Examples

Example 1 Tell whether the transformation is a reflection. If so, identify the line of reflection.

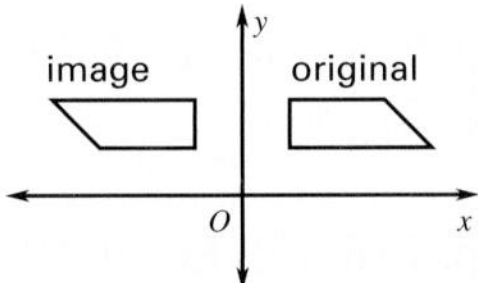

not a reflection

Example 2 $\triangle DEF$ has vertices $D(2, 2)$, $E(1, -1)$, and $F(-2, 1)$. Find the coordinates of the vertices of the image after a reflection in the x-axis. **$D'(2, -2)$, $E'(1, 1)$, $F'(-2, -1)$**

Example 3 Tell how many lines of symmetry each figure has.

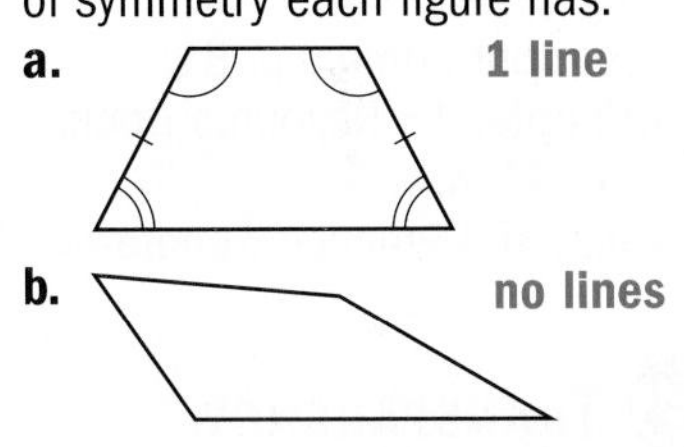

a. **1 line**

b. **no lines**

ALGEBRAIC REASONING

Emphasize the coordinate notation on page 734 to help students see how a reflection in either axis is related to a change in just one of the coordinates.

CONCEPT CHECK

When a point is reflected in the y-axis, what coordinate do the point and its image have in common? **y-coordinate**

DAILY PUZZLER

Which capital letters in the English alphabet look the same when viewed in a mirror? **A, H, I M, O, T, U, V, W, X, Y**

1. See Additional Answers beginning on page AA1.

3 APPLY

ASSIGNMENT GUIDE

Basic Course

Day 1: pp. 736–738 Exs. 8–16, 18, 19, 22, 25–34

Average Course

Day 1: pp. 736–738 Exs. 9–12, 14–18, 20–23, 25–35

Advanced Course

Day 1: pp. 736–738 Exs. 10–13, 15–17, 19–26*, 31–35

Block

pp. 736–738 Exs. 9–12, 14–18, 20–23, 25–35 (with 13.4)

EXTRA PRACTICE

- Student Edition, p. 815
- Chapter 13 Resource Book, pp. 41–43
- Test and Practice Generator

TRANSPARENCY

Even-numbered answers are available on transparencies. A support transparency is available for Exercises 6, 11–13, 18–21, 24, and 33.

HOMEWORK CHECK

When you review students' homework for this lesson, go over the following exercises to check understanding of key concepts.

Basic: 8, 10, 11, 13, 14

Average: 9, 11, 12, 14, 15

Advanced: 10, 11, 12, 16, 17

6.

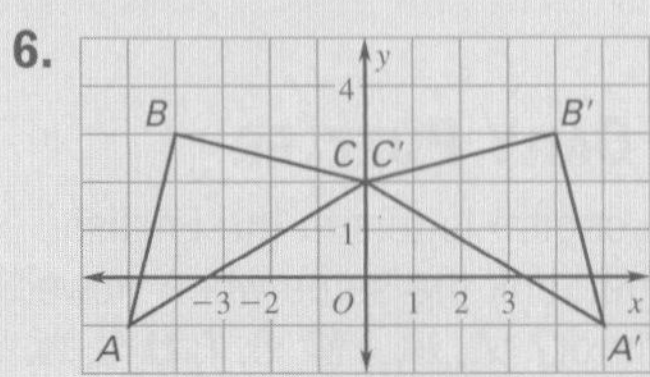

11–13. See Additional Answers beginning on page AA1.

13.5 Exercises

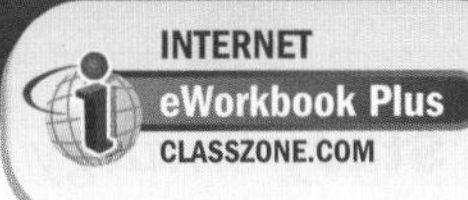

More Practice, p. 815

Guided Practice

Vocabulary Check

1. A figure lies in the first quadrant of a coordinate plane. It is reflected in the x-axis. In which quadrant does the image of the figure lie? **Quadrant IV**

2. How many lines of symmetry does a 3 inch by 4 inch rectangle have? **2 lines of symmetry**

Skill Check **Tell whether the transformation is a reflection. If so, identify the line of reflection.**

3. **4.** no **5.**

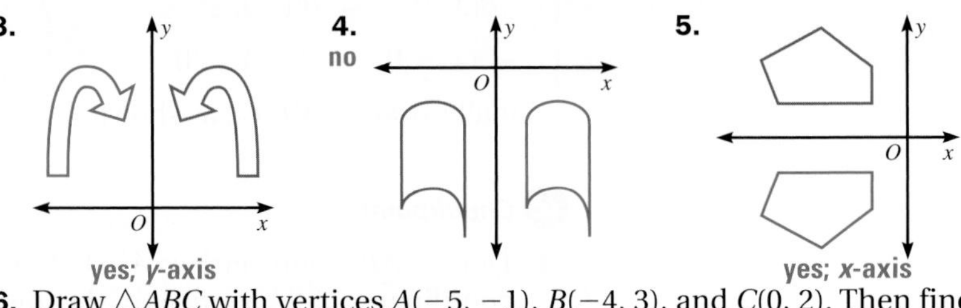

3. **yes; y-axis** 5. **yes; x-axis**

6. Draw $\triangle ABC$ with vertices $A(-5, -1)$, $B(-4, 3)$, and $C(0, 2)$. Then find the coordinates of the vertices of the image after a reflection in the y-axis, and draw the image. **See margin for art; $A'(5, -1)$, $B'(4, 3)$, $C'(0, 2)$.**

7. **Error Analysis** Describe and correct the error in finding the coordinates of the endpoints of the image of $\overline{AB}$ after a reflection in the x-axis.

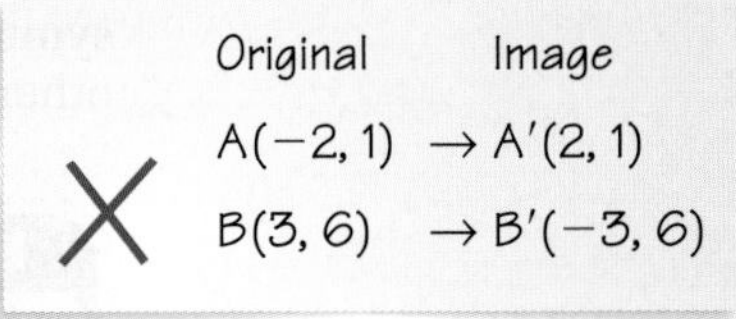

Original
Image
A(−2, 1) → A'(2, 1)
B(3, 6) → B'(−3, 6)

7. ***Sample answer:*** **For a reflection in the x-axis, the y-coordinate is multiplied by −1. The translation shown is a reflection in the y-axis, in which the x-coordinate is multiplied by −1. The correct image points are $A'(-2, -1)$ and $B'(3, -6)$.**

Practice and Problem Solving

Homework *Help*

Example	Exercises
1	8–10
2	11–13
3	14–17

Online Resources CLASSZONE.COM

- More Examples
- eTutorial Plus

Tell whether the transformation is a reflection. If so, identify the line of reflection.

A **8.** **9.** **10.** no

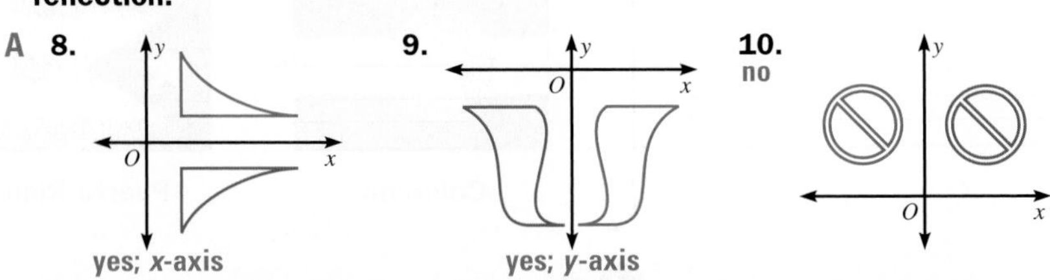

8. **yes; x-axis** 9. **yes; y-axis**

The vertices of a polygon are given. Draw the polygon. Then find the coordinates of the vertices of the image after the specified reflection, and draw the image. **11–13. See margin for art.**

11. $A(1, -2)$, $B(3, -1)$, $C(4, -4)$; reflection in the x-axis **$A'(1, 2)$, $B'(3, 1)$, $C'(4, 4)$**

12. $D(1, 7)$, $E(6, 8)$, $F(5, 4)$, $G(2, 2)$; reflection in the y-axis **$D'(-1, 7)$, $E'(-6, 8)$, $F'(-5, 4)$, $G'(-2, 2)$**

13. $J(-6, 4)$, $K(-4, 7)$, $L(-3, 8)$, $M(0, 5)$, $N(-1, 2)$; reflection in the y-axis **$J'(6, 4)$, $K'(4, 7)$, $L'(3, 8)$, $M'(0, 5)$, $N'(1, 2)$**

Tell how many lines of symmetry the figure has.

14. 
1 line of symmetry

15. 
2 lines of symmetry

16. 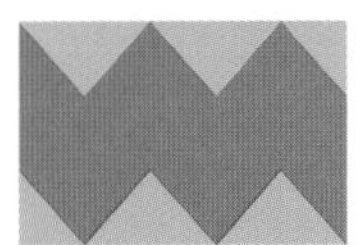
no lines of symmetry

17. Extended Problem Solving The table shows several regular polygons.

Regular polygon	Quadrilateral	Pentagon	Hexagon	Octagon
Drawing of regular polygon				
Lines of symmetry	4	? 5	? 6	? 8

a. Copy and complete the table by drawing the lines of symmetry that each polygon has and recording the number of lines of symmetry. See margin for art.

b. Analyze How is the number of sides of a regular polygon related to the number of lines of symmetry? They are the same.

c. Predict Predict the number of lines of symmetry that a regular 28-gon has. 28 lines of symmetry

Draw the polygon shown. Then find the coordinates of the vertices of the final image after the specified transformations, and draw the final image. 18–19. See margin for art.

B **18.** Reflect the polygon in the x-axis, then translate the image using $(x, y) \to (x + 2, y + 4)$.

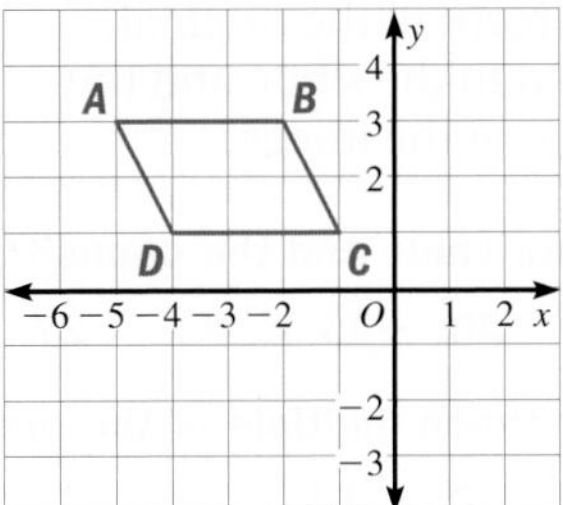

$A''(-3, 1)$, $B''(0, 1)$, $C''(1, 3)$, $D''(-2, 3)$

19. Reflect the polygon in the y-axis, then translate the image using $(x, y) \to (x + 5, y - 1)$.

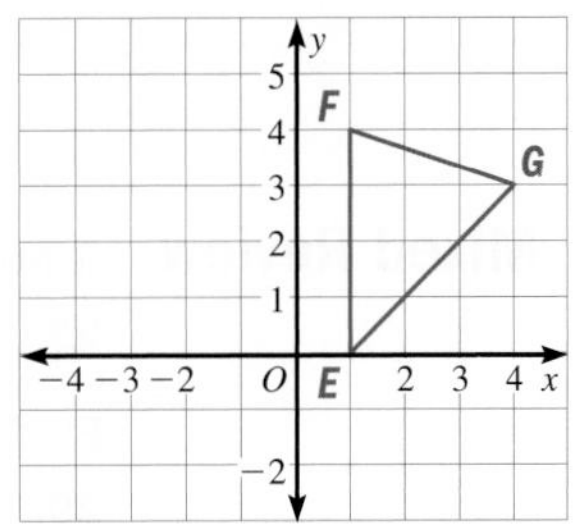

$E''(4, -1)$, $F''(4, 3)$, $G''(1, 2)$

20. Let $\triangle ABC$ have vertices $A(-5, 4)$, $B(-1, 3)$, and $C(-2, 1)$, and let $\triangle DEF$ have vertices $D(0, -4)$, $E(3, -1)$, and $F(6, -6)$.

a. Reflect $\triangle ABC$ in the y-axis, then reflect its image in the x-axis. What are the coordinates of the vertices of the final image? See margin for art; $A''(5, -4)$, $B''(1, -3)$, $C''(2, -1)$.

b. Reflect $\triangle DEF$ in the x-axis, then reflect its image in the y-axis. What are the coordinates of the vertices of the final image? See margin for art; $D''(0, 4)$, $E''(-3, 1)$, $F''(-6, 6)$.

c. Critical Thinking Use coordinate notation to describe how a reflection of a figure in one axis followed by a reflection of its image in the other axis can be performed in one step. $(x, y) \to (-x, -y)$

TEACHING TIP

In Exercises 18 and 19, urge students to read the directions carefully. Point out that the second transformation is to be performed on the first image, not on the original figure.

17a. 

18. 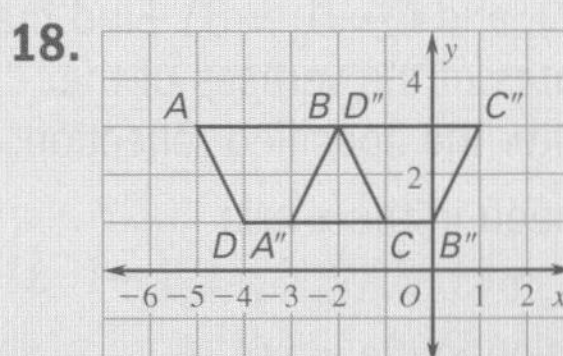

19. 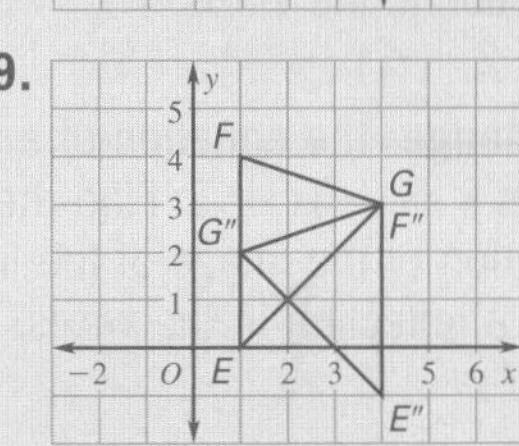

20a. 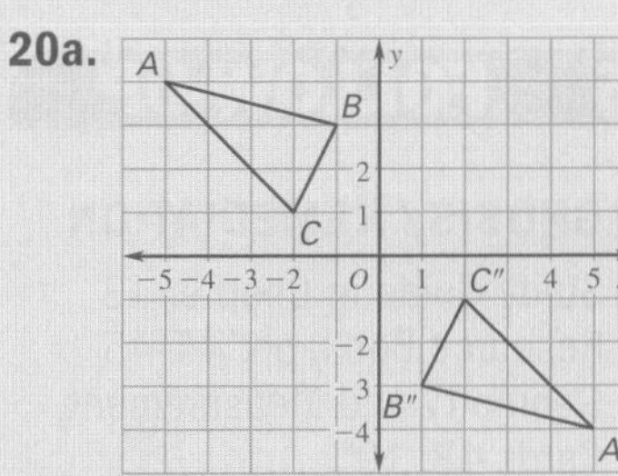

20b. 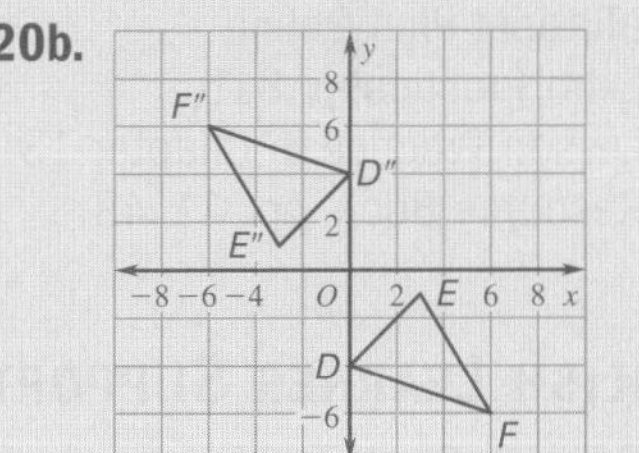

4 ASSESS

ASSESSMENT RESOURCES

For more assessment resources, see:
- Assessment Book
- Test and Practice Generator

MINI-QUIZ

The vertices of $\triangle ABC$ are $A(3, 1)$, $B(2, -2)$, and $C(-1, -3)$. Find the coordinates of the vertices of the image after the specified reflection.

1. reflection in the x-axis **$A'(3, -1)$, $B'(2, 2)$, $C'(-1, 3)$**
2. reflection in the y-axis **$A'(-3, 1)$, $B'(-2, -2)$, $C'(1, -3)$**
3. **Challenge** The equation of a line is $y = -3x + 2$. Find the equation of the image of the line after a reflection in the x-axis. **$y = 3x - 2$**

5 FOLLOW-UP

DIAGNOSIS/REMEDIATION

- Study Guide in Chapter 13 Resource Book, pp. 44–45
- Geometry and Measurement Cards 18, 19
- eTutorial Plus Online
- Extra Practice, p. 815
- Lesson Practice in Chapter 13 Resource Book, pp. 41–43

ENGLISH LEARNER SUPPORT

- Spanish Study Guide
- Multi-Language Visual Glossary
- Chapter Audio Summaries CDs

CHALLENGE

- Challenge Practice in Chapter 13 Resource Book, p. 46
- Teacher's Edition, p. 706F

21a–b, 22, 24b, 33, 35. See Additional Answers beginning on page AA1.

21. In the diagram, $\triangle ABC$ is reflected in the line $x = 3$. Draw the image of $\triangle ABC$ after the specified reflection.

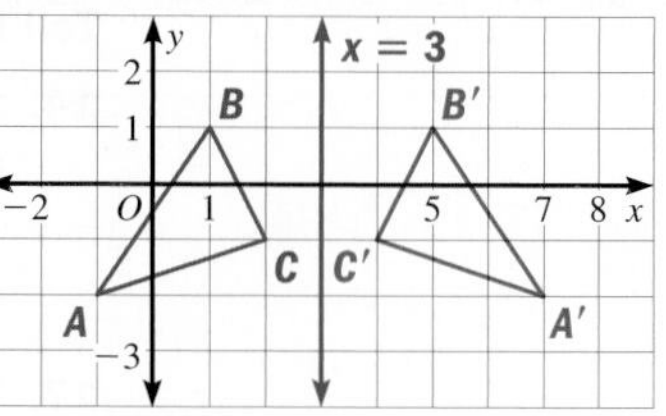

a. Reflection in the line $x = 5$

21a–b. See margin.

b. Reflection in the line $y = -4$

22. Tessellations You can use reflections and translations of a parallelogram to create a tessellation, as shown below. Use this approach to create a tessellation using an equilateral triangle. **See margin.**

1) Draw any parallelogram and reflect it in one side.

2) Translate the new figure repeatedly to create a tessellation.

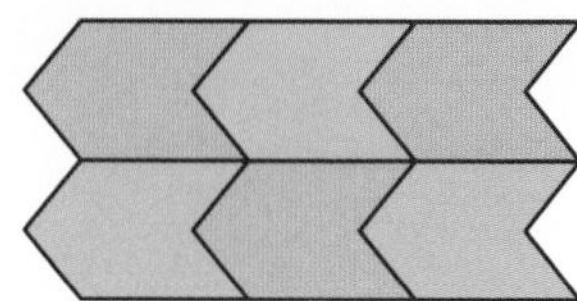

23. *Sample answer:* **They are alike in that both are lines of reflection. They are different in that a line of symmetry has the special property that it reflects a figure back onto itself so that the image and the original look exactly the same.**

23. *Writing* How are a line of reflection and a line of symmetry alike? How are they different?

C **24. Challenge** Use the line shown.

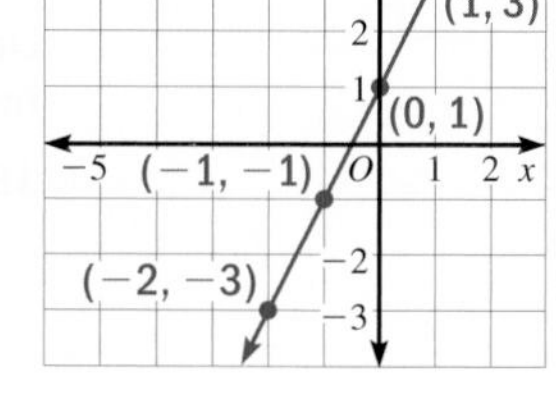

a. What is an equation of the line? **$y = 2x + 1$**

b. Draw the image of the line after a reflection in the y-axis. Then find an equation of the image. **See margin for art; $y = -2x + 1$.**

c. **Compare** How are the slope and the y-intercept of the original line related to the slope and the y-intercept of the image? **The slopes are opposites. The y-intercepts are the same.**

Mixed Review

State the absolute value and the opposite of the number. *(Lesson 1.4)*

25. 71 **71, −71** **26.** −45 **45, 45** **27.** −100 **100, 100** **28.** 265 **265, −265**

Find the least common multiple of the numbers. *(Lesson 4.4)*

29. 6, 11 **66** **30.** 8, 12 **24** **31.** 5, 9, 10 **90** **32.** 4, 12, 15 **60**

33. Draw $\triangle JKL$ with vertices $J(0, 0)$, $K(3, 0)$, and $L(3, -5)$. Then find the coordinates of the vertices of the image after the translation $(x, y) \rightarrow (x - 6, y - 2)$, and draw the image. *(Lesson 13.4)*
See margin for art; $J'(-6, -2)$, $K'(-3, -2)$, $L'(-3, -7)$.

Standardized Test Practice

34. Multiple Choice Each leg of a right triangle has a length of 3 inches. How many lines of symmetry does the triangle have? **A**

A. 1 line **B.** 2 lines **C.** 3 lines **D.** 6 lines

35. **See margin for art; apply the transformation $(x, y) \rightarrow (x, -y)$. That is, keep the original x-coordinates, but multiply the y-coordinates by −1.**

35. Short Response Draw $\overline{AB}$ with endpoints $A(3, 1)$ and $B(2, 3)$. Explain how you would find the coordinates of the endpoints of the image of $\overline{AB}$ after a reflection in the x-axis, and draw the image.

13.5 Reflecting in a Line

Goal Use a graphing calculator to perform a reflection in the line $y = x$.

Example

Reflect the points $A(2, -3)$, $B(3, 1)$, and $C(5, 4)$ in the line $y = x$.

1 Enter the equation $y = x$.

Keystrokes Y= X

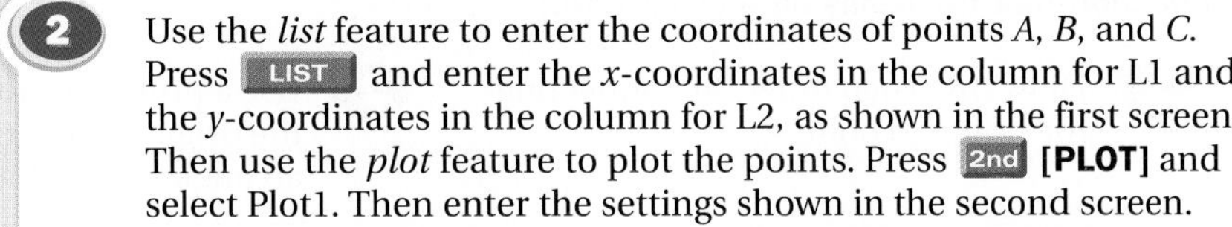

2 Use the *list* feature to enter the coordinates of points A, B, and C. Press LIST and enter the x-coordinates in the column for L1 and the y-coordinates in the column for L2, as shown in the first screen. Then use the *plot* feature to plot the points. Press 2nd **[PLOT]** and select Plot1. Then enter the settings shown in the second screen.

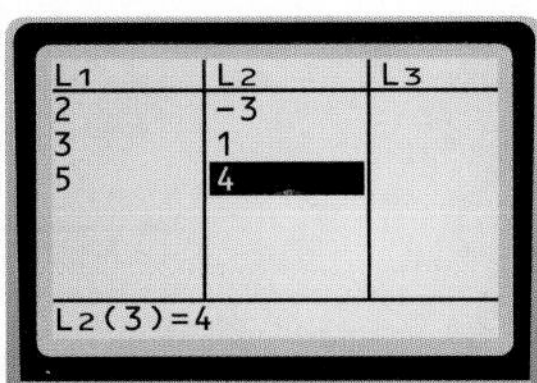

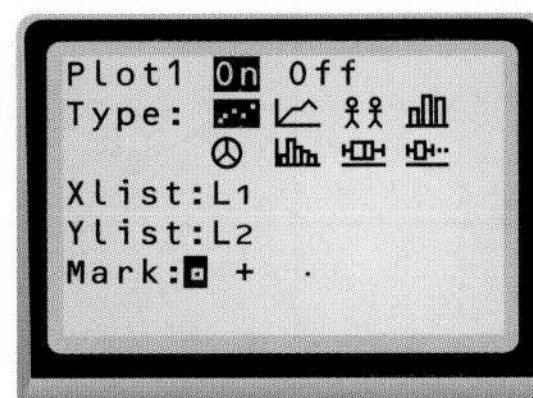

3 To reflect in the line $y = x$, you need to switch the coordinates of each point. Press 2nd **[PLOT]** and select Plot2. Then enter the settings shown in the first screen below, making sure that you switch the places of L1 and L2. Press ZOOM **7** then ZOOM **5** to display the reflection in the line $y = x$, as shown in the second screen below.

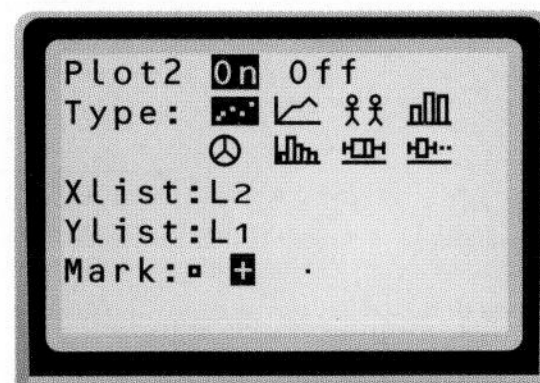

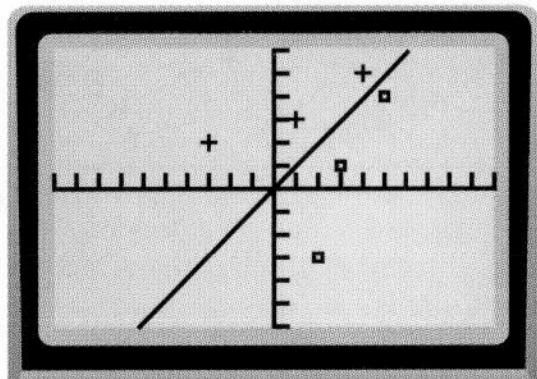

Tech Help

When you use ZOOM **7**, all of the points are displayed on the screen. When you use ZOOM **5**, the line $y = x$ makes a 45° angle with the x- and y-axes on the screen.

Draw Conclusions

1. Reflect the points $D(-1, 4)$, $E(-5, -2)$, and $F(-3, 0)$ in the line $y = x$. Then use the *trace* feature to find the coordinates of D', E', and F'. $D'(4, -1)$, $E'(-2, -5)$, $F'(0, -3)$
2. **Interpret** Use coordinate notation to describe a reflection in the line $y = x$. $(x, y) \to (y, x)$

NCTM CURRICULUM STANDARDS
Standard 3: Apply transformations to math situations

1 PLAN

LEARN THE METHOD

- Students will use a graphing calculator to perform a reflection in the line $y = x$.
- Students can use the skills they learn in this activity to verify their answer to Exercise 20 in Lesson 13.5.

GROUPING

Students should work individually.

2 TEACH

TIPS FOR SUCCESS

Suggest that students rotate their calculators 45° counterclockwise so that the line $y = x$ is positioned vertically. Students may find it easier to see that the points and their images are symmetric over the line $y = x$ when the calculator is oriented this way.

Extra Examples

Example Reflect the points $F(-3, -2)$, $G(-1, 1)$, and $H(1, 4)$ in the line $y = x$.

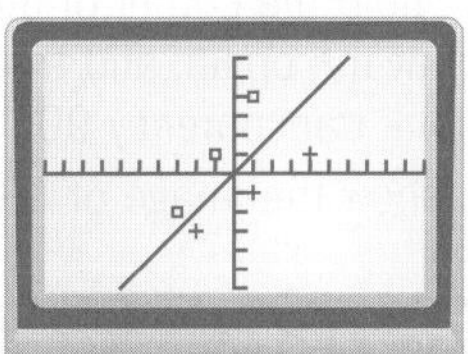

3 CLOSE

ASSESSMENT

1. Reflect the points $K(7, 7)$, $L(-5, 2)$, and $M(-4, -5)$ in the line $y = x$. Then use the *trace* feature to find the coordinates of K', L', and M'. **$K'(7, 7)$, $L'(2, -5)$, $M'(-5, -4)$**

1 PLAN

Investigate the Concept

- Students rotate a segment through a given angle about the origin.
- This activity leads into the study of the rotation of a polygon in Lesson 13.6.

Materials

Each student will need grid paper, a protractor, and a compass. A support transparency is available.

Recommended Time

Work activity: 10 min
Discuss results: 5 min

Grouping

Students should work individually.

2 TEACH

Alternative Strategy

On an overhead projector, position a blank transparency on top of a coordinate plane transparency so a corner of the blank transparency is at the origin. Draw $\overline{AB}$ on the blank transparency, hold the corner of the transparency at the origin, and then rotate the blank transparency 90° clockwise to show the image of $\overline{AB}$.

3 CLOSE

Key Discovery

A 90° clockwise rotation about the origin changes the coordinates (x, y) of a point to $(y, -x)$.

Assessment

1. $C(-5, 6)$ is rotated 90° clockwise about the origin. What are the coordinates of its image? **(6, 5)**

1–3. See Additional Answers beginning on page AA1.

Concept *Activity*

13.6 Rotating a Segment

Goal

Rotate a segment through a given angle about the origin.

Materials

- grid paper
- protractor
- compass

Investigate

Given $\overline{AB}$ with endpoints $A(1, 2)$ and $B(3, 1)$, draw the image of $\overline{AB}$ after a 90° clockwise rotation about the origin. (*Clockwise* refers to the direction that the hands on a clock turn.)

1 Draw $\overline{AB}$. Then draw $\overline{OA}$ connecting the origin to point A.

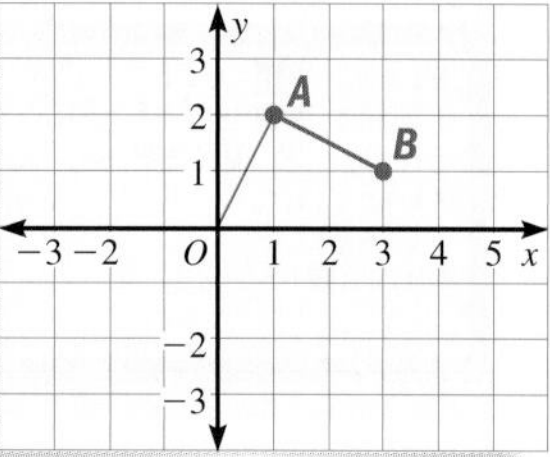

2 Use a protractor to draw a ray from the origin so that the ray creates an angle of 90° clockwise with $\overline{OA}$.

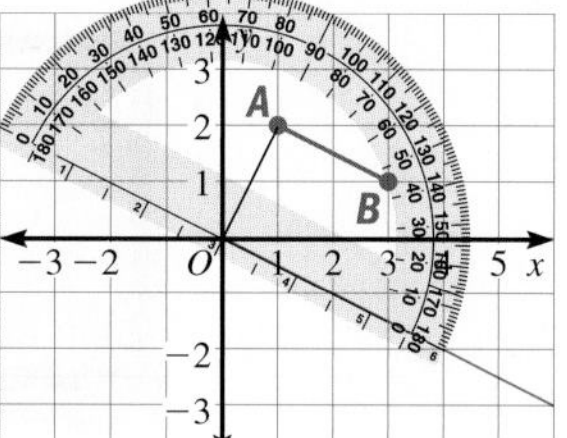

3 Use a compass to copy $\overline{OA}$ on the ray by drawing an arc from A to the ray. Label the point of intersection A'.

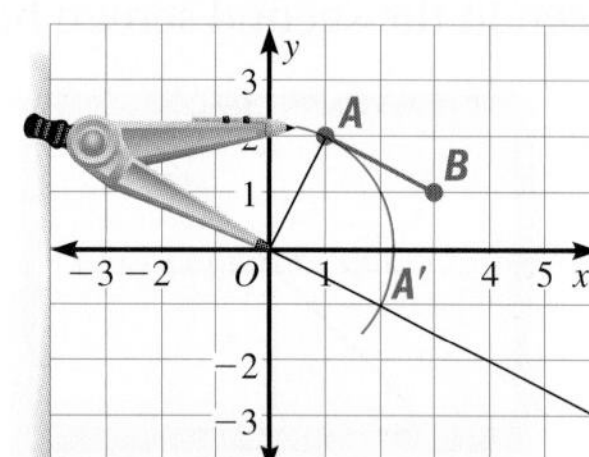

4 Repeat Steps 1–3 for point B. The endpoints of the image, $\overline{A'B'}$, are $A'(2, -1)$ and $B'(1, -3)$.

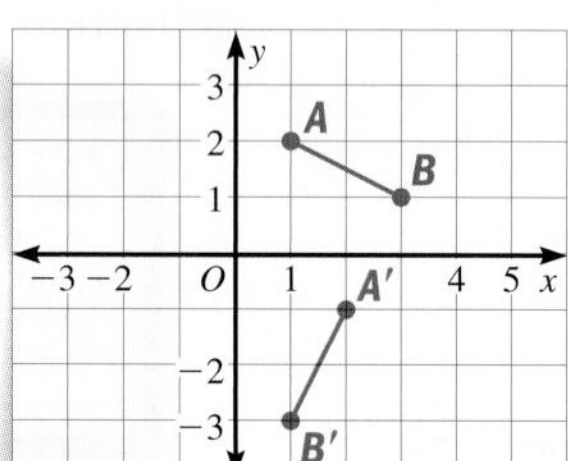

Draw Conclusions

Draw $\overline{AB}$ with the given endpoints. Then draw the image of $\overline{AB}$ after a 90° clockwise rotation about the origin. 1–3. See margin.

1. $A(-3, 1), B(-2, 3)$
2. $A(4, -1), B(3, -4)$
3. $A(-3, -1), B(-2, -4)$
4. **Interpret** Based on your results from Exercises 1–3, use coordinate notation to describe a 90° clockwise rotation about the origin. $(x, y) \rightarrow (y, -x)$

NCTM CURRICULUM STANDARDS

Standard 3: Describe spatial relationships using coordinate geometry; Apply transformations to math situations

LESSON **13.6**

Rotations *and* Symmetry

BEFORE	Now	WHY?
You translated and reflected figures.	You'll rotate figures and identify rotational symmetry.	So you can describe how a CD tray rotates, as in Ex. 17.

Vocabulary
rotation, p. 741
center of rotation, p. 741
angle of rotation, p. 741
rotational symmetry, p. 743

Family Crests A family crest is a design that symbolizes a family's heritage. An example of a family crest for a Japanese family is shown. In Example 4, you will look at the *rotational symmetry* of the design.

A **rotation** is a transformation in which a figure is turned about a fixed point, called the **center of rotation**. The **angle of rotation** is formed by rays drawn from the center of rotation through corresponding points on an original figure and its image. The direction of rotation can be *clockwise* or *counterclockwise*. In a rotation, a figure and its image are congruent.

Reading *Geometry*

Clockwise refers to the direction that the hands on a clock turn. *Counterclockwise* refers to the opposite of the direction that the hands on a clock turn.

45° clockwise rotation

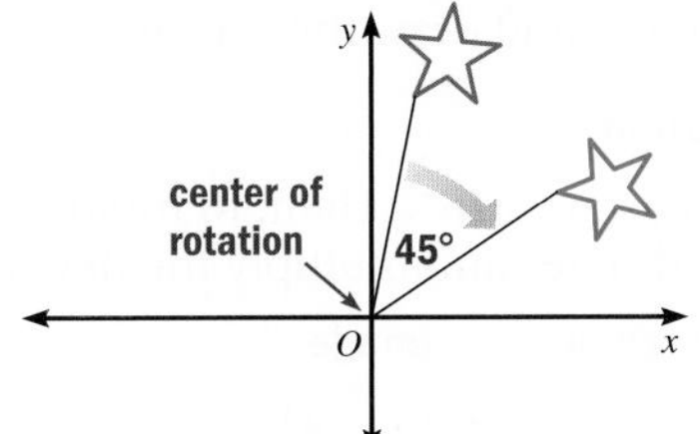

120° counterclockwise rotation

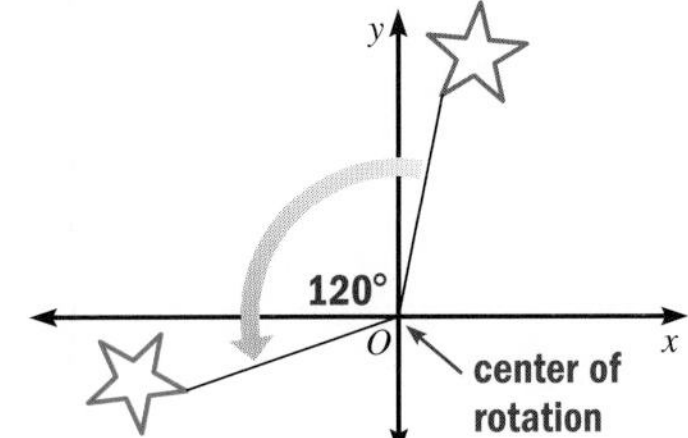

Example 1 *Identifying Rotations*

Tell whether the transformation is a rotation about the origin. If so, give the angle and direction of rotation.

a. 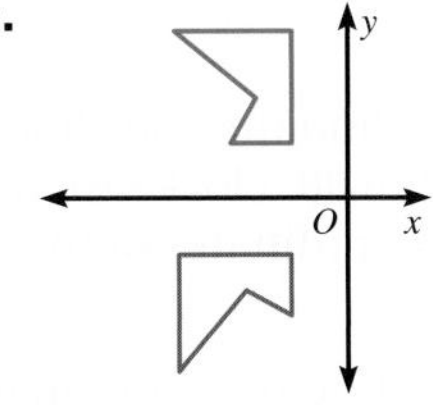

b. 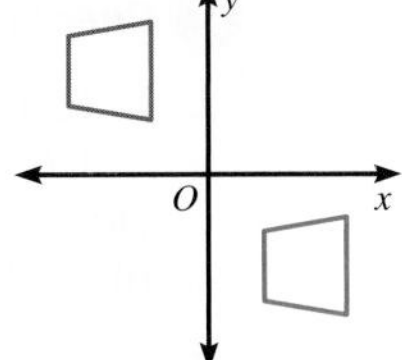

c. 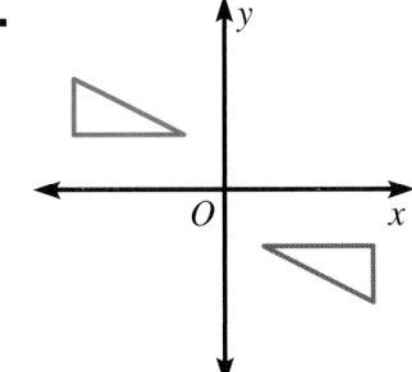

Solution

a. 90° clockwise rotation

b. Not a rotation

c. 180° rotation in either direction

NCTM CURRICULUM STANDARDS
Standard 3: Describe spatial relationships using coordinate geometry; Apply transformations to math situations

1 PLAN

Skill Check
Identify the point correspon-ding to the given ordered pair.

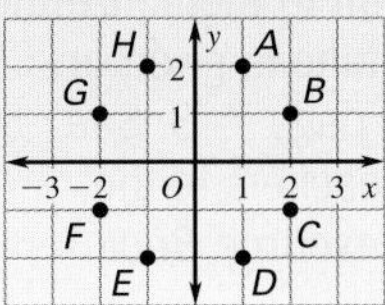

1. (2, −1) C
2. (−1, 2) H
3. (−2, 1) G
4. (−2, −1) F

Lesson Objective

Rotate figures and identify rotational symmetry.

Pacing

Suggested Number of Days
Basic Course: 2 days
Average Course: 2 days
Advanced Course: 2 days
Block: 1 block

Teaching Resources

For a complete list of Teaching Resources, see page 706B.

Transparency

Warm-Up Exercises for this lesson are available on a transparency. A support transparency is available for Examples 2 and 3, and Checkpoint Exercises 1 and 2.

2 TEACH

Motivating the Lesson

Have students draw circular designs that are symmetric horizontally, verti-cally, or both. Later in the lesson you can use some of the designs to illustrate rotational symmetry.

TIPS *for* NEW TEACHERS

Changes in the *x*- and *y*-coordinates as a result of a 90° or 180° rotation may not be intuitive to many students. Encourage them to memorize the coordinate notations given on this page and page 743. See Tips for New Teachers in the *Chapter 13 Resource Book*.

Extra Examples

Example 1 Tell whether the transformation is a rotation about the origin. If so, give the angle and direction of rotation.

a.

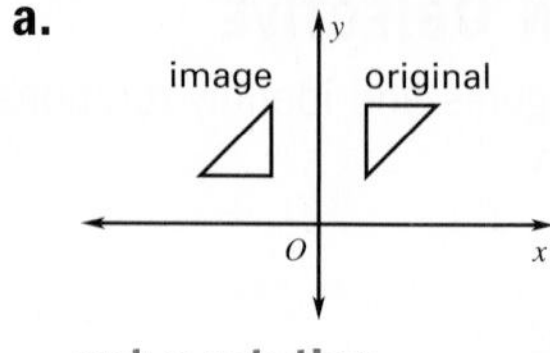

not a rotation

b.

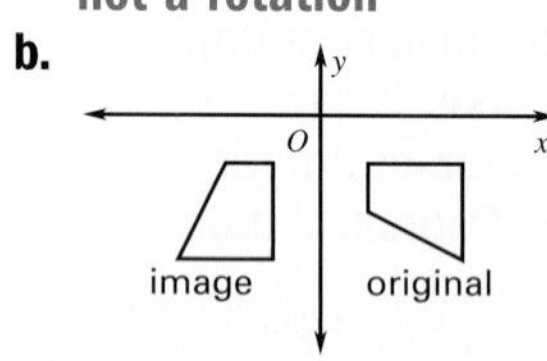

90° clockwise rotation

Example 2 Draw $\triangle PQR$ with vertices $P(0, 2)$, $Q(2, 4)$, and $R(1, 1)$. Then find the coordinates of the vertices of the image after a 90° counterclockwise rotation, and draw the image.

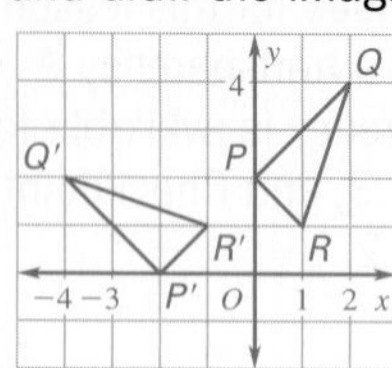

$P'(-2, 0)$, $Q'(-4, 2)$, $R'(-1, 1)$

1, 2. See Additional Answers beginning on page AA1.

Study *Strategy*

Check to see that the coordinate notations for 90° rotations give the correct coordinates of the endpoints of the images of $\overline{AB}$ shown.

90° Rotations In this book, all rotations in the coordinate plane are centered at the origin. You can use coordinate notation to describe a 90° rotation of a figure about the origin.

90° clockwise rotation

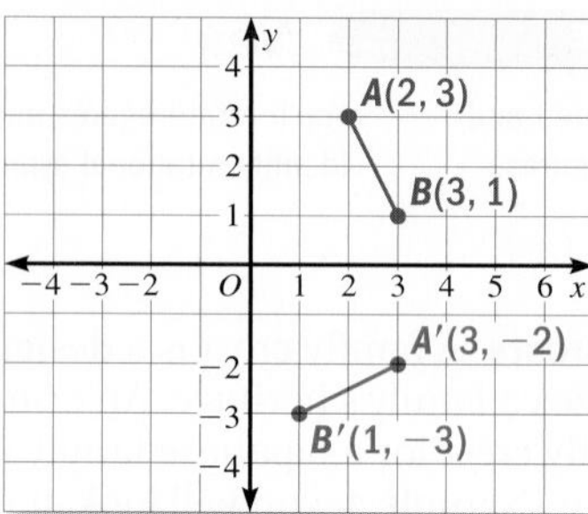

Switch the coordinates, then multiply the new *y*-coordinate by −1.

$(x, y) \to (y, -x)$

90° counterclockwise rotation

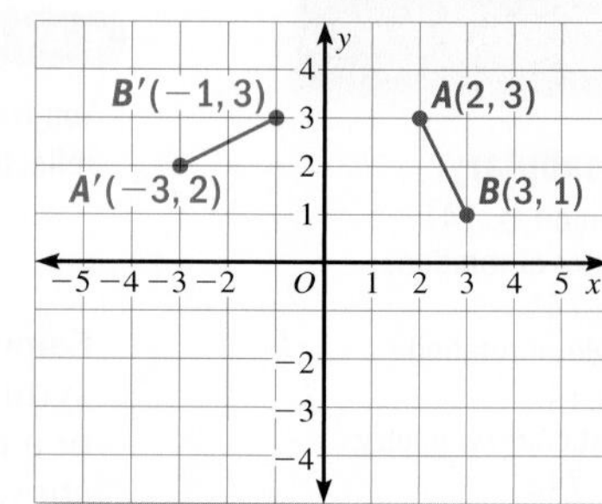

Switch the coordinates, then multiply the new *x*-coordinate by −1.

$(x, y) \to (-y, x)$

Example 2 *Rotating a Triangle*

Draw $\triangle ABC$ with vertices $A(-3, 4)$, $B(-2, 3)$, and $C(-2, 1)$. Then find the coordinates of the vertices of the image after a 90° clockwise rotation, and draw the image.

Solution

First draw $\triangle ABC$. Then, to rotate $\triangle ABC$ 90° clockwise, switch the coordinates and multiply the new *y*-coordinate by −1.

Original		Image
(x, y)	$\to$	$(y, -x)$
$A(-3, 4)$	$\to$	$A'(4, 3)$
$B(-2, 3)$	$\to$	$B'(3, 2)$
$C(-2, 1)$	$\to$	$C'(1, 2)$

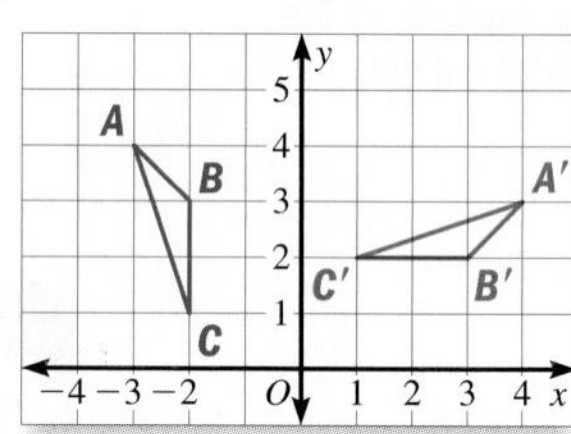

Finally, draw $\triangle A'B'C'$, as shown.

Checkpoint

1. In Example 2, find the coordinates of the vertices of the image of $\triangle A'B'C'$ after a 90° clockwise rotation, and draw the image $\triangle A''B''C''$. How are the coordinates of the vertices of $\triangle A''B''C''$ related to those of $\triangle ABC$?
   $A''(3, -4)$, $B''(2, -3)$, $C''(2, -1)$; see margin for art; they are opposites.
2. In Example 2, find the coordinates of the vertices of the image of $\triangle ABC$ after a 90° counterclockwise rotation, and draw the image.
   $A'(-4, -3)$, $B'(-3, -2)$, $C'(-1, -2)$; see margin for art.
3. **Critical Thinking** A figure lies in the third quadrant of a coordinate plane. In what quadrant does the image lie after a 90° clockwise rotation? after a 90° counterclockwise rotation? **Quadrant II; Quadrant IV**

180° Rotations To rotate a point 180° about the origin, multiply each coordinate by −1. The image is the same whether you rotate the figure clockwise or counterclockwise.

$$(x, y) \rightarrow (-x, -y)$$

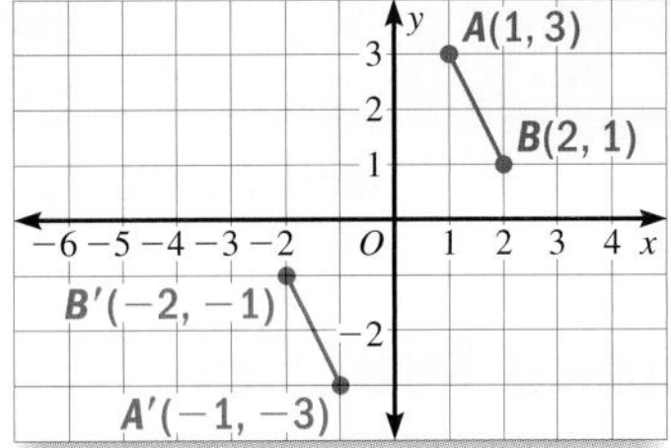

Example 3 *Rotating a Triangle*

Draw $\triangle MNP$ with vertices $M(1, -2)$, $N(4, -1)$, and $P(2, -3)$. Then find the coordinates of the vertices of the image after a 180° rotation, and draw the image.

Solution

First draw $\triangle MNP$. Then, to rotate $\triangle MNP$ 180°, multiply the coordinates by −1.

Original		Image
(x, y)	$\rightarrow$	$(-x, -y)$
$M(1, -2)$	$\rightarrow$	$M'(-1, 2)$
$N(4, -1)$	$\rightarrow$	$N'(-4, 1)$
$P(2, -3)$	$\rightarrow$	$P'(-2, 3)$

Finally, draw $\triangle M'N'P'$, as shown.

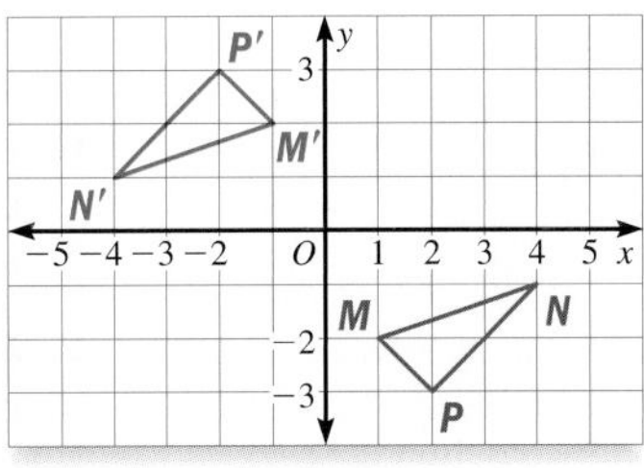

 ***Checkpoint***

4. Draw $\triangle DEF$ with vertices $D(-6, -1)$, $E(0, -2)$, and $F(-5, -4)$. Then find the coordinates of the vertices of the image after a 180° rotation, and draw the image. **See margin for art; $D'(6, 1)$, $E'(0, 2)$, $F'(5, 4)$.**

Rotational Symmetry A figure has **rotational symmetry** if a rotation of 180° or less clockwise (or counterclockwise) about its center produces an image that fits exactly on the original figure.

Example 4 *Identifying Rotational Symmetry*

The family crest shown on page 741 has rotational symmetry for a 90° or 180° clockwise (or counterclockwise) rotation.

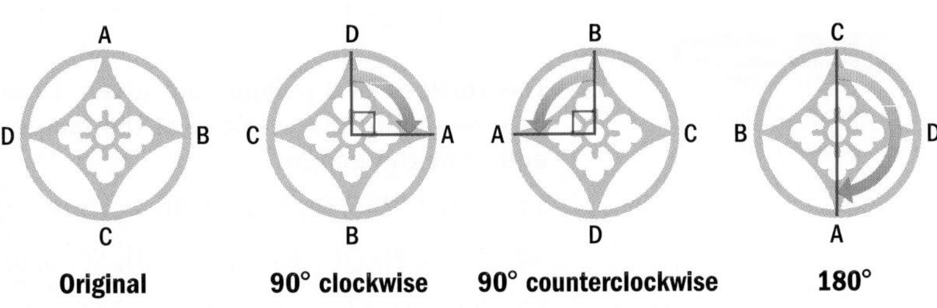

In the **Real World**

Family Crests The family crest shown above has rotational symmetry for a 120° clockwise rotation. Give another angle and direction of rotation that produce rotational symmetry for the crest.
120° counterclockwise

Extra Examples

Example 3 Draw $\triangle KLM$ with vertices $K(-2, 1)$, $L(-1, -1)$, and $M(-4, -1)$. Then find the coordinates of the vertices of the image after a 180° clockwise rotation, and draw the image.
$K'(2, -1)$, $L'(1, 1)$, $M'(4, 1)$

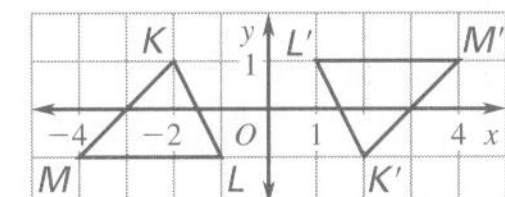

Example 4 Tell whether the figure has rotational symmetry. If so, give each angle and direction of rotation that produce rotational symmetry.

a. 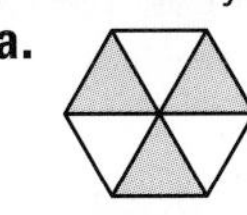 **yes; 120° in either direction**

b.  **no**

Visualize

If students are having difficulty visualizing rotations, consider using pipe cleaners, paper clips, or other thin wire to model the figure so students can actually rotate it around the origin.

Concept Check

What type of transformation results when you switch the coordinates of a point and multiply the new x-coordinate by −1? **a 90° counterclockwise rotation**

Daily Puzzler

Form a regular hexagon using six new pencils. What is the fewest number of new pencils needed to form two rhombuses if you can relocate two of the first six pencils? **1 pencil**

4. See Additional Answers beginning on page AA1.

3 APPLY

ASSIGNMENT GUIDE

Basic Course
Day 1: SRH p. 792 Exs. 1–4; pp. 744–746 Exs. 8–12, 20–22
Day 2: pp. 744–746 Exs. 13–18, 23, 25–30

Average Course
Day 1: pp. 744–746 Exs. 8–12, 20–22, 25–28
Day 2: pp. 744–746 Exs. 13–19, 23, 29, 30

Advanced Course
Day 1: pp. 744–746 Exs. 8–12, 20–22, 27–29
Day 2: pp. 744–746 Exs. 13–19, 23, 24*, 30

Block
pp. 744–746 Exs. 8–23, 25–30

EXTRA PRACTICE

- Student Edition, p. 815
- Chapter 13 Resource Book, pp. 49–51
- Test and Practice Generator

TRANSPARENCY

Even-numbered answers are available on transparencies. A support transparency is available for Exercises 6, 11–13, 18, 20–22, 29, and 30.

HOMEWORK CHECK

When you review students' homework for this lesson, go over the following exercises to check understanding of key concepts.
Basic: 8, 11, 13, 14, 18
Average: 9, 12, 13, 16, 18
Advanced: 10, 12, 13, 17, 19

6, 11–13. See Additional Answers beginning on page AA1.

13.6 Exercises

More Practice, p. 815

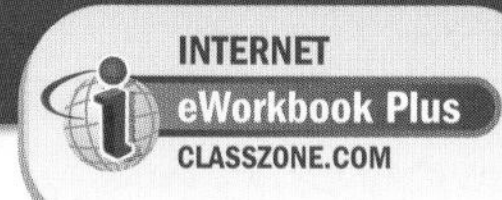

Guided Practice

Vocabulary Check

1. How are rotational symmetry and line symmetry different? **See margin.**
2. Use coordinate notation to describe a 90° counterclockwise rotation. **$(x, y) \rightarrow (-y, x)$**

Skill Check

1. *Sample answer:* In line symmetry, the image that fits exactly on the original figure is formed by reflecting, or flipping, the figure in a line that passes through the center of the figure, while in rotational symmetry the image is formed by turning the original figure a certain angle measure around its center.

Tell whether the transformation is a rotation about the origin. If so, give the angle and direction of rotation.

3. 4. 5. no

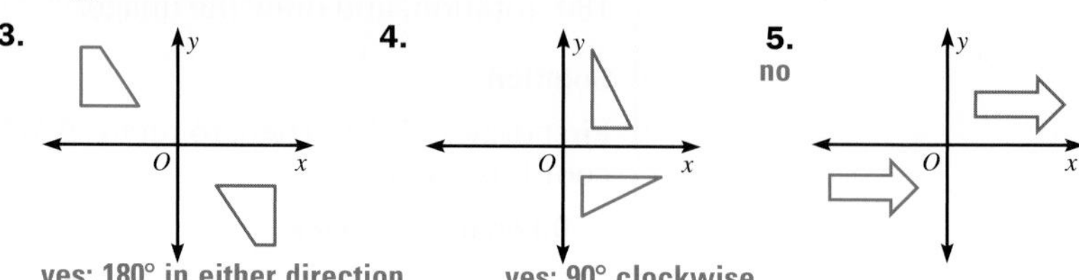

yes; 180° in either direction — yes; 90° clockwise

6. Draw $\triangle ABC$ with vertices $A(3, 2)$, $B(5, 1)$, and $C(6, 4)$. Then find the coordinates of the vertices of the image after a 90° clockwise rotation, and draw the image. **See margin for art; $A'(2, -3)$, $B'(1, -5)$, $C'(4, -6)$.**

7. **Error Analysis** Describe and correct the error in finding the coordinates of the vertices of the image of $\triangle ABC$ after a 90° clockwise rotation.

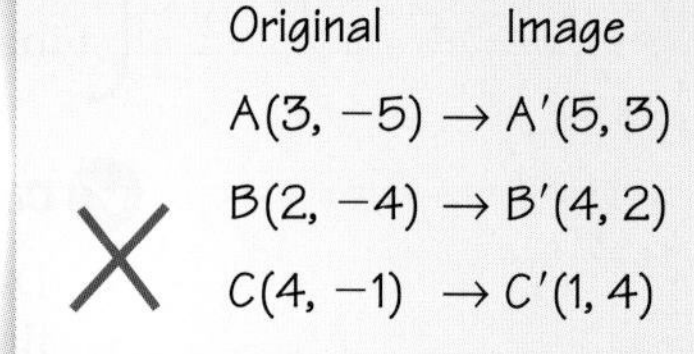

7. *Sample answer:* For a 90° clockwise rotation, the coordinate notation is $(x, y) \rightarrow (y, -x)$. The transformation shown is $(x, y) \rightarrow (-y, x)$, which represents a 90° *counterclockwise* rotation. The correct image points are $A'(-5, -3)$, $B'(-4, -2)$, and $C'(-1, -4)$.

Practice and Problem Solving

Homework Help

Example	Exercises
1	8–10
2	11–12, 18
3	13, 18
4	14–17, 19

Online Resources
CLASSZONE.COM
- More Examples
- eTutorial Plus

Tell whether the transformation is a rotation about the origin. If so, give the angle and direction of rotation.

A 8. no 9. 10.

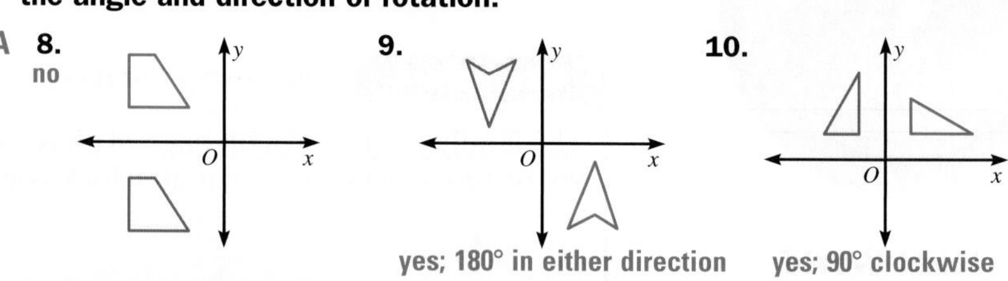

yes; 180° in either direction — yes; 90° clockwise

The vertices of a polygon are given. Draw the polygon. Then find the coordinates of the vertices of the image under the specified rotation, and draw the image. 11–13. See margin for art.

11. $A(1, 3)$, $B(5, 6)$, $C(5, 3)$; 90° counterclockwise rotation **$A'(-3, 1)$, $B'(-6, 5)$, $C'(-3, 5)$**
12. $P(-6, 2)$, $Q(-3, 4)$, $R(-1, 3)$, $S(-5, 0)$; 90° clockwise rotation **$P'(2, 6)$, $Q'(4, 3)$, $R'(3, 1)$, $S'(0, 5)$**
13. $J(2, -1)$, $K(4, -1)$, $L(4, -5)$, $M(3, -6)$, $N(2, -5)$; 180° rotation **$J'(-2, 1)$, $K'(-4, 1)$, $L'(-4, 5)$, $M'(-3, 6)$, $N'(-2, 5)$**

Tell whether the figure has rotational symmetry. If so, give each angle and direction of rotation that produce rotational symmetry.

15. yes; 90° and 180° in either direction

16. yes; 180° in either direction

14. no

15.

16.

17. CD Player Your CD player can hold five compact discs on a rotating tray like the one shown.

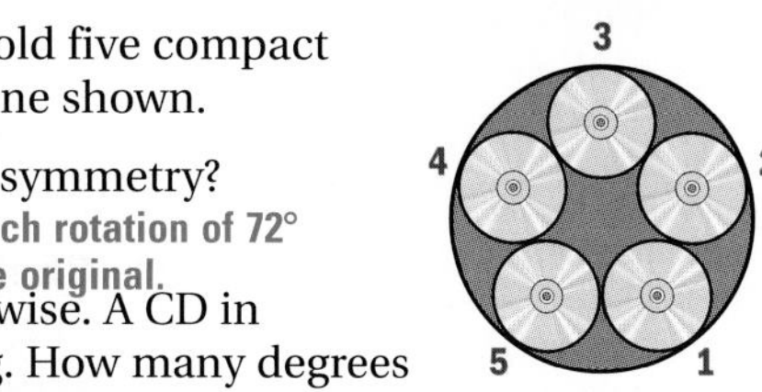

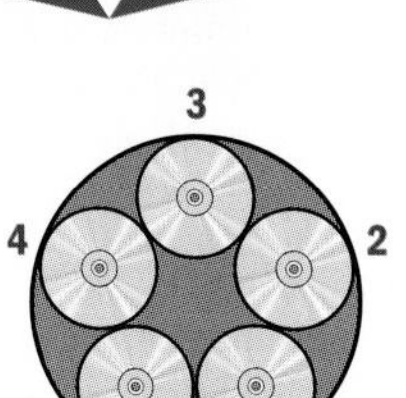

a. Does the tray have rotational symmetry? Explain. Yes. *Sample answer:* Each rotation of 72° will produce an image that fits the original.

b. The tray can move only clockwise. A CD in position 1 is currently playing. How many degrees must the tray rotate to play a CD in position 3? 144°

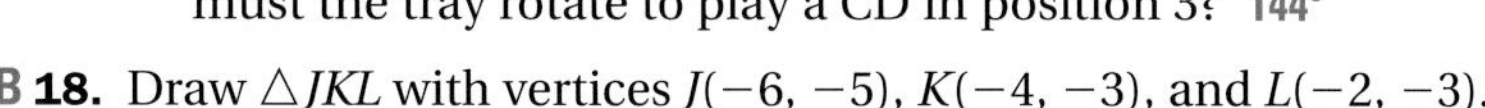

B **18.** Draw $\triangle JKL$ with vertices $J(-6, -5)$, $K(-4, -3)$, and $L(-2, -3)$.

a. You rotate $\triangle JKL$ 90° clockwise, then you rotate its image 180°. Find the coordinates of the final image. Then draw the image. $J''(5, -6)$, $K''(3, -4)$, $L''(3, -2)$; see margin for art.

b. Critical Thinking Use coordinate notation to describe how to rotate $\triangle JKL$ to the final image in part (a) using one rotation. $(x, y) \to (-y, x)$

19. Extended Problem Solving The table shows the first four regular polygons that have an even number of sides.

Regular polygon	Quadrilateral	Hexagon	Octagon	10-gon
Sides	4	? 6	? 8	? 10
Angles of rotation (in either direction)	90°, 180°	60° ? 120°, 180°	45°, ? 90° 135°, 180°	36°,? 72° 108°, 144°, 180°

a. Copy and complete the table by finding the number of sides of each regular polygon and the angles of rotation that produce rotational symmetry.

b. Compare How is the number of sides related to the number of angles of rotation? It is twice the number of angles of rotation.

c. Predict Add a column in the table for a regular 16-gon. sides: 16; angles of rotation: 22.5°, 45°, 67.5°, 90°, 112.5°, 135°, 157.5°, 180°

Draw the polygon shown. Then find the coordinates of the vertices of the final image after the specified transformations, and draw the final image. 20–22. See margin for art.

20. Rotate the polygon 180°, then reflect the image in the y-axis.

21. Rotate the polygon 90° clockwise, then reflect the image in the x-axis.

22. Rotate the polygon 90° counterclockwise, then translate the image using $(x, y) \to (x + 3, y + 4)$.

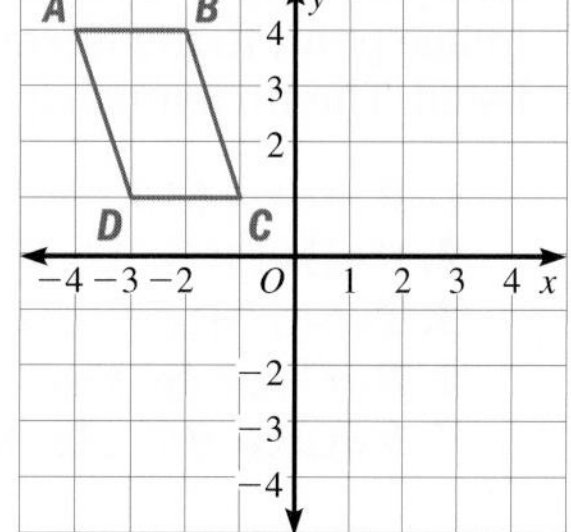

20. $A''(-4, -4)$, $B''(-2, -4)$, $C''(-1, -1)$, $D''(-3, -1)$

21. $A''(4, -4)$, $B''(4, -2)$, $C''(1, -1)$, $D''(1, -3)$

22. $A''(-1, 0)$, $B''(-1, 2)$, $C''(2, 3)$, $D''(2, 1)$

COMMON ERROR

In Exercises 11 and 12, make sure students know which direction is clockwise and which is counterclockwise.

TEACHING TIP

In Exercise 17, students who have not seen multi-disc CD players may need help understanding how the rotating tray works.

18a.

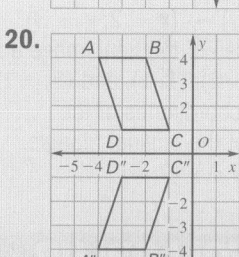

20.

21.

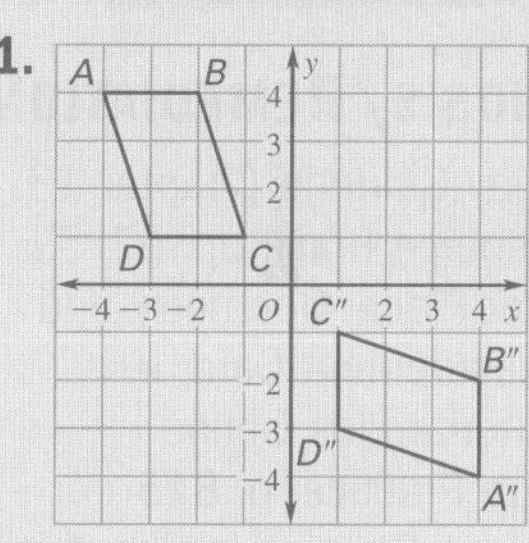

22.

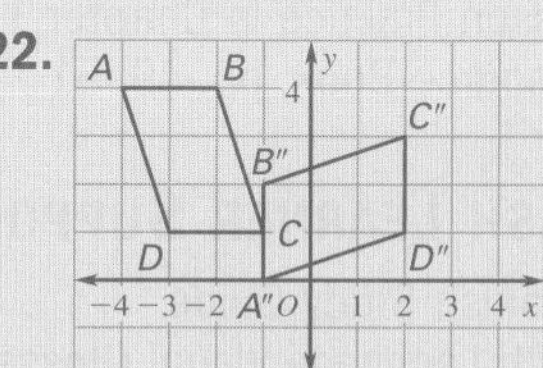

4 ASSESS

Assessment Resources

For more assessment resources, see:

- Assessment Book
- Test and Practice Generator

Mini-Quiz

A triangle has vertices at (1, 2), (3, 0), and (5, 2). Find the coordinates of the vertices of the image under the specified rotation.

1. 90° clockwise rotation **(2, −1), (0, −3), (2, −5)**
2. 180° rotation **(−1, −2), (−3, 0), (−5, −2)**
3. **Challenge** A triangle is rotated 90° counterclockwise about the origin, then its image is translated using $(x, y) \rightarrow (x + 2, y - 3)$. The vertices of the final image are at (−1, −2), (1, 1), and (2, −1). Find the coordinates of the vertices of the original triangle. **(1, 3), (4, 1), (2, 0)**

5 FOLLOW-UP

Diagnosis/Remediation

- Study Guide in Chapter 13 Resource Book, pp. 52-53
- Tutor Place, Geometry and Measurement Card 19
- eTutorial Plus Online
- Extra Practice, p. 815
- Lesson Practice in Chapter 13 Resource Book, pp. 49-51

English Learner Support

- Spanish Study Guide
- Multi-Language Visual Glossary
- Chapter Audio Summaries CDs

Challenge

- Challenge Practice in Chapter 13 Resource Book, p. 55
- Teacher's Edition, p. 706F

23, 29, 30a. See Additional Answers beginning on page AA1.

30b. No. *Sample answer:* In the original order, the transformations are $(x, y) \rightarrow (y, -x) \rightarrow (y, x)$. In reverse order, the transformations are $(x, y) \rightarrow (x, -y) \rightarrow (-y, -x)$, so the image $\triangle A''B''C''$ has coordinates $A''(-2, 6)$, $B''(-5, 2)$, $C''(-1, 4)$, which are not the same as those of the original image.

23. **Tessellations** You can rotate and translate a quadrilateral to create a tessellation, as shown. Use this approach to create a tessellation using a different quadrilateral. **See margin.**

    (1) Draw any quadrilateral and rotate it 180° about the midpoint of one of its sides.

    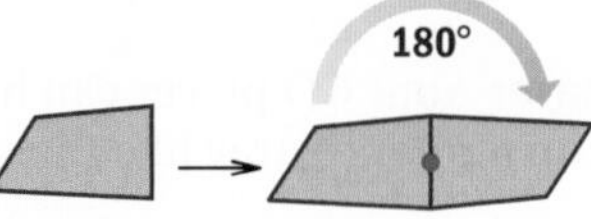

    (2) Translate the new figure repeatedly to form a tessellation.

    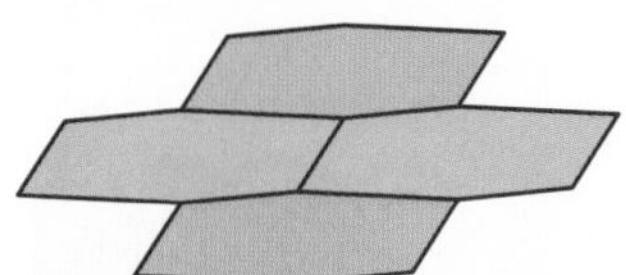

C 24. **Challenge** A triangle is rotated 90° clockwise about the origin, then its image is translated using $(x, y) \rightarrow (x + 3, y - 1)$. The coordinates of the vertices of the final image are (1, −4), (3, −2), and (6, −5). Find the coordinates of the vertices of the original triangle. **(3, −2), (1, 0), (4, 3)**

Mixed Review

A map has a scale of 1 inch : 50 miles. Use the given map distance to find the actual distance. *(Lesson 6.6)*

25. 1.5 inches **75 mi**
26. 3 inches **150 mi**
27. 6 inches **300 mi**
28. 8.5 inches **425 mi**
29. Draw $\triangle PQR$ with vertices $P(-5, -4)$, $Q(-3, 0)$, and $R(-1, -3)$. Then find the coordinates of the vertices of the image after a reflection in the y-axis, and draw the image. *(Lesson 13.5)* **See margin for art; $P'(5, -4)$, $Q'(3, 0)$, $R'(1, -3)$.**

Standardized Test Practice

30. **Extended Response** $\triangle ABC$ has vertices $A(-6, 2)$, $B(-2, 5)$, and $C(-4, 1)$.

    a. Find the coordinates of the vertices of the image of $\triangle ABC$ after a 90° clockwise rotation about the origin, and draw the image $\triangle A'B'C'$. Then find the coordinates of the vertices of the image of $\triangle A'B'C'$ after a reflection in the x-axis, and draw the image $\triangle A''B''C''$. **$A'(2, 6)$, $B'(5, 2)$, $C'(1, 4)$; $A''(2, -6)$, $B''(5, -2)$, $C''(1, -4)$; see margin for art.**

    b. If you switch the order of the transformations, is the image $\triangle A''B''C''$ the same? Justify your answer. **See margin.**

Treasure Hunt

You are located at the point (3, 4) in a coordinate plane. You need to find your way to a treasure chest. Starting at (3, 4), move from one image point to the next by following the order of the transformations listed. The final image point is the location of the treasure chest. **(0, 2)**

1. Rotate 180°.
2. Reflect in the y-axis.
3. Translate 5 units to the left and 4 units up.
4. Reflect in the x-axis.
5. Rotate 90° clockwise.

LESSON

13.7 Dilations

BEFORE	Now	WHY?
You translated, reflected, and rotated figures.	You'll dilate figures in a coordinate plane.	So you can create an illusion of a moving object, as in Ex. 11.

Vocabulary

dilation, p. 747
center of dilation, p. 747
scale factor, p. 747

A **dilation** is a transformation in which a figure stretches or shrinks with respect to a fixed point, called the **center of dilation**. In this book, the origin of a coordinate plane is the center of dilation. In a dilation, a figure and its image are similar.

The **scale factor** of a dilation is the ratio of a side length of the image to the corresponding side length of the original figure. In the diagram, $\overline{A'B'}$ is the image of $\overline{AB}$ after a dilation.

Because $\frac{A'B'}{AB} = 2$, the scale factor is 2.

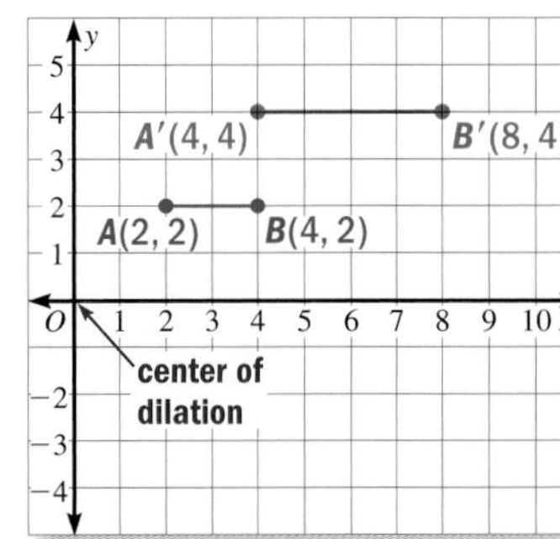

You can describe a dilation with respect to the origin using the notation

$$(x, y) \rightarrow (kx, ky)$$

where k is the scale factor.

Example 1 *Dilating a Quadrilateral*

Draw quadrilateral $ABCD$ with vertices $A(-1, 2)$, $B(3, 1)$, $C(2, -1)$, and $D(-1, -1)$. Then find the coordinates of the vertices of the image after a dilation having a scale factor of 3, and draw the image.

Solution

First draw quadrilateral $ABCD$. Then, to dilate $ABCD$, multiply the x- and y-coordinates of each vertex by 3.

Original		Image
(x, y)	$\rightarrow$	$(3x, 3y)$
$A(-1, 2)$	$\rightarrow$	$A'(-3, 6)$
$B(3, 1)$	$\rightarrow$	$B'(9, 3)$
$C(2, -1)$	$\rightarrow$	$C'(6, -3)$
$D(-1, -1)$	$\rightarrow$	$D'(-3, -3)$

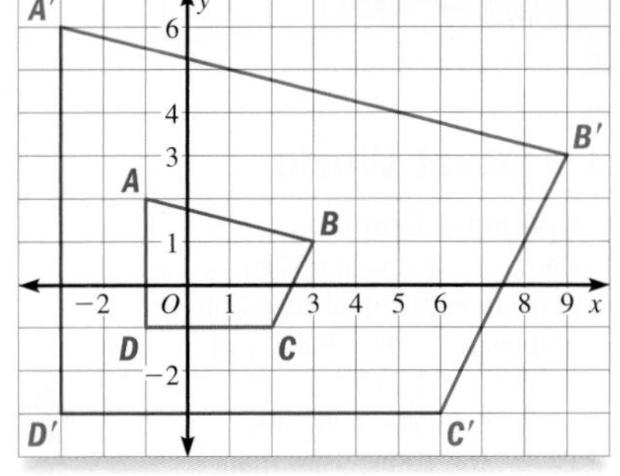

Finally, draw quadrilateral $A'B'C'D'$, as shown.

Study *Strategy*

Notice in Example 1 that when $k > 1$, the new figure is an enlargement of the original figure. As you will see in Example 2, when $k < 1$, the new figure is a reduction of the original figure.

NCTM CURRICULUM STANDARDS

Standard 3: Describe spatial relationships using coordinate geometry; Apply transformations to math situations

1 PLAN

Skill Check

Multiply the coordinates of $(-4, 8)$ by the given value.

1. 4 **(−16, 32)**
2. 6 **(−24, 48)**
3. $\frac{3}{4}$ **(−3, 6)**

Lesson Objective

Dilate figures in a coordinate plane.

Pacing

Suggested Number of Days
Basic Course: 2 days
Average Course: 2 days
Advanced Course: 2 days
Block: 1 block

Teaching Resources

For a complete list of Teaching Resources, see page 706B.

Transparency

Warm-Up Exercises for this lesson are available on a transparency. A support transparency is available for Examples 1–3 and Checkpoint Exercises 1–3.

2 TEACH

Motivating the Lesson

Ask students if they have ever enlarged or reduced a picture or document on a copy machine.

TIPS *for* NEW TEACHERS

Stress that the scale factor is a ratio of corresponding lengths, not the ratio of the areas. See Tips for New Teachers in the *Chapter 13 Resource Book*.

READING STRATEGY

Before discussing Example 1, have a volunteer read the paragraph about scale factors one sentence at a time while you make references to the diagram to the right of the paragraph.

Extra Examples

Example 1 Draw quadrilateral *ABCD* with vertices $A(-1, 2)$, $B(1, 2)$, $C(3, 0)$, and $D(-1, -1)$. Then find the coordinates of the vertices of the image after a dilation having a scale factor of 2, and draw the image. **$A'(-2, 4)$, $B'(2, 4)$, $C'(6, 0)$, $D'(-2, -2)$**

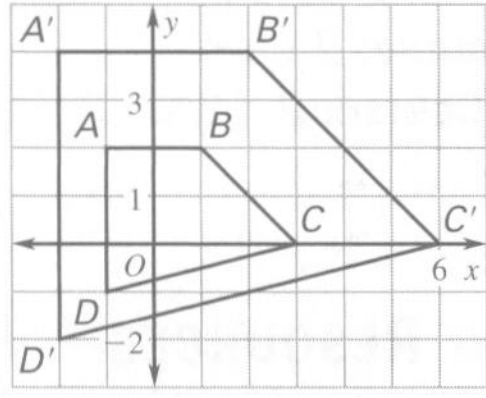

Example 2 Draw quadrilateral *KLMN* with vertices $K(-3, 3)$, $L(6, 3)$, $M(6, 0)$, and $N(3, 0)$. Then find the coordinates of the image after a dilation having a scale factor of $\frac{1}{3}$, and draw the image. **$K'(-1, 1)$, $L'(2, 1)$, $M'(2, 0)$, $N'(1, 0)$**

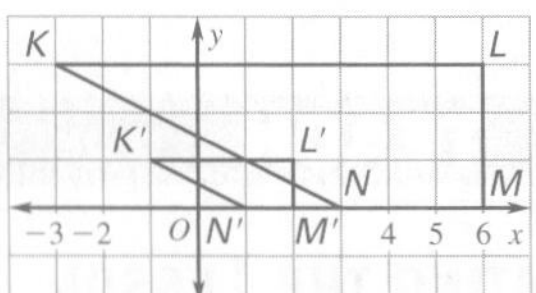

Example 3 A digital photo with dimensions 640 by 460 pixels is reduced to 160 by 115 pixels. Find the scale factor. **0.25**

1, 2. See Additional Answers beginning on page AA1.

Example 2 *Using a Scale Factor Less than 1*

Draw $\triangle PQR$ with vertices $P(4, 4)$, $Q(8, 0)$, and $R(6, -2)$. Then find the coordinates of the vertices of the image after a dilation having a scale factor of 0.5, and draw the image.

Solution

Draw $\triangle PQR$. Then, to dilate $\triangle PQR$, multiply the x- and the y-coordinates of each vertex by 0.5.

Original		Image
(x, y)	$\rightarrow$	$(0.5x, 0.5y)$
$P(4, 4)$	$\rightarrow$	$P'(2, 2)$
$Q(8, 0)$	$\rightarrow$	$Q'(4, 0)$
$R(6, -2)$	$\rightarrow$	$R'(3, -1)$

Finally, draw $\triangle P'Q'R'$, as shown.

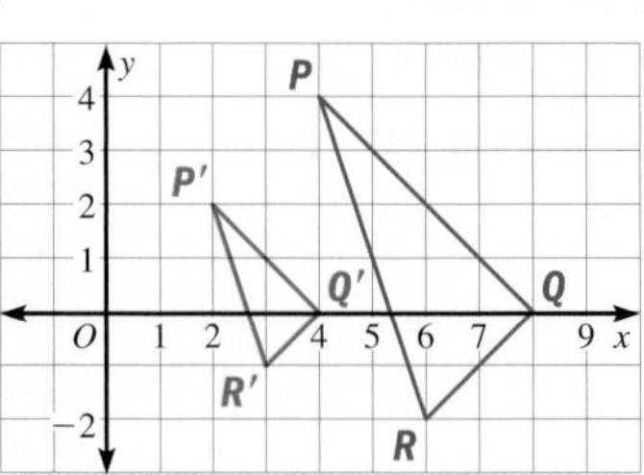

Checkpoint

Draw $\triangle ABC$ with vertices $A(4, 0)$, $B(4, 4)$, and $C(-4, 0)$. Then find the coordinates of the vertices of the image after a dilation having the given scale factor, and draw the image. 1–2. See margin for art.

1. $k = 4$ **$A'(16, 0)$, $B'(16, 16)$, $C'(-16, 0)$** 2. $k = \frac{1}{4}$ **$A'(1, 0)$, $B'(1, 1)$, $C'(-1, 0)$**

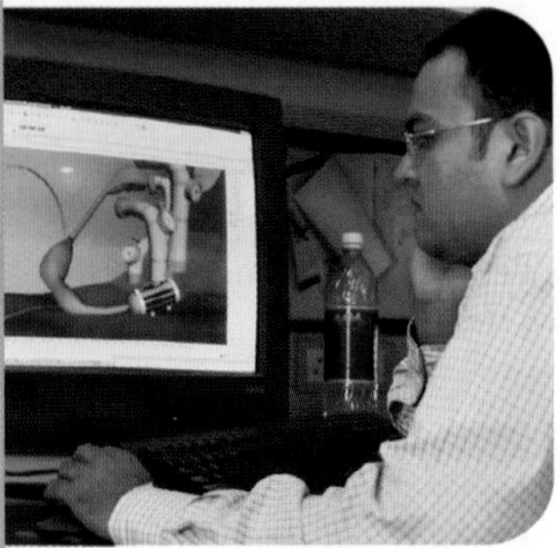

In the **Real World**

Computer Graphics Computer graphics designers may create pictures called bit graphics. A 4 bit graphic can have $2^4 = 16$ colors, and an 8 bit graphic can have $2^8 = 256$ colors. How many colors can a 16 bit graphic have? **65,536 colors**

Example 3 *Finding a Scale Factor*

Computer Graphics An artist uses a computer program to enlarge a design, as shown. What is the scale factor of the dilation?

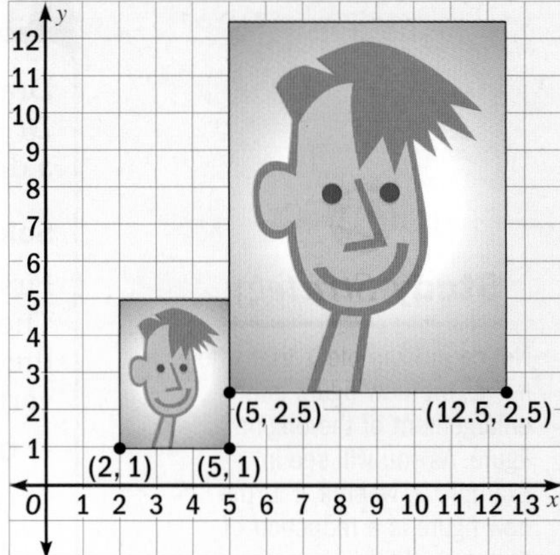

Solution

The width of the original design is $5 - 2 = 3$ units. The width of the image is $12.5 - 5 = 7.5$ units. So, the scale factor is $\frac{7.5 \text{ units}}{3 \text{ units}}$, or 2.5.

Checkpoint

3. Given $\overline{AB}$ with endpoints $A(0.5, 1)$ and $B(1.5, 1)$, let $\overline{A'B'}$ with endpoints $A'(3, 6)$ and $B'(9, 6)$ be the image of $\overline{AB}$ after a dilation. Find the scale factor. **6**

Note *Worthy*

For each transformation that you studied in this chapter, you should include an example in your notebook along with a summary of the characteristics of the transformation.

SUMMARY Transformations in a Coordinate Plane

Translations

In a translation, each point of a figure is moved the same distance in the same direction.

$(x, y) \rightarrow (x + a, y + b)$

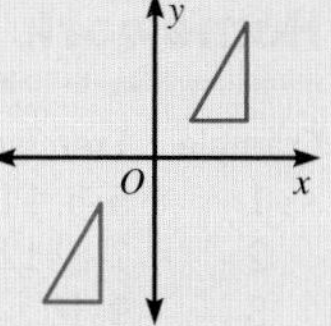

Reflections

In a reflection, a figure is flipped over a line.

Reflection in x-axis: $(x, y) \rightarrow (x, -y)$
Reflection in y-axis (shown): $(x, y) \rightarrow (-x, y)$

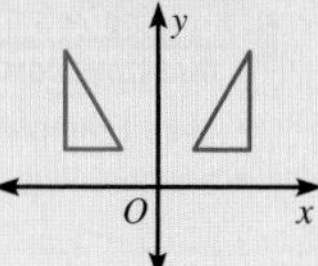

Rotations

In the rotations below, a figure is turned about the origin through a given angle and direction.

90° clockwise rotation (shown): $(x, y) \rightarrow (y, -x)$
90° counterclockwise rotation: $(x, y) \rightarrow (-y, x)$
180° rotation: $(x, y) \rightarrow (-x, -y)$

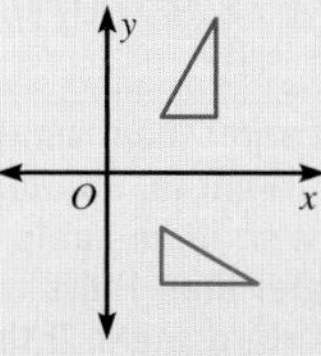

Dilations

In the dilation below, a figure stretches or shrinks with respect to the origin.

$(x, y) \rightarrow (kx, ky)$, where k is the scale factor

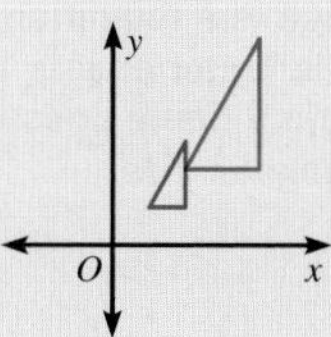

13.7 Exercises

More Practice, p. 815

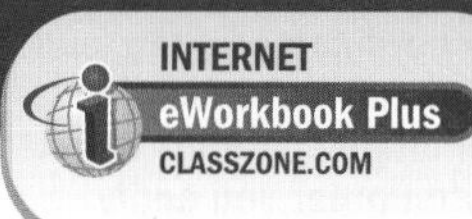

Guided Practice

Vocabulary Check

1. Copy and complete: In a translation, a figure and its image are congruent. In a dilation, a figure and its image are _?_. **similar**

2. Let $P(2, 3)$ be a point on a figure. The figure is dilated by a scale factor of 4. What are the coordinates of P'? **$P'(8, 12)$**

Skill Check

3. Draw $\triangle ABC$ with vertices $A(-2, 0)$, $B(1, 1)$, and $C(2, -1)$. Then find the coordinates of the vertices of the image after a dilation having a scale factor of 3, and draw the image. **See margin for art; $A'(-6, 0)$, $B'(3, 3)$, $C'(6, -3)$.**

4. Given $\overline{AB}$ with endpoints $A(-2, 3)$ and $B(-2, -4)$, let $\overline{A'B'}$ with endpoints $A'(-5, 7.5)$ and $B'(-5, -10)$ be the image of $\overline{AB}$ after a dilation. What is the scale factor of the dilation? **2.5**

COMMON ERROR

Watch for students who expect a figure and its dilated image either to be positioned so that one of them is inside the other (as in Example 1), or to be positioned side by side (as in Example 2). Help students understand why the figures in the two examples appear differently. Inform students that a figure and its image under a dilation can also overlap.

TEACHING TIP

Clarify that a dilation can make a figure either larger or smaller. Students familiar with the everyday usage of the word *dilate* may think that a dilation can only expand a figure.

NOTETAKING

Have students copy the summary information about transformations in a coordinate plane into their notebooks for future reference.

CONCEPT CHECK

A rectangle 3 units wide and 4 units long is transformed by a dilation having a scale factor of 2.5. What are the dimensions of the rectangular image? **7.5 units wide and 10 units long**

DAILY PUZZLER

How many equilateral triangles can you build from 9 new pencils? Explain. **5 triangles; four of the triangles have sides formed by 1 pencil and the other triangle has sides that are each formed by 2 pencils.**

3.

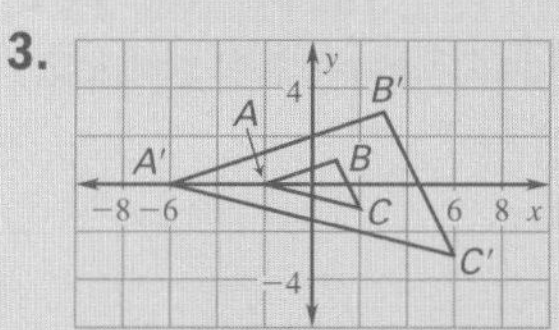

3 APPLY

ASSIGNMENT GUIDE

Basic Course

Day 1: pp. 750–751 Exs. 5–8, 14, 19–24

Day 2: pp. 750–751 Exs. 9–11, 13, 15, 16, 25–27

Average Course

Day 1: pp. 750–751 Exs. 5–8, 12–16, 19–24

Day 2: pp. 750–751 Exs. 9–11, 18, 25–27

Advanced Course

Day 1: pp. 750–751 Exs. 6–8, 12–16, 19, 22–24

Day 2: pp. 750–751 Exs. 9–11, 17*, 18, 25–27

Block

pp. 750–751 Exs. 5–16, 18–27

EXTRA PRACTICE

- Student Edition, p. 815
- Chapter 13 Resource Book, pp. 58–60
- Test and Practice Generator

TRANSPARENCY

Even-numbered answers are available on transparencies. A support transparency is available for Exercises 3, 5–8, 11, 13–18, and 25.

HOMEWORK CHECK

When you review students' homework for this lesson, go over the following exercises to check understanding of key concepts.

Basic: 5, 7, 8, 9, 11
Average: 5, 7, 9, 10, 11
Advanced: 6, 8, 10, 11, 12

5–8, 11a–b, 13a, 14–17, 18b, 25. See Additional Answers beginning on page AA1.

Practice and Problem Solving

Homework *Help*

Example	Exercises
1	5-6, 11-12
2	7-8, 12
3	9-10

- More Examples
- eTutorial Plus

The vertices of a polygon are given. Draw the polygon. Then find the coordinates of the vertices of the image after a dilation having the given scale factor, and draw the image. **5–8. See margin for art.**

A **5.** $A(-1, 2), B(3, 1), C(1, -4); k = 2$ **A′(−2, 4), B′(6, 2), C′(2, −8)**

6. $X(-1, 2), Y(2, 1), Z(-1, -3); k = 3$ **X′(−3, 6), Y′(6, 3), Z′(−3, −9)**

7. $P(-6, 2), Q(2, 2), R(2, 0), S(-6, 0); k = 0.5$ **See margin.**

8. $E(-8, 4), F(4, 4), G(0, -4), H(-4, -4); k = \frac{1}{4}$
E′(−2, 1), F′(1, 1), G′(0, −1), H′(−1, −1)

Find the scale factor of the dilation.

9. **2**

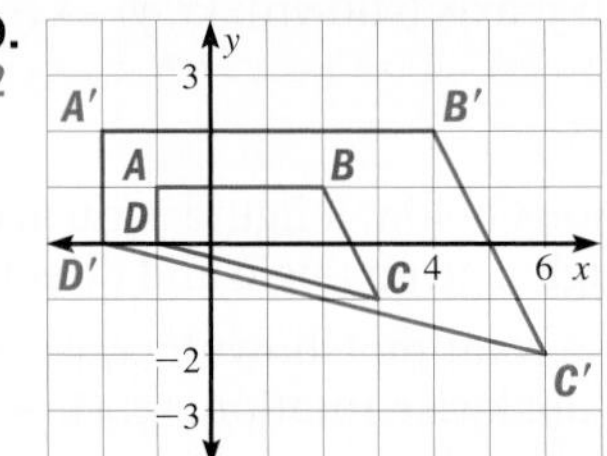

10. $\frac{1}{3}$

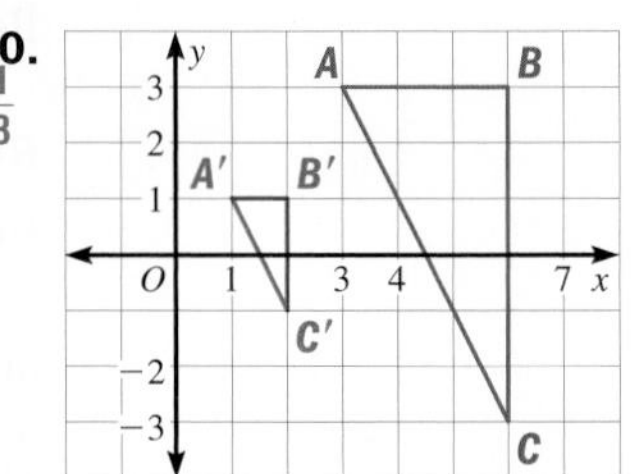

7. **P′(−3, 1), Q′(1, 1), R′(1, 0), S′(−3, 0)**

12. **Larger than; smaller than; congruent to. *Sample answer:* If the scale factor is greater than 1, the image is an enlargement. If the scale factor is less than 1, the image is a reduction. If the scale factor equals 1, the original figure does not change in size.**

11. Illusions You can use dilations to create the illusion of an object moving toward you.

a. Draw rectangle $ABCD$ with vertices $A(-2, -1,), B(-1, -1), C(-1, -1.5)$, and $D(-2, -1.5)$. **11a–b. See margin.**

b. On the same coordinate plane, draw the images of rectangle $ABCD$ using the following scale factors: 2, 4, 8.

12. ***Writing*** Is an image *smaller than, larger than,* or *congruent to* the original figure when the scale factor is 3? 0.5? 1? Explain. **See margin.**

B **13.** Draw $\triangle ABC$ with vertices $A(-2, 4), B(4, 0)$, and $C(2, -4)$.

a. You dilate $\triangle ABC$ using a scale factor of 0.25. You then dilate its image using a scale factor of 2. Find the coordinates of the vertices of the final image, and draw the image.
A″(−1, 2), B″(2, 0), C″(1, −2); see margin for art.

b. Use the scale factors given in part (a) to find the scale factor you could use to dilate $\triangle ABC$ to the final image in one step. **0.5**

c. Critical Thinking Do you get the same final image if you switch the order of the dilations in part (a)? Explain your reasoning.

13c. **Yes. *Sample answer:* Since dilating a figure just multiplies the coordinates by the scale factor, and multiplication is commutative, it does not matter in what order you apply multiple scale factors.**

14. Nesting Dolls The figure is the front view of one of the dolls in a set of nesting dolls. Draw the outline of the figure. Then, on the same coordinate plane, draw the images of the outline after dilations having the following scale factors: $\frac{1}{2}, 1\frac{1}{2}, 2$. **See margin.**

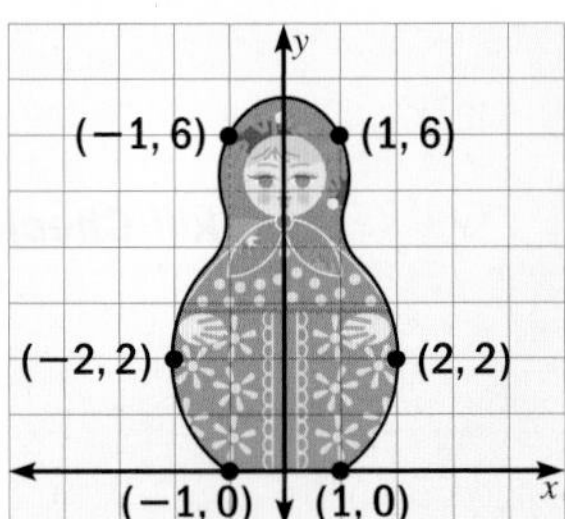

18b. $A'(0, -9)$, $B'(9, 3)$, $C'(9, -9)$; see margin for art; 36 units, 54 square units.

18c. It is the same as the ratio of the perimeters and it is the square root of the ratio of the areas.

In Exercises 15 and 16, $\triangle DEF$ has vertices $D(-2, -4)$, $E(6, 2)$, and $F(0, 4)$. Draw $\triangle DEF$. Then find the coordinates of the vertices of the final image after the specified transformations, and draw the final image. 15–16. See margin for art.

15. Dilate $\triangle DEF$ using a scale factor of 2, then translate its image using $(x, y) \to (x - 2, y + 3)$. $D''(-6, -5)$, $E''(10, 7)$, $F''(-2, 11)$

16. Dilate $\triangle DEF$ using a scale factor of 0.5, then rotate its image 180°. $D''(1, 2)$, $E''(-3, -1)$, $F''(0, -2)$

C **17. Challenge** A triangle is dilated using a scale factor of 2, then its image is reflected in the y-axis. The figure shown is the final image. Find the coordinates of the vertices of the original triangle, and draw the original triangle. $P(2, 1)$, $Q(2, -1)$, $R(0, -1)$; see margin for art.

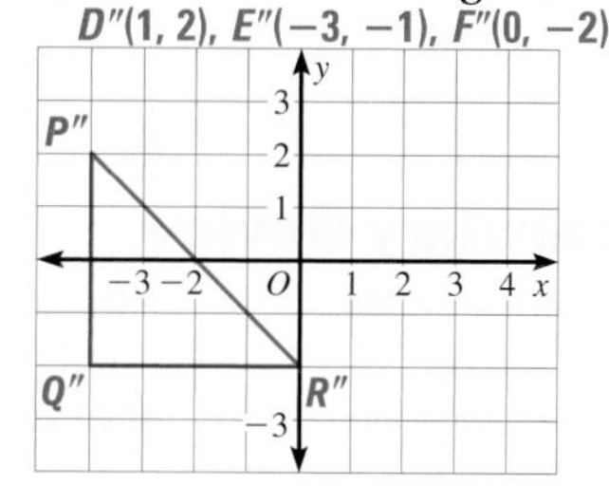

18. Extended Problem Solving Draw $\triangle ABC$ with vertices $A(0, -3)$, $B(3, 1)$, and $C(3, -3)$.

a. Calculate Find the perimeter and the area of $\triangle ABC$. 12 units, 6 square units

b. Find the coordinates of the vertices of the image of $\triangle ABC$ after a dilation having a scale factor of 3, and draw the image. Then find the perimeter and the area of the image.

c. Compare How is the scale factor related to the ratios

$$\frac{\text{Perimeter of image of } \triangle ABC}{\text{Perimeter of } \triangle ABC} \text{ and } \frac{\text{Area of image of } \triangle ABC}{\text{Area of } \triangle ABC}?$$

Mixed Review

Find the number of permutations or combinations. *(Lessons 11.6, 11.7)*

19. ${}_4P_2$ 12 **20.** ${}_8P_5$ 6720 **21.** ${}_9C_9$ 1 **22.** ${}_{25}C_3$ 2300

Write the expression as a polynomial in standard form. *(Lesson 12.1)*

23. $4t + 1 - 6t + t^4 - 4$ $t^4 - 2t - 3$ **24.** $2(b - 6b^2) - 9b$ $-12b^2 - 7b$

25. Draw $\triangle DEF$ with vertices $D(4, 3)$, $E(6, 2)$, and $F(5, 1)$. Then find the coordinates of the vertices of the image after a 90° counterclockwise rotation about the origin, and draw the image. *(Lesson 13.6)* See margin for art; $D'(-3, 4)$, $E'(-2, 6)$, $F'(-1, 5)$.

Standardized Test Practice

26. Multiple Choice Let $P(2, 4)$ be a point on a figure, and let P' be the corresponding point on the image. The figure is dilated by a scale factor of 4. What are the coordinates of P'? D

A. $(-2, 0)$ **B.** $\left(\frac{1}{2}, 1\right)$ **C.** $(6, 8)$ **D.** $(8, 16)$

27. Multiple Choice In the diagram, quadrilateral $A'B'C'D'$ is the image of quadrilateral $ABCD$ after a dilation. What is the scale factor? G

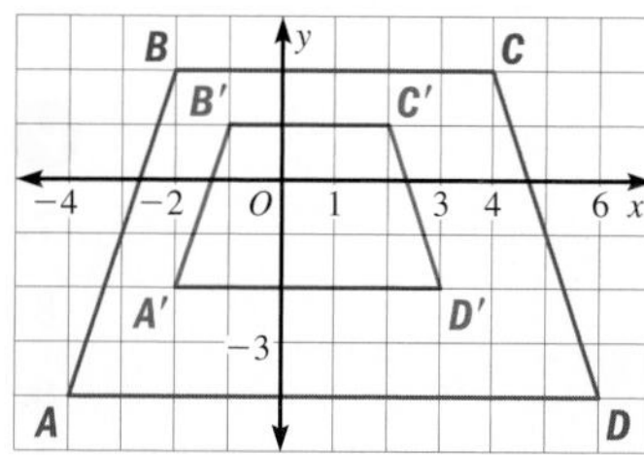

F. $\frac{1}{4}$ **G.** $\frac{1}{2}$

H. 2 **I.** 3

4 ASSESS

Assessment Resources

For more assessment resources, see:
- Assessment Book
- Test and Practice Generator

Mini-Quiz

$\triangle ABC$ has vertices $A(10, 0)$, $B(15, 5)$, and $C(20, -5)$. Find the coordinates of the vertices of the image after the dilation with the given scale factor.

1. 4 $A'(40, 0)$, $B'(60, 20)$, $C'(80, -20)$

2. $\frac{1}{5}$ $A'(2, 0)$, $B'(3, 1)$, $C'(4, -1)$

3. In a dilation, the image of $A(-9, 6)$ is $A'(-3, 2)$. Find the scale factor of the dilation. $\frac{1}{3}$

4. Challenge A triangle is dilated using a scale factor of $\frac{1}{2}$, then its image is reflected in the x-axis to produce an image with vertices $K'(0, -1)$, $L'(2, -2)$, $M'(-1, 0)$. Find the coordinates of the vertices of the original triangle. $K(0, 2)$, $L(4, 4)$, $M(-2, 0)$

5 FOLLOW-UP

Diagnosis/Remediation

- Study Guide in Chapter 13 Resource Book, pp. 61–62
- Tutor Place, Algebra Card 18
- eTutorial Plus Online
- Extra Practice, p. 815
- Lesson Practice in Chapter 13 Resource Book, pp. 58–60

English Learner Support

- Spanish Study Guide
- Multi-Language Visual Glossary
- Chapter Audio Summaries CDs

Challenge

- Challenge Practice in Chapter 13 Resource Book, p. 64
- Teacher's Edition, p. 706F

Additional Resources

The following resources are available to help review the materials in Lessons 13.4–13.7.

Chapter 13 Resource Book
- Lesson Practice
- Study Guide

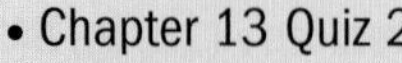

Assessment Book
- Chapter 13 Quiz 2

Technology
- Test and Practice Generator
- eTutorial CD-ROM

Internet
- Classzone
- eWorkbook Plus Online
- eTutorial Plus Online

English Learner Support

- Spanish Study Guide
- Multi-Language Visual Glossary
- Chapter Audio Summaries CDs

2. ***Sample answer:*** **If it has line symmetry, there is at least one line that divides the figure into two parts that are reflections of each other. If it has rotational symmetry, a rotation of 180° or less about the center of the figure produces an image that matches up exactly with the original.**

CHAPTER 13

Chapter Review

Vocabulary Review

1. What is the sum of the measures of two complementary angles? two supplementary angles? **90°; 180°**
2. How can you tell whether a figure has line symmetry? rotational symmetry? **See margin.**
3. Let $P(x, y)$ be a point on a figure. What are the coordinates of P' when the figure is reflected in the x-axis? rotated 180°? dilated using a scale factor of 2? $P'(x, -y)$; $P'(-x, -y)$; $P'(2x, 2y)$
4. How are the measures of two vertical angles related? **They are equal.**

Copy and complete the statement.

5. When a transversal intersects two lines, the angles that lie between the two lines on opposites sides of the transversal are _?_. **alternate interior angles**
6. A(n) _?_ angle of a polygon is an angle that lies inside the polygon. **interior**

13.1 Angle Relationships

Examples on pp. 709–710

Goal

Identify and find measures of complementary, supplementary, and vertical angles.

Example **$\angle 1$ and $\angle 2$ are supplementary angles, and $m\angle 1 = 46°$. Find $m\angle 2$.**

$m\angle 1 + m\angle 2 = 180°$	**Definition of supplementary angles**
$46° + m\angle 2 = 180°$	**Substitute 46° for $m\angle 1$.**
$m\angle 2 = 134°$	**Subtract 46° from each side.**

Use the given information to find $m\angle 2$.

7. $\angle 1$ and $\angle 2$ are complementary angles, and $m\angle 1 = 76°$. **14°**
8. $\angle 1$ and $\angle 2$ are vertical angles, and $m\angle 1 = 84°$. **84°**
9. $\angle 1$ and $\angle 2$ are supplementary angles, and $m\angle 1 = 121°$. **59°**

The following resources are available to help review the materials in this chapter.

Chapter 13 Resource Book

- Chapter Review Games and Activities, p. 65
- Cumulative Practice, Chs. 1–13

English/Spanish Chapter Reviews and Tests

Chapter Audio Summaries CDs

eTutorial CD-ROM

eWorkbook Plus Online

eTutorial Plus Online

13.2 Angles and Parallel Lines

Examples on pp. 716–718

Goal

Identify angles formed when a transversal intersects two lines.

Example **Tell whether ∠1 and ∠8 in the diagram are *corresponding*, *alternate interior*, or *alternate exterior* angles.**

Because ∠1 and ∠8 lie outside lines m and n on opposite sides of the transversal t, they are alternate exterior angles.

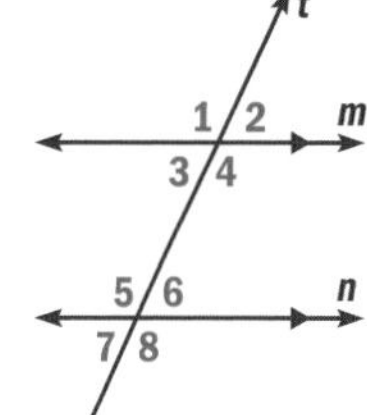

Example **In the diagram, lines *m* and *n* are parallel, and *m*∠1 = 115°. Find *m*∠8.**

Because ∠1 and ∠8 are alternate exterior angles, they have the same measure when formed by parallel lines. So, $m\angle 8 = 115°$.

Tell whether the angles in the diagram above are *corresponding*, *alternate interior*, or *alternate exterior* angles.

10. ∠2 and ∠6 corresponding
11. ∠3 and ∠6 alternate interior
12. ∠2 and ∠7 alternate exterior
13. ∠4 and ∠5 alternate interior

In the diagram above, lines *m* and *n* are parallel, and *m*∠1 = 115°. Find the specified angle measure.

14. $m\angle 2$ 65°
15. $m\angle 4$ 115°
16. $m\angle 5$ 115°
17. $m\angle 7$ 65°

13.3 Angles and Polygons

Examples on pp. 722–724

Goal

Find measures of interior and exterior angles of convex polygons.

Example **Find the measures of an interior angle and an exterior angle of a regular pentagon.**

a. The measure of an interior angle of a regular pentagon is $\frac{(5-2) \cdot 180°}{5} = 108°$.

b. An interior angle and an exterior angle at the same vertex form a straight angle. Because the measure of an interior angle of a regular pentagon is 108°, the measure of an exterior angle is $180° - 108° = 72°$.

Find the measures of an interior angle and an exterior angle of the regular polygon. Round to the nearest tenth, if necessary.

18. Heptagon 128.6°, 51.4°
19. Octagon 135°, 45°
20. 10-gon 144°, 36°
21. 13-gon 152.3°, 27.7°

22. The measures of a triangle's exterior angles, one at each vertex, are 97°, 102°, and $y°$. Find the value of y. 161

23.

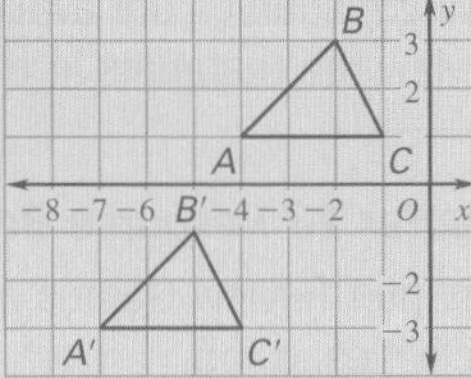

24.

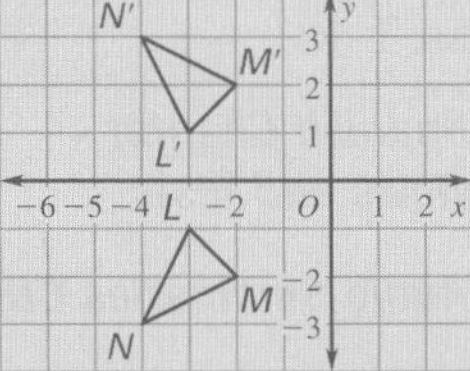

25.

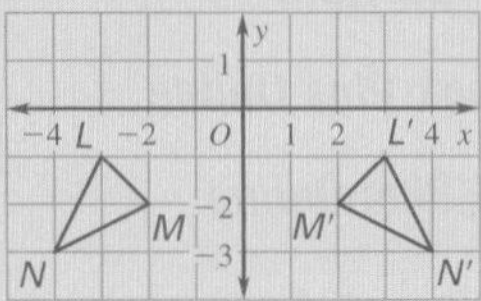

13.4 Translations

Examples on pp. 729–731

Goal

Translate figures in a coordinate plane.

Example **Draw $\triangle ABC$ with vertices $A(-4, 1)$, $B(-2, 3)$, and $C(-1, 1)$. Then find the coordinates of the vertices of the image after the translation $(x, y) \to (x + 5, y - 2)$, and draw the image.**

First draw $\triangle ABC$. Then, to translate $\triangle ABC$, add 5 to the x-coordinate and subtract 2 from the y-coordinate of each vertex.

Original		Image
(x, y)	$\to$	$(x + 5, y - 2)$
$A(-4, 1)$	$\to$	$A'(1, -1)$
$B(-2, 3)$	$\to$	$B'(3, 1)$
$C(-1, 1)$	$\to$	$C'(4, -1)$

Finally, draw $\triangle A'B'C'$, as shown.

23. Draw $\triangle ABC$ given above. Then find the coordinates of the vertices of the image after the translation $(x, y) \to (x - 3, y - 4)$, and draw the image. **See margin for art; $A'(-7, -3)$, $B'(-5, -1)$, $C'(-4, -3)$.**

13.5 Reflections and Symmetry

Examples on pp. 734–735

Goal

Reflect figures in a coordinate plane.

Example **Draw $\triangle DEF$ with vertices $D(1, 3)$, $E(3, 2)$, and $F(2, -1)$. Then find the coordinates of the vertices of the image after a reflection in the y-axis, and draw the image.**

First draw $\triangle DEF$. Then, to reflect $\triangle DEF$ in the y-axis, multiply the x-coordinate of each vertex by -1.

Original		Image
(x, y)	$\to$	$(-x, y)$
$D(1, 3)$	$\to$	$D'(-1, 3)$
$E(3, 2)$	$\to$	$E'(-3, 2)$
$F(2, -1)$	$\to$	$F'(-2, -1)$

Finally, draw $\triangle D'E'F'$, as shown.

Draw $\triangle LMN$ with vertices $L(-3, -1)$, $M(-2, -2)$, and $N(-4, -3)$. Then find the coordinates of the vertices of the image after the specified reflection, and draw the image. **24–25. See margin for art.**

24. Reflection in the x-axis
$L'(-3, 1)$, $M'(-2, 2)$, $N'(-4, 3)$

25. Reflection in the y-axis
$L'(3, -1)$, $M'(2, -2)$, $N'(4, -3)$

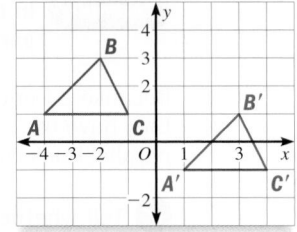

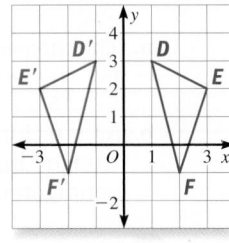

13.6 Rotations and Symmetry

Examples on pp. 741–743

Goal

Rotate figures in a coordinate plane.

Draw $\triangle PQR$ with vertices $P(1, 2)$, $Q(2, 3)$, and $R(3, 1)$. Then find the coordinates of the vertices of the image after a 90° counterclockwise rotation, and draw the image.

First draw $\triangle PQR$. Then, to rotate $\triangle PQR$ 90° counterclockwise, switch the coordinates and multiply the new x-coordinate of each vertex by -1.

Original		Image
(x, y)	$\rightarrow$	$(-y, x)$
$P(1, 2)$	$\rightarrow$	$P'(-2, 1)$
$Q(2, 3)$	$\rightarrow$	$Q'(-3, 2)$
$R(3, 1)$	$\rightarrow$	$R'(-1, 3)$

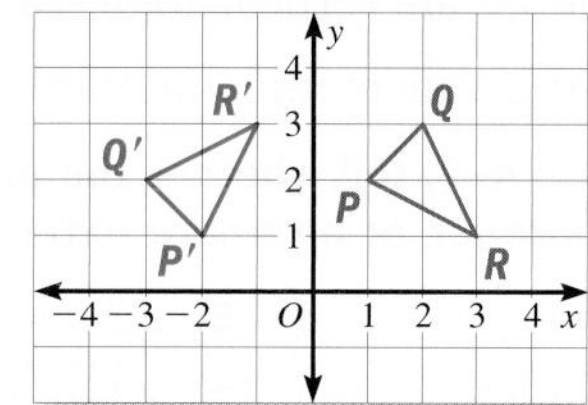

Finally, draw $\triangle P'Q'R'$, as shown.

Draw $\triangle PQR$ given above. Then find the coordinates of the vertices of the image after the specified rotation, and draw the image.
26–27. See margin for art.

26. 90° clockwise rotation
$P'(2, -1)$, $Q'(3, -2)$, $R'(1, -3)$

27. 180° rotation
$P'(-1, -2)$, $Q'(-2, -3)$, $R'(-3, -1)$

13.7 Dilations

Examples on pp. 747–749

Goal

Dilate figures in a coordinate plane.

Draw $\triangle STU$ with vertices $S(-2, -1)$, $T(0, 1)$, and $U(1, -1)$. Then find the coordinates of the vertices of the image after a dilation having a scale factor of 2, and draw the image.

First draw $\triangle STU$. Then, to dilate $\triangle STU$, multiply the coordinates of each vertex by 2.

Original		Image
(x, y)	$\rightarrow$	$(2x, 2y)$
$S(-2, -1)$	$\rightarrow$	$S'(-4, -2)$
$T(0, 1)$	$\rightarrow$	$T'(0, 2)$
$U(1, -1)$	$\rightarrow$	$U'(2, -2)$

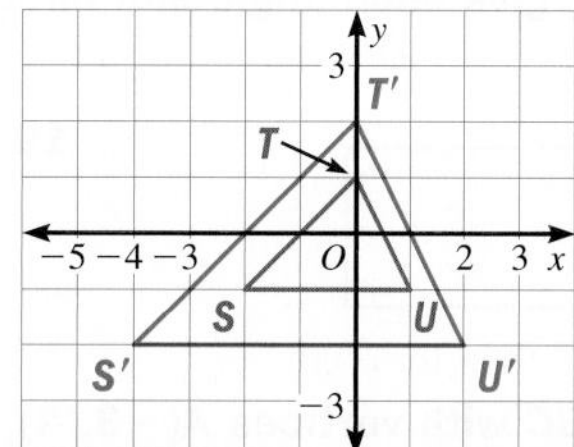

Finally, draw $\triangle S'T'U'$, as shown.

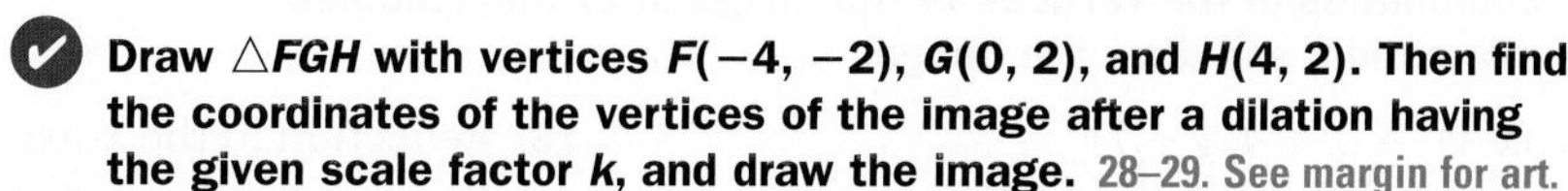

Draw $\triangle FGH$ with vertices $F(-4, -2)$, $G(0, 2)$, and $H(4, 2)$. Then find the coordinates of the vertices of the image after a dilation having the given scale factor k, and draw the image. 28–29. See margin for art.

28. $k = 3$ $F'(-12, -6)$, $G'(0, 6)$, $H'(12, 6)$ **29.** $k = 0.5$ $F'(-2, -1)$, $G'(0, 1)$, $H'(2, 1)$

26.

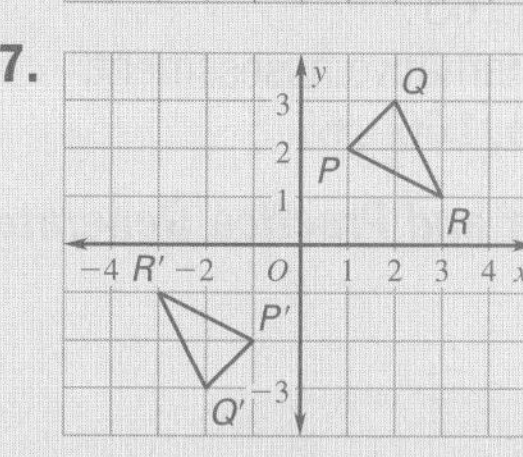

27.

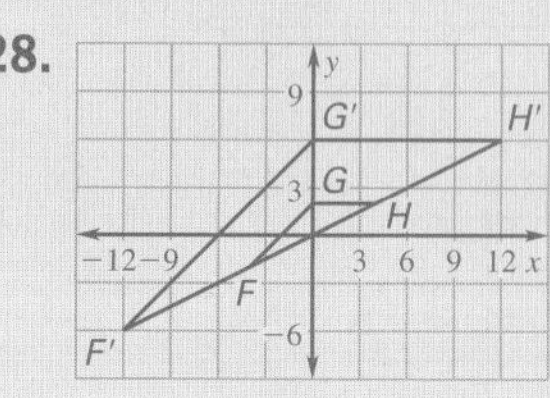

28.

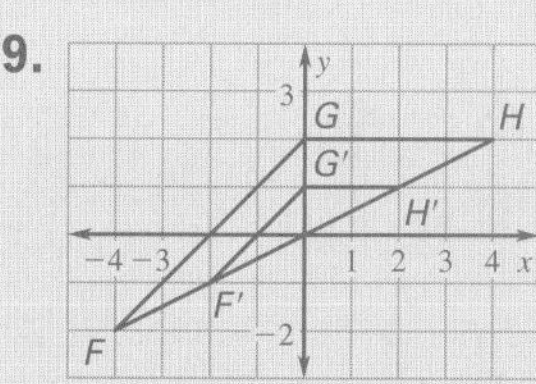

29.

ADDITIONAL RESOURCES

Assessment Book

- Chapter Test (3 levels), pp. 159–164
- Standardized Chapter Test, p. 165
- Alternative Assessment, pp. 166–167

Test and Practice Generator

14.

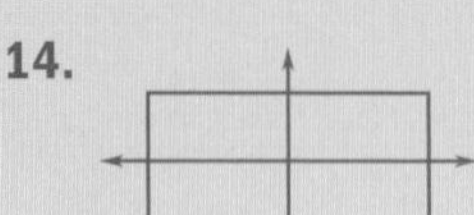

15.

16.

17.

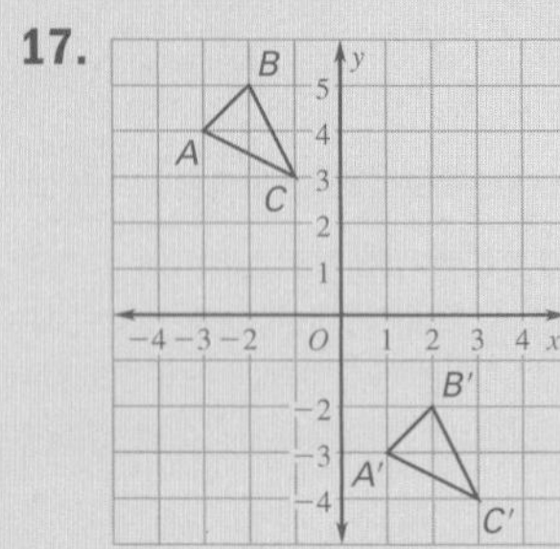

18.

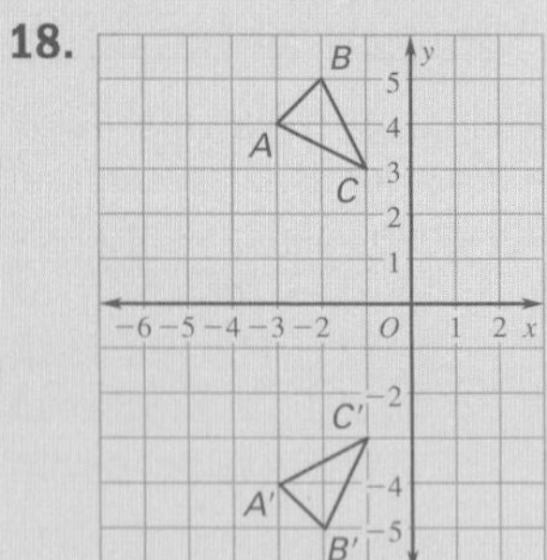

19.

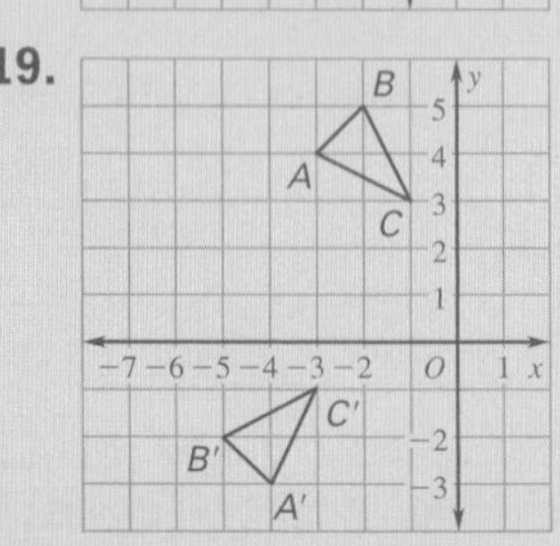

20. See Additional Answers beginning on page AA1.

CHAPTER 13

Chapter Test

Use the given information to find $m\angle 2$.

1. $\angle 1$ and $\angle 2$ are supplementary angles, and $m\angle 1 = 64°$. 116°
2. $\angle 1$ and $\angle 2$ are vertical angles, and $m\angle 1 = 81°$. 81°
3. $\angle 1$ and $\angle 2$ are complementary angles, and $m\angle 1 = 77°$. 13°

In Exercises 4–7, tell whether the angles in the diagram are *corresponding*, *alternate interior*, or *alternate exterior* angles.

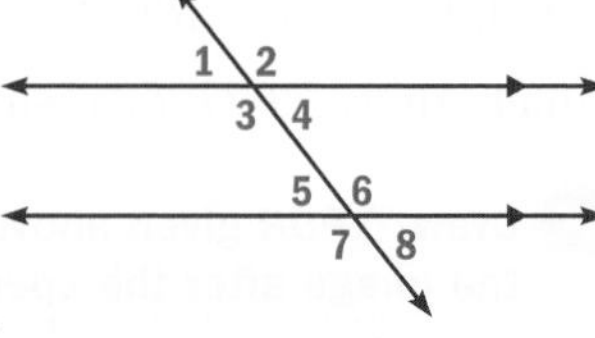

4. $\angle 1$ and $\angle 5$ corresponding
5. $\angle 2$ and $\angle 7$ alternate exterior
6. $\angle 4$ and $\angle 5$ alternate interior
7. $\angle 4$ and $\angle 8$ corresponding
8. If $m\angle 3 = 128°$, find the measures of the other numbered angles in the diagram. $m\angle 1 = 52°$, $m\angle 2 = 128°$, $m\angle 4 = 52°$, $m\angle 5 = 52°$, $m\angle 6 = 128°$, $m\angle 7 = 128°$, $m\angle 8 = 52°$
9. Find the measure of an interior angle of a regular hexagon. 120°
10. Find the measure of an exterior angle of a regular 9-gon. 40°

Find the unknown angle measure in the diagram.

11. 129°

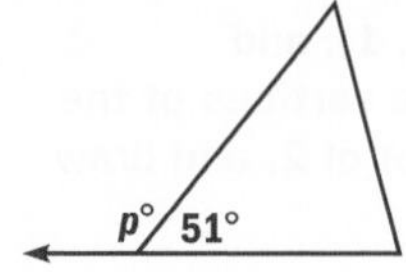

12. 140°

q°, 129°, 141°, 120°, 137°, 143°

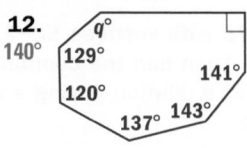

13. 73°

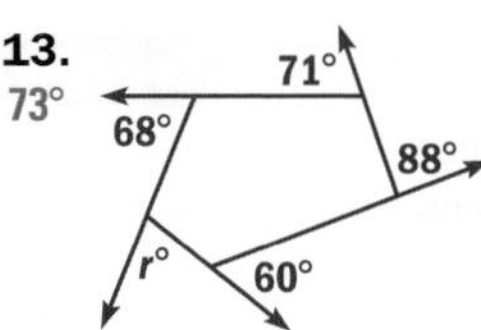

Draw the polygon and any lines of symmetry. If the polygon has rotational symmetry, give each angle and direction of rotation that produce rotational symmetry. 14–16. See margin for art.

14. 180° in either direction

15. no rotational symmetry

16. 120° in either direction

Draw $\triangle ABC$ with vertices $A(-3, 4)$, $B(-2, 5)$, and $C(-1, 3)$. Then find the coordinates of the vertices of the image after the specified transformation, and draw the image. 17–20. See margin for art.

17. $(x, y) \to (x + 4, y - 7)$
$A'(1, -3)$, $B'(2, -2)$, $C'(3, -4)$
18. Reflection in the x-axis
$A'(-3, -4)$, $B'(-2, -5)$, $C'(-1, -3)$
19. 90° counterclockwise rotation
$A'(-4, -3)$, $B'(-5, -2)$, $C'(-3, -1)$
20. Dilation having a scale factor of 2
$A'(-6, 8)$, $B'(-4, 10)$, $C'(-2, 6)$

Additional Resources

Assessment Book
- Standardized Chapter Test, p. 165

Test and Practice Generator

Chapter Standardized Test

Test-Taking Strategy **Think positively when you take a test. A positive attitude can help you stay focused on the questions.**

1. In the diagram, $m\angle 1 = 73°$. What is $m\angle 2$? **B**

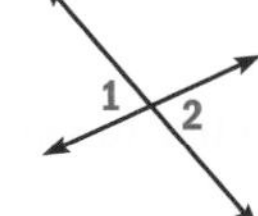

A. 17° **B.** 73° **C.** 107° **D.** 146°

2. If $\angle 3$ and $\angle 4$ are supplementary angles, what could their measures be? **G**

F. $m\angle 3 = 110°$, $m\angle 4 = 110°$
G. $m\angle 3 = 97°$, $m\angle 4 = 83°$
H. $m\angle 3 = 57°$, $m\angle 4 = 33°$
I. $m\angle 3 = 82°$, $m\angle 4 = 41°$

In Exercises 3 and 4, use the diagram.

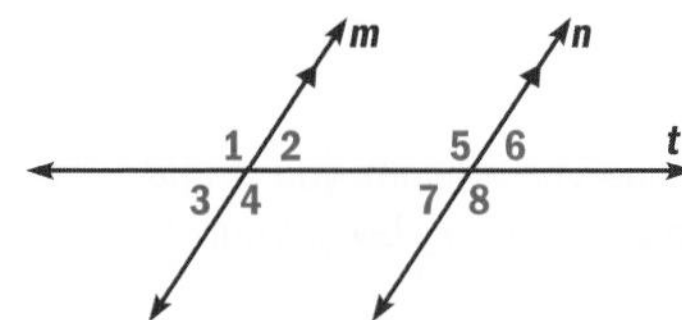

3. Which angles are alternate exterior angles? **B**

A. $\angle 1$ and $\angle 4$ **B.** $\angle 3$ and $\angle 6$
C. $\angle 2$ and $\angle 7$ **D.** $\angle 1$ and $\angle 5$

4. Transversal t intersects parallel lines m and n. If $m\angle 2 = 57°$, what is $m\angle 7$? **G**

F. 33° **G.** 57° **H.** 114° **I.** 123°

5. What is the sum of the measures of the interior angles of a convex octagon? **D**

A. 135° **B.** 360° **C.** 720° **D.** 1080°

6. What is the measure of an exterior angle of a regular pentagon? **F**

F. 72° **G.** 108° **H.** 120° **I.** 540°

In Exercises 7–9, use the diagram.

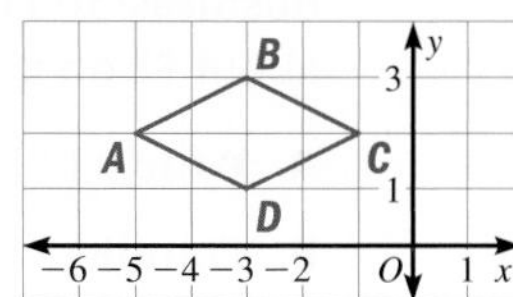

7. What are the coordinates of C' after the translation $(x, y) \to (x + 2, y - 1)$? **A**

A. (1, 1) **B.** (1, 3) **C.** (0, 0) **D.** (0, 4)

8. How many lines of symmetry does quadrilateral $ABCD$ have? **G**

F. 1 **G.** 2 **H.** 4 **I.** 8

9. The coordinates of D' are $(-9, 3)$ after a dilation. What is the scale factor? **D**

A. 0.25 **B.** 0.5 **C.** 2 **D.** 3

10. Short Response The measures of a pentagon's exterior angles, one exterior angle at each vertex, are 67°, 102°, 131°, 28°, and $2x°$. Find the value of x. Explain your reasoning. See margin.

11. Extended Response $\triangle ABC$ has vertices $A(3, 2)$, $B(3, 4)$, and $C(6, 2)$.

a. Find the coordinates of the vertices of the image of $\triangle ABC$ after a reflection in the y-axis, and draw the image $\triangle A'B'C'$. **$A'(-3, 2)$, $B'(-3, 4)$, $C'(-6, 2)$; see art in part b.**

b. Find the coordinates of the vertices of the image of $\triangle A'B'C'$ after a 180° rotation about the origin, and draw the image $\triangle A''B''C''$. **See margin for art; $A''(3, -2)$, $B''(3, -4)$, $C''(6, -2)$.**

c. How can you move $\triangle ABC$ to $\triangle A''B''C''$ using one transformation? Explain your reasoning. See margin.

10. 16. ***Sample answer:*** **The sum of the exterior angles of a convex polygon is 360°, so $67° + 102° + 131° + 28° + 2x° = 360°$, $328° + 2x° = 360°$, $2x° = 32°$, and $x = 16$.**

11b.

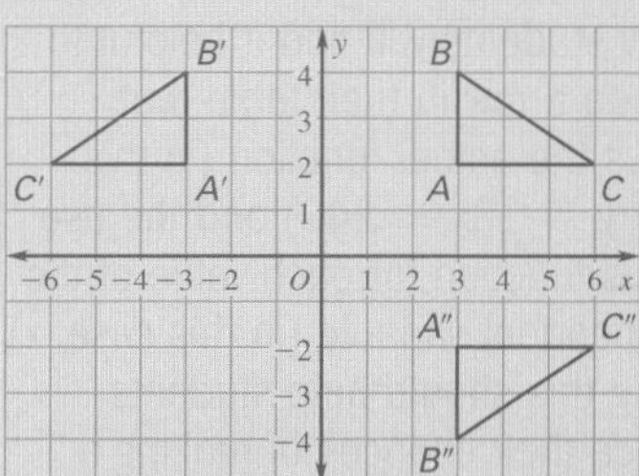

11c. Reflect $\triangle ABC$ in the x-axis. ***Sample answer:*** **Reflection in the y-axis moves the point with coordinates (x, y) to $(-x, y)$. A rotation of 180° in either direction moves $(-x, y)$ to $(-(-x), -y)$, that is to $(x, -y)$. But a reflection in the x-axis moves the point with coordinates (x, y) to $(x, -y)$.**

USING RUBRICS

The rubric given on the pupil page is a sample of a three-level rubric. Other rubrics may contain four, five, or six levels. For more information on rubrics, see the Professional Development Book.

TEST-TAKING TIP

Encourage students to read the question fully before beginning their work on a solution. Suggest that they take a few moments to organize the steps of the solution process in their mind before starting to write down their work. This approach will help organize their solution into a logical sequence of steps leading to their answer.

COMMON ERROR

When drawing graphs of any type, students sometimes forget to label axes or provide titles. Remind students of what constitutes a complete graph, and encourage them to examine their finished graphs for any missing elements that could result in a loss of credit.

VISUALIZE

Many students will find it helpful to include a row in their table that shows the actual function (in this case $y = 13x - 240$) and the use of this function for each value of the independent variable (in this case, x). Doing this should help students reduce their chances of making a computational error, enabling them to earn full credit for their solution.

Unit 4 Chapters 11–13

Building Test-Taking Skills

Scoring Rubric

Full credit
- answer is correct, *and*
- work or reasoning is included

Partial credit
- answer is correct, but reasoning is incorrect, *or*
- answer is incorrect, but reasoning is correct

No credit
- no answer is given, *or*
- answer makes no sense

Strategies for Answering Extended Response Questions

Problem You spend \$240 for a lawn mower to start a lawn mowing business. You charge \$15 per lawn. For each lawn you mow, you spend about \$2 on gas.

a. Write a polynomial you can use to calculate your profit.

b. Complete the table and draw a graph showing how your profit changes as the number of lawns mowed increases.

Lawns	20	30	40	50	60
Profit	?	?	?	?	?

c. If you mow 60 lawns, will your profit be twice as much as if you mow 30 lawns? Explain.

Full credit solution

a. Your profit is the amount you earn minus the amount you spend. You earn \$15 for every lawn and spend \$2 for every lawn. Your start-up cost was \$240.

Let x represent the number of lawns you mow.

The polynomial is correct.

$$\text{Profit} = 15x - (2x + 240)$$
$$= 13x - 240$$

The table and the graph are correct and reflect an understanding of the problem.

b.

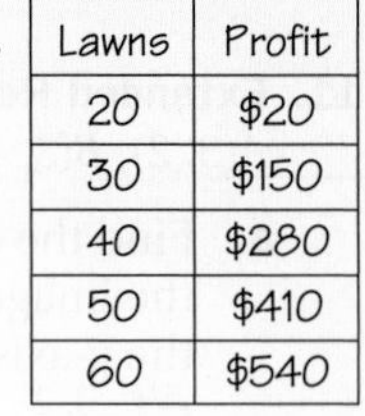

Lawns	Profit
20	\$20
30	\$150
40	\$280
50	\$410
60	\$540

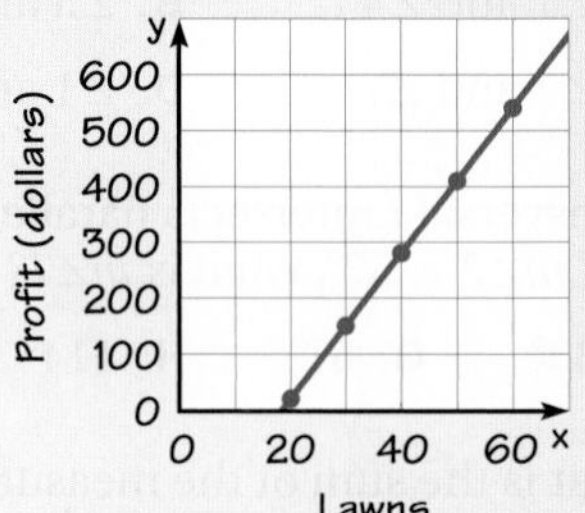

The answer is correct.

The reasoning behind the answer is explained clearly. Extra information is included to support the reasoning.

c. Your profit from mowing 60 lawns is more than twice your profit from mowing 30 lawns. In fact, if you mow 60 lawns you will earn more than three times as much as you earn from mowing 30 lawns. You would earn twice as much for 60 lawns as for 30 lawns if your profit per lawn were constant. Because your start-up cost of \$240 is the same regardless of how many lawns you mow, your profit per lawn increases as you mow more lawns.

Partial credit solution

The polynomial is correct.

a. Polynomial:
$15x - (2x + 240) = 13x - 240$

The table and the graph are correct and reflect an understanding of the problem.

b.

Lawns	Profit
20	\$20
30	\$150
40	\$280
50	\$410
60	\$540

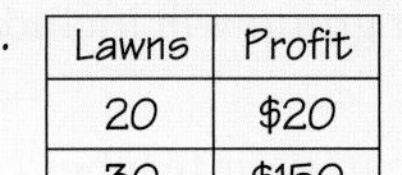

The answer is incorrect.

c. Because \$540 is less than twice \$280, you will earn less than twice as much mowing 60 lawns than mowing 30 lawns.

No credit solution

The polynomial is incorrect.

a. Profit = 15x

The table is incorrect, and there is no graph.

b.

Lawns	20	30	40	50	60
Profit	\$300	\$450	\$600	\$750	\$900

The answer is based on the incorrect table.

c. You will earn twice as much because \$900 is twice \$450.

Checkpoint

1. A student's answer to the problem on page 758 is given below. Score the answer as *full credit, partial credit,* or *no credit.* Explain your choice. If you choose *partial credit* or *no credit,* explain how you would change the answer to earn a score of *full credit.* **See margin.**

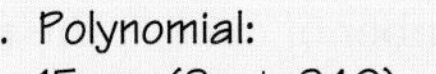

a. Polynomial:
$15x - (2x + 240) = 13x - 240$

b.

Lawns	Profit
20	\$20
30	\$150
40	\$280
50	\$410
60	\$540

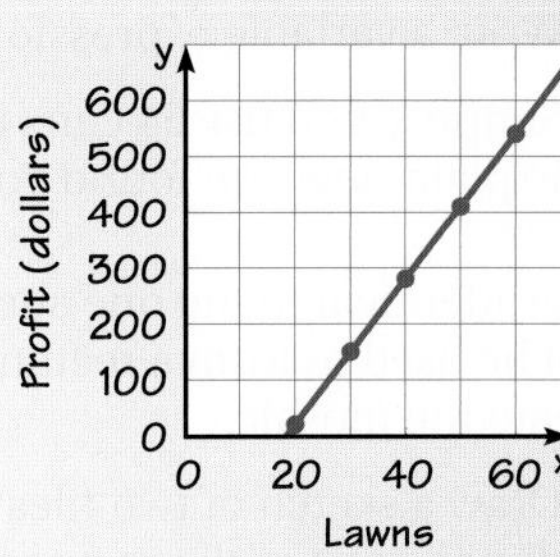

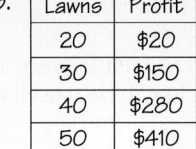

c. You will earn \$390 more mowing 60 lawns than mowing 30 lawns.

Watch *Out*

Scoring is often based on how clearly you explain your reasoning.

1. Partial credit. *Sample answer:* In parts (a) and (b), the polynomial, table, and graph are correct and reflect an understanding of the problem. In part (c), however, the question answered is not the question asked. The student needs to find whether the profit earned from mowing 60 lawns is twice that for mowing 30 lawns, not to find the simple difference in the profits.

1c. No. *Sample answer:* Of all the groups with you in them, only $\frac{286}{1001} \approx 29\%$ also contain your friend, so the probability that your friend is in your group is less than 3 in 10.

2a. Team 1. *Sample answer:* 10 points is the third quartile for Team 1, so about 75%, or 9, of the players scored 10 points or fewer; while for Team 2, 10 points is the median, so about 50%, or 6, of the players scored 10 points.

2b. Team 2. *Sample answer:* At every measure except the upper extreme, the points scored for Team 2 are higher, and even the upper extreme is only 2 points lower for Team 2 than Team 1. There are no outliers, so the mean number of points scored is probably not too far from the median, which would again indicate that Team 2 won the game.

3c. 8 levels. *Sample answer:* I noticed that the total number of cans for 1 level was 1, for 2 levels was 4, for 3 levels was 9, and for 4 levels was 16. I recognized this pattern as n^2, so I found n when $n^2 = 64$.

4a.

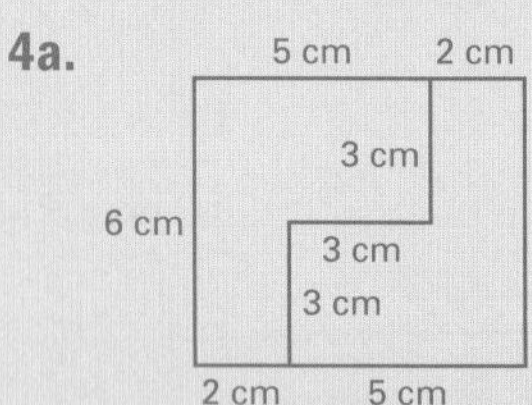

4b. 24 tiles. *Sample answer:* You can fit $4 \cdot 3 = 12$ of the 2-tile rectangles into the space by placing 4 rectangles with their 7 centimeter dimensions along the 28 centimeter side and 3 rectangles with their 6 centimeter dimensions along the 18 centimeter side. So the total number of tiles in the rectangular space is $12 \cdot 2 = 24$.

Unit 4 Practicing Test-Taking Skills

Chapters 11–13

Extended Response

1. You are in a class of 15 students. The teacher randomly selects students to work in groups on their unit projects. Your group will include yourself and 4 other students.

   a. How many different groups of 5 students can your teacher choose that include you? **1001 groups**

   b. Your friend is also in the class. How many different groups of 5 students can your teacher choose that include you and your friend? **286 groups**

   c. Is it likely that you and your friend will be in the same group? Use probability to explain your answer. **See margin.**

2. The box-and-whisker plots show the numbers of points that the players on two basketball teams scored during a game. Each team has 12 players. Use the box-and-whisker plots to justify your answers to the following questions.

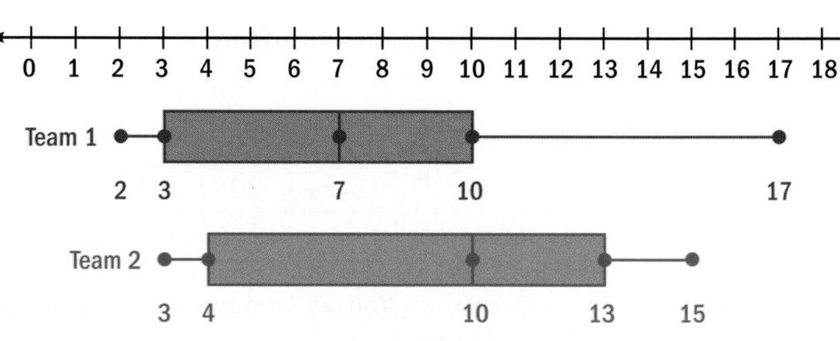

   a. Which team had more players who scored fewer than 10 points? Explain.

   b. Which team do you think won the game? Explain. **2a–b. See margin.**

3. You are stacking cans for a store display. The top level has 1 can. Each level below the top has 2 more cans than the level above it.

   a. Consider the sequence for the number of cans at each level. Write the first 6 terms of this sequence. **1, 3, 5, 7, 9, 11**

   b. Write a variable expression for the number of cans at the nth level. $2n - 1$

   c. Suppose you use 64 cans in your display. How many levels are there? Explain how you found your answer. **See margin.**

4. Tiles identical to the one shown will be used to create a mosaic. Two tiles will be used to form a rectangle. The rectangle will be tessellated to create the mosaic.

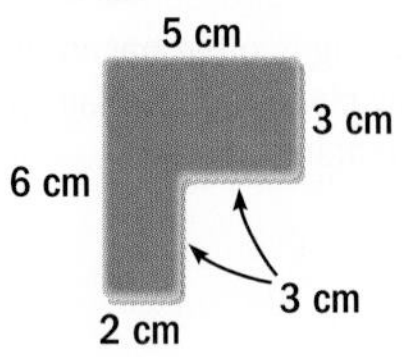

   a. Draw a sketch of two tiles positioned to form a rectangle. Give the dimensions of the rectangle. **See margin for art; 7 cm by 6 cm.**

   b. The mosaic must fit into a rectangular space that is 28 inches long and 18 inches wide. How many tiles fit into the space? Explain. **See margin.**

Multiple Choice

5. A scientist records the lengths of the tails of 45 spider monkeys. Which of the following should *not* be used to display the data? **C**

A. A histogram

B. A stem-and-leaf plot

C. A line graph

D. A box-and-whisker plot

6. What is the value of ${}_9C_5$? **G**

F. 4 **G.** 126 **H.** 252 **I.** 15,120

7. Find the product $(3x - 4)(x + 2)$. **A**

A. $3x^2 + 2x - 8$ **B.** $3x^2 - 2x + 8$

C. $3x^2 - 10x - 8$ **D.** $3x^2 - 10x + 8$

8. What is the degree of the polynomial $x^3 - 6x^3y$? **G**

F. 3 **G.** 4 **H.** 5 **I.** 6

9. What is the measure of ∠1? **C**

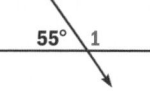

A. 35° **B.** 90°

C. 125° **D.** 180°

55° 1

10. What type of transformation is shown? **G**

F. Translation

G. Dilation

H. Reflection

I. Rotation

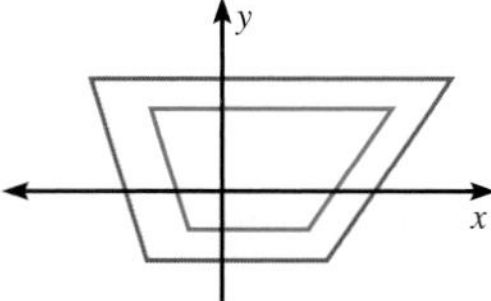

Short Response

11. Draw $\overline{AB}$ with endpoints $A(2, 3)$ and $B(6, 1)$. Find the coordinates of the endpoints of the image after a 90° clockwise rotation, and explain your steps. Then draw the image $\overline{A'B'}$. **See margin.**

12. A game uses tiles with a letter of the alphabet printed on each of them. A player has 7 tiles, each with a different letter. How many arrangements using all 7 tiles are possible? How many arrangements using 5 of the 7 tiles are possible? **5040 arrangements; 2520 arrangements**

13. For each labeled angle, tell whether the angle is complementary, supplementary, or congruent to ∠3. Suppose the measure of ∠3 is 124°. Find the measures of the other angles. **See margin.**

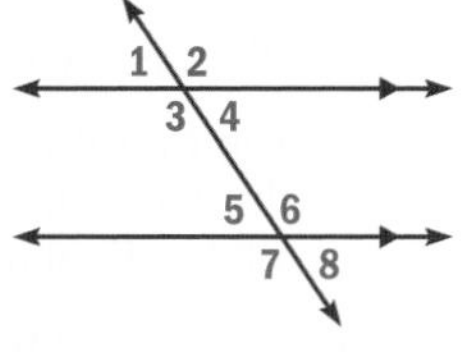

14. A proposition on a voting ballot needs two thirds of the votes to pass. A survey of a random sample of voters finds that 69% of the voters plan to vote for the proposition. The survey's margin of error is ±3%. Can you conclude that the proposition will pass? Explain. **See margin.**

15. A rectangle is 2 inches longer than it is wide. Write polynomial expressions for the length and width of the rectangle's image after dilation by a scale factor of 11. Then write a polynomial expression for the area of the rectangle's image. Write the expressions in standard form. **See margin.**

16. The polygon shown was created by removing a square from the corner of a larger square. Write polynomial expressions for the area and the perimeter of the polygon. Then find the area and perimeter of the polygon if $x = 5$.
$21x^2$, $20x$; 525 square units, 100 units

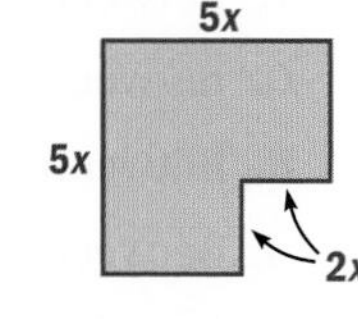

11. $A'(3, -2)$, $B'(1, -6)$. ***Sample answer:*** **A 90° clockwise rotation is represented in coordinate notation by $(x, y) \rightarrow (y, -x)$, so I reversed the coordinates of the original points and found the opposite of the new second coordinate.**

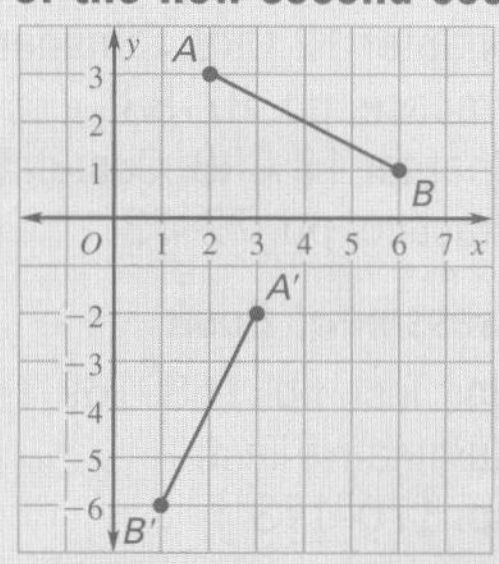

13. **∠1: supplementary, ∠2: congruent, ∠4: supplementary, ∠5: supplementary, ∠6: congruent, ∠7: congruent, ∠8: supplementary; ∠1: 56°, ∠2: 124°, ∠4: 56°, ∠5: 56°, ∠6: 124°, ∠7: 124°, ∠8: 56°**

14. **No. *Sample answer:* The predicted percent voting for the proposition is 66%–72%. Since $\frac{2}{3} = 66\frac{2}{3}\%$, this includes both values for which the proposition will pass and for which it will fail.**

15. **Let w represent the width of the original rectangle; length = $(11w + 22)$ inches, width = $(11w)$ inches; area = $(121w^2 + 242w)$ square inches.**

ADDITIONAL RESOURCES

The following resources are available to help review the materials in this unit:

Chapter Resource Books

- Chapter 11 CRB, Cumulative Practice, pp. 93–94
- Chapter 12 CRB, Cumulative Practice, pp. 87–88
- Chapter 13 CRB, Cumulative Practice, pp. 72–73

Assessment Book

- Unit Test, pp. 168–169
- Cumulative Test, pp. 170–173

8. $\frac{11}{36}$. ***Sample answer:*** **On each roll, the probability that you do *not* roll a 6 is $\frac{5}{6}$. Since these are independent events, the probability that you do not roll a 6 on either roll is $\frac{5}{6} \cdot \frac{5}{6} = \frac{25}{36}$. Rolling a 6 on at least one number cube is complementary to not rolling a 6 on either cube, so the probability is $1 - \frac{25}{36} = \frac{11}{36}$.**

9b. Yes. *Sample answer:* Of the 21 balls, 16 have a mass greater than 4 kilograms, so the probability of choosing one of these balls is $\frac{16}{21}$, or about 76%.

9c. *Sample answer:* It is "typical," because it is very close to the median—only 0.1 kilogram less. Of the 21 balls in the bowling alley, 10 are lighter and 11 are heavier.

Unit 4 Practicing Test-Taking Skills

Chapters 11–13

Cumulative Practice for Chapters 11–13

Chapter 11

Multiple Choice In Exercises 1–7, choose the letter of the correct answer.

1. What is the lower quartile of the data below? *(Lesson 11.2)* **B**

15, 22, 18, 14, 19, 22, 30, 28, 11, 25, 33

A. 11 **B.** 15 **C.** 22 **D.** 28

2. Which of the following *cannot* be used to display numerical data? *(Lesson 11.3)* **H**

F. Histogram
G. Line graph
H. Bar graph
I. Box-and-whisker plot

3. You want to gather information from students at your school. You hand out a survey to students during the lunch period and record the responses that are returned to you. What method of sampling is this? *(Lesson 11.4)* **D**

A. Random **B.** Systematic
C. Stratified **D.** Self-selected

4. A survey found that 28% of a random sample of adults floss regularly. The survey's margin of error was ±4%. In which interval is the actual percent of adults who floss most likely to lie? *(Lesson 11.5)* **I**

F. Between 24% and 28%
G. Between 28% and 32%
H. Between 26% and 30%
I. Between 24% and 32%

5. How many 4-digit numbers include each of the digits 2, 3, 4, and 5? *(Lesson 11.6)* **C**

A. 4 **B.** 14 **C.** 24 **D.** 120

6. You are at a bakery and want to buy 6 different kinds of doughnuts. The bakery sells 10 different kinds of doughnuts. How many combinations are possible? **G** *(Lesson 11.7)*

F. 90 **G.** 210 **H.** 720 **I.** 151,200

7. A game show contestant is trying to guess the last two digits in the price of a car. No digit in the price of the car is used more than once. What is the probability that the contestant correctly guesses the last two digits in the price of the car? *(Lesson 11.9)* **D**

$	1	4	7	?	?

A. $\frac{1}{90}$ **B.** $\frac{1}{56}$ **C.** $\frac{1}{49}$ **D.** $\frac{1}{42}$

8. Short Response A game involves rolling two number cubes to move around a board. In order to win the game on your next turn, you need to roll a 6 on one of the number cubes. What is the probability that you roll a 6 on at least one number cube? Explain your reasoning. *(Lesson 11.8)* **See margin.**

9. Extended Response The stem-and-leaf plot shows the masses (in kilograms) of 21 bowling balls in a bowling alley. *(Lesson 11.1)*

Stem	Leaves
3	5 6 6 6 7
4	4 5 5 6
5	0 4 4 5 5 5 5 8 8 9 9 9

Key: 3 | 5 = 3.5 kg

a. What is the median mass? **5.4 kg**

b. You randomly choose a ball. Do you think the ball's mass will be greater than 4.0 kg? Explain using probability. **9b–c. See margin.**

c. Your friend has her own bowling ball with a mass of 5.3 kg. How does this mass compare with the masses of balls in the bowling alley? Explain.

Chapter 12

Multiple Choice In Exercises 10–20, choose the letter of the correct answer.

10. Write $8x - 5 - 3(2x^2 - 4x + 1)$ as a polynomial in standard form. *(Lesson 12.1)* **B**

A. $-6x^2 - 4x - 8$ **B.** $-6x^2 + 20x - 8$

C. $6x^2 + 4x - 8$ **D.** $-6x^2 + 4x - 8$

11. Find the difference. *(Lesson 12.2)* **H**

$(2x^3 + 7x^2 - x) - (3x^3 - 5x^2 + x)$

F. $-x^3 + 12x^2$ **G.** $-x^3 + 2x^2$

H. $-x^3 + 12x^2 - 2x$ **I.** $-x^3 + 2x^2 - 2x$

12. Which polynomial expression represents the perimeter of the rectangle? *(Lesson 12.2)* **C**

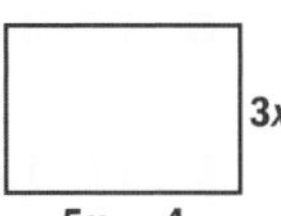

A. $15x^2 - 12x$ **B.** $10x - 8$

C. $16x - 8$ **D.** $8x - 4$

13. Find the product. *(Lesson 12.3)* **I**

$(p^4 + 6p^3 - p + 7)(2p^2)$

F. $2p^6 + 12p^5 - 12p^2$

G. $2p^6 + 12p^5 + 2p^3 + 14p^2$

H. $2p^8 + 12p^6 - 2p^3 + 14p^2$

I. $2p^6 + 12p^5 - 2p^3 + 14p^2$

14. Find the product $(6y + 5)(5y - 6)$. *(Lesson 12.4)* **A**

A. $30y^2 - 11y - 30$ **B.** $30y^2 + 11y - 30$

C. $30y^2 - 30$ **D.** $30y^2 - 11y + 30$

15. Which expression represents the area of the circle? *(Lesson 12.5)* **G**

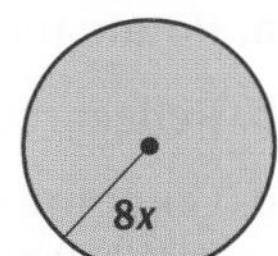

F. $64\pi x$ **G.** $64\pi x^2$

H. $8\pi x$ **I.** $8\pi x^2$

16. Simplify $(a^2b)^4$. *(Lesson 12.5)* **B**

A. a^6b **B.** a^8b^4 **C.** a^2b^4 **D.** a^6b^4

17. Simplify $(2 \times 10^3)^3$. *(Lesson 12.5)* **I**

F. 2×10^5 **G.** 2×10^6

H. 8×10^6 **I.** 8×10^9

18. The graph of which equation is shown? *(Lesson 12.6)* **D**

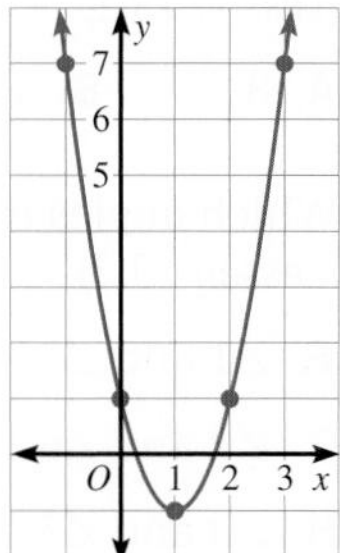

A. $y = -2x^2 - 4x + 1$

B. $y = 2x^2 + 4x + 1$

C. $y = 2x^2 - 4x - 1$

D. $y = 2x^2 - 4x + 1$

19. What is the next term in the sequence 1600, 400, 100, 25, . . . ? *(Lesson 12.8)* **G**

F. 4 **G.** 6.25 **H.** 9 **I.** 16

20. What is the next term in the sequence −9, −3, 3, 9, . . . ? *(Lesson 12.8)* **C**

A. 3 **B.** 12 **C.** 15 **D.** 27

21. Short Response Simplify the expression $\frac{8x^3 - 24x^2 + 20x}{4x}$. Explain your steps. *(Lesson 12.3)* **See margin.**

22. Extended Response You purchase a new snowmobile. The value V (in dollars) of the snowmobile after t years is given by the function $V = 8900(0.75)^t$. *(Lesson 12.7)*

a. Does this function model exponential growth or exponential decay? Explain.

b. Graph the function. **22a–c. See margin.**

c. After how many years will the value of the snowmobile be less than $5000? Explain your reasoning.

Test-Taking Skills

21. $2x^2 - 6x + 5$. *Sample answer:* First I rewrote the quotient by dividing each term in the polynomial by the monomial as $\frac{8x^3}{4x} + \frac{-24x^2}{4x} + \frac{20x}{4x}$. Then I divided numerators and denominators by 4 to get $\frac{2x^3}{x} + \frac{-6x^2}{x} + \frac{5x}{x}$. By the quotient of powers property, this is then $2x^{3-1} - 6x^{2-1} + 5x^{1-1}$, or $2x^2 - 6x^1 + 5x^0 = 2x^2 - 6x + 5$.

22a. Exponential decay. *Sample answer:* For this function, $b = 0.75$ in the exponential form $y = ab^x$. Since $0 < 0.75 < 1$, this represents exponential decay.

22b.

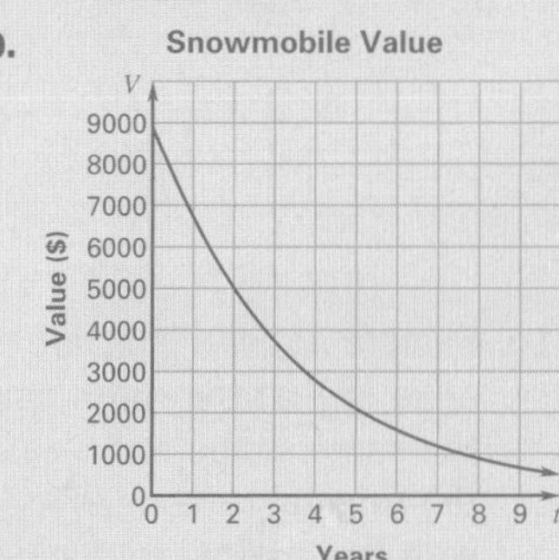

22c. About 2 y. *Sample answer:* Looking at the graph, it appears that the value is about $5000 after 2 years. Substituting $t = 2$ in the formula gives $V = 8900(0.75)^2 = \$5006.25$, which verifies that the value should fall below $5000 in just over 2 years.

30. 145. *Sample answer:* The 125° angle is supplementary with the interior angle at the top of the triangle, so this angle has measure 180° − 125° = 55°. Since the angle measures of a triangle total 180°, the third angle of the triangle has measure 180° − (90° + 55°) = 35°. Finally, the angle with measure $x°$ is supplementary to the angle with measure 35°, so its measure is 180° − 35° = 145°.

31a.

31b.

31c. *Sample answer:* They are alike in that they both have the same shape and size as the original rectangle. As with the original rectangle, they also have the longer dimension oriented horizontally. Both have the images of *A* and *B* on their top segments and the images of *C* and *D* on their bottom segments. They are different in that the orientation of the vertices is switched by the reflection—after the rotation, the vertices are read counterclockwise as in the original rectangle, but after the reflection, they are read clockwise.

Unit 4 Practicing Test-Taking Skills

Chapters 11–13

Cumulative Practice continued

Chapter 13

Multiple Choice In Exercises 23–29, choose the letter of the correct answer.

23. Given that $\angle 3$ and $\angle 4$ are complementary angles and $m\angle 3 = 82°$, find $m\angle 4$. *(Lesson 13.1)* **A**

A. 8° **B.** 18° **C.** 98° **D.** 118°

24. Which angles are congruent? *(Lesson 13.2)* **G**

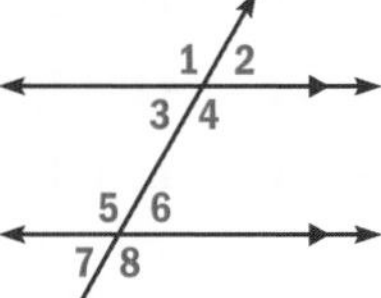

F. $\angle 1$ and $\angle 3$

G. $\angle 2$ and $\angle 6$

H. $\angle 3$ and $\angle 5$

I. $\angle 4$ and $\angle 7$

25. Each angle in a regular octagon measures $(6x + 3)°$. What is the value of x? **B** *(Lesson 13.3)*

A. 7 **B.** 22 **C.** 29.5 **D.** 239.5

26. Which transformation is shown in the graph? *(Lessons 13.4–13.7)* **F**

F. Reflection in the x-axis

G. Dilation using a scale factor of $\frac{1}{2}$

H. Translation of 1 unit to the right and 2 units down

I. 90° clockwise rotation

27. How many lines of symmetry does the figure have? *(Lesson 13.5)* **D**

A. 1 **B.** 2

C. 3 **D.** 4

28. A segment with endpoints $A(3, -3)$ and $B(3, -4)$ is rotated 90° clockwise. Find the coordinates of the image of B. *(Lesson 13.6)* **H**

F. $B'(4, 3)$ **G.** $B'(3, 4)$

H. $B'(-4, -3)$ **I.** $B'(-3, -4)$

29. $\triangle ABC$ has vertices $A(-4, 8)$, $B(0, 2)$, and $C(4, 0)$. Find the coordinates of the vertices of the image after dilation by a scale factor of $\frac{1}{4}$. *(Lesson 13.7)* **C**

A. $A'(-1, 8)$, $B'(0, 2)$, $C'(1, 0)$

B. $A'(-4, -2)$, $B'\left(0, \frac{1}{2}\right)$, $C'(4, 0)$

C. $A'(-1, 2)$, $B'\left(0, \frac{1}{2}\right)$, $C'(1, 0)$

D. $A'(-16, -32)$, $B'(0, 8)$, $C'(16, 0)$

30. Short Response Find the value of x in the diagram. Explain how you found your answer. *(Lesson 13.3)* **See margin.**

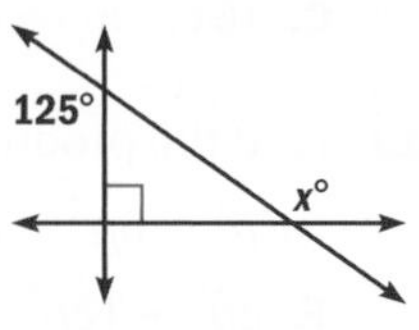

31. Extended Response The vertices of rectangle $ABCD$ have the coordinates shown. *(Lessons 13.5, 13.6)*

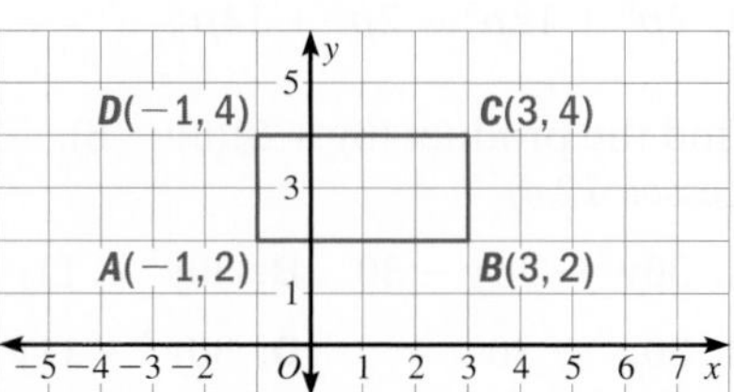

a. Rotate rectangle $ABCD$ 180°. **31a–c. See margin.**

b. Reflect rectangle $ABCD$ in the x-axis.

c. Compare the two images of rectangle $ABCD$ from parts (a) and (b). How are they alike, and how are they different?

End-of-Course Test

Integers, Equations, and Inequalities

Evaluate the expression when $x = 2$, $y = 3$, and $z = 5$.

1. $x + z$ 7 **2.** $0.6z - x$ 1 **3.** $(y + z)^2 - 3$ 61 **4.** $\frac{x + 4y}{7}$ 2

Find the sum, difference, product, or quotient.

5. $-23 + 16$ −7 **6.** $-36 + (-40)$ −76 **7.** $29 - (-17)$ 46 **8.** $-61 - 42$ −103

9. $12(-5)$ −60 **10.** $-15(-7)$ 105 **11.** $\frac{-99}{-11}$ 9 **12.** $\frac{144}{-6}$ −24

State the absolute value and the opposite of the number.

13. 8 8, −8 **14.** −15 15, 15 **15.** −10 10, 10 **16.** 24 24, −24

Plot the point in a coordinate plane. Describe the location of the point. 17–20. See margin for art.

17. $A(-5, -8)$ Quadrant III **18.** $B(-6, 1)$ Quadrant II **19.** $C(0, -3)$ y-axis **20.** $D(4, -2)$ Quadrant IV

Identify the property that the statement illustrates. 21–24. See margin.

21. $(ab) \cdot 1 = ab$ **22.** $x + 0 = x$ **23.** $m + n = n + m$ **24.** $rst = rts$

Evaluate the expression using the distributive property and mental math.

25. 4(93) 372 **26.** 9(104) 936 **27.** 7(8.3) 58.1 **28.** 6(5.9) 35.4

Simplify the expression.

29. $21 + x - 14 + 9x$ $10x + 7$ **30.** $4a + 2a + 3a$ $9a$ **31.** $-4(4m - 2) + 3$ $-16m + 11$ **32.** $6(7n - 4) + 2n$ $44n - 24$

Write the verbal sentence as an equation. Then tell whether 6 is a solution of the equation.

33. The sum of x and 13 is 7. $x + 13 = 7$; no **34.** The product of −11 and z is −66. $-11z = -66$; yes

Solve the equation. Check your solution.

35. $x - 12 = 20$ 32 **36.** $\frac{x}{-6} = -8$ 48 **37.** $7x = -63$ −9 **38.** $4.2 + x = 9.9$ 5.7

39. $5x + 3 = -22$ −5 **40.** $-9x - 4 = 32$ −4 **41.** $5(x + 4) = 60$ 8 **42.** $102 = 6(5 - 3x)$ −4

Solve the inequality. Graph and check your solution. 43–46. See margin for art.

43. $x - 7 \le 19$ $x \le 26$ **44.** $-2x < -16$ $x > 8$ **45.** $4 + 3x > -17$ $x > -7$ **46.** $6x - 8 \ge 7x$ $x \le -8$

End-of-Course Test

ALGEBRAIC REASONING

The following exercises can be used as an Algebra Readiness test.

Exs. 1–4, 21–24, 29–54, 59–66, 78–97, 100–109, 111–113, and 126–137.

17–20.

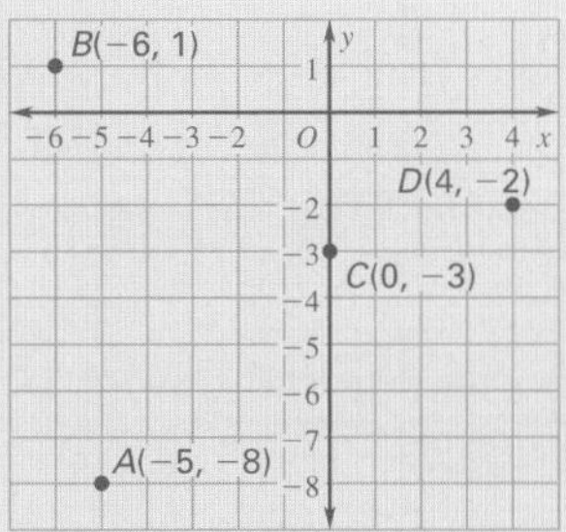

21. identity property of multiplication

22. identity property of addition

23. commutative property of addition

24. commutative property of multiplication

43.

44. 0 2 4 6 8 10 12

45. −9 −8 −7 −6 −5 −4 −3

46. −12 −10 −8 −6 −4 −2 0

78.

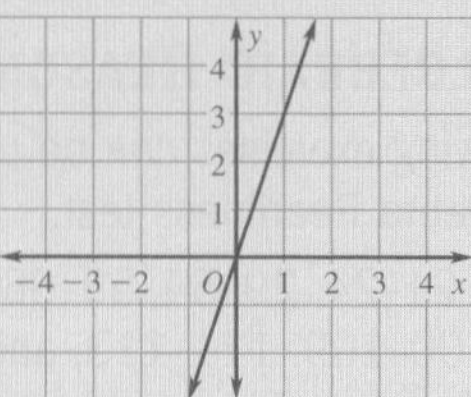

79.

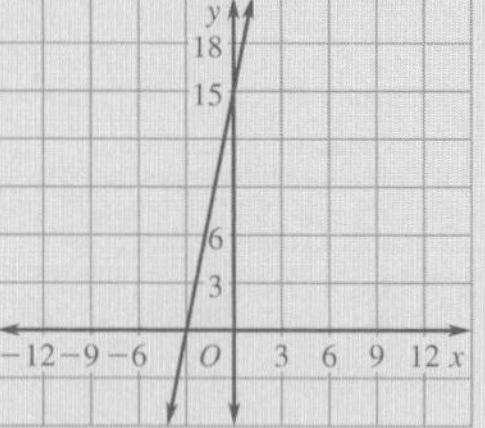

80.

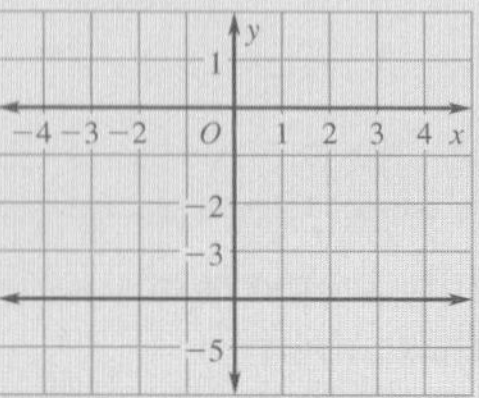

81.

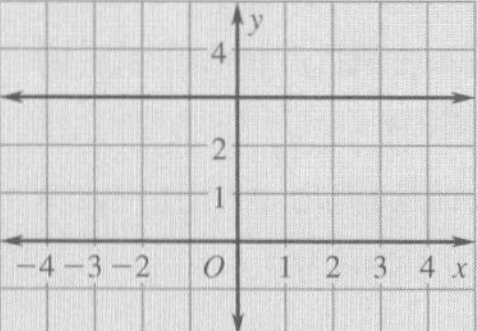

82.

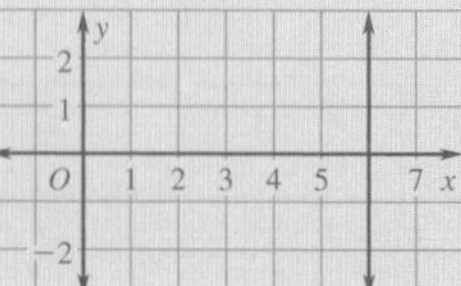

83.

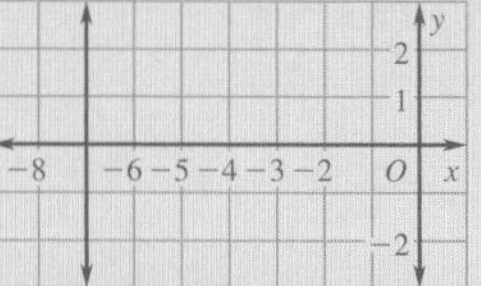

84.

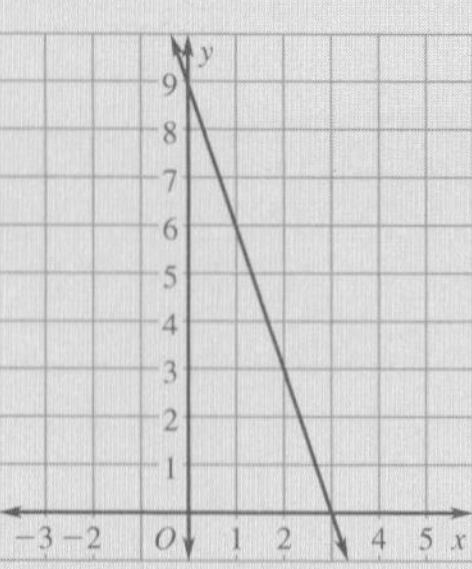

85.

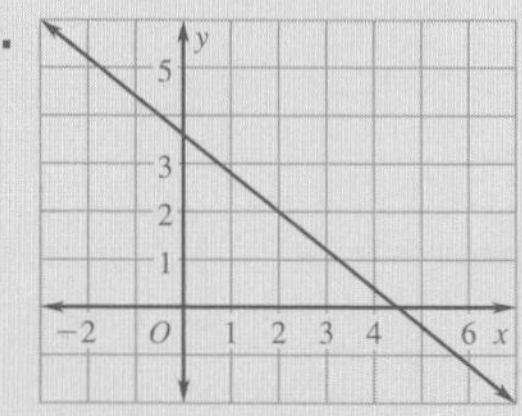

End-of-Course Test

Rational Numbers and Proportions

Find the greatest common factor and the least common multiple of the monomials.

47. $4x$, $6x$ $2x, 12x$ **48.** $15x^2$, $9x$ $3x, 45x^2$ **49.** $20xy^2$, $5y$ $5y, 20xy^2$ **50.** $7x^2y^3$, $5x^3y^4$ $x^2y^3, 35x^3y^4$

Find the product or quotient. Write your answer using only positive exponents.

51. $k^7 \cdot k^3$ k^{10} **52.** $\frac{q^5}{q^2}$ q^3 **53.** $r^{-8} \cdot r^6$ $\frac{1}{r^2}$ **54.** $\frac{s^{-6}}{s^{-3}}$ $\frac{1}{s^3}$

Find the sum, difference, product, or quotient.

55. $-\frac{4}{9} + \frac{5}{9}$ $\frac{1}{9}$ **56.** $-6\frac{2}{3} - 4\frac{7}{8}$ $-11\frac{13}{24}$ **57.** $-2\frac{1}{3} \cdot \left(3\frac{3}{5}\right)$ $-8\frac{2}{5}$ **58.** $-1\frac{2}{5} \div \left(-8\frac{3}{10}\right)$ $\frac{14}{83}$

Solve the equation or inequality by first clearing the fractions or the decimals.

59. $\frac{4}{9}x - 2 > \frac{2}{3}$ $x > 6$ **60.** $-\frac{2}{7}x - \frac{2}{3} \le \frac{1}{7}$ $x \ge -2\frac{5}{6}$ **61.** $1.6x - 2.8 = 5.2$ 5 **62.** $2.5x + 2.79 = 10.21$ 2.968

Solve the proportion.

63. $\frac{8}{120} = \frac{2}{y}$ 30 **64.** $\frac{99}{w} = \frac{9}{14}$ 154 **65.** $\frac{6}{21} = \frac{8}{z}$ 28 **66.** $\frac{1.4}{x} = \frac{11.2}{72}$ 9

Given *ABCD* ~ *EFGH*, find the indicated measure.

67. $m\angle A$ $117°$

68. $m\angle D$ $63°$

69. GH 10.8 cm

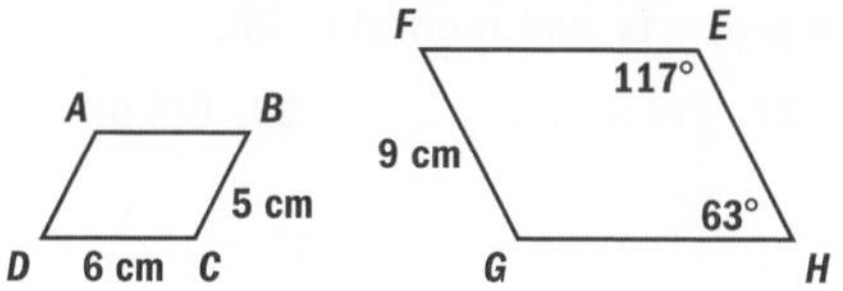

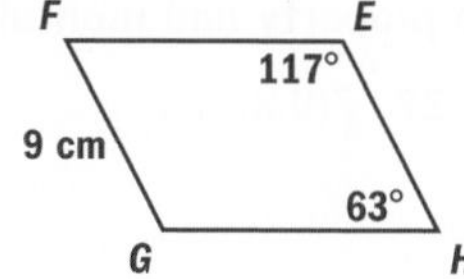

70. Each letter in the word ALGEBRA is written on a separate slip of paper and placed in a hat. A letter is chosen at random from the hat. What is the probability that the chosen letter is a consonant? $\frac{4}{7}$

Use a proportion or the percent equation to answer the question.

71. What percent of 200 is 24? 12% **72.** 11.4 is 9.5% of what number? 120

Identify the percent of change as an *increase* or a *decrease*. Then find the percent of change.

73. Original: 60
New: 75
increase; 25%

74. Original: 95
New: 76
decrease; 20%

75. Original: 32
New: 20
decrease; 37.5%

76. Original: 44
New: 55 increase; 25%

77. A dress shirt is on sale for 20% off the original price of \$32. What is the sale price of the dress shirt? \$25.60

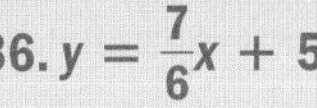

86. $y = \frac{7}{6}x + 5$

87. $y = \frac{5}{2}x + 2$

94. 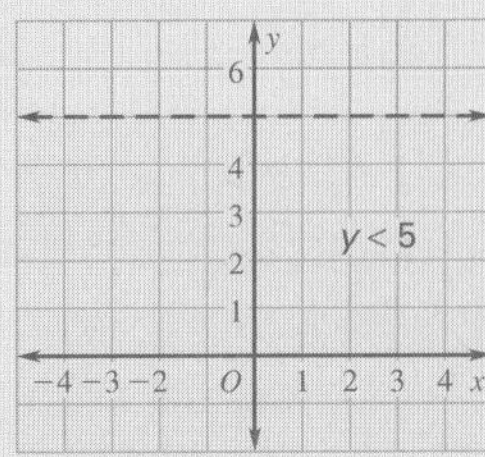

95. 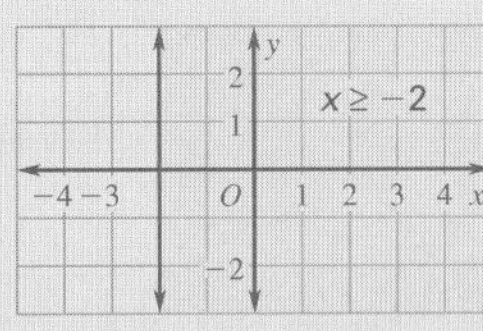

96. 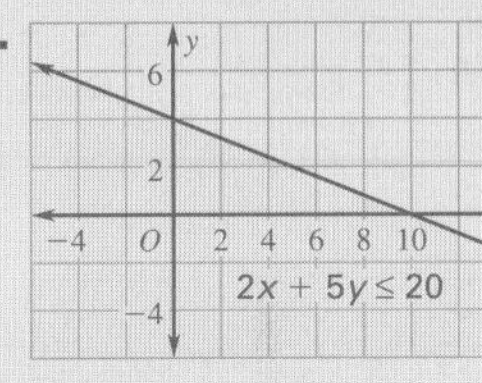

97. 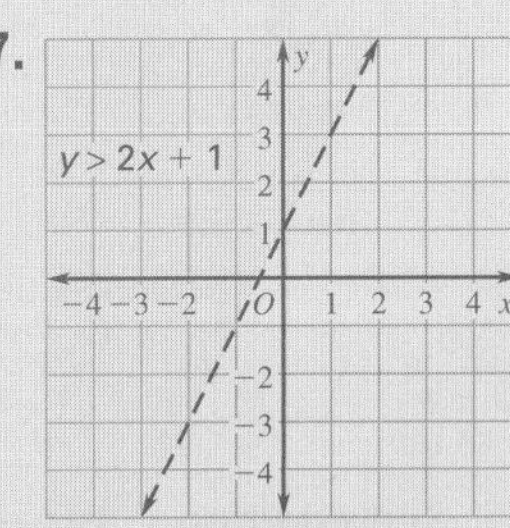

106. (2, 6); $2\sqrt{5}$ units
107. (1, 3); $2\sqrt{193}$ units
108. (7, −7); $2\sqrt{29}$ units
109. (−5.5, 5.5); $3\sqrt{10}$ units

End-of-Course Test

Functions, Geometry, and Measurement

Graph the equation. Then tell whether the equation is a function. 78–85. See margin for art.

78. $y = 3x$ yes **79.** $y = 5x + 15$ yes **80.** $y = -4$ yes **81.** $y = 3$ yes

82. $x = 6$ no **83.** $x = -7$ no **84.** $9x + 3y = 27$ yes **85.** $4x + 5y = 18$ yes

Write an equation of the line through the given points.

86. (0, 5), (6, 12) **87.** (−4, −8), (0, 2) **88.** (3, −7), (0, 11) $y = -6x + 11$ **89.** (0, 1), (10, −2) $y = -\frac{3}{10}x + 1$

86–87. See margin.

Let $f(x) = -3x + 5$ and $g(x) = 4x - 2$. Find the indicated value.

90. $f(4)$ −7 **91.** $g(-10)$ −42 **92.** $f(5) + g(-12)$ −60 **93.** x when $g(x) = 16$ $4\frac{1}{2}$

Graph the inequality in a coordinate plane. 94–97. See margin.

94. $y < 5$ **95.** $x \ge -2$ **96.** $2x + 5y \le 20$ **97.** $y > 2x + 1$

Simplify the expression.

98. $\sqrt{60}$ $2\sqrt{15}$ **99.** $\sqrt{\frac{14}{64}}$ $\frac{\sqrt{14}}{8}$ **100.** $\sqrt{40m^2}$ $2m\sqrt{10}$ **101.** $\sqrt{\frac{25b^2}{36}}$ $\frac{5b}{6}$

Determine whether the triangle with the given side lengths is a right triangle.

102. 6, 8, 10 yes **103.** 5, 12, 15 no **104.** 10, 24, 26 yes **105.** 2, 3, 4 no

Find the midpoint of the segment with the given endpoints. Then find the distance between the points. Write your answer in simplest form. 106–109. See margin.

106. (4, 7), (0, 5) **107.** (8, 15), (−6, −9) **108.** (9, −2), (5, −12) **109.** (−4, 10), (−7, 1)

110. Each leg of a 45°-45°-90° triangle has a length of 12 meters. Find the length of the hypotenuse. Write your answer in simplest form. $12\sqrt{2}$ m

111. In $\triangle ABC$ with right angle at C, $m\angle A = 49°$ and $AB = 25$. Find BC to the nearest tenth. 18.9 units

The angle measures of a polygon are given. Find the value of *x*.

112. Triangle: $3x°$, $(2x + 4)°$, 46° 26 **113.** Quadrilateral: 15°, $8x°$, $4x°$, $(x + 7)°$ 26

Find the area of the figure with the given dimensions. Use 3.14 for π. Round to the nearest whole number.

114. Circle: $r = 23$ in. 1661 in.^{2} **115.** Trapezoid: $h = 6$ in., $b_1 = 26$ in., $b_2 = 16$ in. 126 in.^{2}

Find the surface area and the volume of the solid with the given dimensions. Round to the nearest whole number.

116. Cylinder: $r = 9$ ft, $h = 12$ ft 1188 ft^2, 3054 ft^3 **117.** Cone: $r = 8$ ft, $h = 15$ ft 628 ft^2, 1005 ft^3

118–119. Sample histograms are given.

118.
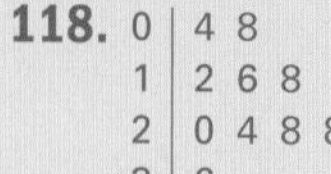

0 | 4 8
1 | 2 6 8
2 | 0 4 8 8
3 | 6
Key: 0 | 4 = 4

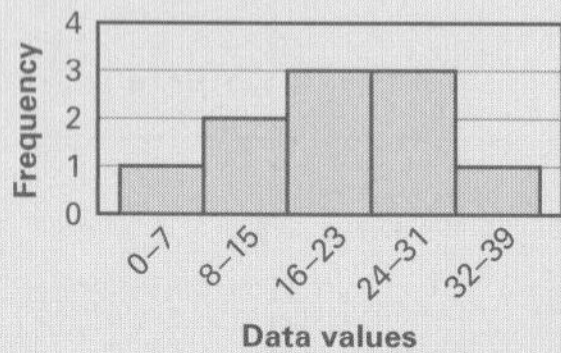

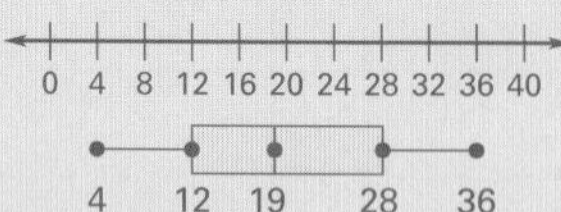

119.
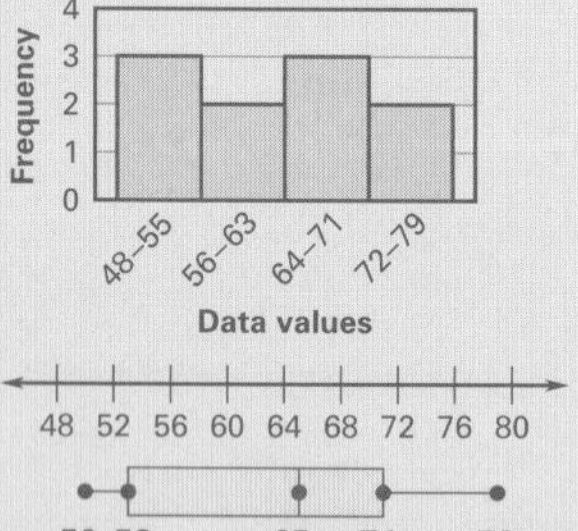

134–137. See Additional Answers beginning on page AA1.

147.
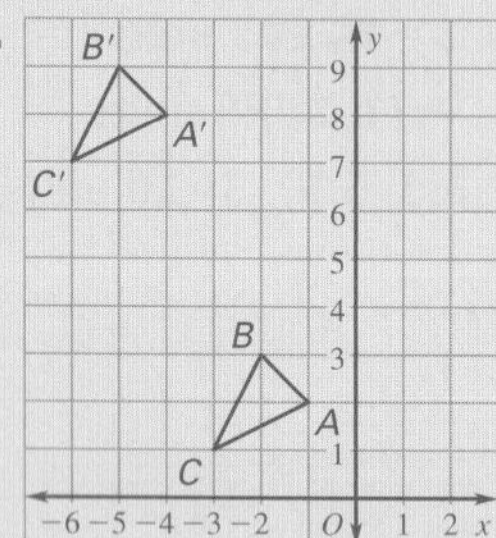

148.
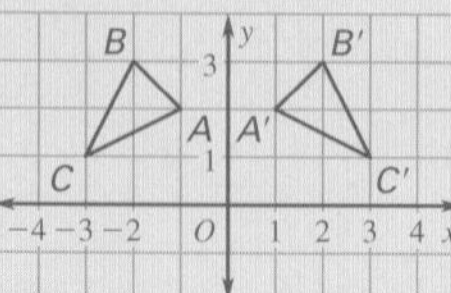

149.
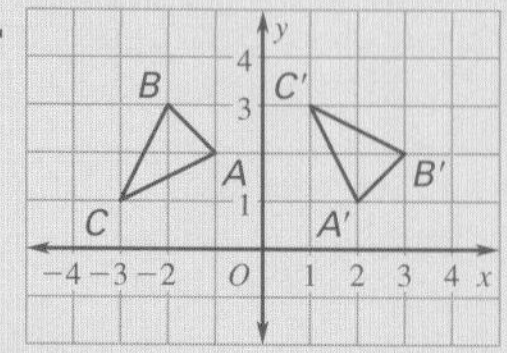

End-of-Course Test

Data Analysis, Polynomials, and Transformations

Make an ordered stem-and-leaf plot, a histogram, and a box-and-whisker plot of the data. 118–119. See margin.

118. 18, 28, 8, 20, 12, 36, 28, 4, 16, 24

119. 71, 53, 67, 74, 50, 68, 51, 63, 79, 60

Evaluate.

120. ${}_8P_3$ 336

121. ${}_{16}C_{10}$ 8008

122. ${}_{20}C_{20}$ 1

123. 5! 120

124. A computer randomly generates whole numbers from 1 to 20. Find the probability that the computer generates a 12 or a multiple of 3. $\frac{3}{10}$

125. A box has 3 red pencils and 5 blue pencils. You randomly choose two pencils. Find the probability that both pencils are blue. $\frac{5}{14}$

Find the sum, difference, or product.

126. $(2x^2 + x + 9) + (3x^2 - 4x - 5)$ $5x^2 - 3x + 4$

127. $(9x^2 + 2x) - (-5x^2 - 6x)$ $14x^2 + 8x$

128. $(-8x - 3)(-7x + 2)$ $56x^2 + 5x - 6$

129. $3x(12x^5 + 16x^3)$ $36x^6 + 48x^4$

Simplify the expression. Write your answer using positive exponents.

130. $(xy)^8$ x^8y^8

131. $(-2x^3)^4$ $16x^{12}$

132. $(x^5)^{-6}$ $\frac{1}{x^{30}}$

133. $(y^{-2})^{-7}$ y^{14}

Make a table of values for the given function. Then graph the function. 134–137. See margin.

134. $y = x^2 + 3$

135. $y = 2x^2 - 4x$

136. $y = 5^x$

137. $y = 3(4)^x$

Tell whether the sequence is *arithmetic* or *geometric*. Then find the common difference or the common ratio, and write the next three terms.

138. 182, 168, 154, 140, . . . arithmetic; common difference: −14; 126, 112, 98

139. 1.7, 5.1, 15.3, 45.9, . . . geometric; common ratio: 3; 137.7, 413.1, 1239.3

Tell whether the angles are *complementary*, *supplementary*, or *neither*.

140. $m\angle 1 = 54°, m\angle 2 = 36°$ complementary

141. $m\angle 3 = 82°, m\angle 4 = 98°$ supplementary

Tell whether the angles in the diagram are *vertical*, *corresponding*, *alternate interior*, or *alternate exterior* angles.

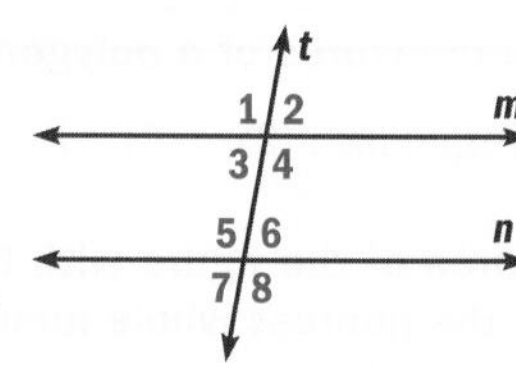

142. $\angle 1$ and $\angle 8$ alternate exterior

143. $\angle 3$ and $\angle 7$ corresponding

144. $\angle 4$ and $\angle 5$ alternate interior

145. $\angle 5$ and $\angle 8$ vertical

146. Find the measure of an exterior angle of a regular 12-gon. 30°

Draw △*ABC* with vertices *A*(−1, 2), *B*(−2, 3), and *C*(−3, 1). Then find the coordinates of the vertices of the image after the specified transformation, and draw the image. 147–149. See margin for art.

147. $(x, y) \to (x - 3, y + 6)$ A′(−4, 8), B′(−5, 9), C′(−6, 7)

148. Reflection in the y-axis A′(1, 2), B′(2, 3), C′(3, 1)

149. 90° clockwise rotation A′(2, 1), B′(3, 2), C′(1, 3)

Contents of Student Resources

6. hundredths, 0.04; 7251.04
7. ten thousands, 40,000; 40,000
9. hundredths, 0.05; 10,064.66
11. thousandths, 0.009; 112.350
13. hundred thousands, 400,000; 500,000

Place Value and Rounding

The **whole numbers** are the numbers 0, 1, 2, 3, ... A **digit** is any of the numbers 0, 1, 2, 3, 4, 5, 6, 7, 8, or 9. **Decimals** are numbers such as 8.56, 234.12, and 6.985, in which the digits in the ones' place and the tenths' place are separated by a decimal point. The value of each digit in a number depends on the position, or place, of the digit within the number. In the number 813,794.0562, the value of 6 is 6×0.001, or 0.006, because 6 is in the thousandths' place.

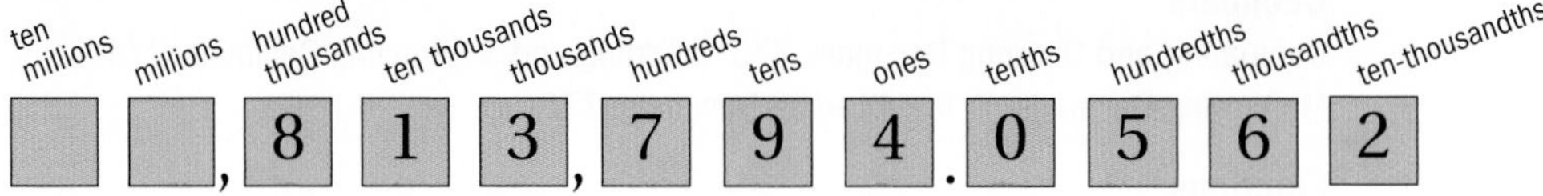

Example **Give the place and value of the red digit in 19.7862.**

Answer The 2 is in the ten-thousandths' place. Its value is 2×0.0001, or 0.0002.

To **round** a number means to approximate it to a given place. When rounding, look at the digit to the right of the given place. If the digit to the right is less than 5, round down by replacing all digits to the right with zeros. If the digit to the right is 5 or greater, round up by adding one to the given digit and replacing all digits to the right with zeros.

Example **Round 88.173 to the place of the red digit.**

Because 7 is in the hundredths' place, round 88.173 to the nearest hundredth. The digit to the right, in the thousandths' place, is 3. Because $3 < 5$, replace the 3 with a 0.

Answer Rounded to the nearest hundredth, 88.173 is 88.170, or 88.17.

Practice

Give the place and value of the red digit. Then round the number to that place.

1. 56.75 tens, 50; 60
2. 19.36 ones, 9; 19
3. 912.756 hundreds, 900; 900
4. 539.52 tenths, 0.5; 539.5
5. 6528.983 thousands, 6000; 7000
6. 7251.041 See margin.
7. 40,192.071 See margin.
8. 504.038 tens, 0; 500
9. 10,064.655 See margin.
10. 357.0815 tenths, 0; 357.1
11. 112.3497 See margin.
12. 46,312.746 tenths, 0.7; 46,312.7
13. 482,615.8 See margin.
14. 54.3852 hundredths, 0.08; 54.39
15. 9172.043 hundreds, 100; 9200
16. 12,099.5186 thousandths, 0.008; 12,099.519

Estimating Sums and Differences

A **sum** is the result of adding two or more numbers. A **difference** is the result of subtracting two numbers. One strategy you can use to estimate a sum or difference is to round to the place of the *leading digit.* The leading digit of a whole number is the leftmost digit.

Example **Estimate the sum 42,143 + 18,672 + 21,047.**

Each number has five digits. The leading digit is in the ten thousands' place. Round each number to the nearest ten thousand.

$$42{,}143 + 18{,}672 + 21{,}047 \approx 40{,}000 + 20{,}000 + 20{,}000$$
$$= 80{,}000$$

The symbol ≈ means "is approximately equal to."

Answer The sum 42,143 + 18,672 + 21,047 is *about* 80,000.

Example **Estimate the difference 812,236 − 587,429.**

Each number has six digits. The leading digit is in the hundred thousands' place. Round each number to the nearest hundred thousand.

$$812{,}236 - 587{,}429 \approx 800{,}000 - 600{,}000$$
$$= 200{,}000$$

Answer The difference 812,236 − 587,429 is *about* 200,000.

For a more accurate estimate of a sum or difference, you can round each number to a place to the right of the leading digit. For instance, in the first example above, you might round to the nearest thousand.

$$42{,}143 + 18{,}672 + 21{,}047 \approx 42{,}000 + 19{,}000 + 21{,}000 = 82{,}000$$

Practice

Estimate the sum or difference by rounding each number to the place of its leading digit.

1. 1704 + 8233 10,000

2. 23,867 + 11,999 30,000

3. 48,119 + 13,974 60,000

4. 462,311 + 109,878 600,000

5. 5284 + 2916 + 4238 12,000

6. 51,098 + 14,235 + 38,794 100,000

7. 7641 − 3244 5000

8. 24,109 − 12,344 10,000

9. 45,098 − 24,672 30,000

10. 89,405 − 43,288 50,000

11. 436,966 − 178,056 200,000

12. 687,005 − 119,684 600,000

13. 219,477 − 105,819 100,000

14. 868,212 − 514,709 400,000

Skills Review Handbook

Estimating Products and Quotients

A **product** is the result of multiplying two or more numbers. Each number multiplied is a **factor** of the product. A **quotient** is the result of dividing a number by a nonzero number. The number being divided is the **dividend**, and the number it is being divided by is the **divisor**. One way to estimate a product or a quotient is to find a low estimate and a high estimate using *compatible numbers*. Compatible numbers are numbers that make a calculation easier.

Example **Find a low and high estimate for the product 783 × 48.**

1) For a low estimate, round both factors *down*.

$$\begin{array}{r} 700 \\ \times\ 40 \\ \hline 28{,}000 \end{array}$$

When rounding down, replace all digits after the first with zeros.

2) For a high estimate, round both factors *up*.

$$\begin{array}{r} 800 \\ \times\ 50 \\ \hline 40{,}000 \end{array}$$

When rounding up, increase the first digit by 1, and replace all digits after the first with zeros.

Answer The product 783 × 48 is between 28,000 and 40,000.

Example **Find a low and high estimate for the quotient 556,772 ÷ 861.**

When the divisor has more than one digit, round it as described below.

1) For a *low* estimate, round the divisor, 861, *up* and replace the dividend, 556,772, with a number that is divisible by 900 and is *less* than 556,772.

$$900\overline{)540{,}000} = 600$$

2) For a *high* estimate, round the divisor, 861, *down* and replace the dividend, 556,772, with a number that is divisible by 800 and is *greater* than 556,772.

$$800\overline{)560{,}000} = 700$$

Answer The quotient 556,772 ÷ 861 is between 600 and 700.

Practice

Find a low and high estimate for the product or quotient. 1–16. Estimates may vary.

1. 787 × 63 42,000; 56,000
2. 97 × 314 27,000; 40,000
3. 925 × 492 360,000; 500,000
4. 206 × 475 80,000; 150,000
5. 955 ÷ 29 30; 50
6. 724 ÷ 87 8; 10
7. 432 ÷ 76 5; 7
8. 3195 ÷ 58 50; 70
9. 293 × 51 10,000; 18,000
10. 7615 × 32 210,000; 320,000
11. 47 × 673 24,000; 35,000
12. 312 × 4918 1,200,000; 2,000,000
13. 4792 ÷ 17 200; 500
14. 21,246 ÷ 419 40; 60
15. 25,421 ÷ 42 500; 700
16. 44,521 ÷ 66 600; 800

Comparing and Ordering Decimals

A **number line** is a line whose points are associated with numbers. You can use a number line to compare and order decimals. First graph the numbers on a number line. Then read the numbers in order as they appear from left to right. Remember that the symbol $<$ means *is less than* and the symbol $>$ means *is greater than*.

Example **Copy and complete the statement using $<$, $>$, or $=$.**

a. 0.543 _?_ 0.54   **b.** 1.12 _?_ 1.21

Solution

a.

0.54   0.543

0.54   0.545   0.55

0.543 is to the right of 0.54, so 0.543 is greater than 0.54.

Answer $0.543 > 0.54$

b.

1.12   1.21

1.1   1.15   1.2

1.12 is to the left of 1.21, so 1.12 is less than 1.21.

Answer $1.12 < 1.21$

Example **Order the numbers 5.1, 5.2, 5.05, 5, 5.12, and 5.15 from least to greatest.**

Graph all the numbers on the same number line.

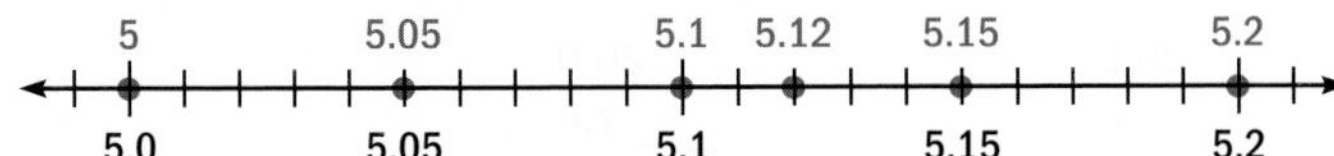

Answer From least to greatest, the numbers are 5, 5.05, 5.1, 5.12, 5.15, and 5.2.

Practice

Copy and complete the statement using $<$, $>$, or $=$.

1. 0.3 _?_ 0.28 $>$
2. 0.57 _?_ 0.6 $<$
3. 0.19 _?_ 0.190 $=$
4. 4.5 _?_ 4.51 $<$
5. 67.2 _?_ 66.9 $>$
6. 1.03 _?_ 1.30 $<$

Order the numbers from least to greatest.

7. 1.3, 1.29, 2.19, 1.9 **1.29, 1.3, 1.9, 2.19**
8. 5.4, 4.55, 5.45, 4.44 **4.44, 4.55, 5.4, 5.45**
9. 0.52, 0.55, 0.49, 0.5 **0.49, 0.5, 0.52, 0.55**
10. 1.0, 0.97, 1.02, 0.99 **0.97, 0.99, 1.0, 1.02**
11. 6.21, 6.19, 6.32, 6.3 **6.19, 6.21, 6.3, 6.32**
12. 8.9, 9.02, 9.1, 8.69 **8.69, 8.9, 9.02, 9.1**

Skills Review Handbook

Adding and Subtracting Decimals

Use a vertical format to add or subtract decimals. Begin by lining up the decimal points. Write zeros as placeholders if necessary. Then add or subtract as you would with whole numbers. Be sure to place the decimal point in the answer.

Example **Find the sum 0.283 + 0.54.**

1) Line up the decimal points and write zero as a placeholder. Add the thousandths.

$$\begin{array}{r} 0.283 \\ +\ 0.540 \\ \hline 3 \end{array}$$

2) Add the hundredths. Regroup 12 hundredths as 1 tenth and 2 hundredths.

$$\begin{array}{r} \scriptstyle 1 \\ 0.283 \\ +\ 0.540 \\ \hline 23 \end{array}$$

3) Add the tenths. Place the decimal point in the answer.

$$\begin{array}{r} \scriptstyle 1 \\ 0.283 \\ +\ 0.540 \\ \hline 0.823 \end{array}$$

Answer 0.283 + 0.54 = 0.823

Example **Find the difference 20 − 2.8.**

1) Start with the tenths. There are no tenths in 20 from which to subtract 8 tenths.

$$\begin{array}{r} 20.0 \\ -\ 2.8 \\ \hline \end{array}$$

2) Move to the ones. There are no ones in 20, so regroup 1 ten as 9 ones and 10 tenths.

$$\begin{array}{r} \scriptstyle 9 \\ \scriptstyle 1\ \cancel{10}\ 10 \\ \cancel{2}\cancel{0}.\cancel{0} \\ -\ 2.8 \\ \hline \end{array}$$

3) Subtract. Place the decimal point in the answer.

$$\begin{array}{r} \scriptstyle 9 \\ \scriptstyle 1\ \cancel{10}\ 10 \\ \cancel{2}\cancel{0}.\cancel{0} \\ -\ 2.8 \\ \hline 17.2 \end{array}$$

Answer 20 − 2.8 = 17.2

✓ **Check** Because addition and subtraction are inverse operations, you can check your answer by adding: 17.2 + 2.8 = 20.

Practice

Find the sum or difference.

1. 4.1 + 2.3 **6.4**
2. 0.37 + 0.55 **0.92**
3. 8.7 − 4.5 **4.2**
4. 2.6 − 0.9 **1.7**
5. 1.34 + 0.9 **2.24**
6. 6.78 + 4.99 **11.77**
7. 41.39 − 23.17 **18.22**
8. 67.38 − 37.46 **29.92**
9. 84.34 + 67.23 **151.57**
10. 28.4 + 3.7 **32.1**
11. 0.67 − 0.43 **0.24**
12. 4.956 − 1.234 **3.722**
13. 3.596 + 5.618 **9.214**
14. 8.95 + 3.476 **12.426**
15. 3.7 − 2.95 **0.75**
16. 8.267 − 6.52 **1.747**

Skills Review Handbook

Multiplying Decimals

To multiply decimals, multiply as you would whole numbers, then place the decimal point in the product. The number of decimal places in the product is equal to the sum of the number of decimal places in the factors.

Example **Find the product 4.94 × 0.45.**

4.94	**2 decimal places**
× 0.45	**+ 2 decimal places**
2470	
1976	
2.2230	**4 decimal places**

After you place the decimal point, you can drop the zero at the end of the product.

Answer $4.94 \times 0.45 = 2.223$

You may need to write zeros as placeholders so that the answer has the correct number of decimal places.

Example **Find the product 3.6 × 0.023.**

3.6	**1 decimal place**
× 0.023	**+ 3 decimal places**
108	
72	
0.0828	**4 decimal places**

Write a zero before the 8 as a placeholder so that the number has four decimal places.

Answer $3.6 \times 0.023 = 0.0828$

Practice

Find the product.

1. 2.4×5.9 14.16 **2.** 1.2×2.3 2.76 **3.** 2.5×6.4 16 **4.** 2.53×0.8 2.024

5. 1.45×0.7 1.015 **6.** 1.4×0.35 0.49 **7.** 0.72×0.06 0.0432 **8.** 0.91×0.6 0.546

9. 15.2×0.004 0.0608 **10.** 13.4×0.65 8.71 **11.** 8.52×3.5 29.82 **12.** 0.05×0.03 0.0015

13. 5.25×1.18 6.195 **14.** 7.2×0.053 0.3816 **15.** 3.06×4.28 13.0968 **16.** 4.33×0.019 0.08227

Dividing Decimals

To divide decimals, multiply both the divisor and the dividend by a power of 10 that will make the divisor a whole number. Then line up the decimal point in the quotient with the decimal point in the dividend.

Example **Find the quotient 7.848 ÷ 0.24.**

$0.24\overline{)7.848}$ **To multiply the divisor and dividend by 100, move both decimal points 2 places to the right.**

```
      32.7
24)784.8
   72
    64
    48
    168
    168
      0
```

Divide as you would with whole numbers. Place the decimal point in the quotient directly above the decimal point in the dividend.

Answer 7.848 ÷ 0.24 = 32.7

You may need to write additional zeros in a dividend to continue dividing. The zeros do not change the value of the dividend.

Example **Find the quotient 7 ÷ 1.4.**

$1.4\overline{)7.0}$

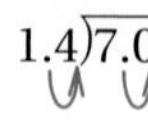

To multiply the divisor and dividend by 10, move both decimal points 1 place to the right. Write a zero as a placeholder.

```
     5
14)70
   70
    0
```

Divide as you would with whole numbers.

Answer 7 ÷ 1.4 = 5

Practice

Find the quotient.

1. 1.2 ÷ 0.3 4 **2.** 2.6 ÷ 0.2 13 **3.** 1.25 ÷ 0.25 5 **4.** 8.84 ÷ 3.4 2.6

5. 51.3 ÷ 2.7 19 **6.** 1.44 ÷ 3.6 0.4 **7.** 4.41 ÷ 2.1 2.1 **8.** 2.52 ÷ 0.7 3.6

9. 4.95 ÷ 5.5 0.9 **10.** 43.25 ÷ 2.5 17.3 **11.** 70.59 ÷ 54.3 1.3 **12.** 160.72 ÷ 32.8 4.9

13. 87.92 ÷ 6.28 14 **14.** 206.08 ÷ 2.3 89.6 **15.** 628.2 ÷ 34.9 18 **16.** 1.593 ÷ 5.9 0.27

17. 6.7 ÷ 0.05 134 **18.** 36.75 ÷ 2.45 15 **19.** 289.25 ÷ 12.5 23.14 **20.** 332.88 ÷ 36.5 9.12

Modeling Fractions

A **fraction** is a number of the form $\frac{a}{b}$ ($b \neq 0$), where a is called the **numerator** and b is called the **denominator.** The number $2\frac{1}{4}$ is a *mixed number.* A **mixed number** is the sum of a whole number and a fraction.

Example **Write a fraction to represent the shaded part of the region.**

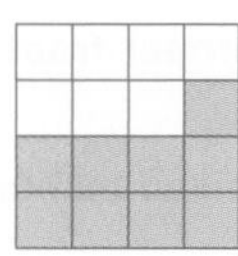

The region is divided into 16 equal parts. Of those, 9 parts are shaded.

Answer The fraction that represents the shaded part of the region is $\frac{9}{16}$.

Example **Write a mixed number to represent the shaded region.**

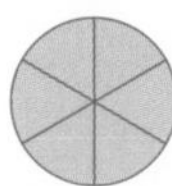
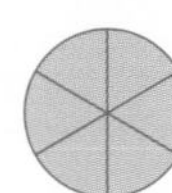
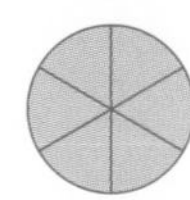
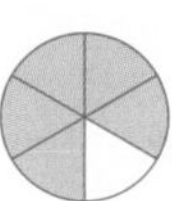

Each circle is divided into 6 equal parts. Three whole circles are shaded, and five parts of the fourth circle are shaded.

Answer The mixed number that represents the shaded region is $3\frac{5}{6}$.

Practice

Write a fraction to represent the shaded part of the set or region.

1. $\frac{1}{3}$    

2. $\frac{5}{12}$ 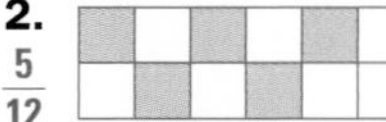

3. $\frac{3}{7}$ 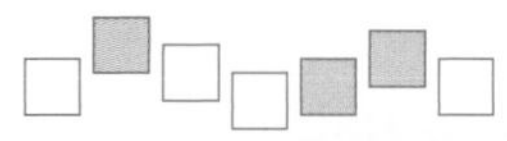

4. $\frac{3}{5}$

5. $\frac{5}{8}$ 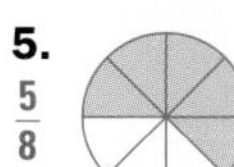

6. $\frac{1}{6}$ 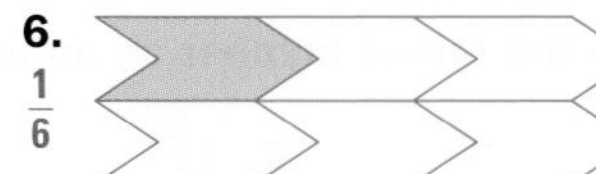

Write a mixed number to represent the shaded region.

7. $2\frac{2}{5}$ 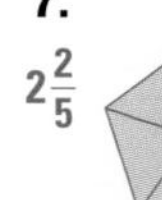 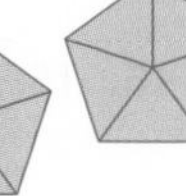 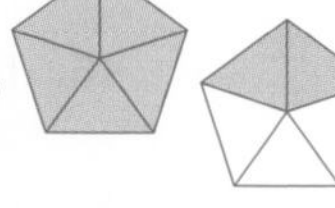

8. $2\frac{1}{8}$ 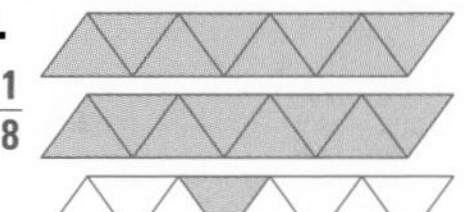

9. $1\frac{5}{6}$ 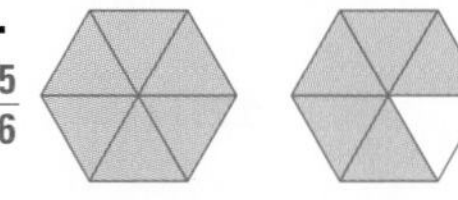

10. $3\frac{3}{4}$ 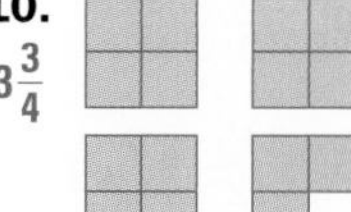

11. $2\frac{1}{3}$ 

12. $1\frac{3}{5}$ 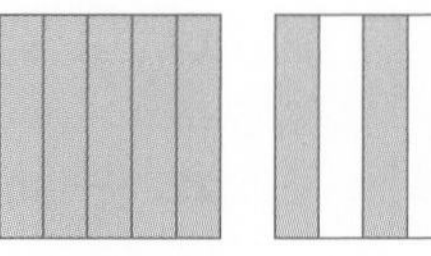

Skills Review Handbook

Skills Review Handbook

Mixed Numbers and Improper Fractions

Recall that a mixed number is the sum of a whole number and a fraction. An **improper fraction**, such as $\frac{21}{8}$, is any fraction in which the numerator is greater than or equal to the denominator.

Example **Write $2\frac{5}{8}$ as an improper fraction.**

$2\frac{5}{8} = 2 + \frac{5}{8}$ **Definition of mixed number**

$= \frac{16}{8} + \frac{5}{8}$ **1 whole = $\frac{8}{8}$, so 2 wholes = $\frac{2 \times 8}{8}$, or $\frac{16}{8}$.**

$= \frac{21}{8}$ **Add.**

Answer The mixed number $2\frac{5}{8}$ is equivalent to the improper fraction $\frac{21}{8}$.

Example **Write $\frac{19}{6}$ as a mixed number.**

$$\begin{array}{r} 3 \text{ R1} \\ 6\overline{)19} \\ \underline{18} \\ 1 \end{array}$$

Divide 19 by 6.

$3 + \frac{1}{6} = 3\frac{1}{6}$ **Write the remainder as a fraction, $\frac{\text{remainder}}{\text{divisor}}$.**

Answer The improper fraction $\frac{19}{6}$ is equivalent to the mixed number $3\frac{1}{6}$.

Practice

Write the mixed number as an improper fraction.

1. $1\frac{9}{10}$ $\frac{19}{10}$ **2.** $1\frac{3}{5}$ $\frac{8}{5}$ **3.** $9\frac{1}{6}$ $\frac{55}{6}$ **4.** $5\frac{1}{9}$ $\frac{46}{9}$ **5.** $3\frac{4}{7}$ $\frac{25}{7}$

6. $4\frac{2}{5}$ $\frac{22}{5}$ **7.** $2\frac{3}{8}$ $\frac{19}{8}$ **8.** $8\frac{1}{2}$ $\frac{17}{2}$ **9.** $6\frac{2}{3}$ $\frac{20}{3}$ **10.** $4\frac{3}{11}$ $\frac{47}{11}$

11. $7\frac{3}{4}$ $\frac{31}{4}$ **12.** $4\frac{7}{13}$ $\frac{59}{13}$ **13.** $8\frac{11}{20}$ $\frac{171}{20}$ **14.** $12\frac{13}{15}$ $\frac{193}{15}$ **15.** $15\frac{7}{9}$ $\frac{142}{9}$

Write the improper fraction as a mixed number.

16. $\frac{14}{5}$ $2\frac{4}{5}$ **17.** $\frac{11}{2}$ $5\frac{1}{2}$ **18.** $\frac{22}{3}$ $7\frac{1}{3}$ **19.** $\frac{29}{9}$ $3\frac{2}{9}$ **20.** $\frac{53}{10}$ $5\frac{3}{10}$

21. $\frac{37}{6}$ $6\frac{1}{6}$ **22.** $\frac{43}{4}$ $10\frac{3}{4}$ **23.** $\frac{31}{8}$ $3\frac{7}{8}$ **24.** $\frac{57}{7}$ $8\frac{1}{7}$ **25.** $\frac{115}{12}$ $9\frac{7}{12}$

Adding and Subtracting Fractions

To add fractions with a common denominator, write the sum of the numerators over the denominator.

Numbers: $\frac{3}{9} + \frac{4}{9} = \frac{3+4}{9} = \frac{7}{9}$ **Model:**

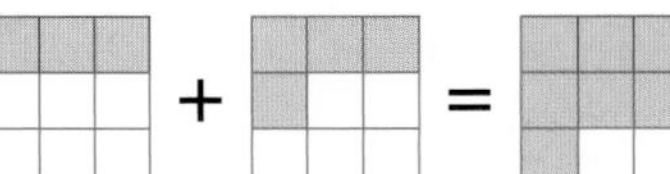

Example **Find the sum $\frac{7}{8} + \frac{4}{8}$.**

$\frac{7}{8} + \frac{4}{8} = \frac{7+4}{8}$ **Write sum of numerators over common denominator.**

$= \frac{11}{8}$ **Add.**

$= 1\frac{3}{8}$ **Write improper fraction as a mixed number.**

To subtract fractions with a common denominator, write the difference of the numerators over the denominator.

Numbers: $\frac{4}{5} - \frac{1}{5} = \frac{4-1}{5} = \frac{3}{5}$ **Model:**

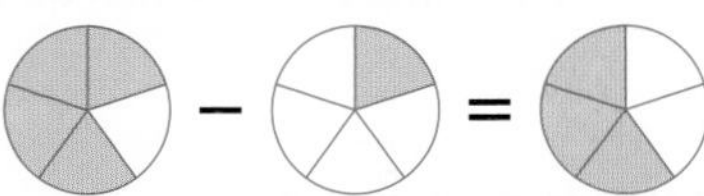

Example **Find the difference $\frac{7}{20} - \frac{4}{20}$.**

$\frac{7}{20} - \frac{4}{20} = \frac{7-4}{20}$ **Write difference of numerators over common denominator.**

$= \frac{3}{20}$ **Subtract.**

Practice

Find the sum or difference.

1. $\frac{2}{5} + \frac{2}{5}$ $\frac{4}{5}$ **2.** $\frac{7}{15} + \frac{6}{15}$ $\frac{13}{15}$ **3.** $\frac{4}{7} - \frac{1}{7}$ $\frac{3}{7}$ **4.** $\frac{8}{9} - \frac{4}{9}$ $\frac{4}{9}$ **5.** $\frac{6}{11} - \frac{5}{11}$ $\frac{1}{11}$

6. $\frac{8}{13} - \frac{3}{13}$ $\frac{5}{13}$ **7.** $\frac{9}{14} + \frac{4}{14}$ $\frac{13}{14}$ **8.** $\frac{3}{20} + \frac{8}{20}$ $\frac{11}{20}$ **9.** $\frac{5}{6} - \frac{4}{6}$ $\frac{1}{6}$ **10.** $\frac{11}{12} - \frac{6}{12}$ $\frac{5}{12}$

11. $\frac{19}{20} - \frac{6}{20}$ $\frac{13}{20}$ **12.** $\frac{22}{27} - \frac{5}{27}$ $\frac{17}{27}$ **13.** $\frac{12}{13} + \frac{9}{13}$ $1\frac{8}{13}$ **14.** $\frac{9}{10} + \frac{8}{10}$ $1\frac{7}{10}$ **15.** $\frac{26}{18} - \frac{7}{18}$ $1\frac{1}{18}$

16. $\frac{17}{16} + \frac{15}{16}$ 2 **17.** $\frac{5}{6} + \frac{1}{6}$ 1 **18.** $\frac{7}{8} + \frac{6}{8}$ $1\frac{5}{8}$ **19.** $\frac{2}{3} + \frac{2}{3}$ $1\frac{1}{3}$ **20.** $\frac{19}{21} - \frac{6}{21}$ $\frac{13}{21}$

Skills Review Handbook

Multiplying Fractions and Whole Numbers

Multiplying a fraction by a whole number can be thought of as repeated addition.

Numbers: $5 \times \frac{3}{4} = \frac{3}{4} + \frac{3}{4} + \frac{3}{4} + \frac{3}{4} + \frac{3}{4}$

$= \frac{15}{4} = 3\frac{3}{4}$

Model:

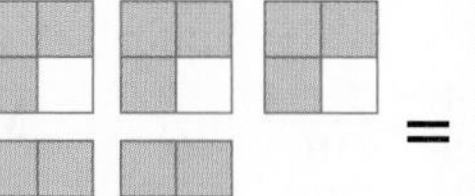

=

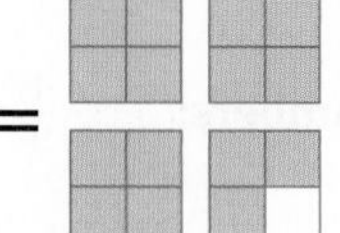

The above example suggests the following rule: To multiply a fraction by a whole number, multiply the numerator of the fraction by the whole number and write the product over the denominator of the fraction. Simplify if possible.

Example **Find the product $18 \times \frac{5}{6}$.**

$18 \times \frac{5}{6} = \frac{18 \times 5}{6}$ — **Write product of whole number and numerator over denominator.**

$= \frac{90}{6}$ — **Multiply.**

$= 15$ — **Write improper fraction as whole number.**

Example **Find the product $\frac{2}{3} \times 14$.**

$\frac{2}{3} \times 14 = \frac{2 \times 14}{3}$ — **Write product of whole number and numerator over denominator.**

$= \frac{28}{3}$ — **Multiply.**

$= 9\frac{1}{3}$ — **Write improper fraction as mixed number.**

Practice

Find the product.

1. $6 \times \frac{1}{2}$ 3 **2.** $10 \times \frac{4}{5}$ 8 **3.** $16 \times \frac{7}{8}$ 14 **4.** $\frac{9}{10} \times 20$ 18

5. $\frac{3}{7} \times 24$ $10\frac{2}{7}$ **6.** $24 \times \frac{1}{5}$ $4\frac{4}{5}$ **7.** $20 \times \frac{3}{5}$ 12 **8.** $\frac{5}{8} \times 16$ 10

9. $\frac{1}{4} \times 9$ $2\frac{1}{4}$ **10.** $\frac{1}{5} \times 21$ $4\frac{1}{5}$ **11.** $12 \times \frac{5}{7}$ $8\frac{4}{7}$ **12.** $\frac{5}{11} \times 24$ $10\frac{10}{11}$

13. $\frac{5}{9} \times 27$ 15 **14.** $\frac{3}{8} \times 15$ $5\frac{5}{8}$ **15.** $\frac{3}{4} \times 12$ 9 **16.** $\frac{5}{6} \times 7$ $5\frac{5}{6}$

Reading Bar Graphs

Data are numbers or facts. A *bar graph* is one way to display data. A **bar graph** uses bars to show how quantities in categories compare.

Example **The bar graph below shows the results of a survey of students who perform community service. More students serve in which location than in any other location? Fewer students serve in which location than in any other location?**

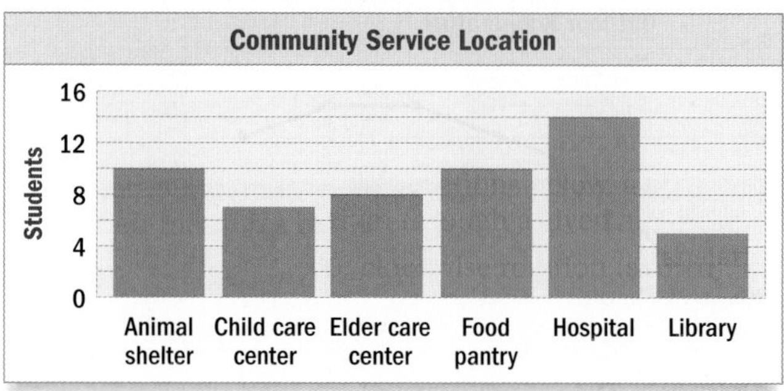

Solution

The longest bar on the graph represents the 14 students who serve in a hospital. So, more students serve in a hospital than in any other location.

The shortest bar on the graph represents the 5 students who serve in a library. So, fewer students serve in a library than in any other location.

Practice

In Exercises 1–3, use the bar graph above to answer the question.

1. How many of the students serve in a food pantry? **10 students**
2. Students serve in equal numbers in which two locations? **animal shelter and food pantry**
3. How many more students serve in a hospital than in an animal shelter? **4 more students**

In Exercises 4–7, use the bar graph, which shows the results of a survey on favorite breakfast foods.

4. Which food was chosen by the greatest number of people? **eggs**
5. Which two foods were chosen by the same number of people? **pancakes and waffles**
6. How many more people chose eggs than chose pancakes? **8 more people**
7. Which foods were chosen by fewer than 12 people? **bagel, pancakes, waffles, muffin**

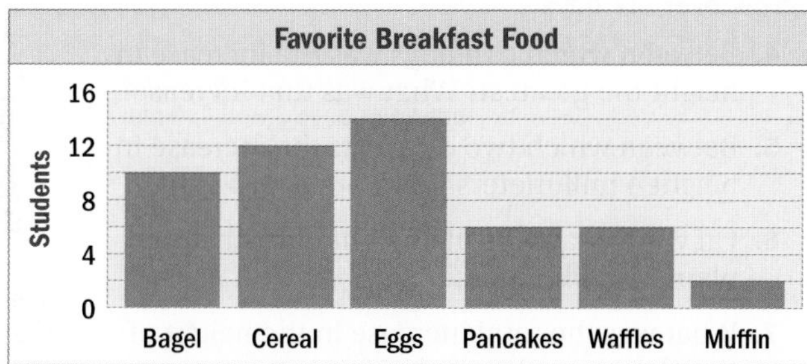

Reading Line Graphs

You can use a *line graph* to display data. A **line graph** uses segments to show how a quantity changes over time.

Example **Students recorded the outdoor temperature every hour from 10 A.M. until 4 P.M. on one day. The line graph below shows the results. Between which two hours did the greatest increase in temperature occur? What was the amount of that increase?**

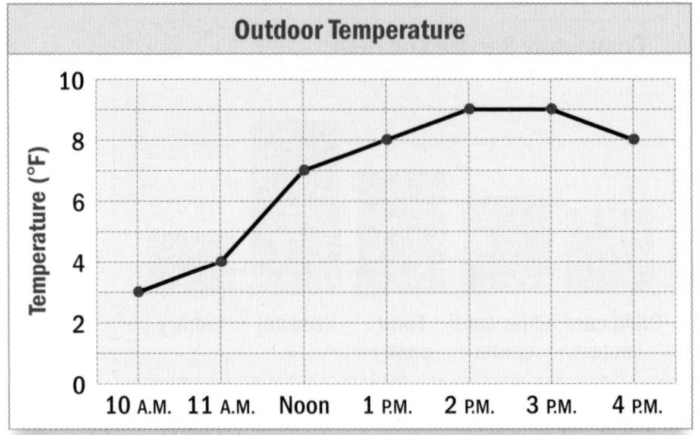

Solution

The steepest segment in the line graph is from 11 A.M. to noon. The temperature was 4°F at 11 A.M. and 7°F at noon, an increase of 3°F.

Practice

In Exercises 1–3, use the line graph above to answer the question.

1. What was the temperature at 1 P.M.? 8°F
2. At what time was the temperature 3°F? 10 A.M.
3. Between which two hours did the temperature decrease? What was the amount of that decrease? between 3 P.M. and 4 P.M.; 1°F

In Exercises 4–7, use the line graph, which shows the height (in millimeters) of a bean plant as it grew over six days.

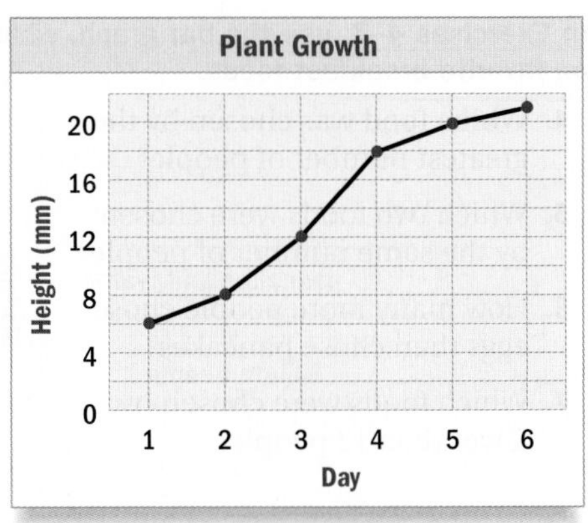

4. Between which two days was the increase in height the greatest? What was that increase? between days 3 and 4; 6 mm
5. Between which two days was the increase in height 4 millimeters? between days 2 and 3
6. On which day was the height of the bean plant 21 millimeters? day 6
7. What was the total increase in the height of the plant over the six days? 15 mm

4. *Sample answer:* There are 10 more homes heated by natural gas than by all other sources in the graph.

Reading Circle Graphs

A **circle graph** displays data as sections of a circle. The entire circle represents all of the data. The sections of the graph may be labeled using the actual data or the data expressed as fractions, decimals, or percents. When expressed as fractions, decimals, or percents, the data have a sum of 1.

Example **The circle graph below shows the results of a survey that asked 100 people how their homes are heated. How many more homes are heated by natural gas than by electricity?**

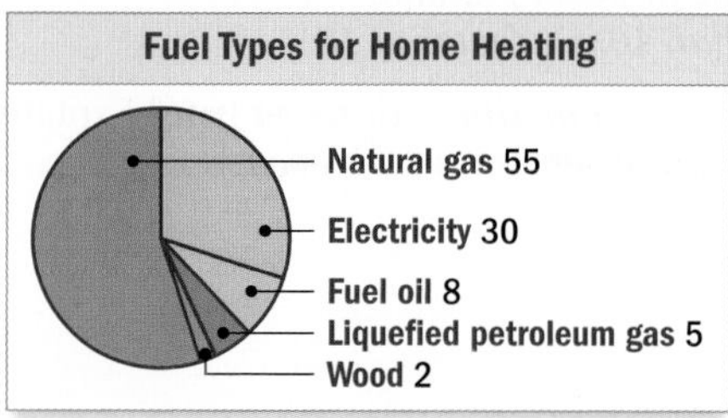

Solution

The graph shows that 55 homes are heated by natural gas and 30 homes are heated by electricity. Because $55 - 30 = 25$, there are 25 more homes that are heated by natural gas than by electricity.

Practice

In Exercises 1–4, use the circle graph above to answer the question.

1. How many homes are heated by liquefied petroleum gas? **5 homes**
2. How many homes are heated by either fuel oil or electricity? **38 homes**
3. How many homes are heated using a source *other* than fuel oil, electricity, or natural gas? **7 homes**
4. How does the number of homes heated by natural gas compare with the total number of homes heated by all other sources in the graph? See margin.

In Exercises 5–8, use the circle graph, which shows the results of a survey that asked 100 people who do not work at home how long their travel time to work is.

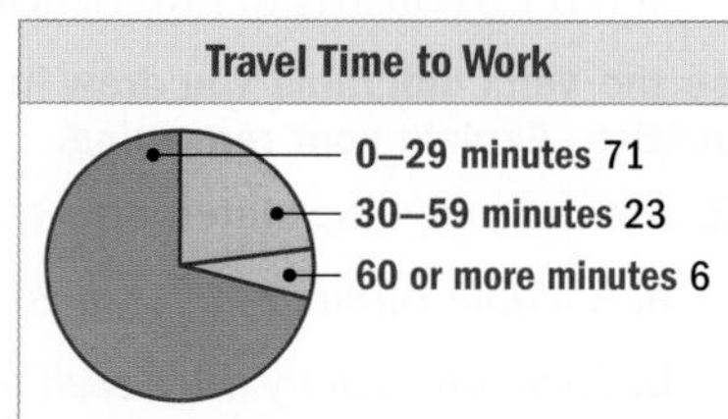

5. How many people have a travel time of 60 or more minutes? **6 people**
6. How many people have a travel time of 30 or more minutes? **29 people**
7. How many people have a travel time of less than 30 minutes? **71 people**
8. How many people have a travel time of less than 1 hour? **94 people**

Skills Review Handbook

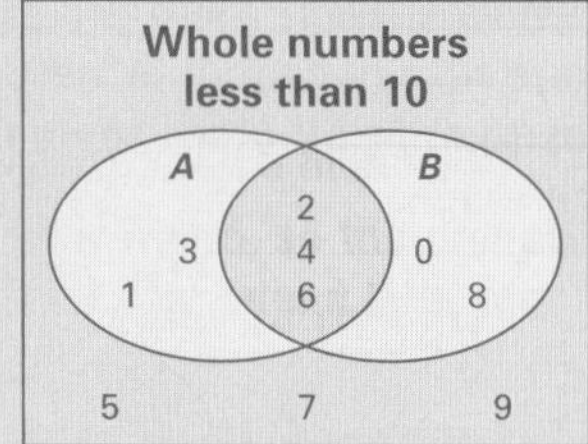

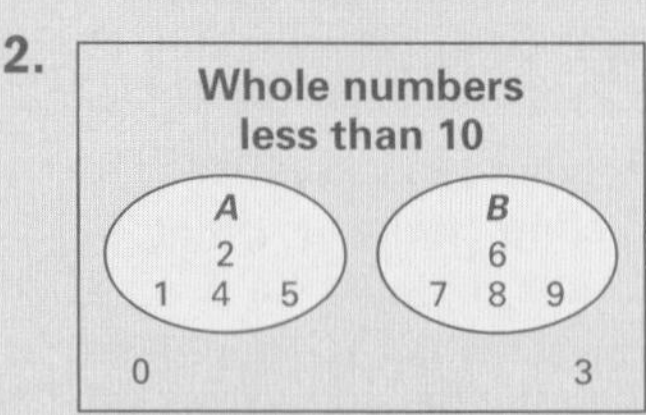

3a. False. *Sample answer:* A counterexample is 2, which is a factor of 20 that is less than 10 and is less than 5.

Skills Review Handbook

Venn Diagrams and Logical Reasoning

A **Venn diagram** uses shapes to show how sets are related. A **counterexample** is an example that shows that a statement is false. You need only a single counterexample to show that a statement is false.

Example **Draw and use a Venn diagram.**

a. Draw a Venn diagram of the whole numbers less than 10 where set *A* consists of factors of 18 and set *B* consists of even numbers.

b. Is the following statement *true* or *false*? Explain.
No even whole number less than 10 is a factor of 18.

c. Is the following statement *always, sometimes,* or *never* true? Explain.
A whole-number factor of 18 that is less than 10 is even.

Solution

a.

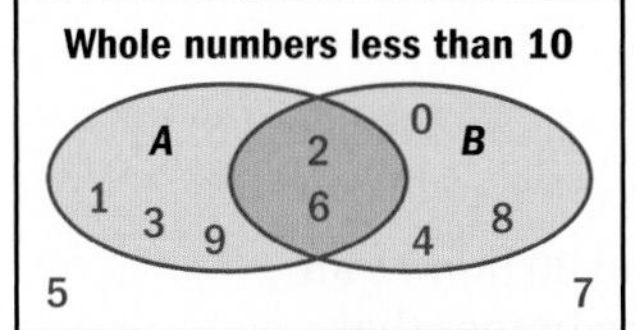

b. False. A counterexample is 2, which is even and a factor of 18.

c. Sometimes. It is true that 2 and 6 are whole-number factors of 18 that are less than 10 and are even, but 1, 3, and 9 are whole-number factors of 18 that are less than 10 and are odd.

Practice

Draw a Venn diagram of the sets described.

1. Of the whole numbers less than 10, set *A* consists of factors of 12 and set *B* consists of even numbers. **1–2. See margin.**

2. Of the whole numbers less than 10, set *A* consists of factors of 20 and set *B* consists of numbers greater than 5.

Use the Venn diagrams you drew in Exercises 1 and 2 to answer the question. Explain your reasoning. **3–4. Sample explanations are given.**

3. Are the following statements *true* or *false*?

   a. *A whole-number factor of 20 that is less than 10 is also greater than 5.* **See margin.**

   b. *There are exactly three even whole numbers less than 10 that are factors of 12.* **True; they are 2, 4, and 6.**

4. Is the following statement *always, sometimes,* or *never* true? Explain.
An even whole number less than 10 is a factor of 12.
Sometimes; 2, 4, and 6 are factors of 12, but 0 and 8 are not.

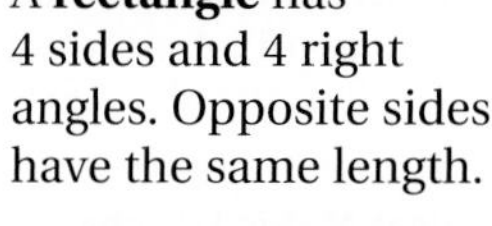

Basic Geometric Figures

A **triangle** is a geometric figure having 3 sides and 3 angles.

A **rectangle** has 4 sides and 4 right angles. Opposite sides have the same length.

A **square** is a rectangle with all four sides the same length.

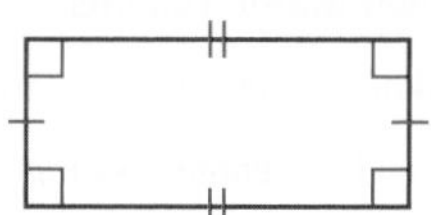

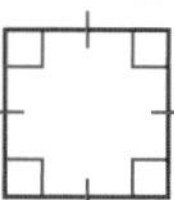

The point where two sides of a figure meet is called a **vertex** (plural: **vertices**). The distance around a figure is called its **perimeter**. If a figure has straight sides, its perimeter is the sum of the lengths of the sides.

Example **Find the perimeter.**

The perimeter is 7 ft + 4 ft + 7 ft + 4 ft = 22 ft.

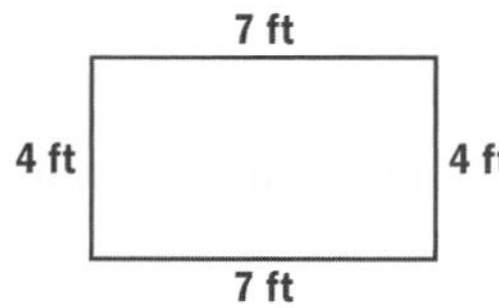

Example **Draw and label a square with a side length of 2 cm. Then find its perimeter.**

Draw a horizontal side 2 cm long.
Then draw the two vertical sides 2 cm long.
Finally, draw the second horizontal side 2 cm long.

The perimeter is 2 cm + 2 cm + 2 cm + 2 cm = 8 cm.

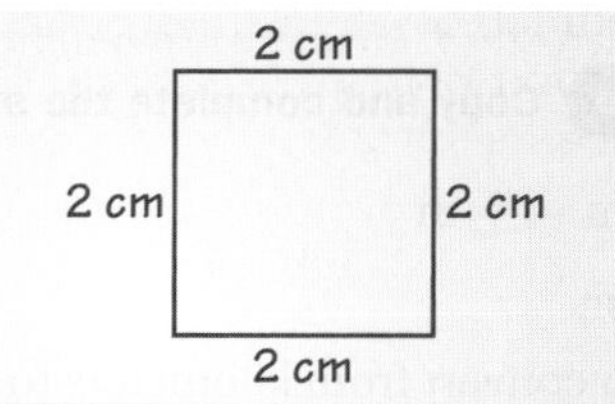

 *Practice*

Find the perimeter.

1. 16 in.
4 in., 4 in., 4 in., 4 in.

2. 12 m

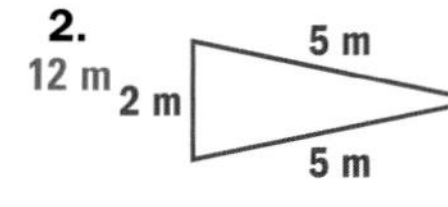

3. 30 ft

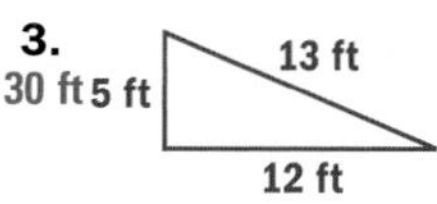

4. 26 cm

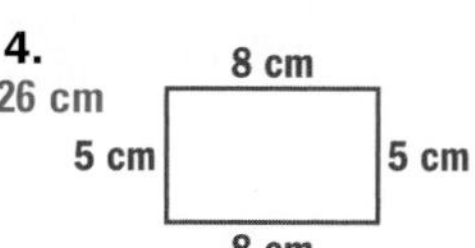

Draw and label the figure described. Then find its perimeter. 5–8. Check students' drawings.

5. A square with sides 3 cm long 12 cm

6. A square with sides 2 in. long 8 in.

7. A rectangle with a length of 4 in. and a width of 1 in. 10 in.

8. A rectangle with a length of 5 cm and a width of 2 cm 14 cm

Skills Review Handbook

Units of Length

Two commonly used systems for measuring length are the U.S. customary system and the metric system. The tables below show equivalent lengths in each system.

Equivalent U.S. Customary Lengths
1 mile (mi) = 5280 feet (ft)
1 yard (yd) = 3 feet (ft)
1 foot (ft) = 12 inches (in.)

Equivalent Metric Lengths
1 kilometer (km) = 1000 meters (m)
1 meter (m) = 100 centimeters (cm)
1 meter (m) = 1000 millimeters (mm)

Each length equivalent can be used to form a **conversion factor** that is equal to 1. Here are some examples:

$$\frac{1\text{ km}}{1000\text{ m}} = 1 \qquad \frac{1000\text{ m}}{1\text{ km}} = 1 \qquad \frac{1\text{ mi}}{5280\text{ ft}} = 1 \qquad \frac{5280\text{ ft}}{1\text{ mi}} = 1$$

The choice of conversion factors depends on **unit analysis**.

- To convert kilometers to meters, multiply by $\frac{1000\text{ m}}{1\text{ km}}$ because

  $\cancel{\text{km}} \times \frac{\text{m}}{\cancel{\text{km}}} = \text{m}$.

- To convert feet to miles, multiply by $\frac{1\text{ mi}}{5280\text{ ft}}$ because

  $\cancel{\text{ft}} \times \frac{\text{mi}}{\cancel{\text{ft}}} = \text{mi}$.

Example **Copy and complete the statement.**

a. 6 km = ? m

b. 108 inches = ? yards

Solution

a. To convert from kilometers to meters, multiply by $\frac{1000\text{ m}}{1\text{ km}}$.

$$6\ \cancel{\text{km}} \times \frac{1000\text{ m}}{1\ \cancel{\text{km}}} = 6000\text{ m}$$

b. To convert from inches to yards, multiply by $\frac{1\text{ yd}}{3\ \cancel{\text{ft}}} \times \frac{1\ \cancel{\text{ft}}}{12\text{ in.}} = \frac{1\text{ yd}}{36\text{ in.}}$.

$$\overset{3}{\cancel{108}}\ \cancel{\text{in.}} \times \frac{1\text{ yd}}{\underset{1}{\cancel{36}}\ \cancel{\text{in.}}} = 3\text{ yd}$$

Practice

Copy and complete.

1. 6000 cm = ? m 60

2. 4830 mm = ? m 4.83

3. 0.9 km = ? cm 90,000

4. 6 ft = ? in. 72

5. 21 ft = ? yd 7

6. 63,360 in. = ? mi 1

Using a Ruler

An **inch ruler** has markings for inches, halves of an inch, fourths of an inch, eighths of an inch, and sixteenths of an inch. As the lengths get shorter, so do the markings.

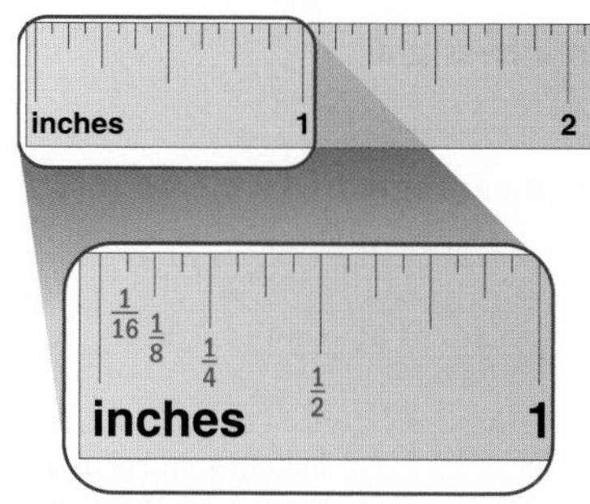

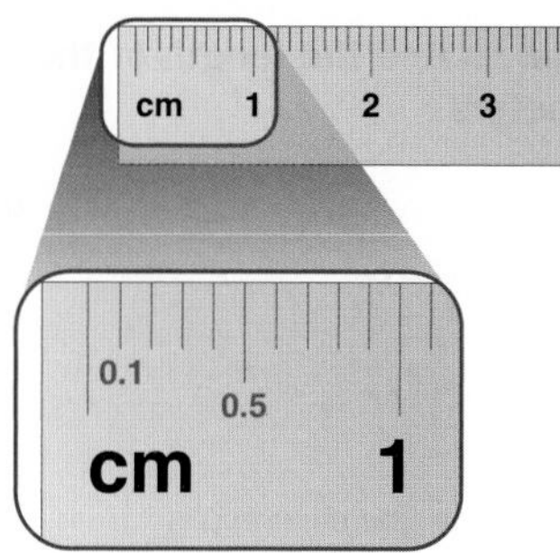

A **centimeter ruler** has markings for centimeters, halves of centimeters, and tenths of a centimeter (also called *millimeters*). Like an inch ruler, as the lengths get shorter, so do the markings.

Example **Use a ruler to draw a segment with the given length.**

a. $2\frac{3}{16}$ inches

b. 5.4 centimeters

Solution

a.

inches 1 2

Start at the leftmost mark on the ruler.

Draw a segment so that the other end is at the third $\frac{1}{16}$ in. mark after 2 in.

b.

cm 1 2 3 4 5 6

Start at the leftmost mark on the ruler.

Draw a segment so that the other end is at the fourth 0.1 cm mark after 5 cm.

Practice

Use a ruler to draw a segment with the given length. **1–16. Check students' work.**

1. $\frac{3}{4}$ inch

2. $2\frac{1}{8}$ inches

3. $3\frac{1}{2}$ inches

4. $\frac{13}{16}$ inch

5. $\frac{7}{8}$ inch

6. $\frac{5}{16}$ inch

7. $1\frac{1}{4}$ inches

8. $4\frac{1}{16}$ inches

9. 3.5 centimeters

10. 6.5 centimeters

11. 3.7 centimeters

12. 4.9 centimeters

13. 1.3 centimeters

14. 2.6 centimeters

15. 5.1 centimeters

16. 4.2 centimeters

Measuring Lengths

You can use an inch ruler or a centimeter ruler to measure lengths of segments.

Example **Use a ruler to find the length of the segment in inches and in centimeters.**

a. Measure in inches.

inches 1 2

Position the ruler so that the 0 mark is at one end of the segment.

The other end is at the fifth $\frac{1}{8}$ in. mark after 1 in.

Answer The segment is $1\frac{5}{8}$ in. long.

b. Measure in centimeters.

cm 1 2 3 4 5

Position the ruler so that the 0 mark is at one end of the segment.

The other end is at the first 0.1 cm mark after 4 cm.

Answer The segment is 4.1 cm long.

Sometimes you want to measure a length to a specified degree of accuracy.

Example **Measure the segment shown to the nearest 0.5 cm.**

To measure the segment to the nearest 0.5 cm, locate the two 0.5 cm marks that are nearest to the end of the segment and choose the closer one.

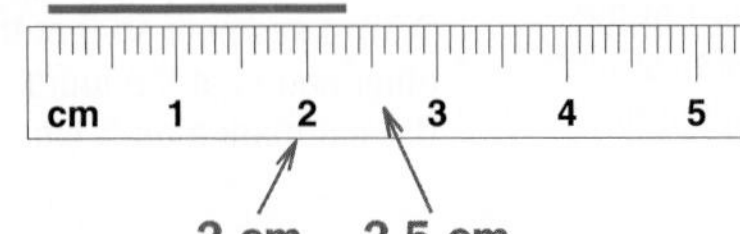

The end of the segment is closer to 2.5 cm.

Answer To the nearest 0.5 cm, the segment is 2.5 cm long.

Practice

Use a ruler to find the length of the segment in inches and in centimeters.

1. ________________ $2\frac{1}{8}$ in., 5.4 cm

2. ________________ $1\frac{5}{16}$ in., 3.3 cm

Find the length of the segment to the specified degree of accuracy.

3. To the nearest $\frac{1}{4}$ inch

________________ $1\frac{1}{2}$ in.

4. To the nearest centimeter

________________ 4 cm

788

Units of Area and Volume

Area is the number of unit squares that are needed to cover a figure.

Unit square

1 unit

1 unit

The area A of a square is given by the formula $A = s^2$, where s is the length of a side.

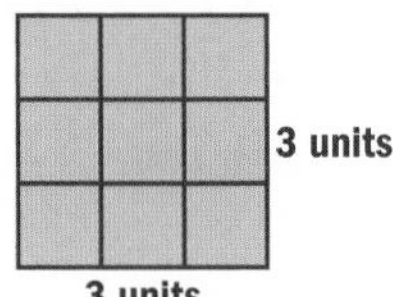

Area = 3^2 = 9 square units

Volume is the number of unit cubes needed to fill a solid.

Unit cube

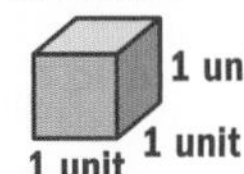

The volume V of a cube is given by the formula $V = s^3$, where s is the length of an edge.

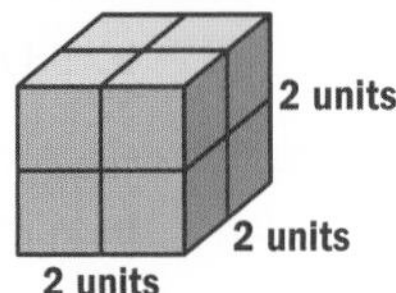

Volume = 2^3 = 8 cubic units

Example **Find the area of the square and the volume of the cube.**

a.

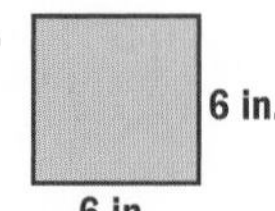

b.

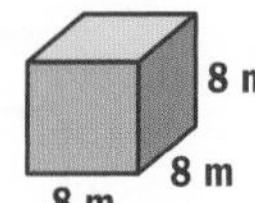

Solution

a. $A = 6^2 = 36 \text{ in.}^2$

The area is 36 square inches.

b. $V = 8^3 = 512 \text{ m}^3$

The volume is 512 cubic meters.

Practice

Find the area of the square.

1.

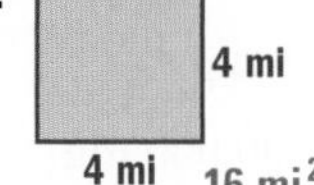

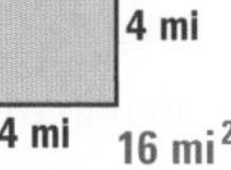

16 mi^2

2.

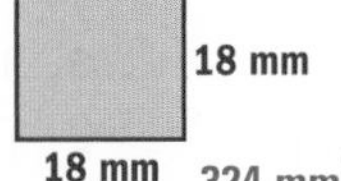

324 mm^2

3.

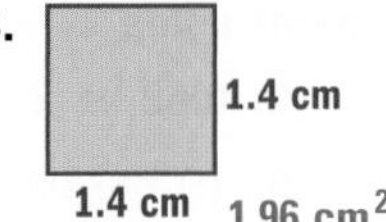

1.96 cm^2

4.

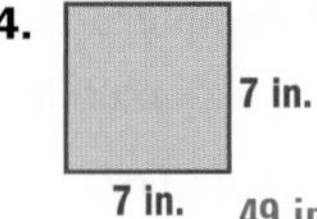

49 in.^2

Find the volume of the cube.

5.

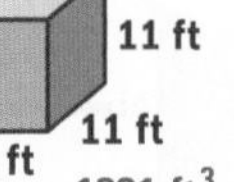

1331 ft^3

6.

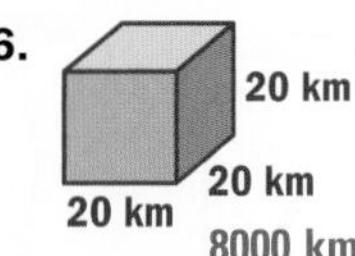

8000 km^3

7.

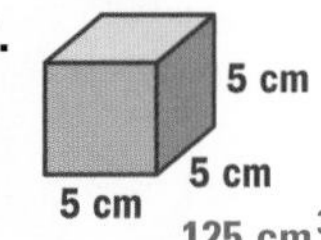

125 cm^3

8.

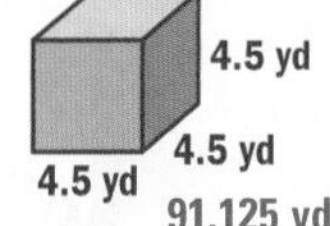

91.125 yd^3

Skills Review Handbook

Units of Weight and Mass

Tables of equivalent weights and masses in the U.S. customary system and the metric system are shown below.

Equivalent U.S. Customary Weights
1 ton (ton) = 2000 pounds (lb)
1 pound (lb) = 16 ounces (oz)

Equivalent Metric Masses
1 kilogram (kg) = 1000 grams (g)
1 gram (g) = 1000 milligrams (mg)

Example **Copy and complete the statement using <, >, or =.**

a. 8 kg _?_ 7900 g

b. 93 oz _?_ 6 lb

Solution

a. $8 \cancel{\text{kg}} \times \frac{1000 \text{ g}}{1 \cancel{\text{kg}}} = 8000 \text{ g}$

Answer So, 8 kg > 7900 g.

b. $6 \cancel{\text{lb}} \times \frac{16 \text{ oz}}{1 \cancel{\text{lb}}} = 96 \text{ oz}$

Answer So, 93 oz < 6 lb.

Example **Find the weight or mass of the object.**

a.

b.

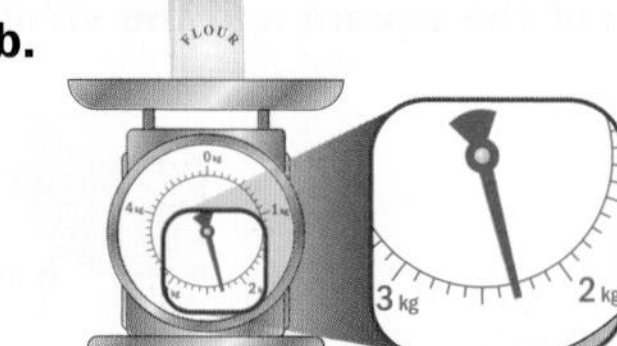

Solution

a. Each pound is divided into sixteenths, so the weight of the squashes is $3\frac{12}{16}$, or $3\frac{3}{4}$ pounds.

b. Each kilogram is divided into tenths, so the mass of the flour is 2.3 kilograms.

Practice

Copy and complete the statement using <, >, or =.

1. 2.5 tons _?_ 4900 lb >

2. 0.62 kg _?_ 622 g <

3. 9400 mg _?_ 9.4 g =

4. 30 lb _?_ 470 oz >

5. 19,217 oz _?_ 0.6 ton >

6. 1.8 kg _?_ 1,790,000 mg >

Find the weight or mass of the object.

7. $1\frac{1}{4}$ lb

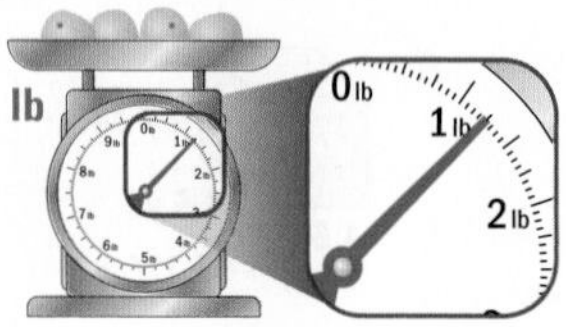

8. 4.5 kg

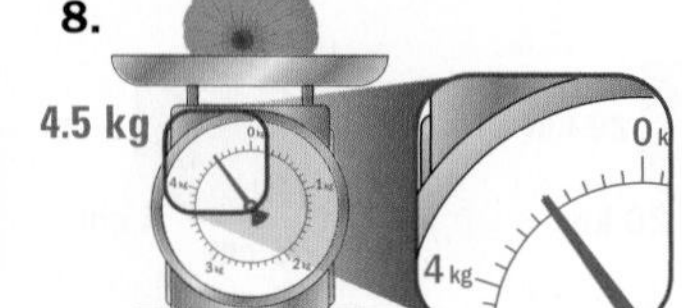

9. $2\frac{1}{2}$ lb

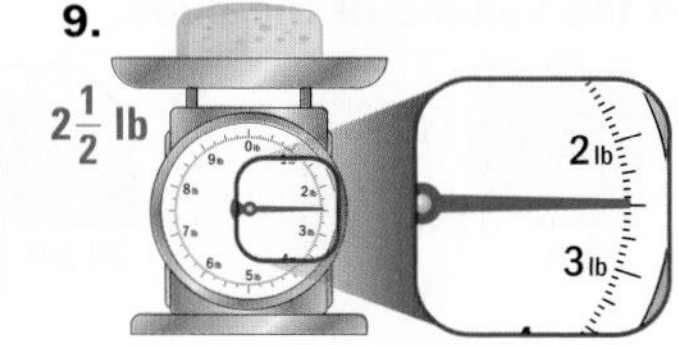

Units of Capacity

Equivalent U.S. Customary Capacities
1 cup (c) = 8 fluid ounces (fl oz)
1 pint (pt) = 2 cups (c)
1 quart (qt) = 2 pints (pt)
1 gallon (gal) = 4 quarts (qt)

Equivalent Metric Capacities
1 kiloliter (kL) = 1000 liters (L)
1 liter (L) = 1000 milliliters (mL)

Example **Copy and complete the statement using $<$, $>$, or $=$.**

a. 9400 mL _?_ 9.6 L

b. 6 gal _?_ 46 pt

Solution

a. $9400 \cancel{\text{mL}} \times \frac{1\text{ L}}{1000 \cancel{\text{mL}}} = 9.4\text{ L}$

Answer So, 9400 mL $<$ 9.6 L.

b. $6 \cancel{\text{gal}} \times \frac{4 \cancel{\text{qt}}}{1 \cancel{\text{gal}}} \times \frac{2\text{ pt}}{1 \cancel{\text{qt}}} = 48\text{ pt}$

Answer So, 6 gal $>$ 46 pt.

Example **Find the amount of liquid in the measuring cup.**

a.

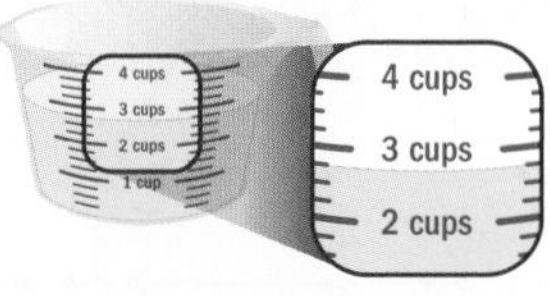

b.

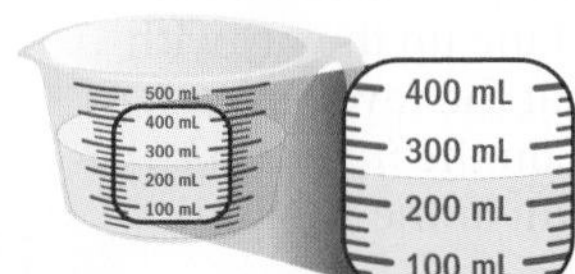

Solution

a. Each cup is divided into fourths, so the liquid is at the $2\frac{3}{4}$ cups level.

b. Each 100 milliliters is divided into fourths, so the liquid is at the 250 milliliters level.

Practice

Copy and complete the statement using $<$, $>$, or $=$.

1. 3 kL _?_ 3010 L $<$

2. 32 fl oz _?_ 1 qt $=$

3. 40 qt _?_ 168 c $<$

4. 1 gal _?_ 128 fl oz $=$

5. 34 pt _?_ 4 gal $>$

6. 34,710 mL _?_ 0.035 kL $<$

Find the amount of liquid in the measuring cup.

7. $3\frac{1}{4}$ c

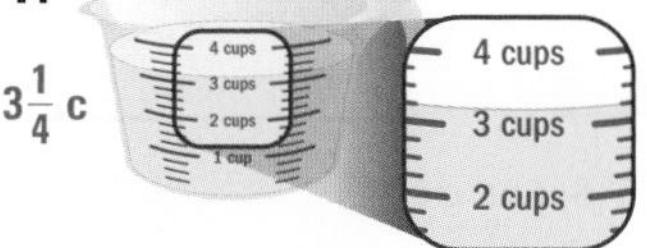

8. 700 mL

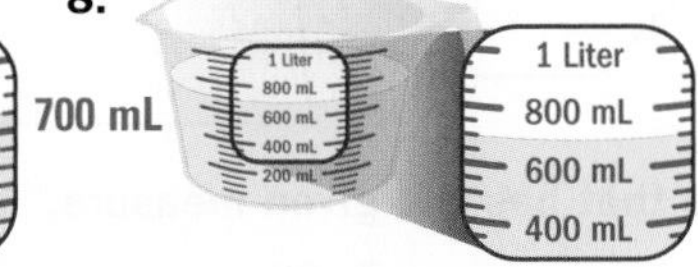

9. $4\frac{1}{2}$ c

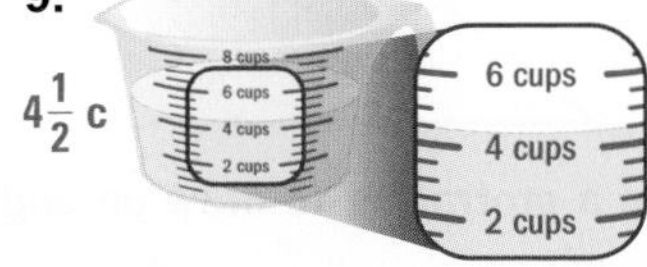

5.

6.

7.

8.

Using a Protractor

A **protractor** is a tool that you can use to draw and measure angles. A unit of measure for angles is the **degree** (°).

Example **Find the measure of the angle.**

1) Place the protractor on the angle so the protractor's center point is on the point where the two rays meet. Line up one ray with the 0° line. Notice that the ray passes through the 0° mark on the *outer scale.*

2) Read where the other ray crosses the outer scale of the protractor. The measure of $\angle ABC$ is 143°. You can write this as $m\angle ABC = 143°$.

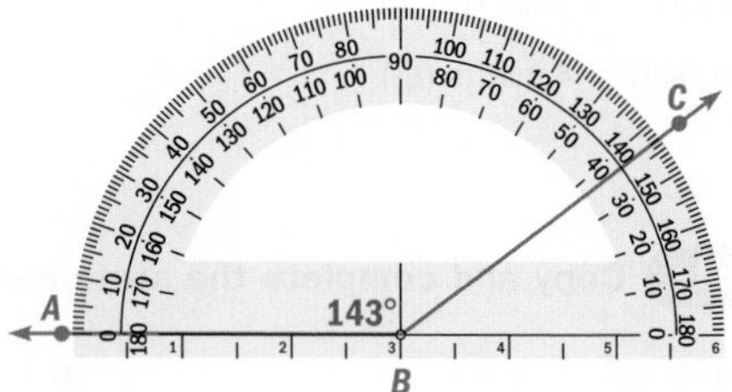

Example **Use a protractor to draw an angle that has a measure of 73°.**

1) Draw and label a ray.

E F

2) Place the center of the protractor at the endpoint of the ray. Line up the ray with the 0° line. Notice that the ray passes through the 0° mark on the *inner scale.* Draw and label a point at the 73° mark on the inner scale.

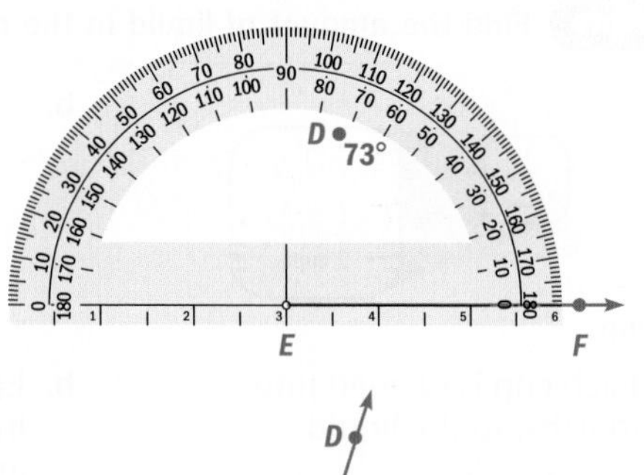

3) Remove the protractor and draw $\overrightarrow{ED}$ to complete the angle.

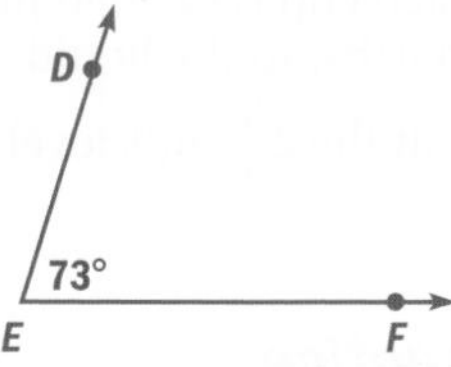

Practice

Use a protractor to measure the angle. Measures may vary. Accept reasonable measures.

1. 38° **2.** 134°

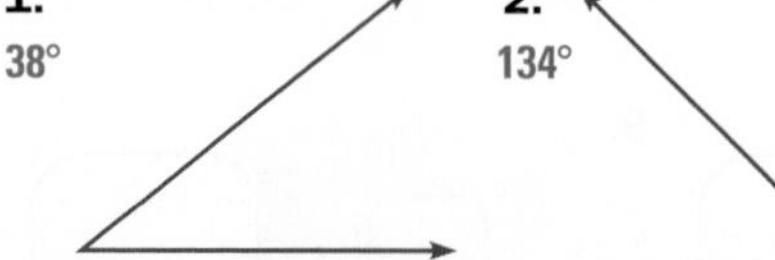

3. 84°

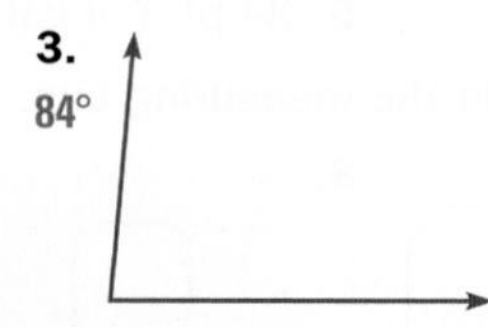

4. 52°

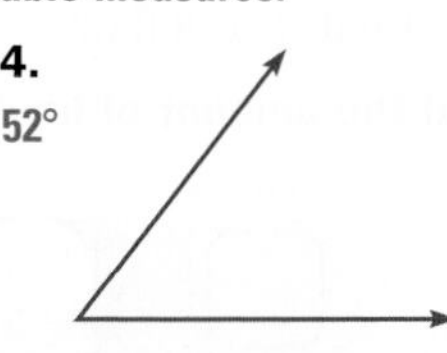

Use a protractor to draw an angle that has the given measure. 5–8. See margin.

5. 55° **6.** 168° **7.** 90° **8.** 77°

Classifying Angles

Classifying Angles	
An **acute angle** has a measure less than 90°: $m\angle ABC < 90°$. 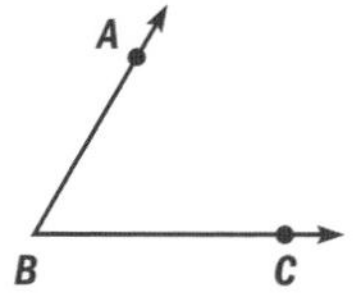	A **right angle** has a measure of exactly 90°: $m\angle ABC = 90°$. 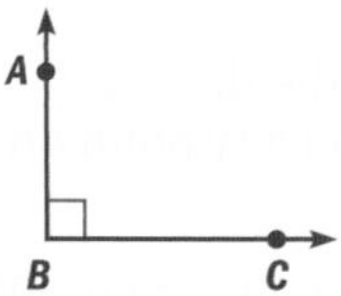
An **obtuse angle** has a measure between 90° and 180°: $m\angle ABC > 90°$ and $m\angle ABC < 180°$. 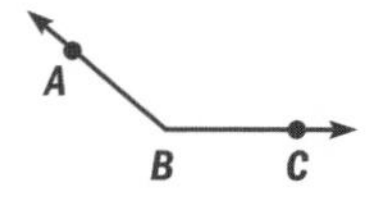	A **straight angle** has a measure of exactly 180°: $m\angle ABC = 180°$. 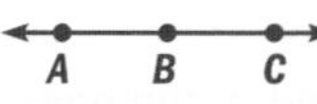

Example **Find the measure of the given angle. Then classify the angle as *acute*, *right*, *obtuse*, or *straight*.**

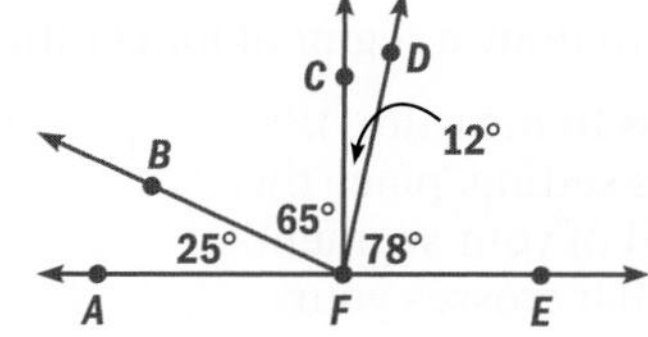

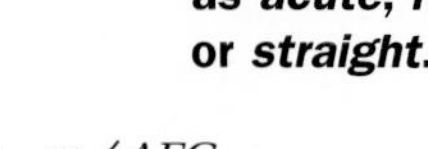

a. $m\angle AFC$

b. $m\angle BFD$

Solution

a. $m\angle AFC = m\angle AFB + m\angle BFC$

$= 25° + 65°$

$= 90°$

Answer $m\angle AFC = 90°$, so $\angle AFC$ is a right angle.

b. $m\angle BFD = m\angle BFC + m\angle CFD$

$= 65° + 12°$

$= 87°$

Answer $m\angle BFD = 87°$, so $\angle BFD$ is an acute angle.

✔ *Practice*

Find the measure of the angle. Then classify the angle as *acute*, *right*, *obtuse*, or *straight*.

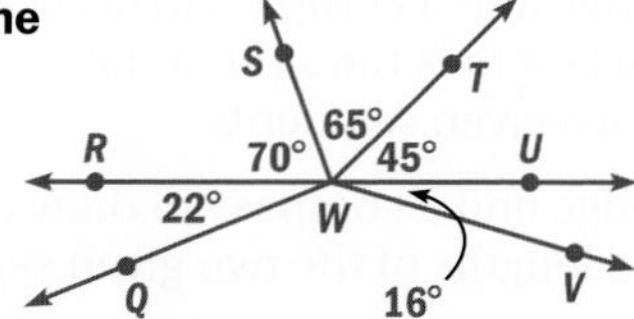

1. $m\angle QWS$ 92°; obtuse
2. $m\angle RWU$ 180°; straight
3. $m\angle TWV$ 61°; acute
4. $m\angle QWT$ 157°; obtuse
5. $m\angle SWV$ 126°; obtuse
6. $m\angle RWT$ 135°; obtuse

Using a Compass

A **compass** is an instrument used to draw circles. A **straightedge** is any object that can be used to draw a segment.

Example **Use a compass to draw a circle with radius 1 cm.**

Recall that the *radius* of a circle is the distance between the center of the circle and any point on the circle.

Use a centimeter ruler to open the compass so that the distance between the point and the pencil is 1 cm.

Place the point on a piece of paper and rotate the pencil around the point to draw the circle.

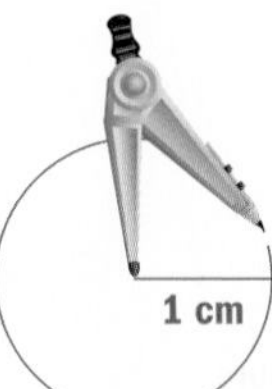

Example **Use a straightedge and a compass to draw a segment whose length is the sum of the lengths of $\overline{AB}$ and $\overline{CD}$.**

A B C D

Solution

Use a straightedge to draw a segment longer than both given segments.

Open your compass to measure $\overline{AB}$. Using this compass setting, place the point at the left end of your segment and make a mark that crosses your segment.

Then open your compass to measure $\overline{CD}$. Using this compass setting, place the point at the first mark you made on your segment and make another mark that crosses your segment.

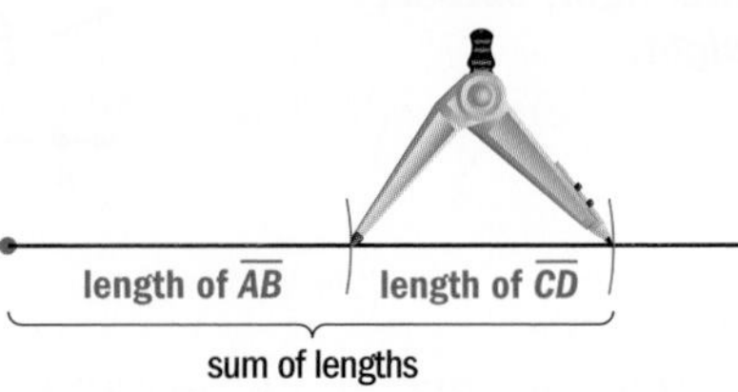

Practice

Use a compass to draw a circle with the given radius. 1–7. Check students' work.

1. 1 inch **2.** 3 cm **3.** 2 inches **4.** 2 cm **5.** 1.7 cm

6. Use a straightedge and a compass to draw a segment whose length is the *sum* of the lengths of the two given segments.

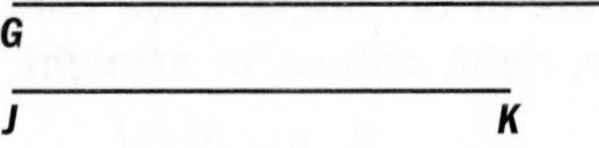

7. Use a straightedge and a compass to draw a segment whose length is the *difference* of the lengths of the two given segments in Exercise 6.

Draw a Diagram

When a problem to be solved is not illustrated, you may find it helpful to draw a diagram that summarizes the information you are given.

Example **Draw a diagram to solve the following problem.**

You are using a word processing program to write a science report. You plan to print the report on paper that is 8.5 inches wide. The left and right margins are each 1 inch wide. On one page of your report, you plan to include a table that is as wide as possible and has 3 columns of equal width. How wide should you make each column?

Solution

Draw a diagram of the sheet of paper with the table.

To find the width of the entire table, subtract the widths of the left and right margins from the width of the paper.

Width of table $= 8.5 - 1 - 1 = 6.5$ in.

Then divide the width of the table by 3 to find the width of each column.

Width of each column $= \frac{6.5}{3} \approx 2.17$ in.

Answer You should make each column about 2.17 inches wide.

Practice

Use the strategy *draw a diagram* to solve the problem.

1. **Paintings** You are hanging 3 paintings on a wall that is 22 feet long. The width of each painting is 2 feet. You want to position the paintings so that the gaps between paintings and between a painting and an end of the wall have the same width. How wide should each gap be? **4 ft**

2. **Travel** Your town is laid out as a grid. Starting at your home, you walk north 6 blocks to buy some snacks at a store. You then walk east 3 blocks to meet a friend, and finally south 2 blocks to a park. What is the shortest distance (in blocks) back to your home? **7 blocks**

3. **Garden** A square garden has sides that are 25 feet long. A path around the garden is 3 feet wide. What is the area of the path? **336 ft^2**

Look for a Pattern

You can solve some problems by looking for, identifying, and extending a pattern.

Example **The table shows the cost of a large pizza at a restaurant for different numbers of toppings. What is the cost of a large pizza with 7 toppings?**

Number of toppings	0	1	2	3	4	5
Cost of large pizza	\$9.00	\$9.75	\$10.50	\$11.25	\$12.00	\$12.75

Solution

Look for a pattern in the costs as the number of toppings increases. Notice that each additional topping increases the cost by \$.75.

Number of toppings	0	1	2	3	4	5
Cost of large pizza	\$9.00	\$9.75	\$10.50	\$11.25	\$12.00	\$12.75

+ \$.75   + \$.75   + \$.75   + \$.75   + \$.75

Because a 7-topping pizza has 2 more toppings than a 5-topping pizza, you can find the cost of a 7-topping pizza by adding 2(\$.75) to the cost of a 5-topping pizza.

Cost of 7-topping pizza = \$12.75 + 2(\$.75) = \$14.25

Answer A large pizza with 7 toppings costs \$14.25.

Practice

Use the strategy *look for a pattern* to solve the problem.

1. **Buses** The table shows part of a bus schedule for a stop near your home. Based on the pattern, when does the 9th bus make a stop? **9:05**

Bus number	1	2	3	4	5	6
Time of bus stop	5:45	6:10	6:35	7:00	7:25	7:50

2. **Logical Reasoning** Find the next number in the list below. Explain your reasoning.

   1, 2, 4, 7, 11, 16, 22, ?

   29. *Sample answer:* Going from one number to the next, the increases are 1, 2, 3, 4, 5, and 6. So, the next increase will be 7, and the missing number will be 22 + 7 = 29.

3. **Stacking Cans** A grocery store clerk stacks cans in the shape of a pyramid. The top 3 layers of cans are shown from above. If the pyramid has 8 layers, how many cans are in the pyramid? **204 cans**

Top layer

Layer 2

Layer 3

Guess, Check, and Revise

An effective way to solve certain problems is to make a reasonable guess of the answer and then check whether the guess is correct. If the guess is not correct, you can revise the guess and try again.

You are saving money for a new bike that costs $275. You already have $80. You can save $15 a week. How long will it take you to save enough money for the bike?

Solution

Guess: Try 10 weeks.

Check: After 10 weeks, you will have saved $80 + 10($15) = $230, which is less than the cost of the bike.

Revise: Try saving for more weeks.

Guess: Try 14 weeks.

Check: After 14 weeks, you will have saved $80 + 14($15) = $290, which is greater than the cost of the bike.

Revise: Try saving for fewer weeks.

Guess: Try 13 weeks.

Check: After 13 weeks, you will have saved $80 + 13($15) = $275, which is equal to the cost of the bike.

Answer It will take you 13 weeks to save enough money for the bike.

Practice

Use the strategy *guess, check, and revise* to solve the problem.

1. **Loan** You are paying back a $132 loan that your parents made to you. You have already repaid $20 and plan to pay back $7 a week from now on. How long will it take you to repay the loan? **16 weeks**
2. **Number Sense** The sum of three consecutive integers is 129. What are the integers? **42, 43, 44**
3. **Trees** A tree farm sold 17 spruce trees for $940. Some of the trees were white spruce, which cost $50 each. The rest were blue spruce, which cost $65 each. How many of each type of tree were sold? **11 white spruce and 6 blue spruce**
4. **Fans** A store sells small fans for $12 each and large fans for $35 each. If the store sells 14 fans for $375, how many of each type of fan are sold? **5 small fans and 9 large fans**
5. **Classroom** The floor of a classroom is a square with an area of 676 square feet. What is the length of a side of the floor? **26 ft**
6. **Geometry** The volume of a cube is 29,791 cubic centimeters. What is the length of an edge of the cube? **31 cm**

Skills Review Handbook

Act It Out

Sometimes you may wish to "act out" a problem using the actual objects described in the problem or other items that represent those objects. The process of acting out the problem may lead you to the solution.

Example **Ben and Paul buy a box of 42 baseball cards at a garage sale. Ben pays twice as much of the cost as Paul, so they agree that Ben should get twice as many of the cards. How many cards should each person get?**

Solution

Use 42 pieces of paper to represent the 42 baseball cards. Divide the pieces into two groups, one for Ben and one for Paul. For every 2 pieces of paper you give to Ben, give 1 piece to Paul.

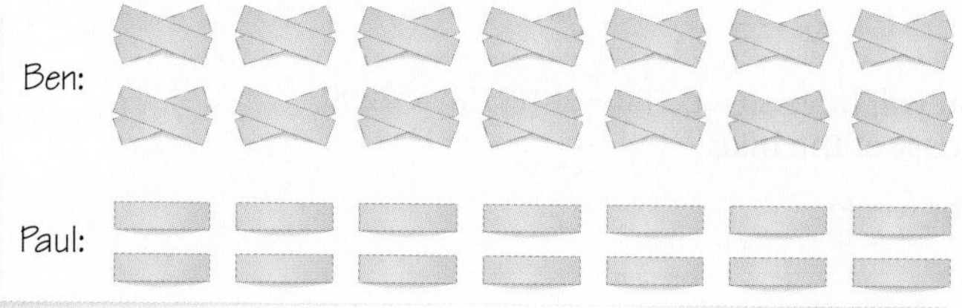

Answer Because Ben has 28 pieces of paper and Paul has 14 pieces, Ben should get 28 baseball cards and Paul should get 14 baseball cards.

Practice

Use the strategy *act it out* to solve the problem.

1. **Computers** Rosa and Kim buy a package of 25 blank CDs to use for backing up their computer files. Rosa has more files to back up, so they agree that she should get 3 CDs for every 2 CDs Kim gets. How many CDs should each person get? **Rosa: 15 CDs, Kim: 10 CDs**
2. **Class Project** Gail, Carlos, and Tonya have a package of 50 sheets of construction paper to use for a class project. Gail takes 6 sheets, Carlos takes twice as many sheets as Gail, and Tonya takes one quarter of the remaining sheets. How many sheets of paper are left? **24 sheets**
3. **Seating** Ann, Bill, Carrie, Devon, Ellie, and Fred are sitting at the table shown. Ellie is sitting in seat 3. Ann is sitting across from Ellie. Carrie is sitting between Ann and Fred. Devon is sitting across from Carrie. In which seat is Bill sitting? **seat 1**

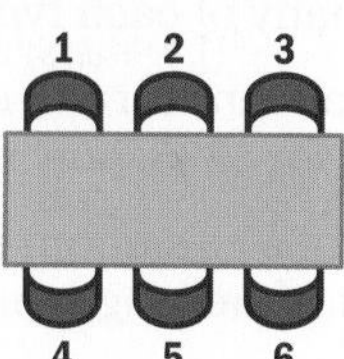

Make a List or Table

Sometimes a problem asks you to generate and record a large amount of information. For such problems, it can be helpful to organize the information using a list or a table.

Example **At a mall, you want to visit the book store, the pet store, the record store, and the shoe store. In how many orders can you visit these stores?**

Solution

Let B represent the book store, P represent the pet store, R represent the record store, and S represent the shoe store. Each arrangement of the letters B, P, R, and S represents an order in which you can visit the stores. You want to find all possible arrangements of the letters.

First list the arrangements that begin with the letter B.

BPRS BPSR BRPS BRSP BSPR BSRP

Similarly, list the arrangements that begin with P, R, and S.

PBRS PBSR PRBS PRSB PSBR PSRB

RBPS RBSP RPBS RPSB RSBP RSPB

SBPR SBRP SPBR SPRB SRBP SRPB

Count the arrangements of the letters. There are 24 arrangements.

Answer There are 24 orders in which you can visit the stores.

Practice

Use the strategy *make a list or table* to solve the problem.

1. **Table Tennis** Aaron, Lori, Mary, and Carlos are playing table tennis at a community center. Each person plays every other person exactly once. How many table tennis matches are played? **6 matches**

2. **Cafeteria** On Mondays, a school cafeteria offers 2 main courses (spaghetti and ham), 3 side dishes (salad, corn, and green beans), and 2 desserts (pie and cake). You can choose 1 main course, 1 side dish, and 1 dessert for your lunch. How many lunches are possible? **12 lunches**

3. **Air Conditioning** The cost of electricity needed to operate a certain air conditioner is $.25 an hour. Copy and complete the table below. How many hours can you run the air conditioner each month if you want to spend at most $35 a month in electricity? **140 h or less**

Hours of operation	20	40	60	80	100	120	140	160	180
Cost of electricity	?	?	?	?	?	?	?	?	?
	$5	**$10**	**$15**	**$20**	**$25**	**$30**	**$35**	**$40**	**$45**

Skills Review Handbook

Solve a Simpler or Related Problem

If a problem seems too difficult, try solving a similar problem that has simpler conditions. Doing so may lead to a solution of the original problem.

Example **A *diameter* of a circle is a segment that passes through the center of the circle and has endpoints on the circle. If you draw 10 diameters of a circle, how many sections are produced?**

Solution

Begin with a simpler task. Find the number of sections produced when you draw 1, 2, or 3 diameters of a circle. Look for a pattern in the results.

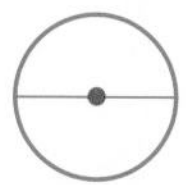

1 diameter
2 sections

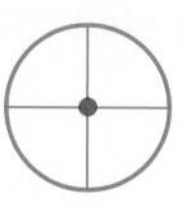

2 diameters
4 sections

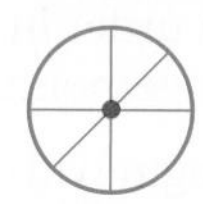

3 diameters
6 sections

In each case, the number of sections is twice the number of diameters.

Answer Based on the pattern, if you draw 10 diameters of a circle, 20 sections are produced.

Practice

Use the strategy *solve a simpler or related problem* to solve the problem.

1. **Restaurant** A restaurant has 12 square tables that seat one person on each side. For a private party, the tables are joined together in a row to form one long table. How many people can be seated at the party? **26 people**

2. **Geometry** The first four figures in a pattern are shown below. Consider the problem of finding the number of squares of different sizes in each figure, where all the sides of each square are segments in the figure. For instance, there is 1 square (a 1×1 square) in the first figure. There are 5 squares (four 1×1 squares and one 2×2 square) in the second figure. Predict the number of squares in the 10th figure of the pattern. **385 squares**

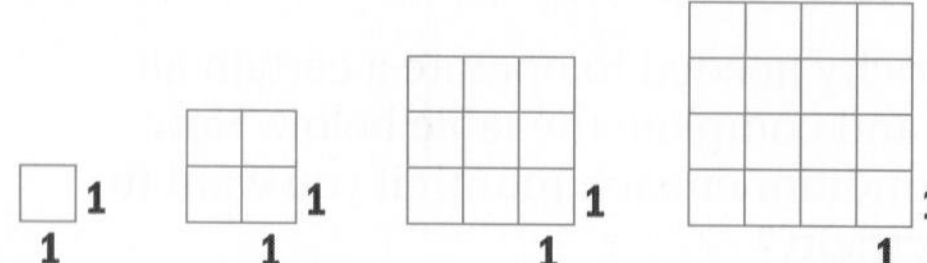

3. **Logical Reasoning** Consider the list of numbers such that the first number is 1 and each number after the first is twice the number before it: 1, 2, 4, 8, 16, ... What is the 15th number in the list? What is the sum of the first 15 numbers? **16,384; 32,767**

Skills Review Handbook

Work Backward

A problem may involve a series of actions where the final result of the actions is known and you need to determine the beginning conditions. It may be helpful to work backward.

Example **At the end of a day, you have $19 in your wallet. You remember spending $14 on dinner, collecting $23 owed you from a friend, and spending $11 on a T-shirt. How much money did you have at the beginning of the day?**

Solution

Work backward from the final amount of money in your wallet, $19. Use the following steps.

1. Add back the $14 spent on dinner to the final amount in your wallet.

   $\$19 + \$14 = \$33$

2. Subtract away the $23 your friend paid you from the result in Step 1.

   $\$33 - \$23 = \$10$

3. Add back the $11 spent on a T-shirt to the result in Step 2.

   $\$10 + \$11 = \$21$

Answer You had $21 at the beginning of the day.

Practice

Use the strategy *work backward* to solve the problem.

1. **Scheduling** On Saturday, you need to be at soccer practice at 3:00 P.M. It takes 25 minutes to walk to the soccer field. Before you leave, you need to mow your lawn, which takes 1 hour 15 minutes. By what time should you start mowing if you are to get to soccer practice on time? **1:20 P.M.**

2. **Finance** The table shows the changes in the price of a share of stock during a certain week. At the end of the week, the price is $23.52. What was the price at the beginning of the week? **$22.60**

Day of week	Monday	Tuesday	Wednesday	Thursday	Friday
Change in price	Down $.18	Up $.41	Up $1.09	Down $.37	Down $.03

3. **Books** You borrow a book from the library to read during your vacation. On the first day of vacation, you read one quarter of the book. On the second day, you read half of the remaining pages. On the third day, you finish the last 120 pages of the book. How many pages does the book have? **320 pages**

Break into Parts

Sometimes a problem cannot be solved in one step. Instead, you need to break the problem into smaller parts in order to find the solution.

Example **Two baseball teams, the Hawks and the Tigers, are playing a best-of-five playoff series. For this type of series, the first team to win three games wins the series. In how many ways can the Hawks win the series?**

Solution

Let W represent a game that the Hawks win, and let L represent a game that they lose. Break the problem into three cases.

Case 1: The Hawks win the series in 3 games.

In this case, there is only 1 possible sequence of wins and losses:

WWW

Case 2: The Hawks win the series in 4 games.

In this case, the Hawks must have 3 wins and 1 loss, and the last game must be a win. There are 3 possible sequences of wins and losses:

LWWW WLWW WWLW

Case 3: The Hawks win the series in 5 games.

In this case, the Hawks must have 3 wins and 2 losses, and the last game must be a win. There are 6 possible sequences of wins and losses:

LLWWW LWLWW LWWLW WLLWW WLWLW WWLLW

Answer The number of ways in which the Hawks can win the series is the sum of the results from the three cases: $1 + 3 + 6 = 10$ ways.

Practice

Use the strategy *break into parts* to solve the problem.

1. **Volleyball** The varsity and junior varsity volleyball teams at a high school are playing a best-of-three series during practice. For this type of series, the first team to win two games wins the series. In how many ways can the varsity team win the series? **3 ways**
2. **Cell Phone** The base cost of a cell phone plan is \$55.25 a month, which includes 600 minutes of calling time. You were billed \$72.40 last month for using 649 minutes. What is the per-minute cost of exceeding the calling time included in the base cost? **\$.35**
3. **Omelets** A diner offers the following ingredients in its omelets: ham, cheese, onion, and mushrooms. How many different omelets with at least 2 ingredients are possible? **11 omelets**

Skills Review Handbook

Extra Practice

Chapter 1

1.1 **Evaluate the expression when $x = 9$, $y = 3$, and $z = 12$.**

1. $17 - x$ 8
2. $8y$ 24
3. $z - y$ 9
4. $\frac{z}{y}$ 4

1.2 **Write the power in words and as a repeated multiplication. Then evaluate the power.**

5. 1^8 See margin for answer.
6. 11^3 11 to the third power, or 11 cubed; 11 • 11 • 11; 1331
7. 5^3 5 to the third power, or 5 cubed; 5 • 5 • 5; 125
8. $(1.3)^2$ 1.3 to the second power, or 1.3 squared; (1.3)(1.3); 1.69

1.3 **Evaluate the expression.**

9. $9 \cdot 6 - 5 \cdot 8$ 14
10. $\frac{49 - 11}{12 + 7}$ 2
11. $6(14 + 4^2)$ 180
12. $72 \div [(15 - 9) \cdot 2]$ 6

1.4 **Graph the integers on a number line. Then write the integers in order from least to greatest.** 13–15. See margin for art.

13. $-7, 0, -3, 9, 4$ −7, −3, 0, 4, 9
14. $-1, -13, -10, 2, 5$ −13, −10, −1, 2, 5
15. $-67, -19, -34, -51$ −67, −51, −34, −19

1.4 **State the absolute value and the opposite of the number.**

16. -98 98, 98
17. 43 43, −43
18. 15 15, −15
19. -3 3, 3

1.5 **Find the sum.**

20. $15 + (-18)$ −3
21. $-17 + 56$ 39
22. $-42 + (-31)$ −73
23. $-28 + 16 + 34$ 22

1.6 **Find the difference.**

24. $6 - 13$ −7
25. $14 - (-9)$ 23
26. $-8 - 15$ −23
27. $-3 - (-22)$ 19

1.7 **Find the product or quotient.**

28. $11(-6)$ −66
29. $-4(-9)$ 36
30. $\frac{-420}{-6}$ 70
31. $-45 \div 15$ −3

1.8 **Give the coordinates of the point.**

32. A (−3, 2)
33. B (1, 1)
34. C (3, 2)
35. D (0, 0)
36. E (−2, −3)
37. F (2, −2)

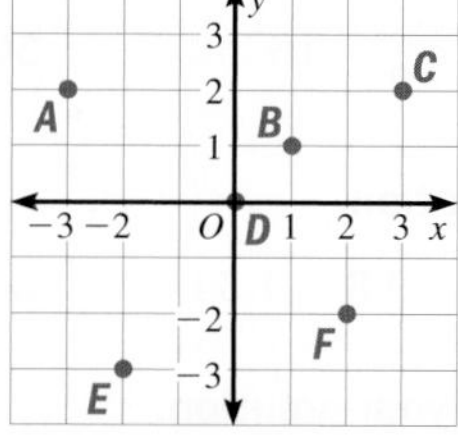

1.8 **Plot the point in a coordinate plane. Describe the location of the point.** 38–41. See margin for art.

38. $M(0, -4)$ *y*-axis
39. $N(5, 6)$ Quadrant I
40. $P(-3, 2)$ Quadrant II
41. $Q(-2, -4)$ Quadrant III

5. 1 to the eighth power; 1 • 1 • 1 • 1 • 1 • 1 • 1 • 1; 1

13.

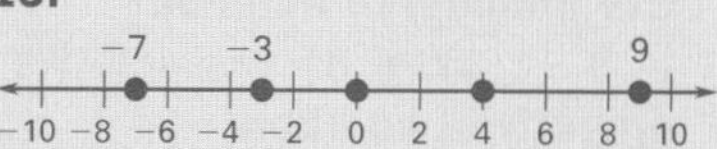

14.

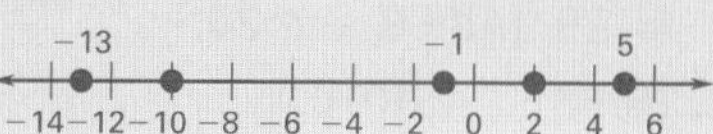

15.

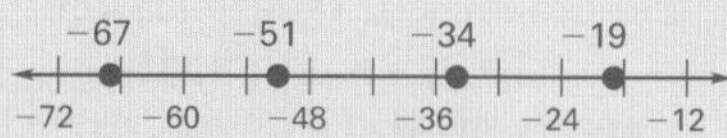

38–41.

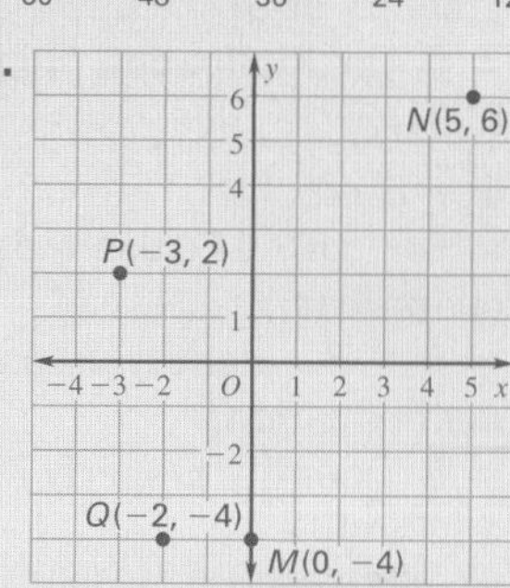

1. $(17 + 9) + 3$
$= (9 + 17) + 3$ [commutative property of addition]
$= 9 + (17 + 3)$ [associative property of addition]
$= 9 + 20$ [Add 17 and 3.]
$= 29$ [Add 9 and 20.]

2. $(5.63)(2.45)(0)$
$= (5.63)[(2.45)(0)]$ [associative property of multiplication]
$= (5.63)(0)$ [multiplication property of 0]
$= 0$ [multiplication property of 0]

3. $0 + 8 \cdot 1$
$= 0 + (8 \cdot 1)$ [Use order of operations.]
$= 0 + 8$ [identity property of multiplication]
$= 8$ [identity property of addition]

4. $2(-18)(5)$
$= -18(2)(5)$ [commutative property of multiplication]
$= -18[(2)(5)]$ [associative property of multiplication]
$= -18(10)$ [Multiply 2 and 5.]
$= -180$ [Multiply -18 and 10.]

Extra Practice

Chapter 2

2.1 Evaluate the expression. Justify each of your steps. 1–4. See margin.

1. $(17 + 9) + 3$ **2.** $(5.63)(2.45)(0)$ **3.** $0 + 8 \cdot 1$ **4.** $2(-18)(5)$

2.1 Evaluate the expression when $x = -7$ and $y = 5$.

5. $8xy$ -280 **6.** $27 + 3y^2 + x$ 95 **7.** $35 + 4x + y$ 12 **8.** $12xy^2$ -2100

2.1 Simplify the expression.

9. $-4(11m)$ $-44m$ **10.** $(3a)(17)$ $51a$ **11.** $b + (-14) + 35$ $b + 21$ **12.** $8 + c + (-5)$ $c + 3$

2.1 Identify the property that the statement illustrates.

13. $-5a + 0 = -5a$ identity property of addition **14.** $4^4 + 21 = 21 + 4^4$ commutative property of addition **15.** $(3 \cdot 5) \cdot 6 = 3 \cdot (5 \cdot 6)$ associative property of multiplication

2.2 Use the distributive property to evaluate the expression.

16. $4(8 - 13)$ -20 **17.** $(6 + 12)3$ 54 **18.** $-9(3 + 10)$ -117 **19.** $(-5 - 2)(-6)$ 42

2.2 Use the distributive property to write an equivalent variable expression.

20. $7(m - 5)$ $7m - 35$ **21.** $-3(5a + 3)$ $-15a - 9$ **22.** $(15 + 4b)(-2)$ $-30 - 8b$ **23.** $(2 - 3z)6$ $12 - 18z$

2.3 Simplify the expression.

24. $d + 7d$ $8d$ **25.** $-5y + 8y - 2y$ y **26.** $6x - (x - 1)$ $5x + 1$ **27.** $2(c + 4) + 3c$ $5c + 8$

28. $4m - 6m - 7m$ $-9m$ **29.** $-3b + 11b$ $8b$ **30.** $-3(r + 2) - 3r$ $-6r - 6$ **31.** $-p + 3(p - 5)$ $2p - 15$

2.4 Solve the equation using mental math.

32. $3 + x = 19$ 16 **33.** $n - 9 = -4$ 5 **34.** $32 = -8u$ -4 **35.** $5 = \frac{55}{g}$ 11

Solve the equation. Check your solution.

2.5

36. $y + 8 = 17$ 9 **37.** $r - 13 = -5$ 8 **38.** $18 = p - 4$ 22 **39.** $-15 = 7 + u$ -22

40. $742 + b = 534$ -208 **41.** $157 = c + 48$ 109 **42.** $173 = x - 23$ 196 **43.** $j - 15 = -47$ -32

2.6

44. $-15z = 0$ 0 **45.** $-78 = 3g$ -26 **46.** $17 = -t$ -17 **47.** $-13w = -91$ 7

48. $\frac{k}{14} = 5$ 70 **49.** $\frac{s}{-9} = 16$ -144 **50.** $-20 = \frac{x}{-17}$ 340 **51.** $-7 = \frac{r}{50}$ -350

2.7 Perform the indicated operation.

52. $6.3 + (-11.9)$ -5.6 **53.** $-9.8 - 1.34$ -11.14 **54.** $13.16 \div (-2.35)$ -5.6 **55.** $3.7(-4.9)$ -18.13

2.7 Solve the equation. Check your solution.

56. $-9.5 = \frac{u}{-2.72}$ 25.84 **57.** $g + 4.6 = 19.3$ 14.7 **58.** $-0.32b = 2.08$ -6.5 **59.** $-12.3 = h - 5.47$ -6.83

Chapter 3

Solve the equation. Check your solution.

3.1 **1.** $6m + 11 = 83$ 12 **2.** $39 = 15a + 24$ 1 **3.** $23 = 19k - 34$ 3 **4.** $59 - 4n = 91$ −8

5. $\frac{x}{8} + 12 = -5$ −136 **6.** $5 = \frac{c}{-4} + 7$ 8 **7.** $\frac{b}{3} - 13 = 14$ 81 **8.** $-8 = -14 - \frac{d}{9}$ −54

3.2 **9.** $11a + 9 - 3a = -7$ −2 **10.** $4r + 41 + 5r = 104$ 7 **11.** $32 = 8(p + 3)$ 1

12. $42 = -7(j - 4)$ −2 **13.** $6(7 - 4y) = 18$ 1 **14.** $-3(2s + 5) = 15$ −5

15. $17 + 5(t + 1) = 37$ 3 **16.** $7h - 4(h - 3) = 33$ 7 **17.** $49 = -6b + 9 + 2b$ −10

3.3 **18.** $14k + 55 = 11k + 94$ 13 **19.** $-4m - 7 = 8 - 9m$ 3 **20.** $23f - 41 = 54f + 21$ −2

21. $16z - 18 = 4 + 5z$ 2 **22.** $d + 3 = 2(9 - d)$ 5 **23.** $4(7c + 2) = 28c$ no solution

24. $6(x + 8) = 5x + 4$ −44 **25.** $12n + 6 = 3(4n + 2)$ all real numbers **26.** $18r - 7 = 3 + 8r$ 1

3.3 **Write the verbal sentence as an equation. Then solve the equation.**

27. Ten plus 7 times a number is equal to 6 less than 5 times the number. $10 + 7x = 5x - 6$; −8

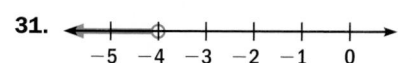

28. Eleven minus 4 times a number is equal to 6 plus the number. $11 - 4x = 6 + x$; 1

3.4 **Write an inequality represented by the graph.**

29.
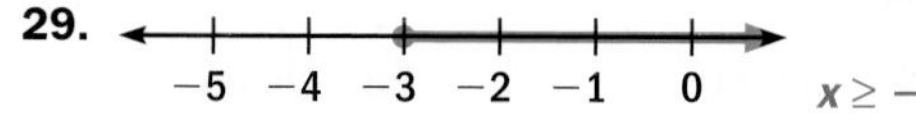

$x \geq -3$

30. −1 0 1 2 3 4 $x > 2$

31. −5 −4 −3 −2 −1 0 $x < -4$

32. −1 0 1 2 3 4 $x \leq 1$

Solve the inequality. Graph your solution. 33–48. See margin for art.

3.4 **33.** $a + 3 < 10$ $a < 7$ **34.** $u + 7 \geq 5$ $u \geq -2$ **35.** $-5 \leq p - 2$ $p \geq -3$ **36.** $41 > g + 45$ $g < -4$

37. $19 \geq b - 29$ $b \leq 48$ **38.** $7.9 < n - 5$ $n > 12.9$ **39.** $k + 3.7 > 4$ $k > 0.3$ **40.** $s + 4.2 \leq 7.8$ $s \leq 3.6$

3.5 **41.** $\frac{b}{8} \leq 13$ $b \leq 104$ **42.** $\frac{a}{-5} < 9$ $a > -45$ **43.** $\frac{x}{4} \geq -2$ $x \geq -8$ **44.** $\frac{d}{7} > 3$ $d > 21$

45. $-5d > 40$ $d < -8$ **46.** $7w \geq 84$ $w \geq 12$ **47.** $-12 < 3t$ $t > -4$ **48.** $-4z \leq -16$ $z \geq 4$

3.5 **Write the verbal sentence as an inequality. Then solve the inequality.**

49. Three times a number is at most 18. $3x \leq 18$; $x \leq 6$

50. Nine times a number is greater than 36. $9x > 36$; $x > 4$

51. A number divided by −2 is less than 10. $\frac{x}{-2} < 10$; $x > -20$

52. A number divided by 5 is at least 20. $\frac{x}{5} \geq 20$; $x \geq 100$

3.6 **Solve the inequality. Graph your solution.** 53–60. See margin for art.

53. $3w + 8 > 17$ $w > 3$ **54.** $8n - 21 \leq -5$ $n \leq 2$ **55.** $43 < 31 - 2z$ $z < -6$ **56.** $9 + 5d \geq 44$ $d \geq 7$

57. $8 + \frac{c}{11} \leq 10$ $c \leq 22$ **58.** $\frac{s}{4} - 9 > -15$ $s > -24$ **59.** $-6r + 3 > 9 - 7r$ $r > 6$ **60.** $3y - 7 \geq -32 + 8y$ $y \leq 5$

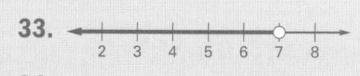

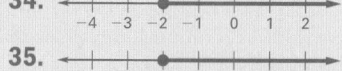

33. 2 3 4 5 6 7 8
34. −4 −3 −2 −1 0 1 2
35. −5 −4 −3 −2 −1 0 1
36. −5 −4 −3 −2 −1 0 1
37. 0 12 24 36 48 60 72
38. 12.6 12.8 13.0
39. 0 0.1 0.2 0.3 0.4 0.5 0.6
40. 3.4 3.5 3.6 3.7 3.8 3.9 4
41. 100 102 104 106
42. −50 −40 −30 −20
43. −12 −10 −8 −6 −4 −2 0
44. 18 19 20 21 22 23 24
45. −12 −10 −8 −6 −4 −2 0
46. 11 12 13 14 15 16 17
47. −6 −5 −4 −3 −2 −1 0
48. 0 1 2 3 4 5 6
53. 0 1 2 3 4 5 6
54. −2 −1 0 1 2 3 4
55. −12 −10 −8 −6 −4 −2 0
56. 3 4 5 6 7 8 9
57. 18 19 20 21 22 23 24
58. −26 −24 −22
59. 0 2 4 6 8 10 12
60. 0 1 2 3 4 5 6

Extra Practice

Chapter 4

4.1 **Tell whether the number is *prime* or *composite*.**

1. 93 composite **2.** 76 composite **3.** 23 prime **4.** 53 prime

4.1 **Write the prime factorization of the number.**

5. 72 $2^3 \cdot 3^2$ **6.** 47 prime **7.** 96 $2^5 \cdot 3$ **8.** 400 $2^4 \cdot 5^2$

4.2 **Find the greatest common factor of the numbers. Then tell whether the numbers are relatively prime.**

9. 51, 63 3; no **10.** 21, 44 1; yes **11.** 32, 110 2; no **12.** 56, 136 8; no

4.2 **Find the greatest common factor of the monomials.**

13. $48y^2, 52y$ $4y$ **14.** $16p, 68p$ $4p$ **15.** $12s, 118s^4$ $2s$ **16.** $3x, 9x^2, 12x^3$ $3x$

4.3 **Write the fraction in simplest form.**

17. $\frac{15}{80}$ $\frac{3}{16}$ **18.** $\frac{8}{84}$ $\frac{2}{21}$ **19.** $\frac{28}{44}$ $\frac{7}{11}$ **20.** $\frac{38}{95}$ $\frac{2}{5}$

21. $\frac{14m^2}{21m^3}$ $\frac{2}{3m}$ **22.** $\frac{36r}{6r^2s}$ $\frac{6}{rs}$ **23.** $\frac{38abc}{4c^2}$ $\frac{19ab}{2c}$ **24.** $\frac{50x^4}{12x}$ $\frac{25x^3}{6}$

4.4 **Find the least common multiple of the numbers.**

25. 10, 15 30 **26.** 21, 28 84 **27.** 32, 60 480 **28.** 18, 45 90

4.4 **Find the least common multiple of the monomials.**

29. $5c, 18c^2$ $90c^2$ **30.** $4s^3, 36s^2$ $36s^3$ **31.** $10n^2p, 16np$ $80n^2p$ **32.** $57z^4, 39z^2$ $741z^4$

4.5 **Find the product or quotient. Write your answer using exponents.**

33. $6^5 \cdot 6^9$ 6^{14} **34.** $12^3 \cdot 12^4 \cdot 12^2$ 12^9 **35.** $\frac{4^{11}}{4^5}$ 4^6 **36.** $\frac{3^8}{3}$ 3^7

4.5 **Simplify.**

37. $4c^3 \cdot 5c^2$ $20c^5$ **38.** $7d^5 \cdot d^2$ $7d^7$ **39.** $\frac{6a^6}{a^3}$ $6a^3$ **40.** $\frac{15r^7}{12r^4}$ $\frac{5r^3}{4}$

4.6 **Write the expression using only positive exponents.**

41. 18^{-4} $\frac{1}{18^4}$ **42.** 7^{-8} $\frac{1}{7^8}$ **43.** s^3t^0 s^3 **44.** $5w^{-2}$ $\frac{5}{w^2}$

4.7 **Write the number in scientific notation.**

45. 16,000,000 1.6×10^7 **46.** 3,120,000,000 3.12×10^9 **47.** 0.00004 4×10^{-5} **48.** 0.0000078 7.8×10^{-6}

4.7 **Write the number in standard form.**

49. 8.23×10^8 823,000,000 **50.** 4.367×10^5 436,700 **51.** 2.1×10^{-3} 0.0021 **52.** 7.893×10^{-7} 0.0000007893

Extra Practice

Chapter 5

5.1 **Show that the number is rational by writing it as a quotient of two integers.** 1–4. Sample answers are given.

1. -4 $\frac{-4}{1}$ or $\frac{4}{-1}$ **2.** 0.58 $\frac{29}{50}$ **3.** $3\frac{5}{16}$ $\frac{53}{16}$ **4.** 70 $\frac{70}{1}$

5.1 **Write the fraction or mixed number as a decimal.**

5. $\frac{3}{5}$ 0.6 **6.** $-\frac{14}{9}$ $-1.\overline{5}$ **7.** $-6\frac{13}{25}$ -6.52 **8.** $2\frac{5}{12}$ $2.41\overline{6}$

5.1 **Write the decimal as a fraction or mixed number.**

9. 0.34 $\frac{17}{50}$ **10.** -3.78 $-3\frac{39}{50}$ **11.** 9.27 $9\frac{27}{100}$ **12.** $0.\overline{5}$ $\frac{5}{9}$

Find the sum or difference.

5.2 **13.** $-\frac{4}{11} + \frac{9}{11}$ $\frac{5}{11}$ **14.** $\frac{7}{18} - \frac{17}{18}$ $-\frac{5}{9}$ **15.** $-4\frac{7}{15} - 2\frac{11}{15}$ $-7\frac{1}{5}$ **16.** $-9\frac{1}{3} + 1\frac{2}{3}$ $-7\frac{2}{3}$

5.3 **17.** $-\frac{3}{4} - \frac{2}{7}$ $-1\frac{1}{28}$ **18.** $\frac{7}{8} + \left(-\frac{3}{16}\right)$ $\frac{11}{16}$ **19.** $-3\frac{1}{6} + 6\frac{5}{22}$ $3\frac{2}{33}$ **20.** $5\frac{2}{9} - 7\frac{8}{15}$ $-2\frac{14}{45}$

5.3 **Simplify the expression.**

21. $\frac{w}{12} + \frac{w}{15}$ $\frac{3w}{20}$ **22.** $\frac{x}{21} - \frac{x}{3}$ $-\frac{2x}{7}$ **23.** $-\frac{5z}{14} + \frac{9z}{28}$ $-\frac{z}{28}$ **24.** $\frac{2y}{25} - \frac{3y}{10}$ $-\frac{11y}{50}$

5.4 **Find the product.**

25. $\frac{3}{7} \cdot \frac{5}{18}$ $\frac{5}{42}$ **26.** $\frac{9}{10}\left(-\frac{5}{21}\right)$ $-\frac{3}{14}$ **27.** $-24 \cdot \left(-\frac{7}{16}\right)$ $10\frac{1}{2}$ **28.** $-3\frac{1}{3} \cdot 5\frac{13}{20}$ $-18\frac{5}{6}$

5.5 **Find the quotient.**

29. $\frac{5}{16} \div \frac{35}{48}$ $\frac{3}{7}$ **30.** $-\frac{11}{12} \div \frac{3}{8}$ $-2\frac{4}{9}$ **31.** $-7\frac{49}{54} \div 5\frac{5}{6}$ $-1\frac{16}{45}$ **32.** $-22 \div \left(-\frac{4}{11}\right)$ $60\frac{1}{2}$

5.6 **Solve the equation. Check your solution.**

33. $\frac{6}{7}a = 18$ 21 **34.** $\frac{5}{14}c = -\frac{1}{2}$ $-1\frac{2}{5}$ **35.** $\frac{2}{7}x - 5 = 17$ 77 **36.** $\frac{4}{9} = \frac{1}{3}x - \frac{5}{9}$ 3

5.7 **Solve the equation by first clearing the fractions or the decimals.**

37. $\frac{1}{4}x + \frac{1}{6} = -\frac{5}{12}$ $-2\frac{1}{3}$ **38.** $\frac{4}{7} = \frac{1}{8}x - 3$ $28\frac{4}{7}$ **39.** $6.8x + 5.3 = 7$ 0.25 **40.** $27.62 = 3.4x - 5.7$ 9.8

5.7 **Solve the inequality.**

41. $-\frac{4}{5}p + 15 > \frac{3}{5}$ $p < 18$ **42.** $\frac{1}{9}m - 2 \geq \frac{2}{3}$ $m \geq 24$ **43.** $\frac{3}{4}z - \frac{3}{8} \leq \frac{1}{4}$ $z \leq \frac{5}{6}$ **44.** $\frac{1}{2} + \frac{4}{11}y < \frac{19}{22}$ $y < 1$

Extra Practice

Chapter 6

6.1 **Find the unit rate.**

1. $\frac{\$13.92}{8 \text{ gallons}}$ $\frac{\$1.74}{1 \text{ gal}}$ **2.** $\frac{58 \text{ mi}}{4 \text{ h}}$ $\frac{14.5 \text{ mi}}{1 \text{ h}}$ **3.** $\frac{15 \text{ L}}{5 \text{ days}}$ $\frac{3 \text{ L}}{1 \text{ day}}$ **4.** $\frac{\$87.50}{5 \text{ tickets}}$ $\frac{\$17.50}{1 \text{ ticket}}$

6.1 **Write the equivalent rate.**

5. $\frac{50 \text{ mi}}{1 \text{ h}} = \frac{? \text{ ft}}{1 \text{ h}}$ 264,000 **6.** $\frac{\$58}{1 \text{ day}} = \frac{? \text{ dollars}}{1 \text{ week}}$ 406 **7.** $\frac{440 \text{ ft}}{1 \text{ min}} = \frac{? \text{ ft}}{1 \text{ h}}$ 26,400 **8.** $\frac{70 \text{ m}}{30 \text{ sec}} = \frac{? \text{ m}}{1 \text{ min}}$ 140

Solve the proportion.

6.2 **9.** $\frac{4}{5} = \frac{x}{20}$ 16 **10.** $\frac{5}{12} = \frac{a}{84}$ 35 **11.** $\frac{z}{15} = \frac{12}{45}$ 4 **12.** $\frac{c}{8} = \frac{28}{32}$ 7

13. $\frac{8}{13} = \frac{w}{52}$ 32 **14.** $\frac{3}{7} = \frac{d}{42}$ 18 **15.** $\frac{b}{6} = \frac{75}{90}$ 5 **16.** $\frac{n}{9} = \frac{56}{72}$ 7

6.3 **17.** $\frac{12}{18} = \frac{2}{p}$ 3 **18.** $\frac{24}{y} = \frac{21}{35}$ 40 **19.** $\frac{36}{g} = \frac{27}{63}$ 84 **20.** $\frac{3.8}{95} = \frac{5.7}{s}$ 142.5

6.4 **In Exercises 21 and 22, the figures are similar. Find the ratio of the lengths of corresponding sides of figure A to figure B.**

21.

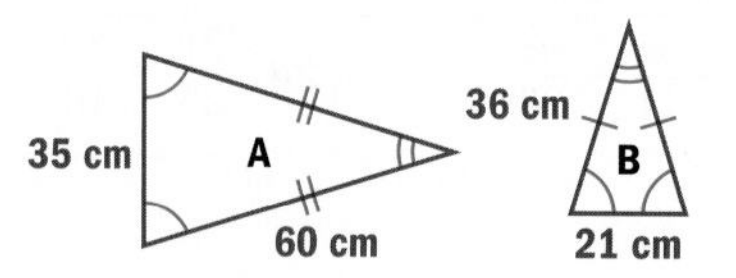

$\frac{5}{3}$

22.

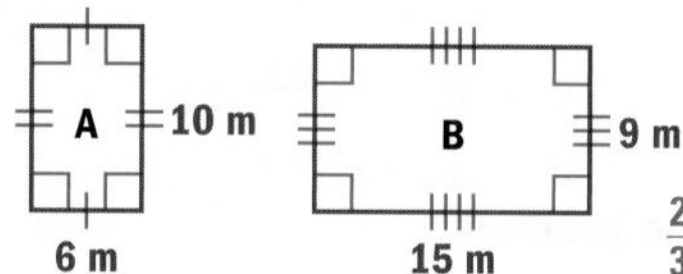

$\frac{2}{3}$

6.5 **23.** Given $LMNP \sim QRST$, find ST.

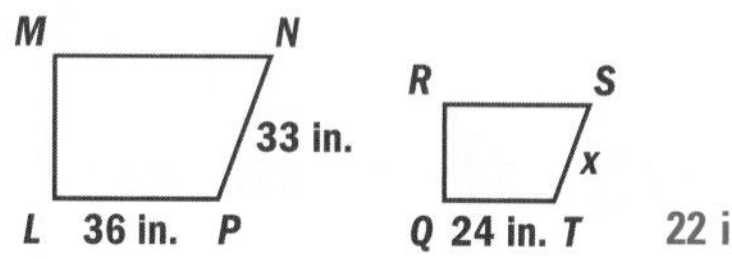

22 in.

24. Given $\triangle ABC \sim \triangle DEF$, find DF.

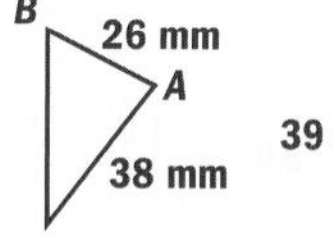

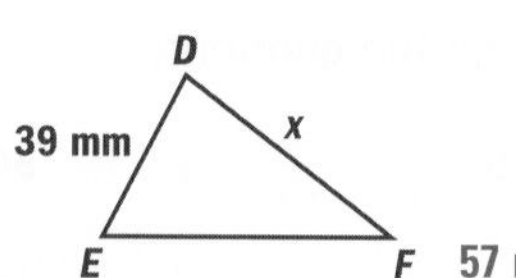

57 mm

6.6 **A map has a scale of 1 inch : 25 miles. Use the given map distance to find the actual distance.**

25. 2 inches 50 mi **26.** 5 inches 125 mi **27.** 0.5 inch 12.5 mi **28.** 6.5 inches 162.5 mi

6.7 **In Exercises 29–32, suppose you roll a number cube. Find the probability of the event.**

29. A multiple of 3 $\frac{1}{3}$ **30.** A multiple of 4 $\frac{1}{6}$ **31.** A factor of 6 $\frac{2}{3}$ **32.** An even number $\frac{1}{2}$

6.8 **33.** You are working on a page for the yearbook and can choose one of 5 action photos, one of 3 group photos, and one of 6 individual photos. How many different groups of 3 photos can you choose? 90 groups

Extra Practice

Chapter 7

7.1 **Write the percent as a fraction or the fraction as a percent.**

1. 43% $\frac{43}{100}$
2. 15% $\frac{3}{20}$
3. $\frac{13}{20}$ 65%
4. $\frac{8}{25}$ 32%

7.1 **Find the percent of the number.**

5. 40% of 300 120
6. 25% of 28 7
7. 75% of 76 57
8. 90% of 430 387

7.2 **Use a proportion to answer the question.**

9. What percent of 140 is 28? 20%
10. 15 is 60% of what number? 25
11. What number is 45% of 180? 81
12. What percent of 136 is 850? 625%

7.3 **Write the decimal as a percent or the percent as a decimal.**

13. 0.045 4.5%
14. 1.34 134%
15. 7% 0.07
16. 0.25% 0.0025

7.3 **Write the fraction as a percent.**

17. $\frac{7}{12}$ $58.\overline{3}\%$
18. $\frac{13}{15}$ $86.\overline{6}\%$
19. $\frac{15}{8}$ 187.5%
20. $\frac{11}{6}$ $183.\overline{3}\%$

7.4 **Use the percent equation to answer the question.**

21. What number is 52% of 625? 325
22. What percent of 72 is 252? 350%
23. 117 is 45% of what number? 260
24. What number is 0.5% of 3400? 17

7.5 **Identify the percent of change as an *increase* or a *decrease*. Then find the percent of change.**

25. Original: 40
New: 62
increase; 55%
26. Original: 650
New: 806
increase; 24%
27. Original: 92
New: 23
decrease; 75%
28. Original: 248
New: 217
decrease; 12.5%

7.6 **Use the given information to find the new price.**

29. Wholesale price: $130
Markup percent: 80%
$234
30. Wholesale price: $14
Markup percent: 120%
$30.80
31. Original price: $24
Discount percent: 30%
$16.80

7.6 **In Exercises 32–34, use the given information to find the total cost.**

32. Original price: $90
Sales tax: 6% $95.40
33. Original price: $65
Sales tax: 5% $68.25
34. Original price: $34
Sales tax: 4% $35.36

7.7 35. A $400 bond earns 2% simple annual interest. After how many years will it earn $72 in interest? 9 y

7.7 36. You deposit $600 into a savings account that earns 3% interest compounded annually. Find the balance of the account after 5 years. Round your answer to the nearest cent. $695.56

Extra Practice

1.

Input Output

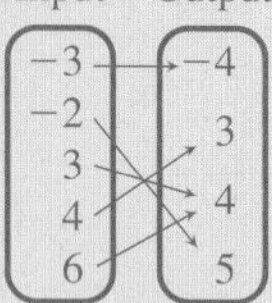

2.

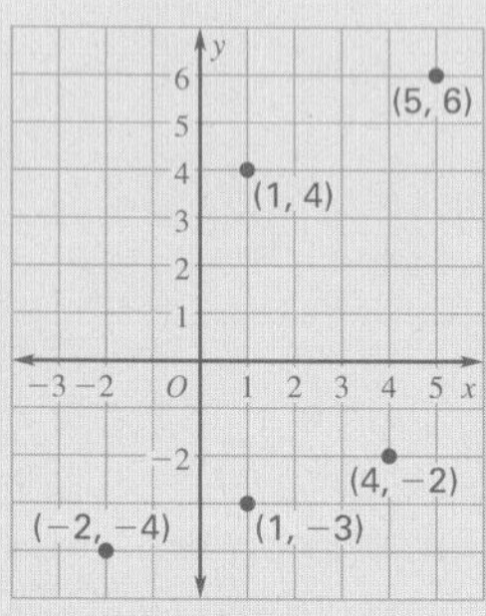

Input Output

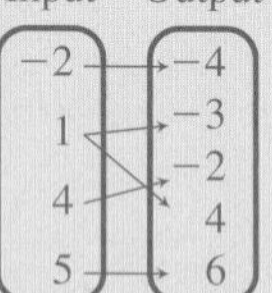

3.

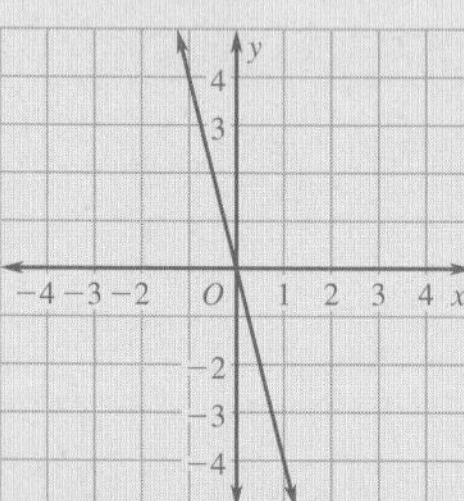

4.

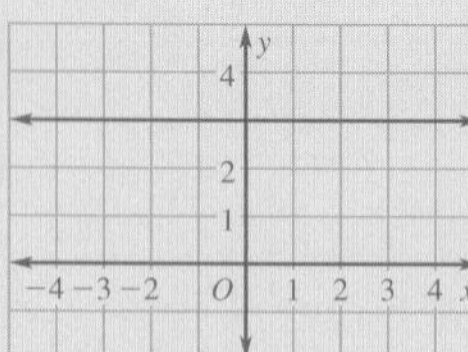

5.

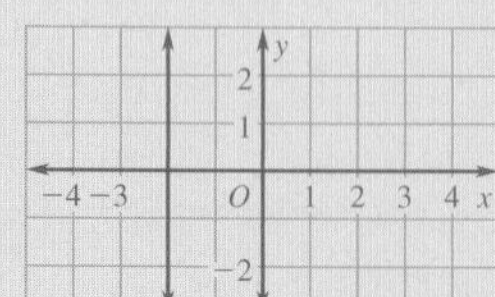

6–10, 19–26, 31–34, 39–42. See Additional Answers beginning on page AA1.

Chapter 8

8.1 **Represent the relation as a graph and as a mapping diagram. Then tell whether the relation is a function. Explain your reasoning.** 1–2. See margin for art.

1. (3, 4), (−2, 5), (4, 3), (6, 4), (−3, −4)
Yes; every input is paired with exactly one output.

2. (5, 6), (1, −3), (4, −2), (1, 4), (−2, −4)
No; the input 1 is paired with two outputs, −3 and 4.

8.2 **Graph the equation. Tell whether the equation is a function.** 3–6. See margin for art.

3. $y = -4x$ yes **4.** $y = 3$ yes **5.** $x = -2$ no **6.** $y = 2x + 3$ yes

8.3 **Find the intercepts of the equation's graph. Then graph the equation.** 7–10. See margin.

7. $x - 2y = 10$ **8.** $2x + 6y = 12$ **9.** $3x + 5y = -15$ **10.** $y = -3x - 6$

8.4 **Find the coordinates of two points on the line with the given equation. Then use the points to find the slope of the line.** 11–14. Sample points are given.

11. $y = -4$ (0, −4), (5, −4); 0

12. $y = \frac{1}{2}x + 7$ (0, 7), (4, 9); $\frac{1}{2}$

13. $x - 3y = 9$ (0, −3), (3, −2); $\frac{1}{3}$

14. $x = 6$ (6, 0), (6, 9); undefined

8.4 **Find the slope of the line through the given points.**

15. (−1, 4), (3, 1) $-\frac{3}{4}$ **16.** (0, 8), (−2, −3) $\frac{11}{2}$ **17.** (5, 6), (9, 10) 1 **18.** (4, −5), (7, −5) 0

8.5 **Identify the slope and *y*-intercept of the line with the given equation. Use the slope and *y*-intercept to graph the equation.** 19–26. See margin for art.

19. $y = 4x - 1$ slope: 4, *y*-intercept: −1

20. $y = -\frac{2}{3}x + 4$ slope: $-\frac{2}{3}$, *y*-intercept: 4

21. $10x - 2y = 4$ slope: 5, *y*-intercept: −2

22. $x + 7y = 21$ slope: $-\frac{1}{7}$, *y*-intercept: 3

23. $y = \frac{1}{4}x + 2$ slope: $\frac{1}{4}$, *y*-intercept: 2

24. $y = -2x - 3$ slope: −2, *y*-intercept: −3

25. $2x + 5y = 15$ slope: $-\frac{2}{5}$, *y*-intercept: 3

26. $3x - 4y = 4$ slope: $\frac{3}{4}$, *y*-intercept: −1

8.6 **Write an equation of the line that is parallel to the given line and passes through the given point.**

27. $y = -4x + 3$; (0, −2) $y = -4x - 2$

28. $y = -\frac{4}{5}x - 2$; (0, 3) $y = -\frac{4}{5}x + 3$

29. $y = \frac{7}{3}x - 6$; (0, −1) $y = \frac{7}{3}x - 1$

30. $y = x + 4$; (0, −5) $y = x - 5$

8.7 **Graph the function.** 31–34. See margin.

31. $f(x) = 6x$ **32.** $g(x) = 3x - 2$ **33.** $h(x) = \frac{1}{4}x + 5$ **34.** $r(x) = -4x - 7$

8.8 **Solve the linear system by graphing.**

35. $y = -4x + 3$, $y = x - 7$ (2, −5)

36. $y = 5x - 2$, $y = -2x + 5$ (1, 3)

37. $2x - 3y = 12$, $x - y = 3$ (−3, −6)

38. $5x + 4y = 20$, $y = 3x + 5$ (0, 5)

8.9 **Graph the inequality in a coordinate plane.** 39–42. See margin.

39. $y \geq 2x - 2$ **40.** $x - 2y > -14$ **41.** $x < -1$ **42.** $y \leq 2$

Extra Practice

Chapter 9

9.1 **Find the square roots of the number.**

1. 49 ± 7 **2.** 2500 ± 50 **3.** 324 ± 18 **4.** 441 ± 21

9.1 **Solve the equation.**

5. $x^2 = 121$ ± 11 **6.** $3y^2 = 75$ ± 5 **7.** $2a^2 = 72$ ± 6 **8.** $6c^2 = 486$ ± 9

9.2 **Simplify the expression.**

9. $\sqrt{162}$ $9\sqrt{2}$ **10.** $\sqrt{\frac{12}{25}}$ $\frac{2\sqrt{3}}{5}$ **11.** $\sqrt{\frac{32a^2}{81}}$ $\frac{4a\sqrt{2}}{9}$ **12.** $\sqrt{54x}$ $3\sqrt{6x}$

9.3 **Find the unknown length. Write your answer in simplest form.**

13. 40

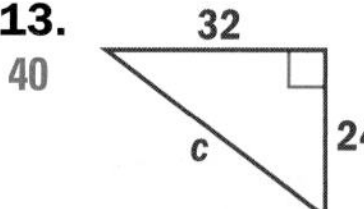

14. 24

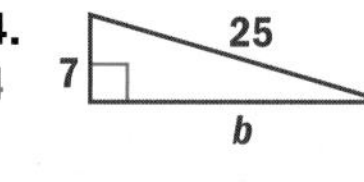

15. $\sqrt{65}$

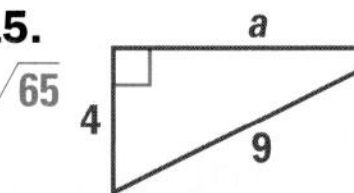

16. $2\sqrt{41}$

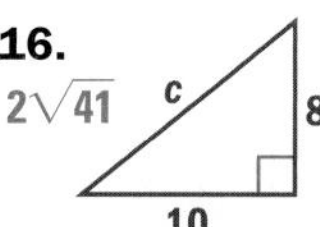

9.4 **Use a number line to order the numbers from least to greatest.**

17. $\sqrt{30}, 5.8, \frac{46}{9}, 2\sqrt{7}$ $\frac{46}{9}, 2\sqrt{7}, \sqrt{30}, 5.8$

18. $\frac{4}{5}, -1.5, -\sqrt{2}, 0$ $-1.5, -\sqrt{2}, 0, \frac{4}{5}$

19. $-\sqrt{36}, -6.9, -3\sqrt{5}, -\frac{19}{3}$ $-6.9, -3\sqrt{5}, -\frac{19}{3}, -\sqrt{36}$

20. $3\sqrt{5}, 7.2, \frac{22}{3}, \sqrt{47}$ $3\sqrt{5}, \sqrt{47}, 7.2, \frac{22}{3}$

9.5 **Find the midpoint of the segment with the given endpoints. Then find the distance between the points. Write your answer in simplest form.**

21. (4, 2), (6, 10) (5, 6); $2\sqrt{17}$ units

22. (−3, 5), (4, 9) (0.5, 7); $\sqrt{65}$ units

23. (0, −4), (−2, 11) (−1, 3.5); $\sqrt{229}$ units

24. (−1, −2), (6, −8) (2.5, −5); $\sqrt{85}$ units

9.6 **Find the unknown lengths. Write your answers in simplest form.**

25.

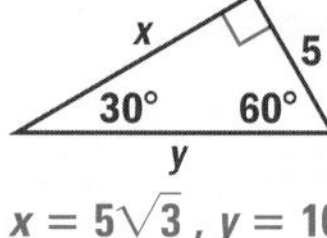

$x = 5\sqrt{3}$, $y = 10$

26.

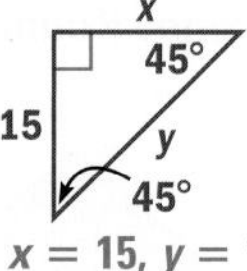

$x = 15$, $y = 15\sqrt{2}$

27.

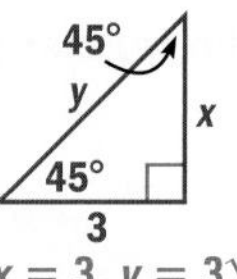

$x = 3$, $y = 3\sqrt{2}$

28.

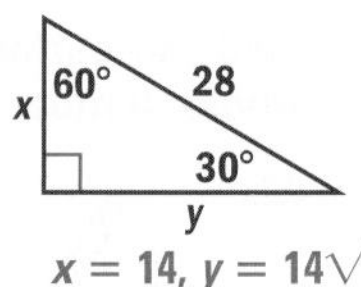

$x = 14$, $y = 14\sqrt{3}$

Find the value of *x*. Round to the nearest tenth.

9.7 **29.** 2.5

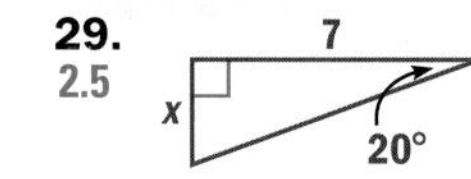

30. 7.0

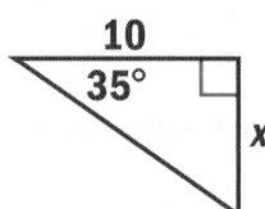

31. 15.0

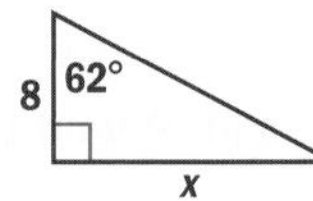

32. 3.3

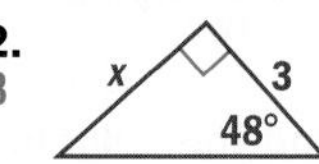

9.8 **33.** 3.9

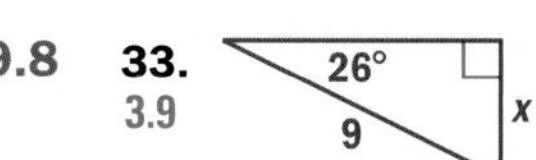

34. 3.8

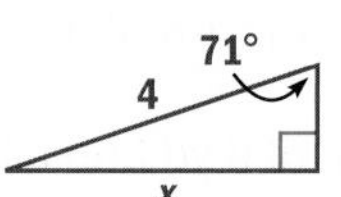

35. 15.5

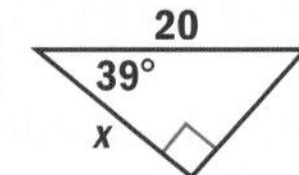

36. 5.0

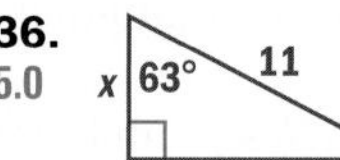

Extra Practice

17–20. Sample nets are given.

17.

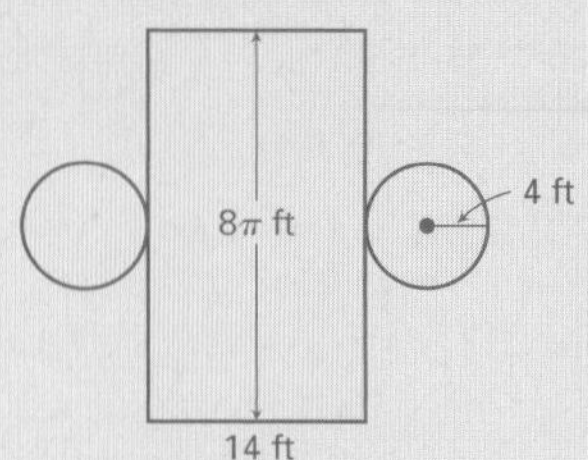

18.

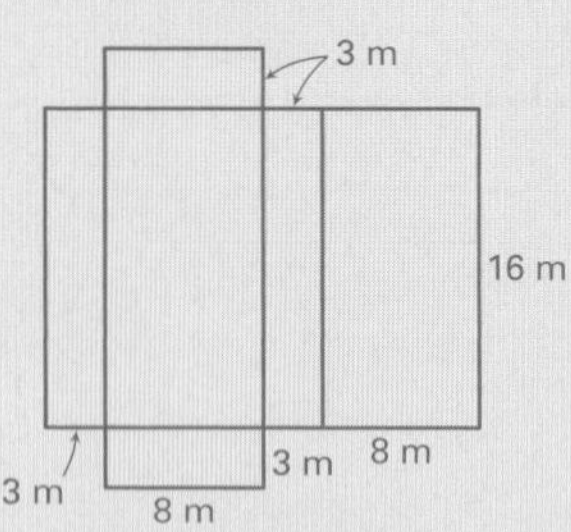

19.

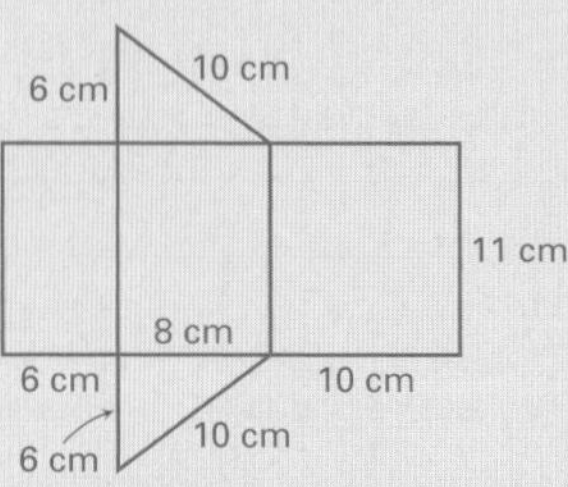

20.

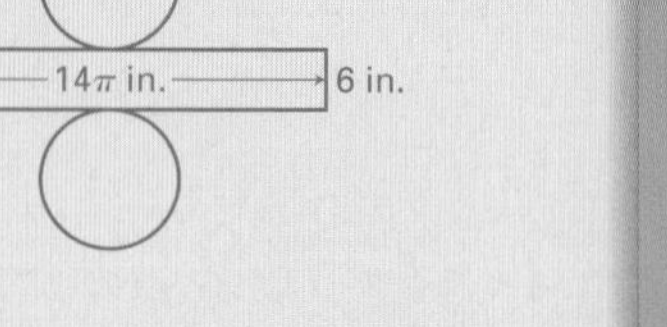

Chapter 10

10.1 Find the value of *x*. Then classify the triangle by its angle measures.

1. 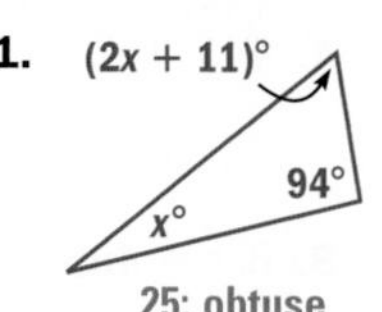

25; obtuse

2. 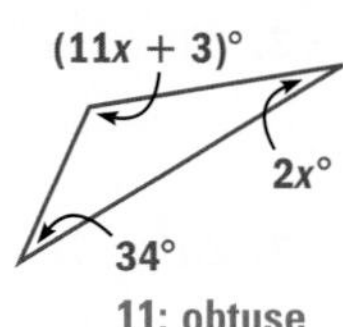

11; obtuse

3. 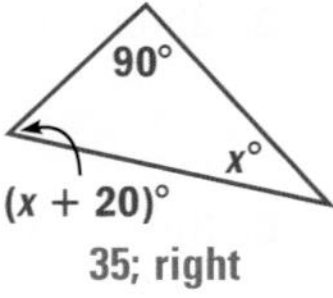

35; right

4. 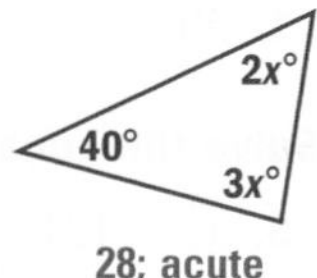

28; acute

10.2 Find the value of *x*.

5. 42 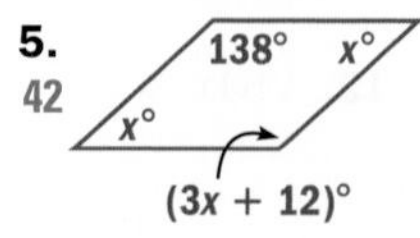

6. 53 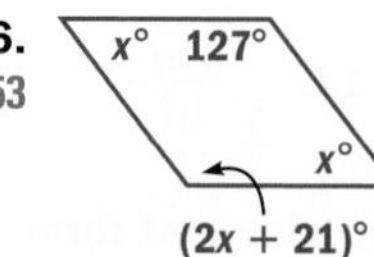

7. 119 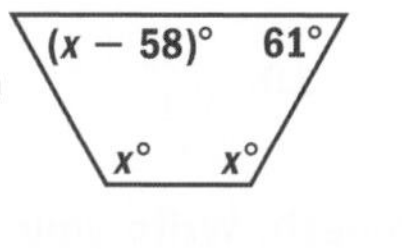

8. 67 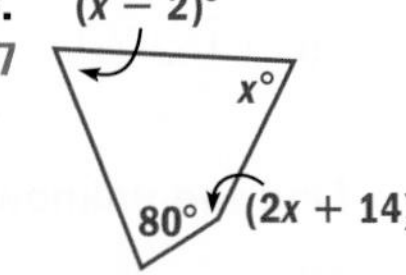

10.3 Find the area of the parallelogram or trapezoid.

9. 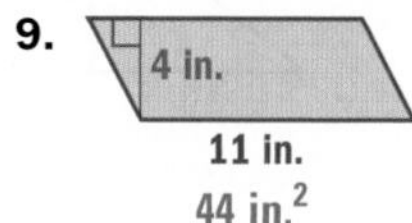

44 in.^{2}

10. 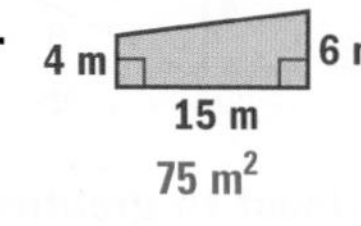

75 m^2

11. 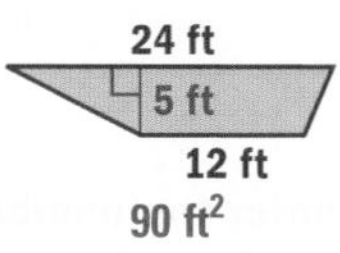

90 ft^2

12. 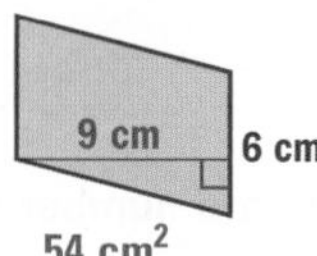

54 cm^2

10.4 For a circle with the given radius *r* or diameter *d*, find the area and circumference of the circle. Round to the nearest whole number.

13. $r = 31$ in. 3018 in.^{2}, 195 in.

14. $r = 3$ m 28 m^2, 19 m

15. $d = 28$ cm 616 cm^2, 88 cm

16. $d = 16$ yd 201 yd^2, 50 yd

10.5 Draw a net for the prism or cylinder. Then find the surface area. Round to the nearest whole number. 17–20. See margin for art.

17. 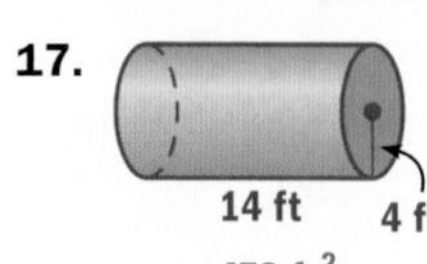

452 ft^2

18. 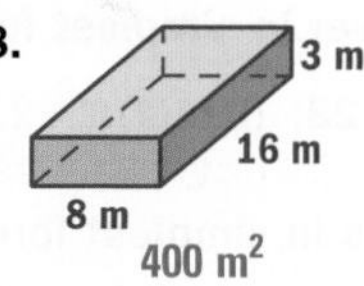

400 m^2

19. 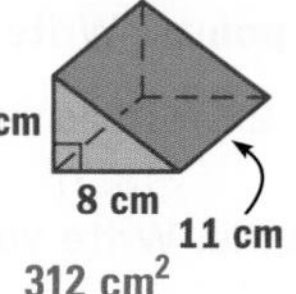

312 cm^2

20. 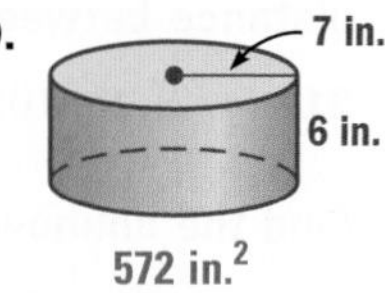

572 in.^{2}

10.6 Find the surface area of the regular pyramid or cone. Round to the nearest whole number.

21. 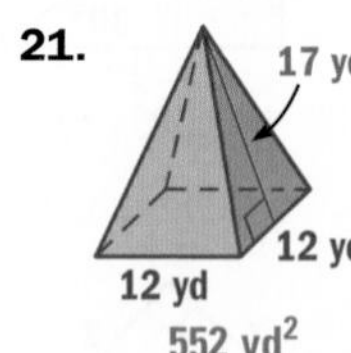

552 yd^2

22. 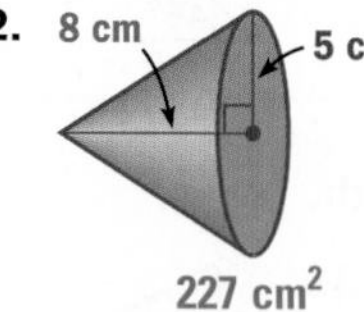

227 cm^2

23. 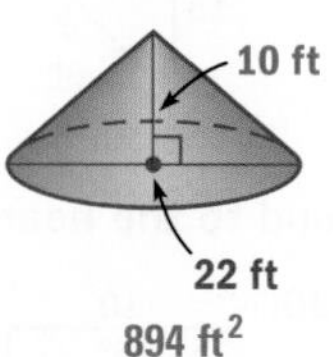

894 ft^2

24. 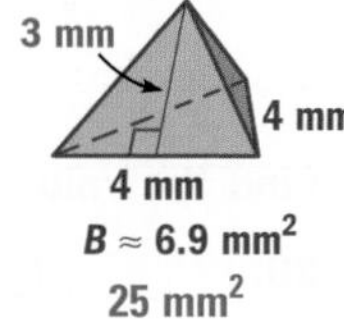

$B \approx 6.9$ mm^2
25 mm^2

Find the volume of the solid. Round to the nearest whole number.

10.7

25. A cylinder with a radius of 4 cm and a height of 5 cm 251 cm^3

26. A rectangular prism with a height of 4 ft, a width of 9 ft, and a length of 11 ft 396 ft^3

10.8

27. A square pyramid with a base side length of 6 yd and a height of 8 yd 96 yd^3

28. A cone with a radius of 7 in. and a height of 10 in. 513 in.^{3}

Extra Practice

Chapter 11

11.1 **1.** Make a stem-and-leaf plot and a histogram of the following numbers of participants in twelve community service days sponsored by a school. See margin for art.

35, 42, 21, 31, 42, 23, 12, 34, 36, 40, 25, 22

1	2
2	1 2 3 5
3	1 4 5 6
4	0 2 2

Key: 1 | 2 = 12

11.2 **2.** Make a box-and-whisker plot of the following monthly average high temperatures (in degrees Fahrenheit) for Atlanta, Georgia. See margin.

53, 57, 65, 73, 80, 87, 89, 88, 82, 73, 63, 55

11.3 **Tell whether the data are *numerical* or *categorical*. Then tell which data display(s) you would use to display the data. Explain your reasoning.** 3–4. See margin.

3. A teacher recorded the test score of each student in a class.

4. A student recorded the colors of the shirts of students in her class.

11.4 **In Exercises 5 and 6, tell whether the question is potentially biased. Explain your answer. If the question is biased, rewrite it so that it is not.**

5. Don't you think that having a school dance is a good idea? See margin.

6. How many times a week do you exercise? No. *Sample answer:* The question is straightforward and can be answered with a simple numerical fact.

11.5 **7.** A town's population is 12,500. In a random sample of 300 townspeople, 204 said they support the building of a new movie theater. Predict the number of townspeople who would support the building of a new movie theater. about 8500 townspeople

11.6 **Evaluate the factorial.**

8. 13! 6,227,020,800 **9.** 0! 1 **10.** 7! 5040 **11.** 2! 2

11.6 **Find the number of permutations.**

12. ${}_4P_4$ 24 **13.** ${}_{13}P_2$ 156 **14.** ${}_{20}P_3$ 6840 **15.** ${}_8P_1$ 8

11.7 **Find the number of combinations.**

16. ${}_7C_4$ 35 **17.** ${}_{12}C_8$ 495 **18.** ${}_{15}C_1$ 15 **19.** ${}_3C_3$ 1

11.8 **In Exercises 20 and 21, events A and B are overlapping. Find *P*(A or B).**

20. $P(A) = \frac{7}{30}, P(B) = \frac{11}{30}, P(A \text{ and } B) = \frac{1}{10}$ $\frac{1}{2}$ **21.** $P(A) = \frac{2}{5}, P(B) = \frac{1}{5}, P(A \text{ and } B) = \frac{1}{20}$ $\frac{11}{20}$

11.9 **22.** A bag contains 5 red marbles, 11 blue marbles, and 6 yellow marbles. You randomly draw a marble from the bag. Then you randomly draw another marble without replacing the first marble. Find the probability of drawing a blue marble, then a red marble. $\frac{5}{42}$

Extra Practice

1. ***Sample:***

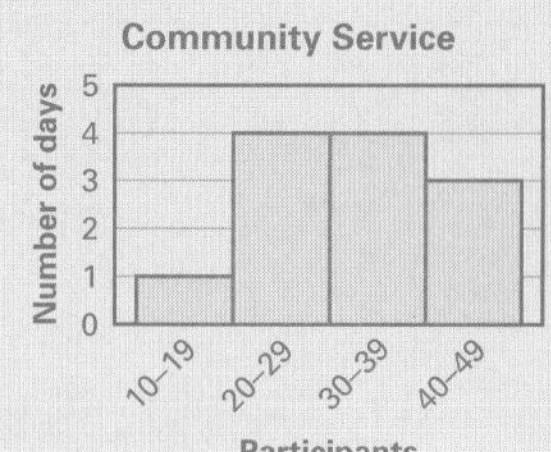

2.

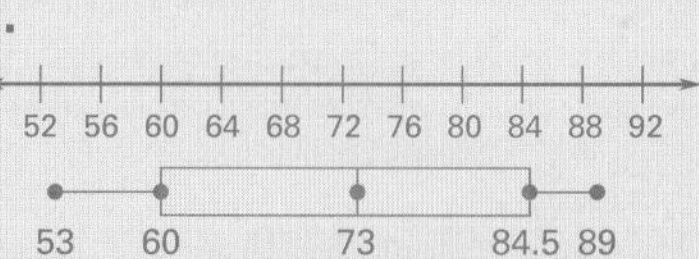

3. Numerical. *Sample answer:* If the data values are few, I might use a stem-and-leaf plot so that I can view all the values. If there are many data values, I might use a histogram, since I can divide the data into equal intervals by test score, or a box-and-whisker plot, since I can calculate the extremes and the quartiles for the data. Either of these displays would provide a convenient pictorial representation.

4. Categorical. *Sample answer:* I would use a bar graph, because it would allow the most direct visual comparison between the numbers of shirts of different colors.

5. Yes. *Sample answer:* It suggests that a person should think that a school dance is a good thing. An alternative question is, "Do you think that a school dance should or should not be held?"

33–36. Sample tables are given.

33.

x	−2	−1	0	1	2
y	16	7	4	7	16

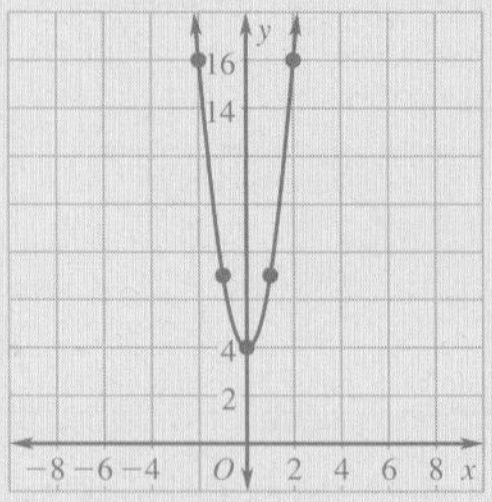

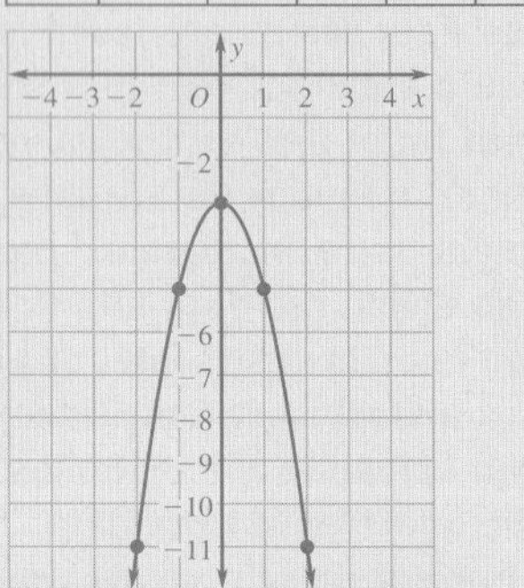

34.

x	−2	−1	0	1	2
y	−11	−5	−3	−5	−11

35.

x	−4	−2	0	2	4
y	−3	3	5	3	−3

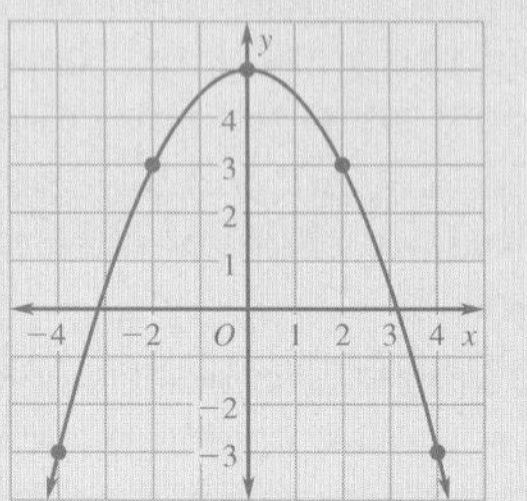

36.

x	−2	−1	0	1	2
y	2	$-\frac{1}{4}$	−1	$-\frac{1}{4}$	2

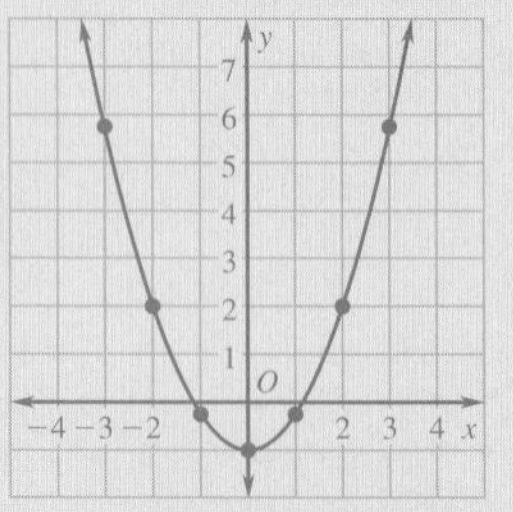

37–40. See Additional Answers beginning on page AA1.

Chapter 12

12.1 Write the expression as a polynomial in standard form.

1. $7x - 3 - 10x + 9$ $-3x + 6$
2. $-2z^2 + 4 - 5z^2$ $-7z^2 + 4$
3. $4y^2 - 2y - 3(y^2 - 6)$ $y^2 - 2y + 18$
4. $5a^2 + 2(2 - 3a^2) + 7$ $-a^2 + 11$

12.2 Find the sum or difference.

5. $(x^2 - 4x + 7) + (-2x^2 + 7x + 9)$ $-x^2 + 3x + 16$
6. $(4c^3 - 6c - 1) + (-5c^2 + 3c - 9)$ $4c^3 - 5c^2 - 3c - 10$
7. $(3w^3 + 4w^2 + 8) - (5w^3 - 4w - 6)$ $-2w^3 + 4w^2 + 4w + 14$
8. $(6s^2 - 8s - 3) - (s^3 + 2s^2 + 7s - 4)$ $-s^3 + 4s^2 - 15s + 1$
9. $(6g^4 - 7g^2) + (4g^3 - 3g^2 + 2)$ $6g^4 + 4g^3 - 10g^2 + 2$
10. $(8n^2 - 5) + (n^2 - 3n)$ $9n^2 - 3n - 5$
11. $(5d^3 + 2) - (4d^3 - 5)$ $d^3 + 7$
12. $(4f^2 - 7f + 11) - (9f^2 - 13)$ $-5f^2 - 7f + 24$

12.3 Find the product.

13. $(8f + 9)4f$ $32f^2 + 36f$
14. $-6p^2(p^3 - 5)$ $-6p^5 + 30p^2$
15. $-2t(t^2 - 3t + 10)$ $-2t^3 + 6t^2 - 20t$
16. $(y^3 + 2y^2 - 3)5y$ $5y^4 + 10y^3 - 15y$

12.3 Find the quotient.

17. $\frac{18n^2 - 21n}{-3n}$ $-6n + 7$
18. $\frac{8r^4 + 2r^3 - 12r^2}{2r}$ $4r^3 + r^2 - 6r$
19. $\frac{5z^6 - z^5 - 3z^4}{z^2}$ $5z^4 - z^3 - 3z^2$
20. $\frac{-6w^6 + 4w^4 + 2w^2}{-2w^2}$ $3w^4 - 2w^2 - 1$

12.4 Find the product.

21. $(x - 4)(3x + 2)$ $3x^2 - 10x - 8$
22. $(4z - 2)(2z - 1)$ $8z^2 - 8z + 2$
23. $(5a + 3)^2$ $25a^2 + 30a + 9$
24. $(-2c - 7)(3c - 8)$ $-6c^2 - 5c + 56$

12.5 Simplify the expression. Write your answer using positive exponents.

25. $(-3g)^3$ $-27g^3$
26. $\left(\frac{5}{a}\right)^4$ $\frac{625}{a^4}$
27. $(6^{-5})^4$ $\frac{1}{6^{20}}$
28. $(b^8)^{-3}$ $\frac{1}{b^{24}}$

12.5 Simplify the expression. Write your answer in scientific notation. Round the decimal part of your answer to the nearest hundredth.

29. $(4.5 \times 10^{-7})^3$ 9.11×10^{-20}
30. $(8.7 \times 10^3)^5$ 4.98×10^{19}
31. $(1.4 \times 10^4)^2$ 1.96×10^8
32. $(6.3 \times 10^{-6})^4$ 1.58×10^{-21}

12.6 Make a table of values for the given function. Then graph the function. 33–36. See margin.

33. $y = 3x^2 + 4$
34. $y = -2x^2 - 3$
35. $y = -\frac{1}{2}x^2 + 5$
36. $y = \frac{3}{4}x^2 - 1$

12.7 Graph the function. 37–40. See margin.

37. $y = 4(3)^x$
38. $y = 6\left(\frac{1}{3}\right)^x$
39. $y = 2\left(\frac{1}{4}\right)^x$
40. $y = 10(4)^x$

12.8 Tell whether the sequence is *arithmetic* or *geometric*. Then find the common difference or the common ratio, and write the next three terms.

41. $-9, -5, -1, 3, \ldots$ arithmetic; common difference: 4; 7, 11, 15
42. $-3, 6, -12, 24, \ldots$ geometric; common ratio: −2; −48, 96, −192
43. $224, 112, 56, 28, \ldots$ geometric; common ratio: $\frac{1}{2}$; 14, 7, $3\frac{1}{2}$
44. $289, 252, 215, 178, \ldots$ arithmetic; common difference: −37; 141, 104, 67

Extra Practice

Chapter 13

13.1 Tell whether the angles are *complementary, supplementary,* or *neither*.

1. $m\angle 1 = 42°$ $m\angle 2 = 48°$ complementary

2. $m\angle 1 = 138°$ $m\angle 2 = 52°$ neither

3. $m\angle 1 = 123°$ $m\angle 2 = 57°$ supplementary

4. $m\angle 1 = 31°$ $m\angle 2 = 59°$ complementary

13.2 Tell whether the angles in the diagram are *corresponding, alternate interior,* or *alternate exterior* angles.

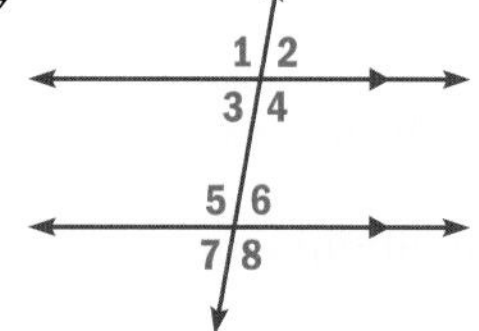

5. $\angle 2$ and $\angle 6$ corresponding

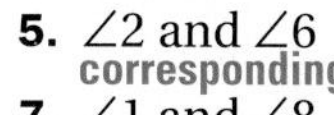

6. $\angle 4$ and $\angle 5$ alternate interior

7. $\angle 1$ and $\angle 8$ alternate exterior

8. $\angle 3$ and $\angle 7$ corresponding

13.3 Find the measure of an interior angle and the measure of an exterior angle for the regular polygon. Round to the nearest tenth, if necessary.

9. Heptagon interior: 128.6°, exterior: 51.4°

10. Hexagon interior: 120°, exterior: 60°

11. 12-gon interior: 150°,exterior: 30°

12. 9-gon interior: 140°, exterior: 40°

13.4 The vertices of a polygon are given. Draw the polygon. Then find the coordinates of the vertices of the image after the specified translation, and draw the image. 13–14. See margin for art.

13. $A(-2, -1), B(-3, 2), C(-1, 4); (x, y) \rightarrow (x + 4, y - 3)$ **$A'(2, -4), B'(1, -1), C'(3, 1)$**

14. $P(1, -2), Q(-1, 1), R(2, 2), S(4, -2); (x, y) \rightarrow (x - 3, y - 1)$ **$P'(-2, -3), Q'(-4, 0), R'(-1, 1), S'(1, -3)$**

13.5 The vertices of a polygon are given. Draw the polygon. Then find the coordinates of the vertices of the image after the specified reflection, and draw the image. 15–16. See margin for art.

15. $A(-3, -1), B(2, -2), C(-1, -4)$; reflection in the x-axis **$A'(-3, 1), B'(2, 2), C'(-1, 4)$**

16. $P(1, 4), Q(4, 3), R(4, 0), S(1, 1)$; reflection in the y-axis **$P'(-1, 4), Q'(-4, 3), R'(-4, 0), S'(-1, 1)$**

13.6 Tell whether the transformation is a rotation about the origin. If so, give the angle and direction of rotation.

17.

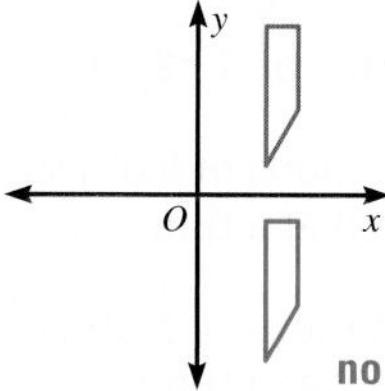

no

18.

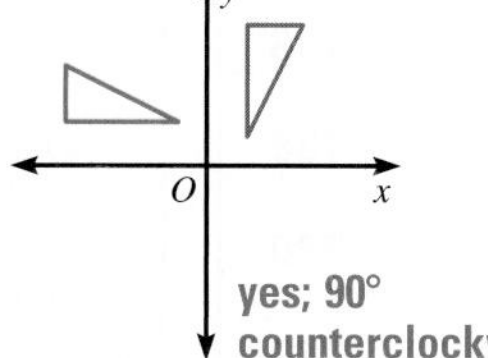

yes; 90° counterclockwise

19.

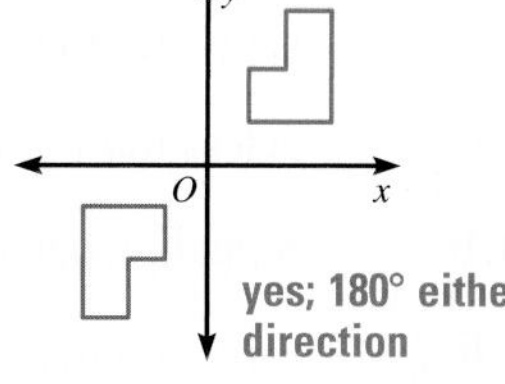

yes; 180° either direction

13.7 The vertices of a polygon are given. Draw the polygon. Then find the coordinates of the vertices of the image after a dilation having the given scale factor, and draw the image. 20–21. See margin for art.

20. $R(-3, 0), S(6, 3), T(3, -3); k = \frac{1}{3}$ **$R'(-1, 0), S'(2, 1), T'(1, -1)$**

21. $A(-2, 2), B(1, 3), C(1, -1), D(-2, -1); k = 2$ **$A'(-4, 4), B'(2, 6), C'(2, -2), D'(-4, -2)$**

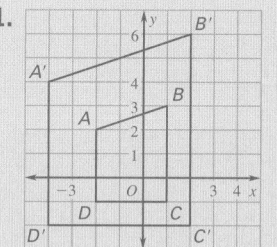

13.

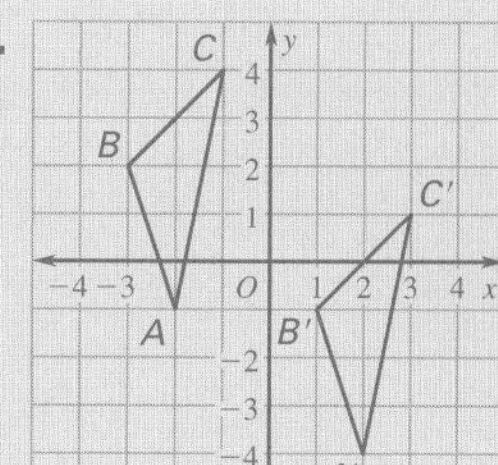

14.

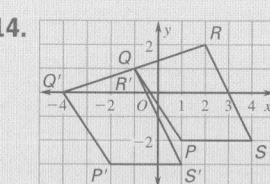

15.

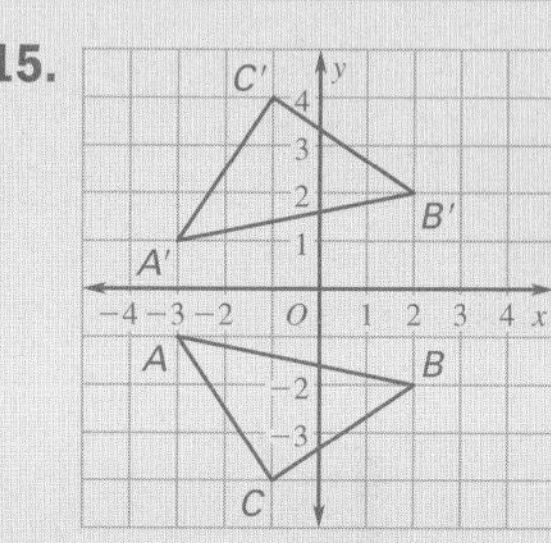

16.

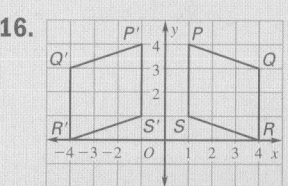

20.

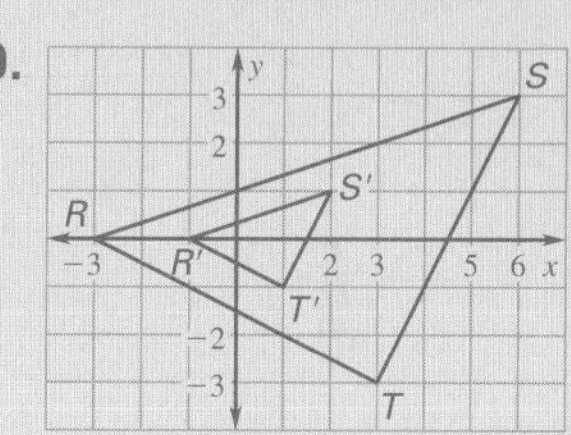

21.

Table of Symbols

Symbol	Meaning	Page
$3 \cdot x$ $3x$ $3(x)$	3 times x	5
$\frac{n}{2}$	n divided by 2	6
...	continues on	9
4^3	4 to the third power, or $4 \cdot 4 \cdot 4$	10
( )	parentheses—a grouping symbol	17
[ ]	brackets—a grouping symbol	17
-3	negative 3	22
$\lvert a \rvert$	absolute value of a number a	23
$-a$	the opposite of a number a	23
(x, y)	ordered pair	47
$=$	equals, is equal to	85
$\stackrel{?}{=}$	is equal to?	85
$\neq$	is not equal to	85
$<$	is less than	138
$>$	is greater than	138
$\geq$	is greater than or equal to	138
$\leq$	is less than or equal to	138
$1.1\overline{6}$	repeating decimal 1.16666. . .	220
$a : b, \frac{a}{b}$	ratio of a to b	269
$\overleftrightarrow{AB}$	line AB	285
$\overline{AB}$	line segment AB, or segment AB	285
AB	length of segment AB	285
$\overrightarrow{AB}$	ray AB	285
$\angle ABC$, $\angle B$	angle ABC, angle with vertex B	285
$m\angle B$	measure of angle B	285
$\triangle ABC$	triangle with vertices A, B, and C	286
$\cong$	is congruent to	286
$\sim$	is similar to	288
%	percent	329
$\parallel$	is parallel to	410
(two parallel lines with arrows)	parallel lines	410
$\perp$	is perpendicular to	410
$f(x)$	the value of the function f at x	426
$\sqrt{a}$	the positive square root of a number a where $a \geq 0$	453
$\pm$	plus or minus	453
$\sqrt[3]{a}$	the cube root of a number a	457
π	pi—a number approximately equal to 3.14	528
3!	3 factorial, or $3 \cdot 2 \cdot 1$	615
${}_8P_3$	permutations of 8 objects taken 3 at a time	616
${}_5C_2$	combinations of 5 objects taken 2 at a time	621
A'	the image of point A	729
$\approx$	is approximately equal to	771
∟	right angle	793

Table of Measures

TIME

60 seconds (sec) = 1 minute (min)
60 minutes = 1 hour (h)
24 hours = 1 day (d)
7 days = 1 week (wk)
4 weeks (approx.) = 1 month

365 days, 52 weeks (approx.), 12 months = 1 year
10 years = 1 decade
100 years = 1 century

METRIC

Length

10 millimeters (mm) = 1 centimeter (cm)
100 cm, 1000 mm = 1 meter (m)
1000 m = 1 kilometer (km)

Area

100 square millimeters (mm^2) = 1 square centimeter (cm^2)
10,000 cm^2 = 1 square meter (m^2)
10,000 m^2 = 1 hectare (ha)

Volume

1000 cubic millimeters (mm^3) = 1 cubic centimeter (cm^3)
1,000,000 cm^3 = 1 cubic meter (m^3)

Liquid Capacity

1000 milliliters (mL), 1000 cubic centimeters (cm^3) = 1 liter (L)
1000 L = 1 kiloliter (kL)

Mass

1000 milligrams (mg) = 1 gram (g)
1000 g = 1 kilogram (kg)
1000 kg = 1 metric ton (t)

Temperature Degrees Celsius (°C)

0°C = freezing point of water
37°C = normal body temperature
100°C = boiling point of water

UNITED STATES CUSTOMARY

Length

12 inches (in.) = 1 foot (ft)
36 in., 3 ft = 1 yard (yd)
5280 ft, 1760 yd = 1 mile (mi)

Area

144 square inches ($in.^2$) = 1 square foot (ft^2)
9 ft^2 = 1 square yard (yd^2)
43,560 ft^2, 4840 yd^2 = 1 acre (A)

Volume

1728 cubic inches ($in.^3$) = 1 cubic foot (ft^3)
27 ft^3 = 1 cubic yard (yd^3)

Liquid Capacity

8 fluid ounces (fl oz) = 1 cup (c)
2 c = 1 pint (pt)
2 pt = 1 quart (qt)
4 qt = 1 gallon (gal)

Weight

16 ounces (oz) = 1 pound (lb)
2000 lb = 1 ton

Temperature Degrees Fahrenheit (°F)

32°F = freezing point of water
98.6°F = normal body temperature
212°F = boiling point of water

Table of Formulas

Geometric Formulas

Rectangle (p. 69)

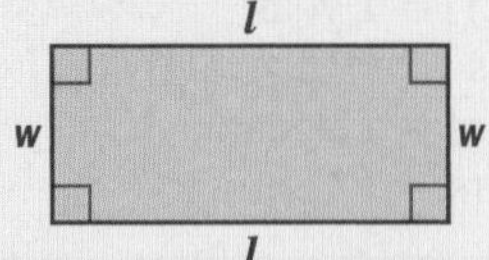

Area
$A = lw$

Perimeter
$P = 2l + 2w$

Square (p. 69)

s
s s
s

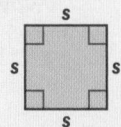

Area
$A = s^2$

Perimeter
$P = 4s$

Triangle (p. 70)

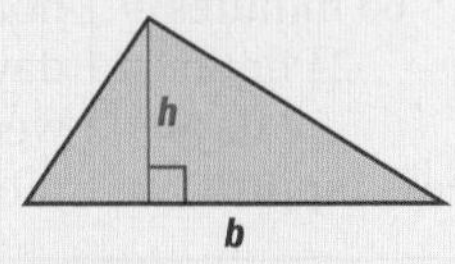

Area
$A = \frac{1}{2}bh$

Pythagorean Theorem (p. 465)

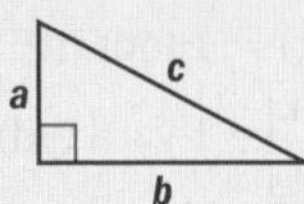

In a right triangle, $a^2 + b^2 = c^2$ where a and b are the lengths of the legs and c is the length of the hypotenuse.

Parallelogram (p. 521)

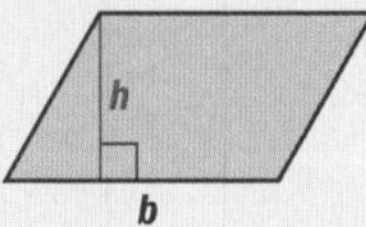

Area
$A = bh$

Trapezoid (p. 522)

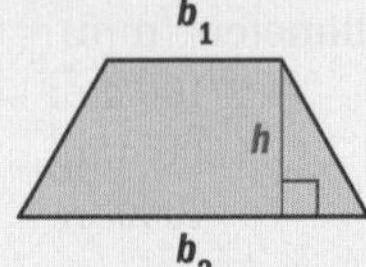

Area
$A = \frac{1}{2}(b_1 + b_2)h$

Circle (pp. 528, 529)

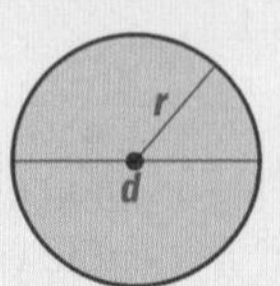

Circumference
$C = \pi d$ or
$C = 2\pi r$

Area
$A = \pi r^2$

Prism (pp. 539, 552)

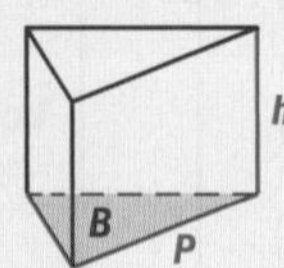

Surface Area
$S = 2B + Ph$

Volume
$V = Bh$

Cylinder (pp. 540, 553)

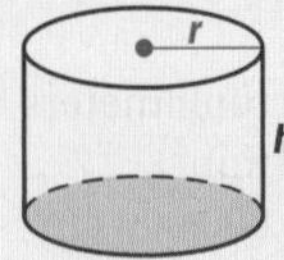

Surface Area
$S = 2\pi r^2 + 2\pi rh$

Volume
$V = \pi r^2 h$

Pyramid (pp. 545, 558)

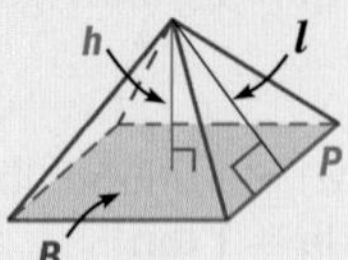

Surface Area
$S = B + \frac{1}{2}Pl$

Volume
$V = \frac{1}{3}Bh$

Cone (pp. 546, 558)

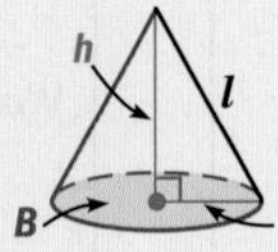

Surface Area
$S = \pi r^2 + \pi rl$

Volume
$V = \frac{1}{3}Bh$
$= \frac{1}{3}\pi r^2 h$

Sphere (pp. 548, 562)

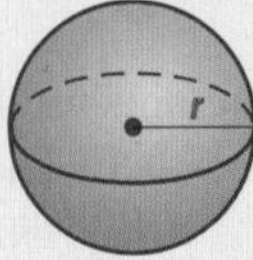

Surface Area
$S = 4\pi r^2$

Volume
$V = \frac{4}{3}\pi r^3$

Other Formulas

Distance traveled (p. 77)	$d = rt$ where d is distance, r is rate, and t is time
Probability of an event (p. 306)	The probability of an event when all the outcomes are equally likely is: $P(\text{event}) = \frac{\text{Number of favorable outcomes}}{\text{Number of possible outcomes}}$
Experimental probability (p. 307)	The experimental probability of an event is: $P(\text{event}) = \frac{\text{Number of successes}}{\text{Number of trials}}$
Simple interest (p. 362)	$I = Prt$ where I is simple interest, P is the principal, r is the annual interest rate (written as a decimal), and t is the time in years
Compound interest (p. 364)	$A = P(1 + r)^t$ where A is the balance, P is the principal, r is the annual interest rate (written as a decimal), and t is the time in years
Distance formula (p. 476)	The distance d between two points (x_1, y_1) and (x_2, y_2) is given by $d = \sqrt{(x_2 - x_1)^2 + (y_2 - y_1)^2}$.
Midpoint formula (p. 478)	The coordinates of the midpoint M of a segment with endpoints $A(x_1, y_1)$ and $B(x_2, y_2)$ are given by $M = \left(\frac{x_1 + x_2}{2}, \frac{y_1 + y_2}{2}\right)$.
Slope formula (p. 478)	If points $A(x_1, y_1)$ and $B(x_2, y_2)$ do not lie on a vertical line, then the slope of $\overleftrightarrow{AB}$ is $\frac{y_2 - y_1}{x_2 - x_1}$.
Permutations (p. 616)	The number of permutations of n objects taken r at a time can be written as ${}_nP_r$ where ${}_nP_r = \frac{n!}{(n - r)!}$.
Combinations (p. 621)	The number of combinations of n objects taken r at a time can be written as ${}_nC_r$ where ${}_nC_r = \frac{{}_nP_r}{r!}$.
Probability of disjoint or overlapping events (pp. 628, 629)	If A and B are disjoint events, then $P(\text{A or B}) = P(\text{A}) + P(\text{B})$. If A and B are overlapping events, then $P(\text{A or B}) = P(\text{A}) + P(\text{B}) - P(\text{A and B})$.
Probability of independent or dependent events (pp. 635, 636)	If A and B are independent events, then $P(\text{A and B}) = P(\text{A}) \cdot P(\text{B})$. If A and B are dependent events, then $P(\text{A and B}) = P(\text{A}) \cdot P(\text{B given A})$.

Table of Formulas

Table of Properties

Properties of Addition and Multiplication

Inverse Properties (pp. 30, 247)	
The sum of a number and its additive inverse, or opposite, is 0.	$a + (-a) = 0$
The product of a nonzero number and its multiplicative inverse, or reciprocal, is 1.	$\frac{a}{b} \cdot \frac{b}{a} = 1 \ (a \neq 0, b \neq 0)$
Commutative Properties (p. 63)	
In a sum, you can add the numbers in any order.	$a + b = b + a$
In a product, you can multiply the numbers in any order.	$ab = ba$
Associative Properties (p. 63)	
Changing the grouping of the numbers in a sum does not change the sum.	$(a + b) + c = a + (b + c)$
Changing the grouping of the numbers in a product does not change the product.	$(ab)c = a(bc)$
Identity Properties (p. 64)	
The sum of a number and the additive identity, 0, is the number.	$a + 0 = a$
The product of a number and the multiplicative identity, 1, is the number.	$a \cdot 1 = a$
Distributive Property (p. 71)	
You can multiply a number and a sum by multiplying each term of the sum by the number and then adding these products. The same property applies to subtraction.	$a(b + c) = ab + ac$ $a(b - c) = ab - ac$

Properties of Equality

Subtraction Property of Equality (p. 91) Subtracting the same number from each side of an equation produces an equivalent equation.	If $x + a = b$, then $x + a - a = b - a$, or $x = b - a$.
Addition Property of Equality (p. 92) Adding the same number to each side of an equation produces an equivalent equation.	If $x - a = b$, then $x - a + a = b + a$, or $x = b + a$.
Division Property of Equality (p. 97) Dividing each side of an equation by the same nonzero number produces an equivalent equation.	If $ax = b$ and $a \neq 0$, then $\frac{ax}{a} = \frac{b}{a}$, or $x = \frac{b}{a}$.
Multiplication Property of Equality (p. 98) Multiplying each side of an equation by the same nonzero number produces an equivalent equation.	If $\frac{x}{a} = b$ and $a \neq 0$, then $a \cdot \frac{x}{a} = a \cdot b$, or $x = ab$.

Properties of Inequality

Addition and Subtraction Properties of Inequality (p. 139) Adding or subtracting the same number on each side of an inequality produces an equivalent inequality.	If $a < b$, then $a + c < b + c$ and $a - c < b - c$. If $a > b$, then $a + c > b + c$ and $a - c > b - c$.
Multiplication and Division Properties of Inequality (pp. 144, 145) Multiplying or dividing each side of an inequality by a *positive* number produces an equivalent inequality. Multiplying or dividing each side of an inequality by a *negative* number and *reversing the direction of the inequality symbol* produces an equivalent inequality.	If $a < b$ and $c > 0$, then $ac < bc$ and $\frac{a}{c} < \frac{b}{c}$. If $a < b$ and $c < 0$, then $ac > bc$ and $\frac{a}{c} > \frac{b}{c}$.

Properties of Exponents

Product of Powers Property (p. 194) To multiply powers with the same base, add their exponents.	$a^m \cdot a^n = a^{m+n}$
Quotient of Powers Property (p. 195) To divide powers with the same nonzero base, subtract the denominator's exponent from the numerator's exponent.	$\frac{a^m}{a^n} = a^{m-n}, a \neq 0$
Power of a Product Property (p. 674) To find the power of a product, find the power of each factor and multiply.	$(ab)^m = a^m b^m$
Power of a Quotient Property (p. 674) To find the power of a quotient, find the power of the numerator and the power of the denominator and divide.	$\left(\frac{a}{b}\right)^m = \frac{a^m}{b^m}, b \neq 0$
Power of a Power Property (p. 675) To find the power of a power, multiply the exponents.	$(a^m)^n = a^{mn}$

Other Properties

Cross Products Property (p. 281) The cross products of a proportion are equal.	If $\frac{a}{b} = \frac{c}{d}$ $(b, d \neq 0)$, then $ad = bc$.
Product Property of Square Roots (p. 458) The square root of a product is equal to the product of the square roots of the factors.	$\sqrt{ab} = \sqrt{a} \cdot \sqrt{b}$, $a \geq 0$ and $b \geq 0$
Quotient Properties of Square Roots (p. 459) The square root of a quotient is equal to the quotient of the square root of the numerator and the square root of the denominator.	$\sqrt{\frac{a}{b}} = \frac{\sqrt{a}}{\sqrt{b}}$, $a \geq 0$ and $b > 0$

Table of Squares and Square Roots

No.	Square	Sq. Root	No.	Square	Sq. Root	No.	Square	Sq. Root
1	1	1.000	**51**	2601	7.141	**101**	10,201	10.050
2	4	1.414	**52**	2704	7.211	**102**	10,404	10.100
3	9	1.732	**53**	2809	7.280	**103**	10,609	10.149
4	16	2.000	**54**	2916	7.348	**104**	10,816	10.198
5	25	2.236	**55**	3025	7.416	**105**	11,025	10.247
6	36	2.449	**56**	3136	7.483	**106**	11,236	10.296
7	49	2.646	**57**	3249	7.550	**107**	11,449	10.344
8	64	2.828	**58**	3364	7.616	**108**	11,664	10.392
9	81	3.000	**59**	3481	7.681	**109**	11,881	10.440
10	100	3.162	**60**	3600	7.746	**110**	12,100	10.488
11	121	3.317	**61**	3721	7.810	**111**	12,321	10.536
12	144	3.464	**62**	3844	7.874	**112**	12,544	10.583
13	169	3.606	**63**	3969	7.937	**113**	12,769	10.630
14	196	3.742	**64**	4096	8.000	**114**	12,996	10.677
15	225	3.873	**65**	4225	8.062	**115**	13,225	10.724
16	256	4.000	**66**	4356	8.124	**116**	13,456	10.770
17	289	4.123	**67**	4489	8.185	**117**	13,689	10.817
18	324	4.243	**68**	4624	8.246	**118**	13,924	10.863
19	361	4.359	**69**	4761	8.307	**119**	14,161	10.909
20	400	4.472	**70**	4900	8.367	**120**	14,400	10.954
21	441	4.583	**71**	5041	8.426	**121**	14,641	11.000
22	484	4.690	**72**	5184	8.485	**122**	14,884	11.045
23	529	4.796	**73**	5329	8.544	**123**	15,129	11.091
24	576	4.899	**74**	5476	8.602	**124**	15,376	11.136
25	625	5.000	**75**	5625	8.660	**125**	15,625	11.180
26	676	5.099	**76**	5776	8.718	**126**	15,876	11.225
27	729	5.196	**77**	5929	8.775	**127**	16,129	11.269
28	784	5.292	**78**	6084	8.832	**128**	16,384	11.314
29	841	5.385	**79**	6241	8.888	**129**	16,641	11.358
30	900	5.477	**80**	6400	8.944	**130**	16,900	11.402
31	961	5.568	**81**	6561	9.000	**131**	17,161	11.446
32	1024	5.657	**82**	6724	9.055	**132**	17,424	11.489
33	1089	5.745	**83**	6889	9.110	**133**	17,689	11.533
34	1156	5.831	**84**	7056	9.165	**134**	17,956	11.576
35	1225	5.916	**85**	7225	9.220	**135**	18,225	11.619
36	1296	6.000	**86**	7396	9.274	**136**	18,496	11.662
37	1369	6.083	**87**	7569	9.327	**137**	18,769	11.705
38	1444	6.164	**88**	7744	9.381	**138**	19,044	11.747
39	1521	6.245	**89**	7921	9.434	**139**	19,321	11.790
40	1600	6.325	**90**	8100	9.487	**140**	19,600	11.832
41	1681	6.403	**91**	8281	9.539	**141**	19,881	11.874
42	1764	6.481	**92**	8464	9.592	**142**	20,164	11.916
43	1849	6.557	**93**	8649	9.644	**143**	20,449	11.958
44	1936	6.633	**94**	8836	9.695	**144**	20,736	12.000
45	2025	6.708	**95**	9025	9.747	**145**	21,025	12.042
46	2116	6.782	**96**	9216	9.798	**146**	21,316	12.083
47	2209	6.856	**97**	9409	9.849	**147**	21,609	12.124
48	2304	6.928	**98**	9604	9.899	**148**	21,904	12.166
49	2401	7.000	**99**	9801	9.950	**149**	22,201	12.207
50	2500	7.071	**100**	10,000	10.000	**150**	22,500	12.247

Table of Trigonometric Ratios

Angle	Sine	Cosine	Tangent
1°	.0175	.9998	.0175
2°	.0349	.9994	.0349
3°	.0523	.9986	.0524
4°	.0698	.9976	.0699
5°	.0872	.9962	.0875
6°	.1045	.9945	.1051
7°	.1219	.9925	.1228
8°	.1392	.9903	.1405
9°	.1564	.9877	.1584
10°	.1736	.9848	.1763
11°	.1908	.9816	.1944
12°	.2079	.9781	.2126
13°	.2250	.9744	.2309
14°	.2419	.9703	.2493
15°	.2588	.9659	.2679
16°	.2756	.9613	.2867
17°	.2924	.9563	.3057
18°	.3090	.9511	.3249
19°	.3256	.9455	.3443
20°	.3420	.9397	.3640
21°	.3584	.9336	.3839
22°	.3746	.9272	.4040
23°	.3907	.9205	.4245
24°	.4067	.9135	.4452
25°	.4226	.9063	.4663
26°	.4384	.8988	.4877
27°	.4540	.8910	.5095
28°	.4695	.8829	.5317
29°	.4848	.8746	.5543
30°	.5000	.8660	.5774
31°	.5150	.8572	.6009
32°	.5299	.8480	.6249
33°	.5446	.8387	.6494
34°	.5592	.8290	.6745
35°	.5736	.8192	.7002
36°	.5878	.8090	.7265
37°	.6018	.7986	.7536
38°	.6157	.7880	.7813
39°	.6293	.7771	.8098
40°	.6428	.7660	.8391
41°	.6561	.7547	.8693
42°	.6691	.7431	.9004
43°	.6820	.7314	.9325
44°	.6947	.7193	.9657
45°	.7071	.7071	1.0000

Angle	Sine	Cosine	Tangent
46°	.7193	.6947	1.0355
47°	.7314	.6820	1.0724
48°	.7431	.6691	1.1106
49°	.7547	.6561	1.1504
50°	.7660	.6428	1.1918
51°	.7771	.6293	1.2349
52°	.7880	.6157	1.2799
53°	.7986	.6018	1.3270
54°	.8090	.5878	1.3764
55°	.8192	.5736	1.4281
56°	.8290	.5592	1.4826
57°	.8387	.5446	1.5399
58°	.8480	.5299	1.6003
59°	.8572	.5150	1.6643
60°	.8660	.5000	1.7321
61°	.8746	.4848	1.8040
62°	.8829	.4695	1.8807
63°	.8910	.4540	1.9626
64°	.8988	.4384	2.0503
65°	.9063	.4226	2.1445
66°	.9135	.4067	2.2460
67°	.9205	.3907	2.3559
68°	.9272	.3746	2.4751
69°	.9336	.3584	2.6051
70°	.9397	.3420	2.7475
71°	.9455	.3256	2.9042
72°	.9511	.3090	3.0777
73°	.9563	.2924	3.2709
74°	.9613	.2756	3.4874
75°	.9659	.2588	3.7321
76°	.9703	.2419	4.0108
77°	.9744	.2250	4.3315
78°	.9781	.2079	4.7046
79°	.9816	.1908	5.1446
80°	.9848	.1736	5.6713
81°	.9877	.1564	6.3138
82°	.9903	.1392	7.1154
83°	.9925	.1219	8.1443
84°	.9945	.1045	9.5144
85°	.9962	.0872	11.4301
86°	.9976	.0698	14.3007
87°	.9986	.0523	19.0811
88°	.9994	.0349	28.6363
89°	.9998	.0175	57.2900

Appendix 1 Use after Lesson 2.6

Vocabulary
absolute value equation, p. 824

Absolute Value Equations

GOAL Solve absolute value equations.

Recall that the *absolute value* of a number a, written $|a|$, is the distance between a and 0 on a number line. An **absolute value equation** is an equation that involves the absolute value of a variable or variable expression. For example, $|x| = 6$ and $|x - 3| = 7$ are absolute value equations. You can solve an absolute value equation using mental math or using algebra.

Example 1 *Using Mental Math*

Use mental math to solve $|x| = 6$.

Ask yourself, "What number(s) are 6 units from the origin?" The number line shows that both -6 and 6 are 6 units from the origin.

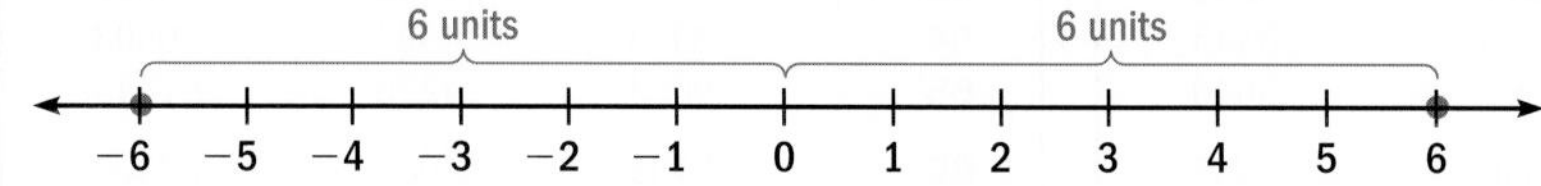

Answer The solutions are 6 and -6.

Example 2 *Solving an Absolute Value Equation*

Solve $|x - 3| = 7$.

Because $|x - 3| = 7$, the expression $x - 3$ can be equal to 7 or -7.

$$|x - 3| = 7$$

$x - 3 = 7$ *or* $x - 3 = -7$ **Expression can equal 7 or −7.**

$x = 10$ *or* $x = -4$ **Add 3 to each side.**

Answer The solutions are 10 and -4.

✓Check Use substitution to check the solutions.

$\lvert x - 3\rvert = 7$	$\lvert x - 3\rvert = 7$	**Write original equation.**
$\lvert 10 - 3\rvert \stackrel{?}{=} 7$	$\lvert -4 - 3\rvert \stackrel{?}{=} 7$	**Substitute for *x*.**
$\lvert 7\rvert \stackrel{?}{=} 7$	$\lvert -7\rvert \stackrel{?}{=} 7$	**Subtract.**
$7 = 7$ ✓	$7 = 7$ ✓	**Simplify. The solution checks.**

Appendix 1

NCTM CURRICULUM STANDARDS
Standard 1: Understand how operations are related
Standard 2: Represent situations using algebraic symbols

Example 3 ***An Equation with No Solution***

Solve $|2x| = -6$.

The absolute value of a real number cannot be negative because a number's distance from 0 on a number line cannot be negative. So, this absolute value equation has no solution.

Isolating Expressions Sometimes you must first isolate the absolute value expression on one side of the equation before solving.

Example 4 ***Isolating an Expression First***

Solve $|4x - 8| + 3 = 23$.

(1) Isolate the absolute value expression on one side of the equation.

$|4x - 8| + 3 = 23$ **Write original equation.**

$|4x - 8| = 20$ **Subtract 3 from each side.**

(2) Solve the revised equation from Step 1.

$|4x - 8| = 20$

$4x - 8 = 20$ *or* $4x - 8 = -20$ **Expression can equal 20 or −20.**

$4x = 28$ *or* $4x = -12$ **Add 8 to each side.**

$x = 7$ *or* $x = -3$ **Divide each side by 4.**

Answer The solutions are 7 and −3. To check the solutions, use substitution.

Appendix 1

Practice

Solve the equation, if possible.

1. $|x| = 4$ 4, −4
2. $|x| = 18$ 18, −18
3. $|2x| = 50$ 25, −25
4. $|3x| = -27$ no solution
5. $|x + 6| = 20$ 14, −26
6. $|x + 5| = 11$ 6, −16
7. $|x - 4| = 6$ 10, −2
8. $|4x - 2| = 22$ 6, −5
9. $|2x + 7| = 17$ 5, −12
10. $|2x - 4| - 8 = 10$ 11, −7
11. $|5 - 4x| - 3 = 4$ 3, −0.5
12. $|3 - 2x| + 9 = 11$ 0.5, 2.5
13. $|6 + x| + 2 = 19$ 11, −23
14. $-|x + 5| = -15$ 10, −20
15. $-|3x + 1| = 15$ no solution

16. Manufacturing A machine is supposed to fill bottles with 12 fluid ounces of water. A bottle is rejected when the actual volume differs from the desired volume by more than 0.5 fluid ounce. The maximum and minimum acceptable volumes are the solutions of $|x - 12| = 0.5$. What are the maximum and minimum acceptable volumes? 12.5 fluid ounces; 11.5 fluid ounces

Appendix 2 Use after Lesson 6.3

Vocabulary
scale drawing, p. 826
scale, p. 826

Proportion Applications

GOAL Use proportions to read maps and convert international currencies.

A **scale drawing** is a diagram of a place or object in which the dimensions are proportional to the actual dimensions of the place or object. The **scale** of a scale drawing is a ratio that tells how the drawing's dimensions and the actual dimensions are related.

Example 1 *Use the Scale of a Map*

Use a metric ruler and the map to estimate the distance between Cleveland and Columbus.

Solution

From the map's scale, 1 centimeter represents 85 kilometers. On the map, the distance between Cleveland and Columbus is 2.4 centimeters. Write and solve a proportion to find the actual distance x between the cities.

$\frac{1}{85} = \frac{2.4}{x}$ ← **centimeters** / ← **kilometers**

$1 \cdot x = 85 \cdot 2.4$ **Cross multiply.**

$x = 204$ **Simplify.**

Answer The actual distance between Cleveland and Columbus is about 204 kilometers.

Example 2 *Convert Currency*

Suppose the exchange rate for purchasing Chinese renminbi using American dollars is \$1.00 (US) to ¥8.00. How many renminbi can the Smith family buy with \$485.00?

Write and solve a proportion.

$\frac{1}{8} = \frac{485}{x}$ ← **dollars** / ← **renminbi**

$1 \cdot x = 8 \cdot 485$ **Cross multiply.**

$x = 3880$ **Simplify.**

Answer The Smiths can buy ¥3880 with \$485.

NCTM CURRICULUM STANDARDS
Standard 2: Represent situations using algebraic symbols; Analyze situations using algebraic symbols
Standard 6: Solve problems in math and other contexts

Appendix 2

Practice

The answers to Exercises 1–4 will vary slightly as they depend on the actual measurements of the student.

The map of the hiking trail has a scale of 1 inch to 3.2 miles. Use a ruler to approximate the actual distance between the two locations.

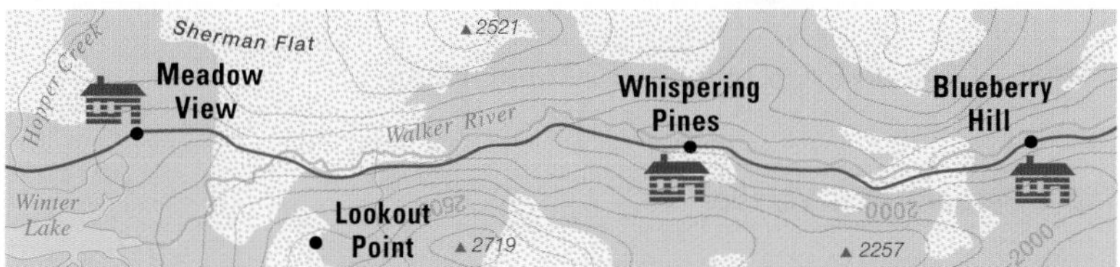

1. Meadow View and Lookout Point 2.8 mi
2. Lookout Point and Whispering Pines 5.2 mi
3. Whispering Pines and Blueberry Hill 4.6 mi
4. Meadow View and Blueberry Hill 12 mi

Using the scale 1 cm : 48 km, predict the distance in centimeters *on the map* for the given actual distance.

5. 24 kilometers 0.5 cm
6. 168 kilometers 3.5 cm
7. 72 kilometers 1.5 cm

Convert the indicated sum of money into US dollars or foreign currency, as indicated, using the given exchange rate.

8. How many Australian dollars (A$) can you buy with $550 (US) at the exchange rate of $1.00 (US) to A$1.34? A$737.00
9. How many New Zealand dollars (NZ$) can you buy with $2250 (US) at the exchange rate of $1.00 (US) to NZ$1.50? NZ$3375.00
10. How many US dollars can you buy with $1350 (Argentine pesos) at the exchange rate of $1.00 (peso) to $0.33 (US)? $445.50 (US)
11. How many US dollars can Peter buy with R2500 (South African rands) at the exchange rate of R1.00 to $0.16 (US)? $400.00
12. How many Israeli new sheqels (₪) can Anna buy with $2500 (US) at the exchange rate of $1.00 to ₪4.70? ₪11,750.00
13. How many US dollars can you buy with Bds$1200 (Barbados dollars) at the exchange rate of Bds$1.00 to $0.51 (US)? $612.00 (US)

Answer the questions about unit prices.

14. Francesca pays $3.88 for 4 ounces of cinnamon. How much does the cinnamon cost per ounce? $.97
15. Nani buys 7 pounds of oats for $6.51. What is the price per pound? $.93
16. You buy $2\frac{1}{2}$ pounds of granola for $6.35. What is the price per pound? $2.54
17. A quart of organic milk costs $1.79. What is the price per gallon? $7.16
18. Michael pays $11.67 for 3 pints of ice cream. Daniel pays $19.35 for 5 pints of ice cream. Who pays less per pint of ice cream, Michael or Daniel? How much less per pint does he pay? Daniel; $.02

Appendix 2

Appendix 3 Use after Lesson 7.4

Using Small *and* Large Percents

GOAL Calculate with very small (< 1%) and very large (> 100%) percents.

Example 1 ***Finding a Percent of a Number***

a. Find 0.4% of 350.

$0.4\% \text{ of } 350 = 0.004 \cdot 350$ **Write percent as decimal.**

$= 1.4$ **Multiply.**

b. Find 0.01% of 800.

$0.01\% \text{ of } 800 = 0.0001 \cdot 8000$ **Write percent as decimal.**

$= 0.08$ **Multiply.**

c. Find 150% of 29.

$150\% \text{ of } 29 = 1.5 \cdot 29$ **Write percent as decimal.**

$= 43.5$ **Multiply.**

d. Find 2800% of 1.1.

$2800\% \text{ of } 1.1 = 28 \cdot 1.1$ **Write percent as decimal.**

$= 30.8$ **Multiply.**

Notice that 0.4% of 350 is less than 1% of 350 (1.4 < 3.5). Also notice that 150% of 29 is greater than 29.

Example 2 ***Finding a Real World Percent***

A zookeeper is recording the growth of a snake at the zoo. The snake was 550 centimeters long when it was previously measured. A new measurement shows that the snake has grown 2.75 centimeters longer. What is the percent of increase?

Solution

a. $\frac{a}{b} = \frac{p}{100}$ **Use $\frac{a}{b} = \frac{p}{100}$ to represent that *a* is *p* percent of *b*.**

$\frac{2.75}{550} = \frac{p}{100}$ **Substitute 2.75 for *a* and 550 for *p*.**

$100 \cdot 2.75 = 550 \cdot p$ **Use cross products property.**

$p = 0.5$ **Solve for *p*.**

Answer The snake has grown 0.5%.

Appendix 3

NCTM CURRICULUM STANDARDS

Standard 1: Compute fluently

Standard 2: Represent situations using algebraic symbols

Standard 6: Solve problems in math and other contexts

Example 3 *Finding a Real World Base*

Your family paid \$900 for a new television. This amount is 180% of the total amount that your friend's family paid for their new television. How much did your friend's family spend on their new television?

Solution

$a = p\% \cdot b$	**Use $a = p\% \cdot b$ to represent that a is p percent of b.**
$900 = 180\% \cdot b$	**Substitute 900 for a and 180 for p.**
$900 = 1.8 \cdot b$	**Write percent as a decimal.**
$500 = b$	**Divide each side by 1.8.**

Answer Your friend's family paid \$500 for their new television.

Practice

Find the percent of the number.

1. 115% of 194 **223.1**
2. 0.08% of 410,000 **328**
3. 0.4% of 900 **3.6**
4. 775% of 76 **589**
5. 0.7% of 680,000 **4760**
6. 355% of 22 **78.1**

Copy and complete each statement using $<$, $>$, or $=$.

7. 150% of 7 _?_ 0.5% of 2100 $=$
8. 180% of 45 _?_ 200% of 40 $>$
9. 0.25% of 800 _?_ 0.5% of 500 $<$
10. 0.1% of 1100 _?_ 105% of 1 $>$
11. 0.9% of 300 _?_ 0.7% of 400 $<$
12. 145% of 40 _?_ 400% of 14.5 $=$

Use a percent equation to answer the question.

13. 621 is what percent of 460? **135%**
14. 138 is 1150% of what number? **12**
15. 4 is 0.8% of what number? **500**
16. 18 is what percent of 4500? **0.4%**
17. 1961 is what percent of 925? **212%**
18. 189 is 135% of what number? **140**
19. 11 is 0.02% of what number? **55,000**
20. 9 is what percent of 1200? **0.75%**
21. 476 is what percent of 280? **170%**
22. 30 is 0.6% of what number? **5000**
23. **Bamboo** A bamboo cane was 36 cm long when it was previously measured. A new measurement shows that the cane has grown 171 cm longer. What is the percent of increase? **21%**
24. **Budget** In one year, a small company paid \$850 for office supplies. This amount is 0.2% of the company's total operating expenses for the year. What were the company's total operating expenses for the year? **\$425,000**
25. **Hurricane** A hurricane's top wind speed was 125 miles per hour when it was previously measured. A new measurement shows that the hurricane's top wind speed has increased by 1 mile per hour. What is the percent of increase? **0.8%**
26. **Park Visits** A park had 6080 visitors in May. This amount is 1520% of the number of visitors it had in January. How many visitors did the park have in January? **400 visitors**

Vocabulary
rationalizing the denominator, p. 831
radicand, p. 832

Operations with Square Roots

GOAL Perform operations with expressions containing square roots.

In Lesson 9.1, you learned that every positive number has two square roots, one positive and one negative. As with any other real number, the real square roots of a number can be plotted on a number line, as shown below.

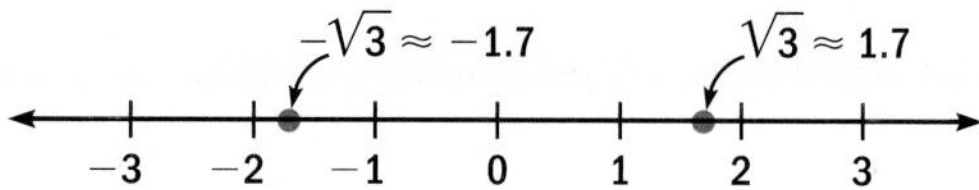

Square roots can also be represented as lengths on a number line. You can use square roots represented as lengths to evaluate sums and differences involving square roots.

Example 1 *Representing Square Roots on a Number Line*

Use a number line to approximate the sum or difference.

a. $3 + \sqrt{7}$

b. $\sqrt{21} - 5$

Solution

a.

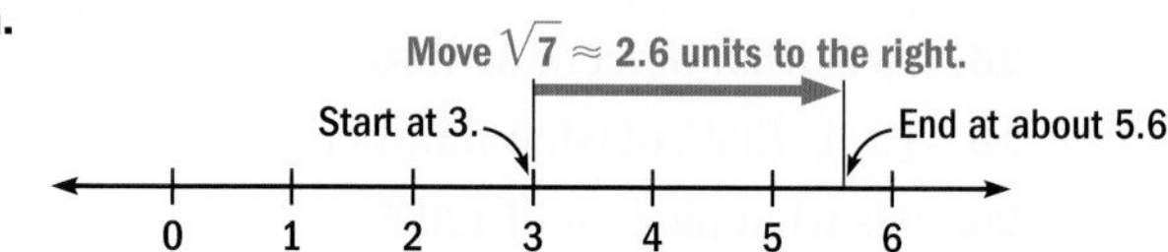

Answer The final position is about 5.6. So, $3 + \sqrt{7} \approx 5.6$.

b.

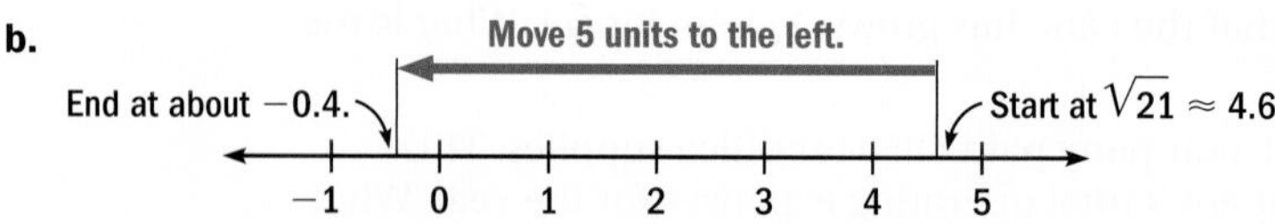

Answer The final position is about −0.4. So, $\sqrt{21} - 5 \approx -0.4$.

Products of Radical Expressions In Lesson 9.2, you used the product property of square roots to simplify radical expressions. This property can also be used to multiply radical expressions, as shown in Example 2.

NCTM CURRICULUM STANDARDS
Standard 1: Understand meanings of operations; Compute fluently

Example 2 *Multiplying Radical Expressions*

a. $\sqrt{15} \cdot \sqrt{6} = \sqrt{15 \cdot 6}$ Product property of square roots

$= \sqrt{90}$ Multiply.

$= \sqrt{9} \cdot \sqrt{10}$ Product property of square roots

$= 3\sqrt{10}$ Simplify.

b. $\sqrt{2x} \cdot \sqrt{8x^3} = \sqrt{2x \cdot 8x^3}$ Product property of square roots

$= \sqrt{16x^4}$ Multiply.

$= \sqrt{16} \cdot \sqrt{x^4}$ Product property of square roots

$= 4x^2$ Simplify.

Quotients of Radical Expressions When you divide two radical expressions, you must rewrite the resulting quotient so that no radical appears in the denominator. Eliminating a radical in a denominator is called **rationalizing the denominator**. In general, you can rationalize the denominator of an expression of the form $\frac{\sqrt{a}}{\sqrt{b}}$ by multiplying the numerator and denominator by $\sqrt{b}$.

$$\frac{\sqrt{a}}{\sqrt{b}} = \frac{\sqrt{a}}{\sqrt{b}} \cdot \frac{\sqrt{b}}{\sqrt{b}}$$

$$= \frac{\sqrt{ab}}{\sqrt{b^2}}$$

$$= \frac{\sqrt{ab}}{b}$$

Example 3 *Dividing Radical Expressions*

a. $\frac{\sqrt{7}}{\sqrt{2}} = \frac{\sqrt{7}}{\sqrt{2}} \cdot \frac{\sqrt{2}}{\sqrt{2}}$ Multiply numerator and denominator by $\sqrt{2}$.

$= \frac{\sqrt{14}}{2}$ Multiply fractions.

b. $\frac{\sqrt{12}}{\sqrt{t}} = \frac{\sqrt{12}}{\sqrt{t}} \cdot \frac{\sqrt{t}}{\sqrt{t}}$ Multiply numerator and denominator by $\sqrt{t}$.

$= \frac{\sqrt{12t}}{t}$ Multiply fractions.

$= \frac{\sqrt{4} \cdot \sqrt{3t}}{t}$ Product property of square roots

$= \frac{2\sqrt{3t}}{t}$ Simplify.

Appendix 4

1. 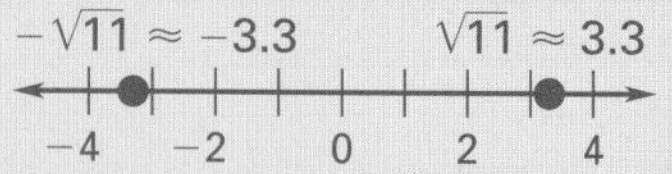

2. 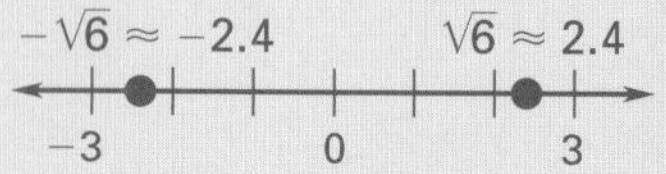

3. 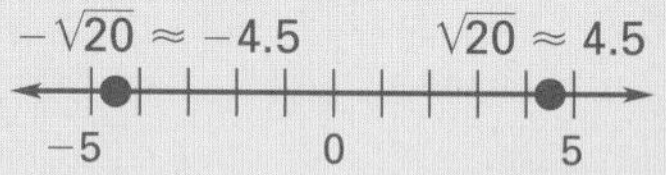

4. 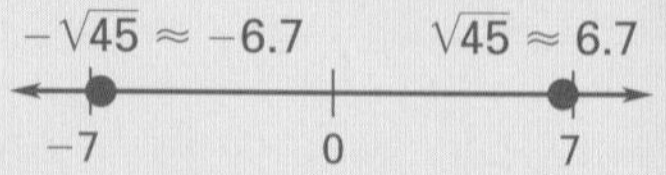

5. 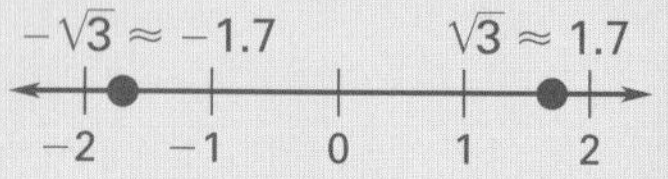

6. 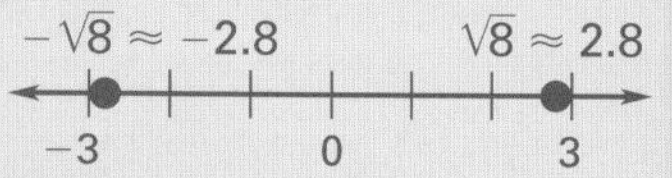

7. 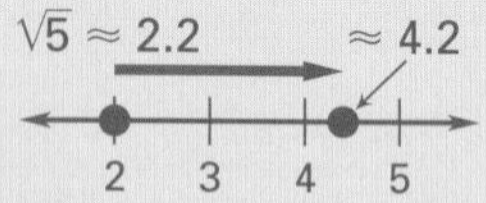

8. 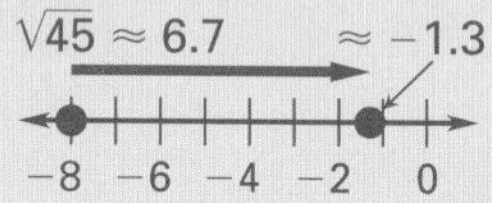

9. 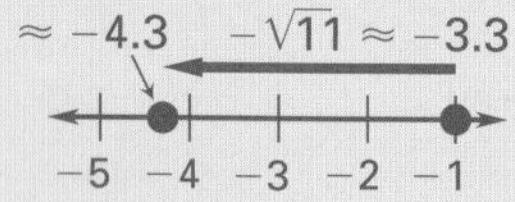

10. 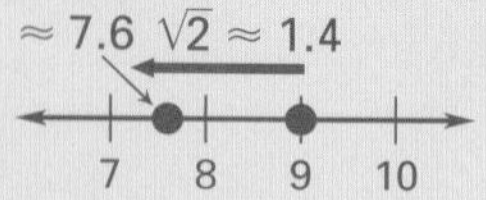

11. 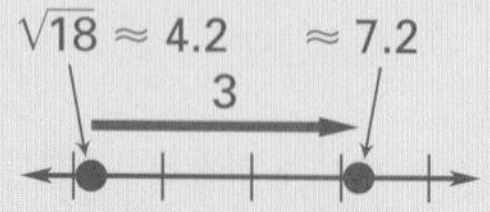

12. 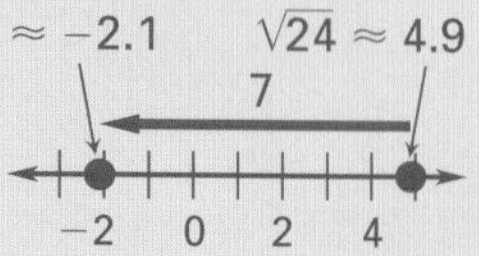

832

Sums and Differences of Radical Expressions You can use the distributive property to add or subtract two square root expressions provided each expression has the same *radicand.* The **radicand** is the expression beneath the radical symbol.

Example 4 *Adding or Subtracting Radical Expressions*

Simplify the expression, if possible.

a. $7\sqrt{3} + 4\sqrt{3}$ **b.** $2\sqrt{5y} - 8\sqrt{5y}$ **c.** $8\sqrt{6t} + 9\sqrt{t}$

Solution

a. $7\sqrt{3} + 4\sqrt{3} = (7 + 4)\sqrt{3}$ **Distributive property**

$= 11\sqrt{3}$ **Simplify.**

b. $2\sqrt{5y} - 8\sqrt{5y} = (2 - 8)\sqrt{5y}$ **Distributive property**

$= -6\sqrt{5y}$ **Simplify.**

c. The radicands $\sqrt{6t}$ and $\sqrt{t}$ are not alike. The expression $8\sqrt{6t} + 9\sqrt{t}$ is already in simplest form.

Practice

Graph the number on a number line. **1–12. See margin.**

1. $\sqrt{11}$ **2.** $\sqrt{6}$ **3.** $\sqrt{20}$

4. $\sqrt{45}$ **5.** $\sqrt{3}$ **6.** $\sqrt{8}$

Use a number line to approximate the sum or difference.

7. $2 + \sqrt{5}$ **8.** $-8 + \sqrt{45}$ **9.** $-1 - \sqrt{11}$

10. $9 - \sqrt{2}$ **11.** $\sqrt{18} + 3$ **12.** $\sqrt{24} - 7$

Simplify the expression, if possible.

13. $\sqrt{14} \cdot \sqrt{30}$ **$2\sqrt{105}$** **14.** $\sqrt{7n} \cdot \sqrt{11n}$ **$n\sqrt{77}$** **15.** $\sqrt{10r^3} \cdot \sqrt{15r^2}$ **$5r^2\sqrt{6r}$**

16. $\dfrac{\sqrt{13}}{\sqrt{5}}$ **$\dfrac{\sqrt{65}}{5}$** **17.** $\dfrac{\sqrt{21}}{\sqrt{3}}$ **$\sqrt{7}$** **18.** $\dfrac{\sqrt{18}}{\sqrt{2x}}$ **$\dfrac{3\sqrt{x}}{x}$**

19. $3\sqrt{7} + 6\sqrt{7}$ **$9\sqrt{7}$** **20.** $8\sqrt{y} + 4\sqrt{2y}$ **in simplest form** **21.** $\sqrt{b} + 5\sqrt{b}$ **$6\sqrt{b}$**

22. $5\sqrt{17} - 2\sqrt{17}$ **$3\sqrt{17}$** **23.** $4\sqrt{m} - \sqrt{m}$ **$3\sqrt{m}$** **24.** $3\sqrt{5s} - 7\sqrt{5s}$ **$-4\sqrt{5s}$**

25. $9\sqrt{3} - 8\sqrt{6}$ **in simplest form** **26.** $\sqrt{27} + 6\sqrt{3}$ **$9\sqrt{3}$** **27.** $8\sqrt{2} \cdot \sqrt{8x}$ **$32\sqrt{x}$**

28. $\dfrac{\sqrt{5}}{2} \cdot \dfrac{10}{\sqrt{2}}$ **$\dfrac{5\sqrt{10}}{2}$** **29.** $\dfrac{\sqrt{3} + 4\sqrt{3}}{\sqrt{7}}$ **$\dfrac{5\sqrt{21}}{7}$** **30.** $\sqrt{28}\,(3\sqrt{2} - 9\sqrt{2})$ **$-12\sqrt{14}$**

Appendix 4

Appendix 5 Use after Lesson 9.3

Vocabulary
truth value, p. 834
truth table, p. 834

Symbolic Notation *and* Truth Tables

GOAL Use symbolic notation to represent logical statements.

Conditional statements can be written using *symbolic notation*, where letters are used to represent statements. An arrow ($\rightarrow$), read "implies," connects the hypothesis and conclusion. To write the negation of a statement p you write the symbol for negation ($\sim$) before the letter. So, "not p" is written $\sim p$.

Symbolic Notation

Let p be "the angle is a right angle" and let q be "the measure of the angle is 90°."

Conditional If p, then q. $p \rightarrow q$

Example: If an angle is a right angle, then its measure is 90°.

Converse If q, then p. $q \rightarrow p$

Example: If the measure of an angle is 90°, then the angle is a right angle.

Inverse If not p, then not q. $\sim p \rightarrow \sim q$

Example: If an angle is not a right angle, then its measure is not 90°.

Contrapositive If not q, then not p. $\sim q \rightarrow \sim p$

If the measure of an angle is not 90°, then the angle is not a right angle.

Biconditional p if and only if q $p \leftrightarrow q$

Example: An angle is a right angle if and only if its measure is 90°.

Example 1 *Use Symbolic Notation*

Let p be "the car is running" and let q be "the key is in the ignition."

a. Write the conditional statement $p \rightarrow q$ in words.
b. Write the converse $q \rightarrow p$ in words.
c. Write the inverse $\sim p \rightarrow \sim q$ in words.
d. Write the contrapositive $\sim q \rightarrow \sim p$ in words.

Solution

a. Conditional: If the car is running, then the key is in the ignition.
b. Converse: If the key is in the ignition, then the car is running.
c. Inverse: If the car is not running, then the key is not in the ignition.
d. Contrapositive: If the key is not in the ignition, then the car is not running.

NCTM CURRICULUM STANDARDS
Standard 7: Recognize reasoning and proof as fundamental to math
Standard 8: Communicate thinking clearly to others

2. If polygon *ABCDE* is equiangular and equilateral, then it is a regular polygon.

3. Polygon *ABCDE* is not equiangular and not equilateral.

4. If polygon *ABCDE* is not a regular polygon, then it is not equiangular and not equilateral.

5. Polygon *ABCDE* is equiangular and equilateral if and only if it is a regular polygon.

6. *Sample answer:* If $x + 5 = 12$, then $x = 7$; if $x = 7$, then $3x = 21$; if $x + 5 = 12$, then $3x = 21$; $p \to q$, $q \to r$, $p \to r$.

7. No; it is false when the hypothesis is true while the conclusion is false.

8.

Converse		
p	q	$q \to p$
T	T	T
T	F	T
F	T	F
F	F	T

9.

Contrapositive				
p	q	$\sim q$	$\sim p$	$\sim q \to \sim p$
T	T	F	F	T
T	F	T	F	F
F	T	F	T	T
F	F	T	T	T

Truth tables The **truth value** of a statement is either true (T) or false (F). You can determine the conditions under which a conditional statement is true by using a **truth table**. The truth table at the right shows the truth values for hypothesis p and conclusion q. The conditional $p \to q$ is only false when a true hypothesis produces a false conclusion.

Conditional		
p	q	$p \to q$
T	T	T
T	F	F
F	T	T
F	F	T

Example 2 *Make a truth table*

Use the truth table above to make a truth table for the inverse of a conditional statement $p \to q$.

Solution

Inverse				
p	q	$\sim p$	$\sim q$	$\sim p \to \sim q$
T	T	F	F	T
T	F	F	T	T
F	T	T	F	F
F	F	T	T	T

Practice

1. **Writing** *Describe* how to use symbolic notation to represent the contrapositive of a conditional statement. $\sim q \to \sim p$

Writing Statements **Use p and q to write the symbolic statement in words.**

p: Polygon *ABCDE* is equiangular and equilateral.

q: Polygon *ABCDE* is a regular polygon. **2–7. See margin.**

2. $p \to q$
3. $\sim p$
4. $\sim q \to \sim p$
5. $p \leftrightarrow q$

6. **Law of Syllogism** The *Law of Syllogism* states that if $p \to q$ and $q \to r$, then $p \to r$. Use the statements p, q, and r below to write a series of conditionals that would satisfy the Law of Syllogism. How could you write your reasoning using symbolic notation?

p: $x + 5 = 12$ q: $x = 7$ r: $3x = 21$

7. **Writing** Is the truth value of a statement always true (T)? *Explain.*

8. **Truth Table** Use the truth table at the top of this page to make a truth table for the converse of a conditional statement $p \to q$. **See margin.**

9. **Truth Table** Use the truth table at the top of this page to make a truth table for the contrapositive of a conditional statement $p \to q$. **See margin.**

Appendix 5

Appendix 6 Use after Lesson 11.3

Vocabulary
Venn diagram, p. 835
intersection, p. 835
union, p. 835

Using Venn Diagrams

GOAL Sort data using Venn diagrams.

A **Venn diagram** groups items within circles to show the relations among them. An **intersection** consists of all items belonging to each of two or more circles. A **union** consists of all items belonging to any of two or more circles.

Example 1 *Sort Data with a Venn Diagram*

Tina, Marvin, Juan, and Cho excel at music. Juan, Cho, and Bea excel at sports. Show these facts in a Venn diagram.

Solution

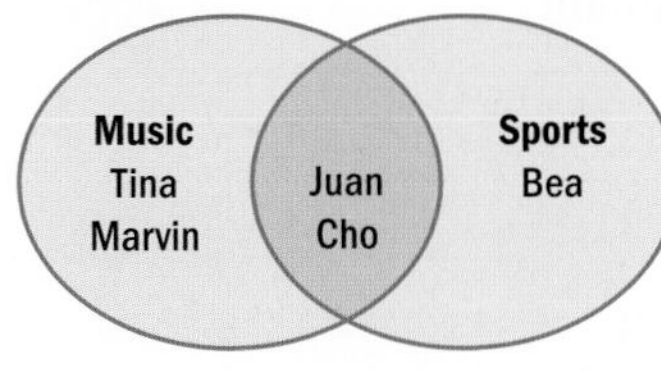

Tina and Marvin excel only at music.

Bea excels only at sports.

Juan and Cho excel at both. This is the intersection.

All five excel at one or at both. This is the union.

Example 2 *Sort Data with a Venn Diagram*

Each person in your group at the Grand Canyon chooses at least one of the following activities: a mule ride, a ranger-led walk, and a conservation film. Of the 75 people in the group, 18 choose all three, 15 choose only the ride, 12 only the walk, 9 only the film, and 5 both the ride and the walk. The total number who choose the mule ride is 48. How many choose the walk and the film?

Solution

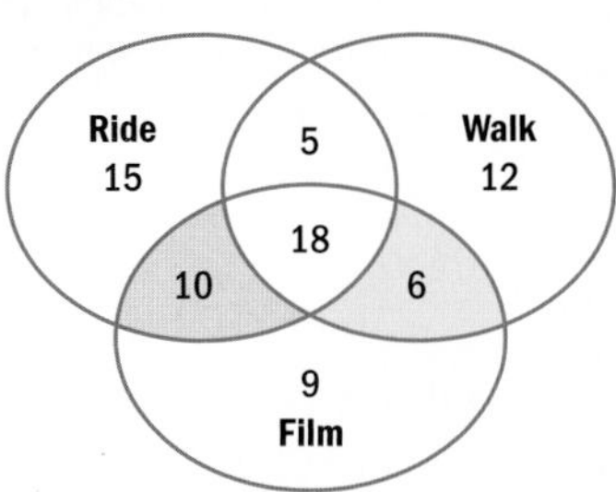

Number who choose the ride and the film $= 48 - (15 + 5 + 18) = \mathbf{10}$

Number who choose the walk and the film $= 75 - (48 + 12 + 9) = \mathbf{6}$

NCTM CURRICULUM STANDARDS

Standard 5: Collect, organize, and display data

Standard 10: Create representations to communicate ideas

1.

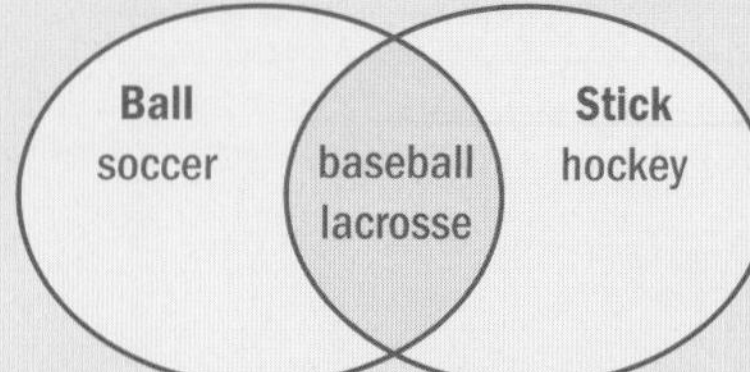

2.

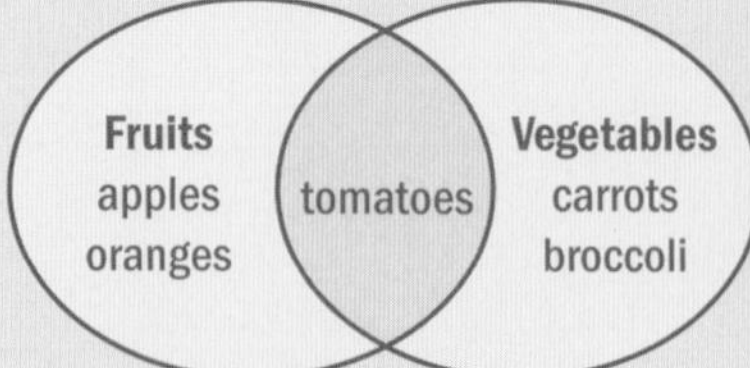

3.

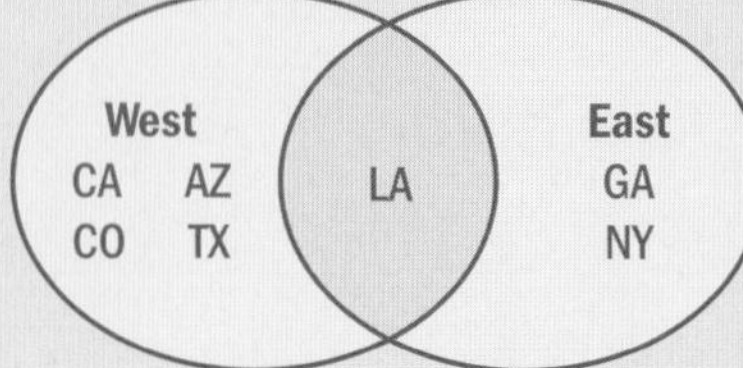

4.

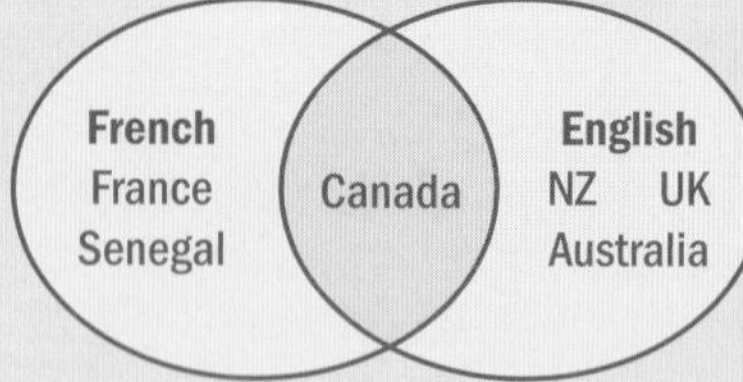

5.

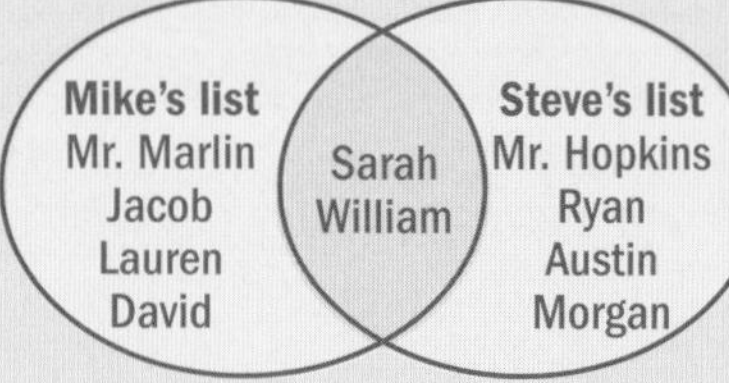

Practice

Create a Venn diagram to show the information presented using the two categories given. 1–5. See margin.

1. Baseball, lacrosse, and soccer are all sports that are played with a *ball*. Baseball, lacrosse, and hockey are all played with a *stick*.
2. According to scientists, apples, oranges, and tomatoes are *fruits*. According to cooks, tomatoes, carrots and broccoli are *vegetables*.
3. The states of California, Arizona, Colorado, Texas, and Louisiana are all *west* of the Mississippi River. Louisiana, Georgia, and New York are *east* of it. The Mississippi River flows through the southern part of Louisiana, effectively dividing the state into two parts.
4. *French* is an official language of France, Senegal (in West Africa), and Canada. English is an official language of Canada, Australia, New Zealand, and the United Kingdom.
5. Mike and Steve won 12 tickets to a basketball game. They each made a list of the people they would like to invite.

   Mike's list: Mike, Steve, Mr. Marlin, Jacob, Sarah, Lauren, David, William

   Steve's list: Mike, Steve, Mr. Hopkins, William, Sarah, Ryan, Austin, Morgan

Use a Venn diagram to solve the problem.

6. In a class of 24 students, 8 are studying only French, 10 are studying only Spanish, and 5 are studying both French and Spanish. How many students are not studying either language? **1 student**
7. Dora made necklaces of red, blue, and yellow beads. Fourteen contain only red beads, 16 contain only blue beads, and 12 contain only yellow beads. Six necklaces contain only blue and yellow beads, and 2 contain only yellow and red beads. Five contain beads of all three colors. If Dora made 30 necklaces that contained blue beads, how many contained blue and red beads? **3 necklaces**
8. **Error Analysis** Thirty-two families live on Oak Lane. Half of the families own a dog. Eight families own a cat, and three own both a dog and a cat. A student says that $\frac{3}{4}$ of the families own a dog or a cat. Describe and correct the error in the student's reasoning.
9. T-shirts, sweatshirts, and hats are being sold at the school store. In one month, 26 students buy T-shirts, and 20 students buy hats. Two students buy all three items, and 3 buy T-shirts and hats, but not sweatshirts. Seventeen buy just T-shirts and 10 buy just hats. How many students buy exactly two of the three items? **12 students**
10. There are 30 students in Mr. Wu's homeroom class. Eighteen of them are taking an art course. Nine are taking just a painting class, 4 are taking just a sculpture class, and 2 are taking both painting and sculpture. What percent of the students in the homeroom class are taking an art course different from painting or sculpture? **10%**

8. The student added 16 and 8 and concluded that 24 out of 32 families own a dog or cat, but this counts the 3 families that own both a dog and a cat twice. There are 13 families that own just a dog, 3 that own both a dog and a cat, and 5 that own just a cat. So, there are $\frac{21}{32}$ families that own a dog or a cat.

Appendix 7 Use after Lesson 12.7

Vocabulary
relation, p. 385
function, p. 386
vertical line test, p. 387

Linear *and* Nonlinear Relations *and* Functions

GOAL Identify linear and nonlinear relations and functions.

Linear Relations You can decide whether a relation is linear by inspecting its graph. A relation is linear if all of its points lie on the same line.

Example 1 *Identifying Linear and Nonlinear Relations*

Tell whether the relation is *linear* or *nonlinear*.

a.

x	−2	−1	0	1	2
y	−4	−2	0	2	4

b. **Input** **Output**

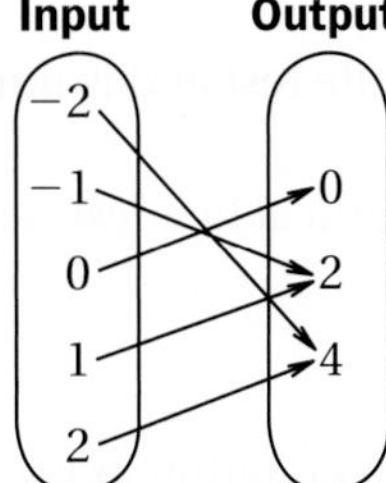

Solution

a. Represent the relation using a graph by plotting the ordered pairs from the table, as shown.

All of the points lie on the line $y = 2x$, so the relation is linear.

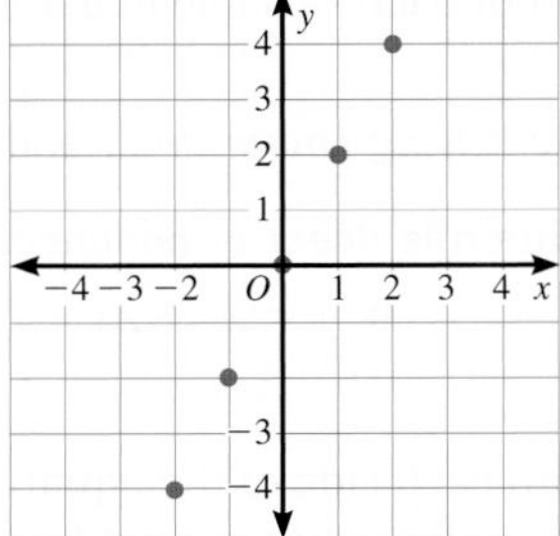

b. Represent the relation using a graph by plotting the ordered pairs from the mapping diagram, as shown.

The points do not all lie on the same line, so the relation is nonlinear.

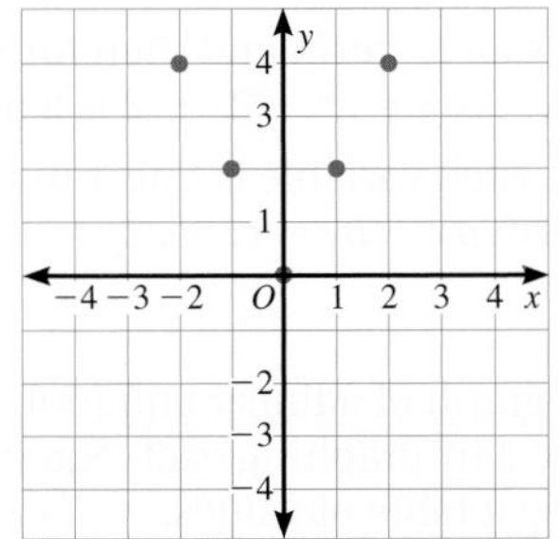

NCTM CURRICULUM STANDARDS

Standard 2: Understand functions; Analyze situations using algebraic symbols; Use models to understand relationships

Identifying Functions Recall from Lesson 8.1 that you can use the vertical line test to tell whether a relation represented by a graph is a function.

Example 2 *Identifying Linear and Nonlinear Functions*

Tell whether the relation represented by the graph is a function. If so, decide whether it is a linear function or a nonlinear function.

a. 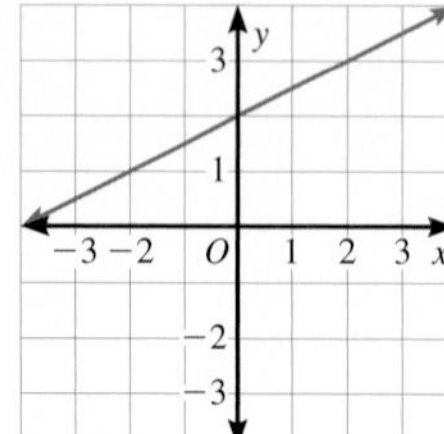

b. 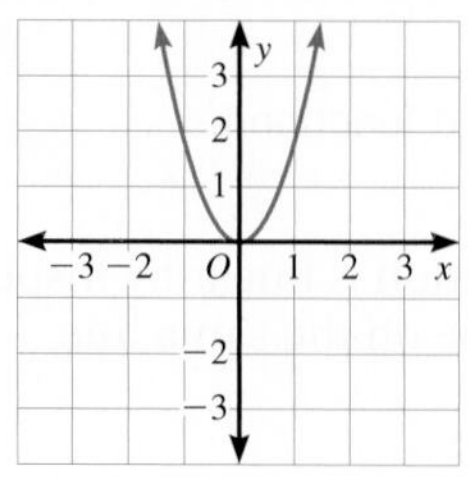

c. 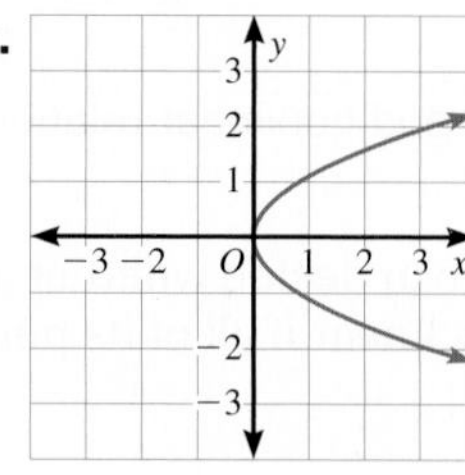

Solution

a. The graph passes the vertical line test and is linear. So, the relation is a linear function.

b. The graph passes the vertical line test and is nonlinear. So, the relation is a nonlinear function.

c. The graph does not pass the vertical line test, so the relation is not a function.

Recognizing Linear Equations A linear equation in two variables is an equation that can be written in the form $ax + by = c$ where a and b are not both zero. The exponent of each variable in a linear equation is one.

Example 3 *Identifying Linear and Nonlinear Equations*

Tell whether the equation is *linear* or *nonlinear*.

a. $y = x + 2$ **b.** $y = x^2 + 2x + 2$ **c.** $xy = 1$

Solution

a. Subtracting x from each side of the equation yields $-x + y = 2$. So, the equation can be written in the form $ax + by = c$, and therefore $y = x + 2$ is a linear equation.

b. The equation has an x^2-term and therefore cannot be written in the form $ax + by = c$. So, $y = x^2 + 2x + 2$ is a nonlinear equation.

c. The exponent of each variable is one, but the equation cannot be written in the form $ax + by = c$. So, $xy = 1$ is a nonlinear equation.

Checking Because the graph of a linear equation is a line, you can check the answers in Example 3 by graphing each equation using a calculator or by making and graphing a table of values.

Practice

Tell whether the relation is *linear* or *nonlinear*.

1.

x	−1	0	1	2	3
y	−8	−2	4	10	16

linear

2.

x	−3	−1	0	1	3
y	−10	−4	−1	4	10

nonlinear

3. 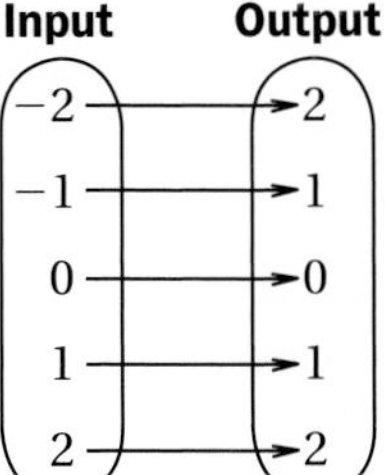

nonlinear

4. 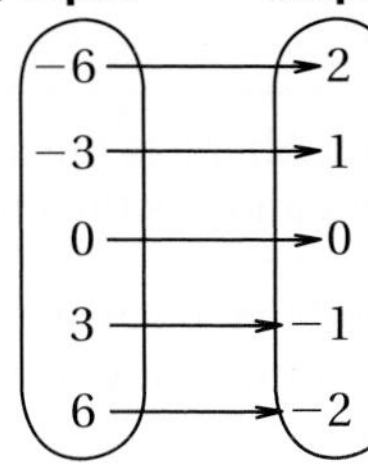

linear

Tell whether the relation represented by the graph is a function. If so, decide whether it is a linear function or a nonlinear function.

5. 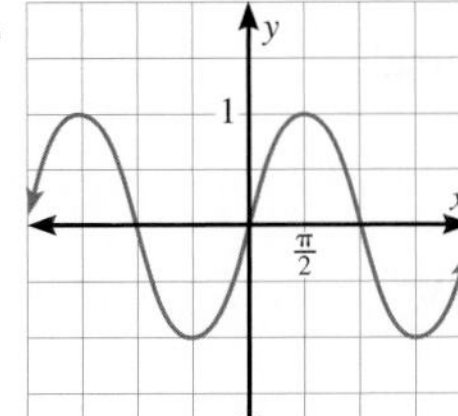

nonlinear function

6. 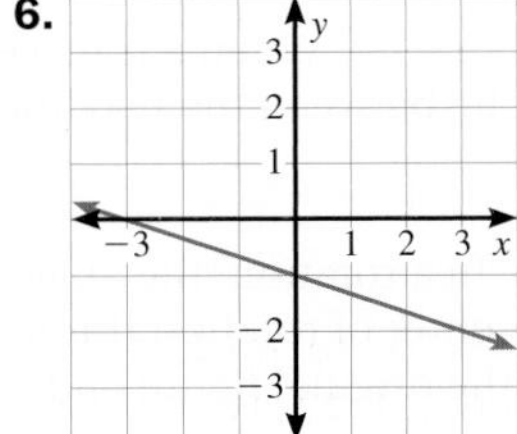

linear function

7. 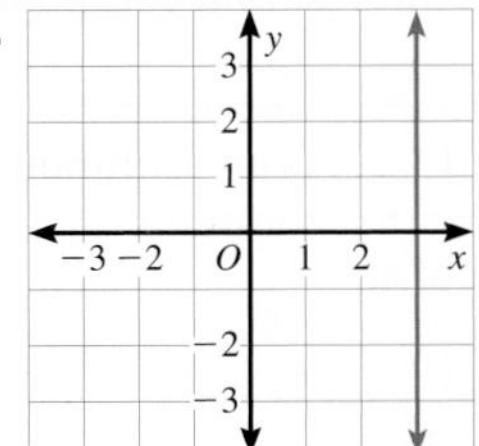

not a function

8. 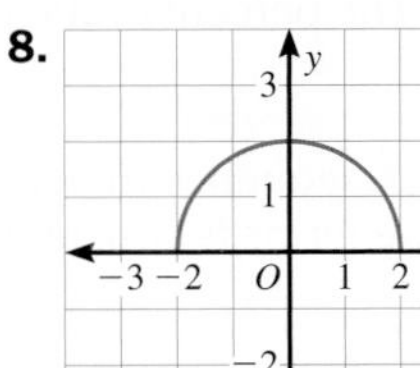

nonlinear function

Tell whether the equation is *linear* or *nonlinear*.

9. $y = 5x^2 - x + 9$ nonlinear
10. $y = 3x - 2$ linear
11. $y - x = 4$ linear
12. $y - x = x^2 + 9$ nonlinear
13. $y = \frac{1}{2}x + 8$ linear
14. $y = \frac{5}{x}$ nonlinear
15. $3y - x = 1$ linear
16. $-4x + y = 5x^4 + 2$ nonlinear
17. $xy - 2x = 8$ nonlinear

18. **Hot Air Balloon** The altitude h (in feet) of a hot air balloon after t minutes in flight is shown in the table. Is h a linear function of t? Explain.

t	0	1	2	3	4
h	250	270	290	310	330

Sample answer: Yes, h is a linear function of t. When t is graphed along the x-axis and h along the y-axis, a graph of the data passes the vertical line test and is linear.

Appendix 7

Glossary

a	Example
absolute value (p. 23) The absolute value of a number a is its distance from 0 on a number line. The absolute value of a number a is written as $\|a\|$.	$\|3\| = 3$ $\|-5\| = 5$ $\|0\| = 0$
additive identity (p. 64) The number 0 is the additive identity, because the sum of any number and 0 is the number.	$-3 + 0 = -3$ $a + 0 = a$
additive inverse (p. 30) The additive inverse of a number a is its opposite, $-a$. The sum of a number and its additive inverse is 0.	The additive inverse of 5 is -5, so $5 + (-5) = 0$.
alternate exterior angles (p. 716) When a transversal intersects two lines, two angles that lie outside the two lines on opposite sides of the transversal.	*See* transversal.
alternate interior angles (p. 716) When a transversal intersects two lines, two angles that lie between the two lines on opposite sides of the transversal.	*See* transversal.
angle of rotation (p. 741) In a rotation, the angle formed by two rays drawn from the center of rotation through corresponding points on the original figure and its image.	*See* rotation.
annual interest rate (p. 362) The percent of the principal earned or paid per year.	*See* simple interest *and* compound interest.
arithmetic sequence (p. 692) A sequence in which the difference between consecutive terms is constant.	1, 5, 9, 13, 17, . . . is an arithmetic sequence with a common difference of 4.
b	
balance of an account (p. 363) The sum of the principal and all interest earned.	*See* simple interest *and* compound interest.
base of a parallelogram (p. 521) The length of any side of the parallelogram.	*See* parallelogram.
base of a power (p. 10) The number or expression that is used as a factor in a repeated multiplication.	In the power 2^7, the base is 2.
bases of a trapezoid (p. 522) The lengths of the parallel sides of the trapezoid.	*See* trapezoid.

	Example
best-fitting line **(p. 421)** The line that lies as close as possible to the points of a scatter plot.	 The best-fitting line for the scatter plot is shown in red.
biased question **(p. 603)** A question that encourages a particular response.	"Don't you think it would be better if the school built a new gymnasium?" is a biased question.
biased sample **(p. 602)** A sample that is not representative of a population.	The members of a school's basketball team are a biased sample for a survey about support for building a new gymnasium.
binomial **(p. 651)** A polynomial with two terms.	$a^2 + 5a$ and $9 - y$ are binomials.
box-and-whisker plot **(p. 588)** A data display that organizes data values into four groups using the lower extreme, lower quartile, median, upper quartile, and upper extreme.	
C	
categorical data **(p. 596)** Data that consist of names, labels, or other nonnumerical values.	A list of eye colors is a set of categorical data.
center of a circle **(p. 528)** The point inside the circle that is the same distance from all points on the circle.	*See* circle.
center of dilation **(p. 747)** The point with respect to which a figure stretches or shrinks when the figure undergoes a dilation.	*See* dilation.
center of rotation **(p. 741)** The point about which a figure is turned when the figure undergoes a rotation.	*See* rotation.
circle **(p. 528)** All points in a plane that are the same distance, called the radius, from a fixed point, called the center.	

	Example
circumference of a circle (p. 528) The distance around the circle.	*See* circle.
coefficient (p. 78) The number part of a term with a variable.	The coefficient of $-7x$ is -7.
combination (p. 620) A selection of objects where the order in which the objects are chosen is not important.	There are 3 combinations of 2 letters chosen from the letters A, H, T: AH AT HT
common difference (p. 692) The difference between consecutive terms of an arithmetic sequence.	*See* arithmetic sequence.
common factor (p. 177) A whole number that is a factor of two or more nonzero whole numbers.	The common factors of 12 and 20 are 1, 2, and 4.
common multiple (p. 187) A whole number that is a multiple of two or more nonzero whole numbers.	The common multiples of 6 and 9 are 18, 36, 54, ...
common ratio (p. 692) The ratio of any term of a geometric sequence to the previous term of the sequence.	*See* geometric sequence.
complementary angles (p. 709) Two angles whose measures have a sum of 90°.	32° 58°
complementary events (p. 630) Two disjoint events such that one event or the other must occur.	When you roll a number cube, the events "roll an odd number" and "roll an even number" are complementary events.
composite number (p. 173) A whole number greater than 1 that has more than two whole number factors.	6 is a composite number, because its whole number factors are 1, 2, 3, and 6.
compound interest (p. 363) Interest that is earned on both the principal and any interest that has been earned previously. The balance A of an account that earns interest compounded annually is $A = P(1 + r)^t$, where P is the principal, r is the annual interest rate (written as a decimal), and t is the time in years.	You deposit \$1000 into an account that earns 3% interest compounded annually. After 5 years, your account balance is $A = P(1 + r)^t = 1000(1 + 0.03)^5 \approx \$1159.27$.
concave (p. 516) A polygon is concave if a segment joining any two interior points does not lie completely within the polygon.	*See* convex.

842

	Example
congruent figures (p. 290) Figures that have the same shape and the same size. Corresponding angles and corresponding sides of congruent figures are congruent.	$\triangle ABC \cong \triangle DEF$
constant term (p. 78) A term that has a number but no variable.	In the expression $8a + 4$, the term 4 is a constant term.
convenience sample (p. 601) A sample in which only members of a population who are easily accessible are selected.	You can select a convenience sample of your school's student population by choosing only students who are in your classes.
convex (p. 516) A polygon is convex if a segment joining any two interior points lies completely within the polygon. A polygon that is not convex is called *concave*.	Convex Concave
coordinate plane (p. 47) A coordinate system formed by the intersection of a horizontal number line called the x-axis and a vertical number line called the y-axis.	y-axis; Quadrant II; Quadrant I; x-axis; origin (0, 0); Quadrant III; Quadrant IV
corresponding angles (p. 716) Two angles that occupy corresponding positions when a transversal intersects two lines.	*See* transversal.
corresponding parts (p. 288) A pair of sides or angles that have the same relative position in two figures.	$\angle A$ and $\angle D$ are corresponding angles. $\overline{AC}$ and $\overline{DF}$ are corresponding sides.
cosine (p. 494) For a right triangle, the cosine of an acute angle A ($\cos A$) is the ratio of the length of the side adjacent to $\angle A$ to the length of the hypotenuse.	*See* trigonometric ratio.

	Example
counting principle (p. 314) If one event can occur in m ways, and for each of these ways a second event can occur in n ways, then the number of ways that the two events can occur together is $m \cdot n$.	You have 3 shirts and 4 pairs of pants. The total number of shirt-and-pants combinations that you can choose from is $3 \cdot 4 = 12$.
cross product (p. 280) The product of the numerator of one ratio and the denominator of another ratio. The cross products of a proportion are equal.	The cross products of the proportion $\frac{2}{3} = \frac{8}{12}$ are $2 \cdot 12 = 24$ and $3 \cdot 8 = 24$.
d	
degree of a polynomial (p. 652) The greatest degree of the terms of the polynomial.	In the polynomial $a^2 + 4a^2b + 5$, the degree of the term a^2 is 2, the degree of the term $4a^2b$ is 3, and the degree of the term 5 is 0. The degree of the polynomial is 3, the greatest degree of the terms.
degree of a term (p. 652) The sum of the exponents of the variables in the term. The degree of a nonzero constant is 0.	*See* degree of a polynomial.
dependent events (p. 634) Two events such that the occurrence of one event affects the probability of the occurrence of the other event.	A bag contains 4 red marbles and 5 green marbles. You randomly choose a marble, do not replace it, then randomly choose a second marble. The events "first marble is red" and "second marble is red" are dependent events.
diagonal of a polygon (p. 518) A segment that joins two vertices of the polygon that are not adjacent.	
diameter of a circle (p. 528) The distance across the circle through the center.	*See* circle.
dilation (p. 747) A transformation in which a figure stretches or shrinks with respect to a fixed point, called the center of dilation.	A′ B′ A B C C′ center of dilation $\triangle ABC$ is dilated with respect to the origin using a scale factor of 3.

	Example
discount **(p. 358)** The decrease from the original price of an item to the sale price.	The original price of a sweater is \$32.99, but the store sells it for \$25.99. The discount is \$7.00.
disjoint events **(p. 627)** Events that have no outcomes in common; also called mutually exclusive events.	When you roll a number cube, the events "roll a 3" and "roll an even number" are disjoint events.
domain of a relation **(p. 385)** The set of all possible inputs for the relation.	*See* relation.
e	
equation **(p. 85)** A mathematical sentence formed by placing an equal sign, =, between two expressions.	$3x - 2 = 12 + 10x$ is an equation.
equation in two variables **(p. 391)** An equation that contains two different variables.	$3x - 4y = 2$ is an equation in two variables.
equivalent equations **(p. 91)** Equivalent equations have the same solution.	$5y - 2 = 8$ and $5y = 10$ are equivalent equations, because the solution of both equations is 2.
equivalent fractions **(p. 182)** Two fractions that represent the same number.	$\frac{4}{8}$ and $\frac{10}{20}$ are equivalent fractions that both represent $\frac{1}{2}$.
equivalent inequalities **(p. 139)** Inequalities that have the same solution.	$3y + 7 > 25$ and $3y > 18$ are equivalent inequalities, because the solution of both inequalities is all numbers greater than 6.
equivalent numerical expressions **(p. 71)** Numerical expressions that have the same value.	$5(10 - 6)$ and $5(10) - 5(6)$ are equivalent numerical expressions, because they each have the value 20.
equivalent ratios **(p. 270)** Two or more ratios that have the same value.	$\frac{3}{4}$, $\frac{9}{12}$, and $\frac{15}{20}$ are equivalent ratios, because they each have the value 0.75.
equivalent variable expressions **(p. 72)** Variable expressions that have the same value for all values of the variable(s).	$5(x + 1) + x$ and $6x + 5$ are equivalent variable expressions.

	Example
evaluate a variable expression (p. 5) To find the value of the variable expression by substituting a number for each variable, and then finding the value of the resulting numerical expression.	The value of $2y - 5$ when $y = 3$ is $2(3) - 5 = 1$.
event (p. 306) An outcome or a collection of outcomes.	An event for rolling a number cube is "roll an even number."
experimental probability (p. 307) A probability based on repeated trials of an experiment. The experimental probability of an event is the ratio of the number of successes (favorable outcomes for the event) to the number of trials.	A basketball player has made 30 out of 36 attempted free throws this season. The experimental probability that she will make a free throw is $\frac{30}{36} = \frac{5}{6}$, or about 0.83.
exponent (p. 10) A number or expression that shows how many times a base is used as a factor in a repeated multiplication.	In the power 2^7, the exponent is 7.
exponential decay (p. 687) A quantity that decreases shows exponential decay if it can be described by an exponential function of the form $y = ab^x$, where $a > 0$ and $0 < b < 1$.	The function $y = \left(\frac{1}{3}\right)^x$ shows exponential decay. *See* exponential function.
exponential function (p. 686) An equation in two variables that can be written in the form $y = ab^x$, where $a \neq 0$, $b > 0$, and $b \neq 1$.	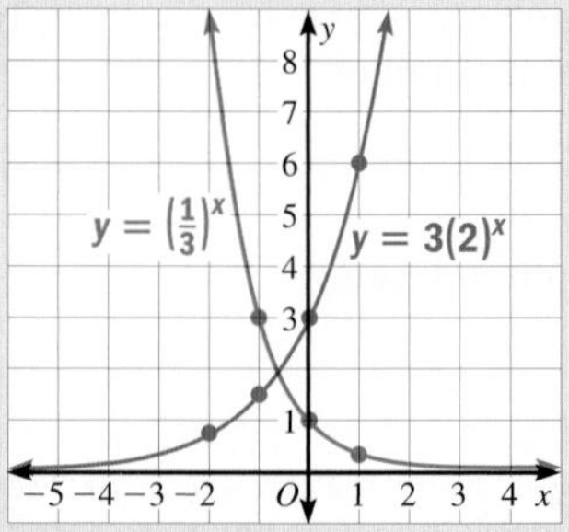 $y = \left(\frac{1}{3}\right)^x$ $y = 3(2)^x$ $y = 3(2)^x$ and $y = \left(\frac{1}{3}\right)^x$ are exponential functions.
exponential growth (p. 687) A quantity that increases shows exponential growth if it can be described by an exponential function of the form $y = ab^x$, where $a > 0$ and $b > 1$.	The function $y = 3(2)^x$ shows exponential growth. *See* exponential function.
exterior angle of a polygon (p. 723) An angle adjacent to an interior angle of the polygon, formed by extending one side of the polygon.	*See* interior angle of a polygon.

	Example
f	
factor tree **(p. 173)** A diagram that can be used to write the prime factorization of a number.	28 → 4 • 7 → 2 • 2 • 7
favorable outcomes **(p. 306)** Outcomes that correspond to a specified event.	When you roll a number cube, the favorable outcomes for the event "roll an even number" are 2, 4, and 6.
frequency **(p. 582)** The number of data values in an interval.	*See* frequency table *and* histogram.
frequency table **(p. 582)** A data display that groups data into intervals.	Interval / Tally / Frequency: 0–9, ǁ, 2; 10–19, , 0; 20–29, ǁǁ, 4
function **(p. 386)** A relation with the property that for each input there is *exactly one* output.	The relation (1, 0), (2, 1), (3, 0), (4, 1), (5, 0) is a function, because each input is paired with exactly one output. The relation (1, 0), (2, 0), (2, 1), (3, 0), (3, 1), (3, 2) is not a function, because the inputs 2 and 3 are each paired with more than one output.
function form of an equation **(p. 393)** An equation in x and y is in function form if it is solved for y.	The equation $y - 2x = 8$ can be written in function form as $y = 2x + 8$.
function notation **(p. 426)** The use of the symbol $f(x)$, instead of y, in an equation to represent the output of the function f for the input x. The symbol $f(x)$ is read "f of x."	The function $y = 3x - 5$ can be written in function notation as $f(x) = 3x - 5$.
g	
geometric sequence **(p. 692)** A sequence in which the ratio of any term to the previous term is constant.	1, 2, 4, 8, 16, . . . is a geometric sequence with a common ratio of 2.

Glossary

	Example
graph of a linear inequality in two variables (p. 436) The set of points in a coordinate plane that represent all the solutions of the inequality.	$y \geq x + 3$ The graph of $y \geq x + 3$ is the shaded half-plane.
graph of an equation in two variables (p. 392) The set of points in a coordinate plane that represent all the solutions of the equation.	$y = -x + 1$
greatest common factor (GCF) (p. 177) The greatest whole number that is a common factor of two or more nonzero whole numbers.	The GCF of 30 and 54 is 6. The GCF of 30, 60, and 75 is 15.

h

half-plane (p. 436) All points on one side of a line in a coordinate plane.	*See* graph of a linear inequality in two variables.
height of a cone (p. 546) The distance between the vertex and the center of the base.	vertex slant height l height h radius r
height of a parallelogram (p. 521) The perpendicular distance between the side whose length is the base and the opposite side.	*See* parallelogram.
height of a pyramid (p. 544) The perpendicular distance between the base and the vertex.	*See* regular pyramid.
height of a trapezoid (p. 522) The perpendicular distance between the sides whose lengths are the bases.	*See* trapezoid.
heptagon (p. 516) A polygon with 7 sides.	

	Example
hexagon (p. 516) A polygon with 6 sides.	
histogram (p. 583) A data display showing data from a frequency table.	
hypotenuse (p. 465) The side of a right triangle that is opposite the right angle.	
I	
image (p. 729) The new figure formed by a transformation. The image of point A is written A'.	*See* translation, reflection, rotation, *and* dilation.
independent events (p. 634) Two events such that the occurrence of one event does not affect the probability of the occurrence of the other event.	You roll a number cube twice. The events "roll a 3 first" and "then roll a 4" are independent events.
inequality (p. 138) A mathematical statement formed by placing an inequality symbol between two expressions.	$4 > -7$ and $5x - 3 \le 2$ are inequalities.
input (p. 385) A number in the domain of a relation.	*See* relation.
integers (p. 22) The numbers . . . , −3, −2, −1, 0, 1, 2, 3, . . . consisting of the negative integers, zero, and the positive integers.	−9 and 23 are integers. −9.25 and $23\frac{1}{2}$ are *not* integers.
interest (p. 362) The amount earned or paid for the use of money.	*See* simple interest *and* compound interest.
interior angle of a polygon (p. 722) An angle inside the polygon.	 $\angle 1$ is an interior angle of $\triangle ABC$. $\angle 2$ is an exterior angle of $\triangle ABC$.

	Example
interquartile range (p. 590) The difference of the upper quartile and the lower quartile of a data set.	*See* box-and-whisker plot.
inverse operations (p. 91) Two operations that undo each other.	Addition and subtraction are inverse operations. Multiplication and division are inverse operations.
irrational number (p. 470) A number that cannot be written as a quotient of two integers. The decimal form of an irrational number neither terminates nor repeats.	$\sqrt{3}$, π, and 0.202002000. . . are irrational numbers.

L

lateral area of a cylinder (p. 540) The area of the curved surface of the cylinder.	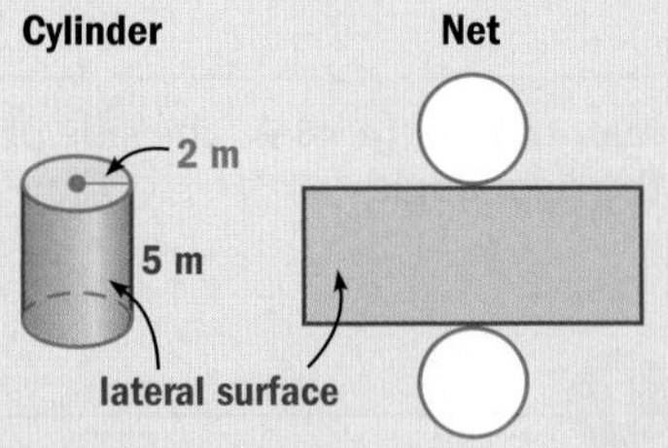 Cylinder / Net: 2 m, 5 m, lateral surface Lateral area $= (2 \cdot \pi \cdot 2)(5)$ $= 20\pi$ $\approx 62.8 \text{ m}^2$
lateral area of a prism (p. 539) The sum of the areas of the lateral faces of the prism.	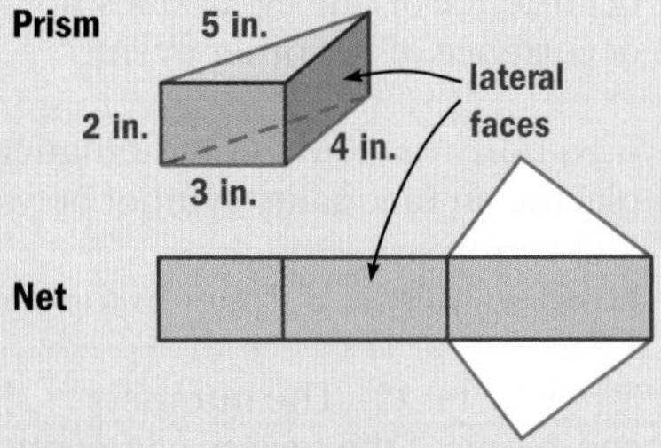 Prism: 5 in., 2 in., 4 in., 3 in., lateral faces; Net Lateral area $= 2(3) + 2(4) + 2(5)$ $= 24 \text{ in.}^2$
lateral faces of a prism (p. 539) The faces of the prism that are not bases.	*See* lateral area of a prism.
lateral surface of a cylinder (p. 540) The curved surface of the cylinder.	*See* lateral area of a cylinder.

	Example
least common denominator (LCD) **(p. 188)** The least common multiple of the denominators of two or more fractions.	The LCD of $\frac{3}{4}$ and $\frac{5}{6}$ is 12, the LCM of 4 and 6.
least common multiple (LCM) **(p. 187)** The least number that is a common multiple of two or more numbers.	The LCM of 6 and 10 is 30. The LCM of 4, 5, and 6 is 60.
legs of a right triangle **(p. 465)** The two sides of a right triangle that form the right angle.	*See* hypotenuse.
like terms **(p. 78)** Terms that have identical variable parts. Two or more constant terms are also like terms.	In the expression $x + 5 - 7x + 1$, x and $-7x$ are like terms, and 5 and 1 are like terms.
linear equation in two variables **(p. 392)** An equation whose graph is a line.	*See* graph of an equation in two variables.
linear inequality in two variables **(p. 436)** An inequality that is the result of replacing the equal sign in a linear equation in two variables with <, ≤, >, or ≥.	$3x - 7y < -1$ and $y \geq x + 4$ are linear inequalities in two variables.
line of reflection **(p. 734)** The line in which a figure is flipped when the figure undergoes a reflection.	*See* reflection.
line of symmetry **(p. 735)** A line that divides a figure into two parts that are reflections of each other in the line.	*See* line symmetry.
line symmetry **(p. 735)** A figure has line symmetry if a line, called the line of symmetry, divides the figure into two parts that are reflections of each other in the line.	A square has 4 lines of symmetry.
lower extreme **(p. 588)** The least value in a data set.	*See* box-and-whisker plot.
lower quartile **(p. 588)** The median of the lower half of an ordered data set.	*See* box-and-whisker plot.

m

margin of error **(p. 610)** The margin of error of a random sample defines an interval centered on a sample percent in which a population percent is most likely to lie.	A prediction that you will get 58% of the votes in an election, with a margin of error of ±4%, means that your percent of the votes is most likely to lie between 54% and 62%.

	Example
markup (p. 357) The increase from the wholesale price of an item to the retail price.	The wholesale price of a gallon of milk is \$2.30, but the store sells it for \$3.19. The markup is \$.89.
maximum value of a function (p. 681) The y-coordinate of the highest point on the graph of the function. A quadratic function $y = ax^2 + bx + c$ has a maximum value when $a < 0$.	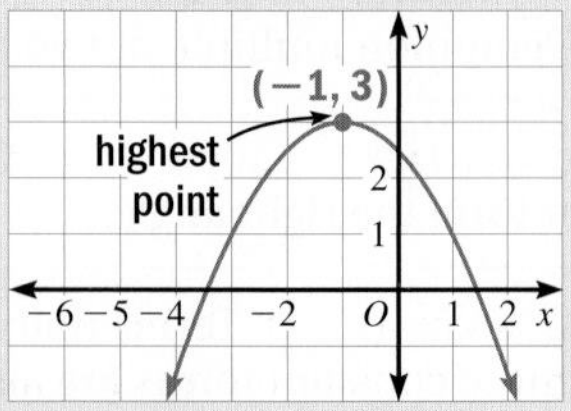 The maximum value of $y = -\frac{1}{2}x^2 - x + \frac{5}{2}$ is 3.
midpoint of a segment (p. 478) The point on the segment that is equally distant from the endpoints.	 M is the midpoint of $\overline{AB}$.
minimum value of a function (p. 681) The y-coordinate of the lowest point on the graph of the function. A quadratic function $y = ax^2 + bx + c$ has a minimum value when $a > 0$.	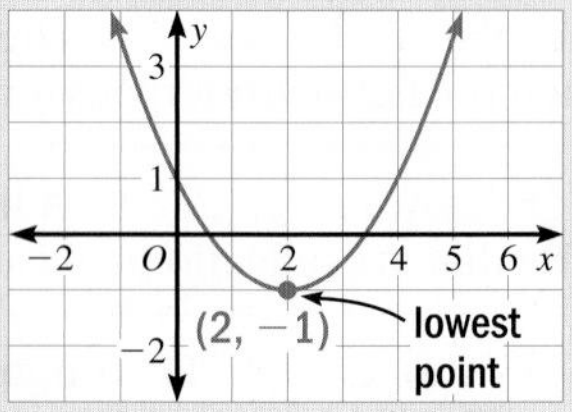 The minimum value of $y = \frac{1}{2}x^2 - 2x + 1$ is -1.
monomial (p. 174) A number, a variable, or the product of a number and one or more variables raised to whole number powers.	$8xy$, $5a^3$, n^2m, p, and 12 are all monomials.
multiple (p. 187) The product of a number and any nonzero whole number.	The multiples of 7 are 7, 14, 21, 28, ...
multiplicative identity (p. 64) The number 1 is the multiplicative identity, because the product of any number and 1 is the number.	$5 \cdot 1 = 5$ $a \cdot 1 = a$
multiplicative inverse (p. 247) The multiplicative inverse of a nonzero number $\frac{a}{b}$, where $a \neq 0$ and $b \neq 0$, is its reciprocal $\frac{b}{a}$. The product of a number and its multiplicative inverse is 1.	The multiplicative inverse of $\frac{5}{3}$ is $\frac{3}{5}$, so $\frac{5}{3} \cdot \frac{3}{5} = 1$.

	Example
mutually exclusive events (p. 627) Events that have no outcomes in common; also called disjoint events.	*See* disjoint events.
n	
negative integers (p. 22) The integers that are less than 0.	$-1, -2, -3, -4, \ldots$
net (p. 538) A two-dimensional representation of a solid. The surface area of a solid is equal to the area of its net.	*See* lateral area of a cylinder *and* lateral area of a prism.
***n* factorial** (p. 615) For any positive integer n, the product of the integers from 1 to n is called n factorial and is written $n!$.	$5! = 5 \cdot 4 \cdot 3 \cdot 2 \cdot 1 = 120$
nonlinear function (p. 680) A function whose graph is not a line.	A quadratic function is a nonlinear function. *See* parabola.
numerical data (p. 596) Data that consist of numbers.	A list of heights is a set of numerical data.
numerical expression (p. 5) An expression that consists of numbers and operations.	$5(2) + 7$ is a numerical expression.
o	
octagon (p. 516) A polygon with 8 sides.	
odds against (p. 308) When all outcomes are equally likely, the ratio of the number of unfavorable outcomes to the number of favorable outcomes is called the odds against an event.	When you randomly choose an integer from 1 to 10, the odds against choosing an integer divisible by 3 are $\frac{7}{3}$, or 7 to 3.
odds in favor (p. 308) When all outcomes are equally likely, the ratio of the number of favorable outcomes to the number of unfavorable outcomes is called the odds in favor of an event.	When you randomly choose an integer from 1 to 10, the odds in favor of choosing an integer divisible by 3 are $\frac{3}{7}$, or 3 to 7.
opposites (p. 23) Two numbers that have the same absolute value but different signs.	-4 and 4 are opposites.

	Example
ordered pair (p. 47) A pair of numbers (x, y) that can be used to represent a point in a coordinate plane. The first number is the x-coordinate, and the second number is the y-coordinate.	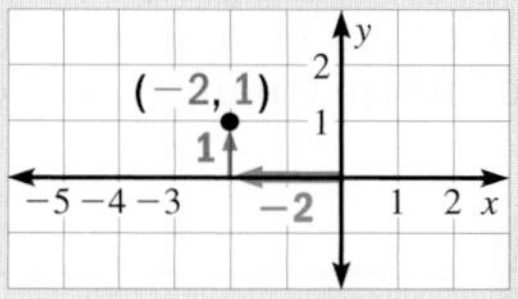 $(-2, 1)$
order of operations (p. 16) A set of rules for evaluating an expression involving more than one operation.	To evaluate $5 - 2^2$, evaluate the power before subtracting: $5 - 2^2 = 5 - 4 = 1$
origin (p. 47) The point (0, 0) where the x-axis and the y-axis meet in a coordinate plane.	*See* coordinate plane.
outcomes (p. 306) The possible results of an experiment.	When you toss a coin, the outcomes are heads and tails.
output (p. 385) A number in the range of a relation.	*See* relation.
overlapping events (p. 627) Events that have one or more outcomes in common.	When you roll a number cube, the events "roll a 3" and "roll an odd number" are overlapping events.

p

parabola (p. 680) A U-shaped curve that is the graph of a quadratic function.	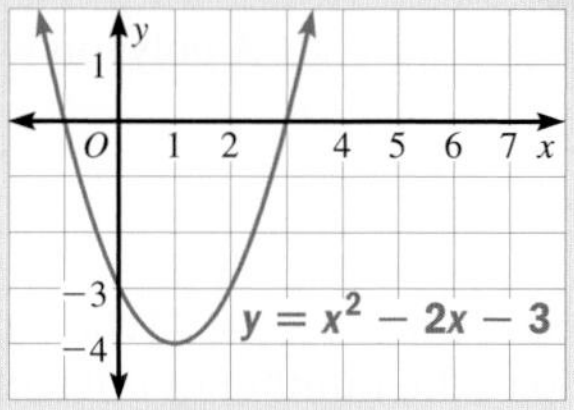 $y = x^2 - 2x - 3$ The graph of $y = x^2 - 2x - 3$ is a parabola.
parallelogram (p. 517) A quadrilateral with both pairs of opposite sides parallel.	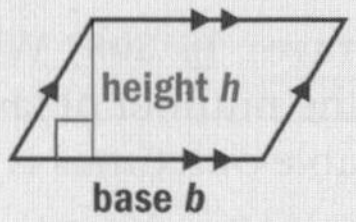 height h base b
pentagon (p. 516) A polygon with 5 sides.	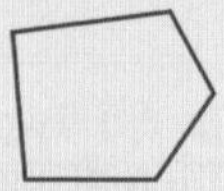
percent (p. 329) A ratio whose denominator is 100. The symbol for percent is %.	$\frac{7}{25} = \frac{7 \cdot 4}{25 \cdot 4} = \frac{28}{100} = 28\%$

	Example
percent of change **(p. 352)** A percent that indicates how much a quantity increases or decreases with respect to the original amount. Percent of change, $p\% = \frac{\text{Amount of increase or decrease}}{\text{Original amount}}$	The percent of change $p\%$ from 12 to 20 is: $p\% = \frac{20 - 12}{12} = \frac{8}{12} \approx 0.667 = 66.7\%$
percent of decrease **(p. 352)** The percent of change in a quantity when the new amount is less than the original amount.	*See* percent of change.
percent of increase **(p. 352)** The percent of change in a quantity when the new amount is greater than the original amount.	*See* percent of change.
perfect square **(p. 454)** A number that is the square of an integer.	36 is a perfect square, because $36 = 6^2$.
permutation **(p. 615)** An arrangement of objects in which order is important.	There are 6 permutations of the 3 letters A, H, T: AHT ATH THA TAH HTA HAT
polygon **(p. 516)** A closed plane figure whose sides are segments that intersect only at their endpoints.	Polygons Not polygons
polynomial **(p. 651)** A sum of monomials.	*See* monomial, binomial, *and* trinomial.
population **(p. 601)** An entire group about which information is gathered.	If a biologist wants to determine the average age of the elephants in a wildlife refuge, the population consists of every elephant in the refuge.
positive integers **(p. 22)** The integers that are greater than 0.	1, 2, 3, 4, . . .
power **(p. 10)** The result of a repeated multiplication of the same factor. A power can be expressed using a base and an exponent.	64 is a power, because $64 = 4 \cdot 4 \cdot 4$, or $64 = 4^3$.
prime factorization **(p. 173)** A whole number written as the product of prime factors.	The prime factorization of 60 is $2 \cdot 2 \cdot 3 \cdot 5 = 2^2 \cdot 3 \cdot 5$.

Glossary

	Example
prime number (p. 173) A whole number greater than 1 that has exactly two whole number factors, 1 and itself.	7 is a prime number, because its only whole number factors are 1 and 7.
principal (p. 362) An amount of money that is deposited or borrowed.	*See* simple interest *and* compound interest.
probability (p. 306) A number from 0 to 1 that measures the likelihood that an event will occur.	*See* experimental probability *and* theoretical probability.
proportion (p. 275) An equation that states that two ratios are equal.	$\frac{2}{7} = \frac{10}{35}$ and $\frac{x}{20} = \frac{4}{5}$ are proportions.
Pythagorean theorem (p. 465) For any right triangle, the sum of the squares of the lengths a and b of the legs equals the square of the length c of the hypotenuse: $a^2 + b^2 = c^2$.	$a = 5$, $c = 13$, $b = 12$ $5^2 + 12^2 = 13^2$
q	
quadrant (p. 47) One of the four regions that a coordinate plane is divided into by the x-axis and the y-axis.	*See* coordinate plane.
quadratic function (p. 679) An equation in two variables that can be written in the form $y = ax^2 + bx + c$, where a, b, and c are constants and $a \neq 0$.	$y = 3x^2 + 5x - 7$ is a quadratic function.
r	
radical expression (p. 454) An expression that involves a radical sign, $\sqrt{\ }$.	$3\sqrt{4a + b}$ is a radical expression.
radius of a circle (p. 528) The distance between the center and any point on the circle.	*See* circle.
random sample (p. 601) A sample in which every member of a population has an equal chance of being selected.	You can select a random sample of your school's student population by having a computer randomly choose 100 student identification numbers.
range of a relation (p. 385) The set of all possible outputs for the relation.	*See* relation.

	Example
ratio (p. 269) A comparison of two numbers using division. The ratio of a to b (where $b \neq 0$) can be written as a to b, as $a : b$, or as $\frac{a}{b}$.	The ratio of 4 to 5 can be written as 4 to 5, as 4 : 5, or as $\frac{4}{5}$.
rational number (p. 219) A number that can be written as a quotient of two integers.	$-\frac{1}{2} = \frac{-1}{2}$, $0 = \frac{0}{1}$, $0.45 = \frac{9}{20}$, $8\frac{3}{4} = \frac{35}{4}$, and $10 = \frac{10}{1}$ are all rational numbers.
real numbers (p. 470) The set of all rational numbers and irrational numbers.	-5, 0, $\frac{2}{3}$, π, 4.37, and 19 are all real numbers.
reciprocals (p. 243) Two nonzero numbers whose product is 1.	5 and $\frac{1}{5}$ are reciprocals.
reflection (p. 734) A transformation in which a figure is reflected, or flipped, in a line, called the line of reflection.	 Reflection in the x-axis
regular polygon (p. 516) A polygon whose sides all have the same length and whose angles all have the same measure.	
regular pyramid (p. 544) A pyramid whose base is a regular polygon and whose lateral faces are all congruent isosceles triangles.	
relation (p. 385) A pairing of numbers in one set (the domain, or set of possible inputs) with numbers in another set (the range, or set of possible outputs). For a relation represented by ordered pairs (x, y), the inputs are the x-coordinates, and the outputs are the y-coordinates.	The set of ordered pairs (1, 0), (2, 1), (3, 0), (4, 1), (5, 0) is a relation. The domain of the relation is the set of inputs: 1, 2, 3, 4, 5. The range of the relation is the set of outputs: 0, 1.

	Example
relatively prime numbers (p. 178) Two or more nonzero whole numbers whose greatest common factor is 1.	10 and 21 are relatively prime because their GCF is 1.
repeating decimal (p. 219) A decimal that has a digit or block of digits that repeats without end. A repeating decimal can be written as a quotient of integers $\frac{a}{b}$, where $b \neq 0$.	0.3333. . . and $6.\overline{15}$ are repeating decimals. $0.3333\ldots = \frac{1}{3}$ $6.\overline{15} = 6\frac{15}{99} = 6\frac{5}{33}$
rhombus (p. 517) A parallelogram with 4 congruent sides.	
rise (p. 404) The vertical change between two points on a line.	*See* slope.
rotation (p. 741) A transformation in which a figure is turned through a given angle, called the angle of rotation, and in a given direction about a fixed point, called the center of rotation.	 45° clockwise rotation about the origin
rotational symmetry (p. 743) A figure has rotational symmetry if a rotation of 180° or less clockwise (or counterclockwise) about its center produces an image that fits exactly on the original figure.	 A square has 180° rotational symmetry. A square also has 90° clockwise (or counterclockwise) rotational symmetry.
run (p. 404) The horizontal change between two points on a line.	*See* slope.

S

	Example
sample (p. 601) A part of a population.	To predict the results of an election, a survey is given to a sample of voters.
scale (p. 300) A ratio that gives the relationship between the dimensions of a scale drawing or a scale model and the actual dimensions of the object.	The scale 1 cm : 100 m means that 1 centimeter in the scale drawing represents an actual distance of 100 meters.
scale drawing (p. 300) A two-dimensional drawing that is similar to the object it represents.	A map is a scale drawing of the land area it shows.
scale factor (p. 747) For a dilation, the ratio of a side length of the image to the corresponding side length of the original figure.	*See* dilation.
scale model (p. 300) A three-dimensional model that is similar to the object it represents.	A globe is a scale model of Earth.
scatter plot (p. 48) A graph in a coordinate plane that displays paired data. Each data pair is plotted as a point.	*See* best-fitting line.
scientific notation (p. 204) A number is written in scientific notation if it has the form $c \times 10^n$ where $1 \le c < 10$ and n is an integer.	In scientific notation, 253,000 is written as 2.53×10^5, and 0.00047 is written as 4.7×10^{-4}.
self-selected sample (p. 601) A sample in which members of a population can select themselves by volunteering.	You put a survey questionnaire in the mailbox of each teacher at your school. The group of all teachers who answer the questionnaire is a self-selected sample of the school's teacher population.
sequence (p. 692) An ordered list of numbers.	1, 5, 9, 13, 17, . . .
similar figures (p. 288) Figures that have the same shape but not necessarily the same size. Corresponding angles of similar figures are congruent, and the ratios of the lengths of corresponding sides are equal. The symbol ~ indicates that two figures are similar.	L 4 m N, 3 m, 5 m, M; P 8 m R, 6 m, 10 m, Q $\triangle LMN \sim \triangle PQR$

	Example
simple interest **(p. 362)** Interest that is earned or paid only on the principal. Simple interest I is the product of the principal P, the annual interest rate r (written as a decimal), and the time t in years: $I = Prt$ The balance A of an account that earns simple annual interest is $A = P + Prt$, or $A = P(1 + rt)$.	You deposit \$500 into a savings account that earns 2.5% simple annual interest. After 3 years, the interest earned is $I = Prt = (500)(0.025)(3) = \$37.50$, and your account balance is $\$500 + \$37.50 = \$537.50$.
simplest form of a fraction **(p. 183)** A fraction is in simplest form when its numerator and denominator are relatively prime.	The simplest form of the fraction $\frac{8}{12}$ is $\frac{2}{3}$.
simplest form of a radical expression **(p. 458)** A radical expression is in simplest form when (1) no factor of the expression under the radical sign is a perfect square other than 1, and (2) there are no fractions under the radical sign and no radical sign in the denominator of any fraction.	In simplest form, $\sqrt{72}$ is written as $6\sqrt{2}$.
sine **(p. 494)** For a right triangle, the sine of an acute angle A ($\sin A$) is the ratio of the length of the side opposite $\angle A$ to the length of the hypotenuse.	*See* trigonometric ratio.
slant height of a cone **(p. 546)** The distance between the vertex and any point on the edge of the base.	*See* height of a cone.
slant height of a pyramid **(p. 544)** The height of a triangular lateral face of the pyramid.	*See* regular pyramid.
slope **(p. 404)** The slope of a nonvertical line is the ratio of the rise (vertical change) to the run (horizontal change) between any two points on the line.	run = 5 rise = −2 The slope of the line shown is: $\text{slope} = \frac{\text{rise}}{\text{run}} = \frac{-2}{5} = -\frac{2}{5}$
slope-intercept form **(p. 412)** The form of a linear equation $y = mx + b$ where m is the slope and b is the y-intercept.	$y = 3x + 7$ is in slope-intercept form. The slope is 3 and the y-intercept is 7.
solution of a linear inequality in two variables **(p. 436)** An ordered pair that produces a true statement when the coordinates of the ordered pair are substituted for the variables in the inequality.	(0, 1) is a solution of the linear inequality $3x - 7y < -1$, because $3(0) - 7(1) < -1$.

	Example
solution of a linear system **(p. 431)** An ordered pair that is a solution of each equation in the system. A solution of a linear system occurs at an intersection point of the graphs of the equations in the system.	$(-1, 3)$ is the solution of this linear system: $y = -2x + 1$ $y = 3x + 6$
solution of an equation **(p. 85)** A number that produces a true statement when it is substituted for the variable in the equation.	The solution of the equation $8 - a = 10$ is -2, because $8 - (-2) = 10$.
solution of an equation in two variables **(p. 391)** An ordered pair that produces a true statement when the coordinates of the ordered pair are substituted for the variables in the equation.	$(2, 1)$ is a solution of the equation $3x - 4y = 2$, because $3(2) - 4(1) = 2$.
solution of an inequality **(p. 138)** The set of all numbers that produce true statements when substituted for the variable in the inequality.	The solution of the inequality $4n < 36$ is $n < 9$, because any number less than 9, when substituted for n, makes $4n < 36$ a true statement.
solving an equation **(p. 86)** Finding all the solutions of the equation.	To solve the equation $3x = 15$, find the number that can be multiplied by 3 to equal 15. Because $3(5) = 15$, the solution of $3x = 15$ is 5.
square root **(p. 453)** A square root of a number n is a number m such that $m^2 = n$. The radical sign, $\sqrt{\ }$, represents a nonnegative square root.	The square roots of 25 are 5 and -5, because $5^2 = 25$ and $(-5)^2 = 25$. So, $\sqrt{25} = 5$ and $-\sqrt{25} = -5$.
standard form of a polynomial **(p. 652)** A polynomial is written in standard form if all like terms are combined and the terms are arranged so that the degree of each term decreases or stays the same from left to right.	The expression $3(x^2 + 5) - x^2 - 3$ can be written as $2x^2 + 12$, a polynomial in standard form.
stem-and-leaf plot **(p. 581)** A display that organizes data based on their digits.	**stems** **leaves** 10 | 8 11 | 2 2 5 12 | 1 3 Key: 10 | 8 = 108
stratified sample **(p. 601)** A sample in which a population is divided into distinct groups. Members are selected from each group.	You can select a stratified sample of your school's student population by choosing 20 students from each grade level.

Glossary

	Example
supplementary angles (p. 709) Two angles whose measures have a sum of 180°.	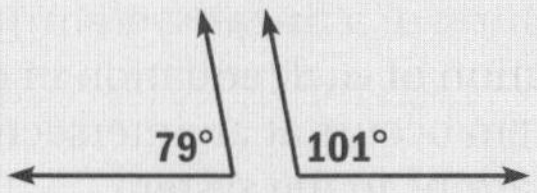 79° 101°
surface area of a solid (p. 538) The sum of the areas of the solid's faces.	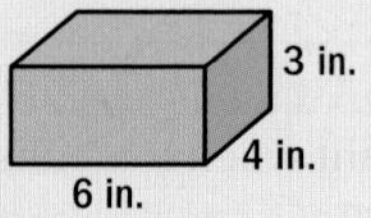 3 in. 4 in. 6 in. Surface area $= 2(6)(4) + 2(6)(3) + 2(4)(3)$ $= 108 \text{ in.}^2$
systematic sample (p. 601) A sample in which a rule is used to select members of a population.	You can select a systematic sample of your school's student population by giving a questionnaire to every tenth student on an alphabetical list of all students at the school.
system of linear equations (p. 431) Two or more linear equations with the same variables; also called a linear system.	The two equations shown below form a linear system: $y = -2x + 1$ $y = 3x + 6$
t	
tangent (p. 489) For a right triangle, the tangent of an acute angle A ($\tan A$) is the ratio of the length of the side opposite $\angle A$ to the length of the side adjacent to $\angle A$.	*See* trigonometric ratio.
terminating decimal (p. 219) A decimal that has a final digit. A terminating decimal can be written as a quotient of integers $\frac{a}{b}$, where $b \neq 0$.	0.8 and 2.307 are terminating decimals. $0.8 = \frac{8}{10} = \frac{4}{5}$ $2.307 = 2\frac{307}{1000} = \frac{2307}{1000}$
terms of an expression (p. 78) The parts of an expression that are added together.	The terms of the expression $5x + (-2x) + 1$ are $5x$, $-2x$, and 1.
terms of a polynomial (p. 651) The monomials that are added together in the polynomial.	The terms of the polynomial $x^2 + 5x - 1$ are x^2, $5x$, and -1.
terms of a sequence (p. 692) The numbers in the sequence.	The fourth term of the sequence 1, 5, 9, 13, 17, . . . is 13.

	Example
tessellation (p. 730) A covering of a plane with a repeating pattern of one or more shapes, with no gaps or overlaps.	
theoretical probability (p. 307) When all outcomes are equally likely, the theoretical probability of an event is the ratio of the number of favorable outcomes to the number of possible outcomes.	A bag of 40 marbles contains 8 blue marbles. The theoretical probability of randomly choosing a blue marble from the bag is $\frac{8}{40} = \frac{1}{5}$, or 0.2.
transformation (p. 729) A change made to the location or to the size of a figure, resulting in a new figure, called the image.	*See* translation, reflection, rotation, *and* dilation.
translation (p. 729) A transformation in which each point of a figure moves the same distance in the same direction.	 $\triangle ABC$ is translated 4 units to the right.
transversal (p. 716) A line that intersects two or more lines at different points.	 Line t is a transversal. $\angle 1$ and $\angle 3$ are corresponding angles. $\angle 2$ and $\angle 3$ are alternate interior angles. $\angle 1$ and $\angle 4$ are alternate exterior angles.
trapezoid (p. 517) A quadrilateral with exactly one pair of parallel sides.	

Glossary

	Example
tree diagram (p. 313) A diagram that uses branching to list all possible choices or outcomes.	H T; H T H T Possibilities: HH HT TH TT
trigonometric ratio (p. 489) A ratio of the lengths of two sides of a right triangle. For an acute angle A of a right triangle, three trigonometric ratios are defined: sine of $\angle A$ ($\sin A$), cosine of $\angle A$ ($\cos A$), and tangent of $\angle A$ ($\tan A$).	B, hypotenuse, c, side opposite $\angle A$, a, C, b, A, side adjacent to $\angle A$ $\sin A = \frac{a}{c}$ $\cos A = \frac{b}{c}$ $\tan A = \frac{a}{b}$
trinomial (p. 651) A polynomial with three terms.	$a^2 + 5a + 6$ is a trinomial.
u	
upper extreme (p. 588) The greatest value in a data set.	*See* box-and-whisker plot.
upper quartile (p. 588) The median of the upper half of an ordered data set.	*See* box-and-whisker plot.
v	
variable (p. 5) A letter that is used to represent one or more numbers.	In the expression $n + 3$, the letter n is the variable.
variable expression (p. 5) An expression that consists of numbers, variables, and operations.	$x - 7$, $\frac{2a}{b}$, and $2t + 3r - 3$ are all variable expressions.
verbal model (p. 6) An expression that describes a problem using words as labels and using math symbols to relate the words.	Distance traveled = Rate of travel • Time traveled
vertical angles (p. 710) A pair of opposite angles formed when two lines intersect at one point.	1, 2, 3, 4 $\angle 1$ and $\angle 3$ are vertical angles. $\angle 2$ and $\angle 4$ are vertical angles.

	Example
vertical line test (p. 387) For a relation represented by a graph, if any vertical line passes through more than one point of the graph, then the relation is not a function. If no vertical line passes through more than one point of the graph, then the relation is a function.	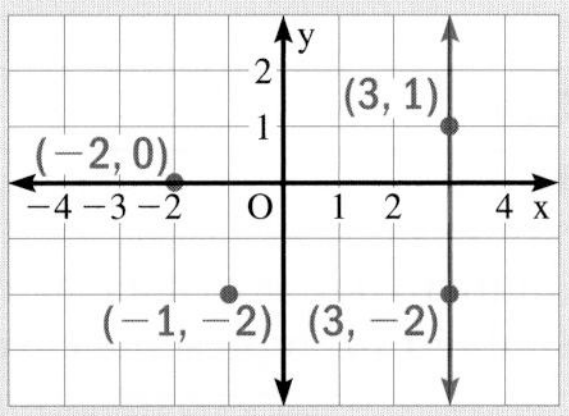 The graph is not a function, because a vertical line passes through two points.

X

***x*-axis (p. 47)** The horizontal number line in a coordinate plane.	*See* coordinate plane.
***x*-coordinate (p. 47)** The first number in an ordered pair representing a point in a coordinate plane.	The *x*-coordinate of the ordered pair (5, −3) is 5.
***x*-intercept (p. 398)** The *x*-coordinate of a point where a graph crosses the *x*-axis.	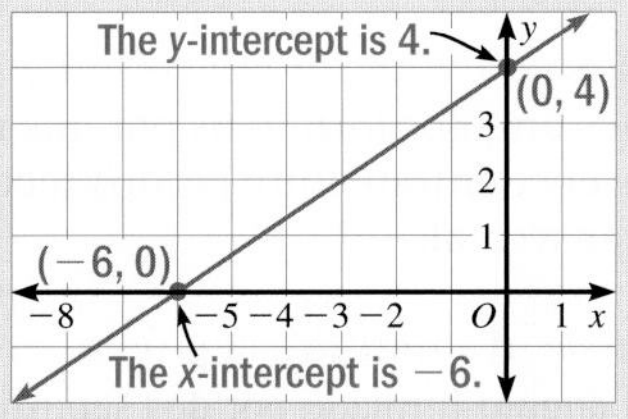

Y

***y*-axis (p. 47)** The vertical number line in a coordinate plane.	*See* coordinate plane.
***y*-coordinate (p. 47)** The second number in an ordered pair representing a point in a coordinate plane.	The *y*-coordinate of the ordered pair (5, −3) is −3.
***y*-intercept (p. 398)** The *y*-coordinate of a point where a graph crosses the *y*-axis.	*See x*-intercept.

Glossary

Glosario

a	Ejemplo
absolute value / valor absoluto **(p. 23)** El valor absoluto de un número a es la distancia entre a y 0 en una recta numérica. El símbolo $\|a\|$ representa el valor absoluto de a.	$\|3\| = 3$ $\|-5\| = 5$ $\|0\| = 0$
additive identity / identidad aditiva **(p. 64)** El número 0 es la identidad aditiva ya que la suma de cualquier número y 0 es ese número.	$-3 + 0 = -3$ $a + 0 = a$
additive inverse / inverso aditivo **(p. 30)** El inverso aditivo de un número a es su opuesto, $-a$. La suma de un número y su inverso aditivo es 0.	El inverso aditivo de 5 es -5, entonces $5 + (-5) = 0$.
alternate exterior angles / ángulos externos alternos **(p. 716)** Dos ángulos formados por dos rectas y una transversal y que se encuentran en el exterior de las dos rectas en lados opuestos de la transversal.	*Ver* transversal / transversal.
alternate interior angles / ángulos internos alternos **(p. 716)** Dos ángulos formados por dos rectas y una transversal y que se encuentran entre las dos rectas en lados opuestos de la transversal.	*Ver* transversal / transversal.
angle of rotation / ángulo de rotación **(p. 741)** En una rotación, el ángulo formado por dos semirrectas trazadas desde el centro de rotación a través de los puntos correspondientes en la figura original y su imagen.	*Ver* rotation / rotación.
annual interest rate / tasa de interés anual **(p. 362)** El porcentaje del capital ganado o pagado por año.	*Ver* simple interest / interés simple *e* compound interest / interés compuesto.
arithmetic sequence / progresión aritmética **(p. 692)** Progresión en la que la diferencia entre los términos consecutivos es constante.	1, 5, 9, 13, 17, . . . es una progresión aritmética en la que la diferencia entre los términos consecutivos es 4.
b	
balance of an account / saldo de una cuenta **(p. 363)** La suma del capital y todo interés ganado.	*Ver* simple interest / interés simple *e* compound interest / interés compuesto.
base of a parallelogram / base de un paralelogramo **(p. 521)** La longitud de cualquier lado del paralelogramo puede usarse como la base.	*Ver* parallelogram / paralelogramo.

Glosario

	Ejemplo
base of a power / base de una potencia **(p. 10)** El número o la expresión que se usa como factor en la multiplicación repetida.	En la potencia 2^7, la base es 2.
bases of a trapezoid / bases de un trapecio **(p. 522)** Las longitudes de los lados paralelos del trapecio.	*Ver* trapezoid / trapecio.
best-fitting line / mejor recta de regresión **(p. 421)** La recta que está situada lo más cerca posible de los puntos de un diagrama de dispersión.	 Se muestra en rojo la mejor recta de regresión del diagrama de dispersión.
biased question / pregunta capciosa **(p. 603)** Pregunta que impulsa a dar una respuesta determinada.	"¿No crees que sería mejor si la escuela construyera un gimnasio nuevo?" es una pregunta capciosa.
biased sample / muestra sesgada **(p. 602)** Muestra que no es representativa de la población.	Los miembros del equipo de baloncesto de una escuela formarían una muestra sesgada si participaran en una encuesta sobre si quieren que se construya un nuevo gimnasio.
binomial / binomio **(p. 651)** Polinomio con dos términos.	$a^2 + 5a$ y $9 - y$ son binomios.
box-and-whisker plot / gráfica de frecuencias acumuladas **(p. 588)** Presentación de datos que organiza los valores de los datos en cuatro grupos usando el extremo inferior, el cuartil inferior, la mediana, el cuartil superior y el extremo superior.	
C	
categorical data / datos categóricos **(p. 596)** Datos que consisten de nombres, etiquetas u otros valores no numéricos.	Una lista de colores de ojos es un conjunto de datos categóricos.
center of a circle / centro de un círculo **(p. 528)** El punto en el interior del círculo que está a la misma distancia de todos los puntos del círculo.	*Ver* circle / círculo.

	Ejemplo
center of dilation / centro de dilatación (p. 747) El punto en torno al cual una figura se amplía o se reduce cuando la figura experimenta una dilatación.	*Ver* dilation / dilatación.
center of rotation / centro de rotación (p. 741) El punto alrededor del cual gira una figura cuando se la hace rotar.	*Ver* rotation / rotación.
circle / círculo (p. 528) El conjunto de todos los puntos de un plano que son equidistantes de un punto dado, llamado centro del círculo.	centro radio r diámetro d circunferencia C
circumference of a circle / circunferencia de un círculo (p. 528) La distancia por el contorno de un círculo.	*Ver* circle / círculo.
coefficient / coeficiente (p. 78) La parte numérica de un término con una variable.	El coeficiente de $-7x$ es -7.
combination / combinación (p. 620) Selección de objetos en la cual el orden en que se eligen los objetos no es importante.	Existen 3 combinaciones de 2 letras tomadas de las letras A, H, T: AH AT HT
common difference / diferencia común (p. 692) La diferencia constante entre los términos consecutivos de una progresión aritmética.	*Ver* arithmetic sequence / progresión aritmética.
common factor / factor común (p. 177) Un número natural que es factor de dos o más números naturales distintos de cero.	Los factores comunes de 12 y 20 son 1, 2 y 4.
common multiple / múltiplo común (p. 187) Un número natural que es múltiplo de dos o más números naturales distintos de cero.	Los múltiplos comunes de 6 y 9 son 18, 36, 54, ...
common ratio / razón común (p. 692) La razón entre cualquier término de una progresión geométrica y el término anterior de la progresión.	*Ver* geometric sequence / progresión geométrica.
complementary angles / ángulos complementarios (p. 709) Dos ángulos cuyas medidas suman 90°.	32° 58°

	Ejemplo
complementary events / sucesos complementarios (p. 630) Dos sucesos disjuntos de modo que debe ocurrir un suceso o el otro.	Cuando lanzas un dado de números, los sucesos "obtener un número impar" y "obtener un número par" son sucesos complementarios.
composite number / número compuesto (p. 173) Un número natural mayor que 1 que tiene factores distintos a sí mismo y a 1.	6 es un número compuesto porque sus factores son 1, 2, 3 y 6.
compound interest / interés compuesto (p. 363) Interés obtenido tanto sobre la inversión inicial como sobre el interés conseguido anteriormente. El saldo A de una cuenta que obtiene interés compuesto anual es $A = P(1 + r)^t$, donde P es el capital, r es la tasa de interés anual (expresada como decimal) y t es el tiempo en años.	Depositas \$1000 en una cuenta al 3% anual de interés compuesto. Después de 5 años, el saldo de la cuenta es $A = P(1 + r)^t = 1000(1 + 0.03)^5 \approx \$1159.27$.
concave / cóncavo (p. 516) Un polígono es cóncavo si un segmento que une dos puntos interiores cualesquiera no está situado completamente dentro del polígono.	*Ver* convex / convexo.
congruent figures / figuras congruentes (p. 290) Figuras que tienen la misma forma y el mismo tamaño. Los ángulos correspondientes y los lados correspondientes de las figuras congruentes son congruentes.	A B C E D F $\triangle ABC \cong \triangle DEF$
constant term / término constante (p. 78) Término que tiene una parte numérica sin variable.	En la expresión $8a + 4$, el término constante es 4.
convenience sample / muestra de conveniencia (p. 601) Muestra en la que se selecciona sólo a los miembros de una población fácilmente accesibles.	Para seleccionar una muestra de conveniencia de la población de estudiantes de una escuela, puedes escoger sólo a los estudiantes que están en tus clases.
convex / convexo (p. 516) Un polígono es convexo si un segmento que une dos puntos interiores cualesquiera está situado completamente dentro del polígono. Un polígono que no es convexo se conoce como *cóncavo*.	Convexo Cóncavo

Glosario

	Ejemplo
coordinate plane / plano de coordenadas (p. 47) Un plano dividido en cuatro cuadrantes por una recta numérica horizontal llamada eje x y una recta numérica vertical llamada eje y.	eje y Cuadrante II, Cuadrante I eje x origen (0, 0) Cuadrante III, Cuadrante IV
corresponding angles / ángulos correspondientes (p. 716) Dos ángulos formados por dos rectas y una transversal y que ocupan posiciones correspondientes.	*Ver* transversal / transversal.
corresponding parts / partes correspondientes (p. 288) Un par de lados o ángulos que tienen la misma posición relativa en dos figuras.	A, B, C, D, E, F $\angle A$ y $\angle D$ son ángulos correspondientes. $\overline{AC}$ y $\overline{DF}$ son lados correspondientes.
cosine / coseno (p. 494) En un triángulo rectángulo, el coseno de un ángulo agudo A (cos A) es la razón entre la longitud del lado adyacente a $\angle A$ y la longitud del hipotenusa.	*See* trigonometric ratio / razón trigonométrica.
counting principle / principio de conteo (p. 314) Si un suceso puede ocurrir de m maneras, y para cada una de estas maneras un segundo suceso puede ocurrir de n maneras, entonces el número de maneras en que los dos sucesos pueden ocurrir juntos es $m \cdot n$.	Tienes 3 camisas y 4 pares de pantalones. El número total de combinaciones de camisas-pantalones que puedes elegir es $3 \cdot 4 = 12$.
cross product / producto cruzado (p. 280) En una proporción, un producto cruzado es el producto del numerador de una de las razones y el denominador de la otra razón. Los productos cruzados de una proporción son iguales.	Los productos cruzados de la proporción $\frac{2}{3} = \frac{8}{12}$ son $2 \cdot 12 = 24$ y $3 \cdot 8 = 24$.

d	Ejemplo
degree of a polynomial / grado de un polinomio (p. 652) El mayor grado de los términos del polinomio.	En el polinomio $a^2 + 4a^2b + 5$, el grado del término a^2 es 2, el grado del término $4a^2b$ es 3 y el grado del término 5 es 0. El grado del polinomio es 3, el grado mayor de los términos.
degree of a term / grado de un término (p. 652) La suma de los exponentes de las variables de un término. El grado de una constante distinta de cero es 0.	*Ver* degree of a polynomial / grado de un polinomio.
dependent events / sucesos dependientes (p. 634) Dos sucesos tales que la ocurrencia de uno de ellos afecta a la ocurrencia del otro.	Una bolsa contiene 4 canicas rojas y 5 verdes. Saca al azar una canica y no la reemplaces; luego saca al azar otra canica. Los sucesos “la primera canica es roja” y “la segunda canica es roja” son sucesos dependientes.
diagonal of a polygon / diagonal de un polígono (p. 518) Segmento que une dos vértices no consecutivos de un polígono.	
diameter of a circle / diámetro de un círculo (p. 528) La distancia que atraviesa el círculo por el centro.	*Ver* circle / círculo.
dilation / dilatación (p. 747) Transformación por la cual una figura se amplía o reduce en torno a un punto fijo, llamado el centro de dilatación.	 $\triangle ABC$ se dilata con respecto al origen usando un factor de escala de 3.
discount / descuento (p. 358) Una cantidad restada del precio habitual de un artículo para obtener el precio de oferta.	El precio original de un abrigo es \$32.99, pero la tienda lo vende a \$25.99. El descuento es \$7.00.
disjoint events / sucesos disjuntos (p. 627) Sucesos que no tienen ningún en común; también se llaman sucesos mutuamente excluyentes.	Al lanzar un dado, los sucesos “obtener un número par” y “obtener un 3” son sucesos disjuntos.

Glosario

	Ejemplo
domain of a relation / dominio de una relación (p. 385) El conjunto de todos los valores de entrada posibles para la relación.	*Ver* relation / relación.
e	
equation / ecuación (p. 85) Un enunciado matemático que se forma colocando un signo de igualdad = entre dos expresiones.	$3x - 2 = 12 + 10x$ es una ecuación.
equation in two variables / ecuación con dos variables (p. 391) Ecuación que tiene dos variables diferentes.	$3x - 4y = 2$ es una ecuación con dos variables.
equivalent equations / ecuaciones equivalentes (p. 91) Ecuaciones que tienen la misma solución o soluciones.	$5y - 2 = 8$ y $5y = 10$ son ecuaciones equivalentes.
equivalent fractions / fracciones equivalentes (p. 182) Fracciones que representan el mismo número.	$\frac{4}{8}$ y $\frac{10}{20}$ son fracciones equivalentes porque ambas representan $\frac{1}{2}$.
equivalent inequalities / desigualdades equivalentes (p. 139) Desigualdades con las mismas soluciones.	$3y + 7 > 25$ y $3y > 18$ son desigualdades equivalentes ya que las soluciones de ambas son todos los números mayores que 6.
equivalent numerical expressions / expresiones numéricas equivalentes (p. 71) Expresiones numéricas que tienen el mismo valor.	$5(10 - 6)$ y $5(10) - 5(6)$ son expresiones numéricas equivalentes porque cada una tiene un valor de 20.
equivalent ratios / razones equivalentes (p. 270) Dos o más razones que tienen el mismo valor.	$\frac{3}{4}$, $\frac{9}{12}$ y $\frac{15}{20}$ son razones equivalentes porque cada una tiene un valor de 0.75.
equivalent variable expressions / expresiones variables equivalentes (p. 72) Expresiones variables que tienen el mismo valor para todos los valores de la/s variable/s.	$5(x + 1) + x$ y $6x + 5$ son expresiones variables equivalentes.
evaluate a variable expression / evaluar una expresión variable (p. 5) Hallar el valor de una expresión variable sustituyendo cada variable por un número y luego hallando el valor de la expresión numérica resultante.	El valor de $2y - 5$ cuando $y = 3$ es $2(3) - 5 = 1$.
event / suceso (p. 306) Caso o colección de casos.	Cuando lanzas un dado, "salir número par" es un suceso.

	Ejemplo
experimental probability / probabilidad experimental **(p. 307)** Una probabilidad basada en el número de ensayos de un experimento. La probabilidad experimental de un suceso es la razón entre el número de sucesos (resultados favorables de un suceso) y el número de ensayos.	Una jugadora de basquetbol ha encestado 30 de los 36 tiros libres que lanzó esta temporada. La probabilidad experimental de que enceste un tiro libre es $\frac{30}{36} = \frac{5}{6}$, o aproximadamente 0.83.
exponent / exponente **(p. 10)** Número o expresión que indica cuántas veces se usa la base como factor en una multiplicación repetida.	En la potencia 2^7, el exponente es 7.
exponential decay / decrecimiento exponencial **(p. 687)** Una cantidad que disminuye muestra decrecimiento exponencial si puede describirse como una función exponencial de la forma $y = ab^x$, donde $a > 0$ y $0 < b < 1$.	La función $y = \left(\frac{1}{3}\right)^x$ muestra decrecimiento exponencial. *Ver* exponential function / función exponencial.
exponential function / función exponencial **(p. 686)** Ecuación con dos variables de la forma $y = ab^x$, donde $a \neq 0$, $b > 0$ y $b \neq 1$.	$y = \left(\frac{1}{3}\right)^x$ $y = 3(2)^x$ $y = 3(2)^x$ e $y = \left(\frac{1}{3}\right)^x$ son funciones exponenciales.
exponential growth / crecimiento exponencial **(p. 687)** Una cantidad que aumenta muestra crecimiento exponencial si puede describirse como una función exponencial de la forma $y = ab^x$, donde $a > 0$ y $b > 1$.	La función $y = 3(2)^x$ muestra crecimiento exponencial. *Ver* exponential function / función exponencial.
exterior angle of a polygon / ángulo externo de un polígono **(p. 723)** Un ángulo adyacente a un ángulo interno del polígono, que se forma extendiendo un lado del polígono.	*Ver* interior angle of a polygon / ángulo interno de un polígono.
f	
factor tree / árbol de factores **(p. 173)** Un diagrama que puede usarse para escribir la descomposición de un número en factores primos.	28 4 • 7 2 • 2 • 7

<table>
<tr><th></th><th>Ejemplo</th></tr>
<tr><td>favorable outcomes / casos favorables (p. 306) Resultados que corresponden a un suceso específico.</td><td>Cuando lanzas un dado de números, los resultados favorables del suceso “obtener un número par” son 2, 4 y 6.</td></tr>
<tr><td>frequency / frecuencia (p. 582) La frecuencia de un intervalo es el número de datos de valores que hay en ese intervalo.</td><td>Ver frequency table / tabla de frecuencias e histogram / histograma.</td></tr>
<tr><td>frequency table / tabla de frecuencias (p. 582) Presentación de datos en la que se agrupan los datos en intervalos iguales.</td><td><table><tr><th>Intervalo</th><th>Marca</th><th>Frecuencia</th></tr><tr><td>0–9</td><td>||</td><td>2</td></tr><tr><td>10–19</td><td></td><td>0</td></tr><tr><td>20–29</td><td>||||</td><td>4</td></tr></table></td></tr>
<tr><td>function / función (p. 386) Una relación con la propiedad de que para cada entrada existe exactamente una salida.</td><td>La relación (1, 0), (2, 1), (3, 0), (4, 1), (5, 0) es una función porque a cada entrada le corresponde exactamente una salida. La relación (1, 0), (2, 0), (2, 1), (3, 0), (3, 1), (3, 2) no es una función porque a las entradas 2 y 3 les corresponde más de una salida.</td></tr>
<tr><td>function form of an equation / forma de función de una ecuación (p. 393) Una ecuación con x e y está en forma de función si resuelve la y.</td><td>La ecuación $y - 2x = 8$ puede escribirse en forma de función como $y = 2x + 8$.</td></tr>
<tr><td>function notation / notación de función (p. 426) El uso del símbolo $f(x)$, en lugar de y, en una ecuación para representar la salida de una función f para la entrada x. El símbolo $f(x)$ se lee “f de x.”</td><td>La función $y = 3x - 5$ puede escribirse como notación de función como $f(x) = 3x - 5$.</td></tr>
<tr><td>g</td><td></td></tr>
<tr><td>geometric sequence / progresión geométrica (p. 692) Progresión en la que la razón entre cualquier término y el término anterior es constante.</td><td>La progresión 1, 2, 4, 8, 16, . . . es una progresión geométrica cuya razón común es 2.</td></tr>
<tr><td>graph of a linear inequality in two variables / gráfica de una desigualdad lineal con dos variables (p. 436) El conjunto de todos los puntos de un plano de coordenadas que representan las soluciones de la desigualdad.</td><td>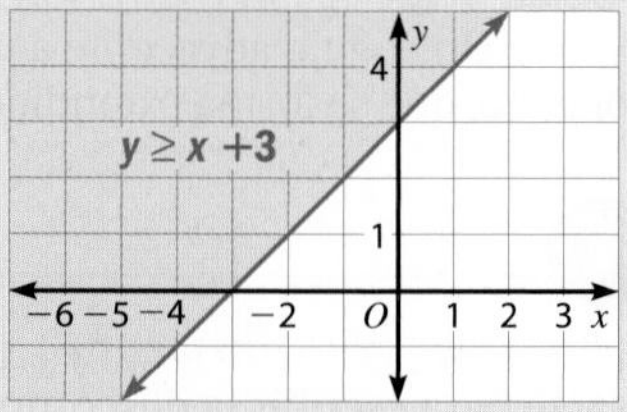

La gráfica de $y \geq x + 3$ es el semiplano sombreado.</td></tr>
</table>

	Ejemplo
graph of an equation in two variables / gráfica de una ecuación con dos variables **(p. 392)** El conjunto de puntos de un plano de coordenadas que representa todas las soluciones de la ecuación.	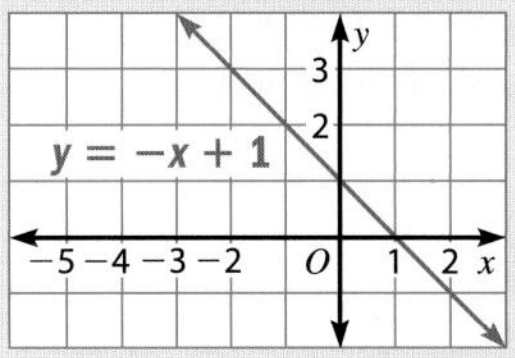 $y = -x + 1$
greatest common factor (GCF) / máximo común divisor (MCD) **(p. 177)** El mayor de los factores comunes de dos o más números naturales distintos de cero.	El MCD de 30 y 54 es 6. El MCD de 30, 60 y 75 es 15.
h	
half-plane / semiplano **(p. 436)** En un plano de coordenadas, la región situada a cada lado de una recta límite.	*Ver* graph of a linear inequality in two variables / gráfica de una desigualdad lineal con dos variables.
height of a cone / altura de un cono **(p. 546)** La distancia entre el vértice y el centro de la base.	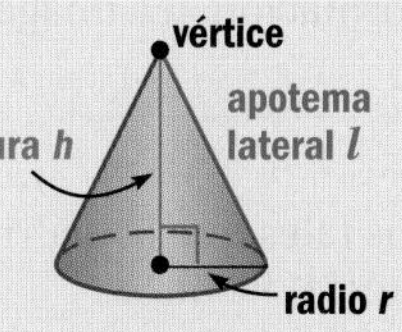 vértice apotema lateral l altura h radio r
height of a parallelogram / altura de un paralelogramo **(p. 521)** La distancia perpendicular entre las bases de un paralelogramo.	*Ver* parallelogram / paralelogramo.
height of a pyramid / altura de una pirámide **(p. 544)** La distancia perpendicular entre la base y el vértice.	*Ver* regular pyramid / pirámide regular.
height of a trapezoid / altura de un trapecio **(p. 522)** La distancia perpendicular entre las bases de un trapecio.	*Ver* trapezoid / trapecio.
heptagon / heptágono **(p. 516)** Un polígono con 7 lados.	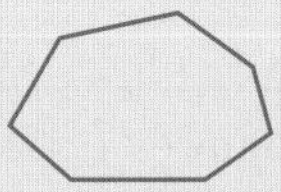
hexagon / hexágono **(p. 516)** Polígono con 6 lados.	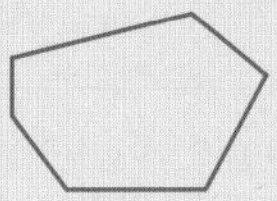

	Ejemplo
histogram / histograma **(p. 583)** Presentación de datos de una tabla de frecuencias.	
hypotenuse / hipotenusa **(p. 465)** El lado de un triángulo rectángulo opuesto al ángulo recto.	
I	
image / imagen **(p. 729)** La nueva figura que resulta tras una transformación. La imagen del punto A se escribe A'.	*Ver* translation / traslación, reflection / reflexión, rotation / rotación *y* dilation / dilatación.
independent events / sucesos independientes **(p. 634)** Dos sucesos tales que la ocurrencia de uno de ellos no afecta a la ocurrencia del otro.	Lanzas un cubo numerado dos veces. Los sucesos “salir primero el 3” y “salir después el 4” son sucesos independientes.
inequality / desigualdad **(p. 138)** Enunciado matemático formado mediante signo de desigualdad entre dos expresiones entre dos expresiones.	$4 > -7$ y $5x - 3 \leq 2$ son desigualdades.
input / entrada **(p. 385)** Número del dominio de una relación.	*Ver* relation / relación.
integers / números enteros **(p. 22)** Los números . . . , −3, −2, −1, 0, 1, 2, 3, . . . que constan de los números enteros negativos, cero y los números enteros positivos.	−9 y 23 son números enteros. −9.25 y $23\frac{1}{2}$ *no* son números enteros.
interest / interés **(p. 362)** La cantidad obtenida o pagada por el uso de dinero.	*Ver* simple interest / interés simple *e* compound interest / interés compuesto.
interior angle of a polygon / ángulo interno de un polígono **(p. 722)** Ángulo que se encuentra dentro del polígono.	$\angle 1$ es una ángulo interno de $\triangle ABC$. $\angle 2$ es una ángulo externo de $\triangle ABC$.

	Ejemplo
interquartile range / rango intercuartílico **(p. 590)** La diferencia entre el cuartil superior y el cuartil inferior de un conjunto de datos.	*Ver* box-and-whisker plot / gráfica de frecuencias acumuladas.
inverse operations / operaciones inversas **(p. 91)** Dos operaciones que se anulan entre sí.	La suma y la resta son operaciones inversas. La multiplicación y la división también son operaciones inversas.
irrational number / número irracional **(p. 470)** Número que no puede escribirse como cociente de dos números enteros. La forma decimal de un número irracional no termina ni se repite.	$\sqrt{3}$, π, y 0.202002000. . . son números irracionales.
L	
lateral area of a cylinder / área lateral de un cilindro **(p. 540)** El área de la superficie curvada del cilindro.	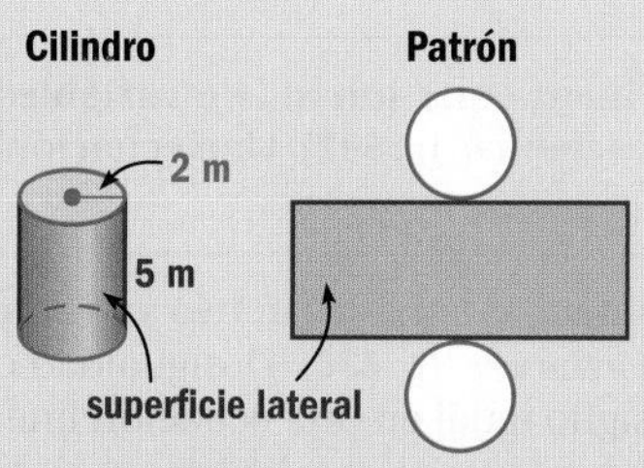 Cilindro, Patrón, 2 m, 5 m, superficie lateral Área lateral $= (2 \cdot \pi \cdot 2)(5)$ $= 20\pi$ $\approx 62.8\ \text{m}^2$
lateral area of a prism / área lateral de un prisma **(p. 539)** La suma de las áreas de las caras laterales del prisma.	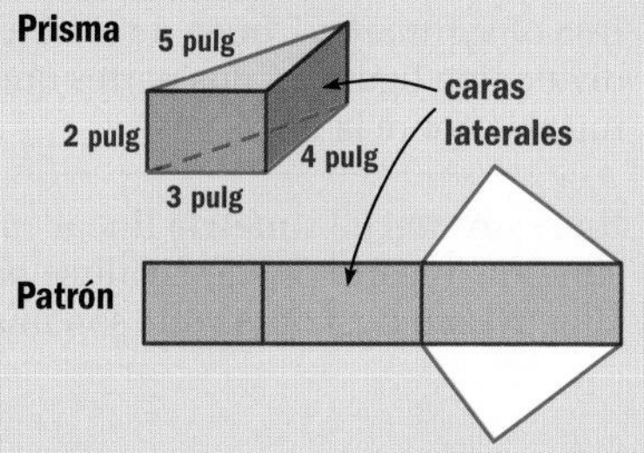 Prisma, 5 pulg, 2 pulg, 3 pulg, 4 pulg, caras laterales, Patrón Área lateral $= 2(3) + 2(4) + 2(5)$ $= 24\ \text{pulg}^2$
lateral faces of a prism / caras laterales de un prisma **(p. 539)** Las caras de un prisma que no son las bases.	*Ver* lateral area of a prism / área lateral de un prisma.
lateral surface of a cylinder / superficie lateral de un cilindro **(p. 540)** La superficie curvada del cilindro.	*Ver* lateral area of a cylinder / área lateral de un cilindro.

	Ejemplo
least common denominator (LCD) / mínimo común denominador (m.c.d.) (p. 188) El múltiplo común menor de los denominadores de dos o más fracciones.	El m.c.d. de $\frac{3}{4}$ y $\frac{5}{6}$ es 12, el m.c.m. de 4 y 6.
least common multiple (LCM) / mínimo común múltiplo (m.c.m.) (p. 187) El menor de los números que es un múltiplo común de dos o más números.	El m.c.m. de 6 y 10 es 30. El m.c.m. de 4, 5 y 6 es 60.
legs of a right triangle / catetos de un triángulo rectángulo (p. 465) En un triángulo rectángulo, los lados adyacentes al ángulo recto.	*Ver* hypotenuse / hipotenusa.
like terms / términos semejantes (p. 78) Términos que tienen las mismas variables. Los términos constantes también son términos semejantes.	En la expresión $x + 5 - 7x + 1$, x y $-7x$ son términos semejantes, y 5 y 1 también son términos semejantes.
linear equation in two variables / ecuación lineal con dos variables (p. 392) Una ecuación cuya gráfica es una recta.	*Ver* graph of an equation in two variables / gráfica de una ecuación con dos variables.
linear inequality in two variables / desigualdad lineal con dos variables (p. 436) Desigualdad que resulta de reemplazar el signo igual en una ecuación lineal con dos variables con $<$, $\leq$, $>$ o $\geq$.	$3x - 7y < -1$ e $y \geq x + 4$ son desigualdades lineales con dos variables.
line of reflection / línea de reflexión (p. 734) La recta sobre la que se voltea una figura cuando dicha figura se refleja.	*Ver* reflection / reflexión.
line of symmetry / línea de simetría (p. 735) Una línea que divide una figura en dos partes que son imágenes reflejas de sí mismas sobre la línea.	*Ver* line symmetry / simetría lineal.
line symmetry / simetría lineal (p. 735) Una figura tiene simetría lineal si puede dividirse por una línea, llamada línea de simetría, en dos partes que son imágenes reflejas entre sí.	Un cuadrado tiene 4 líneas de simetría.
lower extreme / extremo inferior (p. 588) El menor valor en un conjunto de datos.	*Ver* box-and-whisker plot / gráfica de frecuencias acumuladas.
lower quartile / cuartil inferior (p. 588) La mediana de la mitad inferior de un conjunto de datos.	*Ver* box-and-whisker plot / gráfica de frecuencias acumuladas.

m	Ejemplo
margin of error / margen de error **(p. 610)** El margen de error indica un límite acerca de cuánto se preve que diferirían las respuestas obtenidas en una muestra de las obtenidas en la población.	Si una predicción indica que obtendrás el 58% de votos en una elección, con un margen de error del 64%, esto significa que es muy probable que el porcentaje de los votos que obtengas esté entre el 54% y el 62%.
markup / margen de ganancia **(p. 357)** El aumento del precio mayorista de un artículo sobre el precio de venta.	El precio mayorista de un galón de leche es \$2.30, pero la tienda lo vende a \$3.19. El margen de ganancia es \$.89.
maximum value of a function / valor máximo de una función **(p. 681)** La coordenada y del punto más alto en la gráfica de la función. Una función cuadrática $y = ax^2 + bx + c$ tiene un valor máximo cuando $a < 0$.	 El valor máximo de $y = -\frac{1}{2}x^2 - x + \frac{5}{2}$ es 3.
midpoint of a segment / punto medio de un segmento **(p. 478)** El punto del segmento que es equidistante de los extremos.	 M es el punto medio de $\overline{AB}$.
minimum value of a function / valor mínimo de una función **(p. 681)** La coordenada y del punto más bajo en la gráfica de la función. Una función cuadrática $y = ax^2 + bx + c$ tiene un valor mínimo cuando $a > 0$.	 El valor mínimo de $y = \frac{1}{2}x^2 - 2x + 1$ es -1.
monomial / monomio **(p. 174)** Un número, una variable o el producto de un número y una o más variables que tienen exponentes expresados por números naturales.	$8xy$, $5a^3$, n^2m, p y 12 son monomios.
multiple / múltiplo **(p. 187)** Un múltiplo de un número natural es el producto de ese número y cualquier número natural distinto de cero.	Los múltiplos de 7 son 7, 14, 21, 28, ...

	Ejemplo
multiplicative identity / identidad multiplicativa (p. 64) El número 1 es la identidad multiplicativa ya que el producto de cualquier número y 1 es ese número.	$5 \cdot 1 = 5$ $a \cdot 1 = a$
multiplicative inverse / inverso multiplicativo (p. 247) El inverso multiplicativo de un número distinto de cero $\frac{a}{b}$, donde $a \neq 0$ y $b \neq 0$, es su recíproco $\frac{b}{a}$. El producto de un número y su inverso multiplicativo es 1.	El inverso multiplicativo de $\frac{5}{3}$ es $\frac{3}{5}$, entonces $\frac{5}{3} \cdot \frac{3}{5} = 1$.
mutually exclusive events / sucesos mutuamente excluyentes (p. 627) Sucesos que no tienen ningún caso en común.	*Ver* disjoint events / sucesos disjuntos.
n	
negative integers / números enteros negativos (p. 22) Los números enteros menores que 0.	$-1, -2, -3, -4, \ldots$
net / patrón (p. 538) La representación bidimensional de un sólido. El área de la superficie de un sólido es igual al área de su patrón.	*Ver* lateral area of a cylinder / área lateral de un cilindro *y* lateral area of a prism / área lateral de un prisma.
n* factorial / factorial *n (p. 615) Para cualquier número entero positivo *n*, el producto de los números enteros de 1 a *n* se denomina factorial *n* y se escribe *n*!.	$5! = 5 \cdot 4 \cdot 3 \cdot 2 \cdot 1 = 120$
nonlinear function / función no lineal (p. 680) Una función cuya gráfica no es una recta.	Una función cuadrática es una función no lineal. *Ver* parabola / parábola.
numerical data / datos numéricos (p. 596) Datos que consisten de números.	Una lista de alturas es un conjunto de datos numéricos.
numerical expression / expresión numérica (p. 5) Expresión formada por números y operaciones.	$5(2) + 7$ es una expresión numérica.
o	
octagon / octágono (p. 516) Polígono con ocho lados.	
odds against / probabilidad en contra (p. 308) Cuando todos los casos son igualmente posibles, la probabilidad en contra de que ocurra un suceso se define como la razón entre el número de casos desfavorables y el número de casos favorables.	Cuando eliges un número entero al azar de 1 a 10, las probabilidades en contra de que elijas un número entero divisible por 3 son $\frac{7}{3}$ ó 7 a 3.

Glosario

	Ejemplo
odds in favor / probabilidad a favor **(p. 308)** Cuando todos los casos son igualmente posibles, la probabilidad a favor de que ocurra un suceso se define como la razón entre el número de casos favorables y el número de casos desfavorables.	Cuando eliges un número entero al azar de 1 a 10, las probabilidades a favor de que elijas un número entero divisible por 3 son $\frac{3}{7}$ ó 3 a 7.
opposites / opuestos **(p. 23)** Dos números que tienen el mismo valor absoluto pero distinto signo.	-4 y 4 son opuestos.
ordered pair / par ordenado **(p. 47)** Un par de números (x, y) que pueden usarse para representar un punto en un plano de coordenadas. El primer número es la coordenada x, y el segundo número es la coordenada y.	
order of operations / orden de operaciones **(p. 16)** Un conjunto de reglas para evaluar una expresión que incluye más de una operación.	Para evaluar $5 - 2^2$, evalúa la potencia y después resta: $5 - 2^2 = 5 - 4 = 1$
origin / origen **(p. 47)** El punto (0, 0) donde el eje x y el eje y se encuentran en un plano de coordenadas.	*Ver* coordinate plane / plano de coordenadas.
outcomes / casos **(p. 306)** Resultados posibles de un experimento.	Cuando lanzas una moneda, los casos son cara y cruz.
output / salida **(p. 385)** Número que pertenece al rango de una relación.	*Ver* relation / relación.
overlapping events / sucesos superpuestos **(p. 627)** Sucesos que tienen uno o más casos en común.	Al lanzar un dado, los sucesos "obtener un número menor que 3" y "obtener un número par" son sucesos superpuestos.
p	
parabola / parábola **(p. 680)** La gráfica en forma de U de una función cuadrática.	 La gráfica de $y = x^2 - 2x - 3$ es una parábola.

	Ejemplo
parallelogram / paralelogramo **(p. 517)** Cuadrilátero que tiene ambos pares de lados opuestos paralelos.	altura h base b
pentagon / pentágono **(p. 516)** Polígono con cinco lados.	
percent / porcentaje **(p. 329)** Una razón cuyo denominador es 100. El símbolo de porcentaje es %.	$\frac{7}{25} = \frac{7 \cdot 4}{25 \cdot 4} = \frac{28}{100} = 28\%$
percent of change / porcentaje de cambio **(p. 352)** Porcentaje que indica cuánto aumenta o disminuye una cantidad con respecto a la cantidad original. Porcentaje de cambio, $p\% = \frac{\text{Cantidad de aumento o disminución}}{\text{Cantidad original}}$	El porcentaje de cambio, $p\%$, de 12 a 20 es: $p\% = \frac{20 - 12}{12} = \frac{8}{12} \approx 0.667 = 66.7\%$
percent of decrease / porcentaje de disminución **(p. 352)** El porcentaje de cambio de una cantidad cuando la nueva cantidad es menor que la cantidad original.	*Ver* percent of change / porcentaje de cambio.
percent of increase / porcentaje de aumento **(p. 352)** El porcentaje de cambio de una cantidad cuando la nueva cantidad es mayor que la cantidad original.	*Ver* percent of change / porcentaje de cambio.
perfect square / cuadrado perfecto **(p. 454)** Número que es el cuadrado de un número entero.	36 es un cuadrado perfecto ya que $36 = 6^2$.
permutation / permutación **(p. 615)** Disposición de objetos en la que el orden es importante.	Existen 6 permutaciones de las 3 letras A, H, T: AHT ATH THA TAH HTA HAT
polygon / polígono **(p. 516)** Figura plana cerrada cuyos lados son segmentos que se cortan solamente en sus extremos.	Son polígonos No son polígonos
polynomial / polinomio **(p. 651)** Suma de monomios.	*Ver* monomial / monomio, binomial / binomio *y* trinomial / trinomio.

	Ejemplo
population / población (p. 601) El grupo entero sobre el que se desea información.	Una revista invita a sus lectores a enviar por correo las respuestas a un cuestionario sobre la calidad de la revista. La población está formada por todos los lectores de la revista.
positive integers / números enteros positivos (p. 22) Los números enteros mayores que 0.	1, 2, 3, 4, . . .
power / potencia (p. 10) Un producto que se obtiene mediante la multiplicación repetida por el mismo número o expresión. Una potencia se compone de una base y un exponente.	64 es una potencia porque $64 = 4 \cdot 4 \cdot 4$, o $64 = 4^3$.
prime factorization / descomposición en factores primos (p. 173) Número natural escrito como producto de factores primos.	La descomposición en factores primos de 60 es $2 \cdot 2 \cdot 3 \cdot 5 = 2^2 \cdot 3 \cdot 5$.
prime number / número primo (p. 173) Número natural mayor que 1 cuyos únicos factores son 1 y él mismo.	7 es un número primo, porque sus únicos factores son 1 y el mismo número 7.
principal / capital (p. 362) Una cantidad de dinero que se deposita o se pide prestado.	*Ver* simple interest / interés simple *e* compound interest / interés compuesto.
probability / probabilidad (p. 306) Número comprendido entre 0 y 1 que mide la posibilidad de que ocurra un suceso.	*Ver* experimental probability / probabilidad experimental *y* theoretical probability / probabilidad teórica.
proportion / proporción (p. 275) Ecuación que establece que dos razones son iguales.	$\frac{2}{7} = \frac{10}{35}$ y $\frac{x}{20} = \frac{4}{5}$ son proporciones.
Pythagorean theorem / teorema de Pitágoras (p. 465) Para cualquier triángulo rectángulo, la suma de los cuadrados de las longitudes a y b de los catetos es igual al cuadrado de la longitud c de la hipotenusa: $a^2 + b^2 = c^2$.	$a = 5$, $c = 13$, $b = 12$ $5^2 + 12^2 = 13^2$
q	
quadrant / cuadrante (p. 47) Una de las cuatro regiones en las que se divide un plano de coordenadas por el eje x y el eje y.	*Ver* coordinate plane / plano de coordenadas.
quadratic function / función cuadrática (p. 679) Ecuación con dos variables que puede escribirse en la forma $y = ax^2 + bx + c$, donde a, b y c son constantes y $a \neq 0$.	$y = 3x^2 + 5x - 7$ es una función cuadrática.

r	Ejemplo
radical expression / expresión radical (p. 454) Una expresión que involucra un símbolo radical, $\sqrt{\ }$.	$3\sqrt{4a + b}$ es una expresión radical.
radius of a circle / radio de un círculo (p. 528) La distancia desde el centro a cualquier punto del círculo.	*Ver* circle / círculo.
random sample / muestra aleatoria (p. 601) Muestra en la que cada miembro de la población tiene igual probabilidad de ser seleccionado.	Para seleccionar una muestra aleatoria de la población de estudiantes de una escuela, puedes usar la computadora para elegir al azar 100 números de identificación estudiantil.
range of a relation / rango de una relación (p. 385) El conjunto de todas las salidas posibles de una relación.	*Ver* relation / relación.
ratio / razón (p. 269) Comparación entre dos números usando la división. La razón de a a b (donde $b \neq 0$) puede escribirse como a a b, como $a : b$, o como $\frac{a}{b}$.	La razón de 4 a 5 puede escribirse si 4 a 5, si 4 : 5, ó si $\frac{4}{5}$.
rational number / número racional (p. 219) Número que puede escribirse como el cociente de dos números enteros.	$-\frac{1}{2} = \frac{-1}{2}$, $0 = \frac{0}{1}$, $0.45 = \frac{9}{20}$, $8\frac{3}{4} = \frac{35}{4}$ y $10 = \frac{10}{1}$ son todos números racionales.
real numbers / números reales (p. 470) El conjunto de todos los números racionales e irracionales.	$-5, 0, \frac{2}{3}, \pi$, 4.37 y 19 son números reales.
reciprocals / recíprocos (p. 243) Dos números cuyo producto es 1.	5 y $\frac{1}{5}$ son recíprocos.
reflection / reflexión (p. 734) Una transformación que refleja una figura en una línea, llamada línea de reflexión, y crea una imagen espejo de la figura.	Reflexión sobre el eje x
regular polygon / polígono regular (p. 516) Un polígono cuyos lados tienen igual longitud y cuyos ángulos miden lo mismo.	

	Ejemplo
regular pyramid / pirámide regular (p. 544) Pirámide cuya base es un polígono regular y cuyas caras laterales son todos triángulos isósceles congruentes.	vértice altura h apotema lateral l La base es un polígono regular.
relation / relación (p. 385) Correspondencia entre los números de un conjunto (el dominio, o conjunto de entradas posibles) y los números de otro conjunto (el rango, o conjunto de salidas posibles). En una relación representada por pares ordenados (x, y), las entradas son las coordenadas x y las salidas son las coordenadas y.	El conjunto de pares ordenados (1, 0), (2, 1), (3, 0), (4, 1), (5, 0) es una relación. El dominio de la relación es el conjunto de entradas: 1, 2, 3, 4, 5. El rango de la relación es el conjunto de salidas: 0, 1.
relatively prime numbers / números primos relativos (p. 178) Dos o más números enteros positivos distintos de cero cuyo máximo común divisor es 1.	10 y 21 son números primos relativos porque su M.C.D. es 1.
repeating decimal / decimal periódico (p. 219) Un decimal que tiene un dígito o varios dígitos que se repiten indefinidamente. Un decimal periódico puede escribirse como un cociente de números enteros $\frac{a}{b}$, en el que $b \neq 0$.	0.3333. . . y $6.\overline{15}$ son decimales periódicos. $0.3333\ldots = \frac{1}{3}$ $6.\overline{15} = 6\frac{15}{99} = 6\frac{5}{33}$
rhombus / rombo (p. 517) Paralelogramo que tiene los cuatro lados congruentes.	
rise / distancia vertical (p. 404) El cambio vertical entre dos puntos de una recta.	*Ver* slope / pendiente.
rotation / rotación (p. 741) Una transformación que rota una figura por un ángulo dado, llamado ángulo de rotación, y en una dirección dada alrededor de un punto fijo, llamado centro de rotación; también se conoce como giro.	y ángulo de rotación centro de rotación 45° O x 45° de rotación sobre el origen.

	Ejemplo
rotational symmetry / simetría rotacional (p. 743) Una figura tiene simetría rotacional si al girar 180° o menos en sentido de las agujas del reloj (o en contrario) sobre su centro da como resultado una imagen que se corresponde exactamente con la figura original.	90° 180° Un cuadrado tiene simetría rotacional de 180°. Un cuadrado también tiene simetría rotacional al girar 90° en sentido de las agujas del reloj (o en sentido contrario).
run / distancia horizontal (p. 404) El cambio horizontal entre dos puntos de una recta.	*Ver* slope / pendiente.
S	
sample / muestra (p. 601) Una parte de una población.	Para predecir los resultados de una elección, se realiza una encuesta a una muestra de votantes.
scale / escala (p. 300) Razón que relaciona las dimensiones de un dibujo a escala o un modelo a escala con las dimensiones reales.	La escala 1 pulg : 12 pies en un diagrama de planta significa que 1 pulgada en el diagrama de planta representa una distancia real de 12 pies.
scale drawing / dibujo a escala (p. 300) Dibujo bidimensional que es similar al objeto que representa.	Un mapa es un dibujo a escala de la superficie terrestre que muestra.
scale factor / factor de escala (p. 747) En una dilatación, la razón entre una longitud de lado de la imagen y la longitud de lado correspondiente de la figura original.	*Ver* dilation / dilatación.
scale model / modelo a escala (p. 300) Modelo tridimensional que es similar al objeto que representa.	Un globo terráqueo es un modelo a escala de la Tierra.
scatter plot / diagrama de dispersión (p. 48) Gráfica en un plano de coordenadas que muestra pares de datos. Cada par de datos está graficado como un punto.	*Ver* best-fitting line / mejor recta de regresión.
scientific notation / notación científica (p. 204) Un número está escrito en notación científica cuando tiene la forma $c \times 10^n$ donde $1 \le c < 10$ y n es un número entero.	En notación científica, 253,000 se escribe 2.53×10^5, y 0.00047 se escribe 4.7×10^{-4}.

	Ejemplo
self-selected sample / muestra autoseleccionada (p. 601) Muestra en la que los miembros de la población se seleccionan a sí mismos ofreciéndose a participar.	Para obtener una muestra autoseleccionada de la población de estudiantes de una escuela, puedes pedir a los estudiantes que hagan la encuesta que la depositen en un recipiente de recogida.
sequence / progresión (p. 692) Una lista ordenada de números.	1, 5, 9, 13, 17, . . .
similar figures / figuras semejantes (p. 288) Figuras que tienen la misma forma pero no necesariamente el mismo tamaño. Los ángulos correspondientes de las figuras semejantes son congruentes, y las razones de las longitudes de los lados correspondientes son iguales. El símbolo $\sim$ indica que dos figuras son semejantes.	L, 4 m, N, 3 m, 5 m, M; P, 8 m, R, 6 m, 10 m, Q $\triangle LMN \sim \triangle PQR$
simple interest / interés simple (p. 362) Interés obtenido o pagado sólo sobre el capital. El interés simple I es el producto del capital P, la tasa de interés anual r (escrito como decimal), y el tiempo t en años: $I = Prt$ El saldo A de una cuenta que gana interés simple anual es $A = P + Prt$, or $A = P(1 + rt)$.	Depositas \$500 en una caja de ahorro que da un 2.5% de interés simple anual. Después de 3 años, el interés obtenido es $I = Prt = (500)(0.025)(3) = \$37.50$, y el saldo de tu cuenta es $\$500 + \$37.50 = \$537.50$.
simplest form of a fraction / mínima expresión de una fracción (p. 183) Una fracción está en su mínima expresión si el numerador y el denominador son números primos relativos.	La mínima expresión de la fracción $\frac{8}{12}$ es $\frac{2}{3}$.
simplest form of a radical expression / forma simplificada de una expresión radical (p. 458) Una expresión radical está en forma simplificada cuando (1) ningún factor de la expresión bajo el signo radical es un cuadrado perfecto excepto 1, y (2) no hay fracciones debajo del signo radical ni ningún signo radical en el denominador de ninguna fracción.	En forma simplificada, $\sqrt{72}$ se escribe como $6\sqrt{2}$.
sine / seno (p. 494) El seno de un ángulo agudo A de un triángulo rectángulo (sin A) es la razón entre el cateto opuesto $\angle A$ y la hipotenusa.	*Ver* trigonometric ratio / razón trigonométrica.
slant height of a cone / apotema lateral de un cono (p. 546) La distancia entre el vértice y cualquier punto de la arista de la base.	*Ver* height of a cone / altura de un cono.

	Ejemplo
slant height of a pyramid / apotema lateral de una pirámide **(p. 544)** La altura de una cara lateral triangular de la pirámide.	*Ver* regular pyramid / pirámide regular.
slope / pendiente **(p. 404)** La pendiente de una recta no vertical es la razón entre la distancia vertical (cambio vertical) y la distancia horizontal (cambio horizontal) entre dos puntos cualesquiera sobre la recta.	distancia horizontal = 5; distancia vertical = −2 La pendiente de la recta anterior es: pendiente $= \frac{\text{distancia vertical}}{\text{distancia horizontal}} = \frac{-2}{5} = -\frac{2}{5}$
slope-intercept form / forma de pendiente e intersección **(p. 412)** La forma de una ecuación lineal $y = mx + b$ donde m representa la pendiente y b representa la intersección con el eje y.	$y = 3x + 7$ está en la forma de pendiente e intersección. La pendiente es 3 y el punto de intersección de y es 7.
solution of a linear inequality in two variables / solución de una desigualdad lineal con dos variables **(p. 436)** Un par ordenado que produce un enunciado verdadero cuando las coordenadas del par ordenado se sustituyen con las variables de las desigualdad.	(0, 1) es una solución de la desigualdad lineal $3x - 7y < -1$, porque $3(0) - 7(1) < -1$.
solution of a linear system / solución de un sistema lineal **(p. 431)** Un par ordenado que es la solución de cada ecuación en un sistema. Una solución de un sistema lineal se da en un punto de intersección de las gráficas de la ecuaciones del sistema.	(−1, 3) es la solución de este sistema lineal: $y = -2x + 1$ $y = 3x + 6$
solution of an equation / solución de una ecuación **(p. 85)** Un número que, cuando sustituye la variable en la ecuación, hace la ecuación verdadera.	La solución de la ecuación $8 - a = 10$ es −2, ya que $8 - (-2) = 10$.
solution of an equation in two variables / solución de una ecuación con dos variables **(p. 391)** Par ordenado (x, y) que produce una expresión verdadera al sustituir x e y por sus valores en la ecuación.	(2, 1) es una solución de $3x - 4y = 2$, ya que $3(2) - 4(1) = 2$.
solution of an inequality / solución de una desigualdad **(p. 138)** El conjunto de todos los números que, cuando sustituyen la variable en la desigualdad, hacen que la desigualdad sea verdadera.	La solución de la desigualdad $4n < 36$ es $n < 9$, porque cualquier número menor de 9, cuando se reemplaza por n, hace que $4n < 36$, sea un enunciado verdadero.

	Ejemplo
solving an equation / resolver una ecuación **(p. 86)** Hallar todas las soluciones de la ecuación.	Para resolver la ecuación $3x = 15$, halla el número que puede multiplicarse por 3 para obtener 15. Como $3(5) = 15$, la solución de $3x = 15$ es 5.
square root / raíz cuadrada **(p. 453)** La raíz cuadrada de un número n es un número m de modo que $m^2 = n$. El signo radical, $\sqrt{\ }$, representa una raíz cuadrada no negativa.	Las raíces cuadradas de 25 son 5 y -5, ya que $5^2 = 25$ y $(-5)^2 = 25$. Así pues, $\sqrt{25} = 5$ y $-\sqrt{25} = -5$.
standard form of a polynomial / forma usual de un polinomio **(p. 652)** Un polinomio está escrito en forma usual si todos los términos similares están combinados y los términos están ordenados de modo que el grado de cada término disminuye o permanece igual de izquierda a derecha.	La expresión $3(x^2 + 5) - x^2 - 3$ puede escribirse $2x^2 + 12$, a un polinomio en forma usual.
stem-and-leaf plot / tabla arborescente **(p. 581)** Presentación de datos que organiza los datos basándose en sus dígitos.	**raíces** **hojas** 10 | 8 11 | 2 2 5 12 | 1 3 Solución: 10 | 8 = 108
stratified sample / muestra estratificada **(p. 601)** Muestra en la que la población está dividida en grupos diferenciados. Los miembros se seleccionan entre los miembros de cada grupo.	Puedes seleccionar una muestra estratificada de la población de estudiantes de tu escuela escogiendo 20 estudiantes de cada grado.
supplementary angles / ángulos suplementarios **(p. 709)** Dos ángulos cuyas medidas suman 180°.	79° 101°
surface area of a solid / área de la superficie de un sólido **(p. 538)** La suma de las áreas de las caras de un sólido.	3 pulg 4 pulg 6 pulg Área de la superficie $= 2(6)(4) + 2(6)(3) + 2(4)(3)$ $= 108 \text{ pulg}^2$

Glosario

	Ejemplo
systematic sample / muestra sistemática (p. 601) Una muestra en la que se usa una regla para seleccionar a los miembros de una población.	Puedes seleccionar una muestra sistemática de la población de estudiantes de tu escuela dándole un cuestionario a cada décimo estudiante de una lista ordenada alfabéticamente de todos los estudiantes de la escuela.
system of linear equations / sistema de ecuaciones lineales (p. 431) Dos o más ecuaciones lineales con las mismas variables; llamado también sistema lineal.	Las siguientes ecuaciones forman un sistema de ecuaciones lineales: $y = -2x + 1$ $y = 3x + 6$
t	
tangent / tangente (p. 489) En un triángulo rectángulo, la tangente de un ángulo agudo A (tan A) es la razón entre la longitud del lado opuesto $\angle A$ y la longitud del lado adyacente a $\angle A$.	*Ver* trigonometric ratio / razón trigonométrica.
terminating decimal / decimal finito (p. 219) Un decimal que tiene un dígito final. Un decimal finito puede escribirse como un cociente de números enteros $\frac{a}{b}$, en el que $b \neq 0$.	0.8 y 2.307 son decimales finitos. $0.8 = \frac{8}{10} = \frac{4}{5}$ $2.307 = 2\frac{307}{1000} = \frac{2307}{1000}$
terms of an expression / términos de una expresión (p. 78) Las partes de una expresión que se suman.	Los términos de la expresión $5x + (-2x) + 1$ son $5x$, $-2x$ y 1.
terms of a polynomial / términos de un polinomio (p. 651) Los monomios que se suman en el polinomio.	Los términos del polinomio $x^2 + 5x - 1$ son x^2, $5x$ y -1.
terms of a sequence / términos de una progresión (p. 692) Los números de una progresión.	El cuarto término de la progresión 1, 5, 9, 13, 17, . . . es 13.
tessellation / teselado (p. 730) La cobertura de un plano con copias congruentes del mismo patrón de modo que no haya espacios de separación ni superposiciones.	
theoretical probability/probabilidad teórica (p. 307) Cuando todos los casos son igualmente probables, la probabilidad teórica de un suceso es la razón entre el número de casos favorables y el número de casos posibles.	Una bolsa de 40 canicas contiene 8 canicas azules. La probabilidad teórica de tomar al azar una canica azul de la bolsa es: $\frac{8}{40} = \frac{1}{5}$, o 0.2.

	Ejemplo
transformation / transformación **(p. 729)** Cambio en la ubicación o el tamaño de una figura que da como resultado una nueva figura, que se llama imagen.	*Ver* translation / traslación, reflection / reflexión, rotation / rotación *y* dilation / dilatación.
translation / traslación **(p. 729)** Una transformación en la que se mueve cada punto de una figura la misma distancia en la misma dirección.	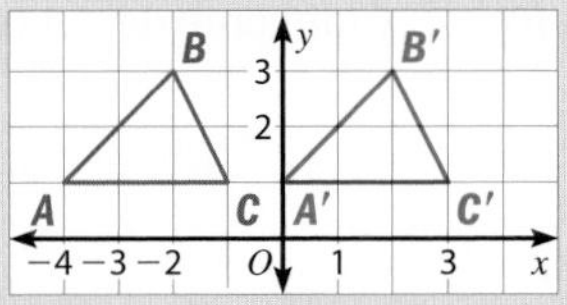 B, B′, A, C, A′, C′, y, x, O, −4, −3, −2, 1, 3, 2, 3 $\triangle ABC$ se traslada 4 unidades a la derecha.
transversal / transversal **(p. 716)** Recta que corta a dos o más rectas en distintos puntos.	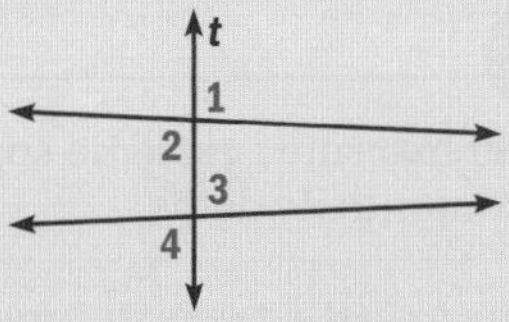 t, 1, 2, 3, 4 La recta t es una transversal. $\angle 1$ y $\angle 3$ son ángulos correspondientes. $\angle 2$ y $\angle 3$ son ángulos internos alternos. $\angle 1$ y $\angle 4$ son ángulos externos alternos.
trapezoid / trapecio **(p. 517)** Cuadrilátero que tiene exactamente un par de lados paralelos.	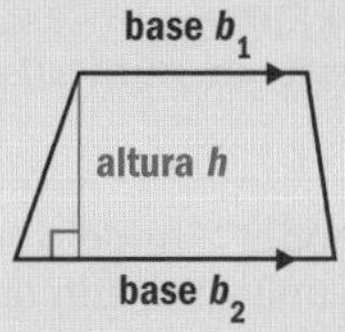 base b_1, altura h, base b_2
tree diagram / diagrama de árbol **(p. 313)** Un diagrama que usa ramas para enumerar todas las opciones o casos posibles.	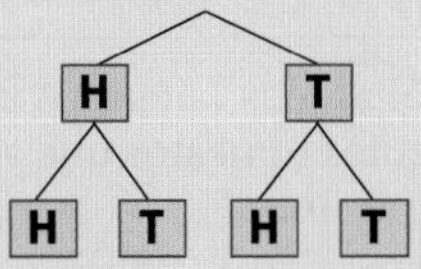 H, T, H, T, H, T Posibilidades: HH HT TH TT

Glosario

Glosario

	Ejemplo
trigonometric ratio / razón trigonométrica **(p. 489)** Una razón entre las longitudes de dos lados de un triángulo rectángulo. En un ángulo agudo A de un triángulo rectángulo, las razones se definen de esta manera: seno de $\angle A$ (sen A), coseno de $\angle A$ (cos A) y tangente de $\angle A$ (tan A).	lado opuesto $\angle A$; hipotenusa; B, C, A, a, b, c; lado adyacente a $\angle A$ sen $A = \frac{a}{c}$ cos $A = \frac{b}{c}$ tan $A = \frac{a}{b}$
trinomial / trinomio **(p. 651)** Polinomio de tres términos.	$a^2 + 5a + 6$ es un trinomio.

u

upper extreme / extremo superior **(p. 588)** El valor mayor de un conjunto de datos.	*Ver* box-and-whisker plot / gráfica de frecuencias acumuladas.
upper quartile / cuartil superior **(p. 588)** La mediana de la mitad superior de un conjunto de datos ordenados.	*Ver* box-and-whisker plot / gráfica de frecuencias acumuladas.

v

variable / variable **(p. 5)** Letra que sirve para representar uno o más números.	En la expresión $n + 3$, la letra n es la variable.
variable expression / expresión variable **(p. 5)** Una expresión que consiste de números, variables y operaciones.	$x - 7$, $\frac{2a}{b}$ y $2t + 3r - 3$ son todas expresiones variables
verbal model / modelo verbal **(p. 6)** Un modelo verbal describe una situación de la vida real mediante palabras que la exponen y símbolos matemáticos que relacionan esas palabras.	Distancia (millas) = Velocidad (millas/hora) • Tiempo (horas)
vertical angles / ángulos opuestos por el vértice **(p. 710)** Par de ángulos opuestos que se forman cuando dos rectas se cortan en un punto.	1, 2, 3, 4 $\angle 1$ y $\angle 3$ son ángulos opuestos. $\angle 2$ y $\angle 4$ son ángulos opuestos.

	Ejemplo
vertical line test / prueba de recta vertical **(p. 387)** En una relación representada por una gráfica, si cualquier recta vertical pasa por más de un punto de la gráfica, entonces la relación no es una función. Si ninguna recta vertical pasa por más de un punto de la gráfica, entonces la relación es una función.	(−2, 0), (3, 1), (−1, −2), (3, −2) La gráfica no es una función porque una recta vertical pasa por dos puntos.

X

x*-axis / eje *x **(p. 47)** La recta numérica horizontal en un plano de coordenadas.	*Ver* coordinate plane / plano de coordenadas.
x*-coordinate / coordenada *x **(p. 47)** El primer número en un par ordenado que representa un punto en un plano de coordenadas.	La coordenada *x* del par ordenado (5, −3) es 5.
x*-intercept / intercepto en *x **(p. 398)** La coordenada *x* de un punto donde la gráfica corta al eje *x*.	El intercepto en *y* es 4. (0, 4) (−6, 0) El intercepto en *x* es −6.

Y

y*-axis / eje *y **(p. 47)** La recta numérica vertical en un plano de coordenadas.	*Ver* coordinate plane / plano de coordenadas.
y*-coordinate / coordenada *y **(p. 47)** El segundo número en un par ordenado que representa un punto en un plano de coordenadas.	La coordenada *y* del par ordenado (5, −3) es −3.
y*-intercept / intercepto en *y **(p. 398)** La coordenada *y* de un punto donde la gráfica corta al eje *y*.	*Ver* *x*-intercept / intercepto en *x*.

Credits

Cover

Bottom left © Jake Martin/Getty Images; *center right* Comstock.

Authors

Larson Meridian Creative Group; *Boswell* Robert C. Jenks/Jenks Studio; *Kanold* McDougal Littell/Houghton Mifflin Co.; *Stiff* Jerry Head Jr.

Photography and Illustration

vi © Julie Houck/Corbis; **vii** © Scott Sroka/National Geographic Image Collection; **viii** © Darryl Torckler/Getty Images; **ix** © Chaco Mohler/Mountain Stock/Sportschrome, Inc.; **x** © Esbin-Anderson/The Image Works; **xi** © Jeremy Woodhouse/Getty Images; **xii** © Jose Luis Pelaez, Inc./Corbis; **xiii** © Sport the Library/Sportschrome, Inc.; **xiv** © Paul A. Souders/Corbis; **xv** #14106 Winged Box Kite courtesy of goflyakite.com; **xvi** © Michael Newman/PhotoEdit; **xvii** © Gale Beery/Index Stock Imagery; **xviii** *Zig Zag Chair* (1995), Designed by Gerrit Rietveld. Philadelphia Museum of Art, purchased with the Fiske Kimball fund and with funds contributed by COLLAB: The Group for Modern and Contemporary Design at the Philadelphia Museum of Art (1995-65-1); **1** © Stephen Simpson/Getty Images; **2–3** © Alison Wright/The Image Works; **5** © Doc White/SeaPics.com, Inc.; **7** Franz Walther/Artville; **8** © Cleve Bryant/PhotoEdit; **9** *top left* © Duomo/Corbis; *top right* © Royalty-Free/Corbis; **11** © Xinhua/Sovfoto; **13** Courtesy of Midwest-Tropical; **15** © Francisco J. Rangel; **16** © Bill Morson; **19** *center left* © David Young-Wolff/PhotoEdit; *center right* © Bill Ross/Corbis; **20** Elizabeth Tustian; **22** © Charles W. Mann/Photo Researchers, Inc.; **25** *bottom left* © David L. Arnold/National Geographic Image Collection; *center right* NASA; **26** © Hugh Rose/AccentAlaska.com; **29** © Julie Houck/Corbis; **30** © Jeffrey L. Rotman/Corbis; **32** © Jeff Vinnick/Getty Images; **33** *top left* © Image Makers/Getty Images; *top right* Image based on illustration from Dr. Michael Studinger/Lamont-Doherty Earth Observatory of Columbia University; **35** © Stella Snead/www.bciusa.com; **37** © William Bacon/Photo Researchers, Inc.; © Antonio Luiz Hamdan/Getty Images; **42** Comstock; **43** © elektraVision/Index Stock Imagery; **45** © Ralph White/Corbis; **46** © Allsport Concepts/Getty Images; **48** © Eric Figge/Index Stock Imagery; **50** *top left* Courtesy of American Honda Motors, Inc; *bottom left* © Jim Sugar/Corbis; **51** Steve Pica/McDougal Littell/Houghton Mifflin Co.; **58** © PhotoDisc; **59** © David Young-Wolff/PhotoEdit; **60–61** © Omni Photo Communinications/Index Stock Imagery; **63** © Chuck Savage/Corbis; **65** © AFP/Getty Images; **67** © Tami Chappell/Reuters; **68** The Granger Collection, New York; **71** © Tom Stewart/Corbis; **72** *top left* © Javier Garcia-Guinea/Reuters; *top right* © Maurice Nimmo/Frank Lane Picture Agency/Corbis; **75** © Scott Sroka/National Geographic Image Collection; **77** © GK Hart/Vikki Hart/PhotoDisc; **78** © David Young-Wolff/PhotoEdit; **80** © Steve Chenn/Corbis; **82** © Ed Young/Corbis; **84** Steve Pica/McDougal Littell/Houghton Mifflin Co.; **85** © Royalty-Free/Corbis; **86** © Reed Saxon/AP Images; **88** © Anthony Bannister/Gallo Images/Corbis; **89** © Corbis; **91** © Joseph Sohm/Visions of America/Corbis; **92** © Kit Houghton/Corbis; **94** Stacy Allison; **95** © Macduff Everton/Corbis; **97, 98** Solar & Heliospheric Observatory (SOHO) (ESA and NASA); **99** © Royalty-Free/Corbis; **100** *top* © Stephen Simpson/Getty Images; *bottom* © Stephen Simpson/Getty Images; **101** © Siede Preis/PhotoDisc; **102** © Gary W. Carter/Corbis; **104** © Frank Cezus/Getty Images; **106** © Roger Ressmeyer/Corbis; **107** *top* © Mark Wagner/Getty Images; *bottom* Steve Pica/McDougal Littell/Houghton Mifflin Co.; **114** *center right* © Ron Chapple/Getty Images; *bottom* Ken O'Donoghue/McDougal Littell/Houghton Mifflin Co.; **115** *top* © Alison Wright/Corbis; *bottom* © Charles O'Rear/Corbis; **116–117** © Steve Hamblin/Alamy; **120** © Michael Newman/PhotoEdit; **122** © EyeWire; **123** © Darryl Torckler/Getty Images; **124** © Robert W. Ginn/PhotoEdit; **125** *bottom left* © SW Productions/Getty Images; *top right* © Steve Cole/PhotoDisc; **128** Stockbyte; **131** © David Young-Wolff/Getty Images; **132** Ken O'Donoghue/McDougal Littell/Houghton Mifflin Co.; **134** © Royalty-Free/Corbis; **138** © Kevin Schafer/Getty Images; **140** © Frank Boxler/AP Images; **141** © Richard Cummins/Corbis; **142** © Richard Hamilton Smith/Corbis; **144** © Bill Brooks/Masterfile; **145** © Jeff Albertson/Corbis; **147** *top left* © Scott Markewitz/Getty Images; *bottom left* © Joe McDonald/Corbis; **148** Steve Pica/McDougal Littell/Houghton Mifflin Co.; **149** *top right* PhotoSpin; *center left* © Tracy Frankel/Getty Images; **150** © AP Images; **152** © Phil Hunt/Getty Images; **153** Jennifer Smith; **167** © AFP/Getty Images; **168–169** NASA; **172** *top right* © Jeff Greenberg/PhotoEdit; *bottom left all* Stockbyte; **175** © Bob Daemmrich/The Image Works; **176** © Mark A. Schneider/Photo Researchers, Inc.; **177** © Oscar C. Williams; **179** Ken O'Donoghue/McDougal Littell/Houghton Mifflin Co.; **180** Photo Courtesy of Robert Murray, The Mars Society; **181** Steve Pica/McDougal Littell/Houghton Mifflin Co.; **185** © Ryan McVay/Getty Images; **186** *top left* © Joel Sartore/National Geographic Image Collection; *top right* © Peter J. Bryant/BPS/Getty Images; **187** © David Zimmerman/Corbis; **188** © Chaco Mohler/Mountain Stock/Sportschrome, Inc.; **190** © Todd Powell/Index Stock Imagery; **194** Tom Bol Photography; **197** T.A. Rector (NRAO/AUI/NSF and NOAO/AURA/NSF) and M. Hanna (NOAO/AURA/NSF); **201** © Peter Weber/Getty Images; **202** © Lucent Technologies' Bell Labs/Science Photo Library/Photo Researchers, Inc.; **203** © Royalty-Free/Corbis; **204** *bottom left* © Ralph C. Eagle, Jr./Photo Researchers, Inc.; *top right* © Scott Bodell/Getty Images; **206** © W. P. Armstrong/Palomar College; **207** © K. H. Kjeldsen/Science Photo Library/Photo Researchers, Inc.; **208** *top left* © ThinkStock LLC/Index Stock Imagery; *center left* © Derek Berwin/Getty Images; **216–217** © Fred Bruemmer/DRK Photo; **220** © Eckart Pott/www.bciusa.com; **223** © Carl Schneider/Getty Images; **225** © Roy Corral/Corbis; **227** Ken O'Donoghue/McDougal Littell/Houghton Mifflin Co.; **228** © Syracuse newspapers/Gary Walts/The Image Works; **229** © Jane Burton/www.bciusa.com; **231** © William S. Kuta/Alamy; **232** © SW Productions/Getty Images; **234** © Suzanne L. Collins and Joseph T. Collins/Photo Researchers, Inc.; **238** © AP Images; **241** © Esbin-Anderson/The Image Works; **244** © Kim Steele/Getty Images; **246** Ken O'Donoghue/McDougal Littell/Houghton Mifflin Co.; **247** © Adam Hart-Davis/Science Photo Library/Photo Researchers, Inc.; **248** © Didier Givois/ImageState; **250** © Barry Winkler/Index Stock Imagery; **251** Steve Pica/McDougal Littell/Houghton Mifflin Co.; **254** © SW Production/Index Stock Imagery; **256** © Don Mason/Corbis; **257** © Mary Kate Denny/PhotoEdit; **264** © PhotoDisc; **265** © Paul T. McMahon; **266–267** © Frank Lloyd Wright Foundation, Scottsdale, AZ/Artists Rights Society (ARS) NY/Art Resource, NY; **266** *inset* Frank Lloyd Wright Foundation, Scottsdale, AZ/Artists Rights Society (ARS) NY/Digital Image © The Museum of Modern Art/Licensed by SCALA/Art Resource, NY; **269** © AP Images; **270** Mike Danzenbaker; **271** Courtesy of Sandia National Laboratories; **273** © Tom McHugh/Photo Researchers, Inc.; **275** © Jeremy Woodhouse/Getty Images; **276** © Don Romero/Index Stock Imagery; **278** © Royalty-Free/Corbis; **281** © Serge Krouglikoff/Getty Images; **283** © Charles O'Rear/Corbis; **284** © Chihuly Studio/Dale Chihuly, "Saffron and Red Tower," 2000. Rutherford, California. Photo: Mark McDonnell; **289** © Duomo/Corbis; **291** © Bob Daemmrich/Stock Boston, LLC; **292** © John Van Hasselt/Corbis Sygma; **293** © Darrell Gulin/Corbis; **294** © Gail Shumway/Getty Images; **296** © George H. H. Huey/Corbis; **297** Steve Pica/McDougal Littell/Houghton Mifflin Co.; **300** © Angelo Hornak/Corbis; **301** © Reuters/Corbis; **303** © Chris Minerva/Index Stock Imagery; **304** Laurie O'Keefe/McDougal Littell/Houghton Mifflin Co.; **305** Frank Siteman/McDougal Littell/Houghton Mifflin Co.; **307** SW Productions/Brand X; **308** © Tony Freeman/PhotoEdit; **313** *top right* © Jon Feingersh/Corbis; *center left* Comstock; **314** © Royalty-Free/Corbis; **316** © Ian Shaw/Getty Images; **317** Frank Siteman/McDougal Littell/Houghton Mifflin Co.; **324** © Tony Freeman/PhotoEdit; **325** © Kwame Zikomo/SuperStock; **326–327** ©

Teacher's Edition Credits

Cover Photography

Bottom left © Jake Martin/Getty Images; *center right* Comstock.

Photography

T3 *Larson* Meridian Creative Group; *Boswell* Robert C. Jenks/Jenks Studio; *Kanold* McDougal Littell/Houghton Mifflin Co.; *Stiff* Jerry Head, Jr.
T44 Meridian Creative Group.

David Young-Wolff/PhotoEdit; **329** © Gary Conner/PhotoEdit; **330** © Kennan Ward/Corbis; **332** © Jose Luis Pelaez, Inc./Corbis; **336** © Jeff Greenberg/PhotoEdit; **338** © AFP/Getty Images; **339** © Kevin R. Morris/Corbis; **340** Laurie O'Keefe/McDougal Littell/Houghton Mifflin Co.; **341** © Tom Brakefield/Corbis; **343** Antiquarian Images; **346** © RNT Productions/Corbis; **348** 2003 stadiumpics.com/Mark Green Photography; **349** Public art sculpture, *Multiple Choice* by Nancy Dwyer. Commissioned by the NYC Dept. of Education, NYC School Construction Authority and NYC Dept. of Cultural Affairs Percent for Art Program; **352** © Witold Skrypczak/SuperStock; **353** © Rob Tringali/Sportschrome, Inc.; **355** © Kevin Fleming/Corbis; **356** © Ben Mangor/SuperStock; **357** *top right* Comstock; *bottom left* © Jason Homa/Getty Images; **358** © Michael Newman/PhotoEdit; **360** © Richard Hamilton Smith/Corbis; **361** Steve Pica/McDougal Littell/Houghton Mifflin Co.; **362** Artville; **363** Patti McConville; **365** © Charles O'Rear/Corbis; **381** © Jonathan Nourok/PhotoEdit; **382–383** © Richard Sisk/Panoramic Images; **385** © Jim Stamates/Getty Images; **386** Eliot Cohen; **389** © NOVASTOCK/PhotoEdit; **390** © Jack W. Greene/Transparencies, Inc./2003; **391** © Chris Johns/National Geographic Image Collection; **392** © Schafer & Hill/Getty Images; **395** © Jeff Rotman/Photo Researchers, Inc.; **396** *top left* Dave Watts/ANTPhoto.com; *top right* Laurie O'Keefe/McDougal Littell/Houghton Mifflin Co.; **399** © Richard Hutchings/Photo Researchers, Inc.; **401** © Chris Sorensen MMIII/All Rights Reserved; **403** *all* RMIP/Richards Haynes/McDougal Littell/Houghton Mifflin Co.; **404** Courtesy of Hyperlite; **406** © Sport the Library/Sportschrome, Inc.; **408** © Roger Ressmeyer/Corbis; **409** © Raymond Gehman/Corbis; **413** Image by Philip E. Long courtesy of Battelle Memorial Institute, Operating and Management Contractor of the Pacific Northwest National Laboratory for the U.S. Department of Energy; **416** © Cops Jim/SYGMA/Corbis; **417** © Bob Daemmrich/Stock Boston, LLC; **418** Steve Pica/McDougal Littell/Houghton Mifflin Co.; **419** © Core Agency/Getty Images; **420** © Akira Kaede/Getty Images; **421** © Robert E. Daemmrich/Getty Images; **423** © www.danheller.com; **424** © AFP/Getty Images; **426** GSFC/NASA; **429** Laurie O'Keefe/McDougal Littell/Houghton Mifflin Co.; **431** © Michael Pole/Corbis; **434** © David Young-Wolff/PhotoEdit; **436** © Donald Nausbaum/Alamy; **438** © Tom Stewart/Corbis; **440** © J. Irwin/RobertStock.com; **448** © PhotoDisc; **449** © David Young-Wolff/PhotoEdit; **450–451** © Mark L. Stephenson/Corbis; **453** © David Lees/Corbis; **455** © Bill Aron/PhotoEdit; **456** © Paul A. Souders/Corbis; **457** © Historical Picture Archive/Corbis; **459** © Tony Freeman/PhotoEdit; **461** © Morton Beebe/Corbis; **465** William H. Harsha Cable Stayed Bridge/2003 ENTRAN; **468** © Donald Graham/Index Stock Imagery; **469** © Craig Jones/Getty Images; **472** © Peter Cade/Getty Images; **473** © Eunice Harris/Photo Researchers, Inc.; **474** Diana Venters; **477** © 2003 Oscar Palmquist/Lightwave; **480** © Michael Newman/PhotoEdit; **481** © Rudi Von Briel/PhotoEdit; **483** © Patrik Giardino/Corbis; **485** © Stuart Darsch; **486** © Will Hart/PhotoEdit; **487** © Antonio M. Rosario/Getty Images; **489** Artville; **492** Stanton's Coffeepot Water Tower courtesy of Wayne Donohue; **495** Dinodia; **497** © Gail Meese/Meese Photo Research; **498** © Steve Bly/Getty Images; **506** Boston Children's Theatre; **506** Ken O'Donoghue/McDougal Littell/Houghton Mifflin Co.; **507** *top right* Brand X Pictures; *bottom right* Lawrence Migdale/McDougal Littell/Houghton Mifflin Co.; **508–509** © Joseph De Sciose/Aurora Photos; **511** © Arthur S. Aubry/Getty Images; **514** © Ludovic Maisant/Corbis; **515** #14106 Winged Box Kite courtesy of goflyakite.com; **516** *bottom left* © C Squared Studios/Getty Images; *bottom right* © Royalty-Free/Corbis; **519** © Kim Karpeles; **522** © Scott Berner/Camerique Inc./RobertStock.com; **525** © George Hall/Corbis; **528** JPL/NASA; **530** © Sally Weigand; **538** © Michael Newman/PhotoEdit; **542** Artville; **543** Erik Seo; **544** © Jonathan Nourok/PhotoEdit; **548** *center left* © Juniors Bildarchiv/Alamy; *bottom left* © 2008 Ripley Entertainment Inc.; **553** Courtesy of www.crestwoodpools.com; **555** Sally McCrae Kuyper; **559** © DesignPics Inc/Index Stock Imagery; **561** *bottom left* © David Young-Wolff/PhotoEdit; *bottom right* Image based on illustration from Greener Products Company; **562** Ken O'Donoghue/McDougal Littell/Houghton Mifflin Co.; **577** © SW Production/Index Stock Imagery; **578–579** © Monika Graff/The Image Works; **581** © AFP/Getty Images; **582** © Tom Stewart/Corbis; **583** © Jeff Greenberg/PhotoEdit; **585** © AP Images; **586** © Reuters/Corbis; **588** © Ed Young/Corbis; **589** © David Carriere/Index Stock Imagery; **591** © Bob Daemmrich/PhotoEdit; **592** © Peter M. Fisher/Corbis; **599** © Mike Chew/Corbis; **601** © Royalty-Free/Getty Images; **603** © David Young-Wolff/PhotoEdit; **604** © Pat Doyle/Corbis; **605** © L. Lefkowitz/Getty Images; **609** © Jose Luis Pelaez, Inc./Corbis; **610** Comstock; **611** © Royalty-Free/Corbis; **612** © TWPhoto/Corbis; **613** © Royalty-Free/Corbis; **616** © GeoStock/Getty Images; **618** © Joe McBride/Corbis; **620** © Michael Newman/PhotoEdit; **622** © Stefan Sollfors/Alamy; **624** © Andersen-Ross/Brand X Pictures/Jupiter; **625** Steve Pica/McDougal Littell/Houghton Mifflin Co.; **628** Ken O'Donoghue/McDougal Littell/Houghton Mifflin Co.; **630** © David Pollack/Corbis; **631** © Andrew Syred/Science Photo Library/Photo Researchers, Inc.; **632** © Charles Gupton/Corbis; **634** Ken O'Donoghue/McDougal Littell/Houghton Mifflin Co.; **638** © PhotoDisc Collection/Getty Images; **639** © Phil Schermeister/Corbis; **646** *bottom left* © Michael Newman/PhotoEdit; *top right* © PhotoDisc; **647** *top right* © Charles Gupton/Corbis; *bottom right* © Paul Conklin/PhotoEdit; **648–649** © Royalty Free/Corbis; **651** © SW Production/Index Stock Imagery; **653** © Dennis MacDonald/PhotoEdit; **654** © Gale Beery/Index Stock Imagery; **655** Digital Vision; **657** Martha Granger/Edge Productions/McDougal Littell/Houghton Mifflin Co.; **658** © HIRB/Index Stock Imagery; **660** © Tom Pantages; **662** © Dale C. Spartas/Corbis; **665** © Jack Hollingsworth/Corbis; **666** © CLEO Photo/Alamy; **669** *top left* © Richard Pasley/Stock Boston, LLC; *top right* © Royalty-Free/Getty Images; **671** © John Post/Panoramic Images; **677** NASA; **678** Courtesy of Metropolitan Museum of Art/Getty Images; **679** © Michael S. Yamashita/Corbis; **683** © Chris Cheadle/Getty Images; **684** © SW Production/Index Stock Imagery; **686** © Tom & Pat Leeson/Photo Researchers, Inc.; **688** © Jeff Lepore/Photo Researchers, Inc.; **690** © Myrleen Ferguson Cate/PhotoEdit; **691** Steve Pica/McDougal Littell/Houghton Mifflin Co.; **693** © Michelle D. Bridwell/PhotoEdit; **696** © Tony Freeman/PhotoEdit; **697** © Scott Camazine/Photo Researchers, Inc.; **704** © PhotoDisc; **705** © Kim Karpeles; **706–707** © Bill Longcore/Photo Researchers, Inc.; **707** © Adam Peiperl/Corbis; **710** © Tom Carter/PhotoEdit; **712** © Branson Reynolds/Index Stock Imagery; **713** Clothespin, 1976 sculpture by Claes Oldenburg. © 2007 Claes Oldenburg and Coosje van Bruggen. Courtesy Oldenburg van Bruggen Foundation. Photo © Robert Holmes/Corbis; **716** © Chris Minerva/Index Stock Imagery; **719** *center left, Zig Zag Chair* (1995), Designed by Gerrit Rietveld. Philadelphia Museum of Art, purchased with the Fiske Kimball fund and with funds contributed by COLLAB: The Group for Modern and Contemporary Design at the Philadelphia Museum of Art (1995-65-1); *center* © C Squared Studios/PhotoDisc; **722** *top right* International Art and Sound/shakerman.com; *bottom left* © Lon C. Diehl/PhotoEdit; © Arthur Thévenart/Corbis; **724** littleasianvillage.com; **726** © DigitalGlobe; **727** © European Central Bank; **729** Vicky Karsala/PhotoDisc/PictureQuest; **732** © George H. H. Huey/Corbis; **733** © Royalty-Free/Corbis; **734** © John Giustina/Getty Images; **741** Douglas Keister; **743** © Royalty-Free/Corbis; **745** © Michael Newman/PhotoEdit; **746** Steve Pica/McDougal Littell/Houghton Mifflin Co.; **748** © Savita Kirloskar/Reuters; **750** Comstock.

All unlisted illustrations by McDougal Littell/Houghton Mifflin Co.

The editors have made every effort to trace the ownership of all copyrighted material found in this book and to make full acknowledgement for its use. Omissions brought to our attention will be corrected in a subsequent edition.

Selected Answers

Chapter 1

1.1 Guided Practice (p. 7) **1.** d **3.** 6 **5.** 8 **7.** 3 **9.** 1 **11.** Step 1: $16d$; Step 2: 196; Step 3: 3136 sunrises

1.1 Practice and Problem Solving (pp. 7–9) **13.** 9 **15.** 2 **17.** 4 **19.** 21 **21.** 12 **23.** 2 **25.** 4 **27.** 8 **29.** 14 **31.** 20 **33–37.** Sample answers are given. **33.** $q - 1$ **35.** $n + 9.4$ **37.** $\frac{n}{41}$ **39.** \$32 **41.** 17.5 **43.** 52.5 **45.** 6 **47.** 1.4 **49.** $12x$ **51. a.** Row 3: 12, 188; Row 4: 16, 184 **b.** $4r$ **c.** $200 - 4r$ **d.** 50 rentals. *Sample answer:* Find the greatest value of r so that $200 - 4r$ is not less than zero. **53.** Yes; when $a = 2$, the value of $2 + a$ is 4 and the value of $2a$ is 4. **55.** The cost with a coupon is \$.50 less than the cost of the item; $n - 0.50$. **57.** 7.9 **59.** 5.2 **61.** 105.6 **63.** 7.6 **65.** 7.8, 7.98, 8.79, 8.9, 9.78, 9.87

1.2 Guided Practice (p. 12) **1.** base: 13; exponent: 5 **3.** 12 squared; 12 • 12; 144 **5.** 1.2 cubed; (1.2)(1.2)(1.2); 1.728 **7.** 36 **9.** 1296 **11.** 2744 $in.^3$

1.2 Practice and Problem Solving (pp. 12–13) **13.** 32^2 **15.** 6^5 **17.** $(5.6)^3$ **19.** z^3 **21.** 8 cubed; 8 • 8 • 8; 512 **23.** 10 to the sixth power; 10 • 10 • 10 • 10 • 10 • 10; 1,000,000 **25.** 9 cubed; 9 • 9 • 9; 729 **27.** 0.2 squared; (0.2)(0.2); 0.04 **29. a.** Row 3: 4^3, 64; Row 4: 4^4, 256 **b.** 262,144 e-mails **c.** stage 10 **31.** 343; 0.064 **33.** 16,807; 0.01024 **35.** *Sample answer:* If you use the base 1 as a factor any number of times, the product is 1. **37. a.** Row 3: 9; Row 4: 16; Row 5: $1 + 3 + 5 + 7 + 9 = 25$; the sum of the first n odd numbers equals n squared. **b.** n^2 **c.** 10,000 **39.** 17.75 **41.** 0.5 **43.** 115 gold medals **45.** 185 **47.** 45

Student Reference (p. 15) **1.** 9:00 A.M. **3.** 24 orders

1.3 Guided Practice (p. 18) **1.** *Sample answer:* Fraction bar, parentheses, brackets **3.** 3 **5.** 44 **7.** 10 **9.** $2(2697) + 3(29) + 4(2) + 5(1) =$ 5494 people

1.3 Practice and Problem Solving (pp. 19–20) **11.** 32 **13.** 20.7 **15.** 6 **17.** 122.5 **19.** 4 **21.** 8 **23.** 9.1 **25.** 7 **27.** 20 **29.** $5 \cdot 72 + 4 \cdot 48$; 552 in. **31.** \$119.93 **33.** 7 **35.** 4.3 **37. a.** 1,310,720 pixels **b.** 1.3 megapixels **c.** No; $\frac{1.3}{8 \cdot 10} \approx 0.016$, $0.016 < 0.017$, so the print will not be clear. **41.** $<$ **43.** 2^8; 256 colors

1.3 Technology Activity (p. 21) **1.** 57 **3.** 9 **5.** 4 **7.** 2 **9.** 396.2652439; for the expression $100 + 87 \div 328 + 296$, the calculator will first do the division $87 \div 328$, then do the additions.

1.4 Guided Practice (p. 24) **1.** 22.5 **3.** −9, −5, −3, 0, 6, 12 **5.** 9 **7.** 12 **9.** 33 **11.** −81 **13.** 4 **15.** 47 **17.** the top of Kilauea

1.4 Practice and Problem Solving (pp. 25–26) **19.** $>$ **21.** $<$

23. 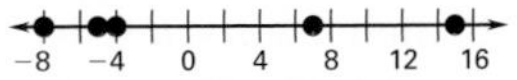

−8, −5, −4, 7, 15

25. 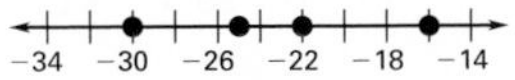

−30, −25, −22, −16

27. 7 **29.** 40 **31.** 42 **33.** 105 **35.** −9 **37.** 11 **39.** 67 **41.** −100 **43.** 8 **45.** 24 **47.** 40 **49.** 13 **51. a.** −3, −8, −12, −37

b. 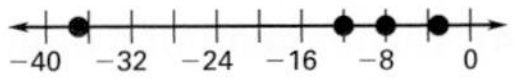

c. Unnamed city, Bay of Bengal **d.** closer to **53. a.** increase **b.** decrease **c.** Wednesday; Saturday **d.** The high temperature consistently rose from Sunday through Wednesday and consistently fell from Wednesday through Saturday. **55.** 15 **57.** 11 **59.** 2 **61.** 7 **63.** 0 **67.** *Sample answer:* 500 **69.** between 42,000 and 56,000 **71.** between 12,000 and 20,000 **73.** 17

1.5 Guided Practice (p. 31) **1.** absolute value **3.** 2 **5.** 8 **7.** −12 **9.** −6 **11.** −12 **13.** The arrow should start at −2 and go 5 units in the positive direction; $-2 + 5 = 3$.

1.5 Practice and Problem Solving (pp. 32–33) **15.** −16 **17.** −10 **19.** −14 **21.** 6 **23.** −9 **25.** −52 **27.** −26 **29.** −102 **31.** 5 **33.** 7 **35.** −24 **37.** −13

39. *Sample answer:* The length of the arrow is the absolute value of the second number. The direction of the arrow is right if the second number is positive and left if the second number is negative. **41.** \$63 **43.** −1915 **45. a.** −3743 m **b.** −4943 m **47.** −24 **49.** 65 **51.** −17 **53.** −18 **55.** Even; the sum of two odd numbers is even. **57.** $x \le 0$; if $x < 0$, then $|x|$ and x are opposites so their sum is 0; if $x = 0$, then $|x|$ and x are both 0 so their sum is 0. **61.** $n + 14.5$ **63.** 4900 yd^2 **65.** <

1.6 Guided Practice (p. 36) **1.** $-15 - x$ **3.** −5 **5.** −13 **7.** −10 **9.** 13 **11.** Step 1: −110; Step 2: −90; Step 3: −20 ft

1.6 Practice and Problem Solving (pp. 36–38) **13.** 9 **15.** 12 **17.** 39 **19.** 52 **21.** −71 **23.** −52 **25.** 10 **27.** −10 **29.** −19 **31.** −10 **33.** 41°C **35.** 25°C **37.** 30 ft **39.** −190 **41.** 235 **43.** −12 **45.** −16 **47.** solution B; 24°C lower **49.** No; if $b = 0$, then $a + b = a - b$ and if $b < 0$, then $a + b < a - b$. **51.** 6 **53.** −2 **55.** 6:40 A.M. **57.** 30 **59.** 6 **61.** 29 **63.** −51

Student Reference (p. 40) **1.** 86; 86; no mode; 24 **3.** 0.6; 0.5; 0.5; 0.6 **5.** 183; 178; no mode; 104

1.7 Guided Practice (p. 44) **1.** The mean of a data set is the sum of the values divided by the number of values. **3.** positive **5.** negative **7.** negative **9.** positive **11.** Step 1: −3; Step 2: 9(−3); −27; Step 3: −5°C

1.7 Practice and Problem Solving (pp. 45–46) **13.** 2 **15.** −132 **17.** −2 **19.** −360 **21.** 17 **23.** −120 **25.** *Sample answer:* The rules are alike in that if the two signs are alike the product or quotient is positive and if the two signs are different the product or quotient is negative. The rules are different for zero: for multiplication, if either factor is zero then the product is zero, but for division you have to check that the divisor is not zero. **27. a.** −20,000 ft **b.** 10 min **29.** −1250 **31.** 5 **33.** −4 **35.** < **37.** 67 ft **39.** 4.5 **41.** −6.4

43. No; the product of an odd number of negative factors is negative, while the product of an even number of negative factors is positive, so $(-1)^n = -1$ is true for any odd positive integer. For example $(-1)^3 = -1$ but $(-1)^4 = 1$. **45.** −21, −12, −5, 0, 13, 31 **47.** 24 **49.** −51

1.8 Guided Practice (p. 49) **1.** −12; 7

3–5.

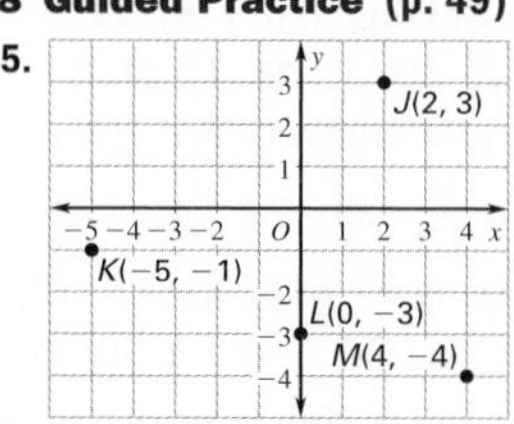

3. Quadrant I **5.** y-axis

7. Step 1: (8, 19), (24, 13), (31, 17), (71, 14), (88, 11), (103, 7), (119, 7), (127, 5), (134, 3)

Step 2:

Step 3: The points generally fall from left to right. We can conclude that as the depth increases the speed tends to decrease.

1.8 Practice and Problem Solving (pp. 49–51) **9.** (0, 3) **11.** (4, 0) **13.** (3, −3) **15.** (−3, −2)

17–23.

17. Quadrant I **19.** Quadrant IV **21.** Quadrant III **23.** Quadrant III **25.** The first number refers to left/right and the second number refers to up/down; the point (2, −8) is 2 units to the right of the origin and 8 units down.

27. a. Mileage (mi/gal); Engine size (L)

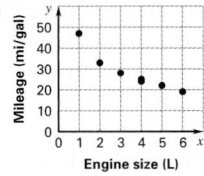

b. The points generally fall from left to right, so we can conclude that as the engine size increases the mileage tends to decrease.

29. a. −5, −3, −1, 1, 3, 5, 7 **b.** (−3, −5), (−2, −3), (−1, −1), (0, 1), (1, 3), (2, 5), (3, 7)

c.

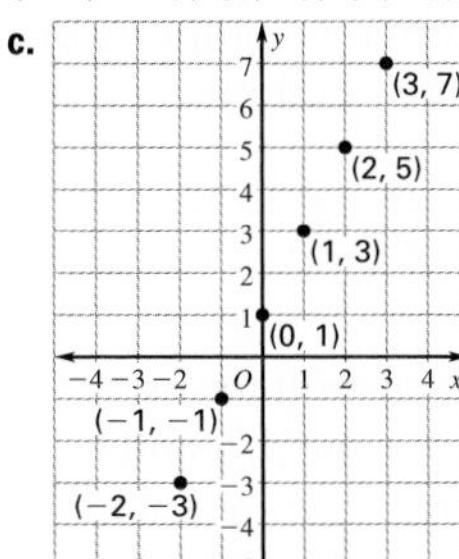

d. The points lie on a line.

31. *Sample answer:* $P(5, 0)$, $Q(5, 5)$, $R(0, 5)$; the distance from O to P is 5 units, the distance from P to Q is 5 units, the distance from Q to R is 5 units, and the distance from R to O is 5 units.
35. $20 - 2c$ **37.** never **39.** −45 **41.** 21

Chapter Review (pp. 52–55)

1.

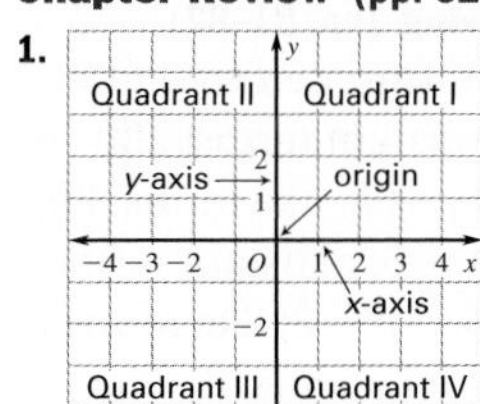

3. The opposite of a nonzero integer has the same absolute value but a different sign. The opposite of zero is zero.

5. 23 **7.** 5 **9.** 13.5 **11.** 8 **13.** 10,000 **15.** 156.25
17. 3125 **19.** 1.728 **21.** 121 **23.** 21
25. −6, −4, −3, 2, 5, 6
27. 18, −18 **29.** 4, −4 **31.** −6 **33.** 11 **35.** 17
37. −12 **39.** 17°F **41.** 0 **43.** 19 **45.** −9 **47.** 31
49. 108 **51.** −51 **53.** 5 **55.** −3 **57.** (1, 2)
59. (−3, −3)

61–63. B(−2, 5); C(0, 4); D(−3, −1); E(4, −2)

61. Quadrant II
63. Quadrant III

Focus on Problem Solving (p. 59) **1.** \$.98; \$5.88
3. 5 c. *Sample answer:* You can find the information in a dictionary or almanac, or on the Internet.
5. yes **7.** Sun.: −6°F, Mon.: +4°F, Tues.: −13°F, Wed.: −13°F, Thu.: +1°F, Fri.: −8°F, Sat.: 0°F; −5°F

Chapter 2

2.1 Guided Practice (p. 66)
1. associative property of addition
3. (26 + 18) + 34
= (18 + 26) + 34 [commutative property of addition]
= 18 + (26 + 34) [associative property of addition]
= 18 + 60 [Add 26 and 34.]
= 78 [Add 18 and 60.]
5. (3.45)(6.26)(0)
= [(3.45)(6.26)](0) [Use order of operations.]
= 0 [multiplication property of zero]

7. 220 **9.** $x + 17$ **11.** $y + 6$ **13.** commutative property of multiplication **15.** *Sample answer:* The conversion factor should be $\frac{1 \text{ pound}}{16 \text{ ounces}}$ so that the common factor of ounces can be divided out. This gives 80 ounces = 80 ounces $\cdot \frac{1 \text{ pound}}{16 \text{ ounces}}$ = 5 pounds.

2.1 Practice and Problem Solving (pp. 66–68)
17. 15(−9)(2)
= [15(−9)](2) [Use order of operations.]
= [−9(15)](2) [commutative property of multiplication]
= −9[(15)(2)] [associative property of multiplication]
= −9(30) [Multiply 15 and 2.]
= −270 [Multiply −9 and 30.]
19. 45 + 29 + 55
= (45 + 29) + 55 [Use order of operations.]
= (29 + 45) + 55 [commutative property of addition]
= 29 + (45 + 55) [associative property of addition]
= 29 + 100 [Add 45 and 55.]
= 129 [Add 29 and 100.]
21. −8100 **23.** 56 **25.** $j - 6$ **27.** $130y$

Selected Answers

29. commutative property of multiplication
31. identity property of multiplication **33.** 7500 g
35. 3 ft^2 **37.** \$140 **39.** 312 yd^2
41. $1.25 + 1.38 + 0.75$

$= (1.25 + 1.38) + 0.75$	[Use order of operations.]
$= (1.38 + 1.25) + 0.75$	[commutative property of addition]
$= 1.38 + (1.25 + 0.75)$	[associative property of addition]
$= 1.38 + 2$	[Add 1.25 and 0.75.]
$= 3.38$	[Add 1.38 and 2.]

43. $4(20)(25)(-5)$

$= 4[(20)(25)](-5)$	[associative property of multiplication]
$= 4[(25)(20)](-5)$	[commutative property of multiplication]
$= [4(25)][(20)(-5)]$	[associative property of multiplication]
$= 100[(20)(-5)]$	[Multiply 4 and 25.]
$= 100(-100)$	[Multiply 20 and −5.]
$= -10{,}000$	[Multiply 100 and −100.]

45. −450 **47. a.** 19.5 m **b.** 6.5 m **49.** Row 1: 5, −5; Row 2: 2, $\frac{1}{2}$; Row 3: 2, 10; Row 4: 4, 16; no. *Sample answer:* The results of evaluating each expression after attempting to apply a commutative or associative property are different from those before applying the property. **51. a.** \$8 **b.** $80x$ **c.** \$2000 **53.** 81 **55.** 1000 **57.** 11 **59.** \$13.13
61–63.

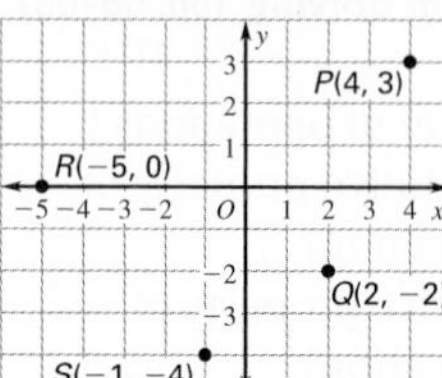

61. Quadrant IV **63.** Quadrant III

Student Reference (p. 70) **1.** 36 ft **3.** 73 in. **5.** 600 cm^2 **7.** 268 ft, 4200 ft^2

2.2 Guided Practice (p. 73) **1.** distributive property **3.** 288 **5.** 17.9 **7.** $2x - 12$ **9.** $20k + 45$ **11. a.** $15(20 + l)$ **b.** $300 + 15l$ **c.** $15(20 + l) = 15(20) + 15(l) = 300 + 15l$

2.2 Practice and Problem Solving (pp. 74–75) **13.** 30 **15.** 18.2 **17.** −81 **19.** 9 **21.** 763 **23.** −1980 **25.** 3.98 **27.** −36.18 **29.** $3y + 27$ **31.** $-7s - 140$ **33.** $-25q + 20$ **35.** $16n + 24$ **37.** 295 inches per year ≈ 300 inches per year, so the total snowfall will be about 5(300) = 1500 inches; 5(295) = 5(300 − 5) = 5(300) − 5(5) = 1500 − 25 = 1475 inches, which is close to the answer obtained by estimation. **39.** $(45a + 63)$ $units^2$ **41.** 65 **43.** 28 **45. a.** $W = 176{,}000 - 4400d$ **b.** 110,000 lb **c.** 110 days **47.** $5m - m^2$ **49.** $-3y^2 - 24y$ **51.** 11 **53.** −139 **55.** −4°F **57.** commutative property of addition **59.** identity property of multiplication

Student Reference (p. 77) **1.** $\frac{17 \text{ m}}{1 \text{ sec}}$ **3.** $\frac{1.5 \text{ in.}}{1 \text{ h}}$ **5.** 150 lb **7.** \$230 **9.** $15x$ Cal

2.3 Guided Practice (p. 80) **1.** constant terms **3.** terms: $6x$, x, 2, 4; like terms: $6x$ and x, 2 and 4; coefficients: 6, 1; constant terms: 2, 4; $7x + 6$ **5.** terms: $5n$, 1, $-n$, −8; like terms: $5n$ and $-n$, 1 and −8; coefficients: 5, −1; constant terms: 1, −8; $4n - 7$ **7.** $-3r - 21$ **9.** *Sample answer:* The distributive property was incorrectly applied. You can rewrite $5a - (3a - 7)$ as $5a + (-1)(3a - 7)$. Applying the distributive property gives $5a + (-1)(3a) - (-1)(7) = 5a - 3a + 7 = 2a + 7$.

2.3 Practice and Problem Solving (pp. 81–82) **11.** terms: $4y$, 23, $-y$, −6; like terms: $4y$ and $-y$, 23 and −6; coefficients: 4, −1; constant terms: 23, −6; $3y + 17$ **13.** terms: $2b$, −8, $4b$, $-6b$; like terms: $2b$, $4b$, and $-6b$; coefficients: 2, 4, −6; constant term: −8; −8 **15.** terms: $8p$, $-5p$, 5, $-p$, −2; like terms: $8p$, $-5p$, and $-p$; 5 and −2; coefficients: 8, −5, and −1; constant terms: 5, −2; $2p + 3$ **17.** $7a$ **19.** $6x$ **21.** $21y$ **23.** $4k - 28$ **25.** $7n + 3$ **27.** $-4w + 17$ **29.** $7q + 13$ **31.** $14(45 - s) + 8s$, $630 - 6s$ **33.** $x + (x + 5) + (2x + 1)$, $4x + 6$ **35.** $2(7y - 5) + 2(2y)$, $18y - 10$ **37. a.** $500x$; $500(800 - x)$, or $400{,}000 - 500x$ **b.** $0.27(500x) + 0.10(400{,}000 - 500x)$, $85x + 40{,}000$ **c.** \$69,750 **39.** $x = 14$ **41.** $n - 3$ **43.** $\frac{n}{6}$ **45.** $-2x - 6$ **47.** $-6m + 30$ **49.** $24t - 56$ **51.** $-24w - 27$

2.3 Technology Activity (p. 83) **1.** $7x + 14$ **3.** $-5x - 4$ **5.** $8x - 15$

7. When $x = 0$, $2(x - 1) + x = 2(0 - 1) + 0 = 2(-1) = -2$ and $4x - 2 = 4(0) - 2 = 0 - 2 = -2$; no. *Sample answer:* Let $Y1 = 2(X - 1) + X$ and $Y2 = 4X - 2$. The pairs of values in each row of the table are not always the same, so the two expressions are not equivalent.

2.4 Guided Practice (p. 87) **1.** solution **3.** $x + 10 = 15$; yes **5.** $-6x = 54$; no **7.** Step 1: $4x$; Step 2: 36 wedges; Step 3: $4x = 36$; Step 4: 9 quesadillas

2.4 Practice and Problem Solving (pp. 87–89) **9.** $26 + y = 43$ **11.** $14m = 56$ **13.** yes **15.** no **21.** 28 **23.** -5 **25.** 5 **27.** -13 **29.** 30 **31.** 231 **33.** about 134 million personal computers **35. a.** $x + 9 + 8 + 5 + 9 = 35$, or $x + 31 = 35$ **b.** 4 cm **37.** *Sample answer:* An expression consists of numbers and/or variables and operations, but has no equal sign or inequality signs. An example is $24x - 7$. An equation uses an equal sign to show that an expression is equal to a number or another expression. An example is $24x - 7 = 17$. **39. a.** $200 + 800x = 13{,}000$ **b.** *Sample:*

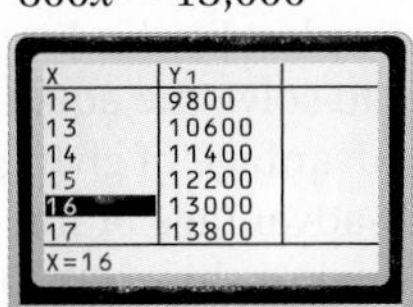

X	Y1
12	9800
13	10600
14	11400
15	12200
16	13000
17	13800

X=16

16; 16 sec

41. -8 **43.** -2 **45.** 985 **47.** $12c + 2$ **49.** $10x - 2$ **51.** -10

2.5 Guided Practice (p. 93) **1.** inverse **3.** 6 **5.** 9 **7.** -9 **9.** The number 8 was subtracted from the left side of the equation, but added to the right side. It should have been subtracted from each side, giving $x + 8 - 8 = 10 - 8$, which simplifies to $x = 2$.

2.5 Practice and Problem Solving (pp. 93–95) **11.** 5 **13.** -8 **15.** 11 **17.** -17 **19.** -29 **21.** 17 **23.** 23 **25.** -226 **27.** 45°C **29.** 3035 ft **31.** You can add -9 to each side of the equation. **33.** -18 **35.** 12 **37.** 4 **39.** 24 cm **41. a.** $190 = x + 45 + \frac{125}{5}$ **b.** 120 mg/dL **c.** borderline **43.** $39 = y + 5$ **47.** 0.3^2 **49.** t^6 **51.** 2401 **53.** 15.625 **55.** 27 **57.** -144 **59.** 7 **61.** 3

2.6 Guided Practice (p. 99) **1.** division **3.** -3 **5.** 24 **7.** Step 1: $8x = 40$, 5 min; Step 2: $5x = 20$, 4 min; Step 3: 9 min

2.6 Practice and Problem Solving (pp. 99–101) **9.** 13 **11.** -4 **13.** -24 **15.** -77 **17.** 19 **19.** 7 **21.** 289 **23.** -3348 **25.** 5 min **27.** 512 sec, or 8 min 32 sec; $37\frac{1}{3}$ sec; about 19.1 sec **29.** -5 **31.** 5 **33.** 104 **35. a.** $100x$ mi **b.** 0; 500; 1000; 1500; 2000; 2500 **c–d.**

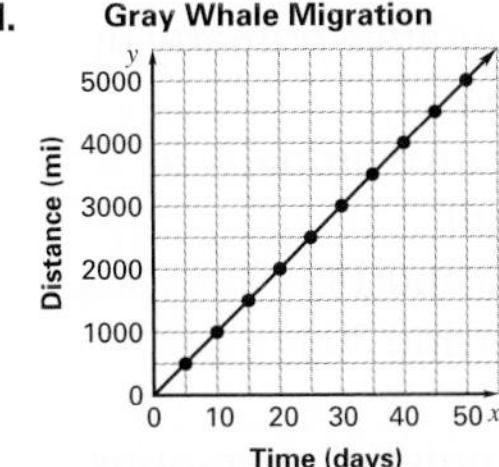

c. *Sample answer:* The points all lie on a straight line that passes through the origin. **d.** 50 days **e.** Solving the equation $100x = 5000$ gives an answer of 50, so the answers are the same. **37.** *Sample answer:* The Montoyas expect to average 50 miles per hour on their trip to the coast. If it is 400 miles to the coast, how long will the trip take? The solution is 8 hours. **41.** 12.81 **43.** 1.499 **45.** 60.0222 **47.** 2.4 **49.** -33 **51.** -2 **53.** 184 **55.** 9

2.7 Guided Practice (p. 105) **1.** absolute value **3.** -1.7 **5.** 3.32 **7.** 5.4 **9.** -41.18 **11.** Step 1: -0.61 m; Step 2: $x - 0.61 = 182.98$; Step 3: 183.59 m

2.7 Practice and Problem Solving (pp. 105–107) **13.** 13.15 **15.** -12.6 **17.** 0.121 **19.** 79.794 **21.** -6.2 **23.** 2.8 **25.** -2.51 **27.** -6.1 **29.** 0.324 **31.** 0.75 **33.** -20.7 **35.** 64.792 **37.** 2.1 m^2 **39.** $-4.5x$ **41.** $2.4 - 7.4n$ **43.** 6.4 ft **45. a.** More money. *Sample answer:* Each year of deficit can be paired with a year in which the surplus was greater than the absolute value of the deficit: 1995 with 2000, 1996 with 1999, and 1997 with 1998. **b.** \$136.7 billion surplus **c.** \$22.8 billion surplus **d.** \$23.6 billion. *Sample answer:* The median and the mean are almost the same. **47. a.** Cessna Skyhawk: 141 mi/h; Boeing 747: 570 mi/h; Concorde: 1346 mi/h **b.** Cessna Skyhawk: 3.9 h; Boeing 747: 1.0 h; Concorde: 0.4 h

Selected Answers

49. terms: $-3p$, 2, p, -4; like terms: $-3p$ and p, 2 and -4; coefficients: -3, 1; constant terms: 2, -4; $-2p - 2$ **51.** terms: 8, $2y$, -1, $-9y$, 3; like terms: 8, -1, and 3, $2y$ and $-9y$; coefficients: 2, -9; constant terms: 8, -1, 3; $10 - 7y$ **53.** 5 **55.** -152

Chapter Review (pp. 108–111) **1.** 0; 1
3. equivalent numerical expressions
5. $16 + 18 + 14$
$= (16 + 18) + 14$ [Use order of operations.]
$= (18 + 16) + 14$ [commutative property of addition]
$= 18 + (16 + 14)$ [associative property of addition]
$= 18 + 30$ [Add 16 and 14.]
$= 48$ [Add 18 and 30.]
7. $4.7 + 2.5 + 2.3$
$= (4.7 + 2.5) + 2.3$ [Use order of operations.]
$= (2.5 + 4.7) + 2.3$ [commutative property of addition]
$= 2.5 + (4.7 + 2.3)$ [associative property of addition]
$= 2.5 + 7$ [Add 4.7 and 2.3.]
$= 9.5$ [Add 2.5 and 7.]
9. $5(-3)(12)$
$= [5(-3)](12)$ [Use order of operations.]
$= [-3(5)](12)$ [commutative property of multiplication]
$= -3[(5)(12)]$ [associative property of multiplication]
$= -3(60)$ [Multiply 5 and 12.]
$= -180$ [Multiply -3 and 60.]
11. 318 **13.** 41.6 **15.** $-2x - 8$ **17.** $28a + 8$
19. terms: $4t$, $13t$, 2; like terms: $4t$ and $13t$; coefficients: 4, 13; constant term: 2 **21.** terms: 12, $-7k$, 9, $-k$; like terms: 12 and 9, $-7k$ and $-k$; coefficients: -7, -1; constant terms: 12, 9
23. $7u + 4$ **25.** 13 **27.** -9 **29.** 3 h **31.** -25
33. 93 **35.** -9 **37.** 32 **39.** 90 fliers **41.** 7.5
43. -2.8 **45.** -3.5 **47.** 8.3

Chapter 3

3.1 Guided Practice (p. 122) **1.** inverse **3.** 5 **5.** 1
7. Step 1: Cost for parts, Number of hours of labor; Step 2: $168 = 78 + 45h$; Step 3: 2 h

3.1 Practice and Problem Solving (pp. 123–124)
9. 3 **11.** 72 **13.** 48 **15.** -24 **17.** -55 **19.** -98
21. \$9 **23.** $5 - 2n = 7$; -1 **25.** $13 + 6n = 67$; 9
27. a. 12 flocks **b.** 2 pigs **c.** No. *Sample answer:* A heifer and two pigs cost $\$500 + 2 \cdot \$120 = \$740$. This leaves $\$755 - \$740 = \$15$, which is less than the \$20 cost of a flock of chicks. **29.** -3.2
31. 18.5 **33.** -4.68 **35. a.** $278 + 50m$; Column 2: \$328, \$378, \$428, \$478
b.

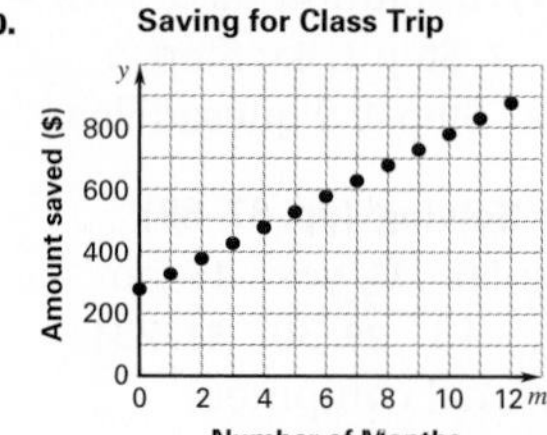

Sample answer: The points lie along a straight line; you can extend the scatter plot either by plotting more points as shown or by drawing a line through the plotted points and estimating what value along the horizontal axis corresponds to a value of \$850 on the vertical axis. **c.** $278 + 50m = 850$, 12 mo
d. *Sample answer:* The scatter plot gives a nice, visual picture of the relationship, and once it is plotted, it is easy to find the time and savings values that relate to each other, but it is time-consuming to make the plot. For finding a single value, it is very simple to solve the equation, and the equation has the advantage of giving an exact value, but it has the disadvantage of not providing a visual image of the relationship. **37.** $66z + 154$
39. $36 - 60y$ **41.** 11 **43.** -28

3.2 Guided Practice (p. 127) **1.** distributive property **3.** -1 **5.** 10 **7.** 3 **9.** Step 1: $2(10) + 2(x + 2) = 28$; Step 2: 2; Step 3: 4 units; Step 4: $2(10) + 2(x + 2) = 2(10) + 2(2 + 2) = 2(10) + 2(4) = 20 + 8 = 28$

3.2 Practice and Problem Solving (pp. 127–129)
11. 3 **13.** 12 **15.** 2 **17.** -3 **19.** 21 **21.** 5 people
23. 3 **25.** 34 **27.** -2 **29.** 2 **31.** 5 **33.** 11
35. 15 **37. a.** $29.50 = 19.50 + 0.25(m - 200)$
b. 240 **c.** 40 min
41–47.

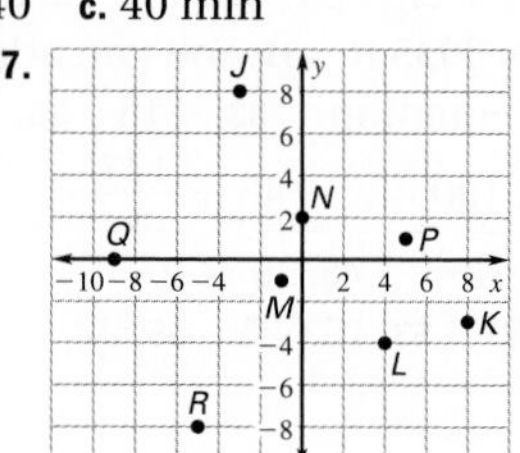

41. Quadrant IV
43. Quadrant III
45. Quadrant I
47. Quadrant III
49. $5b$
51. $5y - 1$
53. $-2x + 11$

Selected Answers

3.3 Guided Practice (p. 133) 1. *Sample answer:* First I would get the variable on only one side of the equation by subtracting $2x$ from each side to obtain $6x + 5 = -7$. Then I would subtract 5 from each side to obtain $6x = -12$, and divide each side by 6 to obtain $x = -2$. **3.** 4 **5.** 9 **7.** 2
9. *Sample answer:* In going from the second to the third statement, the result of subtracting $4x$ from x should have been $-3x$, not $3x$, so the third statement should be $7 = -3x - 2$, followed by $7 + 2 = -3x - 2 + 2$, $9 = -3x$, and $-3 = x$.

3.3 Practice and Problem Solving (pp. 134–135)
11. 9 **13.** −12 **15.** no solution **17.** −4 **19.** all numbers **21.** all numbers **23.** $9 + 2n = 3n - 2$; 11 **25.** $4 - 7n = 12 - 3n$; −2 **27.** 16 times **29.** 288 **31. a.** $700 - 60x$ **b.** $400 + 60x$ **c.** $700 - 60x = 400 + 60x$, 2.5 h **d.** $3\frac{1}{3}$ h, or 3 h 20 min
33. *Sample answer:* Your brother and sister are saving money for a summer camp. Your brother begins with \$5, and saves \$11 each week. Your sister begins with \$23, and saves \$8 each week. Let x be the number of weeks the two of them have been saving. The solution is 6, and indicates after how many weeks your brother and sister will have saved the same amount. **35.** 7 **37.** 2 **39.** 21.78 **41.** −8.9 **45.** −21 **47.** 6 **49.** 5

3.3 Technology Activity (p. 136) 1. 4 **3.** 8 **5.** 1
7. $\frac{2}{5}$, or 0.4. *Sample answer:* If you change the value of ΔTbl to .1, you can see that the solution is $x = 0.4$.

3.4 Guided Practice (p. 140) 1. inequalities that have the same solution **3.** yes **5.** yes
7. $x > -5$; −6 −5 −4 −3 −2 −1 0
9. $x < -1$; −3 −2 −1 0 1 2 3
11. Step 1: $250 + h \geq 1000$;
Step 2: $h \geq 750$; 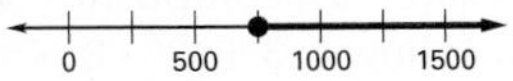 0 500 1000 1500
Step 3: The pilot must log at least 750 additional hours to become a pilot astronaut.

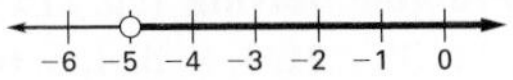

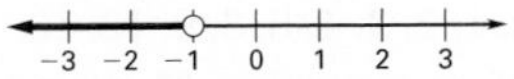

3.4 Practice and Problem Solving (pp. 141–142)
13. $s \leq 55$ **15.** $h \geq 48$ **17.** $x > -1$ **19.** $x \leq 6$
21. $x < 1$; −3 −2 −1 0 1 2 3
23. $-16 < y$, or $y > -16$; −24 −20 −16 −12 −8 −4 0
25. $-29 > g$, or $g < -29$; −31 −29 −27 −25
27. $f \geq -9$; −15 −12 −9 −6 −3 0 3
29. $25.1 \leq p$, or $p \geq 25.1$; 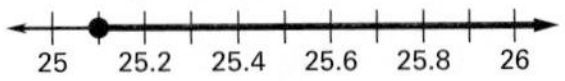
25 25.2 25.4 25.6 25.8 26
31. $b \leq 0$; −3 −2 −1 0 1 2 3
33. $t \geq -411$; −413 −411 −409 −407
35. $n < 51$; 47 48 49 50 51 52 53
37. $q \geq 10$; −5 0 5 10 15 20 25
39. No. *Sample answer:* There are infinitely many solutions—all points to the left or right of a given point, so you can only check sample points; no.
41.  −1 0 1 2 3 4 5
43. $t \geq -6$, $t \leq 15$; $t \geq -6$ and $t \leq 15$; 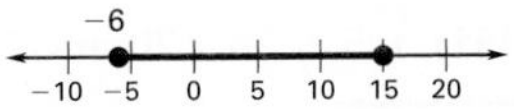
−6
−10 −5 0 5 10 15 20
45. 9.15 m **47.** $5 + 4n = 7n + 11$; −2

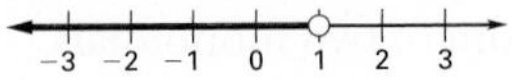

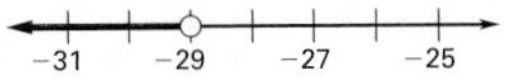

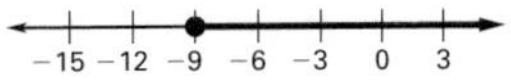

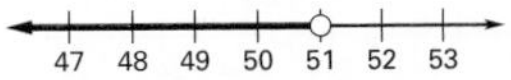

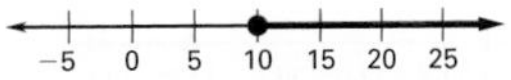

3.5 Guided Practice (p. 146) 1. division property of inequality
3. $v > 16$; 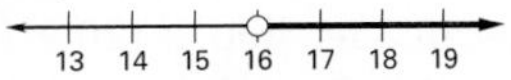 13 14 15 16 17 18 19
5. $u \geq 18$; 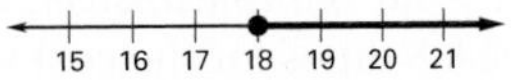 15 16 17 18 19 20 21
7. $a < -7$; −10 −9 −8 −7 −6 −5 −4
9. $r \geq 7$;  4 5 6 7 8 9 10
11. Step 1: $200 \cdot c \geq 500$; Step 2: $c \geq 2.5$, or $c \geq 2\frac{1}{2}$; Step 3: *Sample answer:* You must eat at least $2\frac{1}{2}$ cups of pasta at one meal to get the desired number of calories.

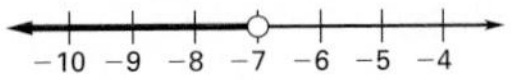

3.5 Practice and Problem Solving (pp. 146–148)
13. $b > 49$; 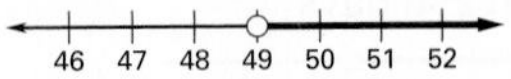 46 47 48 49 50 51 52
15. $y < -3$; −6 −5 −4 −3 −2 −1 0
17. $d \geq -66$; −68 −66 −64 −62
19. $w \leq 17$; 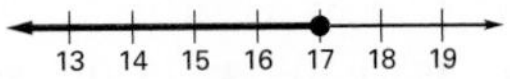 13 14 15 16 17 18 19
21. $h \geq -78$; −80 −78 −76 −74

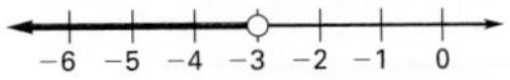

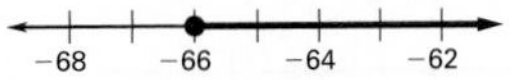

Selected Answers

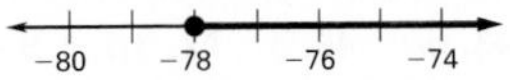

23. $q > -14$;

25. $m < -15$;

27. $n \leq 15$;

29. more than 5 times **31.** $\frac{n}{4} \leq 8$; $n \leq 32$

33. $7n > -35$; $n > -5$ **35.** $3n > -18$; $n > -6$

37. at least 15 pages

39. $b \leq -4.6$;

41. $z < -24.48$;

43. $c \geq -11.2$;

45. less than 30 min **47.** not more than $1.66/ft^2

51. 12.5 **53.** 72.2

55. $x > 84$;

57. $x \leq 59$;

3.6 Guided Practice (p. 151) **1.** $5 + 2n < 20$; $n < 7.5$

3. $x > 0$;

5. $x > 40$;

7. $y \leq 8$;

9. Step 1: $23v + 10v$, or $33v$; Step 2: $120 + 8v < 33v$; Step 3: $4.8 < v$, or $v > 4.8$. *Sample answer:* You must visit the park at least 5 times for the cost with the season pass to be less.

3.6 Practice and Problem Solving (pp. 151–153)

11. yes **13.** no

15. $n \leq -1$;

17. $m < 11$;

19. $b < 12$;

21. $x > 16$;

23. not more than 290 days

25. $b < 1$;

27. $y < 3$;

29. $s \leq 16$;

31. at least 5 sets **35.** (1, 3) **37.** (3, 0) **39.** (−4, 4) **41.** $26a + 13$ **43.** $6a$ **45.** 3 **47.** $3n + 9 = 2n - 7$, −16

Chapter Review (pp. 154–157) **1.** solution of an inequality **3.** equivalent **5.** $2.45 **7.** 14 **9.** 3 **11.** no solution

13. $y < 12$;

15. $x \leq 19$;

17. $-27 < a$, or $a > -27$;

19. $c \leq 8$;

21. $12 < r$, or $r > 12$;

23. $h < -8$;

25. $m > -2$;

27. $6 \geq z$, or $z \leq 6$;

29. $p \leq 168$;

31. $q \leq 1$;

33. $a \geq 2$;

Chapter 4

4.1 Guided Practice (p. 174) **1.** *Sample answer:* Write the number as the product of two whole number factors that are not equal to 1 or the number itself. Continue this process with any composite factors until only prime numbers remain. Write the original number as the product of the prime numbers that remain, using exponents for prime factors that repeat. **3.** 1, 2, 4, 8, 16 **5.** 1, 29 **7.** composite **9.** prime **11.** $2 \cdot 5$ **13.** 5^2 **15.** *Sample answer:* The factor 4 is composite, and equals $2 \cdot 2$. The prime factorization is $60 = 2^2 \cdot 3 \cdot 5$.

4.1 Practice and Problem Solving (pp. 175–176)

17. 1, 53 **19.** 1, 3, 11, 33 **21.** 1, 2, 3, 4, 5, 6, 10, 12, 15, 20, 30, 60 **23.** 1, 2, 3, 4, 6, 8, 9, 12, 16, 18, 24, 36, 48, 72, 144 **25.** composite **27.** prime **29.** composite **31.** composite **33.** Row 2: 20; Row 3: 3, 4; Row 4: 3, 5; $2^2 \cdot 3^2 \cdot 5$ **35.** $2 \cdot 29$ **37.** $5 \cdot 17$ **39.** $2^5 \cdot 5$ **41.** $3 \cdot 5 \cdot 13$ **43.** $2 \cdot 3 \cdot 5 \cdot 7$ **45.** $3^2 \cdot 5^2$ **47.** *Sample answer:* $8x^3y^2$ is a monomial because it is the product only of a number and variables that are raised to whole number powers; $8x^3y^2 + 1$ is not a monomial because it is the sum of two monomials.

49. $19 \cdot m \cdot m \cdot m$ **51.** $3 \cdot 7 \cdot a \cdot b$ **53.** $5 \cdot 7 \cdot r \cdot s \cdot s \cdot s \cdot s \cdot s$ **55.** $2 \cdot 2 \cdot 2 \cdot 5 \cdot m \cdot m \cdot n$ **57.** *Sample answer:* If 5 is the ones digit, then the number must be a multiple of 5. This is because, for example, $15 = 10 + 5 = 5(2 + 1)$, $25 = 20 + 5 = 5(4 + 1)$, and $35 = 30 + 5 = 5(6 + 1)$. **59.** 1, 5, 67, 335 **61.** 1, 3, 67, 201 **63.** 1, 2, 4, 13, 26, 52, w, $2w$, $4w$, $13w$, $26w$, $52w$ **65.** 1, 7, x, y, z, xy, xz, yz, xyz, $7x$, $7y$, $7z$, $7xy$, $7xz$, $7yz$, $7xyz$ **67.** 2^2, 3^2, 2^4, 5^2, $2^2 \cdot 3^2$, 2^6. *Sample answer:* All exponents in the prime factorization of a perfect square must be even. **69.** 1, 2, 3, 6, 9. *Sample answer:* 36, 54, and 72 have 18 as a factor, and also have 1, 2, 3, 6, and 9 as factors. **71.** -8 **73.** 32 **75.** 8 **77.** -63 **79.** $15 + n = 21 - n$; 3 **81.** $8 + n = -3n$; -2

4.2 Guided Practice (p. 179) **1.** *Sample answer:* It is a whole number that is a factor of both numbers. **3.** 7; not relatively prime **5.** 1; relatively prime **7.** $2c$ **9.** $5m$ **11.** Step 1: $225 = 3^2 \cdot 5^2$, $75 = 3 \cdot 5^2$, $120 = 2^3 \cdot 3 \cdot 5$; Step 2: 3 and 5; 15; Step 3: the greatest number of gift bags the owner can make, each with 15 pastel crayons, 5 paintbrushes, and 8 tubes of oil paint

4.2 Practice and Problem Solving (pp. 179–181) **13.** 3 **15.** 12 **17.** 1 **19.** 120 **21.** 11; not relatively prime **23.** 1; relatively prime **25.** 1; relatively prime **27.** 28; not relatively prime **29.** m **31.** $2x$ **33.** 7 bouquets; 9 daisies, 8 lilies, 6 irises, 3 freesias **35.** relatively prime **37.** $2m^2n$ **39.** $4mn$ **41.** x **43.** $9wx$ **45.** s **47.** 15 cm **49. a.** 40 min **b.** 36 space-hours; 37 space-hours **c.** 7560 space-hours **51.** Sometimes. *Sample answer:* Let $a = 4$, $b = 5$, and $c = 8$. Then a and b are relatively prime and b and c are relatively prime, but a and c have common factors of 2 and 4, and therefore are not relatively prime. On the other hand, let $a = 2$, $b = 7$, and $c = 13$. Then a and b are relatively prime, b and c are relatively prime, and a and c are relatively prime. **53.** $\frac{7}{9}$ **55.** $\frac{6}{15}$ **57.** 18 **59.** 15 **61.** 5^3 **63.** $2^2 \cdot 13$

4.3 Guided Practice (p. 184) **1.** *Sample answer:* It means that the numerator and denominator have no whole number common factors other than 1. **3.** *Sample answer:* $\frac{3}{4}$, $\frac{24}{32}$ **5.** *Sample answer:* $\frac{4}{7}$, $\frac{16}{28}$ **7.** $\frac{8}{19}$ **9.** $\frac{21a^2}{11}$ **11.** Step 1: 248 films; Step 2: $\frac{30}{248}$; Step 3: $\frac{15}{124}$

4.3 Practice and Problem Solving (pp. 185–186) **13–19.** Sample answers are given. **13.** $\frac{1}{3}$, $\frac{10}{30}$ **15.** $\frac{6}{7}$, $\frac{36}{42}$ **17.** $\frac{1}{9}$, $\frac{6}{54}$ **19.** $\frac{10}{16}$, $\frac{15}{24}$ **21.** $\frac{5}{7}$ **23.** $\frac{4}{15}$ **25.** $\frac{4}{5}$ **27.** $\frac{12}{19}$ **29.** $\frac{1}{a}$ **31.** $\frac{9cd}{4}$ **33.** $\frac{3}{5w}$ **35.** $\frac{77x^2}{6}$ **37. a.** $\frac{3}{8}$ **b.** $\frac{1}{8}$ **39.** no **41.** $\frac{4}{5}$, $\frac{13}{15}$; no **43.** $\frac{3}{8}$, $\frac{5}{16}$; no **45.** $\frac{7}{9}$, $\frac{7}{9}$; yes **47.** *Sample answer:* Divide the numerator and denominator of each fraction by the GCF of their absolute values. For $\frac{-12}{27}$, divide the numerator and denominator by 3 to get $\frac{-4}{9}$ or $-\frac{4}{9}$. For $\frac{25}{-35}$, divide the numerator and denominator by 5 to get $\frac{5}{-7}$, or $-\frac{5}{7}$. For $\frac{-33}{-55}$, divide the numerator and denominator by 11 to get $\frac{-3}{-5}$, or $\frac{3}{5}$. **49.** 20 **51.** 5 **53. a.** $\frac{96}{216}$; $\frac{4}{9}$ **b.** $\frac{4}{3y}$; $\frac{4}{9}$ **c.** The results are the same. *Sample answer:* The second method; it is easier to simplify the expression before evaluating it because it is easier to identify common factors. Simplifying first also results in an expression that is much easier to evaluate than the original expression, and that can be easily evaluated for any value of y without having to consider the value of x. **d.** (a) $\frac{288}{864}$; $\frac{1}{3}$; (b) $\frac{4}{3y}$; $\frac{1}{3}$. *Sample answer:* The results supporting that the second method is easier are even stronger for the new values of x and y. **55.** 13 **57.** 18 **59.** identity property of multiplication **61.** $2x$ **63.** $5r$

4.4 Guided Practice (p. 189) **1.** *Sample answer:* The least common denominator of two or more fractions is the least common multiple of the denominators of the fractions. **3.** 12 **5.** 72 **7.** $3s^2$ **9.** $45m^2$ **11.** $\frac{3}{4}$ **13.** $\frac{2}{5}$

15. *Sample answer:* When you write the product you will compute to find the LCM, you use the power of each prime factor with the greatest exponent that it has in the given numbers. The power of 2 is 2^4, not 2^5; so the LCM is $2^4 \cdot 3 \cdot 5 = 240$.

4.4 Practice and Problem Solving (pp. 190–191)
17. 24 **19.** 30 **21.** 180 **23.** 462 **25.** 792 **27.** 240 **29.** $63w^2$ **31.** $42x^4$ **33.** $8n^3$ **35.** $33s^2$ **37.** No. *Sample answer:* You can multiply any common multiple that you can find by a whole number greater than 1 to find an even greater common multiple. **39.** $\frac{2}{7}$ **41.** $\frac{11}{15}$ **43.** $\frac{5}{12}$ **45.** $\frac{8}{21}$ **47.** $\frac{7}{6}, \frac{11}{9}, 1\frac{1}{3}$ **49.** $\frac{1}{5}, \frac{3}{10}, \frac{8}{15}$ **51.** $\frac{4}{9}, \frac{7}{15}, \frac{3}{4}$ **53.** $\frac{43}{18}, \frac{12}{5}, 2\frac{5}{12}$ **55.** 25. *Sample answer:* The prime factorization of 12 is $2^2 \cdot 3$. The only additional factor needed is 5^2 to obtain the product $2^2 \cdot 3 \cdot 5^2$ for the LCM 300. Therefore, 5^2 or 25 is the least number that meets the requirements. **57.** $15x^3y^5$ **59.** $495g^4h^3$ **61.** $364ab^2c^3$ **63.** $120d^3ef^2$ **65.** $\frac{4x}{12}, \frac{3x}{12}$ **67.** $\frac{15x^2}{20xy^2}, \frac{8y}{20xy^2}$ **69.** *Sample answer:* $\frac{1}{4}$ **71.** 25 **73.** 625 **75.** $2^2 \cdot 7$ **77.** 3^4 **79.** 8 gift boxes

4.5 Guided Practice (p. 196) **1.** add **3.** 4^{11} **5.** 6^8 **7.** 2^5 **9.** 3^3 **11.** m^7 **13.** x^6 **15.** The coefficients of each expression should have been multiplied to obtain $2x^5 \cdot 2x^4 = 2 \cdot 2 \cdot x^{5+4} = 4x^9$.

4.5 Practice and Problem Solving (pp. 197–198)
17. 9^5 **19.** 8^8 **21.** 8^6 **23.** 9^{10} **25.** b^{15} **27.** $8z^{11}$ **29.** $8r^6$ **31.** z^{14} **33.** $7y^3$ **35.** $\frac{2s^3}{3}$ **37.** = **39.** > **41.** The powers a^7 and b^7 do not have the same base. **43.** 2 **45.** 3 **47.** $4m^5n^7$ **49.** p^7q^4 **51.** $\frac{7m^4n^5}{3}$ **53.** $\frac{7c^4d^5}{6}$ **55.** $\frac{3a^3}{7}$ **57.** $4w^{10}$ **59. a.** 5^{m-n} **b.** *Sample answer:* $m = 4$ and $n = 3$ **c.** Yes. *Sample answer:* Any pair of integers m and n such that m is 1 more than n will result in a true equation. **61.** *Sample answer:* $2^1 \cdot 2^5$, $2^2 \cdot 2^4$, and $2^3 \cdot 2^3$; $\frac{2^7}{2^1}, \frac{2^8}{2^2}$, and $\frac{2^9}{2^3}$ **65.** 7 **67.** 112 **69.** x **71.** 25 **73.** $15x^2y^2$ **75.** $72x^2y^3$

4.6 Guided Practice (p. 201) **1.** $\frac{1}{7^2}$ **3.** $\frac{1}{5^3}$ **5.** $\frac{4}{a^6}$ **7.** 3^{-3} **9.** $4x^{-3}$ **11.** 6^3 **13.** x^8 **15.** Step 1: $\frac{10^{-3}}{10^{-9}}$; Step 2: 10^6

4.6 Practice and Problem Solving (pp. 202–203)
17. 1 **19.** $\frac{1}{20^4}$ **21.** $\frac{18}{f}$ **23.** $\frac{c^3}{d}$ **25.** 19^{-1} **27.** 2^{-6} **29.** $4d^{-1}$ **31.** $9a^2b^{-6}$ **33.** $\frac{1}{5^4}$ **35.** 13^6 **37.** $\frac{15}{t^{11}}$ **39.** $\frac{1}{b^{14}}$ **41.** *Sample answer:* $6^2 = 6 \cdot 6 = 36$, but $6^{-2} = \frac{1}{6^2} = \frac{1}{36}$. **43.** $\frac{1}{2^3}$ **45.** $\frac{1}{16}$ **47.** $\frac{17}{a^4}$ **49.** $2w^8$ **51.** 0.011 **53.** 0.010 **55. a.** 10^{-9} m^2 **b.** 10^{-5} m^2 **57.** $\frac{d^6}{c^6}$ **59.** $\frac{1}{x^8y^6}$ **63.** 5 **65.** −48 **67.** 3^4 **69.** 2^5

4.7 Guided Practice (p. 206) **1.** *Sample answer:* 4.7×10^{-4} **3.** 9.18×10^6 **5.** 7.23×10^5 **7.** 27,800,000 **9.** 0.0000415 **11.** 5×10^{-5} m

4.7 Practice and Problem Solving (pp. 207–208)
13. 4.62×10^7 **15.** 1.7×10^3 **17.** 1.04×10^5 **19.** 2.3×10^{-5} **21.** 1.06×10^{-5} **23.** 5,617,000 **25.** 0.0000000038 **27.** 0.0000006 **29.** 2,280,000,000 **31.** 3.721×10^9 people **33.** 3.34×10^{-10} sec **35.** 0.00003 m **37.** *Sample answer:* The friend did not compare powers of 10. Because $4 \times 10^3 = 4000$ and $2 \times 10^2 = 200$, 4×10^3 is actually 20 times greater than 2×10^2. **39.** 4.2×10^{-4} m, 2.8×10^{-4} m, 2×10^6 dust mites **41.** < **43.** > **45.** 5.4×10^{13} **47.** 5.95×10^{-8} **49.** 1.97×10^3; 8700; 3.98×10^4 **51.** 8.4×10^{-6}; 0.00009; 7.61×10^{-3} **53. a.** 2.07×10^4 plankton **b.** about 7.45×10^7 plankton **c.** about 1.12×10^9 plankton **d.** about 4.47×10^{-4} Cal **55.** −17, −16, 11, 13 **57.** −119, −114, −98, 99 **59.** 20.7 **61.** $x > 5$;

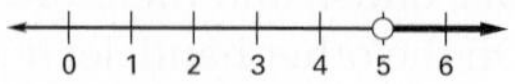

63. $x < -5$;

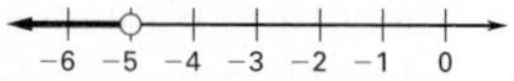

4.7 Technology Activity (p. 209) **1.** 5.46796×10^7 **3.** 1.5×10^{28} kg

Chapter Review (pp. 210–213) **1.** *Sample answer:* prime: 23, composite: 120 **3.** *Sample answer:* $\frac{2}{3}$ and $\frac{10}{15}$; they are equivalent because $\frac{10}{15}$ in simplest form is $\frac{10 \div 5}{15 \div 5} = \frac{2}{3}$. **5.** $3 \cdot 5^2$ **7.** $3 \cdot 43$

Selected Answers

9. $2 \cdot 2 \cdot 3 \cdot 3 \cdot a \cdot a \cdot a \cdot a \cdot b \cdot b \cdot b$ **11.** $2 \cdot 2 \cdot 2 \cdot 3 \cdot 3 \cdot w \cdot w \cdot w \cdot w \cdot w \cdot w \cdot z$ **13.** 2 **15.** 4 **17.** $\frac{2}{9}$ **19.** $\frac{1}{4}$ **21.** $\frac{3a}{2b}$ **23.** $\frac{4}{x}$ **25.** $\frac{1}{12}$ **27.** $\frac{11}{36}$ **29.** the friend's team **31.** 3^{12} **33.** 10^8 **35.** $8c^{11}$ **37.** y^9 **39.** 1 **41.** $\frac{15}{d^9}$ **43.** 6.7×10^7 **45.** 4.28×10^9 **47.** $<$

Chapter 5

5.1 Guided Practice (p. 222) **1.** terminating decimal **3.** terminating decimal **5.** *Sample answer:* If you can write the number as a quotient of two integers, it is rational. Otherwise, it is not rational. **7.** $\frac{-2}{1}$ or $\frac{2}{-1}$ **9.** $\frac{-4}{3}$ or $\frac{4}{-3}$ **11.** 1.8 **13.** -9.625 **15.** $\frac{81}{250}$ **17.** $2\frac{2}{3}$ **19.** Only the "78" repeats, so these are the only digits that should be under the bar: $5.07878\ldots = 5.0\overline{78}$.

5.1 Practice and Problem Solving (pp. 222–224) **21.** $\frac{-29}{1}$ or $\frac{29}{-1}$ **23.** $\frac{-1}{8}$ or $\frac{1}{-8}$ **25.** $\frac{-17}{1}$ or $\frac{17}{-1}$ **27.** $\frac{87}{100}$ **29.** -0.875 **31.** $3.1\overline{6}$ **33.** $-1.\overline{18}$ **35.** -13.7 **37.** $\frac{63}{100}$ **39.** $2\frac{93}{1000}$ **41.** $\frac{19}{1000}$ **43.** $-1\frac{51}{500}$ **45. a.** Nov.: $\frac{8}{25}$, Dec.: $\frac{17}{45}$, Jan.: $\frac{7}{10}$, Feb.: $\frac{39}{55}$, Mar.: $\frac{107}{150}$ **b.** $0.32, 0.3\overline{7}, 0.7, 0.7\overline{09}, 0.71\overline{3}$; March **c.** *Sample answer:* I think it increased recycling efforts. Before January 1, the portion of trash recycled was less than 0.4. After January 1, the portion recycled was at least 0.7. **47.** sometimes **49.** $\frac{8}{9}$ **51.** $-\frac{4}{9}$ **53.** $\frac{4}{33}$ **55.** $\frac{299}{333}$ **57.** $-2, 0.8, \frac{7}{8}, 1\frac{1}{3}, 2.1$ **59.** $-\frac{1}{5}, -0.1, 0.21, 0.\overline{2}, 2.3, \frac{8}{3}$ **61. a.** Maria: 13 at bats, 5 hits; Laura: 13 at bats, 3 hits; Jenny: 12 at bats, 6 hits **b.** Maria: 0.385; Laura: 0.231; Jenny: 0.500 **c.** *Sample answer:* I would rank Jenny first, followed by Maria, then Laura. I think that the higher a person's batting average is, the better the player is at hitting. **63.** *Sample answer:* I do not see any repeating pattern of digits or any sign of termination; $0.\overline{0588235294117647}$; the calculator does not show enough decimal places for the repeating pattern to appear, since the pattern has 16 digits. **67.** $-m - 9$ **69.** 180 **71.** 189

5.2 Guided Practice (p. 227) **1.** numerators **3.** $\frac{8}{9}$ **5.** $-\frac{1}{4}$ **7.** $-12\frac{1}{8}$ **9.** Step 1: $\frac{15}{4}, \frac{7}{4}$; Step 2: $5\frac{1}{2}$; Step 3: No. *Sample answer:* Since $\frac{1}{2} = \frac{2}{4}$, $5\frac{1}{2} > 5\frac{1}{4}$.

5.2 Practice and Problem Solving (pp. 228–229) **11.** $1\frac{1}{19}$ **13.** $1\frac{2}{7}$ **15.** $-\frac{3}{13}$ **17.** $-1\frac{1}{17}$ **19.** -5 **21.** 3 **23.** $-6\frac{2}{9}$ **25.** $-9\frac{1}{7}$ **27.** $1\frac{1}{2}$ h **29.** $\frac{3x}{4}$ **31.** $\frac{1}{p}$ **33.** $-\frac{n}{3}$ **35.** $-\frac{14}{9a}$ **37.** $2\frac{1}{2}$ in. **39.** $\frac{1}{10}$ **41.** $1\frac{1}{5}$ **43.** $-2\frac{5}{14}$ **45.** *Sample answer:* $-\frac{1}{4}$ and $\frac{3}{4}$ **47.** $-\frac{6}{11}$ **49.** $2\frac{7}{9}$ **51.** $6\frac{2}{13}$ **55.** $3s$ **57.** $\frac{13m^2}{16}$ **59.** $18mn$ **61.** $12a^3b$

5.3 Guided Practice (p. 233) **1.** 6 **3.** $-\frac{1}{8}$ **5.** $2\frac{2}{3}$ **7.** $\frac{7a}{30}$ **9.** $\frac{3a}{2}$ **11.** Step 1: $\frac{21}{2}, \frac{14}{3}$; Step 2: $\frac{63}{6}, \frac{28}{6}$; Step 3: $\frac{35}{6}$; $5\frac{5}{6}$ lb

5.3 Practice and Problem Solving (pp. 234–235) **13.** $\frac{1}{6}$ **15.** $-\frac{7}{18}$ **17.** $-\frac{9}{56}$ **19.** $-\frac{1}{55}$ **21.** $-1\frac{7}{36}$ **23.** $-\frac{13}{36}$ **25.** $7\frac{1}{8}$ **27.** $3\frac{23}{26}$ **29.** $5\frac{5}{6}$ **31.** $7\frac{13}{15}$ **33.** length: $4\frac{1}{8}$ in., perimeter: 13 in. **35. a.** small: $\frac{3}{8}$ in., medium: $\frac{3}{8}$ in., large: $\frac{3}{8}$ in., extra large: $\frac{3}{8}$ in. **b.** 3 medium, 2 large, 1 extra large **c.** *Sample answer:* I would make it so that there are no missing measurements in the chart by making small from 21 to $21\frac{1}{2}$, medium from $21\frac{5}{8}$ to $22\frac{1}{4}$, large from $22\frac{3}{8}$ to 23, and extra large from $23\frac{1}{8}$ to 24. **37.** $-\frac{2y}{35}$ **39.** $-\frac{83r}{88}$ **41.** $-\frac{x}{24}$ **43.** $\frac{13w}{36}$ **45.** $9\frac{1}{4}$ **47.** $\frac{7}{24}$ **49.** $-2\frac{13}{30}$ **51.** Yes; yes. *Sample answer:* Using 48, the equivalent fractions are $\frac{42}{48}$ and $\frac{20}{48}$, so the sum is $\frac{62}{48}$. Dividing out the common factor 2 from the numerator and denominator then gives $\frac{31}{24}$, or $1\frac{7}{24}$.

Using the LCD, 24, the equivalent fractions are $\frac{21}{24}$ and $\frac{10}{24}$, so the sum is $\frac{31}{24}$. So using the LCD, you do not have to perform the additional step of simplifying in this case. **53.** 6 **55.** 18 **57.** b^{11} **59.** d^{-2} **61.** 14 ft, $1\frac{1}{2}$ in.

5.4 Guided Practice (p. 239) **1.** numerators, denominators **3.** $\frac{15}{32}$ **5.** $-6\frac{2}{3}$ **7.** *Sample answer:* The product of powers rule was applied incorrectly. To find the product $c^2 \cdot c^4$, you must add the exponents, not multiply them, so the result should be $\frac{4c^6}{35}$.

5.4 Practice and Problem Solving (pp. 240–241) **9.** $-\frac{1}{8}$ **11.** $\frac{7}{16}$ **13.** -16 **15.** $18\frac{3}{4}$ **17.** $40\frac{5}{6}$ **19.** $8\frac{5}{23}$ **21. a.** $98\frac{7}{16}$ ft^2 **b.** Yes. *Sample answer:* Two coats will take enough paint for $2 \cdot 98\frac{7}{16} = 196\frac{7}{8}$ square feet, which is less than the 200 square feet the paint should cover. **23.** $\frac{3a^2}{55}$ **25.** $-\frac{44c^9}{9}$ **27.** $\frac{8x^2}{35}$ **29. a.** $\frac{3}{8} - \frac{3}{64}y$;

Time (y)	1	2	3
Tread depth (in.)	$\frac{21}{64}$	$\frac{9}{32}$	$\frac{15}{64}$

b.

Time (y)	1	2	3	4	5	6	7
Tread depth (in.)	$\frac{21}{64}$	$\frac{9}{32}$	$\frac{15}{64}$	$\frac{3}{16}$	$\frac{9}{64}$	$\frac{3}{32}$	$\frac{3}{64}$

Sample answer: Since $\frac{1}{16} = \frac{4}{64}$ and $\frac{3}{32} = \frac{6}{64}$, there is still sufficient tread left after 6 years but not after 7 years, so the tires should be replaced sometime after 6 years. **31.** 0 **33.** $2\frac{7}{8}$ **35.** $\frac{145}{363}$ **37.** 2.0×10^2 **39.** 2.0×10^{-4} **43.** 6 **45.** -3 **47.** 6.5 **49.** $b > -2$;

5.5 Guided Practice (p. 245) **1.** *Sample answer:* Since $0.25 = \frac{1}{4}$, $0.25 \cdot 4 = \frac{1}{4} \cdot 4 = 1$. **3.** $\frac{1}{8}$ **5.** $\frac{4}{3}$ **7.** $\frac{320}{363}$ **9.** $-\frac{11}{36}$ **11.** $\frac{27}{182}$ **13.** $\frac{1}{65}$ **15.** *Sample answer:* $\frac{25}{4}$ should not have been multiplied by $\frac{1}{2}$, but by its reciprocal, which is 2, to obtain $\frac{25}{4} \cdot \frac{2}{1} = \frac{25}{2} = 12\frac{1}{2}$.

5.5 Practice and Problem Solving (pp. 245–246) **17.** $-1\frac{7}{20}$ **19.** $1\frac{15}{19}$ **21.** $2\frac{20}{53}$ **23.** $-1\frac{13}{99}$ **25.** -99 **27.** $-\frac{8}{189}$ **29.** 6 lanes **31.** 2 **33.** $3\frac{11}{30}$ **35.** $2\frac{17}{39}$ **39.** 6 **41.** 7 **43.** $\frac{7}{15}$ **45.** $\frac{3}{8}$ **47.** $-\frac{2b}{11}$ **49.** $\frac{19d}{18}$

5.6 Guided Practice (p. 249) **1.** the number's reciprocal **3.** -36 **5.** $-1\frac{2}{7}$ **7.** 16 **9.** Step 1: ant A: $10\frac{1}{2} = \frac{3}{4}t$; ant B: $11\frac{3}{8} = \frac{7}{8}t$; Step 2: ant A: $t = 14$ sec; ant B: $t = 13$ sec; Step 3: ant B

5.6 Practice and Problem Solving (pp. 249–251) **11.** 54 **13.** -60 **15.** $-\frac{9}{10}$ **17.** $-\frac{8}{17}$ **19.** $1\frac{9}{10}w = 5$, $2\frac{12}{19}$ ft **21.** 54 **23.** -20 **25.** $3\frac{4}{5}$ **27.** $2\frac{2}{3}$ **29.** $2\frac{1}{3}$ **31.** $8\frac{6}{7}$ min **33.** $-\frac{2}{5}$ **35.** $y > 14$; **37.** $z \geq -3$; **39.** $\frac{5}{12}$ **41.** $-1\frac{1}{36}$

5.6 Technology Activity (p. 252) **1.** 36 **3.** -91 **5.** 112 stitches

5.7 Guided Practice (p. 255) **1.** LCD **3.** $-24\frac{1}{4}$ **5.** 3 **7.** -4 **9.** $x > 2\frac{11}{14}$ **11.** $x < 2\frac{3}{8}$

5.7 Practice and Problem Solving (pp. 256–257) **13.** $\frac{1}{8}$ **15.** $\frac{19}{30}$ **17.** $1\frac{16}{17}$ **19.** $-\frac{7}{27}$ **21.** $-\frac{19}{70}$ **23.** 2.2 **25.** 1.25 **27.** -4 **29.** 1.2 **31.** 5 paychecks **33.** $k \leq -68\frac{8}{9}$ **35.** $r > -\frac{5}{8}$ **37.** $d \geq 1\frac{1}{3}$ **39.** $8 + j - \frac{2}{3}j \leq 18$ or $8 + \frac{1}{3}j \leq 18$, not more than \$30 **41.** 19.95°C **43.** 7 costumes **45.** \$2.73 **47.** 120 **49.** -36 **51.** $\frac{44r}{45}$ **53.** $\frac{7t}{3}$ **55.** 10 h

Chapter Review (pp. 258–261) **1.** *Sample answer:* -7 **3.** *Sample answer:* 18 **5.** *Sample answer:* $\frac{9}{16}$ and $\frac{16}{9}$ **7.** $0.\overline{63}$ **9.** -2.6 **11.** $-\frac{263}{25}$, -5.24, $5.\overline{3}$, $\frac{134}{25}$, $5\frac{9}{20}$ **13.** $-1\frac{2}{7}$ **15.** 15 **17.** $\frac{11}{42}$ **19.** $5\frac{7}{12}$ **21.** $-8\frac{32}{105}$

Selected Answers

23. $-\frac{1}{12}$ **25.** -48 **27.** $\frac{4b^3}{7}$ **29.** $-\frac{3s^5}{5}$ **31.** $-1\frac{27}{29}$ **33.** $-2\frac{1}{2}$ **35.** $-\frac{16}{17}$ **37.** $-\frac{1}{4}$ **39.** $\frac{13}{28}$

Focus on Problem Solving (p. 265) **1.** 4 h **3.** 3 h **5.** about 26 min **7.** 1 h **9.** 3 h

Chapter 6

6.1 Guided Practice (p. 272) **1.** *Sample answer:* A unit rate is a ratio of two quantities that have different units for which the denominator is 1 when expressed in fraction form; $\frac{\$5.20}{1 \text{ lb}}$. **3.** no; 4 to 3; $\frac{4}{3}$, 4 : 3 **5.** no; 3 : 1; $\frac{3}{1}$, 3 to 1 **7.** 1 : 7, 2 to 9, $\frac{7}{28}$, $\frac{3}{10}$, 2 to 6 **9.** Step 1: decorator A: 125 roses, decorator B: 240 roses, decorator C: 240 roses; Step 2: decorator A: \$.96, decorator B: \$.85, decorator C: \$.75; Step 3: decorator C

6.1 Practice and Problem Solving (pp. 272–274) **11.** yes; $\frac{4}{5}$, 4 to 5 **13.** no; $\frac{25}{3}$; 25 to 3, 25 : 3 **15.** no; 3 : 1; $\frac{3}{1}$, 3 to 1 **17.** no; 14 to 5; $\frac{14}{5}$, 14 : 5 **19.** 18 to 6, $\frac{53}{15}$, $\frac{15}{4}$, 19 to 5, 4 : 1 **21.** 9 : 2, 5 : 1, $\frac{100}{19}$, 65 : 12, $\frac{22}{4}$ **23.** $\frac{\$23}{1 \text{ share}}$ **25.** $\frac{14 \text{ mi}}{1 \text{ h}}$ **27.** $\frac{8\frac{2}{3} \text{ points}}{1 \text{ quarter}}$ **29.** $\frac{\frac{5}{8} \text{ win}}{1 \text{ game}}$ **31.** 900 **33.** 2750 **35.** 0.375, or $\frac{3}{8}$ **37.** *Sample answer:* About \$.75 per cookie; I rounded \$11.88 to \$12 and \$12 divided by 16 cookies is \$0.75. **39. a.** 24 gal **b.** 600 mi **c.** \$.06 **d.** No. *Sample answer:* At a rate of \$.06 per mile, gasoline for 350 miles will cost 350 mi $\cdot \frac{\$.06}{1 \text{ mi}} = \$21$. **41.** $\frac{1}{3}$ **43.** $\frac{1}{1}$ **45. a.** 12.5 mi/h **b.** 0.2 mi/min **c.** 1101.1 ft/min **49.** $-\frac{2}{27}$ **51.** 55 stamps; 40 stamps **53.** $y \le -57$

6.2 Guided Practice (p. 277) **1.** *Sample answer:* $\frac{2}{3} = \frac{4}{6}$, or $\frac{2}{4} = \frac{3}{6}$ **3.** 25 **5.** 7 **7.** *Sample answer:* A proportion must use comparable ratios. Because the fraction on the left compares pencils to cost, the fraction on the right must do likewise, so it should be $\frac{30}{x}$, not $\frac{x}{30}$.

6.2 Practice and Problem Solving (pp. 278–279) **9.** 25 **11.** 11 **13.** 70 **15.** 40 **17.** 5 **19.** 18 **21.** 5 **23.** 34 **25.** 15 erasers **27. a.** no **b.** *Sample answer:* $\frac{24}{9} = \frac{x}{15}$, 40 goals **29.** *Sample answer:* $\frac{15}{18} = \frac{5}{6}$; 8 ways; there are 2 ways to arrange the proportion with 15 as the numerator of the first fraction, $\frac{15}{18} = \frac{5}{6}$ or $\frac{15}{5} = \frac{18}{6}$. 15 is 1 of 4 numbers that could be the numerator of the first fraction, so there are 4 • 2 or 8 ways to rearrange the 4 numbers. **31. a.** 1 : 26 **b.** 2 kg **33. a.** $\frac{1}{4}$ **b.** 5 red stripes **35.** It decreases. **37.** $24m^2$ **39.** 1 **41.** $-\frac{3}{16}$ **43.** $\frac{11}{24}$ **45.** $z > 4\frac{8}{15}$ **47.** $x \le 1\frac{29}{35}$

6.3 Guided Practice (p. 282) **1.** 3 • 12 and 4 • 9 **3.** yes **5.** yes **7.** 3 **9.** 2 **11.** Step 1: $\frac{\$.66}{12 \text{ min}}$; Step 2: $\frac{\$1.21}{m \text{ min}}$; Step 3: $\frac{\$.66}{12 \text{ min}} = \frac{\$1.21}{m \text{ min}}$; 22 min

6.3 Practice and Problem Solving (pp. 283–284) **13.** no **15.** no **17.** no **19.** yes **21.** 5 **23.** 25 **25.** 175 **27.** 28 **29.** 0.8 **31.** 3 **33. a.** \$20 **b.** 18 gal **35. a.** 125 g **b.** 36 g **37.** 22 **39.** 6 **41.** *Sample answer:*

$\frac{a}{b} = \frac{c}{d}$	[Given]
$a \cdot d = b \cdot c$	[Form cross products.]
$\frac{ad}{ac} = \frac{bc}{ac}$	[Divide each side by *ac*.]
$\frac{d}{c} = \frac{b}{a}$	[Simplify.]

43. $\frac{3}{5}$. *Sample answer:* Forming cross products gives $4a = 3b$ and $4c = 5b$. I noticed that because $\frac{a}{c} = \frac{4a}{4c}$, I could substitute $3b$ for $4a$ and $5b$ for $4c$ and write $\frac{a}{c} = \frac{3b}{5b} = \frac{3}{5}$. **45–47.** Check students' work. **49.** 5.001×10^6 **51.** 4 to 9 **53.** $\frac{7}{12}$

Student Reference (p. 286) **1.** any three of *M*, *N*, *P*, *R*, *S* **3.** plane *Y* and plane *Z* **5.** any one of $\overline{RS}$, $\overline{MN}$, $\overline{NP}$ **7.** *Sample answer:* quadrilateral *DEFG* **9.** $\angle D$, $\angle E$, $\angle F$, $\angle G$

6.4 Guided Practice (p. 290) **1.** Corresponding angles are congruent and corresponding sides are congruent. **3.** corresponding sides: $\overline{AB}$ and $\overline{DE}$, $\overline{BC}$ and $\overline{EF}$, $\overline{AC}$ and $\overline{DF}$; corresponding angles: $\angle A$ and $\angle D$, $\angle B$ and $\angle E$, $\angle C$ and $\angle F$ **5.** 90°

6.4 Practice and Problem Solving (pp. 291–292) **7.** corresponding angles: $\angle A$ and $\angle D$, $\angle B$ and $\angle E$, $\angle C$ and $\angle F$; corresponding sides: $\overline{AB}$ and $\overline{DE}$, $\overline{BC}$ and $\overline{EF}$, $\overline{AC}$ and $\overline{DF}$ **9.** $\frac{10}{13}$ **11.** $\frac{2}{3}$ **13.** 128° **15.** 18 in. **17.** Sometimes. *Sample answer:* Corresponding angles of similar figures are congruent, but similar figures are congruent only if they are also the same size. **19.** Sometimes. *Sample answer:* All angles are congruent and have measures of 90°, but rectangles are congruent only if they have the same shape and same size. **21. a.** Yes. *Sample answer:* The ratio of the lengths is $\frac{9.41}{6.14} \approx 1.53$, and the ratio of the widths is $\frac{4.00}{2.61} \approx 1.53$, so both ratios are greater than $1\frac{1}{2}$, or 1.5. **b.** Yes. *Sample answer:* The ratio of the lengths is $\frac{4.00}{6.14} \approx 0.65$, and the ratio of the widths is $\frac{1.70}{2.61} \approx 0.65$, so both ratios are less than $\frac{3}{4}$, or 0.75. **c.** no **25.** $\frac{5}{6}$ **27.** $\frac{2}{5xy^3}$ **29.** 6 h

6.5 Guided Practice (p. 295) **1.** $\overline{EH}$ **3.** 4 m **5.** Step 1: *Sample answer:* $\frac{x}{74} = \frac{80}{26}$; Step 2: 228 in.

6.5 Practice and Problem Solving (pp. 295–297) **7.** 15 mm **9.** 12.5 yd **11.** 9 m **13.** 3.75 ft; 12.5 ft **15. a.** $DE = 10$ cm, $FG = 12.5$ cm **b.** $AE = 26$ cm, $AG = 32.5$ cm **19.** −27 **21.** $\frac{2}{5}$ **23.** $\frac{22}{20}$, $\frac{44}{33}$, 35 : 25, 15 to 9, 8 : 3

6.6 Guided Practice (p. 302) **1.** A two-dimensional drawing that is similar to the object it represents. **3.** 200 mi **5.** 1280 mi **7.** 1 : 1008 **9.** 1 : 1200 **11.** Step 1: 1 cm : 0.8 m; Step 2: 1 : 80; Step 3: *Sample answer:* $\frac{1}{80} = \frac{1.5}{l}$, $l = 120$ cm, or 1.2 m; $\frac{1}{80} = \frac{0.5}{w}$, $w = 40$ cm, or 0.4 m

6.6 Practice and Problem Solving (pp. 303–304) **13.** 55 km **15.** 185 km **17.** 7.5 km **19.** 45 km **21.** 30 in. **23.** $4\frac{2}{3}$ in. **25.** 0.5 in. **27.** $\frac{1}{6}$ in. **29.** 1 : 240 **31.** 1 : 360 **33.** 1 : 500,000 **35.** 1 : 340 **37.** 1 : 32 **39. a.** 126 in., or 10 ft 6 in. **b.** 84 in., or 7 ft **c.** 21 in. by $31\frac{1}{2}$ in. **41.** 20 ft **43.** 3 : 2 **45.** head: 2.5 mm, thorax: 3.25 mm, abdomen: 4.25 mm **47.** $17\frac{3}{11}$ **49.** $-15\frac{1}{2}$

6.7 Guided Practice (p. 309) **1.** experimental **3.** $\frac{1}{2}$ **5.** $\frac{2}{3}$

6.7 Practice and Problem Solving (pp. 309–311) **7.** $\frac{1}{4}$ **9.** 3 to 1 **11. a.** $\frac{2}{11}$ **b.** $\frac{5}{11}$ **c.** 6 to 5 **d.** *Sample answer:* RIVER **13.** 15 seeds **15.** *Sample answer:* Write the probability as a ratio. For the odds in favor, write a ratio whose numerator is the numerator of the probability ratio, and whose denominator is the difference in the denominator and numerator of the probability ratio. The odds against are just the reciprocal of the odds in favor. **17.** $\frac{16}{143}$, or about 0.1119 **19. a.** about 400 times **b.** about 20,000 hits **21.** $\frac{5}{6}$; $1 - \frac{1}{n}$. *Sample answer:* In a probability experiment, it is certain that a given event must either occur or not occur. The probability of something that is certain is 1. So, the sum of the probabilities of an event occurring and not occurring is 1. If the probability of an event is $\frac{1}{n}$, then $P(\text{not event}) + \frac{1}{n} = 1$, and $P(\text{not event}) = 1 - \frac{1}{n}$. **23.** −18 **25.** −252 **27.** −2.7, −1.5, $-\frac{3}{5}$, $1\frac{5}{9}$, $\frac{13}{5}$ **29.** 7 m

6.7 Technology Activity (p. 312) **Steps 1–3.** Check work. **1.** Check work. Note that there is a 43% chance that the experiment will require 4 or fewer trials and a 62% chance that it will require 5 or fewer trials. A typical mean might be between 4 and 5.

Selected Answers

6.8 Guided Practice (p. 315)

1. 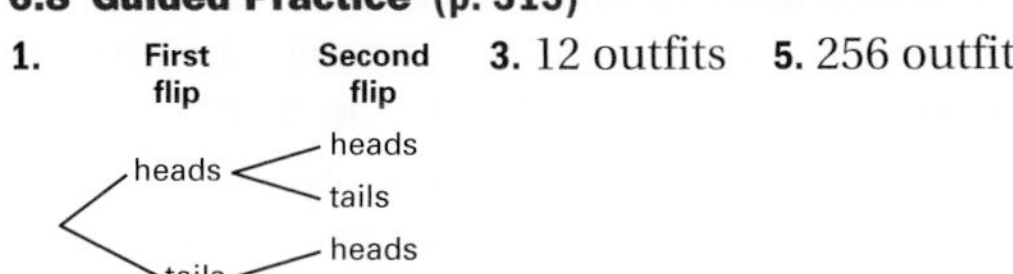

3. 12 outfits **5.** 256 outfits

6.8 Practice and Problem Solving (pp. 315–317)

7. 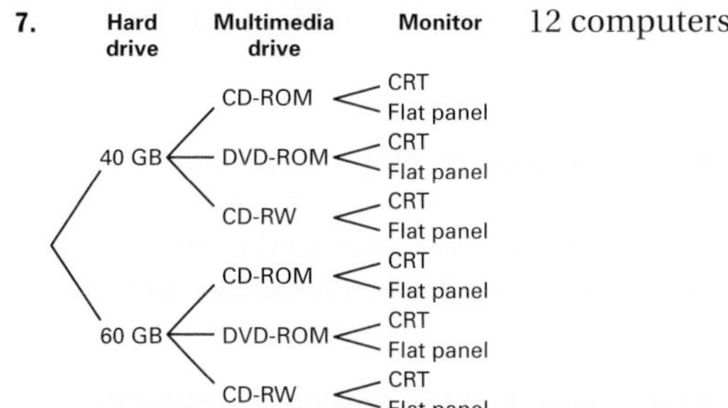

12 computers

9. a. 210 matchups **b.** 64 matchups **c.** No. *Sample answer:* Part b only considers possible matchups. The probability of two teams reaching the finals is not random, but depends at least partially on how good the teams are. **11.** 25 possible outcomes; $\frac{1}{25}$ **13.** 20 possible outcomes; $\frac{1}{5}$ **15.** $\frac{1}{4,569,760,000}$

17a. 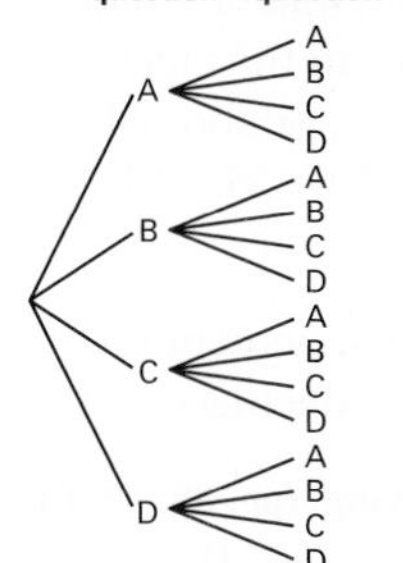

b. $\frac{1}{16}$ **c.** 7 outcomes; $\frac{7}{16}$

19. a. 100,000 phone numbers **b.** 10,000 phone numbers **c.** 5 digits **21.** $-1\frac{1}{4}$ **23.** $\frac{25}{56}$ **25.** 20 **27.** 13.5

Chapter Review (pp. 318–321) **1.** *Sample answer:* You can write the ratios in simplest form or as decimals. If they have the same simplest form or decimal form, they are equivalent. Another way is to find the cross products of the ratios. If the cross products are equal, then the ratios form a proportion, and are equivalent. **3.** *Sample answer:* Congruent figures have the same size and shape. Similar figures have the same shape, but are not necessarily the same size. The lengths of corresponding sides of similar figures have the same ratio, but that ratio is not necessarily 1, as it is for congruent figures. **5.** *Sample answer:* The probability of an event is the ratio of the number of favorable outcomes to the number of possible outcomes, while the odds in favor of an event is the ratio of the number of favorable outcomes to the number of unfavorable outcomes. **7.** $\frac{55 \text{ mi}}{1 \text{ h}}$

9. $\frac{\frac{1}{4}\text{ lap}}{1 \text{ min}}$ or $\frac{0.25 \text{ lap}}{1 \text{ min}}$ **11.** \$8.50 per ticket **13.** 2 **15.** 5 **17.** *Sample answer:* $\frac{5}{6} = \frac{s}{24}$, 20 h **19.** 8.5 **21.** 14 **23.** $\frac{9}{5}$ **25.** 15 cm **27.** 21 yd **29.** 54 yd **31.** $\frac{1}{4}$ **33.** $\frac{1}{8}$ **35.** 18 outfits

Chapter 7

7.1 Guided Practice (p. 331) **1.** 100 **3.** $\frac{13}{20}$ **5.** 48% **7.** Step 1: 114 serves; Step 2: 75 serves; Step 3: 39 serves

7.1 Practice and Problem Solving (pp. 331–333) **9.** $\frac{2}{5}$ **11.** $\frac{27}{100}$ **13.** $\frac{9}{50}$ **15.** $\frac{17}{20}$ **17.** 12% **19.** 70% **21.** 25% **23.** 85% **25.** 75% **27.** $\frac{3}{10}$ **29.** 10% **31.** 50% **33.** 40% **35.** 9 **37.** 15 **39.** 47 **41.** 70 **43.** 600 lb **45.** *Sample answer:* Because $p\% = \frac{p}{100}$, $100\% = \frac{100}{100}$. Simplifying $\frac{100}{100}$ gives 1, so 100% = 1. **47.** $\frac{9}{20}$, 54%, 0.62, $\frac{16}{25}$ **49.** 18 **51.** 18 **53.** 60

55. a. Opponent's side

Your side

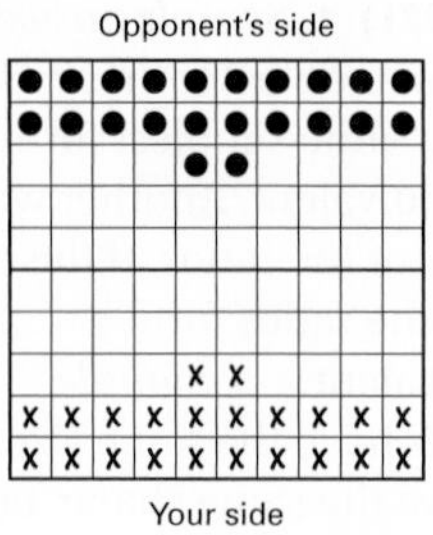

b. 44% **c.** 19 pieces. *Sample answer:* To start the game, there are 44 total pieces on the board. 75% of 44 is 33, so there are 33 pieces remaining. If 14 of these 33 belong to you, then 33 − 14 or 19 pieces belong to the opponent. **57. a.** about 640 students **b.** about 320 students **c.** about 90 students **59. a.** No. *Sample answer:* 40% of x is $0.4x$, and 60% of y is $0.6y$, so their sum is $0.4x + 0.6y$, which is not the same as 100% of $x + y$, which is just $x + y$. **b.** No. *Sample answer:* The average of 40% of x and 60% of y is $\frac{1}{2}(0.4x + 0.6y)$, but 50%, or $\frac{1}{2}$, of the sum of x and y is $\frac{1}{2}(x + y)$. **61.** $-\frac{2}{5}$ **63.** $7\frac{1}{2}$ **65.** 10 **67.** 1

7.2 Guided Practice (p. 337) **3.** 78 **5.** 90% **7.** *Sample answer:* The proportion shown is to find part of a base, not a percent, which is what is being sought. The unknown is the percent, p%, so the proportion should be $\frac{20}{30} = \frac{p}{100}$, which gives $100 \cdot \frac{20}{30} = 100 \cdot \frac{p}{100}$, and $p = 66\frac{2}{3}$%.

7.2 Practice and Problem Solving (pp. 337–339) **9.** 25% **11.** 44 **13.** 50 **15.** 13 teams **17.** 55 paintings **19.** $6\frac{2}{3}$% **21.** *Sample answer:* Biologists have tagged 40% of a herd of elk. If they have tagged 30 elk in the herd, what is the total number of elk in the herd? Solving the proportion gives $x = 75$, so there are 75 elk in the herd. **23.** $12\frac{1}{2}$%, $33\frac{1}{3}$%, $37\frac{1}{2}$%, $62\frac{1}{2}$%, $66\frac{2}{3}$%, $87\frac{1}{2}$% **25. a.** 20%; $62\frac{1}{2}$% **b.** 56% **27.** $4y$ **29.** $5y$ **33.** 0.975 **35.** 0.0015 **37.** $-0.\overline{3}$ **39.** −1.6

7.3 Guided Practice (p. 342) **1.** to the right **3.** 13% **5.** 0.05 **7.** 50% **9.** $116.\overline{6}$% **11.** The decimal point should have been moved two places to the right instead of to the left: 1.5 = 1.50 = 150%.

7.3 Practice and Problem Solving (pp. 342–344) **13.** 28% **15.** 200% **17.** 8.7% **19.** 0.08 **21.** 1.08 **23.** 0.00302 **25.** 15% **27.** $13.\overline{3}$% **29.** 350% **31.** $133.\overline{3}$% **33.** 0.15% **35.** 62.5% **37.** 272 **39.** 42.07 **41.** 480 **43.** 0.175 **45.** about 318 mi/h **47.** 606, 39, 6, 383, 365, 30 **49.** $\frac{3}{4}$, 100%, 150%, $\frac{5}{3}$, 2 **51.** 6.7 **53.** 12 **55.** 2.37 **57.** 0.09 **59. a.** \$36 million **b.** \$263.5 million **c.** \$323.5 million **63.** 0.06 **65.** 15.9 **67.** $\frac{3}{10}$ **69.** 75

7.4 Guided Practice (p. 347) **1.** percent: 40%, base: 80, part of the base: 32 **3.** 15 **5.** 50 **7.** Step 1: percent: 3%, base: \$2000, part of the base: amount of commission; Step 2: a = 3% • \$2000, \$60; Step 3: \$260

7.4 Practice and Problem Solving (pp. 348–349) **9.** 5.6 **11.** 0.5% **13.** 35 **15.** 80% **17.** 144 **19.** 140 students **21.** 50 students **23.** 4.5 **25.** 500 **27.** *Sample answer:* A fraction; a decimal; I would convert 75% to the fraction $\frac{3}{4}$ because 120 is evenly divisible by 4, but because 120 is not evenly divisible by 100, there is no clear advantage to changing 31% to a fraction. **29. a.** Dole **b.** Popular votes. *Sample answer:* The difference in the popular votes was about 49.0% − 40.6%, or about 8%, while the difference in the electoral votes was about 70.4% − 29.6%, or about 41%. **31. a.** \$250,000 **b.** 50% **33.** 471.6 **35.** 12.18 **37.** −6 **39.** 12.5% **41.** $133.\overline{3}$%

7.5 Guided Practice (p. 354) **1.** a percent of decrease **3.** increase; 50% **5.** decrease; 75%

7.5 Practice and Problem Solving (pp. 355–356) **7.** increase; 25% **9.** decrease; 40% **11.** increase; 35% **13.** In the formula for percent of change, the denominator is the original amount, not the new amount, so the denominator should be 90: $p = \frac{90 - 50}{90} = \frac{40}{90} = \frac{4}{9} = 44.\overline{4}$%. **15.** 91.5% decrease **17.** 210 **19.** 25.2 **21.** \$15.75 **23.** Yes. *Sample answer:* A 100% increase represents only a doubling, so if a quantity is more than doubled, the increase is greater than 100%.

25. a. about 50.8% decrease **b.** 1999; about 25.9% **c.** No. *Sample answer:* The graph does not indicate the amount that is made per pair of shoes. Also, it is possible that the decrease might be because the manufacturers are having the shoes made for them outside of the United States. **27.** 300%. *Sample answer:* A decrease of 75% is the same as $100\% - 75\% = 25\%$, or $\frac{1}{4}$, of the original amount. So to return to the original amount requires adding back $\frac{3}{4}$ of the original amount, and $\frac{3}{4}$ is 300% of $\frac{1}{4}$. **29.** 13.55 **31.** 5.44 **33.** 3 **35.** 3 **37.** 65% **39.** 75

7.6 Guided Practice (p. 359) **1.** markup **3.** \$27.30 **5.** \$15.75 **7.** Step 1: discount price: \$27, discount percent: 15%; Step 2: $27 = x - 15\% \cdot x$, or $27 = x \cdot (100\% - 15\%)$; Step 3: about \$31.76

7.6 Practice and Problem Solving (pp. 360–361) **9.** \$187.50 **11.** \$32.40 **13.** \$10.40 **15.** \$82.68 **17.** \$22.50 **19.** about \$26.32 **21.** \$200 **23.** about \$97.73 **25.** \$113.94 **27. a.** about \$1 **b.** *Sample answer:* About \$3; first I rounded the price up to \$20. Then because 10% of \$20 is \$2, and 5% of \$20 is half of 10% of \$20, I estimated the tip as \$2 + \$1 = \$3. **c.** *Sample answer:* About \$24; a high estimate; I rounded the price up to \$20 and the tax up to 5%, and also calculated the tip based on the \$20 price, so I overestimated both the tax and the tip. **d.** \$22.78. *Sample answer:* My estimate was \$1.22 high. **29.** ones, 3; 93 **31.** tenths, 0.9; 1596.0 **33.** 350 **35.** 375 **37.** 0.45 **39.** 1.02

7.7 Guided Practice (p. 364) **1.** the principal, or the amount deposited or borrowed **3.** \$140, \$640 **5.** 1.8% **7.** \$757.70

7.7 Practice and Problem Solving (pp. 365–366) **9.** \$182, \$507 **11.** \$392, \$3592 **13.** \$43.31, \$538.31 **15.** Row 1: 5 y; Row 2: \$9000; Row 3: 4.6% **17.** In the formula, t represents the time in years. Because 6 months = 0.5 year, 0.5 should have been substituted for t: $I = Prt = (200)(0.055)(0.5) = 5.5$. The interest earned is \$5.50. **19.** \$3780.01 **21.** \$1240.95 **23.** account A

25. a. Row 1: \$1050, \$1050; Row 2: \$1100, \$1102.50; Row 3: \$1250, \$1276.28; Row 4: \$1500, \$1628.89; Row 5: \$2000, \$2653.30

b.

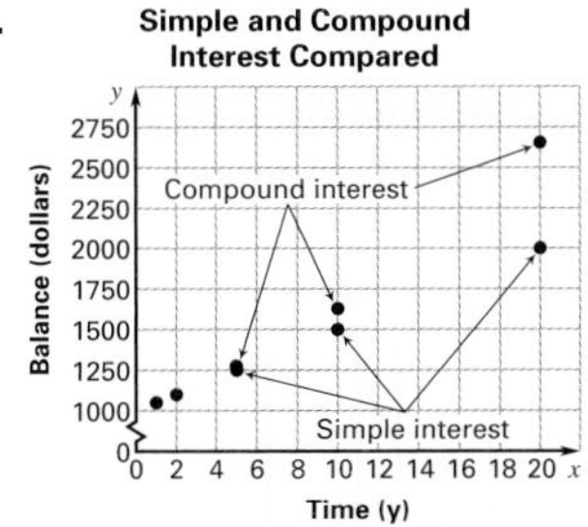

c. *Sample answer:* The points on the simple interest graph lie along a straight line, while the points on the compound interest graph lie on a curve that keeps rising more and more steeply. **27.** 10 y. *Sample answer:* The account will double when the interest earned equals the principal. The interest earned is $P(0.1)t$, so I reasoned that this quantity will equal P when $0.1t = 1$, or when $t = 10$. **29.** −1 **31.** 21 **33.** 36 **35.** \$29.75

7.7 Technology Activity (p. 367) **1.** \$311.93 **3.** \$688.20

Chapter Review (pp. 368–371) **1.** percent **3.** percent of decrease **5.** $\frac{53}{100}$ **7.** $\frac{3}{5}$ **9.** 31% **11.** 62% **13.** 19 **15.** 5 **17.** 150 **19.** 40% **21.** 33 **23.** 58.9% **25.** 48% **27.** 37.5% **29.** $66.\overline{6}\%$ **31.** 33.75 **33.** 472.5 **35.** \$78.75 **37.** 80% **39.** 32 **41.** 5% increase **43.** 62.5% decrease **45.** 388.6 **47.** \$280.50 **49.** \$7789.92

Chapter 8

8.1 Guided Practice (p. 387) **1.** function **3.** domain: 0, 1, 2, 3, 4; range: 0, 2, 4, 6, 8

5.

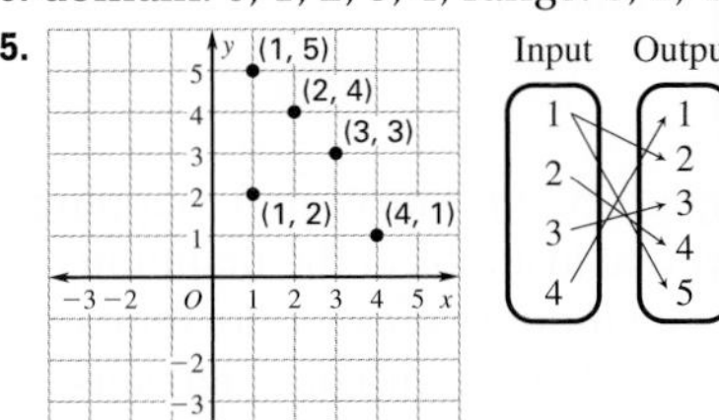

No; the input 1 is paired with two outputs, 2 and 5.

7. *Sample answer:* The relation is a function. A function can have two inputs paired with one output, as in this case, as long as it does not have two outputs paired with one input.

8.1 Practice and Problem Solving (pp. 388–390)
9. domain: 3, 7; range: 3, 6, 9 **11.** domain: 1.5, 2.8, 6.5; range: 0.2, 3.9, 4.3, 6.5

13.

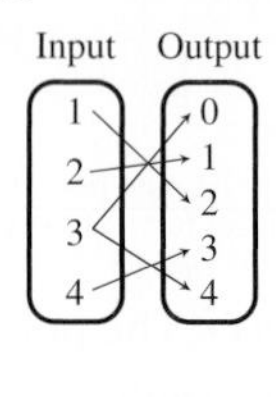

No; the input 3 is paired with two outputs, 0 and 4.

15.

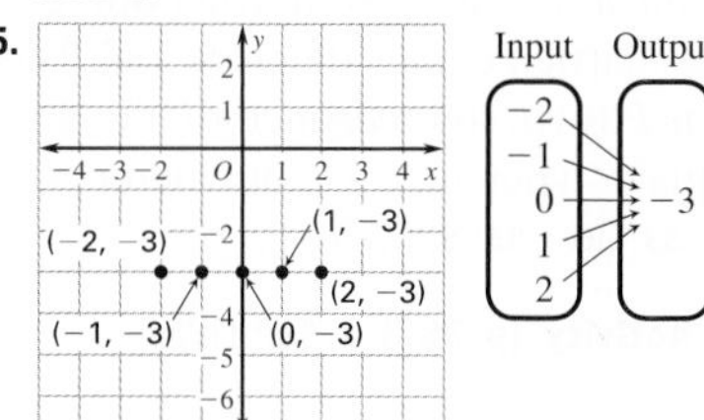

Yes; every input is paired with exactly one output.

17. a. Yes. *Sample answer:* A person can have only one height (output) for any given age (input).
b. No. *Sample answer:* A person can have more than one age (outputs) for a given height (input) because the height of an adult remains the same for many years. **19.** yes **21. a.** domain: 62, 73, 81, 82; range: 604, 1086, 1102, 1199, 1208

b. Input: 62, 73, 81, 82; Output: 604, 1086, 1102, 1199, 1208

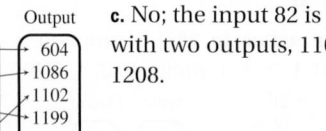

c. No; the input 82 is paired with two outputs, 1102 and 1208.

23. Mapping diagram. *Sample answer:* A mapping diagram allows you to just look at the mapping and see if there is an input that has more than one arrow going from it, whereas with ordered pairs, you need to compare x and y values. **27.** -12
29. -350 **31.** yes **33.** no **35.** \$153, \$1003

8.2 Guided Practice (p. 394) **1.** linear equation
3. yes **5.** no
7.

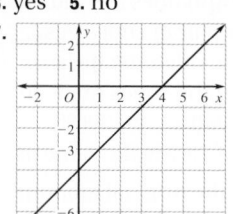

9.

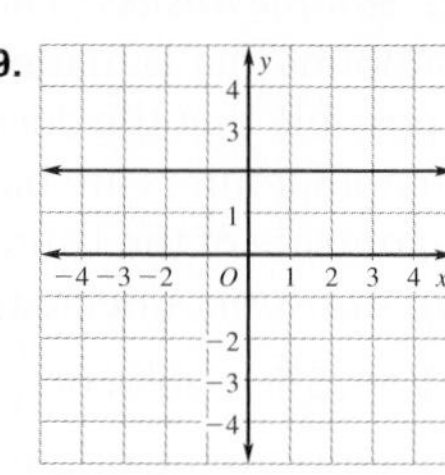

11. Step 1: 0, 120, 240, 360, 480, 600, 720;
Step 2:

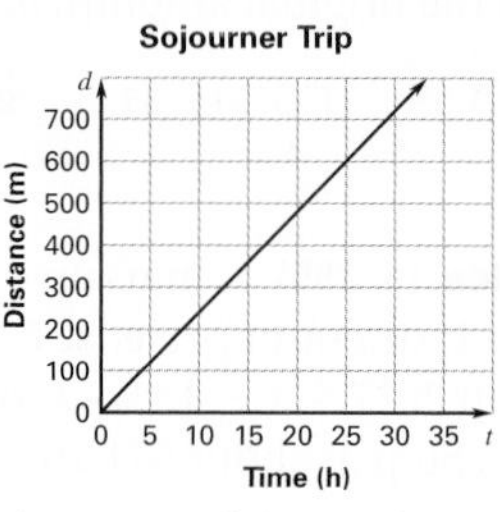

Step 3: about 21; about 21 h

8.2 Practice and Problem Solving (pp. 394–396)
13. yes **15.** no
17.

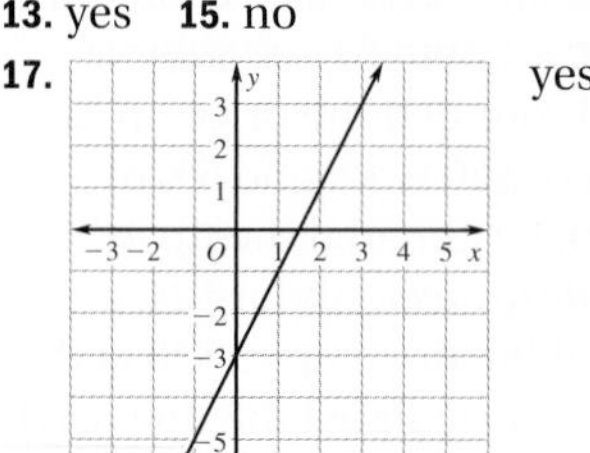

yes

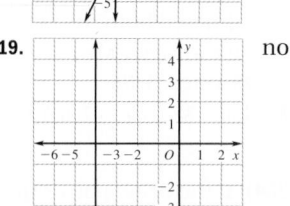

19. no

21.

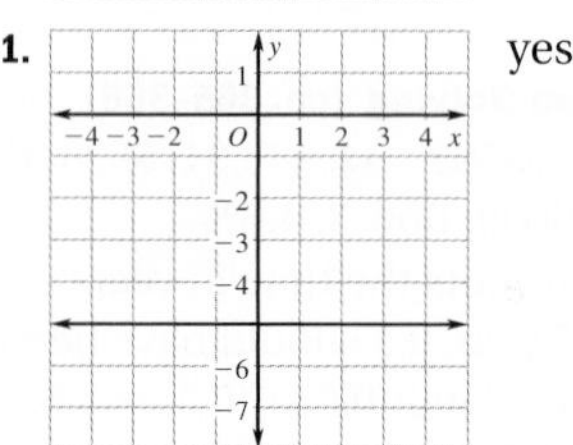

yes

23. 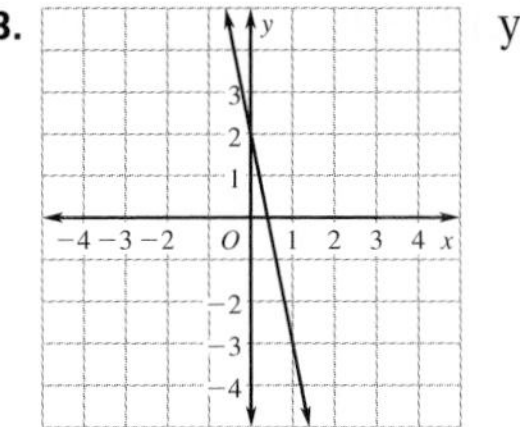 yes

25. $y = -2x + 1$; 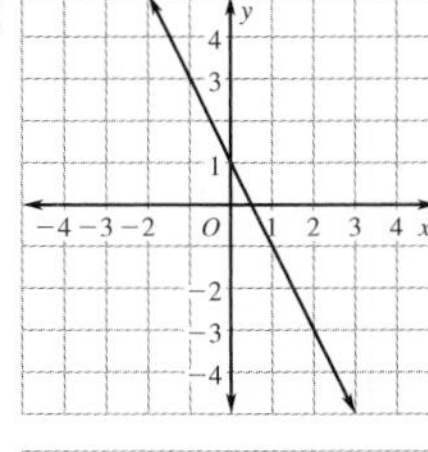

27. $y = -4x - 2$; 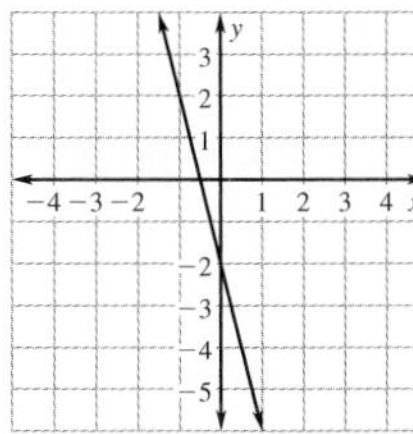

29. $y = -\frac{3}{4}x$; 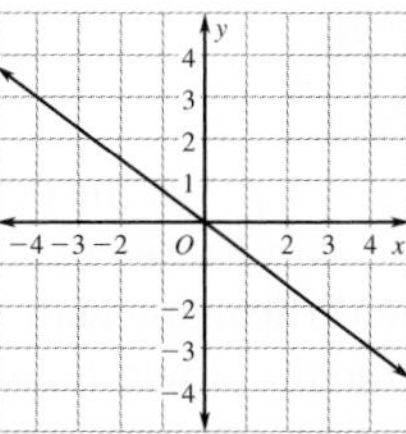

31. $y = -\frac{2}{3}x + 4$; 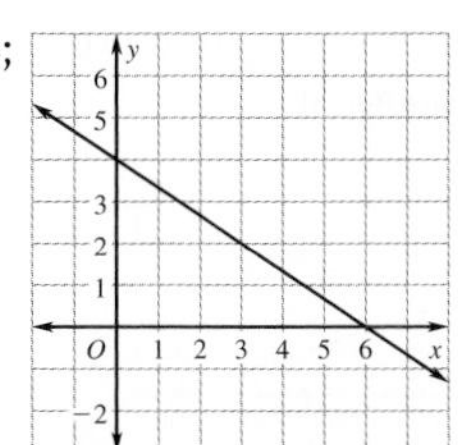

33. 0.355 L **35.** 3 **37.** -5 **39. a.** bigeye thresher: 158 cm, scalloped hammerhead: 194 cm, white shark: 230 cm **b.** bigeye thresher: 63%, scalloped hammerhead: 78%, white shark: 92% **c.** Bigeye thresher. *Sample answer:* The bigeye thresher has the shortest body relative to its total length, so it must have the longest tail relative to its body length.

41. a. $s = \frac{f - 1.19}{2.13}$, or $s \approx \frac{f}{2.13} - 0.56$ **b.** about 0.8 m/sec **43.** -6 **45.** -4 **47.** 3 **49.** 105 **51.** domain: $-2, 0, 2, 4$; range: 1, 2, 3, 4 **53.** domain: 6; range: $-2, 1, 4, 9$

8.2 Technology Activity (p. 397)

1. 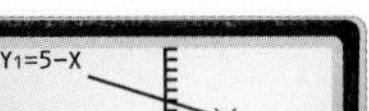
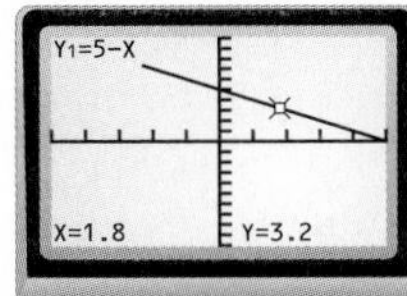

3.2

3. 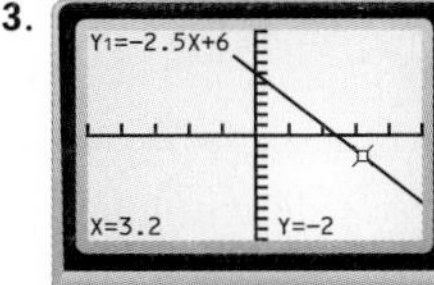

-2

5. 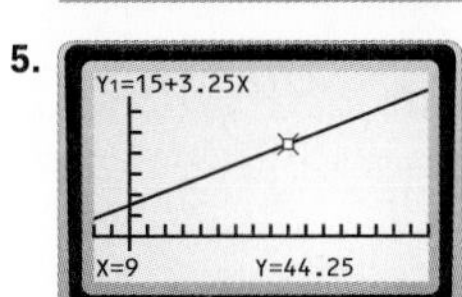

9 games

8.3 Guided Practice (p. 400) **1.** y-intercept, x-intercept **3.** x-intercept: 3; y-intercept: 2 **5.** x-intercept: 0; y-intercept: 0

7. 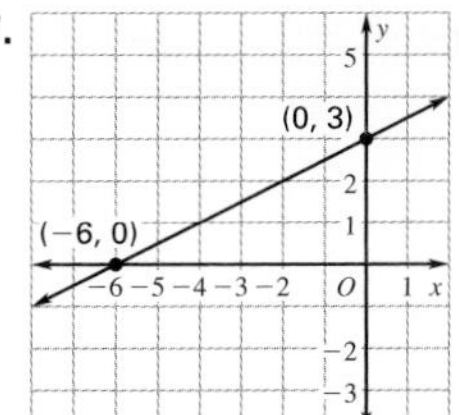

9. Let x be the amount of ground beef and y be the amount of chicken (both in pounds). Then $3x + 5y = 30$.

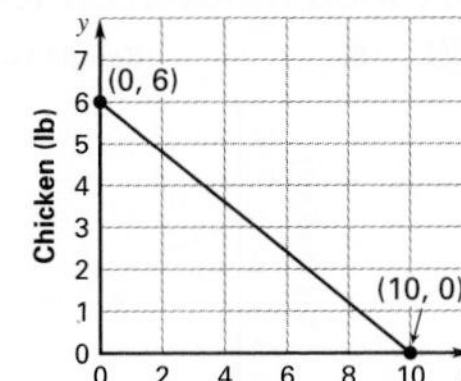

Selected Answers

8.3 Practice and Problem Solving (pp. 400–402)

11. x-intercept: 4; y-intercept: -2;

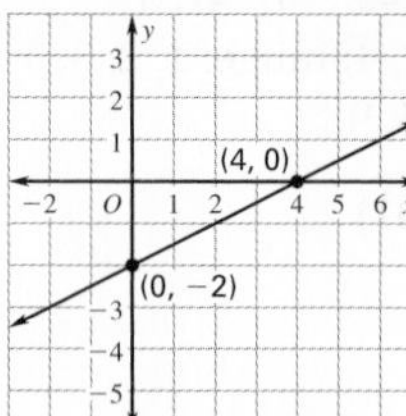

13. x-intercept: -5; y-intercept: -4;

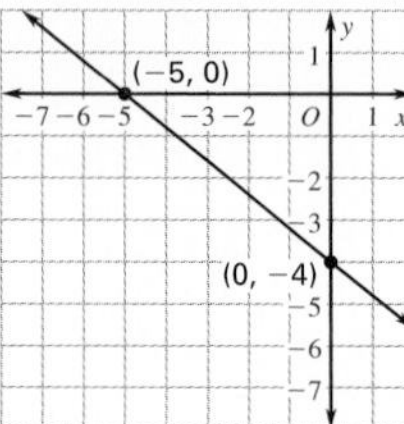

15. x-intercept: -9; y-intercept: 6;

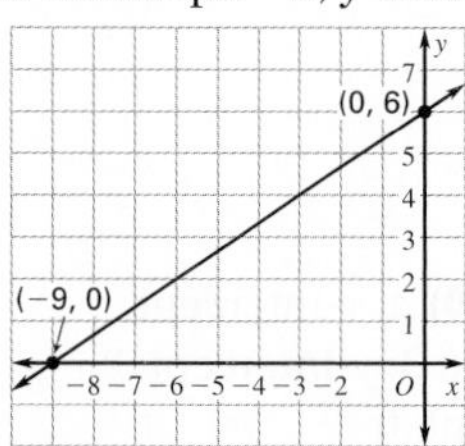

17. x-intercept: 7; y-intercept: 7;

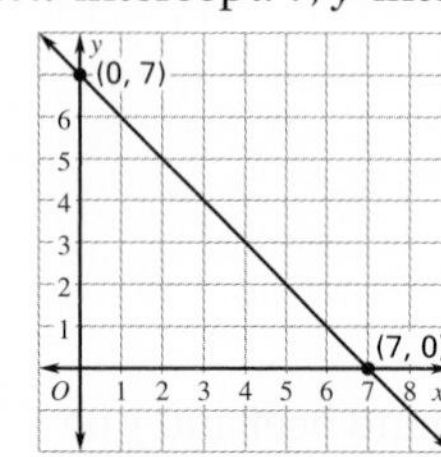

19. a. Let x be the amount of canned food and y be the amount of dry food (both in ounces). Then $40x + 100y = 800$. **b.**

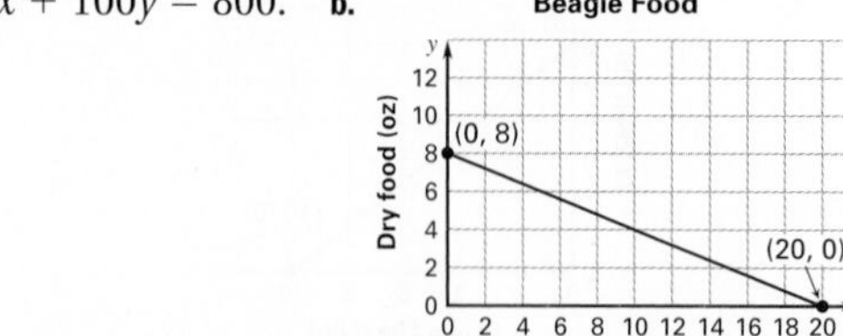

c. *Sample answer:* 0 oz canned and 8 oz dry, 10 oz canned and 4 oz dry, 20 oz canned and 0 oz dry

21. x-intercept: 2; y-intercept: -2;

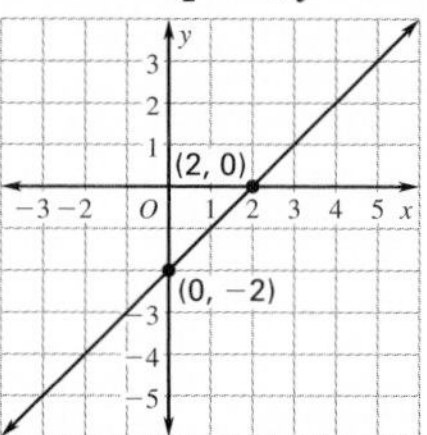

23. x-intercept: -4; y-intercept: 6;

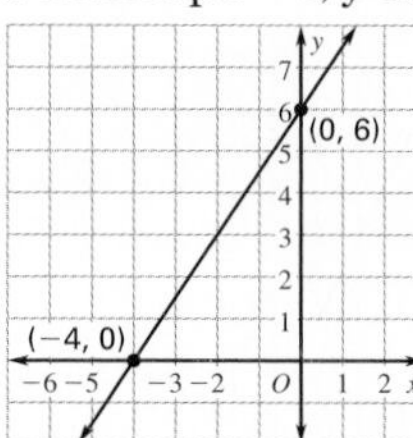

25. x-intercept: 3; y-intercept: 6;

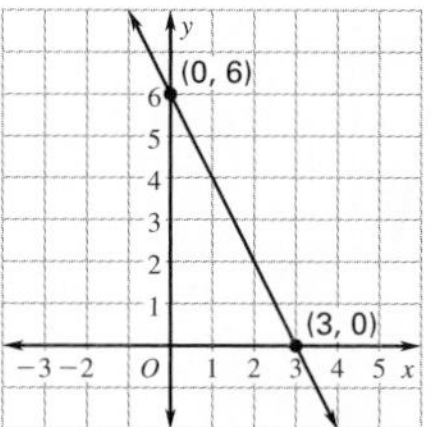

27. *Sample answer:* $y = 3$, $x = 4$; the graph of $y = 3$ is the horizontal line with y-intercept 3, and the graph of $x = 4$ is the vertical line with x-intercept 4. **29. a.** Let x be the time the single-engine plane is rented and y be the time the twin-engine plane is rented (both in hours). Then $60x + 180y = 9000$.

b.

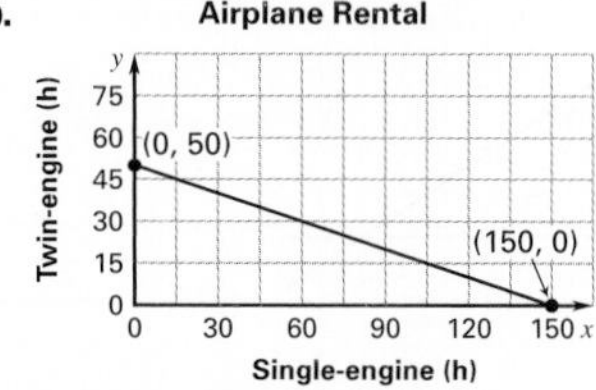

c. about 60 h **d.** $60x + 180(30) = 9000$, $x = 60$ h **31.** *Sample answer:* 12, 24, and 36; they are common multiples of the coefficients. **35.** -1 **37.** 2 **39.** 85% increase **41.** 22% decrease **43.** no **45.** yes

Selected Answers

8.4 Guided Practice (p. 407) **1.** rise, run **3.** *Sample answer:* The x- and y-coordinates of the two points are not used in the same order. If you subtract the second x-coordinate from the first x-coordinate to obtain the denominator $5 - 0$, then you should subtract the second y-coordinate from the first y-coordinate to obtain the numerator $4 - 2$. So, $m = \frac{4-2}{5-0} = \frac{2}{5}$. **5.** positive; $\frac{2}{3}$ **7.** $\frac{5}{12}$. *Sample answer:* $\frac{5}{12} = 0.41\overline{6}$ and $\frac{3}{5} = 0.6$, so the slope of the ramp in Example 1 is greater.

8.4 Practice and Problem Solving (pp. 407–409)
9. negative; $-\frac{3}{4}$ **11–15.** Sample coordinates are given. **11.** $(-2, 0)$ and $(0, 4)$; 2 **13.** $(0, -5)$ and $(4, 1)$; $\frac{3}{2}$ **15.** $(3, 0)$ and $(0, -4)$; $\frac{4}{3}$ **17. a.** 27 **b.** its speed in meters per second **c.** *Sample answer:* It would also start at the origin, but rise less steeply because the gazelle's speed of 22 meters per second is less than the cheetah's speed of 27 meters per second, and the speed is indicated by the slope.

19.

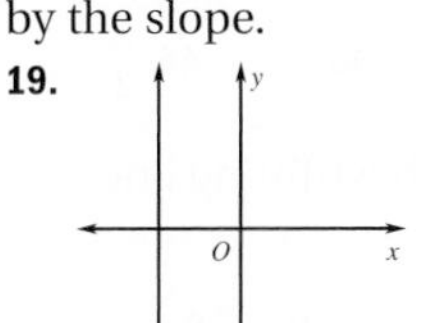

21.

23. -1 **25.** $-\frac{2}{3}$ **27.** 0 **29.** 0 **31.** $\frac{1}{3}$ **33.** undefined **35.** 22 ft **37. a.** No. *Sample answer:* The grade is $\frac{63}{840} = 0.075 = 7.5\%$, which is less than 8%. **b.** 90 ft **39. a.** For any pair of points, the slope is $\frac{1}{2}$; the slope does not depend on which two different points are chosen. **b.** For any pair of points, the slope is $-\frac{2}{3}$; the slope does not depend on which two different points are chosen. **41.** -12 **43.** -11 **45.** 3 **47.** 5

49. x-intercept: 1; y-intercept: -2;

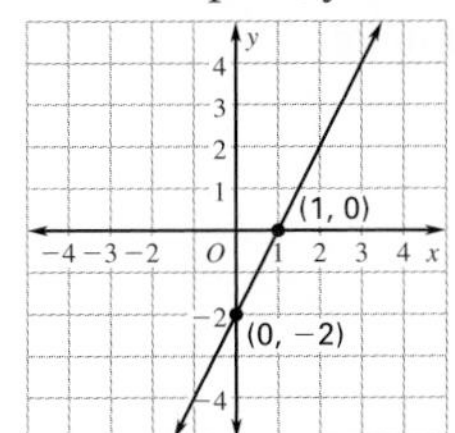

51. x-intercept: -8; y-intercept: -6;

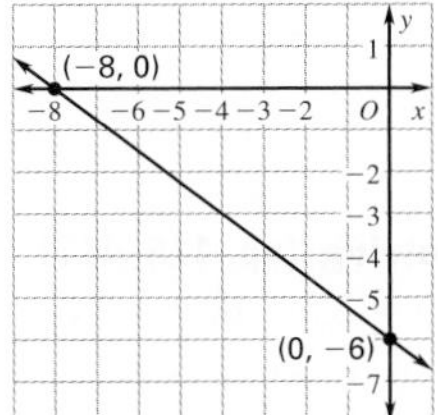

Student Reference (p. 411) **1.** parallel **3.** perpendicular **5.** No; they lie in the same plane. **7.** Yes; they do not lie in the same plane and do not intersect. **9.** *Sample answer:* $\overleftrightarrow{BD}$, $\overleftrightarrow{EG}$

8.5 Guided Practice (p. 415) **1.** slope-intercept **3.** slope: 2; y-intercept: 0;

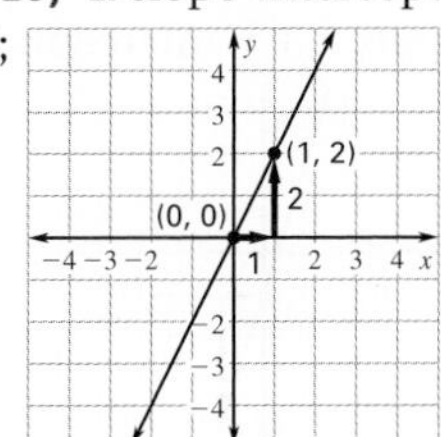

5. slope: $\frac{1}{2}$; y-intercept: -1;

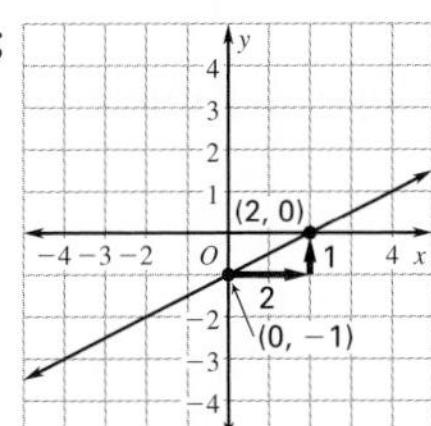

7. parallel: -6; perpendicular: $\frac{1}{6}$

Selected Answers

9. Step 1: $y = 24 + 8x$;
Step 2: slope: 8; y-intercept: 24;

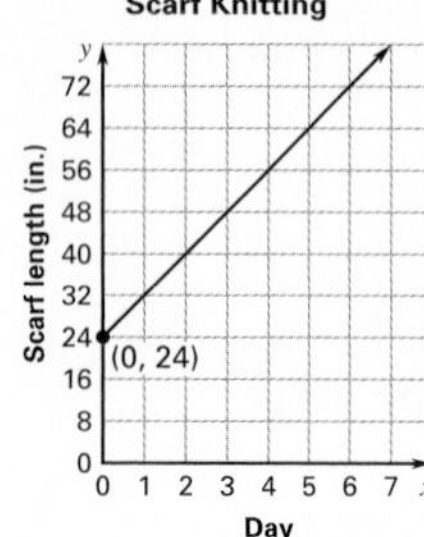

Step 3: about 6 days

8.5 Practice and Problem Solving (pp. 415–417)

13. *Sample answer:* $y = 3x$, $y = 3x + 8$, $y = 3x - 1.1$

15. slope: $\frac{1}{4}$; y-intercept: 1;

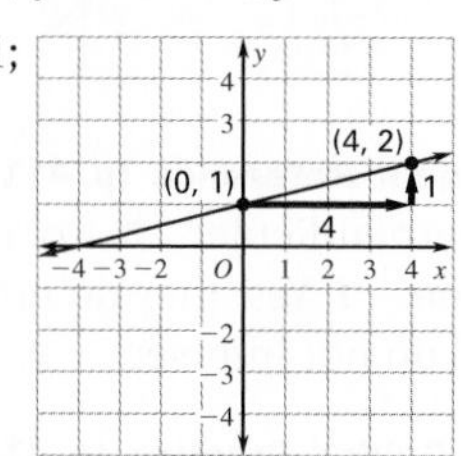

17. slope: -3; y-intercept: -1;

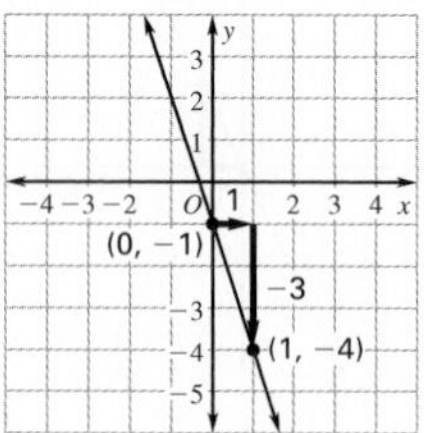

19. slope: $\frac{5}{2}$; y-intercept: 2;

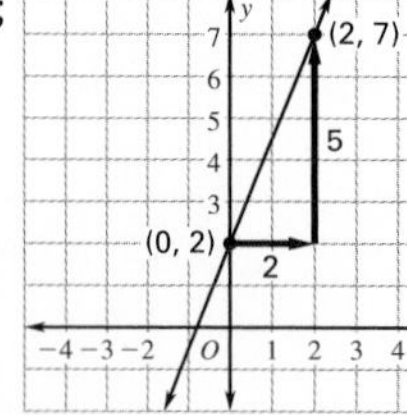

21. a. 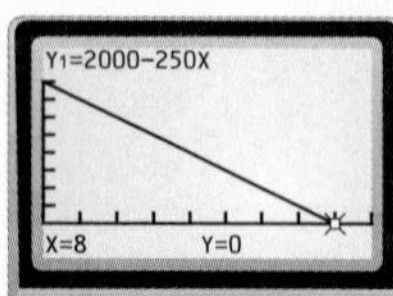

8 min

b. Slope: -250; y-intercept: 2000; the slope represents the rate of descent in feet per minute, and the y-intercept represents the beginning altitude in feet. **23.** parallel: -1; perpendicular: 1 **25.** parallel: $\frac{4}{5}$; perpendicular: $-\frac{5}{4}$ **27.** parallel: $\frac{1}{3}$; perpendicular: -3 **29.** parallel: $-\frac{2}{3}$; perpendicular: $\frac{3}{2}$ **31. a.** $y = 1000 - 50x$

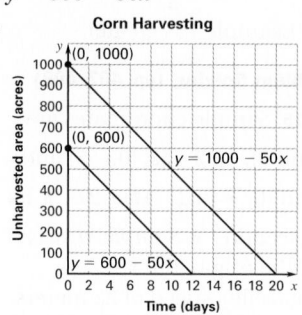

b. $y = 600 - 50x$

c. 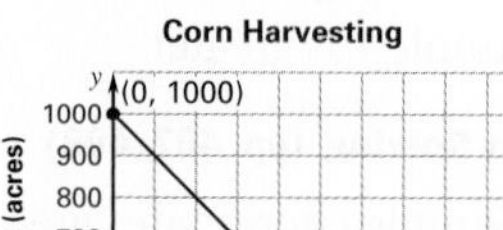

For $y = 1000 - 50x$, the slope is -50 and the y-intercept is 1000. For $y = 600 - 50x$, the slope is -50 and the y-intercept is 600.

d. They are parallel; they have the same slope, -50, and different y-intercepts. **e.** 20 days; 12 days

35. 4 **37.** -7 **39.** 100 **41.** 40% **43.** -2 **45.** $\frac{5}{2}$

8.6 Guided Practice (p. 422) **1.** best-fitting line

3. $y = x + 8$ **5.** $y = \frac{2}{3}x - 5$

7. Step 1:

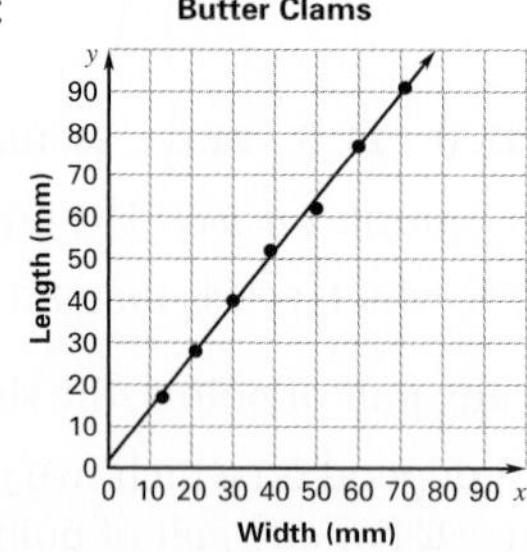

Best-fitting lines may vary.

Step 2: *Sample answer:* Using (10, 14) and (60, 77): $y = 1.26x + 1.4$; Step 3: 109 mm

8.6 Practice and Problem Solving (pp. 422–424)

9. $y = 4x + 10$ **11.** $y = -x - 20$ **13.** $y = \frac{2}{3}x - 2$

15. $y = 2x + 9$ **17.** $y = -11$ **19.** $y = -x + 7$

21. $y = -\frac{1}{3}x + 6$ **23.** $y = 4x + 1$

25. 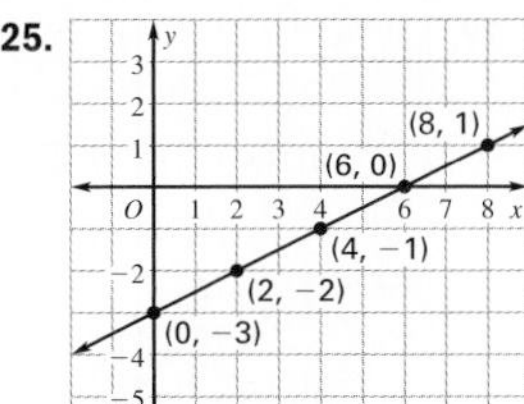

The points lie on a nonvertical line, so the table represents a linear function; $y = \frac{1}{2}x - 3$.

27. $y = 3x$ **29.** $y = \frac{1}{2}x$ **31.** Lisa: no; John: yes. *Sample answer:* Let x represent annual sales and y represent annual earnings. Lisa's earnings would then be $y = 0.02x + 18{,}000$ which does not model the direct variation equation $y = kx$. John's earnings would be $y = 0.06x$ which does model the direct variation equation.

33. a. 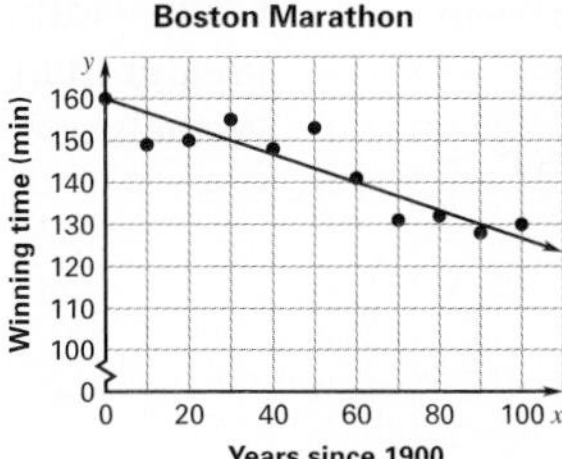

Best-fitting lines may vary.

b. *Sample answer:* Using (0, 160) and (90, 130): $y = -\frac{1}{3}x + 160$ **c.** about 123 min **d.** No. *Sample answer:* The equation predicts a winning time of 0 minutes eventually, which is impossible. I would expect the winning times eventually to level off and decrease very little, if any. **35.** 4 **37.** 8 **39.** 70% **41.** 250%

43. slope: 3; y-intercept: −2;

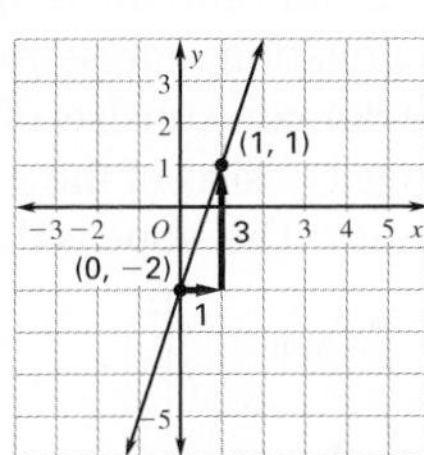

45. slope: $-\frac{3}{2}$; y-intercept: 0;

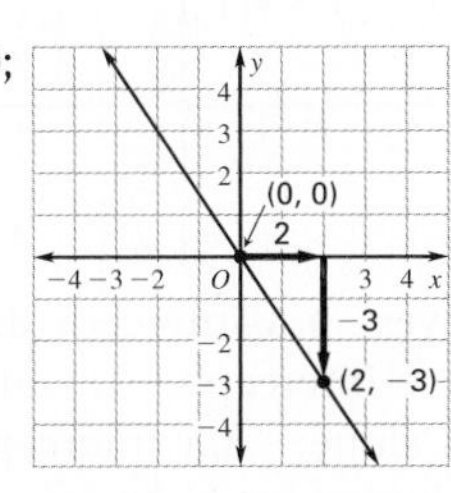

8.6 Technology Activity (p. 425)
1. about 237,000 physicians

8.7 Guided Practice (p. 428) **1.** $f(x) = 4x - 3$ **3.** −52 **5.** 9

7. 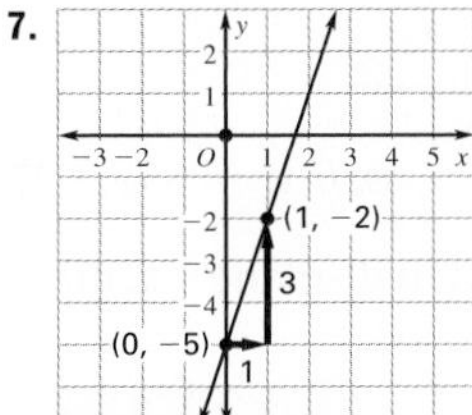

9. $f(x) = -x + 8$

8.7 Practice and Problem Solving (pp. 429–430)
11. 4 **13.** 6 **15.** 61

21. 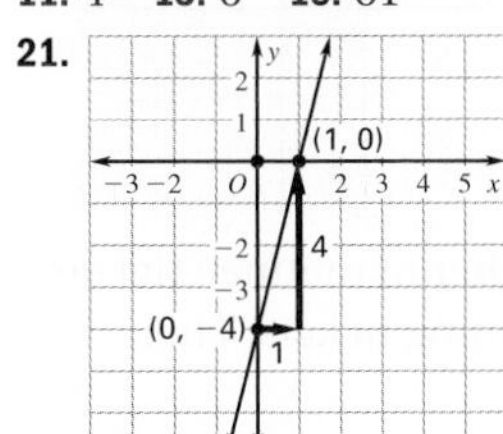

23. $g(x) = -8x$
25. $g(x) = -5x$
27. $r(x) = \frac{2}{3}x - 1$
29. a. $c(x) = 10x + 3000$
b. $i(x) = 50x$
c. $p(x) = 40x - 3000$
d. \$1000
e. 75 birdhouses

33. $10n^{11}$ **35.** $\frac{5c^7}{2}$ **37.** $\frac{16}{25}$ **39.** $\frac{3}{2}$ **41.** $y = \frac{9}{5}x + 3$

8.8 Guided Practice (p. 433) **1.** an ordered pair that is a solution of each equation in the system **3.** (3, 1) **5.** no solution

8.8 Practice and Problem Solving (pp. 434–435)
7. no **9.** yes **11.** (0, 3) **13.** (1, −1) **15.** infinitely many solutions—any point on the line $y = -\frac{1}{2}x + 2$ **17.** no solution **19.** (−3, 1) **21.** (0, 5)
23. Let x be the number of newspaper ads and y be the number of radio ads; $x + y = 50$, $600x + 300y = 24{,}000$; 30 newspaper ads and 20 radio ads.
25. a. Let x be the number of pages and y be the total cost; inkjet: $y = 0.15x + 100$, laser: $y = 0.03x + 400$. **b.** 2500 pages **c.** when fewer than 2500 pages are printed; when more than 2500 pages are printed **d.** The inkjet printer; the laser printer. *Sample answer:* For 3 years, 2 pages per day is $2 \cdot 365 \cdot 3 = 2190$ pages, which is less than 2500, and 4 pages per day is $4 \cdot 365 \cdot 3 = 4380$ pages, which is more than 2500.

27. *Sample answer:* $m = 3$, $b = 5$; for there to be no solution, the lines should be parallel, which means that they must have the same slope but not be the same line.

31. $y \le 7$;

33. $n < 12$;

35. 3.09×10^5 **37.** 7.48×10^{-6} **39.** $h(x) = -5x - 27$

8.9 Guided Practice (p. 439) **1.** half-plane **3.** no **5.** yes

7. $y < 3x + 1$ **9.** $x > -2$

11. Step 1: Let x be the number of matinee tickets and y be the number of evening tickets. Then $5x + 8y \le 40$.

Step 2:

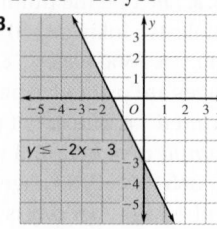

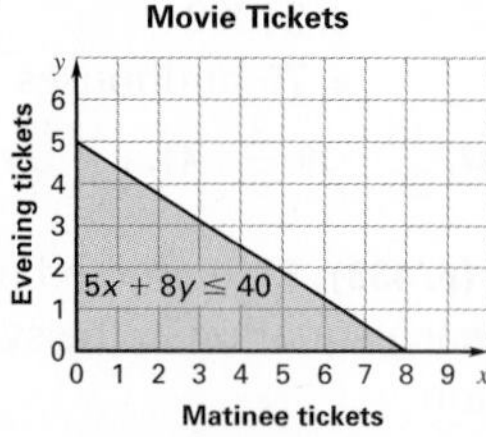

Step 3: *Sample answer:* 0 matinees and 5 evening shows, 3 matinees and 3 evening shows, 6 matinees and 1 evening show

8.9 Practice and Problem Solving (pp. 439–441)
13. The wrong half-plane is shaded. The half-plane to the right and below the boundary should be shaded. **15.** *Sample answer:* $(-2, 3)$, or any other point on the line $y = x + 5$ **17.** no **19.** yes

21. $y > -3x$ **23.** $y \le -2x - 3$

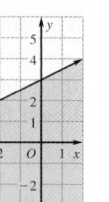

25. $-x + 2y \le 6$ **27.** $4x + 3y < -12$

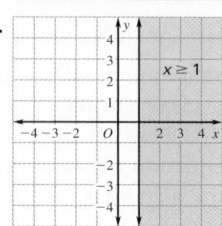

29. $x \ge 1$ **31.** $y \le -1$

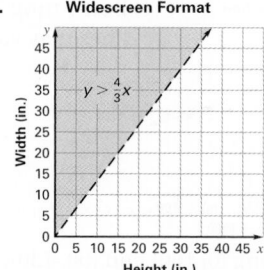

33. a. Widescreen Format; $y > \frac{4}{3}x$; Width (in.); Height (in.) **b.** any width greater than 24 inches

39. 1.2^3 **41.** $\frac{5}{x^2}$ **43.** $\frac{9}{m^5n^4}$ **45.** $(-2, 0)$

Chapter Review (pp. 442–445) **1.** *Sample answer:* In a relation, which pairs numbers in one set with numbers in another set, the domain consists of the inputs and the range consists of the outputs. In a relation represented by ordered pairs (x, y), the domain consists of the x-coordinates and the range consists of the y-coordinates. **3.** *Sample answer:* The slope is the ratio of the rise to the run.

5. $(-5, 6)$, $(-4, 3)$, $(0, 0)$, $(4, -3)$

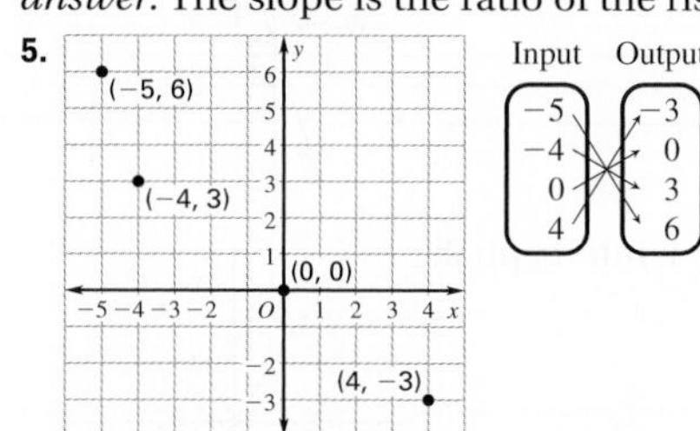

7. yes **9.** x-intercept: 8; y-intercept: -2
11. x-intercept: -1; y-intercept: -5 **13.** 0
15. slope: -3; y-intercept: 2 **17.** slope: 4; y-intercept: 2 **19.** $y = -x - 6$ **21.** -2

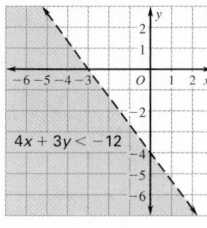

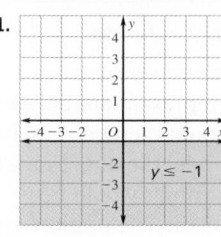

23. 10 **25.** (1, 3)

27. 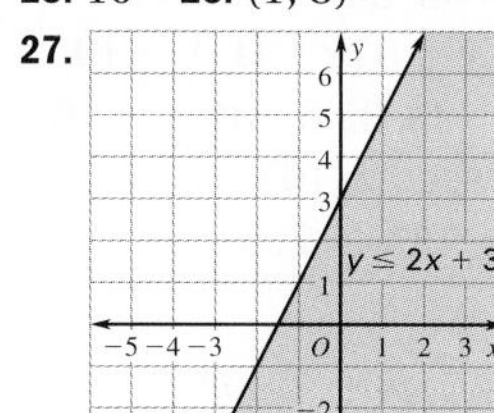

29. 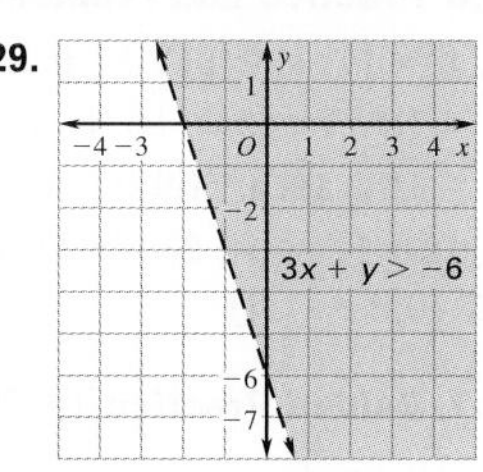

Focus on Problem Solving (p. 449) **1.** *Sample answer:* $\frac{4 \cdot 4}{4 \cdot 4}$, $\frac{4 \div 4}{4 \div 4}$, $4^4 \div 4^4$ **3.** Some possible numbers of coins are 9, 15, and 21. **5.** *Sample answer:* 6 pies and 3 loaves, 4 pies and 6 loaves, 2 pies and 9 loaves **7.** Some possible dimensions of the swimming pool are 150 feet by 100 feet, 125 feet by 120 feet, and 200 feet by 75 feet. **9. a.** No solution. *Sample answer:* For any two consecutive integers, one is even and one is odd. So the sum of two consecutive integers must be odd, but 20 is even. **b.** 4 and 5, or −4 and −5

Chapter 9

9.1 Guided Practice (p. 455) **1.** *Sample answer:* A perfect square is the square of an integer. An example is 169, since $13^2 = 169$. **3.** ±2 **5.** ±11 **7.** 3 **9.** 12 **11.** ±3 **13.** ±19 **15.** Step 1: $A = s^2$; Step 2: $15{,}625 = s^2$, 125 ft

9.1 Practice and Problem Solving (pp. 456–457) **17.** ±13 **19.** ±17 **21.** ±22 **23.** ±30 **25.** 6 **27.** −12 **29.** −9 **31.** 4 **33.** 1.7 **35.** 9.3 **37.** −5.7 **39.** 4.4 **41.** 6 **43.** −72 **45.** ±7 **47.** ±21 **49.** ±4.5 **51.** ±4.7 **53.** *Sample answer:* $x^2 = 2.25$ **59.** 3.2 m/sec **61.** ±18 **63.** ±2.89 **65.** ±6.96 **67. a.** 472 mi/h **b.** 446 mi/h slower **71.** $2 \cdot 7^2$ **73.** $2^2 \cdot 5^2 \cdot 7$ **75.** $\frac{1}{4}$ **77.** $\frac{5}{27}$ **79.** 48 **81.** 6.5%

9.2 Guided Practice (p. 460) **1.** Yes. *Sample answer:* The only perfect square factor of 5 is 1, so it is in simplest form. **3.** $2\sqrt{3}$ **5.** $\frac{9}{2}$ **7.** $10\sqrt{3}$ units

9.2 Practice and Problem Solving (pp. 460–461) **9.** $7\sqrt{2}$ **11.** $12\sqrt{2}$ **13.** $10\sqrt{3x}$ **15.** $\frac{\sqrt{11}}{6}$ **17.** $\frac{4\sqrt{5}}{9}$ **19.** $\frac{\sqrt{z}}{8}$ **21.** $\frac{3\sqrt{7}}{4}$; 2 sec **23.** $5x\sqrt{3y}$ **25.** $60mn\sqrt{2}$

27. a. yours: 4 nautical miles, your friend's: $4\sqrt{13}$ nautical miles **b.** *Sample answer:* For you and your friend on top of the lighthouse to see each other, you must first come close enough to be able to see to the same spot on the ocean. The first moment this happens is at the visual horizon both for you and your friend, so your distance from each other is the sum of your visual horizon and your friend's. **c.** 4, about 14; 18 nautical miles **29.** $y\sqrt{y}$ **31.** a^4 **35.** 180 **37.** 64 **39.** $\frac{2y}{3}$ **41.** $\frac{d}{5c}$ **43.** 7 **45.** 10

Student Reference (p. 463) **1.** 45 **3.** 85 **5.** acute **7.** right **9.** equilateral

9.3 Guided Practice (p. 467) **1.** hypotenuse **3.** 39 **5.** 12

9.3 Practice and Problem Solving (pp. 467–469) **7.** 29 **9.** $\sqrt{34}$ **11.** $2\sqrt{31}$ **13.** no **15.** yes **17.** yes **19.** 36 in. **21. a.** *Sample answer:* Let $n = 5$. Then $2n = 2(5) = 10$, $n^2 - 1 = 5^2 - 1 = 24$, and $n^2 + 1 = 5^2 + 1 = 26$. **b.** *Sample answer:* $10^2 + 24^2 = 100 + 576 = 676 = 26^2$ **23.** *Sample answer:* Mental math; the squares of 1 and 2 can be calculated quickly mentally. **25.** 45 **27.** 10 **29.** 116 **31.** 28.0 m **33.** 16 yd **37.** $\frac{4}{25}$ **39.** $1\frac{3}{40}$ **41.** 1 : 10

9.4 Guided Practice (p. 472) **1.** A number that cannot be written as the quotient of two integers. *Sample answer:* $\sqrt{11}$ **3.** rational **5.** irrational **7.** $<$ **9.** $>$ **11.** irrational

9.4 Practice and Problem Solving (pp. 473–474) **13.** irrational **15.** rational **17.** irrational **19.** irrational **21.** $>$ **23.** $>$ **25.** $-\sqrt{5}, -2, 0, \sqrt{3}, \frac{9}{5}, \sqrt{4}$ **27.** $-\sqrt{18}, -\frac{25}{6}, -\sqrt{\frac{67}{4}}, -4$ **29.** Sometimes. *Sample answer:* For example, $\sqrt{\frac{4}{9}} = \frac{2}{3}$ is rational, but $\sqrt{20}$ is irrational. **31.** Never. *Sample answer:* Any whole number can be written as the quotient of itself and 1, so a whole number is a rational number. **33. a.** $2w$ **b.** $20 = (2w)(w)$, or $20 = 2w^2$ **c.** 3.2 m **d.** 6.3 m **35.** the longer boat; 2 nautical miles per hour **37.** *Sample answer:* $-\sqrt{10}$

39. *Sample answer:* $-\sqrt{101}$ **41.** Sometimes. *Sample answer:* $\sqrt{2} \cdot \sqrt{2} = 2$, which is rational, but $\sqrt{2} \cdot \sqrt{3} = \sqrt{6}$, which is irrational. **45.** 3.375 **47.** $\frac{1}{9}$ **49.** $\frac{3}{5}$ **51.** 6

9.5 Guided Practice (p. 479) **1.** distance **3.** $\sqrt{34}$ units **5.** $\frac{5}{3}$

9.5 Practice and Problem Solving (pp. 479–481)
7. $\sqrt{17}$ units **9.** $\sqrt{10}$ units **11.** $\sqrt{41}$ units **13.** $6\sqrt{5}$ units **15.** 2.5 units **17.** $3\sqrt{2}$ units **19.** (1, 2) **21.** $\left(-\frac{1}{2}, -\frac{3}{2}\right)$ **23.** -1 **25.** $-\frac{3}{2}$ **27.** (5, 3) **29.** $\left(7\frac{1}{2}, 2\right)$ **31.** $\left(4\frac{1}{4}, 2\frac{1}{2}\right)$ **33.** 1 **35.** $\frac{4}{3}$ **37.** $\frac{8}{3}$
39. a. The midpoint between the hospital and the stadium is $\left(\frac{1+9}{2}, \frac{2+6}{2}\right) = (5, 4)$, which matches the coordinates of the Civic Center. **b.** the hospital and the State House **41.** No. *Sample answer:* Since the differences between the x-coordinates and between the y-coordinates are squared in the distance formula, the results are the same. For example, $(2-3)^2 = (-1)^2 = 1$, and $(3-2)^2 = (1)^2 = 1$.
43. $\overline{PQ}$ **45.** $B(-8, 0)$ **47.** $B(17, 12)$
49. No. *Sample answer:* The line through $(-3, 9)$ and $(1, 1)$ has slope -2, the line through $(-3, 9)$ and $(4, -4)$ has slope $-\frac{13}{7}$, and the line through $(1, 1)$ and $(4, -4)$ has slope $-\frac{5}{3}$. Since the lines have different slopes, the three points do not lie on the same line.
51.

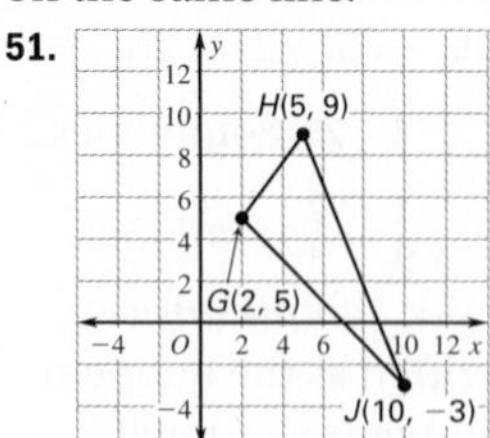

no **53.** $C(2, 2)$ **55.** yes **57.** 131% **59.** > **61.** <

9.6 Guided Practice (p. 485) **1.** $15\sqrt{2}$ units **3.** $6\sqrt{2}$ **5.** $5\sqrt{3}$

9.6 Practice and Problem Solving (pp. 486–487)
7. $x = 11, y = 11\sqrt{2}$ **9.** $x = 5, y = 5\sqrt{2}$ **11.** $x = 10, y = 10\sqrt{3}$ **13. a.** 10 ft **b.** 12 ft **15.** 85 ft **17.** $x = 10, y = 10$ **19. a.** 469 ft **b.** 4.4 ft/sec **c.** 107 sec, or 1 min 47 sec **23.** 7 **25.** 61.25 **27.** $(-2, 5)$ **29.** $(0.8, -1.4)$

9.7 Guided Practice (p. 491) **1. a.** $\overline{BC}$ **b.** $\overline{AC}$ **3.** $\frac{7}{24}$ **5.** $\frac{4}{3}$

9.7 Practice and Problem Solving (pp. 491–493)
7. $\tan A = \frac{11}{60}, \tan B = \frac{60}{11}$ **9.** $\tan A = \frac{24}{7}, \tan B = \frac{7}{24}$ **11.** 2.2460 **13.** 0.2679 **15.** 0.6494 **17.** 57.2900 **19.** 19.6 **21. a.** $d + 1.5$ **b.** 64.0 m **c.** 65.5 m **23.** 137 ft **25.** 175.8 square units
27. *Sample:*

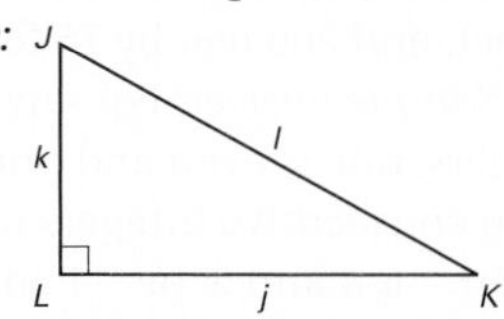

They are reciprocals. *Sample answer:* The side opposite each of the acute angles is the side adjacent to the other. From the drawing, $\tan J = \frac{j}{k}$ and $\tan K = \frac{k}{j}$, and $\frac{j}{k}$ and $\frac{k}{j}$ are reciprocals since $\frac{j}{k} \cdot \frac{k}{j} = 1$.
29. a. About 4400 ft. *Sample answer:* Since $d = rt$, $d = 1100 \cdot 4 = 4400$ feet. **b.** *Sample answer:* Use the fact that triangles *ABD* and *CBD* are right triangles with an acute angle with measure $\frac{x^\circ}{2}$ at your eye. Then you can use the tangent ratio: $\tan \frac{x^\circ}{2} = \frac{s}{d}$. **c.** 384 ft **31.** \$3.12 **33.** $6\sqrt{b}$ **35.** $9fg\sqrt{2}$

9.8 Guided Practice (p. 496) **3.** $\sin J = \frac{40}{41}, \cos J = \frac{9}{41}, \sin L = \frac{9}{41}, \cos L = \frac{40}{41}$

9.8 Practice and Problem Solving (pp. 497–498)
5. $\sin P = \frac{3}{5}, \cos P = \frac{4}{5}, \sin Q = \frac{4}{5}, \cos Q = \frac{3}{5}$ **7.** $\sin A = \frac{12}{13}, \cos A = \frac{5}{13}, \sin B = \frac{5}{13}, \cos B = \frac{12}{13}$ **9.** 0.9272 **11.** 0.9511 **13.** 0.9063 **15.** 0.9998 **17.** 12.1 **19.** 88.2 **21.** 83.4

Selected Answers

23. *Sample:*

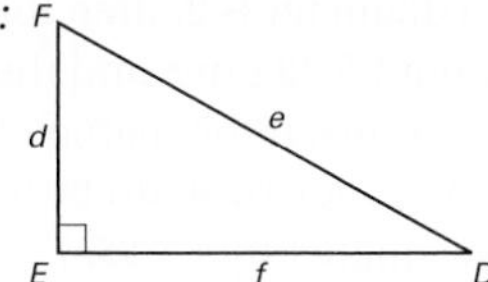

The side opposite each of the acute angles is the side adjacent to the other, so the sine of one acute angle is equal to the cosine of the other acute angle. From the drawing, $\sin D = \frac{d}{e} = \cos F$, and $\sin F = \frac{f}{e} = \cos D$.

25. 4.0 m **27.** *Sample answer:* (1) Use the Pythagorean theorem to write the equation $28^2 + b^2 = 35^2$ and then solve to find that $b = 21$. (2) Use the tangent ratio to write the equation $\tan 37° = \frac{b}{28}$ and solve. (3) Use the sine ratio to write the equation $\sin 37° = \frac{b}{35}$ and solve. (4) Find $m\angle A$: $m\angle A = 90 - 37 = 53°$. Then use the cosine ratio to write the equation $\cos 53° = \frac{b}{35}$ and solve.
31. no **33.** $\angle A$ and $\angle D$, $\angle B$ and $\angle E$, $\angle C$ and $\angle F$, $\overline{AB}$ and $\overline{DE}$, $\overline{BC}$ and $\overline{EF}$, $\overline{AC}$ and $\overline{DF}$
35. irrational **37.** rational

9.8 Technology Activity (p. 499) **1.** 36.9° **3.** 22.6° **5.** 53.1° **7.** 11.5°

Chapter Review (pp. 500–503) **1.** square root **3.** the point on the segment that is equally distant from the endpoints **5.** ±25, ±90 **7.** −5 **9.** 8 **11.** $6\sqrt{2}$ **13.** $\frac{\sqrt{29a}}{10}$ **15.** $3z\sqrt{2}$ **17.** $\frac{a\sqrt{2}}{7}$ **19.** 10 **21.** $\sqrt{58}$ **23.** > **25.** < **27.** $-5.01, -\sqrt{18}, \frac{19}{6}, \sqrt{20}$ **29.** $x = 11, y = 11\sqrt{2}$ **31.** $x = 9\sqrt{3}, y = 9$ **33.** 11.5

Chapter 10

10.1 Guided Practice (p. 513) **1.** 60°, 60°, and 60°; acute **3.** 20; acute **5.** 5 m **7.** *Sample answer:* The measure of the right angle was omitted. The correct equation and solution are $x° + 2x° + 90° = 180°$, $3x = 90$, and $x = 30$.

10.1 Practice and Problem Solving (pp. 513–515) **9.** 15; acute **11.** 23; obtuse **13.** 63; acute **15.** 19 in.; scalene **17.** 28.1 cm; equilateral

19.

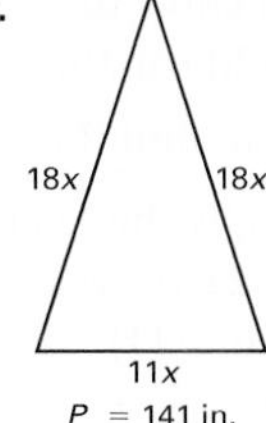

33 in., 54 in., and 54 in.; isosceles

21. a. 49 in., 168 in., 175 in.; scalene **b.** Yes. *Sample answer:* By the converse of the Pythagorean theorem: $49^2 + 168^2 = 2401 + 28{,}224 = 30{,}625 = 175^2$. **23. a.** 24 in., 24 in., 45°, 45° **b.** 48 in. **c.** 36 in.

d. 34 in., 51 in., 68 in.;

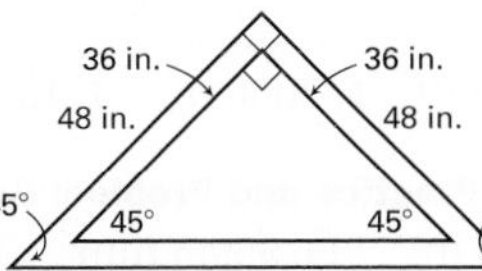

25. Yes. *Sample answer:* There are two possibilities, as shown in the diagram, depending on whether 5 centimeters is the length of one of the congruent sides or the length of the other side.

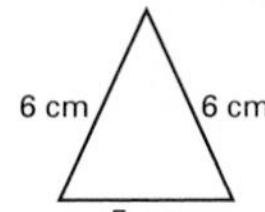

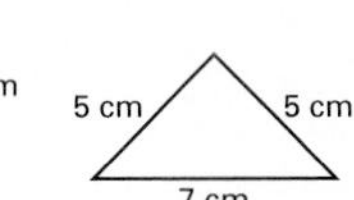

29. $\sin B = \frac{3}{5}$, $\sin C = \frac{4}{5}$, $\cos B = \frac{4}{5}$, $\cos C = \frac{3}{5}$

10.2 Guided Practice (p. 518) **1.** *Sample answer:* A trapezoid has exactly one pair of parallel sides, while a parallelogram has two pairs of parallel sides. **3.** No; it is a circle, which is curved. **5.** trapezoid

10.2 Practice and Problem Solving (pp. 519–520) **7.** yes; 16-gon, concave **9.** No; the top of the figure is curved. **11.** trapezoid **13.** parallelogram **15.** always **17.** never **19.** 90 **21. a.** about $16\frac{5}{8}$ ft, or 16 ft 7.5 in. **b.**

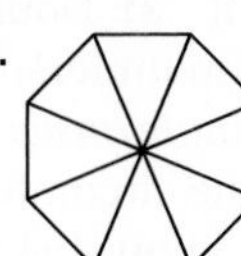

Selected Answers

c. *Sample answer:* You would need to know the height of each triangle. Then you could use the area formula for a triangle, $A = \frac{1}{2}bh$, to find the area of one of the triangles, and multiply the result by 8 to find the area of the octagon. **23.** $m\angle A = 88°$, $m\angle C = 44°$, $m\angle D = 114°$ **25.** (−6, −11) **27.** (3.7, 2.3) **29.** 30°, 45°, 105°; obtuse

10.3 Guided Practice (p. 524)
1. *Sample:* $A = \frac{1}{2}(b_1 + b_2)h$

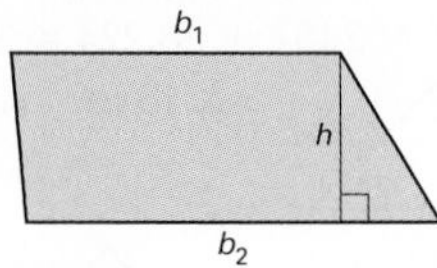

3. 150 ft^2 **5.** 3000 m^2 **7.** 15 m **9.** 20 m

10.3 Practice and Problem Solving (pp. 524–526)
11. 70 in.^{2} **13.** 95.45 mm^2 **15.** 18.36 m^2 **17.** 25 m^2 **19.** 45 m **21.** $1\frac{1}{3}$ yd **23.** 25 ft **25. a.** 136.5 ft^2 **b.** 2747.94 ft^2
27. trapezoid, 20 square units

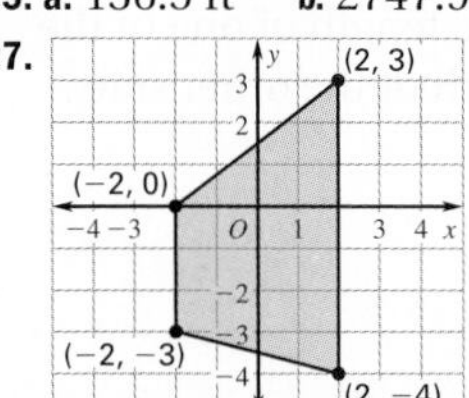

29. It doubles; it doubles; it quadruples. **31.** 156 cm^2 **33.** 16 in.^{2}, 12 in.^{2}; $\frac{4}{3}$ **35.** $1389.15 **37.** 6 **39.** 3 **41.** 107

10.4 Guided Practice (p. 531) **1.** 2.5 cm **3.** 88 cm, 616 cm^2 **5.** 11 ft

10.4 Practice and Problem Solving (pp. 531–533)
7. 113 in. **9.** 132 cm **11.** 100 mm **13.** 6 m, 12 m **15.** 8 in., 16 in. **17.** 201 in.^{2} **19.** 2464 cm^2 **21.** 855 m^2 **23.** 9 m, 18 m **25.** 19 in., 38 in. **27.** 5672 ft^2 **29.** 18,200 ft **31.** Doubling the radius will double the circumference and quadruple the area. *Sample answer:* For example, if the radius is 7, then the circumference is about 44 units and the area is about 154 square units. If the radius is 14, the circumference is about 88 units and the area is about 616 square units. Doubling the diameter will also double the circumference and quadruple the area. For example, if the diameter is 2, then the circumference is about 6.28 units and the area is about 3.14 square units. If the diameter is 4, the circumference is about 12.56 units and the area is about 12.56 square units. **35.** 7 **37.** 170 **39.** undefined **41.** 35 cm^2 **43.** 37.5 in.^{2}

Student Reference (p. 536) **1.** cone **3.** cylinder **5.** *Sample:*

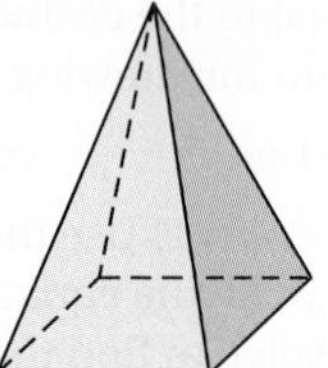

10.5 Guided Practice (p. 541) **1.** $S = 2B + Ph$
3. *Sample answer:* 300 ft^2

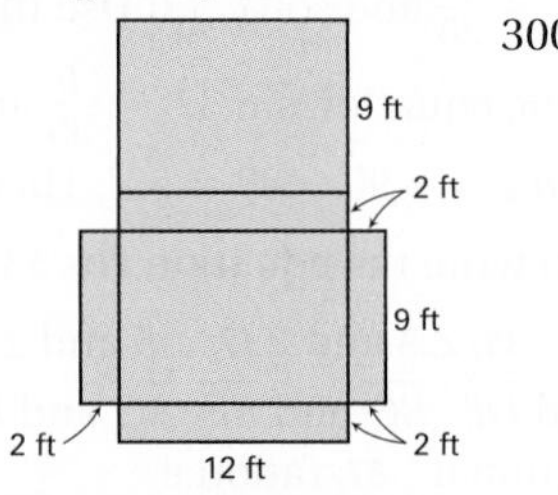

5. *Sample answer:* In this case, the base is not the surface on which the prism is resting, but a triangle with sides 5, 12, and 13: $S = 2B + Ph = 2(0.5 \cdot 5 \cdot 12) + (5 + 12 + 13)(4) = 180$ square centimeters.

10.5 Practice and Problem Solving (pp. 541–543)
7–11. Sample nets are given.
7. 656 yd^2

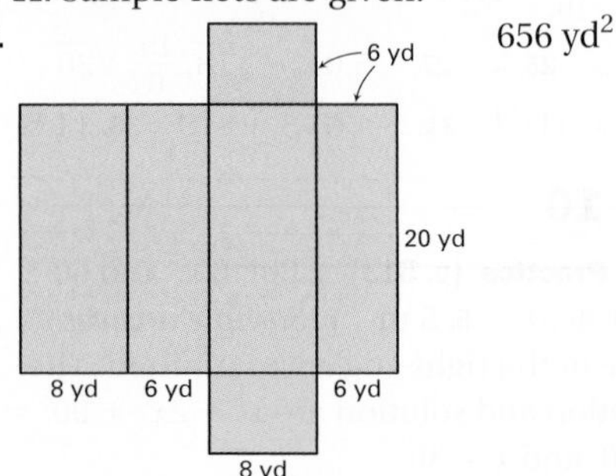

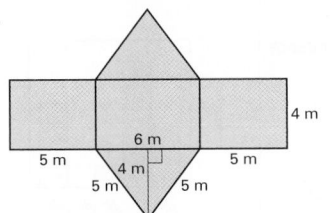

9. 88 m^2

5 m, 6 m, 4 m, 5 m, 4 m, 5 m, 5 m, 5 m

11. 408 $in.^2$

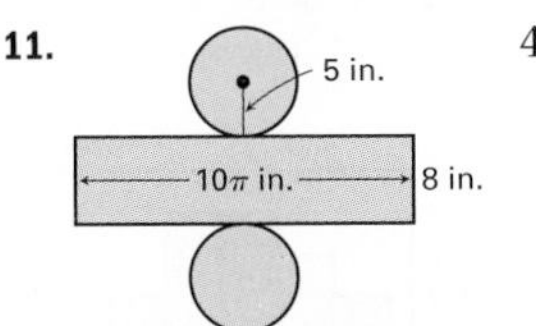

13. 126 $in.^2$ **15.** 384 ft^2 **17. a.** It is quadrupled. *Sample answer:* The area of a base of the original cylinder is πr^2, and of the new cylinder is $\pi(2r)^2 = 4\pi r^2$. **b.** It is doubled. *Sample answer:* The circumference of the original cylinder is $2\pi r$, and of the new cylinder is $2\pi(2r) = 4\pi r$. **c.** It is quadrupled. *Sample answer:* The surface area of the original cylinder is $2\pi r^2 + 2\pi rh$, and of the new cylinder is $2(4\pi r^2) + (4\pi r)(2h) = 4(2\pi r^2) + 4(2\pi rh) = 4(2\pi r^2 + 2\pi rh)$. **19.** 6760 $in.^2$ **21. a.** $S = 4\pi h^2$ **b.** 4 units; 4 units **23.** 15 ft, 11 ft, 11 ft; isosceles **25.** 96.25 m^2 **27.** 264 in. **29.** 641 cm

10.6 Guided Practice (p. 547) **1.** *Sample answer:* The height is the perpendicular distance between the base and the vertex that is not on the base, while the slant height is the height of a lateral face. **3.** 736 $in.^2$ **5.** 352 ft^2

10.6 Practice and Problem Solving (pp. 547–549)
7. 29 yd **9.** 39 m
11. 641 ft^2

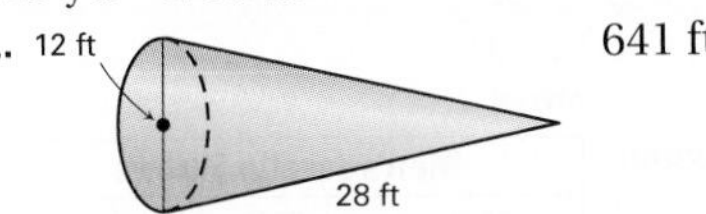

13. Slant height. *Sample answer:* A right triangle can be formed with the pyramid's height, slant height, and half the distance across the base. The pyramid's height would be a leg of the right triangle and the slant height would be the hypotenuse. Since the hypotenuse is always the longest side in a right triangle, the pyramid's slant height is greater than its height. **15.** 7812 mm^2

17. 120 m^2 **19.** 539 $in.^2$ **21.** 2649 $in.^2$ **23.** 72 yd^2 **25.** 11,945,906 mi^2 **27.** 20 ft^2
29. the square pyramid

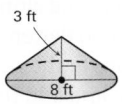

3 ft, 8 ft, 8 ft

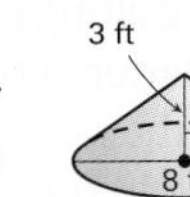

31. 220 m^2 **35.** $12\sqrt{2}$ **37.** $\frac{2\sqrt{6}}{11}$ **39.** 534 cm^2

10.7 Guided Practice (p. 554) **1.** cubic **3.** 120 cm^3 **5.** 1810 ft^3

10.7 Practice and Problem Solving (pp. 555–556)
7. 88 m^3 **9.** 3168 cm^3 **11.** 14 mm^3 **13.** 2040 $in.^3$ **15. a.** red: 42 $in.^3$, blue: 64 $in.^3$, green: 50 $in.^3$ **b.** red: about $.168/$in.^3$, blue: about $.122/$in.^3$, green: $.211/$in.^3$ **c.** The blue candle. *Sample answer:* It has the lowest price per cubic inch of wax. **17.** 8 in. **19.** 948 ft^3 **21. a.** 36π cubic units **b.** 144π cubic units, 72π cubic units, 288π cubic units **c.** *Sample answer:* Doubling the radius quadruples the volume. Doubling the height doubles the volume. Doubling both the radius and the height multiplies the volume by a factor of 8. **25.** yes **27.** $\tan A = \frac{7}{24}$, $\tan B = \frac{24}{7}$ **29.** 144 $in.^2$

10.7 Technology Activity (p. 557)
1. about 0.83; more efficient

10.8 Guided Practice (p. 560) **1.** $V = \frac{1}{3}Bh$ **3.** 20 $in.^3$ **5.** In finding the area of the base, the diameter was used instead of the radius. The correct result is $\frac{1}{3}\pi(4)^2(7) \approx 117$ cm^3.

10.8 Practice and Problem Solving (pp. 561–563)
7. 24 yd^3 **9.** 564 yd^3 **11.** 268 ft^3 **13.** 283 cm^3 **15. a.** $15{,}200\pi$ $in.^3$ **b.** top: $1333\frac{1}{3}\pi$ $in.^3$, bottom: $1066\frac{2}{3}\pi$ $in.^3$ **c.** 48,590 $in.^3$ **d.** Radius. *Sample answer:* In the volume formulas for cylinders and cones, the radius is squared, but the height is not. **17.** 211.67 cm^3 **19.** 36 mm **21.** 299 mm^3 **23.** 14 ft^3 **25.** 4 ft **27.** slope: $\frac{3}{2}$, y-intercept: -1 **29.** slope: 0, y-intercept: $\frac{9}{2}$, or $4\frac{1}{2}$ **31.** 128 $in.^3$

Chapter Review (pp. 564–567) **1.** the lengths of the bases and the height **3.** *Sample answer:* Form a net by imagining cutting along the edges of the prism so that you can flatten it out. Then find the area of the polygons in the net, which represent the faces of the prism, and add the areas. **5.** 24; right **7.** 16; obtuse **9.** yes; square **11.** 6 in.^{2} **13.** 10 m^2 **15.** 108 in.^{2} **17.** 452 in.^{2} **19.** 133 ft^2 **21.** 226 in.^{3} **23.** 336 m^3 **25.** 938 cm^3

Chapter 11

11.1 Guided Practice (p. 584) **1.** 7, 8, and 9

3.

Stem	Leaves
2	1 7 9
3	1 3
4	0 0 1 4 6
5	6 6 8
6	0 2

Key: 2 | 1 = 21

5. Step 1: *Sample answer:*

Earthquakes	Tally	Frequency
5–8	IIII	4
9–12	III	3
13–16	𝍸 II	7
17–20	II	2
21–24	II	2
25–28	I	1

Step 2:

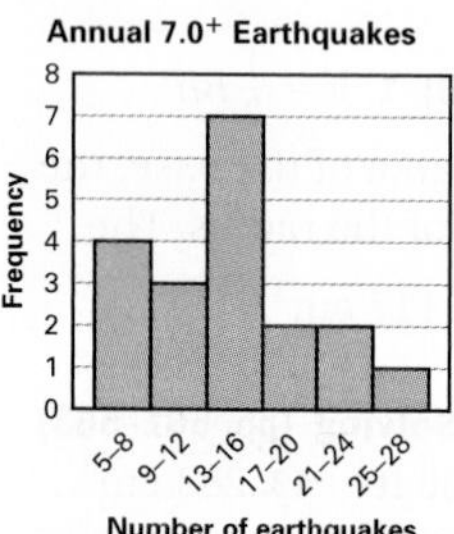

Step 3: *Sample answer:* 9–12; it is the third most frequent interval, after 13–16 and 5–8. Nearly two thirds of the annual numbers of earthquakes, however, are above the interval in which 11 lies.

11.1 Practice and Problem Solving (pp. 584–586)

7.

Stem	Leaves
0	6 9
1	
2	
3	
4	1 4
5	0 4 8
6	1 2 2 3 4 5
7	0 0 1 7

Key: 0 | 6 = 6

9.

Stem	Leaves
12	1 5 6
13	4 5 9
14	1 2
15	0 1 2 7
16	
17	
18	0

Key: 12 | 1 = 12.1

11. *Sample answer:*

Interval	Tally	Frequency
101–120	III	3
121–140	𝍸 I	6
141–160	I	1
161–180		0
181–200	IIII	4

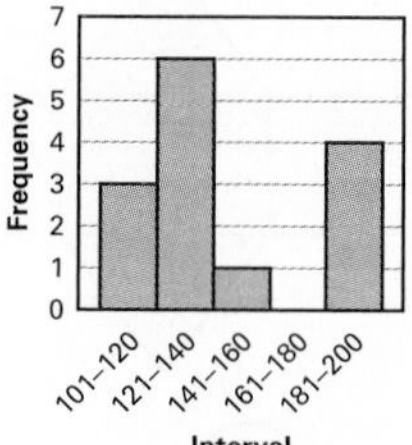

13. *Sample answer:*

Interval	Tally	Frequency
40–49	II	2
50–59	III	3
60–69	IIII	4
70–79	IIII	4
80–89	II	2
90–99	I	1

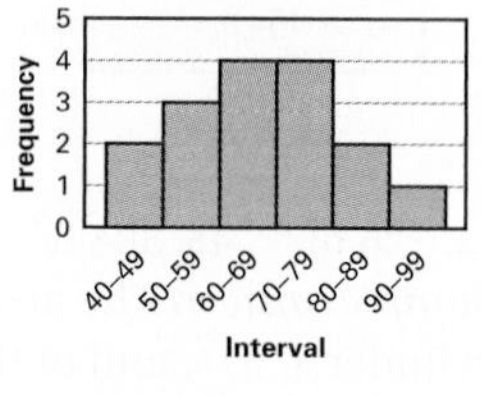

15. a. 25–29 **b.** $33\frac{1}{3}\%$ **c.** *Sample answer:* The vacation days in Shanghai are fewer than for most cities in North America and Europe. At least two thirds of the cities in Europe and North America have more vacation days. **17.** *Sample answer:* 4.6 and 46; in 4.6, the stem 4 represents the ones place and 6 represents the tenths place; in 46, the stem 4 represents the tens place and 6 represents the ones place.

19. *Sample:*

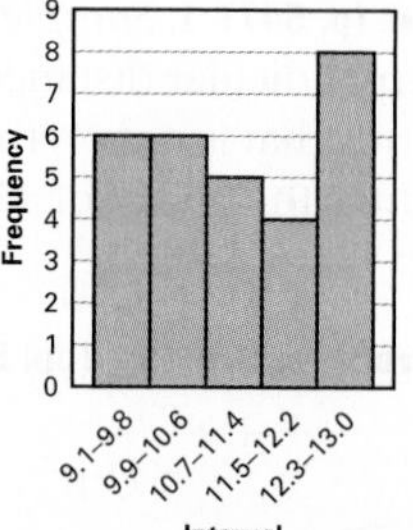

21. a. *Sample answer:*

Men's Javelin Throws		
Meters	**Tally**	**Frequency**
80.00–82.99	III	3
83.00–85.99	II	2
86.00–88.99	II	2
89.00–91.99	II	2
92.00–94.99	I	1

Women's Javelin Throws		
Meters	**Tally**	**Frequency**
58.00–60.99	ll	2
61.00–63.99	𝍸	5
64.00–66.99	ll	2
67.00–69.99	l	1

b. *Sample:*

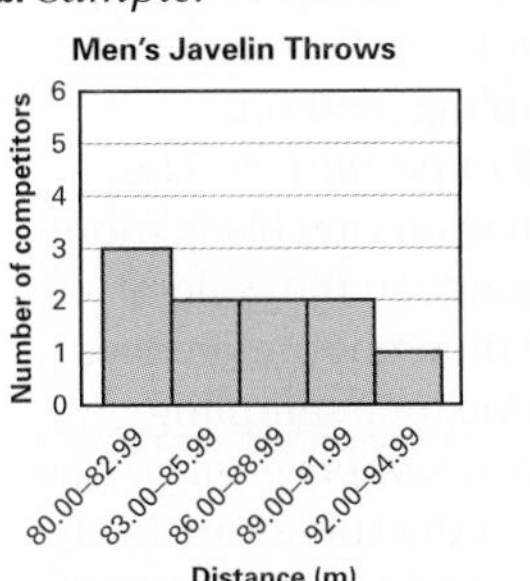

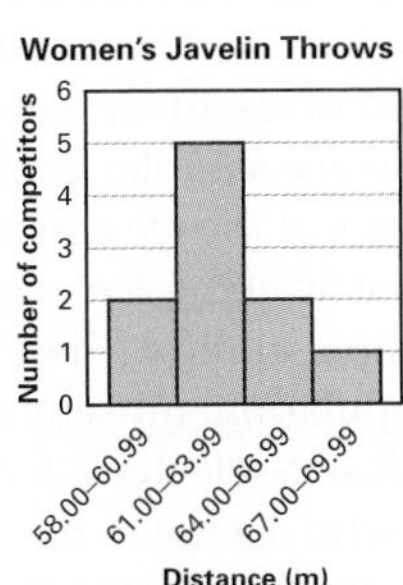

c. *Sample answer:* There is more variation in the distances for the men's throws than in the distances for the women's throws. All the distances for the men's throws are significantly greater than even the greatest distances for the women's throws. **23.** \$34 **25.** -4 **27.** $(-4, 2)$ **29.** $(0.5, 1)$

11.1 Technology Activity (p. 587)

1. *Sample:*

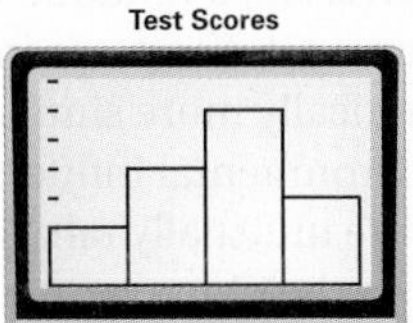

11.2 Guided Practice (p. 590) **1.** 23

3. 0 2 4 6 8 10 12 14 16 18 20

1 7.5 12.5 15.5 18

5. Step 1:

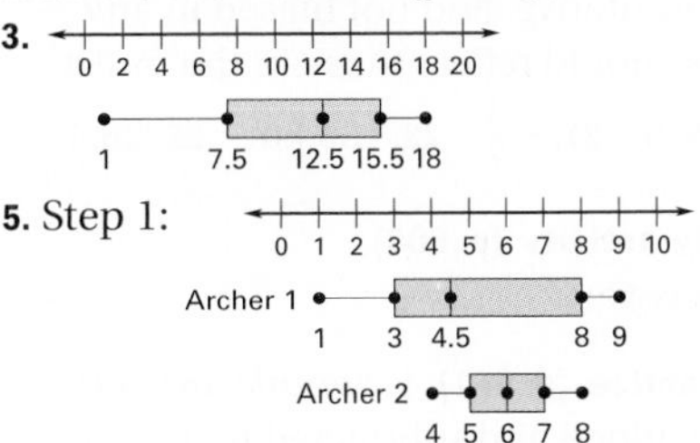

Step 2: Archer 1: 8, 5; Archer 2: 4, 2;
Step 3: Archer 2

11.2 Practice and Problem Solving (pp. 591–592)

7. 14 16 18 20 22 24 26 28

15 18 20 23 26

9. a.

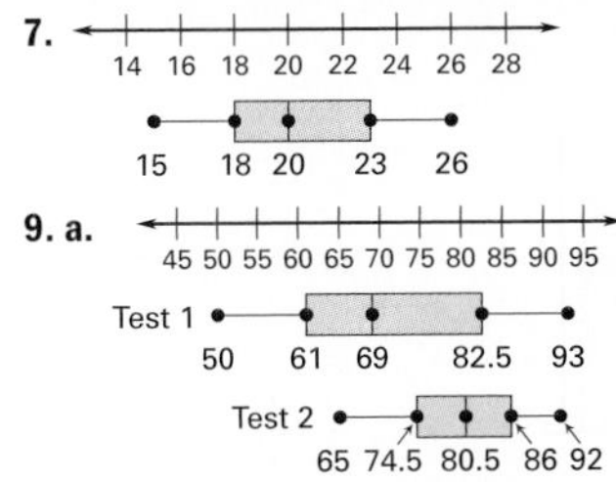

b. *Sample answer:* On test 1, the range was 43, and the interquartile range was 21.5. These are considerably greater than the range of 27 and interquartile range of 11.5 for test 2. **c.** Test 1. *Sample answer:* On test 1, the score of 71 was above the median, but on test 2, the score of 74 was below the median.

11. a.

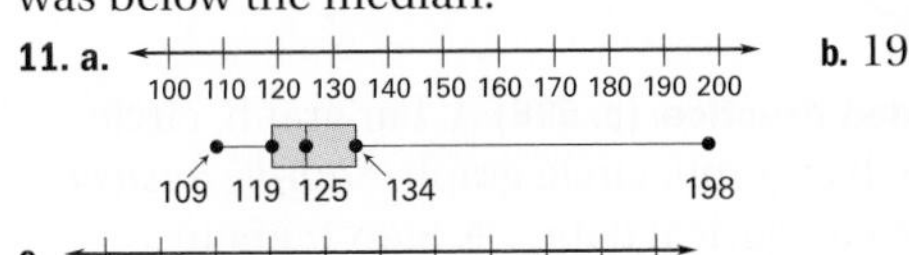

b. 198

c. 100 110 120 130 140 150 160 170 180 190 200

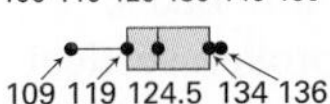

d. *Sample answer:* Though it changes the appearance of the left whisker and the box very little, excluding the outlier greatly shortens the length of the right whisker; from the plot in part (c), you can conclude that all values other than the outlier that are above the upper quartile are very, very close to the upper quartile.

15.

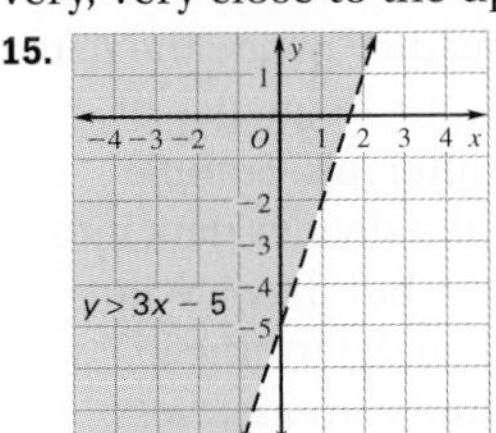

17. 184 m^2 **19.** 90 cm^2

11.2 Technology Activity (p. 593)

1.

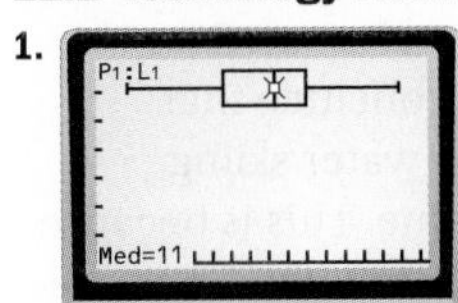

Selected Answers

Student Reference (p. 595)

1.

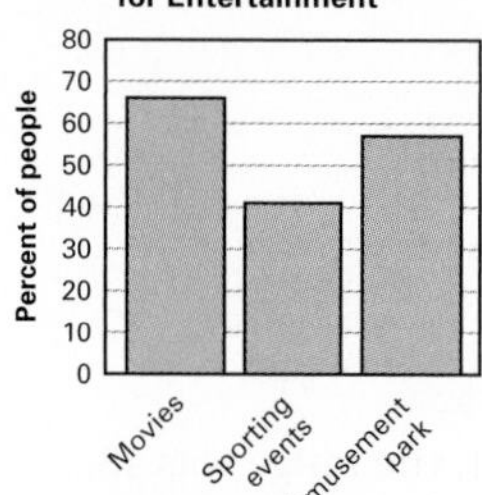

3.

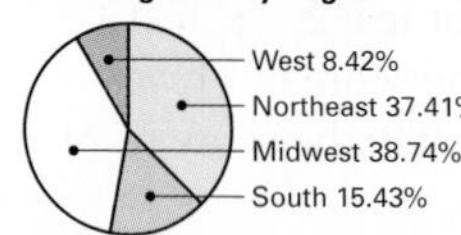

11.3 Guided Practice (p. 598) **1.** bar graph, circle graph **3.** Bar graph, circle graph. *Sample answer:* These are categorical data. **5.** Step 1: about 4 times; Step 2: about 1.4 times more bikes; Step 3: Yes. *Sample answer:* The broken vertical axis exaggerates the differences in the bar heights.

11.3 Practice and Problem Solving (pp. 599–600) **7.** Categorical. *Sample answer:* I would use a bar graph, because it would allow the most direct visual comparison between players' numbers of goals. **9.** stem-and-leaf plot, box-and-whisker plot **11.** stem-and-leaf plot **13.** The extremes, range, and quartiles, and how they divide the data into four equal-sized groups; the frequency of occurrence in chosen equal intervals. *Sample answer:* A box-and-whisker plot divides data into intervals of sorts, the quartiles, but they are not equal. For a histogram, you can determine in what intervals the quartiles and extremes lie, but you cannot determine their exact values. **15.** Histogram. *Sample answer:* There are no stems that correspond to 2-year intervals. **17.** *Sample answer:* You might mistakenly conclude that volleyball is more popular than water skiing, though the numbers are the same. This is because the view at an angle makes the distance along the circle greater for the "Volleyball" section than for the "Water Skiing" section. **19.** $\frac{1}{7}$ **21.** $\frac{1}{3}$ **23.** 8 cm

11.4 Guided Practice (p. 603) **1.** random sample **3.** No. *Sample answer:* Since the movies usually end at different times, it is possible that all the people you interview have gone to the same movie, so they may be inclined to like the same kind of movie.

11.4 Practice and Problem Solving (pp. 604–605) **5.** self-selected **7.** systematic **9.** Population: residents of the town; sampling method: convenience sample; no. *Sample answer:* The customers of the ice cream shops are likely more enthusiastic about ice cream than the general population, and may have different preferences. **11. a.** Population: museum visitors; sampling method: self-selected **b.** No. *Sample answer:* The people who decide to fill out the survey are likely those with strong opinions, and as such may not represent the views of most museum visitors. **13.** *Sample answer:* No; the question is straightforward and can be answered with a simple numerical fact. **15.** *Sample answer:* The sample from several ponds; the turtles from a single pond are likely to be more genetically similar, and are all subject to the availability of food in just that single pond. **17a–d.** Sample answers are given. **17. a.** No; a random sample should be representative. **b.** Yes; trees in one portion might be genetically more similar, as well as subject to local environmental influences. **c.** Yes; if some trees were unusually tall, they would make the average height taller than might be "typical" for the forest. **d.** No; it is the function of a sample to represent a larger population. If the sample is representative, and not biased in any way, the results should reflect those in the forest as a whole. **19.** 6 **21.** $-\frac{4}{7}$ **23.** 150 km **25.** 26.4

11.4 Technology Activity (p. 606)
1–6. Answers may vary.

11.5 Guided Practice (p. 611) **1.** *Sample answer:* It is an amount added and subtracted to a sample percent to determine the upper and lower boundaries for an interval in which the population percent is most likely to lie. **3.** about 975 dog owners

Selected Answers

11.5 Practice and Problem Solving (pp. 612–613)
5. about 1050 families **7.** mayor: leading candidate; treasurer: too close to call; sheriff: leading candidate; controller: too close to call **9.** *Sample answer:* I do not trust the survey or the conclusions. First, the population is just those shoppers at one mall. Also, there is no information as to how the survey was carried out or what sampling method was used to ensure that the survey truly represents even those people at the mall. The survey is even more troublesome because the survey conductor has an interest in the popularity of unusual pets. Finally, no margin of error is given. It seems very likely the interval around the sample percent for mammals, 31%, may overlap the interval around the total sample percent for reptiles and birds, 33%. **11.** No. *Sample answer:* The sample is not random, and represents only a few people of a certain age. Also, because all the students in the classroom are close together, they may be likely to transmit the flu among each other. **13.** 240 students to 384 students **17.** $8m^4$ **19.** 10 **21.** 118.125, or $118\frac{1}{8}$ **23.** 16

11.6 Guided Practice (p. 617) **1.** $6! = 720$ **3.** 60 **5.** 2 **7.** 360 arrangements **9.** *Sample answer:* In this situation, $n = 4$ and $r = 3$. The formula is ${}_nP_r = \frac{n!}{(n-r)!}$, but the quantity shown is $\frac{n!}{r!}$. The correct solution is $\frac{4!}{(4-3)!} = 4! = 24$.

11.6 Practice and Problem Solving (pp. 618–619)
11. 1 **13.** 3,628,800 **15.** 39,916,800 **17.** 479,001,600 **19.** 9 **21.** 6720 **23.** 1 **25.** 13,366,080 **27.** 6720 arrangements **29.** 665,280 choices **31.** $\frac{1}{120}$ **33.** $\frac{30!}{28!}$ **35.** $\frac{12!}{5!}$
37. a. *Sample answer:* This is the number of permutations of 3 digits taken 3 at a time: ${}_3P_3 = 6$; yes. **b.** *Sample answer:* For each of the 3 places, you have the same number of choices, 3. The number of 3-digit numbers is $3 \cdot 3 \cdot 3 = 27$; no. **39. a.** 4 arrangements **b.** 4 arrangements **c.** 8 arrangements **41.** n times. *Sample answer:* $n! = n \cdot (n-1) \cdot (n-2) \cdot \ldots \cdot 1 = n \cdot [(n-1) \cdot (n-2) \cdot \ldots \cdot 1] = n \cdot (n-1)!$ **45.** 52 m **47.** $\sqrt{21}$ ft

11.7 Guided Practice (p. 623) **1.** ${}_{12}C_3$ **3.** 2 **5.** 1 **7.** combinations; 1001 teams

11.7 Practice and Problem Solving (pp. 623–625)
9. 4 sets; winter, spring, and summer; winter, spring, and fall; winter, summer, and fall; spring, summer, and fall **11.** 3 **13.** 35 **15.** 4 **17.** 56 **19.** 220 **21.** 1 **23.** permutations; 120 responses **25.** permutations; 6720 ways **27.** $\frac{1}{210}$ **29.** *Sample answer:* If you choose 4 objects from a group of 5, then for each group of 4 objects chosen, there is 1 object not chosen. Likewise, each time you choose 1 object from 5, there is a group of 4 objects not chosen. Because each group has exactly 1 matching group, there are the same number in each group. Another example is ${}_7C_3 = {}_7C_4 = 35$.
31. a. $\frac{1}{1225}$ **b.** No. *Sample answer:* It multiplies it by 6. If you have 4 of the tickets, then you have ${}_4C_2 = 6$ of the combinations of two tickets in your hand, so the probability that you are holding both winning tickets is $\frac{6}{1225}$. **33.** 9 ways. *Sample answer:* If 8 is the only number greater than 6 that is chosen, then there are ${}_3C_2 = 3$ ways. If 9 is the only number greater than 6 that is chosen, then there are ${}_3C_2 = 3$ ways. If 8 and 9 are both chosen, then there are ${}_3C_1 = 3$ ways. There are $3 + 3 + 3 = 9$ ways total.
37.
93 96 99 102 105 108 111 114 117 120 123
93 97 103 106.5 122
39. 720 ways

11.8 Guided Practice (p. 630) **1.** They have no outcomes in common. **3.** disjoint; $\frac{2}{3}$ **5.** disjoint; $\frac{1}{2}$ **7.** Step 1: disjoint; Step 2: $\frac{3}{14}$; Step 3: $\frac{2}{7}$; Step 4: $\frac{1}{2}$

11.8 Practice and Problem Solving (pp. 631–632)
9. overlapping; $\frac{2}{3}$ **11.** overlapping; $\frac{1}{2}$ **13.** $\frac{3}{5}$ **15.** $\frac{7}{10}$ **17.** $\frac{18}{25}$ **19.** 55% **21.** $\frac{12}{23}$ **23. a.** 85% **b.** 56% **c.** 55% **d.** 49% **25.** $\frac{5}{6}$

Selected Answers

27. They are disjoint. *Sample answer:* P(A and B) = 0 means that A and B will not happen at the same time, therefore events A and B are disjoint. **31.** $\frac{15}{32}$ **33.** $-\frac{65}{288}$ **35.** 462 **37.** 210

11.9 Guided Practice (p. 637) **1.** *Sample answer:* Whether or not one of the events occurs does not affect whether or not the other occurs. **3.** independent **5.** Step 1: dependent; Step 2: $\frac{1}{30}$; Step 3: $\frac{1}{29}$; Step 4: $\frac{1}{870}$

11.9 Practice and Problem Solving (pp. 637–639) **7.** independent **9.** $\frac{5}{34}$ **11. a.** $\frac{7}{59}$ **b.** $\frac{42}{295}$ **c.** $\frac{21}{236}$ **13. a.** $\frac{2}{51}$ **b.** $\frac{5}{51}$ **c.** $\frac{28}{153}$ **d.** $\frac{49}{153}$ **15.** If you do replace it. *Sample answer:* The probability if you replace the red marble is $\frac{1}{2} \cdot \frac{1}{2} = \frac{1}{4} = 0.25$, and the probability if you do not replace it is $\frac{1}{2} \cdot \frac{19}{39} = \frac{19}{78} \approx 0.244$. **17.** 1 in 10^{10}, or $\frac{1}{10{,}000{,}000{,}000}$ **19. a.** BR, RB, RR, BB **b.** BR: $\frac{2}{9} \approx 22\%$, RB: $\frac{20}{87} \approx 23\%$, RR: $\frac{3}{29} \approx 10\%$, BB: $\frac{4}{9} \approx 44\%$ **c.** $\frac{5}{9} \approx 56\%$. *Sample answer:* Since the complement of catching at least one rainbow trout is catching no rainbow trout, I subtracted the probability for BB from 1. **21.** $-3s^2 - 2$ **23.** 15,504 groups

Chapter Review (pp. 640–643) **1.** margin of error

3. **Amount of Purchase ($)**

Stem	Leaves
1	0 2 5 6 6
2	
3	2 2 3 4 4 5 6
4	4 5 8

Key: 1 | 0 = $10

Sample:

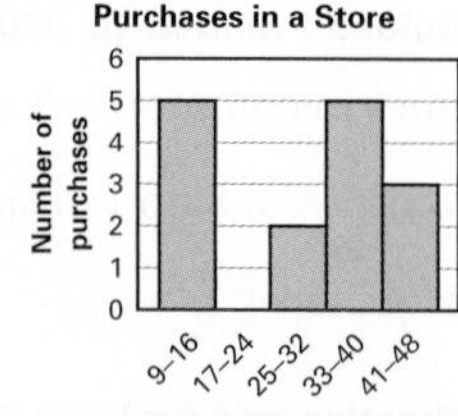

5.

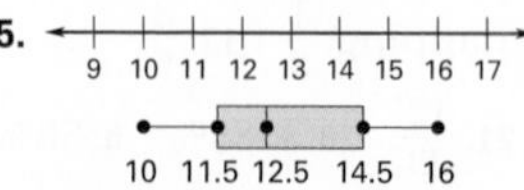

7. population: customers of a pizza parlor; sampling method: convenience sample **9.** 72 **11.** 20,160 **13.** 10; 792 **15.** $\frac{18}{95}$

Chapter 12

12.1 Guided Practice (p. 653) **1.** degree **3.** yes; $5x^3$; monomial **5.** no **7.** 1 **9.** $6x + 12$ **11.** $-z^2 + 10z + 8$ **13.** $2x^2 + 10x$ **15.** 17 **17.** 48

12.1 Practice and Problem Solving (pp. 654–655) **19.** yes; $8a^2$; monomial **21.** yes; $3c^3$, $-2c^2$, and -7; trinomial **23.** no **25.** 2 **27.** 3 **29.** 1 **31.** No. *Sample answer:* In standard form, the degree of each term decreases or stays the same from left to right. The degree of the term $5x^2y$ is 3, so the polynomial in standard form is $5x^2y + 3x^2 + 7$. **33.** $6x + 2$ **35.** $4y + 7$ **37.** $13z^2 - 22z$ **39.** 156 ft; 100 ft **41.** 44 **43.** -52 **45.** 7 **47.** $3x + 15$ **49.** $16x + 16$ **51.** 3 **53.** 4 **55.** 4 **57.** -1 **59. a.** 67 ft; 192 ft **b.** 3259 ft; 7904 ft **c.** about 1361 ft **61.** $n + 4$ **65.** -27 **67.** 135 **69.** 81 m^2

12.2 Guided Practice (p. 659) **1.** like terms **3.** $3x + 11$ **5.** $4a^2 - 4$ **7.** $9z - 5$ **9.** $-2b^2 - b + 7$ **11.** *Sample answer:* When subtracting the second polynomial, the opposite should have been found for each term, not just the first term. So, $(x^2 + 3x - 1) - (x^2 + x + 2) = x^2 + 3x - 1 - x^2 - x - 2 = x^2 - x^2 + 3x - x - 1 - 2 = 2x - 3$.

12.2 Practice and Problem Solving (pp. 660–661) **13.** $-6x - 8$ **15.** $2y^4 - 3y^2 - 9$ **17.** $-4z^3 + z^2 + 3z - 3$ **19.** $4m^2 - 4m + 1$ **21.** $3a^2 + 7a - 2$ **23.** $3b^3 - 4b^2 + 2b$ **25.** $3c^3 + c^2 - 2c + 12$ **27.** $-2d^2 + 4d$ **29.** $15x + y$ **31.** $-6cd - 2$ **33.** $4m - 17n$ **35.** $-11rs + 2r - 3s$ **37.** $3x^2 - 5x - 4$ **39.** $-33x^3 + 670x^2 - 1695x + 31{,}948$ **41.** $21 + 7a$ **43.** $-12t + 60$ **45.** 3^6 **47.** m^{13} **49.** yes

12.3 Guided Practice (p. 664) **1.** distributive **3.** $-6x^3 - 2x^2$ **5.** $8z^3 + 3z^2$ **7.** $30b^3 + 70b^2 + 40b$ **9.** Step 1: $50 = 2l + 2w$; Step 2: $w = 25 - l$; Step 3: $25l - l^2$

12.3 Practice and Problem Solving (pp. 664–666) **11.** $5x^3 - 10x^2$ **13.** $12f^3 - 3f$ **15.** $-g^4 + 6g^3$ **17.** $5d^4 - 35d^3 + 5d^2$ **19.** $-21y^3 - 28y^2 + 14y$ **21.** $6w^4 - 36w^3 + 6w^2$ **23.** $-2z - 5$ **25.** $11m^6 - m^4 - 2m^2$ **27.** $\frac{3n^2}{2} - \frac{n}{2} + 1$ **33.** $3x^2 + x$ **35.** $3x^2 + 4x$ **37.** $18mn + 2n^2 - 8n$ **39.** $5x^2y + 6xy^2 + 8xy$ **41.** $-3mn^2 - 3n^4 - 6n^2$

43. $5c^3 - 35cd^2 + 5cd$ **45. a.** length: $10x + 10$, width: $8x$ **b.** $80x^2 + 80x$; 2400 in.^{2} **c.** *Sample answer:* When $x = 10$, the area is 8800 in.^{2}, which is $3\frac{2}{3}$ times the area when $x = 5$.
47. a. $x(b - x) + b(a - x)$ **b.** $ab - x^2$ **c.** $x(b - x) + b(a - x) = xb - x^2 + ba - bx = bx - bx - x^2 + ab = ab - x^2$ **49.** domain: $-4, 0, 3, 5$; range: $-4, 0, 3, 5$ **51.** domain: 6, 7, 8, 9; range: $-8, 9, 10$ **53.** 10.4 ft **55.** $-3x^2 - 2x + 10$

12.4 Guided Practice (p. 670) **1.** F: First, O: Outer, I: Inner, L: Last **3.** $4a^2 + 11a + 6$ **5.** $-8c^2 + 26c - 20$ **7.** $8y^2 - 14y - 4$ **9.** $3a^2 + 22a + 7$ **11.** $50c^2 - 30c + 4$

12.4 Practice and Problem Solving (pp. 670–672)
13. $3x^2 + 13x + 4$ **15.** $12t^2 - 16t - 16$ **17.** $42p^2 - 38p + 8$ **19.** $-24w^2 + 61w + 8$ **21.** $16m^2 - 56m + 49$ **23.** $-11v^2 - 60v + 36$ **25.** $4x^2 + 38x + 48$ **27.** $3x^2 + 32x + 20$ **29.** Above: $2x$, Row 2: 28
31. *Sample answer:* It is similar because you can use the distributive property. It is different because when you multiply two binomials you have to apply the distributive property twice instead of once and because you may also have to combine like terms to simplify the product.
33. $-2x^2 - 2.6x + 6$ **35.** $g^2 + 16.7g - 14$
37. $36h^2 + \frac{129}{8}h + \frac{15}{32}$ **39.** $22a^2 + 86ab - 8b^2$
41. $-12x^2 + 11xy - 2y^2$ **43. a.** $0.52x^2 + 68.2x + 1750$ **b.** 1750 million pounds **c.** 2406 million pounds **45.** The distributive property. *Sample answer:* First I would use the FOIL method to multiply two of the binomials, but then I would use the distributive property to multiply the result by the third binomial because the result will likely have too many terms for the FOIL method to work, and because algebra tiles and tables would be burdensome with the extra computation.
47. a. length: $11 - 2x$, width: $7 - 2x$, height: x; $x > 0$ and $x < 3.5$ **b.** $4x^3 - 36x^2 + 77x$ **c.** 1.4 in.
49. 5^3 **51.** $\frac{1}{x^7}$ **53.** -3 **55.** 12 **57.** $21x^2 - 28x$
59. $-4s^3 - 40s^2$

12.5 Guided Practice (p. 676) **1.** *Sample answer:* The power of a quotient property states that the power of a quotient is the power of the numerator divided by the power of the denominator. For example, $\left(\frac{2x}{y}\right)^3 = \frac{(2x)^3}{y^3} = \frac{8x^3}{y^3}$. **3.** $-216x^3$ **5.** $\frac{n^2}{49}$
7. 7^6 **9.** y^6 **11.** 1.69×10^{-14} m^2

12.5 Practice and Problem Solving (pp. 677–678)
13. y^6z^6 **15.** $81t^4$ **17.** $6561y^8$ **19.** a^3b^3 **21.** $\frac{p^5}{100{,}000}$
23. $\frac{81}{x^4}$ **25.** 5^8 **27.** $\frac{1}{a^8}$ **29.** 5.83×10^{18} **31.** 4.84×10^{24} **33.** 4.29×10^{-29} **35.** 1.13×10^{10} square light-years **37.** x^8y^4 **39.** d^6e^8 **41.** $\frac{w^{15}}{v^{25}}$ **43.** $-\frac{r^3}{s^{12}}$
45. 0.000045 **47.** 6,000,000 **49.** 55,756,800
51. a. about $21.98r^2$ in.^{3} **b.** $\frac{7}{9}$ in. *Sample answer:* The volumes of oil in each cylinder must be equal. The volume in the cylinder with radius $3r$ is about $3.14(3r)^2h$, so $3.14(3r)^2h = 21.98r^2$. Solving for h gives $h = \frac{7}{9}$ inch. **c.** $9d$ in.

53.
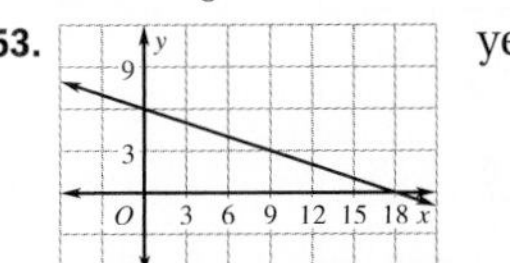

yes

55.
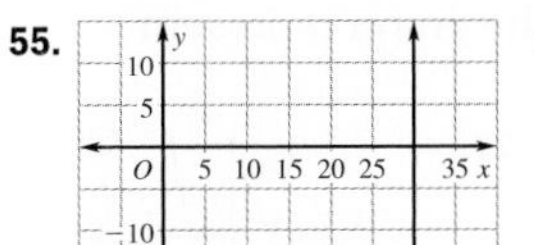

no

57.
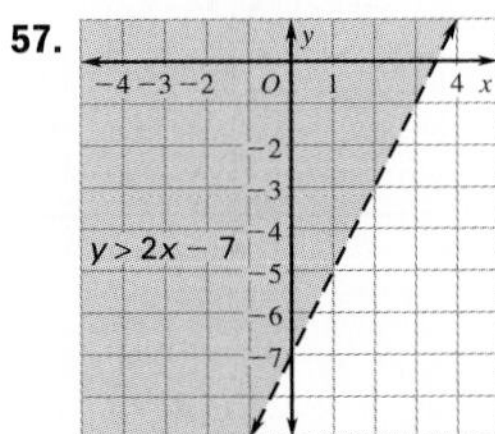

59.
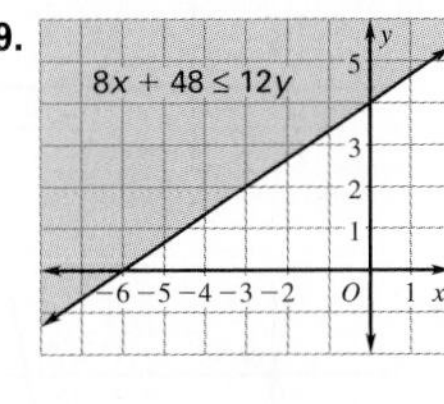

61. $x^2 + 4x - 60$ **63.** $6x^2 - 29x + 35$

12.6 Guided Practice (p. 682) **1.** *Sample answer:* It is a U-shaped graph that opens upward if the coefficient of the x^2-term is positive and downward if the coefficient of the x^2-term is negative.
3. *Sample answer:*

x	−2	−1	0	1	2
y	13	16	17	16	13

Selected Answers

5. *Sample answer:*

x	−4	−3	−2	−1	0
y	0	−9	−12	−9	0

7. Labeled points on the graph represent sample points for a table.

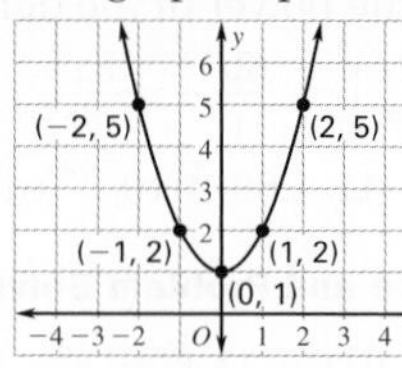

9. maximum **11.** maximum

12.6 Practice and Problem Solving (pp. 682–684)

13–21. Sample tables are given.

13.

x	−5	−4	−3	−2	−1
y	5	8	9	8	5

15.

x	0	1	2	3	4
y	0	−15	−20	−15	0

17.

x	0	1	2	3	4
y	5	2	1	2	5

19.

x	−5	−3	−1	1	3
y	$11\frac{1}{2}$	$5\frac{1}{2}$	$3\frac{1}{2}$	$5\frac{1}{2}$	$11\frac{1}{2}$

21.

x	0	2	4	6	8
y	−6	0	2	0	−6

25–30. Labeled points on the graph represent sample points for a table.

25.

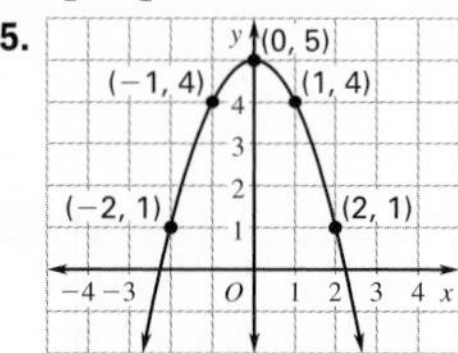

27.

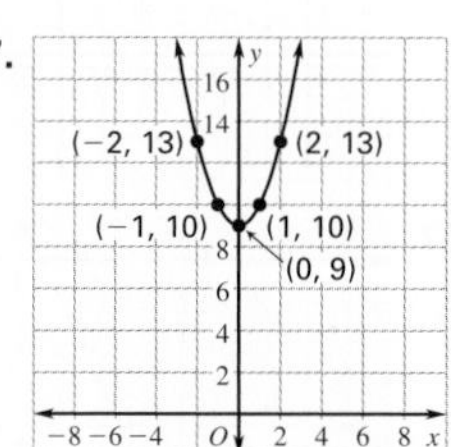

29.

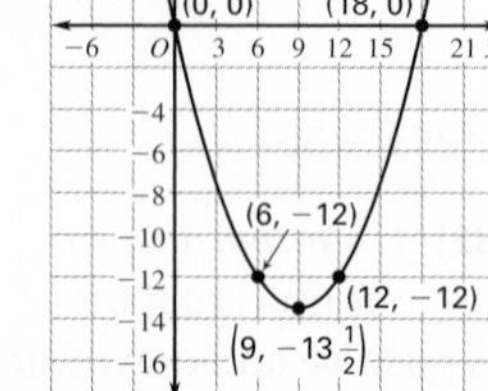

31. maximum **33.** minimum **35.** maximum

37. a. about 13 m/sec to 23 m/sec **b.** above about 31 m/sec

39. maximum;

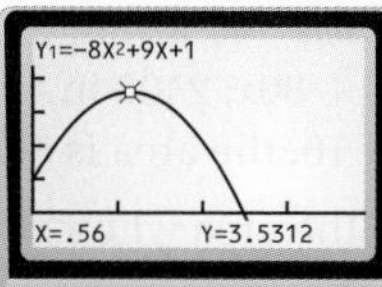

about 3.53

41. maximum;

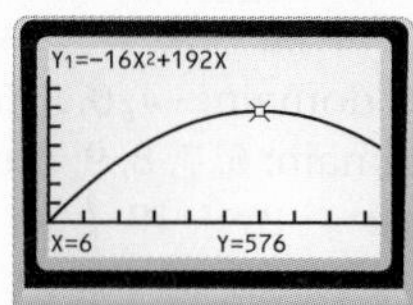

576

43. minimum;

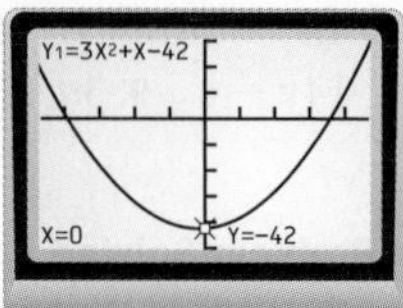

−42

45. *Sample answer:* Substitute $x = 0$ in the equation of the function and solve for y.

47. a.

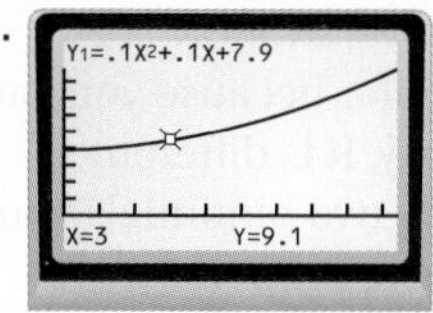

b. 1993 **c.** 1999. *Sample answer:* The graph gets steeper as the year increases, which means that the amount of increase in water consumption gets larger as the year increases.

51. $\frac{5}{b^7}$ **53.**

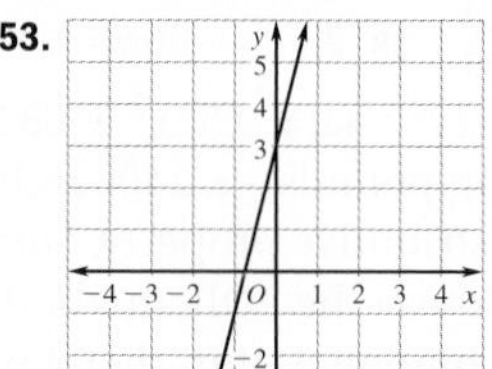

55.

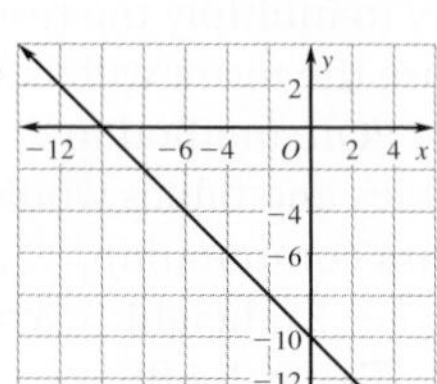

57. $\frac{25}{n^2}$

12.6 Technology Activity (p. 685) **1–5.** Sample answers are given. **1.** Both open up and pass through the origin, but the graph of $y = 4x^2$ is narrower than the graph of $y = x^2$.

Selected Answers

3. Both pass through the origin, but the graph of $y = -0.5x^2$ opens downward and is wider than the graph of $y = x^2$. **5.** If a is positive, the graph opens upward. If a is negative, the graph opens downward. Also, the greater the absolute value of a, the narrower the graph.

12.7 Guided Practice (p. 689) 1. exponential decay **3.** Labeled points on the graph represent sample points for a table.

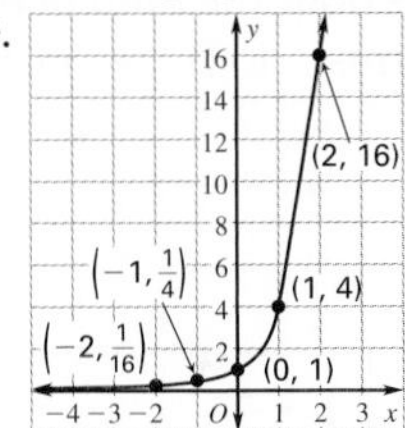

5. Labeled points on the graph represent sample points for a table.

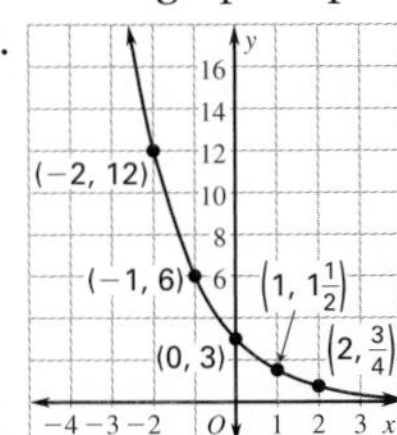

7. Step 1: 25, 12.5, 6.25, 3.125; Step 2: 5 cuts

12.7 Practice and Problem Solving (pp. 689–691)

9–15. Sample tables are given.

9.

x	−2	−1	0	1	2
y	$\frac{2}{9}$	$\frac{2}{3}$	2	6	18

11.

x	−2	−1	0	1	2
y	$\frac{1}{72}$	$\frac{1}{12}$	$\frac{1}{2}$	3	18

13.

x	−2	−1	0	1	2
y	81	27	9	3	1

15.

x	−2	−1	0	1	2
y	40	20	10	5	$\frac{5}{2}$

17.

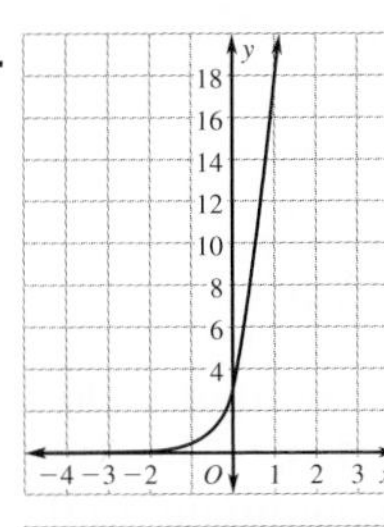

19.

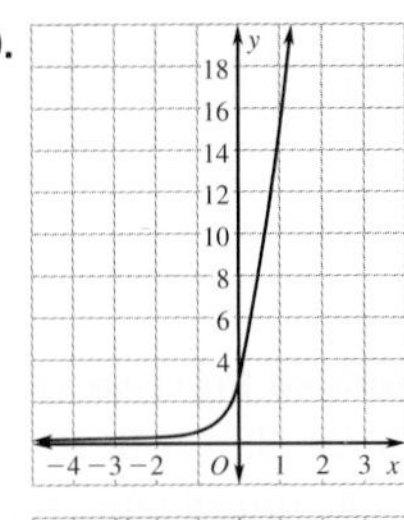

21.

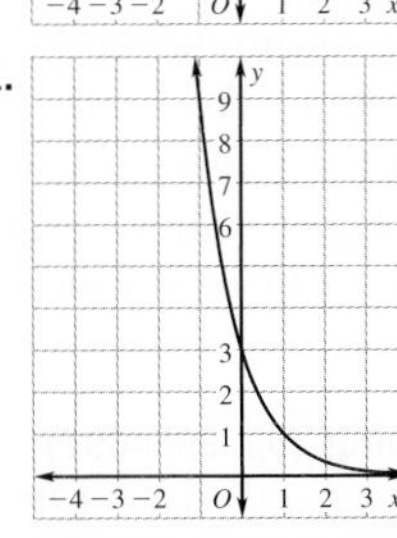

23.

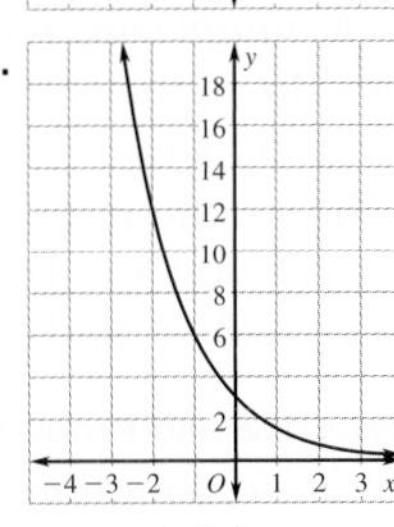

25.

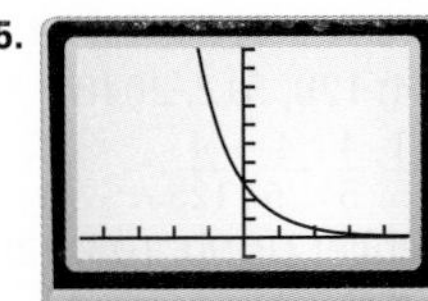

exponential decay

27.

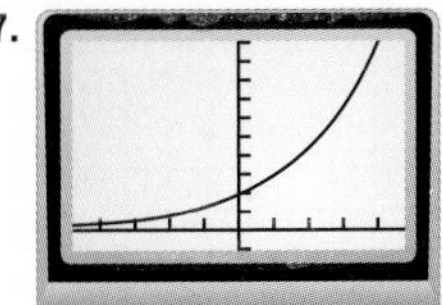

exponential growth

33. $y = 2(3)^x$. *Sample answer:* Since $y = 2(3)^x$ is increasing by powers of 3, it increases faster than $y = 3(2)^x$, which is increasing by powers of 2. **35. a.** Exponential decay. *Sample answer:* It is of the form $y = ab^x$ where $a = 500$ and $b = 0.8$. Since $0 < b < 1$, the function represents exponential decay.

b.

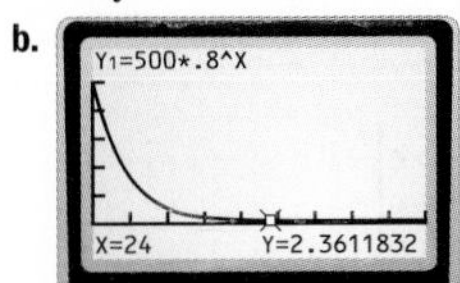

about 2.36 mg

c. after about 6 h; after about 14 h

37. $\sin A = \frac{4}{5}$, $\cos A = \frac{3}{5}$, $\sin B = \frac{3}{5}$, $\cos B = \frac{4}{5}$

39. $\sin J = \frac{5}{13}$, $\cos J = \frac{12}{13}$, $\sin K = \frac{12}{13}$, $\cos K = \frac{5}{13}$

41. 8 **43.** 1

Selected Answers

45.

x	−2	−1	0	1	2
y	9	3	1	3	9

47.

x	−2	−1	0	1	2
y	3	−6	−9	−6	3

12.8 Guided Practice (p. 695) **1.** common ratio **3.** 5; 23, 28, 33 **5.** 8; 16, 24, 32 **7.** 3; −54, −162, −486 **9.** *Sample answer:* The coordinates in the table are not in the correct columns. The first term is 3, so 1 should go under the x and 3 under the y. The second term is 5 so 2 goes under x and 5 under y, and so on. The points plotted should be (1, 3), (2, 5), (3, 7), and (4, 9).

12.8 Practice and Problem Solving (pp. 695–697)
11. geometric; common ratio: −2; −32, 64, −128
13. arithmetic; common difference: 15; 64, 79, 94
15. geometric; common ratio: 4; 128, 512, 2048
17. geometric; common ratio: $\frac{1}{5}$; $\frac{4}{5}, \frac{4}{25}, \frac{4}{125}$
19. arithmetic; common difference: 18; 90, 108, 126
21. geometric; common ratio: $\frac{2}{3}$; 48, 32, $21\frac{1}{3}$
23. arithmetic; 24, 38, 52;

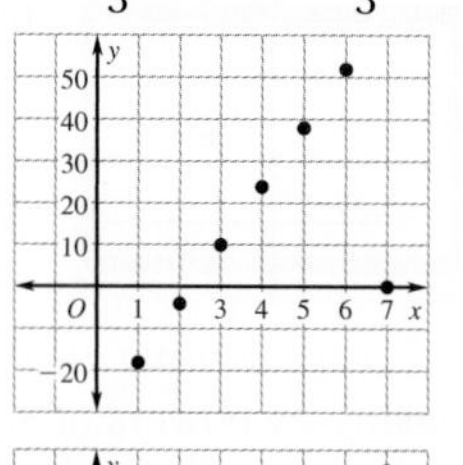

25. arithmetic; 55, 65, 75;

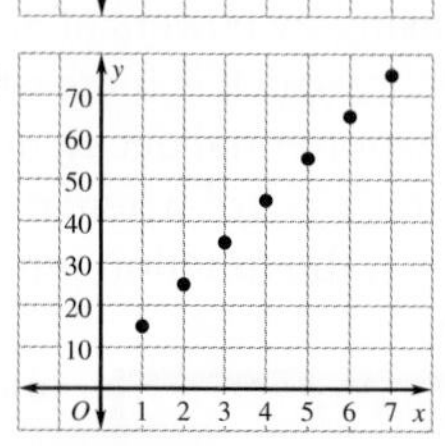

27. geometric; 324, 972, 2916;

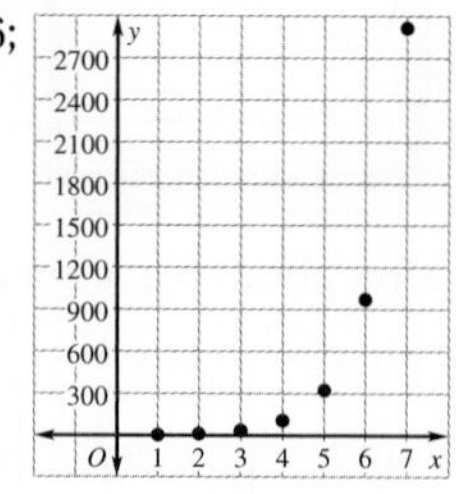

29. a. 36, 45, 54, 63, 72, 81; arithmetic **b.** $9n + 27$ **c.** 23 carts **31. a.** geometric **b.** 12, 4.8, 1.92, 0.768, 0.3072, 0.12288, 0.049152; after 6 bounces
33. 3, 4.5, 6; $-3 + 1.5(n - 1)$, or $1.5n - 4.5$; 13.5
35. 14,641; 161,051; 1,771,561; 11^{n-1}; 214,358,881
37. 8, 4, 2; $128\left(\frac{1}{2}\right)^{n-1}$; $\frac{1}{2}$ **39. a.** Neither. *Sample answer:* The difference between consecutive terms varies, as does the ratio between consecutive terms. **b.** 21, 34, 55, 89, 144
c.

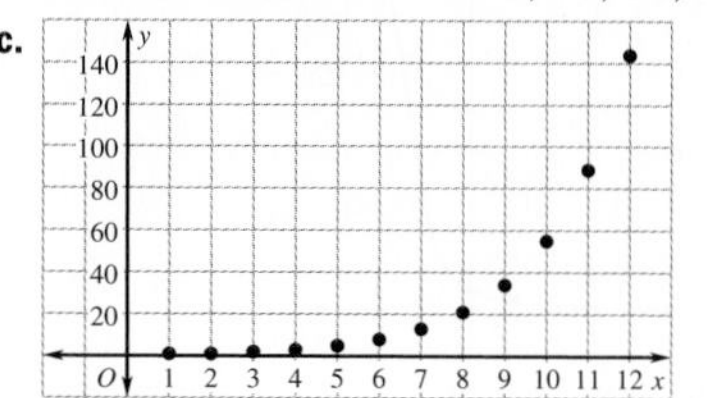

no

41. 6 m **43.** 2
45.

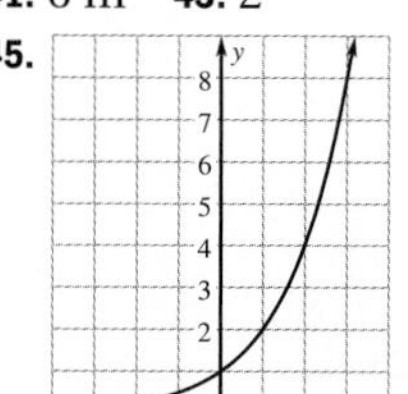

47.

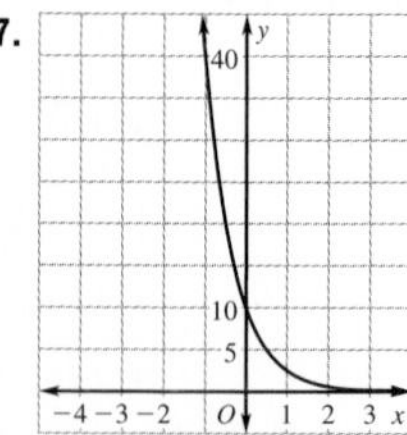

Chapter Review (pp. 698–701) **1.** nonlinear function **3.** arithmetic sequence **5.** *Sample answer:* First find the degree of each term by finding the sum of the exponents of its variables. The degree of the polynomial is the greatest degree of its terms. **7.** *Sample answer:* It is a U-shaped curve that opens downward. **9.** $2x^2 + 3x - 10$ **11.** $8x^2 - 2x + 7$
13. $m^2 - 3m - 10$ **15.** $4a^3 + a^2 + a + 10$
17. $-7z^4 + 42z^2$ **19.** $-9p^3 - 72p^2 - 27p$
21. $-25n^2 + 15n^3$ **23.** $b^2 + 9b + 14$
25. $z^2 - 9z + 20$ **27.** $3c^2 - 17c - 6$ **29.** y^6z^6
31. $\frac{x^4}{16}$ **33.** $625k^4$ **35.** z^{12}
37. Labeled points on the graph represent sample points for a table.

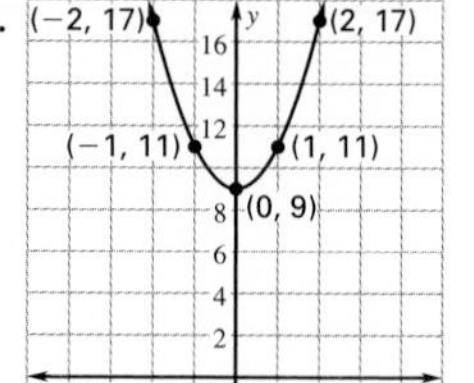

Selected Answers

39. Labeled points on the graph represent sample points for a table.

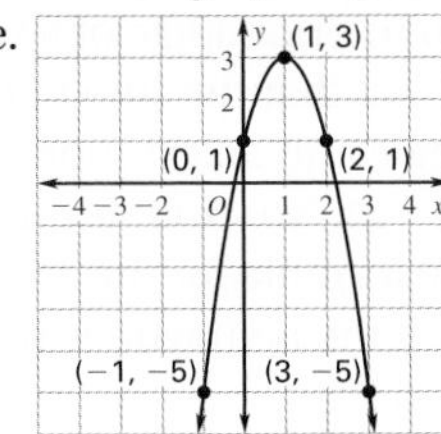

41. arithmetic; common difference: 5; 19, 24, 29
43. geometric; common ratio: 7; 7203; 50,421; 352,947

Focus on Problem Solving (p. 705) **1. a.** Row 2: π, 4π, 9π, 16π; Row 3: 4, 16, 36, 64; Row 4: $\frac{\pi}{4}$, $\frac{\pi}{4}$, $\frac{\pi}{4}$, $\frac{\pi}{4}$; the ratios are the same. **b.** Circle: πr^2; square: $(2r)^2 = 4r^2$; ratio: $\frac{\pi r^2}{4r^2} = \frac{\pi}{4}$; the results are the same.
3. a. \$495; loss **b.** $500 - 500p^2$; loss. *Sample answer:* p^2 is positive, so $500p^2$ is positive. You are subtracting a positive number from 500, so the result is less than 500. **5. a.** $S(1) = \frac{1}{2}$, $S(2) = \frac{3}{4}$, $S(3) = \frac{7}{8}$, $S(4) = \frac{15}{16}$ **b.** $S(n) = 1 - \left(\frac{1}{2}\right)^n$

Chapter 13

13.1 Guided Practice (p. 711) **1.** complementary **3.** neither **5.** complementary **7.** 20°

13.1 Practice and Problem Solving (pp. 711–713) **9.** $\angle A$ and $\angle D$ **11.** neither **13.** complementary **15.** supplementary **17.** 62° **19.** 65° **21.** 140° **23.** 9° **25.** 2 pairs. *Sample answer:* Vertical angles are opposite each other, and meet only at one point. There are only two pairs of angles in this situation for which this is true. Any other pair of angles share a side. **27.** 9; 54° and 54° **29.** yes; right **31.** $m\angle 1 = 180° - x°$, $m\angle 2 = x°$, $m\angle 3 = 180° - x°$; $m\angle 1 = m\angle 3 = 180° - x°$, m(angle labeled $x°$) $= m\angle 2 = x°$ **33.** 45°; 90° **37.** Check students' work. **39.** 10 **41.** −30 **43.** arithmetic

Student Reference (p. 715)

1–3. A ——— B

C ———— D

1.

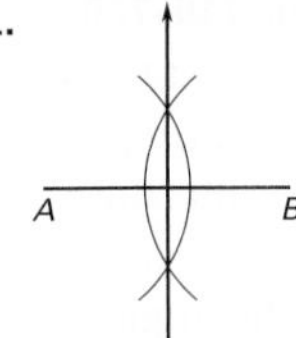

3.

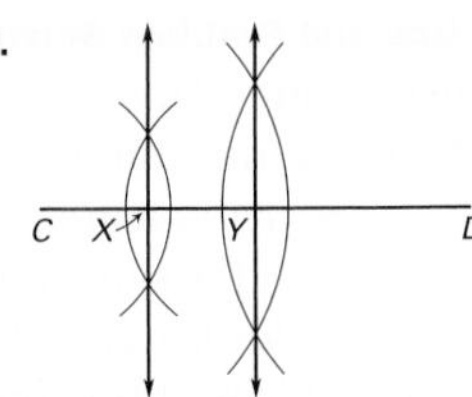

Sample answer: First I copied $\overline{CD}$ and constructed its perpendicular bisector to form two segments with lengths half that of $\overline{CD}$. Then I constructed the perpendicular bisector of one of these segments. The lengths of $\overline{CX}$ and $\overline{XY}$ are one fourth that of $\overline{CD}$.

5.

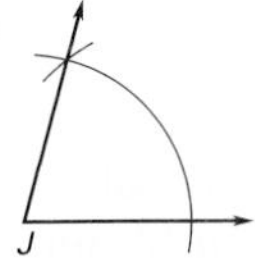

Y J X

$\angle XJY$ has twice the measure of $\angle J$.

7.

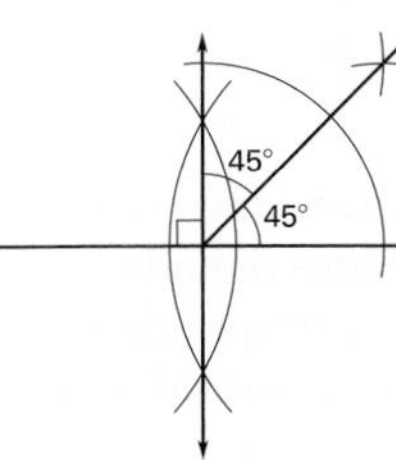

Sample answer: First I drew a segment and constructed its perpendicular bisector, forming four right angles. Then I constructed the angle bisector of one of the right angles to create two 45° angles.

13.2 Guided Practice (p. 718)

1. *Sample:*

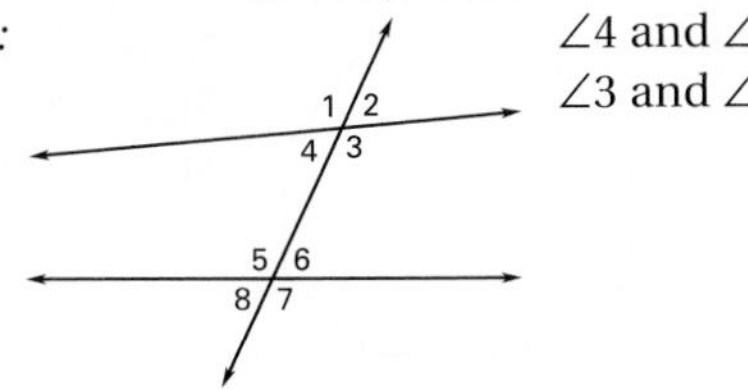

$\angle 4$ and $\angle 6$, $\angle 3$ and $\angle 5$

3. corresponding **5.** alternate exterior
7. $m\angle 2 = 115°$, $m\angle 3 = 115°$, $m\angle 4 = 65°$, $m\angle 5 = 65°$, $m\angle 6 = 115°$, $m\angle 7 = 115°$, $m\angle 8 = 65°$

Selected Answers

13.2 Practice and Problem Solving (pp. 719–720)
9. alternate exterior **11.** corresponding **13.** $\angle 4$, $\angle 5$, $\angle 8$ **15. a.** alternate interior **b.** Yes. *Sample answer:* Because m and n are parallel, alternate interior angles have the same measure. **c.** $m\angle 1 = m\angle 2 = 72°$. *Sample answer:* $\angle 2$ and the angle with measure 108° are supplementary, so $m\angle 2 = 180° - 108° = 72°$. Also, $m\angle 1 = m\angle 2$ as noted.
17. 5 **19.** $m\angle 1 = 90°$, $m\angle 2 = 115°$, $m\angle 3 = 65°$
21. *Sample:*

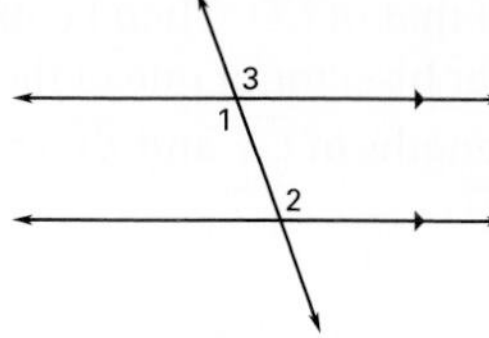

They are the same; they are the measures of corresponding angles formed by a transversal intersecting two parallel lines: $m\angle 1 = m\angle 2$, and $m\angle 1 = m\angle 3$, so $m\angle 2 = m\angle 3$.
23. *Sample:*

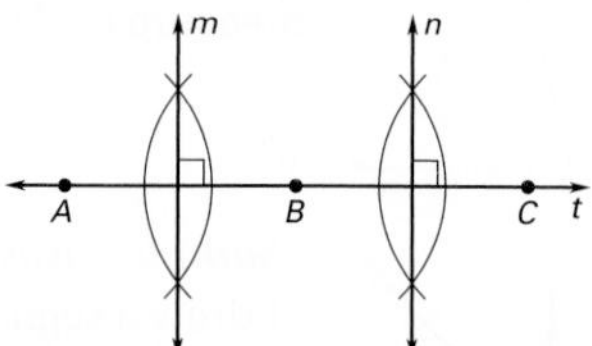

They are parallel. *Sample answer:* Line t is a transversal of lines m and n. Since m and n intersect t in right angles, the corresponding angles have the same measure, so m and n must be parallel. **25.** $\frac{1}{6}$ **27.** $\frac{13}{18}$ **29.** supplementary
31. complementary

13.3 Guided Practice (p. 725)
1. *Sample:*

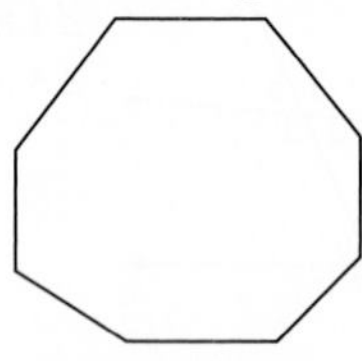

7. Step 1: 360°; Step 2: 69°; Step 3: 111°

13.3 Practice and Problem Solving (pp. 725–727)
9. 900° **11.** Yes. *Sample answer:* For a triangle, $n = 3$, so $(n - 2) \cdot 180° = (3 - 2) \cdot 180° = 180°$, as expected. **13.** interior: 90°, exterior: 90°
15. interior: 108°, exterior: 72° **17.** interior: 156°, exterior: 24° **19.** 78°

21. *Sample answer:* First use the formula for the measure of an interior angle of a regular n-gon. Then use the fact that the sum of the measures of an interior angle and an exterior angle at each vertex is 180°. **23.** No. *Sample answer:* You can only apply the formula for the measure of an interior angle if the pentagon is regular.
25. $x = 70$, $y = 110$
27. a. 90°, 108°, 120°, 128.6°, 135°, 140°, 144°;

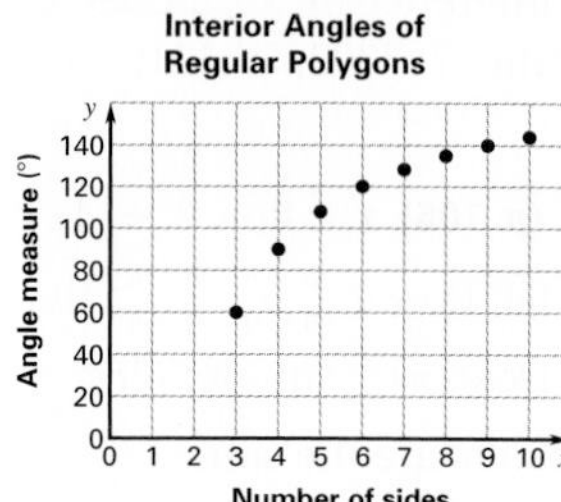

b. decrease **c.** No. *Sample answer:* The numbers in the second row of the table are increasing by a smaller amount each time. The last increment was 4, so this increment will be less than 4, which would make $y < 148°$. **29.** 135
31. *Sample:*

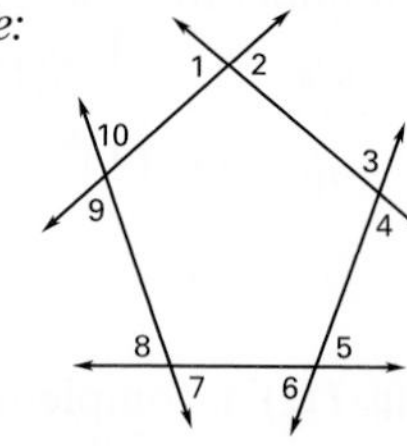

Sample answer: Each combines with the same interior angle to form a straight angle.

33. 11-gon **35.** 17-gon **37.** 5 **39.** −14
41. yes
43. yes **45.** 15

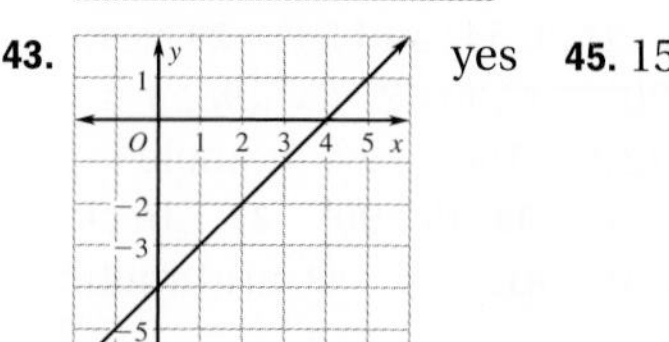

13.4 Guided Practice (p. 731) **1.** image **3.** 3 units left and 4 units down

5. 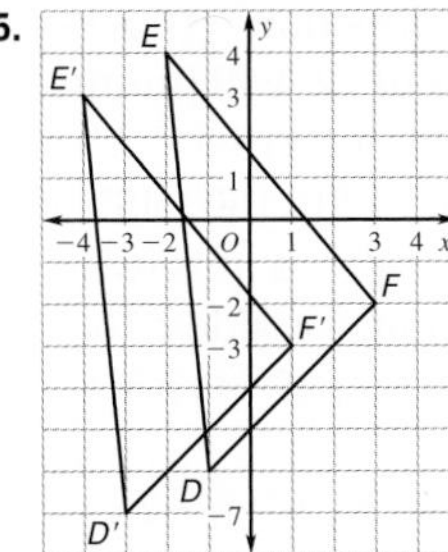 $D'(-3, -7)$, $E'(-4, 3)$, $F'(1, -3)$

13.4 Practice and Problem Solving (pp. 732–733)

7. 5 units left **9.** $A'(-6, -3)$, $B'(-7, 2)$, $C'(-5, 1)$, $D'(-5, -3)$;

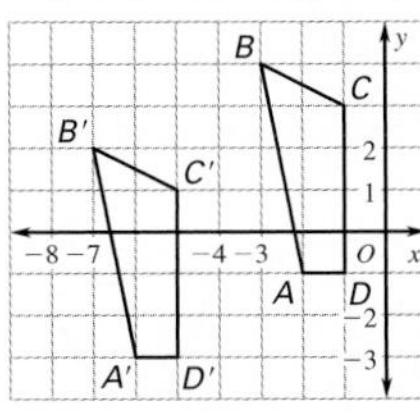

11. *Sample answer:* For the *y*-coordinates, the translation is $y - 4$, which means that 4 should be subtracted from the original *y*-coordinates instead of added. The correct image points are $A'(-1, -6)$ and $B'(5, -1)$.

13. Yes. *Sample:*

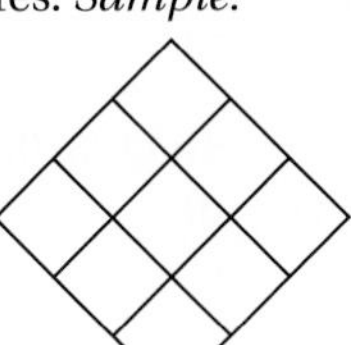

15. Yes. *Sample:*

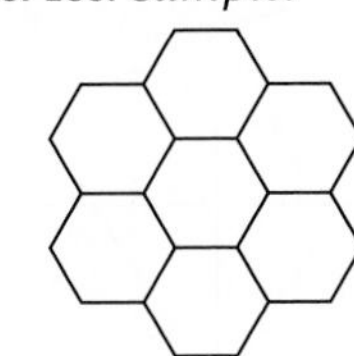

17. *Sample:*

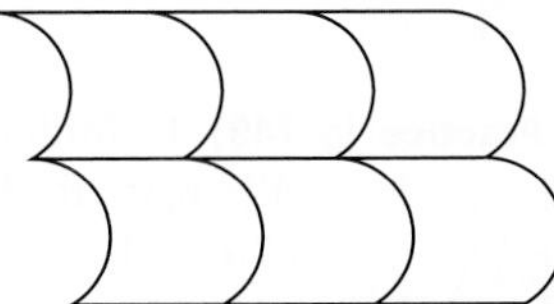

19. Yes. *Sample answer:* Begin with $(2, -7)$. Applying $(x, y) \to (x - 3, y - 4)$ gives $(-1, -11)$. Then applying $(x, y) \to (x + 2, y - 6)$ to $(-1, -11)$ gives $(1, -17)$. If instead you first apply $(x, y) \to (x + 2, y - 6)$ to $(2, -7)$, you get $(4, -13)$. Then applying $(x, y) \to (x - 3, y - 4)$ to $(4, -13)$ gives $(1, -17)$, which is the same result. **23.** -60 **25.** 4 units **27.** $\sqrt{41}$ units

13.5 Guided Practice (p. 736) **1.** Quadrant IV **3.** yes; *y*-axis **5.** yes; *x*-axis **7.** *Sample answer:* For a reflection in the *x*-axis, the *y*-coordinate is multiplied by -1. The translation shown is a reflection in the *y*-axis, in which the *x*-coordinate is multiplied by -1. The correct image points are $A'(-2, -1)$ and $B'(3, -6)$.

13.5 Practice and Problem Solving (pp. 736–738)

9. yes; *y*-axis

11. 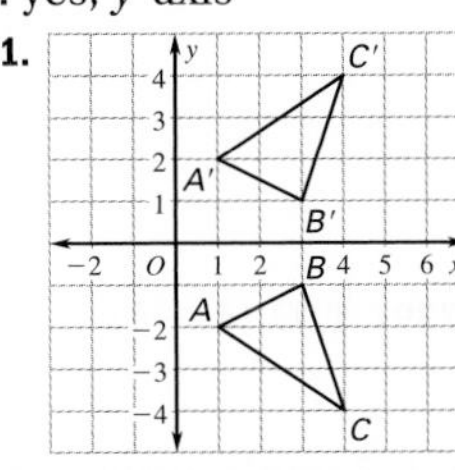 $A'(1, 2)$, $B'(3, 1)$, $C'(4, 4)$

13. $J'(6, 4)$, $K'(4, 7)$, $L'(3, 8)$, $M'(0, 5)$, $N'(1, 2)$

15. 2 lines of symmetry

17. a. 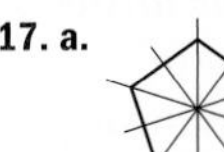 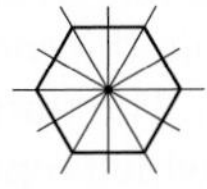 Row 2: 5, 6, 8

b. They are the same. **c.** 28 lines of symmetry

19. 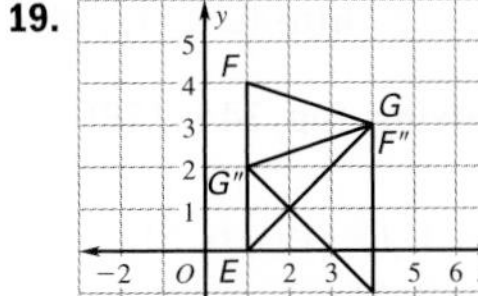 $E''(4, -1)$, $F''(4, 3)$, $G''(1, 2)$

21. a. 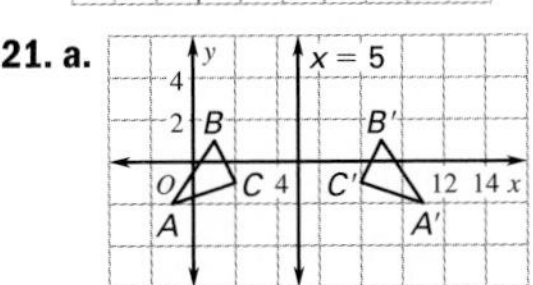

b. 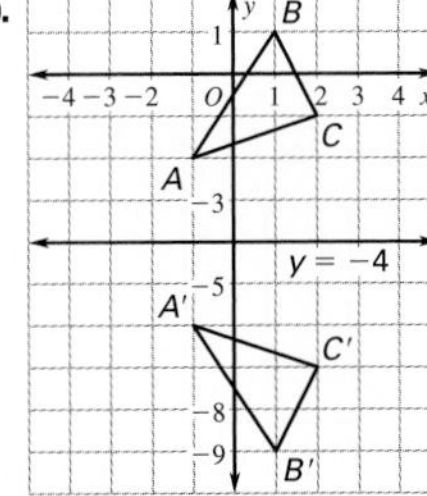

23. *Sample answer:* They are alike in that both are lines of reflection. They are different in that a line of symmetry has the special property that it reflects a figure back onto itself so that the image and the original look exactly the same.
25. 71, −71 **27.** 100, 100 **29.** 66 **31.** 90
33. 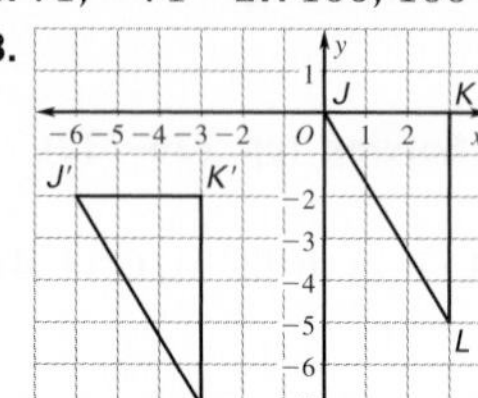
$J'(-6, -2)$, $K'(-3, -2)$, $L'(-3, -7)$

13.5 Technology Activity (p. 739) **1.** $D'(4, -1)$, $E'(-2, -5)$, $F'(0, -3)$

13.6 Guided Practice (p. 744) **1.** *Sample answer:* In line symmetry, the image that fits exactly on the original figure is formed by reflecting, or flipping, the figure in a line that passes through the center of the figure, while in rotational symmetry the image is formed by turning the original figure a certain angle measure around its center. **3.** yes; 180° in either direction **5.** no **7.** *Sample answer:* For a 90° clockwise rotation, the coordinate notation is $(x, y) \to (y, -x)$. The transformation shown is $(x, y) \to (-y, x)$, which represents a 90° *counterclockwise* rotation. The correct image points are $A'(-5, -3)$, $B'(-4, -2)$, and $C'(-1, -4)$.

13.6 Practice and Problem Solving (pp. 744–746)
9. yes; 180° in either direction
11. 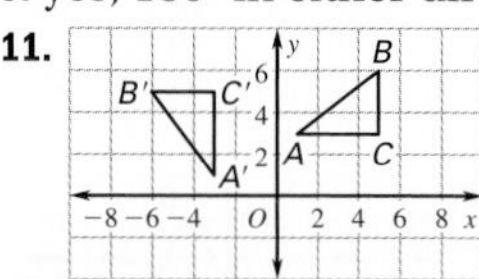
$A'(-3, 1)$, $B'(-6, 5)$, $C'(-3, 5)$
13. 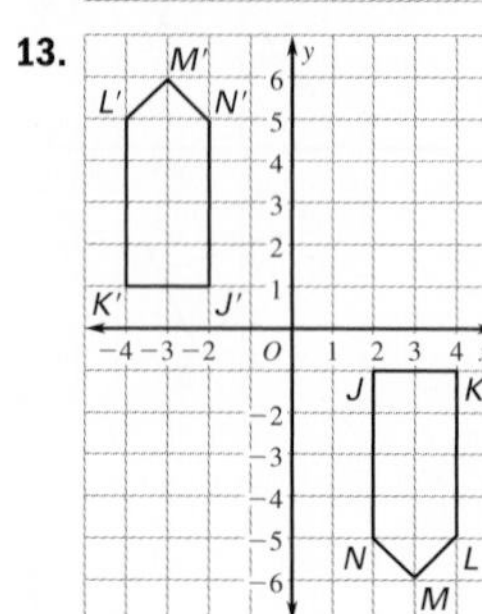
$J'(-2, 1)$, $K'(-4, 1)$, $L'(-4, 5)$, $M'(-3, 6)$, $N'(-2, 5)$

15. yes; 90° and 180° in either direction **17. a.** Yes. *Sample answer:* Each rotation of 72° will produce an image that fits the original. **b.** 144°
19. a. Row 1: 6, 8, 10; Row 2: 60°, 120°, 180°; 45°, 90°, 135°, 180°; 36°, 72°, 108°, 144°, 180° **b.** It is twice the number of angles of rotation. **c.** sides: 16; angles of rotation: 22.5°, 45°, 67.5°, 90°, 112.5°, 135°, 157.5°, 180°
21. 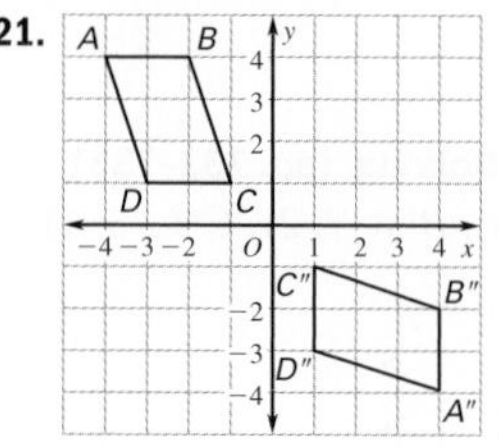
$A''(4, -4)$, $B''(4, -2)$, $C''(1, -1)$, $D''(1, -3)$
23. *Sample:*
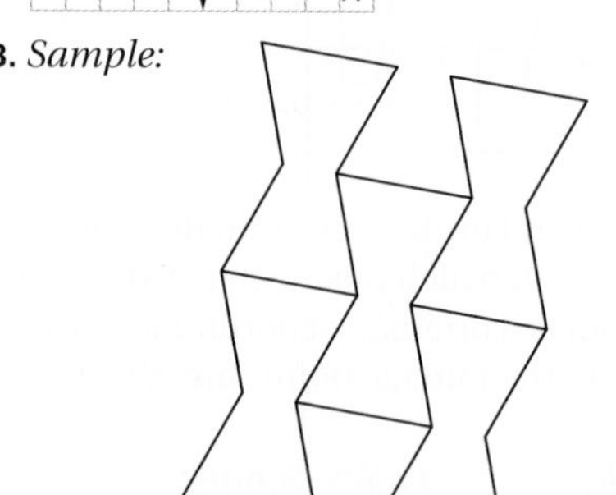
25. 75 mi
27. 300 mi
29. 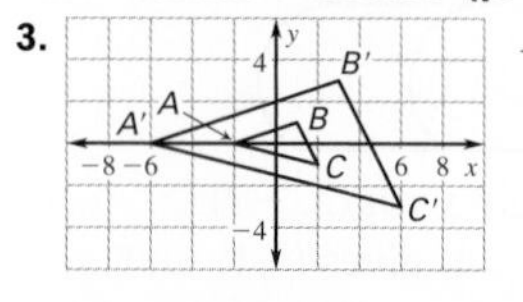
$P'(5, -4)$, $Q'(3, 0)$, $R'(1, -3)$ 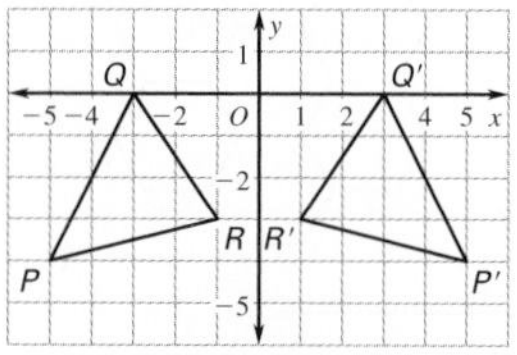

13.7 Guided Practice (p. 749) **1.** similar
3. 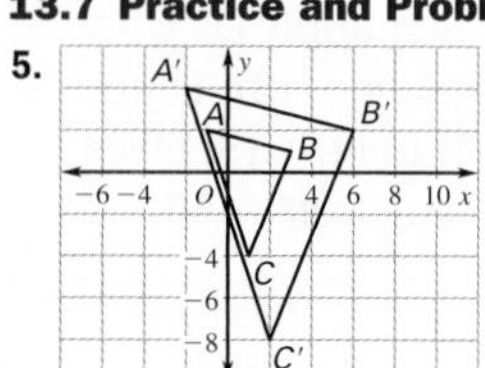
$A'(-6, 0)$, $B'(3, 3)$, $C'(6, -3)$

13.7 Practice and Problem Solving (pp. 750–751)
5. $A'(-2, 4)$, $B'(6, 2)$, $C'(2, -8)$

SA42

7. $P'(-3, 1), Q'(1, 1), R'(1, 0), S'(-3, 0)$

9. 2 **11a–b.**

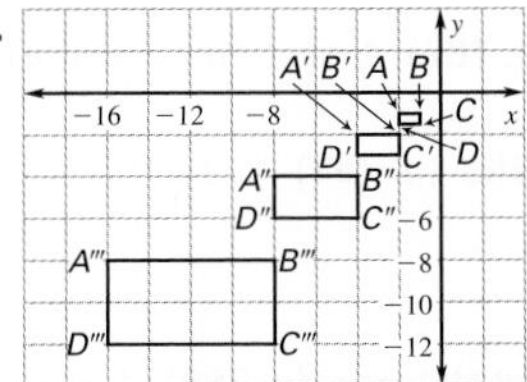

13. a. $A''(-1, 2), B''(2, 0), C''(1, -2)$;

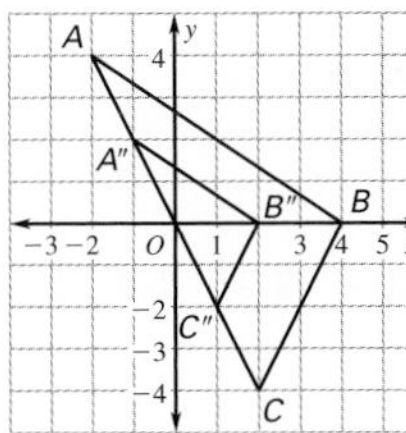

b. 0.5 **c.** Yes. *Sample answer:* Since dilating a figure just multiplies the coordinates by the scale factor, and multiplication is commutative, it does not matter in what order you apply multiple scale factors.

15.

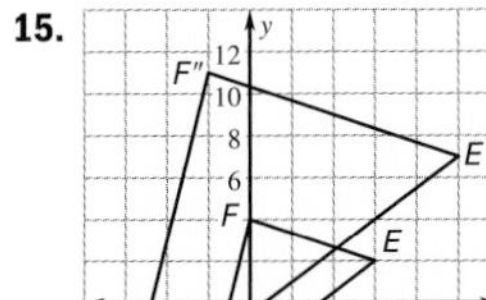

$D''(-6, -5), E''(10, 7), F''(-2, 11)$

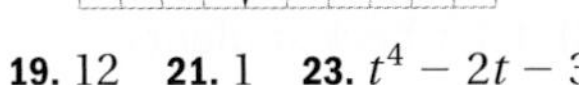

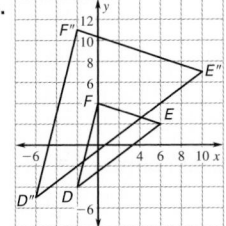

19. 12 **21.** 1 **23.** $t^4 - 2t - 3$

25.

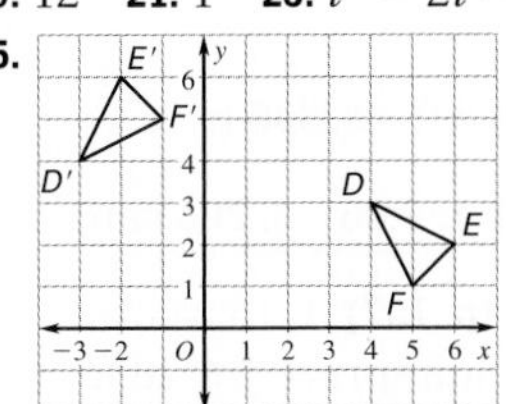

$D'(-3, 4), E'(-2, 6), F'(-1, 5)$

Chapter Review (pp. 752–755) **1.** 90°; 180° **3.** $P'(x, -y)$; $P'(-x, -y)$; $P'(2x, 2y)$ **5.** alternate interior angles **7.** 14° **9.** 59° **11.** alternate interior **13.** alternate interior **15.** 115° **17.** 65° **19.** 135°, 45° **21.** 152.3°, 27.7°

23.

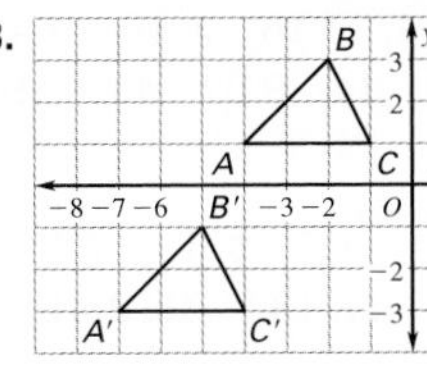

$A'(-7, -3), B'(-5, -1), C'(-4, -3)$

25.

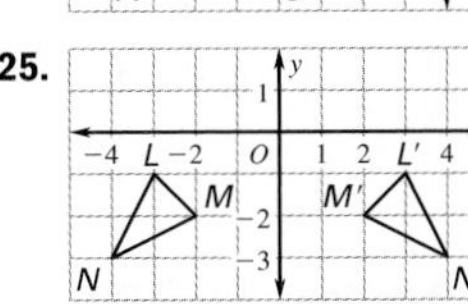

$L'(3, -1), M'(2, -2), N'(4, -3)$

27.

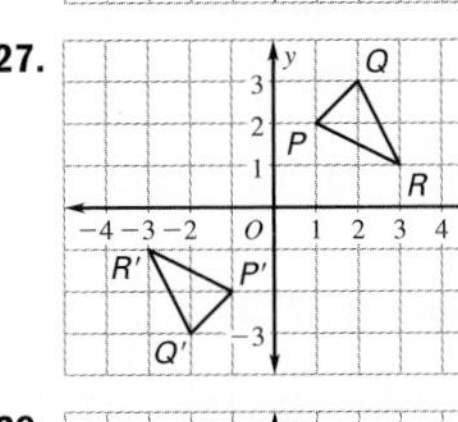

$P'(-1, -2), Q'(-2, -3), R'(-3, -1)$

29.

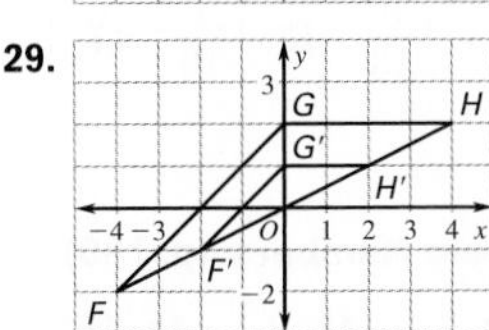

$F'(-2, -1), G'(0, 1), H'(2, 1)$

Skills Review Handbook

Place Value and Rounding (p. 770) **1.** tens, 50; 60 **3.** hundreds, 900; 900 **5.** thousands, 6000; 7000 **7.** ten thousands, 40,000; 40,000 **9.** hundredths, 0.05; 10,064.66 **11.** thousandths, 0.009; 112.350 **13.** hundred thousands, 400,000; 500,000 **15.** hundreds, 100; 9200

Estimating Sums and Differences (p. 771) **1.** 10,000 **3.** 60,000 **5.** 12,000 **7.** 5000 **9.** 30,000 **11.** 200,000 **13.** 100,000

Estimating Products and Quotients (p. 772) **1–15.** Estimates may vary. **1.** 42,000; 56,000 **3.** 360,000; 500,000 **5.** 30; 50 **7.** 5; 7 **9.** 10,000; 18,000 **11.** 24,000; 35,000 **13.** 200; 500 **15.** 500; 700

Comparing and Ordering Decimals (p. 773) **1.** > **3.** = **5.** > **7.** 1.29, 1.3, 1.9, 2.19 **9.** 0.49, 0.5, 0.52, 0.55 **11.** 6.19, 6.21, 6.3, 6.32

Adding and Subtracting Decimals (p. 774) **1.** 6.4 **3.** 4.2 **5.** 2.24 **7.** 18.22 **9.** 151.57 **11.** 0.24 **13.** 9.214 **15.** 0.75

Multiplying Decimals (p. 775) **1.** 14.16 **3.** 16 **5.** 1.015 **7.** 0.0432 **9.** 0.0608 **11.** 29.82 **13.** 6.195 **15.** 13.0968

Dividing Decimals (p. 776) **1.** 4 **3.** 5 **5.** 19 **7.** 2.1 **9.** 0.9 **11.** 1.3 **13.** 14 **15.** 18 **17.** 134 **19.** 23.14

Modeling Fractions (p. 777) **1.** $\frac{1}{3}$ **3.** $\frac{3}{7}$ **5.** $\frac{5}{8}$ **7.** $2\frac{2}{5}$ **9.** $1\frac{5}{6}$ **11.** $2\frac{1}{3}$

Mixed Numbers and Improper Fractions (p. 778) **1.** $\frac{19}{10}$ **3.** $\frac{55}{6}$ **5.** $\frac{25}{7}$ **7.** $\frac{19}{8}$ **9.** $\frac{20}{3}$ **11.** $\frac{31}{4}$ **13.** $\frac{171}{20}$ **15.** $\frac{142}{9}$ **17.** $5\frac{1}{2}$ **19.** $3\frac{2}{9}$ **21.** $6\frac{1}{6}$ **23.** $3\frac{7}{8}$ **25.** $9\frac{7}{12}$

Adding and Subtracting Fractions (p. 779) **1.** $\frac{4}{5}$ **3.** $\frac{3}{7}$ **5.** $\frac{1}{11}$ **7.** $\frac{13}{14}$ **9.** $\frac{1}{6}$ **11.** $\frac{13}{20}$ **13.** $1\frac{8}{13}$ **15.** $1\frac{1}{18}$ **17.** 1 **19.** $1\frac{1}{3}$

Multiplying Fractions and Whole Numbers (p. 780) **1.** 3 **3.** 14 **5.** $10\frac{2}{7}$ **7.** 12 **9.** $2\frac{1}{4}$ **11.** $8\frac{4}{7}$ **13.** 15 **15.** 9

Reading Bar Graphs (p. 781) **1.** 10 students **3.** 4 more students **5.** pancakes and waffles **7.** bagel, pancakes, waffles, muffin

Reading Line Graphs (p. 782) **1.** 8°F **3.** between 3 P.M. and 4 P.M.; 1°F **5.** between days 2 and 3 **7.** 15 mm

Reading Circle Graphs (p. 783) **1.** 5 homes **3.** 7 homes **5.** 6 people **7.** 71 people

Venn Diagrams and Logical Reasoning (p. 784)

1.

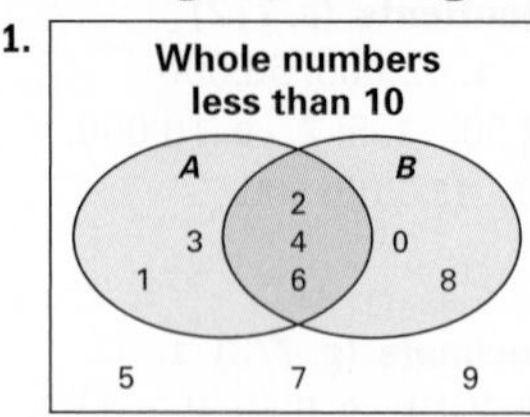

3. a. False. *Sample answer:* A counterexample is 2, which is a factor of 20 that is less than 10 and is less than 5. **b.** True. *Sample answer:* They are 2, 4, and 6.

Basic Geometric Figures (p. 785) **1.** 16 in. **3.** 30 ft **5.** Check students' drawings; 12 cm. **7.** Check students' drawings; 10 in.

Units of Length (p. 786) **1.** 60 **3.** 90,000 **5.** 7

Using a Ruler (p. 787) **1–15.** Check students' work.

Measuring Lengths (p. 788) **1.** $2\frac{1}{8}$ in., 5.4 cm **3.** $1\frac{1}{2}$ in.

Units of Area and Volume (p. 789) **1.** 16 mi^2 **3.** 1.96 cm^2 **5.** 1331 ft^3 **7.** 125 cm^3

Units of Weight and Mass (p. 790) **1.** > **3.** = **5.** > **7.** $1\frac{1}{4}$ lb **9.** $2\frac{1}{2}$ lb

Units of Capacity (p. 791) **1.** < **3.** < **5.** > **7.** $3\frac{1}{4}$ c **9.** $4\frac{1}{2}$ c

Using a Protractor (p. 792) **1.** 38° **3.** 84°

5. **7.**

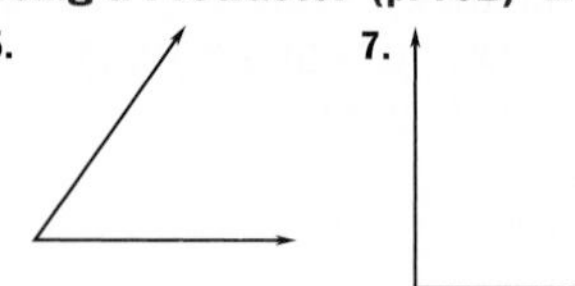

Classifying Angles (p. 793) **1.** 92°; obtuse **3.** 61°; acute **5.** 126°; obtuse

Using a Compass (p. 794) **1–7.** Check students' work.

Draw a Diagram (p. 795) **1.** 4 ft **3.** 336 ft^2

Look for a Pattern (p. 796) **1.** 9:05 **3.** 204 cans

Guess, Check, and Revise (p. 797) **1.** 16 weeks **3.** 11 white spruce and 6 blue spruce **5.** 26 ft

Act It Out (p. 798) **1.** Rosa: 15 CDs, Kim: 10 CDs **3.** seat 1

Make a List or Table (p. 799) **1.** 6 matches **3.** Row 2: \$5, \$10, \$15, \$20, \$25, \$30, \$35, \$40, \$45; 140 h or less

Solve a Simpler or Related Problem (p. 800) **1.** 26 people **3.** 16,384; 32,767

Work Backward (p. 801) **1.** 1:20 P.M. **3.** 320 pages

Break into Parts (p. 802) **1.** 3 ways **3.** 11 omelets

Extra Practice

Chapter 1 (p. 803) **1.** 8 **3.** 9 **5.** 1 to the eighth power; $1 \cdot 1 \cdot 1 \cdot 1 \cdot 1 \cdot 1 \cdot 1 \cdot 1$; 1 **7.** 5 to the third power, or 5 cubed; $5 \cdot 5 \cdot 5$; 125 **9.** 14 **11.** 180

13. $-7, -3, 0, 4, 9$

15. $-67, -51, -34, -19$

17. $43, -43$ **19.** 3, 3 **21.** 39 **23.** 22 **25.** 23 **27.** 19 **29.** 36 **31.** -3 **33.** (1, 1) **35.** (0, 0) **37.** $(2, -2)$

39–41.

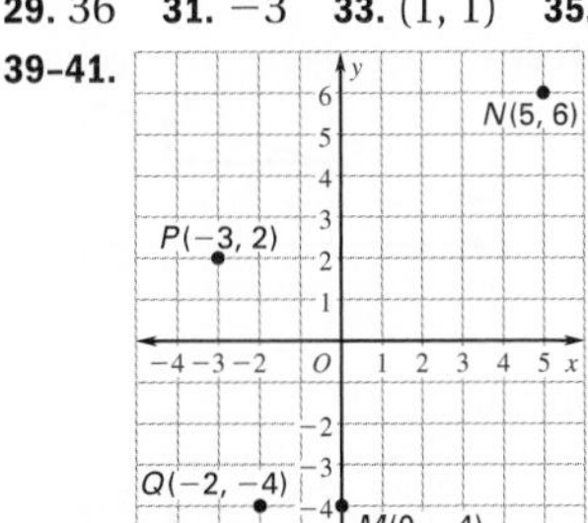

39. Quadrant I **41.** Quadrant III

Chapter 2 (p. 804)

1. $(17 + 9) + 3$
$= (9 + 17) + 3$ [commutative property of addition]
$= 9 + (17 + 3)$ [associative property of addition]
$= 9 + 20$ [Add 17 and 3.]
$= 29$ [Add 9 and 20.]

3. $0 + 8 \cdot 1$
$= 0 + (8 \cdot 1)$ [Use order of operations.]
$= 0 + 8$ [identity property of multiplication]
$= 8$ [identity property of addition]

5. -280 **7.** 12 **9.** $-44m$ **11.** $b + 21$ **13.** identity property of addition **15.** associative property of multiplication **17.** 54 **19.** 42 **21.** $-15a - 9$ **23.** $12 - 18z$ **25.** y **27.** $5c + 8$ **29.** $8b$ **31.** $2p - 15$ **33.** 5 **35.** 11 **37.** 8 **39.** -22 **41.** 109 **43.** -32 **45.** -26 **47.** 7 **49.** -144 **51.** -350 **53.** -11.14 **55.** -18.13 **57.** 14.7 **59.** -6.83

Chapter 3 (p. 805) **1.** 12 **3.** 3 **5.** -136 **7.** 81 **9.** -2 **11.** 1 **13.** 1 **15.** 3 **17.** -10 **19.** 3 **21.** 2 **23.** no solution **25.** all real numbers **27.** $10 + 7x = 5x - 6$; -8 **29.** $x \geq -3$ **31.** $x < -4$

33. $a < 7$;

35. $p \geq -3$;

37. $b \leq 48$;

39. $k > 0.3$;

41. $b \leq 104$;

43. $x \geq -8$;

45. $d < -8$;

47. $t > -4$;

49. $3x \leq 18$; $x \leq 6$ **51.** $\frac{x}{-2} < 10$; $x > -20$

53. $w > 3$;

55. $z < -6$;

57. $c \leq 22$;

59. $r > 6$;

Chapter 4 (p. 806) **1.** composite **3.** prime **5.** $2^3 \cdot 3^2$ **7.** $2^5 \cdot 3$ **9.** 3; no **11.** 2; no **13.** $4y$ **15.** $2s$ **17.** $\frac{3}{16}$ **19.** $\frac{7}{11}$ **21.** $\frac{2}{3m}$ **23.** $\frac{19ab}{2c}$ **25.** 30 **27.** 480 **29.** $90c^2$ **31.** $80n^2p$ **33.** 6^{14} **35.** 4^6 **37.** $20c^5$ **39.** $6a^3$ **41.** $\frac{1}{18^4}$ **43.** s^3 **45.** 1.6×10^7 **47.** 4×10^{-5} **49.** 823,000,000 **51.** 0.0021

Chapter 5 (p. 807) **1.** *Sample answer:* $\frac{-4}{1}$ or $\frac{4}{-1}$ **3.** *Sample answer:* $\frac{53}{16}$ **5.** 0.6 **7.** -6.52 **9.** $\frac{17}{50}$ **11.** $9\frac{27}{100}$ **13.** $\frac{5}{11}$ **15.** $-7\frac{1}{5}$ **17.** $-1\frac{1}{28}$ **19.** $3\frac{2}{33}$ **21.** $\frac{3w}{20}$ **23.** $-\frac{z}{28}$ **25.** $\frac{5}{42}$ **27.** $10\frac{1}{2}$ **29.** $\frac{3}{7}$ **31.** $-1\frac{16}{45}$ **33.** 21 **35.** 77 **37.** $-2\frac{1}{3}$ **39.** 0.25 **41.** $p < 18$ **43.** $z \leq \frac{5}{6}$

Chapter 6 (p. 808) **1.** $\frac{\$1.74}{1 \text{ gal}}$ **3.** $\frac{3 \text{ L}}{1 \text{ day}}$ **5.** 264,000 **7.** 26,400 **9.** 16 **11.** 4 **13.** 32 **15.** 5 **17.** 3 **19.** 84 **21.** $\frac{5}{3}$ **23.** 22 in. **25.** 50 mi **27.** 12.5 mi **29.** $\frac{1}{3}$ **31.** $\frac{2}{3}$ **33.** 90 groups

Chapter 7 (p. 809) **1.** $\frac{43}{100}$ **3.** 65% **5.** 120 **7.** 57 **9.** 20% **11.** 81 **13.** 4.5% **15.** 0.07 **17.** $58.\overline{3}\%$ **19.** 187.5% **21.** 325 **23.** 260 **25.** increase; 55% **27.** decrease; 75% **29.** \$234 **31.** \$16.80 **33.** \$68.25 **35.** 9 y

Chapter 8 (p. 810)

1.

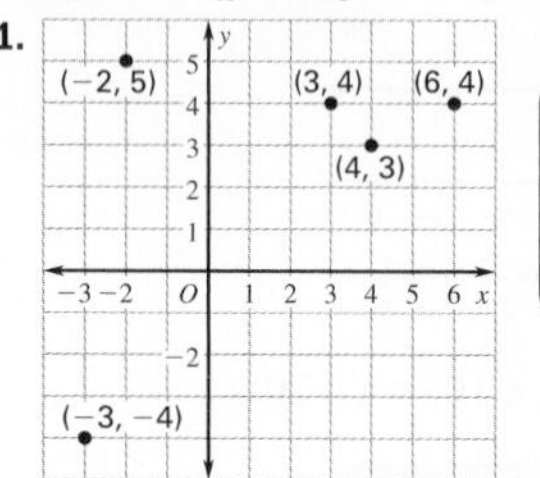

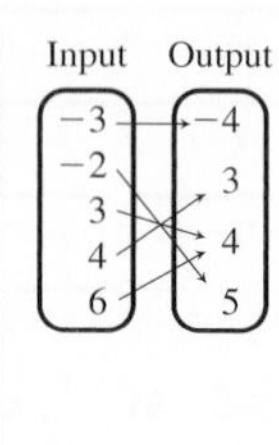

Yes; every input is paired with exactly one output.

3.

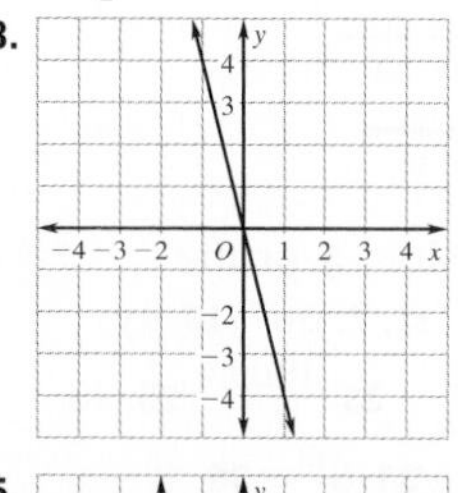

yes

5.

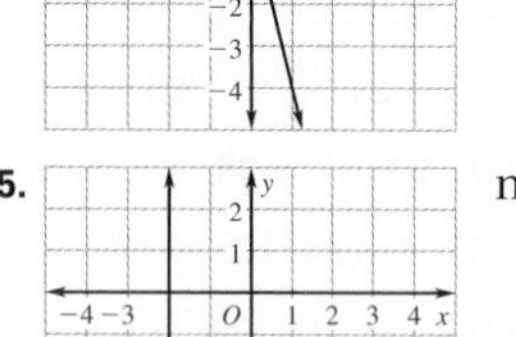

no

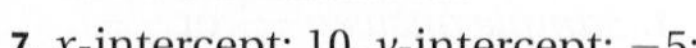

7. x-intercept: 10, y-intercept: −5;

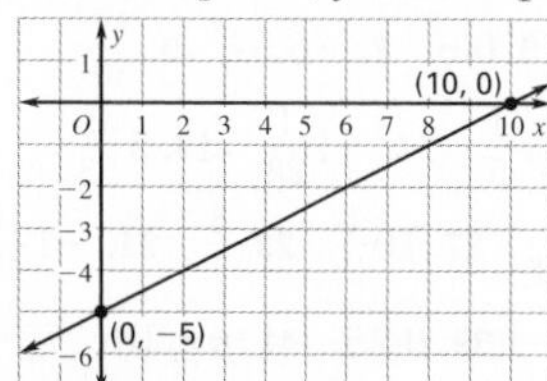

9. x-intercept: −5, y-intercept: −3;

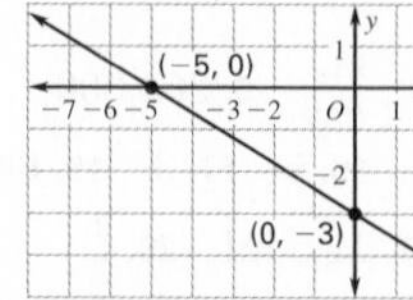

11. *Sample answer:* (0, −4), (5, −4); 0 **13.** *Sample answer:* (0, −3), (3, −2); $\frac{1}{3}$ **15.** $-\frac{3}{4}$ **17.** 1

19. slope: 4, y-intercept: −1;

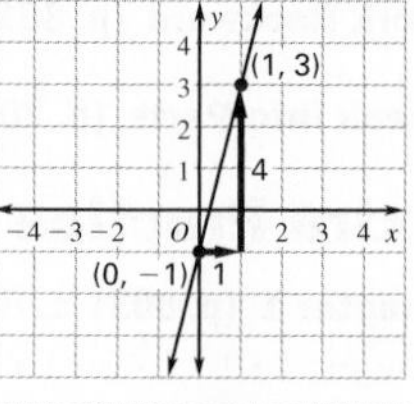

21. slope: 5, y-intercept: −2;

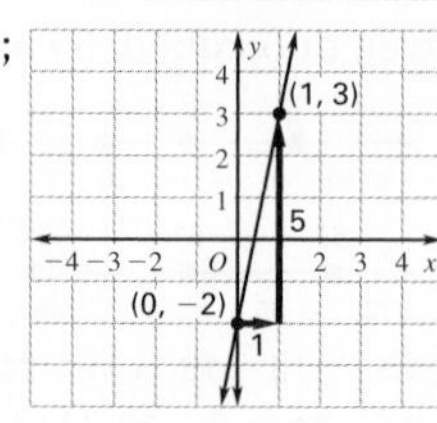

23. slope: $\frac{1}{4}$, y-intercept: 2;

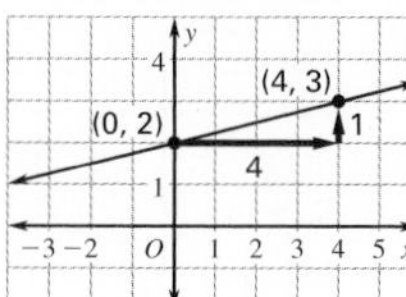

25. slope: $-\frac{2}{5}$, y-intercept: 3;

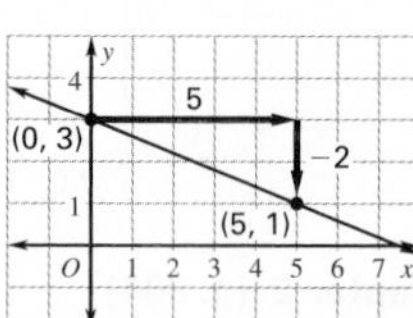

27. $y = -4x - 2$ **29.** $y = \frac{7}{3}x - 1$

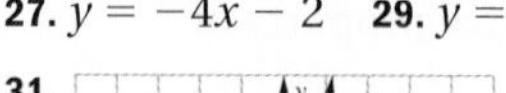

31.

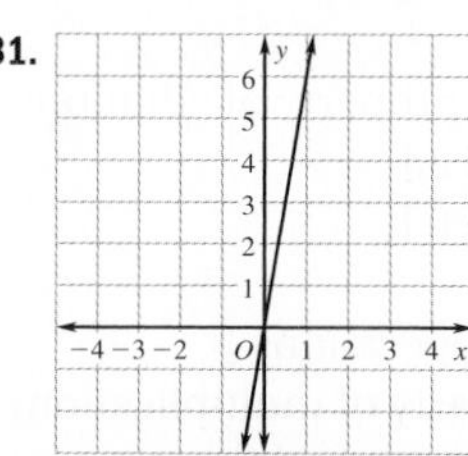

33.

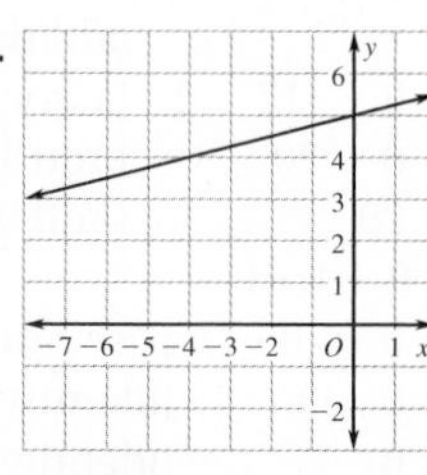

35. (2, −5) **37.** (−3, −6)

39.

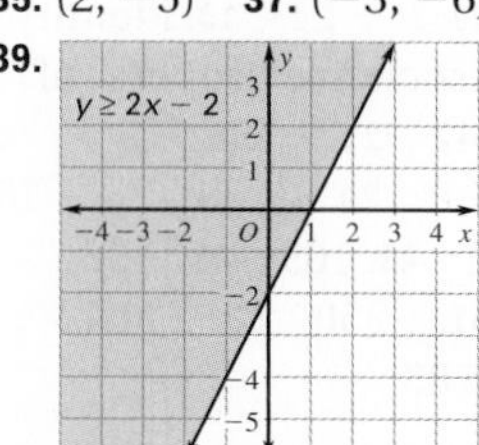

41.

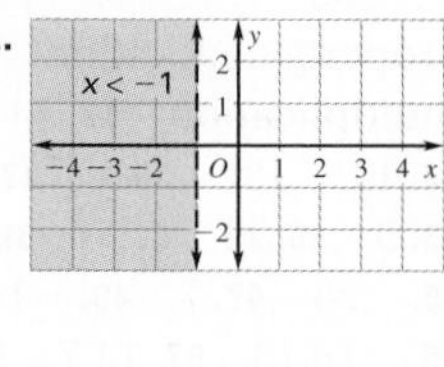

Chapter 9 (p. 811) **1.** ±7 **3.** ±18 **5.** ±11 **7.** ±6 **9.** $9\sqrt{2}$ **11.** $\frac{4a\sqrt{2}}{9}$ **13.** 40 **15.** $\sqrt{65}$

17. $\frac{46}{9}$, $2\sqrt{7}$, $\sqrt{30}$, 5.8 **19.** -6.9, $-3\sqrt{5}$, $-\frac{19}{3}$, $-\sqrt{36}$ **21.** (5, 6); $2\sqrt{17}$ units **23.** $(-1, 3.5)$; $\sqrt{229}$ units **25.** $x = 5\sqrt{3}$, $y = 10$ **27.** $x = 3$, $y = 3\sqrt{2}$ **29.** 2.5 **31.** 15.0 **33.** 3.9 **35.** 15.5

Chapter 10 (p. 812) **1.** 25; obtuse **3.** 35; right **5.** 42 **7.** 119 **9.** 44 in.^{2} **11.** 90 ft^2 **13.** 3018 in.^{2}, 195 in. **15.** 616 cm^2, 88 cm

17. *Sample answer:* 452 ft^2

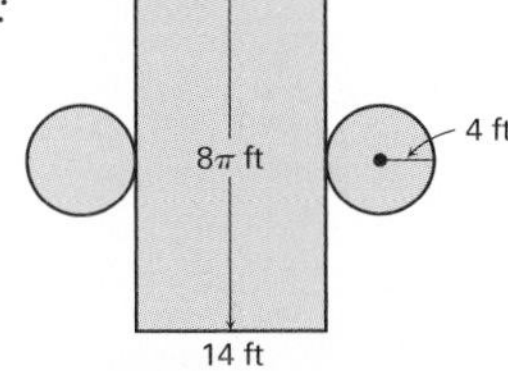

19. *Sample answer:* 312 cm^2

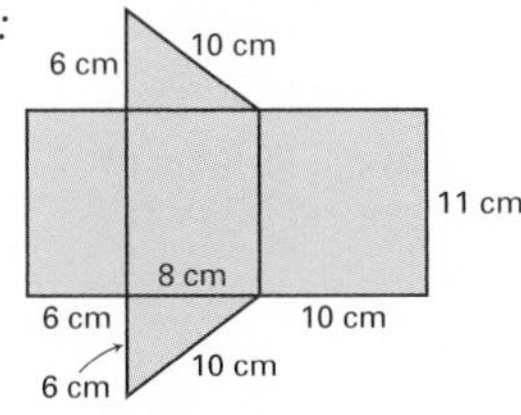

21. 552 yd^2 **23.** 894 ft^2 **25.** 251 cm^3 **27.** 96 yd^3

Chapter 11 (p. 813)

1.

1	2
2	1 2 3 5
3	1 4 5 6
4	0 2 2

Key: 1 | 2 = 12

Sample:

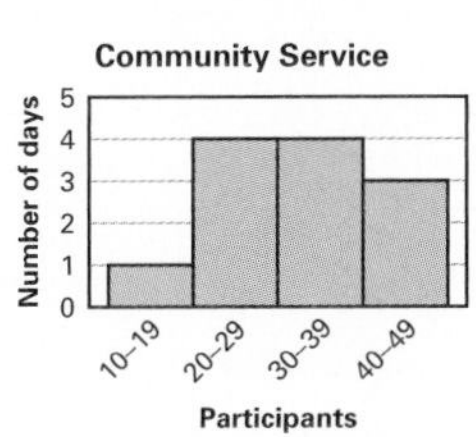

3. Numerical. *Sample answer:* If the data values are few, I might use a stem-and-leaf plot so that I can view all the values. If there are many data values, I might use a histogram, since I can divide the data into equal intervals by test score, or a box-and-whisker plot, since I can calculate the extremes and the quartiles for the data. Either of these displays would provide a convenient pictorial representation. **5.** Yes. *Sample answer:* It suggests that a person should think that a school dance is a good thing. An alternative question is, "Do you think that a school dance should or should not be held?" **7.** about 8500 townspeople **9.** 1 **11.** 2 **13.** 156 **15.** 8 **17.** 495 **19.** 1 **21.** $\frac{11}{20}$

Chapter 12 (p. 814) **1.** $-3x + 6$ **3.** $y^2 - 2y + 18$ **5.** $-x^2 + 3x + 16$ **7.** $-2w^3 + 4w^2 + 4w + 14$ **9.** $6g^4 + 4g^3 - 10g^2 + 2$ **11.** $d^3 + 7$ **13.** $32f^2 + 36f$ **15.** $-2t^3 + 6t^2 - 20t$ **17.** $-6n + 7$ **19.** $5z^4 - z^3 - 3z^2$ **21.** $3x^2 - 10x - 8$ **23.** $25a^2 + 30a + 9$ **25.** $-27g^3$ **27.** $\frac{1}{6^{20}}$ **29.** 9.11×10^{-20} **31.** 1.96×10^8

33. *Sample answer:*

x	−2	−1	0	1	2
y	16	7	4	7	16

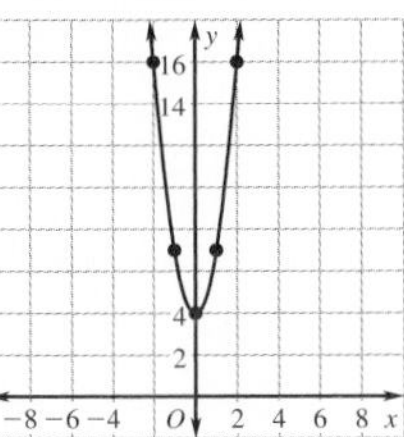

35. *Sample answer:*

x	−4	−2	0	2	4
y	−3	3	5	3	−3

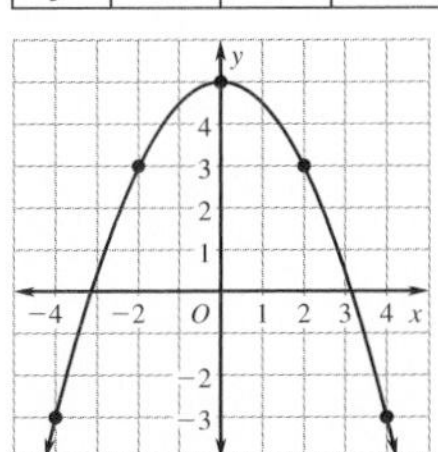

37.

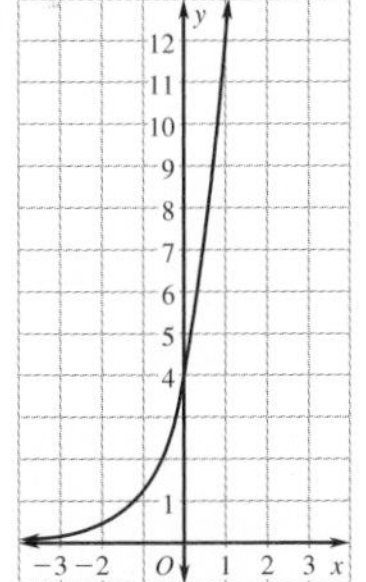

39.

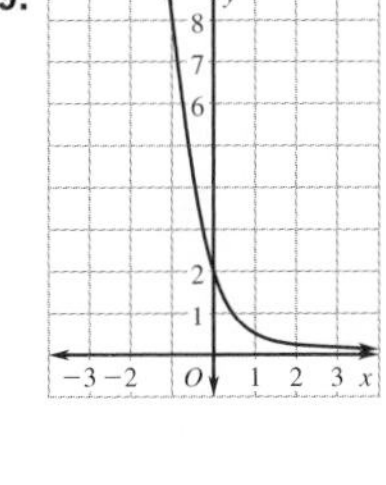

41. arithmetic; common difference: 4; 7, 11, 15

43. geometric; common ratio: $\frac{1}{2}$; 14, 7, $3\frac{1}{2}$

Chapter 13 (p. 815) **1.** complementary **3.** supplementary **5.** corresponding **7.** alternate exterior **9.** interior: 128.6°, exterior: 51.4° **11.** interior: 150°, exterior: 30°

Selected Answers

13. $A'(2, -4)$, $B'(1, -1)$, $C'(3, 1)$;

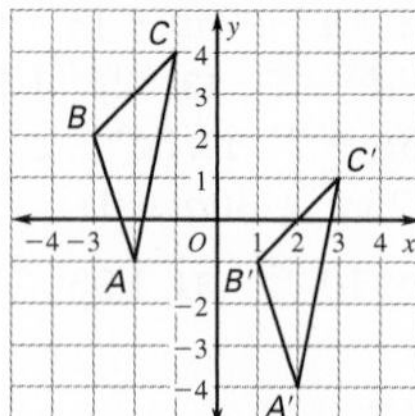

15. $A'(-3, 1)$, $B'(2, 2)$, $C'(-1, 4)$;

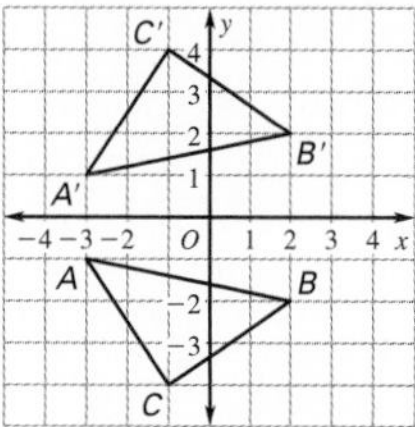

17. no **19.** yes; 180° in either direction

21. $A'(-4, 4)$, $B'(2, 6)$, $C'(2, -2)$, $D'(-4, -2)$;

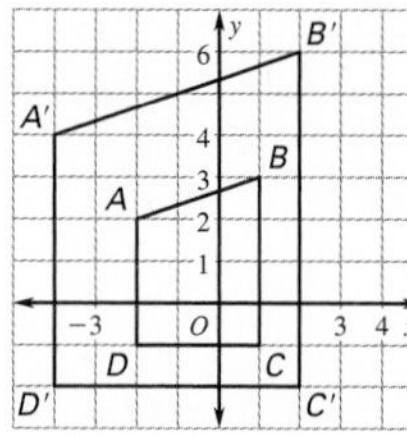

Selected Answers

Teacher's Edition Index

Pupil's Edition in black
Teacher's Edition in blue

Teacher's Edition Index

d

Teacher's Edition Index

e

f

g

Teacher's Edition Index

j

k

l

Teacher's Edition Index

Teacher's Edition Index

Teacher's Edition Index

Teacher's Edition Index

Teacher's Edition Index

Mathematical Rigor and Challenge in *Pre-Algebra*

McDougal Littell Pre-Algebra is designed to meet the needs of students at all ability levels. The student-friendly nature of the text invites students to learn without sacrificing a rigorous approach to mathematical structure. The Practice and Problem Solving pages offer a wide variety of exercises, including many that provide students with challenge:

- **Writing exercises** that require students to explain their reasoning and to justify their answers.
- **Error analysis exercises** that require students to identify and correct errors in reasoning.
- **In-exercise examples** that expand the scope of a lesson.
- **Critical thinking exercises** that help students develop higher-level thinking skills.
- **C-level** and **challenge exercises** that are demanding as well as stimulating.
- **Brain Games** that offer challenge and fun at the same time.

The following are just a few examples that illustrate the *Pre-Algebra* program's attention to critical thinking, challenge, and mathematical structure throughout the book.

Critical Thinking

- In Exercise 43 on page 284, students investigate two proportions involving three variables.
- In Exercise 17 on page 365, students must identify and correct an error in reasoning related to simple interest.
- *See also* Exercises 54–56 on page 33, Exercise 64 on page 224, Exercise 27 on page 356, and Exercise 45 on page 683.

Challenge

- In the example on page 142, students learn how to graph compound inequalities.
- In Exercise 61 on page 203, students explore how to use the quotient of powers property to develop the definitions of zero and negative exponents.
- *See also* Exercise 52 on page 68, Exercise 34 on page 251, Exercise 25 on page 390, and Exercise 34 on page 424.

Mathematical Structure

- On page 476, the Pythagorean theorem is used along with the distance between two points on a horizontal or vertical line to derive the distance formula.
- On pages 483 and 484, the Pythagorean theorem is used to justify the rules for side lengths of special right triangles.
- *See also* pages 63–65, 139, 194–196, and 281.

Additional Answers

Chapter 1

1.3 Practice and Problem Solving (pp. 19–20)

39c.

1.5 Concept Activity (p. 28)

13. *Sample answer:* If the arrows have different lengths, then the sum has the same sign as the number that is shown by the longer arrow. If the arrows are the same length, then the sum is zero.

1.8 Checkpoint (p. 48)

4–7.

P(−1, 1), S(−2, 0), R(0, 0), Q(4, −5)

1.8 Guided Practice (p. 49)

3–6.

J(2, 3), K(−5, −1), L(0, −3), M(4, −4)

7. Step 2:

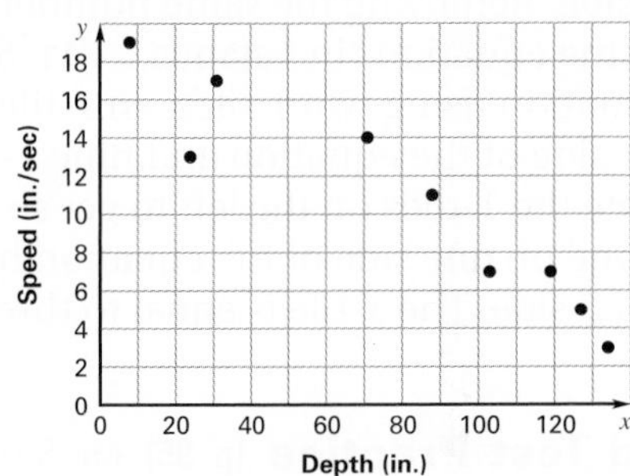

1.8 Practice and Problem Solving (pp. 49–51)

17–24.

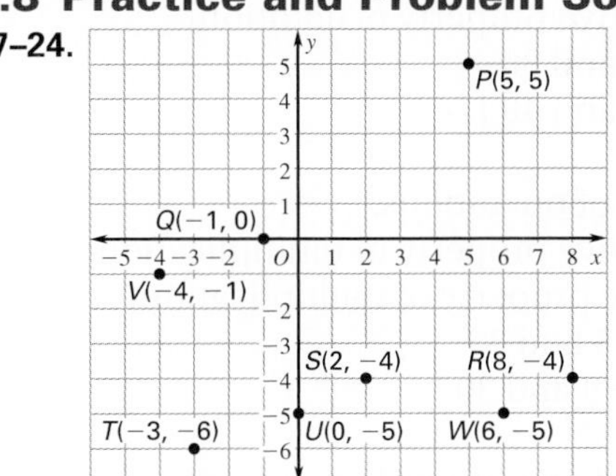

29c.

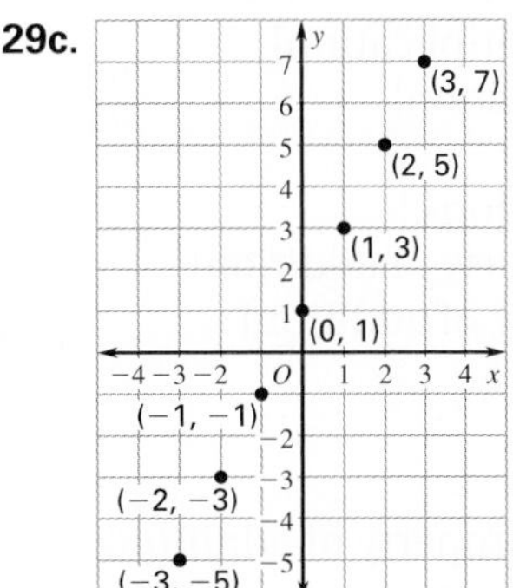

Chapter 2

2.1 Checkpoint (pp. 64–65)

1. $(17 + 36) + 13$

$= (36 + 17) + 13$	[commutative property of addition]
$= 36 + (17 + 13)$	[associative property of addition]
$= 36 + 30$	[Add 17 and 13.]
$= 66$	[Add 36 and 30.]

2. $8(-3)(5)$

$= [8(-3)](5)$	[Use order of operations.]
$= [-3(8)](5)$	[commutative property of multiplication]
$= -3[(8)(5)]$	[associative property of multiplication]
$= -3(40)$	[Multiply 8 and 5.]
$= -120$	[Multiply −3 and 40.]

3. $3.4 + 9.7 + 7.6$

$= (3.4 + 9.7) + 7.6$	[Use order of operations.]
$= (9.7 + 3.4) + 7.6$	[commutative property of addition]
$= 9.7 + (3.4 + 7.6)$	[associative property of addition]
$= 9.7 + 11$	[Add 3.4 and 7.6.]
$= 20.7$	[Add 9.7 and 11.]

2.1 Practice and Problem Solving (pp. 66–67)

16. $32 + 16 + 8$
$= (32 + 16) + 8$ [Use order of operations.]
$= (16 + 32) + 8$ [commutative property of addition]
$= 16 + (32 + 8)$ [associative property of addition]
$= 16 + 40$ [Add 32 and 8.]
$= 56$ [Add 16 and 40.]

17. $15(-9)(2)$
$= [15(-9)](2)$ [Use order of operations.]
$= [-9(15)](2)$ [commutative property of multiplication]
$= -9[(15)(2)]$ [associative property of multiplication]
$= -9(30)$ [Multiply 15 and 2.]
$= -270$ [Multiply −9 and 30.]

18. $7 \cdot 1 + 0$
$= (7 \cdot 1) + 0$ [Use order of operations.]
$= 7 + 0$ [identity property of multiplication]
$= 7$ [identity property of addition]

19. $45 + 29 + 55$
$= (45 + 29) + 55$ [Use order of operations.]
$= (29 + 45) + 55$ [commutative property of addition]
$= 29 + (45 + 55)$ [associative property of addition]
$= 29 + 100$ [Add 45 and 55.]
$= 129$ [Add 29 and 100.]

42. $44 + 19 + 16 + 31$
$= 44 + [19 + 16] + 31$ [associative property of addition]
$= 44 + [16 + 19] + 31$ [commutative property of addition]
$= [44 + 16] + [19 + 31]$ [associative property of addition]
$= 60 + [19 + 31]$ [Add 44 and 16.]
$= 60 + 50$ [Add 19 and 31.]
$= 110$ [Add 60 and 50.]

43. $4(20)(25)(-5)$
$= 4[(20)(25)](-5)$ [associative property of multiplication]
$= 4[(25)(20)](-5)$ [commutative property of multiplication]
$= [4(25)][(20)(-5)]$ [associative property of multiplication]
$= 100[(20)(-5)]$ [Multiply 4 and 25.]
$= 100(-100)$ [Multiply 20 and −5.]
$= -10{,}000$ [Multiply 100 and −100.]

2.1 Mixed Review (p. 68)

60–63.

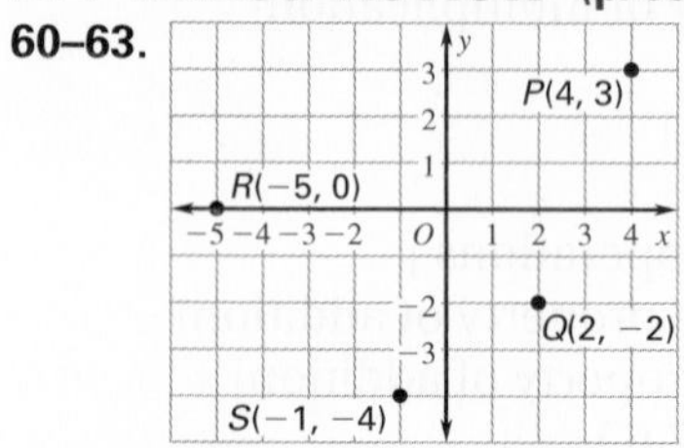

2.3 Guided Practice (p. 80)

9. *Sample answer:* The distributive property was incorrectly applied. You can rewrite $5a - (3a - 7)$ as $5a + (-1)(3a - 7)$. Applying the distributive property gives $5a + (-1)(3a) - (-1)(7) = 5a - 3a + 7 = 2a + 7$.

Mid-Chapter Quiz (p. 84)

1. $29 + 18 + 21$
$= (29 + 18) + 21$ [Use order of operations.]
$= (18 + 29) + 21$ [commutative property of addition]
$= 18 + (29 + 21)$ [associative property of addition]
$= 18 + 50$ [Add 29 and 21.]
$= 68$ [Add 18 and 50.]

2. $1.3 + 6.8 + 2.7$
$= (1.3 + 6.8) + 2.7$ [Use order of operations.]
$= (6.8 + 1.3) + 2.7$ [commutative property of addition]
$= 6.8 + (1.3 + 2.7)$ [associative property of addition]
$= 6.8 + 4$ [Add 1.3 and 2.7.]
$= 10.8$ [Add 6.8 and 4.]

3. $4(9)(-25)$
$= [4(9)](-25)$ [Use order of operations.]
$= [9(4)](-25)$ [commutative property of multiplication]
$= 9[(4)(-25)]$ [associative property of multiplication]
$= 9(-100)$ [Multiply 4 and −25.]
$= -900$ [Multiply 9 and −100.]

4. $5(-7)(-12)$
$= [5(-7)](-12)$ [Use order of operations.]
$= [-7(5)](-12)$ [commutative property of multiplication]
$= -7[(5)(-12)]$ [associative property of multiplication]
$= -7(-60)$ [Multiply 5 and −12.]
$= 420$ [Multiply −7 and −60.]

2.5 Concept Activity (p. 90)

10. *Sample answer:* Before the tiles are removed, the expressions on each side of the equal sign represent the same quantity. If the tiles were removed only from the left side, then it would no longer represent the same quantity as the right side. Removing the same number of tiles from each side keeps the equation "in balance." **11.** *Sample answer:* Model the equation using two 1-tiles, an x-tile, and four 1-tiles on the left side of the equation and nine 1-tiles on the right side. Combine the 1-tiles on the left to get six 1-tiles. Then get the x-tile alone on one side of the equation by removing six 1-tiles from each side. The x-tile is equal to three 1-tiles. So, the solution is 3.

2.5 Standardized Test Practice (p. 95)

65. *Sample answer:* Let x represent the number of employees at the beginning of the year. Write a verbal model.

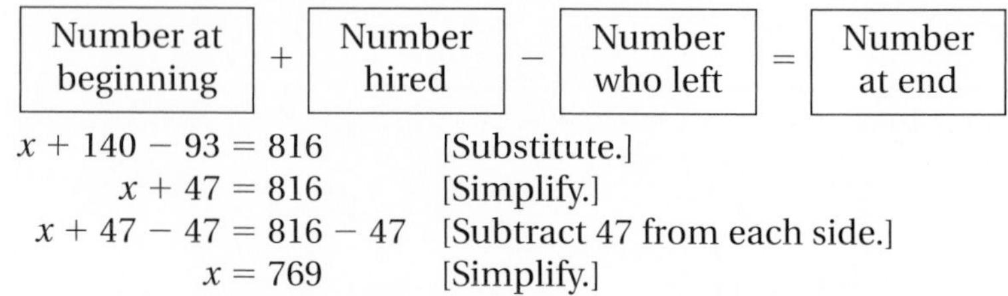

$x + 140 - 93 = 816$ [Substitute.]
$x + 47 = 816$ [Simplify.]
$x + 47 - 47 = 816 - 47$ [Subtract 47 from each side.]
$x = 769$ [Simplify.]

There were 769 employees at the beginning of the year.

2.6 Concept Activity (p. 96) **10.** *Sample answer:* Model the equation by grouping two x-tiles and then three more x-tiles on the left side of the equation and fifteen 1-tiles on the right side. Combine the x-tiles on the left. There are five x-tiles, so divide the x-tiles and 1-tiles into five equal groups. One x-tile is equal to three 1-tiles. The solution is $x = 3$.

Chapter Review (pp. 108–109)

9. $5(-3)(12)$
$= [5(-3)](12)$ [Use order of operations.]
$= [-3(5)](12)$ [commutative property of multiplication]
$= -3[(5)(12)]$ [associative property of multiplication]
$= -3(60)$ [Multiply 5 and 12.]
$= -180$ [Multiply -3 and 60.]

10. $6(13)(0.5)$
$= [6(13)](0.5)$ [Use order of operations.]
$= [13(6)](0.5)$ [commutative property of multiplication]
$= 13[(6)(0.5)]$ [associative property of multiplication]
$= 13(3)$ [Multiply 6 and 0.5.]
$= 39$ [Multiply 13 and 3.]

Chapter Test (p. 112)

2. $15(-7)(4)$
$= [15(-7)](4)$ [Use order of operations.]
$= [-7(15)](4)$ [commutative property of multiplication]
$= -7[(15)(4)]$ [associative property of multiplication]
$= -7(60)$ [Multiply 15 and 4.]
$= -420$ [Multiply -7 and 60.]

3. $5.9 + 10.4 + 2.1$
$= (5.9 + 10.4) + 2.1$ [Use order of operations.]
$= (10.4 + 5.9) + 2.1$ [commutative property of addition]
$= 10.4 + (5.9 + 2.1)$ [associative property of addition]
$= 10.4 + 8$ [Add 5.9 and 2.1.]
$= 18.4$ [Add 10.4 and 8.]

4. $36 \cdot 1 + 0$
$= (36 \cdot 1) + 0$ [Use order of operations.]
$= 36 + 0$ [identity property of multiplication]
$= 36$ [identity property of addition]

Chapter 3

3.1 Practice and Problem Solving (pp. 123–124)

34. *Sample answer:* First adding $2x$ to each side requires three steps: apply the addition property of equality, apply the addition property of equality again, then apply the division property of equality. First subtracting 18 from each side requires only two steps: apply the subtraction property of equality, then apply the division property of equality. The first method has the advantage that you divide both sides by a positive number, while using the second method you must divide both sides by a negative number. Either method gives the same solution, 27.

35b.

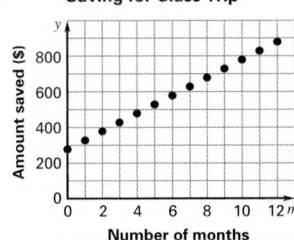

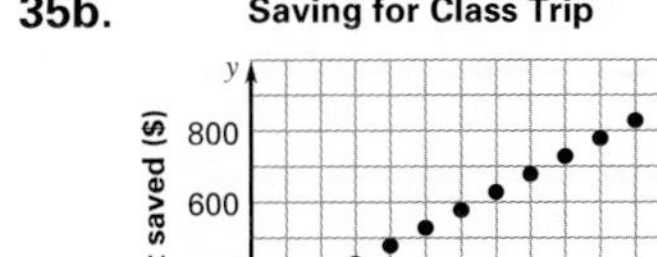

Sample answer: The points lie along a straight line; you can extend the scatter plot either by plotting more points as shown or by drawing a line through the plotted points and estimating what value along the horizontal axis corresponds to a value of \$850 on the vertical axis.

35d. *Sample answer:* The scatter plot gives a nice, visual picture of the relationship, and once it is plotted, it is easy to find the time and savings values that relate to each other, but it is time-consuming to make the plot. For finding a single value, it is very simple to solve the equation, and the equation has the advantage of giving an exact value, but it has the disadvantage of not providing a visual image of the relationship.

36. 6. *Sample answer:* First I multiplied each side by 4 to obtain $x + 2 = 8$. Then I subtracted 2 from each side to obtain $x = 6$. I know this is correct because substituting 6 for x in the original equation gives a left side of $\frac{6 + 2}{4} = \frac{8}{4} = 2$, which agrees with the right side.

3.1 Mixed Review (p. 124)

46. \$25. *Sample answer:* First I wrote a verbal model: Total cost = Amount of down payment + Number of months • Monthly payment. Letting p represent the monthly payment, I then wrote the equation $150 = 25 + 5p$. I subtracted 25 from each side to get $125 = 5p$, and then divided each side by 5 to get $25 = p$.

3.2 Mixed Review (p. 129)

40–47.

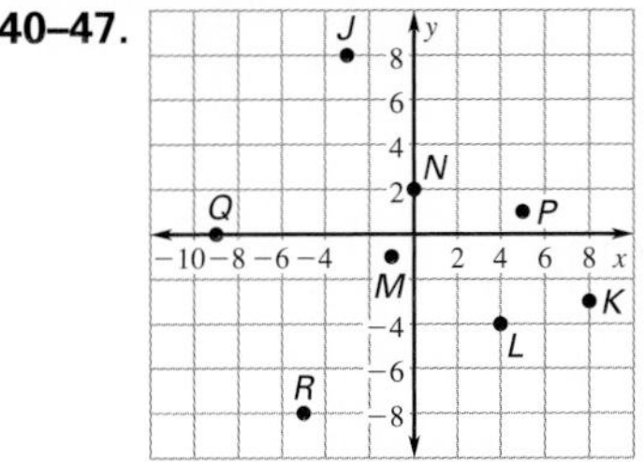

3.3 Concept Activity (p. 130)

4. Yes. *Sample answer:* In one case you are only removing x-tiles first and in the other you are only removing 1-tiles first. Since neither operation has an effect on the tiles of the other operation, it does not matter in which order you do them. **5.** *Sample answer:* If there are variables on both sides of the equation, you must perform an additional operation in order to get the variable on only one side of the equation.

3.4 Checkpoint (p. 139)

1. 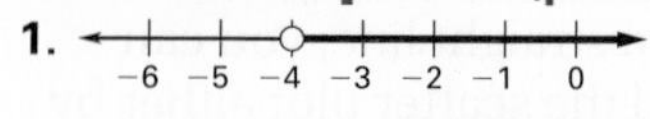

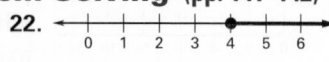

2. 0 2 4 6 8 10 12

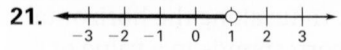

3. −1 0 1 2 3 4 5

4. 0 2 4 6 8 10 12

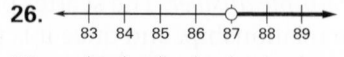

3.4 Practice and Problem Solving (pp. 141–142)

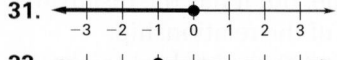

21. −3 −2 −1 0 1 2 3

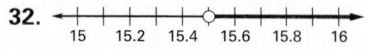

22. 0 1 2 3 4 5 6

23. −24 −20 −16 −12 −8 −4 0

24. −3 −2 −1 0 1 2 3

25. −31 −29 −27 −25

26. 83 84 85 86 87 88 89

27. −15 −12 −9 −6 −3 0 3

28. −6 −5 −4 −3 −2 −1 0

29. 25 25.2 25.4 25.6 25.8 26

30. 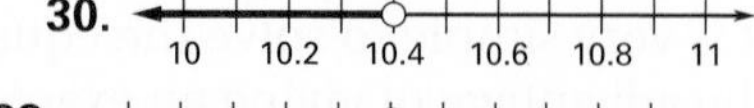

31. −3 −2 −1 0 1 2 3

32. 15 15.2 15.4 15.6 15.8 16

33. −413 −411 −409 −407

34. −3 −2 −1 0 1 2 3

35. 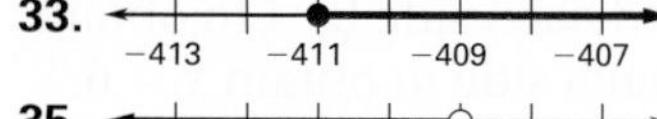

36. 0 8 16 24 32 40 48

37. 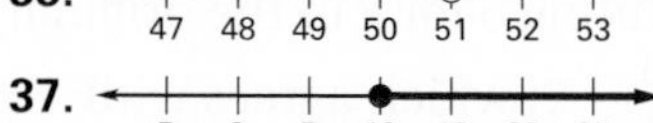

38. −300 −280 −260 −240

39. No. *Sample answer:* There are infinitely many solutions—all points to the left or right of a given point, so you can only check sample points; no.

41. 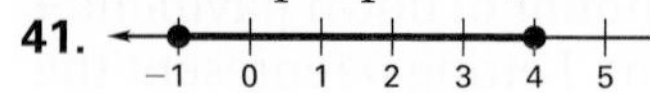

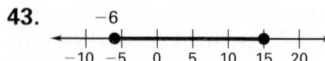

42. 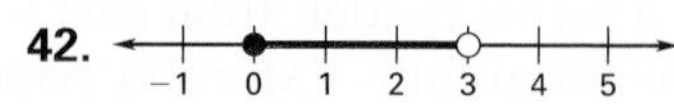

43. −6

−10 −5 0 5 10 15 20

3.5 Concept Activity (p. 143)

1. *Sample answer:*

Step 1: $6 \geq -8$

Step 2: $2 \cdot 6 \overset{?}{\geq} 2 \cdot (-8)$

$12 \overset{?}{\geq} -16$ ✓

Yes, 12 is greater than or equal to −16.

Step 3: $-2 \cdot 6 \overset{?}{\geq} -2 \cdot (-8)$

$-12 \overset{?}{\geq} 16$ ✗

No, −12 is not greater than or equal to 16.

Step 4: $\frac{6}{2} \overset{?}{\geq} \frac{-8}{2}$

$3 \overset{?}{\geq} -4$ ✓

Yes, 3 is greater than or equal to −4.

Step 5: $\frac{6}{-2} \overset{?}{\geq} \frac{-8}{-2}$

$-3 \overset{?}{\geq} 4$ ✗

No, −3 is not greater than or equal to 4.

You could reverse the direction of the inequality symbols.

3.5 Checkpoint (p. 145)

1. 39 40 41 42 43 44 45

2. −48 −32 −16 0

3. −5 −4 −3 −2 −1 0 1

4. 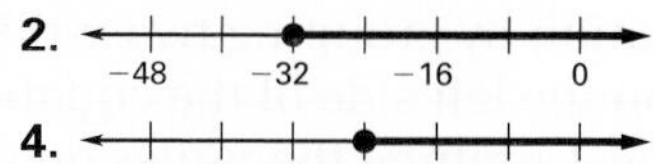

3.5 Practice and Problem Solving (pp. 146–148)

12. −36 −24 −12 0

13. 46 47 48 49 50 51 52

14. 0 6 12 18 24 30 36

15. 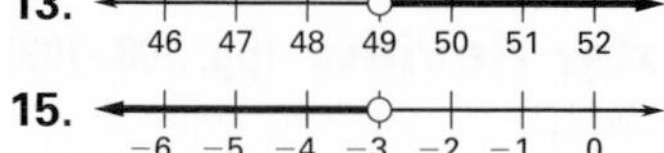

16. 9 10 11 12 13 14 15

17. −68 −66 −64 −62

18. −6 −5 −4 −3 −2 −1 0

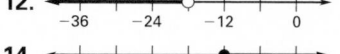

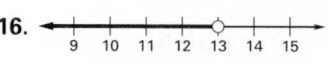

19. 13 14 15 16 17 18 19

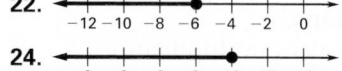

20. 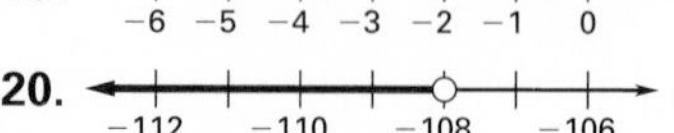

21. 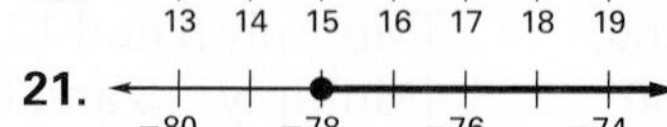

22. −12 −10 −8 −6 −4 −2 0

23. −16 −14 −12 −10

24. 0 3 6 9 12 15 18

25. 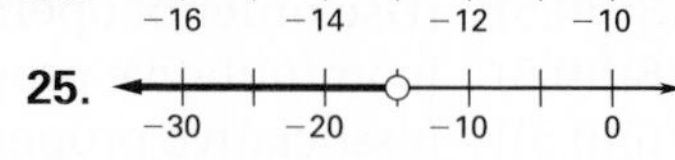

26. 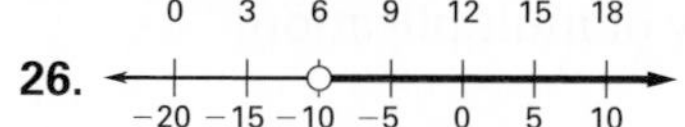

27. 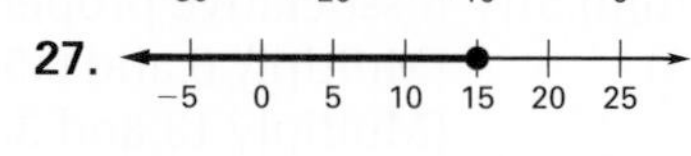

3.5 Mixed Review (p. 148)

55. 82 83 84 85 86 87 88

56. 0 9 18 27 36 45 54

57. 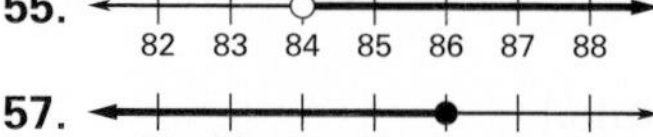

58. 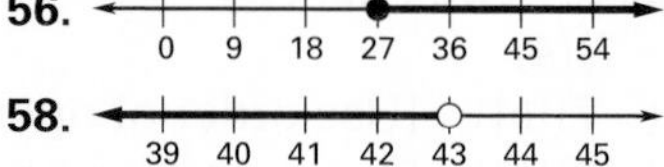

3.6 Guided Practice (p. 151)

3. 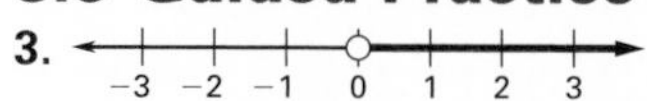

4. 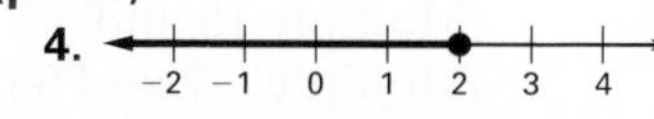

5. 0 10 20 30 40 50 60

6. 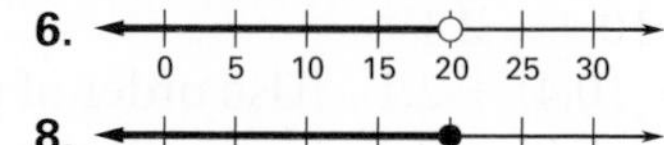

7. 0 2 4 6 8 10 12

8. −3 0 3 6 9 12 15

3.6 Practice and Problem Solving (pp. 151–153)

14. −1 0 1 2 3 4 5

15. 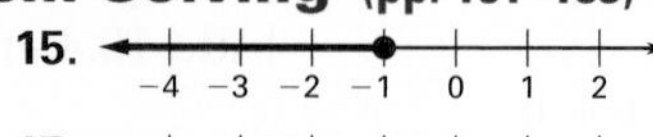

16. 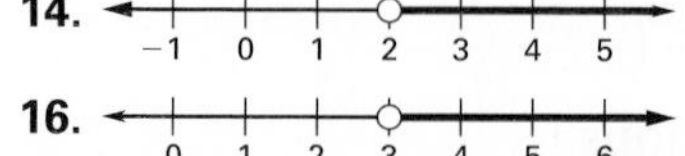

17. 7 8 9 10 11 12 13

18. 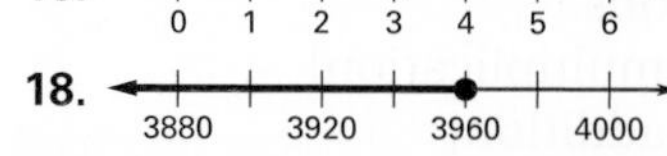

19. 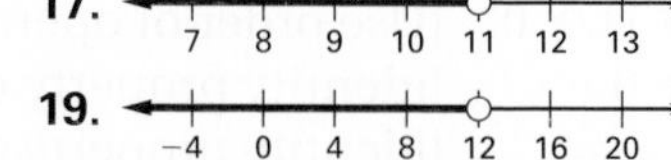

20. 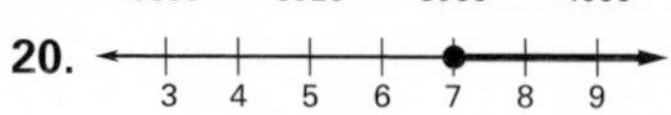

21. 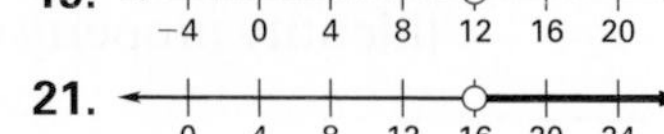

Chapter 4

4.1 Concept Activity (p. 171) **1.** *Sample answer:* The crossed-out numbers are composite because they have whole number factors besides 1 and themselves. The circled numbers are prime because they have only 1 and themselves as factors. **2.** *Sample answer:* All the numbers in the second column after 2 have 2 as a factor, all the numbers in the third column after 3 have 3 as a factor, and all the numbers in the fourth column are multiples of 2.

3. *Sample:* The fourth, sixth, eighth, and tenth columns will have only crossed-out numbers. All the numbers after the first entry in the second and fifth columns will also be crossed out.

1	(2)	(3)	~~4~~	(5)	~~6~~	(7)	~~8~~	~~9~~	~~10~~
(11)	~~12~~	(13)	~~14~~	~~15~~	~~16~~	(17)	~~18~~	(19)	~~20~~
~~21~~	~~22~~	(23)	~~24~~	~~25~~	~~26~~	~~27~~	~~28~~	(29)	~~30~~
(31)	~~32~~	~~33~~	~~34~~	~~35~~	~~36~~	(37)	~~38~~	~~39~~	~~40~~
(41)	~~42~~	(43)	~~44~~	~~45~~	~~46~~	(47)	~~48~~	~~49~~	~~50~~
~~51~~	~~52~~	(53)	~~54~~	~~55~~	~~56~~	~~57~~	~~58~~	(59)	~~60~~

My prediction was correct.

4.1 Practice and Problem Solving (pp. 175–176)

57. *Sample answer:* If 5 is the ones digit, then the number must be a multiple of 5. This is because, for example, $15 = 10 + 5 = 5(2 + 1)$, $25 = 20 + 5 = 5(4 + 1)$, and $35 = 30 + 5 = 5(6 + 1)$. **58.** 1, 2, 3, 4, 5, 6, 8, 10, 12, 15, 16, 20, 24, 30, 40, 48, 60, 80, 120, 240 **59.** 1, 5, 67, 335 **60.** 1, 2, 4, 5, 10, 20, 25, 50, 100, 125, 250, 500 **61.** 1, 3, 67, 201 **62.** 1, 2, 3, 6, a, b, b^2, ab, ab^2, $2a$, $3a$, $6a$, $2b$, $3b$, $6b$, $2b^2$, $3b^2$, $6b^2$, $2ab$, $3ab$, $6ab$, $2ab^2$, $3ab^2$, $6ab^2$ **63.** 1, 2, 4, 13, 26, 52, w, $2w$, $4w$, $13w$, $26w$, $52w$ **64.** 1, 2, r, r^2, r^3, s, rs, r^2s, r^3s, $2r$, $2r^2$, $2r^3$, $2s$, $2rs$, $2r^2s$, $2r^3s$ **65.** 1, 7, x, y, z, xy, xz, yz, xyz, $7x$, $7y$, $7z$, $7xy$, $7xz$, $7yz$, $7xyz$

4.2 Practice and Problem Solving (pp. 179–181)

51. Sometimes. *Sample answer:* Let $a = 4$, $b = 5$, and $c = 8$. Then a and b are relatively prime and b and c are relatively prime, but a and c have common factors of 2 and 4, and therefore are not relatively prime. On the other hand, let $a = 2$, $b = 7$, and $c = 13$. Then a and b are relatively prime, b and c are relatively prime, and a and c are relatively prime.

4.3 Practice and Problem Solving (pp. 185–186)

47. *Sample answer:* Divide the numerator and denominator of each fraction by the GCF of their absolute values. For $\frac{-12}{27}$, divide the numerator and denominator by 3 to get $\frac{-4}{9}$, or $-\frac{4}{9}$. For $\frac{25}{-35}$, divide the numerator and denominator by 5 to get $\frac{5}{-7}$, or $-\frac{5}{7}$. For $\frac{-33}{-55}$, divide the numerator and denominator by 11 to get $\frac{-3}{-5}$, or $\frac{3}{5}$. **53c.** The results are the same. *Sample answer:* The second method; it is easier to simplify the expression before evaluating it because it is easier to identify common factors. Simplifying first also results in an expression that is much easier to evaluate than the original expression, and that can be easily evaluated for any value of y without having to consider the value of x.

4.4 Guided Practice (p. 189)

2. *Sample answer:* The least common denominator is 84. Write equivalent fractions using the LCD. For $\frac{4}{7}$, multiply the numerator and denominator by 12 to get $\frac{48}{84}$. For $\frac{7}{12}$, multiply the numerator and denominator by 7 to get $\frac{49}{84}$. Now compare the numerators. Because $48 < 49$, $\frac{48}{84} < \frac{49}{84}$, and so $\frac{4}{7} < \frac{7}{12}$.

4.4 Practice and Problem Solving (pp. 190–191)

47. $\frac{7}{6}, \frac{11}{9}, 1\frac{1}{3}$ **48.** $\frac{13}{4}, \frac{27}{8}, 3\frac{1}{2}$ **49.** $\frac{1}{5}, \frac{3}{10}, \frac{8}{15}$ **50.** $\frac{9}{22}, \frac{14}{33}, \frac{5}{11}$ **51.** $\frac{4}{9}, \frac{7}{15}, \frac{3}{4}$ **52.** $\frac{7}{10}, \frac{11}{15}, \frac{5}{6}$ **53.** $\frac{43}{18}, \frac{12}{5}, 2\frac{5}{12}$ **54.** $1\frac{1}{3}, 1\frac{13}{33}, \frac{10}{7}$

4.6 Practice and Problem Solving (pp. 202–203)

61b. $\frac{n \text{ factors of } a \rightarrow \not{a}^1 \cdot \not{a}^1 \cdot \not{a}^1 \cdot \ldots \cdot \not{a}^1}{n \text{ factors of } a \rightarrow \not{a}^1 \cdot \not{a}^1 \cdot \not{a}^1 \cdot \ldots \cdot \not{a}^1} = 1$; definition of zero exponent **66.**

43 44 45 46 47 48 49

4.7 Practice and Problem Solving (pp. 207–208)

54a.

n	$n \times 10^{n+1}$	$(n + 1) \times 10^n$
1	1×10^2	2×10^1
2	2×10^3	3×10^2
3	3×10^4	4×10^3
4	4×10^5	5×10^4

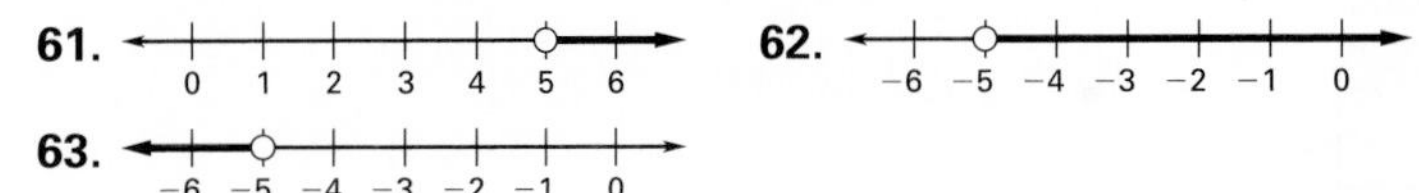

Chapter 5

5.1 Standardized Test Practice (p. 224)

75. $\frac{475}{999}$. *Sample answer:* First I let $x = 0.\overline{475}$. Then I multiplied both sides of $x = 0.\overline{475}$ by $10^3 = 1000$ since there are three repeating digits. This gave the equation $1000x = 475.\overline{475}$. From this I subtracted the equation $x = 0.\overline{475}$ to obtain the new equation $999x = 475$. Solving for x then gave $x = \frac{475}{999}$.

5.2 Practice and Problem Solving (pp. 228–229)

53. $1\frac{7}{8}$. *Sample answer:* First I used the subtraction property of equality to subtract $\frac{7x}{3}$ from each side of the equation and simplified to obtain $\frac{5}{8} = \frac{x}{3}$. Then I used the multiplication property of equality to multiply each side of the new equation by 3 to obtain $\frac{15}{8} = x$, and wrote $\frac{15}{8}$ as a mixed number.

5.3 Concept Activity (p. 230)

5. *Sample answer:* Draw area models for 2 and $\frac{2}{5}$, as shown.

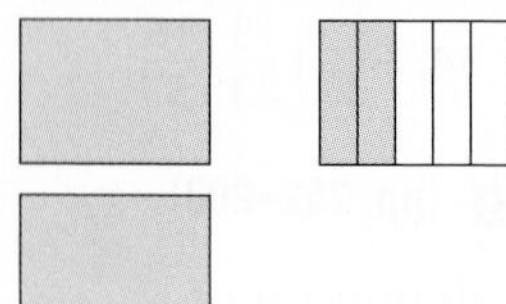

Redraw the models so that one of the models for 1 has the same number of parts as the model for $\frac{2}{5}$.

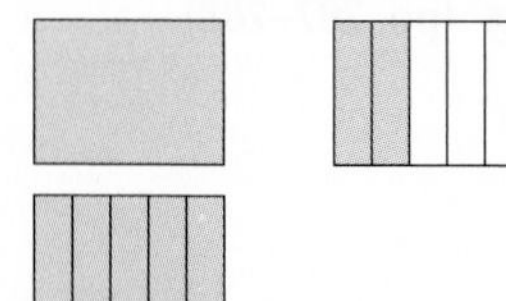

Find the difference of the numbers of shaded parts in the models.

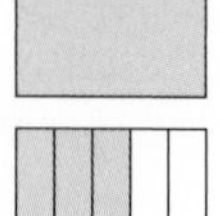

So, $2 - \frac{2}{5} = 1\frac{3}{5}$.

5.3 Practice and Problem Solving (pp. 234–235)

35c. *Sample answer:* I would make it so that there are no missing measurements in the chart by making small from 21 to $21\frac{1}{2}$, medium from $21\frac{5}{8}$ to $22\frac{1}{4}$, large from $22\frac{3}{8}$ to 23, and extra large from $23\frac{1}{8}$ to 24. **51.** Yes; yes. *Sample answer:* Using 48, the equivalent fractions are $\frac{42}{48}$ and $\frac{20}{48}$, so the sum is $\frac{62}{48}$. Dividing out the common factor 2 from the numerator and denominator then gives $\frac{31}{24}$, or $1\frac{7}{24}$. Using the LCD, 24, the equivalent fractions are $\frac{21}{24}$ and $\frac{10}{24}$, so the sum is $\frac{31}{24}$, or $1\frac{7}{24}$. So using the LCD, you do not have to perform the additional step of simplifying in this case.

5.4 Practice and Problem Solving (pp. 240–241)

29a.

Time (y)	1	2	3
Tread depth (in.)	$\frac{21}{64}$	$\frac{9}{32}$	$\frac{15}{64}$

29b.

Time (y)	1	2	3	4	5	6	7
Tread depth (in.)	$\frac{21}{64}$	$\frac{9}{32}$	$\frac{15}{64}$	$\frac{3}{16}$	$\frac{9}{64}$	$\frac{3}{32}$	$\frac{3}{64}$

5.5 Concept Activity (p. 242)

10. *Sample answer:* Multiply the dividend and divisor by $\frac{8}{7}$: $\frac{8}{7}\left(2\frac{3}{5}\right) \div \frac{8}{7}\left(\frac{7}{8}\right) = \frac{8}{7}\left(\frac{13}{5}\right) \div 1 = \frac{8}{7}\left(\frac{13}{5}\right) = \frac{104}{35} = 2\frac{34}{35}$.

5.5 Practice and Problem Solving (pp. 245–246)

36a. *Sample:*

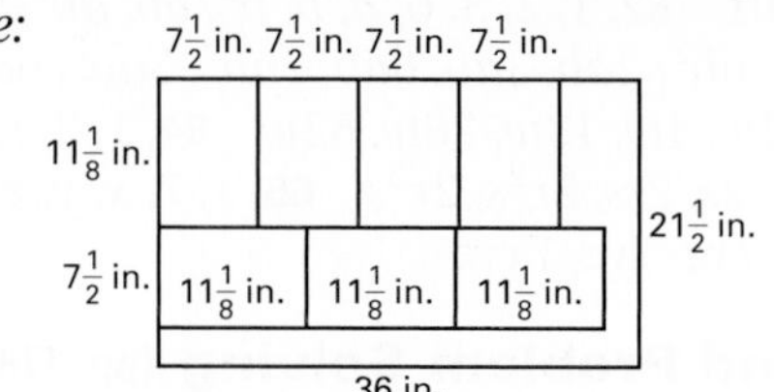

36b. *Sample:*

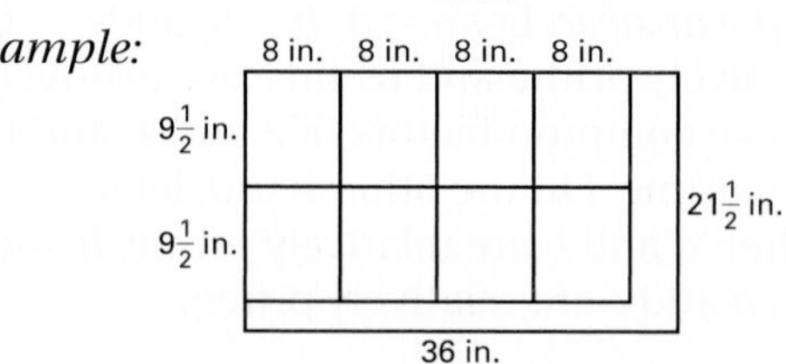

5.5 Standardized Test Practice (p. 246)

50b. 0. *Sample answer:* The average size of the women's shoes sold during the 2-hour period was $8\frac{1}{2}$. A mean deviation of 0 means that, on average, the sizes of the shoes sold during the 2 hours did not differ from the reported average of $8\frac{1}{2}$, so the reported average must have also been the actual average.

5.6 Guided Practice (p. 249)

2. *Sample answer:* Multiply each side by the multiplicative inverse of $\frac{5}{6}$, which is its reciprocal, $\frac{6}{5}$, so that the coefficient of x is 1. This gives $x = \frac{6}{5}\left(\frac{2}{7}\right) = \frac{12}{35}$.

5.6 Practice and Problem Solving (pp. 249–251)

10. *Sample answer:* Each side of the equation should have been multiplied by the multiplicative inverse of $-\frac{1}{6}$, which is -6, not 6, because $6\left(-\frac{1}{6}\right) = -1$, not 1. The second line should be $-6\left(-\frac{1}{6}x\right) = -6\left(\frac{2}{3}\right)$, followed by $x = -4$.

5.7 Practice and Problem Solving (pp. 256–257)

42. *Sample answer:* To solve using multiplicative inverses, your goal is first to isolate the variable term. For $\frac{2}{3}x - 1 = \frac{5}{6}$, this means adding 1, first converting 1 to sixths, to obtain $\frac{2}{3}x = \frac{11}{6}$. You must then multiply each side by the reciprocal of $\frac{2}{3}$, which is $\frac{3}{2}$, and simplify to obtain the solution, $2\frac{3}{4}$. To solve by clearing fractions, your goal is first to eliminate all fractions by multiplying each side by the LCD of the fractions. For $\frac{2}{3}x - 1 = \frac{5}{6}$, this means multiplying by 6 to obtain $4x - 6 = 5$, which you then solve by first isolating the variable term as before. This adds a step, but it allows you to avoid having to add and then multiply fractions. **44.** Yes. *Sample answer:* Any common denominator will work, though using the LCD will help avoid having to perform extra simplification. For example, multiplying each side of $\frac{1}{2}x + \frac{1}{3} = \frac{1}{4}$ by the common denominator 24 gives $12x + 8 = 6$, which has the solution $x = -\frac{1}{6}$, the same as the solution obtained when multiplying each side by the LCD 12 to obtain the equation $6x + 4 = 3$.

46. *Sample answer:*

$$\begin{aligned}
\frac{4}{9}\left(\frac{1}{3}x + 6\right) &= \frac{5}{18}x + \frac{1}{3} \\
54 \cdot \frac{4}{9}\left(\frac{1}{3}x + 6\right) &= 54 \cdot \left(\frac{5}{18}x + \frac{1}{3}\right) \\
24\left(\frac{1}{3}x + 6\right) &= 54\left(\frac{5}{18}x + \frac{1}{3}\right) \\
24\left(\frac{1}{3}x\right) + 24(6) &= 54\left(\frac{5}{18}x\right) - 54\left(\frac{1}{3}\right) \\
8x + 144 &= 15x + 18 \\
8x + 144 - 8x &= 15x + 18 - 8x \\
144 &= 7x + 18 \\
144 - 18 &= 7x + 18 - 18 \\
126 &= 7x \\
\frac{126}{7} &= \frac{7x}{7} \\
18 &= x
\end{aligned}$$

Focus on Problem Solving (p. 265) **6.** Yes. *Sample answer:* You can reason that the sink must fill up because it takes less time for the faucet alone to fill the sink than it does for the drain alone to empty it, so the flow from the faucet is greater than the flow out the drain. Or, to write an equation, note that the faucet fills $\frac{1}{2}$ of the sink per minute, and the drain empties $\frac{1}{3}$ of the sink per minute. So in t minutes, the sink is $\frac{t}{2} - \frac{t}{3}$ full. The equation $\frac{t}{2} - \frac{t}{3} = 1$ represents the time it takes to fill the sink. Since the equation has the solution $t = 6$, the sink will fill in 6 minutes.

8a.

Time (sec)	Heidi's distance traveled (ft)	Josh's distance traveled (ft)
0	400	0
10	620	270
20	840	540
30	1060	810
40	1280	1080
50	1500	1350
60	1720	1620
70	1940	1890
80	2160	2160

Chapter 6

6.3 Practice and Problem Solving (pp. 283–284)

36. *Sample answer:* (1) Use equivalent ratios, realizing that the denominator of the fraction on the right is 4 times that of the fraction on the left. So, multiply the numerator of the fraction on the left by 4 to obtain $x = 24$. (2) Use algebra, multiplying each side by 40 and simplifying. (3) Use cross products, solving $6 \cdot 40 = 10x$ by simplifying and then dividing each side by 10.

41. *Sample answer:*

$$\begin{aligned}
\frac{a}{b} &= \frac{c}{d} && \text{[Given]} \\
a \cdot d &= b \cdot c && \text{[Form cross products.]} \\
\frac{ad}{ac} &= \frac{bc}{ac} && \text{[Divide each side by } ac.] \\
\frac{d}{c} &= \frac{b}{a} && \text{[Simplify.]}
\end{aligned}$$

6.4 Practice and Problem Solving (pp. 291–292)

17. Sometimes. *Sample answer:* Corresponding angles of similar figures are congruent, but similar figures are congruent only if they are also the same size. **18.** Always. *Sample answer:* All angles are congruent and have measures of 90°, and corresponding sides all have the same ratio (the ratio of the side lengths of the two squares). **19.** Sometimes. *Sample answer:* All angles are congruent and have measures of 90°, but rectangles are congruent only if they have the same shape and same size. **20a.** No. *Sample answer:* The ratio of the heights of the computer screens is $\frac{3}{4}$, but the ratio of the widths is $\frac{4}{5}$, and $\frac{3}{4} \neq \frac{4}{5}$. **20b.** Yes; it is similar to the screen of computer 1. *Sample answer:* All angles are congruent and have measures of 90°. The ratio of the heights and of the widths is the same, and equal to $\frac{2}{1}$.

23. *Sample:*

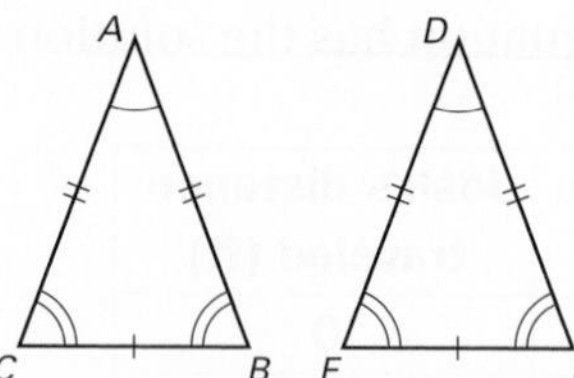

6.6 Concept Activity (p. 299)

2. *Sample:*

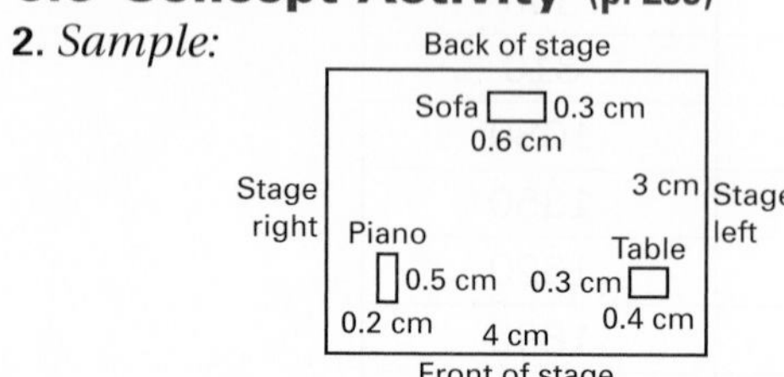

6.6 Standardized Test Practice (p. 304)

51b. *Sample answer:* First rewrite the scale 1 inch : 1 yard as 1 inch : 36 inches, or 1 : 36. To find the dimensions of the deck in the model, convert 15 feet to 80 inches and 12 feet to 144 inches, and then write and solve the proportions $\frac{1}{36} = \frac{l}{180}$ and $\frac{1}{36} = \frac{w}{144}$. The solutions $l = 5$ inches and $w = 4$ inches are then multiplied to find the area: $5 \cdot 4 = 20$ square inches.

6.7 Concept Activity (p. 305)

4. Sample answer is given for an experiment in which after being cut in half the cup lands on its side 14 times, rim side up 15 times, and bottom side up 1 time. In the first experiment, the cup landed on its side far more times than rim side up or bottom side up. In the second experiment, the cup landed rim side up about the same number of times as on its side.

6.8 Checkpoint (p. 313)

1.

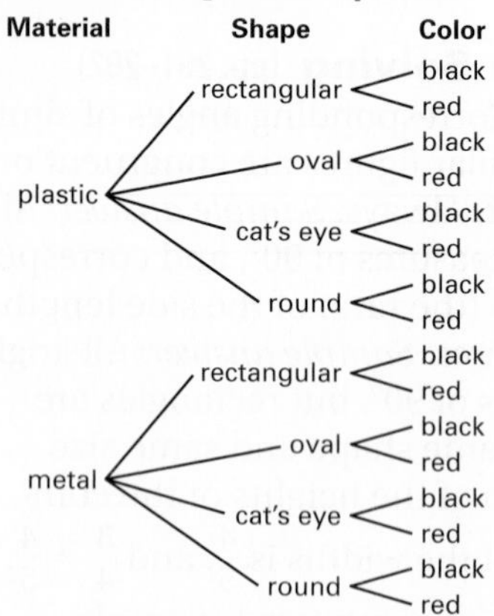

6.8 Guided Practice (p. 315)

6. Step 1:

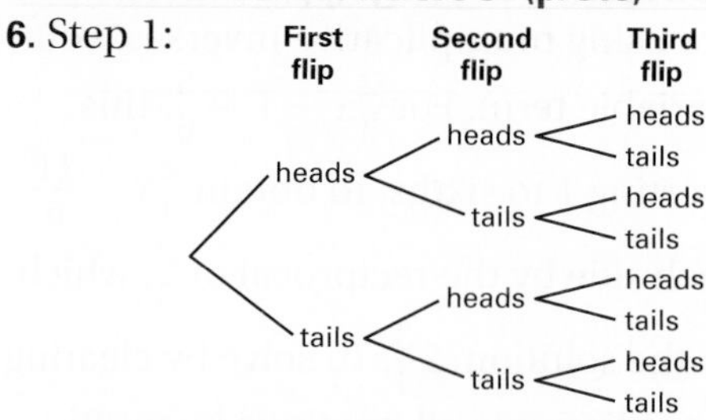

6.8 Practice and Problem Solving (pp. 315–317)

7.

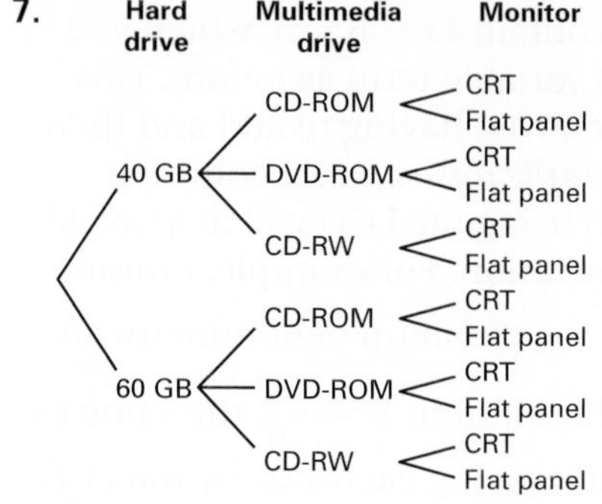

Chapter 7

7.2 Concept Activity (p. 334)

7. *Sample answer:* Draw a percent bar model that has ten equal sections. Label the left side of the model from 0 to b, and label the right side of the model from 0% to 100%. Shade the bar to the 40% mark. On the left-hand side of the model, label the extent of the shading 28 as shown below.

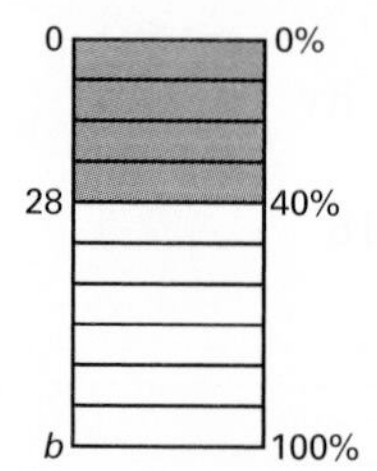

A proportion is $\frac{28}{b} = \frac{40}{100}$, which has the solution $b = 70$.

8.

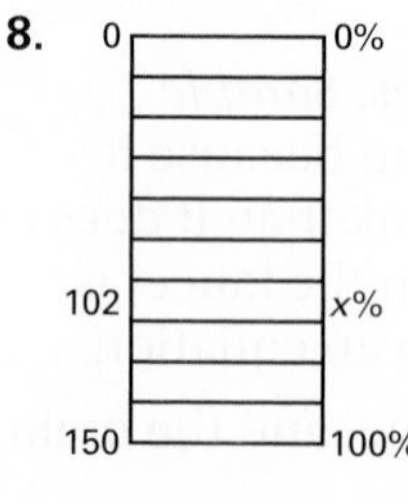

Sample answer: Since you do not know exactly where to place 102 on the left side of the model, and thus where to shade, find what part of the model to shade using the right-hand scale of the model. Let x% represent the extent of the shading on the right-hand scale. A proportion describing x is $\frac{102}{150} = \frac{x}{100}$, which has solution $x = 68$. So, shade to the 68% mark, which corresponds to 102 on the left-hand scale.

Additional Answers

7.3 Brain Game (p. 344) *Sample answer:* At each stage, the grid is two squares shorter along each edge while the shaded portion is always 25% of the entire grid.

7.4 Standardized Test Practice (p. 349) **43.** 50%. *Sample answer:* Originally, there are $0.35 \cdot 20 = 7$ blue marbles in the bag. Adding 6 more blue marbles increases the number of blue marbles to $7 + 6 = 13$, and the total number of marbles to $20 + 6 = 26$. To find the percent of blue marbles, I then solved the percent equation $13 = p\% \cdot 26$, which has the solution $p = 50$.

7.6 Mixed Review (p. 361) **29.** ones, 3; 93 **30.** tenths, 0.0; 341.1 **31.** tenths, 0.9; 1596.0 **32.** hundredths, 0.08; 17,024.98

7.7 Practice and Problem Solving (pp. 365–366)
24. Stays the same; increases. *Sample answer:* In a simple interest account, the interest earned each year is always the same percent of the original principal, but in a compound interest account, the interest earned each year is earned on the amount of the principal increased by any previously-earned interest.
25b.

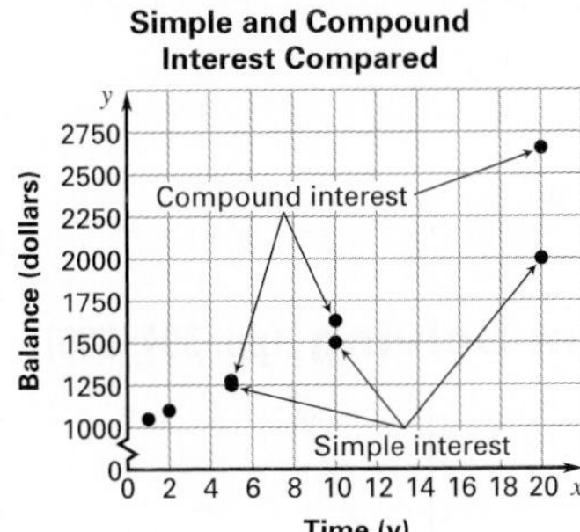

Chapter 8

8.1 Checkpoint (p. 386)
3.

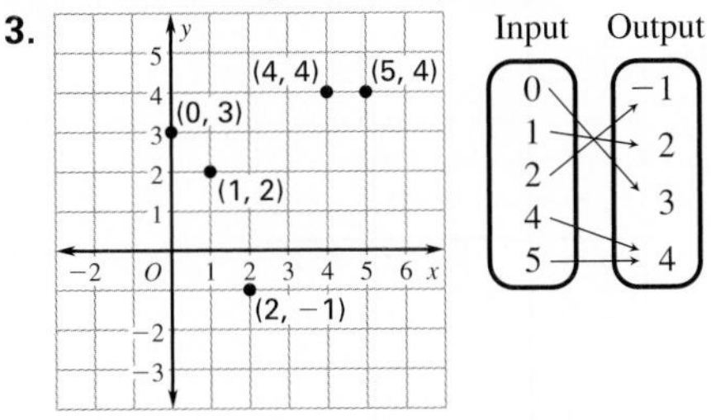

4.

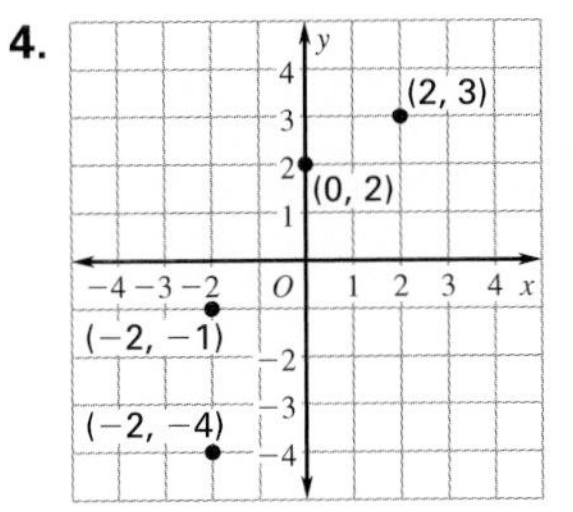

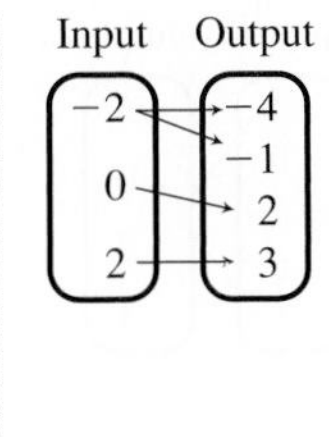

8.1 Guided Practice (p. 387)
2. *Sample:*

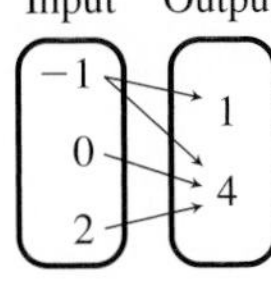

5.

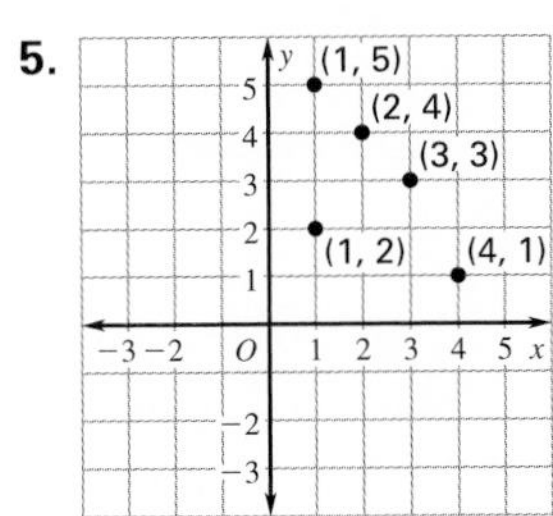

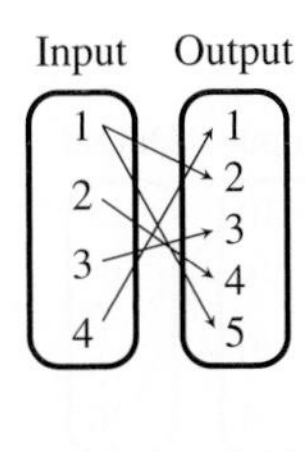

6.

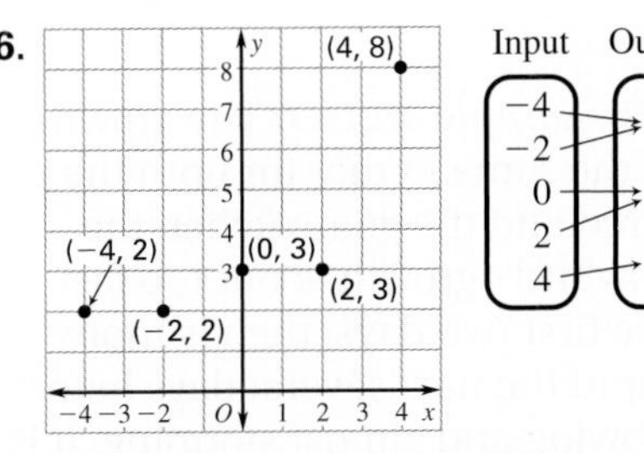

7. *Sample answer:* The relation is a function. A function can have two inputs paired with one output, as in this case, as long as it does not have two outputs paired with one input.

8.1 Practice and Problem Solving (pp. 388–390)
13.

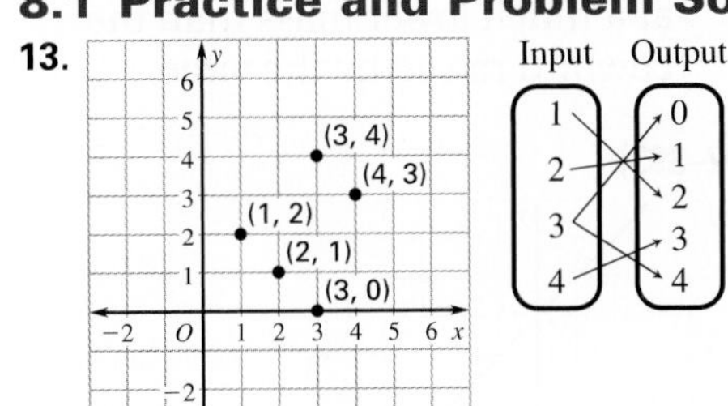

Additional Answers

14.

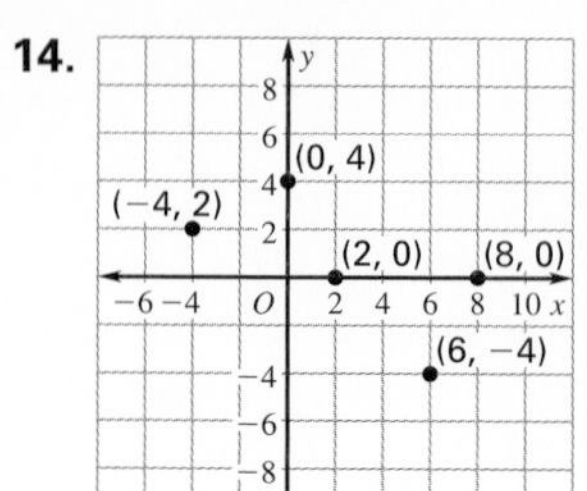

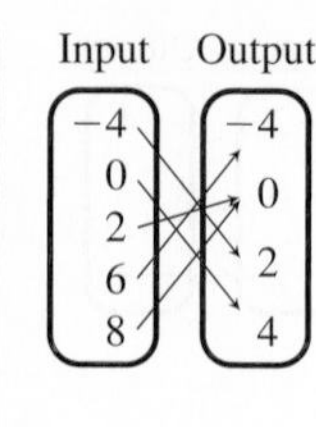

15.

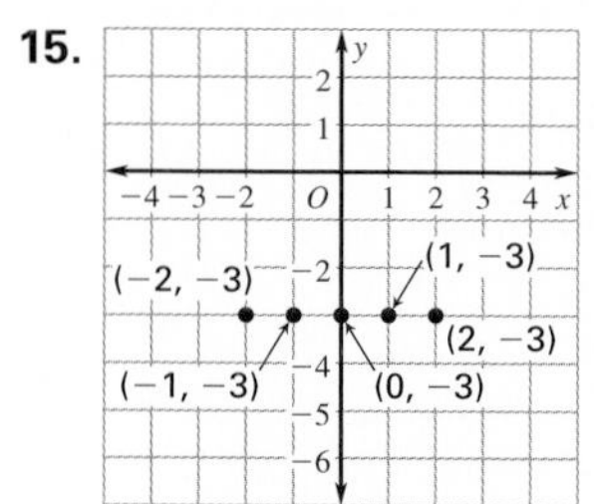

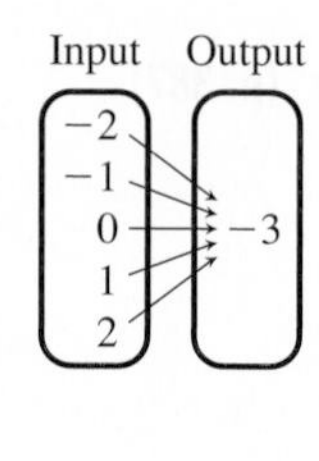

16.

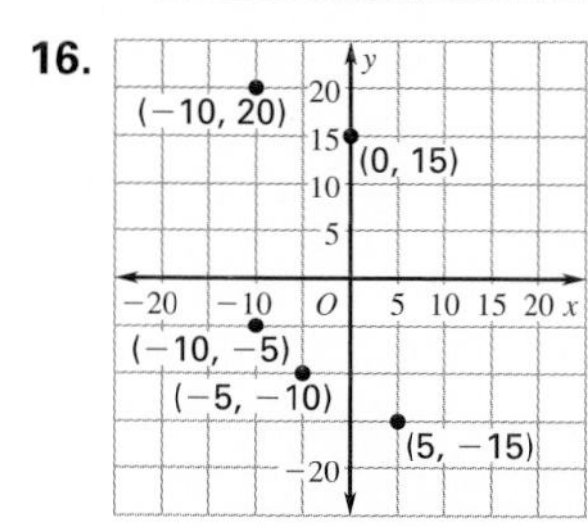

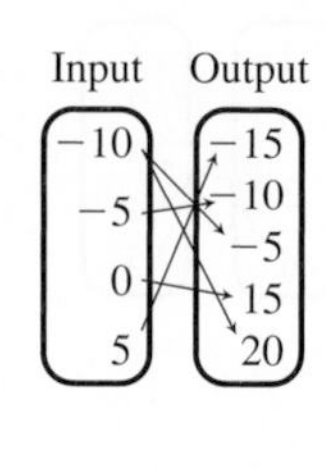

26a.

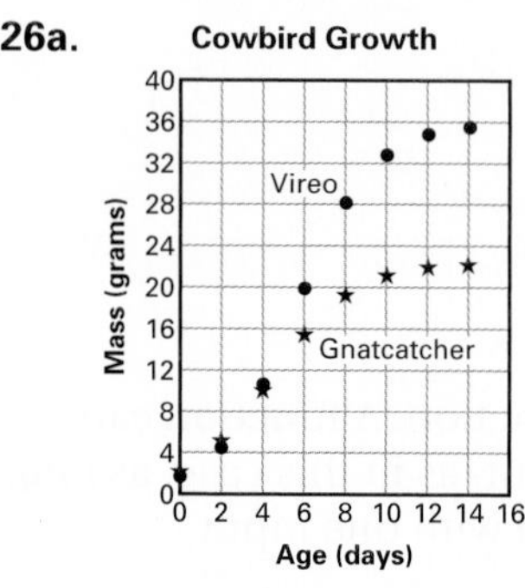

26b. *Sample answer:* The growth is the same in that for both the vireo and the gnatcatcher, the cowbird's growth is not too fast the first two days, then is more rapid the next several days before slowing and almost stopping. It is different in that the growth for the cowbird raised by the gnatcatcher decreases and levels off with the cowbird at an earlier stage and at a much lower mass than the cowbird raised by the vireo.

8.2 Checkpoint (p. 392–393)

5.

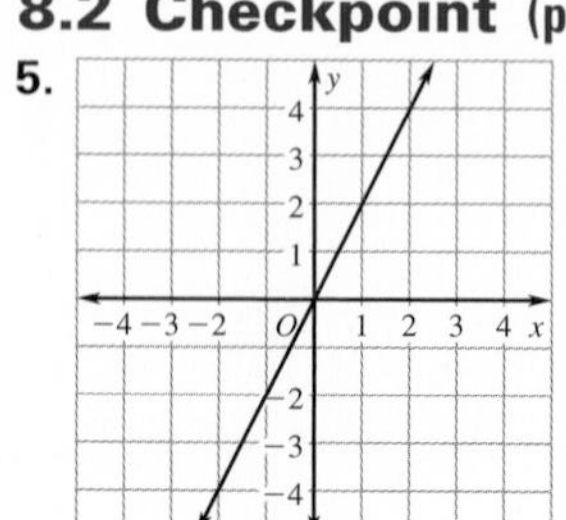

6.

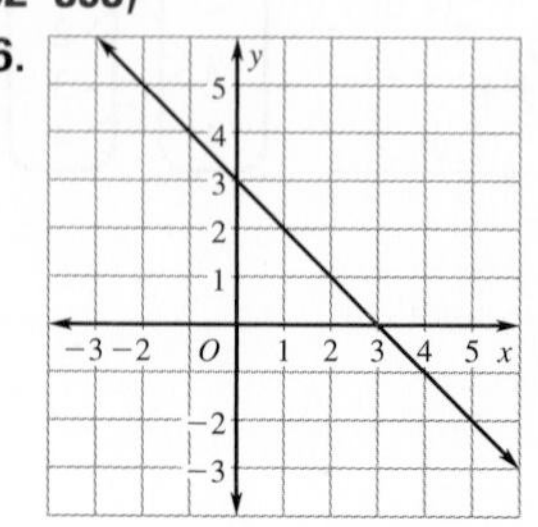

7.

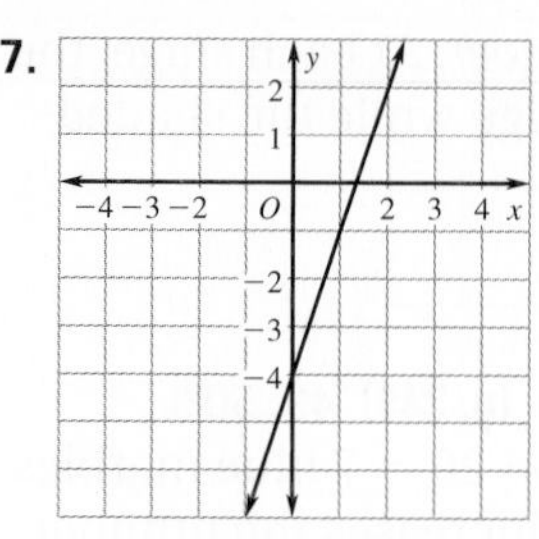

8.

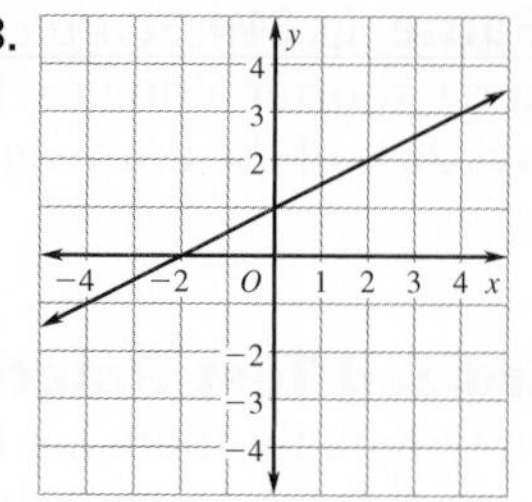

9.

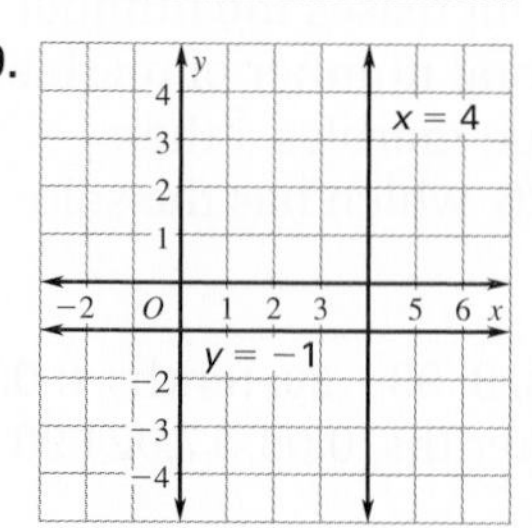

10.

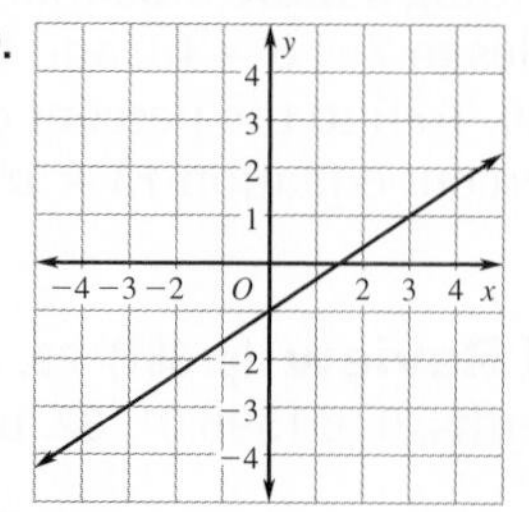

8.2 Guided Practice (p. 394)

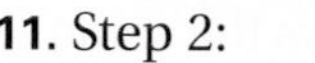

11. Step 2:

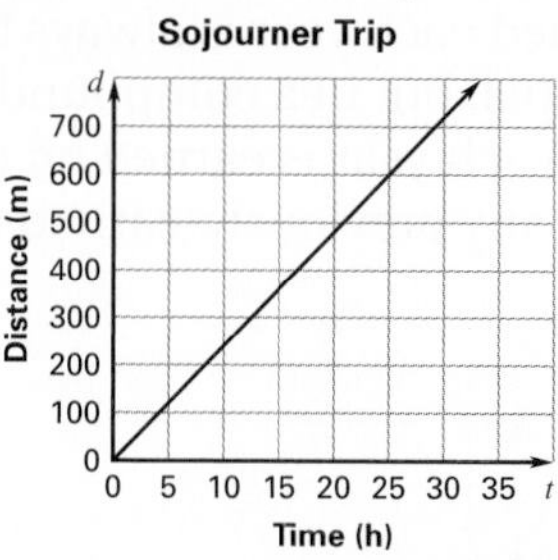

8.2 Practice and Problem Solving (pp. 394–396)

16.

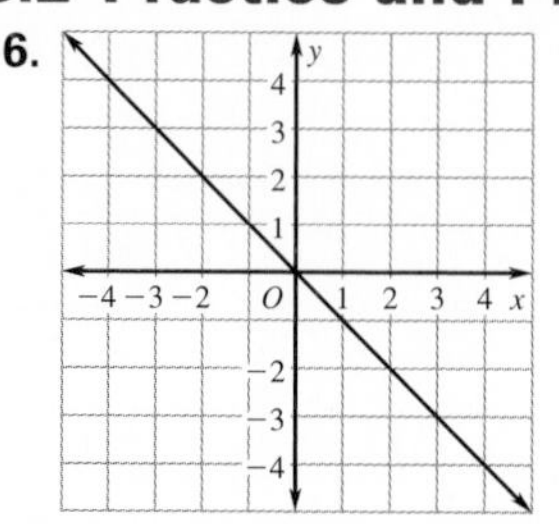

17.

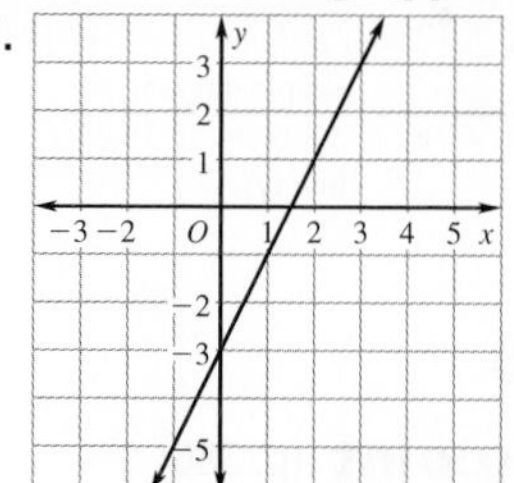

18.

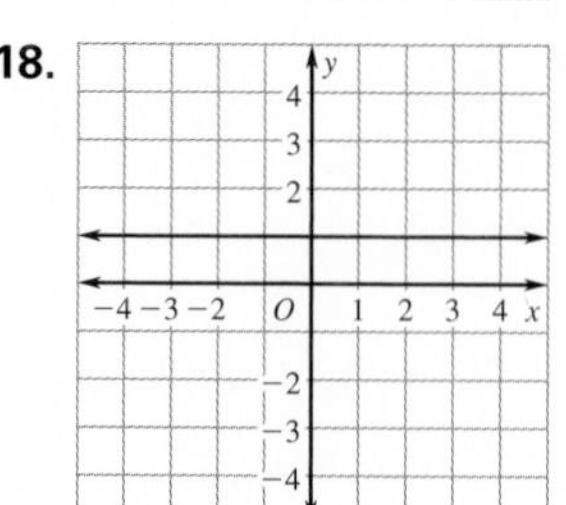

19.

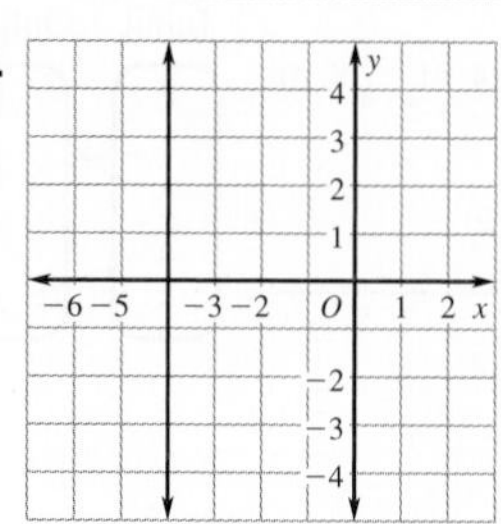

20.

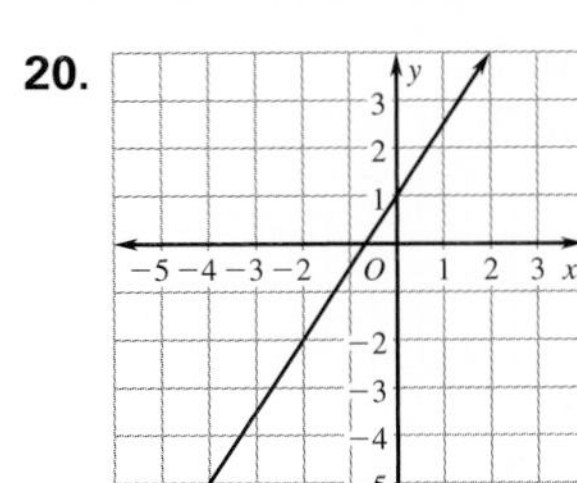

21.

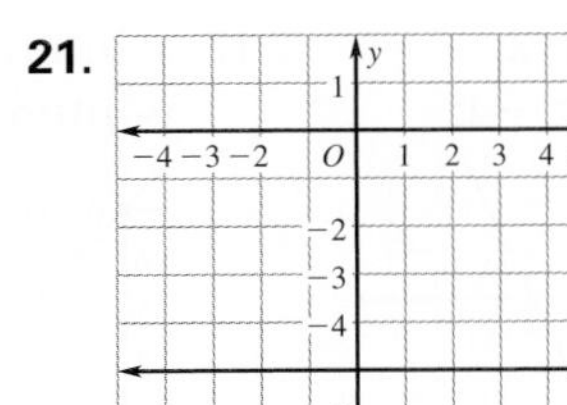

22.

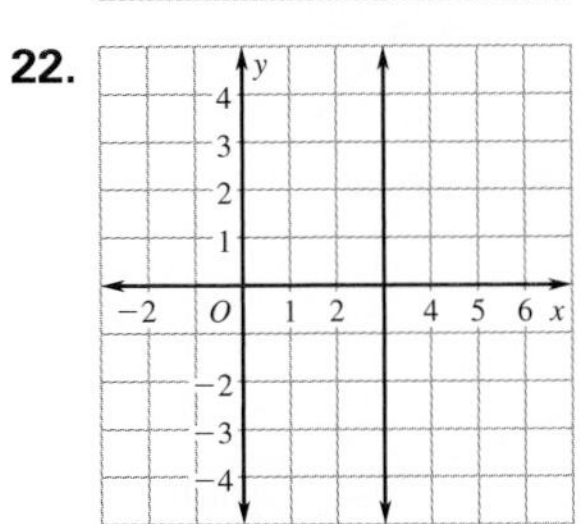

23.

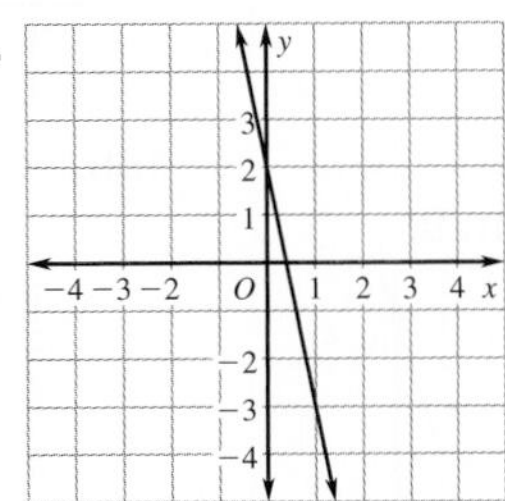

24.

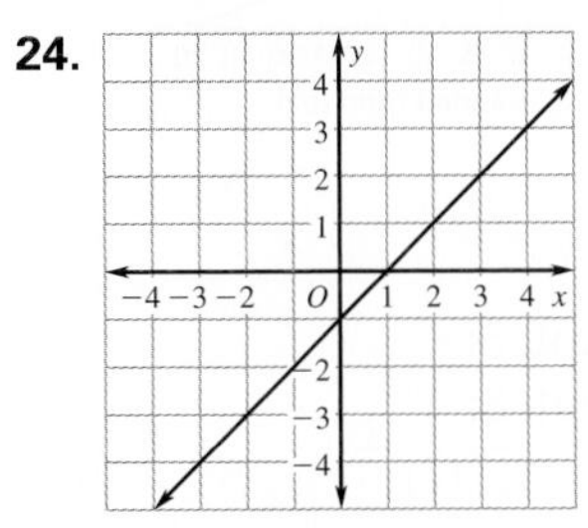

25.

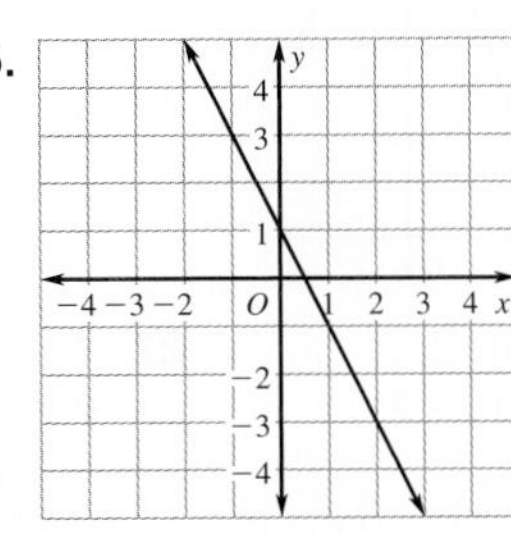

26.

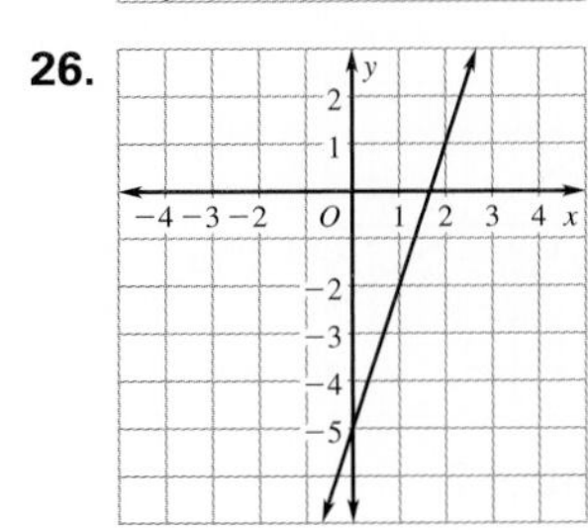

27.

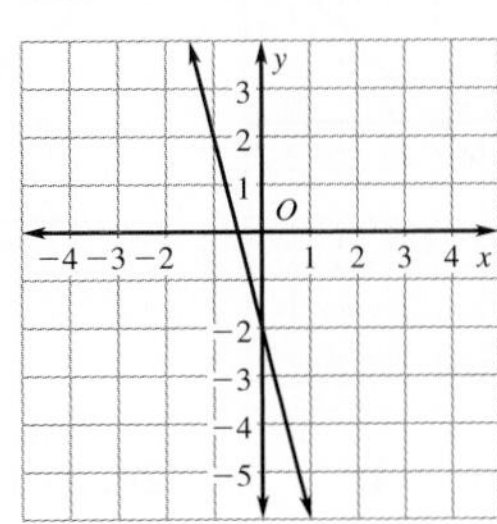

28.

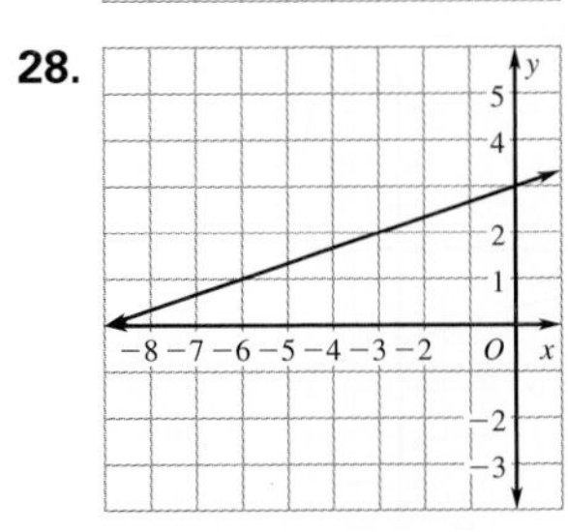

29.

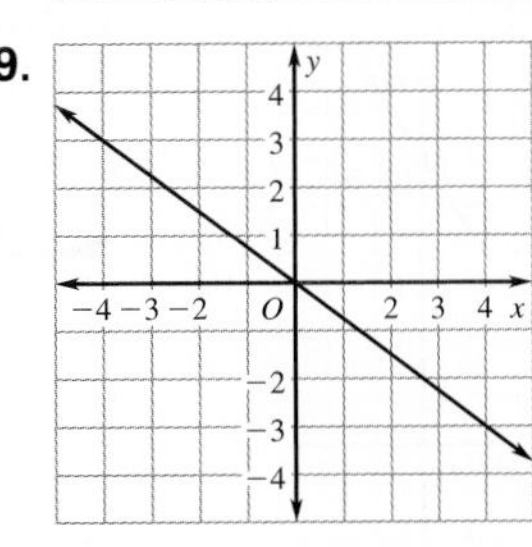

30.

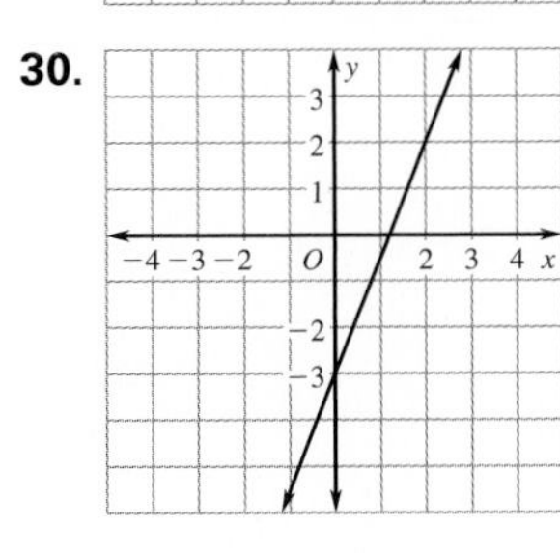

31.

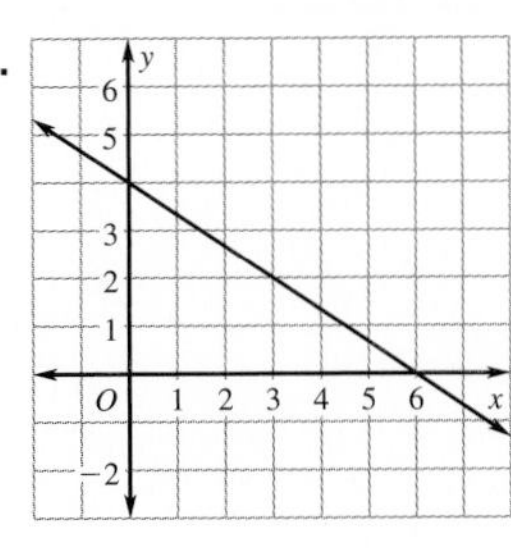

42b.

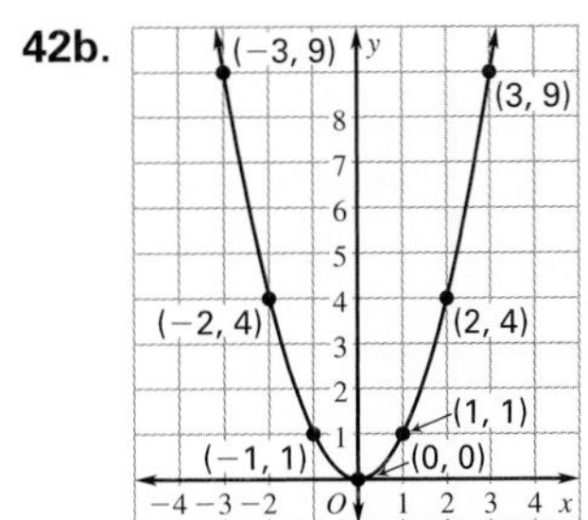

8.2 Technology Activity (p. 397)

1.

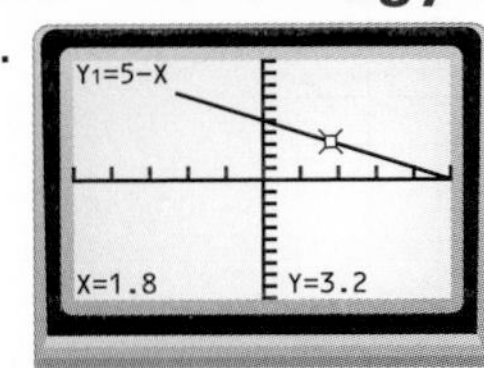

2.

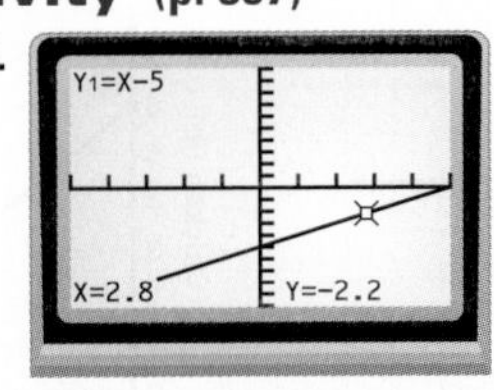

3.

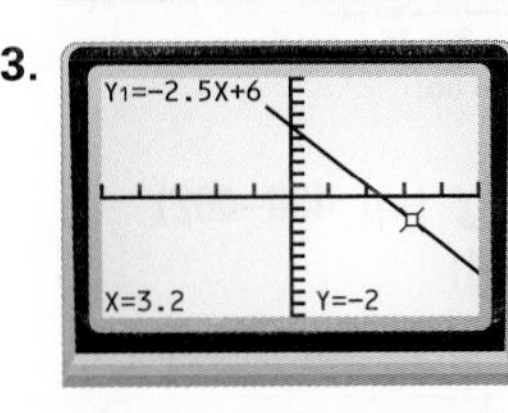

4.

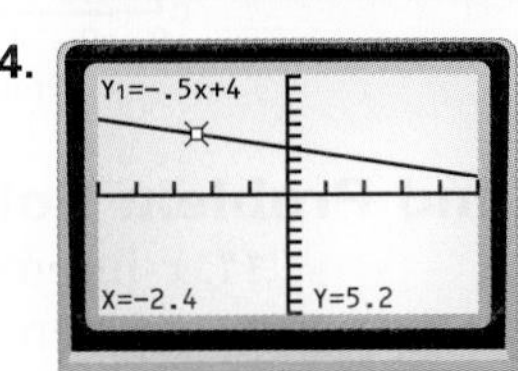

5.

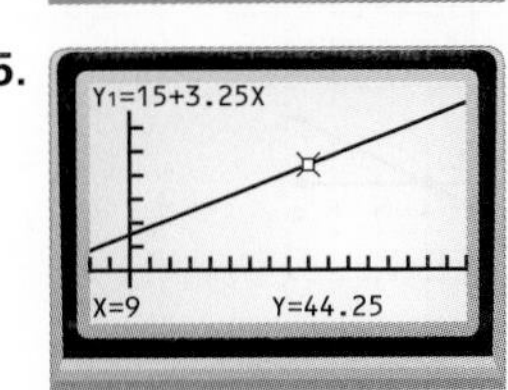

8.3 Checkpoint (p. 399)

1.

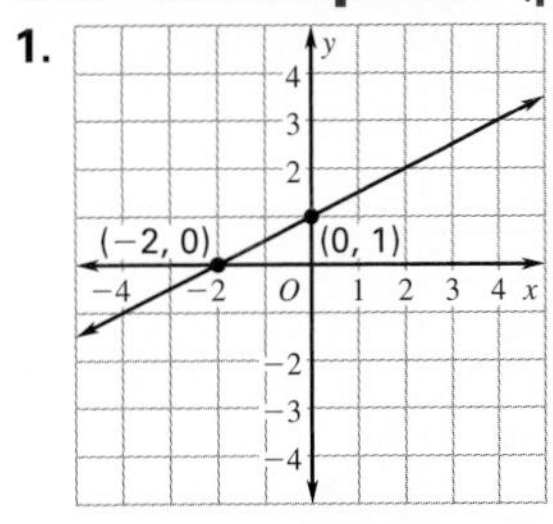

2.

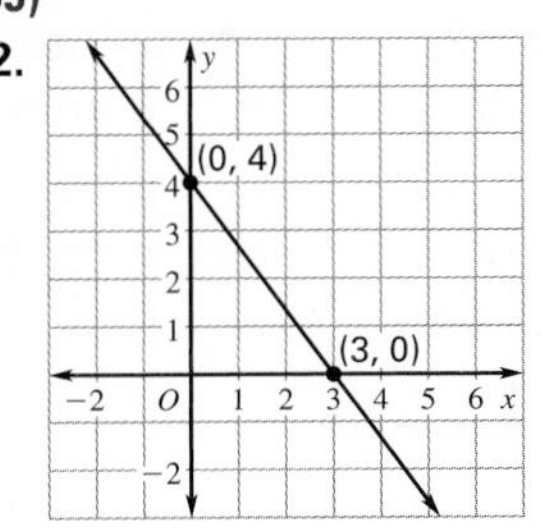

3.

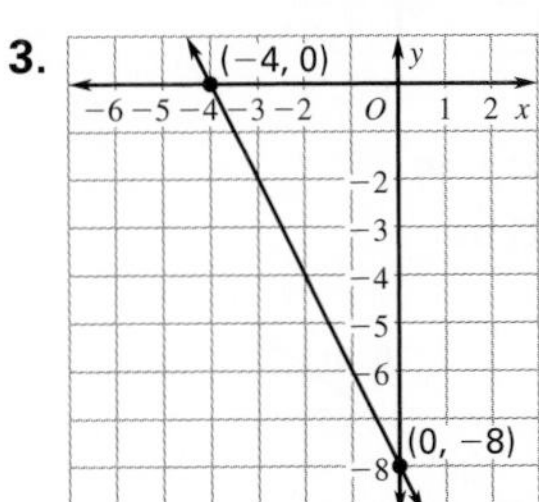

Additional Answers

8.3 Guided Practice (p. 400)

6.

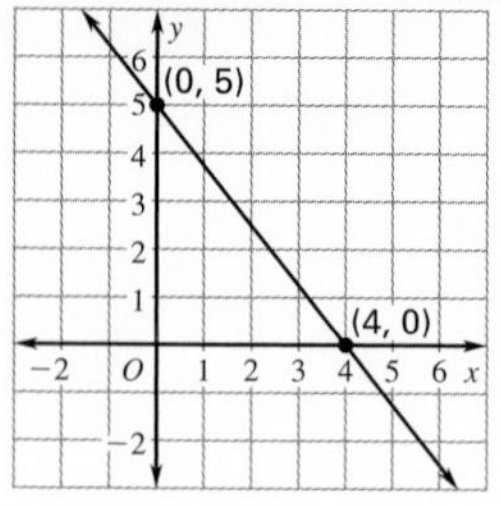

7.

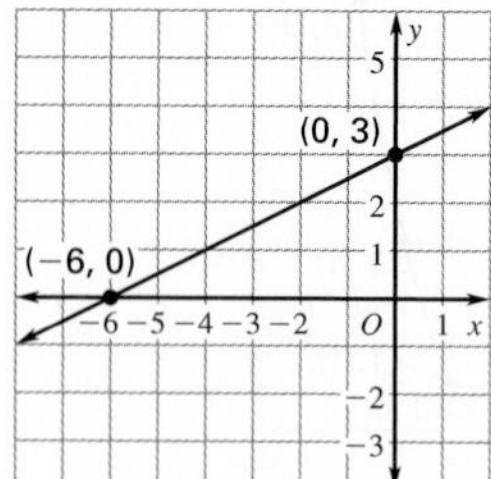

8.

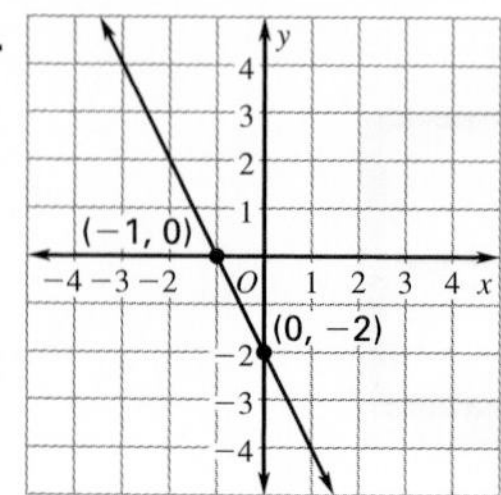

9.

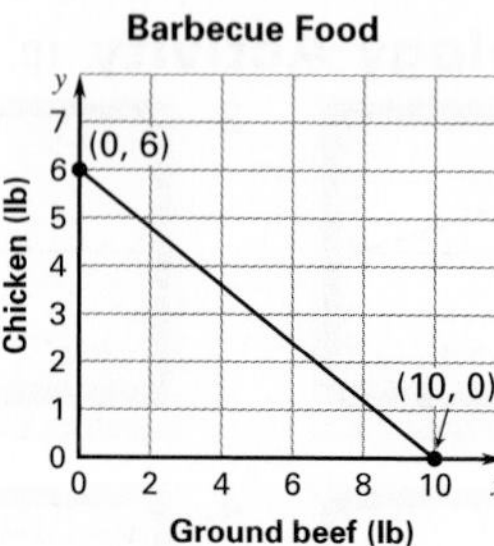

8.3 Practice and Problem Solving (pp. 400–402)

10. x-intercept: 1;
y-intercept: 5;

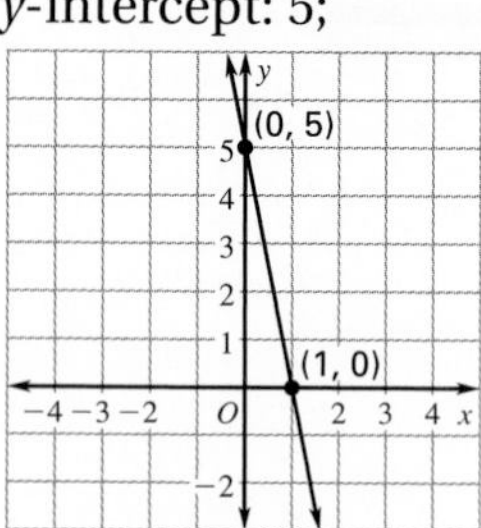

11. x-intercept: 4;
y-intercept: −2;

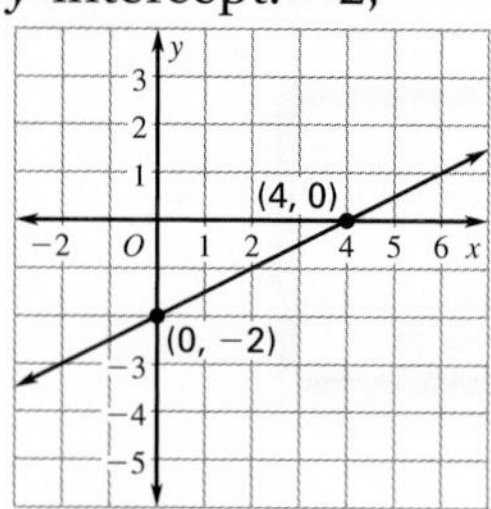

12. x-intercept: −2;
y-intercept: 3;

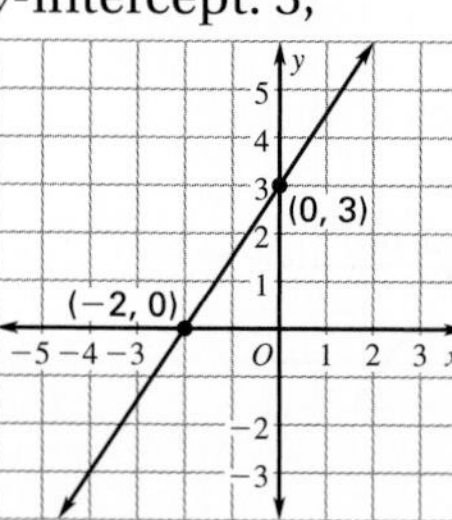

13. x-intercept: −5;
y-intercept: −4;

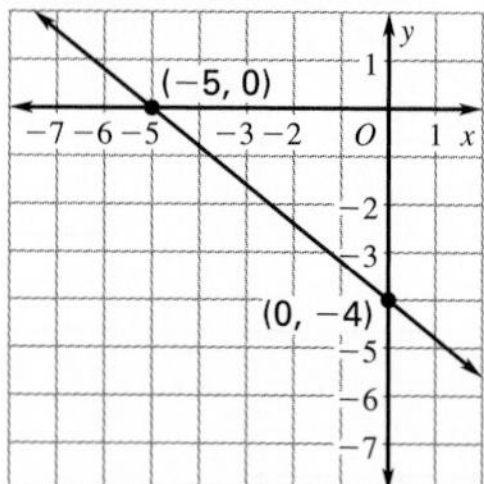

14. x-intercept: 6;
y-intercept: 8;

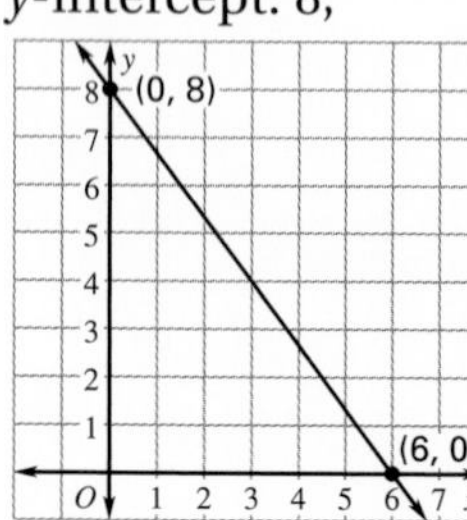

15. x-intercept: −9;
y-intercept: 6;

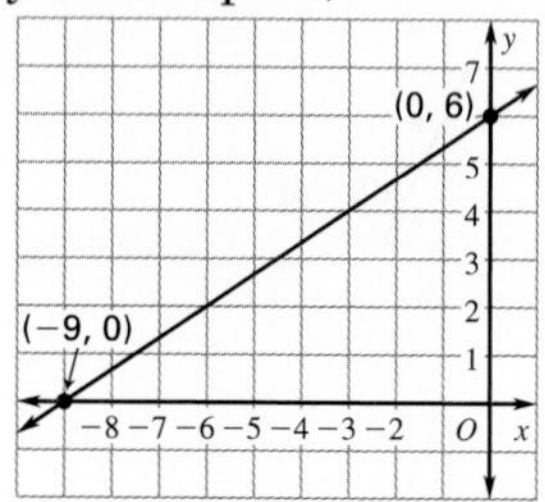

16. x-intercept: 2;
y-intercept: −4;

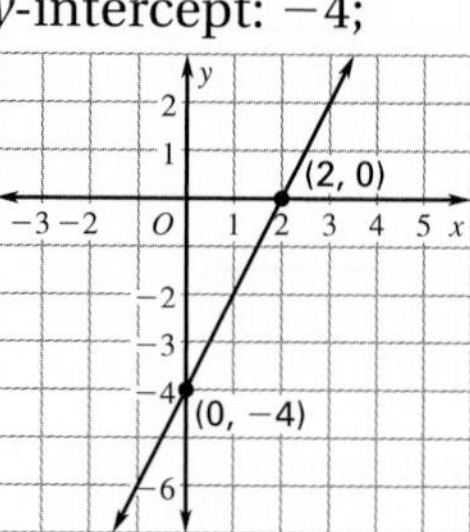

17. x-intercept: 7;
y-intercept: 7;

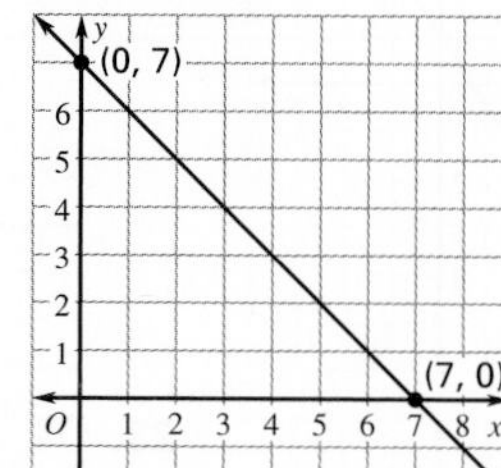

18. x-intercept: −3;
y-intercept: 9;

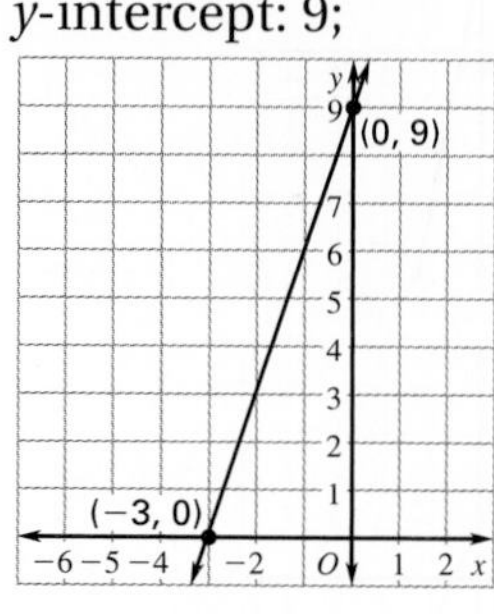

19b.

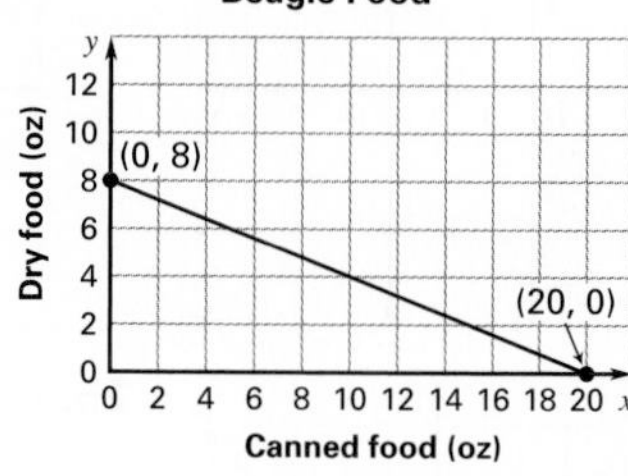

21. x-intercept: 2;
y-intercept: −2;

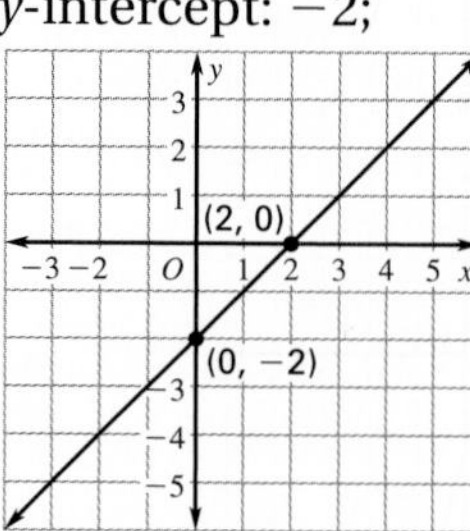

22. x-intercept: 5;
y-intercept: 3;

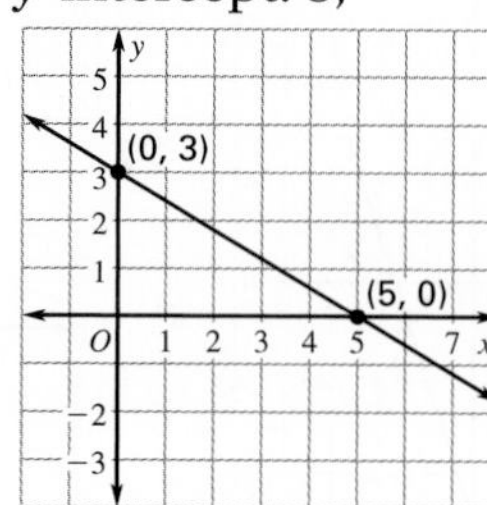

23. x-intercept: −4;
y-intercept: 6;

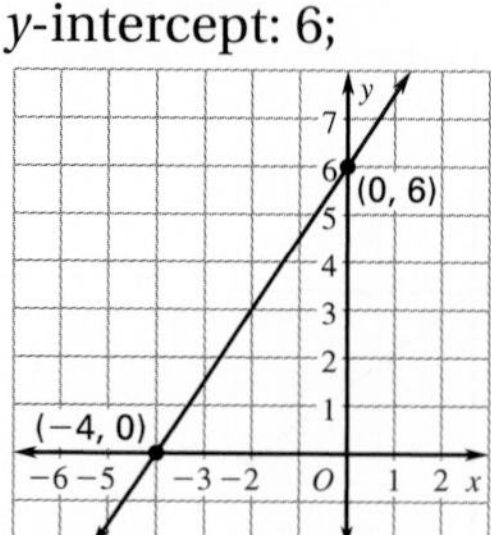

24. x-intercept: −7;
y-intercept: −2;

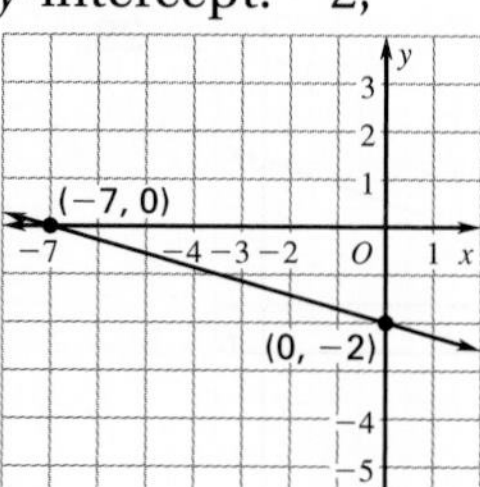

25. x-intercept: 3; y-intercept: 6;

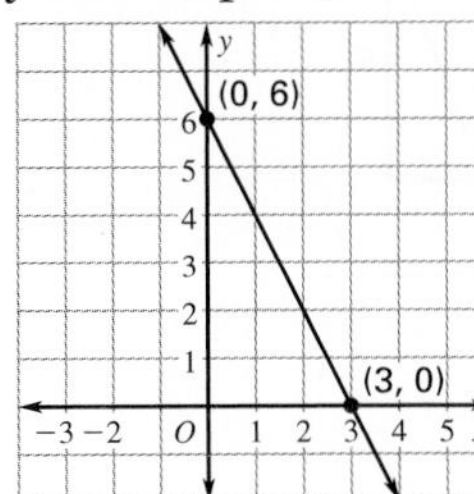

26. x-intercept: $\frac{3}{2}$; y-intercept: $-\frac{7}{2}$;

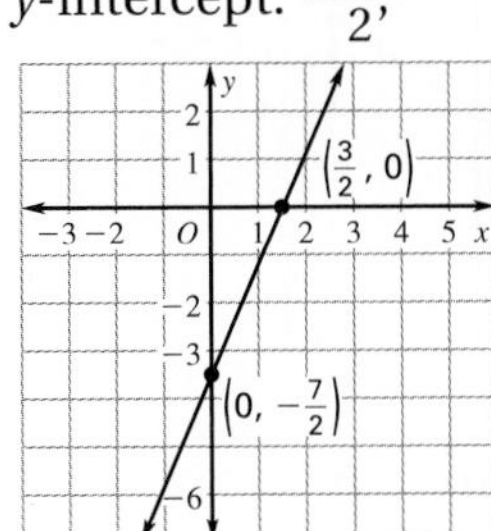

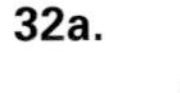

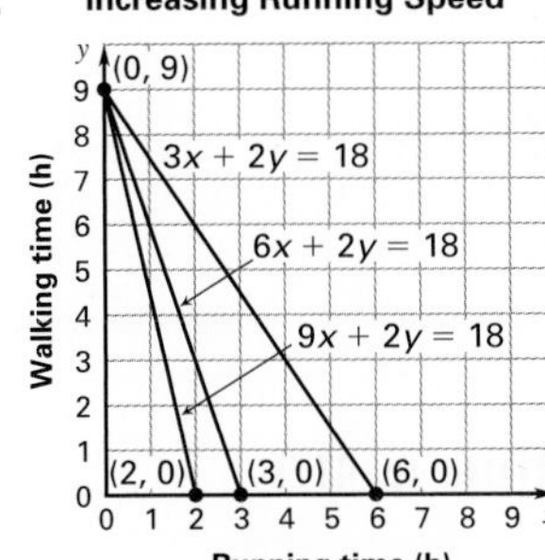

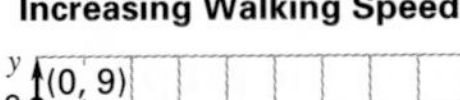

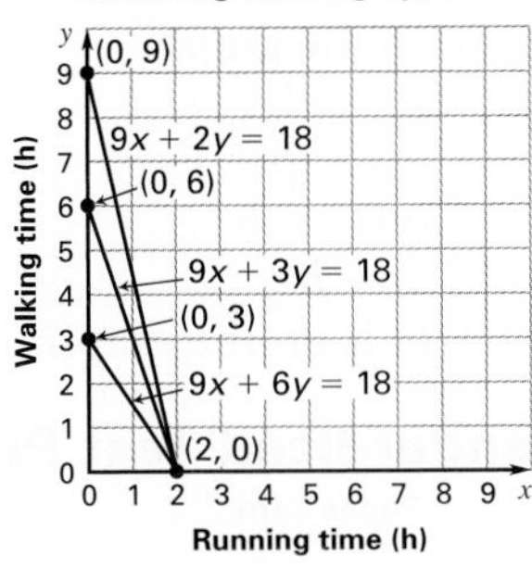

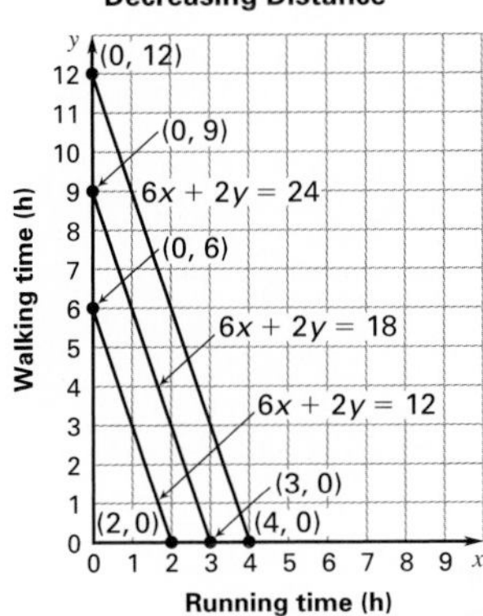

33. x-intercept:

$$\begin{aligned} y &= ax + b \\ 0 - b &= ax + b - b \\ -b &= ax \\ -\frac{b}{a} &= \frac{ax}{a} \\ -\frac{b}{a} &= x \end{aligned}$$

The x-intercept is $-\frac{b}{a}$.

y-intercept:

$$\begin{aligned} y &= ax + b \\ y &= a(0) + b \\ y &= b \end{aligned}$$

The y-intercept is b.

For $y = 3x + 12$, $a = 3$ and $b = 12$. The x-intercept is $-\frac{b}{a} = -\frac{12}{3}$, or -4, and the y-intercept is b, or 12.

8.3 Standardized Test Practice (p. 402)

48.

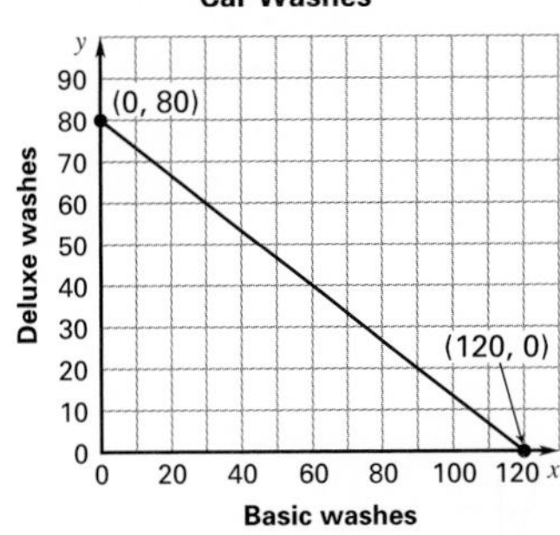

8.4 Concept Activity (p. 403)

2. They are the same. *Sample answer:* A slope of 1 means that the ratio of rise to run is 1, but this can only be true if the rise and run are equal.

8.4 Mixed Review (p. 409)

49.

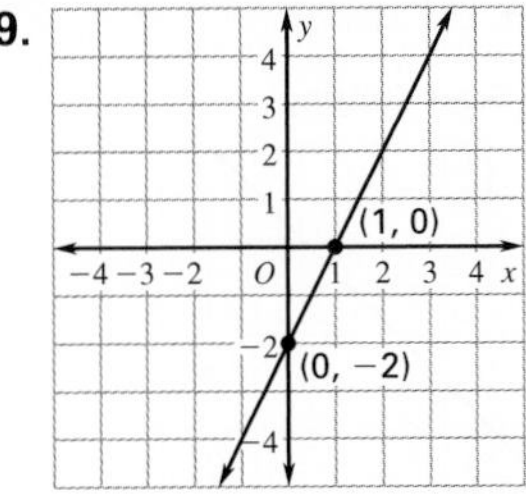

50.

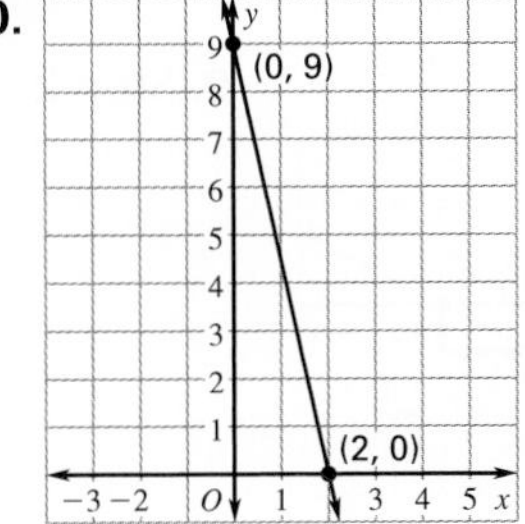

51.

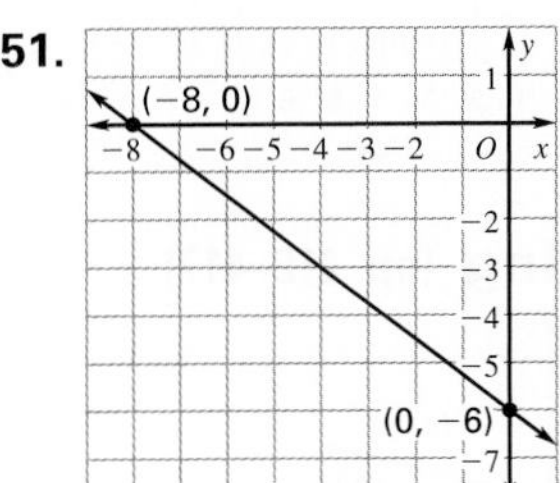

8.5 Checkpoint (pp. 413–414)

1.

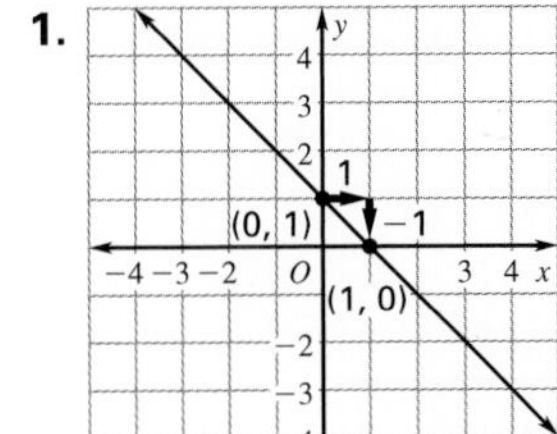

2.

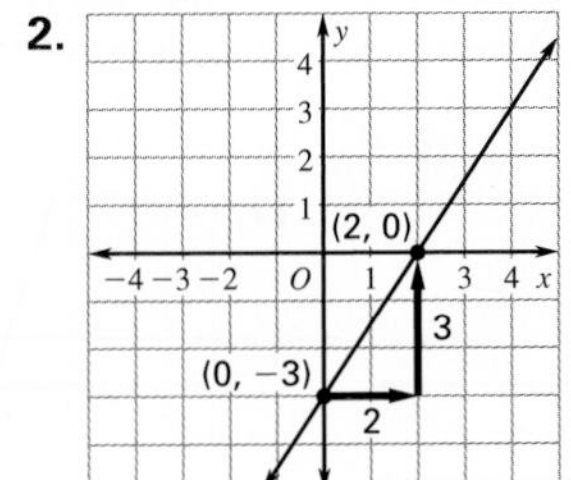

3.

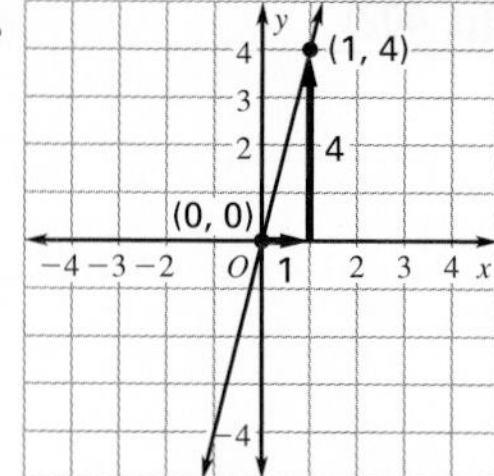

8.5 Guided Practice (p. 415)

3.

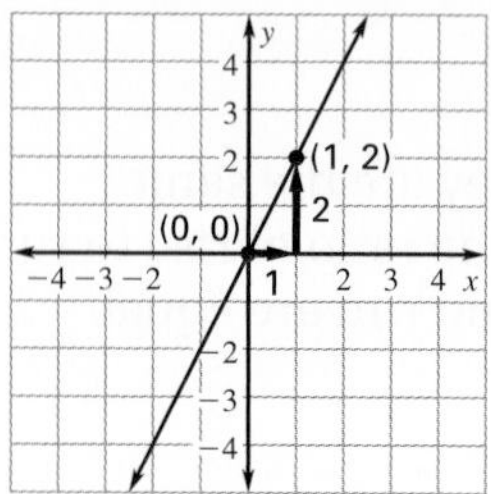

4.

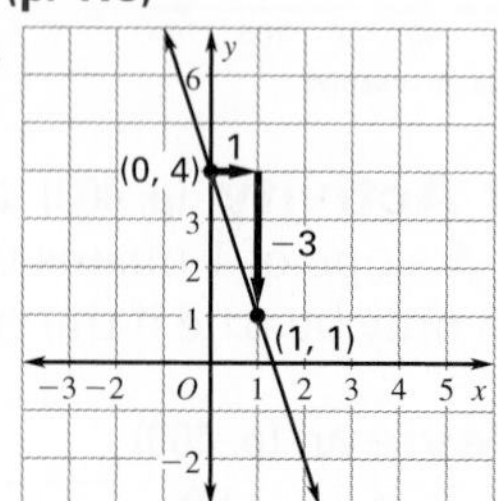

5.

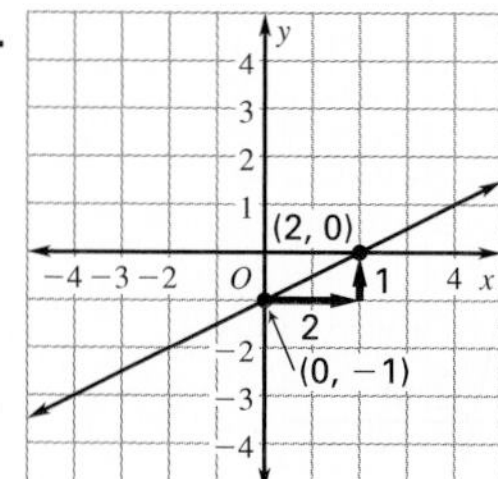

9. Step 2:

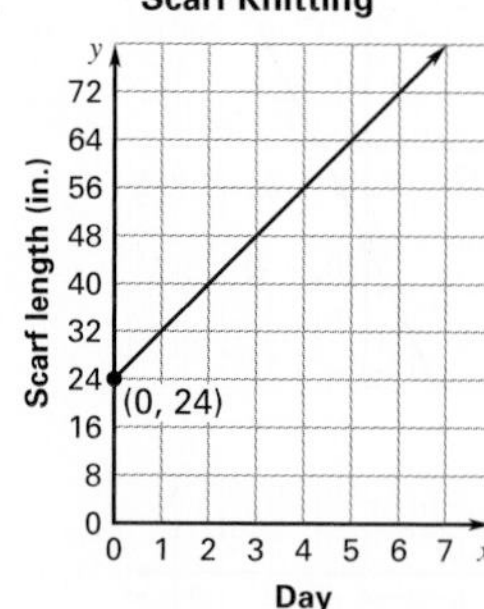

8.5 Practice and Problem Solving (pp. 416–417)

14.

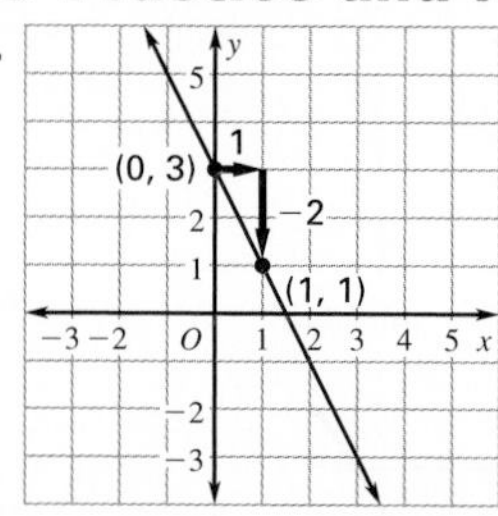

15.

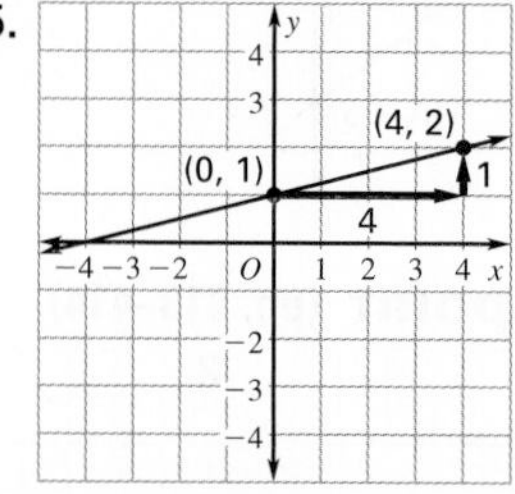

16.

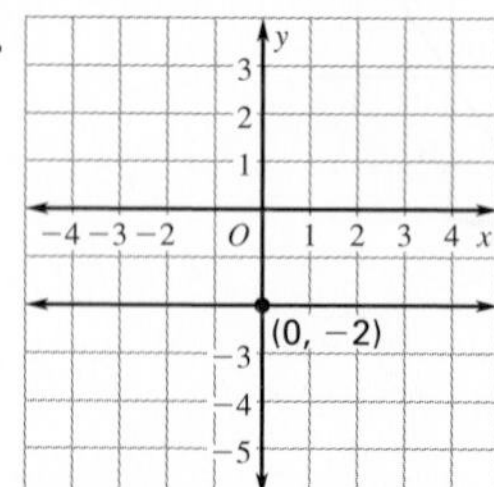

17.

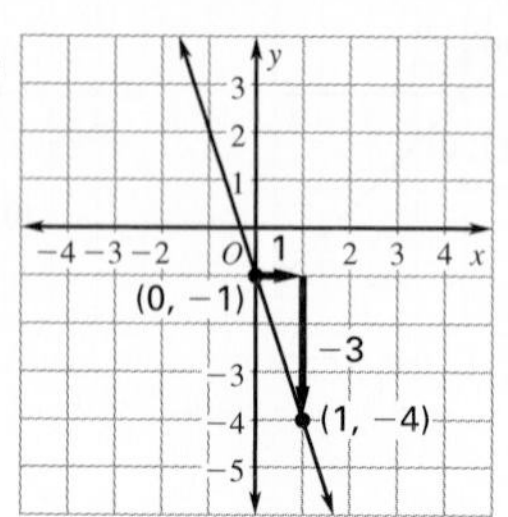

18.

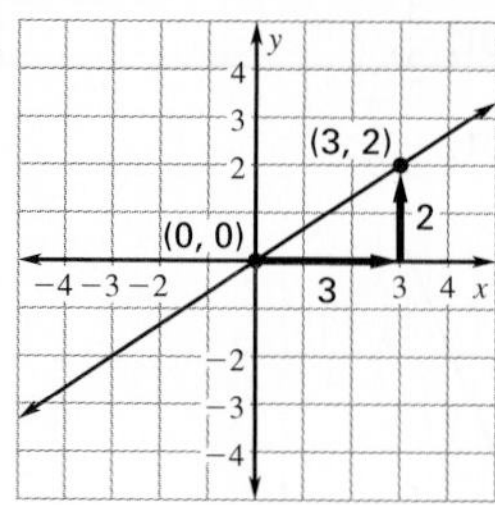

19.

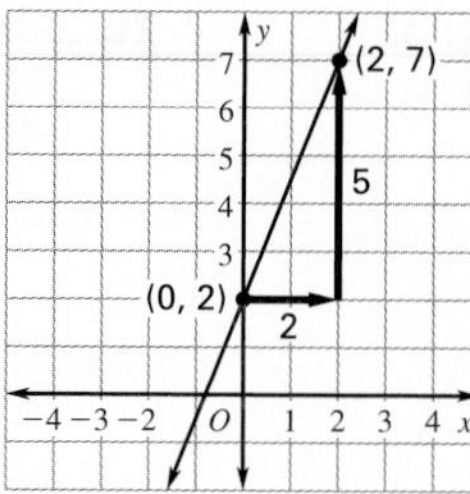

33a. Let $x = 0$:

$y = mx + b$
$y = m(0) + b$
$y = b$

$(0, b)$ is on the graph.

Let $x = 1$:

$y = mx + b$
$y = m(1) + b$
$y = m + b$

$(1, m + b)$ is on the graph.

8.5 Standardized Test Practice (p. 417)

47.

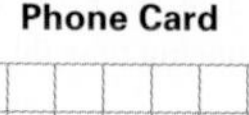

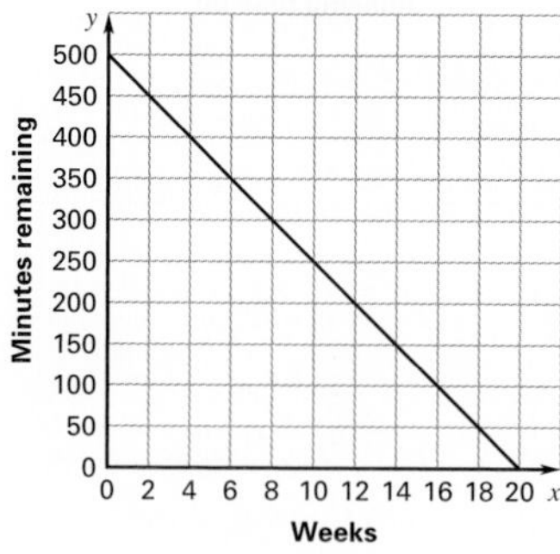

Mid-Chapter Quiz (p. 418)

1.

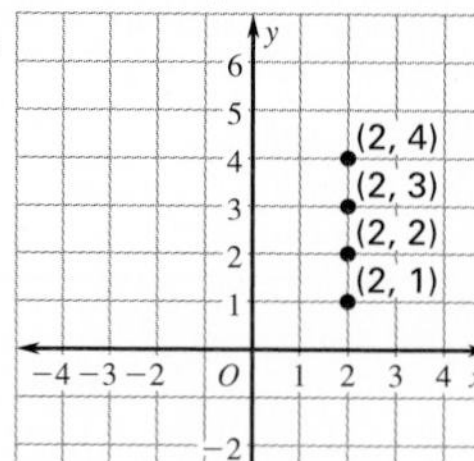

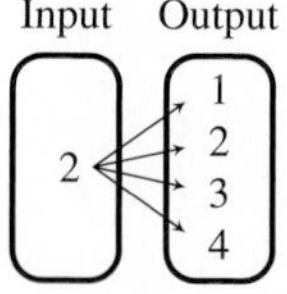

2.

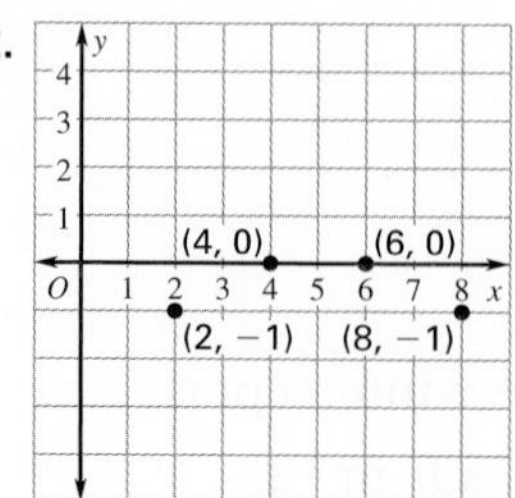

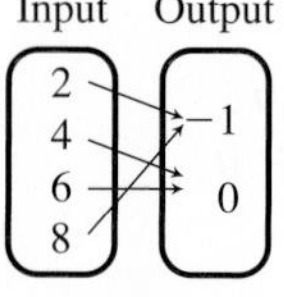

3. 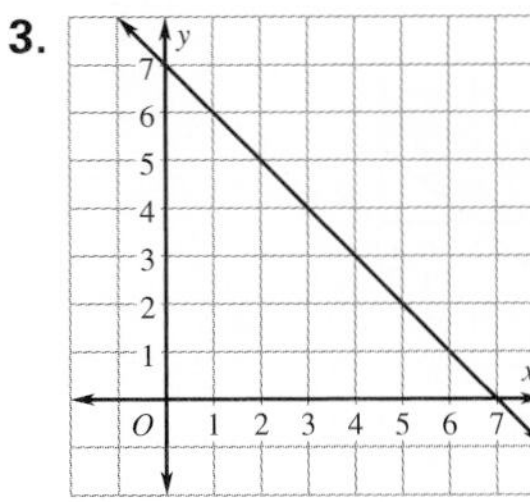

4. 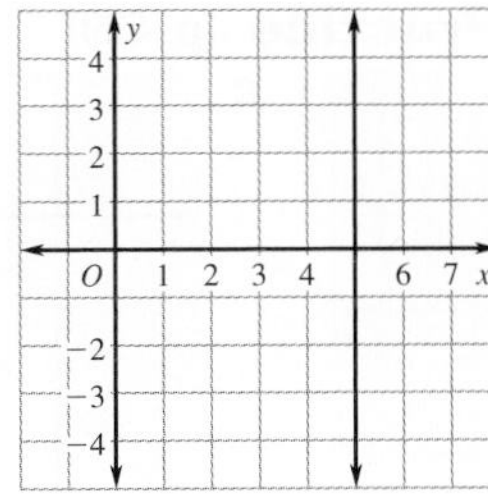

5. 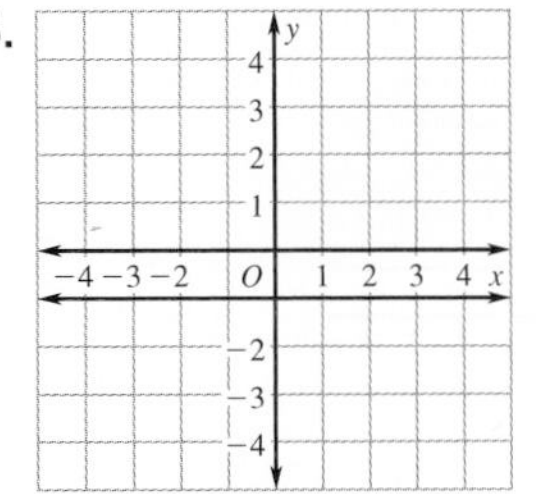

6. 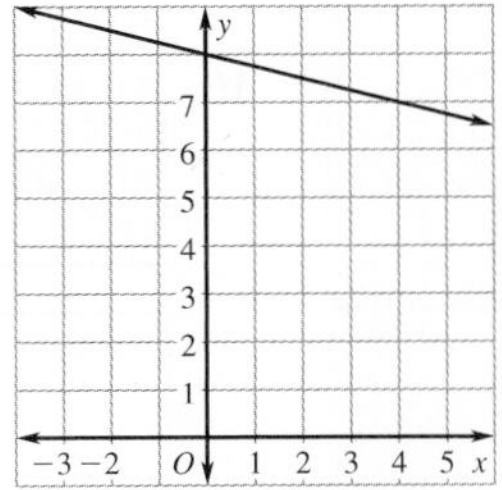

7. 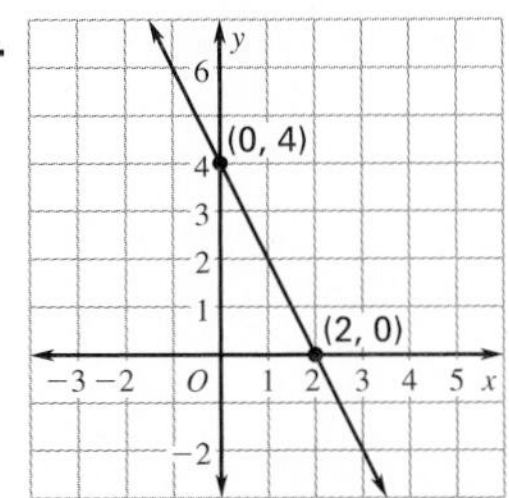

8. 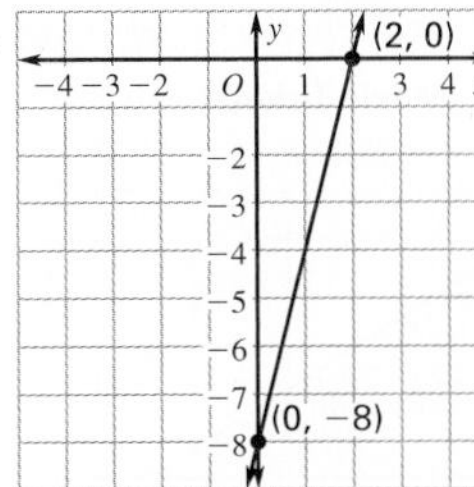

9. 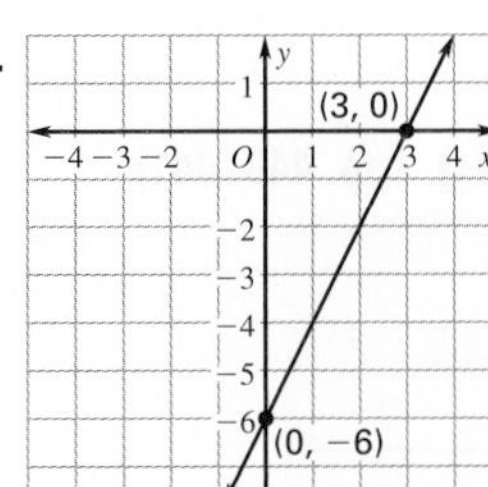

8.6 Practice and Problem Solving (pp. 423–424)

32a. 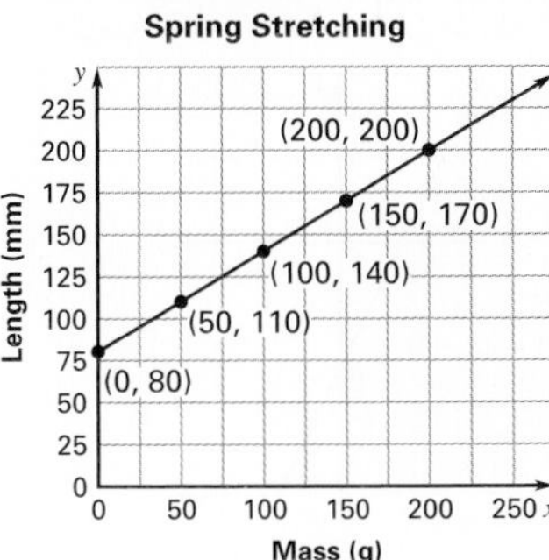

33a. 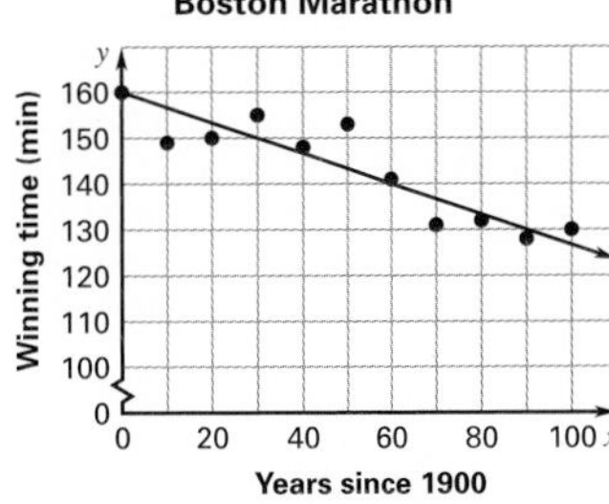

34. $y = \frac{3}{2}x - 4$. *Sample answer:* First I used the points to find the slope: $m = \frac{5 - (-1)}{6 - 2} = \frac{3}{2}$. Then I substituted the slope and the x- and y-values from the point $(2, -1)$ in the slope-intercept equation $y = mx + b$ and solved for b to find the y-intercept: $-1 = \frac{3}{2}(2) + b$, $-1 = 3 + b$, $-4 = b$. Finally, I substituted the values of m and b in the equation $y = mx + b$: $y = \frac{3}{2}x - 4$.

8.6 Mixed Review (p. 424)

43. 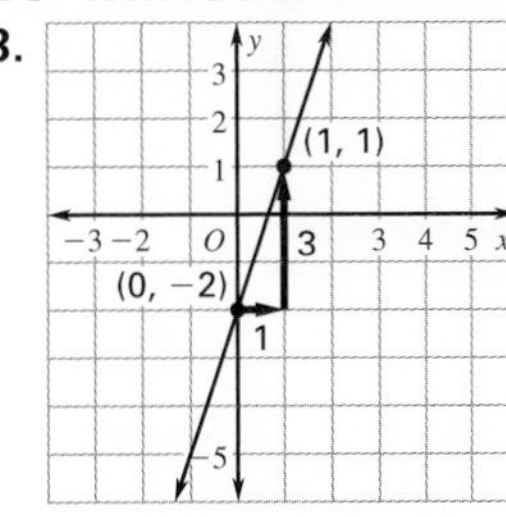

44. 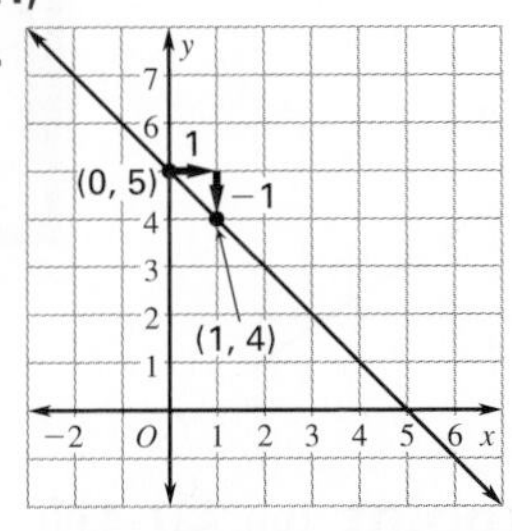

45. 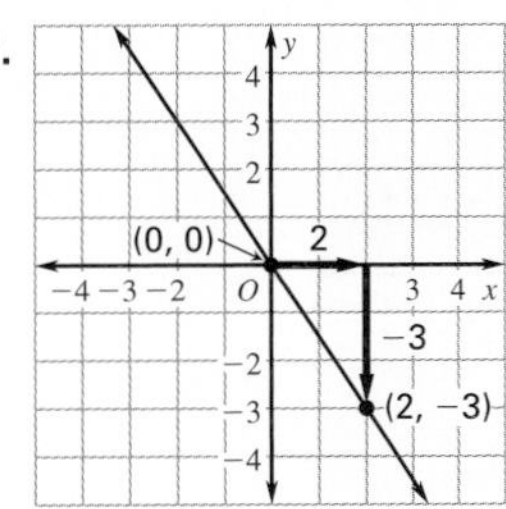

46. 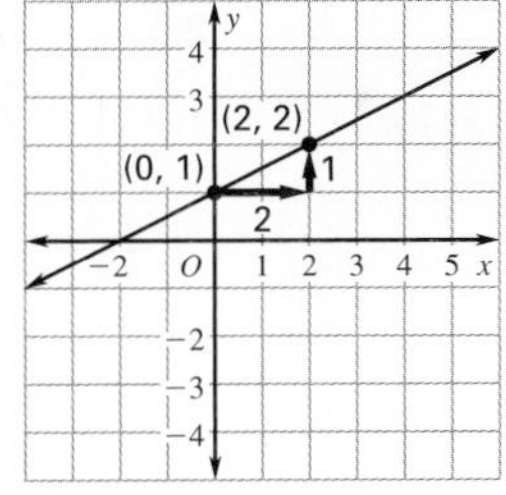

8.7 Checkpoint (p. 427)

4. 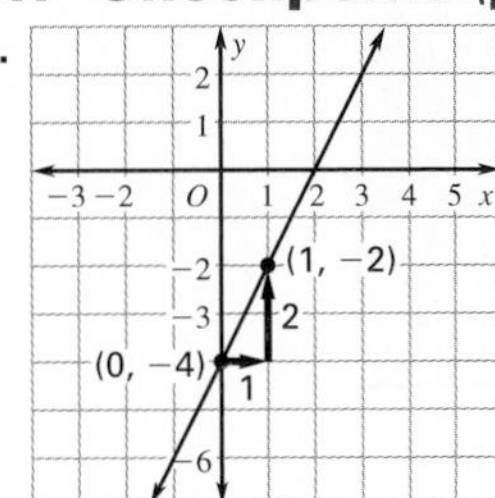

5. 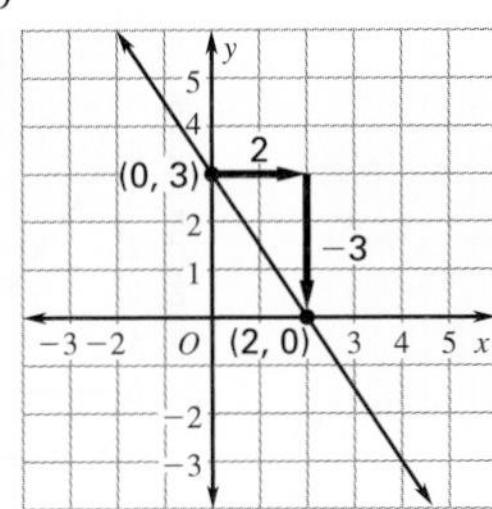

Additional Answers

6.

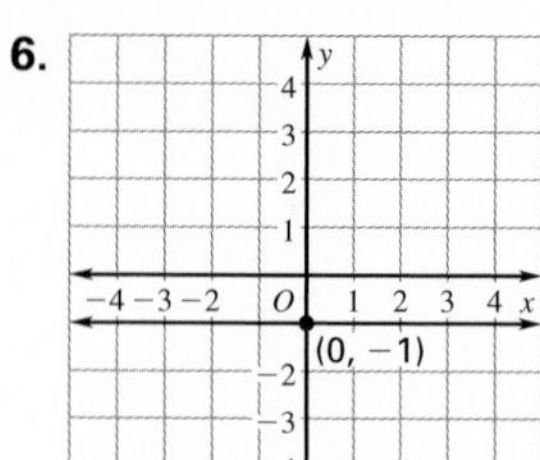

8.7 Practice and Problem Solving (pp. 429–430)

20.

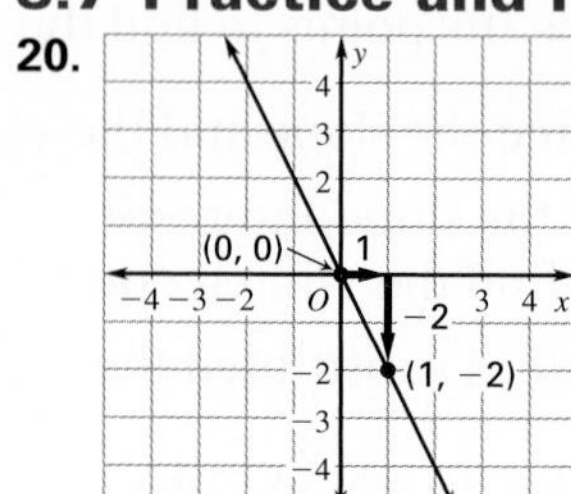

21.

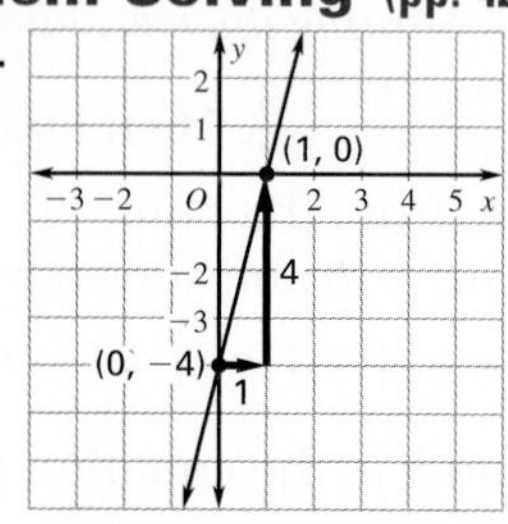

22.

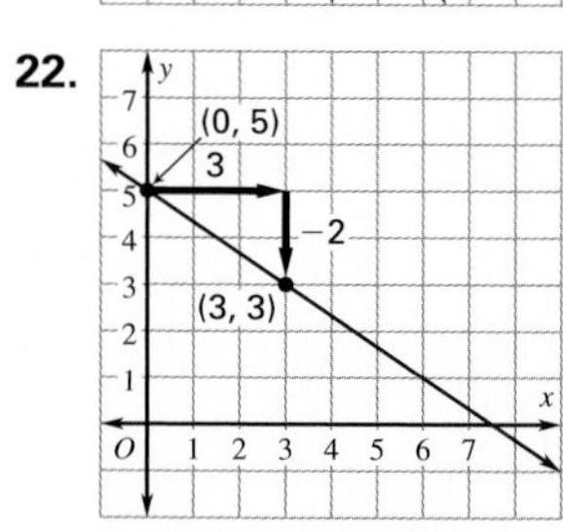

30a.

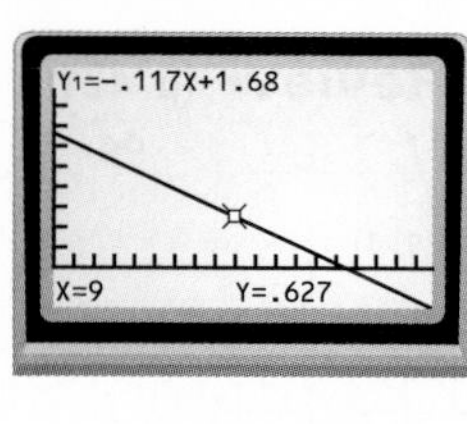

8.9 Checkpoint (pp. 437–438)

1.

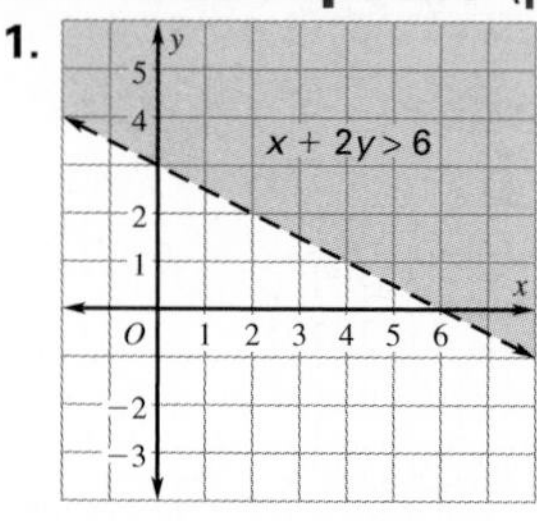

2.

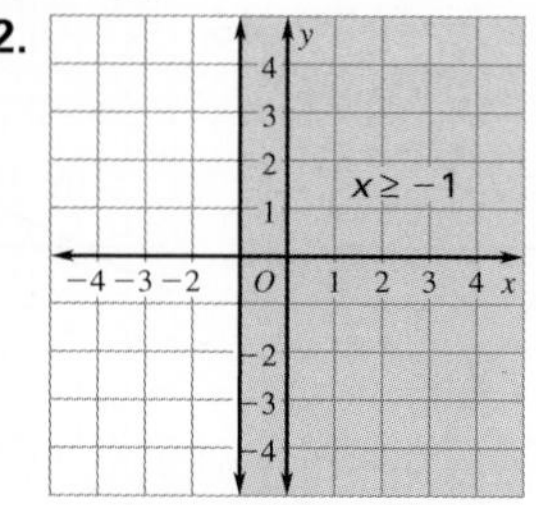

3.

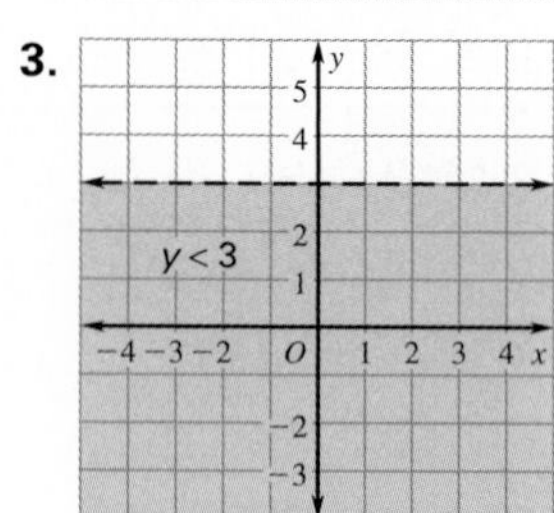

4.

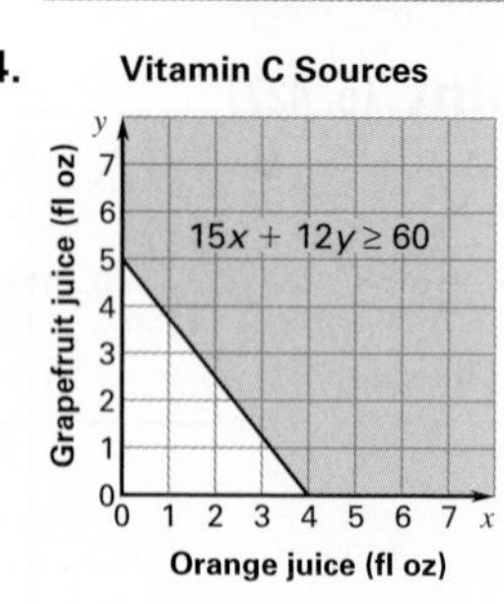

8.9 Guided Practice (p. 439)

7.

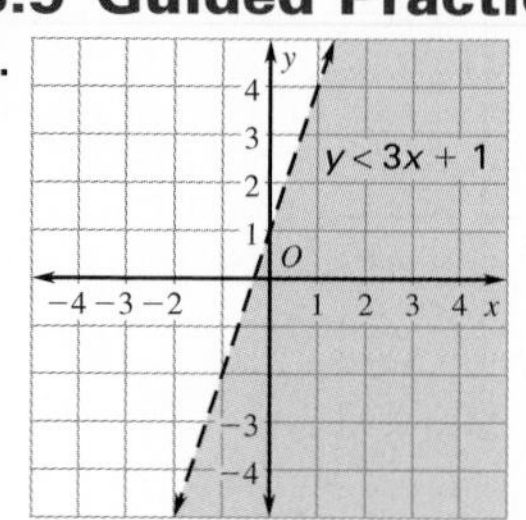

8.

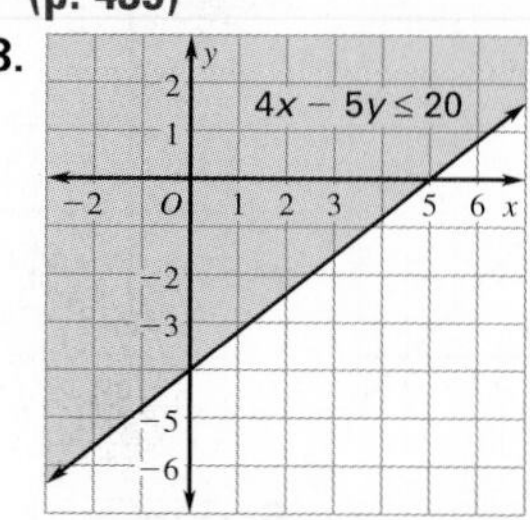

9.

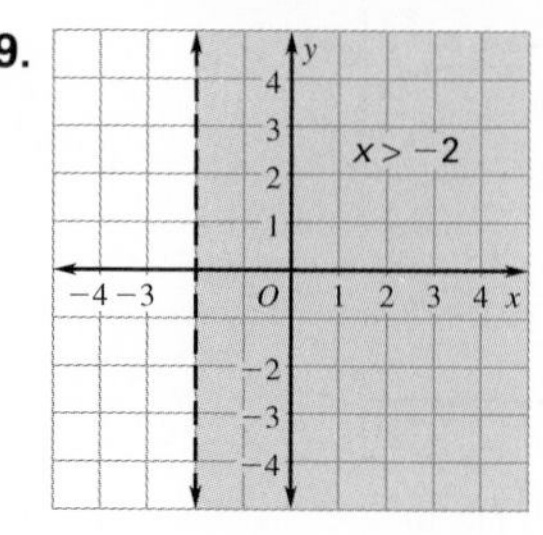

10.

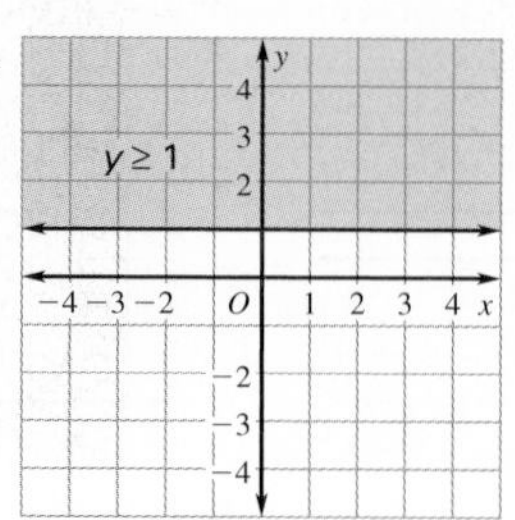

11. Step 2:

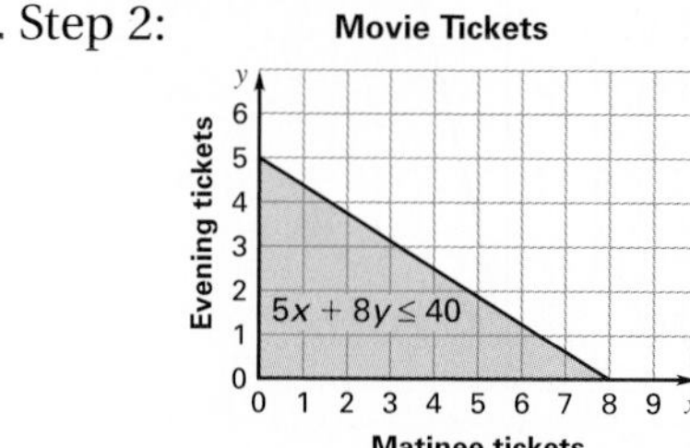

8.9 Practice and Problem Solving (pp. 440–441)

20.

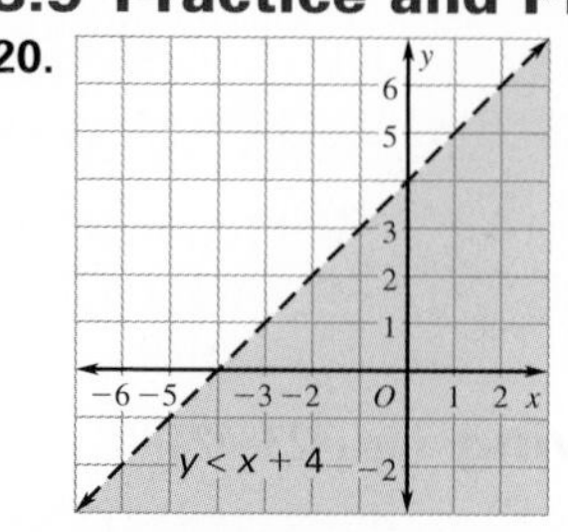

21.

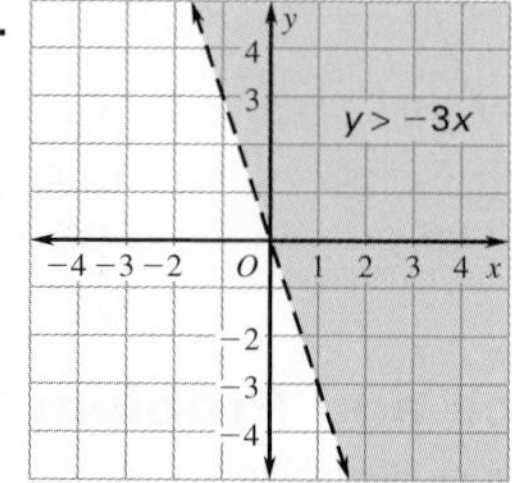

22.

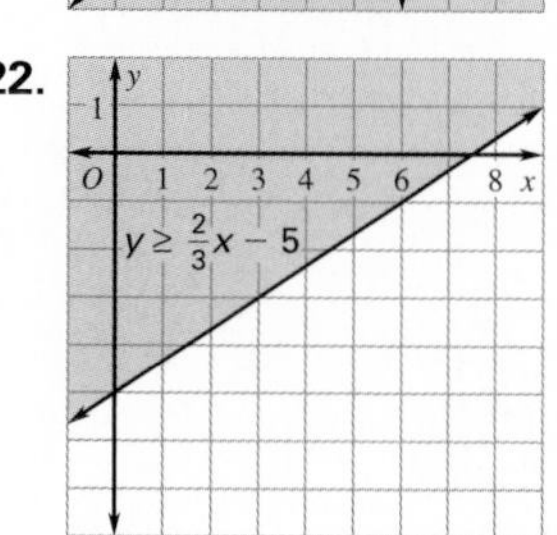

23.

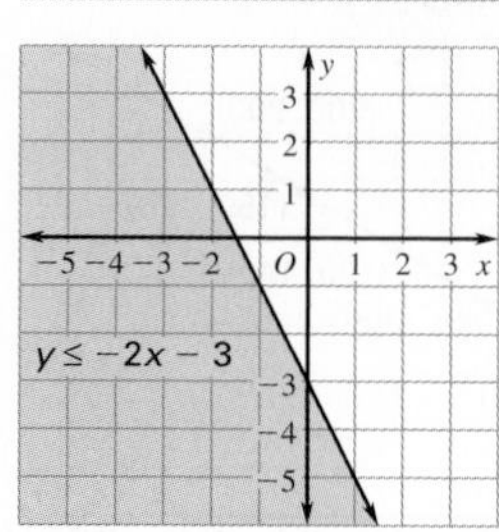

Additional Answers

24.

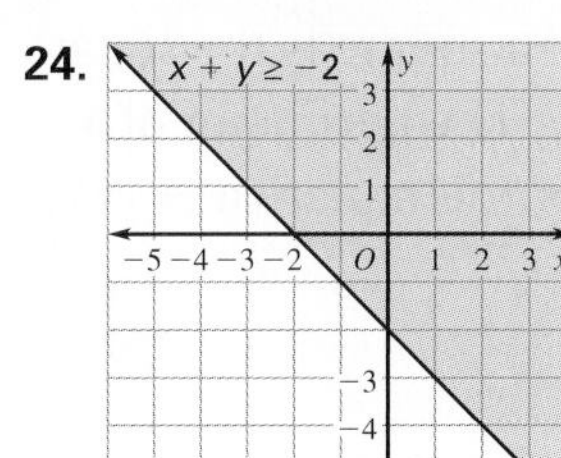

25.

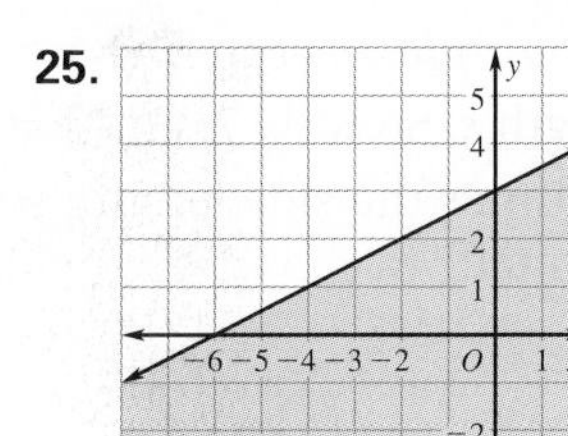

26.

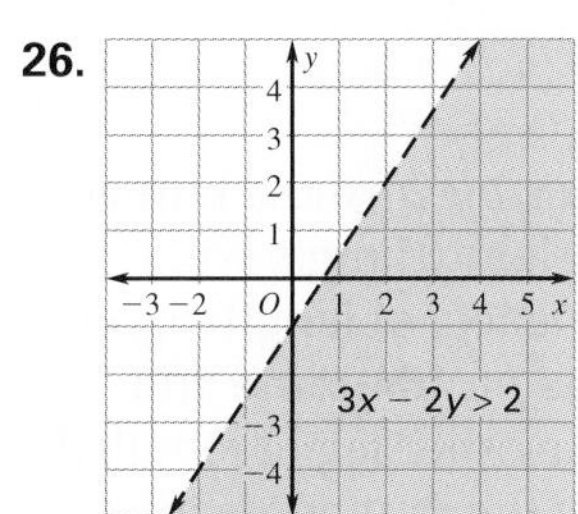

27.

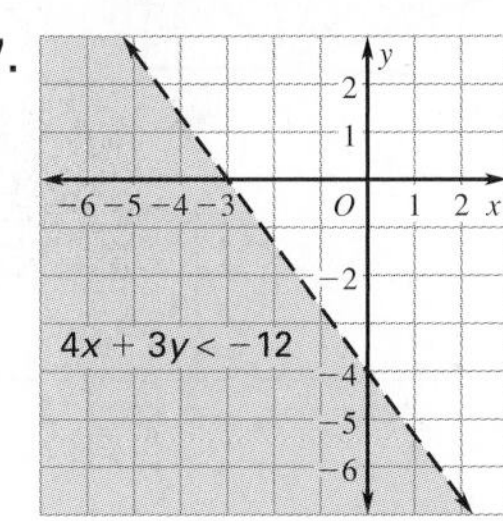

28.

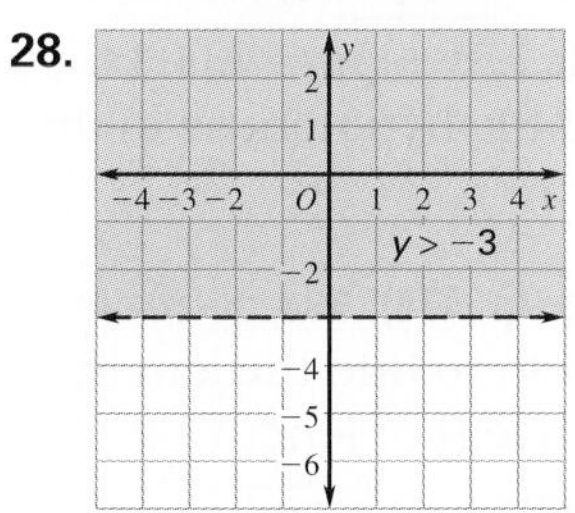

29.

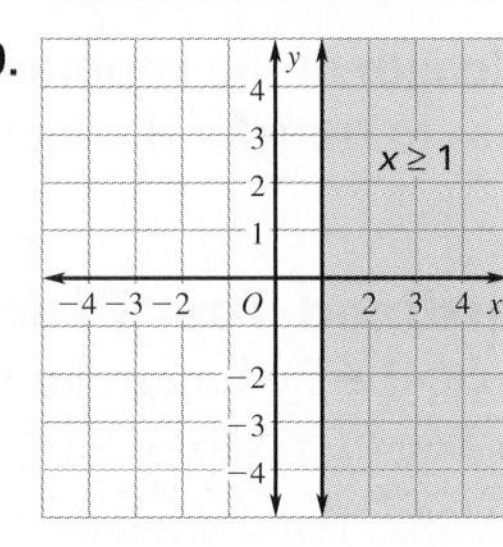

30.

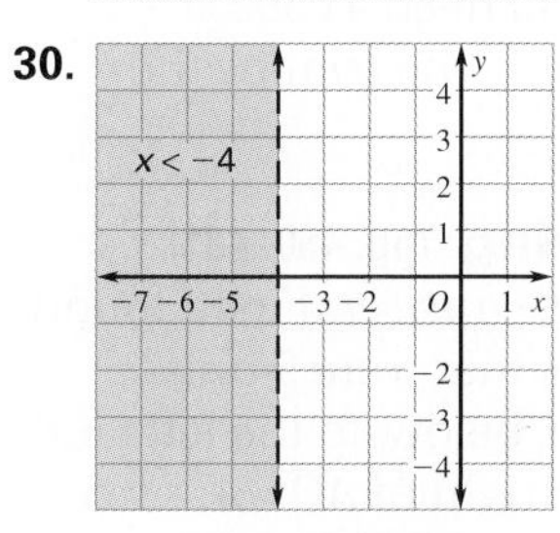

31.

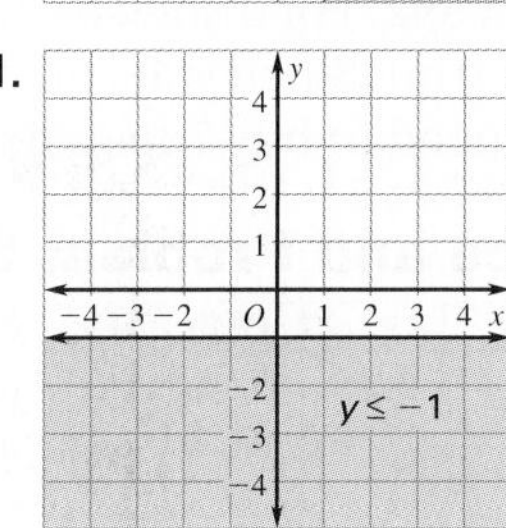

36.

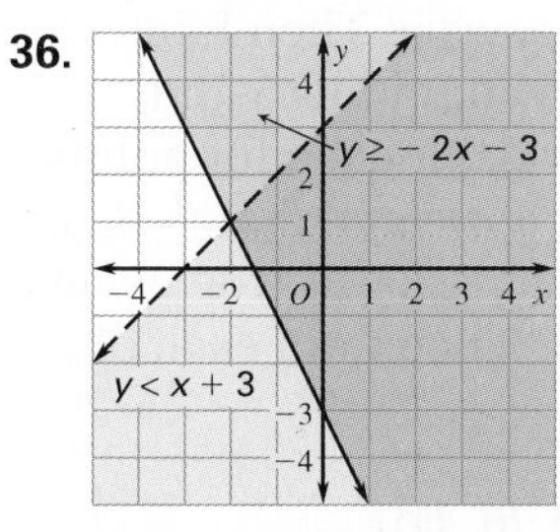

Chapter Test (p. 446)

1.

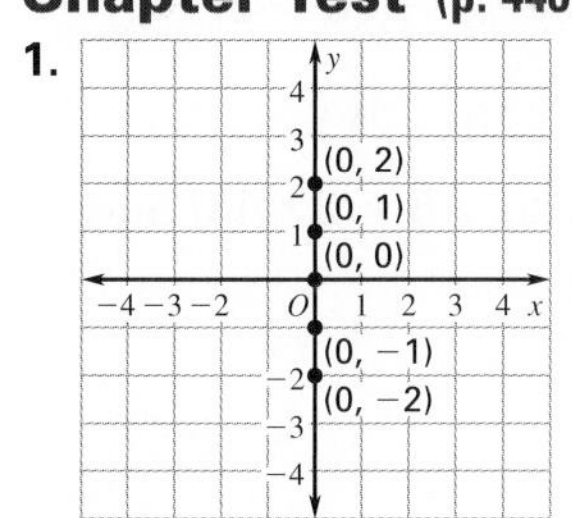

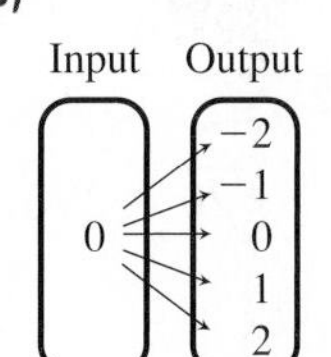

No; the input 0 is paired with five outputs, −2, −1, 0, 1, and 2.

2.

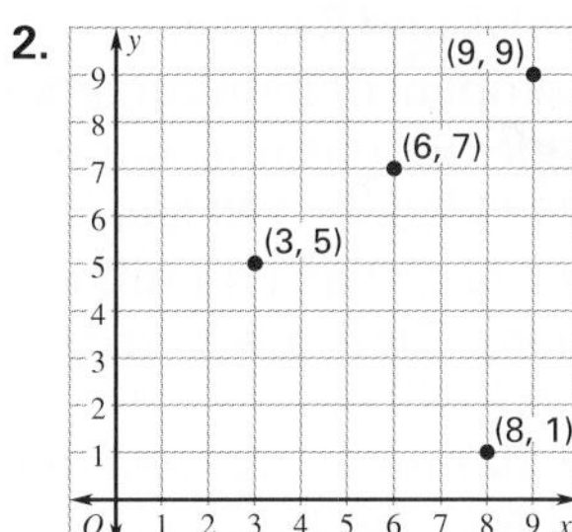

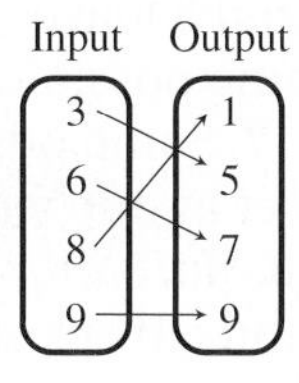

Yes; every input is paired with exactly one output.

13.

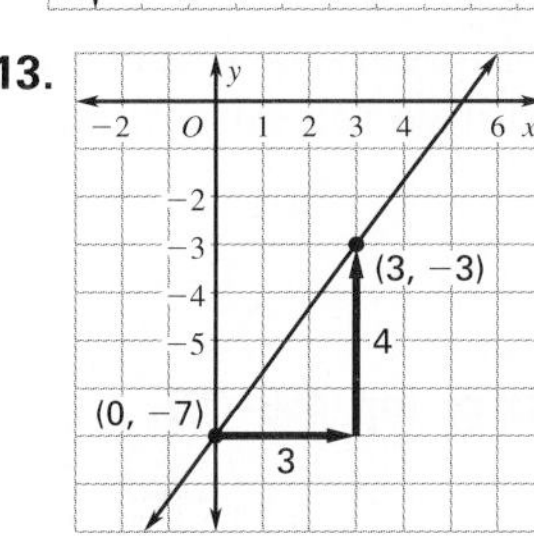

14.

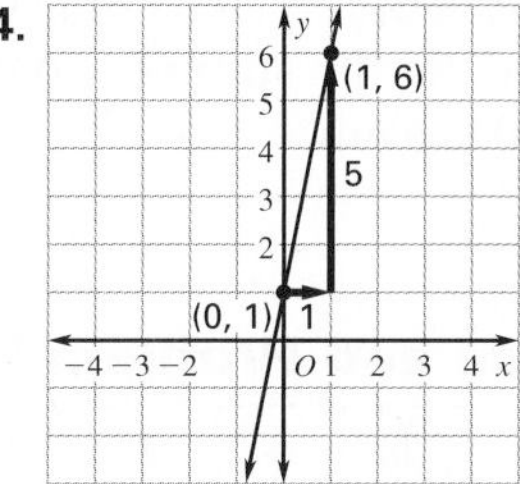

15.

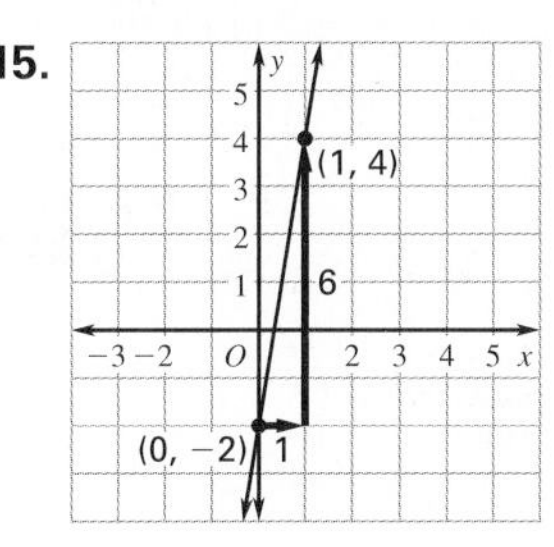

16.

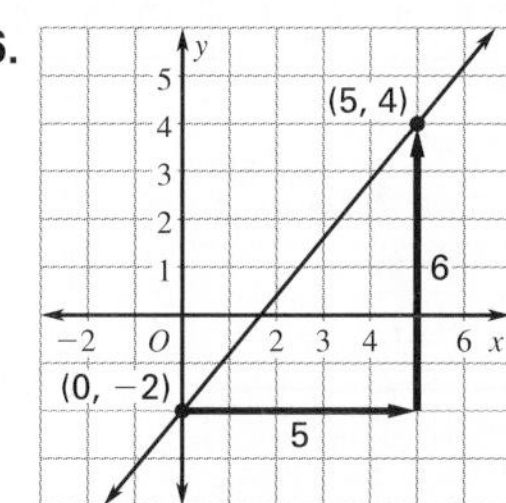

17a.

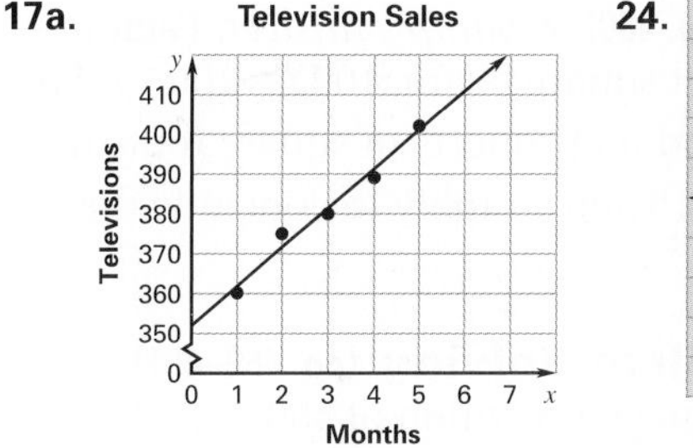

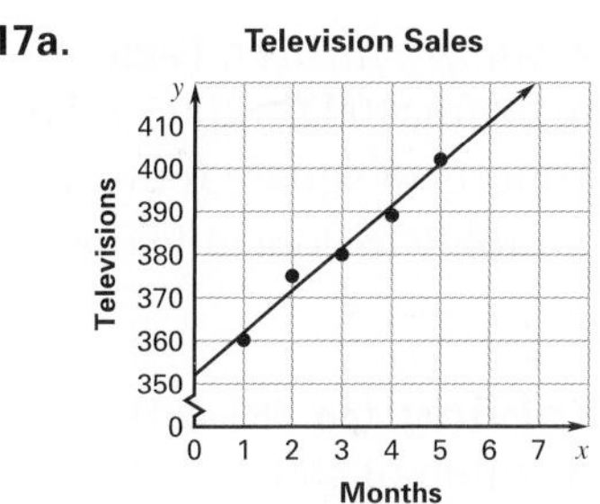

24.

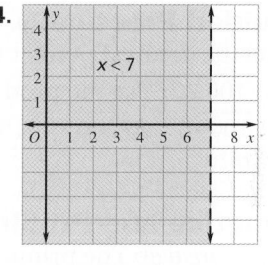

25.

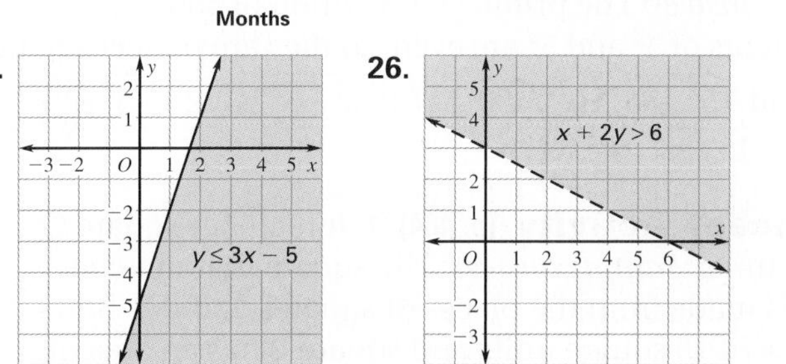

26.

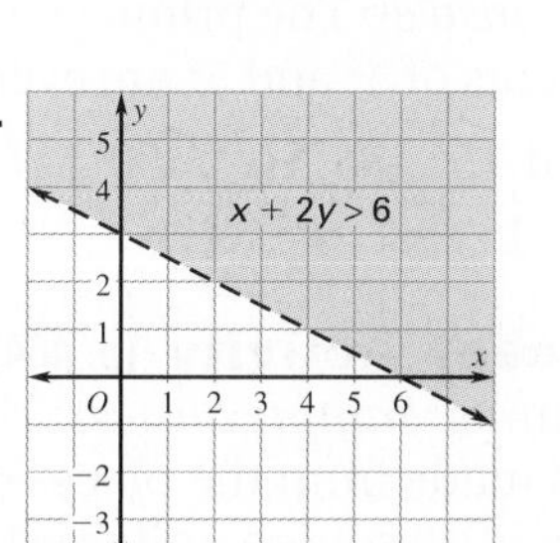

Focus on Problem Solving (p. 449)

4. *Sample:*

16	17	12
11	15	19
18	13	14

5. *Sample answer:* 6 pies and 3 loaves, 4 pies and 6 loaves, 2 pies and 9 loaves **6.** Some possible numbers of hamburgers eaten are 19, 43, and 67. **7.** Some possible dimensions of the swimming pool are 150 feet by 100 feet, 125 feet by 120 feet, and 200 feet by 75 feet. **8.** No. *Sample answer:* Each domino must cover a red square and a black square. There are 32 red squares and only 30 black squares, so there will be two red squares left over for any placement of 30 dominoes. No two red squares are adjacent, so there is no solution. **9a.** No solution. *Sample answer:* For any two consecutive integers, one is even and one is odd. So the sum of two consecutive integers must be odd, but 20 is even.

Chapter 9

9.1 Practice and Problem Solving (pp. 456–457)

66a.

x	0	1	4	9	16	25
y	0	1	2	3	4	5

66b.

9.2 Guided Practice (p. 460)

2. *Sample answer:* Factor 700 using the greatest perfect square factor, 100, as $100 \cdot 7$. So, $\sqrt{700} = \sqrt{100 \cdot 7}$. Use the product property of square roots to rewrite $\sqrt{100 \cdot 7}$ as $\sqrt{100} \cdot \sqrt{7}$. Then simplify to conclude that $\sqrt{700} = 10\sqrt{7}$.

9.2 Practice and Problem Solving (pp. 460–461)

28. *Sample answer:* The prime factorization of 450 is $2 \cdot 3^2 \cdot 5^2$. The exponents of 3^2 and 5^2 are even, so they are perfect squares: $\sqrt{3^2} = 3$ and $\sqrt{5^2} = 5$. So, $\sqrt{450} = \sqrt{2 \cdot 3^2 \cdot 5^2} = \sqrt{2} \cdot \sqrt{3^2} \cdot \sqrt{5^2} = \sqrt{2} \cdot 3 \cdot 5 = 15\sqrt{2}$.

9.3 Concept Activity (p. 464)

1. It matches square C; 25 square units. *Sample answer:* The square that matches square C is made from the pieces of squares A and B. Square A has an area of 16 square units and square B has an area of 9 square units, so the sum of their areas is $16 + 9 = 25$ square units. **2.** 5 units. *Sample answer:* The area A of a square is $A = s^2$. So $25 = s^2$, and $s = \sqrt{25} = 5$ units.

9.4 Practice and Problem Solving (pp. 473–474)

31. Never. *Sample answer:* Any whole number can be written as the quotient of itself and 1, so a whole number is a rational number.

32. Irrational. *Sample answer:* The area of a square is the square of the side length s. So, $s^2 = 7$, and $s = \sqrt{7}$. The perimeter of a square is four times the side length, so for this square it is $4\sqrt{7}$, which is irrational.

42a–b.

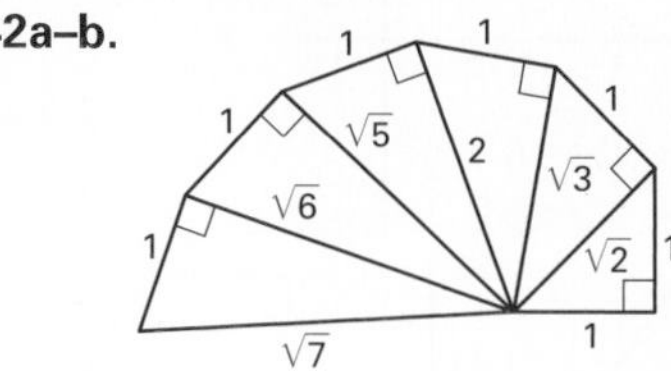

43. *Sample:*

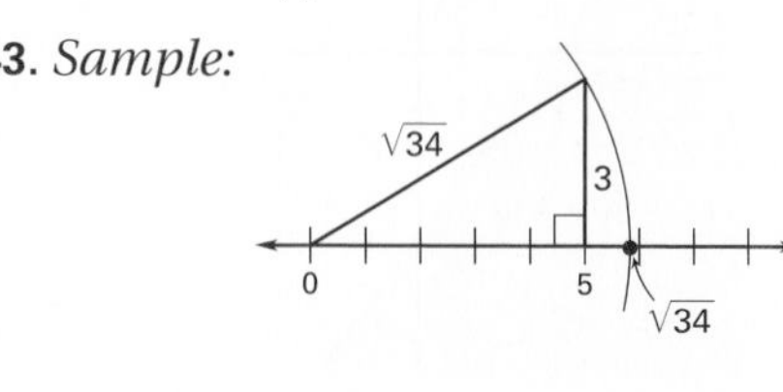

Sample answer: I drew a right triangle with one leg, of length 5, on the number line and the other leg of length 3. By the Pythagorean theorem, the length of the hypotenuse is $\sqrt{5^2 + 3^2} = \sqrt{34}$. I then used a compass to transfer the length of the hypotenuse to the number line.

9.4 Standardized Test Practice (p. 474)

53a. *Sample answer:* First use the Pythagorean theorem to find the length of the hypotenuse of a right triangle with legs of length 14: $\sqrt{14^2 + 14^2} = \sqrt{392}$. For 4 shelves, you will need $4\sqrt{392} \approx 79.2$ inches of trim. Since you can only buy the trim by the foot, you will need to buy 7 feet of trim.

9.5 Practice and Problem Solving (pp. 480–481)

54. *Sample:*

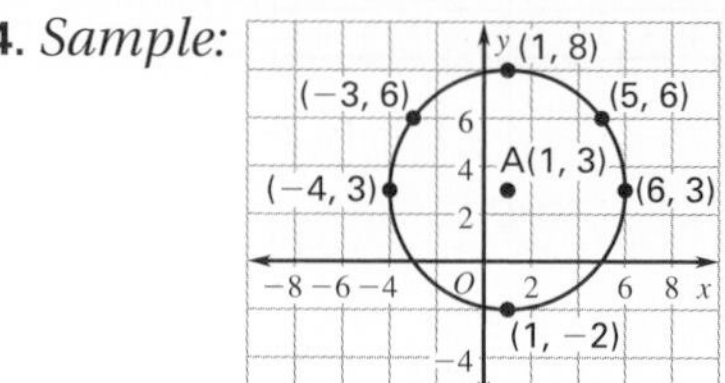

Sample answer: First I found points that were 5 units above, below, to the left, and to the right of $A(1, 3)$, since this was easy. Then I drew a circle with radius 5 and center A. I looked for points with integer coordinates on the circle. It appeared that $(-3, 6)$ and $(5, 6)$ were on the circle. I verified that this was true using the distance formula to show that the distance from each of these points to A was 5 units.

9.5 Standardized Test Practice (p. 481)

63. $M = \left(\frac{1+9}{2}, \frac{2+6}{2}\right) = (5, 4)$; $AB = \sqrt{(9-1)^2 + (6-2)^2} = \sqrt{80} = 4\sqrt{5}$; $AM = \sqrt{(5-1)^2 + (4-2)^2} = \sqrt{20} = 2\sqrt{5}$; $MB = \sqrt{(9-5)^2 + (6-4)^2} = \sqrt{20} = 2\sqrt{5}$; so, $AB = 2 \cdot AM$ and $AB = 2 \cdot MB$.

9.6 Practice and Problem Solving (pp. 486–487)

14. *Sample answer:* Corresponding angles are congruent, and the ratios of the lengths of corresponding sides are equal. For example, if the ratio of the lengths of a pair of corresponding legs is $\frac{a}{b}$, then the ratio of the lengths of the other pair of corresponding legs is also $\frac{a}{b}$ since the legs of a 45°-45°-90° triangle are congruent. Also, the ratio of the lengths of the corresponding hypotenuses is $\frac{a\sqrt{2}}{b\sqrt{2}} = \frac{a}{b}$.

9.7 Concept Activity (p. 488)

2. On the measure of the angle. *Sample answer:* All right triangles with a given acute angle are similar, so the ratio of the lengths of the corresponding sides will always be equal no matter the size of the triangle.

9.8 Practice and Problem Solving (pp. 497–498)

27. *Sample answer:* (1) Use the Pythagorean theorem to write the equation $28^2 + b^2 = 35^2$ and then solve to find that $b = 21$. (2) Use the tangent ratio to write the equation $\tan 37° = \frac{b}{28}$ and solve. (3) Use the sine ratio to write the equation $\sin 37° = \frac{b}{35}$ and solve. (4) Find $m\angle A$: $m\angle A = 90 - 37 = 53°$. Then use the cosine ratio to write the equation $\cos 53° = \frac{b}{35}$ and solve.

Chapter 10

10.1 Practice and Problem Solving (pp. 514–515)

24b. 3 dowels. *Sample answer:* By the Pythagorean theorem, each of the shorter sides has a length of $\sqrt{15^2 + 7.25^2} \approx$ 16.66 inches. Since each dowel is 50 inches long, and $50 \div 3 \approx 16.67$, you can cut 3 pieces from each dowel. Each of the cloth triangles has two of the shorter sides, so there are eight altogether. Since 3 dowels can be cut into a total of 9 pieces, that will provide enough pieces for the kite. **25.** Yes. *Sample answer:* There are two possibilities as shown in the diagram, depending on whether 5 centimeters is the length of one of the congruent sides or the length of the other side.

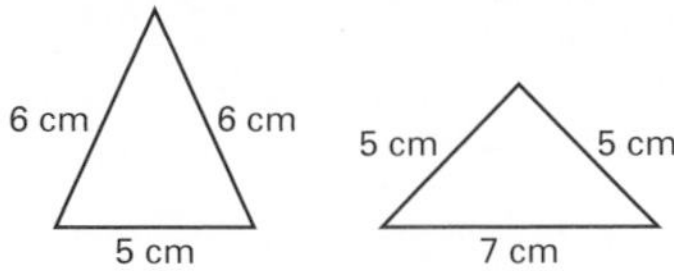

27.

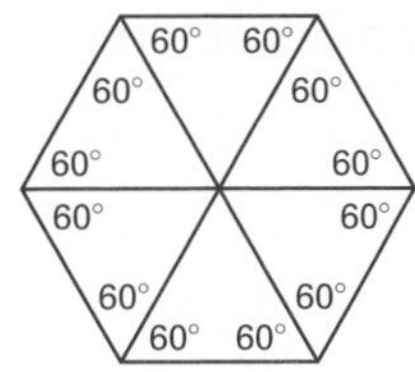

720°. *Sample answer:* Each angle of an equilateral triangle measures 60°. Each angle of the hexagon is made of two of these 60° angles, so its measure is 120°. Since there are six of these 120° angles in the hexagon, the sum of their measures is 6 • 120° = 720°.

10.2 Practice and Problem Solving (pp. 519–520)

24. $m\angle WXY = 135°$, $m\angle XYZ = 120°$. *Sample answer:* The smaller angle that forms part of $\angle WXY$ has a measure of 45° because the sum of the measures of the angles in a triangle is 180°, and $180° - (90° + 45°) = 45°$. Similarly, the smaller angle that forms part of $\angle XYZ$ has a measure of 30° because $180° - (90° + 60°) = 30°$. Let $a°$ represent the measure of each of the congruent angles marked. Then because the sum of the measures of the angles in a convex quadrilateral is 360°, $45° + 45° + a° + a° + 30° + 60° = 360°$, so $2a + 180 = 360$, and $a = 90$. Then $m\angle WXY = 45° + 90° = 135°$, and $m\angle XYZ = 30° + 90° = 120°$.

10.2 Standardized Test Practice (p. 520)

30a–b. *Sample:*

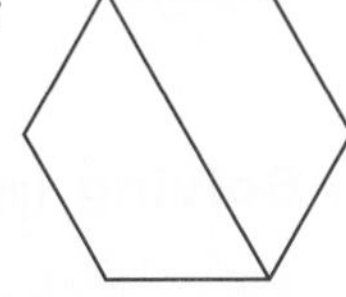

10.2 Brain Game (p. 520)

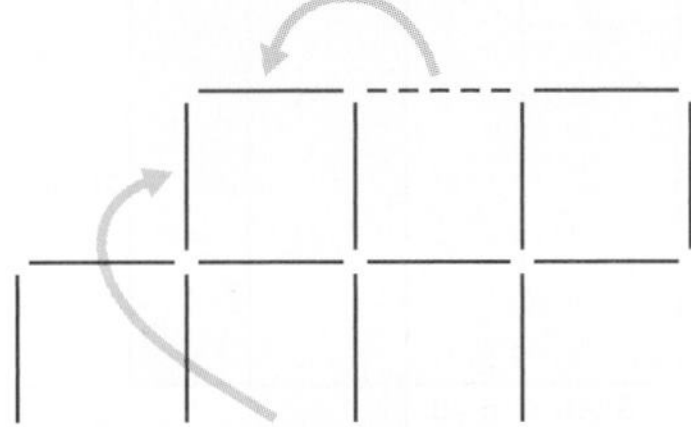

10.5 Concept Activity (p. 537)

1. *Sample answer:* Measure the dimensions of the front, one side, and the top; use the formula for the area of a rectangle to find the area of each; add the areas; and multiply the result by 2, since the back and front have the same area, the top and bottom have the same area, and the sides have the same area.

2. *Sample answer:* It is a rectangle with congruent circles attached to opposite sides.

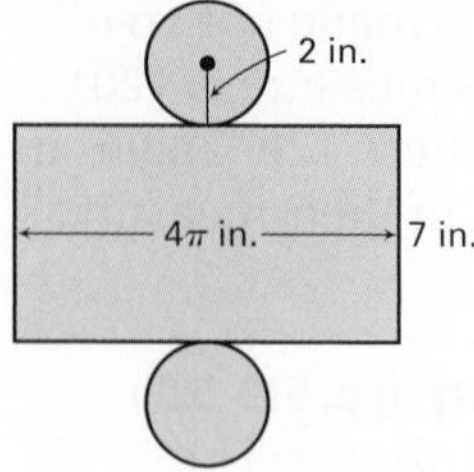

About 113 in.^{2}; the area of the top and bottom can be found by finding the areas of the two circles in the net, each of which has an area of $\pi(2^2) = 4\pi$. The rectangle represents the side. Its width is the height of the cylinder, and its length is the circumference of the cylinder, so its area is $7(4\pi) = 28\pi$. The total surface area is $4\pi + 4\pi + 28\pi = 36\pi$ square inches.

10.5 Guided Practice (p. 541)

4. *Sample:*

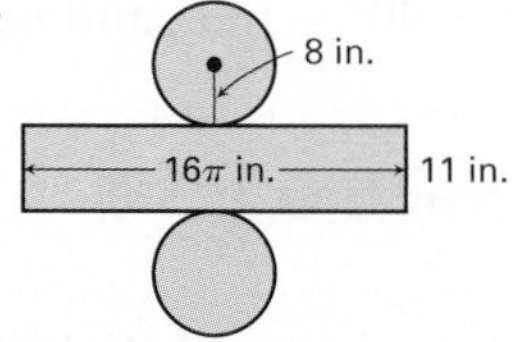

10.5 Practice and Problem Solving (pp. 541–543)

6–11. Sample nets are given.

6.

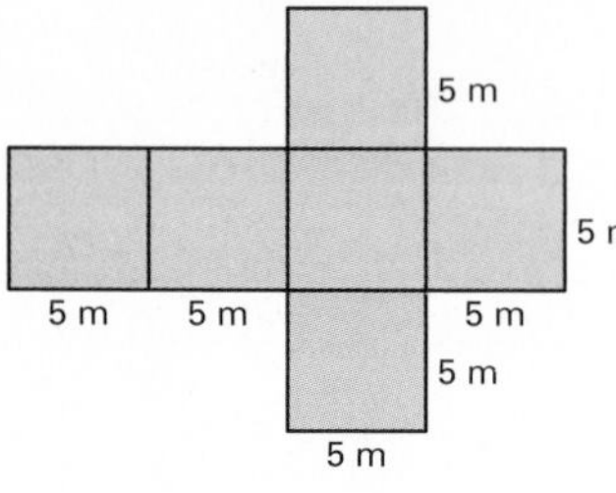

7.

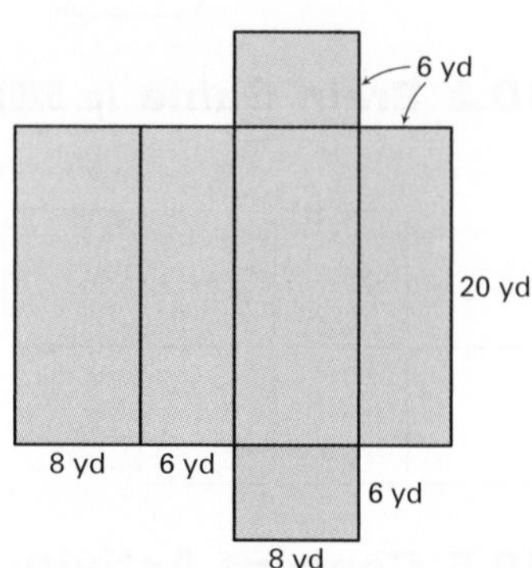

8.

18 ft
16 ft
12 ft
20 ft
12 ft

9.

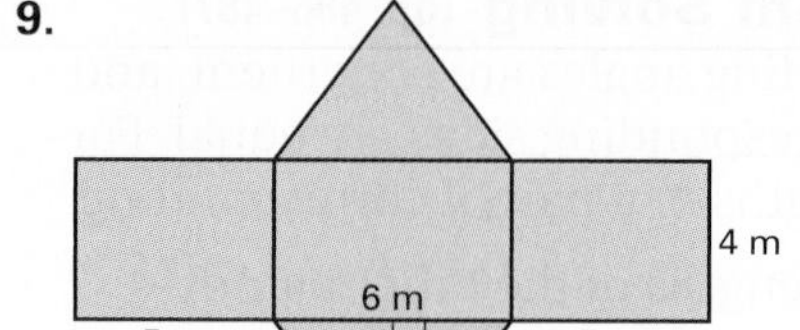

10.

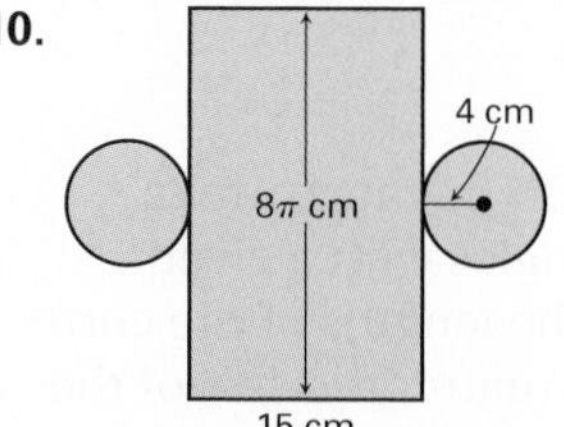

11.

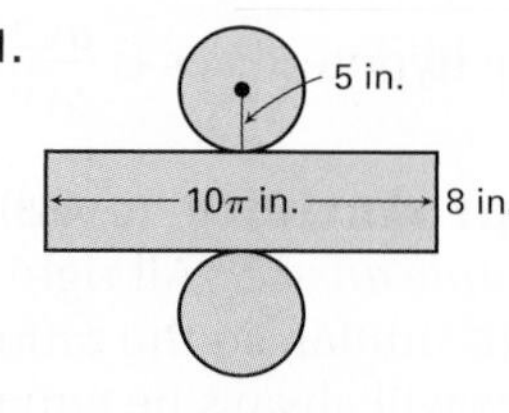

10.6 Practice and Problem Solving (pp. 547–549)

10.

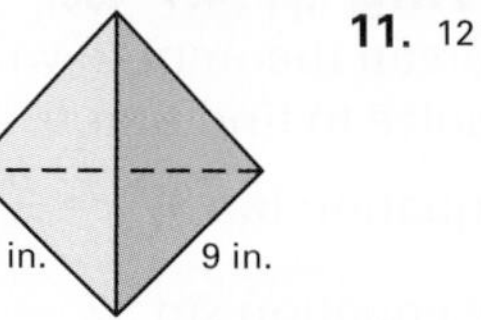

11. 12 ft

28 ft

12.

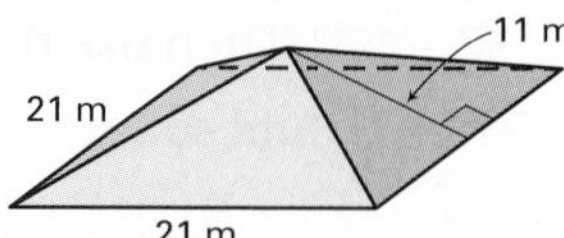

13. Slant height. *Sample answer:* A right triangle can be formed with the pyramid's height, slant height, and half the distance across the base. The pyramid's height would be a leg of the right triangle and the slant height would be the hypotenuse. Since the hypotenuse is always the longest side in a right triangle, the pyramid's slant height is greater than its height.

10.7 Practice and Problem Solving (pp. 555–556)

23.

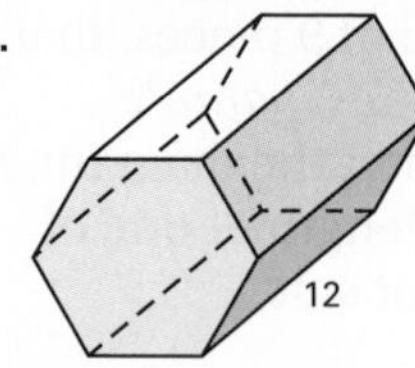

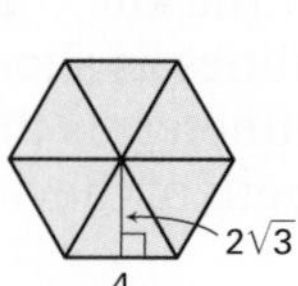

Chapter 11

11.1 Checkpoint (p. 583)

1a. *Sample answer:*

Score	Tally	Frequency
100–109	I	1
110–119	II	2
120–129	III	3
130–139	II	2
140–149	II	2
150–159	II	2
160–169	I	1
170–179	I	1
180–189		0
190–199	I	1

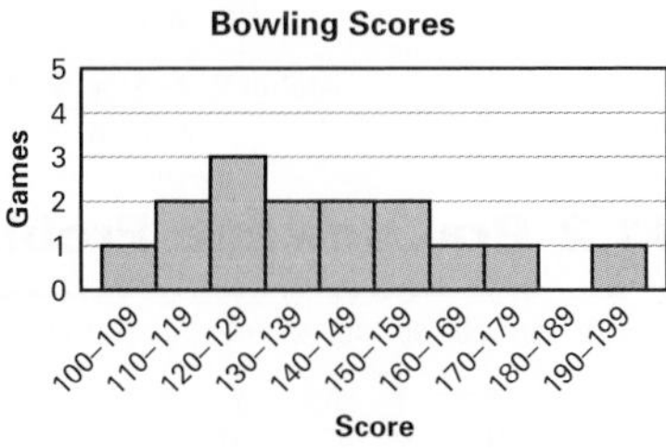

11.1 Guided Practice (p. 584)

4.

Stem	Leaves
1	1 2 6
2	
3	3 3 5
4	2 4 7
5	0 3
6	0 7
7	2 7 9
8	
9	1 8

Key: 1 | 1 = 11

5. Step 1: *Sample answer:*

Earthquakes	Tally	Frequency
5–8	IIII	4
9–12	III	3
13–16	~~IIII~~ II	7
17–20	II	2
21–24	II	2
25–28	I	1

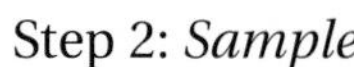
Step 2: *Sample:*

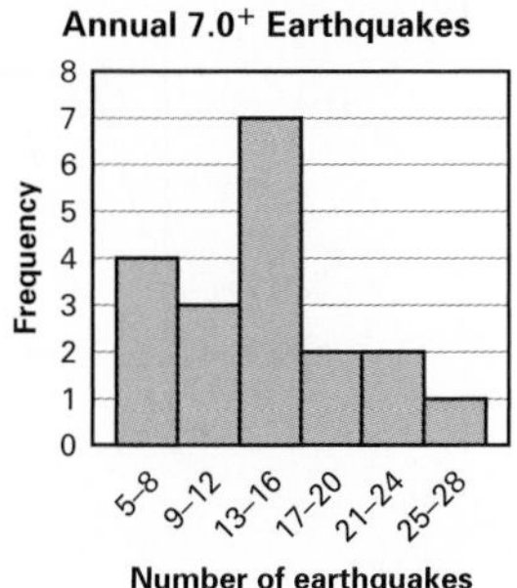

11.1 Practice and Problem Solving (pp. 584–586)

10–13. Sample answers are given.

10.

Interval	Tally	Frequency
1–3	III	3
4–6	IIII	4
7–9	~~IIII~~ I	6
10–12	IIII	4
13–15	I	1
16–18	II	2

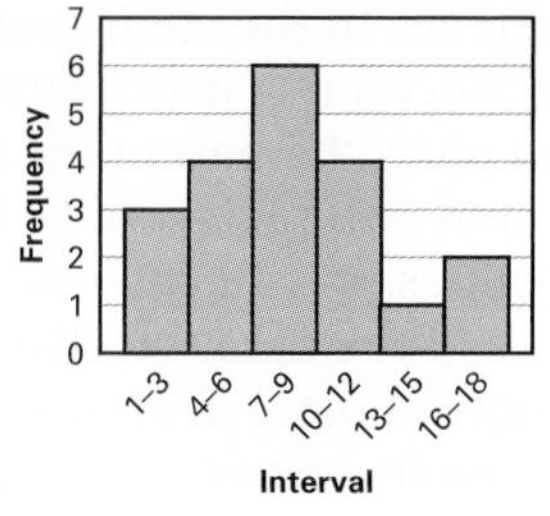

11.

Interval	Tally	Frequency
101–120	III	3
121–140	~~IIII~~ I	6
141–160	I	1
161–180		0
181–200	IIII	4

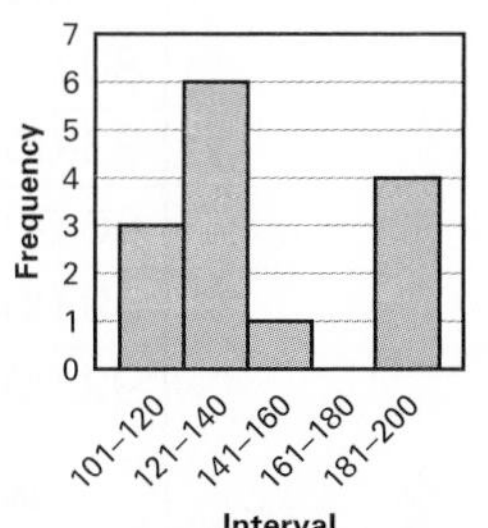

12.

Interval	Tally	Frequency
0–1999	IIII	4
2000–3999	IIII	4
4000–5999	I	1
6000–7999	II	2
8000–9999	I	1

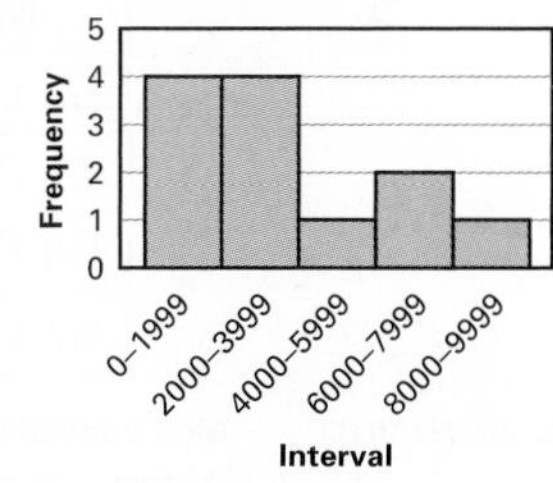

13.

Interval	Tally	Frequency
40–49	II	2
50–59	III	3
60–69	IIII	4
70–79	IIII	4
80–89	II	2
90–99	I	1

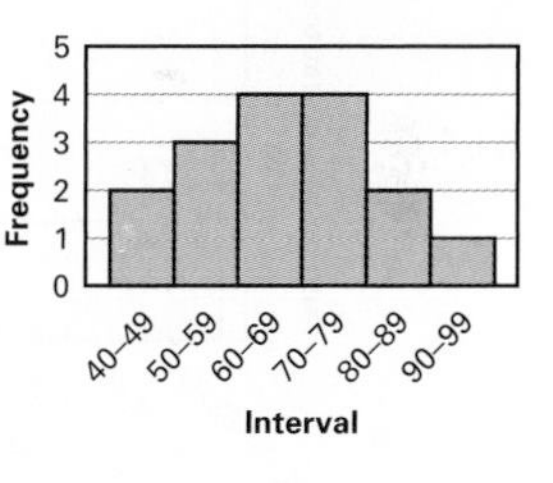

18. *Sample:*

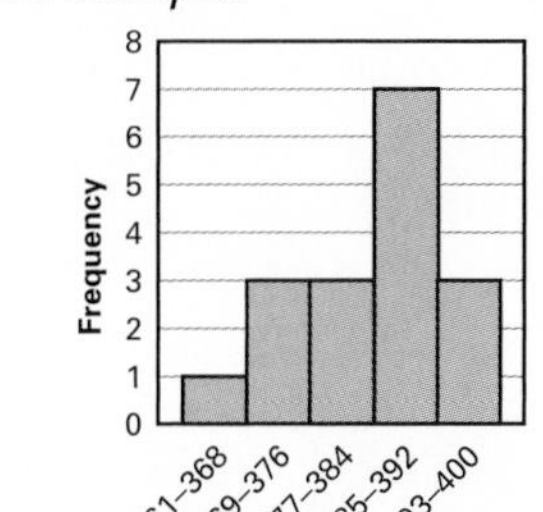

19. *Sample:*

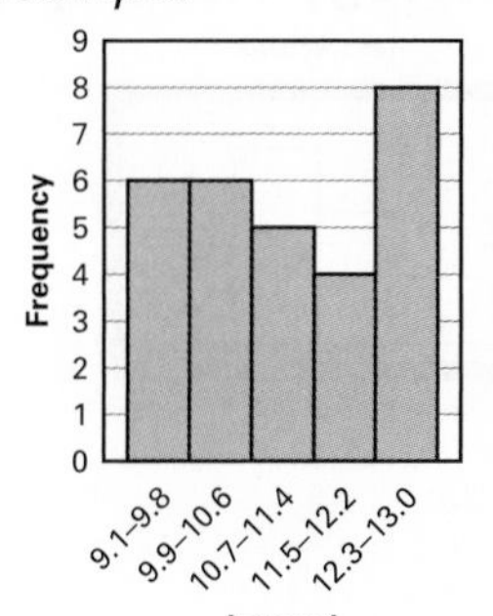

20. *Sample answer:* Stem-and-leaf plots and histograms are similar in that they both give a pictorial view of data grouped in intervals. In the stem-and-leaf plot, the stem plays the part of an interval in a histogram, and the number of leaves for a stem plays the part of the height of a bar in a histogram. Stem-and-leaf plots, unlike histograms, allow you to view all data values, so you can calculate quantities like the range and median of the data set. Histograms, on the other hand, allow you more choices in choosing appropriate intervals.

21a. *Sample answer:*

Men's Javelin Throws		
Meters	**Tally**	**Frequency**
80.00–82.99	III	3
83.00–85.99	II	2
86.00–88.99	II	2
89.00–91.99	II	2
92.00–94.99	I	1

Women's Javelin Throws		
Meters	**Tally**	**Frequency**
58.00-60.99	II	2
61.00-63.99	~~IIII~~	5
64.00-66.99	II	2
67.00-69.99	I	1

21b. *Sample:*

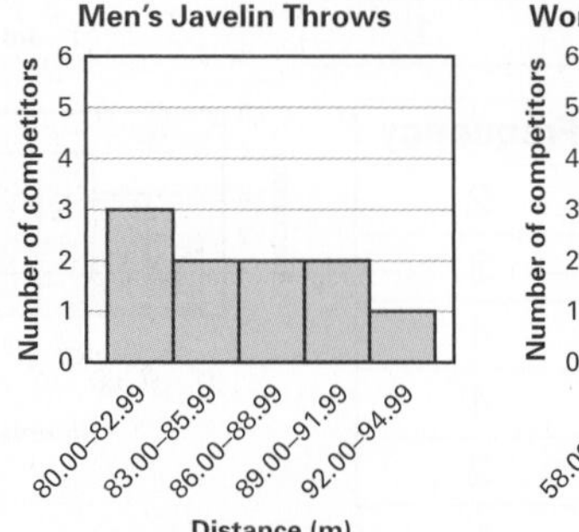

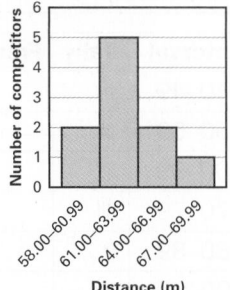

11.1 Technology Activity (p. 587)

1. *Sample:*

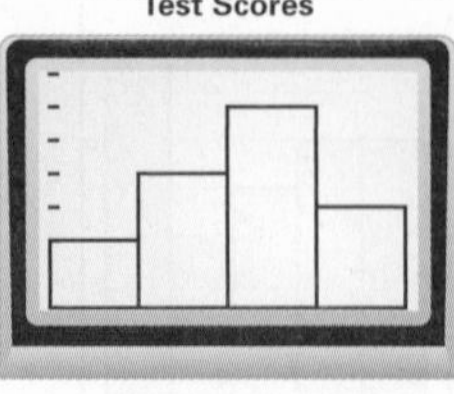

11.2 Guided Practice (p. 590)

5. Step 1:

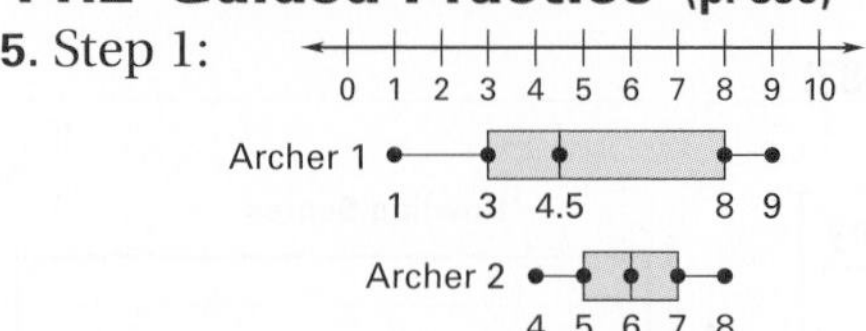

11.2 Practice and Problem Solving (pp. 591–592)

8.
16 32 43 60 95

9a.

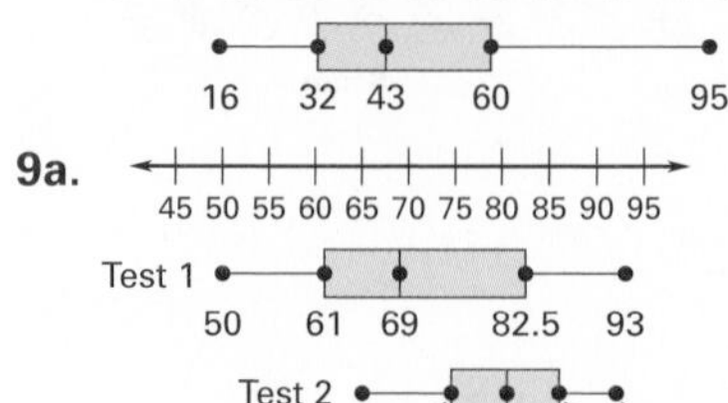

9c. Test 1. *Sample answer:* On test 1, the score of 71 was above the median, but on test 2, the score of 74 was below the median.

11a.

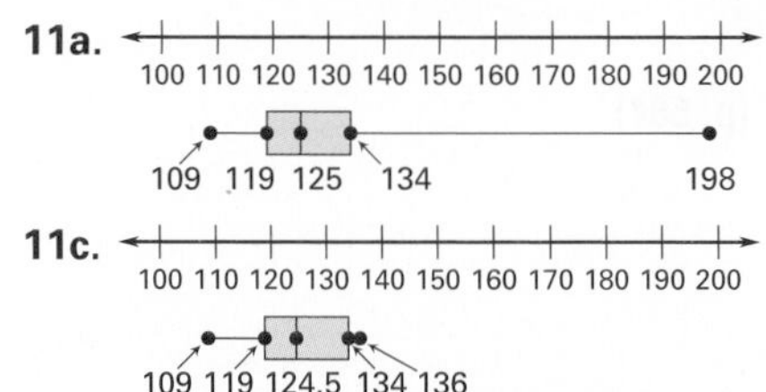

11c.

11d. *Sample answer:* Though it changes the appearance of the left whisker and the box very little, excluding the outlier greatly shortens the length of the right whisker; from the plot in part (c), you can conclude that all values other than the outlier that are above the upper quartile are very, very close to the upper quartile.

12a.

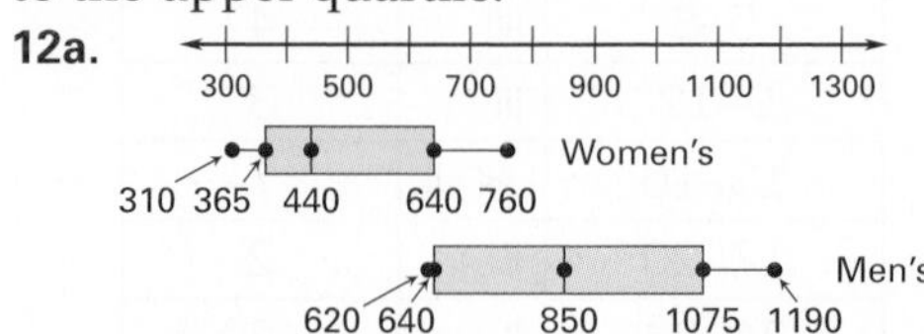

11.2 Mixed Review (p. 592)

14.

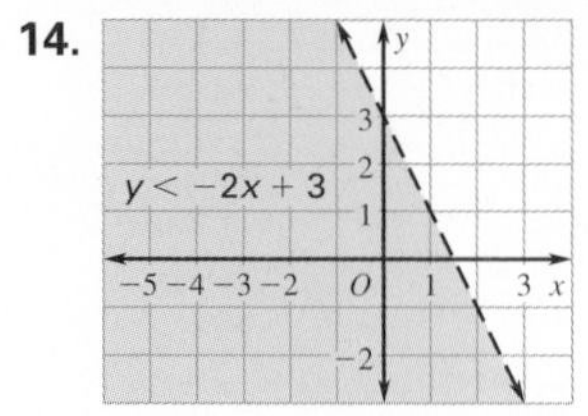

15.

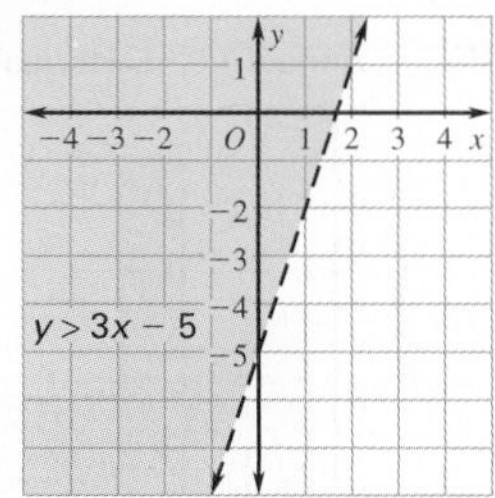

16. 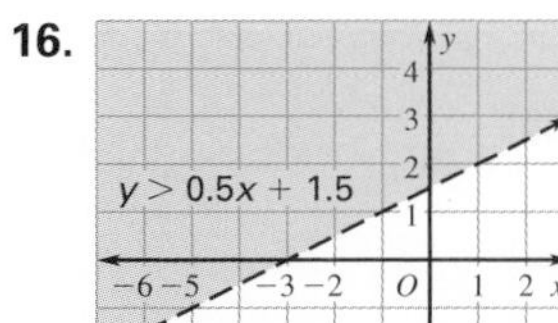

11.2 Technology Activity (p. 593)

1. 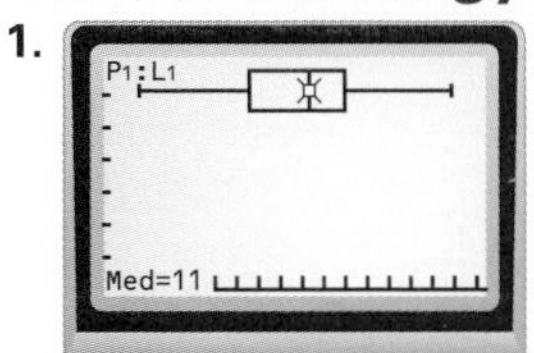

Student Reference (p. 595)

1. 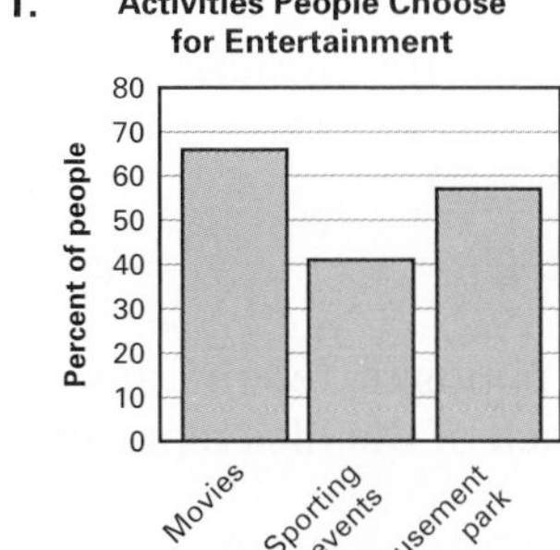

2. 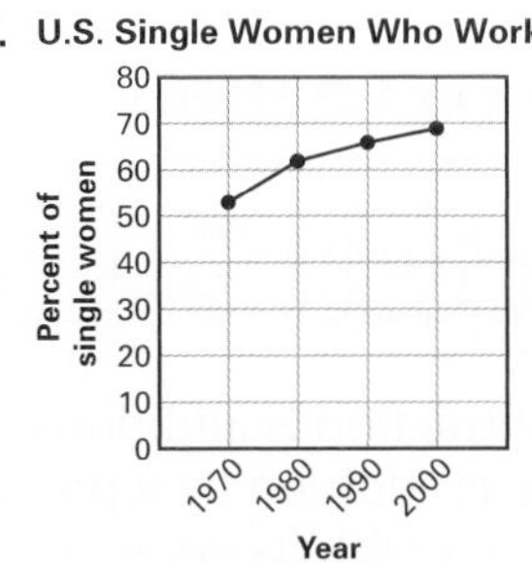

3. 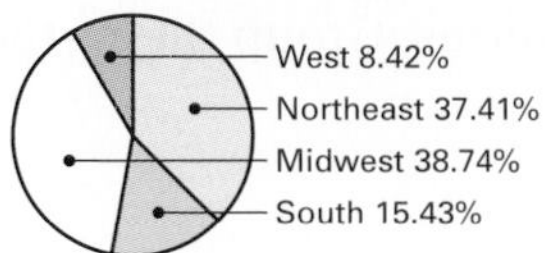

11.3 Practice and Problem Solving (pp. 599–600)

8. Categorical. *Sample answer:* I would use a circle graph, since it provides the best comparison of the production from each source to the total production. **9.** stem-and-leaf plot, box-and-whisker plot **10.** stem-and-leaf plot, box-and-whisker plot **13.** The extremes, range, and quartiles, and how they divide the data into four equal-sized groups; the frequency of occurrence in chosen equal intervals. *Sample answer:* A box-and-whisker plot divides data into intervals of sorts, the quartiles, but they are not equal. For a histogram, you can determine in what intervals the quartiles and extremes lie, but you cannot determine their exact values. **14a.** Yes. *Sample answer:* The intervals have different widths. **14b.** *Sample answer:* You can conclude that the number of people who exercise less than 4 hours per week, between 4 and 8 hours per week, and more than 8 hours per week are approximately equal. You can also conclude that 90% of the people spend at least 2 hours in weekly exercise.

16a. 

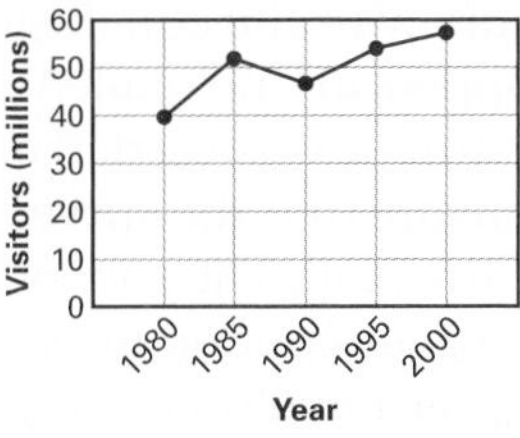

Sample answer: It appears to show an overall gradual increase.

16b. 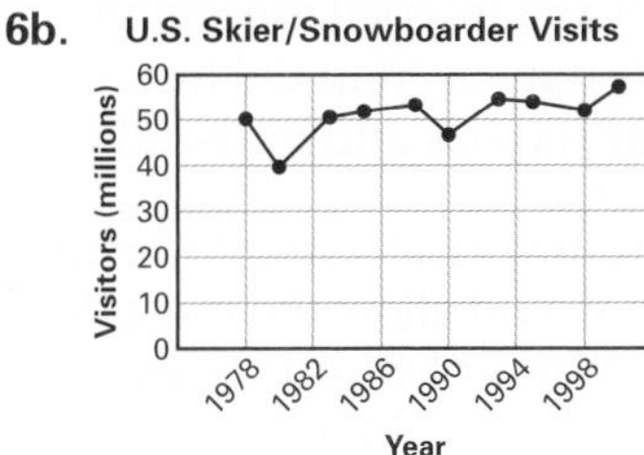

Sample answer: Though there are fluctuations, it appears to show that the number of skier/snowboarder visits is not changing very significantly.

16c. Part (b). *Sample answer:* It reflects more data values.

11.3 Mixed Review (p. 600)

24. 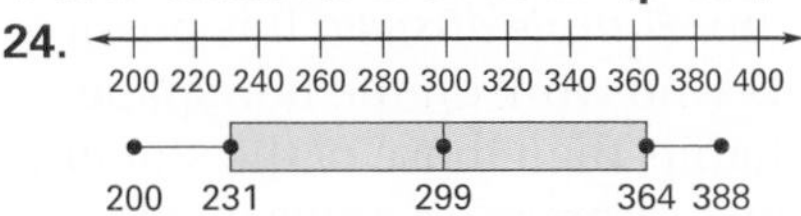

11.4 Guided Practice (p. 603)

4. Step 2: No. *Sample answer:* It gives equal weight to less-populated states, so it is likely to over-represent the views of citizens of those states. Step 3: Yes. *Sample answer:* It does not allow for a response of indifference, and two of the three responses are positive responses, so the question will likely over-represent the proportion of people who really enjoy camping.

11.5 Concept Activity (p. 608)

1. *Sample answer:* In the first sample, the percent of votes for candidate B is greatly overestimated, and the percent of votes for candidates A and C is underestimated. In the second sample, the percent of votes for candidate A matches the election results, with the percent somewhat overestimated for candidate B and somewhat underestimated for candidate C. In the third sample, the percent of votes for candidate B matches the election results, with the percent somewhat underestimated for candidate A and somewhat overestimated for candidate C. The first sample seems to represent the population very poorly, while the second and third samples are fairly representative.

11.5 Guided Practice (p. 611)

2. *Sample answer:* Check who is in the population, what kind of sampling method is used, whether that method provides a sample that represents the population or whether it is biased in some way, whether the survey questions are biased, whether any margin of error is given, whether any data displays could potentially be misleading, and whether the conclusions drawn reflect the data.

11.5 Practice and Problem Solving (pp. 612–613)
9. *Sample answer:* I do not trust the survey or the conclusions. First, the population is just those shoppers at one mall. Also, there is no information as to how the survey was carried out or what sampling method was used to ensure that the survey truly represents even those people at the mall. The survey is even more troublesome because the survey conductor has an interest in the popularity of unusual pets. Finally, no margin of error is given. It seems very likely the interval around the sample percent for mammals, 31%, may overlap the interval around the total sample percent for reptiles and birds, 33%.

Mid-Chapter Quiz (p. 614) **3.** Categorical. *Sample answer:* I would use a bar graph, because it would allow the most direct visual comparison between the numbers of wins for each team. **4.** Categorical. *Sample answer:* I would use a circle graph, since it provides the best way to compare the different ways people travel to school to all of those who travel to school. **5.** Population: all students at the school; sampling method: convenience sample; no. *Sample answer:* It is possible that the small group of students who work on the newspaper have different tastes or eating habits than those of the student body as a whole. **6.** Population: visitors at an amusement park; sampling method: systematic sample; yes. *Sample answer:* There is no reason to think every tenth person would have some particular bias.

11.8 Practice and Problem Solving (pp. 631-632)
29a.

11.9 Concept Activity (p. 633) **1.** *Sample answer:* You could assign, for example, the numbers 1 and 2 to represent the first prize, the numbers 3 and 4 to represent the second prize, and the numbers 5 and 6 to represent the third prize. Then perform the simulation as before, but circle the first occurrence of 1 *or* 2, the first occurrence of 3 *or* 4, and the first occurrence of 5 *or* 6.

Chapter 12

Chapter Prerequisite Skills (p. 650)

10.
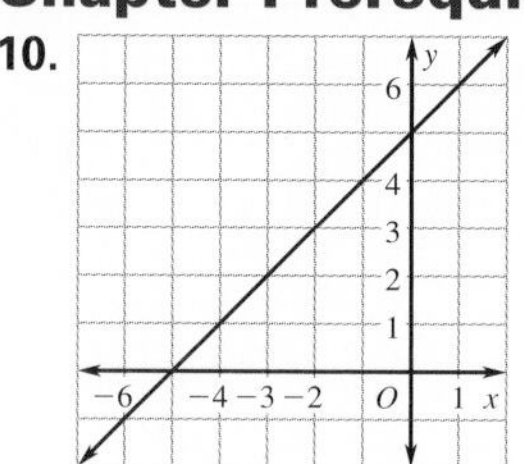

11.
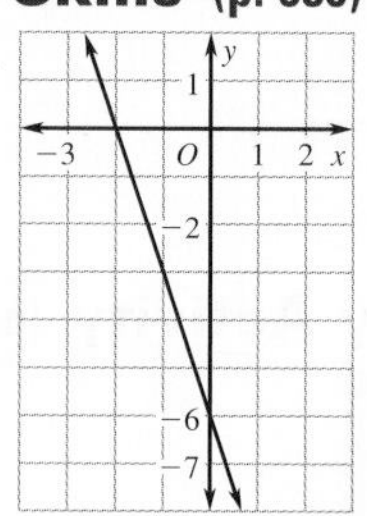

12.
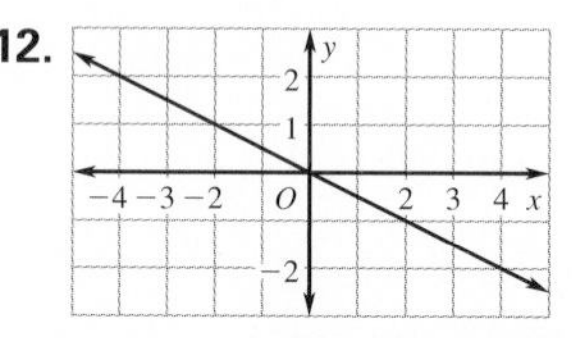

13.
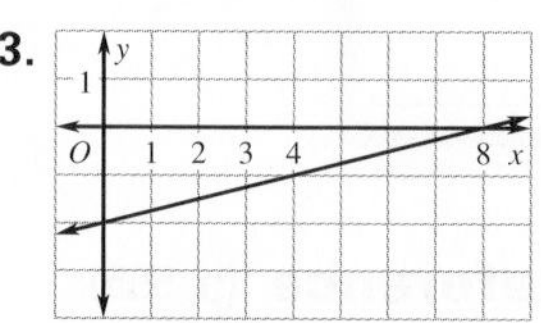

12.2 Concept Activity (p. 656) **3.** *Sample answer:* Use algebra tiles to model $2x^2 + 5x + 2$ and $x^2 + 3x + 1$.

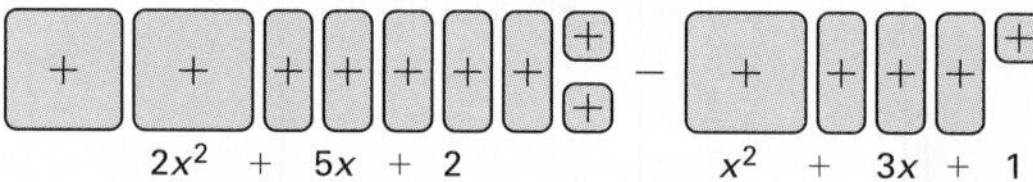

Because subtraction is addition of the opposite, rewrite the subtraction as addition by replacing each of the tiles representing $x^2 + 3x + 1$ with its opposite.

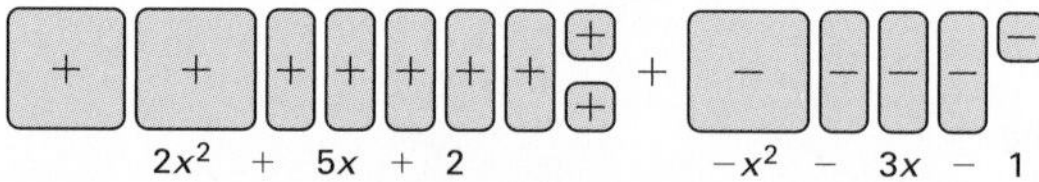

To add the polynomials, combine like terms. Group the x^2-tiles, the x-tiles, and the 1-tiles.

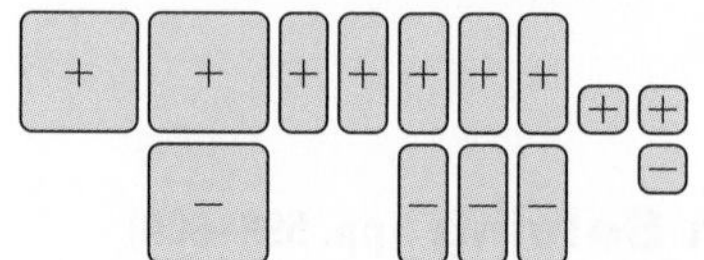

Remove the zero pairs. The difference is $x^2 + 2x + 1$.

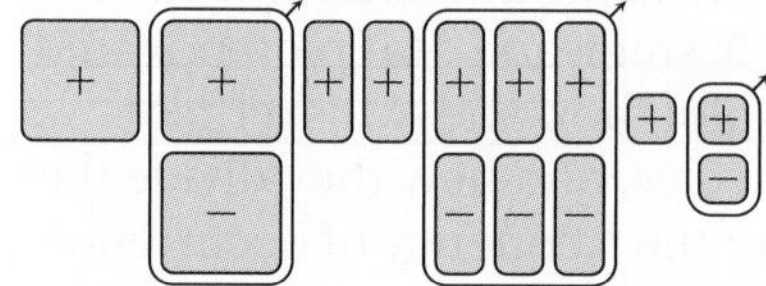

12.3 Practice and Problem Solving (pp. 664–666)
48. It is the sum of the degrees of the monomial and binomial. *Sample answer:* By the product of powers property, exponents of like variables are added, which means that the degree of each term of the product is the sum of the degrees of the two terms that are multiplied. The sum of the degrees of the monomial and the original binomial term with the greatest degree is then the degree of the product binomial. For example, the product of

$4x^2y$, which has degree 3, and $(6y^4 - x^2)$, which has degree 4, is $24x^2y^5 - 4x^4y$, which has degree 7, the sum of the degrees of the monomial and original binomial.

12.3 Standardized Test Practice (p. 666)

56a.

w

l

$2l + 2w = 24$

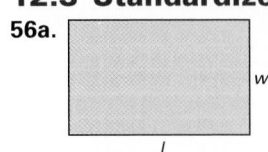

12.4 Concept Activity (p. 667)

1. 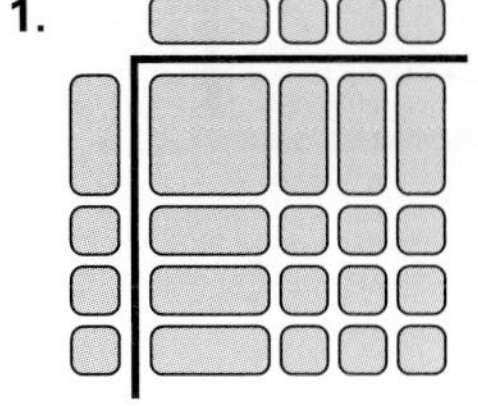

2. 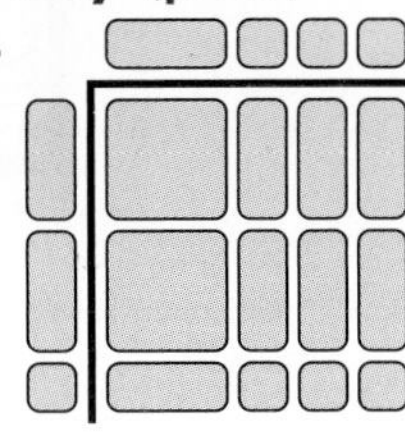

3. 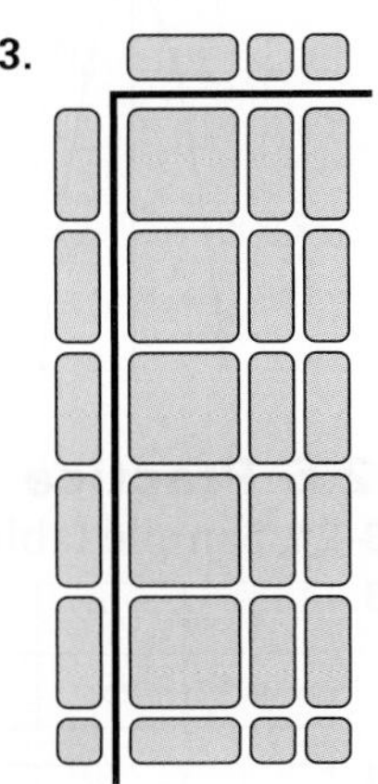

4. **5.** 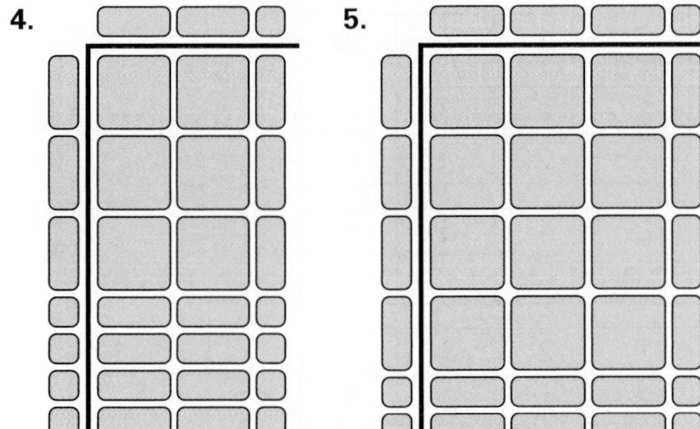

6. 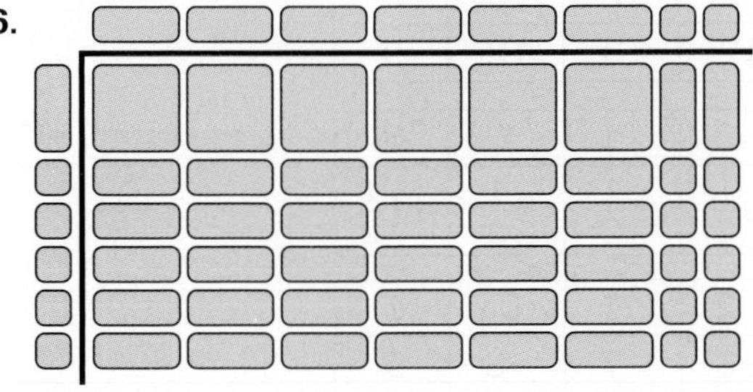

7. *Sample answer:* Place two x-tiles down the left and an x-tile and three 1-tiles along the top and fill in as before to find a product of $2x^2 + 6x$. By the distributive property, $2x(x + 3) = 2x(x) + 2x(3) = 2x^2 + 6x$, as with algebra tiles. The algebra tile model effectively multiplies the two x-tiles on the left by the x-tile on the top and then by the three 1-tiles on the top, and then the results are combined, or added, just as with the distributive property. **8.** *Sample answer:* Distribute $(x + 4)$ to each term of $(3x + 1)$ to obtain $(3x)(x + 4) + (1)(x + 4)$. Then distribute $3x$ and 1 to each term of $(x + 4)$ to obtain $(3x)(x) + (3x)(4) + (1)(x) + (1)(4) = 3x^2 + 12x + x + 4$. Then combine like terms to obtain $3x^2 + 13x + 4$.

12.5 Mixed Review (p. 678)

53.

54. 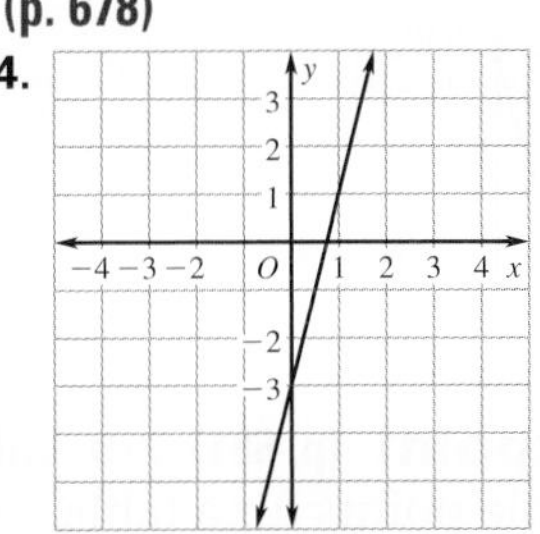

55. 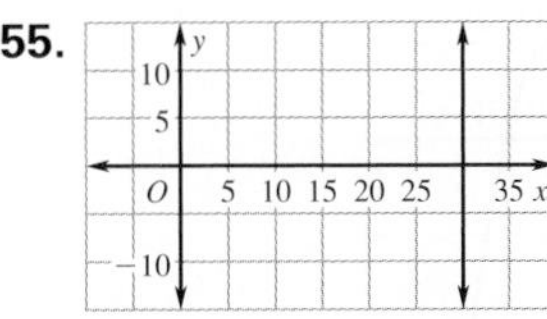

56. 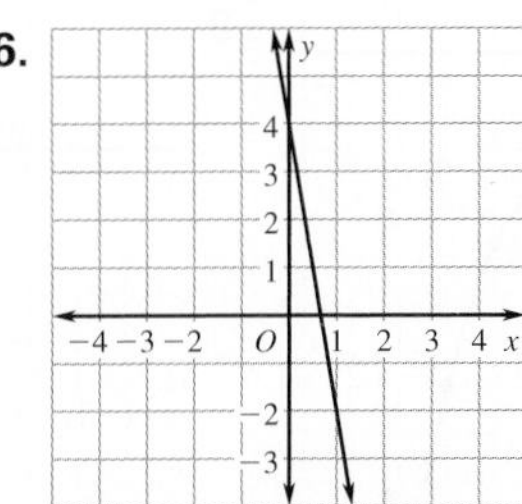

57. 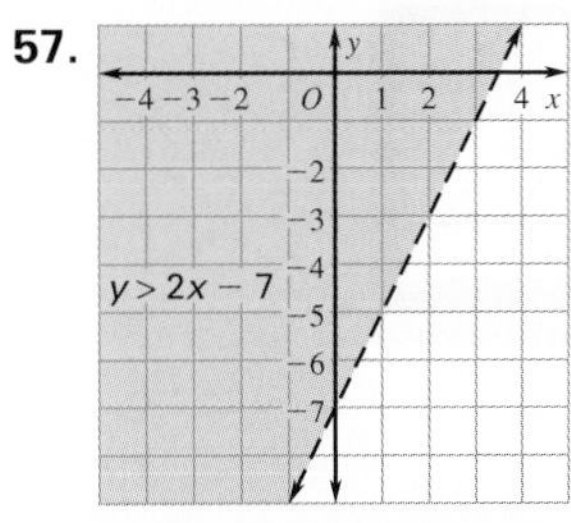

58. 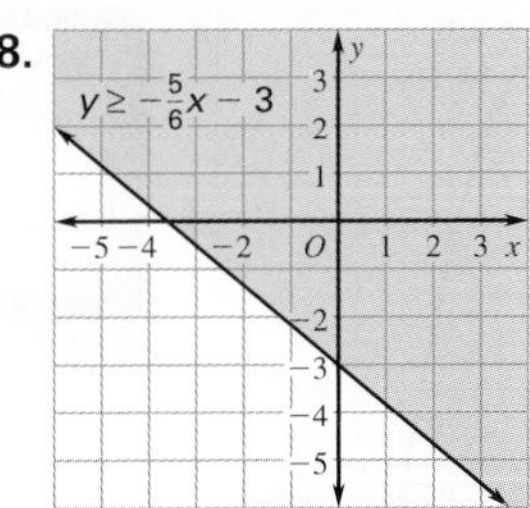

59. 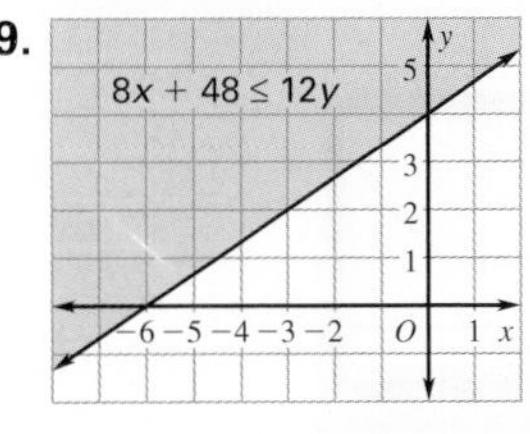

60. 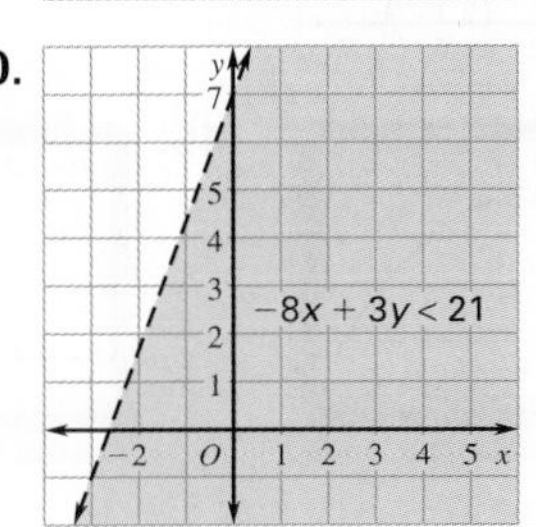

12.6 Checkpoint (p. 680) **4–6.** Labeled points on the graph represent sample points for a table.

4.

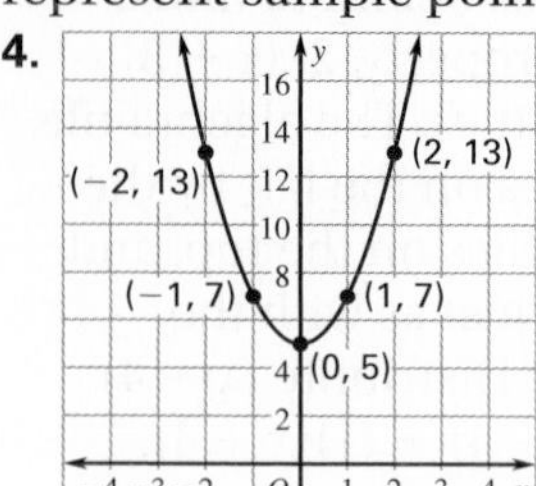

5.

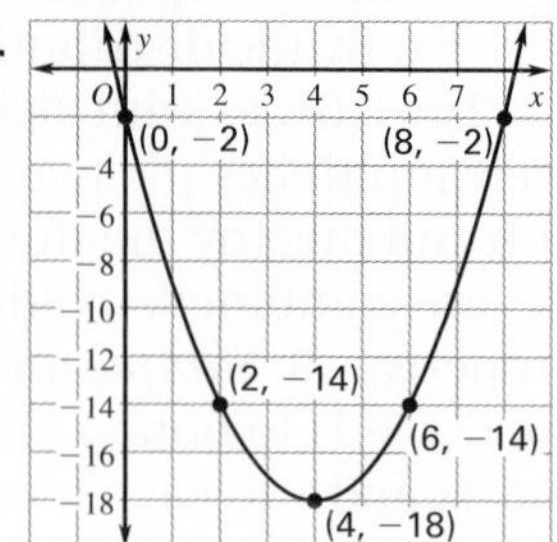

6.

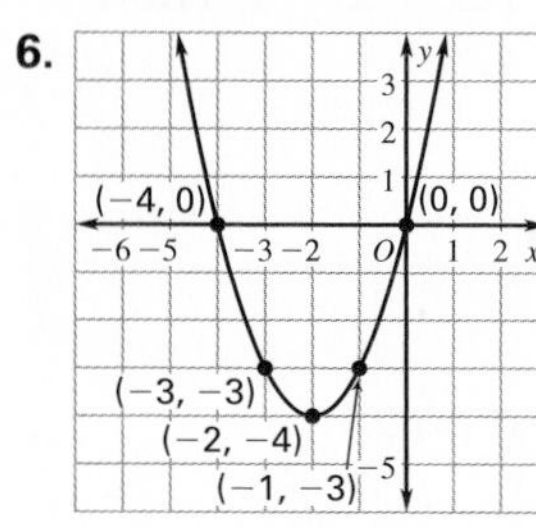

12.6 Checkpoint (p. 681) **7–9.** Labeled points on the graph represent sample points for a table.

7.

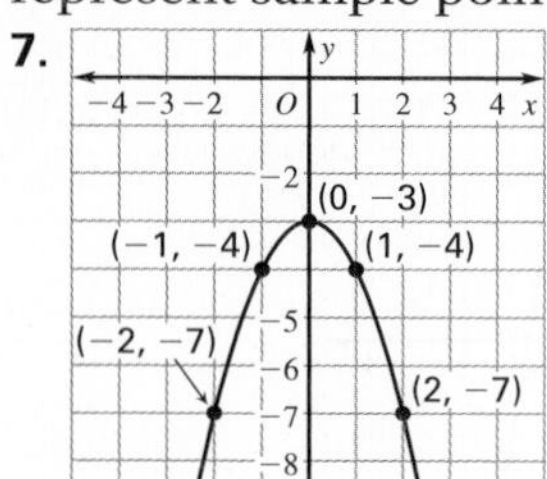

8.

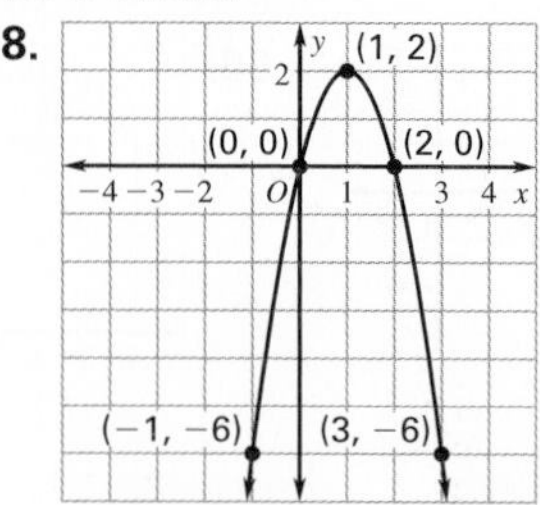

9.

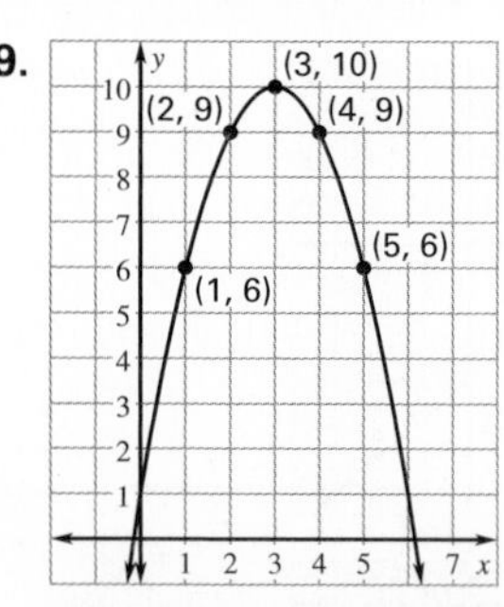

13.

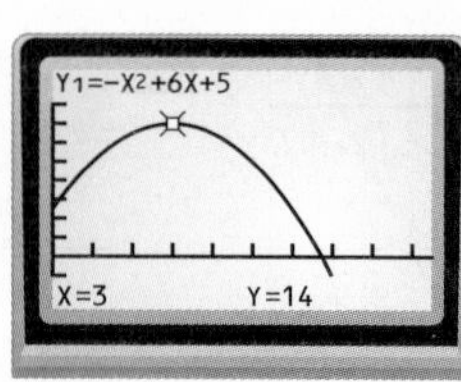

14.

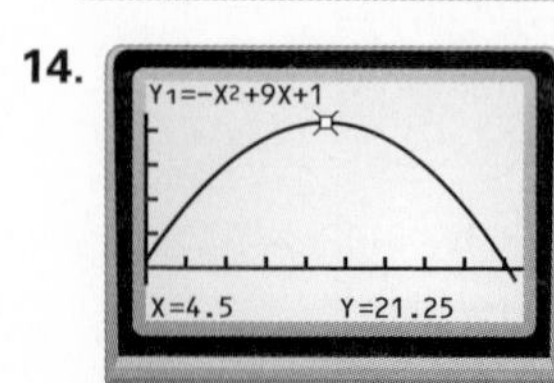

15.

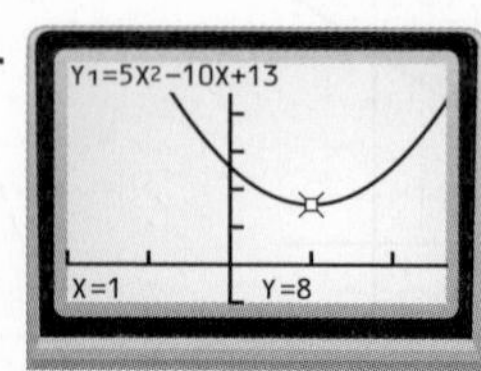

12.6 Guided Practice (p. 682) **1.** *Sample answer:* It is a U-shaped graph that opens upward if the coefficient of the x^2-term is positive and downward if the coefficient of the x^2-term is negative.

6–8. Labeled points on the graph represent sample points for a table.

6.

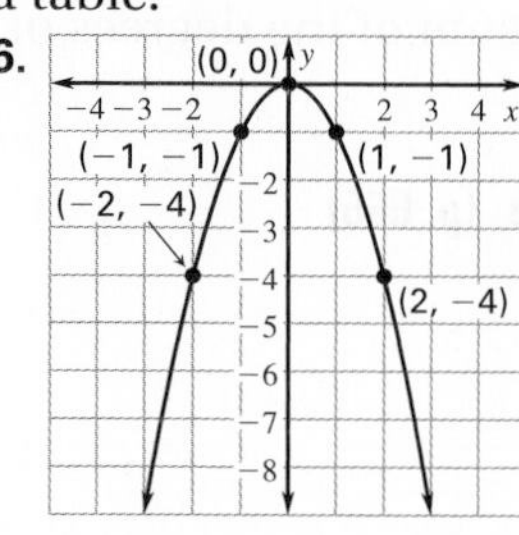

7.

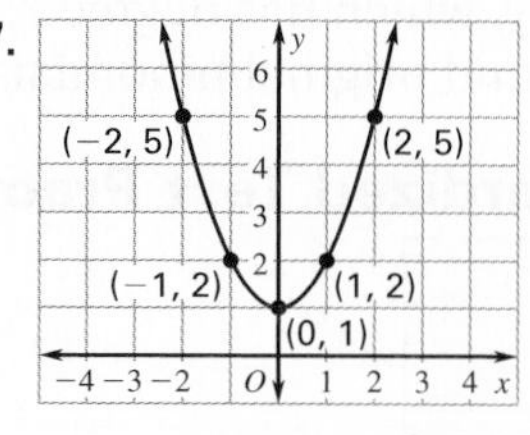

8.

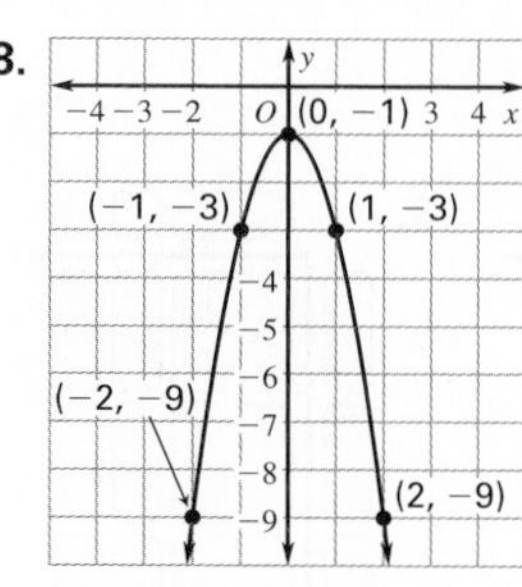

12. Step 1:

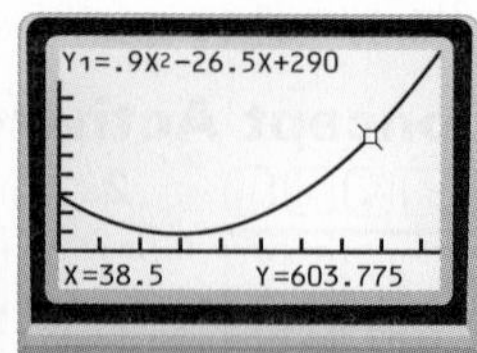

12.6 Practice and Problem Solving (pp. 682–684)

13–21. Sample tables are given.

13.

x	−5	−4	−3	−2	−1
y	5	8	9	8	5

14.

x	−2	−1	0	1	2
y	16	7	4	7	16

15.

x	0	1	2	3	4
y	0	−15	−20	−15	0

16.

x	0	2	4	6	8
y	0	−3	−4	−3	0

17.

x	0	1	2	3	4
y	5	2	1	2	5

18.

x	1	2	3	4	5
y	9	12	13	12	9

19.

x	−5	−3	−1	1	3
y	$11\frac{1}{2}$	$5\frac{1}{2}$	$3\frac{1}{2}$	$5\frac{1}{2}$	$11\frac{1}{2}$

20.

x	−3	−2	−1	0	1
y	9	−3	−7	−3	9

21.

x	0	2	4	6	8
y	−6	0	2	0	−6

38.

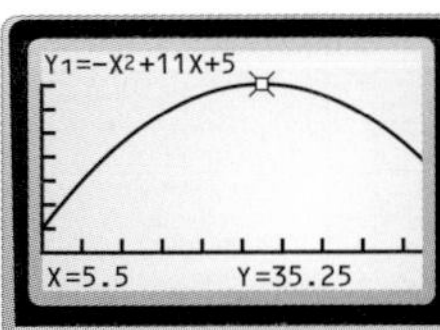

39.

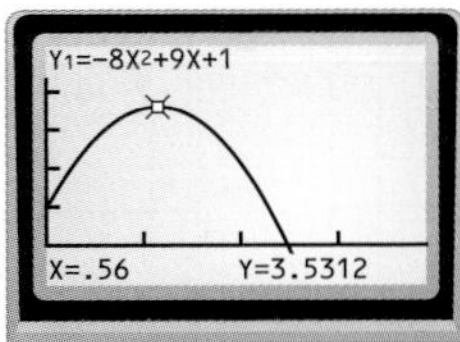

40.

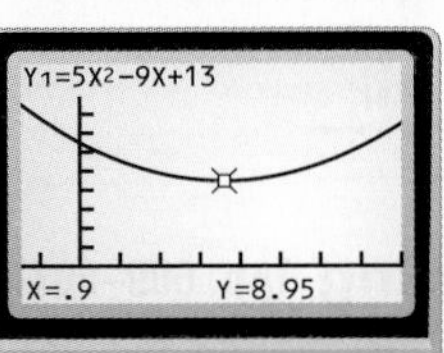

41.

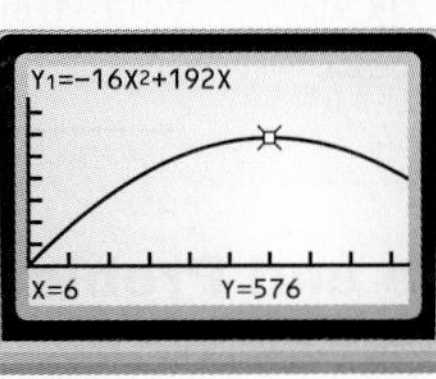

42.

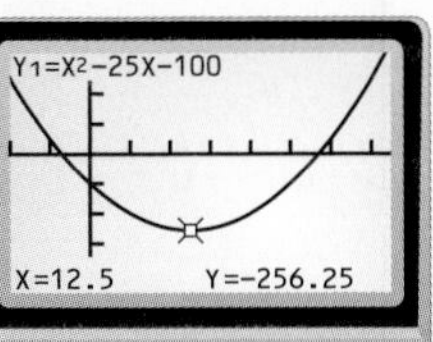

43.

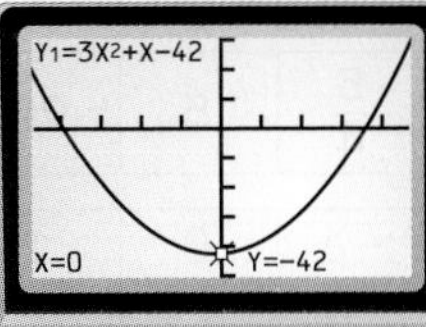

44.

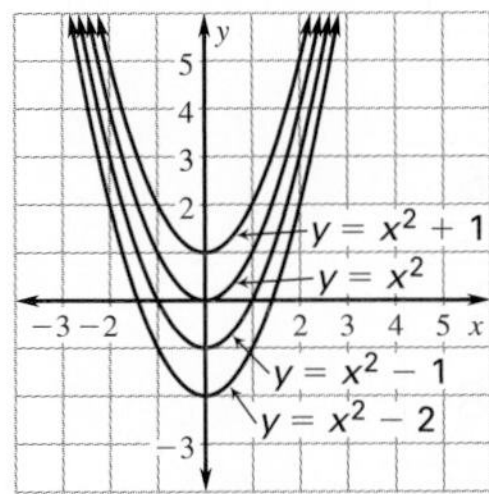

46a. $V = 4\pi r^2$;

r	0	1	2	3	4
V	0	12.56	50.24	113.04	200.96

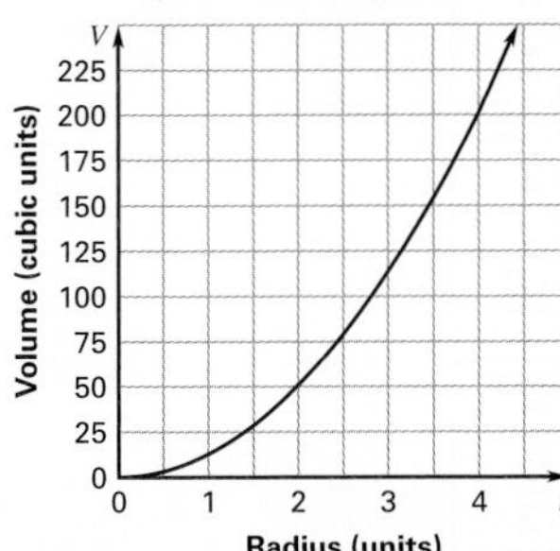

46b. $V = 9\pi h$;

h	0	1	2	3	4
V	0	28.26	56.52	84.78	113.04

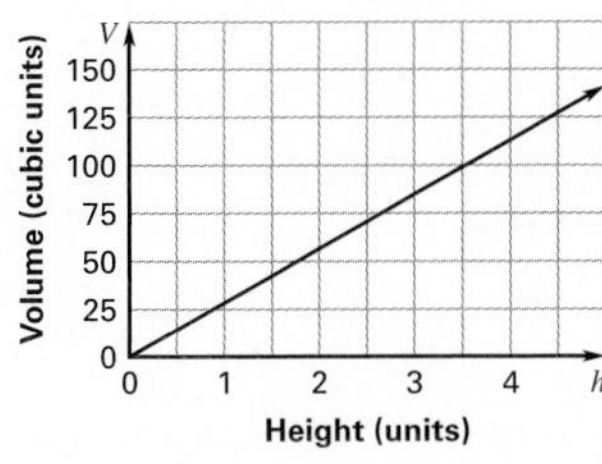

47a.

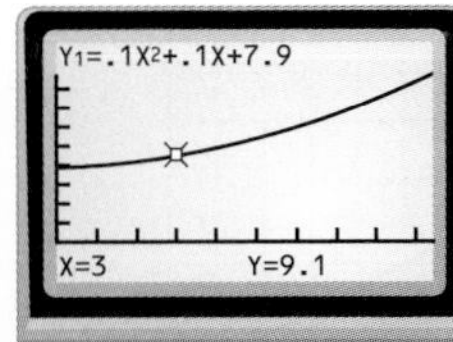

48a.

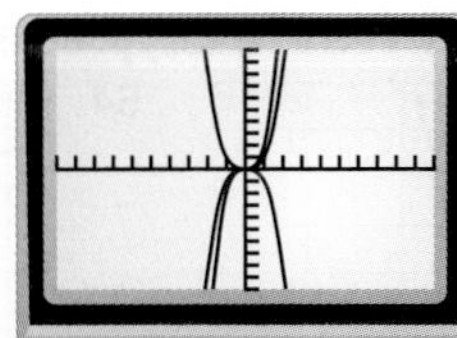

48b. *Sample answer:* The graph of $y = x^3$ rises from left to right. As it approaches the origin from the left, the graph gets less and less steep. To the right of the origin, the graph gets more and more steep. The graph of $y = -x^3$ appears to have the same shape, and also passes through the origin, but it is flipped around so that it falls from left to right. The graph of $y = 2x^3$ looks much like the graph of $y = x^3$, and intersects it at the origin, but it is steeper.

49a. $y = -4x + 3$:

x	0	1	2	3	4	5	6
y	3	−1	−5	−9	−13	−17	−21

$y = -2x^2 + 6x + 4$:

x	0	1	2	3	4	5	6
y	4	8	8	4	−4	−16	−32

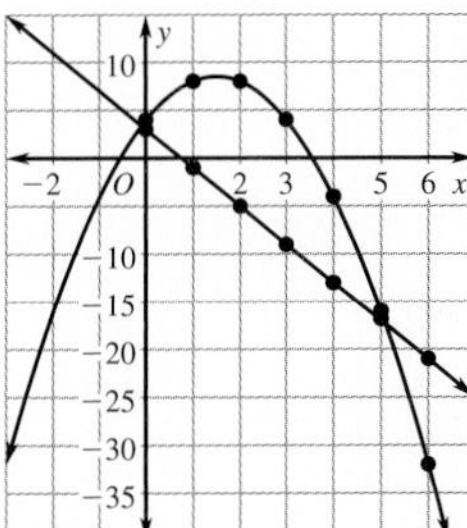

49b. $y = -4x + 3$:

(0, 3) and (1, −1): −4

(1, −1) and (2, −5): −4

(2, −5) and (3, −9): −4

(3, −9) and (4, −13): −4

(4, −13) and (5, −17): −4

(5, −17) and (6, −21): −4

$y = -2x^2 + 6x + 4$:

(0, 4) and (1, 8): 4

(1, 8) and (2, 8): 0

(2, 8) and (3, 4): −4

(3, 4) and (4, −4): −8

(4, −4) and (5, −16): −12

(5, −16) and (6, −32): −16

12.6 Mixed Review (p. 684)

53.

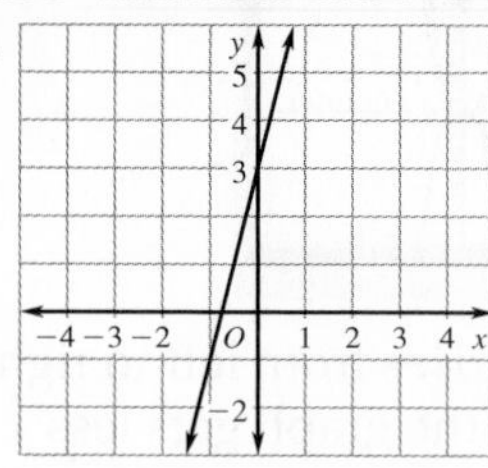

54.

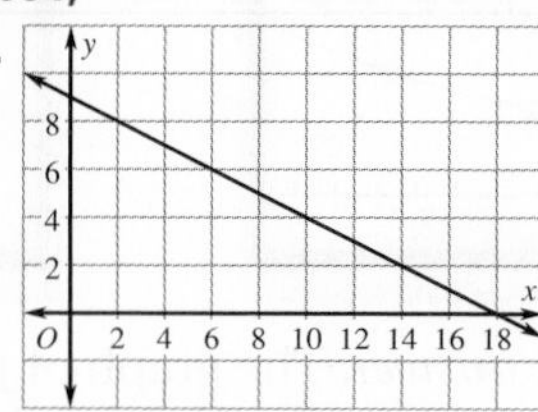

55.

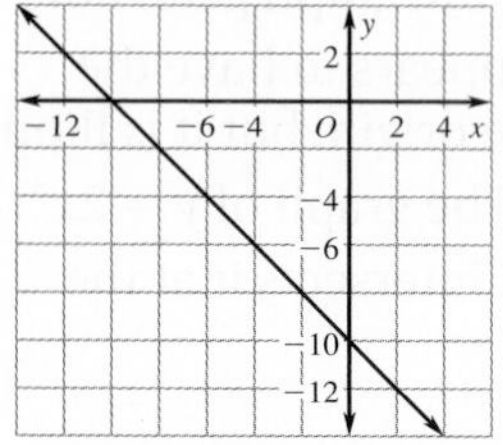

12.7 Checkpoint (p. 687) 1–4. Labeled points on the graph represent sample points for a table.

1.

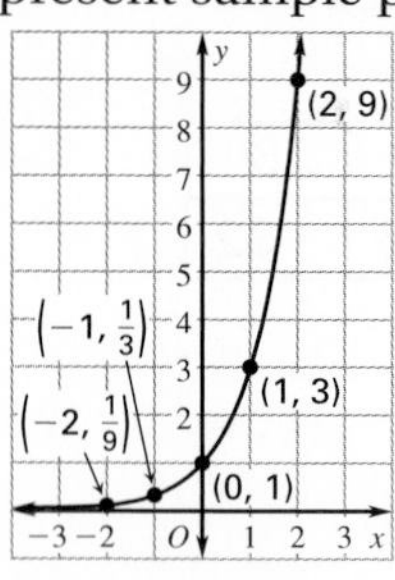

2.

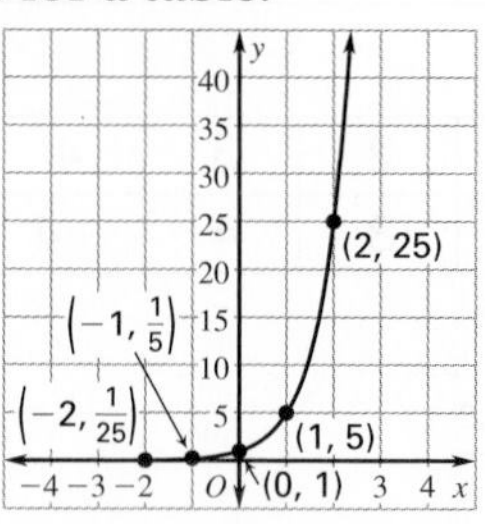

3.

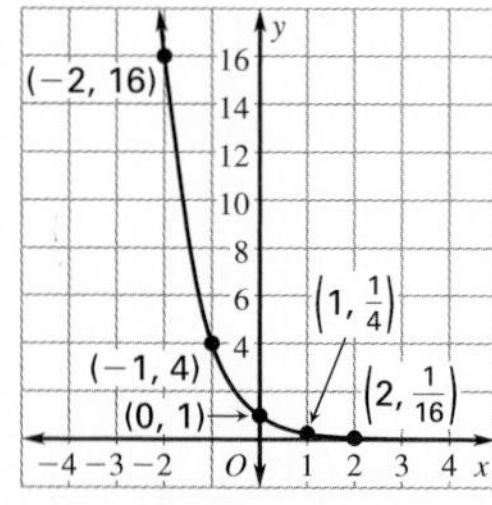

4.

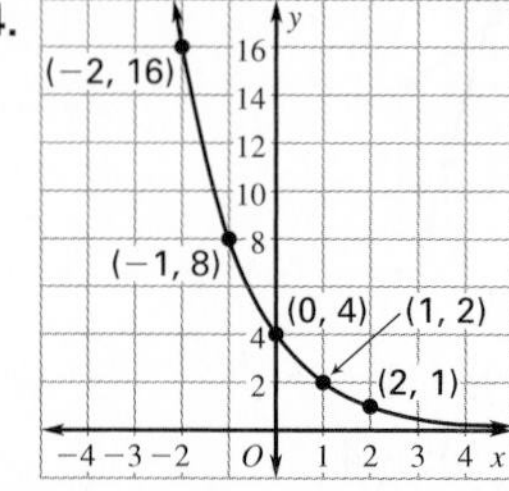

12.7 Guided Practice (p. 689) 3–6. Labeled points on the graph represent sample points for a table.

3.

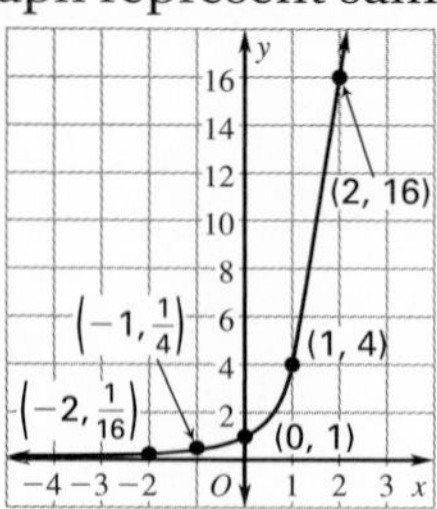

4.

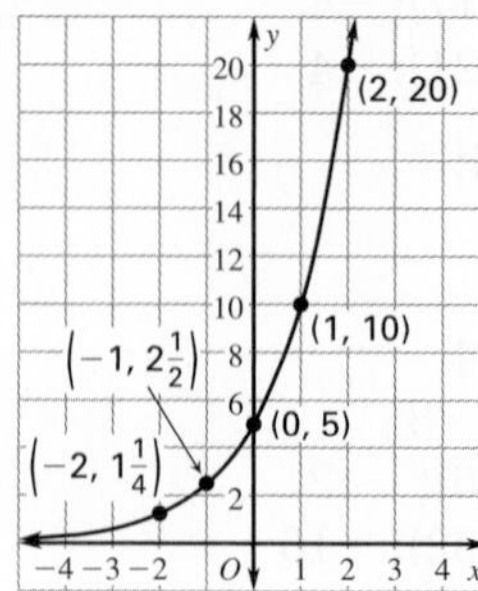

5.

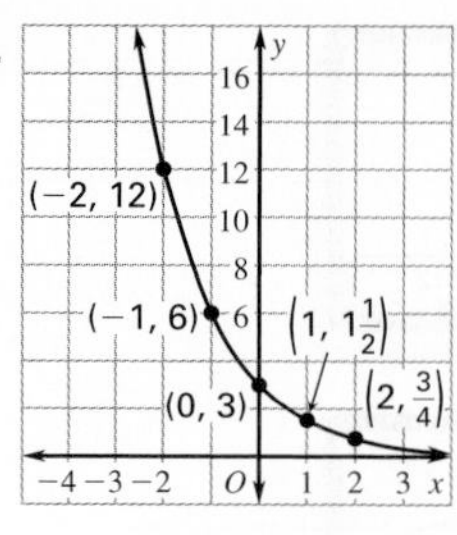

6.

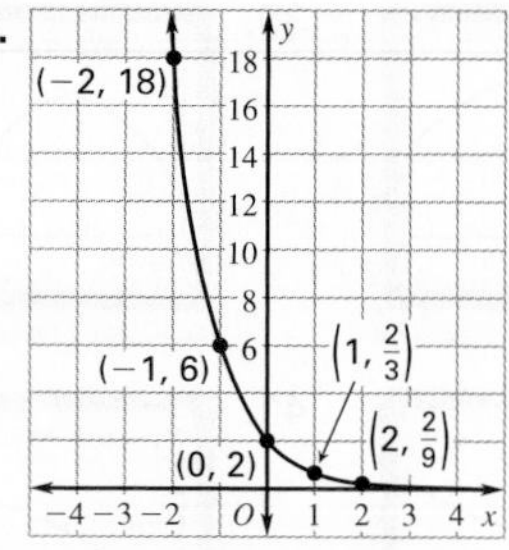

12.7 Practice and Problem Solving (pp. 689–691)

8–15. Sample tables given.

8.

x	−2	−1	0	1	2
y	$\frac{5}{16}$	$\frac{5}{4}$	5	20	80

9.

x	−2	−1	0	1	2
y	$\frac{2}{9}$	$\frac{2}{3}$	2	6	18

10.

x	−2	−1	0	1	2
y	3	6	12	24	48

11.

x	−2	−1	0	1	2
y	$\frac{1}{72}$	$\frac{1}{12}$	$\frac{1}{2}$	3	18

12.

x	−2	−1	0	1	2
y	8	4	2	1	$\frac{1}{2}$

13.

x	−2	−1	0	1	2
y	81	27	9	3	1

14.

x	−2	−1	0	1	2
y	48	12	3	$\frac{3}{4}$	$\frac{3}{16}$

15.

x	−2	−1	0	1	2
y	40	20	10	5	$\frac{5}{2}$

16.

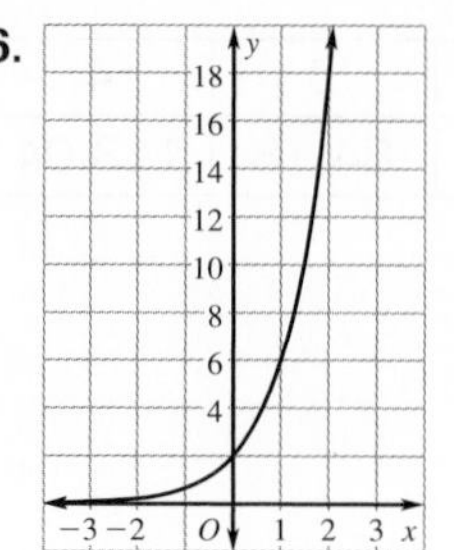

17.

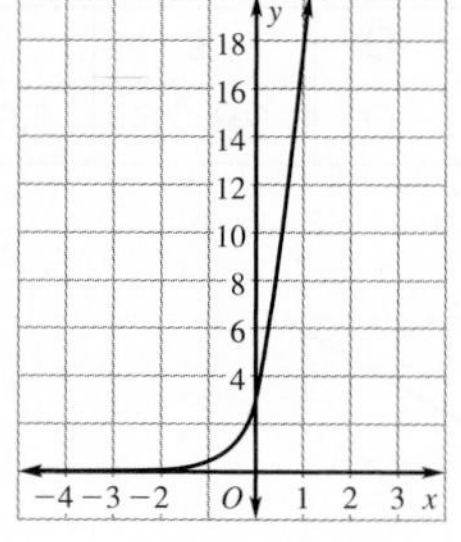

18. 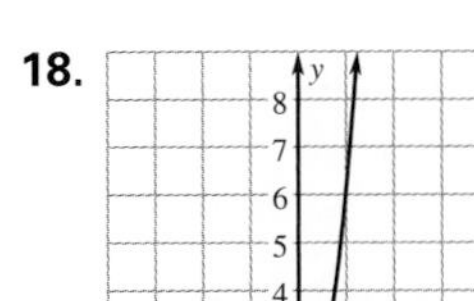

19. 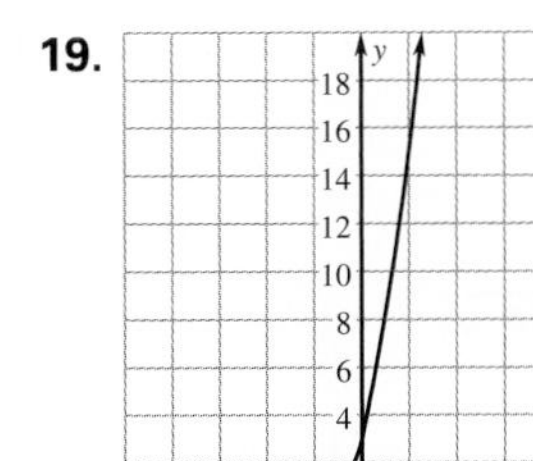

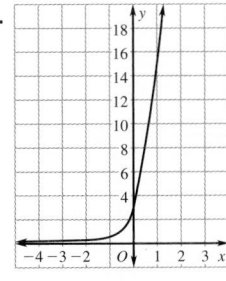

20. 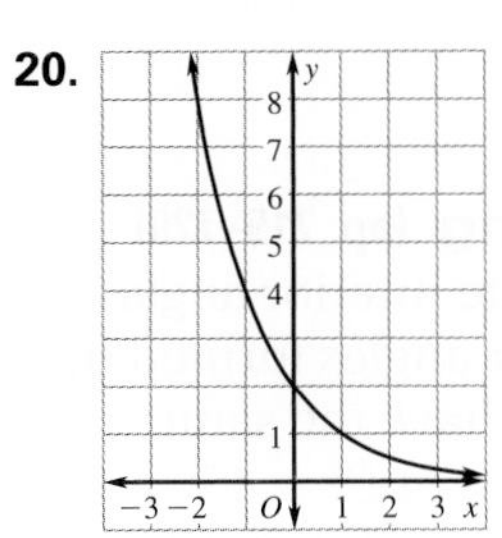

21. 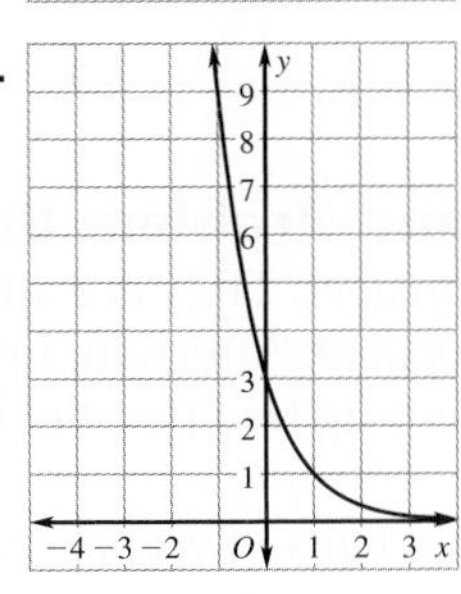

22. 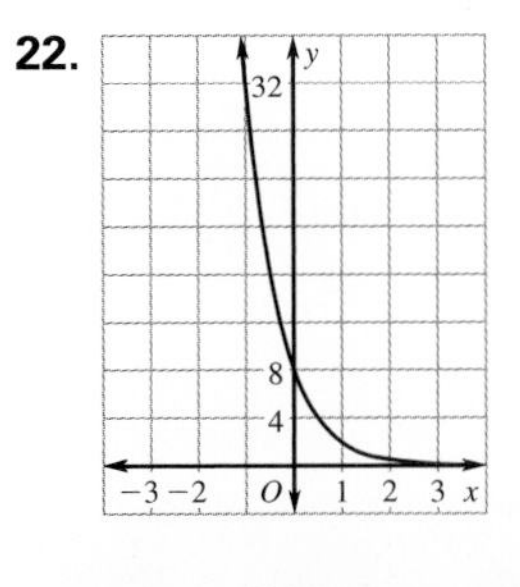

23. 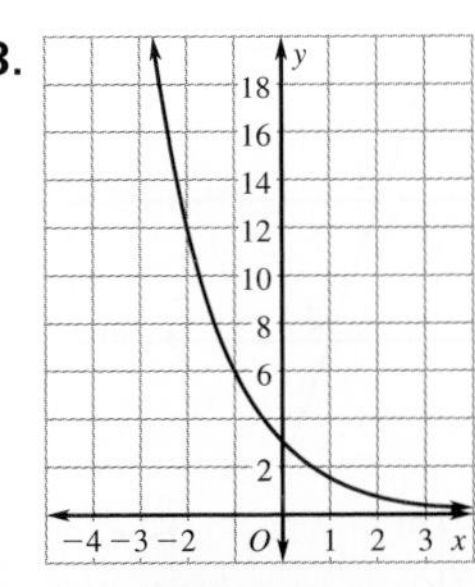

24. 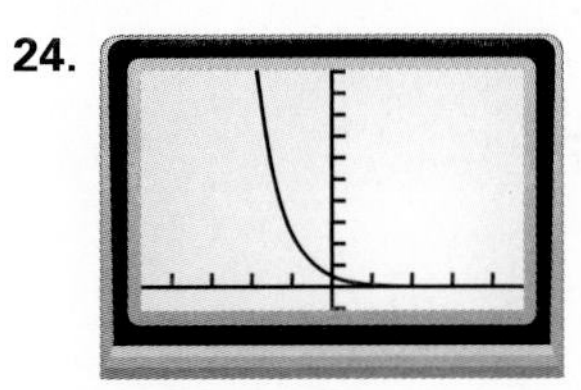

25. 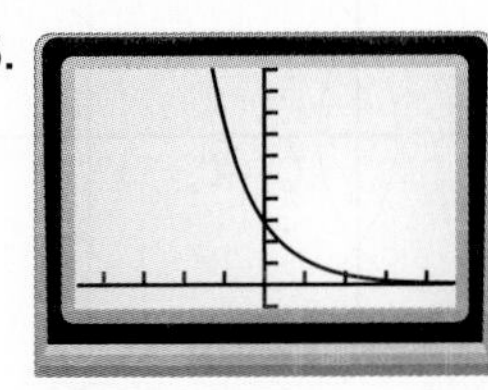

26. 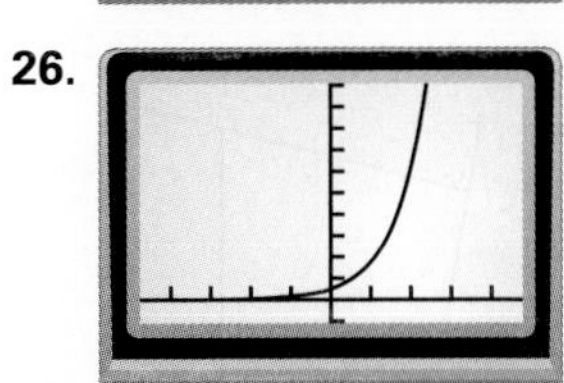

27. 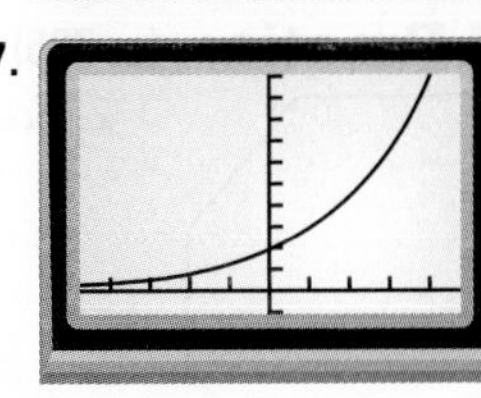

12.8 Checkpoint (p. 694)

4. 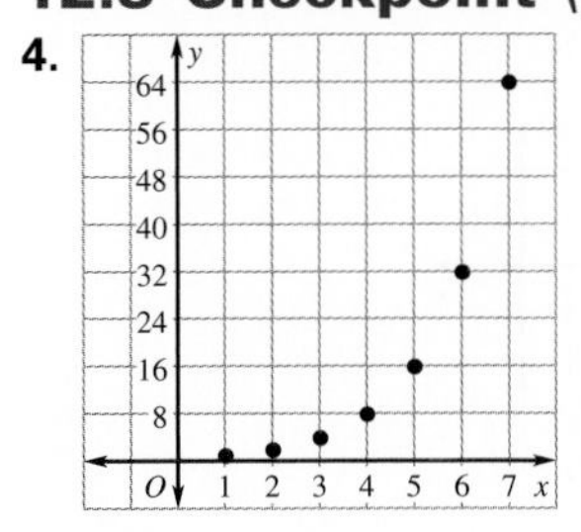

5. 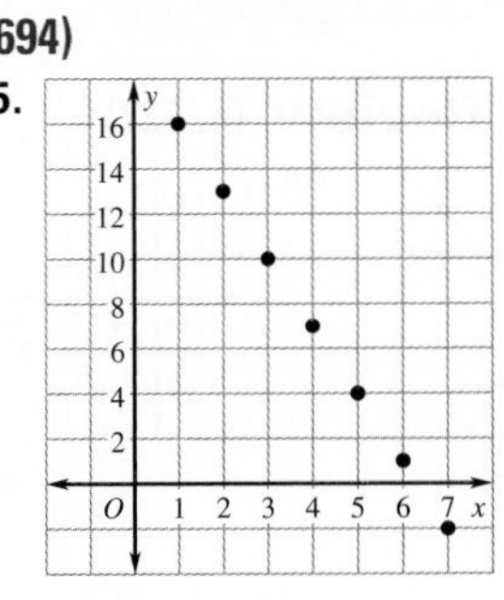

6. 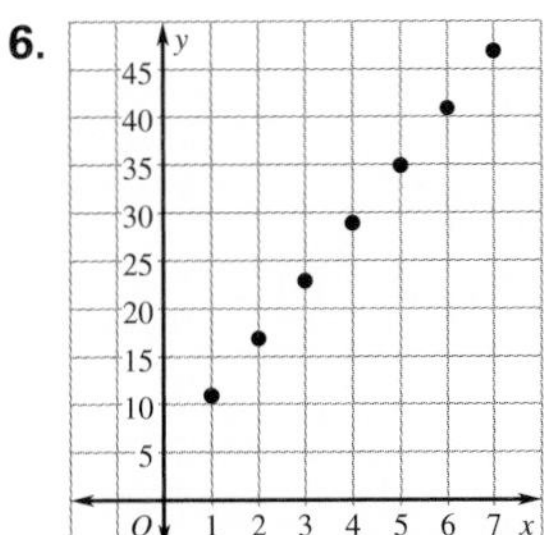

12.8 Practice and Problem Solving (pp. 695–697)

22. 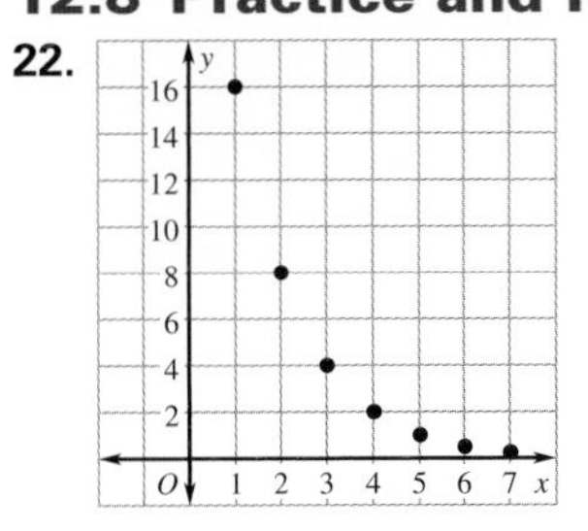

23. 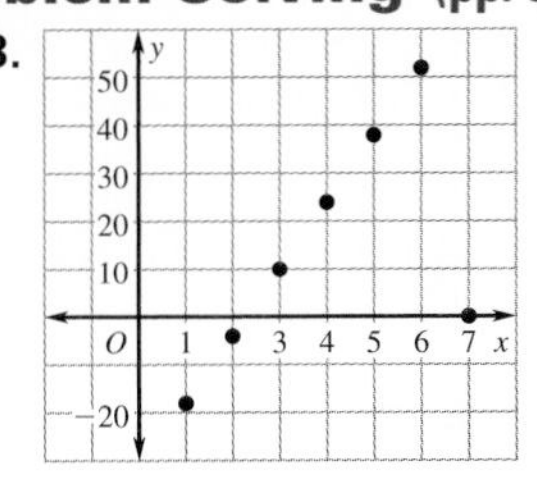

24. 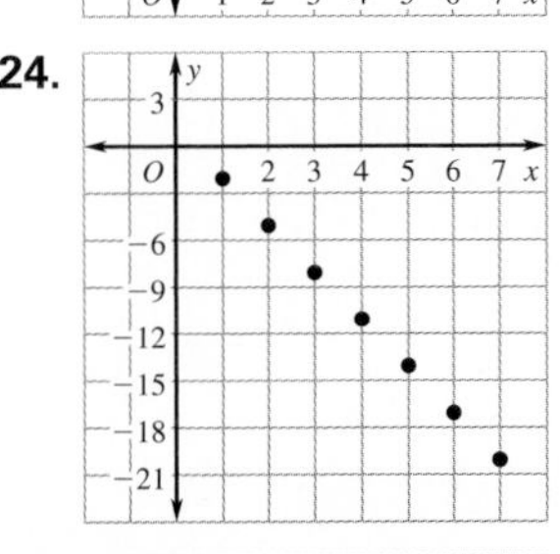

25. 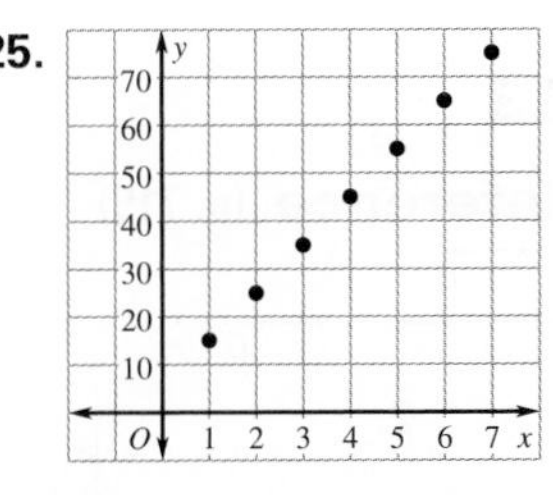

26. 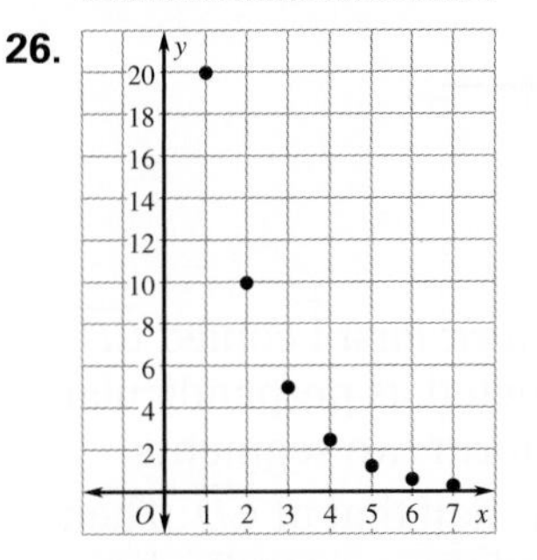

27. 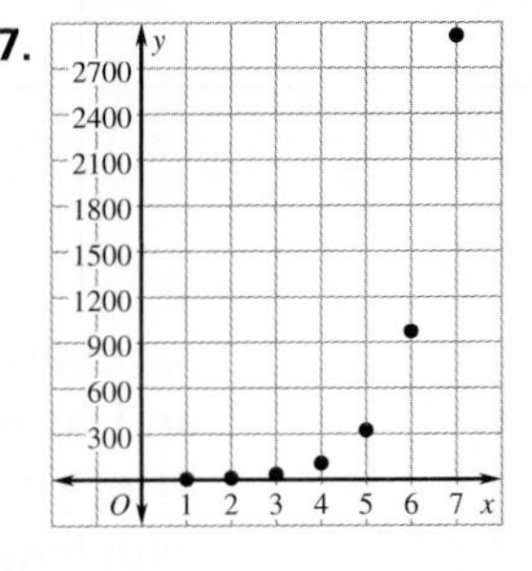

Chapter Test (p. 702)

22. 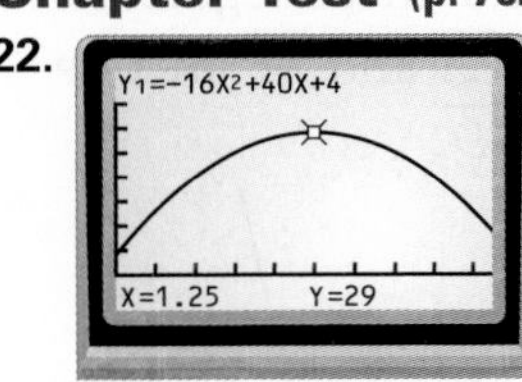

23. 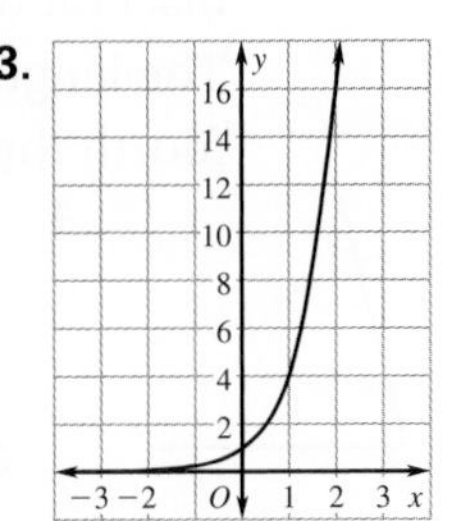

24.

25.

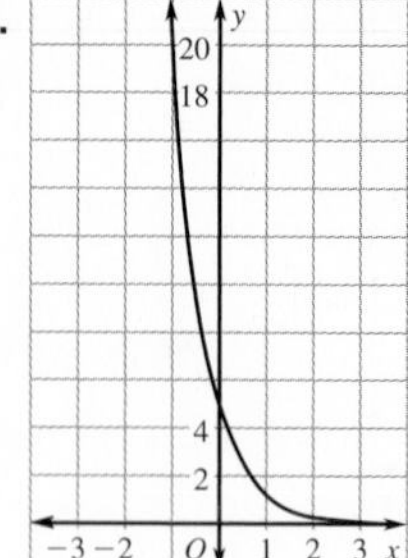

26.

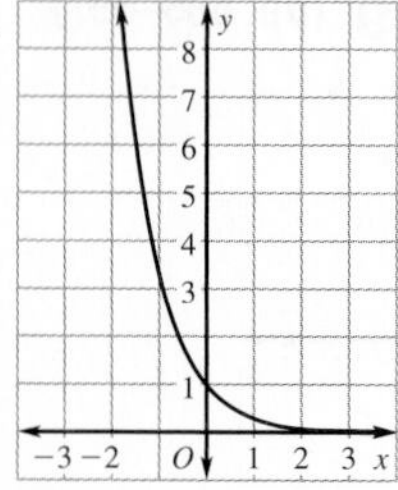

Chapter 13

Student Reference (p. 715)

1–3.

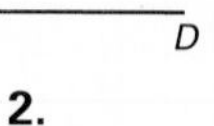

1.

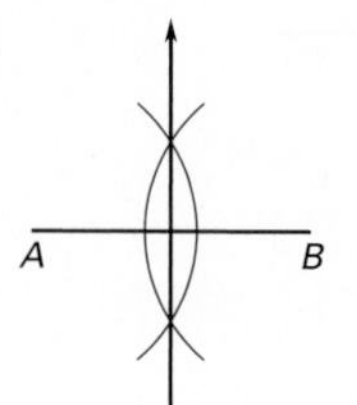

2.

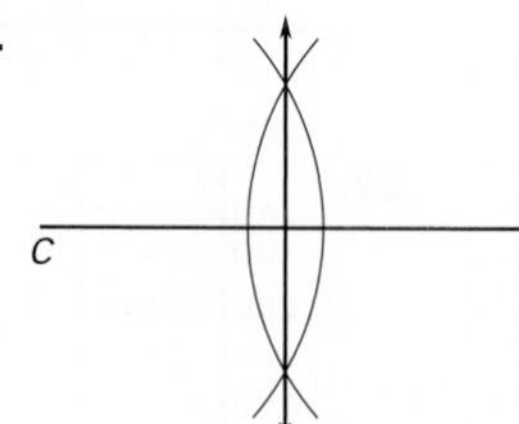

3.

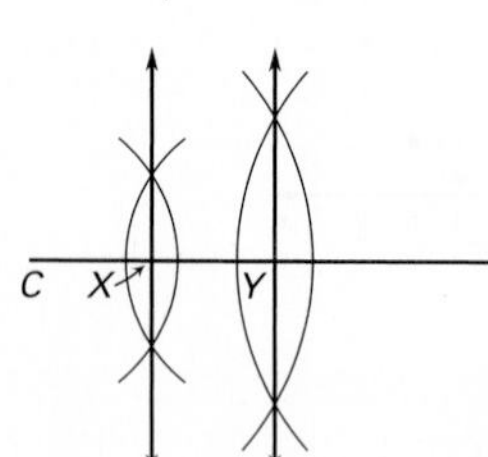

Sample answer: First I copied $\overline{CD}$ and constructed its perpendicular bisector to form two segments with lengths half that of $\overline{CD}$. Then I constructed the perpendicular bisector of one of these segments. The lengths of $\overline{CX}$ and $\overline{XY}$ are one fourth that of $\overline{CD}$.

4–6.

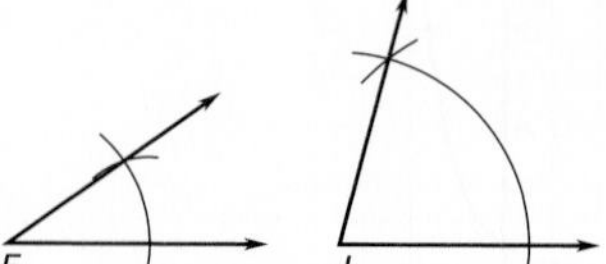

4.

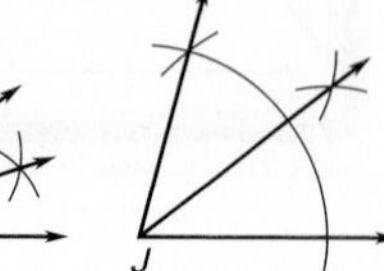

5.

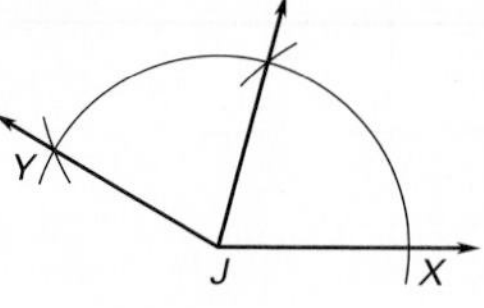

$\angle XJY$ has twice the measure of $\angle J$.

6.

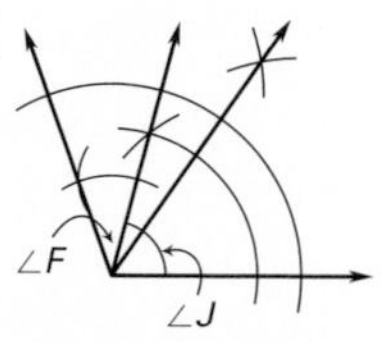

13.2 Practice and Problem Solving (pp. 719–720)

16a. False. *Sample answer:* They are alternate interior angles. **16b.** True. *Sample answer:* Alternate interior angles formed by a transversal intersecting two parallel lines have the same measure. **16c.** True. *Sample answer:* $m\angle 2 = m\angle 3 = 45°$, and $45° + 45° = 90°$ **16d.** False. *Sample answer:* $m\angle 1 + m\angle 2 + m\angle 3 = 95° + 45° + 45° = 185°$

21. *Sample:*

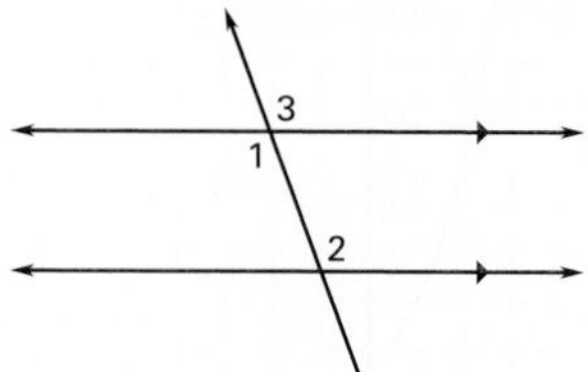

23. *Sample:*

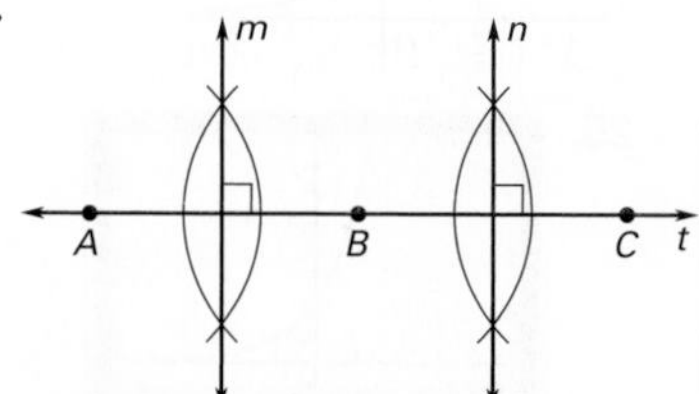

13.3 Guided Practice (p. 725)

1. *Sample:*

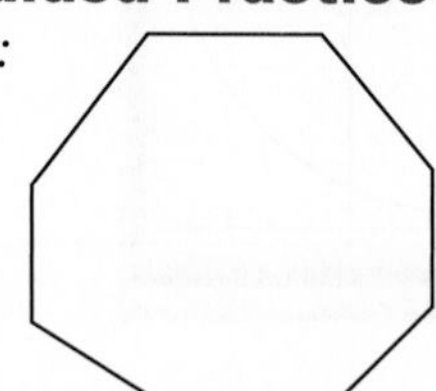

2. *Sample:*

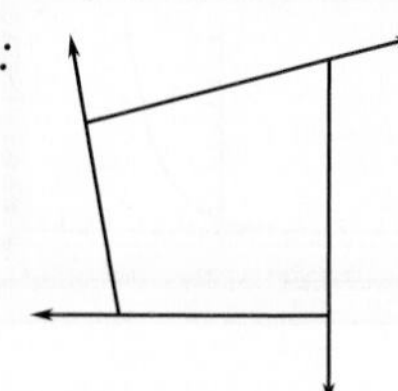

13.3 Mixed Review (p. 727)

43.

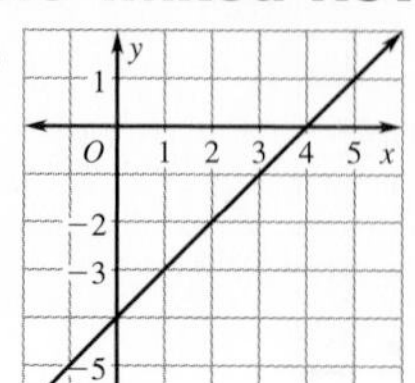

44.

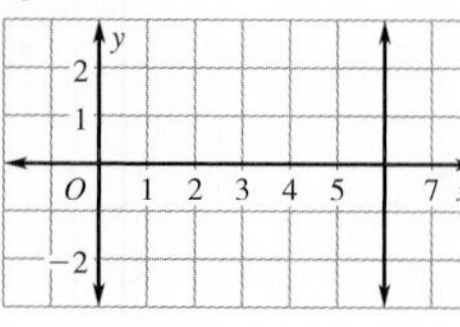

13.4 Guided Practice (p. 731)

5.

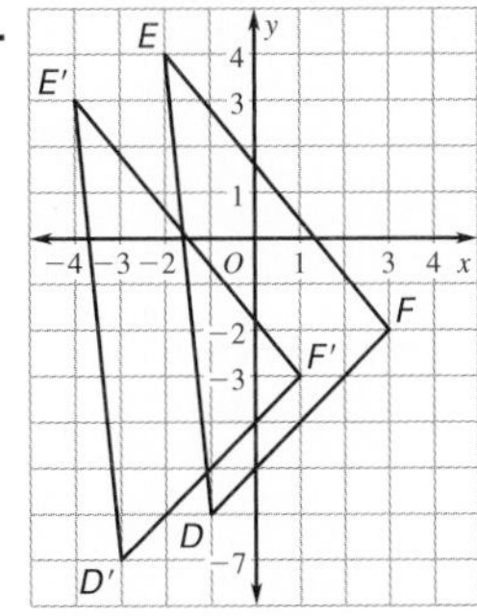

13.4 Practice and Problem Solving (pp. 732–733)

8.

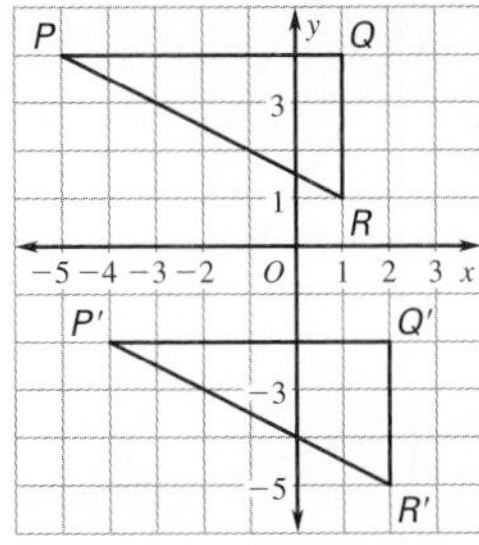

9.

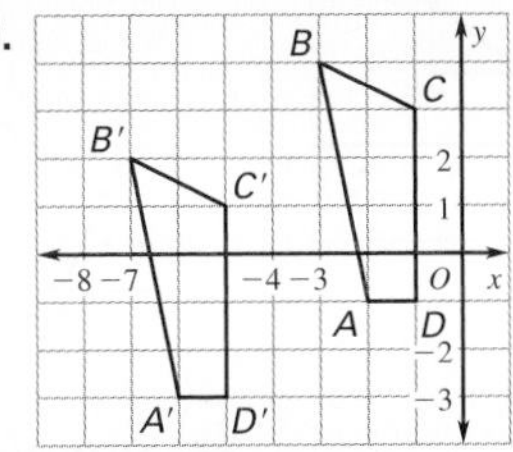

10.

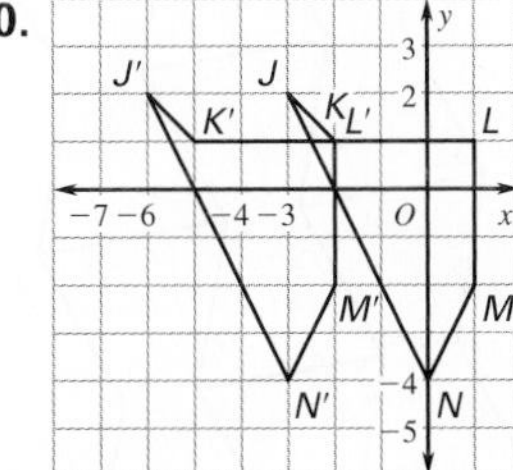

13. *Sample:*

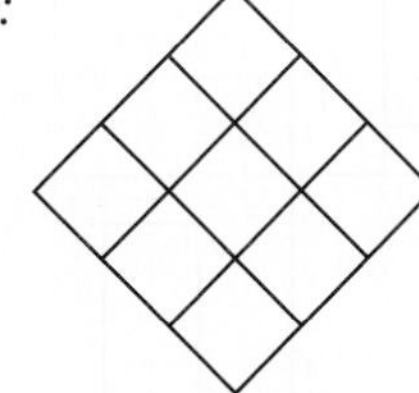

15. *Sample:*

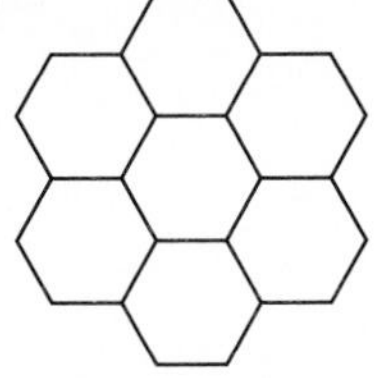

16a–b.

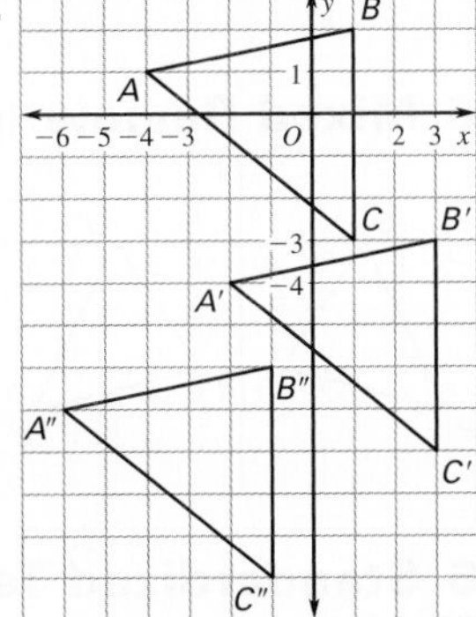

17. *Sample:*

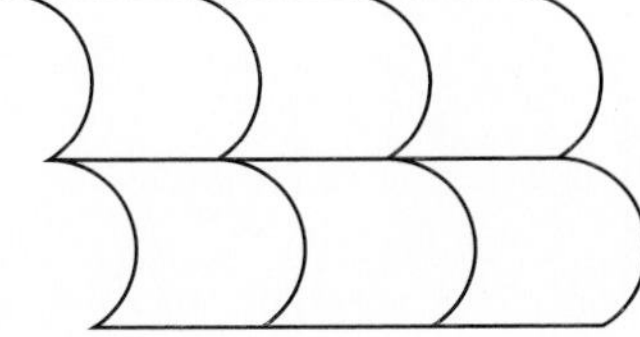

13.5 Checkpoint (p. 735)

1.

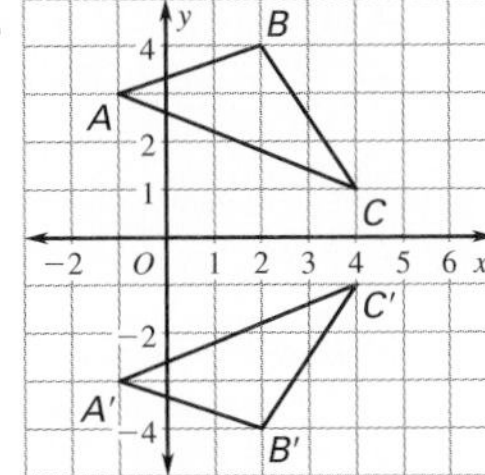

13.5 Practice and Problem Solving (pp. 736–738)

11.

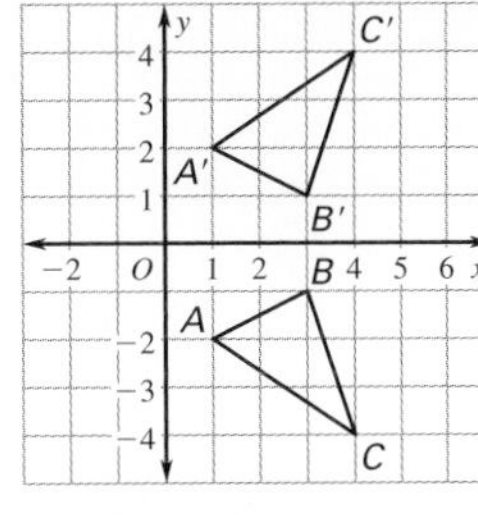

12.

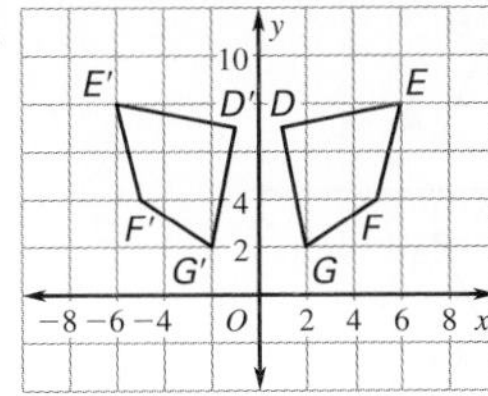

13.

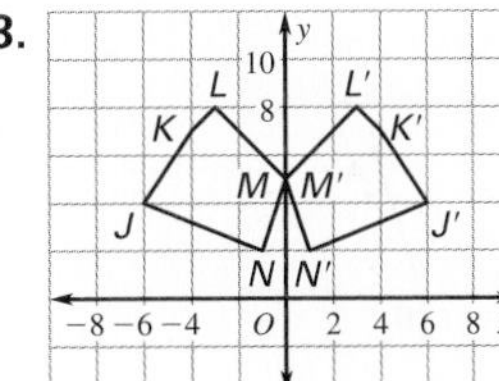

21a.

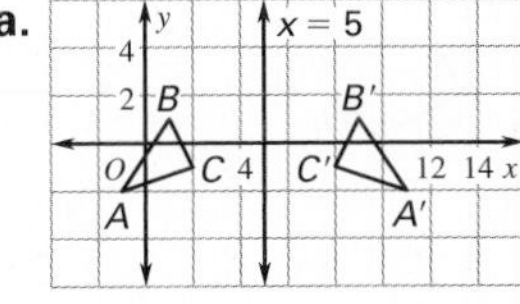

21b.

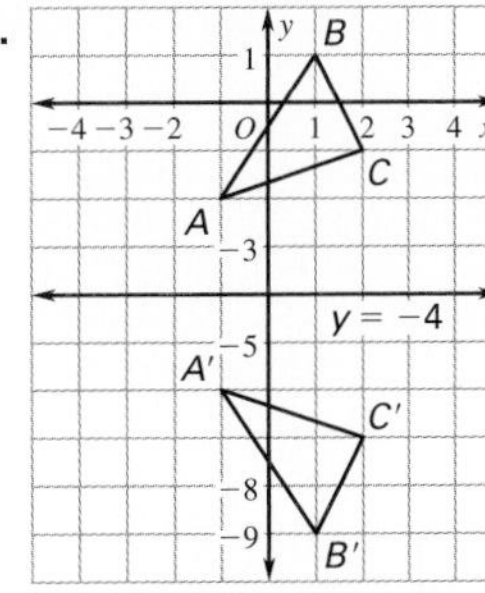

22. *Sample:*

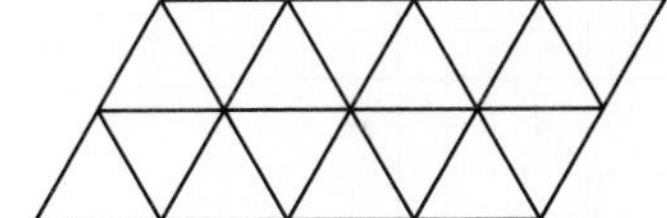

24b.

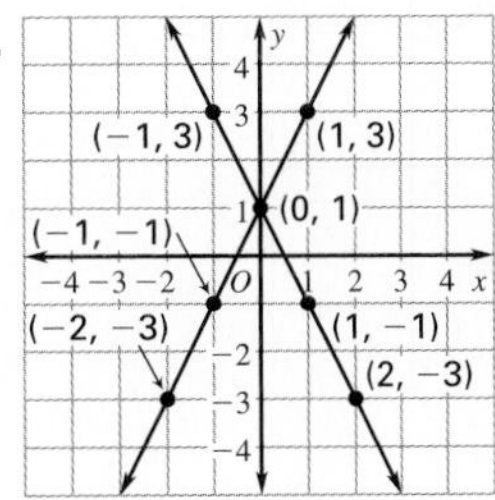

Additional Answers

13.5 Mixed Review (p. 738)

33.

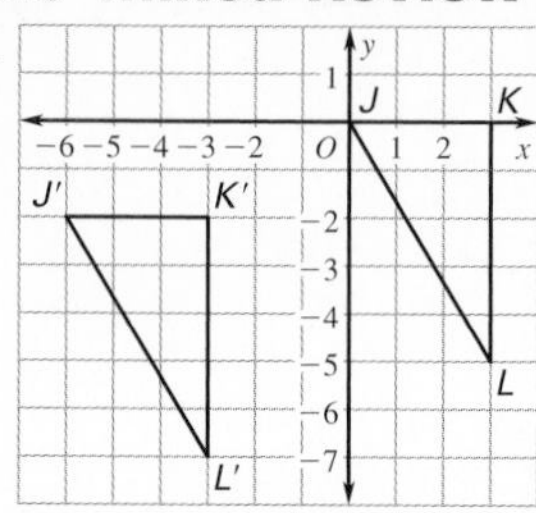

13.5 Standardized Test Practice (p. 738)

35.

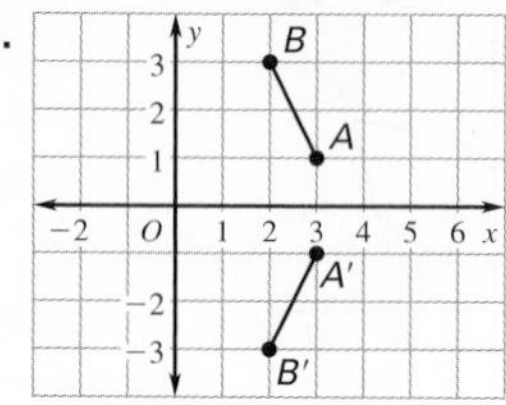

13.6 Concept Activity (p. 740)

1.

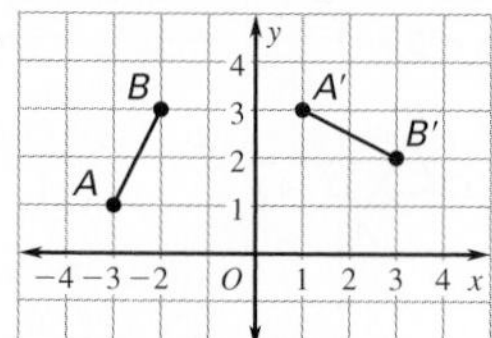

2.

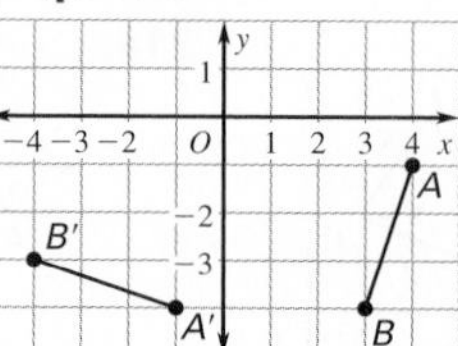

3.

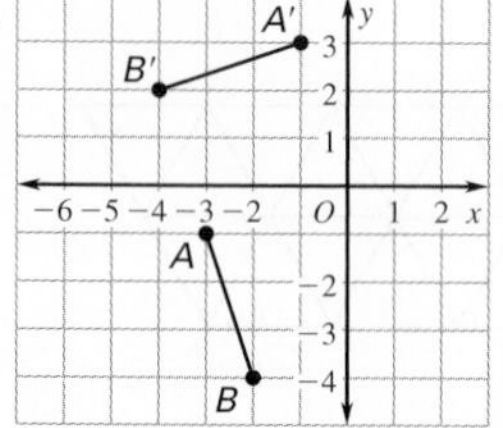

13.6 Checkpoint (pp. 742–743)

1.

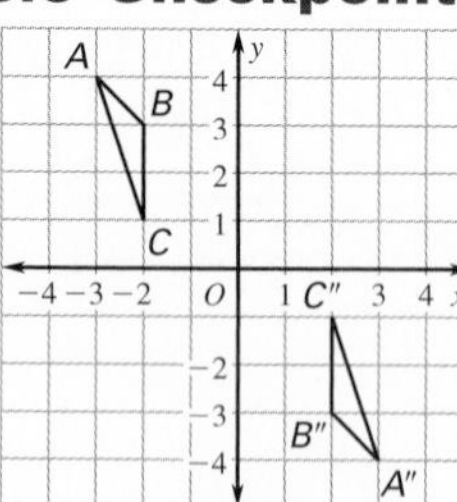

2.

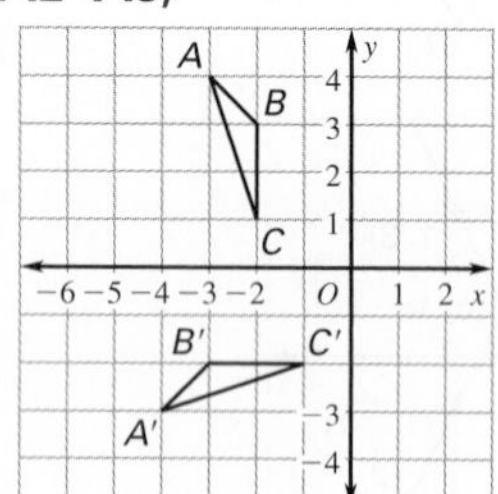

4.

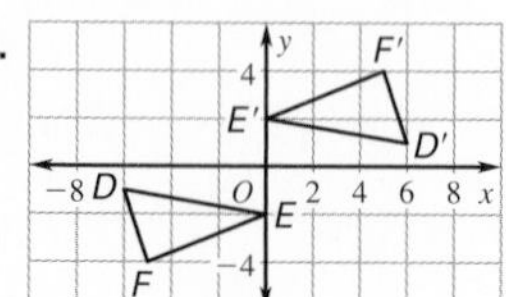

13.6 Guided Practice (p. 744)

6.

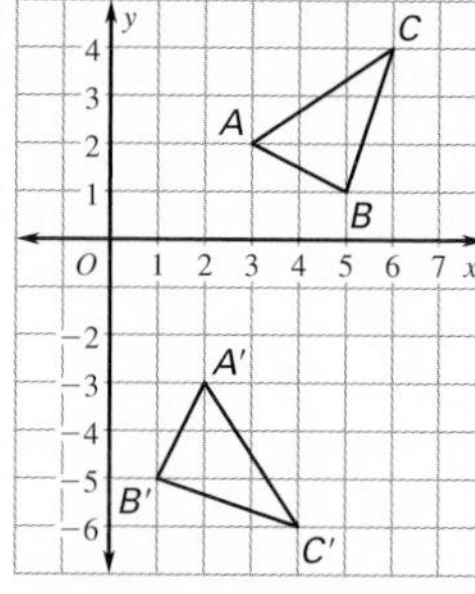

13.6 Practice and Problem Solving (pp. 744–746)

11.

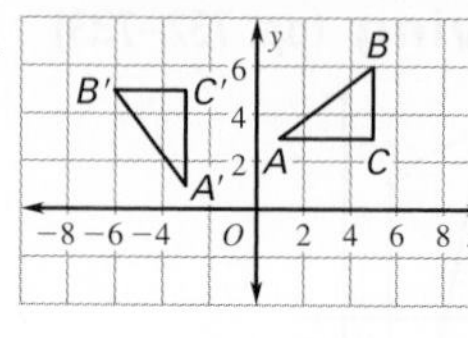

12.

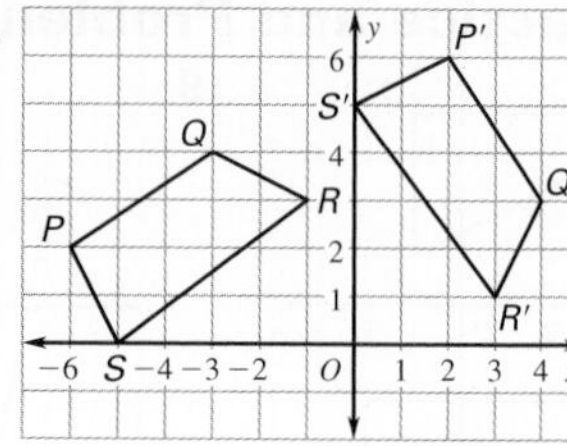

13.

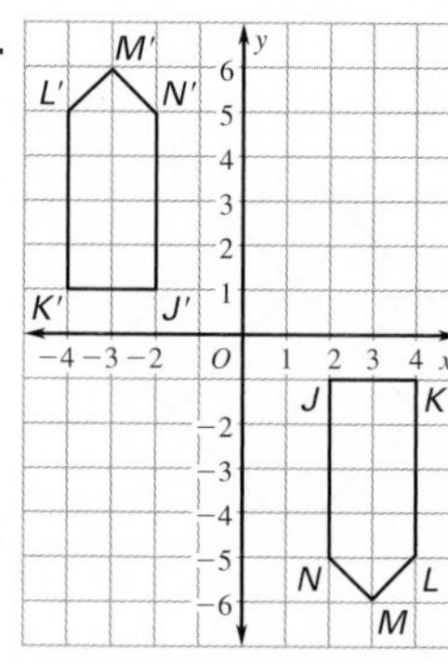

23. *Sample:*

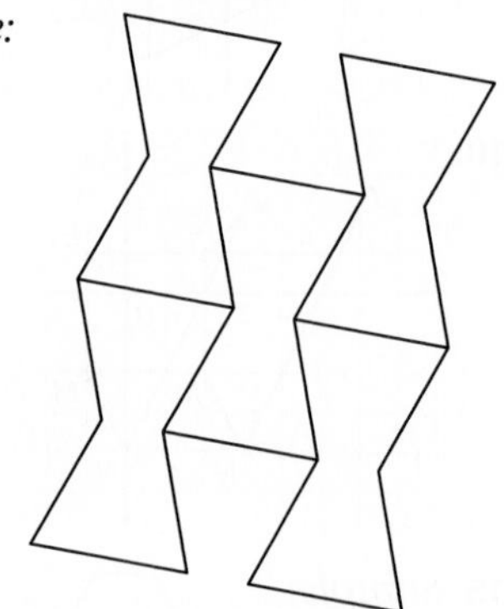

13.6 Mixed Review (p. 746)

29.

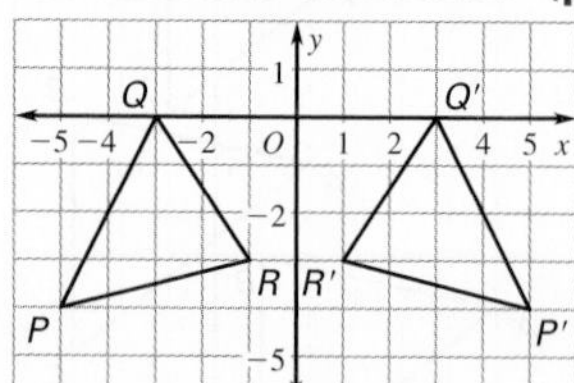

13.6 Standardized Test Practice (p. 746)

30a.

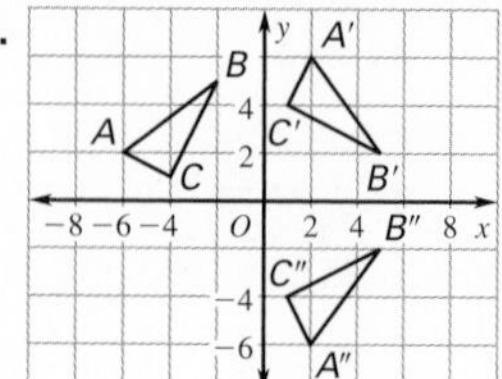

13.7 Checkpoint (p. 748)

1.

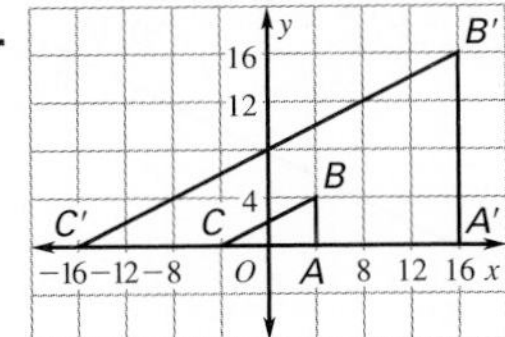

2.

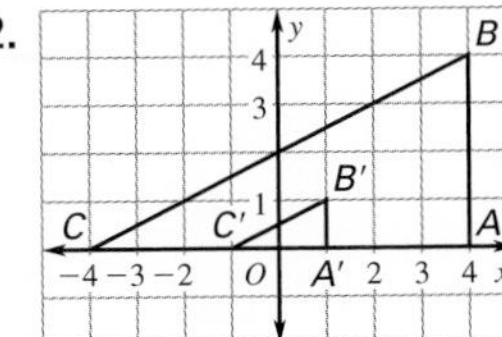

13.7 Practice and Problem Solving (pp. 750–751)

5.

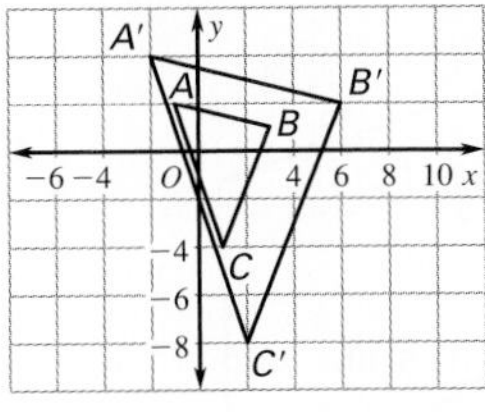

6.

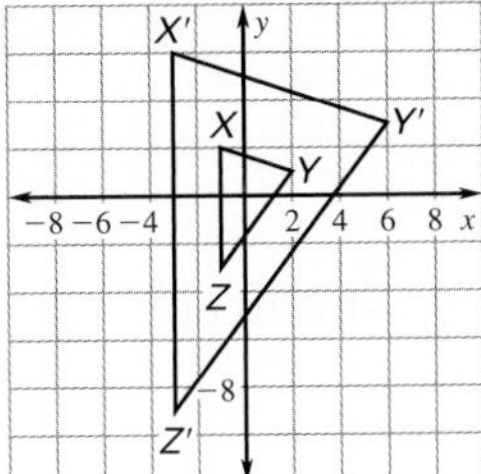

7.

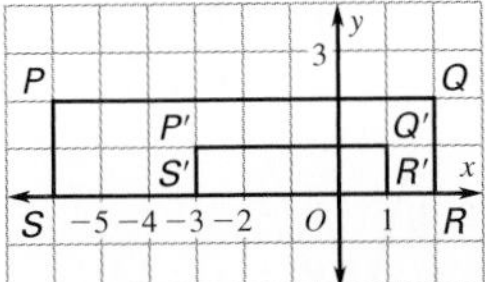

8.

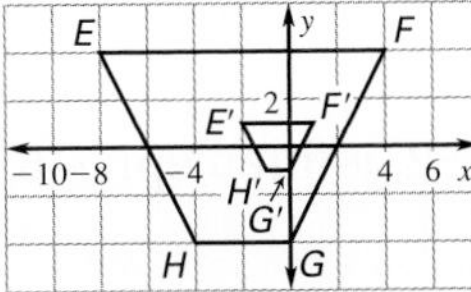

11a–b.

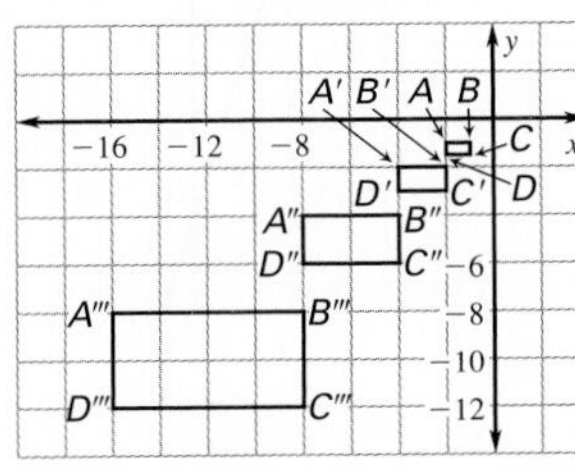

13a.

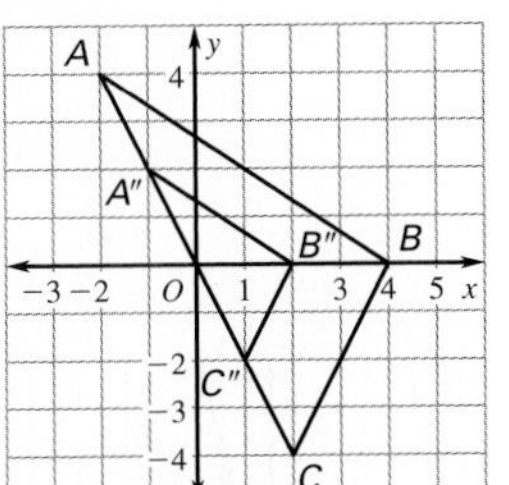

14.

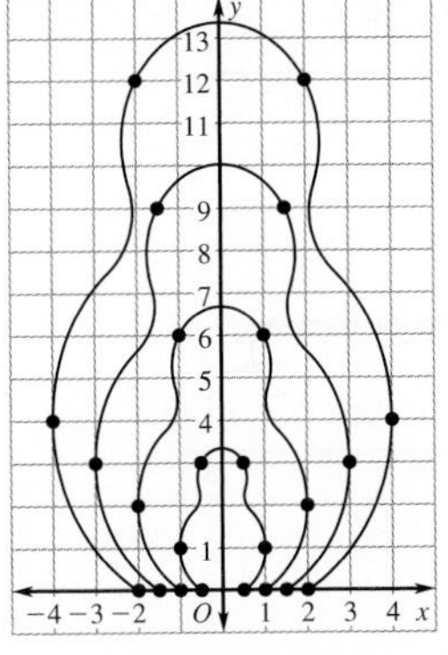

15.

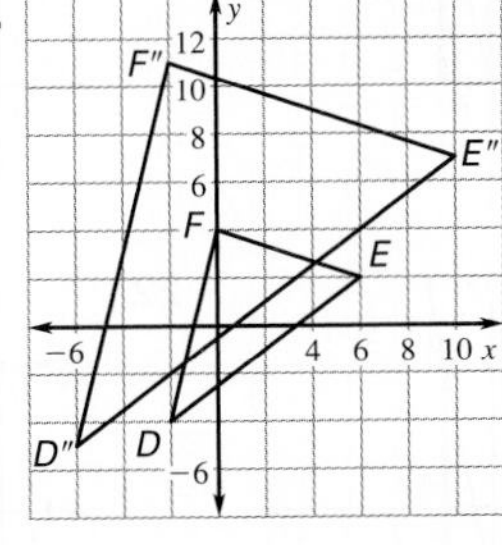

16.

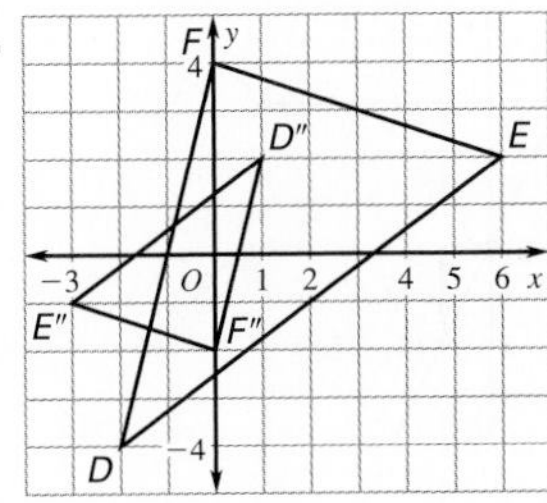

17.

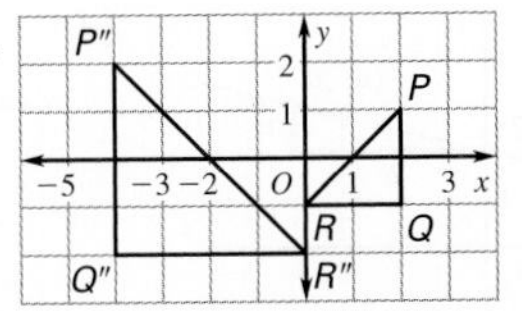

18b.

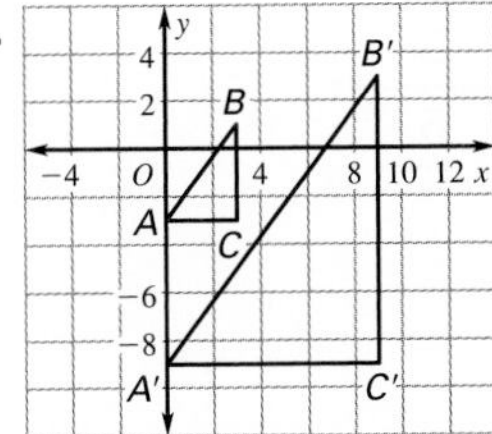

13.7 Mixed Review (p. 751)

25.

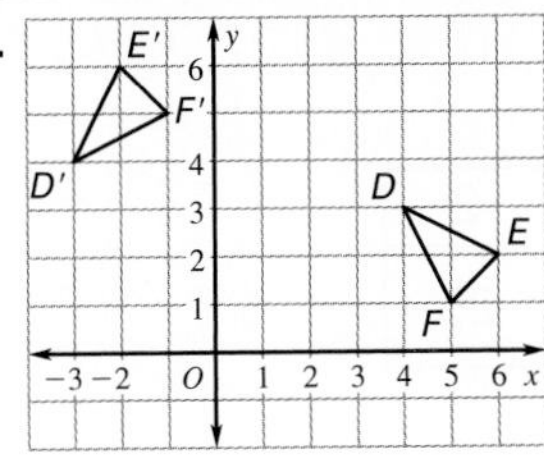

Chapter Test (p. 756)

20.

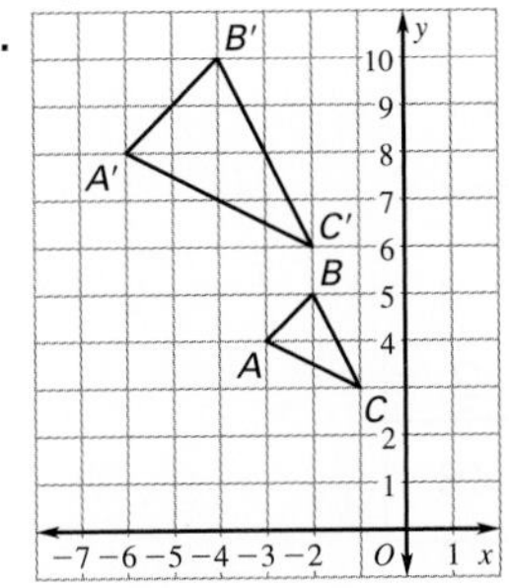

End-of-Course Test

Data Analysis, Polynomials, and Transformations

(p. 768) **134–137.** Sample tables are given.

134.

x	−2	−1	0	1	2
y	7	4	3	4	7

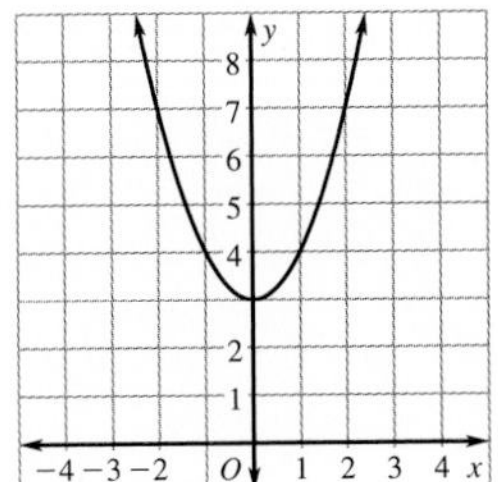

Additional Answers

135.

x	−1	0	1	2	3
y	6	0	−2	0	6

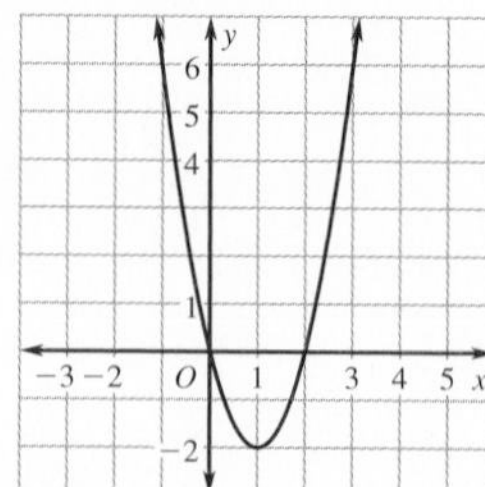

136.

x	−2	−1	0	1	2
y	$\frac{1}{25}$	$\frac{1}{5}$	1	5	25

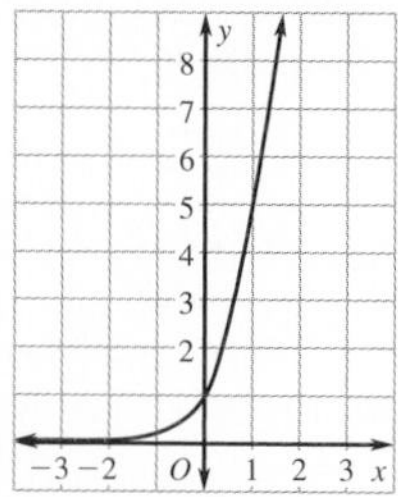

137.

x	−2	−1	0	1	2
y	$\frac{3}{16}$	$\frac{3}{4}$	3	12	48

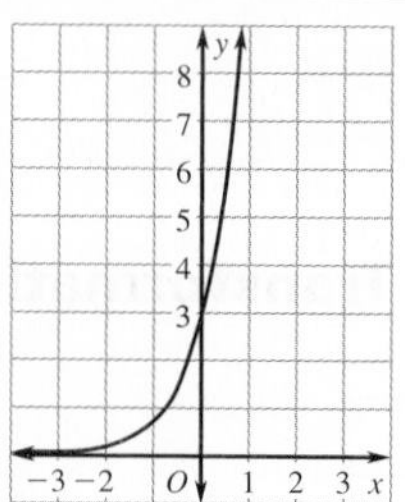

Extra Practice

Chapter 8 (p. 810)

6.

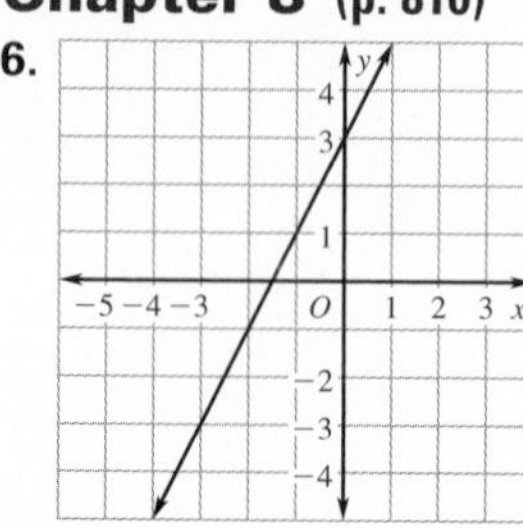

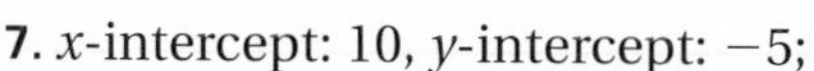

7. x-intercept: 10, y-intercept: -5;

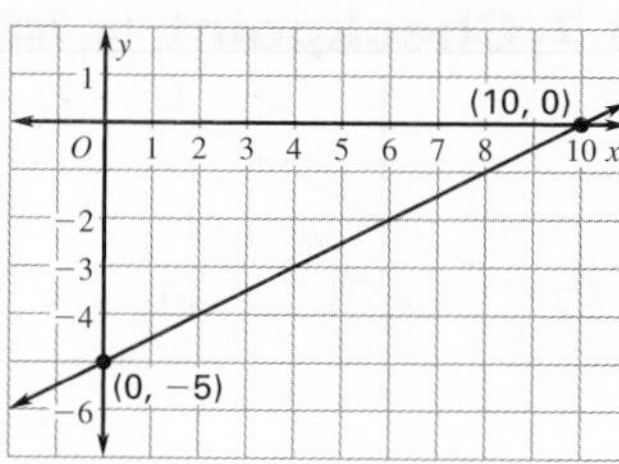

8. x-intercept: 6, y-intercept: 2;

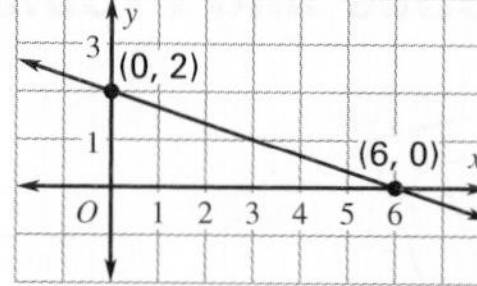

9. x-intercept: -5, y-intercept: -3;

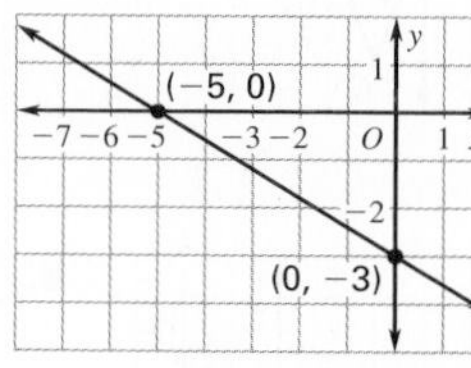

10. x-intercept: -2, y-intercept: -6;

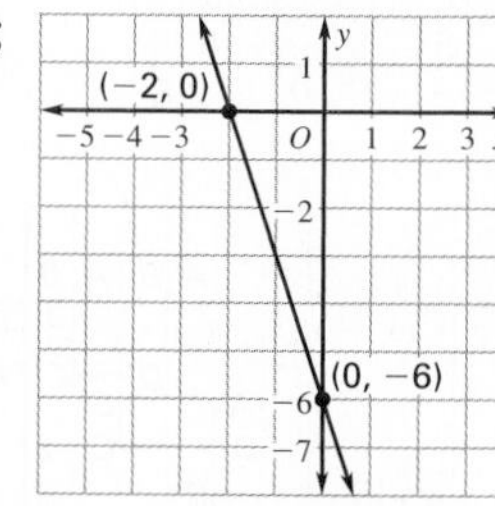

19.

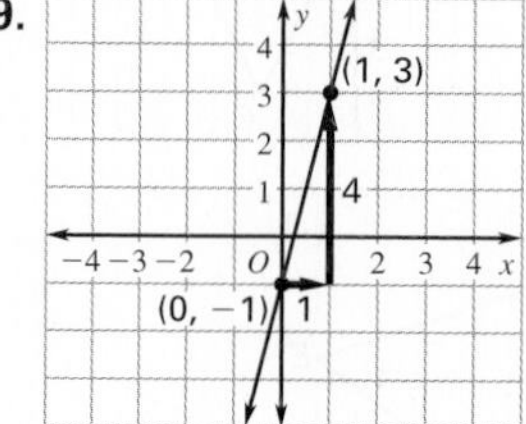

20.

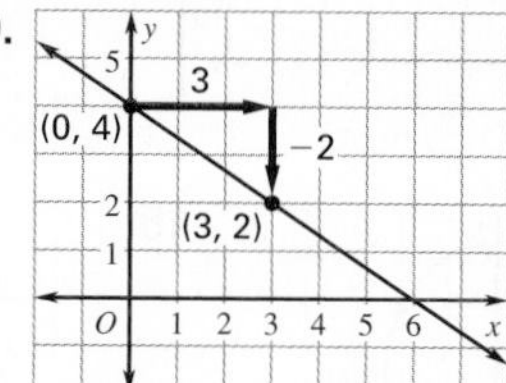

21.

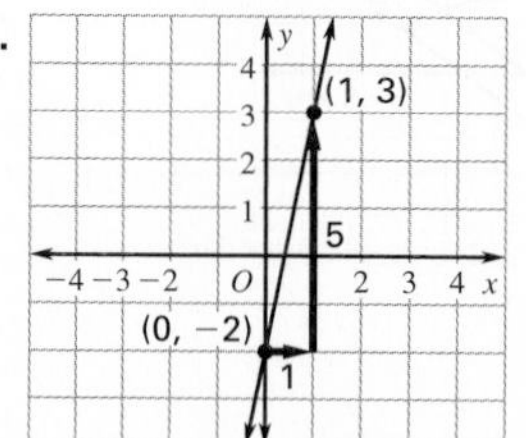

22.

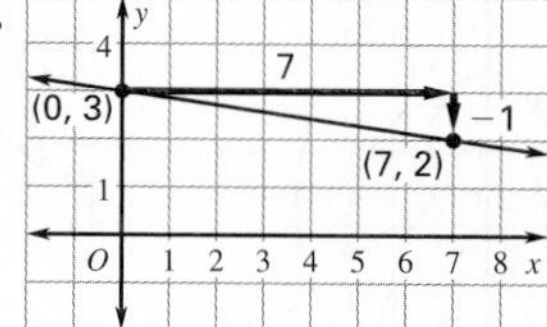

23.

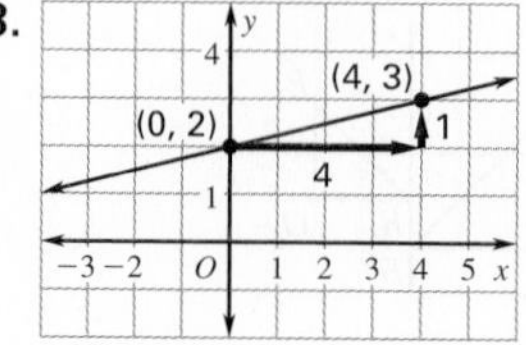

24.

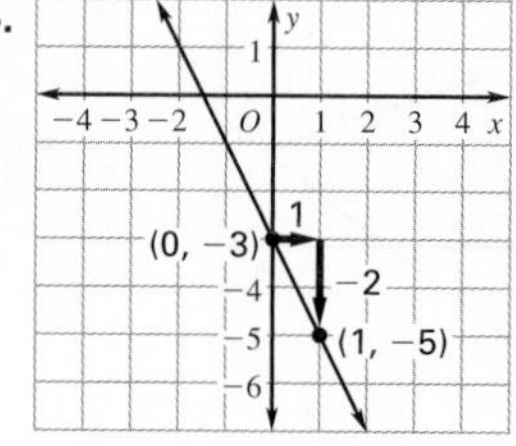

Additional Answers

25.

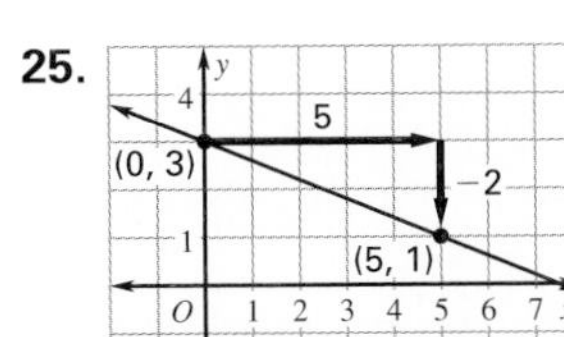

26.

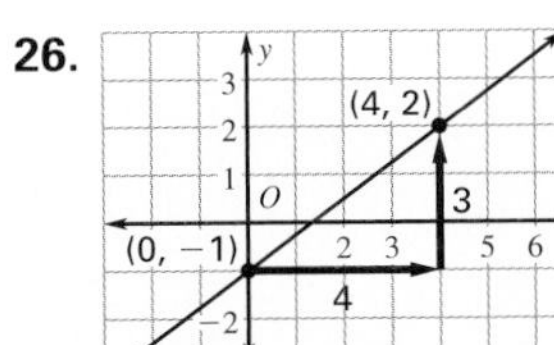

31.

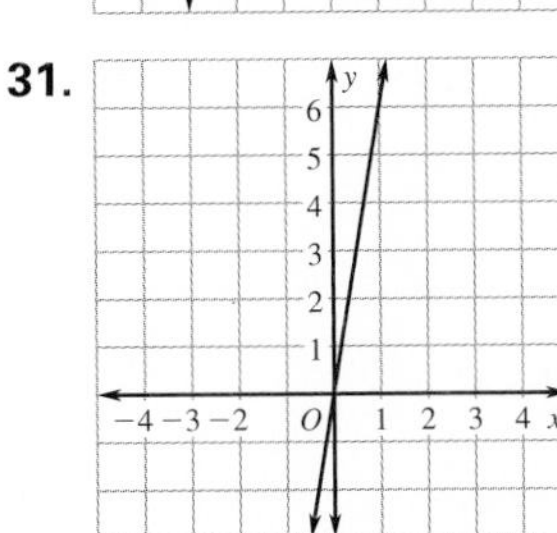

32.

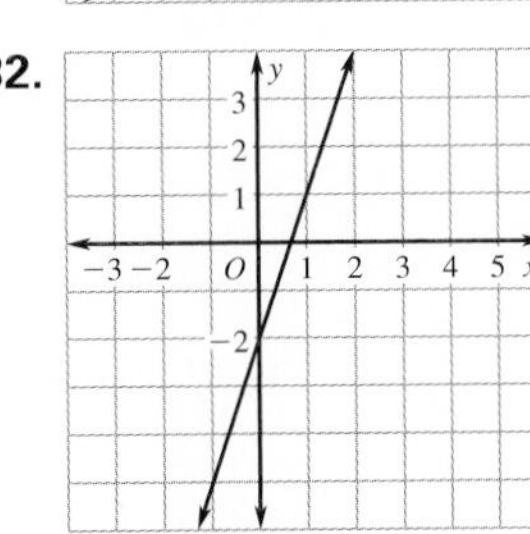

33.

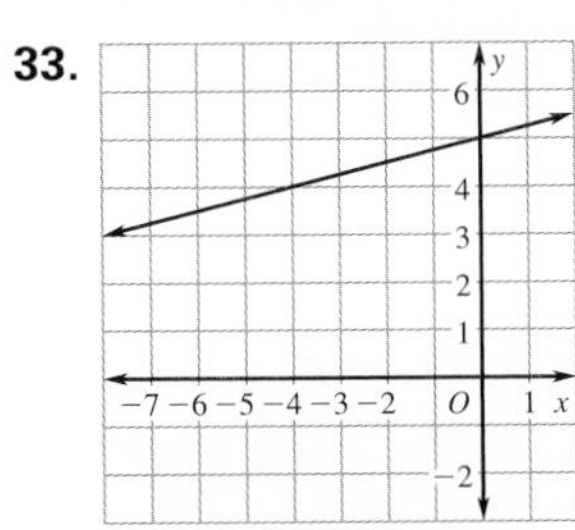

34.

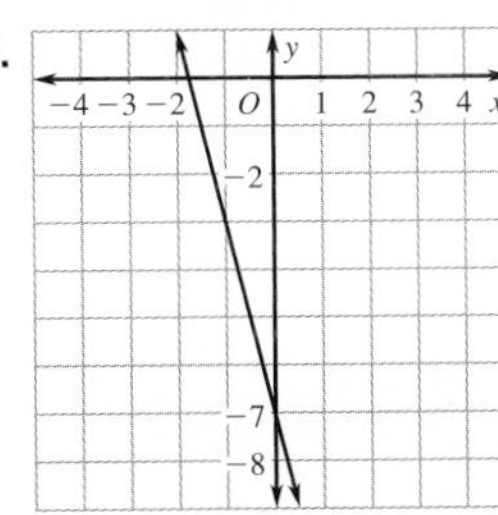

39.

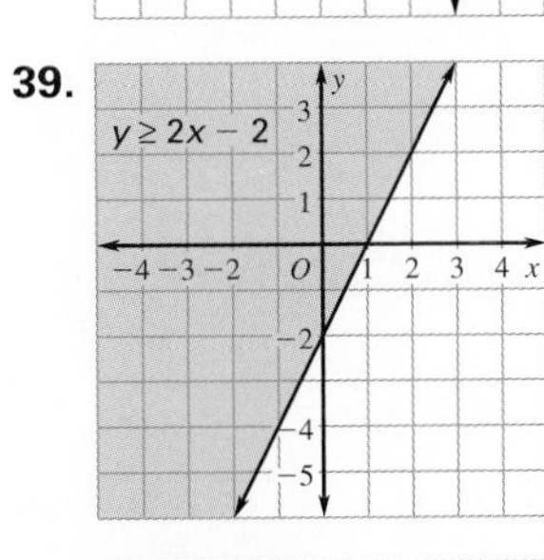

40.

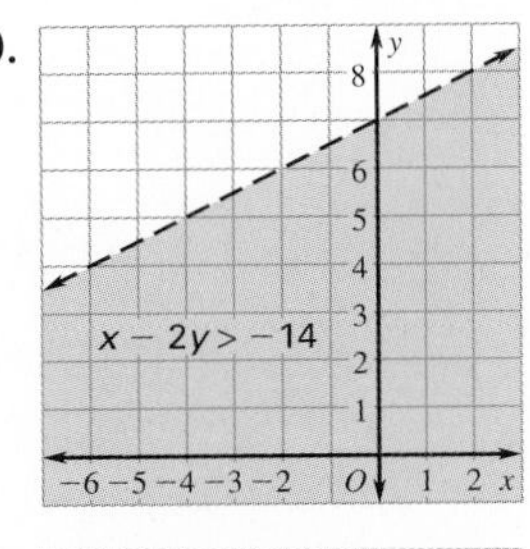

41.

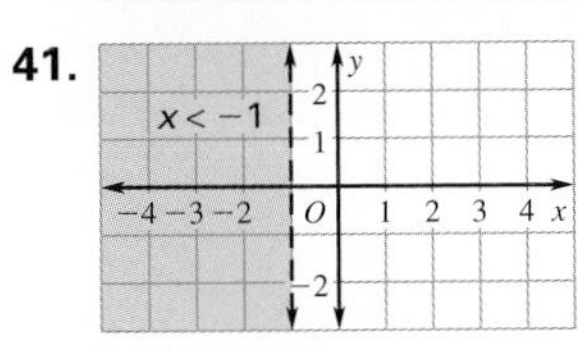

42.

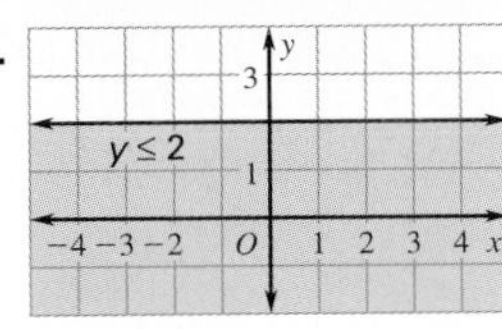

Chapter 12 (p. 814)

37.

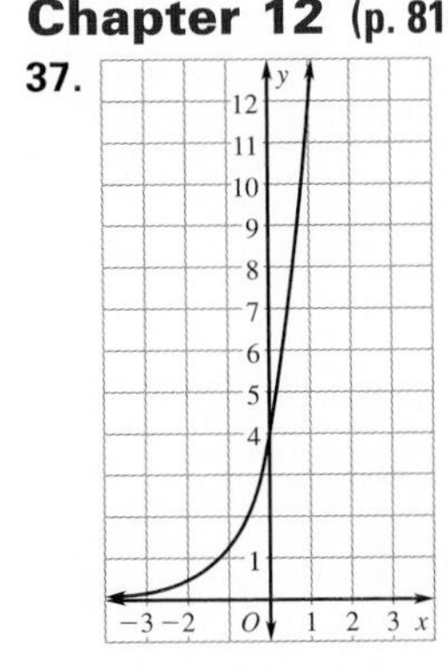

38.

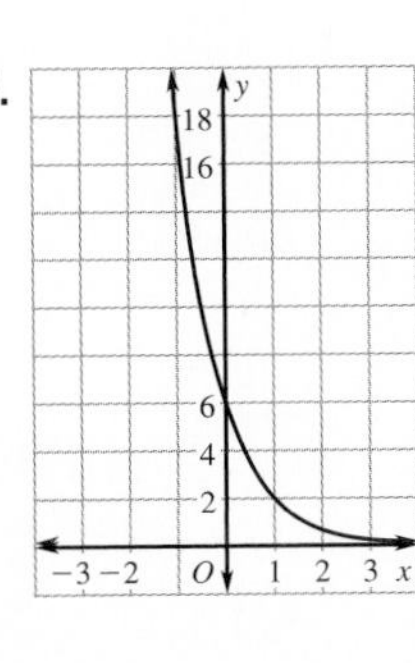

39.

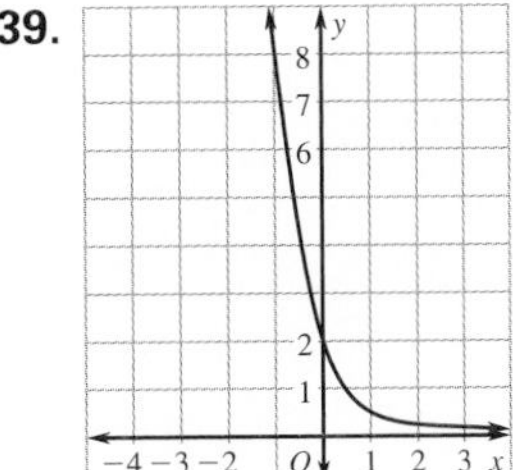

40.

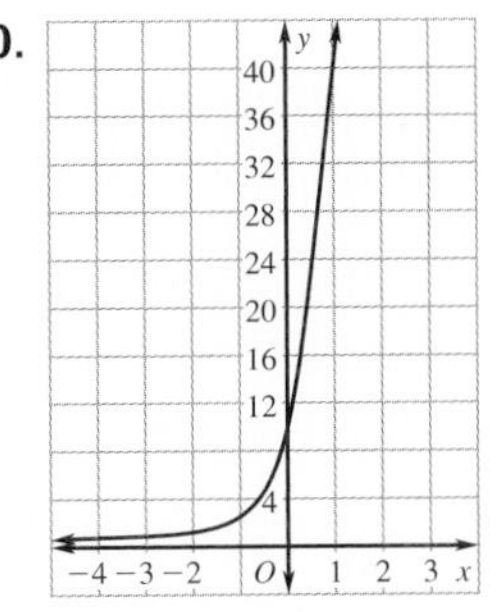

McDougal Littell *Pre-Algebra*

Features	Benefits
Chapter Motivating Application See pp. 2–3, 168–169, 508–509.	These openers draw students into the mathematics by providing ***Math in the Real World***. The dramatic photos ask a relevant math question, setting the stage for the upcoming chapter.
Prerequisite Skills See pp. 39–40, 62, 170, 384, 410–411, 770–802.	The ***Chapter Prerequisite Skills*** page at the beginning of every chapter reviews what students need to know for the chapter. It includes a vocabulary check and a section to teach students how to take notes. The ***Student Reference*** sections throughout the book review key material for use in upcoming lessons. The ***Skills Review Handbook*** reviews material learned in previous courses.
Algebra Preparation See pp. 47, 91, 121, 132, 150, 276, 341, 386, 405, 436, 470, 652, 658, 669, 680, 692.	Through work with real numbers, variables and expressions, equations and inequalities, proportions and formulas, functions, polynomials, sequences, and graphing in the coordinate plane, this course helps students prepare for future mathematics courses.
Before, Now, Why? See pp. 216, 219, 382, 404.	At the start of each chapter and lesson, these lists make a connection to prior knowledge and answer the question, "Why should I learn this?"
Vocabulary and Reading See pp. 268, 269, 275, 290, 318, 516.	The ***Vocabulary*** list at the beginning of each lesson shows students the key review words and new words they should know. Helpful ***Reading Algebra*** and ***Reading Geometry*** notes and questions that help students understand and review vocabulary occur throughout each chapter.
Stepped-Out Examples See pp. 122, 459, 521, 663.	Clear, step-by-step examples, with explanations for each step and color coding to show relationships, help make the math clear and accessible to students.
Notetaking Strand See pp. 4, 118, 132, 145, 150, 282, 708.	***Notetaking Strategies*** appear at the beginning of each chapter. Additional help with notetaking is integrated throughout each chapter.
Focus on Problem Solving See pp. 58–59, 264–265, 448–449, 704–705.	This feature helps students develop problem solving strategies such as identifying relevant and irrelevant information, using multiple methods, solving problems with many or no solutions, and extending and generalizing solutions.
Developing Problem Solving Skills See pp. 122, 123, 251, 279, 394, 395, 435.	***Guided Problem Solving, Extended Problem Solving,*** and ***Challenge*** exercises help students work through real-world problems and prepare students for multi-step problems that appear on high-stakes assessments.
Concept Activities and Projects See pp. 90, 305, 506–507, 646–647.	These optional activities and projects help students develop conceptual understanding through exploration, reflection, and critical thinking. Many activities and projects offer opportunities for cooperative learning.
Building Test-Taking Skills See pp. 107, 113, 160–166, 339, 374–380, 505, 570–576, 758–764.	Throughout the book, students learn how to analyze and respond to multiple choice, short response, and extended response questions. Students can practice test-taking skills on standardized test practice questions in every lesson, in every chapter, and in every unit.